COLLINS

GERMAN ★ ENGLISH
ENGLISH ★ GERMAN
DICTIONARY

BERKLEY BOOKS, NEW YORK

General Editor
R. H. Thomas

The text of this dictionary has been
adapted from the Collins Gem
German–English, English–German
Dictionary

First published in this edition 1982

Editors
Veronika Schnorr, Ute Nicol, Peter Terrell

Assistant Editor
Anne Dickinson

This Berkley book contains the complete
text of the original edition.
It has been completely reset in a typeface
designed for easy reading, and was printed
from new film.

COLLINS GERMAN/ENGLISH ENGLISH/GERMAN
DICTIONARY

A Berkley Book / published by arrangement with
Collins Publishers

PRINTING HISTORY
Collins Gem edition published 1978
Berkley edition / August 1982
Third printing / October 1983

ISBN: 0-425-05450-0

A BERKLEY BOOK ® TM 757,375
Berkley Books are published by The Berkley Publishing Group,
200 Madison Avenue, New York, New York 10016.
The name "BERKLEY" and the stylized "B" with design
are trademarks belonging to Berkley Publishing Corporation.
PRINTED IN THE UNITED STATES OF AMERICA

VORWORT

Der Wörterbuchbenutzer, dem es darum geht, Englisch zu lesen und zu verstehen, findet in diesem Wörterbuch eine ausführliche Erfassung der englischen Gegenwartssprache mit zahlreichen gebräuchlichen Wendungen und Anwendungsbeispielen. Er findet in alphabetischen Listen auch die häufigsten geläufigen Abkürzungen, Kurzwörter und Ortsnamen.

Der Benutzer, der sich verständigen, also auf Englisch ausdrücken will, findet eine klare und ausführliche Behandlung aller Grundwörter mit zahlreichen Hinweisen für eine angebrachte Übersetzung und den korrekten Gebrauch.

INTRODUCTION

The user whose aim is to read and understand German will find a comprehensive and up-to-date wordlist including numerous phrases in current use. He will also find listed alphabetically the main irregular forms with a cross-reference to the basic form where a translation is given, as well as some of the most common abbreviations, acronyms and geographical names in separate alphabetical lists.

The user who wishes to communicate and to express himself in the foreign language will find clear and detailed treatment of all the basic words, with numerous indicators pointing to the appropriate translation, and helping him to use it correctly.

Adjektiv	a	adjective
Abkürzung	abbr	abbreviation
Akkusativ	acc	accusative
Adverb	ad	adverb
Landwirtschaft	Agr	agriculture
Anatomie	Anat	anatomy
Architektur	Archit	architecture
Artikel	art	article
Kunst	Art	art
Astrologie	Astrol	astrology
Astronomie	Astron	astronomy
attributiv	attr	attributive
Kraftfahrzeuge	Aut	automobiles
Hilfsverb	aux	auxiliary
Luftfahrt	Aviat	aviation
Biologie	Biol	biology
Botanik	Bot	botany
britisch	Brit	British
Kartenspiel	Cards	
Chemie	Chem	chemistry
Film	Cine	cinema
Konjunktion	cj	conjunction
umgangssprachlich	col	colloquial
Handel	Comm	commerce
Komparativ	comp	comparative
Kochen und Backen	Cook	cooking
zusammengesetztes Wort	cpd	compound
Dativ	dat	dative
kirchlich	Eccl	ecclesiastical
Elektrizität	Elec	electricity
besonders	esp	especially
und so weiter	etc	et cetera
etwas	etw	something
Euphemismus, Hüllwort	euph	euphemism
Femininum	f	feminine
übertragen	fig	figurative
Finanzwesen	Fin	finance
Genitiv	gen	genitive
Geographie	Geog	geography
Grammatik	Gram	grammar
Geschichte	Hist	history
unpersönlich	impers	impersonal
unbestimmt	indef	indefinite
nicht getrennt gebraucht	insep	inseparable
Interjektion, Ausruf	interj	interjection
interrogativ, fragend	interrog	interrogative
unveränderlich	inv	invariable
unregelmäßig	irreg	irregular
jemand	jd	somebody
jemandem	jdm	(to) somebody
jemanden	jdn	somebody
jemandes	jds	somebody's
Rechtswesen	Jur	law
Sprachwissenschaft	Ling	linguistics
wörtlich	lit	literal
literarisch	liter	literary

Literatur	**Liter**	of literature
Maskulinum	**m**	masculine
Mathematik	**Math**	mathematics
Medizin	**Med**	medicine
Meteorologie	**Met**	meteorology
militärisch	**Mil**	military
Bergbau	**Min**	mining
Musik	**Mus**	music
Substantiv, Hauptwort	**n**	noun
nautisch, Seefahrt	**Naut**	nautical, naval
Nominativ	**nom**	nominative
Neutrum	**nt**	neuter
Zahlwort	**num**	numeral
Objekt	**obj**	object
veraltet	**old**	
sich	**o.s.**	oneself
Parlament	**Parl**	parliament
abschätzig	**pej**	pejorative
Photographie	**Phot**	photography
Physik	**Phys**	physics
Plural	**pl**	plural
Politik	**Pol**	politics
besitzanzeigend	**poss**	possessive
Präfix, Vorsilbe	**pref**	prefix
Präposition	**prep**	preposition
Presse	**Press**	
Typographie	**Print**	printing
Pronomen, Fürwort	**pron**	pronoun
Psychologie	**Psych**	psychology
1. Vergangenheit, Imperfekt	**pt**	past
Partizip Perfekt	**ptp**	past participle
Radio	**Rad**	radio
Eisenbahn	**Rail**	railways
Relativ-	**rel**	relative
Religion	**Rel**	religion
jemand (—en, —em)	**sb**	someone, somebody
Schulwesen	**Sch**	school
Naturwissenschaft	**Sci**	science
schottisch	**Scot**	Scottish
Singular, Einzahl	**sing**	singular
Skisport	**Ski**	skiing
etwas	**sth**	something
Suffix, Nachsilbe	**suff**	suffix
Superlativ	**superl**	superlative
Technik	**Tech**	technology
Nachrichtentechnik	**Tel**	telecommunications
Theater	**Theat**	theatre
Fernsehen	**TV**	television
Hochschulwesen	**Univ**	university
(nord)amerikanisch	**US**	(North) America
gewöhnlich	**usu**	usually
Verb	**v**	verb
intransitives Verb	**vi**	intransitive verb
reflexives Verb	**vr**	reflexive verb
transitives Verb	**vt**	transitive verb
Zoologie	**Zool**	zoology
zwischen zwei Sprechern	**~**	change of speaker
ungefähre Entsprechung	**≈**	cultural equivalent
eingetragenes Warenzeichen	**®**	registered trademark

Regular German noun endings

nom		gen	pl	nom		gen	pl
-ant	m	-anten	-anten	-ion	f	-ion	-ionen
-anz	f	-anz	-anzen	-ist	m	-isten	-isten
-ar	m	-ar(e)s	-are	-ium	nt	-iums	-ien
-chen	nt	-chens	-chen	-ius	m	-ius	-iusse
-ei	f	-ei	-eien	-ive	f	-ive	-iven
-elle	f	-elle	-ellen	-keit	f	-keit	-keiten
-ent	m	-enten	-enten	-lein	nt	-leins	-lein
-enz	f	-enz	-enzen	-ling	m	-lings	-linge
-ette	f	-ette	-etten	-ment	nt	-ments	-mente
-eur	m	-eurs	-eure	-mus	m	-mus	-men
-euse	f	-euse	-eusen	-schaft	f	-schaft	-schaften
-heit	f	-heit	-heiten	-tät	f	-tät	-täten
-ie	f	-ie	-ien	-tor	m	-tors	-toren
-ik	f	-ik	-iken	-ung	f	-ung	-ungen
-in	f	-in	-innen	-ur	f	-ur	-uren
-ine	f	-ine	-inen				

Phonetic symbols
Lautschrift

[:] length mark Längezeichen   ['] stress mark Betonung
['] glottal stop Knacklaut

all vowel sounds are approximate only
alle Vokallaute sind nur ungefähre Entsprechungen

lie	[aɪ]	weit		day	[eɪ]	
now	[aʊ]	Haut		girl	[ɜ:]	
above	[ə]	bitte		board	[ɔ:]	
green	[i:]	viel		root	[u:]	Hut
pity	[ɪ]	Bischof		come	[ʌ]	Butler
rot	[ɒ,ɔ]	Post		salon	[ɔ̃]	Champignon
full	[ʊ]	Pult		avant (garde)	[ɑ̃]	Ensemble
				fair	[ɛə]	mehr
bet	[b]	Ball		beer	[ɪə]	Bier
dim	[d]	dann		toy	[ɔɪ]	Heu
face	[f]	Faß		pure	[ʊə]	
go	[g]	Gast		wine	[w]	
hit	[h]	Herr		thin	[θ]	
you	[j]	ja		this	[ð]	
cat	[k]	kalt				
lick	[l]	Last		Hast	[a]	mash
must	[m]	Mast		Ensemble	[ã]	avant (garde)
nut	[n]	Nuß		Metall	[e]	meths
bang	[ŋ]	lang		häßlich	[ɛ]	
pepper	[p]	Pakt		Cousin	[ɛ̃]	
sit	[s]	Rasse		vital	[i]	
shame	[ʃ]	Schal		Moral	[o]	
tell	[t]	Tal		Champignon	[õ]	salon
vine	[v]	was		ökonomisch	[ø]	
loch	[x]	Bach		gönnen	[œ]	
zero	[z]	Hase		Heu	[ɔɪ]	toy
leisure	[ʒ]	Genie		kulant	[u]	
				physisch	[y]	
bat	[æ]			Müll	[ʏ]	
farm	[ɑ:]	Bahn		ich	[ç]	
set	[e]	Kette				

[*]   r can be pronounced before a vowel; Bindungs-R

A, a [a:] *nt* A, a.

Aal [a:l] *m* -(e)s, -e eel.

Aas [a:s] *nt* -es, -e *or* **Äser** carrion; **~geier** *m* vulture.

ab [ap] *prep* +*dat* from; *ad* off; **links ~** to the left; **~ und zu** *or* **an** now and then *or* again; **von da ~** from then on; **'der Knopf ist ~** the button has come off.

Abänderung ['ap'ɛndərʊŋ] *f* alteration.

abarbeiten ['ap'arbaɪtən] *vr* wear o.s. out, slave away.

Abart ['ap'a:rt] *f* (*Biol*) variety; **a~ig** *a* abnormal.

Abbau ['apbau] *m* -(e)s dismantling; (*Verminderung*) reduction (*gen* in); (*Verfall*) decline (*gen* in); (*Min*) mining; quarrying; (*Chem*) decomposition; **a~en** *vt* dismantle; (*Min*) mine; quarry; (*verringern*) reduce; (*Chem*) break down.

abbeißen ['apbaɪsən] *vt irreg* bite off.

abberufen ['apbəru:fən] *vt irreg* recall.

Abberufung *f* recall.

abbestellen ['apbəʃtɛlən] *vt* cancel.

abbezahlen ['apbətsa:lən] *vt* pay off.

abbiegen ['apbi:gən] *irreg vi* turn off; (*Straße*) bend; *vt* bend; (*verhindern*) ward off.

Abbild ['apbɪlt] *nt* portrayal; (*einer Person*) image, likeness; **a~en** ['apbɪldən] *vt* portray; **~ung** *f* illustration.

Abbitte ['apbɪtə] *f*: **~ leisten** *or* **tun** make one's apologies (*bei* to).

abblasen ['apbla:zən] *vt irreg* blow off; (*fig*) call off.

abblenden ['apblɛndən] *vti* (*Aut*) dip, dim (*US*).

Abblendlicht *nt* dipped *or* dimmed (*US*) headlights *pl.*

abbrechen ['apbrɛçən] *vti irreg* break off; *Gebäude* pull down; *Zelt* take down; (*aufhören*) stop.

abbrennen ['apbrɛnən] *irreg vt* burn off; *Feuerwerk* let off; *vi* (*aux sein*) burn down; **abgebrannt sein** (*col*) be broke.

abbringen ['apbrɪŋən] *vt irreg*: **jdn von etw ~** dissuade sb from sth; **jdn vom Weg ~** divert sb; **ich bringe den Verschluß nicht ab** (*col*) I can't get the top off.

abbröckeln ['apbrœkəln] *vti* crumble off *or* away.

Abbruch ['apbrux] *m* (*von Verhandlungen etc*) breaking off; (*von Haus*) demolition; **jdm/etw ~ tun** harm sb/sth; **a~reif** *a* only fit for demolition.

abbrühen ['apbry:ən] *vt* scald; **abgebrüht** (*col*) hard-boiled.

abbuchen ['apbu:xən] *vt* debit.

abbürsten ['apbyrstən] *vt* brush off.

abdanken ['apdaŋkən] *vi* resign; (*König*) abdicate.

Abdankung *f* resignation; abdication.

abdecken ['apdɛkən] *vt* uncover; *Tisch* clear; *Loch* cover.

abdichten ['apdɪçtən] *vt* seal; (*Naut*) caulk.

abdrängen ['apdrɛŋən] *vt* push off.

abdrehen ['apdre:ən] *vt Gas* turn off; *Licht* switch off; *Film* shoot; **jdm den Hals ~** wring sb's neck; *vi* (*Schiff*) change course.

abdrosseln ['apdrɔsəln] *vt* throttle; (*Aut*) stall; *Produktion* cut back.

Abdruck ['apdruk] *m* (*Nachdrucken*) reprinting; (*Gedrucktes*) reprint; (*Gips—, Wachs—*) impression; (*Finger—*) print; **a~en** *vt* print, publish.

abdrücken ['apdrʏkən] *vt* make an impression of; *Waffe* fire; *Person* hug, squeeze; **jdm die Luft ~** squeeze all the breath out of sb; *vr* leave imprints; (*abstoßen*) push o.s. away.

abebben ['ap'ɛbən] *vi* ebb away.

Abend ['a:bənt] *m* -s, -e evening; **zu ~ essen** have dinner *or* supper; **a~** *ad* evening; **~brot** *nt*, **~essen** *nt* supper; **a~füllend** taking up the whole evening; **~kurs** *m* evening classes *pl*; **~land** *nt* West; **a~lich** *a* evening; **~mahl** *nt* Holy Communion; **~rot** *nt* sunset; **a~s** *ad* in the evening.

Abenteuer ['a:bəntɔʏər] *nt* -s, - adventure; **a~lich** *a* adventurous.

Abenteurer *m* -s, - adventurer; **~in** *f* adventuress.

aber ['a:bər] *cj* but; (*jedoch*) however; **das ist ~ schön** that's really nice; **nun ist ~ Schluß!** now that's enough!; *ad* **tausend und ~ tausend** thousands upon thousands; **A~** *nt* but; **A~glaube** *m* superstition; **~gläubisch** *a* superstitious.

aberkennen ['ap'ɛrkɛnən] *vt irreg*: **jdm etw ~** deprive sb of sth, take sth (away) from sb.

Aberkennung *f* taking away.

aber- *cpd*: **~malig** *a* repeated; **~mals** *ad* once again.

abfahren ['ap-fa:rən] *irreg vi* leave, depart; *vt* take *or* cart away; *Strecke* drive; *Reifen* wear; *Fahrkarte* use.

Abfahrt ['ap-fa:rt] *f* departure; (*Ski*) descent; (*Piste*) run; **~slauf** *m* (*Ski*) descent, run down; **~(s)-tag** *m* day of departure; **~szeit** *f* departure time.

Abfall ['ap-fal] *m* waste; (*von Speisen etc*) rubbish, garbage (*US*); (*Neigung*) slope; (*Verschlechterung*) decline; **~eimer** *m* rubbish bin, garbage can (*US*); **a~en** *vi irreg* (*lit, fig*) fall *or* drop off; (*Pol, vom*

Glauben) break away; (*sich neigen*) fall *or* drop away.

abfällig ['ap-fɛlɪç] *a* disparaging, deprecatory.

abfangen ['ap-faŋən] *vt irreg* intercept; *Person* catch; (*unter Kontrolle bringen*) check.

abfärben ['ap-fɛrbən] *vi* (*lit*) lose its colour; (*Wäsche*) run; (*fig*) rub off.

abfassen ['ap-fasən] *vt* write, draft.

abfertigen ['ap-fɛrtɪgən] *vt* prepare for dispatch, process; (*an der Grenze*) clear; *Kundschaft* attend to; **jdn kurz ~** give sb short shrift.

Abfertigung *f* preparing for dispatch, processing; clearance.

abfeuern ['ap-fɔʏərn] *vt* fire.

abfinden ['ap-fɪndən] *irreg vt* pay off; *vr* come to terms; **sich mit jdm ~/nicht ~** put up with/not get on with sb.

Abfindung *f* (*von Gläubigern*) payment; (*Geld*) sum in settlement.

abflauen ['ap-flaʊən] *vi* (*Wind, Erregung*) die away, subside; (*Nachfrage, Geschäft*) fall *or* drop off.

abfliegen ['ap-fli:gən] *irreg vi* (*Flugzeug*) take off; (*Passagier auch*) fly; *vt Gebiet* fly over.

abfließen ['ap-fli:sən] *vi irreg* drain away.

Abflug ['ap-flu:k] *m* departure; (*Start*) take-off; **~zeit** *f* departure time.

Abfluß ['ap-flus] *m* draining away; (*Öffnung*) outlet.

abfragen ['ap-fra:gən] *vt* test; **jdn** *or* **jdm etw ~** question sb on sth.

Abfuhr ['ap-fu:r] *f* **-, -en** removal; (*fig*) snub, rebuff.

Abführ- ['ap-fy:r] *cpd*: **a~en** *vt* lead away; *Gelder, Steuern* pay; *vi* (*Med*) have a laxative effect; **~mittel** *nt* laxative, purgative.

abfüllen ['ap-fylən] *vt* draw off; (*in Flaschen*) bottle.

Abgabe ['apga:bə] *f* handing in; (*von Ball*) pass; (*Steuer*) tax; (*eines Amtes*) giving up; (*einer Erklärung*) giving; **a~nfrei** *a* tax-free; **a~npflichtig** *a* liable to tax.

Abgang ['apgaŋ] *m* (*von Schule*) leaving; (*Theat*) exit; (*Med: Ausscheiden*) passing; (*Fehlgeburt*) miscarriage; (*Abfahrt*) departure; (*der Post, von Waren*) dispatch.

Abgas ['apga:s] *nt* waste gas; (*Aut*) exhaust.

abgeben ['apge:bən] *irreg vt Gegenstand* hand *or* give in; *Ball* pass; *Wärme* give off; *Amt* hand over; *Schuß* fire; *Erklärung, Urteil* give; (*darstellen, sein*) make; **jdm etw ~** (*überlassen*) let sb have sth; *vr*: **sich mit jdm/etw ~** associate with sb/bother with sth.

abgedroschen ['apgədrɔʃən] *a* hackneyed; *Witz* corny.

abgefeimt ['apgəfaimt] *a* cunning.

abgegriffen ['apgəgrɪfən] *a Buch* well-thumbed; *Redensart* hackneyed.

abgehen ['apge:ən] *irreg vi* go away, leave; (*Theat*) exit; (*Post*) go; (*Med*) be passed; (*Baby*) die; (*Knopf etc*) come off; (*abgezogen werden*) be taken off; (*Straße*) branch off; **etw geht jdm ab** (*fehlt*) sb

lacks sth; *vt Strecke* go *or* walk along.

abgelegen ['apgəle:gən] *a* remote.

abgemacht ['apgəmaxt] *a* fixed; **~!** done.

abgeneigt ['apgənaikt] *a* averse to, disinclined.

Abgeordnete(r) ['apgə'ɔrdnətə(r)] *mf* member of parliament; elected representative.

Abgesandte(r) ['apgəzantə(r)] *mf* delegate; (*Pol*) envoy.

abgeschmackt ['apgəʃmakt] *a* tasteless; **A~heit** *f* lack of taste; (*Bemerkung*) tasteless remark.

abgesehen ['apgəze:ən] *a*: **es auf jdn/etw ~ haben** be after sb/sth; **~ von...** apart from...

abgespannt ['apgəʃpant] *a* tired out.

abgestanden ['apgəʃtandən] *a* stale; *Bier auch* flat.

abgestorben ['apgəʃtɔrbən] *a* numb; (*Biol, Med*) dead.

abgetakelt ['apgəta:kəlt] *a* (*col*) decrepit, past it.

abgetragen ['apgətra:gən] *a* shabby, worn out.

abgewinnen ['apgəvɪnən] *vt irreg*: **jdm Geld ~** win money from sb; **einer Sache etw/Geschmack ~** get sth/pleasure from sth.

abgewöhnen ['apgəvø:nən] *vt*: **jdm/sich etw ~** cure sb of sth/give sth up.

abgleiten ['apglaitən] *vi irreg* slip, slide.

Abgott ['apgɔt] *m* idol.

abgöttisch ['apgœtiʃ] *a*: **~ lieben** idolize.

abgrenzen ['apgrɛntsən] *vt* (*lit, fig*) mark off; fence off.

Abgrund ['apgrunt] *m* (*lit, fig*) abyss.

abgründig ['apgrʏndɪç] *a* unfathomable; *Lächeln* cryptic.

abhacken ['aphakən] *vt* chop off.

abhaken ['apha:kən] *vt* tick off.

abhalten ['aphaltən] *vt irreg Versammlung* hold; **jdn von etw ~** (*fernhalten*) keep sb away from sth; (*hindern*) keep sb from sth.

abhandeln ['aphandəln] *vt Thema* deal with; **jdm die Waren/8 Mark ~** do a deal with sb for the goods/beat sb down 8 marks.

abhanden [ap'handən] *a*: **~ kommen** get lost.

Abhandlung ['aphandluŋ] *f* treatise, discourse.

Abhang ['aphaŋ] *m* slope.

abhängen ['aphɛŋən] *irreg vt Bild* take down; *Anhänger* uncouple; *Verfolger* shake off; *vi* (*Fleisch*) hang; **von jdm/etw ~** depend on sb/sth.

abhängig ['aphɛŋɪç] *a* dependent (*von* on); **A~keit** *f* dependence (*von* on).

abhärten ['aphɛrtən] *vtr* toughen (o.s.) up; **sich gegen etw ~** inure o.s. to sth.

abhauen ['aphaʊən] *irreg vt* cut off; *Baum* cut down; *vi* (*col*) clear off *or* out.

abheben ['aphe:bən] *irreg vt* lift (up); *Karten* cut; *Masche* slip; *Geld* withdraw, take out; *vi* (*Flugzeug*) take off; (*Rakete*) lift off; (*Cards*) cut; *vr* stand out (*von* from), contrast (*von* with).

abhelfen ['aphɛlfən] *vi irreg* (+*dat*) remedy.

abhetzen ['aphɛtsən] *vr* wear *or* tire o.s. out.

Abhilfe ['aphɪlfə] *f* remedy; ~ **schaffen** put things right.

abholen ['aphoːlən] *vt Gegenstand* fetch, collect; *Person* call for; (*am Bahnhof etc*) pick up, meet.

abhorchen ['aphɔrçən] *vt* (*Med*) auscultate, sound.

abhören ['aphøːrən] *vt Vokabeln* test; *Telefongespräch* tap; *Tonband etc* listen to.

Abhörgerät *nt* bug.

Abitur [abiˈtuːr] *nt* **-s, -e** German school leaving examination; ~**i'ent(in** *f*) *m* candidate for school leaving certificate.

abkämmen ['apkɛmən] *vt Gegend* comb, scour.

abkanzeln ['apkantsəln] *vt* (*col*) bawl out.

abkapseln ['apkapsəln] *vr* shut *or* cut o.s. off.

abkaufen ['apkaufən] *vt*: **jdm etw** ~ buy sth from sb.

abkehren ['apkeːrən] *vt Blick* avert, turn away; *vr* turn away.

Abklatsch ['apklatʃ] *m* **-es, -e** (*fig*) (poor) copy.

abklingen ['apklɪŋən] *vi irreg* die away; (*Radio*) fade out.

abknöpfen ['apknœpfən] *vt* unbutton; **jdm etw** ~ (*col*) get sth off sb.

abkochen ['apkɔxən] *vt* boil.

abkommen ['apkɔmən] *vi irreg* get away; **von der Straße/von einem Plan** ~ leave the road/give up a plan; **A** ~ *nt* **-s, -** agreement.

abkömmlich ['apkœmlıç] *a* available, free.

abkratzen ['apkratsən] *vt* scrape off; *vi* (*col*) kick the bucket.

abkühlen ['apkyːlən] *vt* cool down; *vr* (*Mensch*) cool down *or* off; (*Wetter*) get cool; (*Zuneigung*) cool.

Abkunft ['apkʊnft] *f* ~ origin, birth.

abkürzen ['apkyrtsən] *vt* shorten; *Wort auch* abbreviate; **den Weg** ~ take a short cut.

Abkürzung *f* (*Wort*) abbreviation; (*Weg*) short cut.

abladen ['aplaːdən] *vt irreg* unload.

Ablage ['aplaːgə] *f* **-, -n** (*für Akten*) tray; (*für Kleider*) cloakroom; **a** ~ **rn** *vt* deposit; *vr* be deposited; *vi* mature.

ablassen ['aplasən] *irreg vt Wasser, Dampf* let off; (*vom Preis*) knock off; *vi*: **von etw** ~ give sth up, abandon sth.

Ablauf ['aplauf] *m* (*Abfluß*) drain; (*von Ereignissen*) course; (*einer Frist, Zeit*) expiry; **a** ~ **en** *irreg vi* (*abfließen*) drain away; (*Ereignisse*) happen; (*Frist, Zeit, Paß*) expire; **jdm den Rang a** ~ **en** steal a march on sb.

ablegen ['apleːgən] *vt* put *or* lay down; *Kleider* take off; *Gewohnheit* get rid of; *Prüfung* sit; *Zeugnis* give.

Ableger *m* **-s, -** layer; (*fig*) branch, offshoot.

ablehnen ['apleːnən] *vt* reject; *Einladung* decline, refuse; *vi* decline, refuse.

Ablehnung *f* rejection; refusal.

ableiten ['aplaɪtən] *vt Wasser* divert; (*deduzieren*) deduce; *Wort* derive.

Ableitung *f* diversion; deduction; derivation; (*Wort*) derivative.

ablenken ['aplɛŋkən] *vt* turn away, deflect; (*zerstreuen*) distract; *vi* change the subject.

Ablenkung *f* distraction.

ablesen ['apleːzən] *vt irreg* read out; *Meßgeräte* read.

ableugnen ['aplɔygnən] *vt* deny.

ablichten ['aplıçtən] *vt* photocopy; photograph.

abliefern ['apliːfərn] *vt* deliver; **etw bei jdm/einer Dienststelle** ~ hand sth over to sb/in at an office.

Ablieferung *f* delivery; ~**schein** *m* delivery note.

abliegen ['apliːgən] *vi irreg* be some distance away; (*fig*) be far removed.

ablisten ['aplıstən] *vt*: **jdm etw** ~ trick *or* con sb out of sth.

ablösen ['apløːzən] *vt* (*abtrennen*) take off, remove; (*in Amt*) take over from; *Wache* relieve.

Ablösung *f* removal; relieving.

abmachen ['apmaxən] *vt* take off; (*vereinbaren*) agree.

Abmachung *f* agreement.

abmagern ['apmaːgərn] *vi* get thinner.

Abmagerungskur *f* diet; **eine** ~ **machen** go on a diet.

Abmarsch ['apmarʃ] *m* departure; **a** ~ **bereit** *a* ready to start; **a** ~ **ieren** *vi* march off.

abmelden ['apmɛldən] *vt Zeitungen* cancel; *Auto* take off the road; **jdn bei der Polizei** ~ register sb's departure with the police; *vr* give notice of one's departure; (*im Hotel*) check out.

abmessen ['apmɛsən] *vt irreg* measure.

Abmessung *f* measurement.

abmontieren ['apmɔntiːrən] *vt* take off.

abmühen ['apmyːən] *vr* wear o.s. out.

Abnäher ['apnɛːər] *m* **-s, -** dart.

Abnahme ['apnaːmə] *f* **-, -n** removal; (*Comm*) buying; (*Verringerung*) decrease (*gen* in).

abnehmen ['apneːmən] *irreg vt* take off, remove; *Führerschein* take away; *Geld* get (*jdm* out of sb); (*kaufen, col: glauben*) buy (*jdm* from sb); *Prüfung* hold; *Maschen* decrease; **jdm Arbeit** ~ take work off sb's shoulders; *vi* decrease; (*schlanker werden*) lose weight.

Abnehmer *m* **-s, -** purchaser, customer.

Abneigung ['apnaɪgʊŋ] *f* aversion, dislike.

abnorm [ap'nɔrm] *a* abnormal.

abnötigen ['apnøːtıgən] *vt*: **jdm etw/Respekt** ~ force sth from sb/gain sb's respect.

abnutzen ['apnutsən] *vt* wear out.

Abnutzung *f* wear (and tear).

Abonnement [abɔn(e)'mã:] *nt* **-s, -s** subscription.

Abonnent(in *f)* [abɔ'nɛnt(ɪn)] *m* subscriber.

abonnieren [abɔ'niːrən] *vt* subscribe to.

abordnen ['ap'ɔrdnən] *vt* delegate.

Abordnung *f* delegation.

Abort [a'bɔrt] *m* -**(e)s**, -**e** lavatory.

abpacken ['appakən] *vt* pack.

abpassen ['appasən] *vt Person, Gelegenheit* wait for; (*in Größe*) *Stoff etc* adjust.

abpfeifen ['appfaɪfən] *vti irreg (Sport)* **(das Spiel)** ~ blow the whistle (for the end of the game).

Abpfiff ['appfɪf] *m* final whistle.

abplagen ['applaːgən] *vr* wear o.s. out.

Abprall ['appral] *m* rebound; (*von Kugel*) ricochet; **a~en** *vi* bounce off; ricochet.

abputzen ['apputsən] *vt* clean.

abquälen ['ap-kvɛːlən] *vr* drive o.s. frantic; **sich mit etw** ~ struggle with sth.

abraten ['apraːtən] *vi irreg* advise, warn (*jdm von etw* sb against sth).

abräumen ['aprɔymən] *vt* clear up *or* away.

abreagieren ['apreagiːrən] *vt Zorn* work off (*an +dat* on); *vr* calm down.

abrechnen ['aprɛçnən] *vt* deduct, take off; *vi (lit)* settle up; (*fig*) get even.

Abrechnung *f* settlement; (*Rechnung*) bill.

Abrede ['apreːdə] *f:* **etw in** ~ **stellen** deny *or* dispute sth.

abregen ['apreːgən] *vr (col)* calm *or* cool down.

abreiben ['apraɪbən] *vtr irreg* rub off; (*säubern*) wipe; **jdn mit einem Handtuch** ~ towel sb down.

Abreise ['apraɪzə] *f* departure; **a~n** *vi* leave, set off.

abreißen ['apraɪsən] *vt irreg Haus* tear down; *Blatt* tear off.

abrichten ['aprɪçtən] *vt* train.

abriegeln ['apriːgəln] *vt Tür* bolt; *Straße, Gebiet* seal off.

Abriß ['aprɪs] *m* -**sses**, -**sse** (*Übersicht*) outline.

Abruf ['apruːf] *m:* **auf** ~ on call; **a~en** *vt irreg Mensch* call away; (*Comm*) *Ware* request delivery of.

abrunden ['aprʊndən] *vt* round off.

abrüsten ['apryːstən] *vi* disarm.

Abrüstung *f* disarmament.

abrutschen ['aprʊtʃən] *vi* slip; (*Aviat*) sideslip.

Absage ['apzaːgə] *f* -, -**n** refusal; **a~n** *vt* cancel, call off; *Einladung* turn down; *vi* cry off; (*ablehnen*) decline.

absägen ['apzɛːgən] *vt* saw off.

absahnen ['apzaːnən] *vt (lit)* skim; **das beste für sich** ~ take the cream.

Absatz ['apzats] *m (Comm)* sales *pl*; (*Bodensatz*) deposit; (*neuer Abschnitt*) paragraph; (*Treppen—*) landing; (*Schuh—*) heel; **—flaute** *f* slump in the market; **—gebiet** *nt (Comm)* market.

abschaben ['ap-ʃaːbən] *vt* scrape off; *Möhren* scrape.

abschaffen ['ap-ʃafən] *vt* abolish, do away with.

Abschaffung *f* abolition.

abschalten ['ap-ʃaltən] *vti (lit, col)* switch off.

abschattieren ['ap-ʃatiːrən] *vt* shade.

abschätzen ['ap-ʃɛtsən] *vt* estimate; *Lage* assess; *Person* size up.

abschätzig ['ap-ʃɛtsɪç] *a* disparaging, derogatory.

Abschaum ['ap-ʃaʊm] *m* -**(e)s** scum.

Abscheu ['ap-ʃɔy] *m* -**(e)s** loathing, repugnance; **a~erregend** *a* repulsive, loathsome; **a~lich** [ap'ʃɔylɪç] *a* abominable.

abschicken ['ap-ʃɪkən] *vt* send off.

abschieben ['ap-ʃiːbən] *vt irreg* push away; *Person* pack off.

Abschied ['ap-ʃiːt] *m* -**(e)s**, -**e** parting; (*von Armee*) discharge; ~ **nehmen** say good-bye (*von jdm* to sb), take one's leave (*von jdm* of sb); **seinen** ~ **nehmen** (*Mil*) apply for discharge; **zum** ~ on parting; **~sbrief** *m* farewell letter; **~sfeier** *f* farewell party.

abschießen [ap-ʃiːsən] *vt irreg Flugzeug* shoot down; *Geschoß* fire; (*col*) *Minister* get rid of.

abschirmen ['ap-ʃɪrmən] *vt* screen.

abschlagen ['ap-ʃlaːgən] *vt irreg* (*abhacken, Comm*) knock off; (*ablehnen*) refuse; (*Mil*) repel.

abschlägig ['ap-ʃlɛːgɪç] *a* negative.

Abschlagszahlung *f* interim payment.

abschleifen ['ap-ʃlaɪfən] *irreg vt* grind down; *Rost* polish off; *vr* wear off.

Abschlepp- ['ap-ʃlɛp] *cpd:* **~dienst** *m* (*Aut*) breakdown service; **a~en** *vt* take in tow; **~seil** *nt* towrope.

abschließen ['ap-ʃliːsən] *irreg vt Tür* lock; (*beenden*) conclude, finish; *Vertrag, Handel* conclude; *vr (sich isolieren)* cut o.s. off.

Abschluß ['ap-ʃlʊs] *m (Beendigung)* close, conclusion; (*Comm: Bilanz*) balancing; (*von Vertrag, Handel*) conclusion; **zum** ~ in conclusion; **~feier** *f* end-of-term party; **~rechnung** *f* final account.

abschmieren ['ap-ʃmiːrən] *vt (Aut)* grease, lubricate.

abschneiden ['ap-ʃnaɪdən] *irreg vt* cut off; *vi* do, come off.

Abschnitt ['ap-ʃnɪt] *m* section; (*Mil*) sector; (*Kontroll—*) counterfoil; (*Math*) segment; (*Zeit—*) period.

abschnüren ['ap-ʃnyːrən] *vt* constrict.

abschöpfen ['ap-ʃœpfən] *vt* skim off.

abschrauben ['ap-ʃraʊbən] *vt* unscrew.

abschrecken ['ap-ʃrɛkən] *vt* deter, put off; (*mit kaltem Wasser*) plunge in cold water; **~d** *a* deterrent; **~des Beispiel** warning.

abschreiben ['ap-ʃraɪbən] *vt irreg* copy; (*verlorengeben*) write off; (*Comm*) deduct.

Abschreibung *f (Comm)* deduction; (*Wertverminderung*) depreciation.

Abschrift ['ap-ʃrɪft] *f* copy.

abschürfen ['ap-ʃyrfən] *vt* graze.

Abschuß ['ap-ʃʊs] *m (eines Geschützes)* firing; (*Herunterschießen*) shooting down; (*Tötung*) shooting.

abschüssig ['ap-ʃysɪç] *a* steep.

abschütteln ['ap-ʃytəln] *vt* shake off.

abschwächen ['ap-ʃvɛçən] *vt* lessen;

Behauptung, Kritik tone down; *vr* lessen.
abschweifen ['ap-ʃvaɪfən] *vi* wander.
Abschweifung *f* digression.
abschwellen ['ap-ʃvɛlən] *vi* irreg
(*Geschwulst*) go down; (*Lärm*) die down.
abschwenken ['ap-ʃvɛŋkən] *vi* turn away.
abschwören ['ap-ʃvøːrən] *vi* irreg (+*dat*)
renounce.
abseh- ['apze:] *cpd*: ~**bar** a foreseeable;
in ~**barer Zeit** in the foreseeable future;
das Ende ist ~**bar** the end is in sight;
~**en** *irreg vt* Ende, Folgen foresee; **jdm**
etw ~**en** (*erlernen*) copy sth from sb; *vi*:
von etw ~**en** refrain from sth; (*nicht*
berücksichtigen) leave sth out of consideration.
abseits ['apzaɪts] *ad* out of the way; *prep*
+*gen* away from; **A**~ *nt* (*Sport*) offside;
im A~ **stehen** be offside.
Absend- ['apzɛnd] *cpd*: **a**~**en** *vt irreg* send
off, dispatch; ~**er** *m* -**s**, - sender; ~**ung** *f*
dispatch.
absetz- ['apzɛts] *cpd*: ~**bar** a *Beamter* dis-
missible; *Waren* saleable; (*von Steuer*)
deductible; ~**en** *vt* (*niederstellen*, *aus-*
steigen lassen) put down; (*abnehmen*) take
off; (*Comm: verkaufen*) sell; (*Fin: abziehen*)
deduct; (*entlassen*) dismiss; *König* depose;
(*streichen*) drop; (*hervorheben*) pick out; *vr*
(*sich entfernen*) clear off; (*sich ablagern*)
be deposited; **A**~**ung** *f* (*Fin: Abzug*) deduction; (*Entlassung*) dismissal; (*von*
König) deposing; (*Streichung*) dropping.
absichern ['apzɪçərn] *vtr* make safe;
(*schützen*) safeguard.
Absicht ['apzɪçt] *f* intention; **mit** ~ on
purpose; **a**~**lich** a intentional, deliberate;
a~**slos** a unintentional.
absinken ['apzɪŋkən] *vi* irreg sink;
(*Temperatur, Geschwindigkeit*) decrease.
absitzen ['apzɪtsən] *irreg vi* dismount; *vt*
Strafe serve.
absolut [apzo'lu:t] a absolute; **A**~**ismus**
[-'tɪsmʊs] *m* absolutism.
absolvieren [apzɔl'vi:rən] *vt* (*Sch*)
complete.
absonder- ['apzɔndər] *cpd*: ~**lich**
[ap'zɔndərlɪç] a odd, strange; ~**n** *vt*
separate; (*ausscheiden*) give off, secrete; *vr*
cut o.s. off; **A**~**ung** *f* separation; (*Med*)
secretion.
abspalten ['ap-ʃpaltən] *vt* split off.
Abspannung ['ap-ʃpanʊŋ] *f* (*Ermüdung*)
exhaustion.
absparen ['ap-ʃpa:rən] *vt*: **sich** (*dat*) **etw**
~ scrimp and save for sth.
abspeisen ['ap-ʃpaɪzən] *vt* (*fig*) fob off.
abspenstig ['ap-ʃpɛnstɪç]: ~ **machen**
lure away (*jdm* from sb).
absperren ['ap-ʃpɛrən] *vt* block or close
off; *Tür* lock.
Absperrung *f* (*Vorgang*) blocking or
closing off; (*Sperre*) barricade.
abspielen ['ap-ʃpi:lən] *vt* Platte, Tonband
play; (*Sport*) Ball pass; **vom Blatt** ~
(*Mus*) sight-read; *vr* happen.
absplittern ['ap-ʃplɪtərn] *vt* chip off.
Absprache ['ap-ʃpra:xə] *f* arrangement.
absprechen ['ap-ʃprɛçən] *vt* irreg (*verein-*
baren) arrange; **jdm etw** ~ deny sb sth.

abspringen ['ap-ʃprɪŋən] *vi* irreg jump
down/off; (*Farbe, Lack*) flake off; (*Aviat*)
bale out; (*sich distanzieren*) back out.
Absprung ['ap-ʃprʊŋ] *m* jump.
abspülen ['ap-ʃpy:lən] *vt* rinse; *Geschirr*
wash up.
abstammen ['ap-ʃtamən] *vi* be descended;
(*Wort*) be derived.
Abstammung *f* descent; derivation.
Abstand ['ap-ʃtant] *m* distance; (*zeitlich*)
interval; **davon** ~ **nehmen, etw zu tun**
refrain from doing sth; ~ **halten** (*Aut*)
keep one's distance; **mit** ~ **der beste** by
far the best; ~**ssumme** *f* compensation.
abstatten ['ap-ʃtatən] *vt* Dank give; Besuch
pay.
abstauben ['ap-ʃtaubən] *vti* dust; (*col:*
stehlen) pinch; (**den Ball**) ~ (*Sport*) tuck
the ball away.
abstechen ['ap-ʃtɛçən] *irreg vt* cut; *Tier* cut
the throat of; *vi* contrast (*gegen, von* with).
Abstecher *m* -**s**, - detour.
abstecken ['ap-ʃtɛkən] *vt* (*losmachen*)
unpin; *Fläche* mark out.
abstehen ['ap-ʃte:ən] *vi* irreg (*Ohren,*
Haare) stick out; (*entfernt sein*) stand
away.
absteigen ['ap-ʃtaɪgən] *vi* irreg (*vom Rad*
etc) get off, dismount; (*in Gasthof*) put up
(*in* +*dat* at); (*Sport*) be relegated (*in* +*acc*
to).
abstellen ['ap-ʃtɛlən] *vt* (*niederstellen*) put
down; (*entfernt stellen*) pull out; (*hinstellen*)
Auto park; (*ausschalten*) turn or switch off;
Mißstand, Unsitte stop; (*ausrichten*) gear
(*auf* +*acc* to).
Abstellgleis *nt* siding.
abstempeln ['ap-ʃtɛmpəln] *vt* stamp.
absterben ['ap-ʃtɛrbən] *vi* irreg die;
(*Körperteil*) go numb.
Abstieg ['ap-ʃti:k] *m* -(**e**)**s, -e** descent;
(*Sport*) relegation; (*fig*) decline.
abstimmen ['ap-ʃtɪmən] *vi* vote; *vt* Instrument tune (*auf* +*acc* to); *Interessen* match
(*auf* +*acc* with); *Termine, Ziele* fit in (*auf*
+*acc* with); *vr* agree.
Abstimmung *f* vote.
abstinent [apstɪ'nɛnt] a abstemious; (*von*
Alkohol) teetotal.
Abstinenz [apstɪ'nɛnts] *f* abstinence; tee-
totalism; ~**ler** *m* -**s**, - teetotaller.
abstoßen ['ap-ʃto:sən] *vt irreg* push off or
away; (*verkaufen*) unload; (*anekeln*) repel,
repulse; ~**d** a repulsive.
abstrahieren [apstra'hi:rən] *vti* abstract.
abstrakt [ap'strakt] a abstract; *ad*
abstractly, in the abstract; **A**~**ion**
[apstraktsi'o:n] *f* abstraction; **A**~**um** *nt* -**s**,
-**kta** abstract concept/noun.
abstreiten ['ap-ʃtraɪtən] *vt* irreg deny.
Abstrich ['ap-ʃtrɪç] *m* (*Abzug*) cut; (*Med*)
smear; ~**e machen** lower one's sights.
abstufen ['ap-ʃtu:fən] *vt* Hang terrace;
Farben shade; *Gehälter* grade.
abstumpfen ['ap-ʃtʊmpfən] *vt* (*lit, fig*) dull,
blunt; *vi* (*lit, fig*) become dulled.
Absturz ['ap-ʃtʊrts] *m* fall; (*Aviat*) crash.
abstürzen ['ap-ʃtʏrtsən] *vi* fall; (*Aviat*)
crash.

absuchen ['apzuːxən] *vt* scour, search.

absurd [ap'zʊrt] *a* absurd.

Abszeß [aps'tsɛs] *m* **-sses, -sse** abscess.

Abt [apt] *m* **-(e)s, ⁼e** abbot.

abtasten ['aptastən] *vt* feel, probe.

abtauen ['aptaʊən] *vti* thaw.

Abtei [ap'taɪ] *f* **-, -en** abbey.

Abteil [ap'taɪl] *nt* **-(e)s, -e** compartment; **'a~en** *vt* divide up; (*abtrennen*) divide off; **~ung** *f* (*in Firma, Kaufhaus*) department; (*Mil*) unit; **~ungsleiter** *m* head of department.

abtönen ['aptøːnən] *vt* (*Phot*) tone down.

abtragen ['aptraːgən] *vt irreg Hügel, Erde* level down; *Essen* clear away; *Kleider* wear out; *Schulden* pay off.

abträglich ['aptrɛːklɪç] *a* harmful (*dat* to).

abtransportieren ['aptransportiːrən] *vt* take away, remove.

abtreiben ['aptraɪbən] *irreg vt Boot, Flugzeug* drive off course; *Kind* abort; *vi* be driven off course; abort.

Abtreibung *f* abortion; **~sversuch** *m* attempted abortion.

abtrennen ['aptrɛnən] *vt* (*lostrennen*) detach; (*entfernen*) take off; (*abteilen*) separate off.

abtreten ['aptreːtən] *irreg vt* wear out; (*überlassen*) hand over, cede (*jdm* to sb); *vi* go off; (*zurücktreten*) step down.

Abtritt ['aptrɪt] *m* resignation.

abtrocknen ['aptrɔknən] *vti* dry.

abtrünnig ['aptrynɪç] *a* renegade.

abtun ['aptuːn] *vt irreg* take off; (*fig*) dismiss.

aburteilen ['apˈʊrtaɪlən] *vt* condemn.

abverlangen ['apˈfɛrlaŋən] *vt*: **jdm etw ~** demand sth from sb.

abwägen ['apvɛːgən] *vt irreg* weigh up.

abwählen ['apvɛːlən] *vt* vote out (of office).

abwandeln ['apvandəln] *vt* adapt.

abwandern ['apvandərn] *vi* move away.

abwarten ['apvartən] *vt* wait for; *vi* wait.

abwärts ['apvɛrts] *ad* down.

Abwasch ['apvaʃ] *m* **-(e)s** washing-up; **a~en** *vt irreg Schmutz* wash off; *Geschirr* wash (up).

Abwasser ['apvasər] *nt* **-s, -wässer** sewage.

abwechseln ['apvɛksəln] *vir* alternate; (*Personen*) take turns; **~d** *a* alternate.

Abweg ['apveːk] *m*: **auf ~e geraten/führen** go/lead astray; **a~ig** ['apveːgɪç] *a* wrong.

Abwehr ['apveːr] *f* **-** defence; (*Schutz*) protection; (*—dienst*) counter-intelligence (service); **a~en** *vt* ward off; *Ball* stop; **a~ende Geste** dismissive gesture.

abweichen ['apvaɪçən] *vi irreg* deviate; (*Meinung*) differ; **~d** *a* deviant; differing.

abweisen ['apvaɪzən] *vt irreg* turn away; *Antrag* turn down; **~d** *a Haltung* cold.

abwenden ['apvɛndən] *irreg vt* avert; *vr* turn away.

abwerben ['apvɛrbən] *vt irreg* woo away (*jdm* from sb).

abwerfen ['apvɛrfən] *vt irreg* throw off;

Profit yield; (*aus Flugzeug*) drop; *Spielkarte* discard.

abwerten ['apvɛrtən] *vt* (*Fin*) devalue.

abwesend ['apveːzənt] *a* absent.

Abwesenheit ['apveːzənhaɪt] *f* absence.

abwickeln ['apvɪkəln] *vt* unwind; *Geschäft* wind up.

abwiegen ['apviːgən] *vt irreg* weigh out.

abwimmeln ['apvɪməln] *vt* (*col*) *Person* get rid of; *Auftrag* get out of.

abwinken ['apvɪŋkən] *vi* wave it/him *etc* aside.

abwirtschaften ['apvɪrt-ʃaftən] *vi* go downhill.

abwischen ['apvɪʃən] *vt* wipe off or away; (*putzen*) wipe.

abwracken ['apvrakən] *vt Schiff* break (up); **abgewrackter Mensch** wreck of a person.

Abwurf ['apvʊrf] *m* throwing off; (*von Bomben etc*) dropping; (*von Reiter, Sport*) throw.

abwürgen ['apvʏrgən] *vt* (*col*) scotch; *Motor* stall.

abzahlen ['aptsaːlən] *vt* pay off.

abzählen ['aptsɛːlən] *vti* count (up).

Abzahlung *f* repayment; **auf ~ kaufen** buy on hire purchase.

abzapfen ['aptsapfən] *vt* draw off; **jdm Blut/Geld ~** take blood from sb/bleed sb.

abzäunen ['aptsɔʏnən] *vt* fence off.

Abzeichen ['aptsaɪçən] *nt* badge; (*Orden*) decoration.

abzeichnen ['aptsaɪçnən] *vt* draw, copy; *Dokument* initial; *vr* stand out; (*fig: bevorstehen*) loom.

Abziehbild *nt* transfer.

abziehen ['aptsiːən] *irreg vt* take off; *Tier* skin; *Bett* strip; *Truppen* withdraw; (*subtrahieren*) take away, subtract; (*kopieren*) run off; *vi* go away; (*Truppen*) withdraw.

abzielen ['aptsiːlən] *vi* be aimed (*auf +acc* at).

Abzug ['aptsuːk] *m* departure; (*von Truppen*) withdrawal; (*Kopie*) copy; (*Subtraktion*) subtraction; (*Betrag*) deduction; (*Rauch—*) flue; (*von Waffen*) trigger.

abzüglich ['aptsyːklɪç] *prep +gen* less.

abzweigen ['aptsvaɪgən] *vi* branch off; *vt* set aside.

Abzweigung *f* junction.

Accessoires [akseso'aːrs] *pl* accessories *pl*.

ach [ax] *interj* oh; **mit A~ und Krach** by the skin of one's teeth.

Achse ['aksə] *f* **-, -n** axis; (*Aut*) axle; **auf ~ sein** be on the move.

Achsel ['aksəl] *f* **-, -n** shoulder; **~höhle** *f* armpit; **~zucken** *nt* shrug (of one's shoulders).

Achsenbruch *m* (*Aut*) broken axle.

Acht [axt] *f* **-** attention; (*Hist*) proscription; **sich in ~ nehmen** be careful (*vor +dat* of), watch out (*vor +dat* for); **etw außer a~ lassen** disregard sth; **~ *f* -, -en, a~** *num* eight; **a~ Tage a week; a~bar** *a* worthy; **a~e(r,s)** *a* eighth; **~el** *num* eighth; **a~en** *vt* respect; *vi* pay attention (auf +acc to); **darauf a~en, daß** . . . be careful that . . .

ächten ['ɛçtən] vt outlaw, ban.

Achter- cpd: ~**bahn** f big dipper, roller coaster; ~**deck** nt (Naut) afterdeck.

acht- cpd: ~**fach** a eightfold; ~**geben** vi irreg take care (auf +acc of); ~**los** a careless; ~**mal** ad eight times; ~**sam** a attentive.

Achtung ['axtʊŋ] f attention; (Ehrfurcht) respect; interj look out!; (Mil) attention!; ~ **Lebensgefahr/Stufe!** danger/mind the step!

acht- cpd: ~**zehn** num eighteen; ~**zig** num eighty; **A~ziger(in** f) m -s, - octogenarian; **A~zigerjahre** pl eighties pl.

ächzen ['ɛçtsən] vi groan (vor +dat with).

Acker ['akər] m -s, ∺ field; ~**bau** m agriculture; **a~n** vti plough; (col) slog away.

addieren [a'di:rən] vt add (up).

Addition [aditsi'o:n] f addition.

Ade [a'de:] nt -s, -s, **a~** interj farewell, adieu.

Adel ['a:dəl] m -s nobility; **a~ig, adlig** a noble.

Ader ['a:dər] f -, -n vein.

Adjektiv ['atjɛkti:f] nt -s, -e adjective.

Adler ['a:dlər] m -s, - eagle.

Admiral [atmi'ra:l] m -s, -e admiral; ~**i-'tät** f admiralty.

adopt- cpd: ~**ieren** [adɔp'ti:rən] vt adopt; **A~ion** [adɔptsi'o:n] f adoption; **A~iveltern** [adɔp'ti:f-] f adoptive parents pl; **A~ivkind** nt adopted child.

Adress- cpd: ~**ant** [adrɛ'sant] m sender; ~**at** [adrɛ'sa:t] m -en, -en addressee; ~**e** [a'drɛsə] f -, -n address; **a~ieren** [adrɛ'si:rən] vt address (an +acc to).

Advent [at'vɛnt] m -(e)s, -e Advent; ~**skranz** m Advent wreath.

Adverb [at'vɛrp] nt adverb; **a~ial** [atvɛrbi'a:l] a adverbial.

aero- [aero] pref aero-.

Affäre [a'fɛ:rə] f -, -n affair.

Affe ['afə] m -n, -n monkey.

affektiert [afɛk'ti:rt] a affected.

Affen- cpd: **a~artig** a like a monkey; **mit a~artiger Geschwindigkeit** like a flash; ~**hitze** f (col) incredible heat; ~**schande** f (col) crying shame.

affig ['afɪç] a affected.

After ['aftər] m -s, - anus.

Agent [a'gɛnt] m agent; ~**ur** [-'tu:r] f agency.

Aggregat [agre'ga:t] nt -(e)s, -e aggregate; (Tech) unit; ~**zustand** m (Phys) state.

Aggress- cpd: ~**ion** [agrɛsi'o:n] f aggression; **a~iv** [agrɛ'si:f] a aggressive; ~**ivität** [agrɛsivi'tɛ:t] f aggressiveness.

Agitation [agitatsi'o:n] f agitation.

Agrar- [a'gra:r] cpd: ~**politik** f agricultural policy; ~**staat** m agrarian state.

aha [a'ha:] interj aha.

Ahn [a:n] m -en, -en forebear.

ähneln ['ɛ:nəln] vi (+dat) be like, resemble; vr be alike or similar.

ahnen ['a:nən] vt suspect; Tod, Gefahr have a presentiment of; **du ahnst es nicht** you have no idea.

ähnlich ['ɛ:nlɪç] a similar (dat to); **Ä~keit** f similarity.

Ahnung ['a:nʊŋ] f idea, suspicion; presentiment; **a~slos** a unsuspecting.

Ahorn ['a:hɔrn] m -s, -e maple.

Ähre ['ɛ:rə] f -, -n ear.

Akademie [akade'mi:] f academy.

Akademiker(in f) [aka'de:mikər(ɪn)] m -s, - university graduate.

akademisch a academic.

akklimatisieren [aklimati'zi:rən] vr become acclimatized.

Akkord [a'kɔrt] m -(e)s, -e (Mus) chord; **im ~ arbeiten** do piecework; ~**arbeit** f piecework; ~**eon** [a'kɔrdeɔn] nt -s, -s accordion.

Akkusativ ['akuzati:f] m -s, -e accusative (case).

Akrobat(in f) [akro'ba:t(ɪn)] m -en, -en acrobat.

Akt [akt] m -(e)s, -e act; (Art) nude.

Akte ['aktə] f -, -n file; **etw zu den ~n legen** (lit, fig) file sth away; **a~nkundig** a on the files; ~**nschrank** m filing cabinet; ~**ntasche** f briefcase.

Aktie ['aktsiə] f -, -n share; ~**ngesellschaft** f joint-stock company; ~**nkurs** m share price.

Aktion [aktsi'o:n] f campaign; (Polizei-, Such-) action; ~**är** ['nɛ:r] m -s, -e shareholder.

aktiv [ak'ti:f] a active; (Mil) regular; **A~** nt -s (Gram) active (voice); **A~a** [ak'ti:va] pl assets pl; ~**ieren** [-'vi:rən] vt activate; **A~i'tät** f activity; **A~saldo** m (Comm) credit balance.

Aktualität [aktuali'tɛ:t] f topicality; (einer Mode) up-to-dateness.

aktuell [aktu'el] a topical; up-to-date.

Akustik [a'kʊstɪk] f acoustics pl.

akut [a'ku:t] a acute.

Akzent [ak'tsɛnt] m accent; (Betonung) stress.

akzeptieren [aktsep'ti:rən] vt accept.

Alarm [a'larm] m -(e)s, -e alarm; **a~bereit** a standing by; ~**bereitschaft** f stand-by; **a~ieren** [-'mi:rən] vt alarm.

albern ['albərn] a silly.

Album ['album] nt -s, **Alben** album.

Algebra ['algebra] f - algebra.

alias ['a:lias] ad alias.

Alibi ['a:libi] nt -s, -s alibi.

Alimente [ali'mɛntə] pl alimony.

Alkohol ['alkohɔl] m -s, -e alcohol **a~frei** a non-alcoholic; ~**iker(in** f) [alko'ho:likər(ɪn)] m -s, - alcoholic; **a~isch** a alcoholic; ~**verbot** nt ban on alcohol.

All [al] nt -s universe; **a~'abendlich** a every evening; **a~bekannt** a universally known; **a~e(r,s)** a all; **wir a~e** all of us; **a~e beide** both of us/you etc; **a~e vier Jahre** every four years; ad (col: zu Ende) finished; **etw a~e machen** finish sth up.

Allee [a'le:] f -, -n avenue.

allein [a'lain] ad alone; (ohne Hilfe) on

one's own, by oneself; **nicht** ~ (*nicht nur*) not only; *cj* but, only; **A~gang** *m*: **im A~gang** on one's own; **A~herrscher** *m* autocrat; **A~hersteller** *m* sole manufacturer; ~**stehend** *a* single.

alle- *cpd:* ~**mal** *ad* (*jedesmal*) always; (*ohne weiteres*) with no bother; **ein für ~mal** once and for all; ~**nfalls** *ad* at all events; (*höchstens*) at most; ~**rbeste(r,s)** *a* very best; ~**rdings** *ad* (*zwar*) admittedly; (*gewiß*) certainly.

allerg- *cpd:* ~**isch** [a'lɛrgɪʃ] *a* allergic; **A~ie** [-'giː] *f* allergy.

aller- ['alər] *cpd:* ~**hand** *a inv* (*col*) all sorts of; **das ist doch ~hand!** that's a bit thick; ~**hand!** (*lobend*) good show!; **A~-heiligen** *nt* All Saints' Day; ~**höchste(r,s)** *a* very highest; ~**höchstens** *ad* at the very most; ~**lei** *a inv* all sorts of; ~**letzte(r,s)** *a* very last; ~**seits** *ad* on all sides; **prost ~seits!** cheers everyone!; ~**wenigste(r,s)** *a* very least.

alles *pron* everything; ~ **in allem** all in all.

allgemein ['algə'maɪn] *a* general; ~**gültig** *a* generally accepted; **A~heit** *f* (*Menschen*) general public; (*pl: Redensarten*) general remarks *pl*.

Alliierte(r) [ali'iːrtə(r)] *f* mally.

all- *cpd:* ~**jährlich** *a* annual; ~**mählich** *a* gradual; **A~tag** *m* everyday life; ~**täglich** *a,ad* daily; (*gewöhnlich*) commonplace; ~**tags** *ad* on weekdays; ~**'wissend** *a* omniscient; ~**zu** *ad* all too; ~**zuoft** *ad* all too often; ~**zuviel** *ad* too much.

Almosen ['almoːzən] *nt* **-s**, - alms *pl*.

Alpen ['alpən] *pl* Alps *pl*; ~**blume** *f* alpine flower.

Alphabet [alfa'beːt] *nt* **-(e)s, -e** alphabet; **a~isch** *a* alphabetical.

Alptraum ['alptraum] *m* nightmare.

als [als] *cj* (*zeitlich*) when; (*comp*) than; (*Gleichheit*) as; **nichts** ~ nothing but; ~ **ob** as if.

also ['alzoː] *cj* so; (*folglich*) therefore; **ich komme** ~ **morgen** so I'll come tomorrow; ~ **gut** *or* **schön!** okay then; ~**, so was!** well really!; **na** ~! there you are then!

alt [alt] *a* old; **ich bin nicht mehr der** ~**e** I am not the man I was; **alles beim** ~**en lassen** leave everything as it was; **A~** *m* **-s, -e** (*Mus*) alto; **A~ar** [al'taːr] *m* **-(e)s, -äre** altar; ~**bekannt** *a* long-known; **A~'eisen** *nt* scrap iron.

Alter ['altər] *nt* **-s, -** age; (*hohes*) old age; **im** ~ **von** at the age of; **a~n** *vi* grow old, age; ~**na'tive** *f* alternative; ~**sgrenze** *f* age limit; ~**sheim** *nt* old people's home; ~**sversorgung** *f* old age pension; ~**tum** *nt* antiquity.

alt- *cpd:* ~**'hergebracht** *a* traditional; ~**klug** *a* precocious; ~**modisch** *a* old-fashioned; **A~papier** *nt* waste paper; **A~stadt** *f* old town; **A~stimme** *f* alto; **A~'weibersommer** *m* Indian summer.

Aluminium   [alu'miːnium]   *nt*   **-s**

aluminium, aluminum (*US*); ~**folie** *f* tinfoil.

am [am] = **an dem**; ~ **Sterben** on the point of dying; ~ **15. März** on March 15th; ~ **besten/schönsten** best/most beautiful.

Amalgam [amal'gaːm] *nt* **-s, -e** amalgam.

Amateur [ama'tøːr] *m* amateur.

Amboß ['ambɔs] *m* **-sses, -sse** anvil.

ambulant [ambu'lant] *a* outpatient.

Ameise ['aːmaɪzə] *f* **-, -n** ant.

Ampel ['ampəl] *f* **-, -n** traffic lights *pl*.

amphibisch [am'fiːbɪʃ] *a* amphibious.

amputieren [ampu'tiːrən] *vt* amputate.

Amsel ['amzəl] *f* **-, -n** blackbird.

Amt [amt] *nt* **-(e)s, -̈er** office; (*Pflicht*) duty; (*Tel*) exchange; **a~ieren** [am'tiːrən] *vi* hold office; **a~lich** *a* official; ~**sperson** *f* official; ~**srichter** *m* district judge; ~**sstunden** *pl* office hours *pl*; ~**szeit** *f* period of office.

amüsant [amy'zant] *a* amusing.

Amüsement [amyzə'mã:] *nt* amusement.

amüsieren [amy'ziːrən] *vt* amuse; *vr* enjoy o.s.

an [an] *prep +dat* (*räumlich*) at; (*auf, bei*) on; (*nahe bei*) near; (*zeitlich*) on; +*acc* (*räumlich*) (on)to; ~ **Ostern** at Easter; ~ **diesem Ort/Tag** at this place/on this day; ~ **und für sich** actually; *ad:* **von ... ~ from ... on**; ~ **die 5 DM** around 5 marks; **das Licht ist** ~ the light is on.

analog [ana'loːk] *a* analogous; **A~ie** [-'giː] *f* analogy.

Analyse [ana'lyːzə] *f* **-, -n** analysis.

analysieren [analy'ziːrən] *vt* analyse.

Ananas ['ananas] *f* **-, -** *or* **-se** pineapple.

Anarchie [anar'çiː] *f* anarchy.

Anatomie [anato'miː] *f* anatomy.

anbahnen ['anbaːnən] *vtr* open up.

anbändeln ['anbɛndəln] *vi* (*col*) flirt.

Anbau ['anbau] *m* (*Agr*) cultivation; (*Gebäude*) extension; **a~en** *vt* (*Agr*) cultivate; *Gebäudeteil* build on.

anbehalten ['anbəhaltən] *vt irreg* keep on.

anbei [an'baɪ] *ad* enclosed.

anbeißen ['anbaɪsən] *irreg vt* bite into; *vi* (*lit*) bite; (*fig*) swallow the bait; **zum A~** (*col*) good enough to eat.

anbelangen ['anbəlaŋən] *vt* concern; **was mich anbelangt** as far as I am concerned.

anberaumen ['anbəraumən] *vt* fix.

anbeten ['anbeːtən] *vt* worship.

Anbetracht ['anbətraxt] *m*: **in** ~ (+*gen*) in view of.

Anbetung *f* worship.

anbiedern ['anbiːdərn] *vr* make up (*bei* to).

anbieten ['anbiːtən] *irreg vt* offer; *vr* volunteer.

anbinden ['anbɪndən] *irreg vt* tie up; *vi*: **mit jdm** ~ start something with sb; **kurz angebunden** (*fig*) curt.

Anblick ['anblɪk] *m* sight; **a~en** *vt* look at.

anbrechen ['anbrɛçən] *irreg vt* start; *Vorräte* break into; *vi* start; (*Tag*) break; (*Nacht*) fall.

anbrennen ['anbrɛnən] *vi irreg* catch fire; (*Cook*) burn.

anbringen ['anbrɪŋən] *vt irreg* bring; *Ware* sell; (*festmachen*) fasten.

Anbruch ['anbrux] *m* beginning; ~ des Tages/der Nacht dawn/nightfall.

anbrüllen ['anbrʏlən] *vt* roar at.

Andacht ['andaxt] *f* -, -en devotion; (*Gottesdienst*) prayers *pl*.

andächtig ['andɛçtɪç] *a* devout.

andauern ['andaʊərn] *vi* last, go on; ~d a continual.

Andenken ['andɛŋkən] *nt* -s, - memory; souvenir.

andere(r,s) ['andərə(r,z)] *a* other; (*verschieden*) different; **am** ~n **Tage** the next day; **ein** ~s **Mal** another time; **kein** ~r nobody else; **von etw** ~m **sprechen** talk about sth else; ~nteils, ~rseits *ad* on the other hand.

ändern ['ɛndərn] *vt* alter, change; *vr* change.

ander- *cpd:* ~nfalls *ad* otherwise; ~s *ad* differently (*als* from); **wer** ~s? who else?; **jd/irgendwo** ~s *sb*/somewhere else; ~s **aussehen/klingen** look/sound different; ~sartig *a* different; ~seits *ad* on the other hand; ~sfarbig *a* of a different colour; ~sgläubig *a* of a different faith; ~sherum *ad* the other way round; ~swo *ad* elsewhere; ~swoher *ad* from elsewhere; ~swohin *ad* elsewhere.

anderthalb ['andərt'halp] *a* one and a half.

Änderung ['ɛndərʊŋ] *f* alteration, change.

anderweitig ['andər'vaɪtɪç] *a* other; *ad* otherwise; (*anderswo*) elsewhere.

andeuten ['andɔʏtən] *vt* indicate; (*Wink geben*) hint at.

Andeutung *f* indication; hint.

Andrang ['andraŋ] *m* crush.

andrehen ['andre:ən] *vt* turn *or* switch on; (*col*) **jdm etw** ~ unload sth onto sb.

androhen ['andro:ən] *vt:* **jdm etw** ~ threaten sb with sth.

aneignen ['an'aɪgnən] *vt:* **sich** (*dat*) **etw** ~ acquire sth; (*widerrechtlich*) appropriate sth.

aneinander [an'aɪ'nandər] *ad* at/on/to *etc* one another *or* each other; ~fügen *vt* put together; ~geraten *vi irreg* clash; ~legen *vt* put together.

anekeln ['an'e:kəln] *vt* disgust.

Anemone [ane'mo:nə] *f* -, -n anemone.

anerkannt ['an'ɛrkant] *a* recognized, acknowledged.

anerkennen ['an'ɛrkɛnən] *vt irreg* recognize, acknowledge; (*würdigen*) appreciate; ~d *a* appreciative; ~swert *a* praiseworthy.

Anerkennung *f* recognition, acknowledgement; appreciation.

anfachen ['anfaxən] *vt* (*lit*) fan into flame; (*fig*) kindle.

anfahren ['anfa:rən] *irreg vt* deliver; (*fahren gegen*) hit; *Hafen* put into; (*fig*) bawl out; *vi* drive up; (*losfahren*) drive off.

Anfall ['anfal] *m* (*Med*) attack; **a**~en *irreg vt* attack; (*fig*) overcome; *vi* (*Arbeit*) come up; (*Produkt*) be obtained.

anfällig ['anfɛlɪç] *a* delicate; ~ **für etw** prone to sth.

Anfang ['anfaŋ] *m* -(e)s, -fänge beginning, start; **von** ~ **an** right from the beginning; **zu** ~ at the beginning; ~ **Mai** at the beginning of May; **a**~**en** *vti irreg* begin, start; (*machen*) do.

Anfänger(in *f*) ['anfɛŋər(ɪn)] *m* -s, - beginner.

anfänglich ['anfɛŋlɪç] *a* initial.

anfangs *ad* at first; **A**~**buchstabe** *m* initial *or* first letter; **A**~**stadium** *nt* initial stages *pl*.

anfassen ['anfasən] *vt* handle; (*berühren*) touch; *vi* lend a hand; *vr* feel.

anfechten ['anfɛçtən] *vt irreg* dispute; (*beunruhigen*) trouble.

anfertigen ['anfɛrtɪgən] *vt* make.

anfeuern ['anfɔʏərn] *vt* (*fig*) spur on.

anflehen ['anfle:ən] *vt* implore.

anfliegen ['anfli:gən] *irreg vt* fly to; *vi* fly up.

Anflug ['anflu:k] *m* (*Aviat*) approach; (*Spur*) trace.

anfordern ['anfɔrdərn] *vt* demand.

Anforderung *f* demand (*gen* for).

Anfrage ['anfra:gə] *f* inquiry; **a**~**n** *vi* inquire.

anfreunden ['anfrɔʏndən] *vr* make friends.

anfügen ['anfy:gən] *vt* add; (*beifügen*) enclose.

anfühlen ['anfy:lən] *vtr* feel.

anführen ['anfy:rən] *vt* lead; (*zitieren*) quote; (*col: betrügen*) lead up the garden path.

Anführer *m* leader.

Anführung *f* leadership; (*Zitat*) quotation; ~striche, ~zeichen *pl* quotation marks *pl*, inverted commas *pl*.

Angabe ['anga:bə] *f* statement; (*Tech*) specification; (*col: Prahlerei*) boasting; (*Sport*) service; ~**n** *pl* (*Auskunft*) particulars *pl*.

angeben ['ange:bən] *irreg vt* give; (*anzeigen*) inform on; (*bestimmen*) set; *vi* (*col*) boast; (*Sport*) serve.

Angeber *m* -s, - (*col*) show-off; ~**ei** [-'raɪ] *f* (*col*) showing off.

angeblich ['ange:plɪç] *a* alleged.

angeboren ['angəbo:rən] *a* inborn, innate (*jdm in sb*).

Angebot ['angəbo:t] *nt* offer; (*Comm*) supply (*an* +*dat* of).

angebracht ['angəbraxt] *a* appropriate, in order.

angegriffen ['angəgrɪfən] *a* exhausted.

angeheitert ['angəhaɪtərt] *a* tipsy.

angehen ['ange:ən] *irreg vt* concern; (*angreifen*) attack; (*bitten*) approach (*um* for); *vi* (*Feuer*) light; (*col: beginnen*) begin; ~d *a* prospective; **er ist ein** ~**der Vierziger** he is approaching forty.

angehören ['angəhø:rən] *vi* belong (*dat* to).

Angehörige(r) *mf* relative.

Angeklagte(r) ['angəkla:ktə(r)] *mf* accused.

Angel ['aŋəl] *f* -, -**n** fishing rod; (*Tür*—) hinge.

Angelegenheit ['angələ:gənhaıt] *f* affair, matter.

Angel- *cpd*: ~**haken** *m* fish hook; **a**~**n** *vt* catch; *vi* fish; ~**n** *nt* -**s** angling, fishing; ~**rute** *f* fishing rod.

angemessen ['angəmɛsən] *a* appropriate, suitable.

angenehm ['angəne:m] *a* pleasant; ~! (*bei Vorstellung*) pleased to meet you; **jdm** ~ **sein** be welcome.

angenommen ['angənɔmən] *a* assumed; ~, **wir** ... assuming we....

angesehen ['angəze:ən] *a* respected.

angesichts ['angəzıçts] *prep* +*gen* in view of, considering.

angespannt ['angəʃpant] *a* *Aufmerksamkeit* close; *Arbeit* hard.

Angestellte(r) ['angəʃtɛltə(r)] *mf* employee.

angetan ['angəta:n] *a*: **von jdm/etw** ~ **sein** be impressed by sb/sth; **es jdm** ~ **haben** appeal to sb.

angewiesen ['angəvi:zən] *a*: **auf jdn/etw** ~ **sein** be dependent on sb/sth.

angewöhnen ['angəvø:nən] *vt*: **jdm/sich etw** ~ get sb/become accustomed to sth.

Angewohnheit ['angəvo:nhaıt] *f* habit.

angleichen ['anglaıçən] *vtr irreg* adjust (*dat* to).

Angler ['aŋlər] *m* -**s**, - angler.

angreifen ['angraıfən] *vt irreg* attack; (*anfassen*) touch; *Arbeit* tackle; (*beschädigen*) damage.

Angreifer *m* -**s**, - attacker.

Angriff ['angrıf] *m* attack; **etw in** ~ **nehmen** make a start on sth.

Angst [aŋst] *f* -, *̈*e fear; ~ **haben** be afraid *or* scared (*vor* +*dat* of); ~ **haben um jdn/etw** be worried about sb/sth; **nur keine** ~! don't be scared; **a**~ **ist a**~ sb is afraid *or* scared; **jdm a**~ **machen** scare sb; ~**hase** *m* (*col*) chicken, scaredy-cat.

ängst- [ɛŋst] *cpd*: ~**igen** *vt* frighten; *vr* worry (o.s.) (*vor* +*dat*, *um* about); ~**lich** *a* nervous; (*besorgt*) worried; **Ä**~**lichkeit** *f* nervousness.

anhaben ['anha:bən] *vt irreg* have on; **er kann mir nichts** ~ he can't hurt me.

anhalt- ['anhalt] *cpd*: ~**en** *irreg vt* stop; (*gegen etw halten*) hold up (*jdm against* sb); **jdn zur Arbeit/Höflichkeit** ~**en** make sb work/be polite; *vi* stop; (*andauern*) persist; ~**end** a persistent; **A**~**er** *m* -**s**, - hitch-hiker; **per A**~**er fahren** hitch-hike; **A**~**spunkt** *m* clue.

anhand [an'hant] *prep* +*gen* with.

Anhang ['anhaŋ] *m* appendix; (*Leute*) family; supporters *pl*.

anhäng- ['anhɛŋ] *cpd*: ~**en** *vt irreg* hang up; *Wagen* couple up; *Zusatz* add (on); **sich an jdn** ~**en** attach o.s. to sb; **A**~**er** *m* -**s**, - supporter; (*Aut*) trailer; (*am Koffer*) tag; (*Schmuck*) pendant; **A**~**erschaft** *f* supporters *pl*; **A**~**eschloß** *nt* padlock; ~**ig** a (*Jur*) sub judice; ~**ig machen** *Prozeß* bring; ~**lich** a devoted; **A**~**lichkeit** *f* devotion; **A**~**sel** *nt* -**s**, - appendage.

Anhäufung ['anhɔyfuŋ] *f* accumulation.

anheben ['anhe:bən] *vt irreg* lift up; *Preise* raise.

anheimelnd ['anhaıməlnt] *a* comfortable, cosy.

anheimstellen [an'haımʃtɛlən] *vt*: **jdm etw** ~ leave sth up to sb.

Anhieb ['anhi:b] *m*: **auf** ~ at the very first go; (*kurz entschlossen*) on the spur of the moment.

Anhöhe ['anhø:ə] *f* hill.

anhören ['anhø:rən] *vt* listen to; (*anmerken*) hear; *vr* sound.

animieren [ani'mi:rən] *vt* encourage, urge on.

Anis [a'ni:s] *m* -**es**, -**e** aniseed.

ankaufen ['ankaofən] *vt* purchase, buy.

Anker ['aŋkər] *m* -**s**, - anchor; **vor** ~ **gehen** drop anchor; **a**~**n** *vti* anchor; ~**platz** *m* anchorage.

Anklage ['ankla:gə] *f* accusation; (*Jur*) charge; ~**bank** *f* dock; **a**~**n** *vt* accuse; (*Jur*) charge (*gen* with).

Ankläger ['anklɛ:gər] *m* accuser.

Anklang ['anklaŋ] *m*: **bei jdm** ~ **finden** meet with sb's approval.

Ankleide- ['anklaıdə] *cpd*: ~**kabine** *f* changing cubicle; **a**~**n** *vtr* dress.

anklopfen ['anklɔpfən] *vi* knock.

anknüpfen ['anknʏpfən] *vt* fasten *or* tie on; (*fig*) start; *vi* (*anschließen*) refer (*an* +*acc* to).

ankommen ['ankɔmən] *vi irreg* arrive; (*näherkommen*) approach; (*Anklang finden*) go down (*bei* with); **es kommt darauf an** it depends; (*wichtig sein*) that (is what) matters; **es kommt auf ihn an** it depends on him; **es darauf** ~ **lassen** let things take their course; **gegen jdn/etw** ~ cope with sb/sth.

ankündigen ['ankʏndıgən] *vt* announce.

Ankündigung *f* announcement.

Ankunft ['ankunft] *f* -, -**künfte** arrival; ~**szeit** *f* time of arrival.

ankurbeln ['ankurbəln] *vt* (*Aut*) crank; (*fig*) boost.

Anlage ['anla:gə] *f* disposition; (*Begabung*) talent; (*Park*) gardens *pl*; (*Beilage*) enclosure; (*Tech*) plant; (*Fin*) investment; (*Entwurf*) layout.

anlangen ['anlaŋən] *vi* arrive.

Anlaß ['anlas] *m* -**sses**, -**lässe** cause (*zu* for); (*Ereignis*) occasion; **aus** ~ (+*gen*) on the occasion of; ~ **zu etw geben** give rise to sth; **etw zum** ~ **nehmen** take the opportunity of sth.

anlassen *irreg vt* leave on; *Motor* start; *vr* (*col*) start off.

Anlasser *m* -**s**, - (*Aut*) starter.

anläßlich ['anlɛslıç] *prep* +*gen* on the occasion of.

Anlauf ['anlaof] *m* run-up; **a**~**en** *irreg vi* begin; (*Film*) show; (*Sport*) run up; (*Fenster*) mist up; (*Metall*) tarnish; *rot* **a**~**en** colour; **gegen etw a**~**en** run into *or* up against sth; **angelaufen kommen** come running up; *vt* call at.

anläuten ['anlɔytən] *vi* ring.

anlegen ['anle:gən] *vt* put (*an* +*acc*

against/on); (*anziehen*) put on; (*gestalten*) lay out; *Geld* invest; *Gewehr* aim (*auf* +acc at); **es auf etw** (*acc*) ~ be out for sth/to do sth; **sich mit jdm** ~ (*col*) quarrel with sb; *vi* dock.

Anlegestelle *f*, **Anlegeplatz** *m* landing place.

anlehnen ['anle:nən] *vt* lean (*an* +acc against); *Tür* leave ajar; *vr* lean (*an* +acc on).

anleiten ['anlaɪtən] *vt* instruct.

Anleitung *f* instructions *pl*.

anlernen ['anlɛrnən] *vt* teach, instruct.

anliegen ['anli:gən] *vi irreg* (*Kleidung*) cling; **A~** *nt* **-s**, - matter; (*Wunsch*) wish; ~**d** a adjacent; (*beigefügt*) enclosed.

Anlieger *m* **-s**, - resident.

anlügen ['anly:gən] *vt irreg* lie to.

anmachen ['anmaxən] *vt* attach; *Elektrisches* put on; *Salat* dress.

anmaßen ['anma:sən] *vt*: **sich** (*dat*) **etw** ~ lay claim to sth; ~**d** a arrogant.

Anmaßung *f* presumption.

Anmeld- ['anmɛld] *cpd*: ~**eformular** *nt* registration form; **a~en** *vt* announce; *vr* (*sich ankündigen*) make an appointment; (*polizeilich, für Kurs etc*) register; ~**ung** *f* announcement; appointment; registration.

anmerken ['anmɛrkən] *vt* observe; (*anstreichen*) mark; **jdm etw** ~ notice sb's sth; **sich** (*dat*) **nichts** ~ **lassen** not give anything away.

Anmerkung *f* note.

Anmut ['anmu:t] *f* - grace; **a~en** *vt* give a feeling; **a~ig** a charming.

annähen ['annɛ:ən] *vt* sew on.

annähern ['annɛ:ərn] *vr* get closer; ~**d** a approximate.

Annäherung *f* approach; ~**sversuch** *m* advances *pl*.

Annahme ['anna:mə] *f* -, **-n** acceptance; (*Vermutung*) assumption.

annehm- ['anne:m] *cpd*: ~**bar** a acceptable; ~**en** *irreg vt* accept; *Namen* take; *Kind* adopt; (*vermuten*) suppose, assume; **angenommen, das ist so** assuming that is so; *vr* take care (*gen* of); **A~lichkeit** *f* comfort.

annektieren [anɛk'ti:rən] *vt* annex.

Annonce [a'nõ:sə] *f* -, **-n** advertisement.

annoncieren [anõ'si:rən] *vti* advertise.

annullieren [anʊ'li:rən] *vt* annul.

Anode [a'no:də] *f* -, **-n** anode.

anöden ['an'ö:dən] *vt* (*col*) bore stiff.

anonym [ano'ny:m] a anonymous.

Anorak ['anorak] *m* **-s, -s** anorak.

anordnen ['an'ɔrdnən] *vt* arrange; (*befehlen*) order.

Anordnung *f* arrangement; order.

anorganisch ['an'ɔrga:nɪʃ] a inorganic.

anpacken ['anpakən] *vt* grasp; (*fig*) tackle; **mit** ~ lend a hand.

anpassen ['anpasən] *vt* fit (*jdm* on sb); (*fig*) adapt (*dat* to); *vr* adapt.

Anpassung *f* fitting; adaptation; **a~sfähig** a adaptable.

Anpfiff ['anpfɪf] *m* (*Sport*) (starting) whistle; kick-off; (*col*) rocket.

anpöbeln ['anpö:bəln] *vt* abuse.

Anprall ['anpral] *m* collision (*gegen, an* +acc with).

anprangern ['anpraŋərn] *vt* denounce.

anpreisen ['anpraɪzən] *vt irreg* extol.

Anprobe ['anpro:bə] *f* trying on.

anprobieren ['anprobi:rən] *vt* try on.

anrechnen ['anrɛçnən] *vt* charge; (*fig*) count; **jdm etw hoch** ~ value sb's sth greatly.

Anrecht ['anrɛçt] *nt* right (*auf* +acc to).

Anrede ['anre:də] *f* form of address; **a~n** *vt* address; (*belästigen*) accost.

anregen ['anre:gən] *vt* stimulate; **angeregte Unterhaltung** lively discussion; ~**d** a stimulating.

Anregung *f* stimulation; (*Vorschlag*) suggestion.

anreichern ['anraɪçərn] *vt* enrich.

Anreise ['anraɪzə] *f* journey; **a~n** *vi* arrive.

Anreiz ['anraɪts] *m* incentive.

Anrichte ['anrɪçtə] *f* **-**, **-n** sideboard; **a~n** *vt* serve up; **Unheil a~n** make mischief.

anrüchig ['anryçɪç] a dubious.

anrücken ['anrykən] *vi* approach; (*Mil*) advance.

Anruf ['anru:f] *m* call; **a~en** *vt irreg* call out to; (*bitten*) call on; (*Tel*) ring up, phone, call.

anrühren ['anry:rən] *vt* touch; (*mischen*) mix.

ans [ans] = **an das**.

Ansage ['anza:gə] *f* **-**, **-n** announcement; **a~n** *vt* announce; *vr* say one will come; ~**r(in** *f***)** *m* **-s**, - announcer.

ansammeln ['anzaməln] *vtr* collect.

Ansammlung *f* collection; (*Leute*) crowd.

ansässig ['anzɛsɪç] a resident.

Ansatz ['anzats] *m* start; (*Haar—*) hairline; (*Hals—*) base; (*Verlängerungsstück*) extension; (*Veranschlagung*) estimate; **die ersten Ansätze zu etw** the beginnings of sth; ~**punkt** *m* starting point.

anschaffen ['anʃafən] *vt* buy, purchase.

Anschaffung *f* purchase.

anschalten ['anʃaltən] *vt* switch on.

anschau- ['anʃaʊ] *cpd*: ~**en** *vt* look at; ~**lich** a illustrative; **A~ung** *f* (*Meinung*) view; **aus eigener A~ung** from one's own experience; **A~ungsmaterial** *nt* illustrative material.

Anschein ['anʃaɪn] *m* appearance; **allem** ~ **nach** to all appearances; **den** ~ **haben** seem, appear; **a~end** a apparent.

Anschlag ['anʃla:k] *m* notice; (*Attentat*) attack; (*Comm*) estimate; (*auf Klavier*) touch; (*Schreibmaschine*) character; **a~en** ['anʃla:gən] *irreg vt* put up; (*beschädigen*) chip; *Akkord* strike; *Kosten* estimate; *vi* hit (*an* +acc against); (*wirken*) have an effect; (*Glocke*) ring; (*Hund*) bark; ~**zettel** *m* notice.

anschließen ['anʃli:sən] *irreg vt* connect up; *Sender* link up; *vr*: (**sich**) **an etw** (*acc*) ~ adjoin sth; (*zeitlich*) follow sth; *vr* join (*jdm/etw* sb/sth); (*beipflichten*) agree (*jdm/etw* with sb/sth); ~**d** a adjacent; (*zeitlich*) subsequent; *ad* afterwards; ~**d an** (+acc) following.

Anschluß ['anʃlʊs] m (Elec, Rail) connection; (von Wasser etc) supply; **im ~ an** (+acc) following; **~ finden** make friends.

anschmiegsam ['anʃmi:kza:m] a affectionate.

anschmieren ['anʃmi:rən] vt smear; (col) take in.

anschnallen ['anʃnalən] vt buckle on; vr fasten one's seat belt.

anschneiden ['anʃnaidən] vt irreg cut into; Thema broach.

Anschnitt ['anʃnɪt] m first slice.

anschreiben ['anʃraibən] vt irreg write (up); (Comm) charge up; (benachrichtigen) write to; **bei jdm gut/schlecht angeschrieben sein** be well/badly thought of by sb, be in sb's good/bad books.

anschreien ['anʃraiən] vt irreg shout at.

Anschrift ['anʃrɪft] f address.

Anschuldigung ['anʃʊldɪgʊŋ] f accusation.

anschwellen ['anʃvɛlən] vi irreg swell (up).

anschwemmen ['anʃvɛmən] vt wash ashore.

anschwindeln ['anʃvɪndəln] vt lie to.

ansehen ['anze:ən] vt irreg look at; **jdm etw ~** see sth (from sb's face); **jdn/etw als etw ~** look on sb/sth as sth; **~ für** consider; **A~** nt **-s** respect; (Ruf) reputation.

ansehnlich ['anze:nlɪç] a fine-looking; (beträchtlich) considerable.

ansein ['anzain] vi irreg (col) be on.

ansetzen ['anzɛtsən] vt (anfügen) fix on (an +acc to); (anlegen, an Mund etc) put (an +acc to); (festlegen) fix; (entwickeln) develop; Fett put on; Blätter grow; (zubereiten) prepare; **jdn/etw auf jdn/etw ~** set sb/sth on sb/sth; vi (anfangen) start, begin; (Entwicklung) set in; (dick werden) put on weight; **zu etw ~** prepare to do sth; vr (Rost etc) start to develop.

Ansicht ['anzɪçt] f (Anblick) sight; (Meinung) view, opinion; **zur ~** on approval; **meiner ~ nach** in my opinion; **~skarte** f picture postcard; **~ssache** f matter of opinion.

anspannen ['anʃpanən] vt harness; Muskel strain.

Anspannung f strain.

Anspiel ['anʃpiːl] nt (Sport) start; **a~en** vi (Sport) start play; **auf etw** (acc) **a~en** refer or allude to sth; **~ung** f reference, allusion (auf +acc to).

Ansporn ['anʃpɔrn] m **-(e)s** incentive.

Ansprache ['anʃpraːxə] f address.

ansprechen ['anʃprɛçən] irreg vt speak to; (bitten, gefallen) appeal to; **jdn auf etw** (acc) **(hin) ~** ask sb about sth; **etw als etw ~** regard sth as sth; vi react (auf +acc to); **~d** a attractive.

anspringen ['anʃprɪŋən] vi irreg (Aut) start.

Anspruch ['anʃprʊx] m (Recht) claim (auf +acc to); **hohe Ansprüche stellen/haben** demand/ expect a lot; **jdn/etw in ~ nehmen** occupy sb/take

up sth; **a~slos** a undemanding; **a~svoll** a demanding.

anspucken ['anʃpʊkən] vt spit at.

anstacheln ['anʃtaxəln] vt spur on.

Anstalt ['anʃtalt] f **-**, **-en** institution; **~en machen, etw zu tun** prepare to do sth.

Anstand ['anʃtant] m decency.

anständig ['anʃtɛndɪç] a decent; (col) proper; (groß) considerable; **A~keit** f propriety, decency.

anstandslos ad without any ado.

anstarren ['anʃtarən] vt stare at.

anstatt [an'ʃtat] prep +gen instead of; cj: **~ etw zu tun** instead of doing sth.

anstechen ['anʃtɛçən] vt irreg prick; Faß tap.

Ansteck- ['anʃtɛk] cpd: **a~en** vt pin on; (Med) infect; Pfeife light; Haus set fire to; vr: **ich habe mich bei ihm angesteckt** I caught it from him; vi (fig) be infectious; **a~end** a infectious; **~ung** f infection.

anstehen ['anʃte:ən] vi irreg queue (up), line up (US).

anstelle [an'ʃtɛlə] prep +gen in place of; **~n** ['an-] vt (einschalten) turn on; (Arbeit geben) employ; (machen) do; vr queue (up), line up (US); (col) act.

Anstellung f employment; (Posten) post, position.

Anstieg ['anʃtiːk] m **-(e)s**, **-e** climb; (fig: von Preisen etc) increase (gen in).

anstift- ['anʃtɪft] cpd: **~en** vt Unglück cause; **jdn zu etw ~en** put sb up to sth; **A~er** m **-s**, instigator.

anstimmen ['anʃtɪmən] vt Lied strike up with; Geschrei set up; vi strike up.

Anstoß ['anʃtoːs] m impetus; (Ärgernis) offence; (Sport) kick-off; **der erste ~** the initiative; **~ nehmen an** (+dat) take offence at; **a~en** irreg vt push; (mit Fuß) kick; vi knock, bump; (mit der Zunge) lisp; (mit Gläsern) drink (a toast) (auf +acc to); **an etw** (acc) **a~en** (angrenzen) adjoin sth.

anstößig ['anʃtøːsɪç] a offensive, indecent; **A~keit** f indecency, offensiveness.

anstreben ['anʃtreːbən] vt strive for.

anstreichen ['anʃtraiçən] vt irreg paint.

Anstreicher m **-s**, - painter.

anstrengen ['anʃtrɛŋən] vt strain; (Jur) bring; vr make an effort; **angestrengt** ad as hard as one can; **~d** a tiring.

Anstrengung f effort.

Anstrich ['anʃtrɪç] m coat of paint.

Ansturm ['anʃtʊrm] m rush; (Mil) attack.

ansuchen ['anzuːxən] vi: **um etw ~** apply for sth; **A~** nt **-s**, - request.

Antagonismus [antago'nɪsmʊs] m antagonism.

antasten ['antastən] vt touch; Recht infringe upon; Ehre question.

Anteil ['antail] m **-s**, **-e** share (an +dat in); (Mitgefühl) sympathy; **~ nehmen an** (+dat) share in; (sich interessieren) take an interest in; **~nahme** f **-** sympathy.

Antenne [an'tɛnə] f **-**, **-n** aerial; (Zool) antenna.

Anthrazit [antra'tsiːt] m **-s**, **-e** anthracite.

Anti- ['anti] in cpds anti; **~alko'holiker** m

teetotaller; **a~autori'tär** *a* anti-authoritarian; **~biotikum** [antibi'o:tikʊm] *nt* **-s, -ka** antibiotic.

antik [an'ti:k] *a* antique; **A~e** *f* **-, -n** (*Zeitalter*) ancient world; (*Kunstgegenstand*) antique.

Antikörper *m* antibody.

Antilope [anti'lo:pə] *f* **-, -n** antelope.

Antipathie [antipa'ti:] *f* antipathy.

Antiquariat [antikvari'a:t] *nt* **-(e)s, -e** secondhand bookshop.

Antiquitäten [antikvi'tɛ:tən] *pl* antiques *pl*; **~handel** *m* antique business; **~händler** *m* antique dealer.

Antrag ['antra:k] *m* **-(e)s, -träge** proposal; (*Parl*) motion; (*Gesuch*) application.

antreffen ['antrɛfən] *vt irreg* meet.

antreiben ['antraibən] *irreg vt* drive on; *Motor* drive; (*anschwemmen*) wash up; *vi* be washed up.

antreten ['antre:tən] *irreg vt Amt* take up; *Erbschaft* come into; *Beweis* offer; *Reise* start, begin; *vi* (*Mil*) fall in; (*Sport*) line up; **gegen jdn ~** play/fight against sb.

Antrieb ['antri:p] *m* (*lit,fig*) drive; **aus eigenem ~** of one's own accord.

antrinken ['antriŋkən] *vt irreg Flasche, Glas* start to drink from; **sich** (*dat*) **Mut/einen Rausch ~** give oneself Dutch courage/get drunk; **angetrunken sein** be tipsy.

Antritt ['antrɪt] *m* beginning, commencement; (*eines Amts*) taking up.

antun ['antu:n] *vt irreg*: **jdm etw ~** do sth to sb; **sich** (*dat*) **Zwang ~** force o.s.

Antwort ['antvɔrt] *f* **-, -en** answer, reply; **um ~ wird gebeten** RSVP; **a~en** *vi* answer, reply.

anvertrauen ['anfɛrtrauən] *vt*: **jdm etw ~** entrust sb with sth; **sich jdm ~** confide in sb.

anwachsen ['anvaksən] *vi irreg* grow; (*Pflanze*) take root.

Anwalt ['anvalt] *m* **-(e)s, -wälte**, **Anwältin** ['anvɛltɪn] *f* solicitor; lawyer; (*fig*) champion.

Anwandlung ['anvandlʊŋ] *f* caprice; **eine ~ von etw** a fit of sth.

Anwärter ['anvɛrtər] *m* candidate.

anweisen ['anvaizən] *vt irreg* instruct; (*zuteilen*) assign (*jdm etw* sth to sb).

Anweisung *f* instruction; (*Comm*) remittance; (*Post~, Zahlungs~*) money order.

anwend- ['anvɛnd] *cpd*: **~bar** ['anvɛnt-] *a* practicable, applicable; **~en** *vt irreg* use, employ; *Gesetz, Regel* apply; **A~ung** *f* use; application.

Anwesen- ['anve:zən] *cpd*: **a~d** *a* present; **die ~den** those present; **~heit** *f* presence; **~heitsliste** *f* attendance register.

anwidern ['anvi:dərn] *vt* disgust.

Anwuchs ['anvu:ks] *m* growth.

Anzahl ['antsa:l] *f* number (*an +dat* of); **a~en** *vt* pay on account; **~ung** *f* deposit, payment on account.

anzapfen ['antsapfən] *vt* tap; *Person* (*um Geld*) touch.

Anzeichen ['antsaiçən] *nt* sign, indication.

Anzeige ['antsaigə] *f* **-, -n** (*Zeitungs~*) announcement; (*Werbung*) advertisement; (*bei Polizei*) report; **~ erstatten gegen jdn** report sb (to the police); **a~n** *vt* (*zu erkennen geben*) show; (*bekanntgeben*) announce; (*bei Polizei*) report; **~nteil** *m* advertisements *pl*; **~r** *m* indicator.

anzetteln ['antsɛtəln] *vt* (*col*) instigate.

anziehen ['antsi:ən] *irreg vt* attract; *Kleidung* put on; *Mensch* dress; *Schraube, Seil* pull tight; *Knie* draw up; (*Feuchtigkeit*) absorb; *vr* get dressed; **~d** *a* attractive.

Anziehung *f* (*Reiz*) attraction; **~skraft** *f* power of attraction; (*Phys*) force of gravitation.

Anzug ['antsu:k] *m* suit; **im ~ sein** be approaching.

anzüglich ['antsy:klɪç] *a* personal; (*anstößig*) offensive; **A~keit** *f* offensiveness; (*Bemerkung*) personal remark.

anzünden ['antsyndən] *vt* light.

Anzünder *m* lighter.

anzweifeln ['antsvaifəln] *vt* doubt.

apart [a'part] *a* distinctive.

Apathie [apa'ti:] *f* apathy.

apathisch [a'pa:tiʃ] *a* apathetic.

Apfel ['apfəl] *m* **-s, ⁻** apple; **~saft** *m* apple juice; **~sine** [apfəl'zi:nə] *f* **-, -n** orange; **~wein** *m* cider.

Apostel [a'pɔstəl] *m* **-s, -** apostle.

Apostroph [apo'stro:f] *m* **-s, -e** apostrophe.

Apotheke [apo'te:kə] *f* **-, -n** chemist's (shop), drugstore (*US*); **~r(in** *f*) *m* **-s,-** chemist, druggist (*US*).

Apparat [apa'ra:t] *m* **-(e)s, -e** piece of apparatus; camera; telephone; (*Rad, TV*) set; **am ~ bleiben** hold the line; **~ur** [-'tu:r] *f* apparatus.

Appartement [apart[ə]'mã:] *nt* **-s, -s** flat.

Appell [a'pɛl] *m* **-s, -e** (*Mil*) muster, parade; (*fig*) appeal; **a~ieren** [apɛ'li:rən] *vi* appeal (*an +acc* to).

Appetit [ape'ti:t] *m* **-(e)s, -e** appetite; **guten ~** enjoy your meal; **a~lich** *a* appetizing; **~losigkeit** *f* lack of appetite.

Applaus [ap'laus] *m* **-es, -e** applause.

Appretur [apre'tu:r] *f* finish.

Aprikose [apri'ko:zə] *f* **-, -n** apricot.

April [a'prɪl] *m* **-(s), -e** April; **~wetter** *nt* April showers *pl*.

Aquaplaning [akva'pla:nɪŋ] *nt* **-(s)** aquaplaning.

Aquarell [akva'rɛl] *nt* **-s, -e** watercolour.

Aquarium [a'kva:rium] *nt* aquarium.

Äquator [ɛ'kva:tɔr] *m* **-s** equator.

Arbeit ['arbait] *f* **-, -en** work (*no art*); (*Stelle*) job; (*Erzeugnis*) piece of work; (*wissenschaftliche*) dissertation; (*Klassen~*) test; **das war eine ~** that was a hard job; **a~en** *vi* work; *vt* work, make; **~er(in** *f*) *m* **-s, -** worker; (*ungelernt*) labourer; **~erschaft** *f* workers *pl*, labour force; **~geber** *m* **-s, -** employer; **~nehmer** *m* **-s, -** employee; **a~sam** *a* industrious.

Arbeits- *in cpds* labour; **~amt** *nt* employment exchange; **a~fähig** *a* fit for work, able-bodied; **~gang** *m* operation; **~gemeinschaft** *f* study group; **~kräfte** *pl* workers *pl*, *labour*; **a~los** *a* unemployed, out-of-work; **~losigkeit** *f* unemployment; **~platz** *m* job; place of work; **a~scheu** *a* work-shy; **~tag** *m* work(ing) day; **~teilung** *f* division of labour; **a~unfähig** *a* unfit for work; **~zeit** *f* working hours *pl*.

Archäologe [arçɛoˈloːgə] *m* **-n, -n** archaeologist.

Architekt(in *f*) [arçiˈtɛkt(ɪn)] *m* **-en, -en** architect; **~ur** [-ˈtuːr] *f* architecture.

Archiv [arˈçiːf] *nt* **-s, -e** archive.

arg [ark] *a* bad, awful; *ad* awfully, very.

Ärger [ˈɛrgɐr] *m* **-s** (*Wut*) anger; (*Unannehmlichkeit*) trouble; **ä~lich** *a* (*zornig*) angry; (*lästig*) annoying, aggravating; **ä~n** *vt* annoy; *vr* get annoyed; **~nis** *nt* **-ses, -se** annoyance; **öffentliches ~nis erregen** be a public nuisance.

arg- *cpd*: **~listig** *a* cunning, insidious; **~los** *a* guileless, innocent; **A~losigkeit** *f* guilelessness, innocence; **A~ument** [arguˈmɛnt] *nt* argument; **A~wohn** *m* suspicion; **~wöhnisch** *a* suspicious.

Arie [ˈaːriə] *f*-, **-n** aria.

Aristokrat [aristoˈkraːt] *m* **-en,-en** aristocrat; **~ie** [-ˈtiː] *f* aristocracy; **a~isch** *a* aristocratic.

arithmetisch [arɪtˈmeːtɪʃ] *a* arithmetical.

arm [arm] *a* poor; **A~** *m* **-(e)s, -e** arm; (*Fluß~*) branch; **A~atur** *f* (*Elec*) armature; **A~a'turenbrett** *nt* instrument panel; (*Aut*) dashboard; **A~band** *nt* bracelet; **A~banduhr** *f* (wrist) watch; **A~e(r)** *mf* poor man/woman; **die A~en** the poor; **A~ee** [arˈmeː] *f* -, **-n** army; **A~eekorps** *nt* army corps.

Ärmel [ˈɛrməl] *m* **-s,** - sleeve; **etw aus dem ~ schütteln** (*fig*) produce sth just like that.

ärmlich [ˈɛrmlɪç] *a* poor.

armselig *a* wretched, miserable.

Armut [ˈarmuːt] *f* - poverty.

Aroma [aˈroːma] *nt* **-s, Aromen** aroma; **a~tisch** [aroˈmaːtɪʃ] *a* aromatic.

arrangieren [arãˈʒiːrən] *vt* arrange; *vr* come to an arrangement.

Arrest [aˈrɛst] *m* **-(e)s, -e** detention.

arrogant [aroˈgant] *a* arrogant.

Arroganz *f* arrogance.

Arsch [arʃ] *m* **-es, ¨e** (*col*) arse, bum.

Art [aːrt] *f*-, **-en** (*Weise*) way; (*Sorte*) kind, sort; (*Biol*) species; **eine ~ (von) Frucht** a kind of fruit; **Häuser aller ~** houses of all kinds; **es ist nicht seine ~, das zu tun** it's not like him to do that; **ich mache das auf meine ~** I do that my (own) way; **nach ~ des Hauses** à la maison; **a~en** *vi*: **nach jdm a~en** take after sb; **der Mensch ist so geartet, daß . . .** human nature is such that . . .

Arterie [arˈteːriə] *f* artery; **~nverkalkung** *f* arteriosclerosis.

artig [ˈaːrtɪç] *a* good, well-behaved.

Artikel [arˈtiːkəl] *m* **-s,** - article.

Artillerie [artɪləˈriː] *f* artillery.

Arznei [aːrtsˈnaɪ] *f* medicine; **~mittel** *nt* medicine, medicament.

Arzt [aːrtst] *m* **-es, ¨e, Ärztin** [ˈɛːrtstɪn] *f* doctor.

ärztlich [ˈɛːrtstlɪç] *a* medical.

As [as] *nt* **-ses, -se** ace.

Asbest [asˈbɛst] *m* **-(e)s, -e** asbestos.

Asche [ˈaʃə] *f*-, **-n** ash, cinder; **~nbahn** *f* cinder track; **~nbecher** *m* ashtray; **~nbrödel** *nt* Cinderella; **~rmittwoch** *m* Ash Wednesday.

asozial [ˈazotsiaːl] *a* antisocial; *Familien* asocial.

Aspekt [asˈpɛkt] *m* **-(e)s, -e** aspect.

Asphalt [asˈfalt] *m* **-(e)s, -e** asphalt; **a~ieren** [-ˈtiːrən] *vt* asphalt; **~straße** *f* asphalt road.

Assistent(in *f*) [asɪsˈtɛnt(ɪn)] *m* assistant.

Assoziation [asotsiatsiˈoːn] *f* association.

Ast [ast] *m* **-(e)s, ¨e** bough, branch; **~er** *f* -, **-n** aster.

ästhetisch [ɛsˈteːtɪʃ] *a* aesthetic.

Asthma [ˈastma] *nt* **-s** asthma; **~tiker(in** *f*) [astˈmaːtikər(ɪn)] *m* **-s,** - asthmatic.

Astro- [astro] *cpd*: **~'loge** *m* **-n, -n** astrologer; **~lo'gie** *f* astrology; **~'naut** *m* **-en, -en** astronaut; **~'nautik** *f* astronautics; **~'nom** *m* **-en, -en** astronomer; **~no'mie** *f* astronomy.

Asyl [aˈzyːl] *nt* **-s, -e** asylum; (*Heim*) home; (*Obdachlosen~*) shelter.

Atelier [ateliˈeː] *nt* **-s,** - studio.

Atem [ˈaːtəm] *m* **-s** breath; **den ~ anhalten** hold one's breath; **außer ~** out of breath; **a~beraubend** a breath-taking; **a~los** *a* breathless; **~pause** *f* breather; **~zug** *m* breath.

Atheismus [ateˈɪsmʊs] *m* atheism.

Atheist *m* atheist; **a~isch** *a* atheistic.

Äther [ˈɛːtɛr] *m* **-s,** - ether.

Athlet [atˈleːt] *m* **-en, -en** athlete; **~ik** *f* athletics.

Atlas [ˈatlas] *m* **-** *or* **-ses, -se** *or* **Atlanten** atlas.

atmen [ˈaːtmən] *vti* breathe.

Atmosphäre [atmoˈsfɛːrə] *f* -, **-n** atmosphere.

atmosphärisch *a* atmospheric.

Atmung [ˈaːtmʊŋ] *f* respiration.

Atom [aˈtoːm] *nt* **-s, -e** atom; **a~ar** [atoˈmaːr] *a* atomic; **~bombe** *f* atom bomb; **~energie** *f* atomic or nuclear energy; **~kern** *m* atomic nucleus; **~kernforschung** *f* nuclear research; **~kraftwerk** *nt* nuclear power station; **~krieg** *m* nuclear or atomic war; **~macht** *f* nuclear or atomic power; **~müll** *m* atomic waste; **~sperrvertrag** *m* (*Pol*) nuclear non-proliferation treaty; **~versuch** *m* atomic test; **~waffen** *pl* atomic weapons *pl*; **~zeitalter** *nt* atomic age.

Attentat [atɛnˈtaːt] *nt* **-(e)s, -e** (attempted) assassination (*auf* +*acc* of).

Attentäter [atɛnˈtɛːtər] *m* (would-be) assassin.

Attest [aˈtɛst] *nt* **-(e)s, -e** certificate.

attraktiv [atrakˈtiːf] *a* attractive.

Attrappe [aˈtrapə] *f*-, **-n** dummy.

Attribut [atri'bu:t] *nt* **-(e)s, -e** (*Gram*) attribute.

ätzen ['ɛtsən] *vi* be caustic.

auch [aux] *cj* also, too, as well; (*selbst, sogar*) even; (*wirklich*) really; **oder** ~ or; ~ **das ist schön** that's nice too *or* as well; **das habe ich** ~ **nicht gemacht** I didn't do it either; **ich** ~ **nicht** nor I, me neither; ~ **wenn das Wetter schlecht ist** even if the weather is bad; **wer/was** ~ whoever/whatever; **so sieht es** ~ **aus** it looks like it too; ~ **das noch!** not that as well!

auf [auf] *prep* +*acc or dat* (*räumlich*) on; (*hinauf*: +*acc*) up; (*in Richtung*: +*acc*) to; (*nach*) after; ~ **der Reise** on the way; ~ **der Post/dem Fest** at the post office/party; ~ **das Land** into the country; ~ **der Straße** on the road; ~ **dem Land/den ganzen Welt** in the country/the whole world; ~ **deutsch** in German; ~ **Lebenszeit** for sb's lifetime; **bis** ~ **ihn** except for him; ~ **einmal** at once; *ad*: ~ **und ab up and down;** ~ **und davon up and away;** ~**!** (*los*) come on!; ~ **sein** (*col*) (*Person*) be up; (*Tür*) be open; **von Kindheit** ~ from childhood onwards; ~ **daß** so that.

aufatmen ['auf'a:tmən] *vi* heave a sigh of relief.

aufbahren ['aufba:rən] *vt* lay out.

Aufbau ['aufbau] *m* (*Bauen*) building, construction; (*Struktur*) structure; (*aufgebautes Teil*) superstructure; a~**en** *vt* erect, build (up); *Existenz* make; (*gestalten*) construct; (*gründen*) found, base (*auf* +*dat* on).

aufbäumen ['aufbɔymən] *vr* rear; (*fig*) revolt, rebel.

aufbauschen ['aufbauʃən] *vt* puff out; (*fig*) exaggerate.

aufbehalten ['aufbəhaltən] *vt irreg* keep on.

aufbekommen ['aufbəkomən] *vt irreg* (*öffnen*) get open; *Hausaufgaben* be given.

aufbessern ['aufbɛsərn] *vt* *Gehalt* increase.

aufbewahren ['aufbəva:rən] *vt* keep; *Gepäck* put in the left-luggage office.

Aufbewahrung *f* (*safe*)keeping; (*Gepäck*—) left-luggage office; **jdm etw zur** ~ **geben** give sb sth for safekeeping; ~**sort** *m* storage place.

aufbieten ['aufbi:tən] *vt irreg* *Kraft* summon up, exert; *Armee, Polizei* mobilize; *Brautpaar* publish the banns of.

aufblasen ['aufbla:zən] *irreg vt* blow up, inflate; *vr* (*col*) become big-headed.

aufbleiben ['aufblaibən] *vi irreg* (*Laden*) remain open; (*Person*) stay up.

aufblenden ['aufblɛndən] *vt* *Scheinwerfer* turn on full beam.

aufblicken ['aufblikən] *vi* (*lit, fig*) look up (*zu* (*lit*) at, (*fig*) to).

aufblühen ['aufbly:ən] *vi* blossom, flourish.

aufbrauchen ['aufbrauxən] *vt* use up.

aufbrausen ['aufbrauzən] *vi* (*fig*) flare up; ~**d** a hot-tempered.

aufbrechen ['aufbrɛçən] *irreg vt* break *or* prize open; *vi* burst open; (*gehen*) start, set off.

aufbringen ['aufbrɪŋən] *vt irreg* (*öffnen*) open; (*in Mode*) bring into fashion; (*beschaffen*) procure; (*Fin*) raise; (*ärgern*) irritate; **Verständnis für etw** ~ be able to understand sth.

Aufbruch ['aufbrux] *m* departure.

aufbrühen ['aufbry:ən] *vt* *Tee* make.

aufbürden ['aufbyrdən] *vt* burden (*jdm etw* sb with sth).

aufdecken ['aufdɛkən] *vt* uncover.

aufdrängen ['aufdrɛŋən] *vt* force (*jdm* on sb); *vr* intrude (*jdm* on sb).

aufdringlich ['aufdrɪŋlɪç] a pushy.

aufeinander [auf'ai'nandər] *ad* achten after each other; *schießen* at each other; *vertrauen* each other; **A**~**folge** *f* succession, series; ~**folgen** *vi* follow one another; ~**folgend** a consecutive; ~**legen** *vt* lay on top of one another; ~**prallen** *vi* hit one another.

Aufenthalt ['aufɛnthalt] *m* stay; (*Verzögerung*) delay; (*Rail*: *Halten*) stop; (*Ort*) haunt; ~**sgenehmigung** *f* residence permit.

auferlegen ['auf'ɛrle:gən] *vt* impose (*jdm etw* sth upon sb).

Auferstehung ['auf'ɛrʃte:uŋ] *f* resurrection.

aufessen ['auf'ɛsən] *vt irreg* eat up.

auffahr- ['auffa:r] *cpd:* ~**en** *irreg vi* (*Auto*) run, crash (*auf* +*acc* into); (*herankommen*) draw up; (*hochfahren*) jump up; (*wütend werden*) flare up; (*in den Himmel*) ascend; *vt* *Kanonen, Geschütz* bring up; ~**end** a hot-tempered; **A**~**t** *f* (*Haus*—) drive; (*Autobahn*—) slip road; **A**~**unfall** *m* pile-up.

auffallen ['auffalən] *vi irreg* be noticeable; **jdm** ~ strike sb; ~**d** a striking.

auffällig ['auffɛlɪç] a conspicuous, striking.

auffang- ['auffaŋ] *cpd:* ~**en** *vt irreg* catch; *Funkspruch* intercept; *Preise* peg; **A**~**lager** *nt* refugee camp.

auffassen ['auffasən] *vt* understand, comprehend; (*auslegen*) see, view.

Auffassung *f* (*Meinung*) opinion; (*Auslegung*) view, concept; (*also* ~**sgabe**) grasp.

auffindbar ['auffintba:r] a to be found.

auffordern ['auffordərn] *vt* (*befehlen*) call upon, order; (*bitten*) ask.

Aufforderung *f* (*Befehl*) order; (*Einladung*) invitation.

auffrischen ['auffrɪʃən] *vt* freshen up; *Kenntnisse* brush up; *Erinnerungen* reawaken; *vi* (*Wind*) freshen.

aufführen ['auffy:rən] *vt* (*Theat*) perform; (*in einem Verzeichnis*) list, specify; *vr* (*sich benehmen*) behave.

Aufführung *f* (*Theat*) performance; (*Liste*) specification.

Aufgabe ['aufga:bə] *f* -, **-n** task; (*Sch*) exercise; (*Haus*—) homework; (*Verzicht*) giving up; (*von Gepäck*) registration; (*von Post*) posting; (*von Inserat*) insertion.

Aufgang ['aufgaŋ] *m* ascent; (*Sonnen*—) rise; (*Treppe*) staircase.

aufgeben ['aufge:bən] *irreg vt* (*verzichten*) give up; *Paket* send, post; *Gepäck* register;

Bestellung give; *Inserat* insert; *Rätsel, Problem* set; *vi* give up.
Aufgebot ['aʊfgəboːt] *nt* supply; *(von Kräften)* utilization; *(Ehe—)* banns *pl.*
aufgedreht ['aʊfgədreːt] *a (col)* excited.
aufgedunsen ['aʊfgədʊnzən] *a* swollen, puffed up.
aufgehen ['aʊfgeːən] *vi irreg (Sonne, Teig)* rise; *(sich öffnen)* open; *(klarwerden)* become clear *(jdm to sb)*; *(Math)* come out exactly; *(sich widmen)* be absorbed *(in +dat in)*; **in Rauch/Flammen** ~ go up in smoke/flames.
aufgeklärt ['aʊfgəkleːrt] *a* enlightened; *(sexuell)* knowing the facts of life.
aufgelegt ['aʊfgəleːkt] *a*: **gut/schlecht** ~ **sein** be in a good/bad mood; **zu etw** ~ **sein** be in the mood for sth.
aufgeregt ['aʊfgəreːkt] *a* excited.
aufgeschlossen ['aʊfgəʃlɔsən] *a* open, open-minded.
aufgeweckt ['aʊfgəvɛkt] *a* bright, intelligent.
aufgießen ['aʊfgiːsən] *vt irreg Wasser* pour over; *Tee* infuse.
aufgreifen ['aʊfgraɪfən] *vt irreg Thema* take up; *Verdächtige* pick up, seize.
aufgrund [aʊfˈgrʊnt] *prep +gen* on the basis of; *(wegen)* because of.
aufhaben ['aʊfhaːbən] *vt irreg* have on; *Arbeit* have to do.
aufhalsen ['aʊfhalzən] *vt (col)* **jdm etw** ~ **saddle** *or* **lumber sb with sth.**
aufhalten ['aʊfhaltən] *irreg vt Person* detain; *Entwicklung* check; *Tür, Hand* hold open; *Augen* keep open; *vr (wohnen)* live; *(bleiben)* stay; **sich über etw/jdn** ~ go on about sth/sb; **sich mit etw** ~ waste time over.
aufhängen ['aʊfhɛŋən] *irreg vt Wäsche* hang up; *Menschen* hang; *vr* hang o.s.
Aufhänger *m* **-s,** - *(am Mantel)* hook; *(fig)* peg.
aufheben ['aʊfheːbən] *irreg vt (hochheben)* raise, lift; *Sitzung* wind up; *Urteil* annul; *Gesetz* repeal, abolish; *(aufbewahren)* keep; **bei jdm gut aufgehoben sein** be well looked after at sb's; *vr* cancel o.s. out; **viel A**~**(s) machen** make a fuss *(von* about).
aufheitern ['aʊfhaɪtərn] *vtr (Himmel, Miene)* brighten; *Mensch* cheer up.
aufhellen ['aʊfhɛlən] *vtr* clear up; *Farbe, Haare* lighten.
aufhetzen ['aʊfhɛtsən] *vt* stir up *(gegen* against).
aufholen ['aʊfhoːlən] *vt* make up; *vi* catch up.
aufhorchen ['aʊfhɔrçən] *vi* prick up one's ears.
aufhören ['aʊfhøːrən] *vi* stop; ~ **etw zu tun** stop doing sth.
aufklappen ['aʊfklapən] *vt* open.
aufklären ['aʊfkleːrən] *vt Geheimnis etc* clear up; *Person* enlighten; *(sexuell)* tell the facts of life to; *(Mil)* reconnoitre; *vr* clear up.
Aufklärung *f (von Geheimnis)* clearing up; *(Unterrichtung, Zeitalter)* enlightenment; *(sexuell)* sex education; *(Mil, Aviat)* reconnaissance.

aufkleben ['aʊfkleːbən] *vt* stick on.
Aufkleber *m* **-s,** - sticker.
aufknöpfen ['aʊfknœpfən] *vt* unbutton.
aufkommen ['aʊfkɔmən] *vi irreg (Wind)* come up; *(Zweifel, Gefühl)* arise; *(Mode)* start; **für jdn/etw** ~ be liable *or* responsible for sb/sth.
aufladen ['aʊflaːdən] *vt irreg* load.
Auflage ['aʊflaːgə] *f* edition; *(Zeitung)* circulation; *(Bedingung)* condition; **jdm etw zur** ~ **machen** make sth a condition for sb.
auflassen ['aʊflasən] *vt irreg (offen)* leave open; *(aufgesetzt)* leave on.
auflauern ['aʊflaʊərn] *vi*: **jdm** ~ lie in wait for sb.
Auflauf ['aʊflaʊf] *m (Cook)* pudding; *(Menschen—)* crowd.
aufleben ['aʊfleːbən] *vi* revive.
auflegen ['aʊfleːgən] *vt* put on; *Telefon* hang up; *(Print)* print.
auflehnen ['aʊfleːnən] *vt* lean on; *vr* rebel *(gegen* against).
Auflehnung *f* rebellion.
auflesen ['aʊfleːzən] *vt irreg* pick up.
aufleuchten ['aʊflɔʏçtən] *vi* light up.
aufliegen ['aʊfliːgən] *vi irreg* lie on; *(Comm)* be available.
auflockern ['aʊflɔkərn] *vt* loosen; *(fig)* Eintönigkeit etc liven up.
auflösen ['aʊfløːzən] *vt* dissolve; *Haare etc* loosen; *Mißverständnis* sort out; **(in Tränen) aufgelöst sein** be in tears.
Auflösung *f* dissolving; *(fig)* solution.
aufmachen ['aʊfmaxən] *vt* open; *Kleidung* undo; *(zurechtmachen)* do up; *vr* set out.
Aufmachung *f (Kleidung)* outfit, get-up; *(Gestaltung)* format.
aufmerksam ['aʊfmɛrkzaːm] *a* attentive; **jdn auf etw** *(acc)* ~ **machen** point sth out to sb; **A**~**keit** *f* attention, attentiveness.
aufmuntern ['aʊfmʊntərn] *vt (ermutigen)* encourage; *(erheitern)* cheer up.
Aufnahme ['aʊfnaːmə] *f* **-, -n** reception; *(Beginn)* beginning; *(in Verein etc)* admission; *(in Liste etc)* inclusion; *(Notieren)* taking down; *(Phot)* shot; *(auf Tonband etc)* recording; **a**~**fähig** *a* receptive; ~**prüfung** *f* entrance test.
aufnehmen ['aʊfneːmən] *vt irreg* receive; *(hochheben)* pick up; *(beginnen)* take up; *(in Verein etc)* admit; *(in Liste etc)* include; *(fassen)* hold; *(notieren)* take down; *(photographieren)* photograph; *(auf Tonband, Platte)* record; *(Fin: leihen)* take out; **es mit jdm** ~ **können** be able to compete with sb.
aufopfern ['aʊfʔɔpfərn] *vtr* sacrifice; ~**d** *a* selfless.
aufpassen ['aʊfpasən] *vi (aufmerksam sein)* pay attention; **auf jdn/etw** ~ look after *or* watch sb/sth; **aufgepaßt!** look out!
Aufprall ['aʊfpral] *m* **-s, -e** impact; **a**~**en** *vi* hit, strike.
Aufpreis ['aʊfpraɪs] *m* extra charge.
aufpumpen ['aʊfpʊmpən] *vt* pump up.
aufputschen ['aʊfpʊtʃən] *vt (aufhetzen)*

inflame; (*erregen*) stimulate.

aufraffen ['aʊfrafən] *vr* rouse o.s.

aufräumen ['aʊfrɔʏmən] *vti Dinge* clear away; *Zimmer* tidy up.

aufrecht ['aʊfrɛçt] *a* (*lit*, *fig*) upright; ~**erhalten** *vt irreg* maintain.

aufreg- ['aʊfreːg] *cpd*: ~**en** *vt* excite; *vr* get excited; ~**end** *a* exciting; **A**~**ung** *f* excitement.

aufreiben ['aʊfraɪbən] *vt irreg Haut* rub open; (*erschöpfen*) exhaust; ~**d** *a* strenuous.

aufreißen ['aʊfraɪsən] *vt irreg Umschlag* tear open; *Augen* open wide; *Tür* throw open; *Straße* take up.

aufreizen ['aʊfraɪtsən] *vt* incite, stir up; ~**d** *a* exciting, stimulating.

aufrichten ['aʊfrɪçtən] *vt* put up, erect; (*moralisch*) console; *vr* rise; (*moralisch*) take heart (*an* +*dat* from).

aufrichtig ['aʊfrɪçtɪç] *a* sincere, honest; **A**~**keit** *f* sincerity.

aufrücken ['aʊfrʏkən] *vi* move up; (*beruflich*) be promoted.

Aufruf ['aʊfruːf] *m* summons; (*zur Hilfe*) call; (*des Namens*) calling out; **a**~**en** *vt irreg* (*auffordern*) call upon (*zu* for); *Namen* call out.

Aufruhr ['aʊfruːr] *m* -(**e**)**s**, -**e** uprising, revolt; **in** ~ **sein** be in uproar.

aufrührerisch ['aʊfryːrərɪʃ] *a* rebellious.

aufrunden ['aʊfrʊndən] *vt Summe* round up.

Aufrüstung ['aʊfrʏstʊŋ] *f* rearmament.

aufrütteln ['aʊfrʏtəln] *vt* (*lit*, *fig*) shake up.

aufs [aʊfs] = **auf das**.

aufsagen ['aʊfzaːgən] *vt Gedicht* recite; *Freundschaft* put an end to.

aufsammeln ['aʊfzaməln] *vt* gather up.

aufsässig ['aʊfzɛsɪç] *a* rebellious.

Aufsatz ['aʊfzats] *m* (*Geschriebenes*) essay; (*auf Schrank etc*) top.

aufsaugen ['aʊfzaʊgən] *vt irreg* soak up.

aufschauen ['aʊfʃaʊən] *vi* look up.

aufscheuchen ['aʊfʃɔʏçən] *vt* scare or frighten away.

aufschieben ['aʊfʃiːbən] *vt irreg* push open; (*verzögern*) put off, postpone.

Aufschlag ['aʊfʃlaːk] *m* (*Ärmel*—) cuff; (*Jacken*—) lapel; (*Hosen*—) turn-up; (*Aufprall*) impact; (*Preis*—) surcharge; (*Tennis*) service; **a**~**en** *irreg vt* (*öffnen*) open; (*verwunden*) cut; (*hochschlagen*) turn up; (*aufbauen*) *Zelt*, *Lager* pitch, erect; *Wohnsitz* take up; *vi* (*aufprallen*) hit; (*teurer werden*) go up; (*Tennis*) serve.

aufschließen ['aʊfʃliːsən] *irreg vt* open up, unlock; *vi* (*aufrücken*) close up.

Aufschluß ['aʊfʃlʊs] *m* information; **a**~**reich** *a* informative, illuminating.

aufschnappen ['aʊfʃnapən] *vt* (*col*) pick up; *vi* fly open.

aufschneiden ['aʊfʃnaɪdən] *irreg vt Geschwür* cut open; *Brot* cut up; (*Med*) lance; *vi* brag.

Aufschneider *m* -**s**, - boaster, braggart.

Aufschnitt ['aʊfʃnɪt] *m* (slices of) cold meat.

aufschnüren ['aʊfʃnyːrən] *vt* unlace; *Paket* untie.

aufschrauben ['aʊfʃraʊbən] *vt* (*fest*—) screw on; (*lösen*) unscrew.

aufschrecken ['aʊfʃrɛkən] *vt* startle; *vi irreg* start up.

Aufschrei ['aʊfʃraɪ] *m* cry; **a**~**en** *vi irreg* cry out.

aufschreiben ['aʊfʃraɪbən] *vt irreg* write down.

Aufschrift ['aʊfʃrɪft] *f* (*Inschrift*) inscription; (*auf Etikett*) label.

Aufschub ['aʊfʃuːp] *m* -(**e**)**s**, -**schübe** delay, postponement.

aufschwatzen ['aʊfʃvatsən] *vt*: **jdm etw** ~ talk sb into (getting/having *etc*) sth.

Aufschwung ['aʊfʃvʊŋ] *m* (*Elan*) boost; (*wirtschaftlich*) upturn, boom; (*Sport*) circle.

aufsehen ['aʊfzeːən] *vi irreg* (*lit*, *fig*) look up (*zu* (*lit*) at, (*fig*) to); **A**~ *nt* -**s** sensation, stir; ~**erregend** *a* sensational.

Aufseher(in *f*) *m* -**s**, - guard; (*im Betrieb*) supervisor; (*Museums*—) attendant; (*Park*—) keeper.

aufsein ['aʊfzaɪn] *vi irreg* (*col*) be open; (*Person*) be up.

aufsetzen ['aʊfzɛtsən] *vt* put on; *Flugzeug* put down; *Dokument* draw up; *vr* sit upright; *vi* (*Flugzeug*) touch down.

Aufsicht ['aʊfzɪçt] *f* supervision; **die** ~ **haben** be in charge.

aufsitzen ['aʊfzɪtsən] *vi irreg* (*aufrecht hinsitzen*) sit up; (*aufs Pferd*, *Motorrad*) mount, get on; (*Schiff*) run aground; **jdn** ~ **lassen** (*col*) stand sb up; **jdm** ~ (*col*) be taken in by sb.

aufspalten ['aʊfʃpaltən] *vt* split.

aufsparen ['aʊfʃpaːrən] *vt* save (up).

aufsperren ['aʊfʃpɛrən] *vt* unlock; *Mund* open wide.

aufspielen ['aʊfʃpiːlən] *vr* show off; **sich als etw** ~ try to come on as sth.

aufspießen ['aʊfʃpiːsən] *vt* spear.

aufspringen ['aʊfʃprɪŋən] *vi irreg* jump (*auf* +*acc* onto); (*hochspringen*) jump up; (*sich öffnen*) spring open; (*Hände*, *Lippen*) become chapped.

aufspüren ['aʊfʃpyːrən] *vt* track down, trace.

aufstacheln ['aʊfʃtaxəln] *vt* incite.

Aufstand ['aʊfʃtant] *m* insurrection, rebellion.

aufständisch ['aʊfʃtɛndɪʃ] *a* rebellious, mutinous.

aufstechen ['aʊfʃtɛçən] *vt irreg* prick open, puncture.

aufstecken ['aʊfʃtɛkən] *vt* stick on, pin up; (*col*) give up.

aufstehen ['aʊfʃteːən] *vi irreg* get up; (*Tür*) be open.

aufsteigen ['aʊfʃtaɪgən] *vi irreg* (*auf etw*) get onto; (*hochsteigen*) climb; (*Rauch*) rise.

aufstellen ['aʊfʃtɛlən] *vt* (*aufrecht stellen*) put up; (*aufreihen*) line up; (*nominieren*) put up; (*formulieren*) *Programm etc* draw up; (*leisten*) *Rekord* set up.

Aufstellung *f* (*Sport*) line-up; (*Liste*) list.

Aufstieg ['aʊfʃtiːk] *m* -(**e**)**s**, -**e** (*auf Berg*) ascent; (*Fortschritt*) rise; (*beruflich, Sport*) promotion.

aufstoßen ['aʊfʃtoːsən] *irreg vt* push open; *vi* belch.

aufstrebend ['aʊfʃtreːbənt] *a* ambitious; *Land* up-and-coming.

Aufstrich ['aʊfʃtrɪç] *m* spread.

aufstülpen ['aʊfʃtʏlpən] *vt Ärmel* turn up; *Hut* put on.

aufstützen ['aʊfʃtʏtsən] *vr* lean (auf +*acc* on); *vt Körperteil* prop, lean; *Person* prop up.

aufsuchen ['aʊfzuːxən] *vt* (*besuchen*) visit; (*konsultieren*) consult.

auftakeln ['aʊftaːkəln] *vt* (*Naut*) rig (out); *vr* (*col*) deck o.s. out.

Auftakt ['aʊftakt] *m* (*Mus*) upbeat; (*fig*) prelude.

auftanken ['aʊftaŋkən] *vi* get petrol; *vt* refuel.

auftauchen ['aʊftaʊxən] *vi* appear; (*aus Wasser etc*) emerge; (*U-Boot*) surface; (*Zweifel*) arise.

auftauen ['aʊftaʊən] *vti* thaw; (*fig*) relax.

aufteilen ['aʊftaɪlən] *vt* divide up; *Raum* partition.

Aufteilung *f* division; partition.

auftischen ['aʊftɪʃən] *vt* serve (up); (*fig*) tell.

Auftrag ['aʊftraːk] *m* -(e)s, -träge order; (*Anweisung*) commission; (*Aufgabe*) mission; **im ~ von** on behalf of; **a~en** [-gən] *irreg vt Essen* serve; *Farbe* put on; *Kleidung* wear out; **jdm etw a~en** tell sb sth; *vi* (*dick machen*) make you/me *etc* look fat; **dick a~en** (*fig*) exaggerate; **~geber** *m* -s, - (*Comm*) purchaser, customer.

auftreiben ['aʊftraɪbən] *vt irreg* (*col: beschaffen*) raise.

auftreten ['aʊftreːtən] *irreg vt* kick open; *vi* appear; (*mit Füßen*) tread; (*sich verhalten*) behave; **A~** *nt* -s (*Vorkommen*) appearance; (*Benehmen*) behaviour.

Auftrieb ['aʊftriːp] *m* (*Phys*) buoyancy, lift; (*fig*) impetus.

Auftritt ['aʊftrɪt] *m* (*des Schauspielers*) entrance; (*lit, fig: Szene*) scene.

auftun ['aʊftuːn] *irreg vt* open; *vr* open up.

aufwachen ['aʊfvaxən] *vi* wake up.

aufwachsen ['aʊfvaksən] *vi irreg* grow up.

Aufwand ['aʊfvant] *m* -(e)s expenditure; (*Kosten auch*) expense; (*Luxus*) show; **bitte, keinen ~!** please don't go out of your way.

aufwärmen ['aʊfvɛrmən] *vt* warm up; *alte Geschichten* rake up.

aufwärts ['aʊfvɛrts] *ad* upwards; **A~entwicklung** *f* upward trend; **~gehen** *vi irreg* look up.

aufwecken ['aʊfvɛkən] *vt* wake(n) up.

aufweichen ['aʊfvaɪçən] *vt* soften, soak.

aufweisen ['aʊfvaɪzən] *vt irreg* show.

aufwenden ['aʊfvɛndən] *vt irreg* expend; *Geld* spend; *Sorgfalt* devote.

aufwendig *a* costly.

aufwerfen ['aʊfvɛrfən] *irreg vt Fenster etc* throw open; *Probleme* throw up, raise; *vr*: **sich zu etw ~** make o.s. out to be sth.

aufwerten ['aʊfvɛrtən] *vt* (*Fin*) revalue; (*fig*) raise in value.

aufwiegeln ['aʊfviːgəln] *vt* stir up, incite.

aufwiegen ['aʊfviːgən] *vt irreg* make up for.

Aufwind ['aʊfvɪnt] *m* up-current.

aufwirbeln ['aʊfvɪrbəln] *vt* whirl up; **Staub ~** (*fig*) create a stir.

aufwischen ['aʊfvɪʃən] *vt* wipe up.

aufzählen ['aʊftsɛːlən] *vt* count out.

aufzeichnen ['aʊftsaɪçnən] *vt* sketch; (*schriftlich*) jot down; (*auf Band*) record.

Aufzeichnung *f* (*schriftlich*) note; (*Tonband—*) recording; (*Film—*) record.

aufzeigen ['aʊftsaɪgən] *vt* show, demonstrate.

aufziehen ['aʊftsiːən] *vt irreg* (*hochziehen*) raise, draw up; (*öffnen*) pull open; *Uhr* wind; (*col: necken*) tease; (*großziehen*) *Kinder* raise, bring up; *Tiere* rear.

Aufzug ['aʊftsuːk] *m* (*Fahrstuhl*) lift, elevator; (*Aufmarsch*) procession, parade; (*Kleidung*) get-up; (*Theat*) act.

aufzwingen ['aʊftsvɪŋən] *vt irreg*: **jdm etw ~** force sth upon sb.

Aug- ['aʊg] *cpd*: **~apfel** *m* eyeball; (*fig*) apple of one's eye; **~e** *nt* -s, -n eye; (*Fett—*) globule of fat; **unter vier ~en** in private; **~enblick** *m* moment; **im ~enblick** at the moment; **a~enblicklich** *a* (*sofort*) instantaneous; (*gegenwärtig*) present; **~enbraue** *f* eyebrow; **a~enscheinlich** *a* obvious; **~enweide** *f* sight for sore eyes; **~enzeuge** *m* eye witness.

August [aʊˈgʊst] *m* -(e)s *or* -, -e August.

Auktion [aʊktsiˈoːn] *f* auction; **~ator** [-ˈnaːtɔr] *m* auctioneer.

Aula ['aʊla] *f* -, **Aulen** *or* -s assembly hall.

aus [aʊs] *prep* +*dat* out of; (*von ... her*) from; (*Material*) made of; **~ ihr wird nie etwas** she'll never get anywhere; *ad* out; (*beendet*) finished, over; (*ausgezogen*) off; **~ und ein gehen** come and go; (*bei jdm*) visit frequently; **weder ~ noch ein wissen** be at sixes and sevens; **auf etw** (*acc*) **~ sein** be after sth; **vom Fenster ~** out of the window; **von Rom ~** from Rome; **von sich ~** of one's own accord; **A~** *nt* - outfield; **ins A~ gehen** go out.

ausarbeiten ['aʊsʔarbaɪtən] *vt* work out.

ausarten ['aʊsʔartən] *vi* degenerate; (*Kind*) become overexcited.

ausatmen ['aʊsʔaːtmən] *vi* breathe out.

ausbaden ['aʊsbaːdən] *vt*: **etw ~ müssen** (*col*) carry the can for sth.

Ausbau ['aʊsbaʊ] *m* extension, expansion; removal; **a~en** *vt* extend, expand; (*herausnehmen*) take out, remove; **a~fähig** *a* (*fig*) worth developing.

ausbedingen ['aʊsbədɪŋən] *vt irreg*: **sich** (*dat*) **etw ~** insist on sth.

ausbessern ['aʊsbɛsərn] *vt* mend, repair.

ausbeulen ['aʊsbɔʏlən] *vt* beat out.

Ausbeute ['aʊsbɔʏtə] *f* yield; (*Fische*) catch; **a~n** *vt* exploit; (*Min*) work.

ausbild- ['aʊsbɪld] *cpd*: **~en** *vt* educate; *Lehrling, Soldat* instruct, train; *Fähigkeiten* develop; *Geschmack* cultivate; **A~er** *m* -s, - instructor; **A~ung** *f* education; training;

instruction; development, cultivation.

ausbitten ['ausbɪtən] vt irreg: **sich** (dat) **etw** ~ (erbitten) ask for sth; (verlangen) insist on sth.

ausbleiben ['ausblaɪbən] vi irreg (Personen) stay away, not come; (Ereignisse) fail to happen, not happen.

Ausblick ['ausblɪk] m (lit, fig) prospect, outlook, view.

ausbomben ['ausbɔmbən] vt bomb out.

ausbrechen ['ausbrɛçən] irreg vi break out; **in Tränen/Gelächter** ~ burst into tears/out laughing; vt break off.

ausbreiten ['ausbraɪtən] vt spread (out); Arme stretch out; vr spread; (über Thema) expand, enlarge (über +acc on).

ausbrennen ['ausbrɛnən] irreg vt scorch; Wunde cauterize; vi burn out.

ausbringen ['ausbrɪŋən] vt irreg ein Hoch propose.

Ausbruch ['ausbrux] m outbreak; (von Vulkan) eruption; (Gefühls—) outburst; (von Gefangenen) escape.

ausbrüten ['ausbry:tən] vt (lit, fig) hatch.

Ausbuchtung ['ausbuxtuŋ] f bulge; (Küste) projection, protuberance.

ausbuhen ['ausbu:ən] vt boo.

ausbürsten ['ausbyrstən] vt brush out.

Ausdauer ['ausdauər] f perseverance, stamina; **a**~**nd** a persevering.

ausdehnen ['ausde:nən] vtr (räumlich) expand; Gummi stretch; (Nebel) extend; (zeitlich) stretch; (fig) Macht extend.

ausdenken ['ausdɛŋkən] vt irreg (zu Ende denken) think through; **sich** (dat) **etw** ~ think sth up.

ausdiskutieren ['ausdɪskuti:rən] vt talk out.

ausdrehen ['ausdre:ən] vt turn or switch off; Licht auch turn out.

Ausdruck ['ausdruk] m expression, phrase; (Kundgabe, Gesichts—) expression.

ausdrücken ['ausdrykən] vt (also vr: formulieren, zeigen) express; Zigarette put out; Zitrone squeeze.

ausdrücklich a express, explicit.

ausdrucks- cpd: ~**los** a expressionless, blank; ~**voll** a expressive; **A**~**weise** f mode of expression.

auseinander [aus'ai'nandər] ad (getrennt) apart; ~ **schreiben** write as separate words; ~**bringen** vt irreg separate; ~**fallen** vi irreg fall apart; ~**gehen** vi irreg (Menschen) separate; (Meinungen) differ; (Gegenstand) fall apart; (col: dick werden) put on weight; ~**halten** vt irreg tell apart; ~**nehmen** vt irreg take to pieces, dismantle; ~**setzen** vt (erklären) set forth, explain; vr (sich verständigen) come to terms, settle; (sich befassen) concern o.s.; **A**~**setzung** f argument.

auserlesen ['aus'ɛrle:zən] a select, choice.

ausfahren ['ausfa:rən] irreg vi drive out; (Naut) put out (to sea); vt take out; (Tech) Fahrwerk drive out; **ausgefahrene Wege** rutted roads.

Ausfahrt f (des Zuges etc) leaving, departure; (Autobahn—, Garagen—) exit, way out; (Spazierfahrt) drive, excursion.

Ausfall ['ausfal] m loss; (Nichtstattfinden

cancellation; (Mil) sortie; (Fechten) lunge; (radioaktiv) fall-out; **a**~**en** vi irreg (Zähne, Haare) fall or come out; (nicht stattfinden) be cancelled; (wegbleiben) be omitted; (Person) drop out; (Lohn) be stopped; (nicht funktionieren) break down; (Resultat haben) turn out; **wie ist das Spiel ausgefallen?** what was the result of the game?; **a**~**end** a impertinent; ~**straße** f arterial road.

ausfegen ['ausfe:gən] vt sweep out.

ausfeilen ['ausfaɪlən] vt file out; Stil polish up.

ausfertigen ['ausfɛrtɪgən] vt draw up; Rechnung make out; **doppelt** ~ duplicate.

Ausfertigung f drawing up; making out; (Exemplar) copy.

ausfindig machen ['ausfɪndɪç maxən] vt discover.

ausfliegen ['ausfli:gən] vti irreg fly away; **sie sind ausgeflogen** (col) they're out.

ausflippen ['ausflɪpən] vi (col) freak out.

Ausflucht ['ausfluxt] f **-, -flüchte** excuse.

Ausflug ['ausflu:k] m excursion, outing.

Ausflügler ['ausfly:klər] m **-s, -** tripper.

Ausfluß ['ausflus] m outlet; (Med) discharge.

ausfragen ['ausfra:gən] vt interrogate, question.

ausfransen ['ausfranzən] vi fray.

ausfressen ['ausfrɛsən] vt irreg eat up; (aushöhlen) corrode; (col: anstellen) be up to.

Ausfuhr ['ausfu:r] f **-, -en** export, exportation; in cpds export.

ausführ- ['ausfy:r] cpd: ~**bar** a feasible; (Comm) exportable; ~**en** vt (verwirklichen) carry out; Person take out; Hund take for a walk; (Comm) export; (erklären) give details of; ~**lich** a detailed; ad in detail; **A**~**lichkeit** f detail; **A**~**ung** f execution, performance; (Durchführung) completion; (Herstellungsart) version; (Erklärung) explanation.

ausfüllen ['ausfylən] vt fill up; Fragebogen etc fill in; (Beruf) be fulfilling for.

Ausgabe ['ausga:bə] f (Geld) expenditure, outlay; (Aushändigung) giving out; (Gepäck—) left-luggage office; (Buch) edition; (Nummer) issue.

Ausgang ['ausgaŋ] m way out, exit; (Ende) end; (Ausgangspunkt) starting point; (Ergebnis) result; (Ausgehtag) free time, time off; **kein** ~ no exit; ~**sbasis** f, ~**spunkt** m starting point; ~**ssperre** f curfew.

ausgeben ['ausge:bən] irreg vt Geld spend; (austeilen) issue, distribute; vr: **sich für etw/jdn** ~ pass o.s. off as sth/sb.

ausgebucht ['ausgəbu:xt] a fully booked.

ausgedient ['ausgədi:nt] a Soldat discharged; (verbraucht) no longer in use; ~**haben** have done good service.

ausgefallen ['ausgəfalən] a (ungewöhnlich) exceptional.

ausgeglichen ['ausgəglɪçən] a (well-)balanced; **A**~**heit** f balance; (von Mensch) even-temperedness.

Ausgeh- ['ausge:] cpd: ~**anzug** m good suit; **a**~**en** vi irreg go out; (zu Ende gehen) come to an end; (*Benzin*) run out; (*Haare, Zähne*) fall or come out; (*Feuer, Ofen, Licht*) go out; (*Strom*) go off; (*Resultat haben*) turn out; **mir ging das Benzin aus** I ran out of petrol; **auf etw** (*acc*) **a~en** aim at sth; **von etw a~en** (*wegführen*) lead away from sth; (*herrühren*) come from sth; (*zugrunde legen*) proceed from sth; **wir können davon a~en, daß . . .** we can proceed from the assumption that . . ., we can take as our starting point that . . .; **leer a~en** get nothing; **schlecht a~en** turn out badly; **~verbot** *nt* curfew.

ausgelassen ['ausɡəlasən] *a* boisterous, high-spirited; **A~heit** *f* boisterousness, high spirits *pl*, exuberance.

ausgelastet ['ausɡəlastət] *a* fully occupied.

ausgelernt ['ausɡəlɛrnt] *a* trained, qualified.

ausgemacht ['ausɡəmaxt] *a* (*col*) settled; *Dummkopf etc* out-and-out, downright; **es gilt als ~, daß . . .** it is settled that . . .; **es war eine ~e Sache, daß . . .** it was a foregone conclusion that . . .

ausgenommen ['ausɡənɔmən] *prep* +*gen* or *dat, cj* except; **Anwesende sind ~** present company excepted.

ausgeprägt ['ausɡəprɛːkt] *a* prominent.

ausgerechnet ['ausɡərɛçnət] *ad* just, precisely; **~ du/heute** you of all people/today of all days.

ausgeschlossen ['ausɡəʃlɔsən] *a* (*unmöglich*) impossible, out of the question; **es ist nicht ~, daß . . .** it cannot be ruled out that . . .

ausgeschnitten ['ausɡəʃnitən] *a Kleid* low-necked.

ausgesprochen ['ausɡəʃprɔxən] *a Faulheit, Lüge etc* out-and-out; (*unverkennbar*) marked; *ad* decidedly.

ausgezeichnet ['ausɡətsaiçnət] *a* excellent.

ausgiebig ['ausɡiːbɪç] *a Gebrauch* thorough, good; *Essen* generous, lavish; **~ schlafen** have a good sleep.

Ausgleich ['ausɡlaiç] *m* **-(e)s, -e** balance; (*Vermittlung*) reconciliation; (*Sport*) equalization; **zum ~** (+*gen*) in order to offset; **das ist ein guter ~** that's very relaxing; **a~en** *irreg vt* balance (out); reconcile; *Höhe* even up; *vi* (*Sport*) equalize; **~stor** *nt* equalizer.

ausgraben ['ausɡraːbən] *vt irreg* dig up; *Leichen* exhume; (*fig*) unearth.

Ausgrabung *f* excavation; (*Ausgraben auch*) digging up.

Ausguß ['ausɡus] *m* (*Spüle*) sink; (*Abfluß*) outlet; (*Tülle*) spout.

aushaben ['aushaːbən] *vt irreg* (*col*) *Kleidung* have taken off; *Buch* have finished.

aushalten ['aushaltən] *irreg vt* bear, stand; *Geliebte* keep; *vi* hold out; **das ist nicht zum A~** that is unbearable.

aushandeln ['aushandəln] *vt* negotiate.

aushändigen ['aushɛndɪɡən] *vt*: **jdm etw ~** hand sth over to sb.

Aushang ['aushaŋ] *m* notice.

aushängen ['aushɛŋən] *irreg vt Meldung* put up; *Fenster* take off its hinges; *vi* be displayed; *vr* hang out.

Aushängeschild *nt* (shop) sign.

ausharren ['ausharən] *vi* hold out.

ausheben ['aushɛːbən] *vt irreg Erde* lift out; *Grube* hollow out; *Tür* take off its hinges; *Diebesnest* clear out; (*Mil*) enlist.

aushecken ['aushɛkən] *vt* (*col*) concoct, think up.

aushelfen ['aushɛlfən] *vi irreg*: **jdm ~** help sb out.

Aushilfe ['aushɪlfə] *f* help, assistance; (*Person*) (temporary) worker.

Aushilfs- *cpd*: **~kraft** *f* temporary worker; **a~weise** *ad* temporarily, as a stopgap.

ausholen ['aushoːlən] *vi* swing one's arm back; (*zur Ohrfeige*) raise one's hand; (*beim Gehen*) take long strides; **weit ~** (*fig*) be expansive.

aushorchen ['aushɔrçən] *vt* sound out, pump.

aushungern ['aushuŋərn] *vt* starve out.

auskennen ['auskɛnən] *vr irreg* know thoroughly; (*an einem Ort*) know one's way about; (*in Fragen etc*) be knowledgeable.

auskippen ['auskɪpən] *vt* empty.

ausklammern ['ausklamərn] *vt Thema* exclude, leave out.

Ausklang ['ausklaŋ] *m* end.

auskleiden ['ausklaidən] *vr* undress; *vt Wand* line.

ausklingen ['ausklɪŋən] *vi irreg* (*Ton, Lied*) die away; (*Fest*) peter out.

ausklopfen ['ausklɔpfən] *vt Teppich* beat; *Pfeife* knock out.

auskochen ['auskɔxən] *vt* boil; (*Med*) sterilize; **ausgekocht** (*fig*) out-and-out.

auskommen ['auskɔmən] *vi irreg*: **mit jdm ~** get on with sb; **mit etw ~** get by with sth; **A~** *nt* **-s**: **sein A~ haben** get by.

auskosten ['auskɔstən] *vt* enjoy to the full.

auskugeln ['auskuːɡəln] *vt* (*col*) *Arm* dislocate.

auskundschaften ['auskunt-ʃaftən] *vt* spy out; *Gebiet* reconnoitre.

Auskunft ['auskunft] *f* **-, -künfte** information; (*nähere*) details *pl*, particulars *pl*; (*Stelle*) information office; (*Tel*) inquiries; **jdm ~ erteilen** give sb information.

auskuppeln ['auskupəln] *vi* disengage the clutch.

auslachen ['auslaxən] *vt* laugh at, mock.

ausladen ['auslaːdən] *irreg vt* unload; (*col*) *Gäste* cancel an invitation to; *vi* stick out.

Auslage ['auslaːɡə] *f* shop window (display); **~n** *pl* outlay, expenditure.

Ausland ['auslant] *nt* foreign countries *pl*; **im/ins ~** abroad.

Ausländer(in *f*) ['auslɛndər(ɪn)] *m* **-s, -** foreigner.

ausländisch *a* foreign.

Auslands- *cpd*: **~gespräch** *nt* international call; **~korrespondent(in** *f*) *m* foreign correspondent; **~reise** *f* trip abroad.

auslassen ['auslasən] *irreg vt* leave out;

Wort etc auch omit; *Fett* melt; *Kleidungsstück* let out; *Wut, Ärger* vent (*an* +*dat* on); *vr:* **sich über etw** (*acc*) ~ speak one's mind about sth.

Auslassung *f* omission; ~**szeichen** *nt* apostrophe.

Auslauf ['auslauf] *m* (*für Tiere*) run; (*Ausfluß*) outflow, outlet; **a**~**en** *vi irreg* run out; (*Behälter*) leak; (*Naut*) put out (to sea); (*langsam aufhören*) run down.

Ausläufer ['auslɔyfər] *m* (*von Gebirge*) spur; (*Pflanze*) runner; (*Met*) (*von Hoch*) ridge; (*von Tief*) trough.

ausleeren ['ausle:rən] *vt* empty.

auslegen ['ausle:gən] *vt Waren* lay out; *Köder* put down; *Geld* lend; (*bedecken*) cover; *Text etc* interpret.

Auslegung *f* interpretation.

Ausleihe ['auslaɪə] *f* -, -n issuing; (*Stelle*) issue desk; **a**~**n** *vt irreg* (*verleihen*) lend; **sich** (*dat*) **etw a**~**en** borrow sth.

Auslese ['ausle:zə] *f* -, -n selection; (*Elite*) elite; (*Wein*) choice wine; **a**~**n** *vt irreg* select; (*col: zu Ende lesen*) finish.

ausliefern ['ausli:fərn] *vt* deliver (up), hand over; (*Comm*) deliver; **jdm/etw ausgeliefert sein be at the mercy of** sb/sth; *vr:* **sich jdm** ~ give o.s. up to sb.

auslöschen ['auslœʃən] *vt* extinguish; (*fig*) wipe out, obliterate.

auslosen ['auslo:zən] *vt* draw lots for.

auslösen ['auslø:zən] *vt* (*Explosion, Schuß* set off; (*hervorrufen*) cause, produce; *Gefangene* ransom; *Pfand* redeem.

Auslöser *m* -s, - (*Phot*) release.

ausmachen ['ausmaxən] *vt Licht, Radio* turn off; *Feuer* put out; (*entdecken*) make out; (*vereinbaren*) agree; (*beilegen*) settle; (*Anteil darstellen, betragen*) represent; (*bedeuten*) matter; **das macht ihm nichts aus** it doesn't matter to him; **macht es Ihnen etwas aus, wenn . . .?** would you mind if . . .?

ausmalen ['ausma:lən] *vt* paint; (*fig*) describe; **sich** (*dat*) **etw** ~ imagine sth.

Ausmaß ['ausma:s] *nt* dimension; (*fig auch*) scale.

ausmerzen ['ausmɛrtsən] *vt* eliminate.

ausmessen ['ausmɛsən] *vt irreg* measure.

Ausnahme ['ausna:mə] *f* -, -n exception; **eine** ~ **machen** make an exception; ~**fall** *m* exceptional case; ~**zustand** *m* state of emergency.

ausnahms- *cpd:* ~**los** *ad* without exception; ~**weise** *ad* by way of exception, for once.

ausnehmen ['ausne:mən] *irreg vt* take out, remove; *Tier* gut; *Nest* rob; (*col: Geld abnehmen*) clean out; (*ausschließen*) make an exception of; *vr* look, appear; ~**d a** exceptional.

ausnützen ['ausnytsən] *vt Zeit, Gelegenheit* use, turn to good account; *Einfluß* use; *Mensch, Gutmütigkeit* exploit.

auspacken ['auspakən] *vt* unpack.

auspfeifen ['auspfaɪfən] *vt irreg* hiss/boo at.

ausplaudern ['ausplaudərn] *vt Geheimnis* blab.

ausprobieren ['ausprobi:rən] *vt* try (out).

Auspuff ['auspuf] *m* -(e)s, -e (*Tech*) exhaust; ~**rohr** *nt* exhaust (pipe); ~**topf** *m* (*Aut*) silencer.

ausradieren ['ausradi:rən] *vt* erase, rub out.

ausrangieren ['ausrãʒi:rən] *vt* (*col*) chuck out.

ausrauben ['ausraubən] *vt* rob.

ausräumen ['ausrɔymən] *vt Dinge* clear away; *Schrank, Zimmer* empty; *Bedenken* put aside.

ausrechnen ['ausreçnən] *vt* calculate, reckon.

Ausrechnung *f* calculation, reckoning.

Ausrede ['ausre:də] *f* excuse; **a**~**n** *vi* have one's say; *vt:* **jdm etw a**~**n** talk sb out of sth.

ausreichen ['ausraiçən] *vi* suffice, be enough; ~**d a** sufficient, adequate; (*Sch*) adequate.

Ausreise ['ausraizə] *f* departure; **bei der** ~ when leaving the country; ~**erlaubnis** *f* exit visa; **a**~**n** *vi* leave the country.

ausreißen ['ausraisən] *irreg vt* tear or pull out; *vi* (*Riß bekommen*) tear; (*col*) make off, scram.

ausrenken ['ausrɛŋkən] *vt* dislocate.

ausrichten ['ausrɪçtən] *vt Botschaft* deliver; *Gruß* pass on; *Hochzeit etc* arrange; (*erreichen*) get anywhere (*bei* with); (*in gerade Linie bringen*) get in a straight line; (*angleichen*) bring into line; **jdm etw** ~ take a message for sb; **ich werde es ihm** ~ I'll tell him.

ausrotten ['ausrɔtən] *vt* stamp out, exterminate.

ausrücken ['ausrykən] *vi* (*Mil*) move off; (*Feuerwehr, Polizei*) be called out; (*col: weglaufen*) run away.

Ausruf ['ausru:f] *m* (*Schrei*) cry, exclamation; (*Verkünden*) proclamation; **a**~**en** *vt irreg* cry out, exclaim; call out; ~**ezeichen** *nt* exclamation mark.

ausruhen ['ausru:ən] *vtr* rest.

ausrüsten ['ausrystən] *vt* equip, fit out.

Ausrüstung *f* equipment.

ausrutschen ['ausrutʃən] *vi* slip.

Aussage ['ausza:gə] *f* -, -n (*Jur*) statement; **a**~**n** *vt* say, state; *vi* (*Jur*) give evidence.

ausschalten ['ausʃaltən] *vt* switch off; (*fig*) eliminate.

Ausschank ['ausʃaŋk] *m* -(e)s, -schänke dispensing, giving out; (*Comm*) selling; (*Theke*) bar.

Ausschau ['ausʃau] *f:* ~ **halten** look out, watch (*nach* for); **a**~**en** *vi* look out (*nach* for), be on the look-out.

ausscheiden ['ausʃaidən] *irreg vt* separate; (*Med*) give off, secrete; *vi* leave (*aus etw* sth); (*Sport*) be eliminated or knocked out; **er scheidet für den Posten aus** he can't be considered for the job.

Ausscheidung *f* separation; retiral; elimination.

ausschenken ['ausʃɛŋkən] *vt* pour out; (*Comm*) sell.

ausschimpfen ['aʊsʃɪmpfən] *vt* scold, tell off.

ausschlachten ['aʊsʃlaxtən] *vt Auto* cannibalize; (*fig*) make a meal of.

ausschlafen ['aʊsʃlaːfən] *irreg vir* have a long lie (in); *vt* sleep off; **ich bin nicht ausgeschlafen** I didn't have *or* get enough sleep.

Ausschlag ['aʊsʃlaːk] *m* (*Med*) rash; (*Pendel—*) swing; (*Nadel*) deflection; **den ~ geben** (*fig*) tip the balance; **a~en** [-gən] *irreg vt* knock out; (*auskleiden*) deck out; (*verweigern*) decline; *vi* (*Pferd*) kick out; (*Bot*) sprout; (*Zeiger*) be deflected; **a~gebend** *a* decisive.

ausschließen ['aʊsʃliːsən] *vt irreg* shut *or* lock out; (*fig*) exclude; **ich will mich nicht ~** myself not excepted.

ausschließlich *a, ad* exclusive(ly); *prep +gen* excluding, exclusive of.

Ausschluß ['aʊsʃlʊs] *m* exclusion.

ausschmücken ['aʊsʃmʏkən] *vt* decorate; (*fig*) embellish.

ausschneiden ['aʊsʃnaɪdən] *vt irreg* cut out; *Büsche* trim.

Ausschnitt ['aʊsʃnɪt] *m* (*Teil*) section; (*von Kleid*) neckline; (*Zeitungs—*) cutting; (*aus Film etc*) excerpt.

ausschreiben ['aʊsʃraɪbən] *vt irreg* (*ganz schreiben*) write out (in full); (*ausstellen*) write (out); *Stelle, Wettbewerb etc* announce, advertise.

Ausschreitung ['aʊsʃraɪtʊŋ] *f* excess.

Ausschuß ['aʊsʃʊs] *m* committee, board; (*Abfall*) waste, scraps *pl*; (*Comm: also* **~ware** *f*) reject.

ausschütten ['aʊsʃʏtən] *vt* pour out; *Eimer* empty; *Geld* pay; *vr* shake (with laughter).

ausschweifend ['aʊsʃvaɪfənt] *a Leben* dissipated, debauched; *Phantasie* extravagant.

Ausschweifung *f* excess.

ausschweigen ['aʊsʃvaɪgən] *vr irreg* keep silent.

ausschwitzen ['aʊsʃvɪtsən] *vt* exude; (*Mensch*) sweat out.

aussehen ['aʊszeːən] *vi irreg* look; **das sieht nach nichts aus** that doesn't look anything special; **es sieht nach Regen aus** it looks like rain; **es sieht schlecht aus** things look bad; **A~** *nt* **-s** appearance.

aussein ['aʊszaɪn] *vi irreg* (*col*) be out; (*zu Ende*) be over.

außen ['aʊsən] *ad* outside; (*nach —*) outwards; **~ ist es rot** it's red (on the) outside; **A~antenne** *f* outside aerial; **A~bordmotor** *m* outboard motor.

aussenden ['aʊszɛndən] *vt irreg* send out, emit.

Außen- *cpd:* **~dienst** *m* outside *or* field service; (*von Diplomat*) foreign service; **~handel** *m* foreign trade; **~minister** *m* foreign minister; **~ministerium** *nt* foreign office; **~politik** *f* foreign policy; **~seite** *f* outside; **~seiter** *m* **-s, -, ~stehende(r)** *mf* outsider; **~welt** *f* outside world.

außer ['aʊsər] *prep +dat* (*räumlich*) out of; (*abgesehen von*) except; **~ Gefahr sein**

be out of danger; **~ Zweifel** beyond any doubt; **~ Betrieb** out of order; **~ sich** (*dat*) **sein/geraten** be beside o.s.; **~ Dienst** retired; **~ Landes** abroad; *cj* (*ausgenommen*) except; **~ wenn** unless; **~ daß** except; **~amtlich** a unofficial, private; **~dem** *cj* besides, in addition; **~dienstlich** a unofficial.

äußere(r,s) ['ɔʏsərə(r,z)] *a* outer, external.

außer- *cpd:* **~ehelich** a extramarital; **~gewöhnlich** a unusual; **~halb** *prep +gen, ad* outside; **A~kraftsetzung** *f* putting out of action.

äußer- *cpd:* **~lich** a, ad external; **~n** *vt* utter, express; (*zeigen*) show; *vr* give one's opinion; (*sich zeigen*) show itself.

außer- *cpd:* **~ordentlich** a extraordinary; **~planmäßig** a unscheduled; **~'stande** ad not in a position, unable.

äußerst ['ɔʏsərst] *ad* extremely, most; **~e(r,s)** a utmost; (*räumlich*) farthest; *Termin* last possible; *Preis* highest; **~enfalls** ad if the worst comes to the worst.

aussetzen ['aʊszɛtsən] *vt Kind, Tier* abandon; *Boote* lower; *Belohnung* offer; *Urteil, Verfahren* postpone; **jdn/sich etw** (*dat*) **~** lay sb/o.s. open to sth; **jdm/etw ausgesetzt sein** be exposed to sb/sth; **an jdm/etw etwas ~** find fault with sb/sth; *vi* (*aufhören*) stop; (*Pause machen*) drop out.

Aussicht ['aʊszɪçt] *f* view; (*in Zukunft*) prospect; **in ~ sein** be in view; **etw in ~ haben** have sth in view; **a~slos** a hopeless; **~spunkt** *m* viewpoint; **a~sreich** a promising; **~sturm** *m* observation tower.

aussöhnen ['aʊszøːnən] *vt* reconcile; *vr* reconcile o.s., become reconciled.

Aussöhnung *f* reconciliation.

aussondern ['aʊszɔndərn] *vt* separate, select.

aussortieren ['aʊszɔrtiːrən] *vt* sort out.

ausspannen ['aʊsʃpanən] *vt* spread *or* stretch out; *Pferd* unharness; (*col*) *Mädchen* steal (jdm from sb); *vi* relax.

aussparen ['aʊsʃpaːrən] *vt* leave open.

aussperren ['aʊsʃpɛrən] *vt* lock out.

ausspielen ['aʊsʃpiːlən] *vt Karte* lead; *Geldprämie* offer as a prize; **jdn gegen jdn ~** play sb off against sb; *vi* (*Cards*) lead; **ausgespielt haben** be finished.

Aussprache ['aʊsʃpraːxə] *f* pronunciation; (*Unterredung*) (frank) discussion.

aussprechen ['aʊsʃprɛçən] *irreg vt* pronounce; (*zu Ende sprechen*) speak; (*äußern*) say, express; *vr* (*sich äußern*) speak (*über +acc* about); (*sich anvertrauen*) unburden o.s.; (*diskutieren*) discuss; *vi* (*zu Ende sprechen*) finish speaking.

Ausspruch ['aʊsʃprʊx] *m* saying, remark.

ausspülen ['aʊsʃpyːlən] *vt* wash out; *Mund* rinse.

ausstaffieren ['aʊsʃtafiːrən] *vt* equip, kit out; *Zimmer* furnish.

Ausstand ['aʊsʃtant] *m* strike; **in den ~ treten** go on strike.

ausstatten ['aʊsʃtatən] *vt Zimmer etc*

furnish; **jdn mit etw** ~ equip sb or kit sb out with sth.

Ausstattung f (Ausstatten) provision; (Kleidung) outfit; (Aussteuer) dowry; (Aufmachung) make-up; (Einrichtung) furnishing.

ausstechen ['aʊsʃtɛçən] vt irreg Augen, Rasen, Graben dig out; Kekse cut out; (übertreffen) outshine.

ausstehen ['aʊsʃteːən] irreg vt stand, endure; vi (noch nicht dasein) be outstanding.

aussteigen ['aʊsʃtaɪgən] vi irreg get out, alight.

ausstellen ['aʊsʃtɛlən] vt exhibit, display; (col: ausschalten) switch off; Rechnung etc make out; Paß, Zeugnis issue.

Ausstellung f exhibition; (Fin) drawing up; (einer Rechnung) making out; (eines Passes etc) issuing.

aussterben ['aʊsʃtɛrbən] vi irreg die out.

Aussteuer ['aʊsʃtɔyər] f dowry.

ausstopfen ['aʊsʃtɔpfən] vt stuff.

ausstoßen ['aʊsʃtoːsən] vt irreg Luft, Rauch give off, emit; (aus Verein etc) expel, exclude; Auge poke out.

ausstrahlen ['aʊsʃtraːlən] vti radiate; (Rad) broadcast.

Ausstrahlung f radiation; (fig) charisma.

ausstrecken ['aʊsʃtrɛkən] vtr stretch out.

ausstreichen ['aʊsʃtraɪçən] vt irreg cross out; (glätten) smooth out.

ausströmen ['aʊsʃtrøːmən] vi (Gas) pour out, escape; vt give off; (fig) radiate.

aussuchen ['aʊszuːxən] vt select, pick out.

Austausch ['aʊstaʊʃ] m exchange; **a~bar** a exchangeable; **a~en** vt exchange, swop; **~motor** m reconditioned engine.

austeilen ['aʊstaɪlən] vt distribute, give out.

Auster ['aʊstər] f -, -n oyster.

austoben ['aʊstoːbən] vr (Kind) run wild; (Erwachsene) sow one's wild oats.

austragen ['aʊstraːgən] vt irreg Post deliver; Streit etc decide; Wettkämpfe hold.

Austräger ['aʊstrɛːgər] m delivery boy; (Zeitungs—) newspaper boy.

austreiben ['aʊstraɪbən] vt irreg drive out, expel; Geister exorcize.

austreten ['aʊstreːtən] irreg vi (zur Toilette) be excused; **aus etw** ~ leave sth; vt Feuer tread out, trample; Schuhe wear out; Treppe wear down.

austrinken ['aʊstrɪŋkən] irreg vt Glas drain; Getränk drink up; vi finish one's drink, drink up.

Austritt ['aʊstrɪt] m emission; (aus Verein, Partei etc) retirement, withdrawal.

austrocknen ['aʊstrɔknən] vti dry up.

ausüben ['aʊsʔyːbən] vt Beruf practise, carry out; Funktion perform; Einfluß exert; Reiz, Wirkung exercise, have (auf jdn on sb).

Ausübung f practice, exercise.

Ausverkauf ['aʊsferkaʊf] m sale; **a~en** vt sell out; Geschäft sell up; **a~t** a Karten, Artikel sold out; (Theat) Haus full.

Auswahl ['aʊsvaːl] f selection, choice (an +dat of).

auswählen ['aʊsvɛːlən] vt select, choose.

Auswander- ['aʊsvandər] cpd: **~er** m emigrant; **a~n** vi emigrate; **~ung** f emigration.

auswärtig ['aʊsvɛrtɪç] a (nicht am/vom Ort) out-of-town; (ausländisch) foreign; **A~e(s) Amt** nt Foreign Office, State Department (US).

auswärts ['aʊsvɛrts] ad outside; (nach außen) outwards; **~ essen** eat out; **A~spiel** nt away game.

auswechseln ['aʊsvɛksəln] vt change, substitute.

Ausweg ['aʊsveːk] m way out; **a~los** a hopeless.

ausweichen ['aʊsvaɪçən] vi irreg: **jdm/etw** ~ (lit) move aside or make way for sb/sth; (fig) side-step sb/sth; **~d** a evasive.

ausweinen ['aʊsvaɪnən] vr have a (good) cry.

Ausweis ['aʊsvaɪs] m -es, -e identity card, passport; (Mitglieds—, Bibliotheks— etc) card; **a~en** [-zən] irreg vt expel, banish; vr prove one's identity; **~karte** f, **~papiere** pl identity papers pl; **~ung** f expulsion.

ausweiten ['aʊsvaɪtən] vt stretch.

auswendig ['aʊsvɛndɪç] ad by heart; **~lernen** vt learn by heart.

auswert- ['aʊsvɛrt] cpd: **~en** vt evaluate; **A~ung** f evaluation, analysis; (Nutzung) utilization.

auswirk- ['aʊsvɪrk] cpd: **~en** vr have an effect; **A~ung** f effect.

auswischen ['aʊsvɪʃən] vt wipe out; **jdm eins** ~ (col) put one over on sb.

Auswuchs ['aʊsvuːks] m (out)growth; (fig) product.

auswuchten ['aʊsvʊxtən] vt (Aut) balance.

auszacken ['aʊstsakən] vt Stoff etc pink.

auszahlen ['aʊstsaːlən] vt Lohn, Summe pay out; Arbeiter pay off; Miterbe buy out; vr (sich lohnen) pay.

auszählen ['aʊstsɛːlən] vt Stimmen count; (Boxen) count out.

auszeichnen ['aʊstsaɪçnən] vt honour; (Mil) decorate; (Comm) price; vr distinguish o.s.

Auszeichnung f distinction; (Comm) pricing; (Ehrung) awarding of decoration; (Ehre) honour; (Orden) decoration; **mit** ~ with distinction.

ausziehen ['aʊstsiːən] irreg vt Kleidung take off; Haare, Zähne, Tisch etc pull out; (nachmalen) trace; vr undress; vi (aufbrechen) leave; (aus Wohnung) move out.

Auszug ['aʊstsuːk] m (aus Wohnung) removal; (aus Buch etc) extract; (Konto—) statement; (Ausmarsch) departure.

Auto ['aʊto] nt -s, -s (motor-)car; **~fahren** drive; **~bahn** f motorway; **~fahrer(in** f) m motorist, driver; **~fahrt** f drive; **a~gen** [-'geːn] a autogenous; **~'gramm** nt autograph; **~'mat** m -en, -en machine; **a~'matisch** a automatic; **a~'nom** [-'noːm] a autonomous.

Autopsie [aʊtɔ'psiː] f post-mortem, autopsy.

Autor ['aʊtɔr] *m* **-s, -en, Autorin**
[aʊ'toːrɪn] *f* author.
Auto- *cpd:* ~**radio** *nt* car radio; ~**reifen**
m car tyre; ~**rennen** *nt* motor racing.
autoritär [aʊtori'tɛːr] *a* authoritarian.
Autorität *f* authority.
Auto- *cpd:* ~**unfall** *m* car *or* motor
accident; ~**verleih** *m* car hire.
Axt [akst] *f* -, ⁻e axe.

B

B, b [beː] *nt* B, b.
Baby ['beːbi] *nt* **-s, -s** baby;
~**ausstattung** *f* layette; ~**sitter**
['beːbizɪtər] *m* **-s, -** baby-sitter.
Bach [bax] *m* -(e)s, ⁻e stream, brook.
Back- [bak] *cpd:* ~**blech** *nt* baking tray;
~**bord** *nt* -(e)s, -e (*Naut*) port; ~**e** *f* -, -n
cheek; **b~en** *vti irreg* bake; ~**enbart** *m*
sideboards *pl;* ~**enzahn** *m* molar.
Bäcker ['bɛkər] *m* **-s, -** baker; ~**ei** [-'raɪ] *f*
bakery; (~*laden*) baker's (shop).
Back- *cpd:* ~**form** *f* baking tin;
~**hähnchen** *nt* roast chicken; ~**obst** *nt*
dried fruit; ~**ofen** *m* oven; ~**pflaume** *f*
prune; ~**pulver** *nt* baking powder;
~**stein** *m* brick.
Bad [baːt] *nt* -(e)s, ⁻er bath; (*Schwimmen*)
bathe; (*Ort*) spa.
Bade- ['baːdə] *cpd:* ~**anstalt** *f* (swimming) baths *pl;* ~**anzug** *m* bathing suit;
~**hose** *f* bathing *or* swimming trunks *pl;*
~**kappe** *f* bathing cap; ~**mantel** *m* bath-
(ing) robe; ~**meister** *m* baths attendant;
b~n *vi* bathe, have a bath; *vt* bath; ~**ort**
m spa; ~**tuch** *nt* bath towel; ~**wanne** *f*
bath (tub); ~**zimmer** *nt* bathroom.
baff [baf] *a:* ~ **sein** (*col*) be flabbergasted.
Bagatelle [baga'tɛlə] *f* -, -n trifle.
Bagger ['bagər] *m* **-s, -** excavator; (*Naut*)
dredger; **b~n** *vti* excavate; (*Naut*)
dredge.
Bahn [baːn] *f* -, **-en** railway, railroad (*US*);
(*Weg*) road, way; (*Spur*) lane; (*Renn~*)
track; (*Astron*) orbit; (*Stoff~*) length;
b~brechend *a* pioneering; ~**damm** *m*
railway embankment; **b~en** *vt:*
sich/jdm einen Weg b~en clear a
way/a way for sb; ~**fahrt** *f* railway
journey; ~**hof** *m* station; **auf dem** ~**hof**
at the station; ~**hofshalle** *f* station concourse; ~**hofsvorsteher** *m* station-master;
~**hofswirtschaft** *f* station restaurant;
~**linie** *f* (railway) line; ~**steig** *m* platform; ~**steigkarte** *f* platform ticket;
~**strecke** *f* (railway) line; ~**übergang**
m level crossing, grade crossing (*US*);
~**wärter** *m* signalman.
Bahre ['baːrə] *f* -, -n stretcher.
Bajonett [bajo'nɛt] *nt* -(e)s, -e bayonett.
Bakelit ['bake'liːt] *nt* -s Bakelite ®.
Bakterien [bak'teːriən] *pl* bacteria *pl.*
Balance [ba'lãːsə] *f* -, -n balance, equilibrium.
balan'cieren *vti* balance.
bald [balt] *ad* (*zeitlich*) soon; (*beinahe*)
almost; ~ . . . ~ . . . now. . . now. . .; ~**ig**

['baldɪç] *a* early, speedy; ~**möglichst** *ad*
as soon as possible.
Baldrian ['baldriaːn] *m* **-s, -e** valerian.
Balken ['balkən] *m* **-s, -** beam; (*Trag~*)
girder; (*Stütz~*) prop.
Balkon [bal'kõː] *m* **-s, -s** *or* **-e** balcony;
(*Theat*) (dress) circle.
Ball [bal] *m* **-(e)s,** ⁻e ball; (*Tanz*) dance,
ball.
Ballade [ba'laːdə] *f* -, -n ballad.
Ballast ['balast] *m* -(e)s, -e ballast; (*fig*)
weight, burden.
Ballen ['balən] *m* **-s, -** bale; (*Anat*) ball;
b~ *vt* (*formen*) make into a ball; **Faust**
clench; *vr* build up; (*Menschen*) gather.
Ballett [ba'lɛt] *nt* -(e)s, -e ballet;
~**(t)änzer(in** *f*) *m* ballet dancer.
Ball- *cpd:* ~**junge** *m* ball boy; ~**kleid** *nt*
evening dress.
Ballon [ba'lõː] *m* **-s, -s** *or* **-e** balloon.
Ballspiel *nt* ball game.
Ballung ['balʊŋ] *f* concentration; (*von*
Energie) build-up; ~**sgebiet** *nt* conur-
bation.
Bambus ['bambus] *m* **-ses, -se** bamboo;
~**rohr** *nt* bamboo cane.
Bammel ['baməl] *m* **-s** (*col*) **(einen)** ~
haben vor jdm/etw be scared of sb/sth.
banal [ba'naːl] *a* banal; **B~ität**
[banali'tɛːt] *f* banality.
Banane [ba'naːnə] *f* -, -n banana.
Banause [ba'naʊzə] *m* **-n, -n** philistine.
Band [bant] *m* **-(e)s,** ⁻e (*Buch~*) volume;
nt **-(e)s,** ⁻er (*Stoff~*) ribbon, tape;
(*Fließ~*) production line; (*Faß~*) hoop;
(*Ton~*) tape; (*Anat*) ligament; **etw auf** ~
aufnehmen tape sth; **am laufenden** ~
(*col*) non-stop; *nt* **-(e)s, -e** (*Freund-*
schafts~ etc) bond; [bɛnt] *f* -, **-s** band,
group.
Bandage [ban'daːʒə] *f* -, -n bandage.
banda'gieren *vt* bandage.
Bande ['bandə] *f* -, -n band; (*Straßen~*)
gang.
bändigen ['bɛndɪgən] *vt Tier* tame; *Trieb,*
Leidenschaft control, restrain.
Bandit [ban'diːt] *m* **-en, -en** bandit.
Band- *cpd:* ~**maß** *nt* tape measure;
~**säge** *f* band saw; ~**scheibe** *f* (*Anat*)
disc; ~**wurm** *m* tapeworm.
bange ['baŋə] *a* scared; (*besorgt*) anxious;
jdm wird es ~ sb is becoming scared;
jdm ~ **machen** scare sb; **B~macher** *m*
-s, - scaremonger; ~**n** *vi:* **um jdn/etw**
~**n** be anxious *or* worried about sb/sth.
Banjo ['banjo, 'bɛndʒo] *nt* **-s, -s** banjo.
Bank [baŋk] *f* -, ⁻e (*Sitz~*) bench; (*Sand-*
etc) (sand)bank *or* -bar; *f* -, -en (*Geld~*)
bank; ~**anweisung** *f* banker's order;
~**beamte(r)** *m* bank clerk.
Bankett [baŋ'kɛt] *nt* -(e)s, -e (*Essen*) banquet; (*Straßenrand*) verge.
Bankier [baŋki'eː] *m* **-s, -s** banker.
Bank- *cpd:* ~**konto** *m* bank account;
~**note** *f* banknote; ~**raub** *m* bank
robbery.
Bankrott [baŋ'krɔt] *m* -(e)s, -e bankruptcy; ~ **machen** go bankrupt; **b~** *a*
bankrupt.

Bann [ban] *m* -(e)s, -e (*Hist*) ban; (*Kirchen—*) excommunication; (*fig*: *Zauber*) spell; **b~en** *vt* Geister exorcise; *Gefahr* avert; (*bezaubern*) enchant; (*Hist*) banish; **~er** *nt* -s, - banner, flag.

bar [ba:r] *a* (*unbedeckt*) bare; (*frei von*) lacking (*gen* in); (*offenkundig*) utter, sheer; **~e(s) Geld** cash; **etw (in) ~ bezahlen** pay sth (in) cash; **etw für ~e Münze nehmen** (*fig*) take sth at its face value; **B~ f ~, -s bar.**

Bär [bɛ:r] *m* -en, -en bear.

Baracke [ba'rakə] *f* -, -n hut, barrack.

barbarisch [bar'ba:riʃ] *a* barbaric, barbarous.

Bar- *cpd*: **~bestand** *m* money in hand; **b~fuß** *a* barefoot; **~geld** *nt* cash, ready money; **b~geldlos** *a* non-cash; **b~häuptig** *a* bareheaded; **~hocker** *m* bar stool; **~kauf** *m* cash purchase; **~keeper** ['ba:rki:pər] *m* -s, -, **~mann** *m* barman, bartender.

barmherzig [barm'hɛrtsɪç] *a* merciful, compassionate; **B~keit** *f* mercy, compassion.

Barometer [baro'me:tər] *nt* -s, - barometer.

Baron [ba'ro:n] *m* -s, -e baron; **~esse** [baro'nɛsə] *f* -, -n, **~in** *f* baroness.

Barren ['barən] *m* -s, - parallel bars *pl*; (*Gold—*) ingot.

Barriere [bari'ɛ:rə] *f* -, -n barrier.

Barrikade [bari'ka:də] *f* -, -n barricade.

Barsch [barʃ] *m* -(e)s, -e perch; **b~** [barʃ] *a* brusque, gruff.

Bar- *cpd*: **~schaft** *f* ready money; **~scheck** *m* open *or* uncrossed cheque.

Bart [ba:rt] *m* -(e)s, **·e** beard; (*Schlüssel—*) bit.

bärtig ['bɛ:rtɪç] *a* bearded.

Barzahlung *f* cash payment.

Base ['ba:zə] *f* -, -n (*Chem*) base; (*Kusine*) cousin.

basieren [ba'zi:rən] *vt* base; *vi* be based.

Basis ['ba:zɪs] *f* -, **Basen** basis.

basisch [ba:zɪʃ] *a* (*Chem*) alkaline.

Baß [bas] *m* **Basses, Bässe** bass; **~schlüssel** *m* bass clef; **~stimme** *f* bass voice.

Bassin [ba'sɛ̃:] *nt* -s, -s pool.

Bassist [ba'sɪst] *m* bass.

Bast [bast] *m* -(e)s, -e raffia; **b~eln** *vt* make; *vi* do handicrafts.

Bataillon [batal'jo:n] *nt* -s, -e battalion.

Batist [ba'tɪst] *m* -(e)s, -e batiste.

Batterie [bato'ri:] *f* battery.

Bau [bau] *m* -(e)s (*Bauen*) building, construction; (*Aufbau*) structure; (*Körper—*) frame; (*Baustelle*) building site; *pl* **~e** (*Tier—*) hole, burrow; (*Min*) working(s); *pl* **~ten** (*Gebäude*) building; **sich im ~ befinden** be under construction; **~arbeiter** *m* building worker.

Bauch [baux] *m* -(e)s, **Bäuche** belly; (*Anat auch*) stomach, abdomen; **~fell** *nt* peritoneum; **b~ig** *a* bulging; **~muskel** *m* abdominal muscle; **~redner** *m* ventriloquist; **~tanz** *m* belly dance; belly dancing; **~schmerzen** *pl*, **~weh** *nt* stomach-ache.

bauen ['bauən] *vti* build; (*Tech*) construct; **auf jdn/etw ~** depend *or* count upon sb/sth.

Bauer ['bauər] *m* -n *or* -s, -n farmer; (*Schach*) pawn; *nt or m* -s, - (*Vogel—*) cage.

Bäuerin ['bɔʏɤrɪn] *f* farmer; (*Frau des Bauers*) farmer's wife.

bäuerlich *a* rustic.

Bauern- *cpd*: **~brot** *nt* black bread; **~fänge'rei** *f* deception; **~haus** *nt* farmhouse; **~hof** *m* farm(yard); **~schaft** *f* farming community.

Bau- *cpd*: **b~fällig** *a* dilapidated; **~fälligkeit** *f* dilapidation; **~firma** *f* construction firm; **~führer** *m* site foreman; **~gelände** *f* building site; **~genehmigung** *f* building permit; **~herr** *m* purchaser; **~kasten** *m* box of bricks; **~kosten** *pl* construction costs *pl*; **~land** *nt* building land; **~leute** *pl* building workers *pl*; **b~lich** *a* structural.

Baum [baum] *m* -(e)s, **Bäume** tree.

baumeln ['bauməln] *vi* dangle.

bäumen ['bɔʏmən] *vr* rear (up).

Baum- *cpd*: **~schule** *f* nursery; **~stamm** *m* tree trunk; **~stumpf** *m* tree stump; **~wolle** *f* cotton.

Bau- *cpd*: **~plan** *m* architect's plan; **~platz** *m* building site.

Bausch [bauʃ] *m* -(e)s, **Bäusche** (*Watte—*) ball, wad; **in ~ und Bogen** (*fig*) lock, stock and barrel; **b~en** *vtir* puff out; **b~ig** *a* baggy, wide.

Bau- *cpd*: **b~sparen** *vi* insep save with a building society; **~sparkasse** *f* building society; **~stein** *m* building stone, free-stone; **~stelle** *f* building site; **~teil** *m* prefabricated part (of building); **~unternehmer** *m* contractor, builder; **~weise** *f* (method of) construction; **~werk** *nt* building; **~zaun** *m* hoarding.

Bazillus [ba'tsɪlus] *m* -, **Bazillen** bacillus.

beabsichtigen [bə'apzɪçtɪgən] *vt* intend.

beachten [bə'axtən] *vt* take note of; *Vorschrift* obey; *Vorfahrt* observe; **~swert** *a* noteworthy.

beachtlich *a* considerable.

Beachtung *f* notice, attention, observation.

Beamte(r) [bə'amtə(r)] *m* -n, **-n**, **Beamtin** *f* official, civil servant; (*Bank—etc*) employee.

beängstigend [bə'ɛŋstɪgənt] *a* alarming.

beanspruchen [bə'anʃpruxən] *vt* claim; *Zeit, Platz* take up, occupy; *Mensch* take up sb's time.

beanstanden [bə'anʃtandən] *vt* complain about, object to.

Beanstandung *f* complaint.

beantragen [bə'antra:gən] *vt* apply for, ask for.

beantworten [bə'antvɔrtən] *vt* answer.

Beantwortung *f* reply (*gen* to).

bearbeiten [bə'arbaitən] *vt* work; *Material* process; *Thema* deal with; *Land* cultivate; (*Chem*) treat; *Buch* revise; (*col: beeinflussen wollen*) work on.

Bearbeitung *f* processing; treatment; cultivation; revision.

Beatmung [bə'ʔa:tmuŋ] f respiration.

beaufsichtigen [bə'ʔaufzɪçtɪgən] vt supervise.

Beaufsichtigung f supervision.

beauftragen [bə'ʔauftra:gən] vt instruct; **jdn mit etw ~** entrust sb with sth.

bebauen [bə'bauən] vt build on; (Agr) cultivate.

beben ['be:bən] vi tremble, shake; **B~** nt -s - earthquake.

bebildern [bə'bɪldərn] vt illustrate.

Becher ['beçər] nt -s, - mug; (ohne Henkel) tumbler.

Becken ['bɛkən] nt -s, - basin; (Mus) cymbal; (Anat) pelvis.

bedacht [bə'daxt] a thoughtful, careful; **auf etw** (acc) **~ sein** be concerned about sth.

bedächtig [bə'dɛçtɪç] a (umsichtig) thoughtful, reflective; (langsam) slow, deliberate.

bedanken [bə'daŋkən] vr say thank you (bei jdm to sb).

Bedarf [bə'darf] m -(e)s need, requirement; (Comm) demand; supply; **je nach ~** according to demand; **bei ~** if necessary; **~ an etw** (dat) **haben** be in need of sth; **~sartikel** m requisite; **~sfall** m case of need; **~shaltestelle** f request stop.

bedauerlich [bə'dauərlɪç] a regrettable.

bedauern [bə'dauərn] vt be sorry for; (bemitleiden) pity; **B~** nt -s regret; **~swert** a Zustände regrettable; Mensch pitiable, unfortunate.

bedecken [bə'dɛkən] vt cover.

bedeckt a covered; Himmel overcast.

bedenken [bə'dɛŋkən] vt irreg think (over), consider; **B~** nt -s, - (Überlegen) consideration; (Zweifel) doubt; (Skrupel) scruple.

bedenklich a doubtful; (bedrohlich) dangerous, risky.

Bedenkzeit f time for reflection.

bedeuten [bə'dɔytən] vt mean; signify; (wichtig sein) be of importance; **~d** a important; (beträchtlich) considerable.

Bedeutung f meaning; significance; (Wichtigkeit) importance; **b~slos** a insignificant, unimportant; **b~svoll** a momentous, significant.

bedienen [bə'di:nən] vt serve; Maschine work, operate; vr (beim Essen) help o.s.; (gebrauchen) make use (gen of).

Bedienung f service; (Kellnerin) waitress; (Verkäuferin) shop assistant; (Zuschlag) service (charge).

bedingen [bə'dɪŋən] vt (voraussetzen) demand, involve; (verursachen) cause, occasion.

bedingt a limited, conditional; Reflex conditioned.

Bedingung f condition; (Voraussetzung) stipulation; **~sform** f (Gram) conditional; **b~slos** a unconditional.

bedrängen [bə'drɛŋən] vt pester, harass.

Bedrängnis f trouble.

bedrohen [bə'dro:ən] vt threaten.

bedrohlich a ominous, threatening.

Bedrohung f threat, menace.

bedrucken [bə'drukən] vt print on.

bedrücken [bədrʏkən] vt oppress, trouble.

bedürf- [bə'dʏrf] cpd: **~en** vi irreg +gen need, require; **B~nis** nt -ses, -se need; **B~nis nach etw haben** need sth; **B~nisanstalt** f public convenience, comfort station (US); **~nislos** a frugal, modest; **~tig** a in need (gen of), poor, needy.

beehren [bə'ʔe:rən] vt honour; **wir ~ uns** we have pleasure in.

beeilen [bə'ʔailən] vr hurry.

beeindrucken [bə'ʔaindrukən] vt impress, make an impression on.

beeinflussen [bə'ʔainflusən] vt influence.

Beeinflussung f influence.

beeinträchtigen [bə'ʔaintrɛçtɪgən] vt affect adversely; Freiheit infringe upon.

beend(ig)en [bə'ʔɛnd(ɪg)ən] vt end, finish, terminate.

Beend(ig)ung f end(ing), finish(ing).

beengen [bə'ʔɛŋən] vt cramp; (fig) hamper, oppress.

beerben [bə'ʔɛrbən] vt inherit from.

beerdigen [bə'ʔe:rdɪgən] vt bury.

Beerdigung f funeral, burial; **~s-unternehmer** m undertaker.

Beere ['be:rə] f -, -n berry; (Trauben—) grape.

Beet [be:t] nt -(e)s, -e bed.

befähigen [bə'fɛ:ɪgən] vt enable.

befähigt a (begabt) talented; (fähig) capable (für of).

Befähigung f capability; (Begabung) talent, aptitude.

befahrbar [bə'fa:rba:r] a passable; (Naut) navigable.

befahren [bə'fa:rən] vt irreg use, drive over; (Naut) navigate; a used.

befallen [bə'falən] vt irreg come over.

befangen [bə'faŋən] a (schüchtern) shy, self-conscious; (voreingenommen) biased; **B~heit** f shyness; bias.

befassen [bə'fasən] vr concern o.s.

Befehl [bə'fe:l] m -(e)s, -e command, order; **b~en** irreg vt order; **jdm etw b~en** order sb to do sth; vi give orders; **b~igen** vt be in command of; **~sempfänger** m subordinate; **~sform** f (Gram) imperative; **~shaber** m -s, - commanding officer; **~sverweigerung** f insubordination.

befestigen [bə'fɛstɪgən] vt fasten (an +dat to); (stärken) strengthen; (Mil) fortify.

Befestigung f fastening; strengthening; (Mil) fortification.

befeuchten [bə'fɔyçtən] vt damp(en), moisten.

befinden [bə'fɪndən] irreg vr be; (sich fühlen) feel; vt: **jdn/etw für or als etw ~** deem sb/sth to be sth; vi decide (über +acc on), adjudicate; **B~** nt -s health, condition; (Meinung) view, opinion.

befliegen [bə'fli:gən] vt irreg fly to.

befolgen [bə'fɔlgən] vt comply with, follow.

befördern [bə'fœrdərn] vt (senden) transport, send; (beruflich) promote.

Beförderung f transport, conveyance; promotion; ~skosten pl transport costs pl.

befragen [bəˈfraːgən] vt question.

befreien [bəˈfraɪən] vt set free; (erlassen) exempt.

Befreier m -s, - liberator.

Befreiung f liberation, release; (Erlassen) exemption.

befremden [bəˈfrɛmdən] vt surprise, disturb; B~ nt -s surprise, astonishment.

befreunden [bəˈfrɔyndən] vr make friends; (mit Idee etc) acquaint o.s.

befreundet a friendly.

befriedigen [bəˈfriːdɪgən] vt satisfy; ~d a satisfactory.

Befriedigung f satisfaction, gratification.

befristet [bəˈfrɪstət] a limited.

befruchten [bəˈfruxtən] vt fertilize; (fig) stimulate.

Befugnis [bəˈfuːknɪs] f -, -se authorization, powers pl.

befugt a authorized, entitled.

befühlen [bəˈfyːlən] vt feel, touch.

Befund [bəˈfunt] m -(e)s, -e findings pl; (Med) diagnosis.

befürchten [bəˈfyrçtən] vt fear.

Befürchtung f fear, apprehension.

befürwort- [bəˈfyːrvɔrt] cpd: ~en vt support, speak in favour of; B~er m -s, - supporter, advocate; B~ung f support(ing), favouring.

begabt [bəˈgaːpt] a gifted.

Begabung [bəˈgaːbʊŋ] f talent, gift.

begatten [bəˈgatən] vr mate; vt mate or pair (with).

begeben [bəˈgeːbən] vr irreg (gehen) proceed (zu, nach to); (geschehen) occur; B~heit f occurrence.

begegnen [bəˈgeːgnən] vi meet (jdm sb); meet with (etw (dat) sth); (behandeln) treat (jdm sb); Blicke ~ sich eyes meet.

Begegnung f meeting.

begehen [bəˈgeːən] vt irreg Straftat commit; (abschreiten) cover; Straße etc use, negotiate; Feier celebrate.

begehren [bəˈgeːrən] vt desire; ~swert a desirable.

begehrt a in demand; Junggeselle eligible.

begeistern [bəˈgaɪstərn] vt fill with enthusiasm, inspire; vr: sich für etw ~ get enthusiastic about sth.

begeistert a enthusiastic.

Begeisterung f enthusiasm.

Begierde [bəˈgiːrdə] f -, -n desire, passion.

begierig [bəˈgiːrɪç] a eager, keen.

begießen [bəˈgiːsən] vt irreg water; (mit Alkohol) drink to.

Beginn [bəˈgɪn] m -(e)s beginning; zu ~ at the beginning; b~en vti irreg start, begin.

beglaubigen [bəˈglaʊbɪgən] vt countersign.

Beglaubigung f countersignature; ~sschreiben nt credentials pl.

begleichen [bəˈglaɪçən] vt irreg settle, pay.

Begleit- [bəˈglaɪt] cpd: b~en vt accompany; (Mil) escort; ~er m -s, -

companion; (Freund) escort; (Mus) accompanist; ~erscheinung f concomitant (occurrence); ~musik f accompaniment; ~schiff nt escort vessel; ~schreiben nt covering letter; ~umstände pl concomitant circumstances pl; ~ung f company; (Mil) escort; (Mus) accompaniment.

beglücken [bəˈglʏkən] vt make happy, delight.

beglückwünschen [bəˈglʏkvʏnʃən] vt congratulate (zu on).

Beglückwünschung f congratulation, good wishes pl.

begnadigen [bəˈgnaːdɪgən] vt pardon.

Begnadigung f pardon, amnesty.

begnügen [bəˈgnyːgən] vr be satisfied, content o.s.

Begonie [beˈgoːniə] f begonia.

begraben [bəˈgraːbən] vt irreg bury.

Begräbnis [bəˈgrɛːpnɪs] nt -ses, -se burial, funeral.

begradigen [bəˈgraːdɪgən] vt straighten (out).

begreifen [bəˈgraɪfən] vt irreg understand, comprehend.

begreiflich [bəˈgraɪflɪç] a understandable.

Begrenztheit [bəˈgrɛntsthaɪt] f limitation, restriction; (fig) narrowness.

Begriff [bəˈgrɪf] m -(e)s, -e concept, idea; im ~ sein, etw zu tun be about to do sth; schwer von ~ (col) slow, dense; ~sbestimmung f definition; b~sstutzig a dense, slow.

begründ- [bəˈgrʏnd] cpd: ~en vt (Gründe geben) justify; ~et a well-founded, justified; B~ung f justification, reason.

begrüßen [bəˈgryːsən] vt greet, welcome; ~swert a welcome.

Begrüßung f greeting, welcome.

begünstigen [bəˈgʏnstɪgən] vt Person favour; Sache further, promote.

begutachten [bəˈguːtʔaxtən] vt assess.

begütert [bəˈgyːtərt] a wealthy, well-to-do.

behaart [bəˈhaːrt] a hairy.

behäbig [bəˈhɛːbɪç] a (dick) portly, stout; (geruhsam) comfortable.

behaftet [bəˈhaftət] a: mit etw ~ sein be afflicted by sth.

behagen [bəˈhaːgən] vi: das behagt ihm nicht he does not like it; B~ nt -s comfort, ease.

behaglich [bəˈhaːklɪç] a comfortable, cosy; B~keit f comfort, cosiness.

behalten [bəˈhaltən] vt irreg keep, retain; (im Gedächtnis) remember.

Behälter [bəˈhɛltər] m -s, - container, receptacle.

behandeln [bəˈhandəln] vt treat; Thema deal with; Maschine handle.

Behandlung f treatment; (von Maschine) handling.

beharren [bəˈharən] vi: auf etw (dat) ~ stick or keep to sth.

beharrlich [bəˈharlɪç] a (ausdauernd) steadfast, unwavering; (hartnäckig) tenacious, dogged; B~keit f steadfastness; tenacity.

behaupten [bəˈhaʊptən] vt claim, assert,

maintain; *sein Recht* defend; *vr* assert o.s.

Behauptung *f* claim, assertion.

Behausung [bə'hauzʊŋ] *f* dwelling, abode; (*armselig*) hovel.

beheimatet [bə'haimatət] *a* domiciled; *Tier, Pflanze* with its habitat in.

beheizen [bə'haitsən] *vt* heat.

Behelf [bə'hɛlf] *m* **-(e)s, -e** expedient, makeshift; **b~en** *vr irreg:* **sich mit etw b~en** make do with sth; **b~smäßig** *a* improvised, makeshift; (*vorübergehend*) temporary.

behelligen [bə'hɛlɪgən] *vt* trouble, bother.

Behendigkeit [bə'hɛndɪçkait] *f* agility, quickness.

beherbergen [bə'hɛrbɛrgən] *vt* put up, house.

beherrschen [bə'hɛrʃən] *vt Volk* rule, govern; *Situation* control; *Sprache, Gefühle* master; *vr* control o.s.

beherrscht *a* controlled; **B~heit** *f* self-control.

Beherrschung *f* rule; control; mastery.

beherzigen [bə'hɛrtsɪgən] *vt* take to heart.

beherzt *a* spirited, brave.

behilflich [bə'hɪlflɪç] *a* helpful; **jdm ~ sein** help sb (*bei* with).

behindern [bə'hɪndərn] *vt* hinder, impede.

Behinderte(r) *mf* disabled person.

Behinderung *f* hindrance; (*Körper—*) handicap.

Behörde [bə'hø:rdə] *f* **-, -n** authorities *pl.*

behördlich [bə'hø:rtlɪç] *a* official.

behüten [bə'hy:tən] *vt* guard; **jdn vor etw** (*dat*) **~** preserve sb from sth.

behutsam [bə'hu:tza:m] *a* cautious, careful; **B~keit** *f* caution, carefulness.

bei [bai] *prep* +*dat* (*örtlich*) near, by; (*zeitlich*) at, on; (*während*) during; **~m Friseur** at the hairdresser's; **~ uns** at our place; **~ einer Firma arbeiten** work for a firm; **~ Nacht** at night; **~ Nebel** in fog; **~ Regen** if it rains; **etw ~ sich haben** have sth on one; **jdn ~ sich haben** have sb with one; **~ Goethe** in Goethe; **~m Militär** in the army; **~m Fahren** while driving.

beibehalten ['baibəhaltən] *vt irreg* keep, retain.

Beibehaltung *f* keeping, retaining.

Beiblatt ['baiblat] *nt* supplement.

beibringen ['baibrɪŋən] *vt irreg Beweis, Zeugen* bring forward; *Gründe* adduce; **jdm etw ~** (*zufügen*) inflict sth on sb; (*zu verstehen geben*) make sb understand sth; (*lehren*) teach sb sth.

Beichte ['baiçtə] *f* **-, -n** confession; **b~n** *vt* confess; *vi* go to confession.

Beicht- *cpd:* **~geheimnis** *nt* secret of the confessional; **~stuhl** *m* confessional.

beide(s) ['baidə(z)] *pron, a* both; **meine ~n Brüder** my two brothers, both my brothers; **die ersten ~n** the first two; **wir ~** we two; **einer von ~n** one of the two; **alles ~s** both (of them); **~mal** *ad* both times; **~rlei** *a* of both; **~rseitig** *a* mutual, reciprocal; **~rseits** *ad* mutually; *prep* +*gen* on both sides of.

beidrehen [baidre:ən] *vi* heave to.

beieinander [bai'ai'nandər] *ad* together.

Beifahrer ['baifa:rər] *m* passenger; **~sitz** *m* passenger seat.

Beifall ['baifal] *m* **-(e)s** applause; (*Zustimmung*) approval.

beifällig ['baifɛlɪç] *a* approving; *Kommentar* favourable.

Beifilm ['baifilm] *m* supporting film.

beifügen ['baify:gən] *vt* enclose.

beige ['bε:ʒə] *a* beige, fawn.

beigeben ['baige:bən] *irreg vt* (*zufügen*) add; (*mitgeben*) give; *vi* (*nachgeben*) give in (*dat* to).

Beigeschmack ['baigəʃmak] *m* aftertaste.

Beihilfe ['baihilfə] *f* aid, assistance; (*Studien—*) grant; (*Jur*) aiding and abetting.

beikommen ['baikɔmən] *vi irreg* (+*dat*) get at; (*einem Problem*) deal with.

Beil [bail] *nt* **-(e)s, -e** axe, hatchet.

Beilage [baila:gə] *f* (*Buch— etc*) supplement; (*Cook*) vegetables and potatoes *pl.*

beiläufig ['bailɔyfɪç] *a* casual, incidental; *ad* casually, by the way.

beilegen ['baile:gən] *vt* (*hinzufügen*) enclose, add; (*beimessen*) attribute, ascribe; *Streit* settle.

beileibe [bai'laibə] : **~ nicht** *ad* by no means.

Beileid ['bailait] *nt* condolence, sympathy; **herzliches ~** deepest sympathy.

beiliegend ['baili:gənt] *a* (*Comm*) enclosed.

beim [baim] = **bei dem**.

beimessen ['baimɛsən] *vt irreg* attribute, ascribe (*dat* to).

Bein [bain] *nt* **-(e)s, -e** leg; **~bruch** *m* fracture of the leg.

beinah(e) ['baina:(ə)] *ad* almost, nearly.

beinhalten [bə'ɪnhaltən] *vt* contain.

beipflichten ['baipflɪçtən] *vi:* **jdm/etw ~** agree with sb/sth.

Beirat ['baira:t] *m* legal adviser; (*Körperschaft*) advisory council; (*Eltern—*) parents' council.

beirren [bə'ɪrən] *vt* confuse, muddle; **sich nicht ~ lassen** not let o.s. be confused.

beisammen [bai'zamən] *ad* together; **B~sein** *nt* **-s** get-together.

Beischlaf ['baiʃla:f] *m* sexual intercourse.

Beisein ['baizain] *nt* **-s** presence.

beiseite [bai'zaitə] *ad* to one side, aside; **stehen** on one side, aside; **etw ~ legen** (*sparen*) put sth by; **jdn/etw ~ schaffen** put sb/get sth out of the way.

beisetzen ['baizɛtsən] *vt* bury.

Beisetzung *f* funeral.

Beisitzer ['baizɪtsər] *m* **-s, -** (*bei Prüfung*) assessor.

Beispiel ['baiʃpi:l] *nt* **-(e)s, -e** example; **sich an jdm ein ~ nehmen** take sb as an example; **zum ~** for example; **b~haft** *a* exemplary; **b~los** *a* unprecedented, unexampled; **b~sweise** *ad* for instance or example.

beispringen ['baiʃprɪŋən] *vi irreg:* **jdm ~** come to the aid of sb.

beißen ['baisən] *irreg vti* bite; (*stechen:*

Rauch, Säure) burn; *vr* (*Farben*) clash; ~**d**
a biting, caustic; (*fig auch*) sarcastic.
Beißzange ['baɪs-tsaŋə] *f* pliers *pl.*
Beistand ['baɪʃtant] *m* -(e)s, ⸚e support,
help; (*Jur*) adviser.
beistehen ['baɪʃteːən] *vi irreg*: **jdm** ~
stand by sb.
beisteuern ['baɪʃtɔʏərn] *vt* contribute.
beistimmen ['baɪʃtɪmən] *vi* (+*dat*) agree
with.
Beistrich ['baɪʃtrɪç] *m* comma.
Beitrag ['baɪtraːk] *m* -(e)s, ⸚e contribution; (*Zahlung*) fee, subscription;
(*Versicherungs—*) premium; **b**~**en**
['baɪtraːgən] *vt irreg* contribute (*zu* to);
(*mithelfen*) help (*zu* with); ~**szahlende(r)**
mf fee-paying member.
beitreten ['baɪtreːtən] *vi irreg* join (*einem
Verein* a club).
Beitritt ['baɪtrɪt] *m* joining, membership;
~**serklärung** *f* declaration of membership.
Beiwagen ['baɪvaːgən] *m* (*Motorrad—*)
sidecar; (*Straßenbahn—*) extra carriage.
beiwohnen ['baɪvoːnən] *vi*: **einer Sache**
(*dat*) ~ attend *or* be present at sth.
Beiwort ['baɪvɔrt] *nt* adjective.
Beize ['baɪtsə] *f* -, -**n** (*Holz—*) stain; (*Cook*)
marinade.
beizeiten [baɪ'tsaɪtən] *ad* in time.
bejahen [bə'jaːən] *vt Frage* say yes to,
answer in the affirmative; (*gutheißen*)
agree with.
bejahrt [bə'jaːrt] *a* aged, elderly.
bejammern [bə'jamərn] *vt* lament,
bewail; ~**swert** *a* lamentable.
bekämpfen [bə'kɛmpfən] *vt Gegner* fight;
Seuche combat; *vr* fight.
Bekämpfung *f* fight *or* struggle against.
bekannt [bə'kant] *a* (well-)known; (*nicht
fremd*) familiar; **mit jdm** ~ **sein** know
sb; **jdn mit jdm** ~ **machen** introduce sb
to sb; **sich mit etw** ~ **machen**
familiarize o.s. with sth; **das ist mir** ~ I
know that; **es/sie kommt mir** ~ **vor**
it/she seems familiar; **durch etw** ~
werden become famous because of sth;
B~**e(r)** *mf* friend, acquaintance;
B~**enkreis** *m* circle of friends; **B**~**gabe**
f announcement; ~**geben** *vt irreg*
announce publicly; ~**lich** *ad* as is well
known, as you know; ~**machen** *vt*
announce; **B**~**machung** *f* publication;
announcement; **B**~**schaft** *f* acquaintance.
bekehren [bə'keːrən] *vt* convert; *vr*
become converted.
Bekehrung *f* conversion.
bekennen [bə'kɛnən] *vt irreg* confess;
Glauben profess; **Farbe** ~ (*col*) show
where one stands.
Bekenntnis [bə'kɛntnɪs] *nt* -ses, -se admission, confession; (*Religion*) confession,
denomination; ~**schule** *f* denominational
school.
beklagen [bə'klaːgən] *vt* deplore, lament;
vr complain; ~**swert** *a* lamentable,
pathetic.
beklatschen [bə'klatʃən] *vt* applaud, clap.
bekleben [bə'kleːbən] *vt*: **etw mit**

Bildern ~ stick pictures onto sth.
bekleiden [bə'klaɪdən] *vt* clothe; *Amt*
occupy, fill.
Bekleidung *f* clothing; ~**sindustrie** *f*
clothing industry, rag trade.
beklemmen [bə'klɛmən] *vt* oppress.
beklommen [bə'klɔmən] *a* anxious,
uneasy; **B**~**heit** *f* anxiety, uneasiness.
bekommen [bə'kɔmən] *irreg vt* get,
receive; *Kind* have; *Zug* catch, get; *vi*: **jdm**
~ agree with sb.
bekömmlich [bə'kœmlɪç] *a* wholesome,
easily digestible.
bekräftigen [bə'krɛftɪgən] *vt* confirm,
corroborate.
Bekräftigung *f* corroboration.
bekreuzigen [bə'krɔʏtsɪgən] *vr* cross o.s.
bekritteln [bə'krɪtəln] *vt* criticize, pick
holes in.
bekümmern [bə'kʏmərn] *vt* worry,
trouble.
bekunden [bə'kundən] *vt* (*sagen*) state;
(*zeigen*) show.
belächeln [bə'lɛçəln] *vt* laugh at.
beladen [bə'laːdən] *vt irreg* load.
Belag [bə'laːk] *m* -(e)s, ⸚e covering, coating; (*Brot—*) spread; (*Zahn—*) tartar; (*auf
Zunge*) fur; (*Brems—*) lining.
belagern [bə'laːgərn] *vt* besiege.
Belagerung *f* siege; ~**szustand** *m* state
of siege.
Belang [bə'laŋ] *m* -(e)s importance; ~**e**
pl interests *pl*, concerns *pl*; **b**~**en** *vt* (*Jur*)
take to court; **b**~**los** *a* trivial,
unimportant; ~**losigkeit** *f* triviality.
belassen [bə'lasən] *vt irreg* (*in Zustand,
Glauben*) leave; (*in Stellung*) retain; **es**
dabei ~ leave it at that.
belasten [bə'lastən] *vt* (*lit*) burden; (*fig:
bedrücken*) trouble, worry; (*Comm*) *Konto*
debit; (*Jur*) incriminate; *vr* weigh o.s.
down; (*Jur*) incriminate o.s.; ~**d** *a* (*Jur*)
incriminating.
belästigen [bə'lɛstɪgən] *vt* annoy, pester.
Belästigung *f* annoyance, pestering.
Belastung [bə'lastuŋ] *f* (*lit*) load; (*fig:
Sorge etc*) weight; (*Comm*) charge,
debit(ing); (*Jur*) incriminatory evidence;
~**sprobe** *f* capacity test; (*fig*) test;
~**szeuge** *m* witness for prosecution.
belaufen [bə'laufən] *vr irreg* amount (*auf
+acc* to).
belauschen [bə'lauʃən] *vt* eavesdrop on.
belebt [bə'leːpt] *a Straße* crowded.
Beleg [bə'leːk] *m* -(e)s, -e (*Comm*)
receipt; (*Beweis*) documentary evidence,
proof; (*Beispiel*) example; **b**~**en**
[bə'leːgən] *vt* cover; *Kuchen, Brot* spread;
Platz reserve, book; *Kurs, Vorlesung*
register for; (*beweisen*) verify, prove; (*Mil:
mit Bomben*) bomb; ~**schaft** *f* personnel,
staff.
belehren [bə'leːrən] *vt* instruct, teach; **jdn**
eines Besseren ~ teach sb better.
Belehrung *f* instruction.
beleibt [bə'laɪpt] *a* stout, corpulent.
beleidigen [bə'laɪdɪgən] *vt* insult, offend.
Beleidigung *f* insult; (*Jur*) slander, libel.
belesen [bə'leːzən] *a* well-read.

beleuchten [bə'lɔyçtən] *vt* light, illuminate; (*fig*) throw light on.

Beleuchtung *f* lighting, illumination.

belichten [bə'liçtən] *vt* expose.

Belichtung *f* exposure; **~smesser** *m* exposure meter.

Belieben [bə'li:bən] *nt*: **(ganz) nach ~** (just) as you wish.

beliebig [bə'li:bıç] *a* any you like, as you like; **~ viel** as many as you like; **ein ~es Thema** any subject you like *or* want.

beliebt [bə'li:pt] *a* popular; **sich bei jdm ~ machen** make o.s. popular with sb; **B~heit** *f* popularity.

beliefern [bə'li:fərn] *vt* supply.

bellen ['bɛlən] *vi* bark.

belohnen [bə'lo:nən] *vt* reward.

Belohnung *f* reward.

belügen [bə'ly:gən] *vt irreg* lie to, deceive.

belustigen [bə'lustıgən] *vt* amuse.

Belustigung *f* amusement.

bemächtigen [bə'mɛçtıgən] *vr*: **sich einer Sache** (*gen*) **~** take possession of sth, seize sth.

bemalen [bə'ma:lən] *vt* paint.

bemängeln [bə'mɛŋəln] *vt* criticize.

bemannen [bə'manən] *vt* man.

Bemannung *f* manning; (*Naut, Aviat etc*) crew.

bemänteln [bə'mɛntəln] *vt* cloak, hide.

bemerk- [bə'mɛrk] *cpd*: **~bar** *a* perceptible, noticeable; **sich ~bar machen** (*Person*) make *or* get o.s. noticed; (*Unruhe*) become noticeable; **~en** *vt* (*wahrnehmen*) notice, observe; (*sagen*) say, mention; **~enswert** *a* remarkable, noteworthy; **B~ung** *f* remark; (*schriftlich auch*) note.

bemitleiden [bə'mıtlaıdən] *vt* pity.

bemühen [bə'my:ən] *vr* take trouble *or* pains.

Bemühung *f* trouble, pains *pl*, effort.

bemuttern [bə'mutərn] *vt* mother.

benachbart [bə'naxba:rt] *a* neighbouring.

benachrichtigen [bə'na:xrıçtıgən] *vt* inform.

Benachrichtigung *f* notification, information.

benachteiligen [bə'na:xtaılıgən] *vt* (put at a) disadvantage, victimize.

benehmen [bə'ne:mən] *vr irreg* behave; **B~** *nt* **-s** behaviour.

beneiden [bə'naıdən] *vt* envy; **~swert** *a* enviable.

benennen [bə'nɛnən] *vt irreg* name.

Bengel ['bɛŋəl] *m* **-s, -** (little) rascal *or* rogue.

benommen [bə'nɔmən] *a* dazed.

benötigen [bə'nø:tıgən] *vt* need.

benutzen [bə'nutsən], **benützen** [bə'nytsən] *vt* use.

Benutzer *m* **-s, -** user.

Benutzung *f* utilization, use.

Benzin [bɛnt'si:n] *nt* **-s, -e** (*Aut*) petrol, gas(oline) (*US*); **~kanister** *m* petrol can; **~tank** *m* petrol tank; **~uhr** *f* petrol gauge.

beobacht- [bə'o:baxt] *cpd*: **~en** *vt* observe; **B~er** *m* **-s, -** observer; (*eines*

Unfalls) witness; (*Press, TV*) correspondent; **B~ung** *f* observation.

bepacken [bə'pakən] *vt* load, pack.

bepflanzen [bə'pflantsən] *vt* plant.

bequem [bə'kve:m] *a* comfortable; *Ausrede* convenient; *Person* lazy, indolent; **~en** *vr* condescend (*zu* to); **B~lichkeit** *f* convenience, comfort; (*Faulheit*) laziness, indolence.

beraten [bə'ra:tən] *irreg vt* advise; (*besprechen*) discuss, debate; *vr* consult; **gut/schlecht ~ sein** be well/ill advised; **sich ~ lassen** get advice.

Berater *m* **-s, -** adviser.

beratschlagen [bə'ra:t-ʃla:gən] *vti* deliberate (on), confer (about).

Beratung *f* advice, consultation; (*Besprechung*) consultation; **~sstelle** *f* advice centre.

berauben [bə'raubən] *vt* rob.

berechenbar [bə'rɛçənba:r] *a* calculable.

berechnen [bə'rɛçnən] *vt* calculate; (*Comm: anrechnen*) charge; **~d** *a Mensch* calculating, scheming; **B~ung** *f* calculation; (*Comm*) charge.

berechtig- [bə'rɛçtıg] *cpd*: **~en** *vt* entitle, authorize; (*fig*) justify; **~t** [bə'rɛçtıçt] *a* justifiable, justified; **B~ung** *f* authorization; (*fig*) justification.

bereden [bə're:dən] *vtr* (*besprechen*) discuss; (*überreden*) persuade.

beredt [bə're:t] *a* eloquent.

Bereich [bə'raıç] *m* **-(e)s, -e** (*Bezirk*) area; (*Phys*) range; (*Ressort, Gebiet*) sphere.

bereichern [bə'raıçərn] *vt* enrich; *vr* get rich.

Bereifung [bə'raıfuŋ] *f* (set of) tyres *pl*; (*Vorgang*) fitting with tyres.

bereinigen [bə'raınıgən] *vt* settle.

bereisen [bə'raızən] *vt* travel through.

bereit [bə'raıt] *a* ready, prepared; **zu etw ~ sein** be ready for sth; **sich ~erklären** declare o.s. willing; **~en** *vt* prepare, make ready; *Kummer, Freude* cause; **~halten** *vt irreg* keep in readiness; **~legen** *vt* lay out; **~machen** *vtr* prepare, get ready; **~s** *ad* already; **B~schaft** *f* readiness; (*Polizei*) alert; **in B~schaft sein** be on the alert *or* on stand-by; **B~schaftsdienst** *m* emergency service; **~stehen** *vi irreg* (*Person*) be prepared; (*Ding*) be ready; **~stellen** *vt Kisten, Pakete etc* put ready; *Geld etc* make available; *Truppen, Maschinen* put at the ready; **B~ung** *f* preparation; **~willig** *a* willing, ready; **B~willigkeit** *f* willingness, readiness.

bereuen [bə'rɔyən] *vt* regret.

Berg [bɛrk] *m* **-(e)s, -e** mountain, hill; **b~ab** *ad* downhill; **b~an, b~auf** *ad* uphill; **~arbeiter** *m* miner; **~bahn** *f* mountain railway; **~bau** *m* mining; **b~en** ['bɛrgən] *vt irreg* (*retten*) rescue; *Ladung* salvage; (*enthalten*) contain; **~führer** *m* mountain guide; **~gipfel** *m* mountain top, peak, summit; **b~ig** ['bɛrgıç] *a* mountainous, hilly; **~kamm** *m* crest, ridge; **~kette** *f* mountain range; **~mann** *m, pl* **~leute** miner; **~rutsch**

m landslide; ~**schuh** *m* walking boot; ~**steigen** *nt* mountaineering; ~**steiger(in** *f)* *m* -**s,** - mountaineer, climber; ~**ung** ['bεrguŋ] *f (von Menschen)* rescue; *(von Material)* recovery; *(Naut)* salvage; ~**wacht** *f* mountain rescue service; ~**werk** *nt* mine.

Bericht [bə'rɪçt] *m* -**(e)s,** -**e** report, account; **b**~**en** *vti* report; ~**erstatter** *m* -**s,** - reporter, (newspaper) correspondent; ~**erstattung** *f* reporting.

berichtigen [bə'rɪçtɪgən] *vt* correct.
Berichtigung *f* correction.

beritten [bə'rɪtən] *a* mounted.

Bernstein ['bεrnʃtaɪn] *m* amber.

bersten ['bεrstən] *vi irreg* burst, split.

berüchtigt [bə'rʏçtɪçt] *a* notorious, infamous.

berücksichtigen [bə'rʏkzɪçtɪgən] *vt* consider, bear in mind.
Berücksichtigung *f* consideration.

Beruf [bə'ruːf] *m* -**(e)s,** -**e** occupation, profession; *(Gewerbe)* trade; **b**~**en** *irreg vt (in Amt)* appoint *(in +acc* to; *zu* as); *vr:* **sich auf jdn/etw b**~**en** refer *or* appeal to sb/sth; **b**~**en** *a* competent, qualified; **b**~**lich** *a* professional; ~**sausbildung** *f* vocational *or* professional training; ~**sberater** *m* careers adviser; ~**sberatung** *f* vocational guidance; ~**sbezeichnung** *f* job description; ~**sgeheimnis** *nt* professional secret; ~**skrankheit** *f* occupational disease; ~**sleben** *nt* professional life; **b**~**smäßig** *a* professional; ~**srisiko** *nt* occupational hazard; ~**sschule** *f* vocational *or* trade school; ~**ssoldat** *m* professional soldier, regular; ~**ssportler** *m* professional (sportsman); **b**~**stätig** *a* employed; ~**sverkehr** *m* commuter traffic; ~**swahl** *f* choice of a job; ~**ung** *f* vocation, calling; *(Ernennung)* appointment; *(Jur)* appeal; ~**ung einlegen** appeal.

beruhen [bə'ruːən] *vi:* **auf etw** *(dat)* ~ be based on sth; **etw auf sich** ~ **lassen** leave sth at that.

beruhigen [bə'ruːɪgən] *vt* calm, pacify, soothe; *vr (Mensch)* calm (o.s.) down; *(Situation)* calm down.
Beruhigung *f* reassurance; *(der Nerven)* calming; **zu jds** ~ to reassure sb; ~**smittel** *nt* sedative; ~**spille** *f* tranquillizer.

berühmt [bə'ryːmt] *a* famous; **B**~**heit** *f (Ruf)* fame; *(Mensch)* celebrity.

berühren [bə'ryːrən] *vt* touch; *(gefühlsmäßig bewegen)* affect; *(flüchtig erwähnen)* mention, touch on; *vr* meet, touch.
Berührung *f* contact; ~**spunkt** *m* point of contact.

besagen [bə'zaːgən] *vt* mean.
besagt *a Tag etc* in question.

besänftig- [bə'zεnftɪç] *cpd:* ~**en** *vt* soothe, calm; ~**end** *a* soothing; **B**~**ung** *f* soothing, calming.

Besatz [bə'zats] *m* -**es,** -̈**e** trimming, edging; ~**ung** *f* garrison; *(Naut, Aviat)* crew; ~**ungsmacht** *f* occupying power.

besaufen [bə'zaʊfən] *vr irreg (col)* get drunk *or* stoned.

beschädig- [bə'ʃεːdɪg] *cpd:* ~**en** *vt* damage; **B**~**ung** *f* damage; *(Stelle)* damaged spot.

beschaffen [bə'ʃafən] *vt* get, acquire; *a* constituted; **B**~**heit** *f* constitution, nature.
Beschaffung *f* acquisition.

beschäftigen [bə'ʃεftɪgən] *vt* occupy; *(beruflich)* employ; *vr* occupy *or* concern o.s.
beschäftigt *a* busy, occupied.
Beschäftigung *f (Beruf)* employment; *(Tätigkeit)* occupation; *(Befassen)* concern.

beschämen [bə'ʃεːmən] *vt* put to shame; ~**d** *a* shameful; *Hilfsbereitschaft* shaming.
beschämt *a* ashamed.

beschatten [bə'ʃatən] *vt* shade; *Verdächtige* shadow.

beschaulich [bə'ʃaʊlɪç] *a* contemplative.

Bescheid [bə'ʃaɪt] *m* -**(e)s,** -**e** information; *(Weisung)* directions *pl;* ~ **wissen** be well-informed *(über +acc* about); **ich weiß** ~ I know; **jdm** ~ **geben** *or* **sagen** let sb know.

bescheiden [bə'ʃaɪdən] *vr irreg* content o.s.; *a* modest; **B**~**heit** *f* modesty.

bescheinen [bə'ʃaɪnən] *vt irreg* shine on.

bescheinigen [bə'ʃaɪnɪgən] *vt* certify; *(bestätigen)* acknowledge.
Bescheinigung *f* certificate; *(Quittung)* receipt.

bescheißen [bə'ʃaɪsən] *vt irreg (col)* cheat.

beschenken [bə'ʃεŋkən] *vt* give presents to.

bescheren [bə'ʃeːrən] *vt:* **jdm etw** ~ give sb sth as a present; **jdn** ~ give presents to sb.
Bescherung *f* giving of presents; *(col)* mess.

beschildern [bə'ʃɪldərn] *vt* signpost.
beschimpfen [bə'ʃɪmpfən] *vt* abuse.
Beschimpfung *f* abuse, insult.

Beschiß [bə'ʃɪs] *m* -**sses** *(col)* **das ist** ~ that is a swizz *or* a cheat.

Beschlag [bə'ʃlaːk] *m* -**(e)s,** -̈**e** *(Metallband)* fitting; *(auf Fenster)* condensation; *(auf Metall)* tarnish; finish; *(Hufeisen)* horseshoe; **jdn/etw in** ~ **nehmen** *or* **mit** ~ **belegen** monopolize sb/sth; **b**~**en** [bə'ʃlaːgən] *irreg vt* cover; *Pferd* shoe; *Fenster, Metall* cover; **b**~**en sein** be well versed *(in or auf +dat* in); *vir (Fenster etc)* mist over; **b**~**nahmen** *vt* seize, confiscate; requisition; ~**nahmung** *f* confiscation, sequestration.

beschleunigen [bə'ʃlɔʏnɪgən] *vt* accelerate, speed up; *vi (Aut)* accelerate.
Beschleunigung *f* acceleration.

beschließen [bə'ʃliːsən] *vt irreg* decide on; *(beenden)* end, close.

Beschluß [bə'ʃlus] *m* -**sses,** -**schlüsse** decision, conclusion; *(Ende)* close, end.

beschmutzen [bə'ʃmʊtsən] *vt* dirty, soil.

beschneiden [bə'ʃnaɪdən] *vt irreg* cut, prune, trim; *(Rel)* circumcise.

beschönigen [bə'ʃøːnɪgən] *vt* gloss over.

beschränken [bə'ʃrεŋkən] *vt* limit, restrict *(auf +acc* to); *vr* restrict o.s.

beschrankt [bəˈʃraŋkt] a *Bahnübergang* with barrier.
beschränk- [bəˈʃrɛŋk] *cpd:* ~**t** a confined, narrow; *Mensch* limited, narrow-minded; **B**~**theit** *f* narrowness; **B**~**ung** *f* limitation.
beschreiben [bəˈʃraɪbən] *vt irreg* describe; *Papier* write on.
Beschreibung *f* description.
beschriften [bəˈʃrɪftən] *vt* mark, label.
Beschriftung *f* lettering.
beschuldigen [bəˈʃʊldɪgən] *vt* accuse.
Beschuldigung *f* accusation.
beschummeln [bəˈʃʊməln] *vti* (col) cheat.
beschütz- [bəˈʃʏts] *cpd:* ~**en** *vt* protect (*vor* +dat from); **B**~**er** *m* -**s**, - protector **B**~**ung** *f* protection.
Beschwerde [bəˈʃveːrdə] *f* -, -**n** complaint; (*Mühe*) hardship; (*pl:* *Leiden*) pain.
beschweren [bəˈʃveːrən] *vt* weight down; (*fig*) burden; *vr* complain.
beschwerlich a tiring, exhausting.
beschwichtigen [bəˈʃvɪçtɪgən] *vt* soothe, pacify.
Beschwichtigung *f* soothing, calming.
beschwindeln [bəˈʃvɪndəln] *vt* (*betrügen*) cheat; (*belügen*) fib to.
beschwingt [bəˈʃvɪŋt] a cheery, in high spirits.
beschwipst [bəˈʃvɪpst] a tipsy.
beschwören [bəˈʃvøːrən] *vt irreg Aussage* swear to; (*anflehen*) implore; *Geister* conjure up.
beseelen [bəˈzeːlən] *vt* inspire.
besehen [bəˈzeːən] *vt irreg* look at; **genau** ~ examine closely.
beseitigen [bəˈzaɪtɪgən] *vt* remove.
Beseitigung *f* removal.
Besen [ˈbeːzən] *m* -**s**, - broom; ~**stiel** *m* broomstick.
besessen [bəˈzɛsən] a possessed.
besetz- [bəˈzɛts] *cpd:* ~**en** *vt Haus, Land* occupy; *Platz* take, fill; *Posten* fill; *Rolle* cast; (*mit Edelsteinen*) set; ~**t** a full; (*Tel*) engaged, busy; *Platz* taken; *WC* engaged; **B**~**tzeichen** *nt* engaged tone; **B**~**ung** *f* occupation; filling; (*von Rolle*) casting; (*die Schauspieler*) cast.
besichtigen [bəˈzɪçtɪgən] *vt* visit, look at.
Besichtigung *f* visit.
Besied(e)lung [bəˈziːd(ə)lʊŋ] *f* population.
besiegeln [bəˈziːgəln] *vt* seal.
besiegen [bəˈziːgən] *vt* defeat, overcome.
Besiegte(r) [bəˈziːçtə(r)] *m* loser.
besinnen [bəˈzɪnən] *vr irreg* (*nachdenken*) think, reflect; (*erinnern*) remember; **sich anders** ~ change one's mind.
besinnlich a contemplative.
Besinnung *f* consciousness; **zur** ~ **kommen** recover consciousness; (*fig*) come to one's senses; **b**~**slos** a unconscious.
Besitz [bəˈzɪts] *m* -**es** possession; (*Eigentum*) property; **b**~**anzeigend** a (*Gram*) possessive; **b**~**en** *vt irreg* possess, own; *Eigenschaft* have; ~**er(in** *f*) *m* -**s**, - owner, proprietor; ~**ergreifung** *f*, ~**nahme** *f* occupation, seizure.

besoffen [bəˈzɔfən] a (col) drunk, pissed.
besohlen [bəˈzoːlən] *vt* sole.
Besoldung [bəˈzɔldʊŋ] *f* salary, pay.
besondere(r,s) [bəˈzɔndərə(r,z)] a special; (*eigen*) particular; (*gesondert*) separate; (*eigentümlich*) peculiar.
Besonderheit [bəˈzɔndərhaɪt] *f* peculiarity.
besonders [bəˈzɔndərs] ad especially, particularly; (*getrennt*) separately.
besonnen [bəˈzɔnən] a sensible, level-headed; **B**~**heit** *f* prudence.
besorg- [bəˈzɔrg] *cpd:* ~**en** *vt* (*beschaffen*) acquire; (*kaufen auch*) purchase; (*erledigen*) *Geschäfte* deal with; (*sich kümmern um*) take care of; **es jdm** ~ **en** (col) show sb what for; **B**~**nis** *f* -, -**se** anxiety, concern; ~**t** [bəˈzɔrçt] a anxious, worried; **B**~**theit** *f* anxiety, worry; **B**~**ung** *f* acquisition; (*Kauf*) purchase.
bespielen [bəˈʃpiːlən] *vt* record.
bespitzeln [bəˈʃpɪtsəln] *vt* spy on.
besprechen [bəˈʃprɛçən] *vt irreg* discuss; *Tonband etc* record, speak onto; *Buch* review; *vr* discuss, consult.
Besprechung *f* meeting, discussion; (*von Buch*) review.
besser [ˈbɛsər] a better; **nur ein** ~**er . . .** just a glorified . . .; ~**gehen** *vi irreg impers:* **es geht ihm** ~ he feels better; ~**n** *vt* make better, improve; *vr* improve; *Menschen* reform; **B**~**ung** *f* improvement; **gute B**~**ung!** get well soon; **B**~**wisser** *m* -**s**, - know-all.
Bestand [bəˈʃtant] *m* -(**e)s**, ̈**e** (*Fortbestehen*) duration, stability; (*Kassen*—) amount, balance; (*Vorrat*) stock; **eiserne(r)** ~ iron rations *pl*; ~ **haben**, **von** ~ **sein** last long, endure.
beständig [bəˈʃtɛndɪç] a (*ausdauernd*) constant (*auch fig*); *Wetter* settled; *Stoffe* resistant; *Klagen etc* continual.
Bestand- *cpd:* ~**saufnahme** *f* stocktaking; ~**teil** *m* part, component; (*Zutat*) ingredient.
bestärken [bəˈʃtɛrkən] *vt:* **jdn in etw** (*dat*) ~ strengthen or confirm sb in sth.
bestätigen [bəˈʃtɛːtɪgən] *vt* confirm; (*anerkennen, Comm*) acknowledge.
Bestätigung *f* confirmation; acknowledgement.
bestatt- [bəˈʃtat] *cpd:* ~**en** *vt* bury; **B**~**er** *m* -**s**, - undertaker; **B**~**ung** *f* funeral.
bestäuben [bəˈʃtɔybən] *vt* powder, dust; *Pflanze* pollinate.
beste(r,s) [ˈbɛstə(r,z)] a best; **sie singt am** ~**n** she sings best; **so ist es am** ~**n** it's best that way; **am** ~**n gehst du gleich** you'd better go at once; **jdn zum** ~**n haben** pull sb's leg; **etw zum** ~**n geben** tell a joke/story *etc*; **aufs** ~ in the best possible way; **zu jds B**~**n** for the benefit of sb.
bestechen [bəˈʃtɛçən] *vt irreg* bribe.
bestechlich a corruptible; **B**~**keit** *f* corruptibility.
Bestechung *f* bribery, corruption.
Besteck [bəˈʃtɛk] *nt* -(**e)s**, -**e** knife, fork and spoon, cutlery; (*Med*) set of instruments.

bestehen [bə'ʃteːən] *irreg vi* be; exist; (*andauern*) last; *vt Kampf, Probe, Prüfung* pass; ~ **auf** (+*dat*) insist on; ~ **aus** consist of.

bestehlen [bə'ʃteːlən] *vt irreg* rob.

besteigen [bə'ʃtaɪgən] *vt irreg* climb, ascend; *Pferd* mount; *Thron* ascend.

Bestell- [bə'ʃtɛl] *cpd*: ~**buch** *nt* order book; **b**~**en** *vt* order; (*kommen lassen*) arrange to see; (*nominieren*) name; *Acker* cultivate; *Grüße, Auftrag* pass on; ~**schein** *m* order coupon; ~**ung** *f* (*Comm*) order; (*Bestellen*) ordering.

bestenfalls ['bɛstən'fals] *ad* at best.

bestens ['bɛstəns] *ad* very well.

besteuern [bə'ʃtɔʏərn] *vt* tax.

Bestie ['bɛstiə] *f* (*lit, fig*) beast.

bestimm- [bə'ʃtɪm] *cpd*: ~**en** *vt Regeln* lay down; *Tag, Ort* fix; (*beherrschen*) characterize; (*aussersehen*) mean; (*ernennen*) appoint; (*definieren*) define; (*veranlassen*) induce; ~**t** *a* (*entschlossen*) firm; (*gewiß*) certain, definite; *Artikel* definite; *ad* (*gewiß*) definitely, for sure; **B**~**theit** *f* certainty; **B**~**ung** *f* (*Verordnung*) regulation; (*Festsetzen*) determining; (*Verwendungszweck*) purpose; (*Schicksal*) fate; (*Definition*) definition; **B**~**ungsort** *m* destination.

Best- *cpd*: ~**leistung** *f* best performance; **b**~**möglich** *a* best possible.

bestrafen [bə'ʃtraːfən] *vt* punish.

Bestrafung *f* punishment.

bestrahlen [bə'ʃtraːlən] *vt* shine on; (*Med*) treat with X-rays.

Bestrahlung *f* (*Med*) X-ray treatment, radiotherapy.

Bestreben [bə'ʃtreːbən] *nt* ~**s**, **Bestrebung** [bə'ʃtreːbʊŋ] *f* endeavour, effort.

bestreichen [bə'ʃtraɪçən] *vt irreg Brot* spread.

bestreiten [bə'ʃtraɪtən] *vt irreg* (*abstreiten*) dispute; (*finanzieren*) pay for, finance.

bestreuen [bə'ʃtrɔʏən] *vt* sprinkle, dust; *Straße* (spread with) grit.

bestürmen [bə'ʃtʏrmən] *vt* (*mit Fragen, Bitten etc*) overwhelm, swamp.

bestürzen [bə'ʃtʏrtsən] *vt* dismay.

bestürzt *a* dismayed.

Bestürzung *f* consternation.

Besuch [bə'zuːx] *m* **-(e)s, -e** visit; (*Person*) visitor; **einen** ~ **machen bei jdm** pay sb a visit *or* call; ~ **haben** have visitors; **bei jdm auf** *or* **zu** ~ **sein** be visiting sb; **b**~**en** *vt* visit; (*Sch etc*) attend; **gut** ~**t** well-attended; ~**er(in** *f*) *m* **-s,** - visitor, guest; ~**serlaubnis** *f* permission to visit; ~**szeit** *f* visiting hours *pl*.

betagt [bə'taːkt] *a* aged.

betasten [bə'tastən] *vt* touch, feel.

betätigen [bə'tɛːtɪgən] *vt* (*bedienen*) work, operate; *vr* involve o.s.; **sich politisch** ~ be involved in politics; **sich als etw** ~ work as sth.

Betätigung *f* activity; (*beruflich*) occupation; (*Tech*) operation.

betäuben [bə'tɔʏbən] *vt* stun; (*fig*) *Gewissen* still; (*Med*) anaesthetize.

Betäubungsmittel *nt* anaesthetic.

Bete ['beːtə] *f* **-, -n**: **rote** ~ beetroot.

beteiligen [bə'taɪlɪgən] *vr* (*an* +*dat* in) take part *or* participate, share; (*an Geschäft: finanziell*) have a share; *vt*: **jdn** ~ give sb a share *or* interest (*an* +*dat* in).

Beteiligung *f* participation; (*Anteil*) share, interest; (*Besucherzahl*) attendance.

beten ['beːtən] *vti* pray.

beteuern [bə'tɔʏərn] *vt* assert; *Unschuld* protest; **jdm etw** ~ assure sb of sth.

Beteuerung *f* assertion, protest(ation), assurance.

Beton [be'tõ] *m* **-s, -s** concrete.

betonen [bə'toːnən] *vt* stress.

betonieren [beto'niːrən] *vt* concrete.

Betonung *f* stress, emphasis.

betören [bə'tøːrən] *vt* beguile.

Betracht [bə'traxt] *m*: **in** ~ **kommen** be concerned *or* relevant; **nicht in** ~ **kommen** be out of the question; **etw in** ~ **ziehen** consider sth; **außer** ~ **bleiben** not be considered; **b**~**en** *vt* look at; (*fig auch*) consider; ~**er(in** *f*) *m* **-s,** - onlooker.

beträchtlich [bə'trɛçtlɪç] *a* considerable.

Betrachtung *f* (*Ansehen*) examination; (*Erwägung*) consideration.

Betrag [bə'traːk] *m* **-(e)s,** ¨**e** amount; **b**~**en** [bə'traːgən] *irreg vt* amount to; *vr* behave; ~**en** *nt* **-s** behaviour.

betrauen [bə'trauən] *vt*: **jdn mit etw** ~ entrust sb with sth.

betreffen [bə'trɛfən] *vt irreg* concern, affect; **was mich betrifft** as for me; ~**d** *a* relevant, in question.

betreffs [bə'trɛfs] *prep* +*gen* concerning, regarding.

betreiben [bə'traɪbən] *vt irreg* (*ausüben*) practise; *Politik* follow; *Studien* pursue; (*vorantreiben*) push ahead; (*Tech: antreiben*) drive.

betreten [bə'treːtən] *vt irreg* enter; *Bühne etc* step onto; **B**~ **verboten** keep off/out; *a* embarrassed.

Betrieb [bə'triːp] *m* **-(e)s, -e** (*Firma*) firm, concern; (*Anlage*) plant; (*Tätigkeit*) operation; (*Treiben*) traffic; **außer** ~ **sein** be out of order; **in** ~ **sein** be in operation; ~**sausflug** *m* firm's outing; **b**~**sfähig** *a* in working order; ~**sferien** *pl* company holidays *pl*; ~**sklima** *nt* (working) atmosphere; ~**skosten** *pl* running costs *pl*; ~**srat** *m* workers' council; **b**~**ssicher** *a* safe, reliable; ~**sstoff** *m* fuel; ~**sstörung** *f* breakdown; ~**sunfall** *m* industrial accident; ~**swirtschaft** *f* economics.

betrinken [bə'trɪŋkən] *vr irreg* get drunk.

betroffen [bə'trɔfən] *a* (*bestürzt*) amazed, perplexed; **von etw** ~ **werden** *or* **sein** be affected by sth.

betrüben [bə'tryːbən] *vt* grieve.

betrübt [bə'tryːpt] *a* sorrowful, grieved.

Betrug [bə'truːk] *m* **-(e)s** deception; (*Jur*) fraud.

betrügen [bə'tryːgən] *irreg vt* cheat; (*Jur*) defraud; *Ehepartner* be unfaithful to; *vr* deceive o.s.

Betrüger *m* -s, - cheat, deceiver; **b~isch** *a* deceitful; (*Jur*) fraudulent.

betrunken [bə'truŋkən] *a* drunk.

Bett [bɛt] *nt* -(e)s, -en bed; **ins** *or* **zu ~ gehen** go to bed; **~bezug** *m* duvet cover; **~decke** *f* blanket; (*Daunen—*) quilt; (*Überwurf*) bedspread.

Bettel- ['bɛtəl] *cpd*: **b~arm** *a* very poor, destitute; **~ei** [bɛtə'laɪ] *f* begging; **b~n** *vi* beg.

Bett- *cpd*: **b~en** *vt* make a bed for; **b~lägerig** *a* bedridden; **~laken** *nt* sheet.

Bettler(in *f*) ['bɛtlər(ɪn)] *m* -s, - beggar.

Bett- *cpd*: **~nässer** *m* -s, - bedwetter; **~vorleger** *m* bedside rug; **~wäsche** *f*, **~zeug** *nt* bedclothes *pl*, bedding.

beugen ['bɔygən] *vt* bend; (*Gram*) inflect; *vr* (*sich fügen*) bow (*dat* to).

Beule ['bɔylə] *f* -, -n bump, swelling.

beunruhigen [bə'unru:ɪgən] *vt* disturb, alarm; *vr* become worried.

Beunruhigung *f* worry, alarm.

beurkunden [bə'u:rkundən] *vt* attest, verify.

beurlauben [bə'u:rlaubən] *vt* give leave *or* holiday to.

beurteilen [bə'urtaɪlən] *vt* judge; *Buch etc* review.

Beurteilung *f* judgement; review; (*Note*) mark.

Beute ['bɔytə] *f* - booty, loot; **~l** *m* -s, - bag; (*Geld—*) purse; (*Tabak—*) pouch.

bevölkern [bə'fœlkərn] *vt* populate.

Bevölkerung *f* population.

bevollmächtigen [bə'fɔlmɛçtɪgən] *vt* authorize.

Bevollmächtigte(r) *mf* authorized agent.

Bevollmächtigung *f* authorization.

bevor [bə'fo:r] *cj* before; **~munden** *vt insep* dominate; **~stehen** *vi irreg* be in store (*dat* for); **~stehend** *a* imminent, approaching; **~zugen** *vt insep* prefer; **B~zugung** *f* preference.

bewachen [bə'vaxən] *vt* watch, guard.

Bewachung *f* (*Bewachen*) guarding; (*Leute*) guard, watch.

bewaffnen [bə'vafnən] *vt* arm.

Bewaffnung *f* (*Vorgang*) arming; (*Ausrüstung*) armament, arms *pl*.

bewahren [bə'va:rən] *vt* keep; **jdn vor jdm/etw ~** save sb from sth/sth.

bewähren [bə've:rən] *vr* prove o.s.; (*Maschine*) prove its worth.

bewahrheiten [bə'va:rhaɪtən] *vr* come true.

bewährt *a* reliable.

Bewährung *f* (*Jur*) probation; **~sfrist** *f* (period of) probation.

bewaldet [bə'valdət] *a* wooded.

bewältigen [bə'vɛltɪgən] *vt* overcome; *Arbeit* finish; *Portion* manage.

bewandert [bə'vandərt] *a* expert, knowledgeable.

bewässern [bə'vɛsərn] *vt* irrigate.

Bewässerung *f* irrigation.

Beweg- [bə've:g] *cpd*: **b~en** *vtr* move; **jdn zu etw b~en** induce sb to (do) sth;

~grund [bə've:k-] *m* motive; **b~lich** *a* movable, mobile; (*flink*) quick; **b~t** *a* *Leben* eventful; *Meer* rough; (*ergriffen*) touched; **~ung** *f* movement, motion; (*innere*) emotion; (*körperlich*) exercise; **sich** (*dat*) **~ung machen** take exercise; **~ungsfreiheit** *f* freedom of movement *or* action; **b~ungslos** *a* motionless.

Beweis [bə'vaɪs] *m* -es, -e proof; (*Zeichen*) sign; **b~bar** [bə'vaɪz-] *a* provable; **b~en** *vt irreg* prove; (*zeigen*) show; **~führung** *f* reasoning; **~kraft** *f* weight, conclusiveness; **b~kräftig** *a* convincing, conclusive; **~mittel** *nt* evidence.

bewenden [bə'vɛndən] *vi*: **etw dabei ~ lassen** leave sth at that.

Bewerb- [bə'vɛrb] *cpd*: **b~en** *vr irreg* apply (*um* for); **~er(in** *f*) *m* -s, - applicant; **~ung** *f* application.

bewerkstelligen [bə'vɛrkʃtɛlɪgən] *vt* manage, accomplish.

bewerten [bə've:rtən] *vt* assess.

bewilligen [bə'vɪlɪgən] *vt* grant, allow.

Bewilligung *f* granting.

bewirken [bə'vɪrkən] *vt* cause, bring about.

bewirten [bə'vɪrtən] *vt* entertain.

bewirtschaften [bə'vɪrt-ʃaftən] *vt* manage.

Bewirtung *f* hospitality.

bewohn- [bə'vo:n] *cpd*: **~bar** *a* inhabitable; **~en** *vt* inhabit, live in; **B~er(in** *f*) *m* -s, - inhabitant; (*von Haus*) resident.

bewölkt [bə'vœlkt] *a* cloudy, overcast.

Bewölkung *f* clouds *pl*.

Bewunder- [bə'vundər] *cpd*: **~er** *m* -s, - admirer; **b~n** *vt* admire; **b~nswert** *a* admirable, wonderful; **~ung** *f* admiration.

bewußt [bə'vust] *a* conscious; (*absichtlich*) deliberate; **sich** (*dat*) **einer Sache** ~ **sein** be aware of sth; **~los** *a* unconscious; **B~losigkeit** *f* unconsciousness; **~machen** *vt*: **jdm/sich etw ~machen** make sb/o.s. aware of sth; **B~sein** *nt* consciousness; **bei B~sein** conscious.

bezahlen [bə'tsa:lən] *vt* pay (for); **es macht sich bezahlt** it will pay.

Bezahlung *f* payment.

bezaubern [bə'tsaubərn] *vt* enchant, charm.

bezeichnen [bə'tsaɪçnən] *vt* (*kennzeichnen*) mark; (*nennen*) call; (*beschreiben*) describe; (*zeigen*) show, indicate; **~d** *a* characteristic, typical (*für* of).

Bezeichnung *f* (*Zeichen*) mark, sign; (*Beschreibung*) description.

bezeugen [bə'tsɔygən] *vt* testify to.

Bezichtigung *f* [bə'tsɪçtɪgʊŋ] *f* accusation.

beziehen [bə'tsi:ən] *irreg vt* (*mit Überzug*) cover; *Bett* make; *Haus, Position* move into; *Standpunkt* take up; (*erhalten*) receive; *Zeitung* subscribe to, take; **etw auf jdn/etw ~** relate sth to sb/sth; *vr* refer (*auf +acc* to); (*Himmel*) cloud over.

Beziehung *f* (*Verbindung*) connection; (*Zusammenhang*) relation; (*Verhältnis*) relationship; (*Hinsicht*) respect; **~en**

haben (*vorteilhaft*) have connections or contacts; **b~sweise** *ad* or; (*genauer gesagt auch*) that is, or rather.

Bezirk [bə'tsɪrk] *m* **-(e)s, -e** district.

Bezug [bə'tsuːk] *m* **-(e)s, ⁻e** (*Hülle*) covering; (*Comm*) ordering; (*Gehalt*) income, salary; (*Beziehung*) relationship (*zu* to); **in b~ auf** (+*acc*) with reference to; **~ nehmen auf** (+*acc*) refer to.

bezüglich [bə'tsyːklɪç] *prep* +*gen* concerning, referring to; *a* concerning; (*Gram*) relative.

Bezug- *cpd:* **~nahme** *f* reference (*auf* +*acc* to); **~spreis** *m* retail price; **~squelle** *f* source of supply.

bezwecken [bə'tsvɛkən] *vt* aim at.

bezweifeln [bə'tsvaifəln] *vt* doubt, query.

Bibel ['biːbəl] *f* **-, -n** Bible.

Biber ['biːbər] *m* **-s, -** beaver.

Biblio- *cpd:* **~graphie** [bibliogra'fiː] *f* bibliography; **~thek** [biblio'teːk] *f* **-, -en** library; **~thekar(in** *f*) [bibliote'kaːr(ɪn)] *m* **-s, -e** librarian.

biblisch ['biːblɪʃ] *a* biblical.

bieder ['biːdər] *a* upright, worthy; *Kleid etc* plain.

bieg- [biːg] *cpd:* **~bar** *a* flexible; **~en** *irreg vtr* bend; *vi* turn; **~sam** ['biːk-] *a* supple; **B~ung** *f* bend, curve.

Biene ['biːnə] *f* **-, -n** bee; **~nhonig** *m* honey; **~nkorb** *m* beehive; **~nwachs** *nt* beeswax.

Bier [biːr] *nt* **-(e)s, -e** beer; **~brauer** *m* brewer; **~deckel** *m*, **~filz** *m* beer mat; **~krug** *m*, **~seidel** *nt* beer mug.

bieten ['biːtən] *irreg vt* offer; (*bei Versteigerung*) bid; *vr* (*Gelegenheit*) be open (*dat* to); **sich** (*dat*) **etw ~ lassen** put up with sth.

Bikini [bi'kiːni] *m* **-s, -s** bikini.

Bilanz [bi'lants] *f* balance; (*fig*) outcome; **~ ziehen** take stock (*aus* of).

Bild [bɪlt] *nt* **-(e)s, -er** (*lit, fig*) picture; photo; (*Spiegel—*) reflection; **~bericht** *m* pictorial report.

bilden ['bɪldən] *vt* form; (*erziehen*) educate; (*ausmachen*) constitute; *vr* arise; (*erziehen*) educate o.s.

Bilder- ['bɪldər] *cpd:* **~buch** *nt* picture book; **~rahmen** *m* picture frame.

Bild- *cpd:* **~fläche** *f* screen; (*fig*) scene; **~hauer** *m* **-s, -** sculptor; **b~hübsch** *a* lovely, pretty as a picture; **b~lich** *a* figurative; pictorial; **~schirm** *m* television screen; **b~schön** *a* lovely; **~ung** ['bɪldʊŋ] *f* formation; (*Wissen, Benehmen*) education; **~ungslücke** *f* gap in one's education; **~ungspolitik** *f* educational policy; **~weite** *f* (*Phot*) distance.

Billard ['bɪljart] *nt* **-s, -e** billiards; **~ball** *m*, **~kugel** *f* billiard ball.

billig ['bɪlɪç] *a* cheap; (*gerecht*) fair, reasonable; **~en** ['bɪlɪgən] *vt* approve of; **B~ung** *f* approval.

Billion [bɪli'oːn] *f* billion, trillion (*US*).

bimmeln ['bɪməln] *vi* tinkle.

Binde ['bɪndə] *f* **-, -n** bandage; (*Arm—*) band; (*Med*) sanitary towel; **~glied** *nt* connecting link; **b~n** *vt irreg* bind, tie;

~strich *m* hyphen; **~wort** *nt* conjunction.

Bind- *cpd:* **~faden** *m* string; **~ung** *f* bond, tie; (*Ski—*) binding.

binnen ['bɪnən] *prep* +*dat* or *gen* within; **B~hafen** *m* inland harbour; **B~handel** *m* internal trade.

Binse ['bɪnzə] *f* **-, -n** rush, reed; **~nwahrheit** *f* truism.

Bio- [bio] *cpd* bio-; **~graphie** [-gra'fiː] *f* biography; **~loge** [-'loːgə] *m* **-n, -n** biologist; **~logie** [-lo'giː] *f* biology; **b~logisch** [-'loːgɪʃ] *a* biological.

Birke ['bɪrkə] *f* **-, -n** birch.

Birnbaum *m* pear tree.

Birne ['bɪrnə] *f* **-, -n** pear; (*Elec*) (light) bulb.

bis [bɪs] *ad, prep* +*acc* (*räumlich:* — *zu/an* +*acc*) to, as far as; (*zeitlich*) till, until; **Sie haben ~ Dienstag Zeit** you have until or till Tuesday; **~ Dienstag muß es fertig sein** it must be ready by Tuesday; **~ hierher** this far; **~ in die Nacht** into the night; **~ auf weiteres** until further notice; **~ bald/gleich** see you later/soon; **~ auf etw** (*acc*) (*einschließlich*) including sth; (*ausgeschlossen*) except sth; **~ zu** up to; *cj* (*mit Zahlen*) to; (*zeitlich*) until, till; **von ... ~ ...** from ... to ...

Bischof ['bɪʃɔf] *m* **-s, ⁻e** bishop.

bischöflich ['bɪʃøːflɪç] *a* episcopal.

bisher [bɪs'heːr] *ad*, **~ig** *a* till now, hitherto.

Biskuit [bɪs'kviːt] *m* or *nt* **-(e)s, -s** or **-e** biscuit; **~teig** *m* sponge mixture.

bislang [bɪs'laŋ] *ad* hitherto.

Biß [bɪs] *m* **-sses, -sse** bite.

bißchen ['bɪsçən] *a, ad* bit.

Bissen ['bɪsən] *m* **-s, -** bite, morsel.

bissig ['bɪsɪç] *a Hund* snappy; *Bemerkung* cutting, biting.

Bistum ['bɪstuːm] *nt* bishopric.

bisweilen [bɪs'vailən] *ad* at times, occasionally.

Bitte ['bɪtə] *f* **-, -n** request; **b~** *interj* please; (*wie b—?*) (I beg your) pardon; (*als Antwort auf Dank*) you're welcome; **b~ schön!** it was a pleasure; **b~n** *vti irreg* ask (*um* for); **b~nd** *a* pleading, imploring.

bitter ['bɪtər] *a* bitter; **B~böse** *a* very angry; **B~keit** *f* bitterness; **~lich** *a* bitter.

blähen ['blɛːən] *vtr* swell, blow out.

Blähungen *pl* (*Med*) wind.

blam- *cpd:* **~abel** [bla'maːbəl] *a* disgraceful; **B~age** [bla'maːʒə] *f* **-, -n** disgrace; **~ieren** [bla'miːrən] *vr* make a fool of o.s., disgrace o.s.; *vt* let down, disgrace.

blank [blaŋk] *a* bright; (*unbedeckt*) bare; (*sauber*) clean, polished; (*col: ohne Geld*) broke; (*offensichtlich*) blatant.

blanko ['blaŋko] *ad* blank; **B~scheck** *m* blank cheque.

Bläschen ['blɛːsçən] *nt* bubble; (*Med*) spot, blister.

Blase ['blaːzə] *f* **-, -n** bubble; (*Med*) blister; (*Anat*) bladder; **~balg** *m* bellows *pl*; **b~n** *vti irreg* blow.

Blas- *cpd:* **~instrument** *nt* brass or wind instrument; **~kapelle** *f* brass band.

blaß [blas] a pale.

Blässe ['blɛsə] f~ paleness, palour.

Blatt [blat] nt **-(e)s, ̈er** leaf; newspaper; (von Papier) sheet; (Cards) hand; **vom ~ singen/spielen** sight-read.

blättern ['blɛtərn] vi: **in etw** (dat) **~ leaf** through sth.

Blätterteig m flaky or puff pastry.

blau [blau] a blue; (col) drunk, stoned; (Cook) boiled; **Auge** black; **~er Fleck** bruise; **Fahrt ins B~e** mystery tour; **~äugig** a blue-eyed; **B~licht** nt flashing blue light; **~machen** vi (col) skive off work; **B~strumpf** m (fig) bluestocking.

Blech [blɛç] nt **-(e)s, -e** tin, sheet metal; (Back—) baking tray; **~büchse** f, **~dose** f tin, can; **b~en** vti (col) pay; **~schaden** m (Aut) damage to bodywork.

Blei [blai] nt **-(e)s, -e** lead; **~be** f **-, -n** roof over one's head; **b~ben** vi irreg stay, remain, **b~benlassen** vt irreg leave (alone).

bleich [blaiç] a faded, pale; **~en** vt bleach.

Blei- cpd: **b~ern** a leaden; **~stift** m pencil; **~stiftspitzer** m pencil sharpener.

Blende ['blɛndə] f **-, -n** (Phot) aperture; **b~n** vt blind, dazzle; (fig) hoodwink; **b~nd** a (col) grand; **b~nd aussehen** look smashing.

Blick [blik] m **-(e)s, -e** (kurz) glance, glimpse; (Anschauen) look, gaze; (Aussicht) view; **b~en** vi look; **sich b~en lassen** put in an appearance; **~fang** m eye-catching object; **~feld** nt range of vision (auch fig).

blind [blint] a blind; **Glas** etc dull; **~er Passagier** stowaway; **B~darm** m appendix; **B~darmentzündung** f appendicitis; **B~enschrift** ['blindən-] f braille; **B~heit** f blindness; **~lings** ad blindly; **B~schleiche** f slow worm; **~schreiben** vi irreg touch-type.

blink- [bliŋk] cpd: **~en** vi twinkle, sparkle; (Licht) flash, signal; (Aut) indicate; vt flash, signal; **B~er** m **-s, -, B~licht** nt (Aut) indicator.

blinzeln ['blintsəln] vi blink, wink.

Blitz [blits] m **-es, -e** (flash of) lightning; **~ableiter** m lightning conductor; **b~en** vi (aufleuchten) glint, shine; **es blitzt** (Met) there's a flash of lightning; **~licht** nt flashlight; **b~schnell** a, ad as quick as a flash.

Block [blɔk] m **-(e)s, ̈e** (lit, fig) block; (von Papier) pad; **~ade** [blɔ'ka:də] f **-, -n** blockade; **~flöte** f recorder; **b~frei** a (Pol) unaligned; **b~ieren** [blɔ'ki:rən] vt block; vi (Räder) jam; **~schrift** f block letters pl.

blöd [blø:t] a silly, stupid; **~eln** ['blø:dəln] vi (col) fool around; **B~heit** f stupidity; **B~sinn** m nonsense; **~sinnig** a silly, idiotic.

blond [blɔnt] a blond, fair-haired.

bloß [blo:s] a (unbedeckt) bare; (nackt) naked; (nur) mere; ad only, merely; **laß das ~!** just don't do that!

Blöße ['blø:sə] f **-, -n** bareness; nakedness;

(fig) weakness; **sich** (dat) **eine ~ geben** (fig) lay o.s. open to attack.

bloß- cpd: **~legen** vt expose; **~stellen** vt show up.

blühen ['bly:ən] vi (lit) bloom, be in bloom; (fig) flourish.

Blume ['blu:mə] f **-, -n** flower; (von Wein) bouquet; **~nkohl** m cauliflower; **~ntopf** m flowerpot; **~nzwiebel** f bulb.

Bluse ['blu:zə] f **-, -n** blouse.

Blut [blu:t] nt **-(e)s** blood; **b~arm** a anaemic; (fig) penniless; **b~befleckt** a bloodstained; **~buche** f copper beech; **~druck** m blood pressure.

Blüte ['bly:tə] f **-, -n** blossom; (fig) prime; **~zeit** f flowering period; (fig) prime.

Blut- cpd: **~egel** m leech; **b~en** vi bleed.

Blütenstaub m pollen.

Blut- cpd: **~er** m **-s, -** (Med) haemophiliac; **~erguß** m haemorrhage; (auf Haut) bruise; **~gruppe** f blood group; **b~ig** a bloody; **b~jung** a very young; **~probe** f blood test; **~schande** f incest; **~spender** m blood donor; **~übertragung** f blood transfusion; **~ung** f bleeding, haemorrhage; **~vergiftung** f blood poisoning; **~wurst** f black pudding.

Bö(e) ['bø:(ə)] f **-, -en** squall.

Bock [bɔk] m **-(e)s, ̈e** buck, ram; (Gestell) trestle, support; (Sport) buck.

Boden ['bo:dən] m **-s, ̈** ground; (Fuß—) floor; (Meeres—, Faß—) bottom; (Speicher) attic; **b~los** a bottomless; (col) incredible; **~satz** m dregs pl, sediment; **~schätze** pl mineral wealth; **~turnen** nt floor exercises pl.

Bogen ['bo:gən] m **-s, -** (Biegung) curve; (Archit) arch; (Waffe, Mus) bow; (Papier) sheet; **~gang** m arcade; **~schütze** m archer.

Bohle ['bo:lə] f **-, -n** plank.

Bohne ['bo:nə] f **-, -n** bean; **~nkaffee** m pure coffee; **b~rn** vt wax, polish; **~rwachs** nt floor polish.

Bohr- ['bo:r] cpd: **b~en** vt bore; **~er** m **-s, -** drill; **~insel** f oil rig; **~maschine** f drill; **~turm** m derrick.

Boje ['bo:jə] f **-, -n** buoy.

Bolzen ['bɔltsən] m **-s, -** bolt.

Bomb- cpd: **b~ardieren** [bɔmbar'di:rən] vt bombard; (aus der Luft) bomb; **~e** ['bɔmbə] f **-, -n** bomb; **~enangriff** m bombing raid; **~enerfolg** m (col) huge success.

Bonbon [bõ'bõ:] m or nt **-s, -s** sweet.

Boot [bo:t] nt **-(e)s, -e** boat.

Bord [bɔrt] m **-(e)s, -e** (Aviat, Naut) board; **an ~** on board; nt (Brett) shelf; **~ell** [bɔr'dɛl] nt **-s, -e** brothel; **~funkanlage** f radio; **~stein** m kerb(stone).

borgen ['bɔrgən] vt borrow; **jdm etw ~** lend sb sth.

borniert [bɔr'ni:rt] a narrow-minded.

Börse ['bœrzə] f **-, -n** stock exchange; (Geld—) purse.

Borste ['bɔrstə] f **-, -n** bristle.

Borte ['bɔrtə] f **-, -n** edging; (Band) trimming.

bös [bø:s] a bad, evil; (zornig) angry; **~artig** a ['bø:z-] a malicious.

Böschung ['bœʃʊŋ] f slope; (Ufer— etc) embankment.

bos- ['bo:s] cpd: ~**haft** a malicious, spiteful; **B~heit** f malice, spite.

böswillig ['bø:svɪlɪç] a malicious.

Botanik [bo'ta:nɪk] f botany.

botanisch [bo'ta:nɪʃ] a botanical.

Bot- ['bo:t] cpd: ~**e** m -**n**, -**n** messenger; ~**enjunge** m errand boy; ~**schaft** f message, news; (Pol) embassy; ~**schafter** m -**s**, - ambassador.

Bottich ['bɔtɪç] m -**(e)s**, -**e** vat, tub.

Bouillon [bʊ'ljõ:] f -, -**s** consommé.

Bowle ['bo:lə] f -, -**n** punch.

Box- ['bɔks] cpd: **b~en** vi box; ~**er** m -**s**, - boxer; ~**handschuh** m boxing glove; ~**kampf** m boxing match.

boykottieren [bɔykɔ'ti:rən] vt boycott.

Branche ['brã:ʃə] f -, -**n** line of business; ~**nverzeichnis** nt yellow pages pl.

Brand [brant] m -**(e)s**, -**e** fire; (Med) gangrene; **b~en** [brandən] vi surge; (Meer) break; **b~marken** vt brand; (fig) stigmatize; ~**salbe** f ointment for burns; ~**stifter** m arsonist, fire-raiser; ~**stiftung** f arson; ~**ung** f surf; ~**wunde** f burn.

Branntwein ['brantvaɪn] m brandy.

Brat- [bra:t] cpd: ~**apfel** m baked apple; **b~en** vt irreg roast, fry; ~**en** m -**s**, - roast, joint; ~**huhn** nt roast chicken; ~**kartoffeln** pl fried or roast potatoes pl; ~**pfanne** f frying pan; ~**rost** m grill.

Bratsche ['bra:tʃə] f -, -**n** viola.

Brat- cpd: ~**spieß** m spit; ~**wurst** f grilled sausage.

Brauch [braux] m -**(e)s**, **Bräuche** custom; **b~bar** a usable, serviceable; Person capable; **b~en** vt (bedürfen) need; (müssen) have to; (verwenden) use.

Braue ['brauə] f -, -**n** brow; **b~n** vt brew; ~**rei** f brewery.

braun [braun] a brown; (von Sonne auch) tanned.

Bräune ['brɔynə] f -, -**n** brownness; (Sonnen-) tan; **b~n** vt make brown; (Sonne) tan.

braungebrannt a tanned.

Brause ['brauzə] f -, -**n** shower bath; (von Gießkanne) rose; (Getränk) lemonade; **b~n** vi roar; (auch vr: duschen) take a shower; ~**pulver** nt lemonade powder.

Braut [braut] f -, **Bräute** bride; (Verlobte) fiancée.

Bräutigam ['brɔytɪgam] m -**s**, -**e** bridegroom; fiancé.

Braut- cpd: ~**jungfer** f bridesmaid; ~**paar** nt bride and bridegroom, bridal pair.

brav [bra:f] a (artig) good; (ehrenhaft) worthy, honest.

Brech- ['brɛç] cpd: ~**eisen** nt crowbar; **b~en** vti irreg break; Licht refract; (fig) Mensch crush; (speien) vomit; **die Ehe b~en** commit adultery; ~**reiz** m nausea, retching.

Brei [braɪ] m -**(e)s**, -**e** (Masse) pulp; (Cook) gruel; (Hafer-) porridge.

breit [braɪt] a wide, broad; **B~e** f -, -**n** width; breadth; (Geog) latitude; ~**en** vt:

etw über etw (acc) ~**en** spread sth over sth; **B~engrad** m degree of latitude; ~**machen** vr spread o.s. out; ~**schult(e)rig** a broad-shouldered; ~**treten** vt irreg (col) enlarge upon; **B~wandfilm** m wide-screen film.

Brems- ['brɛmz] cpd: ~**belag** m brake lining; ~**e** f -, -**n** brake; (Zool) horsefly; **b~en** vi brake, apply the brakes; vt Auto brake; (fig) slow down; ~**licht** nt brake light; ~**pedal** nt brake pedal; ~**schuh** m brake shoe; ~**spur** f tyre marks pl; ~**weg** m braking distance.

Brenn- ['brɛn] cpd: **b~bar** a inflammable; **b~en** irreg vi burn, be on fire; (Licht, Kerze etc) burn; vt Holz etc burn; Ziegel, Ton fire; Kaffee roast; **darauf b~en, etw zu tun** be dying to do sth; ~**material** nt fuel; ~**(n)essel** f nettle; ~**spiritus** m methylated spirits; ~**stoff** m liquid fuel.

brenzlig ['brɛntslɪç] a smelling of burning, burnt; (fig) precarious.

Brett [brɛt] nt -**(e)s**, -**er** board, plank; (Bord) shelf; (Spiel—) board; **Schwarze(s)** ~ notice board; ~**er** pl (Ski) skis pl; (Theat) boards pl; ~**erzaun** m wooden fence.

Brezel ['bre:tsəl] f -, -**n** bretzel, pretzel.

Brief [bri:f] m -**(e)s**, -**e** letter; ~**beschwerer** m -**s**, - paperweight; ~**kasten** m letterbox; **b~lich** a,ad by letter; ~**marke** f postage stamp; ~**öffner** m letter opener; ~**papier** nt notepaper; ~**tasche** f wallet; ~**träger** m postman; ~**umschlag** m envelope; ~**wechsel** m correspondence.

Brikett [bri'kɛt] nt -**s**, -**s** briquette.

brillant [brɪl'jant] a (fig) sparkling, brilliant; **B~** m -**en**, -**en** brilliant, diamond.

Brille ['brɪlə] f -, -**n** spectacles pl; (Schutz—) goggles pl; (Toiletten—) (toilet) seat.

bringen ['brɪŋən] vt irreg bring; (mitnehmen, begleiten) take; (einbringen) Profit bring in; (veröffentlichen) publish; (Theat, Cine) show; (Rad, TV) broadcast; (in einen Zustand versetzen) get; (col: tun können) manage; **jdn dazu** ~, **etw zu tun** make sb do sth; **jdn nach Hause** ~ take sb home; **jdn um etw** ~ make sb lose sth; **jdn auf eine Idee** ~ give sb an idea.

Brise ['bri:zə] f -, -**n** breeze.

bröckelig ['brœkəlɪç] a crumbly.

Brocken ['brɔkən] m -**s**, - piece, bit; (Fels—) lump of rock.

brodeln ['bro:dəln] vi bubble.

Brokat [bro'ka:t] m -**(e)s**, -**e** brocade.

Brombeere ['brɔmbe:rə] f blackberry, bramble.

bronchial [brɔnçi'a:l] a bronchial.

Bronchien ['brɔnçiən] pl bronchia(l tubes) pl.

Bronze ['brõ:sə] f -, -**n** bronze.

Brosame ['bro:za:mə] f -, -**n** crumb.

Brosche ['brɔʃə] f -, -**n** brooch.

Broschüre [brɔ'ʃy:rə] f -, -**n** pamphlet.

Brot [bro:t] nt -**(e)s**, -**e** bread; (—laib) loaf.

Brötchen ['brøːtçən] *nt* roll.
brotlos ['broːtloːs] *a Person* unemployed; *Arbeit etc* unprofitable.
Bruch [brʊx] *m* -(e)s, ̈e breakage; (*zerbrochene Stelle*) break; (*fig*) split, breach; (*Med Eingeweide*—) rupture, hernia; (*Bein*— *etc*) fracture; (*Math*) fraction; ~**bude** *f* (*col*) shack.
brüchig ['brʏçɪç] *a* brittle, fragile; *Haus* dilapidated.
Bruch- *cpd:* ~**landung** *f* crash landing; ~**strich** *m* (*Math*) line; ~**stück** *nt* fragment; ~**teil** *m* fraction.
Brücke ['brʏkə] *f* -, -n bridge; (*Teppich*) rug.
Bruder ['bruːdər] *m* -s, ̈ brother.
Brüder- ['bryːdər] *cpd:* b~**lich** *a* brotherly; ~**lichkeit** *f* fraternity; ~**schaft** *f* brotherhood, fellowship; ~**schaft trinken** fraternize, address each other as 'du'.
Brühe ['bryːə] *f* -, -n broth, stock; (*pej*) muck.
brüllen ['brʏlən] *vi* bellow, scream.
Brumm- ['brʊm] *cpd:* ~**bär** *m* grumbler; b~**eln** *vti* mumble; b~**en** *vi* (*Bär, Mensch etc*) growl; (*Insekt, Radio*) buzz; (*Motoren*) roar; (*murren*) grumble; *vt* growl; **jdm brummt der Kopf** sb's head is buzzing.
brünett [bry'nɛt] *a* brunette, dark-haired.
Brunnen ['brʊnən] *m* -s, - fountain; (*tief*) well; (*natürlich*) spring; ~**kresse** *f* watercress.
brüsk [brʏsk] *a* abrupt, brusque.
Brust [brʊst] *f* -, ̈e breast; (*Männer*—) chest.
brüsten ['brʏstən] *vr* boast.
Brust- *cpd:* ~**fellentzündung** *f* pleurisy; ~**kasten** *m* chest; ~**schwimmen** *nt* breast-stroke; ~**warze** *f* nipple.
Brüstung ['brʏstʊŋ] *f* parapet.
Brut [bruːt] *f* -, -en brood; (*Brüten*) hatching; b~**al** [bru'taːl] *a* brutal; ~**alität** *f* brutality; ~**apparat** *m*, ~**kasten** *m* incubator.
brüten ['bryːtən] *vi* hatch, brood (*auch fig*).
brutto ['brʊto] *ad* gross; B~**einkommen** *nt*, B~**gehalt** *nt* gross salary; B~**gewicht** *nt* gross weight; B~**lohn** *m* gross wages *pl*.
Bub [buːp] *m* -en, -en boy, lad; ~**e** [buːbə] *m* -n, -n (*Schurke*) rogue; (*Cards*) jack; ~**ikopf** *m* bobbed hair, shingle.
Buch [buːx] *nt* -(e)s, ̈er book; (*Comm*) account book; ~**binder** *m* bookbinder; ~**drucker** *m* printer; ~**e** *f* -, -n beech tree; b~**en** *vt* book; *Betrag* enter.
Bücher- ['byːçər] *cpd:* ~**brett** *nt* bookshelf; ~**ei** [-'raɪ] *f* library; ~**regal** *nt* bookshelves *pl*, bookcase; ~**schrank** *m* bookcase.
Buch- *cpd:* ~**fink** *m* chaffinch; ~**führung** *f* book-keeping, accounting; ~**halter(in** *f*) *m* -s, - book-keeper; ~**handel** *m* book trade; ~**händler(in** *f*) *m* bookseller; ~**handlung** *f* bookshop.
Büchse ['bʏksə] *f* -, -n tin, can; (*Holz*—) box; (*Gewehr*) rifle; ~**nfleisch** *nt* tinned meat; ~**nöffner** *m* tin *or* can opener.
Buch- *cpd:* ~**stabe** *m* -ns, -n letter (of

the alphabet); b~**stabieren** [buːx-ʃta'biːrən] *vt* spell; b~**stäblich** ['buːx-ʃtɛːplɪç] *a* literal.
Bucht [bʊxt] *f* -, -en bay.
Buchung ['buːxʊŋ] *f* booking; (*Comm*) entry.
Buckel ['bʊkəl] *m* -s, - hump.
bücken ['bʏkən] *vr* bend.
Bückling ['bʏklɪŋ] *m* (*Fisch*) kipper; (*Verbeugung*) bow.
Bude ['buːdə] *f* -, -n booth, stall; (*col*) digs *pl*.
Budget [by'dʒeː] *nt* -s, -s budget.
Büffel ['bʏfəl] *m* -s, - buffalo.
Büf(f)ett [by'feː] *nt* -s, -s (*Anrichte*) sideboard; (*Geschirrschrank*) dresser; **kaltes** ~ cold buffet.
Bug [buːk] *m* -(e)s, -e (*Naut*) bow; (*Aviat*) nose.
Bügel ['byːgəl] *m* -s, - (*Kleider*—) hanger; (*Steig*—) stirrup; (*Brillen*—) arm; ~**brett** *nt* ironing board; ~**eisen** *nt* iron; ~**falte** *f* crease; b~**n** *vti* iron.
Bühne ['byːnə] *f* -, -n stage; ~**nbild** *nt* set, scenery.
Buhruf ['buːruːf] *m* boo.
Bulette [bu'lɛtə] *f* meatball.
Bull- ['bʊl] *cpd:* ~**dogge** *f* bulldog; ~**dozer** ['bʊldoːzər] *m* -s, - bulldozer; ~**e** *m* -n, -n bull.
Bummel ['bʊməl] *m* -s, - stroll; (*Schaufenster*—) window-shopping; ~**ant** [-'lant] *m* slowcoach; ~**ei** [-'laɪ] *f* wandering; dawdling; skiving; b~**n** *vi* wander, stroll; (*trödeln*) dawdle; (*faulenzen*) skive, loaf around; ~**streik** *m* go-slow; ~**zug** *m* slow train.
Bummler(in *f*) ['bʊmlər(ɪn)] *m* -s, - (*langsamer Mensch*) dawdler; (*Faulenzer*) idler, loafer.
Bund [bʊnt] *m* -(e)s, ̈e (*Freundschafts*—*etc*) bond; (*Organisation*) union; (*Pol*) confederacy; (*Hosen*—, *Rock*—) waistband; *nt* -(e)s, -e bunch; (*Stroh*—) bundle.
Bünd- ['bʏnt] *cpd:* ~**chen** *nt* ribbing; (*Ärmel*—) cuff; ~**el** *nt* -s, -n bundle, bale; b~**eln** *vt* bundle.
Bundes- ['bʊndəs] *in cpds* Federal (*esp* West German); ~**bahn** *f* Federal Railways *pl*; ~**hauptstadt** *f* Federal capital; ~**kanzler** *m* Federal Chancellor; ~**land** *nt* Land; ~**präsident** *m* Federal President; ~**rat** *m* upper house of West German Parliament; ~**republik** *f* Federal Republic (of West Germany); ~**staat** *m* Federal state; ~**straße** *f* Federal Highway, 'A' road; ~**tag** *m* West German Parliament; ~**verfassungsgericht** *nt* Federal Constitutional Court; ~**wehr** *f* West German Armed Forces *pl*.
Bünd- *cpd:* b~**ig** *a* (*kurz*) concise; ~**nis** *nt* -ses, -se alliance.
Bunker ['bʊŋkər] *m* -s, - bunker.
bunt [bʊnt] *a* coloured; (*gemischt*) mixed; **jdm wird es zu** ~ it's getting too much for sb; B~**stift** *m* coloured pencil, crayon.
Burg [bʊrk] *f* -, -en castle, fort.
Bürge ['bʏrgə] *m* -n, -n guarantor; b~**n** *vi* vouch; ~**r(in** *f*) *m* -s, - citizen; member

of the middle class; ~**rkrieg** *m* civil war;
b~**rlich** *a Rechte* civil; *Klasse* middle-
class; (*pej*) bourgeois; **gut b~rliche
Küche** good home cooking; ~**rmeister**
m mayor; ~**rrecht** *nt* civil rights *pl*;
~**rschaft** *f* population, citizens *pl*;
~**rsteig** *m* pavement; ~**rtum** *nt* citizens
pl.

Bürg- *cpd*: ~**in** *f see* **Bürge**; ~**schaft** *f*
surety; ~**schaft leisten** give security.

Büro [by'ro:] *nt* -**s**, -**s** office;
~**angestellte(r)** *mf* office worker;
~**klammer** *f* paper clip; ~**krat**
[byro'kra:t] *m* -**en**, -**en** bureaucrat;
~**kra'tie** *f* bureaucracy; **b~'kratisch** *a*
bureaucratic; ~**kra'tismus** *m* red tape;
~**schluß** *m* office closing time.

Bursch(e) [burʃ(ə)] *m* -**en**, -**en** lad,
fellow; (*Diener*) servant.

Bürste ['byrstə] *f* -, -**n** brush; **b~n** *vt*
brush.

Bus [bus] *m* -**ses**, -**se** bus.

Busch [buʃ] *m* -(**e**)**s**, -**e** bush, shrub.

Büschel ['byʃəl] *nt* -**s**, - tuft.

buschig *a* bushy.

Busen ['bu:zən] *m* -**s**, - bosom; (*Meer*)
inlet, bay; ~**freund(in** *f*) *m* bosom friend.

Buße ['bu:sə] *f* -, -**n** atonement, penance;
(*Geld*) fine.

büßen ['by:sən] *vti* do penance (for), atone
(for).

Büste ['bystə] *f* -, -**n** bust; ~**nhalter** *m*
bra.

Butter ['butər] *f* - butter; ~**blume** *f*
buttercup; ~**brot** *nt* (piece of) bread and
butter; ~**brotpapier** *nt* greaseproof
paper; ~**dose** *f* butter dish; **b~weich** *a*
soft as butter; (*fig,col*) soft.

Butzen ['butsən] *m* -**s**, - core.

C

(*see also under K and Z; CH under* SCH)

C, c [tse:] *nt* C, c.

Café [ka'fe:] *nt* -**s**, -**s** café.

Cafeteria [kafete'ri:a] *f* -, -**s** cafeteria.

Camp- [kɛmp] *cpd*: **c~en** *vi* camp;
~**er(in** *f*) *m* -**s**, - camper; ~**ing** *nt* -**s**
camping; ~**ingplatz** *m* camp(ing) site.

Caravan ['kɛrəvən] *m* -**s**, -**s** caravan.

Cellist [tʃe'list] *m* cellist.

Cello ['tʃɛlo] *nt* -**s**, -**s** *or* **Celli** cello.

Chamäleon [ka'mɛ:leən] *nt* -**s**, -**s**
chameleon.

Champagner [ʃam'panjər] *m* -**s**, -
champagne.

Champignon ['ʃampinjõ] *m* -**s**, -**s** button
mushroom.

Chance ['ʃã:s(ə)] *f* -, -**n** chance,
opportunity.

Chaos ['ka:ɔs] *nt* -**s**, - chaos.

chaotisch [ka'o:tiʃ] *a* chaotic.

Charakter [ka'raktər] *m* -**s**, -**e**
[karak'te:rə] character; **c~fest** *a* of firm
character; ~**i'sieren** *vt* characterize;
~**istik** [karakte'rɪstɪk] *f* characterization;
c~istisch [karakte'rɪstɪʃ] *a* characteristic, typical (*für* of); **c~los** *a* unprincipled; ~**losigkeit** *f* lack of principle;

~**schwäche** *f* weakness of character;
~**stärke** *f* strength of character; ~**zug**
m characteristic, trait.

charmant [ʃar'mant] *a* charming.

Charme [ʃarm] *m* -**s** charm.

Chassis [ʃa'si:] *nt* -, - chassis.

Chauffeur [ʃɔ'fø:r] *m* chauffeur.

Chauvinismus [ʃovi'nɪsmʊs] *, m*
chauvinism, jingoism.

Chauvinist [ʃovi'nɪst] *m* chauvinist,
jingoist.

Chef [ʃɛf] *m* -**s**, -**s** head; (*col*) boss; ~**arzt**
m head physician; ~**in** *f* (*col*) boss.

Chemie [çe'mi:] *f* - chemistry; ~**faser** *f*
man-made fibre.

Chemikalie [çemi'ka:liə] *f* -, -**n** chemical.

Chemiker(in *f*) ['çe:mikər(ɪn)] *m* -**s**, -
(industrial) chemist.

chemisch ['çe:mɪʃ] *a* chemical; ~**e
Reinigung** dry cleaning.

Chiffre ['ʃɪfər] *f* -, -**n** (*Geheimzeichen*)
cipher; (*in Zeitung*) box number.

Chiffriermaschine [ʃɪfri'rma:ʃi:nə] *f*
cipher machine.

Chips [tʃɪps] *pl* crisps *pl*, chips *pl* (*US*).

Chirurg [çi'rurk] *m* -**en**, -**en** surgeon;
~**ie** [-'gi:] *f* surgery; **c~isch** *a* surgical.

Chlor [klo:r] *nt* -**s** chlorine; ~**o'form** *nt* -**s**
chloroform; **c~ofor'mieren** *vt*
chloroform; ~**ophyll** [kloro'fyl] *nt* -**s**
chlorophyll.

Cholera ['ko:lera] *f* - cholera.

cholerisch [ko'le:rɪʃ] *a* choleric.

Chor [ko:r] *m* -(**e**)**s**, -**e** *or* -**e** choir; (*Musik-
stück, Theat*) chorus; ~**al** [ko'ra:l] *m* -**s**,
-**äle** chorale.

Choreograph [koreo'gra:f] *m* -**en**, -**en**
choreographer; ~**ie** [-'fi:] *f* choreography.

Chor- *cpd*: ~**gestühl** *nt* choir stalls *pl*;
~**knabe** *m* choirboy.

Christ ['krɪst] *m* -**en**, -**en** Christian;
~**baum** *m* Christmas tree; ~**enheit** *f*
Christendom; ~**entum** *nt* Christianity;
~**in** *f* Christian; ~**kind** *nt* ≈ Father
Christmas; (*Jesus*) baby Jesus; **c~lich** *a*
Christian; ~**us** *m* - Christ.

Chrom [kro:m] *nt* -**s** (*Chem*) chromium;
chrome; ~**osom** [kromo'zo:m] *nt* -**s**, -**en**
(*Biol*) chromosome.

Chron- ['kro:n] *cpd*: ~**ik** *f* chronicle;
c~isch *a* chronic; ~**ologie** [-lo'gi:] *f*
chronology; **c~ologisch** [-'lo:gɪʃ] *a*
chronological.

Chrysantheme [kryzan'te:mə] *f* -, -**n**
chrysanthemum.

circa ['tsɪrka] *ad* about, approximately.

Clown [klaun] *m* -**s**, -**s** clown.

Computer [kɔm'pju:tər] *m* -**s**, - computer.

Conférencier [kõferãsi'e:] *m* -**s**, -**s**
compère.

Coupé [ku'pe:] *nt* -**s**, -**s** (*Aut*) coupé, sports
version.

Coupon [ku'põ:] *m* -**s**, -**s** coupon; (*Stoff*—)
length of cloth.

Cousin [ku'zɛ̃:] *m* -**s**, -**s** cousin; ~**e**
[ku'zi:nə] *f* -, -**n** cousin.

Creme [krɛ:m] *f* -, -**s** (*lit, fig*) cream;
(*Schuh*—) polish; (*Zahn*—) paste; (*Cook*)
mousse; **c~farben** *a* cream(-coloured).

Curry(pulver nt) ['kari(pulfər)] m or nt **-s** curry powder.

Cutter(in f) ['katər(ın)] m **-s, -** (Cine) editor.

D

D, d [de:] nt D, d.

da [da:] ad (dort) there; (hier) here; (dann) then; ~, wo where; cj as; **~behalten** vt irreg keep.

dabei [da'baı] ad (räumlich) close to it; (noch dazu) besides; (zusammen mit) with them; (zeitlich) during this; (obwohl doch) but, however; **was ist schon ~?** what of it?; **es ist doch nichts ~, wenn . . .** it doesn't matter if . . .; **bleiben wir ~** let's leave it at that; **es soll nicht ~ bleiben** this isn't the end of it; **es bleibt ~** that's settled; **das Dumme/Schwierige ~** the stupid/difficult part of it; **er war gerade ~, zu gehen** he was just leaving; **~sein** vi irreg (anwesend) be present; (beteiligt) be involved; **~stehen** vi irreg stand around.

Dach [dax] nt **-(e)s, "er** roof; **~boden** m attic, loft; **~decker** m **-s, -** slater, tiler; **~fenster** nt, **~luke** f skylight; **~pappe** f roofing felt; **~rinne** f gutter; **~ziegel** m roof tile.

Dachs [daks] m **-es, -e** badger.

Dackel ['dakəl] m **-s, -** dachshund.

dadurch [da'durç] ad (räumlich) through it; (durch diesen Umstand) thereby, in that way; (deshalb) because of that, for that reason; cj: ~, **daß** because.

dafür [da'fy:r] ad for it; (anstatt) instead; **er kann nichts ~** he can't help it; **er ist bekannt ~** he is well-known for that; **was bekomme ich ~?** what will I get for it?; **D~halten** nt **-s: nach meinem D~halten** in my opinion.

dagegen [da'ge:gən] ad against it; (im Vergleich damit) in comparison with it; (bei Tausch) to it; **ich habe nichts ~** I don't mind; **ich war ~** I was against it; ~ **kann man nichts tun** one can't do anything about it; cj however; **~halten** vt irreg (vergleichen) compare with it; (entgegnen) object to it.

daheim [da'haım] ad at home; **D~** nt **-s** home.

daher [da'he:r] ad (räumlich) from there; (Ursache) from that; ~ **kommt er auch** that's where he comes from too; cj (deshalb) that's why; ~ **die Schwierigkeiten** that's what is causing the difficulties.

dahin [da'hın] ad (räumlich) there; (zeitlich) then; (vergangen) gone; **das tendiert ~** it is tending towards that; **er bringt es noch ~, daß ich . . .** he'll make me . . .; **~gegen** cj on the other hand; **~gehend** ad on this matter; **~gestellt** ad: **~gestellt bleiben** remain to be seen; **~gestellt sein lassen** leave sth open or undecided.

dahinten [da'hıntən] ad over there.

dahinter [da'hıntər] ad behind it;

~**kommen** vi irreg get to the bottom of sth.

Dahlie ['da:liə] f **-, -n** dahlia.

dalassen ['da:lasən] vt irreg leave (behind).

damalig ['da:ma:lıç] a of that time, then.

damals ['da:ma:ls] ad at that time, then.

Damast [da'mast] m **-(e)s, -e** damask.

Dame ['da:mə] f **-, -n** lady; (Schach, Cards) queen; (Spiel) draughts; **d~nhaft** a lady-like; **~nwahl** f ladies' excuse-me; **~spiel** nt draughts.

damit [da'mıt] ad with it; (begründend) by that; **was meint er ~?** what does he mean by that?; **genug ~!** that's enough; ~ **basta!** and that's that; ~ **eilt es nicht** there's no hurry; cj in order that or to.

dämlich ['dɛ:mlıç] a (col) silly, stupid.

Damm [dam] m **-(e)s, "e** dyke; (Stau—) dam; (Hafen—) mole; (Bahn—, Straßen—) embankment.

Dämm- ['dɛm] cpd: **d~en** vt Wasser dam up; Schmerzen keep back; **d~erig** a dim, faint; **d~ern** vi (Tag) dawn; (Abend) fall; **~erung** f twilight; (Morgen—) dawn; (Abend—) dusk.

Dämon [dɛ:mɔn] m **-s, -en** demon; **d~isch** [dɛ'mo:nıʃ] a demoniacal.

Dampf [dampf] m **-(e)s, "e** steam; (Dunst) vapour; **d~en** vi steam.

dämpfen ['dɛmpfən] vt (Cook) steam; (bügeln auch) iron with a damp cloth; (fig) dampen, subdue.

Dampf- cpd: **~er** m **-s, -** steamer; **~kochtopf** m pressure cooker; **~maschine** f steam engine; **~schiff** nt steamship; **~walze** f steamroller.

danach [da'na:x] ad after that; (zeitlich auch) afterwards; (gemäß) accordingly; according to which or that; **er sieht ~ aus** he looks it.

daneben [da'ne:bən] ad beside it; (im Vergleich) in comparison; **~benehmen** vr irreg misbehave; **~gehen** vi irreg miss; (Plan) fail.

Dank [daŋk] m **-(e)s** thanks pl; **vielen** or **schönen ~** many thanks; **jdm ~ sagen** thank sb; **d~** prep +dat or gen thanks to; **d~bar** a grateful; Aufgabe rewarding; **~barkeit** f gratitude; **d~e** interj thank you, thanks; **d~en** vi (+dat) thank; **d~enswert** a Arbeit worthwhile; rewarding; Bemühung kind; **d~sagen** vi express one's thanks.

dann [dan] ad then; ~ **und wann** now and then.

daran [da'ran] ad on it; stoßen against it; **es liegt ~, daß . . .** the cause of it is that . . .; **gut/schlecht ~ sein** be well-/badly off; **das Beste/Dümmste ~** the best/stupidest thing about it; **ich war nahe ~, zu . . .** I was on the point of . . .; **er ist ~ gestorben** he died from or of it; **~gehen** vi irreg start; **~setzen** vt stake; **er hat alles ~gesetzt, von Glasgow wegzukommen** he has done his utmost to get away from Glasgow.

darauf [da'rauf] ad (räumlich) on it; (zielgerichtet) towards it; (danach) afterwards; **es kommt ganz ~ an, ob . . .** it depends whether . . .; **die Tage** ~ the days following or thereafter; **am Tag** ~ the next day; ~**folgend** a Tag, Jahr next, following; ~**hin** [-'hɪn] ad (im Hinblick darauf) in this respect; (aus diesem Grund) as a result; ~**legen** vt lay or put on top.

daraus [da'raus] ad from it; **was ist** ~ **geworden?** what became of it?; ~ **geht hervor, daß** . . . this means that . . .

Darbietung ['da:rbi:tuŋ] f performance.

darin [da'rɪn] ad in (there), in it.

Dar- ['da:r] cpd: **d~legen** vt explain, expound, set forth; ~**legung** f explanation; ~**leh(e)n** nt -s, - loan.

Darm [darm] m -(e)s, ̈-e intestine; (Wurst—) skin; ~**saite** f gut string.

Darstell- ['da:rʃtɛl] cpd: **d~en** vt (abbilden, bedeuten) represent; (Theat) act; (beschreiben) describe; vr appear to be; ~**er(in** f) m -s, - actor/actress; ~**ung** f portrayal, depiction.

darüber [da'ry:bər] ad (räumlich) over/above it; (fahren) over it; (mehr) more; (währenddessen) meanwhile; (sprechen, streiten) about it; ~ **geht nichts** there's nothing like it; **seine Gedanken** ~ his thoughts about or on it.

darum [da'rum] ad (räumlich) round it; ~ **herum** round about (it); **er bittet** ~ he is pleading for it; **es geht** ~, **daß** . . . the thing is that . . .; **er würde viel** ~ **geben, wenn** . . . he would give a lot to . . .; that's why; **ich tue es** ~, **weil** . . . I am doing it because . . .

darunter [da'runtər] ad (räumlich) under it; (dazwischen) among them; (weniger) less; **ein Stockwerk** ~ one floor below (it); **was verstehen Sie** ~? what do you understand by that?; ~**fallen** vi irreg be included; ~**mischen** vt Mehl mix in; vr mingle.

das [das] def art the; pron that; ~ **heißt** that is.

Dasein ['da:zain] nt -s (Leben) life; (Anwesenheit) presence; (Bestehen) existence; **d~** vi irreg be there.

daß [das] cj that.

dasselbe [das'zɛlbə] art, pron the same.

dastehen ['da:ʃte:ən] vi irreg stand there.

Datenverarbeitung ['da:tənfɛr'arbaituŋ] f data processing.

datieren [da'ti:rən] vt date.

Dativ ['da:ti:f] m -s, -e dative.

Dattel ['datəl] f -, -n date.

Datum ['da:tum] nt -s, **Daten** date; (pl: Angaben) data; **das heutige** ~ today's date.

Dauer ['dauər] f -, -n duration; (gewisse Zeitspanne) length; (Bestand, Fortbestehen) permanence; **es war nur von kurzer** ~ it didn't last long; **auf die** ~ in the long run; (auf längere Zeit) indefinitely; ~**auftrag** m standing order; **d~haft** a lasting, durable; ~**haftigkeit** f durability; ~**karte** f season ticket; ~**lauf** m long-distance run; **d~n** vi last; **es hat sehr lang gedauert, bis er** . . . it took him a long time to . . .; **d~nd** a constant; ~**regen** m continuous rain; ~**welle** f perm(anent wave); ~**wurst** f German

salami; ~**zustand** m permanent condition.

Daumen ['daumən] m -s, - thumb; ~**lutscher** m thumb-sucker.

Daune ['daunə] f -, -n down; ~**ndecke** f down duvet or quilt.

davon [da'fɔn] ad of it; (räumlich) away; (weg von) from it; (Grund) because of it; **das kommt** ~! that's what you get; ~ **abgesehen** apart from that; ~ **sprechen/wissen** talk/know of or about it; **was habe ich** ~? what's the point?; ~**gehen** vi irreg leave, go away; ~**kommen** vi irreg escape; ~**laufen** vi irreg run away; ~**tragen** vt irreg carry off; Verletzung receive.

davor [da'fo:r] ad (räumlich) in front of it; (zeitlich) before (that); ~ **warnen** warn about it.

dazu [da'tsu:] ad legen, stellen by it; essen, singen with it; **und** ~ **noch** and in addition; **ein Beispiel/seine Gedanken** ~ one example for/his thoughts on this; **wie komme ich denn** ~? why should I?; ~ **fähig** be capable of it; **sich** ~ **äußern** say sth on it; ~**gehören** vi belong to it; ~**gehörig** a appropriate; ~**kommen** vi irreg (Ereignisse) happen too; (an einen Ort) come along; ~**mal** ['da:tsuma:l] ad in those days.

dazwischen [da'tsvɪʃən] ad in between; (räumlich auch) between (them); (zusammen mit) among them; **der Unterschied** ~ the difference between them; ~**kommen** vi irreg (hineingeraten) get caught in it; **es ist etwas** ~**gekommen** something cropped up; ~**reden** vi (unterbrechen) interrupt; (sich einmischen) interfere; ~**treten** vi irreg intervene.

Debatte [de'batə] f -, -n debate.

Deck [dɛk] nt -(e)s, -s or -e deck; **an** ~ **gehen** go on deck; ~**e** f -, -n cover; (Bett—) blanket; (Tisch—) tablecloth; (Zimmer—) ceiling; **unter einer** ~**e stecken** be hand in glove; ~**el** m -s, - lid; **d~en** vt cover; vr coincide; vi lay the table; ~**mantel** m: **unter dem** ~**mantel von** under the guise of; ~**name** m assumed name; ~**ung** f (Schützen) covering; (Schutz) cover; (Sport) defence; (Übereinstimmen) agreement; **d~ungsgleich** a congruent.

Defekt [de'fɛkt] m -(e)s, -e fault, defect; **d~** a faulty.

defensiv [defɛn'si:f] a defensive.

definieren [defi'ni:rən] vt define.

Definition [definitsi'o:n] f definition.

definitiv [defini'ti:f] a definite.

Defizit ['de:fitsit] nt -s, -e deficit.

deftig ['dɛftɪç] a Essen large; Witz coarse.

Degen ['de:gən] m -s, - sword.

degenerieren [degene'ri:rən] vi degenerate.

degradieren [degra'di:rən] vt degrade.

Dehn- ['de:n] cpd: **d~bar** a elastic; (fig) Begriff loose; ~**barkeit** f elasticity; looseness; **d~en** vtr stretch; ~**ung** f stretching.

Deich [daiç] m -(e)s, -e dyke.

Deichsel ['daɪksəl] f -, -n shaft; d~n vt (fig, col) wangle.

dein [daɪn] pron (D~ in Briefen) your; ~e(r,s) yours; ~er pron or of du of you; ~erseits ad on your part; ~esgleichen pron people like you; ~etwegen, ~etwillen ad (für dich) for your sake; (wegen dir) on your account; ~ige pron: der/die/das ~ige yours.

dekadent [deka'dɛnt] a decadent.

Dekadenz f decadence.

Dekan [de'ka:n] m -s, -e dean.

Deklination [deklinatsi'o:n] f declension.

deklinieren [dekli'ni:rən] vt decline.

Dekolleté [dekɔl'te:] nt -s, -s low neckline.

Deko- [deko] cpd: ~rateur [-ra'tø:r] m window dresser; ~ration [-ratsi'o:n] f decoration; (in Laden) window dressing; d~rativ [-ra'ti:f] a decorative; d~rieren [-'ri:rən] vt decorate; Schaufenster dress.

Delegation [delegatsi'o:n] f delegation.

delikat [deli'ka:t] a (zart, heikel) delicate; (köstlich) delicious.

Delikatesse [delika'tɛsə] f -, -n delicacy; (pl: Feinkost) delicatessen pl; ~n-geschäft nt delicatessen (shop).

Delikt [de'lɪkt] nt -(e)s, -e (Jur) offence.

Delle ['dɛlə] f -, -n (col) dent.

Delphin [dɛl'fi:n] m -s, -e dolphin.

Delta ['dɛlta] nt -s, -s delta.

dem [de(:)m] art dat of der.

Demagoge [dema'go:gə] m -n, -n demagogue.

Demarkationslinie [demarkatsi'o:nli:niə] f demarcation line.

dementieren [demɛn'ti:rən] vt deny.

dem- cpd: ~gemäß, ~nach ad accordingly; ~nächst ad shortly.

Demokrat [demo'kra:t] m -en, -en democrat; ~ie [-'ti:] f democracy; d~isch a democratic; d~isieren [-i'si:rən] vt democratize.

demolieren [demo'li:rən] vt demolish.

Demon- [demon] cpd: ~strant(in f) [-'strant(ɪn)] m demonstrator; ~stration [-stratsi'o:n] f demonstration; d~strativ [-stra'ti:f] a demonstrative; Protest pointed; d~strieren [-'stri:rən] vti demonstrate.

Demoskopie [demosko'pi:] f public opinion research.

Demut ['de:mu:t] f humility.

demütig ['de:my:tɪç] a humble; ~en ['de:my:tɪgən] vt humiliate; D~ung f humiliation.

demzufolge ['de:mtsu'fɔlgə] ad accordingly.

den [de(:)n] art acc of der.

denen ['de:nən] pron dat of diese.

Denk- [dɛŋk] cpd: ~art f mentality; d~bar a conceivable; d~en vti irreg think; ~en nt -s thinking; ~er m -s, - thinker; ~fähigkeit f intelligence; d~faul a lazy; ~fehler m logical error; ~mal nt -s, -er monument; d~würdig a memorable; ~zettel m: jdm einen ~zettel verpassen teach sb a lesson.

denn [dɛn] cj for; ad then; (nach Komparativ) than.

dennoch ['dɛn'nɔx] cj nevertheless.

Denunziant [denuntsi'ant] m informer.

deponieren [depo'ni:rən] vt (Comm) deposit.

Depot [de'po:] nt -s, -s warehouse; (Bus—, Rail) depot; (Bank—) strongroom.

Depression [dɛprɛsi'o:n] f depression.

deprimieren [depri'mi:rən] vt depress.

der [de(:)r] def art the; rel pron that, which; (jemand) who; demon pron this one; ~art ad so; (solcher Art) such; ~artig a such, this sort of.

derb [dɛrp] a sturdy; Kost solid; (grob) coarse; D~heit f sturdiness; solidity; coarseness.

der- cpd: ~'gleichen pron such; ~'jenige pron he; she; it; (rel) the one (who); that (which); ~'maßen ad to such an extent, so; ~'selbe art, pron the same; ~'weil(en) ad in the meantime; ~'zeitig a present, current; (damalig) then.

des [dɛs] art gen of der.

Deserteur [dezɛr'tø:r] m deserter.

desertieren [dezɛr'ti:rən] vi desert.

desgleichen ['dɛs'glaɪçən] pron the same.

deshalb ['dɛs'halp] ad therefore, that's why.

Desinfektion [dezɪnfɛktsi'o:n] f disinfection; ~smittel nt disinfectant.

desinfizieren [dezɪnfi'tsi:rən] vt disinfect.

dessen ['dɛsən] pron gen of der, das; ~ungeachtet ad nevertheless, regardless.

Dessert [dɛ'sɛ:r] nt -s, -s dessert.

Destillation [dɛstilatsi'o:n] f distillation.

destillieren [dɛsti'li:rən] vt distil.

desto ['dɛsto] ad all or so much the; ~ besser all the better.

deswegen ['dɛs've:gən] cj therefore, hence.

Detail [de'taɪ] nt -s, -s detail; d~lieren [deta'ji:rən] vt specify, give details of.

Detektiv [detɛk'ti:f] m -s, -e detective.

Detektor [de'tɛktɔr] m (Tech) detector.

deut- ['dɔyt] cpd: ~en vt interpret, explain; vi point (auf +acc to or at); ~lich a clear; Unterschied distinct; D~lichkeit f clarity; distinctness; D~ung f interpretation.

Devise [de'vi:zə] f -, -n motto, device; (pl: Fin) foreign currency or exchange.

Dezember [de'tsɛmbər] m -(s), - December.

dezent [de'tsɛnt] a discreet.

dezimal [detsi'ma:l] a decimal; D~bruch m decimal (fraction); D~system nt decimal system.

Dia ['di:a] nt -s, -s see **Diapositiv**; ~betes [dia'be:tɛs] m -, - (Med) diabetes; ~gnose [dia'gno:zə] f -, -n diagnosis; d~gonal [diago'na:l] a diagonal; ~gonale f -, -n diagonal.

Dialekt [dia'lɛkt] m -(e)s, -e dialect; ~ausdruck m dialect expression/word; d~frei a pure, standard; d~isch a dialectal; Logik dialectical.

Dialog [dia'lo:k] m -(e)s, -e dialogue.

Diamant [dia'mant] m diamond.

Diapositiv [diapozi'ti:f] *nt* **-s, -e** (*Phot*) slide, transparency.

Diät [di'ɛ:t] *f* - diet; **~en** *pl* (*Pol*) allowance.

dich [dɪç] *pron acc of* **du** you; yourself.

dicht [dɪçt] *a* dense; *Nebel* thick; *Gewebe* close; (*undurchlässig*) (water)tight; (*fig*) concise; *ad*: **~ an/bei** close to; **~bevölkert** a densely or heavily populated; **D~e** *f* -, **-n** density; thickness; closeness; (water)tightness; (*fig*) conciseness; **~en** *vt* (*dicht machen*) make watertight; seal; (*Naut*) caulk; *vti* (*Liter*) compose, write; **D~er(in** *f*) *m* **-s,** - poet; (*Autor*) writer; **~erisch** *a* poetical; **~halten** *vi irreg* (*col*) keep mum; **D~ung** *f* (*Tech*) washer; (*Aut*) gasket; (*Gedichte*) poetry; (*Prosa*) (piece of) writing.

dick [dɪk] *a* thick; (*fett*) fat; **durch ~ und dünn** through thick and thin; **D~e** *f* -, **-n** thickness; fatness; **~fellig** *a* thick-skinned; **~flüssig** *a* viscous; **D~icht** *nt* **-s, -e** thicket; **D~kopf** *m* mule; **D~milch** *f* soured milk.

die [di:] *def art see* **der**.

Dieb(in *f*) [di:p/di:bɪn] *m* **-(e)s, -e** thief; **d~isch** *a* thieving; (*col*) immense; **~stahl** *m* **-(e)s, ²e** theft.

Diele ['di:lə] *f* -, **-n** (*Brett*) board; (*Flur*) hall, lobby; (*Eis—*) ice-cream parlour; (*Tanz—*) dance hall.

dienen ['di:nən] *vi* serve (*jdm* sb).

Diener *m* **-s,** - servant; **~in** *f* (maid)-servant; **~schaft** *f* servants *pl*.

Dienst [di:nst] *m* **-(e)s, -e** service; **außer ~** retired; **~ haben** be on duty; **der öffentliche ~** the civil service; **~ag** *m* Tuesday; **d~ags** *ad* on Tuesdays; **~bote** *m* servant; **d~eifrig** *a* zealous; **d~frei** *a* off duty; **~geheimnis** *nt* professional secret; **~gespräch** *nt* business call; **~grad** *m* rank; **d~habend** *a* Arzt on duty; **d~lich** *a* official; **~mädchen** *nt* domestic servant; **~reise** *f* business trip; **~stelle** *f* office; **d~tuend** *a* on duty; **~vorschrift** *f* service regulations *pl*; **~weg** *m* official channels *pl*; **~zeit** *f* office hours *pl*; (*Mil*) period of service.

dies- [di:s] *cpd*: **~bezüglich** *a* Frage on this matter; **~e(r,s)** [di:zə(r,z)] *pron* this (one); **~elbe** [di:'zɛlbə] *pron, art* the same; **D~elöl** *nt* diesel oil; **~ig** *a* drizzly; **~jährig** *a* this year's; **~mal** *ad* this time; **~seits** *prep* +*gen* on this side; **D~seits** *nt* - this life.

Dietrich ['di:trɪç] *m* **-s, -e** picklock.

differential [dɪfərɛntsi'a:l] *a* differential; **D~getriebe** *nt* differential gear; **D~rechnung** *f* differential calculus.

differenzieren [dɪfərɛn'tsi:rən] *vt* make differences in; **differenziert** complex.

Dikt- [dɪkt] *cpd*: **~aphon** [-a'fo:n] *nt* dictaphone; **~at** [-'ta:t] *nt* **-(e)s, -e** dictation; **~ator** [-'ta:tɔr] *m* dictator; **d~atorisch** [-a'to:rɪʃ] *a* dictatorial; **~atur** [-a'tu:r] *f* dictatorship; **d~ieren** [-'ti:rən] *vt* dictate.

Dilemma [di'lɛma] *nt* **-s, -s** *or* **-ta** dilemma.

Dilettant [dile'tant] *m* dilettante, amateur;

---

d~isch *a* amateurish, dilettante.

Dimension [dimɛnzi'o:n] *f* dimension.

Ding [dɪŋ] *nt* **-(e)s, -e** thing, object; **d~lich** *a* real, concrete; **~sbums** ['dɪŋksbums] *nt* - (*col*) thingummybob.

Diözese [diø'tse:zə] *f*-, **-n** diocese.

Diphtherie [dɪfte'ri:] *f* diphtheria.

Diplom [di'plo:m] *nt* **-(e)s, -e** diploma, certificate; **~at** [-'ma:t] *m* **-en, -en** diplomat; **~atie** [-a'ti:] *f* diplomacy; **d~atisch** [-'ma:tɪʃ] *a* diplomatic; **~ingenieur** *m* qualified engineer.

dir [di:r] *pron dat of* **du** (to) you.

direkt [di'rɛkt] *a* direct; **D~or** *m* director; (*Sch*) principal, headmaster; **D~orium** [-'to:rium] *nt* board of directors; **D~übertragung** *f* live broadcast.

Dirigent [diri'gɛnt] *m* conductor.

dirigieren [diri'gi:rən] *vt* direct; (*Mus*) conduct.

Dirne ['dɪrnə] *f*-, **-n** prostitute.

Diskont [dɪs'kɔnt] *m* **-s, -e** discount; **~satz** *m* rate of discount.

Diskothek [dɪsko'te:k] *f* -, **-en** disco(theque).

Diskrepanz [dɪskre'pants] *f* discrepancy.

diskret [dɪs'kre:t] *a* discreet; **D~ion** [-tsi'o:n] *f* discretion.

Diskussion [dɪskusi'o:n] *f* discussion; debate; **zur ~ stehen** be under discussion.

diskutabel [dɪsku'ta:bəl] *a* debatable.

diskutieren [dɪsku'ti:rən] *vti* discuss; debate.

Dissertation [dɪsɛrtatsi'o:n] *f* dissertation, doctoral thesis.

Distanz [dɪs'tants] *f* distance.

Distel ['dɪstəl] *f* -, **-n** thistle.

Disziplin [dɪstsi'pli:n] *f* discipline.

divers [di'vɛrs] *a* various.

Dividende [divi'dɛndə] *f* -, **-n** dividend.

dividieren [divi'di:rən] *vt* divide (*durch* by).

doch [dɔx] *ad*: **das ist nicht wahr!** ≈ **~!** that's not true! ≈ yes it is!; **nicht ~!** oh no!; **er kam ~ noch** he came after all; *cj* (*aber*) but; (*trotzdem*) all the same.

Docht [dɔxt] *m* **-(e)s, -e** wick.

Dock [dɔk] *nt* **-s, -s** *or* **-e** dock.

Dogge ['dɔgə] *f*-, **-n** bulldog.

Dogma ['dɔgma] *nt* **-s, -men** dogma; **d~tisch** [dɔ'gma:tɪʃ] *a* dogmatic.

Doktor ['dɔktɔr] *m* **-s, -en** [-'to:rən] doctor; **~and** [-'rant] *m* **-en, -en** candidate for a doctorate; **~arbeit** *f* doctoral thesis; **~titel** *m* doctorate.

Dokument [doku'mɛnt] *nt* document; **~arbericht** [-'ta:rbərɪçt] *m* documentary; **~arfilm** *m* documentary (film); **d~arisch** *a* documentary.

Dolch [dɔlç] *m* **-(e)s, -e** dagger.

dolmetschen ['dɔlmɛtʃən] *vti* interpret.

Dolmetscher(in *f*) *m* **-s,** - interpreter.

Dom [do:m] *m* **-(e)s, -e** cathedral.

dominieren [domi'ni:rən] *vt* dominate; *vi* predominate.

Dompfaff ['do:mpfaf] *m* bullfinch.

Dompteur [dɔmp'tø:r] *m*, **Dompteuse** [dɔmp'tø:zə] *f* (*Zirkus*) trainer.

Donner ['dɔnər] m -s, - thunder; **d~n** vi impers thunder; **~stag** m Thursday; **~wetter** nt thunderstorm; (fig) dressing-down; interj good heavens!

doof [do:f] a (col) daft, stupid.

Doppel ['dɔpəl] nt -s, - duplicate; (Sport) doubles; **~bett** nt double bed; **~fenster** nt double glazing; **~gänger** m -s, - double; **~punkt** m colon; **d~sinnig** a ambiguous; **~stecker** m two-way adaptor; **d~t** a double; **in d~ter Ausführung** in duplicate; **~verdiener** pl two-income family; **~zentner** m 100 kilograms; **~zimmer** nt double room.

Dorf [dɔrf] nt -(e)s, ¨er village; **~bewohner** m villager.

Dorn [dɔrn] m -(e)s, -en (Bot) thorn; pl -e (Schnallen—) tongue, pin; **d~ig** a thorny; **~röschen** nt Sleeping Beauty.

dörren ['dœrən] vt dry.

Dörrobst ['dœro:pst] nt dried fruit.

Dorsch [dɔrʃ] m -(e)s, -e cod.

dort [dɔrt] ad there; **~ drüben** over there; **~her** from there; **~hin** (to) there; **~ig** a of that place; in that town.

Dose ['do:zə] f -, -n box; (Blech—) tin, can; **~nöffner** m tin or can opener.

dösen ['dø:zən] vi (col) doze.

Dosis ['do:zıs] f -, **Dosen** dose.

Dotter ['dɔtər] m -s, - egg yolk.

Dozent [do'tsɛnt] m university lecturer.

Drache ['draxə] m -n, -n (Tier) dragon; **~n** m -, - kite.

Draht [dra:t] m -(e)s, ¨e wire; **auf ~ sein** be on the ball; **~gitter** nt wire grating; **~seil** nt cable; **~seilbahn** f cable railway, funicular; **~zange** f pliers pl.

drall [dral] a strapping; Frau buxom.

Drama ['dra:ma] nt -s, **Dramen** drama, play; **~tiker** ['-'ma:tikər] m -s, - dramatist; **d~tisch** ['-'ma:tıʃ] a dramatic.

dran [dran] ad (col) see **daran**.

Drang [draŋ] m -(e)s, ¨e (Trieb) impulse, urge, desire (nach for); (Druck) pressure.

drängeln ['drɛŋəln] vti push, jostle.

drängen ['drɛŋən] vt (schieben) push, press; (antreiben) urge; vi (eilig sein) be urgent; (Zeit) press; **auf etw** (acc) **~** press for sth.

drastisch ['drastıʃ] a drastic.

drauf [drauf] ad (col) see **darauf**; **D~gänger** m -s, - daredevil.

draußen ['drausən] ad outside, out-of-doors.

Dreck [drɛk] m -(e)s mud, dirt; **d~ig** a dirty, filthy.

Dreh- ['dre:] cpd: **~achse** f axis of rotation; **~arbeiten** pl (Cine) shooting; **~bank** f lathe; **d~bar** a revolving; **~buch** nt (Cine) script; **d~en** vti turn, rotate; Zigaretten roll; Film shoot; vr turn; (handeln von) be (um about); **~orgel** f barrel organ; **~tür** f revolving door; **~ung** f (Rotation) rotation; (Um—, Wendung) turn; **~wurm** m (col) **den ~wurm haben/bekommen** be/become dizzy; **~zahl** f rate of revolutions; **~zahlmesser** m rev(olution) counter.

drei [drai] num three; **D~eck** nt triangle; **~eckig** a triangular; **~einhalb** num three and a half; **D~einigkeit** [-'aınıçkaıt] f, **D~faltigkeit** [-'faltıçkaıt] f Trinity; **~erlei** a inv of three kinds; **~fach** a,ad triple, treble; **~hundert** num three hundred; **D~'königsfest** nt Epiphany; **~mal** ad three times, thrice; **~malig** a three times.

dreinreden ['drainre:dən] vi: **jdm ~** (dazwischenreden) interrupt sb; (sich einmischen) interfere with sb.

dreißig ['draisıç] num thirty.

dreist [draist] a bold, audacious; **D~igkeit** f boldness, audacity.

drei- cpd: **~viertel** num three-quarters; **D~viertelstunde** f three-quarters of an hour; **~zehn** num thirteen.

dreschen ['drɛʃən] vt irreg thresh.

dressieren [drɛ'si:rən] vt train.

Drill- ['drıl] cpd: **~bohrer** m light drill; **d~en** vt (bohren) drill, bore; (Mil) drill; (fig) train; **~ing** m triplet.

drin [drın] ad (col) see **darin**.

dringen ['drıŋən] vi irreg (Wasser, Licht, Kälte) penetrate (durch through; in +acc into); **auf etw** (acc) **~** insist on sth; **in jdn ~** entreat sb.

dringend ['drıŋənt], **dringlich** ['drıŋlıç] a urgent.

Dringlichkeit f urgency.

drinnen ['drınən] ad inside, indoors.

dritte(r, s) ['drıtə(r,z)] a third; **D~l** nt -s, - third; **~ns** ad thirdly.

droben ['dro:bən] ad above, up there.

Droge ['dro:gə] f -, -n drug; **d~nabhängig** a addicted to drugs; **~rie** [-'ri:] f chemist's shop.

Drogist [dro'gıst] m pharmacist, chemist.

drohen ['dro:ən] vi threaten (jdm sb).

dröhnen ['drø:nən] vi (Motor) roar; (Stimme, Musik) ring, resound.

Drohung ['dro:uŋ] f threat.

drollig ['drɔlıç] a droll.

Droschke ['drɔʃkə] f -, -n cab; **~nkutscher** m cabman.

Drossel ['drɔsəl] f -, -n thrush.

drüben ['dry:bən] ad over there, on the other side.

drüber ['dry:bər] ad (col) see **darüber**.

Druck [druk] m -(e)s, -e (Phys, Zwang) pressure; (Print) (Vorgang) printing; (Produkt) print; (fig: Belastung) burden, weight; **~buchstabe** m block letter.

Druck- ['dryk] cpd: **~eberger** m -s, - shirker, dodger; **d~en** vti Knopf, Hand press; (zu eng sein) pinch; (fig) Preise keep down; (fig: belasten) oppress, weigh down; **jdm etw in die Hand d~en** press sth into sb's hand; vr: **sich vor etw** (dat) **d~en** get out of (doing) sth; **d~end** a oppressive; **~er** m -s, - button; (Tür—) handle; (Gewehr—) trigger.

Druck- cpd: **~er** m -s, - printer; **~e'rei** f printing works, press; **~erschwärze** f printer's ink; **~fehler** m misprint; **~knopf** m press stud, snap fastener; **~mittel** nt leverage; **~sache** f printed matter; **~schrift** f block or printed letters pl.

drunten ['druntən] ad below, down there.

Drüse ['dry:zə] f -, -n gland.

Dschungel ['dʒʊŋəl] m -s, - jungle.

du [du:] pron (D~ in Briefen) you.

ducken ['dʊkən] vt Kopf, Person duck; (fig) take down a peg or two; vr duck.

Duckmäuser ['dʊkmɔʏzər] m -s, - yes-man.

Dudelsack ['du:dəlzak] m bagpipes pl.

Duell [du'ɛl] nt -s, -e duel.

Duett [du'ɛt] nt -(e)s, -e duet.

Duft [dʊft] m -(e)s, ¨e scent, odour; d~en vi smell, be fragrant; d~ig a Stoff, Kleid delicate, diaphanous; Muster fine.

duld- ['dʊld] cpd: ~en vti suffer; (zulassen) tolerate; ~sam a tolerant.

dumm [dʊm] a stupid; das wird mir zu ~ that's just too much; der D~e sein be the loser; ~dreist a impudent; ~erweise ad stupidly; D~heit f stupidity; (Tat) blunder, stupid mistake; D~kopf m blockhead.

dumpf [dʊmpf] a Ton hollow, dull; Luft close; Erinnerung, Schmerz vague; D~heit f hollowness, dullness; closeness; vagueness; ~ig a musty.

Düne ['dy:nə] f -, -n dune.

Dung [dʊŋ] m -(e)s see Dünger.

düngen ['dyŋən] vt manure.

Dünger m -s, - dung, manure; (künstlich) fertilizer.

dunkel ['dʊŋkəl] a dark; Stimme deep; Ahnung vague; (rätselhaft) obscure; (verdächtig) dubious, shady; im ~n tappen (fig) grope in the dark.

Dünkel ['dʏŋkəl] m -s self-conceit; d~haft a conceited.

Dunkel- cpd: ~heit f darkness; (fig) obscurity; ~kammer f (Phot) dark room; d~n vi impers grow dark; ~ziffer f estimated number of unnotified cases.

dünn [dʏn] a thin; ~flüssig a watery, thin; ~gesät a scarce; D~heit f thinness.

Dunst [dʊnst] m -es, ¨e vapour; (Wetter) haze.

dünsten ['dʏnstən] vt steam.

dunstig ['dʊnstɪç] a vaporous; Wetter hazy, misty.

Duplikat [dupli'ka:t] nt -(e)s, -e duplicate.

Dur [du:r] nt -, - (Mus) major.

durch [dʊrç] prep +acc through; (Mittel, Ursache) by; (Zeit) during; den Sommer ~ during the summer; 8 Uhr ~ past 8 o'clock; ~ und ~ completely; ~arbeiten vti work through; vr work one's way through; ~'aus ad completely; (unbedingt) definitely; ~beißen irreg vt bite through; vr (fig) battle on; ~blättern vt leaf through.

Durchblick ['dʊrçblɪk] m view; (fig) comprehension; d~en vi look through; (col: verstehen) understand (bei etw sth); etw d~en lassen (fig) hint at sth.

durch'bohren vt insep bore through, pierce.

durchbrechen ['dʊrçbrɛçən] vti break; [dʊrç'brɛçən] vt irreg insep Schranken break through; Schallmauer break; Gewohnheit break free from.

durch- ['dʊrç] cpd: ~brennen vi irreg (Draht, Sicherung) burn through; (col) run away; ~bringen irreg vt get through; Geld squander; vr make a living.

Durchbruch ['dʊrçbrʊx] m (Öffnung) opening; (Mil) breach; (von Gefühlen etc) eruption; (der Zähne) cutting; (fig) breakthrough; zum ~ kommen break through.

durch- cpd: ~dacht [dʊrç'daxt] a well thought-out; ~'denken vt irreg insep think out.

durch- ['dʊrç] cpd: ~diskutieren vt talk over, discuss; ~drängen vr force one's way through; ~drehen vt Fleisch mince; vi (col) crack up.

durchdringen ['dʊrçdrɪŋən] vi irreg penetrate, get through; mit etw ~ get one's way with sth; [dʊrç'drɪŋən] vt irreg insep penetrate.

durcheinander [dʊrç'ai'nandər] ad in a mess, in confusion; (col: verwirrt) confused; ~ trinken mix one's drinks; D~ nt -s (Verwirrung) confusion; (Unordnung) mess; ~bringen vt irreg mess up; (verwirren) confuse; ~reden vi talk at the same time.

durch- ['dʊrç] cpd: D~fahrt f transit; (Verkehr) thoroughfare; D~fall m (Med) diarrhoea; ~fallen vi irreg fall through; (in Prüfung) fail; ~finden vr irreg find one's way through.

durch'forschen vt insep explore.

durch- ['dʊrç] cpd: ~fressen vt irreg eat through; ~fragen vr find one's way by asking.

durchführ- ['dʊrçfy:r] cpd: ~bar a feasible, practicable; ~en vt carry out; D~ung f execution, performance.

Durchgang ['dʊrçgaŋ] m passage(way); (bei Produktion, Versuch) run; (Sport) round; (bei Wahl) ballot; ~ verboten no thoroughfare; ~shandel m transit trade; ~slager nt transit camp; ~sstadium nt transitory stage; ~sverkehr m through traffic.

durchgefroren ['dʊrçgefro:rən] a See completely frozen; Mensch frozen stiff.

durchgehen ['dʊrçge:ən] irreg vt (behandeln) go over; vi go through; (ausreißen: Pferd) break loose; (Mensch) run away; mein Temperament ging mit mir durch my temper got the better of me; jdm etw ~ lassen let sb get away with sth; ~d a Zug through; Öffnungszeiten continuous.

durch- ['dʊrç] cpd: ~greifen vi irreg take strong action; ~halten irreg vi last out; vt keep up; ~hecheln vt (col) gossip about; ~kommen vi irreg get through; (überleben) pull through.

durch'kreuzen vt insep thwart, frustrate.

durch ['dʊrç] cpd: ~lassen vt irreg Person let through; Wasser let in; ~lässig a leaky; D~lauf(wasser)erhitzer m -s, - (hot water) geyser.

durch- cpd: ~leben vt insep live or go through, experience; ~lesen vt irreg read through; ~leuchten vt insep X-ray; ~löchern [-'lœçərn] vt insep perforate; (mit Löchern) punch holes in; (mit Kugeln) riddle; '~machen vt go through; die Nacht ~machen make a night of it.

Durch- ['dʊrç] *cpd:* ~**marsch** *m* march through; ~**messer** *m* -**s**, - diameter.
durch'nässen *vt insep* soak (through).
durch- ['dʊrç] *cpd:* ~**nehmen** *vt irreg* go over; ~**numerieren** *vt* number consecutively; ~**pausen** *vt* trace; ~**peitschen** *vt* (*lit*) whip soundly; (*fig*) *Gesetzentwurf, Reform* force through.
durchqueren [dʊrç'kve:rən] *vt insep* cross.
durch- ['dʊrç] *cpd:* **D~reiche** *f* -, (serving) hatch; **D~reise** *f* transit; **auf der D~reise** passing through; *Güter* **in** transit; ~**ringen** *vr irreg* reach after a long struggle; ~**rosten** *vi* rust through.
durchs [dʊrçs] = **durch das.**
Durchsage ['dʊrçza:gə] *f* -, -**n** intercom or radio announcement.
durchschauen ['dʊrçʃauən] *vi* (*lit*) look or see through; [dʊrç'ʃauən] *vt insep Person, Lüge* see through.
durchscheinen ['dʊrçʃaɪnən] *vi irreg* shine through; ~**d** *a* translucent.
Durchschlag ['dʊrçʃla:k] *m* (*Doppel*) carbon copy; (*Sieb*) strainer; **d~en** *irreg vt* (*entzweischlagen*) split (in two); (*sieben*) sieve; (*vi zum Vorschein kommen*) emerge, come out; *vr* get by; **d~end** *a* resounding.
durch ['dʊrç] *cpd:* ~**schlüpfen** *vi* slip through; ~**schneiden** *vt irreg* cut through.
Durchschnitt ['dʊrçʃnɪt] *m* (*Mittelwert*) average; **über/unter dem** ~ above/below average; **im** ~ on average; **d~lich** *a* average; *ad* on average; ~**sgeschwindigkeit** *f* average speed; ~**smensch** *m* average man, man in the street; ~**swert** *m* average.
durch- *cpd:* '**D~schrift** *f* copy; ~'**schwimmen** *vt irreg insep* swim across; '~**sehen** *vt irreg* look through.
durchsetzen ['dʊrçzɛtsən] *vt* enforce; **seinen Kopf** ~ get one's own way; *vr* (*Erfolg haben*) succeed; (*sich behaupten*) get one's way; [dʊrç'zɛtsən] *vt insep* mix.
Durchsicht ['dʊrçzɪçt] *f* looking through, checking; **d~ig** *a* transparent; ~**igkeit** *f* transparence.
durch- *cpd:* '~**sickern** *vi* seep through; (*fig*) leak out; '~**sieben** *vt* sieve; '~**sprechen** *vt irreg* talk over; '~**stehen** *vt irreg* live through; ~**stöbern** [-'ʃtø:bərn] *vt insep* ransack, search through; '~**streichen** *vt irreg* cross out; '~**suchen** *vt insep* search; **D~'suchung** *f* search; ~**tränken** *vt insep* soak; ~**trieben** [-'tri:bən] *a* cunning, wily; '~**wachsen** *a* (*lit*) *Speck* streaky; (*fig: mittelmäßig*) so-so.
durch- ['dʊrç] *cpd:* ~**weg** *ad* throughout, completely; ~**zählen** *vt* count; *vi* count off; ~**ziehen** *irreg vt Faden* draw through; *vi* pass through.
durch- *cpd:* ~**zucken** *vt insep* shoot or flash through; '**D~zug** *m* (*Luft*) draught; (*von Truppen, Vögeln*) passage; '~**zwängen** *vtr* squeeze or force through.
dürfen ['dʏrfən] *vi irreg* be allowed; **darf ich?** may I?; **es darf geraucht werden** you may smoke; **was darf es sein?** what

can I do for you?; **das darf nicht geschehen** that must not happen; **das** ~ **Sie mir glauben** you can believe me; **es dürfte Ihnen bekannt sein, daß . . .** as you will probably know ...
dürftig ['dʏrftɪç] *a* (*ärmlich*) needy, poor; (*unzulänglich*) inadequate.
dürr [dʏr] *a* dried-up; *Land* arid; (*mager*) skinny, gaunt; **D~e** *f* -, -**n** aridity; (*Zeit*) drought; (*Magerkeit*) skinniness.
Durst [dʊrst] *m* -(**e**)**s** thirst; ~ **haben** be thirsty; **d~ig** *a* thirsty.
Dusche ['duʃə] *f* -, -**n** shower; **d~n** *vir* have a shower.
Düse ['dy:zə] *f* -, -**n** nozzle; (*Flugzeug—*) jet; ~**nantrieb** *m* jet propulsion; ~**nflugzeug** *nt* jet (plane); ~**njäger** *m* jet fighter.
Dussel ['dʊsəl] *m* -**s**, - (*col*) twit.
düster ['dy:stər] *a* dark; *Gedanken, Zukunft* gloomy; **D~keit** *f* darkness, gloom; gloominess.
Dutzend ['dʊtsənt] *nt* -**s**, -**e** dozen; **d~(e)mal** *ad* a dozen times; ~**mensch** *m* man in the street; **d~weise** *ad* by the dozen.
duzen ['du:tsən] *vtr* use the familiar form of address or 'du' (*jdn to or* with sb).
Dynamik [dy'na:mɪk] *f* (*Phys*) dynamics; (*fig: Schwung*) momentum; (*von Mensch*) dynamism.
dynamisch [dy'na:mɪʃ] *a* (*lit, fig*) dynamic.
Dynamit [dyna'mi:t] *nt* -**s** dynamite.
Dynamo [dy'na:mo] *m* -**s**, -**s** dynamo.
D-Zug ['de:tsu:k] *m* through train.

E

E, e [e:] *nt* E, e.
Ebbe ['ɛbə] *f* -, -**n** low tide.
eben ['e:bən] *a* level; (*glatt*) smooth; *ad* just; (*bestätigend*) exactly; ~ **deswegen** just because of that; ~**bürtig** *a:* **jdm** ~**bürtig sein** be sb's peer; **E~e** *f* -, -**n** plain; ~**erdig** *a* at ground level; ~**falls** *ad* likewise; **E~heit** *f* levelness; smoothness; ~**so** *ad* just as; ~**sogut** *ad* just as well; ~**sooft** *ad* just as often; ~**soviel** *ad* just as much; ~**soweit** *ad* just as far; ~**sowenig** *ad* just as little.
Eber ['e:bər] *m* -**s**, - boar; ~**esche** *f* mountain ash, rowan.
ebnen ['e:bnən] *vt* level.
Echo ['ɛço] *nt* -**s**, -**s** echo.
echt [ɛçt] *a* genuine; (*typisch*) typical; **E~heit** *f* genuineness.
Eck- ['ɛk] *cpd:* ~**ball** *m* corner (kick); ~**e** *f* -, -**n** corner; (*Math*) angle; **e~ig** *a* angular; ~**zahn** *m* eye tooth.
edel ['e:dəl] *a* noble; **E~metall** *nt* rare metal; **E~stein** *m* precious stone.
Efeu ['e:fɔy] *m* -**s** ivy.
Effekt- [ɛ'fɛkt] *cpd:* ~**en** *pl* stocks *pl*; ~**enbörse** *f* Stock Exchange; ~**hasche'rei** *f* sensationalism; **e~iv** [-'ti:f] *a* effective, actual.
egal [e'ga:l] *a* all the same.
Ego- [ego] *cpd:* ~**ismus** [-'ɪsmʊs] *m* selfishness, egoism; ~**ist** [-'ɪst] *m* egoist;

e~**istisch** *a* selfish, egoistic; e~**zentrisch** [-'tsɛntrɪʃ] *a* egocentric, self-centred.

Ehe ['eːə] *f* -, -**n** marriage; e~ *cj* before; ~**brecher** *m* -**s,** - adulterer; ~**brecherin** *f* adulteress; ~**bruch** *m* adultery; ~**frau** *f* married woman; wife; ~**leute** *pl* married people *pl*; e~**lich** *a* matrimonial; *Kind* legitimate; e~**malig** *a* former; e~**mals** *ad* formerly; ~**mann** *m* married man; husband; ~**paar** *nt* married couple.

eher ['eːər] *ad* (*früher*) sooner; (*lieber*) rather, sooner; (*mehr*) more.

Ehe- *cpd*: ~**ring** *m* wedding ring; ~**scheidung** *f* divorce; ~**schließung** *f* marriage.

eheste(r,s) ['eːəstə(r,z)] *a* (*früheste*) first, earliest; **am** ~**n** (*liebsten*) soonest; (*meist*) most; (*wahrscheinlichst*) most probably.

Ehr- ['eːr] *cpd*: e~**bar** *a* honourable, respectable; ~**e** *f* -, -**n** honour; e~**en** *vt* honour; ~**engast** *m* guest of honour; e~**enhaft** *a* honourable; ~**enmann** *m* man of honour; ~**enmitglied** *nt* honorary member; ~**enplatz** *m* place of honour; ~**enrechte** *pl* civic rights *pl*; e~**enrührig** *a* defamatory; ~**enrunde** *f* lap of honour; ~**ensache** *f* point of honour; e~**envoll** *a* honourable; ~**enwort** *nt* word of honour; e~**erbietig** *a* respectful; ~**furcht** *f* awe, deep respect; ~**gefühl** *nt* sense of honour; ~**geiz** *m* ambition; e~**geizig** *a* ambitious; e~**lich** *a* honest; ~**lichkeit** *f* honesty; e~**los** *a* dishonourable; ~**ung** *f* honour(ing); e~**würdig** *a* venerable.

Ei [ai] *nt* -**(e)s,** -**er** egg; e~ *interj* well, well; (*beschwichtigend*) now, now.

Eich- ['aiç] *cpd*: ~**amt** *nt* Office of Weights and Measures; ~**e** *f* -, -**n** oak (tree); ~**el** *f* -, -**n** acorn; (*Cards*) club; e~**en** *vt* standardize; ~**hörnchen** *nt* squirrel; ~**maß** *nt* standard; ~**ung** *f* standardization.

Eid [ait] *m* -**(e)s,** -**e** oath; ~**echse** ['aidɛksə] *f* -, -**n** lizard; e~**esstattliche Erklärung** affidavit; ~**genosse** *m* Swiss; e~**lich** *a* (sworn) upon oath.

Ei- *cpd*: ~**dotter** *nt* egg yolk; ~**erbecher** *m* eggcup; ~**erkuchen** *m* omelette; pancake; ~**erschale** *f* eggshell; ~**erstock** *m* ovary; ~**eruhr** *f* egg timer.

Eifer ['aifər] *m* -**s** zeal, enthusiasm; ~**sucht** *f* jealousy; e~**süchtig** *a* jealous (*auf* +*acc* of).

eifrig ['aifriç] *a* zealous, enthusiastic.

Eigelb ['aigɛlp] *nt* -**(e)s,** - egg yolk.

eigen ['aigən] *a* own; (-*artig*) peculiar; **mit der/dem ihm** ~**en** . . . with that . . . peculiar to him; **sich** (*dat*) **etw zu** ~ **machen** make sth one's own; E~**art** *f* peculiarity; characteristic; ~**artig** *a* peculiar; E~**bedarf** *m* one's own requirements *pl*; E~**gewicht** *nt* dead weight; ~**händig** *a* with one's own hand; E~**heim** *nt* owner-occupied house; E~**heit** *f* peculiarity; E~**lob** *nt* self-praise; ~**mächtig** *a* high-handed; E~**name** *m* proper name; ~**s** *ad*

expressly, on purpose; E~**schaft** *f* quality, property, attribute; E~**schaftswort** *nt* adjective; E~**sinn** *m* obstinacy; ~**sinnig** *a* obstinate; ~**tlich** *a* actual, real; *ad* actually, really; E~**tor** *nt* own goal; E~**tum** *nt* property; E~**tümer(in** *f*) *m* -**s,** - owner, proprietor; ~**tümlich** *a* peculiar; E~**tümlichkeit** *f* peculiarity; E~**tumswohnung** *f* freehold flat.

eignen ['aignən] *vr* be suited.

Eignung *f* suitability.

Eil- ['ail] *cpd*: ~**bote** *m* courier; ~**brief** *m* express letter; ~**e** *f* - haste; **es hat keine** ~**e** there's no hurry; e~**en** *vi* (*Mensch*) hurry; (*dringend sein*) be urgent; e~**ends** *ad* hastily; e~**fertig** *a* eager, solicitous; ~**gut** *nt* express goods *pl*, fast freight (*US*); e~**ig** *a* hasty, hurried; (*dringlich*) urgent; **es e~ig haben** be in a hurry; ~**zug** *m* semi-fast train, limited stop train.

Eimer ['aimər] *m* -**s,** - bucket, pail.

ein(e) [ain(ə)] *num* one; *indef art* a, an; *ad*: **nicht** ~ **noch aus wissen** not know what to do; ~**e(r,s)** *pron* one; (*jemand*) someone.

einander [ai'nandər] *pron* one another, each other.

einarbeiten ['ainarbaitən] *vr* familiarize o.s. (*in* +*acc* with).

einarmig ['ainarmiç] *a* one-armed.

einatmen ['ainaːtmən] *vti* inhale, breathe in.

einäugig ['ainʼɔygiç] *a* one-eyed.

Einbahnstraße ['ainbaːnʃtraːsə] *f* one-way street.

Einband ['ainbant] *m* binding, cover.

einbändig ['ainbɛndiç] *a* one-volume.

einbau- ['ainbau] *cpd*: ~**en** *vt* build in; *Motor* install, fit; E~**möbel** *pl* built-in furniture.

einbe- ['ainbə] *cpd*: ~**griffen** *a* included, inclusive; ~**rufen** *vt irreg* convene; (*Mil*) call up; E~**rufung** *f* convocation; call-up.

einbett- ['ainbɛt] *cpd*: ~**en** *vt* embed; E~**zimmer** *nt* single room.

einbeziehen ['ainbətsiːən] *vt irreg* include.

einbiegen ['ainbiːgən] *vi irreg* turn.

einbilden ['ainbildən] *vt*: **sich** (*dat*) **etw** ~ imagine sth.

Einbildung *f* imagination; (*Dünkel*) conceit; ~**skraft** *f* imagination.

einbinden ['ainbindən] *vt irreg* bind (up).

einblenden ['ainblɛndən] *vt* fade in.

einbleuen ['ainblɔyən] *vt* (*col*) **jdm etw** ~ hammer sth into sb.

Einblick ['ainblik] *m* insight.

einbrechen ['ainbrɛçən] *vi irreg* (*in Haus*) break in; (*in Land etc*) invade; (*Nacht*) fall; (*Winter*) set in; (*durchbrechen*) break.

Einbrecher *m* -**s,** - burglar.

einbringen ['ainbriŋən] *vt irreg* bring in; *Geld, Vorteil* yield; (*mitbringen*) contribute.

Einbruch ['ainbrux] *m* (*Haus*—) break-in, burglary; (*Eindringen*) invasion; (*des Winters*) onset; (*Durchbrechen*) break; (*Met*) approach; (*Mil*) penetration; ~ **der Nacht** nightfall; e~**ssicher** *a* burglar-proof.

einbürgern ['ainbyrgərn] *vt* naturalize; *vr*

become adopted; **das hat sich so eingebürgert** that's become a custom.

Einbuße ['aɪnbuːsə] f loss, forfeiture.

einbüßen ['aɪnbyːsən] vt lose, forfeit.

eindecken ['aɪndɛkən] vr lay in stocks (mit of).

eindeutig ['aɪndɔʏtɪç] a unequivocal.

eindring- ['aɪndrɪŋ] cpd: ~**en** vi irreg (in +acc) force one's way in(to); (in Haus) break in(to); (in Land) invade; (Gas, Wasser) penetrate; (mit Bitten) pester (auf jdn sb); ~**lich** a forcible, urgent; E~**ling** m intruder.

Eindruck ['aɪndrʊk] m impression; e~**fähig** a impressionable; e~**svoll** a impressive.

eindrücken ['aɪndrʏkən] vt press in.

eineiig ['aɪn''aɪɪç] a Zwillinge identical.

eineinhalb ['aɪn'aɪn'halp] num one and a half.

einengen ['aɪn'ɛŋən] vt confine, restrict.

einer- ['aɪnər] cpd: ~**lei** a (gleichartig) the same kind of; **es ist mir** ~**lei** it is all the same to me; ~**seits** ad on one hand.

einfach ['aɪnfax] a simple; (nicht mehrfach) single; ad simply; E~**heit** f simplicity.

einfädeln ['aɪnfɛːdəln] vt Nadel thread; (fig) contrive.

einfahren ['aɪnfaːrən] irreg vt bring in; Barriere knock down; Auto run in; vi drive in; (Zug) pull in; (Min) go down.

Einfahrt f (Vorgang) driving in; pulling in; (Min) descent; (Ort) entrance.

Einfall ['aɪnfal] m (Idee) idea, notion; (Licht—) incidence; (Mil) raid; e~**en** vi irreg (Licht) fall; (Mil) raid; (einstimmen) join in (in +acc with); (einstürzen) fall in, collapse; **etw fällt jdm ein** sth occurs to sb; **das fällt mir gar nicht ein** I wouldn't dream of it; **sich** (dat) **etwas e~en lassen** have a good idea.

einfältig ['aɪnfɛltɪç] a simple(-minded).

Einfamilienhaus [aɪnfaˈmiːliənhaʊs] nt detached house.

einfangen ['aɪnfaŋən] vt irreg catch.

einfarbig ['aɪnfarbɪç] a all one colour; Stoff etc self-coloured.

einfass- ['aɪnfas] cpd: ~**en** vt set; Beet enclose; Stoff edge, border; Bier barrel; E~**ung** f setting; enclosure; barrelling.

einfetten ['aɪnfɛtən] vt grease.

einfinden ['aɪnfɪndən] vr irreg come, turn up.

einfliegen ['aɪnfliːgən] vt irreg fly in.

einfließen ['aɪnfliːsən] vi irreg flow in.

einflößen ['aɪnfløːsən] vt: **jdm etw** ~ (lit) give sb sth; (fig) instil sth in sb.

Einfluß ['aɪnflʊs] m influence; ~**bereich** m sphere of influence; e~**reich** a influential.

einförmig ['aɪnfœrmɪç] a uniform; E~**keit** f uniformity.

einfrieren ['aɪnfriːrən] irreg vi freeze (in); vt freeze.

einfügen ['aɪnfyːgən] vt fit in; (zusätzlich) add.

Einfuhr ['aɪnfuːr] f - import; ~**artikel** m imported article.

einführ- ['aɪnfyːr] cpd: ~**en** vt bring in; Mensch, Sitten introduce; Ware import; E~**ung** f introduction; E~**ungspreis** m introductory price.

Eingabe ['aɪngaːbə] f petition; (Daten—) input.

Eingang ['aɪngaŋ] m entrance; (Comm: Ankunft) arrival; (Sendung) post; e~**s** ad, prep +gen at the outset (of); ~**sbe-stätigung** f acknowledgement of receipt; ~**shalle** f entrance hall.

eingeben ['aɪngeːbən] vt irreg Arznei give; Daten etc feed; Gedanken inspire.

eingebildet ['aɪngəbɪldət] a imaginary; (eitel) conceited.

Eingeborene(r) ['aɪngəboːrənə(r)] mf native.

Eingebung f inspiration.

einge- ['aɪngə] cpd: ~**denk** prep +gen bearing in mind; ~**fallen** a Gesicht gaunt; ~**fleischt** a inveterate; ~**fleischter Junggeselle** confirmed bachelor; ~**froren** a frozen.

eingehen ['aɪngeːən] irreg vi (Aufnahme finden) come in; (verständlich sein) be comprehensible (jdm to sb); (Sendung, Geld) be received; (Tier, Pflanze) die; (Firma) fold; (schrumpfen) shrink; **auf etw** (acc) ~ go into sth; **auf jdn** ~ respond to sb; vt enter into; Wette make; ~**d** a exhaustive, thorough.

einge- ['aɪngə] cpd: E~**machte(s)** nt preserves pl; ~**meinden** vt incorporate; ~**nommen** a (von) fond (of), partial (to); (gegen) prejudiced; ~**schrieben** a registered; ~**sessen** a old-established; ~**spielt** a: **aufeinander** ~**spielt sein** be in tune with each other; E~**ständnis** nt -ses, -se admission, confession; ~**stehen** vt irreg confess; ~**tragen** a (Comm) registered; E~**weide** nt -s, - innards pl, intestines pl; E~**weihte(r)** mf initiate; ~**wöhnen** vt accustom.

eingießen ['aɪngiːsən] vt irreg pour (out).

eingleisig ['aɪnglaɪzɪç] a single-track.

eingraben ['aɪngraːbən] irreg vt dig in; vr dig o.s. in.

eingreifen ['aɪngraɪfən] vi irreg intervene, interfere; (Zahnrad) mesh.

Eingriff ['aɪngrɪf] m intervention, interference; (Operation) operation.

einhaken ['aɪnhaːkən] vt hook in; vr: **sich bei jdm** ~ link arms with sb; vi (sich einmischen) intervene.

Einhalt ['aɪnhalt] m: ~ **gebieten** (+dat) put a stop to; e~**en** irreg vt Regel keep; vi stop.

einhändig ['aɪnhɛndɪç] a one-handed; ~**en** [-dɪgən] vt hand in.

einhängen ['aɪnhɛŋən] vt hang; Telefon (auch vi) hang up; **sich bei jdm** ~ link arms with sb.

einheim- ['aɪnhaɪm] cpd: ~**isch** a native; ~**sen** vt (col) bring home.

Einheit ['aɪnhaɪt] f unity; (Maß, Mil) unit; e~**lich** a uniform; ~**spreis** m uniform price.

einhellig ['aɪnhɛlɪç] a,ad unanimous.

einholen ['aɪnhoːlən] *vt Tau* haul in; *Fahne, Segel* lower; *(Vorsprung aufholen)* catch up with; *Verspätung* make up; *Rat, Erlaubnis* ask; *vi (einkaufen)* buy, shop.

Einhorn ['aɪnhɔrn] *nt* unicorn.

einhüllen ['aɪnhʏlən] *vt* wrap up.

einig ['aɪnɪç] *a (vereint)* united; **sich** *(dat)* ~ **sein** be in agreement; ~ **werden** agree; ~**e** ['aɪnɪgə] *pl* some; *(mehrere)* several; ~**e(r,s)** *a* some; ~**emal** *ad* a few times; ~**en** *vt* unite; *vr* agree *(auf +acc* on); ~**ermaßen** *ad* somewhat; *(leidlich)* reasonably; ~**es** *pron* something; ~**gehen** *vi irreg* agree; **E**~**keit** *f* unity; *(Übereinstimmung)* agreement; **E**~**ung** *f* agreement; *(Vereinigung)* unification.

einimpfen ['aɪnɪmpfən] *vt* inoculate *(jdm etw* sb with sth); *(fig)* impress *(jdm etw* sth upon sb).

einjährig ['aɪnjɛːrɪç] *a* of or for one year; *(Alter)* one-year-old; *Pflanze* annual.

einkalkulieren ['aɪnkalkuliːrən] *vt* take into account, allow for.

Einkauf ['aɪnkaʊf] *m* purchase; **e**~**en** *vt* buy; *vi* go shopping; ~**sbummel** *m* shopping spree; ~**snetz** *nt* string bag; ~**spreis** *m* cost price.

einkerben ['aɪnkɛrbən] *vt* notch.

einklammern ['aɪnklamərn] *vt* put in brackets, bracket.

Einklang ['aɪnklaŋ] *m* harmony.

einkleiden ['aɪnklaɪdən] *vt* clothe; *(fig)* express.

einklemmen ['aɪnklɛmən] *vt* jam.

einknicken ['aɪnknɪkən] *vt* bend in; *Papier* fold; *vi* give way.

einkochen ['aɪnkɔxən] *vt* boil down; *Obst* preserve, bottle.

Einkommen ['aɪnkɔmən] *nt* **-s, -** income; ~**(s)steuer** *f* income tax.

einkreisen ['aɪnkraɪzən] *vt* encircle.

Einkünfte ['aɪnkʏnftə] *pl* income, revenue.

einlad- ['aɪnlaːd] *cpd:* ~**en** *vt irreg Person* invite; *Gegenstände* load; **jdn ins Kino** ~**en** take sb to the cinema; **E**~**ung** *f* invitation.

Einlage ['aɪnlaːgə] *f (Programm—)* interlude; *(Spar—)* deposit; *(Schuh—)* insole; *(Fußstütze)* support; *(Zahn—)* temporary filling; *(Cook)* noodles *pl,* vegetables *pl etc* in soup; **e**~**rn** *vt* store.

Einlaß ['aɪnlas] *m* **-sses, -lässe** admission.

einlassen *irreg vt* let in; *(einsetzen)* set in; *vr:* **sich mit jdm/auf etw** *(acc)* ~ **get** involved with sb/sth.

Einlauf ['aɪnlaʊf] *m* arrival; *(von Pferden)* finish; *(Med)* enema; **e**~**en** *irreg vi* arrive, come in; *(in Hafen)* enter; *(Sport,* finish; *(Wasser)* run in; *(Stoff)* shrink; *vt Schuhe* break in; **jdm das Haus e**~**en** invade sb's house; *vi (Sport)* warm up; *(Motor, Maschine)* run in.

einleben ['aɪnleːbən] *vr* settle down.

Einlege- ['aɪnleːgə] *cpd:* ~**arbeit** *f* inlay; **e**~**n** *vt (einfügen) Blatt, Sohle* insert; *(Cook)* pickle; *(in Holz etc)* inlay; *Geld* deposit; *Pause* have; *Protest* make; *Veto* use; *Berufung* lodge; **ein gutes Wort bei**

jdm e~**n** put in a good word with sb; ~**sohle** *f* insole.

einleiten ['aɪnlaɪtən] *vt* introduce, start; *Geburt* induce.

Einleitung *f* introduction; induction.

einleuchten ['aɪnlɔʏçtən] *vi* be clear or evident *(jdm* to sb); ~**d** *a* clear.

einliefern ['aɪnliːfərn] *vt* take *(in +acc* into).

einlösen ['aɪnløːzən] *vt Scheck* cash; *Schuldschein, Pfand* redeem; *Versprechen* keep.

einmachen ['aɪnmaxən] *vt* preserve.

einmal ['aɪnmaːl] *ad* once; *(erstens)* first; *(zukünftig)* sometime; **nehmen wir** ~ **an** just let's suppose; **noch** ~ once more; **nicht** ~ not even; **auf** ~ all at once; **es war** ~ once upon a time there was/were; **E**~'**eins** *nt* multiplication tables *pl;* ~**ig** *a* unique; *(einmal geschehend)* single; *(prima)* fantastic.

Einmann- ['aɪn'man] *cpd:* ~**betrieb** *m* one-man business; ~**bus** *m* one-man-operated bus.

Einmarsch ['aɪnmarʃ] *m* entry; *(Mil)* invasion; **e**~**ieren** *vi* march in.

einmengen ['aɪnmɛŋən], **einmischen** ['aɪnmɪʃən] *vr* interfere *(in +acc* with).

einmünden ['aɪnmʏndən] *vi* run *(in +acc* into), join.

einmütig ['aɪnmyːtɪç] *a* unanimous.

Einnahme ['aɪnnaːmə] *f* **-, -n** *(Geld)* takings *pl,* revenue; *(von Medizin)* taking; *(Mil)* capture, taking; ~**quelle** *f* source of income.

einnehmen ['aɪnneːmən] *vt irreg* take; *Stellung, Raum* take up; ~ **für/gegen** persuade in favour of/against; ~**d** *a* charming.

einnicken ['aɪnnɪkən] *vi* nod off.

einnisten ['aɪnnɪstən] *vr* nest; *(fig)* settle o.s.

Einöde ['aɪn'øːdə] *f* **-, -n** desert, wilderness.

einordnen ['aɪn'ɔrdnən] *vt* arrange, fit in; *vr* adapt; *(Aut)* get into lane.

einpacken ['aɪnpakən] *vt* pack (up).

einparken ['aɪnparkən] *vt* park.

einpendeln ['aɪnpɛndəln] *vr* even out.

einpferchen ['aɪnpfɛrçən] *vt* pen in, coop up.

einpflanzen ['aɪnpflantsən] *vt* plant; *(Med)* implant.

einplanen ['aɪnplaːnən] *vt* plan for.

einpräg- ['aɪnprɛːg] *cpd:* ~**en** *vt* impress, imprint; *(beibringen)* impress *(jdm* on sb); **sich** *(dat)* **etw** ~**en** memorize sth; ~**sam** *a* easy to remember; *Melodie* catchy.

einrahmen ['aɪnraːmən] *vt* frame.

einrasten ['aɪnrastən] *vi* engage.

einräumen ['aɪnrɔʏmən] *vt (ordnend)* put away; *(überlassen) Platz* give up; *(zugestehen)* admit, concede.

einrechnen ['aɪnrɛçnən] *vt* include; *(berücksichtigen)* take into account.

einreden ['aɪnreːdən] *vt:* **jdm/sich etw** ~ talk sb/o.s. into believing sth.

einreiben ['aɪnraɪbən] *vt irreg* rub in.

einreichen ['aɪnraɪçən] *vt* hand in; *Antrag* submit.

Einreise ['aɪnraɪzə] *f* entry; ~**bestimmungen** *pl* entry regulations *pl*; ~**erlaubnis** *f*, ~**genehmigung** *f* entry permit; **e~n** *vi* enter (*in ein Land* a country).

einreißen ['aɪnraɪsən] *vt irreg Papier* tear; *Gebäude* pull down; *vi* tear; (*Gewohnheit werden*) catch on.

einrichten ['aɪnrɪçtən] *vt Haus* furnish; (*schaffen*) establish, set up; (*arrangieren*) arrange; (*möglich machen*) manage; *vr* (*in Haus*) furnish one's house; (*sich vorbereiten*) prepare o.s. (*auf +acc* for); (*sich anpassen*) adapt (*auf +acc* to).

Einrichtung *f* (*Wohnungs—*) furnishings *pl*; (*öffentliche Anstalt*) organization; (*Dienste*) service.

einrosten ['aɪnrɔstən] *vi* get rusty.

einrücken ['aɪnrʏkən] *vi* (*Mil*) (*Soldat*) join up; (*in Land*) move in; *vt Anzeige* insert; *Zeile* indent.

Eins [aɪns] *f* -, **-en** one; **e~** *num* one; **es ist mir alles e~** it's all one to me.

einsalzen ['aɪnzaltsən] *vt* salt.

einsam ['aɪnzaːm] *a* lonely, solitary; **E~keit** *f* loneliness, solitude.

einsammeln ['aɪnzaməln] *vt* collect.

Einsatz ['aɪnzats] *m* (*Teil*) inset; (*an Kleid*) insertion; (*Tisch*) leaf; (*Verwendung*) use, employment; (*Spiel—*) stake; (*Risiko*) risk; (*Mil*) operation; (*Mus*) entry; **im ~** in action; **e~bereit** *a* ready for action.

einschalten ['aɪnʃaltən] *vt* (*einfügen*) insert; *Pause* make; (*Elec*) switch on; (*Aut*) *Gang* engage; *Anwalt* bring in; *vr* (*dazwischentreten*) intervene.

einschärfen ['aɪnʃɛrfən] *vt* impress (*jdm etw* sth on sb.)

einschätzen ['aɪnʃɛtsən] *vt* estimate, assess; *vr* rate o.s.

einschenken ['aɪnʃɛŋkən] *vt* pour out.

einschicken ['aɪnʃɪkən] *vt* send in.

einschieben ['aɪnʃiːbən] *vt irreg* push in; (*zusätzlich*) insert.

einschiffen ['aɪnʃɪfən] *vt* take on board; *vr* embark, go on board.

einschlafen ['aɪnʃlaːfən] *vi irreg* fall asleep, go to sleep.

einschläfernd ['aɪnʃlɛːfərnt] *a* (*Med*) soporific; (*langweilig*) boring; *Stimme* lulling.

Einschlag ['aɪnʃlaːk] *m* impact; (*Aut*) lock; (*fig: Beimischung*) touch, hint; **e~en** *irreg vt* knock in; *Fenster* smash, break; *Zähne, Schädel* smash in; *Steuer* turn; (*kürzer machen*) take up; *Ware* pack, wrap up; *Weg, Richtung* take; *vi* hit (*in etw* (*acc*) sth, *auf jdn* sb); (*sich einigen*) agree; (*Anklang finden*) work, succeed.

einschlägig ['aɪnʃlɛːgɪç] *a* relevant.

einschleichen ['aɪnʃlaɪçən] *vr irreg* (*in Haus, Fehler*) creep in, steal in; (*in Vertrauen*) worm one's way in.

einschließen ['aɪnʃliːsən] *irreg vt Kind* lock in; *Häftling* lock up; *Gegenstand* lock away; *Bergleute* cut off; (*umgeben*) surround; (*Mil*) encircle; (*fig*) include, comprise; *vr* lock o.s. in.

einschließlich *ad* inclusive; *prep +gen* inclusive of, including.

einschmeicheln ['aɪnʃmaɪçəln] *vr* ingratiate o.s. (*bei* with).

einschnappen ['aɪnʃnapən] *vi* (*Tür*) click to; (*fig*) be touchy; **eingeschnappt sein** be in a huff.

einschneidend ['aɪnʃnaɪdənt] *a* incisive.

Einschnitt ['aɪnʃnɪt] *m* cutting; (*Med*) incision; (*Ereignis*) incident.

einschränken ['aɪnʃrɛŋkən] *vt* limit, restrict; *Kosten* cut down, reduce; *vr* cut down (on expenditure); ~**d** *a* restrictive.

Einschränkung *f* restriction, limitation; reduction; (*von Behauptung*) qualification.

Einschreib- ['aɪnʃraɪb] *cpd*: ~**(e)brief** *m* recorded delivery letter; **e~en** *irreg vt* write in; *Post* send recorded delivery; *vr* register; (*Univ*) enrol; ~**en** *nt* recorded delivery letter; ~**(e)sendung** *f* recorded delivery packet.

einschreiten ['aɪnʃraɪtən] *vi irreg* step in, intervene; ~ **gegen** take action against.

Einschub ['aɪnʃuːp] *m* **-s**, **ᵁe** insertion.

einschüchtern ['aɪnʃʏçtərn] *vt* intimidate.

einsehen ['aɪnzeːən] *vt irreg* (*hineinsehen in*) realize; *Akten* have a look at; (*verstehen*) see; **E~** *nt* -s understanding; **ein E~ haben** show understanding.

einseifen ['aɪnzaɪfən] *vt* soap, lather; (*fig*) take in, cheat.

einseitig ['aɪnzaɪtɪç] *a* one-sided; **E~keit** *f* one-sidedness.

Einsend- ['aɪnzɛnd] *cpd*: **e~en** *vt irreg* send in; ~**er** *m* **-s**, - sender, contributor; ~**ung** *f* sending in.

einsetzen ['aɪnzɛtsən] *vt* put (in); (*in Amt*) appoint, install; *Geld* stake; (*verwenden*) use; (*Mil*) employ; *vi* (*beginnen*) set in; (*Mus*) enter, come in; *vr* work hard; **sich für jdn/etw** ~ support sb/sth.

Einsicht ['aɪnzɪçt] *f* insight; (*in Akten*) look, inspection; **zu der** ~ **kommen, daß ...** come to the conclusion that ...; **e~ig** *a Mensch* judicious; ~**nahme** *f* -, -**n** examination; **e~slos** *a* unreasonable; **e~svoll** *a* understanding.

Einsiedler ['aɪnziːdlər] *m* hermit.

einsilbig ['aɪnzɪlbɪç] *a* (*lit,fig*) monosyllabic; **E~keit** *f* (*fig*) taciturnity.

einsinken ['aɪnzɪŋkən] *vi irreg* sink in.

Einsitzer ['aɪnzɪtsər] *m* **-s**, - single-seater.

einspannen ['aɪnʃpanən] *vt Werkstück, Papier* put (in), insert; *Pferde* harness; (*col*) *Person* rope in.

einsperren ['aɪnʃpɛrən] *vt* lock up.

einspielen ['aɪnʃpiːlən] *vr* (*Sport*) warm up; **sich aufeinander** ~ become attuned to each other; *vt* (*Film*) *Geld* bring in; *Instrument* play in; **gut eingespielt** smoothly running.

einspringen ['aɪnʃprɪŋən] *vi irreg* (*aushelfen*) help out, step into the breach.

einspritzen ['aɪnʃprɪtsən] *vt* inject.

Einspruch ['aɪnʃprux] *m* protest, objection; ~**srecht** *nt* veto.

einspurig ['aɪnʃpuːrɪç] *a* single-line.

einst [aɪnst] *ad* once; (*zukünftig*) one *or* some day.

Einstand ['aɪnʃtant] *m* (*Tennis*) deuce;

(*Antritt*) entrance (to office).

einstechen ['aɪnʃtɛçən] *vt irreg* stick in.

einstecken ['aɪnʃtɛkən] *vt* stick in, insert; *Brief* post; (*Elec*) *Stecker* plug in; *Geld* pocket; (*mitnehmen*) take; (*überlegen sein*) put in the shade; (*hinnehmen*) swallow.

einstehen ['aɪnʃteːən] *vi irreg* guarantee (*für jdn/etw* sb/sth); (*verantworten*) answer (*für* for).

einsteigen ['aɪnʃtaɪgən] *vi irreg* get in *or* on; (*in Schiff*) go on board; (*sich beteiligen*) come in; (*hineinklettern*) climb in.

einstell- ['aɪnʃtɛl] *cpd:* ~**bar** *a* adjustable; ~**en** *vti* (*aufhören*) stop; *Geräte* adjust; *Kamera etc* focus; *Sender, Radio* tune in; (*unterstellen*) put; (*in Firma*) employ, take on; *vr* (*anfangen*) set in; (*kommen*) arrive; **sich auf jdn/etw** ~**en** adapt to sb/prepare o.s. for sth; **E**~**ung** *f* (*Aufhören*) suspension, cessation; adjustment; focusing; (*von Arbeiter etc*) appointment; (*Haltung*) attitude.

Einstieg ['aɪnʃtiːk] *m* -(e)s, -e entry; (*fig*) approach.

einstig ['aɪnstɪç] *a* former.

einstimm- ['aɪnʃtɪm] *cpd:* ~**en** *vi* join in; *vt* (*Mus*) tune; (*in Stimmung bringen*) put in the mood; ~**ig** *a* unanimous; (*Mus*) for one voice; **E**~**igkeit** *f* unanimity.

einst- ['aɪnst] *cpd:* ~**malig** *a* former; ~**mals** *ad* once, formerly.

einstöckig ['aɪnʃtœkɪç] *a* single-storeyed.

einstudieren ['aɪnʃtudiːrən] *vt* study, rehearse.

einstündig ['aɪnʃtʏndɪç] *a* one-hour.

einstürmen ['aɪnʃtʏrmən] *vi:* **auf jdn** ~ rush at sb; (*Eindrücke*) overwhelm sb.

Einsturz ['aɪnʃtʊrts] *m* collapse; ~**gefahr** *f* danger of collapse.

einstürzen ['aɪnʃtʏrtsən] *vi* fall in, collapse.

einst- ['aɪnst] *cpd:* ~**weilen** *ad* meanwhile; (*vorläufig*) temporarily, for the time being; ~**weilig** *a* temporary.

eintägig ['aɪntɛːgɪç] *a* one-day.

eintauchen ['aɪntaʊxən] *vt* immerse, dip in; *vi* dive.

eintauschen ['aɪntaʊʃən] *vt* exchange.

eintausend ['aɪntaʊzənt] *num* one thousand.

einteil- ['aɪntaɪl] *cpd:* ~**en** *vt* (*in Teile*) divide (up); *Menschen* assign; ~**ig** *a* one-piece.

eintönig ['aɪntøːnɪç] *a* monotonous; **E**~**keit** *f* monotony.

Eintopf(gericht *nt*) ['aɪntɔpf(gərɪçt)] *m* stew.

Eintracht ['aɪntraxt] *f* - concord, harmony.

einträchtig ['aɪntrɛçtɪç] *a* harmonious.

Eintrag ['aɪntraːk] *m* -(e)s, ⁻e entry; *amtlicher* ~ entry in the register; **e**~**en** *irreg vt* (*in Buch*) enter; *Profit* yield; **jdm etw e**~**en** bring sb sth; *vr* put one's name down.

einträglich ['aɪntrɛːklɪç] *a* profitable.

eintreffen ['aɪntrɛfən] *vi irreg* happen; (*ankommen*) arrive.

eintreten ['aɪntreːtən] *irreg vi* occur; (*hineingehen*) enter (*in etw* (*acc*) sth); (*sich*

einsetzen) intercede; (*in Club, Partei*) join (*in etw* (*acc*) sth); (*in Stadium etc*) enter; *vt Tür* kick open.

Eintritt ['aɪntrɪt] *m* (*Betreten*) entrance; (*Anfang*) commencement; (*in Club etc*) joining; ~**sgeld** *nt*, ~**spreis** *m* charge for admission; ~**skarte** *f* (admission) ticket.

eintrocknen ['aɪntrɔknən] *vi* dry up.

einüben ['aɪnʔyːbən] *vt* practise, drill.

einver- ['aɪnfɛr] *cpd:* ~**leiben** *vt* incorporate; *Gebiet* annex; **sich** (*dat*) **etw** ~**leiben** (*fig: geistig*) acquire; **E**~**nehmen** *nt* -s, - agreement, understanding; ~**standen** *interj* agreed; *a:* ~**standen sein** agree, be agreed; **E**~**ständnis** *nt* understanding; (*gleiche Meinung*) agreement.

Einwand ['aɪnvant] *m* -(e)s, ⁻e objection; ~**erer** ['aɪnvandərər] *m* immigrant; **e**~**ern** *vi* immigrate; ~**erung** *f* immigration; **e**~**frei** *a* perfect; *ad* absolutely.

einwärts ['aɪnvɛrts] *ad* inwards.

einwecken ['aɪnvɛkən] *vt* bottle, preserve.

Einwegflasche ['aɪnveːgflaʃə] *f* no-deposit bottle.

einweichen ['aɪnvaɪçən] *vt* soak.

einweih- ['aɪnvaɪ] *cpd:* ~**en** *vt Kirche* consecrate; *Brücke* open; *Gebäude* inaugurate; *Person* initiate (*in* +*acc* in); **E**~**ung** *f* consecration; opening; inauguration; initiation.

einweis- ['aɪnvaɪz] *cpd:* ~**en** *vt irreg* (*in Amt*) install; (*in Arbeit*) introduce; (*in Anstalt*) send; **E**~**ung** *f* installation; introduction; sending.

einwenden ['aɪnvɛndən] *vt irreg* object, oppose (*gegen* to).

einwerfen ['aɪnvɛrfən] *vt irreg* throw in; *Brief* post; *Geld* put in, insert; *Fenster* smash; (*äußern*) interpose.

einwickeln ['aɪnvɪkəln] *vt* wrap up; (*fig col*) outsmart.

einwillig- ['aɪnvɪlɪg] *cpd:* ~**en** *vi* consent, agree (*in* +*acc* to); **E**~**ung** *f* consent.

einwirk- ['aɪnvɪrk] *cpd:* ~**en** *vi:* **auf jdn/etw** ~**en** influence sb/sth; **E**~**ung** *f* influence.

Einwohner ['aɪnvoːnər] *m* -s, - inhabitant; ~'**meldeamt** *nt* registration office; ~**schaft** *f* population, inhabitants *pl*.

Einwurf ['aɪnvʊrf] *m* (*Öffnung*) slot; (*Einwand*) objection; (*Sport*) throw-in.

Einzahl ['aɪntsaːl] *f* singular; **e**~**en** *vt* pay in; ~**ung** *f* paying in.

einzäunen ['aɪntsɔʏnən] *vt* fence in.

einzeichnen ['aɪntsaɪçnən] *vt* draw in.

Einzel ['aɪntsəl] *nt* -s, - (*Tennis*) singles; *in cpds* individual; single; ~**bett** *nt* single bed; ~**fall** *m* single instance, individual case; ~**haft** *f* solitary confinement; ~**heit** *f* particular, detail; **e**~**n** *a* single; (*vereinzelt*) the odd; *ad* singly; **e**~**n angeben** specify; **der/die e**~**ne** the individual; **das e**~**ne** the particular; **ins e**~**ne gehen** go into detail(s); ~**teil** *nt* component (part); ~**zimmer** *nt* single room.

einziehen ['aɪntsiːən] *irreg vt* draw in, take in; *Kopf* duck; *Fühler, Antenne, Fahrgestell* retract; *Steuern, Erkundigungen* collect; (*Mil*) draft, call up; (*aus dem Verkehr ziehen*) withdraw; (*konfiszieren*) confiscate; *vi* move in(to); (*Friede, Ruhe*) come; (*Flüssigkeit*) penetrate.

einzig ['aıntsıç] *a* only; (*ohnegleichen*) unique; **das** ~**e** the only thing; **der/die** ~**e** the only one; ~**artig** *a* unique.

Einzug ['aıntsu:k] *m* entry, moving in.

Eis [aıs] -**es**, - ice; (*Speise*—) ice cream; ~**bahn** *f* ice or skating rink; ~**bär** *m* polar bear; ~**becher** *m* sundae; ~**bein** *nt* pig's trotters *pl*; ~**berg** *m* iceberg; ~**blumen** *pl* ice fern; ~**decke** *f* sheet of ice; ~**diele** *f* ice-cream parlour.

Eisen ['aızən] *nt* -**s**, - iron; ~**bahn** *f* railway, railroad (*US*); ~**bahner** *m* -**s**, - railwayman, railway employee, railroader (*US*); ~**bahnschaffner** *m* railway guard; ~**bahnübergang** *m* level crossing, grade crossing (*US*); ~**bahnwagen** *m* railway carriage; ~**erz** *nt* iron ore; **e**~**haltig** *a* containing iron.

eisern ['aızərn] *a* iron; *Gesundheit* robust; *Energie* unrelenting; *Reserve* emergency.

Eis- *cpd*: **e**~**frei** *a* clear of ice; ~**hockey** *nt* ice hockey; **e**~**ig** ['aızıç] *a* icy; **e**~**kalt** *a* icy cold; ~**kunstlauf** *m* figure skating; ~**laufen** *nt* ice skating; ~**läufer(in** *f*) *m* ice-skater; ~**pickel** *m* ice-axe; ~**schießen** *nt* ≈ curling; ~**schrank** *m* fridge, ice-box (*US*); ~**zapfen** *m* icicle; ~**zeit** *f* ice age.

eitel ['aıtəl] *a* vain; **E**~**keit** *f* vanity.

Eiter ['aıtər] *m* -**s** pus; **e**~**ig** *a* suppurating; **e**~**n** *vi* suppurate.

Ei- [aı] *cpd*: ~**weiß** *nt* -**es**, -**e** white of an egg; ~**zelle** *f* ovum.

Ekel ['e:kəl] *m* -**s** nausea, disgust; *nt* -**s**, - (*col: Mensch*) nauseating person; **e**~**erregend**, **e**~**haft**, **ek(e)lig** *a* nauseating, disgusting; **e**~**n** *vt* disgust; **es ekelt jdn** *or* **jdm** sb is disgusted; *vr* loathe, be disgusted (*vor* +*dat* at).

Ekstase [ɛk'sta:zə] *f* -, -**n** ecstasy.

Ekzem [ɛk'tse:m] *nt* -**s**, -**e** (*Med*) eczema.

Elan [e'lã:] *m* -**s** elan.

elastisch [e'lastıʃ] *a* elastic.

Elastizität [elastizi'tɛ:t] *f* elasticity.

Elch [ɛlç] *m* -**(e)s**, -**e** elk.

Elefant [ele'fant] *m* elephant.

elegant [ele'gant] *a* elegant.

Eleganz [ele'gants] *f* elegance.

Elek- [e'lek] *cpd*: ~**trifizierung** [-trifi'tsi:ruŋ] *f* electrification; ~**triker** [-trikər] *m* -**s**, - electrician; **e**~**trisch** [-trıʃ] *a* electric; **e**~**trisieren** [-tri'zi:rən] *vt* (*lit, fig*) electrify; *Mensch* give an electric shock; *vr* get an electric shock; ~**trizität** [-tritsi'tɛt] *f* electricity; ~**trizitätswerk** *nt* electricity works, power plant.

Elektro- [e'lektro] *cpd*: ~**de** [elɛk'tro:də] *f* -, -**n** electrode; ~**herd** *m* electric cooker; ~**lyse** [-'ly:zə] *f* -, -**n** electrolysis; ~**n** [-ɔn] *nt* -**s**, -**en** electron; ~**nen(ge)hirn** [elɛk'tro:nən-] *nt* electronic brain; ~**nenrechner** *m* computer; **e**~**nisch** *a* electronic; ~**rasierer** *m* -**s**, - electric razor.

Element [ele'mɛnt] *nt* -**s**, -**e** element; (*Elec*) cell, battery; **e**~**ar** [-'ta:r] *a* elementary; (*naturhaft*) elemental.

Elend ['e:lɛnt] *nt* -**(e)s** misery; **e**~ *a* miserable; **e**~**iglich** ['e:lɛnd-] *ad* miserably; ~**sviertel** *nt* slum.

elf [ɛlf] *num* eleven; **E**~ *f* -, -**en** (*Sport*) eleven; **E**~**e** *f* -, -**n** elf; **E**~**enbein** *nt* ivory; **E**~**meter** *m* (*Sport*) penalty (kick).

eliminieren [elimi'ni:rən] *vt* eliminate.

Elite [e'li:tə] *f* -, -**n** elite.

Elixier [elı'ksi:r] *nt* -**s**, -**e** elixir.

Ell- *cpd*: ~**e** ['ɛlə] *f* -, -**n** ell; (*Maß*) yard; ~**(en)bogen** *m* elbow; ~**ipse** [ɛ'lıpsə] *f* -, -**n** ellipse.

Elster ['ɛlstər] *f* -, -**n** magpie.

Elter- ['ɛltər] *cpd*: **e**~**lich** *a* parental; ~**n** *pl* parents *pl*; ~**nhaus** *nt* home; **e**~**nlos** *a* parentless.

Email [e'ma:j] *nt* -**s**, -**s** enamel; **e**~**lieren** [ema'ji:rən] *vt* enamel.

Emanzipation [emantsipatsi'o:n] *f* emancipation.

emanzipieren *vt* emancipate.

Embryo ['ɛmbryo] *m* -**s**, -**s** *or* -**nen** embryo.

Emi- [emi] *cpd*: ~**grant** [-'grant] *m* emigrant; ~**gration** [-gratsi'o:n] *f* emigration; **e**~**grieren** [-'gri:rən] *vi* emigrate.

Empfang [ɛm'pfaŋ] *m* -**(e)s**, ⁼**e** reception; (*Erhalten*) receipt; **in** ~ **nehmen** receive; **e**~**en** *irreg vt* receive; *vi* (*schwanger werden*) conceive.

Empfäng- [ɛm'pfɛŋ] *cpd*: ~**er** *m* -**s**, - receiver; (*Comm*) addressee, consignee; **e**~**lich** *a* receptive, susceptible; ~**nis** *f* -, -**se** conception; ~**nisverhütung** *f* contraception.

Empfangs- *cpd*: ~**bestätigung** *f* acknowledgement; ~**dame** *f* receptionist; ~**schein** *m* receipt; ~**zimmer** *nt* reception room.

empfehlen [ɛm'pfe:lən] *irreg vt* recommend; *vr* take one's leave; ~**swert** *a* recommendable.

Empfehlung *f* recommendation; ~**sschreiben** *nt* letter of recommendation.

empfind- [ɛm'pfınt] *cpd*: ~**en** [ɛm'pfındən] *vt irreg* feel; ~**lich** *a* sensitive; *Stelle* sore; (*reizbar*) touchy; **E**~**lichkeit** *f* sensitiveness; (*Reizbarkeit*) touchiness; ~**sam** *a* sentimental; **E**~**ung** *f* feeling, sentiment; ~**ungslos** *a* unfeeling, insensitive.

empor [ɛm'po:r] *ad* up, upwards.

empören [ɛm'pø:rən] *vt* make indignant; shock; *vr* become indignant; ~**d** *a* outrageous.

empor- *cpd*: ~**kommen** *vi irreg* rise; succeed; **E**~**kömmling** *m* upstart, parvenu.

Empörung *f* indignation.

emsig ['ɛmzıç] *a* diligent, busy.

End- ['ɛnt] *in cpds final*: ~**auswertung** *f* final analysis; ~**bahnhof** ['ɛnt-] *m* terminus; ~**e** *nt* -**s**, -**n** end; **am** ~**e** at the end; (*schließlich*) in the end; **am** ~**e sein** be at the end of one's tether; ~**e Dezember** at the end of December; **zu**

~e sein be finished; e~en *vi* end; e~gültig *a* final, definite; ~ivie [ɛn'diːviə] *f* endive; e~lich *a* final; (*Math*) finite; *ad* finally; e~lich! at last!; e~los *a* endless, infinite; ~spiel *nt* final(s); ~spurt *m* (*Sport*) final spurt; ~station *f* terminus; ~ung *f* ending.

Energie [ɛnɛr'giː] *f* energy; e~los *a* lacking in energy, weak; ~wirtschaft *f* energy industry.

energisch [e'nɛrgɪʃ] *a* energetic.

eng [ɛŋ] *a* narrow; *Kleidung* tight; (*fig*) *Horizont* auch limited; *Freundschaft, Verhältnis* close; ~ an etw (*dat*) close to sth.

Engagement [ãgaʒə'mãː] *nt* -s, -s engagement; (*Verpflichtung*) commitment.

engagieren [ãgaˈʒiːrən] *vt* engage; ein engagierter Schriftsteller a committed writer; *vr* commit o.s.

Enge ['ɛŋə] *f* -, -n (*lit,fig*) narrowness; (*Land*—) defile; (*Meer*—) straits *pl*; jdn in die ~ treiben drive sb into a corner.

Engel ['ɛŋəl] *m* -s, - angel; e~haft *a* angelic; ~macher *m* -s, - (*col*) back-street abortionist.

eng- *cpd*: ~herzig *a* petty; E~paß *m* defile, pass; (*fig, Verkehr*) bottleneck.

en gros [ãˈgro] *ad* wholesale.

engstirnig ['ɛŋʃtɪrnɪç] *a* narrow-minded.

Enkel ['ɛŋkəl] *m* -s, - grandson; ~in *f* granddaughter; ~kind *nt* grandchild.

en masse [ã'mas] *ad* en masse.

enorm [e'nɔrm] *a* enormous.

Ensemble [ã'sãbəl] *nt* -s, -s company, ensemble.

entarten [ɛnt'aːrtən] *vi* degenerate.

entbehr- [ɛnt'beːr] *cpd*: ~en *vt* do without, dispense with; ~lich *a* superfluous; E~ung *f* privation.

entbinden [ɛnt'bɪndən] *irreg vt* release (*gen* from); (*Med*) deliver; *vi* (*Med*) give birth.

Entbindung *f* release; (*Med*) confinement; ~sheim *nt* maternity hospital.

entblößen [ɛnt'bløːsən] *vt* denude, uncover; (*berauben*) deprive (*gen* of).

entdeck- [ɛnt'dɛk] *cpd*: ~en *vt* discover; jdm etw ~en disclose sth to sb; E~er *m* -s, - discoverer; E~ung *f* discovery.

Ente ['ɛntə] *f* -, -n duck; (*fig*) canard, false report.

entehren [ɛnt''eːrən] *vt* dishonour, disgrace.

enteignen [ɛnt''aɪɡnən] *vt* expropriate; *Besitzer* dispossess.

enteisen [ɛnt''aɪzən] *vt* de-ice, defrost.

enterben [ɛnt''ɛrbən] *vt* disinherit.

entfachen [ɛnt'faxən] *vt* kindle.

entfallen [ɛnt'falən] *vi irreg* drop, fall; (*wegfallen*) be dropped; jdm ~ (*vergessen*) slip sb's memory; auf jdn ~ be allotted to sb.

entfalten [ɛnt'faltən] *vt* unfold; *Talente* develop; *vr* open; (*Mensch*) develop one's potential.

Entfaltung *f* unfolding; (*von Talenten*) development.

entfern- [ɛnt'fɛrn] *cpd*: ~en *vt* remove; (*hinauswerfen*) expel; *vr* go away, retire, withdraw; ~t *a* distant; weit davon ~t

sein, etw zu tun be far from doing sth; E~ung *f* distance; (*Wegschaffen*) removal; E~ungsmesser *m* -s, - (*Phot*) rangefinder.

entfesseln [ɛnt'fɛsəln] *vt* (*fig*) arouse.

entfetten [ɛnt'fɛtən] *vt* take the fat from.

entfremd- [ɛnt'frɛmd] *cpd*: ~en *vt* estrange, alienate; E~ung *f* alienation, estrangement.

entfrost- [ɛnt'frɔst] *cpd*: ~en *vt* defrost; E~er *m* -s, - (*Aut*) defroster.

entführ- [ɛnt'fyːr] *cpd*: ~en *vt* carry off, abduct; kidnap; E~er *m* kidnapper; E~ung *f* abduction; kidnapping.

entgegen [ɛnt'geːɡən] *prep* +*dat* contrary to, against; *ad* towards; ~bringen *vt irreg* bring; (*fig*) show (jdm etw sb sth); ~gehen *vi irreg* (+*dat*) go to meet, go towards; ~gesetzt *a* opposite; (*widersprechend*) opposed; ~halten *vt irreg* (*fig*) object; ~kommen *vi irreg* approach; meet (jdm sb); (*fig*) accommodate (jdm sb); E~kommen *nt* obligingness; ~kommend *a* obliging; ~laufen *vi irreg* (+*dat*) run towards or to meet; (*fig*) run counter to; ~nehmen *vt irreg* receive, accept; ~sehen *vi irreg* (+*dat*) await; ~setzen *vt* oppose (*dat* to); ~treten *vi irreg* (+*dat*) (*lit*) step up to; (*fig*) oppose, counter; ~wirken *vi* (+*dat*) counteract.

entgegnen [ɛnt'geːɡnən] *vt* reply, retort.

Entgegnung *f* reply, retort.

entgehen [ɛnt'geːən] *vi irreg* (*fig*) jdm ~ escape sb's notice; sich (*dat*) etw ~ lassen miss sth.

entgeistert [ɛnt'gaɪstərt] *a* thunderstruck.

Entgelt [ɛnt'gɛlt] *nt* -(e)s, -e compensation, remuneration; e~en *vt irreg*: jdm etw e~en repay sb for sth.

entgleisen [ɛnt'glaɪzən] *vi* (*Rail*) be derailed; (*fig: Person*) misbehave; ~ lassen derail.

Entgleisung *f* derailment; (*fig*) faux pas, gaffe.

entgleiten [ɛnt'glaɪtən] *vi irreg* slip (jdm from sb's hand).

entgräten [ɛnt'grɛːtən] *vt* fillet, bone.

Enthaarungsmittel [ɛnt'haːrʊŋsmɪtəl] *nt* depilatory.

enthalten [ɛnt'haltən] *irreg vt* contain; *vr* abstain, refrain (*gen* from).

enthaltsam [ɛnt'haltzaːm] *a* abstinent, abstemious; E~keit *f* abstinence.

enthemmen [ɛnt'hɛmən] *vt*: jdn ~ free sb from his inhibitions.

enthüllen [ɛnt'hʏlən] *vt* reveal, unveil.

Enthusiasmus [ɛntuziˈasmʊs] *m* enthusiasm.

entkernen [ɛnt'kɛrnən] *vt* stone; core.

entkommen [ɛnt'kɔmən] *vi irreg* get away, escape (*dat, aus* from).

entkorken [ɛnt'kɔrkən] *vt* uncork.

entkräften [ɛnt'krɛftən] *vt* weaken, exhaust; *Argument* refute.

entladen [ɛnt'laːdən] *irreg vt* unload; (*Elec*) discharge; *vr* (*Elec, Gewehr*) discharge; (*Ärger etc*) vent itself.

entlang [ɛnt'laŋ] *prep* +*acc* or *dat*, *ad* along; ~ dem Fluß, den Fluß ~ along the river; ~gehen *vi irreg* walk along.

entlarven [ɛnt'larfən] *vt* unmask, expose.

entlassen [ɛnt'lasən] *vt irreg* discharge; *Arbeiter* dismiss.

Entlassung *f* discharge; dismissal.

entlasten [ɛnt'lastən] *vt* relieve; *Achse* relieve the load on; *Angeklagte* exonerate; *Konto* clear.

Entlastung *f* relief; (*Comm*) crediting; ~**szeuge** *m* defence witness.

entledigen [ɛnt'leːdɪgən] *vr*: **sich jds/einer Sache** ~ rid o.s. of sb/sth.

entleeren [ɛnt'leːrən] *vt* empty; evacuate.

entlegen [ɛnt'leːgən] *a* remote.

entlocken [ɛnt'lɔkən] *vt* elicit (*jdm etw* sth from sb).

entlüften [ɛnt'lʏftən] *vt* ventilate.

entmachten [ɛnt'maxtən] *vt* deprive of power.

entmenscht [ɛnt'mɛnʃt] *a* inhuman, bestial.

entmilitarisiert [ɛntmilitari'ziːrt] *a* demilitarized.

entmündigen [ɛnt'mʏndɪgən] *vt* certify.

entmutigen [ɛnt'muːtɪgən] *vt* discourage.

Entnahme [ɛnt'naːmə] *f* -, -n removal, withdrawal.

entnehmen [ɛnt'neːmən] *vt irreg* (+*dat*) take out (*of*), take (from); (*folgern*) infer (from).

entpuppen [ɛnt'pupən] *vr* (*fig*) reveal o.s., turn out (*als* to be).

entrahmen [ɛnt'raːmən] *vt* skim.

entreißen [ɛnt'raisən] *vt irreg* snatch (away) (*jdm etw* sth from sb).

entrichten [ɛnt'rɪçtən] *vt* pay.

entrosten [ɛnt'rɔstən] *vt* derust.

entrüst- [ɛnt'rʏst] *cpd*: ~**en** *vt* incense, outrage; *vr* be filled with indignation; ~**et** *a* indignant, outraged; **E**~**ung** *f* indignation.

entsagen [ɛnt'zaːgən] *vi* renounce (*dat* sth).

entschädigen [ɛnt'ʃɛːdɪgən] *vt* compensate.

Entschädigung *f* compensation.

entschärfen [ɛnt'ʃɛrfən] *vt* defuse; *Kritik* tone down.

Entscheid [ɛnt'ʃait] *m* -(**e)s**, -**e** decision; **e**~**en** *vtir irreg* decide; **e**~**end** *a* decisive; *Stimme* casting; ~**ung** *f* decision; ~**ungsspiel** *nt* play-off.

entschieden [ɛnt'ʃiːdən] *a* decided; (*entschlossen*) resolute; **E**~**heit** *f* firmness, determination.

entschließen [ɛnt'ʃliːsən] *vr irreg* decide.

entschlossen [ɛnt'ʃlɔsən] *a* determined, resolute; **E**~**heit** *f* determination.

Entschluß [ɛnt'ʃlus] *m* decision; **e**~**freudig** *a* decisive; ~**kraft** *f* determination, decisiveness.

entschuld- [ɛnt'ʃuld] *cpd*: ~**bar** *a* excusable; ~**igen** *vt* excuse; *vr* apologize; **E**~**igung** *f* apology; (*Grund*) excuse; **jdn um E**~**igung bitten** apologize to sb; **E**~**igung!** excuse me; (*Verzeihung*) sorry.

entschwinden [ɛnt'ʃvɪndən] *vi irreg* disappear.

entsetz- [ɛnt'zɛts] *cpd*: ~**en** *vt* horrify; (*Mil*) relieve; *vr* be horrified *or* appalled;

E~**en** *nt* -**s** horror, dismay; ~**lich** *a* dreadful, appalling; ~**t** *a* horrified.

entsichern [ɛnt'zɪçərn] *vt* release the safety catch of.

entsinnen [ɛnt'zɪnən] *vr irreg* remember (*gen* sth).

entspannen [ɛnt'ʃpanən] *vtr Körper* relax; (*Pol*) *Lage* ease.

Entspannung *f* relaxation, rest; (*Pol*) détente; ~**spolitik** *f* policy of détente; ~**sübungen** *pl* relaxation exercises *pl*.

entsprechen [ɛnt'ʃprɛçən] *vi irreg* (+*dat*) correspond to; *Anforderungen, Wünschen* meet, comply with; ~**d** *a* appropriate; *ad* accordingly.

entspringen [ɛnt'ʃprɪŋən] *vi irreg* spring (from).

entstehen [ɛnt'ʃteːən] *vi irreg* arise, result.

Entstehung *f* genesis, origin.

entstellen [ɛnt'ʃtɛlən] *vt* disfigure; *Wahrheit* distort.

entstören [ɛnt'ʃtøːrən] *vt* (*Rad*) eliminate interference from; (*Aut*) suppress.

enttäuschen [ɛnt'tɔyʃən] *vt* disappoint.

Enttäuschung *f* disappointment.

entwaffnen [ɛnt'vafnən] *vt* (*lit,fig*) disarm.

Entwarnung [ɛnt'varnuŋ] *f* all clear (signal).

entwässer- [ɛnt'vɛsər] *cpd*: ~**n** *vt* drain; **E**~**ung** *f* drainage.

entweder ['ɛntveːdər] *cj* either.

entweichen [ɛnt'vaiçən] *vi irreg* escape.

entweihen [ɛnt'vaiən] *vt irreg* desecrate.

entwenden [ɛnt'vɛndən] *vt irreg* purloin, steal.

entwerfen [ɛnt'vɛrfən] *vt irreg Zeichnung* sketch; *Modell* design; *Vortrag, Gesetz etc* draft.

entwerten [ɛnt've:rtən] *vt* devalue; (*stempeln*) cancel.

entwickeln [ɛnt'vɪkəln] *vtr* develop (*auch Phot*); *Mut, Energie* show, display.

Entwickler *m* -**s**, - developer.

Entwicklung [ɛnt'vɪkluŋ] *f* development; (*Phot*) developing; ~**sabschnitt** *m* stage of development; ~**shilfe** *f* aid for developing countries; ~**sjahre** *pl* adolescence *sing*; ~**sland** *nt* developing country.

entwirren [ɛnt'vɪrən] *vt* disentangle.

entwischen [ɛnt'vɪʃən] *vi* escape.

entwöhnen [ɛnt'vøːnən] *vt* wean; *Süchtige* cure (*dat, von* of).

Entwöhnung *f* weaning; cure, curing.

entwürdigend [ɛnt'vʏrdɪgənt] *a* degrading.

Entwurf [ɛnt'vurf] *m* outline, design; (*Vertrags—, Konzept*) draft.

entwurzeln [ɛnt'vurtsəln] *vt* uproot.

entziehen [ɛnt'tsiːən] *irreg vt* withdraw, take away (*dat* from); *Flüssigkeit* draw, extract; *vr* escape (*dat* from); (*jds Kenntnis*) be outside; (*der Pflicht*) shirk.

Entziehung *f* withdrawal; ~**sanstalt** *f* drug addiction/alcoholism treatment centre; ~**skur** *f* treatment for drug addiction/alcoholism.

entziffern [ɛnt'tsifərn] *vt* decipher; decode.

entzücken [ɛnt'tsykən] *vt* delight; **E~** *nt* **-s** delight; **~d** *a* delightful, charming.

entzünden [ɛnt'tsyndən] *vt* light, set light to; *(fig, Med)* inflame; *Streit* spark off; *vr (lit, fig)* catch fire; *(Streit)* start; *(Med)* become inflamed.

Entzündung *f (Med)* inflammation.

entzwei [ɛnt'tsvai] *ad* broken; in two; **~brechen** *vti irreg* break in two; **~en** *vt* set at odds; *vr* fall out; **~gehen** *vi irreg* break (in two).

Enzian ['ɛntsiaːn] *m* **-s, -e** gentian.

Enzym [ɛn'tsyːm] *nt* **-s, -e** enzyme.

Epidemie [epide'miː] *f* epidemic.

Epilepsie [epile'psiː] *f* epilepsy.

episch ['eːpiʃ] *a* epic.

Episode [epi'zoːdə] *f* **-,** **-n** episode.

Epoche [e'pɔxə] *f* **-,** **-n** epoch; **e~machend** *a* epoch-making.

Epos ['eːpɔs] *nt* **-s, Epen** epic (poem).

er [eːr] *pron* he; it.

erachten [ɛr'axtən] *vt*: **~** **für** *or* **als** consider (to be); **meines E~s** in my opinion.

erarbeiten [ɛr'arbaitən] *vt (auch sich (dat) ~)* work for, acquire; *Theorie* work out.

erbarmen [ɛr'barmən] *vr* have pity *or* mercy *(gen* on); **E~** *nt* **-s** pity.

erbärmlich [ɛr'bɛrmliç] *a* wretched, pitiful; **E~keit** *f* wretchedness.

erbarmungs- [ɛr'barmuŋs] *cpd:* **~los** *a* pitiless, merciless; **~voll** *a* compassionate; **~würdig** *a* pitiable, wretched.

erbau- [ɛr'bau] *cpd:* **~en** *vt* build, erect; *(fig)* edify; **E~er** *m* **-s, -** builder; **~lich** *a* edifying; **E~ung** *f* construction; *(fig)* edification.

Erbe ['ɛrbə] *m* **-n, -n** heir; *nt* **-s** inheritance; *(fig)* heritage; **e~n** *vt* inherit.

erbeuten [ɛr'bɔytən] *vt* carry off; *(Mil)* capture.

Erb- [ɛrp] *cpd:* **~faktor** *m* gene; **~fehler** *m* hereditary defect; **~folge** *f* (line of) succession; **~in** *f* heiress.

erbittern [ɛr'bitərn] *vt* embitter; *(erzürnen)* incense.

erbittert [ɛr'bitərt] *a Kampf* fierce, bitter.

erblassen [ɛr'blasən] *vi*, **erbleichen** [ɛr'blaiçən] *vi irreg* (turn) pale.

erblich ['ɛrpliç] *a* hereditary.

Erbmasse ['ɛrbmasə] *f* estate; *(Biol)* genotype.

erbosen [ɛr'boːzən] *vt* anger; *vr* grow angry.

erbrechen [ɛr'brɛçən] *vtr irreg* vomit.

Erb- *cpd:* **~recht** *nt* right of succession, hereditary right; law of inheritance; **~schaft** *f* inheritance, legacy.

Erbse ['ɛrpsə] *f* **-, -n** pea.

Erb- *cpd:* **~stück** *nt* heirloom; **~teil** *nt* inherited trait; (portion of) inheritance.

Erd- ['eːrd] *cpd:* **~achse** *f* earth's axis; **~atmosphäre** *f* earth's atmosphere; **~bahn** *f* orbit of the earth; **~beben** *nt* earthquake; **~beere** *f* strawberry;

~boden *m* ground; **~e** *f* **-, -n** earth; **zu ebener ~e** at ground level; **e~en** *vt (Elec)* earth.

erdenkbar [ɛr'dɛŋkbaːr], **erdenklich** [-liç] *a* conceivable.

Erd- *cpd:* **~gas** *nt* natural gas; **~geschoß** *nt* ground floor; **~kunde** *f* geography; **~nuß** *f* peanut; **~oberfläche** *f* surface of the earth; **~öl** *nt* (mineral) oil.

erdreisten [ɛr'draistən] *vr* dare, have the audacity (to do sth).

erdrosseln [ɛr'drɔsəln] *vt* strangle, throttle.

erdrücken [ɛr'drykən] *vt* crush.

Erd- *cpd:* **~rutsch** *m* landslide; **~teil** *m* continent.

erdulden [ɛr'duldən] *vt* endure, suffer.

ereifern [ɛr'aifərn] *vr* get excited.

ereignen [ɛr'aignən] *vr* happen.

Ereignis [ɛr'aignis] *nt* **-ses, -se** event; **e~reich** *a* eventful.

erfahren [ɛr'faːrən] *vt irreg* learn, find out; *(erleben)* experience; *a* experienced.

Erfahrung *f* experience; **e~sgemäß** *ad* according to experience.

erfassen [ɛr'fasən] *vt* seize; *(fig) (einbeziehen)* include, register; *(verstehen)* grasp.

erfind- [ɛr'find] *cpd:* **~en** *vt irreg* invent; **E~er** *m* **-s, -** inventor; **~erisch** *a* inventive; **E~ung** *f* invention; **E~ungsgabe** *f* inventiveness.

Erfolg [ɛr'fɔlk] *m* **-(e)s, -e** success; *(Folge)* result; **e~en** *vi* follow; *(sich ergeben)* result; *(stattfinden)* take place; *(Zahlung)* be effected; **e~los** *a* unsuccessful; **~losigkeit** *f* lack of success; **e~reich** *a* successful; **e~versprechend** *a* promising.

erforder- [ɛr'fɔrdər] *cpd:* **~lich** *a* requisite, necessary; **~n** *vt* require, demand; **E~nis** *nt* **-ses,-se** requirement; prerequisite.

erforsch- [ɛr'fɔrʃ] *cpd:* **~en** *vt Land* explore; *Problem* investigate; *Gewissen* search; **E~er** *m* **-s, -** explorer; investigator; **E~ung** *f* exploration; investigation; searching.

erfragen [ɛr'fraːgən] *vt* inquire after, ascertain.

erfreuen [ɛr'frɔyən] *vr*: **sich ~ an** (+*dat*) enjoy; **sich einer Sache** *(gen)* **~** enjoy sth; *vt* delight.

erfreulich [ɛr'frɔyliç] *a* pleasing, gratifying; **~erweise** *ad* happily, luckily.

erfrieren [ɛr'friːrən] *vi irreg* freeze (to death); *(Glieder)* get frostbitten; *(Pflanzen)* be killed by frost.

erfrischen [ɛr'friʃən] *vt* refresh.

Erfrischung *f* refreshment; **~sraum** *m* snack bar, cafeteria.

erfüllen [ɛr'fʏlən] *vt Raum etc* fill; *(fig) Bitte etc* fulfil; *vr* come true.

ergänzen [ɛr'gɛntsən] *vt* supplement, complete; *vr* complement one another.

Ergänzung *f* completion; *(Zusatz)* supplement.

ergattern [ɛr'gatərn] *vt (col)* get hold of, hunt up.

ergaunern [ɛr'gaunərn] vt (col) **sich** (dat) **etw ~** get hold of sth by underhand methods.

ergeben [ɛr'ge:bən] irreg vt yield, produce; vr surrender; (sich hingeben) give o.s. up, yield (dat to); (folgen) result; a devoted, humble; (dem Trunk) addicted (to); **E~heit** f devotion, humility.

Ergebnis [ɛr'ge:pnɪs] nt **-ses, -se** result; **e~los** a without result, fruitless.

ergehen [ɛr'ge:ən] irreg vi be issued, go out; etw über sich ~ lassen put up with sth; vi impers: **es ergeht ihm gut/schlecht** he's faring or getting on well/badly; vr: **sich in etw** (dat) ~ indulge in sth.

ergiebig [ɛr'gi:bɪç] a productive.

ergötzen [ɛr'gœtsən] vt amuse, delight.

ergreifen [ɛr'graɪfən] vt irreg (lit, fig) seize; Beruf take up; Maßnahmen resort to; (rühren) move; **~d** a moving, affecting.

ergriffen [ɛr'grɪfən] a deeply moved.

Erguß [ɛr'gʊs] m discharge; (fig) outpouring, effusion.

erhaben [ɛr'ha:bən] a (lit) raised, embossed; (fig) exalted, lofty; **über etw** (acc) ~ **sein** be above sth.

erhalten [ɛr'haltən] vt irreg receive; (bewahren) preserve, maintain; **gut ~** in good condition.

erhältlich [ɛr'hɛltlɪç] a obtainable, available.

Erhaltung f maintenance, preservation.

erhängen [ɛr'hɛŋən] vtr hang.

erhärten [ɛr'hɛrtən] vt harden; These substantiate, corroborate.

erhaschen [ɛr'haʃən] vt catch.

erheben [ɛr'he:bən] irreg vt raise; Protest, Forderungen make; Fakten ascertain, establish; vr rise (up); **sich über etw** (acc) ~ rise above sth.

erheblich [ɛr'he:plɪç] a considerable.

erheitern [ɛr'haɪtərn] vt amuse, cheer (up).

Erheiterung f exhilaration; **zur allgemeinen ~** to everybody's amusement.

erhellen [ɛr'hɛlən] vt (lit, fig) illuminate; Geheimnis shed light on; vr brighten, light up.

erhitzen [ɛr'hɪtsən] vt heat; vr heat up; (fig) become heated or aroused.

erhoffen [ɛr'hɔfən] vt hope for.

erhöhen [ɛr'hø:ən] vt raise; (verstärken) increase.

erhol- [ɛr'ho:l] cpd: **~en** vr recover; (entspannen) have a rest; **~sam** a restful; **E~ung** f recovery; relaxation, rest; **~ungsbedürftig** a in need of a rest, run-down; **E~ungsheim** nt convalescent/rest home.

erhören [ɛr'hø:rən] vt Gebet etc hear; Bitte etc yield to.

Erika ['e:rika] ka] f **-, Eriken** heather.

erinnern [ɛr'ɪnərn] vt remind (an +acc of); vr remember (an etw (acc) sth).

Erinnerung f memory; (Andenken) reminder; **~stafel** f commemorative plaque.

erkalten [ɛr'kaltən] vi go cold, cool (down).

erkält- [ɛr'kɛlt] cpd: **~en** vr catch cold; **~et a** with a cold; **~et sein** have a cold; **E~ung** f cold.

erkenn- [ɛr'kɛn] cpd: **~bar** a recognizable; **~en** vt irreg recognize; (sehen, verstehen) see; **~tlich a: sich ~tlich zeigen** show one's appreciation; **E~tlichkeit** f gratitude; (Geschenk) token of one's gratitude; **E~tnis** f **-, -se** knowledge; (das Erkennen) recognition; (Einsicht) insight; **zur E~tnis kommen** realize; **E~ung** f recognition; **E~ungsmarke** f identity disc.

Erker ['ɛrkər] m **-s, -** bay; **~fenster** nt bay window.

erklär- [ɛr'klɛ:r] cpd: **~bar** a explicable; **~en** vt explain; **~lich** a explicable; (verständlich) understandable; **E~ung** f explanation; (Aussage) declaration.

erklecklich [ɛr'klɛklɪç] a considerable.

erklingen [ɛr'klɪŋən] vi irreg resound, ring out.

Erkrankung [ɛr'kraŋkʊŋ] f illness.

erkund- [ɛr'kʊnd] cpd: **~en** vt find out, ascertain; (esp Mil) reconnoitre, scout; **~igen** vr inquire (nach about); **E~igung** f inquiry; **E~ung** f reconnaissance, scouting.

erlahmen [ɛr'la:mən] vi tire; (nachlassen) flag, wane.

erlangen [ɛr'laŋən] vt attain, achieve.

Erlaß [ɛr'las] m **-sses, -lässe** decree; (Aufhebung) remission.

erlassen vt irreg Verfügung issue; Gesetz enact; Strafe remit; **jdm etw ~** release sb from sth.

erlauben [ɛr'laubən] vt allow, permit (jdm etw sb to do sth); vr permit o.s., venture.

Erlaubnis [ɛr'laupnɪs] f **-, -se** permission.

erläutern [ɛr'lɔytərn] vt explain.

Erläuterung f explanation.

Erle ['ɛrlə] f **-, -n** alder.

erleben [ɛr'le:bən] vt experience; Zeit live through; (mit—) witness; (noch mit—) live to see.

Erlebnis [ɛr'le:pnɪs] nt **-ses, -se** experience.

erledigen [ɛr'le:dɪgən] vt take care of, deal with; Antrag etc process; (col: erschöpfen) wear out; (col: ruinieren) finish; (col: umbringen) do in.

erlegen [ɛr'le:gən] vt kill.

erleichter- [ɛr'laɪçtər] cpd: **~n** vt make easier; (fig) Last lighten; (lindern, beruhigen) relieve; **~t** a relieved; **E~ung** f facilitation; lightening; relief.

erleiden [ɛr'laɪdən] vt irreg suffer, endure.

erlernbar a learnable.

erlernen [ɛr'lɛrnən] vt learn, acquire.

erlesen [ɛr'le:zən] a select, choice.

erleuchten [ɛr'lɔyçtən] vt illuminate; (fig) inspire.

Erleuchtung f (Einfall) inspiration.

erlogen [ɛr'lo:gən] a untrue, made-up.

Erlös [ɛr'lø:s] m **-es, -e** proceeds pl.

erlöschen [ɛr'lœʃən] vi (Feuer) go out;

(*Interesse*) cease, die; (*Vertrag, Recht*) expire.

erlösen [ɛr'løːzən] *vt* redeem, save.

Erlösung *f* release; (*Rel*) redemption.

ermächtigen [ɛr'mɛçtɪgən] *vt* authorize, empower.

Ermächtigung *f* authorization; authority.

ermahnen [ɛr'maːnən] *vt* exhort, admonish.

Ermahnung *f* admonition, exhortation.

ermäßigen [ɛr'mɛsɪgən] *vt* reduce.

Ermäßigung *f* reduction.

ermessen [ɛr'mɛsən] *vt irreg* estimate, gauge; E~ *nt* -s estimation; discretion; **in jds E~ liegen** lie within sb's discretion.

ermitteln [ɛr'mɪtəln] *vt* determine; *Täter* trace; *vi*: **gegen jdn ~** investigate sb.

Ermittlung [ɛr'mɪtluŋ] *f* determination; (*Polizei*—) investigation.

ermöglichen [ɛr'møːklɪçən] *vt* make possible (*dat* for).

ermord- [ɛr'mɔrd] *cpd*: ~**en** *vt* murder; E~**ung** *f* murder.

ermüden [ɛr'myːdən] *vti* tire; (*Tech*) fatigue; ~**d** *a* tiring; (*fig*) wearisome.

Ermüdung *f* fatigue; ~**serscheinung** *f* sign of fatigue.

ermuntern [ɛr'muntərn] *vt* rouse; (*ermutigen*) encourage; (*beleben*) liven up; (*aufmuntern*) cheer up.

ermutigen [ɛr'muːtɪgən] *vt* encourage.

ernähr- [ɛr'nɛːr] *cpd*: ~**en** *vt* feed, nourish; *Familie* support; *vr* support o.s., earn a living; **sich ~en von** live on; E~**er** *m* -s, - breadwinner; E~**ung** *f* nourishment; nutrition; (*Unterhalt*) maintenance.

ernennen [ɛr'nɛnən] *vt irreg* appoint.

Ernennung *f* appointment.

erneu- [ɛr'nɔy] *cpd*: ~**ern** *vt* renew; restore; renovate; E~**erung** *f* renewal; restoration; renovation; ~**t** *a* renewed, fresh; *ad* once more.

erniedrigen [ɛr'niːdrɪgən] *vt* humiliate, degrade.

Ernst [ɛrnst] *m* -es seriousness; **das ist mein ~** I'm quite serious; **im ~** in earnest; ~ **machen mit etw** put sth into practice; e~ *a* serious; ~**fall** *m* emergency; e~**gemeint** *a* meant in earnest, serious; e~**haft** *a* serious; ~**haftigkeit** *f* seriousness; e~**lich** *a* serious.

Ernte ['ɛrntə] *f* -, -n harvest; ~**dankfest** *nt* harvest festival; e~**n** *vt* harvest; *Lob etc* earn.

ernüchtern [ɛr'nʏçtərn] *vt* sober up; (*fig*) bring down to earth.

Ernüchterung *f* sobering up; (*fig*) disillusionment.

Erober- [ɛr'oːbər] *cpd*: ~**er** *m* -s, - conqueror; e~**n** *vt* conquer; ~**ung** *f* conquest.

eröffnen [ɛr'œfnən] *vt* open; **jdm etw ~** disclose sth to sb; *vr* present itself.

Eröffnung *f* opening; ~**sansprache** *f* inaugural *or* opening address.

erogen [ɛro'geːn] *a* erogenous.

erörtern [ɛr'œrtərn] *vt* discuss.

Erörterung *f* discussion.

Erotik [e'roːtɪk] *f* eroticism.

erotisch *a* erotic.

erpicht [ɛr'pɪçt] *a* eager, keen (*auf* +*acc* on).

erpress- [ɛr'prɛs] *cpd*: ~**en** *vt Geld etc* extort; *Mensch* blackmail; E~**er** *m* -s, - blackmailer; E~**ung** *f* blackmail; extortion.

erproben [ɛr'proːbən] *vt* test.

erraten [ɛr'raːtən] *vt irreg* guess.

erreg- [ɛr'reːk] *cpd*: ~**bar** *a* excitable; (*reizbar*) irritable; E~**barkeit** *f* excitability; irritability; ~**en** *vt* excite; (*ärgern*) infuriate; (*hervorrufen*) arouse, provoke; *vr* get excited *or* worked up; E~**er** *m* -s, - causative agent; E~**theit** *f* excitement; (*Beunruhigung*) agitation; E~**ung** *f* excitement.

erreichbar *a* accessible, within reach.

erreichen [ɛr'raɪçən] *vt* reach; *Zweck* achieve; *Zug* catch.

errichten [ɛr'rɪçtən] *vt* erect, put up; (*gründen*) establish, set up.

erringen [ɛr'rɪŋən] *vt irreg* gain, win.

erröten [ɛr'røːtən] *vi* blush, flush.

Errungenschaft [ɛr'ruŋənʃaft] *f* achievement; (*col: Anschaffung*) acquisition.

Ersatz [ɛr'zats] *m* -es substitute; replacement; (*Schaden*—) compensation; (*Mil*) reinforcements *pl*; ~**befriedigung** *f* vicarious satisfaction; ~**dienst** *m* (*Mil*) alternative service; ~**mann** *m* replacement; (*Sport*) substitute; **e~pflichtig** *a* liable to pay compensation; ~**reifen** *m* (*Aut*) spare tyre; ~**teil** *nt* spare (part).

ersaufen [ɛr'zaufən] *vi irreg* (*col*) drown.

ersäufen [ɛr'zɔyfən] *vt* drown.

erschaffen [ɛr'ʃafən] *vt irreg* create.

erscheinen [ɛr'ʃaɪnən] *vi irreg* appear.

Erscheinung *f* appearance; (*Geist*) apparition; (*Gegebenheit*) phenomenon; (*Gestalt*) figure.

erschießen [ɛr'ʃiːsən] *vt irreg* shoot (dead).

erschlaffen [ɛr'ʃlafən] *vi* go limp; (*Mensch*) become exhausted.

erschlagen [ɛr'ʃlaːgən] *vt irreg* strike dead.

erschleichen [ɛr'ʃlaɪçən] *vt irreg* obtain by stealth *or* dubious methods.

erschöpf- [ɛr'ʃœpf] *cpd*: ~**en** *vt* exhaust; ~**end** *a* exhaustive, thorough; ~**t** *a* exhausted; E~**ung** *f* exhaustion.

erschrecken [ɛr'ʃrɛkən] *vt* startle, frighten; *vi irreg* be frightened *or* startled; ~**d** *a* alarming, frightening.

erschrocken [ɛr'ʃrɔkən] *a* frightened, startled.

erschüttern [ɛr'ʃʏtərn] *vt* shake; (*ergreifen*) move deeply.

Erschütterung *f* shaking; shock.

erschweren [ɛr'ʃveːrən] *vt* complicate.

erschwingen [ɛr'ʃvɪŋən] *vt irreg* afford.

erschwinglich *a* within one's means.

ersehen [ɛr'zeːən] *vt irreg*: **aus etw ~, daß** gather from sth that.

ersetz- [ɛr'zɛts] *cpd*: ~**bar** *a* replaceable; ~**en** *vt* replace; **jdm Unkosten** *etc* ~**en** pay sb's expenses *etc*.

ersichtlich [ɛrˈzɪçtlɪç] a evident, obvious.

erspar- [ɛrˈʃpaːr] cpd: ~**en** vt Ärger etc spare; Geld save: E~**nis** f-, -**se** saving.

ersprießlich [ɛrˈʃpriːslɪç] a profitable, useful; (angenehm) pleasant.

erst [eːrst] ad (at) first; (nicht früher, nur) only; (nicht bis) not till; ~ **einmal** first.

erstarren [ɛrˈʃtarən] vi stiffen; (vor Furcht) grow rigid; (Materie) solidify.

erstatten [ɛrˈʃtatən] vt Kosten (re)pay; Anzeige etc ~ report sb; Bericht ~ make a report.

Erstaufführung [ˈeːrstauffyːrʊŋ] f first performance.

erstaunen [ɛrˈʃtaunən] vt astonish; vi be astonished; E~ nt -**s** astonishment.

erstaunlich a astonishing.

erst- [ˈeːrst] cpd: E-**ausgabe** f first edition; ~**beste(r,s)** a first that comes along; ~**e(r,s)** a first.

erstechen [ɛrˈʃtɛçən] vt irreg stab (to death).

erstehen [ɛrˈʃteːən] vt irreg buy; vi (a)rise.

ersteigen [ɛrˈʃtaigən] vt irreg climb, ascend.

erstellen [ɛrˈʃtɛlən] vt erect, build.

erst- cpd: ~**emal** ad (the) first time; ~**ens** ad firstly, in the first place; ~**ere(r,s)** pron (the) former.

ersticken [ɛrˈʃtɪkən] vt (lit, fig) stifle; Flammen smother; vi (Mensch) suffocate; (Feuer) be smothered; **in Arbeit** ~ be snowed under with work. **Erstickung** f suffocation.

erst- cpd: ~**klassig** a first-class; E~**kommunion** f first communion; ~**malig** a first; ~**mals** ad for the first time.

erstrebenswert [ɛrˈʃtreːbənsveːrt] a desirable, worthwhile.

erstrecken [ɛrˈʃtrɛkən] vr extend, stretch.

Ersttags- [ˈeːrst-taːgz] cpd: ~**brief** m first-day cover; ~**stempel** m first-day (date) stamp.

ersuchen [ɛrˈzuːxən] vt request.

ertappen [ɛrˈtapən] vt catch, detect.

erteilen [ɛrˈtailən] vt give.

ertönen [ɛrˈtøːnən] vi sound, ring out.

Ertrag [ɛrˈtraːk] m -(e)s, ¨e yield; (Gewinn) proceeds pl; e~**en** vt irreg bear, stand.

erträglich [ɛrˈtrɛːklɪç] a tolerable, bearable.

ertränken [ɛrˈtrɛŋkən] vt drown.

erträumen [ɛrˈtrɔymən] vt: **sich** (dat) **etw** ~ dream of sth, imagine sth.

ertrinken [ɛrˈtrɪŋkən] vi irreg drown; E~ nt -**s** drowning.

erübrigen [ɛrˈyːbrɪgən] vt spare; vr be unnecessary.

erwachen [ɛrˈvaxən] vi awake.

erwachsen [ɛrˈvaksən] a grown-up; E~**e(r)** mf adult; E~**enbildung** f adult education.

erwägen [ɛrˈvɛːgən] vt irreg consider. **Erwägung** f consideration.

erwähn- [ɛrˈvɛːn] cpd: ~**en** vt mention; ~**enswert** a worth mentioning; E~**ung** f mention.

erwärmen [ɛrˈvɛrmən] vt warm, heat; vr get warm, warm up; **sich** ~ **für** warm to.

erwarten [ɛrˈvartən] vt expect; (warten auf) wait for; **etw kaum** ~ **können** hardly be able to wait for sth.

Erwartung f expectation; e~**sgemäß** ad as expected; e~**svoll** a expectant.

erwecken [ɛrˈvɛkən] vt rouse, awake; **den Anschein** ~ give the impression.

erwehren [ɛrˈveːrən] vr fend, ward (gen off); (des Lachens etc) refrain (gen from).

erweichen [ɛrˈvaiçən] vti soften.

Erweis [ɛrˈvais] m -**es**, -**e** proof; e~**en** irreg vt prove; Ehre, Dienst do (jdm sb); vr prove (als to be).

Erwerb [ɛrˈvɛrp] m -(e)s, -**e** acquisition; (Beruf) trade; e~**en** vt irreg acquire; e~**slos** a unemployed; ~**squelle** f source of income; e~**stätig** a (gainfully) employed; e~**sunfähig** a unemployable.

erwidern [ɛrˈviːdərn] vt reply; (vergelten) return.

erwiesen [ɛrˈviːzən] a proven.

erwischen [ɛrˈvɪʃən] vt (col) catch, get.

erwünscht [ɛrˈvʏnʃt] a desired.

erwürgen [ɛrˈvʏrgən] vt strangle.

Erz [eːrts] nt -**es**, -**e** ore.

erzähl- [ɛrˈtsɛːl] cpd: ~**en** vt tell; E~**er** m -**s**, - narrator; E~**ung** f story, tale.

Erz- cpd: ~**bischof** m archbishop; ~**engel** m archangel.

erzeug- [ɛrˈtsɔyg] cpd: ~**en** vt produce; Strom generate; E~**erpreis** m producer's price; E~**nis** nt -**ses**, -**se** product, produce; E~**ung** f production; generation.

erziehen [ɛrˈtsiːən] vt irreg bring up; (bilden) educate, train.

Erziehung f bringing up; (Bildung) education; ~**sbeihilfe** f educational grant; ~**sberechtigte(r)** mf parent; guardian; ~**sheim** nt approved school.

erzielen [ɛrˈtsiːlən] vt achieve, obtain; Tor score.

erzwingen [ɛrˈtsvɪŋən] vt irreg force, obtain by force.

es [ɛs] pron nom, acc it.

Esche [ˈɛʃə] f -, -**n** ash.

Esel [ˈeːzəl] m -**s**, - donkey, ass; ~**sohr** nt dog-ear.

Eskalation [ɛskalatsiˈoːn] f escalation.

eßbar [ˈɛsbaːr] a eatable, edible.

essen [ˈɛsən] vti irreg eat; E~ nt -**s**, - meal; food; E~**szeit** f mealtime; dinner time.

Essig [ˈɛsɪç] m -**s**, -**e** vinegar; ~**gurke** f gherkin.

Eß- [ɛs] cpd: ~**kastanie** f sweet chestnut; ~**löffel** m tablespoon; ~**tisch** m dining table; ~**waren** pl victuals pl, food provisions pl; ~**zimmer** nt dining room.

etablieren [etaˈbliːrən] vr become established; set up business.

Etage [eˈtaːʒə] f -, -**n** floor, storey; ~**nbetten** pl bunk beds pl; ~**nwohnung** f flat.

Etappe [eˈtapə] f -, -**n** stage.

Etat [eˈtaː] m -**s**, -**s** budget; ~**jahr** nt financial year; ~**posten** m budget item.

etepetete [eːtəpeˈteːtə] a (col) fussy.

Ethik [ˈeːtɪk] f ethics sing.

ethisch [ˈeːtɪʃ] a ethical.

Etikett [etiˈkɛt] nt -(e)s, -e label; tag; ~e f etiquette, manners pl; e~ieren [-ˈtiːrən] vt label; tag.

etliche [ˈɛtlɪçə] pron pl some, quite a few; ~s a thing or two.

Etui [ɛtˈviː] nt -s, -s case.

etwa [ˈɛtva] ad (ungefähr) about; (vielleicht) perhaps; (beispielsweise) for instance; **nicht** ~ by no means; ~ig [ˈɛtva-ɪç] a possible; ~s pron something; anything; (ein wenig) a little; ad a little.

Etymologie [etymoloˈgiː] f etymology.

euch [ɔyç] pron acc of **ihr** you; yourselves; dat of **ihr** (to) you.

euer [ˈɔyər] pron gen of **ihr** of you; pron your; ~e(r,s) yours.

Eule [ˈɔylə] f -, -n owl.

eure(r,s) [ˈɔyrə(r,z)] pron your; yours; -rseits ad on your part; ~sgleichen pron people like you; ~twegen, ~twillen ad (für euch) for your sakes; (wegen euch) on your account.

eurige pron: **der/die/das** ~ yours.

Euro- [ɔyro] cpd: ~krat [-ˈkraːt] m -en, -en eurocrat; ~pameister [ɔyˈroːpa-] m European champion.

Euter [ˈɔytər] nt -s, - udder.

evakuieren [evakuˈiːrən] vt evacuate.

evangelisch [evaŋˈgeːlɪʃ] a Protestant.

Evangelium [evaŋˈgeːliʊm] nt gospel.

Eva(s)kostüm [ˈeːfa(s)kɔstyːm] nt: **im** ~ in one's birthday suit.

eventuell [evɛntuˈɛl] a possible; ad possibly, perhaps.

EWG [eːveːˈgeː] f - EEC, Common Market.

ewig [ˈeːvɪç] a eternal; E~keit f eternity.

exakt [ɛˈksakt] a exact.

Examen [ɛˈksaːmən] nt -s, - or **Examina** examination.

Exempel [ɛˈksɛmpəl] nt -s, - example.

Exemplar [ɛksɛmˈplaːr] nt -s, -e specimen; (Buch—) copy; e~isch a exemplary.

exerzieren [ɛksɛrˈtsiːrən] vi drill.

Exil [ɛˈksiːl] nt -s, -e exile.

Existenz [ɛksɪsˈtɛnts] f existence; (Unterhalt) livelihood, living; (pej: Mensch) character; ~kampf m struggle for existence; ~minimum nt -s subsistence level.

existieren [ɛksɪsˈtiːrən] vi exist.

exklusiv [ɛkskluˈziːf] a exclusive; ~e [-ˈziːvə] ad, prep +gen exclusive of, not including.

exorzieren [ɛksɔrˈtsiːrən] vt exorcise.

exotisch [ɛˈksoːtɪʃ] a exotic.

Expansion [ɛkspanziˈoːn] f expansion.

Expedition [ɛkspeditsiˈoːn] f expedition; (Comm) forwarding department.

Experiment [ɛksperiˈmɛnt] nt experiment; e~ell [-ˈtɛl] a experimental; e~ieren [-ˈtiːrən] vi experiment.

Experte [ɛksˈpɛrtə] m -n, -n expert, specialist.

explo- [ɛksplo] cpd: ~dieren [-ˈdiːrən] vi explode; E~sion [ɛksploziˈoːn] f

explosion; ~siv [-ˈziːf] a explosive.

Exponent [ɛkspoˈnɛnt] m exponent.

Export [ɛksˈpɔrt] m -(e)s, -e export; ~eur [-ˈtøːr] m exporter; ~handel m export trade; ~ieren [-ˈtiːrən] vt export; ~land nt exporting country.

Expreß- [ɛksˈprɛs] cpd: ~gut nt express goods pl or freight; ~zug m express (train).

extra [ˈɛkstra] a inv (col: gesondert) separate; (besondere) extra; ad (gesondert) separately; (speziell) specially; (absichtlich) on purpose; (vor Adjektiven, zusätzlich) extra; E~ nt -s, -s extra; E~ausgabe f, E~blatt nt special edition.

Extrakt [ɛksˈtrakt] m -(e)s, -e extract.

extrem [ɛksˈtreːm] a extreme; ~istisch [-ˈmɪstɪʃ] a (Pol) extremist; E~itäten [-ˈteːtən] pl extremities pl.

Exzellenz [ɛkstseˈlɛnts] f excellency.

exzentrisch [ɛksˈtsɛntrɪʃ] a eccentric.

Exzeß [ɛksˈtsɛs] m -sses, -sse excess.

F

F, f [ɛf] nt F, f.

Fabel [ˈfaːbəl] f -, -n fable; f~haft a fabulous, marvellous.

Fabrik [faˈbriːk] f factory; ~ant [-ˈkant] m (Hersteller) manufacturer; (Besitzer) industrialist; ~arbeiter m factory worker; ~at [-ˈkaːt] nt -(e)s, -e manufacture, product; ~ation [-atsiˈoːn] f manufacture, production; ~besitzer m factory owner; ~gelände nt factory premises pl.

Fach [fax] nt -(e)s, ̈-er compartment; (Sachgebiet) subject; **ein Mann vom** ~ an expert; ~arbeiter m skilled worker; ~arzt m (medical) specialist; ~ausdruck m technical term.

Fächer [ˈfɛçər] m -s, - fan.

Fach- cpd: f~kundig a expert, specialist; f~lich a professional; expert; ~mann m, pl -leute specialist; ~schule f technical college; f~simpeln vi talk shop; ~werk nt timber frame.

Fackel [ˈfakəl] f -, -n torch; f~n vi (col) dither.

fad(e) [ˈfaːt, faːdə] a insipid; (langweilig) dull.

Faden [ˈfaːdən] m -s, ̈- thread; ~nudeln pl vermicelli pl; f~scheinig a (lit, fig) threadbare.

fähig [ˈfɛːɪç] a capable (zu, gen of); able; F~keit f ability.

Fähnchen [ˈfɛːnçən] nt pennon, streamer.

fahnden [ˈfaːndən] vi: ~ **nach** search for.

Fahndung f search; ~sliste f list of wanted criminals, wanted list.

Fahne [ˈfaːnə] f -, -n flag, standard; **eine** ~ **haben** (col) smell of drink; ~nflucht f desertion.

Fahrbahn f carriageway (Brit), roadway.

Fähre [ˈfeːrə] f -, -n ferry.

fahren [ˈfaːrən] irreg vt drive; Rad ride; (befördern) drive, take; Rennen drive in; vi (sich bewegen) go; (Schiff) sail; (abfahren) leave; **mit dem Auto/Zug** ~ go or travel by car/train; **mit der Hand** ~ **über**

(+*acc*) pass one's hand over.

Fahr- ['faːr] *cpd*: ∼**er** *m* **-s,** - driver; ∼**erflucht** *f* hit-and-run; ∼**gast** *m* passenger; ∼**geld** *nt* fare; ∼**gestell** *nt* chassis; (*Aviat*) undercarriage; ∼**karte** *f* ticket; ∼**kartenausgabe** *f*, ∼**karten- schalter** *m* ticket office; **f∼lässig** *a* negligent; **f∼lässige Tötung** man- slaughter; ∼**lässigkeit** *f* negligence; ∼**lehrer** *m* driving instructor; ∼**plan** *m* timetable; (*f∼*)**planmäßig** *a* (*Rail*) scheduled; ∼**preis** *m* fare; ∼**prüfung** *f* driving test; ∼**rad** *nt* bicycle; ∼**schein** *m* ticket; ∼**schule** *f* driving school; ∼**schüler(in** *f*) *m* learner (driver); ∼**stuhl** *m* lift, elevator (*US*).

Fahrt [faːrt] *f* -, **-en** journey; (*kurz*) trip; (*Aut*) drive; (*Geschwindigkeit*) speed.

Fährte ['fɛːrtə] *f* -, **-n** track, trail.

Fahrt- *cpd*: ∼**kosten** *pl* travelling expenses *pl*; ∼**richtung** *f* course, direction.

Fahr- *cpd*: ∼**zeug** *nt* vehicle; ∼**zeughalter** *m* -s, - owner of a vehicle.

Fak- [fak] *cpd*: **f∼tisch** *a* actual; ∼**tor** *m* factor; ∼**tum** *nt* -s, -ten fact; ∼**ul'tät** *f* faculty.

Falke ['falkə] *m* -n, -n falcon.

Fall [fal] *m* -(e)s, ̈e (*Sturz*) fall; (*Sachver- halt, Jur, Gram*) case; **auf jeden** ∼, **auf alle** ̈e in any case; (*bestimmt*) definitely; ∼**e** *f* -, **-n** trap; **f∼en** *vi irreg* fall; **etw f∼en lassen** drop sth.

fällen ['fɛlən] *vt* Baum fell; *Urteil* pass.

fallenlassen *vt irreg* Bemerkung make; *Plan* abandon, drop.

fällig ['fɛlɪç] *a* due ; **F∼keit** *f* (*Comm*) maturity.

Fall- *cpd*: ∼**obst** *nt* fallen fruit, windfall; **f∼s** *ad* in case, if; ∼**schirm** *m* para- chute; ∼**schirmjäger** *pl*, ∼**schirm- truppe** *f* paratroops *pl*; ∼**schirm- springer** *m* parachutist; ∼**tür** *f* trap door.

falsch [falʃ] *a* false; (*unrichtig*) wrong.

fälschen ['fɛlʃən] *vt* forge.

Fälscher *m* -s, - forger.

Falsch- *cpd*: ∼**geld** *nt* counterfeit money; ∼**heit** *f* falsity, falseness; (*Unrichtigkeit*) wrongness.

fälsch- *cpd*: ∼**lich** *a* false; ∼**licherweise** *ad* mistakenly; **F∼ung** *f* forgery.

Fältchen ['fɛltçən] *nt* crease, wrinkle.

Falte ['faltə] *f* -, **-n** (*Knick*) fold, crease; (*Haut∼*) wrinkle; (*Rock∼*) pleat; **f∼n** *vt* fold; *Stirn* wrinkle; **f∼nlos** *a* without folds; without wrinkles.

familiär [famili'ɛːr] *a* familiar.

Familie [fa'miːliə] *f* family; ∼**ähnlichkeit** *f* family resemblance; ∼**nkreis** *m* family circle; ∼**nname** *m* surname; ∼**nstand** *m* marital status; ∼**nvater** *m* head of the family.

Fanatiker [fa'naːtikər] *m* -s, - fanatic.

fanatisch *a* fanatical.

Fanatismus [fana'tɪsmʊs] *m* fanaticism.

Fang [faŋ] *m* -(e)s, ̈e catch; (*Jagen*) hunting; (*Kralle*) talon, claw; **f∼en** *irreg vt* catch; *vr* get caught; (*Flugzeug*) level

out; (*Mensch: nicht fallen*) steady o.s.; (*fig*) compose o.s.; (*in Leistung*) get back on form.

Farb- ['farb] *cpd*: ∼**abzug** *m* coloured print; ∼**aufnahme** *f* colour photograph; ∼**band** *m* typewriter ribbon; ∼**e** *f* -, **-n** colour; (*zum Malen etc*) paint; (*Stoff∼*) dye; **f∼echt** *a* colourfast.

färben ['fɛrbən] *vt* colour; *Stoff, Haar* dye.

farben- ['farbən] *cpd*: ∼**blind** *a* colour- blind; ∼**froh** *a*, ∼**prächtig** *a* colourful, gay.

Farb- *cpd*: ∼**fernsehen** *nt* colour tele- vision; ∼**film** *m* colour film; **f∼ig** *a* coloured; ∼**ige(r)** *mf* coloured; ∼**kasten** *m* paint-box; **f∼los** *a* colourless; ∼**photo- graphie** *f* colour photography; ∼**stift** *m* coloured pencil; ∼**stoff** *m* dye; ∼**ton** *m* hue, tone.

Färbung ['fɛrbʊŋ] *f* colouring; (*Tendenz*) bias.

Farn [farn] *m* -(e)s, -e, ∼**kraut** *nt* fern; bracken.

Fasan [fa'zaːn] *m* -(e)s, -e(n) pheasant.

Fasching ['faʃɪŋ] *m* -s, -e *or* -s carnival.

Faschismus [fa'ʃɪsmʊs] *m* fascism.

Faschist *m* fascist.

faseln ['faːzəln] *vi* talk nonsense, drivel.

Faser ['faːzər] *f* -, **-n** fibre; **f∼n** *vi* fray.

Faß [fas] *nt* -sses, **Fässer** -s, barrel; (*Öl*) drum; **Bier vom** ∼ draught beer; **f∼bar** *a* comprehensible; ∼**bier** *nt* draught beer.

fassen ['fasən] *vt* (*ergreifen*) grasp, take; (*inhaltlich*) hold; *Entschluß etc* take; (*verstehen*) understand; *Ring etc* set; (*formulieren*) formulate, phrase; **nicht zu** ∼ unbelievable; *vr* calm down.

faßlich ['faslɪç] *a* intelligible.

Fassung ['fasʊŋ] *f* (*Umrahmung*) mount- ing; (*Lampen∼*) socket; (*Wortlaut*) version; (*Beherrschung*) composure; **jdn aus der** ∼ **bringen** upset sb; **f∼slos** *a* speech- less; ∼**svermögen** *nt* capacity; (*Verständnis*) comprehension.

fast [fast] *ad* almost, nearly.

fasten ['fastən] *vi* fast; **F∼** *nt* -s fasting; **F∼zeit** *f* Lent.

Fastnacht *f* Shrove Tuesday; carnival.

fatal [fa'taːl] *a* fatal; (*peinlich*) embarrassing.

faul [faʊl] *a* rotten; *Person* lazy; *Ausreden* lame; **daran ist etwas** ∼ there's sth fishy about it; ∼**en** *vi* rot; ∼**enzen** *vi* idle; **F∼enzer** *m* -s, - idler, loafer; **F∼heit** *f* laziness; ∼**ig** *a* putrid.

Fäulnis ['fɔʏlnɪs] *f* - decay, putrefaction.

Faust ['faʊst] *f* -, **Fäuste** fist; ∼**handschuh** *m* mitten.

Favorit [favo'riːt] *m* -en, -en favourite.

Februar ['feːbruaːr] *m* -(s), -e February.

fechten ['fɛçtən] *vi irreg* fence.

Feder ['feːdər] *f* -, **-n** feather; (*Schreib∼*) pen nib; (*Tech*) spring; ∼**ball** *m* shuttle- cock; ∼**ballspiel** *nt* badminton; ∼**bett** *nt* continental quilt; ∼**halter** *m* penholder, pen; **f∼leicht** *a* light as a feather; **f∼n** *vi* (*nachgeben*) be springy; (*sich bewegen*) bounce; *vt* spring; ∼**ung** *f* suspension; ∼**vieh** *nt* poultry.

Fee [fe:] f -, -n fairy; f~haft ['fe:ən-] a fairylike.

Fege- ['fe:gə] cpd: ~feuer nt purgatory; f~n vt sweep.

fehl [fe:l] a: ~ am Platz or Ort out of place; ~en vi be wanting or missing; (abwesend sein) be absent; etw fehlt jdm sb lacks sth; du fehlst mir I miss you; was fehlt ihm? what's wrong with him?; F~er m -s, - mistake, error; (Mangel, Schwäche) fault; ~erfrei a faultless; without any mistakes; ~erhaft a incorrect; faulty; F~geburt f miscarriage; ~gehen vi irreg go astray; F~griff m blunder; F~konstruktion f badly designed thing; F~schlag m failure; ~schlagen vi irreg fail; F~schluß m wrong conclusion; F~start m (Sport) false start; F~tritt m false move; (fig) blunder, slip; F~zündung f (Aut) misfire, backfire.

Feier ['faɪər] f -, -n celebration; ~abend m time to stop work; ~abend machen stop, knock off; was machst du am ~abend? what are you doing after work?; jetzt ist ~abend! that's enough!; f~lich a solemn; ~lichkeit f solemnity; pl festivities pl; f~n vti celebrate; ~tag m holiday.

feig(e) ['faɪg(ə)] a cowardly; F~e f -, -n fig; F~heit f cowardice; F~ling m coward.

Feil- [faɪl] cpd: ~e f -, -n file; f~en vti file; f~schen vi haggle.

fein [faɪn] a fine; (vornehm) refined; Gehör etc keen; ~! great!

Feind [faɪnt] m -(e)s, -e enemy; f~lich a hostile; ~schaft f enmity; f~selig a hostile; ~seligkeit f hostility.

Fein- cpd: f~fühlend, f~fühlig a sensitive; ~gefühl nt delicacy, tact; ~heit f fineness; refinement; keenness; ~kostgeschäft nt delicatessen (shop); ~schmecker m -s, - gourmet.

feist [faɪst] a fat.

Feld [fɛlt] nt -(e)s, -er field; (Schach) square; (Sport) pitch; ~blume f wild flower; ~herr m commander; ~webel m -s, - sergeant; ~weg m path; ~zug m (lit, fig) campaign.

Felge ['fɛlgə] f -, -n (wheel) rim; ~nbremse f caliper brake.

Fell [fɛl] nt -(e)s, -e fur; coat; (von Schaf) fleece; (von toten Tieren) skin.

Fels [fɛls] m -en, -en, **Felsen** ['fɛlzən] m -s, - rock; (von Dover etc) cliff; f~enfest a firm; ~envorsprung m ledge; f~ig a rocky; ~spalte f crevice.

feminin [femi'ni:n] a feminine; (pej) effeminate.

Fenster ['fɛnstər] nt -s, - window; ~brett nt windowsill; ~laden m shutter; ~putzer m -s, - window cleaner; ~scheibe f windowpane; ~sims m windowsill.

Ferien ['fe:riən] pl holidays pl, vacation (US); ~ haben be on holiday; ~kurs m holiday course; ~reise f holiday; ~zeit f holiday period.

Ferkel ['fɛrkəl] nt -s, - piglet.

fern [fɛrn] a,ad far-off, distant; ~ von hier a long way (away) from here; F~amt nt (Tel) exchange; F~bedienung f remote control; F~e f -, -n distance; ~er a,ad further; (weiterhin) in future; F~flug m long-distance flight; F~gespräch nt trunk call; F~glas nt binoculars pl; ~halten vtr irreg keep away; F~lenkung f remote control; ~liegen vi irreg; jdm ~liegen be far from sb's mind; F~rohr nt telescope; F~schreiber m teleprinter; ~schriftlich a by telex; F~sehapparat m television set; ~sehen vi irreg watch television; F~sehen nt -s television; im F~sehen on television; F~seher m television; F~sprecher m telephone; F~sprechzelle f telephone box or booth (US).

Ferse ['fɛrzə] f -, -n heel.

fertig ['fɛrtɪç] a (bereit) ready; (beendet) finished; (gebrauchs~) ready-made; F~bau m prefab(ricated house); ~bringen vt irreg (fähig sein) manage, be capable of; (beenden) finish; F~keit f skill; ~machen vt (beenden) finish; (col) Person finish; (körperlich) exhaust; (moralisch) get down; vr get ready; ~stellen vt complete; F~ware f finished product.

Fessel ['fɛsəl] f -, -n fetter; f~n vt bind; (mit Fesseln) fetter; (fig) spellbind; f~nd a fascinating, captivating.

fest [fɛst] a firm; Nahrung solid; Gehalt regular; ad schlafen soundly; F~ nt -(e)s, -e party; festival; ~angestellt a permanently employed; F~beleuchtung f illumination; ~binden vt irreg tie, fasten; ~bleiben vi irreg stand firm; F~essen nt banquet; ~fahren vr irreg get stuck; ~halten irreg vt seize, hold fast; Ereignis record; vr hold on (an +dat to); ~igen vt strengthen; F~igkeit f strength; ~klammern vr cling on (an +dat to); F~land nt mainland; ~legen vt fix; vr commit o.s.; ~lich a festive; ~machen vt fasten; Termin etc fix; F~nahme f -, -n capture; ~nehmen vt irreg capture, arrest; F~rede f address; ~schnallen vt strap down; vr fasten one's seat belt; ~setzen vt fix, settle; F~spiel nt festival; ~stehen vi irreg be certain; ~stellen vt establish; (sagen) remark; F~ung f fortress.

Fett [fɛt] nt -(e)s, -e fat, grease; f~ a fat; Essen etc greasy; f~arm a low fat; f~en vt grease; ~fleck m grease spot or stain; f~gedruckt a bold-type; ~gehalt m fat content; f~ig a greasy, fatty; ~näpfchen nt: ins ~näpfchen treten put one's foot in it.

Fetzen ['fɛtsən] m -s, - scrap.

feucht [fɔʏçt] a damp; Luft humid; F~igkeit f dampness; humidity.

Feuer ['fɔʏər] nt -s, - fire; (zum Rauchen) a light; (fig: Schwung) spirit; ~alarm m fire alarm; ~eifer m zeal; f~fest a fireproof; ~gefahr f danger of fire; f~gefährlich a inflammable; ~leiter f fire escape ladder; ~löscher m -s, - fire extinguisher; ~**melder** *m* -s, - fire alarm; **f~n** *vti* (*lit, fig*) fire; **f~sicher** *a* fireproof; ~**stein** *m* flint; ~**wehr** *f* -, -en fire brigade; ~**werk** *nt* fireworks *pl*; ~**zeug** *nt* (cigarette) lighter.

Fichte ['fɪçtə] *f* -, -n spruce, pine.

fidel [fɪ'de:l] *a* jolly.

Fieber ['fi:bər] *nt* -s, - fever, temperature; **f~haft** *a* feverish; ~**messer** *m*, ~**thermometer** *nt* thermometer.

fies [fi:s] *a* (*col*) nasty.

Figur [fi'gu:r] *f* -, -en figure; (*Schach—*) chessman, chess piece.

Filiale [fili'a:lə] *f* -, -n (*Comm*) branch.

Film [fɪlm] *m* -(e)s, -e film; ~**aufnahme** *f* shooting; **f~en** *vti* film; ~**kamera** *f* cine-camera; ~**vorführgerät** *nt* cineprojector.

Filter ['fɪltər] *m* -s, - filter; **f~n** *vt* filter; ~**mundstück** *nt* filter tip; ~**papier** *nt* filter paper; ~**zigarette** *f* tipped cigarette.

Filz [fɪlts] *m* -es, -e felt; **f~en** *vt* (*col*) frisk; *vi* (*Wolle*) mat.

Finale [fi'na:lə] *nt* -s, -(s) finale; (*Sport*) final(s).

Finanz [fi'nants] *f* finance; ~**amt** *nt* Inland Revenue Office; ~**beamte(r)** *m* revenue officer; **f~iell** [-tsi'el] *a* financial; **f~ieren** [-'tsi:rən] *vt* finance; ~**minister** *m* Chancellor of the Exchequer (*Brit*), Minister of Finance.

Find- ['fɪnd] *cpd*: **f~en** *irreg* *vt* find; (*meinen*) think; *vr* be (found); (*sich fassen*) compose o.s.; **ich finde nichts dabei, wenn . . .** I don't see what's wrong if . . .; **das wird sich f~en** things will work out; ~**er** *m* -s, - finder; ~**erlohn** *m* reward; **f~ig** *a* resourceful.

Finger ['fɪŋər] *m* -s, - finger,; ~**abdruck** *m* fingerprint; ~**handschuh** *m* glove; ~**hut** *m* thimble; (*Bot*) foxglove; ~**ring** *m* ring; ~**spitze** *f* fingertip; ~**zeig** *m* -(e)s, -e hint, pointer.

fingieren [fɪŋ'gi:rən] *vt* feign.

fingiert a made-up, fictitious.

Fink ['fɪŋk] *m* -en, -en finch.

finster ['fɪnstər] *a* dark, gloomy; (*verdächtig*) dubious; (*verdrossen*) grim; *Gedanke* dark; **F~nis** *f* - darkness, gloom.

Finte ['fɪntə] *f* -, -n feint, trick.

firm [fɪrm] *a* well-up; **F~a** *f* -, -men firm; **F~eninhaber** *m* owner of firm; **F~enschild** *nt* (shop) sign; **F~enzeichen** *nt* registered trademark.

Firnis ['fɪrnɪs] *m* -ses, -se varnish.

Fisch [fɪʃ] *m* -(e)s, -e fish; *pl* (*Astrol*) Pisces; **f~en** *vti* fish; ~**er** *m* -s, - fisherman; ~**e'rei** *f* fishing, fishery; ~**fang** *m* fishing; ~**geschäft** *nt* fishmonger's (shop); ~**gräte** *f* fishbone; ~**zug** *m* catch *or* draught of fish.

fix [fɪks] *a* fixed; *Person* alert, smart; ~ **und fertig** finished; (*erschöpft*) done in; ~**ieren** [fɪ'ksi:rən] *vt* fix; (*anstarren*) stare at.

flach [flax] *a* flat; *Gefäß* shallow.

Fläche ['flɛçə] *f* -, -n area; (*Ober—*) surface; ~**ninhalt** *m* surface area.

Flach- *cpd*: ~**heit** *f* flatness; shallowness; ~**land** *nt* lowland.

flackern ['flakərn] *vi* flare, flicker.

Flagge ['flagə] *f* -, -n flag.

flagrant [fla'grant] *a* flagrant; **in** ~**i** red-handed.

Flamme ['flamə] *f* -, -n flame.

Flanell [fla'nɛl] *m* -s, -e flannel.

Flanke ['flaŋkə] *f* -, -n flank; (*Sport: Seite*) wing.

Flasche ['flaʃə] *f* -, -n bottle (*col: Versager*) wash-out; ~**nbier** *nt* bottled beer; ~**nöffner** *m* bottle opener; ~**nzug** *m* pulley.

flatterhaft *a* flighty, fickle.

flattern ['flatərn] *vi* flutter.

flau [flau] *a* weak, listless; *Nachfrage* slack; **jdm ist** ~ sb feels queasy.

Flaum [flaum] *m* -(e)s (*Feder*) down; (*Haare*) fluff.

flauschig ['flauʃɪç] *a* fluffy.

Flausen ['flauzən] *pl* silly ideas *pl*; (*Ausflüchte*) weak excuses *pl*.

Flaute ['flautə] *f* -, -n calm; (*Comm*) recession.

Flechte ['flɛçtə] *f* -, -n plait; (*Med*) dry scab; (*Bot*) lichen; **f~n** *vt irreg* plait; *Kränz* twine.

Fleck [flɛk] *m* -(e)s, -e, **Flecken** *m* -s, - spot; (*Schmutz—*) stain; (*Stoff—*) patch; (*Makel*) blemish; **nicht vom** ~ **kommen** (*lit, fig*) not get any further; **vom** ~ **weg** straight away; **f~enlos** *a* spotless; ~**enmittel** *nt*, ~**enwasser** *nt* stain remover; **f~ig** *a* spotted; stained.

Fledermaus ['fle:dərmaus] *f* bat.

Flegel ['fle:gəl] *m* -s, - flail; (*Person*) lout; **f~haft** *a* loutish, unmannerly; ~**jahre** *pl* adolescence; **f~n** *vr* lounge about.

flehen ['fle:ən] *vi* implore; ~**tlich** *a* imploring.

Fleisch ['flaiʃ] *nt* -(e)s flesh; (*Essen*) meat; ~**brühe** *f* beef tea, stock; ~**er** *m* -s, - butcher; ~**e'rei** *f* butcher's (shop); **f~ig** *a* fleshy; **f~lich** *a* carnal; ~**pastete** *f* meat pie; ~**wolf** *m* mincer; ~**wunde** *f* flesh wound.

Fleiß [flaɪs] *m* -es diligence, industry; **f~ig** *a* diligent, industrious.

flektieren [flɛk'ti:rən] *vt* inflect.

flennen ['flɛnən] *vi* (*col*) cry, blubber.

fletschen ['flɛtʃən] *vt Zähne* show.

flexibel [flɛ'ksi:bəl] *a* flexible.

Flicken ['flɪkən] *m* -s, - patch; **f~** *vt* mend.

Flieder ['fli:dər] *m* -s, - lilac.

Fliege ['fli:gə] *f* -, -n fly; (*Kleidung*) bow tie; **f~n** *vti irreg* fly; **auf jdn/etw f~en** (*col*) be mad about sb/sth; ~**npilz** *m* toadstool; ~**r** *m* -s, - flier, airman; ~**ralarm** *m* air-raid warning.

fliehen ['fli:ən] *vi irreg* flee.

Fliese ['fli:zə] *f* -, -n tile.

Fließ- ['fli:s] *cpd*: ~**arbeit** *f* production-line work; ~**band** *nt* production *or* assembly line; **f~en** *vi irreg* flow; **f~end** *a* flowing; *Rede, Deutsch* fluent; *Übergänge* smooth; -**heck** *nt* fastback; ~**papier** *nt* blotting paper.

flimmern ['flɪmərn] *vi* glimmer.

flink [flɪŋk] *a* nimble, lively; **F~heit** *f* nimbleness, liveliness.

Flinte ['flɪntə] *f* -, -n rifle; shotgun.

Flitter ['flɪtər] *m* -s, - spangle, tinsel; **~wochen** *pl* honeymoon.

flitzen ['flɪtsən] *vi* flit.

Flocke ['flɔkə] *f* -, -n flake.

flockig *a* flaky.

Floh ['floː] *m* -(e)s, ⁻e flea.

florieren [floˈriːrən] *vi* flourish.

Floskel ['flɔskəl] *f* -, -n empty phrase.

Floß [floːs] *nt* -es, ⁻e raft, float.

Flosse ['flɔsə] *f* -, -n fin.

Flöte ['fløːtə] *f* -, -n flute; (*Block—*) recorder.

Flötist(in *f*) [fløˈtɪst(ɪn)] *m* flautist.

flott [flɔt] *a* lively; (*elegant*) smart; (*Naut*) afloat; **F~e** *f* -, -n fleet, navy.

Flöz [fløːts] *nt* -es, -e layer, seam.

Fluch [fluːx] *m* -(e)s, ⁻e curse; **f~en** *vi* curse, swear.

Flucht [fluxt] *f* -, -en flight; (*Fenster—*) row; (*Reihe*) range; (*Zimmer—*) suite; **f~artig** *a* hasty.

flücht- ['flʏçt] *cpd*: **~en** *vir* flee, escape; **~ig** *a* fugitive; (*Chem*) volatile; (*vergänglich*) transitory; (*oberflächlich*) superficial; (*eilig*) fleeting; **F~igkeit** *f* transitoriness; volatility; superficiality; **F~igkeitsfehler** *m* careless slip; **F~ling** *m* fugitive, refugee.

Flug [fluːk] *m* -(e)s, ⁻e flight; **im ~** airborne, in flight; **~abwehr** ['fluːg-] *f* anti-aircraft defence; **~blatt** *nt* pamphlet.

Flügel ['flyːgəl] *m* -s, - wing; (*Mus*) grand piano.

Fluggast *m* airline passenger.

flügge ['flʏgə] *a* (fully-)fledged.

Flug- *cpd*: **~geschwindigkeit** *f* flying or air speed; **~gesellschaft** *f* airline (company); **~hafen** *m* airport; **~höhe** *f* altitude (of flight); **~plan** *m* flight schedule; **~platz** *m* airport; (*klein*) airfield; **~post** *f* airmail; **f~s** [fluks] *ad* speedily; **~schrift** *f* pamphlet; **~strecke** *f* air route; **~verkehr** *m* air traffic; **~wesen** *nt* aviation; **~zeug** *nt* (aero)plane, airplane (*US*); **~zeugentführung** *f* hijacking of a plane; **~zeughalle** *f* hangar; **~zeugträger** *m* aircraft carrier.

Flunder ['flʊndər] *f* -, -n flounder.

flunkern ['flʊŋkərn] *vi* fib, tell stories.

Fluor ['fluːɔr] *nt* -s fluorine.

Flur [fluːr] *m* -(e)s, -e hall; (*Treppen—*) staircase.

Fluß [flʊs] *m* -sses, ⁻sse river; (*Fließen*) flow; **im ~ sein** (*fig*) be in a state of flux.

flüssig ['flʏsɪç] *a* liquid; **~ machen** *vt* *Geld* make available; **F~keit** *f* liquid; (*Zustand*) liquidity.

flüster- ['flʏstər] *cpd*: **~n** *vti* whisper; **F~propaganda** *f* whispering campaign.

Flut [fluːt] *f* -, -en (*lit, fig*) flood; (*Gezeiten*) high tide; **f~en** *vi* flood; **~licht** *nt* floodlight.

Fohlen ['foːlən] *nt* -s, - foal.

Föhn [føːn] *m* -(e)s, -e foehn, warm south wind.

Föhre ['føːrə] *f* -, -n Scots pine.

Folge ['fɔlgə] *f* -, -n series, sequence; (*Fortsetzung*) instalment; (*Auswirkung*) result; **in rascher ~** in quick succession; **etw zur ~ haben** result in sth; **~n haben** have consequences; **einer Sache ~ leisten** comply with sth; **f~n** *vi* follow (*jdm sb*); (*gehorchen*) obey (*jdm sb*); **jdm f~n können** (*fig*) follow or understand sb; **f~nd** *a* following; **f~ndermaßen** *ad* as follows, in the following way; **f~nreich**, **f~nschwer** *a* momentous; **f~richtig** *a* logical; **f~rn** *vt* conclude (*aus* +*dat* from); **~rung** *f* conclusion; **f~widrig** *a* illogical.

folg- *cpd*: **~lich** *ad* consequently; **~sam** *a* obedient.

Folie ['foːliə] *f* -, -n foil.

Folter ['fɔltər] *f* -, -n torture; (*Gerät*) rack; **f~n** *vt* torture.

Fön ® [føːn] *m* -(e)s, -e hair-dryer; **f~en** *vt* (blow) dry.

Fontäne [fɔnˈtɛːnə] *f* -, -n fountain.

foppen ['fɔpən] *vt* tease.

Förder- ['fœrdər] *cpd*: **~band** *nt* conveyor belt; **~korb** *m* pit cage; **f~lich** *a* beneficial.

fordern ['fɔrdərn] *vt* demand.

Förder- *cpd*: **f~n** *vt* promote; (*unterstützen*) help; *Kohle* extract; **~ung** *f* promotion; help; extraction.

Forderung ['fɔrdərʊŋ] *f* demand.

Forelle [foˈrɛlə] *f* trout.

Form [fɔrm] *f* -, -en shape; (*Gestaltung*) form; (*Guß—*) mould; (*Back—*) baking tin; **in ~ sein** be in good form or shape; **in von** in the shape of; **f~alisieren** *vt* formalize; **~alität** *f* formality; **~at** [-ˈmaːt] *nt* -(e)s, -e format; (*fig*) distinction; **~ation** *f* formation; **f~bar** *a* malleable; **~el** *f* -, -n formula; **f~ell** [-ˈmɛl] *a* formal; **f~en** *vt* form, shape; **~fehler** *m* faux-pas, gaffe; (*Jur*) irregularity; **f~ieren** [-ˈmiːrən] *vt* form; *vr* form up.

förmlich ['fœrmlɪç] *a* formal; (*col*) real; **F~keit** *f* formality.

Form- *cpd*: **f~los** *a* shapeless; *Benehmen etc* informal; **~u'lar** *nt* -s, -e form; **f~u'lieren** *vt* formulate.

forsch [fɔrʃ] *a* energetic, vigorous; **~en** *vt* search (*nach* for); *vi* (*wissenschaftlich*) (do) research; **~end** *a* searching; **F~er** *m* -s, - research scientist; (*Natur—*) explorer.

Forschung ['fɔrʃʊŋ] *f* research; **~sreise** *f* scientific expedition.

Forst [fɔrst] *m* -(e)s, -e forest; **~arbeiter** *m* forestry worker; **~wesen** *nt*, **~wirtschaft** *f* forestry.

Förster ['fœrstər] *m* -s, - forester; (*für Wild*) gamekeeper.

fort [fɔrt] *ad* away; (*verschwunden*) gone; (*vorwärts*) on; **und so ~** and so on; **in einem ~** on and on; **~bestehen** *vi irreg* survive; **~bewegen** *vtr* move away; **~bilden** *vr* continue one's education; **~bleiben** *vi irreg* stay away; **~bringen** *vt irreg* take away; **F~dauer** *f* continuance; **~fahren** *vi irreg* depart; (*fort-*

setzen) go on, continue; ~**führen** *vt* continue, carry on; ~**gehen** *vi irreg* go away; ~**geschritten** *a* advance; ~**kommen** *vi irreg* get on; (*wegkommen*) get away; ~**können** *vi irreg* be able to get away; ~**müssen** *vi irreg* have to go; ~**pflanzen** *vr* reproduce; **F**~**pflanzung** *f* reproduction; ~**schaffen** *vt* remove; ~**schreiten** *vi irreg* advance.

Fortschritt ['fɔrt-ʃrɪt] *m* advance; ~**e machen** make progress; **f**~**lich** *ad* progressive.

fort- *cpd:* ~**setzen** *vt* continue; **F**~**setzung** *f* continuation; (*folgender Teil*) instalment; **F**~**setzung folgt** to be continued; ~**während** *a* incessant, continual; ~**ziehen** *irreg vt* pull away; *vi* move on; (*umziehen*) move away.

Foto ['fo:to] *nt* -**s**, -**s** photo(graph); *m* -**s**, -**s** (—*apparat*) camera; ~'**graf** *m* photographer; ~**gra'phie** *f* photography; (*Bild*) photograph; **f**~**gra'phieren** *vt* photograph; *vi* take photographs.

Foul *nt* -**s**, -**s** foul.

Fracht [fraxt] *f* -, -**en** freight; (*Naut*) cargo; (*Preis*) carriage; ~**er** *m* -**s**, -freighter, cargo boat; ~**gut** *nt* freight.

Frack [frak] *m* -(**e**)**s**, ⸚**e** tails *pl*.

Frage ['fra:gə] *f* -, -**n** question; **etw in** ~ **stellen** question sth; **jdm eine** ~ **stellen** ask sb a question, put a question to sb; **nicht in** ~ **kommen** be out of the question; ~**bogen** *m* questionnaire; **f**~**n** *vti* ask; ~**zeichen** *nt* question mark.

frag- *cpd:* ~**lich** *a* questionable, doubtful; ~**los** *ad* unquestionably.

Fragment [fra'gment] *nt* fragment; **f**~**arisch** [-'ta:rɪʃ] *a* fragmentary.

fragwürdig ['fra:kvyrdıç] *a* questionable, dubious.

Fraktion [fraktsi'o:n] *f* parliamentary party.

frank [fraŋk] *a* frank, candid; ~**ieren** [-'ki:rən] *vt* stamp, frank; ~**o** *ad* post-paid; carriage paid.

Franse ['franzə] *f* -, -**n** fringe; **f**~**n** *vi* fray.

Fratze ['fratsə] *f* -, -**n** grimace.

Frau [frau] *f* -, -**en** woman; (*Ehe*—) wife; (*Anrede*) Mrs; ~ **Doktor** Doctor; ~**enarzt** *m* gynaecologist; ~**enbewegung** *f* feminist movement; ~**enzimmer** *nt* female, broad (*US*).

Fräulein ['frɔylaın] *nt* young lady; (*Anrede*) Miss.

fraulich ['fraulıç] *a* womanly.

frech [freç] *a* cheeky, impudent; **F**~**dachs** *m* cheeky monkey; **F**~**heit** *f* cheek, impudence.

Fregatte [fre'gatə] *f* frigate.

frei [fraı] *a* free; *Stelle, Sitzplatz auch* vacant; *Mitarbeiter* freelance; *Geld* available; (*unbekleidet*) bare; **sich** (*dat*) **einen Tag** ~ **nehmen** take a day off; **von etw** ~ **sein** be free of sth; **im F**~**en** in the open air; ~ **sprechen** talk without notes; **F**~**bad** *nt* open-air swimming pool; ~**bekommen** *vt irreg:* **jdn/einen Tag** ~**bekommen** get sb freed/get a day off; **F**~**er** *m* -**s**, - suitor; ~**gebig** *a* generous; **F**~**gebigkeit** *f* generosity; ~**halten** *vt*

irreg keep free; ~**händig** *ad* *fahren* with no hands; **F**~**heit** *f* freedom; ~**heitlich** *a* liberal; **F**~**heitsstrafe** *f* prison sentence; ~**heraus** *ad* frankly; **F**~**karte** *f* free ticket; ~**kommen** *vi irreg* get free; ~**lassen** *vt irreg* (set) free; **F**~**lauf** *m* freewheeling; ~**legen** *vt* expose; ~**lich** *ad* certainly, admittedly; **ja** ~**lich** yes of course; **F**~**lichtbühne** *f* open-air theatre; ~**machen** *vt · Post* frank; **Tage** ~**machen** take days off; *vr* arrange to be free; ~**sinnig** *a* liberal; ~**sprechen** *vt irreg* acquit (*von of*); **F**~**spruch** *m* acquittal; ~**stellen** *vt:* **jdm etw** ~**stellen** leave sth (up) to sb; **F**~**stoß** *m* free kick; **F**~**tag** *m* Friday; ~**tags** *ad* on Fridays; **F**~**übungen** *pl* (physical) exercises *pl*; ~**willig** *a* voluntary; **F**~**willige(r)** *mf* volunteer; **F**~**zeit** *f* spare or free time; ~**zügig** *a* liberal, broad-minded; (*mit Geld*) generous.

fremd [fremt] *a* (*unvertraut*) strange; (*ausländisch*) foreign; (*nicht eigen*) someone else's; **etw ist jdm** ~ sth is foreign to sb; ~**artig** *a* strange; **F**~**e(r)** ['fremdə(r)] *mf* stranger; (*Ausländer*) foreigner; **F**~**enführer** *m* (tourist) guide; **F**~**enlegion** *f* foreign legion; **F**~**enverkehr** *m* tourism; **F**~**enzimmer** *nt* guest room; **F**~**körper** *m* foreign body; ~**ländisch** *a* foreign; **F**~**ling** *m* stranger; **F**~**sprache** *f* foreign language; ~**sprachig** *a* foreign-language; **F**~**wort** *nt* foreign word.

Frequenz [fre'kvents] *f* (*Rad*) frequency.

fressen ['fresən] *vti irreg* eat.

Freude ['frɔydə] *f* -, -**n** joy, delight.

freudig *a* joyful, happy.

freudlos *a* joyless.

freuen ['frɔyən] *vt impers* make happy or pleased; *vr* be glad or happy; **sich auf etw** (*acc*) ~ look forward to sth; **sich über etw** (*acc*) ~ be pleased about sth.

Freund ['frɔynt] *m* -(**e**)**s**, -**e** friend; boyfriend; ~**in** [-dın] *f* friend; girlfriend; **f**~**lich** *a* kind, friendly; **f**~**licherweise** *ad* kindly; ~**lichkeit** *f* friendliness, kindness; ~**schaft** *f* friendship; **f**~**schaftlich** *a* friendly.

Frevel ['fre:fəl] *m* -**s**, - crime, offence (*an* +*dat* against); **f**~**haft** *a* wicked.

Frieden ['fri:dən] *m* -**s**, - peace; **im** ~ **in** peacetime; ~**sschluß** *m* peace agreement; ~**sverhandlungen** *pl* peace negotiations *pl*; ~**svertrag** *m* peace treaty; ~**szeit** *f* peacetime.

fried- ['fri:t] *cpd:* ~**fertig** *a* peaceable; **F**~**hof** *m* cemetery; ~**lich** *a* peaceful.

frieren ['fri:rən] *vti irreg* freeze; **ich friere, es friert mich** I am freezing, I'm cold.

Fries [fri:s] *m* -**es**, -**e** (*Archit*) frieze.

frigid(e) [fri'gi:t, fri'gi:də] *a* frigid.

Frikadelle [frika'dɛlə] *f* meatball.

frisch [frıʃ] *a* fresh; (*lebhaft*) lively; ~ **gestrichen!** wet paint!; **sich** ~ **machen** freshen (o.s.) up; **F**~**e** *f* - freshness; liveliness.

Friseur [fri'zø:r] *m*, **Friseuse** [fri'zø:zə] *f* hairdresser.

Frisier- [fri'ziːr] *cpd*: **f∼en** *vtr* do (one's hair); (*fig*) *Abrechnung* fiddle, doctor; **∼salon** *m* hairdressing salon; **∼tisch** *m* dressing table.

Frisör [fri'zøːr] *m* **-s, e** hairdresser.

Frist [frɪst] *f* **-, -en** period; (*Termin*) deadline; **f∼en** *vt* *Dasein* lead; (*kümmerlich*) eke out; **f∼los** *a* *Entlassung* instant.

Frisur [fri'zuːr] *f* hairdo, hairstyle.

fritieren [fri'tiːrən] *vt* deep fry.

frivol [fri'voːl] *a* frivolous.

froh [froː] *a* happy, cheerful; **ich bin ∼, daß . . .** I'm glad that . . .

fröhlich [frøːlɪç] *a* merry, happy; **F∼keit** *f* merriness, gaiety.

froh- *cpd*: **∼'locken** *vi* exult; (*pej*) gloat; **F∼sinn** *m* cheerfulness.

fromm [frɔm] *a* pious, good; *Wunsch* idle.

Frömm- ['frœm] *cpd*: **∼e'lei** *f* false piety; **∼igkeit** *f* piety.

frönen ['frøːnən] *vi* indulge (*etw* (*dat*) in sth).

Fronleichnam [froːn'laɪçnaːm] *m* **-(e)s** Corpus Christi.

Front [frɔnt] *f* **-, -en** front; **f∼al** [frɔn'taːl] *a* frontal.

Frosch [frɔʃ] *m* **-(e)s, ᵉe** frog; (*Feuerwerk*) squib; **∼mann** *m* frogman; **∼schenkel** *m* frog's leg.

Frost [frɔst] *m* **-(e)s, ᵉe** frost; **∼beule** *f* chilblain.

frösteln ['frœstəln] *vi* shiver.

Frost- *cpd*: **f∼ig** *a* frosty; **∼schutzmittel** *nt* anti-freeze.

Frottee [frɔ'teː] *nt or m* **-(s), -s** towelling.

frottieren [frɔ'tiːrən] *vt* rub, towel.

Frottier(hand)tuch *nt* towel.

Frucht [fruxt] *f* **-, ᵉe** (*lit, fig*) fruit; (*Getreide*) corn; **f∼bar, f∼bringend** *a* fruitful, fertile; **∼barkeit** *f* fertility; **f∼en** *vi* be of use; **f∼los** *a* fruitless; **∼saft** *m* fruit juice.

früh [fryː] *a,ad* early; **heute ∼** this morning; **F∼aufsteher** *m* **-s, -** early riser; **F∼e** *f* - early morning; **∼er** *a* earlier; (*ehemalig*) former; *ad* formerly; **∼er war das anders** that used to be different; **∼estens** *ad* at the earliest; **F∼geburt** *f* premature birth/baby; **F∼jahr** *nt*, **F∼ling** *m* spring; **∼reif** *a* precocious; **F∼stück** *nt* breakfast; **∼stücken** *vi* (have) breakfast; **∼zeitig** *a* early; (*pej*) untimely.

frustrieren [frus'triːrən] *vt* frustrate.

Fuchs [fuks] *m* **-es, ᵉe** fox; **f∼en** (*col*) *vt* rile, annoy; *vr* be annoyed; **f∼teufelswild** *a* hopping mad.

Füchsin ['fʏksɪn] *f* vixen.

fuchteln ['fuxtəln] *vi* gesticulate wildly.

Fuge ['fuːgə] *f* **-, -n** joint; (*Mus*) fugue.

fügen ['fyːgən] *vt* place, join; *vr* be obedient (*in* +*acc* to); (*anpassen*) adapt oneself (*in* +*acc* to); *impers* happen.

fügsam ['fyːkzaːm] *a* obedient.

fühl- ['fyːl] *cpd*: **∼bar** *a* perceptible, noticeable; **∼en** *vtir* feel; **F∼er** *m* **-s, -** feeler.

führen ['fyːrən] *vt* lead; *Geschäft* run; *Name* bear; *Buch* keep; *vi* lead; *vr* behave.

Führer ['fyːrər] *m* **-s,** - leader; (*Fremden∼*) guide; **∼schein** *m* driving licence.

Fuhrmann ['fuːrman] *m, pl* **-leute** carter.

Führung ['fyːruŋ] *f* leadership; (*eines Unternehmens*) management; (*Mil*) command; (*Benehmen*) conduct; (*Museums∼*) conducted tour; **∼szeugnis** *nt* certificate of good conduct.

Fuhrwerk ['fuːrvɛrk] *nt* cart.

Fülle ['fʏlə] *f* - wealth, abundance; **f∼n** *vtr* fill; (*Cook*) stuff; **∼n** *nt* **-s,** - foal; **∼r** *m* **-s, -**, **Füllfederhalter** *m* fountain pen.

Füllung ['fʏluŋ] *f* filling; (*Holz∼*) panel.

fummeln ['fuməln] *vi* (*col*) fumble.

Fund [funt] *m* **-(e)s, -e** find; **∼ament** [-da'mɛnt] *nt* foundation; **f∼amen'tal** *a* fundamental; **∼büro** *nt* lost property office, lost and found; **∼grube** *f* (*fig*) treasure trove; **f∼ieren** [-'diːrən] *vt* back up; **f∼iert** *a* sound.

fünf [fʏnf] *num* five; **∼hundert** *num* five hundred; **∼te** *num* fifth; **F∼tel** *m* **-s, -** fifth; **∼zehn** *num* fifteen; **∼zig** *num* fifty.

fungieren [fuŋ'giːrən] *vi* function; (*Person*) act.

Funk [fuŋk] *m* **-s** radio, wireless; **∼e(n)** *m* **-ns, -n** (*lit, fig*) spark; **f∼eln** *vi* sparkle; **f∼en** *vt* radio; **∼er** *m* **-s, -** radio operator; **∼gerät** *nt* radio set; **∼haus** *nt* broadcasting centre; **∼spruch** *m* radio signal; **∼station** *f* radio station.

Funktion [fuŋktsi'oːn] *f* function; **f∼ieren** [-'niːrən] *vi* work, function.

für [fyːr] *prep* +*acc* for; **was ∼** what kind or sort of; **das F∼ und Wider** the pros and cons *pl*; **Schritt ∼ Schritt** step by step; **F∼bitte** *f* intercession.

Furche ['furçə] *f* **-, -n** furrow; **f∼n** *vt* furrow.

Furcht [furçt] *f* - fear; **f∼bar** *a* terrible, frightful.

fürcht- ['fyrçt] *cpd*: **∼en** *vt* be afraid of, fear; *vr* be afraid (*vor* +*dat* of); **∼erlich** *a* awful.

furcht- *cpd*: **∼los** *a* fearless; **∼sam** *a* timid.

füreinander [fyːr'aɪ'nandər] *ad* for each other.

Furnier [fur'niːr] *nt* **-s, -e** veneer.

fürs [fyːrs] = **für das**.

Fürsorge ['fyːrzɔrgə] *f* care; (*Sozial∼*) welfare; **∼amt** *nt* welfare office; **∼r(in** *f*) *m* **-s,** - welfare worker; **∼unterstützung** *f* social security, welfare benefit (*US*).

Für- *cpd*: **∼sprache** *f* recommendation; (*um Gnade*) intercession; **∼sprecher** *m* advocate.

Fürst [fʏrst] *m* **-en, -en** prince; **∼in** *f* princess; **∼entum** *nt* principality; **f∼lich** *a* princely.

Furt [furt] *f* **-, -en** ford.

Fürwort ['fyːrvɔrt] *nt* pronoun.

Fuß [fuːs] *m* **-es, ᵉe** foot; (*von Glas, Säule etc*) base; (*von Möbel*) leg; **zu ∼** on foot; **∼ball** *m* football; **∼ballspiel** *nt* football match; **∼ballspieler** *m* footballer; **∼boden** *m* floor; **∼bremse** *f* (*Aut*) footbrake; **f∼en** *vi* rest, be based (*auf* +*dat* on); **∼ende** *nt* foot; **∼gänger(in** *f*) *m* **-s, -**

pedestrian; ~**gängerzone** f pedestrian precinct; ~**note** f footnote; ~**pfleger(in** f) m chiropodist; ~**spur** f footprint; ~**tritt** m kick; (Spur) footstep; ~**weg** m footpath.

Futter ['fʊtər] nt -s, - fodder, feed; (Stoff) lining; ~**al** [-'raːl] nt -s, -e case.

füttern ['fʏtərn] vt feed; Kleidung line.

Futur [fu'tuːr] nt -s, -e future.

G

G, g [geː] nt G, g.

Gabe ['gaːbə] f-, -n gift.

Gabel ['gaːbəl] f-, -n fork; ~**frühstück** nt mid-morning snack; ~**ung** f fork.

gackern ['gakərn] vi cackle.

gaffen ['gafən] vi gape.

Gage ['gaːʒə] f-, -n fee; salary.

gähnen ['gɛːnən] vi yawn.

Gala ['gala] f - formal dress; ~**vorstellung** f (Theat) gala performance.

galant [ga'lant] a gallant, courteous.

Galerie [galə'riː] f gallery.

Galgen ['galgən] m -s, - gallows pl; ~**frist** f respite; ~**humor** m macabre humour.

Galle ['galə] f -, -n gall; (Organ) gall-bladder.

Galopp [ga'lɔp] m -s, -s or -e gallop; **g~ieren** [-'piːrən] vi gallop.

galvanisieren [galvani'ziːrən] vt galvanize.

Gamasche [ga'maʃə] f -, -n gaiter; (kurz) spat.

Gammler ['gamlər] m -s, - loafer, layabout.

Gang [gaŋ] m -(e)s, ⸚e walk; (Boten—) errand; (—art) gait; (Abschnitt eines Vorgangs) operation; (Essens—, Ablauf) course; (Flur etc) corridor; (Durch—) passage; (Tech) gear; **in** ~ **bringen** start up; (fig) get off the ground; **in** ~ **sein** in operation; (fig) be underway; [gɛŋ] f-, -s gang; **g~** a: **g~ und gäbe** usual, normal; **g~bar** a passable; Methode practicable.

Gängel- ['gɛŋəl] cpd: ~**band** nt; jdn am ~**band halten** (fig) spoonfeed sb; **g~n** vt spoonfeed.

gängig ['gɛŋɪç] a common, current; Ware in demand, selling well.

Ganove [ga'noːvə] m -n, -n (col) crook.

Gans [gans] f -, ⸚e goose.

Gänse- ['gɛnzə] cpd: ~**blümchen** nt daisy; ~**braten** m roast goose; ~**füßchen** pl (col) inverted commas pl (Brit), quotes pl; ~**haut** f goose pimples pl; ~**marsch** m: **im** ~**marsch** in single file; ~**rich** m -s, -e gander.

ganz [gants] a whole; (vollständig) complete; ~ **Europa** all Europe; **sein** ~**es Geld** all his money; auf quite; (völlig) completely; ~ **und gar nicht** not at all; **es sieht** ~ **so aus** it really looks like it; **aufs G~e gehen** go for the lot.

gänzlich ['gɛntslɪç] a,ad complete(ly), entire(ly).

gar [gaːr] a cooked, done; ad quite; ~ **nicht/nichts/keiner** not/nothing/no-body at all; ~ **nicht schlecht** not bad at all.

Garage [ga'raːʒə] f-, -n garage.

Garantie [garan'tiː] f guarantee; **g~ren** vt guarantee.

Garbe ['garbə] f -, -n sheaf; (Mil) burst of fire.

Garde ['gardə] f-, -n guard(s); **die alte** ~ the old guard; ~**'robe** f -, -n wardrobe; (Abgabe) cloakroom; ~**'robenfrau** f cloakroom attendant; ~**'robenständer** m hallstand.

Gardine [gar'diːnə] f curtain.

gären ['gɛːrən] vi irreg ferment.

Garn [garn] nt -(e)s, -e thread; yarn (auch fig).

Garnele [gar'neːlə] f-, -n shrimp, prawn.

garnieren [gar'niːrən] vt decorate; Speisen garnish.

Garnison [garni'zoːn] f-, -en garrison.

Garnitur [garni'tuːr] f (Satz) set; (Unter-wäsche) set of (matching) underwear; (fig) **erste** ~ top rank; **zweite** ~ second rate.

garstig ['garstɪç] a nasty, horrid.

Garten ['gartən] m -s, ⸚ garden; ~**arbeit** f gardening; ~**bau** m horticulture; ~**fest** nt garden party; ~**gerät** nt gardening tool; ~**haus** nt summerhouse; ~**kresse** f cress; ~**lokal** nt beer garden; ~**schere** f pruning shears pl; ~**tür** f garden gate.

Gärtner(in f) ['gɛrtnər(ɪn)] m -s, - gardener; ~**ei** [-'rai] f nursery; (Gemüse-) market garden (Brit), truck farm (US); **g~n** vi garden.

Gärung ['gɛːrʊŋ] f fermentation.

Gas [gaːs] nt -es, -e gas; ~ **geben** (Aut) accelerate, step on the gas; **g~förmig** a gaseous; ~**herd** m, ~**kocher** m gas cooker; ~**leitung** f gas pipeline; ~**maske** f gasmask; ~**pedal** nt accelerator, gas pedal.

Gasse ['gasə] f-, -n lane, alley; ~**njunge** m street urchin.

Gast [gast] m -es, ⸚e guest; ~**arbeiter(in** f) m foreign worker.

Gästebuch ['gɛstəbuːx] nt visitors' book, guest book.

Gast- cpd: **g~freundlich** a hospitable; ~**geber** m -s, - host; ~**geberin** f hostess; ~**haus** nt, ~**hof** m hotel, inn; **g~ieren** [-'tiːrən] vi (Theat) (appear as a) guest; **g~lich** a hospitable; ~**lichkeit** f hospitality; ~**rolle** f guest role.

gastronomisch [gastro'noːmɪʃ] a gastronomic(al).

Gast- cpd: ~**spiel** nt (Sport) away game; ~**stätte** f restaurant; pub; ~**wirt** m inn-keeper; ~**wirtschaft** f hotel, inn; ~**zimmer** nt (guest) room.

Gas- cpd: ~**vergiftung** f gas poisoning; ~**werk** nt gasworks sing or pl; ~**zähler** m gas meter.

Gatte ['gatə] m -n, -n husband, spouse; **die** ~**n** husband and wife.

Gatter ['gatər] nt -s, - railing, grating; (Eingang) gate.

Gattin f wife, spouse.

Gattung ['gatʊŋ] f genus; kind.
Gaukler ['gaʊklər] m -s, - juggler, conjurer.
Gaul [gaʊl] m -(e)s, **Gäule** horse; nag.
Gaumen ['gaʊmən] m -s, - palate.
Gauner ['gaʊnər] m -s, - rogue; ~**ei** [-'raɪ] f swindle.
Gaze ['ga:zə] f-, -n gauze.
Gebäck [gə'bɛk] nt -(e)s, -e pastry.
Gebälk [gə'bɛlk] nt -(e)s timberwork.
Gebärde [gə'bɛːrdə] f -, -n gesture; g~n vr behave.
gebären [gə'bɛːrən] vt irreg give birth to, bear.
Gebärmutter f uterus, womb.
Gebäude [gə'bɔʏdə] nt -s, - building; ~**komplex** m (building) complex.
Gebein [gə'baɪn] nt -(e)s, -e bones pl.
Gebell [gə'bɛl] nt -(e)s barking.
geben ['ge:bən] irreg vti (jdm etw) give (sb sth or sth to sb); Karten deal; **ein Wort gab das andere** one angry word led to another; v impers **es gibt** there is/are; there will be; **gegeben** given; **zu gegebener Zeit** in good time; vr (sich verhalten) behave, act; (aufhören) abate; **sich geschlagen** ~ admit defeat; **das wird sich schon** ~ that'll soon sort itself out.
Gebet [gə'be:t] nt -(e)s, -e prayer.
Gebiet [gə'bi:t] nt -(e)s, -e area; (Hoheits—) territory; (fig) field; g~en vt irreg command, demand; ~**er** m -s, - master; (Herrscher) ruler; g~**erisch** a imperious.
Gebilde [gə'bɪldə] nt -s, - object, structure; g~t a cultured, educated.
Gebimmel [gə'bɪml] nt -s (continual) ringing.
Gebirge [gə'bɪrgə] nt -s, - mountain chain.
gebirgig a mountainous.
Gebirgszug [gə'bɪrkstsu:k] m mountain range.
Gebiß [gə'bɪs] nt -sses, -sse teeth pl; (künstlich) dentures pl.
geblümt [gə'bly:mt] a flowery.
Geblüt [gə'bly:t] nt -(e)s blood, race.
geboren [gə'bɔːrən] a born; Frau née.
geborgen [gə'bɔrgən] a secure, safe.
Gebot [gə'bo:t] nt -(e)s, -e command(ment Bibl); (bei Auktion) bid.
Gebräu [gə'brɔʏ] nt -(e)s, -e brew, concoction.
Gebrauch [gə'braʊx] m -(e)s, **Gebräuche** use; (Sitte) custom; g~en vt use.
gebräuchlich [gə'brɔʏçlɪç] a usual, customary.
Gebrauchs- cpd: ~**anweisung** f directions pl for use; ~**artikel** m article of everyday use; g~**fertig** a ready for use; ~**gegenstand** m commodity.
gebraucht [gə'braʊxt] a used; G~**wagen** m secondhand or used car.
gebrechlich [gə'brɛçlɪç] a frail; C~**keit** f frailty.
Gebrüder [gə'bry:dər] pl brothers pl.
Gebrüll [gə'brʏl] nt -(e)s roaring.
Gebühr [gə'by:r] f-, -en charge, fee; **nach** ~ fittingly; **über** ~ unduly; g~en vi:

jdm g~**en** be sb's due or due to sb; vr be fitting; g~**end** a,ad fitting(ly), appropriate(ly); ~**enerlaß** m remission of fees; ~**enermäßigung** f reduction of fees; g~**enfrei** a free of charge; g~**enpflichtig** a subject to charges.
Geburt [gə'bu:rt] f -, -en birth; ~**enbeschränkung** f, ~**enkontrolle** f, ~**enregelung** f birth control; ~**enziffer** f birth-rate.
gebürtig [gə'bʏrtɪç] a born in, native of; ~**e Schweizerin** native of Switzerland, Swiss-born.
Geburts- cpd: ~**anzeige** f birth notice; ~**datum** nt date of birth; ~**jahr** nt year of birth; ~**ort** m birthplace; ~**tag** m birthday; ~**urkunde** f birth certificate.
Gebüsch [gə'bʏʃ] nt -(e)s, -e bushes pl.
Gedächtnis [gə'dɛçtnɪs] nt -ses,-se memory; ~**feier** f commemoration; ~**schwund** m loss of memory, failing memory; ~**verlust** m amnesia.
Gedanke [gə'daŋkə] m -ns, -n thought; **sich über etw** (acc) ~**n machen** think about sth; ~**naustausch** m exchange of ideas; g~**nlos** a thoughtless; ~**nlosigkeit** f thoughtlessness; ~**nstrich** m dash; ~**nübertragung** f thought transference, telepathy; g~**nverloren** a lost in thought; g~**nvoll** a thoughtful.
Gedärm [gə'dɛrm] nt -(e)s, -e intestines pl, bowels pl.
Gedeck [gə'dɛk] nt -(e)s, -e cover(ing); (Speisenfolge) menu; **ein** ~ **auflegen** lay a place.
gedeihen [gə'daɪən] vi irreg thrive, prosper.
gedenken [gə'dɛŋkən] vi irreg (sich erinnern) (+gen) remember; (beabsichtigen) intend.
Gedenk- cpd: ~**feier** f commemoration; ~**minute** f minute's silence; ~**tag** m remembrance day.
Gedicht [gə'dɪçt] nt -(e)s, -e poem.
gediegen [gə'di:gən] a (good) quality; Mensch reliable, honest; G~**heit** f quality; reliability, honesty.
Gedränge [gə'drɛŋə] nt -s crush, crowd; **ins** ~ **kommen** (fig) get into difficulties.
gedrängt a compressed; ~ **voll** packed.
gedrungen [gə'drʊŋən] a thickset, stocky.
Geduld [gə'dʊlt] f - patience; g~en [gə'dʊldən] vr be patient; g~**ig** a patient, forbearing; ~**sprobe** f trial of (one's) patience.
gedunsen [gə'dʊnzən] a bloated.
geeignet [gə'aɪgnət] a suitable.
Gefahr [gə'fa:r] f -, -en danger; ~ **laufen, etw zu tun** run the risk of doing sth; **auf eigene** ~ at one's own risk.
gefährden [gə'fɛːrdən] vt endanger.
Gefahren- cpd: ~**quelle** f source of danger; ~**zulage** f danger money.
gefährlich [gə'fɛːrlɪç] a dangerous.
Gefährte [gə'fɛːrtə] m -n, -n, **Gefährtin** f companion.
Gefälle [gə'fɛlə] nt -s, - gradient, incline.
Gefallen [gə'falən] m -s, - favour; nt -s pleasure; **an etw** (dat) ~ **finden** derive

pleasure from sth; **jdm etw zu ~ tun** do sth to please sb; **g~** *vi irreg:* **jdm g~** please sb; **er/es gefällt mir** I like him/it; **das gefällt mir an ihm** that's one thing I like about him; **sich** (*dat*) **etw g~ lassen** put up with sth; *ptp of* **fallen.**

gefällig [gə'fɛlɪç] *a* (*hilfsbereit*) obliging; (*erfreulich*) pleasant; **G~keit** *f* favour; helpfulness; **etw aus G~keit tun** do sth as a favour.

gefälligst *ad* kindly.

gefallsüchtig *a* eager to please.

gefangen [gə'faŋən] *a* captured; (*fig*) captivated; **G~e(r)** *m* prisoner, captive; **G~enlager** *nt* prisoner-of-war camp; **~halten** *vt irreg* keep prisoner; **G~nahme** *f* -, **-n** capture; **G~schaft** *f* captivity.

Gefängnis [gə'fɛŋnɪs] *nt* **-ses, -se** prison; **~strafe** *f* prison sentence; **~wärter** *m* prison warder.

Gefasel [gə'fa:zəl] *nt* **-s** twaddle, drivel.

Gefäß [gə'fɛːs] *nt* **-es, -e** vessel (*auch Anat*), container.

gefaßt [gə'fast] *a* composed, calm; **auf etw** (*acc*) **~ sein** be prepared *or* ready for sth.

Gefecht [gə'fɛçt] *nt* **-(e)s, -e** fight; (*Mil*) engagement.

gefeit [gə'faɪt] *a:* **gegen etw ~ sein** be immune to sth.

Gefieder [gə'fi:dər] *nt* **-s, -** plumage, feathers *pl;* **g~t** *a* feathered.

gefleckt [gə'flɛkt] *a* spotted, mottled.

geflissentlich [gə'flɪsəntlɪç] *a,ad* intentional(ly).

Geflügel [gə'fly:gəl] *nt* **-s** poultry.

Gefolge [gə'fɔlgə] *nt* **-s, -** retinue.

Gefolg- *cpd:* **~schaft** *f* following; (*Arbeiter*) personnel; **~smann** *m* follower.

gefragt [gə'fra:kt] *a* in demand.

gefräßig [gə'frɛːsɪç] *a* voracious.

Gefreite(r) [gə'fraɪtə(r)] *m* **-n, -n** lance corporal; (*Naut*) able seaman; (*Aviat*) aircraftman.

gefrieren [gə'fri:rən] *vi irreg* freeze.

Gefrier- *cpd:* **~fach** *nt* icebox; **~fleisch** *nt* frozen meat; **g~getrocknet** *a* freeze-dried; **~punkt** *m* freezing point; **~schutzmittel** *nt* antifreeze; **~truhe** *f* deep-freeze.

Gefüge [gə'fy:gə] *nt* **-s, -** structure.

gefügig *a* pliant; *Mensch* obedient.

Gefühl [gə'fy:l] *nt* **-(e)s, -e** feeling; **etw im ~ haben** have a feel for sth; **g~los** *a* unfeeling; **g~sbetont** *a* emotional; **~sduselei** [-zdu:zə'laɪ] *f* emotionalism; **g~smäßig** *a* instinctive.

gegebenenfalls [gə'ge:bənənfals] *ad* if need be.

gegen ['ge:gən] *prep* +*acc* against; (*in Richtung auf, jdn betreffend, kurz vor*) towards; (*im Austausch für*) (in return) for; (*ungefähr*) round about; **G~angriff** *m* counter-attack; **G~beweis** *m* counter-evidence.

Gegend ['ge:gənt] *f* -, **-en** area, district.

Gegen- *cpd:* **g~ei'nander** *ad* against one another; **~fahrbahn** *f* oncoming

carriageway; **~frage** *f* counter-question; **~gewicht** *nt* counterbalance; **~gift** *nt* antidote; **~leistung** *f* service in return; **~lichtaufnahme** *f* contre-jour photograph; **~maßnahme** *f* counter-measure; **~probe** *f* cross-check; **~satz** *m* contrast; **~sätze überbrücken** overcome differences; **g~sätzlich** *a* contrary, opposite; (*widersprüchlich*) contradictory; **~schlag** *m* counter attack; **~seite** *f* opposite side; (*Rückseite*) reverse; **g~seitig** *a* mutual, reciprocal; **sich g~seitig helfen** help each other; **~seitigkeit** *f* reciprocity; **~spieler** *m* opponent; **~stand** *m* object; **g~ständlich** *a* objective, concrete; **~stimme** *f* vote against; **~stoß** *m* counterblow; **~stück** *nt* counterpart; **~teil** *nt* opposite; **im ~teil** on the contrary; **ins ~teil umschlagen** swing to the other extreme; **g~teilig** *a* opposite, contrary.

gegenüber [ge:gən''y:bər] *prep* +*dat* opposite; (*zu*) to(wards); (*angesichts*) in the face of; *ad* opposite; **G~** *nt* **-s, -** person opposite; **~liegen** *vr irreg* face each other; **~stehen** *vr irreg* be opposed (to each other); **~stellen** *vt* confront; (*fig*) contrast; **G~stellung** *f* confrontation; (*fig*) contrast; **~treten** *vi irreg* (+*dat*) face.

Gegen- *cpd:* **~verkehr** *m* oncoming traffic; **~vorschlag** *m* counterproposal; **~wart** *f* present; **g~wärtig** *a* present; **das ist mir nicht mehr g~wärtig** that has slipped my mind; *ad* at present; **~wert** *m* equivalent; **~wind** *m* headwind; **~wirkung** *f* reaction; **g~zeichnen** *vti* countersign; **~zug** *m* counter-move; (*Rail*) corresponding train in the other direction.

Gegner ['ge:gnər] *m* **-s, -** opponent; **g~isch** *a* opposing; **~schaft** *f* opposition.

Gehackte(s) [gə'haktə(z)] *nt* mince(d meat).

Gehalt [gə'halt] *m* **-(e)s, -e** content; *nt* **-(e)s, ̈er** salary; **~sempfänger** *m* salary earner; **~serhöhung** *f* salary increase; **~szulage** *f* salary increment.

geharnischt [gə'harnɪʃt] *a* (*fig*) forceful, angry.

gehässig [gə'hɛsɪç] *a* spiteful, nasty; **G~keit** *f* spite(fulness).

Gehäuse [gə'hɔyzə] *nt* **-s, -** case; casing; (*von Apfel etc*) core.

Gehege [gə'he:gə] *nt* **-s, -** enclosure, preserve; **jdm ins ~ kommen** (*fig*) poach on sb's preserve.

geheim [gə'haɪm] *a* secret; **G~dienst** *m* secret service, intelligence service; **~halten** *vt irreg* keep secret; **G~nis** *nt* **-ses, -se** secret; mystery; **G~niskrämer** *m* secretive type; **~nisvoll** *a* mysterious; **G~polizei** *f* secret police; **G~schrift** *f* code, secret writing.

Geheiß [gə'haɪs] *nt* **-es** command; **auf jds ~** at sb's behest.

gehen ['ge:ən] *irreg vti* go; (*zu Fuß —*) walk; **~ nach** (*Fenster*) face; *v impers:* **wie**

geht es (dir)? how are you or things?; **mir/ihm geht es gut** I'm/he's (doing) fine; **geht das?** is that possible?; **geht's noch?** can you manage?; **es geht** not too bad, O.K.; **das geht nicht** that's not on; **es geht um etw** sth is concerned, it's about sth.

geheuer [gə'hɔyər] a: **nicht ~** eery; (fragwürdig) dubious.

Geheul [gə'hɔyl] nt -(e)s howling.

Gehilfe [gə'hılfə] m -n, -n, **Gehilfin** f assistant.

Gehirn [gə'hırn] nt -(e)s, -e brain; **~erschütterung** f concussion; **~wäsche** f brainwashing.

Gehör [gə'hø:r] nt -(e)s hearing; **musikalisches ~** ear; **~ finden** gain a hearing; **jdm ~ schenken** give sb a hearing.

gehorchen [gə'hɔrçən] vi obey (jdm sb).

gehören [gə'hø:rən] vi belong; vr impers be right or proper.

gehörig a proper; **~ zu** or +dat belonging to; part of.

gehorsam [gə'ho:rza:m] a obedient; **G~** m -s obedience.

Gehsteig m, **Gehweg** m ['ge:-] pavement, sidewalk (US).

Geier ['gaıər] m -s, - vulture.

geifern ['gaıfərn] vi salivate; (fig) bitch.

Geige ['gaıgə] f -, -n violin; **~r** m -s, - violinist; **~zähler** m geiger counter.

geil [gaıl] a randy, horny (US).

Geisel ['gaızəl] f -, -n hostage.

Geißel ['gaısəl] f -, -n scourge, whip; **g~n** vt scourge.

Geist [gaıst] m -(e)s, -er spirit; (Gespenst) ghost; (Verstand) mind; **g~erhaft** a ghostly; **g~esabwesend** a absent-minded; **~esblitz** m brainwave; **~esgegenwart** f presence of mind; **~eshaltung** f mental attitude; **g~eskrank** a mentally ill; **~eskranke(r)** mf mentally ill person; **~eskrankheit** f mental illness; **~esstörung** f mental disturbance; **~eswissenschaften** pl arts (subjects) pl; **~eszustand** m state of mind; **g~ig** a intellectual; mental; (Getränke) alcoholic; **g~ig behindert** mentally handicapped; **g~lich** a spiritual, religious; clerical; **~liche(r)** m clergyman; **~lichkeit** f clergy; **g~los** a uninspired, dull; **g~reich** a clever; witty; **g~tötend** a soul-destroying; **g~voll** a intellectual; (weise) wise.

Geiz [gaıts] m -es miserliness, meanness; **g~en** vi be miserly; **~hals** m, **~kragen** m miser; **g~ig** a miserly, mean.

Geklapper [gə'klapər] nt -s rattling.

geknickt [gə'knıkt] a (fig) dejected.

gekonnt [gə'kɔnt] a skilful.

Gekritzel [gə'krıtsəl] nt -s scrawl, scribble.

gekünstelt [gə'kʏnstəlt] a artificial, affected.

Gelächter [gə'lɛçtər] nt -s, - laughter.

geladen [ge'la:dən] a loaded; (Elec) live; (fig) furious.

Gelage [gə'la:gə] nt -s, - feast, banquet.

gelähmt [gə'lɛ:mt] a paralysed.

Gelände [gə'lɛndə] nt -s, - land, terrain; (von Fabrik, Sport—) grounds pl; (Bau—) site; **g~gängig** a able to go cross-country; **~lauf** m cross-country race.

Geländer [gə'lɛndər] nt -s, - railing; (Treppen—) banister(s).

gelangen [gə'laŋən] vi (an +acc or zu) reach; (erwerben) attain; **in jds Besitz ~** to come into sb's possession.

gelassen [gə'lasən] a calm, composed; **G~heit** f calmness, composure.

Gelatine [ʒela'ti:nə] f gelatine.

geläufig [gə'lɔyfıç] a (üblich) common; **das ist mir nicht ~** I'm not familiar with that; **G~keit** f commonness; familiarity.

gelaunt [gə'launt] a: **schlecht/gut ~** in a bad/good mood; **wie ist er ~?** what sort of mood is he in?

Geläut(e) [gə'lɔyt(ə)] nt -(e)s, -(e) ringing; (Läutwerk) chime.

gelb [gɛlp] a yellow; (Ampellicht) amber; **~lich** a yellowish; **G~sucht** f jaundice.

Geld [gɛlt] nt -(e)s, -er money; **etw zu ~ machen** sell sth off; **~anlage** f investment; **~beutel** m, **~börse** f purse; **~einwurf** m slot; **~geber** m -s, - financial backer; **g~gierig** a avaricious; **~mittel** pl capital, means pl; **~schein** m banknote; **~schrank** m safe, strongbox; **~strafe** f fine; **~stück** nt coin; **~verlegenheit** f: **in ~verlegenheit sein/kommen** to be/run short of money; **~verleiher** m -s, - moneylender; **~wechsel** m exchange (of money).

Gelee [ʒe'le:] nt or m -s, -s jelly.

gelegen [gə'le:gən] a situated; (passend) convenient, opportune; **etw kommt jdm ~** sth is convenient for sb.

Gelegenheit [gə'le:gənhaıt] f opportunity; (Anlaß) occasion; **bei jeder ~** at every opportunity; **~sarbeit** f casual work; **~sarbeiter** m casual worker; **~skauf** m bargain.

gelegentlich [gə'le:gəntlıç] a occasional; ad occasionally; (bei Gelegenheit) some time (or other); prep +gen on the occasion of.

gelehrig [gə'le:rıç] a quick to learn, intelligent.

gelehrt a learned; **G~e(r)** mf scholar; **G~heit** f scholarliness.

Geleise [gə'laızə] nt -s, - track; see **Gleis**.

Geleit [gə'laıt] nt -(e)s, -e escort; **g~en** vt escort; **~schutz** m escort.

Gelenk [gə'lɛŋk] nt -(e)s, -e joint; **g~ig** a supple.

gelernt [gə'lɛrnt] a skilled.

Geliebte(r) [gə'li:ptə(r)] mf sweetheart, beloved.

gelind(e) [gə'lınt, gə'lındə] a mild, light; (fig) Wut fierce; **~e gesagt** to put it mildly.

gelingen [gə'lıŋən] vi irreg succeed; **die Arbeit gelingt mir nicht** I'm not being very successful with this piece of work; **es ist mir gelungen, etw zu tun** I succeeded in doing sth.

gellen ['gɛlən] vi shrill.

geloben [gə'lo:bən] *vti* vow, swear.

gelten ['gɛltən] *irreg vt* (*wert sein*) be worth; **etw gilt bei jdm viel/wenig** sb values sth highly/sb doesn't value sth very highly; **jdm viel/wenig** ~ mean a lot/not mean much to sb; **was gilt die Wette?** do you want to bet?; *vi* (*gültig sein*) be valid; (*erlaubt sein*) be allowed; **jdm** ~ (*gemünzt sein auf*) be meant for *or* aimed at sb; **etw** ~ **lassen** accept sth; **als** *or* **für etw** ~ be considered to be sth; **jdm** *or* **für jdn** ~ (*betreffen*) apply to *or* for sb; *v impers* **es gilt, etw zu tun** it is necessary to do sth; ~**d** a prevailing; **etw** ~**d machen** to assert sth; **sich** ~**d machen** make itself/o.s. felt.

Geltung ['gɛltuŋ] *f*: ~ **haben** have validity; **sich/etw** (*dat*) **verschaffen** establish oneself/sth; **etw zur** ~ **bringen** show sth to its best advantage; **zur** ~ **kommen** be seen/heard *etc* to its best advantage; ~**sbedürfnis** *nt* desire for admiration.

Gelübde [gə'lʏpdə] *nt* -**s**, - vow.

gelungen [gə'luŋən] a successful.

gemächlich [gə'mɛːçlɪç] a leisurely.

Gemahl [gə'ma:l] *m* -**(e)s**, -**e** husband; ~**in** *f* wife.

Gemälde [gə'mɛːldə] *nt* -**s**, - picture, painting.

gemäß [gə'mɛːs] *prep* +*dat* in accordance with; a appropriate (*dat* to); ~**igt** a moderate; *Klima* temperate.

gemein [gə'maɪn] a common; (*niederträchtig*) mean; **etw** ~ **haben** (**mit**) have sth in common (with).

Gemeinde [gə'maɪndə] *f* -, -**n** district, community; (*Pfarr*—) parish; (*Kirchen*—) congregation; ~**steuer** *f* local rates *pl*; ~**verwaltung** *f* local administration; ~**vorstand** *m* local council; ~**wahl** *f* local election.

Gemein- *cpd*: **g**~**gefährlich** a dangerous to the public; ~**gut** *nt* public property; ~**heit** *f* commonness; mean thing to do/to say; **g**~**hin** *ad* generally; ~**nutz** *m* public good; ~**platz** *m* commonplace, platitude; **g**~**sam** a joint, common (*auch Math*); **g**~**same Sache mit jdm machen** be in cahoots with sb; *ad* together, jointly; **etw g**~**sam haben** have sth in common; ~**samkeit** *f* community, having in common; ~**schaft** *f* community; **in** ~**schaft mit** jointly *or* together with; **g**~**schaftlich** a *see* **g**~**sam**; ~**schaftsarbeit** *f* teamwork; team effort; ~**schaftserziehung** *f* coeducation; ~**sinn** *m* public spirit; **g**~**verständlich** a generally comprehensible; ~**wohl** *nt* common good.

Gemenge [gə'mɛŋə] *nt* -**s**, - mixture; (*Hand*—) scuffle.

gemessen [gə'mɛsən] a measured.

Gemetzel [gə'mɛtsəl] *nt* -**s**, - slaughter, carnage, butchery.

Gemisch [gə'mɪʃ] *nt* -**es**, -**e** mixture; **g**~**t** a mixed.

Gemse ['gɛmzə] *f* -, -**n** chamois.

Gemunkel [gə'muŋkəl] *nt* -**s** gossip.

Gemurmel [gə'murməl] *nt* -**s** murmur(ing).

Gemüse [gə'my:zə] *nt* -**s**, - vegetables *pl*; ~**garten** *m* vegetable garden; ~**händler** *m* greengrocer.

Gemüt [gə'my:t] *nt* -**(e)s**, -**er** disposition, nature; person; **sich** (*dat*) **etw zu** ~**e führen** (*col*) indulge in sth; **die** ~**er erregen** arouse strong feelings; **g**~**lich** a comfortable, cosy; *Person* good-natured; ~**lichkeit** *f* comfortableness, cosiness; amiability; ~**sbewegung** *f* emotion; ~**smensch** *m* sentimental person; ~**sruhe** *f* composure; ~**szustand** *m* state of mind; **g**~**voll** a warm, tender.

genau [gə'nau] *a,ad* exact(ly), precise(ly); **etw** ~ **nehmen** take sth seriously; ~**genommen** *ad* strictly speaking; **G**~**igkeit** *f* exactness, accuracy.

genehm [gə'ne:m] a agreeable, acceptable; ~**igen** *vt* approve, authorize; **sich** (*dat*) **etw** ~**igen** indulge in sth; **G**~**igung** *f* approval, authorization.

geneigt [gə'naɪkt] a well-disposed, willing; ~ **sein, etw zu tun** be inclined to do sth.

General [gene'ra:l] *m* -**s**, -**e** *or* ~**e** general; ~**direktor** *m* director general; ~**konsulat** *nt* consulate general; ~**probe** *f* dress rehearsal; ~**stabskarte** *f* ordnance survey map; ~**streik** *m* general strike; **g**~**überholen** *vt* thoroughly overhaul.

Generation [generatsi'o:n] *f* generation; ~**skonflikt** *m* generation gap.

Generator [gene'ra:tɔr] *m* generator, dynamo.

genesen [ge'ne:zən] *vi irreg* convalesce, recover, get well; **G**~**de(r)** *mf* convalescent.

Genesung *f* recovery, convalescence.

genetisch [ge'ne:tɪʃ] a genetic.

genial [geni'a:l] a brilliant; **G**~**i'tät** *f* brilliance, genius.

Genick [gə'nɪk] *nt* -**(e)s**, -**e** (back of the) neck; ~**starre** *f* stiff neck.

Genie [ʒe'ni:] *nt* -**s**, -**s** genius.

genieren [ʒe'ni:rən] *vt* bother; **geniert es Sie, wenn . . .?** do you mind if . . .?; *vr* feel awkward *or* self-conscious.

genießbar a edible; drinkable.

genießen [gə'ni:sən] *vt irreg* enjoy; eat; drink.

Genießer *m* -**s**, - epicure; pleasure lover; **g**~**isch** a appreciative; *ad* with relish.

Genosse [gə'nɔsə] *m* -**n**, -**n**, **Genossin** *f* comrade (*esp Pol*), companion; ~**nschaft** *f* cooperative (association).

genug [gə'nu:k] *ad* enough.

Genüge [gə'ny:gə] *f* -: **jdm/etw** ~ **tun** *or* **leisten** satisfy sb/sth; **g**~**n** *vi* be enough, suffice; (+*dat*) satisfied; **g**~**nd** a sufficient.

genügsam [gə'ny:kza:m] a modest, easily satisfied; **G**~**keit** *f* moderation.

Genugtuung [gə'nu:ktu:uŋ] *f* satisfaction.

Genuß [gə'nus] *m* -**sses**, -**sse** pleasure; (*Zusichnehmen*) consumption; **in den** ~ **von etw kommen** receive the benefit of sth; ~**mittel** *pl* (semi-)luxury items *pl*.

genüßlich [gə'nʏslɪç] *ad* with relish.

Geograph [geo'graːf] *m* **-en, -en** geographer; **~ie** [-'fiː] *f* geography; **g~isch** *a* geographical.

Geologe [geo'loːgə] *m* **-n, -n** geologist; **~gie** [-'giː] *f* geology.

Geometrie [geome'triː] *f* geometry.

Gepäck [gə'pɛk] *nt* **-(e)s** luggage, baggage; **~abfertigung** *f*, **~annahme** *f*, **~ausgabe** *f* luggage desk/office; **~aufbewahrung** *f* left-luggage office, checkroom (*US*); **~netz** *nt* luggage-rack; **~träger** *m* porter; (*Fahrrad*) carrier; **~wagen** *m* luggage van, baggage car (*US*).

gepflegt [gə'pfleːkt] *a* well-groomed; *Park etc* well looked after.

Gepflogenheit [gə'pfloːganhait] *f* custom.

Geplapper [gə'plapər] *nt* **-s** chatter.

Geplauder [gə'plaudər] *nt* **-s** chat(ting).

Gepolter [gə'pɔltər] *nt* **-s** din.

gerade [gə'raːdə] *a* straight; *Zahl* even; *ad* (*genau*) exactly; (*örtlich*) straight; (*eben*) just; **warum ~ ich?** why me?; **~ weil** just *or* precisely because; **nicht ~ schön** not exactly nice; **das ist es ja ~** that's just it; **jetzt ~ nicht!** not now!; **~ noch** just; **~ neben** right next to; **~ f~n, -n** straight line; **~aus** *ad* straight ahead; **~heraus** *ad* straight out, bluntly; **~so** *ad* just so; **~so dumm** *etc* just as stupid *etc*; **~so wie** just as; **~zu** *ad* (*beinahe*) virtually, almost.

geradlinig *a* rectilinear.

Gerät [gə'rɛːt] *nt* **-(e)s, -e** device; (*Werkzeug*) tool; (*Sport*) apparatus; (*Zubehör*) equipment *no pl*.

geraten [gə'raːtən] *vi irreg* (*gelingen*) turn out well (*jdm* for sb); (*gedeihen*) thrive; **gut/schlecht ~** turn out well/badly; **an jdn ~** come across sb; **in etw** (*acc*) **~** get into sth; **in Angst ~** get frightened; **nach jdm ~** take after sb.

Geratewohl [gəraːtə'voːl] *nt*: **aufs ~** on the off chance; (*bei Wahl*) at random.

geraum [gə'raum] *a*: **seit ~er Zeit** for some considerable time.

geräumig [gə'rɔymiç] *a* roomy.

Geräusch [gə'rɔyʃ] *nt* **-(e)s, -e** sound, noise; **g~los** *a* silent; **g~voll** *a* noisy.

gerben ['gɛrbən] *vt* tan.

Gerber *m* **-s, -** tanner; **~ei** [-'rai] *f* tannery.

gerecht [gə'rɛçt] *a* just, fair; **jdm/etw ~ werden** do justice to sb/sth; **G~igkeit** *f* justice, fairness.

Gerede [gə'reːdə] *nt* **-s** talk, gossip.

gereizt [gə'raitst] *a* irritable; **G~heit** *f* irritation.

Gericht [gə'riçt] *nt* **-(e)s, -e** court; (*Essen*) dish; **mit jdm ins ~ gehen** (*fig*) judge sb harshly; **über jdn zu ~ sitzen** sit in judgement on sb; **das Letzte ~** the Last Judgement; **g~lich** *a, ad* judicial(ly), legal(ly); **~sbarkeit** *f* jurisdiction; **~shof** *m* court (of law); **~skosten** *pl* (legal) costs *pl*; **~ssaal** *m* courtroom; **~sverfahren** *nt* legal proceedings *pl*; **~sverhandlung** *f* court proceedings *pl*; **~svollzieher** *m* bailiff.

gerieben [gə'riːbən] *a* grated; (*col: schlau*) smart, wily.

gering [gə'rɪŋ] *a* slight, small; (*niedrig*) low; *Zeit* short; **~achten** *vt* think little of; **~fügig** *a* slight, trivial; **~schätzig** *a* disparaging; **G~schätzung** *f* disdain; **~ste(r,s)** *a* slightest, least; **~stenfalls** *ad* at the very least.

gerinnen [gə'rinən] *vi irreg* congeal; (*Blut*) clot; (*Milch*) curdle.

Gerinnsel [gə'rinzəl] *nt* **-s, -** clot.

Gerippe [gə'ripə] *nt* **-s, -** skeleton.

gerissen [gə'risən] *a* wily, smart.

gern(e) ['gɛrn(ə)] *ad* willingly, gladly; **~ haben, ~ mögen** like; **etwas ~ tun** like doing something; **G~egroß** *m* **-, -e** show-off.

Geröll [gə'rœl] *nt* **-(e)s, -e** scree.

Gerste ['gɛrstə] *f* **-, -n** barley; **~nkorn** *nt* (*im Auge*) stye.

Gerte ['gɛrtə] *f* **-, -n** switch, rod; **g~nschlank** *a* willowy.

Geruch [gə'rux] *m* **-(e)s, ̈e** smell, odour; **g~los** *a* odourless; **g~tilgend** *a* deodorant.

Gerücht [gə'rʏçt] *nt* **-(e)s, -e** rumour.

geruhen [gə'ruːən] *vi* deign.

Gerümpel [gə'rʏmpəl] *nt* **-s** junk.

Gerüst [gə'rʏst] *nt* **-(e)s, -e** (*Bau—*) scaffold(ing); frame.

gesamt [gə'zamt] *a* whole, entire; *Kosten* total; *Werke* complete; **im ~en** all in all; **G~ausgabe** *f* complete edition; **~deutsch** *a* all-German; **G~eindruck** *m* general impression; **G~heit** *f* totality, whole.

Gesandte(r) [gə'zantə(r)] *m* envoy.

Gesandtschaft [gə'zant-ʃaft] *f* legation.

Gesang [gə'zaŋ] *m* **-(e)s, ̈e** song; (*Singen*) singing; **~buch** *nt* (*Rel*) hymn book; **~verein** *m* choral society.

Gesäß [gə'zɛːs] *nt* **-es, -e** seat, bottom.

Geschäft [gə'ʃɛft] *nt* **-(e)s, -e** business; (*Laden*) shop; (*—sabschluß*) deal; **~emacher** *m* **-s, -** profiteer; **g~ig** *a* active, busy; (*pej*) officious; **g~lich** *a* commercial; *ad* on business; **~sbericht** *m* financial report; **~sführer** *m* manager; (*Klub*) secretary; **~sjahr** *nt* financial year; **~slage** *f* business conditions *pl*; **~smann** *m* businessman; **g~smäßig** *a* businesslike; **~sreise** *f* business trip; **~sschluß** *m* closing time; **~ssinn** *m* business sense; **~sstelle** *f* office, place of business; **g~stüchtig** *a* efficient; **~sviertel** *nt* business quarter; shopping centre; **~swagen** *m* company car; **~szweig** *m* branch (of a business).

geschehen [gə'ʃeːən] *vi irreg* happen; **es war um ihn ~** that was the end of him.

gescheit [gə'ʃait] *a* clever.

Geschenk [gə'ʃɛŋk] *nt* **-(e)s, -e** present, gift; **~packung** *f* gift pack.

Geschicht- [gə'ʃiçt] *cpd*: **~e** *f* **-, -n** story; (*Sache*) affair; (*Historie*) history; **~enerzähler** *m* storyteller; **g~lich** *a* historical; **~schreiber** *m* historian.

Geschick [gə'ʃik] *nt* **-(e)s, -e** aptitude; (*Schicksal*) fate; **~lichkeit** *f* skill, dexterity; **g~t** *a* skilful.

geschieden [gə'ʃiːdən] a divorced.

Geschirr [gə'ʃɪr] nt -(e)s, -e crockery; pots and pans pl; (Pferd) harness; ~spülmaschine f dishwashing machine; ~tuch nt dish cloth.

Geschlecht [gə'ʃlɛçt] nt -(e)s, -er sex; (Gram) gender; (Art) species; family; g~lich a sexual; ~skrankheit f venereal disease; ~steil nt or m genitals pl; ~sverkehr m sexual intercourse; ~swort nt (Gram) article.

Geschmack [gə'ʃmak] m -(e)s, ¨e taste; nach jds ~ to sb's taste; ~ finden an etw (dat) (come to) like sth; g~los a tasteless; (fig) in bad taste; ~(s)sache f matter of taste; ~sinn m sense of taste; g~voll a tasteful.

Geschmeide [gə'ʃmaɪdə] nt -s, - jewellery.

geschmeidig a supple; (formbar) malleable.

Geschmeiß [gə'ʃmaɪs] nt vermin pl.

Geschmiere [gə'ʃmiːrə] nt -s scrawl; (Bild) daub.

Geschöpf [gə'ʃœpf] nt -(e)s, -e creature.

Geschoß [gə'ʃɔs] nt -sses, -sse (Mil) projectile, missile; (Stockwerk) floor.

geschraubt [gə'ʃraupt] a stilted, artificial.

Geschrei [gə'ʃraɪ] nt -s cries pl, shouting; (fig: Aufhebens) noise, fuss.

Geschütz [gə'ʃyts] nt -es, -e gun, cannon; ein schweres ~ auffahren (fig) bring out the big guns; ~feuer nt artillery fire, gunfire; g~t a protected.

Geschwader [gə'ʃvaːdər] nt -s, - (Naut) squadron; (Aviat) group.

Geschwafel [gə'ʃvaːfəl] nt -s silly talk.

Geschwätz [gə'ʃvɛts] nt -es chatter, gossip; g~ig a talkative; ~igkeit f talkativeness.

geschweige [gə'ʃvaɪgə] ad: ~ (denn) let alone, not to mention.

geschwind [gə'ʃvɪnt] a quick, swift; G~igkeit [-dɪçkaɪt] f speed, velocity; G~igkeitsbegrenzung f speed limit; G~igkeitsmesser m (Aut) speedometer; G~igkeitsüberschreitung f exceeding the speed limit.

Geschwister [gə'ʃvɪstər] pl brothers and sisters pl.

geschwollen [gə'ʃvɔlən] a pompous.

Geschworene(r) [gə'ʃvoːrənə(r)] mf juror; pl jury.

Geschwulst [gə'ʃvulst] f -, ¨e swelling; growth, tumour.

Geschwür [gə'ʃvyːr] nt -(e)s, -e ulcer.

Gesell- [gə'zɛl] cpd: ~e m -n, -n fellow; (Handwerk~) journeyman; g~ig a sociable; ~igkeit f sociability; ~schaft f society; (Begleitung, Comm) company; (Abend—schaft etc) party; g~schaftlich a social; ~schaftsanzug m evening dress; g~schaftsfähig a socially acceptable; ~schaftsreise f group tour; ~schaftsschicht f social stratum.

Gesetz [gə'zɛts] nt -es, -e law; ~buch nt statute book; ~entwurf m, ~esvorlage f bill; g~gebend a legislative; ~geber m -s, - legislator; ~gebung f legislation;

g~lich a legal, lawful; ~lichkeit f legality, lawfulness; g~los a lawless; g~mäßig a lawful; g~t a Mensch sedate; g~tenfalls ad supposing (that); g~widrig a illegal, unlawful.

Gesicht [gə'zɪçt] nt -(e)s, -er face; das zweite ~ second sight; das ist mir nie zu ~ gekommen I've never laid eyes on that; ~sausdruck m (facial) expression; ~sfarbe f complexion; ~spunkt m point of view; ~szüge pl features pl.

Gesindel [gə'zɪndəl] nt -s rabble.

gesinnt [gə'zɪnt] a disposed, minded.

Gesinnung [gə'zɪnʊŋ] f disposition; (Ansicht) views pl; ~sgenosse m like-minded person; ~slosigkeit f lack of conviction; ~swandel m change of opinion, volte-face.

gesittet [gə'zɪtət] a well-mannered.

Gespann [gə'ʃpan] nt -(e)s, -e team; (col) couple; g~t a tense, strained; (begierig) eager; ich bin g~t, ob I wonder if or whether; auf etw/jdn g~t sein look forward to sth/meeting sb.

Gespenst [gə'ʃpɛnst] nt -(e)s, -er ghost, spectre; g~erhaft a ghostly.

Gespiele [gə'ʃpiːlə] m -n, -n, **Gespielin** f playmate.

Gespött [gə'ʃpœt] nt -(e)s mockery; zum ~ werden become a laughing stock.

Gespräch [gə'ʃprɛːç] nt -(e)s, -e conversation; discussion(s); (Anruf) call; zum ~ werden become a topic of conversation; g~ig a talkative; (organisieren) ~igkeit f talkativeness; ~sthema nt subject or topic (of conversation).

Gespür [gə'ʃpyːr] nt -s feeling.

Gestalt [gə'ʃtalt] f -, -en form, shape; (Person) figure; in ~ von in the form of; ~ annehmen take shape; g~en vt (formen) shape, form; (organisieren) arrange, organize; vr turn out (zu to be); ~ung f formation; organization.

geständig [gə'ʃtɛndɪç] a: ~ sein have confessed.

Geständnis [gə'ʃtɛntnɪs] nt -ses, -se confession.

Gestank [gə'ʃtaŋk] m -(e)s stench.

gestatten [gə'ʃtatən] vt permit, allow; ~ Sie? may I?; sich (dat) ~, etw zu tun take the liberty of doing sth.

Geste ['gɛstə] f -, -n gesture.

gestehen [gə'ʃteːən] vt irreg confess.

Gestein [gə'ʃtaɪn] nt -(e)s, -e rock.

Gestell [gə'ʃtɛl] nt -(e)s, -e frame; (Regal) rack, stand.

gestern ['gɛstərn] ad yesterday; ~ abend/morgen yesterday evening/ morning.

gestikulieren [gɛstiku'liːrən] vi gesticulate.

Gestirn [gə'ʃtɪrn] nt -(e)s, -e star; (Stern-bild) constellation.

Gestöber [gə'ʃtøːbər] nt -s, - flurry, blizzard.

Gesträuch [gə'ʃtrɔʏç] nt -(e)s, -e shrubbery, bushes pl.

gestreift [gə'ʃtraɪft] a striped.

gestrig ['gɛstrɪç] a yesterday's.

Gestrüpp [gəˈʃtrʏp] nt -(e)s, -e under-growth.

Gestüt [gəˈʃtyːt] nt -(e)s, -e stud farm.

Gesuch [gəˈzuːx] nt -(e)s, -e petition; (Antrag) application; g~t a (Comm) in demand; wanted; (fig) contrived.

gesund [gəˈzʊnt] a healthy; wieder ~ werden get better; G~heit f health(iness); G~heit! bless you!; ~heitlich a,ad health attr, physical; wie geht es Ihnen ~heitlich? how's your health?; ~heitsschädlich a unhealthy; G~heitswesen nt health service; G~heitszustand nt state of health.

Getöse [gəˈtøːzə] nt -s din, racket.

Getränk [gəˈtrɛŋk] nt -(e)s, -e drink.

getrauen [gəˈtrauən] vr dare, venture.

Getreide [gəˈtraidə] nt -s, - cereals pl, grain; ~speicher m granary.

getrennt [gəˈtrɛnt] a separate.

getreu [gəˈtrɔy] a faithful.

Getriebe [gəˈtriːbə] nt -s, - (Leute) bustle; (Aut) gearbox; ~öl nt transmission oil.

getrost [gəˈtroːst] ad without any bother; ~ sterben die in peace.

Getue [gəˈtuːə] nt -s fuss.

geübt [gəˈyːpt] a experienced.

Gewächs [gəˈvɛks] nt -es, -e growth; (Pflanze) plant.

gewachsen [gəˈvaksən] a: jdm/etw ~ sein be sb's equal/equal to sth.

Gewächshaus nt greenhouse.

gewagt [gəˈvaːkt] a daring, risky.

gewählt [gəˈvɛːlt] a Sprache refined, elegant.

Gewähr [gəˈvɛːr] f - guarantee; keine ~ übernehmen für accept no responsibility for; g~en vt grant; (geben) provide; g~leisten vt guarantee.

Gewahrsam [gəˈvaːrzaːm] m -s, -e safe-keeping; (Polizei~) custody.

Gewähr- cpd: ~smann m informant, source; ~ung f granting.

Gewalt [gəˈvalt] f -, -en power; (große Kraft) force; (~taten) violence; mit aller ~ with all one's might; ~anwendung f use of force; ~herrschaft f tyranny; g~ig a tremendous; Irrtum huge; ~marsch m forced march; g~sam a forcible; g~tätig a violent.

Gewand [gəˈvant] nt -(e)s, ¨er garment.

gewandt [gəˈvant] a deft, skilful; (erfahren) experienced; G~heit f dexterity, skill.

Gewässer [gəˈvɛsər] nt -s, - waters pl.

Gewebe [gəˈveːbə] nt -s, - (Stoff) fabric; (Biol) tissue.

Gewehr [gəˈveːr] nt -(e)s, -e gun; rifle; ~lauf m rifle barrel.

Geweih [gəˈvai] nt -(e)s, -e antlers pl.

Gewerb- [gəˈvɛrb] cpd: ~e nt -s, - trade, occupation; Handel und ~e trade and industry; ~eschule f technical school; g~etreibend a carrying on a trade; industrial; g~lich a industrial; trade attr; g~smäßig a professional; ~szweig m line of trade.

Gewerkschaft [gəˈvɛrkʃaft] f trade union;

~ler m -s, - trade unionist; ~sbund m trade unions federation.

Gewicht [gəˈvɪçt] nt -(e)s, -e weight; (fig) importance; g~ig a weighty.

gewieft [gəˈviːft] a, gewiegt [gəˈviːkt] a shrewd, cunning.

gewillt [gəˈvɪlt] a willing, prepared.

Gewimmel [gəˈvɪməl] nt -s swarm.

Gewinde [gəˈvɪndə] nt -s, - (Kranz) wreath; (von Schraube) thread.

Gewinn [gəˈvɪn] m -(e)s, -e profit; (bei Spiel) winnings pl; etw mit ~ verkaufen sell sth at a profit; ~beteiligung f profit-sharing; g~bringend a profitable; g~en vt irreg win; (erwerben) gain; Kohle, Öl extract; vi win; (profitieren) gain; an etw (dat) g~en gain in sth; g~end a winning, attractive; ~er(in f) m -s, - winner; ~spanne f profit margin; ~sucht f love of gain; ~(n)ummer f winning number; ~ung f winning; gaining; (von Kohle etc) extraction.

Gewirr [gəˈvɪr] nt -(e)s, -e tangle; (von Straßen) maze.

gewiß [gəˈvɪs] a,ad certain(ly).

Gewissen [gəˈvɪsən] nt -s, - conscience; g~haft a conscientious; ~haftigkeit f conscientiousness; g~los a unscrupulous; ~sbisse pl pangs of conscience pl, qualms pl; ~sfrage f matter of conscience; ~sfreiheit f freedom of con-science; ~skonflikt m moral conflict.

gewissermaßen [gəvɪsərˈmaːsən] ad more or less, in a way.

Gewiß- cpd: ~heit f certainty; g~lich ad surely.

Gewitter [gəˈvɪtər] nt -s, - thunderstorm; g~n vi impers: es gewittert there's a thunderstorm; g~schwül a sultry and thundery.

gewitzigt [gəˈvɪtsɪçt] a: ~ sein have learned by experience.

gewitzt [gəˈvɪtst] a shrewd, cunning.

gewogen [gəˈvoːgən] a well-disposed (+dat towards).

gewöhnen [gəˈvøːnən] vt: jdn an etw (acc) ~ accustom sb to sth; (erziehen zu) teach sb sth; vr: sich an etw (acc) ~ get used or accustomed to sth.

Gewohnheit [gəˈvoːnhait] f habit; (Brauch) custom; aus ~ from habit; zur ~ werden become a habit; ~s- in cpds habitual; ~smensch m creature of habit; ~srecht nt common law; ~stier nt (col) creature of habit.

gewöhnlich [gəˈvøːnlɪç] a usual; ordinary; (pej) common; wie ~ as usual.

gewohnt [gəˈvoːnt] a usual; etw ~ sein be used to sth.

Gewöhnung [gəˈvøːnʊŋ] f getting accustomed (an +acc to).

Gewölbe [gəˈvœlbə] nt -s, - vault.

Gewühl [gəˈvyːl] nt -(e)s throng.

Gewürz [gəˈvʏrts] nt -es, -e spice, seasoning; ~nelke f clove.

gezähnt [gəˈtsɛːnt] a serrated, toothed.

Gezeiten [gəˈtsaitən] pl tides pl.

Gezeter [gəˈtseːtər] nt -s clamour, yelling.

gezielt [gəˈtsiːlt] a with a particular aim in mind, purposeful; Kritik pointed.

geziemen [gə'tsiːmən] vr impers be fitting; ~d a proper.

geziert [gə'tsiːrt] a affected; **G~heit** f affectation.

Gezwitscher [gə'tsvɪtʃər] nt -s twitter(ing), chirping.

gezwungen [gə'tsvʊŋən] a forced; ~ermaßen ad of necessity.

Gicht [gɪçt] f- gout; **g~isch** a gouty.

Giebel ['giːbəl] m -s, - gable; ~dach nt gable(d) roof; ~fenster nt gable window.

Gier [giːr] f- greed; **g~ig** a greedy.

Gieß ['giːs] cpd: ~bach m torrent; **g~en** vt irreg pour; Blumen water; Metall cast; Wachs mould; ~e'rei f foundry; ~kanne f watering can.

Gift [gɪft] nt -(e)s, -e poison; **g~ig** a poisonous; (fig: boshaft) venomous; ~zahn m fang.

Gilde ['gɪldə] f -, -n guild.

Ginster ['gɪnstər] m -s, - broom.

Gipfel ['gɪpfəl] m -s, - summit, peak; (fig) height; **g~n** vi culminate; ~treffen nt summit (meeting).

Gips [gɪps] m -es, -e plaster (of Paris); ~abdruck m plaster cast; **g~en** vt plaster; ~figur f plaster figure; ~verband m plaster (cast).

Giraffe [gi'rafə] f -, -n giraffe.

Girlande [gɪr'landə] f -, -n garland.

Giro ['ʒiːro] nt -s, -s giro; ~konto nt current account.

girren ['gɪrən] vi coo.

Gischt [gɪʃt] m -(e)s, -e spray, foam.

Gitarre [gi'tarə] f -, -n guitar.

Gitter ['gɪtər] nt -s, - grating, bars pl; (für Pflanzen) trellis; (Zaun) railing(s); ~bett nt cot; ~fenster nt barred window; ~zaun m railing(s).

Glacéhandschuh [gla'seː:hant-ʃuː] m kid glove.

Gladiole [gladi'oːlə] f -, -n gladiolus.

Glanz [glants] m -es shine, lustre; (fig) splendour.

glänzen ['glɛntsən] vi shine (also fig), gleam; vt polish; ~d a shining; (fig) brilliant.

Glanz~ cpd: ~leistung f brilliant achievement; **g~los** a dull; ~zeit f heyday.

Glas [glaːs] nt -es, "er glass; ~bläser m -s, - glass blower; ~er m -s, - glazier; **g~ieren** [gla'ziːrən] vt glaze; **g~ig** a glassy; ~scheibe f pane; ~ur [gla'zuːr] f glaze; (Cook) icing.

glatt [glat] a smooth; (rutschig) slippery; Absage flat; Lüge downright; **G~eis** nt (black) ice; **jdn aufs G~eis führen** (fig) take sb for a ride.

Glätte ['glɛtə] f -, -n smoothness; slipperiness; **g~n** vt smooth out.

Glatze ['glatsə] f -, -n bald head; **eine ~ bekommen** go bald.

glatzköpfig a bald.

Glaube ['glaubə] m -ns, -n faith (an +acc in); belief (an +acc in); **g~n** vti believe (an +acc in, jdm sb); think; ~nsbekenntnis nt creed.

glaubhaft ['glaubhaft] a credible; **G~igkeit** f credibility.

gläubig ['glɔybɪç] a (Rel) devout; (vertrauensvoll) trustful; **G~e(r)** mf believer; **die G~en** the faithful; **G~er** m -s, - creditor.

glaubwürdig ['glaubvyrdɪç] a credible; Mensch trustworthy; **G~keit** f credibility; trustworthiness.

gleich [glaɪç] a (identisch) (the) same, identical; **es ist mir ~** it's all the same to me; **2 mal 2 ~ 4** 2 times 2 is or equals 4; ad equals; (sofort) straight away; (bald) in a minute; ~ **groß** the same size; ~ **nach/an** right after/at; ~**altrig** a of the same age; ~**artig** a similar; ~**bedeutend** a synonymous; ~**berechtigt** a having equal rights; **G~berechtigung** f equal rights pl; ~**bleibend** a constant; ~**en** vi irreg; **jdm/etw ~en** be like sb/sth; vr be alike; ~**ermaßen** ad equally; ~**falls** ad likewise; **danke ~falls!** the same to you; **G~förmigkeit** f uniformity; ~**gesinnt** a like-minded; **G~gewicht** nt equilibrium, balance; ~**gültig** a indifferent; (unbedeutend) unimportant; **G~gültigkeit** f indifference; **G~heit** f equality; ~**kommen** vi irreg +dat be equal to; **G~mache'rei** f egalitariansim; ~**mäßig** a even, equal; **G~mut** m equanimity; **G~nis** nt -ses, -se parable; ~**sam** ad as it were; ~**sehen** vi irreg (jdm) be or look like (sb); **G~strom** m (Elec) direct current; ~**tun** vi irreg: **es jdm ~tun** match sb; **G~ung** f equation; ~**viel** ad no matter; ~**wohl** ad nevertheless; ~**zeitig** a simultaneous.

Gleis [glaɪs] nt -es, -e track, rails pl; (Bahnsteig) platform.

Gleit- ['glaɪt] cpd: gliding; sliding; **g~en** vi irreg glide; (rutschen) slide; ~**flug** m glide; gliding.

Gletscher ['glɛtʃər] m -s, - glacier; ~spalte f crevasse.

Glied [gliːt] nt -(e)s, -er member; (Arm, Bein) limb; (von Kette) link; (Mil) rank(s); **g~ern** vt organize, structure; ~**erung** f structure, organization; ~**maßen** pl limbs pl.

Glimm- ['glɪm] cpd: **g~en** vi irreg glow, gleam; ~**er** m -s, - glow, gleam; (Mineral) mica; ~**stengel** m (col) fag.

glimpflich ['glɪmpflɪç] a mild, lenient; ~ **davonkommen** get off lightly.

glitzern ['glɪtsərn] vi glitter, twinkle.

Globus ['gloːbus] m - or -ses, **Globen** or -se globe.

Glöckchen ['glœkçən] nt (little) bell.

Glocke ['glɔkə] f -, -n bell; **etw an die große ~ hängen** (fig) shout sth from the rooftops; ~**ngeläut** nt peal of bells; ~**nspiel** nt chime(s); (Mus) glockenspiel.

Glorie ['gloːriə] f -, -n glory; (von Heiligen) halo.

Glosse ['glɔsə] f -, -n comment.

glotzen ['glɔtsən] vi (col) stare.

Glück [glyk] nt -(e)s luck, fortune; (Freude) happiness; ~ **haben** be lucky; **viel ~** good luck; **zum ~** fortunately;

g~en vi succeed; es glückte ihm, es zu bekommen he succeeded in getting it.

gluckern ['glukərn] vi glug.

Glück- cpd: g~lich a fortunate; (froh) happy; g~licherweise ad fortunately; ~sbringer m -s, - lucky charm; g~'selig a blissful; ~sfall m stroke of luck; ~skind nt lucky person; ~ssache f matter of luck; ~sspiel nt game of chance; ~sstern m lucky star; g~strahlend a radiant (with happiness); ~wunsch m congratulations pl, best wishes pl.

Glüh- [gly:] cpd: ~birne f light bulb; g~en vi glow; ~wein m mulled wine; ~würmchen nt glow-worm.

Glut [glu:t] f -, -en (Röte) glow; (Feuers~) fire; (Hitze) heat; (fig) ardour.

Gnade ['gna:də] f -, -n (Gunst) favour; (Erbarmen) mercy; (Milde) clemency; ~nfrist f reprieve, respite; ~ngesuch nt petition for clemency; ~nstoß m coup de grâce.

gnädig ['gnɛ:dɪç] a gracious; (voll Erbarmen) merciful.

Gold [gɔlt] nt -(e)s gold; g~en a golden; ~fisch m goldfish; ~grube f goldmine; ~regen m laburnum; ~schnitt m gilt edging; ~währung f gold standard.

Golf [gɔlf] m -(e)s, -e gulf; nt -s golf; ~platz m golf course; ~schläger m golf club; ~spieler m golfer; ~strom m Gulf Stream.

Gondel ['gɔndəl] f -, -n gondola; (Seilbahn) cable-car.

gönnen ['gœnən] vt: jdm etw ~ not begrudge sb sth; sich (dat) etw ~ allow oneself sth.

Gönner m -s, - patron; g~haft a patronizing; ~miene f patronizing air.

Gosse ['gɔsə] f -, -n gutter.

Gott [gɔt] m -es, "er god; um ~es Willen! for heaven's sake!; ~ sei Dank! thank God!; ~esdienst m service; ~eshaus nt place of worship; ~heit f deity.

Gött- [gœt] cpd: ~in f goddess; g~lich a divine.

Gott- cpd: g~los a godless; ~vertrauen nt trust in God.

Götze ['gœtsə] m -n, -n idol.

Grab [gra:p] nt -(e)s, "er grave; g~en ['gra:bən] vt irreg dig; ~en m -s, "- ditch; (Mil) trench; ~rede f funeral oration; ~stein m gravestone.

Grad [gra:t] m -(e)s, -e degree; ~einteilung f graduation; g~weise ad gradually.

Graf [gra:f] m -en, -en count, earl; ~schaft f county.

Gräfin ['grɛ:fɪn] f countess.

Gram [gra:m] m -(e)s grief, sorrow.

grämen ['grɛ:mən] vr grieve.

Gramm [gram] nt -s, -e gram(me); ~atik [-'matɪk] f grammar; g~atisch a grammatical; ~o'phon nt -s, -e gramophone.

Granat [gra'na:t] m -(e)s, -e (Stein) garnet; ~apfel m pomegranate; ~e f -, -n (Mil) shell; (Hand~) grenade.

Granit [gra'ni:t] m -s, -e granite.

graphisch ['gra:fɪʃ] a graphic; ~e Darstellung graph.

Gras [gra:s] nt -es, "er grass; g~en vi graze; ~halm m blade of grass; g~ig a grassy; ~narbe f turf.

grassieren [gra'si:rən] vi be rampant, rage.

gräßlich ['grɛslɪç] a horrible.

Grat [gra:t] m -(e)s, -e ridge.

Gräte ['grɛ:tə] f -, -n fishbone.

gratis ['gra:tɪs] a,ad free (of charge); G~probe f free sample.

Gratulation [gratulatsi'o:n] f congratulation(s).

gratulieren [gratu'li:rən] vi: jdm ~ (zu etw) congratulate sb (on sth); (ich) gratuliere! congratulations!

grau [grau] a grey; ~en vi (Tag) dawn; vi impers: es graut jdm vor etw sb dreads sth, sb is afraid of sth; vr: sich ~en vor dread, have a horror of; G~en nt -s horror; ~enhaft a horrible; ~haarig a grey-haired; ~meliert a grey-flecked.

grausam ['grauza:m] a cruel; G~keit f cruelty.

Grausen ['grauzən] nt -s horror; g~ vi impers, vr see grauen.

gravieren [gra'vi:rən] vt engrave; ~d a grave.

Grazie ['gra:tsiə] f -, -n grace.

graziös [gratsi'ø:s] a graceful.

greif- [graɪf] cpd: ~bar a tangible, concrete; in ~barer Nähe within reach; ~en vt irreg seize; grip; nach etw ~en reach for sth; um sich ~en (fig) spread; zu etw ~en (fig) turn to sth.

Greis [graɪs] m -es, -e old man; ~enalter nt old age; g~enhaft a senile.

grell [grɛl] a harsh.

Grenz- ['grɛnts] cpd: ~beamte(r) m frontier official; ~e f -, -n boundary; (Staats~) frontier; (Schranke) limit; g~en vi border (an +acc on); g~enlos a boundless; ~fall m borderline case; ~linie f boundary; ~übergang m frontier crossing.

Greuel ['grɔyəl] m -s, - horror, revulsion; etw ist jdm ein ~ sb loathes sth; ~tat f atrocity.

greulich ['grɔylɪç] a horrible.

griesgrämig ['gri:sgrɛ:mɪç] a grumpy.

Grieß [gri:s] m -es, -e (Cook) semolina.

Griff [grɪf] m -(e)s, -e grip; (Vorrichtung) handle; g~bereit a handy.

Griffel ['grɪfəl] m -s, - slate pencil; (Bot) style.

Grille ['grɪlə] f -, -n cricket; (fig) whim; g~n vt grill.

Grimasse [gri'masə] f -, -n grimace.

Grimm [grɪm] m -(e)s fury; g~ig a furious; (heftig) fierce, severe.

grinsen ['grɪnzən] vi grin.

Grippe ['grɪpə] f -, -n influenza, flu.

grob [gro:p] a coarse, gross; Fehler, Verstoß gross; G~heit f coarseness; coarse expression; G~ian ['gro:bia:n] m -s, -e ruffian; ~knochig a large-boned.

Groll [grɔl] m -(e)s resentment; g~en vi

bear ill will (+*dat or mit* towards); (*Donner*) rumble.

groß [gro:s] *a* big, large; (*hoch*) tall; (*fig*) great; **im** ~**en und ganzen** on the whole; *ad* greatly; ~**artig** *a* great, splendid; **G**~**aufnahme** *f* (*Cine*) close-up.

Größe ['grø:sə] *f* -, -**n** size; (*fig*) greatness; (*Länge*) height.

Groß- *cpd:* ~**einkauf** *m* bulk purchase; ~**eltern** *pl* grandparents *pl*; **g**~**enteils** *ad* mostly.

Größen- *cpd:* ~**unterschied** *m* difference in size; ~**wahn** *m* megalomania.

Groß- *cpd:* ~**format** *nt* large size; ~**handel** *m* wholesale trade; ~**händler** *m* wholesaler; **g**~**herzig** *a* generous; ~**macht** *f* great power; ~**maul** *m* braggart; ~**mut** *f* - magnanimity; **g**~**mütig** *a* magnanimous; ~**mutter** *f* grandmother; **g**~**spurig** *a* pompous; ~**stadt** *f* city, large town.

größte(r,s) [grø:stə(r,z)] *a superl* of **groß**; ~**nteils** *ad* for the most part.

Groß- *cpd:* ~**tuer** *m* -**s**, - boaster; **g**~**tun** *vi irreg* boast; ~**vater** *m* grandfather; **g**~**ziehen** *vt irreg* raise; **g**~**zügig** *a* generous; *Planung* on a large scale.

grotesk [gro'tɛsk] *a* grotesque.

Grotte ['grɔtə] *f* -, -**n** grotto.

Grübchen ['gry:pçən] *nt* dimple.

Grube ['gru:bə] *f* -, -**n** pit; mine; ~**narbeiter** *m* miner; ~**ngas** *nt* firedamp.

grübeln ['gry:bəln] *vi* brood.

Grübler ['gry:blər] *m* -**s**, - brooder; **g**~**isch** *a* brooding, pensive.

Gruft [gruft] *f* -, ¨e tomb, vault.

grün [gry:n] *a* green; **G**~**anlage** *f* park.

Grund [grunt] *m* ground; (*von See, Gefäß*) bottom; (*fig*) reason; **im** ~**e genommen** basically; ~**ausbildung** *f* basic training; ~**bedeutung** *f* basic meaning; ~**bedingung** *f* fundamental condition; ~**besitz** *m* land(ed property), real estate; ~**buch** *nt* land register; **g**~**ehrlich** *a* thoroughly honest.

gründ- [grynd] *cpd:* ~**en** *vt* found; ~**en auf** (+*acc*) base on; *vr* be based (*auf* +*dat* on); **G**~**er** *m* -**s**, - founder; ~**lich** *a* thorough; **G**~**ung** *f* foundation.

Grund- *cpd:* **g**~**falsch** *a* utterly wrong; ~**gebühr** *f* basic charge; ~**gedanke** *m* basic idea; ~**gesetz** *nt* constitution; ~**lage** *f* foundation; **g**~**legend** *a* fundamental; **g**~**los** *a* groundless; ~**mauer** *f* foundation wall; ~**regel** *f* basic rule; ~**riß** *m* plan; (*fig*) outline; ~**satz** *m* principle; **g**~**sätzlich** *a,ad* fundamental(ly); *Frage* of principle; (*prinzipiell*) on principle; ~**schule** *f* elementary school; ~**stein** *m* foundation stone; ~**steuer** *f* rates *pl*; ~**stück** *nt* estate; plot; **g**~**verschieden** *a* utterly different; ~**zug** *m* characteristic.

Grün- *cpd:* ~**e** *nt* -**n**; **im** ~**en** in the open air; ~**kohl** *m* kale; ~**schnabel** *m* greenhorn; ~**span** *m* verdigris; ~**streifen** *m* central reservation.

grunzen ['gruntsən] *vi* grunt.

Gruppe ['grupə] *f* -, -**n** group; **g**~**nweise** *ad* in groups.

gruppieren [gru'pi:rən] *vtr* group.

gruselig *a* creepy.

gruseln ['gru:zəln] *vi impers:* **es gruselt jdm vor etw** sth gives sb the creeps; *vr* have the creeps.

Gruß [gru:s] *m* -**es**, ¨e greeting; (*Mil*) salute; **viele e** best wishes; **e an** (+*acc*) regards to.

grüßen ['gry:sən] *vt* greet; (*Mil*) salute; **jdn von jdm** ~ give sb sb's regards; **jdn** ~ **lassen** send sb one's regards.

gucken ['gukən] *vi* look.

Gulasch ['gu:laʃ] *nt* -(**e**)**s**, -**e** goulash.

gültig ['gyltıç] *a* valid; **G**~**keit** *f* validity; **G**~**keitsdauer** *f* period of validity.

Gummi ['gumi] *nt or m* -**s**, -**s** rubber; (~*harze*) gum; (~*band nt*) rubber *or* elastic band; (*Hosen*—) elastic; **g**~**eren** [gu'mi:rən] *vt* gum; ~**knüppel** *m* rubber truncheon; ~**strumpf** *m* elastic stocking.

Gunst [gunst] *f* - favour.

günstig ['gynstıç] *a* favourable.

Gurgel ['gurgəl] *f* -, -**n** throat; **g**~**n** *vi* gurgle; (*im Mund*) gargle.

Gurke ['gurkə] *f* -, -**n** cucumber; **saure** ~ pickled cucumber, gherkin.

Gurt [gurt] *m* -(**e**)**s**, -**e**, **Gurte** *f* -**n** -**n** belt.

Gürtel ['gyrtəl] *m* -**s**, - belt; (*Geog*) zone; ~**reifen** *m* radial tyre.

Guß [gus] *m* -**sses**, **Güsse** casting; (*Regen*—) downpour; (*Cook*) glazing; ~**eisen** *nt* cast iron.

Gut [gu:t] *nt* -(**e**)**s**, ¨er (*Besitz*) possession; (*pl: Waren*) goods *pl*; **g**~ *a* good; *ad* well; **laß es g**~ **sein** that'll do; ~**achten** *nt* -**s**, - (*expert*) opinion; ~**achter** *m* -**s**, - expert; **g**~**artig** *a* good-natured; (*Med*) benign; **g**~**bürgerlich** *a a Küche* (good) plain; ~**dünken** *nt:* **nach** ~**dünken** at one's discretion.

Güte ['gy:tə] *f* - goodness, kindness; (*Qualität*) quality.

Güter- *cpd:* ~**abfertigung** *f* (*Rail*) goods office; ~**bahnhof** *m* goods station; ~**wagen** *m* goods waggon, freight car (*US*); ~ **zug** *m* goods train, freight train (*US*).

Gut- *cpd:* **g**~**gehen** *v impers irreg* work, come off; **es geht jdm g**~ sb's doing fine; **g**~**gelaunt** *a* good-humoured, in a good mood; **g**~**gemeint** *a* well meant; **g**~**gläubig** *a* trusting; ~**haben** *nt* -**s** credit; **g**~**heißen** *vt irreg* approve (of); **g**~**herzig** *a* kind(-hearted).

gütig ['gy:tıç] *a* kind.

gütlich ['gy:tlıç] *a* amicable.

Gut- *cpd:* **g**~**mütig** *a* good-natured; ~**mütigkeit** *f* good nature; ~**sbesitzer** *m* landowner; ~**schein** *m* voucher; **g**~**schreiben** *vt irreg* credit; ~**schrift** *f* credit; ~**sherr** *m* squire; **g**~**tun** *vi irreg:* **jdm g**~**tun** do sb good; **g**~**willig** *a* willing.

Gymnasium [gym'na:zium] *nt* grammar school (*Brit*), high school (*US*).

Gymnastik [gym'nastık] *f* exercises *pl*, keep fit.

H

H, h [ha:] *nt* H, h.

Haar [ha:r] *nt* **-(e)s, -e** hair; **um ein ~** nearly; **~bürste** *f* hairbrush; **h~en** *vir* lose hair; **~esbreite** *f*: **um ~esbreite** by a hair's-breadth; **h~genau** *ad* precisely; **h~ig** *a* hairy; (*fig*) nasty; **~klemme** *f* hair grip; **h~los** a hairless; **~nadel** *f* hairpin; **h~scharf** *ad beobachten* very sharply; *daneben* by a hair's breadth; **~schnitt** *m* haircut; **~schopf** *m* head of hair; **~spalte'rei** *f* hairsplitting; **~spange** *f* hair slide; **h~sträubend** a hair-raising; **~teil** *nt* hairpiece; **~waschmittel** *nt* shampoo.

Habe ['ha:bə] *f*- property.

haben ['ha:bən] *vt, v aux irreg* have; **Hunger/Angst ~** be hungry/afraid; **woher hast du das?** where did you get that from?; **was hast du denn?** what's the matter (with you)?; **H~** *nt* **-s, -** credit.

Habgier *f* avarice; **h~ig** a avaricious.

Habicht ['ha:bɪçt] *m* **-(e)s, -e** hawk.

Habseligkeiten *pl* belongings *pl*.

Hachse ['haksə] *f*-, **-n** (*Cook*) knuckle.

Hacke ['hakə] *f* -, **-n** hoe; (*Ferse*) heel; **h~n** *vt* hack, chop; *Erde* hoe.

Hackfleisch *nt* mince, minced meat.

Häcksel ['hɛksəl] *m or nt* **-s** chopped straw, chaff.

hadern ['ha:dərn] *vi* quarrel.

Hafen ['ha:fən] *m* **-s, ¨** harbour, port; **~arbeiter** *m* docker; **~damm** *m* jetty, mole; **~stadt** *f* port.

Hafer ['ha:fər] *m* **-s, -** oats *pl*; **~brei** *m* porridge; **~flocken** *pl* porridge oats *pl*; **~schleim** *m* gruel.

Haft [haft] *f* - custody; **h~bar** a liable, responsible; **~befehl** *m* warrant (of arrest); **h~en** *vi* stick, cling; **h~en für** be liable *or* responsible for; **h~enbleiben** *vi irreg* stick (*an* +*dat* to); **~pflicht** *f* liability; **~pflichtversicherung** *f* third party insurance; **~schalen** *pl* contact lenses *pl*; **~ung** *f* liability.

Hage- ['ha:gə] *cpd*: **~butte** *f* -, **-n** rose hip; **~dorn** *m* hawthorn.

Hagel ['ha:gəl] *m* **-s** hail; **h~n** *vi impers* hail.

hager ['ha:gər] a gaunt.

Häher ['hɛːər] *m* **-s, -** jay.

Hahn [ha:n] *m* **-(e)s, ¨e** cock; (*Wasser*—) tap, faucet (*US*).

Hähnchen ['hɛːnçən] *nt* cockerel; (*Cook*) chicken.

Hai(fisch) ['haı(fɪʃ)] *m* **-(e)s, -e** shark.

Häkchen ['hɛːkçən] *nt* small hook.

Häkel- ['hɛːkəl] *cpd*: **~arbeit** *f* crochet work; **h~n** *vt* crochet; **~nadel** *f* crochet hook.

Haken ['ha:kən] *m* **-s, -** hook; (*fig*) catch; **~kreuz** *nt* swastika; **~nase** *f* hooked nose.

halb [halp] a half; **~ eins** half past twelve; **ein ~es Dutzend** half a dozen; **H~dunkel** *nt* semi-darkness.

halber ['halbər] *prep* +*gen* (*wegen*) on account of; (*für*) for the sake of.

Halb- *cpd*: **~heit** *f* half-measure; **h~ieren** *vt* halve; **~insel** *f* peninsula; **h~jährlich** a half-yearly; **~kreis** *m* semicircle; **~kugel** *f* hemisphere; **h~laut** a in an undertone; **~links** *m* -, - (*Sport*) inside-left; **~mond** *m* half-moon; (*fig*) crescent; **h~offen** a half-open; **~rechts** *m* -, - (*Sport*) inside-right; **~schuh** *m* shoe; **~tagsarbeit** *f* part-time work; **h~wegs** *ad* half-way; **h~wegs besser** more or less better; **~wüchsige(r)** *mf* adolescent; **~zeit** *f* (*Sport*) half; (*Pause*) half-time.

Halde ['haldə] *f* -, **-n** tip; (*Schlacken*—) slag heap.

Hälfte ['hɛlftə] -, **-n** *f* half.

Halfter ['halftər] *f* -, **¨n**, *or nt* **-s, -** halter; (*Pistolen*—) holster.

Hall [hal] *m* **-(e)s, -e** sound.

Halle ['halə] *f* -, **-n** hall; (*Aviat*) hangar; **h~n** *vi* echo, resound; **~nbad** *nt* indoor swimming pool.

hallo [ha'lo:] *interj* hallo.

Halluzination [halutsinatsi'o:n] *f* hallucination.

Halm ['halm] *m* **-(e)s, -e** blade, stalk.

Hals [hals] *m* **-es, ¨e** neck; (*Kehle*) throat; **~ über Kopf** in a hurry; **~kette** *f* necklace; **~krause** *f* ruff; **~-Nasen-Ohren-Arzt** *m* ear nose and throat specialist; **~schlagader** *f* carotid artery; **~schmerzen** *pl* sore throat; **h~starrig** a stubborn, obstinate; **~tuch** *nt* scarf; **~weh** *nt* sore throat; **~wirbel** *m* cervical vertebra.

Halt [halt] *m* **-(e)s, -e** stop; (*fester* —) hold; (*innerer* —) stability; **h~!** stop!, halt!; **h~bar** a durable; *Lebensmittel* non-perishable; (*Mil*, *fig*) tenable; **~barkeit** *f* durability; (*non-*)perishability; tenability.

halten ['haltən] *irreg vt* keep; (*fest*—) hold; **~ für** regard as; **~ von** think of; *vi* hold; (*frisch bleiben*) keep; (*stoppen*) stop; **an sich ~** restrain oneself; *vr* (*frisch bleiben*) keep; (*sich behaupten*) hold out; **sich rechts/links ~** keep to the right/left.

Halt- *cpd*: **~estelle** *f* stop; **h~los** a unstable; **~losigkeit** *f* instability; **h~machen** *vi* stop; **~ung** *f* posture; (*fig*) attitude; (*Selbstbeherrschung*) composure; **~verbot** *nt* ban on stopping.

Halunke [ha'lʊŋkə] *m* **-n, -n** rascal.

hämisch ['hɛːmɪʃ] a malicious.

Hammel ['haməl] *m* **-s, ¨** *or* **-** wether; **~fleisch** *nt* mutton; **~keule** *f* leg of mutton.

Hammer ['hamər] *m* **-s, ¨** hammer.

hämmern ['hɛmərn] *vti* hammer.

Hampelmann ['hampəlman] *m* (*lit*, *fig*) puppet.

Hamster ['hamstər] *m* **-s, -** hamster; **~ei** [-'raı] *f* hoarding; **~er** *m* **-s, -** hoarder; **h~n** *vi* hoard.

Hand [hant] *f* -, **¨e** hand; **~arbeit** *f* manual work; (*Nadelarbeit*) needlework; **~arbeiter** *m* manual worker; **~besen** *m* brush; **~bremse** *f* handbrake; **~buch** *nt* handbook, manual.

Hände- ['hɛndə] *cpd*: **~druck** *m* handshake; **~klatschen** *nt* clapping, applause.

Handel ['handəl] m -s trade; (Geschäft) transaction; **haben** quarrel.
handeln ['handəln] vi trade; act; ~ **von** be about; vr impers: **sich** ~ **um** be a question of, be about; **h**~ nt -s action.
Handels- cpd: ~**bilanz** f balance of trade; **h**~**einig** a: **mit jdm h**~**einig werden** conclude a deal with sb; ~**kammer** f chamber of commerce; ~**marine** f merchant navy; ~**recht** nt commercial law; ~**reisende(r)** m commercial traveller; ~**schule** f business school; ~**vertreter** m sales representative.
Hand- cpd: ~**feger** m -s, - brush; **h**~**fest** a hefty; **h**~**gearbeitet** a handmade; ~**gelenk** nt wrist; ~**gemenge** nt scuffle; ~**gepäck** nt hand-luggage; **h**~**geschrieben** a handwritten; **h**~**greiflich** a palpable; **h**~**greiflich werden** become violent; ~**griff** m flick of the wrist; **h**~**haben** vt irreg insep handle; ~**karren** m handcart; ~**kuß** m kiss on the hand.
Händler ['hendlər] m -s, - trader, dealer.
handlich ['hantlıç] a handy.
Handlung ['handluŋ] f -, -en act(ion); (in Buch) plot; (Geschäft) shop; ~**sbevollmächtige(r)** mf authorized agent; ~**sweise** f manner of dealing.
Hand- cpd: ~**pflege** f manicure; ~**schelle** f handcuff; ~**schlag** m handshake; ~**schrift** f handwriting; (Text) manuscript; ~**schuh** m glove; ~**tasche** f handbag; ~**tuch** nt towel; ~**werk** nt trade, craft; ~**werker** m -s - craftsman, artisan; ~**werkzeug** nt tools pl.
Hanf [hanf] m -(e)s hemp.
Hang [haŋ] m -(e)s, ²e inclination; (Ab~) slope.
Hänge- ['hɛŋə] in cpds hanging; ~**brücke** f suspension bridge; ~**matte** f hammock.
hängen ['hɛŋən] irreg vi hang; ~ **an** (fig) be attached to; vt hang (an +acc on(to)); **sich** ~ **an** (+acc) hang on to, cling to; ~ **bleiben** vi irreg be caught (an +dat on); (fig) remain, stick.
Hängeschloß nt padlock.
hänseln ['hɛnzəln] vt tease.
hantieren [han'ti:rən] vi work, be busy; **mit etw** ~ handle sth.
hapern ['ha:pərn] vi impers: **es hapert an etw** (dat) sth leaves something to be desired.
Happen ['hapən] m -s, - mouthful.
Harfe ['harfə] f -, -n harp.
Harke ['harkə] f -, -n rake; **h**~n vti rake.
harmlos ['harmlo:s] a harmless; **H**~**igkeit** f harmlessness.
Harmonie [harmo'ni:] f harmony; **h**~**ren** vi harmonize.
Harmonika [har'mo:nika] f -, -s (Zieh~) concertina.
harmonisch [har'mo:nıʃ] a harmonious.
Harmonium [har'mo:nium] nt -s, -nien or -s harmonium.
Harn ['harn] m -(e)s, -e urine; ~**blase** f bladder.
Harnisch ['harnıʃ] m -(e)s, -e armour; **jdn in** ~ **bringen** infuriate sb; **in** ~ **geraten** become angry.

Harpune [har'pu:nə] f -, -n harpoon.
harren ['harən] vi wait (auf +acc for).
hart [hart] a hard; (fig) harsh.
Härte ['hɛrtə] f -, -n hardness; (fig) harshness; **h**~n vtr harden.
hart- cpd: ~**gekocht** a hard-boiled; ~**gesotten** a tough, hard-boiled; ~**herzig** a hard-hearted; ~**näckig** a stubborn; **H**~**näckigkeit** f stubbornness.
Harz [ha:rts] nt -es, -e resin.
Haschee [ha'ʃe:] nt -s, -s hash.
haschen ['haʃən] vt catch, snatch; vi (col) smoke hash.
Haschisch ['haʃıʃ] nt - hashish.
Hase ['ha:zə] m -n, -n hare.
Haselnuß ['ha:zəlnus] f hazelnut.
Hasen- cpd: ~**fuß** m coward; ~**scharte** f harelip.
Haspe ['haspə] f -, -n hinge; ~**l** f -, -n reel, bobbin; (Winde) winch.
Haß [has] m -sses hate, hatred.
hassen ['hasən] vt hate; ~**enswert** a hateful.
häßlich ['hɛslıç] a ugly; (gemein) nasty; **H**~**keit** f ugliness; nastiness.
Hast [hast] f - haste; **h**~en vir rush; **h**~**ig** a hasty.
hätscheln ['hɛtʃəln] vt pamper; (zärtlich) cuddle.
Haube ['haubə] f -, -n hood; (Mütze) cap; (Aut) bonnet, hood (US).
Hauch [haux] m -(e)s, -e breath; (Luft~) breeze; (fig) trace; **h**~en vi breathe; **h**~**fein** a very fine.
Haue ['hauə] f -, -n hoe, pick; (col) hiding; **h**~n vt irreg hew, cut; (col) thrash.
Haufen ['haufən] m -s, - heap; (Leute) crowd; **ein** ~ (x) (col) loads or a lot (of x); **auf einem** ~ in one heap; **h**~**weise** ad in heaps; in droves; **etw h**~**weise haben** have piles of sth.
häufen ['hɔyfən] vt pile up; vr accumulate.
häufig ['hɔyfıç] a,ad frequent(ly); **H**~**keit** f frequency.
Haupt [haupt] nt -(e)s, Häupter head; (Ober~) chief; in cpds main; ~**bahnhof** m central station; **h**~**beruflich** ad as one's main occupation; ~**buch** nt (Comm) ledger; ~**darsteller(in** f) m leading actor/actress; ~**eingang** m main entrance; ~**fach** nt main subject; ~**film** m main film.
Häuptling ['hɔyptlıŋ] m chief(tain).
Haupt- cpd: ~**mann** m, pl -leute (Mil) captain; ~**postamt** nt main post office; ~**quartier** nt headquarters pl; ~**rolle** f leading part; ~**sache** f main thing; **h**~**sächlich** a,ad chief(ly); ~**satz** m main clause; ~**schlagader** f aorta; ~**stadt** f capital; ~**straße** f main street; ~**wort** nt noun.
Haus [haus] nt -es, Häuser house; **nach** ~**e** home; **zu** ~**e** at home; ~**angestellte** f domestic servant; ~**arbeit** f housework; (Sch) homework; ~**arzt** m family doctor; ~**aufgabe** f (Sch) homework; ~**besitzer(in** f) m, ~**eigentümer(in** f) m house-owner.
hausen ['hauzən] vi live (in poverty); (pej) wreak havoc.

Häuser- ['hɔʏzər] *cpd:* ~**block** *m* block (of houses); ~**makler** *m* estate agent.

Haus- *cpd:* ~**frau** *f* housewife; ~**freund** *m* family friend; (*col*) lover; **h**~**gemacht** *a* home-made; ~**halt** *m* household; (*Pol*) budget; **h**~**halten** *vi irreg* keep house; (*sparen*) economize; ~**hälterin** *f* housekeeper; ~**haltsgeld** *nt* housekeeping (money); ~**haltsgerät** *nt* domestic appliance; ~**haltsplan** *m* budget; ~**haltung** *f* housekeeping; ~**herr** *m* host; (*Vermieter*) landlord; **h**~**hoch** *ad:* **h**~**hoch verlieren** lose by a mile.

hausieren [hau'ziːrən] *vi* hawk, peddle.

Hausierer *m* **-s,** **-** hawker, peddlar.

häuslich ['hɔʏslıç] *a* domestic; **H**~**keit** *f* domesticity.

Haus- *cpd:* ~**meister** *m* caretaker, janitor; ~**ordnung** *f* house rules *pl;* ~**putz** *m* house cleaning; ~**schlüssel** *m* front-door key; ~**schuh** *m* slipper; ~**suchung** *f* police raid; ~**tier** *nt* domestic animal; ~**verwalter** *m* caretaker; ~**wirt** *m* landlord; ~**wirtschaft** *f* domestic science.

Haut [haut] *f* **-,** **Häute** skin; (*Tier*—) hide.

häuten ['hɔʏtən] *vt* skin; *vr* slough one's skin.

Haut- *cpd:* **h**~**eng** *a* skin-tight; ~**farbe** *f* complexion.

Haxe ['haksə] *f* **-,** **-n** *see* **Hachse.**

Hebamme ['heːpʔamə] *f* **-,** **-n** midwife.

Hebel ['heːbəl] *m* **-s,** **-** lever.

heben ['heːbən] *vt irreg* raise, lift.

hecheln ['hɛçəln] *vi* (*Hund*) pant.

Hecht [hɛçt] *m* **-(e)s,** **-e** pike.

Heck [hɛk] *nt* **-(e)s,** **-e** stern; (*von Auto*) rear.

Hecke ['hɛkə] *f* **-,** **-n** hedge; ~**nrose** *f* dog rose; ~**schütze** *m* sniper.

Heer [heːr] *nt* **-(e)s,** **-e** army.

Hefe ['heːfə] *f* **-,** **-n** yeast.

Heft [hɛft] *nt* **-(e)s,** **-e** exercise book; (*Zeitschrift*) number; (*von Messer*) haft; **h**~**en** *vt* fasten (*an* +*acc* to); (*nähen*) tack; ~**er** *m* **-s,** **-** folder.

heftig *a* fierce, violent; **H**~**keit** *f* fierceness, violence.

Heft- *cpd:* ~**klammer** *f* paper clip; ~**maschine** *f* stapling machine; ~**pflaster** *nt* sticking plaster; ~**zwecke** *f* drawing pin.

hegen ['heːgən] *vt* nurse; (*fig*) harbour, foster.

Hehl [heːl] *m or nt:* **kein(en)** ~ **aus etw** (*dat*) **machen** make no secret of sth; ~**er** *m* **-s,** **-** receiver (of stolen goods), fence.

Heide ['haidə] *f* **-,** **-n** heath, moor; (—*kraut*) heather; *m* **-n, -n, Heidin** *f* heathen, pagan; ~**kraut** *nt* heather; ~**lbeere** *f* bilberry; **h**~**nmäßig** *a* (*col*) terrific; ~**ntum** *nt* paganism.

heidnisch ['haidnıʃ] *a* heathen, pagan.

heikel ['haikəl] *a* awkward, thorny; (*wählerisch*) fussy.

Heil [hail] *nt* **-(e)s** well-being; (*Seelen*—) salvation; **h**~ *a* in one piece, intact; **h**~ *interj* hail; ~**and** *m* **-(e)s, -e** saviour; **h**~**bar** *a* curable; **h**~**en** *vt* cure; *vi* heal;

h~**froh** *a* very relieved; ~**gymnastin** *f* physiotherapist.

heilig ['hailıç] *a* holy; **H**~**abend** *m* Christmas Eve; **H**~**e(r)** *mf* saint; ~**en** *vt* sanctify, hallow; **H**~**enschein** *m* halo; **H**~**keit** *f* holiness; ~**sprechen** *vt irreg* canonize; **H**~**tum** *nt* shrine; (*Gegenstand*) relic.

Heil- *cpd:* **h**~**los** *a* unholy; ~**mittel** *nt* remedy; **h**~**sam** *a* (*fig*) salutary; ~**sarmee** *f* Salvation Army; ~**ung** *f* cure.

Heim [haim] *nt* **-(e),** **-e** home; **h**~ *ad* home.

Heimat ['haimaːt] *f* **-,** **-en** home (town/country *etc*); ~**land** *nt* homeland; **h**~**lich** *a* native, home *attr;* (*Gefühle*) nostalgic; **h**~**los** *a* homeless; ~**ort** *m* home town/area; ~**vertriebene(r)** *mf* displaced person.

Heim- *cpd:* **h**~**begleiten** *vt* accompany home; **h**~**elig** *a* homely; **h**~**fahren** *vi irreg* drive/go home; ~**fahrt** *f* journey home; ~**gang** *m* return home; (*Tod*) decease; **h**~**gehen** *vi irreg* go home; (*sterben*) pass away; **h**~**isch** *a* (*gebürtig*) native; **sich h**~**isch fühlen** feel at home; ~**kehr** *f* **-, -en** homecoming; **h**~**kehren** *vi irreg* return home; **h**~**lich** *a* secret; ~**lichkeit** *f* secrecy; ~**reise** *f* journey home; **h**~**suchen** *vt* afflict; (*Geist*) haunt; **h**~**tückisch** *a* malicious; **h**~**wärts** *ad* homewards; ~**weg** *m* way home; ~**weh** *nt* homesickness; ~**weh haben be** homesick; **h**~**zahlen** *vt:* **jdm etw h**~**zahlen** pay back sb for sth.

Heirat ['hairaːt] *f* **-, -en** marriage; **h**~**en** *vti* marry; ~**santrag** *m* proposal.

heiser ['haizər] *a* hoarse; **H**~**keit** *f* hoarseness.

heiß [hais] *a* hot; ~**e(r) Draht** hot line; ~**blütig** *a* hot-blooded.

heißen ['haisən] *irreg vi* be called; (*bedeuten*) mean; *vt* command; (*nennen*) name; *v impers* it says; it is said.

Heiß- *cpd:* **h**~**ersehnt** *a* longed for; ~**hunger** *m* ravenous hunger; **h**~**laufen** *vir irreg* overheat.

heiter ['haitər] *a* cheerful; *Wetter* bright; **H**~**keit** *f* cheerfulness; (*Belustigung*) amusement.

Heiz- ['haits] *cpd:* **h**~**bar** *a* heated; *Raum* with heating; **leicht h**~**bar** easily heated; ~**decke** *f* electric blanket; **h**~**en** *vt* heat; ~**er** *m* **-s,** **-** stoker; ~**körper** *m* radiator; ~**öl** *nt* fuel oil; ~**sonne** *f* electric fire; ~**ung** *f* heating; ~**ungsanlage** *f* heating system.

hektisch ['hɛktıʃ] *a* hectic.

Held [hɛlt] *m* **-en, -en** hero; ~**in** *f* heroine.

helfen ['hɛlfən] *irreg vi* help (*jdm* sb, *bei* with); (*nützen*) be of use; **sich** (*dat*) **zu** ~ **wissen** be resourceful; *v impers:* **es hilft nichts, du mußt . . .** it's no use, you have to . . .

Helfer *m* **-s,** **-** helper, assistant; ~**shelfer** *m* accomplice.

hell [hɛl] *a* clear, bright; *Farbe* light; ~**blau** *a* light blue; ~**blond** *a* ash-blond;

H~e *f* - clearness, brightness; H~er *m* -s, - farthing; ~hörig *a* keen of hearing; *Wand* poorly soundproofed; H~igkeit *f* clearness, brightness; lightness; H~seher *m* clairvoyant; ~wach *a* wide-awake.

Helm ['hɛlm] *m* -(e)s, -e (*auf Kopf*) helmet.

Hemd [hɛmt] *nt* -(e)s, -en shirt; (*Unter—*) vest; ~bluse *f* blouse; ~enknopf *m* shirt button.

hemmen ['hɛmən] *vt* check, hold up; **gehemmt sein** be inhibited.

Hemmung *f* check; (*Psych*) inhibition; h~slos *a* unrestrained, without restraint.

Hengst [hɛŋst] *m* -es, -e stallion.

Henkel ['hɛŋkəl] *m* -s, - handle; ~krug *m* jug.

henken ['hɛŋkən] *vt* hang.

Henker *m* -s, - hangman.

Henne ['hɛnə] *f* -, -n hen.

her [heːr] *ad* here; (*Zeit*) ago; ~ **damit!** hand it over!

herab [hɛ'rap] *ad* down(ward(s)); ~hängen *vi irreg* hang down; ~lassen *irreg vt* let down; *vr* condescend; H~lassung *f* condescension; ~sehen *vi irreg* look down (*auf +acc on*); ~setzen *vt* lower, reduce; (*fig*) belittle, disparage; H~setzung *f* reduction; disparagement; ~würdigen *vt* belittle, disparage.

heran [hɛ'ran] *ad:* **näher ~!** come up closer!; ~ **zu mir!** come up to me!; ~bilden *vt* train; ~bringen *vt irreg* bring up (*an +acc to*); ~fahren *vi irreg* drive up (*an +acc to*); ~kommen *vi irreg* (*an +acc*) approach, come near; ~machen *vr:* **sich an jdn ~machen** make up to sb; ~wachsen *vi irreg* grow up; ~ziehen *vt irreg* pull nearer; (*aufziehen*) raise; (*ausbilden*) train; **jdn zu etw ~ziehen** call upon sb to help in sth.

herauf [hɛ'rauf] *ad* up(ward(s)), up here; ~beschwören *vt irreg* conjure up, evoke; ~bringen *vt irreg* bring up; ~ziehen *irreg vt* draw or pull up; *vi* approach; (*Sturm*) gather.

heraus [hɛ'raus] *ad* out; outside; from; ~arbeiten *vt* work out; ~bekommen *vt irreg* get out; (*fig*) find or figure out; ~bringen *vt irreg* bring out; *Geheimnis* elicit; ~finden *vt irreg* find out; ~fordern *vt* challenge; H~forderung *f* challenge; provocation; ~geben *vt irreg* give up, surrender; *Geld* give back; *Buch* edit; (*veröffentlichen*) publish; ~geber *m* -s, - editor; (*Verleger*) publisher; ~gehen *vi irreg:* **aus sich (*dat*) ~gehen** come out of one's shell; ~halten *vr irreg:* **sich aus etw ~halten** keep out of sth; ~hängen *vti irreg* hang out; ~holen *vt* get out (*aus of*); ~kommen *vi irreg* come out; **dabei kommt nichts ~** nothing will come of it; ~nehmen *vt irreg* take out; **sich (*dat*) Freiheiten ~nehmen** take liberties; ~reißen *vt irreg* tear out; pull out; ~rücken *vt Geld* fork out, hand over; **mit etw ~rücken** (*fig*) come out with sth; ~rutschen *vi* slip out; ~schlagen *vt irreg* knock out; (*fig*) obtain; ~stellen *vr*

turn out (*als* to be); ~wachsen *vi irreg* grow out (*aus of*); ~ziehen *vt irreg* pull out, extract.

herb [hɛrp] *a* (slightly) bitter, acid; *Wein* dry; (*fig*) (*schmerzlich*) bitter; (*streng*) stern, austere.

herbei [hɛr'baɪ] *ad* (over) here; ~führen *vt* bring about; ~lassen *vr irreg:* **sich ~lassen zu** condescend or deign to; ~schaffen *vt* procure.

herbemühen ['hɛrbəmyːən] *vr* take the trouble to come.

Herberge ['hɛrbɛrgə] *f* -, -n shelter; hostel, inn.

Herbergsmutter *f*, **Herbergsvater** *m* warden.

her- ['hɛr] *cpd:* ~bitten *vt irreg* ask to come (here); ~bringen *vt irreg* bring here.

Herbst [hɛrpst] *m* -(e)s, -e autumn, fall (*US*); h~lich *a* autumnal.

Herd [heːrt] *m* -(e)s, -e cooker; (*fig, Med*) focus, centre.

Herde ['heːrdə] *f* -, -n herd; (*Schaf—*) flock.

herein [hɛ'raɪn] *ad* in (here); here; ~! come in!; ~bitten *vt irreg* ask in; ~brechen *vi irreg* set in; ~bringen *vt irreg* bring in; ~dürfen *vi irreg* have permission to enter; H~fall *m* letdown; ~fallen *vi irreg* be caught, taken in; ~fallen *auf* (*+acc*) fall for; ~kommen *vi irreg* come in; ~lassen *vt irreg* admit; ~legen *vt:* **jdn ~legen** take sb in; ~platzen *vi* burst in.

Her- ['hɛr] *cpd:* ~fahrt *f* journey here; h~fallen *vi irreg:* **h~fallen über** fall upon; ~gang *m* course of events, circumstances *pl;* h~geben *vt irreg* give, hand (over); **sich zu etw h~geben** lend one's name to sth; h~gehen *vi irreg:* **hinter jdm h~gehen** follow sb; **es geht hoch h~** there are a lot of goings-on; h~halten *vt irreg* hold out; h~halten **müssen** (*col*) have to suffer; h~hören *vi* listen; **hör mal h~!** listen here!

Hering ['heːrɪŋ] *m* -s, -e herring.

her- ['hɛr] *cpd:* ~kommen *vi irreg* come; **komm mal ~!** come here!; ~kömmlich *a* traditional; H~kunft *f* -, -künfte origin; ~laufen *vi irreg;* ~laufen **hinter** (*+dat*) run after; ~leiten *vr* derive; ~machen *vr:* **sich ~machen über** (*+acc*) set about or upon.

Hermelin [hɛrmə'liːn] *m or nt* -s, -e ermine.

hermetisch [hɛr'meːtɪʃ] *a,ad* hermetic(ally).

her- *cpd:* ~'nach *ad* afterwards; ~'nieder *ad* down.

heroisch [he'roːɪʃ] *a* heroic.

Herold ['heːrɔlt] *m* -(e)s, -e herald.

Herr [hɛr] *m* -(e)n, -en master; (*Mann*) gentleman; (*adliger, Rel*) Lord; (*vor Namen*) Mr.; **mein ~!** sir!; **meine ~en!** gentlemen!; ~enbekanntschaft *f* gentleman friend; ~endoppel *nt* men's doubles; ~eneinzel *nt* men's singles; ~enhaus *nt* mansion; h~enlos *a* ownerless.

herrichten ['hɛrrɪçtən] *vt* prepare.

Herr- *cpd:* **~in** *f* mistress; **h~isch** *a* domineering; **h~lich** *a* marvellous, splendid; **~lichkeit** *f* splendour, magnificence; **~schaft** *f* power, rule; *(Herr und Herrin)* master and mistress; **meine ~schaften!** ladies and gentlemen!

herrschen ['hɛrʃən] *vt* rule; *(bestehen)* prevail, be.

Herrscher(in *f)* *m* **-s,** **-** ruler.

Herrschsucht *f* domineering behaviour.

her- ['hɛr] *cpd:* **~rühren** *vi* arise, originate; **~sagen** *vt* recite; **~stammen** *vi* descend, come from; **~stellen** *vt* make, manufacture; **H~steller** *m* **-s, -** manufacturer; **H~stellung** *f* manufacture; **H~stellungskosten** *pl* manufacturing costs *pl*.

herüber [hɛ'ry:bər] *ad* over (here), across.

herum [hɛ'rʊm] *ad* about, (a)round; **um etw ~** around sth; **~ärgern** *vr* get annoyed *(mit* with); **~führen** *vt* show around; **~gehen** *vi irreg* walk or go round *(um etw* sth); walk about; **~irren** *vi* wander about; **~kriegen** *vt* bring or talk around; **~lungern** *vi* lounge about; **~sprechen** *vr irreg* get around, be spread; **~treiben** *vir irreg* drift about; **~ziehen** *vir irreg* wander about.

herunter [hɛ'rʊntər] *ad* downward(s), down (there); **~gekommen** *a* run-down; **~hängen** *vi irreg* hang down; **~holen** *vt* bring down; **~kommen** *vi irreg* come down; *(fig)* come down in the world; **~machen** *vt* take down; *(schimpfen)* abuse, criticise severely.

hervor [hɛr'fo:r] *ad* out, forth; **~brechen** *vi irreg* burst forth, break out; **~bringen** *vt irreg* produce; *Wort* utter; **~gehen** *vi irreg* emerge, result; **~heben** *vt irreg* stress; *(als Kontrast)* set off; **~ragend** *a* excellent; *(lit)* projecting; **~rufen** *vt irreg* cause, give rise to; **~treten** *vi irreg* come out.

Herz [hɛrts] *nt* **-ens, -en** heart; **~anfall** *m* heart attack; **h~en** *vt* caress, embrace; **~enslust** *f:* **nach ~enslust** to one's heart's content; **~fehler** *m* heart defect; **h~haft** *a* hearty; **~infarkt** *m* heart attack; **~klopfen** *nt* palpitation; **h~lich** *a* cordial; **h~lichen Glückwunsch** congratulations *pl*; **h~liche Grüße** best wishes; **~lichkeit** *f* cordiality; **h~los** *a* heartless; **~losigkeit** *f* heartlessness.

Herzog ['hɛrtso:k] *m* **-(e)s,** **ʺe** duke; **~in** *f* duchess; **h~lich** *a* ducal; **~tum** *nt* duchy.

Herz- *cpd:* **~schlag** *m* heartbeat; *(Med)* heart attack; **h~zerreißend** *a* heartrending.

heterogen [hetero'ge:n] *a* heterogeneous.

Hetze ['hɛtsə] *f* **-, -n** *(Eile)* rush; **h~n** *vt* hunt; *(verfolgen)* chase; **jdn/etw auf jdn/etw ~** set sb/sth on sb/sth; *vi (eilen)* rush; **h~n gegen** stir up feeling against; **h~n zu** agitate for; **~rei** *f* agitation; *(Eile)* rush.

Heu [hɔy] *nt* **-(e)s** hay; **~boden** *m* hayloft.

Heuchelei [hɔyçə'lai] *f* hypocrisy.

heucheln ['hɔyçəln] *vt* pretend, feign; *vi* be hypocritical.

Heuchler(in *f)* [hɔyçlər(ın)] *m* **-s, -** hypocrite; **h~isch** *a* hypocritical.

Heuer ['hɔyər] *f* **-, -n** *(Naut)* pay; **h~** *ad* this year.

Heugabel *f* pitchfork.

heulen ['hɔylən] *vi* howl; cry; **das ~de Elend bekommen** get the blues.

heurig ['hɔyrıç] *a* this year's.

Heu- *cpd:* **~schnupfen** *m* hay fever; **~schrecke** *f* grasshopper, locust.

heute ['hɔytə] *ad* today; **~ abend/früh** this evening/morning; **das H~** today.

heutig ['hɔytıç] *a* today's.

heutzutage ['hɔyttsu:ta:gə] *ad* nowadays.

Hexe ['hɛksə] *f* **-, -n** witch; **h~n** *vi* practise witchcraft; **ich kann doch nicht h~n** I can't work miracles; **~nkessel** *m* *(lit, fig)* cauldron; **~nmeister** *m* wizard; **~nschuß** *m* lumbago; **~rei** *f* witchcraft.

Hieb [hi:p] *m* **-(e)s, -e** blow; *(Wunde)* cut, gash; *(Stichelei)* cutting remark; **~e bekommen** get a thrashing.

hier [hi:r] *ad* here; **~auf** *ad* thereupon; *(danach)* after that; **~behalten** *vt irreg* keep here; **~bei** *ad* herewith, enclosed; **~bleiben** *vi irreg* stay here; **~durch** *ad* by this means; *(örtlich)* through here; **~her** *ad* this way, here; **~lassen** *vt irreg* leave here; **~mit** *ad* hereby; **~nach** *ad* hereafter; **~von** *ad* about this, hereof; **~zulande** *ad* in this country.

hiesig ['hi:zıç] *a* of this place, local.

Hilfe ['hılfə] *f* **-, -n** help; aid; **Erste ~** first aid; **~!** help!

Hilf- *cpd:* **h~los** *a* helpless; **~losigkeit** *f* helplessness; **h~reich** *a* helpful; **~saktion** *f* relief measures *pl*; **~sarbeiter** *m* labourer; **h~sbedürftig** *a* needy; **h~sbereit** *a* ready to help; **~skraft** *f* assistant, helper; **~sschule** *f* school for backward children; **~szeitwort** *nt* auxiliary verb.

Himbeere ['hımbe:rə] *f* **-, -n** raspberry.

Himmel ['hıməl] *m* **-s, -** sky; *(Rel, liter)* heaven; **h~angst** *a:* **es ist mir h~angst** I'm scared to death; **h~blau** *a* sky-blue; **~fahrt** *f* Ascension; **h~schreiend** *a* outrageous; **~srichtung** *f* direction.

himmlisch ['hımlıʃ] *a* heavenly.

hin [hın] *ad* there; **~ und her** to and fro; **bis zur Mauer ~** up to the wall; **Geld ~, Geld her** money or no money; **mein Glück ist ~** my happiness has gone.

hinab [hı'nap] *ad* down; **~gehen** *vi* go down; **~sehen** *vi irreg* look down.

hinauf [hı'nauf] *ad* up; **~arbeiten** *vr* work one's way up; **~steigen** *vi irreg* climb.

hinaus [hı'naus] *ad* out; **~befördern** *vt* kick/throw out; **~gehen** *vi irreg* go out; **~gehen über** (+acc) exceed; **~laufen** *vi irreg* run out; **~laufen auf** (+acc) come to, amount to; **~schieben** *vt irreg* put off, postpone; **~werfen** *vt irreg* throw out; **~wollen** *vi* want to go out; **~wollen auf** (+acc) drive at, get at; **~ziehen** *irreg vt* draw out; *vr* be protracted.

Hinblick ['hınblık] *m:* **in** or **im ~ auf** (+acc) in view of.

hinder- ['hındər] *cpd:* **~lich** *a* awkward;

~**n** vt hinder, hamper; **jdn an etw** (dat)
~**n** prevent sb from doing sth; **H~nis** nt
-**ses**, -**se** obstacle.

hindeuten ['hɪndɔytən] vi point (auf +acc
to).

hindurch [hɪn'dʊrç] ad through; across;
(zeitlich) over.

hinein [hɪ'naɪn] ad in; ~**fallen** vi irreg fall
in; ~**fallen in** (+acc) fall into; ~**gehen**
vi irreg go in; ~**gehen in** (+acc) go into,
enter; ~**geraten** vi irreg: ~**geraten in**
(+acc) get into; ~**passen** vi fit in;
~**passen in** (+acc) fit into; ~**reden** vi:
jdm ~**reden** interfere in sb's affairs;
~**steigern** vr get worked up;
~**versetzen** vr: **sich** ~**versetzen in**
(+acc) put oneself in the position of.

hin- ['hɪn] cpd: ~**fahren** irreg vi go; drive;
vt take; drive; **H~fahrt** f journey there;
~**fallen** vi irreg fall down; ~**fällig** a
frail, decrepit; Regel etc unnecessary,
otiose; **H~gabe** f devotion; ~**geben** vr
irreg +dat give oneself up to, devote
oneself to; ~**gehen** vi irreg (Zeit) pass;
~**halten** vt irreg hold out; (warten lassen)
put off, stall.

hinken ['hɪŋkən] vi limp; (Vergleich) be
unconvincing.

hin- ['hɪn] cpd: ~**legen** vt put down; vr lie
down; ~**nehmen** vt irreg (fig) put up
with, take; ~**reichen** vi be adequate; vt:
jdm etw ~**reichen** hand sb sth;
H~reise f journey out; ~**reißen** vt irreg
carry away, enrapture; **sich** ~**reißen
lassen, etw zu tun** get carried away and
do sth; ~**richten** vt execute;
H~richtung f execution; ~**sichtlich**
prep +gen with regard to; **H~spiel** nt
(Sport) first leg; ~**stellen** vt put (down);
vr place o.s.

hintanstellen [hɪnt'anʃtɛlən] vt (fig)
ignore.

hinten ['hɪntən] ad at the back; behind;
~**herum** ad round the back; (fig)
secretly.

hinter ['hɪntər] prep +dat or acc behind;
(nach) after; ~ **jdm hersein** be after sb;
H~achse f rear axle; **H~bein** nt hind
leg; **sich auf die H~beine stellen** get
tough; **H~bliebene(r)** mf surviving
relative; ~**drein** ad afterwards; ~**e(r,s)**
a rear, back; ~**einander** ad one after the
other; **H~gedanke** m ulterior motive;
~**gehen** vt irreg deceive; **H~grund** m
background; **H~halt** m ambush;
~**hältig** a underhand, sneaky; ~**her** ad
afterwards, after; **H~hof** m backyard;
H~kopf m back of one's head; ~'**lassen**
vt irreg leave; **H~'lassenschaft** f
(testator's) estate; ~'**legen** vt deposit;
H~list f cunning, trickery; (Handlung)
trick, dodge; ~**listig** a cunning, crafty;
H~mann m, pl ~**männer** person
behind; **H~rad** nt back wheel;
H~radantrieb m (Aut) rear wheel drive;
~**rücks** ad from behind; **H~teil** nt
behind; **H~treffen** nt: **ins H~treffen
kommen** lose ground; ~'**treiben** vt irreg
prevent, frustrate; **H~tür** f back door;
(fig: Ausweg) escape, loophole; ~'**ziehen**

vt irreg Steuern evade (paying).

hinüber [hɪ'ny:bər] ad across, over;
~**gehen** vi irreg go over or across.

hinunter [hɪ'nʊntər] ad down; ~**bringen**
vt irreg take down; ~**schlucken** vt (lit,
fig) swallow; ~**steigen** vi irreg descend.

hin- ['hɪn] cpd: **H~weg** m journey out;
~'**weghelfen** vi irreg: **jdm über etw**
(acc) ~**weghelfen** help sb to get over
sth; ~'**wegsetzen** vr: **sich** ~**wegsetzen
über** (+acc) disregard; **H~weis** m -**es**,
-**e** (Andeutung) hint; (Anweisung)
instruction; (Verweis) reference;
~**weisen** vi irreg (auf +acc) (anzeigen)
point to; (sagen) point out, refer to;
~**werfen** vt irreg throw down; ~**ziehen**
vr irreg (fig) drag on; ~**zielen** vi aim (auf
+acc at).

hinzu [hɪn'tsu:] ad in addition; ~**fügen** vt
add.

Hirn [hɪrn] nt -(**e**)**s**, -**e** brain(s);
~**gespinst** nt -(**e**)**s**, -**e** fantasy;
h~verbrannt a half-baked, crazy.

Hirsch [hɪrʃ] m -(**e**)**s**, -**e** stag.

Hirse ['hɪrzə] f -, - millet.

Hirt [hɪrt] m -**en**, -**en** herdsman; (Schaf-,
fig) shepherd.

hissen ['hɪsən] vt hoist.

Historiker [hɪs'to:rikər] m -**s**, - historian.

historisch [hɪs'to:rɪʃ] a historical.

Hitze ['hɪtsə] f - heat; ~**beständig** a
heat-resistant; ~**welle** f heatwave.

hitzig a hot-tempered; Debatte heated.

Hitz- cpd: ~**kopf** m hothead; **h~köpfig** a
fiery, hotheaded; ~**schlag** m heatstroke.

Hobel ['ho:bəl] m -**s**, - plane; ~**bank** f carpenter's bench; **h~n** vti plane; ~**späne**
pl wood shavings pl.

hoch [ho:x] a high; **H~** nt -**s**, -**s** (Ruf)
cheer; (Met) anticyclone; ~**achten** vt
respect; **H~achtung** f respect, esteem;
~**achtungsvoll** ad yours faithfully;
H~amt nt high mass; ~**arbeiten** vr
work one's way up; ~**begabt** a extremely
gifted; ~**betagt** a very old, aged;
H~betrieb m intense activity; (Comm)
peak time; ~**bringen** vt irreg bring up;
H~burg f stronghold; **H~deutsch** nt
High German; ~**dotiert** a highly paid;
H~druck m high pressure; **H~ebene** f
plateau; ~**erfreut** a highly delighted;
~**fliegend** a (fig) high-flown; **H~form** f
top form; ~**gradig** a intense, extreme;
~**halten** vt irreg hold up; (fig) uphold,
cherish; **H~haus** nt multi-storey building;
~**heben** vt irreg lift (up);
H~konjunktur f boom; **H~land** nt high-
lands pl; ~**leben** vi: **jdn** ~**leben lassen**
give sb three cheers; **H~mut** m pride;
~**mütig** a proud, haughty; ~**näsig** a
stuck-up, snooty; **H~ofen** m blast
furnace; ~**prozentig** a Alkohol strong;
H~rechnung f projected result;
H~saison f high season; **H~schätzung**
f high esteem; **H~schule** f college; university; **H~sommer** m middle of summer; **H~spannung** f high tension;
H~sprache f standard language;
~**springen** vi irreg jump up; **H~sprung**
m high jump.

höchst [hø:çst] *ad* highly, extremely; ~e(r,s) *a* highest; (äußerste) extreme.
Hochstapler ['ho:xsta:plər] *m* -s, - swindler.
Höchst- *cpd:* **h~ens** *ad* at the most; ~geschwindigkeit *f* maximum speed; **h~persönlich** *ad* in person; ~preis *m* maximum price; **h~wahrscheinlich** *ad* most probably.
Hoch- *cpd* **h~trabend** *a* pompous; ~verrat *m* high treason; ~wasser *nt* high water; (Überschwemmung) floods *pl*; **h~wertig** *a* high-class, first-rate; ~würden *m* Reverend; ~zahl *f* (Math) exponent.
Hochzeit ['hɔxtsait] *f* -, -en wedding; ~sreise *f* honeymoon.
hocken ['hɔkən] *vir* squat, crouch.
Hocker *m* -s, - stool.
Höcker ['hœkər] *m* -s, - hump.
Hode ['ho:də] *m* -n, -n testicle.
Hof [ho:f] *m* -(e)s, ⁺e (Hinter—) yard; (Bauern—) farm; (Königs—) court.
hoffen ['hɔfən] *vi* hope (auf +acc for); ~tlich *ad* I hope, hopefully.
Hoffnung ['hɔfnuŋ] *f* hope; **h~slos** *a* hopeless; ~slosigkeit *f* hopelessness; ~sschimmer *m* glimmer of hope; **h~svoll** *a* hopeful.
höflich ['hø:fliç] *a* polite, courteous; **H~keit** *f* courtesy, politeness.
hohe(r,s) [hø:ə(r,z)] *a see* hoch.
Höhe ['hø:ə] *f* -, -n height; (An—) hill.
Hoheit ['ho:hait] *f* (Pol) sovereignty; (Titel) Highness; ~sgebiet *nt* sovereign territory; ~sgewässer *nt* territorial waters *pl*; ~szeichen *nt* national emblem.
Höhen- ['hø:ən] *cpd:* ~angabe *f* altitude reading; (auf Karte) height marking; ~messer *m* -s, - altimeter; ~sonne *f* sun lamp; ~unterschied *m* difference in altitude; ~zug *m* mountain chain.
Höhepunkt *m* climax.
höher *a,ad* higher.
hohl [ho:l] *a* hollow.
Höhle ['hø:lə] *f* -, -n cave, hole; (Mund—) cavity; (fig, Zool) den.
Hohl- *cpd:* ~heit *f* hollowness; ~maß *nt* measure of volume; ~saum *m* hemstitch.
Hohn [ho:n] *m* -(e)s scorn.
höhnen ['hø:nən] *vt* taunt, scoff at.
höhnisch *a* scornful, taunting.
hold [hɔlt] *a* charming, sweet.
holen ['ho:lən] *vt* get, fetch; (Atem take; jdn/etw ~ lassen send for sb/sth.
Hölle ['hœlə] *f* -, -n hell; ~nangst *f:* eine ~ nangst haben be scared to death.
höllisch ['hœliʃ] *a* hellish, infernal.
holperig ['hɔlpəriç] *a* rough, bumpy.
holpern ['hɔlpərn] *vi* jolt.
Holunder [ho'lundər] *m* -s, - elder.
Holz [hɔlts] *nt* -es, ⁺er wood.
hölzern ['hœltsərn] *a* (lit, fig) wooden.
Holz- *cpd:* ~fäller *m* -s, - lumberjack, woodcutter; **h~ig** *a* woody; ~klotz *m* wooden block; ~kohle *f* charcoal; ~scheit *nt* log; ~schuh *m* clog; ~weg *m* (fig) wrong track; ~wolle *f* fine wood

shavings *pl*; ~wurm *m* woodworm.
homosexuell [homozɛksuˈɛl] *a* homosexual.
Honig ['ho:niç] *m* -s, -e honey; ~wabe *f* honeycomb.
Honorar [hono'ra:r] *nt* -s, -e fee.
honorieren [hono'ri:rən] *vt* remunerate; Scheck honour.
Hopfen ['hɔpfən] *m* -s, - hops *pl*.
hopsen ['hɔpsən] *vi* hop.
Hör- *cpd:* ~apparat *m* hearing aid; **h~bar** *a* audible.
horch [hɔrç] *interj* listen; ~en *vi* listen; (pej) eavesdrop; **H~er** *m* -s, - listener; eavesdropper.
Horde ['hɔrdə] *f* -, -n horde.
hören ['hø:rən] *vti* hear; **H~sagen** *nt:* vom **H~sagen** from hearsay.
Hörer *m* -s, - hearer; (Rad) listener; (Univ) student; (Telefon—) receiver.
Horizont [hori'tsɔnt] *m* -(e)s, -e horizon; **h~al** [-ˈta:l] *a* horizontal.
Hormon [hɔr'mo:n] *nt* -s, -e hormone.
Hörmuschel *f* (Tel) earpiece.
Horn [hɔrn] *nt* -(e)s, ⁺er horn; ~haut *f* horny skin.
Hornisse [hɔr'nisə] *f* -, -n hornet.
Horoskop [horo'sko:p] *nt* -s, -e horoscope.
Hör- *cpd* ~rohr *nt* ear trumpet; (Med) stethoscope; ~saal *m* lecture room; ~spiel *nt* radio play.
Hort [hɔrt] *m* -(e)s, -e hoard; (Sch) nursery school; **h~en** *vt* hoard.
Hose ['ho:zə] *f* -, -n trousers *pl*, pants (US) *pl*; ~nanzug *m* trouser suit; ~nrock *m* culottes *pl*; ~ntasche *f* (trouser) pocket; ~nträger *m* braces *pl*, suspenders (US) *pl*.
Hostie ['hɔstiə] *f* (Rel) host.
Hotel [ho'tɛl] *nt* -s, -s hotel; ~ier [hotɛliˈe:] *m* -s, -s hotelkeeper, hotelier.
Hub [hu:p] *m* -(e)s, ⁺e lift; (Tech) stroke.
hüben ['hy:bən] *ad* on this side, over here.
Hubraum *m* (Aut) cubic capacity.
hübsch [hypʃ] *a* pretty, nice.
Hubschrauber *m* -s, - helicopter.
hudeln ['hu:dəln] *vi* be sloppy.
Huf [hu:f] *m* -(e)s, -e hoof; ~eisen *nt* horseshoe; ~nagel *m* horseshoe nail.
Hüft- ['hyft] *cpd:* ~e *f* -, -n hip; ~gürtel *m*, ~halter *m* -s, - girdle.
Hügel ['hy:gəl] *m* -s, - hill; **h~ig** *a* hilly.
Huhn [hu:n] *nt* -(e)s, ⁺er hen; (Cook) chicken.
Hühner- ['hy:nər] *cpd:* ~auge *nt* corn; ~brühe *f* chicken broth.
Huld [hult] *f* - favour; **h~igen** ['huldigən] *vi* pay homage (jdm to sb); ~igung *f* homage.
Hülle ['hylə] *f* -, -n cover(ing); wrapping; in ~ und Fülle galore; **h~n** *vt* cover, wrap (in +acc with).
Hülse ['hylzə] *f* -, -n husk, shell; ~nfrucht *f* legume.
human [hu'ma:n] *a* humane; ~i'tär *a* humanitarian; **H~i'tät** *f* humanity.
Hummel ['huməl] *f* -, -n bumblebee.
Hummer ['humər] *m* -s, - lobster.
Humor [hu'mo:r] *m* -s, -e humour; ~

haben have a sense of humour; ~**ist** [-'rɪst] m humorist; **h~istisch** a, **h~voll** a humorous.

humpeln ['hʊmpəln] vi hobble.

Humpen ['hʊmpən] m -s, - tankard.

Hund [hʊnt] m -(e)s, -e dog; ~**ehütte** f (dog) kennel; ~**ekuchen** m dog biscuit; **h~emüde** a (col) dog-tired.

hundert ['hʊndərt] num hundred; **H~-'jahrfeier** f centenary; ~**prozentig** a,ad one hundred per cent.

Hündin ['hʏndɪn] f bitch.

Hunger ['hʊŋər] m -s hunger; ~ **haben** be hungry; ~**lohn** m starvation wages pl; **h~n** vi starve; ~**snot** f famine; ~**streik** m hunger strike.

hungrig ['hʊŋrɪç] a hungry.

Hupe ['hu:pə] f -, -n horn, hooter; **h~n** vi hoot, sound one's horn.

hüpfen ['hʏpfən] vi hop, jump.

Hürde ['hʏrdə] f -, -n hurdle; (für Schafe) pen; ~**nlauf** m hurdling.

Hure ['hu:rə] f -, -n whore.

hurtig ['hʊrtɪç] a,ad brisk(ly), quick(ly).

huschen ['hʊʃən] vi flit, scurry.

Husten ['hu:stən] m -s cough; **h~** vi cough; ~**anfall** m coughing fit; ~**bonbon** m or nt cough drop; ~**saft** m cough mixture.

Hut [hu:t] m -(e)s, -e hat; f - care; **auf der ~ sein** be on one's guard.

hüten ['hy:tən] vt guard; vr watch out; **sich ~, zu** take care not to; **sich ~ vor** beware of.

Hütte ['hʏtə] f -, -n hut, cottage; (Eisen—) forge; ~**nwerk** nt foundry.

hutzelig ['hʊtsəlɪç] a shrivelled.

Hyäne [hy'ɛ:nə] f -, -n hyena.

Hyazinthe [hya'tsɪntə] f -, -n hyacinth.

Hydr- cpd: ~**ant** [hy'drant] m hydrant; **h~aulisch** [hy'draʊlɪʃ] a hydraulic; ~**ierung** [hy'dri:rʊŋ] f hydrogenation.

Hygiene [hygi'e:nə] f - hygiene.

hygienisch [hygi'e:nɪʃ] a hygienic.

Hymne ['hʏmnə] f -, -n hymn, anthem.

hyper- ['hypɐ] pref hyper-.

Hypno- [hʏp'no] cpd: ~**se** f -, -n hypnosis; **h~tisch** a hypnotic; ~**tiseur** [-ti'zø:r] hypnotist; **h~ti'sieren** vt hypnotize.

Hypothek [hypo'te:k] f -, -en mortgage.

Hypothese [hypo'te:zə] f -, -n hypothesis.

hypothetisch [hypo'te:tɪʃ] a hypothetical.

Hysterie [hʏste'ri:] f hysteria.

hysterisch [hʏs'te:rɪʃ] a hysterical.

I

I, i [i:] nt I, i.

ich [ɪç] pron I; ~ **bin's!** it's me!; **I~** nt -(s), -(s) self; (Psych) ego.

Ideal [ide'a:l] nt -s, -e ideal; **i~** a ideal; ~**ist** [-'lɪst] m idealist; **i~istisch** [-'lɪstɪʃ] a idealistic.

Idee [i'de:] f -, -n idea; **i~ll** [ide'ɛl] a ideal.

identi- [i'dɛnti] cpd: ~**fizieren** [-fi'tsi:rən] vt identify; ~**sch** a identical; **I~tät** [-'tɛ:t] f identity.

Ideo- [ideo] cpd: ~**loge** [-'lo:gə] m -n, -n

ideologist; ~**logie** [-lo'gi:] f ideology; **i~logisch** [-'lo:gɪʃ] a ideological.

idiomatisch [idio'ma:tɪʃ] a idiomatic.

Idiot [idi'o:t] m -en, -en idiot; **i~isch** a idiotic.

idyllisch [i'dʏlɪʃ] a idyllic.

Igel ['i:gəl] m -s, - hedgehog.

ignorieren [ɪgno'ri:rən] vt ignore.

ihm [i:m] pron dat of **er**, **es** (to) him, (to) it.

ihn [i:n] pron acc of **er** him; it; ~**en** pron dat of **sie** pl (to) them; **I~en** pron dat of **Sie** (to) you.

ihr [i:r] pron nom pl you; dat of **sie** sing (to) her; ~**(e)** poss pron sing her; its; pl their; **I~(e)** poss pron your; ~**e(r,s)** poss pron sing hers; its; pl theirs; **I~e(r,s)** poss pron yours; ~**er** pron gen of **sie** sing/pl of her/them; **I~er** pron gen of **Sie** of you; ~**erseits** ad for her/their part; ~**esgleichen** pron people like her/them; (von Dingen) others like it; ~**etwegen**, ~**etwillen** ad (für sie) for her/its/their sake; (wegen ihr) on her/its/their account; ~**ige** pron: **der/die/das ~ige** hers; its; theirs.

Ikone [i'ko:nə] f -, -n icon.

illegal ['ɪlega:l] a illegal.

Illusion [ɪluzi'o:n] f illusion.

illusorisch [ɪlu'zo:rɪʃ] a illusory.

illustrieren [ɪlʊs'tri:rən] vt illustrate.

Illustrierte f -n, -n picture magazine.

Iltis ['ɪltɪs] m -ses, -se polecat.

im [ɪm] = **in dem**.

imaginär [imagi'nɛ:r] a imaginary.

Imbiß ['ɪmbɪs] m -sses, -sse snack; ~**halle** f, ~**stube** f snack bar.

imitieren [imi'ti:rən] vt imitate.

Imker ['ɪmkər] m -s, - beekeeper.

Immatrikulation [ɪmatrikulatsi'o:n] f (Univ) registration.

immatrikulieren [ɪmatriku'li:rən] vir register.

immer ['ɪmər] ad always; ~ **wieder** again and again; ~ **noch** still; ~ **noch nicht** still not; **für** ~ forever; ~ **wenn ich . . .** everytime I . . .; ~ **schöner/trauriger** more and more beautiful/sadder and sadder; **was/wer (auch)** ~ whatever/whoever; ~**hin** ad all the same; ~**zu** ad all the time.

Immobilien [ɪmo'bi:liən] pl real estate.

immun [ɪ'mu:n] a immune; **I~ität** [-ɪ'tɛ:t] f immunity.

Imperativ ['ɪmperati:f] m -s, -e imperative.

Imperfekt ['ɪmperfɛkt] nt -s, -e imperfect (tense).

Imperialist [ɪmperia'lɪst] m imperialist; **i~isch** a imperialistic.

Impf- [ɪmpf] cpd: **i~en** vt vaccinate; ~**stoff** m vaccine; ~**ung** f vaccination; ~**zwang** m compulsory vaccination.

implizieren [ɪmpli'tsi:rən] vt imply (mit by).

imponieren [ɪmpo'ni:rən] vi impress (jdm sb).

Import [ɪm'pɔrt] m -(e)s, -e import; **i~ieren** [-'ti:rən] vt import.

imposant [ɪmpo'zant] a imposing.

impotent ['ımpɔtɛnt] a impotent.
imprägnieren [ımprɛ'gniːrən] vt
(water)proof.
Improvisation [ımprovizatsi'oːn] f
improvization.
improvisieren [ımprovi'ziːrən] vti
improvize.
Impuls [ım'puls] m -es, -e impulse; **i∼iv**
['ziːf] a impulsive.
imstande [ım'ʃtandə] a: ∼ **sein** be in a
position; (fähig) be able.
in [ın] prep +acc in(to); to; +dat in; ∼
der/die Stadt in/into town; ∼ **der/die
Schule** at/to school.
Inanspruchnahme [ın'anʃpruxnaːmə] f
-, -n demands pl (gen on).
Inbegriff ['ınbəgrıf] m embodiment, per-
sonification; **i∼en** ad included.
inbrünstig ['ınbrynstıç] a ardent.
indem [ın'deːm] cj while; ∼ **man etw
macht** (dadurch) by doing sth.
indes(sen) [ın'dɛs(ən)] ad meanwhile; cj
while.
Indianer(in f) [ındi'aːnər(ın)] m -s, - Red
Indian.
indianisch a Red Indian.
indigniert [ındı'gniːrt] a indignant.
Indikativ ['ındikatiːf] m -s, -e indicative.
indirekt ['ındirɛkt] a indirect.
indiskret ['ındıskreːt] a indiscreet; **I∼ion**
[ındıskretsi'oːn] f indiscretion.
indiskutabel ['ındıskutaːbəl] a out of the
question.
Individu- [ındividu] cpd: ∼**alist** [-a'lıst] m
individualist; **—alität** [-ali'tɛt] f individuality; **i∼ell** ['-ɛl] a individual; ∼**um**
[ındi'viːduum] nt -s, **-en** individual.
Indiz [ın'diːts] nt **-es, -ien** sign (für of);
(Jur) clue; ∼**ienbeweis** m circumstantial
evidence.
indoktrinieren [ındɔktri'niːrən] vt
indoctrinate.
industrialisieren [ındustriali'ziːrən] vt
industrialize.
Industrie [ındus'triː] f industry; in cpds
industrial; ∼**gebiet** nt industrial area;
i∼ll [ındustri'ɛl] a industrial; ∼**zweig** m
branch of industry.
ineinander [ın'aı'nandər] ad in(to) one
another or each other.
Infanterie [ınfantə'riː] f infantry.
Infarkt [ın'farkt] m -(e)s, -e coronary
(thrombosis).
Infektion [ınfɛktsi'oːn] f infection;
∼**skrankheit** f infectious disease.
Infinitiv ['ınfinitiːf] m -s, -e infinitive.
infizieren [ınfi'tsiːrən] vt infect; vr be
infected (bei by).
Inflation [ınfla'tsioːn] f inflation.
inflatorisch [ınfla'toːrıʃ] a inflationary.
infolge [ın'fɔlgə] prep +gen as a result of,
owing to; ∼**dessen** [-'dɛsən] ad
consequently.
Informatik [ınfɔr'maːtık] f information
studies pl.
Information [ınfɔrmatsi'oːn] f
information no pl.
informieren [ınfɔr'miːrən] vt inform; vr
find out (über +acc about).

Infusion [ınfuzi'oːn] f infusion.
Ingenieur [ınʒeni'øːr] m engineer;
∼**schule** f school of engineering.
Ingwer ['ıŋvər] m -s ginger.
Inhaber(in f) ['ınhaːbər(ın)] m -s, -
owner; (Haus—) occupier; (Lizenz—)
licensee, holder; (Fin) bearer.
inhaftieren [ınhaf'tiːrən] vt take into
custody.
inhalieren [ınha'liːrən] vti inhale.
Inhalt ['ınhalt] m -(e)s, -e contents pl;
(eines Buchs etc) content; (Math) area;
volume; **i∼lich** a as regards content;
∼**sangabe** f summary; **i∼slos** a empty;
i∼(s)reich a full; ∼**sverzeichnis** nt
table of contents.
inhuman ['ınhumaːn] a inhuman.
Initiative [ınitsia'tiːvə] f initiative.
Injektion [ınjɛktsi'oːn] f injection.
inklusive [ınklu'ziːvə] prep, ad inclusive
(gen of).
inkognito [ın'kɔgnito] ad incognito.
inkonsequent ['ınkɔnzekvɛnt] a
inconsistent.
inkorrekt ['ınkɔrɛkt] a incorrect.
Inkrafttreten [ın'krafttreːtən] nt -s
coming into force.
Inland ['ınlant] nt -(e)s (Geog) inland;
(Pol, Comm) home (country); ∼**sporto** nt
inland postage.
inmitten [ın'mıtən] prep +gen in the
middle of; ∼ **von** amongst.
innehaben ['ınəhaːbən] vt irreg hold.
innen ['ınən] ad inside; **I∼aufnahme** f
indoor photograph; **I∼einrichtung** f
(interior) furnishings pl; **I∼minister** m
minister of the interior, Home Secretary
(Brit); **I∼politik** f domestic policy;
I∼stadt f town/city centre.
inner- ['ınər] cpd: ∼**e(r,s)** a inner; (im
Körper, inländisch) internal; **I∼e(s)** nt
inside; (Mitte) centre; (fig) heart; **I∼eien**
[-'raıən] pl innards pl; ∼**halb** ad, prep
+gen within; (räumlich) inside; ∼**lich** a
internal; (geistig) inward; **I∼ste(s)** nt
heart; ∼**ste(r,s)** a innermost.
innig ['ınıç] a profound; Freundschaft
intimate.
inoffiziell ['ın'ofitsiɛl] a unofficial.
ins [ıns] = **in das.**
Insasse ['ınzasə] m **-n, -n** (Anstalt)
inmate; (Aut) passenger.
insbesondere [ınsbə'zɔndərə] ad
(e)specially.
Inschrift ['ınʃrıft] f inscription.
Insekt [ın'zɛkt] nt -(e)s, -en insect.
Insel ['ınzəl] f -, -n island.
Inser- cpd: ∼**at** [ınze'raːt] nt -(e)s, -e
advertisement; ∼**ent** [ınze'rɛnt] m adver-
tiser; **i∼ieren** [ınze'riːrən] vti advertise.
insgeheim [ınsgə'haım] ad secretly.
insgesamt [ınsgə'zamt] ad altogether, all
in all.
insofern ['ınzo'fɛrn], **insoweit** ['ınzo'vaıt]
ad in this respect; ∼ **als** in so far as; cj if;
(deshalb) (and) so.
Installateur [ınstala'tøːr] m electrician;
plumber.
Instand- [ın'ʃtant] cpd: ∼**haltung** f main-

tenance; ~**setzung** f overhaul; (eines Gebäudes) restoration.

Instanz [ɪn'stants] f authority; (Jur) court; ~**enweg** m official channels pl.

Instinkt [ɪn'stɪŋkt] m -(e)s, -e instinct; i~**iv** [-'tiːf] a instinctive.

Institut [ɪnsti'tuːt] nt -(e)s, -e institute.

Instrument [ɪnstru'mɛnt] nt instrument.

inszenieren [ɪnstseˈniːrən] vt direct; (fig) stage-manage.

Intell- [ɪntɛl] cpd: i~**ektuell** [-ɛktu'ɛl] a intellectual; i~**igent** [-i'gɛnt] a intelligent; ~**igenz** [-i'gɛnts] f intelligence; (Leute) intelligentsia pl.

Intendant [ɪntɛn'dant] m director.

intensiv [ɪntɛn'ziːf] a intensive.

Interess- cpd: i~**ant** [ɪntɛrɛ'sant] a interesting; i~**anterweise** ad interestingly enough; ~**e** [ɪntɛ'rɛsə] nt -s, -n interest; ~**e haben** be interested (an +dat in); ~**ent** [ɪntɛrɛ'sɛnt] m interested party; i~**ieren** [ɪntɛrɛ'siːrən] vt interest; vr be interested (für in).

Inter- [ɪntɛr] cpd: ~**nat** [-'naːt] nt -(e)s, -e boarding school; i~**national** [-natsio'naːl] a international; i~**nieren** [-'niːrən] vt intern; i~**pretieren** [-pre'tiːrən] vt interpret; ~**punktion** [-puŋktsi'oːn] f punctuation; ~**vall** [-'val] nt -s, -e interval; ~**view** [-'vjuː] nt -s, -s interview; i~**viewen** [-'vjuːəm] vt interview.

intim [ɪn'tiːm] a intimate; I~**ität** [ɪntimi'tɛːt] f intimacy.

intolerant ['ɪntolerant] a intolerant.

intransitiv ['ɪntranzitiːf] a (Gram) intransitive.

Intrige [ɪn'triːgə] f -, -n intrigue, plot.

Invasion [ɪnvazi'oːn] f invasion.

Inventar [ɪnvɛn'taːr] nt -s, -e inventory.

Inventur [ɪnvɛn'tuːr] f stocktaking; ~**machen** stocktake.

investieren [ɪnvɛs'tiːrən] vt invest.

inwiefern [ɪnvi'fɛrn], **inwieweit** [ɪnvi'vaɪt] ad how far, to what extent.

inzwischen [ɪn'tsvɪʃən] ad meanwhile.

irdisch ['ɪrdɪʃ] a earthly.

irgend ['ɪrgənt] ad at all; **wann/was/wer ~** whenever/whatever/whoever; ~**jemand/etwas** somebody/something; anybody/anything; ~**ein(e,s)** a some, any; ~**einmal** ad sometime or other; (fragend) ever; ~**wann** ad sometime; ~**wie** ad somehow; ~**wo** ad somewhere; anywhere.

Ironie [iro'niː] f irony.

ironisch [i'roːnɪʃ] a ironic(al).

irre ['ɪrə] a crazy, mad; I~**(r)** mf lunatic; ~**führen** vt mislead; ~**machen** vt confuse; ~**n** vir be mistaken; (umher—) wander, stray; I~**nanstalt** f lunatic asylum.

irrig ['ɪrɪç] a incorrect, wrong.

Irr- cpd: i~**sinnig** a mad, crazy; (col) terrific; ~**tum** m -s, -tümer mistake, error; i~**tümlich** a mistaken.

Isolation [izolatsi'oːn] f isolation; (Elec) insulation.

Isolator [izo'laːtɔr] m insulator.

Isolier- [izo'liːr] cpd: ~**band** nt insulating tape; i~**en** vt isolate; (Elec) insulate;

~**station** f (Med) isolation ward; ~**ung** f isolation; (Elec) insulation.

J

J, j [jɔt] nt J, j.

ja [jaː] ad yes; **tu das ~ nicht!** don't do that!

Jacht [jaxt] f -, -en yacht.

Jacke ['jakə] f -, -n jacket; (Woll—) cardigan.

Jackett [ʒa'kɛt] nt -s, -s or -e jacket.

Jagd [jaːkt] f -, -en hunt; (Jagen) hunting; ~**beute** f kill; ~**flugzeug** nt fighter; ~**gewehr** nt sporting gun.

jagen ['jaːgən] vi hunt; (eilen) race; vt hunt; (weg—) drive (off); (verfolgen) chase.

Jäger ['jɛːgər] m -s, - hunter.

jäh [jeː] a sudden, abrupt; (steil) steep, precipitous; ~**lings** ad abruptly.

Jahr [jaːr] nt -(e)s, -e year; **j~elang** ad for years; ~**esabonnement** nt annual subscription; ~**esabschluß** m end of the year; (Comm) annual statement of account; ~**esbericht** m annual report; ~**eswechsel** m turn of the year; ~**eszahl** f date, year; ~**eszeit** f season; ~**gang** m age group; (von Wein) vintage; ~**'hundert** nt -s, -e century; ~**'hundertfeier** f centenary.

jährlich ['jɛːrlɪç] a, ad yearly.

Jahr- cpd: ~**markt** m fair; ~**'zehnt** nt decade.

Jähzorn ['jɛːtsɔrn] m sudden anger; hot temper; **j~ig** a hot-tempered.

Jalousie [ʒalu'ziː] f venetian blind.

Jammer ['jamər] m -s misery; **es ist ein ~, daß** ... it is a crying shame that ...

jämmerlich ['jɛmərlɪç] a wretched, pathetic; **J~keit** f wretchedness.

jammer- cpd: ~**n** vi wail; vt impers: **es jammert jdn** it makes sb feel sorry; ~**schade** a: **es ist ~schade** it is a crying shame.

Januar ['januaːr] m -s, -e January.

Jargon [ʒar'gõː] m -s, -s jargon.

jäten ['jɛːtən] vt: Unkraut ~ weed.

jauchzen ['jauxtsən] vi rejoice, shout (with joy).

Jauchzer m -s, - shout of joy.

jaulen ['jaulən] vi howl.

ja- cpd: ~**'wohl** ad yes (of course); **J~wort** nt consent.

Jazz [dʒɛs] m - Jazz.

je [jeː] ad ever; (jeweils) each; ~ **nach** depending on; ~ **nachdem** it depends; ~ ... **desto** or ~ **je** ... the ...

jede(r,s) ['jeːdə(r,z)] a every, each; pron everybody; (— einzelne) each; **ohne ~ x** without any x; ~**nfalls** ad in any case; ~**rmann** pron everone; ~**rzeit** ad at any time; ~**smal** ad every time, each time.

jedoch [je'dɔx] ad however.

jeher ['jeːheːr] ad: **von ~** all along.

jemals ['jeːmaːls] ad ever.

jemand ['jeːmant] pron somebody; anybody.

jene(r,s) ['jeːnə(r,z)] a that; pron that one.

jenseits ['jeːnzaɪts] ad on the other side;

prep +*gen* on the other side of, beyond; **das J**~ the hereafter, the beyond.
jetzig ['jɛtsɪç] *a* present.
jetzt [jɛtst] *ad* now.
je~ *cpd*: ~**weilig** *a* respective; ~**weils**
ad ~**weils zwei zusammen** two at a
time; **zu** ~**weils 5 DM** at 5 marks each;
~**weils das erste** the first each time.
Joch [jɔx] *nt* -**(e)s, -e** yoke.
Jockei ['dʒɔke] *m* -**s, -s** jockey.
Jod [jo:t] *nt* -**(e)s** iodine.
jodeln ['jo:dəln] *vi* yodel.
Joghurt ['jo:gʊrt] *m or nt* -**s, -s** yogurt.
Johannisbeere [jo'hanɪsbe:rə] *f* red-
currant; **schwarze** ~ blackcurrant.
johlen ['jo:lən] *vi* yell.
Jolle ['jɔlə] *f* -, -**n** dinghy.
jonglieren [ʒõ'gli:rən] *vi* juggle.
Joppe ['jɔpə] *f* -, -**n** jacket.
Journal- [ʒʊr'na:l] *cpd*: ~**ismus** [-'lɪsmʊs]
m journalism; ~**ist(in** *f*) [-'lɪst] *m*
journalist; **j**~**istisch** *a* journalistic.
Jubel ['ju:bəl] *m* -**s** rejoicing; **j**~**n** *vi*
rejoice.
Jubiläum [jubi'lɛ:ʊm] *nt* -**s, Jubiläen**
anniversary, jubilee.
jucken ['jʊkən] *vi* itch; *vt* **es juckt mich
am Arm** my arm is itching; **das juckt
mich** that's itchy.
Juckreiz ['jʊkraɪts] *m* itch.
Jude ['ju:də] *m* -**n, -n** Jew; ~**ntum** *nt* -
Judaism; Jewry; ~**nverfolgung** *f*
persecution of the Jews.
Jüd- ['jy:d] *cpd*: ~**in** *f* Jewess; **j**~**isch** *a*
Jewish.
Judo ['ju:do] *nt* -**(s)** judo.
Jugend ['ju:gənt] *f* - youth; ~**herberge** *f*
youth hostel; ~**kriminalität** *f* juvenile
crime; **j**~**lich** *a* youthful; ~**liche(r)** *mf*
teenager, young person; ~**richter** *m*
juvenile court judge.
Juli ['ju:li] *m* -**s, -s** July.
jung [jʊŋ] *a* young; **J**~**e** *m* -**n, -n** boy, lad;
J~**e(s)** *nt* young animal; (*pl*) young *pl*.
Jünger ['jyŋər] *m* -**s, -** disciple; **j**~ *a*
younger.
Jung- *cpd*: ~**fer** *f* -, ~**fer** old
maid; ~**fernfahrt** *f* maiden voyage;
~**frau** *f* virgin; (*Astrol*) Virgo; ~**geselle**
m bachelor.
Jüngling ['jyŋlɪŋ] *m* youth.
jüngst ['jyŋst] *ad* lately, recently; ~**e(r,s)**
a youngest; (*neueste*) latest.
Juni ['ju:ni] *m* -**(s), -s** June.
Junior ['ju:niɔr] *m* -**s, -en** [-'o:rən] junior.
Jurist [ju'rɪst] *m* jurist, lawyer; **j**~**isch** *a*
legal.
Justiz [jʊs'ti:ts] *f* - justice; ~**beamte(r)** *m*
judicial officer; ~**irrtum** *m* miscarriage
of justice.
Juwel [ju've:l] *nt or m* -**s, -en** jewel; ~**ier**
m [-'li:r] *m* -**s, -e** jeweller; ~**iergeschäft**
nt jeweller's (shop).
Jux [jʊks] *m* -**es, -e** joke, lark.

K

K, k [ka:] *nt* K, k.
Kabarett [kaba'rɛt] *nt* -**s, -e** *or* -**s**
cabaret; ~**ist** [-'tɪst] *m* cabaret artiste.
Kabel ['ka:bəl] *nt* -**s, -** (*Elec*) wire; (*stark*)
cable; ~**jau** [-jaʊ] *m* -**s, -e** *or* -**s** cod; **k**~**n**
vti cable.
Kabine [ka'bi:nə] *f* cabin; (*Zelle*) cubicle.
Kabinett [kabi'nɛt] *nt* -**s, -e** (*Pol*) cabinet;
small room.
Kachel ['kaxəl] *f* -, -**n** tile; **k**~**n** *vt* tile;
~**ofen** *m* tiled stove.
Kadaver [ka'da:vər] *m* -**s, -** carcass.
Kadett [ka'dɛt] *m* -**en, -en** cadet.
Käfer ['kɛ:fər] *m* -**s, -** beetle.
Kaffee ['kafe] *m* -**s, -s** coffee; ~**kanne** *f*
coffeepot; ~**klatsch** *m*, ~**kränzchen** *nt*
hen party; coffee morning; ~**löffel** *m*
coffee spoon; ~**mühle** *f* coffee grinder;
~**satz** *m* coffee grounds *pl*.
Käfig ['kɛ:fɪç] *m* -**s, -e** cage.
kahl [ka:l] *a* bald; ~**fressen** *vt irreg* strip
bare; ~**geschoren** *a* shaven, shorn;
K~**heit** *f* baldness; ~**köpfig** *a* bald-
headed.
Kahn [ka:n] *m* -**(e)s, ⸚e** boat, barge.
Kai [kaɪ] *m* -**s, -e** *or* -**s** quay.
Kaiser ['kaɪzər] *m* -**s, -** emperor; ~**in** *f*
empress; **k**~**lich** *a* imperial; ~**reich** *nt*
empire; ~**schnitt** *m* (*Med*) Caesarian
(section).
Kajüte [ka'jy:tə] *f* -, -**n** cabin.
Kakao [ka'ka:o] *m* -**s, -s** cocoa.
Kaktee [kak'te:(ə)] *f* -, -**n, Kaktus**
['kaktus] *m* -, -**se** cactus.
Kalb [kalp] *nt* -**(e)s, ⸚er** calf; **k**~**en**
['kalbən] *vi* calve; ~**fleisch** *nt* veal;
~**sleder** *nt* calf(skin).
Kalender [ka'lɛndər] *m* -**s, -** calendar;
(*Taschen*—) diary.
Kali ['ka:li] *nt* -**s, -s** potash.
Kaliber [ka'li:bər] *nt* -**s, -** (*lit, fig*) calibre.
Kalk [kalk] *m* -**(e)s, -e** lime; (*Biol*)
calcium; ~**stein** *m* limestone.
Kalkulation [kalkulatsi'o:n] *f* calculation.
kalkulieren [kalku'li:rən] *vt* calculate.
Kalorie [kalo'ri:] *f* calorie.
kalt [kalt] *a* cold; **mir ist (es)** ~ I am
cold; ~**bleiben** *vi irreg* be unmoved;
~**blütig** *a* cold-blooded; (*ruhig*) cool;
K~**blütigkeit** *f* cold-bloodedness; coolness.
Kälte ['kɛltə] *f* - cold; coldness; ~**grad** *m*
degree of frost or below zero; ~**welle** *f*
cold spell.
kalt- *cpd*: ~**herzig** *a* cold-hearted;
~**schnäuzig** *a* cold, unfeeling; ~**stellen**
vt chill; (*fig*) leave out in the cold.
Kamel [ka'me:l] *nt* -**s, -e** camel.
Kamera ['kamera] *f* -, -**s** camera.
Kamerad [kamə'ra:t] *m* -**en, -en**
comrade, friend; ~**schaft** *f* comradeship;
k~**schaftlich** *a* comradely.
Kamera- *cpd*: ~**führung** *f* camera work;
~**mann** *m* cameraman.
Kamille [ka'mɪlə] *f* -, -**n** camomile;
~**ntee** *m* camomile tea.

Kamin [ka'mi:n] m -s, -e (außen) chimney; (innen) fireside, fireplace; ~feger, ~kehrer m -s, - chimney sweep.

Kamm [kam] m -(e)s, ¨e comb; (Berg—) ridge; (Hahnen—) crest.

kämmen ['kɛmən] vt comb.

Kammer ['kamər] f -, -n chamber; small bedroom; ~diener m valet.

Kampf [kampf] m -(e)s, ¨e fight, battle; (Wettbewerb) contest; (fig: Anstrengung) struggle; k~bereit a ready for action.

kämpfen ['kɛmpfən] vi fight.

Kämpfer m -s, - fighter, combatant.

Kampfer ['kampfər] m -s camphor.

Kampf- cpd: ~handlung f action; k~los a without a fight; k~lustig a pugnacious; ~richter m (Sport) referee; (Tennis) umpire.

Kanal [ka'na:l] m -s, Kanäle (Fluß) canal; (Rinne, Armel—) channel; (für Abfluß) drain; ~isation [-izatsi'o:n] f sewage system; k~isieren [-i'zi:rən] vt provide with a sewage system.

Kanarienvogel [ka'na:rɪənfo:gəl] m canary.

Kandi- [kandi] cpd: ~dat [-'da:t] m -en, -en candidate; ~datur [-da'tu:r] f candidature, candidacy; k~dieren [-'di:rən] vi stand, run.

Kandis(zucker) ['kandɪs] m - candy.

Känguruh ['kɛŋguru] nt -s, -s kangaroo.

Kaninchen [ka'ni:nçən] nt rabbit.

Kanister [ka'nɪstər] m -s, - can, canister.

Kanne ['kanə] f -, -n (Krug) jug; (Kaffee—) pot; (Milch—) churn; (Gieß—) can.

Kanon ['ka:nɔn] m -s, -s canon.

Kanone [ka'no:nə] f -, -n gun; (Hist) cannon; (fig: Mensch) ace.

Kantate [kan'ta:tə] f -, -n cantata.

Kante ['kantə] f -, -n edge.

Kantine [kan'ti:nə] f canteen.

Kantor ['kantɔr] m choirmaster.

Kanu ['ka:nu] nt -s, -s canoe.

Kanzel ['kantsəl] f -, -n pulpit.

Kanzlei [kants'lai] f chancery; (Büro) chambers pl.

Kanzler ['kantslər] m -s, - chancellor.

Kap [kap] nt -s, -s cape.

Kapazität [kapatsi'tɛ:t] f capacity; (Fachmann) authority.

Kapelle [ka'pɛlə] f (Gebäude) chapel; (Mus) band.

Kaper ['ka:pər] f -, -n caper; k~n vt capture.

kapieren [ka'pi:rən] vti (col) understand.

Kapital [kapi'ta:l] nt -s, -e or -ien capital; ~anlage f investment; ~ismus [-'lɪsmʊs] m capitalism; ~ist [-'lɪst] m capitalist; k~kräftig a wealthy; ~markt m money market.

Kapitän [kapi'tɛ:n] m -s, -e captain.

Kapitel [ka'pɪtəl] nt -s, - chapter.

Kapitulation [kapitulatsi'o:n] f capitulation.

kapitulieren [kapitu'li:rən] vi capitulate.

Kaplan [ka'pla:n] m -s, Kapläne chaplain.

Kappe ['kapə] f -, -n cap; (Kapuze) hood; k~n vt cut.

Kapsel ['kapsəl] f -, -n capsule.

kaputt [ka'pʊt] a (col) smashed, broken; Person exhausted, finished; ~gehen vi irreg break; (Schuhe) fall apart; (Firma) go bust; (Stoff) wear out; (sterben) cop it; ~lachen vr laugh o.s. silly; ~machen vt break; Mensch exhaust, wear out.

Kapuze [ka'pu:tsə] f -, -n hood.

Karaffe [ka'rafə] f -, -n caraffe; (geschliffen) decanter.

Karambolage [karambo'la:ʒə] f -, -n (Zusammenstoß) crash.

Karamel [kara'mɛl] m -s caramel; ~bonbon m or nt toffee.

Karat [ka'ra:t] nt -(e)s, -e carat; ~e nt -s karate.

Karawane [kara'va:nə] f -, -n caravan.

Kardinal [kardi'na:l] m -s, Kardinäle cardinal; ~zahl f cardinal number.

Karfreitag [ka:r'fraita:k] m Good Friday.

karg [kark] a scanty, poor; Mahlzeit auch meagre; ~ mit Worten sein use few words; K~heit f poverty, scantiness; meagreness.

kärglich ['kɛrklɪç] a poor, scanty.

kariert [ka'ri:rt] a Stoff checked; Papier squared.

Karies ['ka:riɛs] f - caries.

Karikatur [karika'tu:r] f caricature; ~ist [-'rɪst] m cartoonist.

karikieren [kari'ki:rən] vt caricature.

Karneval ['karnəval] m -s, -e or -s carnival.

Karo ['ka:ro] nt -s, -s square; (Cards) diamonds; ~As nt ace of diamonds.

Karosse [ka'rɔsə] f -, -n coach, carriage; ~rie [-'ri:] f (Aut) body(work).

Karotte [ka'rɔtə] f -, -n carrot.

Karpfen ['karpfən] m -s, - carp.

Karre ['karə] f -, -n, ~n m -s, - cart, barrow; k~n vt cart, transport.

Karriere [kari'ɛ:rə] f -, -n career; ~ machen get on, get to the top; ~macher m -s, - careerist.

Karte ['kartə] f -, -n card; (Land—) map; (Speise—) menu; (Eintritts—, Fahr—) ticket; alles auf eine ~ setzen put all one's eggs in one basket.

Kartei [kar'tai] f card index; ~karte f index card.

Kartell [kar'tɛl] nt -s, -e cartel.

Karten- cpd: ~haus nt (lit, fig) house of cards; ~spiel nt card game; pack of cards.

Kartoffel [kar'tɔfəl] f -, -n potato; ~brei m, ~püree nt mashed potatoes pl; ~salat m potato salad.

Karton [kar'tõ:] m -s, -s cardboard; (Schachtel) cardboard box; k~iert [karto'ni:rt] a hardback.

Karussell [karu'sɛl] nt -s, -s roundabout (Brit), merry-go-round.

Karwoche [ka:r'vɔxə] f Holy Week.

Kaschemme [ka'ʃɛmə] f -, -n dive.

Käse ['kɛ:zə] m -s, - cheese; ~blatt nt (col) (local) rag; ~kuchen m cheesecake.

Kaserne [ka'zɛrnə] f -, -n barracks pl; ~nhof m parade ground.

Kasino [ka'zi:no] nt -s, -s club; (Mil) officers' mess; (Spiel—) casino.

Kasper ['kaspər] m -s, - Punch; (fig) clown.

Kasse ['kasə] f -, -n (Geldkasten) cashbox; (in Geschäft) till, cash register; (Kino—, Theater— etc) box office; ticket office; (Kranken—) health insurance; (Spar—) savings bank; ~ **machen** count the money; **getrennte ~ führen** pay separately; **an der ~** (in Geschäft) at the desk; **gut bei ~ sein** be in the money; ~**narzt** m panel doctor (Brit); ~**nbestand** m cash balance; ~**npatient** m panel patient (Brit); ~**nprüfung** f audit; ~**nsturz** m: ~**nsturz machen** check one's money; ~**nzettel** m receipt.

Kasserolle [kasə'rɔlə] f -, -n casserole.

Kassette [ka'sɛtə] f small box; (Tonband, Phot) cassette; (Bücher—) case; ~**nrecorder** m -s, - cassette recorder.

kassieren [ka'si:rən] vt take; vi: **darf ich ~?** would you like to pay now?

Kassierer [ka'si:rər] m -s, - cashier; (von Klub) treasurer.

Kastanie [kas'ta:niə] f chestnut; ~**nbaum** m chestnut tree.

Kästchen ['kɛstçən] nt small box, casket.

Kaste ['kastə] f -, -n caste.

Kasten ['kastən] m -s, ~ box (Sport auch), case; (Truhe) chest; ~**wagen** m van.

kastrieren [kas'tri:rən] vt castrate.

Katalog [kata'lo:k] m -(e)s, -e catalogue; **k~isieren** [katalogi'zi:rən] vt catalogue.

Katapult [kata'pʊlt] m or nt -(e)s, -e catapult.

Katarrh [ka'tar] m -s, -e catarrh.

katastrophal [katastro'fa:l] a catastrophic.

Katastrophe [kata'stro:fə] f -, -n catastrophe, disaster.

Kategorie [katego'ri:] f category.

kategorisch [kate'go:rɪʃ] a categorical.

kategorisieren [kategori'zi:rən] vt categorize.

Kater ['ka:tər] m -s, - tomcat; (col) hangover.

Katheder [ka'te:dər] nt -s, - lecture desk.

Kathedrale [kate'dra:lə] f -, -n cathedral.

Kathode [ka'to:də] f -, -n cathode.

Katholik [kato'li:k] m -en, -en Catholic.

katholisch [ka'to:lɪʃ] a Catholic.

Katholizismus [katoli'tsɪsmʊs] m Catholicism.

Kätzchen ['kɛtsçən] nt kitten.

Katze ['katsə] f -, -n cat; **für die Katz** (col) in vain, for nothing; ~**nauge** nt cat's eye; (Fahrrad) rear light; ~**njammer** m (col) hangover; ~**nsprung** m (col) stone's throw; short journey; ~**nwäsche** f lick and a promise.

Kauderwelsch ['kaudərvɛlʃ] nt -(s) jargon; (col) double Dutch.

kauen ['kauən] vti chew.

kauern ['kauərn] vi crouch.

Kauf [kauf] m -(e)s, **Käufe** purchase, buy; (Kaufen) buying; **ein guter ~** a bargain; **etw in ~ nehmen** put up with sth; **k~en** vt buy.

Käufer(in f) ['kɔyfər(ın)] m -s, - buyer.

Kauf- cpd: ~**haus** nt department store; ~**kraft** f purchasing power; ~**laden** m shop, store.

käuflich ['kɔyflıç] a,ad purchasable, for sale; (pej) venal; ~ **erwerben** purchase.

Kauf- cpd: **k~lustig** a interested in buying; ~**mann** m, pl -**leute** business-man; shopkeeper; **k~männisch** a commercial; ~**männische Angestellter** clerk.

Kaugummi ['kaugumi] m chewing gum.

Kaulquappe ['kaulkvapə] f -, -n tadpole.

kaum [kaum] ad hardly, scarcely.

Kaution [kautsi'o:n] f deposit; (Jur) bail.

Kautschuk ['kautʃuk] m -s, -e india-rubber.

Kauz [kauts] m -es, **Käuze** owl; (fig) queer fellow.

Kavalier [kava'li:r] m -s, -e gentleman, cavalier; ~**sdelikt** nt peccadillo.

Kavallerie [kavalə'ri:] f cavalry.

Kavallerist [kavalə'rɪst] m trooper, cavalryman.

Kaviar ['ka:viar] m caviar.

keck [kɛk] a daring, bold; **K~heit** f daring, boldness.

Kegel ['ke:gəl] m -s, - skittle; (Math) cone; ~**bahn** f skittle alley; bowling alley; **k~förmig** a conical; **k~n** vi play skittles.

Kehle ['ke:lə] f -, -n throat.

Kehl- cpd: ~**kopf** m larynx; ~**laut** m guttural.

Kehre ['ke:rə] f -, -n turn(ing), bend; **k~n** vti (wenden) turn; (mit Besen) sweep; **sich an etw** (dat) **nicht k~n** not heed sth.

Kehr- cpd: ~**icht** m -s sweepings pl; ~**maschine** f sweeper; ~**reim** m refrain; ~**seite** f reverse, other side; wrong side; bad side; **k~tmachen** vi turn about, about-turn.

keifen ['kaifən] vi scold, nag.

Keil ['kaıl] m -(e)s, -e wedge; (Mil) arrow-head; **k~en** vt wedge; vr fight; ~**e'rei** f (col) punch-up; ~**riemen** m (Aut) fan belt.

Keim [kaım] m -(e)s, -e bud; (Med, fig) germ; **etw im ~ ersticken** nip sth in the bud; **k~en** vi germinate; **k~frei** a sterile; **k~tötend** a antiseptic, germi-cidal; ~**zelle** f (fig) nucleus.

kein [kaın] a no, not any; ~**e(r,s)** pron no one, nobody; none; ~**esfalls** ad on no account; ~**eswegs** ad by no means; ~**mal** ad not once.

Keks [ke:ks] m or nt -es, -e biscuit.

Kelch [kɛlç] m -(e)s, -e cup, goblet, chalice.

Kelle ['kɛlə] f -, -n ladle; (Maurer—) trowel.

Keller ['kɛlər] m -s, - cellar; ~**assel** f -, -n woodlouse; ~**wohnung** f basement flat.

Kellner ['kɛlnər] m -s, - waiter; ~**in** f waitress.

keltern ['kɛltərn] vt press.

kennen ['kɛnən] vt irreg know; ~**lernen** vt get to know; **sich ~lernen** get to know each other; (zum erstenmal) meet.

Kenn- cpd: ~**er** m -s, - connoisseur; ~**karte** f identity card; **k~tlich** a distinguishable, discernible; **etw k~tlich machen** mark sth; ~**tnis** f -, -se knowledge no pl; **etw zur ~tnis nehmen** note sth; **von etw ~tnis nehmen** take notice of sth; **jdn in ~tnis setzen** inform sb; ~**zeichen** nt mark, characteristic; **k~zeichnen** vt insep characterize; **k~zeichnenderweise** ad characteristically; ~**ziffer** f reference number.

kentern ['kɛntərn] vi capsize.

Keramik [ke'ra:mɪk] f -, -en ceramics pl, pottery.

Kerb- [kɛrb] cpd: ~**e** f -, -n notch, groove; ~**el** m -s, - chervil; **k~en** vt notch; ~**holz** nt: **etw auf dem ~holz haben** have done sth wrong.

Kerker ['kɛrkər] m -s, - prison.

Kerl [kɛrl] m -s, -e chap, bloke (Brit), guy.

Kern [kɛrn] m -(e)s, -e (Obst—) pip, stone; (Nuß—) kernel; (Atom—) nucleus; (fig) heart, core; ~**energie** f nuclear energy; ~**forschung** f nuclear research; ~**frage** f central issue; ~**gehäuse** nt core; **k~gesund** a thoroughly healthy, fit as a fiddle; **k~ig** a robust; (Ausspruch) pithy; ~**kraftwerk** nt nuclear power station; **k~los** a seedless, pipless; ~**physik** f nuclear physics; ~**reaktion** f nuclear reaction; ~**spaltung** f nuclear fission; ~**waffen** pl nuclear weapons pl.

Kerze ['kɛrtsə] f -, -n candle; (Zünd—) plug; **k~ngerade** a straight as a die; ~**nständer** m candle holder.

keß [kɛs] a saucy.

Kessel ['kɛsəl] m -s, - kettle; (von Lokomotive etc) boiler; (Geog) depression; (Mil) encirclement; ~**treiben** nt -s, - (fig) witch hunt.

Kette ['kɛtə] f -, -n chain; **k~n** vt chain; ~**nhund** m watchdog; ~**nladen** m chain store; ~**nrauchen** nt chain smoking; ~**nreaktion** f chain reaction.

Ketzer ['kɛtsər] m -s, - heretic; **k~isch** a heretical.

keuchen ['kɔyçən] vi pant, gasp.

Keuchhusten m whooping cough.

Keule ['kɔylə] f -, -n club; (Cook) leg.

keusch [kɔyʃ] a chaste; **K~heit** f chastity.

Kfz [ka:ɛftseːt] abbr of **Kraftfahrzeug**.

kichern ['kɪçərn] vi giggle.

kidnappen ['kɪdnæpən] vt kidnap.

Kiebitz ['ki:bɪts] m -es, -e peewit.

Kiefer ['ki:fər] m -s, - jaw; f -, -n pine; ~**zapfen** m pine cone.

Kiel [ki:l] m -(e)s, -e (Feder—) quill; (Naut) keel; **k~holen** vt Person keelhaul; Schiff career; ~**wasser** nt wake.

Kieme ['ki:mə] f -, -n gill.

Kies [ki:s] m -es, -e gravel; ~**el** [ki:zəl] m -s, - pebble; ~**elstein** m pebble; ~**grube** f gravel pit; ~**weg** m gravel path.

Kilo ['ki:lo] kilo; ~**gramm** [kilo'gram] nt -s, -e kilogram; ~**meter** [kilo'me:tər] m kilometre; ~**meterzähler** m milometer.

Kimme ['kɪmə] f -, -n notch; (Gewehr) backsight.

Kind [kɪnt] nt -(e)s, -er child; **von ~ auf** from childhood; **sich bei jdm lieb ~ machen** ingratiate o.s. with sb; ~**erbett** ['kɪndərbɛt] nt cot; ~**erei** [kɪndə'raɪ] f childishness; ~**ergarten** m nursery school, playgroup; ~**ergeld** nt family allowance; ~**erlähmung** f poliomyelitis; **k~erleicht** a childishly easy; **k~erlos** a childless; ~**ermädchen** nt nursemaid; **k~erreich** a with a lot of children; ~**erspiel** nt child's play; ~**erstube** f: **eine gute ~erstube haben** be well-mannered; ~**erwagen** m pram, baby carriage (US); ~**esalter** nt infancy; ~**esbeine** pl: **von ~esbeinen an** from early childhood; ~**heit** f childhood; **k~isch** a childish; **k~lich** a childlike; **k~sköpfig** a childish.

Kinn [kɪn] nt -(e)s, -e chin; ~**haken** m (Boxen) uppercut; ~**lade** f jaw.

Kino ['ki:no] nt -s, -s cinema; ~**besucher** m cinema-goer; ~**programm** nt film programme.

Kiosk [ki'ɔsk] m -(e)s, -e kiosk.

Kipp- ['kɪp] cpd: ~**e** f -, -n cigarette end; (col) fag; **auf der ~e stehen** (fig) be touch and go; **k~en** vi topple over, overturn; vt tilt.

Kirch- ['kɪrç] cpd: ~**e** f -, -n church; ~**endiener** m churchwarden; ~**enfest** nt church festival; ~**enlied** nt hymn; ~**gänger** m -s, - churchgoer; ~**hof** m churchyard; **k~lich** a ecclesiastical; ~**turm** m church tower, steeple.

Kirsche ['kɪrʃə] f -, -n cherry.

Kissen ['kɪsən] nt -s, - cushion; (Kopf—) pillow; ~**bezug** m pillowslip.

Kiste ['kɪstə] f -, -n box; chest.

Kitsch [kɪtʃ] m -(e)s trash; **k~ig** a trashy.

Kitt [kɪt] m -(e)s, -e putty; ~**chen** nt (col) clink; ~**el** m -s, - overall, smock; **k~en** vt putty; (fig) Ehe etc cement.

Kitz [kɪts] nt -es, -e kid; (Reh—) fawn.

kitzel- ['kɪtsəl] cpd: ~**ig** a (lit, fig) ticklish; ~**n** vi tickle.

klaffen ['klafən] vi gape.

kläffen ['klɛfən] vi yelp.

Klage ['kla:gə] f -, -n complaint; (Jur) action; **k~n** vi (weh—) lament, wail; (sich beschweren) complain; (Jur) take legal action.

Kläger(in f**)** ['klɛ:gər(ɪn)] m -s, - plaintiff.

kläglich ['klɛ:klɪç] a wretched.

Klamm [klam] f -, -en ravine; **k~ ~** a Finger numb; (feucht) damp.

Klammer ['klamər] f -, -n clamp; (in Text) bracket; (Büro—) clip; (Wäsche—) peg; (Zahn—) brace; **k~n** vr cling (an +acc to).

Klang [klaŋ] m -(e)s, -̈e sound; **k~voll** a sonorous.

Klappe ['klapə] f -, -n valve; (Ofen—) damper; (col: Mund) trap; **k~n** vi (Geräusch) click; vti Sitz etc tip; v impers work.

Klapper ['klapər] f -, -n rattle; **k~ig** a run-down, worn-out; **k~n** vi clatter, rattle;

~**schlange** f rattlesnake; ~**storch** m stork.

Klapp- cpd: ~**messer** nt jack-knife; ~**rad** nt collapsible bicycle; ~**stuhl** m folding chair.

Klaps [klaps] m **-es, -e** slap; **k**~**en** vt slap.

klar [kla:r] a clear; (Naut) ready for sea; (Mil) ready for action; **sich** (dat) **im K**~**en sein über** (+acc) be clear about; **ins K**~**e kommen** get clear.

Klär- ['klɛ:r] cpd: ~**anlage** f purification plant; **k**~**en** vt Flüßigkeit purify; Probleme clarify; vr clear (itself) up.

Klar- cpd: ~**heit** f clarity; ~**inette** [klari'nɛtə] f clarinet; **k**~**legen** vt clear up, explain; **k**~**machen** vt Schiff get ready for sea; **jdm etw k**~**machen** make sth clear to sb; **k**~**sehen** vi irreg see clearly; ~**sichtfolie** f transparent film; **k**~**stellen** vt clarify.

Klärung ['klɛ:rʊŋ] f purification; clarification.

Klasse ['klasə] f **-, -n** class; (Sch auch) form; **k**~ a (col) smashing; ~**narbeit** f test; ~**nbewußtsein** nt class consciousness; ~**ngesellschaft** f class society; ~**nkampf** m class conflict; ~**nlehrer** m form master; **k**~**nlos** a classless; ~**nsprecher(in** f) m form prefect; ~**nzimmer** nt classroom.

klassifizieren [klasifi'tsi:rən] vt classify.

Klassifizierung f classification.

Klassik ['klasɪk] f (Zeit) classical period; (Stil) classicism; ~**er** m **-s, -** classic.

klassisch a (lit, fig) classical.

Klatsch [klatʃ] m **-(e)s, -e** smack, crack; (Gerede) gossip; ~**base** f gossip, scandalmonger; ~**e** f **-, -n** (col) crib; **k**~**en** vi (Geräusch) clash; (reden) gossip; (Beifall) applaud, clap; ~**mohn** m (corn) poppy; **k**~**naß** a soaking wet; ~**spalte** f gossip column.

klauben ['klaubən] vt pick.

Klaue ['klauə] f **-, -n** claw; (col: Schrift) scrawl; **k**~**n** vt claw; (col) pinch.

Klause ['klauzə] f **-, -n** cell; hermitage.

Klausel ['klauzəl] f **-, -n** clause.

Klausur [klau'zu:r] f seclusion; ~**arbeit** f examination paper.

Klaviatur [klavia'tu:r] f keyboard.

Klavier [kla'vi:r] nt **-s, -e** piano.

Kleb- ['kle:b] cpd: ~**emittel** nt glue; **k**~**en** vt stick (an +acc to); **k**~**rig** a sticky; ~**stoff** m glue; ~**streifen** m adhesive tape.

kleckern ['klɛkərn] vi slobber.

Klecks [klɛks] m **-es, -e** blot, stain; **k**~**en** vi blot; (pej) daub.

Klee [kle:] m **-s** clover; ~**blatt** nt cloverleaf; (fig) trio.

Kleid [klaɪt] nt **-(e)s, -er** garment; (Frauen-) dress; pl clothes pl; **k**~**en** ['klaɪdən] vt clothe, dress; (auch vi) suit; vr dress; ~**erbügel** m coat hanger; ~**erbürste** f clothes brush; ~**erschrank** m wardrobe; **k**~**sam** a becoming; ~**ung** f clothing; ~**ungsstück** nt garment.

Kleie ['klaɪə] f **-, -n** bran.

klein [klaɪn] a little, small;

K~**bürgertum** nt petite bourgeoisie; **K**~**e(r,s)** little one; **K**~**format** nt small size; **im K**~**format** small-scale; **K**~**geld** nt small change; ~**gläubig** a of little faith; ~**hacken** vt chop up, mince; **K**~**holz** nt firewood; **K**~**holz aus jdm machen** make mincemeat of sb; **K**~**igkeit** f trifle; **K**~**kind** nt infant; **K**~**kram** m details pl; ~**laut** a dejected, quiet; ~**lich** a petty, paltry; **K**~**lichkeit** f pettiness, paltriness; ~**mütig** a fainthearted; **K**~**od** ['klaɪno:t] nt **-s, -odien** gem, jewel; treasure; ~**schneiden** vt irreg chop up; ~**städtisch** a provincial; ~**stmöglich** a smallest possible.

Kleister ['klaɪstər] m **-s, -** paste; **k**~**n** vt paste.

Klemme ['klɛmə] f **-, -n** clip; (Med) clamp; (fig) jam; **k**~**n** vt (festhalten) jam; (quetschen) pinch, nip; vr catch o.s.; (sich hineinzwängen) squeeze o.s.; **sich hinter jdn/etw k**~**n** get on to sb/get down to sth; vi (Tür) stick, jam.

Klempner ['klɛmpnər] m **-s, -** plumber.

Kleptomanie [klɛptoma'ni:] f kleptomania.

Kleriker ['kle:rikər] m **-s, -** cleric.

Klerus ['kle:rʊs] m **-** clergy.

Klette ['klɛtə] f **-, -n** burr.

Kletter- ['klɛtər] cpd: ~**er** m **-s, -** climber; **k**~**n** vi climb; ~**pflanze** f creeper; ~**seil** nt climbing rope.

klicken ['klɪkən] vi click.

Klient(in f) [kli'ɛnt(ɪn)] m client.

Klima ['kli:ma] nt **-s, -s** or **-te** [kli'ma:tə] climate; ~**anlage** f air conditioning; **k**~**tisieren** [-i'zi:rən] vt air-condition; ~**wechsel** m change of air.

klimpern ['klɪmpərn] vi tinkle; (mit Gitarre) strum.

Klinge ['klɪŋə] f **-, -n** blade, sword.

Klingel ['klɪŋəl] f **-, -n** bell; ~**beutel** m collection bag; **k**~**n** vi ring.

klingen ['klɪŋən] vi irreg sound; (Gläser) clink.

Klinik ['kli:nɪk] f hospital, clinic.

klinisch ['kli:nɪʃ] a clinical.

Klinke ['klɪŋkə] f **-, -n** handle.

Klinker ['klɪŋkər] m **-s, -** clinker.

Klippe ['klɪpə] f **-, -n** cliff; (im Meer) reef; (fig) hurdle; **k**~**nreich** a rocky.

klipp und klar ['klɪp'ʊntkla:r] a clear and concise.

Klips [klɪps] m **-es, -e** clip; (Ohr—) earring.

klirren ['klɪrən] vi clank, jangle; (Gläser) clink; ~**de Kälte** biting cold.

Klischee [kli'ʃe:] nt **-s, -s** (Druckplatte) plate, block; (fig) cliché; ~**vorstellung** f stereotyped idea.

Klo [klo:] nt **-s, -s** (col) loo.

Kloake [klo'a:kə] f **-, -n** sewer.

klobig ['klo:bɪç] a clumsy.

klopfen ['klɔpfən] vti knock; (Herz) thump; **es klopft** sb's knocking; **jdm auf die Schulter** ~ tap sb on the shoulder; vt beat.

Klopfer m **-s, -** (Teppich—) beater; (Tür—) knocker.

Klöppel ['klœpəl] *m* **-s**, **-** (*von Glocke*) clapper; **k~n** *vi* make lace.

Klops [klɔps] *m* **-es**, **-e** meatball.

Klosett [klo'zɛt] *nt* **-s** *or* **-s** lavatory, toilet; ~**papier** *nt* toilet paper.

Kloß [kloːs] *m* **-es**, **:e** (*Erd—*) clod; (*im Hals*) lump; (*Cook*) dumpling.

Kloster ['kloːstɔr] *nt* **-s**, **:** (*Männer—*) monastery; (*Frauen—*) convent.

klösterlich ['kløːstərlɪç] *a* monastic; convent.

Klotz [klɔts] *m* **-es**, **:e** log; (*Hack—*) block; **ein ~ am Bein** (*fig*) drag, millstone round (sb's) neck.

Klub [klʊp] *m* **-s**, **-s** club; ~**sessel** *m* easy chair.

Kluft [klʊft] *f-*, **:e** cleft, gap; (*Geol*) gorge, chasm.

klug [kluːk] *a* clever, intelligent; **K~heit** *f* cleverness, intelligence.

Klümpchen ['klʏmpçən] *nt* clot, blob.

Klumpen ['klʊmpən] *m* **-s**, **-** (*Erd—*) clod; (*Blut—*) lump, clot; (*Gold—*) nugget; (*Cook*) lump; **k~** *vi* go lumpy, clot.

Klumpfuß ['klʊmp-fuːs] *m* club-foot.

knabbern ['knabərn] *vti* nibble.

Knabe ['knaːbə] *m* **-n**, **-n** boy; **k~nhaft** *a* boyish.

Knäckebrot ['knɛkəbroːt] *nt* crispbread.

knacken ['knakən] *vti* (*lit, fig*) crack.

Knall [knal] *m* **-(e)s**, **-e** bang; (*Peitschen—*) crack; ~ **und Fall** (*col*) unexpectedly; ~**bonbon** *m* cracker; ~**effekt** *m* surprise effect, spectacular effect; **k~en** *vi* bang; crack; **k~rot** *a* bright red.

knapp [knap] *a* tight; *Geld* scarce; *Sprache* concise; **K~e** *m* **-n**, **-n** (*Edelmann*) young knight; ~**halten** *vt irreg* stint; **K~heit** *f* tightness; scarcity; conciseness.

knarren ['knarən] *vi* creak.

knattern ['knatərn] *vi* rattle; (*MG*) chatter.

Knäuel ['knɔʏəl] *m or nt* **-s**, **-** (*Woll—*) ball; (*Menschen—*) knot.

Knauf [knaʊf] *m* **-(e)s**, **Knäufe** knob; (*Schwert—*) pommel.

Knauser ['knaʊzɔr] *m* **-s**, **-** miser; **k~ig** *a* miserly; **k~n** *vi* be mean.

knautschen ['knaʊtʃən] *vti* crumple.

Knebel ['kneːbəl] *m* **-s**, **-** gag; **k~n** *vt* gag; (*Naut*) fasten.

Knecht [knɛçt] *m* **-(e)s**, **-e** farm labourer; servant; **k~en** *vt* enslave; ~**schaft** *f* servitude.

kneifen ['knaɪfən] *vti irreg* pinch; (*sich drücken*) back out; **vor etw ~** dodge sth.

Kneipe ['knaɪpə] *f-*, **-n** (*col*) pub.

Knet- [kneːt] *cpd:* **k~en** *vt* knead; *Wachs* mould; ~**masse** *f* Plasticine ®.

Knick [knɪk] *m* **-(e)s**, **-e** (*Sprung*) crack; (*Kurve*) bend; (*Falte*) fold; **k~en** *vti* (*springen*) crack; (*brechen*) break; *Papier* fold; **geknickt sein** be downcast.

Knicks [knɪks] *m* **-es**, **-e** curtsey; **k~en** *vi* curtsey.

Knie [kniː] *nt* **-s**, **-** knee; ~**beuge** *f-*, **-n** knee bend; **k~n** *vi* kneel; ~**fall** *m* genuflection; ~**gelenk** *nt* knee joint; ~**kehle** *f*

back of the knee; ~**scheibe** *f* kneecap; ~**strumpf** *m* knee-length sock.

Kniff [knɪf] *m* **-(e)s**, **-e** (*Zwicken*) pinch; (*Falte*) fold; (*fig*) trick, knack; **k~elig** *a* tricky.

knipsen ['knɪpsən] *vti Fahrkarte* punch; (*Phot*) take a snap (of), snap.

Knirps [knɪrps] *m* **-es**, **-e** little chap; ® (*Schirm*) telescopic umbrella.

knirschen ['knɪrʃən] *vi* crunch; **mit den Zähnen ~** grind one's teeth.

knistern ['knɪstərn] *vi* crackle.

Knitter- ['knɪtər] *cpd:* ~**falte** *f* crease; **k~frei** *a* non-crease; **k~n** *vi* crease.

Knoblauch ['knoːplaʊx] *m* **-(e)s** garlic.

Knöchel ['knœçəl] *m* **-s**, **-** knuckle; (*Fuß—*) ankle.

Knochen ['knɔxən] *m* **-s**, **-** bone; ~**bau** *m* bone structure; ~**bruch** *m* fracture; ~**gerüst** *nt* skeleton.

knöchern ['knœçərn] *a* bone.

knochig ['knɔxɪç] *a* bony.

Knödel ['knøːdəl] *m* **-s**, **-** dumpling.

Knolle ['knɔlə] *f-*, **-n** bulb.

Knopf [knɔpf] *m* **-(e)s**, **:e** button; (*Kragen—*) stud; ~**loch** *nt* buttonhole.

knöpfen ['knœpfən] *vt* button.

Knorpel ['knɔrpəl] *m* **-s**, **-** cartilage, gristle; **k~ig** *a* gristly.

knorrig ['knɔrɪç] *a* gnarled, knotted.

Knospe ['knɔspə] *f-*, **-n** bud; **k~n** *vi* bud.

Knoten ['knoːtən] *m* **-s**, **-** knot; (*Bot*) node; (*Med*) lump; **k~** *vt* knot; ~**punkt** *m* junction.

knuffen ['knʊfən] *vt* (*col*) cuff.

Knüller ['knʏlər] *m* **-s**, **-** (*col*) hit; (*Reportage*) scoop.

knüpfen ['knʏpfən] *vt* tie; *Teppich* knot; *Freundschaft* form.

Knüppel ['knʏpəl] *m* **-s**, **-** cudgel; (*Polizei—*) baton, truncheon; (*Aviat*) (joy)stick; ~**schaltung** *f* (*Aut*) floor-mounted gear change.

knurren ['knʊrən] *vi* (*Hund*) snarl, growl; (*Magen*) rumble; (*Mensch*) mutter.

knusperig ['knʊspərɪç] *a* crisp; *Keks* crunchy.

Koalition [koalitsi'oːn] *f* coalition.

Kobalt ['koːbalt] *nt* **-s** cobalt.

Kobold ['koːbɔlt] *m* **-(e)s**, **-e** goblin, imp.

Kobra ['koːbra] *f-*, **-s** cobra.

Koch [kɔx] *m* **-(e)s**, **:e** cook; ~**buch** *nt* cookery book; **k~en** *vti* cook; *Wasser* boil; ~**er** *m* **-s**, **-** stove, cooker.

Köcher ['kœçər] *m* **-s**, **-** quiver.

Kochgelegenheit ['kɔxgəleːgənhaɪt] *f* cooking facilities *pl.*

Köchin ['kœçɪn] *f* cook.

Koch- *cpd:* ~**löffel** *m* kitchen spoon; ~**nische** *f* kitchenette; ~**platte** *f* boiling ring, hotplate; ~**salz** *nt* cooking salt; ~**topf** *m* saucepan, pot.

Köder ['køːdər] *m* **-s**, **-** bait, lure; **k~n** *vt* lure, entice.

Koexistenz [koɛksɪs'tɛnts] *f* coexistence.

Koffein [kɔfe'iːn] *nt* **-s** caffeine; **k~frei** *a* decaffeinated.

Koffer ['kɔfər] *m* **-s**, **-** suitcase; (*Schrank—*) trunk; ~**radio** *nt* portable radio; ~**raum** m (Aut) boot, trunk (US).

Kognak ['kɔnjak] m -s, -s brandy, cognac.

Kohl [ko:l] m -(e)s, -e cabbage.

Kohle ['ko:lə] f -, -n coal; (Holz—) charcoal; (Chem) carbon; ~**hydrat** nt -(e)s, -e carbohydrate; ~**ndioxyd** nt -(e)s, -e carbon dioxide; ~**ngrube** f coal pit, mine; ~**nhändler** m coal merchant, coalman; ~**nsäure** f carbon dioxide; ~**nstoff** m carbon; ~**papier** nt carbon paper; ~**stift** m charcoal pencil.

Köhler ['kø:lər] m -s, - charcoal burner.

Kohl- cpd: ~**rübe** f turnip; k~**schwarz** a coal-black.

Koje ['ko:jə] f -, -n cabin; (Bett) bunk.

Kokain [koka'i:n] nt -s cocaine.

kokett [ko'kɛt] a coquettish, flirtatious; ~**ieren** [-'ti:rən] vi flirt.

Kokosnuß ['ko:kɔsnus] f coconut.

Koks [ko:ks] m -es, -e coke.

Kolben ['kɔlbən] m -s, - (Gewehr—) rifle butt; (Keule) club; (Chem) flask; (Tech) piston; (Mais—) cob.

Kolchose [kɔl'ço:zə] f -, -n collective farm.

Kolik ['ko:lɪk] f colic, gripe.

Kollaps [kɔ'laps] m -es, -e collapse.

Kolleg [kɔ'le:k] nt -s, -s or -**ien** lecture course; ~**e** [kɔ'le:gə] m -n, -n, -n in f colleague; ~**ium** nt board; (Sch) staff.

Kollekte [kɔ'lɛktə] f -, -n (Rel) collection.

kollektiv [kɔlɛk'ti:f] a collective.

kollidieren [kɔli'di:rən] vi collide; (zeitlich) clash.

Kollision [kɔlizi'o:n] f collision; (zeitlich) clash.

kolonial [koloni'a:l] a colonial; K~**warenhändler** m grocer.

Kolonie [kolo'ni:] f colony.

kolonisieren [koloni'zi:rən] vt colonize.

Kolonist [kolo'nɪst] m colonist.

Kolonne [ko'lɔnə] f -, -n column; (von Fahrzeugen) convoy.

Koloß [ko'lɔs] m -sses, -sse colossus.

kolossal [kolɔ'sa:l] a colossal.

Kombi- ['kɔmbi] cpd: ~**nation** [-natsi'o:n] f combination; (Vermutung) conjecture; (Hemdhose) combinations pl; (Aviat) flying suit; k~**nieren** [-'ni:rən] vt combine; vi deduce, work out; (vermuten) guess; ~**wagen** m station wagon; ~**zange** f (pair of) pliers.

Komet [ko'me:t] m -en, -en comet.

Komfort [kɔm'fo:r] m -s luxury.

Komik ['ko:mɪk] f humour, comedy; ~**er** m -s, - comedian.

komisch ['ko:mɪʃ] a funny.

Komitee [komi'te:] nt -s, -s committee.

Komma ['kɔma] nt -s, -s or -**ta** comma.

Kommand- [kɔ'mand] cpd: ~**ant** [-'dant] m commander, commanding officer; ~**eur** [-'dø:r] m commanding officer; k~**ieren** [-'di:rən] vti command; ~**o** nt -s, -s command, order; (Truppe) detachment, squad; **auf** ~**o** to order.

kommen ['kɔmən] vi irreg come; (näher —) approach; (passieren) happen; (gelangen, geraten) get; (Blumen, Zähne, Tränen etc) appear; (in die Schule, das

Zuchthaus etc) go; ~ **lassen** send for; **das kommt in den Schrank** that goes in the cupboard; **zu sich** ~ come round or to; **zu etw** ~ acquire sth; **um etw** ~ lose sth; **nichts auf jdn/etw** ~ **lassen** have nothing said against sb/sth; **jdm frech** ~ get cheeky with sb; **auf jeden vierten kommt ein Platz** there's one place to every fourth person; **wer kommt zuerst?** who's first?; **unter ein Auto** ~ be run over by a car; **wie hoch kommt das?** what does that cost?; **K**~ nt -s coming.

Kommentar [kɔmɛn'ta:r] m commentary; **kein** ~ no comment; k~**los** a without comment.

Kommentator [kɔmɛn'ta:tɔr] m (TV) commentator.

kommentieren [kɔmɛn'ti:rən] vt comment on.

kommerziell [kɔmɛrtsi'ɛl] a commercial.

Kommilitone [kɔmili'to:nə] m -n, -n fellow student.

Kommiß [kɔ'mɪs] m -sses (life in the) army; ~**brot** nt army bread.

Kommissar [kɔmɪ'sa:r] m police inspector.

Kommission [kɔmɪsi'o:n] f (Comm) commission; (Ausschuß) committee.

Kommode [kɔ'mo:də] f -, -n (chest of) drawers.

Kommune [kɔ'mu:nə] f -, -n commune.

Kommunikation [kɔmunikatsi'o:n] f communication.

Kommunion [kɔmuni'o:n] f communion.

Kommuniqué [kɔmyni'ke:] nt -s, -s communiqué.

Kommunismus [kɔmu'nɪsmus] m communism.

Kommunist [kɔmu'nɪst] m communist; k~**isch** a communist.

kommunizieren [kɔmuni'tsi:rən] vi communicate; (Eccl) receive communion.

Komödiant [komédi'ant] m comedian; ~**in** f comedienne.

Komödie [ko'mé:diə] f comedy.

Kompagnon [kɔmpan'jö:] m -s, -s (Comm) partner.

kompakt [kɔm'pakt] a compact.

Kompanie [kɔmpa'ni:] f company.

Komparativ ['kɔmparati:f] m -s, -e comparative.

Kompaß ['kɔmpas] m -sses, -sse compass.

kompetent [kɔmpe'tɛnt] a competent.

Kompetenz f competence, authority.

komplett [kɔm'plɛt] a complete.

Komplikation [kɔmplikatsi'o:n] f complication.

Kompliment [kɔmpli'mɛnt] nt compliment.

Komplize [kɔm'pli:tsə] m -n, -n accomplice.

komplizieren [kɔmpli'tsi:rən] vt complicate.

Komplott [kɔm'plɔt] nt -(e)s, -e plot.

komponieren [kɔmpo'ni:rən] vt compose.

Komponist [kɔmpo'nɪst] m composer.

Komposition [kɔmpozitsi'o:n] f composition.

Kompost [kɔm'pɔst] *m* -(e)s, -e compost; ~**haufen** *m* compost heap.
Kompott [kɔm'pɔt] *nt* -(e)s, -e stewed fruit.
Kompresse [kɔm'prɛsə] *f* -, -n compress.
Kompressor [kɔm'prɛsɔr] *m* compressor.
Kompromiß [kɔmpro'mɪs] *m* -sses, -sse compromise; **k~bereit** *a* willing to compromise; ~**lösung** *f* compromise solution.
kompromittieren [kɔmprɔmɪ'ti:rən] *vt* compromise.
Kondens- [kɔn'dɛns] *cpd:* ~**ation** [kɔndɛnzatsi'o:n] *f* condensation; ~**ator** [kɔndɛn'za:tɔr] *m* condenser; **k~ieren** [kɔndɛn'zi:rən] *vt* condense; ~**milch** *f* condensed milk; ~**streifen** *m* vapour trail.
Kondition- [kɔndi'tsi:ɔn] *cpd:* ~**alsatz** [kɔnditsio'na:lzats] *m* conditional clause; ~**straining** *int* fitness training.
Konditor [kɔn'di:tɔr] *m* pastrycook; ~**ei** [kɔndito'raɪ] *f* café; cake shop.
kondolieren [kɔndo'li:rən] *vi* condole (*jdm* with sb).
Kondom [kɔn'do:m] *nt* -s, -e condom.
Konfektion [kɔnfɛktsi'o:n] *f* production of ready-made clothing; ~**skleidung** *f* ready-made clothing.
Konferenz [kɔnfe'rɛnts] *f* conference, meeting.
konferieren [kɔnfe'ri:rən] *vi* confer, have a meeting.
Konfession [kɔnfɛsi'o:n] *f* religion; (*christlich*) denomination; **k~ell** [-'nɛl] *a* denominational; **k~slos** *a* non-denominational; ~**sschule** *f* denominational school.
Konfetti [kɔn'fɛti] *nt* -(s) confetti.
Konfirmand [kɔnfɪr'mant] *m* candidate for confirmation.
Konfirmation [kɔnfɪrmatsi'o:n] *f* (*Eccl*) confirmation.
konfirmieren [kɔnfɪr'mi:rən] *vt* confirm.
konfiszieren [kɔnfɪs'tsi:rən] *vt* confiscate.
Konfitüre [kɔnfi'ty:rə] *f* -, -n jam.
Konflikt [kɔn'flɪkt] *m* -(e)s, -e conflict.
konform [kɔn'fɔrm] *a* concurring; ~**gehen** be in agreement.
konfrontieren [kɔnfrɔn'ti:rən] *vt* confront.
konfus [kɔn'fu:s] *a* confused.
Kongreß [kɔn'grɛs] *m* -sses, -sse congress.
Kongruenz [kɔngru'ɛnts] *f* agreement, congruence.
König ['kø:nɪç] *m* -(e)s, -e king; ~**in** ['kø:nɪgɪn] *f* queen; **k~lich** *a* royal; ~**reich** *nt* kingdom; ~**tum** *nt* -(e)s, -tümer kingship.
konisch ['ko:nɪʃ] *a* conical.
Konjugation [kɔnjugatsi'o:n] *f* conjugation.
konjugieren [kɔnju'gi:rən] *vt* conjugate.
Konjunktion [kɔnjuŋktsi'o:n] *f* conjunction.
Konjunktiv ['kɔnjuŋkti:f] *m* -s, -e subjunctive.
Konjunktur [kɔnjuŋk'tu:r] *f* economic situation; (*Hoch*—) boom.
konkav [kɔn'ka:f] *a* concave.

konkret [kɔn'kre:t] *a* concrete.
Konkurrent(in *f*) [kɔnku'rɛnt(ɪn)] *m* competitor.
Konkurrenz [kɔnku'rɛnts] *f* competition; **k~fähig** *a* competitive; ~**kampf** *m* competition; (*col*) rat race.
konkurrieren [kɔnku'ri:rən] *vi* compete.
Konkurs [kɔn'kurs] *m* -es, -e bankruptcy.
können ['kœnən] *vti irreg* be able to, can; (*wissen*) know; ~ **Sie Deutsch?** can you speak German?; **ich kann nicht . . . I** can't *or* cannot . . .; **kann ich gehen?** can I go?; **das kann sein** that's possible; **ich kann nicht mehr** I can't go on; **K~** *nt* -s ability.
konsequent [kɔnze'kvɛnt] *a* consistent.
Konsequenz [kɔnze'kvɛnts] *f* consistency; (*Folgerung*) conclusion.
Konserv- [kɔn'zɛrv] *cpd:* **k~ativ** [-a'ti:f] *a* conservative; ~**atorium** [-a'to:rium] *nt* academy of music, conservatory; (*of f*-, -n tinned food; ~**enbüchse** *f* tin, can; **k~ieren** [-'vi:rən] *vt* preserve; ~**ierung** *f* preservation; ~**ierungsmittel** *nt* preservative.
Konsonant [kɔnzo'nant] *m* consonant.
konstant [kɔn'stant] *a* constant.
Konstitution [kɔnstitutsi'o:n] *f* constitution; **k~ell** [-'nɛl] *a* constitutional.
konstruieren [kɔnstru'i:rən] *vt* construct.
Konstrukteur [kɔnstruk'tø:r] *m* engineer, designer.
Konstruktion [kɔnstruktsi'o:n] *f* construction.
konstruktiv [kɔnstruk'ti:f] *a* constructive.
Konsul ['kɔnzul] *m* -s, -n consul; ~**at** [-'la:t] *nt* consulate.
konsultieren [kɔnzul'ti:rən] *vt* consult.
Konsum [kɔn'zu:m] *m* -s consumption; ~**artikel** *m* consumer article; ~**ent** [-'mɛnt] *m* consumer; **k~ieren** [-'mi:rən] *vt* consume.
Kontakt [kɔn'takt] *m* -(e)s, -e contact; **k~arm** *a* unsociable; **k~freudig** *a* sociable; ~**linsen** *pl* contact lenses *pl*.
Konterfei ['kɔntəfaɪ] *nt* -s, -s picture.
kontern ['kɔntərn] *vti* counter.
Konterrevolution [kɔntərevolutsio:n] *f* counter-revolution.
Kontinent ['kɔntinɛnt] *m* continent.
Kontingent [kɔntɪŋ'gɛnt] *nt* -(e)s, -e quota; (*Truppen*—) contingent.
kontinuierlich [kɔntinu'i:rlɪç] *a* continuous.
Kontinuität [kɔntinui'tɛ:t] *f* continuity.
Konto ['kɔnto] *nt* -s, Konten account; ~**auszug** *m* statement (of account); ~**inhaber(in** *f*) *m* account holder; ~**r** [kɔn'to:r] *nt* -s, -e office; ~**rist** [-'rɪst] *m* clerk, office worker; ~**stand** *m* state of account.
Kontra ['kɔntra] *nt* -s, -s (*Cards*) double; **jdm ~ geben** (*fig*) contradict sb; ~**baß** *m* double bass; ~**hent** [-'hɛnt] *m* contracting party; ~**punkt** *m* counterpoint.
Kontrast [kɔn'trast] *m* -(e)s, -e contrast.
Kontroll- [kɔn'trɔl] *cpd:* ~**e** *f* -, -n control, supervision; (*Paß*—) passport control; ~**eur** [-'lø:r] *m* inspector; **k~ieren**

[-'li:rən] *vt* control, supervise; (*nachprüfen*) check.

Kontur [kɔn'tu:r] *f* contour.

Konvention [kɔnvɛntsi'o:n] *f* convention; **k~ell** [-'nɛl] *a* conventional.

Konversation [kɔnvɛrzatsi'o:n] *f* conversation; **~slexikon** *nt* encyclopaedia.

konvex [kɔn'vɛks] *a* convex.

Konvoi ['kɔnvɔy] *m* **-s, -s** convoy.

Konzentration [kɔntsɛntratsi'o:n] *f* concentration; **~slager** *nt* concentration camp.

konzentrieren [kɔntsɛn'tri:rən] *vtr* concentrate.

konzentriert *a* concentrated; *ad* zuhören, arbeiten intently.

Konzept [kɔn'tsɛpt] *nt* **-(e)s, -e** rough draft; **jdn aus dem ~ bringen** confuse sb.

Konzern [kɔn'tsɛrn] *m* **-s, -e** combine.

Konzert [kɔn'tsɛrt] *nt* **-(e)s, -e** concert; (*Stück*) concerto; **~saal** *m* concert hall.

Konzession [kɔntsɛsi'o:n] *f* licence; (*Zugeständnis*) concession; **k~ieren** [-'ni:rən] *vt* license.

Konzil [kɔn'tsi:l] *nt* **-s, -e** *or* **-ien** council.

konzipieren [kɔntsi'pi:rən] *vt* conceive.

Kopf [kɔpf] *m* **-(e)s, :e** head; **~bedeckung** *f* headgear.

köpfen ['kœpfən] *vt* behead; *Baum* lop; *Ei* take the top off; *Ball* head.

Kopf- *cpd:* **~haut** *f* scalp; **~hörer** *m* headphone; **~kissen** *nt* pillow; **k~los** *a* panic-stricken; **~losigkeit** *f* panic; **k~rechnen** *vi* do mental arithmetic; **~salat** *m* lettuce; **~schmerzen** *pl* headache; **~sprung** *m* header, dive; **~stand** *m* headstand; **~tuch** *nt* headscarf; **k~über** *ad* head over heels; **~weh** *nt* headache; **~zerbrechen** *nt*: **jdm ~zerbrechen machen** give sb a lot of headaches.

Kopie [ko'pi:] *f* copy; **k~ren** *vt* copy.

Koppel ['kɔpəl] *f* **-, -n** (*Weide*) enclosure; *nt* **-s, -** (*Gürtel*) belt; **k~n** *vt* couple; **~ung** *f* coupling; **~ungsmanöver** *nt* docking manoeuvre.

Koralle [ko'ralə] *f* **-, -n** coral; **~nkette** *f* coral necklace; **~nriff** *nt* coral reef.

Korb [kɔrp] *m* **-(e)s, :e** basket; **jdm einen ~ geben** (*fig*) turn sb down; **~ball** *m* basketball; **~stuhl** *m* wicker chair.

Kord [kɔrt] *m* **-(e)s, -e** corduroy.

Kordel ['kɔrdəl] *f* **-, -n** cord, string.

Kork [kɔrk] *m* **-(e)s, -e** cork; **~en** *m* **-s, -** stopper, cork; **~enzieher** *m* **-s, -** cork-screw.

Korn [kɔrn] *nt* **-(e)s, :er** corn, grain; (*Gewehr*) sight; **~blume** *f* cornflower; **~kammer** *f* granary.

Körnchen ['kœrnçən] *nt* grain, granule.

Körper ['kœrper] *m* **-s, -** body; **~bau** *m* build; **k~behindert** *a* disabled; **~gewicht** *nt* weight; **~größe** *f* height; **~haltung** *f* carriage, deportment; **k~lich** *a* physical; **~pflege** *f* personal hygiene; **~schaft** *f* corporation; **~teil** *m* part of the body.

Korps [ko:r] *nt* **-, -** (*Mil*) corps; students' club.

korpulent [kɔrpu'lɛnt] *a* corpulent.

korrekt [kɔ'rɛkt] *a* correct; **K~heit** *f* correctness; **K~or** *m* proofreader; **K~ur** [-'tu:r] *f* (*eines Textes*) proof-reading; (*Text*) proof; (*Sch*) marking, correction.

Korrespond- [kɔrɛspɔnd] *cpd:* **~ent(in** *f)* [-'dɛnt(in)] *m* correspondent; **~enz** [-'dɛnts] *f* correspondence; **k~ieren** [-'di:rən] *vi* correspond.

Korridor ['kɔrido:r] *m* **-s, -e** corridor.

korrigieren [kɔri'gi:rən] *vt* correct.

korrumpieren [kɔrum'pi:rən] *vt* corrupt.

Korruption [kɔruptsi'o:n] *f* corruption.

Korsett [kɔr'zɛt] *nt* **-(e)s, -e** corset.

Kose- ['ko:zə] *cpd:* **~form** *f* pet form; **k~n** *vt* caress; *vi* bill and coo; **~name** *m* pet name; **~wort** *nt* term of endearment.

Kosmetik [kɔs'me:tık] *f* cosmetics *pl*; **~erin** *f* beautician.

kosmetisch *a* cosmetic; *Chirurgie* plastic.

kosmisch ['kɔsmiʃ] *a* cosmic.

Kosmo- [kɔsmo] *cpd:* **~naut** [-'naut] *m* **-en, -en** cosmonaut; **~polit** [-'po'li:t] *m* **-en, -en** cosmopolitan; **k~politisch** [-po'li:tiʃ] *a* cosmopolitan; **~s** *m* **-** cosmos.

Kost [kɔst] *f* **-** (*Nahrung*) food; (*Verpflegung*) board; **k~bar** *a* precious; (*teuer*) costly, expensive; **~barkeit** *f* preciousness; costliness, expensiveness; (*Wertstück*) valuable; **~en** *pl* cost(s); (*Ausgaben*) expenses *pl*; **auf ~ von** at the expense of; **k~en** *vt* cost; *vti* (*versuchen*) taste; **~enanschlag** *m* estimate; **k~enlos** *a* free (of charge); **~geld** *nt* board.

köstlich ['kœstlıç] *a* precious; *Einfall* delightful; *Essen* delicious; **sich ~ amüsieren** have a marvellous time.

Kost- *cpd:* **~probe** *f* taste; (*fig*) sample; **k~spielig** *a* expensive.

Kostüm [kɔs'ty:m] *nt* **-s, -e** costume; (*Damen-*) suit; **~fest** *nt* fancy-dress party; **k~ieren** [kɔsty'mi:rən] *vtr* dress up; **~verleih** *m* costume agency.

Kot [ko:t] *m* **-(e)s** excrement.

Kotelett [kotə'lɛt] *nt* **-(e)s, -e** *or* **-s** cutlet, chop; **~en** *pl* sideboards *pl*.

Köter ['kø:tər] *m* **-s, -** cur.

Kotflügel *m* (*Aut*) wing.

Krabbe ['krabə] *f* **-, -n** shrimp; **k~ln** *vi* crawl.

Krach [krax] *m* **-(e)s, -s** *or* **-e** crash; (*andauernd*) noise; (*col:* Streit) quarrel, row; **k~en** *vi* crash; (*beim Brechen*) crack; *vr* (*col*) row, quarrel.

krächzen ['krɛçtsən] *vi* croak.

Kraft [kraft] *f* **-, :e** strength, power, force; (*Arbeits-*) worker; **in ~ treten** come into effect; **k~** *prep* **+gen** by virtue of; **~ausdruck** *m* swearword; **~fahrer** *m* motor driver; **~fahrzeug** *nt* motor vehicle; **~fahrzeugbrief** *m* logbook; **~fahrzeugsteuer** *f* road tax.

kräftig ['krɛftıç] *a* strong; **~en** [krɛftıgən] *vt* strengthen.

Kraft- *cpd:* **k~los** *a* weak; powerless; (*Jur*) invalid; **~probe** *f* trial of strength; **~rad** *nt* motorcycle; **k~voll** *a* vigorous;

~**wagen** m motor vehicle; ~**werk** nt power station.

Kragen ['kra:gən] m -s, - collar; ~**weite** f collar size.

Krähe ['krɛːə] f -, -n crow; **k**~**n** vi crow.

krakeelen [kra'ke:lən] vi (col) make a din.

Kralle ['kralə] f -, -n claw; (Vogel—) talon; **k**~**n** vt clutch; (krampfhaft) claw.

Kram [kra:m] m -(e)s stuff, rubbish; **k**~**en** vi rummage; ~**laden** m (pej) small shop.

Krampf [krampf] m -(e)s, ⁺e cramp; (zuckend) spasm; ~**ader** f varicose vein; **k**~**haft** a convulsive; (fig) Versuche desperate.

Kran [kra:n] m -(e)s, ⁺e crane; (Wasser—) tap.

Kranich ['kra:nɪç] m -s, -e (Zool) crane.

krank [kraŋk] a ill, sick; **K**~**e(r)** mf sick person; invalid, patient.

kränkeln ['krɛŋkəln] vi be in bad health.

kranken ['kraŋkən] vi: **an etw** (dat) ~ (fig) suffer from sth.

kränken ['krɛŋkən] vt hurt.

Kranken- cpd: ~**bericht** m medical report; ~**geld** nt sick pay; ~**haus** nt hospital; ~**kasse** f health insurance; ~**pfleger** m nursing orderly; ~**schwester** f nurse; ~**versicherung** f health insurance; ~**wagen** m ambulance.

Krank- cpd: **k**~**haft** a diseased; Angst etc morbid; ~**heit** f illness, disease; ~**heitserreger** m disease-carrying agent.

kränk- ['krɛŋk] cpd: ~**lich** a sickly; **K**~**ung** f insult, offence.

Kranz [krants] m -es, ⁺e wreath, garland.

Kränzchen ['krɛntsçən] nt small wreath; ladies' party.

Krapfen ['krapfən] m -s, - fritter; (Berliner) doughnut.

kraß [kras] a crass.

Krater ['kra:tər] m -s, - crater.

Kratz- ['krats] cpd: ~**bürste** f (fig) crosspatch; **k**~**en** vti scratch; ~**er** m -s, - scratch; (Werkzeug) scraper.

Kraul(schwimmen) ['kraul(ʃvɪmən)] nt -s crawl; **k**~**en** vi (schwimmen) do the crawl; vt (streicheln) tickle.

kraus [kraus] a crinkly; Haar frizzy; Stirn wrinkled; **K**~**e** ['krauzə] f -, -n frill, ruffle.

kräuseln ['krɔyzəln] vt Haar make frizzy; Stoff gather; Stirn wrinkle; vr (Haar) go frizzy; (Stirn) wrinkle; (Wasser) ripple.

Kraut [kraut] nt -(e)s, Kräuter plant; (Gewürz) herb; (Gemüse) cabbage.

Krawall [kra'val] m -s, -e row, uproar.

Krawatte [kra'vatə] f -, -n tie.

kreativ [krea'ti:f] a creative.

Kreatur [krea'tu:r] f creature.

Krebs [kre:ps] m -es, -e crab; (Med, Astrol) cancer.

Kredit [kre'di:t] m -(e)s, -e credit.

Kreide ['kraidə] f -, -n chalk; **k**~**bleich** a as white as a sheet.

Kreis [krais] m -es, -e circle; (Stadt— etc) district; **im** ~ **gehen** (lit, fig) go round in circles.

kreischen ['kraiʃən] vi shriek, screech.

Kreis- cpd: ~**el** ['kraizəl] m -s, - top; (Verkehrs—) roundabout; **k**~**en** ['kraizən] vi spin; **k**~**förmig** a circular; ~**lauf** m (Physiol) circulation; (fig: der Natur etc) cycle; ~**säge** f circular saw; ~**stadt** f county town; ~**verkehr** m roundabout traffic.

Kreißsaal ['kraisza:l] m delivery room.

Krem [kre:m] f -, -s cream, mousse.

Krematorium [krema'to:rium] nt crematorium.

Krempe ['krɛmpə] f -, -n brim; ~**l** m -s (col) rubbish.

krepieren [kre'pi:rən] vi (col: sterben) die, kick the bucket.

Krepp [krɛp] m -s, -s or -e crepe; ~**papier** nt crepe paper; ~**sohle** f crepe sole.

Kresse ['krɛsə] f -, -n cress.

Kreuz [krɔyts] nt -es, -e cross; (Anat) small of the back; (Cards) clubs; **k**~**en** vtr cross; vi (Naut) cruise; ~**er** m -s, - (Schiff) cruiser; ~**fahrt** f cruise; ~**feuer** nt (fig) **im** ~**feuer stehen** be caught in the crossfire; ~**gang** m cloisters pl; **k**~**igen** vt crucify; ~**igung** f crucifixion; ~**otter** f adder; ~**ung** f (Verkehrs—) crossing, junction; (Züchten) cross; ~**verhör** nt cross-examination; ~**weg** m crossroads; (Rel) Way of the Cross; ~**worträtsel** nt crossword puzzle; ~**zeichen** nt sign of the cross; ~**zug** m crusade.

Kriech- ['kri:ç] cpd: **k**~**en** vi irreg crawl, creep; (pej) grovel, crawl; ~**er** m -s, - crawler; ~**spur** f crawler lane; ~**tier** nt reptile.

Krieg [kri:k] m -(e)s, -e war; **k**~**en** ['kri:gən] vt (col) get; ~**er** m -s, - warrior; **k**~**erisch** warlike; ~**führung** f warfare; ~**bemalung** f war paint; ~**serklärung** f declaration of war; ~**sfuß** m: **mit jdm/etw auf** ~**sfuß stehen** be at loggerheads with sb/not get on with sth; ~**sgefangene(r)** m prisoner of war; ~**sgefangenschaft** f captivity; ~**sgericht** nt court-martial; ~**sschiff** nt warship; ~**sschuld** f war guilt; ~**sverbrecher** m war criminal; ~**sversehrte(r)** m person disabled in the war; ~**szustand** m state of war.

Krimi ['kri:mi] m -s, -s (col) thriller; **k**~**nal** ['na:l] a criminal; ~**'nalbeamte(r)** m detective; ~**nali'tät** f criminality; ~**'nalpolizei** f detective force, CID (Brit); ~**'nalroman** m detective story; **k**~**nell** ['nɛl] a criminal; ~**'nelle(r)** m criminal.

Krippe ['krɪpə] f -, -n manger, crib; (Kinder—) crèche.

Krise ['kri:zə] f -, -n crisis; **k**~**ln** vi: **es kriselt** there's a crisis; ~**nherd** m trouble spot.

Kristall [krɪs'tal] m -s, -e crystal; nt -s (Glas) crystal.

Kriterium [kri'te:rium] nt criterion.

Kritik [kri'ti:k] f criticism; (Zeitungs—) review, write-up; ~**er** ['kri:tikər] m -s, - critic; **k**~**los** a uncritical.

kritisch ['kri:tiʃ] a critical.

kritisieren [kriti'zi:rən] vti criticize.

kritteln ['krɪtəln] *vi* find fault, carp.
kritzeln ['krɪtsəln] *vti* scribble, scrawl.
Krokodil [kroko'diːl] *nt* **-s, -e** crocodile.
Krokus ['kroːkʊs] *m* **-, -** *or* **-se** crocus.
Krone ['kroːnə] *f* **-, -n** crown; (*Baum—*) top.
krönen ['kroːnən] *vt* crown.
Kron- *cpd:* **~korken** *m* bottle top; **~leuchter** *m* chandelier; **~prinz** *m* crown prince.
Krönung ['kroːnʊŋ] *f* coronation.
Kropf [krɔpf] *m* **-(e)s, ⁺e** (*Med*) goitre; (*im Vogel*) crop.
Kröte ['kroːtə] *f* **-, -n** toad.
Krücke ['krʏkə] *f* **-, -n** crutch.
Krug [kruːk] *m* **-(e)s, ⁺e** jug; (*Bier—*) mug.
Krümel ['kryːməl] *m* **-s, -** crumb; **k~n** *vti* crumble.
krumm [krʊm] *a* (*lit, fig*) crooked; (*kurvig*) curved; **~beinig** a bandy-legged.
krümm- ['krʏm] *cpd:* **~en** *vtr* curve, bend; **K~ung** *f* bend, curve.
krumm- *cpd:* **~lachen** *vr* (*col*) laugh o.s. silly; **~nehmen** *vt irreg* (*col*) **jdm etw ~nehmen** take sth amiss.
Krüppel ['krʏpəl] *m* **-s, -** cripple.
Kruste ['krʊstə] *f* **-, -n** crust.
Kruzifix [krutsi'fɪks] *nt* **-es, -e** crucifix.
Kübel ['kyːbəl] *m* **-s, -** tub; (*Eimer*) pail.
Küche ['kʏçə] *f* **-, -n** kitchen; (*Kochen*) cooking, cuisine.
Kuchen ['kuːxən] *m* **-s, -** cake; **~blech** *nt* baking tray; **~form** *f* baking tin; **~gabel** *f* pastry fork; **~teig** *m* cake mixture.
Küchen- *cpd:* **~herd** *m* range; (*Gas, Elec*) cooker, stove; **~schabe** *f* cockroach; **~nschrank** *m* kitchen cabinet.
Kuckuck ['kʊkʊk] *m* **-s, -e** cuckoo.
Kufe ['kuːfə] *f* **-, -n** (*Faß*) vat; (*Schlitten—*) runner; (*Aviat*) skid.
Kugel ['kuːgəl] *f* **-, -n** ball; (*Math*) sphere; (*Mil*) bullet; (*Erd—*) globe; (*Sport*) shot; **k~förmig** a spherical; **~lager** *nt* ball bearing; **k~n** *vt* roll; (*Sport*) bowl; *vr* (*vor Lachen*) double up; **k~rund** a Gegenstand round; (*col*) *Person* tubby; **~schreiber** *m* ball-point (pen), biro ⁺; **k~sicher** a bulletproof; **~stoßen** *nt* **-s** shot-put.
Kuh [kuː] *f* **-, ⁺e** cow.
kühl [kyːl] a (*lit, fig*) cool; **K~anlage** *f* refrigerating plant; **K~e** *f* **-** coolness; **~en** *vt* cool; **K~er** *m* **-s, -** (*Aut*) radiator; **K~erhaube** (*Aut*) bonnet, hood (*US*); **K~raum** *m* cold-storage chamber; **K~schrank** *m* refrigerator; **K~truhe** *f* freezer; **K~ung** *f* cooling; **K~wagen** *m* (*Rail*) refrigerator van; **K~wasser** *nt* cooling water.
kühn [kyːn] a bold, daring; **K~heit** *f* boldness.
Küken ['kyːkən] *nt* **-s, -** chicken.
kulant [ku'lant] a obliging.
Kuli ['kuːli] *m* **-s, -s** coolie; (*col: Kugelschreiber*) biro ⁺.
Kulisse [ku'lɪsə] *f* **-, -n** scene.
kullern ['kʊlərn] *vi* roll.
Kult [kʊlt] *m* **-(e)s, -e** worship, cult; **mit etw ~ treiben** make a cult out of sth; **k~ivieren** [-i'viːrən] *vt* cultivate;

k~iviert a cultivated, refined; **~ur** [kʊl'tuːr] *f* culture; civilization; (*das Boden*) cultivation; **k~urell** [-u'rɛl] a cultural; **~urfilm** *m* documentary film.
Kümmel ['kʏməl] *m* **-s, -** caraway seed; (*Branntwein*) kümmel.
Kummer [kʊmər] *m* **-s** grief, sorrow.
kümmer- ['kʏmər] *cpd:* **~lich** a miserable, wretched; **~n** *vr:* **sich um jdn ~n** look after sb; **sich um etw ~n** see to sth; *vt* concern; **das kümmert mich nicht** that doesn't worry me.
Kumpan [kʊm'paːn] *m* **-s, -e** mate; (*pej*) accomplice.
Kumpel ['kʊmpəl] *m* **-s, -** (*col*) mate.
kündbar ['kʏntbaːr] a redeemable, recallable; *Vertrag* terminable.
Kunde ['kʊndə] *m* **-n, -n, Kundin** *f* customer; *f* **-, -n** (*Botschaft*) news; **~ndienst** *m* after-sales service.
Kund- *cpd:* **~gabe** *f* announcement; **k~geben** *vt irreg* announce; **~gebung** *f* announcement; (*Versammlung*) rally; **k~ig** a expert, experienced.
Künd- ['kʏnd] *cpd:* **k~igen** *vi* give in one's notice; **jdm k~igen** give sb his notice; *vt* cancel; (**jdm**) **die Stellung/Wohnung ~** give (sb) notice; **~igung** *f* notice; **~igungsfrist** *f* period of notice.
Kundschaft *f* customers *pl*, clientele.
künftig ['kʏnftɪç] a future; *ad* in future.
Kunst [kʊnst] *f* **-, ⁺e** art; (*Können*) skill; **das ist doch keine ~** it's easy; **~akademie** *f* academy of art; **~dünger** *m* artificial manure; **~faser** *f* synthetic fibre; **~fertigkeit** *f* skilfulness; **~geschichte** *f* history of art; **~gewerbe** *nt* arts and crafts *pl*; **~griff** *m* trick, knack; **~händler** *m* art dealer; **~harz** *nt* artificial resin.
Künstler(in *f*) ['kʏnstlər(ɪn)] *m* **-s, -** artist; **k~isch** a artistic; **~name** *m* stagename; pseudonym.
künstlich ['kʏnstlɪç] a artificial.
Kunst- *cpd:* **~sammler** *m* **-s, -** art collector; **~seide** *f* artificial silk; **~stoff** *m* synthetic material; **~stopfen** *nt* **-s** invisible mending; **~stück** *nt* trick; **~turnen** *nt* gymnastics; **k~voll** a ingenious, artistic; **~werk** *nt* work of art.
kunterbunt ['kʊntərbʊnt] a higgledy-piggledy.
Kupfer ['kʊpfər] *nt* **-s, -** copper; **~geld** *nt* coppers *pl*; **k~n** a copper; **~stich** *m* copperplate engraving.
Kuppe ['kʊpə] *f* **-, -n** (*Berg—*) top; (*Finger—*) tip; **~l** *f* **-, -n** cupola, dome; **~lei** *f* (*Jur*) procuring; **k~ln** *vi* (*Jur*) procure; (*Aut*) declutch; *vt* join.
Kupp- ['kʊp] *cpd:* **~ler** *m* **-s, -** pimp; **~lerin** *f* matchmaker; **~lung** *f* coupling; (*Aut*) clutch.
Kur [kuːr] *f*, **-en** cure, treatment.
Kür [kyːr] *f* **-, -en** (*Sport*) free skating/exercises pl.
Kurbel ['kʊrbəl] *f* **-, -n** crank, winch; (*Aut*) starting handle; **~welle** *f* crankshaft.
Kürbis ['kʏrbɪs] *m* **-ses, -se** pumpkin; (*exotisch*) gourd.
Kur- ['kuːr] *cpd:* **~gast** *m* visitor (to a

health resort); **k~ieren** [ku'ri:rən] vt cure; **k~ios** [kuri'o:s] a curious, odd; **~iosi'tät** f curiosity; **~ort** m health resort; **~pfuscher** m quack.

Kurs [kurs] m -es, -e course; (Fin) rate; **hoch im ~ stehen** (fig) be highly thought of; **~buch** nt timetable; **k~ieren** [kur'zi:rən] vi circulate; **k~iv** ad in italics; **~ive** [kur'zi:və] f -, -n italics pl; **~us** ['kurzus] m -, **Kurse** course; **~wagen** m (Rail) through carriage.

Kurve ['kurvə] f -, -n curve; (Straßen— auch) bend; **k~nreich, kurvig** a Straße bendy.

kurz [kurts] a short; **zu ~ kommen** come off badly; **den eren ziehen** get the worst of it; **K~arbeit** f short-time work; **~ärm(e)lig** a short-sleeved.

Kürze ['kyrtsə] f -, -n shortness, brevity; **k~n** vt cut short; (in der Länge) shorten; Gehalt reduce.

kurz- cpd: **~erhand** ad on the spot; **K~fassung** f shortened version; **~fristig** a short-term; **~gefaßt** a concise; **K~geschichte** f short story; **~halten** vt irreg keep short; **~lebig** a shortlived.

kürzlich ['kyrtslıç] ad lately, recently.

Kurz- cpd: **~schluß** m (Elec) short circuit; **~schrift** f shorthand; **k~sichtig** a short-sighted; **~welle** f shortwave.

kuscheln ['kuʃəln] vr snuggle up.

Kusine [ku'zi:nə] f cousin.

Kuß [kus] m -sses, ⸚sse kiss.

küssen ['kysən] vtr kiss.

Küste ['kystə] f -, -n coast; shore; **~nwache** f coastguard (station).

Küster ['kystər] m -s, - sexton, verger.

Kutsche ['kutʃə] f -, -n coach, carriage; **~r** m -s, - coachman.

Kutte ['kutə] f -, -n cowl.

Kuvert [ku'vert] nt -s, -e or -s envelope; cover.

Kybernetik [kybɛr'ne:tık] f cybernetics.

kybernetisch [kybɛr'ne:tıʃ] a cybernetic.

L

L, l [ɛl] nt L, l.

laben ['la:bən] vtr refresh (o.s.); (fig) relish (an etw (dat) sth).

Labor [la'bo:r] nt -s, -e or -s lab; **~ant(in** f) [labo'rant(ın)] m lab(oratory) assistant; **~atorium** [labora'to:rium] nt laboratory.

Labyrinth [laby'rınt] nt -s, -e labyrinth.

Lache ['laxə] f -, -n (Wasser) pool, puddle; (col: Gelächter) laugh.

lächeln ['lɛçəln] vi smile; **L~** nt -s smile.

lachen ['laxən] vi laugh.

lächerlich ['lɛçərlıç] a ridiculous; **L~keit** f absurdity.

Lach- cpd: **~gas** nt laughing gas; **l~haft** a laughable.

Lachs [laks] m -es, -e salmon.

Lack [lak] m -(e)s, -e lacquer, varnish; (von Auto) paint; **l~ieren** [la'ki:rən] vt varnish; Auto spray; **~ierer** [la'ki:rər] m -s, - varnisher; **~leder** nt patent leather.

Lackmus ['lakmus] m or nt - litmus.

Lade ['la:də] f -, -n box, chest; **~baum** m derrick; **~fähigkeit** f load capacity.

laden ['la:dən] vt irreg Lasten load; (Jur) summon; (einladen) invite.

Laden ['la:dən] m -s, ⸚ shop; (Fenster—) shutter; **~besitzer** m shopkeeper; **~dieb** m shoplifter; **~diebstahl** m shoplifting; **~hüter** m -s, - unsaleable item; **~preis** m retail price; **~schluß** m closing time; **~tisch** m counter.

Laderaum m (Naut) hold.

Ladung ['la:duŋ] f (Last) cargo, load; (Beladen) loading; (Jur) summons; (Einladung) invitation; (Spreng—) charge.

Lage ['la:gə] f -, -n position, situation; (Schicht) layer; **in der ~ sein** be in a position; **l~nweise** ad in layers.

Lager ['la:gər] nt -s, - camp; (Comm) warehouse; (Schlaf—) bed; (von Tier) lair; (Tech) bearing; **~arbeiter(in** f) m storehand; **~bestand** m stocks pl; **~geld** nt storage (charges pl); **~haus** nt warehouse, store.

lagern ['la:gərn] vi (Dinge) be stored; (Menschen) camp; (auch vr: rasten) lie down; vt store; (betten) lay down; Maschine bed.

Lager- cpd: **~schuppen** m store shed; **~stätte** f resting place; **~ung** f storage.

Lagune [la'gu:nə] f -, -n lagoon.

lahm [la:m] a lame; **~en** vi be lame, limp.

lähmen ['lɛ:mən] vt paralyse.

lahmlegen vt paralyse.

Lähmung f paralysis.

Laib [laıp] m -s, -e loaf.

Laich [laıç] m -(e)s, -e spawn; **l~en** vi spawn.

Laie ['laıə] m -n, -n layman; **l~nhaft** a amateurish.

Lakai [la'kaı] m -en, -en lackey.

Laken ['la:kən] nt -s, - sheet.

Lakritze [la'krıtsə] f -, -n liquorice.

lallen ['lalən] vti slur; (Baby) babble.

Lamelle [la'mɛlə] f lamella; (Elec) lamina; (Tech) plate.

lamentieren [lamɛn'ti:rən] vi lament.

Lametta [la'mɛta] nt -s tinsel.

Lamm [lam] nt -(e)s, ⸚er lamb; **~fell** nt lambskin; **l~fromm** a like a lamb; **~wolle** f lambswool.

Lampe ['lampə] f -, -n lamp; **~nfieber** nt stage fright; **~nschirm** m lampshade.

Lampion [lãpi'õ:] m -s, -s Chinese lantern.

Land [lant] nt -(e)s, ⸚er land; (Nation, nicht Stadt) country; (Bundes—) state; **auf dem ~(e)** in the country; **~arbeiter** m farm or agricultural worker; **~besitz** m landed property; **~besitzer** m landowner; **~ebahn** f runway; **l~einwärts** ad inland; **l~en** ['landən] vti land.

Ländereien [lɛndə'raıən] pl estates pl.

Landes- ['landəs] cpd: **~farben** pl national colours pl; **~innere(s)** nt inland region; **~tracht** f national costume; **l~üblich** a customary; **~verrat** m high treason; **~verweisung** f banishment; **~währung** f national currency.

Land- cpd: **~gut** nt estate; **~haus** nt

country house; ~**karte** f map; ~**kreis** m administrative region; **l**~**läufig** a customary.

ländlich ['lɛntlɪç] a rural.

Land- cpd: ~**schaft** f countryside; (Art) landscape; **l**~**schaftlich** a scenic; regional; ~**smann** m, ~**smännin** f, pl -**sleute** compatriot, fellow countryman or countrywoman; ~**straße** f country road; ~**streicher** m -**s**, - tramp; ~**strich** m region; ~**tag** m (Pol) regional parliament.

Landung ['landʊŋ] f landing; ~**sboot** nt landing craft; ~**sbrücke** f jetty, pier; ~**sstelle** f landing place.

Land- cpd: ~**vermesser** m surveyor; ~**wirt** m farmer; ~**wirtschaft** f agriculture; ~**zunge** f spit.

lang [laŋ] a long; Mensch tall; ~**atmig** a long-winded; ~**e** ad for a long time; dauern, brauchen a long time.

Länge ['lɛŋə] f -, -**n** length; (Geog) longitude; ~**ngrad** m longitude; ~**nmaß** nt linear measure.

langen ['laŋən] vi (ausreichen) do, suffice; (fassen) reach (nach for); **es langt mir** I've had enough.

lang- cpd: **L**~**eweile** f boredom; ~**lebig** a long-lived.

länglich a longish.

lang- cpd: **L**~**mut** f forbearance, patience; ~**mütig** a forbearing.

längs [lɛŋs] prep +gen or dat along; ad lengthwise.

lang- cpd: ~**sam** a slow; **L**~**samkeit** f slowness; **L**~**schläfer(in** f) m late riser; **L**~**spielplatte** f long-playing record.

längst [lɛŋst] ad **das ist** ~ **fertig** that was finished a long time ago, that has been finished for a long time; ~**e(r,s)** a longest.

lang- cpd: ~**weilig** a boring, tedious; **L**~**welle** f long wave; ~**wierig** a lengthy, long-drawn-out.

Lanze ['lantsə] f -, -**n** lance.

Lanzette [lan'tsɛtə] f lancet.

lapidar [lapi'da:r] a terse, pithy.

Lappalie [la'pa:liə] f trifle.

Lappen ['lapən] m -**s**, - cloth, rag; (Anat) lobe.

läppisch ['lɛpɪʃ] a foolish.

Lapsus ['lapsus] m -, - slip.

Lärche ['lɛrçə] f -, -**n** larch.

Lärm [lɛrm] m -(e)s noise; **l**~**en** vi be noisy, make a noise.

Larve ['larfə] f -, -**n** mask; (Biol) larva.

lasch [laʃ] a slack; Geschmack tasteless.

Lasche ['laʃə] f -, -**n** (Schuh-) tongue; (Rail) fishplate.

Laser ['leɪzə] m -**s**, - laser.

lassen ['lasən] vti irreg leave; (erlauben) let; (aufhören mit) stop; (veranlassen) make; **etw machen** ~ to have sth done; **es läßt sich machen** it can be done; **es läßt sich öffnen** it can be opened, it opens.

lässig ['lɛsɪç] a casual; **L**~**keit** f casualness.

läßlich ['lɛslɪç] a pardonable, venial.

Last [last] f -, -**en** load, burden; (Naut, Aviat) cargo; (usu pl: Gebühr) charge; **jdm zur** ~ **fallen** be a burden to sb; ~**auto** nt lorry, truck; **l**~**en** vi (auf +dat) weigh on.

Laster ['lastə] nt -**s**, - vice.

Lästerer ['lɛstərər] m -**s**, - mocker; (Gottes—) blasphemer.

lasterhaft a immoral.

lästerlich a scandalous.

lästern ['lɛstərn] vti Gott blaspheme; (schlecht sprechen) mock.

Lästerung f jibe; (Gottes—) blasphemy.

lästig ['lɛstɪç] a troublesome, tiresome.

Last- cpd: ~**kahn** m barge; ~**kraftwagen** m heavy goods vehicle; ~**schrift** f debiting; debit item; ~**tier** nt beast of burden; ~**träger** m porter; ~**wagen** m lorry, truck.

latent [la'tɛnt] a latent.

Laterne [la'tɛrnə] f -, -**n** lantern; (Straßen—) lamp, light; ~**npfahl** m lamppost.

Latrine [la'tri:nə] f latrine.

Latsche ['latʃə] f -, -**n** dwarf pine; **l**~**n** ['la:tʃən] vi (col) (gehen) wander, go; (lässig) slouch.

Latte ['latə] f -, -**n** lath; (Sport) goalpost; (quer) crossbar; ~**nzaun** m lattice fence.

Latz [lats] m -**es**, ⁼**e** bib; (Hosen—) flies pl.

Lätzchen ['lɛtsçən] nt bib.

Latzhose f dungarees pl.

lau [lau] a Nacht balmy; Wasser lukewarm.

Laub [laup] nt -(e)s foliage; ~**baum** m deciduous tree; ~**e** ['laubə] f -, -**n** arbour; ~**frosch** m tree frog; ~**säge** f fretsaw.

Lauch [laux] m -(e)s, -**e** leek.

Lauer ['lauər] f: **auf der** ~ **sein** or **liegen**, **l**~**n** vi lie in wait; (Gefahr) lurk.

Lauf [lauf] m -(e)s, **Läufe** run; (Wett—) race; (Entwicklung, Astron) course; (Gewehr) barrel; **einer Sache ihren** ~ **lassen** let sth take its course; ~**bahn** f career; ~**bursche** m errand boy.

laufen ['laufən] vti irreg run; (col: gehen) walk; ~**d** a running; Monat, Ausgaben current; **auf dem** ~**den sein/halten** be/keep up to date; **am** ~**den Band** (fig) continuously; ~ **lassen** vt irreg leave running; ~**lassen** vt irreg Person let go.

Läufer ['lɔʏfər] m -**s**, - (Teppich, Sport) runner; (Fußball) half-back; (Schach) bishop.

Lauf- cpd: ~**kundschaft** f passing trade; ~**masche** f run, ladder (Brit); **im** ~**schritt** at a run; ~**stall** m playpen; ~**steg** m dais; ~**zettel** m circular.

Lauge ['laugə] f -, -**n** soapy water; (Chem) alkaline solution.

Laune ['launə] f -, -**n** mood, humour; (Einfall) caprice; (schlechte) temper; **l**~**nhaft** a capricious, changeable.

launisch a moody; bad-tempered.

Laus [laus] f -, **Läuse** louse; ~**bub** m rascal, imp.

lauschen ['lauʃən] vi eavesdrop, listen in.

lauschig ['lauʃɪç] a snug.

lausen ['lauzən] vt delouse.

laut [laut] a loud; ad loudly; lesen aloud;

prep +*gen or dat* according to; **L~** *m* **-(e)s, -e** sound.

Laute ['lautə] *f* **-, -n** lute.

lauten ['lautən] *vi* say; (*Urteil*) be.

läuten ['lɔytən] *vti* ring, sound.

lauter ['lautər] *a Wasser* clear, pure; *Wahrheit, Charakter* honest; *inv Freude, Dummheit etc* sheer; (*mit pl*) nothing but, only; **L~keit** *f* purity; honesty, integrity.

läutern ['lɔytərn] *vt* purify.

Läuterung *f* purification.

laut- *cpd:* **~hals** *ad* at the top of one's voice; **~los** *a* noiseless, silent; **~malend** *a* onomatopoeic; **L~schrift** *f* phonetics *pl*; **L~sprecher** *m* loudspeaker; **L~sprecherwagen** *m* loudspeaker van; **~stark** *a* vociferous; **L~stärke** *f* (*Rad*) volume.

lauwarm ['lauvarm] *a* (*lit, fig*) lukewarm.

Lava ['la:va] *f* **-, Laven** lava.

Lavendel [la'vɛndəl] *m* **-s, -** lavender.

Lawine [la'vi:nə] *f* avalanche; **~ngefahr** *f* danger of avalanches.

lax [laks] *a* lax.

Lazarett [latsa'rɛt] *nt* **-(e)s, -e** (*Mil*) hospital, infirmary.

Lebe- *cpd:* **~hoch** *nt* three cheers *pl*; **~mann** *m, pl* **~männer** man about town.

leben ['le:bən] *vti* live; **L~** *nt* **-s, -** life; **~d** *a* living; **~dig** [le'bɛndiç] *a* living, alive; (*lebhaft*) lively; **L~digkeit** *f* liveliness.

Lebens- *cpd:* **~alter** *nt* age; **~art** *f* way of life; **~erwartung** *f* life expectancy; **l~fähig** *a* able to live; **l~froh** *a* full of the joys of life; **~gefahr** *f:* **~gefahr!** danger!; **in ~gefahr** dangerously ill; **l~gefährlich** *a* dangerous; *Verletzung* critical; **~haltungskosten** *pl* cost of living *sing*; **~jahr** *nt* year of life; **~lage** *f* situation in life; **~lauf** *m* curriculum vitae; **l~lustig** *a* cheerful, lively; **~mittel** *pl* food *sing*; **~mittelgeschäft** *nt* grocer's; **l~müde** *a* tired of life; **~retter** *m* lifesaver; **~standard** *m* standard of living; **~stellung** *f* permanent post; **~unterhalt** *m* livelihood; **~versicherung** *f* life insurance; **~wandel** *m* way of life; **~weise** *f* way of life, habits *pl*; **~zeichen** *nt* sign of life; **~zeit** *f* lifetime.

Leber ['le:bər] *f* **-, -n** liver; **~fleck** *m* mole; **~tran** *m* cod-liver oil; **~wurst** *f* liver sausage.

Lebe- *cpd:* **~wesen** *nt* creature; **~wohl** *nt* farewell, goodbye.

leb- [le:p] *cpd:* **~haft** *a* lively, vivacious; **L~haftigkeit** *f* liveliness, vivacity; **L~kuchen** *m* gingerbread; **~los** *a* lifeless.

lechzen ['lɛçtsən] *vi:* **nach etw ~** long for sth.

leck [lɛk] *a* leaky, leaking; **L~** *nt* **-(e)s, -e** leak; **~en** *vi* (*Loch haben*) leak; *vti* (*schlecken*) lick.

lecker ['lɛkər] *a* delicious, tasty; **L~bissen** *m* dainty morsel; **L~maul** *nt:* **ein L~maul sein** enjoy one's food.

Leder ['le:dər] *nt* **-s, -** leather; **l~n** *a* leather; **~waren** *pl* leather goods *pl*.

ledig ['le:dɪç] *a* single; **einer Sache ~ sein** be free of sth; **~lich** *ad* merely, solely.

leer [le:r] *a* empty; vacant; **L~e** *f* - emptiness; **~en** *vt* empty; *vr* become empty; **L~gewicht** *nt* weight when empty; **L~lauf** *m* neutral; **~stehend** *a* empty; **L~ung** *f* emptying; (*Post*) collection.

legal [le'ga:l] *a* legal, lawful; **~i'sieren** *vt* legalize; **L~i'tät** *f* legality.

legen ['le:gən] *vt* lay, put, place; *Ei* lay; *vr* lie down; (*fig*) subside.

Legende [le'gɛndə] *f* -, **-n** legend.

leger [le'ʒe:r] *a* casual.

legieren [le'gi:rən] *vt* alloy.

Legierung *f* alloy.

Legislative [legisla'ti:və] *f* legislature.

legitim [legi'ti:m] *a* legitimate; **L~ation** [-atsi'o:n] *f* legitimation; **~ieren** [-'mi:rən] *vt* legitimate; *vr* prove one's identity; **L~i'tät** *f* legitimacy.

Lehm [le:m] *m* **-(e)s, -e** loam; **l~ig** *a* loamy.

Lehne ['le:nə] *f* **-, -n** arm; back; **l~n** *vtr* lean.

Lehnstuhl *m* armchair.

Lehr- *cpd:* **~amt** *nt* teaching profession; **~brief** *m* indentures *pl*; **~buch** *nt* textbook.

Lehre ['le:rə] *f* **-, -n** teaching, doctrine; (*beruflich*) apprenticeship; (*moralisch*) lesson; (*Tech*) gauge; **l~n** *vt* teach; **~r(in** *f)* *m* **-s, -** teacher.

Lehr- *cpd:* **~gang** *m* course; **~jahre** *pl* apprenticeship; **~kraft** *f* teacher; **~ling** *m* apprentice; **~plan** *m* syllabus; **l~reich** *a* instructive; **~satz** *m* proposition; **~stelle** *f* apprenticeship; **~stuhl** *m* chair; **~zeit** *f* apprenticeship.

Leib [laip] *m* **-(e)s, -er** body; **halt ihn mir vom ~!** keep him away from me; **~eserziehung** ['laibəs-] *f* physical education; **~esübung** *f* physical exercise; **l~haftig** *a* personified; *Teufel* incarnate; **l~lich** *a* bodily; *Vater etc* own; **~wache** *f* bodyguard.

Leiche ['laiçə] *f* **-, -n** corpse; **~nbeschauer** *m* **-s, -** doctor who makes out death certificate; **~nhemd** *nt* shroud; **~nträger** *m* bearer; **~nwagen** *m* hearse.

Leichnam ['laiçna:m] *m* **-(e)s, -e** corpse.

leicht [laiçt] *a* light; (*einfach*) easy; **L~athletik** *f* athletics *sing*; **~fallen** *vi irreg:* **jdm ~fallen** be easy for sb; **~fertig** *a* frivolous; **~gläubig** *a* gullible, credulous; **L~gläubigkeit** *f* gullibility, credulity; **~hin** *ad* lightly; **L~igkeit** *f* easiness; **mit L~igkeit** with ease; **~lebig** *a* easy-going; **~machen** *vt:* **es sich** (*dat*) **~machen** make things easy for oneself; **~nehmen** *vt irreg* take lightly; **L~sinn** *m* carelessness; **~sinnig** *a* careless.

Leid [lait] *nt* **-(e)s** grief, sorrow; **l~ a: etw l~ haben** *or* **sein** be tired of sth; **es tut mir/ihm l~** I am/he is sorry; **er/das tut mir l~** I am sorry for him/it; **l~en** ['laidən] *irreg vt* suffer; (*erlauben*) permit; **jdn/etw nicht l~en** *or* **können** not be able to stand sb/sth; **~en** *nt* **-s, -** suffering; (*Krankheit*) complaint; **~enschaft** *f* passion; **l~enschaftlich** *a* passionate.

leider ['laɪdər] *ad* unfortunately; **ja,** ~ yes, I'm afraid so; **~ nicht** I'm afraid not.

leidig ['laɪdɪç] *a* miserable, tiresome.

leidlich *a* tolerable; *ad* tolerably.

Leid- *cpd*: **~tragende(r)** *mf* bereaved; (*Benachteiligter*) one who suffers; **~wesen** *nt*: **zu jds ~wesen** to sb's dismay.

Leier ['laɪər] *f* **-, -n** lyre; (*fig*) old story; **~kasten** *m* barrel organ; **l~n** *vti* Kurbel turn; (*col*) Gedicht rattle off.

Leihbibliothek *f* lending library.

leihen ['laɪən] *vt irreg* lend; **sich** (*dat*) **etw ~** borrow sth.

Leih- *cpd*: **~gebühr** *f* hire charge; **~haus** *nt* pawnshop; **~schein** *m* pawn ticket; (*Buch- etc*) borrowing slip; **~wagen** *m* hired car.

Leim [laɪm] *m* **-(e)s, -e** glue; **l~en** *vt* glue.

Leine ['laɪnə] *f* **-, -n** line, cord; (*Hunde-*) leash, lead; **~n** *nt* **-s, -** linen; **l~n** *a* linen.

Lein- *cpd*: **~tuch** *nt* (*Bett—*) sheet; linen cloth; **~wand** *f* (*Art*) canvas; (*Cine*) screen.

leise ['laɪzə] *a* quiet; (*sanft*) soft, gentle.

Leiste ['laɪstə] *f* **-, -n** ledge; (*Zier—*) strip; (*Anat*) groin.

leisten ['laɪstən] *vt* Arbeit do; Gesellschaft keep; Ersatz supply; (*vollbringen*) achieve; **sich** (*dat*) **etw ~ können** be able to afford sth.

Leistung *f* performance; (*gute*) achievement; **~sdruck** *m* pressure; **l~sfähig** *a* efficient; **~sfähigkeit** *f* efficiency; **~szulage** *f* productivity bonus.

Leit- *cpd*: **~artikel** *m* leading article; **~bild** *nt* model.

leiten ['laɪtən] *vt* lead; Firma manage; (*in eine Richtung*) direct; (*Elec*) conduct.

Leiter ['laɪtər] *m* **-s, -** leader, head; (*Elec*) conductor; *f* **-, -n** ladder.

Leit- *cpd*: **~faden** *m* guide; **~fähigkeit** *f* conductivity; **~motiv** *nt* leitmotiv; **~planke** *f* **-, -n** crash barrier.

Leitung *f* (*Führung*) direction; (*Cine, Theat etc*) production; (*von Firma*) management; directors *pl*; (*Wasser—*) pipe; (*Kabel*) cable; **eine lange ~ haben** be slow on the uptake; **~sdraht** *m* wire; **~smast** *m* telegraph pole; **~srohr** *nt* pipe; **~swasser** *nt* tap water.

Lektion [lɛktsi'o:n] *f* lesson.

Lektor(in *f*) *m* ['lɛktɔr(ɪn)] (*Univ*) lector; (*Verlag*) editor.

Lektüre [lɛk'ty:rə] *f* **-, -n** (*Lesen*) reading; (*Lesestoff*) reading matter.

Lende ['lɛndə] *f* **-, -n** loin; **~nbraten** *m* roast sirloin; **~nstück** *nt* fillet.

lenk- ['lɛŋk] *cpd*: **~bar** *a* Fahrzeug steerable; Kind manageable; **~en** *vt* steer; Kind guide; Blick, Aufmerksamkeit direct (*auf +acc* at); **L~rad** *nt* steering wheel; **L~stange** *f* handlebars *pl*.

Lenz [lɛnts] *m* **-es, -e** (*liter*) spring.

Leopard [leo'part] *m* **-en, -en** leopard.

Lepra ['le:pra] *f* **-** leprosy.

Lerche ['lɛrçə] *f* **-, -n** lark.

lern- [lɛrn] *cpd*: **~begierig** *a* eager to learn; **~en** *vt* learn.

lesbar ['le:sba:r] *a* legible.

Lesbierin ['lɛsbiərin] *f* lesbian.

lesbisch ['lɛsbɪʃ] *a* lesbian.

Lese ['le:zə] *f* **-, -n** gleaning; (*Wein*) harvest; **~buch** *nt* reading book, reader; **l~n** *vti irreg* read; (*ernten*) gather, pick; **~r(in** *f*) *m* **-s, -** reader; **~rbrief** *m* reader's letter; **l~rlich** *a* legible; **~saal** *m* reading room; **~zeichen** *nt* bookmark.

Lesung ['le:zʊŋ] *f* (*Parl*) reading; (*Eccl*) lesson.

letzte(r, s) ['lɛtstə(r,z)] *a* last; (*neueste*) latest; **zum ~nmal** *ad* for the last time; **~ns** *ad* lately; **~re(r,s)** *a* latter.

Leuchte ['lɔyçtə] *f* **-, -n** lamp, light; **l~n** *vi* shine, gleam; **~r** *m* **-s, -** candlestick.

Leucht- *cpd*: **~farbe** *f* fluorescent colour; **~feuer** *nt* beacon; **~käfer** *m* glowworm; **~kugel** *f,* **~rakete** *f* flare; **~reklame** *f* neon sign; **~röhre** *f* strip light; **~turm** *m* lighthouse; **~zifferblatt** *nt* luminous dial.

leugnen ['lɔygnən] *vti* deny.

Leugnung *f* denial.

Leukämie [lɔykɛ'mi:] *f* leukaemia.

Leukoplast [lɔyko'plast] *nt* **-(e)s, -e** elastoplast .

Leumund ['lɔymʊnt] *m* **-(e)s, -e** reputation; **~szeugnis** *nt* character reference.

Leute ['lɔytə] *pl* people *pl*.

Leutnant ['lɔytnant] *m* **-s, -s** *or* **-e** lieutenant.

leutselig ['lɔytze:lɪç] *a* affable; **L~keit** *f* affability.

Lexikon ['lɛksikɔn] *nt* **-s, Lexiken** *or* **Lexika** dictionary.

Libelle [li'bɛlə] *f* **-, -n** dragonfly; (*Tech*) spirit level.

liberal [libe'ra:l] *a* liberal; **L~ismus** [libera'lısmus] *m* liberalism.

Libero ['li:bero] *m* **-s, -s** (*Fußball*) sweeper.

Licht [lɪçt] *nt* **-(e)s, -er** light; **l~ ~** a light, bright; **~bild** *nt* photograph; (*Dia*) slide; **~blick** *m* cheering prospect; **l~empfindlich** *a* sensitive to light; **l~en** *vt* clear; Anker weigh; *vr* clear up; (*Haar*) thin; **l~erloh** *ad*: **l~erloh brennen** blaze; **~hupe** *f* flashing of headlights; **~jahr** *nt* light year; **~maschine** *f* dynamo; **~meß** *f* - Candlemas; **~schalter** *m* light switch.

Lichtung *f* clearing, glade.

Lid [li:t] *nt* **-(e)s, -er** eyelid; **~schatten** *m* eyeshadow.

lieb [li:p] *a* dear; **~äugeln** *vi insep* ogle (*mit jdm/etw* sb/sth).

Liebe ['li:bə] *f* **-, -n** love; **l~bedürftig** *a*: **l~bedürftig sein** need love; **~'lei** *f* flirtation; **l~n** *vt* love; like; **l~nswert** *a* loveable; **l~nswürdig** *a* kind; **l~nswürdigerweise** *ad* kindly; **~nswürdigkeit** *f* kindness.

lieber ['li:bər] *ad* rather, preferably; **ich**

gehe ~ **nicht** I'd rather not go; see **gern, lieb.**

Liebes- cpd: ~**brief** m love letter; ~**dienst** m good turn; ~**kummer** m: ~**kummer haben** be lovesick; ~**paar** nt courting couple, lovers pl.

liebevoll a loving.

lieb- ['li:p] cpd: ~**gewinnen** vt irreg get fond of; ~**haben** vt irreg be fond of; **L**~**haber** m -s, - lover; **L**~**habe'rei** f hobby; ~**kosen** [li:p'ko:zən] vt insep caress; ~**lich** a lovely, charming; **L**~**ling** m darling; **L**~**lings-** in cpds favourite; ~**los** a unloving; **L**~**schaft** f love affair.

Lied [li:t] nt -(e)s, -er song; (Eccl) hymn; ~**erbuch** nt songbook; hymn book.

liederlich ['li:dərlɪç] a slovenly; (Lebenswandel) loose, immoral; **L**~**keit** f slovenliness; immorality.

Lieferant [lifə'rant] m supplier.

liefern ['li:fərn] vt deliver; (versorgen mit) supply; Beweis produce.

Liefer- cpd: ~**schein** m delivery note; ~**termin** m delivery date; ~**ung** f delivery; supply; ~**wagen** m van.

Liege ['li:gə] f -, -n bed.

liegen ['li:gən] vi irreg lie; (sich befinden) be; **mir liegt nichts/viel daran** it doesn't matter to me/it matters a lot to me; **es liegt bei Ihnen, ob . . .** it rests with you whether . . .; **Sprachen** ~ **mir nicht** languages are not my line; **woran liegt es?** what's the cause?; ~**bleiben** vi irreg (Person) stay in bed; stay lying down; (Ding) be left (behind); ~**lassen** vt irreg (vergessen) leave behind; **L**~**schaft** f real estate.

Liege- cpd: ~**sitz** m (Aut) reclining seat; ~**stuhl** m deck chair; ~**wagen** m (Rail) couchette.

Lift [lɪft] m -(e)s, -e or -s lift.

Likör [li'kø:r] m -s, -e liqueur.

lila ['li:la] a purple, lilac; **L**~ nt -s, -s (Farbe) purple, lilac.

Lilie ['li:liə] f lily.

Limonade [limo'na:də] f lemonade.

lind [lɪnt] a gentle, mild; **L**~**e** ['lɪndə] f -, -n lime tree, linden; ~**ern** vt alleviate, soothe; **L**~**erung** f alleviation; ~**grün** a lime green.

Lineal [line'a:l] nt -s, -e ruler.

Linie ['li:niə] f line; ~**nblatt** nt ruled sheet; ~**nflug** m scheduled flight; ~**nrichter** m linesman.

liniieren [lini'i:rən] vt line.

Linke ['lɪŋkə] f -, -n left side; left hand; (Pol) left; **l**~**(r,s)** a left; **l**~ **Masche** purl.

linkisch a awkward, gauche.

links [lɪŋks] ad left; to or on the left; ~ **von mir** on or to my left; **L**~**außen** [lɪŋks''ausən] m -s, - (Sport) outside left; **L**~**händer(in** f) m -s, - left-handed person; **L**~**kurve** f left-hand bend; **L**~**verkehr** m traffic on the left.

Linoleum [li'no:leum] nt -s lino(leum).

Linse ['lɪnzə] f -, -n lentil; (optisch) lens.

Lippe ['lɪpə] f -, -n lip; ~**nstift** m lipstick.

liquidieren [likvi'di:rən] vt liquidate.

lispeln ['lɪspəln] vi lisp.

List [lɪst] f -, -en cunning; trick, ruse.

Liste ['lɪstə] f -, -n list.

listig ['lɪstɪç] a cunning, sly.

Litanei [lita'nai] f litany.

Liter ['li:tər] nt or m -s, - litre.

literarisch [lɪtə'ra:rɪʃ] a literary.

Literatur [lɪtera'tu:r] f literature; ~**preis** m award for literature.

Litfaßsäule ['lɪtfaszɔylə] f advertising pillar.

Lithographie [litogra'fi:] f lithography.

Liturgie [litur'gi:] f liturgy.

liturgisch [li'turgɪʃ] a liturgical.

Litze ['lɪtsə] f -, -n braid; (Elec) flex.

live [laɪf] ad (Rad, TV) live.

Livree [li'vre:] f -, -n livery.

Lizenz [li'tsɛnts] f licence.

Lkw [ɛlka:'ve:] m Lastkraftwagen.

Lob [lo:p] nt -(e)s praise; **l**~**en** ['lo:bən] vt praise; **l**~**enswert** a praiseworthy.

löblich ['lø:plɪç] a praiseworthy, laudable.

Lobrede f eulogy.

Loch [lɔx] nt -(e)s, -er hole; **l**~**en** vt punch holes in; ~**er** m -s, - punch.

löcherig ['lœçərɪç] a full of holes.

Loch- cpd: ~**karte** f punch card; ~**streifen** m punch tape.

Locke ['lɔkə] f -, -n lock, curl; **l**~**n** vt entice; Haare curl; ~**nwickler** m -s, - curler.

locker ['lɔkər] a loose; ~**lassen** vi irreg: **nicht** ~**lassen** not let up; ~**n** vt loosen.

lockig ['lɔkɪç] a curly.

Lock- cpd: ~**ruf** m call; ~**ung** f enticement; ~**vogel** m decoy, bait.

Lodenmantel ['lo:dənmantəl] m thick woollen coat.

lodern ['lo:dərn] vi blaze.

Löffel ['lœfəl] m -s, - spoon; **l**~**n** vt (eat with a) spoon; **l**~**weise** ad by spoonfuls.

Logarithmentafel [loga'rɪtmənta:fəl] f log(arithm) tables pl.

Logarithmus [loga'rɪtmus] m logarithm.

Loge ['lo:ʒə] f -, -n (Theat) box; (Freimaurer) (masonic) lodge; (Pförtner—) office.

logieren [lo'ʒi:rən] vi lodge, stay.

Logik ['lo:gɪk] f logic.

logisch ['lo:gɪʃ] a logical.

Lohn [lo:n] m -(e)s, -e reward; (Arbeits—) pay, wages pl; ~**büro** nt wages office; ~**empfänger** m wage earner.

lohnen ['lo:nən] vt (liter) reward (jdm etw sb for sth); vr impers be worth it; ~**d** a worthwhile.

Lohn- cpd: ~**steuer** f income tax; ~**streifen** m pay slip; ~**tüte** f pay packet.

lokal [lo'ka:l] a local; **L**~ nt -(e)s, -e pub(lic house); ~**i'sieren** vt localize; **L**~**i'sierung** f localization.

Lokomotive [lokomo'ti:və] f -, -n locomotive.

Lokomotivführer m engine driver.

Lorbeer ['lɔrbe:r] m -s, -en (lit, fig) laurel; ~**blatt** nt (Cook) bay leaf.

Lore ['lo:rə] f -, -n (Min) truck.

Los [lo:s] nt -es, -e (Schicksal) lot, fate; lottery ticket.

los [lo:s] a loose; ~! go on!; **etw ~ sein** be rid of sth; **was ist ~?** what's the matter?; **dort ist nichts/viel ~** there's nothing/a lot going on there; **etw ~ haben** (col) be clever; ~**binden** vt irreg untie.

löschen ['lœʃən] vt Feuer, Licht put out, extinguish; Durst quench; (Comm) cancel; Tonband erase; Fracht unload; vi (Feuerwehr) put out a fire; (Papier) blot.

Lösch- cpd: ~**fahrzeug** nt fire engine; fire boat; ~**gerät** nt fire extinguisher; ~**papier** nt blotting paper; ~**ung** f extinguishing; (Comm) cancellation; (Fracht) unloading.

lose ['lo:zə] a loose.

Lösegeld nt ransom.

losen ['lo:zən] vi draw lots.

lösen ['lø:zən] vt loosen; Rätsel etc solve; Verlobung call off; (Chem) dissolve; Partnerschaft break up; Fahrkarte buy; vr (aufgehen) come loose; (Zucker etc) dissolve; (Problem, Schwierigkeit) (re)solve itself.

los- cpd: ~**fahren** vi irreg leave; ~**gehen** vi irreg set out; (anfangen) start; (Bombe) go off; **auf jdn** ~**gehen** make for sb; ~**kaufen** vt Gefangene, Geißeln pay ransom for; ~**kommen** vi irreg: **von etw** ~**kommen** get away from sth; ~**lassen** vt irreg Seil let go of; Schimpfe let loose; ~**laufen** vi irreg run off.

löslich ['lø:slɪç] a soluble; **L~keit** f solubility.

los- cpd: ~**lösen** vtr free; ~**machen** vt loosen; Boot unmoor; vr get free; ~**sagen** vr renounce (von jdm/etw sb/sth); ~**schrauben** vt unscrew; ~**sprechen** vt irreg absolve.

Losung ['lo:zʊŋ] f watchword, slogan.

Lösung ['lø:zʊŋ] f (Lockermachen) loosening; (eines Rätsels, Chem) solution; ~**smittel** nt solvent.

los- cpd: ~**werden** vt irreg get rid of; ~**ziehen** vi irreg (sich aufmachen) set out; **gegen jdn** ~**ziehen** run sb down.

Lot [lo:t] nt -(e)s, -e plummet; **im** ~ vertical; (fig) on an even keel; **l~en** vti plumb, sound.

löten [lø:tən] vt solder.

Lötkolben m soldering iron.

Lotse ['lo:tsə] m -n, -n pilot; (Aviat) air traffic controller; see Schüler~; **l~n** vt pilot; (col) lure.

Lotterie [lɔtə'ri:] f lottery.

Löwe ['lø:və] m -n, -n lion; (Astrol) Leo; ~**nanteil** m lion's share; ~**nmaul** nt snapdragon; ~**nzahn** m dandelion.

Löwin ['lø:vɪn] f lioness.

loyal [loa'ja:l] a loyal; **L~i'tät** f loyalty.

Luchs [lʊks] m -es, -e lynx.

Lücke ['lʏkə] f -, -n gap; ~**nbüßer** m -s, - stopgap; **l~nhaft** a defective, full of gaps; **l~nlos** a complete.

Luder ['lu:dər] nt -s, - (pej: Frau) hussy; (bedauernswert) poor wretch.

Luft [lʊft] f -, ⸚e air; (Atem) breath; **in der** ~ **liegen** be in the air; **jdn wie** ~ **behandeln** ignore sb; ~**angriff** m air raid; ~**ballon** m balloon; ~**blase** f air

bubble; **l~dicht** a airtight; ~**druck** m atmospheric pressure.

lüften ['lʏftən] vti air; Hut lift, raise.

Luft- cpd: ~**fahrt** f aviation; **l~gekühlt** a air-cooled; **l~ig** a Ort breezy; Raum airy; Kleider summery; ~**kissenfahrzeug** nt hovercraft; ~**krieg** m war in the air; aerial warfare; ~**kurort** m health resort; **l~leer** a: ~**leerer Raum** vacuum; ~**linie** f: **in der** ~**linie** as the crow flies; ~**loch** nt air-hole; (Aviat) air-pocket; ~**matratze** f lilo ®, air mattress; ~**pirat** m hijacker; ~**post** f airmail; ~**röhre** f (Anat) wind pipe; ~**schlange** f streamer; ~**schutz** m anti-aircraft defence; ~**schutzkeller** m air-raid shelter; ~**sprung** m: (fig) **einen** ~**sprung machen** jump for joy.

Lüftung ['lʏftʊŋ] f ventilation.

Luft- cpd: ~**verkehr** m air traffic; ~**waffe** f air force; ~**zug** m draught.

Lüge ['ly:gə] f -, -n lie; **jdn/etw** ~**n strafen** give the lie to sb/sth; **l~n** vi irreg lie.

Lügner(in f) m -s, - liar.

Luke ['lu:kə] f -, -n dormer window, hatch.

Lümmel ['lʏməl] m -s, - lout; **l~n** vr lounge (about).

Lump [lʊmp] m -en, -en scamp, rascal.

Lumpen ['lʊmpən] m -s, - rag; **sich nicht l~ lassen** not be mean.

lumpig ['lʊmpɪç] a shabby.

Lunge ['lʊŋə] f -, -n lung; ~**nentzündung** f pneumonia; **l~nkrank** a consumptive.

lungern ['lʊŋərn] vi hang about.

Lunte ['lʊntə] f -, -n fuse; ~ **riechen** smell a rat.

Lupe ['lu:pə] f -, -n magnifying glass; **unter die** ~ **nehmen** (fig) scrutinize.

Lupine [lu'pi:nə] f lupin.

Lust [lʊst] f -, ⸚e joy, delight; (Neigung) desire; ~ **haben zu** or **auf etw** (acc)/**etw zu tun** feel like sth/doing sth.

lüstern ['lʏstərn] a lustful, lecherous.

Lustgefühl nt pleasurable feeling.

lustig ['lʊstɪç] a (komisch) amusing, funny; (fröhlich) cheerful.

Lüstling m lecher.

Lust- cpd: **l~los** a unenthusiastic; ~**mord** m sex(ual) murder; ~**spiel** nt comedy; **l~wandeln** vi stroll about.

lutschen ['lʊtʃən] vti suck; **am Daumen** ~ suck one's thumb.

Lutscher m -s, - lollipop.

luxuriös [lʊksuri'ø:s] a luxurious.

Luxus ['lʊksʊs] m - luxury; ~**artikel** pl luxury goods pl; ~**hotel** nt luxury hotel; ~**steuer** f tax on luxuries.

Lymphe ['lʏmfə] f -, -n lymph.

lynchen ['lʏnçən] vt lynch.

Lyrik ['ly:rɪk] f lyric poetry; ~**er** m -s, - lyric poet.

lyrisch ['ly:rɪʃ] a lyrical.

M

M, m [ɛm] nt M, m.

Mach- [max] cpd: ~**art** f make; **m~bar** a feasible; ~**e** f - (col) show, sham;

m~en *vt* make; (*tun*) do; (*col: reparieren*) fix; (*betragen*) be; **das macht nichts** that doesn't matter; **mach's gut!** good luck!; *vr* come along (nicely); **sich an etw** (*acc*) m~en set about sth; *vi*: **in etw** (*dat*) m~en (*Comm*) be *or* deal in sth.

Macht [maxt] *f* **-s, ⁻e** power; ~**haber** *m* **-s, -** ruler.

mächtig ['mεςtıς] *a* powerful, mighty; (*col: ungeheuer*) enormous.

Macht- *cpd*: **m~los** *a* powerless; ~**probe** *f* trial of strength; ~**stellung** *f* position of power; ~**wort** *nt*: **ein ~wort sprechen** lay down the law.

Machwerk *nt* work; (*schlechte Arbeit*) botched-up job.

Mädchen ['mε:tçən] *nt* girl; **m~haft** *a* girlish; ~**name** *m* maiden name.

Made ['ma:də] *f-*, **-n** maggot.

madig ['ma:dıç] *a* maggoty; **jdm etw ~ machen** spoil sth for sb.

Magazin [maga'tsi:n] *nt* **-s, -e** magazine.

Magd [ma:kt] *f-*, **⁻e** maid(servant).

Magen ['ma:gən] *m* **-s, -** *or* **⁻** stomach; ~**schmerzen** *pl* stomachache.

mager ['ma:gər] *a* lean; (*dünn*) thin; **M~keit** *f* leanness; thinness.

Magie [ma'gi:] *f* magic; ~**r** ['ma:giər] *m* **-s, -** magician.

magisch ['ma:gıʃ] *a* magical.

Magnet [ma'gne:t] *m* **-s** *or* **-en, -en** magnet; **m~isch** *a* magnetic; **m~i-'sieren** *vt* magnetize; ~**nadel** *f* magnetic needle.

Mahagoni [maha'go:ni] *nt* **-s** mahogany.

mähen ['mε:ən] *vti* mow.

Mahl [ma:l] *nt* **-(e)s, -e** meal; **m~en** *vt irreg.* grind; ~**stein** *m* grindstone; ~**zeit** *f* meal; *interj* enjoy your meal.

Mahnbrief *m* reminder.

Mähne ['mε:nə] *f-*, **-n** mane.

Mahn- [ma:n] *cpd*: **m~en** *vt* remind; (*warnend*) warn; (*wegen Schuld*) demand payment from; ~**ung** *f* reminder; admonition, warning.

Mähre ['mε:rə] *f-*, **-n** mare.

Mai [maı] *m* **-(e)s, -e** May; ~**glöckchen** *nt* lily of the valley; ~**käfer** *m* cockchafer.

Mais [maıs] *m* **-es, -e** maize, corn (*US*); ~**kolben** *m* corncob.

Majestät [majεs'tε:t] *f* majesty; **m~isch** *a* majestic.

Major [ma'jo:r] *m* **-s, -e** (*Mil*) major; (*Aviat*) squadron leader.

Majoran [majo'ra:n] *m* **-s, -e** marjoram.

makaber [ma'ka:bər] *a* macabre.

Makel ['ma:kəl] *m* **-s, -** blemish; (*moralisch*) stain; **m~los** *a* immaculate, spotless.

mäkeln ['mε:kəln] *vi* find fault.

Makkaroni [maka'ro:ni] *pl* macaroni *sing.*

Makler ['ma:klər] *m* **-s, -** broker.

Makrele [ma'kre:lə] *f-*, **-n** mackerel.

Makrone [ma'kro:nə] *f-*, **-n** macaroon.

Mal [ma:l] *nt* **-(e)s, -e** mark, sign; (*Zeitpunkt*) time; **m~** ad times; (*col*) see **einmal**; ~**m~** *suff* -times; **m~en** *vti* paint; ~**er** *m* **-s, -** painter; ~**e'rei** *f*

painting; **m~erisch** *a* picturesque; ~**kasten** *m* paintbox; **m~nehmen** *vti irreg* multiply.

Malz [malts] *nt* **-es** malt; ~**bonbon** *nt* cough drop; ~**kaffee** *m* malt coffee.

Mama ['mama:] *f-*, **-s, Mami** ['mami] *f-*, **-s** (*col*) mum(my).

Mammut ['mamʊt] *nt* **-s, -e** *or* **-s** mammoth.

man [man] *pron* one, people *pl,* you.

manche(r,s) ['mançə(r,z)] *a* many a; (*pl*) a number of; *pron* some; ~**rlei** *a inv* various; *pron* a variety of things.

manchmal *ad* sometimes.

Mandant(in *f*) [man'dant(ın)] *m* (*Jur*) client.

Mandarine [manda'ri:nə] *f* mandarin, tangerine.

Mandat [man'da:t] *nt* **-(e)s, -e** mandate.

Mandel ['mandəl] *f-*, **-n** almond; (*Anat*) tonsil.

Manege [ma'ne:ʒə] *f-*, **-n** ring, arena.

Mangel ['maŋəl] *f-*, **-n** mangle; *m* **-s,** lack; (*Knappheit*) shortage (*an* +*dat* of); (*Fehler*) defect, fault; ~**erscheinung** *f* deficiency symptom; **m~haft** *a* poor; (*fehlerhaft*) defective, faulty; **m~n** *vi impers*: **es mangelt jdm an etw** (*dat*) sb lacks sth; *vt Wäsche* mangle; **m~s** *prep* +*gen* for lack of.

Manie [ma'ni:] *f* mania.

Manier [ma'ni:r] *f* - manner; style; (*pej*) mannerism; ~**en** *pl* manners *pl*; **m~iert** [mani'ri:rt] *a* mannered, affected; **m~lich** *a* well-mannered.

Manifest [mani'fεst] *nt* **-es, -e** manifesto.

Maniküre [mani'ky:rə] *f* -, **-n** manicure; **m~n** *vt* manicure.

manipulieren   [manipu'li:rən]   *vt* manipulate.

Manko ['maŋko] *nt* **-s, -s** deficiency; (*Comm*) deficit.

Mann [man] *m* **-(e)s, ⁻er** man; (*Ehe~*) husband; (*Naut*) hand; **seinen ~ stehen** hold one's own.

Männchen ['mεnçən] *nt* little man; (*Tier*) male.

Mannequin [manə'kε̃:] *nt* **-s, -s** fashion model.

mannigfaltig ['manıçfaltıç] *a* various, varied; **M~keit** *f* variety.

männlich ['mεnlıç] *a* (*Biol*) male; (*fig, Gram*) masculine.

Mann- *cpd*: ~**schaft** *f* (*Sport, fig*) team; (*Naut, Aviat*) crew; (*Mil*) other ranks *pl*; ~**sleute** *pl* (*col*) menfolk *pl*; ~**weib** *nt* (*pej*) mannish woman.

Manöver [ma'nø:vər] *nt* **-s, -** manoeuvre.

manövrieren   [manø'vri:rən]   *vti* manoeuvre.

Mansarde [man'zardə] *f-*, **-n** attic.

Manschette [man'ʃεtə] *f* cuff; (*Papier—*) paper frill; (*Tech*) collar; sleeve; ~**nknopf** *m* cufflink.

Mantel ['mantəl] *m* **-s, ⁻** coat; (*Tech*) casing, jacket.

Manuskript [manu'skrıpt] *nt* **-(e)s, -e** manuscript.

Mappe ['mapə] f -, -n briefcase; (Akten—) folder.

Märchen ['mɛːrçən] nt fairy tale; **m~haft** a fabulous; **~prinz** m prince charming.

Marder ['mardər] m -s, - marten.

Margarine [marga'riːnə] f margarine.

Marienkäfer [ma'riːɔnkɛːfər] m ladybird.

Marine [ma'riːnə] f navy; **m~blau** a navy-blue.

marinieren [mari'niːrən] vt marinate.

Marionette [mario'nɛtə] f puppet.

Mark [mark] f -, - (Münze) mark; nt -(e)s (Knochen—) marrow; **durch ~ und Bein gehen** go right through sb; **m~ant** [mar'kant] a striking.

Marke ['markə] f -, -n mark; (Warensorte) brand; (Fabrikat) make; (Rabatt—, Brief—) stamp; (Essens—) ticket; (aus Metall etc) token, disc.

Mark- cpd: **m~ieren** [mar'kiːrən] vt mark; vti (col) act; **~ierung** f marking; **m~ig** ['makiç] a (fig) pithy; **~ise** [mar'kiːzə] f -, -n awning; **~stück** nt one-mark piece.

Markt [markt] m -(e)s, ⁻e market; **~forschung** f market research; **~platz** m market place; **~wirtschaft** f market economy.

Marmelade [marmə'laːdə] f -, -n jam.

Marmor ['marmɔr] m -s, -e marble; **m~ieren** [-'riːrən] vt marble; **m~n** a marble.

Marone [ma'roːnə] f -, -n or **Maroni** chestnut.

Marotte [ma'rɔtə] f -, -n fad, quirk.

Marsch [marʃ] m -(e)s, ⁻e march; **m~** interj march; f -, -en marsh; **~befehl** m marching orders pl; **m~bereit** a ready to move; **m~ieren** [mar'ʃiːrən] vi march.

Marter ['martər] f -, -n torment; **m~n** vt torture.

Märtyrer(in f) ['mɛrtyrər(in)] m -s, - martyr.

März [mɛrts] m -(es), -e March.

Marzipan [martsi'paːn] nt -s, -e marzipan.

Masche ['maʃə] f -, -n mesh; (Strick—) stitch; **das ist die neueste ~** that's the latest dodge; **~ndraht** m wire mesh; **m~nfest** a runproof.

Maschine [ma'ʃiːnə] f machine; (Motor) engine; **m~ll** [maʃi'nɛl] a machine(-); mechanical; **~nbauer** m mechanical engineer; **~ngewehr** nt machine gun; **~npistole** f submachine gun; **~nschaden** m mechanical fault; **~nschlosser** m fitter; **~nschrift** f typescript; **m~schreiben** vi irreg type.

Maschinist [maʃi'nist] m engineer.

Maser ['maːzər] f -, -n grain; speckle; **~n** pl (Med) measles sing; **~ung** f grain(ing).

Maske ['maskə] f -, -n mask; **~nball** m fancy-dress ball; **~rade** [-'raːdə] f masquerade.

maskieren [mas'kiːrən] vt mask; (verkleiden) dress up; vr disguise o.s., dress up.

Maß [maːs] nt -es, -e measure; (Mäßigung) moderation; (Grad) degree, extent; f -, -(e) litre of beer.

Massage [ma'saːʒə] f -, -n massage.

Maß- cpd: **~anzug** m made-to-measure suit; **~arbeit** f (fig) neat piece of work.

Masse ['masə] f -, -n mass; **~nartikel** m mass-produced article; **~ngrab** nt mass grave; **m~nhaft** a loads of; **~nmedien** pl mass media pl.

Mass- cpd: **~eur** [ma'søːr] m masseur; **~euse** [ma'søːzə] f masseuse.

maß- cpd: **~gebend** a authoritative; **~halten** vi irreg exercise moderation.

massieren [ma'siːrən] vt massage; (Mil) mass.

massig ['masiç] a massive; (col) massive amount of.

mäßig ['mɛːsiç] a moderate; **~en** ['mɛːsigən] vt restrain, moderate; **M~keit** f moderation.

massiv [ma'siːf] a solid; (fig) heavy, rough; **M~** nt -s, -e massif.

Maß- cpd: **~krug** m tankard; **m~los** a extreme; **~nahme** f -, -n measure, step; **m~regeln** vt insep reprimand; **~stab** m rule, measure; (fig) standard; (Geog) scale; **m~voll** a moderate.

Mast ['mast] m -(e)s, -e(n) mast; (Elec) pylon.

mästen ['mɛstən] vt fatten.

Material [materi'aːl] nt -s, -ien material(s); **~fehler** m material defect; **~ismus** [-'lismus] m materialism; **~ist** [-'list] m materialist; **m~istisch** [-'listiʃ] a materialistic.

Materie [ma'teːriə] f matter, substance; **m~ll** [materi'ɛl] a material.

Mathematik [matema'tiːk] f mathematics sing; **~er(in** f) [mate'maːtikər(in)] m -s, - mathematician.

mathematisch [mate'maːtiʃ] a mathematical.

Matratze [ma'tratsə] f -, -n mattress.

Matrize [ma'triːtsə] f -, -n matrix; (zum Abziehen) stencil.

Matrose [ma'troːzə] m -n, -n sailor.

Matsch [matʃ] m -(e)s mud; (Schnee—) slush; **m~ig** a muddy; slushy.

matt [mat] a weak; (glanzlos) dull; (Phot) matt; (Schach) mate.

Matte ['matə] f -, -n mat.

Matt- cpd: **~igkeit** f weakness; dullness; **~scheibe** f (TV) screen; **~scheibe haben** (col) be not quite with it.

Mauer ['mauər] f -, -n wall; **m~n** vti build; lay bricks; **~werk** nt brickwork; (Stein) masonry.

Maul [maul] nt -(e)s, **Mäuler** mouth; **m~en** vi (col) grumble; **~esel** m mule; **~korb** m muzzle; **~sperre** f lockjaw; **~tier** nt mule; **~wurf** m mole; **~wurfshaufen** m molehill.

Maurer ['maurər] m -s, - bricklayer.

Maus [maus] f -, **Mäuse** mouse.

mäuschenstill ['mɔysçən'ʃtil] a very quiet.

Maus- [mauz] cpd: **~efalle** f mousetrap; **m~en** vt (col) flinch; vi catch mice; **m~ern** vr moult; **m~(e)tot** a stone dead.

maximal [maksi'maːl] a maximum.

Maxime [ma'ksi:mə] f -, -n maxim.
Mayonnaise [majo'nɛ:zə] f -, -n mayonnaise.
Mechan- [me'ça:n] cpd: ~**ik** f mechanics sing; (Getriebe) mechanics pl; ~**iker** m -s, - mechanic, engineer; m~**isch** a mechanical; m~**i'sieren** vt mechanize; ~**i'sierung** f mechanization; ~**ismus** [meça'nɪsmʊs] m mechanism.
meckern ['mɛkərn] vi bleat; (col) moan.
Medaille [me'daljə] f -, -n medal.
Medaillon [medal'jõ:] nt -s, -s (Schmuck) locket.
Medikament [medika'mɛnt] nt medicine.
meditieren [medi'ti:rən] vi meditate.
Medizin [medi'tsi:n] f -, -en medicine; m~**isch** a medical.
Meer [me:r] nt -(e)s, -e sea; ~**busen** m bay, gulf; ~**enge** f straits pl; ~**esspiegel** m sea level; ~**rettich** m horseradish; ~**schweinchen** nt guinea-pig.
Megaphon [mega'fo:n] nt -s, -e megaphone.
Mehl ['me:l] nt -(e)s, -e flour; m~**ig** a floury.
mehr [me:r] a,ad more; M~**aufwand** m additional expenditure; ~**deutig** a ambiguous; ~**ere** a several; ~**eres** pron several things; ~**fach** a multiple; (wiederholt) repeated; M~**heit** f majority; ~**malig** a repeated; ~**mals** ad repeatedly; ~**stimmig** a for several voices; ~**stimmig singen** harmonize; M~**wertsteuer** f value added tax, VAT; M~**zahl** f majority; (Gram) plural.
meiden ['maidən] vt irreg avoid.
Meile ['mailə] f -, -n mile; ~**nstein** m milestone; m~**nweit** a for miles.
mein [main] pron my; ~**e(r,s)** mine.
Meineid ['main'ait] m perjury.
meinen ['mainən] vti think; (sagen) say; (sagen wollen) mean; **das will ich** ~ I should think so.
mein- cpd: ~**er** pron gen of **ich** of me; ~**erseits** ad for my part; ~**esgleichen** pron people like me; ~**etwegen**, ~**etwillen** ad (für mich) for my sake; (wegen mir) on my account; (von mir aus) as far as I'm concerned; I don't care or mind; ~**ige** pron: **der/die/das** ~**ige** mine.
Meinung ['mainʊŋ] f opinion; **jdm die** ~ **sagen** give sb a piece of one's mind; ~**saustausch** m exchange of views; ~**sumfrage** f opinion poll; ~**sverschiedenheit** f difference of opinion.
Meise ['maizə] f -, -n tit(mouse).
Meißel ['maisəl] m -s, - chisel; m~**n** vt chisel.
meist ['maist] a,ad most(ly); ~**ens** ad generally, usually.
Meister ['maistər] m -s, - master; (Sport) champion; m~**haft** a masterly; m~**n** vt master; ~**schaft** f mastery; (Sport) championship; ~**stück** nt, ~**werk** nt masterpiece.
Melancholie [melaŋko'li:] f melancholy.
melancholisch [melaŋ'ko:lɪʃ] a melancholy.

Melde- ['mɛldə] cpd: ~**frist** f registration period; m~**n** vt report; vr report (bei to); (Sch) put one's hand up; (freiwillig) volunteer; (auf etw, am Telefon) answer; **sich zu Wort** m~**n** ask to speak; ~**pflicht** f obligation to register with the police; ~**stelle** f registration office.
Meldung ['mɛldʊŋ] f announcement; (Bericht) report.
meliert [me'li:rt] a mingled, speckled.
melken ['mɛlkən] vt irreg milk.
Melodie [melo'di:] f melody, tune.
melodisch [me'lo:dɪʃ] a melodious, tuneful.
Melone [me'lo:nə] f -, -n melon; (Hut) bowler (hat).
Membran(e) [mɛm'bra:n(ə)] f -, -en (Tech) diaphragm.
Memoiren [memo'a:rən] pl memoirs pl.
Menge ['mɛŋə] f -, -n quantity; (Menschen—) crowd; (große Anzahl) lot (of); m~**n** vt mix; vr: **sich** m~**n in** (+acc) meddle with; ~**nlehre** f (Math) set theory; ~**nrabatt** m bulk discount.
Mensch [mɛnʃ] m -en, -en human being, man; person; **kein** ~ nobody; nt -(e)s, -er hussy; ~**enalter** nt generation; ~**enfeind** m misanthrope; m~**enfreundlich** a philanthropical; ~**enkenner** m -s, - judge of human nature; ~**enliebe** f philanthropy; m~**enmöglich** a humanly possible; ~**enrecht** nt human rights pl; m~**enscheu** a shy; m~**enunwürdig** a degrading; ~**enverstand** m: **gesunder** ~**enverstand** common sense; ~**heit** f humanity, mankind; m~**lich** a human; (human) humane; ~**lichkeit** f humanity.
Menstruation [mɛnstruatsi'o:n] f menstruation.
Mentalität [mɛntali'tɛ:t] f mentality.
Menü [me'ny:] nt -s, -s menu.
Merk- [mɛrk] cpd: ~**blatt** nt instruction sheet or leaflet; m~**en** vt notice; **sich** (dat) **etw** m~**en** remember sth; m~**lich** a noticeable; ~**mal** nt sign, characteristic; m~**würdig** a odd.
Meß- [mɛs] cpd: m~**bar** a measurable; ~**becher** m measuring cup; ~**buch** nt missal.
Messe ['mɛsə] f -, -n fair; (Eccl) mass; (Mil) mess; m~**n** irreg vt measure; vr compete; ~**r** nt -s, - knife; ~**rspitze** f knife point; (in Rezept) pinch; ~**stand** m exhibition stand.
Meß- cpd: ~**gerät** nt measuring device, gauge; ~**gewand** nt chasuble.
Messing ['mɛsɪŋ] nt -s brass.
Metall [me'tal] nt -s, -e metal; m~**en**, m~**isch** a metallic.
Metaphysik [metafy'zi:k] f metaphysics sing.
Metastase [meta'sta:zə] f -, -n (Med) secondary growth.
Meteor [mete'o:r] nt -s, -e meteor.
Meter ['me:tər] nt or m -s, - metre; ~**maß** nt tape measure.
Methode [me'to:də] f -, -n method.
methodisch [me'to:dɪʃ] a methodical.

Metropole [metro'po:lə] *f* -, -n metropolis.

Metzger ['mɛtsgər] *m* -s, - butcher; ~**ei** [-'raɪ] *f* butcher's (shop).

Meuchelmord ['mɔʏçəlmɔrt] *m* assassination.

Meute ['mɔʏtə] *f* -, -n pack; ~'**rei** *f* mutiny; ~**rer** *m* -s, - mutineer; **m**~**rn** *vi* mutiny.

miauen [mi'auən] *vi* miaow.

mich [mɪç] *pron acc of* **ich** me; myself.

Miene ['mi:nə] *f* -, -n look, expression.

mies [mi:s] *a* (*col*) lousy.

Miet- ['mi:t] *cpd:* ~**auto** *nt* hired car; ~**e** *f* -, -n rent; **zur** ~**e wohnen** live in rented accommodation; **m**~**en** *vt* rent; *Auto* hire; ~**er(in** *f*) *m* -s, - tenant; ~**shaus** *nt* tenement, block of flats; ~**vertrag** *m* tenancy agreement.

Migräne [mi'grɛ:nə] *f* -, -n migraine.

Mikro- *cpd:* ~**be** [mi'kro:bə] *f* -, -n microbe; ~**fon**, ~**phon** [mikro'fo:n] *nt* -s, -e microphone; ~**skop** [mikro'sko:p] *nt* -s, -e microscope; **m**~**skopisch** *a* microscopic.

Milch [mɪlç] *f* - milk; (*Fisch*—) milt, roe; ~**glas** *nt* frosted glass; **m**~**ig** *a* milky; ~**kaffee** *m* white coffee; ~**pulver** *nt* powdered milk; ~**straße** *f* Milky Way; ~**zahn** *m* milk tooth.

mild [mɪlt] *a* mild; *Richter* lenient; (*freundlich*) kind, charitable; **M**~**e** ['mɪldə] *f* -, -n mildness; leniency; ~**ern** *vt* mitigate, soften; *Schmerz* alleviate; ~**ernde Umstände** extenuating circumstances.

Milieu [mili'ö] *nt* -s, -s background, environment; **m**~**geschädigt** *a* maladjusted.

Mili- [mili] *cpd:* **m**~**tant** [-'tant] *a* militant; ~**tär** [-'tɛ:r] *nt* -s military, army; ~**'tärgericht** *nt* military court; **m**~**'tärisch** *a* military; ~**tarismus** [-ta'rɪsmʊs] *m* militarism; **m**~**ta'ristisch** *a* militaristic; ~**'tärpflicht** *f* (compulsory) military service.

Milli- ['mɪli] *cpd:* ~**ardär** [-ar'dɛ:r] *m* multimillionaire; ~**arde** [-'ardə] *f* -, -n milliard; billion (*esp US*); ~**meter** *m* millimetre; ~**on** [-'o:n] *f* -, -en million; ~**onär** [-o'nɛ:r] *m* millionaire.

Milz [mɪlts] *f* -, -en spleen.

Mimik ['mi:mɪk] *f* mime.

Mimose [mi'mo:zə] *f* -, -n mimosa; (*fig*) sensitive person.

minder ['mɪndər] *a* inferior; *ad* less; **M**~**heit** *f* minority; ~**jährig** *a* minor; **M**~**jährigkeit** *f* minority; ~**n** *vtr* decrease, diminish; **M**~**ung** *f* decrease; ~**wertig** *a* inferior; **M**~**wertigkeitsgefühl** *nt*, **M**~**wertigkeitskomplex** *m* inferiority complex.

Mindest- ['mɪndəst] *cpd:* ~**alter** *nt* minimum age; ~**betrag** *m* minimum amount; **m**~**e** *a* least; ~**ens**, **zum** **m**~**en** *ad* at least; ~**lohn** *m* minimum wage; ~**maß** *nt* minimum.

Mine ['mi:nə] *f* -, -n mine; (*Bleistift*—) lead; (*Kugelschreiber*—) refill; ~**nfeld** *nt* minefield.

Mineral [mine'ra:l] *nt* -s, -e *or* -ien mineral; **m**~**isch** *a* mineral; ~**wasser** *nt* mineral water.

Miniatur [minia'tu:r] *f* miniature.

minimal [mini'ma:l] *a* minimal.

Minister [mi'nɪstər] *m* -s, - minister; **m**~**iell** [mɪnɪsteri'ɛl] *a* ministerial; ~**ium** [mɪnɪs'te:rium] *nt* ministry; ~**präsident** *m* prime minister.

minus ['mi:nʊs] *ad* minus; **M**~ *nt* -, - deficit; **M**~**pol** *m* negative pole; **M**~**zeichen** *nt* minus sign.

Minute [mi'nu:tə] *f* -, -n minute; ~**nzeiger** *m* minute hand.

mir [mi:r] *pron dat of* **ich** (to) me; ~ **nichts, dir nichts** just like that.

Misch- ['mɪʃ] *cpd:* ~**ehe** *f* mixed marriage; **m**~**en** *vt* mix; ~**ling** *m* halfcaste; ~**ung** *f* mixture.

Miß- ['mɪs] *cpd:* **m**~'**achten** *vt* disregard; ~'**achtung** *f* disregard; ~**behagen** *nt* discomfort, uneasiness; ~**bildung** *f* deformity; **m**~'**billigen** *vt insep* disapprove of; ~**billigung** *f* disapproval; ~**brauch** *m* abuse; (*falscher Gebrauch*) misuse; **m**~'**brauchen** *vt insep* abuse; misuse (*zu* for); **m**~'**deuten** *vt insep* misinterpret; ~**erfolg** *m* failure.

Misse- ['mɪsə] *cpd:* ~**tat** *f* misdeed; ~**täter(in** *f*) *m* criminal; (*col*) scoundrel.

Miß- *cpd:* **m**~'**fallen** *vi irreg insep* displease (*jdm* sb); ~'**fallen** *nt* -s displeasure; ~**geburt** *f* freak; (*fig*) abortion; ~**geschick** *nt* misfortune; **m**~**glücken** [mɪs'glʏkən] *vi insep* fail; **jdm** **m**~**glückt** **etw** sb does not succeed with sth; ~**griff** *m* mistake; ~**gunst** *f* envy; **m**~**günstig** *a* envious; **m**~'**handeln** *vt insep* ill-treat; ~'**handlung** *f* ill-treatment; ~**helligkeit** *f:* ~**helligkeiten haben** be at variance.

Mission [misi'o:n] *f* mission; ~**ar** [misio'na:r] *m* missionary.

Miß- *cpd:* ~**klang** *m* discord; ~**kredit** *m* discredit; **m**~**lingen** [mɪs'lɪŋən] *vi irreg insep* fail; ~'**lingen** *nt* -s failure; ~**mut** *nt* bad temper; **m**~**mutig** *a* cross; **m**~'**raten** *vi irreg insep* turn out badly; *a* illbred; ~**stand** *m* state of affairs; abuse; ~**stimmung** *f* ill-humour, discord; **m**~'**trauen** *vi insep* mistrust; ~**trauen** *nt* -s distrust, suspicion (*of*); ~**trauensantrag** *m* (*Pol*) motion of no confidence; ~**trauensvotum** *nt* -s, -voten (*Pol*) vote of no confidence; **m**~**trauisch** *a* distrustful, suspicious; ~**verhältnis** *nt* disproportion; ~**verständnis** *nt* misunderstanding; **m**~**verstehen** *vt irreg insep* misunderstand.

Mist [mɪst] *m* -(e)s dung; dirt; (*col*) rubbish; ~**el** *f* -, -n mistletoe; ~**haufen** *m* dungheap.

mit [mɪt] *prep* +*dat* with; (*mittels*) by; ~ **der Bahn** by train; ~ **10 Jahren** at the age of 10; *ad* along, too; **wollen Sie** ~? do you want to come along?

Mitarbeit ['mit'arbaɪt] *f* cooperation; **m**~**en** *vi* cooperate, collaborate; ~**er(in** *f*) *m* collaborator; co-worker; *pl* staff.

Mit- *cpd:* ~**bestimmung** *f* participation in decision-making; (*Pol*) determination;

m~**bringen** vt irreg bring along; ~**bürger(in** f) m fellow citizen; m~**denken** vi irreg follow; **du hast ja** m~**gedacht!** good thinking!

miteinander [mɪt'aɪ'nandər] ad together, with one another.

Mit- cpd: m~**erleben** vt see, witness; ~**esser** ['mɪt'esər] m -s, - blackhead; m~**geben** vt irreg give; ~**gefühl** nt sympathy; m~**gehen** vi irreg go/come along; m~**genommen** a done in, in a bad way; ~**gift** f dowry.

Mitglied ['mɪtgliːt] nt member; ~**sbeitrag** m membership fee; ~**schaft** f membership.

Mit- cpd: m~**halten** vi irreg keep up; ~**hilfe** f help, assistance; m~**hören** vt listen in to; m~**kommen** vi irreg come along; (verstehen) keep up, follow; ~**läufer** m hanger-on; (Pol) fellow-traveller.

Mitleid nt sympathy; (Erbarmen) compassion; ~**enschaft** f: in ~**enschaft ziehen** affect; m~**ig** a sympathetic; m~**slos** a pitiless, merciless.

Mit- cpd: m~**machen** vt join in, take part in; ~**mensch** m fellow man; m~**nehmen** vt irreg take along/away; (anstrengen) wear out, exhaust.

mitsamt [mɪt'zamt] prep +dat together with.

Mitschuld f complicity; m~**ig** a also guilty (an +dat of); ~**ige(r)** mf accomplice.

Mit- cpd: ~**schüler(in** f) m schoolmate; m~**spielen** vi join in, take part; ~**spieler(in** f) m partner; ~**spracherecht** ['mɪtʃpraːxəreçt] nt voice, say.

Mittag ['mɪtaːk] m -(e)s, -e midday, lunchtime; (zu) ~ **essen** have lunch; m~ ad at lunchtime or noon; ~**essen** nt lunch, dinner; m~**s** ad at lunchtime or noon; ~**spause** f lunch break; ~**sschlaf** m early afternoon nap, siesta.

Mittäter(in f) [mɪttɛːtər(ɪn)] m accomplice.

Mitte ['mɪtə] f -, -n middle; **aus unserer** ~ from our midst.

mitteil- ['mɪttaɪl] cpd: ~**en** vt: **jdm etw** ~**en** inform sb of sth, communicate sth to sb; ~**sam** a communicative; M~**ung** f communication.

Mittel ['mɪtəl] nt -s - means; method; (Math) average; (Med) medicine; **ein** ~ **zum Zweck** a means to an end; ~**alter** nt Middle Ages pl; m~**alterlich** a mediaeval; m~**bar** a indirect; ~**ding** nt cross; m~**los** a without means; m~**mäßig** a mediocre, middling; ~**mäßigkeit** f mediocrity; ~**punkt** m centre; m~**s** prep +gen by means of; ~**stand** m middle class; ~**streifen** m central reservation; ~**stürmer** m centre-forward; ~**weg** m middle course; ~**welle** f (Rad) medium wave; ~**wert** m average value, mean.

mitten ['mɪtən] ad in the middle; ~ **auf der Straße/in der Nacht** in the middle of the street/night; ~**hindurch** ad

[-hɪn'dʊrç] through the middle.

Mitternacht ['mɪtərnaxt] f midnight; m~**s** ad at midnight.

mittlere(r,s) ['mɪtlərə(r,z)] a middle; (durchschnittlich) medium, average.

mittlerweile ['mɪtlər'vaɪlə] ad meanwhile.

Mittwoch [mɪtvɔx] m -(e)s, -e Wednesday; m~**s** ad on Wednesdays.

mitunter [mɪt'ʊntər] ad occasionally, sometimes.

Mit- cpd: m~**verantwortlich** a also responsible; ~**verschulden** ['mɪtfɛr-ʃʊldən] nt contributory negligence; m~**wirken** vi contribute (bei to); (Theat) take part (bei in); ~**wirkung** f contribution; participation; ~**wisser** ['mɪtvɪsər] m -s, - sb in the know.

Möbel ['møːbəl] nt -s, - (piece of) furniture; ~**wagen** m furniture or removal van.

mobil [moˈbiːl] a mobile; (Mil) mobilized; M~**iar** [mobiˈliˈaːr] nt -s, -e movable assets pl; M~**machung** f mobilization.

möblieren [møˈbliːrən] vt furnish; **möbliert wohnen** live in furnished accommodation.

Mode ['moːdə] f -, -n fashion.

Modell [moˈdɛl] nt -s, -e model; m~**ieren** [-ˈliːrən] vt (col) model.

Mode- cpd: ~**(n)schau** f fashion show; m~**rn** [moˈdɛrn] a modern; (modisch) fashionable; m~**rnisieren** vt modernize; ~**schmuck** m fashion jewellery; ~**wort** nt fashionable word.

modisch ['moːdɪʃ] a fashionable.

mogeln [moˈgəln] vi (col) cheat.

mögen ['møːgən] vti irreg like; **ich möchte . . .** I would like . . .; **das mag wohl sein** that may well be so.

möglich ['møːklɪç] a possible; ~**erweise** ad possibly; M~**keit** f possibility; **nach** M~**keit** if possible; ~**st** ad as . . . as possible.

Mohn [moːn] m -(e)s, -e (-blume) poppy; (-samen) poppy seed.

Möhre ['møːrə] f -, -n, **Mohrrübe** f carrot.

mokieren [moˈkiːrən] vr make fun (über +acc of).

Mole ['moːlə] f -, -n (harbour) mole; ~**kül** [moleˈkyːl] nt -s, -e molecule.

Molkerei [mɔlkəˈraɪ] f dairy.

Moll [mɔl] nt -, - (Mus) minor (key); m~**ig** a cosy; (dicklich) plump.

Moment [moˈmɛnt] m -(e)s, -e moment; **im** ~ at the moment; nt factor, element; m~**an** [-ˈtaːn] a momentary; ad at the moment.

Monarch [moˈnarç] m -en, -en monarch; ~**ie** [monarˈçiː] f monarchy.

Monat ['moːnat] m -(e)s, -e month; m~**elang** ad for months; m~**lich** a monthly; ~**skarte** f monthly ticket.

Mönch [mœnç] m -(e)s, -e monk.

Mond [moːnt] m -(e)s, -e moon; ~**fähre** f lunar (excursion) module; ~**finsternis** f eclipse of the moon; m~**hell** a moonlit; ~**landung** f moon landing; ~**schein** m moonlight; ~**sonde** f moon probe.

Mono- [mono] *in cpds* mono; **~log** [-'lo:k] *m* **-s, -e** monologue; **~pol** [-'po:l] *nt* **-s, -e** monopoly; **m~polisieren** [-poli'zi:rən] *vt* monopolize; **m~ton** [-'to:n] *a* monotonous; **~tonie** [-to'ni:] *f* monotony.

Monsun [mɔn'zu:n] *m* **-s, -e** monsoon.

Montag ['mo:nta:k] *m* **-(e)s, -e** Monday; **m~s** *ad* on Mondays.

Montage ['mɔn'ta:ʒə] *f* **-, -n** (*Phot etc*) montage; (*Tech*) assembly; (*Einbauen*) fitting.

Monteur [mɔn'tø:r] *m* fitter, assembly man.

montieren [mɔn'ti:rən] *vt* assemble, set up.

Monument [monu'mɛnt] *nt* monument; **m~al** [-'ta:l] *a* monumental.

Moor [mo:r] *nt* **-(e)s, -e** moor.

Moos [mo:s] *nt* **-es, -e** moss.

Moped ['mo:pɛt] *nt* **-s, -s** moped.

Mops [mɔps] *m* **-es, ̈e** pug.

Moral [mo'ra:l] *f* **-, -en** morality; (*einer Geschichte*) moral; **m~isch** *a* moral.

Moräne [mo're:nə] *f* **-, -n** moraine.

Morast [mo'rast] *m* **-(e)s, -e** morass, mire; **m~ig** *a* boggy.

Mord [mɔrt] *m* **-(e)s, -e** murder; **~anschlag** *m* murder attempt.

Mörder ['mœrdər] *m* **-s, -** murderer; **~in** *f* murderess.

Mord- *cpd*: **~kommission** *f* murder squad; **~sglück** *nt* (*col*) amazing luck; **m~smäßig** *a* (*col*) terrific, enormous; **~sschreck** *m* (*col*) terrible fright; **~verdacht** *m* suspicion of murder; **~waffe** *f* murder weapon.

morgen ['mɔrgən] *ad*, **M~** *nt* tomorrow; **~früh** tomorrow morning; **M~** **-s, -**, morning; **M~mantel** *m*, **M~rock** *m* dressing gown; **M~röte** *f* dawn; **~s** *ad* in the morning.

morgig ['mɔrgɪç] *a* tomorrow's; **der ~e Tag** tomorrow.

Morphium ['mɔrfium] *nt* morphine.

morsch [mɔrʃ] *a* rotten.

Morse- ['mɔrzə] *cpd*: **~alphabet** *nt* Morse code; **m~n** *vi* send a message by morse code.

Mörtel ['mœrtəl] *m* **-s, -** mortar.

Mosaik [moza'i:k] *nt* **-s, -en** *or* **-e** mosaic.

Moschee [mɔ'ʃe:] *f* **-, -n** [mɔ'ʃe:ən] mosque.

Moskito [mɔs'ki:to] *m* **-s, -s** mosquito.

Most [mɔst] *m* **-(e)s, -e** (*unfermented*) fruit juice; (*Apfelwein*) cider.

Motel [mo'tɛl] *nt* **-s, -s** motel.

Motiv [mo'ti:f] *nt* **-s, -e** motive; (*Mus*) theme; **m~ieren** [moti'vi:rən] *vt* motivate; **~ierung** *f* motivation.

Motor ['mo:tɔr] *m* **-s, -en** [mo'to:rən] engine; (*esp Elec*) motor; **~boot** *nt* motorboat; **~enöl** *nt* motor oil; **m~isieren** [motori'zi:rən] *vt* motorize; **~rad** *nt* motorcycle; **~roller** *m* motor scooter; **~schaden** *m* engine trouble *or* failure.

Motte ['mɔtə] *f* **-, -n** moth; **~nkugel** *f*, **~npulver** *nt* mothball(s).

Motto ['mɔto] *nt* **-s, -s** motto.

Möwe ['mø:və] *f* **-, -n** seagull.

Mucke ['mʊkə] *f* **-, -n** (*usu pl*) caprice; (*von Ding*) snag, bug; **seine ~n haben** be temperamental.

Mücke ['mʏkə] *f* **-, -n** midge, gnat; **~nstich** *m* midge *or* gnat bite.

mucksen ['mʊksən] *vr* (*col*) budge; (*Laut geben*) open one's mouth.

müde ['my:də] *a* tired.

Müdigkeit ['my:dɪçkaɪt] *f* tiredness.

Muff [mʊf] *m* **-(e)s, -e** (*Handwärmer*) muff; **~el** *m* **-s, -** (*col*) killjoy, sourpuss; **m~ig** *a* *Luft* musty.

Mühe ['my:ə] *f* **-, -n** trouble, pains *pl*; **mit Müh und Not** with great difficulty; **sich** (*dat*) **~ geben** go to a lot of trouble; **m~los** *a* without trouble, easy.

muhen ['mu:ən] *vi* low, moo.

mühevoll *a* laborious, arduous.

Mühle ['my:lə] *f* **-, -n** mill; (*Kaffee—*) grinder.

Müh- *cpd*: **~sal** *f* **-, -e** hardship, tribulation; **m~sam** *a* arduous, troublesome; **m~selig** *a* arduous, laborious.

Mulatte [mu'latə] *m* **-, -n, Mulattin** *f* mulatto.

Mulde ['mʊldə] *f* **-, -n** hollow, depression.

Mull [mʊl] *m* **-(e)s, -e** thin muslin; **~binde** *f* gauze bandage.

Müll [mʏl] *m* **-(e)s** refuse; **~abfuhr** *f* rubbish disposal; (*Leute*) dustmen *pl*; **~abladeplatz** *m* rubbish dump; **~eimer** *m* dustbin, garbage can (*US*); **~er** *m* **-s, -** miller; **~haufen** *m* rubbish heap; **~schlucker** *m* **-s, -** garbage disposal unit; **~wagen** *m* dustcart, garbage truck (*US*).

mulmig ['mʊlmɪç] *a* rotten; (*col*) dodgy; **jdm ist ~** *sb* feels funny.

multiplizieren [multipli'tsi:rən] *vt* multiply.

Mumie ['mu:miə] *f* mummy.

Mumm [mʊm] *m* **-s** (*col*) gumption, nerve.

Mund [mʊnt] *m* **-(e)s, ̈er** ['mʏndər] mouth; **~art** *f* dialect.

Mündel ['mʏndəl] *nt* **-s, -** ward.

münden ['mʏndən] *vi* flow (*in* +*acc* into).

Mund- *cpd*: **~faul** *a* taciturn; **~fäule** *f* (*Med*) ulcerative stomatitis; **~geruch** *m* bad breath; **~harmonika** *f* mouth organ.

mündig ['mʏndɪç] *a* of age; **M~keit** *f* majority.

mündlich ['mʏntlɪç] *a* oral.

Mund- *cpd*: **~stück** *nt* mouthpiece; (*Zigaretten—*) tip; **m~tot** *a*: **jdn m~tot machen** muzzle sb.

Mündung ['mʏnduŋ] *f* mouth; (*Gewehr*) muzzle.

Mund- *cpd*: **~wasser** *nt* mouthwash; **~werk** *nt*: **ein großes ~werk haben** have a big mouth; **~winkel** *m* corner of the mouth.

Munition [munitsi'o:n] *f* ammunition; **~slager** *nt* ammunition dump.

munkeln ['mʊŋkəln] *vi* whisper, mutter.

Münster ['mʏnstər] *nt* **-s, -** minster.

munter ['mʊntər] *a* lively; **M~keit** *f* liveliness.

Münze ['mʏntsə] *f* **-, -n** coin; **m~n** *vt* coin, mint; **auf jdn gemünzt sein** be aimed at sb.

Münzfernsprecher ['myntsfɛrnʃprɛçər] *m* callbox, pay phone (*US*).

mürb(e) ['myrb(ə)] *a Gestein* crumbly; *Holz* rotten; *Gebäck* crisp; **jdn ~ machen** wear sb down; **M~(e)teig** *m* shortcrust pastry.

murmeln ['murməln] *vti* murmer, mutter.

Murmeltier ['murməlti:r] *nt* marmot.

murren ['murən] *vi* grumble, grouse.

mürrisch ['myrɪʃ] *a* sullen.

Mus [mu:s] *nt* **-es, -e** puree.

Muschel ['muʃəl] *f* **-, -n** mussel; (*—schale*) shell; (*Telefon—*) receiver.

Muse ['mu:zə] *f* **-, -n** muse.

Museum [mu'ze:um] *nt* **-s, Museen** museum.

Musik [mu'zi:k] *f* music; (*Kapelle*) band; **m~alisch** [-'ka:lɪʃ] *a* musical; **~box** *f* jukebox; **~er** ['mu:zikər] *m* **-s, -** musician; **~hochschule** *f* music school; **~instrument** *nt* musical instrument; **~truhe** *f* radiogram.

musizieren [muzi'tsi:rən] *vi* make music.

Muskat [mus'ka:t] *m* **-(e)s, -e** nutmeg.

Muskel ['muskəl] *m* **-s, -n** muscle; **~kater** *m*: **einen ~kater haben** be stiff.

Muskulatur [muskula'tu:r] *f* muscular system.

muskulös [musku'lø:s] *a* muscular.

Muß [mus] *nt* - necessity, must.

Muße ['mu:sə] *f* - leisure.

müssen ['mysən] *vi irreg* must, have to; **er hat gehen ~** he (has) had to go.

müßig ['my:sɪç] *a* idle; **M~gang** *m* idleness.

Muster ['mustər] *nt* **-s, -** model; (*Dessin*) pattern; (*Probe*) sample; (*~ohne Wert* free sample; **m~gültig** *a* exemplary; **m~n** *vt Tapete* pattern; (*fig, Mil*) examine; *Truppen* inspect; **~schüler** *m* model pupil; **~ung** *f* (*von Stoff*) pattern; (*Mil*) inspection.

Mut [mu:t] *m* courage; **nur ~!** cheer up!; **jdm ~ machen** encourage sb; **m~ig** *a* courageous; **m~los** *a* discouraged, despondent.

mutmaßlich ['mu:tma:slɪç] *a* presumed; *ad* probably.

Mutter ['mutər] *f* **-, "** mother; *pl* **~n** (*Schrauben—*) nut; **~land** *nt* mother country.

mütterlich ['mytərlɪç] *a* motherly; **~erseits** *ad* on the mother's side.

Mutter- *cpd*: **~liebe** *f* motherly love; **~mal** *nt* birthmark, mole; **~schaft** *f* motherhood, maternity; **~schutz** *m* maternity regulations; **'m~'seelen-a'llein** *a* all alone; **~sprache** *f* native language; **~tag** *m* Mother's Day.

mutwillig ['mu:tvɪlɪç] *a* malicious, deliberate.

Mütze ['mytsə] *f* **-, -n** cap.

mysteriös [mysteri'ø:s] *a* mysterious.

Mystik ['mystɪk] *f* mysticism; **~er** *m* **-s, -** mystic.

Mythos ['my:tɔs] *m* **-, Mythen** myth.

N

N, n [ɛn] *nt* N, n.

na [na] *interj* well.

Nabel ['na:bəl] *m* **-s, -** navel; **~schnur** *f* umbilical cord.

nach [na:x] *prep* **+dat** after; (*in Richtung*) to; (*gemäß*) according to; **~ oben/hinten** up/back; **ihm ~!** after him!; **~ wie vor** still; **~ und ~** gradually; **dem Namen ~** judging by his name; **~äffen** *vt* ape; **~ahmen** *vt* imitate; **N~ahmung** *f* imitation.

Nachbar(in *f*) ['naxba:r(ɪn)] *m* **-s, -n** neighbour; **~haus** *nt*: **im ~haus** next door; **n~lich** *a* neighbourly; **~schaft** *f* neighbourhood; **~staat** *m* neighbouring state.

nach- *cpd*: **~bestellen** *vt* order again; **N~bestellung** *f* (*Comm*) repeat order; **~bilden** *vt* copy; **N~bildung** imitation, copy; **~blicken** *vi* look or gaze after; **~datieren** *vt* postdate.

nachdem [na:x'de:m] *cj* after; (*weil*) since; **je ~ (ob)** it depends (whether).

nach- *cpd*: **~denken** *vi irreg* think (*über* +*acc* about); **N~denken** *nt* **-s** reflection, meditation; **~denklich** *a* thoughtful, pensive.

Nachdruck ['na:xdruk] *m* emphasis; (*Print*) reprint, reproduction.

nachdrücklich ['na:xdrʏklɪç] *a* emphatic.

nacheifern ['na:xaifərn] *vi* emulate (*jdm* sb).

nacheinander [na:x'ai'nandər] *ad* one after the other.

nachempfinden ['na:xɛmpfɪndən] *vt irreg*: **jdm etw ~** feel sth with sb.

Nacherzählung ['na:xɛrtse:luŋ] *f* reproduction (of a story).

Nachfahr ['na:xfa:r] *m* **-s, -en** descendant.

Nachfolge ['na:xfɔlgə] *f* succession; **n~n** *vi* (*lit*) follow (*jdm/etw* sb/sth); **~r(in** *f*) *m* **-s, -** successor.

nach- *cpd*: **~forschen** *vti* investigate; **N~forschung** *f* investigation.

Nachfrage ['na:xfra:gə] *f* inquiry; (*Comm*) demand; **n~n** *vi* inquire.

nach- *cpd*: **~fühlen** *vt* see **~empfinden**; **~füllen** *vt* refill; **~geben** *vi irreg* give way, yield.

Nach- *cpd*: **~gebühr** *f* surcharge; (*Post*) excess postage; **~geburt** *f* afterbirth.

nachgehen ['na:xge:ən] *vi irreg* follow (*jdm* sb); (*erforschen*) inquire (*einer Sache* into sth); (*Uhr*) be slow.

Nachgeschmack ['na:xgəʃmak] *m* aftertaste.

nachgiebig ['na:xgi:bɪç] *a* soft, accommodating; **N~keit** *f* softness.

Nachhall ['na:xhal] *m* resonance; **n~en** *vi* resound.

nachhaltig ['na:xhaltɪç] *a* lasting; *Widerstand* persistent.

nachhelfen ['na:xhɛlfən] *vi irreg* assist, help (*jdm* sb).

nachher [na:x'he:r] *ad* afterwards.

Nachhilfeunterricht ['na:xhɪlfə-ʊntərɪçt] m extra tuition.

nachholen ['na:xho:lən] vt catch up with; *Versäumtes* make up for.

Nachkomme ['na:xkɔmə] m -, -n descendant; n~n vi irreg follow; *einer Verpflichtung* fulfil; ~**nschaft** f descendants pl.

Nachkriegs- ['na:xkri:ks] in cpds postwar; ~**zeit** f postwar period.

Nach- cpd: ~**laß** m -lasses, -lässe (*Comm*) discount, rebate; (*Erbe*) estate; n~**lassen** irreg vt *Strafe* remit; *Summe* take off; *Schulden* cancel; vi decrease, ease off; (*Sturm auch*) die down; (*schlechter werden*) deteriorate; **er hat n~gelassen** he has got worse; n~**lässig** a negligent, careless; ~**lässigkeit** f negligence, carelessness.

nachlaufen ['na:xlaʊfən] vi irreg run after, chase (*jdm* sb).

nachmachen ['na:xmaxən] vt imitate, copy (*jdm etw* sth from sb); (*fälschen*) counterfeit.

Nachmittag ['na:xmɪta:k] m afternoon; **am** ~, n~**s** ad in the afternoon.

Nach- cpd: ~**nahme** f -, -n cash on delivery; **per** ~**nahme** C.O.D.; ~**name** m surname; ~**porto** nt excess postage.

nachprüfen ['na:xpry:fən] vt check, verify.

nachrechnen ['na:xrɛçnən] vt check.

Nachrede ['na:xre:də] f: **üble** ~ libel; slander.

Nachricht ['na:xrɪçt] f -, -en (piece of) news; (*Mitteilung*) message; ~**en** pl news; ~**enagentur** f news agency; ~**endienst** m (*Mil*) intelligence service; ~**ensprecher(in** f) m newsreader; ~**entechnik** f telecommunications sing.

nachrücken ['na:xrʏkən] vi move up.

Nachruf ['na:xru:f] m obituary (notice).

nachsagen ['na:xza:gən] vt repeat; **jdm etw** ~ say sth of sb.

nachschicken ['na:xʃɪkən] vt forward.

Nachschlag- ['na:xʃla:g] cpd: n~**en** vt irreg look up; vi: **jdm n~en** take after sb; ~**ewerk** nt reference boook.

Nach- cpd: ~**schlüssel** m master key; ~**schub** m supplies pl; (*Truppen*) reinforcements pl.

nachsehen ['na:xze:ən] irreg vt (*prüfen*) check; **jdm etw** ~ forgive sb sth; vi look after (*jdm* sb); (*erforschen*) look and see; **das N~ haben** come off worst.

nachsenden ['na:xzɛndən] vt irreg send on, forward.

Nachsicht ['na:xzɪçt] f - indulgence, leniency; n~**ig** a indulgent, lenient.

nachsitzen ['na:xzɪtsən] vi irreg (*Sch*) be kept in.

Nachspeise ['na:xʃpaɪzə] f dessert, sweet, pudding.

Nachspiel ['na:xʃpi:l] nt epilogue; (*fig*) sequel.

nachsprechen ['na:xʃprɛçən] vt irreg repeat (*jdm* after sb).

nächst [nɛːçst] prep +dat (*räumlich*) next to; (*außer*) apart from; ~**beste(r,s)** a first that comes along; (*zweitbeste*) next best;

N~**e(r)** mf neighbour; ~**e(r,s)** next; (*nächstgelegen*) nearest; N~**enliebe** f love for one's fellow men; ~**ens** ad shortly, soon; ~**liegend** a (*lit*) nearest; (*fig*) obvious; ~**möglich** a next possible.

nachsuchen ['na:xzu:xən] vi: **um etw** ~ ask or apply for sth.

Nacht [naxt] f -, ¨e night.

Nachteil ['na:xtaɪl] m disadvantage; n~**ig** a disadvantageous.

Nachthemd nt nightshirt; nightdress.

Nachtigall ['naxtɪgal] f -, -en nightingale.

Nachtisch ['na:xtɪʃ] m see **Nachspeise**.

nächtlich ['nɛçtlɪç] a nightly.

Nach- cpd: ~**trag** m -(e)s, -träge supplement; n~**tragen** vt irreg carry (*jdm* after sb); (*zufügen*) add; **jdm etw** n~**tragen** hold sth against sb; n~**tragend** a resentful; n~**träglich** a,ad later, subsequent(ly); additional(ly); n~**trauern** vi: **jdm/etw** n~**trauern** mourn the loss of sb/sth.

Nacht- cpd: ~**ruhe** f sleep; n~**s** ad by night; ~**schicht** f nightshift; n~**süber** ad during the night; ~**tarif** m off-peak tariff; ~**tisch** m bedside table; ~**topf** m chamberpot; ~**wächter** m night watchman.

Nach- cpd: ~**untersuchung** f checkup; n~**wachsen** vi irreg grow again; ~**wehen** pl afterpains pl; (*fig*) after-effects pl.

Nachweis ['na:xvaɪs] m -es, -e proof; n~**bar** a provable, demonstrable; n~**en** ['na:xvaɪzən] vt irreg prove; **jdm etw** n~**en** point sth out to sb; n~**lich** a evident, demonstrable.

nach- cpd: ~**winken** vi wave (*jdm* after sb); ~**wirken** vi have after-effects; N~**wirkung** f after-effect; N~**wort** nt appendix; N~**wuchs** m offspring; (*beruflich etc*) new recruits pl; ~**zahlen** vti pay extra; N~**zahlung** f additional payment; (*zurückdatiert*) back pay; ~**zählen** vt count again; N~**zügler** m -s, - straggler.

Nacken ['nakən] m -s, - nape of the neck.

nackt [nakt] a naked; *Tatsachen* plain, bare; N~**heit** f nakedness; N~**kultur** f nudism.

Nadel ['na:dəl] f -, -n needle; (*Steck*—) pin; ~**kissen** nt pincushion; ~**öhr** nt eye of a needle; ~**wald** m coniferous forest.

Nagel ['na:gəl] m -s, ¨ nail; ~**feile** f nailfile; ~**haut** f cuticle; ~**lack** m nail varnish; n~**n** vti nail; n~**neu** a brandnew; ~**schere** f nail scissors pl.

nagen ['na:gən] vti gnaw.

Nagetier ['na:gəti:r] nt rodent.

nah(e) ['na:(ə)] a,ad (*räumlich*) near(by); *Verwandte* near; *Freunde* close; (*zeitlich*) near, close; prep +dat near (to), close to; N~**aufnahme** f close-up.

Nähe ['nɛːə] f - nearness, proximity; (*Umgebung*) vicinity; **in der** ~ close by; at hand; **aus der** ~ from close to.

nahe- cpd: ~**bei** ad nearby; ~**gehen** vi irreg grieve (*jdm* sb); ~**kommen** vi irreg get close (*jdm* to sb); ~**legen** vt: **jdm etw** ~**legen** suggest sth to sb; ~**liegen** vi *irreg* be obvious; **~ liegend** *a* obvious; **~n** *vir* approach, draw near.

Näh- ['nɛ:] *cpd:* **n~en** *vti* sew; **n~er** *a,ad* nearer; *Erklärung, Erkundigung* more detailed; **~ere(s)** *nt* details *pl,* particulars *pl;* **~erei** *f* sewing, needlework; **~erin** *f* seamstress; **n~erkommen** *vir irreg* get closer; **n~ern** *vr* approach; **~erungswert** *m* approximate value.

nahe- *cpd:* **~ stehen** *vi irreg* be close (*jdm* to sb); **einer Sache ~ stehen** sympathize with sth; **~ stehend** a close; **~ treten** *vi irreg:* **jdm (zu) ~ treten** offend sb; **~ zu** *ad* nearly.

Näh- *cpd:* **~ garn** *nt* thread; **~ kasten** *m* workbox; **~ maschine** *f* sewing machine; **~ nadel** *f* needle.

nähren ['nɛ:rən] *vtr* feed.

nahrhaft ['na:rhaft] *a* nourishing, nutritious.

Nähr- ['nɛ:r] *cpd:* **~ gehalt** *m* nutritional value; **~ stoffe** *pl* nutrients *pl.*

Nahrung ['na:ruŋ] *f* food; (*fig auch*) sustenance; **~ smittel** *nt* foodstuffs *pl;* **~ smittelindustrie** *f* food industry; **~ ssuche** *f* search for food.

Nährwert *m* nutritional value.

Naht [na:t] *f* **-, -̈e** seam; (*Med*) suture; (*Tech*) join; **n~los** a seamless; **n~los ineinander übergehen** follow without a gap.

Nah- *cpd:* **~ verkehr** *m* local traffic; **~ verkehrszug** *m* local train; **~ ziel** *nt* immediate objective.

naiv [na'i:f] *a* naive; **N~ität** [naivi'tɛ:t] *f* naivety.

Name ['na:mə] *m* **-ns, -n** name; **im ~n von** on behalf of; **n~ns** *ad* by the name of; **n~ntlich** *a* by name; *ad* particularly, especially.

namhaft ['na:mhaft] *a* (*berühmt*) famed, renowned; (*beträchtlich*) considerable; **~ machen** *vt* establish.

nämlich ['nɛ:mlɪç] *ad* that is to say, namely; (*denn*) since; **der/die/das ~e** the same.

Napf [napf] *m* **-(e)s, -̈e** bowl, dish.

Narbe ['narbə] *f* **-, -n** scar.

narbig ['narbɪç] *a* scarred.

Narkose [nar'ko:zə] *f* **-, -n** anaesthetic.

Narr [nar] *m* **-en, -en** fool; **n~en** *vt* fool; **~ heit** *f* foolishness.

Närr- ['nɛr] *cpd:* **~ in** *f* fool; **n~ isch** *a* foolish, crazy.

Narzisse [nar'tsɪsə] *f* **-, -n** narcissus; daffodil.

nasch- ['naʃ] *cpd:* **~ en** *vti* nibble; eat secretly; **~ haft** *a* sweet-toothed.

Nase ['na:zə] *f* **-, -n** nose; **~ nbluten** *nt* **-s** nosebleed; **~ nloch** *nt* nostril; **~ nrücken** *m* bridge of the nose; **~ ntropfen** *pl* nose drops *pl;* **n~ nweis** *a* pert, cheeky; (*neugierig*) nosey.

Nashorn ['na:shɔrn] *nt* rhinoceros.

naß [nas] *a* wet.

Nässe ['nɛsə] *f* wetness; **n~n** *vt* wet.

Naß- *cpd:* **n~ kalt** *a* wet and cold; **~ rasur** *f* wet shave.

Nation [natsi'o:n] *f* nation.

national [natsio'na:l] *a* national;

N~ hymne *f* national anthem; **N~ isieren** [-i'zi:rən] *vt* nationalize; **N~ i'sierung** *f* nationalization; **N~ ismus** [-'lɪsmʊs] *m* nationalism; **~ istisch** [-'lɪstɪʃ] *a* nationalistic; **N~ i'tät** *f* nationality; **N~ mannschaft** *f* national team; **N~ sozialismus** *m* national socialism.

Natron ['na:trɔn] *nt* **-s** soda.

Natter ['natər] *f* **-, -n** adder.

Natur [na'tu:r] *f* nature; (*körperlich*) constitution; **~ alien** [natu'ra:liən] *pl* natural produce; **in ~ alien** in kind; **~ a'lismus** *m* naturalism; **~ erscheinung** *f* natural phenomenon *or* event; **n~ farben** *a* natural coloured; **n~ gemäß** *a* natural; **~ geschichte** *f* natural history; **~ gesetz** *nt* law of nature; **~ katastrophe** *f* natural disaster.

natürlich [na'ty:rlɪç] *a* natural; *ad* naturally; **~ erweise** *ad* naturally, of course; **N~ keit** *f* naturalness.

Natur- *cpd:* **~ produkt** *nt* natural product; **n~ rein** *a* natural, pure; **~ schutzgebiet** *nt* nature reserve; **~ wissenschaft** *f* natural science; **~ wissenschaftler(in** *f)* *m* scientist; **~ zustand** *m* natural state.

nautisch ['nautɪʃ] *a* nautical.

Navelorange ['na:vəlorã:ʒə] *f* navel orange.

Navigation [navigatsi'o:n] *f* navigation; **~ sfehler** *m* navigational error; **~ sinstrumente** *pl* navigation instruments *pl.*

Nazi ['na:tsi] *m* **-s, -s** Nazi.

Nebel ['ne:bəl] *m* **-s, -** fog, mist; **n~ ig** *a* foggy, misty; **~ scheinwerfer** *m* foglamp.

neben ['ne:bən] *prep* +*acc or dat* next to; (*außer*) apart from, besides; **~ an** [ne:bən'an] *ad* next door; **N~ anschluß** *m* (*Tel*) extension; **~ bei** [ne:bən'bai] *ad* at the same time; (*außerdem*) additionally; (*beiläufig*) incidentally; **N~ beschäftigung** *f* sideline; **N~ buhler(in** *f)* *m* **-s, -** rival; **~ einander** [ne:bən'ai'nandər] *ad* side by side; **~ einanderlegen** *vt* put next to each other; **N~ eingang** *m* side entrance; **N~ erscheinung** *f* side effect; **N~ fach** *nt* subsidiary subject; **N~ fluß** *m* tributary; **N~ geräusch** *nt* (*Rad*) atmospherics *pl,* interference; **~ her** [ne:bən'he:r] *ad* (*zusätzlich*) besides; (*gleichzeitig*) at the same time; (*daneben*) alongside; **~ herfahren** *vi irreg* drive alongside; **N~ kosten** *pl* extra charges *pl,* extras *pl;* **N~ produkt** *nt* by-product; **N~ rolle** *f* minor part; **N~ sache** *f* trifle, side issue; **~ sächlich** *a* minor, peripheral; **N~ straße** *f* side street; **N~ zimmer** *nt* adjoining room.

Necessaire [nesɛ'sɛ:r] *nt* **-s, -s** (*Näh—*) needlework box; (*Nagel—*) manicure case.

neck- ['nɛk] *cpd:* **~ en** *vt* tease; **N~ e'rei** *f* teasing; **~ isch** *a* coy; *Einfall, Lied* amusing.

Neffe ['nɛfə] *m* **-n, -n** nephew.

negativ [nega'ti:f] *a* negative; **N~** *nt* **-s, -e** (*Phot*) negative.

Neger ['ne:gər] *m* **-s, -** negro; **~ in** *f* negress.

negieren [ne'gi:rən] vt (bestreiten) deny; (verneinen) negate.

nehmen ['ne:mən] vt irreg take; **jdn zu sich** ~ take sb in; **sich ernst** ~ take o.s. seriously; **nimm dir noch einmal** help yourself.

Neid [nait] m -(e)s envy; **~er** m -s, - envier; **n~isch** a envious, jealous.

neigen ['naigən] vt incline, lean; Kopf bow; vi: **zu etw** ~ tend to sth.

Neigung f (des Geländes) slope; (Tendenz) tendency, inclination; (Vorliebe) liking; (Zuneigung) affection; **~swinkel** m angle of inclination.

nein [nain] ad no.

Nelke ['nɛlkə] f -, -n carnation, pink; (Gewürz) clove.

Nenn- ['nɛn] cpd: **n~en** vt irreg name; (mit Namen) call; **n~enswert** a worth mentioning; **~er** m -s, - denominator; **~ung** f naming; **~wert** m nominal value; (Comm) par.

Neon ['ne:ɔn] nt -s neon; **~licht** nt neon light; **~röhre** f neon tube.

Nerv [nɛrf] m -s, -en nerve; **jdm auf die ~en** gehen get on sb's nerves; **n~enaufreibend** a nerve-racking; **~enbündel** nt bundel of nerves; **~enheilanstalt** f mental home; **n~enkrank** a mentally ill; **~enschwäche** f neurasthenia; **~ensystem** nt nervous system; **~enzusammenbruch** m nervous breakdown; **n~ös** [nɛr'vø:s] a nervous; **~osi'tät** f nervousness; **n~tötend** a nerve-racking; Arbeit soul-destroying.

Nerz [nɛrts] m -es, -e mink.

Nessel ['nɛsəl] f -, -n nettle.

Nest [nɛst] nt -(e)s, -er nest; (col: Ort) dump; **n~eln** vi fumble or fiddle about (an +dat with).

nett [nɛt] a nice; (freundlich auch) kind; **~erweise** ad kindly; **~o** ad net.

Netz [nɛts] nt -es, -e net; (Gepäck~) rack; (Einkaufs~) string bag; (Spinnen~) web; (System) network; **jdm ins ~ gehen** (fig) fall into sb's trap; **~anschluß** m mains connection; **~haut** f retina.

neu [nɔy] a new; Sprache, Geschichte modern; **seit ~estem** (since) recently; **~ schreiben** rewrite, write again; **N~anschaffung** f new purchase or acquisition; **~artig** a new kind of; **N~auflage** f, **N~ausgabe** f new edition; **N~bau** m -s, -ten new building; **~erdings** ad (kürzlich) (since) recently; (von neuem) again; **N~erung** f innovation, new departure; **N~gier** f curiosity; **~gierig** a curious; **N~heit** f newness, novelty; **N~igkeit** f news; **N~jahr** nt New Year; **~lich** ad recently, the other day; **N~ling** m novice; **N~mond** m new moon.

neun [nɔyn] num nine; **~zehn** num nineteen; **~zig** num ninety.

neureich a nouveau riche; **N~e(r)** mf nouveau riche.

Neur- cpd: **~ose** [nɔy'ro:zə] f -, -n neurosis; **~otiker** [nɔy'ro:tikər] m -s, - neurotic; **n~otisch** a neurotic.

Neutr- cpd: **n~al** [nɔy'tra:l] a neutral; **~ali'tät** f neutrality; **n~ali'sieren** vt neutralize; **~on** ['nɔytrɔn] nt -s, -en neutron; **~um** ['nɔytrum] nt -s, -a or -en neuter.

Neu- cpd: **~wert** m purchase price; **~zeit** f modern age; **n~zeitlich** a modern, recent.

nicht [nɪçt] ad not; pref non-; ~ **wahr?** isn't it/he?, don't you etc; ~ **doch!** don't!; ~ **berühren!** do not touch! was du ~ **sagst!** the things you say!; **N~achtung** f disregard; **N~angriffspakt** m non-aggression pact.

Nichte ['nɪçtə] f -, -n niece.

nichtig ['nɪçtɪç] a (ungültig) null, void; (wertlos) futile; **N~keit** f nullity, invalidity; (Sinnlosigkeit) futility.

Nicht- cpd: **~raucher(in** f) m nonsmoker; **n~rostend** a stainless.

nichts [nɪçts] pron nothing; **für ~ und wieder ~** for nothing at all; **N~** nt -s nothingness; (pej: Person) nonentity; **~desto'weniger** ad nevertheless; **N~nutz** m -es, -e good-for-nothing; **~nutzig** a worthless, useless; **~sagend** a meaningless; **N~tun** nt -s idleness.

Nickel ['nɪkəl] nt -s nickel.

nicken ['nɪkən] vi nod.

Nickerchen ['nɪkərçən] nt nap.

nie [ni:] ad never; ~ **wieder** or **mehr** never again; ~ **und nimmer** never ever.

nieder ['ni:dər] low; (gering) inferior; ad down; **N~gang** m decline; **~gehen** vi irreg descend; (Aviat) come down; (Regen) fall; (Boxer) go down; **~geschlagen** a depressed, dejected; **N~geschlagenheit** f depression, dejection; **N~lage** f defeat; (Lager) depot; (Filiale) branch; **~lassen** vr irreg (sich setzen) sit down; (an Ort) settle (down); (Arzt, Rechtsanwalt) set up a practice; **N~lassung** f settlement; (Comm) branch; **~legen** vt lay down; Arbeit stop; Amt resign; **~machen** vt mow down; **N~schlag** m (Chem) precipitate, sediment; (Met) precipitation; rainfall; (Boxen) knockdown; **~schlagen** irreg vt Gegner beat down; Gegenstand knock down; Augen lower; (Jur) Prozeß dismiss; Aufstand put down; vr (Chem) precipitate; **N~schrift** f transcription; **~trächtig** a base, mean; **N~trächtigkeit** f meanness, baseness; outrage; **N~ung** f (Geog) depression; flats pl.

niedlich ['ni:tlɪç] a sweet, nice, cute.

niedrig ['ni:drɪç] a low; Stand lowly, humble; Gesinnung mean.

niemals ['ni:ma:ls] ad never.

niemand ['ni:mant] pron nobody, no one; **N~sland** nt no-man's land.

Niere ['ni:rə] f -, -n kidney; **~nentzündung** f kidney infection.

nieseln ['ni:zəln] vi drizzle.

niesen ['ni:zən] vi sneeze.

Niet [ni:t] m -(e)s, -e, **~e** f -, -n (Tech) rivet; (Los) blank; (Reinfall) flop; (Mensch) failure; **n~en** vt rivet.

Nihil- cpd: **~ismus** [nihi'lɪsmus] m

nihilism; ~ist [nihi'lɪst] m nihilist; n~istisch a nihilistic.

Nikotin [niko'ti:n] nt -s nicotine.

Nilpferd ['ni:lpfe:rt] nt hippopotamus.

nimmersatt ['nɪmərzat] a insatiable; N~ m -(e)s, -e glutton.

nippen ['nɪpən] vti sip.

Nippsachen ['nɪpzaxən] pl knick-knacks pl.

nirgends ['nɪrgənts], **nirgendwo** ['nɪrgəntvo:] ad nowhere.

Nische ['ni:ʃə] f -, -n niche.

nisten ['nɪstən] vi nest.

Nitrat [ni'tra:t] nt -(e)s, -e nitrate.

Niveau [ni'vo:] nt -s, -s level.

Nixe ['nɪksə] f -, -n water nymph.

noch [nɔx] ad still; (in Zukunft) still, yet; one day; (außerdem) else; cj nor; ~ nie never (yet); ~ nicht not yet; immer ~ still; ~ heute today; ~ vor einer Woche only a week ago; und wenn es ~ so schwer ist however hard it is; ~ einmal again; ~ dreimal three more times; ~ und ~ heaps of; (mit Verb) again and again; ~mal(s) ad again, once more; ~malig a repeated.

Nockenwelle ['nɔkənvɛlə] f camshaft.

Nominativ ['no:minati:f] m -s, -e nominative.

nominell [nomi'nɛl] a nominal.

Nonne ['nɔnə] f -, -n nun; ~nkloster nt convent.

Nord(en) ['nɔrd(ən)] m -s north; n~isch a northern; n~ische Kombination (Ski) nordic combination.

nördlich ['nœrtlɪç] a northerly, northern; ~ von, ~ prep +gen (to the) north of.

Nord- cpd: ~pol m North Pole; n~wärts ad northwards.

Nörg- ['nœrg] cpd: ~e'lei f grumbling; n~eln vi grumble; ~ler m -s, - grumbler.

Norm [nɔrm] f -, -en norm; (Größenvorschrift) standard; n~al [nɔr'ma:l] a normal; n~alerweise ad normally; n~ali'sieren vt normalize; vr return to normal; n~en vt standardize.

Not [no:t] f -, ̈-e need; (Mangel) want; (Mühe) trouble; (Zwang) necessity; zur ~ if necessary; (gerade noch) just about; ~ar [no'ta:r] m -s, -e notary; n~ari'ell a notarial; ~ausgang m emergency exit; ~behelf m -s, -e makeshift; ~bremse f emergency brake; n~dürftig a scanty; (behelfsmäßig) makeshift; sich n~dürftig verständigen just about understand each other.

Note ['no:tə] f -, -n note; (Sch) mark; ~nblatt nt sheet of music; ~nschlüssel m clef; ~nständer m music stand.

Not- cpd: ~fall m case of) emergency; n~falls ad if need be; n~gedrungen a necessary, unavoidable; etw ~ gedrungen machen be forced to do sth.

notieren [no'ti:rən] vt note; (Comm) quote.

Notierung f (Comm) quotation.

nötig ['nø:tɪç] a necessary; etw ~ haben need sth; ~en vt compel, force; ~enfalls ad if necessary.

Notiz [no'ti:ts] f -, -en note; (Zeitungs—)

item; ~ nehmen take notice; ~buch nt notebook; ~zettel m piece of paper.

Not- cpd: ~lage f crisis, emergency; n~landen vi make a forced or emergency landing; n~leidend a needy; ~lösung f temporary solution; ~lüge f white lie.

notorisch [no'to:rɪʃ] a notorious.

Not- cpd: ~ruf m emergency call; ~stand m state of emergency; ~standsgesetz nt emergency law; ~unterkunft f emergency accommodation; ~verband m emergency dressing; ~wehr f - self-defence; n~wendig a necessary; ~wendigkeit f necessity; ~zucht f rape.

Novelle [no'vɛlə] f -, -n short story; (Jur) amendment.

November [no'vɛmbər] m -(s), - November.

Nu [nu:] m: im ~ in an instant.

Nuance [ny'ã:sə] f -, -n nuance.

nüchtern ['nyçtərn] a sober; Magen empty; Urteil prudent; N~heit f sobriety.

Nudel ['nu:dəl] f -, -n noodle.

Null [nʊl] f -, -en nought, zero; (pej: Mensch) washout; n~ num zero; Fehler no; n~ Uhr midnight; n~ und nichtig null and void; ~punkt m zero; auf dem ~punkt at zero.

numerieren [nume'ri:rən] vt number.

numerisch [nu'me:rɪʃ] a numerical.

Nummer ['nʊmər] f -, -n number; ~nscheibe f telephone dial; ~nschild nt (Aut) number or license (US) plate.

nun [nu:n] ad now; interj well.

nur [nu:r] ad just, only.

Nuß [nʊs] f -, Nüsse nut; ~baum m walnut tree; hazelnut tree; ~knacker m -s, - nutcracker.

Nüster ['ny:stər] f -, -n nostril.

Nutte ['nʊtə] f -, -n tart.

nutz [nʊts], **nütze** ['nʏtsə] a: zu nichts ~ sein be useless; ~bar a: ~bar machen utilize; N~barmachung v utilization; ~bringend a profitable; ~en, nützen vt use (zu etw for sth); vi be of use; was nützt es? what's the use?, what use is it?; N~en m -s usefulness; profit; von N~en useful.

nützlich ['nʏtslɪç] a useful; N~keit f usefulness.

Nutz- cpd: n~los a useless; ~losigkeit f uselessness; ~nießer m -s, - beneficiary.

Nymphe ['nʏmfə] f -, -n nymph.

O

O, o [o:] nt O, o.

Oase [o'a:zə] f -, -n oasis.

ob [ɔp] cj if, whether; ~ das wohl wahr ist? can that be true?; und ~! you bet!

Obacht ['o:baxt] f: ~ geben pay attention.

Obdach ['ɔpdax] nt -(e)s shelter, lodging; o~los a homeless; ~lose(r) mf homeless person.

Obduktion [ɔpdʊktsi'o:n] f post-mortem.

obduzieren [ɔpdu'tsiːrən] vt do a post mortem on.

O-Beine ['oːbainə] pl bow or bandy legs pl.

oben ['oːbən] ad above; (in Haus) upstairs; **nach ~** up; **von ~** down; **~ ohne** topless; **jdn von ~ bis unten ansehen** look sb up and down; **Befehl von ~** orders from above; **~an** ad at the top; **~auf** ad up above, on the top; a (munter) in form; **~drein** ad into the bargain; **~erwähnt**, **~genannt** a above-mentioned; **~hin** ad cursorily, superficially.

Ober ['oːbər] m -s, - waiter; **~arm** m upper arm; **~arzt** m senior physician; **~aufsicht** f supervision; **~befehl** m supreme command; **~befehlshaber** m commander-in-chief; **~begriff** m generic term; **~bekleidung** f outer clothing; **~'bürgermeister** m lord mayor; **~deck** nt upper or top deck; **o~e(r,s)** a upper; **die ~en** the bosses; (Eccl) the superiors; **~fläche** f surface; **o~flächlich** a superficial; **~geschoß** nt upper storey; **o~halb** ad, prep +gen above; **~haupt** nt head, chief; **~haus** nt upper house; House of Lords; **~hemd** nt shirt; **~herrschaft** f supremacy, sovereignty; **~in** f matron; (Eccl) Mother Superior; **o~irdisch** a above ground; Leitung overhead; **~kellner** m head waiter; **~kiefer** m upper jaw; **~kommando** nt supreme command; **~körper** m trunk, upper part of body; **~leitung** f direction; (Elec) overhead cable; **~licht** nt skylight; **~lippe** f upper lip; **~prima** f -, -primen final year of secondary school; **~schenkel** m thigh; **~schicht** f upper classes pl; **~schule** f grammar school (Brit), high school (US); **~schwester** f (Med) matron; **~sekunda** f -, -sekunden seventh year of secondary school.

Oberst ['oːbərst] m -en or -s, -en or -e colonel; **o~e(r,s)** a very top, topmost.

Ober- cpd: **~stufe** f upper school; **~teil** nt upper part; **~tertia** [-tɛrtsia] f -, -tertien fifth year of secondary school; **~wasser** nt: **~wasser haben/bekommen** be/get on top of (things); **~weite** f bust/chest measurement.

obgleich [ɔp'glaiç] cj although.

Obhut ['ɔphuːt] f - care, protection; **in jds ~ sein** be in sb's care.

obig ['oːbiç] a above.

Objekt [ɔp'jɛkt] nt -(e)s, -e object; **~iv** [-'tiːf] nt -s, -e lens; **o~iv** a objective; **~ivi'tät** f objectivity.

Oblate [o'blaːtə] f -, -n (Gebäck) wafer; (Eccl) host.

obligatorisch [obliga'toːriʃ] a compulsory, obligatory.

Oboe [o'boːə] f -, -n oboe.

Obrigkeit ['oːbriçkait] f (Behörden) authorities pl, administration; (Regierung) government.

obschon [ɔp'ʃoːn] cj although.

Observatorium [ɔpzɛrva'toːrium] nt observatory.

obskur [ɔps'kuːr] a obscure; (verdächtig) dubious.

Obst [oːpst] nt -(e)s fruit; **~bau** m fruit-

growing; **~baum** m fruit tree; **~garten** m orchard; **~händler** m fruiterer, fruit merchant; **~kuchen** m fruit tart.

obszön [ɔps'tsøːn] a obscene; **O~i'tät** f obscenity.

obwohl [ɔp'voːl] cj although.

Ochse ['ɔksə] m -n, -n ox; **o~n** vti (col) cram, swot; **~nschwanzsuppe** f oxtail soup; **~nzunge** f oxtongue.

öd(e) ['øːd(ə)] a Land waste, barren; (fig) dull; **Ö~e** f -, -n desert, waste(land); (fig) tedium.

oder ['oːdər] cj or.

Ofen ['oːfən] m -s, - oven; (Heiz~) fire, heater; (Kohle~) stove; (Hoch~) furnace; (Herd) cooker, stove; **~rohr** nt stovepipe.

offen ['ɔfən] a open; (aufrichtig) frank; Stelle vacant; **~ gesagt** to be honest; **~ bar** a obvious; **~baren** [ɔfən'baːrən] vt reveal, manifest; **O~'barung** f (Rel) revelation; **~bleiben** vi irreg (Fenster) stay open; (Frage, Entscheidung) remain open; **~halten** vt irreg keep open; **O~heit** f candour, frankness; **~herzig** a candid, frank; Kleid revealing; **O~herzigkeit** f frankness; **~kundig** a well-known; (klar) evident; **~lassen** vt irreg leave open; **~sichtlich** a evident, obvious; **~siv** [ɔfɛn'ziːf] a offensive; **O~'sive** f -, -n offensive; **~stehen** vi irreg be open; (Rechnung) be unpaid; **es steht Ihnen ~, es zu tun** you are at liberty to do it.

öffentlich ['œfəntliç] a public; **Ö~keit** f (Leute) public; (einer Versammlung etc) public nature; **in aller Ö~keit** in public; **an die Ö~keit dringen** reach the public ear.

offerieren [ɔfe'riːrən] vt offer.

Offerte [ɔ'fɛrtə] f -, -n offer.

offiziell [ɔfitsi'ɛl] a official.

Offizier [ɔfi'tsiːr] m -s, -e officer; **~skasino** nt officers' mess.

öffnen ['œfnən] vtr open; **jdm die Tür ~** open the door for sb.

Öffner ['œfnər] m -s, - opener.

Öffnung ['œfnuŋ] f opening; **~szeiten** pl opening times pl.

oft [ɔft] ad often.

öfter ['œftər] ad more often or frequently; **~s** ad often, frequently.

oftmals ad often, frequently.

ohne ['oːnə] prep +acc, cj without; **das ist nicht ~** (col) it's not bad; **~ weiteres** without a second thought; (sofort) immediately; **~dies** [oːnə'diːs] ad anyway; **~einander** [oːnəʔaɪ'nandər] ad without each other; **~gleichen** [oːnə'glaiçən] a unsurpassed, without equal; **~hin** [oːnə'hin] ad anyway, in any case.

Ohnmacht ['oːnmaxt] f faint; (fig) impotence; **in ~ fallen** faint.

ohnmächtig ['oːnmɛçtiç] a in a faint, unconscious; (fig) weak, impotent; **sie ist ~** she has fainted.

Ohr [oːr] nt -(e)s, -en ear; (Gehör) hearing.

Öhr [øːr] nt -(e)s, -e eye.

Ohr- cpd: **~enarzt** m ear specialist; **o~enbetäubend** a deafening; **~en-**

schmalz nt earwax; ~**enschmerzen** pl earache; ~**enschützer** m -s, - earmuff; ~**feige** f slap on the face; box on the ears; o~**feigen** vt slap sb's face; box sb's ears; ~**läppchen** nt ear lobe; ~**ringe** pl earrings pl; ~**wurm** m earwig; (Mus) catchy tune.

okkupieren [ɔku'pi:rən] vt occupy.

ökonomisch [øko'no:mɪʃ] a economical.

Oktanzahl [ɔk'ta:ntsa:l] f (bei Benzin) octane.

Oktave [ɔk'ta:fə] f-, -n octave.

Oktober [ɔk'to:bər] m -(s), - October.

ökumenisch [øku'me:nɪʃ] a ecumenical.

Öl [ø:l] nt -(e)s, -e oil; ~**baum** m olive tree; ö~**en** vt oil; (Tech) lubricate; ~**farbe** f oil paint; ~**feld** nt oilfield; ~**film** m film of oil; ~**heizung** f oil-fired central heating; ö~**ig** a oily.

oliv [o'li:f] a olive-green; **O**~**e** [o'li:və] f-, -n olive.

Öl- cpd: ~**meßstab** m dipstick; ~**pest** f oil pollution; ~**sardine** f sardine; ~**scheich** m oil sheik; ~**standanzeiger** m (Aut) oil gauge; ~**ung** f lubrication; oiling; (Eccl) anointment; **die Letzte** ~**ung** Extreme Unction; ~**wechsel** m oil change; ~**zeug** nt oilskins pl.

Olymp- [o'lymp] cpd: ~**iade** [-i'a:də] f Olympic Games pl; ~**iasieger(in** f) [-iazi:gər(ɪn)] m Olympic champion; ~**iateilnehmer(in** f) m, ~**ionike** [-io'ni:kə] m, ~**io'nikin** f Olympic competitor; o~**isch** a Olympic.

Oma [o'ma] f-, -s (col) granny.

Omelett [ɔm(ə)'lɛt] nt -(e)s, -s, **Omelette** f omlet(te).

Omen [o'mεn] nt -s, - or **Omina** omen.

Omnibus [ɔmnibus] m (omni)bus.

Onanie [ona'ni:] f masturbation; o~**ren** vi masturbate.

Onkel [ɔŋkəl] m -s, - uncle.

Opa [o'pa] m -s, -s (col) grandpa.

Opal [o'pa:l] m -s, -e opal.

Oper [o'pər] f-, -n opera; opera house; ~**ation** [operatsi'o:n] f operation; ~**ationssaal** m operating theatre; ~**ette** [ope'rɛtə] f operetta; o~**ieren** [ope'ri:rən] vti operate; ~**nglas** nt opera glasses pl; ~**nhaus** nt opera house; ~**nsänger(in** f) m operatic singer.

Opfer [ɔpfər] nt -s, - sacrifice; (Mensch) victim; o~**n** vt sacrifice; ~**stock** m (Eccl) offertory box; ~**ung** f sacrifice.

Opium [o:pium] nt -s opium.

opponieren [ɔpo'ni:rən] vi oppose (gegen jdn/etw sb/sth).

opportun [ɔpɔr'tu:n] a opportune; **O**~**ismus** [-'nɪsmʊs] m opportunism; **O**~**ist** [-'nɪst] m opportunist.

Opposition [ɔpozitsi'o:n] f opposition; o~**ell** [-'nɛl] a opposing.

Optik [ɔptɪk] f optics sing; ~**er** m -s, - optician.

optimal [ɔpti'ma:l] a optimal, optimum.

Optimismus [ɔpti'mɪsmʊs] m optimism.

Optimist [ɔpti'mɪst] m optimist; o~**isch** a optimistic.

optisch [ɔptɪʃ] a optical.

Orakel [o'ra:kəl] nt -s, - oracle.

Orange [o'rã:ʒə] f-, -n orange; o~ a orange; ~**ade** [orã'ʒa:də] f orangeade; ~**at** [orã'ʒa:t] nt -s, -e candied peel; ~**nmarmelade** f marmelade; ~**nschale** f orange peel.

Orchester [ɔr'kεstər] nt -s, - orchestra.

Orchidee [ɔrçi'de:ə] f-, -n orchid.

Orden [ɔrdən] m -s, - (Eccl) order; (Mil) decoration; ~**sschwester** f nun.

ordentlich [ɔrdəntlɪç] a (anständig) decent, respectable; (geordnet) tidy, neat; (col: annehmbar) not bad; (col: tüchtig) real, proper; ~**er Professor** (full) professor; ad properly; **O**~**keit** f respectability; tidiness, neatness.

Ordinalzahl [ɔrdi'na:ltsa:l] f ordinal number.

ordinär [ɔrdi'nε:r] a common, vulgar.

ordnen [ɔrdnən] vt order, put in order.

Ordner m -s, - steward; (Comm) file.

Ordnung f order; (Ordnen) ordering; (Geordnetsein) tidiness; o~**sgemäß** a proper, according to the rules; o~**shalber** ad as a matter of form; ~**sliebe** f tidiness, orderliness; ~**sstrafe** f fine; o~**swidrig** a contrary to the rules, irregular; ~**szahl** f ordinal number.

Organ [ɔr'ga:n] nt -s, -e organ; (Stimme) voice; ~**isation** [-izatsi'o:n] f organisation; ~**isationstalent** nt organizing ability; (Person) good organizer; ~**isator** [-i'za:tor] m organizer; o~**isch** a organic; o~**isieren** [-i'zi:rən] vt organize, arrange; (col: beschaffen) acquire; vr organize; ~**ismus** [-'nɪsmʊs] m organism; ~**ist** [-'nɪst] m organist; ~**verpflanzung** f transplantation (of organs).

Orgasmus [ɔr'gasmʊs] m orgasm.

Orgel [ɔrgəl] f-, -n organ; ~**pfeife** f organ pipe; **wie die** ~**pfeifen stehen** stand in order of height.

Orgie [ɔrgiə] f orgy.

Orient [o'riεnt] m -s Orient, east; ~**ale** [-'ta:lə] m -n, -n Oriental; o~**alisch** [-'ta:lɪʃ] a oriental; o~**ieren** [-'ti:rən] vt (örtlich) locate; (fig) inform; vr find one's way or bearings; inform oneself; ~**ierung** [-'ti:rʊŋ] f orientation; (fig) information; ~**ierungssinn** m sense of direction.

original [origi'na:l] a original; **O**~ nt -s, -e original; **O**~**fassung** f original version; **O**~**i'tät** f originality.

originell [origi'nεl] a original.

Orkan [ɔr'ka:n] m -(e)s, -e hurricane.

Ornament [ɔrna'mεnt] nt decoration, ornament; o~**al** [-'ta:l] a decorative, ornamental.

Ort [ɔrt] m -(e)s, -e or ̈er place; **an** ~ **und Stelle** on the spot; o~**en** vt locate; **ortho**- [ɔrto] cpd: ~**dox** [-'dɔks] a orthodox; **O**~**graphie** [-gra'fi:] f spelling, orthography; ~**'graphisch** a orthographic; **O**~**päde** [-'pε:də] m -n, -n orthopaedic specialist, orthopaedist; **O**~**pädie** [-pε'di:] f orthopaedics sing; ~**'pädisch** a orthopaedic.

örtlich [œrtlɪç] a local; **Ö**~**keit** f locality.

Ort- cpd: ~**sangabe** f (name of the) town; o~**sansässig** a local; ~**schaft** f village, small town; o~**sfremd** a non-local;

~**sfremde(r)** *mf* stranger; ~**sgespräch** *nt* local (phone)call; ~**sname** *m* place-name; ~**snetz** *nt* (*Tel*) local telephone exchange area; ~**ssinn** *m* sense of direction; ~**szeit** *f* local time; ~**ung** *f* locating.

Öse ['ö:zə] *f* -, -n loop, eye.

Ost- [ɔst] *cpd:* ~**block** *m* (*Pol*) Eastern bloc; ~**en** *m* -s east; **o**~**entativ** [ɔstɛnta'ti:f] a pointed, ostentatious.

Oster- ['o:stər] *cpd:* ~**ei** *nt* Easter egg; ~**fest** *nt* Easter; ~**glocke** *f* daffodil; ~**hase** *m* Easter bunny; ~**montag** *m* Easter Monday; ~**n** *nt* -s, - Easter; ~**sonntag** *m* Easter Day *or* Sunday.

östlich ['œstliç] a eastern, easterly.

Ost- *cpd:* ~**see** *f* Baltic Sea; **o**~**wärts** *ad* eastwards; ~**wind** *m* east wind.

oszillieren [ɔstsi'li:rən] *vi* oscillate.

Otter ['ɔtər] *m* -s, - otter; *f* -, -n (*Schlange*) adder.

Ouvertüre [uver'ty:rə] *f* -, -n overture.

oval [o'va:l] a oval.

Ovation [ovatsi'o:n] *f* ovation.

Ovulation [ovulatsi'o:n] *f* ovulation.

Oxyd [ɔ'ksy:t] *nt* -(e)s, -e oxide; **o**~**ieren** [ɔksy'di:rən] *vti* oxidize; ~**ierung** *f* oxidization.

Ozean ['o:tsea:n] *m* -s, -e ocean; ~**dampfer** *m* (ocean-going) liner; **o**~**isch** [otse'a:niʃ] a oceanic.

Ozon [o'tso:n] *nt* -s ozone.

P

P, p [pe:] *nt* P, p.

Paar [pa:r] *nt* -(e)s, -e pair; (*Ehe—*) couple; **ein p**~ a few; **p**~**en** *vtr* couple; *Tiere* mate; ~**lauf** *m* pair skating; **p**~**mal** *ad:* **ein p**~**mal** a few times; ~**ung** *f* combination; mating; **p**~**weise** *ad* in pairs; in couples.

Pacht [paxt] *f* -, -en lease; **p**~**en** *vt* lease.

Pächter ['pɛçtər] *m* -s, - leaseholder, tenant.

Pack [pak] *m* -(e)s, -e *or* ¨e bundle, pack; *nt* -(e)s (*pej*) mob, rabble.

Päckchen ['pɛkçən] *nt* small package; (*Zigaretten*) packet; (*Post—*) small parcel.

Pack- *cpd:* **p**~**en** *vt* pack; (*fassen*) grasp, seize; (*col: schaffen*) manage; (*fig: fesseln*) grip; ~**en** *m* -s, - bundle; (*fig: Menge*) heaps of; ~**esel** *m* (*lit, fig*) packhorse; ~**papier** *nt* brown paper, wrapping paper; ~**ung** *f* packet; (*Pralinen—*) box; (*Med*) compress.

Pädagog- [pɛda'go:g] *cpd:* ~**e** *m* -n, -n teacher; ~**ik** *f* education; **p**~**isch** a educational, pedagogical.

Paddel ['padəl] *nt* -s, - paddle; ~**boot** *nt* canoe; **p**~**n** *vi* paddle.

paffen ['pafən] *vti* puff.

Page ['pa:ʒə] *m* -n, -n page; ~**nkopf** *m* pageboy.

Paillette [paï'jɛtə] *f* sequin.

Paket [pa'ke:t] *nt* -(e)s, -e packet; (*Post—*) parcel; ~**karte** *f* dispatch note; ~**post** *f* parcel post; ~**schalter** *m* parcels counter.

Pakt [pakt] *m* -(e)s, -e pact.

Palast [pa'last] *m* -es, **Paläste** palace.

Palette [pa'lɛtə] *f* palette; (*Lade—*) pallet.

Palme ['palmə] *f* -, -n palm (tree).

Palmsonntag *m* Palm Sunday.

Pampelmuse ['pampəlmu:zə] *f* -, -n grapefruit.

pampig ['pampiç] a (*col: frech*) fresh.

panieren [pa'ni:rən] *vt* (*Cook*) coat with egg and breadcrumbs.

Paniermehl [pa'ni:rme:l] *nt* breadcrumbs *pl.*

Panik ['pa:nik] *f* panic.

panisch ['pa:niʃ] a panic-stricken.

Panne ['panə] *f* -, -n (*Aut etc*) breakdown; (*Mißgeschick*) slip.

panschen ['panʃən] *vi* splash about; *vt* water down.

Panther ['pantər] *m* -s, - panther.

Pantoffel [pan'tɔfəl] *m* -s, -n slipper; ~**held** *m* (*col*) henpecked husband.

Pantomime [panto'mi:mə] *f* -, -n mime.

Panzer ['pantsər] *m* -s, - armour; (*Platte*) armour plate; (*Fahrzeug*) tank; ~**glas** *nt* bulletproof glass; **p**~**n** *vtr* armour; (*fig*) arm o.s.; ~**schrank** *m* strongbox.

Papa [pa'pa:] *m* -s, -s (*col*) dad, daddy; ~**gei** [-'gai] *m* -s, -en parrot.

Papier [pa'pi:r] *nt* -s, -e paper; (*Wert—*) share; ~**fabrik** *f* paper mill; ~**geld** *nt* paper money; ~**korb** *m* wastepaper basket; ~**krieg** *m* red tape; angry correspondence; ~**tüte** *f* paper bag.

Papp- [pap] *cpd:* ~**deckel** *m*, ~**e** *f* -, -n cardboard; ~**einband** *m* pasteboard; ~**el** *f* -, -n poplar; **p**~**en** *vti* (*col*) stick; ~**enstiel** *m* (*col*): **keinen** ~**enstiel wert sein** to be not worth a thing; **für einen** ~**enstiel bekommen** get for a song; **p**~**erlapapp** *interj* rubbish; **p**~**ig** a sticky; ~**maché** [-ma'fe:] *nt* -s, -s papier-mâché.

Paprika [paprika] *m* -s, -s (*Gewürz*) paprika; (*—schote*) pepper.

Papst [pa:pst] *m* -(e)s, ¨e pope.

päpstlich ['pe:pstliç] a papal.

Parabel [pa'ra:bəl] *f* -, -n parable; (*Math*) parabola.

Parade [pa'ra:də] *f* (*Mil*) parade, review; (*Sport*) parry; ~**marsch** *m* march-past; ~**schritt** *m* goose-step.

Paradies [para'di:s] *nt* -es, -e paradise; **p**~**isch** a heavenly.

paradox [para'dɔks] a paradoxical; **P**~ *nt* -es, -e paradox.

Paragraph [para'gra:f] *m* -en, -en paragraph; (*Jur*) section.

parallel [para'le:l] a parallel; **P**~**e** *f* parallel.

paramilitärisch [paramili'tɛ:riʃ] a para-military.

Paranuß ['pa:ranus] *f* Brazil nut.

paraphieren [para'fi:rən] *vt* *Vertrag* initial.

Parasit [para'zi:t] *m* -en, -en (*lit, fig*) parasite.

parat [pa'ra:t] a ready.

Pärchen ['pɛ:rçən] *nt* couple.

Parfüm [par'fy:m] *nt* -s, -s *or* -e perfume;

~erie [-ə'ri:] f perfumery; ~flasche f
scent bottle; p~ieren [-'mi:rən] vt scent,
perfume.
parieren [pa'ri:rən] vt parry; vi (col) obey.
Parität [pari'tɛ:t] f parity.
Park [park] m -s, -s park; ~anlage f
park; (um Gebäude) grounds pl; p~en vti
park; ~ett [par'kɛt] nt -(e)s, -e parquet
(floor); (Theat) stalls pl; ~haus nt multi-
storey car park; ~lücke f parking space;
~platz m parking place; car park,
parking lot (US); ~scheibe f parking
disc; ~uhr f parking meter; ~verbot nt
no parking.
Parlament [parla'mɛnt] nt parliament;
~arier [-'ta:riər] m -s, - parliamentarian;
p~arisch [-'ta:rɪʃ] a parliamentary;
~sbeschluß m vote of parliament;
~smitglied nt member of parliament;
~ssitzung f sitting (of parliament).
Parodie [paro'di:] f parody; p~ren vt
parody.
Parole [pa'ro:lə] f -, -n password;
(Wahlspruch) motto.
Partei [par'tai] f party; ~ ergreifen für
jdn take sb's side; ~führung f party
leadership; ~genosse m party member;
p~isch a partial, biased; p~los a
neutral; ~nahme f -, -n support, taking
the part of; ~tag m party conference.
Parterre [par'tɛr] nt -s, -s ground floor;
(Theat) stalls pl.
Partie [par'ti:] f part; (Spiel) game;
(Ausflug) outing; (Mann, Frau) catch;
(Comm) lot; mit von der ~ sein join in.
Partikel [par'ti:kəl] f -, -n particle.
Partisan [parti'za:n] m -s or -en, -en
partisan.
Partitur [parti'tu:r] f (Mus) score.
Partizip [parti'tsi:p] nt -s, -ien participle.
Partner(in f) ['partnər] m -s, - partner;
p~schaftlich a as partners.
Party ['pa:rti] f -, -s or Parties party.
Parzelle [par'tsɛlə] f plot, allotment.
Paß [pas] m -sses, -sse pass; (Ausweis)
passport.
Pass- cpd: p~abel [pa'sa:bəl] a passable,
reasonable; ~age [pa'sa:ʒə] f -, -n
passage; ~agier [pasa'ʒi:r] m -s, -e
passenger; p~agierdampfer m passenger
steamer; P~agierflugzeug nt airliner;
~ant [pa'sant] m passer-by.
Paß- cpd: ~amt nt passport office; ~bild
nt passport photograph.
passen ['pasən] vi fit; (Farbe) go (zu with);
(auf Frage, Cards, Sport) pass; das paßt
mir nicht that doesn't suit me; er paßt
nicht zu dir he's not right for you; ~d a
suitable; (zusammen-) matching; (angebracht) fitting; Zeit convenient.
passier- [pa'si:r] cpd: ~bar a passable;
~en vi pass; (durch Sieb) strain; vi
happen; P~schein m pass, permit.
Passion [pasi'o:n] f passion; p~iert
[-'ni:rt] a enthusiastic, passionate; ~sspiel
nt Passion Play.
passiv ['pasi:f] a passive; P~ nt -s, -e
passive; P~a pl (Comm) liabilities pl;
P~i'tät f passiveness.
Paß- cpd: ~kontrolle f passport control;

~stelle f passport office; ~straße f
(mountain) pass; ~zwang m requirement to carry a passport.
Paste ['pastə] f -, -n paste.
Pastell [pas'tɛl] nt -(e)s, -e pastel.
Pastete [pas'te:tə] f -, -n pie.
pasteurisieren [pastöri'zi:rən] vt
pasteurize.
Pastor ['pastɔr] m vicar; pastor, minister.
Pate ['pa:tə] m -n, -n godfather; ~nkind
nt godchild.
Patent [pa'tɛnt] nt -(e)s, -e patent; (Mil)
commission; p~ a clever; ~amt nt
patent office; p~ieren [-'ti:rən] vt patent;
~inhaber m patentee; ~schutz m
patent right.
Pater ['pa:tər] m -s, - or Patres (Eccl)
Father.
pathetisch [pa'te:tɪʃ] a emotional; bombastic.
Pathologe [pato'lo:gə] m -n, -n
pathologist.
pathologisch a pathological.
Pathos ['pa:tɔs] nt - emotiveness,
emotionalism.
Patient(in f) [patsi'ɛnt(ɪn)] m patient.
Patin ['pa:tɪn] f godmother; ~a ['pa:tina] f
- patina.
Patriarch [patri'arç] m -en, -en
patriarch; p~alisch [-'ça:lɪʃ] a
patriarchal.
Patriot [patri'o:t] m -en, -en patriot;
p~isch a patriotic; ~ismus [-'tɪsmʊs] m
patriotism.
Patron [pa'tro:n] m -s, -e patron; (pej)
beggar; ~e f -, -n cartridge; ~enhülse f
cartridge case; ~in f patroness.
Patrouille [pa'trʊljə] f -, -n patrol.
patrouillieren [patrʊl'ji:rən] vi patrol.
patsch [patʃ] interj splash; P~e f -, -n (col:
Händchen) paw; (Fliegen—) swat;
(Feuer—) beater; (Bedrängnis) mess, jam;
~en vti smack, slap; (im Wasser) splash;
~naß a soaking wet.
patzig ['patsɪç] a (col) cheeky, saucy.
Pauke ['paʊkə] f -, -n kettledrum; auf die
~ hauen live it up; p~n vti (Sch) swot,
cram; ~r m -s, - (col) teacher.
pausbäckig ['paʊsbɛkɪç] a chubby-
cheeked.
pauschal [paʊ'ʃa:l] a Kosten inclusive;
Urteil sweeping; P~e f -, -n, P~gebühr f
flat rate; P~preis m all-in price;
P~reise f package tour; P~summe f
lump sum.
Pause ['paʊzə] f -, -n break; (Theat)
interval; (Innehalten) pause; (Kopie)
tracing; p~n vt trace; p~nlos a non-
stop; ~nzeichen nt call sign; (Mus) rest.
pausieren [paʊ'zi:rən] vi make a break.
Pauspapier ['paʊzpapi:r] nt tracing
paper.
Pavian ['pa:via:n] m -s, -e baboon.
Pazifist [patsi'fɪst] m pacifist; p~isch a
pacifist.
Pech [pɛç] nt -s, -e pitch; (fig) bad luck;
~ haben be unlucky; p~schwarz a
pitch-black; ~strähne m (col) unlucky
patch; ~vogel m (col) unlucky person.

Pedal [pe'da:l] *nt* -s, -e pedal.
Pedant [pe'dant] *m* pedant; ~e'rie *f* pedantry; p~isch *a* pedantic.
Peddigrohr ['pɛdɪçro:r] *nt* cane.
Pegel ['pe:gəl] *m* -s, - water gauge; ~stand *m* water level.
peilen ['paɪlən] *vt* get a fix on.
Pein [paɪn] *f* - agony, pain; p~igen *vt* torture; (*plagen*) torment; p~lich *a* (*unangenehm*) embarrassing, awkward, painful; (*genau*) painstaking; P~lichkeit *f* painfulness, awkwardness; scrupulousness.
Peitsche ['paɪtʃə] *f* -, -n whip; p~n *vt* whip; (*Regen*) lash.
Pelikan [pe:lika:n] *m* -s, -e pelican.
Pelle ['pɛlə] *f* -, -n skin; p~n *vt* skin, peel.
Pellkartoffeln *pl* jacket potatoes *pl*.
Pelz [pɛlts] *m* -es, -e fur.
Pendel ['pɛndəl] *nt* -s, - pendulum; ~verkehr *m* shuttle traffic; (*für Pendler*) commuter traffic.
Pendler ['pɛndlər] *m* -s, - commuter.
penetrant [pene'trant] *a* sharp; *Person* pushing.
Penis ['pe:nɪs] *m* -, -se penis.
Pension [penzi'o:n] *f* (*Geld*) pension; (*Ruhestand*) retirement; (*für Gäste*) boarding *or* guest-house; **halbe/volle** ~ half/full board; ~är(in *f*) [-'nɛr(ɪn)] *m* -s, -e pensioner; ~at [-'na:t] *nt* -(e)s, -e boarding school; p~ieren [-'ni:rən] *vt* pension (off); p~iert *a* retired; ~ierung *f* retirement; ~sgast *m* boarder, paying guest.
Pensum ['pɛnzʊm] *nt* -s, **Pensen** quota; (*Sch*) curriculum.
per [pɛr] *prep* +*acc* by, per; (*pro*) per; (*bis*) by.
Perfekt ['pɛrfɛkt] *nt* -(e)s, -e perfect; p~ [pɛr'fɛkt] *a* perfect; ~ionismus [pɛrfɛktsio'nɪsmʊs] *m* perfectionism.
perforieren [pɛrfo'ri:rən] *vt* perforate.
Pergament [pɛrga'mɛnt] *nt* parchment; ~papier *nt* greaseproof paper.
Periode [peri'o:də] *f* -, -n period.
periodisch [peri'o:dɪʃ] *a* periodic; (*dezimal*) recurring.
Peripherie [perife'ri:] *f* periphery; (*um Stadt*) outskirts *pl*; (*Math*) circumference.
Perle ['pɛrlə] *f* -, -n (*lit, fig*) pearl; p~n *vi* sparkle; (*Tropfen*) trickle.
Perlmutt ['pɛrlmʊt] *nt* -s mother-of-pearl.
perplex [pɛr'plɛks] *a* dumbfounded.
Persianer [pɛrzi'a:nər] *m* -s, - Persian lamb.
Person [pɛr'zo:n] *f* -, -en person; **ich für meine** ~ personally I; **klein von** ~ of small build; ~al [-'na:l] *nt* -s personnel; (*Bedienung*) servants *pl*; ~alausweis *m* identity card; ~alien [-'na:liən] *pl* particulars *pl*; ~ali'tät *f* personality; ~alpronomen *nt* personal pronoun; ~enaufzug *m* lift, elevator (*US*); ~enkraftwagen *m* private motorcar; ~enkreis *m* group of people; ~enschaden *m* injury to persons; ~enwaage *f* scales *pl*; ~enzug *m* stopping train; passenger train; p~ifizieren [-ifi'tsi:rən] *vt* personify.

persönlich [pɛr'zø:nlɪç] *a* personal; *ad* in person; personally; P~keit *f* personality.
Perspektive [pɛrspɛk'ti:və] *f* perspective.
Perücke [pe'rʏkə] *f* -, -n wig.
pervers [pɛr'vɛrs] *a* perverse; P~i'tät *f* perversity.
Pessimismus [pɛsi'mɪsmʊs] *m* pessimism.
Pessimist [pɛsi'mɪst] *m* pessimist; p~isch *a* pessimistic.
Pest [pɛst] *f* - plague.
Petersilie [petər'zi:liə] *f* parsley.
Petroleum [pe'tro:leʊm] *nt* -s paraffin, kerosene (*US*).
petzen ['pɛtsən] *vi* (*col*) tell tales.
Pfad [pfa:t] *m* -(e)s, -e path; ~finder *m* -s, - boy scout; ~finderin *f* girl guide.
Pfahl [pfa:l] *m* -(e)s, -e post, stake; ~bau *m* pile dwelling.
Pfand [pfant] *nt* -(e)s, -er pledge, security; (*Flaschen—*) deposit; (*im Spiel*) forfeit; (*fig: der Liebe etc*) pledge; ~brief *m* bond.
pfänden ['pfɛndən] *vt* seize, distrain.
Pfänderspiel *nt* game of forfeits.
Pfand- *cpd*: ~haus *nt* pawnshop; ~leiher *m* -s, - pawnbroker; ~schein *m* pawn ticket.
Pfändung ['pfɛndʊŋ] *f* seizure, distraint.
Pfanne ['pfanə] *f* -, -n (frying) pan.
Pfannkuchen *m* pancake; (*Berliner*) doughnut.
Pfarr- ['pfar] *cpd*: ~ei [-'raɪ] *f* parish; ~er *m* -s, - priest; (*evangelisch*) vicar; minister; ~haus *nt* vicarage; manse.
Pfau [pfaʊ] *m* -(e)s, -en peacock; ~enauge *nt* peacock butterfly.
Pfeffer ['pfɛfər] *m* -s, - pepper; ~korn *nt* peppercorn; ~kuchen *m* gingerbread; ~minz *nt* -es, -e peppermint; ~mühle *f* pepper-mill; p~n *vt* pepper; (*col: werfen*) fling; **gepfefferte Preise/Witze** steep prices/spicy jokes.
Pfeife ['pfaɪfə] *f* -, -n whistle; (*Tabak—, Orgel—*) pipe; p~n *vti irreg* whistle; ~r *m* -s, - piper.
Pfeil [pfaɪl] *m* -(e)s, -e arrow.
Pfeiler ['pfaɪlər] *m* -s, - pillar, prop; (*Brücken—*) pier.
Pfennig ['pfɛnɪç] *m* -(e)s, -e pfennig (*hundredth part of a mark*).
Pferd [pfe:rt] *nt* -(e)s, -e horse; ~erennen *nt* horse-race; horse-racing; ~eschwanz *m* (*Frisur*) ponytail; ~estall *m* stable.
Pfiff [pfɪf] *m* -(e)s, -e whistle; (*Kniff*) trick; ~erling ['pfɪfərlɪŋ] *m* yellow chanterelle; **keinen** ~erling wert not worth a thing; p~ig *a* sly, sharp.
Pfingsten ['pfɪŋstən] *nt* -, -Whitsun.
Pfingstrose ['pfɪŋstro:zə] *f* peony.
Pfirsich ['pfɪrzɪç] *m* -s, -e peach.
Pflanz- ['pflants] *cpd*: ~e *f* -, -n plant; p~en *vt* plant; ~enfett *nt* vegetable fat; ~er *m* -s, - planter; ~ung *f* plantation.
Pflaster ['pflastər] *nt* -s, - plaster; (*Straße*) pavement; p~müde *a* dead on one's feet; p~n *vt* pave; ~stein *m* paving stone.

Pflaume ['pflaumə] f -, -n plum.
Pflege ['pfle:gə] f -, -n care; (von Idee) cultivation; (Kranken—) nursing; **in ~ sein** (Kind) be fostered out; **p~bedürftig** a needing care; **~eltern** pl foster parents pl; **~kind** nt foster child; **p~leicht** a easy-care; **~mutter** f foster mother; **p~n** vt look after; Kranke nurse; Beziehungen foster; **~r** m -s, - orderly; male nurse; **~rin** f nurse, attendant; **~vater** m foster father.
Pflicht [pflıçt] f -, -en duty; (Sport) compulsory section; **p~bewußt** a conscientious; **~fach** nt (Sch) compulsory subject; **~gefühl** nt sense of duty; **p~gemäß** a dutiful; ad as in duty bound; **p~vergessen** a irresponsible; **~versicherung** f compulsory insurance.
Pflock [pflɔk] m -(e)s, -e peg; (für Tiere) stake.
pflücken ['pflʏkən] vt pick; Blumen auch pluck.
Pflug [pflu:k] m -(e)s, -e plough.
pflügen ['pfly:gən] vti plough.
Pforte ['pfɔrtə] f -, -n gate; door.
Pförtner ['pfœrtnər] m -s, - porter, doorkeeper, doorman.
Pfosten ['pfɔstən] m -s, - post.
Pfote ['pfo:tə] f -, -n paw; (col: Schrift) scrawl.
Pfropf [pfrɔpf] m -(e)s, -e (Flaschen—) stopper; (Blut—) clot; **p~en** vt (stopfen) cram; Baum graft; **P~en** m -s, -e see Pfropf.
pfui [pfʊi] interj ugh; (na na) tut tut.
Pfund [pfʊnt] nt -(e)s, -e pound; **p~ig** a (col) great; **p~weise** ad by the pound.
pfuschen ['pfʊʃən] vi (col) be sloppy; **jdm in etw** (acc) **~** interfere in sth.
Pfuscher ['pfʊʃər] m -s, - (col) sloppy worker; (Kur—) quack; **~ei** [-'rai] f (col) sloppy work; (Kur—) quackery.
Pfütze ['pfʏtsə] f -, -n puddle.
Phänomen [fɛno'me:n] nt -s, -e phenomenon; **p~al** [-'na:l] a phenomenal.
Phantasie [fanta'zi:] f imagination; **p~los** a unimaginative; **p~ren** vi fantasize; **p~voll** a imaginative.
phantastisch [fan'tastıʃ] a fantastic.
Pharisäer [fari'zɛ:ər] m -s, - (lit, fig) pharisee.
Pharmazeut(in f) [farma'tsɔyt(ın)] m -en, -en pharmacist.
Phase ['fa:zə] f -, -n phase.
Philanthrop [filan'tro:p] m -en, -en philanthropist; **p~isch** a philanthropic.
Philologe [filo'lo:gə] m -n, -n philologist.
Philologie [filolo'gi:] f philology.
Philosoph [filo'zo:f] m -en, -en philosopher; **~ie** [-'fi:] f philosophy; **p~isch** a philosophical.
Phlegma ['flɛgma] nt -s lethargy; **p~tisch** [flɛ'gma:tıʃ] a lethargic.
Phonet- [fo'ne:t] cpd: **~ik** f phonetics sing; **p~isch** a phonetic.
Phosphor ['fɔsfɔr] m -s phosphorus; **p~eszieren** [fɔsfɔrɛs'tsi:rən] vt phosphoresce.
Photo ['fo:to] nt -s, -s etc see Foto.

Phrase ['fra:zə] f -, -n phrase; (pej) hollow phrase.
Physik [fy'zi:k] f physics sing; **p~alisch** [-'ka:lıʃ] a of physics; **~er(in** f) ['fy:zıkər(ın)] m -s, - physicist.
Physiologe [fyzio'lo:gə] m -n, -n physiologist.
Physiologie [fyziolo'gi:] f physiology.
physisch ['fy:zıʃ] a physical.
Pianist(in f) [pia'nıst(ın)] m pianist.
picheln ['pıçəln] vi (col) booze.
Pickel ['pıkəl] m -s, - pimple; (Werkzeug) pickaxe; (Berg—) ice-axe; **p~ig** a pimply.
picken ['pıkən] vti pick, peck.
Picknick ['pıknık] nt -s, -e or -s picnic; **~ machen** have a picnic.
piepen ['pi:pən], **piepsen** ['pi:psən] vi chirp.
piesacken ['pi:zakən] vt (col) torment.
Pietät [pie'tɛ:t] f piety, reverence; **p~los** a impious, irreverent.
Pigment [pı'gmɛnt] nt pigment.
Pik [pi:k] nt -s, -s (Cards) spades; **einen ~ auf jdn haben** (col) have it in for sb; **p~ant** [pı'kant] a spicy, piquant; (anzüglich) suggestive; **p~iert** [pı'ki:rt] a offended.
Pilger ['pılgər] m -s, - pilgrim; **~fahrt** f pilgrimage.
Pille ['pılə] f -, -n pill.
Pilot [pi'lo:t] m -en, -en pilot.
Pilz [pılts] m -es, -e fungus; (eßbar) mushroom; (giftig) toadstool; **~krankheit** f fungal disease.
pingelig ['pıŋəlıç] a (col) fussy.
Pinguin ['pıŋguˈi:n] m -s, -e penguin.
Pinie ['pi:niə] f pine.
pinkeln ['pıŋkəln] vi (col) pee.
Pinsel ['pınzəl] m -s, - paintbrush.
Pinzette [pın'tsɛtə] f tweezers pl.
Pionier [pio'ni:r] m -s, -e pioneer; (Mil) sapper, engineer.
Pirat [pi'ra:t] m -en, -en pirate; **~ensender** m pirate radio station.
Pirsch [pırʃ] f - stalking.
Piste ['pıstə] f -, -n (Ski) run, piste; (Aviat) runway.
Pistole [pıs'to:lə] f -, -n pistol.
Pizza ['pıtsa] f -, -s pizza.
Pkw [pe:ka:ve:] m -(s), -(s) see Personenkraftwagen.
Plackerei [plakə'rai] f drudgery.
plädieren [plɛ'di:rən] vi plead.
Plädoyer [plɛdoaˈje:] nt -s, -s speech for the defence; (fig) plea.
Plage ['pla:gə] f -, -n plague; (Mühe) nuisance; **~geist** m pest, nuisance; **p~n** vt torment; vr toil, slave.
Plakat [pla'ka:t] nt -(e)s, -e placard; poster.
Plan [pla:n] m -(e)s, -e plan; (Karte) map; **~e** f -, -n tarpaulin; **p~en** vt plan; Mord etc plot; **~er** m -s, - planner; **~et** [pla'ne:t] m -en -en planet; **~etenbahn** f orbit (of a planet); **p~gemäß** according to schedule or plan; (Rail) on time; **p~ieren** [pla'ni:rən] vt plane, level; **~ierraupe** f bulldozer.
Planke ['plaŋkə] f -, -n plank.

Plänkelei [plɛŋkə'laɪ] *f* skirmish(ing).
plänkeln ['plɛŋkəln] *vi* skirmish.
Plankton ['plaŋktɔn] *nt* -s plankton.
Plan- *cpd:* **p~los** *a* *zu Vorgehen* unsystematic; *Umherlaufen* aimless; **p~mäßig** *a* according to plan; systematic; (*Rail*) scheduled.
Plansch- ['planʃ] *cpd:* **~becken** *nt* paddling pool; **p~en** *vi* splash.
Plan- *cpd:* **~soll** *nt* -s output target; **~stelle** *f* post.
Plantage [plan'ta:ʒə] *f* -, -n plantation.
Plan- *cpd:* **~ung** *f* planning; **~wagen** *m* covered wagon; **~wirtschaft** *f* planned economy.
plappern ['plapərn] *vi* chatter.
plärren ['plɛrən] *vi* (*Mensch*) cry, whine; (*Radio*) blare.
Plasma ['plasma] *nt* -s, **Plasmen** plasma.
Plastik ['plastɪk] *f* sculpture; *nt* -s (*Kunststoff*) plastic; **~folie** *f* plastic film.
Plastilin [plasti'li:n] *nt* -s plasticine.
plastisch ['plastɪʃ] *a* plastic; **stell dir das ~ vor!** just picture it!
Platane [pla'ta:nə] *f* -, -n plane (tree).
Platin [pla'ti:n] *nt* -s platinum.
Platitüde [plati'ty:də] *f* -, -n platitude.
platonisch [pla'to:nɪʃ] *a* platonic.
platsch [platʃ] *interj* splash; **~en** *vi* splash; **~naß** *a* drenched.
plätschern ['plɛtʃərn] *vi* babble.
platt [plat] *a* flat; (*col: überrascht*) flabbergasted; (*fig: geistlos*) flat, boring; **~deutsch** *a* low German; **P~e** *f* -, *f* (*Speisen—, Phot, Tech*) plate; (*Stein—*) flag; (*Kachel*) tile; (*Schall—*) record.
Plätt- ['plɛt] *cpd:* **~eisen** *nt* iron; **p~en** *vti* iron.
Platt- *cpd:* **~enspieler** *m* record player; **~enteller** *m* turntable; **~fuß** *m* flat foot; (*Reifen*) flat tyre.
Platz [plats] *m* -es, **¨e** place; (*Sitz—*) seat; (*Raum*) space, room; (*in Stadt*) square; (*Sport—*) playing field; **jdm ~ machen** make room for sb; **p~angst** *f* (*Med*) agoraphobia; (*col*) claustrophobia; **~anweiser(in** *f)* *m* -s, - usher(ette).
Plätzchen ['plɛtsçən] *nt* spot; (*Gebäck*) biscuit.
Platz- *cpd:* **p~en** *vi* burst; (*Bombe*) explode; **vor Wut p~en** (*col*) be bursting with anger; **~karte** *f* seat reservation; **~mangel** *m* lack of space; **~patrone** *f* blank cartridge; **~regen** *m* downpour; **~wunde** *f* cut.
Plauderei [plaʊdə'raɪ] *f* chat, conversation; (*Rad*) talk.
plaudern ['plaʊdərn] *vi* chat, talk.
plausibel [plaʊ'zi:bəl] *a* plausible.
plazieren [pla'tsi:rən] *vt* place; *vr* (*Sport*) be placed; (*Tennis*) be seeded.
Plebejer [ple'be:jər] *m* -s, - plebeian.
plebejisch [ple'be:jɪʃ] *a* plebeian.
pleite ['plaɪtə] *a* (*col*) broke; **P~** *f* -, -n bankruptcy; (*col: Reinfall*) flop; **P~ machen** go bust.
Plenum ['ple:nʊm] *nt* -s plenum.

Pleuelstange ['plɔyəlʃtaŋə] *f* connecting rod.
Plissee [plɪ'se:] *nt* -s, -s pleat.
Plombe ['plɔmbə] *f* -, -n lead seal; (*Zahn—*) filling.
plombieren [plɔm'bi:rən] *vt* seal; *Zahn* fill.
plötzlich ['plœtslıç] *a* sudden; *ad* suddenly.
plump [plʊmp] *a* clumsy; *Hände* coarse; *Körper* shapeless; **~sen** *vi* (*col*) plump down, fall.
Plunder ['plʊndər] *m* -s rubbish.
plündern ['plʏndərn] *vti* plunder; *Stadt* sack.
Plünderung ['plʏndərʊŋ] *f* plundering, sack, pillage.
Plural ['plu:ra:l] *m* -s, -e plural; **p~istisch** [plura'lıstıʃ] *a* pluralistic.
Plus [plʊs] *nt* -, - plus; (*Fin*) profit; (*Vorteil*) advantage; **p~** *ad* plus.
Plüsch [ply:ʃ] *m* -(e)s, -e plush.
Plus- *cpd:* **~pol** *m* (*Elec*) positive pole; **~punkt** *m* point; (*fig*) point in sb's favour; **~quamperfekt** *nt* -s, -e pluperfect.
Po [po:] *m* -s, -s (*col*) bottom, bum.
Pöbel ['pø:bəl] *m* -s mob, rabble; **~ei** [-'laɪ] *f* vulgarity; **p~haft** *a* low, vulgar.
pochen ['pɔxən] *vi* knock; (*Herz*) pound; **auf etw** (*acc*) **~** (*fig*) insist on sth.
Pocken ['pɔkən] *pl* smallpox.
Podium ['po:dium] *nt* podium; **~sdiskussion** *f* panel discussion.
Poesie [poe'zi:] *f* poetry.
Poet [po'e:t] *m* -en, -en poet; **p~isch** *a* poetic.
Pointe ['pʊɛ̃:tə] *f* -, -n point.
Pokal [po'ka:l] *m* -s, -e goblet; (*Sport*) cup; **~spiel** *nt* cup-tie.
Pökel- ['pø:kəl] *cpd:* **~fleisch** *nt* salt meat; **p~n** *vt* pickle, salt.
Pol [po:l] *m* -s, -e pole; **p~ar** [po'la:r] *a* polar; **~arkreis** *m* arctic circle.
Polemik [po'le:mɪk] *f* polemics.
polemisch [po'le:mɪʃ] *a* polemical.
polemisieren [polemi'zi:rən] *vi* polemicize.
Police [po'li:s(ə)] *f* -, -n insurance policy.
Polier [po'li:r] *m* -s, -e foreman; **p~en** *vt* polish.
Poliklinik [poli'kli:nɪk] *f* outpatients.
Politik [poli'ti:k] *f* politics *sing*; (*eine bestimmte*) policy; **~er(in** *f)* [po'li:tikər(ɪn)] *m* -s, - politician.
politisch [po'li:tıʃ] *a* political.
politisieren [politi'zi:rən] *vi* talk politics; *vt* politicize.
Politur [poli'tu:r] *f* polish.
Polizei [poli'tsaɪ] *f* police; **~beamte(r)** *m* police officer; **p~lich** *a* police; **sich p~lich melden** register with the police; **~revier** *nt* police station; **~spitzel** *m* police spy, informer; **~staat** *m* police state; **~streife** *f* police patrol; **~stunde** *f* closing time; **p~widrig** *a* illegal.
Polizist [poli'tsɪst] *m* -en, -en policeman; **~in** *f* policewoman.
Pollen ['pɔlən] *m* -s, - pollen.
Polster ['pɔlstər] *nt* -s, - cushion; (*Polsterung*) upholstery; (*in Kleidung*) padding; (*fig: Geld*) reserves *pl*; **~er** *m* -s,

- upholsterer; ~**möbel** *pl* upholstered furniture; **p**~**n** *vt* upholster; pad; ~**ung** *f* upholstery.

Polter- ['pɔltər] *cpd:* ~**abend** *m* party on eve of wedding; **p**~**n** *vi* (*Krach machen*) crash; (*schimpfen*) rant.

Polygamie [polyga'miː] *f* polygamy.

Polyp [po'lyːp] *m* -en -en polyp; (*pl: Med*) adenoids *pl*; (*col*) cop.

Pomade [po'maːdə] *f* pomade.

Pommes frites [pɔm'frit] *pl* chips *pl*, French fried potatoes *pl*.

Pomp [pɔmp] *m* -(e)s pomp.

Pony ['pɔni] *m* -s, -s (*Frisur*) fringe; *nt* -s, -s (*Pferd*) pony.

Popo [po'poː] *m* -s, -s bottom, bum.

populär [popu'lɛːr] *a* popular.

Popularität [populari'tɛːt] *f* popularity.

Pore ['poːrə] *f* -, -n pore.

Pornographie [pɔrnogra'fiː] *f* pornography.

porös [po'røːs] *a* porous.

Porree ['pɔre] *m* -s, -s leek.

Portal [pɔr'taːl] *nt* -s, -e portal.

Portemonnaie [pɔrtmɔ'neː] *nt* -s, -s purse.

Portier [pɔrti'eː] *m* -s, -s porter; *see* **Pförtner**.

Portion [pɔrtsi'oːn] *f* portion, helping; (*col: Anteil*) amount.

Porto ['pɔrto] *nt* -s, -s postage; **p**~**frei** *a* post-free, (*postage*) prepaid.

Porträt [pɔr'trɛː] *nt* -s, -s portrait; **p**~**ieren** [pɔrtrɛ'tiːrən] *vt* paint, portray.

Porzellan [pɔrtse'laːn] *nt* -s, -e china, porcelain; (*Geschirr*) china.

Posaune [po'zaunə] *f* -, -n trombone.

Pose ['poːzə] *f* -, -n pose.

posieren [po'ziːrən] *vi* pose.

Position [pozitsi'oːn] *f* position; ~**slichter** *pl* (*Aviat*) position lights *pl*.

positiv ['poːzitiːf] *a* positive; **P**~ *nt* -s, -e (*Phot*) positive.

Positur [pozi'tuːr] *f* posture, attitude.

possessiv ['pɔsesiːf] *a* possessive; **P**~(**pronomen**) *nt* -s, -e possessive pronoun.

possierlich [po'siːrlɪç] *a* funny.

Post [pɔst] *f* -, -en post (office); (*Briefe*) mail; ~**amt** *nt* post office; ~**anweisung** *f* postal order, money order; ~**bote** *m* postman; ~**en** *m* -s, - post, position; (*Comm*) item; (*auf Liste*) entry; (*Mil*) sentry; (*Streik*—) picket; ~**fach** *nt* post-office box; ~**karte** *f* postcard; **p**~**lagernd** *ad* poste restante; ~**leitzahl** *f* postal code; ~**scheckkonto** *nt* postal giro account; ~**sparkasse** *f* post office savings bank; ~**stempel** *m* postmark; **p**~**wendend** *ad* by return (of post).

potent [po'tɛnt] *a* potent; (*fig*) high-powered.

Potential [potɛntsi'aːl] *nt* -s, -e potential.

potentiell [potɛntsi'ɛl] *a* potential.

Potenz [po'tɛnts] *f* power; (*eines Mannes*) potency.

Pracht [praxt] *f* - splendour, magnificence.

prächtig ['prɛçtɪç] *a* splendid.

Pracht- *cpd:* ~**stück** *nt* showpiece; **p**~**voll** *a* splendid, magnificent.

Prädikat [prɛdi'kaːt] *nt* -(e)s, -e title; (*Gram*) predicate; (*Zensur*) distinction.

prägen ['prɛːgən] *vt* stamp; *Münze* mint; *Ausdruck* coin; *Charakter* form.

prägnant [prɛ'gnant] *a* precise, terse.

Prägnanz [prɛ'gnants] *f* conciseness, terseness.

Prägung ['prɛːguŋ] *f* minting; forming; (*Eigenart*) character, stamp.

prahlen ['praːlən] *vi* boast, brag.

Prahlerei [praːlə'rai] *f* boasting.

prahlerisch *a* boastful.

Praktik ['praktɪk] *f* practice; **p**~**abel** [-'kaːbəl] *a* practicable; ~**ant(in** *f*) [-'kant(ɪn)] *m* trainee; ~**um** *nt* -s, **Praktika** *or* **Praktiken** practical training.

praktisch ['praktɪʃ] *a* practical, handy; ~**er Arzt** general practitioner.

praktizieren [prakti'tsiːrən] *vti* practise.

Praline [pra'liːnə] *f* chocolate.

prall [pral] *a* firmly rounded; *Segel* taut; *Arme* plump; *Sonne* blazing; ~**en** *vi* bounce, rebound; (*Sonne*) blaze.

Prämie ['prɛːmiə] *f* premium; (*Belohnung*) award, prize; **p**~**ren** [prɛ'miːrən] *vt* give an award to.

Pranger ['praŋər] *m* -s, - (*Hist*) pillory; **jdn an den** ~ **stellen** (*fig*) pillory sb.

Präparat [prɛpa'raːt] *nt* -(e)s, -e (*Biol*) preparation; (*Med*) medicine.

Präposition [prɛpozitsi'oːn] *f* preposition.

Prärie [prɛ'riː] *f* prairie.

Präsens ['prɛːzɛns] *nt* - present tense.

präsentieren [prɛzɛn'tiːrən] *vt* present.

Präservativ [prɛzɛrva'tiːf] *nt* -s, -e contraceptive.

Präsident(in *f*) [prɛzi'dɛnt(ɪn)] *m* president; ~**schaft** *f* presidency; ~**schaftskandidat** *m* presidential candidate.

Präsidium [prɛ'ziːdiʊm] *nt* presidency, chair(manship); (*Polizei*—) police headquarters *pl*.

prasseln ['prasəln] *vi* (*Feuer*) crackle; (*Hagel*) drum; (*Wörter*) rain down.

prassen ['prasən] *vi* live it up.

Präteritum [prɛ'teːritʊm] *nt* -s, **Präterita** preterite.

Pratze ['pratsə] *f* -, -n paw.

Präventiv- [prɛvɛn'tiːf] *in cpds* preventive.

Praxis ['praksɪs] *f* -, **Praxen** practice; (*Behandlungsraum*) surgery; (*von Anwalt*) office.

Präzedenzfall [prɛtse'dɛntsfal] *m* precedent.

präzis [prɛ'tsiːs] *a* precise; **P**~**ion** [prɛtsizi'oːn] *f* precision.

predigen ['preːdigən] *vti* preach.

Prediger *m* -s, - preacher.

Predigt ['preːdɪçt] *f* -, -en sermon.

Preis [prais] *m* -es, -e price; (*Sieges*—) prize; **um keinen** ~ not at any price; ~**elbeere** *f* cranberry; **p**~**en** [praizən] *vi irreg* praise; **p**~**geben** *vt irreg* abandon; (*opfern*) sacrifice; (*zeigen*) expose;

p~gekrönt a prize-winning; ~gericht nt jury; p~günstig a inexpensive; ~lage f price range; p~lich a price, in price; ~sturz m slump; ~träger(in f) m prizewinner; p~wert a inexpensive.

prekär [pre'kɛ:r] a precarious.

Prell- [prɛl] cpd: ~bock m buffers pl; p~en [-en] vt bump; (fig) cheat, swindle; ~ung f bruise.

Premiere [prəmi'ɛ:rə] f-, -n premiere.

Premierminister [prəmi'e:ministər] m prime minister, premier.

Presse ['prɛsə] f-, -n press; ~freiheit f freedom of the press; ~meldung f press report; p~n vt press.

pressieren [prɛ'si:rən] vi (be in a) hurry.

Preß- ['prɛs] cpd: ~luft f compressed air; ~luftbohrer m pneumatic drill.

Prestige [prɛs'ti:ʒə] nt -s prestige.

prickeln ['prikəln] vti tingle, tickle.

Priester ['pri:stər] m -s, - priest.

prima [pri'ma] a first-class, excellent; P~ f-, Primen sixth form, top class.

primär [pri'mɛ:r] a primary.

Primel ['pri:məl] f-, -n primrose.

primitiv [primi'ti:f] a primitive.

Prinz [prints] m -en, -en prince; ~essin [prin'tsɛsin] f princess.

Prinzip [prin'tsi:p] nt -s, -ien principle; p~iell [-i'el] a,ad on principle; p~ienlos a unprincipled.

Priorität [priori'tɛ:t] f priority.

Prise ['pri:zə] f-, -n pinch.

Prisma ['prisma] nt -s, Prismen prism.

privat [pri'va:t] a privat; P~ in cpds private.

pro [pro:] prep +acc per; P~ nt - pro.

Probe ['pro:bə] f-, -n test; (Teststück) sample; (Theat) rehearsal; **jdn auf die ~ stellen** put sb to the test; ~exemplar nt specimen copy; ~fahrt f test drive; p~n vt try; (Theat) rehearse; p~weise ad on approval; ~zeit f probation period.

probieren [pro'bi:rən] vti try; Wein, Speise taste, sample.

Problem [pro'ble:m] nt -s, -e problem; ~atik [-'ma:tik] f problem; p~atisch [-'ma:tiʃ] a problematic; p~los a problem-free.

Produkt [pro'dukt] nt -(e)s, -e product; (Agr) produce no pl; ~ion [produktsi'o:n] f production; output; p~iv [-'ti:f] a productive; ~ivität f productivity.

Produzent [produ'tsɛnt] m manufacturer; (Film) producer.

produzieren [produ'tsi:rən] vt produce.

Professor [pro'fɛsɔr] m professor.

Professur [profɛ'su:r] f chair.

Profil [pro'fi:l] nt -s, -e profile; (fig) image; p~ieren [profi'li:rən] vr create an image for o.s.

Profit [pro'fi:t] m -(e)s, -e profit; p~ieren [profi'ti:rən] vi profit (von from).

Prognose [pro'gno:zə] f-, -n prediction, prognosis.

Programm [pro'gram] nt -s, -e programme; p~(m)äßig a according to plan; p~ieren [-'mi:rən] vt programme; ~ierer(in f) m -s, - programmer.

progressiv [progrɛ'si:f] a progressive.

Projekt [pro'jɛkt] nt -(e)s, -e project; ~or [pro'jɛktɔr] m projector.

projizieren [proji'tsi:rən] vt project.

proklamieren [prokla'mi:rən] vt proclaim.

Prolet [pro'le:t] m -en, -en prole, pleb; ~ariat [-aria't] nt -(e)s, -e proletariat; ~arier [-'ta:riər] m -s, - proletarian.

Prolog [pro'lo:k] m -(e)s, -e prologue.

Promenade [promə'na:də] f promenade.

Promille [pro'milə] nt -(s), - alcohol level.

prominent [promi'nɛnt] a prominent.

Prominenz [promi'nɛnts] f VIPs pl.

Promotion [promotsi'o:n] f doctorate, Ph.D.

promovieren [promo'vi:rən] vi do a doctorate or Ph.D.

prompt [prɔmpt] a prompt.

Pronomen [pro'no:mɛn] nt -s, - pronoun.

Propaganda [propa'ganda] f - propaganda.

Propeller [pro'pɛlər] m -s, - propeller.

Prophet [pro'fe:t] m -en, -en prophet; ~in f prophetess.

prophezeien [profe'tsaiən] vt prophesy.

Prophezeiung f prophecy.

Proportion [proportsi'o:n] f proportion; p~al [-'na:l] a proportional.

Prosa ['pro:za] f - prose; p~isch [pro'za:iʃ] a prosaic.

prosit ['pro:zit] interj cheers.

Prospekt [pro'spɛkt] m -(e)s, -e leaflet, brochure.

prost [pro:st] interj cheers.

Prostituierte [prostitu'i:rtə] f -n, -n prostitute.

Prostitution [prostitutsi'o:n] f prostitution.

Protest [pro'tɛst] m -(e)s, -e protest; ~ant(in f) [protɛs'tant] m Protestant; p~antisch [protɛs'tantiʃ] a Protestant; p~ieren [protɛs'ti:rən] vi protest; ~kundgebung f (protest) rally.

Prothese [pro'te:zə] f -, -n artificial limb; (Zahn~) dentures pl.

Protokoll [proto'kɔl] nt -s, -e register; (von Sitzung) minutes pl; (diplomatisch) protocol; (Polizei~) statement; p~ieren [-'li:rən] vt take down in the minutes.

Proton ['pro:tɔn] nt -s, -en proton.

Protz [prɔts] m -en, -e(n) swank; p~en vi show off; p~ig a ostentatious.

Proviant [provi'ant] m -s, -e provisions pl, supplies pl.

Provinz [pro'vints] f -, -en province; p~iell a provincial.

Provision [provizi'o:n] f (Comm) commission.

provisorisch [provi'zo:riʃ] a provisional.

Provokation [provokatsi'o:n] f provocation.

provozieren [provo'tsi:rən] vt provoke.

Prozedur [protse'du:r] f procedure; (pej) carry-on.

Prozent [pro'tsɛnt] nt -(e)s, -e per cent, percentage; ~rechnung f percentage calculation; ~satz m percentage; p~ual

[-'u'a:l] *a* percentage; as a percentage.

Prozeß [pro'tsɛs] *m* **-sses, -sse** trial, case; **~ kosten** *pl* (legal) costs *pl*.

prozessieren [protsɛ'si:rən] *vi* bring an action, go to law (*mit* against).

Prozession [protsɛsi'o:n] *f* procession.

prüde ['pry:də] *a* prudish; **P~rie** [-'ri:] *f* prudery.

Prüf- ['pry:f] *cpd*: **p~en** *vt* examine, test; (*nach*—) check; **~er** *m* **-s**, - examiner; **~ling** *m* examinee; **~stein** *m* touchstone; **~ung** *f* examination; checking; **~ungsausschuß** *m*, **~ungskommission** *f* examining board.

Prügel ['pry:gəl] *m* **-s**, - cudgel; *pl* beating; **~ei** [-'lai] *f* fight; **~knabe** *m* scapegoat; **p~n** *vt* beat; *vr* fight; **~strafe** *f* corporal punishment.

Prunk [prʊŋk] *m* **-(e)s** pomp, show; **p~voll** *a* splendid, magnificent.

Psalm [psalm] *m* **-s, -en** psalm.

pseudo- [psɔydo] *in cpds* pseudo.

Psych- ['psyç] *cpd*: **~iater** [-i'a:tər] *m* **-s**, - psychiatrist; **p~isch** *a* psychological; **~oanalyse** [-o'analy:zə] *f* psychoanalysis; **~ologe** [-o'lo:gə] *m* **-n**, **-n** psychologist; **~olo'gie** *f* psychology; **p~ologisch** *a* psychological.

Pubertät [puber'tɛ:t] *f* puberty.

Publikum ['pu:blikʊm] *nt* **-s** audience; (*Sport*) crowd.

publizieren [publi'tsi:rən] *vt* publish, publicize.

Pudding ['pʊdɪŋ] *m* **-s, -e** or **-s** blancmange.

Pudel ['pu:dəl] *m* **-s** poodle.

Puder ['pu:dər] *m* **-s**, - powder; **~dose** *f* powder compact; **p~n** *vt* powder; **~zucker** *m* icing sugar.

Puff [pʊf] *m* **-s**, **-e** (*Wäsche*—) linen basket; (*Sitz*—) pouf; *pl* **-e** (*col: Stoß*) push; *pl* **-s** (*col: Bordell*) brothel; **~er** *m* **-s**, - buffer; **~erstaat** *m* buffer state.

Pulli ['pʊli] *m* **-s, -s** (*col*), **Pullover** [pu'lo:vər] *m* **-s**, - pullover, jumper.

Puls [pʊls] *m* **-es**, **-e** pulse; **~ader** *f* artery; **p~ieren** [pʊl'zi:rən] *vi* throb, pulsate.

Pult [pʊlt] *nt* **-(e)s, -e** desk.

Pulver ['pʊlfər] *nt* **-s**, - powder; **p~ig** *a* powdery; **p~isieren** [pʊlveri'zi:rən] *vt* pulverize; **~schnee** *m* powdery snow.

pummelig ['pʊməlɪç] *a* chubby.

Pumpe ['pʊmpə] *f* -, **-n** pump; **p~n** *vt* pump; (*col*) lend; borrow.

Punkt [pʊŋkt] *m* **-(e)s**, **-e** point; (*bei Muster*) dot; (*Satzzeichen*) full stop; **p~ieren** [-'ti:rən] *vt* dot; (*Med*) aspirate.

pünktlich ['pʏŋktlɪç] *a* punctual; **P~keit** *f* punctuality.

Punkt- *cpd*: **~sieg** *m* victory on points; **~zahl** *f* score.

Punsch [pʊnʃ] *m* **-(e)s, -e** punch.

Pupille [pu'pɪlə] *f* -, **-n** pupil.

Puppe ['pʊpə] *f* -, **-n** doll; (*Marionette*) puppet; (*Insekten*—) pupa, chrysalis; **~nspieler** *m* puppeteer; **~nstube** *f* doll's house.

pur [pu:r] *a* pure; (*völlig*) sheer; *Whisky* neat.

Püree [py're:] *nt* **-s**, **-s** mashed potatoes *pl*.

Purzel- ['pʊrtsəl] *cpd*: **~baum** *m* somersault; **p~n** *vi* tumble.

Puste ['pu:stə] *f* - (*col*) puff; (*fig*) steam; **~l** ['pʊstəl] *f* -, **-n** pustule; **p~n** *vi* puff, blow.

Pute ['pu:tə] *f* -, **-n** turkey-hen; **~r** *m* **-s**, - turkey-cock.

Putsch [pʊtʃ] *m* **-(e)s, -e** revolt, putsch; **p~en** *vi* revolt; **~ist** [pu'tʃɪst] *m* rebel.

Putz [pʊts] *m* **-es** (*Mörtel*) plaster, roughcast; **p~en** *vt* clean; *Nase* wipe, blow; *vr* clean oneself; dress oneself up; **~frau** *f* charwoman; **p~ig** *a* quaint, funny; **~lappen** *m* cloth; **~tag** *m* cleaning day; **~zeug** *nt* cleaning things *pl*.

Puzzle ['pasəl] *nt* **-s, -s** jigsaw.

Pyjama [pi'dʒa:ma] *m* **-s, -s** pyjamas *pl*.

Pyramide [pyra'mi:də] *f* -, **-n** pyramid.

Q

Q, q [ku:] *nt* Q, q.

quabb(e)lig ['kvab(ə)lɪç] *a* wobbly; *Frosch* slimy.

Quacksalber ['kvakzalbər] *m* **-s**, - quack (doctor).

Quader ['kva:dər] *m* **-s**, - square stone; (*Math*) cuboid.

Quadrat [kva'dra:t] *nt* **-(e)s, -e** square; **q~isch** *a* square; **~meter** *m* square metre.

quadrieren [kva'dri:rən] *vt* square.

quaken ['kva:kən] *vi* croak; (*Ente*) quack.

quäken ['kvɛ:kən] *vi* screech; **~d** *a* screeching.

Qual [kva:l] *f* -, **-en** pain, agony; (*seelisch*) anguish.

Quäl- [kvɛ:l] *cpd*: **q~en** *vt* torment; *vr* struggle; (*geistig*) torment oneself; **~erei** [-ə'rai] *f* torture, torment; **~geist** *m* pest.

qualifizieren [kvalifi'tsi:rən] *vtr* qualify; (*einstufen*) label.

Qualität [kvali'tɛ:t] *f* quality; **~sware** *f* article of high quality.

Qualle ['kvalə] *f* -, **-n** jellyfish.

Qualm [kvalm] *m* **-(e)s** thick smoke; **q~en** *vti* smoke.

qualvoll ['kva:lfɔl] *a* excruciating, painful, agonizing.

Quant- ['kvant] *cpd*: **~entheorie** *f* quantum theory; **~ität** [-itɛ:t] *f* quantity; **q~itativ** [-ita'ti:f] *a* quantitative; **~um** *nt* **-s, Quanten** quantity, amount.

Quarantäne [karan'tɛ:nə] *f* -, **-n** quarantine.

Quark [kvark] *m* **-s** curd cheese; (*col*) rubbish.

Quarta ['kvarta] *f* -, **Quarten** third year of secondary school; **~l** [kvar'ta:l] *nt* **-s, -e** quarter (year).

Quartier [kvar'ti:r] *nt* **-s**, **-e** accommodation; (*Mil*) quarters *pl*; (*Stadt*—) district.

Quarz [kva:rts] *m* **-es, -e** quartz.

quasseln ['kvasəln] *vi* (*col*) natter.

Quatsch [kvatʃ] *m* **-es** rubbish; **q~en** *vi* chat, natter.

Quecksilber ['kvɛkzɪlbər] *nt* mercury.

Quelle ['kvɛlə] *f* -, **-n** spring; (*eines Flusses*)

source; **q~n** *vi* (*hervor—*) pour *or* gush forth; (*schwellen*) swell.

quengel- ['kvɛŋəl] *cpd*: **Q~ei** [-'laɪ] *f* (*col*) whining; **~ig** *a* (*col*) whining; **~n** *vi* (*col*) whine.

quer [kve:r] *ad* crossways, diagonally; (*rechtwinklig*) at right angles; **~ auf dem Bett** across the bed; **Q~balken** *m* crossbeam; **~feldein** *ad* across country; **Q~flöte** *f* flute; **Q~kopf** *m* awkward customer; **Q~schiff** *nt* transept; **Q~schnitt** *m* cross-section; **~schnittsgelähmt** *a* paralysed below the waist; **Q~straße** *f* intersecting road; **Q~treiber** *m* -s, - obstructionist; **Q~verbindung** *f* connection, link.

quetschen ['kvɛtʃən] *vt* squash, crush; (*Med*) bruise.

Quetschung *f* bruise, contusion.

quieken ['kvi:kən] *vi* squeak.

quietschen ['kvi:tʃən] *vi* squeak.

Quint- ['kvɪnt] *cpd*: **~a** *f* -, **-en** second form in secondary school; **~essenz** [-'ɛsɛnts] *f* quintessence; **~ett** [-'tɛt] *nt* -(e)s, -e quintet.

Quirl [kvɪrl] *m* -(e)s, -e whisk.

quitt [kvɪt] *a* quits, even; **Q~e** *f* -, -n quince; **Q~engelb** *a* sickly yellow; **~ieren** [-'ti:rən] *vt* give a receipt for; *Dienst* leave; **Q~ung** *f* receipt.

Quiz [kvɪs] *nt* -s, - quiz.

Quote ['kvo:tə] *f* -, -n number, rate.

R

R, r [ɛr] *nt* R, r.

Rabatt [ra'bat] *m* -(e)s, -e discount; **~e** *f* -, -n flowerbed, border; **~marke** *f* trading stamp.

Rabe ['ra:bə] *m* -n, -n raven; **~nmutter** *f* bad mother.

rabiat [rabi'a:t] *a* furious.

Rache ['raxə] *f* - revenge, vengeance; **~n** *m* -s, - throat.

rächen ['rɛçən] *vt* avenge, revenge; *vr* take (one's) revenge; **das wird sich ~** you'll pay for that.

Rach- ['rax] *cpd*: **~itis** [ra'xi:tɪs] *f* - rickets *sing*; **~sucht** *f* vindictiveness; **r~süchtig** *a* vindictive.

Racker ['rakər] *m* -s, - rascal, scamp.

Rad [ra:t] *nt* -(e)s, ⁻er wheel; (*Fahr—*) bike; **~ar** ['ra:da:r] *m or nt* -s radar; **~arkontrolle** *f* radar-controlled speed trap; **~au** [ra'dau] *m* -s (*col*) row; **~dampfer** *m* paddle steamer; **r~ebrechen** *vi insep*: **deutsch** *etc* **r~ebrechen** speak broken German *etc*; **r~eln** *vi*, **r~fahren** *vi irreg* cycle; **~fahrer(in** *f*) *m* cyclist; **~fahrweg** *m* cycle track *or* path.

Radier- [ra'di:r] *cpd*: **r~en** *vt* rub out, erase; (*Art*) etch; **~gummi** *m* rubber, eraser; **~ung** *f* etching.

Radieschen [ra'di:sçən] *nt* radish.

radikal [radi'ka:l] *a*, **R~e(r)** *mf* radical.

Radio ['ra:dio] *nt* -s, -s radio, wireless; **r~ak'tiv** *a* radioactive; **~aktivi'tät** *f* radioactivity; **~apparat** *m* radio, wireless set.

Radium ['ra:dium] *nt* -s radium.

Radius ['ra:dius] *m* -, **Radien** radius.

Rad- *cpd*: **~kappe** *f* (*Aut*) hub cap; **~ler(in** *f*) *m* -s, - cyclist; **~rennbahn** *f* cycling (race)track; **~rennen** *nt* cycle race; cycle racing; **~sport** *m* cycling.

raff- [raf] *cpd*: **~en** *vt* snatch, pick up; *Stoff* gather (up); *Geld* pile up, rake in; **R~inade** [-i'na:də] *f* refined sugar; **~inieren** [-i'ni:rən] *vt* refine; **~i'niert** *a* crafty, cunning; *Zucker* refined.

ragen ['ra:gən] *vi* tower, rise.

Rahm [ra:m] *m* -s cream; **~en** *m* -s, - frame(work); **im ~en des Möglichen** within the bounds of possibility; **r~en** *vt* frame; **r~ig** *a* creamy.

Rakete [ra'ke:tə] *f* -, -n rocket; **ferngelenkte ~** guided missile.

rammen ['ramən] *vt* ram.

Rampe ['rampə] *f* -, -n ramp; **~nlicht** *nt* (*Theat*) footlights *pl*.

ramponieren [rampo'ni:rən] *vt* (*col*) damage.

Ramsch [ramʃ] *m* -(e)s, -e junk.

ran [ran] *ad* (*col*) = **heran.**

Rand [rant] *m* -(e)s, ⁻er edge; (*von Brille, Tasse etc*) rim; (*Hut—*) brim; (*auf Papier*) margin; (*Schmutz—, unter Augen*) ring; (*fig*) verge, brink; **außer ~ und Band** wild; **am ~e bemerkt** mentioned in passing; **r~alieren** [randa'li:rən] *vi* (go on the) rampage; **~bemerkung** *f* marginal note; (*fig*) odd comment; **~erscheinung** *f* unimportant side effect, marginal phenomenon.

Rang [raŋ] *m* -(e)s, ⁻e rank; (*Stand*) standing; (*Wert*) quality; (*Theat*) circle; **~abzeichen** *nt* badge of rank; **~älteste(r)** *m* senior officer.

Rangier- [rãʒi:r] *cpd*: **~bahnhof** *m* marshalling yard; **r~en** *vt* (*Rail*) shunt, switch (*US*); *vi* rank, be classed; **~gleis** *nt* siding.

Rang- *cpd*: **~ordnung** *f* hierarchy; (*Mil*) rank; **~unterschied** *m* social distinction; (*Mil*) difference in rank.

Ranke ['raŋkə] *f* -, -n tendril, shoot.

Ränke ['rɛŋkə] *pl* intrigues *pl*; **~schmied** *m* intriguer; **r~voll** *a* scheming.

Ranzen ['rantsən] *m* -s, - satchel; (*col*: *Bauch*) gut, belly.

ranzig ['rantsıç] *a* rancid.

Rappe ['rapə] *m* -n, -n black horse.

Raps [raps] *m* -es, -e (*Bot*) rape.

rar [ra:r] *a* rare; **sich ~ machen** (*col*) keep oneself to oneself; **R~i'tät** *f* rarity; (*Sammelobjekt*) curio.

rasant [ra'zant] *a* quick, rapid.

rasch [raʃ] *a* quick; **~eln** *vi* rustle.

Rasen ['ra:zən] *m* -s, - lawn; grass; **r~ ** *vi* rave; (*schnell*) race; **r~d** *a* furious; **r~de Kopfschmerzen** a splitting head-ache; **~mäher** *m* -s, -, **~mähmaschine** *f* lawnmower; **~platz** *m* lawn.

Raserei [ra:zə'raɪ] *f* raving, ranting; (*Schnelle*) reckless speeding.

Rasier- [ra'zi:r] *cpd*: **~apparat** *m* shaver; **~creme** *f* shaving cream; **r~en** *vtr* shave; **~klinge** *f* razor blade; **~messer** *nt* razor; **~pinsel** *m* shaving brush;

~**seife** f shaving soap or stick; ~**wasser** nt shaving lotion.

Rasse ['rasə] f -, -n race; (Tier—) breed; ~**hund** m thoroughbred dog; ~**l** f -, -n rattle; **r**~**ln** vi rattle, clatter; ~**nhaß** m race or racial hatred; ~**ntrennung** f racial segregation.

Rast [rast] f -, -en rest; **r**~**en** vi rest; ~**haus** nt (Aut) service station; **r**~**los** a tireless; (unruhig) restless; ~**platz** m (Aut) layby.

Rasur [ra'zu:r] f shaving; (Radieren) erasure.

Rat [ra:t] m -(e)s, ~**schläge** (piece of) advice; **jdn zu** ~**e ziehen** consult sb; **keinen** ~ **wissen** not know what to do; ~**e** f -, -n instalment; **r**~**en** vti irreg guess; (empfehlen) advise (jdm sb); **r**~**enweise** ad by instalments; ~**enzahlung** f hire purchase; ~**geber** m -s, - adviser; ~**haus** nt town hall.

ratifizier- [ratifi'tsi:r] cpd: ~**en** vt ratify; **R**~**ung** f ratification.

Ration [ratsi'o:n] f ration; **r**~**al** [-'na:l] a rational; **r**~**ali'sieren** vt rationalize; **r**~**ell** [-'nɛl] a efficient; **r**~**ieren** [-'ni:rən] vt ration.

Rätsel ['rɛːtsəl] nt -s, - puzzle; (Wort—) riddle; **r**~**haft** a mysterious; **es ist mir r**~**haft** it's a mystery to me.

Rats- cpd: ~**herr** m councillor; ~**keller** m town-hall restaurant.

Ratte ['ratə] f -, -n rat; ~**nfänger** m -s, - ratcatcher.

rattern ['ratərn] vi rattle, clatter.

Raub [raup] m -(e)s robbery; (Beute) loot, booty; ~**bau** m ruthless exploitation; **r**~**en** [raubən] vt rob; Mensch kidnap, abduct.

Räuber ['rɔybər] m -s, - robber; **r**~**isch** a thieving.

Raub- cpd: **r**~**gierig** a rapacious; ~**mord** m robbery with murder; ~**tier** nt predator; ~**überfall** m robbery with violence; ~**vogel** m bird of prey.

Rauch ['raux] m -(e)s smoke; **r**~**en** vti smoke; ~**er** m -s, - smoker; ~**erabteil** nt (Rail) smoker.

räuchern ['rɔyçərn] vt smoke, cure.

Rauch- cpd: ~**fahne** f smoke trail; ~**fleisch** nt smoked meat; **r**~**ig** a smoky.

räudig ['rɔydıç] a mangy.

rauf [rauf] ad (col) = herauf; **R**~**bold** m -(e)s, -e rowdy, hooligan; ~**en** vt Haare pull out; vir fight; **R**~**e'rei** f brawl, fight; ~**lustig** a spoiling for a fight, rowdy.

rauh [rau] a rough, coarse; Wetter harsh; ~**haarig** a wire-haired; **R**~**reif** m hoarfrost.

Raum [raum] m -(e)s, Räume space; (Zimmer, Platz) room; (Gebiet) area; ~**bild** nt 3D picture.

räumen ['rɔymən] vt clear; Wohnung, Platz vacate; (wegbringen) shift, move; (in Schrank etc) put away.

Raum- cpd: ~**fahrt** f space travel;

~**inhalt** m cubic capacity, volume.

räumlich ['rɔymlıç] a spatial; **R**~**keiten** pl premises pl.

Raum- cpd: ~**mangel** m lack of space; ~**meter** m cubic metre; ~**pflegerin** f cleaner; ~**schiff** nt spaceship; ~**schiffahrt** f space travel; **r**~**sparend** a space-saving.

Räumung ['rɔymuŋ] f vacating, evacuation; clearing (away); ~**sverkauf** m clearance sale.

raunen ['raunən] vti whisper mysteriously.

Raupe ['raupə] f -, -n caterpillar; (—nkette) (caterpillar) track; ~**nschlepper** m caterpillar tractor.

raus [raus] ad (col) = heraus, hinaus.

Rausch [rauʃ] m -(e)s, Räusche intoxication; **r**~**en** vi (Wasser) rush; (Baum) rustle; (Radio etc) hiss; (Mensch) sweep, sail; **r**~**end** a Beifall thunderous; Fest sumptuous; ~**gift** nt drug; ~**giftsüchtige(r)** mf drug addict.

räuspern ['rɔyspərn] vr clear one's throat.

Raute ['rautə] f -, -n diamond; (Math) rhombus; **r**~**nförmig** a rhombic.

Razzia ['ratsia] f -, Razzien raid.

Reagenzglas [rea'gɛntsgla:s] nt test tube.

reagieren [rea'gi:rən] vi react (auf +acc to).

Reakt- cpd: ~**ion** [reaktsi'o:n] f reaction; **r**~**io'när** a reactionary; ~**ionsgeschwindigkeit** f speed of reaction; ~**or** [re'aktor] m reactor.

real [re'a:l] a real, material; **R**~**ismus** [-'lısmus] m realism; **R**~**ist** [-'lıst] m realist; ~**istisch** a realistic.

Rebe ['re:bə] f -, -n vine.

Rebell [re'bɛl] m -en, -en rebel; ~**i'on** f rebellion; **r**~**isch** a rebellious.

Reb- cpd: ~**ensaft** m grape juice; ~**huhn** ['rɛphu:n] nt partridge; ~**stock** m vine.

Rechen ['rɛçən] m -s, - rake; **r**~ vti rake; ~**aufgabe** f sum, mathematical problem; ~**fehler** m miscalculation; ~**maschine** f calculating machine; ~**schaft** f account; ~**schaftsbericht** m report; ~**schieber** m slide rule.

Rech- ['rɛç] cpd: **r**~**nen** vti calculate; **jdn/etw r**~**nen zu** or **unter** (+acc) count sb/sth among; **r**~**nen mit** reckon with; **r**~**nen auf** (+acc) count on; ~**ner** m -s, calculator; ~**nung** f calculation(s); (Comm) bill, check (US); **jdm/etw** ~**nung tragen** take sb/sth into account; ~**nungsbuch** nt account book; ~**nungsjahr** nt financial year; ~**nungsprüfer** m auditor; ~**nungsprüfung** f audit(ing).

recht [rɛçt] a, ad right; (vor Adjektiv) really, quite; **das ist mir** ~ that suits me; **jetzt erst** ~ now more than ever; ~**haben** be right; **jdm** ~ **geben** agree with sb; **R**~ nt -(e)s, -e right; (Jur) law; **R**~**sprechen** administer justice; **mit R**~ rightly, justly; **von R**~**s wegen** by rights; **R**~**e** f -n, -n right (hand); (Pol) Right; ~**e(r,s)** a right; (Pol) right-wing; **R**~**e(r)** mf right person; **R**~**e(s)** nt right thing; **etwas/nichts R**~**es** something/nothing proper; **R~eck** nt -s, -e rectangle; **~eckig** a rectangular; **~fertigen** vtr insep justify (o.s.); **R~fertigung** f justification; **~haberisch** a dogmatic; **~lich** a, **~mäßig** a legal, lawful.

rechts [reçts] ad on/to the right; **R~anwalt** m, **R~anwältin** f lawyer, barrister; **R~'außen** m -, - (Sport) outside right; **R~beistand** m legal adviser.

Recht- cpd: **r~schaffen** a upright; **~schreibung** f spelling.

Rechts- cpd: **~drehung** f clockwise rotation; **~fall** m (law) case; **~frage** f legal question; **~händer** m -s, - right-handed person; **r~kräftig** a valid, legal; **~kurve** f right-hand bend; **~pflege** f administration of justice; **r~radikal** a (Pol) extreme right-wing; **~spruch** m verdict; **~verkehr** m driving on the right; **r~widrig** a illegal; **~wissenschaft** f jurisprudence.

recht- cpd: **~lich** ['reːtlɪç] a honest; **R~lichkeit** f honesty; **R~ner** m -s, - speaker, orator; **~selig** ['reːtzeːlɪç] a talkative, loquacious; **R~seligkeit** f talkativeness.

reduzieren [redu'tsiːrən] vt reduce.

Reede ['reːdə] f -, -n protected anchorage; **~r** m -s, - shipowner; **~'rei** f shipping line or firm.

reell [re'ɛl] a fair, honest; (Math) real.

Refer- cpd: **~at** [refe'raːt] nt -(e)s, -e report; (Vortrag) paper; (Gebiet) section; **~ent** [refe'rɛnt] m speaker; (Berichterstatter) reporter; (Sachbearbeiter) expert; **~enz** [refe'rɛnts] f reference; **r~ieren** [refe'riːrən] vi: **r~ieren über** (+acc) speak or talk on.

reflektieren [reflɛk'tiːrən] vti reflect; **~ auf** (+acc) be interested in.

Reflex [re'flɛks] m -es, -e reflex; **~bewegung** f reflex action; **r~iv** [-'ksiːf] a (Gram) reflexive.

Reform [re'fɔrm] f -, -en reform; **~a-ti'on** f reformation; **~ator** [-'maːtɔr] m reformer; **r~atorisch** a reformatory, reforming; **~haus** nt health food shop; **r~ieren** [-'miːrən] vt reform.

Refrain [rə'frɛː] m -s, -s refrain, chorus.

Regal [re'gaːl] nt -s, -e (book)shelves pl, bookcase; stand, rack.

rege ['reːgə] a lively, active; Geschäft brisk.

Regel ['reːgəl] f -, -n rule; (Med) period; **r~los** a irregular, unsystematic; **r~mäßig** a regular; **~mäßigkeit** f

regularity; **r~n** vt regulate, control; Angelegenheit settle; vr: **sich von selbst r~n** take care of itself; **r~recht** a regular, proper, thorough; **~ung** f regulation; settlement; **r~widrig** a irregular, against the rules.

regen ['reːgən] vtr move, stir; **R~** m -s, -rain; **R~bogen** m rainbow; **R~bogenhaut** f (Anat) iris; **R~guß** m downpour; **R~mantel** m raincoat, mac(kintosh); **R~menge** f rainfall; **R~schauer** m shower (of rain); **R~schirm** m umbrella.

Regent [re'gɛnt] m regent; **~schaft** f regency.

Regen- cpd: **~tag** m rainy day; **~wurm** m earthworm; **~zeit** f rainy season, rains pl.

Regie [re'ʒiː] f (Film etc) direction; (Theat) production; **r~ren** [re'giːrən] vti govern, rule; **~rung** f government; (Monarchie) reign; **~rungswechsel** m change of government; **~rungszeit** f period in government; (von König) reign.

Regiment [regi'mɛnt] nt -s, -er regiment.

Region [regi'oːn] f region.

Regisseur [reʒɪ'søːr] m director; (Theat) (stage) producer.

Register [re'gɪstər] nt -s, - register; (in Buch) table of contents, index.

Registratur [regɪs'traːtuːr] f registry, record office.

registrieren [regɪs'triːrən] vt register.

reg- ['reːg] cpd: **R~ler** m -s, - regulator, governor; **~los** ['reːkloːs] a motionless; **~nen** vi impers rain; **~nerisch** a rainy; **~sam** ['reːkzaːm] a active.

regulär [regu'lɛːr] a regular.

regulieren [regu'liːrən] vt regulate; (Comm) settle.

Regung ['reːgʊŋ] f motion; (Gefühl) feeling, impulse; **r~slos** a motionless.

Reh [reː] nt -(e)s, -e deer, roe; **~bock** m roebuck; **~kalb** nt, **~kitz** nt fawn.

Reib- ['raɪb] cpd: **~e** f -, -n, **~eisen** nt grater; **r~en** vt irreg rub; (Cook) grate; **~e'rei** f friction no pl; **~fläche** f rough surface; **~ung** f friction; **r~ungslos** a smooth.

reich [raɪç] a rich; **R~** nt -(e)s, -e empire, kingdom; (fig) realm; **das Dritte R~** the Third Reich; **~en** vi reach; (genügen) be enough or sufficient (jdm for sb); vt hold out; (geben) pass, hand; (anbieten) offer; **~haltig** a ample, rich; **~lich** a ample, plenty of; **R~tum** m -s, -tümer wealth; **R~weite** f range.

reif [raɪf] a ripe; Mensch, Urteil mature; **R~** m -(e)s hoarfrost; -(e)s, -e (Ring) ring, hoop; **R~e** f - ripeness; maturity; **~en** vi mature; ripen; **R~en** m -s, - ring, hoop; (Fahrzeug—) tyre; **R~enschaden** m puncture; **R~eprüfung** f school leaving exam; **R~ezeugnis** nt school leaving certificate.

Reihe ['raɪə] f -, -n row; (von Tagen etc, col: Anzahl) series sing; **der ~ nach** in turn; **er ist an der ~** it's his turn; **an die ~ kommen** have one's turn; **r~n** vt set in a row; arrange in series; Perlen string;

~**nfolge** f sequence; **alphabetische**
~**nfolge** alphabetical order; ~**nhaus** nt
terraced house; ~**r** m **-s**, - heron.
Reim [raɪm] m **-(e)s**, **-e** rhyme; **r**~**en** vt
rhyme.

rein [raɪn] ad (col) = **herein, hinein**; a,
ad pure(ly); (sauber) clean; **etw ins** ~**e
schreiben** make a fair copy of sth; **etw
ins** ~**e bringen** clear up sth; **R**~ in cpds
(Comm) net(t); **R**~**(e)machefrau** f
charwoman; **R**~**fall** m (col) let-down;
R~**gewinn** m net profit; **R**~**heit** f
purity; cleanliness; ~**igen** vt clean;
Wasser purify; **R**~**igung** f cleaning;
purification; (Geschäft) cleaners;
chemische R~**igung** dry cleaning; dry
cleaners; ~**lich** a clean; **R**~**lichkeit** f
cleanliness; ~**rassig** a pedigree;
R~**schrift** f fair copy; ~**waschen** vr
irreg clear oneself.

Reis [raɪs] m **-es**, **-e** rice; nt **-es**, **-er** twig,
sprig.
Reise ['raɪzə] f **-**, **-n** journey; (Schiff—)
voyage; ~**n** pl travels pl; ~**andenken** nt
souvenir; ~**büro** nt travel agency;
r~**fertig** a ready to start; ~**führer** m
guide(book); (Mensch) travel guide;
~**gepäck** nt luggage; ~**gesellschaft** f
party of travellers; ~**kosten** pl travelling
expenses pl; ~**leiter** m courier;
~**lektüre** f reading matter for the
journey; **r**~**n** vi travel; go (nach to);
~**nde(r)** mf traveller; ~**paß** m passport;
~**pläne** pl plans pl for a journey;
~**proviant** m provisions pl for the
journey; ~**scheck** m traveller's cheque;
~**tasche** f travelling bag or case;
~**verkehr** m tourist/holiday traffic;
~**wetter** nt holiday weather; ~**ziel** nt
destination.
Reisig ['raɪzɪç] nt **-s** brushwood.
Reiß- [raɪs] cpd: ~**aus nehmen** run
away, flee; ~**brett** nt drawing board;
r~**en** vti irreg tear; (ziehen) pull, drag;
Witz crack; **etw an sich r**~**en** snatch sth
up; (fig) take over sth; **sich um etw
r**~**en** scramble for sth; **r**~**end** a Fluß
torrential; (Comm) rapid; ~**er** m **-s**, - (col)
thriller; **r**~**erisch** a sensationalistic;
~**leine** f (Aviat) ripcord; ~**nagel** m
drawing pin, thumbtack (US); ~**schiene** f
drawing rule, square; ~**verschluß** m
zip(per), zip fastener; ~**zeug** nt geometry
set; ~**zwecke** f = ~**nagel**.
Reit- ['raɪt] cpd: **r**~**en** vti irreg ride;
~**er(in** f) m **-s**, - rider; (Mil) cavalryman,
trooper; ~**er'ei** f cavalry; ~**hose** f riding
breeches pl; ~**pferd** nt saddle horse;
~**stiefel** m riding boot; ~**zeug** nt riding
outfit.
Reiz [raɪts] m **-es**, **-e** stimulus; (angenehm)
charm; (Verlockung) attraction; **r**~**bar** a
irritable; ~**barkeit** f irritability; **r**~**en** vt
stimulate; (unangenehm) irritate;
(verlocken) appeal to, attract; **r**~**end** a
charming; **r**~**los** a unattractive; ~**voll**
a attractive; ~**wäsche** f sexy underwear.
rekeln ['re:kəln] vr stretch out; (lümmeln)
lounge or loll about.
Reklam- cpd: ~**ation** [reklamatsi'o:n] f

complaint; ~**e** [re'kla:mə] f **-**, **-n** advertising; advertisement; ~**e machen für etw**
advertise sth; **r**~**ieren** [rekla'mi:rən] vti
complain (about); (zurückfordern) reclaim.
rekon- [rekon] cpd: ~**struieren**
[stru'i:rən] vt reconstruct; **R**~**valeszenz**
[-vales'tsɛnts] f convalescence.
Rekord [re'kɔrt] m **-(e)s**, **-e** record;
~**leistung** f record performance.
Rekrut [re'kru:t] m **-en**, **-en** recruit;
r~**ieren** [-'ti:rən] vt recruit; vr be
recruited.
Rektor ['rektɔr] m (Univ) rector, vice-
chancellor; (Sch) headmaster; ~**at** [-'ra:t]
nt **-(e)s**, **-e** rectorate, vice-chancellorship;
headship; (Zimmer) rector's etc office.
Relais [rə'lɛ:] nt **-**, - relay.
relativ [rela'ti:f] a relative; **R**~**ität**
[relativi'tɛ:t] f relativity.
relevant [rele'vant] a relevant.
Relief [reli'ɛf] nt **-s**, **-s** relief.
Religion [religi'o:n] f religion; ~**slehre** f,
~**sunterricht** m religious instruction.
religiös [religi'ø:s] a religious.
Relikt [re'lɪkt] nt **-(e)s**, **-e** relic.
Reling ['re:lɪŋ] f **-**, **-s** (Naut) rail.
Reliquie [re'li:kviə] f relic.
Reminiszenz [reminis'tsɛnts] f
reminiscence, recollection.
Remoulade [remu'la:də] f remoulade.
Ren [rɛn] nt **-s**, **-s** or **-e** reindeer.
Rendezvous [rãde'vu:] nt **-**, - rendezvous.
Renn- ['rɛn] cpd: ~**bahn** f racecourse;
(Aut) circuit, race track; **r**~**en** vti irreg
run, race; **R**~**en** nt **-s**, - running;
(Wettbewerb) race; ~**fahrer** m racing
driver; ~**pferd** nt racehorse; ~**platz** m
racecourse; ~**wagen** m racing car.
renovier- [reno'vi:r] cpd: ~**en** vt renovate; **R**~**ung** f renovation.
rentabel [rɛn'ta:bəl] a profitable,
lucrative.
Rentabilität [rɛntabili'tɛ:t] f profitability.
Rente ['rɛntə] f **-**, **-n** pension;
~**nempfänger** m pensioner.
Rentier ['rɛnti:r] nt reindeer.
rentieren [rɛn'ti:rən] vr pay, be profitable.
Rentner(in f) ['rɛntnər(ɪn)] m **-s**, -
pensioner.
Repar- [repa] cpd: ~**ation** [-atsi'o:n] f
reparation; ~**atur** [-ra'tu:r] f repairing;
repair; **r**~**a'turbedürftig** a in need of
repair; ~**a'turwerkstatt** f repair shop;
(Aut) garage; **r**~**ieren** [-'ri:rən] vt repair.
Repertoire [reperto'a:r] nt **-s**, **-s**
repertoire.
Report- cpd: ~**age** [repɔr'ta:ʒə] f **-**, **-n**
(on-the-spot) report; (TV, Rad) live
commentary or coverage; ~**er** [re'pɔrtər]
m **-s**, - reporter, commentator.
Repräsent- cpd: ~**ant** [reprɛzen'tant] m
representative; **r**~**a'tiv** a representative;
Geschenk etc prestigious; **r**~**ieren**
[reprɛzen'ti:rən] vti represent.
Repressalien [reprɛ'sa:liən] pl reprisals
pl.
Reproduktion [reproduktsi'o:n] f
reproduction.

reproduzieren [reprodu'tsi:rən] *vt* reproduce.

Reptil [rɛp'ti:l] *nt* -s, -ien reptile.

Republik [repu'bli:k] *f* republic; ~aner ['-ka:nər] *m* -s, - republican; r~anisch ['-ka:nɪʃ] a republican.

Reserv- *cpd:* ~at [rezɛr'va:t] *nt* -(e)s, -e reservation; ~e [re'zɛrvə] *f* -, -n reserve; ~erad *nt* (Aut) spare wheel; ~espieler *m* reserve; ~etank *m* reserve tank; r~ieren [rezɛr'vi:rən] *vt* reserve; ~ist [rezɛr'vɪst] *m* reservist; ~oir [rezɛrvo'a:r] *nt* -s, -e reservoir.

Residenz [rezi'dɛnts] *f* residence, seat.

Resignation [rezɪgnatsi'o:n] *f* resignation.

resignieren [rezɪ'gni:rən] *vi* resign.

resolut [rezo'lu:t] *a* resolute; R~ion [rezolutsi'o:n] *f* resolution.

Resonanz [rezo'nants] *f* (lit, fig) resonance; ~boden *m* sounding board; ~kasten *m* resonance box.

Resopal * [rezo'pa:l] *nt* -s formica *.

Resozialisierung [rezotsiali'zi:ruŋ] *f* rehabilitation.

Respekt [rɛ'spɛkt] *m* -(e)s respect; r~abel ['-'ta:bəl] a respectable; r~ieren ['-'ti:rən] *vt* respect; r~los a disrespectful; ~sperson *f* person commanding respect; r~voll a respectful.

Ressort [rɛ'so:r] *nt* -s, -s department.

Rest [rɛst] *m* -(e)s, -e remainder, rest; (Über—) remains *pl*; ~er *pl* (Comm) remnants *pl*.

Restaur- *cpd:* ~ant [rɛsto'rã:] *nt* -s, -s restaurant; ~ation [rɛstaoratsi'o:n] *f* restoration; r~ieren [rɛstau'ri:rən] *vt* restore.

Rest- *cpd:* ~betrag *m* remainder, outstanding sum; r~lich a remaining; r~los a complete.

Resultat [rezul'ta:t] *nt* -(e)s, -e result.

Retorte [re'tɔrtə] *f* -, -n retort.

retten ['rɛtən] *vt* save, rescue.

Retter *m* -s, - rescuer, saviour.

Rettich ['rɛtɪç] *m* -s, -e radish.

Rettung *f* rescue; (Hilfe) help; **seine letzte** ~ his last hope; ~sboot *nt* lifeboat; ~sgürtel *m*, ~sring *m* lifebelt, life preserver (US); r~slos a hopeless.

retuschieren [retu'ʃi:rən] *vt* (Phot) retouch.

Reue ['rɔyə] *f* - remorse; (Bedauern) regret; r~n *vt*: **es reut ihn** he regrets (it) or is sorry (about it).

reuig ['rɔyɪç] a penitent.

Revanche [re'vã:ʃə] *f* -, -n revenge; (Sport) return match.

revanchieren [revã'ʃi:rən] *vr* (sich rächen) get one's own back, have one's revenge; (erwidern) reciprocate, return the compliment.

Revers [re've:r] *m or nt* -, - lapel.

revidieren [revi'di:rən] *vt* revise.

Revier [re'vi:r] *nt* -s, -e district; (Jagd—) preserve; police station/beat; (Mil) sickbay.

Revision [revizi'o:n] *f* revision; (Comm) auditing; (Jur) appeal.

Revolte [re'vɔltə] *f* -, -n revolt.

Revolution [revolutsi'o:n] *f* revolution; ~är [-'nɛ:r] *m* -s, -e revolutionary; r~ieren [-'ni:rən] *vt* revolutionize.

Revolver [re'vɔlvər] *m* -s, - revolver.

Rezen- *cpd:* ~sent [-'zɛnt] *m* reviewer, critic; r~sieren [-'zi:rən] *vt* review; ~sion [-zi'o:n] *f* review, criticism.

Rezept [re'tsɛpt] *nt* -(e)s, -e recipe; (Med) prescription; r~pflichtig a available only on prescription.

rezitieren [retsi'ti:rən] *vt* recite.

Rhabarber [ra'barbər] *m* -s rhubarb.

Rhesusfaktor ['re:zusfaktor] *m* rhesus factor.

Rhetorik [re'to:rɪk] *f* rhetoric.

rhetorisch [re'to:rɪʃ] a rhetorical.

Rheuma ['rɔyma] *nt* -s, **Rheumatismus** [rɔyma'tɪsmus] *m* rheumatism.

Rhinozeros [ri'no:tserɔs] *nt* - or -ses, -se rhinoceros.

rhyth- ['rʏt] *cpd:* ~misch a rythmical; R~mus *m* rhythm.

Richt- ['rɪçt] *cpd:* r~en *vt* direct (an +acc at; (fig) to); Waffe aim (auf +acc at); (einstellen) adjust; (instand setzen) repair; (zurechtmachen) prepare; (bestrafen) pass judgement on; *vr:* **sich r~en nach** go by; ~er(in *f*) *m* -s, - judge; r~erlich a judicial; ~ig a right, correct; (echt) proper; ad (col: sehr) really; **der/die** ~ige the right one/person; **das** ~ige the right thing; ~igkeit *f* correctness; ~igstellung *f* correction, rectification; ~preis *m* recommended price; ~ung *f* direction; tendency, orientation.

riechen ['ri:çən] *vti* irreg smell (an etw (dat) sth; nach of); **ich kann das/ihn nicht** ~ (col) I can't stand it/him.

Ried [ri:t] *nt* -(e)s, -e reed; marsh.

Riege ['ri:gə] *f* -, -n team, squad.

Riegel ['ri:gəl] *m* -s, - bolt, bar.

Riemen ['ri:mən] *m* -s, - strap; (Gürtel, Tech) belt; (Naut) oar.

Riese ['ri:zə] *m* -n, -n giant; r~ln *vi* trickle; (Schnee) fall gently; ~nerfolg *m* enormous success; r~ngroß a, r~nhaft a colossal, gigantic, huge.

ries- ['ri:z] *cpd:* ~ig a enormous, huge, vast; R~in *f* giantess.

Riff [rɪf] *nt* -(e)s, -e reef.

Rille ['rɪlə] *f* -, -n groove.

Rind [rɪnt] *nt* -(e)s, -er ox; cow; cattle *pl*; (Cook) beef; ~e *f* ['rɪndə] -, -n rind; (Baum—) bark; (Brot—) crust; ~fleisch *nt* beef; ~sbraten *m* roast beef; ~vieh *nt* cattle *pl*; (col) blockhead, stupid oaf.

Ring [rɪŋ] *m* -(e)s, -e ring; ~buch *nt* loose-leaf book; ~elnatter *f* grass snake; r~en *vi* irreg wrestle; ~en *nt* -s wrestling; ~finger *m* ring finger; r~förmig a ring-shaped; ~kampf *m* wrestling bout; ~richter *m* referee; r~s um ad round; r~sherum ad round about; ~straße *f* ring road; r~sum(her) ad (rundherum) round about; (überall) all round.

Rinn- ['rɪn] *cpd:* ~e *f* -, -n gutter, drain; r~en *vi* irreg run, trickle; ~sal *nt* -s, -e trickle of water; ~stein *m* gutter.

Rippchen ['rɪpçən] *nt* small rib; cutlet.

Rippe ['rɪpə] f -, -n rib; ~**nfellentzündung** f pleurisy.

Risiko ['riːziko] nt -s, -s or **Risiken** risk.

riskant [rɪs'kant] a risky, hazardous.

riskieren [rɪs'kiːrən] vt risk.

Riß [rɪs] m -sses, -sse tear; (in Mauer, Tasse etc) crack; (in Haut) scratch; (Tech) design.

rissig ['rɪsɪç] a torn; cracked; scratched.

Ritt [rɪt] m -(e)s, -e ride; ~**er** m -s, - knight; **r~erlich** a chivalrous; ~**erschlag** m knighting; ~**ertum** nt -s chivalry; ~**erzeit** f age of chivalry; **r~lings** ad astride.

Ritus ['riːtus] m -, **Riten** rite.

Ritze ['rɪtsə] f -, -n crack, chink; **r~n** vt scratch.

Rivale [ri'vaːlə] m -n, -n rival.

Rivalität [rivali'tɛːt] f rivalry.

Rizinusöl ['riːtsinusøːl] nt castor oil.

Robbe ['rɔbə] f -, -n seal.

Robe ['roːbə] f -, -n robe.

Roboter ['rɔbɔtər] m -s, - robot.

röcheln ['rœçəln] vi wheeze.

Rock [rɔk] m -(e)s, ¨e skirt; (Jackett) jacket; (Uniform~) tunic.

Rodel ['roːdəl] m -s, - toboggan; ~**bahn** f toboggan run; **r~n** vi toboggan.

roden ['roːdən] vti clear.

Rogen ['roːgən] m -s, - roe, spawn.

Roggen ['rɔgən] m -s, - rye; ~**brot** nt rye bread, black bread.

roh [roː] a raw; Mensch coarse, crude; **R~bau** m shell of a building; **R~eisen** nt pig iron; **R~ling** m ruffian; **R~material** nt raw material; **R~öl** nt crude oil.

Rohr ['roːr] nt -(e)s, -e pipe, tube; (Bot) cane; (Schilf) reed; (Gewehr~) barrel; ~**bruch** m burst pipe.

Röhre ['røːrə] f -, -n tube, pipe; (Rad etc) valve; (Back~) oven.

Rohr- cpd: ~**geflecht** nt wickerwork; ~**leger** m -s, - plumber; ~**leitung** f pipeline; ~**post** f pneumatic post; ~**stock** m cane; ~**stuhl** m basket chair; ~**zucker** m cane sugar.

Roh- cpd: ~**seide** f raw silk; ~**stoff** m raw material.

Rokoko ['rɔkoko] nt -s rococo.

Roll- ['rɔl] cpd: ~**(l)aden** m shutter; ~**bahn** f, ~**feld** nt (Aviat) runway.

Rolle ['rɔlə] f -, -n roll; (Theat, soziologisch) role; (Garn~ etc) reel, spool; (Walze) roller; (Wäsche~) mangle; **keine** ~ **spielen** not matter; **r~n** vti roll; (Aviat) taxi; Wäsche mangle; ~**nbesetzung** f (Theat) cast; ~**r** m -s, - scooter; (Welle) roller.

Roll- cpd: ~**mops** m pickled herring; ~**schuh** m roller skate; ~**stuhl** m wheelchair; ~**treppe** f escalator.

Roman [ro'maːn] m -'s, -e novel; ~**schreiber** m, ~**schriftsteller** m novelist; ~**tik** [ro'mantɪk] f romanticism; ~**tiker** [ro'mantikər] m -s, - romanticist; **r~tisch** [ro'mantɪʃ] a romantic; ~**ze** [ro'mantsə] f -, -n romance.

Römer ['røːmər] m -s, - wineglass; (Mensch) Roman.

röntgen ['rœntgən] vt X-ray; **R~aufnahme** f, **R~bild** nt X-ray; **R~strahlen** pl X-rays pl.

rosa ['roːza] a pink, rose(-coloured).

Rose ['roːzə] f -, -n rose; ~**nkohl** m Brussels sprouts pl; ~**nkranz** m rosary; ~**nmontag** m Shrove Monday.

Rosette [ro'zɛtə] f rosette; rose window.

rosig ['roːzɪç] a rosy.

Rosine [ro'ziːnə] f raisin, currant.

Roß [rɔs] nt -sses, -sse horse, steed; ~**kastanie** f horse chestnut.

Rost [rɔst] m -(e)s, -e rust; (Gitter) grill, gridiron; (Bett~) springs pl; ~**braten** m roast(ed) meat, joint; **r~en** vi rust.

rösten ['røːstən] vt roast; toast; grill.

Rost- cpd: ~**frei** a rust-free; rustproof; stainless; **r~ig** a rusty; ~**schutz** m rustproofing.

rot [roːt] a red; **R~ation** [rotatsi'oːn] f rotation; ~**bäckig** a red-cheeked; ~**blond** a strawberry blond.

Röte ['røːtə] f - redness; ~**ln** pl German measles sing; **r~n** vtr redden.

rot- cpd: ~**haarig** a red-haired; ~**ieren** [ro'tiːrən] vi rotate; **R~käppchen** nt Little Red Riding Hood; ~**kehlchen** nt robin; **R~stift** m red pencil; **R~wein** m red wine.

Rotz [rɔts] m -es, -e (col) snot.

Roulade [ru'laːdə] f (Cook) beef olive.

Route ['ruːtə] f -, -n route.

Routine [ru'tiːnə] f experience; routine.

Rübe ['ryːbə] f -, -n turnip; **gelbe** ~ carrot; **rote** ~ beetroot; ~**nzucker** m beet sugar.

Rubin [ru'biːn] m -s, -e ruby.

Rubrik [ru'briːk] f heading; (Spalte) column.

Ruck [rʊk] m -(e)s, -e jerk, jolt.

Rück- ['rʏk] cpd: ~**antwort** f reply, answer; **r~bezüglich** a reflexive; **r~blenden** vi flash back; **r~blickend** a retrospective; **r~en** vti move; ~**en** m -s, - back; (Berg~) ridge; ~**endeckung** f backing; ~**enlehne** f back (of chair); ~**enmark** nt spinal cord; ~**enschwimmen** nt backstroke; ~**enwind** m following wind; ~**erstattung** f return, restitution; ~**fahrt** f return journey; ~**fall** m relapse; **r~fällig** a relapsing; **r~fällig werden** relapse; ~**flug** m return flight; ~**frage** f question; ~**gabe** f return; ~**gang** m decline, fall; **r~gängig** a: etw **r~gängig machen** cancel sth; ~**grat** nt -(e)s, -e spine, backbone; ~**griff** m recourse; ~**halt** m backing, reserve; **r~haltlos** a unreserved; ~**kehr** f -, -en return; ~**koppelung** f feedback; ~**lage** f reserve, savings pl; **r~läufig** a declining, falling; ~**licht** nt back light; ~**nahme** f -, -n taking back; ~**porto** nt return postage; ~**reise** f return journey; (Naut) home voyage; ~**ruf** m recall.

Rucksack ['rʊkzak] m rucksack.

Rück- cpd: ~**schau** f reflection;

r~schauend *a, ad* retrospective, in retrospect; ~schluß *m* conclusion; ~schritt *m* retrogression; r~schrittlich *a* reactionary; retrograde; ~seite *f* back; (*von Münze etc*) reverse; ~sicht *f* consideration; ~sicht nehmen auf (+*acc*) show consideration for; r~sichtslos *a* inconsiderate; *Fahren* reckless; (*unbarmherzig*) ruthless; r~sichtsvoll *a* considerate; ~sitz *m* back seat; ~spiegel *m* (*Aut*) rear-view mirror; ~spiel *nt* return match; ~sprache *f* further discussion *or* talk; ~stand *m* arrears *pl*; r~ständig *a* backward, out-of-date; *Zahlungen* in arrears; ~stoß *m* recoil; ~strahler *m* -s, - rear reflector; ~tritt *m* resignation; ~trittbremse *f* pedal brake; ~vergütung *f* repayment; (*Comm*) refund; ~versicherung *f* reinsurance; r~wärtig *a* rear; r~wärts *ad* backward(s), back; ~wärtsgang *m* (*Aut*) reverse gear; ~weg *m* return journey, way back; r~wirkend *a* retroactive; ~wirkung *f* reaction; retrospective effect; ~zahlung *f* repayment; ~zug *m* retreat.

Rüde ['ry:də] *m* -n, -n male dog/fox/wolf; r~ *a* blunt, gruff.

Rudel ['ru:dəl] *nt* -s, - pack; herd.

Ruder ['ru:dər] *nt* -s, - oar; (*Steuer*) rudder; ~boot *nt* rowing boat; ~er *m* -s, - rower; r~n *vt/vi* row.

Ruf [ru:f] *m* -(e)s, -e call, cry; (*Ansehen*) reputation; r~en *vti irreg* call; cry; ~name *m* usual (first) name; ~nummer *f* (tele)phone number; ~zeichen *nt* (*Rad*) call sign; (*Tel*) ringing tone.

Rüge ['ry:gə] *f* -, -n reprimand, rebuke; r~n *vt* reprimand.

Ruhe ['ru:ə] *f* - rest; (*Ungestörtheit*) peace, quiet; (*Gelassenheit, Stille*) calm; (*Schweigen*) silence; sich zur ~ setzen retire; ~! be quiet!, silence!; r~los *a* restless; r~n *vi* rest; ~pause *f* break; ~platz *m* resting place; ~stand *m* retirement; letzte ~stätte *f* final resting place; ~störung *f* breach of the peace; ~tag *m* closing day.

ruhig ['ru:ıç] *a* quiet; (*bewegungslos*) still; *Hand* steady; (*gelassen, friedlich*) calm; *Gewissen* clear; tu das ~ feel free to do that.

Ruhm [ru:m] *m* -(e)s fame, glory.

rühm- ['ry:m] *cpd*: ~en *vt* praise; *vr* boast; ~lich *a* laudable.

ruhm- *cpd*: ~los *a* inglorious; ~reich *a* glorious.

Ruhr ['ru:r] *f* - dysentery.

Rühr- ['ry:r] *cpd*: ~ei *nt* scrambled egg; r~en *vtr* (*lit, fig*) move, stir (*auch Cook*); *vi*: r~en von come *or* stem from; r~en an (+*acc*) touch; (*fig*) touch on; r~end *a* touching, moving; ~ig *a* active, lively; r~selig *a* sentimental, emotional; ~ung *f* emotion.

Ruin [ru'i:n] *m* -s, ~e, *f* -, -n ruin; r~ieren [rui'ni:rən] *vt* ruin.

rülpsen ['rʏlpsən] *vi* burp, belch.

Rum [rum] *m* -s, -s rum.

Rummel ['ruməl] *m* -s (*col*) hubbub; (*Jahrmarkt*) fair; ~platz *m* fairground, fair.

rumoren [ru'mo:rən] *vi* be noisy, make a noise.

Rumpel- ['rumpəl] *cpd*: ~kammer *f* junk room; r~n *vi* rumble; (*holpern*) jolt.

Rumpf [rumpf] *m* -(e)s, -̈e trunk, torso; (*Aviat*) fuselage; (*Naut*) hull.

rümpfen ['rʏmpfən] *vt Nase* turn up.

rund [runt] *a* round; *ad* (*etwa*) around; ~um etw round sth; R~bogen *m* Norman *or* Romanesque arch; R~brief *m* circular; R~e ['rundə] *f* -, -n round; (*in Rennen*) lap; (*Gesellschaft*) circle; ~en *vt* make round; *vr* (*fig*) take shape; ~erneuert *a Reifen* remoulded; R~fahrt *f* (round) trip.

Rundfunk ['runtfuŋk] *m* -(e)s broadcasting; (~anstalt) broadcasting service; im ~ on the radio; ~empfang *m* reception; ~gebühr *f* licence; ~gerät *nt* wireless set; ~sendung *f* broadcast, radio programme.

Rund- *cpd*: r~heraus *ad* straight out, bluntly; r~herum *ad* round about; all round; r~lich *a* plump, rounded; ~reise *f* round trip; ~schreiben *nt* (*Comm*) circular; ~ung *f* curve, roundness.

runter ['runtər] *ad* (*col*) = **herunter, hinunter.**

Runzel ['runtsəl] *f* -, -n wrinkle; r~ig *a* wrinkled; r~n *vt* wrinkle; die Stirn r~n frown.

Rüpel ['ry:pəl] *m* -s, - lout; r~haft *a* loutish.

rupfen ['rupfən] *vt* pluck; R~ *m* -s, - sackcloth.

ruppig ['rupıç] *a* rough, gruff.

Rüsche ['ry:ʃə] *f* -, -n frill.

Ruß [ru:s] *m* -es soot; r~en *vi* smoke; (*Ofen*) be sooty; r~ig *a* sooty.

Rüssel ['rysəl] *m* -s, - snout; (*Elefanten*—) trunk.

rüsten ['rystən] *vtri* prepare; (*Mil*) arm.

rüstig ['rystıç] *a* sprightly, vigorous; R~keit *f* sprightliness, vigour.

Rüstung ['rystuŋ] *f* preparation; arming; (*Ritter*—) armour; (*Waffen etc*) armaments *pl*; ~skontrolle *f* armaments control.

Rüstzeug *nt* tools *pl*; (*fig*) capacity.

Rute ['ru:tə] *f* -, -n rod, switch.

Rutsch [rutʃ] *m* -(e)s, -e slide; (*Erd*—) landslide; ~bahn *f* slide; r~en *vi* slide; (*ausr*—*en*) slip; r~ig *a* slippery.

rütteln ['rʏtəln] *vti* shake, jolt.

S

S,s [ɛs] *nt* S,s.

Saal [za:l] *m* -(e)s, Säle hall; room.

Saat [za:t] *f* -, -en seed; (*Pflanzen*) crop; (*Säen*) sowing.

sabbern ['zabərn] *vi* (*col*) dribble.

Säbel ['zɛ:bəl] *m* -s, - sabre, sword.

Sabotage [zabo'ta:ʒə] *f* -, -n sabotage.

sabotieren [zabo'ti:rən] *vt* sabotage.

Sach- [zax] cpd: ~**bearbeiter** m specialist; s~**dienlich** a relevant, helpful; ~e f -, -n thing; (Angelegenheit) affair, business; (Frage) matter; (Pflicht) task; zur ~e to the point; s~**gemäß** a appropriate, suitable; s~**kundig** a expert; ~**lage** f situation, state of affairs; s~**lich** a matter-of-fact, objective; Irrtum, Angabe factual.

sächlich ['zɛxlɪç] a neuter.

Sach- cpd: ~**schaden** m material damage; s~**t(e)** ad softly, gently; ~**verständige(r)** mf expert.

Sack [zak] m -(e)s, ꞏe sack; s~**en** vi sag, sink; ~**gasse** f cul-de-sac, dead-end street (US).

Sadismus [za'dɪsmus] m sadism.

Sadist [za'dɪst] m sadist; s~**isch** a sadistic.

säen ['zɛːən] vti sow.

Saft [zaft] m -(e)s, ꞏe juice; (Bot) sap; s~**ig** a juicy; s~**los** a dry.

Sage ['zaːgə] f -, -n saga.

Säge ['zɛːgə] f -, -n saw; ~**mehl** nt sawdust; s~**n** vti saw.

sagen ['zaːgən] vti say (jdm to sb), tell (jdm sb); ~**haft** a legendary; (col) great, smashing.

Sägewerk nt sawmill.

Sahne ['zaːnə] f - cream.

Saison [zɛ'zõ] f -, -s season; ~**arbeiter** m seasonal worker.

Saite ['zaɪtə] f -, -n string; ~**ninstrument** nt string instrument.

Sakko ['zako] m or nt -s, -s jacket.

Sakrament [zakramɛnt] nt sacrament.

Sakristei [zakrɪs'taɪ] f sacristy.

Salat [za'laːt] m -(e)s, -e salad; (Kopfsalat) lettuce; ~**soße** f salad dressing.

Salb- ['zalb] cpd: ~**e** f -, -n ointment; ~**ei** [zal'baɪ] m or f -s or - sage; s~**en** vt anoint; ~**ung** f anointing; s~**ungsvoll** a unctuous.

Saldo ['zaldo] m -s, **Salden** balance.

Salmiak [zalmi'ak] m -s sal ammoniac; ~**geist** m liquid ammonia.

Salon [za'lõ] m -s, -s salon.

salopp [za'lɔp] a casual.

Salpeter [zal'peːtər] m -s saltpetre; ~**säure** f nitric acid.

Salut [za'luːt] m -(e)s, -e salute; s~**ieren** [-'tiːrən] vi salute.

Salve ['zalvə] f -, -n salvo.

Salz [zalts] nt -es, -e salt; s~**en** vt irreg salt; s~**ig** a salty; ~**kartoffeln** pl boiled potatoes pl; ~**säure** f hydrochloric acid.

Samen ['zaːmən] m -s, - seed; (Anat) sperm.

Sammel- ['zaməl] cpd: ~**band** m anthology; ~**becken** nt reservoir; ~**bestellung** f collective order; s~**n** vt collect; vr assemble, gather; (konzentrieren) concentrate; ~**name** m collective term; ~**surium** [-'zuːrium] nt hotchpotch.

Sammlung ['zamluŋ] f collection; assembly, gathering; concentration.

Samstag ['zamstaːk] m Saturday; s~**s** ad (on) Saturdays.

Samt [zamt] m -(e)s, -e velvet; s~ prep

+dat (along) with, together with; s~ **und sonders** each and every one (of them).

sämtlich ['zɛmtlɪç] a all (the), entire.

Sand [zant] m -(e)s, -e sand; ~**ale** [zan'daːlə] f -, -n sandal; ~**bank** f sandbank; s~**ig** ['zandɪç] a sandy; ~**kasten** m sandpit; ~**kuchen** m Madeira cake; ~**papier** nt sandpaper; ~**stein** m sandstone; ~**uhr** f hourglass.

sanft [zanft] a soft, gentle; ~**mütig** a gentle, meek.

Sänger(in f) ['zɛŋər(ɪn)] m -s, - singer.

Sani- cpd: s~**eren** [za'niːrən] vt redevelop; Betrieb make financially sound; vr line one's pocket; become financially sound; ~**erung** f redevelopment; making viable; s~**tär** [zani'tɛːr] a sanitary; s~**täre Anlagen** sanitation; ~**täter** [zani'tɛːtər] m -s, - first-aid attendant; (Mil) (medical) orderly.

sanktionieren [zaŋktsio'niːrən] vt sanction.

Saphir ['zaːfiːr] m -s, -e sapphire.

Sardelle [zar'dɛlə] f anchovy.

Sardine [zar'diːnə] f sardine.

Sarg [zark] m -(e)s, ꞏe coffin.

Sarkasmus [zar'kasmus] m sarcasm.

sarkastisch [zar'kastɪʃ] a sarcastic.

Satan ['zaːtan] m -s, -e Satan; devil.

Satellit [zate'liːt] m -en, -en satellite.

Satire [za'tiːrə] f -, -n satire.

satirisch [za'tiːrɪʃ] a satirical.

satt [zat] a full; Farbe rich, deep; jdn/etw ~ **sein** or **haben** be fed up with sb/sth; sich ~ **hören/sehen an** (+dat) see/hear enough of; sich ~ **essen** eat one's fill; ~ **machen** be filling.

Sattel ['zatəl] m -s, ꞏ saddle; (Berg) ridge; s~**fest** a (fig) proficient; s~**n** vt saddle.

sättigen ['zɛtɪgən] vt satisfy; (Chem) saturate.

Satz [zats] m -es, ꞏe (Gram) sentence; (Neben-, Adverbial-) clause; (Theorem) theorem; (Mus) movement; (Tennis, Briefmarken etc) set; (Kaffee) grounds pl; (Comm) rate; (Sprung) jump; ~**gegenstand** m (Gram) subject; ~**lehre** f syntax; ~**teil** m constituent (of a sentence); ~**ung** f statute, rule; s~**ungsgemäß** a statutory; ~**zeichen** nt punctuation mark.

Sau [zau] f -, **Säue** sow; (col) dirty pig.

sauber ['zaubər] a clean; (ironisch) fine; ~**halten** vt irreg keep clean; S~**keit** f cleanness; (einer Person) cleanliness.

säuber- ['zɔybər] cpd: ~**lich** ad neatly; ~**n** vt clean; (Pol etc) purge; S~**ung** f cleaning; purge.

Sauce ['zoːsə] f -, -n sauce, gravy.

sauer ['zauər] a sour; (Chem) acid; (col) cross.

Sauerei [zauə'raɪ] f (col) rotten state of affairs, scandal; (Schmutz etc) mess; (Unanständigkeit) obscenity.

säuerlich ['zɔyərlɪç] a sourish, tart.

Sauer- cpd: ~**milch** f sour milk; ~**stoff** m oxygen; ~**stoffgerät** nt breathing apparatus; ~**teig** m leaven.

saufen ['zaufən] vti irreg (col) drink, booze.

Säufer ['zɔyfər] m -s, - (col) boozer.

Sauferei [zaufəˈraɪ] f drinking, boozing; booze-up.

saugen [ˈzaʊɡən] vti irreg suck.

säugen [ˈzɔʏɡən] vt suckle.

Sauger [zaʊɡər] m -s, - dummy, comforter (US); (auf Flasche) teat; (Staub—) vacuum cleaner, hoover ®.

Säug- [ˈzɔʏɡ] cpd: ~**etier** nt mammal; ~**ling** m infant, baby.

Säule [ˈzɔʏlə] f -, -n column, pillar; ~**ngang** m arcade.

Saum [zaʊm] m -(e)s, **Säume** hem; (Naht) seam.

säumen [ˈzɔʏmən] vt hem; seam; vi delay, hesitate.

Sauna [ˈzaʊna] f -, -s sauna.

Säure [ˈzɔʏrə] f -, -n acid; (Geschmack) sourness, acidity; s~**beständig** a acidproof; s~**haltig** a acidic.

säuseln [ˈzɔʏzəln] vti murmur, rustle.

sausen [ˈzaʊzən] vi blow; (col: eilen) rush; (Ohren) buzz; etw ~ **lassen** (col) give sth a miss.

Saustall [ˈzaʊʃtal] m (col) pigsty.

Saxophon [zaksoˈfoːn] nt -s, -e saxophone.

Schabe [ˈʃaːbə] f -, -n cockroach; s~n vt scrape; ~**rnack** [ˈʃaːbərnak] m -(e)s, -e trick, prank.

schäbig [ˈʃeːbɪç] a shabby; S~**keit** f shabbiness.

Schablone [ʃaˈbloːnə] f -, -n stencil; (Muster) pattern; (fig) convention; s~**nhaft** a stereotyped, conventional.

Schach [ʃax] nt -s, -s chess; (Stellung) check; ~**brett** nt chessboard; ~**figur** f chessman; **'s~'matt** a checkmate; ~**partie** f, ~**spiel** nt game of chess.

Schacht [ʃaxt] m -(e)s, **=e** shaft; ~**el** f -, -n box; (pej: Frau) bag, cow.

schade [ˈʃaːdə] a a pity or shame; **sich** (dat) zu ~ **sein für** etw consider oneself too good for sth; interj (what a) pity or shame.

Schädel [ˈʃeːdəl] m -s, - skull; ~**bruch** m fractured skull.

Schaden [ˈʃaːdən] m -s, = damage; (Verletzung) injury; (Nachteil) disadvantage; s~ vi (+dat) hurt; **einer Sache s~** damage sth; ~**ersatz** m compensation, damages pl; s~**ersatzpflichtig** a liable for damages; ~**freude** f malicious delight; s~**froh** a gloating, with malicious delight.

schadhaft [ˈʃaːthaft] a faulty, damaged.

schäd- [ˈʃeːt] cpd: ~**igen** [ˈʃeːdɪɡən] vt damage; Person do harm to, harm; S~**igung** f damage; harm; ~**lich** a harmful (für to); S~**lichkeit** f harmfulness; S~**ling** m pest; S~**lingsbekämpfungsmittel** nt pesticide.

schadlos [ˈʃaːtloːs] a: **sich ~ halten an** (+dat) take advantage of.

Schaf [ʃaːf] nt -(e)s, -e sheep; ~**bock** m ram.

Schäfchen [ˈʃeːfçən] nt lamb; ~**wolken** pl cirrus clouds pl.

Schäfer [ˈʃeːfər] m -s, -e shepherd; ~**hund** m Alsatian; ~**in** f shepherdess.

schaffen [ˈʃafən] vti irreg create; **sich** (dat) etw ~ get o.s. sth; vt (erreichen) manage, do; (erledigen) finish;

Prüfung pass; (transportieren) take; vi (col: arbeiten) work; **sich an etw** (dat) zu ~ **machen** busy oneself with sth; S~ nt -s (creative) activity; S~**sdrang** m creative urge; energy; S~**skraft** f creativity.

Schaffner(in f) [ˈʃafnər(ɪn)] m -s, - (Bus) conductor/conductress; (Rail) guard.

Schaft [ʃaft] m -(e)s, **=e** shaft; (von Gewehr) stock; (von Stiefel) leg; (Bot) stalk; tree trunk; ~**stiefel** m high boot.

Schakal [ʃaˈkaːl] m -s, -e jackal.

Schäker [ˈʃeːkər] m -s, - flirt; joker; s~n vi flirt; joke.

schal [ʃaːl] a flat; (fig) insipid; S~ m -s, -e or -s scarf.

Schälchen [ˈʃeːlçən] nt cup, bowl.

Schale [ˈʃaːlə] f -, -n skin; (abgeschält) peel; (Nuß—, Muschel—, Ei—) shell; (Geschirr) dish, bowl.

schälen [ˈʃeːlən] vt peel; shell; vr peel.

Schall [ʃal] m -(e)s, -e sound; ~**dämpfer** m -s, - (Aut) silencer; s~**dicht** a soundproof; s~**en** vi (re)sound; s~**end** a resounding, loud; ~**mauer** f sound barrier; ~**platte** f (gramophone) record.

Schalt- [ˈʃalt] cpd: ~**bild** nt circuit diagram; ~**brett** nt switchboard; s~**en** vt switch, turn; vi (Aut) change (gear); (col: begreifen) catch on; s~**en und walten** do as one pleases; ~**er** m -s, - counter; (an Gerät) switch; ~**erbeamte(r)** m counter clerk; ~**hebel** m switch; (Aut) gear-lever; ~**jahr** nt leap year; ~**ung** f switching; (Elec) circuit; (Aut) gear change.

Scham [ʃaːm] f - shame; (—gefühl) modesty; (Organe) private parts pl.

schämen [ˈʃeːmən] vr be ashamed.

Scham- cpd: ~**haare** pl pubic hair; s~**haft** a modest, bashful; s~**los** a shameless.

Schande [ˈʃandə] f - disgrace.

schändlich [ˈʃɛntlɪç] a disgraceful, shameful; S~**keit** f disgracefulness.

Schandtat [ˈʃantaːt] f (col) escapade, shenanigan.

Schändung [ˈʃɛnduŋ] f violation, defilement.

Schank- [ˈʃaŋk] cpd: ~**erlaubnis** f, ~**konzession** f (publican's) licence; ~**tisch** m bar.

Schanze [ˈʃantsə] f -, -n (Mil) fieldwork, earthworks pl; (Sprung—) skijump.

Schar [ʃaːr] f -, -en band, company; (Vögel) flock; (Menge) crowd; **in ~en** in droves; ~**ade** [ʃaˈraːdə] f charade; s~**en** vr assemble, rally; s~**enweise** ad in droves.

scharf [ʃarf] a sharp; Essen hot; Munition live; ~ **nachdenken** think hard; **auf etw** (acc) ~ **sein** (col) be keen on sth; S~**blick** m (fig) penetration.

Schärf- [ˈʃerf] cpd: ~**e** f -, -n sharpness; (Strenge) rigour; s~**en** vt sharpen.

Scharf- cpd: s~**machen** vt (col) stir up; ~**richter** m executioner; ~**schießen** nt firing live ammunition; ~**schütze** m marksman, sharpshooter; ~**sinn** m penetration, astuteness; s~**sinnig** a astute, shrewd.

Scharmützel [ʃarˈmʏtsəl] nt -s, - skirmish.

Scharnier [ʃarˈniːr] nt -s, -e hinge.

Schärpe [ˈʃɛrpə] f -, -n sash.

scharren [ˈʃarən] vti scrape, scratch.

Scharte [ˈʃartə] f -, -n notch, nick; (Berg) wind gap.

schartig [ˈʃartɪç] a jagged.

Schaschlik [ˈʃaʃlɪk] m or nt -s, -s (shish) kebab.

Schatten [ˈʃatən] m -s, - shadow; ~bild nt, ~riß m silhouette; ~seite f shady side, dark side.

schattieren [ʃaˈtiːrən] vti shade.

Schattierung f shading.

schattig [ˈʃatɪç] a shady.

Schatulle [ʃaˈtʊlə] f -, -n casket; (Geld—) coffer.

Schatz [ʃats] m -es, ⁻e treasure; (Person) darling; ~amt nt treasury.

schätz- [ˈʃɛts] cpd: ~bar a assessable; **S~chen** nt darling, love; ~en vt (abschätzen) estimate; Gegenstand value; (würdigen) value, esteem; (vermuten) reckon; ~enlernen vt learn to appreciate; **S~ung** f estimate; estimation; valuation; **nach meiner S~ung ... I** reckon that ...; ~ungsweise ad approximately; it is thought; **S~wert** m estimated value.

Schau [ʃau] f - show; (Ausstellung) display, exhibition; **etw zur ~ stellen** make a show of sth, show sth off; ~bild nt diagram.

Schauder [ˈʃaudər] m -s, -s shudder; (wegen Kälte) shiver; **s~haft** a horrible; **s~n** vi shudder; shiver.

schauen [ˈʃauən] vi look.

Schauer [ˈʃauər] m -s, - (Regen—) shower; (Schreck) shudder; ~geschichte f horror story; **s~lich** a horrific, spine-chilling.

Schaufel [ˈʃaufəl] f -, -n shovel; (Naut) paddle; (Tech) scoop; **s~n** vt shovel, scoop.

Schau- cpd: ~fenster nt shop window; ~fensterauslage f window display; ~fensterbummel m window shopping (expedition); ~fensterdekorateur m window dresser; ~geschäft nt show business; ~kasten m showcase.

Schaukel [ˈʃaukəl] f -, -n swing; **s~n** vi swing, rock; ~pferd nt rocking horse; ~stuhl m rocking chair.

Schaulustige(r) [ˈʃaulʊstɪgə(r)] mf onlooker.

Schaum [ʃaum] m -(e)s, Schäume foam; (Seifen—) lather.

schäumen [ˈʃɔymən] vi foam.

Schaum- cpd: ~gummi m foam (rubber); **s~ig** a frothy, foamy; ~krone f white crest; ~schläger m (fig) windbag; ~wein m sparkling wine.

Schau- cpd: ~platz m scene; **s~rig** a horrific, dreadful; ~spiel nt spectacle; (Theat) play; ~spieler m actor; ~spielerin f actress; **s~spielern** vi insep act.

Scheck [ʃɛk] m -s, -s cheque; ~buch nt cheque book; **s~ig** a dappled, piebald.

scheel [ʃeːl] a (col) dirty; **jdn ~ ansehen** give sb a dirty look.

scheffeln [ˈʃɛfəln] vt amass.

Scheibe [ˈʃaibə] f -, -n disc; (Brot etc) slice; (Glas—) pane (Mil) target; ~nbremse f (Aut) disc brake; ~nwaschanlage f (Aut) windscreen washers pl; ~nwischer m (Aut) windscreen wiper.

Scheich [ʃaiç] m -s, -e or -s sheik(h).

Scheide [ˈʃaidə] f -, -n sheath; (Grenze) boundary; (Anat) vagina; **s~n** irreg vt separate; Ehe dissolve; **sich s~n lassen** get a divorce; vi (de)part.

Scheidung f (Ehe—) divorce; ~sgrund m grounds pl for divorce; ~sklage f divorce suit.

Schein [ʃain] m -(e)s, -e light; (An—) appearance; (Geld) (bank)note; (Bescheinigung) certificate; **zum ~** in pretence; **s~bar** a apparent; **s~en** vi irreg shine; (Anschein haben) seem; **s~heilig** a hypocritical; ~tod m apparent death; ~werfer m -s, - floodlight; spotlight; (Such—) searchlight; (Aut) headlamp.

Scheiß [ˈʃais] in cpds (col) bloody; ~e f - (col) shit.

Scheit [ʃait] nt -(e)s, -e or -er log, billet.

Scheitel [ˈʃaitəl] m -s, - top; (Haar) parting; **s~n** vt part; ~punkt m zenith, apex.

scheitern [ˈʃaitərn] vi fail.

Schelle [ˈʃɛlə] f -, -n small bell; **s~n** vi ring.

Schellfisch [ˈʃɛlfɪʃ] m haddock.

Schelm [ʃɛlm] m -(e)s, -e rogue; **s~isch** a mischievous, roguish.

Schelte [ˈʃɛltə] f -, -n scolding; **s~n** vt irreg scold.

Schema [ˈʃema] nt -s, -s or -ta scheme, plan; (Darstellung) scheme; **nach ~** quite mechanically; **s~tisch** [ʃeˈmaːtɪʃ] a schematic; (pej) mechanical.

Schemel [ˈʃeːməl] m -s, - (foot)stool.

Schenkel [ˈʃɛŋkəl] m -s, - thigh.

schenken [ˈʃɛŋkən] vt (lit, fig) give; Getränk pour; **sich** (dat) **etw ~** (col) skip sth; **das ist geschenkt!** (billig) that's a giveaway!; (nichts wert) that's worthless!

Schenkung [ˈʃɛŋkʊŋ] f gift; ~surkunde f deed of gift.

Scherbe [ˈʃɛrbə] f -, -n broken piece, fragment; (archäologisch) potsherd.

Schere [ˈʃeːrə] f -, -n scissors pl; (groß) shears pl; **s~n** vt irreg cut; Schaf shear; (sich kümmern) bother; vr care; **scher dich (zum Teufel)!** get lost!; ~n-schleifer m -s, - knife-grinder; ~'rei f (col) bother, trouble.

Scherflein [ˈʃɛrflain] nt mite, bit.

Scherz [ʃɛrts] m -es, -e joke; fun; ~frage f conundrum; **s~haft** a joking, jocular.

scheu [ʃɔy] a shy; **S~** f - shyness; (Angst) fear (vor +dat of); (Ehrfurcht) awe; **S~che** f -, -n scarecrow; ~chen vt scare (off); ~en vr: **sich ~en vor** (+dat) be afraid of, shrink from; vt shun; vi (Pferd) shy.

Scheuer- [ˈʃɔyər] cpd: ~bürste f scrubbing brush; ~lappen m floorcloth;

~**leiste** f skirting board; **s~n** vt scour, scrub.

Scheuklappe f blinker.

Scheune [ˈʃɔynə] f -, -n barn.

Scheusal [ˈʃɔyzaːl] nt -s, -e monster.

scheußlich [ˈʃɔyslɪç] a dreadful, frightful; **S~keit** f dreadfulness.

Schi [ʃiː] m see **Ski**.

Schicht [ʃɪçt] f -, -en layer; (Klasse) class, level; (in Fabrik etc) shift; ~**arbeit** f shift work; **s~en** vt layer, stack.

schick [ʃɪk] a stylish, chic; ~**en** vt send; vr resign oneself (in +acc to); v impers (anständig sein) be fitting; ~**lich** a proper, fitting; **S~sal** nt -s, -e fate; ~**salsschlag** m great misfortune, blow.

Schieb- [ˈʃiːb] cpd: ~**edach** nt (Aut) sunshine roof; **s~en** vti irreg push; Schuld put (auf jdn on sb); ~**er** m -s, - slide; (Besteckteil) pusher; (Person) profiteer; ~**etür** f sliding door; ~**lehre** f (Math) calliper rule; ~**ung** f fiddle.

Schieds- [ˈʃiːts] cpd: ~**gericht** nt court of arbitration; ~**richter** m referee, umpire; (Schlichter) arbitrator; **s~richtern** vti insep referee, umpire; arbitrate; ~**spruch** m (arbitration) award.

schief [ʃiːf] a crooked; Ebene sloping; Turm leaning; Winkel oblique; Blick funny; Vergleich distorted; ad crooked(ly); ansehen askance; **etw ~ stellen** slope sth.

Schiefer [ˈʃiːfər] m -s, - slate; ~**dach** nt slate roof; ~**tafel** f (child's) slate.

schief- cpd: ~**gehen** vi irreg (col) go wrong; ~**lachen** vr (col) double up with laughter; ~**liegen** vi irreg (col) be wrong.

schielen [ˈʃiːlən] vi squint; **nach etw ~** (fig) eye sth.

Schienbein nt shinbone.

Schiene [ˈʃiːnə] f -, -n rail; (Med) splint; **s~n** vt put in splints; ~**nstrang** m (Rail etc) (section of) track.

schier [ʃiːr] a pure; Fleisch lean and boneless; (fig) sheer; ad nearly, almost.

Schieß- [ˈʃiːs] cpd: ~**bude** f shooting gallery; ~**budenfigur** f (col) clown, ludicrous figure; **s~en** vti irreg shoot (auf +acc at); (Salat etc) run to seed; Ball kick; Geschoß fire; ~**e'rei** f shooting incident, shoot-up; ~**platz** m firing range; ~**pulver** nt gunpowder; ~**scharte** f embrasure; ~**stand** m rifle or shooting range.

Schiff [ʃɪf] nt -(e)s, -e ship, vessel; (Kirchen—) nave; **s~bar** a navigable; ~**bau** m shipbuilding; ~**bruch** m shipwreck; **s~brüchig** a shipwrecked; ~**chen** nt small boat; (Weben) shuttle; (Mütze) forage cap; ~**er** m -s, - bargeman, boatman; ~**(f)ahrt** f shipping; (Reise) voyage; ~**(f)ahrtslinie** f shipping route; ~**sjunge** m cabin boy; ~**sladung** f cargo, shipload; ~**splanke** f gangplank.

Schikane [ʃiˈkaːnə] f -, -en harassment; dirty trick; **mit allen ~n** with all the trimmings.

schikanieren [ʃikaˈniːrən] vt harass, torment.

Schild [ʃɪlt] m -(e)s, -e shield; (Mützen—) peak, visor; **etw im ~ führen** be up to sth; nt -(e)s, -er sign; nameplate; (Etikett) label; ~**bürger** m duffer, blockhead; ~**drüse** f thyroid gland; **s~ern** [ˈʃɪldərn] vt depict, portray; ~**erung** f description, portrayal; ~**kröte** f tortoise; (Wasser—) turtle.

Schilf [ʃɪlf] nt -(e)s, -e, ~**rohr** nt (Pflanze) reed; (Material) reeds pl, rushes pl.

schillern [ˈʃɪlərn] vi shimmer; ~**d** a iridescent.

Schimmel [ˈʃɪməl] m -s, - mould; (Pferd) white horse; **s~ig** a mouldy; **s~n** vi get mouldy.

Schimmer [ˈʃɪmər] m -s glimmer; **s~n** vi glimmer, shimmer.

Schimpanse [ʃɪmˈpanzə] m -n, -n chimpanzee.

Schimpf [ʃɪmpf] m -(e)s, -e disgrace; **s~en** vti scold; vi curse, complain; ~**wort** nt term of abuse.

Schind- [ˈʃɪnd] cpd: ~**el** f -, -n shingle; **s~en** irreg vt maltreat, drive too hard; (col) **Eindruck s~en** create an impression; vr sweat and strain, toil away (mit at); ~**er** m -s, - knacker; (fig) slave driver; ~**e'rei** f grind, drudgery; ~**luder** nt: ~**luder treiben mit** muck or mess about; Vorrecht abuse.

Schinken [ˈʃɪŋkən] m -s, - ham.

Schippe [ˈʃɪpə] f -, -n shovel; **s~n** vt shovel.

Schirm [ʃɪrm] m -(e)s, -e (Regen—) umbrella; (Sonnen—) parasol, sunshade; (Wand—, Bild—) screen; (Lampen—) (lamp)shade; (Mützen—) peak; (Pilz—) cap; ~**bildaufnahme** f X-ray; ~**herr** m patron, protector; ~**mütze** f peaked cap; ~**ständer** m umbrella stand.

schizophren [ʃitsoˈfreːn] a schizophrenic.

Schlacht [ʃlaxt] f -, -en battle; **s~en** vt slaughter, kill; ~**enbummler** m football supporter; ~**er** m -s, - butcher; ~**feld** nt battlefield; ~**haus** nt, ~**hof** m slaughterhouse, abattoir; ~**plan** m (lit, fig) battle plan; ~**ruf** m battle cry, war cry; ~**schiff** nt battle ship; ~**vieh** nt animals kept for meat; beef cattle.

Schlacke [ˈʃlakə] f -, -n slag.

Schlaf [ʃlaːf] m -(e)s sleep; ~**anzug** m pyjamas pl.

Schläf- [ˈʃleːf] cpd: ~**chen** nt nap; ~**e** f -, -n temple.

schlafen [ˈʃlaːfən] vi irreg sleep; **S~gehen** nt -s going to bed; **S~szeit** f bedtime.

Schläfer(in f) [ˈʃleːfər(ɪn)] m -s, - sleeper.

schlaff [ʃlaf] a slack; (energielos) limp; (erschöpft) exhausted; **S~heit** f slackness; limpness; exhaustion.

Schlaf- cpd: ~**gelegenheit** f sleeping accommodation; ~**lied** nt lullaby; **s~los** a sleepless; ~**losigkeit** f sleeplessness, insomnia; ~**mittel** nt soporific, sleeping pill.

schläfrig [ˈʃleːfrɪç] a sleepy.

Schlaf- cpd: ~**saal** m dormitory; ~**sack** m sleeping bag; ~**tablette** f sleeping pill; **s~trunken** a drowsy, half-asleep; ~**wagen** m sleeping car, sleeper;

s~**wandeln** vi insep sleepwalk; ~**zimmer** nt bedroom.

Schlag [ʃlaːk] m -**(e)s,** ⁝e (lit, fig) blow; stroke (auch Med); (Puls-, Herz—) beat; (pl: Tracht Prügel) beating; (Elec) shock; (Blitz—) bolt, stroke; (Autotür) car door; (col: Portion) helping; (Art) kind, type; **mit einem** ~ all at once; ~ **auf** ~ in rapid succession; ~**ader** f artery; ~**anfall** m stroke; s~**artig** a sudden, without warning; ~**baum** m barrier; s~**en** [ˈʃlaːgən] irreg vti strike, hit; (wiederholt ~, besiegen) beat; (Glocke) ring; Stunde strike; Sahne whip; Schlacht fight; (einwickeln) wrap; **nach jdm** s~**en** (fig) take after sb; vr fight; **sich gut** s~**en** (fig) do well; s~**end** a Beweis convincing; s~**ende Wetter** (Min) firedamp; ~**er** [ˈʃlaːgər] m -s, - (lit, fig) hit; ~**ersänger(in** f) m pop singer.

Schläg- [ˈʃlɛːg] cpd: ~**er** m -s, - brawler; (Sport) bat; (Tennis etc) racket; (golf) club; hockey stick; (Waffe) rapier; ~**e'rei** f fight, punch-up.

Schlag- cpd: s~**fertig** a quick-witted; ~**fertigkeit** f ready wit, quickness of repartee; ~**instrument** nt percussion instrument; s~**instrument** nt percussion instrument; ~**loch** nt pothole; ~**rahm** m, ~**sahne** f (whipped) cream; ~**seite** f (Naut) list; ~**wort** nt slogan, catch phrase; ~**zeile** f headline; ~**zeug** nt percussion, drums pl; ~**zeuger** m -s, - drummer.

Schlamassel [ʃlaˈmasəl] m -s, - (col) mess.

Schlamm [ʃlam] m -**(e)s,** -e mud; s~**ig** a muddy.

Schlamp- [ˈʃlamp] cpd: ~**e** f -, -n (col) slattern, slut; s~**en** vi (col) be sloppy; ~**e'rei** f (col) disorder, untidiness; sloppy work; s~**ig** a (col) slovenly, sloppy.

Schlange [ˈʃlaŋə] f -, -n snake; (Menschen—) queue (Brit), line-up (US); ~ **stehen** (form a) queue, line up.

schlängeln [ˈʃlɛŋəln] vr twist, wind; (Fluß) meander.

Schlangen- cpd: ~**biß** m snake bite; ~**ngift** nt snake venom; ~**linie** f wavy line.

schlank [ʃlank] a slim, slender; S~**heit** f slimness, slenderness; S~**heitskur** f diet.

schlapp [ʃlap] a limp; (locker) slack; S~**e** f -, -n (col) setback; S~**heit** f limpness, slackness; S~**hut** m slouch hat; ~**machen** vi (col) wilt, droop.

Schlaraffenland [ʃlaˈrafənlant] nt land of milk and honey.

schlau [ʃlau] a crafty, cunning.

Schlauch [ʃlaux] m -**(e)s,** **Schläuche** hose; (in Reifen) inner tube; (col: Anstrengung) grind; ~**boot** nt rubber dinghy; s~**en** vt (col) tell on, exhaust; s~**los** a Reifen tubeless.

Schlau- cpd: ~**heit** f, **Schläue** [ˈʃlɔyə] f - cunning; ~**kopf** m clever dick.

schlecht [ʃlɛçt] a bad; ~ **und recht** after a fashion; **jdm ist** ~ sb feels sick or bad; ~**erdings** ad simply; ~**gehen** vi impers irreg: **jdm geht es** ~ sb is in a bad way; S~**heit** f badness; '~**hin** ad simply; **der Dramatiker** ~**hin** THE playwright;

S~**igkeit** f badness; bad deed; ~**machen** vt run down; etw ~ **machen** do sth badly; ~**weg** ad simply.

schlecken [ˈʃlɛkən] vti lick.

Schlegel [ˈʃleːgəl] m -**s,** - (drum)stick; (Hammer) mallet, hammer; (Cook) leg.

Schleie [ˈʃlaiə] f -, -n tench.

schleichen [ˈʃlaiçən] vi irreg creep, crawl; ~**d** a gradual; creeping.

Schleier [ˈʃlaiər] m -**s,** - veil; s~**haft** a (col) **jdm** s~**haft sein** to be a mystery to sb.

Schleif- [ˈʃlaif] cpd: ~**e** f -, -n loop; (Band) bow; s~**en** vt drag; (Mil) Festung raze; vi drag; vt irreg grind; Edelstein cut; (Mil) Soldaten drill; ~**stein** m grindstone.

Schleim [ʃlaim] m -**(e)s,** -e slime; (Med) mucus; (Cook) gruel; s~**ig** a slimy.

Schlemm- [ʃlɛm] cpd: s~**en** vi feast; ~**er** m -s, - gourmet; ~**e'rei** f gluttony, feasting.

schlendern [ˈʃlɛndərn] vi stroll.

Schlendrian [ˈʃlɛndriaːn] m -**(e)s** sloppy way of working.

schlenkern [ˈʃlɛŋkərn] vti swing, dangle.

Schlepp- [ˈʃlɛp] cpd: ~**e** f -, -n train; s~**en** vt drag; Auto, Schiff tow; (tragen) lug; s~**end** a dragging, slow; ~**er** m -s, - tractor; (Schiff) tug; ~**tau** nt towrope; **jdn ins** ~**tau nehmen** (fig) take sb in tow.

Schleuder [ˈʃlɔydər] f -, -n catapult; (Wäsche—) spin-drier; (Butter— etc) centrifuge; s~**n** vt hurl; Wäsche spin-dry; vi (Aut) skid; ~**preis** m give-away price; ~**sitz** m (Aviat) ejector seat; (fig) hot seat; ~**ware** f cheap or cut-price goods pl.

schleunig [ˈʃlɔyniç] a quick, prompt; ~**st** ad straight away.

Schleuse [ˈʃlɔyzə] f -, -n lock; (—ntor) sluice.

Schlich [ʃliç] m -**(e)s,** -e dodge, trick.

schlicht [ʃliçt] a simple, plain; ~**en** vt smooth, dress; Streit settle; S~**er** m -s, - mediator, arbitrator; S~**ung** f settlement; arbitration.

Schlick [ʃlik] m -**(e)s,** -e mud; (Öl—) slick.

Schließ- [ˈʃliːs] cpd: ~**e** f -, -n fastener; s~**en** irreg vtir close, shut; (beenden) close; Freundschaft, Bündnis, Ehe enter into; (folgern) infer (aus +dat from); **etw in sich** s~**en** include sth; ~**fach** nt locker; s~**lich** ad finally; (—doch) after all.

Schliff [ʃlif] m -**(e)s,** -e cut(ting); (fig) polish.

schlimm [ʃlim] a bad; ~**er** a worse; ~**ste(r,s)** a worst; ~**stenfalls** ad at (the) worst.

Schling- [ˈʃliŋ] cpd: ~**e** f -, -n loop; (esp Henkers—) noose; (Falle) snare; (Med) sling; ~**el** m -s, - rascal; s~**en** irreg vt wind; vti (essen) bolt (one's food), gobble; s~**ern** vi roll.

Schlips [ʃlips] m -**es,** -e tie.

Schlitten [ˈʃlitən] m -**s,** - sledge, sleigh; ~**bahn** f toboggan run; ~**fahren** nt -s tobogganing.

schlittern [ˈʃlitərn] vi slide.

Schlittschuh [ˈʃlit-ʃuː] m skate; ~ **laufen** skate; ~**bahn** f skating rink; ~**läufer(in** f) m skater.

Schlitz [ʃlits] m -**es,** -e slit; (für Münze)

slot; (Hosen—) flies pl; s~äugig a slant-eyed; s~en vt slit.

schlohweiß [ˈʃloːvaɪs] a snow-white.

Schloß [ʃlɔs] nt -sses, ¨sser lock; (an Schmuck etc) clasp; (Bau) castle; chateau.

Schlosser [ˈʃlɔsər] m -s, - (Auto—) fitter; (für Schlüssel etc) locksmith; ~ei [-ˈraɪ] f metal (working) shop.

Schlot [ˈʃloːt] m -(e)s, -e chimney; (Naut) funnel.

schlottern [ˈʃlɔtərn] vi shake, tremble; (Kleidung) be baggy.

Schlucht [ʃluxt] f -, -en gorge, ravine.

schluchzen [ˈʃluxtsən] vi sob.

Schluck [ʃluk] m -(e)s, -e swallow; (Menge) drop; ~auf m -s, ~en m -s, -hiccups pl; s~en vti swallow.

schludern [ˈʃluːdərn] vi skimp, do sloppy work.

Schlummer [ˈʃlumər] m -s slumber; s~n vi slumber.

Schlund [ʃlunt] m -(e)s, ¨e gullet; (fig) jaw.

schlüpfen [ˈʃlʏpfən] vi slip; (Vogel etc) hatch (out).

Schlüpfer [ˈʃlʏpfər] m -s, - panties pl, knickers pl.

Schlupfloch [ˈʃlupflɔx] nt hole; hide-out; (fig) loophole.

schlüpfrig [ˈʃlʏpfrɪç] a slippery; (fig) lewd; S~keit f slipperiness; (fig) lewdness.

schlürfen [ˈʃlʊrfən] vti shuffle.

schlürfen [ˈʃlʏrfən] vti slurp.

Schluß [ʃlus] m -sses, ¨sse end; (—folgerung) conclusion; am ~ at the end; ~ machen mit finish with.

Schlüssel [ˈʃlʏsəl] m -s, - (lit, fig) key; (Schraub—) spanner, wrench; (Mus) clef; ~bein nt collarbone; ~blume f cowslip, primrose; ~bund m bunch of keys; ~kind nt latchkey child; ~loch nt keyhole; ~position f key position; ~wort f combination.

schlüssig [ˈʃlʏsɪç] a conclusive.

Schluß- cpd: ~licht nt taillight; (fig) tailender; ~strich m (fig) final stroke; ~verkauf m clearance sale; ~wort nt concluding words pl.

Schmach [ʃmaːx] f - disgrace, ignominy.

schmachten [ˈʃmaːxtən] vi languish; long (nach for).

schmächtig [ˈʃmɛçtɪç] a slight.

schmachvoll a ignominious, humiliating.

schmackhaft [ˈʃmakhaft] a tasty.

schmäh- [ʃmɛː] cpd: ~en vt abuse, revile; ~lich a ignominious, shameful; S~ung f abuse.

schmal [ʃmaːl] a narrow; Person, Buch etc slender, slim; (karg) meagre.

schmälern [ˈʃmɛːlərn] vt diminish; (fig) belittle.

Schmal- cpd: ~film m cine film; ~spur f narrow gauge.

Schmalz [ʃmalts] nt -es, -e dripping, lard; (fig) sentiment, schmaltz; s~ig a (fig) schmaltzy, slushy.

schmarotzen [ʃmaˈrɔtsən] vi sponge; (Bot) be parasitic.

Schmarotzer m -s, - parasite; sponger.

Schmarren [ˈʃmarən] m -s, - (Aus) small

piece of pancake; (fig) rubbish, tripe.

schmatzen [ˈʃmatsən] vi smack one's lips; eat noisily.

Schmaus [ʃmaus] m -es, Schmäuse feast; s~en vi feast.

schmecken [ˈʃmɛkən] vti taste; es schmeckt ihm he likes it.

Schmeichel- [ˈʃmaɪçəl] cpd: ~ei [-ˈlaɪ] f flattery; s~haft a flattering; s~n vi flatter.

schmeißen [ˈʃmaɪsən] vt irreg (col) throw, chuck.

Schmeißfliege f bluebottle.

Schmelz [ʃmɛlts] m -es, -e enamel; (Glasur) glaze; (von Stimme) melodiousness; s~bar a fusible; s~en vti irreg melt; Erz smelt; ~hütte f smelting works pl; ~punkt m melting point; ~wasser nt melted snow.

Schmerz [ʃmɛrts] m -es, -en pain; (Trauer) grief; s~empfindlich a sensitive to pain; s~en vti hurt; ~ensgeld nt compensation; s~haft, s~lich a painful; s~los a painless; s~stillend a soothing.

Schmetterling [ˈʃmɛtərlɪŋ] m butterfly.

schmettern [ˈʃmɛtərn] vti smash; Melodie sing loudly, bellow out; (Trompete) blare.

Schmied [ʃmiːt] m -(e)s, -e blacksmith; ~e [ˈʃmiːdə] f -, -n smithy, forge; ~eeisen nt wrought iron; s~en vt forge; Pläne devise, concoct.

schmiegen [ˈʃmiːgən] vt press, nestle; vr cling, nestle (up) (an +acc to).

schmiegsam [ˈʃmiːkzaːm] a flexible, pliable.

Schmier- [ˈʃmiːr] cpd: ~e f -, -n grease; (Theat) greasepaint, make-up; s~en vt smear; (ölen) lubricate, grease; (bestechen) bribe; vti (schreiben) scrawl; ~fett nt grease; ~fink m messy person; ~geld nt bribe; s~ig a greasy; ~mittel nt lubricant; ~seife f soft soap.

Schminke [ˈʃmɪŋkə] f -, -n make-up; s~n vtr make up.

schmirgel- [ˈʃmɪrgəl] cpd: ~n vt sand (down); S~papier nt emery paper.

Schmöker [ˈʃmøːkər] m -s, - (col) (trashy) old book; s~n vi (col) browse.

schmollen [ˈʃmɔlən] vi sulk, pout; ~d a sulky.

Schmor- [ˈʃmoːr] cpd: ~braten m stewed or braised meat; s~en vt stew, braise.

Schmuck [ʃmuk] m -(e)s, -e jewellery; (Verzierung) decoration.

schmücken [ˈʃmʏkən] vt decorate.

Schmuck- cpd: s~los a unadorned, plain; ~losigkeit f simplicity; ~sachen pl jewels pl, jewellery.

Schmuggel [ˈʃmugəl] m -s smuggling; s~n vti smuggle.

Schmuggler m -s, - smuggler.

schmunzeln [ˈʃmuntsəln] vi smile benignly.

Schmutz [ʃmuts] m -es dirt, filth; s~en vi get dirty; ~fink m filthy creature; ~fleck m stain; s~ig a dirty.

Schnabel [ˈʃnaːbəl] m -s, ¨ beak, bill; (Ausguß) spout.

Schnake [ˈʃnaːkə] f -, -n cranefly; (Stechmücke) gnat.

Schnalle ['ʃnalə] f -, -n buckle, clasp; s~n vt buckle.

schnalzen ['ʃnaltsən] vi snap; (mit Zunge) click.

Schnapp- ['ʃnap] cpd: s~en vt grab, catch; vi snap; ~schloß nt spring lock; ~schuß m (Phot) snapshot.

Schnaps [ʃnaps] m -es, ⁓e spirits pl; schnapps.

schnarchen ['ʃnarçən] vi snore.

schnattern ['ʃnatərn] vi chatter; (zittern) shiver.

schnauben ['ʃnaubən] vi snort; vr blow one's nose.

schnaufen ['ʃnaufən] vi puff, pant.

Schnauz- ['ʃnauts] cpd: ~bart m moustache; ⁓e f -, -n snout, muzzle; (Ausguß) spout; (col) gob.

Schnecke ['ʃnɛkə] f -, -n snail; ~nhaus nt snail's shell.

Schnee ['ʃneː] m -s snow; (Ei—) beaten egg white; ~ball m snowball; ~flocke f snowflake; ~gestöber nt snowstorm; ~glöckchen nt snowdrop; ~kette f (Aut) (snow) chain; ~pflug m snowplough; ~schmelze f -, -n thaw; ~wehe f snowdrift; ~wittchen nt Snow White.

Schneid [ʃnait] m -(e)s (col) pluck; ⁓e f ['ʃnaidə] f -, -n edge; (Klinge) blade; s~en vtr irreg cut (o.s.); (kreuzen) cross, intersect; s~end a cutting; ~er m -s, - tailor; ~erin f dressmaker; s~ern vt make; vi be a tailor; ~ezahn m incisor; s~ig a dashing; (mutig) plucky.

schneien ['ʃnaiən] vi snow.

Schneise ['ʃnaizə] f -, -n clearing.

schnell [ʃnɛl] a,ad quick(ly), fast; ~en vi shoot, fly; S~hefter m -s, - loose-leaf binder; S~igkeit f speed; ~stens ad as quickly as possible; S~straße f expressway; S~zug m fast or express train.

schneuzen ['ʃnɔytsən] vr blow one's nose.

schnippisch ['ʃnɪpɪʃ] a sharp-tongued.

Schnitt [ʃnɪt] m -(e)s, -e cut(ting); (—punkt) intersection; (Quer—) (cross) section; (Durch—) average; (—muster) pattern; (Ernte) crop; (an Buch) edge; (col: Gewinn) profit; ~blumen pl cut flowers pl; ⁓e f -, -n slice; (belegt) sandwich; ~fläche f section; ~lauch m chive; ~muster nt pattern; ~punkt m (point of) intersection; ~wunde f cut.

Schnitz- ['ʃnɪts] cpd: ~arbeit f wood carving; ~el nt -s, - chip; (Cook) escalope; s~en vt carve; ~er m -s, - carver; (col) blunder; ~e'rei f carving; carved woodwork.

schnodderig ['ʃnɔdərɪç] a (col) snotty.

schnöde ['ʃnøːdə] a base, mean.

Schnorchel ['ʃnɔrçəl] m -s, - snorkel.

Schnörkel ['ʃnœrkəl] m -s, - flourish; (Archit) scroll.

schnorren ['ʃnɔrən] vti cadge.

schnüffeln ['ʃnʏfəln] vi sniff.

Schnüffler m -s, - snooper.

Schnuller ['ʃnulər] m -s, - dummy, comforter (US).

Schnupfen ['ʃnupfən] m -s, - cold.

schnuppern ['ʃnupərn] vi sniff.

Schnur [ʃnuːr] f -, ⁓e string, cord; (Elec)

flex; s~gerade a straight (as a die or arrow).

schnüren ['ʃnyːrən] vt tie.

Schnurr- ['ʃnur] cpd: ~bart m moustache; s~en vi purr; (Kreisel) hum.

Schnür- ['ʃnyːr] cpd: ~schuh m lace-up (shoe); ~senkel m shoelace.

schnurstracks ad straight (away).

Schock [ʃɔk] m -(e)s, -e shock; s~ieren [ʃɔˈkiːrən] vt shock, outrage.

Schöffe ['ʃœfə] m -n, -n lay magistrate; ~ngericht nt magistrates' court.

Schöffin f lay magistrate.

Schokolade [ʃokoˈlaːdə] f -, -n chocolate.

Scholle ['ʃɔlə] f -, -n clod; (Eis—) ice floe; (Fisch) plaice.

schon [ʃoːn] ad already; (zwar) certainly; warst du ~ einmal da? have you ever been there?; ich war ~ einmal da I've been there before; das ist ~ immer so that has always been the case; das wird ~ (noch) gut that'll be OK; wenn ich das ~ höre . . . I only have to hear that . . ⁓ ~ der Gedanke the very thought.

schön [ʃøːn] a beautiful; (nett) nice; ~e Grüße best wishes; ~en Dank (many) thanks.

schonen ['ʃoːnən] vt look after; vr take it easy; ~d a careful, gentle.

Schön- cpd: ~geist m cultured person, aesthete; ~heit f beauty; ~heitsfehler m blemish, flaw; ~heitsoperation f cosmetic plastic surgery; s~machen vr make oneself look nice.

Schon- cpd: ~ung f good care; (Nachsicht) consideration; (Forst) plantation of young trees; s~ungslos a unsparing, harsh; ~zeit f close season.

Schöpf- ['ʃœpf] cpd: s~en vt scoop, ladle; (Mut) summon up; (Luft) breath in; ~er m -s, - creator; s~erisch a creative; ~kelle f ladle; ~löffel m skimmer, scoop; ~ung f creation.

Schorf ['ʃɔrf] m -(e)s, -e scab.

Schornstein ['ʃɔrnʃtain] m chimney; (Naut) funnel; ~feger m -s, - chimney sweep.

Schoß [ʃoːs] m -es, ⁓e lap; (Rock—) coat tail; ~hund m pet dog, lapdog.

Schote ['ʃoːtə] f -, -n pod.

Schotter ['ʃɔtər] m -s broken stone, road metal; (Rail) ballast.

schraffieren [ʃraˈfiːrən] vt hatch.

schräg [ʃrɛːk] a slanting, not straight; etw ~ stellen put sth at an angle; ~gegenüber diagonally opposite; S~e f -, -n slant; ~schrift f italics pl; S~streifen m bias binding; S~strich m oblique stroke.

Schramme ['ʃramə] f -, -n scratch; s~n vt scratch.

Schrank [ʃrank] m -(e)s, ⁓e cupboard; (Kleider—) wardrobe; ⁓e f -, -n barrier; s~enlos a boundless; (zügellos) unrestrained; ~enwärter m (Rail) level crossing attendant; ~koffer m trunk.

Schraube ['ʃraubə] f -, -n screw; s~n vt screw; ~nschlüssel m spanner; ~nzieher m -s, - screwdriver.

Schraubstock ['fraubftɔk] m (Tech) vice.
Schrebergarten ['fre:bərgartən] m allotment.

Schreck [frɛk] m -(e)s, -e, ~**en** m -s, - terror; fright; **s~en** vt frighten; scare; ~**gespenst** nt spectre, nightmare; **s~haft** a jumpy, easily frightened; **s~lich** a terrible, dreadful; ~**schuß** m shot fired in the air.

Schrei [frai] m -(e)s, -e scream; (Ruf) shout.

Schreib- ['fraib] cpd: ~**block** m writing pad; **s~en** vti irreg write; (buchstabieren) spell; ~**en** nt -s, - letter, communication; ~**er** m -s, - writer; (Büro~) clerk; **s~faul** a bad about writing letters; ~**fehler** m spelling mistake; ~**maschine** f typewriter; ~**papier** nt notepaper; ~**tisch** m desk; ~**ung** f spelling; ~**waren** pl stationery; ~**weise** f spelling; way of writing; ~**zeug** nt writing materials pl.

schreien ['fraiən] vti irreg scream; (rufen) shout; ~**d** a (fig) glaring; Farbe loud.

Schreiner ['frainər] m -s, - joiner; (Zimmermann) carpenter; (Möbel~) cabinetmaker; ~**ei** [-'rai] f joiner's workshop.

schreiten ['fraitən] vi irreg stride.

Schrift [frift] f -, -en writing; handwriting; (~art) script; (Gedrucktes) pamphlet, work; ~**deutsch** nt written German; ~**führer** m secretary; **s~lich** a written; ad in writing; ~**setzer** m compositor; ~**sprache** f written language; ~**steller(in** f) m -s, - writer; ~**stück** nt document.

schrill [fril] a shrill; ~**en** vi sound or ring shrilly.

Schritt [frit] m -(e)s, -e step; (Gangart) walk; (Tempo) pace; (von Hose) crutch; ~**macher** m -s, pacemaker; ~**(t)empo** nt: **im ~(t)empo** at a walking pace.

schroff [frɔf] a steep; (zackig) jagged; (fig) brusque; (ungeduldig) abrupt.

schröpfen ['frœpfən] vt (fig) fleece.

Schrot [fro:t] m or nt -(e)s, -e (Blei) (small) shot; (Getreide) coarsely ground grain, groats pl; ~**flinte** f shotgun.

Schrott [frɔt] m -(e)s, -e scrap metal; ~**haufen** m scrap heap; **s~reif** a ready for the scrap heap.

schrubben ['frubən] vt scrub.

Schrubber m -s, - scrubbing brush.

Schrulle ['frulə] f -, -n eccentricity, queer idea/habit.

schrumpfen ['frumpfən] vi shrink; (Apfel) shrivel.

Schub- ['fu:b] cpd: ~**fach** nt drawer; ~**karren** m wheelbarrow; ~**lade** f drawer.

schüchtern ['fʏçtərn] a shy; **S~heit** f shyness.

Schuft [fuft] m -(e)s, -e scoundrel; **s~en** vi (col) graft, slave away.

Schuh [fu:] m -(e)s, -e shoe; ~**band** nt shoelace; ~**creme** f shoe polish; ~**löffel** m shoehorn; ~**macher** m -s, - shoemaker.

Schul- ['fu:l] cpd: ~**aufgaben** pl homework; ~**besuch** m school attendance.

Schuld [fult] f -, -en guilt; (Fin) debt; (Verschulden) fault; **s~** a: **s~ sein** or **haben** be to blame (an +dat for); **er ist** or **hat s~** it's his fault; **jdm s~ geben** blame sb; **s~en** ['fuldən] vt owe; **s~enfrei** a free from debt; ~**gefühl** nt feeling of guilt; **s~ig** a guilty (an +dat of); (gebührend) due; **jdm etw s~ig sein** owe sb sth; **jdm etw s~ig bleiben** not provide sb with sth; **s~los** a innocent, without guilt; ~**ner** m -s, - debtor; ~**schein** m promissory note, IOU; ~**spruch** m verdict of guilty.

Schule ['fu:lə] f -, -n school; **s~n** vt train, school.

Schüler(in f) ['fy:lər(in)] m -s, - pupil.

Schul- ['fu:l] cpd: ~**ferien** pl school holidays pl; **s~frei** a: **s~freier Tag** holiday; **s~frei sein** be a holiday; ~**funk** m schools' broadcasts pl; ~**geld** nt school fees pl; ~**hof** m playground; ~**jahr** nt school year; ~**junge** m schoolboy; ~**mädchen** nt schoolgirl; **s~pflichtig** a of school age; ~**schiff** nt (Naut) training ship; ~**stunde** f period, lesson; ~**tasche** f satchel.

Schulter ['fultər] f -, -n shoulder; ~**blatt** nt shoulder blade; **s~n** vt shoulder.

Schul- cpd: ~**ung** f education, schooling; ~**wesen** nt educational system; ~**zeugnis** nt school report.

Schund [funt] m -(e)s trash, garbage; ~**roman** m trashy novel.

Schuppe ['fupə] f -, -n scale; pl (Haar~) dandruff; **s~n** vt scale; vr peel; ~**n** m -s, - shed.

schuppig ['fupiç] a scaly.

Schur [fu:r] f -, -en shearing.

Schür- ['fy:r] cpd: ~**eisen** nt poker; **s~en** vt rake; (fig) stir up; **s~fen** ['fʏrfən] vti scrape, scratch; (Min) prospect, dig; ~**fung** f abrasion; (Min) prospecting; ~**haken** m poker.

Schurke ['furkə] m -n, -n rogue.

Schurz [furts] m -es, -e, **Schürze** ['fʏrtsə] f -, -n apron.

Schuß [fus] m -sses, ²sse shot; (Weben) woof; ~**bereich** m effective range.

Schüssel ['fʏsəl] f -, -n bowl.

Schuß- cpd: ~**linie** f line of fire; ~**verletzung** f bullet wound; ~**waffe** f firearm; ~**weite** f range (of fire).

Schuster ['fu:stər] m -s, - cobbler, shoemaker.

Schutt [fut] m -(e)s rubbish; (Bau~) rubble; ~**abladeplatz** m refuse dump.

Schütt- ['fʏt] cpd: ~**elfrost** m shivering; **s~eln** vtr shake; **s~en** vt pour; (Zucker, Kies etc) tip; (ver~) spill; vi impers pour (down); **s~er** a Haare sparse, thin.

Schutt- cpd: ~**halde** f dump; ~**haufen** m heap of rubble.

Schutz [futs] m protection; (Unterschlupf) shelter; **jdn in ~ nehmen** stand up for sb; ~**anzug** m overalls pl; ~**befohlene(r)** mf charge; ~**blech** nt mudguard; ~**brille** f goggles pl.

Schütze ['fʏtsə] m -n, -n gunman;

(Gewehr—) rifleman; (Scharf—, Sport—) marksman; (Astrol) Sagittarius.

Schutz- cpd: ~**engel** m guardian angel; ~**gebiet** nt protectorate; (Natur—) reserve; ~**haft** f protective custody; ~**impfung** f immunisation; **s~los** a defenceless; ~**mann** m, pl -**leute** or -**männer** policeman; ~**maßnahme** f precaution; ~**patron** m patron saint; ~**umschlag** m (book) jacket; ~**vorrichtung** f safety device.

schwach [ʃvax] a weak, feeble.

Schwäche [ˈʃvɛçə] f -, -n weakness; **s~n** vt weaken.

Schwach- cpd: ~**heit** f weakness; **s~köpfig** a silly, lame-brained.

Schwäch- cpd: **s~lich** a weakly, delicate; ~**ling** m weakling.

Schwach- cpd: ~**sinn** m imbecility; **s~sinnig** a mentally deficient; Idee idiotic; ~**strom** m weak current.

Schwächung [ˈʃvɛçʊŋ] f weakening.

Schwaden [ˈʃvaːdən] m -s, - cloud.

schwafeln [ˈʃvaːfəln] vti blather, drivel.

Schwager [ˈʃvaːgər] m -s, ⸚ brother-in-law.

Schwägerin [ˈʃvɛːgərɪn] f sister-law.

Schwalbe [ˈʃvalbə] f -, -n swallow.

Schwall [ʃval] m -(e)s, -e surge; (Worte) flood, torrent.

Schwamm [ʃvam] m -(e)s, -e sponge; (Pilz) fungus; **s~ig** a spongy; Gesicht puffy.

Schwan [ʃvaːn] m -(e)s, -e swan; **s~en** vi impers: **jdm schwant etw** sb has a foreboding of sth.

schwanger [ˈʃvaŋər] a pregnant.

schwängern [ˈʃvɛŋərn] vt make pregnant.

Schwangerschaft f pregnancy.

Schwank [ʃvaŋk] m -(e)s, -e funny story; **s~en** vi sway; (taumeln) stagger, reel; (Preise, Zahlen) fluctuate; (zögern) hesitate, vacillate; ~**ung** f fluctuation.

Schwanz [ʃvants] m -es, -e tail.

schwänzen [ˈʃvɛntsən] (col) vt skip, cut; vi play truant.

Schwänzer [ˈʃvɛntsər] m -s, - (col) truant.

Schwarm [ʃvarm] m -(e)s, -e swarm; (col) heart-throb, idol.

schwärm- [ˈʃvɛrm] cpd: ~**en** vi swarm; ~**en für** be mad or wild about; **S~erei** f [-ˈraɪ] f enthusiasm; ~**erisch** a impassioned, effusive.

Schwarte [ˈʃvaːrtə] f -, -n hard skin; (Speck—) rind.

schwarz [ʃvarts] a black; **ins S~e treffen** (lit, fig) hit the bull's eye; **S~arbeit** f illicit work, moonlighting; **S~brot** nt black bread.

Schwärze [ˈʃvɛrtsə] f -, -n blackness; (Farbe) blacking; (Drucker—) printer's ink; **s~n** vt blacken.

Schwarz- cpd: **s~fahren** vi irreg travel without paying; drive without a licence; ~**handel** m black-market (trade); **s~hören** vi listen to the radio without a licence.

schwärzlich [ˈʃvɛrtslɪç] a blackish, darkish.

Schwarz- cpd: ~**markt** m black market; **s~sehen** vi irreg (col) see the gloomy side

of things; (TV) watch TV without a licence; ~**seher** m pessimist; (TV) viewer without a licence; **s~weiß** a black and white.

schwatzen [ˈʃvatsən], **schwätzen** [ˈʃvɛtsən] vi chatter.

Schwätzer [ˈʃvɛtsər] m -s, - gasbag; ~**in** f chatterbox, gossip.

schwatzhaft a talkative, gossipy.

Schwebe [ˈʃveːbə] f: **in der ~** (fig) in abeyance; ~**bahn** f overhead railway; ~**balken** m (Sport) beam; **s~n** vi drift, float; (hoch) soar; (unentschieden sein) be in the balance.

Schwefel [ˈʃveːfəl] m -s sulphur; **s~ig** a sulphurous; ~**säure** f sulphuric acid.

Schweif [ʃvaɪf] m -(e)s, -e tail; **s~en** vi wander, roam.

Schweig- [ˈʃvaɪg] cpd: ~**egeld** nt hush money; **s~en** vi irreg be silent; stop talking; ~**en** nt -s silence; **s~sam** [ˈʃvaɪkzaːm] a silent, taciturn; ~**samkeit** f taciturnity, quietness.

Schwein [ʃvaɪn] nt -(e)s, -e pig; (fig) (good) luck; ~**efleisch** nt pork; ~**ehund** m (col) stinker, swine; ~**erei** [-əˈraɪ] f mess; (Gemeinheit) dirty trick; ~**estall** m pigsty; **s~isch** a filthy; ~**sleder** nt pigskin.

Schweiß [ʃvaɪs] m -es sweat, perspiration; **s~en** vti weld; ~**er** m -s, - welder; ~**füße** pl sweaty feet pl; ~**naht** f weld.

schwelen [ˈʃveːlən] vi smoulder.

schwelgen [ˈʃvɛlgən] vi indulge.

Schwelle [ˈʃvɛlə] f -, -n threshold (auch fig); doorstep; (Rail) sleeper; **s~n** vi irreg swell.

Schwellung f swelling.

Schwengel [ˈʃvɛŋəl] m -s, - pump handle; (Glocken-) clapper.

Schwenk- [ˈʃvɛŋk] cpd: **s~bar** a swivel-mounted; **s~en** vt swing; Fahne wave; (abspülen) rinse; vi turn, swivel; (Mil) wheel; ~**ung** f turn; wheel.

schwer [ʃveːr] a heavy; (schwierig) difficult, hard; (schlimm) serious, bad; ad (sehr) very (much); verletzt etc seriously, badly; **S~arbeiter** m manual worker, labourer; **S~e** f -, -n weight, heaviness; (Phys) gravity; ~**elos** a weightless; Kammer zero-G; **S~enöter** m -s, - casanova, ladies' man; ~**erziehbar** a difficult (to bring up); ~**fallen** a irreg: **jdm ~fallen** be difficult for sb; ~**fällig** a ponderous; **S~gewicht** nt heavyweight; (fig) emphasis; ~**hörig** a hard of hearing; **S~industrie** f heavy industry; **S~kraft** f gravity; **S~kranke(r)** mf person who is seriously ill; ~**lich** ad hardly; ~**machen** vt: **jdm/sich etw ~machen** make sth difficult for sb/o.s.; **S~metall** nt heavy metal; ~**mütig** a melancholy; ~**nehmen** vt irreg take to heart; **S~punkt** m centre of gravity; (fig) emphasis, crucial point.

Schwert [ʃveːrt] nt -(e)s, -er sword; ~**lilie** f iris.

schwer- cpd: ~**tun** vi irreg: **sich** (dat or acc) ~**tun** have difficulties; **S~verbrecher(in** f) m criminal, serious offender; ~**verdaulich** a indigestible,

heavy; ~**verletzt** a badly injured;
~**verwundet** a seriously wounded;
~**wiegend** a weighty, important.
Schwester ['ʃvɛstər] f -, -n sister; (Med)
nurse; s~**lich** a sisterly.
Schwieger- ['ʃvi:gər] cpd: ~**eltern** pl
parents-in-law pl; ~**mutter** f mother-in-
law; ~**sohn** m son-in-law; ~**tochter** f
daughter-in-law; ~**vater** m father-in-law.
Schwiele ['ʃvi:lə] f -, -n callus.
schwierig ['ʃvi:rɪç] a difficult, hard;
S~**keit** f difficulty.
Schwimm- ['ʃvɪm] cpd: ~**bad** nt
swimming baths pl; ~**becken** nt
swimming pool; s~**en** vi irreg swim;
(treiben, nicht sinken) float; (fig: unsicher
sein) be all at sea; ~**er** m -s, - swimmer;
(Angeln) float; ~**lehrer** m swimming
instructor; ~**sport** m swimming;
~**weste** f life jacket.
Schwindel ['ʃvɪndl] m -s giddiness; dizzy
spell; (Betrug) swindle, fraud; (Zeug) stuff;
s~**frei** a free from giddiness; s~**n** vi (col:
lügen) fib; **jdm schwindelt es** sb feels
giddy.
schwinden ['ʃvɪndən] vi irreg disappear;
(sich verringern) decrease; (Kräfte)
decline.
Schwind- ['ʃvɪnd] cpd: ~**ler** m -s, -
swindler; (Lügner) liar; s~**lig** a giddy; **mir
ist s~lig** I feel giddy.
Schwing- ['ʃvɪŋ] cpd: s~**en** vti irreg swing;
Waffe etc brandish; (vibrieren) vibrate;
(klingen) sound; ~**er** m -s, - (Boxen)
swing; ~**tür** f swing door(s); ~**ung** f
vibration; (Phys) oscillation.
Schwips [ʃvɪps] m -es, -e: **einen ~
haben** be tipsy.
schwirren ['ʃvɪrən] vi buzz.
schwitzen ['ʃvɪtsən] vi sweat, perspire.
schwören ['ʃvø:rən] vti irreg swear.
schwul [ʃvu:l] a (col) gay, queer.
schwül [ʃvy:l] a sultry, close; S~**e** f - -
sultriness, closeness.
Schwulst [ʃvʊlst] f -(e)s, ˙e bombast.
schwülstig ['ʃvʏlstɪç] a pompous.
Schwund [ʃvʊnt] m -(e)s loss;
(Schrumpfen) shrinkage.
Schwung [ʃvʊŋ] m -(e)s, ˙e swing;
(Triebkraft) momentum; (fig: Energie)
verve, energy; (col: Menge) batch; s~**haft**
a brisk, lively; ~**rad** nt flywheel; s~**voll**
a vigorous.
Schwur [ʃvu:r] m -(e)s, ˙e oath;
~**gericht** nt court with a jury.
sechs [zɛks] num six; ~**hundert** num six
hundred; ~**te(r,s)** a sixth; S~**tel** nt -s -
sixth.
sechzehn ['zɛçtse:n] num sixteen.
sechzig ['zɛçtsɪç] num sixty.
See [ze:] f -, -n sea; m -s, -n lake; ~**bad** nt
seaside resort; ~**fahrt** f seafaring; (Reise)
voyage; ~**gang** m (motion of the) sea;
~**gras** nt seaweed; ~**hund** m seal;
~**igel** [ze:'i:gəl] m sea urchin; s~**krank**
a seasick; ~**krankheit** f seasickness;
~**lachs** m rock salmon.
Seel- ['ze:l] cpd: ~**e** f -, -n soul;
~**enfriede(n)** m peace of mind;
s~**enruhig** ad calmly.

Seeleute ['ze:lɔytə] pl seamen pl.
Seel- cpd: s~**isch** a mental; ~**sorge** f
pastoral duties pl; ~**sorger** m -s, -
clergyman.
See- cpd: ~**macht** f naval power;
~**mann** m, pl -**leute** seaman, sailor;
~**meile** f nautical mile; ~**not** f distress;
~**pferd(chen)** nt sea horse; ~**räuber** m
pirate; ~**rose** f water lily; ~**stern** m
starfish; s~**tüchtig** a seaworthy; ~**weg**
m sea route; **auf dem ~weg** by sea;
~**zunge** f sole.
Segel ['ze:gəl] nt -s, - sail; ~**boot** nt yacht;
~**fliegen** nt -s gliding; ~**flieger** m
glider pilot; ~**flugzeug** nt glider; s~**n** vti
sail; ~**schiff** nt sailing vessel; ~**sport** m
sailing; ~**tuch** nt canvas.
Segen ['ze:gən] m -s, - blessing; s~**sreich**
a beneficial.
Segler ['ze:glər] m -s, - sailor, yachtsman;
(Boot) sailing boat.
segnen ['ze:gnən] vt bless.
Seh- [ze:] cpd: s~**en** vti irreg see; (in
bestimmte Richtung) look; s~**enswert** a
worth seeing; ~**enswürdigkeiten** pl
sights pl (of a town); ~**er** m -s, - seer;
~**fehler** m sight defect.
Sehn- ['ze:n] cpd: ~**e** f -, -n sinew; (an
Bogen) string; s~**en** vr long, yearn (nach
for); s~**ig** a sinewy; s~**lich** a ardent;
~**sucht** f longing; s~**süchtig** a longing.
sehr [ze:r] ad (vor a,ad) very; (mit Verben) a
lot, (very) much; **zu ~** too much.
seicht [zaɪçt] a (lit, fig) shallow.
Seide ['zaɪdə] f -, -n silk; ~**l** nt -s, -
tankard, beer mug; s~**n** a silk;
~**npapier** nt tissue paper.
seidig ['zaɪdɪç] a silky.
Seife ['zaɪfə] f -, -n soap; ~**nlauge** f soap-
suds pl; ~**nschale** f soap dish;
~**nschaum** m lather.
seifig ['zaɪfɪç] a soapy.
seihen ['zaɪən] vt strain, filter.
Seil [zaɪl] nt -(e)s, -e rope; cable; ~**bahn**
f cable railway; ~**hüpfen** nt -s,
~**springen** nt -s skipping; ~**tänzer(in** f)
m tightrope walker; ~**zug** m tackle.
sein [zaɪn] vi irreg be; **laß das ~!** leave
that!; stop that!; **es ist an dir, zu ...** it's
up to you to ...
sein [zaɪn] pron his; its; ~**e(r,s)** his; its;
~**er** pron gen of **er** of him; ~**erseits** ad
for his part; ~**erzeit** ad in those days,
formerly; ~**esgleichen** pron people like
him; ~**etwegen**, ~**etwillen** ad (für ihn)
for his sake; (wegen ihm) on his account;
(von ihm aus) as far as he is concerned;
~**ige** pron: **der/die/das ~** his.
Seismograph [zaɪsmo'gra:f] m -en, -**e**
seismograph.
seit [zaɪt] prep, cj since; **er ist ~ einer
Woche hier** he has been here for a week;
~ **langem** for a long time; ~**dem**
[zaɪt'de:m] ad,cj since.
Seite ['zaɪtə] f -, -n side; (Buch-) page; (Mil)
flank; ~**nansicht** f side view; ~**nhieb** m
(fig) passing shot, dig; ~**nruder** nt (Aviat)
rudder; s~**ns** prep +gen on the part of;
~**nschiff** nt aisle; ~**nsprung** m extramarital escapade; ~**nstechen** nt (a)

stitch; ~**straße** f side road; ~**nwagen** m sidecar; ~**nzahl** f page number; number of pages.

seit- cpd: ~**her** [zaɪt'heːr] ad,cj since (then); ~**lich** a on one or the side; side; ~**wärts** ad sidewards.

Sekretär [zekre'tɛːr] m secretary; (Möbel) bureau; ~**in** f secretary.

Sekretariat [zekretari'aːt] nt -(e)s, -e secretary's office, secretariat.

Sekt [zɛkt] m -(e)s, -e champagne; ~**e** f -, -n sect.

sekundär [zekʊn'dɛːr] a secondary.

Sekunde [ze'kʊndə] f -, -n second.

selber ['zɛlbər] = **selbst**.

selbst [zɛlpst] pron myself; itself; themselves etc; **von** ~ by itself etc; ad even; **S~** nt - self; **S~achtung** f self-respect; ~**ändig** ['zɛlpʃtɛndɪç] a independent; **S~ändigkeit** f independence; **S~auslöser** m (Phot) delayed-action shutter release; **S~bedienung** f self-service; **S~befriedigung** f masturbation; **S~beherrschung** f self-control; ~**bewußt** a (self-)confident; **S~bewußtsein** nt self-confidence; **S~erhaltung** f self-preservation; **S~erkenntnis** f self-knowledge; ~**gefällig** a smug, self-satisfied; ~**gemacht** a home-made; **S~gespräch** nt conversation with oneself; **S~kostenpreis** m cost price; ~**los** a unselfish, selfless; **S~mord** m suicide; **S~mörder(in** f) m suicide; ~**mörderisch** a suicidal; ~**sicher** a self-assured; ~**süchtig** a selfish; ~**tätig** a auto-matic; ~**verständlich** a obvious; ad naturally; **ich halte das für ~verständlich** I take that for granted; **S~vertrauen** nt self-confidence; **S~verwaltung** f autonomy, self-government; **S~zweck** m end in itself.

selig ['zeːlɪç] a happy, blissful; (Rel) blessed; (tot) late; **S~keit** f bliss.

Sellerie ['zɛləriː] m -s, -(s) or f -, -n celery.

selten ['zɛltən] a rare; ad seldom, rarely; **S~heit** f rarity.

Selterswasser ['zɛltərsvasər] nt soda water.

seltsam ['zɛltzaːm] a strange, curious; ~**erweise** ad curiously, strangely; **S~keit** f strangeness.

Semester [ze'mɛstər] nt -s, - semester.

Semi- [zemi] in cpds semi-; ~**kolon** ['koːlon] nt -s, -s semicolon; ~**nar** [-'naːr] nt -s, -e seminary; (Kurs) seminar; (Univ: Ort) department building.

Semmel ['zɛməl] f -, -n roll.

Senat [ze'naːt] m -(e)s, -e senate, council.

Sende- ['zɛndə] cpd: ~**bereich** m range of transmission; ~**folge** f (Serie) series; **s~n** vt irreg send; vti (Rad, TV) transmit, broadcast; ~**r** m -s, - station; (Anlage) transmitter; ~**reihe** f series (of broadcasts); ~**station** f, ~**stelle** f transmitting station.

Sendung ['zɛndʊŋ] f consignment; (Aufgabe) mission; (Rad, TV) transmission; (Programm) programme.

Senf [zɛnf] m -(e)s, -e mustard.

sengen ['zɛŋən] vt singe; vi scorch.

Senk- ['zɛŋk] cpd: ~**blei** nt plumb; ~**e** f -, -n depression; ~**el** m -s, - (shoe)lace; **s~en** vt lower; vr sink, drop gradually; ~**fuß** m flat foot; **s~recht** a vertical, perpendicular; ~**rechte** f -n, -n perpendicular; ~**rechtstarter** m (Aviat) vertical take-off plane; (fig) high-flier.

Sensation [zɛnzatsi'oːn] f sensation; **s~ell** [-'nɛl] a sensational; ~**ssucht** f sensationalism.

Sense ['zɛnzə] f -, -n scythe.

sensibel [zɛn'ziːbəl] a sensitive.

Sensibilität [zɛnzibili'tɛt] f sensitivity.

sentimental [zɛntimɛn'taːl] a sentimental; **S~ität** f sentimentality.

separat [zepa'raːt] a separate.

September [zɛp'ɛmbər] m -(s), - September.

septisch ['zɛptɪʃ] a septic.

Serie ['zeːriə] f series; ~**nherstellung** f mass production; **s~nweise** ad in series.

seriös [zeri'øːs] a serious, bona fide.

Serpentine [zɛrpɛn'tiːn(ə)] f hairpin (bend).

Serum ['zeːrʊm] nt -s, **Seren** serum.

Service [zɛr'viːs] nt -(s), - set, service; ['zøːrvɪs] m -, -s service.

servieren [zɛr'viːrən] vti serve.

Serviette [zɛrvi'ɛtə] f napkin, serviette.

Sessel ['zɛsəl] m -s, - armchair; ~**lift** m chairlift.

seßhaft ['zɛshaft] a settled; (ansässig) resident.

Sets [zɛts] pl tablemats pl.

setzen ['zɛtsən] vt put, set; Baum etc plant; Segel, (Print) set; vr settle; (person) sit down; vi leap.

Setz- [zɛts] cpd: ~**er** m -s, - (Print) compositor; ~**e'rei** f caseroom; ~**ling** m young plant; ~**maschine** f (Print) typesetting machine.

Seuche ['zɔʏçə] f -, -n epidemic; ~**ngebiet** nt infected area.

seufzen ['zɔʏftsən] vti sigh.

Seufzer ['zɔʏftsər] m -s, - sigh.

Sex [zɛks] m -(es) sex; ~**ualität** [-uali'tɛt] f sex, sexuality; **s~uell** [-u'ɛl] a sexual.

Sexta ['zɛksta] f -, **Sexten** first year of secondary school.

sezieren [ze'tsiːrən] vt dissect.

sich [zɪç] pron himself; herself; itself; oneself; yourself; yourselves; themselves; each other.

Sichel ['zɪçəl] f -, -n sickle; (Mond—) crescent.

sicher ['zɪçər] a safe (vor +dat from); (gewiß) certain (+gen of); (zuverlässig) secure, reliable; (selbst—) confident; ~**gehen** vi irreg make sure.

Sicherheit ['zɪçərhaɪt] f safety; security (auch Fin); (Gewißheit) certainty; (Selbst—) confidence; ~**sabstand** m safe distance; ~**sglas** nt safety glass; **s~shalber** ad for safety; to be on the safe side; ~**snadel** f safety pin; ~**sschloß** nt safety lock; ~**sverschluß** m safety clasp; ~**svorkehrung** f safety precaution.

sicher- cpd: ~**lich** ad certainly, surely; ~**n** vt secure; (schützen) protect; Waffe put the safety catch on; **jdm/sich etw ~n** secure sth for sb/(for o.s.); ~**stellen** vt impound; **S~ung** f (Sichern) securing; (Vorrichtung) safety device; (an Waffen) safety catch; (Elec) fuse.

Sicht [zɪçt] f - sight; (Aus—) view; **auf** or **nach ~** (Fin) at sight; **auf lange ~** on a long-term basis; s~**bar** a visible; ~**barkeit** f visibility; s~**en** vt sight; (auswählen) sort out; s~**lich** a evident, obvious; ~**verhältnisse** pl visibility; ~**vermerk** m visa; ~**weite** f visibility.

sickern [ˈzɪkərn] vi trickle, seep.

Sie [ziː] pron sing, pl, nom, acc you.

sie [ziː] pron sing nom she; acc her; pl nom they; acc them.

Sieb [ziːp] nt -(e)s, -e sieve; (Cook) strainer; s~**en** [ˈziːbən] vt sift; Flüssigkeit strain.

sieben [ˈziːbən] num seven; ~**hundert** num seven hundred; **S~sachen** pl belongings pl.

siebte(r,s) [ˈziːptə(r,z)] a seventh; **S~l** nt -s, - seventh.

siebzehn [ˈziːptseːn] num seventeen.

siebzig [ˈziːptsɪç] num seventy.

sied- [ziːd] cpd: ~**eln** vi settle; ~**en** vti boil, simmer; **S~epunkt** m boiling point; **S~ler** m -s, - settler; **S~lung** f settlement; (Häuser—) housing estate.

Sieg [ziːk] m -(e)s, -e victory; ~**el** [ˈziːgəl] nt -s, - seal; ~**ellack** m sealing wax; ~**elring** m signet ring; s~**en** vi be victorious; (Sport) win; ~**er** m -s, - victor; (Sport etc) winner; s~**essicher** a sure of victory; ~**eszug** m triumphal procession; s~**reich** a victorious.

siehe [ziːə] (Imperativ) see; (— da) behold.

siezen [ˈziːtsən] vt address as 'Sie'.

Signal [zɪˈgnaːl] nt -s, -e signal.

Signatur [zɪgnaˈtuːr] f signature.

Silbe [ˈzɪlbə] f -, -n syllable.

Silber [ˈzɪlbər] nt -s silver; ~**bergwerk** nt silver mine; ~**blick** m: **einen ~blick haben** have a slight squint; s~**n** a silver; ~**papier** nt silver paper.

Silhouette [zɪluˈɛtə] f silhouette.

Silo [ˈziːlo] nt or m -s, -s silo.

Silvester(abend m) [zɪlˈvɛstər(aːbənt)] nt -s, - New Year's Eve, Hogmanay (Scot).

simpel [ˈzɪmpəl] a simple; **S~** m -s, - (col) simpleton.

Sims [zɪms] nt or m -es, -e (Kamin—) mantlepiece; (Fenster—) (window)sill.

simulieren [zimuˈliːrən] vti simulate; (vortäuschen) feign.

simultan [zimʊlˈtaːn] a simultaneous.

Sinfonie [zɪnfoˈniː] f symphony.

singen [ˈzɪŋən] vti irreg sing.

Singular [ˈzɪŋgulaːr] m singular.

Singvogel [ˈzɪŋfoːgəl] m songbird.

sinken [ˈzɪŋkən] vi irreg sink; (Preise etc) fall, go down.

Sinn [zɪn] m -(e)s, -e mind; (Wahrnehmungs—) sense; (Bedeutung) sense, meaning; ~ **für etw** sense of sth; **von ~en sein** be out of one's mind;

~**bild** nt symbol; s~**bildlich** a symbolic; s~**en** vi irreg ponder; **auf etw** (acc) s~**en** contemplate sth; ~**enmensch** m sensualist; ~**estäuschung** f illusion; s~**gemäß** a faithful; Wiedergabe in one's own words; s~**ig** a clever; s~**lich** a sensual, sensuous; Wahrnehmung sensory; ~**lichkeit** f sensuality; s~**los** a senseless; meaningless; ~**losigkeit** f senselessness; meaninglessness; s~**voll** a meaningful; (vernünftig) sensible.

Sintflut [ˈzɪntfluːt] f Flood.

Sinus [ˈziːnʊs] m -, - or -**se** (Anat) sinus; (Math) sine.

Siphon [ziˈfõː] m -s, -s siphon.

Sippe [ˈzɪpə] f -, -n clan, kin.

Sippschaft [ˈzɪpʃaft] f (pej) relations pl, tribe; (Bande) gang.

Sirene [ziˈreːnə] f -, -n siren.

Sirup [ˈziːrʊp] m -s, -e syrup.

Sitt- [zɪt] cpd: ~**e** f -, -n custom; pl morals pl; ~**enpolizei** f vice squad; s~**lich** a moral; ~**lichkeit** f morality; ~**lichkeitsverbrechen** nt sex offence; s~**sam** a modest, demure.

Situation [zituatsiˈoːn] f situation.

Sitz [zɪts] m -es, -e seat; **der Anzug hat einen guten ~** the suit is a good fit; s~**en** vi irreg sit; (Bemerkung, Schlag) strike home, tell; (Gelerntes) have sunk in; s~**en bleiben** remain seated; s~**enbleiben** vi irreg (Sch) have to repeat a year; **auf etw** (dat) s~**enbleiben** be lumbered with sth; s~**end** a Tätigkeit sedentary; s~**enlassen** vt irreg (Sch) make (sb) repeat a year; Mädchen jilt; Wartenden stand up; **etw auf sich** (dat) s~**enlassen** take sth lying down; ~**gelegenheit** f place to sit down; ~**platz** m seat; ~**streik** m sit-down strike; ~**ung** f meeting.

Skala [ˈskaːla] f -, Skalen scale.

Skalpell [skalˈpɛl] nt -s, -e scalpel.

Skandal [skanˈdaːl] m -s, -e scandal; s~**ös** [skandaˈløːs] a scandalous.

Skelett [skeˈlɛt] nt -(e)s, -e skeleton.

Skepsis [ˈskɛpsɪs] f - scepticism.

skeptisch [ˈskɛptɪʃ] a sceptical.

Ski, Schi [ʃiː] m -s, -er ski; ~ **laufen** or **fahren** ski; ~**fahrer** m, ~**läufer** m skier; ~**lehrer** m ski instructor; ~**lift** m ski-lift; ~**springen** nt ski-jumping.

Skizze [ˈskɪtsə] f -, -n sketch.

skizzieren [skɪˈtsiːrən] vti sketch.

Sklave [ˈsklaːvə] m -n, -n, **Sklavin** f slave; ~**rei** f slavery.

Skonto [ˈskɔnto] m or nt -s, -s discount.

Skorpion [skɔrpiˈoːn] m -s, -e scorpion; (Astrol) Scorpio.

Skrupel [ˈskruːpəl] m -s, - scruple; s~**los** a unscrupulous.

Slalom [ˈslaːlɔm] m -s, -s slalom.

Smaragd [smaˈrakt] m -(e)s, -e emerald.

Smoking [ˈsmoːkɪŋ] m -s, -s dinner jacket.

so [zoː] ad so; (auf diese Weise) like this; (etwa) roughly; ~ **ein** such a; ~, **das ist fertig** well, that's finished; ~ **etwas!** well, well!; ~.. **wie**... as... as...; ~ **daß** so that, with the result that; cj so; (vor a) as.

Socke ['zɔkə] f -, -n sock.

Sockel ['zɔkəl] m -s, - pedestal, base.

Sodawasser ['zo:davasər] nt soda water.

Sodbrennen ['zo:tbrɛnən] nt -s, - heartburn.

soeben [zo''e:bən] ad just (now).

Sofa ['zo:fa] nt -s, -s sofa.

sofern [zo'fɛrn] cj if, provided (that).

sofort [zo'fɔrt] ad immediately, at once; ~ig a immediate.

Sog [zo:k] m -(e)s, -e suction.

so- cpd: ~**gar** [zo'ga:r] ad even; ~**genannt** ['zo:gənant] a so-called; ~**gleich** [zo'glaiç] ad straight away, at once.

Sohle ['zo:lə] f -, -n sole; (Tal- etc) bottom; (Min) level.

Sohn [zo:n] m -(e)s, ⁻e son.

solang(e) [zo'laŋ(ə)] cj as or so long as.

Solbad ['zo:lba:t] nt saltwater bath.

solch [zɔlç] pron such; **ein** ~**e(r,s)** ... such a ...

Sold [zɔlt] m -(e)s, -e pay; ~**at** [zɔl'da:t] m -en, -en soldier; s~**atisch** a soldierly.

Söldner ['zœldnər] m -s, - mercenary.

solid(e) [zo'li:d(ə)] a solid; Leben, Person staid, respectable; ~**arisch** [zoli'da:rɪʃ] a in/with solidarity; **sich** ~**arisch erklären** declare one's solidarity.

Solist(in f) [zo'lɪst(ɪn)] m soloist.

Soll [zɔl] nt -(s), -(s) (Fin) debit (side); (Arbeitsmenge) quota, target.

sollen ['zɔlən] vi be supposed to; (Verpflichtung) shall, ought to; **du hättest nicht gehen** ~ you shouldn't have gone; **soll ich?** shall I?; **was soll das?** what's that supposed to mean?

Solo ['zo:lo] nt -s, -s or **Soli** solo.

somit [zo'mɪt] cj and so, therefore.

Sommer ['zɔmər] m -s, - summer; s~**lich** a summery; summer; ~**sprossen** pl freckles pl.

Sonate [zo'na:tə] f -, -n sonata.

Sonde ['zɔndə] f -, -n probe.

Sonder- ['zɔndər] in cpds special; ~**angebot** nt special offer; s~**bar** a strange, odd; ~**fahrt** f special trip; ~**fall** m special case; s~**gleichen** a inv without parallel, unparalleled; s~**lich** a particular; (außergewöhnlich) remarkable; (eigenartig) peculiar; ~**ling** m eccentric; s~**n** cj but; **nicht nur ..., s~n auch** not only ..., but also; vt separate; ~**zug** m special train.

sondieren [zɔn'di:rən] vt suss out; Gelände scout out.

Sonett [zo'nɛt] nt -(e)s, -e sonnet.

Sonnabend ['zɔn'a:bənt] m Saturday.

Sonne ['zɔnə] f -, -n sun; s~**n** vt put out in the sun; vr sun oneself; ~**naufgang** m sunrise; s~**nbaden** vi sunbathe; ~**nbrand** m sunburn; ~**nbrille** f sunglasses pl; ~**nfinsternis** f solar eclipse; ~**nschein** m sunshine; ~**nschirm** m parasol, sunshade; ~**nstich** m sunstroke; ~**nuhr** f sundial; ~**nuntergang** m sunset; ~**nwende** f solstice.

sonnig ['zɔnɪç] a sunny.

Sonntag ['zɔnta:k] m Sunday; s~**s** ad (on) Sundays.

sonst [zɔnst] ad otherwise (auch cj); (mit pron, in Fragen) else; (zu anderer Zeit) at other times, normally; ~ **noch etwas?** anything else?; ~ **nichts** nothing else; ~**ig** a other; ~**jemand** pron anybody (at all); ~**wo(hin)** ad somewhere else; ~**woher** ad from somewhere else.

sooft [zo''ɔft] cj whenever.

Sopran [zo'pra:n] m -s, -e soprano; ~**istin** [zopra'nɪstɪn] f soprano.

Sorge ['zɔrgə] f -, -n care, worry; s~**n** vi: **für jdn** s~**n** look after sb; **für etw** s~**n** take care of or see to sth; vr worry (um about); s~**nfrei** a carefree; ~**nkind** nt problem child; s~**nvoll** a troubled, worried; ~**recht** nt custody (of a child).

Sorg- [zɔrk] cpd: ~**falt** f - care(fulness); s~**fältig** a careful; s~**los** a careless; (ohne Sorgen) carefree; s~**sam** a careful.

Sorte ['zɔrtə] f -, -n sort; (Waren—) brand; ~**n** pl (Fin) foreign currency.

sortieren [zɔr'ti:rən] vt sort (out).

Sortiment [zɔrti'mɛnt] nt assortment.

sosehr [zo:ze:r] cj as much as.

Soße ['zo:sə] f -, -n sauce; (Braten—) gravy.

Souffleur [zu'flø:r] m, **Souffleuse** [zu'flø:zə] f prompter.

soufflieren [zu'fli:rən] vti prompt.

souverän [zuvə're:n] a sovereign; (überlegen) superior.

so- cpd: ~**viel** [zo'fi:l] cj as far as; pron as much (wie as); **rede nicht** ~**viel** don't talk so much; ~**weit** [zo'vait] cj as far as; a: ~**weit sein** to be ready; ~**weit, wie** or **als möglich** as far as possible; **ich bin** ~**weit zufrieden** by and large I'm quite satisfied; ~**wenig** [zo've:nɪç] cj little as; pron as little (wie as); ~**wie** [zo'vi:] cj (sobald) as soon as; (ebenso) as well as; ~**wieso** [zovi'zo:] ad anyway; ~**wohl** [zo'vo:l] cj: ~**wohl ... als** or **wie auch** both ... and.

sozial [zotsi'a:l] a social; S~**abgaben** pl national insurance contributions pl; S~**demokrat** m social democrat; ~**isieren** vt socialize; S~**ismus** [-'lɪsmus] m socialism; S~**ist** [-'lɪst] m socialist; ~**istisch** a socialist; S~**politik** f social welfare policy; S~**produkt** nt (gross/net) national product; S~**staat** m welfare state.

Sozio- [zotsio] cpd: ~**loge** [-'lo:gə] m -n, -n sociologist; ~**logie** [-lo'gi:] f sociology; s~**logisch** [-'lo:gɪʃ] a sociological.

Sozius ['zo:tsius] m -, -se (Comm) partner; (Motorrad) pillion rider; ~**sitz** m pillion (seat).

sozusagen [zotsu'za:gən] ad so to speak.

Spachtel ['ʃpaxtəl] m -s, - spatula.

spähen ['ʃpɛ:ən] vi peep, peek.

Spalier [ʃpa'li:r] nt -s, -e (Gerüst) trellis; (Leute) guard of honour.

Spalt [ʃpalt] m -(e)s, -e crack; (Tür—) chink; (fig: Kluft) split; ~**e** f -, -n crack, fissure; (Gletscher—) crevasse; (in Text) column; s~**en** vtr (lit, fig) split; ~**ung** f splitting.

Span [ʃpaːn] **-(e)s, ¨e** shaving; ~**ferkel** nt sucking-pig.

Spange [ʃpaŋə] f **-, -n** clasp; (Haar—) hair slide; (Schnalle) buckle; (Armreif) bangle.

Spann [ʃpan] cpd: ~**beton** m pre-stressed concrete; ~**e** f **-, -n** (Zeit—) space; (Differenz) gap; s~**en** vt (straffen) tighten, tauten; (befestigen) brace; vi be tight; s~**end** a exciting, gripping; ~**kraft** f elasticity; (fig) energy; ~**ung** f tension; (Elec) voltage; (fig) suspense; (unangenehm) tension.

Spar- [ʃpaːr] cpd: ~**buch** nt savings book; ~**büchse** f moneybox; s~**en** vti save; **sich** (dat) **etw** s~**en** save oneself sth; Bemerkung keep sth to oneself; **mit etw** (dat) s~**en** be sparing with sth; **an etw** (dat) s~**en** economize on sth; ~**er** m **-s, -** saver.

Spargel [ʃpargəl] m **-s, -** asparagus.

Spar- cpd: ~**kasse** f savings bank; ~**konto** nt savings account.

spärlich [ʃpɛːrlɪç] a meagre; Bekleidung scanty.

Spar- cpd: ~**maßnahme** f economy measure, cut; s~**sam** a economical, thrifty; ~**samkeit** f thrift, economizing; ~**schwein** nt piggy bank.

Sparte [ʃpartə] f **-, -n** field; line of business; (Press) column.

Spaß [ʃpaːs] m **-es, ¨e** joke; (Freude) fun; **jdm** ~ **machen** be fun (for sb); s~**en** vi joke; **mit ihm ist nicht zu** s~**en** you can't take liberties with him; s~**eshalber** ad for the fun of it; s~**haft**, s~**ig** a funny, droll; ~**macher** m **-s, -** joker, funny man; ~**verderber** m **-s, -** spoilsport.

spät [ʃpɛːt] a, ad late; ~**er** a, ad later; ~**estens** ad at the latest.

Spaten [ʃpaːtən] m **-s, -** spade.

Spatz [ʃpats] m **-en, -en** sparrow.

spazier- [ʃpaˈtsiːr] cpd: ~**en** vi stroll, walk; ~**enfahren** vi irreg go for a drive; ~**engehen** vi irreg go for a walk; S~**gang** m walk; S~**stock** m walking stick; S~**weg** m path, walk.

Specht [ʃpɛçt] m **-(e)s, -e** woodpecker.

Speck [ʃpɛk] m **-(e)s, -e** bacon.

Spediteur [ʃpediˈtøːr] m carrier; (Möbel—) furniture remover.

Spedition [ʃpeditsiˈoːn] f carriage; (—sfirma) road haulage contractor; removal firm.

Speer [ʃpeːr] m **-(e)s, -e** spear; (Sport) javelin.

Speiche [ʃpaɪçə] f **-, -n** spoke.

Speichel [ʃpaɪçəl] m **-s** saliva, spit(tle).

Speicher [ʃpaɪçər] m **-s, -** storehouse; (Dach—) attic, loft; (Korn—) granary; (Wasser—) tank; (Tech) store; s~**n** vt store.

speien [ʃpaɪən] vti irreg spit; (erbrechen) vomit; (Vulkan) spew.

Speise [ʃpaɪzə] f **-, -n** food; ~**eis** [-ʔaɪs] nt ice-cream; ~**kammer** f larder, pantry; ~**karte** f menu; s~**n** vt feed; eat; vi dine; ~**röhre** f gullet, oesophagus; ~**saal** m dining room; ~**wagen** m dining car; ~**zettel** m menu.

Spektakel [ʃpɛkˈtaːkəl] m **-s, -** (col) row; nt **-s, -** spectacle.

Speku- [ʃpeku] cpd: ~**lant** [-ˈlant] m speculator; ~**lation** [-latsiˈoːn] f speculation; s~**lieren** [-ˈliːrən] vi (fig) speculate; **auf etw** (acc) s~**lieren** have hopes of sth.

Spelunke [ʃpeˈlʊŋkə] f **-, -n** dive.

Spende [ʃpɛndə] f **-, -n** donation; s~**n** vt donate, give; ~**r** m **-s, -** donor, donator.

spendieren [ʃpɛnˈdiːrən] vt pay for, buy; **jdm etw** ~ treat sb to sth, stand sb sth.

Sperling [ʃpɛrlɪŋ] m sparrow.

Sperma [ʃpɛrma] nt **-s, Spermen** sperm.

Sperr- [ʃpɛr] cpd: s~**angelweit** [-ʔaŋəlˈvaɪt] a wide open; ~**e** f **-, -n** barrier; (Verbot) ban; s~**en** vt block; (Sport) suspend, bar; (vom Ball) obstruct; (einschließen) lock; (verbieten) ban; vr baulk, jib(e); ~**gebiet** nt prohibited area; ~**holz** nt plywood; s~**ig** a bulky; ~**müll** m bulky refuse; ~**sitz** m (Theat) stalls pl; ~**stunde** f, ~**zeit** f closing time.

Spesen [ʃpeːzən] pl expenses pl.

Spezial- [ʃpetsiˈaːl] in cpds special; s~**i-sieren** vr specialize; ~**isierung** f specialization; ~**ist** [-ˈlɪst] m specialist; ~**ität** f speciality.

speziell [ʃpetsiˈɛl] a special.

spezifisch [ʃpeˈtsiːfɪʃ] a specific.

Sphäre [ˈsfɛːrə] f **-, -n** sphere.

spicken [ʃpɪkən] vt lard; vi (Sch) copy, crib.

Spiegel [ʃpiːgəl] m **-s, -** mirror; (Wasser—) level; (Mil) tab; ~**bild** nt reflection; s~**bildlich** a reversed; ~**ei** [-ʔaɪ] nt fried egg; ~**fechterei** [-fɛçtəˈraɪ] f shadow-boxing, bluff; s~**n** vt mirror, reflect; vr be reflected; vi gleam; (wider—) be reflective; ~**schrift** f mirror-writing; ~**ung** f reflection.

Spiel [ʃpiːl] nt **-(e)s, -e** game; (Schau—) play; (Tätigkeit) play(ing); (Cards) deck; (Tech) (free) play; s~**en** vti play; (um Geld) gamble; (Theat) perform, act; s~**end** ad easily; ~**er** m **-s, -** player; (um Geld) gambler; ~**erei** f trifling pastime; s~**erisch** a playful; Leichtigkeit effortless; s~**erisches Können** skill as a player; acting ability; ~**feld** nt pitch, field; ~**film** m feature film; ~**plan** m (Theat) programme; ~**platz** m playground; ~**raum** m room to manoeuvre, scope; ~**sachen** pl toys pl; ~**verderber** m **-s, -** spoilsport; ~**waren** pl, ~**zeug** nt toys pl.

Spieß [ʃpiːs] m **-es, -e** spear; (Brat—) spit; ~**bürger** m, ~**er** m **-s, -** bourgeois; ~**rutenlaufen** nt running the gauntlet.

Spikes [spaɪks] pl spikes pl; (Aut) studs pl.

Spinat [ʃpiˈnaːt] m **-(e)s, -e** spinach.

Spind [ʃpɪnt] m or nt **-(e)s, -e** locker.

Spinn- [ʃpɪn] cpd: ~**e** f **-, -n** spider; s~**en** vti irreg spin; (col) talk rubbish; (verrückt) be crazy or mad; ~**e'rei** f spinning mill; ~**(en)gewebe** nt cobweb; ~**rad** nt spinning-wheel; ~**webe** f cobweb.

Spion [ʃpiˈoːn] m **-s, -e** spy; (in Tür) spyhole; ~**age** [ʃpioˈnaːʒə] f **-, -n** espionage; s~**ieren** [ʃpioˈniːrən] vi spy.

Spirale [ʃpiˈraːlə] f **-, -n** spiral.

Spirituosen [ʃpiritu'oːzən] *pl* spirits *pl.*

Spiritus ['spiːritus] *m* -, -se (methylated) spirit.

Spital [ʃpi'taːl] *nt* -s, ¨er hospital.

spitz [ʃpits] *a* pointed; *Winkel* acute; *(fig) Zunge* sharp; *Bemerkung* caustic; **S∼** *m* -es, -e spitz; **S∼bogen** *m* pointed arch; **S∼bube** *m* rogue; **S∼e** *f* -, -n point, tip; *(Berg—)* peak; *(Bemerkung)* taunt, dig; *(erster Platz)* lead, top; *(usu pl: Gewebe)* lace; **S∼el** *m* -s, - police informer; **∼en** *vt* sharpen; **S∼en-** *in cpds* top; **S∼enleistung** *f* top performance; **S∼enlohn** *m* top wages *pl;* **S∼ensportler** *m* top-class sportsman; **∼findig** *a* (over)subtle; **∼ig** *a see* spitz; **S∼name** *m* nickname.

Splitter ['ʃplitər] *m* -s, - splinter; **s∼nackt** *a* stark naked.

spontan [ʃpɔn'taːn] *a* spontaneous.

Sport ['ʃpɔrt] *m* -(e)s, -e sport; *(fig)* hobby; **∼lehrer(in** *f)* *m* games *or* P.E. teacher; **∼ler(in** *f)* *m* -s, - sportsman/woman; **s∼lich** *a* sporting; *Mensch* sporty; **∼platz** *m* playing *or* sports field; **∼verein** *m* sports club; **∼wagen** *m* sports car; **∼zeug** *nt* sports gear.

Spott [ʃpɔt] *m* -(e)s mockery, ridicule; **s∼billig** *a* dirt-cheap; **s∼en** *vi* mock *(über +acc* at), ridicule.

spöttisch ['ʃpœtiʃ] *a* mocking.

Sprach- ['ʃpraːx] *cpd:* **s∼begabt** *a* good at languages; **∼e** *f* -, -n language; **∼fehler** *m* speech defect; **∼fertigkeit** *f* fluency; **∼führer** *m* phrasebook; **∼gebrauch** *m* (linguistic) usage; **∼gefühl** *nt* feeling for language; **s∼lich** *a* linguistic; **s∼los** *a* speechless; **∼rohr** *nt* megaphone; *(fig)* mouthpiece.

Spray [spreː] *m or nt* -s, -s spray.

Sprech- ['ʃprɛç] *cpd:* **∼anlage** *f* intercom; **s∼en** *irreg vi* speak, talk *(mit* to); **das spricht für ihn** that's a point in his favour; *vt* say; *Sprache* speak; *Person* speak to; **∼er(in** *f)* *m* -s, - speaker; *(für Gruppe)* spokesman; *(Rad, TV)* announcer; **∼stunde** *f* consultation (hour); (doctor's) surgery; **∼stundenhilfe** *f* (doctor's) receptionist; **∼zimmer** *nt* consulting room, surgery.

spreizen ['ʃpraitsən] *vt* spread; *vr* put on airs.

Spreng- ['ʃprɛŋ] *cpd:* **∼arbeiten** *pl* blasting operations *pl;* **s∼en** *vt* sprinkle; *(mit Sprengstoff)* blow up; *Gestein* blast; *Versammlung* break up; **∼ladung** *f* explosive charge; **∼stoff** *m* explosive(s).

Spreu [ʃprɔy] *f* - chaff.

Sprich- ['ʃpriç] *cpd:* **∼wort** *nt* proverb; **s∼wörtlich** *a* proverbial.

Spring- ['ʃpriŋ] *cpd:* **∼brunnen** *m* fountain; **s∼en** *vi irreg* jump; *(Glas)* crack; *(mit Kopfsprung)* dive; **∼er** *m* -s, - jumper; *(Schach)* knight.

Sprit [ʃprit] *m* -(e)s, -e *(col)* petrol, fuel.

Spritz- ['ʃprits] *cpd:* **∼e** *f* -, -n syringe; injection; *(an Schlauch)* nozzle; **s∼en** *vt* spray; *(Med)* inject; *vi* splash; *(heraus—)* spurt; *(Med)* give injections; **∼pistole** *f* spray gun.

spröde ['ʃprøːdə] *a* brittle; *Person* reserved, coy.

Sproß [ʃprɔs] *m* -sses, -sse shoot; *(Kind)* scion.

Sprosse ['ʃprɔsə] *f* -, -n rung.

Sprößling ['ʃprœsliŋ] *m* offspring *no pl.*

Spruch [ʃprux] *m* -(e)s, ¨e saying, maxim; *(Jur)* judgement.

Sprudel ['ʃpruːdəl] *m* -s, - mineral water; lemonade; **s∼n** *vi* bubble.

Sprüh- ['ʃpryː] *cpd:* **∼dose** *f* aerosol (can); **s∼en** *vti* spray; *(fig)* sparkle; **∼regen** *m* drizzle.

Sprung [ʃpruŋ] *m* -(e)s, ¨e jump; *(Riß)* crack; **∼brett** *nt* springboard; **s∼haft** *a* erratic; *Aufstieg* rapid; **∼schanze** *f* ski-jump.

Spucke ['ʃpukə] *f* - spit; **s∼en** *vti* spit.

Spuk [ʃpuːk] *m* -(e)s, -e haunting; *(fig)* nightmare; **s∼en** *vi (Geist)* walk; **hier spukt es** this place is haunted.

Spule ['ʃpuːlə] *f* -, -n spool; *(Elec)* coil.

Spül- ['ʃpyːl] *cpd:* **∼e** *f* -, -n (kitchen) sink; **s∼en** *vti* rinse; *Geschirr* wash up; *Toilette* flush; **∼maschine** *f* dishwasher; **∼stein** *m* sink; **∼ung** *f* rinsing; flush; *(Med)* irrigation.

Spur [ʃpuːr] *f* -, -en trace; *(Fuß—, Rad—, Tonband—)* track; *(Fährte)* trail; *(Fahr—)* lane; **s∼los** *ad* without (a) trace.

spür- ['ʃpyːr] *cpd:* **∼bar** *a* noticeable, perceptible; **∼en** *vt* feel; **S∼hund** *m* tracker dog; *(fig)* sleuth.

Spurt [ʃpurt] *m* -(e)s, -s *or* -e spurt.

sputen ['ʃpuːtən] *vr* make haste.

Staat [ʃtaːt] *m* -(e)s, -en state; *(Prunk)* show; *(Kleidung)* finery; **mit etw ∼ machen** show off *or* parade sth; **s∼enlos** *a* stateless; **s∼lich** *a* state(-); state-run; **∼sangehörigkeit** *f* nationality; **∼sanwalt** *m* public prosecutor; **∼sbürger** *m* citizen; **∼sdienst** *m* civil service; **s∼seigen** *a* state-owned; **∼sexamen** *nt (Univ)* degree; **s∼sfeindlich** *a* subversive; **∼smann,** *m, pl* -männer statesman; **∼ssekretär** *m* secretary of state.

Stab [ʃtaːp] *m* -(e)s, ¨e rod; *(Gitter—)* bar; *(Menschen)* staff; **∼hochsprung** *m* pole vault; **s∼il** [ʃta'biːl] *a* stable; *Möbel* sturdy; **s∼ilisieren** *vt* stabilize; **∼reim** *m* alliteration.

Stachel ['ʃtaxəl] *m* -s, -n spike; *(von Tier)* spine; *(von Insekten)* sting; **∼beere** *f* gooseberry; **∼draht** *m* barbed wire; **s∼ig** *a* prickly; **∼schwein** *nt* porcupine.

Stadion ['ʃtaːdiɔn] *nt* -s, Stadien stadium.

Stadium ['ʃtaːdium] *nt* stage, phase.

Stadt [ʃtat] *f* -, ¨e town.

Städt- ['ʃtɛːt] *cpd:* **∼chen** *nt* small town; **∼ebau** *m* town planning; **∼er(in** *f)* *m* -s, - town dweller; **s∼isch** *a* municipal; *(nicht ländlich)* urban.

Stadt- *cpd:* **∼mauer** *f* city wall(s); **∼plan** *m* street map; **∼rand** *m* outskirts *pl;* **∼teil** *m* district, part of town.

Staffel ['ʃtafəl] *f* -, -n rung; *(Sport)* relay (team); *(Aviat)* squadron; **∼ei** [-'lai] *f* easel; **s∼n** *vt* graduate; **∼ung** *f* graduation.

Stahl [ʃtaːl] m -(e)s, ⸚e steel; ~helm m steel helmet.

Stall [ʃtal] m -(e)s, ⸚e stable; (Kaninchen—) hutch; (Schweine—) sty; (Hühner—) hen-house.

Stamm [ʃtam] m -(e)s, ⸚e (Baum—) trunk; (Menschen—) tribe; (Gram) stem; ~baum m family tree; (von Tier) pedigree; s~eln vti stammer; s~en vi: s~en von or aus come from; ~gast m regular (customer); ~halter m -s, - son and heir.

stämmig [ʃtɛmɪç] a sturdy; Mensch stocky; S~keit f sturdiness; stockiness.

stampfen [ʃtampfən] vti stamp; (stapfen) tramp; (mit Werkzeug) pound.

Stand [ʃtant] m -(e)s, ⸚e position; (Wasser—, Benzin— etc) level; (Stehen) standing position; (Zustand) state; (Spiel—) score; (Messe— etc) stand; (Klasse) class; (Beruf) profession.

Standard [ʃtandart] m -s, -s standard.

Ständ- [ʃtɛnd] cpd: ~chen f serenade; ~er m -s, - stand.

Stand- [ʃtant] cpd: ~esamt nt registry office; ~esbeamte(r) m registrar; ~esbewußtsein nt status consciousness; s~esgemäß a,ad according to one's social position; ~esunterschied m social difference; s~haft a steadfast; ~haftigkeit f steadfastness; s~halten vi irreg stand firm (jdm/ etw against sb/sth), resist (jdm/ etw sb/sth).

ständig [ʃtɛndɪç] a permanent; (ununterbrochen) constant, continual.

Stand- cpd: ~licht nt sidelights pl, parking lights pl (US); ~ort m location; (Mil) garrison; ~punkt m standpoint.

Stange [ʃtaŋə] f -, -n stick; (Stab) pole, bar; rod; (Zigaretten) carton; von der ~ (Comm) off the peg; eine ~ Geld quite a packet.

Stanniol [ʃtanioːl] nt -s, -e tinfoil.

Stanze [ʃtantsə] f -, -n stanza; (Tech) stamp; s~n vt stamp.

Stapel [ʃtaːpəl] m -s, - pile; (Naut) stocks pl; ~lauf m launch; s~n vt pile (up).

Star [ʃtaːr] m -(e)s -e starling; (Med) cataract; m -s, -s (Film etc) star.

stark [ʃtark] a strong; (heftig, groß) heavy; (Maßangabe) thick.

Stärke [ʃtɛrkə] f -, -n strength; heaviness; thickness; (Cook, Wäsche—) starch; s~n vt strengthen; Wäsche starch.

Starkstrom m heavy current.

Stärkung [ʃtɛrkʊŋ] f strengthening; (Essen) refreshment.

starr [ʃtar] a stiff; (unnachgiebig) rigid; Blick staring; ~en vi stare; ~en vor or von be covered in; Waffen be bristling with; S~heit f rigidity; ~köpfig a stubborn; S~sinn m obstinacy.

Start [ʃtart] m -(e)s, -e start; (Aviat) take-off; ~automatik f (Aut) automatic choke; ~bahn f runway; s~en vti start; take off; ~er m -s, · starter; ~erlaubnis f takeoff clearance; ~zeichen nt start signal.

Station [ʃtatsioːn] f station; hospital ward; s~ieren [-niːrən] vt station.

Statist [ʃtatɪst] m extra, supernumerary;

~ik f statistics; ~iker m -s, - statistician; s~isch a statistical.

Stativ [ʃtatiːf] nt -s, -e tripod.

statt [ʃtat] cj, prep +gen or dat instead of; S~ f- place.

Stätte [ʃtɛtə] f -, -n place.

statt- cpd: ~finden vi irreg take place; ~haft a admissible; ~lich a imposing, handsome.

Statue [ʃtaːtuə] f -, n statue.

Statur [ʃtatuːr] f stature.

Status [ʃtaːtus] m -, - status.

Stau [ʃtau] m -(e)s, -e blockage; (Verkehrs—) (traffic) jam.

Staub [ʃtaup] m -(e)s dust; s~en [ʃtaubən] vi be dusty; ~faden m stamen; s~ig a dusty; ~sauger m vacuum cleaner; ~tuch nt duster.

Staudamm m dam.

Staude [ʃtaudə] f -, -n shrub.

stauen [ʃtauən] vt Wasser dam up; Blut stop the flow of; vr (Wasser) become dammed up; (Med, Verkehr) become congested; (Menschen) collect together; (Gefühle) build up.

staunen [ʃtaunən] vi be astonished; S~ nt -s amazement.

Stauung [ʃtauʊŋ] f (von Wasser) damming-up; (von Blut, Verkehr) congestion.

Stech- [ʃtɛç] cpd: ~becken nt bedpan; s~en vt irreg (mit Nadel etc) prick; (mit Messer) stab; (mit Finger) poke; (Biene etc) sting; (Mücke) bite; (Sonne) burn; (Cards) take; (Art) engrave; Torf, Spargel cut; In See s~en put to sea; ~en nt -s, - (Sport) play-off; jump-off; s~end a piercing, stabbing; Geruch pungent; ~ginster m gorse; ~palme f holly; ~uhr f time clock.

Steck- [ʃtɛk] cpd: ~brief m 'wanted' poster; ~dose f (wall) socket; s~en vt put, insert; Nadel stick; Pflanzen plant; (beim Nähen) pin; vi irreg be; (festsitzen) be stuck; (Nadeln) stick; s~enbleiben vi irreg get stuck; s~enlassen vt irreg leave in; ~enpferd nt hobby-horse; ~er m -s, - plug; ~nadel f pin; ~rübe f swede, turnip; ~zwiebel f bulb.

Steg [ʃteːk] m -(e)s, -e small bridge; (Anlege—) landing stage; ~reif m: aus dem ~reif just like that.

stehen [ʃteːən] vi irreg vi stand (zu by); (sich befinden) be; (in Zeitung) say; (still—) have stopped; jdm ~ suit sb; vi impers: es steht schlecht um things are bad for; wie steht's? how are things?; (Sport) what's the score?; ~ bleiben remain standing; ~bleiben vi irreg (Uhr) stop; (Fehler) stay as it is; ~lassen vt irreg leave; Bart grow.

stehlen [ʃteːlən] vt irreg steal.

steif [ʃtaif] a stiff; S~heit f stiffness.

Steig- [ʃtaik] cpd: ~bügel m stirrup; ~e [ʃtaigə] f -, -n (in Straße) steep road; (Kiste) crate; ~eisen nt crampon; s~en vi irreg rise; (klettern) climb; s~en in (+acc)/auf (+acc) get in/on; s~ern vt raise; (Gram) compare; vi (Auktion) bid; vr increase; ~erung f raising; (Gram) comparison; ~ung f incline, gradient, rise.

steil [ʃtaɪl] *a* steep.
Stein [ʃtaɪn] *m* **-(e)s, -e** stone; *(in Uhr)* jewel; **s~alt** *a* ancient; **~bock** *m (Astrol)* Capricorn; **~bruch** *m* quarry; **~butt** *m* **-s, -e** turbot; **s~ern** *a* (made of) stone; *(fig)* stony; **~gut** *nt* stoneware; **s~hart** *a* hard as stone; **s~ig** *a* stony; **s~igen** *vt* stone; **~kohle** *f* mineral coal; **~metz** *m* **-es, -e** stonemason.
Steiß [ʃtaɪs] *m* **-es, -e** rump.
Stell- [ʃtɛl] *cpd:* **~dichein** *nt* **-(s), -(s)** rendezvous; **~e** *f* **-, -n** place; *(Arbeit)* post, job; *(Amt)* office; **s~en** *vt* put; *Uhr etc* set; *(zur Verfügung ~)* supply; *(fassen)* *Dieb* apprehend; *vr (sich aufstellen)* stand; *(sich einfinden)* present oneself; *(bei Polizei)* give oneself up; *(vorgeben)* pretend (to be); **sich zu etw s~en** have an opinion of sth; **~enangebot** *nt* offer of a post; *(Zeitung)* vacancies; **~engesuch** *nt* application for a post; **~ennachweis** *m*, **~envermittlung** *f* employment agency; **~ung** *f* position; *(Mil)* line; **~ung nehmen zu** comment on; **~ungnahme** *f* **-, -n** comment; **s~vertretend** *a* deputy, acting; **~vertreter** *m* deputy; **~werk** *nt (Rail)* signal box.
Stelze [ʃtɛltsə] *f* **-, -n** stilt.
Stemm- [ʃtɛm] *cpd:* **~bogen** *m (Ski)* stem turn; **s~en** *vt* lift (up); *(drücken)* press; **sich s~en gegen** *(fig)* resist, oppose.
Stempel [ʃtɛmpəl] *m* **-s, -** stamp; *(Bot)* pistil; **~kissen** *nt* inkpad; **s~n** *vt* stamp; *Briefmarke* cancel; **s~n gehen** *(col)* be/go on the dole.
Stengel [ʃtɛŋəl] *m* **-s, -** stalk.
Steno- [ʃteno] *cpd:* **~gramm** [-ˈgram] *nt* shorthand report; **~graphie** [-graˈfiː] *f* shorthand; **s~graphieren** [-graˈfiːrən] *vti* write (in) shorthand; **~typist(in** *f)* [-tyˈpɪst(ɪn)] *m* shorthand typist.
Stepp- [ʃtɛp] *cpd:* **~decke** *f* quilt; **~e** *f* **-, -n** prairie; steppe; **s~en** *vt* stitch; *vi* tapdance.
Sterb- [ʃtɛrb] *cpd:* **~ebett** *nt* deathbed; **~efall** *m* death; **s~en** *vi irreg* die; **~eurkunde** *f* death certificate; **s~lich** [ʃtɛrplɪç] *a* mortal; **~lichkeit** *f* mortality; **~lichkeitsziffer** *f* death rate.
stereo- [ʃteːreo] *in cpds* stereo(-); **~typ** [stereoˈtyːp] *a* stereotype.
steril [ʃteˈriːl] *a* sterile; **~isieren** *vt* sterilize; **S~isierung** *f* sterilization.
Stern [ʃtɛrn] *m* **-(e)s, -e** star; **~bild** *nt* constellation; **~chen** *nt* asterisk; **~schnuppe** *f* **-, -n** meteor, falling star; **~stunde** *f* historic moment.
stet [ʃteːt] *a* steady; **~ig** *a* constant, continual; **~s** *ad* continually, always.
Steuer [ʃtɔʏər] *nt* **-s, -** *(Naut)* helm; *(~ruder)* rudder; *(Aut)* steering wheel; *f* **-, -n** tax; **~bord** *nt* starboard; **~erklärung** *f* tax return; **~klasse** *f* tax group; **~knüppel** *m* control column; *(Aviat)* joystick; **~mann** *m, pl* **-männer** *or* **-leute** helmsman; **s~n** *vti* steer; *Flugzeug* pilot; *Entwicklung, Tonstärke* control; **s~pflichtig** *a* taxable; *Person* liable to pay tax; **~rad** *nt* steering wheel; **~ung** *f* steering *(auch Aut)*; piloting; control;

(Vorrichtung) controls *pl*; **~zahler** *m* **-s, -** taxpayer; **~zuschlag** *m* additional tax.
Steward [ˈstjuːərt] *m* **-s, -s** steward; **~eß** [ˈstjuːɔrdɛs] *f* **-, -essen** stewardess; air hostess.
stibitzen [ʃtiˈbɪtsən] *vt (col)* pilfer, steal.
Stich [ʃtɪç] *m* **-(e)s, -e** *(Insekten—)* sting; *(Messer—)* stab; *(beim Nähen)* stitch; *(Färbung)* tinge; *(Cards)* trick; *(Art)* engraving; **jdn im ~ lassen** leave sb in the lurch; **~el** *m* **-s, -** engraving tool, style; **~e'lei** *f* jibe, taunt; **s~eln** *vi (fig)* jibe; **s~haltig** *a* sound, tenable; **~probe** *f* spot check; **~wahl** *f* final ballot; **~wort** *nt* cue; *(in Wörterbuch)* headword; *(für Vortrag)* note; **~wortverzeichnis** *nt* index.
Stick- [ʃtɪk] *cpd:* **s~en** *vti* embroider; **~e'rei** *f* embroidery; **s~ig** *a* stuffy, close; **~stoff** *m* nitrogen.
Stiefel [ʃtiːfəl] *m* **-s, -** boot.
Stief- [ʃtiːf] *in cpds* step; **~kind** *nt* stepchild; *(fig)* Cinderella; **~mutter** *f* stepmother; **~mütterchen** *nt* pansy.
Stiege [ˈʃtiːgə] *f* **-, -n** staircase.
Stiel [ʃtiːl] *m* **-(e)s, -e** handle; *(Bot)* stalk.
stier [ʃtiːr] *a* staring, fixed; **S~** *m* **-(e)s, -e** bull; *(Astrol)* Taurus; **~en** *vi* stare.
Stift [ʃtɪft] *m* **-(e)s, -e** peg; *(Nagel)* tack; *(Farb—)* crayon; *(Blei—)* pencil; *nt* **-(e)s, -e** *(charitable)* foundation; *(Eccl)* religious institution; **s~en** *vt* found; *Unruhe* cause; *(spenden)* contribute; **~er(in** *f)* *m* **-s, -** founder; **~ung** *f* donation; *(Organisation)* foundation; **~zahn** *m* crown tooth.
Stil [ʃtiːl] *m* **-(e)s, -e** style; **~blüte** *f* howler.
still [ʃtɪl] *a* quiet; *(unbewegt)* still; *(heimlich)* secret; **S~e** *f* **-, -n** stillness, quietness; **in aller S~e** quietly; **~en** *vt* stop; *(befriedigen)* satisfy; *Säugling* breast-feed; **~gestanden** *interj* attention; **~halten** *vi irreg* keep still; **~(l)egen** *vt* close down; **~schweigen** *vi irreg* be silent; **S~schweigen** *nt* silence; **~schweigend** *a,ad* silent(ly); *Einverständnis* tacit(ly); **S~stand** *m* standstill; **~stehen** *vi irreg* stand still.
Stimm- [ʃtɪm] *cpd:* **~abgabe** *f* voting; **~bänder** *pl* vocal chords *pl*; **s~berechtigt** *a* entitled to vote; **~e** *f* **-, -n** voice; *(Wahl—)* vote; **s~en** *vt (Mus)* tune; **das stimmte ihn traurig** that made him feel sad; *vi* be right; **s~en für/gegen** vote for/against; **~enmehrheit** *f* majority (of votes); **~enthaltung** *f* abstention; **~gabel** *f* tuning fork; **s~haft** *a* voiced; **~lage** *f* register; **s~los** *a* voiceless; **~recht** *nt* right to vote; **~ung** *f* mood; atmosphere; **s~ungsvoll** *a* enjoyable; full of atmosphere; **~zettel** *m* ballot paper.
stinken [ˈʃtɪŋkən] *vi irreg* stink.
Stipendium [ʃtiˈpɛndiʊm] *nt* grant.
Stirn [ʃtɪrn] *f* **-, -en** forehead, brow; *(Frechheit)* impudence; **~höhle** *f* sinus; **~runzeln** *nt* frown(ing).
stöbern [ˈʃtøːbərn] *vi* rummage.
stochern [ˈʃtɔxərn] *vi* poke (about).
Stock [ʃtɔk] *m* **-(e)s, ⁻e** stick; *(Bot)* stock; *pl*

-werke storey; **s~-in** cpds vor a (col) completely; **s~en** vi stop, pause; **s~end** a halting; **s~finster** a (col) pitch-dark; **s~taub** a stone-deaf; **~ung** f stoppage; **~werk** nt storey, floor.

Stoff [ʃtɔf] m **-(e)s, -e** (Gewebe) material, cloth; (Materie) matter; (von Buch etc) subject (matter); **s~lich** a material; with regard to subject matter; **~wechsel** m metabolism.

stöhnen [ˈʃtøːnən] vi groan.

stoisch [ˈʃtoːɪʃ] a stoical.

Stollen [ˈʃtɔlən] m **-s, -** (Min) gallery; (Cook) cake eaten at Christmas; (von Schuhen) stud.

stolpern [ˈʃtɔlpərn] vi stumble, trip.

Stolz [ʃtɔlts] m **-es** pride; **s~** a proud; **s~ieren** [ʃtɔlˈtsiːrən] vi strut.

Stopf- [ˈʃtɔpf] cpd: **s~en** vt (hinein—) stuff; (voll—) fill (up); (nähen) darn; vi (Med) cause constipation; **~garn** nt darning thread.

Stoppel [ˈʃtɔpəl] f **-, -n** stubble.

Stopp- [ˈʃtɔp] cpd: **s~en** vti stop; (mit Uhr) time; **~schild** nt stop sign; **~uhr** f stopwatch.

Stöpsel [ˈʃtœpsəl] m **-s, -** plug; (für Flaschen) stopper.

Stör [ʃtøːr] m **-(e)s, -e** sturgeon.

Storch [ʃtɔrç] m **-(e)s, -e** stork.

Stör- [ʃtøːr] cpd: **s~en** vt disturb; (behindern, Rad) interfere with; vr **sich an etw** (dat) **s~en** let sth bother one; **s~end** a disturbing, annoying; **~enfried** m **-(e)s, -e** troublemaker.

störrig [ˈʃtœrɪç], **störrisch** [ˈʃtœrɪʃ] a stubborn, perverse.

Stör- cpd: **~sender** m jammer; **~ung** f disturbance; interference.

Stoß [ʃtoːs] m **-es, -e** (Schub) push; (Schlag) blow; knock; (mit Schwert) thrust; (mit Fuß) kick; (Erd—) shock; (Haufen) pile; **~dämpfer** m **-s, -** shock absorber; **s~en** irreg vt (mit Druck) shove, push; (mit Schlag) knock, bump; (mit Fuß) kick; Schwert etc thrust; (an—) Kopf etc bump; (zerkleinern) pulverize; vr get a knock; **sich s~en an** (+dat) (fig) take exception to; vi: **s~en an** or **auf** (+acc) bump into; (finden) come across; (angrenzen) be next to; **~stange** f (Aut) bumper.

Stotterer [ˈʃtɔtərər] m **-s, -** stutterer.

stottern [ˈʃtɔtərn] vti stutter.

stracks [ʃtraks] ad straight.

Straf- [ˈʃtraːf] cpd: **~anstalt** f penal institution; **~arbeit** f (Sch) punishment; lines pl; **s~bar** a punishable; **~barkeit** f criminal nature; **~e** f **-, -n** punishment; (Jur) penalty; (Gefängnis—) sentence; (Geld—) fine; **s~en** vt punish.

straff [ʃtraf] a tight; (streng) strict; Stil etc concise; Haltung erect; **~en** vt tighten, tauten.

Straf- cpd: **~gefangene(r)** mf prisoner, convict; **~gesetzbuch** nt penal code; **~kolonie** f penal colony.

Sträf- [ˈʃtrɛːf] cpd: **s~lich** a criminal; **~ling** m convict.

Straf- cpd: **~porto** nt excess postage (charge); **~predigt** f severe lecture;

~raum m (Sport) penalty area; **~recht** nt criminal law; **~stoß** m (Sport) penalty (kick); **~tat** f punishable act; **~zettel** m ticket.

Strahl [ʃtraːl] m **-s, -en** ray, beam; (Wasser—) jet; **s~en** vi radiate; (fig) beam; **~enbehandlung, ~entherapie** f radiotherapy; **~ung** f radiation.

Strähne [ˈʃtrɛːnə] f **-, -n** strand.

stramm [ʃtram] a tight; Haltung erect; Mensch robust; **~stehen** vi irreg (Mil) stand to attention.

strampeln [ˈʃtrampəln] vi kick (about), fidget.

Strand [ʃtrant] m **-(e)s, -e** shore; (mit Sand) beach; **~bad** nt open-air swimming pool, lido; **s~en** [ˈʃtrandən] vi run aground; (fig: Mensch) fail; **~gut** nt flotsam; **~korb** m beach chair.

Strang [ʃtraŋ] m **-(e)s, -e** cord, rope; (Bündel) skein; (Schienen—) track; **über die e schlagen** (col) kick over the traces.

Strapaz- cpd: **~e** [ʃtraˈpaːtsə] f **- -n** strain, exertion; **s~ieren** [ʃtrapaˈtsiːrən] vt Material treat roughly, punish; Mensch, Kräfte wear out, exhaust; **s~ierfähig** a hard-wearing; **s~iös** [ʃtrapatsiˈøːs] a exhausting, tough.

Straße [ˈʃtraːsə] f **-, -n** street, road; **~nbahn** f tram, streetcar (US); **~nbeleuchtung** f street lighting; **~nfeger, ~nkehrer** m **-s, -** roadsweeper; **~nsperre** f roadblock; **~nverkehrsordnung** f highway code.

Strateg- [ʃtraˈteːg] cpd: **~e** m **-n, -n** strategist; **~ie** [ʃtrateˈgiː] f strategy; **s~isch** a strategic.

Stratosphäre [ʃtratoˈsfɛːrə] f **-** stratosphere.

sträuben [ˈʃtrɔybən] vt ruffle; vr bristle; (Mensch) resist (gegen etw sth).

Strauch [ʃtraux] m **-(e)s, Sträucher** bush, shrub; **s~eln** vi stumble, stagger.

Strauß [ʃtraus] m **-es, Sträuße** bunch; bouquet; pl **-e** ostrich.

Streb- [ʃtreːb] cpd: **~e** f **-, -n** strut; **~ebalken** m buttress; **s~en** vi strive (nach for), endeavour; **s~en zu** or **nach** (sich bewegen) make for; **~er** m **-s, -** (pej) pusher, climber; (Sch) swot; **s~sam** a industrious; **~samkeit** f industry.

Strecke [ˈʃtrɛkə] f **-, -n** stretch; (Entfernung) distance; (Rail) line; (Math) line; **s~n** vt stretch; Waffen lay down; (Cook) eke out; vr stretch (oneself); vi (Sch) put one's hand up.

Streich [ʃtraiç] m **-(e)s, -e** trick, prank; (Hieb) blow; **s~eln** vt stroke; **s~en** irreg vt (berühren) stroke; (auftragen) spread; (anmalen) paint; (durch—) delete; (nicht genehmigen) cancel; vi (berühren) brush; (schleichen) prowl; **~holz** nt match; **~instrument** nt string instrument.

Streif- [ˈʃtraif] cpd: **~band** nt wrapper; **~e** f **-, -n** patrol; **s~en** vt (leicht berühren) brush against, graze; (Blick) skim over; Thema, Problem touch on; (ab—) take off; vi (gehen) roam; **~en** m **-s, -** (Linie) stripe; (Stück) strip; (Film) film; **~endienst** m patrol duty; **~enwagen** m

patrol car; ~schuß m graze, grazing shot;
~zug m scouting trip.
Streik [ʃtraɪk] m -(e)s, -s strike;
~brecher m -s, - blackleg,
strikebreaker; s~en vi strike; ~kasse f
strike fund; s~posten m (strike) picket.
Streit [ʃtraɪt] m -(e)s, -e argument;
dispute; s~en vir irreg argue; dispute;
~frage f point at issue; s~ig a: jdm etw
s~ig machen dispute sb's right to sth;
~igkeiten pl quarrel, dispute; ~kräfte
pl (Mil) armed forces pl; s~lustig a
quarrelsome; ~sucht f quarrelsomeness.
streng [ʃtrɛŋ] a severe; Lehrer, Maßnahme
strict; Geruch etc sharp; S~e f - severity;
strictness; sharpness; ~genommen ad
strictly speaking; ~gläubig a orthodox,
strict.
Streu [ʃtrɔy] f -, -en litter, bed of straw;
s~en vt strew, scatter, spread; ~ung f
dispersion.
Strich [ʃtrɪç] m -(e)s, -e (Linie) line;
(Feder-, Pinsel-) stroke; (von Geweben)
nap; (von Fell) pile; auf den ~ gehen
(col) walk the streets; jdm gegen den ~
gehen rub sb up the wrong way; einen ~
machen durch (lit) cross out; (fig) foil;
~einteilung f calibration; ~mädchen
nt streetwalker; ~punkt m semicolon;
s~weise ad here and there.
Strick [ʃtrɪk] m -(e)s, -e rope; (col: Kind)
rascal; s~en vti knit; ~jacke f cardigan;
~leiter f rope ladder; ~nadel f knitting
needle; ~waren pl knitwear.
Strieme [ʃtriːmə] f -, -n, **Striemen**
[ʃtriːmən] m -s, - weal.
strikt [ʃtrɪkt] a strict.
strittig [ʃtrɪtɪç] a disputed, in dispute.
Stroh [ʃtroː] nt -(e)s straw; ~blume f
everlasting flower; ~dach nt thatched
roof; ~halm m (drinking) straw;
~mann m, pl ~männer dummy, straw
man; ~witwe f grass widow.
Strolch [ʃtrɔlç] m -(e)s, -e layabout, bum.
Strom [ʃtroːm] m -(e)s, ‐e river; (fig)
stream; (Elec) current; s~abwärts
[-ˈapvɛrts] ad downstream; s~aufwärts
[-ˈaʊfvɛrts] ad upstream.
strömen [ʃtrøːmən] vi stream, pour.
Strom- cpd: ~kreis m circuit;
s~linienförmig a streamlined;
~rechnung f electricity bill; ~sperre f
power cut; ~stärke f amperage.
Strömung [ʃtrøːmʊŋ] f current.
Strophe [ʃtroːfə] f -, -n verse.
strotzen [ʃtrɔtsən] vi: ~vor or von
abound in, be full of.
Strudel [ʃtruːdəl] m -s, - whirlpool, vortex;
(Cook) strudel; s~n vi swirl, eddy.
Struktur [ʃtrʊkˈtuːr] f structure; s~ell
[-ˈrɛl] a structural.
Strumpf [ʃtrʊmpf] m -(e)s, ‐e stocking;
~band nt garter; ~hose f (pair of)
tights.
Strunk [ʃtrʊŋk] m -(e)s, ‐e stump.
struppig [ʃtrʊpɪç] a shaggy, unkempt.
Stube [ʃtuːbə] f -, -n room; ~narrest m
confinement to one's room; (Mil)
confinement to quarters; ~nhocker m

(col) stay-at-home; s~nrein a house-
trained.
Stuck [ʃtʊk] m -(e)s stucco.
Stück [ʃtʏk] nt -(e)s, -e piece; (etwas) bit;
(Theat) play; ~arbeit f piecework;
~chen nt little piece; ~lohn m
piecework wages pl; s~weise ad bit by
bit, piecemeal; (Comm) individually;
~werk nt bits and pieces pl.
Student(in f) [ʃtuˈdɛnt(ɪn)] m student;
s~isch a student, academic.
Studie [ʃtuːdiə] f study.
studieren [ʃtuˈdiːrən] vti study.
Studio [ʃtuːdio] nt -s, -s studio.
Studium [ʃtuːdiʊm] nt studies pl.
Stufe [ʃtuːfə] f -, -n step; (Entwicklungs-)
stage; ~nleiter f (fig) ladder; s~nweise
ad gradually.
Stuhl [ʃtuːl] m -(e)s, ‐e chair; ~gang m
bowel movement.
stülpen [ʃtʏlpən] vt (umdrehen) turn
upside down; (bedecken) put.
stumm [ʃtʊm] a silent; (Med) dumb; S~el
m -s, - stump; (Zigaretten-) stub; S~film
m silent film; S~heit f silence; dumbness.
Stümper [ʃtʏmpər] m -s, - incompetent,
duffer; s~haft a bungling, incompetent;
s~n vi (col) bungle.
stumpf [ʃtʊmpf] a blunt; (teilnahmslos,
glanzlos) dull; Winkel obtuse; S~ m -(e)s,
‐e stump; S~heit f bluntness; dullness;
S~sinn m tediousness; s~sinnig a dull.
Stunde [ʃtʊndə] f -, -n hour; s~n vt: jdm
etw s~en give sb time to pay sth;
~ngeschwindigkeit f average speed per
hour; ~nkilometer pl kilometres per
hour; s~nlang a for hours; ~nlohn m
hourly wage; ~nplan m timetable;
s~nweise a by the hour; every hour.
stündlich [ʃtʏntlɪç] a hourly.
Stups [ʃtʊps] m -es, -e (col) push; ~nase f
snub nose.
stur [ʃtuːr] a obstinate, pigheaded.
Sturm [ʃtʊrm] m -(e)s, ‐e storm, gale; (Mil
etc) attack, assault.
stürm- [ʃtʏrm] cpd: ~en vi (Wind) blow
hard, rage; (rennen) storm; vt (Mil, fig)
storm; v impers es ~t there's a gale
blowing; S~er m -s, - (Sport) forward,
striker; ~isch a stormy.
Sturm- cpd: ~warnung f gale warning;
~wind m storm, gale.
Sturz [ʃtʊrts] m -es, ‐e fall; (Pol)
overthrow.
stürzen [ʃtʏrtsən] vt (werfen) hurl; (Pol)
overthrow; (umkehren) overturn; vr rush;
(hinein-) plunge; vi fall; (Aviat) dive;
(rennen) dash.
Sturz- cpd: ~flug m nose-dive; ~helm m
crash helmet.
Stute [ʃtuːtə] f -, -n mare.
Stütz- [ʃtʏts] cpd: ~balken m brace, joist;
~e f -, -n support; help; s~en vt (lit, fig)
support; Ellbogen etc prop up.
stutz- [ʃtʊts] cpd: ~en vt trim; Ohr,
Schwanz dock; Flügel clip; vi hesitate;
become suspicious; ~ig a perplexed,
puzzled; (mißtrauisch) suspicious.
Stütz- cpd: ~mauer f supporting wall;

~**punkt** *m* point of support; *(von Hebel)* fulcrum; *(Mil, fig)* base.

Styropor ⁿ [ʃtyro'po:r] *nt* **-s** polystyrene.

Subjekt [zup'jɛkt] *nt* **-(e)s, -e** subject; s~**iv** ['-ti:f] *a* subjective; ~**ivi'tät** *f* subjectivity.

Substantiv [zupstan'ti:f] *nt* **-s, -e** noun.

Substanz [zup'stants] *f* substance.

subtil [zup'ti:l] *a* subtle.

subtrahieren [zuptra'hi:rən] *vt* subtract.

Subvention [zupvɛntsi'o:n] *f* subsidy; s~**ieren** [-'ni:rən] *vt* subsidize.

subversiv [zupvɛr'zi:f] *a* subversive.

Such- ['zu:x] *cpd:* ~**aktion** *f* search; ~**e** *f* -, -n search; ~**en** *vti* look (for); seek; *(ver–)* try; ~**er** *m* **-s,** **-** seeker, searcher; *(Phot)* viewfinder.

Sucht [zuxt] *f* -, ⁻**e** mania; *(Med)* addiction, craving.

süchtig ['zyçtiç] *a* addicted; S~**e(r)** *mf* addict.

Süd- [zy:t] *cpd:* ~**en** ['zy:dən] *m* **-s** south; ~**früchte** *pl* Mediterranean fruit; s~**lich** *a* southern; s~**lich von** (to the) south of; s~**wärts** *ad* southwards.

süff- *cpd:* ~**ig** ['zyfiç] *a* Wein pleasant to the taste; ~**isant** [zyfi'zant] *a* smug.

suggerieren [zuge'ri:rən] *vt* suggest *(jdm etw* sth to sb).

Sühne ['zy:nə] *f* -, -n atonement, expiation; s~**n** *vt* atone for, expiate.

Sulfonamid [zulfona'mi:t] *nt* **-(e)s, -e** *(Med)* sulphonamide.

Sultan ['zultan] *m* **-s, -e** sultan; ~**ine** [zulta'ni:nə] *f* sultana.

Sülze ['zyltsə] *f* -, -n brawn.

Summ- [zum] *cpd:* s~**arisch** [zu'ma:rɪʃ] *a* summary; ~**e** *f* -, -n sum, total; s~**en** *vti* buzz; Lied hum; s~**ieren** [zu'mi:rən] *vtr* add up (to).

Sumpf [zumpf] *m* **-(e)s,** ⁻**e** swamp, marsh; s~**ig** *a* marshy.

Sünde ['zyndə] *f* -, -n sin; ~**nbock** *m (col)* scapegoat; ~**nfall** *m* Fall (of man); ~**r(in** *f) m* **-s,** **-** sinner.

Super ['zu:pər] *nt* **-s** *(Benzin)* four star (petrol); ~**lativ** [-lati:f] *m* **-s, -e** superlative; ~**markt** *m* supermarket.

Suppe ['zupə] *f* -, -n soup.

surren ['zurən] *vi* buzz, hum.

Surrogat [zuro'ga:t] *nt* **-(e)s, -e** substitute, surrogate.

suspekt [zus'pɛkt] *a* suspect.

süß [zy:s] *a* sweet; S~**e** *f* - sweetness; ~**en** *vt* sweeten; S~**igkeit** *f* sweetness; *(Bonbon etc)* sweet, candy *(US);* ~**lich** *a* sweetish; *(fig)* sugary; S~**speise** *f* pudding, sweet; S~**stoff** *m* sweetening agent; S~**wasser** *nt* fresh water.

Sylvester [zyl'vɛstər] *nt* **-s,** **-** *see* **Silvester**.

Symbol [zym'bo:l] *nt* **-s, -e** symbol; s~**isch** *a* symbolic(al).

Symmetrie [zyme'tri:] *f* symmetry; ~**achse** *f* symmetric axis.

symmetrisch [zy'me:trɪʃ] *a* symmetrical.

Sympath- *cpd:* ~**ie** [zympa'ti:] *f* liking, sympathy; s~**isch** [zym'pa:tɪʃ] *a* likeable,

congenial; **er ist mir** s~**isch** I like him; s~**i'sieren** *vi* sympathize.

Symptom [zymp'to:m] *nt* **-s, -e** symptom; s~**atisch** [zympto'ma:tɪʃ] *a* symptomatic.

Synagoge [zyna'go:gə] *f* -, -n synagogue.

synchron [zyn'kro:n] *a* synchronous; S~**getriebe** *nt* synchromesh (gears *pl*); ~**i'sieren** *vt* synchronize; Film dub.

Syndikat [zyndi'ka:t] *nt* **-(e)s, -e** combine, syndicate.

Synonym [zyno'ny:m] *nt* **-s, -e** synonym; s~ *a* synonymous.

Syntax ['zyntaks] *f* -, -en syntax.

Synthese [zyn'te:zə] *f* -, -n synthesis.

synthetisch [zyn'te:tɪʃ] *a* synthetic.

Syphilis ['zyfilıs] *f* - syphilis.

System [zys'te:m] *nt* **-s, -e** system; s~**atisch** [zyste'ma:tɪʃ] *a* systematic; s~**ati'sieren** *vt* systematize.

Szene ['stse:nə] *f* -, -n scene; ~**rie** [stsenə'ri:] *f* scenery.

Szepter ['stsɛptər] *nt* **-s,** **-** sceptre.

T

T, t [te:] T, t.

Tabak ['ta:bak] *m* **-s, -e** tobacco.

Tabell- [ta'bɛl] *cpd:* t~**arisch** [tabe'la:rɪʃ] *a* tabular; ~**e** *f* table; ~**enführer** *m* top of the table, league leader.

Tabernakel [tabɛr'na:kəl] *m* **-s,** **-** tabernacle.

Tablette [ta'blɛtə] *f* tablet, pill.

Tachometer [taxo'me:tər] *m* **-s,** **-** *(Aut)* speedometer.

Tadel ['ta:dəl] *m* **-s,** **-** censure, scolding; *(Fehler)* fault, blemish; t~**los** *a* faultless, irreproachable; t~**n** *vt* scold; t~**nswert** *a* blameworthy.

Tafel ['ta:fəl] *f* -, -n table *(auch Math);* *(Anschlag–)* board; *(Wand–)* blackboard; *(Schiefer–)* slate; *(Gedenk–)* plaque; *(Illustration)* plate; *(Schalt–)* panel; *(Schokolade etc)* bar.

Täfel- ['tɛ:fəl] *cpd:* t~**n** *vt* panel; ~**ung** *f* panelling.

Taft [taft] *m* **-(e)s, -e** tafetta.

Tag [ta:k] *m* **-(e)s, -e** day; daylight; **unter/über** ~ *(Min)* underground/on the surface; **an den** ~ **kommen** come to light; **guten** ~! good morning/afternoon!; t~**aus,** t~**ein** ad day in, day out; ~**dienst** *m* day duty; ~**ebuch** ['ta:gəbu:x] *nt* diary, journal; ~**edieb** *m* idler; ~**egeld** *nt* daily allowance; t~**elang** *ad* for days; t~**en** *vi* sit, meet; *v impers:* **es tagt** dawn is breaking; ~**esablauf** *m* course of the day; ~**esanbruch** *m* dawn; ~**eslicht** *nt* daylight; ~**esordnung** *f* agenda; ~**essatz** *m* daily rate; ~**eszeit** *f* time of day; ~**eszeitung** *f* daily (paper).

täglich ['tɛ:kliç] *a,ad* daily.

Tag- *cpd:* t~**süber** *ad* during the day; ~**ung** *f* conference.

Taille ['taljə] *f* -, -n waist.

Takel ['ta:kəl] *nt* **-s,** **-** tackle; t~**n** *vt* rig.

Takt [takt] *m* **-(e)s, -e** tact; *(Mus)* time; ~**gefühl** *nt* tact; ~**ik** *f* tactics *pl;* t~**isch** *a* tactical; t~**los** *a* tactless; ~**losigkeit** *f* tactlessness; ~**stock** m (conductor's) baton; t~**voll** a tactful.

Tal [ta:l] nt -(e)s, ¨er valley.

Talar [ta'la:r] m -s, -e (Jur) robe; (Univ) gown.

Talent [ta'lɛnt] nt -(e)s, -e talent; t~**iert** [talɛn'ti:rt], t~**voll** a talented, gifted.

Taler ['ta:lər] m -s, - taler, florin.

Talg [talk] m -(e)s, -e tallow; ~**drüse** f sebaceous gland.

Talisman ['ta:lɪsman] m -s, -e talisman.

Tal- cpd: ~**sohle** f bottom of a valley; ~**sperre** f dam.

Tamburin [tambu'ri:n] nt -s, -e tambourine.

Tampon ['tampɔn] m -s, -s tampon.

Tang [taŋ] m -(e)s, -e seaweed; ~**ente** [taŋ'gɛntə] f -, -n tangent; t~**ieren** [taŋ'gi:rən] vt (lit) be tangent to; (fig) affect.

Tank [taŋk] m -s, -s tank; t~**en** vi fill up with petrol or gas (US); (Aviat) (re)fuel; ~**er** m -s, -, ~**schiff** nt tanker; ~**stelle** f petrol or gas (US) station; ~**wart** m petrol pump or gas station (US) attendant.

Tanne ['tanə] f -, -n fir; ~**nbaum** m fir tree; ~**nzapfen** m fir cone.

Tante ['tantə] f -, -n aunt.

Tanz [tants] m -es, ¨e dance.

Tänz- ['tɛnts] cpd: t~**eln** vi dance along; ~**er(in** f) m -s, - dancer.

Tanz- cpd: t~**en** vti dance; ~**fläche** f (dance) floor; ~**schule** f dancing school.

Tape- cpd: ~**te** [ta'pe:tə] f -, -n wallpaper; ~**tenwechsel** m (fig) change of scenery; t~**zieren** [tape'tsi:rən] vt (wall)paper; ~**zierer** [tape'tsi:rər] m -s, - (interior) decorator.

tapfer ['tapfər] a brave; **T~keit** f courage, bravery.

tappen ['tapən] vi walk uncertainly or clumsily.

täppisch ['tɛpɪʃ] a clumsy.

Tarif [ta'ri:f] m -s, -e tariff, (scale of) fares/charges; ~**lohn** m standard wage rate.

Tarn- ['tarn] cpd: t~**en** vt camouflage; Person, Absicht disguise; ~**farbe** f camouflage paint; ~**ung** f camouflaging, disguising.

Tasche ['taʃə] f -, -n pocket; handbag; ~**n** in cpds pocket; ~**nbuch** nt paperback; ~**ndieb** m pickpocket; ~**ngeld** nt pocket money; ~**nlampe** f (electric) torch, flashlight (US); ~**nmesser** nt penknife; ~**nspieler** m conjurer; ~**ntuch** nt handkerchief.

Tasse ['tasə] f -, -n cup.

Tast- ['tast] cpd: ~**atur** [-a'tu:r] f keyboard; ~**e** f -, -n push-button control; (an Schreibmaschine) key; t~**en** vt feel, touch; vi feel, grope; vr feel one's way; ~**sinn** m sense of touch.

Tat [ta:t] f -, -en act, deed, action; **in der** ~ indeed, as a matter of fact; ~**bestand** m facts pl of the case; t~**enlos** a inactive.

Tät- ['tɛ:t] cpd: ~**er(in** f) m -s, - perpetrator, culprit; ~**erschaft** f guilt; t~**ig** a active; **in einer Firma t~ig sein** work for a firm; **T~igkeit** f activity;

(Beruf) occupation; t~**lich** a violent; ~**lichkeit** f violence; pl blows pl.

tätowieren [tɛto'vi:rən] vt tattoo.

Tat- cpd: ~**sache** f fact; t~**sächlich** a actual; ad really.

Tatze ['tatsə] f -, -n paw.

Tau [tau] nt -(e)s, -e rope; m -(e)s dew.

taub [taup] a deaf; Nuß hollow; **T~heit** f deafness; ~**stumm** a deaf-and-dumb.

Taube ['taubə] f -, -n dove; pigeon; ~**nschlag** m dovecote.

Tauch- ['taux] cpd: t~**en** vt dip; vi dive; (Naut) submerge; ~**er** m -s, - diver; ~**eranzug** m diving suit; ~**sieder** m -s, - portable immersion heater.

tauen ['tauən] vti, v impers thaw.

Tauf- ['tauf] cpd: ~**becken** nt font; ~**e** f -, -n baptism; t~**en** vt christen, baptize; ~**name** m Christian name; ~**pate** m godfather; ~**patin** f godmother; ~**schein** m certificate of baptism.

Taug- ['taug] cpd: t~**en** vi be of use; t~**en für** do or be good for; **nicht** t~**en** be no good or useless; ~**enichts** m -es, -e good-for-nothing; t~**lich** ['tauklɪç] a suitable; (Mil) fit (for service); ~**lichkeit** f suitability; fitness.

Taumel ['tauməl] m -s dizziness; (fig) frenzy; t~**ig** a giddy, reeling; t~**n** vi reel, stagger.

Tausch [tauʃ] m -(e)s, -e exchange; t~**en** vt exchange, swap; ~**handel** m barter.

täuschen ['tɔyʃən] vt deceive; vi be deceptive; vr be wrong; ~**d** a deceptive.

Täuschung f deception; (optisch) illusion.

tausend ['tauzənt] num (a) thousand; **T~füßler** m -s, - centipede; millipede.

Tau- cpd: ~**tropfen** m dew drop; ~**wetter** nt thaw; ~**ziehen** nt -s, - tug-of-war.

Taxi ['taksi] nt -(s), -(s) taxi; ~**fahrer** m taxi driver.

Tech- ['tɛç] cpd: ~**nik** f technology; (Methode, Kunstfertigkeit) technique; ~**niker** m -s, technician; t~**nisch** a technical; ~**nolo'gie** f technology; t~**no'logisch** a technological.

Tee [te:] m -s, -s tea; ~**kanne** f teapot; ~**löffel** m teaspoon.

Teer [te:r] m -(e)s, -e tar; t~**en** vt tar.

Tee- cpd: ~**sieb** nt tea strainer; ~**wagen** m tea trolley.

Teich [taɪç] m -(e)s, -e pond.

Teig [taɪk] m -(e)s, -e dough; t~**ig** a doughy; ~**waren** pl pasta sing.

Teil [taɪl] m or nt -(e)s, -e part; (An—) share; (Bestand—) component; **zum** ~ partly; t~**bar** a divisible; ~**betrag** m instalment; ~**chen** nt (atomic) particle; t~**en** vtr divide; (mit jdm) share; t~**haben** vi irreg share (an +dat in); ~**haber** m -s, - partner; ~**kaskoversicherung** f third party, fire and theft insurance; ~**nahme** f -, -n participation; (Mitleid) sympathy; t~**nahmslos** a disinterested, apathetic; t~**nehmen** vi irreg take part (an +dat in); ~**nehmer** m -s, - participant; t~**s** ad partly; ~**ung** f division; t~**weise** ad partially, in part;

~zahlung f payment by instalments.
Teint [tɛ̃ː] m -s, -s complexion.

Telefon [tele'foːn] nt -s, -e telephone;
~amt nt telephone exchange; ~anruf
m, ~at [telefo'naːt] nt -(e)s, -e (tele)-
phone call; ~buch nt telephone directory; t~ieren [telefo'niːrən] vi telephone;
t~isch [-ɪʃ] a telephone; Benachrichtigung
by telephone; ~ist(in f) [telefo'nɪst(ɪn)] m
telephonist; ~nummer f (tele)phone
number; ~verbindung f telephone connection; ~zelle f telephone kiosk, callbox; ~zentrale f telephone exchange.

Telegraf [tele'graːf] m -en, -en telegraph; ~enleitung f telegraph line;
~enmast m telegraph pole; ~ie [-'fiː] f
telegraphy; t~ieren [-'fiːrən] vti telegraph, wire; t~isch a telegraphic.

Telegramm [tele'gram] nt -s, -e telegram, cable; ~adresse f telegraphic
address; ~formular nt telegram form.

Tele- cpd: ~graph = ~graf; ~kolleg
['telekɔlek] nt university of the air;
~objektiv ['teːleˈɔpjɛktiːf] nt telephoto
lens; ~pathie [telepa'tiː] f telepathy;
t~pathisch [tele'paːtɪʃ] a telepathic;
~phon = ~fon; ~skop [tele'skoːp] nt
-s, -e telescope.

Teller ['tɛlər] m -s, - plate.

Tempel ['tɛmpəl] m -s, - temple.

Temperafarbe ['tɛmperafarbə] f distemper.

Temperament [tɛmpera'mɛnt] nt
temperament; (Schwung) vivacity, liveliness; t~los a spiritless; t~voll a high-
spirited, lively.

Temperatur [tɛmpera'tuːr] f temperature.

Tempo ['tɛmpo] nt -s, -s speed, pace; pl
Tempi (Mus) tempo; ~! get a move on!;
t~rär [-'rɛːr] a temporary;
~taschentuch ® nt paper handkerchief.

Tendenz [tɛn'dɛnts] f tendency; (Absicht)
intention; t~iös [-i'øːs] a biased, tenden-
tious.

tendieren [tɛn'diːrən] vi show a tendency,
incline (zu to(wards)).

Tenne ['tɛnə] f -, -n threshing floor.

Tennis ['tɛnɪs] nt - tennis; ~platz m
tennis court; ~schläger m tennis racket;
~spieler(in f) m tennis player.

Tenor [te'noːr] m -s, -̈e tenor.

Teppich ['tɛpɪç] m -s, -e carpet; ~boden
m wall-to-wall carpeting; ~kehr-
maschine f carpet sweeper; ~klopfer m
carpet beater.

Termin [tɛr'miːn] m -s, -e (Zeitpunkt)
date; (Frist) time limit, deadline; (Arzt—
etc) appointment; ~kalender m diary,
appointments book; ~ologie [-olo'giː] f
terminology.

Termite [tɛr'miːtə] f -, -n termite.

Terpentin [tɛrpɛn'tiːn] nt -s, -e
turpentine, turps sing.

Terrasse [tɛ'rasə] f -, -n terrace.

Terrine [tɛ'riːnə] f -n tureen.

territorial [tɛritori'aːl] a territorial.

Territorium [tɛri'toːrium] nt territory.

Terror ['tɛror] m -s terror; reign of terror;
t~isieren [tɛrori'ziːrən] vt terrorize;

~ismus [-'rɪsmus] m terrorism; ~ist
[-'rɪst] m terrorist.

Terz [tɛrts] f -, -en (Mus) third; ~ett
[tɛr'tsɛt] nt -(e)s, -e trio.

Tesafilm ® ['teːzafɪlm] m sellotape ®.

Testament [tɛsta'mɛnt] nt will, testament;
(Rel) Testament; t~arisch [-'taːrɪʃ] a
testamentary; ~svollstrecker m
executor (of a will).

Test- [tɛst] cpd: ~at [tɛs'taːt] nt -(e)s, -e
certificate; ~ator [tɛs'taːtor] m testator;
~bild nt (TV) test card; t~en vt test.

Tetanus [te'taːnus] m - tetanus;
~impfung f (anti-)tetanus injection.

teuer ['tɔyər] a dear, expensive; T~ung f
increase in prices; T~ungszulage f cost
of living bonus.

Teufel ['tɔyfəl] m -s, - devil; ~ei [-'laɪ] f
devilry; ~saustreibung f exorcism.

teuflisch ['tɔyflɪʃ] a fiendish, diabolical.

Text [tɛkst] m -(e)s, -e text; (Lieder—)
words pl; t~en vi write the words.

textil [tɛks'tiːl] a textile; T~ien pl textiles
pl; T~industrie f textile industry;
~waren pl textiles pl.

Theater [te'aːtər] nt -s, - theatre; (col)
fuss; ~ spielen (lit, fig) playact;
~besucher m playgoer; ~kasse f box
office; ~stück nt (stage-)play.

theatralisch [tea'traːlɪʃ] a theatrical.

Theke ['teːkə] f -, -n (Schanktisch) bar;
(Ladentisch) counter.

Thema ['teːma] nt -s, Themen or -ta
theme, topic, subject.

Theo- [teo] cpd: ~loge [-'loːgə] m -n, -n
theologian; ~logie [-lo'giː] f theology;
t~logisch [-'loːgɪʃ] a theological;
~retiker [-'reːtikər] m -s, - theorist;
t~retisch [-'reːtɪʃ] a theoretical; ~rie
[-'riː] f theory.

Thera- [tera] cpd: ~peut [-'pɔyt] m -en,
-en therapist; t~peutisch [-'pɔytɪʃ] a
therapeutic; ~pie [-'piː] f therapy.

Therm- cpd: ~albad [tɛrm'aːlbaːt] nt
thermal bath; thermal spa; ~ometer
[tɛrmo'meːtər] nt -s, - thermometer;
~osflasche ['tɛrmɔsflaʃə] f Thermos ®
flask; ~ostat [tɛrmo'staːt] m -(e)s or -en,
-e(n) thermostat.

These ['teːzə] f -, -n thesis.

Thrombose [trɔm'boːzə] f -, -n thrombosis.

Thron [troːn] m -(e)s, -e throne;
~besteigung f accession (to the throne);
~erbe m heir to the throne; ~folge f
succession (to the throne).

Thunfisch ['tuːnfɪʃ] m tuna.

Thymian ['tyːmiaːn] m -s, -e thyme.

Tick [tɪk] m -(e)s, -s tic; (Eigenart) quirk;
(Fimmel) craze; t~en vi tick.

tief [tiːf] a deep; (tiefsinnig) profound;
Ausschnitt, Ton low; T~ nt -s, -s (Met)
depression; T~druck m low pressure;
T~e f -, -n depth; T~ebene f plain;
T~enpsychologie f depth psychology;
T~enschärfe f (Phot) depth of focus;
~ernst a very grave or solemn; T~gang
m (Naut) draught; (geistig) depth;
~gekühlt a frozen; ~greifend a far-
reaching; T~kühlfach nt deep-freeze

compartment; **T~kühltruhe** f deep-freeze, freezer; **T~land** nt lowlands pl; **T~punkt** m low point; (fig) low ebb; **T~schlag** m (Boxen, fig) blow below the belt; **~schürfend** a profound; **T~see** f deep sea; **T~sinn** m profundity; **~sinnig** a profound; melancholy; **T~stand** m low level; **~stapeln** vi be overmodest; **T~start** m (Sport) crouch start; **T~stwert** m minimum or lowest value.

Tiegel ['ti:gǝl] m -s, - saucepan; (Chem) crucible.

Tier [ti:r] nt -(e)s, -e animal; **~arzt** m vet(erinary surgeon); **~garten** m zoo(logical gardens pl); **t~isch** a animal; (lit, fig) brutish; (fig) Ernst etc deadly; **~kreis** m zodiac; **~kunde** f zoology; **t~liebend** a fond of animals; **~quälerei** [-kvɛːləˈrai] f cruelty to animals; **~schutzverein** m society for the prevention of cruelty to animals.

Tiger ['ti:gǝr] m -s, - tiger; **~in** f tigress.

tilgen ['tɪlgǝn] vt erase, expunge; Sünden expiate; Schulden pay off.

Tilgung f erasing, blotting out; expiation; repayment.

Tinktur [tɪŋk'tu:r] f tincture.

Tinte ['tɪntǝ] f -, -n ink; **~nfaß** nt inkwell; **~nfisch** m cuttlefish; **~nfleck** m ink stain, blot; **~nstift** m copying or indelible pencil.

tippen ['tɪpǝn] vti tap, touch; (col: schreiben) type; (col: raten) tip (auf jdn sb); (im Lotto etc) bet (on).

Tipp- [tɪp] cpd: **~fehler** m (col) typing error; **~se** ['tɪ:psǝ] f (col) typist; **t~topp** a (col) tip-top; **~zettel** m (pools) coupon.

Tisch [tɪʃ] m -(e)s, -e table; **bei ~** at table; **vor/nach ~** before/after eating; **unter den ~ fallen** (fig) be dropped; **~decke** f tablecloth; **~ler** m -s, - carpenter, joiner; **~le'rei** f joiner's workshop; (Arbeit) carpentry, joinery; **t~lern** vi do carpentry etc; **~rede** f after-dinner speech; **~tennis** nt table tennis.

Titel ['ti:tǝl] m -s, - title; **~anwärter** m (Sport) challenger; **~bild** nt cover (picture); (von Buch) frontispiece; **~rolle** f title role; **~seite** f cover; (Buch—) title page; **~verteidiger** m defending champion, title holder.

titulieren [titu'li:rǝn] vt entitle; (anreden) address.

Toast [to:st] m -(e)s, -s or -e toast; **~er** m -s, - toaster.

tob- ['to:b] cpd: **~en** vi rage; (Kinder) romp about; **T~sucht** f raving madness; **~süchtig** a maniacal; **~suchtsanfall** m maniacal fit.

Tochter ['tɔxtǝr] f -, ﹎ daughter.

Tod [to:t] m -(e)s, -e death; **t~ernst** a (col) deadly serious; ad in dead earnest; **~esangst** ['to:dǝsaŋst] f mortal fear; **~esanzeige** f obituary (notice); **~esfall** m death; **~eskampf** m throes pl of death; **~esstoß** m death-blow; **~esstrafe** f death penalty; **~estag** m anniversary of death; **~esursache** f cause of death; **~esurteil** nt death sentence;

~esverachtung f utter disgust; **t~krank** a dangerously ill.

tödlich ['tø:tlɪç] a deadly, fatal.

tod- cpd: **~müde** a dead tired; **~schick** a (col) smart, classy; **~sicher** a (col) absolutely or dead certain; **T~sünde** f deadly sin.

Toilette [toa'lɛtǝ] f toilet, lavatory; (Frisiertisch) dressing table; (Kleidung) outfit; **~nartikel** pl toiletries pl, toilet articles pl; **~npapier** nt toilet paper; **~ntisch** m dressing table.

toi, toi, toi ['tɔy, 'tɔy, 'tɔy] interj touch wood.

tolerant [tole'rant] a tolerant.

Toleranz [tole'rants] f tolerance.

tolerieren [tole'ri:rǝn] vt tolerate.

toll [tɔl] a mad; Treiben wild; (col) terrific; **~en** vi romp; **T~heit** f madness, wildness; **T~kirsche** f deadly nightshade; **~kühn** a daring; **T~wut** f rabies.

Tölpel ['tœlpǝl] m -s, - oaf, clod.

Tomate [to'ma:tǝ] f -, -n tomato; **~nmark** nt tomato puree.

Ton [to:n] m -(e)s, -e (Erde) clay; pl ﹎e (Laut) sound; (Mus) note; (Redeweise) tone; (Farb—, Nuance) shade; (Betonung) stress; **~abnehmer** m pick-up; **t~angebend** a leading; **~art** f (musical) key; **~band** nt tape; **~bandgerät** nt tape recorder.

tönen ['tø:nǝn] vi sound; vt shade; Haare tint.

tönern ['tø:nǝrn] a clay.

Ton- cpd: **~fall** m intonation; **~film** m sound film; **t~haltig** a clayey; **~höhe** f pitch; **~ika** f, -iken (Mus), **~ikum** nt -s, -ika (Med) tonic; **~künstler** m musician; **~leiter** f (Mus) scale; **t~los** a soundless.

Tonne ['tɔnǝ] f -, -n barrel; (Maß) ton.

Ton- cpd: **~spur** f soundtrack; **~taube** f clay pigeon; **~waren** pl pottery, earthenware.

Topf [tɔpf] m -(e)s, ﹎e pot; **~blume** f pot plant.

Töpfer ['tœpfǝr] m -s, - potter; **~ei** [-'rai] f piece of pottery; potter's workshop; **~scheibe** f potter's wheel.

topographisch [topo'gra:fɪʃ] a topographic.

topp [tɔp] interj O.K.

Tor [to:r] m -en, -en fool; nt -(e)s, -e gate; (Sport) goal; **~bogen** m archway.

Torf [tɔrf] m -(e)s peat; **~stechen** nt peat-cutting.

Tor- cpd: **~heit** f foolishness; foolish deed; **~hüter** m -s, - goalkeeper.

töricht ['tø:rɪçt] a foolish.

torkeln ['tɔrkǝln] vi stagger, reel.

torpedieren [tɔrpe'di:rǝn] vt (lit, fig) torpedo.

Torpedo [tɔr'pe:do] m -s, -s torpedo.

Torte ['tɔrtǝ] f -, -n cake; (Obst—) flan, tart.

Tortur [tɔr'tu:r] f ordeal.

Tor- cpd: **~verhältnis** nt goal average; **~wart** m -(e)s, -e goalkeeper.

tosen ['to:zǝn] vi roar.

tot [to:t] a dead; **einen ~en Punkt haben** be at one's lowest.

total [to'ta:l] *a* total; ~**itär** [tɔtali'tɛ:r] *a* totalitarian; **T~schaden** *m* (*Aut*) complete write-off.

tot- *cpd:* ~**arbeiten** *vr* work oneself to death; ~**ärgern** *vr* (*col*) get really annoyed.

töten ['tø:tən] *vti* kill.

Tot- *cpd:* ~**enbett** *nt* death bed; **t~enblaß** *a* deathly pale, white as a sheet; ~**engräber** *m* -**s**, - gravedigger; ~**enhemd** *nt* shroud; ~**enkopf** *m* skull; ~**enschein** *m* death certificate; ~**enstille** *f* deathly silence; ~**entanz** *m* danse macabre; ~**e(r)** *mf* dead person; **t~fahren** *vt irreg* run over; **t~geboren** *a* stillborn; **t~lachen** *vr* (*col*) laugh one's head off.

Toto ['to:to] *m or nt* -**s**, -**s** pools *pl*; ~**schein** *m* pools coupon.

tot- *cpd:* ~**sagen** *vt:* **jdn ~ sagen** say that sb is dead; ~**schlagen** *vt irreg* (*lit, fig*) kill; **T~schläger** *m* killer; (*Waffe*) cosh; ~**schweigen** *vt irreg* hush up; ~**stellen** *vr* pretend to be dead; ~**treten** *vt irreg* trample to death.

Tötung ['tø:tʊŋ] *f* killing.

Toupet [tu'pe:] *nt* -**s**, -**s** toupee.

toupieren [tu'pi:rən] *vt* back-comb.

Tour [tu:r] *f* -, -**en** tour, trip; (*Umdrehung*) revolution; (*Verhaltensart*) way; **in einer ~** incessantly; ~**enzahl** *f* number of revolutions; ~**enzähler** *m* rev counter; ~**ismus** [tu'rɪsmʊs] *m* tourism; ~**ist** [tu'rɪst] *m* tourist; ~**istenklasse** *f* tourist class; ~**nee** [tur'ne:] *f* -, -**n** (*Theat etc*) tour; **auf ~nee gehen** go on tour.

Trab [tra:p] *m* -(**e**)**s** trot; ~**ant** [tra'bant] *m* satellite; ~**antenstadt** *f* satellite town; **t~en** *vi* trot.

Tracht [traxt] *f* -, -**en** (*Kleidung*) costume, dress; **eine ~ Prügel** a sound thrashing; **t~en** *vi* strive (*nach* for), endeavour; **jdm nach dem Leben t~en** seek to kill sb.

trächtig ['trɛçtɪç] *a Tier* pregnant; (*fig*) rich, fertile.

Tradition [traditsi'o:n] *f* tradition; **t~ell** [-'nɛl] *a* traditional.

Trag- [tra:g] *cpd:* ~**bahre** *f* stretcher; **t~bar** *a Gerät* portable; *Kleidung* wearable; (*erträglich*) bearable.

träge ['trɛ:gə] *a* sluggish, slow; (*Phys*) inert.

tragen ['tra:gən] *irreg vt* carry; *Kleidung, Brille* wear; *Namen, Früchte* bear; (*erdulden*) endure; **sich mit einem Gedanken ~** have an idea in mind; *vi* (*schwanger sein*) be pregnant; (*Eis*) hold; **zum T~ kommen** have an effect.

Träger ['trɛ:gər] *m* -**s**, - carrier; wearer; bearer; (*Ordens—*) holder; (*an Kleidung*) (*shoulder*) strap; (*Körperschaft etc*) sponsor; ~**rakete** *f* launch vehicle; ~**rock** *m* skirt with shoulder straps.

Trag- ['tra:k] *cpd:* ~**fähigkeit** *f* load-carrying capacity; ~**fläche** *f* (*Aviat*) wing; ~**flügelboot** *nt* hydrofoil.

Trägheit ['trɛ:khaɪt] *f* laziness; (*Phys*) inertia.

Tragi- ['tra:gi] *cpd:* ~**k** *f* tragedy; **t~komisch** *a* tragi-comic; **t~sch** *a* tragic.

Tragödie [tra'gø:diə] *f* tragedy.

Trag- ['tra:k] *cpd:* ~**weite** *f* range; (*fig*) scope; ~**werk** *nt* wing assembly.

Train- [trɛ:n] *cpd:* ~**er** *m* -**s**, - (*Sport*) trainer, coach; (*Fußball*) manager; **t~ieren** [trɛ'ni:rən] *vti* train; *Mensch auch* coach; *Übung* practise; **Fußball t~ieren** do football practice; ~**ing** *nt* -**s**, -**s** training; ~**ingsanzug** *m* track suit.

Traktor ['traktɔr] *m* tractor.

trällern ['trɛlərn] *vti* trill, sing.

trampeln ['trampəln] *vti* trample, stamp.

trampen ['trampən] *vi* hitch-hike.

Tran [tra:n] *m* -(**e**)**s**, -**e** train oil, blubber.

tranchieren [trã'ʃi:rən] *vt* carve.

Tranchierbesteck [trã'ʃi:rbəʃtɛk] *nt* (pair of) carvers.

Träne ['trɛ:nə] *f* -, -**n** tear; **t~n** *vi* water; ~**ngas** *nt* teargas.

Tränke ['trɛŋkə] *f* -, -**n** watering place; **t~n** *vt* (*naß machen*) soak; *Tiere* water.

Trans- *cpd:* ~**formator** [transfɔr'ma:tɔr] *m* transformer; ~**istor** [tran'zɪstɔr] *m* transistor; **t~itiv** ['tranziti:f] *a* transitive; **t~parent** [transpa'rent] *a* transparent; ~**parent** *nt* -(**e**)**s**, -**e** (*Bild*) transparency; (*Spruchband*) banner; **t~pirieren** [transpi'ri:rən] *vi* perspire; ~**plantation** [transplantatsi'o:n] *f* transplantation; (*Haut—*) graft(*ing*); ~**port** [trans'pɔrt] *m* -(**e**)**s**, -**e** transport; **t~portieren** [transpɔr'ti:rən] *vt* transport; ~**portkosten** *pl* transport charges *pl*, carriage; ~**portmittel** *nt* means of transportation; ~**portunternehmen** *nt* carrier.

Trapez [tra'pe:ts] *nt* -**es**, -**e** trapeze; (*Math*) trapezium.

Traube ['traubə] *f* -, -**n** grape; bunch (of grapes); ~**nlese** *f* vintage; ~**nzucker** *m* glucose.

trauen ['trauən] *vi:* **jdm/etw ~** trust sb/sth; *vr* dare; *vt* marry.

Trauer ['trauər] *f* - sorrow; (*für Verstorbenen*) mourning; ~**fall** *m* death, bereavement; ~**marsch** *m* funeral march; **t~n** *vi* mourn (*um* for); ~**rand** *m* black border; ~**spiel** *nt* tragedy.

Traufe ['traufə] *f* -, -**n** eaves *pl*.

träufeln ['trɔyfəln] *vti* drip.

traulich ['traulɪç] *a* cosy, intimate.

Traum [traum] *m* -(**e**)**s**, **Träume** dream; ~**a** *nt* -**s**, -**men** trauma; ~**bild** *nt* vision.

träum- ['trɔym] *cpd:* **t~en** *vti* dream; **T~er** *m* -**s**, - dreamer; **T~e'rei** *f* dreaming; ~**erisch** *a* dreamy.

traumhaft *a* dreamlike; (*fig*) wonderful.

traurig ['traurɪç] *a* sad; **T~keit** *f* sadness.

Trau- ['trau] *cpd:* ~**ring** *m* wedding ring; ~**schein** *m* marriage certificate; ~**ung** *f* wedding ceremony; ~**zeuge** *m* witness (to a marriage).

treffen ['trɛfən] *irreg vti* strike, hit; (*Bemerkung*) hurt; (*begegnen*) meet; *Entscheidung etc* make; *Maßnahmen* take; **er hat es gut getroffen** he did well; ~ **auf** (+ *acc*) come across, meet with; *vr* meet; **es traf sich, daß...** it so happened that...; **es trifft sich gut** it's convenient; **wie es so trifft** as these things happen;

T~ nt -s, - meeting; **~d** a pertinent, apposite.

Treff- cpd: **~er** m -s, - hit; (Tor) goal; (Los) winner; **t~lich** a excellent; **~punkt** m meeting place.

Treib- ['traip] cpd: **~eis** nt drift ice; **t~en** irreg vt drive; Studien etc pursue; Sport do, go in for; **Unsinn t~en** fool around; vi (Schiff etc) drift; (Pflanzen) sprout; (Cook: aufgehen) rise; (Tee, Kaffee) be diuretic; **~en** nt -s activity; **~haus** nt hothouse; **~stoff** m fuel.

trenn- ['trɛn] cpd: **~bar** a separable; **~en** vt separate; (teilen) divide; vr separate; **sich ~en von** part with; **T~schärfe** f (Rad) selectivity; **T~ung** f separation; **T~wand** f partition (wall).

Trepp- ['trɛp] cpd: **t~ab** ad downstairs; **t~auf** ad upstairs; **~e** f -, -n stair(case); **~engeländer** nt banister; **~enhaus** nt staircase.

Tresor [tre'zo:r] m -s, -e safe.

treten ['tre:tən] irreg vi step; (Tränen, Schweiß) appear; **~ nach** kick at; **~ in** (+acc) step in(to); **in Verbindung ~** get in contact; **in Erscheinung ~** appear; vt (mit Fußtritt) kick; (nieder~) tread, trample.

treu [trɔy] a faithful, true; **T~e** f - loyalty, faithfulness; **T~händer** m -s, - trustee; **T~handgesellschaft** f trust company; **~herzig** a innocent; **~lich** ad faithfully; **~los** a faithless.

Tribüne [tri'by:nə] f -, -n grandstand; (Redner~) platform.

Tribut [tri'bu:t] nt -(e)s, -e tribute.

Trichter ['trɪçtər] m -s, - funnel; (in Boden) crater.

Trick [trɪk] m -s, -e or -s trick; **~film** m cartoon.

Trieb [tri:p] m -(e)s, -e urge, drive; (Neigung) inclination; (an Baum etc) shoot; **~feder** f (fig) motivating force; **t~haft** a impulsive; **~kraft** f (fig) drive; **~täter** m sex offender; **~wagen** m (Rail) diesel railcar; **~werk** nt engine.

triefen ['tri:fən] vi drip.

triftig ['trɪftɪç] a good, convincing.

Trigonometrie [trigonome'tri:] f trigonometry.

Trikot [tri'ko:] nt -s, -s vest; (Sport) shirt; m -s, -s (Gewebe) tricot.

Triller ['trɪlər] m -s, - (Mus) trill; **t~n** vi trill, warble; **~pfeife** f whistle.

Trimester [tri'mɛstər] nt -s, - term.

trink- ['trɪŋk] cpd: **~bar** a drinkable; **~en** vti irreg drink; **T~er** m -s, - drinker; **T~geld** nt tip; **T~halm** m (drinking) straw; **T~spruch** m toast; **T~wasser** nt drinking water.

trippeln ['trɪpəln] vi toddle.

Tripper ['trɪpər] m -s, - gonorrhoea.

Tritt [trɪt] m -(e)s, -e step; (Fuß~) kick; **~brett** nt (Rail) step; (Aut) running-board.

Triumph [tri'umf] m -(e)s, -e triumph; **~bogen** m triumphal arch; **t~ieren** [-'fi:rən] vi triumph; (jubeln) exult.

trivial [trivi'a:l] a trivial.

trocken ['trɔkən] a dry; **T~dock** nt dry dock; **T~element** nt dry cell; **T~haube**

f hair-dryer; **T~heit** f dryness; **~legen** vt Sumpf drain; Kind put a clean nappy on; **T~milch** f dried milk.

trocknen ['trɔknən] vti dry.

Troddel ['trɔdəl] f -, -n tassel.

Trödel ['trø:dəl] m -s (col) junk; **t~n** vi (col) dawdle.

Trödler ['trø:dlər] m -s, - secondhand dealer.

Trog [tro:k] -(e)s, -e trough.

Trommel ['trɔməl] f -, -n drum; **~fell** nt eardrum; **t~n** vti drum; **~revolver** m revolver; **~waschmaschine** f tumble-action washing machine.

Trommler ['trɔmlər] m -s, - drummer.

Trompete [trɔm'pe:tə] f -, -n trumpet; **~r** m -s, - trumpeter.

Tropen ['tro:pən] pl tropics pl; **t~beständig** a suitable for the tropics; **~helm** m topee, sun helmet.

Tropf [trɔpf] m -(e)s, -e (col) rogue; **armer ~** poor devil.

tröpfeln ['trœpfəln] vi drop, trickle.

Tropfen ['trɔpfən] m -s, - drop; **t~** vti drip; v impers: **es tropft** a few raindrops are falling; **t~weise** ad in drops.

Tropfsteinhöhle f stalactite cave.

tropisch ['tro:pɪʃ] a tropical.

Trost [tro:st] m -es consolation, comfort; **t~bedürftig** a in need of consolation.

tröst- ['trø:st] cpd: **~en** vt console, comfort; **T~er(in** f) m -s, - comfort(er); **~lich** a comforting.

trost- cpd: **~los** a bleak; Verhältnisse wretched; **T~preis** m consolation prize; **~reich** a comforting.

Tröstung ['trø:stuŋ] f comfort; consolation.

Trott [trɔt] m -(e)s, -e trot; (Routine) routine; **~el** m -s, - (col) fool, dope; **t~en** vi trot; **~oir** [trɔto'a:r] nt -s, -s or -e pavement, sidewalk (US).

Trotz [trɔts] m -es pigheadedness; **etw aus ~ tun** do sth just to show them; **jdm zum ~** in defiance of sb; **t~** prep +gen or dat in spite of; **~alter** nt obstinate phase; **t~dem** ad nevertheless; cj although; **t~ig** a defiant, pig-headed; **~kopf** m obstinate child; **~reaktion** f fit of pique.

trüb [try:p] a dull; Flüssigkeit, Glas cloudy; (fig) gloomy; **~en** ['try:bən] vt cloud; vr become clouded; **T~heit** f dullness; cloudiness; gloom; **T~sal** f -, -e distress; **~selig** a sad, melancholy; **T~sinn** m depression; **~sinnig** a depressed, gloomy.

trudeln ['tru:dəln] vi (Aviat) (go into a) spin.

Trüffel ['tryfəl] f -, -n truffle.

trüg- ['try:g] cpd: **~en** vt irreg deceive; vi be deceptive; **~erisch** a deceptive.

Trugschluß ['tru:gʃlus] m false conclusion.

Truhe ['tru:ə] f -, -n chest.

Trümmer ['trymər] pl wreckage; (Bau~) ruins pl; **~haufen** m heap of rubble.

Trumpf [trumpf] m -(e)s, -e (lit, fig) trump; **t~en** vti trump.

Trunk [truŋk] m -(e)s, -e drink; **t~en** a intoxicated; **~enbold** m -(e)s, -e drunkard; **~enheit** f intoxication;

~**enheit am Steuer** drunken driving; ~**sucht** f alcoholism.

Trupp [trup] m -s, -s troop; ~**e** f -, -n troop; (Waffengattung) force; (Schauspiel—) troupe; ~**en** pl troops pl; ~**enführer** m (military) commander; ~**enteil** m unit; ~**enübungsplatz** m training area.

Truthahn ['truːthaːn] m turkey.

Tube ['tuːbə] f -, -n tube.

Tuberkulose [tubɛrkuˈloːzə] f -, -n tuberculosis.

Tuch [tuːx] nt -(e)s, ¨er cloth; (Hals—) scarf; (Kopf—) headscarf; (Hand—) towel.

tüchtig ['tʏçtɪç] a efficient, (cap)able; (col: kräftig) good, sound; **T~keit** f efficiency, ability.

Tücke ['tʏkə] f -, -n (Arglist) malice; (Trick) trick; (Schwierigkeit) difficulty, problem; **seine ~n haben** be temperamental.

tückisch ['tʏkɪʃ] a treacherous; (böswillig) malicious.

Tugend ['tuːgənt] f -, -en virtue; **t~haft** a virtuous.

Tüll [tʏl] m -s, -e tulle; ~**e** f -, -n spout.

Tulpe ['tʊlpə] f -, -n tulip.

tummeln ['tʊməln] vr romp, gambol; (sich beeilen) hurry.

Tumor ['tuːmɔr] m -s, -e tumour.

Tümpel ['tʏmpəl] m -s, - pool, pond.

Tumult [tuˈmʊlt] m -(e)s, -e tumult.

tun [tuːn] irreg vt (machen) do; (legen) put; **jdm etw ~** (antun) do sth to sb; **etw tut es auch** sth will do; **das tut nichts** that doesn't matter; **das tut nichts zur Sache** that's neither here nor there; vi react; **so ~, als ob** act as if; vr: **es tut sich etwas/viel** something/a lot is happening.

Tünche ['tʏnçə] f -, -n whitewash; **t~n** vt whitewash.

Tunke ['tʊŋkə] f -, -n sauce; **t~n** vt dip, dunk.

tunlichst ['tuːnlɪçst] ad if at all possible; ~ **bald** as soon as possible.

Tunnel ['tʊnəl] m -s, -s or - tunnel.

Tüpfel ['tʏpfəl] m -s, - dot, spot; ~**chen** nt (small) dot; **t~n** vt dot, spot.

tupfen ['tʊpfən] vti dab; (mit Farbe) dot; **T~** m -s, - dot, spot.

Tür [tyːr] f -, -en door.

Turbine [tʊrˈbiːnə] f turbine.

Türkis [tʏrˈkiːs] m -es, -e turquoise; **t~** a turquoise.

Turm [tʊrm] m -(e)s, ¨e tower; (Kirch—) steeple; (Sprung—) diving platform; (Schach) castle, rook.

Türm- ['tʏrm] cpd: ~**chen** nt turret; **t~en** vr tower up; vt heap up; vi (col) scarper, bolt.

Turn- ['tʊrn] cpd: **t~en** vi do gymnastic exercises; vt perform; ~**en** nt -s gymnastics; (Sch) physical education, P.E.; ~**er(in** f) m -s, - gymnast; ~**halle** f gym(nasium); ~**hose** f gym shorts pl.

Turnier [tʊrˈniːr] nt -s, -e tournament.

Turnus ['tʊrnʊs] m -, -se rota; **im ~ in** rotation.

Turn- cpd: ~**verein** m gymnastics club; ~**zeug** nt gym things pl.

Tusche ['tʊʃə] f -, -n Indian ink.

tuscheln ['tʊʃəln] vti whisper.

Tuschkasten m paintbox.

Tüte ['tyːtə] f -, -n bag.

tuten ['tuːtən] vi (Aut) hoot.

TÜV [tʏf] m MOT.

Typ [tyːp] m -s, -en type; ~**e** f -, -n (Print) type.

Typhus ['tyːfʊs] m - typhoid (fever).

typisch ['tyːpɪʃ] a typical (für of).

Tyrann [tyˈran] m -en, -en tyrant; ~**ei** [-ˈnaɪ] f tyranny; **t~isch** a tyrannical; **t~i'sieren** vt tyrannize.

U

U, u [uː] nt U, u.

U-Bahn ['uːbaːn] f underground, tube.

übel ['yːbəl] a bad; (moralisch auch) wicked; **jdm ist ~** sb feels sick; **Ü~** nt -s, - evil; (Krankheit) disease; ~**gelaunt** a bad-tempered, ill-humoured; **Ü~keit** f nausea; ~**nehmen** vt irreg: **jdm eine Bemerkung** etc ~**nehmen** be offended at sb's remark etc; **Ü~stand** m bad state of affairs, abuse; ~**wollend** a malevolent.

üben ['yːbən] vti exercise, practise.

über ['yːbər] prep +dat or acc over; (hoch — auch) above; (quer — auch) across; (Route) via; (betreffend) about; ad over; **den ganzen Tag ~** all day long; **jdm in etw** (dat) ~ **sein** (col) be superior to sb in sth; ~ **und ~** all over; ~**all** [yːbərˈal] ad everywhere.

überanstrengen [yːbərˈʔanʃtrɛŋən] vtr insep overexert (o.s.).

überantworten [yːbərˈʔantvɔrtən] vt insep hand over, deliver (up).

überarbeiten [yːbərˈʔarbaɪtən] vt insep revise, rework; vr overwork (o.s.).

überaus ['yːbərˈaʊs] ad exceedingly.

überbelichten [yːbərbəˈlɪçtən] vt (Phot) overexpose.

über'bieten vt irreg insep outbid; (übertreffen) surpass; Rekord break.

Überbleibsel ['yːbərblaɪpsəl] nt -s, - residue, remainder.

Überblick ['yːbərblɪk] m view; (fig) (Darstellung) survey, overview; (Fähigkeit) overall view, grasp (über +acc of); **ü~en** [-ˈblɪkən] vt insep survey.

überbring- [yːbərˈbrɪŋ] cpd: ~**en** vt irreg insep deliver, hand over; **Ü~er** m -s, - bearer; **Ü~ung** f delivery.

überbrücken [yːbərˈbrʏkən] vt insep bridge (over).

über'dauern vt insep outlast.

über'denken vt irreg insep think over.

überdies [yːbərˈdiːs] ad besides.

überdimensional ['yːbərdimɛnzionaːl] a oversize.

Überdruß ['yːbərdrʊs] m -sses weariness; **bis zum ~** ad nauseam.

überdrüssig ['yːbərdrʏsɪç] a tired, sick (gen of).

übereifrig ['yːbəraɪfrɪç] a overkeen, overzealous.

übereilen [yːbərˈʔaɪlən] vt insep hurry.

übereilt a (over)hasty, premature.

überein- [y:bər'aın] cpd: ~ander [y:bər'aı'nandər] ad one upon the other; sprechen about each other; ~anderschlagen vt irreg fold, cross; ~kommen vi irreg agree; Ü~kunft f -, -künfte agreement; ~stimmen vi agree; Ü~stimmung f agreement.

überempfindlich ['y:bərɛmpfıntlıç] a hypersensitive.

überfahren ['y:bərfa:rən] irreg vt take across; vi (go a)cross; [-'fa:rən] vt insep (Aut) run over; (fig) walk all over.

Überfahrt ['y:bərfa:rt] f crossing.

Überfall ['y:bərfal] m (Bank~, Mil) raid; (auf jdn) assault; ü~en [-'falən] vt irreg insep attack; Bank raid; (besuchen) surprise.

überfällig ['y:bərfɛlıç] a overdue.

über'fliegen vt irreg insep fly over, overfly; Buch skim through.

Überfluß ['y:bərflus] m (super)abundance, excess (an +dat of).

überflüssig ['y:bərflysıç] a superfluous.

über'fordern vt insep demand too much of; Kräfte etc overtax.

über'führen vt insep Leiche etc transport; Täter have convicted (gen of).

Über'führung f transport; conviction; (Brücke) bridge, overpass.

Übergabe ['y:bərga:bə] f handing over; (Mil) surrender.

Übergang ['y:bərgaŋ] m crossing; (Wandel, Überleitung) transition; ~serscheinung f transitory phenomenon; ~slösung f provisional solution, stopgap; ~sstadium nt state of transition; ~szeit f transitional period.

über'geben irreg insep vt hand over; (Mil) surrender; dem Verkehr ~ open to traffic; vr be sick.

übergehen ['y:bərge:ən] irreg vi (Besitz) pass; (zum Feind etc) go over, defect; (überleiten) go on (zu to); (sich verwandeln) turn (in +acc into); [-'ge:ən] vt insep pass over, omit.

Übergewicht ['y:bərgvıçt] nt excess weight; (fig) preponderance.

überglücklich ['y:bərglyklıç] a overjoyed.

übergroß ['y:bərgro:s] a outsize, huge.

überhaben ['y:bərha:bən] vt irreg (col) be fed up with.

überhandnehmen [y:bər'hantne:mən] vi irreg gain the ascendancy.

überhängen ['y:bərhɛŋən] vi irreg overhang.

überhaupt [y:bər'haupt] ad at all; (im allgemeinen) in general; (besonders) especially; ~ nicht not at all.

überheblich [y:bər'he:plıç] a arrogant; Ü~keit f arrogance.

über'holen vt insep overtake; (Tech) overhaul.

überholt a out-of-date, obsolete.

über'hören vt insep not hear; (absichtlich) ignore.

überirdisch ['y:bər'ırdıʃ] a supernatural, unearthly.

überkompensieren ['y:bərkɔmpɛnzı:rən] vt insep overcompensate for.

über'laden vt irreg insep overload; a (fig) cluttered.

über'lassen irreg insep vt: jdm etw ~ leave sth to sb; vr: sich etw (dat) ~ give o.s. over to sth.

über'lasten vt insep overload; Mensch overtax.

überlaufen ['y:bərlaufən] irreg vi (Flüssigkeit) flow over; (zum Feind etc) go over, defect; [-'laufən] insep vt (Schauer etc) come over; ~ sein be inundated or besieged.

Überläufer ['y:bərlɔyfər] m -s, - deserter.

über'leben vt insep survive; Ü~de(r) mf survivor.

über'legen vt insep consider; a superior; Ü~heit f superiority.

Überlegung f consideration, deliberation.

über'liefern vt insep hand down, transmit.

Überlieferung f tradition.

überlisten [y:bər'lıstən] vt insep outwit.

überm ['y:bərm] = über dem.

Übermacht ['y:bərmaxt] f superior force, superiority.

übermächtig ['y:bərmɛçtıç] a superior (in strength); Gefühl etc overwhelming.

übermannen [y:bər'manən] vt insep overcome.

Übermaß ['y:bərma:s] nt excess (an +dat of).

übermäßig ['y:bərmɛ:sıç] a excessive.

Übermensch ['y:bərmɛnʃ] m superman; ü~lich a superhuman.

übermitteln [y:bər'mıtəln] vt insep convey.

übermorgen ['y:bərmɔrgən] ad the day after tomorrow.

Übermüdung [y:bər'my:duŋ] f fatigue, overtiredness.

Übermut ['y:bərmu:t] m exuberance.

übermütig ['y:bərmy:tıç] a exuberant, high-spirited; ~ werden get overconfident.

übernachten [y:bər'naxtən] vi insep spend the night (bei jdm at sb's place).

übernächtigt [y:bər'nɛçtıçt] a tired, sleepy.

Übernahme ['y:bərna:mə] f -, -n taking over or on, acceptance.

über'nehmen irreg insep vt take on, accept; Amt, Geschäft take over; vr take on too much.

über'prüfen vt insep examine, check.

Überprüfung f examination.

überqueren [y:bər'kve:rən] vt insep cross.

überragen [y:bər'ra:gən] vt insep tower above; (fig) surpass; ['y:bərra:gən] vi project, stick out.

überraschen [y:bər'raʃən] vt insep surprise.

Überraschung f surprise.

überreden [y:bər're:dən] vt insep persuade.

überreich ['y:bərraıç] a very/too rich; ~en [-'raıçən] vt insep present, hand over; ~lich a, ad (more than) ample.

überreizt [y:bər'raıtst] a overwrought.

Überreste ['yːbɐrɛstə] *pl* remains *pl*, remnants *pl*.

überrumpeln [yːbɐ'rʊmpəln] *vt insep* take by surprise.

überrunden [yːbɐ'rʊndən] *vt insep* lap.

übers ['yːbɐs] = **über das.**

übersättigen [yːbɐ'zɛtɪgən] *vt insep* satiate.

Überschall- ['yːbɐʃal] *cpd*: ~**flugzeug** *nt* supersonic jet; ~**geschwindigkeit** *f* supersonic speed.

über'schätzen *vtr insep* overestimate.

überschäumen ['yːbɐʃɔʏmən] *vi* froth over; *(fig)* bubble over.

Überschlag ['yːbɐʃlaːk] *m (Fin)* estimate; *(Sport)* somersault; **ü~en** [-'ʃlaːgən] *irreg insep vt (berechnen)* estimate; *(auslassen) Seite* omit; *vr* somersault; *(Stimme)* crack; *(Aviat)* loop the loop; *a* lukewarm, tepid; ['yːbɐʃlaːgən] *irreg vt Beine* cross; *vi (Wellen)* break over; *(Funken)* flash over.

überschnappen ['yːbɐʃnapən] *vi (Stimme)* crack; *(col: Mensch)* flip one's lid.

über'schneiden *vr irreg insep (lit, fig)* overlap; *(Linien)* intersect.

über'schreiben *vt irreg insep* provide with a heading; **jdm etw** ~ transfer *or* make over sth to sb.

über'schreiten *vt irreg insep* cross over; *(fig)* exceed; *(verletzen)* transgress.

Überschrift ['yːbɐʃrɪft] *f* heading, title.

Überschuß ['yːbɐʃʊs] *m* surplus (an +*dat* of).

überschüssig ['yːbɐʃʏsɪç] *a* surplus, excess.

über'schütten *vt insep* **jdn/etw mit etw** ~ *(lit)* pour sth over sb/sth; **jdn mit etw** ~ *(fig)* shower sb with sth.

Überschwang ['yːbɐʃvaŋ] *m* exuberance, excess.

überschwemmen [yːbɐ'ʃvɛmən] *vt insep* flood.

Überschwemmung *f* flood.

überschwenglich ['yːbɐʃvɛŋlɪç] *a* effusive; **Ü~keit** *f* effusion.

Übersee ['yːbɐzeː] *f* **nach/in** ~ overseas; **ü~isch** *a* overseas.

über'sehen *vt irreg insep* look (out) over; *(fig) Folgen* see, get an overall view of; *(nicht beachten)* overlook.

über'senden *vt irreg insep* send, forward.

übersetz- *cpd* ~**en** [yːbɐ'zɛtsən] *vt insep* translate; ['yːbɐzɛtsən] *vi* cross; **Ü~er(in** *f***)** [-'zɛtsər(ɪn)] *m* -**s,** - translator; **Ü~ung** [-zɛtsʊŋ] *f* translation; *(Tech)* gear ratio.

Übersicht ['yːbɐzɪçt] *f* overall view; *(Darstellung)* survey; **ü~lich** *a* clear; *Gelände* open; ~**lichkeit** *f* clarity, lucidity.

übersiedeln ['yːbɐziːdəln] *or* [yːbɐ'ziːdəln] *vi sep or insep* move.

über'spannen *vt insep (zu sehr spannen)* overstretch; *(überdecken)* cover.

überspannt *a* eccentric; *Idee* wild, crazy; **Ü~keit** *f* eccentricity.

überspitzt [yːbɐ'ʃpɪtst] *a* exaggerated.

über'springen *vt irreg insep* jump over; *(fig)* skip.

übersprudeln ['yːbɐʃpruːdəln] *vi* bubble over.

überstehen [yːbɐ'ʃteːən] *irreg vt insep* overcome, get over; *Winter etc* survive, get through; ['yːbɐʃteːən] *vi* project.

über'steigen *vt irreg insep* climb over; *(fig)* exceed.

über'stimmen *vt insep* outvote.

Überstunden ['yːbɐʃtʊndən] *pl* overtime.

über'stürzen *insep vt* rush; *vr* follow (one another) in rapid succession.

überstürzt *a* (over)hasty.

übertölpeln [yːbɐ'tœlpəln] *vt insep* dupe.

über'tönen *vt insep* drown (out).

Übertrag ['yːbɐtraːk] *m* -**(e)s, -träge** *(Comm)* amount brought forward; **ü~bar** [-'traːkbaːr] *a* transferable; *(Med)* infectious; **ü~en** [-'traːgən] *irreg insep vt* transfer *(auf +acc* to); *(Med)* broadcast; *(übersetzen)* render; *Krankheit* transmit; **jdm etw ü~en** assign sth to sb; *vr* spread *(auf +acc* to); *a* figurative; ~**ung** [-'traːgʊŋ] *f* transfer(ence); *(Rad)* broadcast; rendering; transmission.

über'treffen *vt irreg insep* surpass.

über'treiben *vt irreg insep* exaggerate.

Übertreibung *f* exaggeration.

übertreten [yːbɐ'treːtən] *irreg vt insep* cross; *Gebot etc* break; ['yːbɐtreːtən] *vi (über Linie, Gebiet)* step (over); *(Sport)* overstep; *(in anderer Partei)* go over *(in +acc* to); *(zu anderem Glauben)* be converted.

Über'tretung *f* violation, transgression.

übertrieben [yːbɐ'triːbən] *a* exaggerated, excessive.

übertrumpfen [yːbɐ'trʊmpfən] *vt insep* outdo; *(Cards)* overtrump.

übervölkert [yːbɐ'fœlkɐt] *a* overpopulated.

übervoll ['yːbɐfɔl] *a* overfull.

übervorteilen [yːbɐ'fɔrtaɪlən] *vt insep* dupe, cheat.

über'wachen *vt insep* supervise; *Verdächtigen* keep under surveillance.

Überwachung *f* supervision; surveillance.

überwältigen [yːbɐ'vɛltɪgən] *vt insep* overpower; ~**d** *a* overwhelming.

überweisen [yːbɐ'vaɪzən] *vt irreg insep* transfer.

Überweisung *f* transfer.

über'wiegen *vi irreg insep* predominate; ~**d** *a* predominant.

über'winden *irreg insep vt* overcome; *vr* make an effort, bring oneself (to do sth).

Überwindung *f* effort, strength of mind.

Überwurf ['yːbɐvʊrf] *m* wrap, shawl.

Überzahl ['yːbɐtsaːl] *f* superiority, superior numbers *pl*; **in der** ~ **sein** outnumber sb, be numerically superior.

überzählig ['yːbɐtsɛːlɪç] *a* surplus.

über'zeugen *vt insep* convince; ~**d** *a* convincing.

Überzeugung *f* conviction; ~**skraft** *f* power of persuasion.

überziehen [yːbɐ'tsiːən] *irreg vt* put on [-'tsiːən] *vt insep* cover; *Konto* overdraw.

Überzug ['yːbɐtsuːk] *m* cover; *(Belag)* coating.

üblich ['yːplɪç] *a* usual.

U-Boot ['u:bo:t] *nt* submarine.

übrig ['y:brɪç] *a* remaining; **für jdn etwas ~ haben** *(col)* be fond of sb; **die ~en** ['y:brɪgən] the others; **das ~e** the rest; **im ~en** besides; **~bleiben** *vi irreg* remain, be left (over); **~ens** *ad* besides; *(nebenbei bemerkt)* by the way; **~lassen** *vt irreg* leave (over).

Übung ['y:bʊŋ] *f* practice; *(Turn, Aufgabe etc)* exercise; **~ macht den Meister** practice makes perfect.

Ufer ['u:fər] *nt* **-s, -** bank; *(Meeres—)* shore; **~befestigung** *f* embankment.

Uhr [u:r] *f* **-, -en** clock; *(Armband—)* watch; **wieviel ~ ist es?** what time is it?; **1 ~** 1 o'clock; **20 ~** 8 o'clock, 20.00 (twenty hundred) hours; **~band** *nt* watch strap; **~(en)gehäuse** *nt* clock/ watch case; **~kette** *f* watch chain; **~macher** *m* **-s, -** watchmaker; **~werk** *nt* clockwork; works of a watch; **~zeiger** *m* hand; **~zeigersinn** *m*: **im ~zeigersinn** clockwise; **entgegen dem ~zeigersinn** anticlockwise; **~zeit** *f* time (of day).

Uhu ['u:hu] *m* **-s, -s** eagle owl.

UKW [u:ka:'ve:] *abbr* VHF.

Ulk [ʊlk] *m* **-s, -e** lark; **u~ig** *a* funny.

Ulme ['ʊlmə] *f* **-, -n** elm.

Ultimatum [ulti'ma:tʊm] *nt* **-s,** **Ultimaten** ultimatum.

Ultra- *cpd:* **~kurzwellen** [ultra-'kʊrtsvɛlən] *pl* very high frequency; **u~violett** ['ultra-] *a* ultraviolet.

um [ʊm] *prep* +acc (a)round; *(zeitlich)* at; *(mit Größenangabe)* by; *(für)* for; **er schlug ~ sich** he hit about him; **Stunde ~ Stunde** hour after hour; **Auge ~ Auge** an eye for an eye; **~ vieles (besser)** (better) by far; **~ nichts besser** not in the least better; **~ so besser** so much the better; **~ . . . willen** for the sake of; *cj (damit)* (in order) to; **zu klug, ~ zu . . .** clever to . . .; *ad (ungefähr)* about.

umadressieren ['ʊmadrɛsi:rən] *vt* readdress.

umänder- ['ʊm'ɛndər] *cpd:* **~n** *vt* alter; **U~ung** *f* alteration.

umarbeiten ['ʊm'arbaitən] *vt* remodel; *Buch etc* revise, rework.

umarmen ['ʊm'armən] *vt insep* embrace.

Umbau ['ʊmbau] *m* **-(e)s, -e** or **-ten** reconstruction, alteration(s); **u~en** *vt* rebuild, reconstruct.

umbenennen ['ʊmbənɛnən] *vt irreg* rename.

umbiegen ['ʊmbi:gən] *vt irreg* bend (over).

umbilden ['ʊmbɪldən] *vt* reorganize; *(Pol)* Kabinett reshuffle.

umbinden ['ʊmbɪndən] *vt irreg* Krawatte etc put on; ['·bɪndən] *vt irreg insep* tie (sth) round.

umblättern ['ʊmblɛtərn] *vt* turn over.

umblicken ['ʊmblɪkən] *vr* look around.

umbringen ['ʊmbrɪŋən] *vt irreg* kill.

Umbruch ['ʊmbrʊx] *m* radical change; *(Print)* make-up.

umbuchen ['ʊmbu:xən] *vti* change one's reservation/flight *etc*.

umdenken ['ʊmdɛŋkən] *vi irreg* adjust one's views.

um'drängen *vt insep* crowd round.

umdrehen ['ʊmdre:ən] *vtr* turn (round); *Hals* wring.

Um'drehung *f* revolution; rotation.

umeinander [ʊm'ai'nandər] *ad* round one another; *(für einander)* for one another.

umfahren ['ʊmfa:rən] *vt irreg* run over; ['·fa:rən] *insep* drive/sail round.

umfallen ['ʊmfalən] *vi irreg* fall down or over.

Umfang ['ʊmfaŋ] *m* extent; *(von Buch)* size; *(Reichweite)* range; *(Fläche)* area; *(Math)* circumference; **u~reich** *a* extensive; *Buch etc* voluminous.

um'fassen *vt insep* embrace; *(umgeben)* surround; *(enthalten)* include; **~d** *a* comprehensive, extensive.

umform- ['ʊmfɔrm] *cpd:* **~en** *vi* transform; **U~er** *m* **-s, -** *(Elec)* transformer, converter.

Umfrage ['ʊmfra:gə] *f* poll.

umfüllen ['ʊmfylən] *vt* transfer; *Wein* decant.

umfunktionieren ['ʊmfʊŋktsioni:rən] *vt* convert, transform.

Umgang ['ʊmgaŋ] *m* company; *(mit jdm)* dealings *pl*; *(Behandlung)* way of behaving.

umgänglich ['ʊmgɛŋlɪç] *a* sociable.

Umgangs- *cpd:* **~formen** *pl* manners *pl*; **~sprache** *f* colloquial language.

umgeb- [ʊm'ge:b] *cpd:* **~en** *vt irreg insep* surround; **U~ung** *f* surroundings *pl*; *(Milieu)* environment; *(Personen)* people in one's circle.

umgehen ['ʊmge:ən] *irreg vi* go (a)round; *(Gespenst)* haunt; **im Schlosse ~** haunt the castle; **mit jdm grob etc ~** treat sb roughly *etc*; **mit Geld sparsam ~** be careful with one's money; ['·ge:ən] *vt insep* bypass; *(Mil)* outflank; *Gesetz etc* circumvent; *(vermeiden)* avoid; '**~d** *a* immediate.

Um'gehung *f* bypassing; outflanking; circumvention; avoidance; **~sstraße** *f* bypass.

umgekehrt ['ʊmgəke:rt] *a* reverse(d); *(gegenteilig)* opposite; *ad* the other way around; **und ~** and vice versa.

umgraben ['ʊmgra:bən] *vt irreg* dig up.

umgruppieren ['ʊmgrupi:rən] *vt* regroup.

Umhang ['ʊmhaŋ] *m* wrap, cape.

umhängen ['ʊmhɛŋən] *vt* Bild hang somewhere else; **jdm etw ~** put sth on sb.

umhauen ['ʊmhauən] *vt* fell; *(fig)* bowl over.

umher [ʊm'he:r] *ad* about, around; **~gehen** *vi irreg* walk about; **~reisen** *vi* travel about; **~schweifen** *vi* roam about; **~ziehen** *vi irreg* wander from place to place.

umhinkönnen [ʊm'hɪnkœnən] *vi irreg* **ich kann nicht umhin, das zu tun** I can't help doing it.

umhören ['ʊmhø:rən] *vr* ask around.

Umkehr ['ʊmke:r] *f* **-** turning back; *(Änderung)* change; **u~en** *vi* turn back; *vt* turn round, reverse; *Tasche etc* turn inside out; *Gefäß etc* turn upside down.

umkippen ['ʊmkɪpən] *vt* tip over; *vi* overturn; *(fig: Meinung ändern)* change one's mind; *(col: Mensch)* keel over.

Umkleideraum ['ʊmklaɪdəraʊm] *m* changing *or* dressing room.

umkommen ['ʊmkɔmən] *vi irreg* die, perish; *(Lebensmittel)* go bad.

Umkreis ['ʊmkraɪs] *m* neighbourhood; *(Math)* circumcircle; **im ~ von** within a radius of; **u~en** ['ʊm'kraɪzən] *vt insep* circle (round); *(Satellit)* orbit.

umladen ['ʊmla:dən] *vt irreg* transfer, reload.

Umlage ['ʊmla:gə] *f* share of the costs.

Umlauf ['ʊmlaʊf] *m (Geld—)* circulation; *(von Gestirn)* revolution; *(Schreiben)* circular; **~bahn** *f* orbit.

Umlaut ['ʊmlaʊt] *m* umlaut.

umlegen ['ʊmle:gən] *vt* put on; *(verlegen)* move, shift; *Kosten* share out; *(umkippen)* tip over; *(col: töten)* bump off.

umleiten ['ʊmlaɪtən] *vt* divert.

Umleitung *f* diversion.

umlernen ['ʊmlɛrnən] *vi* learn something new; adjust one's views.

umliegend ['ʊmli:gənt] *a* surrounding.

Umnachtung [ʊm'naxtʊŋ] *f* (mental) derangement.

um'rahmen *vt insep* frame.

um'randen *vt insep* border, edge.

umrechnen ['ʊmrɛçnən] *vt* convert.

Umrechnung *f* conversion; **~skurs** *m* rate of exchange.

um'reißen *vt irreg insep* outline, sketch.

um'ringen *vt insep* surround.

Umriß ['ʊmrɪs] *m* outline.

umrühren ['ʊmry:rən] *vti* stir.

ums [ʊms] = **um das.**

umsatteln ['ʊmzatəln] *vi (col)* change one's occupation; switch.

Umsatz ['ʊmzats] *m* turnover.

umschalten ['ʊmʃaltən] *vt* switch.

Umschau ['ʊmʃaʊ] *f* look(ing) round; **~ halten nach** look around for; **u~en** *vr* look round.

Umschlag ['ʊmʃla:k] *m* cover; *(Buchauch)* jacket; *(Med)* compress; *(Brief—)* envelope; *(Wechsel)* change; *(von Hose)* turn-up; **u~en** ['ʊmʃla:gən] *irreg vi* change; *(Naut)* capsize; *vt* knock over; *Ärmel* turn up; *Seite* turn over; *Waren* transfer; **~platz** *m (Comm)* distribution centre.

umschreiben *vt irreg* ['ʊmʃraɪbən] *(neu—)* rewrite; *(übertragen)* transfer *(auf +acc* to); [-'ʃraɪbən] *insep* paraphrase; *(abgrenzen)* circumscribe, define.

umschulen ['ʊmʃu:lən] *vt* retrain; *Kind* send to another school.

umschwärmen [ʊm'ʃvɛrmən] *vt insep* swarm round; *(fig)* surround, idolize.

Umschweife ['ʊmʃvaɪfə] *pl:* **ohne ~** without beating about the bush, straight out.

Umschwung ['ʊmʃvʊŋ] *m* change (around), revolution.

umsehen ['ʊmze:ən] *vr irreg* look around *or* about; *(suchen)* look out *(nach* for).

umseitig ['ʊmzaɪtɪç] *ad* overleaf.

Umsicht ['ʊmzɪçt] *f* prudence, caution; **u~ig** *a* cautious, prudent.

umsonst [ʊm'zɔnst] *ad* in vain; *(gratis)* for nothing.

umspringen ['ʊmʃprɪŋən] *vi irreg* change; *(Wind auch)* veer; **mit jdm ~** treat sb badly.

Umstand ['ʊmʃtant] *m* circumstance; **Umstände** *pl (fig: Schwierigkeiten)* fuss; **in anderen Umständen sein** be pregnant; **Umstände machen** go to a lot of trouble; **unter Umständen** possibly; **mildernde Umstände** *(Jur)* extenuating circumstances.

umständlich ['ʊmʃtɛntlɪç] *a,ad Methode* cumbersome, complicated; *Ausdrucksweise, Erklärung auch* long-winded; *Mensch* ponderous.

Umstands- *cpd:* **~kleid** *nt* maternity dress; **~wort** *nt* adverb.

Umstehende(n) ['ʊmʃte:əndə(n)] *pl* bystanders *pl.*

Umsteig- ['ʊmʃtaɪg] *cpd:* **~ekarte** *f* transfer ticket; **u~en** *vi irreg (Rail)* change.

umstellen ['ʊmʃtɛlən] *vt (an anderen Ort)* change round, rearrange; *(Tech)* convert; *vr* adapt o.s. *(auf +acc* to); [ʊm'ʃtɛlən] *vt insep* surround.

Umstellung [ʊm'ʃtɛlʊŋ] *f* change; *(Umgewöhnung)* adjustment; *(Tech)* conversion.

umstimmen ['ʊmʃtɪmən] *vt (Mus)* retune; **jdn ~** make sb change his mind.

umstoßen ['ʊmʃto:sən] *vt irreg (lit)* overturn; *Plan etc* change, upset.

umstritten [ʊm'ʃtrɪtən] *a* disputed.

Umsturz ['ʊmʃtʊrts] *m* overthrow.

umstürzen ['ʊmʃtʏrtsən] *vt (umwerfen)* overturn; *vi* collapse, fall down; *Wagen* overturn.

umstürzlerisch *a* revolutionary.

Umtausch ['ʊmtaʊʃ] *m* exchange; **u~en** *vt* exchange.

Umtriebe ['ʊmtri:bə] *pl* machinations *pl,* intrigues *pl.*

umtun ['ʊmtu:n] *vr irreg* see; **sich nach etw ~** look for sth.

umwandeln ['ʊmvandəln] *vt* change, convert; *(Elec)* transform.

umwechseln ['ʊmvɛksəln] *vt* change.

Umweg ['ʊmve:k] *m* detour, roundabout way.

Umwelt ['ʊmvɛlt] *f* environment; **~verschmutzung** *f* environmental pollution.

umwenden ['ʊmvɛndən] *vtr irreg* turn (round).

um'werben *vt irreg insep* court, woo.

umwerfen ['ʊmvɛrfən] *vt irreg (lit)* upset, overturn; *Mantel* throw on; *(fig: erschüttern)* upset, throw.

umziehen ['ʊmtsi:ən] *irreg vtr* change; *vi* move.

umzingeln [ʊm'tsɪŋəln] *vt insep* surround, encircle.

Umzug ['ʊmtsu:k] *m* procession; *(Wohnungs—)* move, removal.

unab- ['ʊn'ap] *cpd:* **~'änderlich** *a* irreversible, unalterable; **~hängig** *a* independent; **~hängigkeit** *f* independence; **~kömmlich** *a* indispensable; **zur Zeit ~kömmlich** not free at the moment; **~lässig** *a* incessant, constant; **~sehbar** *a* immeasurable; *Folgen* unforeseeable; *Kosten* incalculable; ~**sichtlich** *a* unintentional; ~'**wendbar** *a* inevitable.

unachtsam ['un'axtza:m] *a* careless; **U**~**keit** *f* carelessness.

unan- ['un'an] *cpd*: ~'**fechtbar** *a* indisputable; ~**gebracht** *a* uncalled-for; ~**gemessen** *a* inadequate; ~**genehm** *a* unpleasant; **U**~**nehmlichkeit** *f* inconvenience; *pl* trouble; ~**sehnlich** *a* unsightly; ~'**ständig** *a* indecent, improper; **U**~**ständigkeit** *f* indecency, impropriety.

unappetitlich ['un'apeti:tlıç] *a* unsavoury.

Unart ['un'a:rt] *f* bad manners *pl*; *(Angewohnheit)* bad habit; **u**~**ig** *a* naughty, badly behaved.

unauf- ['un'auf] *cpd*: ~**fällig** *a* unobtrusive; *Kleidung* inconspicuous; ~-'**findbar** *a* undiscoverable, not to be found; ~**gefordert** *a* unasked; *ad* spontaneously; ~**haltsam** *a* irresistible; ~'**hörlich** *a* incessant, continuous; ~**merksam** *a* inattentive; ~**richtig** *a* insincere.

unaus- ['un'aus] *cpd*: ~'**bleiblich** *a* inevitable, unavoidable; ~**geglichen** *a* volatile; ~'**sprechlich** *a* inexpressible; ~'**stehlich** *a* intolerable; ~'**weichlich** *a* inescapable, ineluctable.

unbändig ['unbɛndıç] *a* extreme, excessive.

unbarmherzig ['unbarmhɛrtsıç] *a* pitiless, merciless.

unbeabsichtigt ['unbə'apzıçtıçt] *a* unintentional.

unbeachtet ['unbə'axtət] *a* unnoticed, ignored.

unbedenklich ['unbədɛŋklıç] *a* unhesitating; *Plan* unobjectionable; *ad* without hesitation.

unbedeutend ['unbədɔʏtənt] *a* insignificant, unimportant; *Fehler* slight.

unbedingt ['unbədıŋt] *a* unconditional; *ad* absolutely; **mußt du** ~ **gehen?** do you really have to go?

unbefangen ['unbəfaŋən] *a* impartial, unprejudiced; *(ohne Hemmungen)* uninhibited; **U**~**heit** *f* impartiality; uninhibitedness.

unbefriedig- ['unbəfri:dıg] *cpd*: ~**end** *a* unsatisfactory; ~**t** [-dıçt] *a* unsatisfied, dissatisfied.

unbefugt ['unbəfu:kt] *a* unauthorized.

unbegabt ['unbəga:pt] *a* untalented.

unbegreiflich ['unbə'graıflıç] *a* inconceivable.

unbegrenzt ['unbəgrɛntst] *a* unlimited.

unbegründet ['unbəgrʏndət] *a* unfounded.

Unbehag- ['unbəha:g] *cpd*: ~**en** *nt* discomfort; **u**~**lich** [-lıç] *a* uncomfortable; *Gefühl* uneasy.

unbeholfen ['unbəhɔlfən] *a* awkward, clumsy; **U**~**heit** *f* awkwardness, clumsiness.

unbeirrt ['unbə'ırt] *a* imperturbable.

unbekannt ['unbəkant] *a* unknown.

unbekümmert ['unbəkʏmərt] *a* unconcerned.

unbeliebt ['unbəli:pt] *a* unpopular; **U**~**heit** *f* unpopularity.

unbequem ['unbəkve:m] *a* *Stuhl*

uncomfortable; *Mensch* bothersome; *Regelung* inconvenient.

unberech- *cpd*: ~**enbar** [unbə'rɛçənba:r] *a* incalculable; *Mensch, Verhalten* unpredictable; ~**tigt** ['unbərɛçtıçt] *a* unjustified; *(nicht erlaubt)* unauthorized.

unberufen [unbə'ru:fən] *interj* touch wood.

unberührt ['unbərʏ:rt] *a* untouched, intact; **sie ist noch** ~ she is still a virgin.

unbescheiden ['unbəʃaıdən] *a* presumptuous.

unbeschreiblich [unbə'ʃraıplıç] *a* indescribable.

unbesonnen ['unbəzɔnən] *a* unwise, rash, imprudent.

unbeständig ['unbəʃtɛndıç] *a* *Mensch* inconstant; *Wetter* unsettled; *Lage* unstable.

unbestechlich [unbə'ʃtɛçlıç] *a* incorruptible.

unbestimmt ['unbəʃtımt] *a* indefinite; *Zukunft auch* uncertain; **U**~**heit** *f* vagueness.

unbeteiligt [unbə'taılıçt] *a* unconcerned, indifferent.

unbeugsam ['unbɔʏkza:m] *a* inflexible, stubborn; *Wille auch* unbending.

unbewacht ['unbəvaxt] *a* unguarded, unwatched.

unbeweglich ['unbəve:klıç] *a* immovable.

unbewußt ['unbəvust] *a* unconscious.

unbrauchbar ['unbrauxba:r] *a* *Arbeit* useless; *Gerät auch* unusable; **U**~**keit** *f* uselessness.

und [unt] *cj* and; ~ **so weiter** and so on.

Undank ['unaŋk] *m* ingratitude; **u**~**bar** *a* ungrateful; ~**barkeit** *f* ingratitude.

undefinierbar [undefi'ni:rba:r] *a* indefinable.

undenkbar [un'dɛŋkba:r] *a* inconceivable.

undeutlich ['undɔʏtlıç] *a* indistinct.

undicht ['undıçt] *a* leaky.

Unding ['undıŋ] *nt* absurdity.

unduldsam ['unduldsa:m] *a* intolerant.

undurch- ['undurç] *cpd*: ~**führbar** [-'fy:rba:r] *a* impracticable; ~**lässig** [-lɛsıç] *a* waterproof, impermeable; ~**sichtig** [-zıçtıç] *a* opaque; *(fig)* obscure.

uneben ['un'e:bən] *a* uneven.

unehelich ['un'e:əlıç] *a* illegitimate.

uneigennützig ['un'aıgənnʏtsıç] *a* unselfish.

uneinig ['un'aınıç] *a* divided; ~ **sein** disagree; **U**~**keit** *f* discord, dissension.

uneins ['un'aıns] *a* at variance, at odds.

unempfindlich ['un'empfıntlıç] *a* insensitive; **U**~**keit** *f* insensitivity.

unendlich [un''ɛntlıç] *a* infinite; **U**~**keit** *f* infinity.

unent- ['un'ɛnt] *cpd*: ~**behrlich** [-'be:rlıç] *a* indispensable; ~**geltlich** [-gɛltlıç] *a* free (of charge); ~**schieden** [-'ʃi:dən] *a* undecided; ~**schieden enden** *(Sport)* end in a draw; ~**schlossen** [-'ʃlɔsən] *a* undecided, irresolute; ~**wegt** [-'ve:kt] *a* unswerving; *(unaufhörlich)* incessant.

uner- [un'er] *cpd*: ~**bittlich** [-bıtlıç] *a* unyielding, inexorable; ~**fahren** [-'fa:rən] *a* inexperienced; ~**freulich** [-frɔʏlıç] *a*

unpleasant; **~gründlich** [-'gryntlɪç] *a*
unfathomable; **~heblich** [-he:plɪç] *a*
unimportant; **~hört** [-hø:rt] *a* unheard-of;
Bitte outrageous; **~läßlich** [-'lɛslɪç] *a*
indispensable; **~laubt** [-laupt] *a*
unauthorized; **~meßlich** [-'mɛslɪç] *a*
immeasurable, immense; **~müdlich**
[-'my:tlɪç] *a* indefatigable; **~sättlich**
[-'zetlɪç] *a* insatiable; **~schöpflich**
[-'ʃœpflɪç] *a* inexhaustible; **~schütterlich**
[-'ʃytɜrlɪç] *a* unshakeable; **~schwinglich**
[-'ʃvɪŋlɪç] *a Preis* exorbitant; too expensive;
~träglich [-'trɛːklɪç] *a* unbearable;
Frechheit insufferable; **~wartet** [-vartɜt]
a unexpected; **~wünscht** [-vynʃt] *a*
undesirable, unwelcome; **~zogen**
[-tso:gɜn] *a* ill-bred, rude.
unfähig ['unfɛ:ɪç] *a* incapable (*zu* of);
incompetent; **U~keit** *f* incapacity;
incompetence.
unfair ['unfɛːr] *a* unfair.
Unfall ['unfal] *m* accident; **~flucht** *f* hit-
and-run (driving); **~stelle** *f* scene of the
accident; **~versicherung** *f* accident
insurance.
unfaßbar [un'fasbaːr] *a* inconceivable.
unfehlbar [un'fe:lbaːr] *a* infallible; *ad*
inevitably; **U~keit** *f* infallibility.
unflätig ['unflɛ:tɪç] *a* rude.
unfolgsam ['unfɔlkza:m] *a* disobedient.
unfrankiert ['unfraŋki:rt] *a* unfranked.
unfrei ['unfraɪ] *a* not free, unfree; **~willig**
a involuntary, against one's will.
unfreundlich ['unfrɔyntlɪç] *a* unfriendly;
U~keit *f* unfriendliness.
Unfriede(n) ['unfri:dɜ(n)] *m* dissension,
strife.
unfruchtbar ['unfruxtbaːr] *a* infertile;
Gespräche unfruitful; **U~keit** *f* infertility;
unfruitfulness.
Unfug ['unfu:k] *m* **-s** (*Benehmen*) mischief;
(*Unsinn*) nonsense; **grober ~** (*Jur*) gross
misconduct; malicious damage.
ungeachtet ['ungə'axtɜt] *prep +gen* notwithstanding.
ungeahnt ['ungə'a:nt] *a* unsuspected,
undreamt-of.
ungebeten ['ungəbe:tɜn] *a* uninvited.
ungebildet ['ungəbɪldɜt] *a* uneducated;
uncultured.
ungebräuchlich ['ungəbrɔyçlɪç] *a*
unusual, uncommon.
ungedeckt ['ungədɛkt] *a Scheck*
uncovered.
Ungeduld ['ungədult] *f* impatience; **u~ig**
[-dɪç] *a* impatient.
ungeeignet ['ungə'aɪgnɜt] *a* unsuitable.
ungefähr ['ungəfɛːr] *a* rough,
approximate; **das kommt nicht von ~**
that's hardly surprising; **~lich** *a* not
dangerous, harmless.
ungehalten ['ungəhaltɜn] *a* indignant.
ungeheuer ['ungəhɔyɜr] *a* huge; *ad* (*col*)
enormously; **U~** *nt* **-s, -** monster; **~lich**
[-'hɔyɜrlɪç] *a* monstrous.
ungehobelt ['ungəho:bɜlt] *a* (*fig*) uncouth.
ungehörig ['ungəhø:rɪç] *a* impertinent,
improper; **U~keit** *f* impertinence.
ungehorsam ['ungəho:rza:m] *a* disobedient; **U~** *m* disobedience.

ungeklärt ['ungəklɛ:rt] *a* not cleared up;
Rätsel unsolved; *Abwasser* untreated.
ungeladen ['ungəla:dən] *a* not loaded;
(*Elec*) uncharged; *Gast* uninvited.
ungelegen ['ungəle:gən] *a* inconvenient.
ungelernt ['ungəlɛrnt] *a* unskilled.
ungelogen ['ungəlo:gən] *ad* really,
honestly.
ungemein ['ungəmaɪn] *a* uncommon.
ungemütlich ['ungəmy:tlɪç] *a* uncomfortable; *Person* disagreeable.
ungenau ['ungənaʊ] *a* inaccurate; **U~ig-
keit** *f* inaccuracy.
ungeniert ['unʒeni:rt] *a* free and easy,
unceremonious; *ad* without embarrassment, freely.
ungenießbar ['ungəni:sba:r] *a* inedible;
undrinkable; (*col*) unbearable.
ungenügend ['ungəny:gənt] *a* insufficient,
inadequate.
ungepflegt ['ungəpfle:kt] *a Garten etc*
untended; *Person* unkempt; *Hände*
neglected.
ungerade ['ungəra:də] *a* uneven, odd.
ungerecht ['ungərɛçt] *a* unjust; **~fertigt**
a unjustified; **U~igkeit** *f* injustice, unfair-
ness.
ungern ['ungɛrn] *ad* unwillingly,
reluctantly.
ungeschehen ['ungəʃe:ən] *a*: **~ machen**
undo.
Ungeschick- ['ungəʃɪk] *cpd*: **~lichkeit** *f*
clumsiness; **u~t** *a* awkward, clumsy.
ungeschminkt ['ungəʃmɪŋkt] *a* without
make-up; (*fig*) unvarnished.
ungesetzlich ['ungəzɛtslɪç] *a* illegal.
ungestempelt ['ungəʃtɛmpəlt] *a Briefmarke* unfranked, uncancelled.
ungestört ['ungəʃtø:rt] *a* undisturbed.
ungestraft ['ungəʃtra:ft] *ad* with impunity.
ungestüm ['ungəʃty:m] *a* impetuous;
tempestuous; **U~** *nt* **-(e)s** impetuosity;
passion.
ungesund ['ungəzunt] *a* unhealthy.
ungetrübt ['ungətry:pt] *a* clear; (*fig*)
untroubled; *Freude* unalloyed.
Ungetüm ['ungəty:m] *nt* **-(e)s, -e**
monster.
ungewiß ['ungəvɪs] *a* uncertain; **U~heit** *f*
uncertainty.
ungewöhnlich ['ungəvø:nlɪç] *a* unusual.
ungewohnt ['ungəvo:nt] *a* unaccustomed.
Ungeziefer ['ungətsi:fər] *nt* **-s** vermin.
ungezogen ['ungətso:gən] *a* rude, impertinent; **U~heit** *f* rudeness, impertinence.
ungezwungen ['ungətsvuŋən] *a* natural,
unconstrained.
ungläubig ['unglɔybɪç] *a* unbelieving; **ein
~er Thomas** a doubting Thomas; **die
U~en** the infidel(s).
unglaub- *cpd*: **~lich** [un'glauplɪç] *a*
incredible; **~würdig** ['unglaupvyrdɪç] *a*
untrustworthy, unreliable; *Geschichte*
improbable.
ungleich ['unglaɪç] *a* dissimilar; unequal;
ad incomparably; **~artig** *a* different;
U~heit *f* dissimilarity; inequality.
Unglück ['ungyk] *nt* **-(e)s, -e** misfortune;
(*Pech*) bad luck; (*~sfall*) calamity,

disaster; (Verkehrs—) accident; **u~lich** a unhappy; (erfolglos) unlucky; (unerfreulich) unfortunate; **u~licherweise** [-'waɪzə] ad unfortunately; **u~selig** a calamitous; Person unfortunate; **~sfall** m accident, calamity.

ungültig ['ʊngyltɪç] a invalid; **U~keit** f invalidity.

ungünstig ['ʊngʏnstɪç] a unfavourable.

ungut ['ʊngut] a Gefühl uneasy; **nichts für ~** no offence.

unhaltbar ['ʊnhaltbaːr] a untenable.

Unheil ['ʊnhaɪl] nt evil; (Unglück) misfortune; **~ anrichten** cause mischief; **u~bar** a incurable; **u~bringend** a fatal, fateful; **u~voll** a disastrous.

unheimlich ['ʊnhaɪmlɪç] a weird, uncanny; ad (col) tremendously.

unhöflich ['ʊnhøːflɪç] a impolite; **U~keit** f impoliteness.

unhygienisch ['ʊnhygiˈeːnɪʃ] a unhygienic.

Uni ['ʊni] f -, -s university; **u~** [y'niː] a self-coloured.

Uniform [uniˈfɔrm] f uniform; **u~iert** [-'miːrt] a uniformed.

uninteressant ['ʊnˈɪntɛrɛsant] a uninteresting.

Universität [univɛrziˈtɛːt] f university.

unkenntlich ['ʊnkɛntlɪç] a unrecognizable.

Unkenntnis ['ʊnkɛntnɪs] f ignorance.

unklar ['ʊnklaːr] a unclear; **im ~en sein über** (+acc) be in the dark about; **U~heit** f unclarity; (Unentschiedenheit) uncertainty.

unklug ['ʊnkluːk] a unwise.

Unkosten ['ʊnkɔstən] pl expense(s).

Unkraut ['ʊnkraʊt] nt weed; weeds pl.

unlängst ['ʊnlɛŋst] ad not long ago.

unlauter ['ʊnlaʊtər] a unfair.

unleserlich ['ʊnleːzərlɪç] a illegible.

unlogisch ['ʊnloːgɪʃ] a illogical.

unlösbar [ʊn'løːsbaːr], **unlöslich** [ʊn'løːslɪç] a insoluble.

Unlust ['ʊnlʊst] f lack of enthusiasm; **u~ig** a unenthusiastic.

unmäßig ['ʊnmɛːsɪç] a immoderate.

Unmenge ['ʊnmɛŋə] f tremendous number, hundreds pl.

Unmensch ['ʊnmɛnʃ] m ogre, brute; **u~lich** a inhuman, brutal; (ungeheuer) awful.

unmerklich [ʊn'mɛrklɪç] a imperceptible.

unmißverständlich ['ʊnmɪsfɛrʃtɛntlɪç] a unmistakable.

unmittelbar ['ʊnmɪtəlbaːr] a immediate.

unmöbliert ['ʊnmøbliːrt] a unfurnished.

unmöglich ['ʊnmøːklɪç] a impossible; **U~keit** f impossibility.

unmoralisch ['ʊnmoraːlɪʃ] a immoral.

Unmut ['ʊnmuːt] m ill humour.

unnachgiebig ['ʊnnaːxɡiːbɪç] a unyielding.

unnahbar [ʊn'naːbaːr] a unapproachable.

unnötig ['ʊnnøːtɪç] a unnecessary; **~erweise** ad unnecessarily.

unnütz ['ʊnnʏts] a useless.

unordentlich ['ʊn'ɔrdəntlɪç] a untidy.

Unordnung ['ʊn'ɔrdnʊŋ] f disorder.

unparteiisch ['ʊnpartaɪʃ] a impartial; **U~e(r)** m umpire; (Fußball) referee.

unpassend ['ʊnpasənt] a inappropriate; Zeit inopportune.

unpäßlich ['ʊnpɛslɪç] a unwell.

unpersönlich ['ʊnpɛrzøːnlɪç] a impersonal.

unpolitisch ['ʊnpoliːtɪʃ] a apolitical.

unpraktisch ['ʊnpraktɪʃ] a unpractical.

unproduktiv ['ʊnprodʊktiːf] a unproductive.

unproportioniert ['ʊnprɔpɔrtsioˈniːrt] a out of proportion.

unpünktlich ['ʊnpʏnktlɪç] a unpunctual.

unrationell ['ʊnratsionɛl] a inefficient.

unrecht ['ʊnrɛçt] a wrong; **U~** nt wrong; **zu U~** wrongly; **U~ haben, im U~ sein** be wrong; **~mäßig** a unlawful, illegal.

unregelmäßig ['ʊnreːɡəlmɛsɪç] a irregular; **U~keit** f irregularity.

unreif ['ʊnraɪf] a Obst unripe; (fig) immature.

unrentabel ['ʊnrɛntaːbəl] a unprofitable.

unrichtig ['ʊnrɪçtɪç] a incorrect, wrong.

Unruh ['ʊnruː] f -, -en (von Uhr) balance; **~e** f -, -n unrest; **~estifter** m troublemaker; **u~ig** a restless.

uns [ʊns] pron acc, dat of **wir** us; ourselves.

unsachlich ['ʊnzaxlɪç] a not to the point, irrelevant; (persönlich) personal.

unsagbar [ʊn'zaːkbaːr], **unsäglich** [ʊn'zɛːklɪç] a indescribable.

unsanft ['ʊnzanft] a rough.

unsauber ['ʊnzaʊbər] a unclean, dirty; (fig) crooked; (Mus) fuzzy.

unschädlich ['ʊnʃɛːtlɪç] a harmless; **jdn/etw ~ machen** render sb/sth harmless.

unscharf ['ʊnʃarf] a indistinct; Bild etc out of focus, blurred.

unscheinbar ['ʊnʃaɪnbaːr] a insignificant; Aussehen, Haus etc. unprepossessing.

unschlagbar [ʊn'ʃlaːkbaːr] a invincible.

unschlüssig ['ʊnʃlʏsɪç] a undecided.

Unschuld ['ʊnʃʊlt] f innocence; **u~ig** [-dɪç] a innocent.

unselbständig ['ʊnzɛlpʃtɛndɪç] a dependent, over-reliant on others.

unser ['ʊnzər] pron our; gen of **wir** of us; **~e(r,s)** ours; **~einer, ~eins, ~esgleichen** pron people like us; **~erseits** ad on our part; **~twegen, ~twillen** ad (für uns) for our sake; (wegen uns) on our account; **~ige** pron: **der/die/das ~ige** ours.

unsicher ['ʊnzɪçər] a uncertain; Mensch insecure; **U~heit** f uncertainty, insecurity.

unsichtbar ['ʊnzɪçtbaːr] a invisible; **U~keit** f invisibility.

Unsinn ['ʊnzɪn] m nonsense; **u~ig** a nonsensical.

Unsitte ['ʊnzɪtə] f deplorable habit.

unsittlich ['ʊnzɪtlɪç] a indecent; **U~keit** f indecency.

unsportlich ['ʊnʃpɔrtlɪç] a not sporty; unfit; Verhalten unsporting.

unsre ['ʊnzrə] = **unsere.**

unsrige ['ʊnzrɪgə] = **unserige.**

unsterblich ['ʊnʃtɛrplɪç] a immortal; **U~keit** f immortality.

Unstimmigkeit ['ʊnʃtɪmɪçkaɪt] f inconsistency; (Streit) disagreement.

unsympathisch ['ʊnzʏmpaːtɪʃ] a unpleasant; **er ist mir ~** I don't like him.

untätig ['ʊntɛːtɪç] a idle.

untauglich ['ʊntaʊklɪç] a unsuitable; (Mil) unfit; **U~keit** f unsuitability; unfitness.

unteilbar [ʊn'taɪlbaːr] a indivisible.

unten ['ʊntən] ad below; (im Haus) downstairs; (an der Treppe etc) at the bottom; **nach ~ down**; **~ am Berg** etc at the bottom of the mountain etc; **ich bin bei ihm ~ durch** (col) he's through with me.

unter ['ʊntər] prep +acc or dat under, below; (bei Menschen) among; (während) during; ad under.

Unter- ['ʊntər] cpd: **~abteilung** f subdivision; **~arm** m forearm.

unterbe- ['ʊntərbə] cpd: **~lichten** vt (Phot) underexpose; **U~wußtsein** nt subconscious; **~zahlt** a underpaid.

unterbieten [ʊntər'biːtən] vt irreg insep (Comm) undercut; Rekord lower, reduce.

unterbinden [ʊntər'bɪndən] vt irreg insep stop, call a halt to.

Unterbodenschutz [ʊntər'boːdənʃʊts] m (Aut) underseal.

unterbrech- [ʊntər'brɛç] cpd: **~en** vt irreg insep interrupt; **U~ung** f interruption.

unterbringen ['ʊntərbrɪŋən] vt irreg (in Koffer) stow; (in Zeitung) place; Person (in Hotel etc) accommodate, put up; (beruflich) fix up (auf, in with).

unterdessen [ʊntər'dɛsən] ad meanwhile.

Unterdruck ['ʊntərdrʊk] m low pressure.

unterdrücken [ʊntər'drʏkən] vt insep suppress; Leute oppress.

untere(r,s) ['ʊntərə(r,z)] a lower.

untereinander [ʊntər'aɪ'nandər] ad with each other; among themselves etc.

unterentwickelt ['ʊntər'ɛntvɪkəlt] a underdeveloped.

unterernährt ['ʊntər'ɛrnɛːrt] a undernourished, underfed.

Unterernährung f malnutrition.

Unter'führung f subway, underpass.

Untergang ['ʊntərgaŋ] m (down-)fall, decline; (Naut) sinking; (von Gestirn) setting.

unter'geben a subordinate.

untergehen ['ʊntərgeːən] vi irreg go down; (Sonne auch) set; (Staat) fall; (Volk) perish; (Welt) come to an end; (im Lärm) be drowned.

Untergeschoß ['ʊntərgəʃɔs] nt basement.

unter'gliedern vt insep subdivide.

Untergrund ['ʊntərgrʊnt] m foundation; (Pol) underground; **~bahn** f underground, tube, subway (US); **~bewegung** f underground (movement).

unterhalb ['ʊntərhalp] prep +gen, ad below; **~ von** below.

Unterhalt ['ʊntərhalt] m maintenance; **u~en** [ʊntər'haltən] irreg insep vt main-

tain; (belustigen) entertain; vr talk; (sich belustigen) enjoy o.s.; **u~end** [ʊntər'haltənt] a entertaining; **~ung** f maintenance; (Belustigung) entertainment, amusement; (Gespräch) talk.

Unterhändler [ʊntər'hɛntlər] m negotiator.

Unterhemd ['ʊntərhɛmt] nt vest, undershirt (US).

Unterhose ['ʊntərhoːzə] f underpants pl.

unterirdisch ['ʊntər'ɪrdɪʃ] a underground.

Unterkiefer ['ʊntərkiːfər] m lower jaw.

unterkommen ['ʊntərkɔmən] vi irreg find shelter; find work; **das ist mir noch nie untergekommen** I've never met with that.

Unterkunft ['ʊntərkʊnft] f **-, -künfte** accommodation.

Unterlage ['ʊntərlaːgə] f foundation; (Beleg) document; (Schreib— etc) pad.

unter'lassen vt irreg insep (versäumen) fail (to do); (sich enthalten) refrain from.

unterlaufen [ʊntər'laʊfən] vi irreg insep happen; a: **mit Blut ~** suffused with blood; (Augen) bloodshot.

unterlegen ['ʊntərleːgən] vt lay or put under; [ʊntər'leːgən] a inferior (dat to); (besiegt) defeated.

Unterleib ['ʊntərlaɪp] m abdomen.

unter'liegen vi irreg insep be defeated or overcome (jdm by sb); (unterworfen sein) be subject to.

Untermiete ['ʊntərmiːtə] f: **zur ~ wohnen** be a subtenant or lodger; **~r(in** f) m subtenant, lodger.

unter'nehmen vt irreg insep undertake; **U~** nt **-s, -** undertaking, enterprise (auch Comm); **~d** a enterprising, daring.

Unternehmer [ʊntər'neːmər] m **-s, -** entrepreneur, businessman.

Unterprima ['ʊntərpriːma] f **-, -primen** eighth year of secondary school.

Unterredung [ʊntər'reːdʊŋ] f discussion, talk.

Unterricht ['ʊntərrɪçt] m **-(e)s, -e** instruction, lessons pl; **u~en** [ʊntər'rɪçtən] insep vt instruct; (Sch) teach; vr inform o.s. (über +acc about).

Unterrock [ʊntərrɔk] m petticoat, slip.

unter'sagen vt insep forbid (jdm etw sb to do sth).

unter'schätzen vt insep underestimate.

unter'scheiden irreg insep vt distinguish; vr differ.

Unter'scheidung f (Unterschied) distinction; (Unterscheiden) differentiation.

Unterschied ['ʊntərʃiːt] m **-(e)s, -e** difference, distinction; **im ~ zu** as distinct from; **u~lich** a varying, differing; (diskriminierend) discriminatory; **u~slos** ad indiscriminately.

unter'schlagen vt irreg insep embezzle; (verheimlichen) suppress.

Unter'schlagung f embezzlement.

Unterschlupf ['ʊntərʃlʊpf] m **-(e)s, -schlüpfe** refuge.

unter'schreiben vt irreg insep sign.

Unterschrift ['ʊntərʃrɪft] f signature.

Unterseeboot ['ʊntərzeːboːt] *nt* submarine.

Untersekunda ['ʊntərzekunda] *f* -, **-sekunden** sixth year of secondary school.

Untersetzer ['ʊntərzɛtsər] *m* tablemat; *(für Gläser)* coaster.

untersetzt [ʊntər'zɛtst] *a* stocky.

unterste(r,s) ['ʊntərstə(r,z)] *a* lowest, bottom.

unterstehen [ʊntər'ʃteːən] *irreg vi insep* be under *(jdm sb)*; *vr* dare; ['ʊntərʃteːən] *vi* shelter.

unterstellen [ʊntər'ʃtələn] *vt insep* subordinate *(dat* to); *(fig)* impute *(jdm etw* sth to sb); ['ʊntərʃtələn] *vt Auto* garage, park; *vr* take shelter.

unter'streichen *vt irreg insep (lit, fig)* underline.

Unterstufe ['ʊntərʃtuːfə] *f* lower grade.

unter'stützen *vt insep* support.

Unter'stützung *f* support, assistance.

unter'suchen *vt insep (Med)* examine; *(Polizei)* investigate.

Unter'suchung *f* examination; investigation, inquiry; **~sausschuß** *m* committee of inquiry; **~shaft** *f* imprisonment on remand.

Untertan ['ʊntərtaːn] *m* -s, **-en** subject.

untertänig ['ʊntərtɛːnɪç] *a* submissive, humble.

Untertasse ['ʊntərtasə] *f* saucer.

untertauchen ['ʊntərtauxən] *vi* dive; *(fig)* disappear, go underground.

Unterteil ['ʊntərtail] *nt or m* lower part, bottom; **u~en** [ʊntər'tailən] *vt insep* divide up.

Untertertia ['ʊntərtɛrtsia] *f* -, **-tertien** fourth year of secondary school.

Unterwäsche ['ʊntərvɛʃə] *f* underwear.

unterwegs [ʊntər'veːks] *ad* on the way.

unter'weisen *vt irreg insep* instruct.

unter'werfen *irreg insep vt* subject; *Volk* subjugate; *vr* submit *(dat* to).

unterwürfig [ʊntər'vyrfɪç] *a* obsequious, servile.

unter'zeichnen *vt insep* sign.

unter'ziehen *irreg insep vt* subject *(dat* to); *vr* undergo *(etw (dat)* sth); *(einer Prüfung)* take.

untreu ['ʊntrɔy] *a* unfaithful; **U~e** *f* unfaithfulness.

untröstlich [ʊn'trøːstlɪç] *a* inconsolable.

Untugend ['ʊntuːgənt] *f* vice, failing.

unüber- ['ʊn'yːbər] *cpd:* **~legt** [-leːkt] *a* ill-considered; *ad* without thinking; **~sehbar** [-zeːbaːr] *a* incalculable.

unum- ['ʊn'ʊm] *cpd:* **~gänglich** ['-gɛŋlɪç] *a* indispensable, vital; absolutely necessary; **~wunden** [-vʊndən] *a* candid; *ad* straight out.

ununterbrochen ['ʊn'ʊntərbrɔxən] *a* uninterrupted.

unver- [ʊn'fɛr] *cpd* **~änderlich** [-'ɛndərlɪç] *a* unchangeable; **~antwortlich** [-'antvɔrtlɪç] *a* irresponsible; *(unentschuldbar)* inexcusable; **~äußerlich** [-'ɔysərlɪç] *a* inalienable; **~besserlich** [-'bɛsərlɪç] *a* incorrigible; **~bindlich**

[-'bɪntlɪç] *a* not binding; *Antwort* curt; *ad (Comm)* without obligation; **~blümt** [-'blyːmt] *a,ad* plain(ly), blunt(ly); **~daulich** ['-dauljç] *a* indigestible; **~dorben** [-'dɔrbən] *a* unspoilt; **~einbar** [-'ainbaːr] *a* incompatible; **~fänglich** ['-fɛŋlɪç] *a* harmless; **~froren** [-'froːrən] *a* impudent; **~hofft** [-'hɔft] *a* unexpected; **~kennbar** [-'kɛnbaːr] *a* unmistakable; **~meidlich** [-'maitlɪç] *a* unavoidable; **~mutet** ['-muːtət] *a* unexpected; **~nünftig** [-'nynftɪç] *a* foolish; **~schämt** ['-ʃɛmt] *a* impudent; **U~schämtheit** *f* impudence, insolence; **~sehens** ['-zeːəns] *ad* all of a sudden; **~sehrt** ['-zeːrt] *a* uninjured; **~söhnlich** [-'zøːnlɪç] *a* irreconcilable; **~ständlich** [-'ʃtɛntlɪç] *a* unintelligible; **~träglich** ['-trɛːklɪç] *a* quarrelsome; *Meinungen, (Med)* incompatible; **~wüstlich** [-'vyːstlɪç] *a* indestructible; *Mensch* irrepressible; **~zeihlich** [-'tsailɪç] *a* unpardonable; **~züglich** [-'tsyːklɪç] *a* immediate.

unvoll- ['ʊnfɔl] *cpd:* **~kommen** *a* imperfect; **~ständig** *a* incomplete.

unvor- ['ʊnfoːr] *cpd:* **~bereitet** *a* unprepared; **~eingenommen** *a* unbiased; **~hergesehen** [-hergəzeːən] *a* unforeseen; **~sichtig** [-zɪçtɪç] *a* careless, imprudent; **~stellbar** [-'ʃtɛlbaːr] *a* inconceivable; **~teilhaft** [-tailhaft] *a* disadvantageous.

unwahr ['ʊnvaːr] *a* untrue; **~haftig** *a* untruthful; **~scheinlich** *a* improbable, unlikely; *ad (col)* incredibly; **U~scheinlichkeit** *f* improbability, unlikelihood.

unweigerlich [ʊn'vaigərlɪç] *a* unquestioning; *ad* without fail.

Unwesen ['ʊnveːzən] *nt* nuisance; *(Unfug)* mischief; **sein ~ treiben** wreak havoc; **u~tlich** *a* inessential, unimportant; **u~tlich besser** marginally better.

Unwetter ['ʊnvɛtər] *nt* thunderstorm.

unwichtig ['ʊnvɪçtɪç] *a* unimportant.

unwider- [ʊnviːdər] *cpd:* **~legbar** [-'leːkbaːr] *a* irrefutable; **~ruflich** [-'ruːflɪç] *a* irrevocable; **~stehlich** [-'ʃteːlɪç] *a* irresistible.

unwill- ['ʊnvɪl] *cpd:* **U~e(n)** *m* indignation; **~ig** *a* indignant; *(widerwillig)* reluctant; **~kürlich** [-kyːrlɪç] *a* involuntary; *ad* instinctively; *lachen* involuntarily.

unwirklich ['ʊnvɪrklɪç] *a* unreal.

unwirsch ['ʊnvɪrʃ] *a* cross, surly.

unwirtlich ['ʊnvɪrtlɪç] *a* inhospitable.

unwirtschaftlich ['ʊnvɪrt-ʃaftlɪç] *a* uneconomical.

unwissen- ['ʊnvɪsən] *cpd:* **~d** *a* ignorant; **U~heit** *f* ignorance; **~schaftlich** *a* unscientific.

unwohl ['ʊnvoːl] *a* unwell, ill; **U~sein** *nt* -s indisposition.

unwürdig ['ʊnvyrdɪç] *a* unworthy *(jds of* sb).

unzählig [ʊn'tsɛːlɪç] *a* innumerable, countless.

unzer- [ʊntsɛr] *cpd* **~brechlich** [-'brɛçlɪç] *a* unbreakable; **~reißbar**

[-'raisba:r] a untearable; ~störbar
[-'ʃtö:rba:r] a indestructible; ~trennlich
[-'trɛnlɪç] a inseparable.
Unzucht ['ʊntsʊxt] f sexual offence.
unzüchtig ['ʊntsʏçtɪç] a immoral; lewd.
unzu- ['ʊntsu] cpd: ~**frieden** a dissatisfied; **U~friedenheit** f discontent;
~**länglich** ['ʊntsu:lɛŋlɪç] a inadequate;
~**lässig** ['ʊntsu:lɛsɪç] a inadmissible;
~**rechnungsfähig** ['ʊntsu:rɛçnʊŋsfɛ:ɪç] a
irresponsible; ~**sammenhängend** a disconnected; Äußerung incoherent;
~**treffend** ['ʊntsu:-] a incorrect;
~**verlässig** ['ʊntsu:-] a unreliable.
unzweideutig ['ʊntsvaɪdɔʏtɪç] adj
unambiguous.

üppig ['ʏpɪç] adj Frau curvaceous; Busen
full, ample; Essen sumptuous, lavish;
Vegetation luxuriant, lush.
uralt ['u:r'alt] a ancient, very old.
Uran [u'ra:n] nt -s uranium.
Ur- ['u:r] in cpds original; ~**aufführung** f
first performance; ~**einwohner** m
original inhabitant; ~**eltern** pl ancestors
pl; ~**enkel(in** f) m great-grandchild;
~**großmutter** f great-grandmother;
~**großvater** m great-grandfather;
~**heber** m -s, - originator; (Autor) author.
Urin [u'ri:n] m -s, -e urine.
ur- cpd: ~**komisch** a incredibly funny;
U~kunde f -, -n document, deed;
~**kundlich** ['u:rkʊntlɪç] a documentary;
~**laub** m -(e)s, -e holiday(s pl), vacation
(US); (Mil etc) leave; ~**lauber** m -s, - holiday-maker, vacationist (US); ~**mensch** m
primitive man.
Urne ['ʊrnə] f -, -n urn.
Ursache ['u:rzaxə] f cause.
Ursprung ['u:rʃprʊŋ] m origin, source;
(von Fluß) source.
ursprünglich [u:rʃprʏŋlɪç] a, ad
original(ly).
Urteil ['ʊrtaɪl] nt -s, -e opinion; (Jur)
sentence, judgement; **u~en** vi judge;
~**sspruch** m sentence, verdict.
Ur- cpd: ~**wald** m jungle; ~**zeit** f prehistoric times pl.
usw [u:svə:] abbr of **und so weiter** etc.
Utensilien [utɛn'zi:liən] pl utensils pl.
Utopie [uto'pi:] f pipedream.
utopisch [u'to:pɪʃ] a utopian.

V

V, v [fau] nt V, v.
vag(e) [va:k, va:gə] a vague.
Vagina [va'gi:na] f -, **Vaginen** vagina.
Vakuum ['va:kuʊm] nt -s, **Vakua** or
Vakuen vacuum.
Vanille [va'nɪljə] f - vanilla.
Variation [variatsi'o:n] f variation.
variieren [vari'i:rən] vti vary.
Vase ['va:zə] f -, -n vase.
Vater ['fa:tər] m -s, ¨ father; ~**land** nt
native country; Fatherland; ~**landsliebe**
f patriotism.
väterlich ['fɛ:tərlɪç] a fatherly; ~**erseits**
ad on the father's side.

Vater- cpd: ~**schaft** f paternity; ~**unser**
nt -s, - Lord's prayer.
Vegetarier(in f) [vege'ta:riər(ɪn)] m -s, -
vegetarian.
Veilchen ['faɪlçən] nt violet.
Vene ['ve:nə] f -, -n vein.
Ventil [vɛn'ti:l] nt -s, -e valve; ~**ator**
[vɛnti'la:tər] m ventilator.
verab- [fɛr'ap] cpd: ~**reden** vt agree,
arrange; vr arrange to meet (mit jdm sb);
V~redung f arrangement; (Treffen)
appointment; ~**scheuen** vt detest, abhor;
~**schieden** vt Gäste say goodbye to;
(entlassen) discharge; Gesetz pass; vr take
one's leave (von of); **V~schiedung** f
leave-taking; discharge; passing.
ver- [fɛr] cpd: ~**achten** [-'axtən] vt
despise; ~**ächtlich** [-'ɛçtlɪç] a contemptuous; (verachtenswert) contemptible;
jdn ~**ächtlich machen** run sb down;
V~achtung f contempt.
verallgemein- [fɛr'algə'maɪn] cpd: ~**ern**
vt generalize; **V~erung** f generalization.
veralten [fɛr'altən] vi become obsolete or
out-of-date.
Veranda [ve'randa] f -, **Veranden**
veranda.
veränder- [fɛr'ɛndər] cpd: ~**lich** a
changeable; **V~lichkeit** f variability,
instability; ~**n** vtr change, alter; **V~ung**
f change, alteration.
veran- [fɛr'an] cpd: ~**lagt** a with a ...
nature; **V~lagung** f disposition, aptitude;
~**lassen** vt cause; **Maßnahmen**
~**lassen** take measures; **sich** ~**laßt**
sehen feel prompted; **V~lassung** f
cause; motive; **auf jds V~lassung (hin)**
at the instance of sb; ~**schaulichen** vt
illustrate; ~**schlagen** v estimate;
~**stalten** vt organize; arrange;
V~stalter m -s, - organizer;
V~staltung f (Veranstalten) organizing;
(Veranstaltetes) event, function.
verantwort- [fɛr'antvɔrt] cpd: ~**en** v
answer for; vr justify o.s.; ~**lich** a
responsible; **V~ung** f responsibility;
~**ungsbewußt** a responsible; ~**ungslos**
a irresponsible.
verarbeiten [fɛr''arbaɪtən] vt process;
(geistig) assimilate; **etw zu etw** ~ make
sth into sth.
Verarbeitung f processing; assimilation.
verärgern [fɛr''ɛrgərn] vt annoy.
verausgaben [fɛr''ausga:bən] vr run out of
money; (fig) exhaust o.s.
veräußern [fɛr''ɔʏsərn] vt dispose of, sell.
Verb [vɛrp] nt -s, -en verb.
Verband [fɛr'bant] m -(e)s, ¨e (Med)
bandage, dressing; (Bund) association,
society; (Mil) unit; ~**(s)kasten** m
medicine chest, first-aid box; ~**stoff** m,
~**zeug** nt bandage, dressing material.
verbannen [fɛr'banən] vt banish.
Verbannung f exile.
verbergen [fɛr'bɛrgən] vtr irreg hide (vor
+dat from).
verbessern [fɛr'bɛsərn] vtr improve;
(berichtigen) correct (o.s.).
Verbesserung f improvement; correction.

verbeugen [fɛr'bɔygən] *vr* bow.
Verbeugung *f* bow.
ver'biegen *vi irreg* bend.
ver'bieten *vt irreg* forbid (*jdm etw* sb to do sth).
ver'binden *irreg vt* connect; *(kombinieren)* combine; *(Med)* bandage; **jdm die Augen** ~ blindfold sb; *vr* combine *(auch Chem)*, join.
verbindlich [fɛr'bɪntlɪç] *a* binding; *(freundlich)* friendly: **V~keit** *f* obligation; *(Höflichkeit)* civility.
Ver'bindung *f* connection; *(Zusammensetzung)* combination; *(Chem)* compound; *(Univ)* club.
verbissen [fɛr'bɪsən] *a* grim, dogged; **V~heit** *f* grimness, doggedness.
ver'bitten *vt irreg*: **sich** *(dat)* **etw** ~ not tolerate sth, not stand for sth.
verbittern [fɛr'bɪtərn] *vt* embitter; *vi* get bitter.
verblassen [fɛr'blasən] *vi* fade.
Verbleib [fɛ'blaip] *m* **-(e)s** whereabouts; **v~en** [fɛr'blaibən] *vi irreg* remain.
Verblendung [fɛr'blɛndʊŋ] *f (fig)* delusion.
verblöden [fɛr'blø:dən] *vi* get stupid.
verblüffen [fɛr'blʏfən] *vt* stagger, amaze.
Verblüffung *f* stupefaction.
ver'blühen *vi* wither, fade.
ver'bluten *vi* bleed to death.
verborgen [fɛr'bɔrgən] *a* hidden.
Verbot [fɛr'bo:t] *nt* **-(e)s, -e** prohibition, ban; **v~en** *a* forbidden; **Rauchen v~en!** no smoking; **v~enerweise** *ad* though it is forbidden; ~**sschild** *nt* prohibitory sign.
Verbrauch [fɛr'braux] *m* **-(e)s** consumption; **v~en** *vt* use up; ~**er** *m* **-s, -** consumer; **v~t** *a* used up, finished; *Luft* stale; *Mensch* worn-out.
Verbrechen [fɛr'breçən] *nt* **-s, -** crime; **v~** *vt irreg* perpetrate.
Verbrecher [fɛr'breçər] *m* **-s, -** criminal; **v~isch** *a* criminal; ~**tum** *nt* **-s** criminality.
ver'breiten *vtr* spread; **sich über etw** *(acc)* ~ expound on sth.
verbreitern [fɛr'braitərn] *vt* broaden.
Verbreitung *f* spread(ing), propagation.
verbrenn- [fɛr'brɛn] *cpd*: ~**bar** *a* combustible; ~**en** *vt irreg* burn; *Leiche* cremate; **V~ung** *f* burning; *(in Motor)* combustion; *(von Leiche)* cremation; **V~ungsmotor** *m* internal combustion engine.
ver'bringen *vt irreg* spend.
Verbrüderung [fɛr'bry:dərʊŋ] *f* fraternization.
verbrühen [fɛr'bry:ən] *vt* scald.
verbuchen [fɛr'bu:xən] *vt* *(Fin)* register; *Erfolg* enjoy; *Mißerfolg* suffer.
verbunden [fɛr'bʊndən] *a* connected; **jdm** ~ **sein** be obliged *or* indebted to sb; **falsch** ~ *(Tel)* wrong number; **V~heit** *f* bond, relationship.
verbünden [fɛr'bʏndən] *vr* ally o.s.
Verbündete(r) [fɛr'bʏndətə(r)] *mf* ally.
ver'bürgen *vr*: **sich** ~ **für** vouch for.
ver'büßen *vt*: **eine Strafe** ~ serve a sentence.

verchromt [fɛr'kro:mt] *a* chromium-plated.
Verdacht [fɛr'daxt] *m* **-(e)s** suspicion.
verdächtig [fɛr'dɛçtɪç] *a* suspicious, suspect; ~**en** [fɛr'dɛçtɪgən] *vt* suspect.
verdammen [fɛr'damən] *vt* damn, condemn.
Verdammnis [fɛr'damnɪs] *f* **-, -se** perdition, damnation.
ver'dampfen *vi* vaporize, evaporate.
ver'danken *vt*: **jdm etw** ~ owe sb sth.
verdauen [fɛr'dauən] *vt (lit, fig)* digest.
verdaulich [fɛr'daulɪç] *a* digestible; **das ist schwer** ~ that is hard to digest.
Verdauung *f* digestion.
Verdeck [fɛr'dɛk] *nt* **-(e)s, -e** *(Aut)* hood; *(Naut)* deck; **v~en** *vt* cover (up); *(verbergen)* hide.
ver'denken *vt irreg*: **jdm etw** ~ blame sb for sth, hold sth against sb.
Verderb- [fɛr'dɛrp] *cpd*: ~**en** [fɛr'dɛrbən] *nt* **-s** ruin; **v~en** *irreg vt* spoil; *(schädigen)* ruin; *(moralisch)* corrupt; **es mit jdm v~en** get into sb's bad books; *vi (Essen)* spoil, rot; *(Mensch)* go to the bad; **v~lich** *a Einfluß* pernicious; *Lebensmittel* perishable; **v~t** *a* depraved; ~**theit** *f* depravity.
verdeutlichen [fɛr'dɔytlɪçən] *vt* make clear.
ver'dichten *vtr* condense.
ver'dienen *vt* earn; *(moralisch)* deserve.
Ver'dienst *m* **-(e)s, -e** earnings *pl*; *nt* **-(e)s, -e** merit; *(Leistung)* service (*um* to).
verdient [fɛr'di:nt] *a* well-earned; *Person* deserving of esteem; **sich um etw** ~ **machen** do a lot for sth.
verdoppeln [fɛr'dɔpəln] *vt* double.
Verdopp(e)lung *f* doubling.
verdorben [fɛr'dɔrbən] *a* spoilt; *(geschädigt)* ruined; *(moralisch)* corrupt.
verdrängen [fɛr'drɛŋən] *vt* oust, displace *(auch Phys)*; *(Psych)* repress.
Verdrängung *f* displacement; *(Psych)* repression.
ver'drehen *vt (lit, fig)* twist; *Augen* roll; **jdm den Kopf** ~ *(fig)* turn sb's head.
verdreifachen [fɛr'draifaxən] *vt* treble.
verdrießlich [fɛr'dri:slɪç] *a* peevish, annoyed.
verdrossen [fɛr'drɔsən] *a* cross, sulky.
ver'drücken *vt (col)* put away, eat; *vr (col)* disappear.
Verdruß [fɛr'drus] *m* **-sses, -sse** annoyance, worry.
ver'duften *vi* evaporate; *vir (col)* disappear.
verdummen [fɛr'dumən] *vt* make stupid; *vi* grow stupid.
verdunkeln [fɛr'dʊŋkəln] *vtr* darken; *(fig)* obscure.
Verdunk(e)lung *f* blackout; *(fig)* obscuring.
verdünnen [fɛr'dʏnən] *vt* dilute.
verdunsten [fɛr'dʊnstən] *vi* evaporate.
verdursten [fɛr'dʊrstən] *vi* die of thirst.
verdutzt [fɛr'dʊtst] *a* nonplussed, taken aback.
verehr- [fɛr''e:r] *cpd*: ~**en** *vt* venerate,

worship *(auch Rel)*; **jdm etw ~ en** present sb with sth; **V~er(in** *f)* *m* **-s, -** admirer, worshipper *(auch Rel)*; **~t** *a* esteemed; **V~ung** *f* respect; *(Rel)* worship.

vereidigen [fɛr'aidigən] *vt* put on oath.

Vereidigung *f* swearing in.

Verein [fɛr'ain] *m* **-(e)s, -e** club, association; **v~bar** *a* compatible; **v~baren** [-ba:rən] *vt* agree upon; **~barung** *f* agreement; **v~fachen** [-faxən] *vt* simplify; **v~heitlichen** *vt* standardize; **v~igen** [-ɪgən] *vtr* unite; **~igung** *f* union; *(Verein)* association; **v~samen** [-za:mən] *vi* become lonely; **v~t** *a* united; **~zelt** *a* isolated.

vereisen [fɛr'aizən] *vi* freeze, ice over; *vt* *(Med)* freeze.

vereiteln [fɛr'aitəln] *vt* frustrate.

ver'eitern *vi* suppurate, fester.

verengen [fɛr'ɛŋən] *vr* narrow.

vererb- [fɛr'ɛrb] *cpd:* **~en** *vt* bequeath; *(Biol)* transmit; **vr** be hereditary; **~lich** [fɛr'ɛrpliç] *a* hereditary; **V~ung** *f* bequeathing; *(Biol)* transmission; *(Lehre)* heredity.

verewigen [fɛr'e:vigən] *vt* immortalize; *vr* *(col)* leave one's name.

ver'fahren *irreg* *vi* act; **~ mit** deal with; *vr* get lost; *a* tangled; **V~** *nt* **-s, -** procedure; *(Tech)* process; *(Jur)* proceedings *pl.*

Verfall [fɛr'fal] *m* **-(e)s** decline; *(von Haus)* dilapidation; *(Fin)* expiry; **v~en** *vi irreg* decline; *(Haus)* be falling down; *(Fin)* lapse; **v~en in** *(+acc)* lapse into; **v~en auf** *(+acc)* hit upon; **einem Laster v~en sein** be addicted to a vice.

verfänglich [fɛr'fɛŋliç] *a* awkward, tricky.

ver'färben *vr* change colour.

Verfasser(in *f)* [fɛr'fasər(in)] *m* **-s, -** author, writer.

Verfassung *f* constitution *(auch Pol)*; **~sgericht** *nt* constitutional court; **v~smäßig** *a* constitutional; **v~swidrig** *a* unconstitutional.

ver'faulen *vi* rot.

ver'fechten *vt irreg* advocate; defend.

Verfechter [fɛr'fɛçtər] *m* **-s, -** champion; defender.

ver'fehlen *vt* miss; **etw für verfehlt halten** regard sth as mistaken.

verfeinern [fɛr'fainərn] *vt* refine.

ver'fliegen *vi irreg* evaporate; *(Zeit)* pass, fly.

verflossen [fɛr'flɔsən] *a* past, former.

ver'fluchen *vt* curse.

verflüchtigen [fɛr'flyçtigən] *vr* vaporize, evaporate; *(Geruch)* fade.

verflüssigen [fɛr'flysigən] *vr* become liquid.

verfolg- [fɛr'fɔlg] *cpd:* **~en** *vt* pursue; *(gerichtlich)* prosecute; *(grausam, esp Pol)* persecute; **V~er** *m* **-s, -** pursuer; **V~ung** *f* pursuit; prosecution; persecution; **V~ungswahn** *m* persecution mania.

verfremden [fɛr'frɛmdən] *vt* alienate, distance.

verfrüht [fɛr'fry:t] *a* premature.

verfüg- [fɛr'fy:g] *cpd:* **~bar** *a* available; **~en** *vt* direct, order; *vr* proceed; *vi:* **~en über** *(+acc)* have at one's disposal; **V~ung** *f* direction, order; **zur V~ung** at one's disposal; **jdm zur V~ung stehen** be available to sb.

verführ- [fɛr'fy:r] *cpd:* **~en** *vt* tempt; *(sexuell)* seduce; **V~er** *m* tempter; seducer; **~erisch** *a* seductive; **V~ung** *f* seduction; *(Versuchung)* temptation.

ver'gammeln *vi (col)* go to seed; *(Nahrung)* go off.

vergangen [fɛr'gaŋən] *a* past; **V~heit** *f* past.

vergänglich [fɛr'gɛŋliç] *a* transitory; **V~keit** *f* transitoriness, impermanence.

vergasen [fɛr'ga:zən] *vt* gasify; *(töten)* gas.

Vergaser *m* **-s, -** *(Aut)* carburettor.

vergeb- [fɛr'ge:b] *cpd:* **~en** *vt irreg* forgive *(jdm etw* sb for sth); *(weggeben)* give away; **~en sein** be occupied; *(col: Mädchen)* be spoken for; **~ens** *ad* in vain; **~lich** [fɛr'ge:pliç] *ad* in vain; *a* vain, futile; **V~ung** *f* forgiveness.

vergegenwärtigen [fɛr'ge:gənvɛrtigən] *vr:* **sich** *(dat)* **etw ~** recall *or* visualize sth.

ver'gehen *irreg vi* pass by *or* away; **jdm vergeht etw** sb loses sth; *vr* commit an offence *(gegen etw* against sth); **sich an jdm ~** *(sexually)* assault sb; **V~** *nt* **-s, -** offence.

ver'gelten *vt irreg* pay back *(jdm etw* sb for sth), repay.

Ver'geltung *f* retaliation, reprisal; **~sschlag** *m (Mil)* reprisal.

vergessen [fɛr'gɛsən] *vt irreg* forget; **V~heit** *f* oblivion.

vergeßlich [fɛr'gɛsliç] *a* forgetful; **V~heit** *f* forgetfulness.

vergeuden [fɛr'gɔydən] *vt* squander, waste.

vergewaltigen [fɛrgə'valtigən] *vt* rape; *(fig)* violate.

Vergewaltigung *f* rape.

vergewissern [fɛrgə'visərn] *vr* make sure.

ver'gießen *vt irreg* shed.

vergiften [fɛr'giftən] *vt* poison.

Vergiftung *f* poisoning.

Vergißmeinnicht [fɛr'gismainniçt] *nt* **-(e)s, -e** forget-me-not.

verglasen [fɛr'gla:zən] *vt* glaze.

Vergleich [fɛr'glaiç] *m* **-(e)s, -e** comparison; *(Jur)* settlement; **im ~ mit** *or* **zu** compared with *or* to; **v~bar** *a* comparable; **v~en** *irreg vt* compare; *vr* reach a settlement.

vergnügen [fɛr'gny:gən] *vr* enjoy *or* amuse o.s.; **V~** *nt* **-s, -** pleasure; **viel V~!** enjoy yourself!

vergnügt [fɛr'gny:kt] *a* cheerful.

Vergnügung *f* pleasure, amusement; **~spark** *m* amusement park; **v~ssüchtig** *a* pleasure-loving.

vergolden [fɛr'gɔldən] *vt* gild.

ver'gönnen *vt* grant.

vergöttern [fɛr'gœtərn] *vt* idolize.

ver'graben *vt* bury.

ver'greifen vr irreg: **sich an jdm ~** lay hands on sb; **sich an etw ~** misappropriate sth; **sich im Ton ~** say the wrong thing.

vergriffen [fɛr'grɪfən] a *Buch* out of print; *Ware* out of stock.

vergrößern [fɛr'grø:sərn] vt enlarge; *(mengenmäßig)* increase; *(Lupe)* magnify.

Vergrößerung f enlargement; increase; magnification; **~sglas** nt magnifying glass.

Vergünstigung [fɛr'gʏnstɪgʊŋ] f concession, privilege.

vergüten [fɛr'gy:tən] vt: **jdm etw ~** compensate sb for sth.

Vergütung f compensation.

verhaften [fɛr'haftən] vt arrest.

Verhaftete(r) mf prisoner.

Verhaftung f arrest; **~sbefehl** m warrant (for arrest).

ver'hallen vi die away.

ver'halten irreg vr be, stand; *(sich benehmen)* behave; *(Math)* be in proportion to; vt hold or keep back; *Schritt* check; **V~** nt **-s** behaviour; **V~sforschung** f behavioural science; **V~smaßregel** f rule of conduct.

Verhältnis [fɛr'hɛltnɪs] nt **-ses, -se** relationship; *(Math)* proportion, ratio; pl *(Umstände)* conditions pl; **über seine ~se leben** live beyond one's means; **v~mäßig** a,ad relative(ly), comparative(ly).

verhandeln [fɛr'handəln] vi negotiate *(über etw (acc)* sth); *(Jur)* hold proceedings; vt discuss; *(Jur)* hear.

Verhandlung f negotiation; *(Jur)* proceedings pl.

ver'hängen vt *(fig)* impose, inflict.

Verhängnis [fɛr'hɛŋnɪs] nt **-ses, -se** fate, doom; **jdm zum ~ werden** be sb's undoing; **v~voll** a fatal, disastrous.

verharmlosen [fɛr'harmlo:zən] vt make light of, play down.

verharren [fɛr'harən] vi remain; *(hartnäckig)* persist.

verhärten [fɛr'hɛrtən] vr harden.

verhaßt [fɛr'hast] a odious, hateful.

verheerend [fɛr'he:rənt] a disastrous, devastating.

verhehlen [fɛr'he:lən] vt conceal.

ver'heilen vi heal.

verheimlichen [fɛr'haɪmlɪçən] vt keep secret *(jdm* from sb).

verheiratet [fɛr'haɪra:tət] a married.

ver'heißen vt irreg: **jdm etw ~** promise sb sth.

ver'helfen vi irreg: **jdm ~ zu** help sb to get.

verherrlichen [fɛr'hɛrlɪçən] vt glorify.

ver'hexen vt bewitch; **es ist wie verhext** it's jinxed.

ver'hindern vt prevent; **verhindert sein** be unable to make it.

Ver'hinderung f prevention.

verhöhnen [fɛr'hø:nən] vt mock, sneer at.

Verhör [fɛr'hø:r] nt **-(e)s, -e** interrogation; *(gerichtlich)* (cross-)examination;

v~en vt interrogate; (cross-)examine; vr misunderstand, mishear.

ver'hungern vi starve, die of hunger.

ver'hüten vt prevent, avert.

Ver'hütung f prevention; **~smittel** nt contraceptive.

verirren [fɛr'ɪrən] vr go astray.

ver'jagen vt drive away or out.

verjüngen [fɛr'jʏŋən] vt rejuvenate; vr taper.

verkalken [fɛr'kalkən] vi calcify; *(col)* become senile.

verkalkulieren [fɛrkalku'li:rən] vr miscalculate.

verkannt [fɛr'kant] a unappreciated.

Verkauf [fɛr'kauf] m sale; **v~en** vt sell.

Verkäufer(in f) [fɛr'kɔyfər(ɪn)] m **-s, -** seller; salesman; *(in Laden)* shop assistant.

verkäuflich [fɛr'kɔyflɪç] a saleable.

Verkehr [fɛr'ke:r] m **-s, -e** traffic; *(Umgang, esp sexuell)* intercourse; *(Umlauf)* circulation; **v~en** vi *(Fahrzeug)* ply, run; *(besuchen)* visit regularly *(bei jdm* sb); **v~en mit** associate with; vtr turn, transform; **~sampel** f traffic lights pl; **~sdelikt** nt traffic offence; **~sinsel** f traffic island; **~sstockung** f traffic jam, stoppage; **~sunfall** m traffic accident; **v~swidrig** a contrary to traffic regulations; **~szeichen** nt traffic sign; **v~t** a wrong; *(umgekehrt)* the wrong way round.

ver'kennen vt irreg misjudge, not appreciate.

ver'klagen vt take to court.

verklären [fɛr'klɛ:rən] vt transfigure; **verklärt lächeln** smile radiantly.

ver'kleben vt glue up, stick; vi stick together.

verkleiden [fɛr'klaɪdən] vtr disguise (o.s.), dress up.

Verkleidung f disguise; *(Archit)* wainscoting.

verkleinern [fɛr'klaɪnərn] vt make smaller, reduce in size.

verklemmt [fɛr'klɛmt] a *(fig)* inhibited.

ver'klingen vi irreg die away.

ver'kneifen vt *(col)* : **sich** *(dat)* **etw ~** *Lachen* stifle; *Schmerz* hide; *(sich versagen)* do without.

verknüpfen [fɛr'knʏpfən] vt tie (up), knot; *(fig)* connect.

Verknüpfung f connection.

verkohlen [fɛr'ko:lən] vti carbonize; vt *(col)* fool.

ver'kommen vi irreg deteriorate, decay; *(Mensch)* go downhill, come down in the world; a *(moralisch)* dissolute, depraved; **V~heit** f depravity.

verkörpern [fɛr'kœrpərn] vt embody, personify.

verköstigen [fɛr'kœstɪgən] vt feed.

verkraften [fɛr'kraftən] vt cope with.

ver'kriechen vr irreg creep away, creep into a corner.

verkrümmt [fɛr'krʏmt] a crooked.

Verkrümmung f bend, warp; *(Anat)* curvature.

verkrüppelt [fɛr'krʏpəlt] a crippled.

verkrustet [fɛr'krustət] a encrusted.

ver'kühlen vr get a chill.

ver'kümmern vi waste away.

verkünden [fɛr'kʏndən] vt proclaim; Urteil pronounce.

verkürzen [fɛr'kʏrtsən] vt shorten; Wort abbreviate; **sich** (dat) **die Zeit** ~ while away the time.

Verkürzung f shortening; abbreviation.

ver'laden vt irreg load.

Verlag [fɛr'la:k] m -(e)s, -e publishing firm.

verlangen [fɛr'laŋən] vt demand; desire; ~ **Sie Herrn X** ask for Mr X; vi ~ **nach** ask for, desire; **V**~ nt -s, - desire (nach for); **auf jds V**~ (**hin**) at sb's request.

verlängern [fɛr'lɛŋərn] vt extend; (länger machen) lengthen.

Verlängerung f extension; (Sport) extra time; ~**sschnur** f extension cable.

verlangsamen [fɛr'laŋza:mən] vtr decelerate, slow down.

Verlaß [fɛr'las] m: **auf ihn/das ist kein** ~ he/it cannot be relied upon.

ver'lassen irreg vt leave; vr depend (auf +acc on); a desolate; Mensch abandoned; **V**~**heit** f loneliness.

verläßlich [fɛr'lɛslɪç] a reliable.

Verlauf [fɛr'lauf] m course; **v**~**en** irreg vi (zeitlich) pass; (Farben) run; vr get lost; (Menschenmenge) disperse.

ver'lauten vi: **etw** ~ **lassen** disclose sth; **wie verlautet** as reported.

ver'leben vt spend.

verlebt [fɛr'le:pt] a dissipated, worn out.

ver'legen vt move; (verlieren) mislay; (abspielen lassen) Handlung set (nach in); Buch publish; vr: **sich auf etw** (acc) ~ take up or to sth; a embarrassed; **nicht** ~ **um** never at a loss for; **V**~**heit** f embarrassment; (Situation) difficulty, scrape.

Verleger [fɛr'le:gər] m -s, - publisher.

Verleih [fɛr'lai] m -(e)s, -e hire service; **v**~**en** vt irreg lend; Kraft, Anschein confer, bestow; Preis, Medaille award; ~**ung** f lending; bestowal; award.

ver'leiten vt lead astray; ~ **zu** talk into, tempt into.

ver'lernen vt forget, unlearn.

ver'lesen irreg vt read out; (aussondern) sort out; vr make a mistake in reading.

verletz- [fɛr'lɛts] cpd: ~**bar** a vulnerable; ~**en** vt (lit, fig) injure, hurt; Gesetz etc violate; ~**end** a (fig) Worte hurtful; ~**lich** a vulnerable, sensitive; **V**~**te(r)** mf injured person; **V**~**ung** f injury; (Verstoß) violation, infringement.

verleugnen [fɛr'lɔygnən] vt deny; Menschen disown.

Verleugnung f denial.

verleumd- [fɛr'lɔymd] cpd: ~**en** vt slander; ~**erisch** a slanderous; **V**~**ung** f slander, libel.

ver'lieben vr fall in love (in jdn with sb).

verliebt [fɛr'li:pt] a in love; **V**~**heit** f being in love.

verlieren [fɛr'li:rən] irreg vti lose; vr get lost; (verschwinden) disappear.

verlob- [fɛr'lo:b] cpd: ~**en** vr get engaged

(mit to); **V**~**te(r)** [fɛr'lo:ptə(r)] mf fiancé(e); **V**~**ung** f engagement.

ver'locken vt entice, lure.

Ver'lockung f temptation, attraction.

verlogen [fɛr'lo:gən] a untruthful; **V**~**heit** f untruthfulness.

verloren [fɛr'lo:rən] a lost; Eier poached; **der** ~**e Sohn** the prodigal son; **etw** ~ **geben** give sth up for lost; ~**gehen** vi irreg get lost.

verlosen [fɛr'lo:zən] vt raffle, draw lots for.

Verlosung f raffle, lottery.

verlottern [fɛr'lɔtərn], **verludern** [fɛr'lu:dərn] vi (col) go to the dogs.

Verlust [fɛr'lust] m -(e)s, -e loss; (Mil) casualty.

ver'machen vt bequeath, leave.

Vermächtnis [fɛr'mɛçtnɪs] nt -ses, -se legacy.

vermählen [fɛr'mɛ:lən] vr marry.

Vermählung f wedding, marriage.

vermehren [fɛr'me:rən] vtr multiply; (Menge) increase.

Vermehrung f multiplying; increase.

ver'meiden vt irreg avoid.

vermeintlich [fɛr'maintlɪç] a supposed.

vermengen [fɛr'mɛŋən] vtr mix; (fig) mix up, confuse.

Vermerk [fɛr'mɛrk] m -(e)s, -e note; (in Ausweis) endorsement; **v**~**en** vt note.

ver'messen irreg vt survey; vr (falsch messen) measure incorrectly; a presumptuous, bold; **V**~**heit** f presumptuousness; recklessness.

Ver'messung f survey(ing).

ver'mieten vt let, rent (out); Auto hire out, rent.

Ver'mieter(in f) m -s, - landlord/ landlady.

Ver'mietung f letting, renting (out); (von Autos) hiring (out).

vermindern [fɛr'mɪndərn] vtr lessen, decrease; Preise reduce.

Verminderung f reduction.

ver'mischen vtr mix, blend.

vermissen [fɛr'mɪsən] vt miss.

vermißt [fɛr'mɪst] a missing.

vermitteln [fɛr'mɪtəln] vi mediate; vt Gespräch connect; **jdm etw** ~ help sb to obtain sth.

Vermittler [fɛr'mɪtlər] m -s, - (Schlichter) agent, mediator.

Vermittlung f procurement; (Stellen—) agency; (Tel) exchange; (Schlichtung) mediation.

ver'mögen vt irreg be capable of; ~ **zu** be able to; **V**~ nt -s, - wealth; (Fähigkeit) ability; **ein V**~ **kosten** cost a fortune; ~**d** a wealthy.

vermuten [fɛr'mu:tən] vt suppose, guess; (argwöhnen) suspect.

vermutlich a supposed, presumed; ad probably.

Vermutung f supposition; suspicion.

vernachlässigen [fɛr'na:xlɛsɪgən] vt neglect.

vernarben [fɛr'narbən] vi heal up.

ver'nehmen vt irreg perceive, hear;

(erfahren) learn; *(Jur)* (cross-)examine; **dem V~ nach** from what I/we *etc* hear.

vernehmlich [fɛr'ne:mlɪç] *a* audible.

Vernehmung *f* (cross-)examination; **v~sfähig** *a* in a condition to be (cross-) examined.

verneigen [fɛr'naɪɡən] *vr* bow.

verneinen [fɛr'naɪnən] *vt* **Frage** answer in the negative; *(ablehnen)* deny; *(Gram)* negate; **~d** *a* negative.

Verneinung *f* negation.

vernichten [fɛr'nɪçtən] *vt* annihilate, destroy; **~d** *a* *(fig)* crushing; **Blick** withering; **Kritik** scathing.

Vernichtung *f* destruction, annihilation.

verniedlichen [fɛr'ni:tlɪçən] *vt* play down.

Vernunft [fɛr'nʊnft] *f* - reason, understanding.

vernünftig [fɛr'nʏnftɪç] *a* sensible, reasonable.

veröden [fɛr'ø:dən] *vi* become desolate; *vt (Med)* remove.

veröffentlichen [fɛr'œfəntlɪçən] *vt* publish.

Veröffentlichung *f* publication.

verordnen [fɛr'ɔrdnən] *vt (Med)* prescribe.

Verordnung *f* order, decree; *(Med)* prescription.

ver'pachten *vt* lease (out).

ver'packen *vt* pack.

Ver'packung *f,* **~smaterial** *nt* packing, wrapping.

ver'passen *vt* miss; **jdm eine Ohrfeige ~** *(col)* give sb a clip round the ear.

verpesten [fɛr'pɛstən] *vt* pollute.

ver'pflanzen *vt* transplant.

Ver'pflanzung *f* transplant(ing).

ver'pflegen *vt* feed, cater for.

Ver'pflegung *f* feeding, catering; *(Kost)* food; *(in Hotel)* board.

verpflichten [fɛr'pflɪçtən] *vt* oblige, bind; *(anstellen)* engage; *vr* undertake; *(Mil)* sign on; *vi* carry obligations; **jdm zu Dank verpflichtet sein** be obliged to sb.

Verpflichtung *f* obligation, duty.

ver'pfuschen *vt (col)* bungle, make a mess of.

verplempern [fɛr'plɛmpərn] *vt (col)* waste.

verpönt [fɛr'pø:nt] *a* disapproved (of), taboo.

verprassen [fɛr'prasən] *vt* squander.

ver'prügeln *vt (col)* beat up, do over.

Verputz [fɛr'pʊts] *m* plaster, roughcast; **v~en** *vt* plaster; *(col)* **Essen** put away.

verquollen [fɛr'kvɔlən] *a* swollen; **Holz** warped.

verrammeln [fɛr'ramɔln] *vt* barricade.

Verrat [fɛr'ra:t] *m* **-(e)s** treachery; *(Pol)* treason; **v~en** *irreg vt* betray; **Geheimnis** divulge; *vr* give o.s. away.

Verräter [fɛr're:tər] *m* **-s,** - traitor; **~in** *f* traitress; **v~isch** *a* treacherous.

ver'rechnen *vt:* **~ mit** set off against; *vr* miscalculate.

Verrechnungsscheck [fɛr'rɛçnʊŋsʃɛk] *m* crossed cheque.

verregnet [fɛr're:ɡnɔt] *a* spoilt by rain, rainy.

ver'reisen *vi* go away (on a journey).

ver'reißen *vt irreg* pull to pieces.

verrenken [fɛr'rɛŋkən] *vt* contort; *(Med)* dislocate; **sich** *(dat)* **den Knöchel ~** sprain one's ankle.

Verrenkung *f* contortion; *(Med)* dislocation, sprain.

ver'richten *vt* do, perform.

verriegeln [fɛr'ri:ɡəln] *vt* bolt up, lock.

verringern [fɛr'rɪŋərn] *vt* reduce; *vr* diminish.

Verringerung *f* reduction; lessening.

ver'rinnen *vi irreg* run out *or* away; *(Zeit)* elapse.

ver'rosten *vi* rust.

verrotten [fɛr'rɔtən] *vi* rot.

ver'rücken *vt* move, shift.

verrückt [fɛr'rʏkt] *a* crazy, mad; **V~e(r)** *mf* lunatic; **V~heit** *f* madness, lunacy.

Verruf [fɛr'ru:f] *m:* **in ~ geraten/bringen** fall/bring into disrepute; **v~en** *a* notorious, disreputable.

Vers [fɛrs] *m* **-es, -e** verse.

ver'sagen *vt:* **jdm/sich** *(dat)* **etw ~** deny sb/o.s. sth; *vi* fail; **V~ nt -s** failure.

Versager [fɛr'za:ɡər] *m* **-s,** - failure.

ver'salzen *vt irreg* put too much salt in; *(fig)* spoil.

ver'sammeln *vtr* assemble, gather.

Ver'sammlung *f* meeting, gathering.

Versand [fɛr'zant] *m* **-(e)s** forwarding; dispatch; *(-abteilung)* dispatch department; **~haus** *nt* mail-order firm.

versäumen [fɛr'zɔymən] *vt* miss; *(unterlassen)* neglect, fail.

Versäumnis *f-,* **-se** neglect; omission.

ver'schaffen *vt:* **jdm/sich etw ~** get *or* procure sth for sb/o.s. **verschämt** [fɛr'ʃɛ:mt] *a* bashful.

verschandeln [fɛr'ʃandəln] *vt (col)* spoil.

verschanzen [fɛr'ʃantsən] *vr:* **sich hinter etw** *(dat)* **~** dig in behind sth; *(fig)* take refuge behind.

verschärfen [fɛr'ʃɛrfən] *vtr* intensify; **Lage** aggravate.

ver'schätzen *vr* be out in one's reckoning.

ver'schenken *vt* give away.

ver'scherzen *vt:* **sich** *(dat)* **etw ~** lose sth, throw away sth.

verscheuchen [fɛr'ʃɔyçən] *vt* frighten away.

ver'schicken *vt* send off; **Sträfling** transport, deport.

ver'schieben *vt irreg* shift; *(Rail)* shunt; **Termin** postpone; *(Comm)* push.

Ver'schiebung *f* shift, displacement; shunting; postponement.

verschieden [fɛr'ʃi:dən] *a* different; *(pl: mehrere)* various; **sie sind ~ groß** they are of different sizes; **~e** *pl* various people/things *pl;* **~es** *pron* various things *pl;* **etwas ~es** something different; **~artig** *a* various, of different kinds; **zwei so ~artige ...** two such differing ...; **V~heit** *f* difference; **~tlich** *ad* several times.

verschlafen [fɛrˈʃlaːfən] *irreg vt* sleep through; *(fig: versäumen)* miss; *vir* oversleep; *a* sleepy.
Verschlag [fɛrˈʃlaːk] *m* shed; **v~en** [fɛrˈʃlaːgən] *vt irreg* board up; *(Tennis)* hit out of play; *Buchseite* lose; **jdm den Atem v~en** take sb's breath away; **an einen Ort v~en werden** wind up in a place; *a* cunning.
verschlampen [fɛrˈʃlampən] *vi* fall into neglect; *vt* lose, mislay.
verschlechtern [fɛrˈʃlɛçtərn] *vt* make worse; *vr* deteriorate, get worse.
Verschlechterung *f* deterioration.
Verschleierung [fɛrˈʃlaɪərʊŋ] *f* veiling; *(fig)* concealment; *(Mil)* screening; **~staktik** *f* smoke-screen tactics *pl*.
Verschleiß [fɛrˈʃlaɪs] *m* **-es, -e** wear and tear; *(Aus)* retail trade; **v~en** *irreg vt* wear out; retail; *vir* wear out.
ver'schleppen *vt* carry off, abduct; *(zeitlich)* drag out, delay.
ver'schleudern *vt* squander; *(Comm)* sell dirt-cheap.
verschließ- [fɛrˈʃliːs] *cpd*: **~bar** *a* lockable; **~en** *irreg vt* close; lock; *vr* **sich einer Sache ~en** close one's mind to sth.
verschlimmern [fɛrˈʃlɪmərn] *vt* make worse, aggravate; *vr* get worse, deteriorate.
Verschlimmerung *f* deterioration.
verschlingen [fɛrˈʃlɪŋən] *vt irreg* devour, swallow up; *Fäden* twist.
verschlossen [fɛrˈʃlɔsən] *a* locked; *(fig)* reserved; **V~heit** *f* reserve.
ver'schlucken *vt* swallow; *vr* choke.
Verschluß [fɛrˈʃlʊs] *m* lock; *(von Kleid etc)* fastener; *(Phot)* shutter; *(Stöpsel)* plug; **unter ~ halten** keep under lock and key.
verschlüsseln [fɛrˈʃlʏsəln] *vt* encode.
verschmähen [fɛrˈʃmɛːən] *vt* disdain, scorn.
ver'schmelzen *vti irreg* merge, blend.
verschmerzen [fɛrˈʃmɛrtsən] *vt* get over.
verschmutzen [fɛrˈʃmʊtsən] *vt* soil; *Umwelt* pollute.
verschneit [fɛrˈʃnaɪt] *a* snowed up, covered in snow.
verschnüren [fɛrˈʃnyːrən] *vt* tie up.
verschollen [fɛrˈʃɔlən] *a* lost, missing.
ver'schonen *vt* spare *(jdn mit etw* sb sth).
verschönern [fɛrˈʃøːnərn] *vt* decorate; *(verbessern)* improve.
verschränken [fɛrˈʃrɛŋkən] *vt* cross, fold.
ver'schreiben *irreg vt* *Papier* use up; *(Med)* prescribe; *vr* make a mistake (in writing); **sich einer Sache ~** devote oneself to sth.
verschrien [fɛrˈʃriːən] *a* notorious.
verschroben [fɛrˈʃroːbən] *a* eccentric, odd.
verschrotten [fɛrˈʃrɔtən] *vt* scrap.
verschüchtert [fɛrˈʃʏçtərt] *a* subdued, intimidated.
verschuld- [fɛrˈʃʊld] *cpd*: **~en** *vt* be guilty of; **V~en** *nt* **-s** fault, guilt; **~et** *a* in debt; **V~ung** *f* fault; *(Geld)* debts *pl*.

ver'schütten *vt* spill; *(zuschütten)* fill; *(unter Trümmer)* bury.
ver'schweigen *vt irreg* keep secret; **jdm etw ~** keep sth from sb.
verschwend- [fɛrˈʃvɛnd] *cpd*: **~en** *vt* squander; **V~er** *m* **-s, -** spendthrift; **~erisch** *a* wasteful, extravagant; **V~ung** *f* waste; extravagance.
verschwiegen [fɛrˈʃviːgən] *a* discreet; *Ort* secluded; **V~heit** *f* discretion; seclusion.
ver'schwimmen *vi irreg* grow hazy, become blurred.
ver'schwinden *vi irreg* disappear, vanish; **V~** *nt* **-s** disappearance.
ver'schwitzen *vt* stain with sweat; *(col)* forget.
verschwommen [fɛrˈʃvɔmən] *a* hazy, vague.
verschwör- [fɛrˈʃvøːr] *cpd*: **~en** *vr irreg* plot, conspire; **V~er** *m* **-s, -** conspirator; **V~ung** *f* conspiracy, plot.
ver'sehen *irreg vt* supply, provide; *Pflicht* carry out; *Amt* fill; *Haushalt* keep; *vr (fig)* make a mistake; **ehe er (es) sich ~ hatte ...** before he knew it ...; **V~** *nt* **-s, -** oversight; **aus V~** by mistake; **~tlich** *ad* by mistake.
Versehrte(r) [fɛrˈzeːrtə(r)] *mf* disabled person.
ver'senden *vt irreg* forward, dispatch.
ver'senken *vt* sink; *vr* become engrossed *(in +acc* in).
versessen [fɛrˈzɛsən] *a*: **~ auf** *(+acc)* mad about.
ver'setzen *vt* transfer; *(verpfänden)* pawn; *(col)* stand up; **jdm einen Tritt/Schlag ~** kick/hit sb; **etw mit etw ~** mix sth with sth; **jdn in gute Laune ~** put sb in a good mood; *vr:* **sich in jdn** *or* **in jds Lage ~** put o.s. in sb's place.
Ver'setzung *f* transfer.
verseuchen [fɛrˈzɔʏçən] *vt* contaminate.
versichern [fɛrˈzɪçərn] *vt* assure; *(mit Geld)* insure; *vr* **sich ~** *(+gen)* make sure of.
Versicherung *f* assurance; insurance; **~spolice** *f* insurance policy.
versiegeln [fɛrˈziːgəln] *vt* seal (up).
ver'siegen *vi* dry up.
ver'sinken *vi irreg* sink.
versöhnen [fɛrˈzøːnən] *vt* reconcile; *vr* become reconciled.
Versöhnung *f* reconciliation.
ver'sorgen *vt* provide, supply *(mit* with); *Familie etc* look after; *vr* look after o.s.
Ver'sorgung *f* provision; *(Unterhalt)* maintenance; *(Alters— etc)* benefit, assistance.
verspäten [fɛrˈʃpɛːtən] *vr* be late.
Verspätung *f* delay; **~ haben** be late.
ver'sperren *vt* bar, obstruct.
Ver'sperrung *f* barrier.
ver'spielen *vti* lose.
verspielt [fɛrˈʃpiːlt] *a* playful; **bei jdm ~ haben** be in sb's bad books.
ver'spotten *vt* ridicule, scoff at.
ver'sprechen *irreg vt* promise; **sich** *(dat)* **etw von etw ~** expect sth from sth; **V~** *nt* **-s, -** promise.

verstaatlichen [fɛr'ʃtaːtlɪçən] *vt* nationalize.

Verstand [fɛr'ʃtant] *m* intelligence; mind; **den ~ verlieren** go out of one's mind; **über jds ~ gehen** go beyond sb; **v~esmäßig** *a* rational; intellectual.

verständig [fɛr'ʃtɛndɪç] *a* sensible; **~en** [fɛr'ʃtɛndɪgən] *vt* inform; *vr* communicate; *(sich einigen)* come to an understanding; **V~keit** *f* good sense; **V~ung** *f* communication; *(Benachrichtigung)* informing; *(Einigung)* agreement.

verständ- [fɛr'ʃtɛnt] *cpd:* **~lich** *a* understandable, comprehensible; **V~lichkeit** *f* clarity, intelligibility; **V~nis** *nt* **-ses, -se** understanding; **~nislos** *a* uncomprehending; **~nisvoll** *a* understanding, sympathetic.

verstärk- [fɛr'ʃtɛrk] *cpd:* **~en** *vt* strengthen; *Ton* amplify; *(erhöhen)* intensify; *vr* intensify; **V~er** *m* **-s, -** amplifier; **V~ung** *f* strengthening; *(Hilfe)* reinforcements *pl*; *(von Ton)* amplification.

verstauchen [fɛr'ʃtauxən] *vt* sprain.

verstauen [fɛr'ʃtauən] *vt* stow away.

Versteck [fɛr'ʃtɛk] *nt* **-(e)s, -e** hiding (place); **v~en** *vtr* hide; **~spiel** *nt* hide-and-seek; **v~t** *a* hidden.

ver'stehen *irreg vt* understand; *vr* get on.

versteifen [fɛr'ʃtaifən] *vt* stiffen, brace; *vr* (fig) insist (*auf +acc* on).

versteigern [fɛr'ʃtaigərn] *vt* auction.

Versteigerung *f* auction.

verstell- [fɛr'ʃtɛl] *cpd:* **~bar** *a* adjustable, variable; **~en** *vt* move, shift; *Uhr* adjust; *(versperren)* block; (fig) disguise; *vr* pretend, put on an act; **V~ung** *f* pretence.

verstiegen [fɛr'ʃtiːgən] *a* exaggerated.

verstimmt [fɛr'ʃtɪmt] *a* out of tune; (fig) cross, put out.

verstockt [fɛr'ʃtɔkt] *a* stubborn; **V~heit** *f* stubbornness.

verstohlen [fɛr'ʃtoːlən] *a* stealthy.

ver'stopfen *vt* block, stop up; *(Med)* constipate.

Ver'stopfung *f* obstruction; *(Med)* constipation.

verstorben [fɛr'ʃtɔrbən] *a* deceased, late.

verstört [fɛr'ʃtøːrt] *a Mensch* distraught.

Verstoß [fɛr'ʃtoːs] *m* infringement, violation *(gegen* of); **v~en** *irreg vt* disown, reject; *vi:* **v~en gegen** offend against.

ver'streichen *irreg vt* spread; *vi* elapse.

ver'streuen *vt* scatter (about).

ver'stricken *vt* (fig) entangle, ensnare; *vr* get entangled (*in +acc* in).

verstümmeln [fɛr'ʃtʏməln] *vt* maim, mutilate *(auch fig).*

verstummen [fɛr'ʃtʊmən] *vi* go silent; *(Lärm)* die away.

Versuch [fɛr'zuːx] *m* **-(e)s, -e** attempt; *(Sci)* experiment; **v~en** *vt* try; *(verlocken)* tempt; *vr:* **sich an etw** *(dat)* **v~en** try one's hand at sth; **~skaninchen** *nt* guinea-pig; **v~sweise** *ad* tentatively; **~ung** *f* temptation.

versunken [fɛr'zʊŋkən] *a* sunken; **~ sein in** *(+acc)* be absorbed *or* engrossed in.

versüßen [fɛr'zyːsən] *vt:* **jdm etw ~** (fig) make sth more pleasant for sb.

vertagen [fɛr'taːgən] *vti* adjourn.

Vertagung *f* adjournment.

ver'tauschen *vt* exchange; *(versehentlich)* mix up.

verteidig- [fɛr'taidɪç] *cpd:* **~en** *vt* defend; **V~er** *m* **-s, -** defender; *(Jur)* defence counsel; **V~ung** *f* defence.

ver'teilen *vt* distribute; *Rollen* assign; *Salbe* spread.

Verteilung *f* distribution, allotment.

verteufelt [fɛr'tɔyfəlt] *a,ad* (col) awful(ly), devilish(ly).

vertiefen [fɛr'tiːfən] *vt* deepen; *vr:* **sich in etw** *(acc)* **~** become engrossed *or* absorbed in sth.

Vertiefung *f* depression.

vertikal [vɛrti'kaːl] *a* vertical.

vertilgen [fɛr'tɪlgən] *vt* exterminate; *(col)* eat up, consume.

vertippen [fɛr'tɪpən] *vr* make a typing mistake.

vertonen [fɛr'toːnən] *vt* set to music.

Vertrag [fɛr'traːk] *m* **-(e)s, ⁻e** contract, agreement; *(Pol)* treaty; **v~en** [fɛr'traːgən] *irreg vt* tolerate, stand; *vr* get along; *(sich aussöhnen)* become reconciled; **v~lich** *a* contractual.

verträglich [fɛr'trɛːklɪç] *a* good-natured, sociable; *Speisen* easily digested; *(Med)* easily tolerated; **V~keit** *f* sociability; good nature; digestibility.

Vertrags- *cpd:* **~bruch** *m* breach of contract; **v~brüchig** *a* in breach of contract; **v~mäßig** *a,ad* stipulated, according to contract; **~partner** *m* party to a contract; **~spieler** *m* (Sport) contract professional; **v~widrig** *a* contrary to contract.

vertrauen [fɛr'trauən] *vi* trust *(jdm* sb); **~ auf** *(+acc)* rely on; **V~** *nt* **-s** confidence; **~erweckend** *a* inspiring trust; **~sselig** *a* too trustful; **~svoll** *a* trustful; **~swürdig** *a* trustworthy.

vertraulich [fɛr'traulɪç] *a* familiar; *(geheim)* confidential; **V~keit** *f* familiarity; confidentiality.

vertraut [fɛr'traut] *a* familiar; **V~e(r)** *mf* confidant, close friend; **V~heit** *f* familiarity.

ver'treiben *vt irreg* drive away; *(aus Land)* expel; *(Comm)* sell; *Zeit* pass.

Ver'treibung *f* expulsion.

vertret- [fɛr'treːt] *cpd:* **~en** *vt irreg* represent; *Ansicht* hold, advocate; **sich** *(dat)* **die Beine ~en** stretch one's legs; **V~er** *m* **-s, -** representative; *(Verfechter)* advocate; **V~ung** *f* representation; advocacy.

Vertrieb [fɛr'triːp] *m* **-(e)s, -e** marketing.

ver'trocknen *vi* dry up.

ver'trödeln *vt* (col) fritter away.

ver'trösten *vt* put off.

vertun [fɛr'tuːn] *irreg vt* (col) waste; *vr* make a mistake.

vertuschen [fɛr'tʊʃən] *vt* hush *or* cover up.

verübeln [fɛr'yːbəln] *vt:* **jdm etw ~** be cross *or* offended with sb on account of sth.

verüben [fɛr'yːbən] *vt* commit.

verun- [fɛr'ʊn] *cpd:* **~glimpfen**

[-glɪmpfən] *vt* disparage; ~**glücken**
[-glʏkən] *vi* have an accident; **tödlich**
~**glücken** be killed in an accident;
~**reinigen** *vt* soil; *Umwelt* pollute;
~**sichern** *vt* rattle; ~**stalten** [-ʃtaltən] *vt*
disfigure; *Gebäude etc* deface; ~**treuen**
[-trɔyən] *vt* embezzle.

verur- [fɛr'uːr] *cpd:* ~**sachen** [-zaxən] *vt*
cause; ~**teilen** [-taɪlən] *vt* condemn;
V~teilung *f* condemnation; *(Jur)*
sentence.

verviel- [fɛr'fiːl] *cpd:* ~**fachen** [-faxən] *vt*
multiply; ~**fältigen** [—fɛltɪgən] *vt* duplicate, copy; **V~fältigung** *f* duplication,
copying.

vervoll- [fɛr'fɔl] *cpd:* ~**kommnen**
[-kɔmnən] *vt* perfect; ~**ständigen**
[-ʃtɛndɪgən] *vt* complete.

ver'wackeln *vt Photo* blur.

ver'wählen *vr (Tel)* dial the wrong
number.

verwahr- [fɛr'vaːr] ~**en** *vt* keep, lock
away; *vr* protest; ~**losen** [-loːzən] *vi*
become neglected; *(moralisch)* go to the
bad; ~**lost** [-loːst] *a* neglected; wayward.

verwaist [fɛr'vaɪst] *a* orphaned.

verwalt- [fɛr'valt] *cpd:* ~**en** *vt* manage;
administer; **V~er** *m* -**s**, - manager;
(Vermögens—) trustee; **V~ung** *f* administration; management; **V~ungsbezirk** *m*
administrative district.

ver'wandeln *vtr* change, transform.

Ver'wandlung *f* change, transformation.

verwandt [fɛr'vant] *a* related *(mit* to);
V~e(r) *mf* relative, relation; **V~schaft** *f*
relationship; *(Menschen)* relations *pl.*

ver'warnen *vt* caution.

Ver'warnung *f* caution.

ver'waschen *a* faded; *(fig)* vague.

verwässern [fɛr'vɛsərn] *vt* dilute, water
down.

ver'wechseln *vt* confuse *(mit* with);
mistake *(mit* for); **zum V~ ähnlich** as
like as two peas.

Ver'wechslung *f* confusion, mixing up.

verwegen [fɛr've:gən] *a* daring, bold;
V~heit *f* daring, audacity, boldness.

Verwehung [fɛr've:uŋ] *f* snow-/ sanddrift.

verweichlich- [fɛr'vaɪçlɪç] *cpd:* ~**en** *vt*
mollycoddle; ~**t** *a* effeminate, soft.

ver'weigern *vt* refuse *(jdm etw* sb sth);
den Gehorsam/die Aussage ~ refuse
to obey/testify.

Ver'weigerung *f* refusal.

verweilen [fɛr'vaɪlən] *vi* stay; *(fig)* dwell
(bei on).

Verweis [fɛr'vaɪs] *m* -**es**, -**e** reprimand,
rebuke; *(Hinweis)* reference; **v~en**
[fɛr'vaɪzən] *vt irreg* refer; **jdm etw v~en**
(tadeln) scold sb for sth; **jdn von der
Schule v~en** expel sb (from school); **jdn
des Landes v~en** deport or expel sb;
~**ung** *f* reference; *(Tadel)* reprimand;
(Landes—) deportation.

ver'welken *vi* fade.

ver'wenden *irreg vt* use; *Mühe, Zeit, Arbeit*
spend; *vr* intercede.

Ver'wendung *f* use.

ver'werfen *vt irreg* reject.

verwerflich [fɛr'vɛrflɪç] *a* reprehensible.

ver'werten *vt* utilize.

Ver'wertung *f* utilization.

verwesen [fɛr've:zən] *vi* decay.

Verwesung *f* decomposition.

ver'wickeln *vt* tangle (up); *(fig)* involve
(in +acc in); *vr* get tangled (up); **sich ~
in** *(+acc) (fig)* get involved in.

Verwicklung *f* complication, entangle-
ment.

verwildern [fɛr'vɪldərn] *vi* run wild.

ver'winden *vt irreg* get over.

verwirklichen [fɛr'vɪrklɪçən] *vt* realize,
put into effect.

Verwirklichung *f* realization.

verwirren [fɛr'vɪrən] *vt* tangle (up); *(fig)*
confuse.

Verwirrung *f* confusion.

verwittern [fɛr'vɪtərn] *vi* weather.

verwitwet [fɛr'vɪtvət] *a* widowed.

verwöhnen [fɛr'vø:nən] *vt* spoil.

Verwöhnung *f* spoiling, pampering.

verworfen [fɛr'vɔrfən] *a* depraved;
V~heit *f* depravity.

verworren [fɛr'vɔrən] *a* confused.

verwund- *cpd:* ~**bar** [fɛr'vuntbaːr] *a*
vulnerable; ~**en** [fɛr'vundən] *vt* wound;
~**erlich** [fɛr'vundərlɪç] *a* surprising;
V~erung [fɛr'vundəruŋ] *f* astonishment;
V~ete(r) *mf* injured (person); **V~ung** *f*
wound, injury.

ver'wünschen *vt* curse.

verwüsten [fɛr'vy:stən] *vt* devastate.

Verwüstung *f* devastation.

verzagen [fɛr'tsa:gən] *vi* despair.

ver'zählen *vr* miscount.

verzehren [fɛr'tse:rən] *vt* consume.

ver'zeichnen *vt* list; *Niederlage, Verlust*
register.

Verzeichnis [fɛr'tsaɪçnɪs] *nt* -**ses**, -**se**
list, catalogue; *(in Buch)* index.

verzeih- [fɛr'tsaɪ] *cpd:* ~**en** *vti irreg* forgive *(jdm etw* sb for sth); ~**lich** *a*
pardonable; **V~ung** *f* forgiveness,
pardon; **V~ung!** sorry!, excuse me!

ver'zerren *vt* distort.

Verzicht [fɛr'tsɪçt] *m* -**(e)s**, -**e** renunciation *(auf +acc* of); **v~en** *vi* forgo, give
up *(auf etw (acc)* sth).

ver'ziehen *irreg vi* move; *vt* put out of
shape; *Kind* spoil; *Pflanzen* thin out; **das
Gesicht** ~ pull a face; *vr* go out of shape;
(Gesicht) contort; *(verschwinden)* disappear.

verzieren [fɛr'tsi:rən] *vt* decorate, ornament.

verzinsen [fɛr'tsɪnzən] *vt* pay interest on.

ver'zögern *vt* delay.

Ver'zögerung *f* delay, time-lag;
~**staktik** *f* delaying tactics *pl.*

verzollen [fɛr'tsɔlən] *vt* declare, pay duty
on.

verzück- [fɛr'tsʏk] *cpd:* ~**en** *vt* send into
ecstasies, enrapture; ~**t** *a* enraptured;
V~ung *f* ecstasy.

verzweif- [fɛr'tsvaɪf] *cpd:* ~**eln** *vi*
despair; ~**elt** *a* desperate; **V~lung** *f*
despair.

verzweigen [fɛr'tsvaɪgən] *vr* branch out.

verzwickt [fɛr'tsvɪkt] a (col) awkward, complicated.

Veto ['ve:to] nt **-s, -s** veto.

Vetter ['fɛtər] m **-s, -n** cousin; **~nwirtschaft** f nepotism.

vibrieren [vi'bri:rən] vi vibrate.

Vieh [fi:] nt **-(e)s** cattle pl; **v~isch** a bestial.

viel [fi:l] a a lot of, much; **~e** pl a lot of, many; ad a lot, much; **~ zuwenig** much too little; **~erlei** a a great variety of; **~es** a a lot; **~fach** a,ad many times; **auf ~fachen Wunsch** at the request of many people; **V~falt** f - variety; **~fältig** a varied, many-sided.

vielleicht [fi'laɪçt] ad perhaps.

viel- cpd: **~mal(s)** ad many times; **danke ~mals** many thanks; **~mehr** ad rather, on the contrary; **~sagend** a significant; **~seitig** a many-sided; **~versprechend** a promising.

vier [fi:r] num four; **V~eck** nt **-(e)s, -e** four-sided figure; (gleichseitig) square; **~eckig** a four-sided; square; **V~taktmotor** m four-stroke engine; **~te(r,s)** ['fi:rtə(r,z)] a fourth; **~teilen** vt quarter; **V~tel** ['fɪrtəl] nt **-s, -** quarter; **~teljährlich** a quarterly; **V~elnote** f crotchet; **V~elstunde** [fɪrtəl'ʃtʊndə] f quarter of an hour; **~zehn** ['fɪrtse:n] num fourteen; **in ~zehn Tagen** in a fortnight; **~zehntägig** a fortnightly; **~zig** ['fɪrtsɪç] num forty.

Vikar [vi'ka:r] m **-s, -e** curate.

Villa ['vɪla] f -, **Villen** villa.

Villenviertel ['vɪlənfɪrtəl] nt (prosperous) residential area.

violett [vio'lɛt] a violet.

Violin- [vio'li:n] cpd: **~bogen** m violin bow; **~e** f -, m violin; **~konzert** nt violin concerto; **~schlüssel** m treble clef.

Virus ['vi:rʊs] m or nt -, **Viren** virus.

Visier [vi'zi:r] nt **-s, -e** gunsight; (am Helm) visor.

Visite [vi'zi:tə] f -, **-n** (Med) visit; **~nkarte** f visiting card.

visuell [vizu'ɛl] a visual.

Visum ['vi:zʊm] nt **-s, Visa** or **Visen** visa.

vital [vi'ta:l] a lively, full of life, vital.

Vitamin [vita'mi:n] nt **-s, -e** vitamin.

Vogel ['fo:gəl] m **-s, -̈** bird; **einen ~ haben** (col) have bats in the belfry; **jdm den ~ zeigen** (col) tap one's forehead (to indicate that one thinks sb stupid); **~bauer** nt birdcage; **~beerbaum** m rowan tree; **~schau** f bird's-eye view; **~scheuche** f -, **-n** scarecrow.

Vokab- cpd: **~el** [vo'ka:bəl] f -, **-n** word; **~ular** [vokabu'la:r] nt **-s, -e** vocabulary.

Vokal [vo'ka:l] m **-s, -e** vowel.

Volk [fɔlk] nt **-(e)s, -̈er** people; nation.

Völker- ['fœlkər] cpd: **~bund** m League of Nations; **~recht** nt international law; **v~rechtlich** a according to international law; **~verständigung** f international understanding; **~wanderung** f migration.

Volks- cpd: **~abstimmung** f referendum; **~hochschule** f adult education classes pl; **~lied** nt folksong; **~republik** f

people's republic; **~schule** f elementary school; **~tanz** m folk dance; **v~tümlich** ['fɔlksty:mlɪç] a popular; **~wirtschaft** f economics.

voll [fɔl] a full; **~ und ganz** completely; **jdn für ~ nehmen** (col) take sb seriously; **~auf** [fɔl'aʊf] ad amply; **~blütig** a full-blooded; **v~'bringen** vt irreg insep accomplish; **v~'enden** vt insep finish, complete; **~ends** ['fɔlɛnts] ad completely; **V~'endung** f completion; **~er** a fuller; (+gen) full of; **V~eyball** ['vɔlibal] m volleyball; **V~gas** nt: **mit V~gas** at full throttle; **V~gas geben** step on it.

völlig ['fœlɪç] a,ad complete(ly).

voll- cpd: **~jährig** a of age; **V~kaskoversicherung** f fully comprehensive insurance; **~'kommen** a perfect; **V~'kommenheit** f perfection; **V~kornbrot** nt wholemeal bread; **~machen** vt fill (up); **V~macht** f -, **-en** authority, full powers pl; **V~mond** m full moon; **V~pension** f full board; **~ständig** a complete; **v~'strecken** vt insep execute; **~tanken** vti fill up; **~zählig** a complete; in full number; **v~'ziehen** vt irreg insep carry out; vr happen; **V~'zug** m execution.

Volt [vɔlt] nt - or **-(e)s, -** volt.

Volumen [vo'lu:mən] nt **-s, -** or **Volumina** volume.

vom [fɔm] = **von dem**.

von [fɔn] prep +dat from; (statt Genitiv, bestehend aus) of; (im Passiv) by; **ein Freund ~ mir** a friend of mine; **~ mir aus** (col) OK by me; **~ wegen!** no way!; **~ei'nander** ad from each other; **~statten** [fɔn'ʃtatən] ad: **~statten gehen** proceed, go.

vor [fo:r] prep +dat or acc before; (räumlich) in front of; **~ Wut/Liebe** with rage/love; **~ 2 Tagen** 2 days ago; **~ allem** above all; **V~abend** m evening before, eve.

voran [fo'ran] ad before, ahead; **~gehen** vi irreg go ahead; **einer Sache** (dat) **~gehen** precede sth; **~gehend** a previous; **~kommen** vi irreg come along, make progress.

Vor- ['fo:r] cpd: **~anschlag** m estimate; **~arbeiter** m foreman.

voraus [fo'raʊs] ad ahead; (zeitlich) in advance; **jdm ~ sein** be ahead of sb; **im ~ in advance; ~bezahlen** vt pay in advance; **~gehen** vi irreg go (on) ahead; (fig) precede; **~haben** vt irreg: **jdm etw ~haben** have the edge on sb in sth; **V~sage** f -, **-n** prediction; **~sagen** vt predict; **~sehen** vt irreg foresee; **~setzen** vt assume; **~gesetzt, daß ...** provided that ...; **V~setzung** f requirement, prerequisite; **V~sicht** f foresight; **aller V~sicht nach** in all probability; **in der V~sicht, daß ...** anticipating that ...; **~sichtlich** ad probably.

vorbauen ['fo:rbaʊən] vt build up in front; vi take precautions (dat against).

Vorbehalt ['fo:rbəhalt] m **-(e)s, -e** reservation, proviso; **v~en** vt irreg:

sich/jdm etw v~en reserve sth (to o.s.)/to sb; v~los *a,ad* unconditional(ly).

vorbei [fɔr'bai] *ad* by, past; ~gehen *vi irreg* pass by, go past.

vorbe- cpd: ~lastet ['fo:rbəlastət] *a (fig)* handicapped; ~reiten ['fo:rbəraitən] *vt* prepare; V~reitung *f* preparation; ~straft ['fo:rbəʃtraft] *a* previously convicted, with a record.

vorbeugen ['fo:rbɔygən] *vtr* lean forward; *vi* prevent (*einer Sache* (dat) sth); ~d *a* preventive.

Vorbeugung *f* prevention; zur ~ gegen for the prevention of.

Vorbild ['fo:rbilt] *nt* model; sich (dat) jdn zum ~ nehmen model o.s. on sb; v~lich *a* model, ideal.

vorbringen ['fo:rbriŋən] *vt irreg* advance, state; (col: nach vorne) bring to the front.

Vorder- ['fɔrdər] cpd: ~achse *f* front axle; ~ansicht *f* front view; v~e(r,s) *a* front; ~grund *m* foreground; v~hand *ad* for the present; ~mann *m, pl* -männer man in front; jdn auf ~mann bringen (col) tell sb to pull his socks up; ~seite *f* front (side); v~ste(r,s) *a* front.

vordrängen ['fo:rdreŋən] *vt* push to the front.

vorehelich ['fo:r'e:əliç] *a* premarital.

voreilig ['fo:r'ailiç] *a* hasty, rash.

voreingenommen ['fo:r'aingənɔmən] *a* biased; V~heit *f* bias.

vorenthalten ['fo:r'enthaltən] *vt irreg*: jdm etw ~ withhold sth from sb.

vorerst ['fo:r'e:rst] *ad* for the moment or present.

Vorfahr ['fo:rfa:r] *m* -en, -en ancestor; v~en *vi irreg* drive (on) ahead; (vors Haus etc) drive up; ~t *f* (Aut) right of way; ~t achten! give way!; ~tsregel *f* right of way; ~tsschild *nt* give way sign.

Vorfall ['fo:rfal] *m* incident; v~en *vi irreg* occur.

vorfinden ['fo:rfindən] *vt irreg* find.

vorführen ['fo:rfy:rən] *vt* show, display; dem Gericht ~ bring before the court.

Vorgabe ['fo:rga:bə] *f* (Sport) start, handicap.

Vorgang ['fo:rgaŋ] *m* course of events; (esp Sci) process; der ~ von etw how sth happens.

Vorgänger(in *f)* ['fo:rgeŋər(in)] *m* -s, - predecessor.

vorgeben ['fo:rge:bən] *vt irreg* pretend, use as a pretext; (Sport) give an advantage or a start of.

vorge- ['fo:rgə] cpd: ~faßt [-fast] *a* preconceived; ~fertigt [-fertiçt] *a* prefabricated; V~fühl [-fyl] *nt* presentiment, anticipation.

vorgehen ['fo:rge:ən] *vi irreg (voraus)* go (on) ahead; (nach vorn) go up front; (handeln) act, proceed; (Uhr) be fast; (Vorrang haben) take precedence; (passieren) go on; V~ *nt* -s action.

Vorgeschmack ['fo:rgəʃmak] *m* foretaste.

Vorgesetzte(r) ['fo:rgəzetstə(r)] *mf* superior.

vorgestern ['fo:rgestərn] *ad* the day before yesterday.

vorgreifen ['fo:rgraifən] *vi irreg* anticipate, forestall.

vorhaben ['fo:rha:bən] *vt irreg* intend; hast du schon was vor? have you got anything on?; V~ *nt* -s, - intention.

vorhalten ['fo:rhaltən] *irreg vt* hold or put up; (fig) reproach (*jdm etw* sb for sth); *vi* last.

Vorhaltung *f* reproach.

vorhanden [fo:r'handən] *a* existing, extant; (erhältlich) available; V~sein *nt* -s existence, presence.

Vorhang ['fo:rhaŋ] *m* curtain.

Vorhängeschloß ['fo:rheŋəʃlɔs] *nt* padlock.

Vorhaut ['fo:rhaut] *f* (Med) foreskin.

vorher [fo:r'he:r] *ad* before(hand); ~bestimmen *vt* Schicksal preordain; ~gehen *vi irreg* precede; ~ig [fo:r'he:riç] *a* previous.

Vorherrschaft ['fo:rherʃaft] *f* predominance, supremacy.

vorherrschen ['fo:rherʃən] *vi* predominate.

vorher- [fo:r'he:r] cpd: V~sage *f* -, -n forecast; ~sagen *vt* forecast, predict; ~sehbar *a* predictable; ~sehen *vt irreg* foresee.

vorhin [fo:r'hin] *ad* not long ago, just now; ~ein [fo:r'hinain] *ad*: im ~ein before-hand.

vorig ['fo:riç] *a* previous, last.

vorjährig ['fo:rje:riç] *a* of the previous year; last year's.

Vorkehrung ['fo:rke:ruŋ] *f* precaution.

vorkommen ['fo:rkɔmən] *vi irreg* come forward; (geschehen, sich finden) occur; (scheinen) seem (to be); sich (dat) dumm etc ~ feel stupid etc; V~ *nt* -s, - occurrence.

Vorkommnis ['fo:rkɔmnis] *nt* -ses, -se occurrence.

Vorkriegs- ['fo:rkri:ks] *in cpds* prewar.

Vorladung ['fo:rla:duŋ] *f* summons.

Vorlage ['fo:rla:gə] *f* model, pattern; (Gesetzes—) bill; (Sport) pass.

vorlassen ['fo:rlasən] *vt irreg* admit; (vorgehen lassen) allow to go in front.

vorläufig ['fo:rlɔyfiç] *a* temporary, provisional.

vorlaut ['fo:rlaut] *a* impertinent, cheeky.

Vorleg- ['fo:rle:g] cpd: v~en *vt* put in front; (fig) produce, submit; jdm etw v~en put sth before sb; ~er *m* -s, - mat.

vorlesen ['fo:rle:zən] *vt irreg* read (out).

Vorlesung *f* (Univ) lecture.

vorletzte(r, s) ['fo:rletstə(r,s)] *a* last but one.

Vorliebe ['fo:rli:bə] *f* preference, partiality.

vorliebnehmen [fo:r'li:pne:mən] *vi irreg*: ~ mit make do with.

vorliegen ['fo:rli:gən] *vi irreg* be (here); etw liegt jdm vor sb has sth; ~d *a* present, at issue.

vormachen ['fo:rmaxən] *vt*: jdm etw ~ show sb how to do sth; (fig) fool sb; have sb on.

Vormachtstellung ['fo:rmaxt∫tɛluŋ] f supremacy, hegemony.

Vormarsch ['fo:rmar∫] m advance.

vormerken ['fo:rmɛrkən] vt book.

Vormittag ['fo:rmıta:k] m morning; **v~s** ad in the morning, before noon.

Vormund ['fo:rmʊnt] m **-(e)s, -e** or **-münder** guardian.

vorn(e) ['fɔrn(ə)] ad in front; **von ~ anfangen** start at the beginning; **nach ~** to the front.

Vorname ['fo:rna:mə] m first or Christian name.

vornan [fɔrn''an] ad at the front.

vornehm ['fo:rne:m] a distinguished; refined; elegant; **~en** vt irreg (fig) carry out; **sich** (dat) **etw ~en** start on sth; (beschließen) decide to do sth; **sich** (dat) **jdn ~en** tell sb off; **~lich** ad chiefly, specially.

vornherein ['fɔrnhɛraın] ad: **von ~** from the start.

Vorort ['fo:r'ɔrt] m suburb; **~zug** m commuter train.

Vorrang ['fo:rraŋ] m precedence, priority; **v~ig** a of prime importance, primary.

Vorrat ['fo:rra:t] m stock, supply; **~skammer** f pantry.

vorrätig ['fo:rrɛ:tıç] a in stock.

Vorrecht ['fo:rrɛçt] nt privilege.

Vorrichtung ['fo:rrıçtʊŋ] f device, contrivance.

vorrücken ['fo:rrʏkən] vi advance; vt move forward.

vorsagen ['fo:rza:gən] vt recite, say out loud; (Sch: zuflüstern) tell secretly, prompt.

Vorsatz ['fo:rzats] m intention; (Jur) intent; **einen ~ fassen** make a resolution.

vorsätzlich ['fo:rzɛtslıç] a,ad intentional(ly); (Jur) premeditated.

Vorschau ['fo:r∫aʊ] f (Rad, TV) (programme) preview; (Film) trailer.

vorschieben ['fo:r∫i:bən] vt irreg push forward; (vor etw) push across; (fig) put forward as an excuse; **jdn ~** use sb as a front.

Vorschlag ['fo:r∫la:k] m suggestion, proposal; **v~en** vt irreg suggest, propose.

vorschnell ['fo:r∫nɛl] ad hastily, too quickly.

vorschreiben ['fo:r∫raıbən] vt irreg prescribe, specify.

Vorschrift ['fo:r∫rıft] f regulation(s); rule(s); (Anweisungen) instruction(s); **Dienst nach ~** work-to-rule; **v~smäßig** a as per regulations/instructions.

Vorschuß ['fo:r∫ʊs] m advance.

vorschweben ['fo:r∫ve:bən] vi: **jdm schwebt etw vor** sb has sth in mind.

vorsehen ['fo:rze:ən] irreg vt provide for, plan; vr take care, be careful; vi be visible.

Vorsehung f providence.

vorsetzen ['fo:rzɛtsən] vt move forward; (vor etw) put in front; (anbieten) offer.

Vorsicht ['fo:rzıçt] f caution, care; **~!** look out!, take care!; (auf Schildern) caution!, danger!; **~, Stufe!** mind the step!; **v~ig** a cautious, careful; **v~shalber** ad just in case.

Vorsilbe ['fo:rzılbə] f prefix.

Vorsitz ['fo:rzıts] m chair(manship); **~ende(r)** mf chairman/-woman.

Vorsorge ['fo:rzɔrgə] f precaution(s), provision(s); **v~n** vi: **v~en für** make provision(s) for.

vorsorglich ['fo:rzɔrklıç] ad as a precaution.

Vorspeise ['fo:r∫paızə] f hors d'oeuvre, appetizer.

Vorspiel ['fo:r∫pi:l] nt prelude.

vorsprechen ['fo:r∫prɛçən] irreg vt say out loud, recite; vi: **bei jdm ~** call on sb.

Vorsprung ['fo:r∫prʊŋ] m projecrion, ledge; (fig) advantage, start.

Vorstadt ['fo:r∫tat] f suburbs pl.

Vorstand ['fo:r∫tant] m executive committee; (Comm) board (of directors); (Person) director, head.

vorstehen ['fo:r∫te:ən] vi irreg project; etw (dat) ~ (fig) be the head of sth.

vorstell- ['fo:r∫tɛl] cpd: **~bar** a conceivable; **~en** vt put forward; (vor etw) put in front; (bekannt machen) introduce; (darstellen) represent; **sich** (dat) **etw ~en** imagine sth; **V~ung** f (Bekanntmachen) introduction; (Theat etc) performance; (Gedanke) idea, thought.

Vorstoß ['fo:r∫to:s] m advance; **v~en** vti irreg push forward.

Vorstrafe ['fo:r∫tra:fə] f previous conviction.

vorstrecken [fo:r∫trɛkən] vt stretch out; **Geld** advance.

Vorstufe ['fo:r∫tu:fə] f first step(s).

Vortag ['fo:rtak] m day before (einer Sache sth).

vortäuschen ['fo:rtɔy∫ən] vt feign, pretend.

Vorteil ['fɔrtaıl] m **-s, -e** advantage (gegenüber over); **im ~ sein** have the advantage; **v~haft** a advantageous.

Vortrag ['fo:rtra:k] m **-(e)s, Vorträge** talk, lecture; (~sart) delivery, rendering; (Comm) balance carried forward; **v~en** vt irreg carry forward (auch Comm); (fig) recite; Rede deliver; Lied perform; Meinung etc express.

vortrefflich [fo:rtrɛflıç] a excellent.

vortreten ['fo:rtre:tən] vi irreg step forward; (Augen etc) protrude.

vorüber [fo:ry:bər] ad past, over; **~gehen** vi irreg pass (by); **~gehen an** (+dat) (fig) pass over; **~gehend** a temporary, passing.

Vorurteil ['fo:r'ʊrtaıl] nt prejudice; **v~sfrei, v~slos** a unprejudiced, openminded.

Vorverkauf ['fo:rfɛrkaʊf] m advance booking.

Vorwahl ['fo:rva:l] f preliminary election; (Tel) dialling code.

Vorwand ['fo:rvant] m **-(e)s, Vorwände** pretext.

vorwärts ['fo:rvɛrts] ad forward; **V~gang** m (Aut etc) forward gear; **~gehen** vi irreg progress; **~kommen** vi irreg get on, make progress.

vorweg [fo:r'vɛk] ad in advance; **V~nahme** f **-, -n** anticipation;

~**nehmen** *vt irreg* anticipate.
vorweisen ['fo:rvaızən] *vt irreg* show, produce.
vorwerfen ['fo:rvɛrfən] *vt irreg:* **jdm etw** ~ reproach sb for sth, accuse sb of sth; **sich** *(dat)* **nichts vorzuwerfen haben** have nothing to reproach o.s. with.
vorwiegend ['fo:rvi:gənt] *a,ad* predominant(ly).
Vorwitz ['fo:rvɪts] *m* cheek; **v~ig** *a* saucy, cheeky.
Vorwort ['fo:rvɔrt] *nt* -(e)s, -e preface.
Vorwurf ['fo:rvurf] *m* reproach; **jdm/sich Vorwürfe machen** reproach sb/o.s.; **v~svoll** *a* reproachful.
vorzeigen ['fo:rtsaigən] *vt* show, produce.
vorzeitig ['fo:rtsaitɪç] *a* premature.
vorziehen ['fo:rtsi:ən] *vt irreg* pull forward; *Gardinen* draw; *(lieber haben)* prefer.
Vorzug ['fo:rtsu:k] *m* preference; *(gute Eigenschaft)* merit, good quality; *(Vorteil)* advantage; *(Rail)* relief train.
vorzüglich [fo:r'tsy:klıç] *a* excellent, first-rate.
vulgär [vul'gɛ:r] *a* vulgar.
Vulkan [vul'ka:n] *m* -s, -e volcano; **v~i-'sieren** *vt* vulcanize.

W

W, w [ve:] *nt* W, w.
Waage ['va:gə] *f* -, -n scales *pl*; *(Astrol)* Libra; **w~recht** *a* horizontal.
wabb(e)lig ['vab(ə)lıç] *a* wobbly.
Wabe ['va:bə] *f* -, -n honeycomb.
wach [vax] *a* awake; *(fig)* alert; **W~e** *f* -, -n guard, watch; **W~e halten** keep watch; **W~e stehen** stand guard; **~en** *vi* be awake; *(W—e halten)* guard.
Wacholder [va'xɔldər] *m* -s, - juniper.
Wachs [vaks] *nt* -es, -e wax.
wachsam ['vaxza:m] *a* watchful, vigilant, alert; **W~keit** *f* vigilance.
Wachs- *cpd:* **~en** *vi irreg* grow; *vt Skier* wax; **~tuch** *nt* oilcloth; **~tum** *nt* -s growth.
Wächter ['vɛçtər] *m* -s, - guard, warder, keeper; *(Parkplatz—)* attendant.
Wacht- [vaxt] *cpd:* **~meister** *m* officer; **~posten** *m* guard, sentry.
wackel- ['vakəl] *cpd:* **~ig** *a* shaky, wobbly; **W~kontakt** *m* loose connection; **~n** *vi* shake; *(fig: Position)* be shaky.
wacker ['vakər] *a* valiant, stout; *ad* well, bravely.
Wade ['va:də] *f* -, -n *(Anat)* calf.
Waffe ['vafə] *f* -, -n weapon; **~l** *f* -, -n waffle; wafer; **~nschein** *m* gun licence; **~nstillstand** *m* armistice, truce.
Wagemut ['va:gəmu:t] *m* daring.
wagen ['va:gən] *vt* venture, dare.
Wagen ['va:gən] *m* -s, - vehicle; *(Auto)* car; *(Rail)* carriage; *(Pferde—)* cart; **~führer** *m* driver; **~heber** *m* -s, - jack.
Waggon [va'gõ:] *m* -s, -s carriage; *(Güter—)* goods van, freight truck (US).
waghalsig ['va:khalzıç] *a* foolhardy.
Wagnis ['va:knıs] *nt* -ses, -se risk.
Wahl ['va:l] *f* -, -en choice; *(Pol)* election;

zweite ~ seconds *pl*; **w~berechtigt** *a* entitled to vote.
wähl- ['vɛ:l] *cpd:* **~bar** *a* eligible; **~en** *vti* choose; *(Pol)* elect, vote (for); *(Tel)* dial; **W~er(in** *f)* *m* -s, voter; **~erisch** *a* fastidious, particular; **W~erschaft** *f* electorate.
Wahl- *cpd:* **~fach** *nt* optional subject; **~gang** *m* ballot; **~kabine** *f* polling booth; **~kampf** *m* election campaign; **~kreis** *m* constituency; **~liste** *f* electoral register; **~lokal** *nt* polling station; **w~los** *ad* at random; **~recht** *nt* franchise; **~spruch** *m* motto; **~urne** *f* ballot box.
Wahn [va:n] *m* -(e)s delusion; folly; **~sinn** *m* madness; **w~sinnig** *a* insane, mad; *ad (col)* incredibly.
wahr [va:r] *a* true; **~en** *vt* maintain, keep.
während ['vɛ:rən] *vi* last; **~d** *prep* +gen during; *cj* while; **~ddessen** [vɛ:rənt'dɛsən] *ad* meanwhile.
wahr- *cpd:* **~haben** *vt irreg:* **etw nicht ~haben wollen** refuse to admit sth; **~haft** *ad (tatsächlich)* truly; **~haftig** [va:r'haftıç] *a* true, real; *ad* really; **W~heit** *f* truth; **~nehmen** *vt irreg* perceive, observe; **W~nehmung** *f* perception; **~sagen** *vi* prophesy, tell fortunes; **W~sager(in** *f)* *m* -s, - fortune teller; **~scheinlich** [va:r'ʃainlıç] *a* probable; *ad* probably; **W~'scheinlichkeit** *f* probability; **aller W~scheinlichkeit nach** in all probability; **W~zeichen** *nt* emblem.
Währung ['vɛ:ruŋ] *f* currency.
Waise ['vaizə] *f* -, -n orphan; **~nhaus** *nt* orphanage; **~nkind** *nt* orphan.
Wald [valt] *m* -(e)s, ¨er wood(s); *(groß)* forest; **w~ig** ['valdıç] *a* wooded.
Wäldchen ['vɛltçən] *nt* copse, grove.
Wal(fisch) ['va:l(fıʃ)] *m* -(e)s, -e whale.
Wall [val] *m* -(e)s, ¨e embankment; *(Bollwerk)* rampart; **w~fahren** *vi irreg* insep go on a pilgrimage; **~fahrer(in** *f)* *m* pilgrim; **~fahrt** *f* pilgrimage.
Wal- ['val] *cpd:* **~nuß** *f* walnut; **~roß** *nt* walrus.
Walze ['valtsə] *f* -, -n *(Gerät)* cylinder; *(Fahrzeug)* roller; **w~n** *vt* roll (out).
wälzen ['vɛltsən] *vt* roll (over); *Bücher* hunt through; *Probleme* deliberate on; *vr* wallow; *(vor Schmerzen)* roll about; *(im Bett)* toss and turn.
Walzer ['valtsər] *m* -s, - waltz.
Wälzer ['vɛltsər] *m* -s, - *(col)* tome.
Wand [vant] *f* -, ¨e wall; *(Trenn—)* partition; *(Berg—)* precipice.
Wandel ['vandəl] *m* -s change; **w~bar** *a* changeable, variable; **w~n** *vtr* change; *vi (gehen)* walk.
Wander- ['vandər] *cpd:* **~bühne** *f* travelling theatre; **~er** *m* -s, - hiker, rambler; **w~n** *vi* hike; *(Blick)* wander; *(Gedanken)* stray; **~preis** *m* challenge trophy; **~schaft** *f* travelling; **~ung** *f* walking tour, hike.
Wand- *cpd:* **~lung** *f* change, transformation; *(Rel)* transubstantiation; **~schirm** *m* (folding) screen; **~schrank**

m cupboard; **~teppich** *m* tapestry; **~verkleidung** *f* wainscoting.
Wange ['vaŋə] *f* -, **-n** cheek.
wankelmütig [vaŋkəlmyːtiç] *a* vacillating, inconstant.
wanken ['vankən] *vi* stagger; *(fig)* waver.
wann [van] *ad* when.
Wanne ['vanə] *f* -, **-n** tub.
Wanze ['vantsə] *f* -, **-n** bug.
Wappen ['vapən] *nt* -s, -, coat of arms, crest; **~kunde** *f* heraldry.
Ware ['vaːrə] *f* -, **-n** ware; **~nhaus** *nt* department store, **~nlager** *nt* stock, store; **~nprobe** *f* sample; **~nzeichen** *nt* trademark.
warm [varm] *a* warm; *Essen* hot.
Wärm- ['vɛrm] *cpd*: **~e** *f* -, **-n** warmth; **w~en** *vtr* warm, heat; **~flasche** *f* hot-water bottle.
warm- *cpd*: **~herzig** *a* warm-hearted; **~laufen** *vi irreg* *(Aut)* warm up; **W~-'wassertank** *m* hot-water tank.
warnen ['varnən] *vt* warn.
Warnung *f* warning.
warten ['vartən] *vi* wait *(auf +acc* for); **auf sich ~ lassen** take a long time.
Wärter(in *f)* ['vɛrtər(in)] *m* -s, - attendant.
Warte- ['vartə] *cpd*: **~saal** *m* *(Rail)*, **~zimmer** *nt* waiting room.
Wartung *f* servicing; service.
warum [va'rum] *ad* why.
Warze ['vartsə] *f* -, **-n** wart.
was [vas] *pron* what; *(col: etwas)* something.
Wasch- ['vaʃ] *cpd*: **w~bar** *a* washable; **~becken** *nt* washbasin; **w~echt** *a* colourfast; *(fig)* genuine.
Wäsche ['vɛʃə] *f* -, **-n** wash(ing); *(Bett—)* linen; *(Unter—)* underclothing; **~'klammer** *f* clothes peg, clothespin *(US)*; **~leine** *f* washing line.
waschen ['vaʃən] *irreg vti* wash; *vr* (have a) wash; **sich** *(dat)* **die Hände ~** wash one's hands; **~ und legen** *Haare* shampoo and set.
Wäsche- *cpd*: **~'rei** *f* laundry; **~schleuder** *f* spin-drier.
Wasch- *cpd*: **~küche** *f* laundry room; **~lappen** *m* face flannel, washcloth *(US)*; *(col)* sissy; **~maschine** *f* washing machine; **~mittel** *nt*, **~pulver** *nt* detergent, washing powder; **~tisch** *m* washhand basin.
Wasser ['vasər] *nt* -s, -, water; **w~dicht** *a* watertight, waterproof; **~fall** *m* waterfall; **~farbe** *f* watercolour; **w~gekühlt** *a* *(Aut)* water-cooled; **~hahn** *m* tap, faucet *(US)*.
wässerig ['vɛsəriç] *a* watery.
Wasser- *cpd*: **~kraftwerk** *nt* hydroelectric power station; **~leitung** *f* water pipe; **~ mann** *m* *(Astrol)* Aquarius; **w~n** *vi* land on the water.
wässern ['vɛsərn] *vti* water.
Wasser- *cpd*: **w~scheu** *a* afraid of the water; **~schi** *nt* water-skiing; **~stand** *m* water level; **~stoff** *m* hydrogen; **~stoffbombe** *f* hydrogen bomb; **~waage** *f*

spirit level; **~welle** *f* shampoo and set; **~zeichen** *nt* watermark.
waten ['vaːtən] *vi* wade.
watscheln ['vaːtʃəln] *vi* waddle.
Watt [vat] *nt* -(e)s, **-en** mud flats *pl*; *nt* -s, - *(Elec)* watt; **~e** *f* -, **-n** cotton wool, absorbent cotton *(US)*; **w~ieren** [va'tiːrən] *vt* pad.
Web- ['veːb] *cpd*: **w~en** *vt irreg* weave; **~er** *m* -s, - weaver; **~e'rei** *f* *(Betrieb)* weaving mill; **~stuhl** *m* loom.
Wechsel ['vɛksəl] *m* -s, - change; *(Comm)* bill of exchange; **~beziehung** *f* correlation; **~geld** *nt* change; **w~haft** *a* *Wetter* variable; **~jahre** *pl* change of life; **~kurs** *m* rate of exchange; **w~n** *vt* change; *Blicke* exchange; *vi* change; vary; *(Geld —)* have change; **~strom** *m* alternating current; **~wirkung** *f* interaction.
wecken ['vɛkən] *vt* wake (up); call.
Wecker ['vɛkər] *m* -s, - alarm clock.
wedeln ['veːdəln] *vi* *(mit Schwanz)* wag; *(mit Fächer)* fan; *(Ski)* wedeln.
weder ['veːdər] *cj* neither; **~ ... noch ...** neither ... nor ...
weg [vɛk] *ad* away, off; **über etw** *(acc)* **~ sein** be over sth; **er war schon ~** he had already left; **Finger ~!** hands off!; **W~** ['veːk] *m* -(e)s, **-e** way; *(Pfad)* path; *(Route)* route; **sich auf den W~ machen** be on one's way; **jdm aus dem W~ gehen** keep out of sb's way; **W~bereiter** *m* -s, - pioneer; **~blasen** *vt irreg* blow away; **~bleiben** *vi irreg* stay away.
wegen ['veːgən] *prep +gen or (col) dat* because of.
weg- ['vɛk] *cpd*: **~fahren** *vi irreg* drive away; leave; **~fallen** *vi irreg* be left out; *(Ferien, Bezahlung)* be cancelled; *(aufhören)* cease; **~gehen** *vi irreg* go away; leave; **~jagen** *vt* chase away; **~lassen** *vt irreg* leave out; **~laufen** *vi irreg* run away or off; **~legen** *vt* put aside; **~machen** *vt* *(col)* get rid of; **~müssen** *vi irreg* *(col)* have to go; **~nehmen** *vt irreg* take away; **~räumen** *vt* clear away; **~schaffen** *vt* clear away; **~schnappen** *vt* snatch away *(jdm etw* sth from sb); **~tun** *vt irreg* put away; **W~weiser** ['veːgvaɪzər] *m* -s, - road sign, signpost; **~werfen** *vt irreg* throw away; **~werfend** *a* disparaging; **~ziehen** *vi irreg* move away.
weh [veː] *a* a sore; **~ tun** hurt, be sore; **jdm/sich ~ tun** hurt sb/o.s.; **~(e)** *interj*: **~(e), wenn du ...** woe betide you if ...; **o ~!** oh dear!; **W~e** *f* -, **-n** drift; *vti* blow; *(Fahnen)* flutter; **W~en** *pl* *(Med)* labour pains *pl*; **~klagen** *vi insep* wail; **~leidig** *a* whiny, whining; **W~mut** *f* melancholy; **~mütig** *a* melancholy.
Wehr [veːr] *nt* -(e)s, **-e** weir; *f*: **sich zur ~ setzen** defend o.s.; **~dienst** *m* military service; **w~en** *vr* defend o.s.; **w~los** *a* defenceless; **~macht** *f* armed forces *pl*; **~pflicht** *f* compulsory military service; **w~pflichtig** *a* liable for military service.
Weib [vaip] *nt* -(e)s, **-er** woman, female; wife; **~chen** *nt* female; **w~isch** *a* ['vaɪbɪʃ]

a sissyish; **w~lich** a feminine.

weich [vaiç] a soft; **W~e f ·, -n** (Rail) points pl; **~en** vi irreg yield, give away; **W~ensteller** m **-s, -** pointsman; **W~heit** f softness; **~lich** a soft, namby-pamby; **W~ling** m weakling.

Weide ['vaidə] f·, **-n** (Baum) willow; (Gras) pasture; **w~n** vi graze; vr: **sich an etw** (dat) **w~n** delight in sth.

weidlich ['vaitliç] ad thoroughly.

weigern ['vaigərn] vr refuse.

Weigerung ['vaigərʊŋ] f refusal.

Weih- ['vai] cpd: **~e f ·, -n** consecration; (Priester—) ordination; **w~en** vt consecrate; ordain; **~er** m **-s, -** pond; **~nacht** f ·, **~nachten** nt · Christmas; **w~nachtlich** a Christmas; **~nachts-abend** m Christmas Eve; **~nachtslied** nt Christmas carol; **~nachtsmann** m Father Christmas, Santa Claus; **zweiter ~nachtstag** m Boxing Day; **~rauch** m incense; **~wasser** nt holy water.

weil [vail] cj because.

Weile ['vailə] f · while, short time.

Wein [vain] m **-(e)s, -e** wine; (Pflanze) vine; **~bau** m cultivation of vines; **~beere** f grape; **~berg** m vineyard; **~bergschnecke** f snail; **~brand** m brandy; **w~en** vti cry; **das ist zum ~en** it's enough to make you cry or weep; **w~erlich** a tearful; **~geist** m spirits of wine; **~lese** f vintage; **~rebe** f vine; **~stein** m tartar; **~stock** m vine; **~traube** f grape.

weise ['vaizə] a wise; **W~(r)** mf wise old man/woman, sage.

Weise ['vaizə] f ·, **-n** manner, way; (Lied) tune; **auf diese ~** in this way; **w~n** vt. irreg show.

Weisheit ['vaishait] f wisdom; **~szahn** m wisdom tooth.

weiß [vais] a white; **W~brot** nt white bread; **~en** vt whitewash; **W~glut** f (Tech) incandescence; **jdn bis zur W~glut bringen** (fig) make sb see red; **W~kohl** m (white) cabbage; **W~wein** m white wine.

Weisung ['vaizʊŋ] f instruction.

weit [vait] a wide; Begriff broad; Reise, Wurf long; **wie ~ ist es ...?** how far is it ...?; **in ~er Ferne** in the far distance; **das geht zu ~** that's going too far; ad far; **~aus** ad by far; **~blickend** a far-seeing; **W~e f ·, -n** width; (Raum) space; (von Entfernung) distance; **~en** vtr widen.

weiter ['vaitər] a wider; broader; farther (away); (zusätzlich) further; **ohne ~es** without further ado; just like that; ad further; **~ nichts/niemand** nothing/nobody else; **~arbeiten** vi go on working; **~bilden** vr continue one's studies; **~empfehlen** vt irreg recommend (to others); **W~fahrt** f continuation of the journey; **~gehen** vi irreg go on; **~hin** ad: **etw ~hin tun** go on doing sth; **~leiten** vt pass on; **~machen** vti continue; **~reisen** vi continue one's journey.

weit- cpd: **~gehend** a considerable; ad largely; **~läufig** a Gebäude spacious; Erklärung lengthy; Verwandter distant;

~schweifig a long-winded; **~sichtig** a (lit) long-sighted; (fig) far-sighted; **W~sprung** m long jump; **~verbreitet** a widespread; **W~winkelobjektiv** nt (Phot) wide-angle lens.

Weizen ['vaitsən] m **-s, -** wheat.

welch [velç] pron: **~ ein(e) ...** what a ...; **~e** indef pron (col: einige) some; **~e(r,s)** rel pron (für Personen) who; (für Sachen) which; interrog pron (adjektivisch) which; (substantivisch) which one.

welk [velk] a withered; **~en** vi wither.

Well- cpd: **~blech** nt corrugated iron; **~e f ·, -n** wave; (Tech) shaft; **~enbereich** m waveband; **~enbrecher** m **-s,** breakwater; **~enlänge** f (lit, fig) wavelength; **~enlinie** f wavy line; **~ensittich** m budgerigar; **~pappe** f corrugated cardboard.

Welt [velt] f ·, **-en** world; **~all** nt universe; **~anschauung** f philosophy of life; **w~berühmt** a world-famous; **w~fremd** a unworldly; **~krieg** m world war; **w~lich** a worldly; (nicht kirchlich) secular; **~macht** f world power; **w~männisch** a sophisticated; **~meister** m world champion; **~raum** m space; **~reise** f trip round the world; **~stadt** f metropolis; **w~weit** a world-wide; **~wunder** nt wonder of the world.

wem [ve:m] pron (dat) to whom.

wen [ve:n] pron (acc) whom.

Wende ['vendə] f ·, **-n** turn; (Veränderung) change; **~kreis** m (Geog) tropic; (Aut) turning circle; **~ltreppe** f spiral staircase; **w~n** vtir irreg turn; **sich an jdn w~n** go/come to sb; **~punkt** m turning point.

Wendung f turn; (Rede—) idiom.

wenig ['ve:niç] a,ad little; **~e** ['ve:nigə] pl few pl; **W~keit** f trifle; **meine W~keit** yours truly, little me; **~ste(r,s)** a least; **~stens** ad at least.

wenn [ven] cj if; (zeitlich) when; **~ auch ...** even if ...; **~ ich doch ...** if only I ...; **~ schon** ad: **na ~ schon** so what?; **~ schon, dennschon!** if a thing's worth doing, it's worth doing properly.

wer [ve:r] pron who.

Werbe- ['verbə] cpd: **~fernsehen** nt commercial television; **~kampagne** f advertising campaign; **w~n** irreg vi win; Mitglied recruit; vi advertise; **um jdn/etw w~n** try to win sb/sth; **für jdn/etw w~n** promote sb/sth.

Werbung f advertising; (von Mitgliedern) recruitment; (um jdn/etw) promotion (um of).

Werdegang ['ve:rdəgaŋ] m development; (beruflich) career.

werden ['ve:rdən] vi irreg become; v aux (Futur) shall, will; (Passiv) be; **was ist aus ihm/aus der Sache geworden?** what became of him/it?; **es ist nichts/gut geworden** it came to nothing/turned out well; **mir wird kalt** I'm getting cold; **das muß anders ~** that will have to change; **zu Eis ~** turn to ice.

werfen ['verfən] vt irreg throw.

Werft [verft] f ·, **-en** shipyard, dockyard.

Werk [vɛrk] nt -(e)s, -e work; (Tätigkeit) job; (Fabrik, Mechanismus) works pl; ans ~ gehen set to work; ~statt f -, -stätten workshop; (Aut) garage; ~student m self-supporting student; ~tag m working day; w~tags ad on working days; w~tägig a working; ~zeug nt tool; ~zeugschrank m tool chest.

Wermut ['ve:rmu:t] m -(e)s wormwood; (Wein) vermouth.

Wert [ve:rt] m -(e)s, -e worth; (Fin) value; ~ legen auf (+acc) attach importance to; es hat doch keinen ~ it's useless; w~ a worth; (geschätzt) dear; worthy; das ist nichts/viel w~ it's not worth anything/it's worth a lot; das ist es/er mir w~ it's/he's worth that to me; ~angabe f declaration of value; w~en vt rate; ~gegenstand m article of value; w~los a worthless; ~losigkeit f worthlessness; ~papier nt security; w~voll a valuable; ~zuwachs m appreciation.

Wesen ['ve:zən] nt -s, - (Geschöpf) being; (Natur, Character) nature; w~tlich a significant; (beträchtlich) considerable.

weshalb [vɛs'halp] ad why.

Wespe ['vɛspə] f -, -n wasp.

wessen ['vɛsən] pron (gen) whose.

West- [vɛst] cpd: ~e f -, -n waistcoat, vest (US); (Woll—) cardigan; ~en m -s west; w~lich a western; ad to the west; w~wärts ad westwards.

weswegen [vɛs've:gən] ad why.

wett [vɛt] a even; W~bewerb m competition; W~e f -, -n bet, wager; W~eifer m rivalry; ~en vt/i bet.

Wetter ['vɛtər] nt -s, - weather; ~bericht m weather report; ~dienst m meteorological service; ~lage f (weather) situation; ~vorhersage f weather forecast; ~warte f -, -n weather station; w~wendisch a capricious.

Wett- cpd: ~kampf m contest; ~lauf m race; w~laufen vi irreg race; w~machen vt make good; ~spiel nt match; ~streit m contest.

wetzen ['vɛtsən] vt sharpen.

Wicht [vɪçt] m -(e)s, -e titch; (pej) worthless creature; w~ig a important; ~igkeit f importance.

wickeln ['vɪkəln] vt wind; Haare set; Kind change; jdn/etw in etw (acc) ~ wrap sb/sth in sth.

Widder ['vɪdər] m -s, - ram; (Astrol) Aries.

wider ['vɪdər] prep +acc against; ~-'fahren vi irreg happen (jdm to sb); ~'legen vt refute.

widerlich ['vi:dərlɪç] a disgusting, repulsive; W~keit f repulsiveness.

wider- ['vi:dər] cpd: ~rechtlich a unlawful; W~rede f contradiction.

Widerruf ['vi:dərru:f] m retraction; countermanding; w~en [vi:dər'ru:fən] vt irreg insep retract; Anordnung revoke; Befehl countermand.

wider'setzen vr insep oppose (jdm/etw sb/sth).

widerspenstig ['vi:dərʃpɛnstɪç] a wilful; W~keit f wilfulness.

widerspiegeln ['vi:dərʃpi:gəln] vt reflect.

wider'sprechen vi irreg insep contradict (jdm sb); ~d a contradictory.

Widerspruch ['vi:dərʃprʊx] m contradiction; w~slos ad without arguing.

Widerstand ['vi:dərʃtant] m resistance; ~sbewegung f resistance (movement); w~sfähig a resistant, tough; w~slos a unresisting.

wider'stehen vi irreg insep withstand (jdm/etw sb/sth).

Wider- ['vi:dər] cpd: ~streit m conflict; w~wärtig a nasty, horrid; ~wille m aversion (gegen to); w~willig a unwilling, reluctant.

widmen ['vɪtmən] vt dedicate; vtr devote (o.s.).

Widmung f dedication.

widrig ['vi:drɪç] a Umstände adverse; Mensch repulsive.

wie [vi:] ad how; cj ~ ich schon sagte as I said; (so) schön ~ ... as beautiful as ...; ~ du like you; singen ~ ein ... sing like a ...

wieder ['vi:dər] ad again; ~ da sein be back (again); gehst du wieder ~? are you off again?; ~ ein(e) ... another ...; W~aufbau [-'aufbau] m rebuilding; W~aufnahme [-'aufna:mə] f resumption; ~aufnehmen vt irreg resume; ~bekommen vt irreg get back; ~bringen vt irreg bring back; ~erkennen vt irreg recognize; W~erstattung f reimbursement; W~gabe f reproduction; ~geben vt irreg (zurückgeben) return; Erzählung etc repeat; Gefühle etc convey; ~gutmachen [-'gu:tmaxən] vt make up for; Fehler put right; W~'gutmachung f reparation; ~'herstellen vt restore; ~'holen vt insep repeat; W~'holung f repetition; W~hören nt : auf W~hören (Tel) goodbye; W~kehr f - return; (von Vorfall) repetition, recurrence; W~kunft f -, =e return; ~sehen vt irreg see again; auf W~sehen goodbye; ~um ad again; (andererseits) on the other hand; ~vereinigen vt reunite; W~wahl f reelection.

Wiege ['vi:gə] f -, -n cradle; w~n vt (schaukeln) rock; vti irreg (Gewicht) weigh; ~nfest nt birthday.

wiehern ['vi:ərn] vi neigh, whinny.

Wiese ['vi:zə] f -, -n meadow; ~l nt -s, - weasel.

wieso [vi:'zo:] ad why.

wieviel [vi:'fi:l] a how much; ~ Menschen how many people; ~mal ad how often; ~te(r,s) a: zum ~ten Mal? how many times?; den W~ten haben wir? what's the date?; an ~ter Stelle? in what place?; der ~te Besucher war er? how many visitors were there before him?

wieweit [vi:vaɪt] ad to what extent.

wild [vɪlt] a wild; W~ nt -(e)s game; ~ern ['vɪldərn] vi poach; ~fremd a (col) quite strange or unknown; W~heit f wildness; W~leder nt suede; W~nis f -, -se wilderness; W~schwein nt (wild) boar.

Wille ['vɪlə] m **-ns, -n** will; w~n prep +gen: **um . . . w~n** for the sake of . . .; **w~nlos** a weak-willed; **w~nsstark** a strong-willed.

will- cpd: ~**ig** a willing; ~**kommen** [vɪl'kɔmən] a welcome; **jdn** ~**kommen heißen** welcome sb; **W~kommen** nt **-s, -** welcome; ~**kürlich** a arbitrary; Bewegung voluntary.

wimmeln ['vɪməln] vi swarm (von with).

wimmern ['vɪmərn] vi whimper.

Wimper ['vɪmpər] f **-, -n** eyelash.

Wind [vɪnt] m **-(e)s, -e** wind; ~**beutel** m cream puff; (fig) windbag; ~**e** ['vɪndə] f **-, -n** (Tech) winch, windlass; (Bot) bindweed; ~**el** ['vɪndəl] f **-, -n** nappy, diaper (US); **w~en** ['vɪndən] vi impers be windy; irreg vt wind; Kranz weave; (ent—) twist; vr wind; (Person) writhe; ~**hose** f whirlwind; ~**hund** m greyhound; (Mensch) fly-by-night; **w~ig** ['vɪndɪç] a windy; (fig) dubious; ~**mühle** f windmill; ~**pocken** pl chickenpox; ~**schutzscheibe** f (Aut) windscreen, windshield (US); ~**stärke** f wind force; ~**stille** f calm; ~**stoß** m gust of wind.

Wink [vɪŋk] m **-(e)s, -e** hint; (mit Kopf) nod; (mit Hand) wave.

Winkel ['vɪŋkəl] m **-s, -** (Math) angle; (Gerät) set square; (in Raum) corner.

winken ['vɪŋkən] vti wave.

winseln ['vɪnzəln] vi whine.

Winter ['vɪntər] m **-s, -** winter; **w~lich** a wintry; ~**sport** m winter sports pl.

Winzer ['vɪntsər] m **-s, -** vine grower.

winzig ['vɪntsɪç] a tiny.

Wipfel ['vɪpfəl] m **-s, -** treetop.

wir [vɪr] pron we; ~ **alle** all of us, we all.

Wirbel ['vɪrbəl] m **-s, -** whirl, swirl; (Trubel) hurly-burly; (Aufsehen) fuss; (Anat) vertebra; **w~n** vi whirl, swirl; ~**säule** f spine; ~**tier** nt vertebrate; ~**wind** m whirlwind.

wirken ['vɪrkən] vi have an effect; (erfolgreich sein) work; (scheinen) seem; vt Wunder work.

wirklich ['vɪrklɪç] a real; **W~keit** f reality.

wirksam ['vɪrkza:m] a effective; **W~keit** f effectiveness, efficacy.

Wirkung ['vɪrkʊŋ] f effect; **w~slos** a ineffective; **w~slos bleiben** have no effect; **w~svoll** a effective.

wirr [vɪr] a confused, wild; **W~en** pl disturbances pl; **W~warr** ['var] m **-s** disorder, chaos.

Wirsing(kohl) ['vɪrzɪŋ(ko:l)] m **-s** savoy cabbage.

Wirt [vɪrt] m **-(e)s, -e** landlord; ~**in** f landlady; ~**schaft** f (Gaststätte) pub; (Haushalt) housekeeping; (eines Landes) economy; (col: Durcheinander) mess; **w~schaftlich** a economical; (Pol) economic; ~**schaftskrise** f economic crisis; ~**schaftsprüfer** m chartered accountant; ~**schaftswunder** nt economic miracle; ~**shaus** nt inn.

Wisch [vɪʃ] m **-(e)s, -e** scrap of paper; **w~en** vt wipe; ~**er** m **-s, -** (Aut) wiper.

wispern ['vɪspərn] vti whisper.

Wißbegier(de) ['vɪsbəgi:r(də)] f thirst for knowledge; **w~ig** a inquisitive, eager for knowledge.

wissen ['vɪsən] vt irreg know; **W~** nt **-s** knowledge; **W~schaft** f science; **W~schaftler(in** f) m **-s,** scientist; ~**schaftlich** a scientific; ~**swert** a worth knowing; ~**tlich** a knowing.

wittern ['vɪtərn] vt scent; (fig) suspect.

Witterung f weather; (Geruch) scent.

Witwe ['vɪtvə] f **-, -n** widow; ~**r** m **-s, -** widower.

Witz [vɪts] m **-es, -e** joke; ~**blatt** nt comic (paper); ~**bold** m **-(e)s, -e** joker, wit; **w~eln** vi joke; **w~ig** a funny.

wo [vo:] ad where; (col: irgendwo) somewhere; **im Augenblick, ~ . . .** the moment (that) . . .; **die Zeit, ~ . . .** the time when . . .; cj (wenn) if; ~**anders** [vo:'andərs] ad elsewhere; ~**bei** [vo:'baɪ] ad (rel) by/with which; (interrog) what . . . in/by/with.

Woche ['vɔxə] f **-, -n** week; ~**nende** nt weekend; **w~nlang** a,ad for weeks; ~**nschau** f newsreel.

wöchentlich ['vœçəntlɪç] a,ad weekly.

wo- cpd: ~**durch** [vo:'dʊrç] ad (rel) through which; (interrog) what . . . through; ~**für** [vo:'fy:r] ad (rel) for which; (interrog) what . . . for.

Woge ['vo:gə] f **-, -n** wave; **w~n** vi heave, surge.

wo- cpd: ~**gegen** [vo:'ge:gən] ad (rel) against which; (interrog) what . . . against; ~**her** [vo:'he:r] ad where . . . from; ~**hin** [vo:'hɪn] ad where . . . to.

wohl [vo:l] ad well; (behaglich) at ease, comfortable; (vermutlich) I suppose, probably; (gewiß) certainly; **er weiß das ~** he knows that perfectly well; **W~** nt **-(e)s** welfare; **zum W~!** cheers!; ~**auf** [vo:l'auf] ad well; **W~behagen** nt comfort; ~**behalten** ad safe and sound; **W~fahrt** f welfare; ~**habend** a wealthy; **W~klang** m melodious sound; ~**schmeckend** a delicious; **W~stand** m prosperity; **W~standsgesellschaft** f affluent society; **W~tat** f relief; act of charity; **W~täter(in** f) m benefactor; ~**tätig** a charitable; ~**tun** vi irreg do good (jdm sb); ~**verdient** a well-earned, well-deserved; ~**weislich** ad prudently; **W~wollen** nt **-s** good will; ~**wollend** a benevolent.

wohn- ['vo:n] cpd: ~**en** vi live; ~**haft** a resident; ~**lich** a comfortable; **W~ort** m domicile; **W~sitz** place of residence; **W~ung** f house; (Etagen—) flat, apartment (US); **W~ungsnot** f housing shortage; **W~wagen** m caravan; **W~zimmer** nt living room.

wölben ['vœlbən] vtr curve.

Wölbung f curve.

Wolf [vɔlf] m **-(e)s, -̈e** wolf.

Wölfin ['vœlfɪn] f she-wolf.

Wolke ['vɔlkə] f **-, -n** cloud; ~**nkratzer** m skyscraper.

wolkig ['vɔlkɪç] a cloudy.

Wolle ['vɔlə] f **-, -n** wool; **w~n** a woollen.

wollen ['vɔlən] vti want.

wollüstig ['vɔlʏstɪç] a lusty, sensual.

wo- cpd: ~**mit** [vo:'mɪt] ad (rel) with which; (interrog) what . . . with; ~**möglich** [vo:'mø:klɪç] ad probably, I suppose; ~**nach** [vo:'na:x] ad (rel) after/for which; (interrog) what . . . for/after.

Wonne ['vɔnə] f -, -**n** joy, bliss.

wo- cpd: ~**ran** [vo:'ran] ad (rel) on/at which; (interrog) what . . . on/at; ~**rauf** [vo:'rauf] ad (rel) on which; (interrog) what . . . on; ~**raus** [vo:'raus] ad (rel) from/out of which; (interrog) what . . . from/out of; ~**rin** [vo:'rɪn] ad (rel) in which; (interrog) what . . . in.

Wort [vɔrt] nt -(**e**)**s**, **¨er**, -**e** word; **jdn beim** ~ **nehmen** take sb at his word; **w**~**brüchig** a not true to one's word.

Wörterbuch ['vœrtərbu:x] nt dictionary.

Wort- cpd: ~**führer** m spokesman; **w**~**getreu** a true to one's word; Übersetzung literal; **w**~**karg** a taciturn; ~**laut** m wording.

wörtlich ['vœrtlɪç] a literal.

Wort- cpd: **w**~**los** a mute; **w**~**reich** a wordy, verbose; ~**schatz** m vocabulary; ~**spiel** nt play on words, pun; ~**wechsel** m dispute.

wo- cpd: ~**rüber** [vo:'ry:bər] ad (rel) over/about which; (interrog) what . . . over/about; ~**rum** [vo:'rum] ad (rel) about/round which; (interrog) what . . . about/round; ~**runter** [vo:'runtər] ad (rel) under which; (interrog) what . . . under; ~**von** [vo:'fɔn] ad (rel) from which; (interrog) what . . . from; ~**vor** [vo:'fɔːr] ad (rel) in front of/before which; (interrog) in front of/before what; of what; ~**zu** [vo:'tsu:] ad (rel) to/for which; (interrog) what . . . for/to; (warum) why.

Wrack [vrak] nt -(**e**)**s**, -**s** wreck.

wringen ['vrɪŋgən] vt irreg wring.

Wucher ['vu:xər] m -**s** profiteering; ~**er** m -**s**, - profiteer; **w**~**isch** a profiteering; **w**~**n** vi (Pflanzen) grow wild; ~**ung** f (Med) growth, tumour.

Wuchs [vu:ks] m -**es** (Wachstum) growth; (Statur) build.

Wucht [vuxt] f - force; **w**~**ig** a solid, massive.

wühlen ['vy:lən] vi scrabble; (Tier) root; (Maulwurf) burrow; (col: arbeiten) slave away; vt dig.

Wulst [vulst] -**es**, **¨e** bulge; (an Wunde) swelling.

wund [vunt] a sore, raw; **W**~**e** ['vundə] f -, -**n** wound.

Wunder ['vundər] nt -**s**, - miracle; **es ist kein** ~ it's no wonder; **w**~**bar** a wonderful, marvellous; ~**kind** nt infant prodigy; **w**~**lich** a odd, peculiar; **w**~**n** vr be surprised (über about at); vt surprise; **w**~**schön** a beautiful; **w**~**voll** a wonderful.

Wundstarrkrampf ['vunt∫tarkrampf] m tetanus, lockjaw.

Wunsch [vun∫] m -(**e**)**s**, **¨e** wish.

wünschen ['vʏn∫ən] vt wish; **sich** (dat) **etw** ~ want sth, wish for sth; ~**swert** a desirable.

Würde ['vʏrdə] f -, -**n** dignity; (Stellung) honour; ~**nträger** m dignitary; **w**~**voll** a dignified.

würdig ['vʏrdɪç] a worthy; (würdevoll) dignified; ~**en** ['vʏrdɪgən] vt appreciate; **jdn keines Blickes** ~**en** not so much as look at sb.

Wurf [vurf] m -**s**, **¨e** throw; (Junge) litter.

Würfel ['vʏrfəl] m -**s**, - dice; (Math) cube; ~**becher** m (dice) cup; **w**~**n** vi play dice; vt dice; ~**spiel** nt game of dice; ~**zucker** m lump sugar.

würgen ['vʏrgən] vti choke.

Wurm [vurm] m -(**e**)**s**, **¨er** worm; **w**~**en** vt (col) rile, nettle; ~**fortsatz** m (Med) appendix; **w**~**ig** a worm-eaten; ~**stichig** a worm-ridden.

Wurst [vurst] f -, **¨e** sausage; **das ist mir** ~ (col) I don't care, I don't give a damn.

Würze ['vʏrtsə] f -, -**n** seasoning, spice.

Wurzel ['vurtsəl] f -, -**n** root.

würz- ['vʏrts] cpd: ~**en** vt season, spice; ~**ig** a spicy.

wüst [vy:st] a untidy, messy; (ausschweifend) wild; (öde) waste; (col: heftig) terrible; **W**~**e** f -, -**n** desert; **W**~**ling** m rake.

Wut [vu:t] f - rage, fury; ~**anfall** m fit of rage.

wüten ['vy:tən] vi rage; ~**d** a furious, mad.

X

X,x [ɪks] nt X,x.

X-Beine ['ɪksbaɪnə] pl knock-knees pl.

x-beliebig [ɪksbə'li:bɪç] a any (whatever).

xerokopieren [kseroko'pi:rən] vt xerox, photocopy.

x-mal ['ɪksma:l] ad any number of times, n times.

Xylophon [ksylo'fo:n] nt -**s**, -**e** xylophone.

Y

Y,y ['ʏpsilɔn] nt Y,y.

Ypsilon nt -(**s**), -**s** the letter Y.

Z

Z,z [tsɛt] nt Z,z.

Zacke ['tsakə] f -, -**n** point; (Berg—) jagged peak; (Gabel—) prong; (Kamm—) tooth.

zackig ['tsakɪç] a jagged; (col) smart; Tempo brisk.

zaghaft ['tsa:khaft] a timid; **Z**~**igkeit** f timidity.

zäh [tsɛː] a tough; Mensch tenacious; Flüssigkeit thick; (schleppend) sluggish; **Z**~**igkeit** f toughness; tenacity.

Zahl [tsa:l] f -, -**en** number; **z**~**bar** a payable; **z**~**en** vti pay; **z**~**en bitte!** the bill please!

zählen ['tsɛːlən] vti count (auf +acc on); ~ **zu** be numbered among.

Zahl- cpd: **z**~**enmäßig** a numerical; ~**er** m -**s**, - payer.

Zähler ['tsɛːlər] m -**s**, - (Tech) meter; (Math) numerator.

Zahl- cpd: **z**~**los** a countless; **z**~**reich** a

numerous; **~tag** m payday; **~ung** f payment; **z~ungsfähig** a solvent; **~wort** nt numeral.

zahm [tsa:m] a tame.

zähmen ['tsɛ:mən] vt tame; (fig) curb.

Zahn [tsa:n] m **-(e)s**, **⁻e** tooth; **~arzt** m dentist; **~bürste** f toothbrush; **z~en** vi cut teeth; **~fäule** f - tooth decay, caries; **~fleisch** nt gums pl; **~pasta**, **~paste** f toothpaste; **~rad** nt cog(wheel); **~radbahn** f rack railway; **~schmelz** m (tooth) enamel; **~schmerzen** pl toothache; **~stein** m tartar; **~stocher** m **-s**, - toothpick.

Zange ['tsaŋə] f **-**, **-n** pliers pl; (Zucker- etc) tongs pl; (Beiß—, Zool) pincers pl; (Med) forceps pl; **~ngeburt** f forceps delivery.

Zank- [tsaŋk] cpd: **~apfel** m bone of contention; **z~en** vir quarrel.

zänkisch ['tsɛŋkɪʃ] a quarrelsome.

Zäpfchen ['tsɛpfçən] nt (Anat) uvula; (Med) suppository.

Zapfen ['tsapfən] m **-s**, - plug; (Bot) cone; (Eis—) icicle; **z~** vt tap; **~streich** m (Mil) tattoo.

zappelig ['tsapəlɪç] a wriggly; (unruhig) fidgety.

zappeln ['tsapəln] vi wriggle; fidget.

zart [tsart] a (weich, leise) soft; Braten etc tender; (fein, schwächlich) delicate; **Z~gefühl** nt tact; **Z~heit** f softness; tenderness; delicacy.

zärtlich ['tsɛ:rtlɪç] a tender, affectionate; **Z~keit** f tenderness; pl caresses pl.

Zauber ['tsaubər] m **-s**, - magic; (—bann) spell; **~ei** ['-rai] f magic; **~er** m **-s**, - magician; conjuror; **z~haft** a magical, enchanting; **~künstler** m conjuror; **z~n** vi conjure, practise magic; **~spruch** m (magic) spell.

zaudern ['tsaudərn] vi hesitate.

Zaum [tsaum] m **-(e)s**, **Zäume** bridle; **etw im ~ halten** keep sth in check.

Zaun [tsaun] m **-(e)s**, **Zäune** fence; **vom ~(e) brechen** (fig) start; **~könig** m wren; **~pfahl** m: **ein Wink mit dem ~pfahl** a broad hint.

Zeche ['tsɛçə] f **-**, **-n** bill; (Bergbau) mine.

Zecke ['tsɛkə] f **-**, **-n** tick.

Zehe ['tse:ə] f **-**, **-n** toe; (Knoblauch—) clove.

zehn [tse:n] num ten; **~te(r,s)** a tenth; **Z~tel** nt **-s**, - tenth (part).

Zeich- ['tsaiç] cpd: **~en** nt **-s**, - sign; **z~nen** vti draw; (kenn—) mark; (unter—) sign; **~ner** m **-s**, - artist; **technischer ~ner** draughtsman; **~nung** f drawing; (Markierung) markings pl.

Zeig- ['tsaig] cpd: **~efinger** m index finger; **z~en** vt show; vi point (auf +acc to, at); vr show o.s.; **es wird sich z~en** time will tell; **es zeigte sich, daß . . .** it turned out that . . .; **~er** m **-s**, - pointer; (Uhr—) hand.

Zeile ['tsailə] f **-**, **-n** line; (Häuser—) row; **~nabstand** m line spacing.

Zeit [tsait] f **-**, **-en** time; (Gram) tense; **zur ~** at the moment; **sich** (dat) **~ lassen** take one's time; **von ~ zu ~** from time to time; **~alter** nt age; **z~gemäß** a in

keeping with the times; **~genosse** m contemporary; **z~ig** a early; **z~'lebens** ad all one's life; **z~lich** a temporal; **~lupe** f slow motion; **~raffer** m **-s** time-lapse photography; **z~raubend** a time-consuming; **~raum** m period; **~rechnung** f time, era; **nach/vor unserer ~rechnung** A.D./B.C.; **~schrift** f periodical; **~ung** f newspaper; **~verschwendung** f waste of time; **~vertreib** m pastime, diversion; **z~weilig** a temporary; **z~weise** ad for a time; **~wort** nt verb; **~zeichen** nt (Rad) time signal; **~zünder** m time fuse.

Zell- ['tsɛl] cpd: **~e** f **-**, **-n** cell; (Telefon—) callbox; **~kern** m cell, nucleus; **~stoff** m cellulose; **~teilung** f cell division.

Zelt [tsɛlt] nt **-(e)s**, **-e** tent; **~bahn** f tarpaulin, groundsheet; **z~en** vi camp.

Zement [tse'mɛnt] m **-(e)s**, **-e** cement; **z~ieren** [-'ti:rən] vt cement.

zensieren [tsɛn'zi:rən] vt censor; (Sch) mark.

Zensur [tsɛn'zu:r] f censorship; (Sch) mark.

Zent- cpd: **~imeter** [tsɛnti'me:tər] m or nt centimetre; **~ner** ['tsɛntnər] m **-s**, - hundredweight.

zentral [tsɛn'tra:l] a central; **Z~e** f **-**, **-n** central office; (Tel) exchange; **Z~heizung** f central heating; **~isieren** [tsɛntrali'zi:rən] vt centralize.

Zentri- [tsɛntri] cpd: **~fugalkraft** [-fu'ga:lkraft] f centrifugal force; **~fuge** [-'fu:gə] f **-**, **-n** centrifuge; (für Wäsche) spin-dryer.

Zentrum ['tsɛntrum] nt **-s**, **Zentren** centre.

Zepter ['tsɛptər] nt **-s**, - sceptre.

zerbrech- [tsɛr'brɛç] cpd: **~en** vti irreg break; **~lich** a fragile.

zerbröckeln [tsɛr'brœkəln] vti crumble (to pieces).

zer'drücken vt squash, crush; Kartoffeln mash.

Zeremonie [tseremo'ni:] f ceremony.

zer'fahren a scatterbrained, distracted.

Zerfall [tsɛr'fal] m decay; **z~en** vi irreg disintegrate, decay; (sich gliedern) fall (in +acc into).

zerfetzen [tsɛr'fɛtsən] vt tear to pieces.

zer'fließen vi irreg dissolve, melt away.

zer'gehen vi irreg melt, dissolve.

zerkleinern [tsɛr'klainərn] vt reduce to small pieces.

zerleg- [tsɛr'le:g] cpd: **~bar** a able to be dismantled; **~en** vt take to pieces; Fleisch carve; Satz analyse.

zerlumpt [tsɛr'lumpt] a ragged.

zermalmen [tsɛr'malmən] vt crush.

zermürben [tsɛr'myrbən] vt wear down.

zer'platzen vi burst.

zerquetschen [tsɛr'kvɛtʃən] vt squash.

Zerrbild ['tsɛrbilt] nt caricature, distorted picture.

zer'reden vt Problem flog to death.

zer'reiben vt irreg grind down.

zer'reißen irreg vt tear to pieces; vi tear, rip.

zerren ['tsɛrən] vt drag; vi tug (an +dat at).

zer'rinnen vi irreg melt away.
zerrissen [tsɛr'rɪsən] a torn, tattered; **Z~heit** f tattered state; (Pol) disunion, discord; (innere ~) disintegration.
zerrütten [tsɛr'rʏtən] vt wreck, destroy.
zerrüttet a wrecked, shattered.
zer'schießen vt irreg shoot to pieces.
zer'schlagen irreg vt shatter, smash; vr fall through.
zerschleißen [tsɛr'ʃlaɪsən] vti irreg wear out.
zer'schneiden vt irreg cut up.
zer'setzen vtr decompose, dissolve.
zersplittern [tsɛr'ʃplɪtərn] vti split (into pieces); (Glas) shatter.
zer'springen vi irreg shatter, burst.
zerstäub- [tsɛr'ʃtɔʏb] cpd: **~en** vt spray; **Z~er** m -s, - atomizer.
zerstör- [tsɛr'ʃtøːr] cpd: **~en** vt destroy; **Z~ung** f destruction.
zer'stoßen vt irreg pound, pulverize.
zer'streiten vr irreg fall out, break up.
zerstreu- [tsɛr'ʃtrɔʏ] cpd: **~en** vtr disperse, scatter; (unterhalten) divert; Zweifel etc dispel; **~t** a scattered; Mensch absent-minded; **Z~theit** f absent-mindedness; **Z~ung** f dispersion; (Ablenkung) diversion.
zerstückeln [tsɛr'ʃtʏkəln] vt cut into pieces.
zer'teilen vt divide into parts.
zer'treten vt irreg crush underfoot.
zertrümmern [tsɛr'trʏmərn] vt shatter; Gebäude etc demolish.
Zerwürfnis [tsɛr'vʏrfnɪs] nt -ses, -se dissension, quarrel.
zerzausen [tsɛr'tsaʊzən] vt Haare ruffle up, tousle.
zetern ['tseːtərn] vi shout, shriek.
Zettel ['tsɛtəl] m -s, - piece of paper, slip; (Notiz~) note; (Formular) form; **~kasten** m card index (box).
Zeug [tsɔʏk] nt -(e)s, -e (col) stuff; (Ausrüstung) gear; **dummes ~** (stupid) nonsense; **das ~ haben zu** have the makings of; **sich ins ~ legen** put one's shoulder to the wheel.
Zeuge ['tsɔʏgə] m -n, -n, **Zeugin** ['tsɔʏgɪn] f witness; **z~n** vi bear witness, testify; **es zeugt von . . .** it testifies to . . .; vt Kind father; **~naussage** f evidence; **~nstand** m witness box.
Zeugnis ['tsɔʏgnɪs] nt -ses, -se certificate; (Sch) report; (Referenz) reference; (Aussage) evidence, testimony; **~ geben von** be evidence of, testify to.
Zeugung ['tsɔʏgʊŋ] f procreation; **z~sunfähig** a sterile.
Zickzack ['tsɪktsak] m -(e)s, -e zigzag.
Ziege ['tsiːgə] f -, -n goat; **~nleder** nt kid.
Ziegel ['tsiːgəl] m -s, - brick; (Dach~) tile; **~ei** ['·laɪ] f brickworks.
ziehen ['tsiːən] irreg vt draw; (zerren) pull; (Schach etc) move; (züchten) rear; **etw nach sich ~** lead to sth, entail sth; vi draw; (um-, wandern) move; (Rauch, Wolke etc) drift; (reißen) pull; v impers: **es zieht** there is a draught, it's draughty; vr

(Gummi) stretch; (Grenze etc) run; (Gespräche) be drawn out.
Ziehharmonika ['tsiː·harmoːnika] f concertina; accordion.
Ziehung ['tsiːʊŋ] f (Los~) drawing.
Ziel [tsiːl] nt -(e)s, -e (einer Reise) destination; (Sport) finish; (Mil) target; (Absicht) goal, aim; **z~en** vi aim (auf +acc at); **~fernrohr** nt telescopic sight; **z~los** a aimless; **~scheibe** f target; **z~strebig** a purposeful.
ziemlich ['tsiːmlɪç] a quite a; fair; ad rather; quite a bit.
zieren ['tsiːrən] vr act coy.
Zier- [tsiːr] cpd: **z~lich** a dainty; **~lichkeit** f daintiness; **~strauch** m flowering shrub.
Ziffer ['tsɪfər] f -, -n figure, digit; **~blatt** nt dial, clock-face.
zig [tsɪk] a (col) umpteen.
Zigarette [tsiga'rɛtə] f cigarette; **~nautomat** m cigarette machine; **~nschachtel** f cigarette packet; **~nspitze** f cigarette holder.
Zigarillo [tsiga'rɪlo] nt or m -s, -s cigarillo.
Zigarre [tsi'garə] f -, -n cigar.
Zigeuner(in f) [tsi'gɔʏnər(ɪn)] m -s, - gipsy.
Zimmer ['tsɪmər] nt -s, - room; **~antenne** f indoor aerial; **~decke** f ceiling; **~herr** m lodger; **~lautstärke** f reasonable volume; **~mädchen** nt chambermaid; **~mann** m carpenter; **z~n** vt make, carpenter; **~pflanze** f indoor plant.
zimperlich ['tsɪmpərlɪç] a squeamish; (pingelig) fussy, finicky.
Zimt [tsɪmt] m -(e)s, -e cinnamon; **~stange** f cinnamon stick.
Zink ['tsɪŋk] nt -(e)s zinc; **~e** f -, -n (Gabel~) prong; (Kamm~) tooth; **z~en** vt Karten mark; **~salbe** f zinc ointment.
Zinn [tsɪn] nt -(e)s (Element) tin; (in ~waren) pewter; **z~oberrot** [tsɪ'noːbərot] a vermilion; **~soldat** m tin soldier; **~waren** pl pewter.
Zins [tsɪns] m -es, -en interest; **~eszins** m compound interest; **~fuß** m, **~satz** m rate of interest; **z~los** a interest-free.
Zipfel ['tsɪpfəl] m -s, - corner; (spitz) tip; (Hemd~) tail; (Wurst~) end; **~mütze** f stocking cap; nightcap.
zirka ['tsɪrka] ad (round) about.
Zirkel ['tsɪrkəl] m -s, - circle; (Math) pair of compasses; **~kasten** m geometry set.
Zirkus ['tsɪrkʊs] m -, -se circus.
Zirrhose [tsɪ'roːzə] f -, -n cirrhosis.
zischeln ['tsɪʃəln] vti whisper.
zischen ['tsɪʃən] vi hiss.
Zitat [tsi'taːt] nt -(e)s, -e quotation, quote.
zitieren [tsi'tiːrən] vt quote.
Zitronat [tsitro'naːt] nt -(e)s, -e candied lemon peel.
Zitrone [tsi'troːnə] f -, -n lemon; **~nlimonade** f lemonade; **~nsaft** m lemon juice; **~nscheibe** f lemon slice.
zittern ['tsɪtərn] vi tremble.
Zitze [tsɪtsə] f -, -n teat, dug.

zivil [tsi'vi:l] *a* civil; *Preis* moderate; **Z~** *nt* **-s** plain clothes *pl*; *(Mil)* civilian clothing; **Z~bevölkerung** *f* civilian population; **Z~courage** *f* courage of one's convictions; **Z~isation** [tsivilizatsi'o:n] *f* civilization; **Z~isationserscheinung** *f* phenomenon of civilization; **Z~isationskrankheit** *f* disease peculiar to civilization; **~i'sieren** *vt* civilize; **Z~ist** [tsivi'list] *m* civilian; **Z~recht** *nt* civil law.

Zölibat [tsøli'ba:t] *nt or m* **-(e)s** celibacy.

Zoll [tsɔl] *m* **-(e)s**, **⁻e** customs *pl*: *(Abgabe)* duty; **~abfertigung** *f* customs clearance; **~amt** *nt* customs office; **~beamte(r)** *m* customs official; **~erklärung** *f* customs declaration; **z~frei** *a* duty-free; **z~pflichtig** *a* liable to duty, dutiable.

Zone ['tso:nə] *f* **-, -n** zone.

Zoo [tso:] *m* **-s, -s** zoo; **~loge** [tsoo'lo:gə] *m* **-n, -n** zoologist; **~lo'gie** *f* zoology; **z~'logisch** *a* zoological.

Zopf [tsɔpf] *m* **-(e)s**, **⁻e** plait; pigtail; **alter ~** antiquated custom.

Zorn [tsɔrn] *m* **-(e)s** anger; **z~ig** *a* angry.

Zote [tso:tə] *f* **-, -n** smutty joke/remark.

zottig ['tsɔtiç] *a* shaggy.

zu [tsu:] *(mit Infinitiv)* to; *prep +dat (bei Richtung, Vorgang)* to; *(bei Orts-, Zeit-, Preisangabe)* at; *(Zweck)* for; **~m Fenster herein** through the window; **~ meiner Zeit** in my time; *ad* too; *(in Richtung)* towards (sb/sth); *a (col)* shut.

zualler- [tsu'alər] *cpd:* **~erst** *ad* first of all; **~letzt** *ad* last of all.

Zubehör ['tsu:bəhø:r] *nt* **-(e)s, -e** accessories *pl*.

Zuber ['tsu:bər] *m* **-s, -** tub.

zubereiten ['tsu:bəraɪtən] *vt* prepare.

zubilligen ['tsu:bɪlɪgən] *vt* grant.

zubinden ['tsu:bɪndən] *vt irreg* tie up.

zubleiben ['tsu:blaɪbən] *vi irreg (col)* stay shut.

zubringen ['tsu:brɪŋən] *vt irreg* spend; *(col) Tür* get shut.

Zubringer *m* **-s, -** *(Tech)* feeder, conveyor; **~straße** *f* approach or slip road.

Zucht [tsʊxt] *f* **-, -en** *(von Tieren)* breed(ing); *(von Pflanzen)* cultivation; *(Rasse)* breed; *(Erziehung)* raising; *(Disziplin)* discipline.

züchten ['tsʏçtən] *vt Tiere* breed; *Pflanzen* cultivate, grow.

Züchter *m* **-s, -** breeder; grower.

Zucht- *cpd:* **~haus** *nt* prison, penitentiary *(US)*; **~hengst** *m* stallion, stud.

züchtig ['tsʏçtɪç] *a* modest, demure; **~en** ['tsʏçtɪgən] *vt* chastise; **Z~ung** *f* chastisement.

zucken ['tsʊkən] *vi* jerk, twitch; *(Strahl etc)* flicker; *vt* shrug.

zücken ['tsʏkən] *vt Schwert* draw; *Geldbeutel* pull out.

Zucker ['tsʊkər] *m* **-s, -** sugar; *(Med)* diabetes; **~dose** *f* sugar bowl; **~guß** *m* icing; **z~krank** *a* diabetic; **z~n** *vt* sugar; **~rohr** *nt* sugar cane; **~rübe** *f* sugar beet.

Zuckung ['tsʊkʊŋ] *f* convulsion, spasm; *(leicht)* twitch.

zudecken ['tsu:dɛkən] *vt* cover (up).

zudem [tsu'de:m] *ad* in addition (to this).

zudrehen ['tsu:dre:ən] *vt* turn off.

zudringlich ['tsu:drɪŋlɪç] *a* forward, pushing, obtrusive; **Z~keit** *f* forwardness, obtrusiveness.

zudrücken ['tsu:drʏkən] *vt* close; **ein Auge ~** turn a blind eye.

zueinander [tsu'aɪ'nandər] *ad* to one other; *(in Verbverbindung)* together.

zuerkennen ['tsu:'ɛrkɛnən] *vt irreg* award *(jdm etw* sth to sb, sb sth).

zuerst [tsu'e:rst] *ad* first; *(zu Anfang)* at first; **~ einmal** first of all.

Zufahrt ['tsu:fa:rt] *f* approach; **~sstraße** *f* approach road; *(von Autobahn etc)* slip road.

Zufall ['tsu:fal] *m* chance; *(Ereignis)* coincidence; **durch ~** by accident; **so ein ~** what a coincidence; **z~en** *vi irreg* close, shut itself; *(Anteil, Aufgabe)* fall *(jdm* to sb).

zufällig ['tsu:fɛlɪç] *a* chance; *ad* by chance; *(in Frage)* by any chance.

Zuflucht ['tsu:flʊxt] *f* recourse; *(Ort)* refuge.

Zufluß ['tsu:flʊs] *m* *(Zufließen)* inflow, influx; *(Geog)* tributary; *(Comm)* supply.

zufolge [tsu'fɔlgə] *prep +dat or gen* judging by; *(laut)* according to.

zufrieden [tsu'fri:dən] *a* content(ed), satisfied; **Z~heit** *f* satisfaction, contentedness; **~stellen** *vt* satisfy.

zufrieren ['tsu:fri:rən] *vi irreg* freeze up or over.

zufügen ['tsu:fy:gən] *vt* add *(dat* to); *Leid etc* cause *(jdm etw* sth to sb).

Zufuhr ['tsu:fu:r] *f* **-, -en** *(Herbeibringen)* supplying; *(Met)* influx; *(Mil)* supplies *pl*.

zuführen ['tsu:fy:rən] *vt (leiten)* bring, conduct; *(transportieren)* convey to; *(versorgen)* supply; *vi:* **auf etw** *(acc)* **~** lead to sth to the full.

Zug [tsu:k] *m* **-(e)s**, **⁻e** *(Eisenbahn)* train; *(Luft—)* draught; *(Ziehen)* pull(ing); *(Gesichts—)* feature; *(Schach etc)* move; *(Klingel—)* pull; *(Schrift—)* stroke; *(Atem—)* breath; *(Charakter—)* trait; *(an Zigarette)* puff, pull, drag; *(Schluck)* gulp; *(Menschengruppe)* procession; *(von Vögeln)* flight; *(Mil)* platoon; **etw in vollen en genießen** enjoy sth to the full.

Zu- ['tsu:] *cpd:* **~gabe** *f* extra; *(in Konzert etc)* encore; **~gang** *m* access, approach; **z~gänglich** *a* accessible; *Mensch* approachable.

Zug- *cpd:* **~abteil** *nt* train compartment; **~brücke** *f* drawbridge.

zugeben ['tsu:ge:bən] *vt irreg (beifügen)* add, throw in; *(zugestehen)* admit; *(erlauben)* permit.

zugehen ['tsu:ge:ən] *vi irreg (schließen)* shut; *v impers (sich ereignen)* go on, proceed; **auf jdn/etw ~** walk towards sb/sth; **dem Ende ~** be finishing.

Zugehörigkeit ['tsu:gəhø:rɪçkaɪt] *f* membership *(zu* of), belonging *(zu* to); **~sgefühl** *nt* feeling of belonging.

zugeknöpft ['tsu:gəknœpft] *a (col)* reserved, stand-offish.

Zügel ['tsy:gəl] *m* **-s, -** rein(s); *(fig auch)*

curb; z~**los** a unrestrained, licentious; ~**losigkeit** f lack of restraint, licentiousness; z~**n** vt curb; *Pferd auch* rein in.

zuge- ['tsu:gə] *cpd:* ~**sellen** vr join (jdm up with); **Z~ständnis** nt -ses, -se concession; ~**stehen** vt irreg admit; *Rechte* concede (jdm to sb).

Zug- *cpd:* ~**führer** m (Rail) inspector; (Mil) platoon commander; **z~ig** a draughty.

zügig ['tsy:gɪç] a speedy, swift.

Zug- *cpd:* ~**luft** f draught; ~**maschine** f traction engine, tractor.

zugreifen ['tsu:graɪfən] vi irreg seize or grab it; (helfen) help; (beim Essen) help o.s.

zugrunde [tsu'grundə] ad: ~ **gehen** collapse; (Mensch) perish; **einer Sache etw** ~ **legen** base sth on sth; **einer Sache** ~ **liegen** be based on sth; ~ **richten** ruin, destroy.

zugunsten [tsu'gunstən] prep +gen or dat in favour of.

zugute [tsu'gu:tə] ad: **jdm etw** ~ **halten** concede sth; **jdm** ~ **kommen** be of assistance to sb.

Zug- *cpd:* ~**verbindung** f train connection; ~**vogel** m migratory bird.

zuhalten ['tsu:haltən] irreg vt hold shut; vi: **auf jdn/etw** ~ make for sb/sth.

Zuhälter ['tsu:hɛltər] m -s, - pimp.

Zuhause [tsu'hausə] nt - home.

Zuhilfenahme [tsu'hɪlfəna:mə] f: **unter** ~ **von** with the help of.

zuhören ['tsu:hø:rən] vi listen (dat to).

Zuhörer m -s, - listener; ~**schaft** f audience.

zujubeln ['tsu:ju:bəln] vi cheer (jdm sb).

zukleben ['tsu:kle:bən] vt paste up.

zuknöpfen ['tsu:knœpfən] vt button up, fasten.

zukommen ['tsu:kɔmən] vi irreg come up (auf +acc to); (sich gehören) be fitting (jdm for sb); (Recht haben auf) be entitled to; **jdm etw** ~ **lassen** give sb sth; **etw auf sich** ~ **lassen** wait and see.

Zukunft ['tsu:kunft] f-, **Zukünfte** future.

zukünftig [tsu:kynftɪç] a future; **mein** ~**er Mann** my husband to be; ad in future.

Zukunfts- *cpd:* ~**aussichten** pl future prospects pl; ~**musik** f (col) wishful thinking; crystal ball gazing; ~**roman** m science-fiction novel.

Zulage ['tsu:la:gə] f bonus, allowance.

zulassen ['tsu:lasən] vt irreg (hereinlassen) admit; (erlauben) permit; Auto license; (col: nicht öffnen) (keep) shut.

zulässig ['tsu:lɛsɪç] a permissible, permitted.

zulaufen ['tsu:laufən] vi irreg run (auf +acc towards); (Tier) adopt (jdm sb); **spitz** ~ come to a point.

zulegen ['tsu:le:gən] vt add; *Geld* put in; *Tempo* accelerate, quicken; (schließen) cover over; **sich** (dat) **etw** ~ (col) get hold of sth.

zuleide [tsu'laɪdə] a: **jdm etw** ~ **tun** hurt or harm sb.

zuleiten ['tsu:laɪtən] vt direct (dat to); (schicken) send.

zuletzt [tsu'lɛtst] ad finally, at last.

zuliebe [tsu'li:bə] ad: **jdm** ~ to please sb.

zum [tsum] = **zu dem**; ~ **dritten Mal** for the third time; ~ **Scherz** as a joke; ~ **Trinken** for drinking.

zumachen ['tsu:maxən] vt shut; *Kleidung* do up, fasten; vi shut; (col) hurry up.

zumal [tsu'ma:l] cj especially (as).

zumeist [tsu'maɪst] ad mostly.

zumindest [tsu'mɪndəst] ad at least.

zumut- *cpd:* ~**bar** ['tsu:mu:tba:r] a reasonable; ~**e wie ist ihm** ~**e?** how does he feel?; ~**en** ['tsu:mu:tən] vt expect, ask (jdm of sb); **Z~ung** [Aut] f unreasonable expectation or demand, impertinence.

zunächst [tsu'nɛ:çst] ad first of all; ~ **einmal** to start with.

zunähen ['tsu:nɛ:ən] vt sew up.

Zunahme ['tsu:na:mə] f-, -n increase.

Zuname ['tsu:na:mə] m surname.

Zünd- [tsynd] *cpd:* z~**en** vi (Feuer) light, ignite; (Motor) fire; (begeistern) fire (with enthusiasm) (bei jdm sb); z~**end** a fiery; ~**er** m -s, - fuse; (Mil) detonator; ~**holz** ['tsynt-] nt match; ~**kerze** f (Aut) spark(ing) plug; ~**schlüssel** m ignition key; ~**schnur** f fuse wire; ~**stoff** m fuel; (fig) dynamite; ~**ung** f ignition.

zunehmen ['tsu:ne:mən] vi irreg increase, grow; (Mensch) put on weight.

zuneigen ['tsu:naɪgən] vi incline, lean; **sich dem Ende** ~ draw to a close; **einer Auffassung** ~ incline towards a view; **jdm zugeneigt sein** be attracted to sb.

Zuneigung f affection.

Zunft [tsunft] f-, **⸚e** guild.

zünftig ['tsynftɪç] a proper, real; *Handwerk* decent.

Zunge ['tsuŋə] f -, -n tongue; (Fisch) sole; z~**nfertig** a glib.

zunichte [tsu'nɪçtə] ad: ~ **machen** ruin, destroy; ~ **werden** come to nothing.

zunutze [tsu'nutsə] ad: **sich** (dat) **etw** ~ **machen** make use of sth.

zuoberst [tsu'o:bərst] ad at the top.

zupfen ['tsupfən] vt pull, pick, pluck; *Gitarre* pluck.

zur [tsu:r] = **zu der**.

zurech- ['tsu:rɛç] *cpd:* ~**nungsfähig** a responsible, accountable; **Z~nungs-fähigkeit** f responsibility, accountability.

zurecht- [tsu'rɛçt] *cpd:* ~**finden** vr irreg find one's way (about); ~**kommen** vi irreg (be able to) deal (mit with); manage; ~**legen** vt get ready; *Ausrede etc* have ready; ~**machen** vt prepare; vr get ready; ~**weisen** vt irreg reprimand; **Z~weisung** f reprimand, rebuff.

zureden ['tsu:re:dən] vi persuade, urge (jdm sb).

zurichten ['tsu:rɪçtən] vt *Essen* prepare; (beschädigen) batter, bash up.

zürnen ['tsʏrnən] vi be angry (jdm with sb).

zurück [tsu'rʏk] ad back; ~**behalten** vt irreg keep back; ~**bekommen** vt irreg get back; ~**bezahlen** vt repay, pay back; ~**bleiben** vi irreg (Mensch) remain behind; (nicht nachkommen) fall behind,

lag; (Schaden) remain; **~bringen** vt irreg
bring back; **~drängen** vt Gefühle repress;
Feind push back; **~drehen** vt turn back;
~erobern vt reconquer; **~fahren** irreg
vi travel back; (vor Schreck) recoil, start; vt
drive back; **~fallen** vi irreg fall back; (in
Laster) relapse; **~finden** vi irreg find
one's way back; **~fordern** vt demand
back; **~führen** vt lead back; etw auf etw
(acc) **~führen** trace sth back to sth;
~geben vt irreg give back; (antworten)
retort with; **~geblieben** a retarded;
~gehen vi irreg go back; (zeitlich) date
back (auf +acc to); (fallen) go down, fall;
~gezogen a retired, withdrawn;
~halten irreg vt hold back; Mensch
restrain; (hindern) prevent; vr (reserviert
sein) be reserved; (im Essen) hold back;
~haltend a reserved; **Z~haltung** f
reserve; **~kehren** vi return; **~kommen**
vi irreg come back; auf etw (acc)
~kommen return to sth; **~lassen** vt
irreg leave behind; **~legen** vt put back;
Geld put by; (reservieren) keep back;
Strecke cover; **~nehmen** vt irreg take
back; **~rufen** vti irreg call back; etw ins
Gedächtnis **~rufen** recall sth;
~schrecken vi shrink (vor +dat from);
~setzen vt put back; (im Preis) reduce;
(benachteiligen) put at a disadvantage;
~stecken vt put back; vi (fig) moderate
(one's wishes); **~stellen** vt put back,
replace; (aufschieben) put off, postpone;
(Mil) turn down; Interessen defer; Ware
keep; **~stoßen** vt irreg repulse; **~treten**
vi irreg step back; (vom Amt) retire;
gegenüber or **hinter** etw **~treten**
diminish in importance in view of sth;
~weisen vt irreg turn down; Mensch
reject; **Z~zahlung** f repayment;
~ziehen irreg vt pull back; Angebot withdraw; vr retire.

Zuruf ['tsu:ru:f] m shout, cry.

Zusage ['tsu:za:gə] f **-**, **-n** promise;
(Annahme) consent; **z~n** vt promise; vi
accept; jdm z~n (gefallen) agree with or
please sb.

zusammen [tsu'zamən] ad together;
Z~arbeit f cooperation; **~arbeiten** vi
cooperate; **~beißen** vt irreg Zähne
clench; **~bleiben** vi irreg stay together;
~brechen vi irreg collapse; (Mensch auch)
break down; **~bringen** vt irreg bring or
get together; Geld get; Sätze put together;
Z~bruch m collapse; **~fahren** vi irreg
collide; (erschrecken) start; **~fassen** vt
summarize; (vereinigen) unite; **~fassend**
a summarizing; ad to summarize;
Z~fassung f summary, résumé;
~finden vir irreg meet (together);
~fließen vi irreg flow together, meet;
Z~fluß m confluence; **~fügen** vt join
(together), unite; **~gehören** vi belong
together; (Paar) match; **~gesetzt** a compound, composite; **~halten** vi irreg stick
together; **Z~hang** m connection; im/aus
dem **Z~hang** in/out of context;
~hängen vi irreg be connected or linked;
~hang(s)los a incoherent, disconnected;
~klappbar a folding, collapsible;

~kommen vi irreg meet, assemble; (sich
ereignen) occur at once or together;
Z~kunft f meeting; **~laufen** vi irreg run
or come together; (Straßen, Flüsse etc) converge, meet; (Farben) run into one
another; **~legen** vt put together; (stapeln)
pile up; (falten) fold; (verbinden) combine,
unite; Termine, Fest amalgamate; Geld
collect; **~nehmen** irreg vt summon up;
alles **~genommen** all in all; vr pull o.s.
together; **~passen** vi go well together,
match; **~prallen** vi collide; **~schlagen**
vt irreg Mensch beat up; Dinge smash up;
(falten) fold; Hände clap; Hacken click;
~schließen vtr irreg join (together);
Z~schluß m amalgamation; **~-
schreiben** vt irreg write together; Bericht
put together; **~schrumpfen** vi shrink,
shrivel up; **Z~sein** nt **-s** get-together;
~setzen vt put together; vr be composed
of; **Z~setzung** f composition; **~stellen**
vt put together; compile; **Z~stellung** f
list; (Vorgang) compilation; **Z~stoß** m
collision; **~stoßen** vi irreg collide;
~treffen vi irreg coincide; Menschen
meet; **Z~treffen** nt meeting; coincidence; **~wachsen** vi irreg grow
together; **~zählen** vt add up; **~ziehen**
irreg vt (verengern) draw together;
(vereinigen) bring together; (addieren) add
up; vr shrink; (sich bilden) form, develop.

Zusatz ['tsu:zats] m addition; **~antrag** m
(Pol) amendment.

zusätzlich ['tsu:zɛtsliç] a additional.

zuschauen ['tsu:ʃauən] vi watch, look on.

Zuschauer m **-s**, **-** spectator; pl (Theat)
audience.

zuschicken ['tsu:ʃikən] vt send, forward
(jdm etw sth to sb).

zuschießen ['tsu:ʃi:sən] irreg vt fire (dat
at); Geld put in; vi: **~ auf** (+acc) rush
towards.

Zuschlag ['tsu:ʃla:k] m extra charge,
surcharge; **z~en** ['tsu:ʃla:gən] irreg vt Tür
slam; Ball hit (jdm to sb); (bei Auktion)
knock down; Steine etc knock into shape; vi
(Fenster, Tür) shut; (Mensch) hit, punch;
~skarte f (Rail) surcharge ticket;
z~spflichtig a subject to surcharge.

zuschließen ['tsu:ʃli:sən] vt irreg lock (up).

zuschmeißen ['tsu:ʃmaisən] vt irreg (col)
slam, bang shut.

zuschneiden ['tsu:ʃnaidən] vt irreg cut out
or to size.

zuschnüren ['tsu:ʃny:rən] vt tie up.

zuschrauben ['tsu:ʃraubən] vt screw down
or up.

zuschreiben ['tsu:ʃraibən] vt irreg (fig)
ascribe, attribute; (Comm) credit.

Zuschrift ['tsu:ʃrift] f letter, reply.

zuschulden [tsu:ʃuldən] ad: sich (dat) etw
~ kommen lassen make o.s. guilty of
sth.

Zuschuß ['tsu:ʃus] m subsidy, allowance.

zuschütten ['tsu:ʃytən] vt fill up.

zusehen ['tsu:ze:ən] vi irreg watch
(jdm/etw sb/sth); (dafür sorgen) take care;
~ds ad visibly.

zusenden ['tsu:zɛndən] vt irreg forward,
send on (jdm etw sth to sb).

zusetzen ['tsuːzɛtsən] *vt (beifügen)* add; *Geld* lose; *vi:* **jdm** ~ harass sb; *(Krankheit)* take a lot out of sb.

zusichern ['tsuːzɪçərn] *vt* assure *(jdm etw* sb of sth).

zusperren ['tsuːʃpɛrən] *vt* bar.

zuspielen ['tsuːʃpiːlən] *vti* pass *(jdm* to sb).

zuspitzen ['tsuːʃpɪtsən] *vt* sharpen; *vr (Lage)* become critical.

zusprechen ['tsuːʃprɛçən] *irreg vt (zuerkennen)* award *(jdm etw* sb sth, sth to sb); **jdm Trost** ~ comfort sb; *vi* speak *(jdm* to sb); **dem Essen/Alkohol** ~ eat/drink a lot.

Zuspruch ['tsuːʃprʊx] *m* encouragement; *(Anklang)* appreciation, popularity.

Zustand ['tsuːʃtant] *m* state, condition; **z~e** [tsuː'ʃtɛndə] *ad:* **z~e bringen** *vt irreg* bring about; **z~e kommen** *vi irreg* come about.

zuständig ['tsuːʃtɛndɪç] *a* competent, responsible; **Z~keit** *f* competence, responsibility.

zustehen ['tsuːʃteːən] *vi irreg:* **jdm** ~ be sb's right.

zustellen ['tsuːʃtɛlən] *vt (verstellen)* block; *Post etc* send.

zustimmen ['tsuːʃtɪmən] *vi* agree *(dat* to).

Zustimmung *f* agreement, consent.

zustoßen ['tsuːʃtoːsən] *vi irreg (fig)* happen *(jdm* to sb).

zutage [tsuː'taːgə] *ad:* ~ **bringen** bring to light; ~ **treten** come to light.

Zutaten ['tsuːtaːtən] *pl* ingredients *pl.*

zuteilen ['tsuːtaɪlən] *vt* allocate, assign.

zutiefst [tsuː'tiːfst] *ad* deeply.

zutragen ['tsuːtraːgən] *irreg vt* bring *(jdm etw* sth to sb); *Klatsch* tell; *vr* happen.

zuträglich ['tsuːtrɛːklɪç] *a* beneficial.

zutrau- ['tsuːtrau] *cpd:* ~**en** *vt* credit *(jdm etw* sb with sth); **Z~en** *nt* -**s** trust *(zu* in); ~**lich** *a* trusting, friendly; **Z~lichkeit** *f* trust.

zutreffen ['tsuːtrɛfən] *vi irreg* be correct; apply; **Z~des bitte unterstreichen** please underline where applicable.

zutrinken ['tsuːtrɪŋkən] *vi irreg* drink to *(jdm* sb).

Zutritt ['tsuːtrɪt] *m* access, admittance.

Zutun ['tsuːtuːn] *nt* -**s** assistance; *vt irreg* add; *(schließen)* shut.

zuverlässig ['tsuːferlɛsɪç] *a* reliable; **Z~keit** *f* reliability.

Zuversicht ['tsuːferzɪçt] *f* - confidence; **z~lich** *a* confident; ~**lichkeit** *f* confidence, hopefulness.

zuviel [tsuː'fiːl] *ad* too much.

zuvor [tsuː'foːr] *ad* before, previously; ~**kommen** *vi irreg* anticipate *(jdm* sb), beat *(sb)* to it; ~**kommend** *a* obliging, courteous.

Zuwachs ['tsuːvaks] *m* -**es** increase, growth; *(col)* addition; **z~en** *vi irreg* become overgrown; *(Wunde)* heal (up).

zuwandern ['tsuːvandərn] *vi* immigrate.

zuwege [tsuː'veːgə] *ad:* **etw** ~ **bringen** accomplish sth; **mit etw** ~ **kommen** manage sth; **gut** ~ **sein** be (doing) well.

zuweilen [tsuː'vaɪlən] *ad* at times, now and then.

zuweisen ['tsuːvaɪzən] *vt irreg* assign, allocate *(jdm* to sb).

zuwenden ['tsuːvɛndən] *irreg vt* turn *(dat* towards); **jdm seine Aufmerksamkeit** ~ give sb one's attention; *vr* devote o.s., turn *(dat* to).

zuwenig [tsuː'veːnɪç] *ad* too little.

zuwerfen ['tsuːvɛrfən] *vt irreg* throw *(jdm* to sb).

zuwider [tsuː'viːdər] *ad:* **etw ist jdm** ~ sb loaths sth, sb finds sth repugnant; *prep* +*dat* contrary to; ~**handeln** *vi* act contrary *(dat* to); **einem Gesetz** ~**handeln** contravene a law; **Z~handlung** *f* contravention; ~**laufen** *vi irreg* run counter *(dat* to).

zuziehen ['tsuːtsiːən] *irreg vt (schließen)* *Vorhang* draw, close; *(herbeirufen)* *Experten* call in; **sich** *(dat)* **etw** ~ *Krankheit* catch; *Zorn* incur; *vi* move in, come.

zuzüglich ['tsuːtsyːklɪç] *prep* +*gen* plus, with the addition of.

Zwang [tsvaŋ] *m* -**(e)s**, **ʹe** compulsion, coercion.

zwängen ['tsvɛŋən] *vtr* squeeze.

Zwang- *cpd:* **z~los** *a* informal; ~**losigkeit** *f* informality; ~**sarbeit** *f* forced labour; *(Strafe)* hard labour; ~**sjacke** *f* straightjacket; ~**slage** *f* predicament, tight corner; **z~släufig** *a* necessary, inevitable; ~**smaßnahme** *f* sanction, coercive measure; **z~sweise** *ad* compulsorily.

zwanzig ['tsvantsɪç] *num* twenty.

zwar [tsvaːr] *ad* to be sure, indeed; **das ist** ~ . . ., **aber** . . . that may be . . . but . . .; **und** ~ **am Sonntag** on Sunday to be precise; **und** ~ **so schnell, daß** . . . in fact so quickly that . . .

Zweck [tsvɛk] *m* -**(e)s**, -**e** purpose, aim; **z~dienlich** *a* practical; expedient; ~**e** *f* -, -**n** hobnail; *(Heft—)* drawing pin, thumbtack *(US);* ~**entfremdung** *f* misuse; **z~los** *a* pointless; **z~mäßig** *a* suitable, appropriate; ~**mäßigkeit** *f* suitability; **z~widrig** *a* unsuitable.

zwei [tsvaɪ] *num* two; ~**deutig** *a* ambiguous; *(unanständig)* suggestive; ~**erlei** *a:* ~**erlei Stoff** two different kinds of material; ~**erlei Meinung** of differing opinions; ~**erlei zu tun haben** have two different things to do; ~**fach** *a* double.

Zweifel ['tsvaɪfəl] *m* -**s**, - doubt; **z~haft** *a* doubtful, dubious; **z~los** *a* doubtless; **z~n** *vi* doubt *(an etw (dat)* sth); ~**sfall** *m:* **im** ~**sfall** in case of doubt.

Zweig [tsvaɪk] *m* -**(e)s**, -**e** branch; ~**geschäft** *nt (Comm)* branch; ~**stelle** *f* branch (office).

zwei- *cpd:* **Z~heit** *f* duality; ~**hundert** *num* two hundred; **Z~kampf** *m* duel; ~**mal** *ad* twice; ~**motorig** *a* twin-engined; ~**reihig** *a (Anzug)* double-breasted; ~**schneidig** *a (fig)* two-edged; **Z~sitzer** *m* -**s**, - two-seater; ~**sprachig** *a* bilingual; ~**spurig** *a (Aut)* two-lane; ~**stimmig** *a* for two voices;

Z~taktmotor *m* two-stroke engine.
zweit- ['tsvait] *cpd*: **~ens** *ad* secondly;
  ~größte(r,s) *a* second largest;
  ~klassig *a* second-class; **~letzte(r,s)** *a*
  last but one, penultimate; **~rangig** *a*
  second-rate; **Z~wagen** *m* second car.
Zwerchfell ['tsvɛrçfɛl] *nt* diaphragm.
Zwerg [tsvɛrk] *m* **-(e)s, -e** dwarf.
Zwetsche ['tsvɛtʃə] *f* **-, -n** plum.
Zwickel ['tsvikəl] *m* **-s, -** gusset.
zwicken ['tsvikən] *vt* pinch, nip.
Zwieback ['tsviːbak] *m* **-(e)s, -e** rusk.
Zwiebel ['tsviːbəl] *f* **-, -n** onion; *(Blumen—)*
  bulb; **z~artig** *a* bulbous.
Zwie- ['tsviː] *cpd*: **~gespräch** *vt* dialogue;
  ~licht *nt* twilight; **z~lichtig** *a* shady,
  dubious; **~spalt** *m* conflict, split;
  z~spältig *a Gefühle* conflicting; *Charakter*
  contradictory; **~tracht** *f* discord, dissension.
Zwilling ['tsviliŋ] *m* **-s, -e** twin; *pl (Astrol)*
  Gemini.
zwingen ['tsviŋən] *vt irreg* force; **~nd** *a*
  Grund etc compelling.
zwinkern ['tsviŋkərn] *vi* blink; *(absichtlich)*
  wink.
Zwirn [tsvirn] *m* **-(e)s, -e** thread.
zwischen ['tsviʃən] *prep +acc or dat*
  between; **Z~bemerkung** *f* (incidental)
  remark; **~blenden** *vt (TV)* insert;
Z~ding *nt* cross; **~durch** [-'durç] *ad* in
between; *(räumlich)* here and there;
Z~ergebnis *nt* intermediate result;
Z~fall *m* incident; **Z~frage** *f* question;
Z~gas *nt*: **Z~gas geben** double-
declutch; **Z~handel** *m* middlemen *pl*;
middleman's trade; **Z~händler** *m*
middleman, agent; **Z~landung** *f* stop,
intermediate landing; **~menschlich** *a*
interpersonal; **Z~raum** *m* space; **Z~ruf**
m interjection, interruption; **Z~spiel** *nt*
interlude; **~staatlich** *f* interstate; international; **Z~station** *f* intermediate
station; **Z~stecker** *m (Elec)* adaptor;
Z~wand *f* partition; **Z~zeit** *f* interval; **in
der Z~zeit** in the interim, meanwhile.
Zwist [tsvist] *m* **-es, -e** dispute, feud.
zwitschern ['tsvitʃərn] *vti* twitter, chirp.
Zwitter ['tsvitər] *m* **-s, -** hermaphrodite.
zwölf [tsvœlf] *num* twelve.
Zyklus ['tsyːklus] *m* **-, Zyklen** cycle.
Zylinder [tsi'lindər] *m* **-s, -** cylinder; *(Hut)*
  top hat; **z~förmig** *a* cylindrical.
Zyniker ['tsyːnikər] *m* **-s, -** cynic.
zynisch ['tsyːniʃ] *a* cynical.
Zynismus [tsy'nismus] *m* cynicism.
Zyste ['tsystə] *f* **-, -n** cyst.

ENGLISH - GERMAN
ENGLISCH - DEUTSCH

A

A, a [eɪ] *n* A *nt*, a *nt*.

a, an [eɪ, ə; æn, ən] *indef art* ein/eine/ein. £1 a metre 1£ pro *or* das Meter.

aback [ə'bæk] *ad*: **to be taken** ~ verblüfft sein.

abandon [ə'bændən] *vt* (*give up*) aufgeben; (*desert*) verlassen; *n* Hingabe *f*.

abashed [ə'bæʃt] *a* verlegen.

abate [ə'beɪt] *vi* nachlassen, sich legen.

abattoir ['æbətwɑː*] *n* Schlachthaus *nt*.

abbey ['æbɪ] *n* Abtei *f*.

abbot ['æbət] *n* Abt *m*.

abbreviate [ə'briːvɪeɪt] *vt* abkürzen.

abbreviation [əbriːvɪ'eɪʃən] *n* Abkürzung *f*.

ABC ['eɪbiː'siː] *n* (*lit, fig*) Abc *nt*.

abdicate ['æbdɪkeɪt] *vt* aufgeben; *vi* abdanken.

abdication [æbdɪ'keɪʃən] *n* Abdankung *f*; (Amts)niederlegung *f*.

abdomen ['æbdəmən] *n* Unterleib *m*.

abdominal [æb'domɪnl] *a* Unterleibs-.

abduct [æb'dʌkt] *vt* entführen; ~**ion** [æb'dʌkʃən] Entführung *f*.

aberration [æbə'reɪʃən] *n* (geistige) Verwirrung *f*.

abet [ə'bet] *vt see* **aid** *vt*.

abeyance [ə'beɪəns] *n*: **in** ~ in der Schwebe; (*disuse*) außer Kraft.

abhor [əb'hɔː*] *vt* verabscheuen.

abhorrent [əb'horənt] *a* verabscheuungswürdig.

abide [ə'baɪd] *vt* vertragen; leiden; ~ **by** *vt* sich halten an (+*acc*).

ability [ə'bɪlɪtɪ] *n* (*power*) Fähigkeit *f*; (*skill*) Geschicklichkeit *f*.

abject ['æbdʒekt] *a* *liar* übel; *poverty* größte(r, s); *apology* zerknirscht.

ablaze [ə'bleɪz] *a* in Flammen; ~ **with lights** hell erleuchtet.

able ['eɪbl] *a* geschickt, fähig; **to be** ~ **to do sth** etw tun können; ~**-bodied** *a* kräftig; *seaman* Voll-; (*Mil*) wehrfähig.

ably ['eɪblɪ] *ad* geschickt.

abnormal [æb'nɔːməl] *a* regelwidrig, abnorm; ~**ity** [æbnɔː'mælɪtɪ] Regelwidrigkeit *f*; (*Med*) krankhafte Erscheinung *f*.

aboard [ə'bɔːd] *ad, prep* an Bord (+*gen*).

abode [ə'bəʊd] *n*: **of no fixed** ~ ohne festen Wohnsitz.

abolish [ə'bolɪʃ] *vt* abschaffen.

abolition [æbə'lɪʃən] *n* Abschaffung *f*.

abominable *a*, **abominably** *ad* [ə'bomɪnəbl, -blɪ] scheußlich.

aborigine [æbə'rɪdʒɪniː] *n* Ureinwohner *m*.

abort [ə'bɔːt] *vt* abtreiben; fehlgebären; ~**ion** [ə'bɔːʃən] Abtreibung *f*; (*miscarriage*) Fehlgeburt *f*; ~**ive** *a* mißlungen.

abound [ə'baʊnd] *vi* im Überfluß vorhanden sein; **to** ~ **in** Überfluß haben an (+*dat*).

about [ə'baʊt] *ad* (*nearby*) in der Nähe; (*roughly*) ungefähr; (*around*) umher, herum; *prep* (*topic*) über (+*acc*); (*place*) um, um . . . herum; **to be** ~ **to go out** ich wollte gerade weggehen.

above [ə'bʌv] *ad* oben; *prep* über; *a* obig; ~ **all** vor allem; ~**board** *a* offen, ehrlich.

abrasion [ə'breɪʒən] *n* Abschürfung *f*.

abrasive [ə'breɪzɪv] *n* Schleifmittel *nt*; *a* Abschleif-; *personality* zermürbend, aufreibend.

abreast [ə'brest] *ad* nebeneinander; **to keep** ~ **of** Schritt halten mit.

abridge [ə'brɪdʒ] *vt* (ab)kürzen.

abroad [ə'brɔːd] *ad* im Ausland; **go ins Ausland**.

abrupt [ə'brʌpt] *a* (*sudden*) abrupt, jäh; (*curt*) schroff.

abscess ['æbsɪs] *n* Geschwür *nt*.

abscond [əb'skond] *vi* flüchten, sich davonmachen.

absence ['æbsəns] *n* Abwesenheit *f*.

absent ['æbsənt] *a* abwesend, nicht da; (*lost in thought*) geistesabwesend; ~**ee** [æbsən'tiː] Abwesende(r) *m*; ~**eeism** [æbsən'tiːɪzəm] Fehlen *nt* (am Arbeitsplatz/in der Schule); ~**-minded** *a* zerstreut.

absolute ['æbsəluːt] *a* absolut; *power* unumschränkt; *rubbish* vollkommen, rein; ~**ly** ['æbsəluːtlɪ] *ad* absolut, vollkommen; ~! ganz bestimmt!

absolve [əb'zolv] *vt* entbinden; freisprechen.

absorb [əb'zɔːb] *vt* aufsaugen, absorbieren; (*fig*) ganz in Anspruch nehmen, fesseln; ~**ent** *a* absorbierend; ~**ent cotton** (*US*) Verbandwatte *f*; ~**ing** *a* aufsaugend; (*fig*) packend.

abstain [əb'steɪn] *vi* (*in vote*) sich enthalten; **to** ~ **from** (*keep from*) sich enthalten (+*gen*).

abstemious [əb'stiːmɪəs] *a* mäßig, enthaltsam.

abstention [əb'stenʃən] *n* (*in vote*) (Stimm)enthaltung *f*.

abstinence ['æbstɪnəns] *n* Enthaltsamkeit *f*.

abstract ['æbstrækt] *a* abstrakt; *n* Abriß *m*; [æb'strækt] *vt* abstrahieren, aussondern.

abstruse [æb'struːs] *a* verworren, abstrus.

absurd [əb'sɜːd] *a* absurd; ~**ity** Unsinnigkeit *f*, Absurdität *f*.

abundance [ə'bʌndəns] *n* Überfluß *m* (*of* an +*dat*).

abundant [ə'bʌndənt] *a* reichlich.

abuse [ə'bju:s] n (*rude language*) Beschimpfung f; (*ill usage*) Mißbrauch m; (*bad practice*) (Amts)mißbrauch m; [ə'bju:z] vt (*misuse*) mißbrauchen.

abusive [ə'bju:sɪv] a beleidigend, Schimpf-.

abysmal [ə'bɪzməl] a scheußlich; *ignorance* bodenlos.

abyss [ə'bɪs] n Abgrund m.

academic [ækə'demɪk] a akademisch; (*theoretical*) theoretisch.

academy [ə'kædəmɪ] n (*school*) Hochschule f; (*society*) Akademie f.

accede [æk'si:d] vi: ~ to *office* antreten; *throne* besteigen; *request* zustimmen (+dat).

accelerate [æk'seləreɪt] vi schneller werden; (*Aut*) Gas geben; vt beschleunigen.

acceleration [ækselə'reɪʃən] n Beschleunigung f.

accelerator [ək'seləreɪtə*] n Gas(pedal) nt.

accent ['æksent] n Akzent m, Tonfall m; (*mark*) Akzent m; (*stress*) Betonung f; ~**uate** [æk'sentjveɪt] vt betonen.

accept [ək'sept] vt (*take*) annehmen; (*agree to*) akzeptieren; ~**able** a annehmbar; ~**ance** Annahme f.

access ['ækses] n Zugang m; ~**ible** [æk'sesɪbl] a (*easy to approach*) zugänglich; (*within reach*) (leicht) erreichbar; ~**ion** [æk'seʃən] (*to throne*) Besteigung f; (*to office*) Antritt m.

accessory [æk'sesərɪ] n Zubehörteil nt; **accessories** pl Zubehör nt; **toilet accessories** pl Toilettenartikel pl.

accident ['æksɪdənt] n Unfall m; (*coincidence*) Zufall m; **by** ~ zufällig; ~**al** [æksɪ'dentl] a unbeabsichtigt; ~**ally** [æksɪ'dentəlɪ] ad zufällig; **to be** ~-**prone** zu Unfällen neigen.

acclaim [ə'kleɪm] vt zujubeln (+dat); n Beifall m.

acclimatize [ə'klaɪmətaɪz] vt: **to become** ~**d** sich gewöhnen (*to* an +acc), sich akklimatisieren.

accolade ['ækəleɪd] n Auszeichnung f.

accommodate [ə'kɒmədeɪt] vt unterbringen; (*hold*) Platz haben für; (*oblige*) (aus)helfen (+dat).

accommodating [ə'kɒmədeɪtɪŋ] a entgegenkommend.

accommodation [ə'kɒmə'deɪʃən] n Unterkunft f.

accompaniment [ə'kʌmpənɪmənt] n Begleitung f.

accompanist [ə'kʌmpənɪst] n Begleiter m.

accompany [ə'kʌmpənɪ] vt begleiten.

accomplice [ə'kʌmplɪs] n Helfershelfer m, Komplize m.

accomplish [ə'kʌmplɪʃ] vt (*fulfil*) durchführen; (*finish*) vollenden; *aim* erreichen; ~**ed** a vollendet, ausgezeichnet; ~**ment** (*skill*) Fähigkeit f; (*completion*) Vollendung f; (*feat*) Leistung f.

accord [ə'kɔ:d] n Übereinstimmung f; **of one's own** ~ freiwillig; vt gewähren; ~**ance**: **in** ~**ance with** in Übereinstimmung mit; ~**ing to** nach, laut (+gen); ~**ingly** ad danach, dementsprechend.

accordion [ə'kɔ:dɪən] n Ziehharmonika f,

Akkordeon nt; ~**ist** Akkordeonspieler m.

accost [ə'kɒst] vt ansprechen.

account [ə'kaʊnt] n (*bill*) Rechnung f; (*narrative*) Bericht m; (*report*) Rechenschaftsbericht m; (*in bank*) Konto nt; (*importance*) Geltung f; **on** ~ auf Rechnung; **of no** ~ ohne Bedeutung; **on no** ~ keinesfalls; **on** ~ **of** wegen; **to take into** ~ berücksichtigen; ~ **for** vt *expenditure* Rechenschaft ablegen für; **how do you** ~ **for that?** wie erklären Sie (sich) das?; ~**able** a verantwortlich; ~**ancy** Buchhaltung f; ~**ant** Wirtschaftsprüfer(in f) m.

accoutrements [ə'ku:trəmənts] npl Ausrüstung f.

accredited [ə'kredɪtɪd] a beglaubigt, akkreditiert.

accretion [ə'kri:ʃən] n Zunahme f.

accrue [ə'kru:] vi erwachsen, sich ansammeln.

accumulate [ə'kju:mjuleɪt] vt ansammeln; vi sich ansammeln.

accumulation [əkju:mju'leɪʃən] n (*act*) Aufhäufung f; (*result*) Ansammlung f.

accuracy ['ækjʊrəsɪ] n Genauigkeit f.

accurate ['ækjʊrɪt] a genau; ~**ly** ad genau, richtig.

accursed, accurst [ə'kɜ:st] a verflucht.

accusation [ækju:'zeɪʃən] n Anklage f, Beschuldigung f.

accusative [ə'kju:zətɪv] n Akkusativ m, vierte(r) Fall m.

accuse [ə'kju:z] vt anklagen, beschuldigen; ~**d** Angeklagte(r) mf.

accustom [ə'kʌstəm] vt gewöhnen (*to* an +acc); ~**ed** a gewohnt.

ace [eɪs] n As nt; (*col*) As nt, Kanone f.

ache [eɪk] n Schmerz m; vi (*be sore*) schmerzen, weh tun; **I** ~ **all over** mir tut es überall weh.

achieve [ə'tʃi:v] vt zustande bringen; *aim* erreichen; ~**ment** Leistung f; (*act*) Erreichen nt.

acid ['æsɪd] n Säure f; a sauer, scharf; ~**ity** [ə'sɪdɪtɪ] Säuregehalt m; (*fig*) Nagelprobe f.

acknowledge [ək'nɒlɪdʒ] vt *receipt* bestätigen; (*admit*) zugeben; ~**ment** Anerkennung f; (*letter*) Empfangsbestätigung f.

acne ['æknɪ] n Akne f.

acorn ['eɪkɔ:n] n Eichel f.

acoustic [ə'ku:stɪk] a akustisch; ~**s** pl Akustik f.

acquaint [ə'kweɪnt] vt vertraut machen; ~**ance** (*person*) Bekannte(r) m; (*knowledge*) Kenntnis f.

acquiesce [ækwɪ'es] vi sich abfinden (*in* mit).

acquire [ə'kwaɪə*] vt erwerben.

acquisition [ækwɪ'zɪʃən] n Errungenschaft f; (*act*) Erwerb m.

acquisitive [ə'kwɪzɪtɪv] a gewinnsüchtig.

acquit [ə'kwɪt] vt (*free*) freisprechen; **to** ~ **o.s.** sich bewähren; ~**tal** Freispruch m.

acre ['eɪkə*] n Morgen m; ~**age** Fläche f.

acrimonious [ækrɪ'məʊnɪəs] a bitter.

acrobat ['ækrəbæt] n Akrobat m.

acrobatics [ækrə'bætɪks] *npl* akrobatische Kunststücke *pl.*

across [ə'krɒs] *prep* über (+*acc*); **he lives ~ the river** er wohnt auf der anderen Seite des Flusses; *ad* hinüber, herüber; **ten metres ~** zehn Meter breit; **he lives ~ from us** er wohnt uns gegenüber; **~-the-board** *a* pauschal.

act [ækt] *n* (*deed*) Tat *f*; (*Jur*) Gesetz *nt*; (*Theat*) Akt *m*; (*Theat: turn*) Nummer *f*; *vi* (*take action*) handeln; (*behave*) sich verhalten; (*pretend*) vorgeben; (*Theat*) spielen; *vt* (*in play*) spielen; **~ing** *a* stellvertretend; *n* Schauspielkunst *f*; (*performance*) Aufführung *f.*

action [ˈækʃən] *n* (*deed*) Tat *f*, Handlung *f*; (*motion*) Bewegung *f*; (*way of working*) Funktionieren *nt*; (*battle*) Einsatz *m*, Gefecht *nt*; (*lawsuit*) Klage *f*, Prozeß *m*; **to take ~** etwas unternehmen.

activate [ˈæktɪveɪt] *vt* in Betrieb setzen, aktivieren.

active [ˈæktɪv] *a* (*brisk*) rege, tatkräftig; (*working*) aktiv; (*Gram*) aktiv, Tätigkeits-; **~ly** *ad* aktiv, tätig.

activist [ˈæktɪvɪst] *n* Aktivist *m.*

activity [æk'tɪvɪtɪ] *n* Aktivität *f*; (*doings*) Unternehmungen *pl*; (*occupation*) Tätigkeit *f.*

actor [ˈæktə*] *n* Schauspieler *m.*

actress [ˈæktrɪs] *n* Schauspielerin *f.*

actual [ˈæktjʊəl] *a* wirklich; **~ly** *ad* tatsächlich; **~ly no** eigentlich nicht.

acumen [ˈækjuːmen] *n* Scharfsinn *m.*

acupuncture [ˈækjupʌŋktʃə*] *n* Akupunktur *f.*

acute [ə'kjuːt] *a* (*severe*) heftig, akut; (*keen*) scharfsinnig; **~ly** *ad* akut, scharf.

ad [æd] *n abbr of* **advertisement**.

adage [ˈædɪdʒ] *n* Sprichwort *nt.*

Adam [ˈædəm] *n* Adam *m*; **~'s apple** Adamsapfel *m.*

adamant [ˈædəmənt] *a* eisern; hartnäckig.

adapt [ə'dæpt] *vt* anpassen; *vi* sich anpassen (*to an* +*acc*); **~able** *a* anpassungsfähig; **~ation** [ædæp'teɪʃən] (*Theat etc*) Bearbeitung *f*; (*adjustment*) Anpassung *f*; **~er** (*Elec*) Zwischenstecker *m.*

add [æd] *vt* (*join*) hinzufügen; *numbers* addieren; **~ up** *vi* (*make sense*) stimmen; **~ up to** *vt* ausmachen.

addendum [ə'dendəm] *n* Zusatz *m.*

adder [ˈædə*] *n* Kreuzotter *f*, Natter *f.*

addict [ˈædɪkt] *n* Süchtige(r) *mf*; **~ed** *a* [ə'dɪktɪd] **~ed to** -süchtig; (*fig*) [ə'dɪkʃən] Sucht *f.*

adding machine [ˈædɪŋməʃiːn] *n* Addiermaschine *f.*

addition [ə'dɪʃən] *n* Anhang *m*, Addition *f*; (*Math*) Addition *f*, Zusammenzählen *nt*; **in ~** zusätzlich, außerdem; **~al** *a* zusätzlich, weiter.

additive [ˈædɪtɪv] *n* Zusatz *m.*

addled [ˈædld] *a* faul, schlecht; (*fig*) verwirrt.

address [ə'dres] *n* Adresse *f*; (*speech*) Ansprache *f*; **form of ~** Anredeform *f*; *vt letter* adressieren; (*speak to*) ansprechen; (*make speech to*) eine Ansprache halten an (+*acc*); **~ee** [ædre'siː] Empfänger(in *f*) *m*, Adressat *m.*

adenoids [ˈædənɔɪdz] *npl* Polypen *pl.*

adept [ˈædept] *a* geschickt; **to be ~ at** gut sein in (+*dat*).

adequacy [ˈædɪkwəsɪ] *n* Angemessenheit *f.*

adequate [ˈædɪkwɪt] *a* angemessen; **~ly** *ad* hinreichend.

adhere [əd'hɪə*] *vi*: **~ to** (*lit*) haften an (+*dat*); (*fig*) festhalten an (+*dat*).

adhesion [əd'hiːʒən] *n* Festhaften *nt*; (*Phys*) Adhäsion *f.*

adhesive [əd'hiːzɪv] *a* klebend; Kleb(e)-; *n* Klebstoff *m.*

adieu [ə'djuː] *n* Adieu *nt*, Lebewohl *nt.*

adjacent [ə'dʒeɪsənt] *n* benachbart.

adjective [ˈædʒəktɪv] *n* Adjektiv *nt*, Eigenschaftswort *nt.*

adjoining [ə'dʒɔɪnɪŋ] *a* benachbart, Neben-.

adjourn [ə'dʒɜːn] *vt* vertagen; *vi* abbrechen.

adjudicate [ə'dʒuːdɪkeɪt] *vti* entscheiden, ein Urteil fällen.

adjudication [ədʒuːdɪ'keɪʃən] *n* Entscheidung *f.*

adjudicator [ə'dʒuːdɪkeɪtə*] *n* Schiedsrichter *m*, Preisrichter *m.*

adjust [ə'dʒʌst] *vt* (*alter*) anpassen; (*put right*) regulieren, richtig stellen; **~able** *a* verstellbar; **~ment** (*rearrangement*) Anpassung *f*; (*settlement*) Schlichtung *f.*

adjutant [ˈædʒətənt] *n* Adjutant *m.*

ad-lib [æd'lɪb] *vi* improvisieren; *n* Improvisation *f*; *a, ad* improvisiert.

administer [əd'mɪnɪstə*] *vt* (*manage*) verwalten; (*dispense*) ausüben; *justice* sprechen; *medicine* geben.

administration [ədmɪnɪs'treɪʃən] *n* Verwaltung *f*; (*Pol*) Regierung *f.*

administrative [əd'mɪnɪstrətɪv] *a* Verwaltungs-.

administrator [əd'mɪnɪstreɪtə*] *n* Verwaltungsbeamte(r) *m.*

admirable [ˈædmərəbl] *a* bewundernswert.

admiral [ˈædmərəl] *n* Admiral *m*; **A~ty** Admiralität *f.*

admiration [ædmɪ'reɪʃən] *n* Bewunderung *f.*

admire [əd'maɪə*] *vt* (*respect*) bewundern; (*love*) verehren; **~r** Bewunderer *m.*

admission [əd'mɪʃən] *n* (*entrance*) Einlaß *f*; (*fee*) Eintritt(spreis) *m*; (*confession*) Geständnis *nt.*

admit [əd'mɪt] *vt* (*let in*) einlassen; (*confess*) gestehen; (*accept*) anerkennen; **~tance** Zulassung *f*; **~tedly** *ad* zugegebenermaßen.

ado [ə'duː] *n*: **without more ~** ohne weitere Umstände.

adolescence [ædə'lesns] *n* Jugendalter *nt.*

adolescent [ædə'lesnt] *a* heranwachsend, jugendlich; *n* Jugendliche(r) *mf.*

adopt [ə'dɒpt] *vt child* adoptieren; *idea* übernehmen; **~ion** [ə'dɒpʃən] (*of child*) Adoption *f*; (*of idea*) Übernahme *f.*

adorable [ə'dɔːrəbl] *a* anbetungswürdig; (*likeable*) entzückend.

adoration [ædo'reɪʃən] n Anbetung f; Verehrung f.

adore [ə'dɔː*] vt anbeten; verehren.

adoring [ə'dɔːrɪŋ] a verehrend.

adorn [ə'dɔːn] vt schmücken.

adornment [ə'dɔːnmənt] n Schmuck m, Verzierung f.

adrenalin [ə'drenəlɪn] n Adrenalin nt.

adrift [ə'drɪft] ad Wind und Wellen preisgegeben.

adroit [ə'drɔɪt] a gewandt.

adulation [ædju'leɪʃən] n Lobhudelei f.

adult ['ædʌlt] a erwachsen; n Erwachsene(r) mf.

adulterate [ə'dʌltəreɪt] vt verfälschen, mischen.

adultery [ə'dʌltərɪ] n Ehebruch m.

advance [ad'vɑːns] n (progress) Vorrücken nt; (money) Vorschuß m; vt (move forward) vorrücken; money vorschießen; argument vorbringen; vi vorwärtsgehen; in ~ im voraus; **in** ~ **of** vor (+dat); ~ **booking** Vorbestellung f, Vorverkauf m; ~**d** a (ahead) vorgerückt; (modern) fortgeschritten; study für Fortgeschrittene; ~**ment** Förderung f; (promotion) Beförderung f.

advantage [ad'vɑːntɪdʒ] n Vorteil m; ~**ous** [ædvən'teɪdʒəs] a vorteilhaft; **to have an** ~ **over sb** jdm gegenüber im Vorteil sein; **to be of** ~ von Nutzen sein; **to take** ~ **of** (misuse) ausnutzen; (profit from) Nutzen ziehen aus.

advent ['ædvent] n Ankunft f; **A** ~ Advent m.

adventure [ad'ventʃə*] n Abenteuer nt.

adventurous [ad'ventʃərəs] a abenteuerlich, waghalsig.

adverb ['ædvɜːb] n Adverb nt, Umstandswort nt.

adversary ['ædvəsərɪ] n Gegner m.

adverse ['ædvɜːs] a widrig.

adversity [ad'vɜːsɪtɪ] n Widrigkeit f, Mißgeschick nt.

advert ['ædvɜːt] n Anzeige f; ~**ise** vt anzeigen; vi annoncieren; ~**isement** [ad'vɜːtɪsmənt] Anzeige f, Annonce f, Inserat nt; ~**ising** Werbung f; ~**ising campaign** Werbekampagne f.

advice [ad'vaɪs] n Rat(schlag) m.

advisable [ad'vaɪzəbl] a ratsam.

advise [ad'vaɪz] vt raten (+dat); ~**r** Berater m.

advisory [ad'vaɪzərɪ] a beratend, Beratungs-.

advocate ['ædvəkeɪt] vt vertreten.

aegis ['iːdʒɪs] n: **under the** ~ **of** unter der Schirmherrschaft von.

aerial ['eərɪəl] n Antenne f; a Luft-.

aero- ['eərəʊ] pref Luft-.

aeroplane ['eərəpleɪn] n Flugzeug nt.

aerosol ['eərəsɒl] n Aerosol nt; Sprühdose f.

aesthetic [ɪs'θetɪk] a ästhetisch; ~**s** Ästhetik f.

afar [ə'fɑː*] ad: **from** ~ aus der Ferne.

affable ['æfəbl] a umgänglich.

affair [ə'feə*] n (concern) Angelegenheit f;

(event) Ereignis nt; (love —) (Liebes)verhältnis nt.

affect [ə'fekt] vt (influence) (ein)wirken auf (+acc); (move deeply) bewegen; **this change doesn't** ~ **us** diese Änderung betrifft uns nicht; ~**ation** [æfek'teɪʃən] Affektiertheit f, Verstellung f; ~**ed** a affektiert, gekünstelt; ~**ion** [ə'fekʃən] Zuneigung f; ~**ionate** [ə'fekʃənɪt] a liebevoll, lieb; ~**ionately** [ə'fekʃənɪtlɪ] ad liebevoll; ~**ionately yours** herzlichst Dein.

affiliated [ə'fɪlɪeɪtɪd] a angeschlossen (to dat).

affinity [ə'fɪnɪtɪ] n (attraction) gegenseitige Anziehung f; (relationship) Verwandtschaft f.

affirmation [æfə'meɪʃən] n Behauptung f.

affirmative [ə'fɜːmətɪv] a bestätigend; n: **in the** ~ (Gram) nicht verneint; **to answer in the** ~ mit Ja antworten.

affix [ə'fɪks] vt aufkleben, anheften.

afflict [ə'flɪkt] vt quälen, heimsuchen; ~**ion** [ə'flɪkʃən] Kummer m; (illness) Leiden nt.

affluence ['æfluəns] n (wealth) Wohlstand m.

affluent ['æfluənt] a wohlhabend, Wohlstands-.

afford [ə'fɔːd] vt (sich) leisten, erschwingen; (yield) bieten, einbringen.

affront [ə'frʌnt] n Beleidigung f; ~**ed** a beleidigt.

afield [ə'fiːld] ad: **far** ~ weit fort.

afloat [ə'fləʊt] a: **to be** ~ schwimmen.

afoot [ə'fʊt] ad im Gang.

aforesaid [ə'fɔːsed] a obengenannt.

afraid [ə'freɪd] a ängstlich; **to be** ~ **of** Angst haben vor (+dat); **to be** ~ **to** sich scheuen; **I am** ~ **I have...** ich habe leider...; **I'm** ~ **so/not** leider/leider nicht.

afresh [ə'freʃ] ad von neuem.

aft [ɑːft] ad achtern.

after ['ɑːftə*] prep nach; (following, seeking) hinter ... (dat) ... her; (in imitation) nach, im Stil von; ad: **soon** ~ bald danach; ~ **all** letzten Endes; ~-**effects** pl Nachwirkungen pl; ~**life** Leben nt nach dem Tode; ~**math** Auswirkungen pl; ~**noon** Nachmittag m; **good** ~**noon!** guten Tag!; ~-**shave** (lotion) Rasierwasser nt; ~**thought** nachträgliche(r) Einfall m; ~**wards** ad danach, nachher.

again [ə'gen] ad wieder, noch einmal; (besides) außerdem, ferner; ~ **and** ~ immer wieder.

against [ə'genst] prep gegen.

age [eɪdʒ] n (of person) Alter nt; (in history) Zeitalter nt; vi altern, alt werden; vt älter machen; **to come of** ~ mündig werden; ~**d** a ... Jahre alt, -jährig; ['eɪdʒɪd] (elderly) betagt; **the** ~**d** die Bejahrten pl; ~ **group** Altersgruppe f; Jahrgang m; ~**less** a zeitlos; ~ **limit** Altersgrenze f.

agency ['eɪdʒənsɪ] n Agentur f; Vermittlung f; (Chem) Wirkung f.

agenda [ə'dʒendə] n Tagesordnung f.

agent ['eɪdʒənt] n (Comm) Vertreter m; (spy) Agent m.

aggravate [ˈægrəveit] vt (make worse) verschlimmern; (irritate) reizen.

aggravating [ˈægrəveitiŋ] a verschlimmernd; ärgerlich.

aggravation [ægrəˈveiʃən] n Verschlimmerung f, Verärgerung f.

aggregate [ˈægrigit] n Summe f.

aggression [əˈgreʃən] n Aggression f.

aggressive a, ~ly ad [əˈgresiv, -li] aggressiv; ~ness Aggressivität f.

aggrieved [əˈgriːvd] a bedrückt, verletzt.

aghast [əˈgɑːst] a entsetzt.

agile [ˈædʒail] a flink; agil; mind rege.

agitate [ˈædʒiteit] vt rütteln; vi agitieren; ~d a aufgeregt.

agitator [ˈædʒiteitə*] n Agitator m; (pej) Hetzer m.

agnostic [ægˈnostik] n Agnostiker (in f) m.

ago [əˈgəu] ad: **two days** ~ vor zwei Tagen; **not long** ~ vor kurzem; **it's so long** ~ es ist schon so lange her.

agog [əˈgog] a, ad gespannt.

agonized [ˈægənaizd] a gequält.

agonizing [ˈægənaiziŋ] a quälend.

agony [ˈægəni] n Qual f.

agree [əˈgriː] vt date vereinbaren; vi (have same opinion, correspond) übereinstimmen (with mit); (consent) zustimmen; (be in harmony) sich vertragen; **to** ~ **to do sth** sich bereit erklären, etw zu tun; **garlic doesn't** ~ **with me** Knoblauch vertrage ich nicht; **I** ~ einverstanden, ich stimme zu; **to** ~ **on sth** sich auf etw (acc) einigen; ~able a (pleasing) liebenswürdig; (willing to consent) einverstanden; ~ably ad angenehm; ~d a vereinbart; ~ment (agreeing) Übereinstimmung f; (contract) Vereinbarung f, Vertrag m.

agricultural [ægriˈkʌltʃərəl] a landwirtschaftlich, Landwirtschafts-.

agriculture [ˈægrikʌltʃə*] n Landwirtschaft f.

aground [əˈgraund] a, ad auf Grund.

ahead [əˈhed] ad vorwärts; **to be** ~ voraus sein.

ahoy [əˈhoi] interj ahoi!

aid [eid] n (assistance) Hilfe f, Unterstützung f; (person) Hilfe f; (thing) Hilfsmittel nt; vt unterstützen, helfen (+dat); ~ **and abet** vti Beihilfe leisten (sb jdm).

aide [eid] n (person) Gehilfe m; (Mil) Adjutant m.

ailing [ˈeiliŋ] a kränkelnd.

ailment [ˈeilmənt] n Leiden nt.

aim [eim] vt gun, camera richten auf (+acc); **that was** ~**ed at you** das war auf dich gemünzt; vi (with gun) zielen; (intend) beabsichtigen; **to** ~ **at sth** etw anstreben; n (intention) Absicht f, Ziel nt; (pointing) Zielen nt, Richten nt; **to take** ~ zielen; ~**less** a, ~**lessly** ad ziellos.

air [ɛə*] n Luft f, Atmosphäre f; (manner) Miene f, Anschein m; (Mus) Melodie f; vt lüften; (fig) an die Öffentlichkeit bringen; ~**bed** Luftmatratze f; ~**-conditioned** a mit Klimaanlage; ~**-conditioning** Klimaanlage f; ~**craft** Flugzeug nt, Maschine f; ~**craft carrier** Flugzeugträger m; ~ **force** Luftwaffe f; ~**gun** Luftgewehr nt; ~ **hostess**

Stewardeß f; ~**ily** ad leichtfertig; ~**letter** Luftpost(leicht)brief m; ~**line** Luftverkehrsgesellschaft f; ~**liner** Verkehrsflugzeug nt; ~**lock** Luftblase f; by ~**mail** mit Luftpost; ~**port** Flughafen m, Flugplatz m; ~ **raid** Luftangriff m; ~**sick** a luftkrank; ~**strip** Landestreifen m; ~**tight** a luftdicht; ~**y** a luftig; manner leichtfertig.

aisle [ail] n Gang m.

ajar [əˈdʒɑː*] ad angelehnt; ein Spalt offen.

alabaster [ˈæləbɑːstə*] n Alabaster m.

à la carte [ælæˈkɑːt] a nach der (Speise)karte, à la carte.

alacrity [əˈlækriti] n Bereitwilligkeit f.

alarm [əˈlɑːm] n (warning) Alarm m; (bell etc) Alarmanlage f; vt erschrecken; ~ **clock** Wecker m; ~**ing** a beängstigend; ~**ist** Bangemacher m.

alas [əˈlæs] interj ach.

album [ˈælbəm] n Album nt.

alcohol [ˈælkəhol] n Alkohol m; ~**ic** [ælkəˈholik] a drink alkoholisch; n Alkoholiker(in f) m; ~**ism** Alkoholismus m.

alcove [ˈælkəuv] n Alkoven m.

alderman [ˈɔːldəmən] n Stadtrat m.

ale [eil] n Ale nt.

alert [əˈlɜːt] a wachsam; n Alarm m; ~**ness** Wachsamkeit f.

algebra [ˈældʒibrə] n Algebra f.

alias [ˈeiliəs] ad alias; n Deckname m.

alibi [ˈælibai] n Alibi nt.

alien [ˈeiliən] n Ausländer m; (foreign) ausländisch; (strange) fremd; ~**ate** vt entfremden; ~**ation** [eiliəˈneiʃən] Entfremdung f.

alight [əˈlait] a, ad brennend; (of building) in Flammen; vi (descend) aussteigen; (bird) sich setzen.

align [əˈlain] vt ausrichten; ~**ment** Ausrichtung f; Gruppierung f.

alike [əˈlaik] a gleich, ähnlich; ad gleich, ebenso.

alimony [ˈæliməni] n Unterhalt m, Alimente pl.

alive [əˈlaiv] a (living) lebend; (lively) lebendig, aufgeweckt; (full of) voll (with von), wimmelnd (with von).

alkali [ˈælkəlai] n Alkali nt.

all [ɔːl] a (every one of) alle; n (the whole) alles, das Ganze; ~ **of the books** alle Bücher; ad (completely) vollkommen, ganz; **it's** ~ **mine** das gehört alles mir; **it's** ~ **over** es ist alles aus or vorbei; ~ **around the edge** rund um den Rand; ~ **at once** auf einmal; ~ **but** alle(s) außer; (almost) fast; ~ **in** alles in allem; ~ **over town** in der ganzen Stadt; ~ **right** okay, in Ordnung; **not at** ~ ganz und gar nicht; (don't mention it) bitte.

allay [əˈlei] vt fears beschwichtigen.

allegation [æliˈgeiʃən] n Behauptung f.

allege [əˈledʒ] vt (declare) behaupten; (falsely) vorgeben; ~**dly** [əˈledʒidli] ad angeblich.

allegiance [əˈliːdʒəns] n Treue f, Ergebenheit f.

allegory [ˈæligəri] n Allegorie f.

all-embracing [ˈɔːlimˈbreisiŋ] a allumfassend.

allergic [ə'lɜːdʒɪk] *a* allergisch (*to* gegen).

allergy ['ælədʒɪ] *n* Allergie *f*.

alleviate [ə'liːvɪeɪt] *vt* erleichtern, lindern.

alleviation [əliːvɪ'eɪʃən] *n* Erleichterung *f*.

alley ['ælɪ] *n* Gasse *f*, Durchgang *m*.

alliance [ə'laɪəns] *n* Bund *m*, Allianz *f*.

allied ['ælaɪd] *a* vereinigt; *powers* alliiert; verwandt (*to* mit).

alligator ['ælɪgeɪtə*] *n* Alligator *m*.

all-important ['ɔːlɪm'pɔːtənt] *a* äußerst wichtig.

all-in ['ɔːlɪn] *a, ad charge* alles inbegriffen, Gesamt-; (*exhausted*) erledigt, kaputt.

alliteration [əlɪtə'reɪʃən] *n* Alliteration *f*, Stabreim *m*.

all-night ['ɔːl'naɪt] *a café, cinema* die ganze Nacht geöffnet, Nacht-.

allocate ['æləkeɪt] *vt* zuweisen, zuteilen.

allocation [ælə'keɪʃən] *n* Zuteilung *f*.

allot [ə'lɒt] *vt* zuteilen; **~ment** (*share*) Anteil *m*; (*plot*) Schrebergarten *m*.

all-out ['ɔːl'aʊt] *a, ad* total.

allow [ə'laʊ] *vt* (*permit*) erlauben, gestatten (*sb* jdm); (*grant*) bewilligen; (*deduct*) abziehen; **~ for** *vt* berücksichtigen, einplanen; **~ances for** berücksichtigen.

alloy ['ælɔɪ] *n* Metallegierung *f*.

all-round ['ɔːl'raʊnd] *a sportsman* allseitig, Allround-.

all-rounder ['ɔːl'raʊndə*] *n* (*Sport*) vielseitige(r) Sportler; (*general*) Allerweltskerl *m*.

all-time ['ɔːl'taɪm] *a record, high ...* aller Zeiten, Höchst-.

allude [ə'luːd] *vi* hinweisen, anspielen (*to* auf +*acc*).

alluring [ə'ljʊərɪŋ] *a* verlockend.

allusion [ə'luːʒən] *n* Anspielung *f*, Andeutung *f*.

alluvium [ə'luːvɪəm] *n* Schwemmland *nt*.

ally ['ælaɪ] *n* Verbündete(r) *mf*; (*Pol*) Alliierte(r) *m*.

almanac ['ɔːlmənæk] *n* Kalender *m*.

almighty [ɔːl'maɪtɪ] *a* allmächtig; **the A~** der Allmächtige.

almond ['ɑːmənd] *n* Mandel *f*.

almost ['ɔːlməʊst] *ad* fast, beinahe.

alms [ɑːmz] *n* Almosen *nt*.

alone [ə'ləʊn] *a, ad* allein.

along [ə'lɒŋ] *prep* entlang, längs; *ad* (*onward*) vorwärts, weiter; **~ with** zusammen mit; **~side** *ad walk* nebenher; *come* nebendran; *be* daneben; *prep* (*walk, compared with*) neben (+*dat*); (*come*) neben (+*acc*); (*be*) entlang, neben (+*dat*); (*of ship*) längsseits (+*gen*); **~ the river** den Fluß entlang; **I knew all ~** ich wußte die ganze Zeit.

aloof [ə'luːf] *a* zurückhaltend; *ad fern*; **~ness** Zurückhaltung *f*, Sich-Fernhalten *nt*.

aloud [ə'laʊd] *ad* laut.

alphabet ['ælfəbet] *n* Alphabet *nt*; **~ical** [ælfə'betɪkl] *a* alphabetisch.

alpine ['ælpaɪn] *a* alpin, Alpen-.

already [ɔːl'redɪ] *ad* schon, bereits.

also ['ɔːlsəʊ] *ad* auch, außerdem.

altar ['ɔːltə*] *n* Altar *m*.

alter ['ɔːltə*] *vti* ändern; *dress* umändern; **~ation** [ɔːltə'reɪʃən] Änderung *f*, Umänderung *f*; (*to building*) Umbau *m*.

alternate [ɒl'tɜːnɪt] *a* abwechselnd; [ɒltə'neɪt] *vi* abwechseln (*with* mit); **~ly** *ad* abwechselnd, wechselweise.

alternative [ɒl'tɜːnətɪv] *a* andere(r, s); *n* (Aus)wahl *f*, Alternative *f*; **what's the ~?** welche Alternative gibt es?; **we have no ~** uns bleibt keine andere Wahl; **~ly** *ad* im anderen Falle.

although [ɔːl'ðəʊ] *cj* obwohl, wenn auch.

altitude ['ælɪtjuːd] *n* Höhe *f*.

alto ['æltəʊ] *n* Alt *m*.

altogether [ɔːltə'geðə*] *ad* (*on the whole*) im ganzen genommen; (*entirely*) ganz und gar.

altruistic [æltrʊ'ɪstɪk] *a* uneigennützig, altruistisch.

aluminium [æljʊ'mɪnɪəm], (US) **aluminum** [ə'luːmɪnəm] *n* Aluminium *nt*.

always ['ɔːlweɪz] *ad immer*; **it was ~ that way** es war schon immer so.

amalgam [ə'mælgəm] *n* Amalgam *nt*; (*fig*) Mischung *f*.

amalgamate [ə'mælgəmeɪt] *vi* (*combine*) sich vereinigen; *vt* (*mix*) amalgamieren.

amalgamation [əmælgə'meɪʃən] *n* Verschmelzung *f*, Zusammenschluß *m*.

amass [ə'mæs] *vt* anhäufen.

amateur ['æmətə*] *n* Amateur *m*; (*pej*) Amateur *m*, Bastler *m*, Stümper *m*; *a* Amateur-, Bastler-; **~ish** *a* (*pej*) dilettantisch, stümperhaft.

amaze [ə'meɪz] *vt* erstaunen, in Staunen versetzen; **~ment** höchste(s) (Er)staunen *nt*.

amazing [ə'meɪzɪŋ] *a* höchst erstaunlich.

ambassador [æm'bæsədə*] *n* Botschafter *m*.

amber ['æmbə*] *n* Bernstein *m*.

ambidextrous [æmbɪ'dekstrəs] *a* beidhändig.

ambiguity [æmbɪ'gjuːɪtɪ] *n* Zweideutigkeit *f*, Unklarheit *f*.

ambiguous [æm'bɪgjʊəs] *a* zweideutig; (*not clear*) unklar.

ambition [æm'bɪʃən] *n* Ehrgeiz *m*.

ambitious [æm'bɪʃəs] *a* ehrgeizig.

ambivalent [æm'bɪvələnt] *n* attitude zwiespältig.

amble ['æmbl] *vi* schlendern.

ambulance ['æmbjʊləns] *n* Krankenwagen *m*.

ambush ['æmbʊʃ] *n* Hinterhalt *m*; *vt* aus dem Hinterhalt angreifen, überfallen.

ameliorate [ə'miːlɪəreɪt] *vt* verbessern.

amelioration [əmiːlɪə'reɪʃən] *n* Verbesserung *f*.

amen ['ɑː'men] *interj* amen.

amenable [ə'miːnəbl] *a* gefügig; (*to reason*) zugänglich (*to dat*); (*to flattery*) empfänglich (*to für*); (*to law*) unterworfen (*to dat*).

amend [ə'mend] *vt law etc* abändern, ergänzen; **to make ~s** etw wiedergutmachen; **~ment** Abänderung *f*.

amenity [ə'miːnɪtɪ] *n* (moderne) Einrichtung *f*.

Americanize [ə'merɪkənaɪz] *vt* amerikanisieren.

amethyst ['æmɪθɪst] *n* Amethyst *m*.

amiable ['eɪmɪəbl] *a* liebenswürdig, sympathisch.

amicable ['æmɪkəbl] *a* freundschaftlich; *settlement* gütlich.

amid(st) [ə'mɪd(st)] *prep* mitten in *or* unter (+*dat*).

amiss [ə'mɪs] *a* verkehrt, nicht richtig; *ad* **to take sth ~** etw übelnehmen.

ammeter ['æmɪtə*] *n* (Aut) Amperemeter *m*.

ammunition [æmju'nɪʃən] *n* Munition *f*.

amnesia [æm'niːzɪə] *n* Gedächtnisverlust *m*.

amnesty ['æmnɪstɪ] *n* Amnestie *f*.

amock [ə'mɒk] *ad see* **amuck**.

amoeba [ə'miːbə] *n* Amöbe *f*.

among(st) [ə'mʌŋ(st)] *prep* unter.

amoral [æ'mɒrəl] *a* unmoralisch.

amorous ['æmərəs] *a* verliebt.

amorphous [ə'mɔːfəs] *a* formlos, gestaltlos.

amount [ə'maʊnt] *n* (of money) Betrag *m*; (of time, energy) Aufwand *m* (of an +*dat*); (of water, sand) Menge *f*; **no ~ of ...** kein(e) ... .; *vi*: **~ to** (total) sich belaufen auf (+*acc*); **this ~s to treachery** das kommt Verrat gleich; **it ~s to the same** es läuft aufs gleiche hinaus; **he won't ~ to much** aus ihm wird nie was.

amp [æmp] *n*, **ampere** ['æmpɛə*] *n* Ampere *nt*.

amphibious [æm'fɪbɪəs] *a* amphibisch, Amphibien-.

amphitheatre ['æmfɪθɪətə*] *n* Amphitheater *nt*.

ample ['æmpl] *a* portion reichlich; *dress* weit, groß; **~ time** genügend Zeit.

amplifier ['æmplɪfaɪə*] *n* Verstärker *m*.

amply ['æmplɪ] *ad* reichlich.

amputate ['æmpjuteɪt] *vt* amputieren, abnehmen.

amuck [ə'mʌk] *ad*: **to run ~** Amok laufen.

amuse [ə'mjuːz] *vt* (entertain) unterhalten; (make smile) belustigen; (occupy) unterhalten; **I'm not ~d** das find' ich gar nicht lustig; **if that ~s you** wenn es dir Spaß macht; **~ment** (feeling) Unterhaltung *f*; (recreation) Zeitvertreib *m*.

amusing [ə'mjuːzɪŋ] *a* amüsant, unterhaltend.

an [æn, ən] *indef art* ein(e).

anaemia [ə'niːmɪə] *n* Anämie *f*.

anaemic [ə'niːmɪk] *a* blutarm.

anaesthetic [ænɪs'θetɪk] *n* Betäubungsmittel *nt*; *under* **~** unter Narkose.

anagram ['ænəgræm] *n* Anagramm *nt*.

analgesic [ænæl'dʒiːsɪk] *n* schmerzlindernde(s) Mittel *nt*.

analogous [ə'næləgəs] *a* analog.

analogy [ə'nælədʒɪ] *n* Analogie *f*.

analyse ['ænəlaɪz] *vt* analysieren.

analysis [ə'næləsɪs] *n* Analyse *f*.

analytic [ænə'lɪtɪk] *a* analytisch.

anarchist ['ænəkɪst] *n* Anarchist(in *f*) *m*.

anarchy ['ænəkɪ] *n* Anarchie *f*.

anathema [ə'næθɪmə] *n* (fig) Greuel *nt*.

anatomical [ænə'tɒmɪkəl] *a* anatomisch.

anatomy [ə'nætəmɪ] *n* (structure) anatomische(r) Aufbau *m*; (study) Anatomie *f*.

ancestor ['ænsestə*] *n* Vorfahr *m*.

ancestral [æn'sestrəl] *n* angestammt, Ahnen-.

ancestry ['ænsɪstrɪ] *n* Abstammung *f*; Vorfahren *pl*.

anchor ['æŋkə*] *n* Anker *m*; *vi* ankern, vor Anker liegen; *vt* verankern; **~age** Ankerplatz *m*.

anchovy ['æntʃəvɪ] *n* Sardelle *f*.

ancient ['eɪnʃənt] *a* alt; *car etc* uralt.

and [ænd, ənd, ən] *cj* und.

anecdote ['ænɪkdəʊt] *n* Anekdote *f*.

anemia [ə'niːmɪə] *n* (US) = **anaemia**.

anemone [ə'neməni] *n* Anemone *f*.

anesthetic [ænɪs'θetɪk] *n* (US) = **anaesthetic**.

anew [ə'njuː] *ad* von neuem.

angel ['eɪndʒəl] *n* Engel *m*; **~ic** [æn'dʒelɪk] *a* engelhaft.

anger ['æŋgə*] *n* Zorn *m*; *vt* ärgern.

angina [æn'dʒaɪnə] *n* Angina *f*, Halsentzündung *f*.

angle ['æŋgl] *n* Winkel *m*; (point of view) Standpunkt *m*; **at an ~** nicht gerade; *vt* stellen; **to ~ for** aussein auf (+*acc*); **~r** Angler *m*.

Anglican ['æŋglɪkən] *a* anglikanisch; *n* Anglikaner(in *f*) *m*.

anglicize ['æŋglɪsaɪz] *vt* anglisieren.

angling ['æŋglɪŋ] *n* Angeln *nt*.

Anglo- ['æŋgləʊ] *pref* Anglo-.

angrily ['æŋgrɪlɪ] *ad* ärgerlich, böse.

angry ['æŋgrɪ] *a* ärgerlich, ungehalten, böse; *wound* entzündet.

anguish ['æŋgwɪʃ] *n* Qual *f*.

angular ['æŋgjʊlə*] *a* eckig, winkelförmig; *face* kantig.

animal ['ænɪməl] *n* Tier *nt*; (living creature) Lebewesen *nt*; *a* tierisch, animalisch.

animate ['ænɪmeɪt] *vt* beleben; ['ænɪmət] *a* lebhaft; **~d** *a* lebendig; *film* Zeichentrick-.

animation [ænɪ'meɪʃən] *n* Lebhaftigkeit *f*.

animosity [ænɪ'mɒsɪtɪ] *n* Feindseligkeit *f*, Abneigung *f*.

aniseed ['ænɪsiːd] *n* Anis *m*.

ankle ['æŋkl] *n* (Fuß)knöchel *m*.

annex ['æneks] *n* Anbau *m*; [ə'neks] *vt* anfügen; (Pol) annektieren, angliedern.

annihilate [ə'naɪəleɪt] *vt* vernichten.

anniversary [ænɪ'vɜːsərɪ] *n* Jahrestag *m*.

annotate ['ænəteɪt] *vt* kommentieren.

announce [ə'naʊns] *vt* ankündigen, anzeigen; **~ment** Ankündigung *f*; (official) Bekanntmachung *f*; **~r** Ansager(in *f*) *m*.

annoy [ə'nɔɪ] *vt* ärgern; **~ance** Ärgernis *nt*, Störung *f*; **~ing** *a* ärgerlich; *person* lästig.

annual ['ænjʊəl] *a* jährlich; *salary* Jahres-; *n* (plant) einjährige Pflanze *f*; (book) Jahrbuch *nt*; **~ly** *ad* jährlich.

annuity [ə'njuːɪtɪ] *n* Jahresrente *f*.

annul [ə'nʌl] *vt* aufheben, annullieren; **~ment** Aufhebung *f*, Annullierung *f*.

anoint [ə'nɔɪnt] vt salben.

anomalous [ə'nɒmələs] a unregelmäßig, anomal.

anomaly [ə'nɒməlɪ] n Abweichung f von der Regel.

anon [ə'nɒn] a = **anonymous.**

anonymity [ænə'nɪmɪtɪ] n Anonymität f.

anonymous [ə'nɒnɪməs] a anonym.

anorak ['ænəræk] n Anorak m, Windjacke f.

another [ə'nʌðə*] a, pron (different) ein(e) andere(r, s); (additional) noch eine(r, s).

answer ['ɑ:nsə*] n Antwort f; vi antworten; (on phone) sich melden; vt person antworten (+dat); letter, question beantworten; telephone gehen an (+acc), abnehmen; door öffnen; ~**able** a beantwortbar; (responsible) verantwortlich, haftbar; ~ **back** vi frech sein; to ~ for sth für etw verantwortlich sein; to ~ to the name of auf den Namen... hören.

ant [ænt] n Ameise f.

antagonism [æn'tægənɪzəm] n Antagonismus m.

antagonist [æn'tægənɪst] n Gegner m, Antagonist m; ~**ic** [æntægə'nɪstɪk] a feindselig.

antagonize [æn'tægənaɪz] vt reizen.

anteater ['æntiːtə*] n Ameisenbär m.

antecedent [æntɪ'siːdənt] n Vorhergehende(s) nt; ~**s** pl Vorleben nt, Vorgeschichte f.

antelope ['æntɪləʊp] n Antilope f.

antenatal [æntɪ'neɪtl] a vor der Geburt.

antenna [æn'tenə] n (Biol) Fühler m; (Rad) Antenne f.

anteroom ['æntɪrʊm] n Vorzimmer nt.

anthem ['ænθəm] n Hymne f.

anthology [æn'θɒlədʒɪ] n Gedichtsammlung f, Anthologie f.

anthropologist [ænθrə'pɒlədʒɪst] n Anthropologe m.

anthropology [ænθrə'pɒlədʒɪ] n Anthropologie f.

anti- ['æntɪ] pref Gegen-, Anti-.

anti-aircraft ['æntɪ'eəkrɑːft] a Flugabwehr-.

antibiotic ['æntɪbaɪ'ɒtɪk] n Antibiotikum nt.

anticipate [æn'tɪsɪpeɪt] vt (expect) trouble, question erwarten, rechnen mit; (look forward to) sich freuen auf (+acc); (do first) vorwegnehmen; (foresee) ahnen, vorhersehen.

anticipation [æntɪsɪ'peɪʃən] n Erwartung f; (foreshadowing) Vorwegnahme f; that was good ~ das war gut vorausgesehen.

anticlimax ['æntɪ'klaɪmæks] n Ernüchterung f.

anticlockwise ['æntɪ'klɒkwaɪz] a entgegen dem Uhrzeigersinn.

antics ['æntɪks] npl Possen pl.

anticyclone ['æntɪ'saɪkləʊn] n Hoch nt, Hochdruckgebiet nt.

antidote ['æntɪdəʊt] n Gegenmittel nt.

antifreeze ['æntɪfriːz] n Frostschutzmittel nt.

antipathy [æn'tɪpəθɪ] n Abneigung f, Antipathie f.

antiquarian [æntɪ'kweərɪən] a altertümlich; n Antiquitätensammler m.

antiquated ['æntɪkweɪtɪd] a antiquiert.

antique [æn'tiːk] n Antiquität f; a antik; (old-fashioned) altmodisch.

antiquity [æn'tɪkwɪtɪ] n Antike f, Altertum nt.

antiseptic [æntɪ'septɪk] n Antiseptikum nt; a antiseptisch.

antisocial [æntɪ'səʊʃl] a person ungesellig; law unsozial.

antithesis [æn'tɪθɪsɪs] n Gegensatz m, Antithese f.

antlers ['æntləz] npl Geweih nt.

anus ['eɪnəs] n After m.

anvil ['ænvɪl] n Amboß m.

anxiety [æŋ'zaɪətɪ] n Angst f; (worry) Sorge f.

anxious ['æŋkʃəs] a ängstlich; (worried) besorgt; ~**ly** ad besorgt; to be ~ to do sth etw unbedingt tun wollen.

any ['enɪ] a: take ~ one nimm irgendein(e,n,s); do you want ~ apples? willst du Äpfel (haben)?; do you want ~? willst du welche?; not ~ keine; ad: ~ faster schneller; ~**body** pron irgend jemand; (everybody) jedermann; ~**how** ad sowieso, ohnehin; (carelessly) einfach so; ~**one** pron = ~**body**; ~**thing** pron irgend etwas; ~**time** ad jederzeit; ~**way** ad sowieso, ohnehin; ~**way, let's stop** na ja or sei's drum, hören wir auf; ~**where** ad irgendwo; (everywhere) überall.

apace [ə'peɪs] ad rasch.

apart [ə'pɑːt] ad (parted) auseinander; (away) beiseite, abseits; ~ **from** außer.

apartheid [ə'pɑːteɪt] n Apartheid f.

apartment [ə'pɑːtmənt] n (US) Wohnung f; ~**s** pl (möblierte Miet)wohnung f.

apathetic [æpə'θetɪk] a teilnahmslos, apathisch.

apathy ['æpəθɪ] n Teilnahmslosigkeit f, Apathie f.

ape [eɪp] n (Menschen)affe m; vt nachahmen.

aperitif [ə'perɪtɪv] n Aperitif m.

aperture ['æpətjʊə*] n Öffnung f; (Phot) Blende f.

apex ['eɪpeks] n Spitze f, Scheitelpunkt m.

aphorism ['æfərɪzəm] n Aphorismus m.

aphrodisiac [æfrəʊ'dɪzɪæk] n Aphrodisiakum nt.

apiece [ə'piːs] ad pro Stück; (per person) pro Kopf.

aplomb [ə'plɒm] n selbstbewußte(s) Auftreten nt.

apocryphal [ə'pɒkrɪfəl] a apokryph, unecht.

apologetic [əpɒlə'dʒetɪk] a entschuldigend; to be ~ sich sehr entschuldigen.

apologize [ə'pɒlədʒaɪz] vi sich entschuldigen.

apology [ə'pɒlədʒɪ] n Entschuldigung f.

apoplexy ['æpəpleksɪ] n Schlaganfall m.

apostle [ə'pɒsl] n Apostel m; (pioneer) Vorkämpfer m.

apostrophe [ə'pɒstrəfɪ] n Apostroph m.

appal [ə'pɔ:l] vt erschrecken; ~**ling** a schrecklich.

apparatus ['æpəreɪtəs] n Apparat m, Gerät nt.

apparent [ə'pærənt] a offenbar; ~**ly** ad anscheinend.

apparition [æpə'rɪʃən] n (ghost) Erscheinung f, Geist m; (appearance) Erscheinen nt.

appeal [ə'pi:l] vi dringend ersuchen; dringend bitten (for um); sich wenden (to an +acc); (to public) appellieren (to an +acc); (Jur) Berufung einlegen; n Aufruf m; (Jur) Berufung f; ~**ing** a ansprechend.

appear [ə'pɪə*] vi (come into sight) erscheinen; (be seen) auftauchen; (seem) scheinen; ~**ance** (coming into sight) Erscheinen nt; (outward show) Äußere(s) nt; to put in or make an ~ance sich zeigen.

appease [ə'pi:z] vt beschwichtigen.

appendage [ə'pendɪdʒ] n Anhang m, Anhängsel nt.

appendicitis [əpendɪ'saɪtɪs] n Blinddarmentzündung f.

appendix [ə'pendɪks] n (in book) Anhang m; (Med) Blinddarm m.

appetite ['æpɪtaɪt] n Appetit m; (fig) Lust f.

appetizing ['æpɪtaɪzɪŋ] a appetitanregend.

applaud [ə'plɔ:d] vti Beifall klatschen (+dat), applaudieren.

applause [ə'plɔ:z] n Beifall m, Applaus m.

apple ['æpl] n Apfel m; ~ tree Apfelbaum m.

appliance [ə'plaɪəns] n Gerät nt.

applicable [ə'plɪkəbl] a anwendbar; (in forms) zutreffend.

applicant ['æplɪkənt] n Bewerber(in f) m.

application [æplɪ'keɪʃən] n (request) Antrag m; (for job) Bewerbung f; (putting into practice) Anwendung f; (hard work) Fleiß m.

applied [ə'plaɪd] a angewandt.

apply [ə'plaɪ] vi (ask) sich wenden (to an +acc), sich melden; (be suitable) zutreffen; vt (place on) auflegen; cream auftragen; (put into practice) anwenden; (devote o.s.) sich widmen (+dat).

appoint [ə'pɔɪnt] vt (to office) ernennen, berufen; (settle) festsetzen; ~**ment** (meeting) Verabredung f; (at hairdresser etc) Bestellung f; (in business) Termin m; (choice for a position) Ernennung f; (Univ) Berufung f.

apportion [ə'pɔ:ʃən] vt zuteilen.

appreciable [ə'pri:ʃəbl] a (perceptible) merklich; (able to be estimated) abschätzbar.

appreciate [ə'pri:ʃɪeɪt] vt (value) zu schätzen wissen; (understand) einsehen; vi (increase in value) im Wert steigen.

appreciation [əpri:ʃɪ'eɪʃən] n Wertschätzung f; (Comm) Wertzuwachs m.

appreciative [ə'pri:ʃɪətɪv] a (showing thanks) dankbar; (showing liking) anerkennend.

apprehend [æprɪ'hend] vt (arrest) festnehmen; (understand) erfassen.

apprehension [æprɪ'henʃən] n Angst f.

apprehensive [æprɪ'hensɪv] a furchtsam.

apprentice [ə'prentɪs] n Lehrling m; ~**ship** Lehrzeit f.

approach [ə'prəʊtʃ] vi sich nähern; vt herantreten an (+acc); problem herangehen an (+acc); n Annäherung f; (to problem) Ansatz m; (path) Zugang m, Zufahrt f; ~**able** a zugänglich.

approbation [æprə'beɪʃən] n Billigung f.

appropriate [ə'prəʊprɪeɪt] vt (take for o.s.) sich aneignen; (set apart) bereitstellen; [ə'prəʊprɪət] a angemessen; remark angebracht; ~**ly** [ə'prəʊprɪətlɪ] ad passend.

approval [ə'pru:vəl] n (show of satisfaction) Beifall m; (permission) Billigung f; (Comm) on ~ bei Gefallen.

approve [ə'pru:v] vti billigen (of acc); I don't ~ of it/him ich halte nichts davon/von ihm.

approximate [ə'prɒksɪmɪt] a annähernd, ungefähr; [ə'prɒksɪmeɪt] vt nahekommen (+dat); ~**ly** ad rund, ungefähr.

approximation [əprɒksɪ'meɪʃən] n Annäherung f.

apricot ['eɪprɪkɒt] n Aprikose f.

April ['eɪprəl] n April m.

apron ['eɪprən] n Schürze f.

apt [æpt] a (suitable) passend; (able) begabt; (likely) geneigt.

aptitude ['æptɪtju:d] n Begabung f.

aqualung ['ækwəlʌŋ] n Unterwasseratmungsgerät nt.

aquarium [ə'kwɛərɪəm] n Aquarium nt.

Aquarius [ə'kwɛərɪəs] n Wassermann m.

aquatic [ə'kwætɪk] a Wasser-.

aqueduct ['ækwɪdʌkt] n Aquädukt nt.

arable ['ærəbl] a bebaubar, Kultur-.

arbiter ['ɑ:bɪtə*] n (Schieds)richter m.

arbitrary ['ɑ:bɪtrərɪ] a willkürlich.

arbitrate ['ɑ:bɪtreɪt] vti schlichten.

arbitration [ɑ:bɪ'treɪʃən] n Schlichtung f; to go to ~ vor ein Schiedsgericht gehen.

arbitrator ['ɑ:bɪtreɪtə*] n Schiedsrichter m, Schlichter m.

arc [ɑ:k] n Bogen m.

arcade [ɑ:'keɪd] n Säulengang m.

arch [ɑ:tʃ] n Bogen m; vt überwölben; back krumm machen; vi sich wölben; a durchtrieben; ~ enemy Erzfeind m.

archaeologist [ɑ:kɪ'ɒlədʒɪst] n Archäologe m.

archaeology [ɑ:kɪ'ɒlədʒɪ] n Archäologie f.

archaic [ɑ:'keɪɪk] a altertümlich.

archbishop ['ɑ:tʃbɪʃəp] n Erzbischof m.

archer ['ɑ:tʃə*] n Bogenschütze m; ~**y** Bogenschießen nt.

archipelago [ɑ:kɪ'pelɪgəʊ] n Archipel m; (sea) Inselmeer nt.

architect ['ɑ:kɪtekt] n Architekt(in f) m; ~**ural** [ɑ:kɪ'tektərəl] a architektonisch; ~**ure** Architektur f.

archives ['ɑ:kaɪvz] npl Archiv nt.

archivist ['ɑ:kɪvɪst] n Archivar m.

archway ['ɑ:tʃweɪ] n Bogen m.

ardent ['ɑ:dənt] a glühend.

ardour ['ɑ:də*] n Eifer m.

arduous ['ɑ:djʊəs] a mühsam.

are [ɑ:*] see be.

area ['ɛərɪə] n Fläche f; (of land) Gebiet nt;

(part of sth) Teil m, Abschnitt m.
arena [ə'ri:nə] n Arena f.
aren't [ɑ:nt] = are not.
arguable ['ɑ:gjʊəbl] a (doubtful)
diskutabel; (possible) it's ~ that ... man
könnte argumentieren daß ...
argue ['ɑ:gju:] vt case vertreten; vi diskutieren; (angrily) streiten; **don't** ~! keine
Widerrede!; **to** ~ **with sb** sich mit jdm
streiten.
argument ['ɑ:gjʊmənt] n (theory)
Argument nt; (reasoning) Argumentation
f; (row) Auseinandersetzung f, Streit m;
~**ative** [ɑ:gjʊ'mentətɪv] a streitlustig; **to
have an** ~ sich streiten.
aria ['ɑ:rɪə] n Arie f.
arid ['ærɪd] a trocken; ~**ity** [ə'rɪdɪtɪ] n
Dürre f.
Aries ['eəri:z] n Widder m.
arise [ə'raɪz] vi irreg aufsteigen; (get up)
aufstehen; (difficulties etc) entstehen;
(case) vorkommen; **to** ~ **out of sth**
herrühren von etw.
aristocracy [ærɪs'tɒkrəsɪ] n Adel m,
Aristokratie f.
aristocrat ['ærɪstəkræt] n Adlige(r) mf,
Aristokrat(in f) m; ~**ic** [ærɪstə'krætɪk] a
adlig, aristokratisch.
arithmetic [ə'rɪθmətɪk] n Rechnen nt,
Arithmetik f.
ark [ɑ:k] n: **Noah's A** ~ die Arche Noah.
arm [ɑ:m] n Arm m; (branch of military service) Zweig m; vt bewaffnen; ~**s** pl
(weapons) Waffen pl; ~**chair** Lehnstuhl
m; ~**ed** a forces Streit-, bewaffnet; robbery
bewaffnet; ~**ful** Armvoll m.
armistice ['ɑ:mɪstɪs] n Waffenstillstand m.
armour ['ɑ:mə*] n (knight's) Rüstung f;
(Mil) Panzerplatte f; ~**y** Waffenlager nt;
(factory) Waffenfabrik f.
armpit ['ɑ:mpɪt] n Achselhöhle f.
army ['ɑ:mɪ] n Armee f, Heer nt; (host)
Heer m.
aroma [ə'rəʊmə] n Duft m, Aroma nt; ~**tic**
[ærə'mætɪk] a aromatisch, würzig.
around [ə'raʊnd] ad ringsherum; (almost)
ungefähr; prep um ... herum; **is he** ~? ist
er hier?
arouse [ə'raʊz] vt wecken.
arrange [ə'reɪndʒ] vt time, meeting
festsetzen; holidays festlegen; flowers, hair,
objects anordnen; **I** ~**d to meet him** ich
habe mit ihm ausgemacht, ihn zu treffen;
it's all ~**d** es ist alles arrangiert;
~**ment** (order) Reihenfolge f; (agreement) Übereinkommen nt; (plan) Vereinbarung f.
array [ə'reɪ] n Aufstellung f.
arrears [ə'rɪəz] npl (of debts) Rückstand
m; (of work) Unerledigte(s) nt; **in** ~ im
Rückstand.
arrest [ə'rest] vt person verhaften; (stop)
aufhalten; n Verhaftung f; **under** ~ in
Haft; **you're under** ~ Sie sind verhaftet.
arrival [ə'raɪvəl] n Ankunft f.
arrive [ə'raɪv] vi ankommen (at in +dat,
bei); **to** ~ **at a decision** zu einer Entscheidung kommen.
arrogance ['ærəgəns] n Überheblichkeit f,
Arroganz f.

arrogant ['ærəgənt] a anmaßend, arrogant.
arrow ['ærəʊ] n Pfeil m.
arse [ɑ:s] n (col) Arsch m.
arsenal ['ɑ:sɪnl] n Waffenlager nt, Zeug-
haus nt.
arsenic ['ɑ:snɪk] n Arsen nt.
arson ['ɑ:sn] n Brandstiftung f.
art [ɑ:t] n Kunst f; ~**s** pl Geisteswissen-
schaften pl; ~ **gallery** Kunstgalerie f.
artery ['ɑ:tərɪ] n Schlagader f, Arterie f.
artful ['ɑ:tfʊl] a verschlagen.
arthritis [ɑ:'θraɪtɪs] n Arthritis f.
artichoke ['ɑ:tɪtʃəʊk] n Artischocke f.
article ['ɑ:tɪkl] n (Press, Gram) Artikel m;
(thing) Gegenstand m, Artikel m; (clause)
Abschnitt m, Paragraph m.
articulate [ɑ:'tɪkjʊlɪt] a (able to express
o.s.) redegewandt; (speaking clearly) deutlich, verständlich; **to be** ~ sich gut ausdrücken können; [ɑ:'tɪkjʊleɪt] vt (connect)
zusammenfügen, gliedern; ~**d vehicle**
Sattelschlepper m.
artifice ['ɑ:tɪfɪs] n (skill) Kunstgriff m;
(trick) Kniff m, List f.
artificial [ɑ:tɪ'fɪʃəl] a künstlich, Kunst-; ~
respiration künstliche Atmung f.
artillery [ɑ:'tɪlərɪ] n Artillerie f.
artisan ['ɑ:tɪsæn] n gelernte(r)
Handwerker m.
artist ['ɑ:tɪst] n Künstler(in f) m; ~**ic**
[ɑ:'tɪstɪk] a künstlerisch; ~**ry** künst-
lerische(s) Können nt.
artless ['ɑ:tlɪs] a ungekünstelt; character
arglos.
arty ['ɑ:tɪ] a: **to be** ~ auf Kunst machen.
as [æz] ad, cj (since) da, weil; (while) als;
(like) wie; (in role of) als; ~ **soon** ~ **he
comes** sobald er kommt; ~ **big** ~ so
groß wie; ~ **well** auch; ~ **well** ~ und
auch; ~ **for him** was ihn anbetrifft; ~ **if,
~ though** als ob; ~ **it were** sozusagen;
old ~ **he was** so alt er auch war.
asbestos [æz'bestəs] n Asbest m.
ascend [ə'send] vi aufsteigen; vt besteigen;
~**ancy** Oberhand f.
ascension [ə'senʃən] n (Eccl) Himmel-
fahrt f.
ascent [ə'sent] n Aufstieg m; Besteigung f.
ascertain [æsə'teɪn] vt feststellen.
ascetic [ə'setɪk] a asketisch.
ascribe [əs'kraɪb] vt zuschreiben (to dat).
ash [æʃ] n (dust) Asche f; (tree) Esche f.
ashamed [ə'ʃeɪmd] a beschämt.
ashen [æʃən] a (pale) aschfahl.
ashore [ə'ʃɔ:*] ad an Land.
ashtray ['æʃtreɪ] n Aschenbecher m.
aside [ə'saɪd] ad beiseite; ~ **from** (US)
abgesehen von; n beiseite gesprochene
Worte pl.
ask [ɑ:sk] vti fragen; permission bitten um;
~ **him his name** frage ihn nach seinem
Namen; **he** ~**ed to see you** er wollte
dich sehen; **you** ~**ed for that!** da bist du
selbst schuld.
askance [əs'kɑ:ns] ad: **to look** ~ **at s.o.**
jdn schief ansehen.
askew [əs'kju:] ad schief.

asleep [ə'sli:p] a, ad: **to be ~** schlafen; **to fall ~** einschlafen.

asp [æsp] n Espe f.

asparagus [əs'pærəgəs] n Spargel m.

aspect ['æspekt] n (appearance) Aussehen nt; Aspekt m.

asphalt ['æsfælt] n Asphalt m.

asphyxiate [əs'fiksieit] vt ersticken.

asphyxiation [əsfiksi'eifən] n Erstickung f.

aspirate ['æspərit] n Hauchlaut m.

aspiration [æspə'reifən] n Trachten nt; **to have ~s towards sth** etw anstreben.

aspire [əs'paiə*] vi streben (to nach).

aspirin ['æsprin] n Aspirin nt.

ass [æs] n (lit, fig) Esel m.

assailant [ə'seilənt] n Angreifer m.

assassin [ə'sæsin] n Attentäter(in f) m; **~ate** vt ermorden; **~ation** [əsæsi'neifən] Ermordung f.

assault [ə'sɔ:lt] n Angriff m; vt überfallen; **woman** herfallen über (+acc).

assemble [ə'sembl] vt versammeln; parts zusammensetzen; vi sich versammeln.

assembly [ə'sembli] n (meeting) Versammlung f; (construction) Zusammensetzung f, Montage f; **~ line** Fließband nt.

assent [ə'sent] n Zustimmung f; vi zustimmen (to dat).

assert [ə'sɜ:t] vt erklären; **~ion** [ə'sɜ:ʃən] Behauptung f; **~ive** a selbstsicher.

assess [ə'ses] vt schätzen; **~ment** Bewertung f, Einschätzung; **~or** Steuerberater m.

asset ['æset] n Vorteil m, Wert m; **~s** pl Vermögen nt; (estate) Nachlaß m.

assiduous [ə'sidjuəs] a fleißig, aufmerksam.

assign [ə'sain] vt zuweisen.

assignment [ə'sainmənt] n Aufgabe f, Auftrag m.

assimilate [ə'simileit] vt sich aneignen, aufnehmen.

assimilation [əsimi'leifən] n Assimilierung f, Aufnahme f.

assist [ə'sist] vt beistehen (+dat); **~ance** Unterstützung f, Hilfe f; **~ant** Assistent(in f) m, Mitarbeiter(in f) m; (in shop) Verkäufer(in f) m.

assizes [ə'saiziz] npl Landgericht nt.

associate [ə'səuʃiit] n (partner) Kollege m, Teilhaber m; (member) außerordentliche(s) Mitglied nt; [ə'səuʃieit] vt verbinden (with mit); vi (keep company) verkehren (with mit).

association [əsəusi'eifən] a Verband m, Verein m; (Psych) Assoziation f; (link) Verbindung f; **~ football** (Brit) Fußball nt.

assorted [ə'sɔ:tid] a gemischt, verschieden.

assortment [ə'sɔ:tmənt] n Sammlung f; (Comm) Sortiment nt (of von), Auswahl f (of an +dat).

assume [ə'sju:m] vt (take for granted) annehmen; (put on) annehmen, sich geben; **~d name** Deckname m.

assumption [ə'sʌmpfən] n Annahme f.

assurance [ə'fuərəns] n (firm statement) Versicherung f; (confidence) Selbstsicherheit f; (insurance) (Lebens)versicherung f.

assure [ə'fuə*] vt (make sure) sicherstellen; (convince) versichern (+dat); **life** versichern.

assuredly [ə'fuəridli] ad sicherlich.

asterisk ['æstərisk] n Sternchen nt.

astern [əs'tɜ:n] ad achtern.

asthma ['æsmə] n Asthma nt; **~tic** [æs'mætik] a asthmatisch; n Asthmatiker(in f) m.

astir [əs'tɜ:*] ad in Bewegung.

astonish [əs'tonif] vt erstaunen; **~ing** a erstaunlich; **~ment** Erstaunen nt.

astound [əs'taund] vt verblüffen; **~ing** a verblüffend.

astray [əs'trei] ad in die Irre; auf Abwege; **a** irregehend.

astride [əs'traid] ad rittlings; prep rittlings auf.

astringent [əs'trindʒənt] a (Med) zusammenziehend; (severe) streng.

astrologer [əs'trolədʒə*] n Astrologe m, Astrologin f.

astrology [əs'trolədʒi] n Astrologie f.

astronaut ['æstrənɔ:t] n Astronaut(in f) m.

astronomer [əs'tronəmə*] n Astronom m.

astronomical [æstrə'nomikəl] a astronomisch; numbers astronomisch; success riesig.

astronomy [əs'tronəmi] n Astronomie f.

astute [əs'tju:t] a scharfsinnig, schlau, gerissen.

asunder [ə'sʌndə*] ad entzwei.

asylum [ə'sailəm] n (home) Heim nt; (refuge) Asyl nt.

at [æt] prep **~ home** zuhause; **~ John's** bei John; **~ table** bei Tisch; **~ school** in der Schule; **~ Easter** an Ostern; **~ 2 o'clock** um 2 Uhr; **~ (the age of) 16** mit 16; **~ £5 a 5 Pfund; ~ 20 mph** mit 20 Meilen pro Stunde; **~ that** darauf; (also) dazu.

ate [et, eit] pt of **eat**.

atheism ['eiθizəm] n Atheismus m.

atheist ['eiθiist] n Atheist(in f) m.

athlete ['æθli:t] n Athlet m, Sportler m.

athletic [æθ'letik] a sportlich, athletisch; **~s** pl Leichtathletik f.

atlas ['ætləs] n Atlas m.

atmosphere ['ætməsfiə*] n Atmosphäre f.

atoll ['ætɔl] n Atoll nt.

atom ['ætəm] n Atom nt; (fig) bißchen nt; **~ic** [ə'tomik] a atomar, Atom-; **~(ic) bomb** Atombombe f; **~ic power** Atomkraft f; **~izer** Zerstäuber m.

atone [ə'təun] vi sühnen (for acc).

atrocious [ə'trəufəs] a gräßlich.

atrocity [ə'trositi] n Scheußlichkeit f; (deed) Greueltat f.

- **attach** [ə'tætʃ] vt (fasten) befestigen; importance etc legen (to auf +acc), beimessen (to dat); **to be ~ed to sb/sth** an jdm/etw hängen; **~é** [ə'tæfei] n Attaché m.

attack [ə'tæk] vti angreifen; n Angriff m; (Med) Anfall m.

attain [ə'tein] vt erreichen; **~ment** Erreichung f; **~ments** pl Kenntnisse pl.

attempt [ə'tempt] n Versuch m; vti versuchen.

attend [ə'tend] vt (go to) teilnehmen (an +dat); lectures besuchen; vi (pay attention) aufmerksam sein; **to ~ to** needs nachkommen (+dat); person sich kümmern um; **~ance** (presence) Anwesenheit f; (people present) Besucherzahl f; **good ~ance** gute Teilnahme; **~ant** n (companion) Begleiter(in f) m; Gesellschafter(in f) m; (in car park etc) Wächter(in f) m; (servant) Bediente(r) mf; a begleitend; (fig) verbunden mit.

attention [ə'tenʃən] n Aufmerksamkeit f; (care) Fürsorge f; (for machine etc) Pflege f.

attentive a, **~ly** ad [ə'tentɪv, -lɪ] aufmerksam.

attenuate [ə'tenjʊeɪt] vt verdünnen.

attest [ə'test] vt bestätigen; **to ~ to** sich verbürgen für.

attic ['ætɪk] n Dachstube f, Mansarde f.

attire [ə'taɪə*] n Gewand nt.

attitude ['ætɪtjuːd] n (position) Haltung f; (mental) Einstellung f.

attorney [ə'tɜːnɪ] n (solicitor) Rechtsanwalt m; (representative) Bevollmächtigte(r) mf; **A~ General** Justizminister m.

attract [ə'trækt] vt anziehen; attention erregen; employees anlocken; **~ion** [ə'trækʃən] n Anziehungskraft f; (thing) Attraktion f; **~ive** a attraktiv; **the idea ~s me** ich finde die Idee attraktiv.

attribute ['ætrɪbjuːt] n Eigenschaft f, Attribut nt; [ə'trɪbjuːt] vt zuschreiben (to dat).

attrition [ə'trɪʃən] n Verschleiß m; **war of ~** Zermürbungskrieg m.

aubergine ['əʊbəʒiːn] n Aubergine f.

auburn ['ɔːbən] a kastanienbraun.

auction ['ɔːkʃən] n Versteigerung f, Auktion f; vt versteigern; **~eer** [ɔːkʃə'nɪə*] Versteigerer m.

audacious [ɔː'deɪʃəs] a (daring) verwegen; (shameless) unverfroren.

audacity [ɔː'dæsɪtɪ] n (boldness) Wagemut m; (impudence) Unverfrorenheit f.

audible ['ɔːdɪbl] a hörbar.

audience ['ɔːdɪəns] n Zuhörer pl, Zuschauer pl; (with king etc) Audienz f.

audit ['ɔːdɪt] n Bücherrevision f; vt prüfen.

audition [ɔː'dɪʃən] n Probe f.

auditorium [ɔːdɪ'tɔːrɪəm] n Zuschauerraum m.

augment [ɔːg'ment] vt vermehren; vi zunehmen.

augur ['ɔːgə*] vti bedeuten, voraussagen; **this ~s well** das ist ein gutes Omen; **~y** ['ɔːgjʊrɪ] Vorbedeutung f, Omen nt.

August ['ɔːgəst] n August m.

august [ɔː'gʌst] a erhaben.

aunt [ɑːnt] n Tante f; **~y, ~ie** Tantchen nt.

au pair ['əʊ' pɛə*] n (also **~ girl**) Au-pair-Mädchen nt.

aura ['ɔːrə] n Nimbus m.

auspices ['ɔːspɪsɪz] npl: **under the ~ of** unter der Schirmherrschaft von.

auspicious [ɔːs'pɪʃəs] a günstig; verheißungsvoll.

austere [os'tɪə*] a streng; room nüchtern.

austerity [os'terɪtɪ] n Strenge f; (Pol) wirtschaftliche Einschränkung f.

authentic [ɔː'θentɪk] a echt, authentisch; **~ate** vt beglaubigen; **~ity** [ɔːθen'tɪsɪtɪ] n Echtheit f.

author ['ɔːθə*] n Autor m, Schriftsteller m; (beginner) Urheber m, Schöpfer m.

authoritarian [ɔːθorɪ'tɛərɪən] a autoritär.

authoritative [ɔː'θorɪtətɪv] a account maßgeblich; manner herrisch.

authority [ɔː'θorɪtɪ] n (power) Autorität f; (expert) Autorität f, Fachmann m; **the authorities** pl die Behörden pl.

authorize ['ɔːθəraɪz] vt bevollmächtigen; (permit) genehmigen.

auto ['ɔːtəʊ] n (US) Auto nt, Wagen m.

autobiographical [ɔːtəbaɪə'græfɪkəl] a autobiographisch.

autobiography [ɔːtəbaɪ'ɒgrəfɪ] n Autobiographie f.

autocracy [ɔː'tokrəsɪ] n Autokratie f.

autocratic [ɔːtə'krætɪk] a autokratisch.

autograph ['ɔːtəgrɑːf] n (of celebrity) Autogramm nt; vt mit Autogramm versehen.

automate ['ɔːtəmeɪt] vt automatisieren, auf Automation umstellen.

automatic [ɔːtə'mætɪk] a automatisch; n Selbstladepistole f; (car) Automatik m; **~ally** ad automatisch.

automation [ɔːtə'meɪʃən] n Automation f.

automaton [ɔː'tomətən] n Automat m, Roboter m.

automobile ['ɔːtəməbiːl] n (US) Auto(mobil) nt.

autonomous [ɔː'tonəməs] a autonom.

autonomy [ɔː'tonəmɪ] n Autonomie f, Selbstbestimmung f.

autopsy ['ɔːtopsɪ] n Autopsie f.

autumn ['ɔːtəm] n Herbst m.

auxiliary [ɔːg'zɪlɪərɪ] a Hilfs-; n Hilfskraft f; (Gram) Hilfsverb nt.

avail [ə'veɪl] vt: **~ o.s. of sth** sich einer Sache bedienen; n: **to no ~** nutzlos; **~ability** [əveɪlə'bɪlɪtɪ] Erhältlichkeit f, Vorhandensein nt; **~able** erhältlich; zur Verfügung stehend; person erreichbar, abkömmlich.

avalanche ['ævəlɑːnʃ] n Lawine f.

avant-garde ['ævɑ̃'gɑːd] a avant-gardistisch; n Avantgarde f.

avarice ['ævərɪs] n Habsucht f, Geiz m.

avaricious [ævə'rɪʃəs] a geizig, habsüchtig.

avenge [ə'vendʒ] vt rächen, sühnen.

avenue ['ævənjuː] n Allee f.

average ['ævərɪdʒ] n Durchschnitt m; a durchschnittlich, Durchschnitts-; vt figures den Durchschnitt nehmen von; (perform) durchschnittlich leisten; (in car etc) im Schnitt fahren; **on ~** durchschnittlich, im Durchschnitt.

averse [ə'vɜːs] a: **to be ~ to** eine Abneigung haben gegen.

aversion [ə'vɜːʃən] n Abneigung f.

avert [ə'vɜːt] vt (turn away) abkehren; (prevent) abwehren.

aviary ['eɪvɪərɪ] n Vogelhaus nt.

aviation [eɪvɪ'eɪʃən] n Luftfahrt f, Flugwesen nt.

aviator ['eɪvɪeɪtə*] n Flieger m.

avid ['ævɪd] a gierig (for auf +acc); ~**ly** ad gierig.

avocado [ævə'kɑːdəʊ] n (also ~ pear) Avocado(birne) f.

avoid [ə'vɔɪd] vt vermeiden; ~**able** a vermeidbar; ~**ance** f Vermeidung f. ˘

avowal [ə'vaʊəl] n Erklärung f.

await [ə'weɪt] vt erwarten, entgegensehen (+dat).

awake [ə'weɪk] a wach; irreg vi aufwachen; vt (auf)wecken; ~**ning** Erwachen nt.

award [ə'wɔːd] n (judgment) Urteil nt; (prize) Preis m; vt zuerkennen.

aware [ə'wɛə*] a bewußt; **to be** ~ sich bewußt sein (of gen); ~**ness** Bewußtsein nt.

awash [ə'wɒʃ] a überflutet.

away [ə'weɪ] ad weg, fort.

awe [ɔː] n Ehrfurcht f; ~-**inspiring**, ~**some** a ehrfurchtgebietend; ~-**struck** a von Ehrfurcht ergriffen.

awful ['ɔːful] a (very bad) furchtbar; ~**ly** ad furchtbar, sehr.

awhile [ə'waɪl] ad eine kleine Weile, ein bißchen.

awkward ['ɔːkwəd] a (clumsy) ungeschickt, linkisch; (embarrassing) peinlich; ~**ness** Ungeschicklichkeit f.

awning ['ɔːnɪŋ] n Markise f.

awry [ə'raɪ] ad, a schief; **to go** ~ (person) fehlgehen; (plans) schiefgehen.

ax (US), **axe** [æks] n Axt f, Beil nt; vt (to end suddenly) streichen.

axiom ['æksɪəm] n Grundsatz m, Axiom nt; ~**atic** [æksɪə'mætɪk] a axiomatisch.

axis ['æksɪs] n Achse f.

axle ['æksl] n Achse f.

ay(e) [aɪ] interj (yes) ja; **the** ~**es** pl die Jastimmen pl.

azure ['eɪʒə*] a himmelblau.

B

B, b [biː] n B nt, b nt.

babble ['bæbl] vi schwätzen; (stream) murmeln; n Geschwätz nt.

babe [beɪb] n Baby nt.

baboon [bə'buːn] n Pavian m.

baby ['beɪbɪ] n Baby nt, Säugling m; ~-**carriage** (US) Kinderwagen m; ~**ish** a kindisch; ~-**sit** vi irreg Kinder hüten, babysitten; ~-**sitter** Babysitter m.

bachelor ['bætʃələ*] n Junggeselle m; **B~ of Arts** Bakkalaureus m der philosophischen Fakultät; **B~ of Science** Bakkalaureus m der Naturwissenschaften.

back [bæk] n (of person, horse) Rücken m; (of house) Rückseite f; (of train) Ende nt; (Ftbl) Verteidiger m; vt (support) unterstützen; (wager) wetten auf (+acc); car rückwärts fahren; vi (go backwards) rückwärts gehen or fahren; a hinter(e, s); ad zurück; (to the rear) nach hinten; ~ **down** vi zurückstecken; ~ **out** vi sich zurückziehen; kneifen (col); ~**biting** Verleumdung f; ~**bone** Rückgrat nt;

(support) Rückhalt m; ~**cloth** Hintergrund m; ~**er** Förderer m; ~**fire** vi (plan) fehlschlagen; (Tech) fehlzünden; ~**ground** Hintergrund m; (information) Hintergrund m, Umstände pl; (person's education) Vorbildung f; ~**hand** (Sport) Rückhand f; a Rückhand-; ~**handed** a shot Rückhand-; compliment zweifelhaft; ~**ing** (support) Unterstützung f; ~**lash** (Tech) tote(r) Gang m; (fig) Gegenschlag m; ~**log** (of work) Rückstand m; ~**number** (Press) alte Nummer f; ~**pay** (Gehalts-, Lohn)nachzahlung f; ~**side** (col) Hintern m; ~**stroke** Rückenschwimmen nt; ~**ward** a (less developed) zurückgeblieben; (primitive) rückständig; ~**wardness** (of child) Unterentwicklung f; (of country) Rückständigkeit f; ~**wards** ad (in reverse) rückwärts; (towards the past) zurück, rückwärts; ~**water** (fig) Kaff nt; cultural ~**water** tiefste Provinz f; ~**yard** Hinterhof m.

bacon ['beɪkən] n Schinkenspeck m.

bacteria [bæk'tɪərɪə] npl Bakterien pl.

bad [bæd] a schlecht, schlimm.

badge [bædʒ] n Abzeichen nt.

badger ['bædʒə*] n Dachs m; vt plagen.

badly ['bædlɪ] ad schlecht, schlimm; ~ **off:** **he is** ~ **off** es geht ihm schlecht.

badminton ['bædmɪntən] n Federballspiel nt.

bad-tempered ['bæd'tempəd] a schlecht gelaunt.

baffle ['bæfl] vt (puzzle) verblüffen.

bag [bæg] n (sack) Beutel m; (paper) Tüte f; (hand—) Tasche f; (suitcase) Koffer m; (booty) Jagdbeute f; (col: old woman) alte Schachtel f; vi sich bauschen; vt (put in sack) in einen Sack stecken; (hunting) erlegen; ~**ful** Sackvoll m; ~**gage** ['bægɪdʒ] Gepäck nt; ~**gy** a bauschig, sackartig; ~**pipes** pl Dudelsack m.

bail [beɪl] n (money) Kaution f; vt prisoner gegen Kaution freilassen; (also ~ **out**) boat ausschöpfen; see **bale**.

bailiff ['beɪlɪf] n Gerichtsvollzieher(in f) m.

bait [beɪt] n Köder m; vt mit einem Köder versehen; (fig) ködern.

bake [beɪk] vti backen; ~**r** Bäcker m; ~**ry** Bäckerei f; ~**r's dozen** dreizehn.

baking ['beɪkɪŋ] n Backen nt; ~ **powder** Backpulver nt.

balance ['bæləns] n (scales) Waage f; (equilibrium) Gleichgewicht nt; (Fin: state of account) Saldo m; (difference) Bilanz f; (amount remaining) Restbetrag m; vt (weigh) wägen; (make equal) ausgleichen; ~**d** a ausgeglichen; ~ **sheet** Bilanz f, Rechnungsabschluß m.

balcony ['bælkənɪ] n Balkon m.

bald [bɔːld] a kahl; statement knapp.

bale [beɪl] n Ballen m; **to** ~ or **bail out** (from a plane) abspringen.

baleful ['beɪlful] a (sad) unglückselig; (evil) böse.

balk [bɔːk] vt (hinder) vereiteln; vi scheuen (at vor +dat).

ball [bɔːl] n Ball m.

ballad ['bæləd] n Ballade f.

ballast ['bæləst] n Ballast m.

ball bearing ['bɔːl'beəriŋ] *n* Kugellager *nt*.

ballerina [bælə'riːnə] *n* Ballerina *f*.

ballet ['bæleɪ] *n* Ballett *nt*.

ballistics [bə'lɪstɪks] *n* Ballistik *f*.

balloon [bə'luːn] *n* (Luft)ballon *m*.

ballot ['bælət] *n* (geheime) Abstimmung *f*.

ball-point (pen) ['bɔːlpɔɪnt('pen)] *n* Kugelschreiber *m*.

ballroom ['bɔːlrʊm] *n* Tanzsaal *m*.

balmy ['bɑːmɪ] *a* lindernd; mild.

balsa ['bɔːlsə] *n* (*also* ~ **wood**) Balsaholz *nt*.

balustrade [bæləs'treɪd] *n* Brüstung *f*.

bamboo [bæm'buː] *n* Bambus *m*.

bamboozle [bæm'buːzl] *vt* übers Ohr hauen.

ban [bæn] *n* Verbot *nt*; *vt* verbieten.

banal [bə'nɑːl] *a* banal.

banana [bə'nɑːnə] *n* Banane *f*.

band [bænd] *n* Band *nt*; (*group*) Gruppe *f*; (*of criminals*) Bande *f*; (*Mus*) Kapelle *f*, Band *f*; *vi* (+*together*) sich zusammentun; ~**age** Verband *m*; (*elastic*) Bandage *f*.

bandit ['bændɪt] *n* Bandit *m*.

bandy ['bændɪ] *vt* wechseln; ~(**-legged**) *a* o-beinig.

bang [bæŋ] *n* (*explosion*) Knall *m*; (*blow*) Hieb *m*; *vti* knallen.

bangle ['bæŋgl] *n* Armspange *f*.

banish ['bænɪʃ] *vt* verbannen.

banister(s) ['bænɪstə*(z)] *n*(*pl*) (Treppen)geländer *nt*.

banjo ['bændʒəʊ] *n* Banjo *nt*.

bank [bæŋk] *n* (*raised ground*) Erdwall *m*; (*of lake etc*) Ufer *nt*; (*Fin*) Bank *f*; *vt* (*tilt: Aviat*) in die Kurve bringen; *money* einzahlen; **to** ~ **on sth** mit etw rechnen; ~**account** Bankkonto *nt*; (*employee*) Bankbeamte(r) *m*; ~ **holiday** gesetzliche(r) Feiertag *m*; ~**ing** Bankwesen *nt*, Bankgeschäft *nt*; ~**note** Banknote *f*; ~**rupt** *n* Zahlungsunfähige(r) *mf*; *vt* bankrott machen; **to go** ~**rupt** Pleite machen; ~**ruptcy** Bankrott *m*.

banner ['bænə*] *n* Banner *nt*.

banns [bænz] *npl* Aufgebot *nt*.

banquet ['bæŋkwɪt] *n* Bankett *nt*, Festessen *nt*.

banter ['bæntə*] *n* Neckerei *f*.

baptism ['bæptɪzəm] *n* Taufe *f*.

baptize [bæp'taɪz] *vt* taufen.

bar [bɑː*] *n* (*rod*) Stange *f*, (*obstacle*) Hindernis *nt*; (*of chocolate*) Tafel *f*; (*of soap*) Stück *nt*; (*for food, drink*) Buffet *nt*, Bar *f*; (*pub*) Wirtschaft *f*; (*Mus*) Takt(strich) *m*; *vt* (*fasten*) verriegeln; (*hinder*) versperren; (*exclude*) ausschließen; **the B~: to be called to the B~** als Anwalt zugelassen werden; ~ **none** ohne Ausnahme.

barbarian [bɑː'beərɪən] *n* Barbar(in *f*) *m*.

barbaric [bɑː'bærɪk] *a* primitiv, unkultiviert.

barbarity [bɑː'bærɪtɪ] *n* Grausamkeit *f*.

barbarous ['bɑːbərəs] *a* grausam, barbarisch.

barbecue ['bɑːbɪkjuː] *n* Barbecue *nt*.

barbed wire ['bɑːbd'waɪə*] *n* Stacheldraht *m*.

barber ['bɑːbə*] *n* Herrenfriseur *m*.

barbiturate [bɑː'bɪtjʊrɪt] *n* Barbiturat *nt*, Schlafmittel *nt*.

bare [beə*] *a* nackt; *trees, country* kahl; (*mere*) bloß; *vt* entblößen; ~**back** *ad* ungesattelt; ~**faced** *a* unverfroren; ~**foot** *a* barfuß; ~**headed** *a* mit bloßem Kopf; ~**ly** *ad* kaum, knapp; ~**ness** Nacktheit *f*; Kahlheit *f*.

bargain ['bɑːgɪn] *n* (*sth cheap*) günstiger Kauf; (*agreement*) (*written*) Kaufvertrag *m*; (*oral*) Geschäft *nt*; **into the** ~ obendrein; ~ **for** *vt* rechnen mit.

barge [bɑːdʒ] *n* Lastkahn *m*; ~ **in** *vi* hereinplatzen.

baritone ['bærɪtəʊn] *n* Bariton *m*.

bark [bɑːk] *n* (*of tree*) Rinde *f*; (*of dog*) Bellen *nt*; *vi* (*dog*) bellen.

barley ['bɑːlɪ] *n* Gerste *f*.

barmaid ['bɑːmeɪd] *n* Bardame *f*.

barman ['bɑːmən] *n* Barkellner *m*.

barn [bɑːn] *n* Scheune *f*.

barnacle ['bɑːnəkl] *n* Entenmuschel *f*.

barometer [bə'rɒmɪtə*] *n* Barometer *nt*.

baron ['bærən] *n* Baron *m*; ~**ess** Baronin *f*; ~**ial** [bə'rəʊnɪəl] *a* freiherrlich.

baroque [bə'rɒk] *a* barock.

barracks ['bærəks] *npl* Kaserne *f*.

barrage ['bærɑːʒ] *n* (*gunfire*) Sperrfeuer *nt*; (*dam*) Staudamm *m*; Talsperre *f*.

barrel ['bærəl] *n* Faß *nt*; (*of gun*) Lauf *m*; ~ **organ** Drehorgel *f*.

barren ['bærən] *a* unfruchtbar.

barricade [bærɪ'keɪd] *n* Barrikade *f*; *vt* verbarrikadieren.

barrier ['bærɪə*] *n* (*obstruction*) Hindernis *nt*; (*fence*) Schranke *f*.

barrister ['bærɪstə*] *n* (*Brit*) Rechtsanwalt *m*.

barrow ['bærəʊ] *n* (*cart*) Schubkarren *m*.

bartender [bɑː'tendə*] *n* (*US*) Barmann *or* -kellner *m*.

barter ['bɑːtə*] *n* Tauschhandel *m*; *vi* Tauschhandel treiben.

base [beɪs] *n* (*bottom*) Boden *m*, Basis *f*; (*Mil*) Stützpunkt *m*; *vt* gründen; **to be** ~**d on** basieren auf (+*dat*); *a* (*low*) gemein; ~**ball** Baseball *m*; ~**less** *a* grundlos; ~**ment** Kellergeschoß *nt*.

bash [bæʃ] *vt* (*col*) (heftig) schlagen.

bashful ['bæʃfʊl] *a* schüchtern.

basic ['beɪsɪk] *a* grundlegend; ~**ally** *ad* im Grunde.

basin ['beɪsn] *n* (*dish*) Schüssel *f*; (*for washing, also valley*) Becken *nt*; (*dock*) (Trocken)becken *nt*.

basis ['beɪsɪs] *n* Basis *f*, Grundlage *f*.

bask [bɑːsk] *vi* sich sonnen.

basket ['bɑːskɪt] *n* Korb *m*; ~**ball** Basketball *m*.

bass [beɪs] *n* (*Mus, also instrument*) Baß *m*; (*voice*) Baßstimme *f*; ~ **clef** Baßschlüssel *m*.

bassoon [bə'suːn] *n* Fagott *nt*.

bastard ['bɑːstəd] *n* Bastard *m*; Arschloch *nt*.

baste [beɪst] *vt* *meat* mit Fett begießen.

bastion ['bæstɪən] *n* (*lit, fig*) Bollwerk *nt*.

bat [bæt] *n* (*Sport*) Schlagholz *nt*; Schläger

m; (*Zool*) Fledermaus *f*; *vt*: **he didn't ~ an eyelid** er hat nicht mit der Wimper gezuckt; **off one's own ~** auf eigene Faust.

batch [bætʃ] *n* (*of letters*) Stoß *m*; (*of samples*) Satz *m*.

bated ['beitid] *a*: **with ~ breath** mit verhaltenem Atem.

bath [bɑ:θ] *n* Bad *nt*; (*tub*) Badewanne *f*; *vt* baden; **~s** [bɑ:ðz] *pl* (Schwimm)bad *nt*; **~chair** Rollstuhl *m*.

bathe [beið] *vti* baden; **~r** Badende(r) *mf*.

bathing ['beiðiŋ] *n* Baden *nt*; **~ cap** Badekappe *f*; **~ costume** Badeanzug *m*.

bathmat ['bɑ:θmæt] *n* Badevorleger *m*.

bathroom ['bɑ:θrʊm] *n* Bad(ezimmer) *nt*.

baths [bɑ:ðz] *npl see* **bath**.

bath towel ['bɑ:θtaʊəl] *n* Badetuch *nt*.

batman ['bætmən] *n* (Offiziers)bursche *m*.

baton ['bæton] *n* (*of police*) Gummiknüppel *m*; (*Mus*) Taktstock *m*.

battalion [bə'tæliən] *n* Bataillon *nt*.

batter ['bætə*] *vt* verprügeln; *n* Schlagteig *m*; (*for cake*) Biskuitteig *m*.

battery ['bætəri] *n* (*Elec*) Batterie *f*; (*Mil*) Geschützbatterie *f*.

battle ['bætl] *n* Schlacht *f*; (*small*) Gefecht *nt*; *vi* kämpfen; **~-axe** (*col*) Xanthippe *f*; **~field** Schlachtfeld *nt*; **~ments** *pl* Zinnen *pl*; **~ship** Schlachtschiff *nt*.

batty ['bæti] *a* (*col*) plemplem.

bauble ['bɔ:bl] *n* Spielzeug *nt*.

bawdy ['bɔ:di] *a* unflätig.

bawl [bɔ:l] *vi* brüllen; **to ~ sb out** jdn zur Schnecke machen.

bay [bei] *n* (*of sea*) Bucht *f*; **at ~** gestellt, in die Enge getrieben; **to keep at ~** unter Kontrolle halten.

bayonet ['beiənet] *n* Bajonett *nt*.

bay window ['bei'windəʊ] *n* Erkerfenster *nt*.

bazaar [bə'zɑ:*] *n* Basar *m*.

bazooka [bə'zu:kə] *n* Panzerfaust *f*.

be [bi:] *vi irreg* sein; (*become, for passive*) werden; (*be situated*) liegen, sein; **the book is 40p** das Buch kostet 40p; **he wants to ~ a teacher** er will Lehrer werden; **how long have you been here?** wie lange sind Sie schon da?; **have you been to Rome?** warst du schon einmal in Rom?, bist du schon einmal in Rom gewesen?; **his name is on the list** sein Name steht auf der Liste; **there is/are** es gibt.

beach [bi:tʃ] *n* Strand *m*; *vt* ship auf den Strand setzen; **~wear** Strandkleidung *f*.

beacon ['bi:kən] *n* (*signal*) Leuchtfeuer *nt*; (*traffic —*) Bake *f*.

bead [bi:d] *n* Perle *f*; (*drop*) Tropfen *m*.

beak [bi:k] *n* Schnabel *m*.

beaker ['bi:kə*] *n* Becher *m*.

beam [bi:m] *n* (*of wood*) Balken *m*; (*of light*) Strahl *m*; (*smile*) strahlende(s) Lächeln *nt*; *vi* strahlen.

bean [bi:n] *n* Bohne *f*.

bear [bɛə*] *vt irreg weight, crops* tragen; (*tolerate*) ertragen; *young* gebären; *n* Bär *m*; **~able** *a* erträglich; **to ~ on** relevant sein für.

beard [biəd] *n* Bart *m*; **~ed** *a* bärtig.

bearer ['bɛərə*] *n* Träger *m*.

bearing ['bɛəriŋ] *n* (*posture*) Haltung *f*; (*relevance*) Relevanz *f*; (*relation*) Bedeutung *f*; (*Tech*) Kugellager *nt*; **~s** *pl* (*direction*) Orientierung *f*.

bearskin ['bɛəskin] *n* Bärenfellmütze *f*.

beast [bi:st] *n* Tier *nt*, Vieh *nt*; (*person*) Bestie *f*; (*nasty person*) Biest *nt*; **~ly** *ad* viehisch; (*col*) scheußlich; **~ of burden** Lasttier *nt*.

beat [bi:t] *n* (*stroke*) Schlag *m*; (*pulsation*) (Herz)schlag *m*; (*police round*) Runde *f*; Revier *nt*; (*Mus*) Takt *m*; Beat *m*; *vt irreg* schlagen; **to ~ about the bush** wie die Katze um den heißen Brei herumgehen; **to ~ time** den Takt schlagen; **~ off** *vt* abschlagen; **~ up** *vt* zusammenschlagen; **~en track** gebahnte(r) Weg *m*; (*fig*) herkömmliche Art und Weise; **off the ~en track** abgelegen; **~er** (*for eggs, cream*) Schneebesen *m*.

beautiful ['bju:tiful] *a* schön; **~ly** *ad* ausgezeichnet.

beautify ['bju:tifai] *vt* verschönern.

beauty ['bju:ti] *n* Schönheit *f*.

beaver ['bi:və*] *n* Biber *m*.

becalm [bi'kɑ:m] *vt*: **to be ~ed** eine Flaute haben.

because [bi'kɔz] *ad*, *cj* weil; *prep*: **~ of** wegen (+*gen* or *col*) dat).

beckon ['bekən] *vti* ein Zeichen geben (*sb* jdm).

become [bi'kʌm] *vt irreg* werden; (*clothes*) stehen (+*dat*).

becoming [bi'kʌmiŋ] *a* (*suitable*) schicklich; *clothes* kleidsam.

bed [bed] *n* Bett *nt*; (*of river*) Flußbett *nt*; (*foundation*) Schicht *f*; (*in garden*) Beet *nt*; **~ and breakfast** Übernachtung *f* mit Frühstück; **~clothes** *pl* Bettwäsche *f*; **~ding** Bettzeug *nt*.

bedeck [bi'dek] *vt* schmücken.

bedlam ['bedləm] *n* (*uproar*) tolle(s) Durcheinander *nt*.

bedraggled [bi'drægld] *a* ramponiert.

bedridden ['bedridn] *a* bettlägerig.

bedroom ['bedrum] *n* Schlafzimmer *nt*.

bedside ['bedsaid] *n*: **at the ~** am Bett.

bed-sitter ['bed'sitə*] *n* Einzimmerwohnung *f*, möblierte(s) Zimmer *nt*.

bedtime ['bedtaim] *n* Schlafenszeit *f*.

bee [bi:] *n* Biene *f*.

beech [bi:tʃ] *n* Buche *f*.

beef [bi:f] *n* Rindfleisch *nt*.

beehive ['bi:haiv] *n* Bienenstock *m*.

beeline ['bi:lain] *n*: **to make a ~ for** schnurstracks zugehen auf (+*acc*).

beer [biə*] *n* Bier *nt*.

beetle ['bi:tl] *n* Käfer *m*.

beetroot ['bi:tru:t] *n* rote Bete *f*.

befall [bi'fɔ:l] *irreg* *vi* sich ereignen; *vt* zustoßen (+*dat*).

befit [bi'fit] *vt* sich schicken für.

before [bi'fɔ:*] *prep* vor; *cj* bevor; *ad* (*of time*) zuvor; früher; **I've done it ~** das hab' ich schon mal getan.

befriend [bi'frend] *vt* sich (jds) annehmen.

beg [beg] *vti* (*implore*) dringend bitten;

alms betteln; ~**gar** Bettler(in *f*) *m*.

begin [bɪ'gɪn] *vti irreg* anfangen, beginnen; (*found*) gründen; **to ~ with** zunächst (einmal); ~**ner** Anfänger *m*; ~**ning** Anfang *m*.

begrudge [bɪ'grʌdʒ] *vt* (be)neiden; **to ~ sb sth** jdm etw mißgönnen.

behalf [bɪ'hɑːf] *n*: **on** or **in** (*US*) ~ **of** im Namen (+*gen*); **on my ~** für mich.

behave [bɪ'heɪv] *vi* sich benehmen.

behaviour, (*US*) **behavior** [bɪ'heɪvjə*] *n* Benehmen *nt*.

behead [bɪ'hed] *vt* enthaupten.

behind [bɪ'haɪnd] *prep* hinter; *ad* (*late*) im Rückstand; (*in the rear*) hinten; *n* (*col*) Hinterteil *nt*.

behold [bɪ'həʊld] *vt irreg* (*old*) erblicken.

beige [beɪʒ] *a* beige.

being [ˈbiːɪŋ] *n* (*existence*) (Da)sein *nt*; (*person*) Wesen *nt*.

belch [beltʃ] *n* Rülpsen *nt*; *vi* rülpsen; *vt smoke* ausspeien.

belfry [ˈbelfrɪ] *n* Glockenturm *m*.

belie [bɪ'laɪ] *vt* Lügen strafen (+*acc*).

belief [bɪ'liːf] *n* Glaube *m* (*in an* +*acc*); (*conviction*) Überzeugung *f*.

believable [bɪ'liːvəbl] *a* glaubhaft.

believe [bɪ'liːv] *vt* glauben (+*dat*); (*think*) glauben, meinen, denken; *vi* (*have faith*) glauben; ~**r** Gläubige(r) *mf*.

belittle [bɪ'lɪtl] *vt* herabsetzen.

bell [bel] *n* Glocke *f*.

belligerent [bɪ'lɪdʒərənt] *a person* streit-süchtig; *country* kriegsführend.

bellow [ˈbeləʊ] *vti* brüllen; *n* Gebrüll *nt*.

bellows [ˈbeləʊz] *npl* (*Tech*) Gebläse *nt*; (*for fire*) Blasebalg *m*.

belly [ˈbelɪ] *n* Bauch *m*; *vi* sich ausbauchen.

belong [bɪ'lɒŋ] *vi* gehören (*to sb* jdm); (*to club*) angehören (+*dat*); **it does not ~ here** es gehört nicht hierher; ~**ings** *pl* Habe *f*.

beloved [bɪ'lʌvɪd] *a* innig geliebt; *n* Geliebte(r) *mf*.

below [bɪ'ləʊ] *prep* unter; *ad* unten.

belt [belt] *n* (*band*) Riemen *m*; (*round waist*) Gürtel *m*; *vt* (*fasten*) mit Riemen befestigen; (*col: beat*) schlagen; *vi* (*col: go fast*) rasen.

bench [bentʃ] *n* (*seat*) Bank *f*; (*workshop*) Werkbank *f*; (*judge's seat*) Richterbank *f*; (*judges*) Richterstand *m*.

bend [bend] *vt irreg* (*curve*) biegen; (*stoop*) beugen; *n* Biegung *f*; (*in road*) Kurve *f*.

beneath [bɪ'niːθ] *prep* unter; *ad* darunter.

benefactor [ˈbenɪfæktə*] *n* Wohltäter(in *f*) *m*.

beneficial [benɪ'fɪʃl] *a* vorteilhaft; (*to health*) heilsam.

beneficiary [benɪ'fɪʃərɪ] *n* Nutznießer(in *f*) *m*.

benefit [ˈbenɪfɪt] *n* (*advantage*) Nutzen *m*; *vt* fördern; *vi* Nutzen ziehen (*from aus*).

benevolence [bɪ'nevələns] *n* Wohlwollen *nt*.

benevolent [bɪ'nevələnt] *a* wohlwollend.

benign [bɪ'naɪn] *a person* gütig; *climate* mild.

bent [bent] *n* (*inclination*) Neigung *f*; *a* (*col:*

dishonest) unehrlich; **to be ~ on** versessen sein auf (+*acc*).

bequeath [bɪ'kwiːð] *vt* vermachen.

bequest [bɪ'kwest] *n* Vermächtnis *nt*.

bereaved [bɪ'riːvd] *n* (*person*) Hinter-bliebene(r) *mf*.

bereavement [bɪ'riːvmənt] *n* schmerz-liche(r) Verlust *m*.

beret [ˈberɪ] *n* Baskenmütze *f*.

berry [ˈberɪ] *n* Beere *f*.

berserk [bə'sɜːk] *a*: **to go ~** wild werden.

berth [bɜːθ] *n* (*for ship*) Ankerplatz *m*; (*in ship*) Koje *f*; (*in train*) Bett *nt*; *vt* am Kai festmachen; *vi* anlegen.

beseech [bɪ'siːtʃ] *vt irreg* anflehen.

beset [bɪ'set] *vt irreg* bedrängen.

beside [bɪ'saɪd] *prep* neben, bei; (*except*) außer; **to be ~ o.s.** außer sich sein (*with* vor +*dat*).

besides [bɪ'saɪdz] *prep* außer, neben; *ad* zudem, überdies.

besiege [bɪ'siːdʒ] *vt* (*Mil*) belagern; (*surround*) umlagern, bedrängen.

besmirch [bɪ'smɜːtʃ] *vt* besudeln.

bespectacled [bɪ'spektɪkld] *a* bebrillt.

bespoke tailor [bɪ'spəʊk'teɪlə*] *n* Maßschneider *m*.

best [best] *a* beste(r, s); *ad* am besten; **at ~** höchstens; **to make the ~ of it** das Beste daraus machen; **for the ~** zum Besten; ~ **man** Trauzeuge *m*.

bestial [ˈbestɪəl] *a* bestialisch.

bestow [bɪ'stəʊ] *vt* verleihen.

bestseller [ˈbest'selə*] *n* Bestseller *m*, meistgekaufte(s) Buch *nt*.

bet [bet] *n* Wette *f*; *vti irreg* wetten.

betray [bɪ'treɪ] *vt* verraten; ~**al** Verrat *m*.

better [ˈbetə*] *a*, *ad* besser; *vt* verbessern; *n*: **to get the ~ of** jdn überwinden; **he thought ~ of it** er hat sich eines Besseren besonnen; **you had ~ leave** Sie gehen jetzt wohl besser; ~ **off** a (*richer*) wohlhabender.

betting [ˈbetɪŋ] *n* Wetten *nt*; ~ **shop** Wett-büro *nt*.

between [bɪ'twiːn] *prep* zwischen; (*among*) unter; *ad* dazwischen.

bevel [ˈbevl] *n* Abschrägung *f*.

beverage [ˈbevərɪdʒ] *n* Getränk *nt*.

beware [bɪ'wɛə*] *vi* sich hüten vor (+*dat*); '~ **of the dog**' 'Vorsicht, bissiger Hund!'

bewildered [bɪ'wɪldəd] *a* verwirrt.

bewildering [bɪ'wɪldərɪŋ] *a* verwirrend.

bewitching [bɪ'wɪtʃɪŋ] *a* bestrickend.

beyond [bɪ'jɒnd] *prep* (*place*) jenseits (+*gen*); (*time*) über . . . hinaus; (*out of reach*) außerhalb (+*gen*); **it's ~ me** das geht über meinen Horizont; *ad* darüber hinaus.

bias [ˈbaɪəs] *n* (*slant*) Neigung *f*; (*prejudice*) Vorurteil *nt*; ~**(s)ed** *a* voreingenommen.

bib [bɪb] *n* Latz *m*.

Bible [ˈbaɪbl] *n* Bibel *f*.

biblical [ˈbɪblɪkl] *a* biblisch.

bibliography [bɪblɪ'ɒgrəfɪ] *n* Biblio-graphie *f*.

bicentenary [baɪsen'tiːnərɪ] *n* Zwei-hundertjahrfeier *f*.

biceps [ˈbaɪseps] *npl* Bizeps *m*.

bicker ['bɪkə*] vi zanken; ~**ing** Gezänk nt, Gekeife nt.

bicycle ['baɪsɪkl] n Fahrrad nt.

bid [bɪd] n (offer) Gebot nt; (attempt) Versuch m; vt irreg (offer) bieten; **to** ~ **farewell** Lebewohl sagen; ~**der** (person) Steigerer m; ~**ding** (command) Geheiß nt.

bide [baɪd] vt: ~ **one's time** abwarten.

big [bɪg] a groß.

bigamy ['bɪgəmɪ] n Bigamie f.

bigheaded ['bɪg'hedɪd] a eingebildet.

bigot ['bɪgət] n Frömmler m; ~**ed** a bigott; ~**ry** Bigotterie f.

bigwig ['bɪgwɪg] n (col) hohe(s) Tier nt.

bike [baɪk] n Rad nt.

bikini [bɪ'ki:nɪ] n Bikini m.

bilateral [baɪ'lætərəl] a bilateral.

bile [baɪl] n (Biol) Galle(nflüssigkeit) f.

bilge [bɪldʒ] n (water) Bilgenwasser nt.

bilingual [baɪ'lɪŋwəl] a zweisprachig.

bilious ['bɪlɪəs] a (sick) gallenkrank; (peevish) verstimmt.

bill [bɪl] n (account) Rechnung f; (Pol) Gesetzentwurf m; (US Fin) Geldschein m; ~ **of exchange** Wechsel m.

billet ['bɪlɪt] n Quartier nt.

billfold ['bɪlfəʊld] n (US) Geldscheintasche f.

billiards ['bɪlɪədz] n Billard nt.

billion ['bɪlɪən] n Billion f; (US) Milliarde f.

billy goat ['bɪlɪgəʊt] n Ziegenbock m.

bin [bɪn] n Kasten m; (dust~) (Abfall)eimer m.

bind [baɪnd] vt irreg (tie) binden; (tie together) zusammenbinden; (oblige) verpflichten; ~**ing** (Buch)einband m; a verbindlich.

binge [bɪndʒ] n (col) Sauferei f.

bingo ['bɪŋgəʊ] n Bingo nt.

binoculars [bɪ'nɒkjʊləz] npl Fernglas nt.

biochemistry ['baɪəʊ'kemɪstrɪ] n Biochemie f.

biographer [baɪ'ɒgrəfə*] n Biograph m.

biographic(al) [baɪəʊ'græfɪk(l)] a biographisch.

biography [baɪ'ɒgrəfɪ] n Biographie f.

biological [baɪə'lɒdʒɪkəl] a biologisch.

biologist [baɪ'ɒlədʒɪst] n Biologe m.

biology [baɪ'ɒlədʒɪ] n Biologie f.

biped ['baɪped] n Zweifüßler m.

birch [bɜ:tʃ] n Birke f.

bird [bɜ:d] n Vogel m; (col: girl) Mädchen nt; ~**'s-eye view** Vogelschau f.

birth [bɜ:θ] n Geburt f; **of good** ~ aus gutem Hause; ~ **certificate** Geburtsurkunde f; ~ **control** Geburtenkontrolle f; ~**day** Geburtstag m; ~**place** Geburtsort m; ~ **rate** Geburtenrate f.

biscuit ['bɪskɪt] n Keks m.

bisect [baɪ'sekt] vt halbieren.

bishop ['bɪʃəp] n Bischof m.

bit [bɪt] n bißchen, Stückchen nt; (horse's) Gebiß nt; **a** ~ **tired** etwas müde.

bitch [bɪtʃ] n (dog) Hündin f; (unpleasant woman) Mißstück nt.

bite [baɪt] vti irreg beißen; n Biß m; (mouthful) Bissen m; ~ **to eat** Happen m.

biting ['baɪtɪŋ] a beißend.

bitter ['bɪtə*] a bitter; memory etc schmerzlich; person verbittert; n (beer) dunkles Bier; **to the** ~ **end** bis zum bitteren Ende; ~**ness** Bitterkeit f; ~**sweet** bittersüß.

bivouac ['bɪvʊæk] n Biwak nt.

bizarre [bɪ'zɑ:*] a bizarr.

blab [blæb] vi klatschen; vt ausplaudern.

black [blæk] a schwarz; night finster; vt schwärzen; shoes wichsen; eye blau schlagen; (industry) boykottieren; ~ **and blue** grün und blau; ~**berry** Brombeere f; ~**bird** Amsel f; ~**board** (Wand)tafel f; ~**currant** schwarze Johannisbeere f; ~**guard** ['blægɑ:d] Schuft m; ~ **leg** Streikbrecher(in f) m; ~**list** schwarze Liste f; ~**mail** Erpressung f; vt erpressen; ~**mailer** Erpresser(in f) m; ~ **market** Schwarzmarkt m; ~**ness** Schwärze f; ~**out** Verdunklung f; (Med) **to have a** ~**out** bewußtlos werden; ~ **sheep** schwarze(s) Schaf nt; ~**smith** Schmied m.

bladder ['blædə*] n Blase f.

blade [bleɪd] n (of weapon) Klinge f; (of grass) Halm m; (of oar) Ruderblatt nt.

blame [bleɪm] n Tadel m, Schuld f; vt tadeln, Vorwürfe machen (+dat) **he is to** ~ er ist daran schuld; ~**less** a untadelig.

blanch [blɑ:ntʃ] vi bleich werden.

blancmange [blə'mɒnʒ] n Pudding m.

bland [blænd] a mild.

blank [blæŋk] a leer, unbeschrieben; look verdutzt; cheque Blanko-; verse Blank-; n (space) Lücke f; Zwischenraum m; (cartridge) Platzpatrone f.

blanket ['blæŋkɪt] n (Woll)decke f.

blankly ['blæŋklɪ] ad leer; look verdutzt.

blare [blɛə*] vti (radio) plärren; (horn) tuten; (Mus) schmettern; n Geplärr nt; Getute nt; Schmettern nt.

blasé ['blɑ:zeɪ] a blasiert.

blaspheme [blæs'fi:m] vti (Gott) lästern.

blasphemous ['blæsfɪməs] a lästernd, lästerlich.

blasphemy ['blæsfəmɪ] n (Gottes)lästerung f, Blasphemie f.

blast [blɑ:st] n Explosion f; (of wind) Windstoß m; vt (blow up) sprengen; ~! (col) verflixt!; ~ **furnace** Hochofen m; ~**-off** (Space) (Raketen)abschuß m.

blatant ['bleɪtənt] a offenkundig.

blaze [bleɪz] n (fire) lodernde(s) Feuer nt; vi lodern; vt: ~ **a trail** Bahn brechen.

blazer ['bleɪzə*] n Klubjacke f, Blazer m.

bleach [bli:tʃ] n Bleichmittel nt; vt bleichen.

bleak [bli:k] a kahl, rauh; future trostlos.

bleary-eyed ['blɪərɪaɪd] a triefäugig; (on waking up) mit verschlafenen Augen.

bleat [bli:t] n (of sheep) Blöken nt; (of goat) Meckern nt; vi blöken; meckern.

bleed [bli:d] vti irreg vi bluten; vt (draw blood) Blut abnehmen; **to** ~ **to death** verbluten.

bleeding ['bli:dɪŋ] a blutend.

blemish ['blemɪʃ] n Makel m; vt verunstalten.

blench [blentʃ] vi zurückschrecken; see **blanch**.

blend [blend] n Mischung f; vt mischen; vi sich mischen.

bless [bles] vt segnen; (give thanks) preisen; (make happy) glücklich machen; ~ **you!** Gesundheit!; ~**ing** Segen m; (at table) Tischgebet nt; (happiness) Wohltat f; Segen m; (good wish) Glück nt.

blight [blait] n (Bot) Mehltau m; (fig) schädliche(r) Einfluß m; vt zunichte machen.

blimey ['blaimi] interj (Brit col) verflucht.

blind [blaind] a blind; corner unübersichtlich; n (for window) Rouleau nt; vt blenden; ~ **alley** Sackgasse f; ~**fold** Augenbinde f; a mit verbundenen Augen; vt die Augen verbinden (sb jdm); ~**ly** a blind; (fig) blindlings; ~**ness** Blindheit f; ~ **spot** (Aut) toter Winkel m; (fig) schwache(r) Punkt m.

blink [bliŋk] vti blinzeln; ~**ers** pl Scheuklappen pl.

bliss [blis] n (Glück)seligkeit f; ~**fully** ad glückselig.

blister ['blistə*] n Blase f; vt Blasen werfen auf (+dat); vi Blasen werfen.

blithe [blaið] a munter; ~**ly** ad fröhlich.

blitz [blits] n Luftkrieg m; vt bombardieren.

blizzard ['blizəd] n Schneesturm m.

bloated ['bləutid] a aufgedunsen; (col: full) nudelsatt.

blob [blob] n Klümpchen nt.

bloc [blok] n (Pol) Block m.

block [blok] n (of wood) Block m, Klotz m; (of houses) Häuserblock m; vt hemmen; ~**ade** [blo'keid] Blockade f; vt blockieren; ~**age** Verstopfung f.

bloke [bləuk] n (col) Kerl m, Typ m.

blonde [blond] a blond; n Blondine f.

blood [blʌd] n Blut nt; ~ **donor** Blutspender m; ~ **group** Blutgruppe f; ~**less** a blutleer; ~ **poisoning** Blutvergiftung f; ~ **pressure** Blutdruck m; ~**shed** Blutvergießen nt; ~**shot** a blutunterlaufen; ~**stained** a blutbefleckt; ~**stream** Blut n, Blutkreislauf m; ~ **thirsty** a blutrünstig; ~ **transfusion** Blutübertragung f; ~**y** a (col) verdammt, saumäßig; (lit) blutig; ~**y-minded** a stur.

bloom [blu:m] n Blüte f; (freshness) Glanz m; vi blühen; in ~ in Blüte.

blossom ['blosəm] n Blüte f; vi blühen.

blot [blot] n Klecks m; vt beklecksen; (ink) (ab)löschen; ~ **out** vt auslöschen.

blotchy ['blotʃi] a fleckig.

blotting paper ['blotiŋpeipə*] n Löschpapier nt.

blouse [blauz] n Bluse f.

blow [bləu] n Schlag m; irreg vt blasen; vi (wind) wehen; **to** ~ **one's top** (vor Wut) explodieren; ~ **over** vi vorübergehen; ~ **up** vi explodieren; vt sprengen; ~**lamp** Lötlampe f; ~**out** (Aut) geplatzte(r) Reifen m; ~-**up** (Phot) Vergrößerung f; ~**y** a windig.

blubber ['blʌbə*] n Walfischspeck m.

bludgeon ['blʌdʒən] vt (fig) zwingen.

blue [blu:] a blau; (col: unhappy) niedergeschlagen; (obscene) pornographisch; joke anzüglich; **to have the** ~**s** traurig

sein; ~**bell** Glockenblume f; ~-**blooded** a blaublütig; ~**bottle** Schmeißfliege f; ~**print** (fig) Entwurf m; ~**s** pl (Mus) Blues m.

bluff [blʌf] vt bluffen, täuschen; n (deception) Bluff m; a gutmütig und derb.

bluish ['blu:iʃ] a bläulich.

blunder ['blʌndə*] n grobe(r) Fehler m, Schnitzer m; vi einen groben Fehler machen.

blunt [blʌnt] a knife stumpf; talk unverblümt; vt abstumpfen; ~**ly** ad frei heraus; ~**ness** Stumpfheit f; (fig) Plumpheit f.

blur [bl3:*] n Fleck m; vi verschwimmen; vt verschwommen machen.

blurb [bl3:b] n Waschzettel m.

blurt [bl3:t] vt: ~ **out** herausplatzen mit.

blush [blʌʃ] vi erröten; n (Scham)röte f; ~**ing** a errötend.

bluster ['blʌstə*] vi (wind) brausen; (person) darauf lospoltern, schwadronieren; ~**y** a sehr windig.

boa ['bəuə] n Boa f.

boar [bɔ:*] n Keiler m, Eber m.

board [bɔ:d] n (of wood) Brett nt; (of card) Pappe f; (committee) Ausschuß m; (of firm) Aufsichtsrat m; (Sch) Direktorium nt; vt train einsteigen in (+acc); ship an Bord gehen (+gen); ~ **and lodging** Unterkunft f und Verpflegung; **to go by the** ~ flachfallen, über Bord gehen; ~ **up** vt mit Brettern vernageln; ~**er** Kostgänger m; (Sch) Internatsschüler(in f) m; ~**ing house** Pension f; ~**ing school** Internat nt; ~ **room** Sitzungszimmer nt.

boast [bəust] vi prahlen; n Großtuerei f, Prahlerei f; ~**ful** a prahlerisch; ~**fulness** Überheblichkeit f.

boat [bəut] n Boot nt; (ship) Schiff nt; ~**er** (hat) Kreissäge f; ~**ing** Bootfahren nt; ~**swain** [bəusn] = **bosun**; ~ **train** Zug m mit Schiffsanschluß.

bob [bob] vi sich auf und nieder bewegen.

bobbin ['bobin] n Spule f.

bobsleigh ['bobslei] n Bob m.

bodice ['bodis] n Mieder nt.

-**bodied** ['bodid] a -gebaut.

bodily ['bodili] a, ad körperlich.

body ['bodi] n Körper m; (dead) Leiche f; (group) Mannschaft f; (Aut) Karosserie f; (trunk) Rumpf m; **in a** ~ in einer Gruppe; **the main** ~ **of the work** der Hauptanteil der Arbeit; ~**guard** Leibwache f; ~**work** Karosserie f.

bog [bog] n Sumpf m; vi: **to get** ~**ged down** sich festfahren.

bogey ['bəugi] n Schreckgespenst nt.

boggle ['bogl] vi stutzen.

bogus ['bəugəs] a unecht, Schein-.

boil [bɔil] vti kochen; n (Med) Geschwür nt; **to come to the** ~ zu kochen anfangen; ~**er** Boiler m; ~**ing point** Siedepunkt m.

boisterous ['bɔistərəs] a ungestüm.

bold [bəuld] a (fearless) unerschrocken; handwriting fest und klar; ~**ly** ad keck; ~**ness** Kühnheit f; (cheekiness) Dreistigkeit f.

bollard ['boləd] n (Naut) Poller m; (on road) Pfosten m.

bolster ['bəʊlstə*] n Polster nt; ~ **up** vt unterstützen.

bolt [bəʊlt] n Bolzen m; (lock) Riegel m; vt verriegeln; (swallow) verschlingen; vi (horse) durchgehen.

bomb [bɒm] n Bombe f; vt bombardieren; ~**ard** [bɒm'bɑːd] vt bombardieren; ~**ardment** [bɒm'bɑːdmənt] Beschießung f; ~**er** Bomber m; ~**ing** Bombenangriff m; ~**shell** (fig) Bombe f.

bombastic [bɒm'bæstɪk] a bombastisch.

bona fide ['bəʊnə'faɪdɪ] a echt.

bond [bɒnd] n (link) Band nt; (Fin) Schuldverschreibung f.

bone [bəʊn] n Knochen m; (of fish) Gräte f; (piece of ~) Knochensplitter m; ~ **of contention** Zankapfel m; vt die Knochen herausnehmen (+dat); fish entgräten; ~**dry** a knochentrocken; ~**r** (US col) Schnitzer m.

bonfire ['bɒnfaɪə*] n Feuer nt im Freien.

bonnet ['bɒnɪt] n Haube f; (for baby) Häubchen nt; (Brit Aut) Motorhaube f.

bonny ['bɒnɪ] a (Scot) hübsch.

bonus ['bəʊnəs] n Bonus m; (annual ~) Prämie f.

bony ['bəʊnɪ] a knochig, knochendürr.

boo [buː] vt auspfeifen.

book [bʊk] n Buch nt; vt ticket etc vorbestellen; person verwarnen; ~**able** a im Vorverkauf erhältlich; ~**case** Bücherregal nt, Bücherschrank m; ~**ing office** (Rail) Fahrkartenschalter m; (Theat) Vorverkaufsstelle f; ~**-keeping** Buchhaltung f; ~**let** Broschüre f; ~**maker** Buchmacher m; ~**seller** Buchhändler m; ~**shop** Buchhandlung f; ~**stall** Bücherstand m; (Rail) Bahnhofsbuchhandlung f; ~**worm** Bücherwurm m.

boom [buːm] n (noise) Dröhnen nt; (busy period) Hochkonjunktur f; vi dröhnen.

boomerang ['buːməræŋ] n Bumerang m.

boon [buːn] n Wohltat f, Segen m.

boorish ['bʊərɪʃ] a grob.

boost [buːst] n Auftrieb m; (fig) Reklame f; vt Auftrieb geben.

boot [buːt] n Stiefel m; (Brit Aut) Kofferraum m; vt (kick) einen Fußtritt geben; to ~ (in addition) obendrein.

booty ['buːtɪ] n Beute f.

booze [buːz] n (col) Alkohol m, Schnaps m; vi saufen.

border ['bɔːdə*] n Grenze f; (edge) Kante f; (in garden) (Blumen)rabatte f; ~ **on** vt grenzen an (+acc); ~**line** Grenze f.

bore [bɔː*] vt bohren; (weary) langweilen; n (person) langweilige(r) Mensch m; (thing) langweilige Sache f; (of gun) Kaliber nt; ~**dom** Langeweile f.

boring ['bɔːrɪŋ] a langweilig.

born [bɔːn] to be ~ geboren werden.

borough ['bʌrə] n Stadt(gemeinde) f, Stadtbezirk m.

borrow ['bɒrəʊ] vt borgen; ~**ing** (Fin) Anleihe f.

bosom ['bʊzəm] n Busen m.

boss [bɒs] n Chef m, Boß m; vt: ~ **around** herumkommandieren; ~**y** a herrisch.

bosun ['bəʊsn] n Bootsmann m.

botanical [bə'tænɪkəl] a botanisch.

botanist ['bɒtənɪst] n Botaniker(in f) m.

botany ['bɒtənɪ] n Botanik f.

botch [bɒtʃ] vt verpfuschen.

both [bəʊθ] a beide(s); ~ **(of) the books** beide Bücher; **I like them** ~ ich mag (sie) beide; pron beide(s); ad: ~ **X and Y** sowohl X wie or als auch Y.

bother ['bɒðə*] vt (pester) quälen; vi (fuss) sich aufregen; (take trouble) sich Mühe machen; n Mühe f, Umstand m.

bottle ['bɒtl] n Flasche f; vt (in Flaschen) abfüllen; ~**neck** (lit, fig) Engpaß m.

bottom ['bɒtəm] n Boden m; (of person) Hintern m; (riverbed) Flußbett nt; **at** ~ im Grunde; **a** unterste(r, s); ~**less** a bodenlos.

bough [baʊ] n Zweig m, Ast m.

boulder ['bəʊldə*] n Felsbrocken m.

bounce [baʊns] vi (ball) hochspringen; (person) herumhüpfen; (cheque) platzen; vt (auf)springen lassen; n (rebound) Aufprall m; ~**r** Rausschmeißer m.

bound [baʊnd] n Grenze f; (leap) Sprung m; vi (spring, leap) (auf)springen; a gebunden, verpflichtet; **out of** ~**s** Zutritt verboten; **to be** ~ **to do sth** verpflichtet sein, etw zu tun, etw tun müssen; **it's** ~ **to happen** es muß so kommen; **to be** ~ **for** . . . nach . . . fahren; ~**ary** Grenze f, Grenzlinie f; ~**less** a grenzenlos.

bouquet [bʊ'keɪ] n Strauß m; (of wine) Blume f.

bourgeois ['bʊəʒwɑː] a kleinbürgerlich, bourgeois.

bout [baʊt] n (of illness) Anfall m; (of contest) Kampf m.

bow[1] [bəʊ] n (ribbon) Schleife f; (weapon, Mus) Bogen m.

bow[2] [baʊ] vi sich verbeugen; (submit) sich beugen (+dat); n Verbeugung f; (of ship) Bug m.

bowels ['baʊəlz] npl Darm m; (centre) Innere m.

bowl [bəʊl] n (basin) Schüssel f; (of pipe) (Pfeifen)kopf m; (wooden ball) (Holz)kugel f; vti (die Kugel) rollen; ~**s** pl (game) Bowls-Spiel nt.

bow-legged ['bəʊlegɪd] a o-beinig.

bowler ['bəʊlə*] n Werfer m; (hat) Melone f.

bowling ['bəʊlɪŋ] n Kegeln nt; ~ **alley** Kegelbahn f; ~ **green** Rasen m zum Bowling-Spiel.

bow tie ['bəʊ'taɪ] n Fliege f.

box [bɒks] n Schachtel f; (bigger) Kasten m; (Theat) Loge f; vt einpacken; **to** ~ **sb's ears** jdm eine Ohrfeige geben; vi boxen; ~**er** Boxer m; ~ **in** vt einpferchen; ~**ing** (Sport) Boxen nt; **B**~**ing Day** zweiter Weihnachtsfeiertag; ~**ing ring** Boxring m; ~ **office** (Theater)kasse f; ~ **room** Rumpelkammer f.

boy [bɔɪ] n Junge m; ~ **scout** Pfadfinder m.

boycott ['bɔɪkɒt] n Boykott m; vt boykottieren.

boyfriend ['bɔɪfrend] n Freund m.

boyish ['bɔɪɪʃ] a jungenhaft.

bra [brɑː] n BH m.

brace [breɪs] n (Tech) Stütze f; (Med) Klammer f; vt stützen; ~s pl Hosenträger pl.

bracelet ['breɪslɪt] n Armband nt.

bracing ['breɪsɪŋ] a kräftigend.

bracken ['brækən] n Farnkraut nt.

bracket ['brækɪt] n Halter m, Klammer f; (in punctuation) Klammer f; (group) Gruppe f; vt einklammern; (fig) in dieselbe Gruppe einordnen.

brag [bræg] vi sich rühmen.

braid [breɪd] n (hair) Flechte f; (trim) Borte f.

Braille [breɪl] n Blindenschrift f.

brain [breɪn] n (Anat) Gehirn nt; (intellect) Intelligenz f, Verstand m; (person) kluge(r) Kopf m; ~s pl Verstand m; ~less a dumm; ~storm verrückte(r) Einfall m; ~wash vt Gehirnwäsche f vornehmen bei; ~wave gute(r) Einfall m, Geistesblitz m; ~y gescheit.

braise [breɪz] vt schmoren.

brake [breɪk] n Bremse f; vti bremsen.

branch [bra:ntʃ] n Ast m; (division) Zweig m; vi (road) sich verzweigen.

brand [brænd] n (Comm) Marke f, Sorte f; (on cattle) Brandmal nt; vt brandmarken; (Comm) eine Schutzmarke geben (+dat).

brandish ['brændɪʃ] vt (drohend) schwingen.

brand-new ['brænd'nju:] a funkelnagelneu.

brandy ['brændɪ] n Weinbrand m, Kognak m.

brash [bræʃ] a unverschämt.

brass [bra:s] n Messing nt; ~ band Blaskapelle f.

brassière ['bræsɪə*] n Büstenhalter m.

brat [bræt] n ungezogene(s) Kind nt, Gör nt.

bravado [brə'va:dəʊ] n Tollkühnheit f.

brave [breɪv] a tapfer; n indianische(r) Krieger m; vt die Stirn bieten (+dat); ~ly ad tapfer; ~ry ['breɪvərɪ] Tapferkeit f.

bravo ['bra:'vəʊ] interj bravo!

brawl [brɔ:l] n Rauferei f; vi Krawall machen.

brawn [brɔ:n] n (Anat) Muskeln pl; (strength) Muskelkraft f; ~y a muskulös, stämmig.

bray [breɪ] n Eselsschrei m; vi schreien.

brazen ['breɪzn] a (shameless) unverschämt; vt: ~ it out sich mit Lügen und Betrügen durchsetzen.

brazier ['breɪzɪə*] n (of workmen) offene(r) Kohlenofen m.

breach [bri:tʃ] n (gap) Lücke f; (Mil) Durchbruch m; (of discipline) Verstoß m (gegen die Disziplin); (of faith) Vertrauensbruch m; vt durchbrechen; ~ of the peace öffentliche Ruhestörung f.

bread [bred] n Brot nt; ~ and butter Butterbrot nt; ~crumbs pl Brotkrumen pl; (Cook) Paniermehl nt; to be on the ~line sich gerade so durchschlagen; ~winner Ernährer m.

breadth [bredθ] n Breite f.

break [breɪk] irreg vt (destroy) (ab- or zer)brechen; promise brechen; nicht einhalten; vi (fall apart) auseinanderbrechen; (collapse) zusammenbrechen; (of dawn) anbrechen; n (gap) Lücke f; (chance) Chance f, Gelegenheit f; (fracture) Bruch m; (rest) Pause f; ~ down vi (car) eine Panne haben; (person) zusammenbrechen; to ~ free or loose sich losreißen; ~ in vt animal abrichten; horse zureiten; vi (burglar) einbrechen; ~ out vi ausbrechen; ~ up vi zerbrechen; (fig) sich zerstreuen; (Sch) in die Ferien gehen; vt brechen; ~able a zerbrechlich; ~age Bruch m, Beschädigung f; ~down (Tech) Panne f; (of nerves) Zusammenbruch m; ~er Brecher m; ~fast ['brekfəst] Frühstück nt; ~through Durchbruch m; ~water Wellenbrecher m.

breast [brest] n Brust f; ~ stroke Brustschwimmen nt.

breath [breθ] n Atem m; out of ~ außer Atem; under one's ~ flüsternd.

breathalize ['breθəlaɪz] vt blasen lassen.

breathe [bri:ð] vti atmen; ~r Verschnaufpause f.

breathless ['breθlɪs] a atemlos.

breath-taking ['breθteɪkɪŋ] a atemberaubend.

breed [bri:d] irreg vi sich vermehren; vt züchten; n (race) Rasse f, Zucht f; ~er (person) Züchter m; ~ing Züchtung f; (upbringing) Erziehung f; (education) Bildung f.

breeze [bri:z] n Brise f.

breezy ['bri:zɪ] a windig; manner munter.

brevity ['brevɪtɪ] n Kürze f.

brew [bru:] vt brauen; plot anzetteln; vi (storm) sich zusammenziehen; ~ery Brauerei f.

bribe ['braɪb] n Bestechungsgeld nt or -geschenk nt; vt bestechen; ~ry ['braɪbərɪ] Bestechung f.

bric-à-brac ['brɪkəbræk] n Nippes pl.

brick [brɪk] n Backstein m; ~layer Maurer m; ~work Mauerwerk nt; ~works Ziegelei f.

bridal ['braɪdl] a Braut-, bräutlich.

bride [braɪd] n Braut f; ~groom Bräutigam m; ~smaid Brautjungfer f.

bridge [brɪdʒ] n Brücke f; (Naut) Kommandobrücke f; (Cards) Bridge nt; (Anat) Nasenrücken m; vt eine Brücke schlagen über (+acc); (fig) überbrücken.

bridle ['braɪdl] n Zaum m; vt (fig) zügeln; horse aufzäumen; ~ path Saumpfad m.

brief [bri:f] a kurz; n (Jur) Akten pl; vt instruieren; ~s pl Schlüpfer m, Slip m; ~case Aktentasche f; ~ing (genaue) Anweisung f; ~ly ad kurz; ~ness Kürze f.

brigade [brɪ'geɪd] n Brigade f.

brigadier [brɪgə'dɪə*] n Brigadegeneral m.

bright [braɪt] a hell; (cheerful) heiter; idea klug; ~en up vt aufhellen; person aufheitern; vi sich aufheitern; ~ly ad hell; heiter.

brilliance ['brɪljəns] n Glanz m; (of person) Scharfsinn m.

brilliant a, ~ly ad ['brɪljənt, -lɪ] glänzend.

brim [brɪm] n Rand m; vi voll sein; ~ful a übervoll.

brine [braɪn] n Salzwasser nt.

bring [brɪŋ] vt irreg bringen; ~ **about** vt zustande bringen; ~ **off** vt davontragen; success erzielen; ~ **round** or **to** vt wieder zu sich bringen; ~ **up** vt aufziehen; question zur Sprache bringen.

brisk [brɪsk] a lebhaft.

bristle ['brɪsl] n Borste f; vi sich sträuben; **bristling with** strotzend vor (+dat).

brittle ['brɪtl] a spröde.

broach [brəʊtʃ] vt subject anschneiden.

broad [brɔːd] a breit; hint deutlich; daylight hellicht; (general) allgemein; accent stark; ~ **cast** n Rundfunkübertragung f; vti irreg übertragen, senden; ~ **casting** Rundfunk m; ~ **en** vt erweitern; vi sich erweitern; ~ **ly** ad allgemein gesagt; ~ **minded** a tolerant.

brocade [brɔ'keɪd] n Brokat m.

broccoli ['brɒkəlɪ] n Spargelkohl m, Brokkoli pl.

brochure ['brəʊʃʊə*] n Broschüre f.

broiler ['brɔɪlə*] n Bratrost m.

broke [brəʊk] a (col) pleite.

broken-hearted ['brəʊkən'hɑːtɪd] a untröstlich.

broker ['brəʊkə*] n Makler m.

bronchitis [brɒŋ'kaɪtɪs] n Bronchitis f.

bronze [brɒnz] n Bronze f; ~**d** a sonnengebräunt.

brooch [brəʊtʃ] n Brosche f.

brood [bruːd] n Brut f; vi brüten; ~**y** a brütend.

brook [brʊk] n Bach m.

broom [bruːm] n Besen m; ~**stick** Besenstiel m.

broth [brɒθ] n Suppe f, Fleischbrühe f.

brothel ['brɒθl] n Bordell m.

brother ['brʌðə*] n Bruder m; ~**hood** Bruderschaft f; ~ **-in-law** Schwager m; ~**ly** a brüderlich.

brow [braʊ] n (eyebrow) (Augen)braue f; (forehead) Stirn f; (of hill) Bergkuppe f; ~**beat** vt irreg einschüchtern.

brown [braʊn] a braun; n Braun nt; vt bräunen; ~**ie** Wichtel m; ~ **paper** Packpapier nt.

browse [braʊz] vi (in books) blättern; (in shop) schmökern, herumschauen.

bruise [bruːz] n Bluterguß m, blaue(r) Fleck m; vti einen blauen Fleck geben/bekommen.

brunette [bru'net] n Brünette f.

brunt [brʌnt] n volle Wucht f.

brush [brʌʃ] n Bürste f; (for sweeping) Handbesen m; (for painting) Pinsel m; (fight) kurze(r) Kampf m; (Mil) Scharmützel nt; (fig) Auseinandersetzung f; vt (clean) bürsten; (sweep) fegen; (touch) streifen; **give sb the** ~**-off** (col) jdm eine Abfuhr erteilen; ~ **aside** vt abtun; ~**wood** Gestrüpp nt.

brusque [bruːsk] a schroff.

Brussels sprout ['brʌsɪz'spraʊt] n Rosenkohl m.

brutal ['bruːtl] a brutal; ~**ity** [bru'tælɪtɪ] n Brutalität f.

brute [bruːt] n (person) Scheusal nt; ~

force rohe Kraft; (violence) nackte Gewalt nt.

brutish ['bruːtɪʃ] a tierisch.

bubble ['bʌbl] n (Luft)blase f; vi sprudeln; (with joy) übersprudeln.

buck [bʌk] n Bock m; (US col) Dollar m; vi bocken; ~ **up** vi (col) sich zusammenreißen.

bucket ['bʌkɪt] n Eimer m.

buckle ['bʌkl] n Schnalle f; vt (an- or zusammen)schnallen; vi (bend) sich verziehen.

bud [bʌd] n Knospe f; vi knospen, keimen.

Buddhism ['bʊdɪzəm] n Buddhismus m.

Buddhist ['bʊdɪst] n Buddhist(in f) m; a buddhistisch.

budding ['bʌdɪŋ] a angehend.

buddy ['bʌdɪ] n (col) Kumpel m.

budge [bʌdʒ] vti (sich) von der Stelle rühren.

budgerigar ['bʌdʒərɪgɑː*] n Wellensittich m.

budget ['bʌdʒɪt] n Budget nt; (Pol) Haushalt m; vi haushalten.

budgie ['bʌdʒɪ] n = **budgerigar.**

buff [bʌf] a colour lederfarben; n (enthusiast) Fan m.

buffalo ['bʌfələʊ] n Büffel m.

buffer ['bʌfə*] n Puffer m.

buffet ['bʌfɪt] n (blow) Schlag m; ['bʊfeɪ] (bar) Imbißraum m, Erfrischungsraum m; (food) (kaltes) Büffet nt; vt ['bʌfɪt] (herum)stoßen.

buffoon [bʌ'fuːn] n Hanswurst m.

bug [bʌg] n (lit, fig) Wanze f; vt verwanzen; ~**bear** Schreckgespenst nt.

bugle ['bjuːgl] n Jagd-, Bügelhorn nt.

build [bɪld] vt irreg bauen; n Körperbau m; ~**er** n Bauunternehmer m; ~**ing** Gebäude nt; ~**ing society** Baugenossenschaft f; ~**-up** Aufbau m; (publicity) Reklame f.

built [bɪlt]: **well-**~ a person gut gebaut; ~**-in** a cupboard eingebaut; ~**-up area** Wohngebiet nt.

bulb [bʌlb] n (Bot) (Blumen)zwiebel f; (Elec) Glühlampe f, Birne f; ~**ous** a knollig.

bulge [bʌldʒ] n (Aus)bauchung f; vi sich (aus)bauchen.

bulk [bʌlk] n Größe f, Masse f; (greater part) Großteil m; ~**head** Schott nt; ~**y** a (sehr) umfangreich; goods sperrig.

bull [bʊl] n (animal) Bulle m; (cattle) Stier m; (papal) Bulle f; ~**dog** Bulldogge f.

bulldoze ['bʊldəʊz] vt planieren; (fig) durchboxen; ~**r** Planierraupe f, Bulldozer m.

bullet ['bʊlɪt] n Kugel f.

bulletin ['bʊlɪtɪn] n Bulletin nt, Bekanntmachung f.

bullfight ['bʊlfaɪt] n Stierkampf m.

bullion ['bʊlɪən] n Barren m.

bullock ['bʊlək] n Ochse m.

bull's-eye ['bʊlzaɪ] n das Schwarze nt.

bully ['bʊlɪ] n Raufbold m; vt einschüchtern.

bum [bʌm] n (col: backside) Hintern m; (tramp) Landstreicher m; (nasty person)

fieser Kerl m; ~ **around** vi herumgammeln.
bumblebee ['bʌmblbi:] n Hummel f.
bump [bʌmp] n (blow) Stoß m; (swelling) Beule f; vti stoßen, prallen; ~**er** (Brit Aut) Stoßstange f; a edition dick; harvest Rekord-.
bumptious ['bʌmpʃəs] a aufgeblasen.
bumpy ['bʌmpɪ] a holprig.
bun [bʌn] n Korinthenbrötchen nt.
bunch [bʌntʃ] n (of flowers) Strauß m; (of keys) Bund m; (of people) Haufen m.
bundle ['bʌndl] n Bündel nt; vt bündeln; ~ **off** vt fortschicken.
bung [bʌŋ] n Spund m; vt (col: throw) schleudern.
bungalow ['bʌŋgələʊ] n einstöckige(s) Haus nt, Bungalow m.
bungle ['bʌŋgl] vt verpfuschen.
bunion ['bʌnɪən] n entzündete(r) Fußballen m.
bunk [bʌŋk] n Schlafkoje f; ~ **bed** Etagenbett nt.
bunker ['bʌŋkə*] n (coal store) Kohlenbunker m; (golf) Sandloch nt.
bunny ['bʌnɪ] n Häschen n.
Bunsen burner ['bʌnsn 'bɜ:nə*] n Bunsenbrenner m.
bunting ['bʌntɪŋ] n Fahnentuch nt.
buoy [bɔɪ] n Boje f; (lifebuoy) Rettungsboje f; ~**ancy** Schwimmkraft f; ~**ant** a (floating) schwimmend; (fig) heiter; ~ **up** vt Auftrieb geben (+dat).
burden ['bɜ:dn] n (weight) Ladung f, Last f; (fig) Bürde f; vt belasten.
bureau [bjʊˈrəʊ] n (desk) Sekretär m; (for information etc) Büro nt.
bureaucracy [bjʊˈrɒkrəsɪ] n Bürokratie f.
bureaucrat ['bjʊrəkræt] n Bürokrat(in f) m; ~**ic** [bjʊrəˈkrætɪk] a bürokratisch.
burglar ['bɜ:glə*] n Einbrecher m; ~ **alarm** Einbruchssicherung f; ~**ize** (US) einbrechen in (+acc); ~**y** Einbruch m.
burgle ['bɜ:gl] vt einbrechen in (+acc).
burial ['berɪəl] n Beerdigung f; ~ **ground** Friedhof m.
burlesque [bɜ:ˈlesk] n Burleske f.
burly ['bɜ:lɪ] a stämmig.
burn [bɜ:n] irreg vt verbrennen; vi brennen; n Brandwunde f; **to** ~ **one's fingers** sich die Finger verbrennen; ~**ing question** brennende Frage f.
burnish ['bɜ:nɪʃ] vt polieren.
burrow ['bʌrəʊ] n (of fox) Bau m; (of rabbit) Höhle f; vi sich eingraben; vt eingraben.
bursar ['bɜ:sə*] n Kassenverwalter m, Quästor m.
burst [bɜ:st] irreg vt zerbrechen; vi platzen; (into tears) ausbrechen; n Explosion f; (outbreak) Ausbruch m; (in pipe) Bruch(stelle f) m.
bury ['berɪ] vt vergraben; (in grave) beerdigen; **to** ~ **the hatchet** das Kriegsbeil begraben.
bus [bʌs] n (Auto)bus m, Omnibus m.
bush [bʊʃ] n Busch m.
bushel ['bʊʃl] n Scheffel m.

bushy ['bʊʃɪ] a buschig.
busily ['bɪzɪlɪ] ad geschäftig.
business ['bɪznɪs] n Geschäft nt; (concern) Angelegenheit f; **it's none of your** ~ es geht dich nichts an; **to mean** ~ es ernst meinen; ~**man** Geschäftsmann m.
bus-stop ['bʌsstɒp] n Bushaltestelle f.
bust [bʌst] n Büste f; a (broken) kaputt-(gegangen); business pleite; **to go** ~ pleite machen.
bustle ['bʌsl] n Getriebe nt; vi hasten.
bustling ['bʌslɪŋ] a geschäftig.
bust-up ['bʌstʌp] n (col) Krach m.
busy ['bɪzɪ] a beschäftigt; road belebt; vt: ~ **o.s.** sich beschäftigen; ~**body** Übereifrige(r) mf.
but [bʌt, bət] cj aber; **not this** ~ **that** nicht dies, sondern das; (only) nur; (except) außer.
butane ['bju:teɪn] n Butan nt.
butcher ['bʊtʃə*] n Metzger m; (murderer) Schlächter m; vt schlachten; (kill) abschlachten.
butler ['bʌtlə*] n Butler m.
butt [bʌt] n (cask) große(s) Faß nt; (target) Zielscheibe f; (thick end) dicke(s) Ende nt; (of gun) Kolben m; (of cigarette) Stummel m; vt (mit dem Kopf) stoßen.
butter ['bʌtə*] n Butter f; vt buttern; ~**fly** Schmetterling m.
buttocks ['bʌtəks] npl Gesäß nt.
button ['bʌtn] n Knopf m; vti zuknöpfen; ~**hole** Knopfloch nt; Blume f im Knopfloch; vt rankriegen.
buttress ['bʌtrɪs] n Strebepfeiler m; Stützbogen m.
buxom ['bʌksəm] a drall.
buy [baɪ] vt irreg kaufen; ~ **up** vt aufkaufen; ~**er** Käufer(in f) m.
buzz [bʌz] n Summen m; vi summen.
buzzard ['bʌzəd] n Bussard m.
buzzer ['bʌzə*] n Summer m.
by [baɪ] prep (near) bei; (via) über (+acc); (past) an (+dat) . . . vorbei; (before) bis; ~ **day/night** tags/nachts; ~ **train/bus** mit dem Zug/Bus; done ~ **sb/sth** von jdm/durch etw gemacht; ~ **oneself** allein; ~ **and large** im großen und ganzen; ~**-election** Nachwahl f; ~**gone** a vergangen; n: let ~**gones be** ~**gones** laß(t) das Vergangene vergangen sein; ~**(e)-law** Verordnung f; ~**pass** Umgehungsstraße f; ~**-product** Nebenprodukt nt; ~**stander** Zuschauer m; ~ **word** Inbegriff m.

C

C, c [si:] n C nt, c nt.
cab [kæb] n Taxi nt; (of train) Führerstand m; (of truck) Führersitz m.
cabaret ['kæbəreɪ] n Kabarett nt.
cabbage ['kæbɪdʒ] n Kohl(kopf) m.
cabin ['kæbɪn] n Hütte f; (Naut) Kajüte f; (Aviat) Kabine f; ~ **cruiser** Motorjacht f.
cabinet ['kæbɪnɪt] n Schrank m; (for china) Vitrine f; (Pol) Kabinett nt; ~**maker** Kunsttischler m.
cable ['keɪbl] n Drahtseil nt, Tau nt; (Tel)

(Leitungs)kabel *nt*; (*telegram*) Kabel *nt*; *vti* kabeln, telegraphieren; ~**car** Seilbahn *f*; ~**gram** (Übersee)telegramm *nt*; ~ **railway** (Draht)seilbahn *f*.

cache [kæʃ] *n* Versteck *nt*; (*for ammunition*) geheimes Munitionslager *nt*; (*for food*) geheimes Proviantlager *nt*; (*supplies of ammunition*) Munitionsvorrat *m*; (*supplies of food*) Lebensmittelvorrat *m*.

cackle ['kækl] *n* Gegacker *nt*; *vi* gacken.

cactus ['kæktəs] *n* Kaktus *m*, Kaktee *f*.

caddie ['kædɪ] *n* Golfjunge *m*.

caddy ['kædɪ] *n* Teedose *f*.

cadence ['keɪdəns] *n* Tonfall *m*; (*Mus*) Kadenz *f*.

cadet [kə'det] *n* Kadett *m*.

cadge [kædʒ] *vt* schmarotzen, nassauern.

Caesarean [siː'zɛərɪən] *a*: ~ **(section)** Kaiserschnitt *m*.

café ['kæfɪ] *n* Café *nt*, Restaurant *nt*.

cafeteria [kæfɪ'tɪərɪə] *n* Selbstbedienungsrestaurant *nt*.

caffein(e) ['kæfiːn] *n* Koffein *nt*.

cage [keɪdʒ] *n* Käfig *m*; *vt* einsperren.

cagey ['keɪdʒɪ] *a* geheimnistuerisch, zurückhaltend.

cajole [kə'dʒəʊl] *vt* überreden.

cake [keɪk] *n* Kuchen *m*; (*of soap*) Stück *nt*; ~**d** verkrustet.

calamine ['kæləmaɪn] *n* Galmei *m*.

calamitous [kə'læmɪtəs] *a* katastrophal, unglückselig.

calamity [kə'læmɪtɪ] *n* Unglück *nt*, (Schicksals)schlag *m*.

calcium ['kælsɪəm] *n* Kalzium *nt*.

calculate ['kælkjʊleɪt] *vt* berechnen, kalkulieren.

calculating ['kælkjʊleɪtɪŋ] *a* berechnend.

calculation [kælkjʊ'leɪʃən] *n* Berechnung *f*.

calculator ['kælkjʊleɪtə*] *n* Rechner *m*.

calculus ['kælkjʊləs] *n* Rechenart *f*.

calendar ['kælɪndə*] *n* Kalender *m*.

calf [kɑːf] *n* Kalb *nt*, (*leather*) Kalbsleder *nt*; (*Anat*) Wade *f*.

calibre, (*US*) **caliber** ['kælɪbə*] *n* Kaliber *nt*.

call [kɔːl] *vt* rufen; (*summon*) herbeirufen; (*name*) nennen; (*meeting*) einberufen; (*awaken*) wecken; (*Tel*) anrufen; *vi* (*for help*) rufen, schreien; (*visit*) vorbeikommen; *n* (*shout*) Schrei *m*, Ruf *m*; (*visit*) Besuch *m*; (*Tel*) Anruf *m*; **on** ~ in Bereitschaft; ~**box** Fernsprechzelle *f*; ~**er** Besucher(in *f*) *m*; (*Tel*) Anrufer *m*; ~**girl** Call-Girl *nt*; ~**ing** (*vocation*) Berufung *f*; **to be** ~**ed** heißen; ~ **for** *vt* rufen (nach); (*fetch*) abholen; (*fig: require*) erfordern, verlangen; ~ **off** *vt meeting* absagen; ~ **on** *vt* besuchen, aufsuchen; (*request*) fragen; ~ **up** *vt* (*Mil*) einziehen, einberufen.

callous *a*, ~**ly** *ad* ['kæləs, -lɪ] herzlos; ~**ness** Herzlosigkeit *f*.

callow ['kæləʊ] *a* unerfahren, noch nicht flügge.

calm [kɑːm] *n* Stille *f*, Ruhe *f*; (*Naut*) Flaute *f*; *vt* beruhigen; *a* still, ruhig; *person* gelassen; ~**ly** *ad* ruhig, still; ~**ness** Stille

f, Ruhe *f*; (*mental*) Gelassenheit *f*; ~ **down** *vi* sich beruhigen; *vt* beruhigen, besänftigen.

calorie ['kælərɪ] *n* Kalorie *f*, Wärmeeinheit *f*.

calve [kɑːv] *vi* kalben.

camber ['kæmbə*] *n* Wölbung *f*.

camel ['kæməl] *n* Kamel *nt*.

cameo ['kæmɪəʊ] *n* Kamee *f*.

camera ['kæmərə] *n* Fotoapparat *m*, Kamera *f*; **in** ~ unter Ausschluß der Öffentlichkeit; ~**man** Kameramann *m*.

camomile ['kæməmaɪl] *n*: ~ **tea** Kamillentee *m*.

camouflage ['kæməflɑːʒ] *n* Tarnung *f*; *vt* tarnen; (*fig*) verschleiern, bemänteln.

camp [kæmp] *n* Lager *nt*, Camp *nt*; (*Mil*) Feldlager *nt*; (*permanent*) Kaserne *f*; (*camping place*) Zeltplatz *m*; *vi* zelten, campen.

campaign [kæm'peɪn] *n* Kampagne *f*; (*Mil*) Feldzug *m*; *vi* (*Mil*) Krieg führen; (*participate*) in den Krieg ziehen; (*fig*) werben, Propaganda machen; (*Pol*) den Wahlkampf führen; **electoral** ~ Wahlkampf *m*.

campbed ['kæmp'bed] *n* Campingbett *nt*.

camper ['kæmpə*] *n* Zeltende(r) *mf*, Camper *m*.

camping ['kæmpɪŋ] *n*: **to go** ~ zelten, Camping machen.

campsite ['kæmpsaɪt] *n* Zeltplatz *m*, Campingplatz *m*.

campus ['kæmpəs] *n* (*Sch*) Schulgelände *nt*; (*Univ*) Universitätsgelände *nt*, Campus *m*.

can [kæn] *v aux irreg* (*be able*) können, fähig sein; (*be allowed*) dürfen, können; *n* Büchse *f*, Dose *f*; (*for water*) Kanne *f*; *vt* konservieren, in Büchsen einmachen.

canal [kə'næl] *n* Kanal *m*.

canary [kə'nɛərɪ] *n* Kanarienvogel *m*; *a* hellgelb.

cancel ['kænsəl] *vt* (*delete*) durchstreichen; (*Math*) kürzen; *arrangement* aufheben; *meeting* absagen; *treaty* annullieren; *stamp* entwerten; ~**lation** [kænsə'leɪʃən] Aufhebung *f*; Absage *f*; Annullierung *f*; Entwertung *f*.

cancer ['kænsə*] *n* (*also Astrol* **C**~) Krebs *m*.

candid ['kændɪd] *a* offen, ehrlich; ~**ly** *ad* ehrlich.

candidate ['kændɪdeɪt] *n* Bewerber(in *f*) *m*; (*Pol*) Kandidat(in *f*) *m*.

candle ['kændl] *n* Kerze *f*; ~**light** Kerzenlicht *nt*; ~**stick** Kerzenleuchter *m*.

candour ['kændə*] *n* Offenheit *f*.

candy ['kændɪ] *n* Kandis(zucker) *m*; (*US*) Bonbons *pl*.

cane [keɪn] *n* (*Bot*) Rohr *nt*; (*for walking*, *Sch*) Stock *m*; *vt* schlagen.

canister ['kænɪstə*] *n* Blechdose *f*.

cannabis ['kænəbɪs] *n* Hanf *m*, Haschisch *nt*.

canned [kænd] *a* Büchsen-, eingemacht.

cannibal ['kænɪbəl] *n* Menschenfresser *m*; ~**ism** Kannibalismus *m*.

cannon ['kænən] *n* Kanone *f*.

cannot ['kænɒt] = can not.

canny ['kænɪ] a (*shrewd*) schlau, erfahren; (*cautious*) umsichtig, vorsichtig.

canoe [kɔ'nuː] n Paddelboot nt, Kanu nt; ~**ing** Kanufahren nt; ~**ist** Kanufahrer(in f) m.

canon ['kænən] n Domherr m; (*in church law*) Kanon m; (*standard*) Grundsatz m.

canonize ['kænɔnaɪz] vt heiligsprechen.

can opener ['kænɔupnə*] n Büchsenöffner m.

canopy ['kænɔpɪ] n Baldachin m.

can't [kænt] = can not.

cantankerous [kæn'tæŋkɔrɔs] a zänkisch, mürrisch.

canteen [kæn'tiːn] n (*in factory*) Kantine f; (*case of cutlery*) Besteckkasten m.

canter ['kæntɔ*] n Kanter m, kurzer leichter Galopp m; vi in kurzem Galopp reiten.

cantilever ['kæntɪliːvɔ*] n Träger m, Ausleger m.

canvas ['kænvɔs] n Segeltuch nt, Zeltstoff m; (*sail*) Segel nt; (*for painting*) Leinwand f; (*painting*) Ölgemälde nt; **under** ~ (*people*) in Zelten; (*boat*) unter Segel.

canvass ['kænvɔs] vt werben; ~**er** Wahlwerber(in f) m.

canyon ['kænjɔn] n Felsenschlucht f.

cap [kæp] n Kappe f, Mütze f; (*lid*) (Verschluß)kappe f, Deckel m; vt verschließen; (*surpass*) übertreffen.

capability [keɪpɔ'bɪlɪtɪ] n Fähigkeit f.

capable ['keɪpɔbl] a fähig; **to be** ~ **of sth** zu etw fähig or imstande sein.

capacity [kɔ'pæsɪtɪ] n Fassungsvermögen nt; (*ability*) Fähigkeit f; (*position*) Eigenschaft f.

cape [keɪp] n (*garment*) Cape nt, Umhang m; (*Geog*) Kap nt.

caper ['keɪpɔ*] n Kaper f.

capital ['kæpɪtl] n (— *city*) Hauptstadt f; (*Fin*) Kapital nt; (— *letter*) Großbuchstabe m; ~**ism** Kapitalismus m; ~**ist** a kapitalistisch; n Kapitalist(in f) m; ~ **punishment** Todesstrafe f.

capitulate [kɔ'pɪtjuleɪt] vi kapitulieren.

capitulation [kɔpɪtju'leɪʃɔn] n Kapitulation f.

capricious [kɔ'prɪʃɔs] a launisch.

Capricorn ['kæprɪkɔːn] n Steinbock m.

capsize [kæp'saɪz] vti kentern.

capstan ['kæpstɔn] n Ankerwinde f, Poller m.

capsule ['kæpsjuːl] n Kapsel f.

captain ['kæptɪn] n Führer m; (*Naut*) Kapitän m; (*Mil*) Hauptmann m; (*Sport*) (Mannschafts)kapitän m; vt anführen.

caption ['kæpʃɔn] n Unterschrift f, Text m.

captivate ['kæptɪveɪt] vt fesseln.

captive ['kæptɪv] n Gefangene(r) mf; a gefangen(gehalten).

captivity [kæp'tɪvɪtɪ] n Gefangenschaft f.

capture ['kæptjuɔ*] vt fassen, gefangennehmen; n Gefangennahme f.

car [kɑː*] n Auto nt, Wagen m.

carafe [kɔ'ræf] n Karaffe f.

caramel ['kærɔmɔl] n Karamelle f.

carat ['kærɔt] n Karat nt.

caravan ['kærɔvæn] n Wohnwagen m; (*in desert*) Karawane f.

caraway ['kærɔweɪ] n: ~ **seed** Kümmel m.

carbohydrate [kɑːbɔu'haɪdreɪt] n Kohlenhydrat nt.

carbon ['kɑːbɔn] n Kohlenstoff m; (— *paper*) Kohlepapier nt; ~ **copy** Durchschlag m.

carburettor ['kɑːbjuretɔ*] n Vergaser m.

carcass ['kɑːkɔs] n Kadaver m.

card [kɑːd] n Karte f; ~**board** Pappe f; ~**board box** Pappschachtel f; ~ **game** Kartenspiel nt.

cardiac ['kɑːdɪæk] a Herz-.

cardigan ['kɑːdɪgɔn] n Strickjacke f.

cardinal ['kɑːdɪnl] a: ~ **number** Kardinalzahl f.

care [kɛɔ*] n Sorge f, Mühe f; (*charge*) Obhut f, Fürsorge f; vi: **I don't** ~ es ist mir egal; **to** ~ **about sb/sth** sich kümmern um jdn/etw; **to take** ~ (*watch*) vorsichtig sein; (*take pains*) darauf achten; **take** ~ **of** vt sorgen für; ~ **for** vt (*look after*) sorgen für; (*like*) mögen, gern haben.

career [kɔ'rɪɔ*] n Karriere f, Laufbahn f; vi rasen.

carefree ['kɛɔfriː] a sorgenfrei.

careful a, ~**ly** ad ['kɛɔful, -fɔlɪ] sorgfältig.

careless a, ~**ly** ad ['kɛɔlɪs, -lɪ] unvorsichtig; ~**ness** Unachtsamkeit f; (*neglect*) Nachlässigkeit f.

caress [kɔ'res] n Liebkosung f; vt liebkosen.

caretaker ['kɛɔteɪkɔ*] n Hausmeister m.

car-ferry ['kɑːferɪ] n Autofähre f.

cargo ['kɑːgɔu] n Kargo m, Schiffsladung f.

caricature ['kærɪkɔtjuɔ*] n Karikatur f; vt karikieren.

carnage ['kɑːnɪdʒ] n Blutbad nt.

carnal ['kɑːnl] a fleischlich, sinnlich.

carnation [kɑː'neɪʃɔn] n Nelke f.

carnival ['kɑːnɪvɔl] n Karneval m, Fastnacht f, Fasching m.

carnivorous [kɑː'nɪvɔrɔs] a fleischfressend.

carol ['kærl] n (Weihnachts)lied nt.

carp [kɑːp] n (*fish*) Karpfen m; ~ **at** vt herumnörgeln an (+dat).

car park ['kɑːpɑːk] n Parkplatz m; Parkhaus nt.

carpenter ['kɑːpɪntɔ*] n Zimmermann m.

carpentry ['kɑːpɪntrɪ] n Zimmerei f.

carpet ['kɑːpɪt] n Teppich m; vt mit einem Teppich auslegen.

carping ['kɑːpɪŋ] a (*critical*) krittelnd, Mecker-.

carriage ['kærɪdʒ] n Wagen m; (*of goods*) Beförderung f; (*bearing*) Haltung f; ~**way** (*on road*) Fahrbahn f.

carrier ['kærɪɔ*] n Träger(in f) m; (*Comm*) Spediteur m; ~ **bag** Tragetasche m; ~ **pigeon** Brieftaube f.

carrion ['kærɪɔn] n Aas nt.

carrot ['kærɔt] n Möhre f, Mohrrübe f, Karotte f.

carry ['kærɪ] vt tragen; vi weit tragen, reichen; ~**cot** Babytragetasche f; **to be**

carried away (fig) hingerissen sein; ~ **on** vti fortführen, weitermachen; ~ **out** vt orders ausführen.

cart [kɑːt] n Wagen m, Karren m; vt schleppen.

cartilage ['kɑːtɪlɪdʒ] n Knorpel m.

cartographer [kɑːˈtɒɡrəfə*] n Kartograph(in f) m.

carton ['kɑːtən] n (Papp)karton m; (of cigarettes) Stange f.

cartoon [kɑːˈtuːn] n (Press) Karikatur f; (Cine) (Zeichen)trickfilm m.

cartridge ['kɑːtrɪdʒ] n (for gun) Patrone f; (film) Rollfilm m; (of record player) Tonabnehmer m.

carve [kɑːv] vti wood schnitzen; stone meißeln; meat (vor)schneiden.

carving ['kɑːvɪŋ] n (in wood etc) Schnitzerei f; ~ **knife** Tranchiermesser nt.

car wash ['kɑːwɒʃ] n Autowäsche f.

cascade [kæsˈkeɪd] n Wasserfall m; vi kaskadenartig herabfallen.

case [keɪs] n (box) Kasten m, Kiste f; (suit—) Koffer m; (Jur, matter) Fall m; in ~ falls, im Falle; **in any** ~ jedenfalls, auf jeden Fall.

cash [kæʃ] n (Bar)geld nt; vt einlösen; ~ **desk** Kasse f; ~ **on delivery** per Nachnahme; ~ **register** Registrierkasse f.

cashmere ['kæʃmɪə*] n Kaschmirwolle f.

casing ['keɪsɪŋ] n Gehäuse nt.

casino [kəˈsiːnəʊ] n Kasino nt.

cask [kɑːsk] n Faß nt.

casket ['kɑːskɪt] n Kästchen nt; (US: coffin) Sarg m.

casserole ['kæsərəʊl] n Kasserole f; (food) Auflauf m.

cassock ['kæsək] n Soutane f, Talar m.

cast [kɑːst] irreg vt werfen; horns etc verlieren; metal gießen; (Theat) besetzen; roles verteilen; n (Theat) Besetzung f; ~ **off** vi (Naut) losmachen; ~**off clothing** abgelegte Kleidung.

castanets [kæstəˈnets] npl Kastagnetten pl.

castaway ['kɑːstəweɪ] n Schiffbrüchige(r) mf.

caste [kɑːst] n Kaste f.

casting ['kɑːstɪŋ] a: ~ **vote** entscheidende Stimme f.

castiron ['kɑːstˈaɪən] n Gußeisen nt; a gußeisern; alibi todsicher.

castle ['kɑːsl] n Burg f; Schloß nt; (country mansion) Landschloß nt; (chess) Turm m.

castor ['kɑːstə*] n (wheel) Laufrolle f; ~ **oil** Rizinusöl nt; ~ **sugar** Streuzucker m.

castrate [kæsˈtreɪt] vt kastrieren.

casual [ˈkæʒjʊl] a arrangement beiläufig; attitude nachlässig; dress leger; meeting zufällig; ~**ly** ad dress zwanglos, leger; remark beiläufig.

casualty ['kæʒjʊltɪ] n Verletzte(r) mf; Tote(r) mf; (department in hospital) Unfallstation f.

cat [kæt] n Katze f.

catalog (US), **catalogue** ['kætəlɒg] n Katalog m; vt katalogisieren.

catalyst ['kætəlɪst] n (lit, fig) Katalysator m.

catapult ['kætəpʌlt] n Katapult nt; Schleuder f.

cataract ['kætərækt] n Wasserfall m; (Med) graue(r) Star m.

catarrh [kəˈtɑː*] n Katarrh m.

catastrophe [kəˈtæstrəfɪ] n Katastrophe f.

catastrophic [kætəsˈtrɒfɪk] a katastrophal.

catch [kætʃ] vt irreg fangen; train etc nehmen; erreichen; (surprise) ertappen; (understand) begreifen; n (of lock) Sperrhaken m; (of fish) Fang m; **to** ~ **a cold** sich erkälten.

catching ['kætʃɪŋ] a (Med, fig) ansteckend.

catch phrase ['kætʃfreɪz] n Schlagwort nt, Slogan m.

catchy ['kætʃɪ] a tune eingängig.

catechism ['kætɪkɪzəm] n Katechismus m.

categorical a, ~**ly** ad [kætəˈɡɒrɪkl, -kəlɪ] kategorisch.

categorize ['kætɪɡəraɪz] vt kategorisieren.

category ['kætɪɡərɪ] n Kategorie f.

cater ['keɪtə*] vi versorgen; ~**ing** Gastronomie f; Bewirtung f; ~ **for** vt (lit) party ausrichten; (fig) eingestellt sein auf (+acc); berücksichtigen.

caterpillar ['kætəpɪlə*] n Raupe f; ~ **track** Gleiskette f.

cathedral [kəˈθiːdrəl] n Kathedrale f, Dom m.

Catholic ['kæθəlɪk] a (Rel) katholisch; n Katholik(in f) m; c~ vielseitig.

cattle ['kætl] npl Vieh nt.

catty ['kætɪ] a gehässig.

cauliflower ['kɒlɪflaʊə*] n Blumenkohl m.

cause [kɔːz] n Ursache f; Grund m; (purpose) Sache f; **in a good** ~ zu einem guten Zweck; vt verursachen.

causeway ['kɔːzweɪ] n Damm m.

caustic ['kɔːstɪk] a ätzend; (fig) bissig.

cauterize ['kɔːtəraɪz] vt ätzen, ausbrennen.

caution ['kɔːʃən] n Vorsicht f; (warning) Warnung f; (Jur) Verwarnung f; vt (ver)warnen.

cautious a, ~**ly** ad ['kɔːʃəs, -lɪ] vorsichtig.

cavalcade [kævəlˈkeɪd] n Kavalkade f.

cavalier [kævəˈlɪə*] a blasiert.

cavalry ['kævəlrɪ] npl Kavallerie f.

cave [keɪv] n Höhle f; ~**man** Höhlenmensch m; ~ **in** vi einstürzen.

cavern ['kævən] n Höhle f; ~**ous** a cheeks hohl; eyes tiefliegend.

cavil ['kævɪl] vi kritteln (at an +dat).

cavity ['kævɪtɪ] n Höhlung f; (in tooth) Loch nt.

cavort [kəˈvɔːt] vi umherspringen.

cease [siːs] vi aufhören; vt beenden; ~**fire** Feuereinstellung f; ~**less** a unaufhörlich.

cedar ['siːdə*] n Zeder f.

cede [siːd] vt abtreten.

ceiling ['siːlɪŋ] n Decke f; (fig) Höchstgrenze f.

celebrate ['selɪbreɪt] vt feiern; anniversary begehen; vi feiern; ~**d** a gefeiert.

celebration [selɪˈbreɪʃən] n Feier f.

celebrity [sɪ'lebrɪti] n gefeierte Persönlichkeit f.
celery ['seləri] n Sellerie m or f.
celestial [sɪ'lestɪəl] a himmlisch.
celibacy ['selibəsɪ] n Zölibat nt or m.
cell [sel] n Zelle f; (Elec) Element nt.
cellar ['selə*] n Keller m.
cellist ['tʃelɪst] n Cellist(in f) m.
cello ['tʃeləʊ] n Cello nt.
cellophane ['seləfeɪn] n Cellophan nt.
cellular ['seljʊlə*] a zellenförmig, zellular.
cellulose ['seljʊləʊs] n Zellulose f.
cement [sɪ'ment] n Zement m; vt (lit) zementieren; (fig) festigen.
cemetery ['semɪtrɪ] n Friedhof m.
cenotaph ['senətɑ:f] n Ehrenmal nt, Zenotaph m.
censor ['sensə*] n Zensor m; ~ship Zensur f.
censure ['senʃə*] vt rügen.
census ['sensəs] n Volkszählung f.
centenary [sen'ti:nərɪ] n Jahrhundertfeier f.
center ['sentə*] n (US) = **centre**.
centigrade ['sentɪgreɪd] a: **10 (degrees)** ~ 10 Grad Celsius.
centilitre, (US) ~**liter** ['sentɪlɪ:tə*] n Zentiliter nt or m.
centimetre, (US) ~**meter** ['sentɪmɪ:tə*] n Zentimeter nt.
centipede ['sentɪpi:d] n Tausendfüßler m.
central ['sentrəl] a zentral ; ~ **heating** Zentralheizung f; ~**ize** vt zentralisieren.
centre ['sentə*] n Zentrum nt; ~ **of gravity** Schwerpunkt m; **to** ~ **on** (sich) konzentrieren auf (+acc).
century ['sentjʊrɪ] n Jahrhundert nt.
ceramic [sɪ'ræmɪk] a keramisch.
cereal ['sɪərɪəl] n (any grain) Getreide nt; (at breakfast) Getreideflocken pl.
ceremonial [serɪ'məʊnɪəl] a zeremoniell.
ceremony ['serɪmənɪ] n Feierlichkeiten pl, Zeremonie f.
certain ['sɜ:tən] a sicher; (particular) gewiß; **for** ~ ganz bestimmt; ~**ly** ad sicher, bestimmt; ~**ty** Gewißheit f.
certificate [sə'tɪfɪkɪt] n Bescheinigung f; (Sch etc) Zeugnis nt.
certify ['sɜ:tɪfaɪ] vti bescheinigen.
cessation [se'seɪʃən] n Einstellung f, Ende nt.
chafe [tʃeɪf] vti (wund)reiben, scheuern.
chaffinch ['tʃæfɪntʃ] n Buchfink m.
chain [tʃeɪn] n Kette f; vt (also ~ **up**) anketten; mit Ketten fesseln; ~ **reaction** Kettenreaktion f; ~ **smoker** Kettenraucher(in f) m; ~ **store** Kettenladen m.
chair [tʃeə*] n Stuhl m; (arm—) Sessel m; (Univ) Lehrstuhl m; vt: **to** ~ **a meeting** in einer Versammlung den Vorsitz führen; ~**lift** Sessellift m; ~**man** Vorsitzende(r) m; (of firm) Präsident m.
chalet ['ʃæleɪ] n Chalet nt.
chalice ['tʃælɪs] n (Abendmahls)kelch m.
chalk [tʃɔ:k] n Kreide f.
challenge ['tʃælɪndʒ] n Herausforderung f; vt auffordern; (contest) bestreiten; ~**r** Herausforderer m.
challenging ['tʃælɪndʒɪŋ] a statement herausfordernd; work anspruchsvoll.

chamber ['tʃeɪmbə*] n Kammer f; ~ **of commerce** Handelskammer f; ~**maid** Zimmermädchen nt; ~ **music** Kammermusik f; ~**pot** Nachttopf m.
chameleon [kə'mi:lɪən] n Chamäleon nt.
chamois ['ʃæmwɑ:] n Gemse f; ~ **leather** ['ʃæmɪ'leðə*] Sämischleder nt.
champagne [ʃæm'peɪn] n Champagner m, Sekt m.
champion ['tʃæmpɪən] n (Sport) Sieger(in f) m, Meister m; (of cause) Verfechter(in f) m; ~**ship** Meisterschaft f.
chance [tʃɑ:ns] n (luck, fate) Zufall m; (possibility) Möglichkeit f; (opportunity) Gelegenheit f, Chance f; (risk) Risiko nt; a zufällig; vt: **to** ~ **it** es darauf ankommen lassen; **by** ~ zufällig; **to take a** ~ ein Risiko eingehen; **no** ~ keine Chance.
chancel ['tʃɑ:nsəl] n Altarraum m, Chor m.
chancellor ['tʃɑ:nsələ*] n Kanzler m; **C**~ **of the Exchequer** Schatzkanzler m.
chancy ['tʃɑ:nsɪ] a (col) riskant.
chandelier [ʃændɪ'lɪə*] n Kronleuchter m.
change [tʃeɪndʒ] vt verändern; money wechseln; vi sich verändern; (trains) umsteigen; (colour etc) sich verwandeln; (clothes) sich umkleiden; n Veränderung f; (money) Wechselgeld nt; (coins) Kleingeld nt; ~**able** a weather wechselhaft; ~**over** Umstellung f, Wechsel m.
changing ['tʃeɪndʒɪŋ] a veränderlich; ~**room** Umkleideraum m.
channel ['tʃænl] n (stream) Bachbett nt; (Naut) Straße f; Meerenge f; (Rad, TV) Kanal m; (fig) Weg m; vt (hindurch)leiten, lenken; **through official** ~**s** durch die Instanzen; **the (English) C**~ der Ärmelkanal; **C**~ **Islands** Kanalinseln pl.
chant [tʃɑ:nt] n liturgische(r) Gesang m; Sprechgesang m, Sprechchor m; vt intonieren.
chaos ['keɪɒs] n Chaos nt, Durcheinander nt.
chaotic [keɪ'ɒtɪk] a chaotisch.
chap [tʃæp] n (col) Bursche m, Kerl m; vt skin rissig machen; vi (hands etc) aufspringen.
chapel ['tʃæpəl] n Kapelle f.
chaperon ['ʃæpərəʊn] n Anstandsdame f, vt begleiten.
chaplain ['tʃæplɪn] n Geistliche(r) m, Pfarrer m, Kaplan m.
chapter ['tʃæptə*] n Kapitel nt.
char [tʃɑ:*] vt (burn) verkohlen; vi (cleaner) putzen gehen.
character ['kærɪktə*] n Charakter m, Wesen nt; (Liter) Figur f, Gestalt f; (Theat) Person f, Rolle f; (peculiar person) Original nt; (in writing) Schriftzeichen nt; ~**istic** [kærɪktə'rɪstɪk] a charakteristisch, bezeichnend (of für); n Kennzeichen nt, Eigenschaft f; ~**ize** vt charakterisieren, kennzeichnen.
charade [ʃə'rɑ:d] n Scharade f.
charcoal ['tʃɑ:kəʊl] n Holzkohle f.
charge [tʃɑ:dʒ] n (cost) Preis m; (Jur) Anklage f; (Mil) Angriff m; vt gun, battery laden; price verlangen; (Mil) angreifen; vi (rush)

angreifen, (an)stürmen; **to be in** ~ **of** verantwortlich sein für; **to take** ~ (die Verantwortung) übernehmen.

chariot ['tʃærɪət] n (Streit)wagen m.

charitable ['tʃærɪtəbl] a wohltätig; (lenient) nachsichtig.

charity ['tʃærɪtɪ] n (institution) Wohlfahrtseinrichtung f, Hilfswerk nt; (attitude) Nächstenliebe f, Wohltätigkeit f.

charlady ['tʃɑːleɪdɪ] n Reinemachefrau f, Putzfrau f.

charlatan ['ʃɑːlətən] n Scharlatan m, Schwindler(in f) m.

charm [tʃɑːm] n Charme m, gewinnende(s) Wesen nt; (in superstition) Amulett nt; Talisman m; vt bezaubern; ~**ing** a reizend, liebenswürdig, charmant.

chart [tʃɑːt] n Tabelle f; (Naut) Seekarte f.

charter ['tʃɑːtə*] vt (Naut, Aviat) chartern; n Schutzbrief m; (cost) Schiffsmiete f; ~**flight** Charterflug m; ~**ed accountant** Wirtschaftsprüfer(in f) m.

charwoman ['tʃɑːwʊmən] n Reinemachefrau f, Putzfrau f.

chary ['tʃɛərɪ] a zurückhaltend (of sth mit etw).

chase [tʃeɪs] vt jagen, verfolgen; n Jagd f.

chasm ['kæzəm] n Kluft f.

chassis ['ʃæsɪ] n Chassis nt, Fahrgestell nt.

chaste [tʃeɪst] a keusch.

chastity ['tʃæstɪtɪ] n Keuschheit f.

chat [tʃæt] vi plaudern, sich (zwanglos) unterhalten; n Plauderei f.

chatter ['tʃætə*] vi schwatzen; (teeth) klappern; n Geschwätz nt; ~**box** Quasselstrippe f.

chatty ['tʃætɪ] a geschwätzig.

chauffeur ['ʃəʊfə*] n Chauffeur m, Fahrer m.

cheap [tʃiːp] a billig; joke billig; (of poor quality) minderwertig; **to** ~**en o.s.** sich herablassen; ~**ly** a billig.

cheat [tʃiːt] vti betrügen; (Sch) mogeln; (of Betrüger(in f) m; ~**ing** Betrug m.

check [tʃek] vt prüfen; (look up, make sure) nachsehen; (control) kontrollieren; (restrain) zügeln; (stop) anhalten; n (examination, restraint) Kontrolle f; (restaurant bill) Rechnung f; (pattern) Karo(muster) nt; (US) = **cheque**; ~**ers** (US) Damespiel nt; ~**list** Kontroll-liste f; ~**mate** Schachmatt nt; ~**point** Kontrollpunkt m; ~**up** (Nach)prüfung f; (Med) (ärztliche) Untersuchung f.

cheek [tʃiːk] n Backe f, Wange f; (fig) Frechheit f, Unverschämtheit f; ~**bone** Backenknochen m; ~**y** a frech, übermütig.

cheep [tʃiːp] n Pieps(er) nt.

cheer [tʃɪə*] n Beifallsruf m, Hochruf m; ~**s!** Prost!; vt zujubeln; (encourage) ermuntern, aufmuntern; vi jauchzen, Hochrufe ausbringen; ~**ful** a fröhlich; ~**fulness** Fröhlichkeit f, Munterkeit f; ~**ing** Applaus m; a aufheiternd; ~**io** interj tschüs!; ~**less** a prospect trostlos; person verdrießlich; ~ **up** vt ermuntern; vi: ~ **up!** Kopf hoch!

cheese [tʃiːz] n Käse m; ~**board**

(gemischte) Käseplatte f; ~**cake** Käsekuchen m.

cheetah ['tʃiːtə] n Gepard m.

chef [ʃef] n Küchenchef m.

chemical ['kemɪkəl] a chemisch.

chemist ['kemɪst] n (Med) Apotheker m, Drogist m; (Chem) Chemiker m; ~**ry** Chemie f; ~**'s (shop)** (Med) Apotheke f, Drogerie f.

cheque [tʃek] n Scheck m; ~**book** Scheckbuch nt; ~ **card** Scheckkarte f.

chequered ['tʃekəd] a (fig) bewegt.

cherish ['tʃerɪʃ] vt person lieben; hope hegen; memory bewahren.

cheroot [ʃəˈruːt] n Zigarillo nt or m.

cherry ['tʃerɪ] n Kirsche f.

chervil ['tʃɜːvɪl] n Kerbel m.

chess [tʃes] n Schach nt; ~**board** Schachbrett nt; ~**man** Schachfigur f; ~**player** Schachspieler(in f) m.

chest [tʃest] n Brust f, Brustkasten m; (box) Kiste f, Kasten m; **to get sth off one's** ~ seinem Herzen Luft machen; ~ **of drawers** Kommode f.

chestnut ['tʃesnʌt] n Kastanie f; ~ **(tree)** Kastanienbaum m.

chew [tʃuː] vti kauen; ~**ing gum** Kaugummi m.

chic [ʃiːk] a schick, elegant.

chicanery [ʃɪˈkeɪnərɪ] n Schikane f.

chick [tʃɪk] n Küken nt; ~**en** Huhn nt; (food: roast) Hähnchen nt; ~**enpox** Windpocken pl; ~**pea** Kichererbse f.

chicory ['tʃɪkərɪ] n Zichorie f; (plant) Chicorée f.

chief [tʃiːf] n (Ober)haupt nt; Anführer m; (Comm) Chef m; a höchst, Haupt-; ~**ly** ad hauptsächlich.

chieftain ['tʃiːftən] n Häuptling m.

chilblain ['tʃɪlbleɪn] n Frostbeule f.

child [tʃaɪld] n Kind nt; ~**birth** Entbindung f; ~**hood** Kindheit f; ~**ish** a kindisch; ~**like** a kindlich; ~**ren** ['tʃɪldrən] npl of **child**; ~**'s play** (fig) Kinderspiel nt.

chill [tʃɪl] n Kühle f; (Med) Erkältung f; ~**y** a kühl, frostig.

chime [tʃaɪm] n Glockenschlag m, Glockenklang m; vi ertönen, (er)klingen.

chimney ['tʃɪmnɪ] n Schornstein m, Kamin m.

chimpanzee [tʃɪmpænˈziː] n Schimpanse m.

chin [tʃɪn] n Kinn m.

china ['tʃaɪnə] n Porzellan nt.

chink [tʃɪŋk] n (opening) Ritze f, Spalt m; (noise) Klirren nt.

chintz [tʃɪnts] n Kattun m.

chip [tʃɪp] n (of wood etc) Splitter m; (potato) ~**s** pl Pommes frites pl; (US: crisp) Chip m; vt absplittern; ~ **in** vi Zwischenbemerkungen machen.

chiropodist [kɪˈropədɪst] n Fußpfleger(in f) m.

chirp [tʃɜːp] n Zwitschern nt; vi zwitschern.

chisel ['tʃɪzl] n Meißel m.

chit [tʃɪt] n Notiz f; ~**chat** Plauderei f.

chivalrous ['ʃɪvəlrəs] a ritterlich.

chivalry ['ʃɪvəlrɪ] n Ritterlichkeit f; (honour) Ritterschaft f.

chive [tʃaɪv] n Schnittlauch m.
chloride ['klɔːraɪd] n Chlorid nt.
chlorine ['klɔːriːn] n Chlor nt.
chock [tʃɒk] n Keil m; ~-a-block a vollgepfropft.
chocolate ['tʃɒklɪt] n Schokolade f.
choice [tʃɔɪs] n Wahl f; (of goods) Auswahl f; a auserlesen, Qualitäts-.
choir ['kwaɪəʳ] n Chor m; ~boy Chorknabe m.
choke [tʃəʊk] vi ersticken; vt erdrosseln; (block) (ab)drosseln; n (Aut) Starterklappe f.
cholera ['kɒlərə] n Cholera f.
choose [tʃuːz] vt irreg wählen; (decide) beschließen.
chop [tʃɒp] vt (zer)hacken; wood spalten; vi: to ~ and change schwanken; n Hieb m; (meat) Kotelett nt; ~py a bewegt; ~sticks pl (Eß)stäbchen pl.
choral ['kɔːrəl] a Chor-.
chord [kɔːd] n Akkord m; (string) Saite f.
chore [tʃɔːʳ] n Pflicht f; harte Arbeit f.
choreographer [kɒrɪ'ɒgrəfəʳ] n Choreograph(in f) m.
chorister ['kɒrɪstəʳ] n Chorsänger(in f) m.
chortle ['tʃɔːtl] vi glucksen, tief lachen.
chorus ['kɔːrəs] n Chor m; (in song) Refrain m.
chow [tʃaʊ] n (dog) Chow-Chow m.
Christ [kraɪst] n Christus m.
christen ['krɪsn] vt taufen; ~ing Taufe f.
Christian ['krɪstɪən] a christlich; n Christ(in f) m; ~ name Vorname m; ~ity [krɪstɪ'ænɪtɪ] Christentum nt.
Christmas ['krɪsməs] n Weihnachten pl; ~ card Weihnachtskarte f; ~ tree Weihnachtsbaum m.
chrome [krəʊm] n = chromium plating.
chromium ['krəʊmɪəm] n Chrom nt; ~ plating Verchromung f.
chronic ['krɒnɪk] a (Med) chronisch; (terrible) scheußlich.
chronicle ['krɒnɪkl] n Chronik f.
chronological [krɒnə'lɒdʒɪkəl] a chronologisch.
chrysalis ['krɪsəlɪs] n (Insekten)puppe f.
chrysanthemum [krɪs'ænθɪməm] n Chrysantheme f.
chubby ['tʃʌbɪ] a child pausbäckig; adult rundlich.
chuck [tʃʌk] vt werfen; n (Tech) Spannvorrichtung f.
chuckle ['tʃʌkl] vi in sich hineinlachen.
chum [tʃʌm] n (child) Spielkamerad m; (adult) Kumpel m.
chunk [tʃʌŋk] n Klumpen m; (of food) Brocken m.
church [tʃɜːtʃ] n Kirche f; (clergy) Geistlichkeit f; ~yard Kirchhof m.
churlish ['tʃɜːlɪʃ] a grob.
churn [tʃɜːn] n Butterfaß nt; (for transport) (große) Milchkanne f; ~ out vt (col) produzieren.
chute [ʃuːt] n Rutsche f.
cicada [sɪ'kɑːdə] n Zikade f.
cider ['saɪdəʳ] n Apfelwein m.
cigar [sɪ'gɑːʳ] n Zigarre f; ~ette [sɪgə'ret]

Zigarette f; ~ette case Zigarettenetui nt; ~ette end Zigarettenstummel m; ~ette holder Zigarettenspitze f.
cinch [sɪntʃ] n (col) klare(r) Fall m; (easy) Kinderspiel nt.
cinder ['sɪndəʳ] n Zinder m.
Cinderella [sɪndə'relə] n Aschenbrödel nt.
cine ['sɪnɪ] n: ~-camera Filmkamera f; ~ film Schmalfilm m.
cinema ['sɪnəmə] n Kino nt.
cine-projector [sɪnɪprə'dʒektəʳ] n Filmvorführapparat m.
cinnamon ['sɪnəmən] n Zimt m.
cipher ['saɪfəʳ] n (code) Chiffre f; (numeral) Ziffer f.
circle ['sɜːkl] n Kreis m; vi kreisen; vt umkreisen; (attacking) umzingeln.
circuit ['sɜːkɪt] n Umlauf m; (Elec) Stromkreis m; ~ous [sɜː'kjuːɪtəs] a weitschweifig.
circular ['sɜːkjʊləʳ] a (kreis)rund, kreisförmig; n Rundschreiben nt.
circularize ['sɜːkjʊləraɪz] vt (inform) benachrichtigen; letter herumschicken.
circulate ['sɜːkjʊleɪt] vi zirkulieren; vt in Umlauf setzen.
circulation [sɜːkjʊ'leɪʃən] n (of blood) Kreislauf m; (of newspaper) Auflage f; (of money) Umlauf m.
circumcise ['sɜːkəmsaɪz] vt beschneiden.
circumference [sɜː'kʌmfərəns] n (Kreis)umfang m.
circumspect ['sɜːkəmspekt] a umsichtig.
circumstances ['sɜːkəmstənsəz] npl (facts connected with sth) Umstände pl; (financial condition) Verhältnisse pl.
circumvent [sɜːkəm'vent] vt umgehen.
circus ['sɜːkəs] n Zirkus m.
cissy ['sɪsɪ] n Weichling m.
cistern ['sɪstən] n Zisterne f; (of W.C.) Spülkasten m.
citation [saɪ'teɪʃən] n Zitat nt.
cite [saɪt] vt zitieren, anführen.
citizen ['sɪtɪzn] n Bürger(in f) m; (of nation) Staatsangehörige(r) mf; ~ship Staatsangehörigkeit f.
citrus ['sɪtrəs] adj: ~ fruit Zitrusfrucht f.
city ['sɪtɪ] n Großstadt f; (centre) Zentrum nt, City f.
civic ['sɪvɪk] a städtisch, Bürger-.
civil ['sɪvɪl] a (of town) Bürger-; (of state) staatsbürgerlich; (not military) zivil; (polite) höflich; ~ engineer Bauingenieur m; ~ engineering Hoch- und Tiefbau m; ~ian [sɪ'vɪlɪən] n Zivilperson f; a zivil, Zivil-; ~ization [sɪvɪlaɪ'zeɪʃən] n Zivilisation f, Kultur f; ~ized a zivilisiert; Kultur-; ~ law bürgerliche(s) Recht, Zivilrecht m; ~ rights pl Bürgerrechte pl; ~ servant Staatsbeamte(r) m; ~ service Staatsdienst m; ~ war Bürgerkrieg m.
clad [klæd] a gekleidet; ~ in gehüllt in (+acc).
claim [kleɪm] vt beanspruchen; (have opinion) behaupten; n (demand) Forderung f, (right) Anspruch m; Behauptung f; ~ant Antragsteller(in f) m.

clairvoyant [kleə'vɔɪənt] n Hellseher(in f) m; a hellseherisch.

clam [klæm] n Venusmuschel f.

clamber ['klæmbə*] vi kraxeln.

clammy ['klæmɪ] a feucht(kalt); klamm.

clamorous ['klæmərəs] a lärmend, laut.

clamp [klæmp] n Schraubzwinge f; vt einspannen.

clan [klæn] n Sippe f, Clan m.

clang [klæŋ] n Klang m; Scheppern nt; vi klingen; scheppern.

clap [klæp] vi klatschen; vt Beifall klatschen (+dat); ~ping (Beifall)klatschen nt.

claret ['klærɪt] n rote(r) Bordeaux(wein) m.

clarification [klærɪfɪ'keɪʃən] n Erklärung f.

clarify ['klærɪfaɪ] vt klären, erklären.

clarinet [klærɪ'net] n Klarinette f.

clarity ['klærɪtɪ] n Klarheit f.

clash [klæʃ] n (fig) Konflikt m, Widerstreit m; (sound) Knall m; vi zusammenprallen; (colours) sich beißen; (argue) sich streiten.

clasp [klɑːsp] n Klammer f, Haken m; (on belt) Schnalle f; vt umklammern.

class [klɑːs] n Klasse f; vt einordnen, einstufen; ~-conscious a klassenbewußt.

classic ['klæsɪk] n Klassiker(in f) m; a (traditional) klassisch; ~al a klassisch.

classification [klæsɪfɪ'keɪʃən] n Klassifizierung f; Einteilung f.

classify ['klæsɪfaɪ] vt klassifizieren, einteilen.

classroom ['klɑːsrʊm] n Klassenzimmer nt.

classy ['klɑːsɪ] a (col) todschick.

clatter ['klætə*] n Klappern nt, Rasseln nt; (of feet) Getrappel nt; vi klappern, rasseln; (feet) trappeln.

clause [klɔːz] n (Jur) Klausel f; (Gram) Satz(teil) m, Satzglied nt.

claustrophobia [klɔːstrə'fəʊbɪə] n Platzangst f, Klaustrophobie f.

claw [klɔː] n Kralle f; vt (zer)kratzen.

clay [kleɪ] n Lehm m; (for pots) Ton m.

clean [kliːn] a sauber; (fig) schuldlos; shape ebenmäßig; cut glatt; vt saubermachen, reinigen, putzen; ~er (person) Putzfrau f; (for grease etc) Scheuerpulver nt; ~ers pl Chemische Reinigung f; ~ing Reinigen nt, Säubern nt; ~liness ['klenlɪnɪs] Sauberkeit f, Reinlichkeit f; ~ly a reinlich; ~se [klenz] vt reinigen, säubern; ~-shaven a glattrasiert; ~-up Reinigung f; ~ out vt gründlich putzen; ~ up vt aufräumen.

clear ['klɪə*] a water klar; glass durchsichtig; sound deutlich, klar, hell; meaning genau, klar; (certain) klar, sicher; road frei; to stand ~ of sth etw frei halten; vt road etc freimachen; vi (become clear) klarwerden; ~ance ['klɪərns] (removal) Räumung f; (free space) Lichtung f; (permission) Freigabe f; ~-cut a scharf umrissen; case eindeutig; ~ing Lichtung f; ~ly ad klar, deutlich, zweifellos; ~way (Brit) (Straße f mit) Halteverbot nt; ~ up vi (weather) sich aufklären; vt reinigen, säubern; (solve) aufklären.

clef [klef] n Notenschlüssel m.

clench [klentʃ] vt teeth zusammenbeißen; fist ballen.

clergy ['klɜːdʒɪ] n Geistliche(n) pl; ~man Geistliche(r) m.

clerical ['klerɪkəl] a (office)Schreib-, Büro-; (Eccl) geistlich, Pfarr(er)-; ~ error Schreibfehler m.

clerk [klɑːk, US klɜːk] n (in office) Büroangestellte(r) mf; (US: salesman) Verkäufer(in f) m.

clever ['klevə*] a, ~ly ad ['klevə*, -əlɪ] klug, geschickt, gescheit.

cliché ['kliːʃeɪ] n Klischee nt.

click [klɪk] vi klicken; n Klicken nt; (of door) Zuklinken nt.

client ['klaɪənt] n Klient(in f) m; ~ele [kliːɑ̃'tel] Kundschaft f.

cliff [klɪf] n Klippe f.

climate ['klaɪmɪt] n Klima nt.

climatic [klaɪ'mætɪk] a klimatisch.

climax ['klaɪmæks] n Höhepunkt m.

climb [klaɪm] vt besteigen; vi steigen, klettern; n Aufstieg m; ~er Bergsteiger m, Kletterer m; (fig) Streber m; ~ing Bergsteigen nt, Klettern nt.

clinch [klɪntʃ] vt (decide) entscheiden; deal festmachen; n (boxing) Clinch m.

cling [klɪŋ] vi irreg anhaften, anhängen.

clinic ['klɪnɪk] n Klinik f; ~al a klinisch.

clink [klɪŋk] n (of coins) Klimpern nt; (of glasses) Klirren nt; (col: prison) Knast m; vi klimpern; vt klimpern mit; glasses anstoßen.

clip [klɪp] n Spange f; paper ~ (Büro-, Heft)klammer f; vt papers heften; hair, hedge stutzen; ~pers pl (instrument) (for hedge) Heckenschere f; (for hair) Haarschneidemaschine f.

clique [kliːk] n Clique f, Gruppe f.

cloak [kləʊk] n lose(r) Mantel m, Umhang m; ~-room (for coats) Garderobe f; (W.C.) Toilette f.

clobber ['klɒbə*] n (col) Klamotten pl; vt schlagen.

clock [klɒk] n Uhr f; ~wise ad im Uhrzeigersinn; ~work Uhrwerk nt; like ~work wie am Schnürchen.

clog [klɒg] n Holzschuh m; vt verstopfen.

cloister ['klɔɪstə*] n Kreuzgang m.

close [kləʊs] a nahe; march genau, gründlich; weather schwül; ad knapp; ~ly ad gedrängt, dicht; ~ to prep in der Nähe (+gen); I had a ~ shave das war knapp; ~-up Nahaufnahme f.

close [kləʊz] vt schließen, abschließen; vi sich schließen; (end) Ende nt, Schluß m; to ~ with sb jdn angreifen; ~ down vt Geschäft aufgeben; vi eingehen; ~d a road gesperrt; shop etc geschlossen; ~d shop Gewerkschaftszwang m.

closet ['klɒzɪt] n Abstellraum m, Schrank m.

closure ['kləʊʒə*] n Schließung f.

clot [klɒt] n Klumpen m; (of blood) Blutgerinnsel nt; (fool) Blödmann m; vi gerinnen.

cloth [klɒθ] n (material) Stoff m, Tuch nt;

(*for washing etc*) Lappen *m*, Tuch *nt*.
clothe [kləʊð] *vt* kleiden, bekleiden; ~s *pl*
Kleider *pl*, Kleidung *f*; see **bedclothes**;
~s **brush** Kleiderbürste *f*; ~s **line**
Wäscheleine *f*; ~s **peg** Wäscheklammer
f.
clothing [ˈkləʊðɪŋ] *n* = **clothes**.
cloud [klaʊd] *n* Wolke *f*; ~**burst** Wolken-
bruch *m*; ~**y** *a* wolkig, bewölkt.
clout [klaʊt] (*col*) *n* Schlag *m*; *vt* hauen.
clove [kləʊv] *n* Gewürznelke *f*; ~ **of**
garlic Knoblauchzehe *f*.
clover [ˈkləʊvə*] *n* Klee *m*; ~**leaf** Kleeblatt *nt*.
clown [klaʊn] *n* Clown *m*, Hanswurst *m*; *vi*
kaspern, sich albern benehmen.
cloy [klɔɪ] *vi*: **it** ~**s** es übersättigt einen.
club [klʌb] *n* Knüppel *m*; (*society*) Klub *m*;
(*golf*) Golfschläger *m*; (*Cards*) Kreuz *nt*; *vt*
prügeln; ~ **together** *vi* (*with money etc*)
zusammenlegen; ~**house** Klubhaus *nt*.
cluck [klʌk] *vi* glucken.
clue [kluː] *n* Anhaltspunkt *m*, Fingerzeig *m*,
Spur *f*; **he hasn't a** ~ er hat keine
Ahnung.
clump [klʌmp] *n* Gebüsch *nt*.
clumsy [ˈklʌmzɪ] *a person* ungelenk, unbeholfen; *object, shape* unförmig.
cluster [ˈklʌstə*] *n* Traube *f*; (*of trees etc*)
Gruppe *f*; ~ **round** *vi* sich scharen um;
umschwarmen.
clutch [klʌtʃ] *n* feste(r) Griff *m*; (*Aut*)
Kupplung *f*; *vt* sich festklammern an
(+*dat*); *book* an sich klammern.
clutter [ˈklʌtə*] *vt* vollpropfen; *desk etc*
übersäen; *n* Unordnung *f*.
coach [kəʊtʃ] *n* Omnibus *m*, (Überland)bus
m; (*old*) Kutsche *f*; (*Rail*) (Personen)
wagen *m*; (*trainer*) Trainer *m*; *vt* (*Sch*)
Nachhilfeunterricht geben (+*dat*); (*Sport*)
trainieren.
coagulate [kəʊˈægjʊleɪt] *vi* gerinnen.
coal [kəʊl] *n* Kohle *f*.
coalesce [kəʊəˈles] *vi* sich verbinden.
coal face [ˈkəʊlfeɪs] *n* (Abbau)sohle *f*,
Streb *m*; **at the** ~ vor Ort.
coalfield [ˈkəʊlfiːld] *n* Kohlengebiet *nt*.
coalition [kəʊəˈlɪʃən] *n* Zusammenschluß
m; (*Pol*) Koalition *f*.
coalmine [ˈkəʊlmaɪn] *n* Kohlenbergwerk
nt; ~**r** Bergarbeiter *m*.
coarse [kɔːs] *a* (*lit*) grob; (*fig*) ordinär.
coast [kəʊst] *n* Küste *f*; ~**al** *a* Küsten-;
~**er** Küstenfahrer *m*; ~**guard** Küsten-
wache *f*; ~**line** Küste(nlinie) *f*.
coat [kəʊt] *n* Mantel *m*; (*on animals*) Fell *nt*,
Pelz *m*; (*of paint*) Schicht *f*; *vt* über-
streichen; (*cover*) bedecken; ~ **of arms**
Wappen *nt*; ~**hanger** Kleiderbügel *m*;
~**ing** Schicht *f*, Überzug *m*; (*of paint*)
Schicht *f*.
coax [kəʊks] *vt* beschwatzen.
cobble(stone)s [ˈkɒbl(stəʊn)z] *npl*
Pflastersteine *pl*.
cobra [ˈkɒbrə] *n* Kobra *f*.
cobweb [ˈkɒbweb] *n* Spinnennetz *nt*.
cocaine [kəˈkeɪn] *n* Kokain *nt*.
cock [kɒk] *n* Hahn *m*; *vt* ears spitzen; *gun*
den Hahn spannen; ~**erel** junge(r) Hahn

m; ~**-eyed** *a* (*fig*) verrückt.
cockle [ˈkɒkl] *n* Herzmuschel *f*.
cockney [ˈkɒknɪ] *n* echte(r) Londoner *m*.
cockpit [ˈkɒkpɪt] *n* (*Aviat*) Pilotenkanzel *f*.
cockroach [ˈkɒkrəʊtʃ] *n* Küchenschabe *f*.
cocktail [ˈkɒkteɪl] *n* Cocktail *m*; ~
cabinet Hausbar *f*; ~ **party** Cocktail-
party *f*; ~ **shaker** Mixbecher *m*.
cocoa [ˈkəʊkəʊ] *n* Kakao *m*.
coconut [ˈkəʊkənʌt] *n* Kokosnuß *f*.
cocoon [kəˈkuːn] *n* Puppe *f*, Kokon *m*.
cod [kɒd] *n* Kabeljau *m*.
code [kəʊd] *n* Kode *m*; (*Jur*) Kodex *m*; **in**
~ verschlüsselt, in Kode.
codeine [ˈkəʊdiːn] *n* Kodein *nt*.
codify [ˈkəʊdɪfaɪ] *vt message* verschlüsseln;
(*Jur*) kodifizieren.
coeducational [kəʊedjʊˈkeɪʃənl] *a* koedu-
kativ, gemischt.
coerce [kəʊˈɜːs] *vt* nötigen, zwingen.
coercion [kəʊˈɜːʃən] *n* Zwang *m*, Nötigung
f.
coexistence [kəʊɪgˈzɪstəns] *n* Koexistenz *f*.
coffee [ˈkɒfɪ] *n* Kaffee *m*; ~ **bar**
Kaffeeausschank *m*, Café *nt*.
coffin [ˈkɒfɪn] *n* Sarg *m*.
cog [kɒg] *n* (Rad)zahn *m*.
cogent [ˈkəʊdʒənt] *a* triftig, überzeugend,
zwingend.
cognac [ˈkɒnjæk] *n* Kognak *m*.
coherent [kəʊˈhɪərnt] *a* zusammenhängend, einheitlich.
coil [kɔɪl] *n* Rolle *f*; (*Elec*) Spule *f*; *vt*
aufrollen, aufwickeln.
coin [kɔɪn] *n* Münze *f*; *vt* prägen; ~**age**
(*word*) Prägung *f*.
coincide [kəʊɪnˈsaɪd] *vi* (*happen together*)
zusammenfallen; (*agree*) übereinstimmen;
~**nce** [kəʊˈɪnsɪdəns] Zufall *m*; **by a**
strange ~**nce** merkwürdigerweise;
~**ntal** [kəʊɪnsɪˈdentl] *a* zufällig.
coke [kəʊk] *n* Koks *m*.
colander [ˈkʌləndə*] *n* Durchschlag *m*.
cold [kəʊld] *a* kalt; **I'm** ~ mir ist kalt, ich
friere; *n* Kälte *f*; (*illness*) Erkältung *f*; **to**
have ~ **feet** (*fig*) kalte Füße haben,
Angst haben; **to give sb the** ~ **shoulder**
jdm die kalte Schulter zeigen; ~**ly** *ad* kalt;
(*fig*) gefühllos; ~ **sore** Erkältungs-
bläschen *nt*.
coleslaw [ˈkəʊlslɔː] *n* Krautsalat *m*.
colic [ˈkɒlɪk] *n* Kolik *f*.
collaborate [kəˈlæbəreɪt] *vi* zusammenarbeiten.
collaboration [kəlæbəˈreɪʃən] *n* Zusammenarbeit *f*; (*Pol*) Kollaboration *f*.
collaborator [kəˈlæbəreɪtə*] *n* Mitarbeiter
m; (*Pol*) Kollaborateur *m*.
collage [kɒˈlɑːʒ] *n* Collage *f*.
collapse [kəˈlæps] *vi* (*people*) zusammenbrechen; (*things*) einstürzen; *n* Zusammenbruch *m*, Einsturz *m*.
collapsible [kəˈlæpsəbl] *a* zusammenklappbar, Klapp-.
collar [ˈkɒlə*] *n* Kragen *m*; ~**bone**
Schlüsselbein *nt*.
collate [kɒˈleɪt] *vt* zusammenstellen und
vergleichen.
colleague [ˈkɒliːg] *n* Kollege *m*, Kollegin *f*.

collect [kə'lekt] vt sammeln; (fetch) abholen; vi sich sammeln; ~ **call** (US) R-Gespräch nt; ~**ed** a gefaßt; ~**ion** [kə'lekʃən] Sammlung f; (Eccl) Kollekte f; ~**ive** a gemeinsam; (Pol) kollektiv; ~**or** Sammler m; (tax —or) (Steuer)einnehmer m.

college ['kɒlidʒ] n (Univ) College nt; (Tech) Fach-, Berufsschule f.

collide [kə'laid] vi zusammenstoßen; kollidieren, im Widerspruch stehen (with zu).

collie ['kɒli] n schottische(r) Schäferhund m, Collie m.

colliery ['kɒliəri] n (Kohlen)bergwerk nt, Zeche f.

collision [kə'liʒən] n Zusammenstoß m; (of opinions) Konflikt m.

colloquial [kə'loukwiəl] a umgangssprachlich.

collusion [kə'luːʒən] n geheime(s) Einverständnis nt, Zusammenspiel nt.

colon ['koulon] n Doppelpunkt m.

colonel ['kɜːnl] n Oberst m.

colonial [kə'lounial] a Kolonial-.

colonize ['kɒlənaiz] vt kolonisieren.

colonnade [kɒlə'neid] n Säulengang m.

colony ['kɒləni] n Kolonie f.

color ['kʌlə*] (US) = **colour**.

Colorado beetle [kɒlə'rɑːdou 'biːtl] n Kartoffelkäfer m.

colossal [kə'losl] a kolossal, riesig.

colour ['kʌlə*] n Farbe f; **off** ~ nicht wohl; vt (lit, fig) färben; vi sich verfärben; ~**s** pl Fahne f; ~ **bar** Rassenschranke f; ~**-blind** a farbenblind; ~**ed** a farbig; ~**ed** (**wo**)**man** Farbige(r) mf; ~ **film** Farbfilm m; ~**ful** a bunt; ~ **scheme** Farbgebung f; ~ **television** Farbfernsehen nt.

colt [koult] n Fohlen nt.

column ['kɒləm] n Säule f; (Mil) Kolonne f; (of print) Spalte f; ~**ist** ['kɒləmnist] Kolumnist m.

coma ['koumə] n Koma nt.

comb [koum] n Kamm m; vt kämmen; (search) durchkämmen.

combat ['kɒmbæt] n Kampf m; vt bekämpfen.

combination [kɒmbi'neiʃən] n Verbindung f, Kombination f.

combine [kəm'bain] vt verbinden; vi sich vereinigen; ['kɒmbain] n (Comm) Konzern m, Verband f; ~ **harvester** Mähdrescher m.

combustible [kəm'bʌstibl] a brennbar, leicht entzündlich.

combustion [kəm'bʌstʃən] n Verbrennung f.

come [kʌm] irreg vi kommen; (reach) ankommen, gelangen; ~ **about** vi geschehen; ~ **across** vt (find) stoßen auf (+acc); ~ **away** vi (person) weggehen; (handle etc) abgehen; ~ **by** vi vorbeikommen; vt (find) zu etw kommen; ~ **down** vi (price) fallen; ~ **forward** vi (volunteer) sich melden; ~ **from** vt (result) kommen von; **where do you ~ from?** wo kommen Sie her?; **I ~ from London** ich komme aus London; ~ **in for**

vt abkriegen; ~ **into** vi eintreten in (+acc); (inherit) erben; ~ **of** vi: **what came of it?** was ist daraus geworden?; ~ **off** vi (handle) abgehen; (happen) stattfinden; (succeed) klappen; ~ **off it!** laß den Quatsch!; ~ **on** vi (progress) vorankommen; **how's the book coming on?** was macht das Buch?; ~ **on!** komm!; (hurry) beeil dich!; (encouraging) los!; ~ **out** vi herauskommen; ~ **out with** vt herausrücken mit; ~ **round** vi (visit) vorbeikommen; (Med) wieder zu sich kommen; ~ **to** vi (Med) wieder zu sich kommen; (bill) sich belaufen auf; ~ **up** vi hochkommen; (problem) auftauchen; ~ **upon** vt stoßen auf (+acc); ~ **up to** vi (approach) zukommen auf (+acc); (water) reichen bis; (expectation) entsprechen (+dat); ~ **up with** sich etw einfallen lassen; ~**back** Wiederauftreten nt, Comeback nt.

comedian [kə'miːdiən] n Komiker m.

comedown ['kʌmdaun] n Abstieg m.

comedy ['kɒmədi] n Komödie f.

comet ['kɒmit] n Komet m.

comfort ['kʌmfət] n Bequemlichkeit f; (of body) Behaglichkeit f; (of mind) Trost m; vt trösten; ~**s** pl Annehmlichkeiten pl; ~**able** a bequem, gemütlich; ~ **station** (US) öffentliche Toilette f.

comic ['kɒmik] n Comic(heft) nt; (comedian) Komiker m; a (also ~**al**) komisch, humoristisch.

coming ['kʌmiŋ] n Kommen nt, Ankunft f.

comma ['kɒmə] n Komma nt.

command [kə'mɑːnd] n Befehl m; (control) Führung f; (Mil) Kommando nt, (Ober)befehl m; vt befehlen (+dat); (Mil) kommandieren, befehligen; (be able to get) verfügen über (+acc); vi befehlen; ~**er** [kəmən'diə*] vt (Mil) requirieren; ~**er** Befehlshaber m, Kommandant m; ~**ing officer** Kommandeur m; ~**ment** Gebot nt; ~**o** (Mitglied einer) Kommandotruppe f.

commemorate [kə'meməreit] vt gedenken (+gen).

commemoration [kəmemə'reiʃən] n: **in ~ of** zum Gedächtnis or Andenken an (+acc).

commemorative [kə'memərətiv] a Gedächtnis-; Gedenk-.

commence [kə'mens] vti beginnen; ~**ment** Beginn m.

commend [kə'mend] vt (recommend) empfehlen; (praise) loben; ~**able** a empfehlenswert, lobenswert; ~**ation** [kɒmən'deiʃən] Empfehlung f; (Sch) Lob nt.

commensurate [kə'mensjurit] a vergleichbar, entsprechend (with dat).

comment ['kɒment] n (remark) Bemerkung f; (note) Anmerkung f; (opinion) Stellungnahme f; vi etw sagen (on zu); sich äußern (on zu); ~**ary** ['kɒməntri] Kommentar m; Erläuterungen pl; ~**ator** ['kɒmənteitə*] Kommentator m.

commerce ['kɒmɜːs] n Handel m.

commercial [kə'mɜːʃəl] a kommerziell, geschäftlich; training kaufmännisch; n (TV) Fernsehwerbung f; ~**ize** vt kommerzialisieren; ~ **television** Werbefernsehen *nt*; ~ **vehicle** Lieferwagen *m*.

commiserate [kə'mɪzəreɪt] *vi* Mitleid haben.

commission [kə'mɪʃən] *n* Auftrag *m*; (*fee*) Provision *f*; (*Mil*) Offizierspatent *nt*; (*of offence*) Begehen *nt*; (*reporting body*) Kommission *f*; *vt* bevollmächtigen, beauftragen; **out of** ~ außer Betrieb; ~**aire** [kəmɪʃə'nɛə*] Portier *m*; ~**er** (Regierungs)bevollmächtigte(r) *m*.

commit [kə'mɪt] *vt crime* begehen; (*undertake*) sich verpflichten; (*entrust*) übergeben, anvertrauen; **I don't want to** ~ **myself** ich will mich nicht festlegen; ~**ment** Verpflichtung *f*.

committee [kə'mɪtɪ] *n* Ausschuß *m*, Komitee *nt*.

commodious [kə'məʊdɪəs] *a* geräumig.

commodity [kə'mɒdɪtɪ] *n* Ware *f*; (Handels-, Gebrauchs)artikel *m*.

commodore ['kɒmədɔː*] *n* Flotillenadmiral *m*.

common ['kɒmən] *a cause* gemeinsam; (*public*) öffentlich, allgemein; *experience* allgemein, alltäglich; (*pej*) gewöhnlich; (*widespread*) üblich, häufig, gewöhnlich; *n* Gemeindeland *nt*; öffentliche Anlage *f*; ~**ly** *ad* im allgemeinen, gewöhnlich; **C~ Market** Gemeinsame(r) Markt *m*; ~**place** *a* alltäglich; *n* Gemeinplatz *m*; ~**room** Gemeinschaftsraum *m*; ~**sense** gesunde(r) Menschenverstand *m*; **the C~wealth** das Commonwealth.

commotion [kə'məʊʃən] *n* Aufsehen *nt*, Unruhe *f*.

communal ['kɒmjuːnl] *a* Gemeinde-; Gemeinschafts-.

commune ['kɒmjuːn] *n* Kommune *f*; *vi* sich mitteilen (*with dat*), vertraulich verkehren.

communicate [kə'mjuːnɪkeɪt] *vt* (*transmit*) übertragen; *vi* (*be in touch*) in Verbindung stehen; (*make self understood*) sich verständlich machen.

communication [kəmjuːnɪ'keɪʃən] *n* (*message*) Mitteilung *f*; (*Rad, TV etc*) Kommunikationsmittel *nt*; (*making understood*) Kommunikation *f*; ~**s** *pl* (*transport etc*) Verkehrswege *pl*; ~ **cord** Notbremse *f*.

communion [kə'mjuːnɪən] *n* (*group*) Gemeinschaft *f*; (*Rel*) Religionsgemeinschaft *f*; (**Holy**) C~ Heilige(s) Abendmahl *nt*, Kommunion *f*.

communiqué [kə'mjuːnɪkeɪ] *n* Kommuniqué *nt*, amtliche Verlautbarung *f*.

communism ['kɒmjunɪzəm] *n* Kommunismus *m*.

communist ['kɒmjunɪst] *n* Kommunist(in *f*) *m*; *a* kommunistisch.

community [kə'mjuːnɪtɪ] *n* Gemeinschaft *f*; (*public*) Gemeinwesen *nt*; ~ **centre** Gemeinschaftszentrum *nt*; ~ **chest** (*US*) Wohltätigkeitsfonds *m*.

commutation ticket [kɒmju'teɪʃən'tɪkɪt] *n* (*US*) Zeitkarte *f*.

commute [kə'mjuːt] *vi* pendeln; ~**r** Pendler *m*.

compact [kəm'pækt] *a* kompakt, fest,

dicht; ['kɒmpækt] *n* Pakt *m*, Vertrag *m*; (*for make-up*) Puderdose *f*.

companion [kəm'pænɪən] *n* Begleiter(in *f*) *m*; ~**ship** Gesellschaft *f*.

company ['kʌmpənɪ] *n* Gesellschaft *f*; (*Comm also*) Firma *f*, (*Mil*) Kompanie *f*; **to keep sb** ~ jdm Gesellschaft leisten.

comparable ['kɒmpərəbl] *a* vergleichbar.

comparative [kəm'pærətɪv] *a* (*relative*) verhältnismäßig, relativ; (*Gram*) steigernd; ~**ly** *ad* verhältnismäßig.

compare [kəm'pɛə*] *vt* vergleichen; *vi* sich vergleichen lassen.

comparison [kəm'pærɪsn] *n* Vergleich *m*; (*object*) Vergleichsgegenstand *m*; **in** ~ (**with**) im Vergleich (mit *or* zu).

compartment [kəm'pɑːtmənt] *n* (*Rail*) Abteil *nt*; (*in drawer etc*) Fach *nt*.

compass ['kʌmpəs] *n* Kompaß *m*; ~**es** *pl* Zirkel *m*.

compassion [kəm'pæʃən] *n* Mitleid *nt*; ~**ate** *a* mitfühlend.

compatible [kəm'pætɪbl] *a* vereinbar, im Einklang; **we're not** ~ wir vertragen uns nicht.

compel [kəm'pel] *vt* zwingen; ~**ling** *a argument* zwingend.

compendium [kəm'pendɪəm] *n* Kompendium *nt*.

compensate ['kɒmpenseɪt] *vt* entschädigen; **to** ~ **for** Ersatz leisten für, kompensieren.

compensation [kɒmpen'seɪʃən] *n* Entschädigung *f*; (*money*) Schadenersatz *m*; Entschädigung *f*; (*Jur*) Abfindung *f*; (*Psych etc*) Kompensation *f*.

compère ['kɒmpɛə*] *n* Conférencier *m*.

compete [kəm'piːt] *vi* sich bewerben; konkurrieren, sich messen mit.

competence ['kɒmpɪtəns] *n* Fähigkeit *f*; (*Jur*) Zuständigkeit *f*.

competent ['kɒmpɪtənt] *a* kompetent, fähig; (*Jur*) zuständig.

competition [kɒmpɪ'tɪʃən] *n* Wettbewerb *m*; (*Comm*) Konkurrenz *f*.

competitive [kəm'petɪtɪv] *a* Konkurrenz-; (*Comm*) konkurrenzfähig.

competitor [kəm'petɪtə*] *n* Mitbewerber(in *f*) *m*; (*Comm*) Konkurrent(in *f*) *m*; (*Sport*) Teilnehmer(in *f*) *m*.

compile [kəm'paɪl] *vt* zusammenstellen.

complacency [kəm'pleɪsnsɪ] *n* Selbstzufriedenheit *f*, Gleichgültigkeit *f*.

complacent [kəm'pleɪsnt] *a* selbstzufrieden, gleichgültig.

complain [kəm'pleɪn] *vi* sich beklagen, sich beschweren (*about* über +*acc*); ~**t** Beschwerde *f*; (*Med*) Leiden *nt*.

complement ['kɒmplɪmənt] *n* Ergänzung *f*; (*ship's crew etc*) Bemannung *f*; ~**ary** [kɒmplɪ'mentərɪ] *a* Komplementär-, (sich) ergänzend.

complete [kəm'pliːt] *a* vollständig, vollkommen, ganz; *vt* vervollständigen; (*finish*) beenden; ~**ly** *ad* vollständig, ganz.

completion [kəm'pliːʃən] *n* Vervollständigung *f*; (*of building*) Fertigstellung *f*.

complex ['kɒmpleks] *a* kompliziert, verwickelt; *n* Komplex *m*.

complexion [kəm'plekʃən] *n* Gesichts-

farbe f, Teint m; (fig) Anstrich m,
Aussehen nt.

complexity [kɔm'plɛksɪtɪ] n Verwicklung
f, Kompliziertheit f.

compliance [kɔm'plaɪəns] n Fügsamkeit f,
Einwilligung f.

complicate ['kɔmplɪkeɪt] vt komplizieren,
verwickeln; ~d a kompliziert, verwickelt.

complication [kɔmplɪ'keɪʃən] a Komplikation f, Erschwerung f.

compliment ['kɔmplɪmənt] n Kompliment nt; ['kɔmplɪment] vt ein Kompliment
machen (sb jdm); ~s pl Grüße pl,
Empfehlung f; ~ary [kɔmplɪ'mentərɪ] a
schmeichelhaft; (free) Frei-, Gratis-.

comply [kɔm'plaɪ] vi: ~ **with** erfüllen
(+acc); entsprechen (+dat).

component [kɔm'pəʊnənt] a Teil-;
Bestandteil m.

compose [kɔm'pəʊz] vt (arrange) zusammensetzen; music komponieren; poetry
schreiben; thoughts sammeln; features
beherrschen; ~d a ruhig, gefaßt; **to be**
~**d of** bestehen aus; ~**r** Komponist(in f)
m.

composite ['kɔmpəzɪt] a zusammengesetzt.

composition [kɔmpə'zɪʃən] n (Mus)
Komposition f; (Sch) Aufsatz m; (composing) Zusammensetzung f, Gestaltung f;
(structure) Zusammensetzung f, Aufbau m.

compositor [kɔm'pɔzɪtə*] n Schriftsetzer
m.

compos mentis ['kɔmpɔs'mentɪs] a klar
im Kopf.

compost ['kɔmpɔst] n Kompost m; ~
heap Komposthaufen m.

composure [kɔm'pəʊʒə*] n Gelassenheit f,
Fassung f.

compound ['kɔmpaʊnd] n (Chem) Verbindung f; (mixture) Gemisch nt; (enclosure) eingezäunte(s) Gelände nt; (Ling)
Kompositum nt; a zusammengesetzt; ~
fracture komplizierte(r) Bruch m; ~
interest Zinseszinsen pl.

comprehend [kɔmprɪ'hend] vt begreifen;
(include) umfassen, einschließen.

comprehension [kɔmprɪ'henʃən] n
Fassungskraft f, Verständnis nt.

comprehensive [kɔmprɪ'hensɪv] a umfassend; ~ **school** Gesamtschule f.

compress [kɔm'pres] vt zusammen-
drücken, komprimieren; ['kɔmpres] n
(Med) Kompresse f, Umschlag m; ~**ion**
[kɔm'preʃən] Komprimieren nt.

comprise [kɔm'praɪz] vt (also **be** ~**d of**)
umfassen, bestehen aus.

compromise ['kɔmprəmaɪz] n Kompromiß m, Verständigung f; vt reputation
kompromittieren; vi einen Kompromiß
schließen.

compulsion [kɔm'pʌlʃən] n Zwang m.

compulsive [kɔm'pʌlsɪv] a Gewohnheits-.

compulsory [kɔm'pʌlsərɪ] a (obligatory)
obligatorisch, Pflicht-.

computer [kɔm'pjuːtə*] n Computer m,
Rechner m.

comrade ['kɔmrɪd] n Kamerad m; (Pol)
Genosse m; ~**ship** Kameradschaft f.

concave ['kɔn'keɪv] a konkav, hohl-
geschliffen.

conceal [kɔn'siːl] vt secret verschweigen;
to ~ **o.s.** sich verbergen.

concede [kɔn'siːd] vt (grant) gewähren;
point zugeben; vi (admit) zugeben.

conceit [kɔn'siːt] n Eitelkeit f, Einbildung f;
~**ed** a eitel, eingebildet.

conceivable [kɔn'siːvəbl] a vorstellbar.

conceive [kɔn'siːv] vt idea ausdenken;
imagine sich vorstellen; vti baby
empfangen.

concentrate ['kɔnsəntreɪt] vi sich konzentrieren (on auf +acc); vt (gather) konzentrieren.

concentration [kɔnsən'treɪʃən] n Konzentration f; ~ **camp** Konzentrationslager
nt, KZ nt.

concentric [kɔn'sentrɪk] a konzentrisch.

concept ['kɔnsept] n Begriff m; ~**ion**
[kɔn'sepʃən] (idea) Vorstellung f; (Physiol)
Empfängnis f.

concern [kɔn'sɜːn] n (affair) Angelegenheit f; (Comm) Unternehmen nt, Konzern
m; (worry) Sorge f, Unruhe f; vt (interest)
angehen; (be about) handeln von; (have
connection with) betreffen; ~**ed** a
(anxious) besorgt; ~**ing** prep betreffend,
hinsichtlich (+gen).

concert ['kɔnsət] n Konzert nt; **in** ~
(with) im Einverständnis (mit); ~**ed**
[kɔn'sɜːtɪd] a gemeinsam; (Fin) konzer-
tiert; ~ **hall** Konzerthalle f.

concertina [kɔnsə'tiːnə] n Hand-
harmonika f.

concerto [kɔn'tʃɜːtəʊ] n Konzert nt.

concession [kɔn'seʃən] n (yielding)
Zugeständnis nt; (right to do sth)
Genehmigung f.

conciliation [kɔnsɪlɪ'eɪʃən] n Versöhnung
f; (official) Schlichtung f.

conciliatory [kɔn'sɪlɪətrɪ] a vermittelnd;
versöhnlich.

concise [kɔn'saɪs] a knapp, gedrängt.

conclave ['kɔnkleɪv] n Konklave nt.

conclude [kɔn'kluːd] vt (end) beenden;
treaty (ab)schließen; (decide) schließen,
folgern; vi (finish) schließen.

conclusion [kɔn'kluːʒən] n (Ab)schluß m;
in ~ zum Schluß, schließlich.

conclusive [kɔn'kluːsɪv] a überzeugend,
schlüssig; ~**ly** ad endgültig.

concoct [kɔn'kɔkt] vt zusammenbrauen.

concord ['kɔŋkɔːd] n Eintracht f.

concourse ['kɔŋkɔːs] n (Bahnhofs)halle f,
Vorplatz m.

concrete ['kɔŋkriːt] n Beton m; a konkret.

concur [kɔn'kɜː*] vi übereinstimmen.

concurrently [kɔn'kʌrəntlɪ] ad gleichzeitig.

concussion [kɔn'kʌʃən] n (Gehirn)er-
schütterung f.

condemn [kɔn'dem] vt verdammen; (Jur)
verurteilen; building abbruchreif erklären;
~**ation** [kɔndem'neɪʃən] Verurteilung f;
(of object) Verwerfung f.

condensation [kɔnden'seɪʃən] n Kon-
densation f.

condense [kɔn'dens] vi (Chem) kondensieren; *vt* (*fig*) zusammendrängen; ~**d milk** Kondensmilch *f.*

condescend [kɔndɪ'send] *vi* sich herablassen; ~**ing** a herablassend.

condition [kən'dɪʃən] *n* (*state*) Zustand *m*, Verfassung *f*; (*presupposition*) Bedingung *f*; *vt* *hair etc* behandeln; (*regulate*) regeln; **on ~ that . . .** unter der Bedingung, daß . . .; ~**ed to** gewöhnt an (+*acc*); ~**ed reflex** bedingter Reflex; ~**s** *pl* (*circumstances, weather*) Verhältnisse *f*; ~**al** a bedingt; (*Gram*) Bedingungs-.

condolences [kən'dəʊlənsɪz] *npl* Beileid *nt.*

condone [kən'dəʊn] *vt* gutheißen.

conducive [kən'djuːsɪv] a dienlich (*to dat*).

conduct ['kɔndʌkt] *n* (*behaviour*) Verhalten *nt*; (*management*) Führung *f*; [kən'dʌkt] *vt* führen, leiten; (*Mus*) dirigieren; ~**ed tour** Führung *f*; ~**or** [kən'dʌktə*] (*of orchestra*) Dirigent *m*; (*in bus*) Schaffner *m*; ~**ress** [kən'dʌktrɪs] (*in bus*) Schaffnerin *f.*

conduit ['kɔndɪt] *n* (*water*) Rohrleitung *f*; (*Elec*) Isolierrohr *nt.*

cone [kəʊn] *n* (*Math*) Kegel *m*; (*for ice cream*) (Waffel)tüte *f*; (*fir*) Tannenzapfen *m.*

confectioner [kən'fekʃənə*] *n* Konditor *m*; ~'**s** (**shop**) Konditorei *f*; ~**y** (*cakes*) Konfekt *nt*, Konditorwaren *pl*; (*sweets*) Süßigkeiten *pl.*

confederation [kənfedə'reɪʃən] *n* Bund *m.*

confer [kən'fɜː*] *vt* *degree* verleihen; *vi* (*discuss*) konferieren, verhandeln; ~**ence** ['kɔnfərəns] Konferenz *f.*

confess [kən'fes] *vti* gestehen; (*Eccl*) beichten; ~**ion** [kən'feʃən] Geständnis *nt*; (*Eccl*) Beichte *f*; ~**ional** [kən'feʃənl] Beichtstuhl *m*; ~**or** (*Eccl*) Beichtvater *m.*

confetti [kən'fetɪ] *n* Konfetti *nt.*

confide [kən'faɪd] *vt:* ~ **in** (sich) anvertrauen (+*dat*); (*trust*) vertrauen (+*dat*); ~**nce** ['kɔnfɪdəns] Vertrauen *nt*; (*assurance*) Selbstvertrauen *nt*; (*secret*) vertrauliche Mitteilung *f*, Geheimnis *nt*; ~**nce trick** ['kɔnfɪdənstrɪk] Schwindel *m.*

confident ['kɔnfɪdənt] a (*sure*) überzeugt; sicher; (*self-assured*) selbstsicher; ~**ial** [kɔnfɪ'denʃəl] a (*secret*) vertraulich, geheim; (*trusted*) Vertrauens-.

confine [kən'faɪn] *vt* (*limit*) begrenzen, einschränken; (*lock up*) einsperren; ~**s** ['kɔnfaɪnz] *pl* Grenze *f*; ~**d** a *space* eng, begrenzt; ~**ment** (*of room*) Beengtheit *f*; (*in prison*) Haft *f*; (*Med*) Wochenbett *nt.*

confirm [kən'fɜːm] *vt* bestätigen; ~**ation** [kɔnfə'meɪʃən] Bestätigung *f*; (*Rel*) Konfirmation *f*; ~**ed** a unverbesserlich, hartnäckig; *bachelor* eingefleischt.

confiscate ['kɔnfɪskeɪt] *vt* beschlagnahmen, konfiszieren.

confiscation [kɔnfɪs'keɪʃən] *n* Beschlagnahme *f.*

conflagration [kɔnflə'greɪʃən] *n* Feuersbrunst *f.*

conflict ['kɔnflɪkt] *n* Kampf *m*; (*of words, opinions*) Konflikt *m*, Streit *m*; [kən'flɪkt] *vi* im Widerspruch stehen; ~**ing** [kən'flɪktɪŋ] a gegensätzlich; *testimony* sich widersprechend.

conform [kən'fɔːm] *vi* sich anpassen (*to dat*); (*to rules*) sich fügen (*to dat*); (*to general trends*) sich richten (*to nach*); ~**ist** Konformist(in *f*) *m.*

confront [kən'frʌnt] *vt* *enemy* entgegentreten (+*dat*); *sb with sth* konfrontieren; *sb with sb* gegenüberstellen (*with dat*); ~**ation** [kɔnfrʌn'teɪʃən] Gegenüberstellung *f*; (*quarrel*) Konfrontation *f.*

confuse [kən'fjuːz] *vt* verwirren; (*sth with sth*) verwechseln.

confusing [kən'fjuːzɪŋ] a verwirrend.

confusion [kən'fjuːʒən] *n* (*disorder*) Verwirrung *f*; (*tumult*) Aufruhr *m*; (*embarrassment*) Bestürzung *f.*

congeal [kən'dʒiːl] *vi* (*freeze*) gefrieren; (*clot*) gerinnen.

congenial [kən'dʒiːnɪəl] a (*agreeable*) angenehm.

congenital [kən'dʒenɪtəl] a angeboren.

conger eel ['kɔŋgər'iːl] *n* Meeraal *m.*

congested [kən'dʒestɪd] a überfüllt.

congestion [kən'dʒestʃən] *n* Stauung *f*; Stau *m.*

conglomeration [kɔnglɔmə'reɪʃən] *n* Anhäufung *f.*

congratulate [kən'grætjuleɪt] *vt* beglückwünschen (*on zu*).

congratulations [kən'grætjʊ'leɪʃənz] *npl* Glückwünsche *pl*; ~**!** gratuliere!, herzlichen Glückwunsch!

congregate ['kɔŋgrɪgeɪt] *vi* sich versammeln.

congregation [kɔŋgrɪ'geɪʃən] *n* Gemeinde *f.*

congress ['kɔŋgres] *n* Kongreß *m*; ~**ional** [kən'greʃənl] a Kongreß-; ~**man** (*US*) Mitglied *nt* des amerikanischen Repräsentantenhauses.

conical ['kɔnɪkəl] a kegelförmig, konisch.

conifer ['kɔnɪfə*] *n* Nadelbaum *m*; ~**ous** [kə'nɪfərəs] a zapfentragend.

conjecture [kən'dʒektʃə*] *n* Vermutung *f*; *vti* vermuten.

conjugal ['kɔndʒugəl] a ehelich.

conjunction [kən'dʒʌŋkʃən] *n* Verbindung *f*; (*Gram*) Konjunktion *f*, Verbindungswort *nt.*

conjunctivitis [kəndʒʌŋktɪ'vaɪtɪs] *n* Bindehautentzündung *f.*

conjure ['kʌndʒə*] *vti* zaubern; ~ **up** *vt* heraufbeschwören; ~**r** Zauberer *m*; (*entertainer*) Zauberkünstler(in *f*) *m.*

conjuring ['kʌndʒərɪŋ] *n:* ~ **trick** Zauberkunststück *nt.*

conk [kɔŋk]: ~ **out** *vi* (*col*) stehenbleiben, streiken.

connect [kə'nekt] *vt* verbinden; *train* koppeln; ~**ion** [kə'nekʃən] Verbindung *f*; (*relation*) Zusammenhang *m*; **in** ~**ion with** in Verbindung mit.

connexion [kə'nekʃən] *n* = **connection**.

connoisseur [kɔnɪ'sɜː*] *n* Kenner *m.*

connotation [kɔnə'teɪʃən] *n* Konnotation *f.*

conquer ['kɔŋkə*] *vt* (*overcome*) überwinden, besiegen; (*Mil*) besiegen; *vi* siegen; ~**or** Eroberer *m.*

conquest ['kɔŋkwest] *n* Eroberung *f.*

conscience ['kɔnʃəns] *n* Gewissen *nt.*

conscientious [kɒnʃi'enʃəs] a gewissenhaft; ~ **objector** Wehrdienstverweigerer m (aus Gewissensgründen).

conscious ['kɒnʃəs] a bewußt; (Med) bei Bewußtsein; ~**ness** Bewußtsein nt.

conscript ['kɒnskrɪpt] n Wehrpflichtige(r) m; ~**ion** [kən'skrɪpʃən] Wehrpflicht f.

consecrate ['kɒnsɪkreɪt] vt weihen.

consecutive [kən'sekjutɪv] a aufeinanderfolgend.

consensus [kən'sensəs] n allgemeine Übereinstimmung f.

consent [kən'sent] n Zustimmung f; vi zustimmen (to dat).

consequence ['kɒnsɪkwəns] n (importance) Bedeutung f, Konsequenz f; (result, effect) Wirkung f.

consequently ['kɒnsɪkwəntlɪ] ad folglich.

conservation [kɒnsə'veɪʃən] n Erhaltung f, Schutz m.

conservative [kən'sɜːvətɪv] a konservativ; (cautious) mäßig, vorsichtig; **C~** a party konservativ; n Konservative(r) mf.

conservatory [kən'sɜːvətrɪ] n (greenhouse) Gewächshaus nt; (room) Wintergarten m.

conserve [kən'sɜːv] vt erhalten.

consider [kən'sɪdə*] vt überlegen; (take into account) in Betracht ziehen; (regard) halten für; ~**able** a beträchtlich; ~**ate** a rücksichtsvoll, aufmerksam; ~**ation** [kənsɪdə'reɪʃən] Rücksicht(nahme) f; (thought) Erwägung f; (reward) Entgelt nt; ~**ing** prep in Anbetracht (+gen); cf da; on no ~**ation** unter keinen Umständen.

consign [kən'saɪn] vt übergeben; ~**ment** (of goods) Sendung f, Lieferung f.

consist [kən'sɪst] vi bestehen (of aus).

consistency [kən'sɪstənsɪ] n (of material) Festigkeit f; (of argument) Folgerichtigkeit f; (of person) Konsequenz f.

consistent [kən'sɪstənt] a gleichbleibend, stetig; argument folgerichtig; **she's not** ~ sie ist nicht konsequent.

consolation [kɒnsə'leɪʃən] n Trost m; ~ **prize** Trostpreis m.

console [kən'səul] vt trösten.

consolidate [kən'sɒlɪdeɪt] vt festigen.

consommé [kən'sɒmeɪ] n Fleischbrühe f.

consonant ['kɒnsənənt] n Konsonant m, Mitlaut m.

consortium [kən'sɔːtɪəm] n Gruppe f, Konsortium nt.

conspicuous [kən'spɪkjuəs] a (prominent) auffallend; (visible) deutlich, sichtbar.

conspiracy [kən'spɪrəsɪ] n Verschwörung f, Komplott nt.

conspire [kən'spaɪə*] vi sich verschwören.

constable ['kʌnstəbl] n Polizist(in f) m.

constabulary [kən'stæbjulərɪ] n Polizei f.

constancy ['kɒnstənsɪ] n Beständigkeit f, Treue f.

constant ['kɒnstənt] a dauernd; ~**ly** ad (continually) andauernd; (faithfully) treu, unwandelbar.

constellation [kɒnstə'leɪʃən] n (temporary) Konstellation f; (permanent) Sternbild nt.

consternation [kɒnstə'neɪʃən] n (dismay) Bestürzung f.

constipated ['kɒnstɪpeɪtɪd] a verstopft.

constipation [kɒnstɪ'peɪʃən] n Verstopfung f.

constituency [kən'stɪtjuənsɪ] n Wahlkreis m.

constituent [kən'stɪtjuənt] n (person) Wähler m; (part) Bestandteil m.

constitute ['kɒnstɪtjuːt] vt ausmachen.

constitution [kɒnstɪ'tjuːʃən] n Verfassung f; ~**al** a Verfassungs-; monarchy konstitutionell.

constrain [kən'streɪn] vt zwingen; ~**t** Zwang m; (Psych) Befangenheit f.

constrict [kən'strɪkt] vt zusammenziehen; ~**ion** [kən'strɪkʃən] Zusammenziehung f; (of chest) Zusammenschnürung f, Beklemmung f.

construct [kən'strʌkt] vt bauen; ~**ion** [kən'strʌkʃən] (action) (Er)bauen nt, Konstruktion f; (building) Bau m; **under** ~**ion** im Bau befindlich; ~**ive** a konstruktiv.

construe [kən'struː] vt (interpret) deuten.

consul ['kɒnsl] n Konsul m; ~**ate** ['kɒnsjulət] Konsulat nt.

consult [kən'sʌlt] vt um Rat fragen; doctor konsultieren; book nachschlagen in (+dat); ~**ant** (Med) Facharzt m; (other specialist) Gutachter m; ~**ation** [kɒnsəl'teɪʃən] Beratung f; (Med) Konsultation f; ~**ing room** Sprechzimmer nt.

consume [kən'sjuːm] vt verbrauchen; food verzehren, konsumieren; ~**r** Verbraucher m.

consummate ['kɒnsʌmeɪt] vt vollenden; marriage vollziehen.

consumption [kən'sʌmpʃən] n Verbrauch m; (of food) Konsum m.

contact ['kɒntækt] n (touch) Berührung f; (connection) Verbindung f; (person) Kontakt m, Beziehung f; vt sich in Verbindung setzen mit; ~ **lenses** pl Kontaktlinsen pl.

contagious [kən'teɪdʒəs] a ansteckend.

contain [kən'teɪn] vt enthalten; **to** ~ **o.s.** sich zügeln; ~**er** Behälter m; (transport) Container m.

contaminate [kən'tæmɪneɪt] vt verunreinigen; (germs) infizieren.

contamination [kəntæmɪ'neɪʃən] n Verunreinigung f.

contemplate ['kɒntəmpleɪt] vt (nachdenklich) betrachten; (think about) überdenken; (plan) vorhaben.

contemplation [kɒntem'pleɪʃən] n Betrachtung f; (Rel) Meditation f.

contemporary [kən'tempərərɪ] a zeitgenössisch; n Zeitgenosse m.

contempt [kən'tempt] n Verachtung f; ~**ible** a verächtlich, nichtswürdig; ~**uous** a voller Verachtung (of für).

contend [kən'tend] vt (fight) kämpfen (um); (argue) behaupten; ~**er** (for post) Bewerber(in f) m; (Sport) Wettkämpfer(in f) m.

content [kən'tent] a zufrieden; vt befriedigen; ['kɒntent] n (also ~**s**) Inhalt m; ~**ed** a zufrieden.

contention [kən'tenʃən] n (dispute) Streit

m; (*argument*) Behauptung *f*.
contentment [kən'tentmənt] *n* Zufriedenheit *f*.
contest ['kɔntest] *n* (Wett)kampf *m*; [kən'test] *vt* (*dispute*) bestreiten; (*Pol*) kandidieren (*in dat*); ~**ant** [kən'testənt] Bewerber(in *f*) *m*.
context ['kɔntekst] *n* Zusammenhang *m*.
continent ['kɔntinənt] *n* Kontinent *m*, Festland *nt*; the C~ das europäische Festland, der Kontinent; ~**al** [kɔntɪ'nentl] *a* kontinental; *n* Bewohner(in *f*) *m* des Kontinents.
contingency [kən'tɪndʒənsɪ] *n* Möglichkeit *f*.
contingent [kən'tɪndʒənt] *n* (*Mil*) Kontingent *nt*; *a* abhängig (*upon* von).
continual [kən'tɪnjʊəl] *a* (*endless*) fortwährend; (*repeated*) immer wiederkehrend; ~**ly** *ad* immer wieder.
continuation [kəntɪnju'eɪʃən] *n* Verlängerung *f*; Fortsetzung *f*.
continue [kən'tɪnjuː] *vi* (*go on*) anhalten; (*last*) fortbestehen; shall we ~? wollen wir weitermachen?; if this ~s wenn das so weitergeht; the rain ~d es regnete weiter; *vt* fortsetzen; to ~ doing sth fortfahren, etw zu tun.
continuity [kɔntɪ'njuɪtɪ] *n* Kontinuität *nt*; (*wholeness*) Zusammenhang *m*.
continuous [kən'tɪnjʊəs] *a* ununterbrochen.
contort [kən'tɔːt] *vt* verdrehen; ~**ion** [kən'tɔːʃən] Verzerrung *f*; ~**ionist** [kən'tɔːʃənɪst] Schlangenmensch *m*.
contour ['kɔntʊə*] *n* Umriß *m*; (*height*) Höhenlinie *f*.
contraband ['kɔntrəbænd] *n* Schmuggelware *f*.
contraception [kɔntrə'sepʃən] *n* Empfängnisverhütung *f*.
contraceptive [kɔntrə'septɪv] *n* empfängnisverhütende(s) Mittel *nt*; *a* empfängnisverhütend.
contract ['kɔntrækt] *n* (*agreement*) Vertrag *m*, Kontrakt *m*; [kən'trækt] *vi* (*to do sth*) sich vertraglich verpflichten; (*muscle*) sich zusammenziehen; (*become smaller*) schrumpfen; ~**ion** [kən'trækʃən] (*shortening*) Verkürzung *f*; ~**or** [kən'træktə*] Unternehmer *m*; (*supplier*) Lieferant *m*.
contradict [kɔntrə'dɪkt] *vt* widersprechen (+*dat*); ~**ion** [kɔntrə'dɪkʃən] Widerspruch *m*.
contralto [kən'træltəʊ] *n* (tiefe) Altstimme *f*.
contraption [kən'træpʃən] *n* (*col*) komische Konstruktion *f*, komische(s) Ding *nt*.
contrary ['kɔntrərɪ] *a* entgegengesetzt; *wind* ungünstig, Gegen-; (*obstinate*) widerspenstig, eigensinnig; *n* Gegenteil *nt*; on the ~ im Gegenteil.
contrast ['kɔntrɑːst] *n* Kontrast *m*; [kən'trɑːst] *vt* entgegensetzen; ~**ing** [kən'trɑːstɪŋ] *a* Kontrast-.
contravene [kɔntrə'viːn] *vt* verstoßen gegen.

contribute [kən'trɪbjuːt] *vti* beitragen; *money* spenden.
contribution [kɔntrɪ'bjuːʃən] *n* Beitrag *m*.
contributor [kən'trɪbjʊtə*] *n* Beitragende(r) *mf*.
contrite ['kɔntraɪt] *a* zerknirscht.
contrivance [kən'traɪvəns] *n* Vorrichtung *f*, Kniff *m*, Erfindung *f*.
contrive [kən'traɪv] *vt* zustande bringen; to ~ to do sth es schaffen, etw zu tun.
control [kən'trəʊl] *vt* (*direct, test*) kontrollieren; *n* Kontrolle *f*; (*business*) Leitung *f*; ~s *pl* (*of vehicle*) Steuerung *f*; (*of engine*) Schalttafel *f*; ~ point Kontrollstelle *f*; out of ~ außer Kontrolle; under ~ unter Kontrolle.
controversial [kɔntrə'vɜːʃəl] *a* umstritten, kontrovers.
controversy ['kɔntrəvɜːsɪ] *n* Meinungsstreit *m*, Kontroverse *f*.
convalesce [kɔnvə'les] *vi* gesund werden; ~**nce** Genesung *f*; ~**nt** *a* auf dem Wege der Besserung; *n* Genesende(r) *mf*.
convector [kən'vektə*] *n* Heizlüfter *m*.
convene [kən'viːn] *vt* zusammenrufen; *vi* sich versammeln.
convenience [kən'viːnɪəns] *n* Annehmlichkeit *f*; (*thing*) bequeme Einrichtung *f*; see public.
convenient [kən'viːnɪənt] *a* günstig.
convent ['kɔnvənt] *n* Kloster *nt*.
convention [kən'venʃən] *n* Versammlung *f*; (*Pol*) Übereinkunft *f*; (*custom*) Konvention *f*; ~**al** *a* herkömmlich, konventionell.
converge [kən'vɜːdʒ] *vi* zusammenlaufen.
conversant [kən'vɜːsənt] *a* vertraut; (*in learning*) bewandert (*with* in +*dat*).
conversation [kɔnvə'seɪʃən] *n* Unterhaltung *f*; ~**al** *a* Unterhaltungs-.
converse [kən'vɜːs] *vi* sich unterhalten; ['kɔnvɜːs] *a* gegenteilig; ~**ly** [kən'vɜːslɪ] *ad* umgekehrt.
conversion [kən'vɜːʃən] *n* Umwandlung *f*; (*esp Rel*) Bekehrung *f*; ~ table Umrechnungstabelle *f*.
convert [kən'vɜːt] *vt* (*change*) umwandeln; (*Rel*) bekehren; ['kɔnvɜːt] *n* Bekehrte(r) *mf*, Konvertit(in *f*) *m*; ~**ible** (*Aut*) Kabriolett *nt*; *a* umwandelbar; (*Fin*) konvertierbar.
convex ['kɔn'veks] *a* konvex.
convey [kən'veɪ] *vt* (*carry*) befördern; *feelings* vermitteln; ~**or belt** Fließband *nt*.
convict [kən'vɪkt] *vt* verurteilen; ['kɔnvɪkt] *n* Häftling *m*; ~**ion** [kən'vɪkʃən] (*verdict*) Verurteilung *f*; (*belief*) Überzeugung *f*.
convince [kən'vɪns] *vt* überzeugen.
convincing [kən'vɪnsɪŋ] *a* überzeugend.
convivial [kən'vɪvɪəl] *a* festlich, froh.
convoy ['kɔnvɔɪ] *n* (*of vehicles*) Kolonne *f*; (*protected*) Konvoi *m*.
convulse [kən'vʌls] *vt* zusammenzucken lassen; to be ~d with laughter sich vor Lachen krümmen.
convulsion [kən'vʌlʃən] *n* (*esp Med*) Zuckung *f*, Krampf *m*.
coo [kuː] *vi* (*dove*) gurren.
cook [kʊk] *vti* kochen; *n* Koch *m*, Köchin *f*;

~**book** Kochbuch *nt;* ~**er** Herd *m;* ~**ery** Kochkunst *f;* ~**ery book** = ~**book;** ~**ie** (*US*) Plätzchen *nt;* ~**ing** Kochen *nt.*

cool [ku:l] *a* kühl; *vti* (ab)kühlen; ~ **down** *vti* (*fig*) (sich) beruhigen; ~**ing-tower** Kühlturm *m;* ~**ness** Kühle *f;* (*of temperament*) kühle(r) Kopf.

coop [ku:p] *n* Hühnerstall *m; vt:* ~ **up** (*fig*) einpferchen.

co-op [ˈkəʊɒp] *n* = **cooperative.**

cooperate [kəʊˈɒpəreɪt] *vi* zusammenarbeiten.

cooperation [kəʊɒpəˈreɪʃən] *n* Zusammenarbeit *f.*

cooperative [kəʊˈɒpərətɪv] *a* hilfsbereit; (*Comm*) genossenschaftlich; *n* (*of farmers*) Genossenschaft *f;* (— *store*) Konsumladen *m.*

coordinate [kəʊˈɔːdɪneɪt] *vt* koordinieren.

coordination [kəʊɔːdɪˈneɪʃən] *n* Koordination *f.*

coot [ku:t] *n* Wasserhuhn *nt.*

cop [kɒp] *n* (*col*) Polyp *m,* Bulle *m.*

cope [kəʊp] *vi* fertig werden, schaffen (*with acc*).

co-pilot [ˈkəʊpaɪlət] *n* Kopilot *m.*

copious [ˈkəʊpɪəs] *a* reichhaltig.

copper [ˈkɒpə*] *n* Kupfer *nt;* Kupfermünze *f;* (*col: policeman*) Polyp *m,* Bulle *m.*

coppice [ˈkɒpɪs], **copse** [kɒps] *n* Unterholz *nt.*

copulate [ˈkɒpjuleɪt] *vi* sich paaren.

copy [ˈkɒpɪ] *n* (*imitation*) Nachahmung *f;* (*of book etc*) Exemplar *nt;* (*of newspaper*) Nummer *f; vt* kopieren, abschreiben; ~**cat** Nachäffer *m;* ~**right** Copyright *nt;* ~**right reserved** alle Rechte vorbehalten, Nachdruck verboten.

coral [ˈkɒrəl] *n* Koralle *f;* ~ **reef** Korallenriff *nt.*

cord [kɔːd] *n* Schnur *f,* Kordel *f; see* **vocal.**

cordial [ˈkɔːdɪəl] *a* herzlich; *n* Fruchtsaft *m;* ~**ly** *ad* herzlich.

cordon [ˈkɔːdn] *n* Absperrkette *f.*

corduroy [ˈkɔːdərɔɪ] *n* Kord(samt) *m.*

core [kɔː*] *n* Kern *m; vt* entkernen.

cork [kɔːk] *n* (*bark*) Korkrinde *f;* (*stopper*) Korken *m;* ~**age** Korkengeld *nt;* ~**screw** Korkenzieher *m.*

corm [kɔːm] *n* Knolle *f.*

cormorant [ˈkɔːmərənt] *n* Kormoran *m.*

corn [kɔːn] *n* Getreide *nt,* Korn *nt;* (*US: maize*) Mais *m;* (*on foot*) Hühnerauge *nt.*

cornea [ˈkɔːnɪə] *n* Hornhaut *f.*

corned beef [ˈkɔːndˈbiːf] *n* Corned Beef *nt.*

corner [ˈkɔːnə*] *n* Ecke *f;* (*nook*) Winkel *m;* (*on road*) Kurve *f; vt* in die Enge treiben; *vi* (*Aut*) in die Kurve gehen; ~**flag** Eckfahne *f;* ~ **kick** Eckball *m;* ~**stone** Eckstein *m.*

cornet [ˈkɔːnɪt] *n* (*Mus*) Kornett *nt;* (*for ice cream*) Eistüte *f.*

cornflour [ˈkɔːnflaʊə*] *n* Maizena *nt,* Maismehl *nt.*

cornice [ˈkɔːnɪs] *n* Gesims *nt.*

cornstarch [ˈkɔːnstɑːtʃ] *n* (*US*) = **cornflour.**

cornucopia [kɔːnjuˈkəʊpɪə] *n* Füllhorn *nt.*

corny [ˈkɔːnɪ] *a joke* blöd(e).

corollary [kəˈrɒlərɪ] *n* Folgesatz *m.*

coronary [ˈkɒrənərɪ] *a* (*Med*) Koronar-; *n* Herzinfarkt *m;* ~ **thrombosis** Koronarthrombose *f.*

coronation [kɒrəˈneɪʃən] *n* Krönung *f.*

coroner [ˈkɒrənə*] *n* Untersuchungsrichter *m* und Leichenbeschauer *m.*

coronet [ˈkɒrənɪt] *n* Adelskrone *f.*

corporal [ˈkɔːpərəl] *n* Obergefreite(r) *m; a:* ~ **punishment** Prügelstrafe *f.*

corporate [ˈkɔːpərɪt] *a* gemeinschaftlich, korporativ.

corporation [kɔːpəˈreɪʃən] *n* Gemeinde *f,* Stadt *f;* (*esp business*) Körperschaft *f,* Aktiengesellschaft *f.*

corps [kɔː*] *n* (Armee)korps *nt.*

corpse [kɔːps] *n* Leiche *f.*

corpulent [ˈkɔːpjulənt] *a* korpulent.

Corpus Christi [ˈkɔːpəsˈkrɪstɪ] *n* Fronleichnamsfest *nt.*

corpuscle [ˈkɔːpʌsl] *n* Blutkörperchen *nt.*

corral [kəˈrɑːl] *n* Pferch *m,* Korral *m.*

correct [kəˈrekt] *a* (*accurate*) richtig; (*proper*) korrekt; *vt mistake* berichtigen; *pupil* tadeln; ~**ion** [kəˈrekʃən] Berichtigung *f;* ~**ly** *ad* richtig; korrekt.

correlate [ˈkɒrɪleɪt] *vt* aufeinander beziehen; *vi* korrelieren.

correlation [kɒrɪˈleɪʃən] *n* Wechselbeziehung *f.*

correspond [kɒrɪˈspɒnd] *vi* übereinstimmen; (*exchange letters*) korrespondieren; ~**ence** (*similarity*) Entsprechung *f;* Briefwechsel *m,* Korrespondenz *f;* ~**ence course** Fernkurs *m;* ~**ent** (*Press*) Berichterstatter *m;* ~**ing** *a* entsprechend, gemäß (*to dat*).

corridor [ˈkɒrɪdɔː*] *n* Gang *m.*

corroborate [kəˈrɒbəreɪt] *vt* bestätigen, erhärten.

corroboration [kərɒbəˈreɪʃən] *n* Bekräftigung *f.*

corrode [kəˈrəʊd] *vt* zerfressen; *vi* rosten.

corrosion [kəˈrəʊʒən] *n* Rost *m,* Korrosion *f.*

corrugated [ˈkɒrəgeɪtɪd] *a* gewellt; ~ **cardboard** Wellpappe *f;* ~ **iron** Wellblech *nt.*

corrupt [kəˈrʌpt] *a* korrupt; *vt* verderben; (*bribe*) bestechen; ~**ion** [kəˈrʌpʃən] (*of society*) Verdorbenheit *f;* (*bribery*) Bestechung *f.*

corset [ˈkɔːsɪt] *n* Korsett *nt.*

cortège [kɔːˈteːʒ] *n* Zug *m;* (*of funeral*) Leichenzug *m.*

cortisone [ˈkɔːtɪzəʊn] *n* Kortison *nt.*

cosh [kɒʃ] *n* Totschläger *m; vt* über den Schädel hauen.

cosignatory [ˈkəʊsɪgnətərɪ] *n* Mitunterzeichner(in *f*) *m.*

cosine [ˈkəʊsaɪn] *n* Kosinus *m.*

cosiness [ˈkəʊzɪnɪs] *n* Gemütlichkeit *f.*

cosmetic [kɒzˈmetɪk] *n* Schönheitsmittel *nt,* kosmetische(s) Mittel *nt;* *a* kosmetisch.

cosmic [ˈkɒzmɪk] *a* kosmisch.

cosmonaut [ˈkɒzmənɔːt] *n* Kosmonaut(in *f*) *m.*

cosmopolitan [kɔzmə'pɔlɪtən] a international; city Welt-.

cosmos ['kɔzmɔs] n Weltall nt, Kosmos m.

cost [kɔst] n Kosten pl, Preis m; vt irreg kosten; **it ~ him his life/job** es kostete ihm sein Leben/seine Stelle; **at all ~s** um jeden Preis; **~ of living** Lebenshaltungskosten pl.

co-star ['kəustɑ:*] n zweite(r) or weitere(r) Hauptdarsteller(in f) m.

costing ['kɔstɪŋ] n Kostenberechnung f.

costly ['kɔstlɪ] a kostspielig.

cost price ['kɔst'praɪs] n Selbstkostenpreis m.

costume ['kɔstju:m] n Kostüm nt; (fancy dress) Maskenkostüm nt; (for bathing) Badeanzug m; **~ jewellery** Modeschmuck m.

cosy ['kəuzɪ] a behaglich, gemütlich.

cot [kɔt] n Kinderbett(chen) nt.

cottage ['kɔtɪdʒ] n kleine(s) Haus nt (auf dem Land); **~ cheese** Hüttenkäse m.

cotton ['kɔtn] n (material) Baumwollstoff m; a dress etc Baumwoll-, Kattun-; **~ wool** Watte f.

couch [kautʃ] n Couch f; vt (in Worte) fassen, formulieren.

cougar ['ku:gə*] n Puma m.

cough [kɔf] vi husten; n Husten m; **~ drop** Hustenbonbon nt.

could [kud] pt of **can**; **~n't = could not**.

council ['kaunsl] n (of town) Stadtrat m; **~ estate/house** Siedlung f/Haus nt des sozialen Wohnungsbaus; **~lor** ['kaunsɪlə*] Stadtrat m.

counsel ['kaunsl] n (barrister) Anwalt m, Rechtsbeistand m; (advice) Rat(schlag) m; **~lor** Berater m.

count [kaunt] vti zählen; vi (be important) zählen, gelten; n (reckoning) Abrechnung f; (nobleman) Graf m; **~down** Countdown m; **~ on** vt zählen auf (+acc); **~ up** vt zusammenzählen.

counter ['kauntə*] n (in shop) Ladentisch m; (in café) Tresen m, Theke f; (in bank, post office) Schalter m; vt entgegnen; ad entgegen; **~act** [kauntə'rækt] vt entgegenwirken (+dat); **~attack** Gegenangriff m; **~balance** vt aufwiegen; **~clockwise** ad entgegen dem Uhrzeigersinn; **~espionage** Spionageabwehr f; **~feit** Fälschung f; vt fälschen; a gefälscht, unecht; **~foil** (Kontroll)abschnitt m; **~part** (object) Gegenstück nt; (person) Gegenüber nt.

countess ['kauntɪs] n Gräfin f.

countless ['kauntlɪs] a zahllos, unzählig.

countrified ['kʌntrɪfaɪd] a ländlich.

country ['kʌntrɪ] n Land nt; **in the ~** auf dem Land(e); **~ dancing** Volkstanztanzen m; **~ house** Landhaus nt; **~man** (national) Landsmann m; (rural) Bauer m; **~side** Landschaft f.

county ['kauntɪ] n Landkreis m; (Brit) Grafschaft f; **~ town** Kreisstadt f.

coup [ku:] n Coup m; **~ d'état** Staatsstreich m, Putsch m.

coupé [ku:'peɪ] n (Aut) Coupé nt.

couple ['kʌpl] n Paar nt; **a ~ of** ein paar; vt koppeln.

couplet ['kʌplɪt] n Reimpaar nt.

coupling ['kʌplɪŋ] n Kupplung f.

coupon ['ku:pɔn] n Gutschein m.

courage ['kʌrɪdʒ] n Mut m; **~ous** [kə'reɪdʒəs] a mutig.

courier ['kurɪə*] n (for holiday) Reiseleiter m; (messenger) Kurier m, Eilbote m.

course [kɔ:s] n (race) Strecke f, Bahn f; (of stream) Lauf m; (of action) Richtung f; (of lectures) Vortragsreihe f; (of study) Studiengang m; **summer ~** Sommerkurs m; (Naut) Kurs m; (in meal) Gang m; **of ~** natürlich; **in the ~ of** im Laufe (+gen); **in due ~** zu gegebener Zeit; see **golf**.

court [kɔ:t] n (royal) Hof m; (Jur) Gericht nt; vt gehen mit; see **tennis**.

courteous ['kɜ:tɪəs] a höflich, zuvorkommend.

courtesan [kɔ:tɪ'zæn] n Kurtisane f.

courtesy ['kɜ:təsɪ] n Höflichkeit f.

courthouse ['kɔ:thaus] n (US) Gerichtsgebäude nt.

courtier ['kɔ:tɪə*] n Höfling m.

court-martial ['kɔ:t'mɑ:ʃəl] n Kriegsgericht nt; vt vor ein Kriegsgericht stellen.

courtroom ['kɔ:trum] n Gerichtssaal m.

courtyard ['kɔ:tjɑ:d] n Hof m.

cousin ['kʌzn] n Cousin m, Vetter m; Kusine f.

cove [kəuv] n kleine Bucht f.

covenant ['kʌvənənt] n feierliche(s) Abkommen nt.

cover ['kʌvə*] vt (spread over) bedecken; (shield) abschirmen; (include) sich erstrecken über (+acc); (protect) decken; n (lid) Deckel m; (for bed) Decke f; (Mil) Bedeckung f; **~age** ['kʌvrɪdʒ] (Press) (reports) Berichterstattung f; (distribution) Verbreitung f; **~ charge** Bedienungsgeld nt; **~ing** Bedeckung f; **~ing letter** Begleitbrief m.

covet ['kʌvɪt] vt begehren.

covetous ['kʌvɪtəs] a begehrlich.

cow [kau] n Kuh f.

coward ['kauəd] n Feigling m; **~ice** ['kauədɪs] Feigheit f; **~ly** a feige.

cowboy ['kaubɔɪ] n Cowboy m.

cower ['kauə*] vi kauern; (movement) sich kauern.

co-worker ['kəu'wɜ:kə*] n Mitarbeiter(in f) m.

cowshed ['kauʃed] n Kuhstall m.

coxswain ['kɔksn] n (abbr **cox**) Steuermann m.

coy [kɔɪ] a schüchtern; girl spröde.

coyote [kɔɪ'əutɪ] n Präriewolf m.

crab [kræb] n Krebs m; **~apple** Holzapfel m.

crack [kræk] n Riß m, Sprung m; (noise) Knall m; vt (break) springen lassen; joke reißen; vi (noise) knallen, knacken; a erstklassig; troops Elite-; **~er** (firework) Knallkörper m, Kracher m; (biscuit) Keks m; (Christmas —) Knallbonbon m; **~ up** vi (fig) zusammenbrechen.

crackle ['krækl] vi knistern; (fire) prasseln.

crackling ['kræklɪŋ] n Knistern n; (rind) Kruste f (des Schweinebratens).

cradle ['kreɪdl] n Wiege f.

craft [krɑːft] n (skill) (Hand- or Kunst)-
fertigkeit f; (trade) Handwerk nt;
(cunning) Verschlagenheit f; (Naut)
Fahrzeug nt, Schiff nt; ~sman
gelernte(r) Handwerker m; ~smanship
(quality) handwerkliche Ausführung f;
(ability) handwerkliche(s) Können nt; ~y
a schlau, gerieben.

crag [kræg] n Klippe f; ~gy a schroff,
felsig.

cram [kræm] vt vollstopfen; (col) (teach)
einpauken; vi (learn) pauken.

cramp [kræmp] n Krampf m; vt (hinder)
einengen, hemmen.

crampon ['kræmpən] n Steigeisen nt.

cranberry ['krænbərɪ] n Preiselbeere f.

crane [kreɪn] n (machine) Kran m; (bird)
Kranich m.

cranium ['kreɪnɪəm] n Schädel m.

crank [kræŋk] n (lever) Kurbel f; (person)
Spinner m; vt ankurbeln; ~shaft Kurbel-
welle f.

cranky ['kræŋkɪ] a verschroben.

cranny ['krænɪ] n Ritze f.

crap [kræp] n (col) Mist m, Scheiße f.

craps [kræps] n (US) Würfelspiel nt.

crash [kræʃ] n (noise) Krachen nt; (with
cars) Zusammenstoß m; (with plane)
Absturz m; vi stürzen; (cars) zusammenstoßen; (plane) abstürzen; (economy)
zusammenbrechen; (noise) knallen; a
course Schnell-; ~ helmet Sturzhelm m;
~ landing Bruchlandung f.

crass [kræs] a kraß.

crate [kreɪt] n (lit, fig) Kiste f.

crater ['kreɪtə*] n Krater m.

cravat(e) [krə'væt] n Krawatte f.

crave [kreɪv] vi verlangen (for nach).

craving ['kreɪvɪŋ] n Verlangen nt.

crawl [krɔːl] vi kriechen; (baby) krabbeln;
n Kriechen nt; (swim) Kraul m.

crayon ['kreɪən] n Buntstift m.

craze [kreɪz] n Fimmel m.

crazy ['kreɪzɪ] a (foolish) verrückt; (insane)
wahnsinnig; (eager for) versessen (auf
+acc); ~ paving Mosaikpflaster nt.

creak [kriːk] n Knarren nt; vi quietschen,
knarren.

cream [kriːm] n (from milk) Rahm m,
Sahne f; (polish, cosmetic) Creme f;
(colour) Cremefarbe f; (fig: people) Elite f;
~ cake (small) Sahnetörtchen nt; (big)
Sahnekuchen m; ~ cheese Rahmquark
m; ~ery Molkerei f; ~y a sahnig.

crease [kriːs] n Falte f; vt falten; (untidy)
zerknittern.

create [krɪ'eɪt] vt erschaffen; (cause)
verursachen.

creation [krɪ'eɪʃən] n Schöpfung f.

creative [krɪ'eɪtɪv] a schöpferisch, kreativ.

creator [krɪ'eɪtə*] n Schöpfer m.

creature ['kriːtʃə*] n Geschöpf nt.

credence ['kriːdəns] n Glauben m.

credentials [krɪ'denʃəlz] npl Beglau-
bigungsschreiben nt.

credibility [kredɪ'bɪlɪtɪ] n Glaubwürdig-
keit f.

credible ['kredɪbl] a person glaubwürdig;
story glaubhaft.

credit ['kredɪt] n (Comm) Kredit m;
Guthaben nt; vt Glauben schenken (+dat);
to sb's ~**s** zu jds Ehren; ~**able** a rühmlich; ~
card Kreditkarte m; ~**or** Gläubiger m.

credulity [krɪ'djuːlɪtɪ] n Leichtgläubigkeit
f.

creed [kriːd] n Glaubensbekenntnis nt.

creek [kriːk] n (inlet) kleine Bucht f; (US:
river) kleine(r) Wasserlauf m.

creep [kriːp] vi irreg kriechen; ~**er**
Kletterpflanze f, ~**y** a (frightening)
gruselig.

cremate [krɪ'meɪt] vt einäschern.

cremation [krɪ'meɪʃən] n Einäscherung f.

crematorium [kremə'tɔːrɪəm] n Krematorium nt.

creosote ['krɪəsəʊt] n Kreosot nt.

crepe [kreɪp] n Krepp m; ~ **bandage**
Elastikbinde f.

crescent ['kresnt] n (of moon) Halbmond
m.

cress [kres] n Kresse f.

crest [krest] n (of cock) Kamm m; (of
wave) Wellenkamm m; (coat of arms)
Wappen nt; ~**fallen** a niedergeschlagen.

cretin ['kretɪn] n Idiot m.

crevasse [krɪ'væs] n Gletscherspalte f.

crevice ['krevɪs] n Riß m; (in rock) Fels-
spalte f.

crew [kruː] n Besatzung f, Mannschaft f;
~**cut** Bürstenschnitt m; ~**neck**
runde(r) Ausschnitt m.

crib [krɪb] n (bed) Krippe f; (translation)
wortwörtliche Übersetzung f, Klatsche f.

crick [krɪk] n Muskelkrampf m.

cricket ['krɪkɪt] n (insect) Grille f; (game)
Kricket nt; ~**er** Kricketspieler m.

crime [kraɪm] n Verbrechen nt.

criminal ['krɪmɪnl] n Verbrecher m; a
kriminell, strafbar.

crimp [krɪmp] vt hair drehen.

crimson ['krɪmzn] n Karmesin nt; a
leuchtend rot.

cringe [krɪndʒ] vi sich ducken.

crinkle ['krɪŋkl] vt zerknittern; vi knittern.

crinkly ['krɪŋklɪ] a hair kraus.

cripple ['krɪpl] n Krüppel m; vt lahmlegen;
(Med) lähmen, verkrüppeln.

crisis ['kraɪsɪs] n Krise f.

crisp [krɪsp] a knusprig; n Chip m.

criss-cross ['krɪskrɒs] a gekreuzt, Kreuz-.

criterion [kraɪ'tɪərɪən] n Kriterium nt.

critic ['krɪtɪk] n Kritiker(in f) m; ~**al** a
kritisch; ~**ally** ad kritisch; ill gefährlich;
~**ism** ['krɪtɪsɪzəm] Kritik f; ~**ize**
['krɪtɪsaɪz] vt kritisieren; (comment)
beurteilen.

croak [krəʊk] vi krächzen; (frog) quaken; n
Krächzen nt; Quaken nt.

crochet ['krəʊʃeɪ] n Häkelei f.

crockery ['krɒkərɪ] n Geschirr nt.

crocodile ['krɒkədaɪl] n Krokodil nt.

crocus ['krəʊkəs] n Krokus m.

croft [krɒft] n kleine(s) Pachtgut nt; ~**er**
Kleinbauer m.

crony ['krəʊnɪ] n (col) Kumpel m.

crook [kruk] n (*criminal*) Gauner m, Schwindler m; (*stick*) Hirtenstab m; ~ed ['krukɪd] a krumm.

crop [krop] n (*harvest*) Ernte f; (*col: series*) Haufen m; ~ **up** vi auftauchen; (*thing*) passieren.

croquet ['krəʊkeɪ] n Krocket nt.

croquette [krəʊ'ket] n Krokette f.

cross [krɒs] n Kreuz nt; (*Biol*) Kreuzung f; vt road überqueren; *legs* übereinander legen; (*write*) einen Querstrich ziehen; (*Biol*) kreuzen; *cheque* als Verrechnungsscheck kennzeichnen; a (*annoyed*) ärgerlich, böse; ~**bar** Querstange f; ~**breed** Kreuzung f; ~-**country** (**race**) Geländelauf m; ~-**examination** Kreuzverhör nt; ~-**examine** vt ins Kreuzverhör nehmen; ~-**eyed** a: **to be** ~-**eyed** schielen; ~**ing** n (*crossroads*) (Straßen)kreuzung f; (*of ship*) Überfahrt f; (*for pedestrians*) Fußgängerüberweg m; ~ **out** vt streichen; **to be at** ~ **purposes** von verschiedenen Dingen reden; ~-**reference** Querverweis m; ~-**roads** Straßenkreuzung f; (*fig*) Scheideweg m; ~ **section** Querschnitt m; ~-**wind** Seitenwind m; ~-**word** (**puzzle**) Kreuzworträtsel nt.

crotch [krɒtʃ] n Zwickel m; (*Anat*) Unterleib nt.

crotchet ['krɒtʃɪt] n Viertelnote f.

crotchety ['krɒtʃɪtɪ] a *person* launenhaft.

crouch [krautʃ] vi hocken.

crouton ['kruːtɔ̃] n geröstete(r) Brotwürfel m.

crow [krəʊ] n Krähen nt; vi krähen.

crowbar ['krəʊbɑː] n Stemmeisen nt.

crowd [kraud] n Menge f, Gedränge nt; vt (*fill*) überfüllen; vi drängen; ~ed a überfüllt.

crown [kraun] n Krone f; (*of head, hat*) Kopf m; vt krönen; ~ **jewels** pl Kronjuwelen pl; ~ **prince** Kronprinz m.

crow's-nest ['krəʊznest] n Krähennest nt, Ausguck m.

crucial ['kruːʃəl] a entscheidend.

crucifix ['kruːsɪfɪks] n Kruzifix nt; ~**ion** [kruːsɪ'fɪkʃən] Kreuzigung f.

crucify ['kruːsɪfaɪ] vt kreuzigen.

crude [kruːd] a (*raw*) roh; *humour, behaviour* grob, unfein; ~**ly** ad grob; ~**ness** Roheit f.

crudity ['kruːdɪtɪ] n = **crudeness**.

cruel ['kruəl] a grausam; (*distressing*) schwer; (*hard-hearted*) hart, gefühllos; ~**ty** Grausamkeit f.

cruet ['kruːɪt] n Gewürzständer m, Menage f.

cruise [kruːz] n Kreuzfahrt f; vi kreuzen; ~**r** (*Mil*) Kreuzer m.

cruising-speed ['kruːzɪŋspiːd] n Reisegeschwindigkeit f.

crumb [krʌm] n Krume f; (*fig*) Bröckchen nt.

crumble ['krʌmbl] vti zerbröckeln.

crumbly ['krʌmblɪ] a krümelig.

crumpet ['krʌmpɪt] n Tee(pfann)kuchen m.

crumple ['krʌmpl] vt zerknittern.

crunch [krʌntʃ] n Knirschen nt; (*fig*) der entscheidende Punkt; vt knirschen; ~**y** a knusprig.

crusade [kruː'seɪd] n Kreuzzug m; ~**r** Kreuzfahrer m.

crush [krʌʃ] n Gedränge nt; vt zerdrücken; (*rebellion*) unterdrücken, niederwerfen; vi (*material*) knittern; ~**ing** a überwältigend.

crust [krʌst] n (*of bread*) Rinde f, Kruste f; (*Med*) Schorf m.

crutch [krʌtʃ] n Krücke f; see also **crotch.**

crux [krʌks] n (*crucial point*) der springende Punkt, Haken m (*col*).

cry [kraɪ] vi (*call*) ausrufen; (*shout*) schreien; (*weep*) weinen; n (*call*) Schrei m; ~**ing** a (*fig*) himmelschreiend; ~ **off** vi (*plötzlich*) absagen.

crypt [krɪpt] n Krypta f.

cryptic ['krɪptɪk] a (*secret*) geheim; (*mysterious*) rätselhaft.

crystal ['krɪstl] n Kristall m; (*glass*) Kristallglas nt; (*mineral*) Bergkristall m; ~-**clear** a kristallklar; ~**lize** vti (*lit*) kristallisieren; (*fig*) klären.

cub [kʌb] n Junge(s) nt; (*young Boy Scout*) Wölfling m.

cubbyhole ['kʌbɪhəʊl] n Eckchen nt.

cube [kjuːb] n Würfel m; (*Math*) Kubikzahl f.

cubic ['kjuːbɪk] a würfelförmig; *centimetre etc* Kubik-.

cubicle ['kjuːbɪkl] n Kabine f.

cubism ['kjuːbɪzəm] n Kubismus m.

cuckoo ['kuku:] n Kuckuck m; ~ **clock** Kuckucksuhr f.

cucumber ['kjuːkʌmbə*] n Gurke f.

cuddle ['kʌdl] vti herzen, drücken (*col*); n enge Umarmung f.

cuddly ['kʌdlɪ] a anschmiegsam; *teddy* zum Drücken.

cudgel ['kʌdʒəl] n Knüppel m.

cue [kjuː] n Wink m; (*Theat*) Stichwort nt; Billardstock m.

cuff [kʌf] n (*of shirt, coat etc*) Manschette f; Aufschlag m; (*US*) = **turn-up**; ~**link** Manschettenknopf m.

cuisine [kwiː'ziːn] n Kochkunst f, Küche f.

cul-de-sac ['kʌldəsæk] n Sackgasse f.

culinary ['kʌlɪnərɪ] a Koch-.

culminate ['kʌlmɪneɪt] vi gipfeln.

culmination [kʌlmɪ'neɪʃən] n Höhepunkt m.

culpable ['kʌlpəbl] a strafbar, schuldhaft.

culprit ['kʌlprɪt] n Täter m.

cult [kʌlt] n Kult m.

cultivate ['kʌltɪveɪt] vt (*Agr*) bebauen; *mind* bilden; ~**d** a (*Agr*) bebaut; (*cultured*) kultiviert.

cultivation [kʌltɪ'veɪʃən] n (*Agr*) Bebauung f; (*of person*) Bildung f.

cultural ['kʌltʃərəl] a kulturell, Kultur-.

culture ['kʌltʃə*] n (*refinement*) Kultur f, Bildung f; (*of community*) Kultur f; ~**d** a gebildet, kultiviert.

cumbersome ['kʌmbəsəm] a *task* beschwerlich; *object* schwer zu handhaben.

cummmberbund ['kʌməbʌnd] n Kummerbund m.

cumulative ['kjuːmjulətɪv] a gehäuft; **to be ~** sich häufen.

cunning ['kʌnɪŋ] n Verschlagenheit f; a schlau.

cup [kʌp] n Tasse f; (prize) Pokal m; **~board** ['kʌbəd] Schrank m; **~ final** Meisterschaftsspiel nt; **~ful** Tasse(voll) f.

cupola ['kjuːpələ] n Kuppel f.

curable ['kjuərəbəl] a heilbar.

curator [kjuˈreɪtə*] n Kustos m.

curb [kɜːb] vt zügeln; n Zaum m; (on spending etc) Einschränkung f.

cure [kjuə*] n Heilmittel nt; (process) Heilverfahren nt; **there's no ~ for ...** es gibt kein Mittel gegen ...; vt heilen.

curfew ['kɜːfjuː] n Ausgangssperre f; Sperrstunde f.

curiosity [kjuərɪˈɒsɪti] n Neugier f; (for knowledge) Wißbegierde f; (object) Merkwürdigkeit f.

curious ['kjuərɪəs] a neugierig; (strange) seltsam; **~ly** ad besonders.

curl [kɜːl] n Locke f; vti locken; **~er** Lockenwickler m.

curlew ['kɜːljuː] n Brachvogel m.

curly ['kɜːli] a lockig.

currant ['kʌrənt] n Korinthe f; Johannisbeere f.

currency ['kʌrənsi] n Währung f; (of ideas) Geläufigkeit f.

current ['kʌrənt] n Strömung f; a expression gängig, üblich; issue neueste; **~ account** Girokonto nt; **~ affairs** pl Zeitgeschehen nt; **~ly** ad zur Zeit.

curriculum [kəˈrɪkjuləm] n Lehrplan m; **~ vitae** Lebenslauf m.

curry ['kʌri] n Currygericht nt; **~ powder** Curry(pulver) nt.

curse [kɜːs] vi (swear) fluchen (at auf +acc); vt (insult) verwünschen; n Fluch m.

cursory ['kɜːsəri] a flüchtig.

curt [kɜːt] a schroff.

curtail [kɜːˈteɪl] vt abkürzen; rights einschränken.

curtain ['kɜːtn] n Vorhang m, Gardine f; (Theat) Vorhang m.

curtsy ['kɜːtsi] n Knicks m; vi knicksen.

cushion ['kuʃən] n Kissen nt; vt polstern.

custard ['kʌstəd] n Vanillesoße f.

custodian [kʌsˈtəudiən] n Kustos m, Verwalter(in f) m.

custody ['kʌstədi] n Aufsicht f; (police) Polizeigewahrsam m.

custom ['kʌstəm] n (tradition) Brauch m; (business dealing) Kundschaft f; **~s** (taxes) Einfuhrzoll m; **C~s** Zollamt nt; **~ary** a üblich; **~er** Kunde m, Kundin f; **~-made** a speziell angefertigt; **C~s officer** Zollbeamte(r) mf.

cut [kʌt] vt irreg schneiden; wages kürzen; prices heruntersetzen; **I ~ my hand** ich habe mir in die Hand geschnitten; n Schnitt m; (wound) Schnittwunde f; (in book, income etc) Kürzung f; (share) Anteil m.

cute [kjuːt] a reizend, niedlich.

cuticle ['kjuːtɪkl] n (on nail) Nagelhaut f.

cutlery ['kʌtləri] n Besteck nt.

cutlet ['kʌtlɪt] n (pork) Kotelett nt; (veal) Schnitzel nt.

cutout ['kʌtaut] n (Elec) Sicherung f.

cut-price ['kʌtpraɪs] a verbilligt.

cutting ['kʌtɪŋ] a schneidend; n (from paper) Ausschnitt m.

cyanide ['saɪənaɪd] n Zyankali nt.

cybernetics [saɪbəˈnetɪks] n Kybernetik f.

cyclamen ['sɪkləmən] n Alpenveilchen nt.

cycle ['saɪkl] n Fahrrad nt; (series) Reihe f; (of songs) Zyklus m; vi radfahren.

cycling ['saɪklɪŋ] n Radfahren nt; (Sport) Radsport m.

cyclist ['saɪklɪst] n Radfahrer(in f) m.

cyclone ['saɪkləun] n Zyklon m.

cygnet ['sɪgnɪt] n junge(r) Schwan m.

cylinder ['sɪlɪndə*] n Zylinder m; (Tech) Walze f; **~ block** Zylinderblock m; **~ capacity** Zylindervolumen nt, Zylinderinhalt m; **~ head** Zylinderkopf m.

cymbals ['sɪmbəlz] npl Becken nt.

cynic ['sɪnɪk] n Zyniker(in f) m; **~al** a zynisch; **~ism** Zynismus m.

cypress ['saɪprɪs] n Zypresse f.

cyst [sɪst] n Zyste f.

czar [zɑː*] n Zar m; **~ina** [zɑːˈriːnə] Zarin f.

D

D, d [diː] n D nt, d nt.

dab [dæb] vt wound, paint betupfen; n (little bit) bißchen nt; (of paint) Tupfer m; (smear) Klecks m.

dabble ['dæbl] vi (splash) plätschern; (fig) **to ~ in sth** in etw (dat) machen.

dachshund ['dækshund] n Dackel m.

dad(dy) [dæd, -i] n Papa m, Vati m; **daddy-long-legs** Weberknecht m.

daffodil ['dæfədɪl] n Osterglocke f.

daft [dɑːft] a (col) blöd(e), doof.

dagger ['dægə*] n Dolch m.

dahlia ['deɪlɪə] n Dahlie f.

daily ['deɪli] a täglich; n (Press) Tageszeitung f; (woman) Haushaltshilfe f.

dainty ['deɪnti] a zierlich; (attractive) reizend.

dairy ['dɛəri] n (shop) Milchgeschäft nt; (on farm) Molkerei f; a Milch-.

daisy ['deɪzi] n Gänseblümchen nt.

dally ['dæli] vi tändeln.

dam [dæm] n (Stau)damm m; vt stauen.

damage ['dæmɪdʒ] n Schaden m; vt beschädigen; **~s** (Jur) Schaden(s)ersatz m.

dame [deɪm] n Dame f; (col) Weibsbild nt.

damn [dæm] vt verdammen, verwünschen; a (col) verdammt; **~ it!** verflucht!; **~ing** a vernichtend.

damp [dæmp] a feucht; n Feuchtigkeit f; (also **~en**) befeuchten; (discourage) dämpfen; **~ness** Feuchtigkeit f.

damson ['dæmzən] n Damaszenerpflaume f.

dance [dɑːns] n Tanz m; (party) Tanz(abend) m; vi tanzen; **~ hall** Tanzlokal nt; **~r** Tänzer m.

dancing ['dɑːnsɪŋ] n Tanzen nt.

dandelion ['dændɪlaɪən] n Löwenzahn m.

dandruff ['dændrəf] n (Kopf)schuppen pl.

dandy ['dændɪ] n Dandy m.

danger ['deɪndʒə*] n Gefahr f; ~! (sign) Achtung!; **in** ~ in Gefahr; **on the** ~**-list** in Lebensgefahr; ~**ous** a, ~**ously** ad gefährlich.

dangle ['dæŋgl] vi baumeln; vt herabhängen lassen.

dapper ['dæpə*] a elegant.

dare [dɛə*] vt herausfordern; vi: ~ **(to) do sth** es wagen, etw zu tun; **I** ~ **say** ich würde sagen.

daring ['dɛərɪŋ] a (audacious) verwegen; (bold) wagemutig; dress gewagt; n Mut m.

dark [dɑːk] a dunkel; (fig) düster, trübe; (deep colour) dunkel-; n Dunkelheit f; **after** ~ nach Anbruch der Dunkelheit; **D~ Ages** (finsteres) Mittelalter nt; ~**en** vti verdunkeln; ~**ness** Finsternis nt; ~**room** Dunkelkammer f.

darling ['dɑːlɪŋ] n Liebling m; a lieb.

darn [dɑːn] n Gestopfte(s) nt; vt stopfen.

dart [dɑːt] n (leap) Satz m; (weapon) Pfeil m; vi sausen; ~**s** (game) Pfeilwerfen nt; ~**board** Zielscheibe f.

dash [dæʃ] n Sprung m; (mark) (Gedanken)strich m; vt (lit) schmeißen; vi stürzen; ~**board** Armaturenbrett nt; ~**ing** a schneidig.

data ['deɪtə] npl Einzelheiten pl, Daten pl; ~ **processing** Datenverarbeitung f.

date [deɪt] n Datum nt; (for meeting etc) Termin m; (with person) Verabredung f; (fruit) Dattel f; vt letter etc datieren; person gehen mit; ~**d** a altmodisch; ~**-line** Datumsgrenze f.

dative ['deɪtɪv] n Dativ m; a Dativ-.

daub [dɔːb] vt beschmieren; paint schmieren.

daughter ['dɔːtə*] n Tochter f; ~**-in-law** Schwiegertochter f.

daunt [dɔːnt] vt entmutigen.

davenport ['dævnpɔːt] n Sekretär m; (US: sofa) Sofa nt.

dawdle ['dɔːdl] vi trödeln.

dawn [dɔːn] n Morgendämmerung f; vi dämmern; (fig) dämmern (on dat).

day [deɪ] n Tag m; (daylight) Tageslicht nt; ~ **by** ~ Tag für Tag, täglich; **one** ~ eines Tages; ~**break** Tagesanbruch m; ~**dream** n Wachtraum m, Träumerei f; vi irreg (mit offenen Augen) träumen; ~**light** Tageslicht nt; ~**time** Tageszeit f.

daze [deɪz] vt betäuben; n Betäubung f; ~**d** a benommen.

dazzle ['dæzl] vt blenden; n Blenden nt.

deacon ['diːkən] n Diakon m; Kirchenvorsteher m.

dead [ded] a tot, gestorben; (without feeling) gefühllos; (without movement) leer, verlassen; ~ **centre** genau in der Mitte; ad völlig; **the** ~ pl die Toten pl; ~**en** vt pain abtöten; sound ersticken; ~ **end** Sackgasse f; ~ **heat** tote(s) Rennen nt; ~**line** Frist(ablauf) m, Stichtag m; ~**lock** Stillstand m; ~**ly** a tödlich; ~**pan** a undurchdringlich.

deaf [def] a taub; ~**-aid** Hörgerät nt; ~**en** vt taub machen; ~**ening** a ohrenbetäubend; ~**ness** Taubheit f; ~**-mute** Taubstumme(r) m.

deal [diːl] n Geschäft nt; vti irreg austeilen; **a great** ~ **of** sehr viel; **to** ~ **with** person behandeln; department sich befassen mit; ~**er** (Comm) Händler m; (Cards) Kartengeber m; ~**ings** pl (Fin) Geschäfte pl; (relations) Beziehungen pl, Geschäftsverkehr m.

dean [diːn] n (Protestant) Superintendent m; (Catholic) Dechant m; (Univ) Dekan m.

dear [dɪə*] a lieb; (expensive) teuer; n Liebling m; ~ **me!** du liebe Zeit!; **D~ Sir** Sehr geehrter Herr!; **D~ John** Lieber John!; ~**ly** ad love herzlich; pay teuer.

dearth [dɜːθ] n Mangel m (of an +dat).

death [deθ] n Tod m; (end) Ende nt; (statistic) Sterbefall m; ~**bed** Sterbebett nt; ~ **certificate** Totenschein m; ~ **duties** (Brit) Erbschaftssteuer f; ~**ly** a totenähnlich, Toten-; ~ **penalty** Todesstrafe f; ~ **rate** Sterblichkeitsziffer f.

debar [dɪˈbɑː*] vt ausschließen.

debase [dɪˈbeɪs] vt entwerten.

debatable [dɪˈbeɪtəbl] a anfechtbar.

debate [dɪˈbeɪt] n Debatte f, Diskussion f; vt debattieren, diskutieren; (consider) überlegen.

debauched [dɪˈbɔːtʃt] a ausschweifend.

debauchery [dɪˈbɔːtʃərɪ] n Ausschweifungen pl.

debit ['debɪt] n Schuldposten m; vt belasten.

debris ['debriː] n Trümmer pl.

debt [det] n Schuld f; **to be in** ~ verschuldet sein; ~**or** Schuldner m.

début ['deɪbuː] n Debüt nt.

decade ['dekeɪd] n Jahrzehnt nt.

decadence ['dekədəns] n Verfall m, Dekadenz f.

decadent ['dekədənt] a dekadent.

decanter [dɪˈkæntə*] n Karaffe f.

decarbonize [diːˈkɑːbənaɪz] vt entkohlen.

decay [dɪˈkeɪ] n Verfall m; vi verfallen; teeth, meat etc faulen; leaves etc verrotten.

decease [dɪˈsiːs] n Hinscheiden nt; ~**d** verstorben.

deceit [dɪˈsiːt] n Betrug m; ~**ful** a falsch.

deceive [dɪˈsiːv] vt täuschen.

decelerate [diːˈseləreɪt] vti (sich) verlangsamen, die Geschwindigkeit verringern.

December [dɪˈsembə*] n Dezember m.

decency ['diːsənsɪ] n Anstand m.

decent [diːsənt] a (respectable) anständig; (pleasant) annehmbar.

decentralization [diːsentrəlaɪˈzeɪʃən] n Dezentralisierung f.

deception [dɪˈsepʃən] n Betrug m.

deceptive [dɪˈseptɪv] a täuschend, irreführend.

decibel ['desɪbel] n Dezibel nt.

decide [dɪˈsaɪd] vt entscheiden; vi sich entscheiden; **to** ~ **on sth** etw beschließen; ~**d** a bestimmt, entschieden; ~**dly** ad entschieden.

deciduous [dɪˈsɪdjuəs] a jedes Jahr abfallend, Laub-.

decimal ['desɪməl] a dezimal; n Dezimalzahl f; ~ **point** Komma nt (eines

Dezimalbruches); ~ **system** Dezimal-system *nt.*

decimate ['desɪmeɪt] *vt* dezimieren.

decipher [dɪ'saɪfə*] *vt* entziffern.

decision [dɪ'sɪʒən] *n* Entscheidung *f,* Entschluß *m.*

decisive [dɪ'saɪsɪv] *a* entscheidend, ausschlaggebend.

deck [dek] *n* (*Naut*) Deck *nt;* (*of cards*) Pack *m;* ~**chair** Liegestuhl *m;* ~**hand** Matrose *m.*

declaration [deklə'reɪʃən] *n* Erklärung *f.*

declare [dɪ'klɛə*] *vt* (*state*) behaupten; *war* erklären; (*Customs*) verzollen.

decline [dɪ'klaɪn] *n* (*decay*) Verfall *m;* (*lessening*) Rückgang *m,* Niedergang *m; vt invitation* ausschlagen, ablehnen; *vi* (*of strength*) nachlassen; (*say no*) ablehnen.

declutch ['di:'klʌtʃ] *vi* auskuppeln.

decode ['di:'kəʊd] *vt* entschlüsseln.

decompose [di:kəm'pəʊz] *vi* (sich) zersetzen.

decomposition [di:kɒmpə'zɪʃən] *n* Zersetzung *f.*

decontaminate [di:kən'tæmɪneɪt] *vt* entgiften.

décor ['deɪkɔ:*] *n* Ausstattung *f.*

decorate ['dekəreɪt] *vt room* tapezieren; streichen; (*adorn*) (aus)schmücken; *cake* verzieren; (*honour*) auszeichnen.

decoration [dekə'reɪʃən] *n* (*of house*) (Wand)dekoration *f;* (*medal*) Orden *m.*

decorative ['dekərətɪv] *a* dekorativ, Schmuck-.

decorator ['dekəreɪtə*] *n* Maler *m,* Anstreicher *m.*

decorum [dɪ'kɔ:rəm] *n* Anstand *m.*

decoy ['di:kɔɪ] *n* (*lit, fig*) Lockvogel *m.*

decrease [di:'kri:s] *n* Abnahme *f; vt* vermindern; *vi* abnehmen.

decree [dɪ'kri:] *n* Verfügung *f,* Erlaß *m.*

decrepit [dɪ'krepɪt] *a* hinfällig.

dedicate ['dedɪkeɪt] *vt* (*to God*) weihen; *book* widmen.

dedication [dedɪ'keɪʃən] *n* (*devotion*) Ergebenheit *f.*

deduce [dɪ'dju:s] *vt* ableiten, schließen (*from* aus).

deduct [dɪ'dʌkt] *vt* abziehen; ~**ion** [dɪ'dʌkʃən] (*of money*) Abzug *m;* (*conclusion*) (Schluß)folgerung *f.*

deed [di:d] *n* Tat *f;* (*document*) Urkunde *f.*

deep [di:p] *a* tief; ~**en** *vt* vertiefen; ~-**freeze** Tiefkühlung *f;* ~-**seated** *a* tiefsitzend; ~-**set** *a* tiefliegend.

deer [dɪə*] *n* Reh *nt;* (*with antlers*) Hirsch *m.*

deface [dɪ'feɪs] *vt* entstellen.

defamation [defə'meɪʃən] *n* Verleumdung *f.*

default [dɪ'fɔ:lt] *n* Versäumnis *nt; vi* versäumen; **by** ~ durch Nichterscheinen *nt;* ~**er** Schuldner *m,* Zahlungsunfähige(r) *m.*

defeat [dɪ'fi:t] *n* (*overthrow*) Vernichtung *f;* (*battle*) Niederlage *f; vt* schlagen, zu Fall bringen; ~**ist** *a* defätistisch.

defect ['di:fekt] *n* Defekt *m,* Fehler *m;* [dɪ'fekt] *vi* überlaufen; ~**ive** [dɪ'fektɪv] *a* fehlerhaft, schadhaft.

defence [dɪ'fens] *n* (*Mil, Sport*) Verteidigung *f;* (*excuse*) Rechtfertigung *f;* ~**less** *a* wehrlos.

defend [dɪ'fend] *vt* verteidigen; ~**ant** Angeklagte(r) *m;* ~**er** Verteidiger *m.*

defensive [dɪ'fensɪv] *a* defensiv, Schutz-.

defer [dɪ'fɜ:*] *vt* verschieben; ~**ence** ['defərəns] Hochachtung *f,* Rücksichtnahme *f;* ~**ential** [defə'renʃəl] *a* ehrerbietig.

defiance [dɪ'faɪəns] *n* Trotz *m,* Unnachgiebigkeit *f;* **in** ~ **of the order** dem Befehl zum Trotz.

defiant [dɪ'faɪənt] *a* trotzig, unnachgiebig.

deficiency [dɪ'fɪʃənsɪ] *n* Unzulänglichkeit *f,* Mangel *m.*

deficient [dɪ'fɪʃənt] *a* unzureichend.

deficit ['defɪsɪt] *n* Defizit *nt,* Fehlbetrag *m.*

defile [dɪ'faɪl] *vt* beschmutzen; *n* ['di:faɪl] Schlucht *f.*

define [dɪ'faɪn] *vt* bestimmen; (*explain*) definieren.

definite ['defɪnɪt] *a* bestimmt; (*clear*) klar, eindeutig; ~**ly** *ad* bestimmt.

definition [defɪ'nɪʃən] *n* Definition *f;* (*Phot*) Schärfe *f.*

definitive [dɪ'fɪnɪtɪv] *a* definitiv, endgültig.

deflate [di:'fleɪt] *vt* die Luft ablassen aus.

deflation [di:'fleɪʃən] *n* (*Fin*) Deflation *f.*

deflect [dɪ'flekt] *vt* ablenken.

deform [dɪ'fɔ:m] *vt* deformieren, entstellen; ~**ed** *a* deformiert; ~**ity** Verunstaltung *f,* Mißbildung *f.*

defraud [dɪ'frɔ:d] *vt* betrügen.

defray [dɪ'freɪ] *vt* bestreiten.

defrost [di:'frɒst] *vt fridge* abtauen; *food* auftauen.

deft [deft] *a* geschickt.

defunct [dɪ'fʌŋkt] *a* verstorben.

defy [dɪ'faɪ] *vt* (*challenge*) sich widersetzen (+*dat*); (*resist*) trotzen (+*dat*), sich stellen gegen.

degenerate [dɪ'dʒenəreɪt] *vi* degenerieren; [dɪ'dʒenərɪt] *a* degeneriert.

degradation [degrə'deɪʃən] *n* Erniedrigung *f.*

degrading [dɪ'greɪdɪŋ] *a* erniedrigend.

degree [dɪ'gri:] *n* Grad *m;* (*Univ*) akademische(r) Grad *m;* **by** ~**s** allmählich; **to take one's** ~ sein Examen machen.

dehydrated [di:haɪ'dreɪtɪd] *a* getrocknet, Trocken-.

de-ice [di:'aɪs] *vt* enteisen, auftauen.

deign [deɪn] *vi* sich herablassen.

deity ['di:ɪtɪ] *n* Gottheit *f.*

dejected [dɪ'dʒektɪd] *a* niedergeschlagen.

dejection [dɪ'dʒekʃən] *n* Niedergeschlagenheit *f.*

delay [dɪ'leɪ] *vt* (*hold back*) aufschieben; **the flight was** ~**ed** die Maschine hatte Verspätung; *vi* (*linger*) sich aufhalten, zögern; *n* Aufschub *m,* Verzögerung *f;* **without** ~ unverzüglich; ~**ed** *a action* verzögert.

delegate ['delɪgɪt] *n* Delegierte(r) *mf;* Abgeordnete(r) *mf;* ['delɪgeɪt] *vt* delegieren.

delegation [delɪ'geɪʃən] n Abordnung f; (foreign) Delegation f.

delete [dɪ'liːt] vt (aus)streichen.

deliberate [dɪ'lɪbərɪt] a (intentional) bewußt, überlegt; (slow) bedächtig; [dɪ'lɪbəreɪt] vi (consider) überlegen; (debate) sich beraten; ~ly ad vorsätzlich.

deliberation [dɪlɪbə'reɪʃən] n Überlegung f, Beratung f.

delicacy ['delɪkəsɪ] n Zartheit f; (weakness) Anfälligkeit f; (tact) Zartgefühl nt; (food) Delikatesse f.

delicate ['delɪkɪt] a (fine) fein; (fragile) zart; (situation) heikel; (Med) empfindlich; ~ly ad bedenklich.

delicatessen [delɪkə'tesn] n Feinkostgeschäft nt.

delicious [dɪ'lɪʃəs] a köstlich, lecker, delikat.

delight [dɪ'laɪt] n Wonne f; vt entzücken; ~ful a entzückend, herrlich.

delinquency [dɪ'lɪŋkwənsɪ] n Straffälligkeit f, Delinquenz f.

delinquent [dɪ'lɪŋkwənt] n Straffällige(r) mf; a straffällig.

delirious [dɪ'lɪrɪəs] a irre, im Fieberwahn.

delirium [dɪ'lɪrɪəm] n Fieberwahn m, Delirium nt.

deliver [dɪ'lɪvə*] vt goods (ab)liefern; letter bringen, zustellen; verdict aussprechen; speech halten; ~y (Ab)lieferung f; (of letter) Zustellung f; (of speech) Vortragsweise f; ~y van Lieferwagen m.

delouse ['diː'laus] vt entlausen.

delta ['deltə] n Delta nt.

delude [dɪ'luːd] vt täuschen.

deluge ['deljuːdʒ] n Überschwemmung f; (fig) Flut f; vt (fig) überfluten.

delusion [dɪ'luːʒən] n (Selbst)täuschung f.

de luxe [dɪ'lʌks] a Luxus-.

demand [dɪ'mɑːnd] vt verlangen; n (request) Verlangen nt; (Comm) Nachfrage f; **in** ~ begehrt, gesucht; **on** ~ auf Verlangen; ~ing a anspruchsvoll.

demarcation [diːmɑː'keɪʃən] n Abgrenzung f.

demeanour [dɪ'miːnə*] n Benehmen nt.

demented [dɪ'mentɪd] a wahnsinnig.

demi- ['demɪ] pref halb-.

demise [dɪ'maɪz] n Ableben nt.

demobilization ['diːməubɪlaɪ'zeɪʃn] n Demobilisierung f.

democracy [dɪ'mɒkrəsɪ] n Demokratie f.

democrat ['deməkræt] n Demokrat m; ~ic a, ~ically ad [demə'krætɪk, -lɪ] demokratisch.

demolish [dɪ'mɒlɪʃ] vt (lit) abreißen; (destroy) zerstören; (fig) vernichten.

demolition [demə'lɪʃən] n Abbruch m.

demon ['diːmən] n Dämon m.

demonstrate ['demənstreɪt] vti demonstrieren.

demonstration [demən'streɪʃən] n Demonstration f; (proof) Beweisführung f.

demonstrative [dɪ'mɒnstrətɪv] a demonstrativ.

demonstrator ['demənstreɪtə*] n (Pol) Demonstrant(in f) m.

demoralize [dɪ'mɒrəlaɪz] vt demoralisieren.

demote [dɪ'məut] vt degradieren.

demure [dɪ'mjuə*] a ernst.

den [den] n (of animal) Höhle f, Bau m; Bude f; ~ **of vice** Lasterhöhle f.

denationalize [diː'næʃnəlaɪz] vt reprivatisieren.

denial [dɪ'naɪəl] n Leugnung f; official ~ Dementi nt.

denigrate ['denɪgreɪt] vt verunglimpfen.

denim ['denɪm] a Denim-; ~s pl Denim-Jeans.

denomination [dɪnɒmɪ'neɪʃən] n (Eccl) Bekenntnis nt; (type) Klasse f; (Fin) Wert m.

denominator [dɪ'nɒmɪneɪtə*] n Nenner; **common** ~ gemeinsame(r) Nenner m.

denote [dɪ'nəut] vt bedeuten.

denounce [dɪ'nauns] vt brandmarken.

dense [dens] a dicht, dick; (stupid) schwer von Begriff; ~ly ad dicht.

density ['densɪtɪ] n Dichte f.

dent [dent] n Delle f; vt einbeulen.

dental ['dentl] a Zahn-; ~ **surgeon** = **dentist**.

dentifrice ['dentɪfrɪs] n Zahnputzmittel nt.

dentist ['dentɪst] n Zahnarzt m/-ärztin f; ~ry Zahnmedizin f.

denture ['dentʃə*] n künstliche(s) Gebiß nt.

denude [dɪ'njuːd] vt entblößen.

deny [dɪ'naɪ] vt leugnen; rumour widersprechen (+dat); knowledge verleugnen; help abschlagen; **to ~ o.s. sth** sich etw versagen.

deodorant [diː'əudərənt] n Desodorans nt.

depart [dɪ'pɑːt] vi abfahren.

department [dɪ'pɑːtmənt] n (Comm) Abteilung f, Sparte f; (Univ, Sch) Fachbereich m; (Pol) Ministerium nt, Ressort nt; ~al [dɪ'pɑːtməntl] a Fach-; ~ **store** Warenhaus nt.

departure [dɪ'pɑːtʃə*] n (of person) Weggang m; (on journey) Abreise f; (of train) Abfahrt f; (of plane) Abflug m; **new** ~ Neuerung f.

depend [dɪ'pend] vi: **it** ~**s** es kommt darauf an; ~ **on** vt abhängen von; parents etc angewiesen sein auf (+acc); ~**able** a zuverlässig; ~**ence** n Abhängigkeit f; ~**ent** n (person) Familienangehörige(r) mf; a bedingt (on durch).

depict [dɪ'pɪkt] vt schildern.

depleted [dɪ'pliːtɪd] a aufgebraucht.

deplorable [dɪ'plɔːrəbl] a bedauerlich.

deplore [dɪ'plɔː*] vt mißbilligen.

deploy [dɪ'plɔɪ] vt einsetzen.

depopulation ['diːpɒpju'leɪʃən] n Entvölkerung f.

deport [dɪ'pɔːt] vt deportieren; ~**ation** [diːpɔː'teɪʃən] Abschiebung f; ~**ation order** Ausweisung f; ~**ment** Betragen nt.

depose [dɪ'pəuz] vt absetzen.

deposit [dɪ'pɒzɪt] n (in bank) Guthaben nt; (down payment) Anzahlung f; (security) Kaution f; (Chem) Niederschlag m; vt (in bank) deponieren; (put down) niederlegen;

~ account Sparkonto *nt*; **~or** Konto-
inhaber *m*.
depot ['depəʊ] *n* Depot *nt*.
deprave [dɪ'preɪv] *vt* (moralisch)
verderben; **~d** *a* verworfen.
depravity [dɪ'prævɪtɪ] *n* Verworfenheit *f*.
deprecate ['deprɪkeɪt] *vt* mißbilligen.
depreciate [dɪ'priːʃɪeɪt] *vi* im Wert sinken.
depreciation [dɪpriːʃɪ'eɪʃən] *n* Wert-
minderung *f*.
depress [dɪ'pres] *vt* (*press down*) niederdrücken; (*in mood*) deprimieren; **~ed** *a*
person niedergeschlagen, deprimiert;
~ed area Notstandsgebiet *nt*; **~ing** *a*
deprimierend; **~ion** [dɪ'preʃən] (*mood*)
Depression *f*; (*in trade*) Wirtschaftskrise *f*;
(*hollow*) Vertiefung *f*; (*Met*) Tief(druck-
gebiet) *nt*.
deprivation [deprɪ'veɪʃən] *n* Entbehrung *f*,
Not *f*.
deprive [dɪ'praɪv] *vt* berauben (*of* +*gen*);
~d *a child* sozial benachteiligt; *area*
unterentwickelt.
depth [depθ] *n* Tiefe *f*; **in the ~s of**
despair in tiefster Verzweiflung; **to be**
out of one's ~ den Boden unter den
Füßen verloren haben; **~ charge**
Wasserbombe *f*.
deputation [depjʊ'teɪʃən] *n* Abordnung *f*.
deputize ['depjʊtaɪz] *vi* vertreten (*for*
+*acc*).
deputy ['depjʊtɪ] *a* stellvertretend; *n*
(Stell)vertreter *m*.
derail [dɪ'reɪl] *vt* entgleisen lassen; **to be**
~ed entgleisen; **~ment** Entgleisung *f*.
deranged [dɪ'reɪndʒd] *a* irr, verrückt.
derby ['dɑːbɪ] *n* (US) Melone *f*.
derelict ['derɪlɪkt] *a* verlassen; *building*
baufällig.
deride [dɪ'raɪd] *vt* auslachen.
derision [dɪ'rɪʒən] *n* Hohn *m*, Spott *m*.
derisory [dɪ'raɪsərɪ] *a* spöttisch.
derivation [derɪ'veɪʃən] *n* Ableitung *f*.
derivative [dɪ'rɪvətɪv] *n* Abgeleitete(s) *nt*;
a abgeleitet.
derive [dɪ'raɪv] *vt* (*get*) gewinnen;
(*deduce*) ableiten; *vi* (*come from*)
abstammen.
dermatitis [dɜːmə'taɪtɪs] *n* Hautent-
zündung *f*.
derogatory [dɪ'rɒgətərɪ] *a* geringschätzig.
derrick ['derɪk] *n* Drehkran *m*.
desalination [diːsælɪ'neɪʃən] *n* Entsalzung
f.
descend [dɪ'send] *vti* hinuntersteigen; **to**
~ from abstammen von; **~ant** Nachkomme *m*.
descent [dɪ'sent] *n* (*coming down*) Abstieg
m; (*origin*) Abstammung *f*.
describe [dɪs'kraɪb] *vt* beschreiben.
description [dɪs'krɪpʃən] *n* Beschreibung
f; (*sort*) Art *f*.
descriptive [dɪs'krɪptɪv] *a* beschreibend;
word anschaulich.
desecrate ['desɪkreɪt] *vt* schänden.
desegregation [diːsegrə'geɪʃən] *n*
Aufhebung *f* der Rassentrennung.
desert[1] ['dezət] *n* Wüste *f*.
desert[2] [dɪ'zɜːt] *vt* verlassen; (*temporarily*)

im Stich lassen; *vi* (*Mil*) desertieren; **~er**
Deserteur *m*; **~ion** [dɪ'zɜːʃən] (*of wife*)
böswillige(s) Verlassen *nt*; (*Mil*) Fahnen-
flucht *f*.
deserve [dɪ'zɜːv] *vt* verdienen.
deserving [dɪ'zɜːvɪŋ] *a person* würdig;
action verdienstvoll.
design [dɪ'zaɪn] *n* (*plan*) Entwurf *m*; (*drawing*) Zeichnung *f*; (*planning*) Gestaltung *f*,
Design *nt*; *vt* entwerfen; (*intend*)
bezwecken; **to have ~s on sb/sth** es auf
jdn/etw abgesehen haben.
designate ['dezɪgneɪt] *vt* bestimmen;
['dezɪgnɪt] *a* designiert.
designation [dezɪg'neɪʃən] *n* Bezeichnung
f.
designer [dɪ'zaɪnə*] *n* Designer *m*; (*Theat*)
Bühnenbildner(in *f*) *m*.
desirability [dɪzaɪərə'bɪlɪtɪ] *n* Erwünscht-
heit *f*.
desirable [dɪ'zaɪərəbl] *n* wünschenswert;
woman begehrenswert.
desire [dɪ'zaɪə*] *n* Wunsch *m*, Verlangen
nt; (*lust*) begehren, wünschen; (*ask for*)
verlangen, wollen.
desirous [dɪ'zaɪərəs] *a* begierig (*of* auf
+*acc*).
desist [dɪ'zɪst] *vi* Abstand nehmen,
aufhören.
desk [desk] *n* Schreibtisch *m*.
desolate ['desəlɪt] *a* öde; (*sad*) trostlos.
desolation [desə'leɪʃən] *n* Trostlosigkeit *f*.
despair [dɪs'peə*] *n* Verzweiflung *f*; *vi*
verzweifeln (*of* an +*dat*).
despatch [dɪs'pætʃ] = dispatch.
desperate ['despərɪt] *a* verzweifelt;
situation hoffnungslos; **to be ~ for sth**
etw unbedingt brauchen; **~ly** *ad* verzweifelt.
desperation [despə'reɪʃən] *n* Verzweiflung
f.
despicable [dɪs'pɪkəbl] *a* abscheulich.
despise [dɪs'paɪz] *vt* verachten.
despite [dɪs'paɪt] *prep* trotz (+*gen*).
despondent [dɪs'pɒndənt] *a* mutlos.
dessert [dɪ'zɜːt] *n* Nachtisch *m*; **~spoon**
Dessertlöffel *m*.
destination [destɪ'neɪʃən] *n* (*of person*)
(Reise)ziel *nt*; (*of goods*) Bestimmungsort
m.
destine ['destɪn] *vt* (*set apart*) bestimmen.
destiny ['destɪnɪ] *n* Schicksal *nt*.
destitute ['destɪtjuːt] *a* notleidend.
destitution [destɪtjuːʃən] *n* Elend *f*.
destroy [dɪs'trɔɪ] *vt* zerstören; **~er** (*Naut*)
Zerstörer *m*.
destruction [dɪs'trʌkʃən] *n* Zerstörung *f*.
destructive [dɪs'trʌktɪv] *a* zerstörend.
detach [dɪ'tætʃ] *vt* loslösen; **~able** *a*
abtrennbar; **~ed** *a* attitude distanziert,
objektiv; *house* Einzel-; **~ment** (*Mil*)
Abteilung *f*, Sonderkommando *nt*; (*fig*)
Abstand *m*, Unvoreingenommenheit *f*.
detail ['diːteɪl] *n* Einzelheit *f*, Detail *nt*;
(*minor part*) unwichtige Einzelheit *f*; *vt*
(*relate*) ausführlich berichten; (*appoint*)
abkommandieren; **in ~** ausführlichst, bis
ins kleinste.

detain [dɪˈteɪn] vt aufhalten; (*imprison*) in Haft halten.

detect [dɪˈtekt] vt entdecken; ~**ion** [dɪˈtekʃən] Aufdeckung f; ~**ive** Detektiv m; ~**ive story** Krimi(nalgeschichte f) m; ~**or** Detektor m.

détente [ˈdeɪtɑ̃nt] n Entspannung f.

detention [dɪˈtenʃən] n Haft f; (*Sch*) Nachsitzen nt.

deter [dɪˈtɜː*] vt abschrecken.

detergent [dɪˈtɜːdʒənt] n Waschmittel nt; Reinigungsmittel nt.

deteriorate [dɪˈtɪərɪəreɪt] vi sich verschlechtern.

deterioration [dɪtɪərɪəˈreɪʃən] n Verschlechterung f.

determination [dɪtɜːmɪˈneɪʃən] n Entschlossenheit f.

determine [dɪˈtɜːmɪn] vt bestimmen; ~**d** a entschlossen.

deterrent [dɪˈterənt] n Abschreckungsmittel nt; a abschreckend.

detest [dɪˈtest] vt verabscheuen; ~**able** a abscheulich.

dethrone [diːˈθrəʊn] vt entthronen.

detonate [ˈdetəneɪt] vt detonieren.

detonator [ˈdetəneɪtə*] n Sprengkapsel f.

detour [ˈdeɪtʊə*] n Umweg m; (*on road sign*) Umleitung f.

detract [dɪˈtrækt] vi schmälern (*from acc*).

detriment [ˈdetrɪmənt] n: to the ~ of zum Schaden (+*gen*); ~**al** [detrɪˈmentl] a schädlich.

deuce [djuːs] n (*tennis*) Einstand m.

devaluation [dɪvæljʊˈeɪʃən] n Abwertung f.

devalue [ˈdiːˈvæljuː] vt abwerten.

devastate [ˈdevəsteɪt] vt verwüsten.

devastating [ˈdevəsteɪtɪŋ] a verheerend.

develop [dɪˈveləp] vt entwickeln; *resources* erschließen; vi sich entwickeln; ~**er** (*Phot*) Entwickler m; (*of land*) Bauunternehmer m; ~**ing a country** Entwicklungs-; ~**ment** Entwicklung f.

deviant [ˈdiːvɪənt] a abweichend; n Abweichler m.

deviate [ˈdiːvɪeɪt] vi abweichen.

deviation [diːvɪˈeɪʃən] n Abweichung f.

device [dɪˈvaɪs] n Vorrichtung f, Gerät nt.

devil [ˈdevl] n Teufel m; ~**ish** a teuflisch.

devious [ˈdiːvɪəs] a *route* gewunden; *means* krumm; *person* verschlagen.

devise [dɪˈvaɪz] vt entwickeln.

devoid [dɪˈvɔɪd] a: ~ of ohne, bar (+*gen*).

devolution [diːvəˈluːʃən] n Dezentralisierung f.

devote [dɪˈvəʊt] vt widmen (*to dat*); ~**d** a ergeben; ~**e** [devəʊˈtiː] Anhänger(in f) m, Verehrer(in f) m.

devotion [dɪˈvəʊʃən] n (*piety*) Andacht f; (*loyalty*) Ergebenheit f, Hingabe f.

devour [dɪˈvaʊə*] vt verschlingen.

devout [dɪˈvaʊt] a andächtig.

dew [djuː] n Tau m.

dexterity [deksˈterɪtɪ] n Geschicklichkeit f.

diabetes [daɪəˈbiːtiːz] n Zuckerkrankheit f.

diabetic [daɪəˈbetɪk] a zuckerkrank; n Diabetiker m.

diagnose [ˈdaɪəgnəʊz] vt (*Med*) diagnostizieren; feststellen.

diagnosis [daɪəgˈnəʊsɪs] n Diagnose f.

diagonal [daɪˈægənl] a diagonal, schräg; n Diagonale f.

diagram [ˈdaɪəgræm] n Diagramm nt, Schaubild nt.

dial [ˈdaɪəl] n (*Tel*) Wählscheibe f; (*of clock*) Zifferblatt nt; vt wählen; ~**ling tone** Amtszeichen nt.

dialect [ˈdaɪəlekt] n Dialekt m.

dialogue [ˈdaɪəlɒg] n Gespräch nt; (*Liter*) Dialog m.

diameter [daɪˈæmɪtə*] n Durchmesser m.

diametrically [daɪəˈmetrɪklɪ] ad: ~ **opposed to** genau entgegengesetzt (+*dat*).

diamond [ˈdaɪəmənd] n Diamant m; (*Cards*) Karo nt.

diaper [ˈdaɪəpə*] n (*US*) Windel f.

diaphragm [ˈdaɪəfræm] n Zwerchfell nt.

diarrhoea [daɪəˈrɪːə] n Durchfall m.

diary [ˈdaɪərɪ] n Taschenkalender m; (*account*) Tagebuch nt.

dice [daɪs] n Würfel pl; vt (*Cook*) in Würfel schneiden.

dicey [ˈdaɪsɪ] a (*col*) riskant.

dichotomy [dɪˈkɒtəmɪ] n Kluft f.

dictate [dɪkˈteɪt] vt diktieren; (*of circumstances*) gebieten; [ˈdɪkteɪt] n Mahnung f, Gebot nt.

dictation [dɪkˈteɪʃən] n Diktat nt.

dictator [dɪkˈteɪtə*] n Diktator m.

dictatorship [dɪkˈteɪtəʃɪp] n Diktatur f.

diction [ˈdɪkʃən] n Ausdrucksweise f.

dictionary [ˈdɪkʃənrɪ] n Wörterbuch nt.

diddle [ˈdɪdl] vt (*col*) übers Ohr hauen.

didn't [ˈdɪdənt] = **did not**.

die [daɪ] vi sterben; (*end*) aufhören; ~ **away** vi schwächer werden; ~ **down** vi nachlassen; ~ **out** vi aussterben; (*fig*) nachlassen.

diesel [ˈdiːzəl]: ~ **engine** Dieselmotor m.

diet [ˈdaɪət] n Nahrung f, Kost f; (*special food*) Diät f; (*slimming*) Abmagerungskur f; vi eine Abmagerungskur machen.

differ [ˈdɪfə*] vi sich unterscheiden; (*disagree*) anderer Meinung sein; **we** ~ **wir sind unterschiedlicher Meinung;** ~**ence** Unterschied m; (*disagreement*) (Meinungs)unterschied m; ~**ent** a verschieden; **that's** ~**ent** das ist anders; ~**ential** [dɪfəˈrenʃəl] (*Aut*) Differentialgetriebe nt; (*in wages*) Lohnstufe f; ~**entiate** [dɪfəˈrenʃɪeɪt] vti unterscheiden; ~**ently** ad verschieden, unterschiedlich.

difficult [ˈdɪfɪkəlt] a schwierig; ~**y** Schwierigkeit f; **with** ~**y** nur schwer.

diffidence [ˈdɪfɪdəns] n mangelnde(s) Selbstvertrauen nt.

diffident [ˈdɪfɪdənt] a schüchtern.

diffuse [dɪˈfjuːs] a langatmig; [dɪˈfjuːz] vt verbreiten.

dig [dɪg] vti irreg *hole* graben; *garden* (um)graben; *claws* senken; n (*prod*) Stoß m; ~ **in** vi (*Mil*) sich eingraben; (*to food*) sich hermachen über (+*acc*); ~ **in!** greif zu!; ~ **up** vt ausgraben; (*fig*) aufgabeln.

digest [daɪˈdʒest] vt (*lit, fig*) verdauen;

['daɪdʒest] n Auslese f; ~ible a verdaulich; ~ion Verdauung f.

digit ['dɪdʒɪt] n einstellige Zahl f; (Anat) Finger m; Zehe f; ~al computer Einzahlcomputer m.

dignified ['dɪgnɪfaɪd] a würdevoll.

dignify ['dɪgnɪfaɪ] vt Würde verleihen (+dat).

dignitary ['dɪgnɪtərɪ] n Würdenträger m.

dignity ['dɪgnɪtɪ] n Würde f.

digress [daɪ'gres] vi abschweifen; ~ion [daɪ'greʃən] Abschweifung f.

digs [dɪgz] npl (Brit col) Bude f.

dilapidated [dɪ'læpɪdeɪtɪd] a baufällig.

dilate [daɪ'leɪt] vti (sich) weiten.

dilatory ['dɪlətərɪ] a hinhaltend.

dilemma [daɪ'lemə] n Dilemma nt.

dilettante [dɪlɪ'tæntɪ] n Dilettant m.

diligence ['dɪlɪdʒəns] n Fleiß m.

diligent ['dɪlɪdʒənt] a fleißig.

dill [dɪl] n Dill m.

dilly-dally ['dɪlɪdælɪ] vi (col) herumtrödeln.

dilute [daɪ'luːt] vt verdünnen; a verdünnt.

dim [dɪm] a trübe, matt; (stupid) schwer von Begriff; **to take a ~ view of sth** etw mißbilligen; vt verdunkeln.

dime [daɪm] n (US) Zehncentstück nt.

dimension [dɪ'menʃən] n Dimension f; ~s pl Maße pl.

diminish [dɪ'mɪnɪʃ] vti verringern.

diminutive [dɪ'mɪnjutɪv] a winzig; n Verkleinerungsform f.

dimly ['dɪmlɪ] ad trübe.

dimple ['dɪmpl] n Grübchen nt.

dim-witted ['dɪm'wɪtɪd] a (col) dämlich.

din [dɪn] n Getöse nt.

dine [daɪn] vi speisen; ~r Tischgast m; (Rail) Speisewagen m.

dinghy ['dɪŋgɪ] n kleine(s) Ruderboot nt; Dinghy nt.

dingy ['dɪndʒɪ] a armselig.

dining car ['daɪnɪŋkaː*] n Speisewagen m.

dining room ['daɪnɪŋrum] n Eßzimmer nt; (in hotel) Speisezimmer nt.

dinner ['dɪnə*] n Mittagessen nt, Abendessen nt; (public) Festessen nt; ~ jacket Smoking m; ~ party Tischgesellschaft f; ~ time Tischzeit f.

dinosaur ['daɪnəsɔː*] n Dinosaurier m.

diocese ['daɪəsɪs] n Diözese f, Sprengel m.

dip [dɪp] n (hollow) Senkung f; (bathe) kurze(s) Bad(en) nt; vt eintauchen; (Aut) abblenden; vi (slope) sich senken, abfallen.

diphtheria [dɪf'θɪərɪə] n Diphterie f.

diphthong ['dɪfθɒŋ] n Diphthong m.

diploma [dɪ'pləumə] n Urkunde f, Diplom nt.

diplomat ['dɪpləmæt] n Diplomat(in f) m; ~ic [dɪplə'mætɪk] a diplomatisch; ~ic corps diplomatische(s) Korps nt.

dipstick ['dɪpstɪk] n Ölmeßstab m.

dire [daɪə*] a schrecklich.

direct [daɪ'rekt] a direkt; vt leiten; film die Regie führen (+gen); jury anweisen; (aim) richten, lenken; (tell way) den Weg erklären (+dat); (order) anweisen; ~ current Gleichstrom m; ~ hit Volltreffer m; ~ion [dɪ'rekʃən] Führung f,

Leitung f; (course) Richtung f; (Cine) Regie f; ~ions pl (for use) Gebrauchsanleitung f; (orders) Anweisungen pl; ~ional [dɪ'rekʃənl] a Richt-; ~ive Direktive f; ~ly (in straight line) gerade, direkt; (at once) unmittelbar, sofort; ~or Direktor m, Leiter m; (of film) Regisseur m; ~ory Adreßbuch nt; (Tel) Telefonbuch nt.

dirt [dɜːt] n Schmutz m, Dreck m; ~ road unbefestigte Straße; ~y a schmutzig, dreckig; gemein; vt beschmutzen; ~ cheap a spottbillig.

disability [dɪsə'bɪlɪtɪ] n Körperbehinderung f.

disabled [dɪs'eɪbld] a körperbehindert.

disabuse [dɪsə'bjuːz] vt befreien.

disadvantage [dɪsəd'vɑːntɪdʒ] n Nachteil m; ~ous [dɪsædvɑːn'teɪdʒəs] a ungünstig.

disagree [dɪsə'griː] vi nicht übereinstimmen; (quarrel) (sich) streiten; (food) nicht bekommen (with dat); ~able a person widerlich; task unangenehm; ~ment (between persons) Streit m; (between things) Widerspruch m.

disallow [dɪsə'lau] vt nicht zulassen.

disappear [dɪsə'pɪə*] vi verschwinden; ~ance Verschwinden nt.

disappoint [dɪsə'pɔɪnt] vt enttäuschen; ~ing a enttäuschend; ~ment Enttäuschung f.

disapproval [dɪsə'pruːvəl] n Mißbilligung f.

disapprove [dɪsə'pruːv] vi mißbilligen (of acc); **she ~s** sie mißbilligt es.

disarm [dɪs'ɑːm] vt entwaffnen; (Pol) abrüsten; ~ament Abrüstung f.

disaster [dɪ'zɑːstə*] n Unglück nt; Katastrophe f.

disastrous [dɪ'zɑːstrəs] a verhängnisvoll.

disband [dɪs'bænd] vt auflösen.

disbelief ['dɪsbə'liːf] n Ungläubigkeit f.

disc [dɪsk] n Scheibe f; (record) (Schall)-platte f.

discard ['dɪskɑːd] vt ablegen.

disc brake ['dɪsk breɪk] n Scheibenbremse f.

discern [dɪ'sɜːn] vt unterscheiden (können), erkennen; ~ing a scharfsinnig.

discharge [dɪs'tʃɑːdʒ] vt ship entladen; duties nachkommen (+dat); (dismiss) entlassen; gun abschießen; n (of ship) Entladung f; ['dɪstʃɑːdʒ] (Med) Ausfluß m.

disciple [dɪ'saɪpl] n Jünger m.

disciplinary ['dɪsɪplɪnərɪ] a disziplinarisch.

discipline ['dɪsɪplɪn] n Disziplin f; vt (train) schulen; (punish) bestrafen.

disc jockey ['dɪskdʒɒkɪ] n Diskjockey m.

disclaim [dɪs'kleɪm] vt nicht anerkennen; (Pol) dementieren.

disclose [dɪs'kləuz] vt enthüllen.

disclosure [dɪs'kləuʒə*] n Enthüllung f.

disco ['dɪskəu] n abbr of **discotheque**.

discoloured [dɪs'kʌləd] a verfärbt, verschossen.

discomfort [dɪs'kʌmfət] n Unbehagen nt; (embarrassment) Verlegenheit f.

disconcert [dɪskən'sɜːt] vt aus der

Fassung bringen; (*puzzle*) verstimmen.

disconnect ['dɪskə'nekt] *vt* abtrennen.

discontent ['dɪskən'tent] *n* Unzufriedenheit *f*; ~**ed** *a* unzufrieden.

discontinue ['dɪskən'tɪnjuː] *vt* einstellen; *vi* aufhören.

discord ['dɪskɔːd] *n* Zwietracht *f*; (*noise*) Dissonanz *f*; ~**ant** [dɪs'kɔːdənt] *a* uneinig; *noise* mißtönend.

discotheque ['dɪskəʊtek] *n* Diskothek *f*.

discount ['dɪskaʊnt] *n* Rabatt *m*; [dɪs'kaʊnt] *vt* außer acht lassen.

discourage [dɪs'kʌrɪdʒ] *vt* entmutigen; (*prevent*) abraten, abhalten.

discouraging [dɪs'kʌrɪdʒɪŋ] *a* entmutigend.

discourteous [dɪs'kɜːtɪəs] *a* unhöflich.

discover [dɪs'kʌvə*] *vt* entdecken; ~**y** Entdeckung *f*.

discredit [dɪs'kredɪt] *vt* in Verruf bringen.

discreet *a*, ~**ly** *ad* [dɪskriːt, -lɪ] taktvoll, diskret.

discrepancy [dɪs'krepənsɪ] *n* Unstimmigkeit *f*, Diskrepanz *f*.

discretion [dɪs'kreʃən] *n* Takt *m*, Diskretion *f*; (*decision*) Gutdünken *nt*; **to leave sth to sb's** ~ etw jds Gutdünken überlassen.

discriminate [dɪs'krɪmɪneɪt] *vi* unterscheiden; **to** ~ **against** diskriminieren.

discriminating [dɪs'krɪmɪneɪtɪŋ] *a* klug; *taste* anspruchsvoll.

discrimination [dɪskrɪmɪ'neɪʃən] *n* Urteilsvermögen *nt*; (*pej*) Diskriminierung *f*.

discus ['dɪskəs] *n* Diskus *m*.

discuss [dɪs'kʌs] *vt* diskutieren, besprechen; ~**ion** [dɪs'kʌʃən] Diskussion *f*, Besprechung *f*.

disdain [dɪs'deɪn] *vt* verachten, für unter seiner Würde halten; *n* Verachtung *f*; ~**ful** *a* geringschätzig.

disease [dɪ'ziːz] *n* Krankheit *f*; ~**d** *a* erkrankt.

disembark [dɪsɪm'bɑːk] *vt* aussteigen lassen; *vi* von Bord gehen.

disenchanted ['dɪsɪn'tʃɑːntɪd] *a* desillusioniert.

disengage [dɪsɪn'geɪdʒ] *vt* (*Aut*) auskuppeln.

disentangle ['dɪsɪn'tæŋgl] *vt* entwirren.

disfavour [dɪs'feɪvə*] *n* Ungunst *f*.

disfigure [dɪs'fɪgə*] *vt* entstellen.

disgrace [dɪs'greɪs] *n* Schande *f*; (*thing*) Schandfleck *m*; *vt* Schande bringen über (+*acc*); (*less strong*) blamieren; ~**ful** *a* schändlich, unerhört; **it's** ~**ful** es ist eine Schande.

disgruntled [dɪs'grʌntld] *a* verärgert.

disguise [dɪs'gaɪz] *vt* verkleiden; *feelings* verhehlen; *voice* verstellen; *n* Verkleidung *f*; **in** ~ verkleidet, maskiert.

disgust [dɪs'gʌst] *n* Abscheu *f*; *vt* anwidern; ~**ing** *a* abscheulich; (*terrible*) gemein.

dish [dɪʃ] *n* Schüssel *f*; (*food*) Gericht *nt*; ~ **up** *vt* auftischen; ~ **cloth** Spüllappen *m*.

dishearten [dɪs'hɑːtn] *vt* entmutigen.

dishevelled [dɪ'ʃevəld] *a* *hair* zerzaust; *clothing* ungepflegt.

dishonest [dɪs'ɒnɪst] *a* unehrlich; ~**y** Unehrlichkeit *f*.

dishonour [dɪs'ɒnə*] *n* Unehre *f*; *vt cheque* nicht einlösen; ~**able** *a* unehrenhaft.

dishwasher ['dɪʃwɒʃə*] *n* Geschirrspülmaschine *f*.

disillusion [dɪsɪ'luːʒən] *vt* enttäuschen, desillusionieren.

disinfect [dɪsɪn'fekt] *vt* desinfizieren; ~**ant** Desinfektionsmittel *nt*.

disingenuous [dɪsɪn'dʒenjʊəs] *a* unehrlich.

disinherit [dɪsɪn'herɪt] *vt* enterben.

disintegrate [dɪs'ɪntɪgreɪt] *vi* sich auflösen.

disinterested [dɪs'ɪntrɪstɪd] *a* uneigennützig; (*col*) uninteressiert.

disjointed [dɪs'dʒɔɪntɪd] *a* unzusammenhängend.

disk [dɪsk] *n* = **disc.**

dislike [dɪs'laɪk] *n* Abneigung *f*; *vt* nicht leiden können.

dislocate ['dɪsləʊkeɪt] *vt* auskugeln; (*upset*) in Verwirrung bringen.

dislodge [dɪs'lɒdʒ] *vt* verschieben; (*Mil*) aus der Stellung werfen.

disloyal ['dɪs'lɔɪəl] *a* treulos.

dismal ['dɪzməl] *a* trostlos, trübe.

dismantle [dɪs'mæntl] *vt* demontieren.

dismay [dɪs'meɪ] *n* Bestürzung *f*; *vt* bestürzen.

dismiss [dɪs'mɪs] *vt employee* entlassen; *idea* von sich weisen; (*send away*) wegschicken; (*Jur*) *complaint* abweisen; ~**al** Entlassung *f*.

disobedience [dɪsə'biːdɪəns] *n* Ungehorsam *m*.

disobedient [dɪsə'biːdɪənt] *a* ungehorsam.

disobey ['dɪsə'beɪ] *vt* nicht gehorchen (+*dat*).

disorder [dɪs'ɔːdə*] *n* (*confusion*) Verwirrung *f*; (*commotion*) Aufruhr *m*; (*Med*) Erkrankung *f*.

disorderly [dɪs'ɔːdəlɪ] *a* (*untidy*) unordentlich; (*unruly*) ordnungswidrig.

disorganized [dɪs'ɔːgənaɪzd] *a* unordentlich.

disown [dɪs'əʊn] *vt son* verstoßen; **I** ~ **you** ich will nichts mehr mit dir zu tun haben.

disparaging [dɪs'pærɪdʒɪŋ] *a* geringschätzig.

disparity [dɪs'pærɪtɪ] *n* Verschiedenheit *f*.

dispassionate [dɪs'pæʃnɪt] *a* gelassen, unparteiisch.

dispatch [dɪs'pætʃ] *vt goods* abschicken, abfertigen; *n* Absendung *f*; (*esp Mil*) Meldung *f*.

dispel [dɪs'pel] *vt* zerstreuen.

dispensable [dɪs'pensəbl] *a* entbehrlich.

dispensary [dɪs'pensərɪ] *n* Apotheke *f*.

dispensation [dɪspen'seɪʃən] *n* (*Eccl*) Befreiung *f*.

dispense [dɪs'pens]: ~ **with** *vt* verzichten auf (+*acc*); ~**r** (*container*) Spender *m*.

dispensing [dɪs'pensɪŋ] *a*: ~ **chemist** Apotheker *m*.

dispersal [dɪs'pɜːsəl] *n* Zerstreuung *f*.

disperse [dɪs'pɜːs] *vt* zerstreuen; *vi* sich verteilen.

dispirited [dɪsˈpɪrɪtɪd] a nieder-geschlagen.

displace [dɪsˈpleɪs] vt verschieben; ~d a: ~ **person** Verschleppte(r) mf.

display [dɪsˈpleɪ] n (of goods) Auslage f; (of feeling) Zurschaustellung f; (Mil) Entfaltung f; vt zeigen, entfalten.

displease [dɪsˈpliːz] vt mißfallen (+dat).

displeasure [dɪsˈpleʒə*] n Mißfallen nt.

disposable [dɪsˈpəʊzəbl] a container etc Wegwerf-.

disposal [dɪsˈpəʊzəl] n (of property) Verkauf m; (throwing away) Beseitigung f; **to be at one's** ~ einem zur Verfügung stehen.

dispose [dɪsˈpəʊz]: ~ **of** vt loswerden.

disposed [dɪsˈpəʊzd] a geneigt.

disposition [dɪspəˈzɪʃən] n Wesen nt, Natur f.

disproportionate [dɪsprəˈpɔːʃnɪt] a unverhältnismäßig.

disprove [dɪsˈpruːv] vt widerlegen.

dispute [dɪsˈpjuːt] n Streit m; vt bestreiten.

disqualification [dɪskwɒlɪfɪˈkeɪʃən] n Disqualifizierung f.

disqualify [dɪsˈkwɒlɪfaɪ] vt disqualifizieren.

disquiet [dɪsˈkwaɪət] n Unruhe f.

disregard [dɪsrɪˈɡɑːd] vt nicht (be-)achten.

disreputable [dɪsˈrepjʊtəbl] a verrufen.

disrepute [ˈdɪsrɪˈpjuːt] n Verruf m.

disrespectful [dɪsrɪsˈpektfʊl] a respektlos.

disrupt [dɪsˈrʌpt] vt stören; programme unterbrechen; ~**ion** [dɪsˈrʌpʃən] Störung f, Unterbrechung f.

dissatisfaction [ˈdɪssætɪsˈfækʃən] n Unzufriedenheit f.

dissatisfied [ˈdɪsˈsætɪsfaɪd] a unzufrieden.

dissect [dɪˈsekt] vt zerlegen, sezieren.

disseminate [dɪˈsemɪneɪt] vt verbreiten.

dissent [dɪˈsent] n abweichende Meinung f; vi nicht übereinstimmen.

dissident [ˈdɪsɪdənt] a andersdenkend; n Dissident m.

dissimilar [ˈdɪˈsɪmɪlə*] a unähnlich (to dat).

dissipate [ˈdɪsɪpeɪt] vt (waste) verschwenden; (scatter) zerstreuen; ~**d** a ausschweifend.

dissipation [dɪsɪˈpeɪʃən] n Ausschweifung f.

dissociate [dɪˈsəʊʃɪeɪt] vt trennen.

dissolute [ˈdɪsəluːt] a liederlich.

dissolve [dɪˈzɒlv] vt auflösen; vi sich auflösen.

dissuade [dɪˈsweɪd] vt abraten (+dat).

distance [ˈdɪstəns] n Entfernung f; **in the** ~ in der Ferne.

distant [ˈdɪstənt] a entfernt, fern; (with time) fern; (formal) distanziert.

distaste [dɪsˈteɪst] n Abneigung f; ~**ful** a widerlich.

distemper [dɪsˈtempə*] n (paint) Temperafarbe f; (Med) Staupe f.

distend [dɪsˈtend] vti (sich) ausdehnen.

distil [dɪsˈtɪl] vt destillieren; ~**lery** Brennerei f.

distinct [dɪsˈtɪŋkt] a (separate) getrennt; (clear) klar, deutlich; ~**ion** [dɪsˈtɪŋkʃən]

Unterscheidung f; (eminence) Berühmtheit f; (in exam) Auszeichnung f; ~**ive** a bezeichnend; ~**ly** ad deutlich.

distinguish [dɪsˈtɪŋɡwɪʃ] vt unterscheiden; ~**ed** a (eminent) berühmt; ~**ing** a unterscheidend, bezeichnend.

distort [dɪsˈtɔːt] vt verdrehen; (misrepresent) entstellen; ~**ion** [dɪsˈtɔːʃən] Verzerrung f.

distract [dɪsˈtrækt] vt ablenken; (bewilder) verwirren; ~**ing** a verwirrend; ~**ion** [dɪsˈtrækʃən] Zerstreutheit f; (distress) Raserei f; (diversion) Zerstreuung f.

distraught [dɪsˈtrɔːt] a bestürzt.

distress [dɪsˈtres] n Not f; (suffering) Qual f; vt quälen; ~**ing** a erschütternd; ~ **signal** Notsignal nt.

distribute [dɪsˈtrɪbjuːt] vt verteilen.

distribution [dɪstrɪˈbjuːʃən] n Verteilung f.

distributor [dɪsˈtrɪbjʊtə*] n Verteiler m.

district [ˈdɪstrɪkt] n (of country) Kreis m; (of town) Bezirk m; ~ **attorney** (US) Oberstaatsanwalt m; ~ **nurse** (Brit) Kreiskrankenschwester f.

distrust [dɪsˈtrʌst] n Mißtrauen nt; vt mißtrauen (+dat).

disturb [dɪsˈtɜːb] vt stören; (agitate) erregen; ~**ance** Störung f; ~**ing** a beunruhigend.

disuse [ˈdɪsˈjuːs] n Nichtgebrauch m; **to fall into** ~ außer Gebrauch kommen.

disused [ˈdɪsˈjuːzd] a aufgegeben, außer Gebrauch.

ditch [dɪtʃ] n Graben m; vt im Stich lassen.

dither [ˈdɪðə*] vi verdattert sein.

ditto [ˈdɪtəʊ] n dito, ebenfalls.

divan [dɪˈvæn] n Liegesofa nt.

dive [daɪv] n (into water) Kopfsprung m; (Aviat) Sturzflug m; vi tauchen; ~**r** Taucher m.

diverge [daɪˈvɜːdʒ] vi auseinandergehen.

diverse [daɪˈvɜːs] a verschieden.

diversification [daɪvɜːsɪfɪˈkeɪʃən] n Verzweigung f.

diversify [daɪˈvɜːsɪfaɪ] vt (ver)ändern; vi variieren.

diversion [daɪˈvɜːʃən] n Ablenkung f; (traffic) Umleitung f.

diversity [daɪˈvɜːsɪtɪ] n Verschiedenheit f; (variety) Mannigfaltigkeit f.

divert [daɪˈvɜːt] vt ablenken; traffic umleiten.

divide [dɪˈvaɪd] vt teilen; vi sich teilen.

dividend [ˈdɪvɪdend] n Dividende f; (fig) Gewinn m.

divine [dɪˈvaɪn] a göttlich; vt erraten.

diving board [ˈdaɪvɪŋbɔːd] n Sprungbrett nt.

divinity [dɪˈvɪnɪtɪ] n Gottheit f, Gott m; (subject) Religion f.

divisible [dɪˈvɪzəbl] a teilbar.

division [dɪˈvɪʒən] n Teilung f; (Math) Division f, Teilung f; (Mil) Division f; (part) Teil m, Abteilung f; (in opinion) Uneinigkeit f.

divorce [dɪˈvɔːs] n (Ehe)scheidung f; vt scheiden; ~**d** a geschieden; **to get** ~**d** sich scheiden lassen; ~**e** [dɪvɔːˈsiː] Geschiedene(r) mf.

divulge [daɪ'vʌldʒ] vt preisgeben.
dizziness ['dɪzɪnəs] n Schwindelgefühl nt.
dizzy ['dɪzɪ] a schwindlig.
do [duː] irreg vt tun, machen; vi (proceed) vorangehen; (be suitable) passen; (be enough) genügen; n (party) Party f; **how ~ you ~?** guten Tag! etc.
docile ['dəʊsaɪl] a gefügig; dog gutmütig.
dock [dɒk] n Dock nt; (Jur) Anklagebank f; vi ins Dock gehen; **~er** Hafenarbeiter m.
docket ['dɒkɪt] n Inhaltsvermerk m.
dockyard ['dɒkjɑːd] n Werft f.
doctor ['dɒktə*] n Arzt m, Ärztin f; (Univ) Doktor m.
doctrinaire [dɒktrɪ'nɛə*] a doktrinär.
doctrine ['dɒktrɪn] n Doktrin f.
document ['dɒkjʊmənt] n Dokument nt; **~ary** [dɒkjʊ'mentərɪ] Dokumentarbericht m; (film) Dokumentarfilm m; a dokumentarisch; **~ation** ↘ [dɒkjʊmen'teɪʃən] dokumentarische(r) Nachweis m.
doddering ['dɒdərɪŋ], **doddery** ['dɒdərɪ] a zittrig.
dodge [dɒdʒ] n Kniff m; vt umgehen; ausweichen (+dat); **~m** Boxauto nt.
dodo ['dəʊdəʊ] n Dronte f: **as dead as the ~** von Anno dazumal.
dog [dɒg] n Hund m; **~ biscuit** Hundekuchen m; **~ collar** Hundehalsband nt; (Eccl) Kragen m des Geistlichen; **~-eared** a mit Eselsohren; **~fish** Hundsfisch m; **~ food** Hundefutter nt.
dogged ['dɒgɪd] a hartnäckig.
dogma ['dɒgmə] n Dogma nt; **~tic** [dɒg'mætɪk] a dogmatisch.
doings ['duːɪŋz] npl (activities) Treiben nt.
do-it-yourself ['duːɪtjɔː'self] n Do-it-yourself nt; a zum Selbermachen.
doldrums ['dɒldrəmz] npl: **to be in the ~** Flaute haben; (person) deprimiert sein.
dole [dəʊl] n (Brit) Stempelgeld nt; **to be on the ~** stempeln gehen; **~ out** vt ausgeben, austeilen.
doleful ['dəʊlful] a traurig.
doll [dɒl] n Puppe f; vt: **~ o.s. up** sich aufdonnern.
dollar ['dɒlə*] n Dollar m.
dollop ['dɒləp] n Brocken m.
dolphin ['dɒlfɪn] n Delphin m, Tümmler m.
domain [dəʊ'meɪn] n Sphäre f, Bereich m.
dome [dəʊm] n Kuppel f.
domestic [də'mestɪk] a häuslich; (within country) Innen-, Binnen-; animal Haus-; **~ated** a person häuslich; animal zahm.
domicile ['dɒmɪsaɪl] n (ständiger) Wohnsitz m.
dominant ['dɒmɪnənt] a vorherrschend.
dominate ['dɒmɪneɪt] vt beherrschen.
domination [dɒmɪ'neɪʃən] n (Vor)herrschaft f.
domineering [dɒmɪ'nɪərɪŋ] a herrisch, überheblich.
dominion [də'mɪnɪən] n (rule) Regierungsgewalt f; (land) Staatsgebiet nt mit Selbstverwaltung.
dominoes ['dɒmɪnəʊz] n Domino(spiel) nt.
don [dɒn] n akademische(r) Lehrer m.
donate [dəʊ'neɪt] vt (blood, little money) spenden; (lot of money) stiften.

donation [dəʊ'neɪʃən] n Spende f.
donkey ['dɒŋkɪ] n Esel m.
donor ['dəʊnə*] n Spender m.
don't [dəʊnt] = **do not**.
doom [duːm] n böse(s) Geschick nt; (downfall) Verderben nt; vt: **to be ~ed** zum Untergang verurteilt sein.
door [dɔː*] n Tür f; **~bell** Türklingel f; **~-handle** Türklinke f; **~man** Türsteher m; **~mat** Fußmatte f; **~step** Türstufe f; **~way** Türöffnung f.
dope [dəʊp] n (drug) Aufputschmittel nt.
dopey ['dəʊpɪ] a (col) bekloppt.
dormant ['dɔːmənt] a schlafend, latent.
dormitory ['dɔːmɪtrɪ] n Schlafsaal m.
dormouse ['dɔːmaʊs] n Haselmaus f.
dosage ['dəʊsɪdʒ] n Dosierung f.
dose [dəʊs] n Dosis f; vt dosieren.
dossier ['dɒsɪeɪ] n Dossier m, Aktenbündel nt.
dot [dɒt] n Punkt m; **on the ~** pünktlich.
dote [dəʊt]: **~ on** vt vernarrt sein in (+acc).
double ['dʌbl] a, ad doppelt; n Doppelgänger m; vt verdoppeln; (fold) zusammenfalten; vi (in amount) sich verdoppeln; **at the ~** im Laufschritt; **~s** (tennis) Doppel nt; **~ bass** Kontrabaß m; **~ bed** Doppelbett nt; **~-breasted** a zweireihig; **~cross** n Betrug m; vt hintergehen; **~decker** Doppeldecker m; **~room** Doppelzimmer nt.
doubly ['dʌblɪ] ad doppelt.
doubt [daʊt] n Zweifel m; vi zweifeln; vt bezweifeln; **without ~** zweifellos; **~ful** a zweifelhaft, fraglich; **~less** ad ohne Zweifel, sicherlich.
dough [dəʊ] n Teig m; **~nut** Krapfen m, Pfannkuchen m.
dove [dʌv] n Taube f; **~tail** n Schwalbenschwanz m, Zinke f; vt verzahnen, verzinken.
dowdy ['daʊdɪ] a unmodern, schlampig.
down [daʊn] n (fluff) Flaum m; (hill) Hügel m; ad unten; (motion) herunter; hinunter; prep **he came ~ the street** er kam die Straße herunter; **to go ~ the street** die Straße hinuntergehen; **he lives ~ the street** er wohnt unten an der Straße; vt niederschlagen; **~ with X!** nieder mit X!; **~-and-out** a abgerissen; n Tramp m; **~-at-heel** a schäbig; **~cast** a niedergeschlagen; **~fall** Sturz m; **~-hearted** a niedergeschlagen, mutlos; **~hill** ad bergab; **~pour** Platzregen m; **~right** a völlig, ausgesprochen; **~stairs** ad unten; (motion) nach unten; a untere(r, s); **~stream** ad flußabwärts; **~town** ad in die/der Innenstadt; a (US) im Geschäftsviertel, City-; **~ward** a sinkend, Abwärts-; **~wards** ad abwärts, nach unten.
dowry ['daʊrɪ] n Mitgift f.
doze [dəʊz] vi dösen; n Schläfchen nt, Nickerchen nt.
dozen ['dʌzn] n Dutzend nt.
drab [dræb] a düster, eintönig.
draft [drɑːft] n Skizze f, Entwurf m; (Fin) Wechsel m; (US Mil) Einberufung f; vt skizzieren.
drag [dræg] vt schleifen, schleppen; river

mit einem Schleppnetz absuchen; *vi* sich (dahin)schleppen; *n* (*bore*) etwas Blödes; (*hindrance*) Klotz *m* am Bein; **in ~** als Tunte; **~ on** *vi* sich in die Länge ziehen.

dragon ['drægən] *n* Drache *m*; **~fly** Libelle *f*.

drain [dreın] *n* (*lit*) Abfluß *m*; (*ditch*) Abflußgraben *m*; (*fig: burden*) Belastung *f*; *vt* ableiten; (*exhaust*) erschöpfen; *vi* (*of water*) abfließen; **~age** Kanalisation *f*; **~pipe** Abflußrohr *nt*.

drama ['drɑːmə] *n* (*lit, fig*) Drama *nt*; **~tic** [drə'mætık] *a* dramatisch; **~tist** Dramatiker *m*.

drape [dreıp] *vt* drapieren; *npl* **~s** (*US*) Vorhänge *pl*; **~r** Tuchhändler *m*.

drastic ['dræstık] *a* drastisch.

draught [drɑːft] *n* Zug *m*; (*Naut*) Tiefgang *m*; **~s** Damespiel *nt*; (*beer*) **on ~** vom Faß; **~board** Zeichenbrett *nt*; **~sman** technische(r) Zeichner *m*; **~y** *a* zugig.

draw [drɔː] *irreg vt* ziehen; *crowd* anlocken; *picture* zeichnen; *money* abheben; *water* schöpfen; *vi* (*Sport*) unentschieden spielen; *n* (*Sport*) Unentschieden *nt*; (*lottery*) Ziehung *f*; **to ~ to a close** (*speech*) zu Ende kommen; (*year*) zu Ende gehen; **~out** *vi* (*train*) ausfahren; (*lengthen*) sich hinziehen; *vt money* abheben; **~ up** *vi* (*stop*) halten; *vt document* aufsetzen; **~back** (*disadvantage*) Nachteil *m*; (*obstacle*) Haken *m*; **~bridge** Zugbrücke *f*; **~er** Schublade *f*; **~ing** Zeichnung *f*; Zeichnen *nt*; **~ing pin** Reißzwecke *f*; **~ing room** Salon *m*.

drawl [drɔːl] *n* schleppende Sprechweise *f*; *vi* gedehnt sprechen.

drawn [drɔːn] *a game* unentschieden; *face* besorgt.

dread [dred] *n* Furcht *f*, Grauen *nt*; *vt* fürchten; sich grauen vor (+*dat*); **~ful a** furchtbar.

dream [driːm] *n* Traum *m*; (*fancy*) Wunschtraum *m*; *vti irreg* träumen (*about* von); *a house etc* Traum-; **~er** Träumer *m*; **~ world** Traumwelt *f*; **~y** *a* verträumt.

dreary ['drıərı] *a* trostlos, öde.

dredge [dredʒ] *vt* ausbaggern; (*with flour etc*) mit Mehl *etc* bestreuen; **~r** Baggerschiff *nt*; (*for flour etc*) (Mehl *etc*)streuer *m*.

dregs [dregz] *npl* Bodensatz *m*; (*fig*) Abschaum *m*.

drench [drentʃ] *vt* durchnässen.

dress [dres] *n* Kleidung *f*; (*garment*) Kleid *nt*; *vt* anziehen; (*Med*) verbinden; (*Agr*) düngen; *food* anrichten; **to get ~ed** sich anziehen; **~ up** *vi* sich fein machen; **~ circle** erste(r) Rang *m*; **~er** (*furniture*) Anrichte *f*, Geschirrschrank *m*; **she's a smart ~er** sie zieht sich elegant an; **~ing** (*Med*) Verband *m*; (*Cook*) Soße *f*; **~ing gown** Morgenrock *m*; **~ing room** (*Theat*) Garderobe *f*; (*Sport*) Umkleideraum *m*; **~ing table** Toilettentisch *m*; **~maker** Schneiderin *f*; **~making** Schneidern *nt*; **~ rehearsal** Generalprobe *f*; **~ shirt** Frackhemd *nt*.

dribble ['drıbl] *vi* tröpfeln; *vt* sabbern.

drift [drıft] *n* Trift *f*, Strömung *f*; (*snow-*) Schneewehe *f*; (*fig*) Richtung *f*; *vi* getrieben werden; (*aimlessly*) sich treiben lassen; **~wood** Treibholz *nt*.

drill [drıl] *n* Bohrer *m*; (*Mil*) Drill *m*; *vt* bohren; (*Mil*) ausbilden; *vi* (*Mil*) exerzieren; bohren (*for* nach); **~ing** Bohren *nt*; (*hole*) Bohrloch *nt*; (*Mil*) Exerzieren *nt*.

drink [drıŋk] *n* Getränk *nt*; (*spirits*) Drink *m*; *vti irreg* trinken; **~able** *a* trinkbar; **~er** Trinker *m*; **~ing water** Trinkwasser *nt*.

drip [drıp] *n* Tropfen *m*; (*dripping*) Tröpfeln *nt*; *vi* tropfen; **~-dry** *a* bügelfrei; **~ping** Bratenfett *nt*; **~ping wet** *a* triefend.

drive [draıv] *n* Fahrt *f*; (*road*) Einfahrt *f*; (*campaign*) Aktion *f*; (*energy*) Schwung *m*, Tatkraft *f*; (*Sport*) Schlag *m*; *irreg vt car* fahren; *animals* treiben; *nail* einschlagen; *ball* schlagen; (*power*) antreiben; (*force*) treiben; *vi* fahren; **to ~ sb mad** jdn verrückt machen; **what are you driving at?** worauf willst du hinaus?; **~-in** *a* Drive-in-.

drivel ['drıvl] *n* Faselei *f*.

driver ['draıvə*] *n* Fahrer *m*; **~'s license** (*US*) Führerschein *m*.

driving ['draıvıŋ] *a rain* stürmisch; **~ instructor** Fahrlehrer *m*; **~ lesson** Fahrstunde *f*; **~ licence** (*Brit*) Führerschein *m*; **~ school** Fahrschule *f*; **~ test** Fahrprüfung *f*.

drizzle ['drızl] *n* Nieselregen *m*; *vi* nieseln.

droll [drəʊl] *a* drollig.

dromedary ['dromıdərı] *n* Dromedar *nt*.

drone [drəʊn] *n* (*sound*) Brummen *nt*; (*bee*) Drohne *f*.

drool [druːl] *vi* sabbern.

droop [druːp] *vi* (*shoulder*) herabhängen.

drop [drop] *n* (*of liquid*) Tropfen *m*; (*fall*) Fall *m*; *vt* fallen lassen; (*lower*) senken; (*abandon*) aufgeben; *vi* (*fall*) herunterfallen; **~ off** *vi* (*sleep*) einschlafen; **~ out** *vi* (*withdraw*) ausscheiden; **~out** Ausgeflippte(r) *mf*, Drop-out *mf*.

dross [dros] *n* Unrat *m*.

drought [draʊt] *n* Dürre *f*.

drove [drəʊv] *n* (*crowd*) Herde *f*.

drown [draʊn] *vt* ertränken; *sound* übertönen; *vi* ertrinken.

drowsy ['draʊzı] *a* schläfrig.

drudge [drʌdʒ] *n* Kuli *m*; **~ry** ['drʌdʒərı] Plackerei *f*.

drug [drʌg] *n* (*Med*) Arznei *f*; (*narcotic*) Rauschgift *nt*; *vt* betäuben; **~ addict** Rauschgiftsüchtige(r) *mf*; **~gist** (*US*) Drogist *m*; **~store** (*US*) Drogerie *f*.

drum [drʌm] *n* Trommel *f*; **~mer** Trommler *m*.

drunk [drʌŋk] *a* betrunken; *n* Betrunkene(r) *m*; Trinker(in *f*) *m*; **~ard** Trunkenbold *m*; **~en** *a* betrunken; **~enness** Betrunkenheit *f*.

dry [draı] *a* trocken; *vt* (ab)trocknen; *vi* trocknen, trocken werden; **~ up** *vi* austrocknen; (*dishes*) abtrocknen; **~-clean** *vt* chemisch reinigen; **~-cleaning** chemische Reinigung *f*; **~er** Trockner *m*;

~**ness** Trockenheit *f*; ~ **rot** Hausschwamm *m*.

dual ['dju:əl] *a* doppelt; ~ **carriageway** zweispurige Fahrbahn *f*; ~ **nationality** doppelte Staatsangehörigkeit *f*; ~**-purpose** *a* Mehrzweck-.

dubbed [dʌbd] *a* film synchronisiert.

dubious ['dju:biəs] *a* zweifelhaft.

duchess ['dʌtʃɪs] *n* Herzogin *f*.

duck [dʌk] *n* Ente *f*; *vt* (ein)tauchen; *vi* sich ducken; ~**ling** Entchen *nt*.

duct [dʌkt] *n* Röhre *f*.

dud [dʌd] *n* Niete *f*; *a* wertlos, miserabel; *cheque* ungedeckt.

due [dju:] *a* fällig; (*fitting*) angemessen; **the train is** ~ der Zug soll ankommen; *n* Gebühr *f*; (*right*) Recht *nt*; *ad south etc* genau, gerade; ~ **to** infolge (+*gen*), wegen (+*gen*).

duel ['djuəl] *n* Duell *nt*.

duet [dju:'et] *n* Duett *nt*.

duke [dju:k] *n* Herzog *m*.

dull [dʌl] *a* colour, weather trübe; (*stupid*) schwer von Begriff; (*boring*) langweilig; *vt* (*soften, weaken*) abstumpfen.

duly ['dju:lɪ] *ad* ordnungsgemäß, richtig; (*on time*) pünktlich.

dumb [dʌm] *a* (*lit*) stumm; (*col: stupid*) doof, blöde.

dummy ['dʌmɪ] *n* Schneiderpuppe *f*; (*substitute*) Attrappe *f*; (*teat*) Schnuller *m*; *a* Schein-.

dump [dʌmp] *n* Abfallhaufen *m*; (*Mil*) Stapelplatz *m*; (*col: place*) Nest *nt*; *vt* abladen, auskippen; ~**ing** (*Comm*) Schleuderexport *m*; (*of rubbish*) Schuttabladen *nt*.

dumpling ['dʌmplɪŋ] *n* Kloß *m*, Knödel *m*.

dunce [dʌns] *n* Dummkopf *m*.

dune [dju:n] *n* Düne *f*.

dung [dʌŋ] *n* Mist *m*; (*Agr*) Dünger *m*.

dungarees [dʌŋgə'ri:z] *npl* Arbeitsanzug *m*, Arbeitskleidung *f*.

dungeon ['dʌndʒən] *n* Kerker *m*.

dupe [dju:p] *n* Gefoppte(r) *m*; *vt* hintergehen, anführen.

duplicate ['dju:plɪkɪt] *a* doppelt; *n* Duplikat *nt*; ['dju:plɪkeɪt] *vt* verdoppeln; (*make copies*) kopieren; **in** ~ in doppelter Ausführung.

duplicator ['dju:plɪkeɪtə*] *n* Vervielfältigungsapparat *m*.

durability [djuərə'bɪlɪtɪ] *n* Haltbarkeit *f*.

durable ['djuərəbl] *a* haltbar.

duration [djuə'reɪʃən] *n* Dauer *f*.

during ['djuərɪŋ] *prep* während (+*gen*).

dusk [dʌsk] *n* Abenddämmerung *f*.

dust [dʌst] *n* Staub *m*; *vt* abstauben; (*sprinkle*) bestäuben; ~**bin** (*Brit*) Mülleimer *m*; ~**er** Staubtuch *nt*; ~**man** (*Brit*) Müllmann *m*; ~ **storm** Staubsturm *m*; ~**y** *a* staubig.

dutiable ['dju:tɪəbl] *a* zollpflichtig.

duty ['dju:tɪ] *n* Pflicht *f*; (*job*) Aufgabe *f*; (*tax*) Einfuhrzoll *m*; **on** ~ im Dienst, diensthabend; ~**-free** *a* zollfrei; ~**-free articles** zollfreie Waren *pl*.

dwarf [dwɔ:f] *n* Zwerg *m*.

dwell [dwel] *vi irreg* wohnen; ~ **on** *vt* ver-

weilen bei; ~**ing** Wohnung *f*.

dwindle ['dwɪndl] *vi* schwinden.

dye [daɪ] *n* Farbstoff *m*; *vt* färben.

dying ['daɪɪŋ] *a* person sterbend; *moments* letzt.

dynamic [daɪ'næmɪk] *a* dynamisch; ~**s** Dynamik *f*.

dynamite ['daɪnəmaɪt] *n* Dynamit *nt*.

dynamo ['daɪnəməʊ] *n* Dynamo *m*.

dynasty ['dɪnəstɪ] *n* Dynastie *f*.

dysentery ['dɪsntrɪ] *n* Ruhr *f*.

dyspepsia [dɪs'pepsɪə] *n* Verdauungsstörung *f*.

E

E, e [i:] *n* E *nt*, e *nt*.

each [i:tʃ] *a* jeder/jede/jedes; *pron* (ein) jeder/(eine) jede/(ein) jedes; ~ **other** einander, sich.

eager *a*, ~**ly** *ad* ['i:gə*, -lɪ] eifrig; ~**ness** Eifer *m*; Ungeduld *f*.

eagle ['i:gl] *n* Adler *m*.

ear [ɪə*] *n* Ohr *nt*; (*of corn*) Ähre *f*; ~**ache** Ohrenschmerzen *pl*; ~**drum** Trommelfell *nt*.

earl [ɜ:l] *n* Graf *m*.

early ['ɜ:lɪ] *a, ad* früh; **you're** ~ du bist früh dran.

earmark ['ɪəma:k] *vt* vorsehen.

earn [ɜ:n] *vt* verdienen.

earnest ['ɜ:nɪst] *a* ernst; **in** ~ im Ernst.

earnings ['ɜ:nɪŋz] *npl* Verdienst *m*.

earphones ['ɪəfəʊnz] *npl* Kopfhörer *pl*.

earplug ['ɪəplʌg] *n* Ohropax ' *nt*.

earring ['ɪərɪŋ] *n* Ohrring *m*.

earshot ['ɪəʃɒt] *n* Hörweite *f*.

earth [ɜ:θ] *n* Erde *f*; (*Elec*) Erdung *f*; *vt* erden; ~**enware** Steingut *nt*; ~**quake** Erdbeben *nt*.

earthy ['ɜ:θɪ] *a* roh; (*sensual*) sinnlich.

earwig ['ɪəwɪg] *n* Ohrwurm *m*.

ease [i:z] *n* (*simplicity*) Leichtigkeit *f*; (*social*) Ungezwungenheit *f*; *vt* pain lindern; *burden* erleichtern; **at** ~ ungezwungen; (*Mil*) rührt euch!; **to feel at** ~ sich wohl fühlen; ~ **off** *or* **up** *vi* nachlassen.

easel ['i:zl] *n* Staffelei *f*.

easily ['i:zɪlɪ] *ad* leicht.

east [i:st] *n* Osten *m*; *a* östlich; *ad* nach Osten.

Easter ['i:stə*] *n* Ostern *nt*.

eastern ['i:stən] *a* östlich; orientalisch.

eastward(s) ['i:stwəd(z)] *ad* ostwärts.

easy ['i:zɪ] *a* task einfach; *life* sorglos; *manner* ungezwungen, natürlich; *ad* leicht.

eat [i:t] *vt irreg* essen; (*animals*) fressen; (*destroy*) zer)fressen; ~ **away** *vt* (*corrode*) zerfressen; ~**able** *a* genießbar.

eaves [i:vz] *npl* (überstehender) Dachrand *m*.

eavesdrop ['i:vzdrɒp] *vi* horchen, lauschen; **to** ~ **on sb** jdn belauschen.

ebb [eb] *n* Ebbe *f*; *vi* ebben.

ebony ['ebənɪ] *n* Ebenholz *nt*.

ebullient [ɪ'bʌlɪənt] *a* sprudelnd, temperamentvoll.

eccentric [ɪk'sentrɪk] *a* exzentrisch, über-

spannt; n exzentrische(r) Mensch m.
ecclesiastical [ɪklɪːzɪˈæstɪkəl] a kirchlich, geistlich.
echo [ˈekəʊ] n Echo nt; vt zurückwerfen; (fig) nachbeten; vi widerhallen.
eclipse [ɪˈklɪps] n Verfinsterung f, Finsternis f; vt verfinstern.
ecology [ɪˈkɒlədʒɪ] n Ökologie f.
economic [iːkəˈnɒmɪk] a (volks)wirtschaftlich, ökonomisch; ~al a wirtschaftlich; person sparsam; ~s Volkswirtschaft f.
economist [ɪˈkɒnəmɪst] n Volkswirt(schaftler) m.
economize [ɪˈkɒnəmaɪz] vi sparen (on an +dat).
economy [ɪˈkɒnəmɪ] n (thrift) Sparsamkeit f; (of country) Wirtschaft f.
ecstasy [ˈekstəsɪ] n Ekstase f.
ecstatic [eksˈtætɪk] a hingerissen.
ecumenical [iːkjuˈmenɪkəl] a ökumenisch.
eczema [ˈeksɪmə] n Ekzem nt.
Eden [ˈiːdn] n (Garten m) Eden nt.
edge [edʒ] n Rand m; (of knife) Schneide f; **on** ~ nervös; (nerves) überreizt.
edging [ˈedʒɪŋ] n Einfassung f.
edgy [ˈedʒɪ] a nervös.
edible [ˈedɪbl] a eßbar.
edict [ˈiːdɪkt] n Erlaß m.
edifice [ˈedɪfɪs] n Gebäude nt.
edit [ˈedɪt] vt edieren, redigieren; ~ion [ɪˈdɪʃən] Ausgabe f; ~or (of newspaper) Redakteur m; (of book) Lektor m; ~orial [edɪˈtɔːrɪəl] a Redaktions-; n Leitartikel m.
educate [ˈedjʊkeɪt] vt erziehen, (aus)bilden.
education [edjʊˈkeɪʃən] n (teaching) Unterricht m; (system) Schulwesen nt; (schooling) Erziehung f; Bildung f; ~al a pädagogisch.
eel [iːl] n Aal m.
eerie [ˈɪərɪ] a unheimlich.
efface [ɪˈfeɪs] vt auslöschen.
effect [ɪˈfekt] n Wirkung f, vt bewirken; **in** ~ in der Tat; ~s pl (sound, visual) Effekte pl; ~ive a wirksam, effektiv.
effeminate [ɪˈfemɪnət] a weibisch.
effervescent [efəˈvesnt] a (lit, fig) sprudelnd.
efficiency [ɪˈfɪʃənsɪ] n Leistungsfähigkeit f.
efficient a, ~ly ad [ɪˈfɪʃənt, -lɪ] tüchtig; (Tech) leistungsfähig; method wirksam.
effigy [ˈefɪdʒɪ] n Abbild nt.
effort [ˈefət] n Anstrengung f; **to make an** ~ sich anstrengen; ~**less** a mühelos.
effrontery [ɪˈfrʌntərɪ] n Unverfrorenheit f.
egalitarian [ɪgælɪˈtɛərɪən] a Gleichheits-, egalitär.
egg [eg] n Ei nt; ~ **on** vt anstacheln; ~**cup** Eierbecher m; ~**plant** Aubergine f; ~**shell** Eierschale f.
ego [ˈiːgəʊ] n Ich nt, Selbst nt.
egotism [ˈegəʊtɪzəm] n Ichbezogenheit f.
egotist [ˈegəʊtɪst] n Egozentriker m.
eiderdown [ˈaɪdədaʊn] n Daunendecke f.
eight [eɪt] num acht; ~**een** num achtzehn; ~**h** [eɪtθ] a achte(r,s); n Achtel nt; ~**y** num achtzig.
either [ˈaɪðə*] cj ~ ... **or** entweder ... oder;

pron ~ **of the two** eine(r,s) von beiden; **I don't want** ~ ich will keins von beiden; a **on** ~ **side** auf beiden Seiten; ad **I don't** ~ ich auch nicht.
eject [ɪˈdʒekt] vt ausstoßen, vertreiben; ~**or seat** Schleudersitz m.
elaborate [ɪˈlæbərɪt] a sorgfältig ausgearbeitet, ausführlich; [ɪˈlæbəreɪt] vt sorgfältig ausarbeiten; ~**ly** ad genau, ausführlich.
elaboration [ɪlæbəˈreɪʃən] n Ausarbeitung f.
elapse [ɪˈlæps] vi vergehen.
elastic [ɪˈlæstɪk] n Gummiband nt; a elastisch; ~ **band** Gummiband nt.
elated [ɪˈleɪtɪd] a froh, in gehobener Stimmung.
elation [ɪˈleɪʃən] n gehobene Stimmung f.
elbow [ˈelbəʊ] n Ellbogen m.
elder [ˈeldə*] a älter; n Ältere(r) mf; ~**ly** a ältere(r,s).
elect [ɪˈlekt] vt wählen; a zukünftig; ~**ion** Wahl f; ~**ioneering** [ɪlekʃəˈnɪərɪŋ] Wahlpropaganda f; ~**or** Wähler m; ~**oral** a Wahl-; ~**orate** Wähler pl, Wählerschaft f.
electric [ɪˈlektrɪk] a elektrisch, Elektro-; ~**al** a elektrisch; ~ **blanket** Heizdecke f; ~ **chair** elektrische(r) Stuhl m; ~ **cooker** Elektroherd m; ~ **current** elektrische(r) Strom m; ~ **fire** elektrische(r) Heizofen m; ~**ian** [ɪlekˈtrɪʃən] Elektriker m; ~**ity** [ɪlekˈtrɪsɪtɪ] Elektrizität f.
electrification [ɪlektrɪfɪˈkeɪʃən] n Elektrifizierung f.
electrify [ɪˈlektrɪfaɪ] vt elektrifizieren; (fig) elektrisieren.
electro- [ɪˈlektrəʊ] pref Elektro-.
electrocute [ɪˈlektrəʊkjuːt] vt elektrisieren; durch elektrischen Strom töten.
electrode [ɪˈlektrəʊd] n Elektrode f.
electron [ɪˈlektrɒn] n Elektron nt.
electronic [ɪlekˈtrɒnɪk] a elektronisch, Elektronen-; ~**s** Elektronik f.
elegance [ˈelɪgəns] n Eleganz f.
elegant [ˈelɪgənt] a elegant.
elegy [ˈelɪdʒɪ] n Elegie f.
element [ˈelɪmənt] n Element nt; (fig) Körnchen nt; ~**ary** [elɪˈmentərɪ] a einfach; (primary) grundlegend, Anfangs-.
elephant [ˈelɪfənt] n Elefant m.
elevate [ˈelɪveɪt] vt emporheben.
elevation [elɪˈveɪʃən] n (height) Erhebung f; (of style) Niveau nt; (Archit) (Quer)schnitt m.
elevator [ˈelɪveɪtə*] n (US) Fahrstuhl m, Aufzug m.
eleven [ɪˈlevn] num elf; n (team) Elf f.
elf [elf] n Elfe f.
elicit [ɪˈlɪsɪt] vt herausbekommen.
eligible [ˈelɪdʒəbl] a wählbar; **he's not** ~ er kommt nicht in Frage; **to be** ~ **for a pension/competition** pensions-/teilnahmeberechtigt sein; ~ **bachelor** gute Partie f.
eliminate [ɪˈlɪmɪneɪt] vt ausschalten; beseitigen.
elimination [ɪlɪmɪˈneɪʃən] n Ausschaltung f; Beseitigung f.
elite [eɪˈliːt] n Elite f.
elm [elm] n Ulme f.

elocution [elə'kju:ʃən] n Sprecherziehung f; (clarity) Artikulation f.

elongated ['i:lɒŋgeɪtɪd] a verlängert.

elope [ɪ'ləup] vi entlaufen; ~**ment** Entlaufen nt.

eloquence ['eləkwəns] n Beredsamkeit f.

eloquent a, ~**ly** ad ['eləkwənt, -lɪ] redegewandt.

else [els] ad sonst; ~**where** ad anderswo, woanders; **who** ~? wer sonst?; **sb** ~ jd anders; **or** ~ sonst.

elucidate [ɪ'lu:sɪdeɪt] vt erläutern.

elude [ɪ'lu:d] vt entgehen (+dat).

elusive [ɪ'lu:sɪv] a schwer faßbar.

emaciated [ɪ'meɪsɪeɪtɪd] a abgezehrt.

emanate ['eməneɪt] vi ausströmen (from aus).

emancipate [ɪ'mænsɪpeɪt] vt emanzipieren; slave freilassen.

emancipation [ɪmænsɪ'peɪʃən] n Emanzipation f; Freilassung f.

embalm [ɪm'bɑ:m] vt einbalsamieren.

embankment [ɪm'bæŋkmənt] n (of river) Uferböschung f; (of road) Straßendamm m.

embargo [ɪm'bɑ:gəu] n Embargo nt.

embark [ɪm'bɑ:k] vi sich einschiffen; ~ **on** vt unternehmen; ~**ation** [embɑ:'keɪʃən] Einschiffung f.

embarrass [ɪm'bærəs] vt in Verlegenheit bringen; ~**ed** a verlegen; ~**ing** a peinlich; ~**ment** Verlegenheit f.

embassy ['embəsɪ] n Botschaft f.

embed [ɪm'bed] vt einbetten.

embellish [ɪm'belɪʃ] vt verschönern.

embers ['embəz] npl Glut(asche) f.

embezzle [ɪm'bezl] vt unterschlagen; ~**ment** Unterschlagung f.

embitter [ɪm'bɪtə*] vt verbittern.

emblem ['embləm] n Emblem nt, Abzeichen nt.

embodiment [ɪm'bɒdɪmənt] n Verkörperung f.

embody [ɪm'bɒdɪ] vt ideas verkörpern; new features (in sich) vereinigen.

emboss [ɪm'bɒs] vt prägen.

embrace [ɪm'breɪs] vt umarmen; (include) einschließen; n Umarmung f.

embroider [ɪm'brɔɪdə*] vt (be)sticken; story ausschmücken; ~**y** Stickerei f.

embryo ['embrɪəu] n (lit) Embryo m; (fig) Keim m.

emerald ['emərəld] n Smaragd m; a smaragdgrün.

emerge [ɪ'mɜ:dʒ] vi auftauchen; (truth) herauskommen; ~**nce** Erscheinen nt; ~**ncy** n Notfall m; a action Not-; ~**ncy exit** Notausgang m.

emery ['emərɪ] n: ~ **paper** Schmirgelpapier nt.

emetic [ɪ'metɪk] n Brechmittel nt.

emigrant ['emɪgrənt] n Auswanderer m, Emigrant m; a Auswanderungs-.

emigrate ['emɪgreɪt] vi auswandern, emigrieren.

emigration [emɪ'greɪʃən] n Auswanderung f, Emigration f.

eminence ['emɪnəns] n hohe(r) Rang m; **E**~ Eminenz f.

eminent ['emɪnənt] a bedeutend.

emission [ɪ'mɪʃən] n (of gases) Ausströmen nt.

emit [ɪ'mɪt] vt von sich (dat) geben.

emotion [ɪ'məuʃən] n Emotion f, Gefühl nt; ~**al** a person emotional; scene ergreifend; ~**ally** ad gefühlsmäßig; behave emotional; sing ergreifend.

emotive [ɪ'məutɪv] a gefühlsbetont.

emperor ['empərə*] n Kaiser m.

emphasis ['emfəsɪs] n (Ling) Betonung f; (fig) Nachdruck m.

emphasize ['emfəsaɪz] vt betonen.

emphatic a, ~**ally** ad [ɪm'fætɪk, -əlɪ] nachdrücklich; **to be** ~ **about sth** etw nachdrücklich betonen.

empire ['empaɪə*] n Reich nt.

empirical [em'pɪrɪkəl] a empirisch.

employ [ɪm'plɔɪ] vt (hire) anstellen; (use) verwenden; ~**ee** [emplɔɪ'i:] Angestellte(r) mf; ~**er** Arbeitgeber(in f) m; ~**ment** Beschäftigung f; **in** ~**ment** beschäftigt.

empress ['emprɪs] n Kaiserin f.

emptiness ['emptɪnɪs] n Leere f.

empty ['emptɪ] a leer; vt contents leeren; container ausleeren; ~-**handed** a mit leeren Händen.

emu ['i:mju:] n Emu m.

emulate ['emjuleɪt] vt nacheifern (+dat).

enable [ɪ'neɪbl] vt ermöglichen; **it** ~**s us to** . . . das ermöglicht es uns, zu . . .

enamel [ɪ'næməl] n Email nt; (of teeth) (Zahn)schmelz m.

enamoured [ɪ'næməd] a verliebt sein (of in +dat).

encase [ɪn'keɪs] vt einschließen; (Tech) verschalen.

enchant [ɪn'tʃɑ:nt] vt bezaubern; ~**ing** a entzückend.

encircle [ɪn'sɜ:kl] vt umringen.

enclose [ɪn'kləuz] vt einschließen; (in letter) beilegen (in, with dat); ~**d** (in letter) beiliegend, anbei.

enclosure [ɪn'kləuʒə*] n Einfriedung f; (in letter) Anlage f.

encore ['ɒŋkɔ:*] n Zugabe f; ~! da capo!

encounter [ɪn'kauntə*] n Begegnung f; (Mil) Zusammenstoß m; vt treffen; resistance stoßen auf (+acc).

encourage [ɪn'kʌrɪdʒ] vt ermutigen; ~**ment** Ermutigung f, Förderung f.

encouraging [ɪn'kʌrɪdʒɪŋ] a ermutigend, vielversprechend.

encroach [ɪn'krəutʃ] vi eindringen ((up)on in +acc), überschreiten ((up)on acc).

encyclop(a)edia [ensaɪkləu'pi:dɪə] n Konversationslexikon nt.

end [end] n Ende nt, Schluß m; (purpose) Zweck m; a End-; vt beenden; vi zu Ende gehen; ~ **up** vi landen.

endanger [ɪn'deɪndʒə*] vt gefährden.

endeavour [ɪn'devə*] n Bestrebung f; vi sich bemühen.

ending ['endɪŋ] n Ende nt.

endless ['endlɪs] a endlos; plain unendlich.

endorse [ɪn'dɔ:s] vt unterzeichnen; (approve) unterstützen; ~**ment** Bestätigung f; (of document) Unterzeichnung f; (on licence) Eintrag m.

endow [ɪn'dau] vt: ~ **sb with sth** jdm etw verleihen; (with money) jdm etw stiften.

end product ['endprɒdʌkt] n Endprodukt nt.

endurable [ɪn'djuərəbl] a erträglich.

endurance [ɪn'djuərəns] n Ausdauer f; (suffering) Ertragen nt.

endure [ɪn'djuə*] vt ertragen; vi (last) (fort)dauern.

enemy ['enɪmɪ] n Feind m; a feindlich.

energetic [enə'dʒetɪk] a tatkräftig.

energy ['enədʒɪ] n (of person) Energie f, Tatkraft f; (Phys) Energie f.

enervating ['enɜːveɪtɪŋ] a nervenaufreibend.

enforce [ɪn'fɔːs] vt durchsetzen; obedience erzwingen.

engage [ɪn'geɪdʒ] vt (employ) einstellen; (in conversation) verwickeln; (Mil) angreifen; (Tech) einrasten lassen, einschalten; ~**d** a verlobt; (Tel, toilet) besetzt; (busy) beschäftigt, unabkömmlich; **to get** ~**d** sich verloben; ~**ment** (appointment) Verabredung f; (to marry) Verlobung f; (Mil) Gefecht nt; ~**ment ring** Verlobungsring m.

engaging [ɪn'geɪdʒɪŋ] a einnehmend.

engender [ɪn'dʒendə*] vt hervorrufen.

engine ['endʒɪn] n (Aut) Motor m; (Rail) Lokomotive f; ~**er** [endʒɪ'nɪə*] Ingenieur m; (US Rail) Lokomotivführer m; ~**ering** [endʒɪ'nɪərɪŋ] Technik f; Maschinenbau m; ~ **failure**, ~ **trouble** Maschinenschaden m; (Aut) Motorschaden m.

engrave [ɪn'greɪv] vt (carve) einschneiden; (fig) tief einprägen; (print) gravieren.

engraving [ɪn'greɪvɪŋ] n Stich m.

engrossed [ɪn'grəust] a vertieft.

engulf [ɪn'gʌlf] vt verschlingen.

enhance [ɪn'hɑːns] vt steigern, heben.

enigma [ɪ'nɪgmə] n Rätsel nt; ~**tic** [enɪg'mætɪk] a rätselhaft.

enjoy [ɪn'dʒɔɪ] vt genießen; privilege besitzen; ~**able** a erfreulich; ~**ment** Genuß m, Freude f.

enlarge [ɪn'lɑːdʒ] vt erweitern; (Phot) vergrößern; **to** ~ **on sth** etw weiter ausführen; ~**ment** Vergrößerung f.

enlighten [ɪn'laɪtn] vt aufklären; ~**ment** Aufklärung f.

enlist [ɪn'lɪst] vt gewinnen; vi (Mil) sich melden.

enmity ['enmɪtɪ] n Feindschaft f.

enormity [ɪ'nɔːmɪtɪ] n Ungeheuerlichkeit f.

enormous a, ~**ly** ad [ɪ'nɔːməs, -lɪ] ungeheuer.

enough [ɪ'nʌf] a genug; ad genug, genügend; ~**!** genug!; **that's** ~**!** das reicht!

enquire [ɪn'kwaɪə*] = **inquire**.

enrich [ɪn'rɪtʃ] vt bereichern.

enrol [ɪn'rəul] vt (Mil) anwerben; vi (register) sich anmelden; ~**ment** (for course) Anmeldung f; (Univ) Einschreibung f.

en route [ɑːn'ruːt] ad unterwegs.

ensign ['ensaɪn] n (Naut) Flagge f; (Mil) Fähnrich m.

enslave [ɪn'sleɪv] vt versklaven.

ensue [ɪn'sjuː] vi folgen, sich ergeben.

ensuing [ɪn'sjuːɪŋ] a (nach)folgend.

ensure [ɪn'ʃuə*] vt garantieren.

entail [ɪn'teɪl] vt mit sich bringen.

enter ['entə*] vt eintreten in (+dat), betreten; club beitreten (+dat); (in book) eintragen; vi hereinkommen, hineingehen; ~ **for** vt sich beteiligen an (+dat); ~ **into** vt agreement eingehen; argument sich einlassen auf (+acc); ~ **upon** vt beginnen.

enterprise ['entəpraɪz] n (in person) Initiative f, Unternehmungsgeist m; (Comm) Unternehmen nt, Betrieb m.

enterprising ['entəpraɪzɪŋ] a unternehmungslustig.

entertain [entə'teɪn] vt guest bewirten; (amuse) unterhalten; ~**er** Unterhaltungskünstler(in f) m; ~**ing** a unterhaltend, amüsant; ~**ment** (amusement) Unterhaltung f; (show) Veranstaltung f.

enthralled [ɪn'θrɔːld] a gefesselt.

enthusiasm [ɪn'θuːzɪæzəm] n Begeisterung f.

enthusiast [ɪn'θuːzɪæst] n Enthusiast m, Schwärmer(in f) m; ~**ic** [ɪnθuːzɪ'æstɪk] a begeistert.

entice [ɪn'taɪs] vt verleiten, locken.

entire [ɪn'taɪə*] a ganz; ~**ly** ad ganz, völlig; ~**ty** [ɪn'taɪərətɪ]: **in its** ~**ty** in seiner Gesamtheit.

entitle [ɪn'taɪtl] vt (allow) berechtigen; (name) betiteln.

entity ['entɪtɪ] n Ding nt, Wesen nt.

entrance ['entrəns] n Eingang m; (entering) Eintritt m; [ɪn'trɑːns] vt hinreißen; ~ **examination** Aufnahmeprüfung f; ~ **fee** Eintrittsgeld nt.

entrancing [ɪn'trɑːnsɪŋ] a bezaubernd.

entrant ['entrənt] n (for exam) Kandidat m; (into job) Anfänger m; (Mil) Rekrut m; (in race) Teilnehmer m.

entreat [ɪn'triːt] vt anflehen, beschwören; ~**y** flehende Bitte f, Beschwörung f.

entrée ['ɒntreɪ] n Zwischengang m.

entrenched [ɪn'trentʃt] a (fig) verwurzelt.

entrust [ɪn'trʌst] vt anvertrauen (sb with sth jdm etw).

entry ['entrɪ] n Eingang m; (Theat) Auftritt m; (in account) Eintragung f; (in dictionary) Eintrag m; '**no** ~' 'Eintritt verboten'; (for cars) 'Einfahrt verboten'; ~ **form** Anmeldeformular nt.

enunciate [ɪ'nʌnsɪeɪt] vt (deutlich) aussprechen.

envelop [ɪn'veləp] vt einhüllen; ~**e** ['envələup] n Umschlag m.

enviable ['envɪəbl] a beneidenswert.

envious ['envɪəs] a neidisch.

environment [ɪn'vaɪərənmənt] n Umgebung f; (ecology) Umwelt f; ~**al** [ɪnvaɪərən'mentl] a Umwelt-.

envisage [ɪn'vɪzɪdʒ] vt sich (dat) vorstellen; (plan) ins Auge fassen.

envoy ['envɔɪ] n Gesandte(r) mf.

envy ['envɪ] n Neid m; (object) Gegenstand m des Neides; vt beneiden (sb sth jdn um etw).

enzyme ['enzaɪm] n Enzym nt.
ephemeral [ɪ'femərəl] a kurzlebig, vorübergehend.
epic ['epɪk] n Epos nt; (film) Großfilm m; a episch; (fig) heldenhaft.
epidemic [epɪ'demɪk] n Epidemie f.
epigram ['epɪɡræm] n Epigramm nt.
epilepsy ['epɪlepsɪ] n Epilepsie f.
epileptic [epɪ'leptɪk] a epileptisch; n Epileptiker(in f) m.
epilogue ['epɪlɒɡ] n (of drama) Epilog m; (of book) Nachwort nt.
episode ['epɪsəʊd] n (incident) Vorfall m; (story) Episode f.
epistle [ɪ'pɪsl] n Brief m.
epitaph ['epɪtɑːf] n Grab(in)schrift f.
epitome [ɪ'pɪtəmɪ] n Inbegriff m.
epitomize [ɪ'pɪtəmaɪz] vt verkörpern.
epoch ['iːpɒk] n Epoche f.
equable ['ekwəbl] a ausgeglichen.
equal ['iːkwl] a gleich; ~ to the task der Aufgabe gewachsen; n Gleichgestellte(r) mf; vt gleichkommen (+dat); two times two ~s four zwei mal zwei ist (gleich) vier; without ~ ohne seinesgleichen; ~ity [ɪ'kwɒlɪtɪ] Gleichheit f; (equal rights) Gleichberechtigung f; ~ize vt gleichmachen; vi (Sport) ausgleichen; ~izer (Sport) Ausgleich(streffer) m; ~ly ad gleich; ~s sign Gleichheitszeichen nt.
equanimity [ekwə'nɪmɪtɪ] n Gleichmut m.
equate [ɪ'kweɪt] vt gleichsetzen.
equation [ɪ'kweɪʒən] n Gleichung f.
equator [ɪ'kweɪtə*] n Äquator m; ~ial [ekwə'tɔːrɪəl] a Äquator-.
equilibrium [iːkwɪ'lɪbrɪəm] n Gleichgewicht nt.
equinox ['iːkwɪnɒks] n Tag- und Nachtgleiche f.
equip [ɪ'kwɪp] vt ausrüsten; ~ment Ausrüstung f; (Tech) Gerät nt.
equitable ['ekwɪtəbl] a gerecht, billig.
equity ['ekwɪtɪ] n Billigkeit f, Gerechtigkeit f.
equivalent [ɪ'kwɪvələnt] a gleichwertig (to dat), entsprechend (to dat); n (amount) gleiche Menge f; (in money) Gegenwert m; Äquivalent nt.
equivocal [ɪ'kwɪvəkəl] a zweideutig; (suspect) fragwürdig.
era ['ɪərə] n Epoche f, Ära f.
eradicate [ɪ'rædɪkeɪt] vt ausrotten.
erase [ɪ'reɪz] vt ausradieren; tape löschen; ~r Radiergummi m.
erect [ɪ'rekt] a aufrecht; vt errichten; ~ion Errichtung f; (Physiol) Erektion f.
ermine ['ɜːmɪn] n Hermelin(pelz) m.
erode [ɪ'rəʊd] vt zerfressen; land auswaschen.
erosion [ɪ'rəʊʒən] n Auswaschen nt, Erosion f.
erotic [ɪ'rɒtɪk] a erotisch; ~ism [ɪ'rɒtɪsɪzəm] Erotik f.
err [ɜː*] vi sich irren.
errand ['erənd] n Besorgung f; ~ boy Laufbursche m.
erratic [ɪ'rætɪk] a sprunghaft; driving unausgeglichen.
erroneous [ɪ'rəʊnɪəs] a irrig, irrtümlich.

error ['erə*] n Fehler m.
erudite ['erʊdaɪt] a gelehrt.
erudition [erʊ'dɪʃən] n Gelehrsamkeit f.
erupt [ɪ'rʌpt] vi ausbrechen; ~ion Ausbruch m.
escalate ['eskəleɪt] vt steigern; vi sich steigern.
escalator ['eskəleɪtə*] n Rolltreppe f.
escapade [eskə'peɪd] n Eskapade f, Streich m.
escape [ɪs'keɪp] n Flucht f; (of gas) Entweichen nt; vti entkommen (+dat); (prisoners) fliehen; (leak) entweichen; to ~ notice unbemerkt bleiben; the word ~s me das Wort ist mir entfallen.
escapism [ɪs'keɪpɪzəm] n Flucht f (vor der Wirklichkeit).
escort ['eskɔːt] n (person accompanying) Begleiter m; (guard) Eskorte f; [ɪs'kɔːt] vt lady begleiten; (Mil) eskortieren.
especially [ɪs'peʃəlɪ] ad besonders.
espionage ['espɪɒnɑːʒ] n Spionage f.
esplanade [esplə'neɪd] n Esplanade f, Promenade f.
Esquire [ɪs'kwaɪə*] n (in address) J. Brown, Esq Herrn J. Brown.
essay ['eseɪ] n Aufsatz m; (Liter) Essay m.
essence ['esəns] n (quality) Wesen nt; (extract) Essenz f, Extrakt m.
essential [ɪ'senʃəl] a (necessary) unentbehrlich; (basic) wesentlich; n Hauptbestandteil m, Allernötigste(s) nt; ~ly ad in der Hauptsache, eigentlich.
establish [ɪs'tæblɪʃ] vt (set up) gründen, einrichten; (prove) nachweisen; ~ment (setting up) Einrichtung f; (business) Unternehmen nt; the E~ment das Establishment.
estate [ɪs'teɪt] n Gut nt; (housing —) Siedlung f; (will) Nachlaß m; ~ agent Grundstücksmakler m; ~ car (Brit) Kombiwagen m.
esteem [ɪs'tiːm] n Wertschätzung f.
estimate ['estɪmət] n (opinion) Meinung f; (of price) (Kosten)voranschlag m; ['estɪmeɪt] vt schätzen.
estimation [estɪ'meɪʃən] n Einschätzung f; (esteem) Achtung f.
estuary ['estjʊərɪ] n Mündung f.
etching ['etʃɪŋ] n Kupferstich m.
eternal a, ~ly ad [ɪ'tɜːnl, -nlɪ] ewig.
eternity [ɪ'tɜːnɪtɪ] n Ewigkeit f.
ether ['iːθə*] n (Med) Äther m.
ethical ['eθɪkəl] a ethisch.
ethics ['eθɪks] npl Ethik f.
ethnic ['eθnɪk] a Volks-, ethnisch.
etiquette ['etɪket] n Etikette f.
Eucharist ['juːkərɪst] n heilige(s) Abendmahl nt.
eulogy ['juːlədʒɪ] n Lobrede f.
eunuch ['juːnək] n Eunuch m.
euphemism ['juːfɪmɪzəm] n Euphemismus m.
euphoria [juː'fɔːrɪə] n Taumel m, Euphorie f.
euthanasia [juːθə'neɪzɪə] n Euthanasie f.
evacuate [ɪ'vækjʊeɪt] vt place räumen; people evakuieren; (Med) entleeren.

evacuation [ɪˌvækjuˈeɪʃən] n Evakuierung f; Räumung f; Entleerung f.

evade [ɪˈveɪd] vt (escape) entkommen (+dat); (avoid) meiden; duty sich entziehen (+dat).

evaluate [ɪˈvæljueɪt] vt bewerten; information auswerten.

evangelical [iːvænˈdʒelɪkəl] a evangelisch.

evangelist [ɪˈvændʒəlɪst] n Evangelist m.

evaporate [ɪˈvæpəreɪt] vi verdampfen; vt verdampfen lassen; ~d milk Kondensmilch f.

evaporation [ɪvæpəˈreɪʃən] n Verdunstung f.

evasion [ɪˈveɪʒən] n Umgehung f; (excuse) Ausflucht f.

evasive [ɪˈveɪzɪv] a ausweichend.

even [ˈiːvən] a eben; gleichmäßig; score etc unentschieden; number gerade; vt (ein)-ebnen, glätten; ad ~ you selbst or sogar du; **he ~ said** ... er hat sogar gesagt ...; **~ as he spoke** (gerade) da er sprach; **~ if** sogar or selbst wenn, wenn auch; **~ so** dennoch; **~ out** or **up** vi sich ausgleichen; vt ausgleichen; **get ~** sich revanchieren.

evening [ˈiːvnɪŋ] n Abend m; **in the ~** abends, am Abend; **~ class** Abendschule f; **~ dress** (man's) Gesellschaftsanzug m; (woman's) Abendkleid nt.

evenly [ˈiːvənlɪ] ad gleichmäßig.

evensong [ˈiːvənsɒŋ] n (Rel) Abendandacht f.

event [ɪˈvent] n (happening) Ereignis nt; (Sport) Disziplin f; (horses) Rennen nt; **the next ~** der nächste Wettkampf; **in the ~ of** im Falle (+gen); **~ful** a ereignisreich.

eventual [ɪˈventʃuəl] a (final) schließlich; **~ity** [ɪventʃuˈælɪtɪ] Möglichkeit f; **~ly** ad (at last) am Ende; (given time) schließlich.

ever [ˈevə*] ad (always) immer; (at any time) je(mals); **~ so big** sehr groß; **~ so many** sehr viele; **~green** a immergrün; n Immergrün nt; **~-lasting** a immerwährend.

every [ˈevrɪ] a jeder/jede/jedes; **~ day** jeden Tag; **~ other day** jeden zweiten Tag; **~body** pron jeder, alle pl; **~day** a (daily) täglich; (commonplace) alltäglich, Alltags-; **~one** = **~body**; **~so often** hin und wieder; **~thing** pron alles; **~where** ad überall.

evict [ɪˈvɪkt] vt ausweisen; **~ion** Ausweisung f.

evidence [ˈevɪdəns] n (sign) Spur f; (proof) Beweis m; (testimony) Aussage f; **in ~** (obvious) zu sehen.

evident [ˈevɪdənt] a augenscheinlich; **~ly** ad offensichtlich.

evil [ˈiːvl] a böse, übel; n Übel nt; Unheil nt; (sin) Böse(s) nt.

evocative [ɪˈvɒkətɪv] a **to be ~ of sth** an etw (acc) erinnern.

evoke [ɪˈvəʊk] vt hervorrufen.

evolution [iːvəˈluːʃən] n Entwicklung f; (of life) Evolution f.

evolve [ɪˈvɒlv] vt entwickeln; vi sich entwickeln.

ewe [juː] n Mutterschaf nt.

ex- [eks] a Ex-, Alt-, ehemalig.

exact a, **~ly** ad [ɪgˈzækt, -lɪ] genau; vt (demand) verlangen; (compel) erzwingen; money, fine einziehen; punishment vollziehen; **~ing** a anspruchsvoll; **~itude** Genauigkeit f; **~ness** Genauigkeit f, Richtigkeit f.

exaggerate [ɪgˈzædʒəreɪt] vti übertreiben; **~d** a übertrieben.

exaggeration [ɪgzædʒəˈreɪʃən] n Übertreibung f.

exalt [ɪgˈzɔːlt] vt (praise) verherrlichen.

exam [ɪgˈzæm] n Prüfung f.

examination [ɪgzæmɪˈneɪʃən] n Untersuchung f; (Sch, Univ) Prüfung f, Examen nt; (customs) Kontrolle f.

examine [ɪgˈzæmɪn] vt untersuchen; (Sch) prüfen; (consider) erwägen; **~r** Prüfer m.

example [ɪgˈzɑːmpl] n Beispiel nt; **for ~** zum Beispiel.

exasperate [ɪgˈzɑːspəreɪt] vt zum Verzweifeln bringen.

exasperating [ɪgˈzɑːspəreɪtɪŋ] a ärgerlich, zum Verzweifeln bringend.

exasperation [ɪgzɑːspəˈreɪʃən] n Verzweiflung f.

excavate [ˈekskəveɪt] vt (hollow out) aushöhlen; (unearth) ausgraben.

excavation [ekskəˈveɪʃən] n Ausgrabung f.

excavator [ˈekskəveɪtə*] n Bagger m.

exceed [ɪkˈsiːd] vt überschreiten; hopes übertreffen; **~ingly** ad in höchstem Maße.

excel [ɪkˈsel] vi sich auszeichnen; vt übertreffen; **~lence** [ˈeksələns] Vortrefflichkeit f; **His E~lency** [ˈeksələnsɪ] Seine Exzellenz f; **~lent** [ˈeksələnt] a ausgezeichnet.

except [ɪkˈsept] prep (also ~ **for**) außer (+dat); vt ausnehmen; **~ing** prep = **except**; **~ion** [ɪkˈsepʃən] Ausnahme f; **to take ~ion to** Anstoß nehmen an (+dat); **~ional** a, **~ionally** ad [ɪkˈsepʃənl, -nəlɪ] außergewöhnlich.

excerpt [ˈeksɜːpt] n Auszug m.

excess [ɪkˈses] n Übermaß nt (of an +dat); Exzeß m; a money Nach-; baggage Mehr-; **~es** pl Ausschweifungen pl, Exzesse pl; (violent) Ausschreitungen pl; **~ weight** (of thing) Mehrgewicht nt; (of person) Übergewicht nt; **~ive** a, **~ively** ad übermäßig.

exchange [ɪksˈtʃeɪndʒ] n Austausch m; (Fin) Wechselstube f; (Tel) Vermittlung f, Zentrale f; (Post Office) (Fernsprech)amt nt; vt goods tauschen; greetings austauschen; money, blows wechseln; see **rate**.

exchequer [ɪksˈtʃekə*] n Schatzamt nt.

excisable [ekˈsaɪzɪbl] a (verbrauchs)-steuerpflichtig.

excise [ˈeksaɪz] n Verbrauchssteuer f; [ekˈsaɪz] vt (Med) herausschneiden.

excitable [ɪkˈsaɪtəbl] a erregbar, nervös.

excite [ɪkˈsaɪt] vt erregen; **~d** a aufgeregt; **to get ~d** sich aufregen; **~ment** Aufgeregtheit f; (of interest) Erregung f.

exciting [ɪkˈsaɪtɪŋ] a aufregend; book, film spannend.

exclaim [ɪksˈkleɪm] vi ausrufen.

exclamation [ekskləˈmeɪʃən] n Ausruf m.

~ **mark** Ausrufezeichen *nt.*

exclude [ɪks'kluːd] *vt* ausschließen.

exclusion [ɪks'kluːʒən] *n* Ausschluß *m.*

exclusive [ɪks'kluːsɪv] *a* (*select*) exklusiv; (*sole*) ausschließlich, Allein-; ~ **of** exklusive (+*gen*); ~**ly** *ad* nur, ausschließlich.

excommunicate [ekskə'mjuːnɪkeɪt] *vt* exkommunizieren.

excrement ['ekskrɪmənt] *n* Kot *m.*

excruciating [ɪks'kruːʃieɪtɪŋ] *a* qualvoll.

excursion [ɪks'kɜːʃən] *n* Ausflug *m.*

excusable [ɪks'kjuːzəbl] *a* entschuldbar.

excuse [ɪks'kjuːs] *n* Entschuldigung *f*; [ɪks'kjuːz] *vt* entschuldigen; ~ **me!** entschuldigen Sie!

execute ['eksɪkjuːt] *vt* (*carry out*) ausführen; (*kill*) hinrichten.

execution [eksɪ'kjuːʃən] *n* Ausführung *f*; (*killing*) Hinrichtung *f*; ~**er** Scharfrichter *m.*

executive [ɪg'zekjutɪv] *n* (*Comm*) leitende(r) Angestellte(r) *m*, Geschäftsführer *m*; (*Pol*) Exekutive *f*; *a* Exekutiv-, ausführend.

executor [ɪg'zekjutə*] *n* Testamentsvollstrecker *m.*

exemplary [ɪg'zemplərɪ] *a* musterhaft.

exemplify [ɪg'zemplɪfaɪ] *vt* veranschaulichen.

exempt [ɪg'zempt] *a* befreit; *vt* befreien; ~**ion** [ɪg'zempʃən] Befreiung *f.*

exercise ['eksəsaɪz] *n* Übung *f*; *vt power* ausüben; *muscle, patience* üben; *dog* ausführen; ~ **book** (Schul)heft *nt.*

exert [ɪg'zɜːt] *vt influence* ausüben; ~ **o.s.** sich anstrengen; ~**ion** Anstrengung *f.*

exhaust [ɪg'zɔːst] *n* (*fumes*) Abgase *pl*; (*pipe*) Auspuffrohr *nt*; *vt* (*weary*) ermüden; (*use up*) erschöpfen; ~**ed** *a* erschöpft; ~**ing** *a* anstrengend; ~**ion** Erschöpfung *f*; ~**ive** *a* erschöpfend.

exhibit [ɪg'zɪbɪt] *n* (*Art*) Ausstellungsstück *nt*; (*Jur*) Beweisstück *nt*; *vt* ausstellen; ~**ion** [eksɪ'bɪʃən] (*Art*) Ausstellung *f*; (*of temper etc*) Zurschaustellung *f*; ~**ionist** [eksɪ'bɪʃənɪst] Exhibitionist *m*; ~**or** Aussteller *m.*

exhilarating [ɪg'zɪləreɪtɪŋ] *a* erhebend.

exhilaration [ɪgzɪlə'reɪʃən] *n* erhebende(s) Gefühl *nt.*

exhort [ɪg'zɔːt] *vt* ermahnen; beschwören.

exile ['eksaɪl] *n* Exil *nt*; (*person*) im Exil Lebende(r) *mf*; *vt* verbannen; **in** ~ im Exil.

exist [ɪg'zɪst] *vi* existieren; (*live*) leben; ~**ence** Existenz *f*; (*way of life*) Leben *nt*, Existenz *f*; ~**ing** *a* vorhanden, bestehend.

exit ['eksɪt] *n* Ausgang *m*; (*Theat*) Abgang *m.*

exonerate [ɪg'zɒnəreɪt] *vt* entlasten.

exorbitant [ɪg'zɔːbɪtənt] *a* übermäßig; *price* Phantasie-.

exotic [ɪg'zɒtɪk] *a* exotisch.

expand [ɪks'pænd] *vt* (*spread*) ausspannen; *operations* ausdehnen; *vi* sich ausdehnen.

expanse [ɪks'pæns] *n* weite Fläche *f*, Weite *f.*

expansion [ɪks'pænʃən] *n* Erweiterung *f.*

expatriate [eks'pætrɪeɪt] *a* Exil-; *n* im Exil Lebende(r) *mf*; *vt* ausbürgern.

expect [ɪks'pekt] *vt* erwarten; (*suppose*) annehmen; *vi*: **to be** ~**ing** ein Kind erwarten; ~**ant** *a* (*hopeful*) erwartungsvoll; *mother* werdend; ~**ation** [ekspek'teɪʃən] (*hope*) Hoffnung *f*; ~**ations** *pl* Erwartungen *pl*; (*prospects*) Aussicht *f.*

expedience [ɪks'piːdɪəns], **expediency** [ɪks'piːdɪənsɪ] *n* Zweckdienlichkeit *f.*

expedient [ɪks'piːdɪənt] *a* zweckdienlich; *n* (Hilfs)mittel *nt.*

expedite ['ekspɪdaɪt] *vt* beschleunigen.

expedition [ekspɪ'dɪʃən] *n* Expedition *f.*

expel [ɪks'pel] *vt* ausweisen; *student* (ver)weisen.

expend [ɪks'pend] *vt money* ausgeben; *effort* aufwenden; ~**able** *a* entbehrlich; ~**iture** Kosten *pl*, Ausgaben *pl.*

expense [ɪks'pens] *n* (*cost*) Auslage *f*, Ausgabe *f*; (*high cost*) Aufwand *m*; ~**s** *pl* Spesen *pl*; **at the** ~ **of** auf Kosten von; ~ **account** Spesenkonto *nt.*

expensive [ɪks'pensɪv] *a* teuer.

experience [ɪks'pɪərɪəns] *n* (*incident*) Erlebnis *nt*; (*practice*) Erfahrung *f*; *vt* erfahren, erleben; *hardship* durchmachen; ~**d** *a* erfahren.

experiment [ɪks'perɪmənt] *n* Versuch *m*, Experiment *m*; [ɪks'perɪment] *vi* experimentieren; ~**al** [ɪksperɪ'mentl] *a* versuchsweise, experimentell.

expert ['ekspɜːt] *n* Fachmann *m*; (*official*) Sachverständige(r) *m*; *a* erfahren; (*practised*) gewandt; ~**ise** [ekspɜː'tiːz] Sachkenntnis *f.*

expiration [ekspaɪə'reɪʃən] *n* (*breathing*) Ausatmen *nt*; (*fig*) Ablauf *m.*

expire [ɪks'paɪə*] *vi* (*end*) ablaufen; (*die*) sterben; (*ticket*) verfallen.

expiry [ɪks'paɪərɪ] *n* Ablauf *m.*

explain [ɪks'pleɪn] *vt* (*make clear*) erklären; (*account for*) begründen; ~ **away** *vt* wegerklären.

explanation [eksplə'neɪʃən] *n* Erklärung *f.*

explanatory [ɪks'plænətərɪ] *a* erklärend.

explicable [eks'plɪkəbl] *a* erklärlich.

explicit [ɪks'plɪsɪt] *a* (*clear*) ausdrücklich; (*outspoken*) deutlich; ~**ly** *ad* deutlich.

explode [ɪks'pləʊd] *vi* explodieren; *vt bomb* zur Explosion bringen; *theory* platzen lassen.

exploit ['eksplɔɪt] *n* (Helden)tat *f*; [ɪks'plɔɪt] *vt* ausbeuten; ~**ation** [eksplɔɪ'teɪʃən] Ausbeutung *f.*

exploration [eksplɔː'reɪʃən] *n* Erforschung *f.*

exploratory [eks'plɔrətərɪ] *a* sondierend, Probe-.

explore [ɪks'plɔː*] *vt* (*travel*) erforschen; (*search*) untersuchen; ~**r** Forschungsreisende(r) *mf*, Erforscher(in *f*) *m.*

explosion [ɪks'pləʊʒən] *n* (*lit*) Explosion *f*; (*fig*) Ausbruch *m.*

explosive [ɪks'pləʊzɪv] *a* explosiv, Spreng-; *n* Sprengstoff *m.*

exponent [eks'pəʊnənt] *n* Exponent *m.*

export [eks'pɔːt] *vt* exportieren; ['ekspɔːt] *n* Export *m*; *a trade* Export-; ~**ation**

[ekspɔː'teɪʃən] Ausfuhr f; ~er Exporteur m.

expose [ɪks'pəʊz] vt (to danger etc) aussetzen (to dat); imposter entlarven; lie aufdecken.

exposé [eks'pəʊzeɪ] n (of scandal) Enthüllung f.

exposed [ɪks'pəʊzd] a position exponiert.

exposure [ɪks'pəʊʒə⁺] m (Med) Unterkühlung f; (Phot) Belichtung f; ~ meter Belichtungsmesser m.

expound [ɪks'paʊnd] vt entwickeln.

express [ɪks'pres] a ausdrücklich; (speedy) Expreß-, Eil-; n (Rail) Zug m; vt ausdrücken; **to ~ o.s.** sich ausdrücken; ~ion [ɪks'preʃən] (phrase) Ausdruck m; (look) (Gesichts)ausdruck m; ~ive a ausdrucksvoll; ~ly ad ausdrücklich, extra.

expropriate [eks'prəʊprɪeɪt] vt enteignen.

expulsion [ɪks'pʌlʃən] n Ausweisung f.

exquisite [eks'kwɪzɪt] a erlesen; ~ly ad ausgezeichnet.

extend [ɪks'tend] vt visit etc verlängern; building vergrößern, ausbauen; hand ausstrecken; welcome bieten.

extension [ɪks'tenʃən] n Erweiterung f; (of building) Anbau m; (Tel) Nebenanschluß m, Apparat m.

extensive [ɪks'tensɪv] a knowledge umfassend; use weitgehend.

extent [ɪks'tent] n Ausdehnung f; (fig) Ausmaß nt.

extenuating [eks'tenjueɪtɪŋ] a mildernd.

exterior [eks'tɪərɪə⁺] a äußere(r,s), Außen-; n Äußere(s) nt.

exterminate [eks'tɜːmɪneɪt] vt ausrotten.

extermination [ekstɜːmɪ'neɪʃən] n Ausrottung f.

external [eks'tɜːnl] a äußere(r,s), Außen-; ~ly ad äußerlich.

extinct [ɪks'tɪŋkt] a ausgestorben; ~ion [ɪks'tɪŋkʃən] Aussterben nt.

extinguish [ɪks'tɪŋgwɪʃ] vt (aus)löschen; ~er Löschgerät nt.

extort [ɪks'tɔːt] vt erpressen (sth from sb jdn um etw); ~ion [ɪks'tɔːʃən] Erpressung f; ~ionate [ɪks'tɔːʃənɪt] a überhöht, erpresserisch.

extra ['ekstrə] a zusätzlich; ad besonders; (work) Sonderarbeit f; (benefit) Sonderleistung f; (charge) Zuschlag m; (Theat) Statist m.

extract [ɪks'trækt] vt (heraus)ziehen; (select) auswählen; n ['ekstrækt] (from book etc) Auszug m; (Cook) Extrakt m; ~ion (Heraus)ziehen nt; (origin) Abstammung f.

extradite ['ekstrədaɪt] vt ausliefern.

extradition [ekstrə'dɪʃən] n Auslieferung f.

extraneous [eks'treɪnɪəs] a unwesentlich; influence äußere(r,s).

extraordinary [ɪks'trɔːdnrɪ] a außerordentlich; (amazing) erstaunlich.

extravagance [ɪks'trævəgəns] n Verschwendung f; (lack of restraint) Zügellosigkeit f; (an —) Extravaganz f.

extravagant [ɪks'trævəgənt] a extravagant.

extreme [ɪks'triːm] a edge äußerste(r,s), hinterste(r,s); cold äußerste(r,s); behaviour

außergewöhnlich, übertrieben; n Extrem nt, das Äußerste; ~s pl (excesses) Ausschreitungen pl; (opposites) Extreme pl; ~ly ad äußerst, höchst.

extremist [ɪks'triːmɪst] a extremistisch; n Extremist(in f) m.

extremity [ɪks'tremɪtɪ] n (end) Spitze f, äußerste(s) Ende nt; (hardship) bitterste Not f; (Anat) Hand f, Fuß m.

extricate ['ekstrɪkeɪt] vt losmachen, befreien.

extrovert ['ekstrəʊvɜːt] n Extravertierte(r) mf; a extravertiert.

exuberance [ɪg'zuːbərəns] n Überschwang m.

exuberant [ɪg'zuːbərənt] a ausgelassen.

exude [ɪg'zjuːd] vt absondern; vi sich absondern.

exult [ɪg'zʌlt] vi frohlocken; ~ation [egzʌl'teɪʃən] Jubel m.

eye [aɪ] n Auge nt; (of needle) Öhr nt; vt betrachten; (up and down) mustern; **to keep an ~ on** aufpassen auf (+acc); **in the ~s of** in den Augen (+gen); **up to the ~s in** bis zum Hals in; ~**ball** Augapfel m; ~**bath** Augenbad nt; ~**brow** Augenbraue f; ~**lash** Augenwimper f; ~**lid** Augenlid nt; **that was an ~opener** das hat mir die Augen geöffnet; ~**shadow** Lidschatten m; ~**sight** Sehkraft f; ~**sore** Schandfleck m; ~**wash** (lit) Augenwasser nt; (fig) Schwindel m; Quatsch m; ~ **witness** Augenzeuge m.

F

F,f [ef] n F nt, f nt.

fable ['feɪbl] n Fabel f.

fabric ['fæbrɪk] n Stoff m, Gewebe nt; (fig) Gefüge nt.

fabricate ['fæbrɪkeɪt] vt fabrizieren.

fabulous ['fæbjuləs] a (imaginary) legendär, sagenhaft; (unbelievable) unglaublich; (wonderful) fabelhaft, unglaublich.

façade [fə'sɑːd] n (lit, fig) Fassade f.

face [feɪs] n Gesicht nt; (grimace) Grimasse f; (surface) Oberfläche f; (of clock) Zifferblatt nt; vt (point towards) liegen nach; situation sich gegenübersehen (+dat); difficulty mutig entgegentreten (+dat); **in the ~ of** angesichts (+gen); **to ~ up to sth** einer Sache ins Auge sehen; ~ **cream** Gesichtscreme f; ~ **powder** (Gesichts)puder m.

facet ['fæsɪt] n Seite f, Aspekt m; (of gem) Kristallfläche f, Schliff m.

facetious [fə'siːʃəs] a schalkhaft; (humorous) witzig; ~ly ad spaßhaft, witzig.

face to face [feɪstə'feɪs] ad Auge in Auge, direkt.

face value ['feɪs 'væljuː] n Nennwert m; (fig) **to take sth at its ~** etw für bare Münze nehmen.

facial ['feɪʃəl] a Gesichts-.

facile ['fæsaɪl] a oberflächlich; (US: easy) leicht.

facilitate [fə'sɪlɪteɪt] vt erleichtern.

facility [fə'sɪlɪtɪ] n (ease) Leichtigkeit f;

(skill) Gewandtheit f; **facilities** pl Einrichtungen pl.

facing ['feɪsɪŋ] a zugekehrt; prep gegenüber.

facsimile [fæk'sɪmɪlɪ] n Faksimile nt.

fact [fækt] n Tatsache f; **in** ~ in der Tat.

faction ['fækʃən] n Splittergruppe f.

factor ['fæktə*] n Faktor m.

factory ['fæktərɪ] n Fabrik f.

factual ['fæktjʊəl] a Tatsachen-, sachlich.

faculty ['fækəltɪ] n Fähigkeit f; (Univ) Fakultät f; (US: teaching staff) Lehrpersonal nt.

fade [feɪd] vi (lose colour) verschießen, verblassen; (grow dim) nachlassen, schwinden; (sound, memory) schwächer werden; (wither) verwelken; vt material verblassen lassen; ~ a verwelkt; colour verblichen; **to** ~ **in/out** (Cine) ein-/ausblenden.

fag [fæg] n Plackerei f; (col: cigarette) Kippe f; ~**ged** a (exhausted) erschöpft.

Fahrenheit ['færənhaɪt] n Fahrenheit.

fail [feɪl] vt exam nicht bestehen; student durchfallen lassen; (courage) verlassen; (memory) im Stich lassen; vi (supplies) zu Ende gehen; (student) durchfallen; (eyesight) nachlassen; (light) schwächer werden; (crop) fehlschlagen; (remedy) nicht wirken; ~ **to do sth** (neglect) es unterlassen, etw zu tun; (be unable) es nicht schaffen, etw zu tun; **without** ~ ganz bestimmt, unbedingt; ~**ing** n Fehler m, Schwäche f; prep in Ermangelung (+gen); ~**ing this** falls nicht, sonst; ~**ure** (person) Versager m; (act) Versagen nt; (Tech) Defekt m.

faint [feɪnt] a schwach, matt; n Ohnmacht f; vi ohnmächtig werden; ~**hearted** a mutlos, kleinmütig; ~**ly** ad schwach; ~**ness** Schwäche f; (Med) Schwächegefühl nt.

fair [fɛə*] a schön; hair blond; skin hell; weather schön, trocken; (just) gerecht, fair; (not very good) leidlich, mittelmäßig; conditions günstig, gut; (sizeable) ansehnlich; ad play ehrlich, fair; (n Comm) Messe f; (fun —) Jahrmarkt m; ~**ly** ad (honestly) gerecht, fair; (rather) ziemlich; ~**ness** Schönheit f; (of hair) Blondheit f; (of game) Ehrlichkeit f, Fairneß f; ~**way** (Naut) Fahrrinne f.

fairy ['fɛərɪ] n Fee f; ~**land** Märchenland nt; ~ **tale** Märchen nt.

faith [feɪθ] n Glaube m; (trust) Vertrauen nt; (sect) Bekenntnis nt, Religion f; ~**ful** a, ~**fully** ad treu; **yours** ~**fully** hochachtungsvoll.

fake [feɪk] n (thing) Fälschung f; (person) Schwindler m; a vorgetäuscht; vt fälschen.

falcon ['fɔːlkən] n Falke m.

fall [fɔːl] n Fall m, Sturz m; (decrease) Fallen nt; (of snow) (Schnee)fall m; (US: autumn) Herbst m; vi irreg (lit, fig) fallen; (night) hereinbrechen; ~**s** pl (waterfall) Fälle pl; ~ **back on** vt in Reserve haben; ~ **down** vi (person) hinfallen; (building) einstürzen; ~ **flat** vi (lit) nicht hinfallen; (joke) nicht ankommen; **the plan fell flat** aus dem Plan wurde nichts; ~ **for** vt trick

hereinfallen auf (+acc); person sich verknallen in (+acc); ~ **off** vi herunterfallen (von); (diminish) sich vermindern; ~ **out** vi sich streiten; ~ **through** vi (plan) ins Wasser fallen.

fallacy ['fæləsɪ] n Trugschluß m.

fallible ['fæləbl] a fehlbar.

fallout ['fɔːlaʊt] n radioaktive(r) Niederschlag m.

fallow ['fæləʊ] a brach(liegend).

false [fɔːls] a falsch; (artificial) gefälscht, künstlich; **under** ~ **pretences** unter Vorspiegelung falscher Tatsachen; ~ **alarm** Fehlalarm m; ~**ly** ad fälschlicherweise; ~ **teeth** pl Gebiß nt.

falter ['fɔːltə*] vi schwanken; (in speech) stocken.

fame [feɪm] n Ruhm m.

familiar [fə'mɪlɪə*] a vertraut, bekannt; (intimate) familiär; **to be** ~ **with** vertraut sein mit, gut kennen; ~**ize** [fəmɪlɪ'ærɪtɪ] Vertrautheit f; ~**ize** vt vertraut machen.

family ['fæmɪlɪ] n Familie f; (relations) Verwandtschaft f; ~ **allowance** Kindergeld nt; ~ **business** Familienunternehmen nt; ~ **doctor** Hausarzt m; ~ **life** Familienleben nt; ~ **planning** Geburtenkontrolle f.

famine ['fæmɪn] n Hungersnot f.

famished ['fæmɪʃt] a ausgehungert.

famous ['feɪməs] a berühmt.

fan [fæn] n (folding) Fächer m; (Elec) Ventilator m; (admirer) begeisterte(r) Anhänger m; Fan m; vt fächeln; ~ **out** vi sich (fächerförmig) ausbreiten.

fanatic [fə'nætɪk] n Fanatiker(in f) m; ~**al** a fanatisch.

fan belt ['fænbɛlt] n Keilriemen m.

fancied ['fænsɪd] a beliebt, populär.

fanciful ['fænsɪful] a (odd) seltsam; (imaginative) phantasievoll.

fancy ['fænsɪ] n (liking) Neigung f; (imagination) Phantasie f, Einbildung f; a schick, ausgefallen; vt (like) gern haben; wollen; (imagine) sich einbilden; (just) ~ (**that**)! stellen Sie sich (das nur) vor!; ~ **dress** Verkleidung f, Maskenkostüm nt; ~**-dress ball** Maskenball m.

fanfare ['fænfɛə*] n Fanfare f.

fang [fæŋ] n Fangzahn m; (snake's) Giftzahn m.

fanlight ['fænlaɪt] n Oberlicht nt.

fantastic [fæn'tæstɪk] a phantastisch.

fantasy ['fæntəzɪ] n Phantasie f.

far [fɑː*] a weit; ad weit entfernt; (very much) weitaus, (sehr) viel; ~ **away**, ~ **off** weit weg; **by** ~ bei weitem; **so** ~ soweit; bis jetzt; ~**away** a weit entfernt; **the F**~ **East** der Ferne Osten.

farce [fɑːs] n Schwank m, Posse f; (fig) Farce f.

farcical ['fɑːsɪkəl] a possenhaft; (fig) lächerlich.

fare [fɛə*] n Fahrpreis m; Fahrgeld nt; (food) Kost f; vi: **he is faring well** es ergeht ihm gut; ~**well** Abschied(sgruß) m; interj lebe wohl!; a Abschieds-.

far-fetched ['fɑː'fɛtʃt] a weit hergeholt.

farm [fɑːm] n Bauernhof m, Farm f; vt

bewirtschaften; *vi* Landwirt *m* sein; ~**er**
Bauer *m*, Landwirt *m*; ~**hand** Landarbeiter *m*; ~**house** Bauernhaus *nt*; ~**ing**
Landwirtschaft *f*; ~**land** Ackerland *nt*;
~**yard** Hof *m*.

far-reaching ['fɑː'riːtʃɪŋ] *a* weitgehend.
far-sighted ['fɑː'saɪtɪd] *a* weitblickend.
fart [fɑːt] *n* (*col*) Furz *m*; *vi* (*col*) furzen.
farther ['fɑːðə*] *a*, *ad* weiter.
farthest ['fɑːðɪst] *a* weiteste(r,s),
fernste(r,s); *ad* am weitesten.
fascinate ['fæsɪneɪt] *vt* faszinieren,
bezaubern.
fascinating ['fæsɪneɪtɪŋ] *a* faszinierend,
spannend.
fascination [fæsɪ'neɪʃən] *n* Faszination *f*,
Zauber *m*.
fascism ['fæʃɪzəm] *n* Faschismus *m*.
fascist ['fæʃɪst] *n* Faschist *m*; *a*
faschistisch.
fashion ['fæʃən] *n* (*of clothes*) Mode *f*;
(*manner*) Art *f* (und Weise *f*); *vt* machen,
gestalten; **in** ~ in Mode; **out of** ~ unmodisch; ~**able** *a* **clothes** modern,
modisch; *place* elegant; ~ **show** Mode(n)-
schau *f*.
fast [fɑːst] *a* schnell; (*firm*) fest; *dye*
waschecht; **to be** ~ (*clock*) vorgehen; *ad*
schnell; (*firmly*) fest; *n* Fasten *nt*; *vi* fasten.
fasten ['fɑːsn] *vt* (*attach*) befestigen; *seat
belt* festmachen; (*with rope*) zuschnüren; *vi*
sich schließen lassen; ~**er**, ~**ing**
Verschluß *m*.
fastidious [fæs'tɪdɪəs] *a* wählerisch.
fat [fæt] *a* dick, fett; *n* (*on person*) Fett *nt*,
Speck *m* (*col*); (*on meat*) Fett *nt*; (*for cooking*) (Braten)fett *nt*.
fatal ['feɪtl] *a* tödlich; (*disastrous*) verhängnisvoll; ~**ism** Fatalismus *m*,
Schicksalsglaube *m*; ~**ity** [fə'tælɪtɪ] (*road
death etc*) Todesopfer *nt*; ~**ly** *ad* tödlich.
fate [feɪt] *n* Schicksal *nt*; ~**ful** *a* (*prophetic*) schicksalsschwer; (*important*)
schicksalhaft.
father ['fɑːðə*] *n* Vater *m*; (*Rel*) Pater *m*;
~**-in-law** Schwiegervater *m*; ~**ly** *a*
väterlich.
fathom ['fæðəm] *n* Klafter *m*; *vt* ausloten;
(*fig*) ergründen.
fatigue [fə'tiːg] *n* Ermüdung *f*; *vt* ermüden.
fatness ['fætnɪs] *n* Dicke *f*.
fatten ['fætn] *vt* dick machen; *animals*
mästen; *vi* dick werden.
fatty ['fætɪ] *a* food fettig.
fatuous ['fætjʊəs] *a* albern, affig.
faucet ['fɔːsɪt] *n* (*US*) Wasserhahn *m*.
fault [fɔːlt] *n* (*defect*) Defekt *m*; (*Elec*)
Störung *f*; (*blame*) Fehler *m*, Schuld *f*;
(*Geog*) Verwerfung *f*; **it's your** ~ du bist
daran schuld; **at** ~ schuldig, im Unrecht;
vt: ~ **sth** etwas an etw (*dat*) auszusetzen
haben; ~**less** *a* fehlerfrei, tadellos; ~**y** *a*
fehlerhaft, defekt.
fauna ['fɔːnə] *n* Fauna *f*.
favour, (*US*) **favor** ['feɪvə*] *n* (*approval*)
Wohlwollen *nt*; (*kindness*) Gefallen *m*; *vt*
(*prefer*) vorziehen; **in** ~ **of** für; zugunsten
(+*gen*); ~**able** *a*, ~**ably** *ad* günstig; ~**ite**
['feɪvərɪt] *a* Lieblings-; *n* Günstling *m*;
(*child*) Liebling *m*; (*Sport*) Favorit *m*;

~**itism** (*Sch*) Bevorzugung *f*; (*Pol*)
Günstlingswirtschaft *f*.
fawn [fɔːn] *a* rehbraun; *n* (*colour*)
Rehbraun *nt*; (*animal*) (Reh)kitz *nt*.
fawning ['fɔːnɪŋ] *a* kriecherisch.
fear [fɪə*] *n* Furcht *f*; *vt* fürchten; **no** ~!
keine Angst!; ~**ful** *a* (*timid*) furchtsam;
(*terrible*) fürchterlich; ~**less** *a*, ~**lessly**
ad furchtlos; ~**lessness** Furchtlosigkeit *f*.
feasibility [fiːzə'bɪlɪtɪ] *n* Durchführbarkeit
f.
feasible ['fiːzəbl] *a* durchführbar, machbar.
feast [fiːst] *n* Festmahl *nt*; (*Rel*) Kirchenfest *nt*; *vi* sich gütlich tun (*on an* +*dat*); ~
day kirchliche(r) Feiertag *m*.
feat [fiːt] *n* Leistung *f*.
feather ['feðə*] *n* Feder *f*.
feature ['fiːtʃə*] *n* (Gesichts)zug *m*;
(*important part*) Grundzug *m*; (*Cine, Press*)
Feature *nt*; *vt* darstellen; (*advertising etc*)
groß herausbringen; **featuring X** mit X;
vi vorkommen; ~ **film** Spielfilm *m*;
~**less** *a* nichtssagend.
February ['februərɪ] *n* Februar *m*.
federal ['fedərəl] *a* Bundes-.
federation [fedə'reɪʃən] *n* (*society*)
Verband *m*; (*of states*) Staatenbund *m*.
fed-up [fed'ʌp] *a*: **to be** ~ **with sth** etw
satt haben; **I'm** ~ ich habe die Nase voll.
fee [fiː] *n* Gebühr *f*.
feeble ['fiːbl] *a* person schwach; *excuse*
lahm; ~**-minded** *a* geistesschwach.
feed [fiːd] *n* (*for baby*) Essen *nt*; (*for
animals*) Futter *nt*; *vt irreg* füttern;
(*support*) ernähren; **to** ~ **on** leben von,
fressen; ~**back** (*Tech*) Rückkopplung *f*;
(*information*) Feedback *nt*.
feel [fiːl] *n*: **it has a soft** ~ es fühlt sich
weich an; **to get the** ~ **of sth** sich an etw
(*acc*) gewöhnen; *irreg vt* (*sense*) fühlen;
(*touch*) anfassen; (*think*) meinen; *vi*
(*person*) sich fühlen; (*thing*) sich anfühlen;
I ~ **cold** mir ist kalt; **I** ~ **like a cup of
tea** ich habe Lust auf eine Tasse Tee;
~**er** Fühler *m*; ~**ing** Gefühl *nt*; (*opinion*)
Meinung *f*.
feet [fiːt] *npl of* **foot**.
feign [feɪn] *vt* vortäuschen; ~**ed** *a* vorgetäuscht, Schein-.
feint [feɪnt] *n* Täuschungsmanöver *nt*.
feline ['fiːlaɪn] *a* Katzen-, katzenartig.
fell [fel] *vt* tree fällen; *n* (*hill*) kahle(r) Berg
m; *a*: **with one** ~ **swoop** auf einem
Schlag; auf einen Streich.
fellow ['feləʊ] *n* (*companion*) Gefährte *m*,
Kamerad *m*; (*man*) Kerl *m*; ~ **citizen**
Mitbürger(in *f*) *m*; ~ **countryman**
Landsmann *m*; ~ **feeling** Mitgefühl *nt*;
~ **men** *pl* Mitmenschen *pl*; ~**ship**
(*group*) Körperschaft *f*; (*friendliness*)
Gemeinschaft *f*, Kameradschaft *f*; (*scholarship*) Forschungsstipendium *nt*; ~
worker Mitarbeiter(in *f*) *m*.
felony ['felənɪ] *n* schwere(s) Verbrechen
nt.
felt [felt] *n* Filz *m*.
female ['fiːmeɪl] *n* (*of animals*) Weibchen
nt; *a* weiblich.

feminine ['feminɪn] a (Gram) weiblich; qualities fraulich.

femininity [femɪ'nɪnɪtɪ] n Weiblichkeit f; (quality) Fraulichkeit f.

feminist ['femɪnɪst] n Feminist(in f) m.

fence [fens] n Zaun m; (crook) Hehler m; vi fechten; ~ **in** vt einzäunen; ~ **off** vt absperren.

fencing ['fensɪŋ] n Zaun m; (Sport) Fechten nt.

fend [fend] vi: ~ **for o.s.** sich (allein) durchschlagen.

fender ['fendə*] n Kaminvorsetzer m; (US Aut) Kotflügel m.

ferment [fə'ment] vi (Chem) gären; ['fɜːment] n (excitement) Unruhe f; ~**ation** [fɜːmen'teɪʃən] Gärung f.

fern [fɜːn] n Farn m.

ferocious [fə'rəʊʃəs] a wild, grausam; ~**ly** ad wild.

ferocity [fə'rɒsɪtɪ] n Wildheit f, Grimmigkeit f.

ferry ['ferɪ] n Fähre f; vt übersetzen.

fertile ['fɜːtaɪl] a fruchtbar.

fertility [fə'tɪlɪtɪ] n Fruchtbarkeit f.

fertilization [fɜːtɪlaɪ'zeɪʃən] n Befruchtung f.

fertilize ['fɜːtɪlaɪz] vt (Agr) düngen; (Biol) befruchten; ~**r** (Kunst)dünger m.

fervent ['fɜːvənt] a admirer glühend; hope innig.

festival ['festɪvəl] n (Rel etc) Fest nt; (Art, Mus) Festspiele pl; Festival nt.

festive ['festɪv] a festlich; **the ~ season** (Christmas) die Festzeit f.

festivity [fes'tɪvɪtɪ] n Festlichkeit f.

fetch [fetʃ] vt holen; (in sale) einbringen, erzielen.

fetching ['fetʃɪŋ] a einnehmend, reizend.

fête [feɪt] n Fest nt.

fetish ['fiːtɪʃ] n Fetisch m.

fetters ['fetəz] npl (lit, fig) Fesseln pl.

fetus ['fiːtəs] n (US) = **foetus**.

feud [fjuːd] n Fehde f; vi sich befehden; ~**al** a lehnsherrlich, Feudal-; ~**alism** Lehenswesen nt, Feudalismus m.

fever ['fiːvə*] n Fieber nt; ~**ish** a (Med) fiebrig, Fieber-; (fig) fieberhaft; ~**ishly** ad (fig) fieberhaft.

few [fjuː] a wenig; pron wenige; **a** ~ a, pron einige; ~**er** weniger; ~**est** wenigste(r,s); **a good** ~ ziemlich viele.

fiancé [fɪ'ãːnseɪ] n Verlobte(r) m; ~**e** Verlobte f.

fiasco [fɪ'æskəʊ] n Fiasko nt, Reinfall m.

fib [fɪb] n Flunkerei f; vi flunkern.

fibre, (US) **fiber** ['faɪbə*] n Faser f, Fiber f; (material) Faserstoff m; ~**glass** Glaswolle f.

fickle ['fɪkl] a unbeständig, wankelmütig; ~**ness** Unbeständigkeit f, Wankelmut m.

fiction ['fɪkʃən] n (novels) Romanliteratur f; (story) Erdichtung f; ~**al** a erfunden.

fictitious [fɪk'tɪʃəs] a erfunden, fingiert.

fiddle ['fɪdl] n Geige f, Fiedel f; (trick) Schwindelei f, vt accounts frisieren; ~ **with** vi herumfummeln an (+dat); ~**r** Geiger m.

fidelity [fɪ'delɪtɪ] n Treue f.

fidget ['fɪdʒɪt] vi zappeln; n Zappelphilipp m; ~**y** a nervös, zappelig.

field [fiːld] n Feld nt; (range) Gebiet nt; ~ **day** (gala) Paradetag m; ~ **marshal** Feldmarschall m; ~**work** (Mil) Schanze f; (Univ) Feldforschung f.

fiend [fiːnd] n Teufel m; (beast) Unhold m; Fanatiker(in f) m; ~**ish** a teuflisch.

fierce a, ~**ly** ad [fɪəs, -lɪ] wild; ~**ness** Wildheit f.

fiery ['faɪərɪ] a glühend; (blazing) brennend; (hot-tempered) hitzig, heftig.

fifteen [fɪf'tiːn] num fünfzehn.

fifth [fɪfθ] a fünfte(r,s); n Fünftel nt.

fifty ['fɪftɪ] num fünfzig; ~-~ halbe halbe, fifty fifty (col).

fig [fɪg] n Feige f.

fight [faɪt] n Kampf m; (brawl) Schlägerei f; (argument) Streit m; irreg vt kämpfen gegen; sich schlagen mit; (fig) bekämpfen; vi kämpfen; sich schlagen; streiten; ~**er** Kämpfer(in f) m; (plane) Jagdflugzeug nt; ~**ing** Kämpfen nt; (war) Kampfhandlungen pl.

figment ['fɪgmənt] n ~ **of imagination** reine Einbildung f.

figurative ['fɪgərətɪv] a bildlich.

figure ['fɪgə*] n Form f; (of person) Figur f; (person) Gestalt f; (illustration) Zeichnung f; (number) Ziffer f; vt (US: imagine) glauben; vi (appear) eine Rolle spielen, erscheinen; (US: make sense) stimmen; ~ **out** vt verstehen, herausbekommen; ~**head** (Naut, fig) Galionsfigur f; ~ **skating** Eiskunstlauf m.

filament ['fɪləmənt] n Faden m; (Elec) Glühfaden m.

file [faɪl] n (tool) Feile f; (dossier) Akte f; (folder) Aktenordner m; (row) Reihe f; vt metal, nails feilen; papers abheften; claim einreichen; vi: ~ **in/out** hintereinander hereinkommen/hinausgehen; **in single** ~ einer hinter dem anderen.

filing ['faɪlɪŋ] n Feilen nt; ~**s** pl Feilspäne pl; ~ **cabinet** Aktenschrank m.

fill [fɪl] vt füllen; (occupy) ausfüllen; (satisfy) sättigen; n: **to eat one's** ~ sich richtig satt essen; **to have had one's** ~ genug haben; **to** ~ **the bill** (fig) allen Anforderungen genügen; ~ **in** vt hole (auf)füllen; form ausfüllen; ~ **up** vt container auffüllen; form ausfüllen.

fillet ['fɪlɪt] n Filet nt; vt als Filet herrichten.

filling ['fɪlɪŋ] n (Cook) Füllung f; (for tooth) (Zahn)plombe f; ~ **station** Tankstelle f.

fillip ['fɪlɪp] n Anstoß m, Auftrieb m.

film [fɪlm] n Film m; (layer) Häutchen nt, Film m; vt scene filmen; ~ **star** Filmstar m; ~**strip** Filmstreifen m.

filter ['fɪltə*] n Filter m; (for traffic) Verkehrsfilter m; vt filtern; vi durchsickern; ~ **tip** Filter m, Filtermundstück nt; ~-**tipped cigarette** Filterzigarette f.

filth [fɪlθ] n (lit) Dreck m; (fig) Unflat m; ~**y** a dreckig; (behaviour) gemein; weather scheußlich.

fin [fɪn] n Flosse f.

final ['faɪnl] a letzte(r,s); End-; (conclusive) endgültig; n (Ftbl etc) Endspiel nt; ~**s** pl

(*Univ*) Abschlußexamen *nt*; (*Sport*) Schlußrunde *f*; ~**e** [fiˈnɑːli] (*Theat*) Schlußszene *f*; (*Mus*) Finale *nt*; ~**ist** (*Sport*) Schlußrundenteilnehmer *m*; ~**ize** *vt* endgültige Form geben (+*dat*); abschließen; ~**ly** *ad* (*lastly*) zuletzt; (*eventually*) endlich; (*irrevocably*) endgültig.

finance [faiˈnæns] *n* Finanzwesen *nt*; ~**s** *pl* Finanzen *pl*; (*income*) Einkünfte *pl*; *vt* finanzieren.

financial [faiˈnænʃəl] *a* Finanz-; finanziell; ~**ly** *ad* finanziell.

financier [faiˈnænsiə*] *n* Finanzier *m*.

find [faind] *irreg vt* finden; (*realize*) erkennen; *n* Fund *m*; **to** ~ **sb guilty** jdn für schuldig erklären; **to** ~ **out** herausfinden; ~**ings** *pl* (*Jur*) Ermittlungsergebnis *nt*; (*of report*) Feststellung *f*, Befund *m*.

fine [fain] *a* fein; (*thin*) dünn, fein; (*good*) gut; *clothes* elegant; *weather* schön; *ad* (*well*) gut; (*small*) klein; *n* (*Jur*) Geldstrafe *f*; *vt* (*Jur*) mit einer Geldstrafe belegen; **to cut it** ~ (*fig*) knapp rechnen; ~ **arts** *pl* die schönen Künste *pl*; ~**ness** *n* Feinheit *f*; ~**ry** [ˈfainəri] Putz *m*; ~**sse** [fiˈnes] Finesse *f*.

finger [ˈfiŋgə*] *n* Finger *m*; *vt* befühlen; ~**nail** Fingernagel *m*; ~**print** Fingerabdruck *m*; ~**stall** Fingerling *m*; ~**tip** Fingerspitze *f*; **to have sth at one's** ~**tips** etw parat haben.

finicky [ˈfiniki] *a* pingelig.

finish [ˈfiniʃ] *n* Ende *nt*; (*Sport*) Ziel *nt*; (*of object*) Verarbeitung *f*; (*of paint*) Oberflächenwirkung *f*; *vt* beenden; *book* zu Ende lesen; **to be** ~**ed with sth** fertig sein mit etw; *vi* aufhören; (*Sport*) ans Ziel kommen; ~**ing line** Ziellinie *f*; ~**ing school** Mädchenpensionat *nt*.

finite [ˈfainait] *a* endlich, begrenzt; (*Gram*) finit.

fiord [fjɔːd] *n* Fjord *m*.

fir [fɜː*] *n* Tanne *f*, Fichte *f*.

fire [faiə*] *n* (*lit, fig*) Feuer *nt*; (*damaging*) Brand *m*, Feuer *nt*; **to set** ~ **to sth** etw in Brand stecken; **to be on** ~ brennen; *vt* (*Aut*) zünden; *gun* abfeuern; (*fig*) *imagination* entzünden; (*dismiss*) hinauswerfen; *vi* (*Aut*) zünden; **to** ~ **at sb** auf jdn schießen; ~ **away!** schieß los!; ~ **alarm** Feueralarm *m*; ~**arm** Schußwaffe *f*; ~ **brigade** Feuerwehr *f*; ~ **engine** Feuerwehrauto *nt*; ~ **escape** Feuerleiter *f*; ~ **extinguisher** Löschgerät *nt*; ~**man** Feuerwehrmann *m*; ~**place** offene(r) Kamin *m*; ~**proof** *a* feuerfest; ~**side** Kamin *m*; ~ **station** Feuerwehrwache *f*; ~**wood** Brennholz *nt*; ~**works** *pl* Feuerwerk *nt*.

firing [ˈfaiəriŋ] *n* Schießen *nt*; ~ **squad** Exekutionskommando *nt*.

firm *a*, ~**ly** *ad* [fɜːm,-li] fest; (*determined*) entschlossen; *n* Firma *f*; ~**ness** Festigkeit *f*; Entschlossenheit *f*.

first [fɜːst] *a* erste(r,s); *ad* zuerst; *arrive* als erste(r); *happen* zum erstenmal; *n* (*person: in race*) Erste(r) *mf*; (*Univ*) Eins *f*; (*Aut*) erste(r) Gang *m*; **at** ~ zuerst, anfangs; ~

of all zu allererst; ~ **aid** Erste Hilfe *f*; ~**-aid kit** Verbandskasten *m*; ~**-class** *a* erstklassig; (*travel*) erste(r) Klasse; ~**-hand** *a* aus erster Hand; ~ **lady** (*US*) First Lady *f*; ~**ly** *ad* erstens; ~ **name** Vorname *m*; ~ **night** Premiere *f*; Erstaufführung *f*; ~**-rate** *a* erstklassig.

fiscal [ˈfiskəl] *a* fiskalisch, Finanz-.

fish [fiʃ] *n* Fisch *m*; *vt* *river* angeln in (+*dat*); *sea* fischen in (+*dat*); *vi* fischen; angeln; ~ **out** *vt* herausfischen; **to go** ~**ing** angeln gehen; (*in sea*) fischen gehen; ~**erman** Fischer *m*; ~**ery** Fischgrund *m*; ~ **finger** Fischstäbchen *nt*; ~ **hook** Angelhaken *m*; ~**ing boat** Fischerboot *nt*; ~**ing line** Angelschnur *f*; ~**ing rod** Angel(rute) *f*; ~**ing tackle** Angelzeug *nt*; ~ **market** Fischmarkt *m*; ~**monger** Fischhändler *m*; ~ **slice** Fischvorlegemesser *nt*; ~**y** *a* (*col*: *suspicious*) faul.

fission [ˈfiʃən] *n* Spaltung *f*.

fissure [ˈfiʃə*] *n* Riß *m*.

fist [fist] *n* Faust *f*.

fit [fit] *a* (*Med*) gesund; (*Sport*) in Form, fit; (*suitable*) geeignet; *vt* passen (+*dat*); (*insert, attach*) einsetzen; *vi* (*correspond*) passen (zu); (*clothes*) passen; (*in space, gap*) hineinpassen; *n* (*of clothes*) Sitz *m*; (*Med, of anger*) Anfall *m*; (*of laughter*) Krampf *m*; ~ **in** *vi* sich einfügen; *vt* einpassen; ~ **out** *vt*, ~ **up** *vt* ausstatten; ~**fully**, **by** ~**s and starts** *move* ruckweise; *work* unregelmäßig; ~**ment** Einrichtungsgegenstand *m*; ~**ness** (*suitability*) Eignung *f*; (*Med*) Gesundheit *f*; (*Sport*) Fitneß *f*; ~**ter** (*Tech*) Monteur *m*; ~**ting** *a* passend; *n* (*of dress*) Anprobe *f*; (*piece of equipment*) (Ersatz)teil *nt*; ~**tings** *pl* Zubehör *nt*.

five [faiv] *num* fünf; ~**r** (*Brit*) Fünf-Pfund-Note *f*.

fix [fiks] *vt* befestigen; (*settle*) festsetzen; (*repair*) richten, reparieren; *drink* zurechtmachen; *n*: **in a** ~ in der Klemme; ~**ed** *a* repariert; *time* abgemacht; **it was** ~**ed** (*dishonest*) das war Schiebung; ~**ture** [ˈfikstʃə*] Installationsteil *m*; (*Sport*) Spiel *nt*.

fizz [fiz] *n* Sprudeln *nt*; *vi* sprudeln.

fizzle [ˈfizl] *vi* zischen; ~ **out** *vi* verpuffen.

fizzy [ˈfizi] *a* Sprudel-, sprudelnd.

fjord [fjɔːd] *n* = *fiord*.

flabbergasted [ˈflæbəgɑːstid] *a* (*col*) platt.

flabby [ˈflæbi] *a* wabbelig.

flag [flæg] *n* Fahne *f*; *vi* (*strength*) nachlassen; (*spirit*) erlahmen; ~ **down** *vt* stoppen, abwinken.

flagon [ˈflægən] *n* bauchige (Wein)flasche *f*, Krug *m*.

flagpole [ˈflægpəʊl] *n* Fahnenstange *f*.

flagrant [ˈfleigrənt] *a* offenkundig; *offence* schamlos; *violation* flagrant.

flagstone [ˈflægstəʊn] *n* Steinplatte *f*.

flair [flɛə*] *n* (*talent*) Talent *nt*; (*of style*) Schick *m*.

flake [fleik] *n* (*of snow*) Flocke *f*, (*of rust*) Schuppe *f*; *vi* (*also* ~ **off**) abblättern.

flamboyant [flæmˈbɔiənt] *a* extravagant; *colours* brillant; *gesture* großartig.

flame [fleɪm] n Flamme f.

flaming ['fleɪmɪŋ] a (col) verdammt; row irre.

flamingo [fləˈmɪŋgəʊ] n Flamingo m.

flan [flæn] n Obsttorte f.

flank [flæŋk] n Flanke f; vt flankieren.

flannel ['flænl] n Flanell m; (face —) Waschlappen m; (col) Geschwafel nt; ~s pl Flanellhose f.

flap [flæp] n Klappe f; (col: crisis) (helle) Aufregung f; vt wings schlagen mit; vi lose herabhängen; flattern; (col: panic) sich aufregen.

flare [flɛə*] n (signal) Leuchtsignal nt; (in skirt etc) Weite f; ~ up vi aufflammen; (fig) aufbrausen; (revolt) (plötzlich) ausbrechen.

flared [flɛəd] a trousers ausgestellt.

flash [flæʃ] n Blitz m; (news —) Kurzmeldung f; (Phot) Blitzlicht nt; vt aufleuchten lassen; message durchgeben; vi aufleuchten; **in a** ~ im Nu; **to** ~ **by** or **past** vorbeirasen; ~**back** Rückblende f; ~ **bulb** Blitzlichtbirne f; ~**er** (Aut) Blinker m.

flashy ['flæʃɪ] a (pej) knallig.

flask [flɑːsk] n Reiseflasche f; (Chem) Kolben m; (vacuum —) Thermosflasche f.

flat [flæt] a flach; (dull) matt; (Mus) erniedrigt; beer schal; tyre platt; **A** ~ as; ad (Mus) zu tief; n (rooms) Wohnung f; (Mus) b nt; (Aut) Reifenpanne f, Platte(r) m; ~ **broke** a (col) völlig pleite; ~**footed** a plattfüßig; ~**ly** ad glatt; ~**ness** Flachheit f; ~**ten** vt (also ~**ten out**) platt machen, (ein)ebnen.

flatter ['flætə*] vt schmeicheln (+dat); ~**er** Schmeichler(in f) m; ~**ing** a schmeichelhaft; ~**y** Schmeichelei f.

flatulence ['flætjʊləns] n Blähungen pl.

flaunt [flɔːnt] vt prunken mit.

flavour, (US) **flavor** ['fleɪvə*] n Geschmack m; vt würzen; ~**ing** Würze f.

flaw [flɔː] n Fehler m; (in argument) schwache(r) Punkt m; ~**less** a einwandfrei.

flax [flæks] n Flachs m; ~**en** a flachsfarben.

flea [fliː] n Floh m.

flee [fliː] irreg vi fliehen; vt fliehen vor (+dat); country fliehen aus.

fleece [fliːs] n Schaffell nt, Vlies nt; vt (col) schröpfen.

fleet [fliːt] n Flotte f.

fleeting ['fliːtɪŋ] a flüchtig.

flesh [fleʃ] n Fleisch nt; (of fruit) Fruchtfleisch nt; ~ **wound** Fleischwunde f.

flex [fleks] n (Leitungs)kabel nt; vt beugen, biegen; ~**ibility** [fleksɪˈbɪlɪtɪ] Biegsamkeit f; (fig) Flexibilität f; ~**ible** a biegsam; plans flexibel.

flick [flɪk] n Schnippen nt; (blow) leichte(r) Schlag m; vt leicht schlagen; ~ **through** vt durchblättern; **to** ~ **sth off** etw wegschnippen.

flicker ['flɪkə*] n Flackern nt; (of emotion) Funken m; vi flackern.

flier ['flaɪə*] n Flieger m.

flight [flaɪt] n Fliegen nt; (journey) Flug m; (fleeing) Flucht f; ~ **of stairs** Treppe f;

to take ~ die Flucht ergreifen; **to put to** ~ in die Flucht schlagen; ~ **deck** Flugdeck nt; ~**y** a flatterhaft.

flimsy ['flɪmzɪ] a nicht stabil, windig; (thin) hauchdünn; excuse fadenscheinig.

flinch [flɪntʃ] vi zurückschrecken (away from vor +dat).

fling [flɪŋ] vt irreg schleudern.

flint [flɪnt] n (in lighter) Feuerstein m.

flip [flɪp] vt werfen; **he** ~**ped the lid off** er klappte den Deckel auf.

flippancy ['flɪpənsɪ] n Leichtfertigkeit f.

flippant ['flɪpənt] a schnippisch; **to be about sth** etw nicht ernst nehmen.

flirt [flɜːt] vi flirten; n kokette(s) Mädchen nt; **he/she is a** ~ er/sie flirtet gern; ~**ation** [flɜːˈteɪʃən] Flirt m.

flit [flɪt] vi flitzen.

float [fləʊt] n (Fishing) Schwimmer m; (esp in procession) Plattformwagen m; vi schwimmen; (in air) schweben; vt schwimmen lassen; (Comm) gründen; currency floaten; ~**ing** a (lit) schwimmend; (fig) votes unentschieden.

flock [flɒk] n (of sheep, Rel) Herde f; (of birds) Schwarm m; (of people) Schar f.

flog [flɒg] vt prügeln; peitschen; (col: sell) verkaufen.

flood [flʌd] n Überschwemmung f; (fig) Flut f; **the F**~ die Sintflut f; **to be in Hochwasser haben**; vt (lit, fig) überschwemmen; ~**ing** Überschwemmung f; ~**light** n Flutlicht nt; vt anstrahlen; ~**lighting** Beleuchtung f.

floor [flɔː*] n (of building) (Fuß)boden m; (storey) Stock m; vt person zu Boden schlagen; **ground** ~ (Brit), **first** ~ (US) Erdgeschoß nt; **first** ~ (Brit), **second** ~ (US) erste(r) Stock m; ~**board** Diele f; ~ **show** Kabarettvorstellung f; ~**walker** (Comm) Abteilungsaufseher m.

flop [flɒp] n Plumps m; (failure) Reinfall m; vi (fail) durchfallen; **the project** ~**ped** aus dem Plan wurde nichts.

floppy ['flɒpɪ] a hängend; ~ **hat** Schlapphut m.

flora ['flɔːrə] n Flora f; ~**l** a Blumen-.

florid ['flɒrɪd] a style blumig.

florist ['flɒrɪst] n Blumenhändler(in f) m; ~'**s (shop)** Blumengeschäft nt.

flotsam ['flɒtsəm] n Strandgut nt.

flounce [flaʊns] n (on dress) Besatz m; vi: ~ **in/out** hinein-/hinausstürmen.

flounder ['flaʊndə*] vi herumstrampeln; (fig) ins Schleudern kommen.

flour ['flaʊə*] n Mehl nt.

flourish ['flʌrɪʃ] vi blühen; gedeihen; vt (wave) schwingen; n (waving) Schwingen nt; (of trumpets) Tusch m, Fanfare f; ~**ing** a blühend.

flout [flaʊt] vt mißachten, sich hinwegsetzen über (+acc).

flow [fləʊ] n Fließen nt; (of sea) Flut f; vi fließen.

flower ['flaʊə*] n Blume f; vi blühen; ~**bed** Blumenbeet nt; ~**pot** Blumentopf m; ~**y** a style blumenreich.

flowing ['fləʊɪŋ] a fließend; hair wallend; style flüssig.

flu [fluː] n Grippe f.

fluctuate ['flʌktjʊeɪt] vi schwanken.
fluctuation [flʌktjʊ'eɪʃən] n Schwankung f.
fluency ['fluːənsɪ] n Flüssigkeit f; **his ~ in English** seine Fähigkeit, fließend Englisch zu sprechen.
fluent a **~ly** ad ['fluːənt,-lɪ] speech flüssig; **to be ~ in German** fließend Deutsch sprechen.
fluff [flʌf] n Fussel f; **~y** a flaumig; pastry flockig.
fluid ['fluːɪd] n Flüssigkeit f; a (lit) flüssig; (fig) plans veränderbar.
fluke [fluːk] n (col) Dusel m.
fluorescent [flʊə'resnt] a fluoreszierend, Leucht-.
fluoride ['flʊəraɪd] n Fluorid nt.
flurry ['flʌrɪ] n (of activity) Aufregung f; (of snow) Gestöber nt.
flush [flʌʃ] n Erröten nt; (of excitement) Glühen nt; (Cards) Sequenz f; vt (aus)spülen; vi erröten; a glatt; **~ed** a rot.
fluster ['flʌstə*] n Verwirrung f; **~ed** a verwirrt.
flute [fluːt] n Querflöte f.
fluted ['fluːtɪd] a gerillt.
flutter ['flʌtə*] n (of wings) Flattern nt; (of excitement) Beben nt; vi flattern; (person) rotieren.
flux [flʌks] n: **in a state of ~** in Fluß.
fly [flaɪ] n (insect) Fliege f; (on trousers, also **flies**) (Hosen)schlitz m; irreg vt fliegen; vi fliegen; (flee) fliehen; (flag) wehen; **~ open** vi auffliegen; **let ~** vti (shoot) losschießen; (verbally) loswettern; insults loslassen; **~ing** n Fliegen nt; **with ~ing colours** mit fliegenden Fahnen; **~ing saucer** fliegende Untertasse f; **~ing start** gute(r) Start m; **~ing visit** Stippvisite f; **~over** (Brit) Überführung f; **~paper** Fliegenfänger m; **~past** Luftparade f; **~sheet** (for tent) Regendach nt; **~swatter** Fliegenwedel m; **~wheel** Schwungrad nt.
foal [fəʊl] n Fohlen nt.
foam [fəʊm] n Schaum m; (plastic etc) Schaumgummi m; vi schäumen.
fob [fɒb] n: **~ off** vt andrehen (sb with sth jdm etw); (with promise) abspeisen.
focal ['fəʊkəl] a im Brennpunkt (stehend), Brennpunkt-.
focus ['fəʊkəs] n Brennpunkt m; (fig) Mittelpunkt m; vt attention konzentrieren; camera scharf einstellen; vi sich konzentrieren (on auf +acc); **in ~** scharf eingestellt; **out of ~** unscharf (eingestellt).
fodder ['fɒdə*] n Futter nt.
foe [fəʊ] n (liter) Feind m, Gegner m.
foetus ['fiːtəs] n Fötus m.
fog [fɒg] n Nebel m; vt issue verunklären, verwirren; **~gy** a neblig, trüb.
foible ['fɔɪbl] n Schwäche f, Faible nt.
foil [fɔɪl] vt vereiteln; n (metal, also fig) Folie f; (fencing) Florett nt.
fold [fəʊld] n (bend, crease) Falte f; (Agr) Pferch m; (for sheep) Pferch m; vt falten; **~ up** vt map etc zusammenfalten; vi (business) eingehen; **~er** (pamphlet) Broschüre f; (portfolio) Schnellhefter m; **~ing** a chair etc zusammenklappbar, Klapp-.

foliage ['fəʊlɪdʒ] n Laubwerk nt.
folio ['fəʊlɪəʊ] n Foliant m.
folk [fəʊk] n Volk nt; a Volks-; **~s** pl Leute pl; **~lore** (study) Volkskunde f; (tradition) Folklore f; **~song** Volkslied nt; (modern) Folksong m.
follow ['fɒləʊ] vt folgen (+dat); (obey) befolgen; fashion mitmachen; profession nachgehen (+dat); (understand) folgen können (+dat); vi folgen; (result) sich ergeben; **as ~s** wie im folgenden; **~ up** vt (weiter) verfolgen; **~er** Anhänger(in f) m; **~ing** a folgend; n Folgende(s) nt; (people) Gefolgschaft f.
folly ['fɒlɪ] n Torheit f.
fond [fɒnd] a: **to be ~ of** gern haben; **~ly** ad (with love) liebevoll; (foolishly) törichterweise; **~ness** Vorliebe f; (for people) Liebe f.
font [fɒnt] n Taufbecken nt.
food [fuːd] n Essen nt, Nahrung f; (for animals) Futter nt; **~ mixer** Küchenmixer m; **~poisoning** Lebensmittelvergiftung f; **~stuffs** pl Lebensmittel pl.
fool [fuːl] n Narr m, Närrin f; (jester) (Hof)narr m, Hanswurst m; (food) Mus nt; vt (deceive) hereinlegen; vi (behave like a ~) (herum)albern; **~hardy** a tollkühn; **~ish** a, **~ishly** ad dumm; albern; **~ishness** Dummheit f; **~proof** a idiotensicher.
foot [fʊt] n Fuß m; (of animal) Pfote f; **to put one's ~ in it** ins Fettnäpfchen treten; **on ~** zu Fuß; vt bill bezahlen; **~ball** Fußball m; **~baller** Fußballer m; **~brake** Fußbremse f; **~bridge** Fußgängerbrücke f; **~hills** pl Ausläufer pl; **~hold** Halt m; Stütze f; **~ing** (lit) Halt m; (fig) Verhältnis nt; **to get a ~ing in society** in der Gesellschaft Fuß fassen; **to be on a good ~ing with sb** mit jdm auf gutem Fuß stehen; **~light** Rampenlicht nt; **~man** Bediente(r) m; **~-and-mouth** (disease) Maul- und Klauenseuche f; **~note** Fußnote f; **~path** Fußweg m; **~rest** Fußstütze f; **~sore** a fußkrank; **~step** Schritt m; **in his father's ~steps** in den Fußstapfen seines Vaters; **~wear** Schuhzeug nt.
fop [fɒp] n Geck m.
for [fɔː*] prep für; cj denn; **what ~?** wozu?
forage ['fɒrɪdʒ] n (Vieh)futter nt; vi nach Nahrung suchen.
foray ['fɒreɪ] n Raubzug m.
forbearing [fɔ'bɛərɪŋ] a geduldig.
forbid [fə'bɪd] vt irreg verbieten; **~den** a verboten; **~ding** a einschüchternd, abschreckend.
force [fɔːs] n Kraft f, Stärke f; (compulsion) Zwang m; (Mil) Truppen pl; vt zwingen; lock aufbrechen; plant hochzüchten; **in ~** rule gültig; group in großer Stärke; **the F~s** pl die Armee; vi a smile gezwungen; landing Not-; **~ful** a speech kraftvoll; personality resolut.
forceps ['fɔːseps] npl Zange f.
forcible ['fɔːsəbl] a (convincing) wirksam, überzeugend; (violent) gewaltsam.
forcibly ['fɔːsəblɪ] ad unter Zwang, zwangsweise.
ford [fɔːd] n Furt f; vt durchwaten.

fore [fɔː*] a vorder, Vorder-; n: **to the ~ in** den Vordergrund.

forearm ['fɔːrɑːm] n Unterarm m.

foreboding [fɔː'bəʊdɪŋ] n Vorahnung f.

forecast ['fɔːkɑːst] n Vorhersage f; vt irreg voraussagen.

forecourt ['fɔːkɔːt] n (of garage) Vorplatz m.

forefathers ['fɔːfɑːðəz] npl Vorfahren pl.

forefinger ['fɔːfɪŋgə*] n Zeigefinger m.

forefront ['fɔːfrʌnt] n Spitze f.

forego [fɔː'gəʊ] vt irreg verzichten auf (+acc); ~**ing** a vorangehend; ~**ne con-clusion** ausgemachte Sache.

foreground ['fɔːgraʊnd] n Vordergrund m.

forehead ['fɔrɪd] n Stirn f.

foreign ['fɔrɪn] a Auslands-; country, accent ausländisch; trade Außen-; body Fremd-; ~**er** Ausländer(in f) m; ~ **exchange** Devisen pl; ~ **minister** Außenminister m.

foreman ['fɔːmən] n Vorarbeiter m.

foremost ['fɔːməʊst] a erste(r,s).

forensic [fə'rensɪk] a gerichtsmedizinisch.

forerunner ['fɔːrʌnə*] n Vorläufer m.

foresee [fɔː'siː] vt irreg vorhersehen; ~**able** a absehbar.

foreshore ['fɔːʃɔː*] n Küste f, Küstenland nt.

foresight ['fɔːsaɪt] n Voraussicht f.

forest ['fɔrɪst] n Wald m.

forestall [fɔː'stɔːl] vt zuvorkommen (+dat).

forestry ['fɔrɪstrɪ] n Forstwirtschaft f.

foretaste ['fɔːteɪst] n Vorgeschmack m.

foretell [fɔː'tel] vt irreg vorhersagen.

forever [fə'revə*] ad für immer.

forewarn [fɔː'wɔːn] vt vorherwarnen.

foreword ['fɔːwɜːd] n Vorwort nt.

forfeit ['fɔːfɪt] n Einbuße f; vt verwirken.

forge [fɔːdʒ] n Schmiede f; vt fälschen; iron schmieden; ~ **ahead** vi Fortschritte machen; ~**r** Fälscher m; ~**ry** Fälschung f.

forget [fə'get] vti irreg vergessen; ~**ful** a vergeßlich; ~**fulness** Vergeßlichkeit f.

forgive [fə'gɪv] vt irreg verzeihen (sb for sth jdm etw).

forgiveness [fə'gɪvnəs] n Verzeihung f.

forgo [fɔː'gəʊ] see **forego.**

fork [fɔːk] n Gabel f; (in road) Gabelung f; vi (road) sich gabeln; ~ **out** (col: pay) blechen; ~**ed** a gegabelt; lightning zick-zackförmig.

forlorn [fə'lɔːn] a person verlassen; hope vergeblich.

form [fɔːm] n Form f; (type) Art f; (figure) Gestalt f; (Sch) Klasse f; (bench) (Schul-)bank f; (document) Formular nt; vt formen; (be part of) bilden.

formal ['fɔːməl] a character, formell; occasion offiziell; ~**ity** [fɔː'mælɪtɪ] Förm-lichkeit f; (of occasion) offizielle(r) Charakter m; ~**ities** pl Formalitäten pl; ~**ly** ad (ceremoniously) formell; (officially) offiziell.

format ['fɔːmæt] n Format nt.

formation [fɔː'meɪʃən] n Bildung f; Gestal-tung f; (Aviat) Formation f.

formative ['fɔːmətɪv] a years formend.

former ['fɔːmə*] a früher; (opposite of latter) erstere(r,s); ~**ly** ad früher.

Formica ® [fɔː'maɪkə] n Resopal ® nt.

formidable ['fɔːmɪdəbl] a furchtbar; gewaltig.

formula ['fɔːmjʊlə] n Formel f; ~**te** ['fɔːmjʊleɪt] vt formulieren.

forsake [fə'seɪk] vt irreg im Stich lassen, verlassen; habit aufgeben.

fort [fɔːt] n Feste f, Fort nt.

forte ['fɔːtɪ] n Stärke f, starke Seite f.

forth [fɔːθ] ad: **and so ~** und so weiter; ~**coming** a kommend; character entgegenkommend; ~**right** a offen, gerade heraus.

fortification [fɔːtɪfɪ'keɪʃən] n Befestigung f.

fortify ['fɔːtɪfaɪ] vt (ver)stärken; (protect) befestigen.

fortitude ['fɔːtɪtjuːd] n Seelenstärke f, Mut m.

fortnight ['fɔːtnaɪt] n zwei Wochen pl, vierzehn Tage pl; ~**ly** a zweiwöchentlich; ad alle vierzehn Tage.

fortress ['fɔːtrɪs] n Festung f.

fortuitous [fɔː'tjuːɪtəs] a zufällig.

fortunate ['fɔːtʃənɪt] a glücklich; ~**ly** ad glücklicherweise, zum Glück.

fortune ['fɔːtʃən] n Glück nt; (money) Ver-mögen nt; ~**teller** Wahrsager(in f) m.

forty ['fɔːtɪ] num vierzig.

forum ['fɔːrəm] n Forum nt.

forward ['fɔːwəd] a vordere(r,s); movement vorwärts; person vorlaut; planning Voraus-; ad vorwärts; n (Sport) Stürmer m; vt (send) schicken; (help) fördern; ~**s** ad vorwärts.

fossil ['fɒsl] n Fossil nt, Versteinerung f.

foster ['fɒstə*] vt talent fördern; ~ **child** Pflegekind nt; ~ **mother** Pflegemutter f.

foul [faʊl] a schmutzig; language gemein; weather schlecht; n (Sport) Foul nt; vt mechanism blockieren; (dirty) foulen.

found [faʊnd] vt (establish) gründen; ~**ation** [faʊn'deɪʃən] (act) Gründung f; (fig) Fundament nt; ~**ations** pl Fundament nt.

founder ['faʊndə*] n Gründer(in f) m; vi sinken.

foundry ['faʊndrɪ] n Gießerei f, Eisenhütte f.

fount [faʊnt] n (liter) Quell m; ~**ain** (Spring)brunnen m; ~**ain pen** Füllfederhalter m.

four [fɔː*] num vier; ~**on all** ~s auf allen vieren; ~**some** Quartett nt; ~**teen** num vierzehn; ~**th** a vierte(r,s).

fowl [faʊl] n Huhn nt; (food) Geflügel nt.

fox [fɒks] n Fuchs m; ~**ed** a verblüfft; ~**hunting** Fuchsjagd f; ~**trot** Foxtrott m.

foyer ['fɔɪeɪ] n Foyer nt, Vorhalle f.

fracas ['frækɑː] n Radau m.

fraction ['frækʃən] n (Math) Bruch m; (part) Bruchteil m.

fracture ['fræktʃə*] n (Med) Bruch m; vt brechen.

fragile ['frædʒaɪl] a zerbrechlich.

fragment ['frægmənt] n Bruchstück nt, Fragment nt; (small part) Stück nt, Splitter m; ~ary [fræg'mentəri] a bruchstückhaft, fragmentarisch.

fragrance ['freigrəns] n Duft m.

fragrant ['freigrənt] a duftend.

frail [freil] a schwach, gebrechlich.

frame [freim] n Rahmen m; (body) Gestalt f; vt einrahmen; (make) gestalten, machen; (col: incriminate) to ~ sb jdm etw anhängen; ~ of mind Verfassung f; ~work Rahmen m; (of society) Gefüge nt.

franchise ['fræntʃaiz] n (aktives) Wahlrecht nt.

frank [fræŋk] a offen; ~furter Saitenwürstchen nt; ~ly ad offen gesagt; ~ness Offenheit f.

frankincense ['fræŋkinsens] n Weihrauch m.

frantic ['fræntik] a effort verzweifelt; ~with worry außer sich vor Sorge; ~ally ad außer sich; verzweifelt.

fraternal [frə'tɜ:nl] a brüderlich.

fraternity [frə'tɜ:niti] n (club) Vereinigung f; (spirit) Brüderlichkeit f; (US Sch) Studentenverbindung f.

fraternization [frætənai'zeiʃən] n Verbrüderung f.

fraternize ['frætənaiz] vi fraternisieren.

fraud [frɔ:d] n (trickery) Betrug m; (trick) Schwindel m, Trick m; (person) Schwindler(in f) m.

fraudulent ['frɔ:djulənt] a betrügerisch.

fraught [frɔ:t] a voller (with gen).

fray [frei] n Rauferei f; vti ausfransen.

freak [fri:k] n Monstrosität f; (crazy person) Irre(r) mf; (storm etc) Ausnahmeerscheinung f; a storm, conditions anormal; animal monströs; ~ out vi (col) durchdrehen.

freckle ['frekl] n Sommersprosse f; ~d a sommersprossig.

free [fri:] a frei; (loose) lose; (liberal) freigebig; to get sth ~ etw umsonst bekommen; you're ~ to . . . es steht dir frei zu . . .; vt (set free) befreien; (unblock) freimachen; ~dom Freiheit f; ~-for-all allgemeine(r) Wettbewerb m; (fight) allgemeine(s) Handgemenge nt; ~ kick Freistoß m; ~lance a frei; artist freischaffend; ~ly ad frei; lose; (generously) reichlich; admit offen; ~mason Freimaurer m; ~masonry Freimaurerei f; ~ trade Freihandel m; ~way (US) Autobahn f; ~wheel vi im Freilauf fahren.

freesia ['fri:ʒə] n Freesie f.

freeze [fri:z] irreg vi gefrieren; (feel cold) frieren; vt (lit, fig) einfrieren; n (fig, Fin) Stopp m; ~r Tiefkühltruhe f; (in fridge) Gefrierfach nt.

freezing ['fri:ziŋ] a eisig; (~ cold) eiskalt; ~ point Gefrierpunkt m.

freight [freit] n (goods) Fracht f; (money charged) Fracht(gebühr) f; ~ car (US) Güterwagen m; ~er (Naut) Frachtschiff nt.

French [frentʃ] a: ~ fried potatoes pl Pommes frites pl; ~ window Verandatür f; see appendix.

frenzy ['frenzi] n Raserei f, wilde Aufregung f.

frequency ['fri:kwənsi] n Häufigkeit f; (Phys) Frequenz f.

frequent a ~ly ad ['fri:kwənt,-li] häufig; [fri:'kwent] vt (regelmäßig) besuchen.

fresco ['freskəu] n Fresko nt.

fresh [freʃ] a frisch; (new) neu; (cheeky) frech; ~en (also ~en up) vi (sich) auffrischen; (person) sich frisch machen; vt auffrischen; ~ly ad gerade; ~ness Frische f; ~water a fish Süßwasser-.

fret [fret] vi sich (dat) Sorgen machen (about über+acc).

friar ['fraiə*] n Klosterbruder m.

friction ['frikʃən] n (lit, fig) Reibung f.

Friday ['fraidei] n Freitag m; see good.

fridge [fridʒ] n Kühlschrank m.

fried [fraid] a gebraten.

friend [frend] n Bekannte(r) mf; (more intimate) Freund(in f) m; ~liness Freundlichkeit f; ~ly a freundlich; relations freundschaftlich; ~ship Freundschaft f.

frieze [fri:z] n Fries m.

frigate ['frigit] n Fregatte f.

fright [frait] n Schrecken m; you look a ~ (col) du siehst unmöglich aus!; ~en vt erschrecken; to be ~ened Angst haben; ~ening a schrecklich; ängstigend; ~ful a, ~fully ad (col) schrecklich, furchtbar.

frigid ['fridʒid] a kalt, eisig; woman frigide; ~ity [fri'dʒiditi] Kälte f; Frigidität f.

frill [fril] n Rüsche f.

fringe [frindʒ] n Besatz m; (hair) Pony m; (fig) äußere(r) Rand m, Peripherie f.

frisky ['friski] a lebendig, ausgelassen.

fritter ['fritə*] n: ~ away vt vertun, verplempern.

frivolity [fri'voliti] n Leichtfertigkeit f, Frivolität f.

frivolous ['frivələs] a frivol, leichtsinnig.

frizzy ['frizi] a kraus.

fro [frəu] see to.

frock [frɒk] n Kleid nt.

frog [frɒg] n Frosch m; ~man Froschmann m.

frolic ['frɒlik] n lustige(r) Streich m; vi ausgelassen sein.

from [frɒm] prep von; (place) aus; (judging by) nach; (because of) wegen (+gen).

front [frʌnt] n Vorderseite f; (of house) Fassade f; (promenade) Strandpromenade f; (Mil, Pol, Met) Front f; (fig: appearances) Fassade f; a (forward) vordere(r,s), Vorder-; (first) vorderste(r,s); page erste(r,s); door Eingangs-, Haus-; in ~ ad vorne; in ~ of prep vor; ~age Vorderfront f; ~al a frontal, Vorder-; ~ier ['frʌntiə*] Grenze f; ~ room (Brit) Vorderzimmer nt, Wohnzimmer nt; ~wheel drive Vorderradantrieb m.

frost [frɒst] n Frost m; ~bite Erfrierung f; ~ed a glass Milch-; ~y a frostig.

froth [frɒθ] n Schaum m; ~y a schaumig.

frown [fraun] n Stirnrunzeln nt; vi die Stirn runzeln.

frozen ['frəuzn] a food gefroren; (Fin) assets festgelegt.

frugal ['fru:gəl] a sparsam, bescheiden.

fruit [fru:t] *n* (*particular*) Frucht *f*; **I like** ~ ich esse gern Obst; ~**erer** Obsthändler *m*; ~**ful** a fruchtbar; ~**ion** [fru:'ıʃən] Verwirklichung *f*; **to come to** ~**ion** in Erfüllung gehen; ~ **machine** Spielautomat *m*; ~ **salad** Obstsalat *m*.

frustrate [frʌs'treıt] *vt* vereiteln; ~**d** a gehemmt; (*Psych*) frustriert.

frustration [frʌs'treıʃən] *n* Behinderung *f*; Frustration *f.*

fry [fraı] *vt* braten; **small** ~ *pl* kleine Leute *pl*; (*children*) Kleine(n) *pl*; ~**ing pan** Bratpfanne *f.*

fuchsia ['fju:ʃə] *n* Fuchsie *f.*

fuddy-duddy ['fʌdıdʌdı] *n* altmodische(r) Kauz *m.*

fudge [fʌdʒ] *n* Karamellen *pl.*

fuel [fjʊəl] *n* Treibstoff *m*; (*for heating*) Brennstoff *m*; (*for cigarette lighter*) Benzin *nt*; ~ **oil** (*diesel fuel*) Heizöl *nt*; ~ **tank** Tank *m.*

fugitive ['fju:dʒıtıv] *n* Flüchtling *m*; (*from prison*) Flüchtige(r) *mf.*

fulfil [fʊl'fıl] *vt* duty erfüllen; *promise* einhalten; ~**ment** Erfüllung *f*; Einhaltung *f.*

full [fʊl] a *box, bottle, price* voll; *person* (*satisfied*) satt; *member, power, employment, moon* Voll-; (*complete*) vollständig, Voll-; *speed* höchste(r, s); *skirt* weit; **in** ~ vollständig, ungekürzt; ~**back** Verteidiger *m*; ~**ness** Fülle *f*; ~ **stop** Punkt *m*; ~-**time** *a job* Ganztags-; *ad work* hauptberuflich; ~**y** *ad* völlig; ~**y-fledged** a (*lit, fig*) flügge; a ~**y-fledged teacher** ein vollausgebildeter Lehrer.

fumble ['fʌmbl] *vi* herumfummeln (*with, at* an+*dat*).

fume [fju:m] *vi* rauchen, qualmen; (*fig*) wütend sein, kochen (*col*); ~**s** *pl* Abgase *pl*; Qualm *m.*

fumigate ['fju:mıgeıt] *vt* ausräuchern.

fun [fʌn] *n* Spaß *m*; **to make** ~ **of** sich lustig machen über (+*acc*).

function ['fʌŋkʃən] *n* Funktion *f*; (*occasion*) Veranstaltung *f*, Feier *f*; *vi* funktionieren; ~**al** a funktionell, praktisch.

fund [fʌnd] *n* (*money*) Geldmittel *pl*, Fonds *m*; (*store*) Schatz *m*, Vorrat *m.*

fundamental [fʌndə'mentl] a fundamental, grundlegend; ~**s** *pl* Grundbegriffe *pl*; ~**ly** *ad* im Grunde.

funeral ['fju:nərəl] *n* Beerdigung *f*; a Beerdigungs-.

fungus ['fʌŋgəs] *n, pl* **fungi** *or* **funguses** Pilz *m.*

funicular [fju:'nıkjʊlə*] *n* (Draht)seilbahn *f.*

funnel ['fʌnl] *n* Trichter *m*; (*Naut*) Schornstein *m.*

funnily ['fʌnılı] *ad* komisch; ~ **enough** merkwürdigerweise.

funny ['fʌnı] a komisch; ~ **bone** Musikantenknochen *m.*

fur [f3:*] *n* Pelz *m*; ~ **coat** Pelzmantel *m.*

furious a, ~**ly** *ad* ['fjʊərıəs, -lı] wütend; *attempt* heftig.

furlong ['f3:lɒŋ] *n* = 220 yards.

furlough ['f3:ləʊ] *n* (*US*) Urlaub *m.*

furnace ['f3:nıs] *n* (Brenn)ofen *m.*

furnish ['f3:nıʃ] *vt* einrichten, möblieren;

(*supply*) versehen; ~**ings** *pl* Einrichtung *f.*

furniture ['f3:nıtʃə*] *n* Möbel *pl.*

furrow ['fʌrəʊ] *n* Furche *f.*

furry ['f3:rı] a pelzartig; *tongue* pelzig; *animal* Pelz-.

further ['f3:ðə*] *comp of* **far**; a weitere(r,s); *ad* weiter; *vt* fördern; ~ **education** Weiterbildung *f*; Erwachsenenbildung *f*; ~**more** *ad* ferner.

furthest ['f3:ðıst] *superl of* **far**.

furtive a, ~**ly** *ad* ['f3:tıv, -lı] verstohlen.

fury ['fjʊərı] *n* Wut *f*, Zorn *m.*

fuse [fju:z] *n* (*Elec*) Sicherung *f*; (*of bomb*) Zünder *m*; *vt* verschmelzen; *vi* (*Elec*) durchbrennen; ~ **box** Sicherungskasten *m.*

fuselage ['fju:zəla:ʒ] *n* Flugzeugrumpf *m.*

fusion ['fju:ʒən] *n* Verschmelzung *f.*

fuss [fʌs] *n* Theater *nt*; ~**y** a (*difficult*) heikel; (*attentive to detail*) kleinlich.

futile ['fju:taıl] a zwecklos, sinnlos.

futility [fju:'tılıtı] *n* Zwecklosigkeit *f.*

future ['fju:tʃə*] a zukünftig; *n* Zukunft *f*; **in (the)** ~ in Zukunft, zukünftig.

futuristic [fju:tʃə'rıstık] a futuristisch.

fuze [fju:z] (*US*) = **fuse**.

fuzzy ['fʌzı] a (*indistinct*) verschwommen; *hair* kraus.

G

G, g [dʒi:] *n* G *nt*, g *nt.*

gabble ['gæbl] *vi* plappern.

gable ['geıbl] *n* Giebel *m.*

gadget ['gædʒıt] *n* Vorrichtung *f*; ~**ry** Kinkerlitzchen *pl.*

gaffe [gæf] *n* Fauxpas *m.*

gag [gæg] *n* Knebel *m*; (*Theat*) Gag *m*; *vt* knebeln; (*Pol*) mundtot machen.

gaiety ['geıtı] *n* Fröhlichkeit *f.*

gaily ['geılı] *ad* lustig, fröhlich.

gain [geın] *vt* (*obtain*) erhalten; (*win*) gewinnen; *vi* (*improve*) gewinnen (*in* an +*dat*); (*make progress*) Vorsprung gewinnen; (*clock*) vorgehen; *n* Gewinn *m*; ~**ful employment** Erwerbstätigkeit *f.*

gala ['ga:lə] *n* Fest *nt.*

galaxy ['gæləksı] *n* Sternsystem *nt.*

gale [geıl] *n* Sturm *m.*

gallant ['gælənt] a tapfer, ritterlich; (*polite*) galant; ~**ry** Tapferkeit *f*, Ritterlichkeit *f*; Galanterie *f.*

gall-bladder ['gɔ:lblædə*] *n* Gallenblase *f.*

gallery ['gælərı] *n* Galerie *f.*

galley ['gælı] *n* (*ship's kitchen*) Kombüse *f*; (*ship*) Galeere *f.*

gallon ['gælən] *n* Gallone *f.*

gallop ['gæləp] *n* Galopp *m*; *vi* galoppieren.

gallows ['gæləʊz] *npl* Galgen *m.*

gallstone ['gɔ:lstəʊn] *n* Gallenstein *m.*

gamble ['gæmbl] *vi* (*um Geld*) spielen; *vt* (*risk*) aufs Spiel setzen; *n* Risiko *nt*; ~**r** Spieler(in *f*) *m.*

gambling ['gæmblıŋ] *n* Glücksspiel *nt.*

game [geım] *n* Spiel *nt*; (*hunting*) Wild *nt*; a bereit (*for* zu); (*brave*) mutig; ~**keeper** Wildhüter *m.*

gammon ['gæmən] *n* geräucherte(r) Schinken *m.*

gander ['gændə*] n Gänserich m.
gang [gæŋ] n (of criminals, youths) Bande f; (of workmen) Kolonne f.
gangrene ['gæŋgri:n] n Brand m.
gangster ['gæŋstə*] n Gangster m.
gangway ['gæŋweɪ] n (Naut) Laufplanke f.
gaol [dʒeɪl] n = **jail**.
gap [gæp] n (hole) Lücke f; (space) Zwischenraum m.
gape [geɪp] vi glotzen.
gaping ['geɪpɪŋ] a wound klaffend; hole gähnend.
garage ['gæra:ʒ] n Garage f; (for repair) (Auto)reparaturwerkstatt f; (for petrol) Tankstelle f; vt einstellen.
garbage ['ga:bɪdʒ] n Abfall m; ~ **can** (US) Mülltonne f.
garbled ['ga:bld] a story verdreht.
garden ['ga:dn] n Garten m; vi gärtnern; ~**er** Gärtner(in f) m; ~**ing** Gärtnern nt; ~ **party** Gartenfest nt.
gargle ['ga:gl] vi gurgeln; n Gurgelmittel nt.
gargoyle ['ga:gɔɪl] n Wasserspeier m.
garish ['gɛərɪʃ] a grell.
garland ['ga:lənd] n Girlande f.
garlic ['ga:lɪk] n Knoblauch m.
garment ['ga:mənt] n Kleidungsstück nt.
garnish ['ga:nɪʃ] vt food garnieren; n Garnierung f.
garret ['gærɪt] n Dachkammer f, Mansarde f.
garrison ['gærɪsən] n Garnison f; vt besetzen.
garrulous ['gærʊləs] a geschwätzig.
garter ['ga:tə*] n Strumpfband nt.
gas [gæs] n Gas nt; (Med) Betäubungsmittel nt; (esp US: petrol) Benzin nt; **to step on the** ~ Gas geben; vt vergasen; ~ **cooker** Gasherd m; ~ **cylinder** Gasflasche f; ~ **fire** Gasofen m, Gasheizung f.
gash [gæʃ] n klaffende Wunde f; vt tief verwunden.
gasket ['gæskɪt] n Dichtungsring m.
gasmask ['gæsma:sk] n Gasmaske f.
gas meter ['gæsmi:tə*] n Gaszähler m.
gasoline ['gæsəli:n] n (US) Benzin nt.
gasp [ga:sp] vi keuchen; (in astonishment) tief Luft holen; n Keuchen nt.
gas ring ['gæsrɪŋ] n Gasring m.
gas station ['gæssteɪʃən] n (US) Tankstelle f.
gas stove ['gæs'stəʊv] n Gaskocher m.
gassy ['gæsɪ] a drink sprudelnd.
gastric ['gæstrɪk] a Magen-; ~ **ulcer** Magengeschwür nt.
gastronomy [gæs'trɒnəmɪ] n Kochkunst f.
gate [geɪt] n Tor nt; (barrier) Schranke f; ~**crash** vt party platzen in (+acc); ~**way** Toreingang m.
gather ['gæðə*] vt people versammeln; things sammeln; vi (understand) annehmen; (deduce) schließen (from aus); (assemble) sich versammeln; ~**ing** Versammlung f.
gauche [gəʊʃ] a linkisch.
gaudy ['gɔːdɪ] a schreiend.
gauge [geɪdʒ] n Normalmaß nt; (Rail) Spurweite f; (dial) Anzeiger m; (measure)

Maß nt; vt (lit) (ab)messen; (fig) abschätzen.
gaunt [gɔːnt] a hager.
gauntlet ['gɔːntlɪt] n (knight's) Fehdehandschuh m; Handschuh m.
gauze [gɔːz] n Mull m, Gaze f.
gawk [gɔːk] vi dumm (an)glotzen (at acc).
gay [geɪ] a lustig; (coloured) bunt; (col) schwul.
gaze [geɪz] n Blick m; vi (an)blicken (at acc).
gazelle [gə'zel] n Gazelle f.
gazetteer [gæzɪ'tɪə*] n geographische(s) Lexikon nt.
gear [gɪə*] n Getriebe nt; (equipment) Ausrüstung f; (Aut) Gang m; **to be out of/in** ~ aus-/eingekuppelt sein; ~**box** Getriebe(gehäuse) nt; ~-**lever**, ~**shift** (US) Schalthebel m.
geese [gi:s] pl of **goose**.
gelatin(e) ['dʒelətɪn] n Gelatine f.
gem [dʒem] n Edelstein m; (fig) Juwel nt.
Gemini ['dʒemini:] n Zwillinge pl.
gen [dʒen] n (col: information) Infos pl (on über +acc).
gender ['dʒendə*] n (Gram) Geschlecht nt.
gene [dʒi:n] n Gen nt.
general ['dʒenərəl] n General m; a allgemein; ~ **election** allgemeine Wahlen pl; ~**ization** Verallgemeinerung f; ~**ize** vi verallgemeinern; ~**ly** ad allgemein, im allgemeinen.
generate ['dʒenəreɪt] vt erzeugen.
generation [dʒenə'reɪʃən] n Generation f; (act) Erzeugung f.
generator ['dʒenəreɪtə*] n Generator m.
generosity [dʒenə'rɒsɪtɪ] n Großzügigkeit f.
generous a, ~**ly** ad ['dʒenərəs, -lɪ] (noble-minded) hochherzig; (giving freely) großzügig.
genetics [dʒɪ'netɪks] n Genetik f, Vererbungslehre f.
genial ['dʒi:nɪəl] a freundlich, jovial.
genitals ['dʒenɪtlz] npl Geschlechtsteile pl, Genitalien pl.
genitive ['dʒenɪtɪv] n Genitiv m, Wesfall m.
genius ['dʒi:nɪəs] n Genie nt.
genocide ['dʒenəʊsaɪd] n Völkermord m.
genteel [dʒen'ti:l] a (polite) wohlanständig; (affected) affektiert.
gentile ['dʒentaɪl] n Nichtjude m.
gentle ['dʒentl] a sanft, zart; ~**man** Herr m; (polite) Gentleman m; ~**ness** Zartheit f, Milde f.
gently ['dʒentlɪ] ad zart, sanft.
gentry ['dʒentrɪ] n Landadel m.
gents [dʒents] n: '**G**~' (lavatory) 'Herren'.
genuine ['dʒenjʊɪn] a echt, wahr; ~**ly** ad wirklich, echt.
geographer [dʒɪ'ɒgrəfə*] n Geograph(in f) m.
geographical [dʒɪə'græfɪkəl] a geographisch.
geography [dʒɪ'ɒgrəfɪ] n Geographie f, Erdkunde f.
geological [dʒɪəʊ'lɒdʒɪkəl] a geologisch.
geologist [dʒɪ'ɒlədʒɪst] n Geologe m, Geologin f.

geology [dʒɪ'ɔlədʒɪ] n Geologie f.
geometric(al) [dʒɪə'metrɪk(əl)] a geometrisch.
geometry [dʒɪ'ɔmɪtrɪ] n Geometrie f.
geranium [dʒɪ'reɪnɪəm] n Geranie f.
germ [dʒɜːm] n Keim m; (Med) Bazillus m.
germination [dʒɜːmɪ'neɪʃən] n Keimen nt.
gesticulate [dʒes'tɪkjuleɪt] vi gestikulieren.
gesticulation [dʒestɪkju'leɪʃən] n Gesten pl, Gestikulieren nt.
gesture ['dʒestʃə*] n Geste f.
get [get] vt irreg (receive) bekommen, kriegen; (become) werden; (go. travel) kommen; (arrive) ankommen; **to ~ sb to do sth** jdn dazu bringen, etw zu tun, jdn etw machen lassen; **~ along** vi (people) (gut) zurechtkommen; (depart) sich (acc) auf den Weg machen; **~ at** vt facts herausbekommen; **to ~ at sb** (nag) an jdm herumnörgeln; **~ away** vi (leave) sich (acc) davonmachen; (escape) entkommen (from dat); **~ away with you!** laß den Quatsch!; **~ down** vi (her)untergehen; vt (depress) fertigmachen; **~ in** vi (train) ankommen; (arrive home) heimkommen; **~ off** vi (from train etc) aussteigen (aus); (from horse) absteigen (von); **~ on** vi (progress) vorankommen; (be friends) auskommen; (age) alt werden; vt train etc einsteigen (in +acc); horse aufsteigen (auf +acc); **~ out** vi (of house) herauskommen; (of vehicle) aussteigen; vt (take out) herausholen; **~ over** vt illness sich (acc) erholen von; surprise verkraften; news fassen; loss sich abfinden mit; **I couldn't ~ over her** ich konnte sie nicht vergessen; **~ up** vi aufstehen; **~away** Flucht f.
geyser ['giːzə*] n Geiser m; (heater) Durchlauferhitzer m.
ghastly ['gɑːstlɪ] a (horrible) gräßlich; (pale) totenbleich.
gherkin ['gɜːkɪn] n Gewürzgurke f.
ghetto ['getəʊ] n G(h)etto nt.
ghost [gəʊst] n Gespenst nt, Geist m; **~ly** a gespenstisch; **~ story** Gespenstergeschichte f.
giant ['dʒaɪənt] n Riese m; a riesig, Riesen-.
gibberish ['dʒɪbərɪʃ] n dumme(s) Geschwätz nt.
gibe [dʒaɪb] n spöttische Bemerkung f.
giblets ['dʒɪblɪts] npl Geflügelinnereien pl.
giddiness ['gɪdɪnəs] n Schwindelgefühl nt.
giddy ['gɪdɪ] a schwindlig; (frivolous) leichtsinnig.
gift [gɪft] n Geschenk nt; (ability) Begabung f; **~ed** a begabt.
gigantic [dʒaɪ'gæntɪk] a riesenhaft, ungeheuer groß.
giggle ['gɪgl] vi kichern; n Gekicher nt.
gild [gɪld] vt vergolden.
gill¹ [gɪl] n (1/4 pint) Viertelpinte f.
gill² [gɪl] n (of fish) Kieme f.
gilt [gɪlt] n Vergoldung f; a vergoldet.
gimlet ['gɪmlɪt] n Handbohrer m.
gimmick ['gɪmɪk] n (for sales, publicity) Gag m; **it's so ~y** es ist alles nur ein Gag.

gin [dʒɪn] n Gin m.
ginger ['dʒɪndʒə*] n Ingwer m; **~ ale, ~ beer** Ingwerbier nt; **~bread** Pfefferkuchen m; **~-haired** a rothaarig.
gingerly ['dʒɪndʒəlɪ] ad behutsam.
gipsy ['dʒɪpsɪ] n Zigeuner(in f) m.
giraffe [dʒɪ'rɑːf] n Giraffe f.
girder ['gɜːdə*] n (steel) Eisenträger m; (wood) Tragebalken m.
girdle ['gɜːdl] n (woman's) Hüftgürtel m; vt umgürten.
girl [gɜːl] n Mädchen nt; **~friend** Freundin f; **~ish** a mädchenhaft.
girth [gɜːθ] n (measure) Umfang m; (strap) Sattelgurt m.
gist [dʒɪst] n Wesentliche(s) nt, Quintessenz f.
give [gɪv] irreg vt geben; vi (break) nachgeben; **~ away** vt (give free) verschenken; (betray) verraten; **~ back** vt zurückgeben; **~ in** vi (yield) aufgeben; (agree) nachgeben; vt (hand in) abgeben; **~ up** vti aufgeben; **~ way** vi (traffic) Vorfahrt lassen; (to feelings) nachgeben (+dat).
glacier ['glæsɪə*] n Gletscher m.
glad [glæd] a froh; **I was ~ to hear . . .** ich habe mich gefreut, zu hören . . .; **~den** vt erfreuen.
gladiator ['glædɪeɪtə*] n Gladiator m.
gladioli [glædɪ'əʊlaɪ] npl Gladiolen pl.
gladly ['glædlɪ] ad gern(e).
glamorous ['glæmərəs] a bezaubernd; life reizvoll.
glamour ['glæmə*] n Zauber m, Reiz m.
glance [glɑːns] n flüchtige(r) Blick m; vi schnell (hin)blicken (at auf +acc); **~ off** vi (fly off) abprallen von.
glancing ['glɑːnsɪŋ] a blow abprallend, Streif-.
gland [glænd] n Drüse f; **~ular fever** Drüsenentzündung f.
glare [gleə*] n (light) grelle(s) Licht nt; (stare) wilde(r) Blick m; vi grell scheinen; (angrily) böse ansehen (at acc).
glaring ['gleərɪŋ] a injustice schreiend; mistake kraß.
glass [glɑːs] n Glas nt; (mirror) Spiegel m; **~es** pl Brille f; **~house** Gewächshaus nt; **~ware** Glaswaren pl; **~y** a glasig.
glaze [gleɪz] vt verglasen; (finish with a ~) glasieren; n Glasur f.
glazier ['gleɪzɪə*] n Glaser m.
gleam [gliːm] n Schimmer m; vi schimmern; **~ing** a schimmernd.
glee [gliː] n Frohsinn m; **~ful** a fröhlich.
glen [glen] n Bergtal nt.
glib [glɪb] a (rede)gewandt; (superficial) oberflächlich; **~ly** ad glatt.
glide [glaɪd] vi Gleiten nt; (Aviat) Segelflug m; **~r** (Aviat) Segelflugzeug nt.
gliding ['glaɪdɪŋ] n Segelfliegen nt.
glimmer ['glɪmə*] n Schimmer m; **~ of hope** Hoffnungsschimmer m.
glimpse [glɪmps] n flüchtige(r) Blick m; vt flüchtig erblicken.
glint [glɪnt] n Glitzern nt; vi glitzern.
glisten ['glɪsn] vi glänzen.

glitter ['glɪtə*] vi funkeln; n Funkeln nt; ~ing a glitzernd.

gloat over ['gləʊtəʊvə*] vt sich weiden an (+dat).

global ['gləʊbl] a global.

globe [gləʊb] n Erdball m; (sphere) Globus m; ~-trotter Weltenbummler(in f) m, Globetrotter(in f) m.

gloom [glu:m] n (also ~iness) (darkness) Dunkel nt, Dunkelheit f; (depression) düstere Stimmung f; ~ily ad, ~y a düster.

glorification [glɔːrɪfɪ'keɪʃən] n Verherrlichung f.

glorify ['glɔːrɪfaɪ] vt verherrlichen; just a glorified cafe nur ein besseres Café.

glorious ['glɔːrɪəs] a glorreich; (splendid) prächtig.

glory ['glɔːrɪ] n Herrlichkeit f; (praise) Ruhm m; to ~ in sich sonnen in (+dat).

gloss [glɒs] n (shine) Glanz m; ~ paint Ölfarbe f; ~ over vt übertünchen.

glossary ['glɒsərɪ] n Glossar nt.

glossy ['glɒsɪ] a surface glänzend.

glove [glʌv] n Handschuh m.

glow [gləʊ] vi glühen, leuchten; n (heat) Glühen nt; (colour) Röte f; (feeling) Wärme f.

glower ['glaʊə*] vi: ~ at finster anblicken.

glucose ['glu:kəʊs] n Traubenzucker m.

glue [glu:] n Klebstoff m, Leim m; vt leimen, kleben.

glum [glʌm] a bedrückt.

glut [glʌt] n Überfluß m; vt überladen.

glutton ['glʌtn] n Vielfraß m; (fig) Unersättliche(r) mf; ~ous a gierig; ~y Völlerei f, Unersättlichkeit f.

glycerin(e) ['glɪsəriːn] n Glyzerin nt.

gnarled [nɑːld] a knorrig.

gnat [næt] n Stechmücke f.

gnaw [nɔː] vt nagen an (+dat).

gnome [nəʊm] n Gnom m.

go [gəʊ] vi irreg gehen; (travel) reisen, fahren; (depart: train) (ab)fahren; (money) ausgehen; (vision) verschwinden; (smell) verfliegen; (disappear) (fort)gehen; (be sold) kosten; (at auction) weggehen; (work) gehen, funktionieren; (fit, suit) passen (with zu); (become) werden; (break etc) nachgeben; n (energy) Schwung m; (attempt) Versuch m; can I have another ~? darf ich noch mal?; ~ ahead vi (proceed) weitergehen; ~ along with vt (agree to support) zustimmen (+dat), unterstützen; ~ away vi (depart) weggehen; ~ back vi (return) zurückgehen; ~ back on vt promise nicht halten; ~ by vi (years, time) vergehen; ~ down vi (sun) untergehen; ~ for vt (fetch) holen (gehen); (like) mögen; (attack) sich stürzen auf (+acc); ~ in vi hineingehen; ~ into (enter) hineingehen in (+acc); (study) sich befassen mit; ~ off vi (depart) weggehen; (lights) ausgehen; (milk etc) sauer werden; (explode) losgehen; vt (dislike) nicht mehr mögen; ~ on vi (continue) weitergehen; (col: complain) meckern; (lights) angehen; to ~ on with sth mit etw weitermachen; ~ out vi

(fire, light) ausgehen; (of house) hinausgehen; ~ over vt (examine, check) durchgehen; ~ up vi (price) steigen; ~ without vt sich behelfen ohne; food entbehren.

goad [gəʊd] vt anstacheln; n Treibstock m.

go-ahead ['gəʊəhed] a zielstrebig; (progressive) fortschrittlich; n grünes Licht nt.

goal [gəʊl] n Ziel nt; (Sport) Tor nt; ~keeper Torwart m; ~-post Torpfosten m.

goat [gəʊt] n Ziege f.

gobble ['gɒbl] vt hinunterschlingen.

go-between ['gəʊbɪtwiːn] n Mittelsmann m.

goblet ['gɒblɪt] n Kelch(glas nt) m.

goblin ['gɒblɪn] n Kobold m.

god [gɒd] n Gott m; ~child Patenkind nt; ~dess Göttin f; ~father Pate m; ~forsaken a gottverlassen; ~mother Patin f; ~send Geschenk nt des Himmels.

goggle ['gɒgl] vi (stare) glotzen; to ~ at anglotzen; ~s pl Schutzbrille f.

going ['gəʊɪŋ] n (condition of ground) Straßenzustand m; (horse-racing) Bahn f; it's hard ~ es ist schwierig; a rate gängig; concern gutgehend; ~s-on pl Vorgänge pl.

gold [gəʊld] n Gold nt; ~en a golden; Gold-; ~-fish Goldfisch m; ~ mine Goldgrube f.

golf [gɒlf] n Golf nt; ~ club (society) Golfklub m; (stick) Golfschläger m; ~ course Golfplatz m; ~er Golfspieler(in f) m.

gondola ['gɒndələ] n Gondel f.

gong [gɒŋ] n Gong m.

good [gʊd] n (benefit) Wohl nt; (moral excellence) Güte f; a gut; (suitable) passend; ~s pl Ware(n pl) f, Güter pl; a ~ deal of ziemlich viel; a ~ many ziemlich viele; ~-bye! auf Wiedersehn!; G~ Friday Karfreitag m; ~-looking a gutaussehend; ~ morning! guten Morgen!; ~ness Güte f, (virtue) Tugend f; ~ will (favour) Wohlwollen nt; (Comm) Firmenansehen nt.

goose [guːs] n Gans f; ~berry [guzbərɪ] Stachelbeere f; ~flesh, ~ pimples pl Gänsehaut f.

gore [gɔː*] vt durchbohren; aufspießen; n Blut nt.

gorge [gɔːdʒ] n Schlucht f; vti (sich voll)fressen.

gorgeous ['gɔːdʒəs] a prächtig; person bildhübsch.

gorilla [gə'rɪlə] n Gorilla m.

gorse [gɔːs] n Stechginster m.

gory ['gɔːrɪ] a blutig.

go-slow ['gəʊ'sləʊ] n Bummelstreik m.

gospel ['gɒspəl] n Evangelium nt.

gossamer ['gɒsəmə*] n Spinnfäden pl.

gossip ['gɒsɪp] n Klatsch m; (person) Klatschbase f; vi klatschen.

goulash ['guːlæʃ] n Gulasch nt or m.

gout [gaʊt] n Gicht f.

govern ['gʌvən] vt regieren, verwalten; (Gram) bestimmen; ~ess Gouvernante f; ~ing a leitend; (fig) bestimmend; ~ment Regierung f; a Regierungs-; ~or Gouverneur m.

gown 264 grill

gown [gaʊn] n Gewand nt; (Univ) Robe f.
grab [græb] vt packen; an sich reißen; n plötzliche(r) Griff m; (crane) Greifer m.
grace [greɪs] n Anmut f; (favour) Güte f, Gefälligkeit f; (blessing) Gnade f; (prayer) Tischgebet nt; (Comm) Zahlungsfrist f; vt (adorn) zieren; (honour) auszeichnen; **5 days' ~** 5 Tage Aufschub m; **~ful** a ~fully ad anmutig, graziös.
gracious [ˈɡreɪʃəs] a gnädig; (kind, courteous) wohlwollend, freundlich.
gradation [ɡrəˈdeɪʃən] n (Ab)stufung f.
grade [ɡreɪd] n Grad m; (slope) Gefälle nt; **to make the ~** es schaffen; vt (classify) einstufen; **~ crossing** (US) Bahnübergang m.
gradient [ˈɡreɪdɪənt] n Steigung f; Gefälle nt.
gradual a, **~ly** ad [ˈɡrædjʊəl,-lɪ] allmählich.
graduate [ˈɡrædjʊɪt] n: **to be a ~** das Staatsexamen haben; [ˈɡrædjʊeɪt] vi das Staatsexamen machen or bestehen.
graduation [ɡrædjʊˈeɪʃən] n Erlangung f eines akademischen Grades.
graft [ɡrɑːft] n (on plant) Pfropfreis nt; (hard work) Schufterei f; (Med) Verpflanzung f; (unfair self-advancement) Schiebung f; vt propfen; (fig) aufpropfen; (Med) verpflanzen.
grain [ɡreɪn] n Korn nt, Getreide nt; (particle) Körnchen nt, Korn nt; (in wood) Maserung f.
grammar [ˈɡræmə*] n Grammatik f.
grammatical [ɡrəˈmætɪkəl] a grammatisch.
gram(me) [ɡræm] n Gramm nt.
gramophone [ˈɡræməfəʊn] n Grammophon nt.
granary [ˈɡrænərɪ] n Kornspeicher m.
grand [ɡrænd] a großartig; **~daughter** Enkelin f; **~eur** [ˈɡrændjə*] Erhabenheit f; **~father** Großvater m; **~iose** a (imposing) großartig; (pompous) schwülstig; **~mother** Großmutter f; **~ piano** Flügel m; **~son** Enkel m; **~stand** Haupttribüne f; **~ total** Gesamtsumme f.
granite [ˈɡrænɪt] n Granit m.
granny [ˈɡrænɪ] n Oma f.
grant [ɡrɑːnt] vt gewähren; (allow) zugeben; n Unterstützung f; (Univ) Stipendium nt; **to take sth/sb for ~ed** jdn/etw als selbstverständlich (an)nehmen.
granulated [ˈɡrænjʊleɪtɪd] a sugar raffiniert.
granule [ˈɡrænjuːl] n Körnchen nt.
grape [ɡreɪp] n (Wein)traube f; **~fruit** Pampelmuse f, Grapefruit f; **~ juice** Traubensaft m.
graph [ɡrɑːf] n Schaubild nt; **~ic** a (descriptive) anschaulich, lebendig; drawing graphisch.
grapple [ˈɡræpl] vi sich raufen; **~ with** (lit, fig) kämpfen mit.
grasp [ɡrɑːsp] vt ergreifen; (understand) begreifen; n Griff m; (possession) Gewalt f; (of subject) Beherrschung f; **~ing** a habgierig.
grass [ɡrɑːs] n Gras nt; **~hopper** Heuschrecke f; **~land** Weideland nt; **~**

roots pl (fig) Basis f; **~ snake** Ringelnatter f; **~y** a grasig, Gras-.
grate [ɡreɪt] n Feuerrost m, Kamin m; vi kratzen; (sound) knirschen; (on nerves) zerren (on an +dat); vt dieses reiben.
grateful a, **~ly** ad [ˈɡreɪtfʊl, -fəlɪ] dankbar.
grater [ˈɡreɪtə*] n (in kitchen) Reibe f.
gratification [ɡrætɪfɪˈkeɪʃən] n Befriedigung f.
gratify [ˈɡrætɪfaɪ] vt befriedigen.
gratifying [ˈɡrætɪfaɪŋ] a erfreulich.
grating [ˈɡreɪtɪŋ] n (iron bars) Gitter nt; a noise knirschend.
gratitude [ˈɡrætɪtjuːd] n Dankbarkeit f.
gratuitous [ɡrəˈtjuːɪtəs] a (uncalled-for) grundlos, überflüssig; (given free) unentgeltlich, gratis.
gratuity [ɡrəˈtjuːɪtɪ] n (Geld)geschenk nt; (Comm) Gratifikation f.
grave [ɡreɪv] n Grab nt; a (serious) ernst, schwerwiegend; (solemn) ernst, feierlich; **~digger** Totengräber m.
gravel [ˈɡrævəl] n Kies m.
gravely [ˈɡreɪvlɪ] ad schwer, ernstlich.
gravestone [ˈɡreɪvstəʊn] n Grabstein m.
graveyard [ˈɡreɪvjɑːd] n Friedhof m.
gravitate [ˈɡrævɪteɪt] vi streben; (fig) tendieren.
gravity [ˈɡrævɪtɪ] n Schwerkraft f; (seriousness) Schwere f, Ernst m.
gravy [ˈɡreɪvɪ] n (Braten)soße f.
gray [ɡreɪ] a = **grey**.
graze [ɡreɪz] vi grasen; vt (touch) streifen; (Med) abschürfen; n (Med) Abschürfung f.
grease [ɡriːs] n (fat) Fett nt; (lubricant) Schmiere f; vt (ab)schmieren; einfetten; **~ gun** Schmierspritze f; **~proof** a paper Butterbrot-.
greasy [ˈɡriːsɪ] a fettig.
great [ɡreɪt] a groß; (important) groß, bedeutend; (distinguished) groß, hochstehend; (col: good) prima; **~grandfather** Urgroßvater m; **~grandmother** Urgroßmutter f; **~ly** ad sehr; **~ness** Größe f.
greed [ɡriːd] n (also **~iness**) Gier f (for nach); (meanness) Geiz m; **~ily** ad gierig; **~y** a gefräßig, gierig; **~y for money** geldgierig.
green [ɡriːn] a grün; n (village ~) Dorfwiese f, **~grocer** Obst- und Gemüsehändler m; **~house** Gewächshaus nt; **~ish** a grünlich; **~ light** (lit, fig) grüne(s) Licht nt.
greet [ɡriːt] vt grüßen; **~ing** Gruß m, Begrüßung f.
gregarious [ɡrɪˈɡɛərɪəs] a gesellig.
grenade [ɡrɪˈneɪd] n Granate f.
grey [ɡreɪ] a grau; **~haired** a grauhaarig; **~hound** Windhund m; **~ish** a gräulich.
grid [ɡrɪd] n Gitter nt; (Elec) Leitungsnetz nt; (on map) Gitternetz nt; **~iron** Bratrost m.
grief [ɡriːf] n Gram m, Kummer m.
grievance [ˈɡriːvəns] n Beschwerde f.
grieve [ɡriːv] vi sich grämen; vt betrüben.
grill [ɡrɪl] n (on cooker) Grill m; vt grillen;

(*question*) in die Mangel nehmen.
grille [grɪl] n (*on car etc*) (Kühler)gitter nt.
grim [grɪm] a grimmig; *situation* düster.
grimace [grɪ'meɪs] n Grimasse f; vi Grimassen schneiden.
grime [graɪm] n Schmutz m.
grimly ['grɪmlɪ] ad grimmig, finster.
grimy ['graɪmɪ] a schmutzig.
grin [grɪn] n Grinsen nt; vi grinsen.
grind [graɪnd] vt irreg mahlen; (*sharpen*) schleifen; *teeth* knirschen mit; n (*bore*) Plackerei f.
grip [grɪp] n Griff m; (*mastery*) Griff m, Gewalt f; (*suitcase*) kleine(r) Handkoffer m; vt packen.
gripes [graɪps] npl (*bowel pains*) Bauchschmerzen pl, Bauchweh nt.
gripping ['grɪpɪŋ] a (*exciting*) spannend.
grisly ['grɪzlɪ] a gräßlich.
gristle ['grɪsl] n Knorpel m.
grit [grɪt] n Splitt m; (*courage*) Mut m, Mumm m; vt *teeth* knirschen mit; *road* (mit Splitt be)streuen.
groan [grəʊn] n Stöhnen nt; vi stöhnen.
grocer ['grəʊsə*] n Lebensmittelhändler m; ~ies pl Lebensmittel pl.
grog [grɒg] n Grog m.
groggy ['grɒgɪ] a benommen; (*boxing*) angeschlagen.
groin [grɔɪn] n Leistengegend f.
groom [gru:m] n Bräutigam m; (*for horses*) Pferdeknecht m; to ~ o.s. (*of man*) sich zurechtmachen, sich pflegen; (*well*) ~ed gepflegt; to ~ sb for a career jdn auf eine Laufbahn vorbereiten.
groove [gru:v] n Rille f, Furche f.
grope [grəʊp] vi tasten.
gross [grəʊs] a (*coarse*) dick, plump; (*bad*) grob, schwer; (*Comm*) brutto; Gesamt-; n Gros nt; ~ly ad höchst, ungeheuerlich.
grotesque [grəʊ'tesk] a grotesk.
grotto ['grɒtəʊ] n Grotte f.
ground [graʊnd] n Boden m, Erde f; (*land*) Grundbesitz m; (*reason*) Grund m; ~s pl (*dregs*) Bodensatz m; (*around house*) (Garten)anlagen pl; vt (*run ashore*) auf Strand setzen; *aircraft* stillegen; (*instruct*) die Anfangsgründe beibringen (+dat); vi (*run ashore*) stranden, auflaufen; ~ floor (*Brit*) Erdgeschoß nt, Parterre nt; ~ing (*instruction*) Anfangsunterricht m; ~sheet Zeltboden m; ~work Grundlage f.
group [gru:p] n Gruppe f; vti (sich) gruppieren.
grouse [graʊs] n (*bird*) schottische(s) Moorhuhn nt; (*complaint*) Nörgelei f; vi (*complain*) meckern.
grove [grəʊv] n Gehölz nt, Hain m.
grovel ['grɒvl] vi auf dem Bauch kriechen; (*fig*) kriechen.
grow [grəʊ] irreg vi wachsen, größer werden; (*grass*) wachsen; (*become*) werden; it ~s on you man gewöhnt sich daran; vt (*raise*) anbauen, ziehen; ~ up vi aufwachsen; (*mature*) erwachsen werden; ~er Züchter m; ~ing a wachsend; (*fig*) zunehmend.
growl [graʊl] vi knurren; n Knurren nt.

grown-up ['grəʊn'ʌp] a erwachsen; n Erwachsene(r) mf.
growth [grəʊθ] n Wachstum nt, Wachsen nt; (*increase*) Anwachsen nt, Zunahme f; (*of beard etc*) Wuchs m.
grub [grʌb] n Made f, Larve f; (*col: food*) Futter nt; ~by a schmutzig, schmuddelig.
grudge [grʌdʒ] n Groll m; vt misgönnen (*sb sth* jdm etw); to bear sb a ~ einen Groll gegen jdn hegen.
grudging ['grʌdʒɪŋ] a neidisch, (*unwilling*) widerwillig.
gruelling ['grʊəlɪŋ] a *climb, race* mörderisch.
gruesome ['gru:səm] a grauenhaft.
gruff [grʌf] a barsch.
grumble ['grʌmbl] vi murren, schimpfen; n Brummen nt, Murren nt.
grumpy ['grʌmpɪ] a verdrießlich.
grunt [grʌnt] vi grunzen; n Grunzen nt.
guarantee [gærən'ti:] n (*promise to pay*) Gewähr f; (*promise to replace*) Garantie f; vt gewährleisten; garantieren.
guarantor [gærən'tɔ:*] n Gewährsmann m, Bürge m.
guard [gɑ:d] n (*defence*) Bewachung f; (*sentry*) Wache f; (*Rail*) Zugbegleiter m; to be on ~ Wache stehen; to be on one's ~ aufpassen; vt bewachen, beschützen; ~ed a vorsichtig, zurückhaltend; ~ian Vormund m; (*keeper*) Hüter m; ~'s van (*Brit Rail*) Dienstwagen m.
guerrilla [gə'rɪlə] n Guerilla(kämpfer) m; ~ warfare Guerillakrieg m.
guess [ges] vti (er)raten, schätzen; n Vermutung f; ~work Raterei f; good ~ gut geraten.
guest [gest] n Gast m; ~-house Pension f; ~ room Gastzimmer nt.
guffaw [gʌ'fɔ:] n schallende(s) Gelächter nt; vi schallend lachen.
guidance ['gaɪdəns] n (*control*) Leitung f; (*advice*) Rat m, Beratung f.
guide [gaɪd] n Führer m; vt führen; girl ~ Pfadfinderin f; ~book Reiseführer m; ~d missile Fernlenkgeschoß nt; ~lines pl Richtlinien pl.
guild [gɪld] n (*Hist*) Gilde f; (*society*) Vereinigung f; ~hall (*Brit*) Stadthalle f.
guile [gaɪl] n Arglist f; ~less a arglos.
guillotine [gɪlə'ti:n] n Guillotine f.
guilt [gɪlt] n Schuld f; ~y a schuldig.
guise [gaɪz] n (*appearance*) Verkleidung f; in the ~ of (*things*) in der Form (+gen); (*people*) gekleidet als.
guitar [gɪ'tɑ:*] n Gitarre f; ~ist Gitarrist (in f) m.
gulf [gʌlf] n Golf m; (*fig*) Abgrund m.
gull [gʌl] n Möwe f.
gullet [gʌlɪt] n Schlund m.
gullible ['gʌlɪbl] a leichtgläubig.
gully ['gʌlɪ] n (*Wasser*)rinne f; (*gorge*) Schlucht f.
gulp [gʌlp] vi hinunterschlucken; (*gasp*) schlucken; n große(r) Schluck m.
gum [gʌm] n (*around teeth*) Zahnfleisch nt; (*glue*) Klebstoff m; (*chewing* ~) Kaugummi m; vt gummieren, kleben; ~boots pl Gummistiefel pl.

gumption ['gʌmpʃən] n (col) Mumm m.

gum tree ['gʌmtriː] n Gummibaum m; up a ~ (col) in der Klemme.

gun [gʌn] n Schußwaffe f; ~fire Geschützfeuer nt; ~man bewaffnete(r) Verbrecher m; ~ner Kanonier m, Artillerist m; ~powder Schießpulver nt; ~shot Schuß m; ~ down vt niederknallen.

gurgle ['gɜːgl] n Gluckern nt; vi gluckern.

gush [gʌʃ] n Strom m, Erguß m; vi (rush out) hervorströmen; (fig) schwärmen.

gusset ['gʌsɪt] n Keil m, Zwickel m.

gust [gʌst] n Windstoß m, Bö f.

gusto ['gʌstəʊ] n Genuß m, Lust f.

gut [gʌt] n (Anat) Gedärme pl; (string) Darm m; ~s pl (fig) Schneid m.

gutter ['gʌtə*] n Dachrinne f; (in street) Gosse f.

guttural ['gʌtərəl] a guttural, Kehl-.

guy [gaɪ] n (rope) Halteseil nt; (man) Typ m, Kerl m.

guzzle ['gʌzl] vti (drink) saufen; (eat) fressen.

gym(nasium) [dʒɪm'neɪzɪəm] n Turnhalle f.

gymnast ['dʒɪmnæst] n Turner(in f) m; ~ics [dʒɪm'næstɪks] Turnen nt, Gymnastik f.

gyn(a)ecologist [gaɪnɪ'kɒlədʒɪst] n Frauenarzt m/-ärztin f, Gynäkologe m, Gynäkologin f.

gyn(a)ecology [gaɪnɪ'kɒlədʒɪ] n Gynäkologie f, Frauenheilkunde f.

gypsy ['dʒɪpsɪ] n = gipsy.

gyrate [dʒaɪ'reɪt] vi kreisen.

H

H, h [eɪtʃ] n H nt, h nt.

haberdashery [hæbə'dæʃərɪ] n Kurzwaren pl.

habit ['hæbɪt] n (An)gewohnheit f; (monk's) Habit nt or m.

habitable ['hæbɪtəbl] a bewohnbar.

habitat ['hæbɪtæt] n Lebensraum m.

habitation [hæbɪ'teɪʃən] n Bewohnen nt; (place) Wohnung f.

habitual [hə'bɪtjʊəl] a üblich, gewohnheitsmäßig; ~ly ad gewöhnlich.

hack [hæk] vt hacken; n Hieb m; (writer) Schreiberling m.

hackney cab ['hæknɪ'kæb] n Taxi nt.

hackneyed ['hæknɪd] a abgedroschen.

haddock ['hædək] n Schellfisch m.

hadn't ['hædnt] = had not.

haemorrhage, (US) hemo~ ['hemərɪdʒ] n Blutung f.

haemorrhoids, (US) hemo~ ['hemərɪdz] Hämorrhoiden pl.

haggard ['hægəd] a abgekämpft.

haggle ['hægl] vi feilschen.

haggling ['hæglɪŋ] n Feilschen nt.

hail [heɪl] n Hagel m; vt umjubeln; to ~ sb as emperor jdn zum Kaiser ausrufen; vi hageln; ~storm Hagelschauer m.

hair [heə*] n Haar nt, Haare pl; (one ~) Haar nt; ~brush Haarbürste f; ~cut Haarschnitt m; to get a ~cut sich (dat) die Haare schneiden lassen; ~do Frisur f;

~dresser Friseur m, Friseuse f; ~drier Trockenhaube f; (hand) Fön m; ~net Haarnetz nt; ~ oil Haaröl nt; ~piece (lady's) Haarteil nt; (man's) Toupet m; ~pin (lit) Haarnadel f; (bend) Haarnadelkurve f; ~raising a haarsträubend; ~'s breadth Haaresbreite f; ~ style Frisur f; ~y a haarig.

hake [heɪk] n Seehecht m.

half [haːf] n Hälfte f; a halb, zur Hälfte; ad halb, zur Hälfte; ~back Läufer m; ~breed, ~caste Mischling m; ~hearted a lustlos, unlustig; ~hour halbe Stunde f; ~penny ['heɪpnɪ] halbe(r) Penny m; ~price halbe(r) Preis m; ~time Halbzeit f; ~way ad halbwegs, auf halbem Wege.

halibut ['hælɪbət] n Heilbutt m.

hall [hɔːl] n Saal m; (entrance ~) Hausflur m; (building) Halle f.

hallmark ['hɔːlmɑːk] n (lit, fig) Stempel m.

hallo [hʌ'ləʊ] see hello.

hallucination [həluːsɪ'neɪʃən] n Halluzination f.

halo ['heɪləʊ] n (of saint) Heiligenschein m; (of moon) Hof m.

halt [hɔːlt] n Halt m; vti anhalten.

halve [haːv] vt halbieren.

ham [hæm] n Schinken m; ~ sandwich Schinkenbrötchen nt; ~burger Frikadelle f.

hamlet ['hæmlɪt] n Weiler m.

hammer ['hæmə*] n Hammer m; vt hämmern.

hammock ['hæmək] n Hängematte f.

hamper ['hæmpə*] vt (be)hindern; n Picknickkorb m; Geschenkkorb m.

hand [hænd] n Hand f; (of clock) (Uhr)zeiger m; (worker) Arbeiter m; vt (pass) geben; to give sb a ~ jdm helfen; at first ~ aus erster Hand; to ~ zur Hand; in ~ (under control) in fester Hand, unter Kontrolle; (being done) im Gange; (extra) übrig; ~bag Handtasche f; ~ball Handball m; ~book Handbuch nt; ~brake Handbremse f; ~ cream Handcreme f; ~cuffs pl Handschellen pl; ~ful Handvoll f; (col: person) Plage f.

handicap ['hændɪkæp] n Handikap nt; vt benachteiligen.

handicraft ['hændɪkrɑːft] n Kunsthandwerk nt.

handkerchief ['hæŋkətʃɪf] n Taschentuch nt.

handle ['hændl] n (of door etc) Klinke f; (of cup etc) Henkel m; (for winding) Kurbel f; vt (touch) anfassen; (deal with) things sich befassen mit; people umgehen mit; ~bars pl Lenkstange f.

hand-luggage ['hændlʌgɪdʒ] n Handgepäck nt.

handmade ['hændmeɪd] a handgefertigt.

handshake ['hændʃeɪk] n Händedruck f.

handsome ['hænsəm] a gutaussehend; (generous) großzügig.

handwriting ['hændraɪtɪŋ] n Handschrift f.

handy ['hændɪ] a praktisch; shops leicht erreichbar.

handyman ['hændɪmən] n Mädchen nt für

alles; (*do-it-yourself*) Bastler *m*; (*general* ~) Gelegenheitsarbeiter *m*.

hang [hæŋ] *irreg vt* aufhängen; (*execute*) hängen; **to ~ sth on sth** etw an etw (*acc*) hängen; *vi* (*droop*) hängen; **~ about** *vi* sich herumtreiben.

hangar ['hæŋɔ*] *n* Hangar *m*, Flugzeughalle *f*.

hanger ['hæŋɔ*] *n* Kleiderbügel *m*.

hanger-on ['hæŋɔr'ɒn] *n* Anhänger(in *f*) *m*.

hangover ['hæŋɔuvɔ*] *n* Kater *m*.

hank [hæŋk] *n* Strang *m*.

hanker ['hæŋkɔ*] *vi* sich sehnen (*for, after* nach).

haphazard ['hæp'hæzɔd] *a* wahllos, zufällig.

happen ['hæpən] *vi* sich ereignen, passieren; **~ing** *n* Ereignis *nt*; (*Art*) Happening *nt*.

happily ['hæpɪlɪ] *ad* glücklich; (*fortunately*) glücklicherweise.

happiness ['hæpɪnɪs] *n* Glück *nt*.

happy ['hæpɪ] *a* glücklich; **~-lucky** *a* sorglos.

harass ['hærɔs] *vt* bedrängen, plagen.

harbour, (*US*) **harbor** ['hɑːbɔ*] *n* Hafen *m*.

hard [hɑːd] *a* (*firm*) hart, fest; (*difficult*) schwer, schwierig; (*physically*) schwer; (*harsh*) hart(herzig), gefühllos; **at work** hart; *try* sehr; *push, hit* fest; **~ by** (*close*) dicht *or* nahe an(+*dat*); **he took it ~** er hat es schwer genommen; **~back** *n* kartonierte Ausgabe; **~-boiled** *a* hartgekocht; **~en** *vt* erhärten; (*fig*) verhärten; *vi* hart werden; (*fig*) sich verhärten; **~-hearted** *a* hartherzig; **~ly** *ad* kaum; **~ship** Not *f*; (*injustice*) Unrecht *nt*; **~-up** *a* knapp bei Kasse; **~ware** Eisenwaren *pl*.

hardy ['hɑːdɪ] *a* (*strong*) widerstandsfähig; (*brave*) verwegen.

hare [heɔ*] *n* Hase *m*.

harem ['hɑːriːm] *n* Harem *m*.

harm [hɑːm] *n* Schaden *m*; Leid *nt*; *vt* schaden (+*dat*); **it won't do any ~** es kann nicht schaden; **~ful** *a* schädlich; **~less** *a* harmlos, unschädlich.

harmonica [hɑːˈmɒnɪkɔ] *n* Mundharmonika *f*.

harmonious [hɑːˈmɔʊnɪɔs] *a* harmonisch.

harmonize ['hɑːmɔnaɪz] *vt* abstimmen; *vi* harmonieren.

harmony ['hɑːmɔnɪ] *n* Harmonie *f*; (*fig also*) Einklang *m*.

harness ['hɑːnɪs] *n* Geschirr *nt*; *vt horse* anschirren; (*fig*) nutzbar machen.

harp [hɑːp] *n* Harfe *f*; **to ~ on about sth** auf etw (*dat*) herumreiten; **~ist** Harfenspieler(in *f*) *m*.

harpoon [hɑːˈpuːn] *n* Harpune *f*.

harrow ['hærəʊ] *n* Egge *f*; *vt* eggen.

harrowing ['hærəʊɪŋ] *a* nervenaufreibend.

harsh [hɑːʃ] *a* (*rough*) rauh, grob; (*severe*) schroff, streng; **~ly** *ad* rauh, barsch; **~ness** Härte *f*.

harvest ['hɑːvɪst] *n* Ernte *f*; (*time*) Erntezeit *f*; *vt* ernten.

harvester ['hɑːvɪstɔ*] *n* Mähbinder *m*.

hash [hæʃ] *vt* kleinhacken; *n* (*mess*) Kuddelmuddel *m*; (*meat cooked*) Haschee *nt*; (*raw*) Gehackte(s) *nt*.

hashish ['hæʃɪʃ] *n* Haschisch *nt*.

haste [heɪst] *n* (*speed*) Eile *f*; (*hurry*) Hast *f*; **~n** ['heɪsn] *vt* beschleunigen; *vi* eilen, sich beeilen.

hasty *a*, **hastily** *ad* [heɪstɪ, -lɪ] hastig; (*rash*) vorschnell.

hat [hæt] *n* Hut *m*.

hatbox ['hætbɒks] *n* Hutschachtel *f*.

hatch [hætʃ] *n* (*Naut*) Luke *f*; (*in house*) Durchreiche *f*; *vi* brüten; (*young*) ausschlüpfen; *vt brood* ausbrüten; *plot* aushecken.

hatchet ['hætʃɪt] *n* Beil *nt*.

hate [heɪt] *vt* hassen; **I ~ queuing** ich stehe nicht gern Schlange; *n* Haß *m*; **~ful** *a* verhaßt.

hatred ['heɪtrɪd] *n* Haß *m*; (*dislike*) Abneigung *f*.

hat trick ['hættrɪk] *n* Hattrick *m*.

haughty *a*, **haughtily** *ad* [hɔːtɪ, -lɪ] hochnäsig, überheblich.

haul [hɔːl] *vt* ziehen, schleppen; *n* (*pull*) Zug *m*; (*catch*) Fang *m*; (*transport*) Transport *m*; (*Comm*) Spedition *f*; **~ier** Transportunternehmer *m*, Spediteur *m*.

haunch [hɔːntʃ] *n* Lende *f*; **to sit on one's ~es** hocken.

haunt [hɔːnt] *vt* (*ghost*) spuken in (+*dat*), umgehen in (+*dat*); (*memory*) verfolgen; *pub* häufig besuchen; **the castle is ~ed** in dem Schloß spukt es; *n* Lieblingsplatz *m*.

have [hæv] *vt irreg* haben; (*at meal*) essen; trinken; (*col: trick*) hereinlegen; **to ~ sth done** etw machen lassen; **to ~ to do sth** etw tun müssen; **to ~ sb on** jdn auf den Arm nehmen.

haven ['heɪvn] *n* Hafen *m*; (*fig*) Zufluchtsort *m*.

haversack ['hævɔsæk] *n* Rucksack *m*.

havoc ['hævɔk] *n* Verwüstung *f*.

hawk [hɔːk] *n* Habicht *m*.

hay [heɪ] *n* Heu *nt*; **~ fever** Heuschnupfen *m*; **~stack** Heuschober *m*.

haywire ['heɪwaɪɔ*] *a* (*col*) durcheinander.

hazard ['hæzɔd] *n* (*chance*) Zufall *m*; (*danger*) Wagnis *nt*, Risiko *nt*; *vt* aufs Spiel setzen; **~ous** *a* gefährlich, riskant.

haze [heɪz] *n* Dunst *m*; (*fig*) Unklarheit *f*.

hazelnut ['heɪzlnʌt] *n* Haselnuß *f*.

hazy ['heɪzɪ] *a* (*misty*) dunstig, diesig; (*vague*) verschwommen.

he [hiː] *pron* er.

head [hed] *n* Kopf *m*; (*top*) Spitze *f*; (*leader*) Leiter *m*; *a* Kopf-; (*leading*) Ober-; *vt* (an)führen, leiten; **~ for** Richtung nehmen auf (+*acc*), zugehen auf (+*acc*); **~ache** Kopfschmerzen *pl*, Kopfweh *nt*; **~ing** Überschrift *f*; **~lamp** Scheinwerfer *m*; **~land** Landspitze *f*; **~light = ~lamp**; **~line** Schlagzeile *f*; **~long** *ad* kopfüber; **~master** (*of primary school*) Rektor *m*; (*of secondary school*) Direktor *m*; **~mistress** Rektorin *f*; Direktorin *f*; **~-on** *a* Frontal-; **~quarters** *pl* Zentrale *f*; (*Mil*) Hauptquartier *nt*; **~rest**

Kopfstütze f; ~**room** (of bridges etc) lichte Höhe f; Platz m für den Kopf; ~**s** (on coin) Kopf m, Wappen nt; ~**scarf** Kopftuch nt; ~**strong** a eigenwillig; ~**waiter** Oberkellner m; ~**way** Fahrt f (voraus); (fig) Fortschritte pl; ~**wind** Gegenwind m; ~**y** a (rash) hitzig; (intoxicating) stark, berauschend.

heal [hi:l] vt heilen; vi verheilen.

health [helθ] n Gesundheit f; **your** ~! prost!; ~**y** a gesund.

heap [hi:p] n Haufen m; vt häufen.

hear [hɪə*] irreg vt hören; (listen to) anhören; vi hören; ~**ing** Gehör nt; (Jur) Verhandlung f; **to give sb a** ~**ing** jdn anhören; ~**ing aid** Hörapparat m; ~**say** Hörensagen nt.

hearse [hɜːs] n Leichenwagen m.

heart [hɑːt] n Herz nt; (centre also) Zentrum nt; (courage) Mut m; **by** ~ auswendig; **the** ~ **of the matter** der Kern des Problems; ~ **attack** Herzanfall m; ~**beat** Herzschlag m; ~**breaking** a herzzerbrechend; ~**broken** a (ganz)gebrochen; ~**burn** Sodbrennen nt; ~ **failure** Herzschlag m; ~**felt** a aufrichtig.

hearth [hɑːθ] n Herd m.

heartily [ˈhɑːtɪlɪ] ad herzlich; eat herzhaft.

heartless [ˈhɑːtlɪs] a herzlos.

hearty [ˈhɑːtɪ] a kräftig; (friendly) freundlich.

heat [hi:t] n Hitze f; (of food, water etc) Wärme f; (Sport) Ausscheidungsrunde f; (excitement) Feuer nt; **in the** ~ **of the moment** in der Hitze des Gefechts; vt house heizen; substance heiß machen, erhitzen; ~ **up** vi warm werden; vt aufwärmen; ~**ed** a erhitzt; (fig) hitzig; ~**er** (Heiz)ofen m.

heath [hi:θ] n (Brit) Heide f.

heathen [ˈhiːðən] n Heide m; a heidnisch, Heiden-.

heather [ˈheðə*] n Heidekraut nt, Erika f.

heating [ˈhiːtɪŋ] n Heizung f.

heatstroke [ˈhiːtstrəʊk] n Hitzschlag m.

heatwave [ˈhiːtweɪv] n Hitzewelle f.

heave [hi:v] vt hochheben; sigh ausstoßen; vi wogen; (breast) sich heben; n heben nt.

heaven [hevn] n Himmel m; (bliss) (der siebte) Himmel m; ~**ly** a himmlisch; ~**ly body** Himmelskörper m.

heavy, heavily [ˈhevɪ, -lɪ] schwer.

heckle [hekl] vt unterbrechen; vi dazwischenrufen, störende Fragen stellen.

hectic [ˈhektɪk] a hektisch.

he'd [hi:d] = **he had; he would.**

hedge [hedʒ] n Hecke f; vt einzäunen; **to** ~ **one's bets** sich absichern; vi (fig) ausweichen.

hedgehog [ˈhedʒhɒg] n Igel m.

heed [hi:d] vt beachten; n Beachtung f; ~**ful** a achtsam; ~**less** a achtlos.

heel [hi:l] n Ferse f; (of shoe) Absatz m; vt shoes mit Absätzen versehen.

hefty [ˈheftɪ] a person stämmig; portion reichlich; bite kräftig; weight schwer.

heifer [ˈhefə*] n Färse f.

height [haɪt] n (of person) Größe f; (of object) Höhe f; (high place) Gipfel m; ~**en** vt erhöhen.

heir [ɛə*] n Erbe m; ~**ess** [ˈɛərɪs] Erbin f; ~**loom** Erbstück nt.

helicopter [ˈhelɪkɒptə*] n Hubschrauber m.

hell [hel] n Hölle f; interj verdammt!

he'll [hi:l] = **he will, he shall.**

hellish [ˈhelɪʃ] a höllisch, verteufelt.

hello [hʌˈləʊ] interj (greeting) Hallo; (surprise) hallo, he.

helm [helm] n Ruder nt, Steuer nt.

helmet [ˈhelmɪt] n Helm m.

helmsman [ˈhelmzmən] n Steuermann m.

help [help] n Hilfe f; vt helfen (+dat); **I can't** ~ **it** ich kann nichts dafür; **I couldn't** ~ **laughing** ich mußte einfach lachen; ~ **yourself** bedienen Sie sich; ~**er** Helfer m; ~**ful** a hilfreich; ~**ing** Portion f; ~**less** a hilflos.

hem [hem] n Saum m; ~ **in** vt einschließen; (fig) einengen.

hemisphere [ˈhemɪsfɪə*] n Halbkugel f; Hemisphäre f.

hemline [ˈhemlaɪn] n Rocklänge f.

hemp [hemp] n Hanf m.

hen [hen] n Henne f.

hence [hens] ad von jetzt an; (therefore) daher.

henchman [ˈhentʃmən] n Anhänger m, Gefolgsmann m.

henpecked [ˈhenpekt] a: **to be** ~ **unter dem Pantoffel stehen;** ~ **husband** Pantoffelheld m.

her [hɜː*] pron (acc) sie; (dat) ihr; a ihr.

herald [ˈherəld] n Herold m; (fig) (Vor)bote m; vt verkünden, anzeigen.

heraldry [ˈherəldrɪ] n Wappenkunde f.

herb [hɜːb] n Kraut nt.

herd [hɜːd] n Herde f.

here [hɪə*] ad hier; (to this place) hierher; ~**after** ad hernach, künftig; n Jenseits nt; ~**by** ad hiermit.

hereditary [hɪˈredɪtərɪ] a erblich.

heredity [hɪˈredɪtɪ] n Vererbung f.

heresy [ˈherəsɪ] n Ketzerei f.

heretic [ˈheretɪk] n Ketzer m; ~**al** [hɪˈretɪkəl] a ketzerisch.

herewith [ˈhɪəˈwɪð] ad hiermit; (Comm) anbei.

heritage [ˈherɪtɪdʒ] n Erbe nt.

hermetically [hɜːˈmetɪkəlɪ] ad luftdicht, hermetisch.

hermit [ˈhɜːmɪt] n Einsiedler m.

hernia [ˈhɜːnɪə] n Bruch m.

hero [ˈhɪərəʊ] n Held m; ~**ic** [hɪˈrəʊɪk] a heroisch.

heroin [ˈherəʊɪn] n Heroin nt.

heroine [ˈherəʊɪn] n Heldin f.

heroism [ˈherəʊɪzəm] n Heldentum nt.

heron [ˈherən] n Reiher m.

herring [ˈherɪŋ] n Hering m.

hers [hɜːz] pron ihre(r,s).

herself [hɜːˈself] pron sich (selbst); (emphatic) selbst; **she's not** ~ mit ihr ist etwas los or nicht in Ordnung.

he's [hi:z] = **he is, he has.**

hesitant [ˈhezɪtənt] a zögernd; speech stockend.

hesitate [ˈhezɪteɪt] vi zögern; (feel doubtful) unschlüssig sein.

hesitation [hezı'teıʃən] n Zögern nt, Schwanken nt.

het up [het'ʌp] a (col) aufgeregt.

hew [hju:] vt irreg hauen, hacken.

hexagon ['heksəgən] n Sechseck nt; ~**al** [hek'sægənəl] a sechseckig.

heyday ['heıdeı] n Blüte f, Höhepunkt m.

hi [haı] interj he, hallo.

hibernate ['haıbəneıt] vi Winterschlaf halten.

hibernation [haıbə'neıʃən] n Winterschlaf m.

hiccough, hiccup ['hıkʌp] vi den Schluckauf haben; ~**s** pl Schluckauf m.

hide [haıd] n (skin) Haut f, Fell nt; irreg vt verstecken; (keep secret) verbergen; vi sich verstecken; ~-**and-seek** Versteckspiel nt.

hideous ['hıdıəs] a abscheulich; ~**ly** ad scheußlich.

hiding ['haıdıŋ] n (beating) Tracht f Prügel; **to be in** ~ sich versteckt halten; ~ **place** Versteck nt.

hierarchy ['haıərɑːkı] n Hierarchie f.

high [haı] a hoch; importance groß; spirits Hoch-; wind stark; living extravagant, üppig; ad hoch; ~**brow** n Intellektuelle(r) mf; a (betont) intellektuell; (pej) hochgestochen; ~**chair** Hochstuhl m, Sitzer m; ~-**handed** a eigenmächtig; ~-**heeled** a hochhackig; ~-**jack** = **hijack**; ~-**level** a meeting wichtig, Spitzen-; ~-**light** (fig) Höhepunkt m; ~-**ly** ad in hohem Maße, höchst; praise in hohen Tönen; ~**ly strung** a überempfindlich, reizbar; **H~ Mass** Hochamt nt; ~**ness** Höhe f; **H~ness** Hoheit f; ~-**pitched** a voice hoch, schrill, hell; ~ **school** Oberschule f; ~-**speed** a Schnell-; ~ **tide** Flut f; ~-**way** Landstraße f.

hijack ['haıdʒæk] vt hijacken, entführen.

hike [haık] vi wandern; n Wanderung f; ~**r** Wanderer m.

hiking ['haıkıŋ] n Wandern nt.

hilarious [hı'lɛərıəs] a lustig; zum Schreien komisch.

hilarity [hı'lærıtı] n Lustigkeit f.

hill [hıl] n Berg m; ~**side** (Berg)hang m; ~**top** Bergspitze f; ~**y** a hügelig.

hilt [hılt] n Heft nt; **up to the** ~ ganz und gar.

him [hım] pron (acc) ihn; (dat) ihm.

himself [hım'self] pron sich (selbst); (emphatic) selbst; **he's not** ~ mit ihm ist etwas los or nicht in Ordnung.

hind [haınd] a hinter, Hinter-; n Hirschkuh f.

hinder ['hındə*] vt (stop) hindern; (delay) behindern.

hindrance ['hındrəns] n (delay) Behinderung f; (obstacle) Hindernis nt.

hinge [hındʒ] n Scharnier nt; (on door) Türangel f; vt mit Scharnieren versehen; vi (fig) abhängen (on von).

hint [hınt] n Tip m, Andeutung f; (trace) Anflug m; vi andeuten (at acc), anspielen (at auf +acc).

hip [hıp] n Hüfte f.

hippopotamus [hıpə'pɒtəməs] n Nilpferd nt.

hire ['haıə*] vt worker anstellen; car mieten; n Miete f; **for** ~ taxi frei; **to have for** ~ verleihen; ~ **purchase** Teilzahlungskauf m.

his [hız] poss a sein; poss pron seine(r,s).

hiss [hıs] vi zischen; n Zischen nt.

historian [hıs'tɔːrıən] n Geschichtsschreiber m; Historiker m.

historic [hıs'tɒrık] a historisch.

historical [hıs'tɒrıkəl] a historisch, geschichtlich.

history ['hıstərı] n Geschichte f; (personal) Entwicklung f, Werdegang m.

hit [hıt] vt irreg schlagen; (injure) treffen, verletzen; n (blow) Schlag m, Stoß m; (success) Erfolg m, Treffer m; (Mus) Hit m.

hitch [hıtʃ] vt festbinden; (pull up) hochziehen; n (loop) Knoten m; (difficulty) Schwierigkeit f, Haken m.

hitch-hike ['hıtʃhaık] vi trampen, per Anhalter fahren; ~**r** Tramper m.

hitherto ['hıðə'tu:] ad bislang.

hive [haıv] n Bienenkorb m.

hoard [hɔːd] n Schatz m; vt horten, hamstern.

hoarding ['hɔːdıŋ] n Bretterzaun m; (for advertising) Reklamewand f.

hoarfrost ['hɔː'frɒst] n (Rauh)reif m.

hoarse [hɔːs] a heiser, rauh.

hoax [həʊks] n Streich m.

hobble ['hɒbl] vi humpeln.

hobby ['hɒbı] n Steckenpferd nt, Hobby nt.

hobo ['həʊbəʊ] n (US) Tippelbruder m.

hock [hɒk] n (wine) weiße(r) Rheinwein m.

hockey ['hɒkı] n Hockey nt.

hoe [həʊ] n Hacke f; vt hacken.

hog [hɒg] n Schlachtschwein nt; vt mit Beschlag belegen.

hoist [hɔıst] n Winde f; vt hochziehen.

hold [həʊld] irreg vt halten; (keep) behalten; (contain) enthalten; (be able to contain) fassen; (keep back) zurück(be)-halten; breath anhalten; meeting abhalten; vi (withstand pressure) standhalten, aushalten; n (grasp) Halt m; (claim) Anspruch m; (Naut) Schiffsraum m; ~ **back** vt zurückhalten; ~ **down** vt niederhalten; job behalten; ~ **out** vt hinhalten, bieten; vi aushalten; ~ **up** vt (delay) aufhalten; (rob) überfallen; ~**all** Reisetasche f; ~**er** Behälter m; ~**ing** (share) (Aktien)anteil m; ~**up** (in traffic) Stockung f; (robbery) Überfall m.

hole [həʊl] n Loch nt; vt durchlöchern.

holiday ['hɒlədı] n (day) Feiertag m; freie(r) Tag m; (vacation) Urlaub m; (Sch) Ferien pl; ~-**maker** Feriengast m, Urlauber(in f) m.

holiness ['həʊlınıs] n Heiligkeit f.

hollow ['hɒləʊ] a hohl; (fig) leer; n Vertiefung f; (in rock) Höhle f; ~ **out** vt aushöhlen.

holly ['hɒlı] n Stechpalme f.

holster ['həʊlstə*] n Pistolenhalfter m.

holy ['həʊlı] a heilig; (religious) fromm.

homage ['hɒmıdʒ] n Huldigung f; **to pay** ~ **to** huldigen (+dat).

home [həʊm] n Heim nt, Zuhause nt; (insti-

tution) Heim *nt*, Anstalt *f*; *a* einheimisch; (*Pol*) inner; *ad* heim, nach Hause; **at ~** zu Hause; **~coming** Heimkehr *f*; **~less** *a* obdachlos; **~ly** *a* häuslich; (*US*: *ugly*) unscheinbar; **~made** *a* selbstgemacht; **~sick** *a*: **to be ~ sick** Heimweh haben; **~ward(s)** *a* heimwärts; **~work** Hausaufgaben *pl*.

homicide ['hɒmɪsaɪd] *n* (*US*) Totschlag *m*, Mord *m*.

homoeopathy [həʊmɪ'ɒpəθɪ] *n* Homöopathie *f*.

homogeneous [hɒmə'dʒiːnɪəs] *a* homogen, gleichartig.

homosexual ['hɒməʊ'seksjʊəl] *a* homosexuell; *n* Homosexuelle(r) *m*.

hone [həʊn] *n* Schleifstein *m*; *vt* feinschleifen.

honest ['ɒnɪst] *a* ehrlich; (*upright*) aufrichtig; **~ly** *ad* ehrlich; **~y** Ehrlichkeit *f*.

honey ['hʌnɪ] *n* Honig *m*; **~comb** Honigwabe *f*; **~moon** Flitterwochen *pl*, Hochzeitsreise *f*.

honk [hɒŋk] *n* (*Aut*) Hupensignal *nt*; *vi* hupen.

honorary ['ɒnərərɪ] *a* Ehren-.

honour, (*US*) **honor** ['ɒnə*] *vt* ehren; *cheque* einlösen; *debts* begleichen; *contract* einhalten; *n* (*respect*) Ehre *f*; (*reputation*) Ansehen *nt*, gute(r) Ruf *m*; (*sense of right*) Ehrgefühl *nt*; **~s** *pl* (*titles*) Auszeichnungen *pl*; **~able** *a* ehrenwert, rechtschaffen; *intention* ehrenhaft.

hood [hʊd] *n* Kapuze *f*; (*Aut*) Verdeck *nt*; (*US Aut*) Kühlerhaube *f*; **~wink** *vt* reinlegen.

hoof [huːf] *n* Huf *m*.

hook [hʊk] *n* Haken *m*; *vt* einhaken; **~-up** Gemeinschaftssendung *f*.

hooligan ['huːlɪgən] *n* Rowdy *m*.

hoop [huːp] *n* Reifen *m*.

hoot [huːt] *vi* (*Aut*) hupen; **to ~ with laughter** schallend lachen; *n* (*shout*) Johlen *nt*; (*Aut*) Hupen *nt*; **~er** (*Naut*) Dampfpfeife *f*; (*Aut*) (Auto)hupe *f*.

hop[1] [hɒp] *vi* hüpfen, hopsen; *n* (*jump*) Hopser *m*.

hop[2] [hɒp] *n* (*Bot*) Hopfen *m*.

hope [həʊp] *vi* hoffen; **I ~ that** ... hoffentlich ...; *n* Hoffnung *f*; **~ful** *a* hoffnungsvoll; (*promising*) vielversprechend; **~less** *a* hoffnungslos; (*useless*) unmöglich.

horde [hɔːd] *n* Horde *f*.

horizon [hə'raɪzn] *n* Horizont *m*; **~tal** [hɒrɪ'zɒntl] *a* horizontal.

hormone ['hɔːməʊn] *n* Hormon *nt*.

horn [hɔːn] *n* Horn *nt*; (*Aut*) Hupe *f*; **~ed** *a* gehörnt, Horn-.

hornet ['hɔːnɪt] *n* Hornisse *f*.

horny ['hɔːnɪ] *a* schwielig; (*US*) scharf.

horoscope ['hɒrəskəʊp] *n* Horoskop *nt*.

horrible *a*, **horribly** *ad* ['hɒrɪbl, -blɪ] fürchterlich.

horrid *a*, **~ly** *ad* ['hɒrɪd, -lɪ] abscheulich, scheußlich.

horrify ['hɒrɪfaɪ] *vt* entsetzen.

horror ['hɒrə*] *n* Schrecken *m*; (*great dislike*) Abscheu *m* (*of* vor + *dat*).

hors d'oeuvre [ɔː'dɜːvr] *n* Vorspeise *f*.

horse [hɔːs] *n* Pferd *nt*; **on ~back** beritten; **~ chestnut** Roßkastanie *f*; **~-drawn** *a* von Pferden gezogen, Pferde-; **~power** Pferdestärke *f*, PS *nt*; **~-racing** Pferderennen *nt*; **~shoe** Hufeisen *nt*.

horsy ['hɔːsɪ] *a* pferdenärrisch.

horticulture ['hɔːtɪkʌltʃə*] *n* Gartenbau *m*.

hose(pipe) ['həʊz(paɪp)] *n* Schlauch *m*.

hosiery ['həʊzɪərɪ] *n* Strumpfwaren *pl*.

hospitable [hɒs'pɪtəbl] *a* gastfreundlich.

hospital ['hɒspɪtl] *n* Krankenhaus *nt*.

hospitality [hɒspɪ'tælɪtɪ] *n* Gastlichkeit *f*, Gastfreundschaft *f*.

host [həʊst] *n* Gastgeber *m*; (*innkeeper*) (Gast)wirt *m*; (*large number*) Heerschar *f*; (*Eccl*) Hostie *f*.

hostage ['hɒstɪdʒ] *n* Geisel *f*.

hostel ['hɒstəl] *n* Herberge *f*.

hostess ['həʊstes] *n* Gastgeberin *f*.

hostile ['hɒstaɪl] *a* feindlich.

hostility [hɒs'tɪlɪtɪ] *n* Feindschaft *f*; **hostilities** *pl* Feindseligkeiten *pl*.

hot [hɒt] *a* heiß; *drink, food, water* warm; (*spiced*) scharf; (*angry*) hitzig; **~ air** (*col*) Gewäsch *nt*; **~bed** (*lit*) Mistbeet *nt*; (*fig*) Nährboden *m*; **~-blooded** *a* heißblütig; **~ dog** heiße(s) Würstchen *nt*.

hotel [həʊ'tel] *n* Hotel *nt*; **~ier** Hotelier *m*.

hotheaded ['hɒt'hedɪd] *a* hitzig, aufbrausend.

hothouse ['hɒthaʊs] *n* (*lit, fig*) Treibhaus *nt*.

hot line ['hɒtlaɪn] *n* (*Pol*) heiße(r) Draht *m*.

hotly ['hɒtlɪ] *ad* *argue* hitzig; *pursue* dicht.

hot news ['hɒt'njuːz] *n* das Neueste vom Neuen.

hotplate ['hɒtpleɪt] *n* Kochplatte *f*.

hot-water bottle [hɒt'wɔːtəbɒtl] *n* Wärmflasche *f*.

hound [haʊnd] *n* Jagdhund *m*; *vt* jagen, hetzen.

hour ['aʊə*] *n* Stunde *f*; (*time of day*) (Tages)zeit *f*; **~ly** *a* stündlich.

house [haʊs] *n* Haus *nt*; [haʊz] *vt* (*accommodate*) unterbringen; (*shelter*) aufnehmen; **~boat** Hausboot *nt*; **~breaking** Einbruch *m*; **~hold** Haushalt *m*; **~keeper** Haushälterin *f*; **~keeping** Haushaltung *f*; **~wife** Hausfrau *f*; **~work** Hausarbeit *f*.

housing ['haʊzɪŋ] *n* (*act*) Unterbringung *f*; (*houses*) Wohnungen *pl*; (*Pol*) Wohnungsbau *m*; (*covering*) Gehäuse *nt*; **~ estate** (Wohn)siedlung *f*.

hovel ['hɒvəl] *n* elende Hütte *f*; Loch *nt*.

hover ['hɒvə*] *vi* (*bird*) schweben; (*person*) wartend herumstehen; **~craft** Luftkissenfahrzeug *nt*.

how [haʊ] *ad* wie; **~ many** wie viele; **~ much** wieviel; **~ever** *ad* (*but*) (je)doch, aber; **~ever you phrase it** wie Sie es auch ausdrücken.

howl [haʊl] *n* Heulen *nt*; *vi* heulen.

howler ['haʊlə*] *n* grobe(r) Schnitzer *m*.

hub [hʌb] *n* Radnabe *f*; (*of the world*) Mittelpunkt *m*; (*of commerce*) Zentrum *nt*.

hubbub ['hʌbʌb] *n* Tumult *m*.

hub cap ['hʌbkæp] n Radkappe f.
huddle ['hʌdl] vi sich zusammendrängen; n Grüppchen nt.
hue [hju:] n Färbung f, Farbton m; ~ **and cry** Zetergeschrei nt.
huff [hʌf] n Eingeschnapptsein nt; **to go into a** ~ einschnappen.
hug [hʌg] vt umarmen; (fig) sich dicht halten an (+acc); n Umarmung f.
huge [hju:dʒ] a groß, riesig.
hulk [hʌlk] n (ship) abgetakelte(s) Schiff nt; (person) Koloß m; ~**ing** a ungeschlacht.
hull [hʌl] n Schiffsrumpf m.
hullo [hʌ'ləʊ] see **hello**.
hum [hʌm] vi summen; (bumblebee) brummen; vt summen; n Summen nt.
human ['hju:mən] a menschlich; n (also ~ **being**) Mensch m.
humane [hju:'meɪn] a human.
humanity [hju:'mænɪtɪ] n Menschheit f; (kindliness) Menschlichkeit f.
humble ['hʌmbl] a demütig; (modest) bescheiden; vt demütigen.
humbly ['hʌmblɪ] ad demütig.
humdrum ['hʌmdrʌm] a eintönig, langweilig.
humid ['hju:mɪd] a feucht; ~**ity** [hju:'mɪdɪtɪ] Feuchtigkeit f.
humiliate [hju:'mɪlɪeɪt] vt demütigen.
humiliation [hju:mɪlɪ'eɪʃən] n Demütigung f.
humility [hju:'mɪlɪtɪ] n Demut f.
humorist ['hju:mərɪst] n Humorist m.
humorous ['hju:mərəs] a humorvoll, komisch.
humour, (US) **humor** ['hju:mə*] n (fun) Humor m; (mood) Stimmung f; vt nachgeben (+dat); bei Stimmung halten.
hump [hʌmp] n Buckel m.
hunch [hʌntʃ] n (presentiment) (Vor)-ahnung f; vt shoulders hochziehen; ~**back** Bucklige(r) m.
hundred ['hʌndrɪd] num, a, n hundert; ~**weight** Zentner m.
hunger ['hʌŋgə*] n Hunger m; (fig) Verlangen nt (for nach); vi hungern.
hungry a, **hungrily** ad ['hʌŋgrɪ, -lɪ] hungrig; **to be** ~ Hunger haben.
hunt [hʌnt] vi jagen; (search) suchen (for acc); vi jagen; n Jagd f; ~**er** Jäger m; ~**ing** Jagen nt, Jagd f.
hurdle ['hɜ:dl] n (lit, fig) Hürde f.
hurl [hɜ:l] vt schleudern.
hurrah [hʊ'rɑ:], **hurray** [hʊ'reɪ] n Hurra nt.
hurricane ['hʌrɪkən] n Orkan m.
hurried ['hʌrɪd] a eilig; (hasty) übereilt; ~**ly** ad übereilt, hastig.
hurry ['hʌrɪ] n Eile f; **to be in a** ~ es eilig haben, vi sich beeilen; ~! mach schnell!; vt (an)treiben; job übereilen.
hurt [hɜ:t] irreg vt weh tun (+dat); (injure, fig) verletzen; vi weh tun; ~**ful** a schädlich; remark verletzend.
hurtle ['hɜ:tl] vt schleudern; vi sausen.
husband ['hʌzbənd] n (Ehe)mann m, Gatte m.

hush [hʌʃ] n Stille f; vt zur Ruhe bringen; vi still sein; ~ interj pst, still.
husk [hʌsk] n Spelze f.
husky ['hʌskɪ] a voice rauh; figure stämmig; n Eskimohund m.
hustle ['hʌsl] vt (push) stoßen; (hurry) antreiben, drängen; n (Hoch)betrieb m; ~ **and bustle** Geschäftigkeit f.
hut [hʌt] n Hütte f.
hutch [hʌtʃ] n (Kaninchen)stall m.
hyacinth ['haɪəsɪnθ] n Hyazinthe f.
hybrid ['haɪbrɪd] n Kreuzung f; a Misch-.
hydrant ['haɪdrənt] n Hydrant m.
hydraulic [haɪ'drɔlɪk] a hydraulisch.
hydroelectric ['haɪdrəʊɪ'lektrɪk] a hydroelektrisch.
hydrofoil ['haɪdrəʊfɔɪl] n Tragflügel m; Tragflügelboot nt.
hydrogen ['haɪdrədʒən] n Wasserstoff m.
hyena [haɪ'i:nə] n Hyäne f.
hygiene ['haɪdʒi:n] n Hygiene f.
hygienic [haɪ'dʒi:nɪk] a hygienisch.
hymn [hɪm] n Kirchenlied nt.
hyphen ['haɪfən] n Bindestrich m; Trennungszeichen nt.
hypnosis [hɪp'nəʊsɪs] n Hypnose f.
hypnotism ['hɪpnətɪzəm] n Hypnotismus m.
hypnotist ['hɪpnətɪst] n Hypnotiseur m.
hypnotize ['hɪpnətaɪz] vt hypnotisieren.
hypochondriac [haɪpəʊ'kɒndrɪæk] n eingebildete(r) Kranke(r) mf.
hypocrisy [hɪ'pɒkrɪsɪ] n Heuchelei f, Scheinheiligkeit f.
hypocrite ['hɪpəkrɪt] n Heuchler m, Scheinheilige(r) m.
hypocritical [hɪpə'krɪtɪkəl] a scheinheilig, heuchlerisch.
hypothesis [haɪ'pɒθɪsɪs] n Hypothese f.
hypothetic(al) [haɪpəʊ'θetɪk(əl)] a hypothetisch.
hysteria [hɪs'tɪərɪə] n Hysterie f.
hysterical [hɪs'terɪkəl] a hysterisch.
hysterics [hɪs'terɪks] npl hysterische(r) Anfall m.

I

I, i [aɪ] n I nt, i nt; **I** pron ich.
ice [aɪs] n Eis nt; vt (Cook) mit Zuckerguß überziehen; vi (also ~ **up**) vereisen; ~**axe** Eispickel m; ~**berg** Eisberg m; ~**box** (US) Kühlschrank m; ~**cream** Eis nt; ~**cold** a eiskalt; ~**cube** Eiswürfel m; ~ **hockey** Eishockey nt; ~**rink** (Kunst)eisbahn f.
icicle ['aɪsɪkl] n Eiszapfen m.
icing ['aɪsɪŋ] n (on cake) Zuckerguß m; (on window) Vereisung f.
icon ['aɪkɒn] n Ikone f.
icy ['aɪsɪ] a (slippery) vereist; (cold) eisig.
I'd [aɪd] = **I would**; **I had**.
idea [aɪ'dɪə] n Idee f; **no** ~ keine Ahnung; **my** ~ **of a holiday** wie ich mir einen Urlaub vorstelle.
ideal [aɪ'dɪəl] n Ideal nt; a ideal; ~**ism** Idealismus m; ~**ist** Idealist m; ~**ly** ad ideal(erweise).

identical [aı'dentıkəl] a identisch; *twins* eineiig.

identification [aıdentıfı'keıʃən] n Identifizierung f.

identify [aı'dentıfaı] vt identifizieren; (*regard as the same*) gleichsetzen.

identity [aı'dentıtı] n Identität f; ~ **card** Personalausweis m; ~ **papers** pl (Ausweis)papiere pl.

ideology [aıdı'ɔlədʒı] n Ideologie f.

idiocy ['ıdıəsı] n Idiotie f.

idiom ['ıdıəm] n (*expression*) Redewendung f; (*dialect*) Idiom nt.

idiosyncrasy [ıdıə'sıŋkrəsı] n Eigenart f.

idiot ['ıdıət] n Idiot(in f) m; ~**ic** [ıdı'ɔtık] a idiotisch.

idle ['aıdl] a (*doing nothing*) untätig, müßig; (*lazy*) faul; (*useless*) vergeblich, nutzlos; *machine* still(stehend); *threat, talk* leer; ~**ness** Müßiggang m; Faulheit f; ~**r** Faulenzer m.

idol ['aıdl] n Idol nt; ~**ize** vt vergöttern.

idyllic [ı'dılık] a idyllisch.

if [ıf] cj wenn, falls; (*whether*) ob; ~ **only** . . . wenn . . . doch nur; ~ **not** falls nicht.

igloo ['ıglu:] n Iglu m or nt.

ignite [ıg'naıt] vt (an)zünden.

ignition [ıg'nıʃən] n Zündung f; ~ **key** (*Aut*) Zündschlüssel m.

ignoramus [ıgnə'reıməs] n Ignorant m.

ignorance ['ıgnərəns] n Unwissenheit f, Ignoranz f.

ignorant ['ıgnərənt] a unwissend.

ignore [ıg'nɔ:*] vt ignorieren.

ikon ['aıkɔn] n = **icon**.

I'll [aıl] = **I will, I shall**.

ill [ıl] a krank; (*evil*) schlecht, böse; n Übel nt; ~**-advised** a schlecht beraten, unklug; ~**-at-ease** a unbehaglich.

illegal a, ~**ly** ad [ı'li:gəl, -ı] illegal.

illegible [ı'ledʒəbl] a unleserlich.

illegitimate [ılı'dʒıtımət] a unzulässig; *child* unehelich.

ill-fated ['ıl'feıtıd] a unselig.

ill-feeling ['ıl'fi:lıŋ] n Verstimmung f.

illicit [ı'lısıt] a verboten.

illiterate [ı'lıtərət] a ungebildet.

ill-mannered ['ıl'mænəd] a ungehobelt.

illness ['ılnəs] n Krankheit f.

illogical [ı'lɔdʒıkəl] a unlogisch.

ill-treat ['ıl'tri:t] vt mißhandeln.

illuminate [ı'lu:mıneıt] vt beleuchten.

illumination [ılu:mı'neıʃən] n Beleuchtung f.

illusion [ı'lu:ʒən] n Illusion f.

illusive [ı'lu:sıv], **illusory** [ı'lu:sərı] a illusorisch, trügerisch.

illustrate ['ıləstreıt] vt *book* illustrieren; (*explain*) veranschaulichen.

illustration [ıləs'treıʃən] n Illustration f; (*explanation*) Veranschaulichung f.

illustrious [ı'lʌstrıəs] a berühmt.

ill will ['ıl'wıl] n Groll m.

I'm [aım] = **I am**.

image ['ımıdʒ] n Bild nt; (*likeness*) Abbild nt; (*public —*) Image nt; ~**ry** Symbolik f.

imaginable [ı'mædʒınəbl] a vorstellbar.

imaginary [ı'mædʒınərı] a eingebildet; *world* Phantasie-.

imagination [ımædʒı'neıʃən] n Einbildung f; (*creative*) Phantasie f.

imaginative [ı'mædʒınətıv] a phantasiereich, einfallsreich.

imagine [ı'mædʒın] vt sich vorstellen; (*wrongly*) sich einbilden.

imbalance [ım'bæləns] n Unausgeglichenheit f.

imbecile ['ımbəsi:l] n Schwachsinnige(r) mf.

imbue [ım'bju:] vt durchdringen.

imitate ['ımıteıt] vt nachmachen, imitieren.

imitation [ımı'teıʃən] n Nachahmung f, Imitation f.

imitator [ımı'teıtə*] n Nachahmer m.

immaculate [ı'mækjulıt] a makellos; *dress* tadellos; (*Eccl*) unbefleckt.

immaterial [ımə'tıərıəl] a unwesentlich.

immature [ımə'tjʊə*] a unreif.

immaturity [ımə'tjʊərıtı] n Unreife f.

immediate [ı'mi:dıət] a (*instant*) sofortig; (*near*) unmittelbar; *relatives* nächste(r, s); *needs* dringlich; ~**ly** ad sofort; (*in position*) unmittelbar.

immense [ı'mens] a unermeßlich; ~**ly** ad ungeheuerlich; *grateful* unheimlich.

immerse [ı'mɜ:s] vt eintauchen.

immersion heater [ı'mɜ:ʃənhi:tə*] n Heißwassergerät nt.

immigrant ['ımıgrənt] n Einwanderer m.

immigration [ımı'greıʃən] n Einwanderung f.

imminent ['ımınənt] a bevorstehend; *danger* drohend.

immobilize [ı'məʊbılaız] vt lähmen.

immoderate [ı'mɔdərət] a maßlos, übertrieben.

immoral [ı'mɔrəl] a unmoralisch; (*sexually*) unsittlich; ~**ity** [ımə'rælıtı] Verderbtheit f.

immortal [ı'mɔ:tl] a unsterblich; n Unsterbliche(r) mf; ~**ity** [ımɔ:'tælıtı] Unsterblichkeit f; (*of book etc*) Unvergänglichkeit f; ~**ize** vt unsterblich machen.

immune [ı'mju:n] a (*secure*) geschützt (*from gegen*), sicher (*from vor +dat*); (*Med*) immun.

immunity [ı'mju:nıtı] n (*Med, Jur*) Immunität f; (*fig*) Freiheit f.

immunization [ımjunaı'zeıʃən] n Immunisierung f.

immunize ['ımjunaız] vt immunisieren.

impact ['ımpækt] n (*lit*) Aufprall m; (*force*) Wucht f; (*fig*) Wirkung f.

impair [ım'pɛə*] vt beeinträchtigen.

impale [ım'peıl] vt aufspießen.

impartial [ım'pɑ:ʃəl] a unparteiisch; ~**ity** [ımpɑ:ʃı'ælıtı] Unparteilichkeit f.

impassable [ım'pɑ:səbl] a unpassierbar.

impassioned [ım'pæʃnd] a leidenschaftlich.

impatience [ım'peıʃəns] n Ungeduld f.

impatient [ım'peıʃənt] a, ~**ly** ad [ım'peıʃənt, -lı] ungeduldig; **to be** ~ **to do sth** es nicht erwarten können, etw zu tun.

impeccable [ɪm'pekəbl] a tadellos.

impede [ɪm'piːd] vt (be)hindern.

impediment [ɪm'pedɪmənt] n Hindernis nt; (in speech) Sprachfehler m.

impending [ɪm'pendɪŋ] a bevorstehend.

impenetrable [ɪm'penɪtrəbl] a (lit, fig) undurchdringlich; forest unwegsam; theory undurchsichtig; mystery unerforschlich.

imperative [ɪm'perətɪv] a (necessary) unbedingt erforderlich; n (Gram) Imperativ m, Befehlsform f.

imperceptible [ɪmpə'septəbl] a nicht wahrnehmbar.

imperfect [ɪm'pɜːfɪkt] a (faulty) fehlerhaft; (incomplete) unvollständig; ∼ion [ɪmpə'fekʃən] Unvollkommenheit f; (fault) Fehler m; (faultiness) Fehlerhaftigkeit f.

imperial [ɪm'pɪərɪəl] a kaiserlich; ∼ism Imperialismus m.

imperil [ɪm'perɪl] vt gefährden.

impersonal [ɪm'pɜːsnl] a unpersönlich.

impersonate [ɪm'pɜːsəneɪt] vt sich ausgeben als; (for amusement) imitieren.

impersonation [ɪmpɜːsə'neɪʃən] n Verkörperung f; (Theat) Imitation f.

impertinence [ɪm'pɜːtɪnəns] n Unverschämtheit f.

impertinent [ɪm'pɜːtɪnənt] a unverschämt, frech.

imperturbable [ɪmpə'tɜːbəbl] a unerschütterlich, gelassen.

impervious [ɪm'pɜːvɪəs] a undurchlässig; (fig) unempfänglich (to für).

impetuous [ɪm'petjʊəs] a heftig, ungestüm.

impetus ['ɪmpɪtəs] n Triebkraft f; (fig) Auftrieb m.

impinge [ɪm'pɪndʒ]: ∼ on vt beeinträchtigen; (light) fallen auf (+acc).

implausible [ɪm'plɔːzəbl] a unglaubwürdig, nicht überzeugend.

implement ['ɪmplɪmənt] n Werkzeug nt, Gerät nt; ['ɪmplɪment] vt ausführen.

implicate ['ɪmplɪkeɪt] vt verwickeln, hineinziehen.

implication [ɪmplɪ'keɪʃən] n (meaning) Bedeutung f; (effect) Auswirkung f; (hint) Andeutung f; (in crime) Verwicklung f; by ∼ folglich.

implicit [ɪm'plɪsɪt] a (suggested) unausgesprochen; (utter) vorbehaltlos.

implore [ɪm'plɔː*] vt anflehen.

imply [ɪm'plaɪ] vt (hint) andeuten; (be evidence for) schließen lassen auf (+acc); **what does that** ∼? was bedeutet das?

impolite [ɪmpə'laɪt] a unhöflich.

impolitic [ɪm'pɒlɪtɪk] a undiplomatisch.

imponderable [ɪm'pɒndərəbl] a unwägbar.

import [ɪm'pɔːt] vt einführen, importieren; ['ɪmpɔːt] n Einfuhr f, Import m; (meaning) Bedeutung f, Tragweite f.

importance [ɪm'pɔːtəns] n Bedeutung f; (influence) Einfluß m.

important [ɪm'pɔːtənt] a wichtig; (influential) bedeutend, einflußreich.

import duty ['ɪmpɔːtdjuːtɪ] n Einfuhrzoll m.

imported [ɪm'pɔːtɪd] a eingeführt, importiert.

importer [ɪm'pɔːtə*] n Importeur m.

import licence ['ɪmpɔːtlaɪsəns] n Einfuhrgenehmigung f.

impose [ɪm'pəʊz] vti auferlegen (on dat); penalty, sanctions verhängen (on gegen); to ∼ ~ (o.s.) on sb sich jdm aufdrängen; to ∼ on sb's kindness jds Liebenswürdigkeit ausnützen.

imposing [ɪm'pəʊzɪŋ] a eindrucksvoll.

imposition [ɪmpə'zɪʃən] n (of burden, fine) Auferlegung f; (Sch) Strafarbeit f.

impossibility [ɪmpɒsə'bɪlɪtɪ] n Unmöglichkeit f.

impossible a, **impossibly** ad [ɪm'pɒsəbl, -blɪ] unmöglich.

impostor [ɪm'pɒstə*] n Betrüger m; Hochstapler m.

impotence ['ɪmpətəns] Impotenz f.

impotent ['ɪmpətənt] a machtlos; (sexually) impotent.

impound [ɪm'paʊnd] vt beschlagnahmen.

impoverished [ɪm'pɒvərɪʃt] a verarmt.

impracticable [ɪm'præktɪkəbl] a undurchführbar.

impractical [ɪm'præktɪkəl] a unpraktisch.

imprecise [ɪmprɪ'saɪs] a ungenau.

impregnable [ɪm'pregnəbl] a castle uneinnehmbar.

impregnate ['ɪmpregneɪt] vt (saturate) sättigen; (fertilize) befruchten; (fig) durchdringen.

impresario [ɪmpre'sɑːrɪəʊ] n Impresario m.

impress [ɪm'pres] vt (influence) beeindrucken; (imprint) (auf)drücken; to ∼ sth on sb jdm etw einschärfen; ∼ion Eindruck m; (on wax, footprint) Abdruck m; (of stamp) Aufdruck m; (of book) Auflage f; (take-off) Nachahmung f; I was under the ∼ion ich hatte den Eindruck; ∼ionable a leicht zu beeindrucken(d); ∼ionist Impressionist m; ∼ive a eindrucksvoll.

imprison [ɪm'prɪzn] vt ins Gefängnis schicken; ∼ment Inhaftierung f; Gefangenschaft f; 3 years' ∼ment eine Gefängnisstrafe von 3 Jahren.

improbable [ɪm'prɒbəbl] a unwahrscheinlich.

impromptu [ɪm'prɒmptjuː] a, ad aus dem Stegreif, improvisiert.

improper [ɪm'prɒpə*] a (indecent) unanständig; (wrong) unrichtig, falsch; (unsuitable) unpassend.

impropriety [ɪmprə'praɪətɪ] n Ungehörigkeit f.

improve [ɪm'pruːv] vt verbessern; vi besser werden; ∼ment (Ver)besserung f; (of appearance) Verschönerung f.

improvisation [ɪmprəvaɪ'zeɪʃən] n Improvisation f.

improvise ['ɪmprəvaɪz] vti improvisieren.

imprudence [ɪm'pruːdəns] n Unklugheit f.

imprudent [ɪm'pruːdənt] a unklug.

impudent ['ɪmpjʊdənt] a unverschämt.

impulse ['ɪmpʌls] n (desire) Drang m; (driving force) Antrieb m, Impuls m; **my first** ∼ **was to . . .** ich wollte zuerst . . .

impulsive [ɪm'pʌlsɪv] a impulsiv.
impunity [ɪm'pjuːnɪtɪ] n Straflosigkeit f.
impure [ɪm'pjuə*] a (dirty) unrein; (mixed) gemischt; (bad) schmutzig, unanständig.
impurity [ɪm'pjuərɪtɪ] n Unreinheit f; (Tech) Verunreinigung f.
in [ɪn] prep in; (made of) aus; ~ Dickens/a child bei Dickens/einem Kind; ~ him you'll have ... an ihm hast du ...; ~ doing this he has ... dadurch, daß er das tat, hat er ...; ~ saying that I mean ... wenn ich das sage, meine ich ...; I haven't seen him ~ years ich habe ihn seit Jahren nicht mehr gesehen; 15 pence ~ the £ 15 Pence per Pfund; blind ~ the left eye auf dem linken Auge or links blind; ~ itself an sich; ~ that, ~ so or as far as insofern als; ad hinein; to be ~ zuhause sein; (train) da sein; (in fashion) in (Mode) sein; to have it ~ for sb es auf jdn abgesehen haben; ~s and outs pl Einzelheiten pl; to know the ~s and outs sich auskennen.
inability [ɪnə'bɪlɪtɪ] n Unfähigkeit f.
inaccessible [ɪnæk'sesəbl] a unzugänglich.
inaccuracy [ɪn'ækjurəsɪ] n Ungenauigkeit f.
inaccurate [ɪn'ækjurɪt] a ungenau; (wrong) unrichtig.
inaction [ɪn'ækʃən] n Untätigkeit f.
inactive [ɪn'æktɪv] a untätig.
inactivity [ɪnæk'tɪvɪtɪ] n Untätigkeit f.
inadequacy [ɪn'ædɪkwəsɪ] n Unzulänglichkeit f; (of punishment) Unangemessenheit f.
inadequate [ɪn'ædɪkwət] a unzulänglich; punishment unangemessen.
inadvertently [ɪnəd'vɜːtəntlɪ] ad unabsichtlich.
inadvisable [ɪnəd'vaɪzəbl] a nicht ratsam.
inane [ɪ'neɪn] a dumm, albern.
inanimate [ɪn'ænɪmət] a leblos.
inapplicable [ɪnə'plɪkəbl] a unzutreffend.
inappropriate [ɪnə'prəuprɪət] a clothing ungeeignet; remark unangebracht.
inapt [ɪn'æpt] a unpassend; (clumsy) ungeschickt; ~itude Untauglichkeit f.
inarticulate [ɪnɑː'tɪkjulət] a unklar; to be ~ sich nicht ausdrücken können.
inartistic [ɪnɑː'tɪstɪk] a unkünstlerisch.
inasmuch as [ɪnəz'mʌtʃəz] ad da, weil; (in so far as) soweit.
inattention [ɪnə'tenʃən] n Unaufmerksamkeit f.
inattentive [ɪnə'tentɪv] a unaufmerksam.
inaudible [ɪn'ɔːdəbl] a unhörbar.
inaugural [ɪ'nɔːgjurəl] a Eröffnungs-; (Univ) Antritts-.
inaugurate [ɪ'nɔːgjureɪt] vt (open) einweihen; (admit to office) (feierlich) einführen.
inauguration [ɪnɔːgju'reɪʃən] n Eröffnung f; (feierliche) Amtseinführung f.
inborn [ɪn'bɔːn] a angeboren.
inbred [ɪn'bred] a quality angeboren; they are ~ bei ihnen herrscht Inzucht.
inbreeding [ɪn'briːdɪŋ] n Inzucht f.
incalculable [ɪn'kælkjuləbl] a person

unberechenbar; consequences unabsehbar.
incapability [ɪnkeɪpə'bɪlɪtɪ] n Unfähigkeit f.
incapable [ɪn'keɪpəbl] a unfähig (of doing sth etw zu tun); (not able) nicht einsatzfähig.
incapacitate [ɪnkə'pæsɪteɪt] vt untauglich machen; ~d behindert; machine nicht gebrauchsfähig.
incapacity [ɪnkə'pæsɪtɪ] n Unfähigkeit f.
incarcerate [ɪn'kɑːsəreɪt] vt einkerkern.
incarnate [ɪn'kɑːnɪt] a menschgeworden; (fig) leibhaftig.
incarnation [ɪnkɑː'neɪʃən] n (Eccl) Menschwerdung f; (fig) Inbegriff m.
incendiary [ɪn'sendɪərɪ] a brandstifterisch, Brand-; (fig) aufrührerisch; n Brandstifter m; (bomb) Brandbombe f.
incense ['ɪnsens] n Weihrauch m; [ɪn'sens] vt erzürnen.
incentive [ɪn'sentɪv] n Anreiz m.
incessant a, ~ly ad [ɪn'sesnt, -lɪ] unaufhörlich.
incest ['ɪnsest] n Inzest m.
inch [ɪntʃ] n Zoll m.
incidence ['ɪnsɪdəns] n Auftreten nt; (of crime) Quote f.
incident ['ɪnsɪdənt] n Vorfall m; (disturbance) Zwischenfall m; ~al [ɪnsɪ'dentl] a music Begleit-; expenses Neben-; (unplanned) zufällig; (unimportant) nebensächlich; remark beiläufig; ~al to sth mit etw verbunden; ~ally [ɪnsɪ'dentəlɪ] ad (by chance) nebenbei; (by the way) nebenbei bemerkt, übrigens.
incinerator [ɪn'sɪnəreɪtə*] n Verbrennungsofen m.
incision [ɪn'sɪʒən] n Einschnitt m.
incisive [ɪn'saɪsɪv] a style treffend; person scharfsinnig.
incite [ɪn'saɪt] vt anstacheln.
inclement [ɪn'klemənt] a weather rauh.
inclination [ɪnklɪ'neɪʃən] n Neigung f.
incline ['ɪnklaɪn] n Abhang m; [ɪn'klaɪn] vt neigen; (fig) veranlassen; to be ~d to do sth Lust haben, etw zu tun; (have tendency) dazu neigen, etw zu tun; vi sich neigen.
include [ɪn'kluːd] vt einschließen; (on list, in group) aufnehmen.
including [ɪn'kluːdɪŋ] prep: ~ X X inbegriffen.
inclusion [ɪn'kluːʒən] n Aufnahme f, Einbeziehung f.
inclusive [ɪn'kluːsɪv] a einschließlich; (Comm) inklusive.
incognito [ɪnkɒg'niːtəu] ad inkognito.
incoherent [ɪnkəu'hɪərənt] a zusammenhanglos.
income ['ɪnkʌm] n Einkommen nt; (from business) Einkünfte pl; ~ tax Lohnsteuer f; (of self-employed) Einkommensteuer f.
incoming ['ɪnkʌmɪŋ] a ankommend; (succeeding) folgend; mail eingehend; tide steigend.
incomparable [ɪn'kɒmpərəbl] a unvergleichlich.
incompatible [ɪnkəm'pætəbl] a unvereinbar; people unverträglich.

incompetence [ɪn'kɒmpɪtəns] n Unfähigkeit f.

incompetent [ɪn'kɒmpɪtənt] a unfähig; (not qualified) nicht berechtigt.

incomplete [ɪnkəm'pliːt] a unvollständig.

incomprehensible [ɪnkɒmprɪ'hensəbl] a unverständlich.

inconceivable [ɪnkən'siːvəbl] a unvorstellbar.

inconclusive [ɪnkən'kluːsɪv] a nicht schlüssig.

incongruity [ɪnkɒŋ'gruːɪtɪ] n Seltsamkeit f; (of remark etc) Unangebrachtsein nt.

incongruous [ɪn'kɒŋgruəs] a seltsam; remark unangebracht.

inconsequential [ɪnkɒnsɪ'kwenʃəl] a belanglos.

inconsiderable [ɪnkən'sɪdərəbl] a unerheblich.

inconsiderate [ɪnkən'sɪdərət] a rücksichtslos; (hasty) unüberlegt.

inconsistency [ɪnkən'sɪstənsɪ] n innere(r) Widerspruch m; (state) Unbeständigkeit f.

inconsistent [ɪnkən'sɪstənt] a unvereinbar; behaviour inkonsequent; action, speech widersprüchlich; person, work unbeständig.

inconspicuous [ɪnkən'spɪkjuəs] a unauffällig.

inconstancy [ɪn'kɒnstənsɪ] n Unbeständigkeit f.

inconstant [ɪn'kɒnstənt] a unbeständig.

incontinence [ɪn'kɒntɪnəns] n (Med) Unfähigkeit f, Stuhl und Harn zurückzuhalten; (fig) Zügellosigkeit f.

incontinent [ɪn'kɒntɪnənt] a (Med) nicht fähig, Stuhl und Harn zurückzuhalten; (fig) zügellos.

inconvenience [ɪnkən'viːnɪəns] n Unbequemlichkeit f; (trouble to others) Unannehmlichkeiten pl.

inconvenient [ɪnkən'viːnɪənt] a ungelegen; journey unbequem.

incorporate [ɪn'kɔːrpəreɪt] vt (include) aufnehmen; (unite) vereinigen.

incorporated [ɪn'kɔːrpəreɪtɪd] a eingetragen; (US) GmbH.

incorrect [ɪnkə'rekt] a unrichtig; behaviour inkorrekt.

incorrigible [ɪn'kɒrɪdʒəbl] a unverbesserlich.

incorruptible [ɪnkə'rʌptəbl] a unzerstörbar; person unbestechlich.

increase ['ɪnkriːs] n Zunahme f, Erhöhung f; (pay —) Gehaltserhöhung f; (in size) Vergrößerung f; [ɪn'kriːs] vt erhöhen; wealth, rage vermehren; business erweitern; vi zunehmen; (prices) steigen; (in size) größer werden; (in number) sich vermehren.

increasingly [ɪn'kriːsɪŋlɪ] ad zunehmend.

incredible a, **incredibly** ad [ɪn'kredəbl, -blɪ] unglaublich.

incredulity [ɪnkrɪ'djuːlɪtɪ] n Ungläubigkeit f.

incredulous [ɪn'kredjuləs] a ungläubig.

increment ['ɪnkrɪmənt] n Zulage f.

incriminate [ɪn'krɪmɪneɪt] vt belasten.

incubation [ɪnkju'beɪʃən] n Ausbrüten nt; ~ **period** Inkubationszeit f.

incubator ['ɪnkjubeɪtə*] n Brutkasten m.

incur [ɪn'kɜː*] vt sich zuziehen; debts machen.

incurable [ɪn'kjuərəbl] a unheilbar; (fig) unverbesserlich.

incursion [ɪn'kɜːʃən] n (feindlicher) Einfall m.

indebted [ɪn'detɪd] a (obliged) verpflichtet (to sb jdm); (owing) verschuldet.

indecency [ɪn'diːsnsɪ] n Unanständigkeit f.

indecent [ɪn'diːsnt] a unanständig.

indecision [ɪndɪ'sɪʒən] n Unschlüssigkeit f.

indecisive [ɪndɪ'saɪsɪv] a battle nicht entscheidend; result unentschieden; person unentschlossen.

indeed [ɪn'diːd] ad tatsächlich, in der Tat.

indefinable [ɪndɪ'faɪnəbl] a undefinierbar; (vague) unbestimmt.

indefinite [ɪn'defɪnɪt] a unbestimmt; ~**ly** ad auf unbestimmte Zeit; wait unbegrenzt lange.

indelible [ɪn'deləbl] a unauslöschlich; ~ **pencil** Tintenstift m.

indemnify [ɪn'demnɪfaɪ] vt entschädigen; (safeguard) versichern.

indentation [ɪnden'teɪʃən] n Einbuchtung f; (Print) Einrückung f.

independence [ɪndɪ'pendəns] n Unabhängigkeit f.

independent [ɪndɪ'pendənt] a (free) unabhängig; (unconnected) unabhängig von.

indescribable [ɪndɪs'kraɪbəbl] a unbeschreiblich.

index ['ɪndeks] n Index m (also Eccl), Verzeichnis nt; ~ **finger** Zeigefinger m.

indicate ['ɪndɪkeɪt] vt anzeigen; (hint) andeuten.

indication [ɪndɪ'keɪʃən] n Anzeichen nt; (information) Angabe f.

indicative [ɪn'dɪkətɪv] n (Gram) Indikativ m.

indicator ['ɪndɪkeɪtə*] n (sign) (An)-zeichen nt; (Aut) Richtungsanzeiger m.

indict [ɪn'daɪt] vt anklagen; ~**able** a person strafrechtlich verfolgbar; offence strafbar; ~**ment** Anklage f.

indifference [ɪn'dɪfrəns] n (lack of interest) Gleichgültigkeit f; (unimportance) Unwichtigkeit f.

indifferent [ɪn'dɪfrənt] a (not caring) gleichgültig; (unimportant) unwichtig; (mediocre) mäßig.

indigenous [ɪn'dɪdʒɪnəs] a einheimisch; **a plant ~ to X** eine in X vorkommende Pflanze.

indigestible [ɪndɪ'dʒestəbl] a unverdaulich.

indigestion [ɪndɪ'dʒestʃən] n Verdauungsstörung f; verdorbene(r) Magen m.

indignant [ɪn'dɪgnənt] a ungehalten, entrüstet.

indignation [ɪndɪg'neɪʃən] n Entrüstung f.

indignity [ɪn'dɪgnɪtɪ] n Demütigung f.

indigo ['ɪndɪgəu] n Indigo m or nt; a indigoblau.

indirect a, ~**ly** ad [ɪndɪ'rekt, -lɪ] indirekt; answer nicht direkt; **by ~ means** auf Umwegen.

indiscernible [ɪndɪ'sɔːnəbl] *a* nicht wahrnehmbar.

indiscreet [ɪndɪs'kriːt] *a* (*insensitive*) unbedacht; (*improper*) taktlos; (*telling secrets*) indiskret.

indiscretion [ɪndɪs'kreʃən] *n* Taktlosigkeit *f*; Indiskretion *f*.

indiscriminate [ɪndɪs'krɪmɪnət] *a* wahllos; kritiklos.

indispensable [ɪndɪs'pensəbl] *a* unentbehrlich.

indisposed [ɪndɪs'pəʊzd] *a* unpäßlich.

indisposition [ɪndɪspə'zɪʃən] *n* Unpäßlichkeit *f*.

indisputable [ɪndɪs'pjuːtəbl] *a* unbestreitbar; *evidence* unanfechtbar.

indistinct [ɪndɪs'tɪŋkt] *a* undeutlich.

indistinguishable [ɪndɪs'tɪŋɡwɪʃəbl] *a* nicht unterscheidbar; *difference* unmerklich.

individual [ɪndɪ'vɪdjʊəl] *n* Einzelne(r) *mf*, Individuum *nt*; *a* individuell; *case* Einzel-; (*of, for one person*) eigen, individuell; (*characteristic*) eigentümlich; **~ist** Individualist *m*; **~ity** [ɪndɪvɪdju'ælɪtɪ] Individualität *f*; **~ly** *ad* einzeln, individuell.

indoctrinate [ɪn'dɒktrɪneɪt] *vt* indoktrinieren.

indoctrination [ɪndɒktrɪ'neɪʃən] *n* Indoktrination *f*.

indolence ['ɪndələns] *n* Trägheit *f*.

indolent ['ɪndələnt] *a* träge.

indoor ['ɪndɔː*] *a* Haus-; Zimmer-; Innen-; (*Sport*) Hallen-; **~s** *ad* drinnen, im Haus; **to go ~s** hinein *or* ins Haus gehen.

indubitable [ɪn'djuːbɪtəbl] *a* unzweifelhaft.

indubitably [ɪn'djuːbɪtəblɪ] *ad* zweifellos.

induce [ɪn'djuːs] *vt* dazu bewegen, veranlassen; *reaction* herbeiführen; **~ment** Veranlassung *f*; (*incentive*) Anreiz *m*.

induct [ɪn'dʌkt] *vt* in sein Amt einführen.

indulge [ɪn'dʌldʒ] *vt* (*give way*) nachgeben (+*dat*); (*gratify*) frönen (+*dat*); **to ~ o.s. in sth** sich (*dat*) etw gönnen; *vi* frönen (*in dat*), sich gönnen (*in acc*); **~nce** Nachsicht *f*; (*enjoyment*) (übermäßiger) Genuß *m*; **~nt** *a* nachsichtig; (*pej*) nachgiebig.

industrial [ɪn'dʌstrɪəl] *a* Industrie-, industriell; *dispute, injury* Arbeits-; (*in*) Industrielle(r) *mf*; **~ize** *vt* industrialisieren.

industrious [ɪn'dʌstrɪəs] *a* fleißig.

industry ['ɪndəstrɪ] *n* Industrie *f*; (*diligence*) Fleiß *m*; **hotel ~** Hotelgewerbe *nt*.

inebriated [ɪ'niːbrɪeɪtɪd] *a* betrunken, berauscht.

inedible [ɪn'edɪbl] *a* ungenießbar.

ineffective [ɪnɪ'fektɪv], **ineffectual** [ɪnɪ'fektʃʊəl] *a* unwirksam, wirkungslos; *person* untauglich.

inefficiency [ɪnɪ'fɪʃənsɪ] *n* Ineffizienz *f*.

inefficient [ɪnɪ'fɪʃənt] *a* ineffizient; (*ineffective*) unwirksam.

inelegant [ɪn'elɪɡənt] *a* unelegant.

ineligible [ɪn'elɪdʒəbl] *a* nicht berechtigt; *candidate* nicht wählbar.

ineluctable [ɪnɪ'lʌktəbl] *a* unausweichlich.

inept [ɪ'nept] *a* *remark* unpassend; *person* ungeeignet.

inequality [ɪnɪ'kwɒlɪtɪ] *n* Ungleichheit *f*.

ineradicable [ɪnɪ'rædɪkəbl] *a* unausrottbar; *mistake* unabänderlich; *guilt* tiefsitzend.

inert [ɪ'nɜːt] *a* träge; (*Chem*) inaktiv; (*motionless*) unbeweglich.

inertia [ɪ'nɜːʃə] *n* Trägheit *f*.

inescapable [ɪnɪs'keɪpəbl] *a* unvermeidbar.

inessential [ɪnɪ'senʃəl] *a* unwesentlich.

inestimable [ɪn'estɪməbl] *a* unschätzbar.

inevitability [ɪnevɪtə'bɪlɪtɪ] *n* Unvermeidlichkeit *f*.

inevitable [ɪn'evɪtəbl] *a* unvermeidlich.

inexact [ɪnɪɡ'zækt] *a* ungenau.

inexcusable [ɪnɪks'kjuːzəbl] *a* unverzeihlich.

inexhaustible [ɪnɪɡ'zɔːstəbl] *a* *wealth* unerschöpflich; *talker* unermüdlich; *curiosity* unstillbar.

inexorable [ɪn'eksərəbl] *a* unerbittlich.

inexpensive [ɪnɪks'pensɪv] *a* preiswert.

inexperience [ɪnɪks'pɪərɪəns] *n* Unerfahrenheit *f*; **~d** *a* unerfahren.

inexplicable [ɪnɪks'plɪkəbl] *a* unerklärlich.

inexpressible [ɪnɪks'presəbl] *a* *pain, joy* unbeschreiblich; *thoughts* nicht ausdrückbar.

inextricable [ɪnɪks'trɪkəbl] *a* un(auf)lösbar.

infallibility [ɪnfælə'bɪlɪtɪ] *n* Unfehlbarkeit *f*.

infallible [ɪn'fæləbl] *a* unfehlbar.

infamous ['ɪnfəməs] *a* *place* verrufen; *deed* schändlich; *person* niederträchtig.

infamy ['ɪnfəmɪ] *n* Verrufenheit *f*; Niedertracht *f*; (*disgrace*) Schande *f*.

infancy ['ɪnfənsɪ] *n* frühe Kindheit *f*; (*fig*) Anfangsstadium *nt*.

infant ['ɪnfənt] *n* kleine(s) Kind *nt*, Säugling *m*; **~ile** *a* kindisch, infantil; **~ school** Vorschule *f*.

infantry ['ɪnfəntrɪ] *n* Infanterie *f*; **~man** Infanterist *m*.

infatuated [ɪn'fætjʊeɪtɪd] *a* vernarrt; **to become ~ with** sich vernarren in (+*acc*).

infatuation [ɪnfætju'eɪʃən] *n* Vernarrtheit *f* (*with in* +*acc*).

infect [ɪn'fekt] *vt* anstecken (*also fig*), infizieren; **~ion** Ansteckung *f*, Infektion *f*; **~ious** [ɪn'fekʃəs] *a* ansteckend.

infer [ɪn'fɜː*] *vt* schließen; **~ence** [ɪnfərəns] *n* Schlußfolgerung *f*.

inferior [ɪn'fɪərɪə*] *a* *rank* untergeordnet, niedriger; *quality* minderwertig; (*in*) untergebene(r) *m*; **~ity** [ɪnfɪərɪ'ɒrɪtɪ] Minderwertigkeit *f*; (*in rank*) untergeordnete Stellung *f*; **~ity complex** Minderwertigkeitskomplex *m*.

infernal [ɪn'fɜːnl] *a* höllisch.

inferno [ɪn'fɜːnəʊ] *n* Hölle *f*, Inferno *nt*.

infertile [ɪn'fɜːtaɪl] *a* unfruchtbar.

infertility [ɪnfɜː'tɪlɪtɪ] *n* Unfruchtbarkeit *f*.

infest [ɪn'fest] *vt* plagen, heimsuchen; **to be ~ed with** wimmeln von.

infidel ['ɪnfɪdəl] n Ungläubige(r) mf.
infidelity [ɪnfɪ'delɪtɪ] n Untreue f.
in-fighting ['ɪnfaɪtɪŋ] n Nahkampf m.
infiltrate ['ɪnfɪltreɪt] vt infiltrieren; spies einschleusen; (liquid) durchdringen; vi (Mil, liquid) einsickern; (Pol) unterwandern (into acc).
infinite ['ɪnfɪnɪt] a unendlich.
infinitive [ɪn'fɪnɪtɪv] n Infinitiv m, Nennform f.
infinity [ɪn'fɪnɪtɪ] n Unendlichkeit f.
infirm [ɪn'fɜːm] a schwach, gebrechlich; (irresolute) willensschwach.
infirmary [ɪn'fɜːmərɪ] n Krankenhaus nt.
infirmity [ɪn'fɜːmɪtɪ] n Schwäche f, Gebrechlichkeit f.
inflame [ɪn'fleɪm] vt (Med) entzünden; person reizen; anger erregen.
inflammable [ɪn'flæməbl] a feuergefährlich.
inflammation [ɪnflə'meɪʃən] n Entzündung f.
inflate [ɪn'fleɪt] vt aufblasen; tyre aufpumpen; prices hochtreiben.
inflation [ɪn'fleɪʃən] n Inflation f; ~ary increase inflationistisch; situation inflationär.
inflexible [ɪn'fleksəbl] a person nicht flexibel; opinion starr; thing unbiegsam.
inflict [ɪn'flɪkt] vt zufügen (sth on sb jdm etw); punishment auferlegen (on dat); wound beibringen (on dat); ~ion [ɪn'flɪkʃən] Zufügung f; Auferlegung f; (suffering) Heimsuchung f.
inflow ['ɪnfləʊ] n Einfließen nt, Zustrom m.
influence ['ɪnflʊəns] n Einfluß m; vt beeinflussen.
influential [ɪnflʊ'enʃəl] a einflußreich.
influenza [ɪnflʊ'enzə] n Grippe f.
influx ['ɪnflʌks] n (of water) Einfluß m; (of people) Zustrom m; (of ideas) Eindringen nt.
inform [ɪn'fɔːm] vt informieren; to keep sb ~ed jdn auf dem laufenden halten.
informal [ɪn'fɔːməl] a zwanglos; ~ity [ɪnfɔː'mælɪtɪ] Ungezwungenheit f.
information [ɪnfə'meɪʃən] n Auskunft f, Information f.
informative [ɪn'fɔːmətɪv] a informativ; person mitteilsam.
informer [ɪn'fɔːmə*] n Denunziant(in f) m.
infra-red ['ɪnfrə'red] a infrarot.
infrequent [ɪn'friːkwənt] a selten.
infringe [ɪn'frɪndʒ] vt law verstoßen gegen; ~ upon vt verletzen; ~ment Verstoß m, Verletzung f.
infuriate [ɪn'fjʊərɪeɪt] vt wütend machen.
infuriating [ɪn'fjʊərɪeɪtɪŋ] a ärgerlich.
ingenious [ɪn'dʒiːnɪəs] a genial; thing raffiniert.
ingenuity [ɪndʒɪ'njuːɪtɪ] n Findigkeit f, Genialität f; Raffiniertheit f.
ingot ['ɪŋgət] n Barren m.
ingratiate [ɪn'greɪʃɪeɪt] vt einschmeicheln (o.s. with sb sich bei jdm).
ingratitude [ɪn'grætɪtjuːd] n Undankbarkeit f.
ingredient [ɪn'griːdɪənt] n Bestandteil m; (Cook) Zutat f.

inhabit [ɪn'hæbɪt] vt bewohnen; ~ant Bewohner(in f) m; (of island, town) Einwohner(in f) m.
inhale [ɪn'heɪl] vt einatmen; (Med, cigarettes) inhalieren.
inherent [ɪn'hɪərənt] a innewohnend (in dat).
inherit [ɪn'herɪt] vt erben; ~ance Erbe nt, Erbschaft f.
inhibit [ɪn'hɪbɪt] vt hemmen; (restrain) hindern; ~ion [ɪnhɪ'bɪʃən] Hemmung f.
inhospitable [ɪnhɒs'pɪtəbl] a person ungastlich; country unwirtlich.
inhuman [ɪn'hjuːmən] a unmenschlich.
inimitable [ɪ'nɪmɪtəbl] a unnachahmlich.
iniquity [ɪ'nɪkwɪtɪ] n Ungerechtigkeit f.
initial [ɪ'nɪʃəl] a anfänglich, Anfangs-; n Anfangsbuchstabe m, Initiale f; vt abzeichnen; (Pol) paraphieren; ~ly ad anfangs.
initiate [ɪ'nɪʃɪeɪt] vt einführen; negotiations einleiten; (instruct) einweihen.
initiation [ɪnɪʃɪ'eɪʃən] n Einführung f; Einleitung f.
initiative [ɪ'nɪʃətɪv] n Initiative f.
inject [ɪn'dʒekt] vt einspritzen; (fig) einflößen; ~ion Spritze f, Injektion f.
injure ['ɪndʒə*] vt verletzen; (fig) schaden (+dat).
injury ['ɪndʒərɪ] n Verletzung f.
injustice [ɪn'dʒʌstɪs] n Ungerechtigkeit f.
ink [ɪŋk] n Tinte f.
inkling ['ɪŋklɪŋ] n (dunkle) Ahnung f.
inlaid ['ɪn'leɪd] a eingelegt, Einlege-.
inland ['ɪnlænd] a Binnen-; (domestic) Inlands-; ad landeinwärts; ~ revenue (Brit) Fiskus m.
in-law ['ɪnlɔː] n angeheiratete(r) Verwandte(r) mf.
inlet ['ɪnlet] n Öffnung f, Einlaß m; (bay) kleine Bucht f.
inmate ['ɪnmeɪt] n Insasse m.
inn [ɪn] n Gasthaus nt, Wirtshaus nt.
innate [ɪ'neɪt] a angeboren, eigen (+dat).
inner ['ɪnə*] a inner, Innen-; (fig) verborgen, innerste(r,s).
innocence ['ɪnəsns] n Unschuld f; (ignorance) Unkenntnis f.
innocent ['ɪnəsnt] a unschuldig.
innocuous [ɪ'nɒkjuəs] a harmlos.
innovation [ɪnəʊ'veɪʃən] n Neuerung f.
innuendo [ɪnju'endəʊ] n (versteckte) Anspielung f.
innumerable [ɪ'njuːmərəbl] a unzählig.
inoculation [ɪnɒkjʊ'leɪʃən] n Impfung f.
inopportune [ɪn'ɒpətjuːn] a remark unangebracht; visit ungelegen.
inordinately [ɪ'nɔːdɪnɪtlɪ] ad unmäßig.
inorganic [ɪnɔː'gænɪk] a unorganisch; (Chem) anorganisch.
in-patient ['ɪnpeɪʃənt] n stationäre(r) Patient(in f) m.
input ['ɪnpʊt] n (Elec) (Auf)ladung f; (Tech) zugeführte Menge f; (labour) angewandte Arbeitsleistung f; (money) Investitionssumme f.
inquest ['ɪnkwest] n gerichtliche Untersuchung f.
inquire [ɪn'kwaɪə*] vi sich erkundigen; vt

price sich erkundigen nach; ~ **into** *vt* untersuchen.

inquiring [ɪnˈkwaɪərɪŋ] *a mind* wissensdurstig.

inquiry [ɪnˈkwaɪərɪ] *n* (*question*) Erkundigung *f*, Nachfrage *f*; (*investigation*) Untersuchung *f*; ~ **office** Auskunft(sbüro *nt*) *f*.

inquisitive [ɪnˈkwɪzɪtɪv] *a* neugierig; *look* forschend.

inroad [ˈɪnrəʊd] *n* (*Mil*) Einfall *m*; (*fig*) Eingriff *m*.

insane [ɪnˈseɪn] *a* wahnsinnig; (*Med*) geisteskrank.

insanitary [ɪnˈsænɪtərɪ] *a* unhygienisch, gesundheitsschädlich.

insanity [ɪnˈsænɪtɪ] *n* Wahnsinn *m*.

insatiable [ɪnˈseɪʃəbl] *a* unersättlich.

inscription [ɪnˈskrɪpʃən] *n* (*on stone*) Inschrift *f*; (*in book*) Widmung *f*.

inscrutable [ɪnˈskruːtəbl] *a* unergründlich.

insect [ˈɪnsekt] *n* Insekt *nt*; ~**icide** [ɪnˈsektɪsaɪd] Insektenvertilgungsmittel *nt*.

insecure [ɪnsɪˈkjʊə*] *a person* unsicher; *thing* nicht fest *or* sicher.

insecurity [ɪnsɪˈkjʊərɪtɪ] *n* Unsicherheit *f*.

insensible [ɪnˈsensɪbl] *a* gefühllos; (*unconscious*) bewußtlos; (*imperceptible*) unmerklich; ~ **of** *or* **to** sth unempfänglich für etw.

insensitive [ɪnˈsensɪtɪv] *a* (*to pain*) unempfindlich; (*without feelings*) gefühllos.

inseparable [ɪnˈsepərəbl] *a people* unzertrennlich; *word* untrennbar.

insert [ɪnˈsɜːt] *vt* einfügen; *coin* einwerfen; (*stick into*) hineinstecken; *advert* aufgeben; [ˈɪnsɜːt] *n* Beifügung *f*; (*in book*) Einlage *f*; (*in magazine*) Beilage *f*; ~**ion** Einfügung *f*; (*Press*) Inserat *nt*.

inshore [ˈɪnʃɔː*] *n* Küsten-; [ˈɪnˈʃɔː*] *ad* an der Küste.

inside [ˈɪnˈsaɪd] *n* Innenseite *f*, Innere(s) *nt*; *a* inner(e,s), Innen-; *ad* (*place*) innen; (*direction*) nach innen, hinein; *prep* (*place*) in (+*dat*); (*direction*) in (+*acc*) ... hinein; (*time*) innerhalb (+*gen*); ~ **forward** (*Sport*) Halbstürmer *m*; ~ **out** *ad* linksherum; *know* in- und auswendig; ~**r** Eingeweihte(r) *mf*; (*member*) Mitglied *nt*.

insidious [ɪnˈsɪdɪəs] *a* heimtückisch.

insight [ˈɪnsaɪt] *n* Einsicht *f*; Einblick *m* (*into* in +*acc*).

insignificant [ɪnsɪgˈnɪfɪkənt] *a* unbedeutend.

insincere [ɪnsɪnˈsɪə*] *a* unaufrichtig, falsch.

insincerity [ɪnsɪnˈserɪtɪ] *n* Unaufrichtigkeit *f*.

insinuate [ɪnˈsɪnjʊeɪt] *vt* (*hint*) andeuten; **to** ~ **o.s. into** sth sich in etw (*acc*) einschleichen.

insinuation [ɪnsɪnjʊˈeɪʃən] *n* Anspielung *f*.

insipid [ɪnˈsɪpɪd] *a* fad(e).

insist [ɪnˈsɪst] *vi* bestehen (*on* auf +*acc*); ~**ence** Bestehen *nt*; ~**ent** *a* hartnäckig; (*urgent*) dringend.

insolence [ˈɪnsələns] *n* Frechheit *f*.

insolent [ˈɪnsələnt] *a* frech.

insoluble [ɪnˈsɒljʊbl] *a* unlösbar; (*Chem*) unlöslich.

insolvent [ɪnˈsɒlvənt] *a* zahlungsunfähig.

insomnia [ɪnˈsɒmnɪə] *n* Schlaflosigkeit *f*.

inspect [ɪnˈspekt] *vt* besichtigen, prüfen; (*officially*) inspizieren; ~**ion** Besichtigung *f*, Inspektion *f*; ~**or** (*official*) Aufsichtsbeamte(r) *m*, Inspektor *m*; (*police*) Polizeikommissar *m*; (*Rail*) Kontrolleur *m*.

inspiration [ɪnspɪˈreɪʃən] *n* Inspiration *f*.

inspire [ɪnˈspaɪə*] *vt respect* einflößen (*in dat*); *hope* wecken (*in* in +*dat*); *person* inspirieren; **to** ~ **sb to do sth** jdn dazu anregen, etw zu tun; ~**d** *a* begabt, einfallsreich.

inspiring [ɪnˈspaɪərɪŋ] *a* begeisternd.

instability [ɪnstəˈbɪlɪtɪ] *n* Unbeständigkeit *f*, Labilität *f*.

install [ɪnˈstɔːl] *vt* (*put in*) einbauen, installieren; *telephone* anschließen; (*establish*) einsetzen; ~**ation** [ɪnstəˈleɪʃən] (*of person*) (Amts)einsetzung *f*; (*of machinery*) Einbau *m*, Installierung *f*; (*machines etc*) Anlage *f*.

instalment, (*US*) **installment** [ɪnˈstɔːlmənt] *n* Rate *f*; (*of story*) Fortsetzung *f*; **to pay in** ~**s** auf Raten zahlen.

instance [ˈɪnstəns] *n* Fall *m*; (*example*) Beispiel *nt*; **for** ~ zum Beispiel.

instant [ˈɪnstənt] *n* Augenblick *m*; *a* augenblicklich, sofortig; ~ **coffee** Pulverkaffee *m*; ~**ly** *ad* sofort.

instead [ɪnˈsted] *ad* stattdessen; ~ **of** *prep* anstatt (+*gen*).

instigation [ɪnstɪˈgeɪʃən] *n* Veranlassung *f*; (*of crime etc*) Anstiftung *f*.

instil [ɪnˈstɪl] *vt* (*fig*) beibringen (*in sb* jdm).

instinct [ˈɪnstɪŋkt] *n* Instinkt *m*; ~**ive** *a*, ~**ively** *ad* [ɪnˈstɪŋktɪv, -lɪ] instinktiv.

institute [ˈɪnstɪtjuːt] *n* Institut *nt*; (*society also*) Gesellschaft *f*; *vt* einführen; *search* einleiten.

institution [ɪnstɪˈtjuːʃən] *n* (*custom*) Einrichtung *f*, Brauch *m*; (*society*) Institution *f*; (*home*) Anstalt *f*; (*beginning*) Einführung *f*, Einleitung *f*.

instruct [ɪnˈstrʌkt] *vt* anweisen; (*officially*) instruieren; ~**ion** [ɪnˈstrʌkʃən] Unterricht *m*; ~**ions** *pl* Anweisungen *pl*; (*for use*) Gebrauchsanweisung *f*; ~**ive** *a* lehrreich; ~**or** Lehrer *m*; (*Mil*) Ausbilder *m*.

instrument [ˈɪnstrʊmənt] *n* (*tool*) Instrument *nt*, Werkzeug *nt*; (*Mus*) (Musik)instrument *nt*; ~**al** [ɪnstrʊˈmentl] *a* (*Mus*) Instrumental-; (*helpful*) behilflich (*in* bei); ~**alist** [ɪnstrʊˈmentəlɪst] Instrumentalist *m*; ~ **panel** Armaturenbrett *nt*.

insubordinate [ɪnsəˈbɔːdənət] *a* aufsässig, widersetzlich.

insubordination [ˈɪnsəbɔːdɪˈneɪʃən] *n* Gehorsamsverweigerung *f*.

insufferable [ɪnˈsʌfərəbl] *a* unerträglich.

insufficient *a*, ~**ly** *ad* [ɪnsəˈfɪʃnt, -lɪ] ungenügend.

insular [ˈɪnsjʊlə*] *a* (*fig*) engstirnig; ~**ity** [ɪnsjʊˈlærɪtɪ] (*fig*) Engstirnigkeit *f*.

insulate [ˈɪnsjʊleɪt] *vt* (*Elec*) isolieren; (*fig*) abschirmen (*from* vor +*dat*).

insulating tape ['ɪnsjuleɪtɪŋteɪp] *n* Isolierband *nt*.

insulation [ɪnsju'leɪʃən] *n* Isolierung *f*.

insulator ['ɪnsjuleɪtə*] *n* Isolator *m*.

insulin ['ɪnsjulɪn] *n* Insulin *nt*.

insult ['ɪnsʌlt] *n* Beleidigung *f*; [ɪn'sʌlt] *vt* beleidigen; ~**ing** [ɪn'sʌltɪŋ] *a* beleidigend.

insuperable [ɪn'su:pərəbl] *a* unüberwindlich.

insurance [ɪn'ʃuərəns] *n* Versicherung *f*; ~ **agent** Versicherungsvertreter *m*; ~ **policy** Versicherungspolice *f*.

insure [ɪn'ʃuə*] *vt* versichern.

insurmountable [ɪnsə'mauntəbl] *a* unüberwindlich.

insurrection [ɪnsə'rekʃən] *n* Aufstand *m*.

intact [ɪn'tækt] *a* intakt, unangetastet, ganz.

intake ['ɪnteɪk] *n* (*place*) Einlaßöffnung *f*; (*act*) Aufnahme *f*; (*amount*) aufgenommene Menge *f*; (*Sch*) Neuaufnahme *f*.

intangible [ɪn'tændʒəbl] *a* unfaßbar; *thing* nicht greifbar.

integer ['ɪntɪdʒə*] *n* ganze Zahl *f*.

integral ['ɪntɪgrəl] *a* (*essential*) wesentlich; (*complete*) vollständig; (*Math*) Integral-.

integrate ['ɪntɪgreɪt] *vt* vereinigen; *people* eingliedern, integrieren.

integration [ɪntɪ'greɪʃən] *n* Eingliederung *f*, Integration *f*.

integrity [ɪn'tegrɪtɪ] *n* (*honesty*) Redlichkeit *f*, Integrität *f*.

intellect ['ɪntɪlekt] *n* Intellekt *m*; ~**ual** [ɪntɪ'lektjuəl] *a* geistig, intellektuell; *n* Intellektuelle(r) *mf*.

intelligence [ɪn'telɪdʒəns] *n* (*understanding*) Intelligenz *f*; (*news*) Information *f*; (*Mil*) Geheimdienst *m*.

intelligent [ɪn'telɪdʒənt] *a* intelligent; *beings* vernunftbegabt; ~**ly** *ad* klug; *write, speak* verständlich.

intelligible [ɪn'telɪdʒəbl] *a* verständlich.

intemperate [ɪn'tempərət] *a* unmäßig.

intend [ɪn'tend] *vt* beabsichtigen; **that was** ~**ed for you** das war für dich gedacht.

intense [ɪn'tens] *a* stark, intensiv; *person* ernsthaft; ~**ly** *ad* äußerst; *study* intensiv.

intensify [ɪn'tensɪfaɪ] *vt* verstärken, intensivieren.

intensity [ɪn'tensɪtɪ] *n* Intensität *f*, Stärke *f*.

intensive *a*, ~**ly** *ad* [ɪn'tensɪv, -lɪ] intensiv.

intent [ɪn'tent] *n* Absicht *f*; **to all** ~**s and purposes** praktisch; ~**ly** *ad* aufmerksam; *look* forschend; **to be** ~ **on doing sth** fest entschlossen sein, etw zu tun.

intention [ɪn'tenʃən] *n* Absicht *f*; **with good** ~**s** mit guten Vorsätzen; ~**al** *a*, ~**ally** *ad* absichtlich.

inter [ɪn'tɜ:*] *vt* beerdigen.

inter- ['ɪntə*] *pref* zwischen-, Zwischen-.

interact [ɪntər'ækt] *vi* aufeinander einwirken; ~**ion** Wechselwirkung *f*.

intercede [ɪntə'si:d] *vi* sich verwenden; (*in argument*) vermitteln.

intercept [ɪntə'sept] *vt* abfangen; ~**ion** Abfangen *nt*.

interchange ['ɪntə'tʃeɪndʒ] *n* (*exchange*) Austausch *m*; (*on roads*) Verkehrskreuz *nt*; [ɪntə'tʃeɪndʒ] *vt* austauschen; ~**able** [ɪntə'tʃeɪndʒəbl] *a* austauschbar.

intercom ['ɪntəkɔm] *n* (Gegen)sprechanlage *f*.

interconnect [ɪntəkə'nekt] *vt* miteinander verbinden; *vi* miteinander verbunden sein; (*roads*) zusammenführen.

intercontinental ['ɪntəkɔntɪ'nentl] *a* interkontinental.

intercourse ['ɪntəkɔ:s] *n* (*exchange*) Verkehr *m*, Beziehungen *pl*; (*sexual*) Geschlechtsverkehr *m*.

interdependence [ɪntədɪ'pendəns] *n* gegenseitige Abhängigkeit *f*.

interest ['ɪntrest] *n* Interesse *nt*; (*Fin*) Zinsen *pl*; (*Comm: share*) Anteil *m*; (*group*) Interessengruppe *f*; **to be of** ~ **von** Interesse sein; *vt* interessieren; ~**ed** *a* (*having claims*) beteiligt; (*attentive*) interessiert; **to be** ~**ed in** sich interessieren für; ~**ing** *a* interessant.

interfere [ɪntə'fɪə*] *vi* (*meddle*) sich einmischen (**with** in + *acc*) stören (**with** *acc*); (**with** *an object*) sich zu schaffen machen (**with** an +*dat*); ~**nce** Einmischung *f*; (*TV*) Störung *f*.

interim ['ɪntərɪm] *a* vorläufig; *n*: **in the** ~ inzwischen.

interior [ɪn'tɪərɪə*] *n* Innere(s) *nt*; *a* innere(r,s), Innen-.

interjection [ɪntə'dʒekʃən] *n* Ausruf *m*; (*Gram*) Interjektion *f*.

interlock [ɪntə'lɔk] *vi* ineinandergreifen; *vt* zusammenschließen, verzahnen.

interloper ['ɪntələupə*] *n* Eindringling *m*.

interlude ['ɪntəlu:d] *n* Pause *f*; (*in entertainment*) Zwischenspiel *nt*.

intermarriage [ɪntə'mærɪdʒ] *n* Mischehe *f*.

intermarry [ɪntə'mærɪ] *vi* untereinander heiraten.

intermediary [ɪntə'mi:dɪərɪ] *n* Vermittler *m*.

intermediate [ɪntə'mi:dɪət] *a* Zwischen-, Mittel-.

interminable [ɪn'tɜ:mɪnəbl] *a* endlos.

intermission [ɪntə'mɪʃən] *n* Pause *f*.

intermittent [ɪntə'mɪtənt] *a* periodisch, stoßweise; ~**ly** *ad* mit Unterbrechungen.

intern [ɪn'tɜ:n] *vt* internieren; ['ɪntɜ:n] *n* (*US*) Assistenzarzt *m*/-ärztin *f*.

internal [ɪn'tɜ:nl] *a* (*inside*) innere(r,s); (*domestic*) Inlands-; ~**ly** *ad* innen; (*Med*) innerlich; intern; ~ **revenue** (*US*) Sozialprodukt *nt*.

international [ɪntə'næʃnəl] *a* international; *n* (*Sport*) Nationalspieler *m*; (*match*) internationale(s) Spiel *nt*.

internment [ɪn'tɜ:nmənt] *n* Internierung *f*.

interplanetary [ɪntə'plænɪtərɪ] *a* interplanetar.

interplay ['ɪntəpleɪ] *n* Wechselspiel *nt*.

Interpol ['ɪntəpɔl] *n* Interpol *f*.

interpret [ɪn'tɜ:prɪt] *vt* (*explain*) auslegen, interpretieren; (*translate*) verdolmetschen; (*represent*) darstellen; ~**ation** Deutung *f*, Interpretation *f*; (*translation*)

Dolmetschen *nt*; ~**er** Dolmetscher(in *f*) *m*.

interrelated [ɪntərɪˈleɪtɪd] *a* untereinander zusammenhängend.

interrogate [ɪnˈterəgeɪt] *vt* befragen; (*Jur*) verhören.

interrogation [ɪntərəˈgeɪʃən] *n* Verhör *nt*.

interrogative [ɪntəˈrɒgətɪv] *a* fragend, Frage-.

interrogator [ɪnˈterəgeɪtə*] *n* Vernehmungsbeamte(r) *m*.

interrupt [ɪntəˈrʌpt] *vt* unterbrechen; ~**ion** Unterbrechung *f*.

intersect [ɪntəˈsekt] *vt* (durch)schneiden; *vi* sich schneiden; ~**ion** (*of roads*) Kreuzung *f*; (*of lines*) Schnittpunkt *m*.

intersperse [ɪntəˈspɜːs] *vt* (*scatter*) verstreuen; **to** ~ **sth with sth** etw mit etw durchsetzen.

intertwine [ɪntəˈtwaɪn] *vti* (sich) verflechten.

interval [ˈɪntəvəl] *n* Abstand *m*; (*break*) Pause *f*; (*Mus*) Intervall *nt*; **at** ~**s** hier und da; (*time*) dann und wann.

intervene [ɪntəˈviːn] *vi* dazwischenliegen; (*act*) einschreiten (*in gegen*), eingreifen (*in* in +*acc*).

intervening [ɪntəˈviːnɪŋ] *a* dazwischenliegend.

intervention [ɪntəˈvenʃən] *n* Eingreifen *nt*, Intervention *f*.

interview [ˈɪntəvjuː] *n* (*Press etc*) Interview *nt*; (*for job*) Vorstellungsgespräch *nt*; *vt* interviewen; ~**er** Interviewer *m*.

intestate [ɪnˈtesteɪt] *a* ohne Hinterlassung eines Testaments.

intestinal [ɪnˈtestɪnl] *a* Darm-.

intestine [ɪnˈtestɪn] *n* Darm *m*; ~**s** *pl* Eingeweide *nt*.

intimacy [ˈɪntɪməsɪ] *n* vertraute(r) Umgang *m*, Intimität *f*.

intimate [ˈɪntɪmət] *a* (*inmost*) innerste(r,s); *knowledge* eingehend; (*familiar*) vertraut; *friends* eng; [ˈɪntɪmeɪt] *vt* andeuten; ~**ly** *ad* vertraut, eng.

intimidate [ɪnˈtɪmɪdeɪt] *vt* einschüchtern.

intimidation [ɪntɪmɪˈdeɪʃən] *n* Einschüchterung *f*.

into [ˈɪntu] *prep* (*motion*) in (+*acc*) . . . hinein; **5** ~ **25** 25 durch 5.

intolerable [ɪnˈtɒlərəbl] *a* unerträglich.

intolerance [ɪnˈtɒlərəns] *n* Intoleranz *f*.

intolerant [ɪnˈtɒlərənt] *a* intolerant.

intonation [ɪntəˈneɪʃən] *n* Intonation *f*.

intoxicate [ɪnˈtɒksɪkeɪt] *vt* betrunken machen; (*fig*) berauschen; ~**d** *a* betrunken; (*fig*) trunken.

intoxication [ɪntɒksɪˈkeɪʃən] *n* Rausch *m*.

intractable [ɪnˈtræktəbl] *a* schwer zu handhaben(d); *problem* schwer lösbar.

intransigent [ɪnˈtrænsɪdʒənt] *a* unnachgiebig.

intransitive [ɪnˈtrænsɪtɪv] *a* intransitiv.

intravenous [ɪntrəˈviːnəs] *a* intravenös.

intrepid [ɪnˈtrepɪd] *a* unerschrocken.

intricacy [ˈɪntrɪkəsɪ] *n* Kompliziertheit *f*.

intricate [ˈɪntrɪkət] *a* kompliziert.

intrigue [ɪnˈtriːg] *n* Intrige *f*; *vt* faszinieren.

intriguing [ɪnˈtriːgɪŋ] *a* faszinierend.

intrinsic [ɪnˈtrɪnsɪk] *a* innere(r,s); *difference* wesentlich.

introduce [ɪntrəˈdjuːs] *vt person* vorstellen (*to sb* jdm); *sth new* einführen; *subject* anschneiden; **to** ~ **sb to sth** jdn in etw (*acc*) einführen.

introduction [ɪntrəˈdʌkʃən] *n* Einführung *f*; (*to book*) Einleitung *f*.

introductory [ɪntrəˈdʌktərɪ] *a* Einführungs-, Vor-.

introspective [ɪntrəʊˈspektɪv] *a* nach innen gekehrt.

introvert [ˈɪntrəʊvɜːt] *n* Introvertierte(r) *mf*; *a* introvertiert.

intrude [ɪnˈtruːd] *vi* stören (*on acc*); ~**r** Eindringling *m*.

intrusion [ɪnˈtruːʒən] *n* Störung *f*; (*coming into*) Eindringen *nt*.

intrusive [ɪnˈtruːsɪv] *a* aufdringlich.

intuition [ɪnˈtjuːʃən] *n* Intuition *f*.

intuitive *a*, ~**ly** *ad* [ɪnˈtjuːɪtɪv, -lɪ] intuitiv.

inundate [ˈɪnʌndeɪt] *vt* (*lit*, *fig*) überschwemmen.

invade [ɪnˈveɪd] *vt* einfallen in (+*acc*); ~**r** Eindringling *m*.

invalid [ˈɪnvəlɪd] *n* (*disabled*) Kranke(r) *mf*; Invalide *m*; *a* (*ill*) krank; (*disabled*) invalide; [ɪnˈvælɪd] *a* (*not valid*) ungültig; ~**ate** [ɪnˈvælɪdeɪt] *vt passport* (für) ungültig erklären; (*fig*) entkräften.

invaluable [ɪnˈvæljʊəbl] *a* unschätzbar.

invariable [ɪnˈveərɪəbl] *a* unveränderlich.

invariably [ɪnˈveərɪəblɪ] *ad* ausnahmslos.

invasion [ɪnˈveɪʒən] *n* Invasion *f*, Einfall *m*.

invective [ɪnˈvektɪv] *n* Beschimpfung *f*.

invent [ɪnˈvent] *vt* erfinden; ~**ion** [ɪnˈvenʃən] Erfindung *f*; ~**ive** *a* erfinderisch; ~**iveness** Erfindungsgabe *f*; ~**or** Erfinder *m*.

inventory [ˈɪnvəntrɪ] *n* (Bestands-) verzeichnis *nt*, Inventar *nt*.

inverse [ˈɪnvɜːs] *n* Umkehrung *f*; *a*, ~**ly** [ɪnˈvɜːs, -lɪ] *ad* umgekehrt.

invert [ɪnˈvɜːt] *vt* umdrehen; ~**ed commas** *pl* Anführungsstriche *pl*.

invertebrate [ɪnˈvɜːtɪbrət] *n* wirbellose(s) Tier *nt*.

invest [ɪnˈvest] *vt* (*Fin*) anlegen, investieren; (*endue*) ausstatten.

investigate [ɪnˈvestɪgeɪt] *vt* untersuchen.

investigation [ɪnvestɪˈgeɪʃən] *n* Untersuchung *f*.

investigator [ɪnˈvestɪgeɪtə*] *n* Untersuchungsbeamte(r) *m*.

investiture [ɪnˈvestɪtʃə*] *n* Amtseinsetzung *f*.

investment [ɪnˈvestmənt] *n* Investition *f*.

investor [ɪnˈvestə*] *n* (Geld)anleger *m*.

inveterate [ɪnˈvetərət] *a* unverbesserlich.

invigorating [ɪnˈvɪgəreɪtɪŋ] *a* stärkend.

invincible [ɪnˈvɪnsəbl] *a* unbesiegbar.

inviolate [ɪnˈvaɪələt] *a* unverletzt.

invisible [ɪnˈvɪzəbl] *a* unsichtbar; *ink* Geheim-.

invitation [ɪnvɪˈteɪʃən] *n* Einladung *f*.

invite [ɪnˈvaɪt] *vt* einladen; *criticism, discussion* herausfordern.

inviting [ɪnˈvaɪtɪŋ] *a* einladend.

invoice ['ɪnvɔɪs] n Rechnung f, Lieferschein m; vt goods in Rechnung stellen (sth for sb jdm etw acc).

invoke [ɪn'vəuk] vt anrufen.

involuntary a, **involuntarily** ad [ɪn'vɒləntərɪ, -lɪ] (unwilling) unfreiwillig; (unintentional) unabsichtlich.

involve [ɪn'vɒlv] vt (entangle) verwickeln; (entail) mit sich bringen; ~d a verwickelt; **the person** ~d die betreffende Person; ~ment Verwicklung f.

invulnerable [ɪn'vʌlnərəbl] a unverwundbar; (fig) unangreifbar.

inward ['ɪnwəd] a innere(r,s); curve Innen-; ~(s) ad nach innen; ~ly ad im Innern.

iodine ['aɪədi:n] n Jod nt.

iota [aɪ'əutə] n (fig) bißchen nt.

irascible [ɪ'ræsɪbl] a reizbar.

irate [aɪ'reɪt] a zornig.

iris ['aɪərɪs] n Iris f.

irk [ɜːk] vt verdrießen.

irksome ['ɜːksəm] a lästig.

iron ['aɪən] n Eisen nt; (for ironing) Bügeleisen nt; (golf club) Golfschläger m, Metallschläger m; a eisern; vt bügeln; ~s pl (chains) Hand-/Fußschellen pl; ~ out vt (lit, fig) ausbügeln; differences ausgleichen; **I~ Curtain** Eiserne(r) Vorhang m.

ironic(al) [aɪ'rɒnɪk(əl)] a ironisch; coincidence etc witzig; ~ally ad ironisch; witzigerweise.

ironing ['aɪənɪŋ] n Bügeln nt; (laundry) Bügelwäsche f; ~ board Bügelbrett nt.

ironmonger ['aɪənmʌŋgə*] n Eisenwarenhändler m; ~'s (shop) Eisenwarenhandlung f.

iron ore ['aɪənɔː*] n Eisenerz nt.

ironworks ['aɪənwɜːks] n Eisenhütte f.

irony ['aɪərənɪ] n Ironie f; **the** ~ **of it was ...** das Witzige daran war ...

irrational [ɪ'ræʃənl] a vernünftig, irrational.

irreconcilable [ɪrekən'saɪləbl] a unvereinbar.

irredeemable [ɪrɪ'di:məbl] a (Comm) money nicht einlösbar; loan unkündbar; (fig) rettungslos.

irrefutable [ɪrɪ'fju:təbl] a unwiderlegbar.

irregular [ɪ'regjulə*] a unregelmäßig; shape ungleich(mäßig); (fig) unüblich; behaviour ungehörig; ~ity [ɪregju'lærɪtɪ] Unregelmäßigkeit f; Ungleichmäßigkeit f; (fig) Vergehen nt.

irrelevance [ɪ'reləvəns] n Belanglosigkeit f.

irrelevant [ɪ'reləvənt] a belanglos, irrelevant.

irreligious [ɪrɪ'lɪdʒəs] a ungläubig.

irreparable [ɪ'repərəbl] a nicht gutzumachen(d).

irreplaceable [ɪrɪ'pleɪsəbl] a unersetzlich.

irrepressible [ɪrɪ'presəbl] a nicht zu unterdrücken(d); joy unbändig.

irreproachable [ɪrɪ'prəutʃəbl] a untadelig.

irresistible [ɪrɪ'zɪstəbl] a unwiderstehlich.

irresolute [ɪ'rezəlu:t] a unentschlossen.

irrespective [ɪrɪ'spektɪv] : ~ **of** prep ungeachtet (+gen).

irresponsibility ['ɪrɪspɒnsə'bɪlɪtɪ] n Verantwortungslosigkeit f.

irresponsible [ɪrɪ'spɒnsəbl] a verantwortungslos.

irretrievably [ɪrɪ'tri:vəblɪ] ad unwiederbringlich; lost unrettbar.

irreverence [ɪ'revərəns] n Mißachtung f.

irreverent [ɪ'revərənt] a respektlos.

irrevocable [ɪ'revəkəbl] a unwiderrufbar.

irrigate ['ɪrɪgeɪt] vt bewässern.

irrigation [ɪrɪ'geɪʃən] n Bewässerung f.

irritability [ɪrɪtə'bɪlɪtɪ] n Reizbarkeit f.

irritable ['ɪrɪtəbl] a reizbar.

irritant ['ɪrɪtənt] n Reizmittel nt.

irritate ['ɪrɪteɪt] vt irritieren, reizen (also Med).

irritating ['ɪrɪteɪtɪŋ] a irritierend, aufreizend.

irritation [ɪrɪ'teɪʃən] n (anger) Ärger m; (Med) Reizung f.

is [ɪz] see be.

Islam ['ɪzlɑːm] n Islam m.

island ['aɪlənd] n Insel f; ~er Inselbewohner(in f) m.

isle [aɪl] n (kleine) Insel f.

isn't ['ɪznt] = is not.

isobar ['aɪsəubɑː*] n Isobare f.

isolate ['aɪsəuleɪt] vt isolieren; ~d a isoliert; case Einzel-.

isolation [aɪsəu'leɪʃən] n Isolierung f; **to treat sth in** ~ etw vereinzelt or isoliert behandeln.

isolationism [aɪsəu'leɪʃənɪzəm] n Isolationismus m.

isotope ['aɪsətəup] n Isotop nt.

issue ['ɪʃuː] n (matter) Problem nt, Frage f; (outcome) Resultat nt, Ausgang m; (of newspaper, shares) Ausgabe f; (offspring) Nachkommenschaft f; (of river) Mündung f; **that's not at** ~ das steht nicht zur Debatte; **to make an** ~ **out of sth** ein Theater machen wegen etw (dat); vt ausgeben; warrant erlassen; documents ausstellen; orders erteilen; books herausgeben; verdict aussprechen; **to** ~ **sb with sth** etw (acc) an jdn ausgeben.

isthmus ['ɪsməs] n Landenge f.

it [ɪt] pron (nom, acc) es; (dat) ihm.

italic [ɪ'tælɪk] a kursiv; ~s pl Kursivschrift f; **in** ~s kursiv gedruckt.

itch [ɪtʃ] n Juckreiz m; (fig) brennende(s) Verlangen nt; vi jucken; **to be** ~**ing to do sth** darauf brennen, etw zu tun; ~**ing** Jucken nt; ~**y** a juckend.

it'd ['ɪtd] = it would; it had.

item ['aɪtəm] n Gegenstand m; (on list) Posten m; (in programme) Nummer f; (in agenda) (Programm)punkt m; (in newspaper) (Zeitungs)notiz f; ~**ize** vt verzeichnen.

itinerant [ɪ'tɪnərənt] a person umherreisend.

itinerary [aɪ'tɪnərərɪ] n Reiseroute f; (records) Reisebericht m.

it'll ['ɪtl] = it will; it shall.

its [ɪts] poss a (masculine, neuter) sein; (feminine) ihr; poss pron seine(r,s); ihre(r,s).

it's [ɪts] = it is; it has.

itself [ɪt'self] *pron* sich (selbst); (*emphatic*) selbst.

I've [aɪv] = **I have.**

ivory ['aɪvərɪ] *n* Elfenbein *nt*; ~ **tower** (*fig*) Elfenbeinturm *m*.

ivy ['aɪvɪ] *n* Efeu *nt*.

J

J, j [dʒeɪ] *n* J *nt*, j *nt*.

jab [dʒæb] *vti* (hinein)stechen; *n* Stich *m*, Stoß *m*; (*col*) Spritze *f*.

jabber ['dʒæbə*] *vi* plappern.

jack [dʒæk] *n* (Wagen)heber *m*; (*Cards*) Bube *m*; ~ **up** *vt* aufbocken.

jackdaw ['dʒækdɔ:] *n* Dohle *f*.

jacket ['dʒækɪt] *n* Jacke *f*, Jackett *nt*; (*of book*) Schutzumschlag *m*; (*Tech*) Ummantelung *f*.

jack-knife ['dʒæknaɪf] *n* Klappmesser *nt*; *vi* (*truck*) sich quer stellen.

jackpot ['dʒækpɒt] *n* Haupttreffer *m*.

jade [dʒeɪd] *n* (*stone*) Jade *m*.

jaded ['dʒeɪdɪd] *a* ermattet.

jagged ['dʒægɪd] *a* zackig; *blade* scharfig.

jail [dʒeɪl] *n* Gefängnis *nt*; *vt* einsperren; ~**break** Gefängnisausbruch *m*; ~**er** Gefängniswärter *m*.

jam [dʒæm] *n* Marmelade *f*; (*crowd*) Gedränge *nt*; (*col: trouble*) Klemme *f*; *see* **traffic;** *vt people* zusammendrängen; (*wedge*) einklemmen; (*cram*) hineinzwängen; (*obstruct*) blockieren; **to** ~ **on the brakes** auf die Bremse treten.

jamboree [dʒæmbə'ri:] *n* (Pfadfinder)-treffen *nt*.

jangle ['dʒæŋgl] *vti* klimpern; (*bells*) bimmeln.

janitor ['dʒænɪtə*] *n* Hausmeister *m*.

January ['dʒænjʊərɪ] *n* Januar *m*.

jar [dʒɑ:*] *n* Glas *nt*; *vi* kreischen; (*colours etc*) nicht harmonieren.

jargon ['dʒɑ:gən] *n* Fachsprache *f*, Jargon *m*.

jarring ['dʒɑ:rɪŋ] *a sound* kreischend; *colour* unharmonisch.

jasmin(e) ['dʒæzmɪn] *n* Jasmin *m*.

jaundice ['dʒɔ:ndɪs] *n* Gelbsucht *f*; ~**d** *a* (*fig*) mißgünstig.

jaunt [dʒɔ:nt] *n* Spritztour *f*; ~**y** *a* (*lively*) munter; (*brisk*) flott; *attitude* unbekümmert.

javelin ['dʒævlɪn] *n* Speer *m*.

jaw [dʒɔ:] *n* Kiefer *m*; ~**s** *pl* (*fig*) Rachen *m*.

jaywalker ['dʒeɪwɔ:kə*] *n* unvorsichtige(r) Fußgänger *m*, Verkehrssünder *m*.

jazz [dʒæz] *n* Jazz *m*; ~ **up** *vt* (*Mus*) aufjazzen; (*enliven*) aufpolieren; ~ **band** Jazzkapelle *f*; ~**y** *a colour* schreiend, auffallend.

jealous ['dʒeləs] *a* (*envious*) mißgünstig; *husband* eifersüchtig; (*watchful*) bedacht (*of* auf +*acc*); ~**ly** *ad* mißgünstig, eifersüchtig; *sorgsam*; ~**y** Mißgunst *f*, Eifersucht *f*.

jeans [dʒi:nz] *npl* Jeans *pl*.

jeep [dʒi:p] *n* Jeep *m*.

jeer [dʒɪə*] *vi* höhnisch lachen (*at* über +*acc*), verspotten (*at sb* jdn); *n* Hohn *m*; (*remark*) höhnische Bemerkung *f*; ~**ing** *a* höhnisch.

jelly ['dʒelɪ] *n* Gelee *nt*; (*on meat*) Gallert *nt*; (*dessert*) Grütze *f*; ~**fish** Qualle *f*.

jemmy ['dʒemɪ] *n* Brecheisen *nt*.

jeopardize ['dʒepədaɪz] *vt* gefährden.

jeopardy ['dʒepədɪ] *n* Gefahr *f*.

jerk [dʒɜ:k] *n* Ruck *m*; (*col: idiot*) Trottel *m*; *vt* ruckartig bewegen; *vi* sich ruckartig bewegen; (*muscles*) zucken.

jerkin ['dʒɜ:kɪn] *n* Wams *nt*.

jerky ['dʒɜ:kɪ] *a movement* ruckartig; *writing* zitterig; *ride* rüttelnd.

jersey ['dʒɜ:zɪ] *n* Pullover *m*.

jest [dʒest] *n* Scherz *m*; **in** ~ im Spaß; *vi* spaßen.

jet [dʒet] *n* (*stream: of water etc*) Strahl *m*; (*spout*) Düse *f*; (*Aviat*) Düsenflugzeug *nt*; ~**-black** *a* rabenschwarz; ~ **engine** Düsenmotor *m*.

jetsam ['dʒetsəm] *n* Strandgut *nt*.

jettison ['dʒetɪsn] *vt* über Bord werfen.

jetty ['dʒetɪ] *n* Landesteg *m*, Mole *f*.

Jew [dʒu:] *n* Jude *m*.

jewel ['dʒu:əl] *n* (*lit, fig*) Juwel *nt*; (*stone*) Edelstein *m*; ~**(l)er** Juwelier *m*; ~**(l)er's (shop)** Schmuckwarengeschäft *nt*, Juwelier *m*; ~**(le)ry** Schmuck *m*, Juwelen *pl*.

Jewess ['dʒu:ɪs] *n* Jüdin *f*.

Jewish ['dʒu:ɪʃ] *a* jüdisch.

jib [dʒɪb] *n* (*Naut*) Klüver *m*; *vi* sich scheuen (*at* vor +*dat*).

jibe [dʒaɪb] *n* spöttische Bemerkung *f*.

jiffy ['dʒɪfɪ] *n* (*col*) **in a** ~ sofort.

jigsaw (puzzle) ['dʒɪgsɔ:(pʌzl)] *n* Puzzle(-spiel) *nt*.

jilt [dʒɪlt] *vt* den Laufpaß geben (+*dat*).

jingle ['dʒɪŋgl] *n* (*advertisement*) Werbesong *m*; (*verse*) Reim *m*; *vti* klimpern; (*bells*) bimmeln.

jinx [dʒɪŋks] *n* Fluch *m*; **to put a** ~ **on sth** etw verhexen.

jitters ['dʒɪtəz] *npl* (*col*) **to get the** ~ einen Bammel kriegen.

jittery ['dʒɪtərɪ] *a* (*col*) nervös.

jiujitsu [dʒu:'dʒɪtsu:] *n* Jiu-Jitsu *nt*.

job [dʒɒb] *n* (*piece of work*) Arbeit *f*; (*occupation*) Stellung *f*, Arbeit *f*; (*duty*) Aufgabe *f*; (*difficulty*) Mühe *f*; **what's your** ~? was machen Sie von Beruf?; **it's a good** ~ **he . . .** es ist ein Glück, daß er . . .; **just the** ~ genau das Richtige; ~**bing** *a* (*in factory*) Akkord-; (*freelance*) Gelegenheits-; ~**less** *a* arbeitslos.

jockey ['dʒɒkɪ] *n* Jockei *m*; *vi*: **to** ~ **for position** sich in eine gute Position drängeln.

jocular ['dʒɒkjʊlə*] *a* scherzhaft, witzig.

jodhpurs ['dʒɒdpə:z] *npl* Reithose *f*.

jog [dʒɒg] *vt* (an)stoßen; *vi* (*run*) einen Dauerlauf machen.

john [dʒɒn] *n* (*US col*) Klo *nt*.

join [dʒɔɪn] *vt* (*put together*) verbinden (*to* mit); *club* beitreten (+*dat*); *person* sich anschließen (+*dat*); *vi* (*unite*) sich vereinigen; (*bones*) zusammenwachsen; ~

Verbindungsstelle f, Naht f; ~ **in** vi mitmachen; ~ **up** vi (Mil) zur Armee gehen; ~**er** Schreiner m; ~**ery** Schreinerei f; ~**t** n (Tech) Fuge f; (of bones) Gelenk nt; (of meat) Braten m; (col: place) Lokal nt; a, ~**tly** ad gemeinsam.

joist [dʒɔɪst] n Träger m.

joke [dʒəʊk] n Witz m; **it's no** ~ es ist nicht zum Lachen; vi spaßen, Witze machen; **you must be joking** das ist doch wohl nicht dein Ernst; ~**r** Witzbold m; (Cards) Joker m.

joking ['dʒəʊkɪŋ] a scherzhaft; ~**ly** ad zum Spaß; **talk** im Spaß, scherzhaft.

jollity ['dʒɒlɪtɪ] n Fröhlichkeit f.

jolly ['dʒɒlɪ] a lustig, vergnügt; ad (col) ganz schön; ~ **good!** prima!; **to** ~ **sb along** jdn ermuntern.

jolt [dʒɒult] n (shock) Schock m; (jerk) Stoß m, Rütteln nt; vt (push) stoßen; (shake) durchschütteln; (fig) aufrütteln; vi holpern.

jostle ['dʒɒsl] vt anrempeln.

jot [dʒɒt] n: **not one** ~ kein Jota nt; ~ **down** vt schnell aufschreiben, notieren; ~**ter** Notizbuch nt; (Sch) Schulheft nt.

journal ['dʒɜːnl] n (diary) Tagebuch nt; (magazine) Zeitschrift f; ~**ese** ['dʒɜːnə'liːz] Zeitungsstil m; ~**ism** Journalismus m; ~**ist** Journalist(in f) m.

journey ['dʒɜːnɪ] n Reise f.

jovial ['dʒəʊvɪəl] a jovial.

joy [dʒɔɪ] n Freude f; ~**ful** a freudig; (gladdening) erfreulich; ~**fully** ad freudig; ~**ous** a freudig; ~ **ride** Schwarzfahrt f; ~**stick** Steuerknüppel m.

jubilant ['dʒuːbɪlənt] a triumphierend.

jubilation [dʒuːbɪ'leɪʃən] n Jubel m.

jubilee ['dʒuːbɪliː] n Jubiläum nt.

judge [dʒʌdʒ] n Richter m; (fig) Kenner m; vt (Jur) person die Verhandlung führen über (+acc); case verhandeln; (assess) beurteilen; (criticize) verurteilen; vi ein Urteil abgeben; **as far as I can** ~ soweit ich das beurteilen kann; **judging by sth** nach etw zu urteilen; ~**ment** (Jur) Urteil nt; (Eccl) Gericht nt; (opinion) Ansicht f; (ability) Urteilsvermögen nt.

judicial [dʒuː'dɪʃəl] a gerichtlich, Justiz-.

judicious [dʒuː'dɪʃəs] a weis(e).

judo ['dʒuːdəʊ] n Judo nt.

jug [dʒʌg] n Krug m.

juggernaut ['dʒʌgənɔːt] n (truck) Fernlastwagen m.

juggle ['dʒʌgl] vi jonglieren; vt facts verdrehen; figures frisieren; ~**r** Jongleur m.

jugular ['dʒʌgjʊlə*] a vein Hals-.

juice [dʒuːs] n Saft m.

juiciness ['dʒuːsɪnɪs] n Saftigkeit f.

juicy ['dʒuːsɪ] a (lit, fig) saftig; story schlüpfrig.

jukebox ['dʒuːkbɒks] n Musikautomat m.

July [dʒuː'laɪ] n Juli m.

jumble ['dʒʌmbl] n Durcheinander nt; vt (also ~ **up**) durcheinanderwerfen; facts durcheinanderbringen; ~ **sale** (Brit) Basar m, Flohmarkt m.

jumbo (jet) ['dʒʌmbəʊ(dʒet)] n Jumbo(-Jet) m.

jump [dʒʌmp] vi springen; (nervously) zusammenzucken; **to** ~ **to conclusions** voreilige Schlüsse ziehen; vt überspringen; **to** ~ **the gun** (fig) voreilig handeln; **to** ~ **the queue** sich vordrängeln; n Sprung m; **to give sb a** ~ jdn erschrecken; ~**ed-up** a (col) eingebildet; ~**er** Pullover m; ~**y** a nervös.

junction ['dʒʌŋkʃən] n (of roads) (Straßen)kreuzung f; (Rail) Knotenpunkt m.

juncture ['dʒʌŋktʃə*] n: **at this** ~ in diesem Augenblick.

June [dʒuːn] n Juni m.

jungle ['dʒʌŋgl] n Dschungel m, Urwald m.

junior ['dʒuːnɪə*] a (younger) jünger; (after name) junior; (Sport) Junioren-; (lower position) untergeordnet; (for young people) Junioren-; n Jüngere(r) m.

junk [dʒʌŋk] n (rubbish) Plunder m; (ship) Dschunke f; ~**shop** Ramschladen m.

junta ['dʒʌntə] n Junta f.

jurisdiction [dʒʊərɪs'dɪkʃən] n Gerichtsbarkeit f; (range of authority) Zuständigkeit(sbereich m) f.

jurisprudence [dʒʊərɪs'pruːdəns] n Rechtswissenschaft f, Jura no art.

juror ['dʒʊərə*] n Geschworene(r) mf; Schöffe m, Schöffin f; (in competition) Preisrichter m.

jury ['dʒʊərɪ] n (court) Geschworene pl; (in competition) Jury f, Preisgericht nt; ~**man** = juror.

just [dʒʌst] a gerecht; ad (recently, now) gerade, eben; (barely) gerade noch; (exactly) genau, gerade; (only) nur, bloß; (a small distance) gleich; (absolutely) einfach; ~ **as I arrived** gerade als ich ankam; ~ **as nice** genauso nett; ~ **as well** um so besser; ~ **about** so etwa; ~ **now** soeben, gerade; **not** ~ **now** nicht im Moment; ~ **try** versuch es bloß or mal.

justice ['dʒʌstɪs] n (fairness) Gerechtigkeit f; (magistrate) Richter m; ~ **of the peace** Friedensrichter m.

justifiable ['dʒʌstɪfaɪəbl] a berechtigt.

justifiably ['dʒʌstɪfaɪəblɪ] ad berechtigterweise, zu Recht.

justification [dʒʌstɪfɪ'keɪʃən] n Rechtfertigung f.

justify ['dʒʌstɪfaɪ] vt rechtfertigen.

justly ['dʒʌstlɪ] ad say mit Recht; condemn gerecht.

justness ['dʒʌstnəs] n Gerechtigkeit f.

jut [dʒʌt] vi (also ~ **out**) herausragen, vorstehen.

juvenile ['dʒuːvənaɪl] a (young) jugendlich; (for the young) Jugend-; n Jugendliche(r) mf; ~ **delinquency** Jugendkriminalität f; ~ **delinquent** jugendliche(r) Straftäter(in f) m.

juxtapose ['dʒʌkstəpəʊz] vt nebeneinanderstellen.

juxtaposition [dʒʌkstəpə'zɪʃən] n Nebeneinanderstellung f.

K

K, k [keɪ] n K nt, k nt.

kaleidoscope [kə'laɪdəskəup] n Kaleidoskop nt.

kangaroo [kæŋgə'ruː] n Känguruh nt.

kayak ['kaɪæk] n Kajak m or nt.

keel [kiːl] n Kiel m; **on an even ~** (fig) im Lot.

keen [kiːn] a eifrig, begeistert; intelligence, wind, blade scharf; sight, hearing gut; price günstig; **~ly** ad leidenschaftlich; (sharply) scharf; **~ness** Schärfe f; (eagerness) Begeisterung f.

keep [kiːp] irreg vt (retain) behalten; (have) haben; animals, one's word halten; (support) versorgen; (maintain in state) halten; (preserve) aufbewahren; (restrain) abhalten; vi (continue in direction) sich halten; (food) sich halten; (remain: quiet etc) sein, bleiben; **it ~s happening** es passiert immer wieder; n Unterhalt m; (tower) Burgfried m; **~ back** vt fernhalten; secret verschweigen; **~ on** vi: **~ on doing sth** etw immer weiter tun; vt anbehalten; hat aufbehalten; **~ out** vt draußen lassen, nicht hereinlassen; **'~ out!'** 'Eintritt verboten!'; **~ up** vi Schritt halten; vt aufrechterhalten; (continue) weitermachen; **~ing** (care) Obhut f; **in ~ing (with)** in Übereinstimmung (mit).

keg [keg] n Faß nt.

kennel ['kenl] n Hundehütte f.

kerb(stone) ['kɜːbstəʊn] n Bordstein m.

kernel ['kɜːnl] n Kern m.

kerosene ['kerəsiːn] n Kerosin nt.

kestrel ['kestrəl] n Turmfalke m.

ketchup ['ketʃəp] n Ketchup nt or m.

kettle ['ketl] n Kessel m; **~drum** Pauke f.

key [kiː] n Schlüssel m; (solution, answers) Schlüssel m, Lösung f; (of piano, typewriter) Taste f; (Mus) Tonart f; (explanatory note) Zeichenerklärung f; a position etc Schlüssel-; **~board** (of piano, typewriter) Tastatur f; **~hole** Schlüsselloch nt; **~note** Grundton m; **~ ring** Schlüsselring m.

khaki ['kɑːkɪ] n K(h)aki nt; a k(h)aki-(farben).

kick [kɪk] vt einen Fußtritt geben (+dat), treten; vi treten; (baby) strampeln; (horse) ausschlagen; n (Fuß)tritt m; (thrill) Spaß m; **~ around** vt person herumstoßen; **~ off** vi (Sport) anstoßen; **~ up** vt (col) schlagen; **~-off** (Sport) Anstoß m.

kid [kɪd] n (child) Kind nt; (goat) Zicklein nt; (leather) Glacéleder nt; vt auf den Arm nehmen; vi Witze machen.

kidnap ['kɪdnæp] vt entführen, kidnappen; **~per** Kidnapper m, Entführer m; **~ping** Entführung f, Kidnapping nt.

kidney ['kɪdnɪ] n Niere f.

kill [kɪl] vt töten, umbringen; chances ruinieren; vi töten; n Tötung f; (hunting) (Jagd)beute f; **~er** Mörder m.

kiln [kɪln] n Brennofen m.

kilo ['kiːləʊ] n Kilo nt; **~gram(me)** Kilogramm nt; **~metre**, (US) **~meter** Kilometer m; **~watt** Kilowatt nt.

kilt [kɪlt] n Schottenrock m.

kimono [kɪ'məʊnəʊ] n Kimono m.

kin [kɪn] n Verwandtschaft f, Verwandte(n) pl.

kind [kaɪnd] a freundlich, gütig; n Art f; **~ of** eine Art von; **(two) of a ~** (zwei) von der gleichen Art; **in ~** auf dieselbe Art; (in goods) in Naturalien.

kindergarten ['kɪndəgɑːtn] n Kindergarten m.

kind-hearted ['kaɪnd'hɑːtɪd] a gutherzig.

kindle ['kɪndl] vt (set on fire) anzünden; (rouse) reizen, (er)wecken.

kindliness ['kaɪndlɪnəs] n Freundlichkeit f, Güte f.

kindly ['kaɪndlɪ] a freundlich; ad liebenswürdig(erweise); **would you ~ ...?** wären Sie so freundlich und ...?

kindness ['kaɪndnəs] n Freundlichkeit f.

kindred ['kɪndrɪd] a verwandt; **~ spirit** Gleichgesinnte(r) mf.

kinetic [kɪ'netɪk] a kinetisch.

king [kɪŋ] n König m; **~dom** Königreich nt; **~fisher** Eisvogel m; **~pin** (Tech) Bolzen m; (Aut) Achsschenkelbolzen m; (fig) Stütze f; **~-size** a cigarette Kingsize.

kink [kɪŋk] n Knick m; **~y** a (fig) exzentrisch.

kiosk ['kiːɒsk] n (Tel) Telefonhäuschen nt.

kipper ['kɪpə*] n Räucherhering m.

kiss [kɪs] n Kuß m; vt küssen; vi: **they ~ed** sie küßten sich.

kit [kɪt] n Ausrüstung f; (tools) Werkzeug nt; **~bag** Seesack m.

kitchen ['kɪtʃɪn] n Küche f; **~ garden** Gemüsegarten m; **~ sink** Spülbecken nt; **~ware** Küchengeschirr nt.

kite [kaɪt] n Drachen m.

kith [kɪθ] n: **~ and kin** Blutsverwandte pl; **with ~ and kin** mit Kind und Kegel.

kitten ['kɪtn] n Kätzchen nt.

kitty ['kɪtɪ] n (money) (gemeinsame) Kasse f.

kleptomaniac [kleptəʊ'meɪnɪæk] n Kleptomane m, Kleptomanin f.

knack [næk] n Dreh m, Trick m.

knapsack ['næpsæk] n Rucksack m; (Mil) Tornister m.

knave [neɪv] n (old) Schurke m.

knead [niːd] vt kneten.

knee [niː] n Knie nt; **~cap** Kniescheibe f; **~-deep** a knietief.

kneel [niːl] vi irreg knien.

knell [nel] n Grabgeläute nt.

knickers ['nɪkəz] npl Schlüpfer m.

knife [naɪf] n Messer nt; vt erstechen.

knight [naɪt] n Ritter m; (chess) Springer m, Pferd nt; **~hood** Ritterwürde f.

knit [nɪt] vti stricken; vi (bones) zusammenwachsen; (people) harmonieren; **~ting** (occupation) Stricken nt; (work) Strickzeug nt; **~ting machine** Strickmaschine f; **~ting needle** Stricknadel f; **~wear** Strickwaren pl.

knob [nɒb] n Knauf m; (on instrument) Knopf m; (of butter etc) kleine(s) Stück nt.

knock [nɒk] vt schlagen; (criticize) heruntermachen; vi klopfen; (knees) zittern; n Schlag m; (on door) Klopfen nt;

~ **off** vt (do quickly) hinhauen; (col: steal) klauen; vi (finish) Feierabend machen; ~ **out** vt ausschlagen; (boxing) k.o. schlagen; ~**er** (on door) Türklopfer m; ~-**kneed** a x-beinig; ~**out** (lit) K.o.-Schlag m; (fig) Sensation f.

knot [nɒt] n Knoten m; (in wood) Astloch nt; (group) Knäuel nt or m; vt (ver)knoten; ~**ted** a verknotet.

knotty ['nɒtɪ] a knorrig; problem kompliziert.

know [nəʊ] vti irreg wissen; (be able to) können; (be acquainted with) kennen; (recognize) erkennen; **to ~ how to do sth** wissen, wie man etw macht, etw tun können; **you ~** nicht (wahr); **to be well ~n** bekannt sein; ~**all** Alleswisser m; ~-**how** Kenntnis f, Know-how nt; ~**ing** a schlau; look, smile wissend; ~**ingly** ad wissend; (intentionally) wissentlich.

knowledge ['nɒlɪdʒ] n Wissen nt, Kenntnis f; ~**able** a informiert.

knuckle ['nʌkl] n Fingerknöchel m.

kudos ['kjuːdɒs] n Ehre f.

L

L, l [el] n L nt, l nt.

lab [læb] n (col) Labor nt.

label ['leɪbl] n Etikett nt, Schild nt; vt mit einer Aufschrift versehen, etikettieren.

laboratory [ləˈbɒrətərɪ] n Laboratorium nt.

laborious a, ~**ly** ad [ləˈbɔːrɪəs, -lɪ] mühsam.

labour, (US) **labor** ['leɪbə*] n Arbeit f; (workmen) Arbeitskräfte pl; (Med) Wehen pl; a (Pol) Labour-; **hard ~** Zwangsarbeit f; ~**er** Arbeiter m; ~-**saving** a arbeitssparend.

laburnum [ləˈbɜːnəm] n Goldregen m.

labyrinth ['læbərɪnθ] n (lit, fig) Labyrinth nt.

lace [leɪs] n (fabric) Spitze f; (of shoe) Schnürsenkel m; (braid) Litze f; vt (also ~ up) (zu)schnüren.

lacerate ['læsəreɪt] vt zerschneiden, tief verwunden.

lack [læk] vt nicht haben; sb ~s sth jdm fehlt etw (nom); vi: **to be ~ing** fehlen; sb **is ~ing in sth** es fehlt jdm an etw (dat); n Mangel m; **for ~ of** aus Mangel an (+dat).

lackadaisical [lækəˈdeɪzɪkəl] a lasch.

lackey ['lækɪ] n Lakei m.

lacklustre, (US) **lackluster** ['læklʌstə*] a glanzlos, matt.

laconic [ləˈkɒnɪk] a lakonisch.

lacquer ['lækə*] n Lack m.

lacrosse [ləˈkrɒs] n Lacrosse nt.

lacy ['leɪsɪ] a spitzenartig, Spitzen-.

lad [læd] n (boy) Junge m; (young man) Bursche m.

ladder ['lædə*] n (lit) Leiter f; (fig) Stufenleiter f; (Brit: in stocking) Laufmasche f; vt Laufmaschen bekommen in (+dat).

laden ['leɪdn] a beladen, voll.

ladle ['leɪdl] n Schöpfkelle f.

lady ['leɪdɪ] n Dame f; (title) Lady f; **'Ladies'** (lavatory) 'Damen'; ~**bird**, (US)

~**bug** Marienkäfer m; ~-**in-waiting** Hofdame f; ~**like** a damenhaft, vornehm.

lag [læg] n (delay) Verzug m; (time ~) Zeitabstand m; vi (also ~ **behind**) zurückbleiben; vt pipes verkleiden.

lager ['lɑːgə*] n Lagerbier nt, helles Bier nt.

lagging ['lægɪŋ] n Isolierung f.

lagoon [ləˈguːn] n Lagune f.

laid [leɪd]: **to be ~ up** ans Bett gefesselt sein.

lair [lɛə*] n Lager nt.

laissez-faire ['leɪseɪˈfɛə*] n Laisser-faire nt.

laity ['leɪtɪ] n Laien pl.

lake [leɪk] n See m.

lamb [læm] n Lamm nt; (meat) Lammfleisch nt; ~ **chop** Lammkotelett nt; ~'**s wool** Lammwolle f.

lame [leɪm] a lahm; person also gelähmt; excuse faul.

lament [ləˈment] n Klage f; vt beklagen; ~**able** ['læməntəbl] a bedauerlich; (bad) erbärmlich; ~**ation** [læmənˈteɪʃən] Wehklage f.

laminated ['læmɪneɪtɪd] a beschichtet.

lamp [læmp] n Lampe f; (in street) Straßenlaterne f; ~**post** Laternenpfahl m; ~**shade** Lampenschirm m.

lance [lɑːns] n Lanze f; vt (Med) aufschneiden; ~ **corporal** Obergefreite(r) m.

lancet ['lɑːnsɪt] n Lanzette f.

land [lænd] n Land nt; vi (from ship) an Land gehen; (Aviat, end up) landen; vt (obtain) gewinnen, kriegen; passengers absetzen; goods abladen; troops, space probe landen; ~**ed** a Land-; ~**ing** Landung f; (on stairs) (Treppen)absatz m; ~**ing craft** Landungsboot nt; ~**ing stage** Landesteg m; ~**ing strip** Landebahn f; ~**lady** (Haus)wirtin f; ~**locked** a landumschlossen, Binnen-; ~**lord** (of house) Hauswirt m, Besitzer m; (of pub) Gastwirt m; (of land) Grundbesitzer m; ~**lubber** Landratte f; ~**mark** Wahrzeichen nt; (fig) Meilenstein m; ~**owner** Grundbesitzer m; ~**scape** Landschaft f; ~**slide** (Geog) Erdrutsch m; (Pol) überwältigende(r) Sieg m.

lane [leɪn] n (in town) Gasse f; (in country) Weg m; Sträßchen nt; (of motorway) Fahrbahn f, Spur f; (Sport) Bahn f.

language ['læŋgwɪdʒ] n Sprache f; (style) Ausdrucksweise f.

languid ['læŋgwɪd] a schlaff, matt.

languish ['læŋgwɪʃ] vi schmachten; (pine) sich sehnen (for nach).

languor ['læŋgə*] n Mattigkeit f.

languorous ['læŋgərəs] a schlaff, träge.

lank [læŋk] a dürr; ~**y** a schlacksig.

lantern ['læntən] n Laterne f.

lanyard ['lænjəd] n (Naut) Taljereep nt; (Mil) Kordel f.

lap [læp] n Schoß m; (Sport) Runde f; vt auflecken; vi (water) plätschern; ~**dog** Schoßhund m.

lapel [ləˈpel] n Rockaufschlag m, Revers nt or m.

lapse [læps] n (mistake) Irrtum m; (moral) Fehltritt m; (time) Zeitspanne f.

larceny ['lɑːsənɪ] n Diebstahl m.

lard [lɑːd] n Schweineschmalz nt.

larder ['lɑːdə*] n Speisekammer f.

large [lɑːdʒ] a groß; **at ~** auf freiem Fuß; **by and ~** im großen und ganzen; **~ly** ad zum größten Teil; **~scale** a groß angelegt, Groß-; **~sse** [lɑː'ʒes] Freigebigkeit f.

lark [lɑːk] n (bird) Lerche f; (joke) Jux m; **~ about** vi (col) herumalbern.

larva ['lɑːvə] n Larve f.

laryngitis [lærɪn'dʒaɪtɪs] n Kehlkopfentzündung f.

larynx ['lærɪŋks] n Kehlkopf m.

lascivious a, **~ly** ad [lə'sɪvɪəs, -lɪ] wollüstig.

lash [læʃ] n Peitschenhieb m; vt (beat against) schlagen an (+acc); (rain) schlagen gegen; (whip) peitschen; (bind) festbinden; **~ out** vi (with fists) um sich schlagen; (spend money) sich in Unkosten stürzen; vt money etc springen lassen; **~ing** (beating) Tracht f Prügel; (tie) Schleife f; **~ings of** (col) massenhaft.

lass [læs] n Mädchen nt.

lassitude ['læsɪtjuːd] n Abgespanntheit f.

lasso [læ'suː] n Lasso nt; vt mit einem Lasso fangen.

last [lɑːst] a letzte(r, s); ad zuletzt; (last time) das letztemal; n (person) Letzte(r) mf; (thing) Letzte(s) nt; (for shoe) (Schuh)leisten m; vi (continue) dauern; (remain good) sich halten; (money) ausreichen; **at ~** endlich; **~ night** gestern abend; **~ing** a dauerhaft, haltbar; shame etc andauernd; **~-minute** a in letzter Minute.

latch [lætʃ] n Riegel m; **~key** Hausschlüssel m.

late [leɪt] a spät; zu spät; (recent) jüngste(r, s); (former) frühere(r,s); (dead) verstorben; ad spät; (after proper time) zu spät; **to be ~** zu spät kommen; **of ~** in letzter Zeit; **~ in the day** (lit) spät; (fig) reichlich spät; **~comer** Nachzügler m; **~ly** ad in letzter Zeit.

lateness ['leɪtnəs] n (of person) Zuspätkommen nt; (of train) Verspätung f; **~ of the hour** die vorgerückte Stunde.

latent ['leɪtənt] a latent.

lateral ['lætərəl] a seitlich.

latest ['leɪtɪst] n (news) Neu(e)ste(s) nt; **at the ~** spätestens.

latex ['leɪteks] n Milchsaft m.

lath [læθ] n Latte f, Leiste f.

lathe [leɪð] n Drehbank f.

lather ['lɑːðə*] n (Seifen)schaum m; vt einschäumen; vi schäumen.

latitude ['lætɪtjuːd] n (Geog) Breite f; (freedom) Spielraum m.

latrine [lə'triːn] n Latrine f.

latter ['lætə*] a (second of two) letztere; (coming at end) letzte(r, s), später; **~ly** ad in letzter Zeit; **~-day** a modern.

lattice work ['lætɪswɜːk] n Lattenwerk nt, Gitterwerk nt.

laudable ['lɔːdəbl] a löblich.

laugh [lɑːf] n Lachen nt; vi lachen; **~ at** vt lachen über (+acc); **~ off** vt lachend abtun; **~able** a lachhaft; **~ing** a lachend;

~ing stock Zielscheibe f des Spottes; **~ter** Lachen nt, Gelächter nt.

launch [lɔːntʃ] n (of ship) Stapellauf m; (of rocket) Raketenabschuß m; (boat) Barkasse f; (pleasure boat) Vergnügungsboot nt; vt (set afloat) vom Stapel laufen lassen; rocket (ab)schießen; (set going) in Gang setzen, starten; **~ing** Stapellauf m; **~(ing) pad** Abschußrampe f.

launder ['lɔːndə*] vt waschen und bügeln; **~ette** [lɔːndə'ret] Waschsalon m.

laundry ['lɔːndrɪ] n (place) Wäscherei f; (clothes) Wäsche f.

laureate ['lɔːrɪət] a see poet.

laurel ['lɔrəl] n Lorbeer m.

lava ['lɑːvə] n Lava f.

lavatory ['lævətrɪ] n Toilette f.

lavender ['lævɪndə*] n Lavendel m.

lavish ['lævɪʃ] n (extravagant) verschwenderisch; (generous) großzügig; vt money verschwenden (on auf +acc); attentions, gifts überschütten mit (on sb jdn); **~ly** ad verschwenderisch.

law [lɔː] n Gesetz nt; (system) Recht nt; (of game etc) Regel f; (as studies) Jura no art; **~-abiding** a gesetzestreu; **~breaker** Gesetzesübertreter m; **~ court** Gerichtshof m; **~ful** a gesetzlich, rechtmäßig; **~fully** ad rechtmäßig; **~less** a gesetzlos.

lawn [lɔːn] n Rasen m; **~mower** Rasenmäher m; **~ tennis** Rasentennis m.

law school ['lɔːskuːl] n Rechtsakademie f.

law student ['lɔːstjuːdənt] n Jurastudent m.

lawsuit ['lɔːsuːt] n Prozeß m.

lawyer ['lɔːjə*] n Rechtsanwalt m Rechtsanwältin f.

lax [læks] a lax.

laxative ['læksətɪv] n Abführmittel nt.

laxity ['læksɪtɪ] n Laxheit f.

lay [leɪ] n Laien-; vt irreg (place) legen; table decken; fire anrichten; egg legen; trap stellen; money wetten; **~ aside** vt zurücklegen; **~ by** vt (set aside) beiseite legen; **~ down** vt hinlegen; rules vorschreiben; arms strecken; **~ off** vt workers (vorübergehend) entlassen; **~ on** vt auftragen; concert etc veranstalten; **~ out** vt (her)auslegen; money ausgeben; corpse aufbahren; **~ up** vt (store) aufspeichern; supplies anlegen; (save) zurücklegen; **~about** Faulenzer m; **~-by** Parkbucht f; (bigger) Rastplatz m; **~er** Schicht f; **~ette** [leɪ'et] Babyausstattung f; **~man** Laie m; **~out** Anlage f; (Art) Layout nt.

laze [leɪz] vi faulenzen.

lazily ['leɪzɪlɪ] ad träge, faul.

laziness ['leɪzɪnəs] n Faulheit f.

lazy ['leɪzɪ] a faul; (slow-moving) träge.

lead¹ [led] n Blei nt; (of pencil) (Bleistift)mine f; a bleiern, Blei-.

lead² [liːd] n (front position) Führung f; (distance, time ahead) Vorsprung f; (example) Vorbild nt; (clue) Tip m; (of police) Spur f; (Theat) Hauptrolle f; (dog's) Leine f; vt irreg vt (give) führen; group etc leiten; vi (be first) führen; **~ astray** vt irreführen; **~ away** vt wegführen; prisoner abführen; **~ back** vi zurück-

führen; ~ **on** vt anführen; ~ **to** vt (street)
(hin)führen nach; (result in) führen zu; ~
up to vt (drive) führen zu; (speaker etc)
hinführen auf (+ acc); ~**er** Führer m,
Leiter m; (of party) Vorsitzende(r) m;
(Press) Leitartikel m; ~**ership** (office)
Leitung f; (quality) Führerschaft f; ~**ing** a
führend; ~**ing lady** (Theat) Haupt-
darstellerin f; ~**ing light** (person)
führende(r) Geist m; ~**ing man** (Theat)
Hauptdarsteller m.

leaf [liːf] n Blatt nt; (of table) Ausziehplatte;
~**let** Blättchen nt; (advertisement)
Prospekt m; (pamphlet) Flugblatt nt; (for
information) Merkblatt nt; ~**y** a belaubt.

league [liːg] n (union) Bund m, Liga f;
(Sport) Liga f, Tabelle f; (measure) 3
englische Meilen.

leak [liːk] n undichte Stelle f; (in ship) Leck
nt; vi liquid etc durchlassen; vi (pipe etc)
undicht sein; (liquid etc) auslaufen; ~ **out**
vi (liquid etc) auslaufen; (information)
durchsickern.

leaky [ˈliːkɪ] a undicht.

lean [liːn] a mager; n Magere(s) nt; irreg vi
sich neigen; **to** ~ **against sth** an etw
(dat) angelehnt sein; sich an etw (acc)
anlehnen; vt (an)lehnen; ~ **back** vi sich
zurücklehnen; ~ **forward** vi sich
vorbeugen; ~ **on** vi sich stützen auf
(+acc); ~ **over** vi sich hinüberbeugen; ~
towards vt neigen zu; ~**ing** Neigung f;
~**-to** Anbau m.

leap [liːp] n Sprung m; vi irreg vi springen; by
~**s and bounds** schnell; ~**frog** Bock-
springen nt; ~ **year** Schaltjahr nt.

learn [lɜːn] vti irreg lernen; (find out)
erfahren, hören; ~**ed** [ˈlɜːnɪd] a gelehrt;
~**er** Anfänger(in f) m; (Aut) Fahr-
schüler(in f) m; ~**ing** Gelehrsamkeit f.

lease [liːs] n (of property) Mietvertrag m;
(of land) Pachtvertrag m; vt mieten;
pachten.

leash [liːʃ] n Leine f.

least [liːst] a kleinste(r, s); (slightest)
geringste(r, s); n Mindeste(s) nt; **at** ~
zumindest; **not in the** ~! durchaus nicht!

leather [ˈleðə*] n Leder nt; a ledern,
Leder-; ~**y** a zäh, ledern.

leave [liːv] irreg vt verlassen; (~ behind)
zurücklassen; (forget) vergessen; (allow to
remain) lassen; (after death) hinterlassen;
(entrust) überlassen (to sb jdm); **to be left**
(remain) übrigbleiben; vi weggehen, weg-
fahren; (for journey) abreisen; (bus, train)
abfahren; n Erlaubnis f; (Mil) Urlaub m; **on**
~ auf Urlaub; **to take one's** ~ of
Abschied nehmen von; ~ **off** vi aufhören;
~ **out** vt auslassen.

lecherous [ˈletʃərəs] a lüstern.

lectern [ˈlektɜːn] n Lesepult nt.

lecture [ˈlektʃə*] n Vortrag m; (Univ)
Vorlesung f; vi einen Vortrag halten;
(Univ) lesen; ~**r** Vortragende(r) mf;
(Univ) Dozent(in f) m.

ledge [ledʒ] n Leiste f; (window ~) Sims m
or nt; (of mountain) (Fels)vorsprung m.

ledger [ˈledʒə*] n Hauptbuch nt.

lee [liː] n Windschatten m; (Naut) Lee f.

leech [liːtʃ] n Blutegel m.

leek [liːk] n Lauch m.

leer [lɪə*] n schiefe(r) Blick m; vi schielen
(at nach).

leeway [ˈliːweɪ] n (fig) Rückstand m; (freedom) Spielraum m.

left [left] a linke(r, s); ad links; nach links; n
(side) linke Seite f; **the L** ~ (Pol) die Linke
f; ~**-hand drive** Linkssteuerung f;
~**-handed** a linkshändig; ~**-hand side**
linke Seite f; ~**-luggage (office)** Gepäck-
aufbewahrung f; ~**-overs** pl Reste pl,
Überbleibsel pl; ~ **wing** linke(r) Flügel
m; ~**-wing** a linke(r, s).

leg [leg] n Bein nt; (of meat) Keule f; (stage)
Etappe f.

legacy [ˈlegəsɪ] n Erbe nt, Erbschaft f.

legal [ˈliːgəl] a gesetzlich, rechtlich;
(allowed) legal, rechtsgültig; **to take** ~
action prozessieren; ~**ize** vt legalisieren;
~**ly** ad gesetzlich; legal; ~ **tender**
gesetzliche(s) Zahlungsmittel nt.

legation [lɪˈgeɪʃən] n Gesandtschaft f.

legend [ˈledʒənd] n Legende f; ~**ary** a
legendär.

-legged [ˈlegɪd] a -beinig.

leggings [ˈlegɪŋz] npl (hohe) Gamaschen
pl; (for baby) Gamaschenhose f.

legibility [ledʒɪˈbɪlɪtɪ] n Leserlichkeit f.

legible a, **legibly** ad [ˈledʒəbl, -blɪ] leserlich.

legion [ˈliːdʒən] n Legion f.

legislate [ˈledʒɪsleɪt] vi Gesetze geben.

legislation [ledʒɪsˈleɪʃən] n Gesetzgebung
f.

legislative [ˈledʒɪslətɪv] a gesetzgebend.

legislator [ˈledʒɪsleɪtə*] n Gesetzgeber m.

legislature [ˈledʒɪslətʃə*] n Legislative f.

legitimacy [lɪˈdʒɪtɪməsɪ] n Rechtmäßig-
keit f; (of birth) Ehelichkeit f.

legitimate [lɪˈdʒɪtɪmət] a rechtmäßig,
legitim; child ehelich.

legroom [ˈlegrʊm] n Platz m für die Beine.

leisure [ˈleʒə*] n Freizeit f; a Freizeit-; **to
be at** ~ Zeit haben; ~**ly** a gemächlich.

lemming [ˈlemɪŋ] n Lemming m.

lemon [ˈlemən] n Zitrone f; (colour) Zitro-
nengelb nt; ~**ade** [lemɔˈneɪd] Limonade f.

lend [lend] vt irreg leihen; **to** ~ **sb sth** jdm
etw leihen; **it** ~**s itself to** es eignet sich
zu; ~**er** Verleiher m; ~**ing library** Leihbibliothek f.

length [leŋθ] n Länge f; (section of road, pipe
etc) Strecke f; (of material) Stück nt; ~ **of
time** Zeitdauer f; **at** ~ (lengthily) ausführlich; (at last) schließlich; ~**en** vt
verlängern; vi länger werden; ~**ways** ad
längs; ~**y** a sehr lang; langatmig.

leniency [ˈliːnɪənsɪ] n Nachsicht f.

lenient [ˈliːnɪənt] a nachsichtig; ~**ly** ad
milde.

lens [lenz] n Linse f; (Phot) Objektiv nt.

Lent [lent] n Fastenzeit f.

lentil [ˈlentɪl] n Linse f.

Leo [ˈliːəʊ] n Löwe m.

leopard [ˈlepəd] n Leopard m.

leotard [ˈliːəʊtɑːd] n Trikot nt, Gymnastik-
anzug m.

leper [ˈlepə*] n Leprakranke(r) mf.

leprosy [ˈleprəsɪ] n Lepra f.

lesbian ['lezbɪən] a lesbisch; n Lesbierin f.

less [les] a, ad, n weniger.

lessen ['lesn] vi abnehmen; vt verringern, verkleinern.

lesser ['lesə*] a kleiner, geringer.

lesson ['lesn] n (Sch) Stunde f; (unit of study) Lektion f; (fig) Lehre f; (Eccl) Lesung f; ~s start at 9 der Unterricht beginnt um 9.

lest [lest] cj damit ... nicht.

let [let] n: without ~ or hindrance völlig unbehindert; vt irreg lassen; (lease) vermieten; ~'s go! gehen wir!; ~ down vt hinunterlassen; (disappoint) enttäuschen; ~ go vi loslassen; vt things loslassen; person gehen lassen; ~ off vt gun abfeuern; steam ablassen; (forgive) laufen lassen; ~ out vt herauslassen; scream fahren lassen; ~ up vi nachlassen; (stop) aufhören; ~-down Enttäuschung f.

lethal ['li:θəl] a tödlich.

lethargic [le'θɑ:dʒɪk] a lethargisch, träge.

lethargy ['leθədʒɪ] n Lethargie f, Teilnahmslosigkeit f.

letter ['letə*] n (of alphabet) Buchstabe m; (message) Brief m; ~s pl (literature) (schöne) Literatur f; ~box Briefkasten m; ~ing Beschriftung f.

lettuce ['letɪs] n (Kopf)salat m.

let-up ['letʌp] n (col) Nachlassen nt.

leukaemia, (US) **leukemia** [lu:'ki:mɪə] n Leukämie f.

level ['levl] a ground eben; (at same height) auf gleicher Höhe; (equal) gleich gut; head kühl; **to do one's ~ best** sein möglichstes tun; ad auf gleicher Höhe; **to draw ~ with** gleichziehen mit; n (instrument) Wasserwaage f; (altitude) Höhe f; (flat place) ebene Fläche f; (position on scale) Niveau nt; (amount, degree) Grad m; **talks on a high ~** Gespräche auf hoher Ebene; **profits keep on the same ~** Gewinne halten sich auf dem gleichen Stand; **on the moral ~** aus moralischer Sicht; **on the ~** (lit) auf gleicher Höhe; (fig: honest) ehrlich; vt ground einebnen; building abreißen; town dem Erdboden gleichmachen; blow versetzen (at sb jdm); remark richten (at gegen); ~ off or out vi flach or eben werden; (fig) sich ausgleichen; (plane) horizontal fliegen; vt ground planieren; differences ausgleichen; ~ crossing Bahnübergang m; ~-headed a vernünftig.

lever ['li:və*], (US) ['levə*] n Hebel m; (fig) Druckmittel nt; vt (hoch)stemmen; ~age Hebelkraft f; (fig) Einfluß m.

levity ['levɪtɪ] n Leichtfertigkeit f.

levy ['levɪ] n (of taxes) Erhebung f; (tax) Abgaben pl; (Mil) Aushebung f; vt erheben; (Mil) ausheben.

lewd [lu:d] a unzüchtig, unanständig.

liability [laɪə'bɪlɪtɪ] n (burden) Belastung f; (duty) Pflicht f; (debt) Verpflichtung f; (proneness) Anfälligkeit f; (responsibility) Haftung f.

liable ['laɪəbl] a (responsible) haftbar; (prone) anfällig; **to be ~ for** etw (dat) unterliegen; **it's ~ to happen** es kann leicht vorkommen.

liaison [li:'eɪzɒn] n Verbindung f.

liar ['laɪə*] n Lügner m.

libel ['laɪbəl] n Verleumdung f; vt verleumden; ~(l)ous a verleumderisch.

liberal ['lɪbərəl] a (generous) großzügig; (open-minded) aufgeschlossen; (Pol) liberal; n liberal denkende(r) Mensch m; L~ (Pol) Liberale(r) mf; ~ly ad (abundantly) reichlich.

liberate ['lɪbəreɪt] vt befreien.

liberation [lɪbə'reɪʃən] n Befreiung f.

liberty ['lɪbətɪ] n Freiheit f; (permission) Erlaubnis f; **to be at ~ to do sth** etw tun dürfen; **to take liberties with** sich (dat) Freiheiten herausnehmen gegenüber.

Libra ['li:brə] n Waage f.

librarian [laɪ'breərɪən] n Bibliothekar(in f) m.

library ['laɪbrərɪ] n Bibliothek f; (lending ~) Bücherei f.

libretto [lɪ'bretəʊ] n Libretto nt.

lice [laɪs] npl of **louse**.

licence, (US) **license** ['laɪsəns] n (permit) Erlaubnis f, amtliche Zulassung f; (driving ~) Führerschein m; (excess) Zügellosigkeit f; ~ **plate** (US Aut) Nummernschild nt.

license ['laɪsəns] vt genehmigen, konzessionieren; ~e [laɪsən'si:] Konzessionsinhaber m.

licentious [laɪ'senʃəs] a ausschweifend.

lichen ['laɪkən] n Flechte f.

lick [lɪk] vt lecken; vi (flames) züngeln; n Lecken nt; (small amount) Spur f.

licorice ['lɪkərɪs] n Lakritze f.

lid [lɪd] n Deckel m; (eye—) Lid nt.

lido ['li:dəʊ] n Freibad nt.

lie [laɪ] n Lüge f; vi lügen; irreg (rest, be situated) liegen; (put o.s. in position) sich legen; **to ~ idle** stillstehen; ~ **detector** Lügendetektor m.

lieu [lu:] n: **in ~ of** anstatt (+gen).

lieutenant [lef'tenənt], (US) [lu:'tenənt] n Leutnant m.

life [laɪf] n Leben nt; (story) Lebensgeschichte f; (energy) Lebendigkeit f; ~ **assurance** Lebensversicherung f; ~**belt** Rettungsring m; ~**boat** Rettungsboot nt; ~**guard** Bademärter m; ~ **Rettungs-schwimmer** m; ~ **jacket** Schwimmweste f; ~**less** a (dead) leblos, tot; (dull) langweilig; ~**like** a lebensnah, naturgetreu; ~**line** (lit) Rettungsleine f; (fig) Rettungsanker m; ~**long** a lebenslang; ~ **preserver** Totschläger m; ~**raft** Rettungsfloß nt; ~**sized** a in Lebensgröße f; ~ **span** Lebensspanne f; ~**time** Lebenszeit f.

lift [lɪft] vt hochheben; vi sich heben; n (raising) (Hoch)heben nt; (elevator) Aufzug m, Lift m; **to give sb a ~** jdn mitnehmen; ~**-off** Abheben nt (vom Boden).

ligament ['lɪgəmənt] n Sehne f, Band nt.

light [laɪt] n Licht nt; (lamp) Lampe f; (flame) Feuer nt; ~**s** pl (Aut) Beleuchtung f; **in the ~ of** angesichts (+gen); vt irreg beleuchten; lamp anmachen; fire, cigarette anzünden; (brighten) erleuchten, erhellen; a (bright) hell, licht; (pale) hell-; (not heavy, easy) leicht; punishment milde; taxes niedrig; touch leicht; ~ **up** vi (lamp) angehen; (face) aufleuchten; vt (illuminate) beleuchten; *lights* anmachen; ~ **bulb** Glühbirne *f*; ~**en** *vi (brighten)* hell werden; *(lightning)* blitzen; *vt (give light to)* erhellen; *hair* aufhellen; *gloom* aufheitern; *(make less heavy)* leichter machen; *(fig)* erleichtern; ~**er** *(cigarette —)* Feuerzeug *nt*; *(boat)* Leichter *m*; ~**-headed** *a (thoughtless)* leichtsinnig; *(giddy)* schwindlig; ~**-hearted** *a* leichtherzig, fröhlich; ~**house** Leuchtturm *m*; ~**ing** Beleuchtung *f*; ~**ing-up time** Zeit *f* des Einschaltens ~ der Straßen-/Autobeleuchtung; ~**ly** *ad* leicht; *(irresponsibly)* leichtfertig; ~ **meter** *(Phot)* Belichtungsmesser *m*; ~**ness** *(of weight)* Leichtigkeit *f*; *(of colour)* Helle *f*; *(light)* Helligkeit *f*; ~**ning** Blitz *m*; ~**ning conductor** Blitzableiter *m*; ~**weight** *a suit* leicht; ~**weight boxer** Leichtgewicht *nt*; ~**year** Lichtjahr *nt*.

lignite ['lɪgnaɪt] *n* Lignit *m*.

like [laɪk] *vt* mögen, gernhaben; **would you** ~ **...?** hatten Sie gern ...?; **would you** ~ **to** ...? möchten Sie gern...?; *prep* wie; **what's it/he** ~? wie ist es/er?; **that's just** ~ him das sieht ihm ähnlich; ~ **that/this** so; *a (similar)* ähnlich; *(equal)* gleich; *n* Gleiche(s) *nt*; ~**able** *a* sympathisch; ~**lihood** Wahrscheinlichkeit *f*; ~**ly** *a (probable)* wahrscheinlich; *(suitable)* geeignet; *ad* wahrscheinlich; ~**-minded** *a* gleichgesinnt; ~**n** *vt* vergleichen *(to* mit*)*; ~**wise** *ad* ebenfalls.

liking ['laɪkɪŋ] *n* Zuneigung *f*; *(taste for)* Vorliebe *f*.

lilac ['laɪlək] *n* Flieder *m*.

lilting ['lɪltɪŋ] *a accent* singend; *tune* munter.

lily ['lɪlɪ] *n* Lilie *f*; ~ **of the valley** Maiglöckchen *nt*.

limb [lɪm] *n* Glied *nt*.

limber ['lɪmbə*] *: ~ **up** *vi* sich auflockern; *(fig)* sich vorbereiten.

limbo ['lɪmbəʊ] *n*: **to be in** ~ *(fig)* in der Schwebe sein.

lime [laɪm] *n (tree)* Linde *f*; *(fruit)* Limone *f*; *(substance)* Kalk *m*; ~ **juice** Limonensaft *m*; ~ **light** *(fig)* Rampenlicht *nt*.

limerick ['lɪmərɪk] *n* Limerick *m*.

limestone ['laɪmstəʊn] *n* Kalkstein *m*.

limit ['lɪmɪt] *n* Grenze *f*; *(col)* Höhe *f*; *vt* begrenzen, einschränken; ~**ation** Grenzen *pl*, Einschränkung *f*; ~**ed** *a* beschränkt; ~**ed company** Gesellschaft *f* mit beschränkter Haftung, GmbH *f*.

limousine ['lɪməziːn] *n* Limousine *f*.

limp [lɪmp] *n* Hinken *nt*; *vi* hinken; *a (without firmness)* schlaff.

limpet ['lɪmpɪt] *n (lit)* Napfschnecke *f*; *(fig)* Klette *f*.

limpid ['lɪmpɪd] *a* klar.

limply ['lɪmplɪ] *ad* schlaff.

line [laɪn] *n* Linie *f*; *(rope)* Leine *f*, Schnur *f*; *(on face)* Falte *f*; *(row)* Reihe *f*; *(of hills)* Kette *f*; *(US: queue)* Schlange *f*; *(company)* Linie *f*, Gesellschaft *f*; *(Rail)* Strecke *f*; *(pl)* Geleise *pl*; *(Tel)* Leitung *f*; *(written)* Zeile *f*; *(direction)* Richtung *f*; *(fig: business)* Branche *f*, Beruf *m*; *(range of items)* Kollektion *f*; **it's a bad** ~ *(Tel)* die Verbindung

ist schlecht; **hold the** ~ bleiben Sie am Apparat; **in** ~ **with** in Übereinstimmung mit; *vt coat* füttern; *(border)* säumen; ~ **up** *vi* sich aufstellen; *vt* aufstellen; *(prepare)* sorgen für; *support* mobilisieren; *surprise* planen.

linear ['lɪnɪə*] *a* gerade; *(measure)* Längen-.

linen ['lɪnɪn] *n* Leinen *nt*; *(sheets etc)* Wäsche *f*.

liner ['laɪnə*] *n* Überseedampfer *m*.

linesman ['laɪnzmən] *n (Sport)* Linienrichter *m*.

line-up ['laɪnʌp] *n* Aufstellung *f*.

linger ['lɪŋgə*] *vi (remain long)* verweilen; *(taste)* (zurück)bleiben; *(delay)* zögern, verharren.

lingerie ['lænʒəri:] *n* Damenunterwäsche *f*.

lingering ['lɪŋgərɪŋ] *a* lang; *doubt* zurückbleibend; *disease* langwierig; *taste* nachhaltend; *look* lang.

lingo ['lɪŋgəʊ] *n (col)* Sprache *f*.

linguist ['lɪŋgwɪst] *n* Sprachkundige(r) *mf*; *(Univ)* Sprachwissenschaftler(in *f*) *m*.

linguistic [lɪŋ'gwɪstɪc] *a* sprachlich; sprachwissenschaftlich; ~**s** Sprachwissenschaft *f*, Linguistik *f*.

liniment ['lɪnɪmənt] *n* Einreibemittel *nt*.

lining ['laɪnɪŋ] *n (of clothes)* Futter *nt*.

link [lɪŋk] *n* Glied *nt*; *(connection)* Verbindung *f*; *vt* verbinden; ~**s** *pl* Golfplatz *m*; ~**-up** *(Tel)* Verbindung *f*; *(of spaceships)* Kopplung *f*.

lino ['laɪnəʊ] *n*, **linoleum** [lɪ'nəʊlɪəm] *n* Linoleum *nt*.

linseed oil ['lɪnsi:d'ɔɪl] *n* Leinöl *nt*.

lint [lɪnt] *n* Verbandstoff *m*.

lintel ['lɪntl] *n (Archit)* Sturz *m*.

lion ['laɪən] *n* Löwe *m*; ~**ess** Löwin *f*.

lip [lɪp] *n* Lippe *f*; *(of jug)* Tülle *f*, Schnabel *m*; ~**read** *vi irreg* von den Lippen ablesen; **to pay** ~ **service (to)** ein Lippenbekenntnis ablegen (zu); ~**stick** Lippenstift *m*.

liquefy ['lɪkwɪfaɪ] *vt* verflüssigen.

liqueur [lɪ'kjʊə*] *n* Likör *m*.

liquid ['lɪkwɪd] *n* Flüßigkeit *f*; *a* flüssig; ~**ate** *vt* liquidieren; ~**ation** Liquidation *f*.

liquor ['lɪkə*] *n* Alkohol *m*, Spirituosen *pl*.

lisp [lɪsp] *n* Lispeln *nt*; *vti* lispeln.

list [lɪst] *n* Liste *f*, Verzeichnis *nt*; *(of ship)* Schlagseite *f*; *vt (write down)* eine Liste machen von; *(verbally)* aufzählen; *vi (ship)* Schlagseite haben.

listen ['lɪsn] *vi* hören, horchen; ~ **to** *vt* zuhören (+ *dat*); ~**er** (Zu)hörer(in *f*) *m*.

listless *a*, ~**ly** *ad* ['lɪstləs, -lɪ] lustlos, teilnahmslos; ~**ness** Lustlosigkeit *f*, Teilnahmslosigkeit *f*.

litany ['lɪtənɪ] *n* Litanei *f*.

literacy ['lɪtərəsɪ] *n* Fähigkeit *f* zu lesen und zu schreiben.

literal ['lɪtərəl] *a* eigentlich, buchstäblich; *translation* wortwörtlich; ~**ly** *ad* wörtlich; buchstäblich.

literary ['lɪtərərɪ] *a* literarisch, Literatur-.

literate ['lɪtərət] a des Lesens und Schreibens kundig.
literature ['lɪtrətʃə*] n Literatur f.
lithograph ['lɪθəʊgrɑːf] n Lithographie f.
litigate ['lɪtɪgeɪt] vi prozessieren.
litmus ['lɪtməs] n: ~ **paper** Lackmuspapier nt.
litre, (US) **liter** ['liːtə*] n Liter m.
litter ['lɪtə*] n (rubbish) Abfall m; (of animals) Wurf m; vt in Unordnung bringen; **to be ~ed with** übersät sein mit.
little ['lɪtl] a klein; (unimportant) unbedeutend; ad, n wenig; **a ~** ein bißchen; **the ~** das wenige.
liturgy ['lɪtədʒɪ] n Liturgie f.
live¹ [lɪv] vi leben; (last) fortleben; (dwell) wohnen; vt life führen; **~ down** vt Gras wachsen lassen über (+acc); **I'll never ~ it down** das wird man mir nie vergessen; **~ on** vi weiterleben; **~ on sth** von etw leben; **~ up to** vt standards gerecht werden (+dat); principles anstreben; hopes entsprechen (+dat).
live² [laɪv] a lebendig; (burning) glühend; (Mil) scharf; (Elec) geladen; broadcast live.
livelihood ['laɪvlɪhʊd] n Lebensunterhalt m.
liveliness ['laɪvlɪnəs] n Lebendigkeit f.
lively ['laɪvlɪ] a lebhaft, lebendig.
liver ['lɪvə*] n (Anat) Leber f; **~ish** a (bad-tempered) gallig.
livery ['lɪvərɪ] n Livree f.
livestock ['laɪvstɒk] n Vieh nt, Viehbestand m.
livid ['lɪvɪd] a (lit) bläulich; (furious) fuchsteufelswild.
living ['lɪvɪŋ] n (Lebens)unterhalt m; a lebendig; language etc lebend; wage ausreichend; **~ room** Wohnzimmer nt.
lizard ['lɪzəd] n Eidechse f.
llama ['lɑːmə] n Lama nt.
load [ləʊd] n (burden) Last f; (amount) Ladung f, Fuhre f; **~s of** (col) massenhaft; vt (be)laden; (fig) überhäufen; camera Film einlegen in (+acc); gun laden.
loaf [ləʊf] n Brot nt, Laib m; vi herumlungern, faulenzen.
loam [ləʊm] n Lehmboden m.
loan [ləʊn] n Leihgabe f; (Fin) Darlehen nt; vt leihen; **on ~** geliehen.
loathe [ləʊð] vt verabscheuen.
loathing ['ləʊðɪŋ] n Abscheu f.
lobby ['lɒbɪ] n Vorhalle f; (Pol) Lobby f; vt politisch beeinflussen (wollen).
lobe [ləʊb] n Ohrläppchen nt.
lobster ['lɒbstə*] n Hummer m.
local ['ləʊkəl] a ortsansässig, hiesig, Orts-; anaesthetic örtlich; n (pub) Stammwirtschaft f; **the ~s** pl die Ortsansässigen pl; **~ colour** Lokalkolorit nt; **~ity** [ləʊ'kælɪtɪ] Ort m; **~ly** ad örtlich, am Ort.
locate [ləʊ'keɪt] vt ausfindig machen; (establish) errichten.
location [ləʊ'keɪʃən] n Platz m, Lage f; **on ~** (Cine) auf Außenaufnahme.
loch [lɒx] n (Scot) See m.
lock [lɒk] n Schloß nt; (Naut) Schleuse f; (of hair) Locke f; vt (fasten) (ver)schließen; vi

(door etc) sich schließen (lassen); (wheels) blockieren.
locker ['lɒkə*] n Spind m.
locket ['lɒkɪt] n Medaillon nt.
locomotive [ləʊkə'məʊtɪv] n Lokomotive f.
locust ['ləʊkəst] n Heuschrecke f.
lodge [lɒdʒ] n (gatehouse) Pförtnerhaus nt; (freemasons') Loge f; vi (in Untermiete) wohnen (with bei); (get stuck) stecken(bleiben); vt protest einreichen; **~r** (Unter)mieter m.
lodgings ['lɒdʒɪŋz] n (Miet)wohnung f; Zimmer nt.
loft [lɒft] n (Dach)boden m.
lofty ['lɒftɪ] a hoch(ragend); (proud) hochmütig.
log [lɒg] n Klotz m; (Naut) Log nt.
logarithm ['lɒgərɪðəm] n Logarithmus m.
logbook ['lɒgbʊk] n Bordbuch nt, Logbuch nt; (for lorry) Fahrtenschreiber m; (Aut) Kraft-fahrzeugbrief m.
loggerheads ['lɒgəhedz] n: **to be at ~** sich in den Haaren liegen.
logic ['lɒdʒɪk] n Logik f; **~al** a logisch; **~ally** ad logisch(erweise).
logistics [lɒ'dʒɪstɪks] npl Logistik f.
loin [lɔɪn] n Lende f.
loiter ['lɔɪtə*] vi herumstehen, sich herumtreiben.
loll [lɒl] vi sich rekeln.
lollipop ['lɒlɪpɒp] n (Dauer)lutscher m.
lone [ləʊn] a einsam.
loneliness ['ləʊnlɪnəs] n Einsamkeit f.
lonely ['ləʊnlɪ] a einsam.
long [lɒŋ] a lang; distance weit; ad lange; **two-day-~** zwei Tage lang; vi sich sehnen (for nach); **~ ago** vor langer Zeit; **before ~** bald; **as ~ as** solange; **in the ~ run** auf die Dauer; **~-distance** a Fern-; **~-haired** a langhaarig; **~hand** Langschrift f; **~ing** Verlangen nt, Sehnsucht f; a sehnsüchtig; **~ish** a ziemlich lang; **~itude** Längengrad m; **~-jump** Weitsprung m; **~-lost** a längst verloren geglaubt; **~-playing** record Langspielplatte f; **~-range** a Langstrecken-, Fern-; **~-sighted** a weitsichtig; **~-standing** a alt, seit langer Zeit bestehend; **~-suffering** a schwer geprüft; **~-term** a langfristig; **~ wave** Langwelle f; **~-winded** a langatmig.
loo [luː] n (col) Klo nt.
loofah ['luːfə*] n (plant) Luffa f; (sponge) Luffa(schwamm) m.
look [lʊk] vi schauen, blicken; (seem) aussehen; (face) liegen nach, gerichtet sein nach; n Blick m; **~s** pl Aussehen nt; **~ after** vt (care for) sorgen für; (watch) aufpassen auf (+acc); **~ down on** vt (fig) herabsehen auf (+acc); **~ for** vt (seek) suchen (nach); (expect) erwarten; **~ forward to** vt sich freuen auf (+acc); **~ out for** vt Ausschau halten nach; (be careful) achtgeben auf (+acc); **~ to** vt (take care of) achtgeben auf (+acc); (rely on) sich verlassen auf (+acc); **~ up** vi aufblicken; (improve) sich bessern; vt word nachschlagen; person besuchen; vt **~ up to** vt aufsehen zu; **~-out** (watch) Ausschau f;

(person) Wachposten *m; (place)* Ausguck *m;*
(prospect) Aussichten *pl.*

loom [luːm] *n* Webstuhl *m; vi* sich
abzeichnen.

loop [luːp] *n* Schlaufe *f,* Schleife *f; vt*
schlingen; ~**hole** *(fig)* Hintertürchen *nt.*

loose [luːs] *a* lose, locker; *(free)* frei;
(inexact) unpräzise; *vt* lösen, losbinden; **to
be at a** ~ **end** nicht wissen, was man tun
soll; ~**ly** *ad* locker, lose; ~**ly speaking**
grob gesagt; ~**n** *vt* lockern, losmachen;
~**ness** Lockerheit *f.*

loot [luːt] *n* Beute *f; vt* plündern; ~**ing**
Plünderung *f.*

lop [lɒp] ~ **off** *vt* abhacken.

lop-sided ['lɒp'saɪdɪd] *a* schief.

lord [lɔːd] *n (ruler)* Herr *m,* Gebieter *m;*
(Brit, title) Lord *m;* the **L**~ *(Gott)* der
Herr *m;* ~**ly** *a* vornehm; *(proud)* stolz.

lore [lɔː*] *n* Überlieferung *f.*

lorry ['lɒrɪ] *n* Lastwagen *m.*

lose [luːz] *irreg vt* verlieren; *chance* verpassen; ~ **out** *on* zu kurz kommen bei; *vi*
verlieren; ~**r** Verlierer *m.*

losing ['luːzɪŋ] *a* Verlierer-; *(Comm)*
verlustbringend.

loss [lɒs] *n* Verlust *m;* **at a** ~ *(Comm)* mit
Verlust; *(unable)* außerstande; **I am at a**
~ **for words** mir fehlen die Worte.

lost [lɒst] *a* verloren; ~ **cause** aus-
sichtslose Sache *f;* ~ **property**
Fundsachen *pl.*

lot [lɒt] *n (quantity)* Menge *f; (fate, at
auction)* Los *nt; (col: people, things)* Haufen
m; the ~ alles; *(people)* alle; **a** ~ **of** viel;
pl viele; ~**s of** massenhaft, viel(e).

lotion ['ləʊʃən] *n* Lotion *f.*

lottery ['lɒtərɪ] *n* Lotterie *f.*

loud [laʊd] *a* laut; *(showy)* schreiend; *ad*
laut; ~**ly** *ad* laut; ~**ness** Lautheit *f;*
~**speaker** Lautsprecher *m.*

lounge [laʊndʒ] *n (in hotel)* Gesellschafts-
raum *m; (in house)* Wohnzimmer *nt; (on
ship)* Salon *m; vi* sich herumlümmeln; ~
suit Straßenanzug *m.*

louse [laʊs] *n* Laus *f.*

lousy ['laʊzɪ] *a (lit)* verlaust; *(fig)* lausig,
miserabel.

lout [laʊt] *n* Lümmel *m.*

lovable ['lʌvəbl] *a* liebenswert.

love [lʌv] *n* Liebe *f; (person)* Liebling *m,*
Schatz *m; (Sport)* null; *vt* person lieben;
activity gerne mögen; **to** ~ **to do sth** etw
(sehr) gerne tun; **to make** ~ sich lieben;
to make ~ **to/with sb** jdn lieben; ~
affair (Liebes)verhältnis *nt;* ~ **letter**
Liebesbrief *m;* ~ **life** Liebesleben *nt;* ~**ly**
a schön; *person, object also* entzückend,
reizend; ~-**making** Liebe *f;* ~**r** Lieb-
haber *m;* Geliebte *f; (of books etc)* Lieb-
haber *m;* the ~**rs** die Liebenden, das
Liebespaar; ~**song** Liebeslied *nt.*

loving ['lʌvɪŋ] *a* liebend, liebevoll; ~**ly** *ad*
liebevoll.

low [ləʊ] *a* niedrig; *rank* niedere(r, s); *level,
note, neckline usw (intelligence, density)*
gering; *(vulgar)* ordinär; *(not loud)* leise;
(depressed) gedrückt; *ad (not high)* niedrig;
(not loudly) leise; *n (low point)* Tiefstand *m;*

(Met) Tief *nt;* ~-**cut** *a dress* tiefaus-
geschnitten.

lower ['ləʊə*] *vt* herunterlassen; *eyes, gun*
senken; *(reduce)* herabsetzen, senken.

lowly ['ləʊlɪ] *a* bescheiden.

loyal ['lɔɪəl] *a (true)* treu; *(to king)* loyal,
treu; ~**ly** *ad* treu; loyal; ~**ty** Treue *f;*
Loyalität *f.*

lozenge ['lɒzɪndʒ] *n* Pastille *f.*

lubricant ['luːbrɪkənt] *n* Schmiermittel *nt.*

lubricate ['luːbrɪkeɪt] *vt* (ab)schmieren,
ölen.

lubrication [luːbrɪ'keɪʃən] *n* (Ein- or
Ab)schmierung *f.*

lucid ['luːsɪd] *a* klar; *(sane)* bei klarem
Verstand; *mind* klar; ~**ity** ['luːsɪdɪtɪ]
Klarheit *f;* ~**ly** *ad* klar.

luck [lʌk] *n* Glück *nt; bad* ~ Pech *nt;* ~**ily**
ad glücklicherweise, zum Glück; ~**y** *a*
glücklich, Glücks-; **to be** ~ Glück haben.

lucrative ['luːkrətɪv] *a* einträglich.

ludicrous ['luːdɪkrəs] *a* grotesk.

ludo ['luːdəʊ] *n* Mensch ärgere dich nicht
nt.

lug [lʌg] *vt* schleppen.

luggage ['lʌgɪdʒ] *n* Gepäck *nt;* ~ **rack**
Gepäcknetz *nt.*

lugubrious [luː'guːbrɪəs] *a* traurig.

lukewarm ['luːkwɔːm] *a* lauwarm; *(indifferent)* lau.

lull [lʌl] *n* Flaute *f; vt* einlullen; *(calm)*
beruhigen; ~**aby** ['lʌləbaɪ] Schlaflied *nt.*

lumbago [lʌm'beɪgəʊ] *n* Hexenschuß *m.*

lumber ['lʌmbə*] *n* Plunder *m; (wood)* Holz
nt; ~**jack** Holzfäller *m.*

luminous ['luːmɪnəs] *a* leuchtend, Leucht-.

lump [lʌmp] *n* Klumpen *m; (Med)*
Schwellung *f; (in breast)* Knoten *m; (of
sugar)* Stück *m; vt* zusammentun; *(judge together)* in einen Topf werfen; ~ **sum**
Pauschalsumme *f;* ~**y** klumpig; **to go** ~**y**
klumpen.

lunacy ['luːnəsɪ] *n* Irrsinn *m.*

lunar ['luːnə*] *a* Mond-.

lunatic ['luːnətɪk] *n* Wahnsinnige(r) *mf; a*
wahnsinnig, irr.

lunch [lʌntʃ] *n (also* ~**eon** [-ən]) Mittagessen *nt;* ~ **hour** Mittagspause *f;*
~**time** Mittagszeit *f;* ~**eon meat**
Frühstücksfleisch *nt.*

lung [lʌŋ] *n* Lunge *f;* ~ **cancer** Lungen-
krebs *m.*

lunge [lʌndʒ] *vi* (los)stürzen.

lupin ['luːpɪn] *n* Lupine *f.*

lurch [lɜːtʃ] *vi* taumeln; *(Naut)* schlingern; *n*
Taumeln *nt; (Naut)* plötzliche(s)
Schlingern *nt.*

lure [ljʊə*] *n* Köder *m; (fig)* Lockung *f; vt*
(ver)locken.

lurid ['ljʊərɪd] *a (shocking)* grausig, widerlich; *colour* grell.

lurk [lɜːk] *vi* lauern.

luscious ['lʌʃəs] *a* köstlich; *colour* satt.

lush [lʌʃ] *a* satt; *vegetation* üppig.

lust [lʌst] *n* sinnliche Begierde *f (for* nach);
(sensation) Wollust *f; (greed)* Gier *f; vi*
gieren *(after* nach); ~**ful** *a* wollüstig,
lüstern.

lustre, *(US)* **luster** ['lʌstə*] *n* Glanz *m.*

lusty ['lʌstɪ] *a* gesund und munter; *old person* rüstig.
lute [luːt] *n* Laute *f*.
luxuriant [lʌg'zjuərɪənt] *a* üppig.
luxurious [lʌg'zjuərɪəs] *a* luxuriös, Luxus-.
luxury ['lʌkʃərɪ] *n* Luxus *m*; **the little luxuries** die kleinen Genüsse.
lying ['laɪɪŋ] *n* Lügen *nt*; *a* verlogen.
lynch [lɪntʃ] *vt* lynchen.
lynx [lɪŋks] *n* Luchs *m*.
lyre ['laɪə*] *n* Leier *f*.
lyric ['lɪrɪk] *n* Lyrik *f*; *(pl: words for song)* (Lied)text *m*; *a* lyrisch; ~**al** *a* lyrisch, gefühlvoll.

M

M, m [em] *n* M *nt*, m *nt*.
mac [mæk] *n* (Brit col) Regenmantel *m*.
macabre [mə'kɑːbr] *a* makaber.
macaroni [mækə'rəʊnɪ] *n* Makkaroni *pl*.
mace [meɪs] *n* Amtsstab *m*; *(spice)* Muskat *m*.
machine [mə'ʃiːn] *n* Maschine *f*; *vt* dress etc mit der Maschine nähen; maschinell herstellen/bearbeiten; ~**gun** Maschinengewehr *nt*; ~**ry** [mə'ʃiːnərɪ] Maschinerie *f*, Maschinen *pl*; ~ **tool** Werkzeugmaschine *f*.
machinist [mə'ʃiːnɪst] *n* Machinist *m*.
mackerel ['mækrəl] *n* Makrele *f*.
mackintosh ['mækɪntɒʃ] *n* Regenmantel *m*.
macro- ['mækrəʊ] *pref* Makro-, makro-.
mad [mæd] *a* verrückt; *dog* tollwütig; *(angry)* wütend; ~ **about** *(fond of)* verrückt nach, versessen auf *(+acc)*.
madam ['mædəm] *n* gnädige Frau *f*.
madden ['mædn] *vt* verrückt machen; *(make angry)* ärgern; ~**ing** *a* ärgerlich.
made-to-measure ['meɪdtə'meʒə*] *a* Maß-.
made-up ['meɪd'ʌp] *a story* erfunden.
madly ['mædlɪ] *ad* wahnsinnig.
madman ['mædmən] *n* Verrückte(r) *m*, Irre(r) *m*.
madness ['mædnəs] *n* Wahnsinn *m*.
Madonna [mə'dɒnə] *n* Madonna *f*.
madrigal ['mædrɪgəl] *n* Madrigal *nt*.
magazine ['mægəziːn] *n* Zeitschrift *f*; *(in gun)* Magazin *nt*.
maggot ['mægət] *n* Made *f*.
magic ['mædʒɪk] *n* Zauberei *f*, Magie *f*; *(fig)* Zauber *m*; *a* magisch, Zauber-; ~**al** *a* magisch; ~**ian** [mə'dʒɪʃən] Zauberer *m*.
magistrate ['mædʒɪstreɪt] *n* (Friedens)richter *m*.
magnanimity [mægnə'nɪmɪtɪ] *n* Großmut *f*.
magnanimous [mæg'nænɪməs] *a* großmütig.
magnate ['mægneɪt] *n* Magnat *m*.
magnet ['mægnɪt] *n* Magnet *m*; ~**ic** [mæg'netɪk] *a* magnetisch; *(fig)* anziehend, unwiderstehlich; ~**ism** Magnetismus *m*; *(fig)* Ausstrahlungskraft *f*.
magnification [mægnɪfɪ'keɪʃən] *n* Vergrößerung *f*.

magnificence [mæg'nɪfɪsəns] *n* Großartigkeit *f*.
magnificent *a*, ~**ly** *ad* [mæg'nɪfɪsənt, -lɪ] großartig.
magnify ['mægnɪfaɪ] *vt* vergrößern; ~**ing glass** Vergrößerungsglas *nt*, Lupe *f*.
magnitude ['mægnɪtjuːd] *n* *(size)* Größe *f*; *(importance)* Ausmaß *nt*.
magnolia [mæg'nəʊlɪə] *n* Magnolie *f*.
magpie ['mægpaɪ] *n* Elster *f*.
maharajah [mɑːhə'rɑːdʒə] *n* Maharadscha *m*.
mahogany [mə'hogənɪ] *n* Mahagoni *nt*; *a* Mahagoni-.
maid [meɪd] *n* Dienstmädchen *nt*; **old** ~ alte Jungfer *f*; ~**en** *(liter)* Maid *f*; *a flight, speech* Jungfern-; ~**en name** Mädchenname *m*.
mail [meɪl] *n* Post *f*; *vt* aufgeben; ~ **box** *(US)* Briefkasten *m*; ~**ing list** Anschreibeliste *f*; ~ **order** Bestellung *f* durch die Post; ~ **order firm** Versandhaus *nt*.
maim [meɪm] *vt* verstümmeln.
main [meɪn] *a* hauptsächlich, Haupt-; *n* *(pipe)* Hauptleitung *f*; **in the** ~ im großen und ganzen; ~**land** Festland *nt*; ~ **road** Hauptstraße *f*; ~**stay** *(fig)* Hauptstütze *f*.
maintain [meɪn'teɪn] *vt* machine, roads instand halten; *(support)* unterhalten; *(keep up)* aufrechterhalten; *(claim)* behaupten; *innocence* beteuern.
maintenance ['meɪntənəns] *n* *(Tech)* Wartung *f*; *(of family)* Unterhalt *m*.
maisonette [meɪzə'net] *n* kleine(s) Eigenheim *nt*; Wohnung *f*.
maize [meɪz] *n* Mais *m*.
majestic [mə'dʒestɪk] *a* majestätisch.
majesty ['mædʒɪstɪ] *n* Majestät *f*.
major ['meɪdʒə*] *n* Major *m*; *a* *(Mus)* Dur; *(more important)* Haupt-; *(bigger)* größer.
majority [mə'dʒɒrɪtɪ] *n* Mehrheit *f*; *(Jur)* Volljährigkeit *f*.
make [meɪk] *vt irreg* machen; *(appoint)* ernennen (zu); *(cause to do sth)* veranlassen; *(reach)* erreichen; *(in time)* schaffen; *(earn)* verdienen; **to** ~ **sth happen** etw geschehen lassen; *n* Marke *f*, Fabrikat *nt*; ~ **for** *vi* gehen/fahren nach; ~ **out** *vi* zurechtkommen; *vt* *(write out)* ausstellen; *(understand)* verstehen; *(pretend)* (so) tun (als ob); ~ **up** *vt* *(make)* machen, herstellen; *face* schminken; *quarrel* beilegen; *story* etc erfinden; *vi sich* versöhnen; ~ **up for** *vt* wiedergutmachen; *(Comm)* vergüten; ~**believe** *n* it's ~**believe** es ist nicht wirklich; *a* Phantasie-, ersonnen; ~**r** *(Comm)* Hersteller *m*; ~**shift** *a* behelfsmäßig, Not-; ~**-up** Schminke *f*, Make-up *nt*.
making ['meɪkɪŋ] *n:* **in the** ~ im Entstehen; **to have the** ~**s of** das Zeug haben zu.
maladjusted ['mælə'dʒʌstɪd] *a* fehlangepaßt, umweltgestört.
malaise [mæ'leɪz] *n* Unbehagen *nt*.
malaria [mə'lɛərɪə] *n* Malaria *f*.
male [meɪl] *n* Mann *m*; *(animal)* Männchen *nt*; *a* männlich.
malevolence [mə'levələns] *n* Böswilligkeit *f*.

malevolent [mə'levələnt] a übelwollend.

malfunction [mæl'fʌŋkʃən] vi versagen, nicht funktionieren.

malice ['mælɪs] n Bosheit f.

malicious a, ~ly ad [mə'lɪʃəs, -lɪ] böswillig, gehässig.

malign [mə'laɪn] vt verleumden.

malignant [mə'lɪgnənt] a bösartig.

malinger [mə'lɪŋgə*] vi simulieren; ~er Drückeberger m, Simulant m.

malleable ['mælɪəbl] a formbar.

mallet ['mælɪt] n Holzhammer m.

malnutrition ['mælnju'trɪʃən] n Unterernährung f.

malpractice ['mæl'præktɪs] n Amtsvergehen nt.

malt [mɔːlt] n Malz nt.

maltreat [mæl'triːt] vt mißhandeln.

mammal ['mæməl] n Säugetier nt.

mammoth ['mæməθ] a Mammut-, Riesen-.

man [mæn] n, pl **men** Mann m; (human race) der Mensch, die Menschen pl; vt bemannen.

manage ['mænɪdʒ] vi zurechtkommen; vt (control) führen, leiten; (cope with) fertigwerden mit; to ~ to do sth etw schaffen; ~able a person, animal lenksam, fügsam; object handlich; ~ment (control) Führung f, Leitung f; (directors) Management nt; ~r Geschäftsführer m, (Betriebs)leiter m; ~ress ['mænɪdʒə'res] Geschäftsführerin f; ~rial [mænə'dʒɪərɪəl] a leitend; problem etc Management-.

managing ['mænɪdʒɪŋ] a: ~ **director** Betriebsleiter m.

mandarin ['mændərɪn] n (fruit) Mandarine f; (Chinese official) Mandarin m.

mandate ['mændeɪt] n Mandat nt.

mandatory ['mændətərɪ] a obligatorisch.

mandolin(e) ['mændəlɪn] n Mandoline f.

mane [meɪn] n Mähne f.

maneuver [mə'nuːvə*] (US) = **manoeuvre**.

manful a, ~ly ad ['mænfʊl, -fəlɪ] beherzt; mannhaft.

mangle ['mæŋgl] vt verstümmeln.

mango ['mæŋgəʊ] n Mango(pflaume) f.

mangrove ['mæŋgrəʊv] n Mangrove f.

mangy ['meɪndʒɪ] a dog räudig.

manhandle ['mænhændl] vt grob behandeln.

manhole ['mænhəʊl] n (Straßen)schacht m.

manhood ['mænhʊd] n Mannesalter f; (manliness) Männlichkeit f.

man-hour ['mæn'aʊə*] n Arbeitsstunde f.

manhunt ['mænhʌnt] n Fahndung f.

mania ['meɪnɪə] n (craze) Sucht f, Manie f; (madness) Wahn m; ~c ['meɪnɪæk] Wahnsinnige(r) mf, Verrückte(r) mf.

manicure ['mænɪkjʊə*] n Maniküre f; vt maniküren; ~ **set** Necessaire nt.

manifest ['mænɪfest] vt offenbaren; a offenkundig; ~ation (showing) Ausdruck m, Bekundung f; (sign) Anzeichen nt; ~ly ad offenkundig; ~o [mænɪ'festəʊ] Manifest nt.

manipulate [mə'nɪpjʊleɪt] vt handhaben; (fig) manipulieren.

manipulation [mənɪpjʊ'leɪʃən] n Manipulation f.

mankind [mæn'kaɪnd] n Menschheit f.

manliness ['mænlɪnəs] n Männlichkeit f.

manly ['mænlɪ] a männlich; mannhaft.

man-made ['mæn'meɪd] a fibre künstlich.

manner ['mænə*] n Art f, Weise f; (style) Stil m; in such a ~ so; in a ~ of speaking sozusagen; ~s pl Manieren pl; ~ism (of person) Angewohnheit f; (of style) Manieriertheit f.

manoeuvrable [mə'nuːvrəbl] a manövrierfähig.

manoeuvre [mə'nuːvə*] vti manövrieren; n (Mil) Feldzug m; (general) Manöver nt, Schachzug m; ~s pl Truppenübungen pl, Manöver nt.

manor ['mænə*] n Landgut nt; ~ **house** Herrenhaus nt.

manpower ['mænpaʊə*] n Arbeitskräfte pl.

manservant ['mænsɜːvənt] n Diener m.

mansion ['mænʃən] n Herrenhaus nt, Landhaus nt.

manslaughter ['mænslɔːtə*] n Totschlag m.

mantelpiece ['mæntlpiːs] n Kaminsims m.

mantle ['mæntl] n (cloak) lange(r) Umhang m.

manual ['mænjʊəl] a manuell, Hand-; n Handbuch nt.

manufacture [mænju'fæktʃə*] vt herstellen; n Herstellung f; ~r Hersteller m.

manure [mə'njʊə*] n Dünger m.

manuscript ['mænjuskrɪpt] n Manuskript nt.

many ['menɪ] a viele; as ~ as 20 sage und schreibe 20; ~ a good soldier so mancher gute Soldat; ~'s the time oft.

map [mæp] n (Land)karte f; (of town) Stadtplan m; vt eine Karte machen von; ~ out (fig) ausarbeiten.

maple ['meɪpl] n Ahorn m.

mar [mɑː*] vt verderben, beeinträchtigen.

marathon ['mærəθən] n (Sport) Marathonlauf m; (fig) Marathon m.

marauder [mə'rɔːdə*] n Plünderer m.

marble ['mɑːbl] n Marmor m; (for game) Murmel f.

March [mɑːtʃ] n März m.

march [mɑːtʃ] vi marschieren; n Marsch m; ~-past Vorbeimarsch m.

mare [mɛə*] n Stute f; ~'s **nest** Windei nt.

margarine [mɑːdʒə'riːn] n Margarine f.

margin ['mɑːdʒɪn] n Rand m; (extra amount) Spielraum m; (Comm) Spanne f; ~al a note Rand-; difference etc geringfügig; ~ally ad nur wenig.

marigold ['mærɪgəʊld] n Ringelblume f.

marijuana [mærɪ'hwɑːnə] n Marihuana f.

marina [mə'riːnə] n Yachthafen m.

marine [mə'riːn] a Meeres-, See-; n (Mil) Marineinfanterist m; (fleet) Marine f; ~r ['mærɪnə*] Seemann m.

marionette [mærɪə'net] n Marionette f.

marital ['mærɪtl] a ehelich, Ehe-.

maritime ['mærɪtaɪm] a See-.

marjoram ['mɑːdʒərəm] n Majoram

mark [mɑːk] n (coin) Mark f; (spot) Fleck m; (scar) Kratzer m; (sign) Zeichen nt; (target) Ziel nt; (Sch) Note f; **quick off the ~** blitzschnell; **on your ~s** auf die Plätze; vt (make mark) Flecken/Kratzer machen auf (+acc); (indicate) markieren, bezeichnen; (note) sich (dat) merken; exam korrigieren; **to ~ time** (lit, fig) auf der Stelle treten; **~ out** vt bestimmen; area abstecken; **~ed** a deutlich; **~edly** ['mɑːkɪdlɪ] ad merklich; **~er** (in book) (Lese)zeichen nt; (on road) Schild nt.

market ['mɑːkɪt] n Markt m; (stock —) Börse f; vt (Comm: new product) auf dem Markt bringen; (sell) vertreiben; **~ day** Markttag m; **~ garden** (Brit) Handelsgärtnerei f; **~ing** Marketing nt; **~ place** Marktplatz m.

marksman ['mɑːksmən] n Scharfschütze m; **~ship** Treffsicherheit f.

marmalade ['mɑːməleɪd] n Orangenmarmelade f.

maroon [mə'ruːn] vt aussetzen; a (colour) kastanienbraun.

marquee [mɑː'kiː] n große(s) Zelt nt.

marquess, marquis ['mɑːkwɪs] n Marquis m.

marriage ['mærɪdʒ] n Ehe f; (wedding) Heirat f; (fig) Verbindung f.

married ['mærɪd] a person verheiratet; couple, life Ehe-.

marrow ['mærəʊ] n (Knochen)mark nt; (vegetable) Kürbis m.

marry ['mærɪ] vt (join) trauen; (take as husband, wife) heiraten; vi (also **get married**) heiraten.

marsh [mɑːʃ] n Marsch f, Sumpfland nt.

marshal ['mɑːʃəl] n (US) Bezirkspolizeichef m; vt (an)ordnen, arrangieren.

marshy ['mɑːʃɪ] a sumpfig.

martial ['mɑːʃəl] a kriegerisch; **~ law** Kriegsrecht nt.

martyr ['mɑːtə*] n (lit, fig) Märtyrer(in f) m; vt zum Märtyrer machen; **~dom** Martyrium nt.

marvel ['mɑːvəl] n Wunder nt; vi sich wundern (at über +acc); **~lous,** (US) **~ous** a, **~lously,** (US) **~ously** ad wunderbar.

Marxism ['mɑːksɪzəm] n Marxismus m.

Marxist ['mɑːksɪst] n Marxist(in f) m.

marzipan [mɑːzɪ'pæn] n Marzipan nt.

mascara [mæs'kɑːrə] n Wimperntusche f.

mascot ['mæskət] n Maskottchen nt.

masculine ['mæskjʊlɪn] a männlich; n Maskulinum nt.

masculinity [mæskjʊ'lɪnɪtɪ] n Männlichkeit f.

mashed [mæʃt] a: **~ potatoes** pl Kartoffelbrei m or -püree nt.

mask [mɑːsk] n (lit, fig) Maske f; vt maskieren, verdecken.

masochist ['mæzəʊkɪst] n Masochist(in f) m.

~ason ['meɪsn] n (stone—) Steinmetz m; (—) Freimaurer m; **~ic** [mə'sɒnɪk] a **~urer-; ~ry** Mauerwerk nt.

~de [mæskə'reɪd] n Maskerade f; **~ieren,** sich verkleiden; **to ~ ~n** als.

mass [mæs] n Masse f; (greater part) Mehrheit f; (Rel) Messe f; **~es of** massenhaft; vt sammeln, anhäufen; vi sich sammeln.

massacre ['mæsəkə*] n Blutbad nt; vt niedermetzeln, massakrieren.

massage ['mæsɑːʒ] n Massage f; vt massieren.

masseur [mæ'sɜː*] n Masseur m.

masseuse [mæ'sɜːz] n Masseuse f.

massive ['mæsɪv] a gewaltig, massiv.

mass media ['mæs'miːdɪə] npl Massenmedien pl.

mass-produce ['mæsprə'djuːs] vt serienmäßig herstellen.

mass production ['mæsprə'dʌkʃən] n Serienproduktion f, Massenproduktion f.

mast [mɑːst] n Mast m.

master ['mɑːstə*] n Herr m; (Naut) Kapitän m; (teacher) Lehrer m; (artist) Meister m; vt meistern; language etc beherrschen; **~ly** a meisterhaft; **~mind** n Kapazität f; vt geschickt lenken; **M~ of Arts** Magister Artium m; **~piece** Meisterstück nt; (Art) Meisterwerk nt; **~ stroke** Glanzstück nt; **~y** Können nt; **to gain ~y over sb** die Oberhand gewinnen über jdn.

masturbate ['mæstəbeɪt] vi masturbieren, onanieren.

masturbation [mæstə'beɪʃən] n Masturbation f, Onanie f.

mat [mæt] n Matte f; (for table) Untersetzer m; vi sich verfilzen; vt verfilzen.

match [mætʃ] n Streichholz nt; (sth corresponding) Pendant nt; (Sport) Wettkampf m; (ball games) Spiel nt; **it's a good ~** es paßt gut (for zu); **to be a ~ for sb** sich mit jdm messen können; jdm gewachsen sein; **he's a good ~** er ist eine gute Partie; vt (be alike, suit) passen zu; (equal) gleichkommen (+dat); (Sport) antreten lassen; vi zusammenpassen; **~box** Streichholzschachtel f; **~ing** a passend; **~less** a unvergleichlich; **~maker** Kuppler(in f) m.

mate [meɪt] n (companion) Kamerad m; (spouse) Lebensgefährte m; (of animal) Weibchen nt/Männchen nt; (Naut) Schiffsoffizier m; vi (chess) (schach)matt sein; (animals) sich paaren; vt (chess) matt setzen.

material [mə'tɪərɪəl] n Material nt; (for book, cloth) Material nt, Stoff m; a (important) wesentlich; damage Sach-; comforts etc materiell; **~s** pl Materialien pl; **~istic** a materialistisch; **~ize** vi sich verwirklichen, zustande kommen; **~ly** ad grundlegend.

maternal [mə'tɜːnl] a mütterlich, Mutter-; **~ grandmother** Großmutter mütterlicherseits.

maternity [mə'tɜːnɪtɪ] a Schwangeren-; dress Umstands-; benefit Wochen-.

matey ['meɪtɪ] a (Brit col) kameradschaftlich.

mathematical a, **~ly** ad [mæθə'mætɪkəl, -ɪ] mathematisch.

mathematician [mæθəmə'tɪʃən] n Mathematiker m.

mathematics [mæθə'mætɪks] n Mathematik f.

maths [mæθs] n Mathe f.
matinee ['mætineɪ] n Matinee f.
mating ['meɪtɪŋ] n Paarung f; ~ **call** Lockruf m.
matins ['mætɪnz] n (Früh)mette f.
matriarchal [meɪtrɪ'ɑːkl] a matriarchalisch.
matrimonial [mætrɪ'məʊnɪəl] a ehelich, Ehe-.
matrimony ['mætrɪmənɪ] n Ehestand m.
matron ['meɪtrən] n (Med) Oberin f; (Sch) Hausmutter f; ~**ly** a matronenhaft.
matt [mæt] a paint matt.
matter ['mætə*] n (substance) Materie f; (affair) Sache f, Angelegenheit f; (content) Inhalt m; (Med) Eiter m; vi darauf ankommen; **it doesn't** ~ es macht nichts; **no** ~ **how/what** egal wie/was; **what is the** ~? was ist los?; **as a** ~ **of fact** eigentlich; ~**-of-fact** a sachlich, nüchtern.
mattress ['mætrəs] n Matratze f.
mature [mə'tjʊə*] a reif; vi reif werden.
maturity [mə'tjʊərɪtɪ] n Reife f.
maudlin ['mɔːdlɪn] a weinerlich; gefühlsduselig.
maul [mɔːl] vt übel zurichten.
mausoleum [mɔːsə'liːəm] n Mausoleum nt.
mauve [məʊv] a mauve.
mawkish ['mɔːkɪʃ] a kitschig; taste süßlich.
maxi ['mæksɪ] pref Maxi-.
maxim ['mæksɪm] n Maxime f.
maximize ['mæksɪmaɪz] vt maximieren.
maximum ['mæksɪməm] a höchste(r, s), Höchst-, Maximal-; n Höchstgrenze f, Maximum nt.
May [meɪ] n Mai m.
may [meɪ] v aux (be possible) können; (have permission) dürfen; **I** ~ **come** ich komme vielleicht, es kann sein, daß ich komme; **we** ~ **as well go** wir können ruhig gehen; ~ **you be very happy** ich hoffe, ihr seid glücklich; ~**be** ad vielleicht.
Mayday ['meɪdeɪ] n (message) SOS nt.
mayonnaise [meɪə'neɪz] n Mayonnaise f.
mayor [mɛə*] n Bürgermeister m; ~**ess** (wife) (die) Frau f Bürgermeister; (lady —) Bürgermeisterin f.
maypole ['meɪpəʊl] n Maibaum m.
maze [meɪz] n (lit) Irrgarten m; (fig) Wirrwarr nt; **to be in a** ~ (fig) durcheinander sein.
me [miː] pron (acc) mich; (dat) mir; **it's** ~ ich bin's.
meadow ['medəʊ] n Wiese f.
meagre, (US) **meager** ['miːgə*] a dürftig, spärlich.
meal [miːl] n Essen nt, Mahlzeit f; (grain) Schrotmehl nt; **to have a** ~ essen (gehen); ~**time** Essenszeit f; ~**y-mouthed** a: **to be** ~**y-mouthed** d(a)rum herumreden.
mean [miːn] a (stingy) geizig; (spiteful) gemein; (shabby) armselig, schäbig; (average) durchschnittlich, Durchschnitts-; irreg vt (signify) bedeuten; (intend) vorhaben, beabsichtigen; (be resolved) entschlossen sein; **he** ~**s well** er meint es gut; **I** ~ **it!** ich meine das ernst!; **do you**

~ **me?** meinen Sie mich?; **it** ~**s nothing to me** es sagt mir nichts; n (average) Durchschnitt m; ~**s** pl Mittel pl; (wealth) Vermögen nt; **by** ~**s of** durch; **by all** ~**s** selbstverständlich; **by no** ~**s** keineswegs.
meander [mɪ'ændə*] vi sich schlängeln.
meaning ['miːnɪŋ] n Bedeutung f; (of life) Sinn m; ~**ful** a bedeutungsvoll; life sinnvoll; ~**less** a sinnlos.
meanness ['miːnnəs] n (stinginess) Geiz m; (spitefulness) Gemeinheit f; (shabbiness) Schäbigkeit f.
meantime ['miːntaɪm] ad, **meanwhile** ['miːnwaɪl] ad inzwischen, mittlerweile; **for the** ~ vorerst.
measles ['miːzlz] n Masern pl; **German** ~ Röteln pl.
measly ['miːzlɪ] a (col) poplig.
measurable ['meʒərəbl] a meßbar.
measure ['meʒə*] vti messen; n Maß nt; (step) Maßnahme f; **to be a** ~ **of sth** etw erkennen lassen; ~**d** a (slow) gemessen; ~**ment** (way of measuring) Messung f; (amount measured) Maß nt.
meat [miːt] n Fleisch nt; ~**y** a (lit) fleischig; (fig) gehaltvoll.
mechanic [mɪ'kænɪk] n Mechaniker m; ~**s** Mechanik f; ~**al** a mechanisch.
mechanism ['mekənɪzəm] n Mechanismus m.
mechanization [mekənaɪ'zeɪʃən] n Mechanisierung f.
mechanize ['mekənaɪz] vt mechanisieren.
medal ['medl] n Medaille f; (decoration) Orden m; ~**lion** [mɪ'dælɪən] Medaillon nt; ~**list**, (US) ~**ist** Medaillengewinner(in f) m.
meddle ['medl] vi sich einmischen (in in +acc); (tamper) hantieren (with an +dat); ~ **with sb** sich mit jdm einlassen.
media ['miːdɪə] npl Medien pl.
mediate ['miːdɪeɪt] vi vermitteln.
mediation [miːdɪ'eɪʃən] n Vermittlung f.
mediator ['miːdɪeɪtə*] n Vermittler m.
medical ['medɪkəl] a medizinisch; Medizin-; ärztlich; n (ärztliche) Untersuchung f.
medicated ['medɪkeɪtɪd] a medizinisch.
medicinal [me'dɪsɪnl] a medizinisch, Heil-.
medicine ['medsɪn] n Medizin f; (drugs) Arznei f; ~ **chest** Hausapotheke f.
medieval [medɪ'iːvəl] a mittelalterlich.
mediocre [miːdɪ'əʊkə*] a mittelmäßig.
mediocrity [miːdɪ'ɒkrɪtɪ] n Mittelmäßigkeit f; (person also) kleine(r) Geist m.
meditate ['medɪteɪt] vi nachdenken (on über +acc); meditieren (on über +acc).
meditation [medɪ'teɪʃən] n Nachsinnen nt; Meditation f.
medium ['miːdɪəm] a mittlere(r, s), Mittel-, mittel-; n Mitte f; (means) Mittel nt; (person) Medium nt.
medley ['medlɪ] n Gemisch nt.
meek a, ~**ly** ad [miːk, -lɪ] sanft(mütig); (pej) duckmäuserisch.
meet [miːt] irreg vt (encounter) treffen, begegnen (+dat); (by arrangement) sich treffen mit; difficulties stoßen auf (+acc);

(become acquainted with) kennenlernen; *(fetch)* abholen; *(join)* zusammentreffen mit; *(river)* fließen in (+acc); *(satisfy)* entsprechen (+dat); *debt* bezahlen; **pleased to ~ you!** angenehm!; *vi* sich treffen; *(become acquainted)* sich kennenlernen; *(join)* sich treffen; *(rivers)* ineinanderfließen; *(roads)* zusammenlaufen; *~* **with** *vt* *problems* stoßen auf (+acc); *(US: people)* zusammentreffen mit; *~***ing** Sitzung *f*; *(business —)* Besprechung *f*, Konferenz *f*; *(discussion)* Sitzung *f*; *(assembly)* Versammlung *f*; *~***ing place** Treffpunkt *m*.

megaphone ['megəfəʊn] *n* Megaphon *nt*.

melancholy ['melənkəlɪ] *n* Melancholie *f*; *a* *person* melancholisch, schwermütig; *sight, event* traurig.

mellow ['meləʊ] *a* mild, weich; *fruit* reif, weich; *(fig)* gesetzt; *vi* reif werden.

melodious [mɪ'ləʊdɪəs] *a* wohlklingend.

melodrama ['melədrɑːmə] *n* Melodrama *nt*; *~***tic** [melədrə'mætɪk] *a* melodramatisch.

melody ['melədɪ] *n* Melodie *f*.

melon ['melən] *n* Melone *f*.

melt [melt] *vi* schmelzen; *(anger)* verfliegen; *vt* schmelzen; *~* **away** *vi* dahinschmelzen; *~* **down** *vt* einschmelzen; *~***ing point** Schmelzpunkt *m*; *~***ing pot** *(fig)* Schmelztiegel *m*; **to be in the *~***ing pot** in der Schwebe sein.

member ['membə*] *n* Mitglied *nt*; *(of tribe, species)* Angehörige(r) *m*; *(Anat)* Glied *nt*; *~***ship** Mitgliedschaft *f*.

membrane ['membreɪn] *n* Membrane *f*.

memento [mə'mentəʊ] *n* Andenken *nt*.

memo ['meməʊ] *n* Notiz *f*, Mitteilung *f*.

memoirs ['memwɑː*z] *npl* Memoiren *pl*.

memorable ['memərəbl] *a* denkwürdig.

memorandum [memə'rændəm] *n* Notiz *f*, Mitteilung *f*; *(Pol)* Memorandum *nt*.

memorial [mɪ'mɔːrɪəl] *n* Denkmal *nt*; *a* Gedenk-.

memorize ['meməraɪz] *vt* sich einprägen.

memory ['memərɪ] *n* Gedächtnis *nt*; *(of computer)* Speicher *m*; *(sth recalled)* Erinnerung *f*; **in ~ of** zur Erinnerung an (+acc); **from ~** aus dem Kopf.

men [men] *npl of* **man.**

menace ['menɪs] *n* Drohung *f*; Gefahr *f*; *vt* bedrohen.

menacing *a*, *~***ly** *ad* ['menɪsɪŋ, -lɪ] drohend.

ménage [me'nɑːʒ] *n* Haushalt *m*.

menagerie [mɪ'nædʒərɪ] *n* Tierschau *f*.

mend [mend] *vt* reparieren, flicken; *n* ausgebesserte Stelle *f*; **on the ~** auf dem Wege der Besserung.

menial ['miːnɪəl] *a* niedrig, untergeordnet.

meningitis [menɪn'dʒaɪtɪs] *n* Hirnhautentzündung *f*, Meningitis *f*.

menopause ['menəʊpɔːz] *n* Wechseljahre *pl*, Menopause *f*.

menstrual ['menstrʊəl] *a* Monats-, Menstruations-.

menstruate ['menstrʊeɪt] *vi* menstruieren.

menstruation [menstrʊ'eɪʃən] *n* Menstruation *f*.

mental ['mentl] *a* geistig, Geistes-; *arithmetic* Kopf-; *hospital* Nerven-; *cruelty* seelisch; *(col: abnormal)* verrückt; *~***ity** [men'tælɪtɪ] Mentalität *f*; *~***ly** *ad* geistig; *~***ly ill** geisteskrank.

mentholated ['menθəleɪtɪd] *a* Menthol-.

mention ['menʃən] *n* Erwähnung *f*; *vt* erwähnen; *names* nennen; **don't ~ it!** bitte (sehr), gern geschehen.

menu ['menjuː] *n* Speisekarte *f*; *(food)* Speisen *pl*.

mercantile ['mɜːkəntaɪl] *a* Handels-.

mercenary ['mɜːsɪnərɪ] *a person* geldgierig; *(Mil)* Söldner-; *n* Söldner *m*.

merchandise ['mɜːtʃəndaɪz] *n* (Handels)ware *f*.

merchant ['mɜːtʃənt] *n* Kaufmann *m*; *a* Handels-; *~* **navy** Handelsmarine *f*.

merciful ['mɜːsɪful] *a* gnädig, barmherzig; *~***ly** ['mɜːsɪfəlɪ] *ad* gnädig; *(fortunately)* glücklicherweise.

merciless *a*, *~***ly** *ad* ['mɜːsɪləs, -lɪ] erbarmungslos.

mercurial [mɜː'kjʊərɪəl] *a* quecksilbrig, Quecksilber-.

mercury ['mɜːkjʊrɪ] *n* Quecksilber *nt*.

mercy ['mɜːsɪ] *n* Erbarmen *nt*; Gnade *f*; *(blessing)* Segen *m*; **at the ~ of** ausgeliefert (+dat).

mere *a*, *~***ly** *ad* [mɪə*, 'mɪəlɪ] bloß.

merge [mɜːdʒ] *vt* verbinden; *(Comm)* fusionieren; *vi* verschmelzen; *(roads)* zusammenlaufen; *(Comm)* fusionieren; **to ~ into** übergehen in (+acc); *~***r** *(Comm)* Fusion *f*.

meridian [mə'rɪdɪən] *n* Meridian *m*.

meringue [mə'ræŋ] *n* Baiser *nt*, Schaumgebäck *nt*.

merit ['merɪt] *n* Verdienst *nt*; *(advantage)* Vorzug *m*; **to judge on ~** nach Leistung beurteilen; *vt* verdienen.

mermaid ['mɜːmeɪd] *n* Wassernixe *f*, Meerjungfrau *f*.

merrily ['merɪlɪ] *ad* lustig.

merriment ['merɪmənt] *n* Fröhlichkeit *f*; *(laughter)* Gelächter *nt*.

merry ['merɪ] *a* fröhlich; *(col)* angeheitert; *~***-go-round** Karussell *nt*.

mesh [meʃ] *n* Masche *f*; *vi* *(gears)* ineinandergreifen.

mesmerize ['mezməraɪz] *vt* hypnotisieren; *(fig)* faszinieren.

mess [mes] *n* Unordnung *f*; *(dirt)* Schmutz *m*; *(trouble)* Schwierigkeiten *pl*; *(Mil)* Messe *f*; **to look a ~** fürchterlich aussehen; **to make a ~ of sth** etw verpfuschen; *~* **about** *vi* *(tinker with)* herummurksen *(with* an *+dat)*; *(play fool)* herumalbern; *(do nothing in particular)* herumgammeln; *~* **up** *vt* verpfuschen; *(make untidy)* in Unordnung bringen.

message ['mesɪdʒ] *n* Mitteilung *f*, Nachricht *f*; **to get the ~** kapieren.

messenger ['mesɪndʒə*] *n* Bote *m*.

messy ['mesɪ] *a* schmutzig; *(untidy)* unordentlich.

metabolism [me'tæbəlɪzəm] *n* Stoffwechsel *m*.

metal ['metl] *n* Metall *nt*; *~***lic** [mɪ'tælɪk] *a* metallisch;   ~**lurgy**   [me'tæləd ʒɪ] Metallurgie f.

metamorphosis [metə'mɔːfəsɪs] n Metamorphose f.

metaphor ['metəfə:*] n Metapher f; ~**ical** [metə'fɒrɪkəl] a bildlich, metaphorisch.

metaphysics [metə'fɪzɪks] n Metaphysik f.

meteor ['miːtɪə*] n Meteor m; ~**ic** [miːtɪ'ɒrɪk] a meteorisch, Meteor-; ~**ite** Meteorit m; ~**ological** [miːtɪərə'lɒdʒɪkəl] a meteorologisch; ~**ology** [miːtɪə'rɒlədʒɪ] Meteorologie f.

meter ['miːtə*] n Zähler m; (US) = **metre**.

method ['meθəd] n Methode f; ~**ical** [mɪ'θɒdɪkəl] a methodisch; ~**ology** [meθə'dɒlədʒɪ] Methodik f.

methylated spirit ['meθɪleɪtɪd' spɪrɪt] n (also **meths**) (Brenn)spiritus m.

meticulous [mɪ'tɪkjʊləs] a (über)genau.

metre ['miːtə*] n Meter m or nt; (verse) Metrum nt.

metric ['metrɪk] a (also ~**al**) metrisch; ~**ation** Umstellung f auf das Dezimalsystem; ~ **system** Dezimalsystem nt.

metronome ['metrənəʊm] n Metronom nt.

metropolis [me'trɒpəlɪs] n Metropole f.

mettle ['metl] n Mut m.

mezzanine ['mezəniːn] n Hochparterre nt.

miaow [miː'aʊ] vi miauen.

mice [maɪs] npl of **mouse**.

mickey ['mɪkɪ] n: to take the ~ out of sb (col) jdn auf den Arm nehmen.

microbe ['maɪkrəʊb] n Mikrobe f.

microfilm ['maɪkrəʊfɪlm] n Mikrofilm m; vt auf Mikrofilm aufnehmen.

microphone ['maɪkrəfəʊn] n Mikrophon nt.

microscope ['maɪkrəskəʊp] n Mikroskop nt.

microscopic [maɪkrə'skɒpɪk] a mikroskopisch.

mid [mɪd] a mitten in (+dat); **in the** ~ **eighties** Mitte der achtziger Jahre; **in** ~ **course** mittendrin.

midday ['mɪd'deɪ] n Mittag m.

middle ['mɪdl] n Mitte f; (waist) Taille f; **in the** ~ **of** mitten in (+dat); a mittlere(r, s), Mittel-; ~-**aged** a mittleren Alters; **the M** ~ **Ages** pl das Mittelalter; ~-**class** Mittelstand m or -klasse f; a Mittelstands-, Mittelklassen-; **the M** ~ **East** der Nahe Osten; ~**man** (Comm) Zwischenhändler m; ~ **name** zweiter Vorname m; ~-**of-the-road** a gemäßigt.

middling ['mɪdlɪŋ] a mittelmäßig.

midge [mɪdʒ] n Mücke f.

midget ['mɪdʒɪt] n Liliputaner(in f) m; a Kleinst-.

midnight ['mɪdnaɪt] n Mitternacht f.

midriff ['mɪdrɪf] n Taille f.

midst [mɪdst] n **in the** ~ **of** persons mitten unter (+dat); things mitten in (+dat); **in our** ~ unter uns.

midsummer ['mɪd'sʌmə*] n Hochsommer m; **M**~**'s Day** Sommersonnenwende f.

midway ['mɪd'weɪ] ad auf halbem Wege; a Mittel-.

midweek ['mɪd'wiːk] a, ad in der Mitte der Woche.

midwife ['mɪdwaɪf] n Hebamme f; ~**ry** ['mɪdwɪfərɪ] Geburtshilfe f.

midwinter ['mɪd'wɪntə*] n tiefste(r) Winter m.

might [maɪt] n Macht f, Kraft f; pt of **may**; **I** ~ **come** ich komme vielleicht; ~**ily** ad mächtig; ~**n't** = **might not**; ~**y** a, ad mächtig.

migraine ['miːgreɪn] n Migräne f.

migrant ['maɪgrənt] n (bird) Zugvogel m; (worker) Saison- or Wanderarbeiter m; a Wander-; bird Zug-.

migrate [maɪ'greɪt] vi (ab)wandern; (birds) (fort)ziehen.

migration [maɪ'greɪʃən] n Wanderung f, Zug m.

mike [maɪk] n = **microphone**.

mild [maɪld] a mild; medicine, interest leicht; person sanft.

mildew ['mɪldjuː] n (on plants) Mehltau m; (on food) Schimmel m.

mildly ['maɪldlɪ] ad leicht; **to put it** ~ gelinde gesagt.

mildness ['maɪldnəs] n Milde f.

mile [maɪl] n Meile f; ~**age** Meilenzahl f; ~**stone** (lit, fig) Meilenstein m.

milieu ['miːljɜː] n Milieu nt.

militant ['mɪlɪtənt] n Militante(r) mf; a militant.

militarism ['mɪlɪtərɪzəm] n Militarismus m.

military ['mɪlɪtərɪ] a militärisch, Militär-, Wehr-; n Militär nt.

militate ['mɪlɪteɪt] vi sprechen; entgegenwirken (against dat).

militia [mɪ'lɪʃə] n Miliz f, Bürgerwehr f.

milk [mɪlk] n Milch f; vt (lit, fig) melken; ~ **chocolate** Milchschokolade f; ~**ing** Melken nt; ~**man** Milchmann m; ~ **shake** Milchmixgetränk nt; **M**~**y Way** Milchstraße f.

mill [mɪl] n Mühle f; (factory) Fabrik f; vt mahlen; vi (move around) umherlaufen; ~**ed** a gemahlen.

millennium [mɪ'lenɪəm] n Jahrtausend nt.

miller ['mɪlə*] n Müller m.

millet ['mɪlɪt] n Hirse f.

milligram(me) ['mɪlɪgræm] n Milligramm nt.

millilitre, (US) ~**liter** ['mɪlɪliːtə*] n Milliliter m.

millimetre, (US) ~**meter** ['mɪlɪmiːtə*] n Millimeter m.

milliner ['mɪlɪnə*] n Hutmacher(in f) m; ~**y** (hats) Hüte pl, Modewaren pl; (business) Hutgeschäft nt.

million ['mɪljən] n Million f; ~**aire** [mɪljə'nɛə*] Millionär(in f) m.

millwheel ['mɪlwiːl] n Mühlrad nt.

milometer [maɪ'lɒmɪtə*] n Kilometerzähler m.

mime [maɪm] n Pantomime f; (actor) Mime m, Mimin f; vti mimen.

mimic ['mɪmɪk] n Mimiker m; vti nachahmen; ~**ry** ['mɪmɪkrɪ] Nachahmung f; (Biol) Mimikry f.

mince [mɪns] vt (zer)hacken; vi (walk)

trippeln; n *(meat)* Hackfleisch nt; ∼**meat** süße Pastetenfüllung f; ∼ **pie** gefüllte (süße) Pastete f.

mincing ['mɪnsɪŋ] a *manner* affektiert.

mind [maɪnd] n Verstand m, Geist m; *(opinion)* Meinung f; **on my** ∼ auf dem Herzen; **to my** ∼ meiner Meinung nach; **to be out of one's** ∼ wahnsinnig sein; **to bear** *or* **keep in** ∼ bedenken, nicht vergessen; **to change one's** ∼ es sich *(dat)* anders überlegen; **to make up one's** ∼ sich entschließen; **to have sth in** ∼ an etw *(acc)* denken; etw beabsichtigen; **to have a good** ∼ **to do sth** große Lust haben, etw zu tun; vt aufpassen auf *(+acc)*; *(object to)* etwas haben gegen; vi etwas dagegen haben; **I don't** ∼ **the rain** der Regen macht mir nichts aus; **do you** ∼ **if I ...** macht es Ihnen etwas aus, wenn ich ...; **do you** ∼! na hören Sie mal!; **never** ∼! macht nichts!; **'**∼ **the step'** 'Vorsicht Stufe'; ∼ **your own business** kümmern Sie sich um Ihre eigenen Angelegenheiten; ∼**ful** a achtsam *(of auf +acc)*; ∼**less** a achtlos, dumm.

mine [maɪn] *poss pron* meine(r, s); n *(coal—)* Bergwerk nt; *(Mil)* Mine f; *(source)* Fundgrube f; vt abbauen; *(Mil)* verminen; vi Bergbau betreiben; **to** ∼ **for sth** etw gewinnen; ∼ **detector** Minensuchgerät nt; ∼**field** Minenfeld nt; ∼**er** Bergarbeiter m.

mineral ['mɪnərəl] a mineralisch, Mineral-; n Mineral nt; ∼ **water** Mineralwasser nt.

minesweeper ['maɪnswiːpə*] n Minensuchboot nt.

mingle ['mɪŋgl] vt vermischen; vi sich mischen *(with unter +acc)*.

mingy ['mɪndʒɪ] a *(col)* knickerig.

mini ['mɪnɪ] *pref* Mini-, Klein-.

miniature ['mɪnɪtʃə*] a Miniatur-, Klein-; n Miniatur f; **in** ∼ en miniature.

minibus ['mɪnɪbʌs] n Kleinbus m, Minibus m.

minicab ['mɪnɪkæb] n Kleintaxi nt.

minim ['mɪnɪm] n halbe Note f.

minimal ['mɪnɪml] a kleinste(r, s), minimal, Mindest-.

minimize ['mɪnɪmaɪz] vt auf das Mindestmaß beschränken; *(belittle)* herabsetzen.

minimum ['mɪnɪməm] n Minimum nt; a Mindest-.

mining ['maɪnɪŋ] n Bergbau m; a Bergbau-, Berg-.

minion ['mɪnjən] n *(pej)* Trabant m.

miniskirt ['mɪnɪskɜːt] n Minirock m.

minister ['mɪnɪstə*] n *(Pol)* Minister m; *(Eccl)* Geistliche(r) m, Pfarrer m; ∼**ial** [mɪnɪs'tɪərɪəl] a ministeriell, Minister-.

ministry ['mɪnɪstrɪ] n *(government body)* Ministerium nt; *(Eccl)* *(office)* geistliche(s) Amt nt; *(all ministers)* Geistlichkeit f.

mink [mɪŋk] n Nerz m.

minnow ['mɪnəʊ] n Elritze f.

minor ['maɪnə*] a kleiner; *operation* leicht; *problem, poet* unbedeutend; *(Mus)* Moll; **Smith** ∼ Smith der Jüngere; n *(Brit: under*

18) Minderjährige(r) mf; ∼**ity** [maɪ'nɒrɪtɪ] Minderheit f.

minster ['mɪnstə*] n Münster nt, Kathedrale f.

minstrel ['mɪnstrəl] n *(Hist)* Spielmann m, Minnesänger m.

mint [mɪnt] n Minze f; *(sweet)* Pfefferminzbonbon nt; *(place)* Münzstätte f; a *condition* (wie) neu; *stamp* ungestempelt; ∼ **sauce** Minzsoße f.

minuet [mɪnjʊ'et] n Menuett nt.

minus ['maɪnəs] n Minuszeichen nt; *(amount)* Minusbetrag m; prep minus, weniger.

minute [maɪ'njuːt] a winzig, sehr klein; *(detailed)* minuziös; ['mɪnɪt] n Minute f; *(moment)* Augenblick m; ∼**s** pl Protokoll nt; ∼**ly** [maɪ'njuːtlɪ] ad *(in detail)* genau.

miracle ['mɪrəkl] n Wunder nt; ∼ **play** geistliche(s) Drama nt.

miraculous [mɪ'rækjʊləs] a wunderbar; ∼**ly** ad auf wunderbare Weise.

mirage ['mɪrɑːʒ] n Luftspiegelung f, Fata Morgana f.

mirror ['mɪrə*] n Spiegel m; vt (wider)spiegeln.

mirth [mɜːθ] n Freude f; Heiterkeit f.

misadventure [mɪsəd'ventʃə*] n Mißgeschick nt, Unfall m.

misanthropist [mɪ'zænθrəpɪst] n Menschenfeind m.

misapprehension ['mɪsæprɪ'henʃən] n Mißverständnis nt; **to be under the** ∼ **that . . .** irrtümlicherweise annehmen, daß. .

misappropriate ['mɪsə'prəʊprɪeɪt] vt *funds* veruntreuen.

misappropriation ['mɪsəprəʊprɪ'eɪʃən] n Veruntreuung f.

misbehave ['mɪsbɪ'heɪv] vi sich schlecht benehmen.

miscalculate ['mɪs'kælkjʊleɪt] vt falsch berechnen.

miscalculation ['mɪskælkjʊ'leɪʃən] n Rechenfehler m.

miscarriage ['mɪskærɪdʒ] n *(Med)* Fehlgeburt f; ∼ **of justice** Fehlurteil nt.

miscellaneous [mɪsɪ'leɪnɪəs] a verschieden.

miscellany [mɪsɪ'selənɪ] n *(bunte)* Sammlung f.

mischance [mɪs'tʃɑːns] n Mißgeschick nt.

mischief ['mɪstʃɪf] n Unfug m; *(harm)* Schaden m.

mischievous a, ∼**ly** ad ['mɪstʃɪvəs, -lɪ] *person* durchtrieben; *glance* verschmitzt; *rumour* bösartig.

misconception ['mɪskən'sepʃən] n fälschliche Annahme f.

misconduct [mɪs'kɒndʌkt] n Vergehen nt.

misconstrue ['mɪskən'struː] vt mißverstehen.

miscount ['mɪs'kaʊnt] vt falsch (be)rechnen.

misdemeanour, *(US)* **misdemeanor** [mɪsdɪ'miːnə*] n Vergehen nt.

misdirect ['mɪsdɪ'rekt] vt *person* irreleiten; *letter* fehlleiten.

miser ['maɪzə*] n Geizhals m.

miserable ['mɪzərəbl] *a (unhappy)* unglücklich; *headache, weather* fürchterlich; *(poor)* elend; *(contemptible)* erbärmlich.

miserably ['mɪzərəblɪ] *ad* unglücklich; *fail* kläglich.

miserly ['maɪzəlɪ] *a* geizig.

misery ['mɪzərɪ] *n* Elend *nt*, Qual *f*.

misfire ['mɪs'faɪə*] *vi (gun)* versagen; *(engine)* fehlzünden; *(plan)* fehlgehen.

misfit ['mɪsfɪt] *n* Außenseiter *m*.

misfortune [mɪs'fɔːtʃən] *n* Unglück *nt*.

misgiving [mɪs'gɪvɪŋ] *n (often pl)* Befürchtung *f*, Bedenken *pl*.

misguided ['mɪs'gaɪdɪd] *a* fehlgeleitet; *opinions* irrig.

mishandle ['mɪs'hændl] *vt* falsch handhaben.

mishap ['mɪshæp] *n* Unglück *nt*; *(slight)* Panne *f*.

mishear ['mɪs'hɪə*] *vt irreg* mißverstehen.

misinform ['mɪsɪn'fɔːm] *vt* falsch unterrichten.

misinterpret ['mɪsɪn'tɜːprɪt] *vt* falsch auffassen; **~ation** ['mɪsɪntɜːprɪ'teɪʃən] falsche Auslegung *f*.

misjudge ['mɪs'dʒʌdʒ] *vt* falsch beurteilen.

mislay [mɪs'leɪ] *vt irreg* verlegen.

mislead [mɪs'liːd] *vt irreg (deceive)* irreführen; **~ing** *a* irreführend.

mismanage ['mɪs'mænɪdʒ] *vt* schlecht verwalten; **~ment** Mißwirtschaft *f*.

misnomer ['mɪs'nəʊmə*] *n* falsche Bezeichnung *f*.

misogynist [mɪ'sɒdʒɪnɪst] *n* Weiberfeind *m*.

misplace ['mɪs'pleɪs] *vt* verlegen.

misprint ['mɪsprɪnt] *n* Druckfehler *m*.

mispronounce ['mɪsprə'naʊns] *vt* falsch aussprechen.

misread ['mɪs'riːd] *vt irreg* falsch lesen.

misrepresent ['mɪsreprɪ'zent] *vt* falsch darstellen.

miss [mɪs] *vt (fail to hit, catch)* verfehlen; *(not notice)* verpassen; *(be too late)* versäumen, verpassen; *(omit)* auslassen; *(regret the absence of)* vermissen; **I ~ you** du fehlst mir; *vi* fehlen; *n (shot)* Fehlschuß *m*; *(failure)* Fehlschlag *m*; *(title)* Fräulein *nt*.

missal ['mɪsəl] *n* Meßbuch *nt*.

misshapen ['mɪs'ʃeɪpən] *a* mißgestaltet.

missile ['mɪsaɪl] *n* Geschoß *nt*, Rakete *f*.

missing ['mɪsɪŋ] *a person* vermißt; *thing* fehlend; **to be ~** fehlen.

mission ['mɪʃən] *n (work)* Auftrag *n*, Mission *f*; *(people)* Delegation *f*; *(Rel)* Mission *f*; **~ary** Missionar(in *f*) *m*.

misspent ['mɪs'spent] *a youth* vergeudet.

mist [mɪst] *n* Dunst *m*, Nebel *m*; *vi (also ~ over, ~ up)* sich beschlagen.

mistake [mɪs'teɪk] *n* Fehler *m*; *vt irreg (misunderstand)* mißverstehen; *(mix up)* verwechseln *(for mit)*; **~n** *a idea* falsch; **~n identity** Verwechslung *f*; **to be ~n** sich irren.

mister ['mɪstə*] *n (abbr* **Mr**) Herr *m*.

mistletoe ['mɪsltəʊ] *n* Mistel *f*.

mistranslation ['mɪstræns'leɪʃən] *n* falsche Übersetzung *f*.

mistreat [mɪs'triːt] *vt* schlecht behandeln.

mistress ['mɪstrɪs] *n (teacher)* Lehrerin *f*; *(in house)* Herrin *f*; *(lover)* Geliebte *f*; *(abbr* **Mrs**) Frau *f*.

mistrust ['mɪs'trʌst] *vt* mißtrauen (*+dat*).

misty ['mɪstɪ] *a* neblig.

misunderstand ['mɪsʌndə'stænd] *vti irreg* mißverstehen, falsch verstehen; **~ing** Mißverständnis *nt*; *(disagreement)* Meinungsverschiedenheit *f*.

misunderstood ['mɪsʌndə'stʊd] *a person* unverstanden.

misuse ['mɪs'juːs] *n* falsche(r) Gebrauch *m*; ['mɪs'juːz] *vt* falsch gebrauchen.

mite [maɪt] *n* Milbe *f*; *(fig)* bißchen *nt*.

mitigate ['mɪtɪgeɪt] *vt pain* lindern; *punishment* mildern.

mitre, *(US)* **miter** ['maɪtə*] *n (Eccl)* Mitra *f*.

mitt(en) ['mɪt(n)] *n* Fausthandschuh *m*.

mix [mɪks] *vt (blend)* (ver)mischen; *vi (liquids)* sich (ver)mischen lassen; *(people) (get on)* sich vertragen; *(associate)* Kontakt haben; **he ~es well** er ist kontaktfreudig; *n (mixture)* Mischung *f*; **~ed** *a* gemischt; **~er** *(for food)* Mixer *m*; **~ture** *(assortment)* Mischung *f*; *(Med)* Saft *m*; **~-up** Durcheinander *nt*, Verwechslung *f*; **~ up** *vt (mix)* zusammenmischen; *(confuse)* verwechseln; **to be ~ed up in sth** in etw *(dat)* verwickelt sein; **~-ed-up** *a papers, person* durcheinander.

moan [məʊn] *n* Stöhnen *nt*; *(complaint)* Klage *f*; *vi* stöhnen; *(complain)* maulen; **~ing** Stöhnen *nt*; Gemaule *nt*.

moat [məʊt] *n* (Burg)graben *m*.

mob [mɒb] *n* Mob *m*; *(the masses)* Pöbel *m*; *vt star* herfallen über *(+acc)*.

mobile ['məʊbaɪl] *a* beweglich; *library etc* fahrbar; *n (decoration)* Mobile *nt*; **~ home** Wohnwagen *m*.

mobility [məʊ'bɪlɪtɪ] *n* Beweglichkeit *f*.

moccasin ['mɒkəsɪn] *n* Mokassin *m*.

mock [mɒk] *vt* verspotten; *(defy)* trotzen *(+dat)*; *a* Schein-; **~ery** Spott *m*; *(person)* Gespött *nt*; **~ing** *a tone* spöttisch; **~ing bird** Spottdrossel *f*; **~-up** Modell *nt*.

mode [məʊd] *n (Art f und)* Weise *f*.

model ['mɒdl] *n* Modell *nt*; *(example)* Vorbild *nt*; *(in fashion)* Mannequin *nt*; *vt (make)* formen, modellieren, bilden; *(clothes)* vorführen; *a railway* Modell-; *(perfect)* Muster-; vorbildlich; **~ling**, *(US)* **~ing** ['mɒdlɪŋ] *(— making)* Basteln *nt*.

moderate ['mɒdərət] *a* gemäßigt; *(fairly good)* mittelmäßig; *n (Pol)* Gemäßigte(r) *mf*; ['mɒdəreɪt] *vi* sich mäßigen; *vt* mäßigen; **~ly** ['mɒdərətlɪ] *ad* mäßig.

moderation [mɒdə'reɪʃən] *n* Mäßigung *f*; **in ~** mit Maßen.

modern ['mɒdən] *a* modern; *history, languages* neuere(r, s); *Greek etc* Neu-; **~ity** [mɒ'dɜːnɪtɪ] Modernität *f*; **~ization** [mɒdənaɪ'zeɪʃən] Modernisierung *f*; **~ize** *vt* modernisieren.

modest *a.* **~ly** *ad* ['mɒdɪst, -lɪ] *attitude* bescheiden; *meal, home* einfach; *(chaste)* schamhaft; ~y Bescheidenheit f; *(chastity)* Schamgefühl *nt.*

modicum ['mɒdɪkəm] *n* bißchen *nt.*

modification [mɒdɪfɪ'keɪʃən] *n* (Ab)änderung *f.*

modify ['mɒdɪfaɪ] *vt* abändern; *(Gram)* modifizieren.

modulation [mɒdju'leɪʃən] *n* Modulation *f.*

module ['mɒdjʊl] *n* (Raum)kapsel *f.*

mohair ['məʊheə*] *n* Mohair *m*; *a* Mohair-.

moist [mɔɪst] *a* feucht; ~en ['mɔɪsn] *vt* befeuchten; ~ure Feuchtigkeit *f*; ~urizer Feuchtigkeitscreme *f.*

molar ['məʊlə*] *n* Backenzahn *m.*

molasses [mə'læsɪz] *npl* Melasse *f.*

mold [məʊld] *(US)* = **mould.**

mole [məʊl] *n (spot)* Leberfleck *m; (animal)* Maulwurf *m; (pier)* Mole *f.*

molecular [mə'lekjʊlə*] *a* molekular, Molekular-.

molecule ['mɒlɪkjuːl] *n* Molekül *nt.*

molest [məʊ'lest] *vt* belästigen.

mollusc ['mɒləsk] *n* Molluske *f*, Weichtier *nt.*

mollycoddle ['mɒlɪkɒdl] *vt* verhätscheln.

molt [məʊlt] *(US)* = **moult.**

molten ['məʊltən] *a* geschmolzen.

moment ['məʊmənt] *n* Moment *m*, Augenblick *m; (importance)* Tragweite *f*; ~ of truth Stunde *f* der Wahrheit; **any** ~ jeden Augenblick; ~**arily** ['məʊmən-'terəlɪ] *ad* momentan; ~**ary** *a* kurz; ~**ous** [məʊ'mentəs] *a* folgenschwer; ~**um** [məʊ'mentəm] Schwung *m.*

monarch ['mɒnək] *n* Herrscher(in *f*) *m*; ~**ist** Monarchist(in *f*) *m*; ~**y** Monarchie *f.*

monastery ['mɒnəstrɪ] *n* Kloster *nt.*

monastic [mə'næstɪk] *a* klösterlich, Kloster-.

Monday ['mʌndeɪ] *n* Montag *m.*

monetary ['mʌnɪtərɪ] *a* geldlich, Geld-; *(of currency)* Währungs-, monetär.

money ['mʌnɪ] *n* Geld *nt*; ~**ed** *a* vermögend; ~**lender** Geldverleiher *m*; ~**making** *a* einträglich, lukrativ; *n* Gelderwerb *m*; ~ **order** Postanweisung *f.*

mongol ['mɒŋgəl] *n (Med)* mongoloide(s) Kind *nt*; *a* mongolisch; *(Med)* mongoloid.

mongoose ['mɒŋguːs] *n* Mungo *m.*

mongrel ['mʌŋgrəl] *n* Promenadenmischung *f*; *a* Misch-.

monitor ['mɒnɪtə*] *n (Sch)* Klassenordner *m; (television* —) Monitor *m*; *vt broadcasts* abhören; *(control)* überwachen.

monk [mʌŋk] *n* Mönch *m.*

monkey ['mʌŋkɪ] *n* Affe *m*; ~ **nut** Erdnuß *f*; ~ **wrench** *(Tech)* Engländer *m*, Franzose *m.*

mono- ['mɒnəʊ] *pref* Mono-.

monochrome ['mɒnəkrəʊm] *a* schwarzweiß.

monocle ['mɒnəkl] *n* Monokel *nt.*

monogram ['mɒnəgræm] *n* Monogramm *nt.*

monolithic [mɒnəʊ'lɪθɪk] *a* monolithisch.

monologue ['mɒnəlɒg] *n* Monolog *m.*

monopolize [mə'nɒpəlaɪz] *vt* beherrschen.

monopoly [mə'nɒpəlɪ] *n* Monopol *nt.*

monorail ['mɒnəʊreɪl] *n* Einschienenbahn *f.*

monosyllabic ['mɒnəʊsɪ'læbɪk] *a* einsilbig.

monotone ['mɒnətəʊn] *n* gleichbleibende(r) Ton(fall) *m.*

monotonous [mə'nɒtənəs] *a* eintönig, monoton.

monotony [mə'nɒtənɪ] *n* Eintönigkeit *f*, Monotonie *f.*

monseigneur [mɒnsen'jɜː*], **monsignor** [mɒn'siːnjə*] *n* Monsignore *m.*

monsoon [mɒn'suːn] *n* Monsun *m.*

monster ['mɒnstə*] *n* Ungeheuer *nt*; *(person)* Scheusal *nt*; *a (col)* Riesen-.

monstrosity [mɒns'trɒsɪtɪ] *n* Ungeheuerlichkeit *f*; *(thing)* Monstrosität *f.*

monstrous ['mɒnstrəs] *a (shocking)* gräßlich, ungeheuerlich; *(huge)* riesig.

montage [mɒn'tɑːʒ] *n* Montage *f.*

month [mʌnθ] *n* Monat *m*; ~**ly** *a* monatlich, Monats-; *ad* einmal im Monat; *n (magazine)* Monatsschrift *f.*

monument ['mɒnjʊmənt] *n* Denkmal *nt*; ~**al** [mɒnjʊ'mentl] *a (huge)* gewaltig; *ignorance* ungeheuer.

moo [muː] *vi* muhen.

mood [muːd] *n* Stimmung *f*, Laune *f*; **to be in the** ~ **for** aufgelegt sein zu; **I am not in the** ~ **for laughing** mir ist nicht zum Lachen zumute; ~**ily** *ad* launisch; ~**iness** Launenhaftigkeit *f*; ~**y** *a* launisch.

moon [muːn] *n* Mond *m*; ~**beam** Mondstrahl *m*; ~**less** *a* mondlos; ~**light** Mondlicht *nt*; ~**lit** *a* mondhell; ~**shot** Mondflug *m.*

moor [mʊə*] *n* Heide *f*, Hochmoor *nt*; *vt ship* festmachen, verankern; *vi* anlegen; ~**ings** *pl* Liegeplatz *m*; ~**land** Heidemoor *nt.*

moose [muːs] *n* Elch *m.*

moot [muːt] *vt* aufwerfen; *a:* ~ **point** strittige(r) Punkt *m.*

mop [mɒp] *n* Mop *m*; *vt* (auf)wischen; ~ **of hair** Mähne *f.*

mope [məʊp] *vi* Trübsal blasen.

moped ['məʊped] *n (Brit)* Moped *nt.*

moping ['məʊpɪŋ] *a* trübselig.

moquette [mə'ket] *n* Plüschgewebe *nt.*

moral ['mɒrəl] *a* moralisch; *values* sittlich; *(virtuous)* tugendhaft; *n* Moral *f*; ~**s** *pl* Moral *f*; ~**e** [mɒ'rɑːl] Moral *f*, Stimmung *f*; ~**ity** [mə'rælɪtɪ] Sittlichkeit *f*; ~**ly** *ad* moralisch.

morass [mə'ræs] *n* Sumpf *m.*

morbid ['mɔːbɪd] *a* morbid, krankhaft; *jokes* makaber.

more [mɔː*] *a, n, pron, ad* mehr; ~ **or less** mehr oder weniger; ~ **than ever** mehr denn je; **a few** ~ noch ein paar; ~ **beautiful** schöner; ~**over** *ad* überdies.

morgue [mɔːg] *n* Leichenschauhaus *nt.*

moribund ['mɒrɪbʌnd] *a* aussterbend.

morning ['mɔːnɪŋ] *n* Morgen *m*; *a* morgendlich, Morgen-, Früh-; **in the** ~ am Morgen; ~ **sickness** (Schwangerschafts)erbrechen *nt.*

moron ['mɔːrɒn] *n* Schwachsinnige(r) *m*; ~**ic** [mə'rɒnɪk] *a* schwachsinnig.

morose [mə'rəʊs] a mürrisch.
morphine ['mɔːfiːn] n Morphium nt.
Morse [mɔːs] n (also ~ **code**) Morse-alphabet nt.
morsel ['mɔːsl] n Stückchen nt, bißchen nt.
mortal ['mɔːtl] a sterblich; (deadly) tödlich; (very great) Todes-; n (human being) Sterbliche(r) mf; ~**ity** [mɔː'tælɪtɪ] Sterblichkeit f; (death rate) Sterblichkeits-ziffer f; ~**ly** ad tödlich.
mortar ['mɔːtə*] n (for building) Mörtel m; (bowl) Mörser m; (Mil) Granatwerfer m.
mortgage ['mɔːgɪdʒ] n Hypothek f; vt eine Hypothek aufnehmen (+acc).
mortification [mɔːtɪfɪ'keɪʃən] n Beschämung f.
mortified ['mɔːtɪfaɪd] a: **I was** ~ es war mir schrecklich peinlich.
mortuary ['mɔːtjʊərɪ] n Leichenhalle f.
mosaic [məʊ'zeɪɪk] n Mosaik nt.
mosque [mɒsk] n Moschee f.
mosquito [mɒs'kiːtəʊ] n Moskito m.
moss [mɒs] n Moos nt; ~**y** a bemoost.
most [məʊst] a meiste(r, s); ~ **men** die meisten Männer; ad am meisten; (very) höchst; n das meiste, der größte Teil; (people) die meisten; ~ **of the time** meistens, die meiste Zeit; ~ **of the winter** fast den ganzen Winter über; the ~ **beautiful** der/die/das Schönste; **at the** (**very**) ~ allerhöchstens; **to make the** ~ **of** das Beste machen aus; ~**ly** ad größtenteils.
motel [məʊ'tel] n Motel nt.
moth [mɒθ] n Nachtfalter m; (wool-eating) Motte f; ~**ball** Mottenkugel f; ~-**eaten** a mottenzerfressen.
mother ['mʌðə*] n Mutter f; vt bemuttern; a tongue Mutter-; country Heimat-; ~**hood** Mutterschaft f; ~-**in-law** Schwieger-mutter f; ~**ly** a mütterlich; ~-**to-be** werdende Mutter f.
mothproof ['mɒθpruːf] a mottenfest.
motif [məʊ'tiːf] n Motiv nt.
motion ['məʊʃən] n Bewegung f; (in meet-ing) Antrag m; vti winken (+dat), zu ver-stehen geben (+dat); ~**less** a regungslos; ~ **picture** Film m.
motivated ['məʊtɪveɪtɪd] a motiviert.
motivation [məʊtɪ'veɪʃən] n Motivierung f.
motive ['məʊtɪv] n Motiv nt, Beweggrund m; a treibend.
motley ['mɒtlɪ] a bunt.
motor ['məʊtə*] n Motor m; (car) Auto nt; vi (im Auto) fahren; a Motor-; ~**bike** Motor-rad nt; ~**boat** Motorboot nt; ~**car** Auto nt; ~**cycle** Motorrad nt; ~**cyclist** Motor-radfahrer(in f) m; ~**ing** n Autofahren nt; a Auto-; ~**ist** ['məʊtərɪst] Autofahrer(in f) m; ~ **oil** Motorenöl nt; ~ **racing** Auto-rennen nt; ~ **scooter** Motorroller m; ~ **vehicle** Kraftfahrzeug nt; ~**way** (Brit) Autobahn f.
mottled ['mɒtld] a gesprenkelt.
motto ['mɒtəʊ] n Motto nt, Wahlspruch m.
mould [məʊld] n Form f; (mildew) Schimmel m; vt (lit, fig) formen; ~**er** vi (decay) vermodern; ~**ing** Formen nt; ~**y** a schimmelig.
moult [məʊlt] vi sich mausern.

mound [maʊnd] n (Erd)hügel m.
mount [maʊnt] n (liter: hill) Berg m; (horse) Pferd nt; (for jewel etc) Fassung f; vt horse steigen auf (+acc); (put in setting) fassen; exhibition veranstalten; attack unter-nehmen; vi (also ~ **up**) sich häufen; (on horse) aufsitzen; ~**ain** ['maʊntɪn] Berg m; ~**aineer** [maʊntɪ'nɪə*] Bergsteiger(in f) m; ~**aineering** Bergsteigen nt; **to go** ~**aineering** klettern gehen; ~**ainous** a bergig; ~**ainside** Berg(ab)hang m.
mourn [mɔːn] vt betrauen, beklagen; vi trauern (for um); ~**er** Trauernde(r) mf; ~**ful** a traurig; ~**ing** (grief) Trauer f; **in** ~**ing** (period etc) in Trauer; (dress) in Trauerkleidung f.
mouse [maʊs] n, pl **mice** Maus f; ~**trap** Mausefalle f.
moustache [məs'tɑːʃ] n Schnurrbart m.
mousy ['maʊsɪ] a colour mausgrau; person schüchtern.
mouth [maʊθ] n Mund m; (general) Öffnung f; (of river) Mündung f; (of harbour) Ein-fahrt f; [maʊð] vt words affektiert sprechen; **down in the** ~ nieder-geschlagen; ~**ful** Mundvoll m; ~ **organ** Mundharmonika f; ~**piece** (lit) Mund-stück nt; (fig) Sprachrohr nt; ~**wash** Mundwasser nt; ~**watering** a lecker, appetitlich.
movable ['muːvəbl] a beweglich.
move [muːv] n (movement) Bewegung f; (in game) Zug m; (step) Schritt m; (of house) Umzug m; vt bewegen; object rücken; people transportieren; (in job) versetzen; (emotionally) bewegen, ergreifen; **to** ~ **sb to do sth** jdn veranlassen, etw zu tun; vi sich bewegen; (change place) gehen; (vehicle, ship) fahren; (take action) etwas unternehmen; (go to another house) umziehen; **to get a** ~ **on** sich beeilen; **on the** ~ in Bewegung; **to** ~ **house** umziehen; **to** ~ **closer to or towards sth** sich etw (dat) nähern; ~ **about** vi sich hin- und herbewegen; (travel) unterwegs sein; ~ **away** vi weggehen; ~ **back** vi zurückgehen; (to the rear) zurückweichen; ~ **forward** vi vorwärtsgehen; sich vorwärtsbewegen; vt vorschieben; time vorverlegen; ~ **in** vi (to house) einziehen; (troops) einrücken; ~ **on** vi weitergehen; vt weitergehen lassen; ~ **out** vi (of house) ausziehen; (troops) abziehen; ~ **up** vi auf-steigen; (in job) befördert werden; vt nach oben bewegen; (in job) befördern; (Sch) versetzen; ~**ment** Bewegung f; (Mus) Satz m; (of clock) Uhrwerk nt.
movie ['muːvɪ] n Film m; **the** ~**s** (the cinema) das Kino; ~ **camera** Film-kamera f.
moving ['muːvɪŋ] a beweglich; force treibend; (touching) ergreifend.
mow [məʊ] vt irreg mähen; ~ **down** vt (fig) niedermähen; ~**er** (machine) Mäh-maschine f; (lawn-) Rasenmäher m.
Mr [mɪstə*] Herr m.
Mrs ['mɪsɪz] Frau f.
Ms [mɪz] n Frau f.
much [mʌtʃ] a viel; ad sehr; viel; n viel, eine Menge f; ~ **better** viel besser; ~

the same size so ziemlich gleich groß; **how ~?** wieviel?; **too ~** zuviel; **~ to my surprise** zu meiner großen Überraschung; **~ as I should like to** so gern ich möchte.

muck [mʌk] n (lit) Mist m; (fig) Schmutz m; **~ about** (col) vi herumlungern; (meddle) herumalbern (with an +dat); vt **~ sb about** mit jdm treiben, was man will; **~ up** vt (col: ruin) vermasseln; (dirty) dreckig machen; **~y** a (dirty) dreckig.

mucus ['mjuːkəs] n Schleim m.

mud [mʌd] n Schlamm m; (fig) Schmutz m.

muddle ['mʌdl] n Durcheinander nt; vt (also **~ up**) durcheinanderbringen; **~ through** vi sich durchwursteln.

muddy ['mʌdɪ] a schlammig.

mudguard ['mʌdgaːd] n Schutzblech nt.

mudpack ['mʌdpæk] n Moorpackung f.

mud-slinging ['mʌdslɪŋɪŋ] n (col) Verleumdung f.

muff [mʌf] n Muff m.

muffin ['mʌfɪn] n süße(s) Teilchen nt.

muffle ['mʌfl] vt sound dämpfen; (wrap up) einhüllen.

mufti ['mʌftɪ] n: **in ~** in Zivil.

mug [mʌg] n (cup) Becher m; (col: face) Visage f; (col: fool) Trottel m; vt überfallen und ausrauben; **~ging** Überfall m.

muggy ['mʌgɪ] a weather schwül.

mulatto [mjuːˈlætəʊ] n Mulatte m, Mulattin f.

mule [mjuːl] n Maulesel m.

mull [mʌl]: **~ over** vt nachdenken über (+acc).

mulled [mʌld] a wine Glüh-.

multi- ['mʌltɪ] pref Multi-, multi-.

multicoloured, (US) **multicolored** ['mʌltɪˈkʌləd] a mehrfarbig.

multifarious [mʌltɪˈfɛərɪəs] a mannigfaltig.

multilateral ['mʌltɪˈlætərəl] a multilateral.

multiple ['mʌltɪpl] n Vielfache(s) nt; a mehrfach; (many) mehrere; **~ sclerosis** multiple Sklerose f; **~ store** Kaufhauskette f.

multiplication [mʌltɪplɪˈkeɪʃən] n Multiplikation f.

multiply ['mʌltɪplaɪ] vt multiplizieren (by mit); vi (Biol) sich vermehren.

multiracial [mʌltɪˈreɪʃəl] a gemischtrassig; **~ policy** Rassenintegration f.

multitude ['mʌltɪtjuːd] n Menge f.

mum¹ [mʌm] a: **to keep ~** den Mund halten (about über +acc).

mum² [mʌm] n (col) Mutti f.

mumble ['mʌmbl] vti murmeln; n Gemurmel nt.

mummy ['mʌmɪ] n (dead body) Mumie f; (col) Mami f.

mumps [mʌmps] n Mumps m.

munch [mʌntʃ] vti mampfen.

mundane ['mʌnˈdeɪn] a weltlich; (fig) profan.

municipal [mjuːˈnɪsɪpəl] a städtisch, Stadt-; **~ity** [mjuːnɪsɪˈpælɪtɪ] Stadt f mit Selbstverwaltung.

munificence [mjuːˈnɪfɪsns] n Freigebigkeit f.

munitions [mjuːˈnɪʃənz] npl Munition f.

mural ['mjuərəl] n Wandgemälde nt.

murder ['mɜːdə*] n Mord m; **it was ~** (fig) es war möderisch; **to get away with ~** (fig) sich alles erlauben können; vt ermorden; **~er** Mörder m; **~ess** Mörderin f; **~ous** a Mord-; (fig) mörderisch.

murk [mɜːk] n Dunkelheit f **~y** a finster.

murmur ['mɜːmə*] n Murmeln nt; (of water, wind) Rauschen nt; **without a ~** ohne zu murren; vti murmeln.

muscle ['mʌsl] n Muskel m.

muscular ['mʌskjʊlə*] a Muskel-; (strong) muskulös.

muse [mjuːz] vi (nach)sinnen; **M~** Muse f.

museum [mjuːˈzɪəm] n Museum nt.

mushroom ['mʌʃrʊm] n Champignon m; Pilz m; vi (fig) emporschießen.

mushy ['mʌʃɪ] a breiig; (sentimental) gefühlsduselig.

music ['mjuːzɪk] n Musik f; (printed) Noten pl; **~al** a melodisch; (person) musikalisch; n (show) Musical nt; **~al box** Spieldose f; **~al instrument** Musikinstrument nt; **~ally** ad musikalisch; sing melodisch; **~ hall** (Brit) Varieté nt; **~ian** [mjuːˈzɪʃən] Musiker(in f) m.

muslin ['mʌzlɪn] n Musselin m.

mussel ['mʌsl] n Miesmuschel f.

must [mʌst] v aux müssen; (in negation) dürfen; n Muß nt; **the film is a ~** den Film muß man einfach gesehen haben.

mustache ['mʌstæʃ] (US) = **moustache**.

mustard ['mʌstəd] n Senf m.

muster ['mʌstə*] vt (Mil) antreten lassen; courage zusammennehmen.

mustiness ['mʌstɪnəs] n Muffigkeit f.

mustn't ['mʌsnt] = **must not**.

musty ['mʌstɪ] a muffig.

mute [mjuːt] a stumm; n (person) Stumme(r) mf; (Mus) Dämpfer m.

mutilate ['mjuːtɪleɪt] vt verstümmeln.

mutilation [mjuːtɪˈleɪʃən] n Verstümmelung f.

mutinous ['mjuːtɪnəs] a meuterisch.

mutiny ['mjuːtɪnɪ] n Meuterei f; vi meutern.

mutter ['mʌtə*] vti murmeln.

mutton ['mʌtn] n Hammelfleisch nt.

mutual ['mjuːtjʊəl] a gegenseitig; beiderseitig; **~ly** ad gegenseitig; auf beiden Seiten; für beide Seiten.

muzzle ['mʌzl] n (of animal) Schnauze f; (for animal) Maulkorb m; (of gun) Mündung f; vt einen Maulkorb anlegen (+dat).

my [maɪ] poss a mein.

myopic [maɪˈɒpɪk] a kurzsichtig.

myrrh [mɜː*] n Myrrhe f.

myself [maɪˈself] pron mich (acc); mir (dat); (emphatic) selbst; **I'm not ~** mit mir ist etwas nicht in Ordnung.

mysterious [mɪsˈtɪərɪəs] a geheimnisvoll, mysteriös; **~ly** ad auf unerklärliche Weise.

mystery ['mɪstərɪ] n (secret) Geheimnis nt;

(sth difficult) Rätsel *nt;* ~ **play** Mysterien-
spiel *nt.*

mystic ['mɪstɪk] *n* Mystiker *m; a* mystisch;
~**al** *a* mystisch; ~**ism** ['mɪstɪsɪzəm]
Mystizismus *m.*

mystification [mɪstɪfɪ'keɪʃən] *n* Verblüffung *f.*

mystify ['mɪstɪfaɪ] *vt* ein Rätsel sein
(+dat); verblüffen.

mystique [mɪs'tiːk] *n* geheimnisvolle
Natur *f.*

myth [mɪθ] *n* Mythos *m; (fig)* Erfindung *f;*
~**ical** *a* mythisch, Sagen-; ~**ological**
[mɪθə'lɒdʒɪkəl] *a* mythologisch; ~**ology**
[mɪ'θɒlədʒɪ] Mythologie *f.*

N

N, n [en] *n* N *nt,* n *nt.*

nab [næb] *vt (col)* schnappen.

nadir ['neɪdɪə*] *n* Tiefpunkt *m.*

nag [næg] *n (horse)* Gaul *m; (person)*
Nörgler(in *f) m; vti* herumnörgeln (sb an
jdm*);* ~**ging** *a doubt* nagend; *n* Nörgelei *f.*

nail [neɪl] *n* Nagel *m; vt* nageln; ~ **down** *vt
(lit, fig)* festnageln; ~**brush** Nagelbürste *f;*
~**file** Nagelfeile *f;* ~ **polish** Nagellack
m; ~ **scissors** *pl* Nagelschere *f.*

naive *a,* ~**ly** *ad* [naɪ'iːv, -lɪ] naiv.

naked ['neɪkɪd] *a* nackt; ~**ness** Nacktheit
f.

name [neɪm] *n* Name *m; (reputation)* Ruf
m; vt nennen; *sth new* benennen; *(appoint)*
ernennen; **what's your** ~? wie heißen
Sie?; **in the** ~ **of** im Namen *(+gen); (for
the sake of)* um *(+gen)* willen; ~ **dropping: he's always** ~ **dropping** er wirft
immer mit großen Namen um sich;
~**less** *a* namenlos; ~**ly** *ad* nämlich;
~**sake** Namensvetter *m.*

nanny ['nænɪ] *n* Kindermädchen *nt.*

nap [næp] *n (sleep)* Nickerchen *nt; (on
cloth)* Strich *m;* **to have a** ~ ein
Nickerchen machen.

napalm ['neɪpɑːm] *n* Napalm *nt.*

nape [neɪp] *n* Nacken *m.*

napkin ['næpkɪn] *n (at table)* Serviette *f;
(Brit: for baby)* Windel *f.*

nappy ['næpɪ] *n (Brit: for baby)* Windel *f.*

narcissism [nɑː'sɪsɪzəm] *n* Narzißmus *m.*

narcotic [nɑː'kɒtɪk] *n* Betäubungsmittel *nt.*

narrate [nə'reɪt] *vt* erzählen.

narration [nə'reɪʃən] *n* Erzählung *f.*

narrative ['nærətɪv] *n* Erzählung *f; a*
erzählend.

narrator [nə'reɪtə*] *n* Erzähler(in *f) m.*

narrow ['nærəu] *a* eng, schmal; *(limited)*
beschränkt; *vi* sich verengen; **to** ~ **sth
down to sth** etw auf etw *(acc)* einschränken; ~**ly** *ad miss* knapp; *escape net*
knapper Not; ~**-minded** *a* engstirnig;
~**-mindedness** Engstirnigkeit *f.*

nasal ['neɪzəl] *a* Nasal-.

nastily ['nɑːstɪlɪ] *ad* böse, schlimm.

nastiness ['nɑːstɪnəs] *n* Ekligkeit *f.*

nasty ['nɑːstɪ] *a* ekelhaft, fies; *business,
wound* schlimm; **to turn** ~ gemein
werden.

nation ['neɪʃən] *n* Nation *f,* Volk *nt;* ~**al**

['næʃənl] *a* national, National-, Landes-; *n*
Staatsangehörige(r) *mf;* ~**al anthem**
Nationalhymne *f;* ~**alism** ['næʃnəlɪzəm]
Nationalismus *m;* ~**alist** ['næʃnəlɪst] *n*
Nationalist(in *f) m; a* nationalistisch;
~**ality** [næʃə'nælɪtɪ] Staatsangehörigkeit *f.*
Nationalität *f;* ~**alization** [næʃnə-
laɪ'zeɪʃən] Verstaatlichung *f;* ~**alize**
['næʃnəlaɪz] *vt* verstaatlichen; ~**ally**
['næʃnəlɪ] *ad* national, auf Staatsebene;
~**-wide** *a, ad* allgemein, landesweit.

native ['neɪtɪv] *n (born in)* Einheimische(r)
mf; (original inhabitant) Eingeborene(r) *mf;
a (coming from a certain place)* einheimisch; *(of the original inhabitants)* Ein-
geborenen-; *(belonging to birth)* heimatlich,
Heimat-; *(inborn)* angeboren, natürlich; **a**
~ **of Germany** ein gebürtiger
Deutscher; ~ **language** Muttersprache *f.*

natter ['nætə*] *vi (col: chat)* quatschen; *n*
Gequatsche *nt.*

natural ['nætʃrəl] *a* natürlich; Natur-; *(inborn)* (an)geboren; ~**ist** Naturkundler(in
f) m; ~**ize** *vt foreigner* einbürgern,
naturalisieren; *plant etc* einführen; ~**ly** *ad*
natürlich; ~**ness** Natürlichkeit *f.*

nature ['neɪtʃə*] *n* Natur *f;* **by** ~ von
Natur (aus).

naught [nɔːt] *n* Null *f.*

naughtily ['nɔːtɪlɪ] *ad* unartig.

naughtiness ['nɔːtɪnəs] *n* Unartigkeit *f.*

naughty ['nɔːtɪ] *a child* unartig, ungezogen;
action ungehörig.

nausea ['nɔːsɪə] *n (sickness)* Übelkeit *f; (disgust)* Ekel *m;* ~**te** ['nɔːsɪeɪt] *vt* anekeln.

nauseating ['nɔːsɪeɪtɪŋ] *a* ekelerregend;
job widerlich.

nautical ['nɔːtɪkəl] *a* nautisch, See-; *expression* seemännisch.

naval ['neɪvəl] *a* Marine-, Flotten-.

nave [neɪv] *n* Kirchen(haupt)schiff *nt.*

navel ['neɪvəl] *n* Nabel *m.*

navigable ['nævɪgəbl] *a* schiffbar.

navigate ['nævɪgeɪt] *vt ship etc* steuern; *vi
(sail)* (zu Schiff) fahren.

navigation [nævɪ'geɪʃən] *n* Navigation *f.*

navigator ['nævɪgeɪtə*] *n* Steuermann *m;
(explorer)* Seefahrer *m; (Aviat)* Navigator
m; (Aut) Beifahrer(in *f) m.*

navvy ['nævɪ] *n* Straßenarbeiter *m; (on railway)* Streckenarbeiter *m.*

navy ['neɪvɪ] *n* Marine *f,* Flotte *f; (warships
etc)* (Kriegs)flotte *f;* ~**-blue** Marineblau
nt; a marineblau.

nay [neɪ] *ad (old) (no)* nein; *(even)* ja sogar.

neap [niːp] *a:* ~ **tide** Nippflut *f.*

near [nɪə*] *a* nah; **the holidays are** ~ es
sind bald Ferien; *ad* in der Nähe; **to come**
~**er** näher kommen; *(time)* näher rücken;
prep (also ~ **to)** *(space)* in der Nähe
(+gen); (time) um *(+acc)* ... herum; *vt* sich
nähern *(+dat);* **at hand** nicht weit weg;
~**by** *a* nahe (gelegen); *ad* in der Nähe;
~**ly** *ad* fast; **a** ~ **miss** knapp daneben;
~**ness** Nähe *f;* ~**side** *(Aut)* Beifahrerseite *f; a* auf der Beifahrerseite; **a** ~
thing knapp.

neat *a,* ~**ly** *ad* ['niːt, -lɪ] *(tidy)* ordentlich;
(clever) treffend; *solution* sauber; *(pure)*

unverdünnt, rein; ~**ness** Ordentlichkeit *f*, Sauberkeit *f*.

nebulous ['nebjuləs] *a* nebelhaft, verschwommen.

necessarily ['nesɪsərɪlɪ] *ad* unbedingt; notwendigerweise.

necessary ['nesɪsərɪ] *a* notwendig, nötig.

necessitate [nɪ'sesɪteɪt] *vt* erforderlich machen.

necessity [nɪ'sesɪtɪ] *n (need)* Not *f; (compulsion)* Notwendigkeit *f*; **in case of** ~ im Notfall; **necessities of life** Bedürfnisse *pl* des Lebens.

neck [nek] *n* Hals *m*; ~ **and** ~ Kopf an Kopf; ~**lace** ['neklɪs] Halskette *f*; ~**line** Ausschnitt *m*; ~**tie** *(US)* Krawatte *f*.

nectar ['nektə*] *n* Nektar *m*.

née [neɪ] *a* geborene.

need [niːd] *n* Bedarf *m no pl (for an +dat)*; Bedürfnis *nt (for für); (want)* Mangel *m; (necessity)* Notwendigkeit *f; (poverty)* Not *f; vt* brauchen; **to** ~ **to do** tun müssen; **if** ~ **be** wenn nötig; **to be in** ~ **of** brauchen; **there is no** ~ **for you to come** du brauchst nicht zu kommen; **there's no** ~ es ist nicht nötig.

needle [niːdl] *n* Nadel *f*.

needless *a*, ~**ly** *ad* ['niːdlɪs, -lɪ] unnötig.

needlework ['niːdlwəːk] *n* Handarbeit *f*.

needy ['niːdɪ] *a* bedürftig.

negation [nɪ'geɪʃən] *n* Verneinung *f*.

negative ['negətɪv] *a (Phot)* Negativ *nt; a* negativ; *answer* abschlägig.

neglect [nɪ'glekt] *vt (leave undone)* versäumen; *(take no care of)* vernachlässigen; *n* Vernachlässigung *f*.

negligée ['neglɪʒeɪ] *n* Negligé *nt*.

negligence ['neglɪdʒəns] *n* Nachlässigkeit *f*.

negligent *a*, ~**ly** *ad* ['neglɪdʒənt, -lɪ] nachlässig, unachtsam.

negligible ['neglɪdʒəbl] *a* unbedeutend, geringfügig.

negotiable [nɪ'gəʊʃɪəbl] *a cheque* übertragbar, einlösbar.

negotiate [nɪ'gəʊʃɪeɪt] *vi* verhandeln; *vt treaty* abschließen, aushandeln; *difficulty* überwinden; *corner* nehmen.

negotiation [nɪgəʊʃɪ'eɪʃən] *n* Verhandlung *f*.

negotiator [nɪ'gəʊʃɪeɪtə*] *n* Unterhändler *m*.

Negress ['niːgres] *n* Negerin *f*.

Negro ['niːgrəʊ] *n* Neger *m; a* Neger-.

neighbour, *(US)* **neighbor** ['neɪbə*] *n* Nachbar(in *f) m;* ~**hood** Nachbarschaft *f;* Umgebung *f;* ~**ing** *a* benachbart, angrenzend; ~**ly** *a* freundlich.

neither ['naɪðə*] *a, pron* keine(r, s) (von beiden); *cj* weder; **he can't do it, and** ~ **can I** er kann es nicht und ich auch nicht.

neo- ['niːəʊ] *pref* neo-.

neon ['niːɒn] *n* Neon *nt;* ~ **light** Neonlicht *nt*.

nephew ['nefjuː] *n* Neffe *m*.

nerve [nɜːv] *n* Nerv *m; (courage)* Mut *m; (impudence)* Frechheit *f;* ~-**racking** *a* nervenaufreibend.

nervous ['nɜːvəs] *a (of the nerves)* Nerven-;

(timid) nervös, ängstlich; ~ **breakdown** Nervenzusammenbruch *m;* ~**ly** *ad* nervös; ~**ness** Nervosität *f*.

nest [nest] *n* Nest *nt*.

nestle ['nesl] *vi* sich kuscheln; *(village)* sich schmiegen.

net [net] *n* Netz *nt; a:* ~(**t**) netto, Netto-, Rein-; ~**ball** Netzball *m*.

netting ['netɪŋ] *n* Netz(werk) *nt*, Drahtgeflecht *nt*.

network ['netwəːk] *n* Netz *nt*.

neurosis [njʊə'rəʊsɪs] *n* Neurose *f*.

neurotic [njʊə'rɒtɪk] *a* neurotisch; *n* Neurotiker(in *f) m*.

neuter ['njuːtə*] *a (Biol)* geschlechtslos; *(Gram)* sächlich; *n (Biol)* kastrierte(s) Tier *nt; (Gram)* Neutrum *nt*.

neutral ['njuːtrəl] *a* neutral; ~**ity** [njuː'trælɪtɪ] Neutralität *f*.

never ['nevə*] *ad* nie(mals); **well I** ~ na so was!; ~-**ending** *a* endlos; ~**theless** [nevəðə'les] *ad* trotzdem, dennoch.

new [njuː] *a* neu; **they are still** ~ **to the work** die Arbeit ist ihnen noch neu; ~ **from** frisch aus *or* von; ~**born** *a* neugeboren; ~**comer** Neuankömmling *m;* ~**ly** *ad* frisch, neu; ~ **moon** Neumond *m;* ~**ness** Neuheit *f*.

news [njuːz] *n* Nachricht *f; (Rad, TV)* Nachrichten *pl;* ~**agent** Zeitungshändler *m;* ~**flash** Kurzmeldung *f;* ~**letter** Rundschreiben *nt;* ~**paper** Zeitung *f;* ~**reel** Wochenschau *f*.

New Year ['njuː'jɪə*] *n* Neujahr *nt;* ~'**s Day** Neujahrstag *m;* ~'**s Eve** Silvester(abend *m) m*.

next [nekst] *a* nächste(r, s); *ad (after)* dann, darauf; *(next time)* das nächstemal; *prep:* ~ **to** (gleich) neben *(+dat);* ~ **to nothing** so gut wie nichts; **to do sth** ~ etw als nächstes tun; **what** ~! was denn noch (alles)?; **the** ~ **day** am nächsten *or* folgenden Tag; ~ **door** *ad* nebenan; ~ **year** nächstes Jahr; ~ **of kin** Familienangehörige(r) *mf*.

nib [nɪb] *n* Spitze *f*.

nibble ['nɪbl] *vt* knabbern an *(+dat)*.

nice [naɪs] *a* hübsch, nett, schön; *(subtle)* fein; ~-**looking** *a* hübsch, gutaussehend; ~**ly** *ad* gut, fein, nett.

nick [nɪk] *n* Einkerbung *f;* **in the** ~ **of time** gerade rechtzeitig.

nickel ['nɪkl] *n* Nickel *nt; (US)* Nickel *m* (5 cents).

nickname ['nɪkneɪm] *n* Spitzname *m*.

nicotine ['nɪkətiːn] *n* Nikotin *nt*.

niece [niːs] *n* Nichte *f*.

niggardly ['nɪgədlɪ] *a* schäbig; *person* geizig.

niggling ['nɪglɪŋ] *a* pedantisch; *doubt, worry* quälend; *detail* kleinlich.

night [naɪt] *n* Nacht *f; (evening)* Abend *m;* **good** ~! gute Nacht!; **at** *or* **by** ~ nachts; abends; ~**cap** *(drink)* Schlummertrunk *m;* ~**club** Nachtlokal *nt;* ~**dress** Nachthemd *nt;* ~**fall** Einbruch *m* der Nacht; ~**ie** *(col)* Nachthemd *nt;* ~**ingale** Nachtigall *f;* ~ **life** Nachtleben *nt;* ~**ly** *a, ad* jeden Abend; jede Nacht; ~**mare** Alptraum *m;* ~ **school** Abendschule *f;*

~time Nacht *f;* **at ~ time** nachts; **~watchman** Nachtwächter *m.*

nil [nɪl] *n* Nichts *nt,* Null *f (also Sport).*

nimble ['nɪmbl] *a* behend(e), flink; *mind* beweglich.

nimbly ['nɪmblɪ] *ad* flink.

nine [naɪn] *n* Neun *f;* *a* neun; **~teen** *n* Neunzehn *f;* *a* neunzehn; **~ty** *n* Neunzig *f;* *a* neunzig.

ninth [naɪnθ] *a* neunte(r, s); *n* Neuntel *nt.*

nip [nɪp] *vt* kneifen; *n* Kneifen *nt.*

nipple ['nɪpl] *n* Brustwarze *f.*

nippy ['nɪpɪ] *a (col) person* flink; *car* flott; *(cold)* frisch.

nit [nɪt] *n* Nisse *f.*

nitrogen ['naɪtrədʒən] *n* Stickstoff *m.*

no [nəu] *a* kein; *ad* nein; *n* Nein *nt;* **~ further** nicht weiter; **~ more time** keine Zeit mehr; **in ~ time** schnell.

nobility [nəu'bɪlɪtɪ] *n* Adel *m;* **the ~ of this deed** diese edle Tat.

noble ['nəubl] *a rank* adlig; *(splendid)* nobel, edel; *a* Adlige(r) *mf;* **~man** Edelmann *m,* Adlige(r) *m.*

nobly ['nəublɪ] *ad* edel, großmütig.

nobody ['nəubədɪ] *pron* niemand, keiner; *n* Niemand *m.*

nod [nɒd] *vi* nicken; **~ off** einnicken; *n* Nicken *nt.*

noise [nɔɪz] *n (sound)* Geräusch *nt; (unpleasant, loud)* Lärm *m.*

noisily ['nɔɪzɪlɪ] *ad* lärmend, laut.

noisy ['nɔɪzɪ] *a* laut; *crowd* lärmend.

nomad ['nəumæd] *n* Nomade *m;* **~ic** [nəu'mædɪk] *a* nomadisch.

no-man's land ['nəumænzlænd] *n (lit, fig)* Niemandsland *nt.*

nominal ['nɒmɪnl] *a* nominell; *(Gram)* Nominal-.

nominate ['nɒmɪneɪt] *vt (suggest)* vorschlagen; *(in election)* aufstellen; *(appoint)* ernennen.

nomination [nɒmɪ'neɪʃən] *n (election)* Nominierung *f; (appointment)* Ernennung *f.*

nominee [nɒmɪ'niː] *n* Kandidat(in *f) m.*

non- [nɒn] *pref* Nicht-, un-; **~-alcoholic** *a* alkoholfrei.

nonchalant ['nɒnʃələnt] *a* lässig.

nondescript ['nɒndɪskrɪpt] *a* mittelmäßig.

none [nʌn] *a, pron* kein(e, r, s); *ad:* **~ the wiser** keineswegs klüger; **~ of your cheek!** sei nicht so frech!

nonentity [nɒ'nentɪtɪ] *n* Null *f (col).*

nonetheless [nʌnðə'les] *ad* nichtsdestoweniger.

non-fiction [nɒn'fɪkʃən] *n* Sachbücher *pl.*

nonplussed [nɒn'plʌst] *a* verdutzt.

nonsense ['nɒnsəns] *n* Unsinn *m.*

non-stop [nɒn'stɒp] *a* pausenlos, Nonstop-.

noodles ['nuːdlz] *npl* Nudeln *pl.*

nook [nuk] *n* Winkel *m,* Eckchen *nt.*

noon [nuːn] *n* (12 Uhr) Mittag *m.*

no one ['nəuwʌn] *pron* = **nobody.**

noose [nuːs] *n* Schlinge *f.*

norm [nɔːm] *n* Norm *f,* Regel *f.*

normal ['nɔːməl] *a* normal; **~ly** *ad* normal; *(usually)* normalerweise.

north [nɔːθ] *n* Norden *m;* *a* nördlich, Nord-; *ad* nördlich, nach *or* im Norden; **~-east**

Nordosten *m;* **~ern** ['nɔːðən] *a* nördlich, Nord-; **~ward(s)** *ad* nach Norden; **~-west** Nordwesten *m.*

nose [nəuz] *n* Nase *f;* **~bleed** Nasenbluten *nt;* **~-dive** Sturzflug *m;* **~y** *a* neugierig.

nostalgia [nɒs'tældʒɪə] *n* Sehnsucht *f,* Nostalgie *f.*

nostalgic [nɒs'tældʒɪk] *a* wehmütig, nostalgisch.

nostril ['nɒstrɪl] *n* Nasenloch *nt; (of animal)* Nüster *f.*

not [nɒt] *ad* nicht; **he is ~ an expert** er ist kein Experte; **~ at all** keineswegs; *(don't mention it)* gern geschehen.

notable ['nəutəbl] *a* bemerkenswert.

notably ['nəutəblɪ] *ad (especially)* besonders; *(noticeably)* bemerkenswert.

notch [nɒtʃ] *n* Kerbe *f,* Einschnitt *m.*

note [nəut] *n (Mus)* Note *f,* Ton *m; (short letter)* Nachricht *f; (Pol)* Note *f; (comment, attention)* Notiz *f; (of lecture etc)* Aufzeichnung *f; (bank—)* Schein *m; (fame)* Ruf *m,* Ansehen *nt; vt (observe)* bemerken; *(write down)* notieren; **to take ~s** of sich Notizen machen über *(+acc);* **~book** Notizbuch *nt;* **~-case** Brieftasche *f;* **~d** *a* bekannt; **~paper** Briefpapier *nt.*

nothing ['nʌθɪŋ] *n* nichts; **for ~** umsonst; **it is ~ to me** es bedeutet mir nichts.

notice ['nəutɪs] *n (announcement)* Anzeige *f,* Bekanntmachung *f; (attention)* Beachtung *f; (warning)* Ankündigung *f; (dismissal)* Kündigung *f; vt* bemerken; **to take ~ of** beachten; **to bring sth to sb's ~** jdn auf etw *(acc)* aufmerksam machen; **take no ~!** kümmere dich nicht darum!; **~able** *a* merklich; **~ board** Anschlagtafel *f.*

notification [nəutɪfɪ'keɪʃən] *n* Benachrichtigung *f.*

notify ['nəutɪfaɪ] *vt* benachrichtigen.

notion ['nəuʃən] *n (idea)* Vorstellung *f,* Idee *f; (fancy)* Lust *f.*

notorious [nəu'tɔːrɪəs] *a* berüchtigt.

notwithstanding [nɒtwɪð'stændɪŋ] *ad* trotzdem; *prep* trotz.

nougat ['nuːgɑː] *n* weiße(r) Nougat *m.*

nought [nɔːt] *n* Null *f.*

noun [naun] *n* Hauptwort *nt,* Substantiv *nt.*

nourish ['nʌrɪʃ] *vt* nähren; **~ing** *a* nahrhaft; **~ment** Nahrung *f.*

novel ['nɒvəl] *n* Roman *m;* *a* neu(artig); **~ist** Schriftsteller(in *f) m;* **~ty** Neuheit *f.*

November [nəu'vembə*] *n* November *m.*

novice ['nɒvɪs] *n* Neuling *m; (Eccl)* Novize *m.*

now [nau] *ad* jetzt; **right ~** jetzt, gerade; **do it right ~** tun Sie es sofort; **~ and then, ~ and again** ab und zu, manchmal; **~, ~** na, na; **~ ... ~** *or* **then** bald ... bald, mal ... mal; **~adays** *ad* heutzutage.

nowhere ['nəuwɛə*] *ad* nirgends.

nozzle ['nɒzl] *n* Düse *f.*

nuance ['njuːɑːns] *n* Nuance *f.*

nuclear ['njuːklɪə*] *a energy etc* Atom-, Kern-.

nucleus ['njuːklɪəs] *n* Kern *m.*

nude [njuːd] *a* nackt; *n (person)* Nackte(r) *mf; (Art)* Akt *m;* **in the ~** nackt.

nudge [nʌdʒ] *vt* leicht anstoßen.

nudist ['nju:dɪst] n Nudist(in f) m.
nudity ['nju:dɪtɪ] n Nacktheit f.
nuisance ['nju:sns] n Ärgernis nt; **that's a** ~ das ist ärgerlich; **he's a** ~ er geht einem auf die Nerven.
null [nʌl] a: ~ **and void** null und nichtig; ~**ify** vt für null und nichtig erklären.
numb [nʌm] a taub, gefühllos; vt betäuben.
number ['nʌmbə*] n Nummer f; (numeral also) Zahl f; (quantity) (An)zahl f; (Gram) Numerus m; (of magazine also) Ausgabe f; vt (give a number to) numerieren; (amount to) sein; **his days are** ~**d** seine Tage sind gezählt; ~ **plate** (Brit Aut) Nummernschild nt.
numbness ['nʌmnəs] n Gefühllosigkeit f.
numbskull ['nʌmskʌl] n Idiot m.
numeral ['nju:mərəl] n Ziffer f.
numerical [nju:'merɪkəl] a order zahlenmäßig.
numerous ['nju:mərəs] a zahlreich.
nun [nʌn] n Nonne f.
nurse [nɜːs] n Krankenschwester f; (for children) Kindermädchen nt; vt patient pflegen; doubt etc hegen; ~**ry** (for children) Kinderzimmer nt; (for plants) Gärtnerei f; (for trees) Baumschule f; ~**ry rhyme** Kinderreim m; ~**ry school** Kindergarten m.
nursing ['nɜːsɪŋ] n (profession) Krankenpflege f; ~ **home** Privatklinik f.
nut [nʌt] n Nuß f; (screw) Schraubenmutter f; (col) Verrückte(r) mf; ~**s** a (col: crazy) verrückt.
nutcase ['nʌtkeɪs] n (col) Verrückte(r) mf.
nutcrackers ['nʌtkrækəz] npl Nußknacker m.
nutmeg ['nʌtmeg] n Muskat(nuß f) m.
nutrient ['nju:trɪənt] n Nährstoff m.
nutrition [nju:'trɪʃən] n Nahrung f.
nutritious [nju:'trɪʃəs] a nahrhaft.
nutshell ['nʌtʃel] n: **in a** ~ in aller Kürze.
nylon ['naɪlɒn] n Nylon nt; a Nylon-.

O

O, o [əʊ] n O nt, o nt; (Tel) Null f; see **oh**.
oaf [əʊf] n Trottel m.
oak [əʊk] n Eiche f; a Eichen(holz)-.
oar [ɔː*] n Ruder nt.
oasis [əʊ'eɪsɪs] n Oase-f.
oath [əʊθ] n (statement) Eid m, Schwur m; (swearword) Fluch m.
oatmeal ['əʊtmiːl] n Haferschrot m.
oats [əʊts] n pl Hafer m; (Cook) Haferflocken pl.
obedience [ə'biːdɪəns] n Gehorsam m.
obedient [ə'biːdɪənt] a gehorsam, folgsam.
obelisk ['ɒbɪlɪsk] n Obelisk m.
obesity [əʊ'biːsɪtɪ] n Korpulenz f, Fettleibigkeit f.
obey [ə'beɪ] vti gehorchen (+dat), folgen (+dat).
obituary [ə'bɪtjʊərɪ] n Nachruf m.
object ['ɒbdʒɪkt] n (thing) Gegenstand m, Objekt nt; (of feeling etc) Gegenstand m; (purpose) Ziel nt; (Gram) Objekt nt; [əb'dʒekt] vi dagegen sein, Einwände haben (to gegen); (morally) Anstoß nehmen (to an +acc); ~**ion** [əb'dʒekʃən] (reason against) Einwand m, Einspruch m; (dislike) Abneigung f; ~**ionable** [əb'dʒekʃnəbl] a nicht einwandfrei; language anstößig; ~**ive** [əb'dʒektɪv] n Ziel nt; a objektiv; ~**ively** [əb'dʒektɪvlɪ] ad objektiv; ~**ivity** [ɒbdʒɪk'tɪvɪtɪ] Objektivität f; ~**or** [əb'dʒektə*] Gegner(in f) m.
obligation [ɒblɪ'geɪʃən] n (duty) Pflicht f; (promise) Verpflichtung f; **no** ~ unverbindlich; **be under an** ~ verpflichtet sein.
obligatory [ɒ'blɪgətərɪ] a bindend, obligatorisch; **it is** ~ **to . . .** es ist Pflicht, zu . . .
oblige [ə'blaɪdʒ] vt (compel) zwingen; (do a favour) einen Gefallen tun (+dat); **you are not** ~**d to do it** Sie sind nicht verpflichtet, es zu tun; **much** ~**d** herzlichen Dank.
obliging [ə'blaɪdʒɪŋ] a entgegenkommend.
oblique [ə'bliːk] a schräg, schief; n Schrägstrich m.
obliterate [ə'blɪtəreɪt] vt auslöschen.
oblivion [ə'blɪvɪən] n Vergessenheit f.
oblivious [ə'blɪvɪəs] a nicht bewußt (of gen); **he was** ~ **of it** er hatte es nicht bemerkt.
oblong ['ɒblɒŋ] n Rechteck nt; a länglich.
obnoxious [əb'nɒkʃəs] a abscheulich, widerlich.
oboe ['əʊbəʊ] n Oboe f.
obscene [əb'siːn] a obszön, unanständig.
obscenity [əb'senɪtɪ] n Obszönität f; **obscenities** Zoten pl.
obscure [əb'skjʊə*] a unklar; (indistinct) undeutlich; (unknown) unbekannt, obskur; (dark) düster; vt verdunkeln; view verbergen; (confuse) verwirren.
obscurity [əb'skjʊərɪtɪ] n Unklarheit f; (being unknown) Verborgenheit f; (darkness) Dunkelheit f.
obsequious [əb'siːkwɪəs] a servil.
observable [əb'zɜːvəbl] a wahrnehmbar, sichtlich.
observance [əb'zɜːvəns] n Befolgung f.
observant [əb'zɜːvənt] a aufmerksam.
observation [ɒbzə'veɪʃən] n (noticing) Beobachtung f; (surveillance) Überwachung f; (remark) Bemerkung f.
observatory [əb'zɜːvətrɪ] n Sternwarte f, Observatorium nt.
observe [əb'zɜːv] vt (notice) bemerken; (watch) beobachten; customs einhalten; ~**er** Beobachter(in f) m.
obsess [əb'ses] vt verfolgen, quälen; **to be** ~**ed with an idea** von einem Gedanken besessen sein; ~**ion** [əb'seʃən] Besessenheit f, Wahn m; ~**ive** a krankhaft.
obsolescence [ɒbsə'lesns] n Veralten nt.
obsolescent [ɒbsə'lesnt] a veraltend.
obsolete ['ɒbsəliːt] a überholt, veraltet.
obstacle ['ɒbstəkl] n Hindernis nt; ~ **race** Hindernisrennen nt.
obstetrics [ɒb'stetrɪks] n Geburtshilfe f.
obstinacy ['ɒbstɪnəsɪ] n Hartnäckigkeit f, Sturheit f.
obstinate a, ~**ly** ad ['ɒbstɪnət, -lɪ] hartnäckig, stur.

obstreperous [əb'strepərəs] a aufmüpfig.
obstruct [əb'strʌkt] vt versperren; *pipe*
verstopfen; *(hinder)* hemmen; **~ion**
[əb'strʌkʃən] Versperrung f; Verstopfung f;
(obstacle) Hindernis nt; **~ive** a hemmend.
obtain [əb'teɪn] vt erhalten, bekommen;
result erzielen; **~able** a erhältlich.
obtrusive [əb'truːsɪv] a aufdringlich.
obtuse [əb'tjuːs] a begriffsstutzig; *angle*
stumpf.
obviate ['ɒbvɪeɪt] vt beseitigen; *danger*
abwenden.
obvious ['ɒbvɪəs] a offenbar, offensichtlich; **~ly** ad offensichtlich.

occasion [ə'keɪʒən] n Gelegenheit f;
(special event) große(s) Ereignis nt;
(reason) Grund m, Anlaß m; **on ~**
gelegentlich, zu veranlassen; **~al** a,
~ally ad gelegentlich; **very ~ally** sehr
selten.
occult [ɒ'kʌlt] n the **~** der Okkultismus; a
okkult.
occupant ['ɒkjupənt] n Inhaber(in f) m; *(of
house etc)* Bewohner(in f) m.
occupation [ɒkju'peɪʃən] n *(employment)*
Tätigkeit f, Beruf m; *(pastime)*
Beschäftigung f, *(of country)* Besetzung f,
Okkupation f; **~al a** hazard Berufs-;
therapy Beschäftigungs-.
occupier ['ɒkjupaɪə*] n Bewohner(in f) m.
occupy ['ɒkjupaɪ] vt *(take possession of)*
besetzen; *seat* belegen; *(live in)* bewohnen;
position, office bekleiden; *position in sb's life*
einnehmen; *time* beanspruchen; *mind*
beschäftigen.
occur [ə'kɜː*] vi *(happen)* vorkommen,
geschehen; *(appear)* vorkommen; *(come to
mind)* einfallen *(to dat)*; **~rence** *(event)*
Ereignis nt; *(appearing)* Auftreten nt.
ocean ['əuʃən] n Ozean m, Meer nt;
~-going a Hochsee-.
ochre ['əukə*] n Ocker m or nt.
o'clock [ə'klɒk] ad: **it is 5 ~** es ist 5 Uhr.
octagonal [ɒk'tægənl] a achteckig.
octane ['ɒkteɪn] n Oktan nt.
octave ['ɒktɪv] n Oktave f.
October [ɒk'təubə*] n Oktober m.
octopus ['ɒktəpəs] n Krake f; *(small)*
Tintenfisch m.
oculist ['ɒkjulɪst] n Augenarzt m/-ärztin f.
odd [ɒd] a *(strange)* sonderbar; *(not even)*
ungerade; *(the other part missing)* einzeln;
(about) ungefähr; *(surplus)* übrig; *(casual)*
Gelegenheits-, zeitweilig; **~ity** *(strangeness)* Merkwürdigkeit f; *(queer person)*
seltsame(r) Kauz m; *(thing)* Kuriosität f;
~ly ad seltsam; **~ly enough** merkwürdigerweise; **~ment** Rest m, Einzel-
stück nt; **~s** pl Chancen pl; *(betting)*
Gewinnchancen pl; **it makes no ~s** es
spielt keine Rolle; **at ~s** uneinig; **~s and
ends** pl Reste pl; Krimskrams m.
ode [əud] n Ode f.
odious ['əudɪəs] a verhaßt; *action* abscheulich.
odour, *(US)* **odor** ['əudə*] n Geruch m;
~less a geruchlos.
of [ɒv, əv] prep von; *(indicating material)*
aus; **the first ~ May** der erste Mai;
within a month ~ his death einen

Monat nach seinem Tod; **a girl ~ ten** ein
zehnjähriges Mädchen; **fear ~ God**
Gottesfurcht f; **love ~ money** Liebe f
zum Geld; **the six ~ us** wir sechs.
off [ɒf] ad *(absent)* weg, fort; *(switch)*
aus(geschaltet), ab(geschaltet); *(milk)*
sauer; **I'm ~** ich gehe jetzt; **the button's
~** der Knopf ist ab; **to be well-/badly ~**
reich/arm sein; prep von; *(distant from)*
ab(gelegen) von; **3% ~** 3% Nachlaß or
Abzug; **just ~ Piccadilly** gleich bei
Piccadilly; **I'm ~ smoking** ich rauche
nicht mehr.
offal ['ɒfəl] n Innereien pl.
off-colour ['ɒf'kʌlə*] a nicht wohl.
offence, *(US)* **offense** [ə'fens] n *(crime)*
Vergehen nt, Straftat f; *(insult)* Beleidigung
f.
offend [ə'fend] vt beleidigen; **~er**
Gesetzesübertreter m; **~ing** a verletzend.
offensive [ə'fensɪv] a *(unpleasant)* übel,
abstoßend; *weapon* Kampf-; *remark* verletzend; n Angriff m, Offensive f.
offer ['ɒfə*] n Angebot f, **on ~** zum Verkauf angeboten; vt anbieten; *reward* aussetzen; *opinion* äußern; *resistance* leisten;
~ing Gabe f; *(collection)* Kollekte f.
offhand ['ɒf'hænd] a lässig; ad ohne
weiteres.
office ['ɒfɪs] n Büro nt; *(position)* Amt nt;
(duty) Aufgabe f; *(Eccl)* Gottesdienst m; **~
block** Büro(hoch)haus nt; **~ boy** Lauf-
junge m; **~r** *(Mil)* Offizier m; *(public ~)*
Beamte(r) m im öffentlichen Dienst; **~
work** Büroarbeit f; **~ worker** Büro-
angestellte(r) mf.
official [ə'fɪʃəl] a offiziell, amtlich; n
Beamte(r) m; *(Pol)* amtliche(r) Sprecher
m; *(of club etc)* Funktionär m, Offizielle(r)
m; **~ly** ad offiziell.
officious [ə'fɪʃəs] a aufdringlich.
offing ['ɒfɪŋ] n: **in the ~** in (Aus)sicht.
off-licence ['ɒflaɪsəns] n Wein- und
Spirituosenhandlung f.
off-peak ['ɒfpiːk] a *heating* Speicher-;
charges verbilligt.
off-season ['ɒfsiːzn] a außer Saison.
offset ['ɒfset] vt *irreg* ausgleichen.
offshore ['ɒfʃɔː*] ad in einiger Entfernung
von der Küste; a küstennah, Küsten-.
offside ['ɒf'saɪd] a *(Sport)* im Abseits
(stehend); ad abseits; n *(Aut)* Fahrerseite f.
offspring ['ɒfsprɪŋ] n Nachkommenschaft
f; *(one)* Sprößling m.
offstage ['ɒf'steɪdʒ] ad hinter den Kulissen.
off-the-cuff ['ɒfðəkʌf] a unvorbereitet, aus
dem Stegreif.
often ['ɒfən] ad oft.
ogle ['əugl] vt liebäugeln mit.
oh [əu] *interj* oh, ach.
oil [ɔɪl] n Öl nt; vt ölen; **~can** Ölkännchen
nt; **~field** Ölfeld nt; **~-fired** a Öl-; **~
level** Ölstand nt; **~ painting** Ölgemälde
nt; **~ refinery** Ölraffinerie f, **~-rig**
Ölplattform f; **~skins** pl Ölzeug nt; **~
tanker** (Öl)tanker m; **~ well** Ölquelle f;
~y a ölig; *(dirty)* ölbeschmiert; *manners*
schleimig.
ointment ['ɔɪntmənt] n Salbe f.
O.K., okay ['əu'keɪ] *interj* in Ordnung, O.K.;

a in Ordnung; **that's ~ with** *or* **by me** ich bin damit einverstanden; *n* Zustimmung *f*; *vt* genehmigen.

old [ɔʊld] *a* alt; *(former also)* ehemalig; **in the ~ days** früher; **any ~ thing** irgend etwas; **~ age** Alter *nt*; **~en** *a* (*liter*) alt, vergangen; **~-fashioned** *a* altmodisch; **~ maid** alte Jungfer *f*.

olive ['ɒlɪv] *n* (*fruit*) Olive *f*; (*colour*) Olive *nt*; *a* Oliven-; (*coloured*) olivenfarbig; **~ branch** Ölzweig *m*; **~ oil** Olivenöl *nt*.

Olympic [əʊ'lɪmpɪk] *a* olympisch; **~ Games, ~s** *pl* Olympische Spiele *pl*.

omelet(te) ['ɒmlɪt] *n* Omelett *nt*.

omen ['əʊmən] *n* Zeichen *nt*, Omen *nt*.

ominous ['ɒmɪnəs] *a* bedrohlich.

omission [əʊ'mɪʃən] *n* Auslassung *f*; (*neglect*) Versäumnis *nt*.

omit [əʊ'mɪt] *vt* auslassen; (*fail to do*) versäumen.

on [ɒn] *prep* auf; **~ TV** im Fernsehen; **I have it ~ me** ich habe es bei mir; **a ring ~ his finger** ein Ring am Finger; **~ the main road/the bank of the river** an der Hauptstraße/dem Flußufer; **~ foot** zu Fuß; **a lecture ~ Dante** eine Vorlesung über Dante; **~ the left** links; **~ the right** rechts; **~ Sunday** am Sonntag; **~ Sundays** sonntags; **~ hearing this, he** left als er das hörte, ging er; *ad* (dar)auf; **she had nothing ~** sie hatte nichts an; *(no plans)* sie hatte nichts vor; **what's ~ at the cinema?** was läuft im Kino?; **move ~** weitergehen; **go ~** mach weiter; **the light is ~** das Licht ist an; **you're ~** (*col*) akzeptiert; **it's not ~** (*col*) das ist nicht drin; **~ and off** hin und wieder.

once [wʌns] *ad* einmal; *cj* wenn ... einmal; **~ you've seen him** wenn du ihn erst einmal gesehen hast; **~ she had seen him** sobald sie ihn gesehen hatte; **at ~** sofort; *(at the same time)* gleichzeitig; **all at ~** plötzlich; **~ more** noch einmal; **more than ~** mehr als einmal; **~ in a while** ab und zu; **~ and for all** ein für allemal; **~ upon a time** es war einmal.

oncoming ['ɒnkʌmɪŋ] *a traffic* Gegen-, entgegenkommend.

one [wʌn] *a* ein; *(only)* einzig; *n* Eins *f*; *pron* eine(r, s); *(people, you)* man; **this ~, that ~** das; dieser/diese/dieses; **~ day** eines Tages; **the blue ~** der/die/das blaue; **which ~** welche(r, s); **he is ~ of us** er ist einer von uns; **~ by ~** einzeln; **~ another** einander; **~-man** *a* Einmann-; **~self** *pron* sich (selber); **~-way** *a street* Einbahn-.

ongoing ['ɒngəʊɪŋ] *a* stattfindend, momentan; *(progressing)* sich entwickelnd.

onion ['ʌnjən] *n* Zwiebel *f*.

onlooker ['ɒnlʊkə*] *n* Zuschauer(in *f*) *m*.

only ['əʊnlɪ] *ad* nur, bloß; *a* einzige(r, s); **~ yesterday** erst gestern; **~ just arrived** gerade erst angekommen.

onset ['ɒnset] *n* (*beginning*) Beginn *m*.

onshore ['ɒnʃɔ:*] *ad an Land; a* Küsten-.

onslaught ['ɒnslɔːt] *n* Angriff *m*.

onto ['ɒntʊ] *prep* = **on to.**

onus ['əʊnəs] *n* Last *f*, Pflicht *f*.

onwards [ˌɒnwədz] *ad* (*place*) voran, vorwärts; **from that day ~** von dem Tag an; **from today ~** ab heute.

onyx ['ɒnɪks] *n* Onyx *m*.

ooze [uːz] *vi* sickern.

opacity [əʊ'pæsɪtɪ] *n* Undurchsichtigkeit *f*.

opal ['əʊpəl] *n* Opal *m*.

opaque [əʊ'peɪk] *a* undurchsichtig.

open ['əʊpən] *a* offen; *(public)* öffentlich; *mind* aufgeschlossen; *sandwich* belegt; **in the ~ (air)** im Freien; **to keep a day ~** einen Tag freihalten; *vt* öffnen, aufmachen; *trial, motorway, account* eröffnen; *vi* (*begin*) anfangen; (*shop*) aufmachen; (*door, flower*) aufgehen; (*play*) Premiere haben; **~ out** ausbreiten; *hole, business* erweitern; *vi* (*person*) aus sich herausgehen; **~ up** *vt route* erschließen; *(shop, prospects)* eröffnen; **~-air** *a* Frei(luft)-; **~er** Öffner *m*; **~ing** (*hole*) Öffnung *f*, Loch *nt*; (*beginning*) Eröffnung *f*, Anfang *m*; (*good chance*) Gelegenheit *f*; **~ly** *ad* offen; (*publicly*) öffentlich; **~-minded** *a* aufgeschlossen; **~-necked** *a* offen.

opera ['ɒpərə] *n* Oper *f*; **~ glasses** *pl* Opernglas *nt*; **~ house** Opernhaus *nt*.

operate ['ɒpəreɪt] *vt machine* bedienen; *brakes, light* betätigen; *vi* (*machine*) laufen, in Betrieb sein; (*person*) arbeiten; (*Med*) **to ~ on** operieren.

operatic [ɒpə'rætɪk] *a* Opern-.

operation [ɒpə'reɪʃən] *n* (*working*) Betrieb *m*, Tätigkeit *f*; (*Med*) Operation *f*; (*undertaking*) Unternehmen *nt*; (*Mil*) Einsatz *m*; **in full ~** in vollem Gang; **to be in ~** (*Jur*) in Kraft sein; (*machine*) in Betrieb sein; **~al** *a* einsatzbereit.

operative ['ɒpərətɪv] *a* wirksam; *law* rechtsgültig; (*Med*) operativ; *n* Mechaniker *m*; Agent *m*.

operator ['ɒpəreɪtə*] *n* (*of machine*) Arbeiter *m*; (*Tel*) Telefonist(in *f*) *m*; **phone the ~** rufen Sie die Vermittlung *or* das Fernamt an.

operetta [ɒpə'retə] *n* Operette *f*.

opinion [ə'pɪnjən] *n* Meinung *f*; **in my ~** meiner Meinung nach; **a matter of ~** Ansichtssache; **~ated** *a* starrsinnig.

opium ['əʊpɪəm] *n* Opium *nt*.

opponent [ə'pəʊnənt] *n* Gegner *m*.

opportune ['ɒpətjuːn] *a* günstig; *remark* passend.

opportunist [ɒpə'tjuːnɪst] *n* Opportunist *m*.

opportunity [ɒpə'tjuːnɪtɪ] *n* Gelegenheit *f*, Möglichkeit *f*.

oppose [ə'pəʊz] *vt* entgegentreten (+*dat*); *argument, idea* ablehnen; *plan* bekämpfen; **~d** *a*: **to be ~d to sth** gegen etw sein; **as ~d to** im Gegensatz zu.

opposing [ə'pəʊzɪŋ] *a* gegnerisch; *points of view* entgegengesetzt.

opposite ['ɒpəzɪt] *a house* gegenüberliegend; *direction* entgegengesetzt; *ad* gegenüber; *prep* gegenüber; **~ me** mir gegenüber; **~ in** Gegenteil *nt*; **~ number** (*person*) Pendant *nt*; (*Sport*) Gegenspieler *m*.

opposition [ɒpə'zɪʃən] *n* (*resistance*) Widerstand *m*; (*Pol*) Opposition *f*; (*contrast*) Gegensatz *m*.

oppress [ə'pres] vt unterdrücken; *(heat etc)* bedrücken; ~**ion** [ə'preʃən] Unterdrückung f; ~**ive** a authority, law ungerecht; *burden, thought* bedrückend; *heat* drückend.

opt [ɒpt] vi: ~ **for sth** sich entscheiden für etw; **to** ~ **to do sth** sich entscheiden, etw zu tun; ~ **out of** vi sich drücken vor *(+dat); (of society)* ausflippen aus *(+dat).*

optical ['ɒptɪkl] a optisch.

optician [ɒp'tɪʃən] n Optiker m.

optimism ['ɒptɪmɪzəm] n Optimismus m.

optimist ['ɒptɪmɪst] n Optimist m; ~**ic** ['ɒptɪ'mɪstɪk] a optimistisch.

optimum ['ɒptɪməm] a optimal.

option ['ɒpʃən] n Wahl f; *(Comm)* Vorkaufsrecht m, Option f; ~**al** a freiwillig; *subject* wahlfrei; ~**al extras** Extras auf Wunsch.

opulence ['ɒpjʊləns] n Reichtum m.

opulent ['ɒpjʊlənt] a sehr reich.

opus ['əʊpəs] n Werk nt, Opus nt.

or [ɔː*] cj oder; **he could not read** ~ **write** er konnte weder lesen noch schreiben.

oracle ['ɒrəkl] n Orakel nt.

oral ['ɔːrəl] a mündlich; n *(exam)* mündliche Prüfung f, Mündliche(s) nt.

orange ['ɒrɪndʒ] n *(fruit)* Apfelsine f, Orange f; *(colour)* Orange nt; a orange.

orang-outang, orang-utan [ɔː'ræŋ-u:'tæn] n Orang-Utan m.

oration [ɔː'reɪʃən] n feierliche Rede f.

orator ['ɒrətə*] n Redner(in) f.

oratorio [ɒrə'tɔːrɪəʊ] n Oratorium nt.

orbit ['ɔːbɪt] n Umlaufbahn f; **2** ~**s** 2 Umkreisungen; vt **be in** ~ *(die Erde/den Mond etc)* umkreisen; vi umkreisen.

orchard ['ɔːtʃəd] n Obstgarten m.

orchestra ['ɔːkɪstrə] n Orchester nt; ~**l** [ɔː'kestrəl] a Orchester-, orchestral; ~**te** ['ɔːkɪstreɪt] vt orchestrieren.

orchid ['ɔːkɪd] n Orchidee f.

ordain [ɔː'deɪn] vt *(Eccl)* weihen; *(decide)* verfügen.

ordeal [ɔː'diːl] n schwere Prüfung f, Qual f.

order ['ɔːdə*] n *(sequence)* Reihenfolge f; *(good arrangement)* Ordnung f; *(command)* Befehl m; *(Jur)* Anordnung f; *(peace)* Ordnung f, Ruhe f; *(condition)* Zustand m; *(rank)* Klasse f; *(Comm)* Bestellung f; *(Eccl, honour)* Orden m; **out of** ~ außer Betrieb; **in** ~ **to do sth** um etw zu tun; **in** ~ **that** damit; **holy** ~**s** Priesterweihe f; vt *(arrange)* ordnen; *(command)* befehlen *(sth etw acc, sb jdm); (Comm)* bestellen; ~**form** Bestellschein m; ~**ly** n *(Mil)* Offiziersbursche m; *(Mil Med)* Sanitäter m; *(Med)* Pfleger m; a *(tidy)* ordentlich; *(wellbehaved)* ruhig; ~**ly officer** diensthabender Offizier.

ordinal ['ɔːdɪnl] a Ordnungs-, Ordinal-.

ordinarily ['ɔːdnrɪlɪ] ad gewöhnlich.

ordinary ['ɔːdnrɪ] a *(usual)* gewöhnlich, normal; *(commonplace)* gewöhnlich, alltäglich.

ordination [ɔːdɪ'neɪʃən] n Priesterweihe f; *(Protestant)* Ordination f.

ordnance ['ɔːdnəns] n Artillerie f, Munition f; ~ **factory** Munitionsfabrik f.

ore [ɔː*] n Erz nt.

organ ['ɔːgən] n *(Mus)* Orgel f; *(Biol, fig)* Organ nt; ~**ic** [ɔː'gænɪk] a organisch; ~**ism** ['ɔːgənɪzm] Organismus m; ~**ist** Organist(in f) m.

organization [ɔːgənaɪ'zeɪʃən] n Organisation f; *(make-up)* Struktur f.

organize ['ɔːgənaɪz] vt organisieren; ~**r** Organisator m, Veranstalter m.

orgasm ['ɔːgæzm] n Orgasmus m.

orgy ['ɔːdʒɪ] n Orgie f.

Orient ['ɔːrɪənt] n Orient m.

oriental [ɔːrɪ'entəl] a orientalisch; n Orientale m, Orientalin f.

orientate ['ɔːrɪenteɪt] vt orientieren.

orifice ['ɒrɪfɪs] n Öffnung f.

origin ['ɒrɪdʒɪn] n Ursprung m; *(of the world)* Anfang m, Entstehung f.

original [ə'rɪdʒɪnl] a *(first)* ursprünglich; *painting* original; *idea* originell; n Original nt; ~**ity** [ərɪdʒɪ'nælɪtɪ] Originalität f; ~**ly** ad ursprünglich; originell.

originate [ə'rɪdʒɪneɪt] vi entstehen; **to** ~ **from** stammen aus; in's Leben rufen.

originator [ə'rɪdʒɪneɪtə*] n *(of movement)* Begründer m; *(of invention)* Erfinder m.

ornament ['ɔːnəmənt] n Schmuck m; *(on mantelpiece)* Nippesfigur f; *(fig)* Zierde f; ~**al** [ɔːnə'mentl] a schmückend, Zier-; ~**ation** Verzierung f.

ornate [ɔː'neɪt] a reich verziert; *style* überladen.

ornithologist [ɔːnɪ'θɒlədʒɪst] n Ornithologe m, Ornithologin f.

ornithology [ɔːnɪ'θɒlədʒɪ] n Vogelkunde f, Ornithologie f.

orphan ['ɔːfən] n Waise f, Waisenkind nt; vt zur Waise machen; ~**age** Waisenhaus nt.

orthodox ['ɔːθədɒks] a orthodox.

orthopaedic, *(US)* **orthopedic** [ɔːθəʊ'piːdɪk] a orthopädisch.

oscillation [ɒsɪ'leɪʃən] n Schwingung f, Oszillation f.

ostensible a, **ostensibly** ad [ɒs'tensəbl, -blɪ] vorgeblich, angeblich.

ostentation [ɒsten'teɪʃən] n Zurschaustellen nt.

ostentatious [ɒsten'teɪʃəs] a großtuerisch, protzig.

ostracize ['ɒstrəsaɪz] vt ausstoßen.

ostrich ['ɒstrɪtʃ] n Strauß m.

other ['ʌðə*] a andere(r, s); **the** ~ **day** neulich; **every** ~ **day** jeden zweiten Tag; **any person** ~ **than him** alle außer ihm; **there are 6** ~**s** da sind noch 6; pron andere(r, s); ad: ~ **than** anders als; ~**wise** ad *(in a different way)* anders; *(in other ways)* sonst, im übrigen; *(or else)* sonst.

otter ['ɒtə*] n Otter m.

ought [ɔːt] v aux sollen; **he behaves as he** ~ er benimmt sich, wie es sich gehört; **you** ~ **to do that** Sie sollten das tun; **he** ~ **to win** er müßte gewinnen; **that** ~ **to do** das müßte or dürfte reichen.

ounce [aʊns] n Unze f.

our [aʊə*] poss a unser; ~**s** poss pron unsere(r, s); ~**selves** pron uns (selbst); *(emphatic)* (wir) selbst.

oust [aʊst] vt verdrängen.

out [aʊt] ad hinaus/heraus; (not indoors) draußen; (not alight) aus; (unconscious) bewußtlos; (results) bekanntgegeben; **to eat/go** ~ auswärts essen/ausgehen; **that fashion's** ~ das ist nicht mehr Mode; **the ball was** ~ der Ball war aus; **the flowers are** ~ die Blumen blühen; **he was** ~ **in his calculations** seine Berechnungen waren nicht richtig; **to be** ~ **for sth** auf etw (acc) aus sein; ~ **loud** ad laut; ~ **of** prep aus; (away from) außerhalb (+gen); **to be** ~ **of milk** etc keine Milch etc mehr haben; **made** ~ **of wood** aus Holz gemacht; ~ **of danger** außer Gefahr; ~ **of place** fehl am Platz; ~ **of curiosity** aus Neugier; **nine** ~ **of ten** neun von zehn; ~ **and** ~ durch und durch; ~**-of-bounds** a verboten; ~**-of-date** a veraltet; ~**-of-doors** ad im Freien; ~**-of-the-way** a (off the general route) abgelegen; (unusual) ungewöhnlich.

outback ['aʊtbæk] n Hinterland nt.

outboard (motor) ['aʊtbɔːd ('məʊtə*)] n Außenbordmotor m.

outbreak ['aʊtbreɪk] n Ausbruch m.

outbuilding ['aʊtbɪldɪŋ] n Nebengebäude nt.

outburst ['aʊtbɜːst] n Ausbruch m.

outcast ['aʊtkɑːst] n Ausgestoßene(r) mf.

outclass [aʊt'klɑːs] vt übertreffen.

outcome ['aʊtkʌm] n Ergebnis nt.

outcry ['aʊtkraɪ] n Protest m.

outdated ['aʊt'deɪtɪd] a veraltet, überholt.

outdo [aʊt'duː] vt irreg übertrumpfen.

outdoor ['aʊtdɔː*] a Außen-; (Sport) im Freien.

outdoors ['aʊt'dɔːz] ad draußen, im Freien; **to go** ~ ins Freie or nach draußen gehen.

outer ['aʊtə*] a äußere(r, s); ~ **space** Weltraum m.

outfit ['aʊtfɪt] n Ausrüstung f; (set of clothes) Kleidung f; ~**ters** (for men's clothes) Herrenausstatter m.

outgoings ['aʊtgəʊɪŋz] npl Ausgaben pl.

outgrow [aʊt'grəʊ] vt irreg clothes herauswachsen aus; habit ablegen.

outing ['aʊtɪŋ] n Ausflug m.

outlandish [aʊt'lændɪʃ] a eigenartig.

outlaw ['aʊtlɔː] n Geächtete(r) m; vt ächten; (thing) verbieten.

outlay ['aʊtleɪ] n Auslage f.

outlet ['aʊtlet] n Auslaß m, Abfluß m; (Comm) Absatzmarkt m; (for emotions) Ventil nt.

outline ['aʊtlaɪn] n Umriß m.

outlive [aʊt'lɪv] vt überleben.

outlook ['aʊtlʊk] n (lit, fig) Aussicht f; (attitude) Einstellung f.

outlying ['aʊtlaɪɪŋ] a entlegen; district Außen-.

outmoded [aʊt'məʊdɪd] a veraltet.

outnumber [aʊt'nʌmbə*] vt zahlenmäßig überlegen sein (+dat).

outpatient ['aʊtpeɪʃənt] n ambulante(r) Patient(in f) m.

outpost ['aʊtpəʊst] n (Mil, fig) Vorposten m.

output ['aʊtpʊt] n Leistung f, Produktion f.

outrage ['aʊtreɪdʒ] n (cruel deed) Aus-

schreitung f, Verbrechen nt; (indecency) Skandal m; vt morals verstoßen gegen; person empören; ~**ous** [aʊt'reɪdʒəs] a unerhört, empörend.

outright ['aʊtraɪt] ad (at once) sofort; (openly) ohne Umschweife; **to refuse** ~ rundweg ablehnen; a denial völlig; sale Total-; winner unbestritten.

outset ['aʊtset] n Beginn m.

outside ['aʊt'saɪd] n Außenseite f; **on the** ~ außen; **at the very** ~ höchstens; a äußere(r, s), Außen-; price Höchst-; chance gering; ad außen; **to go** ~ nach draußen or hinaus gehen; prep außerhalb (+gen); ~**r** Außenseiter(in f) m.

outsize ['aʊtsaɪz] a übergroß.

outskirts ['aʊtskɜːts] npl Stadtrand m.

outspoken [aʊt'spəʊkən] a offen, freimütig.

outstanding [aʊt'stændɪŋ] a hervorragend; debts etc ausstehend.

outstay [aʊt'steɪ] vt: ~ **one's welcome** länger bleiben als erwünscht.

outstretched [aʊt'stretʃt] a ausgestreckt.

outward ['aʊtwəd] a äußere(r, s); journey Hin-; freight ausgehend; ad nach außen; ~**ly** ad äußerlich.

outweigh [aʊt'weɪ] vt (fig) überwiegen.

outwit [aʊt'wɪt] vt überlisten.

outworn [aʊt'wɔːn] a expression abgedroschen.

oval ['əʊvəl] a oval; n Oval nt.

ovary ['əʊvərɪ] n Eierstock m.

ovation [əʊ'veɪʃən] n Beifallssturm m.

oven ['ʌvn] n Backofen m.

over ['əʊvə*] ad (across) hinüber/herüber; (finished) vorbei; (left) übrig; (again) wieder, noch einmal; prep über; (in every part of) in; pref (excessively) übermäßig; **famous the world** ~ in der ganzen Welt berühmt; **five times** ~ fünfmal; **the weekend** über's Wochenende; ~ **coffee** bei einer Tasse Kaffee; ~ **the phone** am Telephon; **all** ~ (everywhere) überall; (finished) vorbei; ~ **and** ~ immer wieder; ~ **and above** darüber hinaus.

over- ['əʊvə*] pref über-.

overact ['əʊvər'ækt] vi übertreiben.

overall ['əʊvərɔːl] n (Brit) (for woman) Kittelschürze f; a situation allgemein; length Gesamt-; ad insgesamt; ~**s** pl (for man) Overall m.

overawe [əʊvər'ɔː] vt (frighten) einschüchtern; (make impression) überwältigen.

overbalance [əʊvə'bæləns] vi Übergewicht bekommen.

overbearing [əʊvə'bɛərɪŋ] a aufdringlich.

overboard ['əʊvəbɔːd] ad über Bord.

overcast ['əʊvəkɑːst] a bedeckt.

overcharge ['əʊvə'tʃɑːdʒ] vt zuviel verlangen von.

overcoat ['əʊvəkəʊt] n Mantel m.

overcome [əʊvə'kʌm] vt irreg überwinden; (sleep, emotion) übermannen; ~ **by the song** vom Lied gerührt.

overcrowded [əʊvə'kraʊdɪd] a überfüllt.

overcrowding [əʊvə'kraʊdɪŋ] n Überfüllung f.

overdo ['ouvə'du:] vt irreg (cook too much) verkochen; (exaggerate) übertreiben.
overdose ['ouvədous] n Überdosis f.
overdraft ['ouvədra:ft] n (Konto)Überziehung f; **to have an ~** sein Konto überzogen haben.
overdrawn ['ouvə'drɔ:n] a account überzogen.
overdrive ['ouvədraɪv] n (Aut) Schnellgang m.
overdue ['ouvə'dju:] a überfällig.
overenthusiastic ['ouvərɪnθju:zɪ'æstɪk] a zu begeistert.
overestimate ['ouvər'estɪmeɪt] vt überschätzen.
overexcited ['ouvərɪk'saɪtɪd] a überreizt; children aufgeregt.
overexertion ['ouvərɪg'zɜ:ʃən] n Überanstrengung f.
overexpose ['ouvərɪks'pəuz] vt (Phot) überbelichten.
overflow [ouvə'fləu] vi überfließen; ['ouvəfləu] n (excess) Überschuß m; (outlet) Überlauf m.
overgrown ['ouvə'grəun] a garden verwildert.
overhaul [ouvə'hɔ:l] vt car überholen; plans überprüfen; ['ouvəhɔ:l] n Überholung f.
overhead ['ouvəhed] a Hoch-; wire oberirdisch; lighting Decken-; ['ouvə'hed] ad oben; **~s** pl allgemeine Unkosten pl.
overhear [ouvə'hɪə*] vt irreg (mit an)hören.
overjoyed [ouvə'dʒɔɪd] a überglücklich.
overland ['ouvəlænd] a Überland-; [ouvə'lænd] ad travel über Land.
overlap [ouvə'læp] vi sich überschneiden; (objects) sich teilweise decken; ['ouvəlæp] n Überschneidung f.
overload [ouvə'ləud] vt überladen.
overlook [ouvə'luk] vt (view from above) überblicken; (not to notice) übersehen; (pardon) hinwegsehen über (+acc).
overlord ['ouvələ:d] n Lehnsherr m.
overnight [ouvə'naɪt] a journey Nacht-; ad über Nacht; **~ bag** Reisetasche f; **~ stay** Übernachtung f.
overpass ['ouvəpɑ:s] n Überführung f.
overpower [ouvə'pauə*] vt überwältigen; **~ing** a überwältigend.
overrate [ouvə'reɪt] vt überschätzen.
override [ouvə'raɪd] vt irreg order, decision aufheben; objection übergehen.
overriding [ouvə'raɪdɪŋ] a Haupt-, vorherrschend.
overrule [ouvə'ru:l] vt verwerfen; **we were ~d** unser Vorschlag wurde verworfen.
overseas ['ouvə'si:z] ad nach/in Übersee; a überseeisch, Übersee-.
overseer ['ouvəsɪə*] n Aufseher m.
overshadow [ouvə'ʃædəu] vt überschatten.
overshoot ['ouvə'ʃu:t] vt irreg runway hinausschießen über (+acc).
oversight ['ouvəsaɪt] n (mistake) Versehen nt.
oversimplify ['ouvə'sɪmplɪfaɪ] vt zu sehr vereinfachen.
oversleep ['ouvə'sli:p] vi irreg verschlafen.

overspill ['ouvəspɪl] n (Bevölkerungs)überschuß m.
overstate ['ouvə'steɪt] vt übertreiben; **~ment** Übertreibung f.
overt [ou'vɜ:t] a offen(kundig).
overtake [ouvə'teɪk] vti irreg überholen.
overthrow [ouvə'θrəu] vt irreg (Pol) stürzen.
overtime ['ouvətaɪm] n Überstunden pl.
overtone ['ouvətəun] n (fig) Note f.
overture ['ouvətjuə*] n Ouvertüre f; **~s** pl (fig) Angebot nt.
overturn [ouvə'tɜ:n] vti umkippen.
overweight ['ouvə'weɪt] a zu dick, zu schwer.
overwhelm [ouvə'welm] vt überwältigen; **~ing** a überwältigend.
overwork [ouvə'wɜ:k] n Überarbeitung f; vt überlasten; vi sich überarbeiten.
overwrought ['ouvə'rɔ:t] a überreizt.
owe [ou] vt schulden; **to ~ sth to sb** money jdm etw schulden; favour etc jdm etw verdanken.
owing to ['ouɪŋ'tu:] prep wegen (+gen).
owl [aul] n Eule f.
own [oun] vt besitzen; (admit) zugeben; **who ~s that?** wem gehört das?; a eigen; **I have money of my ~** ich habe selbst Geld; n Eigentum nt; **all my ~** mein Eigentum, on one's ~ allein; **~ up** vi zugeben (to sth etw acc); **~er** Besitzer(in f) m, Eigentümer(in f) m; **~ership** Besitz m.
ox [ɒks] n Ochse m.
oxide ['ɒksaɪd] n Oxyd nt.
oxtail ['ɒksteɪl] n: **~ soup** Ochsenschwanzsuppe f.
oxyacetylene ['ɒksɪə'setɪli:n] a Azetylensauerstoff-.
oxygen ['ɒksɪdʒən] n Sauerstoff m; **~ mask** Sauerstoffmaske f; **~ tent** Sauerstoffzelt nt.
oyster ['ɔɪstə*] n Auster f.
ozone ['əuzəun] n Ozon nt.

P

P, p [pi:] n P nt, p nt.
pa [pɑ:] n (col) Papa m.
pace [peɪs] n Schritt m; (speed) Geschwindigkeit f, Tempo nt; vi schreiten; **to keep ~ with** Schritt halten mit; **~-maker** Schrittmacher m.
pacification [pæsɪfɪ'keɪʃən] n Befriedung f.
pacifism ['pæsɪfɪzəm] n Pazifismus m.
pacifist ['pæsɪfɪst] n Pazifist m.
pacify ['pæsɪfaɪ] vt befrieden; (calm) beruhigen.
pack [pæk] n Packen m; (of wolves) Rudel nt; (of hounds) Meute f; (of cards) Spiel nt; (gang) Bande f; vti case packen; clothes einpacken; **~age** Paket nt; **~age tour** Pauschalreise; f; **~et** Päckchen nt; **~horse** Packpferd nt; **~ ice** Packeis nt; **~ing** (action) Packen nt; (material) Verpackung f; **~ing case** (Pack)kiste f.
pact [pækt] n Pakt m, Vertrag m.
pad [pæd] n (of paper) (Schreib)block m;

(for inking) Stempelkissen *nt; (padding)* Polster *nt; vt* polstern.

paddle ['pædl] *n* Paddel *nt; vt boat* paddeln; *vi (in sea)* plantschen.

paddling pool ['pædlɪŋ puːl] *n* Plantschbecken *nt.*

paddock ['pædək] *n* Koppel *f.*

paddy ['pædɪ] *n* — **field** Reisfeld *nt.*

padlock ['pædlɒk] *n* Vorhängeschloß *nt.*

padre ['pɑːdrɪ] *n* Militärgeistliche(r) *m.*

paediatrics [piːdɪ'ætrɪks] *n* Kinderheilkunde *f.*

pagan ['peɪgən] *a* heidnisch.

page [peɪdʒ] *n* Seite *f; (person)* Page *m; vt (in hotel etc)* ausrufen lassen.

pageant ['pædʒənt] *n* Festzug *m;* —**ry** Gepränge *nt.*

pagoda [pə'gəʊdə] *n* Pagode *f.*

pail [peɪl] *n* Eimer *m.*

pain [peɪn] *n* Schmerz *m,* Schmerzen *pl;* —**s** *(efforts)* große Mühe *f,* große Anstrengungen *pl;* **to be at** —**s to do sth** sich *(dat)* Mühe geben, etw zu tun; —**ed** *expression* gequält; —**ful** *a (physically)* schmerzhaft; *(embarrassing)* peinlich; *(difficult)* mühsam; —**killing drug** schmerzstillendes *nt* Mittel *nt;* —**less** *a* schmerzlos; —**staking** *a* gewissenhaft.

paint [peɪnt] *n* Farbe *f; vt* anstreichen; *picture* malen; —**brush** Pinsel *m;* —**er** Maler *m; (decorator)* Maler *m,* Anstreicher *m;* —**ing** *(act)* Malen *nt; (Art)* Malerei *f; (picture)* Bild *nt,* Gemälde *nt.*

pair [pɛə*] *n* Paar *nt;* — **of scissors** Schere *f;* — **of trousers** Hose *f.*

pajamas *(US)* [pə'dʒɑːməz] *npl* Schlafanzug *m.*

pal [pæl] *n (col)* Kumpel *m; (woman)* (gute) Freundin *f.*

palace ['pæləs] *n* Palast *m,* Schloß *nt.*

palatable ['pælətəbl] *a* schmackhaft.

palate ['pælɪt] *n* Gaumen *m; (taste)* Geschmack *m.*

palaver [pə'lɑːvə*] *n (col)* Theater *nt.*

pale [peɪl] *a face* blaß, bleich; *colour* hell, blaß; —**ness** Blässe *f.*

palette ['pælɪt] *n* Palette *f.*

palisade [pælɪ'seɪd] *n* Palisade *f.*

pall [pɔːl] *n* Bahr- or Leichentuch *nt; (of smoke)* (Rauch)wolke *f; vi* jeden Reiz verlieren, verblassen; —**bearer** Sargträger *m.*

pallid ['pælɪd] *a* blaß, bleich.

pally ['pælɪ] *a (col)* befreundet.

palm [pɑːm] *n (of hand)* Handfläche *f; (also* — **tree)** Palme *f;* —**ist** Handleserin *f;* **P** — **Sunday** Palmsonntag *m.*

palpable ['pælpəbl] *a (lit, fig)* greifbar.

palpably ['pælpəblɪ] *ad* offensichtlich.

palpitation [pælpɪ'teɪʃən] *n* Herzklopfen *nt.*

paltry ['pɔːltrɪ] *a* armselig.

pamper ['pæmpə*] *vt* verhätscheln.

pamphlet ['pæmflət] *n* Broschüre *f.*

pan [pæn] *n* Pfanne *f; vi (Cine)* schwenken.

pan- [pæn] *pref* Pan-, All-.

panacea [pænə'sɪə] *n (fig)* Allheilmittel *nt.*

panache [pə'næʃ] *n* Schwung *m.*

pancake ['pænkeɪk] *n* Pfannkuchen *m.*

panda ['pændə] *n* Panda *m.*

pandemonium [pændɪ'məʊnɪəm] *n* Hölle *f; (noise)* Höllenlärm *m.*

pander ['pændə*] *vi* sich richten *(to* nach).

pane [peɪn] *n* (Fenster)scheibe *f.*

panel ['pænl] *n (of wood)* Tafel *f; (TV)* Diskussionsteilnehmer *pl;* —**ing** *(US),* —**ling** Täfelung *f.*

pang [pæŋ] *n* Stich *m,* Qual *f;* —**s of conscience** Gewissensbisse *pl.*

panic ['pænɪk] *n* Panik *f; a* panisch; *vi* von panischem Schrecken erfaßt werden, durchdrehen; **don't** — (nur) keine Panik; —**ky** *a person* überängstlich.

pannier ['pænɪə*] *n* (Trage)korb *m; (on bike)* Satteltasche *f.*

panorama [pænə'rɑːmə] *n* Rundblick *m,* Panorama *nt.*

panoramic [pænə'ræmɪk] *a* Panorama-.

pansy ['pænzɪ] *n (flower)* Stiefmütterchen *nt; (col)* Schwule(r) *m.*

pant [pænt] *vi* keuchen; *(dog)* hecheln.

pantechnicon [pæn'teknɪkən] *n* Möbelwagen *m.*

panther ['pænθə*] *n* Panther *m.*

panties ['pæntɪz] *npl* (Damen)slip *m.*

pantomime ['pæntəmaɪm] *n* Märchenkomödie *f* um Weihnachten.

pantry ['pæntrɪ] *n* Vorratskammer *f.*

pants [pænts] *npl* Unterhose *f; (trousers)* Hose *f.*

papal ['peɪpəl] *a* päpstlich.

paper ['peɪpə*] *n* Papier *nt; (newspaper)* Zeitung *f; (essay)* Vortrag *m,* Referat *nt; a* Papier-, aus Papier; *vt wall* tapezieren; —**s** *pl (identity)* Ausweis(papiere *pl) m;* —**back** Taschenbuch *nt;* — **bag** Tüte *f;* —**clip** Büroklammer *f;* —**weight** Briefbeschwerer *m;* —**work** Schreibarbeit *f.*

papier-mâché ['pæpɪer'mæʃeɪ] *n* Papiermaché *nt.*

paprika ['pæprɪkə] *n* Paprika *m.*

papyrus [pə'paɪərəs] *n* Papyrus *m.*

par [pɑː*] *n (Comm)* Nennwert *m; (Golf)* Par *m;* **on a** — **with** ebenbürtig *(+dat);* **to be on a** — **with sb** sich mit jdm messen können; **below** — unter (jds) Niveau.

parable ['pærəbl] *n* Parabel *f; (Rel)* Gleichnis *nt.*

parachute ['pærəʃuːt] *n* Fallschirm *m; vi* (mit dem Fallschirm) abspringen.

parachutist ['pærəʃuːtɪst] *n* Fallschirmspringer *m.*

parade [pə'reɪd] *n* Parade *f; vt* aufmarschieren lassen; *vi* paradieren, vorbeimarschieren.

paradise ['pærədaɪs] *n* Paradies *nt.*

paradox ['pærədɒks] *n* Paradox *nt;* —**ical** [pærə'dɒksɪkəl] *a* paradox, widersinnig; —**ically** [pærə'dɒksɪkəlɪ] *ad* paradoxerweise.

paraffin ['pærəfɪn] *n* Paraffin *nt.*

paragraph ['pærəgrɑːf] *n* Absatz *m,* Paragraph *m.*

parallel ['pærəlel] *a* parallel; *n* Parallele *f.*

paralysis [pə'rælɪsɪs] *n* Lähmung *f.*

paralyze ['pærəlaɪz] *vt* lähmen.

paramount ['pærəmaunt] *a* höchste(r, s), oberste(r, s).

paranoia [pærə'nɔɪə] n Paranoia f.

parapet ['pærəpɪt] n Brüstung f.

paraphernalia ['pærəfə'neɪlɪə] n Zubehör nt, Utensilien pl.

paraphrase ['pærəfreɪz] vt umschreiben.

paraplegic [pærə'pli:dʒɪk] n Querschnittsgelähmte(r) mf.

parasite ['pærəsaɪt] n (lit, fig) Schmarotzer m, Parasit m.

parasol ['pærəsɒl] n Sonnenschirm m.

paratrooper ['pærətru:pə*] n Fallschirmjäger m.

parcel ['pɑ:sl] n Paket nt; vt (also ~ up) einpacken.

parch [pɑ:tʃ] vt (aus)dörren; **I'm ~ed** ich bin am Verdursten.

parchment ['pɑ:tʃmənt] n Pergament nt.

pardon ['pɑ:dn] n Verzeihung f; vt (Jur) begnadigen; ~ **me!, I beg your ~!** verzeihen Sie bitte!; (objection) aber ich bitte Sie!; ~ **me?** (US), **(I beg your) ~?** wie bitte?

parent ['pɛərənt] n Elternteil m; ~**al** [pə'rentl] a elterlich, Eltern-; ~**hood** Elternschaft f; ~**s** pl Eltern pl; ~**ship** Mutterschiff nt.

parenthesis [pə'renθɪsɪs] n Klammer f; (sentence) Parenthese f.

parish ['pærɪʃ] n Gemeinde f; ~**ioner** [pə'rɪʃənə*] Gemeindemitglied nt.

parity ['pærɪtɪ] n (Fin) Umrechnungskurs m, Parität f.

park [pɑ:k] n Park m; vti parken; ~**ing** Parken nt; 'no ~**ing'** Parken verboten; ~**ing lot** (US) Parkplatz m; ~**ing meter** Parkuhr f; ~**ing place** Parkplatz m.

parliament ['pɑ:ləmənt] n Parlament nt; ~**ary** [pɑ:lə'mentərɪ] a parlamentarisch, Parlaments-.

parlour, (US) **parlor** ['pɑ:lə*] n Salon m, Wohnzimmer nt.

parlous ['pɑ:ləs] a state schlimm.

parochial [pə'rəʊkɪəl] a Gemeinde-, gemeindlich; (narrow-minded) eng(stirnig), Provinz-.

parody ['pærədɪ] n Parodie f; vt parodieren.

parole [pə'rəʊl] n: **on ~** (prisoner) auf Bewährung.

parquet ['pɑ:keɪ] n Parkett(fußboden m) nt.

parrot ['pærət] n Papagei m; ~ **fashion** ad wie ein Papagei.

parry ['pærɪ] vt parieren, abwehren.

parsimonious a, ~**ly** ad [pɑ:sɪ'məʊnɪəs, -lɪ] knauserig.

parsley ['pɑ:slɪ] n Petersilie m.

parsnip ['pɑ:snɪp] n Pastinake f, Petersilienwurzel f.

parson ['pɑ:sn] n Pfarrer m.

part [pɑ:t] n (piece) Teil m, Stück nt; (Theat) Rolle f; (of machine) Teil nt; a Teil-; ad = **partly**; vt trennen; hair scheiteln; vi (people) sich trennen, Abschied nehmen; **for my ~** ich für meinen Teil; **for the most ~** meistens, größtenteils; ~ **with** vt hergeben; (renounce) aufgeben; **in ~ exchange** in Zahlung; ~**ial** ['pɑ:ʃəl] a (incomplete) teilweise, Teil-; (biased) ein-

genommen, parteiisch; eclipse partiell; **to be ~ial to** eine (besondere) Vorliebe haben für; ~**ially** ['pɑ:ʃəlɪ] ad teilweise, zum Teil.

participate [pɑ:'tɪsɪpeɪt] vi teilnehmen (in an +dat).

participation [pɑ:tɪsɪ'peɪʃən] n Teilnahme f; (sharing) Beteiligung f.

participle ['pɑ:tɪsɪpl] n Partizip nt, Mittelwort nt.

particular [pə'tɪkjʊlə*] a bestimmt, speziell; (exact) genau; (fussy) eigen; n Einzelheit f; ~**s** pl (details) Einzelheiten pl; Personalien pl; ~**ly** ad besonders.

parting ['pɑ:tɪŋ] n (separation) Abschied m, Trennung f; (of hair) Scheitel m; a Abschieds-.

partisan [pɑ:tɪ'zæn] n Parteigänger m; (guerrilla) Partisan m; a Partei-, Partisanen-.

partition [pɑ:'tɪʃən] n (wall) Trennwand f; (division) Teilung f.

partly ['pɑ:tlɪ] ad zum Teil, teilweise.

partner ['pɑ:tnə*] n Partner m; (Comm also) Gesellschafter m, Teilhaber m; vt der Partner sein von; ~**ship** Partnerschaft f, Gemeinschaft f; (Comm) Teilhaberschaft f.

partridge ['pɑ:trɪdʒ] n Rebhuhn m.

part-time ['pɑ:t'taɪm] a (half-day only) halbtägig, Halbtags-; (part of the week only) nebenberuflich; ad halbtags; nebenberuflich.

party ['pɑ:tɪ] n (Pol, Jur) Partei f; (group) Gesellschaft f; (celebration) Party f; a dress Gesellschafts-, Party-; politics Partei-.

pass [pɑ:s] vt vorbeikommen an (+dat); (on foot) vorbeigehen an (+dat); vorbeifahren an (+dat); (surpass) übersteigen; (hand on) weitergeben; (approve) gelten lassen, genehmigen; time verbringen; exam bestehen; vi (go by) vorbeigehen, vorbeifahren; (years) vergehen; (be successful) bestehen; in (mountains) Paß m; (permission) Durchgangs- or Passierschein m; (Sport) Paß m, Abgabe f; (in exam) Bestehen nt; **to get a ~** bestehen; ~ **away** vi (euph) verscheiden; ~ **by** vi vorbeigehen; vorbeifahren; (years) vergehen; ~ **for** vi gehalten werden für; ~ **out** vi (faint) ohnmächtig werden; ~**able** a road passierbar, befahrbar; (fairly good) passabel, leidlich; ~**ably** ad leidlich, ziemlich; ~**age** ['pæsɪdʒ] (corridor) Gang m, Korridor m; (in book) (Text)stelle f; (voyage) Überfahrt f; ~**ageway** Passage f, Durchgang m.

passenger ['pæsɪndʒə*] n Passagier m; (on bus) Fahrgast m; (in aeroplane also) Fluggast m.

passer-by [pɑ:sə'baɪ] n Passant(in f) m.

passing ['pɑ:sɪŋ] n (death) Ableben nt; a car vorbeifahrend; thought, affair momentan; **in ~** en passant.

passion ['pæʃən] n Leidenschaft f; ~**ate** a, ~**ately** ad leidenschaftlich.

passive ['pæsɪv] n Passiv nt; a Passiv-, passiv.

Passover ['pɑ:səʊvə*] n Passahfest nt.

passport ['pɑ:spɔ:t] n (Reise)paß m.

password ['pɑːswɜːd] n Parole f, Kennwort nt, Losung f.

past [pɑːst] n Vergangenheit f; ad vorbei; prep **to go ~ sth** an etw (dat) vorbeigehen; **to be ~ 10** (with age) über 10 sein; (with time) nach 10 sein; **a years vergangen;** president etc ehemalig.

paste [peɪst] n (for pastry) Teig m; (fish — etc) Paste f; (glue) Kleister m; vt kleben; (put — on) mit Kleister bestreichen.

pastel ['pæstəl] a colour Pastell-.

pasteurized ['pæstəraɪzd] a pasteurisiert.

pastille ['pæstɪl] n Pastille f.

pastime ['pɑːstaɪm] n Hobby nt, Zeitvertreib m.

pastor ['pɑːstə*] n Pastor m, Pfarrer m.

pastoral ['pɑːstərəl] a literature Schäfer-, Pastoral-.

pastry ['peɪstrɪ] n Blätterteig m; (tarts etc) Stückchen pl; Tortengebäck nt.

pasture ['pɑːstʃə*] n Weide f.

pasty ['pæstɪ] n (Fleisch)pastete f; ['peɪstɪ] a bläßlich, käsig.

pat [pæt] n leichte(r) Schlag m, Klaps m; vt tätscheln.

patch [pætʃ] n Fleck m; vt flicken; **~ of fog** Nebelfeld nt; **a bad ~** eine Pechsträhne; **~work** Patchwork nt; **~y** a (irregular) ungleichmäßig.

pate [peɪt] n Schädel m.

patent ['peɪtənt] n Patent nt; vt patentieren lassen; (by authorities) patentieren; a offenkundig; **~ leather** Lackleder nt; **~ly** ad offensichtlich; **~ medicine** pharmazeutische(s) Präparat nt.

paternal [pə'tɜːnl] a väterlich; **his ~ grandmother** seine Großmutter väterlicherseits; **~istic** [pətɜːnə'lɪstɪk] a väterlich, onkelhaft.

paternity [pə'tɜːnɪtɪ] n Vaterschaft f.

path [pɑːθ] n Pfad m; Weg m; (of the sun) Bahn f.

pathetic a, **~ally** ad [pə'θetɪk, -lɪ] (very bad) kläglich; **it's ~** es ist zum Weinen.

pathological [pæθə'lɒdʒɪkəl] a krankhaft, pathologisch.

pathologist [pə'θɒlədʒɪst] n Pathologe m.

pathology [pə'θɒlədʒɪ] n Pathologie f.

pathos ['peɪθɒs] n Rührseligkeit f.

pathway ['pɑːθweɪ] n Pfad m, Weg m.

patience ['peɪʃəns] n Geduld f; (Cards) Patience f.

patient ['peɪʃənt] n Patient(in f) m, Kranke(r) mf; a, **~ly** ad geduldig.

patio ['pætɪəʊ] n Innenhof m; (outside) Terrasse f.

patriotic [pætrɪ'ɒtɪk] a patriotisch.

patriotism ['pætrɪətɪzəm] n Patriotismus m.

patrol [pə'trəʊl] n Patrouille f; (police) Streife f; vt patrouillieren in (+dat); vi (police) die Runde machen; (Mil) patrouillieren; **on ~** (police) auf Streife; **~ car** Streifenwagen m; **~man** (US) (Streifen)polizist m.

patron ['peɪtrən] n (in shop) (Stamm)kunde m; (in hotel) (Stamm)gast m; (supporter) Förderer m; **~age** ['pætrənɪdʒ] Förderung f; Schirmherrschaft f; (Comm) Kundschaft f; **~ize** also ['pætrənaɪz] vt (support) unterstützen; shop besuchen; ['pætrənaɪz] (treat condescendingly) von oben herab behandeln; **~izing** a attitude herablassend; **~ saint** Schutzheilige(r) mf, Schutzpatron(in f) m.

patter ['pætə*] n (sound) (of feet) Trappeln nt; (of rain) Prasseln nt; (sales talk) Art f zu reden, Gerede nt; vi (feet) trappeln; (rain) prasseln.

pattern ['pætən] n Muster nt; (sewing) Schnittmuster nt; (knitting) Strickanleitung f; vt **~ sth on sth** etw nach etw bilden.

paunch [pɔːntʃ] n dicke(r) Bauch m, Wanst m.

pauper ['pɔːpə*] n Arme(r) mf.

pause [pɔːz] n Pause f; vi innehalten.

pave [peɪv] vt pflastern; **to ~ the way for** den Weg bahnen für; **~ment** (Brit) Bürgersteig m.

pavilion [pə'vɪlɪən] n Pavillon m; (Sport) Klubhaus m.

paving ['peɪvɪŋ] n Straßenpflaster nt.

paw [pɔː] n Pfote f; (of big cats) Tatze f, Pranke f; vt (scrape) scharren; (handle) betatschen.

pawn [pɔːn] n Pfand nt; (chess) Bauer m; vt versetzen, verpfänden; **~broker** Pfandleiher m; **~shop** Pfandhaus nt.

pay [peɪ] n Bezahlung f, Lohn m; **to be in sb's ~** von jdm bezahlt werden; irreg vt bezahlen; **it would ~ you to ...** es würde sich für dich lohnen, zu ...; **to ~ attention** achtgeben (to auf +acc); vi zahlen; (be profitable) sich bezahlt machen; **it doesn't ~** es lohnt sich nicht; **~ for** vt bezahlen für; **~ up** vi bezahlen, seine Schulden begleichen; **~able** a zahlbar, fällig; **~day** Zahltag m; **~ee** [peɪ'iː] Zahlungsempfänger m; **~ing** a einträglich, rentabel; **~load** Nutzlast f; **~ment** Bezahlung f; **~ packet** Lohntüte f; **~roll** Lohnliste f.

pea [piː] n Erbse f; **~ souper** (col) Suppe f, Waschküche f.

peace [piːs] n Friede(n) m; **~able** a, **~ably** ad friedlich; **~ful** a friedlich, ruhig; **~-keeping** a Friedens-; **~-keeping role** Vermittlerrolle f; **~ offering** Friedensangebot nt; **~time** Friede(n) m.

peach [piːtʃ] n Pfirsich m.

peacock ['piːkɒk] n Pfau m.

peak [piːk] n Spitze f; (of mountain) Gipfel m; (fig) Höhepunkt m; (of cap) (Mützen)schirm m; **~ period** Stoßzeit f, Hauptzeit f.

peal [piːl] n (Glocken)läuten nt.

peanut ['piːnʌt] n Erdnuß f; **~ butter** Erdnußbutter f.

pear [peə*] n Birne f.

pearl [pɜːl] n Perle f.

peasant ['pezənt] n Bauer m.

peat [piːt] n Torf m.

pebble ['pebl] n Kiesel m.

peck [pek] vti picken; n (with beak) Schnabelhieb m; (kiss) flüchtige(r) Kuß m; **~ish** a (col) ein bißchen hungrig.

peculiar [pɪ'kjuːlɪə*] a (odd) seltsam; **~ to** charakteristisch für; **~ity** [pɪkjʊlɪ'ærɪtɪ] (singular quality) Besonderheit f; (strange-

ness) Eigenartigkeit *f;* ~**ly** *ad* seltsam; *(especially)* besonders.

pecuniary [pɪ'kjuːnɪərɪ] *a* Geld-, finanziell, pekuniär.

pedal ['pedl] *n* Pedal *nt; vti (cycle)* fahren, radfahren.

pedant ['pedənt] *n* Pedant *m.*

pedantic [pɪ'dæntɪk] *a* pedantisch.

pedantry ['pedəntrɪ] *n* Pedanterie *f.*

peddle ['pedl] *vt* hausieren gehen mit.

pedestal ['pedɪstl] *n* Sockel *m.*

pedestrian [pɪ'destrɪən] *n* Fußgänger *m; a* Fußgänger-; *(humdrum)* langweilig; ~ **crossing** Fußgängerüberweg *m;* ~ **precinct** Fußgängerzone *f.*

pediatrics [piːdɪ'ætrɪks] *n (US)* = **paediatrics.**

pedigree ['pedɪgriː] *n* Stammbaum *m; a animal* reinrassig, Zucht-.

pee [piː] *vi (col)* pissen, pinkeln.

peek [piːk] *n* flüchtige(r) Blick *m; vi* gucken.

peel [piːl] *n* Schale *f; vt* schälen; *vi (paint etc)* abblättern; *(skin)* sich schälen; ~**ings** *pl* Schalen *pl.*

peep [piːp] *n (look)* neugierige(r) Blick *m; (sound)* Piepsen *nt; vi (look)* neugierig gucken; ~**hole** Guckloch *nt.*

peer [pɪə*] *vi* spähen; angestrengt schauen *(at* auf *+acc); (peep)* gucken; *n (nobleman)* Peer *m; (equal)* Ebenbürtige(r) *m;* **his** ~**s** seinesgleichen; ~**age** Peerswürde *f;* ~**less** *a* unvergleichlich.

peeve [piːv] *vt (col)* verärgern; ~**d** *a* ärgerlich; *person* sauer.

peevish ['piːvɪʃ] *a* verdrießlich, brummig; ~**ness** Verdrießlichkeit *f.*

peg [peg] *n* Stift *m; (hook)* Haken *m; (stake)* Pflock *m;* **clothes** ~ Wäscheklammer *f;* **off the** ~ von der Stange.

pejorative [pɪ'dʒɒrɪtɪv] *a* pejorativ, herabsetzend.

pekinese [piːkɪ'niːz] *n* Pekinese *m.*

pelican ['pelɪkən] *n* Pelikan *m.*

pellet ['pelɪt] *n* Kügelchen *nt.*

pelmet ['pelmɪt] *n* Blende *f,* Schabracke *f.*

pelt [pelt] *vt* bewerfen; *n* Pelz *m,* Fell *nt;* ~ **down** *vi* niederprasseln.

pelvis ['pelvɪs] *n* Becken *nt.*

pen [pen] *n (fountain* ~*)* Federhalter *m; (ball-point)* Kuli *m; (for sheep)* Pferch *m;* **have you got a** ~**?** haben Sie etwas zum Schreiben?

penal ['piːnl] *a* Straf-; ~**ize** *vt (make punishable)* unter Strafe stellen; *(punish)* bestrafen; *(disadvantage)* benachteiligen; ~**ty** ['penltɪ] Strafe *f; (Ftbl)* Elfmeter *m;* ~**ty area** Strafraum *m;* ~**ty kick** Elfmeter *m.*

penance ['penəns] *n* Buße *f.*

pence [pens] *npl (pl of* penny*)* Pence *pl.*

penchant [pɑ̃ːʃɑ̃ːŋ] *n* Vorliebe *f,* Schwäche *f.*

pencil ['pensl] *n* Bleistift *m;* ~ **sharpener** Bleistiftspitzer *m.*

pendant ['pendənt] *n* Anhänger *m.*

pending ['pendɪŋ] *prep* bis (zu); *a* unentschieden, noch offen.

pendulum ['pendjʊləm] *n* Pendel *nt.*

penetrate ['penɪtreɪt] *vt* durchdringen; *(enter into)* eindringen in *(+acc).*

penetrating ['penɪtreɪtɪŋ] *a* durchdringend; *analysis* scharfsinnig.

penetration [penɪ'treɪʃən] *n* Durchdringen *nt;* Eindringen *nt.*

penfriend ['penfrend] *n* Brieffreund(in *f) m.*

penguin ['peŋgwɪn] *n* Pinguin *m.*

penicillin [penɪ'sɪlɪn] *n* Penizillin *nt.*

peninsula [pɪ'nɪnsjʊlə] *n* Halbinsel *f.*

penis ['piːnɪs] *n* Penis *m,* männliche(s) Glied *nt.*

penitence ['penɪtəns] *n* Reue *f.*

penitent ['penɪtənt] *a* reuig; ~**iary** [penɪ'tenʃərɪ] *(US)* Zuchthaus *nt.*

penknife ['pennaɪf] *n* Federmesser *nt.*

pen name ['penneɪm] *n* Pseudonym *nt.*

pennant ['penənt] *n* Wimpel *m; (official* ~*)* Stander *m.*

penniless ['penɪləs] *a* mittellos, ohne einen Pfennig.

penny ['penɪ] *n* Penny *m.*

pension ['penʃən] *n* Rente *f; (for civil servants, executives etc)* Ruhegehalt *nt,* Pension *f;* ~**able** *a person* pensionsberechtigt; *job* mit Renten- or Pensionsanspruch; ~**er** Rentner(in *f) m; (civil servant, executive)* Pensionär *m;* ~ **fund** Rentenfonds *m.*

pensive ['pensɪv] *a* nachdenklich.

pentagon ['pentəgən] *n* Fünfeck *nt.*

Pentecost ['pentɪkɒst] *n* Pfingsten *pl or nt.*

penthouse ['penthaʊs] *n* Dachterrassenwohnung *f.*

pent-up ['pentʌp] *a feelings* angestaut.

penultimate [pɪ'nʌltɪmət] *a* vorletzte(r, s).

people ['piːpl] *n (nation)* Volk *nt; (inhabitants)* Bevölkerung *f; (persons)* Leute *pl;* ~ **think** man glaubt; *vt* besiedeln.

pep [pep] *n (col)* Schwung *m,* Schmiß *m;* ~ **up** *vt* aufmöbeln.

pepper ['pepə*] *n* Pfeffer *m; (vegetable)* Paprika *m; vt (pelt)* bombardieren; ~**mint** *(plant)* Pfefferminze *f; (sweet)* Pfefferminz *nt.*

peptalk ['peptɔːk] *n (col)* Anstachelung *f.*

per [pɜː*] *prep* pro; ~ **annum** pro Jahr; ~ **cent** Prozent *nt.*

perceive [pə'siːv] *vt (realize)* wahrnehmen, spüren; *(understand)* verstehen.

percentage [pə'sentɪdʒ] *n* Prozentsatz *m.*

perceptible [pə'septəbl] *a* merklich, wahrnehmbar.

perception [pə'sepʃən] *n* Wahrnehmung *f; (insight)* Einsicht *f.*

perceptive [pə'septɪv] *a person* aufmerksam; *analysis* tiefgehend.

perch [pɜːtʃ] *n* Stange *f; (fish)* Flußbarsch *m; vi* sitzen, hocken.

percolator ['pɜːkəleɪtə*] *n* Kaffeemaschine *f.*

percussion [pə'kʌʃən] *n (Mus)* Schlagzeug *nt.*

peremptory [pə'remptərɪ] *a* schroff.

perennial [pə'renɪəl] *a* wiederkehrend; *(everlasting)* unvergänglich; *n* perennierende Pflanze *f.*

perfect ['pɜːfɪkt] *a* vollkommen; *crime,*

solution perfekt; *(Gram)* vollendet; *n (Gram)* Perfekt *nt;* [pəˈfekt] *vt* vervollkommnen; ~**ion** [pəˈfekʃən] Vollkommenheit *f;* ~**ionist** [pəˈfekʃənɪst] Perfektionist *m;* ~**ly** *ad* vollkommen, perfekt; *(quite)* ganz, einfach.

perforate [ˈpɜːfəreɪt] *vt* durchlöchern; ~**d** *a* durchlöchert, perforiert.

perforation [pɜːfəˈreɪʃən] *n* Perforation *f.*

perform [pəˈfɔːm] *vt (carry out)* durch- or ausführen; *task* verrichten; *(Theat)* spielen, geben; *vi (Theat)* auftreten; ~**ance** Durchführung *f; (efficiency)* Leistung *f; (show)* Vorstellung *f;* ~**er** Künstler(in *f*) *m;* ~**ing** *a animal* dressiert.

perfume [ˈpɜːfjuːm] *n* Duft *m; (lady's)* Parfüm *nt.*

perfunctory [pəˈfʌŋktərɪ] *a* oberflächlich, mechanisch.

perhaps [pəˈhæps] *ad* vielleicht.

peril [ˈperɪl] *n* Gefahr *f;* ~**ous** *a,* ~**ously** *ad* gefährlich.

perimeter [pəˈrɪmɪtə*] *n* Peripherie *f; (of circle etc)* Umfang *m.*

period [ˈpɪərɪəd] *n* Periode *f,* Zeit *f; (Gram)* Punkt *m; (Med)* Periode *f;* *a costume historisch;* ~**ic(al)** [pɪərɪˈɒdɪk(əl)] *a* periodisch; ~**ical** *n* Zeitschrift *f;* ~**ically** [pɪərɪˈɒdɪkəlɪ] *ad* periodisch.

peripheral [pəˈrɪfərəl] *a* Rand-, peripher.

periphery [pəˈrɪfərɪ] *n* Peripherie *f,* Rand *m.*

periscope [ˈperɪskəʊp] *n* Periskop *nt,* Sehrohr *nt.*

perish [ˈperɪʃ] *vi* umkommen; *(material)* unbrauchbar werden; *(fruit)* verderben; ~ **the thought!** daran wollen wir nicht denken; ~**able** *a fruit* leicht verderblich; ~**ing** *a (col: cold)* eisig.

perjure [ˈpɜːdʒə*] *vr:* ~ **o.s.** einen Meineid leisten.

perjury [ˈpɜːdʒərɪ] *n* Meineid *m.*

perk [pɜːk] *n (col: fringe benefit)* Vorteil *m,* Vergünstigung *f;* ~ **up** *vi* munter werden; *vt* ears spitzen; ~**y** *a (cheerful)* keck.

perm [pɜːm] *n* Dauerwelle *f.*

permanence [ˈpɜːmənəns] *n* Dauer(haftigkeit) *f,* Beständigkeit *f.*

permanent *a,* ~**ly** *ad* [ˈpɜːmənənt, —lɪ] dauernd, ständig.

permissible [pəˈmɪsəbl] *a* zulässig.

permission [pəˈmɪʃən] *n* Erlaubnis *f,* Genehmigung *f.*

permissive [pəˈmɪsɪv] *a* nachgiebig; *society etc* permissiv.

permit [ˈpɜːmɪt] *n* Zulassung *f,* Erlaubnis(schein *m*) *f;* [pəˈmɪt] *vt* erlauben, zulassen.

permutation [pɜːmjuːˈteɪʃən] *n* Veränderung *f; (Math)* Permutation *f.*

pernicious [pɜːˈnɪʃəs] *a* schädlich.

perpendicular [pɜːpənˈdɪkjʊlə*] *a* senkrecht.

perpetrate [ˈpɜːpɪtreɪt] *vt* begehen, verüben.

perpetual *a,* ~**ly** *ad* [pəˈpetjʊəl, -ɪ] dauernd, ständig.

perpetuate [pəˈpetjʊeɪt] *vt* verewigen, bewahren.

perpetuity [pɜːpɪˈtjuːɪtɪ] *n* Ewigkeit *f.*

perplex [pəˈpleks] *vt* verblüffen; ~**ed** *a* verblüfft, perplex; ~**ing** *a* verblüffend; ~**ity** Verblüffung *f.*

persecute [ˈpɜːsɪkjuːt] *vt* verfolgen.

persecution [pɜːsɪˈkjuːʃən] *n* Verfolgung *f.*

perseverance [pɜːsɪˈvɪərəns] *n* Ausdauer *f.*

persevere [pɜːsɪˈvɪə*] *vi* beharren, durchhalten.

persist [pəˈsɪst] *vi (in belief etc)* bleiben *(in* bei*); (rain, smell)* andauern; *(continue)* nicht aufhören; ~**ence** Beharrlichkeit *f;* ~**ent** *a,* ~**ently** *ad* beharrlich; *(unending)* ständig.

person [ˈpɜːsn] *n* Person *f,* Mensch *m; (Gram)* Person *f;* **on one's** ~ bei sich; **in** ~ persönlich; ~**able** *a* gut aussehend; ~**al** *a* persönlich; *(private)* privat; *(of body)* körperlich, Körper-; ~**ality** [pɜːsəˈnælɪtɪ] Persönlichkeit *f;* ~**ally** *ad* persönlich; ~**ification** [pɜːsɒnɪfɪˈkeɪʃən] Verkörperung *f;* ~**ify** [pɜːˈsɒnɪfaɪ] *vt* verkörpern, personifizieren.

personnel [pɜːsəˈnel] *n* Personal *nt; (in factory)* Belegschaft *f;* ~ **manager** Personalchef *m.*

perspective [pəˈspektɪv] *n* Perspektive *f.*

Perspex ® [ˈpɜːspeks] *n* Plexiglas ® *nt.*

perspicacity [pɜːspɪˈkæsɪtɪ] *n* Scharfsinn *m.*

perspiration [pɜːspəˈreɪʃən] *n* Transpiration *f.*

perspire [pəsˈpaɪə*] *vi* transpirieren.

persuade [pəˈsweɪd] *vt* überreden; *(convince)* überzeugen.

persuasion [pəˈsweɪʒən] *n* Überredung *f,* Überzeugung *f.*

persuasive *a,* ~**ly** *ad* [pəˈsweɪsɪv, -lɪ] überzeugend.

pert [pɜːt] *a* keck.

pertain [pɜːˈteɪn] *vt* gehören *(to* zu).

pertaining: ~ **to** betreffend *(+acc).*

pertinent [ˈpɜːtɪnənt] *a* relevant.

perturb [pəˈtɜːb] *vt* beunruhigen.

perusal [pəˈruːzəl] *n* Durchsicht *f.*

peruse [pəˈruːz] *vt* lesen.

pervade [pɜːˈveɪd] *vt* erfüllen, durchziehen.

pervasive [pɜːˈveɪsɪv] *a* durchdringend; *influence etc* allgegenwärtig.

perverse *a,* ~**ly** *ad* [pəˈvɜːs, -lɪ] pervers; *(obstinate)* eigensinnig; ~**ness** Perversität *f;* Eigensinn *m.*

perversion [pəˈvɜːʃən] *n* Perversion *f; (of justice)* Verdrehung *f.*

perversity [pəˈvɜːsɪtɪ] *n* Perversität *f.*

pervert [ˈpɜːvɜːt] *n* perverse(r) Mensch *m;* [pəˈvɜːt] *vt* verdrehen; *(morally)* verderben.

pessimism [ˈpesɪmɪzəm] *n* Pessimismus *m.*

pessimist [ˈpesɪmɪst] *n* Pessimist *m;* ~**ic** [pesɪˈmɪstɪk] *a* pessimistisch.

pest [pest] *n* Plage *f; (insect)* Schädling *m; (fig) (person)* Nervensäge *f; (thing)* Plage *f.*

pester [ˈpestə*] *vt* plagen.

pesticide [ˈpestɪsaɪd] *n* Insektenvertilgungsmittel *nt.*

pestle [ˈpesl] *n* Stößel *m.*

pet [pɛt] n (animal) Haustier nt; (person) Liebling m; vt liebkosen, streicheln.

petal ['pɛtl] n Blütenblatt nt.

peter out ['piːtə aʊt] vi allmählich zu Ende gehen.

petite [pə'tiːt] a zierlich.

petition [pə'tɪʃən] n Bittschrift f.

petrel ['pɛtrəl] n Sturmvogel m.

petrified ['pɛtrɪfaɪd] a versteinert; person starr (vor Schreck).

petrify ['pɛtrɪfaɪ] vt versteinern; person erstarren lassen.

petrol ['pɛtrəl] n (Brit) Benzin nt, Kraftstoff m; ~engine Benzinmotor m; ~eum [pɪ'trəʊlɪəm] Petroleum nt; ~ pump (in car) Benzinpumpe f; (at garage) Zapfsäule f, Tanksäule f; ~ station Tankstelle f; ~tank Benzintank m.

petticoat ['pɛtɪkəʊt] n Petticoat m.

pettifogging ['pɛtɪfɒgɪŋ] a kleinlich.

pettiness ['pɛtɪnəs] n Geringfügigkeit f; (meanness) Kleinlichkeit f.

petty ['pɛtɪ] a (unimportant) geringfügig, unbedeutend; (mean) kleinlich; ~ cash Portokasse f; ~ officer Maat m.

petulant ['pɛtjʊlənt] a leicht reizbar.

pew [pjuː] n Kirchenbank f.

pewter ['pjuːtə*] n Zinn nt.

phallic ['fælɪk] a phallisch, Phallus-.

phantom ['fæntəm] n Phantom nt, Geist m.

pharmacist ['fɑːməsɪst] n Pharmazeut m; (druggist) Apotheker m.

pharmacy ['fɑːməsɪ] n Pharmazie f; (shop) Apotheke f.

phase [feɪz] n Phase f; ~ out vt langsam abbauen; model auslaufen lassen; person absetzen.

pheasant ['fɛznt] n Fasan m.

phenomenal a, ~ly ad [fɪ'nɒmɪnl, -nəlɪ] phänomenal.

phenomenon [fɪ'nɒmɪnən] n Phänomen nt; common ~ häufige Erscheinung f.

phial ['faɪəl] n Fläschchen nt, Ampulle f.

philanderer [fɪ'lændərə*] n Schwerenöter m.

philanthropic [fɪlən'θrɒpɪk] a philanthropisch.

philanthropist [fɪ'lænθrəpɪst] n Philanthrop m, Menschenfreund m.

philatelist [fɪ'lætəlɪst] n Briefmarkensammler m, Philatelist m.

philately [fɪ'lætəlɪ] n Briefmarkensammeln nt, Philatelie f.

philosopher [fɪ'lɒsəfə*] n Philosoph m.

philosophical [fɪlə'sɒfɪkəl] a philosophisch.

philosophize [fɪlɒsəfaɪz] vi philosophieren.

philosophy [fɪ'lɒsəfɪ] n Philosophie f; Weltanschauung f.

phlegm [flɛm] n (Med) Schleim m; (calmness) Gelassenheit f; ~atic [flɛg'mætɪk] a gelassen.

phobia ['fəʊbɪə] n krankhafte Furcht f, Phobie f.

phoenix ['fiːnɪks] n Phönix m.

phone [fəʊn] n (abbr of **telephone**) Telefon nt; vti telefonieren, anrufen.

phonetics [fəʊ'nɛtɪks] n Phonetik f,

Laut(bildungs)lehre f; pl Lautschrift f.

phon(e)y ['fəʊnɪ] a (col) unecht; excuse faul; money gefälscht; n (person) Schwindler m; (thing) Fälschung; (pound note) Blüte f.

phonograph ['fəʊnəgrɑːf] n (US) Grammophon nt.

phonology [fəʊ'nɒlədʒɪ] n Phonologie f, Lautlehre f.

phosphate ['fɒsfeɪt] n Phosphat nt.

phosphorus ['fɒsfərəs] n Phosphor m.

photo ['fəʊtəʊ] n (abbr of **photograph**) Foto nt.

photocopier ['fəʊtəʊ'kɒpɪə*] n Kopiergerät nt.

photocopy ['fəʊtəʊkɒpɪ] n Fotokopie f; vt fotokopieren.

photoelectric ['fəʊtəʊɪ'lɛktrɪk] a fotoelektrisch.

photo finish ['fəʊtəʊ'dʒenɪk] a fotogen.

photogenic ['fəʊtəʊ'dʒenɪk] a fotogen.

photograph ['fəʊtəgrɑːf] n Fotografie f, Aufnahme f; vt fotografieren, aufnehmen; ~er [fə'tɒgrəfə] Fotograf m; ~ic ['fəʊtə'græfɪk] a fotografisch; ~y [fə'tɒgrəfɪ] Fotografie f, Fotografieren nt; (of film, book) Aufnahmen pl.

photostat ['fəʊtəʊstæt] n Fotokopie f.

phrase [freɪz] n (kurzer) Satz m; (Gram) Phrase f; (expression) Redewendung f, Ausdruck m; vt ausdrücken, formulieren; ~book Sprachführer m.

physical a, ~ly ad ['fɪzɪkəl, -ɪ] physikalisch; (bodily) körperlich, physisch; ~ training Turnen nt.

physician [fɪ'zɪʃən] n Arzt m.

physicist ['fɪzɪsɪst] n Physiker(in f) m.

physics ['fɪzɪks] n Physik f.

physiology [fɪzɪ'ɒlədʒɪ] n Physiologie f.

physiotherapist [fɪzɪə'θerəpɪst] n Heilgymnast(in f) m.

physiotherapy [fɪzɪə'θerəpɪ] n Heilgymnastik f, Physiotherapie f.

physique [fɪ'ziːk] n Körperbau m; (in health) Konstitution f.

pianist ['pɪənɪst] n Pianist(in f) m.

piano ['pjɑːnəʊ] n Klavier nt, Piano nt; ~-accordion Akkordeon nt.

piccolo ['pɪkələʊ] n Pikkoloflöte f.

pick [pɪk] n (tool) Pickel m; (choice) Auswahl f; the ~ of das Beste von; vt (gather) (auf)lesen, sammeln; fruit pflücken; (choose) aussuchen; (Mus) zupfen; to ~ one's nose in der Nase bohren; to ~ sb's pocket jdm bestehlen; to ~ at one's food im Essen herumstochern; ~ on vt person herumfahren auf (+dat); why ~ on me? warum ich?; ~ out vt auswählen; ~ up vi (improve) sich erholen; vt (lift up) aufheben; (learn) (schnell) mitbekommen; word aufschnappen; (collect) abholen; girl (sich dat) anlachen; speed gewinnen an (+dat); ~ axe Pickel m.

picket ['pɪkɪt] n (stake) Pfahl m, Pflock m; (guard) Posten m; (striker) Streikposten m; vt factory (Streik)posten aufstellen vor (+dat); vi (Streik)posten stehen; ~ing Streikwache f; ~ line Streikpostenlinie f.

pickle ['pıkl] n *(salty mixture)* Pökel m; *(col)* Klemme f; vt *(in Essig)* einlegen; einpökeln.

pick-me-up ['pıkmi:ʌp] a Schnäpschen nt.

pickpocket ['pıkpɔkıt] n Taschendieb m.

pickup ['pıkʌp] n *(on record player)* Tonabnehmer m; *(small truck)* Lieferwagen m.

picnic ['pıknık] n Picknick nt; vi picknicken.

pictorial [pık'tɔ:rıəl] a in Bildern; n Illustrierte f.

picture ['pıktʃə*] n Bild nt; *(likeness also)* Abbild nt; *(in words also)* Darstellung f; **in the ～** *(fig)* im Bild; vt darstellen; *(fig: paint)* malen; *(visualize)* sich *(dat)* vorstellen; **the ～s** *(Brit)* Kino nt; **～ book** Bilderbuch nt; **～sque** [pıktʃə'resk] a malerisch.

piddling ['pıdlıŋ] a *(col)* lumpig; *task* pingelig.

pidgin ['pıdʒın] a: **～ English** Pidgin-Englisch nt.

pie [paı] n *(meat)* Pastete f; *(fruit)* Torte f.

piebald ['paıbɔ:ld] a gescheckt.

piece [pi:s] n Stück nt; **to go to ～s** *(work, standard)* wertlos werden; **he's gone to ～s** er ist vollkommen fertig; **in ～s** entzwei, kaputt; *(taken apart)* auseinandergenommen; **a ～ of cake** *(col)* ein Kinderspiel nt; **～meal** ad stückweise, Stück für Stück; **～work** Akkordarbeit f; **～ together** vt zusammensetzen.

pier [pıə*] n Pier m, Mole f.

pierce [pıəs] vt durchstechen, durchbohren *(also look)*; durchdringen *(also fig)*.

piercing ['pıəsıŋ] a durchdringend; *cry also* gellend; *look also* durchbohrend.

piety ['paıətı] n Frömmigkeit f.

pig [pıg] n Schwein nt.

pigeon ['pıdʒən] n Taube f; **～hole** *(compartment)* Ablegefach nt; vt ablegen; *idea* zu den Akten legen.

piggy bank ['pıgıbæŋk] n Sparschwein nt.

pigheaded ['pıg'hedıd] a dickköpfig.

piglet ['pıglət] n Ferkel nt, Schweinchen nt.

pigment ['pıgmənt] n Farbstoff m, Pigment nt *(also Biol)*; **～ation** [pıgmən'teıʃən] Färbung f, Pigmentation f.

pigmy ['pıgmı] n = **pygmy.**

pigskin ['pıgskın] n Schweinsleder nt; a schweinsledern.

pigsty ['pıgstaı] n *(lit, fig)* Schweinestall m.

pigtail ['pıgteıl] n Zopf m.

pike [paık] n Pike f; *(fish)* Hecht m.

pilchard ['pıltʃəd] n Sardine f.

pile [paıl] n Haufen m; *(of books, wood)* Stapel m, Stoß m; *(in ground)* Pfahl m; *(of bridge)* Pfeiler m; *(on carpet)* Flausch m; vti *(also ～ up)* sich anhäufen.

piles [paılz] npl Hämorrhoiden pl.

pile-up ['paılʌp] n *(Aut)* Massenzusammenstoß m.

pilfer ['pılfə*] vt stehlen, klauen; **～ing** Diebstahl m.

pilgrim ['pılgrım] n Wallfahrer(in f) m, Pilger(in f) m; **～age** Wallfahrt f, Pilgerfahrt f.

pill [pıl] n Tablette f, Pille f; **the P～** die *(Antibaby)*pille.

pillage ['pılıdʒ] vt plündern.

pillar ['pılə*] n Pfeiler m, Säule f *(also fig)*; **～ box** *(Brit)* Briefkasten m.

pillion ['pıljən] n Soziussitz m; **～ passenger** Soziusfahrer m.

pillory ['pılərı] n Pranger m; vt an den Pranger stellen; *(fig)* anprangern.

pillow ['pıləʊ] n Kissen nt; **～case** Kissenbezug m.

pilot ['paılət] n Pilot m; *(Naut)* Lotse m; a *scheme etc* Versuchs-; vt führen; *ship* lotsen; **～ light** Zündflamme f.

pimp [pımp] n Zuhälter m.

pimple ['pımpl] n Pickel m.

pimply ['pımplı] a pick(e)lig.

pin [pın] n Nadel f; *(sewing)* Stecknadel f; *(Tech)* Stift m, Bolzen m; vt stecken, heften *(to an +acc)*; *(keep in one position)* pressen, drücken; **～s and needles** Kribbeln nt; **I have ～s and needles in my leg** mein Bein ist *(mir)* eingeschlafen; **～ down** vt *(fig)* person festnageln *(to auf +acc)*.

pinafore ['pınəfɔ:*] n Schürze f; **～ dress** Kleiderrock m.

pincers ['pınsəz] npl Kneif- or Beißzange f; *(Med)* Pinzette f.

pinch [pıntʃ] n Zwicken, Kneifen nt; *(of salt)* Prise f; vti zwicken, kneifen; *(shoe)* drücken; vt *(col: steal)* klauen; *(arrest)* schnappen; **at a ～** notfalls, zur Not; **to feel the ～** die Not or es zu spüren bekommen.

pincushion ['pınkuʃən] n Nadelkissen nt.

pine [paın] n *(also ～ tree)* Kiefer f, Föhre f, Pinie f; vi: **～ for** sich sehnen or verzehren nach; **～ away** sich zu Tode sehnen.

pineapple ['paınæpl] n Ananas f.

ping [pıŋ] n Peng nt; Kling nt; **～-pong** Pingpong nt.

pink [pıŋk] n *(plant)* Nelke f; *(colour)* Rosa nt; a rosa inv.

pinnacle ['pınəkl] n Spitze f.

pinpoint ['pınpɔınt] vt festlegen.

pinstripe ['pınstraıp] n Nadelstreifen m.

pint [paınt] n Pint nt.

pinup ['pınʌp] n Pin-up-girl nt.

pioneer [paıə'nıə*] n Pionier m; *(fig also)* Bahnbrecher m.

pious ['paıəs] a fromm; *literature* geistlich.

pip [pıp] n Kern m; *(sound)* Piepen nt; *(on uniform)* Stern m; **to give sb the ～** *(col)* jdn verrückt machen.

pipe [paıp] n *(smoking)* Pfeife f; *(Mus)* Flöte f; *(tube)* Rohr nt; *(in house)* (Rohr)leitung f vti *(durch Rohre)* leiten; *(Mus)* blasen; **～ down** vi *(be quiet)* die Luft anhalten, **～-dream** Luftschloß nt; **～-line** *(for oil)* Pipeline f; **～r** Pfeifer m; *(bagpipes)* Dudelsackbläser m; **～ tobacco** Pfeifentabak m.

piping ['paıpıŋ] n Leitungsnetz nt; *(on cake)* Dekoration f; *(on uniform)* Tresse f; ad: **～ hot** siedend heiß.

piquant ['pi:kənt] a pikant.

pique [pi:k] n gekränkte(r) Stolz m; **～d** a pikiert.

piracy ['paıərəsı] n Piraterie f, Seeräuberei f; (plagiarism) Plagiat nt.

pirate ['paɪərɪt] n Pirat m, Seeräuber m; (plagiarist) Plagiator m; ~ **radio** Schwarzsender m; (exterritorial) Piratensender m.

pirouette [pɪru'et] n Pirouette f; vi pirouettieren, eine Pirouette drehen.

Pisces ['paɪsiːz] n Fische pl.

pissed [pɪst] a (col) blau, besoffen.

pistol ['pɪstl] n Pistole f.

piston ['pɪstən] n Kolben m.

pit [pɪt] n Grube f; (Theat) Parterre nt; (orchestra —) Orchestergraben m; vt (mark with scars) zerfressen; (compare) o.s. messen (against mit); sb/sth messen (against an +dat); **the ~s** pl (motor racing) die Boxen.

pitch [pɪtʃ] n Wurf m; (of trader) Stand m; (Sport) (Spiel)feld nt; (slope) Neigung f; (degree) Stufe f; (Mus) Tonlage f; (substance) Pech nt; **perfect ~** absolute(s) Gehör nt; **to queer sb's ~** (col) jdm alles verderben; vt werfen, schleudern; (set up) aufschlagen; song anstimmen; **~ed too high** zu hoch; vi (fall) (längelang) hinschlagen; (Naut) rollen; **~-black** a pechschwarz; **~ed battle** offene Schlacht f.

pitcher ['pɪtʃə*] n Krug m.

pitchfork ['pɪtʃfɔːk] n Heugabel f.

piteous ['pɪtɪəs] a kläglich, erbärmlich.

pitfall ['pɪtfɔːl] n (fig) Falle f.

pith [pɪθ] n Mark nt; (of speech) Kern m.

pithead ['pɪthed] n Schachtkopf m.

pithy ['pɪθɪ] a prägnant.

pitiable ['pɪtɪəbl] a bedauernswert; (contemptible) jämmerlich.

pitiful a, **~ly** ad ['pɪtɪful, -fəlɪ] mitleidig; (deserving pity) bedauernswert; (contemptible) jämmerlich.

pitiless a, **~ly** ad ['pɪtɪləs, -lɪ] erbarmungslos.

pittance ['pɪtəns] n Hungerlohn m.

pity ['pɪtɪ] n (sympathy) Mitleid nt; (shame) Jammer m; **to have** or **take ~ on sb** Mitleid mit jdm haben; **for ~'s sake** um Himmels willen; **what a ~!** wie schade!; **it's a ~** es ist schade; vt Mitleid haben mit; **I ~ you** du tust mir leid; **~ing** a mitleidig.

pivot ['pɪvət] n Drehpunkt m; (pin) (Dreh)zapfen m; (fig) Angelpunkt m; vi sich drehen (on um).

pixie ['pɪksɪ] n Elf(e f) m.

placard ['plækɑːd] n Plakat nt, Anschlag m; vt anschlagen.

placate [plə'keɪt] vt beschwichtigen, besänftigen.

place [pleɪs] n Platz m; (spot) Stelle f; (town etc) Ort m; vt setzen, stellen, legen; order aufgeben; (Sport) plazieren; (identify) unterbringen; **in ~** am rechten Platz; **out of ~** nicht am rechten Platz; (fig) remark unangebracht; **in ~ of** anstelle von; **in the first/second** etc ~ erstens/zweitens etc; **to give ~ to** Platz machen (+dat); **to invite sb to one's ~** jdn zu sich (nach Hause) einladen; **to keep sb in his ~** jdn in seinen Schranken halten; **to put sb in his ~** jdn in seine Schranken (ver)weisen; **~ of worship** Stätte f des Gebets; **~ mat** Platzdeckchen nt.

placid ['plæsɪd] a gelassen, ruhig; **~ity** [plə'sɪdɪtɪ] Gelassenheit f, Ruhe f.

plagiarism ['pleɪdʒɪərɪzəm] n Plagiat nt.

plagiarist ['pleɪdʒɪərɪst] n Plagiator m.

plagiarize ['pleɪdʒɪəraɪz] vt abschreiben, plagiieren.

plague [pleɪg] n Pest f; (fig) Plage f; vt plagen.

plaice [pleɪs] n Scholle f.

plaid [plæd] n Plaid nt.

plain a, **~ly** ad [pleɪn, -lɪ] (clear) klar, deutlich; (simple) einfach, schlicht; (not beautiful) einfach, nicht attraktiv; (honest) offen; n Ebene f; **in ~ clothes** (police) in Zivil(kleidung); **it is ~ sailing** das ist ganz einfach; **~ness** Einfachheit f.

plaintiff ['pleɪntɪf] n Kläger m.

plait [plæt] n Zopf m; vt flechten.

plan [plæn] n Plan m; vti planen; (intend also) vorhaben; **~ out** vt vorbereiten; **according to ~** planmäßig.

plane [pleɪn] n Ebene f; (Aviat) Flugzeug nt; (tool) Hobel m; (tree) Platane f; a eben, flach; vt hobeln.

planet ['plænɪt] n Planet m.

planetarium [plænɪ'teərɪəm] n Planetarium nt.

planetary ['plænɪtərɪ] a planetarisch.

plank [plæŋk] n Planke f, Brett nt; (Pol) Programmpunkt m.

plankton ['plæŋktən] n Plankton nt.

planner ['plænə*] n Planer m.

planning ['plænɪŋ] n Planen nt, Planung f.

plant [plɑːnt] n Pflanze f; (Tech) (Maschinen)anlage f; (factory) Fabrik f, Werk nt; vt pflanzen; (set firmly) stellen.

plantain ['plæntɪn] n (Mehl)banane f.

plantation [plæn'teɪʃən] n Pflanzung f, Plantage f.

planter ['plɑːntə*] n Pflanzer m.

plaque [plæk] n Gedenktafel f.

plasma ['plæzmə] n Plasma nt.

plaster ['plɑːstə*] n Gips m; (whole surface) Verputz m; (Med) Pflaster nt; (for fracture: also ~ **of Paris**) Gipsverband m; **in ~** (leg etc) in Gips; vt (glaze; hole zugipsen; ceiling verputzen; (fig: with pictures etc) bewor verkleben; **~ed** a (col) besoffen; **~er** Gipser m.

plastic ['plæstɪk] n Kunststoff m; a (made of plastic) Kunststoff-, Plastik-; (soft) formbar, plastisch; (Art) plastisch, bildend; **p~ine** ['plæstɪsiːn] Plastilin nt; **~ surgery** plastische Chirurgie f; Schönheitsoperation f.

plate [pleɪt] n Teller m; (gold/silver) vergoldete(s)/versilberte(s) Tafelgeschirr nt; (flat sheet) Platte f; (in book) (Bild)tafel f; vt überziehen, plattieren; **to silver-/gold-~** versilbern/vergolden.

plateau ['plætəu] n, pl **~x** Hochebene f, Plateau nt.

plateful ['pleɪtful] n Teller(voll) m.

plate glass ['pleɪt'glɑːs] n Tafelglas nt.

platform ['plætfɔːm] n (at meeting) Plattform f, Podium nt; (stage) Bühne f; (Rail) Bahnsteig m; (Pol) Partieprogramm nt; **~ ticket** Bahnsteigkarte f.

platinum ['plætɪnəm] n Platin nt.

platitude ['plætɪtjuːd] n Gemeinplatz m, Platitüde f.

platoon [plə'tuːn] n (Mil) Zug m.

platter ['plætə*] n Platte f.

plausibility [plɔːzə'bɪlɪtɪ] n Plausibilität f.

plausible a, **plausibly** ad ['plɔːzəbl, -blɪ] plausibel, einleuchtend; liar überzeugend.

play [pleɪ] n Spiel nt (also Tech); (Theat) (Theater)stück nt, Schauspiel nt; vti spielen; another team spielen gegen; (put sb in a team) einsetzen, spielen lassen; **to ~ a joke on sb** jdm einen Streich spielen; **to ~ sb off against sb else** jdn gegen jdn anders ausspielen; **to ~ a part in** (fig) eine Rolle spielen bei; **~ down** vt bagatellisieren, herunterspielen; **~ up** vi (cause trouble) frech werden; (bad leg etc) weh tun; vt person plagen; **to ~ up to sb** jdm flattieren; **~acting** Schauspielerei f; **~boy** Playboy m; **~er** Spieler(in f) m; **~ful** a spielerisch, verspielt; **~goer** Theaterfreund m; **~ground** Spielplatz m; **~group** Kindergarten m; **~ing card** Spielkarte f; **~ing field** Sportplatz m; **~mate** Spielkamerad m; **~-off** (Sport) Entscheidungsspiel nt; **~pen** Laufstall m; **~thing** Spielzeug nt; **~wright** Theaterschriftsteller m.

plea [pliː] n (dringende) Bitte f, Gesuch nt; (Jur) Antwort f des Angeklagten; (excuse) Ausrede f, Vorwand m; (objection) Einrede f; **~ of guilty** Geständnis nt.

plead [pliːd] vt (as be agreeable to) anführen; (Jur) sb's case vertreten; vi (beg) dringend bitten (with sb jdn); (Jur) plädieren; **to ~ guilty** schuldig plädieren.

pleasant a, **~ly** ['pleznt, -lɪ] angenehm; freundlich; **~ness** Angenehme(s) nt; (of person) angenehme(s) Wesen nt, Freundlichkeit f; **~ry** Scherz m.

please [pliːz] vt (be agreeable to) gefallen (+dat); **~!** bitte!; **~ yourself!** wie du willst!; **do what you ~** mach was du willst; **~d** a zufrieden; (glad) erfreut (with über +acc).

pleasing ['pliːzɪŋ] a erfreulich.

pleasurable a, **pleasurably** ad ['pleʒərəbl, -blɪ] angenehm, erfreulich.

pleasure ['pleʒə*] n Vergnügen nt, Freude f; (old: will) Wünsche pl; **it's a ~** gern geschehen; **they take (no/great) ~ in doing ...** es macht ihnen (keinen/ großen) Spaß zu...; **~ ground** Vergnügungspark m; **~-seeking** a vergnügungshungrig; **~ steamer** Vergnügungsdampfer m.

pleat [pliːt] n Falte f.

plebeian [plɪ'biːən] n Plebejer(in f) m; a plebejisch.

plebiscite ['plebɪsɪt] n Volksentscheid m, Plebiszit nt.

plebs [plebz] npl Plebs m, Pöbel m.

plectrum ['plektrəm] n Plektron nt.

pledge [pledʒ] n Pfand nt; (promise) Versprechen nt vt verpfänden; (promise) geloben, versprechen; **to take the ~** dem Alkohol abschwören.

plenipotentiary [plenɪpə'tenʃərɪ] m Bevollmächtiger m; a bevollmächtigt; **~ power** Vollmacht f.

plentiful ['plentɪful] a reichlich.

plenty ['plentɪ] n Fülle f, Überfluß m; ad (col) ganz schön; **~ of** eine Menge, viel; **in ~** reichlich, massenhaft; **to be ~** genug sein, reichen.

plethora ['pleθərə] n Überfülle f.

pleurisy ['pluərɪsɪ] n Rippenfellentzündung f.

pliability [plaɪə'bɪlɪtɪ] n Biegsamkeit f; (of person) Beeinflußbarkeit f.

pliable ['plaɪəbl] a biegsam; person beeinflußbar.

pliers ['plaɪəz] npl (Kneif)zange f.

plight [plaɪt] n (Not)lage f; (schrecklicher) Zustand m.

plimsolls ['plɪmsɔlz] npl Turnschuhe pl.

plinth [plɪnθ] n Säulenplatte f, Plinthe f.

plod [plɒd] vi (work) sich abplagen; (walk) trotten; **~der** Arbeitstier nt; **~ding** a schwerfällig.

plonk [plɒŋk] n (col: wine) billige(r) Wein m; vt: **~ sth down** etw hinknallen.

plot [plɒt] n Komplott nt, Verschwörung f; (story) Handlung f; (of land) Stück nt Land, Grundstück nt; vt markieren; curve zeichnen; movements nachzeichnen; vi (plan secretly) sich verschwören, ein Komplott schmieden; **~ter** Verschwörer m; **~ting** Intrigen pl.

plough, (US) **plow** [plau] n Pflug m; vt pflügen; (col) exam candidate durchfallen lassen; **~ back** vt (Comm) wieder in das Geschäft stecken; **~ through** vt water durchpflügen; book sich kämpfen durch; **~ing** Pflügen nt.

ploy [plɔɪ] n Masche f.

pluck [plʌk] vt fruit pflücken; guitar zupfen; goose rupfen; n Mut m; **to ~ up courage** all seinen Mut zusammennehmen; **~y** a beherzt.

plug [plʌg] n Stöpsel m; (Elec) Stecker m; (of tobacco) Pfriem m; (col: publicity) Schleichwerbung f; (Aut) Zündkerze f; vt (zu)stopfen; (col: advertise) Reklame machen für; **to ~ in a lamp** den Stecker einer Lampe einstecken.

plum [plʌm] n Pflaume f, Zwetschge f; a job etc Bomben-.

plumage ['pluːmɪdʒ] n Gefieder nt.

plumb [plʌm] n Lot nt; out of ~ nicht im Lot; a senkrecht; ad (exactly) genau; vt ausloten; (fig) sondieren; mystery ergründen.

plumber ['plʌmə*] n Klempner m, Installateur m.

plumbing ['plʌmɪŋ] n (craft) Installieren nt; (fittings) Leitungen pl, Installationen pl.

plumbline ['plʌmlaɪn] n Senkblei nt.

plume [pluːm] n Feder f; (of smoke etc) Fahne f; vt (bird) putzen.

plummet ['plʌmɪt] n Senkblei nt; vi (ab)stürzen.

plump [plʌmp] a rundlich, füllig; vi plumpsen, sich fallen lassen; vt plumpsen lassen; **to ~ for** (col: choose) wählen, sich entscheiden für; **~ness** Rundlichkeit f.

plunder ['plʌndə*] n Plünderung f; (loot) Beute f; vt plündern; things rauben.

plunge [plʌndʒ] n Sprung m, Stürzen nt; vt stoßen; vi (sich) stürzen; (ship) rollen; **a room ~d into darkness** ein in Dunkelheit getauchtes Zimmer.

plunging ['plʌndʒɪŋ] a neckline offenherzig.

pluperfect ['pluː'pɜːfɪkt] n Plusquamperfekt nt, Vorvergangenheit f.

plural ['pluərəl] a Plural-, Mehrzahl-; n Plural m, Mehrzahl f; **~istic** [pluərə'lɪstɪk] a pluralistisch.

plus [plʌs] prep plus, und; a Plus-.

plush [plʌʃ] a (also **~y:** col: luxurious) feudal; n Plüsch m.

ply [plaɪ] n as in: **three-~** wood dreischichtig; wool Dreifach-; vt trade (be)treiben; (with questions) zusetzen (+dat); (ship, taxi) befahren; vi (ship, taxi) verkehren; **~wood** Sperrholz nt.

pneumatic [njuː'mætɪk] a pneumatisch; (Tech) Luft-; **~ drill** Preßlufthammer m; **~ tyre** Luftreifen m.

pneumonia [njuː'məʊnɪə] n Lungenentzündung f.

poach [pəʊtʃ] vt (Cook) pochieren; game stehlen; vi (steal) wildern (for nach); **~ed** a egg pochiert, verloren; **~er** Wilddieb m; **~ing** Wildern nt.

pocket ['pɒkɪt] n Tasche f; (of ore) Ader f; (of resistance) (Widerstands)nest nt; air **~** Luftloch nt; vt einstecken, in die Tasche stecken; **to be out of ~** kein Geld haben; **~book** Taschenbuch nt; **~ful** Tasche(voll) f; **~ knife** Taschenmesser nt; **~ money** Taschengeld nt.

pockmarked ['pɒkmɑːkt] a face pockennarbig.

pod [pɒd] Hülse f; (of peas also) Schote f.

podgy ['pɒdʒɪ] a pummelig.

poem ['pəʊɪm] n Gedicht nt.

poet ['pəʊɪt] n Dichter m, Poet m; **~ic** [pəʊ'etɪk] a poetisch, dichterisch; beauty malerisch, stimmungsvoll; **~ laureate** Hofdichter m; **~ry** Poesie f; (poems) Gedichte pl.

poignant a, **~ly** ad ['pɔɪnjənt, -lɪ] scharf, stechend; (touching) ergreifend, quälend.

point [pɔɪnt] n Punkt m (also in discussion, scoring); (spot also) Stelle f; (sharpened tip) Spitze f; (moment) (Zeit)punkt m, Moment m; (purpose) Zweck m; (idea) Argument nt; (decimal) Dezimalstelle f; (personal characteristic) Seite f; vt zeigen mit; gun richten; vi zeigen; **~s** pl (Rail) Weichen pl; **~ of view** Stand- or Gesichtspunkt m; **what's the ~?** was soll das?; **you have a ~ there** da hast du recht; **three ~ two** drei Komma zwei; **~ to** vt hinweisen auf (+acc); **~ to** vt zeigen auf (+acc); **~-blank** ad (at close range) aus nächster Entfernung; (bluntly) unverblümt; **~ duty** Verkehrsregelungsdienst m; **~ed** a, **~er** **edly** ad spitz, scharf; (fig) gezielt; **~er** Zeigestock m; (on dial) Zeiger m; **~less** a, **~lessly** ad zwecklos, sinnlos; **~lessness** Zwecklosigkeit f, Sinnlosigkeit f.

poise [pɔɪz] n Haltung f; (fig also) Gelassenheit f; vti balancieren; knife, pen bereithalten; o.s. sich bereitmachen; **~d** a beherrscht.

poison ['pɔɪzn] n (lit, fig) Gift nt; vt vergiften; **~ing** Vergiftung f; **~ous** a giftig, Gift-.

poke [pəʊk] vt stoßen; (put) stecken; fire schüren; hole bohren; n Stoß m; **to ~ one's nose into** seine Nase stecken in (+acc); **to ~ fun at sb** sich über jdn lustig machen; **~ about** vi herumstochern; herumwühlen; **~r** Schürhaken m; (Cards) Poker nt; **~r-faced** a undurchdringlich.

poky ['pəʊkɪ] a eng.

polar ['pəʊlə*] a Polar-, polar; **~ bear** Eisbär m; **~ization** [pəʊləraɪ'zeɪʃən] n Polarisation f; **~ize** vt polarisieren; vi sich polarisieren.

pole [pəʊl] n Stange f, Pfosten m; (flag-, telegraph —) Mast m; (Elec, Geog) Pol m; (Sport) (vaulting —) Stab m; (ski —) Stock m; **~s apart** durch Welten getrennt; **~cat** (US) Skunk m; **~ star** Polarstern m; **~ vault** Stabhochsprung m.

polemic [pɒ'lemɪk] n Polemik f.

police [pə'liːs] n Polizei f; vt polizeilich überwachen; kontrollieren; **~ car** Polizeiwagen m; **~man** Polizist m; **~ state** Polizeistaat m; **~ station** (Polizei)revier nt, Wache f; **~woman** Polizistin f.

policy ['pɒlɪsɪ] n Politik f; (of business also) Usus m; (insurance) (Versicherungs)police f; (prudence) Klugheit f; (principle) Grundsatz m; **~ decision/statement** Grundsatzentscheidung f/-erklärung f.

polio ['pəʊlɪəʊ] n (spinale) Kinderlähmung f, Polio f.

polish ['pɒlɪʃ] n Politur f; (for floor) Wachs nt; (for shoes) Creme f; (nail —) Lack m; (shine) Glanz m; (of furniture) Politur f; (fig) Schliff m; vt polieren; shoes putzen; (fig) den letzten Schliff geben (+dat), aufpolieren; **~ off** vt (col: work) erledigen; food wegputzen; drink hinunterschütten; **~ up** vt essay aufpolieren; knowledge auffrischen; **~ed** a glänzend (also fig); manners verfeinert.

polite a, **~ly** ad [pə'laɪt, -lɪ] höflich; society fein; **~ness** Höflichkeit f, Feinheit f.

politic ['pɒlɪtɪk] a (prudent) diplomatisch; **~al** a, **~ally** ad [pə'lɪtɪkəl, -ɪ] politisch; **~al science** Politologie f; **~ian** [pɒlɪ'tɪʃən] Politiker m, Staatsmann m; **~s** pl Politik f.

polka ['pɒlkə] n Polka f; **~ dot** Tupfen m.

poll [pəʊl] n Abstimmung f; (in election) Wahl f; (votes cast) Wahlbeteiligung f; (opinion —) Umfrage f; vt votes erhalten, auf sich vereinigen.

pollen ['pɒlən] n Blütenstaub m, Pollen m; **~ count** Pollenkonzentration f.

pollination [pɒlɪ'neɪʃən] n Befruchtung f.

polling booth ['pəʊlɪŋbuːð] n Wahlkabine f.

polling day ['pəʊlɪŋ deɪ] n Wahltag m.

polling station ['pəʊlɪŋ steɪʃən] n Wahllokal nt.

pollute [pə'luːt] vt verschmutzen, verunreinigen.

pollution [pə'luːʃən] n Verschmutzung f.

polo ['pəʊləʊ] n Polo nt.

poly- [pɒlɪ] pref Poly-.

polygamy [pɒ'lɪgəmɪ] n Polygamie f.

polytechnic [pɒlɪ'teknɪk] n technische Hochschule f.

polythene ['pɒlɪθiːn] n Plastik nt; ~ **bag** Plastiktüte f.

pomegranate ['pɒmɔgrænɪt] n Granatapfel m.

pommel ['pʌml] vt mit den Fäusten bearbeiten; n Sattelknopf m.

pomp [pɒmp] n Pomp m, Prunk m.

pompous a, ~**ly** ad ['pɒmpəs, -lɪ] aufgeblasen; language geschwollen.

ponce [pɒns] n (col) (pimp) Louis m; (queer) Schwule m.

pond [pɒnd] n Teich m, Weiher m.

ponder ['pɒndə*] vt nachdenken or nachgrübeln über (+acc); ~**ous** a schwerfällig.

pontiff ['pɒntɪf] n Pontifex m.

pontificate [pɒn'tɪfɪkeɪt] vi (fig) geschwollen reden.

pontoon [pɒn'tuːn] n Ponton m; (Cards) 17-und-4 nt.

pony ['pəʊnɪ] n Pony nt; ~**tail** Pferdeschwanz m.

poodle ['puːdl] n Pudel m.

pooh-pooh [puː'puː] vt die Nase rümpfen über (+acc).

pool [puːl] n (swimming ~) Schwimmbad nt; (private) Swimming-pool m; (of spilt liquid, blood) Lache f; (fund) (gemeinsame) Kasse f; (billiards) Poolspiel nt; vt money etc zusammenlegen.

poor [pʊə*] a arm; (not good) schlecht, schwach; **the** ~ pl die Armen pl; ~**ly** ad schlecht, schwach; dressed ärmlich; a schlecht, elend.

pop [pɒp] n Knall m; (music) Popmusik f; (drink) Limo(nade) f; (US col) Pa m; vt (put) stecken; balloon platzen lassen; vi knallen; ~ **in/out** (person) vorbeikommen/hinausgehen; hinein-/hinausspringen; ~ **concert** Popkonzert nt; ~**corn** Puffmais m.

Pope [pəʊp] n Papst m.

poplar ['pɒplə*] n Pappel f.

poplin ['pɒplɪn] n Popelin m.

poppy ['pɒpɪ] n Mohn m; ~**cock** (col) Quatsch m.

populace ['pɒpjʊlɪs] n Volk nt.

popular ['pɒpjʊlə*] a beliebt, populär; (of the people) volkstümlich, Populär-; (widespread) allgemein; ~**ity** [pɒpjʊ'lærɪtɪ] Beliebtheit f, Popularität f; ~**ize** f popularisieren; ~**ly** ad allgemein, überall.

populate ['pɒpjʊleɪt] vt bevölkern; town bewohnen.

population [pɒpjʊ'leɪʃən] n Bevölkerung f; (of town) Einwohner pl.

populous ['pɒpjʊləs] a dicht besiedelt.

porcelain ['pɔːslɪn] n Porzellan nt.

porch [pɔːtʃ] n Vorbau m, Veranda f; (in church) Vorhalle f.

porcupine ['pɔːkjʊpaɪn] n Stachelschwein nt.

pore [pɔː*] n Pore f; ~ **over** vt brüten or hocken über (+dat).

pork [pɔːk] n Schweinefleisch nt.

pornographic a, ~**ally** ad [pɔːnə'græfɪk, -əlɪ] pornographisch.

pornography [pɔː'nɒgrəfɪ] n Pornographie f.

porous ['pɔːrəs] a porös; skin porig.

porpoise ['pɔːpəs] n Tümmler m.

porridge ['pɒrɪdʒ] n Porridge m, Haferbrei m.

port [pɔːt] n Hafen m; (town) Hafenstadt f; (Naut: left side) Backbord nt; (opening for loads) Luke f; (wine) Portwein m.

portable ['pɔːtəbl] a tragbar; radio Koffer-; typewriter Reise-.

portal ['pɔːtl] n Portal nt.

portcullis [pɔːt'kʌlɪs] n Fallgitter nt.

portend [pɔː'tend] vt anzeigen, hindeuten auf (+acc).

portent ['pɔːtent] n schlimme(s) Vorzeichen nt; ~**ous** [pɔː'tentəs] a schlimm, ominös; (amazing) ungeheuer.

porter ['pɔːtə*] n Pförtner(in f) m; (for luggage) (Gepäck)träger m.

porthole ['pɔːthəʊl] n Bullauge nt.

portico ['pɔːtɪkəʊ] n Säulengang m.

portion ['pɔːʃən] n Teil m, Stück nt; (of food) Portion f.

portly ['pɔːtlɪ] a korpulent, beleibt.

portrait ['pɔːtrɪt] n Porträt nt, Bild(nis) nt.

portray [pɔː'treɪ] vt darstellen; (describe) schildern; ~**al** Darstellung f, Schilderung f.

pose [pəʊz] n Stellung f, Pose f (also affectation); vi posieren, sich in Positur setzen; vt stellen; **to** ~ **as** sich ausgeben als; ~**r** knifflige Frage f.

posh [pɒʃ] a (col) (piek)fein.

position [pə'zɪʃən] n Stellung f; (place) Position f, Lage f; (job) Stelle f; (attitude) Standpunkt m, Haltung f; **to be in a** ~ **to do sth** in der Lage sein, etw zu tun; vt aufstellen.

positive a, ~**ly** ad ['pɒzɪtɪv, -lɪ] positiv; (convinced) sicher; (definite) eindeutig.

posse ['pɒsɪ] n (US) Aufgebot nt.

possess [pə'zes] vt besitzen; **what** ~**ed you to . . .?** was ist in dich gefahren, daß...?; ~**ed a** besessen; ~**ion** [pə'zeʃən] Besitz m; ~**ive** a besitzergreifend, eigensüchtig; (Gram) Possessiv-, besitzanzeigend; ~**ively** ad besitzergreifend, eigensüchtig; ~**or** Besitzer m.

possibility [pɒsə'bɪlɪtɪ] n Möglichkeit f.

possible ['pɒsəbl] a möglich; **if** ~ wenn möglich, möglichst; **as big as** ~ so groß wie möglich, möglichst groß.

possibly ['pɒsəblɪ] ad möglicherweise, vielleicht; **as soon as I** ~ **can** sobald ich irgendwie kann.

post [pəʊst] n Post f; (pole) Pfosten m, Pfahl m; (place of duty) Posten m; (job) Stelle f; vt notice anschlagen; letters aufgeben; soldiers aufstellen; ~**age** Postgebühr f, Porto nt; ~**al** a Post-; ~**al order** Postanweisung f; ~**card** Postkarte f; ~**date** vt cheque nachdatieren; ~**er** Plakat nt, Poster m; ~**e restante** Aufbewahrungsstelle f für postlagernde Sendungen; **to send sth** ~**e restante** etw postlagernd schicken.

posterior [pɒs'tɪərɪə*] n (col) Hintern m.

posterity [pɒs'terɪtɪ] n Nachwelt f; (descendants) Nachkommenschaft f.

postgraduate ['pəust'grædjuıt] n Weiterstudierender(in f) m.

posthumous a, ~ly ad ['pɒstjuməs, -lı] post(h)um.

postman ['pəustmən] n Briefträger m, Postbote m.

postmark ['pəustmɑːk] n Poststempel m.

postmaster ['pəustmɑːstə*] n Postmeister m; P~ **General** Postminister m.

post-mortem ['pəust'mɔːtəm] n Autopsie f.

post office ['pəustɒfıs] n Postamt nt, Post f (also organization).

postpone [pə'spəun] vt verschieben, aufschieben; ~**ment** Verschiebung f, Aufschub m.

postscript ['pəusskrıpt] n Nachschrift f, Postskript nt; (in book) Nachwort nt.

postulate ['pɒstjuleıt] vt voraussetzen; (maintain) behaupten.

postulation [pɒstju'leıʃən] n Voraussetzung f; Behauptung f.

posture ['pɒstʃə*] n Haltung f; vi posieren.

postwar ['pəust'wɔː*] a Nachkriegs-.

posy ['pəuzı] n Blumenstrauß m.

pot [pɒt] n Topf m; (tea—) Kanne f; (col: marijuana) Hasch m; vt plant eintopfen.

potash ['pɒtæʃ] n Pottasche f.

potato [pə'teıtəu] n, pl -es Kartoffel f.

potency ['pəutənsı] n Stärke f, Potenz f.

potent ['pəutənt] a stark; argument zwingend.

potentate ['pəutənteıt] n Machthaber m.

potential [pə'tenʃəl] a potentiell; he is a ~ **virtuoso** er hat das Zeug zum Virtuosen; n Potential nt; ~**ly** ad potentiell.

pothole ['pɒthəul] n Höhle f; (in road) Schlagloch nt; ~**r** Höhlenforscher m.

potholing ['pɒthəulıŋ] n: to go ~ Höhlen erforschen.

potion ['pəuʃən] n Trank m.

potluck ['pɒt'lʌk] n: to take ~ with sth etw auf gut Glück nehmen.

potpourri [pəu'purı] n Potpourri nt.

potshot ['pɒtʃɒt] n: to take a ~ at sth auf etw (acc) ballern.

potted ['pɒtıd] a food eingelegt, eingemacht; plant Topf-; (fig: book, version) konzentriert.

potter ['pɒtə*] n Töpfer m; vi herumhantieren, herumwursteln; ~**y** Töpferwaren pl, Steingut nt; (place) Töpferei f.

potty ['pɒtı] a (col) verrückt; n Töpfchen nt.

pouch [pautʃ] n Beutel m; (under eyes) Tränensack m; (for tobacco) Tabaksbeutel m.

pouffe [puːf] n Sitzkissen nt.

poultice ['pəultıs] n Packung f.

poultry ['pəultrı] n Geflügel nt; ~ **farm** Geflügelfarm f.

pounce [pauns] vi sich stürzen (on auf +acc); n Sprung m, Satz m.

pound [paund] n (Fin, weight) Pfund nt; (for cars, animals) Auslösestelle f; (for stray animals) (Tier)asyl nt; (col) Halunken, hämmern; vt (zer)stampfen; ~**ing** starke(s) Klopfen nt, Hämmern nt; (Zer)stampfen nt.

pour [pɔː*] vt gießen, schütten; vi gießen;

(crowds etc) strömen; ~ **away** vt, ~ **off** vt abgießen; ~**ing rain** strömende(r) Regen m.

pout [paut] n Schnute f, Schmollmund m; vi eine Schnute ziehen, schmollen.

poverty ['pɒvətı] n Armut f; ~-**stricken** a verarmt, sehr arm.

powder ['paudə*] n Pulver nt; (cosmetic) Puder m; vt pulverisieren; (sprinkle) bestreuen; to ~ **one's nose** sich (dat) die Nase pudern; ~ **room** Damentoilette f; ~**y** a pulverig, Pulver-.

power [pauə*] n Macht f (also Pol); (ability) Fähigkeit f; (strength) Stärke f; (authority) Macht f, Befugnis f; (Math) Potenz f; (Elec) Strom m; vt betreiben, antreiben; ~ **cut** Stromausfall m; ~**ful** a person mächtig; engine, government stark; ~**less** a machtlos; ~ **line** (Haupt)stromleitung f; ~ **point** elektrische(r) Anschluß m; ~ **station** Elektrizitätswerk nt.

powwow ['pauwau] n Besprechung f; vi eine Besprechung abhalten.

practicability [præktıkə'bılıtı] n Durchführbarkeit f.

practicable ['præktıkəbl] a durchführbar.

practical a, ~**ly** ad ['præktıkəl, -ı] praktisch; ~ **joke** Streich m.

practice ['præktıs] n Übung f; (reality) Praxis m; (custom) Brauch m; (in business) Usus m; (doctor's, lawyer's) Praxis f; **in** ~ (in reality) in der Praxis; **out of** ~ außer Übung.

practise, (US) **practice** ['præktıs] vt üben; profession ausüben; to ~ **law/medicine** als Rechtsanwalt/Arzt arbeiten; vi (sich) üben; (doctor, lawyer) praktizieren; ~**d** a erfahren.

practising, (US) **practicing** ['præktısıŋ] a praktizierend; Christian etc aktiv.

practitioner [præk'tıʃənə*] n praktische(r) Arzt m.

pragmatic [præg'mætık] a pragmatisch.

pragmatism ['prægmətızəm] n Pragmatismus m.

pragmatist ['prægmətıst] n Pragmatiker m.

prairie ['prɛərı] n Prärie f, Steppe f.

praise [preız] n Lob nt, Preis m; vt loben; (worship) (lob)preisen, loben; ~**worthy** a lobenswert.

pram [præm] n Kinderwagen m.

prance [prɑːns] vi (horse) tänzeln; (person) stolzieren; (gaily) herumhüpfen.

prank [præŋk] n Streich m.

prattle ['prætl] vi schwatzen, plappern.

prawn [prɔːn] n Garnele f, Krabbe f.

pray [preı] vi beten; ~**er** [prɛə*] Gebet nt; ~**er book** Gebetbuch nt.

pre- [priː] pref prä-, vor(her)-.

preach [priːtʃ] vi predigen; ~**er** Prediger m.

preamble [priː'æmbl] n Einleitung f.

prearrange ['priːə'reındʒ] vt vereinbaren, absprechen; ~**d** a vereinbart; ~**ment** Vereinbarung f, vorherige Absprache f.

precarious a, ~**ly** ad [prı'kɛərıəs, -lı] prekär, unsicher.

precaution [prı'kɔːʃən] n (Vorsichts)maßnahme f, Vorbeugung f; ~**ary**

a measure vorbeugend, Vorsichts-.

precede [prɪ'siːd] *vti* vorausgehen (+*dat*); *(be more important)* an Bedeutung übertreffen; **~nce** ['presɪdəns] Priorität *f*, Vorrang *m*; **to take ~nce over** den Vorrang haben vor (+*dat*); **~nt** ['presɪdənt] Präzedenzfall *m*.

preceding [prɪ'siːdɪŋ] *a* vorhergehend.

precept ['priːsept] *n* Gebot *nt*, Regel *f*.

precinct ['priːsɪŋkt] *n* Gelände *f*; *(district)* Bezirk *m*; *(shopping —)* Einkaufszone *f*.

precious ['preʃəs] *a* kostbar, wertvoll; *(affected)* preziös, geziert.

precipice ['presɪpɪs] *n* Abgrund *m*.

precipitate *a*, **~ly** *ad* [prɪ'sɪpɪtɪt, -lɪ] überstürzt, übereilt; *vt* [prɪ'sɪpɪteɪt] hinunterstürzen; *events* heraufbeschwören.

precipitation [prɪsɪpɪ'teɪʃən] *n* Niederschlag *m*.

precipitous *a*, **~ly** *ad* [prɪ'sɪpɪtəs, -lɪ] abschüssig; *action* überstürzt.

précis ['preɪsiː] *n (kurze)* Übersicht *f*, Zusammenfassung *f*; *(Sch)* Inhaltsangabe *f*.

precise *a*, **~ly** *ad* [prɪ'saɪs, -lɪ] genau, präzis.

preclude [prɪ'kluːd] *vt* ausschließen; *person* abhalten.

precocious [prɪ'kəʊʃəs] *a* frühreif.

preconceived ['priːkən'siːvd] *a idea* vorgefaßt.

precondition ['priːkən'dɪʃən] *n* Vorbedingung *f*, Voraussetzung *f*.

precursor [priː'kɜːsə*] *n* Vorläufer *m*.

predator ['predətə*] *n* Raubtier *nt*; **~y** *a* Raub-; räuberisch.

predecessor ['priːdɪsesə*] *n* Vorgänger *m*.

predestination [priːdestɪ'neɪʃən] *n* Vorherbestimmung *f*, Prädestination *f*.

predestine [priː'destɪn] *vt* vorherbestimmen.

predetermine ['priːdɪ'tɜːmɪn] *vt* vorherentscheiden, vorherbestimmen.

predicament [prɪ'dɪkəmənt] *n* mißliche Lage *f*; **to be in a ~** in der Klemme sitzen.

predicate ['predɪkət] *n* Prädikat *nt*, Satzaussage *f*.

predict [prɪ'dɪkt] *vt* voraussagen; **~ion** [prɪ'dɪkʃən] Voraussage *f*.

predominance [prɪ'dɒmɪnəns] *n (in power)* Vorherrschaft *f*; *(fig)* Vorherrschen *nt*, Überwiegen *nt*.

predominant [prɪ'dɒmɪnənt] *a* vorherrschend; *(fig also)* überwiegend; **~ly** *ad* überwiegend, hauptsächlich.

predominate [prɪ'dɒmɪneɪt] *vi* vorherrschen; *(fig also)* überwiegen.

pre-eminent [priː'emɪnənt] *a* hervorragend, herausragend.

pre-empt [priː'empt] *vt action, decision* vorwegnehmen.

preen [priːn] *vt* putzen; **to ~ o.s. on sth** sich *(dat)* etwas auf etw *(acc)* einbilden.

prefab ['priːfæb] *n* Fertighaus *nt*.

prefabricated ['priː'fæbrɪkeɪtɪd] *a* vorgefertigt, Fertig-.

preface ['prefɪs] *n* Vorwort *nt*, Einleitung *f*.

prefect ['priːfekt] *n* Präfekt *m*; *(Sch)* Aufsichtsschüler(in *f*) *m*.

prefer [prɪ'fɜː*] *vt* vorziehen, lieber mögen; **to ~ to do sth** etw lieber tun; **~able** ['prefərəbl] *a* vorzuziehen(d) (*to dat*); **~ably** ['prefərəblɪ] *ad* vorzugsweise, am liebsten; **~ence** ['prefərəns] Präferenz *f*, Vorzug *m*; **~ential** [prefə'renʃəl] *a* bevorzugt, Vorzugs-.

prefix ['priːfɪks] *n* Vorsilbe *f*, Präfix *nt*.

pregnancy ['pregnənsɪ] *n* Schwangerschaft *f*.

pregnant ['pregnənt] *a* schwanger; **~ with meaning** *(fig)* bedeutungsschwer *or* -voll.

prehistoric ['priːhɪs'tɒrɪk] *a* prähistorisch, vorgeschichtlich.

prehistory ['priː'hɪstərɪ] *n* Urgeschichte *f*.

prejudge ['priːdʒʌdʒ] *vt* vorschnell beurteilen.

prejudice ['predʒudɪs] *n* Vorurteil *nt*; Voreingenommenheit *f*; *(harm)* Schaden *m*; *vt* beeinträchtigen; **~d** *a person* voreingenommen.

prelate ['prelət] *n* Prälat *m*.

preliminary [prɪ'lɪmɪnərɪ] *a* einleitend, Vor-; **the preliminaries** *pl* die vorbereitenden Maßnahmen *pl*.

prelude ['preljuːd] *n* Vorspiel *nt*; *(Mus)* Präludium *nt*; *(fig also)* Auftakt *m*.

premarital ['priː'mærɪtl] *a* vorehelich.

premature ['premətʃʊə*] *a* vorzeitig, verfrüht; *birth* Früh-; *decision* voreilig; **~ly** *ad* vorzeitig; verfrüht; voreilig.

premeditate [priː'medɪteɪt] *vt* im voraus planen; **~d** *a* geplant; *murder* vorsätzlich.

premeditation [priːmedɪ'teɪʃən] *n* Planung *f*.

premier ['premɪə*] *a* erste(r, s), oberste(r, s), höchste(r, s); *n* Premier *m*.

premiere [premɪ'eə*] *n* Premiere *f*; Uraufführung *f*.

premise ['premɪs] *n* Voraussetzung *f*, Prämisse *f*; **~s** *pl* Räumlichkeiten *pl*; *(grounds)* Grundstück *nt*.

premium ['priːmɪəm] *n* Prämie *f*; **to sell at a ~** mit Gewinn verkaufen.

premonition [premə'nɪʃən] *n* Vorahnung *f*.

preoccupation [priːɒkjʊ'peɪʃən] *n* Sorge *f*.

preoccupied [priː'ɒkjʊpaɪd] *a look* geistesabwesend; **to be ~ with** mit dem Gedanken an etw *(acc)* beschäftigt sein.

prep [prep] *n (Sch: study)* Hausaufgabe *f*.

prepaid ['priː'peɪd] *a* vorausbezahlt; *letter* frankiert.

preparation ['prepə'reɪʃən] *n* Vorbereitung *f*.

preparatory [prɪ'pærətərɪ] *a* Vor-(bereitungs)-.

prepare [prɪ'peə*] *vt* vorbereiten *(for auf +acc)*; *vi* sich vorbereiten; **to be ~d to ...** bereit sein zu ...

preponderance [prɪ'pɒndərəns] *n* Übergewicht *nt*.

preposition [prepə'zɪʃən] *n* Präposition *f*, Verhältniswort *nt*.

preposterous [prɪ'pɒstərəs] *a* absurd, widersinnig.

prerequisite ['pri:'rekwɪzɪt] *n.* (unerläßliche) Voraussetzung *f.*

prerogative [prɪ'rɒgətɪv] *n* Vorrecht *nt,* Privileg *nt.*

presbytery ['prezbɪtərɪ] *n (house)* Presbyterium *nt; (Catholic)* Pfarrhaus *nt.*

prescribe [prɪs'kraɪb] *vt* vorschreiben, anordnen; *(Med)* verschreiben.

prescription [prɪs'krɪpʃən] *n* Vorschrift *f; (Med)* Rezept *nt.*

prescriptive [prɪs'krɪptɪv] *a* normativ.

presence ['prezns] *n* Gegenwart *f,* Anwesenheit *f;* ~ **of mind** Geistesgegenwart *f.*

present ['preznt] *a* anwesend; *(existing)* gegenwärtig, augenblicklich; *n* Gegenwart *f;* **at** ~ im Augenblick; Präsens *nt (Gram); (gift)* Geschenk *nt;* [prɪ'zent] *vt* vorlegen; *(introduce)* vorstellen; *(show)* zeigen; *(give)* überreichen; **to** ~ **sb with sth** jdm etw überreichen; ~**able** [prɪ'zentəbl] *a* präsentabel; ~**ation** Überreichung *f;* ~**-day** *a* heutig, gegenwärtig, modern; ~**ly** *ad* bald; *(at present)* im Augenblick; ~ **participle** Partizip *nt* des Präsens, Mittelwort *nt* der Gegenwart; ~ **tense** Präsens *nt,* Gegenwart *f.*

preservation [prezə'veɪʃən] *n* Erhaltung *f.*

preservative [prɪ'zɜ:vətɪv] *n* Konservierungsmittel *nt.*

preserve [prɪ'zɜ:v] *vt* erhalten, schützen; *food* einmachen, konservieren; *n (jam)* Eingemachte(s) *nt; (hunting)* Schutzgebiet *nt.*

preside [prɪ'zaɪd] *vi* den Vorsitz haben.

presidency ['prezɪdənsɪ] *n (Pol)* Präsidentschaft *f.*

president ['prezɪdənt] *n* Präsident *m;* ~**ial** [prezɪ'denʃəl] *a* Präsidenten-; *election* Präsidentschafts-; *system* Präsidial-.

press [pres] *n* Presse *f; (printing house)* Druckerei *f;* **to give the clothes a** ~ die Kleider bügeln; *vt* drücken, pressen; *(iron)* bügeln; *(urge)* (be)drängen; *vi (push)* drücken, pressen; **to be** ~**ed for time** unter Zeitdruck stehen; **to be** ~**ed for money/space** wenig Geld/Platz haben; **to** ~ **for sth** drängen auf etw *(acc);* ~ **on** *vi* vorwärtsdrängen; ~ **agency** Presseagentur *f;* ~ **conference** Pressekonferenz *f;* ~ **cutting** Zeitungsausschnitt *m;* ~**ing** *a* dringend; ~**-stud** Druckknopf *m.*

pressure ['preʃə*] *n* Druck *m;* ~ **cooker** Schnellkochtopf *m;* ~ **gauge** Druckmesser *m;* ~ **group** Interessenverband *m,* Pressure Group *f.*

pressurized ['preʃəraɪzd] *a* Druck-.

prestige [pres'ti:ʒ] *n* Ansehen *nt,* Prestige *nt.*

prestigious [pres'tɪdʒəs] *a* Prestige-.

presumably [prɪ'zju:məblɪ] *ad* vermutlich.

presume [prɪ'zju:m] *vti* annehmen; *(dare)* sich erlauben.

presumption [prɪ'zʌmpʃən] *n* Annahme *f; (impudent behaviour)* Anmaßung *f.*

presumptuous [prɪ'zʌmptjuəs] *a* anmaßend.

presuppose [pri:sə'pəuz] *vt* voraussetzen.

presupposition [pri:sʌpə'zɪʃən] *n* Voraussetzung *f.*

pretence [prɪ'tens] *n* Vorgabe *f,* Vortäuschung *f; (false claim)* Vorwand *m.*

pretend [prɪ'tend] *vt* vorgeben, so tun als ob ...; *vi* so tun; **to** ~ **to sth** Anspruch erheben auf etw *(acc).*

pretense [prɪ'tens] *n (US)* = **pretence.**

pretension [prɪ'tenʃən] *n* Anspruch *m; (impudent claim)* Anmaßung *f.*

pretentious [prɪ'tenʃəs] *a* angeberisch.

pretext ['pri:tekst] *n* Vorwand *m.*

prettily ['prɪtɪlɪ] *ad* hübsch, nett.

pretty ['prɪtɪ] *a* hübsch, nett; *ad (col)* ganz schön.

prevail [prɪ'veɪl] *vi* siegen *(against, over* über +*acc); (custom)* vorherrschen; **to** ~ **upon sb to do sth** jdn dazu bewegen, etw zu tun; ~**ing** *a* vorherrschend.

prevalent ['prevələnt] *a* vorherrschend.

prevarication [prɪværɪ'keɪʃən] *n* Ausflucht *f.*

prevent [prɪ'vent] *vt (stop)* verhindern, verhüten; **to** ~ **sb from doing sth** jdn (daran) hindern, etw zu tun; ~**able** *a* verhütbar; ~**ative** Vorbeugungsmittel *nt;* ~**ion** [prɪ'venʃən] Verhütung *f,* Schutz *m (of* gegen); ~**ive** *a* vorbeugend, Schutz-.

preview ['pri:vju:] *n* private Voraufführung *f; (trailer)* Vorschau *f; vt film* privat vorführen.

previous ['pri:vɪəs] *a* früher, vorherig; ~**ly** *ad* früher.

prewar ['pri:'wɔ:*] *a* Vorkriegs-.

prey [preɪ] *n* Beute *f;* ~ **on** *vt* Jagd machen auf *(+acc); mind* nagen an *(+dat);* **bird/beast of** ~ Raubvogel *m/*Raubtier *nt.*

price [praɪs] *n* Preis *m; (value)* Wert *m; vt* schätzen; *(label)* auszeichnen; ~**less** *a (lit, fig)* unbezahlbar; ~ **list** Preisliste *f;* ~**y** *a (col)* teuer.

prick [prɪk] *n* Stich *m; vti* stechen; **to** ~ **up one's ears** die Ohren spitzen.

prickle ['prɪkl] *n* Stachel *m,* Dorn *m; vi* brennen.

prickly ['prɪklɪ] *a* stachelig; *(fig) person* reizbar; ~ **heat** Hitzebläschen *pl;* ~ **pear** Feigenkaktus *m; (fruit)* Kaktusfeige *f.*

pride [praɪd] *n* Stolz *m; (arrogance)* Hochmut *m;* **to** ~ **o.s. on sth** auf etw *(acc)* stolz sein.

priest [pri:st] *n* Priester *m;* ~**ess** Priesterin *f;* ~**hood** Priesteramt *nt.*

prig [prɪg] *n* Selbstgefällige(r) *mf.*

prim *a,* ~**ly** *ad* [prɪm, -lɪ] prüde.

prima donna ['pri:mə 'dɒnə] *n* Primadonna *f.*

primarily ['praɪmərɪlɪ] *ad* vorwiegend, hauptsächlich.

primary ['praɪmərɪ] *a* Haupt-, Grund-, primär; ~ **colour** Grundfarbe *f;* ~ **education** Grundschul(aus)bildung *f;* ~ **election** Vorwahl *f;* ~ **school** Grundschule *f,* Volksschule *f.*

primate ['praɪmɪt] *n (Eccl)* Primas *m; (Biol)* Primat *m.*

prime [praɪm] *a* oberste(r, s), erste(r, s), wichtigste(r, s); *(excellent)* erstklassig, prima *inv; vt* vorbereiten; *gun* laden; *n (of*

life) beste(s) Alter nt; ~ **minister**
Premierminister m, Ministerpräsident m;
~**r** Elementarlehrbuch nt, Fibel f.
primeval [praɪˈmiːvəl] a vorzeitlich; forests
Ur-.
primitive [ˈprɪmɪtɪv] a primitiv.
primrose [ˈprɪmrəʊz] n (gelbe) Primel f.
primula [ˈprɪmjʊlə] n Primel f.
primus (stove) [ˈpraɪməs (stəʊv)] n
Primuskocher m.
prince [prɪns] n Prinz m; (ruler) Fürst m;
~**ss** [prɪnˈses] Prinzessin f; Fürstin f.
principal [ˈprɪnsɪpəl] a Haupt-;
wichtigste(r, s); n (Sch) (Schul)direktor m,
Rektor m; (money) (Grund)kapital nt;
~**ity** [prɪnsɪˈpælɪt] Fürstentum nt; ~**ly** ad
hauptsächlich.
principle [ˈprɪnsəpl] n Grundsatz m,
Prinzip nt; **in/on** ~ im/aus Prinzip,
prinzipiell.
print [prɪnt] n Druck m; (made by feet,
fingers) Abdruck m; (Phot) Abzug m;
(cotton) Kattun m; vt drucken; name in
Druckbuchstaben schreiben; Photo
abziehen; ~**ed matter** Drucksache f;
~**er** Drucker m; ~**ing** Drucken nt; (of
photos) Abziehen nt; ~**ing press** Drucker-
presse f; **is the book still in** ~? wird das
Buch noch gedruckt?; **out of** ~ vergriffen.
prior [ˈpraɪə*] a früher; ~ **to** sth vor etw
(dat); ~ **to going abroad, she had . . .**
bevor sie ins Ausland ging, hatte sie ...; n
Prior m; ~**ess** Priorin f; ~**ity** [praɪˈɒrɪtɪ]
Vorrang m; Priorität f; ~**y** Kloster nt.
prise [praɪz] vt: ~ **open** aufbrechen.
prism [ˈprɪzəm] n Prisma nt.
prison [ˈprɪzn] n Gefängnis nt; ~**er**
Gefangene(r) mf; ~**er of war** Kriegs-
gefangene(r) m; **to be taken** ~**er** in
Gefangenschaft geraten.
prissy [ˈprɪsɪ] a (col) etepetete.
pristine [ˈprɪstiːn] a makellos.
privacy [ˈprɪvəsɪ] n Ungestörtheit f, Ruhe
f; Privatleben nt.
private [ˈpraɪvɪt] a privat, Privat-; (secret)
vertraulich, geheim; soldier einfach; n
einfache(r) Soldat m; **in** ~ privat, unter
vier Augen; ~ **eye** Privatdetektiv m; ~**ly**
ad privat; vertraulich, geheim.
privet [ˈprɪvɪt] n Liguster m.
privilege [ˈprɪvɪlɪdʒ] n Vorrecht nt, Vergünstigung f, Privileg nt; ~**d** a bevorzugt,
privilegiert.
privy [ˈprɪvɪ] a geheim, privat; ~ **council**
Geheime(r) Staatsrat m.
prize [praɪz] n Preis m; a example erstklassig; idiot Voll-; vt (hoch)schätzen; ~
fighting Preisboxen nt; ~ **giving** Preis-
verteilung f; ~ **money** Geldpreis m;
~**winner** Preisträger(in f) m; (of money)
Gewinner(in f) m.
pro- [prəʊ] pref pro-; n: the ~**s and cons**
pl das Für und Wider.
pro [prəʊ] n (professional) Profi m.
probability [prɒbəˈbɪlɪtɪ] n Wahrscheinlichkeit f; **in all** ~ aller Wahrscheinlichkeit nach.
probable a, **probably** ad [ˈprɒbəbl, -blɪ]
wahrscheinlich.

probation [prəˈbeɪʃən] n Probe(zeit) f;
(Jur) Bewährung f; **on** ~ auf Probe; auf
Bewährung; ~ **officer** Bewährungshelfer
m; ~**ary** a Probe-; ~**er** (nurse) Lern-
schwester f; Pfleger m in der Ausbildung;
(Jur) auf Bewährung freigelassene(r)
Gefangene(r) m.
probe [prəʊb] n Sonde f; (enquiry) Untersuchung f; vti untersuchen, erforschen,
sondieren.
probity [ˈprəʊbɪtɪ] n Rechtschaffenheit f.
problem [ˈprɒbləm] n Problem nt; ~**atic**
[prɒblɪˈmætɪk] a problematisch.
procedural [prəˈsiːdjʊrəl] a verfahrens-
mäßig, Verfahrens-.
procedure [prəˈsiːdʒə*] n Verfahren nt,
Vorgehen nt.
proceed [prəˈsiːd] vi (advance) vorrücken;
(start) anfangen; (carry on) fortfahren; (set
about) vorgehen; (come from) entstehen
(from aus); (Jur) gerichtlich vorgehen;
~**ings** pl Verfahren nt; (record of things)
Sitzungsbericht m; ~**s** [ˈprəʊsiːdz] pl Erlös
m, Gewinn m.
process [ˈprəʊses] n Vorgang m, Prozeß m;
(method also) Verfahren nt; vt bearbeiten;
food verarbeiten; film entwickeln; ~**ing**
(Phot) Entwickeln nt.
procession [prəˈseʃən] n Prozession f,
Umzug m.
proclaim [prəˈkleɪm] vt verkünden,
proklamieren; **to** ~ **sb king** jdn zum
König ausrufen.
proclamation [prɒkləˈmeɪʃən] n
Verkündung f, Proklamation f; Ausrufung
f.
procrastination [prəʊkræstɪˈneɪʃən] n
Hinausschieben nt.
procreation [prəʊkrɪˈeɪʃən] n (Er)zeugung
f.
procure [prəˈkjʊə*] vt beschaffen.
prod [prɒd] vt stoßen; **to** ~ **sb** (fig)
bohren; n Stoß m.
prodigal [ˈprɒdɪgəl] a verschwenderisch
(of mit); **the** ~ **son** der verlorene Sohn.
prodigious [prəˈdɪdʒəs] a gewaltig,
erstaunlich; (wonderful) wunderbar.
prodigy [ˈprɒdɪdʒɪ] n Wunder nt; **a child**
~ ein Wunderkind.
produce [ˈprɒdjuːs] n (Agr)
(Boden)produkte pl, (Natur)erzeugnis nt;
[prəˈdjuːs] vt herstellen, produzieren;
(cause) hervorrufen; (farmer) erzeugen;
(yield) liefern, bringen; play inszenieren;
~**r** Erzeuger m; Hersteller m, Produzent
m (also Cine).
product [ˈprɒdʌkt] n Produkt nt, Erzeugnis
nt; ~**ion** [prəˈdʌkʃən] Produktion f, Herstellung f; (thing) Erzeugnis nt, Produkt nt;
(Theat) Inszenierung f; ~**ion line**
Fließband nt; ~**ive** a produktiv; (fertile)
ertragreich, fruchtbar; **to be** ~**ive of**
führen zu, erzeugen.
productivity [prɒdʌkˈtɪvɪtɪ] n
Produktivität f; (Comm) Leistungsfähigkeit
f; (fig) Fruchtbarkeit f.
prof [prɒf] n (col) Professor m.
profane [prəˈfeɪn] a weltlich, profan,
Profan-.
profess [prəˈfes] vt bekennen; (show)

zeigen; *(claim to be)* vorgeben; **~ion** [prɔ'feʃən] Beruf *m; (declaration)* Bekenntnis *nt;* **~ional** [prɔ'feʃənl] Fachmann *m; (Sport)* Berufsspieler(in *f*) *m; a* Berufs-; *(expert)* fachlich; *player* professionell; **~ionalism** [prɔ'feʃnəlɪzəm] *(fachliches)* Können *nt;* Berufssportlertum *nt;* **~or** Professor *m.*

proficiency [prɔ'fɪʃənsɪ] *n* Fertigkeit *f,* Können *nt.*

proficient [prɔ'fɪʃnt] *a* fähig.

profile ['prəʊfaɪl] *n* Profil *nt; (fig: report)* Kurzbiographie *f.*

profit ['prɒfɪt] *n* Gewinn *m,* Profit *m; vi* profitieren *(by, from* von), Nutzen *or* Gewinn ziehen *(by, from* aus); **~ability** [prɒfɪtə'bɪlɪtɪ] Rentabilität *f;* **~able** *a* einträglich, rentabel; **~ably** *ad* nützlich; **~eering** [prɒfɪ'tɪərɪŋ] Profitmacherei *f.*

profound [prɔ'faʊnd] *a* tief; *knowledge* profund; *book, thinker* tiefschürfend; **~ly** *ad* zutiefst.

profuse [prɔ'fjuːs] *a* überreich; **to be ~ in** überschwenglich sein bei; **~ly** *ad* überschwenglich; *sweat* reichlich.

profusion [prɔ'fjuːʒən] *n* Überfülle *f,* Überfluß *m (of an* +*dat).*

progeny ['prɒdʒɪnɪ] *n* Nachkommenschaft *f.*

programme, *(US)* **program** ['prəʊgræm] *n* Programm *nt; vt* planen; *computer* programmieren.

programming, *(US)* **programing** ['prəʊgræmɪŋ] *n* Programmieren *nt,* Programmierung *f.*

progress ['prəʊgres] *n* Fortschritt *m;* **to be in ~** im Gang sein; **to make ~** Fortschritte machen; [prɔ'gres] *vi* fortschreiten, weitergehen; **~ion** [prɔ'greʃən] Fortschritt *m,* Progression *f; (walking etc)* Fortbewegung *f;* **~ive** [prɔ'gresɪv] *a* fortschrittlich, progressiv; **~ively** [prɔ'gresɪvlɪ] *ad* zunehmend.

prohibit [prɔ'hɪbɪt] *vt* verbieten; **~ion** [prəʊɪ'bɪʃən] Verbot *nt; (US)* Alkoholverbot *nt,* Prohibition *f;* **~ive** *a price etc* unerschwinglich.

project ['prɒdʒekt] *n* Projekt *nt;* [prɔ'dʒekt] *vt* vorausplanen; *(Psych)* hineinprojizieren; *film etc* projizieren; *personality, voice* zum Tragen bringen; *vi (stick out)* hervorragen, (her)vorstehen; **~ile** [prɔ'dʒektaɪl] Geschoß *nt,* Projektil *nt;* **~ion** [prɔ'dʒekʃən] Projektion *f; (sth prominent)* Vorsprung *m;* **~or** [prɔ'dʒektə*] Projektor *m,* Vorführgerät *nt.*

proletarian [prəʊlə'tɛərɪən] *a* proletarisch, Proletarier-; *n* Proletarier(in *f*) *m.*

proletariat [prəʊlə'tɛərɪət] *n* Proletariat *nt.*

proliferate [prɔ'lɪfəreɪt] *vi* sich vermehren.

proliferation [prɔlɪfə'reɪʃən] *n* Vermehrung *f.*

prolific [prɔ'lɪfɪk] *a* fruchtbar; *author etc* produktiv.

prologue ['prəʊlɒg] *n* Prolog *m; (event)* Vorspiel *nt.*

prolong [prɔ'lɒŋ] *vt* verlängern; **~ed** *a* lang.

prom [prɒm] *n abbr of* **promenade** *and* **promenade concert;** *(US: college ball)* Studentenball *m.*

promenade [prɒmɪ'nɑːd] *n* Promenade *f;* **~ concert** Promenadenkonzert *nt,* Stehkonzert *nt;* **~ deck** Promenadendeck *nt.*

prominence ['prɒmɪnəns] *n (große)* Bedeutung *f,* Wichtigkeit *f; (sth standing out)* vorspringende(r) Teil *m.*

prominent ['prɒmɪnənt] *a* bedeutend; *politician* prominent; *(easily seen)* herausragend, auffallend.

promiscuity [prɒmɪs'kjuːɪtɪ] *n* Promiskuität *f.*

promiscuous [prɔ'mɪskjʊəs] *a* lose; *(mixed up)* wild.

promise ['prɒmɪs] *n* Versprechen *nt; (hope)* Aussicht *f (of* auf + *acc);* **to show ~** vielversprechend sein; **a writer of ~** ein vielversprechender Schriftsteller; *vti* versprechen; **the ~d land** das Gelobte Land.

promising ['prɒmɪsɪŋ] *a* vielversprechend.

promontory ['prɒməntrɪ] *n* Vorsprung *m.*

promote [prɔ'məʊt] *vt* befördern; *(help on)* fördern, unterstützen; **~r** *(in sport, entertainment)* Veranstalter *m; (for charity etc)* Organisator *m.*

promotion [prɔ'məʊʃən] *n (in rank)* Beförderung *f; (furtherance)* Förderung *f; (Comm)* Werbung *f (of* für).

prompt [prɒmpt] *a* prompt, schnell; **to be ~ to do sth** etw sofort tun; *ad (punctually)* genau; **at two o'clock ~** punkt zwei Uhr; *vt* veranlassen; *(Theat)* einsagen *(+dat),* soufflieren *(+dat);* **~er** *(Theat)* Souffleur *m,* Souffleuse *f;* **~ly** *ad* sofort; **~ness** Schnelligkeit *f,* Promptheit *f.*

promulgate ['prɒməlgeɪt] *vt* (öffentlich) bekanntmachen, verkünden; *beliefs* verbreiten.

prone [prəʊn] *a* hingestreckt; **to be ~ to sth** zu etw neigen.

prong [prɒŋ] *n* Zinke *f.*

pronoun ['prəʊnaʊn] *n* Pronomen *nt,* Fürwort *nt.*

pronounce [prɔ'naʊns] *vt* aussprechen; *(Jur)* verkünden; *vi (give an opinion)* sich äußern *(on* zu); **~d** *a* ausgesprochen; **~ment** Erklärung *f.*

pronto ['prɒntəʊ] *ad (col)* fix, pronto.

pronunciation [prɔnʌnsɪ'eɪʃən] *n* Aussprache *f.*

proof [pruːf] *n* Beweis *m; (Print)* Korrekturfahne *f; (of alcohol)* Alkoholgehalt *m;* **to put to the ~** unter Beweis stellen; *a* sicher; *alcohol* prozentig; **rain~** regendicht.

prop [prɒp] *n* Stütze *f (also fig); (Min)* Stempel *m; (Theat)* Requisit *nt; vt (also ~ up)* (ab)stützen.

propaganda [prɒpə'gændə] *n* Propaganda *f.*

propagate ['prɒpəgeɪt] *vt* fortpflanzen; *news* propagieren, verbreiten.

propagation [prɒpə'geɪʃən] *n* Fortpflanzung *f;* *(of knowledge also)* Verbreitung *f.*

propel [prə'pel] *vt* (an)treiben; ∼ler Propeller *m;* ∼ling pencil Drehbleistift *m.*

propensity [prə'pensıtı] *n* Tendenz *f.*

proper ['propə*] *a* richtig; *(seemly)* schicklich; ∼ly *ad* richtig; ∼ly speaking genau genommen; it is not ∼ to ... es schickt sich nicht, zu ...; ∼ noun Eigenname *m.*

property ['propətı] *n* Eigentum *nt*, Besitz *m*, Gut *nt;* *(quality)* Eigenschaft *f;* *(land)* Grundbesitz *m;* *(Theat)* properties *pl* Requisiten *pl;* ∼ owner Grundbesitzer *m.*

prophecy ['profısı] *n* Prophezeiung *f.*

prophesy ['profısaı] *vt* prophezeien, vorhersagen.

prophet ['profıt] *n* Prophet *m;* ∼ic [prə'fetık] *a* prophetisch.

proportion [prə'pɔ:ʃən] *n* Verhältnis *nt*, Proportion *f;* *(share)* Teil *m;* *vt* abstimmen *(to* auf *+acc);* ∼al *a*, ∼ally *ad* proportional, verhältnismäßig; to be ∼al to entsprechen *(+dat);* ∼ate *a*, ∼ately *ad* verhältnismäßig; ∼ed *a* proportioniert.

proposal [prə'pəuzl] *n* Vorschlag *m*, Antrag *m;* *(of marriage)* Heiratsantrag *m.*

propose [prə'pəuz] *vt* vorschlagen; *toast* ausbringen; *vi* *(offer marriage)* einen Heiratsantrag machen; ∼r Antragsteller *m.*

proposition [propə'zıʃən] *n* Angebot *nt;* *(Math)* Lehrsatz *m;* *(statement)* Satz *m.*

propound [prə'paund] *vt theory* vorlegen.

proprietary [prə'praıətərı] *a* Eigentums-; *medicine* gesetzlich geschützt.

proprietor [prə'praıətə*] *n* Besitzer *m*, Eigentümer *m.*

props [props] *npl* Requisiten *pl.*

propulsion [prə'pʌlʃən] *n* Antrieb *m.*

pro-rata [prəu'rɑ:tə] *ad* anteilmäßig.

prosaic [prə'zeıık] *a* prosaisch, alltäglich.

prose [prəuz] *n* Prosa *f.*

prosecute ['prosıkju:t] *vt* (strafrechtlich) verfolgen.

prosecution [prosı'kju:ʃən] *n* Durchführung *f;* *(Jur)* strafrechtliche Verfolgung *f;* *(party)* Anklage *f;* Staatsanwaltschaft *f.*

prosecutor ['prosıkju:tə*] *n* Vertreter *m* der Anklage; Public P∼ Staatsanwalt *m.*

prospect ['prospekt] *n* Aussicht *f;* [prəs'pekt] *vi* suchen *(for* nach); ∼ing [prəs'pektıŋ] *(for minerals)* Suche *f;* ∼ive [prəs'pektıv] *a* möglich; ∼or [prəs'pektə*] (Gold)sucher *m;* ∼us [prəs'pektəs] (Werbe)prospekt *m.*

prosper ['prospə*] *vi* blühen, gedeihen; *(person)* erfolgreich sein; ∼ity [pros'perıtı] Wohlstand *m;* ∼ous *a* wohlhabend, reich; *business* gutgehend, blühend.

prostitute ['prostıtju:t] *n* Prostituierte *f.*

prostrate ['prostreıt] *a* ausgestreckt (liegend); ∼ with grief/exhaustion von Schmerz/Erschöpfung übermannt.

protagonist [prəu'tægonıst] *n* Hauptperson *f*, Held *m.*

protect [prə'tekt] *vt* (be)schützen; ∼ion [prə'tekʃən] Schutz *m;* ∼ive *a* Schutz-,

(be)schützend; ∼or (Be)schützer *m.*

protégé ['proteʒeı] *n* Schützling *m.*

protein ['prəuti:n] *n* Protein *nt*, Eiweiß *nt.*

protest ['prəutest] *n* Protest *m;* [prə'test] *vi* protestieren *(against* gegen*);* to ∼ that ... beteuern ...; P∼ant *a* protestantisch; *n* Protestant(in *f*) *m.*

protocol ['prəutəkol] *n* Protokoll *nt.*

prototype ['prəutəutaıp] *n* Prototyp *m.*

protracted [prə'træktıd] *a* sich hinziehend.

protractor [prə'træktə*] *n* Winkelmesser *m.*

protrude [prə'tru:d] *vi* (her)vorstehen.

protuberance [prə'tju:bərəns] *n* Auswuchs *m.*

protuberant [prə'tju:bərənt] *a* (her)vorstehend.

proud *a*, ∼ly *ad* [praud, -lı] stolz *(of* auf *+acc).*

prove [pru:v] *vt* beweisen; *vi* sich herausstellen, sich zeigen.

proverb ['provə:b] *n* Sprichwort *nt;* ∼ial *a*, ∼ially *ad* [prə'və:bıəl, -ı] sprichwörtlich.

provide [prə'vaıd] *vt* versehen; *(supply)* besorgen; *person* versorgen; ∼ for *vt* sorgen für, sich kümmern um; *emergency* Vorkehrungen treffen für; blankets will be ∼d Decken werden gestellt; ∼d (that) *cj* vorausgesetzt (daß); P∼nce ['provıdəns] die Vorsehung.

providing [prə'vaıdıŋ] *cj* = **provided (that).**

province ['provıns] *n* Provinz *f;* *(division of work)* Bereich *m;* the ∼s die Provinz.

provincial [prə'vınʃəl] *a* provinziell, Provinz-; *n* Provinzler(in *f*) *m.*

provision [prə'vıʒən] *n* Vorkehrung *f*, Maßnahme *f;* *(condition)* Bestimmung *f;* ∼s *pl* *(food)* Vorräte *pl*, Proviant *m;* ∼al *a*, ∼ally *ad* vorläufig, provisorisch.

proviso [prə'vaızəu] *n* Vorbehalt *m*, Bedingung *f.*

provocation [provə'keıʃən] *n* Provokation *f*, Herausforderung *f.*

provocative [prə'vokətıv] *a* provokativ, herausfordernd.

provoke [prə'vəuk] *vt* provozieren; *(cause)* hervorrufen.

prow [prau] *n* Bug *m;* ∼ess überragende(s) Können *nt;* *(valour)* Tapferkeit *f.*

prowl [praul] *vt streets* durchstreifen; *vi* herumstreichen; *(animal)* schleichen; *n:* on the ∼ umherstreifend; *(police)* auf der Streife; ∼er Eindringling *m.*

proximity [prok'sımıtı] *n* Nähe *f.*

proxy ['proksı] *n* (Stell)vertreter *m*, Bevollmächtigte(r) *m;* *(document)* Vollmacht *f;* to vote by ∼ Briefwahl machen.

prudence ['pru:dəns] *n* Klugheit *f*, Umsicht *f.*

prudent *a*, ∼ly *ad* ['pru:dənt, -lı] klug, umsichtig.

prudish ['pru:dıʃ] *a* prüde; ∼ness Prüderie *f.*

prune [pru:n] *n* Backpflaume *f;* *vt* ausputzen; *(fig)* zurechtstutzen.

pry [praɪ] vi seine Nase stecken (into in +acc).

psalm [sɑːm] n Psalm m.

pseudo ['sjuːdəʊ] a Pseudo-; (false) falsch, unecht; ~**nym** ['sjuːdənɪm] Pseudonym nt, Deckname m.

psyche ['saɪkɪ] n Psyche f.

psychiatric [saɪkɪ'ætrɪk] a psychiatrisch.

psychiatrist [saɪ'kaɪətrɪst] n Psychiater m.

psychiatry [saɪ'kaɪətrɪ] n Psychiatrie f.

psychic(al) ['saɪkɪk(əl)] a übersinnlich; person paranormal begabt; **you must be ~** du kannst wohl hellsehen.

psychoanalyse, (US) **psychoanalyze** [saɪkəʊ'ænəlaɪz] vt psychoanalytisch behandeln.

psychoanalysis [saɪkəʊə'nælɪsɪs] n Psychoanalyse f.

psychoanalyst [saɪkəʊ'ænəlɪst] n Psychoanalytiker(in f) m.

psychological a, ~**ly** ad [saɪkə'lɒdʒɪkəl, -ɪ] psychologisch.

psychologist [saɪ'kɒlədʒɪst] n Psychologe m, Psychologin f.

psychology [saɪ'kɒlədʒɪ] n Psychologie f.

psychopath ['saɪkəʊpæθ] n Psychopath(in f) m.

psychosomatic ['saɪkəʊsəʊ'mætɪk] a psychosomatisch.

psychotherapy ['saɪkəʊ'θerəpɪ] n Psychotherapie f.

psychotic [saɪ'kɒtɪk] a psychotisch; ~ Psychotiker(in f) m.

pub [pʌb] n Wirtschaft f, Kneipe f.

puberty ['pjuːbətɪ] n Pubertät f.

pubic ['pjuːbɪk] a Scham-.

public a, ~**ly** ad ['pʌblɪk, -lɪ] öffentlich; n (also **general** ~) Öffentlichkeit f; ~**an** Wirt m; ~**ation** [pʌblɪ'keɪʃən] Publikation f, Veröffentlichung f; ~ **company** Aktiengesellschaft f; ~ **convenience** öffentliche Toiletten pl; ~ **house** Lokal nt, Kneipe f; ~**ity** [pʌb'lɪsɪtɪ] Publicity f, Werbung f; ~ **opinion** öffentliche Meinung f; ~ **relations** pl Public Relations pl; ~ **school** (Brit) Privatschule f, Internatsschule f; ~-**spirited** a mit Gemeinschaftssinn; **to be** ~-**spirited** Gemeinschaftssinn haben.

publish ['pʌblɪʃ] vt veröffentlichen, publizieren; event bekanntgeben; ~**er** Verleger m; ~**ing** Herausgabe f, Verlegen nt; (business) Verlagswesen nt.

puce [pjuːs] a violettbraun.

puck [pʌk] n Puck m, Scheibe f.

pucker ['pʌkə*] vt face verziehen; lips kräuseln.

pudding ['pʊdɪŋ] n (course) Nachtisch m; Pudding m.

puddle ['pʌdl] n Pfütze f.

puerile ['pjʊəraɪl] a kindisch.

puff [pʌf] n (of wind etc) Stoß m; (cosmetic) Puderquaste f; vt blasen, pusten; pipe paffen; vi keuchen, schnaufen; (smoke) paffen; ~**ed** a (col: out of breath) außer Puste.

puffin ['pʌfɪn] n Papageitaucher m.

puff pastry, (US) **puff paste** ['pʌf'peɪstrɪ, 'pʌf'peɪst] n Blätterteig m.

puffy ['pʌfɪ] a aufgedunsen.

pull [pʊl] n Ruck m; Zug m; (influence) Beziehung f; vt ziehen; trigger abdrücken; vi ziehen; **to ~ a face** ein Gesicht schneiden; **to ~ sb's leg** jdn auf den Arm nehmen; **to ~ to pieces** (lit) in Stücke reißen; (fig) verreißen; **to ~ one's weight** sich in die Riemen legen; **to ~ o.s. together** sich zusammenreißen; ~ **apart** vt (break) zerreißen; (dismantle) auseinandernehmen; fighters trennen; ~ **down** vt house abreißen; ~ **in** vi hineinfahren; (stop) anhalten; (Rail) einfahren; ~ **off** vt deal etc abschließen; ~ **out** vi (car) herausfahren; (fig: partner) aussteigen; vt herausziehen; ~ **round**, ~ **through** vi durchkommen; ~ **up** vi anhalten.

pulley ['pʊlɪ] n Rolle f, Flaschenzug m.

pullover ['pʊləʊvə*] n Pullover m.

pulp [pʌlp] n Brei m; (of fruit) Fruchtfleisch nt.

pulpit ['pʊlpɪt] n Kanzel f.

pulsate [pʌl'seɪt] vi pulsieren.

pulse [pʌls] n Puls m.

pulverize ['pʌlvəraɪz] vt pulverisieren, in kleine Stücke zerlegen (also fig).

puma ['pjuːmə] n Puma m.

pummel ['pʌml] vt mit den Fäusten bearbeiten.

pump [pʌmp] n Pumpe f; (shoe) leichter (Tanz)schuh m; vt pumpen; ~ **up** vt tyre aufpumpen.

pumpkin ['pʌmpkɪn] n Kürbis m.

pun [pʌn] n Wortspiel nt.

punch [pʌntʃ] n (tool) Stanze f; Locher m; (blow) (Faust)schlag m; (drink) Punsch m, Bowle f; vt stanzen; lochen; (strike) schlagen, boxen; ~-**drunk** a benommen; ~-**up** (col) Keilerei f.

punctual ['pʌŋktjʊəl] a pünktlich; ~**ity** [pʌŋktjʊ'ælɪtɪ] Pünktlichkeit f.

punctuate ['pʌŋktjʊeɪt] vt mit Satzzeichen versehen, interpunktieren; (fig) unterbrechen.

punctuation [pʌŋktjʊ'eɪʃən] n Zeichensetzung f, Interpunktion f.

puncture ['pʌŋktʃə*] n Loch nt; (Aut) Reifenpanne f; vt durchbohren.

pundit ['pʌndɪt] n Gelehrte(r) m.

pungent ['pʌndʒənt] a scharf.

punish ['pʌnɪʃ] vt bestrafen; (in boxing etc) übel zurichten; ~**able** a strafbar; ~**ment** Strafe f; (action) Bestrafung f.

punitive ['pjuːnɪtɪv] a strafend.

punt [pʌnt] n Stechkahn m.

punter ['pʌntə*] n (better) Wetter m.

puny ['pjuːnɪ] a kümmerlich.

pup [pʌp] n = **puppy**.

pupil ['pjuːpl] n Schüler(in f) m; (in eye) Pupille f.

puppet ['pʌpɪt] n Puppe f; Marionette f.

puppy ['pʌpɪ] n junge(r) Hund m.

purchase ['pɜːtʃɪs] n Kauf m, Anschaffung f; (grip) Halt m; vt kaufen, erwerben; ~**r** Käufer(in f) m.

pure [pjʊə*] a pur; rein (also fig); ~**ly** ['pjʊəlɪ] ad rein; (only) nur; (with a also) rein.

purée ['pjuəreɪ] n Püree nt.

purgatory ['pɜːgətərɪ] n Fegefeuer nt.

purge [pɜːdʒ] n Säuberung f (also Pol); (medicine) Abführmittel nt; vt reinigen; body entschlacken.

purification [pjuərɪfɪ'keɪʃən] n Reinigung f.

purify ['pjuərɪfaɪ] vt reinigen.

purist ['pjuərɪst] n Purist m.

puritan ['pjuərɪtən] n Puritaner m; ~ical [pjuərɪ'tænɪkəl] a puritanisch.

purity ['pjuərɪtɪ] n Reinheit f.

purl [pɜːl] n linke Masche f; vt links stricken.

purple ['pɜːpl] a violett; face dunkelrot; n Violett nt.

purpose ['pɜːpəs] n Zweck m, Ziel nt; (of person) Absicht f; on ~ absichtlich; ~ful a zielbewußt, entschlossen; ~ly ad absichtlich.

purr [pɜː*] n Schnurren nt; vi schnurren.

purse [pɜːs] n Portemonnaie nt, Geldbeutel m; vt lips zusammenpressen, schürzen.

purser ['pɜːsə*] n Zahlmeister m.

pursue [pə'sjuː] vt verfolgen, nachjagen (+dat); study nachgehen (+dat); ~r Verfolger m.

pursuit [pə'sjuːt] n Jagd f (of nach), Verfolgung f; (occupation) Beschäftigung f.

purveyor [pɜː'veɪə*] n Lieferant m.

pus [pʌs] n Eiter m.

push [puʃ] n Stoß m, Schub m; (energy) Schwung m; (Mil) Vorstoß m; vt stoßen, schieben; button drücken; idea durchsetzen; vi stoßen, schieben; at a ~ zur Not; ~ aside vt beiseiteschieben; ~ off vi (col) abschieben; ~ on vi weitermachen; ~ through vt durchdrücken; policy durchsetzen; ~ up vt total erhöhen; prices hochtreiben; ~chair (Kinder)-sportwagen m; ~ing a aufdringlich; ~over (col) Kinderspiel nt; ~y a (col) aufdringlich.

puss [pus] n Mieze(katze) f.

put [put] vt irreg setzen, stellen, legen; (express) ausdrücken, sagen; (write) schreiben; ~ about vi (turn back) wenden; vt (spread) verbreiten; ~ across vt (explain) erklären; ~ away vt weglegen; (store) einstielegen; ~ back vt zurückstellen or -legen; ~ by vt zurücklegen, sparen; ~ down vt hinstellen or -legen; (stop) niederschlagen; animal einschläfern; (in writing) niederschreiben; ~ forward vt idea vorbringen; clock vorstellen; ~ off vt verlegen, verschieben; (discourage) abbringen von; it ~ me off smoking das hat mir die Lust am Rauchen verdorben; ~ on vt clothes etc anziehen; light etc anschalten, anmachen; play etc aufführen; brake anziehen; ~ out vt hand etc (her)ausstrecken; news, rumour verbreiten; light etc ausschalten, ausmachen; ~ up vt tent aufstellen; building errichten; price erhöhen; person unterbringen; to ~ up with sich abfinden mit; I won't ~ up with it das laß ich mir nicht gefallen.

putrid ['pjuːtrɪd] a faul.

putsch [putʃ] n Putsch m.

putt [pʌt] vt (golf) putten, einlochen; n (golf)

Putten nt, leichte(r) Schlag m; ~er Putter m.

putty ['pʌtɪ] n Kitt m; (fig) Wachs nt.

put-up ['putʌp] a: ~ job abgekartete(s) Spiel nt.

puzzle ['pʌzl] n Rätsel nt; (toy) Geduldspiel nt; vt verwirren; vi sich den Kopf zerbrechen.

puzzling ['pʌzlɪŋ] a rätselhaft, verwirrend.

pygmy ['pɪgmɪ] n Pygmäe m; (fig) Zwerg m.

pyjamas [pɪ'dʒɑːməz] npl Schlafanzug m, Pyjama m.

pylon ['paɪlən] n Mast m.

pyramid ['pɪrəmɪd] n Pyramide f.

python ['paɪθən] n Pythonschlange f.

Q

Q, q [kjuː] n Q nt, q nt.

quack [kwæk] n Quacken nt; (doctor) Quacksalber m.

quad [kwɒd] abbr of quadrangle, quadruple, quadruplet.

quadrangle ['kwɒdræŋgl] n (court) Hof m; (Math) Viereck nt.

quadruped ['kwɒdruped] n Vierfüßler m.

quadruple ['kwɒ'druːpl] a vierfach; vi sich vervierfachen; vt vervierfachen.

quadruplet ['kwɒ'druːplət] n Vierling m.

quagmire ['kwægmaɪə*] n Morast m.

quaint [kweɪnt] a kurios; malerisch; ~ly ad kurios; ~ness malerischer Anblick m; Kuriosität f.

quake [kweɪk] vi beben, zittern; Q~r Quäker m.

qualification [kwɒlɪfɪ'keɪʃən] n Qualifikation f; (sth which limits) Einschränkung f.

qualified ['kwɒlɪfaɪd] a (competent) qualifiziert; (limited) bedingt.

qualify ['kwɒlɪfaɪ] vt (prepare) befähigen; (limit) einschränken; vi sich qualifizieren.

qualitative ['kwɒlɪtətɪv] a qualitativ.

quality ['kwɒlɪtɪ] n Qualität f; (characteristic) Eigenschaft f; a Qualitäts-.

qualm [kwɑːm] n Bedenken nt, Zweifel m.

quandary ['kwɒndərɪ] n Verlegenheit f; to be in a ~ in Verlegenheit sein.

quantitative ['kwɒntɪtətɪv] a quantitativ.

quantity ['kwɒntɪtɪ] n Menge f, Quantität f.

quarantine ['kwɒrəntiːn] n Quarantäne f.

quarrel ['kwɒrəl] n Streit m; vi sich streiten; ~some a streitsüchtig.

quarry ['kwɒrɪ] n Steinbruch m; (animal) Wild nt; (fig) Opfer nt.

quart [kwɔːt] n Quart nt.

quarter ['kwɔːtə*] n Viertel nt; (of year) Quartal nt, Vierteljahr nt; vt (divide) vierteln, in Viertel teilen; (Mil) einquartieren; ~s pl (esp Mil) Quartier nt; ~ of an hour Viertelstunde f; ~ past three viertel nach drei; ~ to three dreiviertel drei, viertel vor drei; ~-deck Achterdeck nt; ~ final Viertelfinale nt; ~ly a vierteljährlich; ~master Quartiermeister m.

quartet(te) [kwɔː'tet] n Quartett nt.

quartz [kwɔːts] n Quarz m.

quash [kwɒʃ] vt verdict aufheben.

quasi [kwɑːzɪ] *ad* quasi.

quaver ['kweɪvə*] *n (Mus)* Achtelnote *f; vi (tremble)* zittern.

quay [kiː] *n* Kai *m.*

queasiness ['kwiːzɪnəs] *n* Übelkeit *f.*

queasy ['kwiːzɪ] *a* übel; **he feels** ~ ihm ist übel.

queen [kwiːn] *n* Königin *f;* ~ **mother** Königinmutter *f.*

queer [kwɪə*] *a* seltsam, sonderbar, kurios; ~ **fellow** komische(r) Kauz *m; n (col: homosexual)* Schwule(r) *m.*

quell [kwel] *vt* unterdrücken.

quench [kwentʃ] *vt thirst* löschen, stillen; *(extinguish)* löschen.

query ['kwɪərɪ] *n (question)* (An)frage *f; (question mark)* Fragezeichen *nt; vt* in Zweifel ziehen, in Frage stellen.

quest [kwest] *n* Suche *f.*

question ['kwestʃən] *n* Frage *f; vt (ask)* (be)fragen; *suspect* verhören; *(doubt)* in Frage stellen, bezweifeln; **beyond** ~ ohne Frage; **out of the** ~ ausgeschlossen; ~**able** *a* zweifelhaft; ~**er** Fragesteller *m;* ~**ing** *a* fragend; ~ **mark** Fragezeichen *nt;* ~**naire** Fragebogen *m; (enquiry)* Umfrage *f.*

queue [kjuː] *n* Schlange *f; vi (also* ~ **up)** Schlange stehen.

quibble ['kwɪbl] *n* Spitzfindigkeit *f; vi* kleinlich sein.

quick *a,* ~**ly** *ad* [kwɪk, -lɪ] *a* schnell; *n (of nail)* Nagelhaut *f; (old: the living)* die Lebenden; **to the** ~ *(fig)* bis ins Innerste; ~**en** *vt (hasten)* beschleunigen; *(stir)* anregen; *vi* sich beschleunigen; ~**-fire** *questions etc* Schnellfeuer-; ~**ness** Schnelligkeit *f; (mental)* Scharfsinn *m;* ~**sand** Treibsand *m;* ~**step** Quickstep *m;* ~-**witted** *a* schlagfertig, hell.

quid [kwɪd] *n (Brit col: £1)* Pfund *nt.*

quiet ['kwaɪət] *a (without noise)* leise; *(peaceful, calm)* still, ruhig; *n* Stille *f,* Ruhe *f;* ~**en** *(also* ~**en down)** *vi* ruhig werden; *vt* beruhigen; ~**ly** *ad* leise, ruhig; ~**ness** Ruhe *f,* Stille *f.*

quill [kwɪl] *n (of porcupine)* Stachel *m; (pen)* Feder *f.*

quilt [kwɪlt] *n* Steppdecke *f;* ~**ing** Füllung *f,* Wattierung *f.*

quin [kwɪn] *abbr of* **quintuplet.**

quince [kwɪns] *n* Quitte *f.*

quinine ['kwɪniːn] *n* Chinin *f.*

quinsy ['kwɪnzɪ] *n* Mandelentzündung *f.*

quintet(te) [kwɪn'tet] *n* Quintett *nt.*

quintuplet [kwɪn'tjuːplət] *n* Fünfling *m.*

quip [kwɪp] *n* witzige Bemerkung *f; vi* witzeln.

quirk [kwɜːk] *n (oddity)* Eigenart *f.*

quit [kwɪt] *irreg vt* verlassen; *vi* aufhören.

quite [kwaɪt] *ad (completely)* ganz, völlig; *(fairly)* ziemlich; ~ **(so)!** richtig!

quits [kwɪts] *a* quitt.

quiver ['kwɪvə*] *vi* zittern; *n (for arrows)* Köcher *m.*

quiz [kwɪz] *n (competition)* Quiz *nt; (series of questions)* Befragung *f; vt* prüfen; ~**zical** *a* fragend, verdutzt.

quoit [kwɔɪt] *n* Wurfring *m.*

quorum ['kwɔːrəm] *n* beschlußfähige Anzahl *f.*

quota ['kwəʊtə] *n* Anteil *m; (Comm)* Quote *f.*

quotation [kwəʊ'teɪʃən] *n* Zitat *nt; (price)* Kostenvoranschlag *m;* ~ **marks** *pl* Anführungszeichen *pl.*

quote [kwəʊt] *n see* **quotation;** *vi (from book)* zitieren; *vt (from book)* zitieren; *price* angeben.

quotient ['kwəʊʃənt] *n* Quotient *m.*

R

R, r [ɑː*] *n* R *nt, r nt.*

rabbi ['ræbaɪ] *n* Rabbiner *m; (title)* Rabbi *m.*

rabbit ['ræbɪt] *n* Kaninchen *nt;* ~ **hutch** Kaninchenstall *m.*

rabble ['ræbl] *n* Pöbel *m.*

rabies ['reɪbiːz] *n* Tollwut *f.*

raccoon [rə'kuːn] *n* Waschbär *m.*

race [reɪs] *n (species)* Rasse *f; (competition)* Rennen *nt; (on foot also)* Wettlauf *m; (rush)* Hetze *f; vt* um die Wette laufen mit; *horses* laufen lassen; *vi (run)* rennen; *(in contest)* am Rennen teilnehmen; ~**course** *(for horses)* Rennbahn *f;* ~**horse** Rennpferd *nt;* ~ **meeting** *(for horses)* (Pferde)rennen *nt;* ~ **relations** *pl* Beziehungen *pl* zwischen den Rassen; ~**track** *(for cars etc)* Rennstrecke *f.*

racial ['reɪʃəl] *a* Rassen-; ~ **discrimination** Rassendiskriminierung *f;* ~**ism** Rassismus *m;* ~**ist** *a* rassistisch; *n* Rassist *m.*

racing ['reɪsɪŋ] *n* Rennen *nt;* ~ **car** Rennwagen *m;* ~ **driver** Rennfahrer *m.*

racism ['reɪsɪzəm] *n* Rassismus *m.*

racist ['reɪsɪst] *n* Rassist *m; a* rassistisch.

rack [ræk] *n* Ständer *m,* Gestell *nt; vt* (zer)martern; **to go to** ~ **and ruin** verfallen.

racket ['rækɪt] *n (din)* Krach *m; (scheme)* (Schwindel)geschäft *nt; (tennis)* (Tennis)schläger *m.*

racquet ['rækɪt] *n* = **racket** *(tennis).*

racy ['reɪsɪ] *a* gewagt; *style* spritzig.

radar ['reɪdɑː*] *n* Radar *nt or m.*

radiance ['reɪdɪəns] *n* strahlende(r) Glanz *m.*

radiant ['reɪdɪənt] *a (bright)* strahlend; *(giving out rays)* Strahlungs-.

radiate ['reɪdɪeɪt] *vti* ausstrahlen; *(roads, lines)* strahlenförmig wegführen.

radiation [reɪdɪ'eɪʃən] *n* (Aus)strahlung *f.*

radiator ['reɪdɪeɪtə*] *n (for heating)* Heizkörper *m; (Aut)* Kühler *m;* ~ **cap** Kühlerdeckel *m.*

radical *a,* ~**ly** *ad* ['rædɪkəl, -ɪ] radikal.

radio ['reɪdɪəʊ] *n* Rundfunk *m,* Radio *nt; (set)* Radio *nt,* Radioapparat *m;* ~**active** *a* radioaktiv; ~**activity** Radioaktivität *f;* ~**grapher** [reɪdɪ'ɒgrəfə*] Röntgenassistent(in *f) m;* ~**graphy** [reɪdɪ'ɒgrəfɪ] Radiographie *f,* Röntgenphotographie *f;* ~**logy** [reɪdɪ'ɒlədʒɪ] Strahlenkunde *f;* ~ **station** Rundfunkstation *f;* ~ **telephone** Funksprechanlage *f;* ~ **telescope** Radio-

teleskop *nt;* ~ **therapist** Radiologie-
assistent(in *f*) *m.*

radish ['rædɪʃ] *n (big)* Rettich *m; (small)*
Radieschen *nt.*

radium ['reɪdɪəm] *n* Radium *nt.*

radius ['reɪdɪəs] *n* Radius *m,* Halbkreis *m;
(area)* Umkreis *m.*

raffia ['ræfɪə] *n* (Raffia)bast *m.*

raffish ['ræfɪʃ] *a* liederlich; *clothes* gewagt.

raffle ['ræfl] *n* Verlosung *f,* Tombola *f.*

raft [rɑːft] *n* Floß *nt.*

rafter ['rɑːftə*] *n* Dachsparren *m.*

rag [ræg] *n (cloth)* Lumpen *m,* Lappen *m;
(col: newspaper)* Käseblatt *nt; (Univ: for
charity)* studentische Sammelaktion *f; vt
auf den Arm nehmen;* ~ **bag** *(fig)*
Sammelsurium *nt.*

rage [reɪdʒ] *n* Wut *f; (desire)* Sucht *f;
(fashion)* große Mode *f;* **to be in a** ~
wütend sein; *vi* wüten, toben.

ragged ['rægɪd] *a edge* gezackt; *clothes*
zerlumpt.

raging ['reɪdʒɪŋ] *a* tobend; *thirst* Heiden-.

raid [reɪd] *n* Überfall *m; (Mil)* Angriff *m;
(by robbers)* Razzia *f; vt* überfallen; ~ **er**
(person) (Bank)räuber *m; (Naut)* Kaper-
schiff *nt.*

rail [reɪl] *n* Schiene *f,* Querstange *f; (on
stair)* Geländer *nt; (of ship)* Reling *f; (Rail)*
Schiene *f;* **by** ~ per Bahn; ~ **ing(s)**
Geländer *nt;* ~ **road** *(US),* ~ **way** *(Brit)*
Eisenbahn *f;* ~ **road** *or* ~ **way station**
Bahnhof *m.*

rain [reɪn] *n* Regen *m; vti* regnen; **the** ~ **s**
pl die Regenzeit; ~ **bow** Regenbogen *m;*
~ **coat** Regenmantel *m;* ~ **drop** Regen-
tropfen *m;* ~ **fall** Niederschlag *m;*
~ **storm** heftige(r) Regenguß *m;* ~ **y** *a*
region, season Regen-; *day* regnerisch, verregnet.

raise [reɪz] *n (esp US: increase)* (Lohn- or
Gehalts- or Preis)erhöhung *f, vt (lift)*
(hoch)heben; *(increase)* erhöhen; *question*
aufwerfen; *doubts* äußern; *funds*
beschaffen; *family* großziehen; *livestock*
züchten; *(build)* errichten.

raisin ['reɪzən] *n* Rosine *f.*

rajah ['rɑːdʒə] *n* Radscha *m.*

rake [reɪk] *n* Rechen *m,* Harke *f; (person)*
Wüstling *m; vt* rechen, harken; *(with gun)*
(mit Feuer) bestreichen; *(search)*
(durch)suchen; **to** ~ **in** *or* **together**
zusammenscharren.

rakish ['reɪkɪʃ] *a* verwegen.

rally ['rælɪ] *n (Pol etc)* Kundgebung *f; (Aut)*
Sternfahrt *f,* Rallye *f; (improvement)*
Erholung *f; vt (Mil)* sammeln; *vi* Kräfte
sammeln; ~ **round** *vti* (sich) scharen um;
(help) zu Hilfe kommen *(+dat).*

ram [ræm] *n* Widder *m; (instrument)*
Ramme *f; vt (strike)* rammen; *(stuff)*
(hinein)stopfen.

ramble ['ræmbl] *n* Wanderung *f,* Ausflug
m; vi (wander) umherstreifen; *(talk)*
schwafeln; ~ **r** Wanderer *m; (plant)*
Kletterrose *f.*

rambling ['ræmblɪŋ] *a plant* Kletter-;
speech weitschweifig; *town* ausgedehnt.

ramification [ræmɪfɪˈkeɪʃən] *n*
Verästelung *f;* ~ **s** *pl* Tragweite *f.*

ramp [ræmp] *n* Rampe *f.*

rampage [ræmˈpeɪdʒ] *n:* **to be on the** ~
(also ~ *vi)* randalieren.

rampant ['ræmpənt] *a (heraldry)* auf-
gerichtet; **to be** ~ überhandnehmen.

rampart ['ræmpɑːt] *n* (Schutz)wall *m.*

ramshackle ['ræmʃækl] *a* baufällig.

ranch [rɑːntʃ] *n* Ranch *f;* ~ **er** Rancher *m.*

rancid ['rænsɪd] *a* ranzig.

rancour, *(US)* **rancor** ['ræŋkə*] *n* Ver-
bitterung *f,* Groll *m.*

random ['rændəm] *a* ziellos, wahllos; *n:* **at**
~ aufs Geratewohl.

randy ['rændɪ] *a (Brit)* geil, scharf.

range [reɪndʒ] *n* Reihe *f; (of mountains)*
Kette *f; (Comm)* Sortiment *nt; (selection)*
(große) Auswahl *f (of an +dat); (reach)*
(Reich)weite *f; (of gun)* Schußweite *f; (for
shooting practice)* Schießplatz *m; (stove)*
(großer) Herd *m; vt (set in row)* anordnen,
aufstellen; *(roam)* durchstreifen; *vi (extend)* sich erstrecken; *prices ranging
from £5 to £10* Preise, die sich zwischen
5£ und 10£ bewegen; ~ **r** Förster *m.*

rank [ræŋk] *n (row)* Reihe *f; (for taxis)*
Stand *m; (Mil)* Dienstgrad *m,* Rang *m;
(social position)* Stand *m; vt* einschätzen; *vi
(have)* ~ gehören *(among* zu); *a (strong-
smelling)* stinkend; *(extreme)* krass; **the**
~ **s** *pl (Mil)* die Mannschaften *pl;* **the** ~
and file *(fig)* die breite Masse.

rankle ['ræŋkl] *vi* nagen.

ransack ['rænsæk] *vt (plunder)* plündern;
(search) durchwühlen.

ransom ['rænsəm] *n* Lösegeld *nt;* **to hold
sb to** ~ jdn gegen Lösegeld festhalten.

rant [rænt] *vi* hochtrabend reden; ~ **ing**
Wortschwall *m.*

rap [ræp] *n* Schlag *m; vt* klopfen.

rape [reɪp] *n* Vergewaltigung *f; vt* vergewaltigen.

rapid ['ræpɪd] *a* rasch, schnell; ~ **s** *pl*
Stromschnellen *pl;* ~ **ity** [rəˈpɪdɪtɪ]
Schnelligkeit *f;* ~ **ly** *ad* schnell.

rapier ['reɪpɪə*] *n* Florett *nt.*

rapist ['reɪpɪst] *n* Vergewaltiger *m.*

rapport [ræˈpɔː*] *n* gute(s) Verhältnis *nt.*

rapprochement [ræˈprɒʃmɑ̃ː] *n*
(Wieder)annäherung *f.*

rapt [ræpt] *a* hingerissen.

rapture ['ræptʃə*] *n* Entzücken *nt.*

rapturous ['ræptʃərəs] *a applause*
stürmisch; *expression* verzückt.

rare [rɛə*] *a* selten, rar; *(especially good)*
vortrefflich; *(underdone)* nicht durchgebraten; ~ **fied** ['rɛərɪfaɪd] *a air, atmosphere* dünn; ~ **ly** *ad* selten.

rarity ['rɛərɪtɪ] *n* Seltenheit *f.*

rascal ['rɑːskəl] *n* Schuft *m; (child)* Strick
m.

rash [ræʃ] *a* übereilt; *(reckless)*
unbesonnen; *n* (Haut)ausschlag *m.*

rasher ['ræʃə*] *n* Speckscheibe *f.*

rashly ['ræʃlɪ] *ad* vorschnell, unbesonnen.

rashness ['ræʃnəs] *n* Voreiligkeit *f; (recklessness)* Unbesonnenheit *f.*

rasp [rɑːsp] *n* Raspel *f.*

raspberry ['rɑːzbərɪ] *n* Himbeere *f.*

rasping ['rɑːspɪŋ] *a noise* kratzend.

rat [ræt] n (animal) Ratte f; (person) Halunke m.

ratable ['reɪtəbl] a: ~ **value** Grundsteuer f.

ratchet ['rætʃɪt] n Sperrad nt.

rate [reɪt] n (proportion) Ziffer f, Rate f; (price) Tarif m, Gebühr f; (speed) Geschwindigkeit f; vt (ein)schätzen; ~s pl (Brit) Grundsteuer f, Gemeindeabgaben pl; **at any** ~ jedenfalls; (at least) wenigstens; **at this** ~ wenn es so weitergeht; ~ **of exchange** (Wechsel)kurs m; ~**payer** Steuerzahler(in f) m; see **first**.

rather ['rɑːðə*] ad (in preference) lieber, eher; (to some extent) ziemlich; ~! und ob!

ratification [rætɪfɪ'keɪʃən] n Ratifikation f.

ratify ['rætɪfaɪ] vt bestätigen; (Pol) ratifizieren.

rating ['reɪtɪŋ] n Klasse f; (sailor) Matrose m.

ratio ['reɪʃɪəʊ] n Verhältnis nt.

ration ['ræʃən] n (usually pl) Ration f; vt rationieren.

rational a, ~**ly** ad ['ræʃənl, -nəlɪ] rational, vernünftig; ~**e** [ræʃə'nɑːl] Grundprinzip nt; ~**ization** [ræʃnəlaɪ'zeɪʃən] Rationalisierung f; ~**ize** ['ræʃnəlaɪz] vt rationalisieren.

rationing ['ræʃnɪŋ] n Rationierung f.

rat race ['rætreɪs] n Konkurrenzkampf m.

rattle ['rætl] n (sound) Rattern nt, Rasseln nt; (toy) Rassel f; vi ratteln, klappern; ~**snake** Klapperschlange f.

raucous a, ~**ly** ad ['rɔːkəs, -lɪ] heiser, rauh.

ravage ['rævɪdʒ] vt verheeren; ~s pl verheerende Wirkungen pl; **the** ~s **of time** der Zahn der Zeit.

rave [reɪv] vi (talk wildly) phantasieren; (rage) toben.

raven ['reɪvn] n Rabe m.

ravenous ['rævənəs] a heißhungrig; appetite unersättlich.

ravine [rə'viːn] n Schlucht f, Klamm f.

raving ['reɪvɪŋ] a tobend; ~ **mad** total verrückt.

ravioli [rævɪ'əʊlɪ] n Ravioli pl.

ravish ['rævɪʃ] vt (delight) entzücken; (Jur) woman vergewaltigen; ~**ing** a hinreißend.

raw [rɔː] a roh; (tender) wund(gerieben); wound offen; (inexperienced) unerfahren; ~ **material** Rohmaterial nt.

ray [reɪ] n (of light) (Licht)strahl m; (gleam) Schimmer m.

rayon ['reɪən] n Kunstseide f, Reyon nt or m.

raze [reɪz] vt dem Erdboden gleichmachen.

razor ['reɪzə*] n Rasierapparat m; ~ **blade** Rasierklinge f.

re- [riː] pref wieder-.

re [riː] prep (Comm) betreffs (+ gen).

reach [riːtʃ] n Reichweite f; (of river) Flußstrecke f; **within** ~ (shops etc) in erreichbarer Weite or Entfernung; vt erreichen; (pass on) reichen, geben; vi (try to get) langen (for nach); (stretch) sich erstrecken; ~ **out** vi die Hand ausstrecken.

react [riː'ækt] vi reagieren; ~**ion** [riː'ækʃən] Reaktion f; ~**ionary** [riː'ækʃənrɪ] a reaktionär; ~**or** Reaktor m.

read [riːd] vti irreg lesen; (aloud) vorlesen; **it** ~s **as follows** es lautet folgendermaßen; ~**able** a leserlich; (worth ~ing) lesenswert; ~**er** (person) Leser(in f) m; (book) Lesebuch nt; ~**ership** Leserschaft f.

readily ['redɪlɪ] ad (willingly) bereitwillig; (easily) prompt.

readiness ['redɪnəs] n (willingness) Bereitwilligkeit f; (being ready) Bereitschaft f.

reading ['riːdɪŋ] n Lesen nt; (interpretation) Deutung f, Auffassung f; ~ **lamp** Leselampe f; ~ **matter** Lesestoff m, Lektüre f; ~ **room** Lesezimmer nt, Lesesaal m.

readjust ['riːə'dʒʌst] vt wieder in Ordnung bringen; neu einstellen; **to** ~ **(o.s.) to sth** sich wieder anpassen an etw (acc); ~**ment** Wiederanpassung f.

ready ['redɪ] a (prepared) bereit, fertig; (willing) bereit, willens; (in condition to) reif; (quick) schlagfertig; money verfügbar, bar; ad bereit; n: **at the** ~ bereit; ~-**made** a gebrauchsfertig, Fertig-; clothes Konfektions-; ~ **reckoner** Rechentabelle f.

real [rɪəl] a wirklich; (actual) eigentlich; (true) wahr; (not fake) echt; ~ **estate** Grundbesitz m; ~**ism** Realismus m; ~**ist** Realist m; ~**istic** a, ~**istically** ad realistisch; ~**ity** [rɪ'ælɪtɪ] (real existence) Wirklichkeit f, Realität f; (facts) Tatsachen pl; ~**ization** (understanding) Erkenntnis f; (fulfilment) Verwirklichung f; ~**ize** vt (understand) begreifen; (make real) verwirklichen; money einbringen; **I didn't** ~**ize** . . .; ich wußte nicht, . . .; ~**ly** ad wirklich.

realm [relm] n Reich nt.

ream [riːm] n Ries nt.

reap [riːp] vt ernten; ~**er** Mähmaschine f.

reappear ['riːə'pɪə*] vi wieder erscheinen; ~**ance** Wiedererscheinen nt.

reapply ['riːə'plaɪ] vi wiederholt beantragen (for acc); (for job) sich erneut bewerben (for um).

reappoint ['riːə'pɔɪnt] vt wieder anstellen; wiederernennen.

reappraisal ['riːə'preɪzəl] n Neubeurteilung f.

rear [rɪə*] a hintere(r, s), Rück-; n Rückseite f; (last part) Schluß m; vt (bring up) aufziehen; vi (horse) sich aufbäumen; ~-**engined** a mit Heckmotor; ~**guard** Nachhut f.

rearm ['riː'ɑːm] vt wiederbewaffnen; vi wiederaufrüsten; ~**ament** Wiederaufrüstung f.

rearrange ['riːə'reɪndʒ] vt umordnen; plans ändern.

rear-view ['rɪəvjuː] a: ~ **mirror** Rückspiegel m.

reason ['riːzn] n (cause) Grund m; (ability to think) Verstand m; (sensible thoughts) Vernunft f; vi (think) denken; (use arguments) argumentieren; **to** ~ **with sb** mit jdm diskutieren; ~**able** a vernünftig; ~**ably** ad vernünftig; (fairly) ziemlich;

one could ~**ably suppose** man könnte doch (mit gutem Grund) annehmen; ~**ed** *a argument* durchdacht; ~**ing** Urteilen *nt; (argumentation)* Beweisführung *f.*

reassemble ['ri:ə'sembl] *vt* wieder versammeln; *(Tech)* wieder zusammensetzen, wieder zusammenbauen; *vi* sich wieder versammeln.

reassert ['ri:ə'sə:t] *vt* wieder geltend machen.

reassurance ['ri:ə'ʃuərəns] *n* Beruhigung *f; (confirmation)* nochmalige Versicherung *f.*

reassure ['ri:ə'ʃuə*] *vt* beruhigen; *(confirm)* versichern *(sb* jdm).

reassuring ['ri:ə'ʃuəriŋ] *a* beruhigend.

reawakening ['ri:ə'weiknıŋ] *n* Wiedererwachen *nt.*

rebate ['ri:beit] *n* Rabatt *m; (money back)* Rückzahlung *f.*

rebel ['rebl] *n* Rebell *m; a* Rebellen-; ~**lion** [rɪ'beljən] rebellion *f,* Aufstand *m;* ~**lious** [rɪ'beljəs] *a* rebellisch; *(fig)* widerspenstig.

rebirth ['ri:'bə:θ] *n* Wiedergeburt *f.*

rebound [rɪ'baund] *vi* zurückprallen; ['ri:baund] *n* Rückprall *m;* **on the** ~ *(fig)* als Reaktion.

rebuff [rɪ'bʌf] *n* Abfuhr *f; vt* abblitzen lassen.

rebuild ['ri:'bɪld] *vt irreg* wiederaufbauen; *(fig)* wiederherstellen; ~**ing** Wiederaufbau *m.*

rebuke [rɪ'bju:k] *n* Tadel *m; vt* tadeln, rügen.

rebut [rɪ'bʌt] *vt* widerlegen.

recalcitrant [rɪ'kælsɪtrənt] *a* widerspenstig.

recall [rɪ'kɔ:l] *vt (call back)* zurückrufen; *(remember)* sich erinnern an (+*acc*).

recant [rɪ'kænt] *vi* (öffentlich) widerrufen.

recap ['ri:kæp] *n* kurze Zusammenfassung *f; vti* information wiederholen.

recapture ['ri:'kæptʃə*] *vt* wieder (ein)fangen.

recede [rɪ'si:d] *vi* zurückweichen.

receding [rɪ'si:dɪŋ] *a:* ~ **hair** Stirnglatze *f.*

receipt [rɪ'si:t] *n (document)* Quittung *f; (receiving)* Empfang *m;* ~**s** *pl* Einnahmen *pl.*

receive [rɪ'si:v] *vt* erhalten; *visitors etc* empfangen; ~**r** *(Tel)* Hörer *m.*

recent ['ri:snt] *a* vor kurzem (geschehen), neuerlich; *(modern)* neu; ~**ly** *ad* kürzlich, neulich.

receptacle [rɪ'septəkl] *n* Behälter *m.*

reception [rɪ'sepʃən] *n* Empfang *m; (welcome)* Aufnahme *f; (in hotel)* Rezeption *f;* ~**ist** *(in hotel)* Empfangschef *m/*-dame *f; (Med)* Sprechstundenhilfe *f.*

receptive [rɪ'septɪv] *a* aufnahmebereit.

recess [rɪ'ses] *n (break)* Ferien *pl; (hollow)* Nische *f;* ~**es** *pl* Winkel *m;* ~**ion** [rɪ'seʃən] Rezession *f.*

recharge ['ri:'tʃɑːdʒ] *vt battery* aufladen.

recipe ['resɪpɪ] *n* Rezept *nt.*

recipient [rɪ'sɪpɪənt] *n* Empfänger *m.*

reciprocal [rɪ'sɪprəkəl] *a* gegenseitig; *(mutual)* wechselseitig.

reciprocate [rɪ'sɪprəkeit] *vt* erwidern.

recital [rɪ'saitl] *n (Mus)* Konzert *nt,* Vortrag *m.*

recitation [resɪ'teiʃən] *n* Rezitation *f.*

recite [rɪ'sait] *vt* vortragen, aufsagen; *(give list of also)* aufzählen.

reckless *a,* ~**ly** *ad* ['rekləs, -lı] leichtsinnig; *driving* fahrlässig; ~**ness** Rücksichtslosigkeit *f.*

reckon ['rekən] *vt (count)* (be- or er)rechnen; *(consider)* halten für; *vi (suppose)* annehmen; ~ **on** *vt* rechnen mit; ~**ing** *(calculation)* Rechnen *nt.*

reclaim [rɪ'kleim] *vt land* abgewinnen *(from dat); expenses* zurückverlangen.

reclamation [reklə'meiʃən] *n (of land)* Gewinnung *f.*

recline [rɪ'klain] *vi* sich zurücklehnen.

reclining [rɪ'klainıŋ] *a* verstellbar, Liege-.

recluse [rɪ'klu:s] *n* Einsiedler *m.*

recognition [rekəg'nɪʃən] *n (recognizing)* Erkennen *nt; (acknowledgement)* Anerkennung *f.*

recognizable ['rekəgnaizəbl] *a* erkennbar.

recognize ['rekəgnaiz] *vt* erkennen; *(Pol, approve)* anerkennen.

recoil [rɪ'kɔil] *n* Rückstoß *m; vi (in horror)* zurückschrecken; *(rebound)* zurückprallen.

recollect [rekə'lekt] *vt* sich erinnern an (+*acc*); ~**ion** Erinnerung *f.*

recommend [rekə'mend] *vt* empfehlen; ~**ation** Empfehlung *f.*

recompense ['rekəmpens] *n (compensation)* Entschädigung *f; (reward)* Belohnung *f; vt* entschädigen; belohnen.

reconcilable ['rekənsailəbl] *a* vereinbar.

reconcile ['rekənsail] *vt facts* vereinbaren, in Einklang bringen; *people* versöhnen.

reconciliation [rekənsılı'eiʃən] *n* Versöhnung *f.*

reconditioned ['ri:kən'dɪʃənd] *a* überholt, erneuert.

reconnaissance [rɪ'kɒnɪsəns] *n* Aufklärung *f.*

reconnoitre, *(US)* **reconnoiter** [rekə'nɔitə*] *vt* erkunden; *vi* aufklären.

reconsider ['ri:kən'sɪdə*] *vti* von neuem erwägen, (es) überdenken.

reconstitute ['ri:'kɒnstɪtju:t] *vt* neu bilden.

reconstruct ['ri:kən'strʌkt] *vt* wiederaufbauen; *crime* rekonstruieren; ~**ion** ['ri:kən'strʌkʃən] Rekonstruktion *f.*

record ['rekɔ:d] *n* Aufzeichnung *f; (Mus)* Schallplatte *f; (best performance)* Rekord *m; a time* Rekord-; [rɪ'kɔ:d] *vt* aufzeichnen; *(Mus etc)* aufnehmen; ~ **card** *(in file)* Karteikarte *f;* ~**ed music** Musikaufnahmen *pl;* ~**er** [rɪ'kɔ:də*] *(officer)* Protokollführer *m; (Mus)* Blockflöte *f;* ~**holder** *(Sport)* Rekordinhaber *m;* ~**ing** [rɪ'kɔ:dɪŋ] *(Mus)* Aufnahme *f;* ~ **library** Schallplattenarchiv *nt;* ~ **player** Plattenspieler *m.*

recount ['ri:kaunt] *n* Nachzählung *f; vt (count again)* nachzählen; [rɪ'kaunt] *(tell)* berichten.

recoup [rɪ'ku:p] *vt* wettmachen.

recourse [rɪ'kɔ:s] *n* Zuflucht *f.*

recover [rɪ'kʌvə*] vt (get back) zurückerhalten; ['riː'kʌvə*] quilt etc neu überziehen; vi sich erholen; ~y Wiedererlangung f; (of health) Genesung f.

recreate ['riːkrɪ'eɪt] vt wiederherstellen.

recreation [rekrɪ'eɪʃən] n Erholung f; Freizeitbeschäftigung f; ~al a Erholungs-.

recrimination [rɪkrɪmɪ'neɪʃən] n Gegenbeschuldigung f.

recruit [rɪ'kruːt] n Rekrut m; vt rekrutieren; ~ing office Wehrmeldeamt nt; ~ment Rekrutierung f.

rectangle ['rektæŋgl] n Rechteck nt.

rectangular [rek'tæŋgjulə*] a rechteckig, rechtwinklig.

rectify ['rektɪfaɪ] vt berichtigen.

rectory ['rektərɪ] n Pfarrhaus nt.

recuperate [rɪ'kuːpəreɪt] vi sich erholen.

recur [rɪ'kɜː*] vi sich wiederholen; ~rence Wiederholung f; ~rent a wiederkehrend.

red [red] n Rot nt; (Pol) Rote(r) m; a rot; **in the** ~ in den roten Zahlen; **R~ Cross** Rote(s) Kreuz nt; ~**den** vti (sich) röten; (blush) erröten; ~**dish** a rötlich.

redecorate ['riː'dekəreɪt] vt renovieren.

redecoration ['riːdekə'reɪʃən] n Renovierung f.

redeem [rɪ'diːm] vt (Comm) einlösen; (set free) freikaufen; (compensate) retten; **to** ~ **sb from sin** jdn von seinen Sünden erlösen.

redeeming [rɪ'diːmɪŋ] a virtue, feature rettend.

redeploy ['riːdɪ'plɔɪ] vt resources umverteilen.

red-haired ['red'hɛəd] a rothaarig.

red-handed [red'hændɪd] ad auf frischer Tat.

redhead ['redhed] n Rothaarige(r) mf.

red herring ['red'herɪŋ] n Ablenkungsmanöver nt.

red-hot ['red'hot] a rotglühend; (excited) hitzig; tip heiß.

redirect ['riːdaɪ'rekt] vt umleiten.

rediscovery ['riːdɪs'kʌvərɪ] n Wiederentdeckung f.

redistribute ['riːdɪs'trɪbjuːt] vt neu verteilen.

red-letter day ['red'letədeɪ] n (lit, fig) Festtag m.

redness ['rednəs] n Röte f.

redo ['riː'duː] vt irreg nochmals tun or machen.

redolent ['redəulənt] a: ~ **of** riechend nach; (fig) erinnernd an (+acc).

redouble [riː'dʌbl] vt verdoppeln.

red tape ['red'teɪp] n Bürokratismus m.

reduce [rɪ'djuːs] vt price herabsetzen (to auf +acc); speed, temperature vermindern; photo verkleinern; **to** ~ **sb to tears/silence** jdn zum Weinen/ Schweigen bringen.

reduction [rɪ'dʌkʃən] n Herabsetzung f; Verminderung f; Verkleinerung f; (amount of money) Nachlaß m.

redundancy [rɪ'dʌndənsɪ] n Überflüssigkeit f; (of workers) Entlassung f.

redundant [rɪ'dʌndənt] a überflüssig;

workers ohne Arbeitsplatz; **to be made** ~ arbeitslos werden.

reed [riːd] n Schilf nt; (Mus) Rohrblatt nt.

reef [riːf] n Riff nt.

reek [riːk] vi stinken (of nach).

reel [riːl] n Spule f, Rolle f; vt (wind) wickeln, spulen; (stagger) taumeln.

re-election ['riːɪ'lekʃən] n Wiederwahl f.

re-engage ['riːɪn'geɪdʒ] vt wieder einstellen.

re-enter ['riː'entə*] vti wieder eintreten (in +acc).

re-entry ['riː'entrɪ] n Wiedereintritt m.

re-examine ['riːɪg'zæmɪn] vt neu überprüfen.

ref [ref] n (col) Schiri m.

refectory [rɪ'fektərɪ] n (Univ) Mensa f; (Sch) Speisesaal m; (Eccl) Refektorium nt.

refer [rɪ'fɜː*] vt: ~ **sb to sb/sth** jdn an jdn/etw verweisen; vi: ~ **to** hinweisen auf (+acc); (to book) nachschlagen in (+dat); (mention) sich beziehen auf (+acc).

referee [refə'riː] n Schiedsrichter m; (for job) Referenz f; vt schiedsrichtern.

reference ['refrəns] n (mentioning) Hinweis m; (allusion) Anspielung f; (for job) Referenz f; (in book) Verweis m; (number, code) Aktenzeichen nt; Katalognummer f; **with** ~ **to** in bezug auf (+acc); ~ **book** Nachschlagewerk nt.

referendum [refə'rendəm] n Volksabstimmung f.

refill ['riː'fɪl] vt nachfüllen; ['riː'fɪl] n Nachfüllung f; (for pen) Ersatzpatrone f; Ersatzmine f.

refine [rɪ'faɪn] vt (purify) raffinieren, läutern; (fig) bilden, kultivieren; ~**d** a gebildet, kultiviert; ~**ment** Bildung f, Kultiviertheit f; ~**ry** Raffinerie f.

reflect [rɪ'flekt] vt light reflektieren; (fig) (wider)spiegeln, zeigen; vi (meditate) nachdenken (on über +acc); ~**ion** Reflexion f; (image) Spiegelbild nt; (thought) Überlegung f, Gedanke m; ~**or** Reflektor m.

reflex [rɪ'fleks] n Reflex m; ~**ive** [rɪ'fleksɪv] a (Gram) Reflexiv-, rückbezüglich, reflexiv.

reform [rɪ'fɔːm] n Reform f; vt person bessern; **the R~ation** [refə'meɪʃən] die Reformation; ~**er** Reformer m; (Eccl) Reformator m.

refrain [rɪ'freɪn] vi unterlassen (from acc).

refresh [rɪ'freʃ] vt erfrischen; ~**er course** Wiederholungskurs m; ~**ing** a erfrischend; ~**ments** pl Erfrischungen pl.

refrigeration [rɪfrɪdʒə'reɪʃən] n Kühlung f.

refrigerator [rɪ'frɪdʒəreɪtə*] n Kühlschrank m.

refuel ['riː'fjuəl] vti auftanken; ~**ling** Auftanken nt.

refuge ['refjuːdʒ] n Zuflucht f; ~**e** [refjuˈdʒiː] Flüchtling m.

refund ['riː'fʌnd] n Rückvergütung f; [rɪ'fʌnd] vt zurückerstatten, rückvergüten.

refurbish ['riː'fɜːbɪʃ] vt aufpolieren.

refurnish ['riː'fɜːnɪʃ] vt neu möblieren.

refusal [rɪ'fjuːzəl] n (Ver)weigerung f; (official) abschlägige Antwort f.

refuse ['refju:s] n Abfall m, Müll m; [rɪ'fju:z] vt abschlagen; vi sich weigern.

refute [rɪ'fju:t] vt widerlegen.

regain [rɪ'geɪn] vt wiedergewinnen; *consciousness* wiedererlangen.

regal ['ri:gəl] a königlich; ~**ia** [rɪ'geɪlɪə] pl Insignien pl; (of mayor etc) Amtsornat m.

regard [rɪ'gɑ:d] n Achtung f; vt ansehen; ~**s** pl Grüße pl; ~**ing, as** ~**s,** with ~ to bezüglich (+gen), in bezug auf (+acc); ~**less** a ohne Rücksicht (of auf +acc); ad unbekümmert, ohne Rücksicht auf die Folgen.

regatta [rɪ'gætə] n Regatta f.

regency ['ri:dʒənsɪ] n Regentschaft f.

regent ['ri:dʒənt] n Regent m.

régime [reɪ'ʒi:m] n Regime nt.

regiment ['redʒɪmənt] n Regiment nt; ~**al** [redʒɪ'mentl] a Regiments-; ~**ation** Reglementierung f.

region ['ri:dʒən] n Gegend f, Bereich m; ~**al** a örtlich, regional.

register ['redʒɪstə*] n Register nt, Verzeichnis nt, Liste f; vt (list) registrieren, eintragen; emotion zeigen; (write down) eintragen; vi (at hotel) sich eintragen; (with police) sich melden (with bei); (make impression) wirken, ankommen; ~**ed** a design eingetragen; letter Einschreibe-, eingeschrieben.

registrar [redʒɪs'trɑ:*] n Standesbeamte(r) m.

registration [redʒɪs'treɪʃən] n (act) Erfassung f, Registrierung f; (number) Autonummer f, polizeiliche(s) Kennzeichen nt.

registry office ['redʒɪstrɪɒfɪs] n Standesamt nt.

regret [rɪ'gret] n Bedauern nt; **to have no** ~**s** nichts bedauern; vt bedauern; ~**ful** a traurig; **to be** ~**ful about sth** etw bedauern; ~**fully** ad mit Bedauern, ungern; ~**table** a bedauerlich.

regroup [ri:'gru:p] vt umgruppieren; vi sich umgruppieren.

regular ['regjulə*] a regelmäßig; (usual) üblich; (fixed by rule) geregelt; (col) regelrecht; n (client etc) Stammkunde m; (Mil) Berufssoldat m; ~**ity** [regju'lærɪtɪ] Regelmäßigkeit f; ~**ly** ad regelmäßig.

regulate ['regjuleɪt] vt regeln, regulieren.

regulation [regju'leɪʃən] n (rule) Vorschrift f; (control) Regulierung f; (order) Anordnung f, Regelung f.

rehabilitation ['ri:həbɪlɪ'teɪʃən] n (of criminal) Resozialisierung f.

rehash ['ri:'hæʃ] vt (col) aufwärmen.

rehearsal [rɪ'hɜ:səl] n Probe f.

rehearse [rɪ'hɜ:s] vt proben.

reign [reɪn] n Herrschaft f; vi herrschen; ~**ing** a monarch herrschend; champion gegenwärtig.

reimburse [ri:ɪm'bɜ:s] vt entschädigen, zurückzahlen (sb for sth jdm etw).

rein [reɪn] n Zügel m.

reincarnation ['ri:ɪnkɑ:'neɪʃən] n Wiedergeburt f.

reindeer ['reɪndɪə*] n Ren nt.

reinforce [ri:ɪn'fɔ:s] vt verstärken; ~**d** a verstärkt; concrete Eisen-; ~**ment**

Verstärkung f; ~**ments** pl (Mil) Verstärkungstruppen pl.

reinstate ['ri:ɪn'steɪt] vt wiedereinsetzen.

reissue ['ri:'ɪʃu:] vt neu herausgeben.

reiterate [ri:'ɪtəreɪt] vt wiederholen.

reject ['ri:dʒekt] n (Comm) Ausschuß(artikel) m; [rɪ'dʒekt] vt ablehnen; (throw away) ausrangieren; ~**ion** [rɪ'dʒekʃən] Zurückweisung f.

rejoice [rɪ'dʒɔɪs] vi sich freuen.

rejuvenate [rɪ'dʒu:vɪneɪt] vt verjüngen.

rekindle ['ri:'kɪndl] vt wieder anfachen.

relapse [rɪ'læps] n Rückfall m.

relate [rɪ'leɪt] vt (tell) berichten, erzählen; (connect) verbinden; ~**d** a verwandt (to mit).

relating [rɪ'leɪtɪŋ] prep: ~ **to** bezüglich (+gen).

relation [rɪ'leɪʃən] n Verwandte(r) mf; (connection) Beziehung f; ~**ship** Verhältnis nt, Beziehung f.

relative ['relətɪv] n Verwandte(r) mf; a relativ, bedingt; ~**ly** ad verhältnismäßig; ~ **pronoun** Verhältniswort nt, Relativpronomen nt.

relax [rɪ'læks] vi (slacken) sich lockern; (muscles, person) sich entspannen; (be less strict) freundlicher werden; vt (ease) lockern, entspannen; ~**!** reg' dich nicht auf!; ~**ation** [ri:læk'seɪʃən] Entspannung f; ~**ed** a entspannt, locker; ~**ing** a entspannend.

relay ['ri:leɪ] n (Sport) Staffel f; vt message weiterleiten; (Rad, TV) übertragen.

release [rɪ'li:s] n (freedom) Entlassung f; (Tech) Auslöser m; vt befreien; prisoner entlassen; report, news verlautbaren, bekanntgeben.

relent [rɪ'lent] vi nachgeben; ~**less** a, ~**lessly** ad unnachgiebig.

relevance ['reləvəns] n Bedeutung f, Relevanz f.

relevant ['reləvənt] a wichtig, relevant.

reliability [rɪlaɪə'bɪlɪtɪ] n Zuverlässigkeit f.

reliable a, **reliably** ad [rɪ'laɪəbl, -blɪ] zuverlässig.

reliance [rɪ'laɪəns] n Abhängigkeit f (on von).

relic ['relɪk] n (from past) Überbleibsel nt; (Rel) Reliquie f.

relief [rɪ'li:f] n Erleichterung f; (help) Hilfe f, Unterstützung f; (person) Ablösung f; (Art) Relief nt; (distinctness) Hervorhebung f.

relieve [rɪ'li:v] vt (ease) erleichtern; (bring help) entlasten; person ablösen; **to** ~ **sb of sth** jdm etw abnehmen.

religion [rɪ'lɪdʒən] n Religion f.

religious [rɪ'lɪdʒəs] a religiös; ~**ly** ad religiös; (conscientiously) gewissenhaft.

reline ['ri:'laɪn] vt brakes neu beschuhen.

relinquish [rɪ'lɪŋkwɪʃ] vt aufgeben.

relish ['relɪʃ] n Würze f, pikante Beigabe f; vt genießen.

relive ['ri:'lɪv] vt noch einmal durchleben.

reluctance [rɪ'lʌktəns] n Widerstreben nt, Abneigung f.

reluctant [rɪ'lʌktənt] a widerwillig; ~ly ad ungern.

rely [rɪ'laɪ]: ~ on vt sich verlassen auf (+acc).

remain [rɪ'meɪn] vi (be left) übrigbleiben; (stay) bleiben; ~der Rest m; ~ing a übrig(geblieben); ~s pl Überreste pl; (dead body) sterbliche Überreste pl.

remand [rɪ'maːnd] n: on ~ in Untersuchungshaft; vt: ~ in custody in Untersuchungshaft schicken.

remark [rɪ'maːk] n Bemerkung f; vt bemerken; ~able a, ~ably ad bemerkenswert.

remarry ['riː'mærɪ] vi sich wieder verheiraten.

remedial [rɪ'miːdɪəl] a Heil-; teaching Hilfsschul-.

remedy ['remədɪ] n Mittel nt; vt pain abhelfen (+dat); trouble in Ordnung bringen.

remember [rɪ'membə*] vt sich erinnern an (+acc); ~ me to them grüße sie von mir.

remembrance [rɪ'membrəns] n Erinnerung f; (official) Gedenken nt.

remind [rɪ'maɪnd] vt erinnern; ~er Mahnung f.

reminisce [remɪ'nɪs] vi in Erinnerungen schwelgen; ~nces [remɪ'nɪsənsɪz] pl Erinnerungen pl; ~nt a erinnernd (of an +acc), Erinnerungen nachrufend (of an +acc).

remit [rɪ'mɪt] vt money überweisen (to an +acc); ~tance Geldanweisung f.

remnant ['remnənt] n Rest m.

remorse [rɪ'mɔːs] n Gewissensbisse pl; ~ful a reumütig; ~less a, ~lessly ad unbarmherzig.

remote [rɪ'məʊt] a abgelegen, entfernt; (slight) gering; ~ control Fernsteuerung f; ~ly ad entfernt; ~ness Entlegenheit f.

removable [rɪ'muːvəbl] a entfernbar.

removal [rɪ'muːvəl] n Beseitigung f; (of furniture) Umzug m; (from office) Entlassung f; ~ van Möbelwagen m.

remove [rɪ'muːv] vt beseitigen, entfernen; (dismiss) entlassen; ~r (for paint etc) Fleckenentferner m; ~rs pl Möbelspedition f.

remuneration [rɪmjuːnə'reɪʃən] n Vergütung f, Honorar nt.

Renaissance [rə'neɪsɑːns]: the ~ die Renaissance.

rename ['riː'neɪm] vt umbenennen.

rend [rend] vt irreg zerreißen.

render ['rendə*] vt machen; (translate) übersetzen; ~ing (Mus) Wiedergabe f.

rendezvous ['rɒndɪvuː] n Verabredung f, Rendezvous nt.

renegade ['renɪgeɪd] n Überläufer m.

renew [rɪ'njuː] vt erneuern; contract, licence verlängern; (replace) ersetzen; ~al Erneuerung f; Verlängerung f.

renounce [rɪ'naʊns] vt (give up) verzichten auf (+acc); (disown) verstoßen.

renovate ['renəʊveɪt] vt renovieren; building restaurieren.

renovation [renəʊ'veɪʃən] n Renovierung f; Restauration f.

renown [rɪ'naʊn] n Ruf m; ~ed a namhaft.

rent [rent] n Miete f; (for land) Pacht f; vt (hold as tenant) mieten; pachten; (let) vermieten; verpachten; car etc mieten; (firm) vermieten; ~al Miete f; Pacht f, Pachtgeld nt.

renunciation [rɪnʌnsɪ'eɪʃən] n Verzicht m (of auf +acc).

reopen ['riː'əʊpən] vt wiedereröffnen.

reorder ['riː'ɔːdə*] vt wieder bestellen.

reorganization ['riːɔːgənaɪ'zeɪʃən] n Neugestaltung f; (Comm etc) Umbildung f.

reorganize ['riː'ɔːgənaɪz] vt umgestalten, reorganisieren.

rep [rep] n (Comm) Vertreter m; (Theat) Repertoire nt.

repair [rɪ'pɛə*] n Reparatur f; in good ~ in gutem Zustand; vt reparieren; damage wiedergutmachen; ~ kit Werkzeugkasten m; ~ man Mechaniker m; ~ shop Reparaturwerkstatt f.

repartee [repaː'tiː] n Witzeleien pl.

repay [riː'peɪ] vt irreg zurückzahlen; (reward) vergelten; ~ment Rückzahlung f; (fig) Vergelten nt.

repeal [rɪ'piːl] n Aufhebung f; vt aufheben.

repeat [rɪ'piːt] n (Rad, TV) Wiederholung(ssendung) f; vt wiederholen; ~edly ad wiederholt.

repel [rɪ'pel] vt (drive back) zurückschlagen; (disgust) abstoßen; ~lent a abstoßend; n: insect ~lent Insektenmittel nt.

repent [rɪ'pent] vti bereuen; ~ance Reue f.

repercussion [riːpə'kʌʃən] n Auswirkung f; (of rifle) Rückstoß m.

repertoire ['repətwaː*] n Repertoire nt.

repertory ['repətərɪ] n Repertoire nt.

repetition [repə'tɪʃən] n Wiederholung f.

repetitive [rɪ'petɪtɪv] a sich wiederholend.

rephrase [riː'freɪz] vt anders formulieren.

replace [rɪ'pleɪs] vt ersetzen; (put back) zurückstellen; ~ment Ersatz m.

replenish [rɪ'plenɪʃ] vt (wieder) auffüllen.

replete [rɪ'pliːt] a (zum Platzen) voll.

replica ['replɪkə] n Kopie f.

reply [rɪ'plaɪ] n Antwort f, Erwiderung f; vi antworten, erwidern.

report [rɪ'pɔːt] n Bericht m; (Sch) Zeugnis nt; (of gun) Knall m; vt (tell) berichten; (give information against) melden; (to police) anzeigen; vi (make report) Bericht erstatten; (present o.s.) sich melden; ~er Reporter m.

reprehensible [reprɪ'hensɪbl] a tadelnswert.

represent [reprɪ'zent] vt darstellen, zeigen; (act) darstellen; (speak for) vertreten; ~ation Darstellung f; (being represented) Vertretung f; ~ative a n (person) Vertreter m; a räpräsentativ.

repress [rɪ'pres] vt unterdrücken; ~ion [rɪ'preʃən] Unterdrückung f; ~ive a Unterdrückungs-; (Psych) Hemmungs-.

reprieve [rɪ'priːv] n Aufschub m; (cancellation) Begnadigung f; (fig) Atempause f; vt Gnadenfrist gewähren (+dat); begnadigen.

reprimand ['reprɪmaːnd] n Verweis m; vt

einen Verweis erteilen *(+dat).*

reprint ['ri:prɪnt] *n* Neudruck *m;* ['ri:'prɪnt] *vt* wieder abdrucken.

reprisal [rɪ'praɪzəl] *n* Vergeltung *f.*

reproach [rɪ'prəʊtʃ] *n (blame)* Vorwurf *m,* Tadel *m; (disgrace)* Schande *f; beyond* ~ über jeden Vorwurf erhaben; *vt* Vorwürfe machen *(+dat),* tadeln; ~**ful** *a* vorwurfsvoll.

reproduce [ri:prə'dju:s] *vt* reproduzieren; *vi (have offspring)* sich vermehren.

reproduction [ri:prə'dʌkʃən] *n* Wiedergabe *f; (Art, Phot)* Reproduktion *f; (breeding)* Fortpflanzung *f.*

reproductive [ri:prə'dʌktɪv] *a* reproduktiv; *(breeding)* Fortpflanzungs-.

reprove [rɪ'pru:v] *vt* tadeln.

reptile ['reptaɪl] *n* Reptil *nt.*

republic [rɪ'pʌblɪk] *n* Republik *f;* ~**an** *a* republikanisch; *n* Republikaner *m.*

repudiate [rɪ'pju:dɪeɪt] *vt* zurückweisen, nicht anerkennen.

repugnance [rɪ'pʌgnəns] *n* Widerwille *m.*

repugnant [rɪ'pʌgnənt] *a* widerlich.

repulse [rɪ'pʌls] *vt (drive back)* zurückschlagen; *(reject)* abweisen.

repulsion [rɪ'pʌlʃən] *n* Abscheu *m.*

repulsive [rɪ'pʌlsɪv] *a* abstoßend.

repurchase ['ri:'pɜ:tʃəs] *vt* zurückkaufen.

reputable ['repjʊtəbl] *a* angesehen.

reputation [repjʊ'teɪʃən] *n* Ruf *m.*

repute [rɪ'pju:t] *n* hohe(s) Ansehen *nt;* ~**d** *a,* ~**dly** *ad* angeblich.

request [rɪ'kwest] *n (asking)* Ansuchen *nt; (demand)* Wunsch *m;* **at sb's** ~ auf jds Wunsch; *vt thing* erbitten; *person* ersuchen.

requiem ['rekwɪem] *n* Requiem *nt.*

require [rɪ'kwaɪə*] *vt (need)* brauchen; *(wish)* wünschen; **to be** ~**d to do sth** etw tun müssen; ~**ment** *(condition)* Anforderung *f; (need)* Bedarf *m.*

requisite ['rekwɪzɪt] *n* Erfordernis *nt; a* erforderlich.

requisition [rekwɪ'zɪʃən] *n* Anforderung *f; vt* beschlagnahmen; *(order)* anfordern.

reroute ['ri:'ru:t] *vt* umleiten.

rescind [rɪ'sɪnd] *vt* aufheben.

rescue ['reskju:] *n* Rettung *f; vt* retten; ~ **party** Rettungsmannschaft *f;* ~**r** Retter *m.*

research [rɪ'sɜ:tʃ] *n* Forschung *f; vi* Forschungen anstellen *(into* über *+acc); vt* erforschen; ~**er** Forscher *m;* ~ **work** Forschungsarbeit *f;* ~ **worker** wissenschaftliche(r) Mitarbeiter(in *f*) *m.*

resemblance [rɪ'zembləns] *n* Ähnlichkeit *f.*

resemble [rɪ'zembl] *vt* ähneln *(+dat).*

resent [rɪ'zent] *vt* übelnehmen; ~**ful** *a* nachtragend, empfindlich; ~**ment** Verstimmung *f,* Unwille *m.*

reservation [rezə'veɪʃən] *n (of seat)* Reservierung *f; (Theat)* Vorbestellung *f; (doubt)* Vorbehalt *m; (land)* Reservat *nt.*

reserve [rɪ'zɜ:v] *n (store)* Vorrat *m,* Reserve *f; (manner)* Zurückhaltung *f; (game* ~*)* Naturschutzgebiet *nt; (native* ~*)* Reservat *nt; (Sport)* Ersatzspieler(in *f*) *m; vt* reservieren; *judgement* sich *(dat)* vor-

behalten; ~**s** *pl (Mil)* Reserve *f;* **in** ~ in Reserve; ~**d** *a* reserviert; **all rights** ~**d** alle Rechte vorbehalten.

reservist [rɪ'zɜ:vɪst] *n* Reservist *m.*

reservoir ['rezəvwɑ:*] *n* Reservoir *nt.*

reshape ['ri:'ʃeɪp] *vt* umformen.

reshuffle ['ri:'ʃʌfl] *vt (Pol)* umbilden.

reside [rɪ'zaɪd] *vi* wohnen, ansässig sein; ~**nce** ['rezɪdəns] *(house)* Wohnung *f,* Wohnsitz *m; (living)* Wohnen *nt,* Aufenthalt *m;* ~**nt** ['rezɪdənt] *(in house)* Bewohner *m; (in area)* Einwohner *m; a* wohnhaft, ansässig; ~**ntial** [rezɪ'denʃəl] *a* Wohn-.

residue ['rezɪdju:] *n* Rest *m; (Chem)* Rückstand *m; (fig)* Bodensatz *m.*

resign [rɪ'zaɪn] *vt office* aufgeben, zurücktreten von; **to be** ~**ed to sth, to** ~ **o.s. to sth** sich mit etw abfinden; *(vi from office)* zurücktreten; ~**ation** [rezɪg'neɪʃən] *(resigning)* Aufgabe *f; (Pol)* Rücktritt *m; (submission)* Resignation *f;* ~**ed** *a* resigniert.

resilience [rɪ'zɪlɪəns] *n* Spannkraft *f,* Elastizität *f; (of person)* Unverwüstlichkeit *f.*

resilient [rɪ'zɪlɪənt] *a* unverwüstlich.

resin ['rezɪn] *n* Harz *nt.*

resist [rɪ'zɪst] *vt* widerstehen *(+dat);* ~**ance** Widerstand *m;* ~**ant** *a* widerstandsfähig *(to* gegen*); (to stains etc)* abstoßend.

resolute *a,* ~**ly** *ad* ['rezəlu:t, -lɪ] entschlossen, resolut.

resolution [rezə'lu:ʃən] *n (firmness)* Entschlossenheit *f; (intention)* Vorsatz *m; (decision)* Beschluß *m; (personal)* Entschluß *m.*

resolve [rɪ'zɒlv] *n* Vorsatz *m,* Entschluß *m; vt (decide)* beschließen; **it** ~**d itself** es löste sich; ~**d** *a* (fest) entschlossen.

resonant ['rezənənt] *a* widerhallend; *voice* volltönend.

resort [rɪ'zɔ:t] *n (holiday place)* Erholungsort *m; (help)* Zuflucht *f; vi* Zuflucht nehmen *(to* zu*);* **as a last** ~ als letzter Ausweg.

resound [rɪ'zaʊnd] *vi* widerhallen; ~**ing** *a* nachhallend; *success* groß.

resource [rɪ'sɔ:s] *n* Findigkeit *f;* ~**s** *pl (of energy)* Energiequellen *pl; (of money)* Quellen *pl; (of a country etc)* Bodenschätze *pl;* ~**ful** *a* findig; ~**fulness** Findigkeit *f.*

respect [rɪs'pekt] *n* Respekt *m; (esteem)* (Hoch)achtung *f; vt* achten, respektieren; ~**s** *pl* Grüße *pl;* **with** ~ **to** in bezug auf *(+acc),* hinsichtlich *(+gen);* **in** ~ **of** in bezug auf *(+acc);* **in this** ~ in dieser Hinsicht; ~**ability** [rɪspektə'bɪlɪtɪ] Anständigkeit *f,* Achtbarkeit *f;* ~**able** *a (decent)* angesehen, achtbar; *(fairly good)* leidlich; ~**ed** *a* angesehen; ~**ful** *a* höflich; ~**fully** *ad* ehrerbietig; *(in letter)* mit vorzüglicher Hochachtung; ~**ing** *prep* betreffend; ~**ive** *a* jeweilig; ~**ively** *ad* beziehungsweise.

respiration [respɪ'reɪʃən] *n* Atmung *f,* Atmen *nt.*

respiratory [rɪs'pɪrətərɪ] *a* Atmungs-.

respite ['respaɪt] *n* Ruhepause *f;* **without** ~ ohne Unterlaß.

resplendent [rɪsˈplendənt] a strahlend.

respond [rɪsˈpɒnd] vi antworten; (react) reagieren (to auf +acc).

response [rɪsˈpɒns] n Antwort f; Reaktion f; (to advert etc) Resonanz f.

responsibility [rɪspɒnsəˈbɪlɪtɪ] n Verantwortung f.

responsible [rɪsˈpɒnsəbl] a verantwortlich; (reliable) verantwortungsvoll.

responsibly [rɪsˈpɒnsəblɪ] ad verantwortungsvoll.

responsive [rɪsˈpɒnsɪv] a empfänglich.

rest [rest] n Ruhe f; (break) Pause f; (remainder) Rest m; **the ~ of them** die übrigen; vi sich ausruhen; (be supported) (auf)liegen; (remain) liegen (with bei).

restaurant [ˈrestərɔ̃ːŋ] n Restaurant nt, Gaststätte f; **~ car** Speisewagen m.

rest cure [ˈrestkjuə*] n Erholung f.

restful [ˈrestfʊl] a erholsam, ruhig.

rest home [ˈresthəʊm] n Erholungsheim nt.

restitution [restɪˈtjuːʃən] n Rückgabe f, Entschädigung f.

restive [ˈrestɪv] a unruhig; (disobedient) störrisch.

restless [ˈrestləs] a unruhig; **~ly** ad ruhelos; **~ness** Ruhelosigkeit f.

restock [ˈriːˈstɒk] vt auffüllen.

restoration [restəˈreɪʃən] n Wiederherstellung f; Neueinführung f; Wiedereinsetzung f; Rückgabe f; Restauration f; **the R~** die Restauration.

restore [rɪsˈtɔː*] vt order wiederherstellen; customs wieder einführen; person to position wiedereinsetzen; (give back) zurückgeben; paintings restaurieren.

restrain [rɪsˈtreɪn] vt zurückhalten; curiosity etc beherrschen; **~ed** a style etc gedämpft, verhalten; **~t** (restraining) Einschränkung f; (being restrained) Beschränkung f; (self-control) Zurückhaltung f.

restrict [rɪsˈtrɪkt] vt einschränken; **~ed** a beschränkt; **~ion** [rɪsˈtrɪkʃən] Einschränkung f; **~ive** a einschränkend.

rest room [ˈrestrum] n (US) Toilette f.

result [rɪˈzʌlt] n Resultat nt, Folge f; (of exam, game) Ergebnis nt; vi zur Folge haben (in acc); **~ant** a (daraus) entstehend or resultierend.

resume [rɪˈzjuːm] vt fortsetzen; (occupy again) wieder einnehmen.

résumé [ˈreɪzjuːmeɪ] n Zusammenfassung f.

resumption [rɪˈzʌmpʃən] n Wiederaufnahme f.

resurgence [rɪˈsɜːdʒəns] n Wiedererwachen nt.

resurrection [rezəˈrekʃən] n Auferstehung f.

resuscitate [rɪˈsʌsɪteɪt] vt wiederbeleben.

resuscitation [rɪsʌsɪˈteɪʃən] n Wiederbelebung f.

retail [ˈriːteɪl] n Einzelhandel m; a Einzelhandels-, Laden-; [ˈriːteɪl] vt im kleinen verkaufen; vi im Einzelhandel kosten; **~er** [ˈriːteɪlə*] Einzelhändler m, Kleinhändler m; **~ price** Ladenpreis m.

retain [rɪˈteɪn] vt (keep) (zurück)behalten; (pay) unterhalten; **~er** (servant) Gefolgsmann m; (fee) (Honorar)vorschuß m.

retaliate [rɪˈtælɪeɪt] vi zum Vergeltungsschlag ausholen.

retaliation [rɪtælɪˈeɪʃən] n Vergeltung f.

retarded [rɪˈtɑːdɪd] a zurückgeblieben.

retention [rɪˈtenʃən] n Behalten nt.

retentive [rɪˈtentɪv] a memory gut.

rethink [ˈriːˈθɪŋk] vt irreg nochmals durchdenken.

reticence [ˈretɪsəns] n Schweigsamkeit f.

reticent [ˈretɪsənt] a schweigsam.

retina [ˈretɪnə] n Netzhaut f.

retinue [ˈretɪnjuː] n Gefolge nt.

retire [rɪˈtaɪə*] vi (from work) in den Ruhestand treten; (withdraw) sich zurückziehen; (go to bed) schlafen gehen; **~d** a person pensioniert, im Ruhestand; **~ment** Ruhestand m.

retiring [rɪˈtaɪərɪŋ] a zurückhaltend, schüchtern.

retort [rɪˈtɔːt] n (reply) Erwiderung f; (Sci) Retorte f; vi (scharf) erwidern.

retrace [rɪˈtreɪs] vt zurückverfolgen.

retract [rɪˈtrækt] vt statement zurücknehmen; claws einziehen; **~able** a aerial ausziehbar.

retrain [ˈriːˈtreɪn] vt umschulen; **~ing** Umschulung f.

retreat [rɪˈtriːt] n Rückzug m; (place) Zufluchtsort m; vi sich zurückziehen.

retrial [ˈriːˈtraɪəl] n Wiederaufnahmeverfahren nt.

retribution [retrɪˈbjuːʃən] n Strafe f.

retrieval [rɪˈtriːvəl] n Wiedergewinnung f.

retrieve [rɪˈtriːv] vt wiederbekommen; (rescue) retten; **~r** Apportierhund m.

retroactive [retrəʊˈæktɪv] a rückwirkend.

retrograde [ˈretrəʊgreɪd] a step Rück-; policy rückschrittlich.

retrospect [ˈretrəʊspekt] n: **in ~** im Rückblick, rückblickend; **~ive** [retrəʊˈspektɪv] a rückwirkend; rückblickend.

return [rɪˈtɜːn] n Rückkehr f; (profits) Ertrag m, Gewinn m; (report) amtliche(r) Bericht m; (rail ticket etc) Rückfahrkarte f; (plane) Rückflugkarte f; (bus) Rückfahrschein m; a **by ~ of post** postwendend; journey, match Rück-; vi zurückkehren or -kommen; vt zurückgeben, zurücksenden; (pay back) zurückzahlen; (elect) wählen; verdict aussprechen; **~able** a bottle etc mit Pfand.

reunion [riːˈjuːnjən] n Wiedervereinigung f; (Sch etc) Treffen nt.

reunite [ˈriːjuːˈnaɪt] vt wiedervereinigen.

rev [rev] n Drehzahl f; vti (also **~ up**) (den Motor) auf Touren bringen.

revamp [ˈriːˈvæmp] vt aufpolieren.

reveal [rɪˈviːl] vt enthüllen; **~ing** a aufschlußreich.

reveille [rɪˈvælɪ] n Wecken nt.

revel [ˈrevl] vi genießen (in acc).

revelation [revəˈleɪʃən] n Offenbarung f.

reveller [ˈrevələ*] n Schwelger m.

revelry [ˈrevlrɪ] n Rummel m.

revenge [rɪˈvendʒ] *n* Rache *f; vt* rächen;
~**ful** *a* rachsüchtig.

revenue [ˈrevənjuː] *n* Einnahmen *pl,*
Staatseinkünfte *pl.*

reverberate [rɪˈvɜːbəreɪt] *vi* widerhallen.

reverberation   [rɪvɜːbəˈreɪʃən]   *n*
Widerhall *m.*

revere [rɪˈvɪə*] *vt* (ver)ehren; ~**nce**
[ˈrevərəns] Ehrfurcht *f;* [ˈrevərənd] **R**~**nd**
. . . Hochwürden . . .; ~**nt** [ˈrevərənt] *a*
ehrfurchtsvoll.

reverie [ˈrevərɪ] *n* Träumerei *f.*

reversal [rɪˈvɜːsəl] *n* Umkehrung *f.*

reverse [rɪˈvɜːs] *n* Rückseite *f; (Aut: gear)*
Rückwärtsgang *m; a* order, direction entgegengesetzt; *vt* umkehren; *vi (Aut)* rückwärts fahren.

reversion [rɪˈvɜːʃən] *n* Umkehrung *f.*

revert [rɪˈvɜːt] *vi* zurückkehren.

review [rɪˈvjuː] *n (Mil)* Truppenschau *f; (of
book)* Besprechung *f,* Rezension *f; (maga-
zine)* Zeitschrift *f;* **to be under** ~ untersucht werden; *vt* Rückschau halten auf
(+acc); (Mil) mustern; *book* besprechen,
rezensieren; *(reexamine)* von neuem untersuchen; ~**er** *(critic)* Rezensent *m.*

revise [rɪˈvaɪz] *vt* durchsehen, verbessern;
book überarbeiten; *(reconsider)* ändern,
revidieren.

revision [rɪˈvɪʒən] *n* Durchsicht *f,* Prüfung
f; (Comm) Revision *f; (of book)* verbesserte
Ausgabe *f; (Sch)* Wiederholung *f.*

revisit [riːˈvɪzɪt] *vt* wieder besuchen.

revitalize [riːˈvaɪtəlaɪz] *vt* neu beleben.

revival [rɪˈvaɪvəl] *n* Wiederbelebung *f;
(Rel)* Erweckung *f; (Theat)* Wiederaufnahme *f.*

revive [rɪˈvaɪv] *vt* wiederbeleben; *(fig)*
wieder auffrischen; *vi* wiedererwachen;
(fig) wieder aufleben.

revoke [rɪˈvəuk] *vt* aufheben.

revolt [rɪˈvəult] *n* Aufstand *m,* Revolte *f; vi*
sich auflehnen; *vt* entsetzen; ~**ing** *a*
widerlich.

revolution   [revəˈluːʃən]   *n*   *(turn)*
Umdrehung *f; (change)* Umwälzung *f; (Pol)*
Revolution *f;* ~**ary** *a* revolutionär; *n*
Revolutionär *m;* ~**ize** *vt* revolutionieren.

revolve [rɪˈvolv] *vi* kreisen; *(on own axis)*
sich drehen; ~**r** Revolver *m.*

revue [rɪˈvjuː] *n* Revue *f.*

revulsion [rɪˈvʌlʃən] *n (disgust)* Ekel *m.*

reward [rɪˈwɔːd] *n* Belohnung *f; vt*
belohnen; ~**ing** *a* lohnend.

reword [riːˈwɜːd] *vt* anders formulieren.

rewrite [riːˈraɪt] *vt irreg* umarbeiten, neu
schreiben.

rhapsody [ˈræpsədɪ] *n* Rhapsodie *f; (fig)*
Schwärmerei *f.*

rhetoric [ˈretərɪk] *n* Rhetorik *f,* Redekunst
f; ~**al** [rɪˈtorɪkəl] *a* rhetorisch.

rheumatic [ruːˈmætɪk] *a* rheumatisch.

rheumatism   [ˈruːmətɪzəm]   *n*
Rheumatismus *m,* Rheuma *nt.*

rhinoceros [raɪˈnosərəs] *n* Nashorn *nt,*
Rhinozeros *nt.*

rhododendron   [rəudəˈdendrən]   *n*
Rhododendron *m.*

rhubarb [ˈruːbɑːb] *n* Rhabarber *m.*

rhyme [raɪm] *n* Reim *m.*

rhythm [ˈrɪðəm] *n* Rhythmus *m;* ~**ic(al)**
a, ~**ically** *ad* [ˈrɪðmɪk(l), -l] rhythmisch.

rib [rɪb] *n* Rippe *f; vt (mock)* hänseln, aufziehen.

ribald [ˈrɪbəld] *a* saftig.

ribbon [ˈrɪbən] *n* Band *nt.*

rice [raɪs] *n* Reis *m;* ~ **pudding** Milchreis
m.

rich [rɪtʃ] *a* reich, wohlhabend; *(fertile)*
fruchtbar; *(splendid)* kostbar; *food* reichhaltig; ~**es** *pl* Reichtum *m,* Reichtümer
pl; ~**ly** *ad* reich; *deserve* völlig; ~**ness**
Reichtum *m; (of food)* Reichhaltigkeit *f; (of
colours)* Sattheit *f.*

rick [rɪk] *n* Schober *m.*

rickets [ˈrɪkɪts] *n* Rachitis *f.*

rickety [ˈrɪkɪtɪ] *a* wack(e)lig.

rickshaw [ˈrɪkʃɔː] *n* Riksha *f.*

ricochet [ˈrɪkəʃeɪ] *n* Abprallen *nt; (shot)*
Querschläger *m; vi* abprallen.

rid [rɪd] *vt irreg* befreien *(of* von*);* **to get** ~
of loswerden; **good** ~**dance!** den/die/das
wären wir los!

riddle [ˈrɪdl] *n* Rätsel *nt; vt (esp passive)*
durchlöchern.

ride [raɪd] *n (in vehicle)* Fahrt *f; (on horse)*
Ritt *m; irreg vt horse* reiten; *bicycle* fahren;
vi fahren; reiten; *(ship)* vor Anker liegen;
~**r** Reiter *m; (addition)* Zusatz *m.*

ridge [rɪdʒ] *n (of hills)* Bergkette *f; (top)*
Grat *m,* Kamm *m; (of roof)* Dachfirst *m.*

ridicule [ˈrɪdɪkjuːl] *n* Spott *m; vt* lächerlich
machen.

ridiculous *a,* ~**ly** *ad* [rɪˈdɪkjuləs, -lɪ]
lächerlich.

riding [ˈraɪdɪŋ] *n* Reiten *nt;* **to go** ~ reiten
gehen; ~ **habit** Reitkleid *nt;* ~ **school**
Reitschule *f.*

rife [raɪf] *a* weit verbreitet.

riffraff [ˈrɪfræf] *n* Gesindel *nt,* Pöbel *m.*

rifle [ˈraɪfl] *n* Gewehr *nt; vt* berauben; ~
range Schießstand *m.*

rift [rɪft] *n* Ritze *f,* Spalte *f; (fig)* Bruch *m.*

rig [rɪg] *n (outfit)* Takelung *f; (fig)* Aufmachung *f; (oil* ~*)* Bohrinsel *f; vt election
etc* manipulieren; ~**ging** Takelage *f;* ~
out *vt* ausstatten; ~ **up** *vt* zusammenbasteln, konstruieren.

right [raɪt] *a (correct, just)* richtig, recht;
(right side) rechte*(r, s); n* Recht *nt; (not left,
Pol)* Rechte *f; ad (on the right)* rechts; *(to
the right)* nach rechts; *look, work* richtig,
recht; *(directly)* gerade; *(exactly)* genau; *vt*
in Ordnung bringen, korrigieren; *interj* gut;
~ **away** sofort; **to be** ~ recht haben; **all**
~! gut!, in Ordnung!, schön!; ~ **now** in
diesem Augenblick, eben; **by** ~**s** von
Rechts wegen; ~ **to the end** bis ans
Ende; **on the** ~ rechts; ~ **angle**
Rechteck *nt;* ~**eous** [ˈraɪtʃəs] *a* rechtschaffen; ~**eousness** Rechtschaffenheit
f; ~**ful** *a* rechtmäßig; ~**fully** *ad* rechtmäßig; *(justifiably)* zu Recht; ~**-hand
drive: to have** ~**-hand drive** das Steuer
rechts haben; ~**-handed** *a* rechtshändig;
~**-hand man** rechte Hand *f;* ~**-hand
side** rechte Seite *f;* ~**ly** *ad* mit Recht;
~**-minded** *a* rechtschaffen; ~ **of way**
Vorfahrt *f;* ~**-wing** rechte(r) Flügel *m.*

rigid ['rɪdʒɪd] a (stiff) starr, steif; (strict) streng; ~**ity** [rɪ'dʒɪdɪtɪ] Starrheit f, Steifheit f; Strenge f; ~**ly** starr, steif; (fig) hart, unbeugsam.

rigmarole ['rɪgmərəul] n Gewäsch nt.

rigor mortis ['rɪgə'mɔːtɪs] n Totenstarre f.

rigorous a, ~**ly** ad ['rɪgərəs, -lɪ] streng.

rigour, (US) **rigor** ['rɪgə*] n Strenge f, Härte f.

rig-out ['rɪgaut] n (col) Aufzug m.

rile [raɪl] vt ärgern.

rim [rɪm] n (edge) Rand m; (of wheel) Felge f; ~**less** a randlos; ~**med** a gerändert.

rind [raɪnd] n Rinde f.

ring [rɪŋ] n Ring m; (of people) Kreis m; (arena) Ring m, Manege f; (of telephone) Klingeln nt, Läuten nt; **to give sb a** ~ jdn anrufen; **it has a familiar** ~ es klingt bekannt; vti irreg **bell** läuten; (also ~ **up**) anrufen; ~ **off** vi aufhängen; ~ **binder** Ringbuch nt; ~**leader** Anführer m, Rädelsführer m; ~**lets** pl Ringellocken pl; ~ **road** Umgehungsstraße f.

rink [rɪŋk] n (ice ~) Eisbahn f.

rinse [rɪns] n Spülen nt; vt spülen.

riot ['raɪət] n Aufruhr m; vi randalieren; ~**er** Aufrührer m; ~**ous** a, ~**ously** ad aufrührerisch; (noisy) lärmend.

rip [rɪp] n Schlitz m, Riß m; vti (zer)reißen.

ripcord ['rɪpkɔːd] n Reißleine f.

ripe [raɪp] a fruit reif; cheese ausgereift; ~**n** vti reifen, reif werden (lassen); ~**ness** Reife f.

riposte [rɪ'pɒst] n Nachstoß m; (fig) schlagfertige Antwort f.

ripple ['rɪpl] n kleine Welle f; vt kräuseln; vi sich kräuseln.

rise [raɪz] n (slope) Steigung f; (esp in wages) Erhöhung f; (growth) Aufstieg m; vi irreg aufstehen; (sun) aufgehen; (smoke) aufsteigen; (mountain) sich erheben; (ground) ansteigen; (prices) steigen; (in revolt) sich erheben; **to give** ~ **to** Anlaß geben zu; **to** ~ **to the occasion** sich der Lage gewachsen zeigen.

risk [rɪsk] n Gefahr f, Risiko nt; vt (venture) wagen; (chance loss of) riskieren, aufs Spiel setzen; ~**y** a gewagt, gefährlich, riskant.

risqué ['riːskeɪ] a gewagt.

rissole ['rɪsəul] n Fleischklößchen nt.

rite [raɪt] n Ritus m; **last** ~**s** pl Letzte Ölung f.

ritual ['rɪtjuəl] n Ritual nt; a ritual, Ritual-; (fig) rituell.

rival ['raɪvəl] n Rivale m, Konkurrent m; a rivalisierend; vt rivalisieren mit; (Comm) konkurrieren mit; ~**ry** Rivalität f, Konkurrenz f.

river ['rɪvə*] n Fluß m, Strom m; ~**bank** Flußufer nt; ~**bed** Flußbett nt; ~**side** n Flußufer nt; a am Ufer gelegen, Ufer-.

rivet ['rɪvɪt] n Niete f; vt (fasten) (ver)nieten.

road [rəud] n Straße f; ~**block** Straßensperre f; ~**hog** Verkehrsrowdy m; ~**map** Straßenkarte f; ~ **side** n Straßenrand m; a an der Landstraße (gelegen); ~ **sign** Straßenschild nt; ~ **user** Verkehrsteilnehmer m; ~**way** Fahrbahn f; ~**worthy** a verkehrssicher.

roam [rəum] vi (umher)streifen; vt durchstreifen.

roar [rɔː*] n Brüllen nt, Gebrüll nt; vi brüllen; ~**ing** a fire Bomben-, prasselnd; trade schwunghaft, Bomben-.

roast [rəust] n Braten m; vt braten, rösten, schmoren.

rob [rɒb] vt bestehlen, berauben; bank ausrauben; ~**ber** Räuber m; ~**bery** Raub m.

robe [rəub] n (dress) Gewand nt; (US) Hauskleid nt; (judge's) Robe f; vt feierlich ankleiden.

robin ['rɒbɪn] n Rotkehlchen nt.

robot ['rəubɒt] n Roboter m.

robust [rəu'bʌst] a stark, robust.

rock [rɒk] n Felsen m; (piece) Stein m; (bigger) Fels(brocken) m; (sweet) Zuckerstange f; vti wiegen, schaukeln; **on the** ~**s** drink mit Eis(würfeln); marriage gescheitert; ship aufgelaufen; ~-**bottom** (fig) Tiefpunkt m; ~ **climber** (Steil)kletterer m; **to go** ~ **climbing** (steil)klettern gehen; ~**ery** Steingarten m.

rocket ['rɒkɪt] n Rakete f.

rock face ['rɒkfeɪs] n Felswand f.

rocking chair ['rɒkɪŋtʃeə*] n Schaukelstuhl m.

rocking horse ['rɒkɪŋhɔːs] n Schaukelpferd nt.

rocky ['rɒkɪ] a felsig.

rococo [rəu'kəukəu] a Rokoko-; n Rokoko nt.

rod [rɒd] n (bar) Stange f; (stick) Rute f.

rodent ['rəudənt] n Nagetier nt.

rodeo ['rəudɪəu] n Rodeo m or nt.

roe [rəu] n (deer) Reh nt; (of fish) Rogen m.

rogue [rəug] n Schurke m; (hum) Spitzbube m.

roguish ['rəugɪʃ] a schurkisch; hum schelmisch.

role [rəul] n Rolle f.

roll [rəul] n Rolle f; (bread) Brötchen nt, Semmel f; (list) (Namens)liste f, Verzeichnis nt; (of drum) Wirbel m; vt (turn) rollen, (herum)wälzen; grass etc walzen; vi (swing) schlingern; (sound) (g)rollen; ~ **by** vi (time) verfließen; ~ **in** vi (mail) hereinkommen; ~ **over** vi sich (herum)drehen; ~ **up** vi (arrive) kommen, auftauchen; vt carpet aufrollen; ~ **call** Namensaufruf m; ~**ed** a umbrella zusammengerollt; ~**er** Rolle f, Walze f; (road ~er) Straßenwalze f; ~**er skates** pl Rollschuhe pl.

rollicking ['rɒlɪkɪŋ] a ausgelassen.

rolling ['rəulɪŋ] a landscape wellig; ~ **pin** Nudel- or Wellholz nt; ~ **stock** Wagenmaterial nt.

Roman ['rəumən] a römisch; n Römer(in f) m; ~ **Catholic** a römisch-katholisch; n Katholik(in f) m.

romance [rəu'mæns] n Romanze f; (story) (Liebes)roman m; vi aufschneiden, erfinden; ~**r** (storyteller) Aufschneider m.

romantic [rəu'mæntɪk] a romantisch; R~**ism** [rəu'mæntɪsɪzm] Romantik f.

romp [rɒmp] n Tollen nt; vi (also ~ **about**) herumtollen; ~**ers** pl Spielanzug m.

rondo ['rɒndəu] n (Mus) Rondo nt.

roof [ru:f] n Dach nt; (of mouth) Gaumen nt; vt überdachen, überdecken; **~ing** Deckmaterial nt.

rook [ruk] n (bird) Saatkrähe f; (chess) Turm m; vt (cheat) betrügen.

room [rum] n Zimmer nt, Raum m; (space) Platz m; (fig) Spielraum m; **~s** pl Wohnung f; **~iness** Geräumigkeit f; **~-mate** Mitbewohner(in f) m; **~ service** Zimmerbedienung f; **~y** a geräumig.

roost [ru:st] n Hühnerstange f; vi auf der Stange hocken.

root [ru:t] n (lit, fig) Wurzel f; vt einwurzeln; **~ed** a (fig) verwurzelt; **~ about** vi (fig) herumwühlen; **~ for** vt Stimmung machen für; **~ out** vt ausjäten; (fig) ausrotten.

rope [rəʊp] n Seil nt, Strick m; vt (tie) festschnüren; **to ~ sb in** jdn gewinnen; **~ off** vt absperren; **to know the ~s** sich auskennen; **~ ladder** Strickleiter f.

rosary ['rəʊzərɪ] n Rosenkranz m.

rose [rəʊz] n Rose f; a Rosen-, rosenrot.

rosé ['rəʊzeɪ] n Rosé m.

rosebed ['rəʊzbed] n Rosenbeet nt.

rosebud ['rəʊzbʌd] n Rosenknospe f.

rosebush ['rəʊzbʊʃ] n Rosenstock m, Rosenstrauch m.

rosemary ['rəʊzmərɪ] n Rosmarin m.

rosette [rəʊ'zet] n Rosette f.

roster ['rɒstə*] n Dienstplan m.

rostrum ['rɒstrəm] n Rednerbühne f.

rosy ['rəʊzɪ] a rosig.

rot [rɒt] n Fäulnis f; (nonsense) Quatsch m, Blödsinn m; vti verfaulen (lassen).

rota ['rəʊtə] n Dienstliste f.

rotary ['rəʊtərɪ] a rotierend, sich drehend.

rotate [rəʊ'teɪt] vt rotieren lassen; (two or more things in order) turnusmäßig wechseln; vi rotieren.

rotating [rəʊ'teɪtɪŋ] a rotierend.

rotation [rəʊ'teɪʃən] n Umdrehung f, Rotation f; **in ~** der Reihe nach, abwechselnd.

rotor ['rəʊtə*] n Rotor m.

rotten ['rɒtn] a faul, verfault; (fig) schlecht, gemein.

rotund [rəʊ'tʌnd] a rund; person rundlich.

rouge [ru:ʒ] n Rouge nt.

rough [rʌf] a (not smooth) rauh; path uneben; (violent) roh, grob; crossing stürmisch; wind rauh; (without comforts) hart, unbequem; (unfinished, makeshift) grob; (approximate) ungefähr; n (grass) unebene(r) Boden m; (person) Rowdy m, Rohling m; **to ~ it** primitiv leben; **to play ~** (Sport) hart spielen; **to sleep ~** im Freien schlafen; **~ out** vt entwerfen, flüchtig skizzieren; **~en** vt aufrauhen; **~ly** ad grob; (about) ungefähr; **~ness** Rauheit f; (of manner) Ungeschliffenheit f.

roulette [ru:'let] n Roulette nt.

round [raʊnd] a rund; figures abgerundet, aufgerundet; ad (in a circle) rundherum; prep um . . . herum; n Runde f; (of ammunition) Magazin nt; (song) Kanon m; **theatre in the ~** Rundtheater nt; vt corner biegen um; **~ off** vt abrunden; **~ up** vt (end) abschließen; figures aufrunden; **~ of**

applause Beifall m; **~about** n (traffic) Kreisverkehr m; (merry-go-round) Karussell nt; a auf Umwegen; **~ed a** gerundet; **~ly** ad (fig) gründlich; **~-shouldered** a mit abfallenden Schultern; **~sman** (general) Austräger m; (milk ~) Milchmann m; **~up** Zusammentreiben nt, Sammeln nt.

rouse [raʊz] vt (waken) (auf)wecken; (stir up) erregen.

rousing ['raʊzɪŋ] a welcome stürmisch; speech zündend.

rout [raʊt] n wilde Flucht f; Überwältigung f; vt in die Flucht schlagen.

route [ru:t] n Weg m, Route f.

routine [ru:'ti:n] n Routine f; a Routine-.

rover ['rəʊvə*] n Wanderer m.

roving ['rəʊvɪŋ] a reporter im Außendienst.

row [rəʊ] n (line) Reihe f; vti boat rudern.

row [raʊ] n (noise) Lärm m, Krach m, Radau m; (dispute) Streit m; (scolding) Krach m; vi sich streiten.

rowboat ['rəʊbəʊt] n (US) Ruderboot nt.

rowdy ['raʊdɪ] a rüpelhaft; n (person) Rowdy m.

rowing ['rəʊɪŋ] n Rudern nt; (Sport) Rudersport m; **~ boat** Ruderboot nt.

rowlock ['rɒlək] n Rudergabel f.

royal ['rɔɪəl] a königlich, Königs-; **~ist** n Royalist m; a königstreu; **~ty** (family) königliche Familie f; (for invention) Patentgebühr f; (for book) Tantieme f.

rub [rʌb] n (problem) Haken m; **to give sth a ~** etw (ab)reiben; vt reiben; **~ off** vi (lit, fig) abfärben (on auf +acc); **to ~ it in** darauf herumreiten.

rubber ['rʌbə*] n Gummi m; (Brit) Radiergummi m; **~ band** Gummiband nt; **~ plant** Gummibaum m; **~y** a gummiartig, wie Gummi.

rubbish ['rʌbɪʃ] n (waste) Abfall m; (nonsense) Blödsinn m, Quatsch m; **~ dump** Müllabladeplatz m.

rubble ['rʌbl] n (Stein)schutt m.

ruby ['ru:bɪ] n Rubin m; a rubinrot.

rucksack ['rʌksæk] n Rucksack m.

rudder ['rʌdə*] n Steuerruder nt.

ruddy ['rʌdɪ] a (colour) rötlich; (col: bloody) verdammt.

rude, a, **~ly** ad [ru:d, -lɪ] unhöflich, unverschämt; shock hart; awakening unsanft; (unrefined, rough) grob; **~ness** Unhöflichkeit f, Unverschämtheit f; Grobheit f.

rudiment ['ru:dɪmənt] n Grundlage f; **~ary** [ru:dɪ'mentərɪ] a rudimentär.

ruff [rʌf] n Halskrause f.

ruffian ['rʌfɪən] n Rohling m.

ruffle ['rʌfl] vt kräuseln; durcheinanderbringen.

rug [rʌg] n Brücke f; (in bedroom) Bettvorleger m; (for knees) (Reise)decke f.

rugged ['rʌgɪd] a coastline zerklüftet; features markig.

ruin ['ru:ɪn] n Ruine f; (downfall) Ruin m; vt ruinieren; **~s** pl Trümmer pl; **~ation** Zerstörung f, Ruinierung f; **~ous** a ruinierend.

rule [ru:l] n Regel f; (government) Herrschaft *f*, Regierung *f*; *(for measuring)* Lineal *nt*; *vti (govern)* herrschen über *(+acc)*, regieren; *(decide)* anordnen, entscheiden; *(make lines)* linieren; **as a** ~ in der Regel; ~**d** *a paper* liniert; ~**r** Lineal *nt*; Herrscher *m*.

ruling ['ru:lɪŋ] *a party* Regierungs-; *class* herrschend.

rum [rʌm] *n* Rum *m*; *a (col)* komisch.

rumble ['rʌmbl] *n* Rumpeln *nt*; *(of thunder)* Rollen *nt*; *vi* rumpeln; grollen.

ruminate ['ru:mɪneɪt] *vi* grübeln; *(cows)* wiederkäuen.

rummage ['rʌmɪdʒ] *n* Durchsuchung *f*; *vi* durchstöbern.

rumour, *(US)* **rumor** ['ru:mə*] *n* Gerücht *nt*; *vt*: **it is** ~**ed that** man sagt *or* man munkelt, daß.

rump [rʌmp] *n* Hinterteil *nt*; *(of fowl)* Bürzel *m*; ~ **steak** Rumpsteak *nt*.

rumpus ['rʌmpəs] *n* Spektakel *m*, Krach *m*.

run [rʌn] *n* Lauf *m*; *(in car)* (Spazier)fahrt *f*; *(series)* Serie *f*, Reihe *f*; *(of play)* Spielzeit *f*; *(sudden demand)* Ansturm *m*, starke Nachfrage *f*; *(for animals)* Auslauf *m*; *(Ski* —) (Ski)abfahrt *f*; *(in stocking)* Laufmasche *f*; *irreg vt (cause to run)* laufen lassen; *car, train, bus* fahren; *(pay for)* unterhalten; *race, distance* laufen, rennen; *(manage)* leiten, verwalten, führen; *knife* stoßen; *(pass) hand, eye* gleiten lassen; *vi* laufen; *(move quickly also)* rennen; *(bus, train)* fahren; *(flow)* fließen, laufen; *(colours)* (ab)färben; **on the** ~ auf der Flucht; **in the long** ~ auf die Dauer; **to** ~ **riot** Amok laufen; **to** ~ **a risk** ein Risiko eingehen; ~ **about** *vi (children)* umherspringen; ~ **across** *vt (find)* stoßen auf *(+acc)*; ~ **away** *vi* weglaufen; ~ **down** *vi (clock)* ablaufen; *vt (with car)* überfahren; *(talk against)* heruntermachen; **to be** ~- **down** erschöpft *or* abgespannt sein; **to** ~ **for president** für die Präsidentschaft kandidieren; ~ **off** *vi* fortlaufen; ~ **out** *vt (person)* hinausrennen; *(liquid)* auslaufen; *(lease)* ablaufen; *(money)* ausgehen; **he ran out of money/petrol** ihm ging das Geld/Benzin aus; ~ **over** *vt (in accident)* überfahren; *(read quickly)* überfliegen; ~- **through** *vt instructions* durchgehen; ~ **up** *vt debt, bill* machen; ~ **up against** *vt* difficulties stoßen auf *(+acc)*; ~**about** *(small car)* kleine(r) Flitzer *m*; ~**away** *a horse* ausgebrochen; *person* flüchtig.

rung [rʌŋ] *n* Sprosse *f*.

runner ['rʌnə*] *n* Läufer(in *f*) *m*; *(messenger)* Bote *m*; *(for sleigh)* Kufe *f*; ~**up** Zweite(r) *mf*.

running ['rʌnɪŋ] *n (of business)* Leitung *f*; *(of machine)* Laufen *nt*, Betrieb *m*; *a water* fließend; *commentary* laufend; **3 days** ~ 3 Tage lang *or* hintereinander.

run-of-the-mill ['rʌnəvðə'mɪl] *a* gewöhnlich, alltäglich.

runny ['rʌnɪ] *a* dünn.

runway ['rʌnweɪ] *n* Startbahn *f*, Landebahn *f*, Rollbahn *f*.

rupture ['rʌptfə*] *n (Med)* Bruch *m*; *vt*: ~ **o.s.** sich *(dat)* einen Bruch zuziehen.

rural ['ruərəl] *a* ländlich, Land-.

ruse [ru:z] *n* Kniff *m*, List *f*.

rush [rʌʃ] *n* Eile *f*, Hetze *f*; *(Fin)* starke Nachfrage *f*; *vt (carry along)* auf dem schnellsten Wege schaffen *or* transportieren; *(attack)* losstürmen auf *(+acc)*; **don't** ~ **me** dräng mich nicht; *vi (hurry)* eilen, stürzen; **to** ~ **into sth** etw überstürzen; ~**es** *pl (Bot)* Schilf(rohr) *nt*; ~ **hour** Hauptverkehrszeit *f*.

rusk [rʌsk] *n* Zwieback *m*.

rust [rʌst] *n* Rost *m*; *vi* rosten.

rustic ['rʌstɪk] *a* bäuerlich, ländlich, Bauern-.

rustle ['rʌsl] *n* Rauschen *nt*, Rascheln *nt*; *vi* rauschen, rascheln; *vt* rascheln lassen; *cattle* stehlen.

rustproof ['rʌstpru:f] *a* nichtrostend, rostfrei.

rusty ['rʌstɪ] *a* rostig.

rut [rʌt] *n (in track)* Radspur *f*; *(of deer)* Brunst *f*; *(fig)* Trott *m*.

ruthless *a*, ~**ly** *ad* ['ru:θləs, -lɪ] erbarmungslos; rücksichtslos; ~**ness** Unbarmherzigkeit *f*, Rücksichtslosigkeit *f*.

rye [raɪ] *n* Roggen *m*; ~ **bread** Roggenbrot *nt*.

S

S, s [es] *n* S *nt*, s *nt*.

sabbath ['sæbəθ] *n* Sabbat *m*.

sabbatical [sə'bætɪkəl] *a*: ~ **year** Beurlaubungs- *or* Forschungsjahr *nt*.

sabotage ['sæbətɑ:ʒ] *n* Sabotage *f*; *vt* sabotieren.

sabre, *(US)* **saber** ['seɪbə*] *n* Säbel *m*.

saccharin(e) ['sækərɪn] *n* Saccharin *nt*.

sachet ['sæʃeɪ] *n (of shampoo)* Briefchen *nt*, Kissen *nt*.

sack [sæk] *n* Sack *m*; **to give sb the** ~ *(col)* jdn hinauswerfen; *vt (col)* hinauswerfen; *(pillage)* plündern; ~**ful** Sack(voll) *m*; ~**ing** *(material)* Sackleinen *nt*; *(col)* Rausschmiß *m*.

sacrament ['sækrəmənt] *n* Sakrament *nt*.

sacred ['seɪkrɪd] *a building, music etc* geistlich, Kirchen-; *altar, oath* heilig.

sacrifice ['sækrɪfaɪs] *n* Opfer *nt*; *vt (lit, fig)* opfern.

sacrilege ['sækrɪlɪdʒ] *n* Schändung *f*.

sacrosanct ['sækrəusæŋkt] *a* sakrosankt.

sad [sæd] *a* traurig; ~**den** *vt* traurig machen, betrüben.

saddle ['sædl] *n* Sattel *m*; *vt (burden)* aufhalsen *(sb with sth* jdm etw); ~**bag** Satteltasche *f*.

sadism ['seɪdɪzəm] *n* Sadismus *m*.

sadist ['seɪdɪst] *n* Sadist *m*; ~**ic** [sə'dɪstɪk] *a* sadistisch.

sadly ['sædlɪ] *ad* betrübt, beklagenswert; *(very)* arg.

sadness ['sædnəs] *n* Traurigkeit *f*.

safari [sə'fɑ:rɪ] *n* Safari *f*.

safe [seɪf] *a (free from danger)* sicher; *(careful)* vorsichtig; **it's** ~ **to say** man kann ruhig behaupten; **in** ~ Safe *m*, Tresor *m*, Geldschrank *m*; ~**guard** *n* Sicherung *f*; *vt* sichern, schützen; ~**keeping** sichere Verwahrung *f*; ~**ly** *ad* sicher; *arrive*

wohlbehalten; ~ness Zuverlässigkeit f;
~ty Sicherheit f; ~ty belt Sicherheitsgurt m; ~ty curtain eiserne(r) Vorhang
m; ~ty first (slogan) Sicherheit geht vor;
~ty pin Sicherheitsnadel f.

sag [sæg] vi (durch)sacken, sich senken.

saga ['sɑːgə] n Sage f.

sage [seidʒ] n (herb) Salbei m; (man)
Weise(r) m.

Sagittarius [sadʒɪ'tɛərɪəs] n Schütze m.

sago ['seigəu] n Sago m.

said [sed] a besagt.

sail [seil] n Segel nt; (trip) Fahrt f; vt
segeln; vi segeln; mit dem Schiff fahren;
(begin voyage) (person) abfahren; (ship)
auslaufen; (fig: cloud etc) dahinsegeln;
~boat (US) Segelboot nt; ~ing Segeln
nt; to go ~ing segeln gehen; ~ing ship
Segelschiff nt; ~or Matrose m, Seemann
m.

saint [seint] n Heilige(r) mf; ~liness
Heiligkeit f; ~ly a heilig, fromm.

sake [seik] n: for the ~ of um (+gen)
willen; for your ~ um deinetwillen,
deinetwegen, wegen dir.

salad ['sæləd] n Salat m; ~ cream
gewürzte Mayonnaise f; ~ dressing
Salatsoße f; ~ oil Speiseöl nt, Salatöl nt.

salami [sə'lɑːmɪ] n Salami f.

salaried ['sælərɪd] a: ~ staff
Gehaltsempfänger pl.

salary ['sælərɪ] n Gehalt nt.

sale [seil] n Verkauf m; (reduced prices)
Schlußverkauf m; ~room Verkaufsraum
m; ~sman Verkäufer m; (representative)
Vertreter m; ~smanship Geschäfts-
tüchtigkeit f; ~swoman Verkäuferin f.

salient ['seiliənt] a hervorspringend,
bemerkenswert.

saliva [sə'laivə] n Speichel m.

sallow ['sæləu] a fahl; face bleich.

salmon ['sæmən] n Lachs m.

salon ['sælɔ̃:ŋ] n Salon m.

saloon [sə'luːn] n (Aut) Limousine f; (ship's
lounge) Salon m.

salt [sɔːlt] n Salz nt; vt (cure) einsalzen;
(flavour) salzen; ~cellar Salzfaß nt; ~
mine Salzbergwerk nt; ~y a salzig.

salubrious [sə'luːbrɪəs] a gesund; district
etc ersprießlich.

salutary ['sæljutərɪ] a gesund, heilsam.

salute [sə'luːt] n (Mil) Gruß m, Salut m;
(with guns) Salutschüsse pl; vt (Mil)
salutieren.

salvage ['sælvɪdʒ] n (from ship) Bergung f;
(property) Rettung f; vt bergen; retten.

salvation [sæl'veiʃən] n Rettung f; S~
Army Heilsarmee f.

salver ['sælvə*] n Tablett nt.

salvo ['sælvəu] n Salve f.

same [seim] a (similar) gleiche(r,s);
(identical) derselbe/dieselbe/ dasselbe; all
or just the ~ trotzdem; it's all the ~ to
me das ist mir egal; they all look the ~
to me für mich sehen sie alle gleich aus;
the ~ to you gleichfalls; at the ~ time
zur gleichen Zeit, gleichzeitig; (however)
zugleich, andererseits.

sampan ['sæmpæn] n Sampan m.

sample ['sɑːmpl] n (specimen) Probe f;
(example of sth) Muster nt, Probe f; vt
probieren.

sanatorium [sænə'tɔːrɪəm] n Sanatorium
nt.

sanctify ['sæŋktɪfaɪ] vt weihen.

sanctimonious [sæŋktɪ'məunɪəs] a
scheinheilig.

sanction ['sæŋkʃən] n Sanktion f.

sanctity ['sæŋktɪtɪ] n Heiligkeit f; (fig)
Unverletzlichkeit f.

sanctuary ['sæŋktjuərɪ] n Heiligtum nt;
(for fugitive) Asyl nt; (refuge) Zufluchtsort
m; (for animals) Naturpark m, Schutzgebiet nt.

sand [sænd] n Sand m; vt mit Sand
bestreuen; furniture schmirgeln; ~s pl
Sand m.

sandal ['sændl] n Sandale f.

sandbag ['sændbæg] n Sandsack m.

sand dune ['sænddjuːn] n (Sand)düne f.

sandpaper ['sændpeipə*] n Sandpapier nt.

sandpit ['sændpɪt] n Sandkasten m.

sandstone ['sændstəun] n Sandstein m.

sandwich ['sænwɪdʒ] n Sandwich m or nt;
vt einklemmen.

sandy ['sændɪ] a sandig, Sand-; (colour)
sandfarben; hair rotblond.

sane [sein] a geistig gesund or normal;
(sensible) vernünftig, gescheit.

sanguine ['sæŋgwɪn] a (hopeful) zuver-
sichtlich.

sanitarium [sænɪ'tɛərɪəm] n (US) =
sanatorium.

sanitary ['sænɪtərɪ] a hygienisch (ein-
wandfrei); (against dirt) hygienisch,
Gesundheits-; ~ napkin (US), ~ towel
(Monats)binde f.

sanitation [sænɪ'teɪʃən] n sanitäre
Einrichtungen pl; Gesundheitswesen nt.

sanity ['sænɪtɪ] n geistige Gesundheit f;
(good sense) gesunde(r) Verstand m,
Vernunft f.

Santa Claus [sæntə'klɔːz] n Nikolaus m,
Weihnachtsmann m.

sap [sæp] n (of plants) Saft m; vt strength
schwächen; health untergraben.

sapling ['sæplɪŋ] n junge(r) Baum m.

sapphire ['sæfaɪə*] n Saphir m.

sarcasm ['sɑːkæzəm] n Sarkasmus m.

sarcastic [sɑː'kæstɪk] a sarkastisch.

sarcophagus [sɑː'kɔfəgəs] n Sarkophag m.

sardine [sɑː'diːn] n Sardine f.

sardonic [sɑː'dɔnɪk] a zynisch.

sari ['sɑːrɪ] n Sari m.

sash [sæʃ] n Schärpe f.

Satan ['seitn] n Satan m, Teufel m; s~ic
[sə'tænɪk] a satanisch, teuflisch.

satchel ['sætʃəl] n (Sch) Schulranzen m,
Schulmappe f.

satellite ['sætəlaɪt] n Satellit m; (fig)
Trabant m; a Satelliten-.

satin ['sætɪn] n Satin m; a Satin-.

satire ['sætaɪə*] n Satire f.

satirical [sə'tɪrɪkəl] a satirisch.

satirize ['sætəraɪz] vt (durch Satire) verspotten.

satisfaction [sætɪs'fækʃən] n Befriedigung
f, Genugtuung f.

satisfactorily [sætɪsˈfæktərɪlɪ] *ad* zufriedenstellend.
satisfactory [sætɪsˈfæktərɪ] *a* zufriedenstellend, befriedigend.
satisfy [ˈsætɪsfaɪ] *vt* befriedigen, zufriedenstellen; (*convince*) überzeugen; *conditions* erfüllen; ~**ing** *a* befriedigend; *meal* sättigend.
saturate [ˈsætʃəreɪt] *vt* (durch)tränken.
saturation [sætʃəˈreɪʃən] *n* Durchtränkung *f*; (*Chem, fig*) Sättigung *f*.
Saturday [ˈsætədeɪ] *n* Samstag *m*, Sonnabend *m*.
sauce [sɔːs] *n* Soße *f*, Sauce *f*; ~**pan** Kasserolle *f*; ~**r** Untertasse *f*.
saucily [ˈsɔːsɪlɪ] *ad* frech.
sauciness [ˈsɔːsɪnəs] *n* Frechheit *f*.
saucy [ˈsɔːsɪ] *a* frech, keck.
sauna [ˈsɔːnə] *n* Sauna *f*.
saunter [ˈsɔːntə*] *vi* schlendern; *n* Schlendern *nt*.
sausage [ˈsɒsɪdʒ] *n* Wurst *f*; ~ **roll** Wurst *f* im Schlafrock, Wurstpastete *f*.
savage [ˈsævɪdʒ] *a* (*fierce*) wild, brutal, grausam; (*uncivilized*) wild, primitiv; *n* Wilde(r) *mf*; *vt* (*animals*) zerfleischen; ~**ly** *ad* grausam; ~**ry** Roheit *f*, Grausamkeit *f*.
save [seɪv] *vt* retten; *money, electricity etc* sparen; *strength etc* aufsparen; **to ~ you the trouble of** um dir Mühe zu ersparen; *n* (*Sport*) (Ball)abwehr *f*; *prep, cj* außer, ausgenommen.
saving [ˈseɪvɪŋ] *a* rettend; *n* Sparen *nt*, Ersparnis *f*; ~**s** *pl* Ersparnisse *pl*; ~**s bank** Sparkasse *f*.
saviour [ˈseɪvjə*] *n* Retter *m*; (*Eccl*) Heiland *m*, Erlöser *m*.
savoir-faire [ˈsævwaːˈfɛə*] *n* Gewandtheit *f*.
savour, (*US*) **savor** [ˈseɪvə*] *n* Wohlgeschmack *m*; *vt* (*taste*) schmecken; (*fig*) genießen; *vi* schmecken (*of* nach), riechen (*of* nach); ~**y** *a* schmackhaft; *food* pikant, würzig.
savvy [ˈsævɪ] *n* (*col*) Grips *m*.
saw [sɔː] *n* (*tool*) Säge *f*; *vti irreg* sägen; ~**dust** Sägemehl *nt*; ~**mill** Sägewerk *nt*.
saxophone [ˈsæksəfəʊn] *n* Saxophon *nt*.
say [seɪ] *n* Meinung *f*; (*right*) Mitspracherecht *nt*; **to have no/a ~ in sth** (kein) Mitspracherecht bei etw haben; **let him have his ~** laß ihn doch reden; *vti irreg* sagen; **I couldn't ~** schwer zu sagen; **how old would you ~ he is?** wie alt schätzt du ihn?; **you don't ~!** was du nicht sagst!; **don't ~ you forgot** sag bloß nicht, daß du es vergessen hast; **there are,** ~**, 50** es sind, sagen wir mal, 50. . .; **that is to ~** das heißt; (*more precisely*) beziehungsweise, mit anderen Worten; **to ~ nothing of . . .** ganz zu schweigen von. . .; ~**ing** Sprichwort *nt*; ~**-so** (*col*) Ja *nt*, Zustimmung *f*.
scab [skæb] *n* Schorf *m*; (*of sheep*) Räude *f*; (*pej*) Streikbrecher *m*.
scabby [ˈskæbɪ] *a* *sheep* räudig; *skin* schorfig.
scaffold [ˈskæfəʊld] *n* (*for execution*) Schafott *nt*; ~**ing** (Bau)gerüst *nt*.

scald [skɔːld] *n* Verbrühung *f*; *vt* (*burn*) verbrühen; (*clean*) (ab)brühen; ~**ing** *a* brühheiß.
scale [skeɪl] *n* (*of fish*) Schuppe *f*; (*Mus*) Tonleiter *f*; (*dish for measuring*) Waagschale *f*; (*on map, size*) Maßstab *m*; (*gradation*) Skala *f*; *vt* (*climb*) erklimmen; ~**s** *pl* (*balance*) Waage *f*; **on a large ~** (*fig*) im großen, in großem Umfang; ~ **drawing** maßstabgerechte Zeichnung *f*.
scallop [ˈskɒləp] *n* Kammuschel *f*.
scalp [skælp] *n* Kopfhaut *f*; *vt* skalpieren.
scalpel [ˈskælpəl] *n* Skalpell *nt*.
scamp [skæmp] *vt* schlud(e)rig machen, hinschlampen.
scamper [ˈskæmpə*] *vi* huschen.
scan [skæn] *vt* (*examine*) genau prüfen; (*quickly*) überfliegen; *horizon* absuchen; *poetry* skandieren.
scandal [ˈskændl] *n* (*disgrace*) Skandal *m*; (*gossip*) böswillige(r) Klatsch *m*; ~**ize** *vt* schockieren; ~**ous** *a* skandalös, schockierend.
scant [skænt] *a* knapp; ~**ily** *ad* knapp, dürftig; ~**iness** Knappheit *f*; ~**y** knapp, unzureichend.
scapegoat [ˈskeɪpgəʊt] *n* Sündenbock *m*.
scar [skɑː*] *n* Narbe *f*; *vt* durch Narben entstellen.
scarce [skɛəs] *a* selten, rar; *goods* knapp; ~**ly** *ad* kaum; ~**ness** Seltenheit *f*.
scarcity [ˈskɛəsɪtɪ] *n* Mangel *m*, Knappheit *f*.
scare [skɛə*] *n* Schrecken *m*, Panik *f*; *vt* erschrecken; ängstigen; **to be ~d** Angst haben; ~**crow** Vogelscheuche *f*; ~**monger** Bangemacher *m*.
scarf [skɑːf] *n* Schal *m*; (*on head*) Kopftuch *nt*.
scarlet [ˈskɑːlət] *a* scharlachrot; *n* Scharlachrot *nt*; ~ **fever** Scharlach *m*.
scarred [skɑːd] *a* narbig.
scary [ˈskɛərɪ] *a* (*col*) schaurig.
scathing [ˈskeɪðɪŋ] *a* scharf, vernichtend.
scatter [ˈskætə*] *n* Streuung *f*; *vt* (*sprinkle*) (ver)streuen; (*disperse*) zerstreuen; *vi* sich zerstreuen; ~**brained** *a* flatterhaft, schusselig; ~**ing (of)** ein paar.
scavenger [ˈskævɪndʒə*] *n* (*animal*) Aasfresser *m*.
scene [siːn] *n* (*of happening*) Ort *m*; (*of play, incident*) Szene *f*; (*canvas etc*) Bühnenbild *nt*; (*view*) Anblick *m*; (*argument*) Szene *f*, Auftritt *m*; **on the ~** am Ort, dabei; **behind the ~s** hinter den Kulissen; ~**ry** [ˈsiːnərɪ] (*Theat*) Bühnenbild *nt*; (*landscape*) Landschaft *f*.
scenic [ˈsiːnɪk] *a* landschaftlich, Landschafts-.
scent [sent] *n* Parfüm *nt*; (*smell*) Duft *m*; (*sense*) Geruchsinn *m*; *vt* parfümieren.
sceptic [ˈskeptɪk] *n* Skeptiker *m*; ~**al** *a* skeptisch; ~**ism** [ˈskeptɪsɪzəm] Skepsis *f*.
sceptre, (*US*) **scepter** [ˈseptə*] *n* Zepter *nt*.
schedule [ˈʃedjuːl] *n* (*list*) Liste *f*, Tabelle *f*; (*plan*) Programm *nt*; *vt*: **it is ~d for 2** es soll um 2 abfahren/stattfinden *etc*; **on ~** pünktlich, fahrplanmäßig; **behind ~** mit Verspätung.

scheme [ski:m] *n* Schema *nt*; (*dishonest*) Intrige *f*; (*plan of action*) Plan *m*, Programm *nt*; *vi* sich verschwören, intriguieren; *vt* planen.

scheming ['ski:mɪŋ] *a* intrigierend, ränkevoll.

schism ['skɪzəm] *n* Spaltung *f*; (*Eccl*) Schisma *nt*, Kirchenspaltung *f*.

schizophrenic [skɪtsəʊ'frenɪk] *a* schizophren.

scholar ['skolə*] *n* Gelehrte(r) *m*; (*holding scholarship*) Stipendiat *m*; ~**ly** *a* gelehrt; ~**ship** Gelehrsamkeit *f*, Belesenheit *f*; (*grant*) Stipendium *nt*.

school [sku:l] *n* Schule *f*; (*Univ*) Fakultät *f*, *vt* schulen; *dog* trainieren; ~**book** Schulbuch *nt*; ~**boy** Schüler *m*, Schuljunge *m*; ~**days** *pl* (alte) Schulzeit *f*; ~**girl** Schülerin *f*, Schulmädchen *nt*; ~**ing** Schulung *f*, Ausbildung *f*; ~**master** Lehrer *m*; ~**mistress** Lehrerin *f*; ~**room** Klassenzimmer *nt*; ~**teacher** Lehrer(in *f*) *m*.

schooner ['sku:nə*] *n* Schoner *m*; (*glass*) große(s) Sherryglas *nt*.

sciatica [saɪ'ætɪkə] *n* Ischias *m or nt*.

science ['saɪəns] *n* Wissenschaft *f*; (*natural* ~) Naturwissenschaft *f*; ~ **fiction** Science-fiction *f*.

scientific [saɪən'tɪfɪk] *a* wissenschaftlich; (*natural sciences*) naturwissenschaftlich.

scientist ['saɪəntɪst] *n* Wissenschaftler(in *f*) *m*.

scintillating ['sɪntɪleɪtɪŋ] *a* sprühend.

scissors ['sɪzəz] *npl* Schere *f*; **a pair of** ~ eine Schere.

scoff [skɒf] *vt* (*eat*) fressen; *vi* (*mock*) spotten (*at* über +*acc*).

scold [skəʊld] *vt* schimpfen.

scone [skɒn] *n* weiche(s) Teegebäck *nt*.

scoop [sku:p] *n* Schaufel *f*; (*news*) sensationelle Erstmeldung *f*; *vt* (*also* ~ **out** *or* **up**) schaufeln.

scooter ['sku:tə*] *n* Motorroller *m*; (*child's*) Roller *m*.

scope [skəʊp] *n* Ausmaß *nt*; (*opportunity*) (Spiel)raum *m*, Bewegungsfreiheit *f*.

scorch [skɔ:tʃ] *n* Brandstelle *f*, *vt* versengen, verbrennen; ~**er** (*col*) heiße(r) Tag *m*; ~**ing** *a* brennend, glühend.

score [skɔ:*] *n* (*in game*) Punktzahl *f*, (Spiel)ergebnis *nt*; (*Mus*) Partitur *f*; (*line*) Kratzer *m*; (*twenty*) 20, 20 Stück; **on that** ~ in dieser Hinsicht; **what's the** ~? wie steht's?; *vt goal* schießen; *points* machen; (*mark*) einkerben, zerkratzen, einritzen; *vi* (*keep record*) Punkte zählen; ~**board** Anschreibetafel *f*; ~**card** (*Sport*) Punktliste *f*; ~**r** Torschütze *m*; (*recorder*) (Auf)schreiber *m*.

scorn ['skɔ:n] *n* Verachtung *f*; *vt* verhöhnen; ~**ful** *a*, ~**fully** *ad* höhnisch, verächtlich.

Scorpio ['skɔ:pɪəʊ] *n* Skorpion *m*.

scorpion ['skɔ:pɪən] *n* Skorpion *m*.

scotch [skɒtʃ] *vt* (*end*) unterbinden.

scoundrel ['skaʊndrəl] *n* Schurke *m*, Schuft *m*.

scour ['skaʊə*] *vt* (*search*) absuchen;

(*clean*) schrubben; ~**er** Topfkratzer *m*.

scourge [skɜ:dʒ] *n* (*whip*) Geißel *f*; (*plague*) Qual *f*.

scout [skaʊt] *n* (*Mil*) Späher *m*, Aufklärer *m*; *vi* (*reconnoitre*) auskundschaften; *see* **boy.**

scowl [skaʊl] *n* finstere(r) Blick *m*; *vi* finster blicken.

scraggy ['skrægɪ] *a* dürr, hager.

scram [skræm] *vi* (*col*) verschwinden, abhauen.

scramble ['skræmbl] *n* (*climb*) Kletterei *f*; (*struggle*) Kampf *m*; *vi* klettern; (*fight*) sich schlagen; ~**d eggs** *pl* Rührei *nt*.

scrap [skræp] *n* (*bit*) Stückchen *nt*; (*fight*) Keilerei *f*; *a* Abfall-; *vt* verwerfen; *vi* (*fight*) streiten, sich prügeln; ~**book** Einklebealbum *nt*; ~**s** *pl* (*waste*) Abfall *m*.

scrape [skreɪp] *n* Kratzen *nt*; (*trouble*) Klemme *f*; *vt* kratzen; *car* zerkratzen; (*clean*) abkratzen; *vi* (*make harsh noise*) kratzen; ~**r** Kratzer *m*.

scrap heap ['skræphi:p] *n* Abfallhaufen *m*; (*for metal*) Schrotthaufen *m*.

scrap iron ['skræp'aɪən] *n* Schrott *m*.

scrappy ['skræpɪ] *a* zusammengestoppelt.

scratch ['skrætʃ] *n* (*wound*) Kratzer *m*, Schramme *f*; **to start from** ~ ganz von vorne anfangen; *a* (*improvised*) zusammengewürfelt; *vt* kratzen; *car* zerkratzen; *vi* (sich) kratzen.

scrawl [skrɔ:l] *n* Gekritzel *nt*; *vti* kritzeln.

scream [skri:m] *n* Schrei *m*; *vi* schreien.

scree ['skri:] *n* Geröll(halde *f*) *nt*.

screech [skri:tʃ] *n* Schrei *m*; *vi* kreischen.

screen [skri:n] *n* (*protective*) Schutzschirm *m*; (*film*) Leinwand *f*; (*TV*) Bildschirm *m*; (*against insects*) Fliegengitter *nt*; (*Eccl*) Lettner *m*; *vt* (*shelter*) (be)schirmen; *film* zeigen, vorführen.

screw [skru:] *n* Schraube *f*; (*Naut*) Schiffsschraube *f*; *vt* (*fasten*) schrauben; (*vulgar*) bumsen; **to** ~ **money out of sb** (*col*) jdm das Geld aus der Tasche ziehen; ~**driver** Schraubenzieher *m*; ~**y** *a* (*col*) verrückt.

scribble ['skrɪbl] *n* Gekritzel *nt*; *vt* kritzeln.

scribe [skraɪb] *n* Schreiber *m*; (*Jewish*) Schriftgelehrte(r) *m*.

script [skrɪpt] *n* (*handwriting*) Handschrift *f*; (*for film*) Drehbuch *nt*; (*Theat*) Manuskript *nt*, Text *m*.

Scripture ['skrɪptʃə*] *n* Heilige Schrift *f*.

scriptwriter ['skrɪptraɪtə*] *n* Textverfasser *m*.

scroll [skrəʊl] *n* Schriftrolle *f*.

scrounge [skraʊndʒ] *vt* schnorren; *n*: **on the** ~ beim Schnorren.

scrub [skrʌb] *n* (*clean*) Schrubben *nt*; (*in countryside*) Gestrüpp *nt*; *vt* (*clean*) schrubben; (*reject*) fallenlassen.

scruff [skrʌf] *n* Genick *nt*, Kragen *m*; ~**y** *a* unordentlich, vergammelt.

scrum(mage) ['skrʌm(ɪdʒ)] *n* Getümmel *nt*.

scruple ['skru:pl] *n* Skrupel *m*, Bedenken *nt*.

scrupulous *a*, ~**ly** *ad* ['skru:pjʊləs, -lɪ] peinlich genau, gewissenhaft.

scrutinize ['skru:tınaız] *vt* genau prüfen *or* untersuchen.

scrutiny ['skru:tını] *n* genaue Untersuchung *f.*

scuff [skʌf] *vt shoes* abstoßen.

scuffle ['skʌfl] *n* Handgemenge *nt.*

scullery ['skʌlərı] *n* Spülküche *f;* Abstellraum *m.*

sculptor ['skʌlptə*] *n* Bildhauer *m.*

sculpture ['skʌlptʃə*] *n* (*art*) Bildhauerei *f;* (*statue*) Skulptur *f.*

scum [skʌm] *n* (*lit, fig*) Abschaum *m.*

scurrilous ['skʌrıləs] *a* unflätig.

scurry ['skʌrı] *vi* huschen.

scurvy ['skɜ:vı] *n* Skorbut *m.*

scuttle ['skʌtl] *n* Kohleneimer *m; vt ship* versenken; *vi* (*scamper*) (+ *away, off*) sich davonmachen.

scythe [saıð] *n* Sense *f.*

sea [si:] *n* Meer *nt* (*also fig*), See *f;* a Meeres-, See-; ~ **bird** Meervogel *m;* ~**board** Küste *f;* ~ **breeze** Seewind *m;* ~**dog** Seebär *m;* ~**farer** Seefahrer *m;* ~**faring** a seefahrend; ~**food** Meeresfrüchte *pl;* ~ **front** Strandpromenade *f;* ~**going** a seetüchtig, Hochsee-; ~**gull** Möwe *f.*

seal [si:l] *n* (*animal*) Robbe *f,* Seehund *m;* (*stamp, impression*) Siegel *nt; vt* versiegeln.

sea level ['si:levl] *n* Meeresspiegel *m.*

sealing wax ['si:lıŋwæks] *n* Siegellack *m.*

sea lion ['si:laıən] *n* Seelöwe *m.*

seam [si:m] *n* Saum *m;* (*edges joining*) Naht *f;* (*layer*) Schicht *f;* (*of coal*) Flöz *nt.*

seaman ['si:mən] *n* Seemann *m.*

seamless ['si:mlıs] *a* nahtlos.

seamy ['si:mı] *a people, café* zwielichtig; *life* anrüchig; ~ **side of life** dunkle Seite *f* des Lebens.

seaport ['si:pɔ:t] *n* Seehafen *m,* Hafenstadt *f.*

search [sɜ:tʃ] *n* Suche *f* (*for* nach); *vi* suchen; *vt* (*examine*) durchsuchen; ~**ing** *a* look forschend, durchdringend; ~**light** Scheinwerfer *m;* ~ **party** Suchmannschaft *f.*

seashore ['si:ʃɔ:*] *n* Meeresküste *f.*

seasick ['si:sık] *a* seekrank; ~**ness** Seekrankheit *f.*

seaside ['si:saıd] *n* Küste *f;* **at the** ~ an der See; **to go to the** ~ an die See fahren.

season ['si:zn] *n* Jahreszeit *f;* (*eg Christmas*) Zeit *f,* Saison *f;* *vt* (*flavour*) würzen; ~**al** a Saison-; ~**ing** Gewürz *nt,* Würze *f;* ~ **ticket** (*Rail*) Zeitkarte *f;* (*Theat*) Abonnement *nt.*

seat [si:t] *n* Sitz *m,* Platz *m;* (*in Parliament*) Sitz *m;* (*part of body*) Gesäß *nt;* (*part of garment*) Sitzfläche *f,* Hosenboden *m;* (*place*) setzen; (*have space for*) Sitzplätze bieten für; ~ **belt** Sicherheitsgurt *m;* ~**ing** Anweisen *nt* von Sitzplätzen.

sea water ['si:wɔ:tə*] *n* Meerwasser *nt,* Seewasser *nt.*

seaweed ['si:wi:d] *n* (*See*)tang *m,* Alge *f.*

seaworthy ['si:wɜ:ðı] *a* seetüchtig.

secede [sı'si:d] *vi* sich lossagen.

secluded [sı'klu:dıd] *a* abgelegen, ruhig.

seclusion [sı'klu:ʒən] *n* Zurückgezogenheit *f.*

second ['sekənd] *a* zweite(r,s); *ad* (*in position*) an zweiter Stelle; (*Rail*) zweite(r) Klasse; *n* Sekunde *f;* (*person*) Zweite(r) *m;* (*Comm: imperfect*) zweite Wahl *f;* (*Sport*) Sekundant *m; vt* (*support*) unterstützen; ~**ary** *a* zweitrangig; ~**ary education** Sekundarstufe *f;* ~**ary school** höhere Schule *f,* Mittelschule *f;* ~**er** Unterstützer *m;* ~**hand** *a* aus zweiter Hand; *car etc* gebraucht; ~**ly** *ad* zweitens; **it is** ~ **nature to him** es ist ihm zur zweiten Natur geworden; ~**rate** *a* mittelmäßig; **to have** ~ **thoughts** es sich (*dat*) anders überlegen.

secrecy ['si:krəsı] *n* Geheimhaltung *f.*

secret ['si:krət] *n* Geheimnis *nt; a* geheim, heimlich, Geheim-; **in** ~ geheim, heimlich.

secretarial [sekrə'tɛərıəl] *a* Sekretärs-.

secretariat [sekrə'tɛərıət] *n* Sekretariat *nt.*

secretary ['sekrətrı] *n* Sekretär(in *f*) *m;* (*government*) Staatssekretär(in *f*) *m;* Minister *m.*

secretive ['si:krətıv] *a* geheimtuerisch.

secretly ['si:krətlı] *ad* heimlich.

sect [sekt] *n* Sekte *f;* ~**arian** [sek'tɛərıən] *a* (*belonging to a sect*) Sekten-.

section ['sekʃən] *n* Teil *m,* Ausschnitt *m;* (*department*) Abteilung *f;* (*of document*) Abschnitt *m,* Paragraph *m;* ~**al** *a* (*regional*) partikularistisch.

sector ['sektə*] *n* Sektor *m.*

secular ['sekjulə*] *a* weltlich, profan.

secure [sı'kjuə*] *a* (*safe*) sicher; (*firmly fixed*) fest; *vt* (*make firm*) befestigen, sichern; (*obtain*) sichern; ~**ly** *ad* sicher, fest.

security [sı'kjuərıtı] *n* Sicherheit *f;* (*pledge*) Pfand *nt;* (*document*) Sicherheiten *pl;* (*national* ~) Staatssicherheit *f;* ~ **guard** Sicherheitsbeamte(r) *m; see* **social.**

sedate [sı'deıt] *a* (*calm*) gelassen; (*serious*) gesetzt; *vt* (*Med*) ein Beruhigungsmittel geben (+*dat*).

sedation [sı'deıʃən] *n* (*Med*) Einfluß *m* von Beruhigungsmitteln.

sedative ['sedətıv] *n* Beruhigungsmittel *nt; a* beruhigend, einschläfernd.

sedentary ['sedntrı] *a job* sitzend.

sediment ['sedımənt] *n* (*Boden*)satz *m;* ~**ary** [sedı'mentərı] *a* (*Geol*) Sediment-.

seduce [sı'dju:s] *vt* verführen.

seduction [sı'dʌkʃən] *n* Verführung *f.*

seductive [sı'dʌktıv] *a* verführerisch.

see [si:] *irreg vt* sehen; (*understand*) (ein)-sehen, erkennen; (*find out*) sehen, herausfinden; (*make sure*) dafür sorgen (daß); (*accompany*) begleiten, bringen; (*visit*) besuchen; **to** ~ **a doctor** zum Arzt gehen; *vi* (*be aware*) sehen; (*find out*) nachsehen; **I** ~ ach so, ich verstehe; **let me** ~ warte mal; **we'll** ~ werden (mal) sehen; *n* (*Eccl*) (*R.C.*) Bistum *nt;* (*Protestant*) Kirchenkreis *m;* **to** ~ **sth through** etw durchfechten; **to** ~ **through sb/sth** jdn/etw durchschauen; **to** ~ **to it** dafür sorgen; **to** ~ **sb off** jdn zum Zug *etc* begleiten.

seed [si:d] *n* Samen *m*, (Samen)korn *nt*; *vt* (*Tennis*) plazieren; ~**ling** Setzling *m*; ~**y** *a* (*ill*) flau, angeschlagen; *clothes* schäbig; *person* zweifelhaft.

seeing ['si:ɪŋ] *cj* da.

seek [si:k] *vt irreg* suchen.

seem [si:m] *vi* scheinen; ~**ingly** *ad* anscheinend; ~**ly** *a* geziemend.

seep [si:p] *vi* sickern.

seer [sɪə*] *n* Seher *m*.

seesaw ['si:sɔ:] *n* Wippe *f*.

seethe [si:ð] *vi* kochen; (*with crowds*) wimmeln von.

see-through ['si:θru:] *a dress* durchsichtig.

segment ['segmənt] *n* Teil *m*; (*of circle*) Ausschnitt *m*.

segregate ['segrɪgeɪt] *vt* trennen, absondern.

segregation [segrɪ'geɪʃən] *n* Rassentrennung *f*.

seismic ['saɪzmɪk] *a* seismisch, Erdbeben-.

seize [si:z] *vt* (*grasp*) (er)greifen, packen; *power* ergreifen; (*take legally*) beschlagnahmen; *point* erfassen, begreifen; ~ **up** *vi* (*Tech*) sich festfressen.

seizure ['si:ʒə*] *n* (*illness*) Anfall *m*.

seldom ['seldəm] *ad* selten.

select [sɪ'lekt] *a* ausgewählt; *vt* auswählen; ~**ion** [sɪ'lekʃən] Auswahl *f*; ~**ive** *a person* wählerisch.

self [self] *n* Selbst *nt*, Ich *nt*; ~**-adhesive** *a* selbstklebend; ~**-appointed** *a* selbsternannt; ~**-assurance** Selbstsicherheit *f*; ~**-assured** *a* selbstbewußt; ~**-coloured**, (*US*) ~**-colored** *a* einfarbig; ~**-confidence** Selbstvertrauen *nt*, Selbstbewußtsein *nt*; ~**-confident** *a* selbstsicher; ~**-conscious** *a* gehemmt, befangen; ~**-contained** *a* (*complete*) (in sich) geschlossen; *person* verschlossen; ~**-defeating** *a*: **to be** ~**-defeating** ein Widerspruch in sich sein; ~**-defence**, (*Jur*) Notwehr *f*; ~**-employed** *a* frei(schaffend); ~**-evident** *a* offensichtlich; ~**-explanatory** *a* für sich (selbst) sprechend; ~**-indulgent** *a* zügellos; ~**-interest** Eigennutz *m*; ~**-ish** *a*, ~**-ishly** *ad* egoistisch, selbstsüchtig; ~**-ishness** Egoismus *m*, Selbstsucht *f*; ~**-lessly** *ad* selbstlos; ~**-made** *a* selbstgemacht; ~**-pity** Selbstmitleid *nt*; ~**-portrait** Selbstbildnis *nt*; ~**-propelled** *a* mit Eigenantrieb; ~**-reliant** *a* unabhängig; ~**-respect** Selbstachtung *f*; ~**-respecting** *a* mit Selbstachtung; ~**-righteous** *a* selbstgerecht; ~**-satisfied** *a* selbstzufrieden; ~**-service** *a* Selbstbedienungs-; ~**-sufficient** *a* selbstgenügsam; ~**-supporting** *a* (*Fin*) Eigenfinanzierungs-; *person* eigenständig.

sell [sel] *irreg vt* verkaufen; *vi* verkaufen; (*goods*) sich verkaufen (lassen); ~**er** Verkäufer *m*; ~**ing price** Verkaufspreis *m*.

semantic [sɪ'mæntɪk] *a* semantisch; ~**s** Semantik *f*.

semaphore ['seməfɔ:*] *n* Winkzeichen *pl*.

semi ['semɪ] *n* = ~**-detached house**;

~**circle** Halbkreis *m*; ~**colon** Semikolon *nt*; ~**conscious** *a* halbbewußt; ~**detached house** Zweifamilienhaus *nt*, Doppelhaus *nt*; ~**final** Halbfinale *nt*.

seminar ['semɪnɑ:*] *n* Seminar *nt*.

semiquaver ['semɪkweɪvə*] *n* Sechzehntel *nt*.

semiskilled ['semɪ'skɪld] *a* angelernt.

semitone ['semɪtəun] *n* Halbton *m*.

semolina [seməˈli:nə] *n* Grieß *m*.

senate ['senət] *n* Senat *m*.

senator ['senətə*] *n* Senator *m*.

send [send] *vt irreg* senden, schicken; (*col: inspire*) hinreißen; ~ **away** *vt* wegschicken; ~ **away for** *vt* holen lassen; ~ **back** *vt* zurückschicken; ~ **for** *vt* holen lassen; ~ **off** *vt goods* abschicken; *player* vom Feld schicken; ~ **out** *vt invitation* aussenden; ~ **up** *vt* hinaufsenden; (*col*) verulken; ~**er** Absender *m*; ~**-off** Verabschiedung *f*; ~**-up** (*col*) Verulkung *f*.

senile ['si:naɪl] *a* senil, Alters-.

senility [sɪ'nɪlɪtɪ] *n* Altersschwachheit *f*.

senior ['si:nɪə*] *a* (*older*) älter; (*higher rank*) Ober-; *n* (*older person*) Ältere(r) *m*; (*higher ranking*) Rangälteste(r) *m*; ~**ity** [si:nɪ'ɒrɪtɪ] (*of age*) höhere(s) Alter *nt*; (*in rank*) höhere(r) Dienstgrad *m*.

sensation [sen'seɪʃən] *n* Empfindung *f*, Gefühl *nt*; (*excitement*) Sensation *f*, Aufsehen *nt*; ~**al** *a* sensationell, Sensations-.

sense [sens] *n* Sinn *m*; (*understanding*) Verstand *m*, Vernunft *f*; (*meaning*) Sinn *m*, Bedeutung *f*; (*feeling*) Gefühl *nt*; **to make** ~ Sinn ergeben; *vt* fühlen, spüren; ~**less** *a* sinnlos; (*unconscious*) besinnungslos; ~**lessly** *ad* (*stupidly*) sinnlos.

sensibility [sensɪ'bɪlɪtɪ] *n* Empfindsamkeit *f*; (*feeling hurt*) Empfindlichkeit *f*.

sensible *a*, **sensibly** *ad* ['sensəbl, -blɪ] vernünftig.

sensitive ['sensɪtɪv] *a* empfindlich (*to* gegen); (*easily hurt*) sensibel, feinfühlig; *film* lichtempfindlich.

sensitivity [sensɪ'tɪvɪtɪ] *n* Empfindlichkeit *f*; (*artistic*) Feingefühl *nt*; (*tact*) Feinfühligkeit *f*.

sensual ['sensjuəl] *a* sinnlich.

sensuous ['sensjuəs] *a* sinnlich, sinnenfreudig.

sentence ['sentəns] *n* Satz *m*; (*Jur*) Strafe *f*; Urteil *nt*; *vt* verurteilen.

sentiment ['sentɪmənt] *n* Gefühl *nt*; (*thought*) Gedanke *m*, Gesinnung *f*; ~**al** [sentɪ'mentl] *a* sentimental; (*of feelings rather than reason*) gefühlsmäßig; ~**ality** [sentɪmen'tælɪtɪ] Sentimentalität *f*.

sentinel ['sentɪnl] *n* Wachtposten *m*.

sentry ['sentrɪ] *n* (Schild)wache *f*.

separable ['sepərəbl] *a* (ab)trennbar.

separate ['seprət] *a* getrennt, separat; ['sepəreɪt] *vt* trennen; *vi* sich trennen; ~**ly** *ad* getrennt.

separation [sepə'reɪʃən] *n* Trennung *f*.

sepia ['si:pɪə] *n* Sepia-.

September [sep'tembə*] *n* September *m*.

septic ['septɪk] *a* vereitert, septisch.

sequel ['si:kwəl] *n* Folge *f*.

sequence ['si:kwəns] n (Reihen)folge f.

sequin ['si:kwɪn] n Paillette f.

serenade [serə'neɪd] n Ständchen nt, Serenade f; vt ein Ständchen bringen (+dat).

serene a, **~ly** ad [sə'ri:n, -lɪ] heiter, gelassen, ruhig.

serenity [sɪ'renɪtɪ] n Heiterkeit f, Gelassenheit f, Ruhe f.

serf [sɜːf] n Leibeigene(r) mf.

serge [sɜːdʒ] n Serge f.

sergeant ['sɑːdʒənt] n Feldwebel m; (police) (Polizei)wachtmeister m.

serial ['sɪərɪəl] n Fortsetzungsroman m; (TV) Fernsehserie f; a number (fort)-laufend; **~ize** vt in Fortsetzungen veröffentlichen / senden.

series ['sɪərɪz] n Serie f, Reihe f.

serious ['sɪərɪəs] a ernst; injury schwer; development ernstzunehmend; **I'm ~** das meine ich ernst; **~ly** ad ernst(haft); hurt schwer; **~ness** Ernst m, Ernsthaftigkeit f.

sermon ['sɜːmən] n Predigt f.

serpent ['sɜːpənt] n Schlange f.

serrated [se'reɪtɪd] a gezackt; **~ knife** Sägemesser nt.

serum ['sɪərəm] n Serum nt.

servant ['sɜːvənt] n Bedienstete(r) mf, Diener(in f) m; see **civil**.

serve [sɜːv] vt dienen (+dat); guest, customer bedienen; food servieren; writ zustellen (on sb jdm); vi dienen, nützen; (at table) servieren; (tennis) geben, aufschlagen; **it ~s him right** das geschieht ihm recht; **that'll ~ the purpose** das reicht; **that'll ~ as a table** das geht als Tisch; **~ out** or **up** vt food auftragen, servieren.

service ['sɜːvɪs] n (help) Dienst m; (trains etc) Verkehrsverbindungen pl; (hotel) Service m, Bedienung f; (set of dishes) Service nt; (Rel) Gottesdienst m; (Mil) Waffengattung f; (car) Inspektion f; (for TVs etc) Kundendienst m; (tennis) Aufschlag m; **to be of ~ to sb** jdm einen großen Dienst erweisen; **can I be of ~?** kann ich Ihnen behilflich sein?; vt (Aut, Tech) warten, überholen; **the S~s** pl (armed forces) Streitkräfte pl; **~able** a brauchbar; **~ area** (on motorway) Raststätte f; **~ charge** Bedienung f; **~man** (soldier etc) Soldat m; **~ station** (Groß)tankstelle f.

servicing ['sɜːvɪsɪŋ] n Wartung f.

serviette [sɜːvɪ'et] n Serviette f.

servile ['sɜːvaɪl] a sklavisch, unterwürfig.

session ['seʃən] n Sitzung f; (Pol) Sitzungsperiode f.

set [set] n (collection of things) Satz m, Set nt; (Rad, TV) Apparat m; (tennis) Satz m; (group of people) Kreis m; (Cine) Szene f; (Theat) Bühnenbild nt; a festgelegt; (ready) bereit; **~ phrase** feststehende(r) Ausdruck m; **~ square** Zeichendreieck nt; irreg vt (place) setzen, stellen, legen; (arrange) (an)ordnen; table decken; time, price festsetzen; alarm, watch stellen; jewels (ein)fassen; task stellen; exam ausarbeiten; **to ~ one's hair** die Haare eindrehen; vi (sun) untergehen; (become hard) fest

werden; (bone) zusammenwachsen; **to ~ on fire** anstecken; **to ~ free** freilassen; **to ~ sth going** etw in Gang bringen; **to ~ sail** losfahren; **~ about** vt task anpacken; **~ aside** vt beseitelegen; **~ back** vt zurückwerfen; **~ down** vt absetzen; **~ off** vi ausbrechen; vt (explode) zur Explosion bringen; alarm losgehen lassen; (show up well) hervorheben; **~ out** vi aufbrechen; vt (arrange) anlegen, arrangieren; (state) darlegen; **~ up** vt organization aufziehen; record aufstellen; monument erstellen; **~back** Rückschlag m.

settee [se'ti:] n Sofa nt.

setting ['setɪŋ] n (Mus) Vertonung f; (scenery) Hintergrund m.

settle ['setl] vt beruhigen; (pay) begleichen, bezahlen; (agree) regeln; vi (also ~ down) sich einleben; (come to rest) sich niederlassen; (sink) sich setzen; (calm down) sich beruhigen; **~ment** Regelung f; (payment) Begleichung f; (colony) Siedlung f, Niederlassung f; **~r** Siedler m.

setup ['setʌp] n (arrangement) Aufbau m, Gliederung f; (situation) Situation f, Lage f.

seven ['sevn] num sieben; **~teen** num siebzehn; **~th** a siebte(r,s) n Siebtel nt; **~ty** num siebzig.

sever ['sevə*] vt abtrennen.

several ['sevrəl] a mehrere, verschiedene; pron mehrere.

severance ['sevərəns] n Abtrennung f; (fig) Abbruch m.

severe [sɪ'vɪə*] a (strict) streng; (serious) schwer; climate rauh; (plain) streng, schmucklos; **~ly** ad (strictly) streng, strikt; (seriously) schwer, ernstlich.

severity [sɪ'verɪtɪ] n Strenge f; Schwere f; Ernst m.

sew [səʊ] vti irreg nähen; **~ up** vt zunähen.

sewage ['sju:ɪdʒ] n Abwässer pl.

sewer ['sjʊə*] n (Abwasser)kanal m.

sewing ['səʊɪŋ] n Näharbeit f; **~ machine** Nähmaschine f.

sex [seks] n Sex m; (gender) Geschlecht nt; **~ act** Geschlechtsakt m.

sextant ['sekstənt] n Sextant m.

sextet [seks'tet] n Sextett nt.

sexual ['seksjʊəl] a sexuell, geschlechtlich, Geschlechts-; **~ly** ad geschlechtlich, sexuell.

sexy ['seksɪ] a sexy.

shabbily ['ʃæbɪlɪ] ad schäbig.

shabbiness ['ʃæbɪnəs] n Schäbigkeit f.

shabby ['ʃæbɪ] a (lit, fig) schäbig.

shack [ʃæk] n Hütte f.

shackle ['ʃækl] vt fesseln; **~s** pl (lit, fig) Fesseln pl, Ketten pl.

shade [ʃeɪd] n Schatten m; (for lamp) Lampenschirm m; (colour) Farbton m; (small quantity) Spur f, Idee f; vt abschirmen.

shadow ['ʃædəʊ] n Schatten m; vt (follow) beschatten; a: **~ cabinet** (Pol) Schattenkabinett nt; **~y** a schattig.

shady ['ʃeɪdɪ] a schattig; (fig) zwielichtig.

shaft [ʃɑːft] n (of spear etc) Schaft m; (in

mine) Schacht *m*; (*Tech*) Welle *f*; (*of light*) Strahl *m*.

shaggy ['ʃægɪ] *a* struppig.

shake [ʃeɪk] *irreg vt* schütteln, rütteln; (*shock*) erschüttern; **to ~ hands** die Hand geben (*with dat*); **they shook hands** sie gaben sich die Hand; **to ~ one's head** den Kopf schütteln; *vi* (*move*) schwanken; (*tremble*) zittern, beben; *n* (*jerk*) Schütteln *nt*, Rütteln *nt*; **~ off** *vt* abschütteln; **~ up** *vt* (*lit*) aufschütteln; (*fig*) aufrütteln; **~-up** Aufrüttelung *f*; (*Pol*) Umgruppierung *f*.

shakily ['ʃeɪkɪlɪ] *ad* zitternd, unsicher.

shakiness ['ʃeɪkɪnəs] *n* Wackeligkeit *f*.

shaky ['ʃeɪkɪ] *a* zittrig; (*weak*) unsicher.

shale [ʃeɪl] *n* Schiefer(ton) *m*.

shall [ʃæl] *v aux irreg* werden; (*must*) sollen.

shallow ['ʃæləʊ] *a* flach, seicht (*also fig*); **~s** *pl* flache Stellen *pl*.

sham [ʃæm] *n* Täuschung *f*, Trug *m*, Schein *m*; *a* unecht, falsch.

shambles ['ʃæmblz] *n sing* Durcheinander *nt*.

shame [ʃeɪm] *n* Scham *f*; (*disgrace, pity*) Schande *f*; *vt* beschämen; **what a ~!** wie schade!; **~ on you!** schäm dich!; **~faced** *a* beschämt; **~ful** *a*, **~fully** *ad* schändlich; **~less** *a* schamlos; (*immodest*) unverschämt.

shampoo [ʃæm'puː] *n* Schampoon *nt*; *vt* schampunieren; **~ and set** Waschen *nt* und Legen.

shamrock ['ʃæmrɒk] *n* Kleeblatt *nt*.

shandy ['ʃændɪ] *n* Radlermaß *m*.

shan't [ʃɑːnt] = **shall not**.

shanty ['ʃæntɪ] *n* (*cabin*) Hütte *f*, Baracke *f*; **~ town** Elendsviertel *nt*.

shape [ʃeɪp] *n* Form *f*, Gestalt *f*; *vt* formen, gestalten; **to take ~** Gestalt annehmen; **~less** *a* formlos; **~ly** *a* wohlgeformt, wohlproportioniert.

share [ʃɛə*] *n* (An)teil *m*; (*Fin*) Aktie *f*; *vt* teilen; **~holder** Aktionär *m*.

shark [ʃɑːk] *n* Hai(fisch) *m*; (*swindler*) Gauner *m*.

sharp [ʃɑːp] *a* scharf; *pin* spitz; *person* clever; *child* aufgeweckt; (*unscrupulous*) gerissen, raffiniert; (*Mus*) erhöht; **~ practices** *pl* Machenschaften *pl*; *n* (*Mus*) Kreuz *nt*; *ad* (*Mus*) zu hoch; **nine o'clock ~** Punkt neun; **look ~!** mach schnell!; **~en** *vt* schärfen; *pencil* spitzen; **~ener** Spitzer *m*; **~-eyed** *a* scharfsichtig; **~ness** Schärfe *f*; **~-witted** *a* scharfsinnig, aufgeweckt.

shatter ['ʃætə*] *vt* zerschmettern; (*fig*) zerstören; *vi* zerspringen; **~ed** *a* (*lit, fig*) kaputt; **~ing** *a* *experience* furchtbar.

shave [ʃeɪv] *n* Rasur *f*, Rasieren *nt*; **to have a ~** sich rasieren (lassen); *vt* rasieren; *vi* sich rasieren; **~n** *a* *head* geschoren; **~r** (*Elec*) Rasierapparat *m*, Rasierer *m*.

shaving ['ʃeɪvɪŋ] *n* (*action*) Rasieren *nt*; **~s** *pl* (*of wood etc*) Späne *pl*; **~ brush** Rasierpinsel *m*; **~ cream** Rasierkrem *f*; **~ point** Rasiersteckdose *f*; **~ soap** Rasierseife *f*.

shawl [ʃɔːl] *n* Schal *m*, Umhang *m*.

she [ʃiː] *pron* sie; *a* weiblich; **~-bear** Bärenweibchen *nt*.

sheaf [ʃiːf] *n* Garbe *f*.

shear [ʃɪə*] *vt irreg* scheren; **~ off** *vt* abscheren; **~s** *pl* Heckenschere *f*.

sheath [ʃiːθ] *n* Scheide *f*; **~e** [ʃiːð] *vt* einstecken; (*Tech*) verkleiden.

shed [ʃed] *n* Schuppen *m*; (*for animals*) Stall *m*; *vt irreg leaves etc* abwerfen, verlieren; *tears* vergießen.

she'd [ʃiːd] = **she had; she would**.

sheep [ʃiːp] *n* Schaf *nt*; **~dog** Schäferhund *m*; **~ish** *a* verschämt, betreten; **~skin** Schaffell *nt*.

sheer [ʃɪə*] *a* bloß, rein; (*steep*) steil, jäh; (*transparent*) (hauch)dünn, durchsichtig; *ad* (*directly*) direkt.

sheet [ʃiːt] *n* Bettuch *nt*, Bettlaken *nt*; (*of paper*) Blatt *nt*; (*of metal etc*) Platte *f*; (*of ice*) Fläche *f*; **~ lightning** Wetterleuchten *nt*.

sheik(h) [ʃeɪk] *n* Scheich *m*.

shelf [ʃelf] *n* Bord *nt*, Regal *nt*.

she'll [ʃiːl] = **she will; she shall**.

shell [ʃel] *n* Schale *f*; (*sea-*) Muschel *f*; (*explosive*) Granate *f*; (*of building*) Mauern *pl*; *vt peas* schälen; (*fire on*) beschießen; **~fish** Schalentier *nt*; (*as food*) Meeresfrüchte *pl*.

shelter ['ʃeltə*] *n* Schutz *m*; Bunker *m*; *vt* schützen, bedecken; *refugees* aufnehmen; *vi* sich unterstellen; **~ed** *a life* behütet; *spot* geschützt.

shelve [ʃelv] *vt* aufschieben; *vi* abfallen.

shelving ['ʃelvɪŋ] *n* Regale *pl*.

shepherd ['ʃepəd] *n* Schäfer *m*; *vt* treiben, führen; **~ess** Schäferin *f*.

sheriff ['ʃerɪf] *n* Sheriff *m*.

sherry ['ʃerɪ] *n* Sherry *m*.

she's [ʃiːz] = **she is; she has**.

shield [ʃiːld] *n* Schild *m*; (*fig*) Schirm *m*, Schutz *m*; *vt* (be)schirmen; (*Tech*) abschirmen.

shift [ʃɪft] *n* Veränderung *f*, Verschiebung *f*; (*work*) Schicht *f*; *vt* (ver)rücken, verschieben; *office* verlegen; *arm* wegnehmen; *vi* sich verschieben; (*col*) schnell fahren; **~ work** Schichtarbeit *f*; **~y** *a* verschlagen.

shilling ['ʃɪlɪŋ] *n* (*old*) Shilling *m*.

shilly-shally ['ʃɪlɪʃælɪ] *vi* zögern.

shimmer ['ʃɪmə*] *n* Schimmer *m*; *vi* schimmern.

shin [ʃɪn] *n* Schienbein *nt*.

shine [ʃaɪn] *n* Glanz *m*, Schein *m*; *irreg vt* polieren; **to ~ a torch on sb** jdn (mit einer Lampe) anleuchten; *vi* scheinen; (*fig*) glänzen.

shingle ['ʃɪŋgl] *n* Schindel *f*; (*on beach*) Strandkies *m*; **~s** *pl* (*Med*) Gürtelrose *f*.

shining ['ʃaɪnɪŋ] *a light* strahlend.

shiny ['ʃaɪnɪ] *a* glänzend.

ship [ʃɪp] *n* Schiff *nt*; *vt* an Bord bringen, verladen; (*transport as cargo*) verschiffen; **~-building** Schiffbau *m*; **~ canal** Seekanal *m*; **~ment** Verladung *f*, (*goods shipped*) Schiffsladung *f*; **~per** Verschiffer *m*; **~ping** (*act*) Verschiffung *f*; (*ships*) Schiffahrt *f*; **~shape** *a* in Ordnung;

~**wreck** Schiffbruch m; (destroyed ship) Wrack nt; ~**yard** Werft f.

shirk [ʃɔːk] vt ausweichen (+dat).

shirt [ʃɔːt] n (Ober)hemd nt; **in** ~**-sleeves** in Hemdsärmeln; ~**y** a (col) mürrisch.

shiver ['ʃɪvə*] n Schauer m; vi frösteln, zittern.

shoal [ʃəʊl] n (Fisch)schwarm m.

shock [ʃɒk] n Stoß m, Erschütterung f; (mental) Schock m; (Elec) Schlag m; vt erschüttern; (offend) schockieren; ~**absorber** Stoßdämpfer m; ~**ing** a unerhört, schockierend; ~**proof** a watch stoßsicher.

shoddiness ['ʃɒdɪnəs] n Schäbigkeit f.

shoddy ['ʃɒdɪ] a schäbig.

shoe [ʃuː] n Schuh m; (of horse) Hufeisen nt; vt irreg horse beschlagen; ~**brush** Schuhbürste f; ~**horn** Schuhlöffel m; ~**lace** Schnürsenkel m.

shoot [ʃuːt] n (branch) Schößling m; irreg vt gun abfeuern; goal, arrow schießen; (kill) erschießen; film drehen, filmen; **shot in the leg** ins Bein getroffen; vi (gun, move quickly) schießen; **don't** ~! nicht schießen!; ~**down** vt abschießen; ~**ing** Schießerei f; ~**ing star** Sternschnuppe f.

shop [ʃɒp] n Geschäft nt, Laden m; (workshop) Werkstatt f; vi (also **go** ~**ping**) einkaufen gehen; ~ **assistant** Verkäufer(in f) m; ~**keeper** Geschäftsinhaber m; ~**lifter** Ladendieb m; ~**lifting** Ladendiebstahl m; ~**per** Käufer(in f) m; ~**ping** Einkaufen nt, Einkauf m; ~**ping bag** Einkaufstasche f; ~**ping centre**, (US) ~**ping center** Einkaufszentrum nt; ~**soiled** a angeschmutzt; ~ **steward** Betriebsrat m; ~ **window** Schaufenster nt; see **talk**.

shore [ʃɔː*] n Ufer nt; (of sea) Strand m, Küste f; vt: ~ **up** abstützen.

short [ʃɔːt] a kurz; person klein; (curt) kurz angebunden; (measure) zu knapp; **to be** ~ **of** zu wenig . . . haben; **two** ~ zwei zu wenig; n (Elec: —circuit) Kurzschluß m; ad (suddenly) plötzlich; vi (Elec) einen Kurzschluß haben; **to cut** ~ abkürzen; **to fall** ~ nicht erreichen; **for** ~ kurz; ~**age** Knappheit f, Mangel m; ~**bread** Mürbegebäck nt, Heidesand m; ~**circuit** Kurzschluß m; vi einen Kurzschluß haben; ~**coming** Fehler m, Mangel m; ~**cut** Abkürzung f; ~**en** vt (ab)kürzen; clothes kürzer machen; ~**hand** Stenographie f, Kurzschrift f; ~**hand typist** Stenotypistin f; ~**list** engere Wahl f; ~**lived** a kurzlebig; ~**ly** ad bald; ~**ness** Kürze f; ~**s** pl Shorts pl; ~**sighted** a (lit, fig) kurzsichtig; ~**sightedness** Kurzsichtigkeit f; ~ **story** Kurzgeschichte f; ~**tempered** a leicht aufbrausend; ~**term** a effect kurzfristig; ~ **wave** (Rad) Kurzwelle f.

shot [ʃɒt] n (from gun) Schuß m; (person) Schütze m; (try) Versuch m; (injection) Spritze f; (Phot) Aufnahme f, Schnappschuß m; **like a** ~ wie der Blitz; ~**gun** Schrotflinte f.

should [ʃʊd] v aux: **I** ~ **go now** ich sollte jetzt gehen; **I** ~ **say** ich würde sagen; **I**

~ **like to** ich möchte gerne, ich würde gerne.

shoulder ['ʃəʊldə*] n Schulter f; vt rifle schultern; (fig) auf sich nehmen; ~ **blade** Schulterblatt nt.

shouldn't ['ʃʊdnt] = **should not**.

shout [ʃaʊt] n Schrei m; (call) Ruf m; vt rufen; vi schreien, laut rufen; **to** ~ **at** anbrüllen; ~**ing** Geschrei nt.

shove [ʃʌv] n Schubs m, Stoß m; vt schieben, stoßen, schubsen; ~ **off** vi (Naut) abstoßen; (fig col) abhauen.

shovel ['ʃʌvl] n Schaufel f; vt schaufeln.

show [ʃəʊ] n (display) Schau f; (exhibition) Ausstellung f; (Cine, Theat) Vorstellung f, Show f; irreg vt zeigen; kindness erweisen; vi zu sehen sein; **to** ~ **sb in** jdn hereinführen; **to** ~ **sb out** jdn hinausbegleiten; ~ **off** vi (pej) angeben, protzen; vt (display) ausstellen; ~ **up** vi (stand out) sich abheben; (arrive) erscheinen; vt aufzeigen; (unmask) bloßstellen; ~ **business** Showbusineß nt; ~**down** Kraftprobe f, endgültige Auseinandersetzung f.

shower ['ʃaʊə*] n Schauer m; (of stones) (Stein)hagel m; (of sparks) (Funken)regen m; (— bath) Dusche f; **to have a** ~ duschen; vt (fig) überschütten; ~**proof** a wasserabstoßend; ~**y** a weather regnerisch.

showground ['ʃəʊgraʊnd] n Ausstellungsgelände nt.

showing ['ʃəʊɪŋ] n (of film) Vorführung f.

show jumping ['ʃəʊdʒʌmpɪŋ] n Turnierreiten nt.

showmanship ['ʃəʊmənʃɪp] n Talent nt als Showman.

show-off ['ʃəʊɒf] n Angeber m.

showpiece ['ʃəʊpiːs] n Paradestück nt.

showroom ['ʃəʊrʊm] n Ausstellungsraum m.

shrapnel ['ʃræpnl] n Schrapnell nt.

shred [ʃred] n Fetzen m; vt zerfetzen; (Cook) raspeln; **in** ~**s** in Fetzen.

shrewd a, ~**ly** ad [ʃruːd, -lɪ] scharfsinnig, clever; ~**ness** Scharfsinn m.

shriek [ʃriːk] n Schrei m; vti kreischen, schreien.

shrill [ʃrɪl] a schrill, gellend.

shrimp [ʃrɪmp] n Krabbe f, Garnele f.

shrine [ʃraɪn] n Schrein m.

shrink [ʃrɪŋk] irreg vi schrumpfen, eingehen; vt einschrumpfen lassen; ~**age** Schrumpfung f; ~ **away** vi zurückschrecken (from vor +dat).

shrivel ['ʃrɪvl] vti (also ~ **up**) schrumpfen, schrumpeln.

shroud [ʃraʊd] n Leichentuch nt; vt umhüllen, (ein)hüllen.

Shrove Tuesday ['ʃrəʊv'tjuːzdeɪ] n Fastnachtsdienstag m.

shrub [ʃrʌb] n Busch m, Strauch m; ~**bery** Gebüsch nt.

shrug [ʃrʌg] n Achselzucken nt; vi die Achseln zucken; ~ **off** vi auf die leichte Schulter nehmen.

shrunken ['ʃrʌŋkən] a eingelaufen.

shudder ['ʃʌdə*] n Schauder m; vi schaudern.

shuffle ['ʃʌfl] n (Cards) (Karten)mischen

nt; *vt* cards mischen; *vi* (*walk*) schlurfen.
shun [ʃʌn] *vt* scheuen, (ver)meiden.
shunt [ʃʌnt] *vt* rangieren.
shut [ʃʌt] *irreg vt* schließen, zumachen; *vi* sich schließen (lassen); ~ **down** *vti* schließen; ~ **off** *vt* supply abdrehen; ~ **up** *vi* (*keep quiet*) den Mund halten; *vt* (*close*) zuschließen; (*silence*) zum Schweigen bringen; ~ **up!** halt den Mund!; ~**ter** Fensterladen *m*, Rolladen *m*; (*Phot*) Verschluß *m*.
shuttlecock [ˈʃʌtlkɒk] *n* Federball *m*; Federballspiel *nt*.
shuttle service [ˈʃʌtlsɜːvɪs] *n* Pendelverkehr *m*.
shy *a*. ~**ly** *ad* [ʃaɪ, -lɪ] schüchtern, scheu; ~**ness** Schüchternheit *f*, Zurückhaltung *f*.
Siamese [saɪəˈmiːz] *a*: ~ **cat** Siamkatze *f*; ~ **twins** *pl* siamesische Zwillinge *pl*.
sick [sɪk] *a* krank; *humour* schwarz; *joke* makaber; **I feel** ~ mir ist schlecht; **I was** ~ ich habe gebrochen; **to be** ~ **of sb/sth** jdn/etw satt haben; ~ **bay** (*Schiffs*)lazarett *nt*; ~**bed** Krankenbett *nt*; ~**en** *vt* (*disgust*) krankmachen; *vi* krank werden; ~**ening** *a sight* widerlich; (*annoying*) zum Weinen.
sickle [ˈsɪkl] *n* Sichel *f*.
sick leave [ˈsɪkliːv] *n*: **to be on** ~ krank geschrieben sein.
sick list [ˈsɪklɪst] *n* Krankenliste *f*.
sickly [ˈsɪklɪ] *a* kränklich, blaß; (*causing nausea*) widerlich.
sickness [ˈsɪknəs] *n* Krankheit *f*; (*vomiting*) Übelkeit *f*, Erbrechen *nt*.
sick pay [ˈsɪkpeɪ] *n* Krankengeld *nt*.
side [saɪd] *n* Seite *f*; *a door, entrance* Seiten-, Neben-; **by the** ~ **of** neben; **on all** ~**s** von allen Seiten; **to take** ~**s (with)** Partei nehmen (für); *vi*: ~ **with sb** es halten mit jdm; ~**board** Anrichte *f*, Sideboard *nt*; ~**boards**, ~**burns** *pl* Koteletten *pl*; ~ **effect** Nebenwirkung *f*; ~**light** (*Aut*) Parkleuchte *f*, Standlicht *nt*; ~**line** (*Sport*) Seitenlinie *f*; (*fig: hobby*) Nebenbeschäftigung *f*; ~ **road** Nebenstraße *f*; ~ **show** Nebenausstellung *f*; ~**track** *vt* (*fig*) ablenken; ~**walk** (*US*) Bürgersteig *m*; ~**ways** *ad* seitwärts.
siding [ˈsaɪdɪŋ] *n* Nebengleis *nt*.
sidle [ˈsaɪdl] *vi*: ~ **up** sich heranmachen (*to an* +*acc*.)
siege [siːdʒ] *n* Belagerung *f*.
siesta [sɪˈestə] *n* Siesta *f*.
sieve [sɪv] *n* Sieb *nt*; *vt* sieben.
sift [sɪft] *vt* sieben; (*fig*) sichten.
sigh [saɪ] *n* Seufzer *m*; *vi* seufzen.
sight [saɪt] *n* (*power of seeing*) Sehvermögen *nt*, Augenlicht *nt*; (*view*) (An)blick *m*; (*scene*) Aussicht *f*, Blick *m*; (*of gun*) Zielvorrichtung *f*, Korn *nt*; ~**s** *pl* (*of city etc*) Sehenswürdigkeiten *pl*; **in** ~ in Sicht; **out of** ~ außer Sicht; ~**seeing** Besuch *m* von Sehenswürdigkeiten; **to go** ~**seeing** Sehenswürdigkeiten besichtigen; ~**seer** Tourist *m*.
sign [saɪn] *n* Zeichen *nt*; (*notice, road — etc*) Schild *nt*; *vt* unterschreiben; ~ **out** *vi* sich austragen; ~ **up** *vi* (*Mil*) sich verpflichten; *vt* verpflichten.

signal [ˈsɪgnl] *n* Signal *nt*; *vt* ein Zeichen geben (+*dat*).
signatory [ˈsɪgnətrɪ] *n* Signatar *m*.
signature [ˈsɪgnətʃə*] *n* Unterschrift *f*; ~ **tune** Erkennungsmelodie *f*.
signet ring [ˈsɪgnətrɪŋ] *n* Siegelring *m*.
significance [sɪgˈnɪfɪkəns] *n* Bedeutung *f*.
significant [sɪgˈnɪfɪkənt] *a* (*meaning sth*) bedeutsam; (*important*) bedeutend, wichtig; ~**ly** *ad* bezeichnenderweise.
signify [ˈsɪgnɪfaɪ] *vt* bedeuten; (*show*) andeuten, zu verstehen geben.
sign language [ˈsaɪnlæŋgwɪdʒ] *n* Zeichensprache *f*, Fingersprache *f*.
signpost [ˈsaɪnpəʊst] *n* Wegweiser *m*, Schild *nt*.
silence [ˈsaɪləns] *n* Stille *f*, Ruhe *f*; (*of person*) Schweigen *nt*; *vt* zum Schweigen bringen; ~**r** (*on gun*) Schalldämpfer *m*; (*Aut*) Auspufftopf *m*.
silent [ˈsaɪlənt] *a* still; *person* schweigsam; ~**ly** *ad* schweigend, still.
silhouette [sɪluːˈet] *n* Silhouette *f*, Umriß *m*; (*picture*) Schattenbild *nt*; *vt*: **to be** ~**d against sth** sich als Silhouette abheben gegen etw.
silk [sɪlk] *n* Seide *f*; *a* seiden, Seiden-; ~**y** *a* seidig.
silliness [ˈsɪlɪnəs] *n* Albernheit *f*, Dummheit *f*.
silly [ˈsɪlɪ] *a* dumm, albern.
silo [ˈsaɪləʊ] *n* Silo *m*.
silt [sɪlt] *n* Schlamm *m*, Schlick *m*.
silver [ˈsɪlvə*] *n* Silber *nt*; *a* silbern, Silber-; ~ **paper** Silberpapier *nt*; ~**-plate** Silber(geschirr) *nt*; ~**-plated** *a* versilbert; ~**smith** Silberschmied *m*; ~**ware** Silber *nt*; ~**y** *a* silbern.
similar [ˈsɪmɪlə*] *a* ähnlich (*to dat*); ~**ity** [sɪmɪˈlærɪtɪ] Ähnlichkeit *f*; ~**ly** *ad* in ähnlicher Weise.
simile [ˈsɪmɪlɪ] *n* Vergleich *m*.
simmer [ˈsɪmə*] *vti* sieden (lassen).
simple [ˈsɪmpl] *a* einfach; *dress also* schlicht; ~**(-minded)** *a* naiv, einfältig.
simplicity [sɪmˈplɪsɪtɪ] *n* Einfachheit *f*; (*of person*) Einfältigkeit *f*.
simplification [sɪmplɪfɪˈkeɪʃən] *n* Vereinfachung *f*.
simplify [ˈsɪmplɪfaɪ] *vt* vereinfachen.
simply [ˈsɪmplɪ] *ad* einfach; (*only*) bloß, nur.
simulate [ˈsɪmjuleɪt] *vt* simulieren.
simulation [sɪmjuˈleɪʃən] *n* Simulieren *nt*.
simultaneous *a*, ~**ly** *ad* [sɪməlˈteɪnɪəs, -lɪ] gleichzeitig.
sin [sɪn] *n* Sünde *f*; *vi* sündigen.
since [sɪns] *ad* seither; *prep* seit, seitdem; *cj* (*time*) seit; (*because*) da, weil.
sincere [sɪnˈsɪə*] *a* aufrichtig, ehrlich, offen; ~**ly** aufrichtig; **yours** ~**ly** mit freundlichen Grüßen.
sincerity [sɪnˈserɪtɪ] *n* Aufrichtigkeit *f*.
sinecure [ˈsaɪnɪkjʊə*] *n* einträgliche(r) Ruheposten *m*.
sinew [ˈsɪnjuː] *n* Sehne *f*; (*of animal*) Flechse *f*.
sinful [ˈsɪnful] *a* sündig, sündhaft.
sing [sɪŋ] *vti irreg* singen.

singe [sɪndʒ] vt versengen.

singer ['sɪŋə*] n Sänger(in f) m.

singing ['sɪŋɪŋ] n Singen nt, Gesang m.

single ['sɪŋgl] a (one only) einzig; bed, room Einzel-, einzeln; (unmarried) ledig; ticket einfach; (having one part only) einzeln; n (ticket) einfache Fahrkarte f; ~s (tennis) Einzel nt; ~ **out** vt aussuchen, auswählen; ~-**breasted** a einreihig; **in** ~ **file** hintereinander; ~-**handed** a allein; ~-**minded** a zielstrebig.

singlet ['sɪŋglət] n Unterhemd nt.

singly ['sɪŋglɪ] ad einzeln, allein.

singular ['sɪŋgjulə*] a (Gram) Singular-; (odd) merkwürdig, seltsam; n (Gram) Einzahl f, Singular m; ~**ly** ad besonders, höchst.

sinister ['sɪnɪstə*] a (evil) böse; (ghostly) unheimlich.

sink [sɪŋk] n Spülbecken nt, Ausguß m; irreg vt ship versenken; (dig) einsenken; vi sinken; ~ **in** vi (news etc) eingehen (+dat); ~**ing** a feeling flau.

sinner ['sɪnə*] n Sünder(in f) m.

sinuous ['sɪnjuəs] a gewunden, sich schlängelnd.

sinus ['saɪnəs] n (Anat) Nasenhöhle f, Sinus m.

sip [sɪp] n Schlückchen nt; vt nippen an (+dat).

siphon ['saɪfən] n Siphon(flasche f) m; ~ **off** vt absaugen; (fig) abschöpfen.

sir [sɜː*] n (respect) Herr m; (knight) Sir m; **yes S**~ ja(wohl, mein Herr).

siren ['saɪərən] n Sirene f.

sirloin ['sɜːlɔɪn] n Lendenstück nt.

sirocco [sɪ'rɒkəu] n Schirokko m.

sissy ['sɪsɪ] n = **cissy**.

sister ['sɪstə*] n Schwester f; (nurse) Oberschwester f; (nun) Ordensschwester f; ~-**in-law** Schwägerin f.

sit [sɪt] irreg vi sitzen; (hold session) tagen, Sitzung halten; vt exam machen; **to** ~ **tight** abwarten; ~ **down** vi sich hinsetzen; ~ **up** vi (after lying) sich aufsetzen; (straight) sich gerade setzen; (at night) aufbleiben.

site [saɪt] n Platz m; vt plazieren, legen.

sit-in ['sɪtɪn] n Sit-in nt.

siting ['saɪtɪŋ] n (location) Platz m, Lage f.

sitting ['sɪtɪŋ] n (meeting) Sitzung f, Tagung f; ~ **room** Wohnzimmer nt.

situated ['sɪtjueɪtɪd] a: **to be** ~ liegen.

situation [sɪtju'eɪʃən] n Situation f, Lage f; (place) Lage f; (employment) Stelle f.

six [sɪks] num sechs; ~**teen** num sechzehn; ~**th** a sechste(r,s); n Sechstel nt; ~**ty** num sechzig.

size [saɪz] n Größe f; (of project) Umfang m; (glue) Kleister m; ~ **up** vt (assess) abschätzen, einschätzen; ~**able** a ziemlich groß, ansehnlich.

sizzle ['sɪzl] n Zischen nt; vi zischen; (Cook) brutzeln.

skate [skeɪt] n Schlittschuh m; vi Schlittschuh laufen; ~**r** Schlittschuhläufer(in f) m.

skating ['skeɪtɪŋ] n Eislauf m; **to go** ~ Eislaufen gehen; ~ **rink** Eisbahn f.

skeleton ['skelɪtn] n Skelett nt; (fig) Gerüst nt; ~ **key** Dietrich m.

skeptic ['skeptɪk] n (US) = **sceptic**.

sketch [sketʃ] n Skizze f; (Theat) Sketch m; vt skizzieren, eine Skizze machen von; ~**book** Skizzenbuch nt; ~**ing** Skizzieren nt; ~ **pad** Skizzenblock m; ~**y** a skizzenhaft.

skewer ['skjuə*] n Fleischspieß m.

ski [skiː] n Ski m, Schi m; vi Ski or Schi laufen; ~ **boot** Skistiefel m.

skid [skɪd] n (Aut) Schleudern nt; vi rutschen; (Aut) schleudern.

skidmark ['skɪdmɑːk] n Rutschspur f.

skier ['skiːə*] n Skiläufer(in f) m.

skiing ['skiːɪŋ] n: **to go** ~ Skilaufen gehen.

ski-jump ['skiːdʒʌmp] n Sprungschanze f; vi Ski springen.

ski-lift ['skiːlɪft] n Skilift m.

skilful a, ~**ly** ad ['skɪlful, -fəlɪ] geschickt.

skill [skɪl] n Können nt, Geschicklichkeit f; ~**ed** a geschickt; worker Fach-, gelernt.

skim [skɪm] vt liquid abschöpfen; milk entrahmen; (read) überfliegen; (glide over) gleiten über (+acc).

skimp [skɪmp] vt (do carelessly) oberflächlich tun; ~**y** a work schlecht gemacht; dress knapp.

skin [skɪn] n Haut f; (peel) Schale f; vt abhäuten, schälen; ~-**deep** a oberflächlich; ~ **diving** Schwimmtauchen nt; ~**ny** a dünn; ~-**tight** a dress eng hauteng.

skip [skɪp] n Sprung m, Hopser m; vi hüpfen, springen; (with rope) Seil springen; vt (pass over) übergehen.

ski pants ['skiːpænts] npl Skihosen pl.

skipper ['skɪpə*] n (Naut) Schiffer m, Kapitän m; (Sport) Mannschaftskapitän m; vt führen.

skipping rope ['skɪpɪŋrəup] n Hüpfseil nt.

skirmish ['skɜːmɪʃ] n Scharmützel nt.

skirt [skɜːt] n Rock m; vt herumgehen um; (fig) umgehen.

ski run ['skiːrʌn] n Skiabfahrt f.

skit [skɪt] n Parodie f.

ski tow ['skiːtəu] n Schlepplift m.

skittle ['skɪtl] n Kegel m; ~**s** (game) Kegeln nt.

skive [skaɪv] vi (Brit col) schwänzen.

skulk [skʌlk] vi sich herumdrücken.

skull [skʌl] n Schädel m; ~ **and crossbones** Totenkopf m.

skunk [skʌŋk] n Stinktier nt.

sky [skaɪ] n Himmel m; ~-**blue** a himmelblau; n Himmelblau nt; ~**light** Dachfenster nt, Oberlicht nt; ~**scraper** Wolkenkratzer m.

slab [slæb] n (of stone) Platte f; (of chocolate) Tafel f.

slack [slæk] a (loose) lose, schlaff, locker; business flau; (careless) nachlässig, lasch; vi nachlässig sein; n (in rope etc) durchhängende(s) Teil nt; **to take up the** ~ straffziehen; ~**s** pl Hose(n pl) f; ~**en** (also ~ **off**) vi schlaff/locker werden; (become slower) nachlassen, stocken; vt (loosen) lockern; ~**ness** Schlaffheit f.

slag [slæg] n Schlacke f; ~ **heap** Halde f.

slalom ['slɑːləm] n Slalom m.

slam [slæm] *n* Knall *m*; *vt door* zuschlagen, zuknallen; (*throw down*) knallen; *vi* zuschlagen.

slander ['slɑːndə•] *n* Verleumdung *f*; *vt* verleumden; ~**ous** *a* verleumderisch.

slang [slæŋ] *n* Slang *m*; Jargon *m*.

slant [slɑːnt]` *n* (*lit*) Schräge *f*; (*fig*) Tendenz *f*, Einstellung *f*; *vt* schräg legen; *vi* schräg liegen; ~**ing** *a* schräg.

slap [slæp] *n* Schlag *m*, Klaps *m*; *vt* schlagen, einen Klaps geben (+*dat*); *ad* (*directly*) geradewegs; ~**dash** *a* salopp; ~**stick** (*comedy*) Klamauk *m*; ~-**up** *a* meal erstklassig, prima.

slash [slæʃ] *n* Hieb *m*, Schnittwunde *f*; *vt* (auf)schlitzen; *expenditure* radikal kürzen.

slate [sleɪt] *n* (*stone*) Schiefer *m*; (*roofing*) Dachziegel *m*; *vt* (*criticize*) verreißen.

slaughter ['slɔːtə•] *n* (*of animals*) Schlachten *nt*; (*of people*) Gemetzel *nt*; *vt* schlachten; *people* niedermetzeln.

slave [sleɪv] *n* Sklave *m* Sklavin *f*; *vi* schuften, sich schinden; ~**ry** Sklaverei *f*; (*work*) Schinderei *f*.

slavish *a*, ~**ly** *ad* ['sleɪvɪʃ, -lɪ] sklavisch.

slay [sleɪ] *vt irreg* ermorden.

sleazy ['sliːzɪ] *a place* schmierig.

sledge ['sledʒ] *n* Schlitten *m*; ~**hammer** Schmiedehammer *m*.

sleek [sliːk] *a* glatt, glänzend; *shape* rassig.

sleep [sliːp] *n* Schlaf *m*; *vi irreg* schlafen; **to go to** ~ einschlafen; ~ **in** *vi* ausschlafen; (*oversleep*) verschlafen; ~**er** (*person*) Schläfer *m*; (*Rail*) Schlafwagen *m*; (*beam*) Schwelle *f*; ~**ily** *ad* schläfrig; ~**iness** Schläfrigkeit *f*; ~**ing bag** Schlafsack *m*; ~**ing car** Schlafwagen *m*; ~**ing pill** Schlaftablette *f*; ~**less** *a night* schlaflos; ~**lessness** Schlaflosigkeit *f*; ~**walker** Schlafwandler *m*; ~**y** schläfrig.

sleet [sliːt] *n* Schneeregen *m*.

sleeve [sliːv] *n* Ärmel *m*; (*of record*) Umschlag *m*; ~**less** *garment* ärmellos.

sleigh [sleɪ] *n* Pferdeschlitten *m*.

sleight [slaɪt] *n*: ~ **of hand** Fingerfertigkeit *f*.

slender ['slendə•] *a* schlank; (*fig*) gering.

slice [slaɪs] *n* Scheibe *f*; *vt* in Scheiben schneiden.

slick [slɪk] *a* (*clever*) raffiniert, aalglatt; *n* Ölteppich *m*.

slide [slaɪd] *n* Rutschbahn *f*; (*Phot*) Dia- (positiv) *nt*; (*for hair*) (Haar-)spange *f*; (*fall in prices*) (Preis)rutsch *m*; *vt irreg vt* schieben; *vi* (*slip*) gleiten, rutschen; **to let things** ~ die Dinge schleifen lassen; ~ **rule** Rechenschieber *m*.

sliding ['slaɪdɪŋ] *a door* Schiebe-.

slight [slaɪt] *a* zierlich; (*trivial*) geringfügig; (*small*) leicht, gering; *n* Kränkung *f*; *vt* (*offend*) kränken; ~**ly** *ad* etwas, ein bißchen.

slim [slɪm] *a* schlank; *book* dünn; *chance* gering; *vi* eine Schlankheitskur machen.

slime [slaɪm] *n* Schlamm *m*; Schleim *m*.

slimming ['slɪmɪŋ] *n* Schlankheitskur *f*.

slimness ['slɪmnəs] *n* Schlankheit *f*.

slimy ['slaɪmɪ] *a* glitschig; (*dirty*) schlammig; *person* schmierig.

sling [slɪŋ] *n* Schlinge *f*; (*weapon*) Schleuder *f*; *vt irreg* werfen; (*hurl*) schleudern.

slip [slɪp] *n* (*slipping*) Ausgleiten *nt*, Rutschen *nt*; (*mistake*) Flüchtigkeitsfehler *m*; (*petticoat*) Unterrock *m*; (*of paper*) Zettel *m*; **to give sb the** ~ jdn entwischen; ~ **of the tongue** Versprecher *m*; ~ (*put*) stecken, schieben; **it** ~**ped my mind** das ist mir entfallen, ich habe es vergessen; *vi* (*lose balance*) ausrutschen; (*move*) gleiten, rutschen; (*make mistake*) einen Fehler machen; (*decline*) nachlassen; **to let things** ~ die Dinge schleifen lassen; ~ **away** *vi* sich wegstehlen; ~ **by** *vi* (*time*) verstreichen; ~ **in** *vt* hineingleiten lassen; *vi* (*errors*) sich einschleichen; ~ **out** *vi* hinausschlüpfen; ~**per** Hausschuh *m*; ~**pery** *a* glatt; (*tricky*) aalglatt, gerissen; ~-**road** Auffahrt *f*/Ausfahrt *f*; ~**shod** *a* schlampig; ~**stream** Windschatten *m*; ~-**up** Panne *f*; ~**way** Auslaufbahn *f*.

slit [slɪt] *n* Schlitz *m*; *vt irreg* aufschlitzen.

slither ['slɪðə•] *vi* schlittern; (*snake*) sich schlängeln.

slob [slɒb] *n* (*col*) Klotz *m*.

slog [slɒg] *n* (*great effort*) Plackerei *f*; *vi* (*work hard*) schuften.

slogan ['sləʊgən] *n* Schlagwort *nt*; (*Comm*) Werbespruch *m*.

slop [slɒp] *vi* überschwappen; *vt* verschütten.

slope [sləʊp] *n* Neigung *f*, Schräge *f*; (*of mountains*) (Ab)hang *m*; *vi*: ~ **down** sich senken; ~ **up** ansteigen.

sloping ['sləʊpɪŋ] *a* schräg; *shoulders* abfallend; *ground* abschüssig.

sloppily ['slɒpɪlɪ] *ad* schlampig.

sloppiness ['slɒpɪnəs] *n* Matschigkeit *f*; (*of work*) Nachlässigkeit *f*.

sloppy ['slɒpɪ] *a* (*wet*) matschig; (*careless*) schlampig; (*silly*) rührselig.

slot [slɒt] *n* Schlitz *m*; *vt*: ~ **sth in** etw einlegen; ~ **machine** Automat *m*.

slouch [slaʊtʃ] *vi* krumm dasitzen or dastehen.

slovenly ['slʌvnlɪ] *a* schlampig; *speech* salopp.

slow [sləʊ] *a* langsam; **to be** ~ (*clock*) nachgehen; (*stupid*) begriffsstutzig sein; ~ **down** *vi* langsamer werden; ~ **down!** mach langsam!; *vt* aufhalten, langsamer machen, verlangsamen; ~ **up** *vi* sich verlangsamen, sich verzögern; *vt* aufhalten, langsamer machen; ~**ly** *ad* langsam; allmählich; **in** ~ **motion** in Zeitlupe.

sludge [slʌdʒ] *n* Schlamm *m*, Matsch *m*.

slug [slʌg] *n* Nacktschnecke *f*; (*col: bullet*) Kugel *f*; ~**gish** *a* träge; (*Comm*) schleppend; ~**gishly** *ad* träge; ~**gishness** Langsamkeit *f*, Trägheit *f*.

sluice [sluːs] *n* Schleuse *f*.

slum [slʌm] *n* Elendsviertel *nt*, Slum *m*.

slumber ['slʌmbə•] *n* Schlummer *m*.

slump [slʌmp] *n* Rückgang *m*; *vi* fallen, stürzen.

slur [slɜː•] *n* Undeutlichkeit *f*; (*insult*) Verleumdung *f*; *vt* (*also* ~ **over**) hin-weggehen über (+*acc*); ~**red** [slɜːd] a *pro-nunciation* undeutlich.

slush [slʌʃ] *n* (*snow*) Schneematsch *m*; (*mud*) Schlamm *m*; ~**y** a (*lit*) matschig; (*fig: sentimental*) schmalzig.

slut [slʌt] *n* Schlampe *f*.

sly a, ~**ly** [slaɪ, -lɪ] ad schlau, verschlagen; ~**ness** Schlauheit *f*.

smack [smæk] *n* Klaps *m*; *vt* einen Klaps geben (+*dat*); **to ~ one's lips** schmatzen, sich (*dat*) die Lippen lecken; *vi* ~ **of** riechen nach.

small [smɔːl] a klein; ~ **change** Kleingeld *nt*; ~**holding** Kleinlandbesitz *m*; ~ **hours** *pl* frühe Morgenstunden *pl*; ~**ish** a ziemlich klein; ~**ness** Kleinheit *f*; ~**pox** Pocken *pl*; ~**-scale** a klein, in kleinem Maßstab; ~ **talk** Konversation *f*, Geplauder *nt*.

smarmy [ˈsmɑːmɪ] a (*col*) schmierig.

smart a, ~**ly** ad [smɑːt, -lɪ] (*fashionable*) elegant, schick; (*neat*) adrett; (*clever*) clever; (*quick*) scharf; *vi* brennen, schmerzen; ~**en up** *vi* sich in Schale werfen; *vt* herausputzen; ~**ness** Gescheitheit *f*; Eleganz *f*.

smash [smæʃ] *n* Zusammenstoß *m*; (*tennis*) Schmetterball *m*; *vt* (*break*) zer-schmettern; (*destroy*) vernichten; *vi* (*break*) zersplittern, zerspringen; ~**ing** a (*col*) toll, großartig.

smattering [ˈsmætərɪŋ] *n* oberflächliche Kenntnis *f*.

smear [smɪə*] *n* Fleck *m*; *vt* beschmieren.

smell [smel] *n* Geruch *m*; (*sense*) Geruchs-sinn *m*; *vti irreg* riechen (*of* nach); ~**y** a übelriechend.

smile [smaɪl] *n* Lächeln *nt*; *vi* lächeln.

smirk [smɜːk] *n* blöde(s) Grinsen *nt*; *vi* blöde grinsen.

smith [smɪθ] *n* Schmied *m*; ~**y** [ˈsmɪðɪ] Schmiede *f*.

smock [smɒk] *n* Kittel *m*.

smog [smɒg] *n* Smog *m*.

smoke [sməʊk] *n* Rauch *m*; *vt* rauchen; *food* räuchern; *vi* rauchen; ~**r** Raucher *m*; (*Rail*) Raucherabteil *nt*; ~ **screen** Rauchwand *f*.

smoking [ˈsməʊkɪŋ] *n* Rauchen *nt*; '**no ~**' 'Rauchen verboten'.

smoky [ˈsməʊkɪ] a rauchig; *room* verraucht; *taste* geräuchert.

smolder [ˈsməʊldə*] *vi* US) = **smoulder**.

smooth [smuːð] a glatt; *movement* geschmeidig; *person* glatt, gewandt; *vt* (*also* ~ **out**) glätten, glattstreichen; ~**ly** ad glatt, eben; (*fig*) reibungslos; ~**ness** Glätte *f*.

smother [ˈsmʌðə*] *vt* ersticken.

smoulder [ˈsməʊldə*] *vi* glimmen, schwelen.

smudge [smʌdʒ] *n* Schmutzfleck *m*; *vt* beschmieren.

smug [smʌg] a selbstgefällig.

smuggle [ˈsmʌgl] *vt* schmuggeln; ~**r** Schmuggler *m*.

smuggling [ˈsmʌglɪŋ] *n* Schmuggel *m*.

smugly [ˈsmʌglɪ] ad selbstgefällig.

smugness [ˈsmʌgnəs] *n* Selbstgefälligkeit *f*.

smutty [ˈsmʌtɪ] a (*fig: obscene*) obszön, schmutzig.

snack [snæk] *n* Imbiß *m*; ~ **bar** Imbißstube *f*.

snag [snæg] *n* Haken *m*; (*in stocking*) gezogene(r) Faden *m*.

snail [sneɪl] *n* Schnecke *f*.

snake [sneɪk] *n* Schlange *f*.

snap [snæp] *n* Schnappen *nt*; (*photograph*) Schnappschuß *m*; a *decision* schnell; (*break*) zerbrechen; (*Phot*) knipsen; **to ~ one's fingers** mit den Fingern schnipsen; *vi* (*break*) brechen; (*bite*) schnappen; (*speak*) anfauchen; ~ **out of it!** raff dich auf!; ~ **off** *vt* (*break*) abbrechen; ~ **up** *vt* aufschnappen; ~**py** a flott; ~**shot** Schnappschuß *m*.

snare [snɛə*] *n* Schlinge *f*; *vt* mit einer Schlinge fangen.

snarl [snɑːl] *n* Zähnefletschen *nt*; *vi* (*dog*) knurren; (*engine*) brummen, dröhnen.

snatch [snætʃ] *n* (*grab*) Schnappen *nt*; (*small amount*) Bruchteil *m*; *vt* schnappen, packen.

sneak [sniːk] *vi* schleichen.

sneakers [ˈsniːkəz] *npl* (*US*) Freizeit-schuhe *pl*.

sneer [snɪə*] *n* Hohnlächeln *nt*; *vi* höhnisch grinsen; spötteln.

sneeze [sniːz] *n* Niesen *nt*; *vi* niesen.

snide [snaɪd] a (*col: sarcastic*) schneidend.

sniff [snɪf] *n* Schnüffeln *nt*; *vi* schnieben; (*smell*) schnüffeln; *vt* schnuppern.

snigger [ˈsnɪgə*] *n* Kichern *nt*; *vi* hämisch kichern.

snip [snɪp] *n* Schnippel *m*, Schnipsel *m*; *vt* schnippeln.

sniper [ˈsnaɪpə*] *n* Heckenschütze *m*.

snippet [ˈsnɪpɪt] *n* Schnipsel *m*; (*of conversation*) Fetzen *m*.

snivelling [ˈsnɪvlɪŋ] a weinerlich.

snob [snɒb] *n* Snob *m*; ~**bery** Snobismus *m*; ~**ish** a versnobt; ~**bishness** Versnobtheit *f*, Snobismus *m*.

snooker [ˈsnuːkə*] *n* Snooker *nt*.

snoop [snuːp] *vi*: ~ **about** herum-schnüffeln.

snooty [ˈsnuːtɪ] a (*col*) hochnäsig; *restaurant* stinkfein.

snooze [snuːz] *n* Nickerchen *nt*; *vi* ein Nickerchen machen, dösen.

snore [snɔː*] *vi* schnarchen.

snoring [ˈsnɔːrɪŋ] *n* Schnarchen *nt*.

snorkel [ˈsnɔːkl] *n* Schnorchel *m*.

snort [snɔːt] *n* Schnauben *nt*; *vi* schnauben.

snotty [ˈsnɒtɪ] a (*col*) rotzig.

snout [snaʊt] *n* Schnauze *f*; (*of pig*) Rüssel *m*.

snow [snəʊ] *n* Schnee *m*; *vi* schneien; ~**ball** Schneeball *m*; ~**-blind** a schnee-blind; ~**bound** a eingeschneit; ~**drift** Schneewehe *f*; ~**drop** Schneeglöckchen *nt*; ~**fall** Schneefall *m*; ~**flake** Schnee-flocke *f*; ~**line** Schneegrenze *f*; ~**man** Schneemann *m*; ~**plough**, (*US*) ~**plow** Schneepflug *m*; ~**storm** Schneesturm *m*.

snub [snʌb] *vt* schroff abfertigen; *n* Verweis *m*, schroffe Abfertigung *f*; a ~**-nosed** stupsnasig.

snuff [snʌf] n Schnupftabak m; ~**box** Schnupftabakdose f.

snug [snʌg] a gemütlich, behaglich.

so [səu] ad so; cj daher, folglich, also; ~ **as to** um zu; **or** ~ so etwa; ~ **long!** (goodbye) tschüß!; ~ **many** so viele; ~ **much** soviel; ~ **that** damit.

soak [səuk] vt durchnässen; (leave in liquid) einweichen; ~ **in** vi einsickern in (+acc); ~**ing** Einweichen nt; ~**ing wet** a klatschnaß.

soap [səup] n Seife f; ~**flakes** pl Seifenflocken pl; ~ **powder** Waschpulver nt; ~**y** a seifig, Seifen-.

soar [sɔ:*] vi aufsteigen; (prices) in die Höhe schnellen.

sob [sɒb] n Schluchzen nt; vi schluchzen.

sober [ˈsəubə*] a (lit, fig) nüchtern; ~ **up** vi nüchtern werden; ~**ly** ad nüchtern.

so-called [ˈsəuˈkɔːld] a sogenannt.

soccer [ˈsɒkə*] n Fußball m.

sociability [səufəˈbɪlɪtɪ] n Umgänglichkeit f.

sociable [ˈsəufəbl] a umgänglich, gesellig.

social [ˈsəufəl] a sozial; (friendly, living with others) gesellig; ~**ism** Sozialismus m; ~**ist** Sozialist(in f) m; a sozialistisch; ~**ly** ad gesellschaftlich, privat; ~ **science** Sozialwissenschaft f; ~ **security** Sozialversicherung f; ~ **welfare** Fürsorge f; ~ **work** Sozialarbeit f; ~ **worker** Sozialarbeiter(in f) m.

society [səˈsaɪətɪ] n Gesellschaft f; (fashionable world) die große Welt.

sociological [səusɪəˈlɒdʒɪkəl] a soziologisch.

sociologist [səusɪˈɒlədʒɪst] n Soziologe m, Soziologin f.

sociology [səusɪˈɒlədʒɪ] n Soziologie f.

sock [sɒk] n Socke f; vt (col) schlagen.

socket [ˈsɒkɪt] n (Elec) Steckdose f; (of eye) Augenhöhle f; (Tech) Rohransatz m.

sod [sɒd] n Rasenstück nt; (col) Saukerl m.

soda [ˈsəudə] n Soda f; ~ **water** Mineralwasser nt, Soda(wasser) nt.

sodden [ˈsɒdn] a durchweicht.

sofa [ˈsəufə] n Sofa nt.

soft [sɒft] a weich; (not loud) leise, gedämpft; (kind) weichherzig, gutmütig; (weak) weich, nachgiebig; ~ **drink** alkoholfreie(s) Getränk nt; ~**en** [ˈsɒfn] vt weich machen; blow abschwächen, mildern; vi weich werden; ~**hearted** a weichherzig; ~**ly** ad sanft; leise; ~**ness** Weichheit f; (fig) Sanftheit f.

soggy [ˈsɒgɪ] a ground sumpfig; bread aufgeweicht.

soil [sɔɪl] n Erde f, Boden m; vt beschmutzen; ~**ed** a beschmutzt, schmutzig.

solace [ˈsɒləs] n Trost m.

solar [ˈsəulə*] a Sonnen-; ~ **system** Sonnensystem nt.

solder [ˈsɒldə*] vt löten; n Lötmetall nt.

soldier [ˈsəuldʒə*] n Soldat m.

sole [səul] n Sohle f; (fish) Seezunge f; vt besohlen; a alleinig, Allein-; ~**ly** ad ausschließlich, nur.

solemn [ˈsɒləm] a feierlich; (serious) feierlich, ernst.

solicitor [səˈlɪsɪtə*] n Rechtsanwalt m.

solid [ˈsɒlɪd] a (hard) fest; (of same material) rein, massiv; (not hollow) massiv, stabil; (without break) voll, ganz; (reliable) solide, zuverlässig; (sensible) solide, gut; (united) eins, einig; meal kräftig; n Feste(s) nt; ~**arity** [sɒlɪˈdærɪtɪ] Solidarität f, Zusammenhalt m; ~ **figure** (Math) Körper m; ~**ify** [səˈlɪdɪfaɪ] vi fest werden, sich verdichten, erstarren; vt fest machen, verdichten; ~**ity** [səˈlɪdɪtɪ] Festigkeit f; ~**ly** ad (fig) behind einmütig; work ununterbrochen.

soliloquy [səˈlɪləkwɪ] n Monolog m.

solitaire [sɒlɪˈtɛə*] n (Cards) Patience f; (gem) Solitär m.

solitary [ˈsɒlɪtərɪ] a einsam, einzeln.

solitude [ˈsɒlɪtjuːd] n Einsamkeit f.

solo [ˈsəuləu] n Solo nt; ~**ist** Soloist(in f) m.

solstice [ˈsɒlstɪs] n Sonnenwende f.

soluble [ˈsɒljubl] a substance löslich; problem (auf)lösbar.

solution [səˈluːʃən] n (lit, fig) Lösung f; (of mystery) Erklärung f.

solve [sɒlv] vt (auf)lösen.

solvent [ˈsɒlvənt] a (Fin) zahlungsfähig.

sombre, (US) **somber** a, ~**ly** ad [ˈsɒmbə*, -əlɪ] düster.

some [sʌm] a people etc einige; water etc etwas; (unspecified) (irgend)ein; (remarkable) toll, enorm; that's ~ **house** das ist vielleicht ein Haus; pron (amount) etwas; (number) einige; ~**body** pron (irgend) jemand; he is ~**body** er ist jemand or wer; ~**day** ad irgendwann; ~**how** ad (in a certain way) irgendwie; (for a certain reason) aus irgendeinem Grunde; ~**one** pron = **somebody**; ~**place** ad (US) = **somewhere**.

somersault [ˈsʌməsɔːlt] n Purzelbaum m; Salto m; vi Purzelbäume schlagen; einen Salto machen.

something [ˈsʌmθɪŋ] pron (irgend) etwas.

sometime [ˈsʌmtaɪm] ad (irgend) einmal; ~**s** ad manchmal, gelegentlich.

somewhat [ˈsʌmwɒt] ad etwas, ein wenig, ein bißchen.

somewhere [ˈsʌmwɛə*] ad irgendwo; (to a place) irgendwohin.

son [sʌn] n Sohn m.

sonata [səˈnɑːtə] n Sonate f.

song [sɒŋ] n Lied nt; ~**writer** Texter m.

sonic [ˈsɒnɪk] a Schall-; ~ **boom** Überschallknall m.

son-in-law [ˈsʌnɪnlɔː] n Schwiegersohn m.

sonnet [ˈsɒnɪt] n Sonett nt.

sonny [ˈsʌnɪ] n (col) Kleine(r) m.

soon [suːn] ad bald; **too** ~ zu früh; **as** ~ **as possible** so bald wie möglich; ~ **er** ad (time) eher, früher; (for preference) lieber; **no** ~**er** kaum.

soot [sut] n Ruß m.

soothe [suːð] vt person beruhigen; pain lindern.

soothing [ˈsuːðɪŋ] a (for person) beruhigend; (for pain) lindernd.

sop [sɒp] n (bribe) Schmiergeld nt.

sophisticated [sə'fɪstɪkeɪtɪd] *a person* kultiviert, weltgewandt; *machinery* differenziert, hochentwickelt; *plan* ausgeklügelt.

sophistication [səfɪstɪ'keɪʃən] *n* Weltgewandtheit *f*, Kultiviertheit *f*; *(Tech)* technische Verfeinerung *f*.

sophomore ['sɒfəmɔ:*] *n (US)* College-Student *m* im 2. Jahr.

soporific [sɒpə'rɪfɪk] *a* einschläfernd, Schlaf-.

sopping ['sɒpɪŋ] *a (very wet)* patschnaß, triefend.

soppy ['sɒpɪ] *a (col)* schmalzig.

soprano [sə'prɑ:nəʊ] *n* Sopran *m*.

sordid ['sɔ:dɪd] *a (dirty)* schmutzig; *(mean)* niederträchtig.

sore [sɔ:*] *a* schmerzend; *point* wund; **to be ~** weh tun; *(angry)* böse sein; *n* Wunde *f*; **~ly** *ad* tempted stark, sehr; **~ness** Schmerzhaftigkeit *f*, Empfindlichkeit *f*.

sorrow ['sɒrəʊ] *n* Kummer *m*, Leid *nt*; **~ful** *a* sorgenvoll; **~fully** *ad* traurig, betrübt, kummervoll.

sorry ['sɒrɪ] *a* traurig, erbärmlich; **(I'm) ~** es tut mir leid; **I feel ~ for him** er tut mir leid.

sort [sɔ:t] *n* Art *f*, Sorte *f*; *vt (also ~ out)* papers sortieren, sichten; *problems* in Ordnung bringen.

so-so ['səʊ'səʊ] *ad* so(-so) la-la, mäßig.

soufflé ['su:fleɪ] *n* Auflauf *m*, Soufflé *nt*.

soul [səʊl] *n* Seele *f*; *(music)* Soul *m*; **~-destroying** *a* trostlos; **~ful** *a* seelenvoll; **~less** *a* seelenlos, gefühllos.

sound [saʊnd] *a (healthy)* gesund; *(safe)* sicher, solide; *(sensible)* vernünftig; *theory* stichhaltig; *(thorough)* tüchtig, gehörig; *n (noise)* Geräusch *nt*, Laut *m*; *(Geog)* Meerenge *f*, Sund *m*; *vt* erschallen lassen; *alarm* (Alarm) schlagen; *(Med)* abhorchen; **to ~ one's horn** hupen; *vi (make a sound)* schallen, tönen; *(seem)* klingen; **~ out** *vt opinion* erforschen; *person* auf den Zahn fühlen (+dat); **~ barrier** Schallmauer *f*; **~ing** *(Naut etc)* Lotung *f*; **~ly** *ad sleep* fest, tief; *beat* tüchtig; **~proof** *a room* schalldicht; *vt* schalldicht machen; **~-track** Tonstreifen *m*; Filmmusik *f*.

soup [su:p] *n* Suppe *f*; **in the ~** *(col)* in der Tinte; **~spoon** Suppenlöffel *m*.

sour ['saʊə*] *a (lit, fig)* sauer.

source [sɔ:s] *n (lit, fig)* Quelle *f*.

sourness ['saʊənəs] *n* Säure *f*; *(fig)* Bitterkeit *f*.

south [saʊθ] *n* Süden *m*; *a* Süd-, südlich; *ad* nach Süden, südwärts; **~-east** Südosten *m*; **~erly** ['sʌðəlɪ] *a* südlich; **~ern** ['sʌðən] *a* südlich, Süd-; **~ward(s)** *ad* südwärts, nach Süden; **~-west** Südwesten *m*.

souvenir [su:və'nɪə*] *n* Andenken *nt*, Souvenir *nt*.

sovereign ['sɒvrɪn] *n (ruler)* Herrscher *m*; *a (independent)* souverän; **~ty** Oberhoheit *f*, Souveränität *f*.

sow [saʊ] *n* Sau *f*; [səʊ] *vt irreg (lit, fig)* säen.

soya bean ['sɔɪə'bi:n] *n* Sojabohne *f*.

spa [spɑ:] *n (spring)* Mineralquelle *f*; *(place)* Kurort *m*, Bad *nt*.

space [speɪs] *n* Platz *m*, Raum *m*; *(universe)* Weltraum *m*, All *nt*; *(length of time)* Abstand *m*; **~ out** *vt* Platz lassen zwischen; *(typing)* gesperrt schreiben; **~craft** Raumschiff *nt*; **~man** Raumfahrer *m*.

spacious ['speɪʃəs] *a* geräumig, weit.

spade [speɪd] *n* Spaten *m*; **~s** *(Cards)* Pik *nt*, Schippe *f*; **~work** *(fig)* Vorarbeit *f*.

spaghetti [spə'getɪ] *n* Spaghetti *pl*.

span [spæn] *n* Spanne *f*; Spannweite *f*; *vt* überspannen.

spaniel ['spænjəl] *n* Spaniel *m*.

spank [spæŋk] *vt* verhauen, versohlen.

spanner ['spænə*] *n* Schraubenschlüssel *m*.

spar [spɑ:*] *n (Naut)* Sparren *m*; *vi (boxing)* einen Sparring machen.

spare [spɛə*] *a* Ersatz-; *n* **~ part**; *vt lives, feelings* verschonen; *trouble* ersparen; **4 to ~** 4 übrig; **~ part** Ersatzteil *nt*; **~ time** Freizeit *f*.

spark [spɑ:k] *n* Funken *m*; **~(ing) plug** Zündkerze *f*.

sparkle ['spɑ:kl] *n* Funkeln *nt*, Glitzern *nt*; *(gaiety)* Lebhaftigkeit *f*, Schwung *m*; *vi* funkeln, glitzern.

sparkling ['spɑ:klɪŋ] *a* funkelnd, sprühend; *wine* Schaum-; *conversation* spritzig, geistreich.

sparrow ['spærəʊ] *n* Spatz *m*.

sparse *a*, **~ly** *ad* [spɑ:s, -lɪ] spärlich, dünn.

spasm ['spæzəm] *n (Med)* Krampf *m*; *(fig)* Anfall *m*; **~odic** [spæz'mɒdɪk] *a* krampfartig, spasmodisch; *(fig)* sprunghaft.

spastic ['spæstɪk] *a* spastisch.

spate [speɪt] *n (fig)* Flut *f*, Schwall *m*; **in ~** *river* angeschwollen.

spatter ['spætə*] *n* Spritzer *m*; *vt* bespritzen, verspritzen; *vi* spritzen.

spatula ['spætjʊlə] *n* Spatel *m*; *(for building)* Spachtel *f*.

spawn [spɔ:n] *vi* laichen.

speak [spi:k] *irreg vt* sprechen, reden; *truth* sagen; *language* sprechen; *vi* sprechen *(to mit or zu)*; **~ for** *vi* sprechen or eintreten für; **~ up** *vi* lauter sprechen; **~er** Sprecher *m*, Redner *m*; **loud~** Lautsprecher *m*; **not to be on ~ing terms** nicht miteinander sprechen.

spear [spɪə*] *n* Speer *m*, Lanze *f*, Spieß *m*; *vt* aufspießen, durchbohren.

spec [spek] *n (col)* **on ~** auf gut Glück.

special ['speʃəl] *a* besondere(r,s); speziell; *n (Rail)* Sonderzug *m*; **~ist** Spezialist *m*; *(Tech)* Fachmann *m*; *(Med)* Facharzt *m*; **~ity** [speʃɪ'ælɪtɪ] Spezialität *f*; *(study)* Spezialgebiet *nt*; **~ize** *vi* sich spezialisieren *(in auf +acc)*; **~ly** *ad* besonders; *(explicitly)* extra, ausdrücklich.

species ['spi:ʃi:z] *n* Art *f*.

specific [spə'sɪfɪk] *a* spezifisch, eigentümlich, besondere(r,s); **~ally** *ad* genau, spezifisch; **~ations** *pl* [spesɪfɪ'keɪʃənz] genaue Angaben *pl*; *(Tech)* technische Daten *pl*.

specify ['spesɪfaɪ] *vt* genau angeben.

specimen ['spesɪmɪn] n Probe f, Muster nt.

speck [spek] n Fleckchen nt; **~led** a gesprenkelt.

specs [speks] npl (col) Brille f.

spectacle ['spektəkl] n Schauspiel nt; **~s** pl Brille f.

spectacular [spek'tækjʊlə*] a aufsehenerregend, spektakulär.

spectator [spek'teɪtə*] n Zuschauer m.

spectre, (US) **specter** ['spektə*] n Geist m, Gespenst nt.

spectrum ['spektrəm] n Spektrum nt.

speculate ['spekjʊleɪt] vi vermuten, spekulieren (also Fin).

speculation [spekjʊ'leɪʃən] n Vermutung f, Spekulation f (also Fin).

speculative ['spekjʊlətɪv] a spekulativ.

speech [spiːtʃ] n Sprache f; (address) Rede f, Ansprache f; (manner of speaking) Sprechweise f; **~ day** (Sch) (Jahres)schlußfeier f; **~less** a sprachlos; **~ therapy** Sprachheilpflege f.

speed [spiːd] n Geschwindigkeit f; (gear) Gang m; vi irreg rasen; (Jur) (zu) schnell fahren; **~ up** vt beschleunigen; vi schneller werden/ fahren; **~boat** Schnellboot nt; **~ily** ad schnell, schleunigst; **~ing** zu schnelles Fahren; **~ limit** Geschwindigkeitsbegrenzung f; **~ometer** [spɪ'dɒmɪtə*] Tachometer m; **~way** (bike racing) Motorradrennstrecke f; **~y** a schnell, zügig.

spell [spel] n (magic) Bann m, Zauber m; (period of time) Zeit f, Zeitlang f, Weile f; **sunny ~s** pl Aufheiterungen pl; **rainy ~s** pl vereinzelte Schauer pl; vt irreg buchstabieren; (imply) bedeuten; **how do you . . .?** wie schreibt man . . .?; **~bound** a (wie) gebannt; **~ing** Buchstabieren nt; **English ~ing** die englische Rechtschreibung.

spend [spend] vt irreg money ausgeben; time verbringen; **~ing money** Taschengeld nt.

spent [spent] a patience erschöpft.

sperm [spɜːm] n (Biol) Samenflüssigkeit f.

spew [spjuː] vt (er)brechen.

sphere [sfɪə*] n (globe) Kugel f; (fig) Sphäre f, Gebiet nt.

spherical ['sferɪkəl] a kugelförmig.

sphinx [sfɪŋks] n Sphinx f.

spice [spaɪs] n Gewürz nt; vt würzen.

spiciness ['spaɪsɪnəs] n Würze f.

spick-and-span ['spɪkən'spæn] a blitzblank.

spicy ['spaɪsɪ] a würzig, pikant (also fig).

spider ['spaɪdə*] n Spinne f; **~y** a writing krakelig.

spike [spaɪk] n Dorn m, Spitze f; **~s** pl Spikes pl.

spill [spɪl] irreg vt verschütten; vi sich ergießen.

spin [spɪn] n Umdrehung f; (trip in car) Spazierfahrt f; (Aviat) (Ab)trudeln nt; (on ball) Drall m; irreg vt thread spinnen; (like top) schnell drehen, (herum)wirbeln; vi sich drehen; **~ out** vt (in die Länge ziehen; story ausmalen.

spinach ['spɪnɪtʃ] n Spinat m.

spinal ['spaɪnl] a spinal, Rückgrat-, Rückenmark-; **~ cord** Rückenmark nt.

spindly ['spɪndlɪ] a spindeldürr.

spin-drier ['spɪn'draɪə*] n Wäscheschleuder f.

spin-dry [spɪn'draɪ] vt schleudern.

spine [spaɪn] n Rückgrat nt; (thorn) Stachel m; **~less** a (lit, fig) rückgratlos.

spinet [spɪ'net] n Spinett nt.

spinner ['spɪnə*] n (of thread) Spinner m.

spinning ['spɪnɪŋ] n (of thread) (Faden)spinnen nt; **~ wheel** Spinnrad nt.

spinster ['spɪnstə*] n unverheiratete Frau f; (pej) alte Jungfer f.

spiral ['spaɪərəl] n Spirale f; a gewunden, spiralförmig, Spiral-; vi sich ringeln; **~ staircase** Wendeltreppe f.

spire ['spaɪə*] n Turm m.

spirit ['spɪrɪt] n Geist m; (humour, mood) Stimmung f; (courage) Mut m; (verve) Elan m; (alcohol) Alkohol m; **~s** pl Spirituosen pl; **in good ~s** gut aufgelegt; **~ed** a beherzt; **~ level** Wasserwaage f; **~ual** a geistig, seelisch; (Rel) geistlich; n Spiritual nt; **~ualism** Spiritismus m.

spit [spɪt] n (for roasting) (Brat)spieß m; (saliva) Spucke f; vi irreg spucken; (rain) sprühen; (make a sound) zischen; (cat) fauchen.

spite [spaɪt] n Gehässigkeit f; vt ärgern, kränken; **in ~ of** trotz (+gen or dat); **~ful** a gehässig.

splash [splæʃ] n Spritzer m; (of colour) (Farb)fleck m; vt bespritzen; vi spritzen; **~down** Wasserlandung f.

spleen [spliːn] n (Anat) Milz f.

splendid a, **~ly** ad ['splendɪd, -lɪ] glänzend, großartig.

splendour, (US) **splendor** ['splendə*] n Pracht f.

splice [splaɪs] vt spleißen.

splint [splɪnt] n Schiene f.

splinter ['splɪntə*] n Splitter m; vi (zer)splittern.

split [splɪt] n Spalte f; (fig) Spaltung f; (division) Trennung f; irreg vt spalten; vi (divide) reißen; vt sich spalten; (col: depart) abhauen; **~ up** vi sich trennen; vt aufteilen, teilen; **~ting** a headache rasend, wahnsinnig.

splutter ['splʌtə*] vi spritzen; (person, engine) stottern.

spoil [spɔɪl] irreg vt (ruin) verderben; child verwöhnen, verziehen; vi (food) verderben; **~s** pl Beute f; **~sport** Spielverderber m.

spoke [spəʊk] n Speiche f; **~sman** Sprecher m, Vertreter m.

sponge [spʌndʒ] n Schwamm m; vt mit dem Schwamm abwaschen; vi auf Kosten leben (on gen); **~ bag** Kulturbeutel m; **~ cake** Rührkuchen m; **~r** (col) Schmarotzer m.

spongy ['spʌndʒɪ] a schwammig.

sponsor ['spɒnsə*] n Bürge m; (in advertising) Sponsor m; vt bürgen für; födern; **~ship** Bürgschaft f; (public) Schirmherrschaft f.

spontaneity [spɒntə'neɪɪtɪ] n Spontanität f.

spontaneous a, **~ly** ad [spɒn'teɪnɪəs, -lɪ] spontan.

spooky ['spuːkɪ] a (col) gespenstisch.

spool [spuːl] n Spule f, Rolle f.

spoon [spuːn] n Löffel m; **~-feed** vt irreg (lit) mit dem Löffel füttern; (fig) hochpäppeln; **~ful** Löffel(voll) m.

sporadic [spə'rædɪk] a vereinzelt, sporadisch.

sport [spɔːt] n Sport m; (fun) Spaß m; (person) feine(r) Kerl m; **~ing** a (fair) sportlich, fair; **~s car** Sportwagen m; **~(s) coat**, **~(s) jacket** Sportjackett nt; **~sman** Sportler m; (fig) anständige(r) Kerl m; **~smanship** Sportlichkeit f; (fig) Anständigkeit f; **~s page** Sportseite f; **~swear** Sportkleidung f; **~swoman** Sportlerin f; **~y** a sportlich.

spot [spɒt] n Punkt m, (dirty) Fleck(en) m; (place) Stelle f, Platz m; (Med) Pickel m, Pustel f, (small amount) Schluck m, Tropfen m; vt erspähen; mistake bemerken; **~ check** Stichprobe f; **~less** a, **~ly** ad fleckenlos; **~light** Scheinwerferlicht nt; (lamp) Scheinwerfer m; **~ted** a gefleckt; dress gepunktet; **~ty** a face pickelig.

spouse [spauz] n Gatte m/Gattin f.

spout [spaut] n (of pot) Tülle f; (jet) Wasserstrahl m; vi speien, spritzen.

sprain [spreɪn] n Verrenkung f; vt verrenken.

sprawl [sprɔːl] n (of city) Ausbreitung f; vi sich strecken.

spray [spreɪ] n Spray nt; (off sea) Gischt f; (instrument) Zerstäuber m; Spraydose f; (of flowers) Zweig m; vt besprühen, sprayen.

spread [spred] n (extent) Verbreitung f; (of wings) Spannweite f; (col: meal) Schmaus m; (for bread) Aufstrich m; vt irreg ausbreiten; (scatter) verbreiten; butter streichen.

spree [spriː] n lustige(r) Abend m; (shopping) Einkaufsbummel m; **to go out on a ~** einen draufmachen.

sprig [sprɪg] n kleine(r) Zweig m.

sprightly ['spraɪtlɪ] a munter, lebhaft.

spring [sprɪŋ] n (leap) Sprung m; (metal) Feder f; (season) Frühling m; (water) Quelle f; vi irreg (leap) springen; **~ up** vi (problem) entstehen, auftauchen; **~board** Sprungbrett nt; **~-clean** vt Frühjahrsputz machen in (+dat); **~-cleaning** Frühjahrsputz m; **~iness** Elastizität f; **~time** Frühling m; **~y** a federnd, elastisch.

sprinkle ['sprɪŋkl] n Prise f; vt salt streuen; liquid sprenkeln.

sprinkling ['sprɪŋklɪŋ] n Spur f, ein bißchen.

sprint [sprɪnt] n Kurzstreckenlauf m; Sprint m; vi sprinten; **~er** Sprinter m, Kurzstreckenläufer m.

sprite [spraɪt] n Elfe f, Kobold m.

sprout [spraut] vi sprießen; n see **Brussels**.

spruce [spruːs] n Fichte f; a schmuck, adrett.

spry [spraɪ] a flink, rege.

spud [spʌd] n (col) Kartoffel f.

spur [spɜː*] n Sporn m; (fig) Ansporn m; vt (also ~ on) (fig) anspornen; **on the ~ of the moment** spontan.

spurious ['spjuərɪəs] a falsch, unecht, Pseudo-.

spurn [spɜːn] vt verschmähen.

spurt [spɜːt] n (jet) Strahl m; (acceleration) Spurt m; vt spritzen; vi (jet) steigen; (liquid) schießen; (run) spurten.

spy [spaɪ] n Spion m; vi spionieren; vt erspähen; **to ~ on sb** jdm nachspionieren; **~ing** Spionage f.

squabble ['skwɒbl] n Zank m; vi sich zanken.

squabbling ['skwɒblɪŋ] n Zankerei f.

squad [skwɒd] n (Mil) Abteilung f; (police) Kommando nt.

squadron ['skwɒdrən] n (cavalry) Schwadron f; (Naut) Geschwader nt; (air force) Staffel f.

squalid ['skwɒlɪd] a schmutzig, verkommen.

squall [skwɔːl] n Bö f, Windstoß m; **~y** a weather stürmisch; wind böig.

squalor ['skwɒlə*] n Verwahrlosung f, Schmutz m.

squander ['skwɒndə*] vt verschwenden.

square [skwɛə*] n (Math) Quadrat nt; (open space) Platz m; (instrument) Winkel m; (col: person) Spießer m; a viereckig, quadratisch; (fair) ehrlich, reell; (meal) reichlich; (col) ideas, tastes spießig; ad (exactly) direkt, gerade; vt (arrange) ausmachen, aushandeln; (Math) ins Quadrat erheben; (bribe) schmieren; vi (agree) übereinstimmen; **all ~** quitt; **2 metres ~** 2 Meter im Quadrat; **2 metres 2 ~** Quadratmeter; **~ly** ad fest, gerade.

squash [skwɒʃ] n (drink) Saft m; vt zerquetschen.

squat [skwɒt] a untersetzt, gedrungen; vi hocken; **~ter** Squatter m, Siedler m ohne Rechtstitel; Hausbesetzer m.

squaw [skwɔː] n Squaw f.

squawk [skwɔːk] n Kreischen nt; vi kreischen.

squeak [skwiːk] n Gequiek(s)e nt; vi quiek(s)en; (spring, door etc) quietschen; **~y** a quiek(s)end; quietschend.

squeal [skwiːl] n schrille(r) Schrei m; (of brakes etc) Quietschen nt; vi schrill schreien.

squeamish ['skwiːmɪʃ] a empfindlich; **that made me ~** davon wurde mir übel; **~ness** Überempfindlichkeit f.

squeeze [skwiːz] n (lit) Pressen nt; (Pol) Geldknappheit f, wirtschaftliche(r) Engpaß m; vt pressen, drücken; orange auspressen; **~ out** vt ausquetschen.

squid [skwɪd] n Tintenfisch m.

squint [skwɪnt] n Schielen nt; vi schielen.

squire ['skwaɪə*] n Gutsherr m.

squirm [skwɜːm] vi sich winden.

squirrel ['skwɪrəl] n Eichhörnchen nt.

squirt [skwɜːt] n Spritzer m, Strahl m; vti spritzen.

stab [stæb] n (blow) Stoß m, Stich m; (col: try) Versuch m; vt erstechen; **~bing** Messerstecherei f.

stability [stə'bılıtı] *n* Festigkeit *f*, Stabilität *f*.

stabilization [steıbəlaı'zeıʃən] *n* Festigung *f*, Stabilisierung *f*.

stabilize ['steıbəlaız] *vt* festigen, stabilisieren; ~**r** Stabilisator *m*.

stable ['steıbl] *n* Stall *m*; *vt* im Stall unterbringen; *a* fest, stabil; *person* gefestigt.

staccato [stə'ka:təʊ] *a* stakkato.

stack [stæk] *n* Stoß *m*, Stapel *m*; *vt* (auf-)stapeln.

stadium ['steıdıəm] *n* Stadion *nt*.

staff [sta:f] *n* (*stick, Mil*) Stab *m*; (*personnel*) Personal *nt*; (*Sch*) Lehrkräfte *pl*; *vt* (*with people*) besetzen.

stag [stæg] *n* Hirsch *m*.

stage [steıdʒ] *n* Bühne *f*; (*of journey*) Etappe *f*; (*degree*) Stufe *f*; (*point*) Stadium *nt*; *vt* (*put on*) aufführen; *play* inszenieren; *demonstration* veranstalten; **in ~s** etappenweise; ~**coach** Postkutsche *f*; ~ **door** Bühneneingang *m*; ~ **manager** Spielleiter *m*, Intendant *m*.

stagger ['stægə*] *vi* wanken, taumeln; *vt* (*amaze*) verblüffen; *hours* staffeln; ~**ing** *a* unglaublich.

stagnant ['stægnənt] *a* stagnierend; *water* stehend.

stagnate [stæg'neıt] *vi* stagnieren.

stagnation [stæg'neıʃən] *n* Stillstand *m*, Stagnation *f*.

staid [steıd] *a* gesetzt.

stain [steın] *n* Fleck *m*; (*colouring for wood*) Beize *f*; *vt* beflecken, Flecken machen auf (+*acc*); beizen; ~**ed glass window** buntes Glasfenster *nt*; ~**less** *a* (*steel*) rostfrei, nichtrostend; ~ **remover** Fleckentferner *m*.

stair [steə*] *n* (Treppen)stufe *f*; ~**case** Treppenhaus *nt*, Treppe *f*; ~**s** *pl* Treppe *f*; ~**way** Treppenaufgang *m*.

stake [steık] *n* (*post*) Pfahl *m*, Pfosten *m*; (*money*) Einsatz *m*; *vt* (*bet money*) setzen; **to be at** ~ auf dem Spiel stehen.

stalactite ['stæləktaıt] *n* Stalaktit *m*.

stalagmite ['stæləgmaıt] *n* Stalagmit *m*.

stale [steıl] *a* alt; *beer* schal; *bread* altbacken; ~**mate** (*chess*) Patt *nt*; (*fig*) Stillstand *m*.

stalk [stɔ:k] *n* Stengel *m*, Stiel *m*; *vt game* sich anpirschen an (+*acc*), jagen; *vi* (*walk*) stolzieren.

stall [stɔ:l] *n* (*in stable*) Stand *m*, Box *f*; (*in market*) (Verkaufs)stand *m*; *vt* (*Aut*) (den Motor) abwürgen; *vi* (*Aut*) stehenbleiben; (*avoid*) Ausflüchte machen, ausweichen; ~**s** *pl* (*Theat*) Parkett *nt*.

stallion ['stælıən] *n* Zuchthengst *m*.

stalwart ['stɔ:lwət] *a* standhaft; *n* treue(r) Anhänger *m*.

stamina ['stæmınə] *n* Durchhaltevermögen *nt*, Zähigkeit *f*.

stammer ['stæmə*] *n* Stottern *nt*; *vti* stottern, stammeln.

stamp [stæmp] *n* Briefmarke *f*; (*with foot*) Stampfen *nt*; (*for document*) Stempel *m*; *vi* stampfen; *vt* (*mark*) stempeln; *mail* frankieren; *foot* stampfen mit; ~ **album** Briefmarkenalbum *nt*; ~ **collecting** Briefmarkensammeln *nt*.

stampede [stæm'pi:d] *n* panische Flucht *f*.

stance [stæns] *n* (*posture*) Haltung *f*, Stellung *f*; (*opinion*) Einstellung *f*.

stand [stænd] *n* Standort *m*, Platz *m*; (*for objects*) Gestell *nt*; (*seats*) Tribüne *f*; **to make a** ~ Widerstand leisten; *irreg vi* stehen; (*rise*) aufstehen; (*decision*) feststehen; **to** ~ **still** still stehen; *vt* setzen, stellen; (*endure*) aushalten; *person* ausstehen, leiden können; *nonsense* dulden; **it** ~**s to reason** es ist einleuchtend; ~ **by** *vi* (*be ready*) bereitstehen; *vt opinion* treu bleiben (+*dat*); ~ **for** *vt* (*signify*) stehen für; (*permit, tolerate*) hinnehmen; ~ **in for** *vt* einspringen für; ~ **out** *vi* (*be prominent*) hervorstechen; ~ **up** *vi* (*rise*) aufstehen; ~ **up for** *vt* sich einsetzen für.

standard ['stændəd] *n* (*measure*) Standard *m*, Norm *f*; (*flag*) Standarte *f*, Fahne *f*; *a size etc* Normal-, Durchschnitts-; ~**ization** Vereinheitlichung *f*; ~**ize** *vt* vereinheitlichen, normen; ~ **lamp** Stehlampe *f*; ~ **of living** Lebensstandard *m*; ~ **time** Ortszeit *f*.

stand-by ['stændbaı] *n* Reserve *f*; ~ **flight** Standby-Flug *m*.

stand-in ['stændın] *n* Ersatz(mann) *m*, Hilfskraft *f*.

standing ['stændıŋ] *a* (*erect*) stehend; (*permanent*) ständig, dauernd; *invitation* offen; *n* (*duration*) Dauer *f*; (*reputation*) Ansehen *nt*; ~ **jump** Sprung *m* aus dem Stand; ~ **order** (*at bank*) Dauerauftrag *m*; ~ **orders** *pl* (*Mil*) Vorschrift; ~ **room** only nur Stehplatz.

stand-offish ['stænd'ɒfıʃ] *a* zurückhaltend, sehr reserviert.

standpoint ['stændpɔınt] *n* Standpunkt *m*.

standstill ['stændstıl] *n*: **to be at a** ~ stillstehen; **to come to a** ~ zum Stillstand kommen.

stanza ['stænzə] *n* (*verse*) Strophe *f*; (*poem*) Stanze *f*.

staple ['steıpl] *n* (*clip*) Krampe *f*; (*in paper*) Heftklammer *f*; (*article*) Haupterzeugnis *nt*; *a* Grund-, Haupt-; *vt* (*fest*)klammern; ~**r** Heftmaschine *f*.

star [sta:*] *n* Stern *m*; (*person*) Star *m*; *vi* die Hauptrolle spielen; *vt actor* in der Hauptrolle zeigen.

starboard ['sta:bəd] *n* Steuerbord *nt*; *a* Steuerbord-.

starch [sta:tʃ] *n* Stärke *f*; *vt* stärken; ~**y** *a* stärkehaltig; (*formal*) steif.

stardom ['sta:dəm] *n* Berühmtheit *f*.

stare [steə*] *n* starre(r) Blick *m*; *vi* starren (*at* auf +*acc*); ~ **at** *vt* anstarren.

starfish ['sta:fıʃ] *n* Seestern *m*.

staring ['steərıŋ] *a eyes* starrend.

stark [sta:k] *a* öde; *ad*: ~ **naked** splitternackt.

starless ['sta:ləs] *a* sternlos.

starlight ['sta:laıt] *n* Sternenlicht *nt*.

starling ['sta:lıŋ] *n* Star *m*.

starlit ['sta:lıt] *a* sternklar.

starring ['sta:rıŋ] *a* mit . . . in der Hauptrolle.

star-studded ['sta:stʌdıd] *a* mit Spitzenstars.

starry ['stɑːrɪ] a Sternen-; ~**-eyed** a (*innocent*) blauäugig.

start [stɑːt] n Beginn m, Anfang m, Start m; (*Sport*) Start m; (*lead*) Vorsprung m; **to give a** ~ zusammenfahren; **to give sb a** ~ jdn zusammenfahren lassen; vt in Gang setzen, anfangen; *car* anlassen; vi anfangen; (*car*) anspringen; (*on journey*) aufbrechen; (*Sport*) starten; ~ **over** vi (*US*) wieder anfangen; ~ **up** vi anfangen; (*startled*) auffahren; vt beginnen; *car* anlassen; *engine* starten; ~**er** m (*Aut*) Anlasser m; (*for race*) Starter m; ~**ing handle** Anlaßkurbel f, ~**ing point** Ausgangspunkt m.

startle ['stɑːtl] vt erschrecken.

startling ['stɑːtlɪŋ] a erschreckend.

starvation [stɑːˈveɪʃən] n Verhungern nt; **to die of** ~ verhungern.

starve [stɑːv] vi verhungern; vt verhungern lassen; **to be** ~**d of affection** unter Mangel an Liebe leiden; ~ **out** vt aushungern.

starving ['stɑːvɪŋ] a (ver)hungernd.

state [steɪt] n (*condition*) Zustand m; (*Pol*) Staat m; (*col: anxiety*) (schreckliche) Verfassung f; vt erklären; *facts* angeben; ~**control** staatliche Kontrolle f, ~**d** a festgesetzt; ~**liness** Pracht f, Würde f; ~**ly** a würdevoll, erhaben; ~**ment** Aussage f; (*Pol*) Erklärung f; ~ **secret** Staatsgeheimnis nt; ~**sman** Staatsmann m.

static ['stætɪk] n Statik f; a statisch.

station ['steɪʃən] n (*Rail etc*) Bahnhof m; (*police etc*) Station f, Wache f; (*in society*) gesellschaftliche Stellung f; vt aufstellen; **to be** ~**ed** stationiert sein.

stationary ['steɪʃənərɪ] a stillstehend; *car* parkend.

stationer ['steɪʃənə*] n Schreibwarenhändler m; ~'**s (shop)** Schreibwarengeschäft nt; ~**y** Schreibwaren pl.

station master ['steɪʃənmɑːstə*] n Bahnhofsvorsteher m.

station wagon ['steɪʃənwægən] n Kombiwagen m.

statistic [stəˈtɪstɪk] n Statistik f; ~**al** a statistisch; ~**s** pl Statistik f.

statue ['stætjuː] n Statue f.

statuesque [stætjʊˈesk] a statuenhaft.

stature ['stætʃə*] n Wuchs m, Statur f; (*fig*) Größe f.

status ['steɪtəs] n Stellung f, Status m; **the** ~ **quo** der Status quo; ~ **symbol** Statussymbol nt.

statute ['stætjuːt] n Gesetz nt.

statutory ['stætjʊtərɪ] a gesetzlich.

staunch a, ~**ly** ad [stɔːntʃ, -lɪ] treu, zuverlässig; *Catholic* standhaft, erz-.

stave [steɪv]: ~ **off** vt *attack* abwehren; *threat* abwenden.

stay [steɪ] n Aufenthalt m; (*support*) Stütze f; (*for tent*) Schnur f; vi bleiben; (*reside*) wohnen; **to** ~ **put** an Ort und Stelle bleiben; **to** ~ **with friends** bei Freunden untergebracht sein; **to** ~ **the night** übernachten; ~ **behind** vi zurückbleiben; ~ **in** vi (*at home*) zu Hause bleiben; ~ **on** vi (*continue*) länger bleiben; ~ **up** vi (*at night*) aufbleiben.

steadfast ['stedfəst] a standhaft, treu.

steadily ['stedɪlɪ] ad stetig, regelmäßig.

steadiness ['stedɪnəs] n Festigkeit f; (*fig*) Beständigkeit f.

steady ['stedɪ] a (*firm*) fest, stabil; (*regular*) gleichmäßig; (*reliable*) zuverlässig, beständig; *hand* ruhig; *job, boyfriend* fest; vt festigen; **to** ~ **o.s.** sich stützen.

steak [steɪk] n Steak nt; (*fish*) Filet nt.

steal [stiːl] irreg vti stehlen; vi sich stehlen; ~**th** [stelθ] Heimlichkeit f; ~**thy** ['stelθɪ] a verstohlen, heimlich.

steam [stiːm] n Dampf m; vt (*Cook*) im Dampfbad erhitzen; vi dampfen; (*ship*) dampfen, fahren; ~ **engine** Dampfmaschine f; ~**er** Dampfer m; ~**roller** Dampfwalze f; ~**y** a dampfig.

steel [stiːl] n Stahl m; a Stahl-; (*fig*) stählern; ~**works** Stahlwerke pl.

steep [stiːp] a steil; *price* gepfeffert; vt einweichen.

steeple ['stiːpl] n Kirchturm m; ~**chase** Hindernisrennen nt; ~**jack** Turmarbeiter m.

steeply ['stiːplɪ] ad steil.

steepness ['stiːpnəs] n Steilheit f.

steer [stɪə*] n Mastochse m; vti steuern; *car etc* lenken; ~**ing** (*Aut*) Steuerung f; ~**ing column** Lenksäule f; ~**ing wheel** Steuer- or Lenkrad nt.

stellar ['stelə*] a Stern(en)-.

stem [stem] n (*Biol*) Stengel m, Stiel m; (*of glass*) Stiel m; vt aufhalten; ~ **from** vi abstammen von.

stench [stentʃ] n Gestank m.

stencil ['stensl] n Schablone f; (*paper*) Matrize f; vt (auf)drucken.

stenographer [steˈnɒɡrəfə*] n Stenograph(in f) m.

step [step] n Schritt m; (*stair*) Stufe f; **to take** ~**s** Schritte unternehmen; vi treten, schreiten; ~ **=** ~ **ladder**; ~ **down** vi (*fig*) abtreten; ~ **up** vt steigern; ~**-brother** Stiefbruder m; ~**-child** Stiefkind nt; ~**-father** Stiefvater m; ~**-ladder** Trittleiter f; ~**-mother** Stiefmutter f.

steppe [step] n Steppe f.

stepping stone ['stepɪŋstəʊn] n Stein m; (*fig*) Sprungbrett nt.

stereo ['stɪərɪəʊ] n Stereoanlage f; ~**phonic** a stereophonisch; ~**type** n Prototyp m; vt stereotypieren; (*fig*) stereotyp machen.

sterile ['steraɪl] a steril, keimfrei; *person* unfruchtbar; (*after operation*) steril.

sterility [steˈrɪlɪtɪ] n Unfruchtbarkeit f, Sterilität f.

sterilization [sterɪlaɪˈzeɪʃən] n Sterilisation f.

sterilize ['sterɪlaɪz] vt (*make unproductive*) unfruchtbar machen; (*make germfree*) sterilisieren, keimfrei machen.

sterling ['stɜːlɪŋ] a (*Fin*) Sterling-; *silver* von Standardwert; *character* bewährt, gediegen; **£** ~ Pfund Sterling; ~ **area** Sterlingblock m.

stern a, ~**ly** ad [stɜːn, -lɪ] streng; n Heck nt, Achterschiff nt; ~**ness** Strenge f.

stethoscope ['steθəskəʊp] n Stethoskop nt, Hörrohr nt.

stevedore ['sti:vədɔ:*] n Schauermann m.

stew [stju:] n Eintopf m; vti schmoren.

steward ['stju:əd] n Steward m; (in club) Kellner m; (organizer) Verwalter m; ~ess Stewardess f.

stick [stɪk] n Stock m, Stecken m; (of chalk etc) Stück nt; irreg vt (stab) stechen; (fix) stecken; (put) stellen; (gum) (an)kleben; (col: tolerate) vertragen; vi (stop) steckenbleiben; (get stuck) klemmen; (hold fast) kleben, haften; ~ out vi (project) hervorstehen aus; ~ up vi (project) in die Höhe stehen; ~ up for vt (defend) eintreten für; ~er Klebezettel m, Aufkleber m.

stickleback ['stɪklbæk] n Stichling m.

stickler ['stɪklə*] n Pedant m (for in +acc).

stick-up ['stɪkʌp] n (col) (Raub)überfall m.

sticky ['stɪkɪ] a klebrig; atmosphere stickig.

stiff [stɪf] a steif; (difficult) schwierig, hart; paste dick, zäh; drink stark; ~en vt versteifen, (ver)stärken; vi sich versteifen; ~ness Steifheit f.

stifle ['staɪfl] vt yawn etc unterdrücken.

stifling ['staɪflɪŋ] a atmosphere drückend.

stigma ['stɪgmə] n (disgrace) Stigma nt.

stile [staɪl] n Steige f.

still [stɪl] a still; ad (immer) noch; (anyhow) immerhin; ~born a totgeboren; ~ life Stilleben nt; ~ness Stille f.

stilt [stɪlt] n Stelze f.

stilted ['stɪltɪd] a gestelzt.

stimulant ['stɪmjʊlənt] n Anregungsmittel nt, Stimulans nt.

stimulate ['stɪmjʊleɪt] vt anregen, stimulieren.

stimulating ['stɪmjʊleɪtɪŋ] a anregend, stimulierend.

stimulation [stɪmjʊ'leɪʃən] n Anregung f, Stimulation f.

stimulus ['stɪmjʊləs] n Anregung f, Reiz m.

sting [stɪŋ] n Stich m; (organ) Stachel m; vti irreg stechen; (on skin) brennen.

stingily ['stɪndʒɪlɪ] ad knickerig, geizig.

stinginess ['stɪndʒɪnəs] n Geiz m.

stinging nettle ['stɪŋɪŋnetl] n Brennessel f.

stingy ['stɪndʒɪ] a geizig, knauserig.

stink [stɪŋk] n Gestank m; vi irreg stinken; ~er (col) (person) gemeine(r) Hund m; (problem) böse Sache f; ~ing a (fig) widerlich; ~ing rich steinreich.

stint [stɪnt] n Pensum nt; (period) Betätigung f; vt einschränken, knapphalten.

stipend ['staɪpend] n Gehalt nt.

stipulate ['stɪpjʊleɪt] vt festsetzen.

stipulation [stɪpjʊ'leɪʃən] n Bedingung f.

stir [stɜ:*] n Bewegung f; (Cook) Rühren nt; (sensation) Aufsehen nt; vt (um)rühren; vi sich rühren; ~ up vt mob aufhetzen; fire entfachen; mixture umrühren; dust aufwirbeln; to ~ things up Ärger machen; ~ring a ergreifend.

stirrup ['stɪrəp] n Steigbügel m.

stitch [stɪtʃ] n (with needle) Stich m; (Med) Faden m; (of knitting) Masche f; (pain)

Stich m, Stechen nt; vt nähen.

stoat [stəʊt] n Wiesel nt.

stock [stɒk] n Vorrat m; (Comm) (Waren)lager nt; (live~) Vieh nt; (Cook) Brühe f; (Fin) Grundkapital nt; a stets vorrätig; (standard) Normal-; vt versehen, versorgen; (in shop) führen; **in** ~ auf Vorrat; **to take** ~ Inventur machen; (fig) Bilanz ziehen; **to** ~ **up with** Reserven anlegen von; ~**ade** [stɒ'keɪd] Palisade f; ~**broker** Börsenmakler m; ~ **exchange** Börse f.

stocking ['stɒkɪŋ] n Strumpf m.

stockist ['stɒkɪst] n Händler m.

stock market ['stɒkmɑ:kɪt] n Börse f, Effektenmarkt m.

stockpile ['stɒkpaɪl] n Vorrat m; **nuclear** ~ Kernwaffenvorräte pl; vt aufstapeln.

stocktaking ['stɒkteɪkɪŋ] n Inventur f, Bestandsaufnahme f.

stocky ['stɒkɪ] a untersetzt.

stodgy ['stɒdʒɪ] a füllend, stopfend; (fig) langweilig, trocken.

stoic ['stəʊɪk] n Stoiker m; ~**al** a stoisch; ~**ism** ['stəʊɪsɪzəm] Stoizismus m; (fig) Gelassenheit f.

stoke [stəʊk] vt schüren; ~**r** Heizer m.

stole [stəʊl] n Stola f; ~ **n** a gestohlen.

stolid ['stɒlɪd] a schwerfällig; silence stur.

stomach ['stʌmək] n Bauch m, Magen m; **I have no** ~ **for it** das ist nichts für mich; vt vertragen; ~**-ache** Magen- or Bauchschmerzen pl.

stone [stəʊn] n Stein m; (seed) Stein m, Kern m; (weight) Gewichtseinheit f = 6.35 kg; a steinern, Stein-; vt entkernen; (kill) steinigen; ~**-cold** a eiskalt; ~**-deaf** a stocktaub; ~**mason** Steinmetz m; ~**work** Mauerwerk nt.

stony ['stəʊnɪ] a steinig.

stool [stu:l] n Hocker m.

stoop [stu:p] vi sich bücken.

stop [stɒp] n Halt m; (bus~) Haltestelle f; (punctuation) Punkt m; vt stoppen, anhalten; (bring to end) aufhören (mit), sein lassen; vi aufhören; (clock) stehenbleiben; (remain) bleiben; **to** ~ **doing sth** aufhören, etw zu tun; ~ **it!** hör auf (damit)!; ~ **dead** vi plötzlich aufhören, innehalten; ~ **in** vi (at home) zu Hause bleiben; ~ **off** vi kurz haltmachen; ~ **out** vi (of house) ausbleiben; ~ **over** vi übernachten, über Nacht bleiben; ~ **up** vi (at night) aufbleiben; vt hole zustopfen, verstopfen; ~**-lights** pl (Aut) Bremslichter pl; ~**over** (on journey) Zwischenaufenthalt m; ~**page** ['stɒpɪdʒ] (An)halten nt; (traffic) Verkehrsstockung f; (strike) Arbeitseinstellung f; ~**per** Propfen m, Stöpsel m; ~**-press** letzte Meldung f; ~**watch** Stoppuhr f.

storage ['stɔːrɪdʒ] n Lagerung f.

store [stɔː*] n Vorrat m; (place) Lager nt, Warenhaus nt; (large shop) Kaufhaus nt; vt lagern; ~ **up** vt sich eindecken mit; ~**room** Lagerraum m, Vorratsraum m.

storey ['stɔːrɪ] n (Brit) Stock m, Stockwerk nt.

stork [stɔːk] n Storch m.

storm [stɔːm] n (lit, fig) Sturm m; vti stürmen; **to take by** ~ im Sturm

nehmen; ~-**cloud** Gewitterwolke *f*; ~**y** a
stürmisch.

story ['stɔːrɪ] *n* Geschichte *f*, Erzählung *f*;
(*lie*) Märchen *nt*: (*US: storey*) Stock *m*,
Stockwerk *nt*; ~**book** Geschichtenbuch
nt; ~**teller** Geschichtenerzähler *m*.

stout [staʊt] *a* (*bold*) mannhaft, tapfer; (*too
fat*) beleibt, korpulent; ~**ness** Festigkeit
f; (*of body*) Korpulenz *f*.

stove [stəʊv] *n* (Koch)herd *m*; (*for heating*)
Ofen *m*.

stow [stəʊ] *vt* verstauen; ~**away** blinde(r)
Passagier *m*.

straddle ['strædl] *vt horse, fence* rittlings
sitzen auf (+*dat*); (*fig*) überbrücken.

strafe [strɑːf]   *vt*   beschießen,
bombardieren.

straggle ['strægl] *vi* (*branches etc*)
wuchern; (*people*) nachhinken; ~**r**
Nachzügler *m*.

straight [streɪt] *a* gerade; (*honest*) offen,
ehrlich; (*in order*) in Ordnung; *drink pur*,
unverdünnt;   *ad* (*direct*) direkt,
geradewegs; *n* (*Sport*) Gerade *f*; ~**away**
ad sofort, unverzüglich; ~ **off** *ad* sofort;
direkt nacheinander; ~ **on** *ad* geradeaus;
~**en** *vt* (*also* ~**en out**) (*lit*) gerade
machen; (*fig*) in Ordnung bringen,
klarstellen; ~**forward**   *a*   einfach,
unkompliziert.

strain [streɪn] *n* Belastung *f*; (*streak, trace*)
Zug *m*; (*of music*) Fetzen *m*; *vt* überanstrengen; (*stretch*) anspannen; *muscle*
zerren; (*filter*) (durch)seihen; **don't** ~
yourself überanstrenge dich nicht; *vi*
(*make effort*) sich anstrengen; ~**ed** *a*
laugh gezwungen; *relations* gespannt; ~**er**
Sieb *nt*.

strait [streɪt] *n* Straße *f*, Meerenge *f*;
~**ened** *a circumstances* beschränkt;
~-**jacket** Zwangsjacke *f*; ~-**laced** *a*
engherzig, streng.

strand [strænd] *n* (*lit, fig*) Faden *m*; (*of
hair*) Strähne *f*; **to be** ~**ed** (*lit, fig*)
gestrandet sein.

strange [streɪndʒ] *a* fremd; (*unusual*)
merkwürdig, seltsam; ~**ly** *ad* merkwürdig;   fremd;   ~**ly   enough**
merkwürdigerweise; ~**ness** Fremdheit *f*;
~**r** Fremde(r) *mf*; **I'm a** ~**r here** ich bin
hier fremd.

strangle ['stræŋgl]   *vt* erdrosseln,
erwürgen; ~**hold** (*fig*) Unklammerung *f*.

strangulation   [stræŋgjʊ'leɪʃən]   *n*
Erdrosseln *nt*.

strap [stræp] *n* Riemen *m*; (*on clothes*)
Träger *m*; *vt* (*fasten*) festschnallen; ~**less**
a dress trägerlos; ~**ping** *a* stramm.

stratagem ['strætədʒəm] *n* (Kriegs)list *f*.

strategic *a*, ~**ally** *ad* [strə'tiːdʒɪk, -əlɪ]
strategisch.

strategist ['strætədʒɪst] *n* Stratege *m*.

strategy ['strætədʒɪ] *n* Kriegskunst *f*; (*fig*)
Strategie *f*.

stratosphere   ['strætəʊsfɪə*]   *n*
Stratosphäre *f*.

stratum ['strɑːtəm] *n* Schicht *f*.

straw [strɔː] *n* Stroh *nt*; (*single stalk,
drinking* —) Strohhalm *m*; a Stroh-;
~**berry** Erdbeere *f*.

stray [streɪ] *n* verirrte(s) Tier *nt*; *vi* herum-
streunen; *a animal* verirrt; *thought* zufällig.

streak [striːk] *n* Streifen *m*; (*in character*)
Einschlag *m*; (*in hair*) Strähne *f*; ~ **of bad
luck** Pechsträhne *f*; *vt* streifen; ~**y** *a*
gestreift; *bacon* durchwachsen.

stream [striːm] *n* (*brook*) Bach *m*; (*fig*)
Strom *m*; (*flow of liquid*) Strom *m*, Flut *f*; *vi*
strömen, fluten; ~**er** (*pennon*) Wimpel *m*;
(*of. paper*) Luftschlange *f*; ~-**lined** *a*
stromlinienförmig; (*effective*) rationell.

street [striːt] *n* Straße *f*; ~**car** (*US*)
Straßenbahn *f*; ~ **lamp** Straßenlaterne *f*.

strength [streŋθ] *n* Stärke *f* (*also fig*);
Kraft *f*; ~**en** *vt* (ver)stärken.

strenuous ['strenjʊəs] *a* anstrengend; ~**ly**
ad angestrengt.

stress [stres] *n* Druck *m*; (*mental*) Streß *m*;
(*Gram*) Betonung *f*; *vt* betonen.

stretch [stretʃ] *n* Stück *nt*, Strecke *f*; *vt*
ausdehnen, strecken; *vi* sich erstrecken;
(*person*) sich strecken; **at a** ~ (*continuously*) ununterbrochen; ~ **out** *vi* sich
ausstrecken;   *vt*   ausstrecken;   ~**er**
Tragbahre *f*.

stricken ['strɪkən] *a person* befallen,
ergriffen; *city, country* heimgesucht.

strict [strɪkt] *a* (*exact*) genau; (*severe*)
streng; ~**ly** *ad* streng, genau; ~**ly
speaking** streng *or* genau genommen;
~**ness** Strenge *f*.

stride [straɪd] *n* lange(r) Schritt *m*; *vi irreg*
schreiten.

strident ['straɪdənt] *a* schneidend, durchdringend.

strife [straɪf] *n* Streit *m*.

strike [straɪk] *n* Streik *m*, Ausstand *m*; (*discovery*) Fund *m*; (*attack*) Schlag *m*; *irreg vt*
(*hit*) schlagen; treffen; (*collide*) stoßen
gegen; (*come to mind*) einfallen (+*dat*);
(*stand out*) auffallen; (*find*) stoßen auf
(+*acc*), finden; *vi* (*stop work*) streiken;
(*attack*) zuschlagen; (*clock*) schlagen; ~
down *vt* (*lay low*) niederschlagen; ~ **out**
vt (*cross out*) ausstreichen; ~ **up** *vt music*
anstimmen; *friendship* schließen; ~ **pay**
Streikgeld *nt*; ~**r** Streikende(r) *mf*.

striking *a*, ~**ly** *ad* ['straɪkɪŋ, -lɪ]
auffallend, bemerkenswert.

string [strɪŋ] *n* Schnur *f*, Kordel *f*, Bindfaden *m*; (*row*) Reihe *f*; (*Mus*) Saite *f*; ~-
bean grüne Bohne *f*.

stringency ['strɪndʒənsɪ] *n* Schärfe *f*.

stringent ['strɪndʒənt] *a* streng, scharf.

strip [strɪp] *n* Streifen *m*; *vt* (*uncover*)
abstreifen, abziehen; *clothes* ausziehen;
(*Tech*) auseinandernehmen; *vi* (*undress*)
sich ausziehen; ~-**cartoon** Bildserie *f*.

stripe [straɪp] *n* Streifen *m*; ~**d** *a*
gestreift.

strip light ['strɪplaɪt] *n* Leuchtröhre *f*.

stripper ['strɪpə*] *n* Stripteasetänzerin *f*.

striptease ['strɪptiːz] *n* Striptease *nt*.

strive [straɪv] *vi irreg* streben (*for nach*).

stroke [strəʊk] *n* Schlag *m*, Hieb *m*; (*swim,
row*) Stoß *m*; (*Tech*) Hub *m*; (*Med*)
Schlaganfall *m*; (*caress*) Streichein *nt*; *vt*
streicheln; **at a** ~ mit einem Schlag; **on
the** ~ **of 5** Schlag 5.

stroll [strəʊl] *n* Spaziergang *m*; *vi*

spazierengehen, schlendern.

strong [strɒŋ] *a* stark; (*firm*) fest; **they are 50 ~** sie sind 50 Mann stark; **~hold** Hochburg *f*; **~ly** *ad* stark; **~room** Tresor *m*.

structural ['strʌktʃərəl] *a* strukturell.

structure ['strʌktʃə*] *n* Struktur *f*, Aufbau *m*; (*building*) Gebäude *nt*, Bau *m*.

struggle ['strʌgl] *n* Kampf *m*, Anstrengung *f*; *vi* (*fight*) kämpfen; **to ~ to do sth** sich (ab)mühen etw zu tun.

strum [strʌm] *vt guitar* klimpern auf (+*dat*).

strung [strʌŋ] *see* **highly**.

strut [strʌt] *n* Strebe *f*, Stütze *f*; *vi* stolzieren.

strychnine ['strɪknɪːn] *n* Strychnin *nt*.

stub [stʌb] *n* Stummel *m*; (*of cigarette*) Kippe *f*.

stubble ['stʌbl] *n* Stoppel *f*.

stubbly ['stʌblɪ] *a* stoppelig, Stoppel-.

stubborn *a*, **~ly** *ad* ['stʌbən, -lɪ] stur, hartnäckig; **~ness** Sturheit *f*, Hartnäckigkeit *f*.

stubby ['stʌbɪ] *a* untersetzt.

stucco ['stʌkəʊ] *n* Stuck *m*.

stuck-up ['stʌk'ʌp] *a* hochnäsig.

stud [stʌd] *n* (*nail*) Beschlagnagel *m*; (*button*) Kragenknopf *m*; (*number of horses*) Stall *m*; (*place*) Gestüt *nt*; **~ded with** übersät mit.

student ['stjuːdənt] *n* Student(in *f*) *m*; (*US also*) Schüler(in *f*) *m*; **fellow ~** Kommilitone *m*, Kommilitonin *f*.

studied ['stʌdɪd] *a* absichtlich.

studio ['stjuːdɪəʊ] *n* Studio *nt*; (*for artist*) Atelier *nt*.

studious *a*, **~ly** *ad* ['stjuːdɪəs, -lɪ] lernbegierig.

study ['stʌdɪ] *n* Studium *nt*; (*investigation also*) Untersuchung *f*; (*room*) Arbeitszimmer *nt*; (*essay etc*) Studie *f*; *vt* studieren; *face* erforschen; *evidence* prüfen; *vi* studieren; **~ group** Arbeitsgruppe *f*.

stuff [stʌf] *n* Stoff *m*; (*col*) Zeug *nt*; **that's hot ~!** das ist Klasse!; *vt* stopfen, füllen; *animal* ausstopfen; **to ~ o.s.** sich vollstopfen; **~ed full** vollgepfropft; **~iness** Schwüle *f*; Spießigkeit *f*; **~ing** Füllung *f*; **~y** *a room* schwül; *person* spießig.

stumble ['stʌmbl] *vi* stolpern; **to ~ on** zufällig stoßen auf (+*acc*).

stumbling block ['stʌmblɪŋblɒk] *n* Hindernis *nt*, Stein *m* des Anstoßes.

stump [stʌmp] *n* Stumpf *m*; *vt* umwerfen.

stun [stʌn] *vt* betäuben; (*shock*) niederschmettern.

stunning ['stʌnɪŋ] *a* betäubend; *news* überwältigend, umwerfend; **~ly beautiful** traumhaft schön.

stunt [stʌnt] *n* Kunststück *nt*, Trick *m*; *vt* verkümmern lassen; **~ed** *a* verkümmert.

stupefy ['stjuːpɪfaɪ] *vt* betäuben; (*by news*) bestürzen; **~ing** *a* betäubend; bestürzend.

stupendous [stjuːˈpendəs] *a* erstaunlich, enorm.

stupid *a*, **~ly** *ad* ['stjuːpɪd, -lɪ] dumm; **~ity** [stjuːˈpɪdɪtɪ] Dummheit *f*.

stupor ['stjuːpə*] *n* Betäubung *f*.

sturdily ['stɜːdɪlɪ] *ad* kräftig, stabil.

sturdiness [ʃtɜːdɪnəs] *n* Robustheit *f*.

sturdy ['stɜːdɪ] *a* kräftig, robust.

stutter ['stʌtə*] *n* Stottern *nt*; *vi* stottern.

sty [staɪ] *n* Schweinestall *m*.

stye [staɪ] *n* Gerstenkorn *nt*.

style [staɪl] *n* Stil *m*; (*fashion*) Mode *f*; **hair ~** Frisur *f*; **in ~** mit Stil; *vt hair* frisieren.

styling ['staɪlɪŋ] *n* (*of car etc*) Formgebung *f*.

stylish *a*, **~ly** *ad* ['staɪlɪʃ, -lɪ] modisch, schick, flott.

stylized ['staɪlaɪzd] *a* stilisiert.

stylus ['staɪləs] *n* (*Grammophon*)nadel *f*.

styptic ['stɪptɪk] *a*: **~ pencil** blutstillende(r) Stift *m*.

suave [swɑːv] *a* zuvorkommend.

sub- [sʌb] *pref* Unter-.

subconscious ['sʌbˈkɒnʃəs] *a* unterbewußt; *n*: **the ~** das Unterbewußte.

subdivide ['sʌbdɪˈvaɪd] *vt* unterteilen.

subdivision ['sʌbdɪvɪʒən] *n* Unterteilung *f*; (*department*) Unterabteilung *f*.

subdue [səbˈdjuː] *vt* unterwerfen; **~d** *a lighting* gedämpft; *person* still.

subject ['sʌbdʒɪkt] *n* (*of kingdom*) Untertan *m*; (*citizen*) Staatsangehörige(r) *mf*; (*topic*) Thema *nt*; (*Sch*) Fach *nt*; (*Gram*) Subjekt *nt*, Satzgegenstand *m*; [səbˈdʒekt] *vt* (*subdue*) unterwerfen, abhängig machen; (*expose*) aussetzen; **to be ~ to** unterworfen sein (+*dat*); (*exposed*) ausgesetzt sein (+*dat*); **~ion** [səbˈdʒekʃən] (*conquering*) Unterwerfung *f*; (*being controlled*) Abhängigkeit *f*; **~ive** *a*, **~ively** *ad* [səbˈdʒektɪv, -lɪ] subjektiv; **~ matter** Thema *nt*.

sub judice [sʌbˈdjuːdɪsɪ] *a* in gerichtliche(r) Untersuchung.

subjunctive [səbˈdʒʌŋktɪv] *n* Konjunktiv *m*, Möglichkeitsform *f*; *a* Konjunktiv-, konjunktivisch.

sublet ['sʌbˈlet] *vt irreg* untervermieten.

sublime [səˈblaɪm] *a* erhaben.

submarine [sʌbməˈriːn] *n* Unterseeboot *nt*, U-Boot *nt*.

submerge [səbˈmɜːdʒ] *vt* untertauchen; (*flood*) überschwemmen; *vi* untertauchen.

submission [səbˈmɪʃən] *n* (*obedience*) Ergebenheit *f*, Gehorsam *m*; (*claim*) Behauptung *f*; (*of plan*) Unterbreitung *f*.

submit [səbˈmɪt] *vt* behaupten; *plan* unterbreiten; *vi* (*give in*) sich ergeben.

subnormal ['sʌbˈnɔːml] *a* minderbegabt.

subordinate [səˈbɔːdɪnət] *a* untergeordnet; *n* Untergebene(r) *mf*.

subpoena [səˈpiːnə] *n* Vorladung *f*; *vt* vorladen.

subscribe [səbˈskraɪb] *vi* spenden, Geld geben; (*to view etc*) unterstützen, beipflichten (+*dat*); (*to newspaper*) abonnieren (*to acc*); **~r** (*to periodical*) Abonnent *m*; (*Tel*) Telefonteilnehmer *m*.

subscription [səbˈskrɪpʃən] *n* Abonnement *nt*; (*Mitglieds*)beitrag *m*.

subsequent ['sʌbsɪkwənt] *a* folgend, später; **~ly** *ad* später.

subside [səb'saɪd] *vi* sich senken; ~**nce** [sʌb'saɪdəns] Senkung *f*.

subsidiary [səb'sɪdɪərɪ] *n* Neben-; *n* (*company*) Zweig *m*, Tochtergesellschaft *f*.

subsidize ['sʌbsɪdaɪz] *vt* subventionieren.

subsidy ['sʌbsɪdɪ] *n* Subvention *f*.

subsistence [səb'sɪstəns] *n* Unterhalt *m*; ~ **level** Existenzminimum *nt*.

substance ['sʌbstəns] *n* Substanz *f*, Stoff *m*; (*most important part*) Hauptbestandteil *m*.

substandard ['sʌb'stændəd] *a* unterdurch-schnittlich.

substantial [səb'stænʃəl] *a* (*strong*) fest, kräftig; (*important*) wesentlich; ~**ly** *ad* erheblich.

substantiate [səb'stænʃɪeɪt] *vt* begründen, belegen.

substation ['sʌbsteɪʃən] *n* (*Elec*) Nebenwerk *nt*.

substitute ['sʌbstɪtjuːt] *n* Ersatz *m*; *vt* ersetzen.

substitution [sʌbstɪ'tjuːʃən] *n* Ersetzung *f*.

subterfuge ['sʌbtəfjuːdʒ] *n* Vorwand *f*; Tricks *pl*.

subterranean [sʌbtə'reɪnɪən] *a* unterirdisch.

subtitle ['sʌbtaɪtl] *n* Untertitel *m*.

subtle ['sʌtl] *a* fein; (*sly*) raffiniert; ~**ty** subtile Art *f*, Raffinesse *f*.

subtly ['sʌtlɪ] *ad* fein, raffiniert.

subtract [səb'trækt] *vt* abziehen, sub-trahieren; ~**ion** [səb'trækʃən] Abziehen *nt*, Subtraktion *f*.

subtropical ['sʌb'trɒpɪkəl] *a* subtropisch.

suburb ['sʌbɜːb] *n* Vorort *m*; ~**an** [sə'bɜːbən] *a* Vorort(s)-, Stadtrand-; ~**ia** [sə'bɜːbɪə] Vorstadt *f*.

subvention [səb'venʃən] *n* (*US*) Unter-stützung *f*, Subvention *f*.

subversive [səb'vɜːsɪv] *a* subversiv.

subway ['sʌbweɪ] *n* (*US*) U-Bahn *f*, Unter-grundbahn *f*; (*Brit*) Unterführung *f*.

sub-zero ['sʌb'zɪərəʊ] *a* unter Null, unter dem Gefrierpunkt.

succeed [sək'siːd] *vi* gelingen (+*dat*), Erfolg haben; **he** ~**ed** es gelang ihm; *vt* (*nach*)folgen (+*dat*); ~**ing** *a* (*nach*)-folgend.

success [sək'ses] *n* Erfolg *m*; ~**ful** *a*, ~**fully** *ad* erfolgreich; ~**ion** [sək'seʃən] (*Aufeinander*)folge *f*; (*to throne*) Nach-folge *f*; ~**ive** *a* [sək'sesɪv] aufeinander-folgend; ~**or** Nachfolger(in *f*) *m*.

succinct [sək'sɪŋkt] *a* kurz und bündig, knapp.

succulent ['sʌkjʊlənt] *a* saftig.

succumb [sə'kʌm] *vi* zusammenbrechen (*to* unter +*dat*); (*yield*) nachgeben; (*die*) erliegen.

such [sʌtʃ] *a* solche(r, s); ~ *a* so ein; ~ **a** lot so viel; ~ **is** life so ist das Leben; ~ **is my wish** das ist mein Wunsch; ~ **as** wie; *pron* solch; ~ **as I have** die, die ich habe; ~**like** *a* derartig; *pron* dergleichen.

suck [sʌk] *vt* saugen; *ice cream etc* lecken; *toffee etc* lutschen; *vi* saugen; ~**er** (*col*) Idiot *m*, Dummkopf *m*.

suckle ['sʌkl] *vt* säugen; *child* stillen; *vi* saugen.

suction ['sʌkʃən] *n* Saugen *nt*, Saugkraft *f*.

sudden *a*, ~**ly** *ad* ['sʌdn, -lɪ] plötzlich; **all of a** ~ ganz plötzlich, auf einmal; ~**ness** Plötzlichkeit *f*.

sue [suː] *vt* verklagen.

suède [sweɪd] *n* Wildleder *nt*; *a* Wildleder-.

suet [suɪt] *n* Nierenfett *nt*.

suffer ['sʌfə*] *vt* (er)leiden; (*old: allow*) zulassen, dulden; *vi* leiden; ~**er** Leidende(r) *mf*; ~**ering** Leiden *nt*.

suffice [sə'faɪs] *vi* genügen.

sufficient *a*, ~**ly** *ad* [sə'fɪʃənt, -lɪ] ausreichend.

suffix ['sʌfɪks] *n* Nachsilbe *f*.

suffocate ['sʌfəkeɪt] *vti* ersticken.

suffocation [sʌfə'keɪʃən] *n* Ersticken *nt*.

suffragette [sʌfrə'dʒet] *n* Suffragette *f*.

sugar ['ʃʊgə*] *n* Zucker *m*; *vt* zuckern; ~ **beet** Zuckerrübe *f*; ~ **cane** Zuckerrohr *nt*; ~**y** *a* süß.

suggest [sə'dʒest] *vt* vorschlagen; (*show*) schließen lassen auf (+*acc*); **what does this painting** ~ **to you?** was drückt das Bild für dich aus?; ~**ion** [sə'dʒestʃən] Vorschlag *m*; ~**ive** *a* anregend; (*indecent*) zweideutig; **to be** ~**ive of sth** an etw (*acc*) erinnern.

suicidal [suɪ'saɪdl] *a* selbstmörderisch; **that's** ~ das ist Selbstmord.

suicide ['suɪsaɪd] *n* Selbstmord *m*; **to commit** ~ Selbstmord begehen.

suit [suːt] *n* Anzug *m*; (*Cards*) Farbe *f*; *vt* passen (+*dat*); *clothes* stehen (+*dat*); (*adapt*) anpassen; ~ **yourself** mach doch, was du willst; ~**ability** [suːtə'bɪlɪtɪ] Eignung *f*; ~**able** *a* geeignet, passend; ~**ably** *ad* passend, angemessen; ~**case** (Hand)koffer *m*.

suite [swiːt] *n* (*of rooms*) Zimmerflucht *f*; (*of furniture*) Einrichtung *f*; (*Mus*) Suite *f*; **three-piece** ~ Couchgarnitur *f*.

sulfur ['sʌlfə*] *n* (*US*) = **sulphur**.

sulk [sʌlk] *vi* schmollen; ~**y** *a* schmollend.

sullen ['sʌlən] *a* (*gloomy*) düster; (*bad-tempered*) mürrisch, verdrossen.

sulphur ['sʌlfə*] *n* Schwefel *m*.

sulphuric [sʌl'fjʊərɪk] *a:* ~ **acid** Schwefelsäure *f*.

sultan ['sʌltən] *n* Sultan *m*; ~**a** [sʌl'tɑːnə] (*woman*) Sultanin *f*; (*raisin*) Sultanine *f*.

sultry ['sʌltrɪ] *a* schwül.

sum [sʌm] *n* Summe *f*; (*money also*) Betrag *m*; (*arithmetic*) Rechenaufgabe *f*; ~**s** *pl* Rechnen *nt*; ~ **up** *vti* zusammenfassen; ~**marize** *vt* kurz zusammenfassen; ~**mary** Zusammenfassung *f*; (*of book etc*) Inhaltsangabe *f*.

summer ['sʌmə*] *n* Sommer *m*; *a* Sommer-; ~**house** (*in garden*) Garten-haus *nt*; ~**time** Sommerzeit *f*.

summing-up ['sʌmɪŋ'ʌp] *n* Zusammen-fassung *f*.

summit ['sʌmɪt] *n* Gipfel *m*; ~ **conference** Gipfelkonferenz *f*.

summon ['sʌmən] *vt* bestellen, kommen lassen; (*Jur*) vorladen; (*gather up*) auf-bieten, aufbringen; ~**s** (*Jur*) Vorladung *f*.

sump [sʌmp] *n* Ölwanne *f*.

sumptuous ['sʌmptjuəs] *a* prächtig;
~**ness** Pracht *f.*

sun [sʌn] *n* Sonne *f*; ~**bathe** *vi* sich
sonnen; ~**bathing** Sonnenbaden *nt*;
~**burn** Sonnenbrand *m*; **to be** ~**burnt**
einen Sonnenbrand haben.

Sunday ['sʌndeɪ] *n* Sonntag *m.*

sundial ['sʌndaɪəl] *n* Sonnenuhr *f.*

sundown ['sʌndaʊn] *n* Sonnenuntergang
m.

sundry ['sʌndrɪ] *a* verschieden; *n*:
sundries *pl* Verschiedene(s) *nt*; **all and**
~ **alle.**

sunflower ['sʌnflaʊə*] *n* Sonnenblume *f.*

sunglasses ['sʌnglɑːsɪz] *npl* Sonnenbrille *f.*

sunken ['sʌŋkən] *a* versunken; *eyes*
eingesunken.

sunlight ['sʌnlaɪt] *n* Sonnenlicht *nt.*

sunlit ['sʌnlɪt] *a* sonnenbeschienen.

sunny ['sʌnɪ] *a* sonnig.

sunrise ['sʌnraɪz] *n* Sonnenaufgang *m.*

sunset ['sʌnset] *n* Sonnenuntergang *m.*

sunshade ['sʌnʃeɪd] *n* Sonnenschirm *m.*

sunshine ['sʌnʃaɪn] *n* Sonnenschein *m.*

sunspot ['sʌnspɒt] *n* Sonnenfleck *m.*

sunstroke ['sʌnstrəʊk] *n* Hitzschlag *m.*

sun tan ['sʌntæn] *n* (Sonnen)bräune *f*; `to
get a` ~ braun werden.

suntrap ['sʌntræp] *n* sonnige(r) Platz *m.*

sunup ['sʌnʌp] *n* (*col*) Sonnenaufgang *m.*

super ['suːpə*] *a* (*col*) prima, klasse;
Super-, Über-.

superannuation [suːpərænjʊeɪʃən] *n*
Pension *f.*

superb *a*, ~**ly** *ad* [suː'pɜːb, -lɪ]
ausgezeichnet, hervorragend.

supercilious [suːpə'sɪlɪəs] *a* herablassend.

superficial *a*, ~**ly** *ad* [suːpə'fɪʃəl, -ɪ] oberflächlich.

superfluous [suː'pɜːflʊəs] *a* überflüssig.

superhuman [suːpə'hjuːmən] *a effort* über-
menschlich.

superimpose [suːpərɪm'pəʊz] *vt*
übereinanderlegen.

superintendent [suːpərɪn'tendənt] *n*
Polizeichef *m.*

superior [suː'pɪərɪə*] *a* (*higher*) höher-
(stehend); (*better*) besser; (*proud*)
überlegen; *n* Vorgesetzte(r) *mf*; ~**ity**
[sʊpɪərɪ'ɒrɪtɪ] Überlegenheit *f.*

superlative [suː'pɜːlətɪv] *a* höchste(r,s); *n*
(*Gram*) Superlativ *m.*

superman ['suːpəmæn] *n* Übermensch *m.*

supermarket ['suːpəmɑːkɪt] *n* Supermarkt
m.

supernatural [suːpə'nætʃərəl] *a*
übernatürlich.

superpower ['suːpəpaʊə*] *n* Weltmacht *f.*

supersede [suːpə'siːd] *vt* ersetzen.

supersonic ['suːpə'sɒnɪk] *n* Überschall-.

superstition [suːpə'stɪʃən] *n* Aberglaube
m.

superstitious [suːpə'stɪʃəs] *a* aber-
gläubisch.

supervise ['suːpəvaɪz] *vt* beaufsichtigen,
kontrollieren.

supervision [suːpə'vɪʒən] *n* Aufsicht *f.*

supervisor ['suːpəvaɪzə*] *n* Auf-
sichtsperson *f*; ~**y** *a* Aufsichts-.

supper ['sʌpə*] *n* Abendessen *nt.*

supple ['sʌpl] *a* gelenkig, geschmeidig;
wire biegsam.

supplement ['sʌplɪmənt] *n* Ergänzung *f*;
(*in book*) Nachtrag *m*; [sʌplɪ'ment] *vt*
ergänzen; ~**ary** [sʌplɪ'mentərɪ] *a*
ergänzend, Ergänzungs-, Zusatz-.

supplier [sə'plaɪə*] *n* Lieferant *m.*

supply [sə'plaɪ] *vt* liefern; *n* Vorrat *m*;
(*supplying*) Lieferung *f*; **supplies** *pl* (*food*)
Vorräte *pl*; (*Mil*) Nachschub *m*; ~ **and
demand** Angebot *nt* und Nachfrage.

support [sə'pɔːt] *n* Unterstützung *f*; (*Tech*)
Stütze *f*; *vt* (*hold up*) stützen, tragen;
(*provide for*) ernähren; (*speak in favour of*)
befürworten, unterstützen; ~**er** Anhänger
m; ~**ing** *a programme* Bei-; *role* Neben-.

suppose [sə'pəʊz] *vti* annehmen, denken,
glauben; **I** ~ **so** ich glaube schon; ~ **he
comes** . . . angenommen, er kommt . . .;
~**dly** [sə'pəʊzɪdlɪ] *ad* angeblich.

supposing [sə'pəʊzɪŋ] *cj* angenommen.

supposition [sʌpə'zɪʃən] *n* Voraussetzung
f.

suppress [sə'pres] *vt* unterdrücken; ~**ion**
[sə'preʃən] Unterdrückung *f*; ~**or** (*Elec*)
Entstörungselement *nt.*

supra- ['suːprə] *pref* Über-.

supremacy [su'preməsɪ] *n* Vorherrschaft
f, Oberhoheit *f.*

supreme *a*, ~**ly** *ad* [su'priːm, -lɪ]
oberste(r,s), höchste(r,s).

surcharge ['sɜːtʃɑːdʒ] *n* Zuschlag *m.*

sure [ʃʊə*] *a* sicher, gewiß; **to be** ~ sicher
sein; **to be** ~ **about sth** sich (*dat*) einer
Sache sicher sein; **we are** ~ **to win** wir
werden ganz sicher gewinnen; *ad* sicher;
~**!** (*of course*) ganz bestimmt!, natürlich!,
klar!; **to make** ~ **of** sich vergewissern
(+*gen*); ~**-footed** *a* sicher (auf den
Füßen); ~**ly** *ad* (*certainly*) sicherlich,
gewiß; ~**ly it's wrong** das ist doch wohl
falsch; ~**ly not!** das ist doch wohl nicht
wahr!; ~**ty** Sicherheit *f*; (*person*) Bürge *m.*

surf [sɜːf] *n* Brandung *f.*

surface ['sɜːfɪs] *n* Oberfläche *f*; *vt roadway*
teeren; *vi* auftauchen; ~ **mail**
gewöhnliche Post *f*, Post per Bahn *f.*

surfboard ['sɜːfbɔːd] *n* Wellenreiterbrett
nt.

surfeit ['sɜːfɪt] *n* Übermaß *nt.*

surfing ['sɜːfɪŋ] *n* Wellenreiten *nt*, Surfing
nt.

surge [sɜːdʒ] *n* Woge *f*; *vi* wogen.

surgeon ['sɜːdʒən] *n* Chirurg (in *f*) *m.*

surgery ['sɜːdʒərɪ] *n* Praxis *f*; (*room*)
Sprechzimmer *nt*; (*time*) Sprechstunde *f*;
(*treatment*) operative(r) Eingriff *m*,
Operation *f*; **he needs** ~ er muß operieren
werden.

surgical ['sɜːdʒɪkəl] *a* chirurgisch.

surly ['sɜːlɪ] *a* verdrießlich, grob.

surmise [sɜː'maɪz] *vt* vermuten.

surmount [sɜː'maʊnt] *vt* überwinden.

surname ['sɜːneɪm] *n* Zuname *m.*

surpass [sɜː'pɑːs] *vt* übertreffen.

surplus ['sɜːpləs] *n* Überschuß *m*; *a* überschüssig, Über(schuß)-.

surprise [sə'praɪz] n Überraschung f; vt überraschen.

surprising [sə'praɪzɪŋ] a überraschend; ~ly ad überraschend(erweise).

surrealism [sə'rɪəlɪzəm] n Surrealismus m.

surrealist [sə'rɪəlɪst] a surrealistisch; n Surrealist m.

surrender [sə'rendə*] n Übergabe f; Kapitulation f; vi sich ergeben, kapitulieren; vt übergeben.

surreptitious a. ~ly ad [sʌrəp'tɪʃəs, -lɪ] verstohlen.

surround [sə'raʊnd] vt umgeben; (come all round) umringen; ~ed by umgeben von; ~ing a countryside umliegend; n: ~ings pl Umgebung f, (environment) Umwelt f.

surveillance [sɜː'veɪləns] n Überwachung f.

survey ['sɜːveɪ] n Übersicht f; [sɜː'veɪ] vt überblicken; land vermessen; ~ing [sə'veɪɪŋ] (of land) (Land)vermessung f; ~or [sə'veɪə*] Land(ver)messer m.

survival [sə'vaɪvəl] n Überleben nt; (sth from earlier times) Überbleibsel nt.

survive [sə'vaɪv] vti überleben.

survivor [sə'vaɪvə*] n Überlebende(r) mf.

susceptible [sə'septəbl] a empfindlich (to gegen); empfänglich (to für).

suspect ['sʌspekt] n Verdächtige(r) mf; a verdächtig; [səs'pekt] vt verdächtigen; (think) vermuten.

suspend [səs'pend] vt verschieben; (from work) suspendieren; (hang up) aufhängen; (Sport) sperren; n: ~ers pl Strumpfhalter m; (men's) Sockenhalter m; (US) Hosenträger m.

suspense [səs'pens] n Spannung f.

suspension [səs'penʃən] n (hanging) (Auf-)hängen nt, Aufhängung f; (postponing) Aufschub m; (from work) Suspendierung f; (Sport) Sperrung f; (Aut) Federung f; ~bridge Hängebrücke f.

suspicion [səs'pɪʃən] n Mißtrauen nt; Verdacht m.

suspicious a. ~ly ad [səs'pɪʃəs, -lɪ] mißtrauisch; (causing suspicion) verdächtig; ~ness Mißtrauen nt.

sustain [səs'teɪn] vt (hold up) stützen, tragen; (maintain) aufrechterhalten; (confirm) bestätigen; (Jur) anerkennen; injury davontragen; ~ed a effort anhaltend.

sustenance ['sʌstɪnəns] n Nahrung f.

swab [swɒb] n (Med) Tupfer m; vt decks schrubben; wound abtupfen.

swagger ['swægə*] vi stolzieren; (behave) prahlen, angeben.

swallow ['swɒləʊ] n (bird) Schwalbe f; (of food etc) Schluck m; vt (ver)schlucken; ~ up vt verschlingen.

swamp [swɒmp] n Sumpf m; vt überschwemmen; ~y a sumpfig.

swan [swɒn] n Schwan m; ~ song Schwanengesang m.

swap [swɒp] n Tausch m; vt (ein)tauschen (for gegen); vi tauschen.

swarm [swɔːm] n Schwarm m; vi wimmeln (with von).

swarthy ['swɔːðɪ] a dunkel, braun.

swastika ['swɒstɪkə] n Hakenkreuz nt.

swat [swɒt] vt totschlagen.

sway [sweɪ] vi schwanken; (branches) schaukeln, sich wiegen; vt schwenken; (influence) beeinflussen, umstimmen.

swear [swɛə*] vi irreg (promise) schwören; (curse) fluchen; to ~ to sth schwören auf etw (acc); ~word Fluch m.

sweat [swet] n Schweiß m; vi schwitzen; ~er n Pullover m; ~y a verschwitzt.

swede [swiːd] n Steckrübe f.

sweep [swiːp] n (cleaning) Kehren nt; (wide curve) Bogen m; (with arm) schwungvolle Bewegung f; (chimney —) Schornsteinfeger m; irreg vt fegen, kehren; vi (road) sich dahinziehen; (go quickly) rauschen; ~ away vt wegfegen; (river) wegspülen; ~ past vi vorbeisausen; ~ up vt zusammenkehren; ~ing a gesture schwungvoll; statement verallgemeinernd; ~stake Toto nt.

sweet [swiːt] n (course) Nachtisch m; (candy) Bonbon nt; a, ~ly ad süß; ~corn Zuckermais m; ~en vt süßen; (fig) versüßen; ~heart Liebste(r) mf; ~ness Süße f; ~ pea Gartenwicke f; to have a ~ tooth ein Leckermaul sein.

swell [swel] n Seegang m; a (col) todschick; irreg vt numbers vermehren; vi (also ~ up) (an)schwellen; ~ing Schwellung f.

sweltering ['sweltərɪŋ] a drückend.

swerve [swɜːv] n Ausschwenken nt; vti ausscheren, zur Seite schwenken.

swift [swɪft] n Mauersegler m; a, ~ly ad geschwind, schnell, rasch; ~ness Schnelligkeit f.

swig [swɪg] n Zug m.

swill [swɪl] n (for pigs) Schweinefutter nt; vt spülen.

swim [swɪm] n: to go for a ~ schwimmen gehen; irreg vi schwimmen; my head is ~ming mir dreht sich der Kopf; vt (cross) (durch)schwimmen; ~mer Schwimmer(in f) m; ~ming Schwimmen nt; to go ~ming schwimmen gehen; ~ming baths pl Schwimmbad nt; ~ming cap Badehaube f, Badekappe f; ~ming costume Badeanzug m; ~ming pool Schwimmbecken nt; (private) Swimming-Pool m; ~suit Badeanzug m.

swindle ['swɪndl] n Schwindel m, Betrug m; vt betrügen; ~r Schwindler m.

swine [swaɪn] n (lit, fig) Schwein nt.

swing [swɪŋ] n (child's) Schaukel f; (swinging) Schwingen nt, Schwung m; (Mus) Swing m; irreg vt schwingen, (herum-)schwenken; vi schwingen, pendeln, schaukeln; (turn quickly) schwenken; in full ~ in vollem Gange; ~ bridge Drehbrücke f; ~ door Schwingtür f.

swipe [swaɪp] n Hieb m; vt (col) (hit) hart schlagen; (steal) klauen.

swirl [swɜːl] n Wirbel m; vi wirbeln.

switch [swɪtʃ] n (Elec) Schalter m; (change) Wechsel m; vti (change) schalten; (change) wechseln; ~ off vt ab- or ausschalten; ~ on vt an- or einschalten; ~back Achterbahn f; ~board

Vermittlung f, Zentrale f; (board) Schaltbrett nt.

swivel ['swɪvl] vti (also ~ round) (sich) drehen.

swollen ['swəʊlən] a geschwollen.

swoon [swuːn] vi (old) in Ohnmacht fallen.

swoop [swuːp] n Sturzflug m; (esp by police) Razzia f; vi (also ~ **down**) stürzen.

swop [swɒp] = **swap**.

sword [sɔːd] n Schwert nt; ~**fish** Schwertfisch m; ~**sman** Fechter m.

sworn [swɔːn] a: ~ **enemies** pl Todfeinde pl.

sycamore ['sɪkəmɔː*] n (US) Platane f; (Brit) Bergahorn m.

sycophantic [sɪkə'fæntɪk] a schmeichlerisch, kriecherisch.

syllable ['sɪləbl] n Silbe f.

syllabus ['sɪləbəs] n Lehrplan m.

symbol ['sɪmbəl] n Symbol nt; ~**ic(al)** [sɪm'bɒlɪk(əl)] a symbolisch; ~**ism** symbolische Bedeutung f; (Art) Symbolismus m; ~**ize** vt versinnbildlichen, symbolisieren.

symmetrical a, ~**ly** ad [sɪ'metrɪkəl, -lɪ] symmetrisch, gleichmäßig.

symmetry ['sɪmɪtrɪ] n Symmetrie f.

sympathetic [sɪmpə'θetɪk], ~**ally** ad [-əlɪ] mitfühlend.

sympathize ['sɪmpəθaɪz] vi sympathisieren; mitfühlen; ~**r** Mitfühlende(r) mf; (Pol) Sympathisant m.

sympathy ['sɪmpəθɪ] n Mitleid nt, Mitgefühl nt; (condolence) Beileid nt.

symphonic [sɪm'fɒnɪk] a sinfonisch.

symphony ['sɪmfənɪ] n Sinfonie f; ~ **orchestra** Sinfonieorchester nt.

symposium [sɪm'pəʊzɪəm] n Tagung f.

symptom ['sɪmptəm] n Symptom nt, Anzeichen nt; ~**atic** [sɪmptə'mætɪk] a (fig) bezeichnend (of für).

synagogue ['sɪnəgɒg] n Synagoge f.

synchromesh ['sɪŋkrəʊ'meʃ] n Synchronschaltung f.

synchronize ['sɪŋkrənaɪz] vt synchronisieren; vi gleichzeitig sein or ablaufen.

syndicate ['sɪndɪkət] n Konsortium nt, Verband m, Ring m.

syndrome ['sɪndrəʊm] n Syndrom nt.

synonym ['sɪnənɪm] n Synonym nt; ~**ous** [sɪ'nɒnɪməs] a gleichbedeutend.

synopsis [sɪ'nɒpsɪs] n Abriß m, Zusammenfassung f.

syntactic [sɪn'tæktɪk] a syntaktisch.

syntax ['sɪntæks] n Syntax f.

synthesis ['sɪnθəsɪs] n Synthese f.

synthetic a, ~**ally** ad [sɪn'θetɪk, -əlɪ] synthetisch, künstlich.

syphilis ['sɪfɪlɪs] n Syphilis f.

syphon ['saɪfən] = **siphon**.

syringe [sɪ'rɪndʒ] n Spritze f.

syrup ['sɪrəp] n Sirup m; (of sugar) Melasse f.

system ['sɪstəm] n System nt; ~**atic** a, ~**atically** ad [sɪstə'mætɪk, -əlɪ] systematisch, planmäßig.

T

T, t [tiː] n T nt, t nt; **to a** ~ genau.

ta [tɑː] interj (Brit col) danke.

tab [tæb] n Schlaufe f, Aufhänger m; (name ~) Schild nt.

tabby ['tæbɪ] n (female cat) (weibliche) Katze f; a (black-striped) getigert.

tabernacle ['tæbənækl] n Tabernakel nt or m.

table ['teɪbl] n Tisch m; (list) Tabelle f, Tafel f; **to lay sth on the** ~ (fig) etw zur Diskussion stellen; vt (Parl: propose) vorlegen, einbringen.

tableau ['tæbləʊ] n lebende(s) Bild nt.

tablecloth ['teɪblklɒθ] n Tischtuch nt, Tischdecke f.

table d'hôte ['tɑːbl'dəʊt] n Tagesmenu nt.

tablemat ['teɪblmæt] n Untersatz m.

tablespoon ['teɪblspuːn] n Eßlöffel m; ~**ful** Eßlöffel(voll) m.

tablet ['tæblət] n (Med) Tablette f; (for writing) Täfelchen nt; (of paper) Schreibblock m; (of soap) Riegel m.

table talk ['teɪbltɔːk] n Tischgespräch nt.

table tennis ['teɪbltenɪs] n Tischtennis nt.

table wine ['teɪblwaɪn] n Tafelwein m.

taboo [tə'buː] n Tabu nt; a tabu.

tabulate ['tæbjʊleɪt] vt tabellarisch ordnen.

tacit a, ~**ly** ad ['tæsɪt, -lɪ] stillschweigend; ~**urn** a schweigsam, wortkarg.

tack [tæk] n (small nail) Stift m; (US: thumb~) Reißzwecke f; (stitch) Heftstich m; (Naut) Lavieren nt; (course) Kurs m.

tackle ['tækl] n (for lifting) Flaschenzug m; (Naut) Takelage f; (Sport) Tackling nt; vt (deal with) anpacken, in Angriff nehmen; person festhalten; player angehen; **he couldn't** ~ **it** er hat es nicht bewältigt.

tacky ['tækɪ] a klebrig.

tact [tækt] n Takt m; ~**ful** a, ~**fully** ad taktvoll.

tactical ['tæktɪkəl] a taktisch.

tactics ['tæktɪks] npl Taktik f.

tactless a, ~**ly** ad ['tæktləs, -lɪ] taktlos.

tadpole ['tædpəʊl] n Kaulquappe f.

taffeta ['tæfɪtə] n Taft m.

taffy ['tæfɪ] n (US) Sahnebonbon nt.

tag [tæg] n (label) Schild nt, Anhänger m; (maker's name) Etikett nt; (phrase) Floskel f, Spruch m; ~ **along** vi mitkommen; ~ **question** Bestätigungsfrage f.

tail [teɪl] n Schwanz m; (of list) Schluß m; (of comet) Schweif m; ~**s** (of coin) Zahl(seite) f; vt folgen (+dat); ~ **off** vi abfallen, schwinden; ~ **end** Schluß m, Ende nt.

tailor ['teɪlə*] n Schneider m; ~**ing** Schneidern nt, Schneiderarbeit f; ~**-made** a (lit) maßgeschneidert; (fig) wie auf den Leib geschnitten (for sb jdm).

tailwind ['teɪlwɪnd] n Rückenwind m.

tainted ['teɪntɪd] a verdorben.

take [teɪk] vt irreg nehmen; prize entgegennehmen; trip, exam machen; (capture) person fassen; town einnehmen; disease bekommen; (carry to a place) bringing; (*Math: subtract*) abziehen (*from von*); (*extract*) quotation entnehmen (*from dat*); (*get for o.s.*) sich (*dat*) nehmen; (*gain, obtain*) bekommen; (*Fin, Comm*) einnehmen; (*record*) aufnehmen; (*consume*) zu sich nehmen; (*Phot*) aufnehmen, machen; (*put up with*) hinnehmen; (*respond to*) aufnehmen; (*understand, interpret*) auffassen; (*assume*) annehmen; (*contain*) fassen, Platz haben für; (*Gram*) stehen mit; **it ~s 4 hours** man braucht 4 Stunden; **it ~s him 4 hours** er braucht 4 Stunden; **to ~ sth from sb** jdm etw wegnehmen; **to ~ part in** teilnehmen an (+*dat*); **to ~ place** stattfinden; **~ after** *vt* ähnlich sein (+*dat*); **~ back** *vt* (*return*) zurückbringen; (*retract*) zurücknehmen; (*remind*) zurückversetzen (*to* in +*acc*); **~ down** *vt* (*pull down*) abreißen; (*write down*) aufschreiben; **~ in** *vt* (*deceive*) hereinlegen; (*understand*) begreifen; (*include*) einschließen; **~ off** *vi* (*plane*) starten; *vt* (*remove*) wegnehmen, abmachen; *clothing* ausziehen; (*imitate*) nachmachen; **~ on** *vt* (*undertake*) übernehmen; (*engage*) einstellen; (*opponent*) antreten gegen; **~ out** *vt girl, dog* ausführen; (*extract*) herausnehmen; *insurance* abschließen; *licence* sich (*dat*) geben lassen; *book* ausleihen; (*remove*) entfernen; **to ~ sth out on sb** etw an jdm auslassen; **~ over** *vt* übernehmen; *vi* ablösen (*from acc*); **~ to** *vt* (*like*) mögen; (*adopt as practice*) sich (*dat*) angewöhnen; **~ up** *vt* (*raise*) aufnehmen; *hem* kürzer machen; (*occupy*) in Anspruch nehmen; (*absorb*) aufsaugen; (*engage in*) sich befassen mit; **to ~ sb up on sth** jdn beim Wort nehmen; **to be ~n with** begeistert sein von; **~off** (*Aviat*) Abflug *m*, Start *m*; (*imitation*) Nachahmung *f*; **~over** (*Comm*) Übernahme *f*; **~over bid** Übernahmeangebot *nt*.

takings ['teɪkɪŋz] *npl* (*Comm*) Einnahmen *pl*.

talc [tælk] *n* (*also* **~um powder**) Talkumpuder *m*.

tale [teɪl] *n* Geschichte *f*, Erzählung *f*.

talent ['tælənt] *n* Talent *nt*, Begabung *f*; **~ed** a talentiert, begabt.

talk [tɔ:k] *n* (*conversation*) Gespräch *nt*; (*rumour*) Gerede *nt*; (*speech*) Vortrag *m*; *vi* sprechen, reden; (*gossip*) klatschen, reden; **~ing of . . .** da wir gerade von . . . sprechen; **~ about impertinence!** so eine Frechheit!; **to ~ sb into doing sth** jdn überreden, etw zu tun; **to ~ shop** fachsimpeln; **~ over** *vt* besprechen; **~ative** a redselig, gesprächig; **~er** Schwätzer *m*.

tall [tɔ:l] a groß; *building* hoch; **~boy** Kommode *f*; **~ness** Größe *f*; Höhe *f*; **~story** übertriebene Geschichte *f*.

tally ['tælɪ] *n* Abrechnung *f*; *vi* übereinstimmen.

talon ['tælən] *n* Kralle *f*.

tambourine [tæmbə'ri:n] *n* Tamburin *nt*.

tame [teɪm] a zahm; (*fig*) fade, langweilig;

vt zähmen; **~ness** Zahmheit *f*; (*fig*) Langweiligkeit *f*.

tamper ['tæmpə*]: **~ with** *vt* herumpfuschen an (+*dat*); *documents* fälschen.

tampon ['tæmpən] *n* Tampon *m*.

tan [tæn] *n* (*on skin*) (Sonnen)bräune *f*; (*colour*) Gelbbraun *nt*; a (*colour*) (gelb)braun.

tandem ['tændəm] *n* Tandem *nt*.

tang [tæŋ] *n* Schärfe *f*, scharfe(r) Geschmack *m* or Geruch *m*.

tangent ['tændʒənt] *n* Tangente *f*.

tangerine [tændʒə'ri:n] *n* Mandarine *f*.

tangible ['tændʒəbl] a (*lit*) greifbar; (*real*) handgreiflich.

tangle ['tæŋgl] *n* Durcheinander *nt*; (*trouble*) Schwierigkeiten *pl*; *vt* verwirren.

tango ['tæŋgəʊ] *n* Tango *m*.

tank [tæŋk] *n* (*container*) Tank *m*, Behälter *m*; (*Mil*) Panzer *m*.

tankard ['tæŋkəd] *n* Seidel *nt*, Deckelkrug *m*.

tanker ['tæŋkə*] *n* (*ship*) Tanker *m*; (*vehicle*) Tankwagen *m*.

tankful ['tæŋkful] *n* volle(r) Tank *m*.

tanned [tænd] a *skin* gebräunt, sonnenverbrannt.

tantalizing ['tæntəlaɪzɪŋ] a verlockend; (*annoying*) quälend.

tantamount ['tæntəmaʊnt] a gleichbedeutend (*to* mit).

tantrum ['tæntrəm] *n* Wutanfall *m*.

tap [tæp] *n* Hahn *m*; (*gentle blow*) leichte(r) Schlag *m*, Klopfen *nt*; *vt* (*strike*) klopfen; *supply* anzapfen.

tap-dance ['tæpdɑ:ns] *vi* steppen.

tape [teɪp] *n* Band *nt*; (*magnetic*) (Ton)band *nt*; (*adhesive*) Klebstreifen *m*; *vt* (*record*) (auf Band) aufnehmen; **~measure** Maßband *nt*.

taper ['teɪpə*] *n* (dünne) Wachskerze *f*; *vi* spitz zulaufen.

tape recorder ['teɪprɪkɔ:də*] *n* Tonbandgerät *nt*.

tapered ['teɪpəd], **tapering** ['teɪpərɪŋ] a spitz zulaufend.

tapestry ['tæpɪstrɪ] *n* Wandteppich *m*, Gobelin *m*.

tapioca [tæpɪ'əʊkə] *n* Tapioka *f*.

tappet ['tæpɪt] *n* (*Aut*) Nocke *f*.

tar [tɑ:*] *n* Teer *m*.

tarantula [tə'ræntjʊlə] *n* Tarantel *f*.

tardy ['tɑ:dɪ] a langsam, spät.

target ['tɑ:gɪt] *n* Ziel *nt*; (*board*) Zielscheibe *f*.

tariff ['tærɪf] *n* (*duty paid*) Zoll *m*; (*list*) Tarif *m*.

tarmac ['tɑ:mæk] *n* (*Aviat*) Rollfeld *nt*.

tarn [tɑ:n] *n* Gebirgssee *m*.

tarnish ['tɑ:nɪʃ] *vt* (*lit*) matt machen; (*fig*) beflecken.

tarpaulin [tɑ:'pɔ:lɪn] *n* Plane *f*, Persenning *f*.

tarry ['tærɪ] *vi* (*liter*) bleiben; (*delay*) säumen.

tart [tɑ:t] *n* (Obst)torte *f*; (*col*) Nutte *f*; a scharf, sauer; *remark* scharf, spitz.

tartan ['tɑ:tən] *n* schottisch-karierte(r) Stoff *m*; Schottenkaro *nt*.

tartar ['tɑːtə*] n Zahnstein m; ~(e) **sauce** Remouladensoße f.

tartly ['tɑːtlɪ] ad spitz.

task [tɑːsk] n Aufgabe f; (duty) Pflicht f; ~ **force** Sondertrupp m.

tassel ['tæsəl] n Quaste f.

taste [teɪst] n Geschmack m; (sense) Geschmackssinn m; (small quantity) Kostprobe f; (liking) Vorliebe f; vt schmecken; (try) versuchen; vi schmecken (of nach); ~**ful** a, ~**fully** ad geschmackvoll; ~**less** a (insipid) ohne Geschmack, fade; (in bad taste) geschmacklos; ~**lessly** ad geschmacklos.

tastily ['teɪstɪlɪ] ad schmackhaft.

tastiness ['teɪstɪnəs] n Schmackhaftigkeit f.

tasty ['teɪstɪ] a schmackhaft.

tata ['tæ'tɑː] interj (Brit col) tschüß.

tattered ['tætəd] a zerrissen, zerlumpt.

tatters ['tætəz] npl: **in** ~ in Fetzen.

tattoo [tə'tuː] n (Mil) Zapfenstreich m; (on skin) Tätowierung f; vt tätowieren.

tatty ['tætɪ] a (col) schäbig.

taunt [tɔːnt] n höhnische Bemerkung f; vt verhöhnen.

Taurus ['tɔːrəs] n Stier m.

taut [tɔːt] a straff.

tavern ['tævən] n Taverne f.

tawdry ['tɔːdrɪ] a (bunt und) billig.

tawny ['tɔːnɪ] a gelbbraun.

tax [tæks] n Steuer f; vt besteuern; (strain) strapazieren; strength angreifen; ~**ation** [tæk'seɪʃən] Besteuerung f; ~ **collector** Steuereinnehmer m; ~-**free** a steuerfrei.

taxi ['tæksɪ] n Taxi nt; vi (plane) rollen.

taxidermist ['tæksɪdɜːmɪst] n Tierausstopfer m.

taxi driver ['tæksɪ draɪvə*] n Taxifahrer m.

taxi rank ['tæksɪræŋk] n Taxistand m.

taxpayer ['tækspeɪə*] n Steuerzahler m.

tax return ['tæksrɪ'tɜːn] n Steuererklärung f.

tea [tiː] n Tee m; (meal) (frühes) Abendessen nt; ~ **bag** Tee(aufguß)beutel m; ~ **break** Teepause f; ~ **cake** Rosinenbrötchen nt.

teach [tiːtʃ] vti irreg lehren; (Sch also) unterrichten; (show) zeigen, beibringen (sb sth jdm etw); **that'll** ~ **him!** das hat er nun davon!; ~**er** Lehrer(in f) m; ~-**in** Teach-in nt; ~**ing** (teacher's work) Unterricht m, Lehren nt; (doctrine) Lehre f.

tea cosy ['tiːkəʊzɪ] n Teewärmer m.

teacup ['tiːkʌp] n Teetasse f.

teak [tiːk] n Teakbaum m; a Teak(holz)-.

tea leaves ['tiːliːvz] npl Teeblätter pl.

team [tiːm] n (workers) Team nt; (Sport) Mannschaft f; (animals) Gespann nt; ~ **spirit** Gemeinschaftsgeist m; (Sport) Mannschaftsgeist m; ~**work** Zusammenarbeit f, Teamwork nt.

tea party ['tiːpɑːtɪ] n Kaffeeklatsch m.

teapot ['tiːpɒt] n Teekanne f.

tear [tɛə*] n Riß m; irreg vt zerreißen; muscle zerren; **I am torn between . . .** ich

schwanke zwischen . . .; vi (zer)reißen; (rush) rasen, sausen.

tear [tɪə*] n Träne f; **in** ~**s** in Tränen (aufgelöst); ~**ful** a weinend; voice weinerlich; ~ **gas** Tränengas nt.

tearing ['tɛərɪŋ] a: **to be in a** ~ **hurry** es schrecklich eilig haben.

tearoom ['tiːrʊm] n Teestube f.

tease [tiːz] n Hänsler m; vt necken, aufziehen; animal quälen; **I was only teasing** ich habe nur Spaß gemacht.

tea set ['tiːset] n Teeservice nt.

teashop ['tiːʃɒp] n Café nt.

teaspoon ['tiːspuːn] n Teelöffel m; ~**ful** Teelöffel(voll) m.

tea strainer ['tiːstreɪnə*] n Teesieb nt.

teat [tiːt] n (of woman) Brustwarze f; (of animal) Zitze f; (of bottle) Sauger m.

tea towel ['tiːtaʊəl] n Küchenhandtuch nt.

tea urn ['tiːɜːn] n Teemaschine f.

technical ['teknɪkəl] a technisch; knowledge, terms Fach-; ~**ity** [teknɪ'kælɪtɪ] technische Einzelheit f; (Jur) Formsache f; ~**ly** ad technisch; speak spezialisiert; (fig) genau genommen.

technician [tek'nɪʃən] n Techniker m.

technique [tek'niːk] n Technik f.

technological [teknə'lɒdʒɪkəl] a technologisch.

technologist [tek'nɒlədʒɪst] n Technologe m.

technology [tek'nɒlədʒɪ] n Technologie f.

teddy (bear) ['tedɪ(bɛə*)] n Teddybär m.

tedious a, ~**ly** ad ['tiːdɪəs, -lɪ] langweilig, ermüdend.

tedium ['tiːdɪəm] n Langweiligkeit f.

tee [tiː] n (golf) Abschlagstelle f; (object) Tee nt.

teem [tiːm] vi (swarm) wimmeln (with von); (pour) gießen.

teenage ['tiːneɪdʒ] a fashions etc Teenager-, jugendlich; ~**r** Teenager m, Jugendliche(r) mf.

teens [tiːnz] npl Jugendjahre pl.

teeter ['tiːtə*] vi schwanken.

teeth [tiːθ] npl of **tooth**.

teethe [tiːð] vi zahnen.

teething ring ['tiːðɪŋrɪŋ] n Beißring m.

teetotal ['tiː'təʊtl] a abstinent; ~**ler**, (US) ~**er** Antialkoholiker m, Abstinenzler m.

telecommunications ['telɪkəmjuːnɪ'keɪʃənz] npl Fernmeldewesen nt.

telegram ['telɪgræm] n Telegramm nt.

telegraph ['telɪgrɑːf] n Telegraph m; ~**ic** [telɪ'græfɪk] a address Telegramm-; ~ **pole** Telegraphenmast m.

telepathic [telɪ'pæθɪk] a telepathisch.

telepathy [tə'lepəθɪ] n Telepathie f, Gedankenübertragung f.

telephone ['telɪfəʊn] n Telefon nt, Fernsprecher m; vi telefonieren; vt anrufen; message telefonisch mitteilen; ~ **booth**, ~ **box** Telefonhäuschen nt, Fernsprechzelle f; ~ **call** Telefongespräch nt, Anruf m; ~ **directory** Telefonbuch nt; ~ **exchange** Telefonvermittlung f, Telefonzentrale f; ~ **number** Telefonnummer f.

telephonist [tə'lefənɪst] n Telefonist(in f) m.

telephoto lens ['telɪ'fəʊtəʊ'lenz] *n* Tele-objektiv *nt*.

teleprinter ['telɪprɪntə*] *n* Fernschreiber *m*.

telescope ['telɪskəʊp] *n* Teleskop *nt*, Fernrohr *nt*; *vt* ineinanderschieben.

telescopic [telɪs'kopɪk] *a* teleskopisch; *aerial etc* ausziehbar.

televiewer ['telɪvjuːə*] *n* Fernsehteil-nehmer(in *f*) *m*.

televise ['telɪvaɪz] *vt* durch das Fernsehen übertragen.

television ['telɪvɪʒən] *n* Fernsehen *nt*; **to watch** ~ fernsehen; ~ **(set)** Fern-sehapparat *m*, Fernseher *m*; **on** ~ im Fernsehen.

telex ['teleks] *n* Telex *nt*.

tell [tel] *irreg vt story* erzählen; *secret* ausplaudern; (*say, make known*) sagen (*sth to sb* jdm etw); (*distinguish*) erkennen (*sb by sth* jdn an etw dat); (*be sure*) wissen; (*order*) sagen, befehlen (*sb* jdm); **to** ~ **a lie** lügen; **to** ~ **sb about sth** jdm von etw erzählen; *vi* (*be sure*) wissen; (*divulge*) es verraten; (*have effect*) sich auswirken; ~ **off** *vt* schimpfen; ~ **on** *vt* verraten, ver-petzen; ~ **er** Kassenbeamte(r) *mf*; ~ **ing** verräterisch; *blow* hart; *moment* der Wahrheit; ~ **tale** *a* verräterisch.

telly ['telɪ] *n* (*col*) Fernseher *m*.

temerity [tɪ'merɪtɪ] *n* (Toll)kühnheit *f*.

temper ['tempə*] *n* (*disposition*) Tempera-ment *nt*, Gemütsart *f*; (*anger*) Gereiztheit *f*, Zorn *m*; **to be in a (bad)** ~ wütend or gereizt sein; *vt* (*tone down*) mildern; *metal* härten; **quick** ~ **ed** jähzornig, auf-brausend; ~ **ament** Temperament *nt*, Veranlagung *f*; ~ **amental** [tempərə'mentl] *a* (*moody*) launisch.

temperance ['tempərəns] *n* Mäßigung *f*; (*abstinence*) Enthaltsamkeit *f*; ~ **hotel** alkoholfreie(s) Hotel *nt*.

temperate ['tempərət] *a* gemäßigt.

temperature ['temprɪtʃə*] *n* Temperatur *f*; (*Med: high* —) Fieber *nt*.

tempered ['tempəd] *a steel* gehärtet.

tempest ['tempɪst] *n* (*wilder*) Sturm *m*; ~ **uous** [tem'pestjʊəs] *a* stürmisch; (*fig*) ungestüm.

template ['templət] *n* Schablone *f*.

temple ['templ] *n* Tempel *m*; (*Anat*) Schläfe *f*.

tempo ['tempəʊ] *n* Tempo *nt*.

temporal ['tempərəl] *a* (*of time*) zeitlich; (*worldly*) irdisch, weltlich.

temporarily ['tempərərɪlɪ] *ad* zeitweilig, vorübergehend.

temporary ['tempərərɪ] *a* vorläufig; *road, building* provisorisch.

tempt [tempt] *vt* (*persuade*) verleiten, in Versuchung führen; (*attract*) reizen, (ver-)locken; ~ **ation** [temp'teɪʃən] Versuchung *f*; ~ **ing** *a person* verführerisch; *object, situation* verlockend.

ten [ten] *num* zehn.

tenable ['tenəbl] *a* haltbar; **to be** ~ (*post*) vergeben werden.

tenacious *a*, ~ **ly** *ad* [tə'neɪʃəs, -lɪ] zäh, hartnäckig.

tenacity [tə'næsɪtɪ] *n* Zähigkeit *f*, Hart-näckigkeit *f*.

tenancy ['tenənsɪ] *n* Mietverhältnis *nt*; Pachtverhältnis *nt*.

tenant ['tenənt] *n* Mieter *m*; (*of larger property*) Pächter *m*.

tend [tend] *vt* (*look after*) sich kümmern um; *vi* neigen, tendieren (*to* zu); **to** ~ **to do sth** (*things*) etw gewöhnlich tun; ~ **ency** Tendenz *f*; (*of person also*) Neigung *f*.

tender ['tendə*] *a* (*soft*) weich, zart; (*delicate*) zart; (*loving*) liebevoll, zärtlich; *n* (*Comm: offer*) Kostenanschlag *m*; ~ **ize** *vt* weich machen; ~ **ly** *ad* liebevoll; *touch also* zart; ~ **ness** Zartheit *f*; (*being loving*) Zärtlichkeit *f*.

tendon ['tendən] *n* Sehne *f*.

tenement ['tenəmənt] *n* Mietshaus *nt*.

tenet ['tenət] *n* Lehre *f*.

tennis ['tenɪs] *n* Tennis *nt*; ~ **ball** Tennis-ball *m*; ~ **court** Tennisplatz *m*; ~ **racket** Tennisschläger *m*.

tenor ['tenə*] *n* (*voice*) Tenor(stimme *f*) *m*; (*singer*) Tenor *m*; (*meaning*) Sinn *m*, wesentliche(r) Inhalt *m*.

tense [tens] *a* angespannt; (*stretched tight*) gespannt, straff; *n* Zeitform *f*; ~ **ly** *ad* (an)gespannt; ~ **ness** Spannung *f*; (*strain*) Angespanntheit *f*.

tension ['tenʃən] *n* Spannung *f*; (*strain*) (An)gespanntheit *f*.

tent [tent] *n* Zelt *nt*.

tentacle ['tentəkl] *n* Fühler *m*; (*of sea animals*) Fangarm *m*.

tentative ['tentətɪv] *a movement* unsicher; *offer* Probe-; *arrangement* vorläufig; *suggestion* unverbindlich; ~ **ly** *ad* versuchsweise; *try, move* vorsichtig.

tenterhooks ['tentəhʊks] *npl*: **to be on** ~ auf die Folter gespannt sein.

tenth [tenθ] *a* zehnte(r,s); *n* Zehntel *nt*.

tent peg ['tentpeg] *n* Hering *m*.

tent pole ['tentpəʊl] *n* Zeltstange *f*.

tenuous ['tenjʊəs] *a* fein; *air* dünn; *con-nection, argument* schwach.

tenure ['tenjʊə*] *n* (*of land*) Besitz *m*; (*of office*) Amtszeit *f*.

tepid ['tepɪd] *a* lauwarm.

term [tɜːm] *n* (*period of time*) Zeit(raum *m*) *f*; (*limit*) Frist *f*; (*Sch*) Quartal *nt*; (*Univ*) Trimester *nt*; (*expression*) Aus-druck *m*; *vt* (be)nennen; ~ **s** *pl* (*con-ditions*) Bedingungen *pl*; (*relationship*) Beziehungen *pl*; **to be on good** ~ **s with sb** mit jdm gut auskommen; ~ **inal** (*Rail, bus* ~ *inal*; *also* ~ **inus**) Endstation *f*; (*Aviat*) Terminal *m*; *a* Schluß-; (*Med*) unheilbar; ~ **inal cancer** Krebs *m* im Endstadium; ~ **inate** *vt* beenden; *vi* enden, aufhören (*in auf* +*dat*); ~ **ination** [tɜːmɪ'neɪʃən] Ende *nt*; (*act*) Beendigung *f*; ~ **inology** [tɜːmɪ'nɒlədʒɪ] Terminologie *f*.

termite ['tɜːmaɪt] *n* Termite *f*.

terrace ['terəs] *n* (*of houses*) Häuserreihe *f*; (*in garden etc*) Terrasse *f*; ~ **d** *a garden* terrassenförmig angelegt; *house* Reihen-.

terracotta ['terə'kɒtə] *n* Terrakotta *f*.

terrain [te'reɪn] *n* Gelände *nt*, Terrain *nt*.

terrible ['terəbl] *a* schrecklich, entsetzlich, fürchterlich.
terribly ['terəblɪ] *ad* fürchterlich.
terrier ['terɪə*] *n* Terrier *m*.
terrific *a*, ~**ally** *ad* [təˈrɪfɪk, -lɪ] unwahrscheinlich; ~! klasse!
terrify ['terɪfaɪ] *vt* erschrecken; ~**ing** *a* erschreckend, grauenvoll.
territorial [terɪˈtɔːrɪəl] *a* Gebiets-, territorial; ~ **waters** *pl* Hoheitsgewässer *pl*.
territory ['terɪtərɪ] *n* Gebiet *nt*.
terror ['terə*] *n* Schrecken *m*; (*Pol*) Terror *m*; ~**ism** Terrorismus *m*; ~**ist** Terrorist-(in *f*) *m*; ~**ize** *vt* terrorisieren.
terse [tɜːs] *a* knapp, kurz, bündig.
Terylene ['terɪliːn] *n* Terylen(e) *nt*.
test [test] *n* Probe *f*; (*examination*) Prüfung *f*; (*Psych*, *Tech*) Test *m*; *vt* prüfen; (*Psych*) testen.
testament ['testəmənt] *n* Testament *nt*.
test card ['testkɑːd] *n* (*TV*) Testbild *nt*.
test case ['testkeɪs] *n* (*Jur*) Präzedenzfall *m*; (*fig*) Musterbeispiel *nt*.
test flight ['testflaɪt] *n* Probeflug *m*.
testicle ['testɪkl] *n* Hoden *m*.
testify ['testɪfaɪ] *vi* aussagen; bezeugen (*to acc*).
testimonial [testɪˈməʊnɪəl] *n* (*of character*) Referenz *f*.
testimony ['testɪmənɪ] *n* (*Jur*) Zeugenaussage *f*; (*fig*) Zeugnis *nt*.
test match ['testmætʃ] *n* (*Sport*) Länderkampf *m*.
test paper ['testpeɪpə*] *n* schriftliche (Klassen)arbeit *f*.
test pilot ['testpaɪlət] *n* Testpilot *m*.
test tube ['testtjuːb] *n* Reagenzglas *nt*.
testy ['testɪ] *a* gereizt; reizbar.
tetanus ['tetənəs] *n* Wundstarrkrampf *m*, Tetanus *m*.
tether ['teðə*] *vt* anbinden; **to be at the end of one's** ~ völlig am Ende sein.
text [tekst] *n* Text *m*; (*of document*) Wortlaut *m*; ~**book** Lehrbuch *nt*.
textile ['tekstaɪl] *n* Gewebe *nt*; ~**s** *pl* Textilien *pl*.
texture ['tekstʃə*] *n* Beschaffenheit *f*, Struktur *f*.
than [ðæn] *prep*, *cj* als.
thank [θæŋk] *vt* danken (+*dat*); **you've him to** ~ **for your success** Sie haben Ihren Erfolg ihm zu verdanken; ~**ful** *a* dankbar; ~**fully** *ad* (*luckily*) zum Glück; ~**less** *a* undankbar; ~**s** *pl* Dank *m*; ~**s to dank** (+*gen*); ~ **you**, ~**s** *interj* danke, dankeschön; **T**~**sgiving** (*US*) (Ernte)dankfest *nt*.
that [ðæt] *a* der/die/das, jene(r,s); *pron* das; *cj* daß; **and** ~**'s** ~ und damit Schluß; ~ **is** das heißt; **after** ~ danach; **at** ~ dazu noch; ~ **big** so groß.
thatched [θætʃt] *a* strohgedeckt.
thaw [θɔː] *n* Tauwetter *nt*; *vi* tauen; (*frozen foods*, *fig*: *people*) auftauen; *vt* (auf)tauen lassen.
the [ðiː, ðə] *def art* der/die/das; **to play** ~ **piano** Klavier spielen; ~ **sooner** ~ **better** je eher desto besser.
theatre, (*US*) **theater** ['θɪətə*] *n* Theater

nt; (*for lectures etc*) Saal *m*; (*Med*) Operationssaal *m*; ~**goer** Theaterbesucher(in *f*) *m*.
theatrical [θɪˈætrɪkəl] *a* Theater-; *career* Schauspieler-; (*showy*) theatralisch.
theft [θeft] *n* Diebstahl *m*.
their [ðɛə*] *poss a* ihr; ~**s** *poss pron* ihre(r,s).
them [ðem, ðəm] *pron* (*acc*) sie; (*dat*) ihnen.
theme [θiːm] *n* Thema *nt*; (*Mus*) Motiv *nt*; ~ **song** Titelmusik *f*.
themselves [ðəmˈselvz] *pl pron* (*reflexive*) sich (selbst); (*emphatic*) selbst.
then [ðen] *ad* (*at that time*) damals; (*next*) dann; *cj* also, folglich; (*furthermore*) ferner; *a* damalig; **from** ~ **on** von da an; **before** ~ davor; **by** ~ bis dahin; **not till** ~ erst dann.
theologian [θɪəˈləʊdʒən] *n* Theologe *m*, Theologin *f*.
theological [θɪəˈlɒdʒɪkəl] *a* theologisch.
theology [θɪˈɒlədʒɪ] *n* Theologie *f*.
theorem ['θɪərəm] *n* Grundsatz *m*, Theorem *nt*.
theoretical *a*, ~**ly** *ad* [θɪəˈretɪkəl, -ɪ] theoretisch.
theorize ['θɪəraɪz] *vi* theoretisieren.
theory ['θɪərɪ] *n* Theorie *f*.
therapeutic(al) [θerəˈpjuːtɪk(əl)] *a* (*Med*) therapeutisch; erholsam.
therapist ['θerəpɪst] *n* Therapeut(in *f*) *m*.
therapy ['θerəpɪ] *n* Therapie *f*, Behandlung *f*.
there [ðɛə*] *ad* dort; (*to a place*) dorthin; *interj* (*see*) na also; (*to child*) (sei) ruhig, na na; ~ **is eit** es gibt; ~ **are** es sind, es gibt; ~**abouts** *ad* so ungefähr; ~**after** [ðɛərˈɑːftə*] *ad* danach, später; ~**by** *ad* dadurch; ~**fore** *ad* daher, deshalb; ~**'s** = **there is**.
thermal ['θɜːməl] *a springs* Thermal-; (*Phys*) thermisch.
thermodynamics [θɜːməʊdaɪˈnæmɪks] *n* Thermodynamik *f*.
thermometer [θəˈmɒmɪtə*] *n* Thermometer *nt*.
thermonuclear ['θɜːməʊˈnjuːklɪə*] *a* thermonuklear.
Thermos ® ['θɜːməs] *n* Thermosflasche *f*.
thermostat ['θɜːməstæt] *n* Thermostat *m*.
thesaurus [θɪˈsɔːrəs] *n* Synonymwörterbuch *nt*.
these [ðiːz] *pl pron*, *a* diese.
thesis ['θiːsɪs] *n* (*for discussion*) These *f*; (*Univ*) Dissertation *f*, Doktorarbeit *f*.
they [ðeɪ] *pl pron* sie; (*people in general*) man; ~**'d** = **they had**; **they would**; ~**'ll** = **they shall**, **they will**; ~**'re** = **they are**; ~**'ve** = **they have**.
thick [θɪk] *a* dick; *forest* dicht; *liquid* dickflüssig; (*slow*, *stupid*) dumm, schwer von Begriff; *n*: **in the** ~ **of** mitten in (+*dat*); ~**en** *vi* (*fog*) dichter werden; *vt sauce etc* verdicken; ~**ness** (*of object*) Dicke *f*, Dichte *f*; Dickflüssigkeit *f*; (*of person*) Dummheit *f*; ~**set** *a* untersetzt; ~**skinned** *a* dickhäutig.
thief [θiːf] *n* Dieb(in *f*) *m*.

thieving ['θi:vɪŋ] n Stehlen nt; a diebisch.

thigh [θaɪ] n Oberschenkel m; ~**bone** Oberschenkelknochen m.

thimble ['θɪmbl] n Fingerhut m.

thin [θɪn] a dünn; person also mager; (not abundant) spärlich; fog, rain leicht; excuse schwach.

thing [θɪŋ] n Ding nt; (affair) Sache f; my ~s pl meine Sachen pl.

think [θɪŋk] vti irreg denken; (believe) meinen, denken; **to** ~ **of doing sth** vorhaben or beabsichtigen, etw zu tun; ~ **over** vt überdenken; ~ **up** vt sich (dat) ausdenken; ~**ing** a denkend.

thinly ['θɪnlɪ] ad dünn; disguised kaum.

thinness ['θɪnnəs] n Dünnheit f; Magerkeit f; Spärlichkeit f.

third [θɜ:d] a dritte(r,s); n (person) Dritte(r) mf; (part) Drittel nt; ~**ly** ad drittens; ~ **party insurance** Haftpflichtversicherung f. ~**rate** a minderwertig.

thirst [θɜ:st] n (lit, fig) Durst m; (fig) Verlangen nt; ~**y** a person durstig; work durstig machend; **to be** ~**y** Durst haben.

thirteen ['θɜ:'ti:n] num dreizehn.

thirty ['θɜ:tɪ] num dreißig.

this [ðɪs] a diese(r,s); pron dies/das; **it was** ~ **long** es war so lang.

thistle ['θɪsl] n Distel f.

thong [θɒŋ] n (Leder)riemen m.

thorn [θɔ:n] n Dorn m, Stachel m; (plant) Dornbusch m; ~**y** a dornig; problem schwierig.

thorough ['θʌrə] a gründlich; contempt tief; ~**bred** Vollblut nt; a reinrassig, Vollblut-; ~**fare** Straße f; ~**ly** ad gründlich; (extremely) vollkommen, äußerst; ~**ness** Gründlichkeit f.

those [ðəʊz] pl pron die (da), jene; a die, jene; ~ **who** diejenigen, die.

though [ðəʊ] cj obwohl; ad trotzdem; **as** ~ als ob.

thought [θɔ:t] n (idea) Gedanke m; (opinion) Auffassung f; (thinking) Denken nt, Denkvermögen nt; ~**ful** a (thinking) gedankenvoll, nachdenklich; (kind) rücksichtsvoll, aufmerksam; ~**less** a gedankenlos, unbesonnen; (unkind) rücksichtslos.

thousand ['θaʊzənd] num tausend.

thrash [θræʃ] vt (lit) verdreschen; (fig) (vernichtend) schlagen.

thread [θred] n Faden m, Garn nt; (on screw) Gewinde nt; (in story) Faden m, Zusammenhang m; vt needle einfädeln; vi: ~ **one's way** sich hindurchschlängeln; ~**bare** a (lit, fig) fadenscheinig.

threat [θret] n Drohung f; (danger) Bedrohung f, Gefahr f; ~**en** vt bedrohen; vi drohen; **to** ~**en sb with sth** jdm etw androhen; ~**ening** a drohend; letter Droh-.

three [θri:] num drei; ~-**dimensional** a dreidimensional; ~**fold** a dreifach; ~-**piece suit** dreiteilige(r) Anzug m; ~-**piece suite** dreiteilige Polstergarnitur f; ~**ply** a wool dreifach; wood dreischichtig; ~-**quarter** [θri:'kwɔːtə*] a dreiviertel; ~-**wheeler** Dreiradwagen m.

thresh [θreʃ] vti dreschen; ~**ing machine** Dreschmaschine f.

threshold ['θreʃhəʊld] n Schwelle f.

thrift [θrɪft] n Sparsamkeit f; ~**y** a sparsam.

thrill [θrɪl] n Reiz m, Erregung f; **it gave me quite a** ~ **to** ... es war ein Erlebnis für mich, zu ...; vt begeistern, packen; vi beben, zittern; ~**er** Krimi m; ~**ing** a spannend, packend; news aufregend.

thrive [θraɪv] vi gedeihen (on bei).

thriving ['θraɪvɪŋ] a blühend, gut gedeihend.

throat [θrəʊt] n Hals m, Kehle f.

throb [θrɒb] n Pochen nt, Schlagen -nt; (Puls)schlag m; vi klopfen, pochen.

throes [θrəʊz] npl: **in the** ~ **of** mitten in (+dat).

thrombosis [θrɒm'bəʊsɪs] n Thrombose f.

throne [θrəʊn] n Thron m; (Eccl) Stuhl m.

throttle ['θrɒtl] n Gashebel m; **to open the** ~ Gas geben; vt erdrosseln.

through [θru:] prep durch; (time) während (+gen); (because of) aus, durch; ad durch; **to put sb** ~ (Tel) jdn verbinden (to mit); a ticket, train durchgehend; (finished) fertig; ~**out** [θru:'aʊt] prep (place) überall in (+dat); (time) während (+gen); ad überall; die ganze Zeit; **we're** ~ es ist aus zwischen uns.

throw [θrəʊ] n Wurf m; vt irreg werfen; ~ **out** vt hinauswerfen; rubbish wegwerfen; plan verwerfen; ~ **up** vti (vomit) speien; ~**away** a (disposable) Wegwerf-; bottle Einweg-; ~-**in** Einwurf m.

thru [θru:] (US) = **through**.

thrush [θrʌʃ] n Drossel f.

thrust [θrʌst] n (Tech) Schubkraft f; vti irreg (push) stoßen; (fig) sich drängen; **to** ~ **oneself on sb** sich jdm aufdrängen; ~**ing** a person aufdringlich, unverfroren.

thud [θʌd] n dumpfe(r) (Auf)schlag m.

thug [θʌg] n Schlägertyp m.

thumb [θʌm] n Daumen m; vt book durchblättern; **a well-~ed book** ein abgegriffenes Buch; **to** ~ **a lift** per Anhalter fahren (wollen); ~ **index** Daumenregister nt; ~**nail** Daumennagel m; ~**tack** (US) Reißzwecke f.

thump [θʌmp] n (blow) Schlag m; (noise) Bums m; vi hämmern, pochen; vt schlagen auf (+acc).

thunder ['θʌndə*] n Donner m; vi donnern; vt brüllen; ~**ous** a stürmisch; ~**storm** Gewitter nt, Unwetter nt; ~**struck** a wie vom Donner gerührt; ~**y** a gewitterschwül.

Thursday ['θɜ:zdeɪ] n Donnerstag m.

thus [ðʌs] ad (in this way) so; (therefore) somit, also, folglich.

thwart [θwɔ:t] vt vereiteln, durchkreuzen; person hindern.

thyme [taɪm] n Thymian m.

thyroid ['θaɪrɔɪd] n Schilddrüse f.

tiara [tɪ'ɑ:rə] n Diadem nt; (pope's) Tiara f.

tic [tɪk] n Tick m.

tick [tɪk] n (sound) Ticken nt; (mark) Häkchen nt; **in a** ~ (col) sofort; vi ticken; vt abhaken.

ticket ['tɪkɪt] n (for travel) Fahrkarte f; (for entrance) (Eintritts)karte f; (price —) Preisschild nt; (luggage —) (Gepäck)-schein m; (raffle —) Los nt; (parking —) Strafzettel m; (permission) Parkschein m; **~ collector** Fahrkartenkontrolleur m; **~ holder** Karteninhaber m; **~ office** (Rail etc) Fahrkartenschalter m; (Theat etc) Kasse f.

ticking-off ['tɪkɪŋ'ɒf] n (col) Anschnauzer m.

tickle ['tɪkl] n Kitzeln nt; vt kitzeln; (amuse) amüsieren; **that ~d her fancy** das gefiel ihr.

ticklish ['tɪklɪʃ] a (lit, fig) kitzlig.

tidal ['taɪdl] a Flut-, Tide-.

tidbit ['tɪdbɪt] n (US) Leckerbissen m.

tiddlywinks ['tɪdlɪwɪŋks] n Floh-(hüpf)spiel nt.

tide [taɪd] n Gezeiten pl, Ebbe f und Flut; **the ~ is in/out** es ist Flut/Ebbe.

tidily ['taɪdɪlɪ] ad sauber, ordentlich.

tidiness ['taɪdɪnəs] n Ordnung f.

tidy ['taɪdɪ] a ordentlich; vt aufräumen, in Ordnung bringen.

tie [taɪ] n (necktie) Kravatte f, Schlips m; (sth connecting) Band nt; (Sport) Unentschieden nt; vt (fasten, restrict) binden; knot schnüren, festbinden; vi (Sport) unentschieden spielen; (in competition) punktgleich sein; **~ down** vt (lit) festbinden; (fig) binden; **~ up** vt dog anbinden; parcel verschnüren; boat festmachen; person fesseln; **I am ~d up right now** ich bin im Moment beschäftigt.

tier [tɪə*] n Reihe f, Rang m; (of cake) Etage f.

tiff [tɪf] n kleine Meinungsverschiedenheit f.

tiger ['taɪgə*] n Tiger m.

tight [taɪt] a (close) eng, knapp; schedule gedrängt; (firm) fest, dicht; screw festsitzend; control streng; (stretched) stramm, (an)gespannt; (col) blau, stramm; **~s** pl Strumpfhose f; **~en** vt anziehen, anspannen; restrictions verschärfen; vi sich spannen; **~-fisted** a knauserig; **~ly** ad eng; fest, dicht; stretched straff; **~ness** Enge f; Festigkeit f, Straffheit f; (of money) Knappheit f; **~-rope** Seil nt.

tile [taɪl] n (in roof) Dachziegel m; (on wall or floor) Fliese f; **~d** a roof gedeckt, Ziegel-; floor, wall mit Fliesen belegt.

till [tɪl] n Kasse f; vt bestellen; prep,cj bis; **not ~** (in future) nicht vor; (in past) erst.

tiller ['tɪlə*] n Ruderpinne f.

tilt [tɪlt] vt kippen, neigen; vi sich neigen.

timber ['tɪmbə*] n Holz nt; (trees) Baumbestand m.

time [taɪm] n Zeit f; (occasion) Mal nt; (rhythm) Takt m; vt zur rechten Zeit tun, zeitlich einrichten; (Sport) stoppen; **I have no ~ for people like him** mit Leute wie ihn habe ich nichts übrig; **in 2 weeks' ~** in 2 Wochen; **for the ~ being** vorläufig; **at all ~s** immer; **at one ~** früher; **at no ~** nie; **at ~s** manchmal; **by the ~** bis; **this ~** diesmal, dieses Mal; **to have a good ~** viel Spaß haben, sich amüsieren; **in ~** (soon enough) rechtzeitig; (after some

time) mit der Zeit; (Mus) im Takt; **on ~** pünktlich, rechtzeitig; **five ~s** fünfmal; **local ~** Ortszeit f; **what ~ is it?** wieviel Uhr ist es?, wie spät ist es?; **~keeper** Zeitnehmer m; **~-lag** (in travel) Verzögerung f; (difference) Zeitunterschied m; **~less** a beauty zeitlos; **~ limit** Frist f; **~ly** a rechtzeitig; günstig; **~-saving** a zeitsparend; **~ switch** Zeitschalter m; **~ table** Fahrplan m; (Sch) Stundenplan m; **~ zone** Zeitzone f.

timid ['tɪmɪd] a ängstlich, schüchtern; **~ity** [tɪ'mɪdɪtɪ] Ängstlichkeit f; **~ly** ad ängstlich.

timing ['taɪmɪŋ] n Wahl f des richtigen Zeitpunkts, Timing nt; (Aut) Einstellung f.

timpani ['tɪmpənɪ] npl Kesselpauken pl.

tin [tɪn] n (metal) Blech nt; (container) Büchse f, Dose f; **~foil** Staniolpapier nt.

tinge [tɪndʒ] n (colour) Färbung f; (fig) Anflug m; vt färben, einen Anstrich geben (+dat).

tingle ['tɪŋgl] n Prickeln nt; vi prickeln.

tinker ['tɪŋkə*] n Kesselflicker m; **~ with** vt herumpfuschen an (+dat).

tinkle ['tɪŋkl] n Klingeln nt; vi klingeln.

tinned [tɪnd] a food Dosen-, Büchsen-.

tinny ['tɪnɪ] a Blech-, blechern.

tin opener ['tɪnəupnə*] n Dosen- or Büchsenöffner m.

tinsel ['tɪnsəl] n Rauschgold nt; Lametta nt.

tint [tɪnt] n Farbton m; (slight colour) Anflug m; (hair) Tönung f.

tiny ['taɪnɪ] a winzig.

tip [tɪp] n (pointed end) Spitze f; (money) Trinkgeld nt; (hint) Wink m, Tip m; **it's on the ~ of my tongue** es liegt mir auf der Zunge; vt (slant) kippen; hat antippen; (~ over) umkippen; waiter ein Trinkgeld geben (+dat); **~-off** Hinweis m, Tip m; **~ped** a cigarette Filter-.

tipple ['tɪpl] n (drink) Schnäpschen nt.

tipsy ['tɪpsɪ] a beschwipst.

tiptoe ['tɪptəu] n: **on ~** auf Zehenspitzen.

tiptop ['tɪp'tɒp] a: **in ~ condition** tipptopp, erstklassig.

tire ['taɪə*] n (US) = **tyre**; vti ermüden, müde machen/werden; **~ a müde; to be ~d of sth** etw satt haben; **~dness** Müdigkeit f; **~less** a, **~lessly** ad unermüdlich; **~some** a lästig.

tiring ['taɪərɪŋ] a ermüdend.

tissue ['tɪʃu:] n Gewebe nt; (paper handkerchief) Papiertaschentuch nt; **~ paper** Seidenpapier nt.

tit [tɪt] n (bird) Meise f; (col: breast) Titte f; **~ for tat** wie du mir, so ich dir.

titbit ['tɪtbɪt] n Leckerbissen m.

titillate ['tɪtɪleɪt] vt kitzeln.

titillation [tɪtɪ'leɪʃən] n Kitzeln nt.

titivate ['tɪtɪveɪt] vt schniegeln.

title ['taɪtl] n Titel m; (in law) Rechtstitel m, Eigentumsrecht nt; **~ deed** Eigentumsurkunde f; **~ role** Hauptrolle f.

tittle-tattle ['tɪtltætl] n Klatsch m.

titter ['tɪtə*] vi kichern.

titular ['tɪtjʊlə*] a Titular-, nominell; possessions Titel-.

to [tu:, tə] prep (towards) zu; (with countries,

towns) nach; (*indir obj*) dat; (*as far as*) bis; (*next to, attached to*) an (+*dat*); (*per*) pro; *cj* (*in order to*) um... zu; *ad* ~ **and fro** hin und her; **to go** ~ **school/the theatre/bed** in die Schule/ins Theater/ins Bett gehen; **I have never been** ~ **Germany** ich war noch nie in Deutschland; **to give sth** ~ **sb** jdm etw geben; ~ **this day** bis auf den heutigen Tag; **20 (minutes)** ~ **4** 20 (Minuten) vor 4; **superior** ~ **sth** besser als etw; **they tied him** ~ **a tree** sie banden ihn an einen Baum.

toad [təʊd] *n* Kröte *f*; ~**stool** Giftpilz *m*; ~**y** Speichellecker *m*, Kriecher *m*; *vi* kriechen (*to* vor +*dat*).

toast [təʊst] *n* (*bread*) Toast *m*; (*drinking*) Trinkspruch *m*; *vt* trinken auf (+*acc*); *bread* toasten; (*warm*) wärmen; ~**er** Toaster *m*; ~**master** Zeremonienmeister *m*; ~**rack** Toastständer *m*.

tobacco [təˈbækəʊ] *n* Tabak *m*; ~**nist** [təˈbækənɪst] Tabakhändler *m*; ~**nist's (shop)** Tabakladen *m*.

toboggan [təˈbɒgən] *n* (Rodel)schlitten *m*.

today [təˈdeɪ] *ad* heute; (*at the present time*) heutzutage; *n* (*day*) heutige(r) Tag *m*; (*time*) Heute *nt*, heutige Zeit *f*.

toddle [ˈtɒdl] *vi* watscheln.

toddler [ˈtɒdlə*] *n* Kleinkind *nt*.

toddy [ˈtɒdɪ] *n* (Whisky)grog *m*.

to-do [təˈduː] *n* Aufheben *nt*, Theater *nt*.

toe [təʊ] *n* Zehe *f*; (*of sock, shoe*) Spitze *f*; *vt*: ~ **the line** (*fig*) sich einfügen; ~ **hold** Halt *m* für die Fußspitzen; ~**nail** Zehennagel *m*.

toffee [ˈtɒfɪ] *n* Sahnebonbon *nt*; ~ **apple** kandierte(r) Apfel *m*.

toga [ˈtəʊgə] *n* Toga *f*.

together [təˈgeðə*] *ad* zusammen; (*at the same time*) gleichzeitig; ~**ness** (*company*) Beisammensein *nt*; (*feeling*) Zusammengehörigkeitsgefühl *nt*.

toil [tɔɪl] *n* harte Arbeit *f*, Plackerei *f*; *vi* sich abmühen, sich plagen.

toilet [ˈtɔɪlət] *n* Toilette *f*; *a* Toiletten-; ~ **bag** Waschbeutel *m*; ~ **paper** Toilettenpapier *nt*; ~**ries** [ˈtɔɪlətrɪz] *pl* Toilettenartikel *pl*; ~ **roll** Rolle *f* Toilettenpapier; ~ **soap** Toilettenseife *f*; ~ **water** Toilettenwasser *nt*.

token [ˈtəʊkən] *n* Zeichen *nt*; (*gift* —) Gutschein *m*.

tolerable [ˈtɒlərəbl] *a* (*bearable*) erträglich; (*fairly good*) leidlich.

tolerably [ˈtɒlərəblɪ] *ad* ziemlich, leidlich.

tolerance [ˈtɒlərəns] *n* Toleranz *f*.

tolerant *a*, ~**ly** *ad* [ˈtɒlərənt, -lɪ] tolerant; (*patient*) geduldig.

tolerate [ˈtɒləreɪt] *vt* dulden; *noise* ertragen.

toleration [tɒləˈreɪʃən] *n* Toleranz *f*.

toll [təʊl] *n* Gebühr *f*; **it took a heavy** ~ **of human life** es forderte *or* kostete viele Menschenleben; *vi* (*bell*) läuten; ~**bridge** gebührenpflichtige Brücke *f*; ~ **road** gebührenpflichtige Autostraße *f*.

tomato [təˈmɑːtəʊ] *n*, *pl* -**es** Tomate *f*.

tomb [tuːm] *n* Grab(mal) *nt*.

tombola [tɒmˈbəʊlə] *n* Tombola *f*.

tomboy [ˈtɒmbɔɪ] *n* Wildfang *m*; **she's a** ~ sie ist sehr burschikos.

tombstone [ˈtuːmstəʊn] *n* Grabstein *m*.

tomcat [ˈtɒmkæt] *n* Kater *m*.

tome [təʊm] *n* (*volume*) Band *m*; (*big book*) Wälzer *m*.

tomorrow [təˈmɒrəʊ] *n* Morgen *nt*; *ad* morgen.

ton [tʌn] *n* Tonne *f*; ~**s of** (*col*) eine Unmenge von.

tonal [ˈtəʊnl] *a* tonal; Klang-.

tone [təʊn] *n* Ton *m*; *vi* (*harmonize*) passen (zu), harmonisieren (mit); *vt* eine Färbung geben (+*dat*); ~ **down** *vt* *criticism, demands* mäßigen; *colours* abtönen; ~-**deaf** *a* ohne musikalisches Gehör.

tongs [tɒŋz] *npl* Zange *f*; (*curling* —) Lockenstab *m*.

tongue [tʌŋ] *n* Zunge *f*; (*language*) Sprache *f*; **with** ~ **in cheek** ironisch, scherzhaft; ~-**tied** *a* stumm, sprachlos; ~-**twister** Zungenbrecher *m*.

tonic [ˈtɒnɪk] *n* (*Med*) Stärkungsmittel *nt*; (*Mus*) Grundton *m*, Tonika *f*; ~ **water** Tonic(water) *nt*.

tonight [təˈnaɪt] *n* heutige(r) Abend *m*; diese Nacht *f*; *ad* heute abend; heute nacht.

tonnage [ˈtʌnɪdʒ] *n* Tonnage *f*.

tonsil [ˈtɒnsl] *n* Mandel *f*; ~**itis** [tɒnsɪˈlaɪtɪs] Mandelentzündung *f*.

too [tuː] *ad* zu; (*also*) auch.

tool [tuːl] *n* (*lit, fig*) Werkzeug *nt*; ~**box** Werkzeugkasten *m*; ~**kit** Werkzeug *nt*.

toot [tuːt] *n* Hupen *nt*; *vi* tuten; (*Aut*) hupen.

tooth [tuːθ] *n*, *pl* **teeth** Zahn *m*; ~**ache** Zahnschmerzen *pl*, Zahnweh *nt*; ~**brush** Zahnbürste *f*; ~**paste** Zahnpasta *f*; ~**pick** Zahnstocher *m*; ~ **powder** Zahnpulver *nt*.

top [tɒp] *n* Spitze *f*; (*of mountain*) Gipfel *m*; (*of tree*) Wipfel *m*; (*toy*) Kreisel *m*; (—*gear*) vierte(r) Gang *m*; *a* oberste(r,s); *vt* *list* an erster Stelle stehen auf (+*dat*); **to** ~ **it all, he said** ... und er setzte dem noch die Krone auf, indem er sagte ...; **from** ~ **to toe** von Kopf bis Fuß; ~**coat** Mantel *m*; ~**flight** *a* erstklassig, prima; ~ **hat** Zylinder *m*; ~-**heavy** *a* oben schwerer als unten, kopflastig.

topic [ˈtɒpɪk] *n* Thema *nt*, Gesprächsgegenstand *m*; ~**al** *a* aktuell.

topless [ˈtɒpləs] *a* *dress* oben ohne.

top-level [ˈtɒpˈlevl] *a* auf höchster Ebene.

topmost [ˈtɒpməʊst] *a* oberste(r,s), höchste(r,s).

topple [ˈtɒpl] *vti* stürzen, kippen.

top-secret [ˈtɒpˈsiːkrət] *a* streng geheim.

topsy-turvy [ˈtɒpsɪˈtɜːvɪ] *ad* durcheinander; *a* auf den Kopf gestellt.

torch [tɔːtʃ] *n* (*Elec*) Taschenlampe *f*; (*with flame*) Fackel *f*.

torment [ˈtɔːment] *n* Qual *f*; [tɔːˈment] *vt* (*annoy*) plagen; (*distress*) quälen.

torn [tɔːn] *a* hin- und hergerissen.

tornado [tɔːˈneɪdəʊ] *n* Tornado *m*, Wirbelsturm *m*.

torpedo [tɔːˈpiːdəʊ] *n* Torpedo *m*.

torpor [ˈtɔːpə*] *n* Erstarrung *f*.

torrent ['tɔrənt] n Sturzbach m; ~ial [tə'renʃəl] a wolkenbruchartig.

torso ['tɔːsəʊ] n Torso m.

tortoise ['tɔːtəs] n Schildkröte f.

tortuous ['tɔːtjʊəs] a (winding) gewunden; (deceitful) krumm, unehrlich.

torture ['tɔːtʃə*] n Folter f; vt foltern.

Tory ['tɔːrɪ] n Tory m; a Tory-, konservativ.

toss [tɒs] vt werfen, schleudern; n (of coin) Hochwerfen nt; to ~ a coin, to ~ up for sth etw mit einer Münze entscheiden.

tot [tɒt] n (small quantity) bißchen nt; (small child) Knirps m.

total ['təʊtl] n Gesamtheit f, Ganze(s) nt; a ganz, gesamt, total; vt (add up) zusammenzählen; (amount to) sich belaufen auf; ~itarian [təʊtælɪ'tɛərɪən] a totalitär; ~ity [təʊ'tælɪtɪ] Gesamtheit f; ~ly ad gänzlich, total.

totem pole ['təʊtəmpəʊl] n Totempfahl m.

totter ['tɒtə*] vi wanken, schwanken, wackeln.

touch [tʌtʃ] n Berührung f, (sense of feeling) Tastsinn m; (small amount) Spur f; (style) Stil m; vt (feel) berühren; (come against) leicht anstoßen; (emotionally) bewegen, rühren; in ~ with in Verbindung mit; ~ on vt topic berühren, erwähnen; ~ up vt paint auffrischen; ~-and-go a riskant, knapp; ~down Landen nt, Niedergehen nt; ~iness Empfindlichkeit f; ~ing a rührend, ergreifend; ~line Seitenlinie f; ~y a empfindlich, reizbar.

tough [tʌf] a (strong) zäh, widerstandsfähig; (difficult) schwierig, hart; meat zäh; ~ luck Pech nt; n Schläger(typ) m; ~en vt zäh machen; (make strong) abhärten; vi zäh werden; ~ness Zähigkeit f, Härte f.

toupée ['tuːpeɪ] n Toupet nt.

tour ['tʊə*] n Reise f, Tour f, Fahrt f; vi umherreisen; (Theat) auf Tour sein/gehen; ~ing Umherreisen nt; (Theat) Tournee f; ~ism Fremdenverkehr m, Tourismus m; ~ist Tourist(in f); a (class) Touristen-; ad Touristenklasse; ~ist office Verkehrsamt nt.

tournament ['tʊənəmənt] n Tournier nt.

tousled ['taʊzld] a zerzaust.

tow [təʊ] n Schleppen nt; vt (ab)schleppen.

toward(s) [tə'wɔːd(z)] prep (with time) gegen; (in direction of) nach; he walked ~ me/the town er kam auf mich zu/er ging auf die Stadt zu; my feelings ~ him meine Gefühle ihm gegenüber.

towel ['taʊəl] n Handtuch nt.

tower ['taʊə*] n Turm m; ~ over vi (lit, fig) überragen; ~ing a hochragend; rage rasend.

town [taʊn] n Stadt f; ~ clerk Stadtdirektor m; ~ hall Rathaus nt; ~ planner Stadtplaner m.

towpath ['təʊpɑːθ] n Leinpfad m.

towrope ['təʊrəʊp] n Abschlepptau nt.

toxic ['tɒksɪk] a giftig, Gift-.

toy [tɔɪ] n Spielzeug nt; ~ with vt spielen mit; ~shop Spielwarengeschäft nt.

trace [treɪs] n Spur f; vt (follow a course) nachspüren (+dat); (find out) aufspüren; (copy) zeichnen, durchpausen.

track [træk] n (mark) Spur f; (path) Weg

m, Pfad m; (race—) Rennbahn f; (Rail) Gleis nt; vt verfolgen; to keep ~ of sb jdn im Auge behalten; to keep ~ of an argument einer Argumentation folgen können; to keep ~ of the situation die Lage verfolgen; to make ~s (for) gehen (nach); ~ down vt aufspüren; ~er dog Spürhund m; ~less a pfadlos.

tract [trækt] n (of land) Gebiet nt; (booklet) Abhandlung f, Traktat nt.

tractor ['træktə*] n Traktor m.

trade [treɪd] n (commerce) Handel m; (business) Geschäft nt, Gewerbe nt; (people) Geschäftsleute pl; (skilled manual work) Handwerk nt; vi handeln (in mit); vt tauschen; ~ in vt in Zahlung geben; ~mark Warenzeichen nt; ~ name Handelsbezeichnung f; ~r Händler m; ~sman (shopkeeper) Geschäftsmann m; (workman) Handwerker m; (delivery man) Lieferant m; ~ union Gewerkschaft f; ~unionist Gewerkschaftler(in f) m.

trading ['treɪdɪŋ] n Handel m; ~ estate Industriegelände nt; ~ stamp Rabattmarke f.

tradition [trə'dɪʃən] n Tradition f; ~al a traditionell, herkömmlich; ~ally ad üblicherweise, schon immer.

traffic ['træfɪk] n Verkehr m; (esp in drugs) Handel m (in mit); vi esp drugs handeln; ~ circle (US) Kreisverkehr m; ~ jam Verkehrsstauung f; ~ lights pl Verkehrsampeln pl.

tragedy ['trædʒədɪ] n (lit, fig) Tragödie f.

tragic ['trædʒɪk] a tragisch; ~ally ad tragisch, auf tragische Weise.

trail [treɪl] n (track) Spur f, Fährte f; (of meteor) Schweif m; (of smoke) Rauchfahne f; (of dust) Staubwolke f; (road) Pfad m, Weg m; vt animal verfolgen; person folgen (+dat); (drag) schleppen; vi (hang loosely) schleifen; (plants) sich ranken; (be behind) hinterherhinken; (Sport) weit zurückliegen; (walk) zuckeln; on the ~ auf der Spur; ~ behind vi zurückbleiben; ~er Anhänger m; (US: caravan) Wohnwagen m; (for film) Vorschau f.

train [treɪn] n Zug m; (of dress) Schleppe f; (series) Folge f, Kette f; vt (teach) person ausbilden; animal abrichten; mind schulen; (Sport) trainieren; (aim) richten (on auf +acc); plant wachsen lassen, ziehen; vi (exercise) trainieren; (study) ausgebildet werden; ~ed a eye geschult; person, voice ausgebildet; ~ee Anlernling m; Lehrling m; Praktikant(in f) m; ~er (Sport) Trainer m; Ausbilder m; ~ing (for occupation) Ausbildung f; (Sport) Training nt; in ~ing im Training; ~ing college Pädagogische Hochschule f, Lehrerseminar nt; (for priests) Priesterseminar nt.

traipse [treɪps] vi latschen.

trait [treɪ(t)] n Zug m, Merkmal nt.

traitor ['treɪtə*] n Verräter m.

trajectory [trə'dʒektərɪ] n Flugbahn f.

tram(car) ['træm(kɑː*)] n Straßenbahn f; ~line Straßenbahnschiene f; (route) Straßenbahnlinie f.

tramp [træmp] n Landstreicher m; vi

(walk heavily) stampfen, stapfen; *(travel on foot)* wandern; **~le** ['træmpl] *vt* (nieder)-trampeln; *vi* (herum)trampeln; **~oline** Trampolin *nt.*

trance [trɑ:ns] *n* Trance *f.*

tranquil ['træŋkwɪl] *a* ruhig, friedlich; **~ity** [træŋ'kwɪlɪtɪ] Ruhe *f;* **~izer** Beruhigungsmittel *nt.*

trans- [trænz] *pref* Trans-.

transact [træn'zækt] *vt* (durch)führen, abwickeln; **~ion** Durchführung *f,* Abwicklung *f; (piece of business)* Geschäft *nt,* Transaktion *f.*

transatlantic ['trænzət'læntɪk] *a* transatlantisch.

transcend [træn'send] *vt* übersteigen.

transcendent [træn'sendənt] *a* transzendent.

transcript ['trænskrɪpt] *n* Abschrift *f,* Kopie *f, (Jur)* Protokoll *nt;* **~ion** [træn'skrɪpʃən] Transkription *f; (product)* Abschrift *f.*

transept ['trænsept] *n* Querschiff *nt.*

transfer ['trænsfə*] *n (transferring)* Übertragung *f, (of business)* Umzug *m; (being transferred)* Versetzung *f; (design)* Abziehbild *nt; (Sport)* Transfer *m; (player)* Transferspieler *m;* [træns'fɜ:*] *vt* business verlegen; person versetzen; prisoner überführen; drawing übertragen; money überweisen; **~able** [træns'fɜ:rəbl] *a* übertragbar.

transform [træns'fɔ:m] *vt* umwandeln, verändern; **~ation** [trænsfə'meɪʃən] Umwandlung *f,* Veränderung *f,* Verwandlung *f;* **~er** *(Elec)* Transformator *m.*

transfusion [træns'fju:ʒən] *n* Blut-übertragung *f,* Transfusion *f.*

transient ['trænziənt] *a* kurz(lebig).

transistor [træn'zɪstə*] *n (Elec)* Transistor *m; (radio)* Transistorradio *nt.*

transit ['trænzɪt] *n:* **in ~** unterwegs, auf dem Transport.

transition [træn'zɪʃən] *n* Übergang *m;* **~al** *a* Übergangs-.

transitive *a,* **~ly** *ad* ['trænzɪtɪv, -lɪ] transitiv.

transitory ['trænzɪtɔrɪ] *a* vorübergehend.

translate [trænz'leɪt] *vti* übersetzen.

translation [trænz'leɪʃən] *n* Übersetzung *f.*

translator [trænz'leɪtə*] *n* Übersetzer(in *f) m.*

transmission [trænz'mɪʃən] *n (of information)* Übermittlung *f; (Elec, Med, TV)* Übertragung *f; (Aut)* Getriebe *nt; (process)* Übersetzung *f.*

transmit [trænz'mɪt] *vt* message übermitteln; *(Elec, Med, TV)* übertragen; **~ter** Sender *m.*

transparency [træns'pɛərənsɪ] *n* Durchsichtigkeit *f,* Transparenz *f; (Phot also* [-'pærənsɪ] Dia(positiv) *nt.*

transparent [træns'pærənt] *a (lit)* durchsichtig; *(fig)* offenkundig.

transplant [træns'plɑ:nt] *vt* umpflanzen; *(Med)* verpflanzen; *(fig)* person verpflanzen; ['trænsplɑ:nt] *n (Med)* Transplantation *f; (organ)* Transplantat *nt.*

transport ['trænspɔ:t] *n* Transport *m,* Beförderung *f; (vehicle)* fahrbare(r)

Untersatz *m;* **means of ~** Transportmittel *nt;* [træns'pɔ:t] *vt* befördern; transportieren; **~able** [træns'pɔ:təbl] *a* transportabel; **~ation** [trænspɔ:'teɪʃən] Transport *m,* Beförderung *f; (means)* Beförderungsmittel *nt; (cost)* Transportkosten *pl.*

transverse ['trænzvɜ:s] *a* Quer-; *position* horizontal; *engine* querliegend.

transvestite [trænz'vestaɪt] *n* Transvestit *m.*

trap [træp] *n* Falle *f; (carriage)* zweirädrige(r) Einspänner *m; (col: mouth)* Klappe *f; vt* fangen; person in eine Falle locken; **the miners were ~ed** die Bergleute waren eingeschlossen; **~door** Falltür *f.*

trapeze [trə'pi:z] *n* Trapez *nt.*

trapper ['træpə*] *n* Fallensteller *m,* Trapper *m.*

trappings ['træpɪŋz] *npl* Aufmachung *f.*

trash [træʃ] *n (rubbish)* wertlose(s) Zeug *nt,* Plunder *m; (nonsense)* Mist *m,* Blech *nt;* **~ can** *(US)* Mülleimer *m;* **~y** *a* wertlos; *novel etc* Schund-.

trauma ['trɔ:mə] *n* Trauma *nt;* **~tic** [trɔ:'mætɪk] *a* traumatisch.

travel ['trævl] *n* Reisen *nt; vi* reisen, eine Reise machen; *vt distance* zurücklegen; country bereisen; **~ler,** *(US)* **~er** Reisende(r) *mf; (salesman)* Handlungsreisende(r) *m;* **~ler's cheque,** *(US)* **~er's check** Reisescheck *m;* **~ling,** *(US)* **~ing** Reisen *nt;* **~ling bag** Reisetasche *f;* **~ sickness** Reisekrankheit *f.*

traverse [træ'vɜ:s] *vt (cross)* durchqueren; *(lie across)* überspannen.

travesty ['trævəstɪ] *n* Zerrbild *nt,* Travestie *f;* **a ~ of justice** ein Hohn *m* auf die Gerechtigkeit.

trawler ['trɔ:lə*] *n* Fischdampfer *m,* Trawler *m.*

tray [treɪ] *n (tea ~)* Tablett *nt; (receptacle)* Schale *f; (for mail)* Ablage *f.*

treacherous ['tretʃərəs] *a* verräterisch; *memory* unzuverlässig; *road* tückisch.

treachery ['tretʃərɪ] *n* Verrat *m; (of road)* tückische(r) Zustand *m.*

treacle ['tri:kl] *n* Sirup *m,* Melasse *f.*

tread [tred] *n* Schritt *m,* Tritt *m; (of stair)* Stufe *f; (on tyre)* Profil *nt; vi irreg* treten; *(walk)* gehen; **~ on** *vt* treten auf *(+acc).*

treason ['tri:zn] *n* Verrat *m (to* an *+dat).*

treasure ['treʒə*] *n* Schatz *m; vt* schätzen; **~ hunt** Schatzsuche *f;* **~r** Kassenverwalter *m,* Schatzmeister *m.*

treasury ['treʒərɪ] *n (Pol)* Finanzministerium *nt.*

treat [tri:t] *n* besondere Freude *f; (school ~ etc)* Fest *nt; (outing)* Ausflug *m; vt (deal with)* behandeln; *(entertain)* bewirten; **to ~ sb to sth** jdn zu etw einladen, jdm etw spendieren.

treatise ['tri:tɪz] *n* Abhandlung *f.*

treatment ['tri:tmənt] *n* Behandlung *f.*

treaty ['tri:tɪ] *n* Vertrag *m.*

treble ['trebl] *a* dreifach; *vt* verdreifachen; *n (voice)* Sopran *m; (music)* Diskant *m;* **~ clef** Violinschlüssel *m.*

tree [tri:] *n* Baum *m*; ~-**lined** *a* baumbestanden; ~ **trunk** Baumstamm *m*.

trek [trek] *n* Treck *m*, Zug *m*; *vi* trecken.

trellis ['trelɪs] *n* Gitter *nt*; (*for gardening*) Spalier *nt*.

tremble ['trembl] *vi* zittern; (*ground*) beben.

trembling ['tremblɪŋ] *n* Zittern *nt*; *a* zitternd.

tremendous [trə'mendəs] *a* gewaltig, kolossal; (*col: very good*) prima; ~**ly** *ad* ungeheuer, enorm; (*col*) unheimlich.

tremor ['tremə*] *n* Zittern *nt*; (*of earth*) Beben *nt*.

trench [trentʃ] *n* Graben *m*; (*Mil*) Schützengraben *m*.

trend [trend] *n* Richtung *f*, Tendenz *f*; *vi* sich neigen, tendieren; ~**y** *a* (*col*) modisch.

trepidation [trepɪ'deɪʃən] *n* Beklommenheit *f*.

trespass ['trespəs] *vi* widerrechtlich betreten (*on* *acc*); '~**ers will be prosecuted**' 'Betreten verboten.'

tress [tres] *n* Locke *f*.

trestle ['tresl] *n* Bock *m*; ~ **table** Klapptisch *m*.

tri- [traɪ] *pref* Drei-, drei-.

trial ['traɪəl] *n* (*Jur*) Prozeß *m*, Verfahren *nt*; (*test*) Versuch *m*, Probe *f*; (*hardship*) Prüfung *f*; **by** ~ **and error** durch Ausprobieren.

triangle ['traɪæŋgl] *n* Dreieck *nt*; (*Mus*) Triangel *f*.

triangular [traɪ'æŋgjulə*] *a* dreieckig.

tribal ['traɪbəl] *a* Stammes-.

tribe [traɪb] *n* Stamm *m*; ~**sman** Stammesangehörige(r) *m*.

tribulation [trɪbju'leɪʃən] *n* Not *f*, Mühsal *f*.

tribunal [traɪ'bju:nl] *n* Gericht *nt*; (*inquiry*) Untersuchungsausschuß *m*.

tributary ['trɪbjutərɪ] *n* Nebenfluß *m*.

tribute ['trɪbju:t] *n* (*admiration*) Zeichen *nt* der Hochachtung.

trice [traɪs] *n*: **in a** ~ im Nu.

trick [trɪk] *n* Trick *m*; (*mischief*) Streich *m*; (*habit*) Angewohnheit *f*; (*Cards*) Stich *m*; *vt* überlisten, beschwindeln; ~**ery** Betrügerei *f*, Tricks *pl*.

trickle ['trɪkl] *n* Tröpfeln *nt*; (*small river*) Rinnsal *nt*; *vi* tröpfeln; (*seep*) sickern.

tricky ['trɪkɪ] *a problem* schwierig; *situation* kitzlig.

tricycle ['traɪsɪkl] *n* Dreirad *nt*.

tried [traɪd] *a* erprobt, bewährt.

trier ['traɪə*] *n*: **to be a** ~ sich (*dat*) ernsthaft Mühe geben.

trifle ['traɪfl] *n* Kleinigkeit *f*; (*Cook*) Trifle *m*; *ad*: **a** ~ ein bißchen.

trifling ['traɪflɪŋ] *a* geringfügig.

trigger ['trɪgə*] *n* Drücker *m*; ~ **off** *vt* auslösen.

trigonometry [trɪgə'nɒmətrɪ] *n* Trigonometrie *f*.

trilby ['trɪlbɪ] *n* weiche(r) Filzhut *m*.

trill [trɪl] *n* (*Mus*) Triller *m*.

trilogy ['trɪlədʒɪ] *n* Trilogie *f*.

trim [trɪm] *a* ordentlich, gepflegt; *figure*

schlank; *n* (gute) Verfassung *f*; (*embellishment, on car*) Verzierung *f*; **to give sb's hair a** ~ jdm die Haare etwas schneiden; *vt* (*clip*) schneiden; *trees* stutzen; (*decorate*) besetzen; *sails* trimmen; ~**mings** *pl* (*decorations*) Verzierung(en *pl*) *f*; (*extras*) Zubehör *nt*.

Trinity ['trɪnɪtɪ] *n*: **the** ~ die Dreieinigkeit.

trinket ['trɪŋkɪt] *n* kleine(s) Schmuckstück *nt*.

trio ['tri:əʊ] *n* Trio *nt*.

trip [trɪp] *n* (kurze) Reise *f*; (*outing*) Ausflug *m*; (*stumble*) Stolpern *nt*; *vi* (*walk quickly*) trippeln; (*stumble*) stolpern; ~ **over** *vt* stolpern über (+*acc*); ~ **up** *vi* stolpern; (*fig also*) einen Fehler machen; *vt* zu Fall bringen; (*fig*) hereinlegen.

tripe [traɪp] *n* (*food*) Kutteln *pl*; (*rubbish*) Mist *m*.

triple ['trɪpl] *a* dreifach; ~**ts** ['trɪpləts] *pl* Drillinge *pl*.

triplicate ['trɪplɪkət] *n*: **in** ~ in dreifacher Ausfertigung.

tripod ['traɪpɒd] *n* Dreifuß *m*; (*Phot*) Stativ *nt*.

tripper ['trɪpə*] *n* Ausflügler(in *f*) *m*.

trite [traɪt] *a* banal.

triumph ['traɪʌmf] *n* Triumph *m*; *vi* triumphieren; ~**al** [traɪ'ʌmfəl] *a* triumphal, Sieges-; ~**ant** [traɪ'ʌmfənt] *a* triumphierend; (*victorious*) siegreich; ~**antly** *ad* triumphierend; siegreich.

trivial ['trɪvɪəl] *a* gering(fügig), trivial; ~**lity** [trɪvɪ'ælɪtɪ] *n* Trivialität *f*, Nebensächlichkeit *f*.

trolley ['trɒlɪ] *n* Handwagen *m*; (*in shop*) Einkaufswagen *m*; (*for luggage*) Kofferkuli *m*; (*table*) Teewagen *m*; ~ **bus** O(berleitungs)bus *m*.

trollop ['trɒləp] *n* Hure *f*; (*slut*) Schlampe *f*.

trombone [trɒm'bəʊn] *n* Posaune *f*.

troop [tru:p] *n* Schar *f*; (*Mil*) Trupp *m*; ~**s** *pl* Truppen *pl*; ~ **in/out** *vi* hinein-/hinausströmen; ~**er** *n* Kavallerist *m*; ~**ship** Truppentransporter *m*.

trophy ['trəʊfɪ] *n* Trophäe *f*.

tropic ['trɒpɪk] *n* Wendekreis *m*; **the** ~**s** *pl* die Tropen *pl*; ~**al** *a* tropisch.

trot [trɒt] *n* Trott *m*; *vi* trotten.

trouble ['trʌbl] *n* (*worry*) Sorge *f*, Kummer *m*; (*in country, industry*) Unruhen *pl*; (*effort*) Umstand *m*, Mühe *f*; *vt* (*disturb*) beunruhigen, stören, belästigen; **to** ~ **to do sth** sich bemühen, etw zu tun; **to make** ~ Schwierigkeiten or Unannehmlichkeiten machen; **to have** ~ **with** Ärger haben mit; **to be in** ~ Probleme or Ärger haben; ~**d** *a person* beunruhigt; *country* geplagt; ~**-free** *a* sorglos; ~**maker** Unruhestifter *m*; ~**shooter** Vermittler *m*; ~**some** *a* lästig, unangenehm; *child* schwierig.

trough [trɒf] *n* (*vessel*) Trog *m*; (*channel*) Rinne *f*, Kanal *m*; (*Met*) Tief *nt*.

trounce [traʊns] *vt* (*esp Sport*) vernichtend schlagen.

troupe [tru:p] *n* Truppe *f*.

trousers ['traʊzəz] *npl* (lange) Hose *f*, Hosen *pl*.

trousseau ['tru:səʊ] n Aussteuer f.

trout [traʊt] n Forelle f.

trowel ['traʊəl] n Kelle f.

truant ['truːənt] n: **to play ~** (die Schule) schwänzen.

truce [truːs] n Waffenstillstand m.

truck [trʌk] n Lastwagen m, Lastauto nt; (Rail) offene(r) Güterwagen m; (barrow) Gepäckkarren m; **to have no ~ with sb** nichts zu tun haben wollen mit jdm; **~ driver** Lastwagenfahrer m; **~ farm** (US) Gemüsegärtnerei f.

truculent ['trʌkjʊlənt] a trotzig.

trudge [trʌdʒ] vi sich (mühselig) dahinschleppen.

true [truː] a (exact) wahr; (genuine) echt; friend treu.

truffle ['trʌfl] n Trüffel f.

truly ['truːlɪ] ad (really) wirklich; (exactly) genau; (faithfully) treu; **yours ~** Ihr sehr ergebener.

trump [trʌmp] n (Cards) Trumpf m; **~ed-up** erfunden.

trumpet ['trʌmpɪt] n Trompete f; vt ausposaunen; vi trompeten.

truncated [trʌŋ'keɪtɪd] a verstümmelt.

truncheon ['trʌntʃən] n Gummiknüppel m.

trundle ['trʌndl] vt schieben; vi: **~ along** (person) dahinschlendern; (vehicle) entlangrollen.

trunk [trʌŋk] n (of tree) (Baum)stamm m; (Anat) Rumpf m; (box) Truhe f, Überseekoffer m; (of elephant) Rüssel m; **~s** pl Badehose f; **~ call** Ferngespräch nt.

truss [trʌs] n (Med) Bruchband nt.

trust [trʌst] n (confidence) Vertrauen nt; (for property etc) Treuhandvermögen nt; vt (rely on) vertrauen (+dat), sich verlassen auf (+acc); (hope) hoffen; **~ him to break it!** er muß es natürlich kaputt machen, typisch!; **to ~ sth to sb** jdm etw anvertrauen; **~ed** a treu; **~ee** [trʌs'tiː] Vermögensverwalter m; **~ful** a, **~ing** a vertrauensvoll; **~worthy** a vertrauenswürdig; account glaubwürdig; **~y** a treu, zuverlässig.

truth [truːθ] n Wahrheit f; **~ful** a ehrlich; **~fully** ad wahrheitsgemäß; **~fulness** Ehrlichkeit f; (of statement) Wahrheit f.

try [traɪ] n Versuch m; **to have a ~** es versuchen; vt (attempt) versuchen; (test) (aus)probieren; (Jur) person unter Anklage stellen; case verhandeln; (strain) anstrengen; courage, patience auf die Probe stellen; vi (make effort) versuchen, sich bemühen; **~ on** vt dress anprobieren; hat aufprobieren; **~ out** vt ausprobieren; **~ing** a schwierig; **~ing for** anstrengend für.

tsar [zɑː*] n Zar m.

T-shirt ['tiː:ʃɜːt] n T-shirt nt.

T-square ['tiːskwɛə*] n Reißschiene f.

tub [tʌb] n Wanne f, Kübel m; (for margarine etc) Becher m.

tuba ['tjuːbə] n Tuba f.

tubby ['tʌbɪ] a rundlich, klein und dick.

tube [tjuːb] n (pipe) Röhre f, Rohr nt; (for toothpaste etc) Tube f; (in London) U-Bahn

f; (Aut: for tyre) Schlauch m; **~less** a (Aut) schlauchlos.

tuber ['tjuːbə*] n Knolle f.

tuberculosis [tjubɜːkjuˈləʊsɪs] n Tuberkulose f.

tube station ['tjuːbsteɪʃən] n U-Bahn-station f.

tubular ['tjuːbjʊlə*] a röhrenförmig.

tuck [tʌk] n (fold) Falte f, Einschlag m; vt (put) stecken; (gather) fälteln, einschlagen; **~ away** vt wegstecken; **~ in** vt hineinstecken; blanket etc feststecken; person zudecken; vi (eat) hineinhauen, zulangen; **~ up** vt child warm zudecken; **~ shop** Süßwarenladen m.

Tuesday ['tjuːzdeɪ] n Dienstag m.

tuft [tʌft] n Büschel m.

tug [tʌg] n (jerk) Zerren nt, Ruck m; (Naut) Schleppdampfer m; vti zerren, ziehen; boat schleppen; **~-of-war** Tauziehen nt.

tuition [tjuˈɪʃən] n Unterricht m.

tulip ['tjuːlɪp] n Tulpe f.

tumble ['tʌmbl] n (fall) Sturz m; vi (fall) fallen, stürzen; **~ to** vt kapieren; **~down** a baufällig; **~r** (glass) Trinkglas nt, Wasserglas nt; (for drying) Trockenautomat m.

tummy ['tʌmɪ] n (col) Bauch m.

tumour ['tjuːmə*] n Tumor m, Geschwulst f.

tumult ['tjuːmʌlt] n Tumult m; **~uous** [tjuˈmʌltjuəs] a lärmend, turbulent.

tumulus ['tjuːmjʊləs] n Grabhügel m.

tuna ['tjuːnə] n Thunfisch m.

tundra ['tʌndrə] n Tundra f.

tune [tjuːn] n Melodie f; vt (put in tune) stimmen; (Aut) richtig einstellen; **to sing in ~/out of ~** richtig/falsch singen; **to be out of ~** with nicht harmonieren mit; **~ in** vi einstellen (to acc); **~ up** vi (Mus) stimmen; **~r** (person) (Instrumenten)stimmer m; (radio set) Empfangsgerät nt, Steuergerät nt; (part) Tuner m, Kanalwähler m; **~ful** a melodisch.

tungsten ['tʌŋstən] n Wolfram nt.

tunic ['tjuːnɪk] n Waffenrock m; (loose garment) lange Bluse f.

tuning ['tjuːnɪŋ] n (Rad, Aut) Einstellen nt; (Mus) Stimmen nt.

tunnel ['tʌnl] n Tunnel m, Unterführung f; vi einen Tunnel anlegen.

tunny ['tʌnɪ] n Thunfisch m.

turban ['tɜːbən] n Turban m.

turbid ['tɜːbɪd] a trübe; (fig) verworren.

turbine ['tɜːbaɪn] n Turbine f.

turbot ['tɜːbət] n Steinbutt m.

turbulence ['tɜːbjʊləns] n (Aviat) Turbulenz f.

turbulent ['tɜːbjʊlənt] a stürmisch.

tureen [tjʊriːn] n Terrine f.

turf [tɜːf] n Rasen m; (piece) Sode f.

turgid ['tɜːdʒɪd] a geschwollen.

turkey ['tɜːkɪ] n Puter m, Truthahn m.

turmoil ['tɜːmɔɪl] n Aufruhr m, Tumult m.

turn [tɜːn] n (rotation) (Um)drehung f; (performance) (Programm)nummer f; (Med) Schock m; vt (rotate) drehen; (change position of) umdrehen, wenden; page umblättern; (transform) verwandeln;

(*direct*) zuwenden; *vi* (*rotate*) sich drehen;
(*change direction*) (*in car*) abbiegen;
(*wind*) drehen; (— *round*) umdrehen,
wenden; (*become*) werden; (*leaves*) sich
verfärben; (*milk*) sauer werden; (*weather*)
umschlagen; (*become*) werden; **to make a
~ to the left** nach links abbiegen; **the ~
of the tide** der Gezeitenwechsel; **the ~
of the century** die Jahrhundertwende; **to
take a ~ for the worse** sich zum
Schlechten wenden; **it's your ~** du bist
dran or an der Reihe; **in ~, by ~s**
abwechselnd; **to take ~s** sich
abwechseln; **to do sb a good/bad ~** jdm
einen guten/schlechten Dienst erweisen;
it gave me quite a ~ das hat mich
schön erschreckt; **to ~ sb loose** jdn los-
or freilassen; **~ back** *vt* umdrehen; *person*
zurückschicken; *clock* zurückstellen; *vi*
umkehren; **~ down** *vt* (*refuse*) ablehnen;
(*fold down*) umschlagen; **~ in** *vi* (*go to
bed*) ins Bett gehen; *vt* (*fold inwards*) einwärts biegen; **~ into** *vi* sich verwandeln
in (+*acc*); **~ off** *vi* abbiegen; *vt* ausschalten; *tap* zudrehen; *machine, electricity*
abstellen; **~ on** *vt* (*light*) anschalten, einschalten; *tap* aufdrehen; *machine* anstellen;
~ out *vt* (*prove to be*) sich herausstellen,
sich erweisen; (*people*) sich entwickeln;
how did the cake ~ out? wie ist der
Kuchen geworden?; *vt light* ausschalten;
gas abstellen; (*produce*) produzieren; **~ to**
vt sich zuwenden (+*dat*); **~ up** *vi*
auftauchen; (*happen*) passieren, sich
ereignen; *vt collar* hochklappen, hoch-
stellen; *nose* rümpfen; (*increase*) *radio*
lauter stellen; *heat* höher drehen; **~about**
Kehrtwendung *f.*; **~ed-up a** *nose* Stups-;
~ing (*in road*) Abzweigung *f.*; **~ing
point** Wendepunkt *m.*

turnip [ˈtəːnɪp] *n* Steckrübe *f.*

turnout [ˈtəːnaʊt] *n* (Besucher)zahl *f.*;
(*Comm*) Produktion *f.*

turnover [ˈtəːnəʊvə*] *n* Umsatz *m.*; (*of
staff*) Wechsel *m.*; (*Cook*) Tasche *f.*

turnpike [ˈtəːnpaɪk] *n* (*US*) gebührenpflichtige Straße *f.*

turnstile [ˈtəːnstaɪl] *n* Drehkreuz *nt.*

turntable [ˈtəːnteɪbl] *n* (*of record-player*)
Plattenteller *m.*; (*Rail*) Drehscheibe *f.*

turn-up [ˈtəːnʌp] *n* (*on trousers*) Aufschlag
m.

turpentine [ˈtəːpəntaɪn] *n* Terpentin *nt.*

turquoise [ˈtəːkwɔɪz] *n* (*gem*) Türkis *m.*;
(*colour*) Türkis *nt.*; *a* türkisfarben.

turret [ˈtʌrɪt] *n* Turm *m.*

turtle [ˈtəːtl] *n* Schildkröte *f.*

tusk [tʌsk] *n* Stoßzahn *m.*

tussle [ˈtʌsl] *n* Balgerei *f.*

tutor [ˈtjuːtə*] *n* (*teacher*) Privatlehrer *m.*;
(*college instructor*) Tutor *m.*; **~ial**
[tjuːˈtɔːrɪəl] *n* (*Univ*) Kolloquium *nt.*,
Seminarübung *f.*

tuxedo [tʌkˈsiːdəʊ] *n* (*US*) Smoking *m.*

TV [ˈtiːˈviː] *n* Fernseher *m.*; *a* Fernseh-.

twaddle [ˈtwɒdl] *n* (*col*) Gewäsch *nt.*

twang [twæŋ] *n* scharfe(r) Ton *m.*; (*of
voice*) Näseln *nt.*; *vt* zupfen; *vi* klingen;
(*talk*) näseln.

tweed [twiːd] *n* Tweed *m.*

tweezers [ˈtwiːzəz] *npl* Pinzette *f.*

twelfth [twelfθ] *a* zwölfte(r,s); **T~ Night**
Dreikönigsabend *m.*

twelve [twelv] *num a* zwölf.

twenty [ˈtwentɪ] *num a* zwanzig.

twerp [twəːp] *n* (*col*) Knülch *m.*

twice [twaɪs] *ad* zweimal; **~ as much**
doppelt soviel; **~ my age** doppelt so alt
wie ich.

twig [twɪg] *n* dünne(r) Zweig *m.*; *vt* (*col*)
kapieren, merken.

twilight [ˈtwaɪlaɪt] *n* Dämmerung *f.*,
Zwielicht *nt.*

twill [twɪl] *n* Köper *m.*

twin [twɪn] *n* Zwilling *m.*; *a* Zwillings-; (*very
similar*) Doppel-.

twine [twaɪn] *n* Bindfaden *m.*; *vi* binden.

twinge [twɪndʒ] *n* stechende(r) Schmerz
m., Stechen *nt.*

twinkle [ˈtwɪŋkl] *n* Funkeln *nt.*, Blitzen *nt.*;
vi funkeln.

twin town [ˈtwɪntaʊn] *n* Partnerstadt *f.*

twirl [twəːl] *n* Wirbel *m.*; *vti* (*herum*)-
wirbeln.

twist [twɪst] *n* (*twisting*) Biegen *nt.*,
Drehung *f.*; (*bend*) Kurve *f.*; *vt* (*turn*)
drehen; (*make crooked*) verbiegen;
(*distort*) verdrehen; *vi* (*wind*) sich drehen;
(*curve*) sich winden.

twit [twɪt] *n* (*col*) Idiot *m.*

twitch [twɪtʃ] *n* Zucken *nt.*; *vi* zucken.

two [tuː] *num a* zwei; **to break in ~** in
zwei Teile brechen; **~ by ~** zu zweit; **to
be in ~ minds** nicht genau wissen; **to
put ~ and ~ together** seine Schlüsse
ziehen; **~-door** *a* zweitürig; **~-faced** *a*
falsch; **~-fold** *a, ad* zweifach, doppelt;
~-piece *a* zweiteilig; **~-seater** (*plane,
car*) Zweisitzer *m.*; **~some** Paar *nt.*;
~-way *a traffic* Gegen-.

tycoon [taɪˈkuːn] *n* (Industrie)magnat *m.*

type [taɪp] *n* Typ *m.*, Art *f.*; (*Print*) Type *f.*;
vti maschineschreiben, tippen; **~-cast** *a*
(*Theat, TV*) auf eine Rolle festgelegt;
~script maschinegeschriebene(r) Text
m.; **~writer** Schreibmaschine *f.*;
~written *a* maschinegeschrieben.

typhoid [ˈtaɪfɔɪd] *n* Typhus *m.*

typhoon [taɪˈfuːn] *n* Taifun *m.*

typhus [ˈtaɪfəs] *n* Flecktyphus *m.*

typical *a*, **~ly** *ad* [ˈtɪpɪkəl, -klɪ] typisch (*of*
für).

typify [ˈtɪpɪfaɪ] *vt* typisch sein für.

typing [ˈtaɪpɪŋ] *n* Maschineschreiben *nt.*

typist [ˈtaɪpɪst] *n* Maschineschreiber(in *f*)
m, Tippse *f* (*col*).

tyranny [ˈtɪrənɪ] *n* Tyrannei *f*, Gewaltherr-
schaft *f.*

tyrant [ˈtaɪərənt] *n* Tyrann *m.*

tyre [taɪə*] *n* Reifen *m.*

U

U, u [juː] *n* U *nt*, u *nt.*

ubiquitous [juːˈbɪkwɪtəs] *adj* überall zu
finden(d); allgegenwärtig.

udder [ˈʌdə*] *n* Euter *nt.*

ugh [əːh] *interj* hu.

ugliness [ˈʌglɪnəs] *n* Häßlichkeit *f.*

ugly [ˈʌglɪ] a häßlich; (bad) böse, schlimm.

ukulele [juːkəˈleɪlɪ] n Ukulele f.

ulcer [ˈʌlsə*] n Geschwür nt.

ulterior [ʌlˈtɪərɪə*] a: ~ **motive** Hintergedanke m.

ultimate [ˈʌltɪmət] a äußerste(r,s), allerletzte(r,s); ~**ly** ad schließlich, letzten Endes.

ultimatum [ʌltɪˈmeɪtəm] n Ultimatum nt.

ultra- [ˈʌltrə] pref ultra-.

ultraviolet [ʌltrəˈvaɪələt] a ultraviolett.

umbilical cord [ʌmˈbɪklɪkl kɔːd] n Nabelschnur f.

umbrage [ˈʌmbrɪdʒ] n: **to take** ~ Anstoß nehmen (at an +dat).

umbrella [ʌmˈbrelə] n Schirm m.

umpire [ˈʌmpaɪə*] n Schiedsrichter m; vti schiedsrichtern.

umpteen [ˈʌmptiːn] num (col) zig.

un- [ʌn] pref un-.

unabashed [ʌnəˈbæʃt] a unerschrocken.

unabated [ʌnəˈbeɪtɪd] a unvermindert.

unable [ʌnˈeɪbl] a außerstande; **to be** ~ **to do sth** etw nicht tun können.

unaccompanied [ˈʌnəˈkʌmpənɪd] a ohne Begleitung.

unaccountably [ʌnəˈkauntəblɪ] ad unerklärlich.

unaccustomed [ʌnəˈkʌstəmd] a nicht gewöhnt (to an +acc); (unusual) ungewohnt.

unadulterated [ˈʌnəˈdʌltəreɪtəd] a rein, unverfälscht.

unaided [ˈʌnˈeɪdɪd] a selbständig, ohne Hilfe.

unanimity [juːnəˈnɪmɪtɪ] n Einstimmigkeit f.

unanimous a, ~**ly** ad [juːˈnænɪməs, -lɪ] einmütig; vote einstimmig.

unattached [ʌnəˈtætʃt] a ungebunden.

unattended [ʌnəˈtendɪd] a person unbeaufsichtigt; thing unbewacht.

unattractive [ʌnəˈtræktɪv] a unattraktiv.

unauthorized [ʌnˈɔːθəraɪzd] a unbefugt.

unavoidable a, **unavoidably** ad [ʌnəˈvɔɪdəbl, -blɪ] unvermeidlich.

unaware [ʌnəˈweə*] a: **to be** ~ **of sth** sich (dat) einer Sache nicht bewußt sein; ~**s** ad unversehens.

unbalanced [ˈʌnˈbælənst] a unausgeglichen; (mentally) gestört.

unbearable [ʌnˈbɛərəbl] a unerträglich.

unbeatable [ʌnˈbiːtəbl] a unschlagbar.

unbeaten [ʌnˈbiːtn] a ungeschlagen.

unbecoming [ʌnbɪˈkʌmɪŋ] a dress unkleidsam; behaviour unpassend, unschicklich.

unbeknown [ʌnbɪˈnəʊn] ad ohne jedes Wissen (to gen).

unbelief [ʌnbɪˈliːf] n Unglaube m.

unbelievable [ʌnbɪˈliːvəbl] a unglaublich.

unbend [ʌnˈbend] irreg vt geradebiegen, gerademachen; vi aus sich herausgehen.

unbounded [ʌnˈbaʊndɪd] a unbegrenzt.

unbreakable [ʌnˈbreɪkəbl] a unzerbrechlich.

unbridled [ʌnˈbraɪdld] a ungezügelt.

unbroken [ʌnˈbrəʊkən] a period

ununterbrochen; spirit ungebrochen; record unübertroffen.

unburden [ʌnˈbɜːdn] vt: ~ **o.s.** (jdm) sein Herz ausschütten.

unbutton [ʌnˈbʌtn] vt aufknöpfen.

uncalled-for [ʌnˈkɔːldfɔː*] a unnötig.

uncanny [ʌnˈkænɪ] a unheimlich.

unceasing [ʌnˈsiːsɪŋ] a unaufhörlich.

uncertain [ʌnˈsɜːtn] a unsicher; (doubtful) ungewiß; (unreliable) unbeständig; (vague) undeutlich, vage; ~**ty** Ungewißheit f.

unchanged [ʌnˈtʃeɪndʒd] a unverändert.

uncharitable [ʌnˈtʃærɪtəbl] a hartherzig; remark unfreundlich.

uncharted [ʌnˈtʃɑːtɪd] a nicht verzeichnet.

unchecked [ʌnˈtʃekt] a ungeprüft; (not stopped) advance ungehindert.

uncivil [ʌnˈsɪvɪl] a unhöflich, grob.

uncle [ʌŋkl] n Onkel m.

uncomfortable [ʌnˈkʌmfətəbl] a unbequem, ungemütlich.

uncompromising [ʌnˈkɒmprəmaɪzɪŋ] kompromißlos, unnachgiebig.

unconditional [ˈʌnkənˈdɪʃənl] a bedingungslos.

uncongenial [ˈʌnkənˈdʒiːnɪəl] a unangenehm.

unconscious [ʌnˈkɒnʃəs] a (Med) bewußtlos; (not aware) nicht bewußt; (not meant) unbeabsichtigt; **the** ~ das Unbewußte; ~**ly** ad unwesentlich, unbewußt; ~**ness** Bewußtlosigkeit f.

uncontrollable [ʌnkənˈtrəʊləbl] a unkontrollierbar, unbändig.

uncork [ʌnˈkɔːk] vt entkorken.

uncouth [ʌnˈkuːθ] a grob, ungehobelt.

uncover [ʌnˈkʌvə*] vt aufdecken.

unctuous [ˈʌŋktjʊəs] a salbungsvoll.

undaunted [ʌnˈdɔːntɪd] a unerschrocken.

undecided [ˈʌndɪˈsaɪdɪd] a unschlüssig.

undeniable [ʌndɪˈnaɪəbl] a unleugbar.

undeniably [ʌndɪˈnaɪəblɪ] ad unbestreitbar.

under [ˈʌndə*] prep unter; ad darunter; ~ **repair** in Reparatur; ~**-age** a minderjährig.

undercarriage [ˈʌndəkærɪdʒ] n Fahrgestell nt.

underclothes [ˈʌndəkləʊðz] npl Unterwäsche f.

undercoat [ˈʌndəkəʊt] n (paint) Grundierung f.

undercover [ˈʌndəkʌvə*] a Geheim-.

undercurrent [ˈʌndəkʌrənt] n Unterströmung f.

undercut [ˈʌndəkʌt] vt irreg unterbieten.

underdeveloped [ˈʌndədɪˈveləpt] a Entwicklungs-, unterentwickelt.

underdog [ˈʌndədɒg] n Unterlegene(r) mf.

underdone [ˈʌndəˈdʌn] a (Cook) nicht gar, nicht durchgebraten.

underestimate [ˈʌndərˈestɪmeɪt] vt unterschätzen.

underexposed [ˈʌndərɪksˈpəʊzd] a unterbelichtet.

underfed [ˈʌndəˈfed] a unterernährt.

underfoot [ˈʌndəˈfʊt] ad unter den Füßen.

undergo [ˈʌndəˈgəʊ] vt irreg experience

durchmachen; *operation, test* sich unterziehen (+*dat*).

undergraduate ['ʌndə'grædjuət] *n* Student(in *f*) *m*.

underground ['ʌndəgraʊnd] *n* Untergrundbahn *f*, U-Bahn *f*; *a press etc* Untergrund-.

undergrowth ['ʌndəgrəʊθ] *n* Gestrüpp *nt*, Unterholz *nt*.

underhand ['ʌndəhænd] *a* hinterhältig.

underlie [ʌndə'laɪ] *vt irreg* (*form the basis of*) zugrundeliegen (+*dat*).

underline [ʌndə'laɪn] *vt* unterstreichen; (*emphasize*) betonen.

underling ['ʌndəlɪŋ] *n* Handlanger *m*.

undermine [ʌndə'maɪn] *vt* unterhöhlen; (*fig*) unterminieren, untergraben.

underneath [ʌndə'niːθ] *ad* darunter; *prep* unter.

underpaid [ʌndə'peɪd] *a* unterbezahlt.

underpants ['ʌndəpænts] *npl* Unterhose *f*.

underpass ['ʌndəpɑːs] *n* Unterführung *f*.

underplay ['ʌndə'pleɪ] *vt* herunterspielen.

underprice ['ʌndə'praɪs] *vt* zu niedrig ansetzen.

underprivileged [ʌndə'prɪvɪlɪdʒd] *a* benachteiligt, unterprivilegiert.

underrate [ʌndə'reɪt] *vt* unterschätzen.

undershirt ['ʌndəʃɜːt] *n* (*US*) Unterhemd *nt*.

undershorts ['ʌndəʃɔːts] *npl* (*US*) Unterhose *f*.

underside ['ʌndəsaɪd] *n* Unterseite *f*.

underskirt ['ʌndəskɜːt] *n* Unterrock *m*.

understand [ʌndə'stænd] *vt irreg* verstehen; **I ~ that . . .** ich habe gehört, daß . . .; **am I to ~ that . . .?** soll das (etwa) heißen, daß . . .?; **what do you ~ by that?** was verstehen Sie darunter?; **it is understood that . . .** es wurde vereinbart, daß . . .; **to make o.s. understood** sich verständlich machen; **is that understood?** is das klar?; **~able** *a* verständlich; **~ing** Verständnis *nt*; *a* verständnisvoll.

understatement ['ʌndəsteɪtmənt] *n* Untertreibung *f*, Understatement *nt*.

understudy ['ʌndəstʌdɪ] *n* Ersatz(schau)spieler(in *f*) *m*.

undertake [ʌndə'teɪk] *irreg vt* unternehmen; *vi* (*promise*) sich verpflichten; **~r** Leichenbestatter *m*; **~r's** Beerdigungsinstitut *nt*.

undertaking [ʌndə'teɪkɪŋ] *n* (*enterprise*) Unternehmen *nt*; (*promise*) Verpflichtung *f*.

underwater ['ʌndə'wɔːtə*] *ad* unter Wasser; *a* Unterwasser-.

underwear ['ʌndəweə*] *n* Unterwäsche *f*.

underweight ['ʌndə'weɪt] *a*: **to be ~** Untergewicht haben.

underworld ['ʌndəwɜːld] *n* (*of crime*) Unterwelt *f*.

underwriter ['ʌndəraɪtə*] *n* Assekurant *m*.

undesirable [ʌndɪ'zaɪərəbl] *a* unerwünscht.

undies ['ʌndɪz] *npl* (*col*) (Damen)unterwäsche *f*.

undiscovered ['ʌndɪs'kʌvəd] *a* unentdeckt.

undisputed ['ʌndɪs'pjuːtɪd] *a* unbestritten.

undistinguished ['ʌndɪs'tɪŋgwɪʃt] *a* unbekannt, nicht ausgezeichnet.

undo ['ʌn'duː] *vt irreg* (*unfasten*) öffnen, aufmachen; *work* zunichte machen; **~ing** Verderben *nt*.

undoubted [ʌn'daʊtɪd] *a* unbezweifelt; **~ly** *ad* zweifellos, ohne Zweifel.

undress ['ʌn'dres] *vti* (sich) ausziehen.

undue ['ʌndjuː] *a* übermäßig.

undulating ['ʌndjuleɪtɪŋ] *a* wellenförmig; *country* wellig.

unduly ['ʌn'djuːlɪ] *ad* übermäßig.

unearth ['ʌn'ɜːθ] *vt* (*dig up*) ausgraben; (*discover*) ans Licht bringen; **~ly** *a* schauerlich.

unease [ʌn'iːz] *n* Unbehagen *nt*; (*public*) Unruhe *f*.

uneasy [ʌn'iːzɪ] *a* (*worried*) unruhig; *feeling* ungut; (*embarrassed*) unbequem; **I feel ~ about it** mir ist nicht wohl dabei.

uneconomic(al) ['ʌniːkə'nɒmɪk(əl)] *a* unwirtschaftlich.

uneducated ['ʌn'edjukeɪtɪd] *a* ungebildet.

unemployed ['ʌnɪm'plɔɪd] *a* arbeitslos; **the ~** die Arbeitslosen *pl*.

unemployment ['ʌnɪm'plɔɪmənt] *n* Arbeitslosigkeit *f*.

unending [ʌn'endɪŋ] *a* endlos.

unenviable ['ʌn'envɪəbl] *a* wenig beneidenswert.

unerring ['ʌn'ɜːrɪŋ] *a* unfehlbar.

uneven ['ʌn'iːvən] *a surface* uneben; *quality* ungleichmäßig.

unexploded ['ʌnɪks'pləʊdɪd] *a* nicht explodiert.

unfailing [ʌn'feɪlɪŋ] *a* nie versagend.

unfair *a*, **~ly** *ad* ['ʌn'feə*, -əlɪ] ungerecht, unfair.

unfaithful ['ʌn'feɪθfʊl] *a* untreu.

unfasten ['ʌn'fɑːsn] *vt* öffnen, aufmachen.

unfavourable, (*US*) **unfavorable** ['ʌn'feɪvərəbl] *a* ungünstig.

unfeeling [ʌn'fiːlɪŋ] *a* gefühllos, kalt.

unfinished ['ʌn'fɪnɪʃt] *a* unvollendet.

unfit ['ʌn'fɪt] *a* ungeeignet (*for* zu, für); (*in bad health*) nicht fit.

unflagging [ʌn'flægɪŋ] *a* unermüdlich.

unflappable ['ʌn'flæpəbl] *a* unerschütterlich.

unflinching [ʌn'flɪntʃɪŋ] *a* unerschrocken.

unfold [ʌn'fəʊld] *vt* entfalten; *paper* auseinanderfalten; *vi* (*develop*) sich entfalten.

unforeseen ['ʌnfɔː'siːn] *a* unvorhergesehen.

unforgivable ['ʌnfə'gɪvəbl] *a* unverzeihlich.

unfortunate [ʌn'fɔːtʃnət] *a* unglücklich, bedauerlich; **~ly** *ad* leider.

unfounded ['ʌn'faʊndɪd] *a* unbegründet.

unfriendly ['ʌn'frendlɪ] *a* unfreundlich.

unfurnished ['ʌn'fɜːnɪʃt] *a* unmöbliert.

ungainly [ʌn'geɪnlɪ] *a* linkisch.

ungodly [ʌn'gɒdlɪ] *a hour* nachtschlafend; *row* heillos.

unguarded ['ʌn'gɑːdɪd] *a moment* unbewacht.

unhappiness [ʌn'hæpɪnəs] *n* Unglück *nt*, Unglückseligkeit *f*.

unhappy [ʌn'hæpɪ] *a* unglücklich.

unharmed ['ʌn'hɑːmd] *a* wohlbehalten, unversehrt.

unhealthy [ʌn'helθɪ] *a* ungesund.

unheard-of [ʌn'hɜːdɒv] *a* unerhört.

unhurt ['ʌn'hɜːt] *a* unverletzt.

unicorn ['juːnɪkɔːn] *n* Einhorn *nt*.

unidentified ['ʌnaɪ'dentɪfaɪd] *a* unbekannt, nicht identifiziert.

unification [juːnɪfɪ'keɪʃən] *n* Vereinigung *f*.

uniform ['juːnɪfɔːm] *n* Uniform *f*; *a* einheitlich; **~ity** [juːnɪ'fɔːmɪtɪ] Einheitlichkeit *f*.

unify ['juːnɪfaɪ] *vt* vereinigen.

unilateral ['juːnɪ'lætərəl] *a* einseitig.

unimaginable [ʌnɪ'mædʒɪnəbl] *a* unvorstellbar.

uninjured ['ʌn'ɪndʒəd] *a* unverletzt.

unintentional ['ʌnɪn'tenʃənl] *a* unabsichtlich.

union ['juːnjən] *n* (*uniting*) Vereinigung *f*; (*alliance*) Bund *m*, Union *f*; (*trade* ~) Gewerkschaft *f*; **U~ Jack** Union Jack *m*.

unique [juː'niːk] *a* einzig(artig).

unison ['juːnɪzn] *n* Einstimmigkeit *f*; **in ~** einstimmig.

unit ['juːnɪt] *n* Einheit *f*.

unite [juː'naɪt] *vt* vereinigen; *vi* sich vereinigen; **~d** *a* vereinigt; (*together*) vereint; **U~d Nations** Vereinte Nationen *pl*.

unit trust ['juːnɪt'trʌst] *n* (*Brit*) Treuhandgesellschaft *f*.

unity ['juːnɪtɪ] *n* Einheit *f*; (*agreement*) Einigkeit *f*.

universal *a*, **~ly** *ad* [juːnɪ'vɜːsəl, -ɪ] allgemein.

universe ['juːnɪvɜːs] *n* (Welt)all *nt*, Universum *nt*.

university [juːnɪ'vɜːsɪtɪ] *n* Universität *f*.

unjust ['ʌn'dʒʌst] *a* ungerecht.

unjustifiable [ʌn'dʒʌstɪfaɪəbl] *a* ungerechtfertigt.

unkempt ['ʌn'kempt] *a* ungepflegt, verwahrlost.

unkind [ʌn'kaɪnd] *a* unfreundlich.

unknown ['ʌn'nəʊn] *a* unbekannt (*to dat*).

unladen ['ʌn'leɪdn] *a weight* Leer-, unbeladen.

unleash ['ʌn'liːʃ] *vt* entfesseln.

unleavened ['ʌn'levnd] *a* ungesäuert.

unless [ən'les] *cj* wenn nicht, es sei denn . . .

unlicensed ['ʌn'laɪsənst] *a* (*to sell alcohol*) unkonzessioniert.

unlike ['ʌn'laɪk] *a* unähnlich; *prep* im Gegensatz zu.

unlimited [ʌn'lɪmɪtɪd] *a* unbegrenzt.

unload ['ʌn'ləʊd] *vt* entladen.

unlock ['ʌn'lɒk] *vt* aufschließen.

unmannerly [ʌn'mænəlɪ] *a* unmanierlich.

unmarried ['ʌn'mærɪd] *a* unverheiratet, ledig.

unmask ['ʌn'mɑːsk] *vt* demaskieren; (*fig*) entlarven.

unmistakable ['ʌnmɪs'teɪkəbl] *a* unverkennbar.

unmistakably ['ʌnmɪs'teɪkəblɪ] *ad* unverwechselbar, unverkennbar.

unmitigated [ʌn'mɪtɪgeɪtɪd] *a* ungemildert, ganz.

unnecessary ['ʌn'nesəsərɪ] *a* unnötig.

unobtainable ['ʌnəb'teɪnəbl] *a*: **this number is ~** kein Anschluß unter dieser Nummer.

unoccupied ['ʌn'ɒkjʊpaɪd] *a seat* frei.

unopened ['ʌn'əʊpənd] *a* ungeöffnet.

unorthodox ['ʌn'ɔːθədɒks] *a* unorthodox.

unpack ['ʌn'pæk] *vti* auspacken.

unpalatable [ʌn'pælətəbl] *a truth* bitter.

unparalleled [ʌn'pærəleld] *a* beispiellos.

unpleasant [ʌn'pleznt] *a* unangenehm.

unplug ['ʌn'plʌg] *vt* den Stecker herausziehen von.

unpopular ['ʌn'pɒpjʊlə*] *a* unbeliebt, unpopulär.

unprecedented [ʌn'presɪdəntɪd] *a* noch nie dagewesen; beispiellos.

unqualified ['ʌn'kwɒlɪfaɪd] *a success* uneingeschränkt, voll; *person* unqualifiziert.

unravel [ʌn'rævəl] *vt* (*disentangle*) auffasern, entwirren; (*solve*) lösen.

unreal ['ʌn'rɪəl] *a* unwirklich.

unreasonable [ʌn'riːznəbl] *a* unvernünftig; *demand* übertrieben; **that's ~** das ist zuviel verlangt.

unrelenting ['ʌnrɪ'lentɪŋ] *a* unerbittlich.

unrelieved ['ʌnrɪ'liːvd] *a monotony* ungemildert.

unrepeatable ['ʌnrɪ'piːtəbl] *a* nicht zu wiederholen(d).

unrest [ʌn'rest] *n* (*discontent*) Unruhe *f*; (*fighting*) Unruhen *pl*.

unroll ['ʌn'rəʊl] *vt* aufrollen.

unruly [ʌn'ruːlɪ] *a child* undiszipliniert; schwer lenkbar.

unsafe ['ʌn'seɪf] *a* nicht sicher.

unsaid ['ʌn'sed] *a*: **to leave sth ~** etw ungesagt sein lassen.

unsatisfactory ['ʌnsætɪs'fæktərɪ] *a* unbefriedigend; unzulänglich.

unsavoury, (*US*) **unsavory** ['ʌn'seɪvərɪ] *a* (*fig*) widerwärtig.

unscrew ['ʌn'skruː] *vt* aufschrauben.

unscrupulous [ʌn'skruːpjʊləs] *a* skrupellos.

unselfish ['ʌn'selfɪʃ] *a* selbstlos, uneigennützig.

unsettled ['ʌn'setld] *a* unstet; *person* rastlos; *weather* wechselhaft; *dispute* nicht beigelegt.

unshaven ['ʌn'ʃeɪvn] *a* unrasiert.

unsightly [ʌn'saɪtlɪ] *a* unansehnlich.

unskilled ['ʌn'skɪld] *a* ungelernt.

unsophisticated ['ʌnsə'fɪstɪkeɪtɪd] *a* einfach, natürlich.

unsound ['ʌn'saʊnd] *a ideas* anfechtbar.

unspeakable [ʌn'spiːkəbl] *a joy* unsagbar; *crime* scheußlich.

unstuck ['ʌn'stʌk] *a*: **to come ~** (*lit*) sich lösen; (*fig*) ins Wasser fallen.

unsuccessful ['ʌnsək'sesful] a erfolglos.

unsuitable ['ʌn'su:təbl] a unpassend.

unsuspecting ['ʌnsəs'pektɪŋ] a nichtsahnend.

unswerving [ʌn'swɜ:vɪŋ] a loyalty unerschütterlich.

untangle ['ʌn'tæŋgl] vt entwirren.

untapped ['ʌn'tæpt] a resources ungenützt.

unthinkable [ʌn'θɪŋkəbl] a unvorstellbar.

untidy [ʌn'taɪdɪ] a unordentlich.

untie ['ʌn'taɪ] vt aufmachen, aufschnüren.

until [ən'tɪl] prep, cj bis.

untimely [ʌn'taɪmlɪ] a death vorzeitig.

untold ['ʌn'təʊld] a unermeßlich.

untoward [ʌntə'wɔ:d] a widrig, ungünstig.

untranslatable ['ʌn'trænsleɪtəbl] a unübersetzbar.

untried ['ʌn'traɪd] a plan noch nicht ausprobiert.

unused [ʌn'ju:zd] a unbenutzt.

unusual a, ~ly [ʌn'ju:ʒʊəl, -ɪ] ungewöhnlich.

unveil [ʌn'veɪl] vt enthüllen.

unwary [ʌn'weərɪ] a unbedacht(sam).

unwavering [ʌn'weɪvərɪŋ] a standhaft, unerschütterlich.

unwell ['ʌn'wel] a unpäßlich.

unwieldy [ʌn'wi:ldɪ] a unhandlich, sperrig.

unwilling ['ʌn'wɪlɪŋ] a unwillig.

unwind ['ʌn'waɪnd] irreg vt (lit) abwickeln; vi (relax) sich entspannen.

unwitting [ʌn'wɪtɪŋ] a unwissentlich.

unwrap ['ʌn'ræp] vt aufwickeln, auspacken.

unwritten ['ʌn'rɪtn] a ungeschrieben.

up [ʌp] prep auf; ad nach oben, hinauf; (out of bed) auf; **it is ~ to you** es liegt bei Ihnen; **what is he ~ to?** was hat er vor?; **he is not ~ to it** er kann es nicht (tun); **what's ~?** was ist los?; **~ to** (temporally) bis; **~-and-coming** a im Aufstieg; **the ~s and downs** das Auf und Ab.

upbringing ['ʌpbrɪŋɪŋ] n Erziehung f.

update [ʌp'deɪt] vt auf den neuesten Stand bringen.

upend [ʌp'end] vt auf Kante stellen.

upgrade [ʌp'greɪd] vt höher einstufen.

upheaval [ʌp'hi:vəl] n Umbruch m.

uphill ['ʌp'hɪl] a ansteigend; (fig) mühsam; ad bergauf.

uphold [ʌp'həʊld] vt irreg unterstützen.

upholstery [ʌp'həʊlstərɪ] n Polster nt; Polsterung f.

upkeep ['ʌpki:p] n Instandhaltung f.

upon [ə'pɒn] prep auf.

upper ['ʌpə*] n (on shoe) Oberleder nt; a obere(r,s), höhere(r,s); **the ~ class** die Oberschicht; **~-class** a vornehm; **~most** a oberste(r,s), höchste(r,s).

upright ['ʌpraɪt] a (erect) aufrecht; (honest) aufrecht, rechtschaffen; n Pfosten m.

uprising [ʌp'raɪzɪŋ] n Aufstand m.

uproar ['ʌprɔ:*] n Aufruhr m.

uproot ['ʌp'ru:t] vt ausreißen; tree entwurzeln.

upset ['ʌpset] n Aufregung f; [ʌp'set] vt irreg (overturn) umwerfen; (disturb) aufregen, bestürzen; plans durcheinanderbringen; ~ting a bestürzend.

upshot ['ʌpʃɒt] n (End)ergebnis nt, Ausgang m.

upside-down ['ʌpsaɪd'daʊn] ad verkehrt herum; (fig) drunter und drüber.

upstairs ['ʌp'steəz] ad oben, im oberen Stockwerk; **go** nach oben; **a room** obere(r,s), Ober-; n obere(s) Stockwerk nt.

upstart ['ʌpstɑ:t] n Emporkömmling m.

upstream ['ʌp'stri:m] ad stromaufwärts.

uptake ['ʌpteɪk] n: **to be quick on the ~** schnell begreifen; **to be slow on the ~** schwer von Begriff sein.

uptight ['ʌp'taɪt] a (col) (nervous) nervös; (inhibited) verklemmt.

up-to-date ['ʌptə'deɪt] a clothes modisch, modern; information neueste(r,s); **to bring sth up to date** etw auf den neuesten Stand bringen.

upturn ['ʌptɜ:n] n (in luck) Aufschwung m.

upward ['ʌpwəd] a nach oben gerichtet; ~(s) ad aufwärts.

uranium [jʊə'reɪnɪəm] n Uran nt.

urban ['ɜ:bən] a städtisch, Stadt-.

urbane [ɜ:'beɪn] a höflich, weltgewandt.

urchin ['ɜ:tʃɪn] n (boy) Schlingel m; (sea ~) Seeigel m.

urge [ɜ:dʒ] n Drang m; vt drängen, dringen in (+acc); ~ **on** vt antreiben.

urgency ['ɜ:dʒənsɪ] n Dringlichkeit f.

urgent a, ~ly ad ['ɜ:dʒənt, -lɪ] dringend.

urinal ['jʊərɪnl] n (Med) Urinflasche f; (public) Pissoir nt.

urinate ['jʊərɪneɪt] vi urinieren, Wasser lassen.

urine ['jʊərɪn] n Urin m, Harn m.

urn [ɜ:n] n Urne f; (tea ~) Teemaschine f.

us [ʌs] pron uns.

usage ['ju:zɪdʒ] n Gebrauch m; (esp Ling) Sprachgebrauch m.

use [ju:s] n Verwendung f; (custom) Brauch m, Gewohnheit f; (employment) Gebrauch m; (point) Zweck m; **in ~** in Gebrauch; **out of ~** außer Gebrauch; **it's no ~** es hat keinen Zweck; **what's the ~?** was soll's?; [ju:z] vt gebrauchen; ~d **to** [ju:st] gewöhnt an (+acc); **she ~d to live here** sie hat früher mal hier gewohnt; ~ **up** [ju:z] vt aufbrauchen, verbrauchen; ~d [ju:zd] a car Gebraucht-; ~**ful** a nützlich; ~**fulness** Nützlichkeit f; ~**less** a nutzlos, unnütz; ~**lessly** ad nutzlos; ~**lessness** Nutzlosigkeit f; ~**r** ['ju:zə*] Benutzer m.

usher ['ʌʃə*] n Platzanweiser m; ~**ette** [ʌʃə'ret] Platzanweiserin f.

usual ['ju:ʒʊəl] a gewöhnlich, üblich; ~ly ad gewöhnlich.

usurp [ju:'zɜ:p] vt an sich reißen; ~**er** Usurpator m.

usury ['ju:ʒʊrɪ] n Wucher m.

utensil [ju:'tensl] n Gerät nt, Utensil nt.

uterus ['ju:tərəs] n Gebärmutter f, Uterus m.

utilitarian [ju:tɪlɪ'teərɪən] a Nützlichkeits-.

utility [ju:'tɪlɪtɪ] n (usefulness) Nützlichkeit f; (also public ~) öffentliche(r) Versorgungsbetrieb m.

utilization [ju:tɪlaɪ'zeɪʃən] n Nutzbarmachung f, Benutzung f.

utilize ['ju:tɪlaɪz] *vt* nutzbar machen; benützen.

utmost ['ʌtməʊst] *a* äußerste(r,s); *n*: **to do one's ~** sein möglichstes tun.

utter ['ʌtə•] *a* äußerste(r,s) höchste(r,s), völlig; *vt* äußern, aussprechen; **~ance** Äußerung *f*; **~ly** *ad* äußerst, absolut, völlig.

U-turn ['ju:'tɜ:n] *n* (Aut) Kehrtwendung *f*.

V

V, v [vi:] *n* V *nt*, v *nt*.

vacancy ['veɪkənsɪ] *n* (job) offene Stelle *f*; (room) freies Zimmer *nt*.

vacant ['veɪkənt] *a* leer; (unoccupied) frei; house leerstehend, unbewohnt; (stupid) (gedanken)leer; '**~**' (on door) 'frei'.

vacate [və'keɪt] *vt* seat frei machen; room räumen.

vacation [və'keɪʃən] *n* Ferien *pl*, Urlaub *m*; **~ist** (US) Ferienreisende(r) *mf*.

vaccinate ['væksɪneɪt] *vt* impfen.

vaccination [væksɪ'neɪʃən] *n* Impfung *f*.

vaccine ['væksi:n] *n* Impfstoff *m*.

vacuum ['vækjʊm] *n* luftleere(r) Raum *m*, Vakuum *nt*; **~ bottle** (US), **~ flask** (Brit) Thermosflasche *f*; **~ cleaner** Staubsauger *m*.

vagary ['veɪgərɪ] *n* Laune *f*.

vagina [və'dʒaɪnə] *n* Scheide *f*, Vagina *f*.

vagrant ['veɪgrənt] *n* Landstreicher *m*.

vague [veɪg] *a* unbestimmt, vage; outline verschwommen; (absent-minded) geistesabwesend; **~ly** *ad* unbestimmt, vage; understand, correct ungefähr; **~ness** Unbestimmtheit *f*; Verschwommenheit *f*.

vain [veɪn] *a* (worthless) eitel, nichtig; attempt vergeblich; (conceited) eitel, eingebildet; **in ~** vergebens, umsonst; **~ly** *ad* vergebens, vergeblich; eitel, eingebildet.

valentine ['væləntaɪn] *n* Valentinsgruß *m*.

valiant *a*, **~ly** *ad* ['væliənt, -lɪ] tapfer.

valid ['vælɪd] *a* gültig; argument stichhaltig; objection berechtigt; **~ity** [və'lɪdɪtɪ] Gültigkeit *f*; Stichhaltigkeit *f*.

valise [və'li:z] *n* Reisetasche *f*.

valley ['vælɪ] *n* Tal *nt*.

valuable ['væljʊəbl] *a* wertvoll; time kostbar; **~s** *pl* Wertsachen *pl*.

valuation [væljʊ'eɪʃən] *n* (Fin) Schätzung *f*; Beurteilung *f*.

value ['vælju:] *n* Wert *m*; (usefulness) Nutzen *m*; *vt* (prize) (hoch)schätzen, werthalten; (estimate) schätzen; **~d** *a* (hoch)geschätzt; **~less** *a* wertlos; **~r** Schätzer *m*.

valve [vælv] *n* Ventil *nt*; (Biol) Klappe *f*; (Rad) Röhre *f*.

vampire ['væmpaɪə•] *n* Vampir *m*.

van [væn] *n* Lieferwagen *m*; Kombiwagen *m*.

vandal ['vændəl] *n* Vandale *m*; **~ism** mutwillige Beschädigung *f*, Vandalismus *m*.

vanilla [və'nɪlə] *n* Vanille *f*.

vanish ['vænɪʃ] *vi* verschwinden.

vanity ['vænɪtɪ] *n* Eitelkeit *f*, Einbildung *f*; **~ case** Schminkkoffer *m*.

vantage ['va:ntɪdʒ] *n*: **~ point** gute(r) Aussichtspunkt *m*.

vapour, (US) **vapor** ['veɪpə•] *n* (mist) Dunst *m*; (gas) Dampf *m*.

variable ['veərɪəbl] *a* wechselhaft, veränderlich; speed, height regulierbar.

variance ['veərɪəns] *n*: **to be at ~** uneinig sein.

variant ['veərɪənt] *n* Variante *f*.

variation [veərɪ'eɪʃən] *n* Variation *f*, Veränderung *f*; (of temperature, prices) Schwankung *f*.

varicose ['værɪkəʊs] *a*: **~ veins** Krampfadern *pl*.

varied ['veərɪd] *a* verschieden, unterschiedlich; life abwechslungsreich.

variety [və'raɪətɪ] *n* (difference) Abwechslung *f*, (varied collection) Vielfalt *f*; (Comm) Auswahl *f*; (sorte) Sorte *f*, Art *f*; **~ show** Varieté *nt*.

various ['veərɪəs] *a* verschieden; (several) mehrere.

varnish ['va:nɪʃ] *n* Lack *m*; (on pottery) Glasur *f*; *vt* lackieren; truth beschönigen.

vary ['veərɪ] *vt* (alter) verändern; (give variety to) abwechslungsreicher gestalten; *vi* sich (ver)ändern; (prices) schwanken; (weather) unterschiedlich sein; **to ~ from sth** sich von etw unterscheiden; **~ing** *a* unterschiedlich; veränderlich.

vase [va:z] *n* Vase *f*.

vast [va:st] *a* weit, groß, riesig; **~ly** *ad* wesentlich; grateful, amused äußerst; **~ness** Unermeßlichkeit *f*, Weite *f*.

vat [væt] *n* große(s) Faß *nt*.

Vatican ['vætɪkən] *n*: **the ~** der Vatikan.

vaudeville ['vəʊdəvɪl] *n* (US) Varieté *nt*.

vault [vɔ:lt] *n* (of roof) Gewölbe *nt*; (tomb) Gruft *f*; (in bank) Tresorraum *m*; (leap) Sprung *m*; *vt* überspringen.

vaunted ['vɔ:ntɪd] *a* gerühmt, gepriesen.

veal [vi:l] *n* Kalbfleisch *nt*.

veer [vɪə•] *vi* sich drehen; (of car) ausscheren.

vegetable ['vedʒətəbl] *n* Gemüse *nt*; (plant) Pflanze *f*.

vegetarian [vedʒɪ'teərɪən] *n* Vegetarier(in *f*) *m*; *a* vegetarisch.

vegetate ['vedʒɪteɪt] *vi* (dahin)-vegetieren.

vegetation [vedʒɪ'teɪʃən] *n* Vegetation *f*.

vehemence ['vi:ɪməns] *n* Heftigkeit *f*.

vehement ['vi:ɪmənt] *a* heftig; feelings leidenschaftlich.

vehicle ['vi:ɪkl] *n* Fahrzeug *nt*; (fig) Mittel *nt*.

vehicular [vɪ'hɪkjʊlə•] *a* Fahrzeug-; traffic Kraft-.

veil [veɪl] *n* (lit, fig) Schleier *m*; *vt* verschleiern.

vein [veɪn] *n* Ader *f*; (Anat) Vene *f*; (mood) Stimmung *f*.

velocity [vɪ'lɒsɪtɪ] *n* Geschwindigkeit *f*.

velvet ['velvɪt] *n* Samt *m*.

vendetta [ven'detə] *n* Fehde *f*; (in family) Blutrache *f*.

vending machine ['vendɪŋməʃi:n] *n* Automat *m*.

vendor ['vendɔː*] n Verkäufer m.

veneer [vəˈnɪə*] n (lit) Furnier(holz) nt; (fig) äußere(r) Anstrich m.

venerable ['venərəbl] a ehrwürdig.

venereal [vɪˈnɪərɪəl] a disease Geschlechts-.

venetian [vɪˈniːʃən] a: ~ blind Jalousie f.

vengeance ['vendʒəns] n Rache f; with a ~ gewaltig.

venison ['venɪsn] n Reh(fleisch) nt.

venom ['venəm] n Gift nt; ~ous a, ~ously ad giftig, gehässig.

vent [vent] n Öffnung f; (in coat) Schlitz m; (fig) Ventil nt; vt emotion abreagieren.

ventilate ['ventɪleɪt] vt belüften; question erörtern.

ventilation [ventɪˈleɪʃən] n (Be)lüftung f, Ventilation f.

ventilator ['ventɪleɪtə*] n Ventilator m.

ventriloquist [venˈtrɪləkwɪst] n Bauchredner m.

venture ['ventʃə*] n Unternehmung f, Projekt nt; vt wagen; life aufs Spiel setzen; vi sich wagen.

venue ['venjuː] n Schauplatz m; Treffpunkt m.

veranda(h) [vəˈrændə] a Veranda f.

verb [vɜːb] n Zeitwort nt, Verb nt; (spoken) mündlich; translation wörtlich; (of a verb) verbal, Verbal-; ~ally ad mündlich; (as a verb) verbal; ~atim [vɜːˈbeɪtɪm] ad Wort für Wort; a wortwörtlich.

verbose [vɜːˈbəʊs] a wortreich.

verdict ['vɜːdɪkt] n Urteil nt.

verge [vɜːdʒ] n Rand m; on the ~ of doing sth im Begriff, etw zu tun; vi: ~ on grenzen an (+acc).

verger ['vɜːdʒə*] n Kirchendiener m, Küster m.

verification [verɪfɪˈkeɪʃən] n Bestätigung f; (checking) Überprüfung f; (proof) Beleg m.

verify ['verɪfaɪ] vt (über)prüfen; (confirm) bestätigen; theory beweisen.

vermin ['vɜːmɪn] npl Ungeziefer nt.

vermouth ['vɜːməθ] n Wermut m.

vernacular [vəˈnækjʊlə*] n Landessprache f; (dialect) Dialekt m, Mundart f; (jargon) Fachsprache f.

versatile ['vɜːsətaɪl] a vielseitig.

versatility [vɜːsəˈtɪlɪtɪ] n Vielseitigkeit f.

verse [vɜːs] n (poetry) Poesie f; (stanza) Strophe f; (of Bible) Vers m; in ~ in Versform; ~d a: ~d in bewandert in (+dat), beschlagen in (+dat).

version ['vɜːʃən] n Version f; (of car) Modell nt.

versus ['vɜːsəs] prep gegen.

vertebra ['vɜːtɪbrə] n (Rücken)wirbel m.

vertebrate ['vɜːtɪbrət] a animal Wirbel-.

vertical ['vɜːtɪkəl] a senkrecht, vertikal; ~ly ad senkrecht, vertikal.

vertigo ['vɜːtɪgəʊ] n Schwindel m, Schwindelgefühl nt.

verve [vɜːv] n Schwung m.

very ['verɪ] ad sehr; a (extreme) äußerste(r,s); the ~ book genau das Buch; at that ~ moment gerade or

genau in dem Augenblick; at the ~ latest allerspätestens; the ~ same day noch am selben Tag; the ~ thought der Gedanke allein, der bloße Gedanke.

vespers ['vespəz] npl Vesper f.

vessel ['vesl] n (ship) Schiff nt; (container) Gefäß nt.

vest [vest] n Unterhemd nt; (US: waistcoat) Weste f; vt: ~ sb with sth or sth in sb jdm etw verleihen; ~ed a: ~ed interests pl finanzielle Beteiligung f; (people) finanziell Beteiligte pl; (fig) persönliche(s) Interesse nt.

vestibule ['vestɪbjuːl] n Vorhalle f.

vestige ['vestɪdʒ] n Spur f.

vestry ['vestrɪ] n Sakristei f.

vet [vet] n Tierarzt m/-ärztin f; vt genau prüfen.

veteran ['vetərən] n Veteran m; a altgedient.

veterinary ['vetɪnərɪ] a Veterinär-; ~ surgeon Tierarzt m/-ärztin f.

veto ['viːtəʊ] n Veto nt; power of ~ Vetorecht nt; vt sein Veto einlegen gegen.

vex [veks] vt ärgern; ~ed a verärgert; ~ed question umstrittene Frage f; ~ing a ärgerlich.

via ['vaɪə] prep über (+acc).

viability [vaɪəˈbɪlɪtɪ] n (of plan, scheme) Durchführbarkeit f; (of company) Rentabilität f; (of life forms) Lebensfähigkeit f.

viable ['vaɪəbl] a plan durchführbar; company rentabel; plant, economy lebensfähig.

viaduct ['vaɪədʌkt] n Viadukt m.

vibrate [vaɪˈbreɪt] vi zittern, beben; (machine, string) vibrieren; (notes) schwingen.

vibration [vaɪˈbreɪʃən] n Schwingung f; (of machine) Vibrieren nt; (of voice, ground) Beben nt.

vicar ['vɪkə*] n Pfarrer m; ~age n Pfarrhaus nt.

vice [vaɪs] n (evil) Laster nt; (Tech) Schraubstock m; pref: ~chairman stellvertretende(r) Vorsitzende(r) m; ~president Vizepräsident m; ~ versa ad umgekehrt.

vicinity [vɪˈsɪnɪtɪ] n Umgebung f; (closeness) Nähe f.

vicious ['vɪʃəs] a gemein, böse; ~ circle Teufelskreis m; ~ness Bösartigkeit f, Gemeinheit f.

vicissitudes [vɪˈsɪsɪtjuːdz] npl Wechselfälle pl.

victim ['vɪktɪm] n Opfer nt; ~ization [vɪktɪmaɪˈzeɪʃən] n Benachteiligung f; ~ize vt benachteiligen.

victor ['vɪktə*] n Sieger m.

Victorian [vɪkˈtɔːrɪən] a viktorianisch; (fig) (sitten)streng.

victorious [vɪkˈtɔːrɪəs] a siegreich.

victory ['vɪktərɪ] n Sieg m.

video ['vɪdɪəʊ] a Fernseh-, Bild-.

vie [vaɪ] vi wetteifern.

view [vjuː] n (sight) Sicht f, Blick m; (scene) Aussicht f; (opinion) Ansicht f, Meinung f; (intention) Absicht f; to have sth in ~ etw beabsichtigen; in ~ of wegen (+gen), angesichts (+gen); vt situation betrachten; house besichtigen; ~er (viewfinder) Sucher m; (Phot: small projector) Gucki m; (TV) Fernsehteilnehmer(in f) m; ~finder Sucher m; ~point Standpunkt m.

vigil ['vɪdʒɪl] n (Nacht)wache f; ~ance Wachsamkeit f; ~ant a wachsam; ~antly ad aufmerksam.

vigorous a, ~ly ad ['vɪgərəs, -lɪ] kräftig; protest energisch, heftig.

vigour, (US) **vigor** ['vɪgə*] n Kraft f, Vitalität f; (of protest) Heftigkeit f.

vile [vaɪl] a (mean) gemein; (foul) abscheulich.

vilify ['vɪlɪfaɪ] vt verleumden.

villa ['vɪlə] n Villa f.

village ['vɪlɪdʒ] n Dorf nt; ~r Dorfbewohner(in f) m.

villain ['vɪlən] n Schurke m, Bösewicht m.

vindicate ['vɪndɪkeɪt] vt rechtfertigen; (clear) rehabilitieren.

vindication [vɪndɪ'keɪʃən] n Rechtfertigung f; Rehabilitation f.

vindictive [vɪn'dɪktɪv] a nachtragend, rachsüchtig.

vine [vaɪn] n Rebstock m, Rebe f.

vinegar ['vɪnɪgə*] n Essig m.

vineyard ['vɪnjəd] n Weinberg m.

vintage ['vɪntɪdʒ] n (of wine) Jahrgang m; ~ car Vorkriegsmodell nt; ~ wine edle(r) Wein m; ~ year besondere(s) Jahr nt.

viola [vɪ'əʊlə] n Bratsche f.

violate ['vaɪəleɪt] vt promise brechen; law übertreten; rights, rule, neutrality verletzen; sanctity, woman schänden.

violation [vaɪə'leɪʃən] n Verletzung f; Übertretung f.

violence ['vaɪələns] n (force) Heftigkeit f; (brutality) Gewalttätigkeit f.

violent a, ~ly ad ['vaɪələnt, -lɪ] (strong) heftig; (brutal) gewalttätig, brutal; contrast kraß; death gewaltsam.

violet ['vaɪələt] n Veilchen nt; a veilchenblau, violett.

violin [vaɪə'lɪn] n Geige f, Violine f.

viper ['vaɪpə*] n Viper f; (fig) Schlange f.

virgin ['vɜːdʒɪn] n Jungfrau f; a jungfräulich, unberührt; ~ity [vɜː'dʒɪnɪtɪ] Unschuld f.

Virgo ['vɜːgəʊ] n Jungfrau f.

virile ['vɪraɪl] a männlich; (fig) kraftvoll.

virility [vɪ'rɪlɪtɪ] n Männlichkeit f.

virtual ['vɜːtjʊəl] a eigentlich; **it was a ~ disaster** es war geradezu eine Katastrophe; ~ly ad praktisch, fast.

virtue ['vɜːtjuː] n (moral goodness) Tugend f; (good quality) Vorteil m, Vorzug m; **by ~ of** aufgrund (+gen).

virtuoso [vɜːtjʊ'əʊzəʊ] n Virtuose m.

virtuous ['vɜːtjʊəs] a tugendhaft.

virulence ['vɪrjʊləns] n Bösartigkeit f.

virulent ['vɪrjʊlənt] a (poisonous) bösartig; (bitter) scharf, geharnischt.

virus ['vaɪərəs] n Virus m.

visa ['viːzə] n Visum nt, Sichtvermerk m.

vis-à-vis ['viːzəviː] prep gegenüber.

visibility [vɪzɪ'bɪlɪtɪ] n Sichtbarkeit f; (Met) Sicht(weite) f.

visible ['vɪzəbl] a sichtbar.

visibly ['vɪzəblɪ] ad sichtlich.

vision ['vɪʒən] n (ability) Sehvermögen nt; (foresight) Weitblick m; (in dream, image) Vision f; ~ary Hellseher m; (dreamer) Phantast m; a phantastisch.

visit ['vɪzɪt] n Besuch m; vt besuchen; town, country fahren nach; ~ing a professor Gast-; ~ing card Visitenkarte f; ~or (in house) Besucher(in f) m; (in hotel) Gast m; ~or's book Gästebuch nt.

visor ['vaɪzə*] n Visier nt; (on cap) Schirm m; (Aut) Blende f.

vista ['vɪstə] n Aussicht f.

visual ['vɪzjʊəl] a Seh-, visuell; ~ aid Anschauungsmaterial nt; ~ize vt (imagine) sich (dat) vorstellen; (expect) erwarten; ~ly ad visuell.

vital ['vaɪtl] a (important) unerläßlich; (necessary for life) Lebens-, lebenswichtig; (lively) vital; ~ity [vaɪ'tælɪtɪ] Vitalität f, Lebendigkeit f; ~ly ad äußerst, ungeheuer.

vitamin ['vɪtəmɪn] n Vitamin nt.

vitiate ['vɪʃɪeɪt] vt verunreinigen; theory etc ungültig machen.

vivacious [vɪ'veɪʃəs] a lebhaft.

vivacity [vɪ'væsɪtɪ] n Lebhaftigkeit f, Lebendigkeit f.

vivid a, ~ly ad ['vɪvɪd, -lɪ] (graphic) lebendig, deutlich; memory lebhaft; (bright) leuchtend.

vivisection [vɪvɪ'sekʃən] n Vivisektion f.

vocabulary [vəʊ'kæbjʊlərɪ] n Wortschatz m, Vokabular nt.

vocal ['vəʊkəl] a Vokal-, Gesang-; (fig) lautstark; ~ cord Stimmband nt; ~ist Sänger(in f) m.

vocation [vəʊ'keɪʃən] n (calling) Berufung f; ~al a Berufs-.

vociferous a, ~ly ad [vəʊ'sɪfərəs, -lɪ] lautstark.

vodka ['vodkə] n Wodka m.

vogue [vəʊg] n Mode f.

voice [vɔɪs] n (lit) Stimme f; (fig) Mitspracherecht nt; (Gram) Aktionsart f; **active/passive** ~ Aktiv nt/Passiv nt; **with one** ~ einstimmig; vt äußern; ~d consonant stimmhafte(r) Konsonant m.

void [vɔɪd] n Leere f; a (empty) leer; (lacking) ohne (of acc), bar (of gen); (Jur) ungültig; see **null**.

volatile ['volətaɪl] a gas flüchtig; person impulsiv; situation brisant.

volcanic [vol'kænɪk] a vulkanisch, Vulkan-.

volcano [vol'keɪnəʊ] n Vulkan m.

volition [və'lɪʃən] n Wille m; **of one's own** ~ aus freiem Willen.

volley ['volɪ] n (of guns) Salve f; (of stones) Hagel m; (of words) Schwall m; (tennis) Flugball m; ~ball Volleyball m.

volt [vəʊlt] n Volt nt; ~age (Volt)spannung f.

volte-face [volt'fɑːs] n (Kehrt)wendung f.

voluble ['voljʊbl] a redselig.

volume ['voljuːm] n (book) Band m; (size)

Umfang m; (space) Rauminhalt m,
Volumen nt; (of sound) Lautstärke f.

voluntary a, **voluntarily** ad ['vɔlɔntərɪ,
-lɪ] freiwillig.

volunteer [vɔlən'tɪə*] n Freiwillige(r) mf;
vi sich freiwillig melden; vt anbieten.

voluptuous [vɔ'lʌptjuɔs] a sinnlich,
wollüstig.

vomit ['vɔmɪt] n Erbrochene(s) nt; (act)
Erbrechen nt; vt speien; vi sich übergeben.

vote [vəut] n Stimme f; (ballot) Wahl f,
Abstimmung f; (result) Wahl- or Abstim-
mungsergebnis nt; (right to vote)
Wahlrecht nt; vti wählen; ~r Wähler(in f)
m.

voting ['vəutɪŋ] n Wahl f; low ~ geringe
Wahlbeteiligung f.

vouch [vautʃ]: ~ for vt bürgen für.

voucher ['vautʃə*] n Gutschein m.

vow [vau] n Versprechen nt; (Rel) Gelübde
nt; vt geloben; vengeance schwören.

vowel ['vauəl] n Vokal m, Selbstlaut m.

voyage ['vɔɪɪdʒ] n Reise f.

vulgar ['vʌlgə*] a (rude) vulgär; (of
common people) allgemein, Volks-; ~ity
[vʌl'gærɪtɪ] Gewöhnlichkeit f, Vulgarität f.

vulnerability [vʌlnərə'bɪlɪtɪ] n Verletz-
lichkeit f.

vulnerable ['vʌlnərəbl] a (easily injured)
verwundbar; (sensitive) verletzlich.

vulture ['vʌltʃə*] n Geier m.

W

W, w ['dʌblju:] n W nt, w nt.

wad [wɔd] n (bundle) Bündel nt; (of paper)
Stoß m; (of money) Packen m.

wade [weɪd] vi waten.

wafer ['weɪfə*] n Waffel f; (Eccl) Hostie f.

waffle ['wɔfl] n Waffel f; (col: empty talk)
Geschwafel nt; vi (col) schwafeln.

waft [wɑ:ft] vti wehen.

wag [wæg] vt tail wedeln mit; vi (tail)
wedeln; **her tongue never stops** ~**ging**
ihr Mund steht nie still.

wage [weɪdʒ] n (Arbeits)lohn m; vt führen;
~**s** pl Lohn m; ~ **claim** Lohnforderung f;
~ **earner** Lohnempfänger(in f) m; ~
freeze Lohnstopp m.

wager ['weɪdʒə*] n Wette f; vti wetten.

waggle ['wægl] vt tail wedeln mit; vi
wedeln.

wag(g)on ['wægən] n (horse-drawn) Fuhrwerk nt; (US Aut) Wagen m; (Brit Rail)
Waggon m.

wail [weɪl] n Wehgeschrei nt; vi
wehklagen, jammern.

waist [weɪst] n Taille f; ~**coat** Weste f;
~**line** Taille f.

wait [weɪt] n Wartezeit f; vi warten (for auf
+acc); **to** ~ **for sb to do sth** darauf
warten, daß jd etw tut; ~ **and see!**
abwarten!; **to** ~ **at table** servieren; ~**er**
Kellner m; (as address) Herr Ober m;
~**ing list** Warteliste f, ~**ing room**
(Med) Wartezimmer nt; (Rail) Wartesaal
m; ~**ress** Kellnerin f; (as address)
Fräulein nt.

waive [weɪv] vt verzichten auf (+acc).

wake [weɪk] irreg vt wecken; vi aufwachen;
to ~ **up to** (fig) sich bewußt werden
(+gen); n (Naut) Kielwasser nt; (for dead)
Totenwache f; **in the** ~ **of** unmittelbar
nach; ~**n** vt aufwecken.

walk [wɔ:k] n Spaziergang m; (way of walking) Gang m; (route) Weg m; ~**s of life** pl
Sphären pl; **to take sb for a** ~ mit jdm
einen Spaziergang machen; **a 10-minute**
~ 10 Minuten zu Fuß; vi gehen; (stroll)
spazierengehen; (longer) wandern; ~**er**
Spaziergänger m; (hiker) Wanderer m;
~**ie-talkie** tragbare(s) Sprechfunkgerät
nt; ~**ing** n Gehen nt; Spazieren(gehen) nt;
Wandern nt; a Wander-; ~**ing stick**
Spazierstock m; ~**out** Streik m; ~**over**
(col) leichter Sieg m.

wall [wɔ:l] n (inside) Wand f; (outside)
Mauer f; ~**ed** a von Mauern umgeben.

wallet ['wɔlɪt] n Brieftasche f.

wallow ['wɔləu] vi sich wälzen or suhlen.

wallpaper ['wɔ:lpeɪpə*] n Tapete f.

walnut ['wɔ:lnʌt] n Walnuß f; (tree)
Walnußbaum m; (wood) Nußbaumholz nt.

walrus ['wɔ:lrəs] n Walroß nt.

waltz [wɔ:lts] n Walzer m; vi Walzer
tanzen.

wan [wɔn] a bleich.

wand [wɔnd] n Stab m.

wander ['wɔndə*] vi (roam) (herum)-
wandern; (fig) abschweifen; ~**er**
Wanderer m; ~**ing** a umherziehend;
thoughts abschweifend.
weifend.

wane [weɪn] vi abnehmen; (fig) schwinden.

want [wɔnt] n (lack) Mangel m (of an
+dat); (need) Bedürfnis nt; **for** ~ **of** aus
Mangel an (+dat); mangels (+gen); vt
(need) brauchen; (desire) wollen; (lack)
nicht haben; **I** ~ **to go** ich will gehen; **he**
~**s confidence** ihm fehlt das Selbstvertrauen.

wanton ['wɔntən] a mutwillig, zügellos.

war [wɔ:*] n Krieg m.

ward [wɔ:d] n (in hospital) Station f; (child)
Mündel nt; (of city) Bezirk m; **to** ~ **off**
abwenden, abwehren.

warden ['wɔ:dən] n (guard) Wächter m,
Aufseher m; (in youth hostel) Herbergsvater m; (Univ) Heimleiter m.

warder ['wɔ:də*] n Gefängnis-wärter m.

wardrobe ['wɔ:drəub] n Kleiderschrank
m; (clothes) Garderobe f.

ware [wɛə*] n Ware f; ~**house** Lagerhaus
nt.

warfare ['wɔ:fɛə*] n Krieg m; Kriegs-
führung f.

warhead ['wɔ:hed] n Sprengkopf m.

warily ['wɛərɪlɪ] ad vorsichtig.

warlike ['wɔ:laɪk] a kriegerisch.

warm [wɔ:m] a warm; welcome herzlich;
vti wärmen; ~ **up** vt aufwärmen; vi warm
werden; ~**-hearted** a warmherzig; ~**ly**
ad warm; herzlich; ~**th** Wärme f, Herz-
lichkeit f.

warn [wɔ:n] vt warnen (of, against vor
+dat); ~**ing** Warnung f; **without** ~**ing**
unerwartet; ~**ing light** Warnlicht nt.

warp [wɔ:p] vt verziehen; ~**ed** a (lit)
wellig; (fig) pervers.

warrant ['wɒrənt] n Haftbefehl m.
warranty ['wɒrəntɪ] n Garantie f.
warrior ['wɒrɪə•] n Krieger m.
warship ['wɔːʃɪp] n Kriegsschiff nt.
wart [wɔːt] n Warze f.
wartime ['wɔːtaɪm] n Kriegszeit f, Krieg m.
wary ['wɛərɪ] a vorsichtig; mißtrauisch.
was [wɒz, wəz] pt of **be**.
wash [wɒʃ] n Wäsche f; **to give sth a ~** etw waschen; **to have a ~** sich waschen; vt waschen; (dishes) abwaschen; vi sich waschen; (do washing) waschen; **~ away** vt abwaschen, wegspülen; **~able** a waschbar; **~basin** Waschbecken nt; **~er** (Tech) Dichtungsring m; (machine) Wasch- or Spülmaschine f; **~ing** Wäsche f; **~ing machine** Waschmaschine f; **~ing powder** Waschpulver nt; **~ing-up** Abwasch m; **~ leather** Waschleder nt; **~-out** (col) (event) Reinfall m; (person) Niete f; **~room** Waschraum m.
wasn't ['wɒznt] = **was not**.
wasp [wɒsp] n Wespe f.
wastage ['weɪstɪdʒ] n Verlust m; **natural ~** Verschleiß m.
waste [weɪst] n (wasting) Verschwendung f; (what is wasted) Abfall m; **~s** pl Einöde f; a (useless) Überschüssig, Abfall-; vt object verschwenden; time, life vergeuden; vi: **~ away** verfallen; **~ful** a, **~fully** ad verschwenderisch; process auswendig; **~ land** Ödland nt; **~ paper basket** Papierkorb m.
watch [wɒtʃ] n Wache f; (for time) Uhr f; **to be on the ~ (for sth)** (auf etw acc) aufpassen; vt ansehen; (observe) beobachten; (be careful of) aufpassen auf (+acc); (guard) bewachen; **to ~ TV** fernsehen; **to ~ sb doing sth** jdm bei etw zuschauen; **~ it!** paß bloß auf!; vi zusehen; (guard) Wache halten; **to ~ for sb/sth** nach jdm/etw Ausschau halten; **~ out!** paß auf!; **~dog** (lit) Wachthund m; (fig) Wächter m; **~ful** a wachsam; **~maker** Uhrmacher m; **~man** (Nacht)wächter m; **~strap** Uhrarmband nt.
water ['wɔːtə•] n Wasser nt; **~s** pl Gewässer nt; vt (be)gießen; (river) bewässern; horses tränken; vi (eye) tränen; **my mouth is ~ing** mir läuft das Wasser im Mund zusammen; **~ down** vt verwässern; **~ closet** (Wasser)klosett nt; **~colour**, (US) **~color** (painting) Aquarell nt; (paint) Wasserfarbe f; **~cress** (Brunnen)kresse f; **~fall** Wasserfall m; **~ hole** Wasserloch nt; **~ing can** Gießkanne f; **~ level** Wasserstand m; **~lily** Seerose f; **~line** Wasserlinie f; **~logged** a ground voll Wasser; wood mit Wasser vollgesogen; **~melon** Wassermelone f; **~ polo** Wasserball(spiel) ·nt; **~proof** a wasserdicht; **~shed** Wasserscheide f; **~-skiing** Wasserschilaufen nt; **to go ~-skiing** wasserschilaufen gehen; **~tight** a wasserdicht; **~works** pl Wasserwerk nt; **~y** a wäss(e)rig.
watt [wɒt] n Watt nt.
wave [weɪv] n Welle f; (with hand) Winken

nt; vt (move to and fro) schwenken; hand, flag winken mit; hair wellen; vi (person) winken; (flag) wehen; (hair) sich wellen; **to ~ to sb** jdm zuwinken; **to ~ sb good-bye** jdm zum Abschied winken; **~length** (lit, fig) Wellenlänge f.
waver ['weɪvə•] vi (hesitate) schwanken; (flicker) flackern.
wavy ['weɪvɪ] a wellig.
wax [wæks] n Wachs nt; (sealing ~) Siegellack m; (in ear) Ohrenschmalz nt; vt floor (ein)wachsen; vi (moon) zunehmen; **~works** pl Wachsfigurenkabinett nt.
way [weɪ] n Weg m; (road also) Straße f; (method) Art und Weise f, Methode f; (direction) Richtung f; (habit) Eigenart f, Gewohnheit f; (distance) Entfernung f; (condition) Zustand m; **a long ~ away** or **off** weit weg; **to lose one's ~** sich verirren; **to make ~ for sb/sth** jdm/etw Platz machen; **to be in a bad ~** schlecht dransein; **do it this ~** machen Sie es so; **give ~** (Aut) Vorfahrt achten!; **~ of thinking** Meinung f; **to get one's own ~** seinen Willen bekommen; **one ~ or another** irgendwie; **under ~** im Gange; **in a ~** in gewisser Weise; **in the ~** im Wege; **by the ~** übrigens; **by ~ of** (via) über (+acc); (in order to) um ... zu; (instead of) als; **'~ in'** 'Eingang'; **'~ out'** 'Ausgang'; **~lay** vt irreg auflauern (+dat); **~ward** a eigensinnig.
we [wiː] pl pron wir.
weak a, **~ly** ad [wiːk, -lɪ] schwach; **~en** vt schwächen, entkräften; vi schwächer werden; nachlassen; **~ling** Schwächling m; **~ness** Schwäche f.
wealth [welθ] n Reichtum m; (abundance) Fülle f; **~y** a reich.
wean [wiːn] vt entwöhnen.
weapon ['wepən] n Waffe f.
wear [wɛə•] n (clothing) Kleidung f; (use) Verschleiß m; vt irreg vi (have on) tragen; smile etc haben; (use) abnutzen; vi (last) halten; (become old) (sich) verschleißen; (clothes) sich abtragen; **~ and tear** Abnutzung f, Verschleiß m; **~ away** vt verbrauchen; vi schwinden; **~ down** vt people zermürben; **~ off** vi sich verlieren; **~ out** vt verschleißen; person erschöpfen; **~er** Träger(in f) m.
wearily ['wɪərɪlɪ] ad müde.
weariness ['wɪərɪnəs] n Müdigkeit f.
weary ['wɪərɪ] a (tired) müde; (tiring) ermüdend; vt ermüden; vi überdrüssig werden (of gen).
weasel ['wiːzl] n Wiesel nt.
weather ['weðə•] n Wetter nt; vt verwittern lassen; (resist) überstehen; **~-beaten** a verwittert; skin wettergegerbt; **~cock** Wetterhahn m; **~ forecast** Wettervorhersage f.
weave [wiːv] vt irreg weben; **to ~ one's way through sth** sich durch etw durchschlängeln; **~r** Weber(in f) m.
weaving ['wiːvɪŋ] n Weben nt, Weberei f.
web [web] n Netz nt; (membrane) Schwimmhaut f; **~bed** a Schwimm-, schwimmhäutig; **~bing** Gewebe nt.
wed [wed] vt irreg (old) heiraten.

we'd [wiːd] = **we had; we would**.

wedding ['wedɪŋ] n Hochzeit f; ~ **day** Hochzeitstag m; ~ **present** Hochzeitsgeschenk nt; ~ **ring** Trau- or Ehering m.

wedge [wedʒ] n Keil m; (of cheese etc) Stück nt; vt (fasten) festklemmen; (pack tightly) einkeilen.

Wednesday ['wenzdeɪ] n Mittwoch m.

wee [wiː] a (esp Scot) klein, winzig.

weed [wiːd] n Unkraut nt; vt jäten; ~-**killer** Unkrautvertilgungsmittel nt.

week [wiːk] n Woche f; a ~ **today** heute in einer Woche; ~**day** Wochentag m; ~**end** Wochenende nt; ~**ly** a, ad wöchentlich; wages, magazine Wochen-.

weep [wiːp] vi irreg weinen.

weigh [weɪ] vti wiegen; ~ **down** vt niederdrücken; ~ **up** vt prüfen, abschätzen; ~**bridge** Brückenwaage f.

weight [weɪt] n Gewicht nt; **to lose/put on** ~ abnehmen/ zunehmen; ~**lessness** Schwerelosigkeit f; ~-**lifter** Gewichtheber m; ~**y** a (heavy) gewichtig; (important) schwerwiegend.

weir [wɪə*] n (Stau)wehr nt.

weird [wɪəd] a seltsam.

welcome ['welkəm] n Willkommen nt, Empfang m; vt begrüßen.

welcoming ['welkəmɪŋ] a Begrüßungs-; freundlich.

weld [weld] n Schweißnaht f; vt schweißen; ~**er** Schweißer m; ~**ing** Schweißen nt.

welfare ['welfɛə*] n Wohl nt; (social) Fürsorge f; ~ **state** Wohlfahrtsstaat m.

well [wel] n Brunnen m; (oil —) Quelle f; a (in good health) gesund; **are you** ~? geht es Ihnen gut?; interj nun, na schön; (starting conversation) nun, tja; ~, ~! na, na!; ad gut; ~ **over 40** weit über 40; **it may** ~ **be** es kann wohl sein; **it would be (as)** ~ **to** ... es wäre wohl gut, zu ...; **you did** ~ (not) **to** ... Sie haben gut daran getan, (nicht) zu ...; **very** ~ (O.K.) nun gut.

we'll [wiːl] = **we will, we shall**.

well-behaved ['welbɪ'heɪvd] a wohlerzogen.

well-being ['welbiːɪŋ] n Wohl nt, Wohlergehen nt.

well-built ['wel'bɪlt] a kräftig gebaut.

well-developed ['weldɪ'veləpt] a girl gut entwickelt; economy hochentwickelt.

well-earned ['wel'ɜːnd] a rest wohlverdient.

well-heeled ['wel'hiːld] a (col: wealthy) gut gepolstert.

wellingtons ['welɪŋtənz] npl Gummistiefel pl.

well-known ['wel'nəʊn] a person weithin bekannt.

well-meaning ['wel'miːnɪŋ] a person wohlmeinend; action gutgemeint.

well-off ['wel'ɒf] a gut situiert.

well-read ['wel'red] a (sehr) belesen.

well-to-do ['weltə'duː] a wohlhabend.

well-wisher ['welwɪʃə*] n wohlwollende(r) Freund m, Gönner m.

wench [wentʃ] n (old) Maid f, Dirne f.

went [went] pt of **go**.

were [wɜː*] pt pl of **be**.

we're [wɪə*] = **we are**.

weren't [wɜːnt] = **were not**.

west [west] n Westen m; a West-, westlich; ad westwärts, nach Westen; ~**erly** a westlich; ~**ern** a westlich, West-; n (Cine) Western m; ~**ward(s)** ad westwärts.

wet [wet] a naß; ~ **blanket** (fig) Triefel m; ~**ness** Nässe f, Feuchtigkeit f; '~ **paint**' 'frisch gestrichen'.

we've [wiːv] = **we have**.

whack [wæk] n Schlag m; vt schlagen.

whale [weɪl] n Wal m.

wharf [wɔːf] n Kai m.

what [wɒt] pron, interj was; a welche(r,s); ~ **a hat!** was für ein Hut!; ~ **money I had** das Geld, das ich hatte; ~ **about ...?** (suggestion) wie wär's mit ...?; ~ **about it?, so** ~? na und?; **well,** ~ **about him?** was ist mit ihm?; **and** ~ **about me?** und ich?; ~ **for?** wozu?; ~**ever** a: ~**ever he says** egal, was er sagt; **no reason** ~**ever** überhaupt kein Grund.

wheat [wiːt] n Weizen m.

wheel [wiːl] n Rad nt; (steering —) Lenkrad nt; (disc) Scheibe f; vt schieben; vi (revolve) sich drehen; ~**barrow** Schubkarren m; ~**chair** Rollstuhl m.

wheeze [wiːz] n Keuchen nt; vi keuchen.

when [wen] ad interrog wann; ad,cj (with present tense) wenn; (with past tense) als; (with indir question) wann; ~**ever** ad wann immer; immer wenn.

where [wɛə*] ad (place) wo; (direction) wohin; ~ **from** woher; ~**abouts** ['wɛərə'baʊts] ad wo; n Aufenthalt m, Verbleib m; ~**as** [wɛər'æz] cj während, wo ... doch; ~**ever** [wɛər'evə*] ad wo (immer).

whet [wet] vt appetite anregen.

whether ['weðə*] cj ob.

which [wɪtʃ] a (from selection) welche(r,s); rel pron der/die/das; (rel: which fact) was; (interrog) welche(r,s); ~**ever** (book) he takes welches (Buch) er auch nimmt.

whiff [wɪf] n Hauch m.

while [waɪl] n Weile f; cj während; **for a** ~ eine Zeitlang.

whim [wɪm] n Laune f.

whimper ['wɪmpə*] n Wimmern nt; vi wimmern.

whimsical ['wɪmzɪkəl] a launisch.

whine [waɪn] n Gewinsel nt, Gejammer nt; vi heulen, winseln.

whip [wɪp] n Peitsche f; (Parl) Einpeitscher m; vt (beat) peitschen; (snatch) reißen; ~-**round** (col) Geldsammlung f.

whirl [wɜːl] n Wirbel m; vti (herum)-wirbeln; ~**pool** Wirbel m; ~**wind** Wirbelwind m.

whirr [wɜː*] vi schwirren, surren.

whisk [wɪsk] n Schneebesen m; vt cream etc schlagen.

whisker ['wɪskə*] n (of animal) Barthaare pl; ~**s** pl (of man) Backenbart m.

whisk(e)y ['wɪskɪ] n Whisky m.

whisper ['wɪspə*] n Flüstern nt; vi flüstern; (leaves) rascheln; vt flüstern, munkeln.

whist [wɪst] n Whist nt.

whistle ['wɪsl] n Pfiff m; (instrument) Pfeife f; vti pfeifen.

white [waɪt] n Weiß nt; (of egg) Eiweiß nt; (of eye) Weiße(s) nt; a weiß; (with fear) blaß; ~**collar worker** Angestellte(r) m; ~ **lie** Notlüge f; ~**ness** Weiß nt; ~**wash** n (paint) Tünche f; (fig) Ehrenrettung f; vt weißen, tünchen; (fig) reinwaschen.

whiting ['waɪtɪŋ] n Weißfisch m.

Whitsun ['wɪtsn] n Pfingsten nt.

whittle ['wɪtl] vt: ~ **away** or **down** stutzen, verringern.

whizz [wɪz] vi sausen, zischen, schwirren; ~ **kid** (col) Kanone f.

who [huː] pron (interrog) wer; (rel) der/die/das; ~**ever** [huː'evə*] pron wer immer; jeder, der/jede, das.

whole [həʊl] a ganz; (uninjured) heil; n Ganze(s) nt; **the ~ of the year** das ganze Jahr; **on the ~** im großen und ganzen; ~**hearted** a rückhaltlos; ~**heartedly** ad von ganzem Herzen; ~**sale** Großhandel m; a trade Großhandels-; destruction vollkommen, Massen; ~**saler** Großhändler m; ~**some** a bekömmlich, gesund.

wholly ['həʊlɪ] ad ganz, völlig.

whom [huːm] pron (interrog) wen; (rel) den/die/das/die pl.

whooping cough ['huːpɪŋkɒf] n Keuchhusten m.

whopper ['wɒpə*] n (col) Mordsding nt; faustdicke Lüge f.

whopping ['wɒpɪŋ] a (col) kolossal, Riesen-.

whore ['hɔː*] n Hure f.

whose [huːz] pron (interrog) wessen; (rel) dessen/deren/ dessen/deren pl.

why [waɪ] ad warum; interj nanu; **that's ~** deshalb.

wick [wɪk] n Docht m.

wicked ['wɪkɪd] a böse; ~**ness** Bosheit f, Schlechtigkeit f.

wicker ['wɪkə*] n Weidengeflecht nt, Korbgeflecht nt.

wicket ['wɪkɪt] n Tor nt, Dreistab m; (playing pitch) Spielfeld nt.

wide [waɪd] a breit; plain weit; (in firing) daneben; ~ **of** weitab von; ad weit; daneben; ~**angle** a lens Weitwinkel-; ~**awake** a hellwach; ~**ly** ad weit; known allgemein; ~**n** vt erweitern; ~**ness** Breite f, Ausdehnung f; ~**open** a weit geöffnet; ~**spread** a weitverbreitet.

widow ['wɪdəʊ] n Witwe f; ~**ed** a verwitwet; ~**er** Witwer m.

width [wɪdθ] n Breite f, Weite f.

wield [wiːld] vt schwingen, handhaben.

wife [waɪf] n (Ehe)frau f, Gattin f.

wig [wɪg] n Perücke f.

wiggle ['wɪgl] n Wackeln nt; vt wackeln mit; vi wackeln.

wigwam ['wɪgwæm] n Wigwam m, Indianerzelt nt.

wild [waɪld] a wild; (violent) heftig; plan, idea verrückt; **the ~s** pl die Wildnis; ~**erness** ['wɪldənəs] Wildnis f, Wüste f; ~**goose chase** fruchtlose(s) Unternehmen nt; ~**life** Tierwelt f; ~**ly** ad wild, ungestüm; exaggerated irrsinnig.

wilful ['wɪlfʊl] a (intended) vorsätzlich; (obstinate) eigensinnig.

will [wɪl] v aux: **he ~ come** er wird kommen; **I ~ do it!** ich werde es tun; n (power to choose) Wille m; (wish) Wunsch m, Bestreben nt; (Jur) Testament nt; vt wollen; ~**ing** a gewillt, bereit; ~**ingly** ad bereitwillig, gern; ~**ingness** (Bereit)willigkeit f.

willow ['wɪləʊ] n Weide f.

will power ['wɪl'paʊə*] n Willenskraft f.

wilt [wɪlt] vi (ver)welken.

wily ['waɪlɪ] a gerissen.

win [wɪn] n Sieg m; irreg vt gewinnen; vi (be successful) siegen; **to ~ sb over** jdn gewinnen, jdn dazu bringen.

wince [wɪns] n Zusammenzucken nt; vi zusammenzucken, zurückfahren.

winch [wɪntʃ] n Winde f.

wind [waɪnd] irreg vt rope winden; bandage wickeln; **to ~ one's way** sich schlängeln; vi (turn) sich winden; (change direction) wenden; ~ **up** vt clock aufziehen; debate (ab)schließen.

wind [wɪnd] n Wind m; (Med) Blähungen pl; ~**break** Windschutz m; ~**fall** unverhoffte(r) Glücksfall m.

winding ['waɪndɪŋ] a road gewunden, sich schlängelnd.

wind instrument ['wɪndɪnstrumənt] n Blasinstrument nt.

windmill ['wɪndmɪl] n Windmühle f.

window ['wɪndəʊ] n Fenster nt; ~ **box** Blumenkasten m; ~ **cleaner** Fensterputzer m; ~ **ledge** Fenstersims m; ~**pane** Fensterscheibe f; ~**shopping** Schaufensterbummel m; ~**sill** Fensterbank f.

windpipe ['wɪndpaɪp] n Luftröhre f.

windscreen ['wɪndskriːn], (US) **windshield** ['wɪndʃiːld] n Windschutzscheibe f; ~ **wiper** Scheibenwischer m.

windswept ['wɪndswept] a vom Wind gepeitscht; person zersaust.

windy ['wɪndɪ] a windig.

wine [waɪn] n Wein m; ~**glass** Weinglas nt; ~ **list** Weinkarte f; ~ **merchant** Weinhändler m; ~ **tasting** Weinprobe f; ~ **waiter** Weinkellner m.

wing [wɪŋ] n Flügel m; (Mil) Gruppe f; ~**s** pl (Theat) Seitenkulisse f; ~**er** (Sport) Flügelstürmer m.

wink [wɪŋk] n Zwinkern nt; vi zwinkern, blinzeln; **to ~ at sb** jdm zublinzeln; **forty ~s** Nickerchen nt.

winner ['wɪnə*] n Gewinner m; (Sport) Sieger m.

winning ['wɪnɪŋ] a team siegreich, Sieger-; goal entscheidend; n: ~**s** pl Gewinn m; ~**post** Ziel nt.

winter ['wɪntə*] n Winter m; a clothes Winter-; vi überwintern; ~ **sports** pl Wintersport m.

wintry ['wɪntrɪ] a Winter-, winterlich.

wipe [waɪp] n Wischen nt; vt wischen, abwischen; ~ **out** vt debt löschen; (destroy) auslöschen.

wire ['waɪə*] n Draht m; (telegram) Telegramm nt; vt telegrafieren (sb jdm, sth etw); ~**less** Radio(apparat m) nt.

wiry ['waɪərɪ] *a* drahtig.
wisdom ['wɪzdəm] *n* Weisheit *f*; (*of decision*) Klugheit *f*; ~ **tooth** Weisheitszahn *m*.
wise [waɪz] *a* klug, weise; ~**crack** Witzelei *f*; ~**ly** *ad* klug, weise.
wish [wɪʃ] *n* Wunsch *m*; *vt* wünschen; **he ~es us to do it** er möchte, daß wir es tun; **with best ~es** herzliche Grüße; **to ~ sb goodbye** jdn verabschieden; **to ~ to do sth** etw tun wollen; ~**ful thinking** Wunschdenken *nt*.
wisp [wɪsp] *n* (Haar)strähne *f*; (*of smoke*) Wölkchen *nt*.
wistful ['wɪstful] *a* sehnsüchtig.
wit [wɪt] *n* (*also* ~**s**) Verstand *m no pl*; (*amusing ideas*) Witz *m*; (*person*) Witzbold *m*; **at one's ~s' end** mit seinem Latein am Ende; **to have one's ~s about one** auf dem Posten sein.
witch [wɪtʃ] *n* Hexe *f*; ~**craft** Hexerei *f*.
with [wɪð, wɪθ] *prep* mit; (*in spite of*) trotz (+*gen or dat*); ~ **him it's ...** bei ihm ist es . . .; **to stay ~ sb** bei jdm wohnen; **I have no money ~ me** ich habe kein Geld bei mir; **shaking ~ fright** vor Angst zitternd.
withdraw [wɪð'drɔː] *irreg vt* zurückziehen; *money* abheben; *remark* zurücknehmen; *vi* sich zurückziehen; ~**al** Zurückziehung *f*; Abheben *nt*; Zurücknahme *f*; ~**al symptoms** *pl* Entzugserscheinungen *pl*.
wither ['wɪðə*] *vi* (ver)welken; ~**ed** *a* verwelkt, welk.
withhold [wɪð'həʊld] *vt irreg* vorenthalten (*from sb* jdm).
within [wɪð'ɪn] *prep* innerhalb (+*gen*).
without [wɪð'aʊt] *prep* ohne; **it goes ~ saying** es ist selbstverständlich.
withstand [wɪð'stænd] *vt irreg* widerstehen (+*dat*).
witness ['wɪtnəs] *n* Zeuge *m*; Zeugin *f*; *vt* (*see*) sehen, miterleben; (*sign document*) beglaubigen; *vi* aussagen; ~ **box**, (*US*) ~**stand** Zeugenstand *m*.
witticism ['wɪtɪsɪzəm] *n* witzige Bemerkung *f*.
witty *a*, **wittily** *ad* ['wɪtɪ, -lɪ] witzig, geistreich.
wizard ['wɪzəd] *n* Zauberer *m*.
wobble ['wɒbl] *vi* wackeln.
woe [wəʊ] *n* Weh *nt*, Leid *nt*, Kummer *m*.
wolf [wʊlf] *n* Wolf *m*.
woman ['wʊmən] *n*, *pl* **women** Frau *f*; *a* ~**in** *f*.
womb [wuːm] *n* Gebärmutter *f*.
women ['wɪmɪn] *npl of* **woman**.
wonder ['wʌndə*] *n* (*marvel*) Wunder *nt*; (*surprise*) Staunen *nt*, Verwunderung *f*; *vi* sich wundern; **I ~ whether ...** ich frage mich, ob . . .; ~**ful** *a* wunderbar, herrlich; ~**fully** *ad* wunderbar.
won't [wəʊnt] = **will not**.
wood [wʊd] *n* Holz *nt*; (*forest*) Wald *m*; ~**carving** Holzschnitzerei *f*; ~**ed** *a* bewaldet, waldig, Wald-; ~**en** *a* (*lit, fig*) hölzern; ~**pecker** Specht *m*; ~**wind** Blasinstrumente *pl*; ~**work** Holzwerk *nt*; (*craft*) Holzarbeiten *pl*; ~**worm** Holzwurm *m*.

wool [wʊl] *n* Wolle *f*; ~**len**, (*US*) ~**en** *a* Woll-; ~**ly**, (*US*) ~**y** *a* wollig; (*fig*) schwammig.
word [wɜːd] *n* Wort *nt*; (*news*) Bescheid *m*; **to have a ~ with sb** mit jdm reden; **to have ~s with sb** Worte wechseln mit jdm; **by ~ of mouth** mündlich; *vt* formulieren; ~**ing** Wortlaut *m*, Formulierung *f*.
work [wɜːk] *n* Arbeit *f*; (*Art, Liter*) Werk *nt*; *vi* arbeiten; *machine* funktionieren; (*medicine*) wirken; (*succeed*) klappen; ~**s** (*factory*) Fabrik *f*, Werk *nt*; (*of watch*) Werk *nt*; ~ **off** *vt debt* abarbeiten; *anger* abreagieren; ~ **on** *vi* weiterarbeiten; *vt* (*be engaged in*) arbeiten an (+*dat*); (*influence*) bearbeiten; ~ **out** *vi* (*sum*) aufgehen; (*plan*) klappen; *vt problem* lösen; *plan* ausarbeiten; ~ **up to** *vt* hinarbeiten auf (+*acc*); **to get ~ed up** sich aufregen; ~**able** *a soil* bearbeitbar; *plan* ausführbar; ~**er** Arbeiter(in *f*) *m*; ~**ing class** Arbeiterklasse *f*; ~**ing-class** *a* Arbeiter-; ~**ing man** Werktätige(r) *m*; ~**man** Arbeiter *m*; ~**manship** Arbeit *f*, Ausführung *f*; ~**shop** Werkstatt *f*.
world [wɜːld] *n* Welt *f*; (*animal* — *etc*) Reich *nt*; **out of this ~** himmlisch; **to come into the ~** auf die Welt kommen; **to do sb/sth the ~ of good** jdm/etw sehr gut tun; **to be the ~ to sb** jds ein und alles sein; **to think the ~ of sb** große Stücke auf jdn halten; ~**-famous** *a* weltberühmt; ~**ly** *a* weltlich, irdisch; ~**-wide** *a* weltweit.
worm [wɜːm] *n* Wurm *m*.
worn [wɔːn] *a clothes* abgetragen; ~**-out** *a object* abgenutzt; *person* völlig erschöpft.
worried ['wʌrɪd] *a* besorgt, beunruhigt.
worrier ['wʌrɪə*] *n*: **he is a ~** er macht sich (*dat*) ewig Sorgen.
worry ['wʌrɪ] *n* Sorge *f*, Kummer *m*; *vt* quälen, beunruhigen; *vi* (*feel uneasy*) sich sorgen, sich (*dat*) Gedanken machen; ~**ing** *a* beunruhigend.
worse [wɜːs] *a comp of* **bad** schlechter, schlimmer; *ad comp of* **badly** schlimmer, ärger; *n* Schlimmere(s) *nt*, Schlechtere(s) *nt*; ~**n** *vt* verschlimmern; *vi* sich verschlechtern.
worship ['wɜːʃɪp] *n* Anbetung *f*, Verehrung *f*; (*religious service*) Gottesdienst *m*; (*title*) Hochwürden *f*; *vt* anbeten; ~**per** Gottesdienstbesucher(in *f*) *m*.
worst [wɜːst] *a superl of* **bad** schlimmste(r,s), schlechteste(r,s); *ad superl of* **badly** am schlimmsten, am ärgsten; *n* Schlimmste(s) *nt*, Ärgste(s) *nt*.
worsted ['wʊstɪd] *n* Kammgarn *nt*.
worth [wɜːθ] *n* Wert *m*; **£10 ~ of food** Essen für 10 £; *a* wert; ~ **seeing** sehenswert; **it's ~ £10** es ist 10 £ wert; ~**less** *a* wertlos; *person* nichtsnutzig; ~**while** *a* lohnend, der Mühe wert; *ad*: **it's not ~while going** es lohnt sich nicht, dahin zu gehen; ~**y** [wɜːðɪ] *a* (*having worth*) wertvoll; wert (*of gen*), würdig (*of gen*).
would [wʊd] *v aux*: **she ~ come** sie würde kommen; **if you asked he ~**

come wenn Sie ihn fragten, würde er kommen; ~ **you like a drink?** möchten Sie etwas trinken?; ~-**be** a angeblich; ~**n't** = ~ **not**.

wound [wu:nd] n (lit, fig) Wunde f; vt verwunden, verletzen (also fig).

wrangle ['ræŋgl] n Streit m; vi sich zanken.

wrap [ræp] n (stole) Umhang m, Schal m; vt (also ~ **up**) einwickeln; **deal** abschließen; ~**per** Umschlag m, Schutzhülle f; ~**ping paper** Einwickelpapier nt.

wreath [ri:θ] n Kranz m.

wreck [rek] n Schiffbruch m; (ship) Wrack nt; (sth ruined) Ruine f, Trümmerhaufen m; **a nervous** ~ ein Nervenbündel nt; vt zerstören; ~**age** Wrack nt, Trümmer pl.

wren [ren] n Zaunkönig m.

wrench [rentʃ] n (spanner) Schraubenschlüssel m; (twist) Ruck m, heftige Drehung f; vt reißen, zerren.

wrestle ['resl] vi ringen.

wrestling ['resliŋ] n Ringen nt; ~ **match** Ringkampf m.

wretched ['retʃid] a hovel elend; (col) verflixt; **I feel** ~ mir ist elend.

wriggle ['rigl] n Schlängeln nt; vi sich winden.

wring [riŋ] vt irreg wringen.

wrinkle ['riŋkl] n Falte f, Runzel f; vt runzeln; vi sich runzeln; (material) knittern.

wrist [rist] n Handgelenk nt; ~**watch** Armbanduhr f.

writ [rit] n gerichtliche(r) Befehl m.

write [rait] vti irreg schreiben; ~ **down** vt niederschreiben, aufschreiben; ~ **off** vt (dismiss) abschreiben; ~ **out** vt essay abschreiben; cheque ausstellen; ~ **up** vt schreiben; ~-**off: it is a off** das kann man abschreiben; ~**r** Verfasser m; (author) Schriftsteller m; ~-**up** Besprechung f.

writing ['raitiŋ] n (act) Schreiben nt; (hand—) (Hand)schrift f; ~**s** pl Schriften pl, Werke pl; ~ **paper** Schreibpapier.

wrong [roŋ] a (incorrect) falsch; (morally) unrecht; (out of order) nicht in Ordnung; **he was** ~ **in doing** that es war nicht recht von ihm, das zu tun; **what's** ~ **with your leg?** was ist mit deinem Bein los?; **to go** ~ (plan) schiefgehen; (person) einen Fehler machen; n Unrecht m; vt Unrecht tun (+dat); ~**ful** a unrechtmäßig; ~**ly** ad falsch; accuse zu Unrecht.

wrought [rɔ:t] a: ~ **iron** Schmiedeeisen nt.

wry [rai] a schief, krumm; (ironical) trocken; **to make a** ~ **face** das Gesicht verziehen.

X

X, x [eks] n X nt, x nt.

Xmas ['eksməs] n (col) Weihnachten f.

X-ray ['eks'rei] n Röntgenaufnahme f; vt röntgen.

xylophone ['zailəfəun] n Xylophon nt.

Y

Y, y [wai] n Y nt, y nt.

yacht [jɔt] n Jacht f; ~**ing** (Sport)segeln nt; ~**sman** Sportsegler m.

Yank [jæŋk] n (col) Ami m.

yap [jæp] vi (dog) kläffen; (people) quasseln.

yard [jɑ:d] n Hof m; (measure) (englische) Elle f, Yard nt, 0,91 m; ~**stick** (fig) Maßstab m.

yarn [jɑ:n] n (thread) Garn nt; (story) (Seemanns)garn nt.

yawn [jɔ:n] n Gähnen nt; vi gähnen.

year ['jiə*] n Jahr nt; ~**ly** a, ad jährlich.

yearn [jɜ:n] vi sich sehnen (for nach); ~**ing** Verlangen nt, Sehnsucht f.

yeast [ji:st] n Hefe f.

yell [jel] n gellende(r) Schrei m; vi laut schreien.

yellow ['jeləu] a gelb; n Gelb nt; ~ **fever** Gelbfieber nt.

yelp [jelp] n Gekläff nt; vi kläffen.

yeoman ['jəumən] n: **Y~ of the Guard** Leibgardist m.

yes [jes] ad ja; n Ja nt, Jawort nt; ~**man** Jasager m.

yesterday ['jestədei] ad gestern; n Gestern nt; **the day before** ~ vorgestern.

yet [jet] ad noch; (in question) schon; (up to now) bis jetzt; **and** ~ **again** und wieder or noch einmal; **as** ~ bis jetzt; (in past) bis dahin; cj doch, dennoch.

yew [ju:] n Eibe f.

Yiddish ['jidiʃ] n Jiddisch nt.

yield [ji:ld] n Ertrag m; vt result, crop hervorbringen; interest, profit abwerfen; (concede) abtreten; vi nachgeben; (Mil) sich ergeben.

yodel ['jəudl] vi jodeln.

yoga ['jəugə] n Joga m.

yoghurt ['jɒgət] n Joghurt m.

yoke [jəuk] n (lit, fig) Joch nt.

yolk [jəuk] n Eidotter m, Eigelb nt.

yonder ['jɒndə*] ad dort drüben, da drüben; a jene(r, s) dort.

you [ju:] pron (familiar) (sing) (nom) du; (acc) dich; (dat) dir; (pl) (nom) ihr; (acc, dat) euch; (polite) (nom, acc) Sie; (dat) Ihnen; (indef) (nom) man; (acc) einen; (dat) einem.

you'd [ju:d] = **you had; you would**.

you'll [ju:l] = **you will, you shall**.

young [jʌŋ] a jung; npl die Jungen; ~**ish** a ziemlich jung; ~**ster** Junge m, junge(r) Bursche m/junge(s) Mädchen nt.

your ['jɔ:*] poss a (familiar) (sing) dein; (pl) euer, eure pl; (polite) Ihr.

you're ['juə*] = **you are**.

yours ['jɔ:z] poss pron (familiar) (sing) deine(r, s); (pl) eure(r, s); (polite) Ihre(r, s).

yourself [jɔ:'self] pron (emphatic) selbst; (familiar) (sing) (acc) dich (selbst); (dat) dir (selbst); (pl) euch (selbst); (polite) sich (selbst); **you're not** ~ mit dir/Ihnen ist etwas nicht in Ordnung.

youth [ju:θ] n Jugend f; (young man)

junge(r) Mann *m*; (*young people*) Jugend *f*;
~**ful** *a* jugendlich; ~ **hostel** Jugend-
herberge *f*.
you've [ju:v] = **you have**.

Z

Z, z [zɛd] *n* Z *nt*, z *nt*.
zany ['zeɪnɪ] *a* komisch.
zeal [zi:l] *n* Eifer *m*; ~**ous** ['zeləs] *a* eifrig.
zebra ['zi:brə] *n* Zebra *nt*; ~ **crossing**
['zi:brə'krɒsɪŋ] Zebrastreifen *m*.
zenith ['zenɪθ] *n* Zenit *m*.
zero ['zɪərəʊ] *n* Null *f*; (*on scale*) Nullpunkt
m; ~ **hour** die Stunde X.
zest [zest] *n* Begeisterung *f*.

zigzag ['zɪgzæg] *n* Zickzack *m*; *vi* im
Zickzack laufen/fahren.
zinc [zɪŋk] *n* Zink *nt*.
Zionism ['zaɪənɪzəm] *n* Zionismus *m*.
zip [zɪp] *n* (*also* ~ **fastener**, ~**per**)
Reißverschluß *m*; *vt* (*also* ~ **up**) den
Reißverschluß zumachen (+*gen*).
zither ['zɪðə*] *n* Zither *f*.
zodiac ['zəʊdɪæk] *n* Tierkreis *m*.
zombie ['zɒmbɪ] *n* Trantüte *f*.
zone [zəʊn] *n* Zone *f*; (*area*) Gebiet *nt*.
zoo [zu:] *n* Zoo *m*; ~**logical** [zəʊə'lɒdʒɪkəl]
a zoologisch; ~**logist** [zu:'ɒlədʒɪst]
Zoologe *m*; ~**logy** [zu:'ɒlədʒɪ] Zoologie *f*.
zoom [zu:m] *vi* (*engine*) surren; (*plane*) aufsteigen; (*move fast*) brausen; (*prices*) hoch-
schnellen; ~ **lens** Zoomobjektiv *nt*.

Länder, Völker und Sprachen

ich bin Deutscher/Engländer/Albanier I am German/English/Albanian

ein Deutscher/Engländer/Albanier a German/an Englishman/an Albanian;
eine Deutsche/Engländerin/Albanierin a German (woman/girl)/an English
woman/girl/an Albanian (woman/girl)

sprechen Sie Deutsch/Englisch/Albanisch? do you speak German/English/
Albanian?

Adria (die), Adriatische(s) Meer the Adriatic.
Afrika Africa; **Afrikaner(in** *f*) *m* African; **afrikanisch** *a* African.
Ägäis (die), Ägäische(s) Meer the Aegean.
Ägypten Egypt; **Ägypter(in** *f*) *m* Egyptian; **ägyptisch** *a* Egyptian.
Albanien Albania; **Albanier(in** *f*) *m* Albanian; **albanisch** *a* Albanian.
Algerien Algeria; **Algerier(in** *f*) *m* Algerian; **algerisch** *a* Algerian.
Alpen *pl* (**die**) the Alps *pl*.
Amazonas (der) the Amazon.
Amerika America; **Amerikaner(in** *f*) *m* American; **amerikanisch** *a* American.
Anden *pl* (**die**) the Andes *pl*.
Antarktis (die) the Antarctic.
Antillen *pl* (**die**) the Antilles *pl*.
Antwerpen Antwerp.
Arabien Arabia; **Araber** *m* Arab, Arabian; **arabisch** *a* Arab, Arabic, Arabian.
Argentinien Argentina, the Argentine; **Argentinier(in** *f*) *m* Argentinian;
   argentinisch *a* Argentinian.
Ärmelkanal (der) the English Channel.
Armenien Armenia; **Armenier(in** *f*) *m* Armenian; **armenisch** *a* Armenian.
Asien Asia; **Asiat(in** *f*) *m* Asian; **asiatisch** *a* Asian, Asiatic.
Athen Athens; **Athener(in** *f*) *m* Athenian; **athenisch** *a* Athenian.
Äthiopien Ethiopia; **Äthiopier(in** *f*) *m* Ethiopian; **äthiopisch** *a* Ethiopian.
Atlantik (der), Atlantische(r) Ozean the Atlantic (Ocean).
Ätna (der) Mount Etna.
Australien Australia; **Australier(in** *f*) *m* Australian; **australisch** *a* Australian.
Azoren *pl* (**die**) the Azores *pl*.
Balkan (der) the Balkans *pl*.
Basel Basle.
Bayern Bavaria; **Bayer(in** *f*) *m* Bavarian; **bayerisch** *a* Bavarian.
Belgien Belgium; **Belgier(in** *f*) *m* Belgian; **belgisch** *a* Belgian.
Belgrad Belgrade.
Birma Burma; **Birmane** *m*, **Birmanin** *f* Burmese; **Birmanisch** *a* Burmese.
Biskaya (die) the Bay of Biscay.
Bodensee (der) Lake Constance.
Böhmen Bohemia; **Böhme** *m*, **Böhmin** *f* Bohemian; **böhmisch** *a* Bohemian.
Bolivien Bolivia; **Bolivianer(in** *f*) *m* Bolivian; **bolivianisch, bolvisch** *a* Bolivian.
Brasilien Brazil; **Brasilianer(in** *f*) *m* Brazilian; **brasilianisch** *a* Brazilian.
Braunschweig Brunswick.
Brite *m*, **Britin** *f* Briton; **britisch** *a* British.
Brüssel Brussels.
Bulgarien Bulgaria; **Bulgare** *m*, **Bulgarin** *f* Bulgarian, Bulgar; **bulgarisch** *a*
   Bulgarian.
Burgund Burgundy; **burgundisch, Burgunder** *a* Burgundian.
Calais: Straße von Calais (die) the Straits of Dover *pl*.
Chile Chile; **Chilene** *m*, **Chilenin** *f* Chilean; **chilenisch** *a* Chilean.
China China; **Chinese** *m*, **Chinesin** *f* Chinese; **chinesisch** *a* Chinese.
Dänemark Denmark; **Däne** *m*, **Dänin** *f* Dane; **dänisch** *a* Danish.
Deutsche Demokratische Republik (die) German Democratic Republic, East
   Germany.
Deutschland Germany; **Deutsche(r)** *mf* German; **deutsch** *a* German.
Dolomiten *pl* (**die**) the Dolomites *pl*.
Donau (die) the Danube.
Dünkirchen Dunkirk.

Eismeer (das) the Arctic.
Elfenbeinküste (die) the Ivory Coast.
Elsaß (das) Alsace; **Elsässer(in** f**)** m Alsatian; **elsässisch** a Alsatian.
Engadin (das) the Engadine.
England England; **Engländer(in** f**)** m Englishman/-woman; **englisch** a English.
Estland Estonia; **Este** m, **Estin** f Estonian; **estnisch** a Estonian.
Etsch (die) the Adige.
Euphrat (der) the Euphrates.
Eurasien Eurasia.
Europa Europe; **Europäer(in** f**)** m European; **europäisch** a European.
Ferne(r) Osten (der) the Far East.
Finnland Finland; **Finne** m, **Finnin** f Finn; **finnisch** a Finnish.
Flandern Flanders; **Flame** m, **Flämin** or **Flamin** f Fleming; **flämisch** a Flemish.
Florenz Florence; **Florentiner(in** f**)** m Florentine; **florentinisch** a Florentine.
Frankreich France; **Franzose** m, **Französin** f Frenchman/-woman; **französisch** a French.
Friesland Frisia; **Friese** m, **Friesin** f Frisian; **friesisch** a Frisian.
Genf Geneva.
Genfer See Lake Geneva.
Genua Genoa; **Genuese** m, **Genuesin** f Genoan; **genuesisch** a Genoan.
Griechenland Greece; **Grieche** m, **Griechin** f Greek; **griechisch** a Greek.
Großbritannien Great Britain; **Brite** m, **Britin** f Briton; **britisch, großbritannisch** a British.
Guinea Guinea.
Haag (der), Den Haag the Hague.
Hannover Hanover; **Hannoveraner(in** f**)** m Hanoverian; **Hannoveraner, hannoversch** a Hanoverian.
Hebriden pl **(die)** the Hebrides pl.
Helgoland Heligoland.
Hessen Hesse; **Hesse** m, **Hessin** f Hessian; **hessisch** a Hessian.
Holland Holland; **Holländer(in** f**)** m Dutchman/-woman; **holländisch** a Dutch.
Iberische Halbinsel (die) the Iberian Peninsula.
Indien India; **Inder(in** f**)** m, **Indianer(in** f**)** m Indian; **indisch, indianisch** a Indian.
Indonesien Indonesia; **Indonesier(in** f**)** m Indonesian; **indonesisch** a Indonesian.
Irak (auch **der)** Iraq; **Iraker(in** f**)** m Iraqi; **irakisch** a Iraqi.
Iran (auch **der)** Iran; **Iraner(in** f**)** m Iranian; **iranisch** a Iranian.
Irland Ireland; **Ire** m, **Irin** f Irishman/-woman; **irisch** a Irish.
Island Iceland; **Isländer(in** f**)** m Icelander; **isländisch** a Icelandic.
Israel Israel; **Israeli** mf Israeli; **israelisch** a Israeli.
Italien Italy; **Italiener(in** f**)** m Italian; **italienisch** a Italian.
Japan Japan; **Japaner(in** f**)** m Japanese; **japanisch** a Japanese.
Jemen (auch **der)** the Yemen; **Jemenit(in** f**)** m Yemeni; **jemenitisch** a Yemeni.
Jordanien Jordan; **Jordanier(in** f**)** m Jordanian; **jordanisch** a Jordanian.
Jugoslawien Yugoslavia; **Jugoslawe** m, **Jugoslawin** f Yugoslavian; **jugoslawisch** a Yugoslavian.
Kanada Canada; **Kanadier(in** f**)** m Canadian; **kanadisch** a Canadian.
Kanalinseln pl **(die)** the Channel Islands pl.
Kanarische Inseln pl **(die)** the Canary Islands pl, the Canaries pl.
Kap der Guten Hoffnung (das) the Cape of Good Hope.
Kapstadt Cape Town.
Karibische Inseln pl **(die)** the Caribbean Islands pl.
Karpaten pl **(die)** the Carpathians pl.
Kaspische(s) Meer the Caspian Sea.
Kleinasien Asia Minor.
Köln Cologne.
Konstanz Constance.
Kreml (der) the Kremlin.
Kreta Crete; **Kreter(in** f**)** m Cretan; **kretisch** a Cretan.
Krim (die) the Crimea.
Kroatien Croatia; **Kroate** m, **Kroatin** f Croatian; **kroatisch** a Croatian.
Lappland Lapland; **Lappe** m, **Lappin** f Laplander; **lappisch** a Lapp.
Lateinamerika Latin America.
Lettland Latvia; **Lette** m, **Lettin** f Latvian; **lettisch** a Latvian.
Libanon the Lebanon; **Libanese** m, **Libanesin** f Lebänese; **libanesisch** a Lebanese.
Libyen Libya; **Libyer(in** f**)** m Libyan; **libyisch** a Libyan.
Lissabon Lisbon.
Litauen Lithuania; **Litauer(in** f**)** m Lithuanian; **litauisch** a Lithuanian.
Livland Livonia; **Livländer(in** f**)** m Livonian; **livländisch** a Livonian.
London London; **Londoner(in** f**)** m Londoner; **Londoner** a London.

Lothringen Lorraine.
Lüneburger Heide (die) the Lüneburg Heath.
Luxemburg Luxembourg.
Maas (die) the Meuse.
Mähren Moravia.
Mailand Milan; **Mailänder(in** *f***)** *m* Milanese; **mailändisch** *a* Milanese.
Mallorca Majorca.
Mandschurei (die) Manchuria; **Mandschure** *m*, **Mandschurin** *f* Manchurian; **mandschurisch** *a* Manchurian.
Marokko Morocco; **Marokkaner(in** *f***)** *m* Moroccan; **marokkanisch** *a* Moroccan.
Mazedonien Macedonia; **Mazedonier(in** *f***)** *m* Macedonian; **mazedonisch** *a* Macedonian.
Mittelamerika Central America.
Mitteleuropa Central Europe.
Mittelmeer (das) the Mediterranean.
Moldau (die) Moldavia.
Mongolei (die) Mongolia; **Mongole** *m*, **Mongolin** *f* Mongol(ian); **mongolisch** *a* Mongol(ian).
Moskau Moscow; **Moskauer(in** *f***)** *m* Muscovite; **moskauisch** *a* Muscovite.
München Munich.
Nahe(r) Osten (der) the Near East.
Neapel Naples; **Neapolitaner(in** *f***)** *m* Neapolitan; **neapolitanisch** *a* Neapolitan.
Neufundland Newfoundland; **Neufundländer(in** *f***)** *m* Newfoundlander; **neufundländisch** *a* Newfoundland.
Neuguinea New Guinea.
Neuseeland New Zealand; **Neuseeländer(in** *f***)** *m* New Zealander; **neuseeländisch** *a* New Zealand.
Niederlande *pl* **(die)** the Netherlands; **Niederländer(in** *f***)** *m* Dutchman/-woman; **niederländisch** *a* Dutch.
Niedersachsen Lower Saxony.
Niederrhein Lower Rhine.
Nil (der) the Nile.
Nordirland Northern Ireland.
Nordsee (die) the North Sea.
Norwegen Norway; **Norweger(in** *f***)** *m* Norwegian; **norwegisch** *a* Norwegian.
Nord-Ostsee-Kanal (der) the Kiel Canal.
Nordrhein-Westfalen North Rhine-Westphalia.
Nürnberg Nuremberg.
Oberbayern Upper Bavaria.
Ostasien Eastern Asia.
Ostende Ostend.
Ostsee (die) the Baltic.
Österreich Austria; **Österreicher(in** *f***)** *m* Austrian; **österreichisch** *a* Austrian.
Palästina Palestine; **Palästinenser(in** *f***)** *m* Palestinian; **palästinensisch** *a* Palestinian.
Paris Paris; **Pariser(in** *f***)** *m* Parisian; **Pariser** *a* Parisian.
Pazifik (der), Pazifische(r) Ozean the Pacific.
Peloponnes (der *or* **die)** the Peloponnese.
Persien Persia; **Perser(in** *f***)** *m* Persian; **persisch** *a* Persian.
Philippinen *pl* **(die)** the Philippines *pl*.
Polen Poland; **Pole** *m*, **Polin** *f* Pole; **polnisch** *a* Polish.
Pommern Pomerania; **Pommer(in** *f***)** *m* Pomeranian; **pommerisch** *a* Pomeranian.
Portugal Portugal; **Portugiese** *m*, **Portugiesin** *f* Portuguese; **portugiesisch** *a* Portuguese.
Prag Prague.
Preußen Prussia; **Preuße** *m*, **Preußin** *f* Prussian; **preußisch** *a* Prussian.
Pyrenäen *pl* **(die)** the Pyrenees *pl*.
Rhein (der) the Rhine; **rheinisch** *a* Rhenish.
Rhodesien Rhodesia; **Rhodesier(in** *f***)** *m* Rhodesian; **rhodesisch** *a* Rhodesian.
Rhodos Rhodes.
Rom Rome; **Römer(in** *f***)** *m* Roman; **römisch** *a* Roman.
Rote(s) Meer the Red Sea.
Rumänien Ro(u)mania; **Rumäne** *m*, **Rumänin** *f* Ro(u)manian; **rumänisch** *a* Ro(u)manian.
Rußland Russia; **Russe** *m*, **Russin** *f* Russian; **russisch** *a* Russian.
Saarland the Saar.
Sachsen Saxony; **Sachse** *m*, **Sächsin** *f* Saxon; **sächsisch** *a* Saxon.
Sardinien Sardinia; **Sardinier(in** *f***)** *m*, **Sarde** *m*, **Sardin** *f* Sardinian; **sardinisch, sardisch** *a* Sardinian.
Schlesien Silesia; **Schlesier(in** *f***)** *m* Silesian; **schlesisch** *a* Silesian.

Schottland Scotland; **Schotte** *m*, **Schottin** *f* Scot, Scotsman/-woman; **schottisch** *a* Scottish, Scots, Scotch.
Schwaben Swabia; **Schwabe** *m*, **Schwäbin** *f* Swabian; **schwäbisch** *a* Swabian.
Schwarzwald (der) the Black Forest.
Schweden Sweden; **Schwede** *m*, **Schwedin** *f* Swede; **schwedisch** *a* Swedish.
Schweiz (die) Switzerland; **Schweizer(in** *f)* *m* Swiss; **schweizerisch** *a* Swiss.
Serbien Serbia; **Serbe** *m*, **Serbin** *f* Serbian; **serbisch** *a* Serbian.
Sibirien Siberia; **sibirisch** *a* Siberian.
Sizilien Sicily; **Sizilianer(in** *f)* *m*, **Sizilier(in** *f)* *m* Sicilian; **sizilisch, sizilianisch** *a* Sicilian.
Skandinavien Scandinavia; **Skandinavier(in** *f)* *m* Scandinavian; **skandinavisch** *a* Scandinavian.
Slowakei (die) Slovakia; **Slowake** *m*, **Slowakin** *f* Slovak; **slowakisch** *a* Slovak.
Sowjetunion (die) the Soviet Union; **Sowjetbürger(in** *f)* *m* Soviet; **sowjetisch** *a* Soviet.
Spanien Spain; **Spanier(in** *f)* *m* Spaniard; **spanisch** *a* Spanish.
Steiermark Styria; **Steiermärker(in** *f)* *m*, **Steirer** *m*, **Steierin** *f* Styrian; **steiermärkisch, steirisch** *a* Styrian.
Stille(r) Ozean the Pacific.
Syrien Syria; **Syrer(in** *f)* *m* Syrian; **syrisch** *a* Syrian.
Teneriffa Tenerife.
Themse (die) the Thames.
Thüringen Thuringia; **Thüringer(in** *f)* *m* Thuringian; **thüringisch** *a* Thuringian.
Tirol the Tyrol; **Tiroler(in** *f)* *m* Tyrolean; **tirolisch** *a* Tyrolean.
Tschechoslowakei (die) Czechoslovakia; **Tscheche** *m*, **Tschechin** *f*, **Tschechoslowake** *m*, **Tschechoslowakin** *f* Czech, Czechoslovak(ian); **tschechisch, tschechoslowakisch** *a* Czech, Czechoslovak(ian).
Toscana (die) Tuscany.
Trient Trent.
Tunesien Tunisia; **Tunesier(in** *f)* *m* Tunisian; **tunesisch** *a* Tunisian.
Türkei (die) Turkey; **Türke** *m*, **Türkin** *f* Turk; **türkisch** *a* Turkish.
Ungarn Hungary; **Ungar(in** *f)* *m* Hungarian; **ungarisch** *a* Hungarian.
Venedig Venice; **Venetianer(in** *f)* *m* Venetian; **venetianisch** *a* Venetian.
Vereinigte Staaten *pl* **(die)** the United States *pl*.
Vesuv (der) Vesuvius.
Vierwaldstättersee (der) Lake Lucerne.
Vogesen *pl* **(die)** the Vosges *pl*.
Volksrepublik China (die) the People's Republic of China.
Vorderasien the Near East.
Warschau Warsaw.
Weichsel (die) the Vistula.
Westfalen Westphalia; **Westfale** *m*, **Westfälin** *f* Westphalian; **westfälisch** *a* Westphalian.
Westindien the West Indies; **westindisch** *a* West Indian.
Wien Vienna; **Wiener(in** *f)* *m* Viennese; **Wiener** *a* Viennese.
Zypern Cyprus; **Zyprer(in** *f)* *m*, **Zyprier(in** *f)* *m*, **Zypriot(in** *f)* *m* Cypriot; **zyprisch, zypriotisch** *a* Cypriot.

Countries, nationalities and languages

I am German/English/Albanian ich bin Deutscher/Engländer/Albaner

a German/an Englishman/an Albanian ein Deutscher/Engländer/Albaner; **a German (woman/girl)/an English woman/girl/an Albanian (woman/girl)** eine Deutsche/Engländerin/Albanierin

do you speak German/English/Albanian? sprechen Sie Deutsch/Englisch/Albanisch?

the Adriatic die Adria.
the Aegean die Ägäis.
Afghanistan Afghanistan *nt*; **Afghan** *n* Afghane *m*, Afghanin *f*; *a* afghanisch.
Africa Afrika *nt*; **African** *n* Afrikaner(in *f*) *m*; *a* afrikanisch.
Albania Albanien *nt*; **Albanian** *n* Albanier(in *f*) *m*; *a* albanisch.

398

Algeria Algerien *nt*; **Algerian** *n* Algerier(in *f*) *m*; *a* algerisch.
the Alps *pl* die Alpen *pl*.
America Amerika *nt*; **American** *n* Amerikaner(in *f*) *m*; *a* amerikanisch.
the Andes *pl* die Anden *pl*.
Angola Angola *nt*; **Angolan** *n* Angolaner(in *f*) *m*; *a* angolanisch.
the Antarctic die Antarktis; **Antarctic** *a* antarktisch.
Arabia Arabien *nt*; **Arab, Arabian** *n* Araber(in *f*) *m*; *a* arabisch.
the Arctic die Arktis; **Arctic** *a* arktisch.
Argentina, the Argentine Argentinien *nt*; **Argentinian** *n* Argentinier(in *f*) *m*; *a* argentinisch.
Asia Asien *nt*; **Asian** *n* Asiat(in *f*) *m*; *a* asiatisch.
Asia Minor Kleinasien *nt*.
Athens Athen *nt*.
the Atlantic (Ocean) der Atlantik, der Atlantische Ozean.
Australia Australien *nt*; **Australian** *n* Australier(in *f*) *m*; *a* australisch.
Austria Österreich *nt*; **Austrian** *n* Österreicher(in *f*) *m*; *a* österreichisch.
the Baltic die Ostsee.
Bavaria Bayern *nt*; **Bavarian** *n* Bayer(in *f*) *m*; *a* bay(e)risch.
the Bay of Biscay (der Golf von) Biskaya *f*.
Belgium Belgien *nt*; **Belgian** *n* Belgier(in *f*) *m*; *a* belgisch.
the Black Forest der Schwarzwald.
Bolivia Bolivien *nt*; **Bolivian** *n* Bolivianer(in *f*) *m*, Bolivier(in *f*) *m*; *a* boliv(ian)isch.
Brazil Brasilien *nt*; **Brazilian** *n* Brasilianer(in *f*) *m*; *a* brasilianisch.
Britain Großbritannien *nt*; **Briton** *n* Brite *m*, Britin *f*; **British** *a* britisch.
Brittany die Bretagne; **Breton** *n* Bretone *m*, Bretonin *f*; *a* bretonisch.
Brussels Brüssel *nt*.
Bulgaria Bulgarien *nt*; **Bulgarian, Bulgar** *n* Bulgare *m*, Bulgarin *f*; **Bulgarian** *a* bulgarisch.
Burma Birma *nt*; **Burmese** *n* Birmane *m*, Birmanin *f*; *a* birmanisch.
California Kalifornien *nt*; **Californian** *n* Kalifornier(in *f*) *m*; *a* kalifornisch.
Cambodia Kambodscha *nt*; **Cambodian** *n* Kambodschaner(in *f*) *m*; *a* kambodschanisch.
Canada Kanada *nt*; **Canadian** *n* Kanadier(in *f*) *m*; *a* kanadisch.
the Canary Islands *pl* die Kanarischen Inseln *pl*.
the Caribbean die Karibik; **Caribbean** *a* karibisch.
Central America Zentralamerika *nt*.
the Channel Islands *pl* die Kanalinseln *pl*, die Normannischen Inseln *pl*.
Chile Chile *nt*; **Chilean** *n* Chilene *m*, Chilenin *f*; *a* chilenisch.
China China *nt*; **Chinese** *n* Chinese *m*, Chinesin *f*; *a* chinesisch.
Cologne Köln *nt*.
Colombia Kolumbien *nt*; **Colombian** *n* Kolumbianer(in *f*) *m*, Kolumbier(in *f*) *m*; *a* kolumb(ian)isch.
Lake Constance der Bodensee.
Cornish *a* von/aus Cornwall.
Corsica Korsika *nt*; **Corsican** *n* Korse *m*, Korsin *f*; *a* korsisch.
Crete Kreta *nt*; **Cretan** *n* Kreter(in *f*) *m*; *a* kretisch.
Cuba Kuba *nt*; **Cuban** *n* Kubaner(in *f*) *m*; *a* kubanisch.
Cyprus Zypern *nt*; **Cypriot** *n* Zypriot(in *f*) *m*; *a* zypriotisch.
Czechoslovakia die Tschechoslowakei; **Czech, Czechoslovak(ian)** *n* Tscheche *m*, Tschechin *f*; *a* tschechisch.
Denmark Dänemark *nt*; **Dane** *n* Däne *m*, Dänin *f*; **Danish** *a* dänisch.
Dutch *a see* Holland.
East Germany Deutsche Demokratische Republik *f*; **East German** *n* Staatsbürger(in *f*) *m* der Deutschen Demokratischen Republik; **he is an East German** er ist aus der DDR; *a* der DDR; **East German towns** Städte (in) der DDR.
Ecuador Ecuador *nt*; **Ecuadorian** *n* Ecuadorianer(in *f*) *m*; *a* ecuadorianisch.
Egypt Ägypten *nt*; **Egyptian** *n* Ägypter(in *f*) *m*; *a* ägyptisch.
Eire ['eərə] (Republik *f*) Irland *nt*.
England England *nt*; **Englishman/-woman** *n* Engländer(in *f*) *m*; **English** *a* englisch.
the English Channel der Ärmelkanal.
Ethiopia Äthiopien *nt*; **Ethiopian** *n* Äthiopier(in *f*) *m*; *a* äthiopisch.
Europe Europa *nt*; **European** *n* Europäer(in *f*) *m*; *a* europäisch.
Fiji (Islands *pl*) die Fidschiinseln *pl*; **Fijian** *n* Fidschianer(in *f*) *m*; *a* fidschianisch.
Filipino *n see* **the Philippines.**
Finland Finnland *nt*; **Finn** *n* Finne *m*, Finnin *f*; **Finnish** *a* finnisch.
Flanders Flandern *nt*; **Fleming** *n* Flame *m*, Flämin *f*; **Flemish** *a* flämisch.
Florence Florenz *nt*; **Florentine** *n* Florentiner(in *f*) *m*; *a* florentinisch.

France Frankreich *nt* ; **Frenchman/-woman** *n* Franzose *m*, Französin *f*; **French** *a* französisch.
Geneva Genf *nt* ; **Lake Geneva** der Genfer See.
Germany Deutschland *nt* ; **German** *n* Deutsche(r) *m*, Deutsche *f*; *a* deutsch.
Ghana Ghana *nt* ; **Ghanaian** *n* Ghanaer(in *f*) *m* ; *a* ghanaisch.
Great Britain Großbritannien *nt*.
Greece Griechenland *nt* ; **Greek** *n* Grieche *m*, Griechin *f*; *a* griechisch.
the Hague Den Haag.
Haiti Haiti *nt* ; **Haitian** *n* Haitianer(in *f*) *m*, Haitier(in *f*) *m* ; *a* haitianisch, haitisch.
Hawaii Hawaii *nt* ; **Hawaiian** *n* Hawaiier(in *f*) *m* ; *a* hawaiisch.
the Hebrides *pl* die Hebriden *pl*.
the Himalayas *pl* der Himalaja.
Holland Holland *nt* ; **Dutchman/-woman** *n* Holländer(in *f*) *m* ; **Dutch** *a* holländisch, niederländisch.
Hungary Ungarn *nt* ; **Hungarian** *n* Ungar(in *f*) *m* ; *a* ungarisch.
Iceland Island *nt* ; **Icelander** *n* Isländer(in *f*) *m* ; **Icelandic** *a* isländisch.
India Indien *nt* ; **Indian** *n* Inder(in *f*) *m* ; *a* indisch.
Indonesia Indonesien *nt* ; **Indonesian** *n* Indonesier(in *f*) *m* ; *a* indonesisch.
Iran (der) Iran; **Iranian** *n* Iraner(in *f*) *m* ; *a* iranisch.
Iraq (der) Irak; **Iraqi** *n* Iraker(in *f*) *m* ; *a* irakisch.
Ireland Irland *nt* ; **Irishman/-woman** *n* Ire *m*, Irin *f*; **Irish** *a* irisch.
Israel Israel *nt* ; **Israeli** *n* Israeli *mf*; *a* israelisch.
Italy Italien *nt* ; **Italian** *n* Italiener(in *f*) *m* ; *a* italienisch.
Jamaica Jamaika *nt* ; **Jamaican** *n* Jamaikaner(in *f*) *m*, Jamaiker(in *f*) *m* ; *a* jamaikanisch, jamaikisch.
Japan Japan *nt* ; **Japanese** *n* Japaner(in *f*) *m* ; *a* japanisch.
Jordan Jordanien *nt* ; **Jordanian** *n* Jordanier(in *f*) *m* ; *a* jordanisch.
Kenya Kenia *nt* ; **Kenyan** *n* Kenianer(in *f*) *m* ; *a* kenianisch.
the Kiel Canal der Nord-Ostsee-Kanal.
Korea Korea *nt* ; **Korean** *n* Koreaner(in *f*) *m* ; *a* koreanisch.
Laos Laos *nt* ; **Laotian** *n* Laote *m*, Laotin *f*; *a* laotisch.
Lapland Lappland *nt* ; **Lapp** *n* Lappe *m*, Lappin *f*; *a* lappisch.
Latin America Lateinamerika *nt*.
Lebanon (der) Libanon; **Lebanese** *n* Libanese *m*, Libanesin *f*; *a* libanesisch.
Liberia Liberia *nt* ; **Liberian** *n* Liberianer(in *f*) *m* ; *a* liberianisch.
Libya Libyen *nt* ; **Libyan** *n* Libyer(in *f*) *m* ; *a* libysch.
Lisbon Lissabon *nt*.
London London *nt* ; **Londoner** *n* Londoner(in *f*) *m* ; **London** *a* Londoner *inv*.
Luxembourg Luxemburg *nt* ; **Luxembourger** *n* Luxemburger(in *f*) *m*.
Majorca Mallorca *nt* ; **Majorcan** *n* Bewohner(in *f*) *m* Mallorcas; *a* mallorkinisch.
Malaysia Malaysia *nt* ; **Malaysian** *n* Malaysier(in *f*) *m* ; *a* malaysisch.
Malta Malta *nt* ; **Maltese** *n* Malteser(in *f*) *m* ; *a* maltesisch.
the Mediterranean (Sea) das Mittelmeer.
Mexico Mexiko *nt* ; **Mexican** *n* Mexikaner(in *f*) *m* ; *a* mexikanisch.
Milan Mailand *nt* ; **Milanese** *n* Mailänder(in *f*) *m* ; *a* mailändisch.
Mongolia die Mongolei; **Mongolian** *n* Mongole *m*, mongolin *f*; *a* mongolisch.
Morocco Marokko *nt* ; **Moroccan** *n* Marokkaner(in *f*) *m* ; *a* marrokkanisch.
Moscow Moskau *nt* ; **Muscovite** *n* Moskauer(in *f*) *m* ; *a* moskauisch.
Munich München *nt*.
Naples Neapel *nt* ; **Neapolitan** *n* Neapolitaner(in *f*) *m* ; *a* neapolitanisch.
the Netherlands *pl* die Niederlande *pl*.
New Zealand Neuseeland *nt* ; **New Zealander** *n* Neuseeländer(in *f*) *m* ; **New Zealand** *a* neuseeländisch.
Nigeria Nigeria *nt* ; **Nigerian** *n* Nigerianer(in *f*) *m* ; *a* nigerianisch.
Normandy die Normandie; **Norman** *n* Normanne *m*, Normannin *f*; *a* normannisch.
Northern Ireland Nordirland *nt*.
the North Sea die Nordsee.
Norway Norwegen *nt* ; **Norwegian** *n* Norweger(in *f*) *m* ; *a* norwegisch.
the Pacific (Ocean) der Pazifik, der Pazifische *or* Stille Ozean.
Pakistan Pakistan *nt* ; **Pakistani** *n* Pakistaner(in *f*) *m* ; *a* pakistanisch.
Palestine Palästina *nt* ; **Palestinian** *n* Palästinenser(in *f*) *m* ; *a* palästinensisch.
Paraguay Paraguay *nt* ; **Paraguayan** *n* Paraguayer(in *f*) *m* ; *a* paraguayisch.
Paris Paris *nt* ; **Parisian** *n* Pariser(in *f*) *m* ; *a* Pariser *inv*.
the People's Republic of China die Volksrepublik China.
Persia Persien *nt* ; **Persian** *n* Perser(in *f*) *m* ; *a* persisch.
Peru Peru *nt* ; **Peruvian** *n* Peruaner(in *f*) *m* ; *a* peruanisch.
the Philippines *pl* die Philippinen *pl* ; **Filipino** *n* Philippiner(in *f*) *m* ; *a*, **Philippine** *a* philippinisch.
Poland Polen *nt* ; **Pole** *n* Pole *m*, Polin *f*; **Polish** *a* polnisch.

400

Portugal Portugal *nt*; **Portuguese** *n* Portugiese *m*, Portugiesin *f*; *a* portugiesisch.
Puerto Rico Puerto Rico *nt*; **Puerto-Rican** *n* Puertoricaner(in *f*) *m*; *a* puertoricanisch.
the Pyrenees *pl* die Pyrenäen *pl*; **Pyrenean** *a* pyrenäisch.
the Red Sea das Rote Meer.
Rhodes Rhodos *nt*.
Rhodesia Rhodesien *nt*; **Rhodesian** *n* Rhodesier(in *f*) *m*; *a* rhodesisch.
Rome Rom *nt*; **Roman** *n* Römer(in *f*) *m*; *a* römisch.
Ro(u)mania Rumänien *nt*; **Ro(u)manian** *n* Rumäne *m*, Rumänin *f*; *a* rumänisch.
Russia Rußland *nt*; **Russian** *n* Russe *m*, Russin *f*; *a* russisch.
the Sahara die Sahara.
Sardinia Sardinien *nt*; **Sardinian** *n* Sarde *m*, Sardin *f*; *a* sardisch.
Saudi Arabia Saudi-Arabien *nt*; **Saudi (Arabian)** *n* Saudiaraber(in *f*) *m*; *a* saudiarabisch.
Scandinavia Skandinavien *nt*; **Scandinavian** *n* Skandinave *m* Skandinavin *f*; *a* skandinavisch.
Scotland Schottland *nt*; **Scot, Scotsman/-woman** *n* Schotte *m*, Schottin *f*; **Scottish, Scots, Scotch** *a* schottisch.
Siberia Sibirien *nt*; **Siberian** *n* Sibirier(in *f*) *m*; *a* sibirisch.
Sicily Sizilien *nt*; **Sicilian** *n* Sizilianer(in *f*) *m*, Sizilier(in *f*) *m*; *a* sizilianisch, sizilisch.
South Africa Südafrika *nt*; **South African** *n* Südafrikaner(in *f*) *m*; *a* südafrikanisch.
the Soviet Union die Sowjetunion.
Spain Spanien *nt*; **Spaniard** *n* Spanier(in *f*) *m*; **Spanish** *a* spanisch.
Sri Lanka Sri Lanka *nt*; **Sri Lankan** *n* Ceylonese *m*, Ceylonesin *f*; *a* ceylonesisch.
the Sudan der Sudan; **Sudanese** *n* Sudanese *m*, Sudanesin *f*, Sudaner(in *f*) *m*; *a* sudanesisch.
the Suez Canal der Suez-Kanal.
Sweden Schweden *nt*; **Swede** *n* Schwede *m*, Schwedin *f*; **Swedish** *a* schwedisch.
Switzerland die Schweiz; **Swiss** *n* Schweizer(in *f*) *m*; *a* Schweizer *inv*, schweizerisch.
Syria Syrien *nt*; **Syrian** *n* Syrer(in *f*) *m*, Syrier(in *f*) *m*; *a* syrisch.
Tahiti Tahiti *nt*; **Tahitian** *n* Tahitianer(in *f*) *m*; *a* tahitianisch.
Taiwan Taiwan *nt*; **Taiwanese** *n* Taiwanese(r) *m*, Taiwanesin *f*; *a* taiwanesisch.
Tanzania Tansania *nt*; **Tanzanian** *n* Tansanier(in *f*) *m*; *a* tansanisch.
Tenerife Teneriffa *nt*.
Thailand Thailand *nt*; **Thai** *n* Thailänder(in *f*) *m*; *a* thailändisch.
the Thames die Themse.
the Tyrol Tirol *nt*; **Tyrolean** *n* Tiroler(in *f*) *m*; *a* Tiroler *inv*.
Tunisia Tunesien *nt*; **Tunisian** *n* Tunesier(in *f*) *m*; *a* tunesisch.
Turkey die Türkei; **Turk** *n* Türke *m*, Türkin *f*; **Turkish** *a* türkisch.
Uganda Uganda *nt*; **Ugandan** *n* Ugander(in *f*) *m*; *a* ugandisch.
the United Kingdom das Vereinigte Königreich.
the United States *pl* **(of America)** die Vereinigten Staaten *pl* (von Amerika).
Uruguay Uruguay *nt*; **Uruguayan** *n* Uruguayer(in *f*) *m*; *a* uruguayisch.
Venezuela Venezuela *nt*; **Venezuelan** *n* Venezolaner(in *f*) *m*; *a* venezolanisch.
Venice Venedig *nt*; **Venetian** *n* Venezianer(in *f*) *m*; *a* venezianisch.
Vienna Wien *nt*; **Viennese** *n* Wiener(in *f*) *m*; *a* wienerisch, Wiener *inv*.
Vietnam Vietnam *nt*; **Vietnamese** *n* Vietnamese *m*, Vietnamesin *f*; *a* vietnamesisch.
Wales Wales *nt*; **Welshman/-woman** *n* Waliser(in *f*) *m*; **Welsh** *a* walisisch.
Warsaw Warschau *nt*.
West Germany die Bundesrepublik (Deutschland); **West German** *n* Bundesdeutsche(r) *m*, Bundesdeutsche *f*; *a* Bundes-, der Bundesrepublik.
the West Indies *pl* Westindien *nt*; **West Indian** *n* Westinder(in *f*) *m*; *a* westindisch.
the Yemen (der) Jemen; **Yemeni, Yemenite** *n* Jemenit(in *f*) *m*; *a* jemenitisch.
Yugoslavia Jugoslawien *nt*; **Yugoslav(ian)** *n* Jugoslawe *m*, Jugoslawin *f*; *a* jugoslawisch.
Zaire Zaire *nt*.
Zambia Sambia *nt*; **Zambian** *n* Sambier(in *f*) *m*; *a* sambisch.

Deutsche Abkürzungen

Abf.	Abfahrt *departure, dep*
Abk.	Abkürzung *abbreviation, abbr*
Abs.	Absatz *paragraph;* Absender *sender*
Abt.	Abteilung *department, dept*
AG	Aktiengesellschaft *(Brit) (public) limited company, Ltd, (US) corporation, inc*
Ank.	Ankunft *arrival, arr* .
Anm.	Anmerkung *note*
b.a.w.	bis auf weiteres *until further notice*
Best. Nr.	Bestellnummer *order number*
Betr.	Betreff, betrifft *re*
Bhf.	Bahnhof *station*
BRD	Bundesrepublik Deutschland *Federal Republic of Germany*
b.w.	bitte wenden *please turn over, pto*
bzgl.	bezüglich *with reference to, re*
bzw.	beziehungsweise *(see text)*
ca.	circa, ungefähr *approximately, approx*
Cie., Co.	Kompanie *company, co*
DDR	Deutsche Demokratische Republik *German Democratic Republic, GDR*
d.h.	das heißt *that is, i.e.*
d.J.	dieses Jahres *of this year*
d.M.	dieses Monats *instant, inst*
DM	Deutsche Mark *German Mark, Deutschmark*
EDV	elektronische Datenverarbeitung *electronic data processing, EDP*
einschl.	einschließlich *inclusive, including, incl*
Einw.	Einwohner *inhabitant*
empf.	empfohlen(er Preis) *recommended (price)*
ev.	evangelisch *Protestant*
evtl.	eventuell *perhaps, possibly*
EWG	Europäische Wirtschaftsgemeinschaft *European Economic Community, EEC*
e. Wz.	eingetragenes Warenzeichen *registered trademark*
Expl.	Exemplar *sample, copy*
Fa.	Firma *firm;* in Briefen: *Messrs*
ff.	folgende Seiten *pages, pp*
Ffm.	Frankfurt am Main
fl. W.	fließendes Wasser *running water*
Forts.	Fortsetzung *continued, cont'd*
geb.	geboren *born;* geborene *née;* gebunden *bound.*
Gebr.	Gebrüder *Brothers, Bros*
ges. gesch.	gesetzlich geschützt *registered*
GmbH	Gesellschaft mit beschränkter Haftung *(Brit) (private) limited company, Ltd, (US) corporation, inc*
Hbf.	Hauptbahnhof *central station*
hl.	heilig *holy*
Hrsg.	Herausgeber *editor, ed*
i.A.	im Auftrag *for;* in Briefen auch: *pp*
Ing.	Ingenieur *engineer*
Inh.	Inhaber *proprietor, prop;* Inhalt *contents*
i.V.	in Vertretung *by proxy, on behalf of;* im Vorjahre *in the last or previous year;* in Vorbereitung *in preparation*
Jh.	Jahrhundert *century, cent*
jr., jun.	junior, der Jüngere *junior, jun, jr*
kath.	katholisch *Catholic, Cath*
kfm.	kaufmännisch *commercial*
Kfz.	*(see text)*
KG	Kommanditgesellschaft *limited partnership*
led.	ledig *single*
Lkw.	*(see text)*

402

lt.	laut *according to*
m. E.	meines Erachtens *in my opinion*
Mehrw. St.	Mehrwertsteuer *value-added tax, VAT*
Mrd.	Milliarde *thousand millions, (US) billion*
n. Chr.	nach Christus *AD*
Nr.	Numero, Nummer *number, no*
NS	Nachschrift *postscript, PS;* nationalsozialistisch *National Socialist*
OHG	Offene Handelsgesellschaft *general partnership*
PKW, Pkw.	*(see text)*
Pl.	Platz *square*
Postf.	Postfach *post-office box, PO box*
PS	Pferdestärken *horsepower, HP;* Nachschrift *postscript, PS*
S.	Seite *page, p*
s.	siehe *see*
sen.	senior, der Ältere *senior, sen, sr*
s.o.	siehe oben *see above*
St.	Stück *piece;* Sankt *Saint, St*
Std., Stde.	Stunde *hour, hr*
stdl.	stündlich *every hour*
Str.	Straße *street, St*
s.u.	siehe unten *see below*
tägl.	täglich *daily, per day*
Tsd.	Tausend *thousand*
u.	und *and*
u.a.	und andere(s) *and others;* unter anderem/anderen *among other things, inter alia/among others*
U.A.w.g.	Um Antwort wird gebeten *an answer is requested;* auf Einladung: *RSVP*
UdSSR	Union der Sozialistischen Sowjetrepubliken *Union of Soviet Socialist Republics, USSR*
u.E.	unseres Erachtens *in our opinion*
USA	Vereinigte Staaten (von Amerika) *United States (of America), USA.*
usf.	und so fort *and so forth, etc*
usw.	und so weiter *etcetera, etc*
u.U.	unter Umständen *possibly*
v. Chr.	vor Christus *BC*
Verf., Vf.	Verfasser *author*
verh.	verheiratet *married*
Verl.	Verlag *publishing firm;* Verleger *publisher*
vgl.	vergleiche *compare, cf, cp*
v.H.	vom Hundert *per cent*
Wz.	Warenzeichnen *registered trademark*
z.B.	zum Beispiel *for example or instance, eg*
z.H(d)	zu Händen *for the attention of*
z.T.	zum Teil *partly*
zw.	zwischen *between; among*
z.Z(t).	zur Zeit *at the time, at present, for the time being*

English abbreviations

AD	after (the birth of) Christ *Anno Domini, nach Christi, A.D., n. Chr.*
AGM	annual general meeting *Jahresvollversammlung*
am	before midday (ante meridiem) *vormittags, vorm.;* 1.00am. *1.00 Uhr*
arr	arrival, arrives *Ankunft, Ank.*
asst	assistant *Assistent, Mitarbeiter*
Ave	avenue *Straße, Str.*
BA	Bachelor of Arts *Bakkalaureus der Philosophischen Fakultät*
B and B	bed and breakfast *Zimmer mit Frühstück,* in catalogue: *Zi. m Fr.,* as sign: *Fremdenzimmer*
BAOR	British Army of the Rhine *(britische) Rheinarmee*
BC	before (the birth of) Christ *vor Christi Geburt, v. Chr.*
BO	body odour *Körpergeruch*
Bros	[brɔs] brothers *Gebrüder, Gebr.*
BSc	Bachelor of Science *Bakkalaureus der Naturwissenschaftlichen Fakultät*

Cantab	['kæntæb] Cambridge University (Cantabrigiensis) *Cambridge*
CBI	Confederation of British Industry *Bundesverband der britischen Industrie*
cc	cubic centimetres *Kubikzentimeter, ccm.*
CD	Diplomatic Corps (French: Corps Diplomatique) *Diplomatisches Corps, CD*
CIA	Central Intelligence Agency *CIA*
CID	Criminal Investigation Department *Kriminalpolizei*
cif	cost insurance and freight *Kosten, Versicherung und Fracht einbegriffen*
C-in-C	Commander-in-Chief *Oberkommandierender*
cm	centimetre(s) *Zentimeter, cm*
c/o	care of *bei, c/o*
COD	cash on delivery *gegen Nachnahme*
C of E	Church of England *anglikanische Kirche*
cwt	hundredweight ≈ *Zentner, ztr.*
DA	(*US*) District Attorney *Bezirksstaatsanwalt*
dep	depart(s) *Abfahrt, Abf.*
dept	department *Abteilung, Abt.*
DJ	dinner jacket *Smoking* ; disc jockey *Diskjockey*
ed	edited by *herausgegeben, hrsg.*; editor *Herausgeber, Hrsg.*
EEC	European Economic Community *Europäische Wirtschaftsgemeinschaft, EWG*
eg	for example (exempli gratia) *zum Beispiel, z.B.*
ESP	extrasensory perception *übersinnliche Wahrnehmung*
ETA	estimated time of arrival *voraussichtliche Ankunft*
etc	etcetera, and so on *und so weiter, usw., etc.*
FBI	Federal Bureau of Investigation *FBI*
fig	figure, illustration *Abbildung, Abb.*
fob	free on board *frei Schiff*
gbh	grievous bodily harm *schwere Körperverletzung*
GI	(government issue) private in the American Army *amerikanischer Soldat, GI*
govt	government *Regierung*
GP	General Practitioner *praktischer Arzt*
GPO	General Post Office *Britische Post; Hauptpostamt*
HM	His/Her Majesty *Seine/Ihre Majestät*
HMS	His/Her Majesty's Ship *Schiff der Königlichen Marine*
hp	(*Brit*) hire purchase *Abzahlungskauf*; horsepower *Pferdestärke, PS*
HQ	headquarters *Hauptquartier*
hr(s)	hour(s) *Stunde(n), Std.*
HRH	His/Her Royal Highness *Seine/Ihre Hoheit*
ID	identification *Ausweis*
i.e.	that is (id est) *das heißt, d.h.*
IOU	I owe you *Schuldschein*
JP	Justice of the Peace *Friedensrichter*
km	kilometre(s) *Kilometer, km*
kph	kilometres per hour *Stundenkilometer, km/h*
LA	Los Angeles
lb	pound (weight) *Pfund, Pfd.*
LP	long-playing (record), long-player *Langspielplatte, LP*
Ltd	limited (in names of businesses) *Gesellschaft mit beschränkter Haftung, GmbH*
MA	Master of Arts *Magister Artium, M.A.*
max	maximum *maximal, max*
MI5	department of British Intelligence Service (originally Military Intelligence) *Britischer Geheimdienst*
min	minimum *minimal*
MIT	Massachusetts Institute of Technology
mm	millimetre(s) *Millimeter, mm*
mod cons	[mɔd'kɔnz] modern conveniences (cooker, lights, *etc*) *mit allem Komfort*
MOT	Ministry of Transport (used for the roadworthiness test of motor vehicles) *Technischer Überwachungsverein, TÜV*
MP	Member of Parliament *Abgeordneter*; military policeman *Militärpolizist, MP*
mpg	miles per gallon *Meilen pro Gallone, Benzinverbrauch*
mph	miles per hour *Meilen pro Stunde*
Mr	['mɪstə] Mister *Herr*
Mrs	['mɪsɪz] Mistress *Frau*
Ms	[mɔz] *Frau*

404

NAAFI	['næfɪ] (*Brit*) Navy, Army and Air Force Institutes (canteen services) *Kantine*
NATO	['neɪtəʊ] North Atlantic Treaty Organization *Nordatlantikpakt, NATO*
NB	note well (nota bene) *notabene, NB*
NCO	non-commissioned officer *Unteroffizier, Uffz.*
no(s)	number(s) *Nummer(n), Nr.*
o.n.o.	or nearest offer *oder höchstes Angebot*
Oxon	['ɔksən] Oxford University (Oxonia) *Oxford*
oz	ounce(s) (onza) *Unze*
p	page *Seite, S.*; (new) pence *Pence, p*
PA	public address (system) *Lautsprecheranlage*
pa	per year (per annum) *pro Jahr, jährlich, jhrl.*
PC	police constable *Polizeibeamter*; Privy Councillor *Mitglied des Geheimen Staatsrats*
PhD	Doctor of Philosophy *Doktor der Philosophie, Dr. phil.*
PM	Prime Minister *Premierminister*
pm	afternoon (post meridiem) *nachmittags, nachm.*; 10.00pm *22.00 Uhr*
pop	population *Einwohner, Einw.*
POW	prisoner of war *Kriegsgefangener*
pp	pages *Seiten, ff.*; pro persona, for *im Auftrag, i.A.*
PRO	public relations officer *PR-Chef*
PS	postscript *Nachschrift, PS*
pto	please turn over *bitte wenden, b.w.*
QC	Queen's Counsel *Anwalt der königlichen Anwaltskammer*
RADA	Royal Academy of Dramatic Art
RAF	Royal Air Force *britische Luftwaffe*
Rd	road *Straße, Str.*
Rev	Reverend *Herr Pfarrer*
RIP	rest in peace (requiescat in pace) *ruhe in Frieden, R.I.P.*
RSVP	please reply (written on invitations, French: répondez s'il vous plaît) *um Antwort wird gebeten, u.A.w.g.*
Rt Hon	Right Honourable *Anrede für Grafen etc, Abgeordnete und Minister*
s.a.e.	stamped addressed envelope *vorfrankierter Umschlag*
SOS	(save our souls) *SOS*
Sq	square (in town) *Platz, Pl.*
ss	steamship *Dampfer*
St	saint *Sankt, St.*; street *Straße, Str.*
st	stone (weight) *6,35 kg*
STD	subscriber trunk dialling *Selbstwählfernverkehr*
TB	tuberculosis *Tuberkulose, TB*
Tel	telephone *Telefon, Tel.*
TUC	Trades Union Congress *Gewerkschaftsbund*
UFO	['juːfəʊ] unidentified flying object *unbekanntes Flugobjekt, Ufo*
UK	United Kingdom *Vereinigtes Königreich*
UN	United Nations *Vereinte Nationen*
USA	United States of America *Vereinigte Staaten von Amerika, USA*; United States Army *Amerikanische Armee*
USAF	United States Air Force *Amerikanische Luftwaffe*
USN	United States Navy *Amerikanische Marine*
USSR	Union of Soviet Socialist Republics *Sowjetunion, UdSSR*
VAT	[*also* væt] value added tax *Mehrwertsteuer, Mehrw.St.*
VD	venereal disease *Geschlechtskrankheit*
VHF	very high frequency *Ultrakurzwelle, UKW*
VIP	very important person *wichtige Persönlichkeit, VIP*
viz	[vɪz] namely (videlicet) *nämlich*
VSO	voluntary service overseas *Entwicklungshilfe*
WASP	(*US*) White Anglo-Saxon Protestant
WC	water closet *Toilette, WC*
ZIP	[zɪp] (*US*) Zone Improvement Plan (postal code) *Postleitzahl, PLZ*

German irregular verbs
* with 'sein'

infinitive	present indicative (2nd, 3rd sing.)	preterite	past participle
aufschrecken*	schrickst auf, schrickt auf	schrak or schreckte auf	aufgeschreckt
ausbedingen	bedingst aus, bedingt aus	bedang or bedingte aus	ausbedungen
backen	bäckst, bäckt	backte or buk	gebacken
befehlen	befiehlst, befiehlt	befahl	befohlen
beginnen	beginnst, beginnt	begann	begonnen
beißen	beißt, beißt	biß	gebissen
bergen	birgst, birgt	barg	geborgen
bersten*	birst, birst	barst	geborsten
bescheißen*	bescheißt, bescheißt	beschiß	beschissen
bewegen	bewegst, bewegt	bewog	bewogen
biegen	biegst, biegt	bog	gebogen
bieten	bietest, bietet	bot	geboten
binden	bindest, bindet	band	gebunden
bitten	bittest, bittet	bat	gebeten
blasen	bläst, bläst	blies	geblasen
bleiben*	bleibst, bleibt	blieb	geblieben
braten	brätst, brät	briet	gebraten
brechen*	brichst, bricht	brach	gebrochen
brennen	brennst, brennt	brannte	gebrannt
bringen	bringst, bringt	brachte	gebracht
denken	denkst, denkt	dachte	gedacht
dreschen	drisch(e)st, drischt	drasch	gedroschen
dringen*	dringst, dringt	drang	gedrungen
dürfen	darfst, darf	durfte	gedurft
empfehlen	empfiehlst, empfiehlt	empfahl	empfohlen
erbleichen*	erbleichst, erbleicht	erbleichte	erblichen
erlöschen*	erlischst, erlischt	erlosch	erloschen
erschrecken*	erschrickst, erschrickt	erschrak	erschrocken
essen	ißt, ißt	aß	gegessen
fahren*	fährst, fährt	fuhr	gefahren
fallen*	fällst, fällt	fiel	gefallen
fangen	fängst, fängt	fing	gefangen
fechten	fichtst, ficht	focht	gefochten
finden	findest, findet	fand	gefunden
flechten	flichst, flicht	flocht	geflochten
fliegen*	fliegst, fliegt	flog	geflogen
fliehen*	fliehst, flieht	floh	geflohen
fließen*	fließt, fließt	floß	geflossen
fressen	frißt, frißt	fraß	gefressen
frieren	frierst, friert	fror	gefroren
gären*	gärst, gärt	gor	gegoren
gebären	gebierst, gebiert	gebar	geboren
geben	gibst, gibt	gab	gegeben
gedeihen*	gedeihst, gedeiht	gedieh	gediehen
gehen*	gehst, geht	ging	gegangen
gelingen*	——, gelingt	gelang	gelungen
gelten	giltst, gilt	galt	gegolten
genesen*	gene(se)st, genest	genas	genesen
genießen	genießt, genießt	genoß	genossen
geraten*	gerätst, gerät	geriet	geraten
geschehen*	——, geschieht	geschah	geschehen
gewinnen	gewinnst, gewinnt	gewann	gewonnen
gießen	gießt, gießt	goß	gegossen
gleichen	gleichst, gleicht	glich	geglichen

infinitive	present indicative (2nd, 3rd sing.)	preterite	past participle
gleiten*	gleitest, gleitet	glitt	geglitten
glimmen	glimmst, glimmt	glomm	geglommen
graben	gräbst, gräbt	grub	gegraben
greifen	greifst, greift	griff	gegriffen
haben	hast, hat	hatte	gehabt
halten	hältst, hält	hielt	gehalten
hängen	hängst, hängt	hing	gehangen
hauen	haust, haut	hieb	gehauen
heben	hebst, hebt	hob	gehoben
heißen	heißt, heißt	hieß	geheißen
helfen	hilfst, hilft	half	geholfen
kennen	kennst, kennt	kannte	gekannt
klimmen	klimmst, klimmt	klomm	geklommen
klingen	klingst, klingt	klang	geklungen
kneifen	kneifst, kneift	kniff	gekniffen
kommen*	kommst, kommt	kam	gekommen
können	kannst, kann	konnte	gekonnt
kriechen*	kriechst, kriecht	kroch	gekrochen
laden	lädst, lädt	lud	geladen
lassen	läßt, läßt	ließ	gelassen
laufen*	läufst, läuft	lief	gelaufen
leiden	leidest, leidet	litt	gelitten
leihen	leihst, leiht	lieh	geliehen
lesen	liest, liest	las	gelesen
liegen*	liegst, liegt	lag	gelegen
lügen	lügst, lügt	log	gelogen
mahlen	mahlst, mahlt	mahlte	gemahlen
meiden	meidest, meidet	mied	gemieden
melken	milkst, milkt	molk	gemolken
messen	mißt, mißt	maß	gemessen
mißlingen*	——, mißlingt	mißlang	mißlungen
mögen	magst, mag	mochte	gemocht
müssen	mußt, muß	mußte	gemußt
nehmen	nimmst, nimmt	nahm	genommen
nennen	nennst, nennt	nannte	genannt
pfeifen	pfeifst, pfeift	pfiff	gepfiffen
preisen	preist, preist	pries	gepriesen
quellen*	quillst, quillt	quoll	gequollen
raten	rätst, rät	riet	geraten
reiben	reibst, reibt	rieb	gerieben
reißen*	reißt, reißt	riß	gerissen
reiten*	reitest, reitet	ritt	geritten
rennen*	rennst, rennt	rannte	gerannt
riechen	riechst, riecht	roch	gerochen
ringen	ringst, ringt	rang	gerungen
rinnen*	rinnst, rinnt	rann	geronnen
rufen	rufst, ruft	rief	gerufen
salzen	salzt, salzt	salzte	gesalzen
saufen	säufst, säuft	soff	gesoffen
saugen	saugst, saugt	sog	gesogen
schaffen	schaffst, schafft	schuf	geschaffen
schallen	schallst, schallt	scholl	geschollen
scheiden*	scheidest, scheidet	schied	geschieden
scheinen	scheinst, scheint	schien	geschienen
schelten	schiltst, schilt	schalt	gescholten
scheren	scherst, schert	schor	geschoren
schieben	schiebst, schiebt	schob	geschoben
schießen	schießt, schießt	schoß	geschossen
schinden	schindest, schindet	schund	geschunden
schlafen	schläfst, schläft	schlief	geschlafen
schlagen	schlägst, schlägt	schlug	geschlagen
schleichen*	schleichst, schleicht	schlich	geschlichen
schleifen	schleifst, schleift	schliff	geschliffen
schließen	schließt, schließt	schloß	geschlossen
schlingen	schlingst, schlingt	schlang	geschlungen
schmeißen	schmeißt, schmeißt	schmiß	geschmissen
schmelzen*	schmilzt, schmilzt	schmolz	geschmolzen
schneiden	schneidest, schneidet	schnitt	geschnitten
schreiben	schreibst, schreibt	schrieb	geschrieben

infinitive	(2nd, 3rd sing.)	preterite	participle
schreien	schreist, schreit	schrie	geschrie(e)n
schreiten	schreitest, schreitet	schritt	geschritten
schweigen	schweigst, schweigt	schwieg	geschwiegen
schwellen*	schwillst, schwillt	schwoll	geschwollen
schwimmen*	schwimmst, schwimmt	schwamm	geschwommen
schwinden*	schwindest, schwindet	schwand	geschwunden
schwingen	schwingst, schwingt	schwang	geschwungen
schwören	schwörst, schwört	schwur	geschworen
sehen	siehst, sieht	sah	gesehen
sein*	bist, ist	war	gewesen
senden	sendest, sendet	sandte	gesandt
singen	singst, singt	sang	gesungen
sinken*	sinkst, sinkt	sank	gesunken
sinnen	sinnst, sinnt	sann	gesonnen
sitzen*	sitzt, sitzt	saß	gesessen
sollen	sollst, soll	sollte	gesollt
speien	speist, speit	spie	gespie(e)n
spinnen	spinnst, spinnt	spann	gesponnen
sprechen	sprichst, spricht	sprach	gesprochen
sprießen*	sprießt, sprießt	sproß	gesprossen
springen*	springst, springt	sprang	gesprungen
stechen	stichst, sticht	stach	gestochen
stecken	steckst, steckt	steckte *or* stak	gesteckt
stehen	stehst, steht	stand	gestanden
stehlen	stiehlst, stiehlt	stahl	gestohlen
steigen*	steigst, steigt	stieg	gestiegen
sterben*	stirbst, stirbt	starb	gestorben
stinken	stinkst, stinkt	stank	gestunken
stoßen	stößt, stößt	stieß	gestoßen
streichen	streichst, streicht	strich	gestrichen
streiten*	streitest, streitet	stritt	gestritten
tragen	trägst, trägt	trug	getragen
treffen	triffst, trifft	traf	getroffen
treiben*	treibst, treibt	trieb	getrieben
treten*	trittst, tritt	trat	getreten
trinken	trinkst, trinkt	trank	getrunken
trügen	trügst, trügt	trog	getrogen
tun	tust, tut	tat	getan
verderben	verdirbst, verdirbt	verdarb	verdorben
verdrießen	verdrießt, verdrießt	verdroß	verdrossen
vergessen	vergißt, vergißt	vergaß	vergessen
verlieren	verlierst, verliert	verlor	verloren
verschleißen	verschleißt, verschleißt	verschliß	verschlissen
wachsen*	wächst, wächst	wuchs	gewachsen
wägen	wägst, wägt	wog	gewogen
waschen	wäschst, wäscht	wusch	gewaschen
weben	webst, webt	wob	gewoben
weichen*	weichst, weicht	wich	gewichen
weisen	weist, weist	wies	gewiesen
wenden	wendest, wendet	wandte	gewandt
werben	wirbst, wirbt	warb	geworben
werden*	wirst, wird	wurde	geworden
werfen	wirfst, wirft	warf	geworfen
wiegen	wiegst, wiegt	wog	gewogen
winden	windest, windet	wand	gewunden
wissen	weißt, weiß	wußte	gewußt
wollen	willst, will	wollte	gewollt
wringen	wringst, wringt	wrang	gewrungen
zeihen	zeihst, zeiht	zieh	geziehen
ziehen*	ziehst, zieht	zog	gezogen
zwingen	zwingst, zwingt	zwang	gezwungen

English irregular verbs

present	pt	ptp
arise (arising)	arose	arisen
awake (awaking)	awoke	awaked
be (am, is, are; being)	was, were	been
bear	bore	born(e)
beat	beat	beaten
become (becoming)	became	become
befall	befell	befallen
begin (beginning)	began	begun
behold	beheld	beheld
bend	bent	bent
beseech	besought	besought
beset (besetting)	beset	beset
bet (betting)	bet (also betted)	bet (also betted)
bid (bidding)	bid	bid
bind	bound	bound
bite (biting)	bit	bitten
bleed	bled	bled
blow	blew	blown
break	broke	broken
breed	bred	bred
bring	brought	brought
build	built	built
burn	burnt or burned	burnt (also burned)
burst	burst	burst
buy	bought	bought
can	could	(been able)
cast	cast	cast
catch	caught	caught
choose (choosing)	chose	chosen
cling	clung	clung
come (coming)	came	come
cost	cost	cost
creep	crept	crept
cut (cutting)	cut	cut
deal	dealt	dealt
dig (digging)	dug	dug
do (3rd person; he/she/it/does)	did	done
draw	drew	drawn
dream	dreamed (dreamt)	dreamed (dreamt)
drink	drank	drunk
drive (driving)	drove	driven
dwell	dwelt	dwelt
eat	ate	eaten

present	pt	ptp
fall	fell	fallen
feed	fed	fed
feel	felt	felt
fight	fought	fought
find	found	found
flee	fled	fled
fling	flung	flung
fly (flies)	flew	flown
forbid (forbidding)	forbade	forbidden
forecast	forecast	forecast
forego	forewent	foregone
foresee	foresaw	foreseen
foretell	foretold	foretold
forget (forgetting)	forgot	forgotten
forgive (forgiving)	forgave	forgiven
forsake (forsaking)	forsook	forsaken
freeze (freezing)	froze	frozen
get (getting)	got	got, (US) gotten
give (giving)	gave	given
go (goes)	went	gone
grind	ground	ground
grow	grew	grown
hang	hung (also hanged)	hung (also hanged)
have (has; having)	had	had
hear	heard	heard
hide (hiding)	hid	hidden
hit (hitting)	hit	hit
hold	held	held
hurt	hurt	hurt
keep	kept	kept
kneel	knelt (also kneeled)	knelt (also kneeled)
know	knew	known
lay	laid	laid
lead	led	led
lean	leant (also leaned)	leant (also leaned)
leap	leapt (also leaped)	leapt (also leaped)
learn	learnt (also learned)	learnt (also learned)
leave (leaving)	left	left
lend	lent	lent
let (letting)	let	let
lie (lying)	lay	lain
light	lit (also lighted)	lit (also lighted)
lose (losing)	lost	lost

present	pt	ptp	present	pt	ptp
make (making)	made	made	spell	spelt (also spelled)	spelt (also spelled)
may	might	——	spend	spent	spent
mean	meant	meant	spill	spilt (also spilled)	spilt (also spilled)
meet	met	met	spin (spinning)	spun	spun
mistake (mistaking)	mistook	mistaken	spit (spitting)	spat	spat
mow	mowed	mown (also mowed)	split (splitting)	split	split
must	(had to)	(had to)	spoil	spoiled (also spoilt)	spoiled (also spoilt)
pay	paid	paid	spread	spread	spread
put (putting)	put	put	spring	sprang	sprung
quit (quitting)	quit (also quitted)	quit (also quitted)	stand	stood	stood
read	read	read	steal	stole	stolen
rend	rent	rent	stick	stuck	stuck
rid (ridding)	rid	rid	sting	stung	stung
ride (riding)	rode	ridden	stink	stank	stunk
ring	rang	rung	stride (striding)	strode	stridden
rise (rising)	rose	risen	strike (striking)	struck	struck (also stricken)
run (running)	ran	run	strive (striving)	strove	striven
saw	sawed	sawn	swear	swore	sworn
say	said	said	sweep	swept	swept
see	saw	seen	swell	swelled	swollen (also swelled)
seek	sought	sought	swim (swimming)	swam	swum
sell	sold	sold	swing	swung	swung
send	sent	sent	take (taking)	took	taken
set (setting)	set	set	teach	taught	taught
shake (shaking)	shook	shaken	tear	tore	torn
shall	should	——	tell	told	told
shear	sheared	shorn (also sheared)	think	thought	thought
shed (shedding)	shed	shed	throw	threw	thrown
shine (shining)	shone	shone	thrust	thrust	thrust
shoot	shot	shot	tread	trod	trodden
show	showed	shown	wake (waking)	woke (also waked)	woken (also waked)
shrink	shrank	shrunk	waylay	waylaid	waylaid
shut (shutting)	shut	shut	wear	wore	worn
sing	sang	sung	weave (weaving)	wove (also weaved)	woven (also weaved)
sink	sank	sunk	wed (wedding)	wedded (also wed)	wedded (also wed)
sit (sitting)	sat	sat	weep	wept	wept
slay	slew	slain	win (winning)	won	won
sleep	slept	slept	wind	wound	wound
slide (sliding)	slid	slid	withdraw	withdrew	withdrawn
sling	slung	slung	withhold	withheld	withheld
slit (slitting)	slit	slit	withstand	withstood	withstood
smell	smelt (also smelled)	smelt (also smelled)	wring	wrung	wrung
sow	sowed	sown (also sowed)	write (writing)	wrote	written
speak	spoke	spoken			
speed	sped (also speeded)	sped (also speeded)			

CHARLES DICKENS

of Two Cities

WITH AN AFTERWORD BY
Edgar Johnson

Revised and Updated Bibliography

A SIGNET CLASSIC

NEW AMERICAN LIBRARY

NEW YORK AND SCARBOROUGH, ONTARIO

𝒞

SIGNET CLASSIC TRADEMARK REG. U.S. PAT. OFF. AND FOREIGN COUNTRIES
REGISTERED TRADEMARK—MARCA REGISTRADA
HECHO EN CHICAGO, U.S.A.

SIGNET, SIGNET CLASSIC, MENTOR, ONYX, PLUME, MERIDIAN AND
NAL BOOKS are published *in the United States* by
NAL PENGUIN INC.,
1633 Broadway, New York, New York 10019,
in Canada by The New American Library of Canada Limited,
81 Mack Avenue, Scarborough, Ontario M1L 1M8

31   32   33   34   35   36   37   38

PRINTED IN THE UNITED STATES OF AMERICA

THIS TALE IS INSCRIBED
TO THE
LORD JOHN RUSSELL
IN REMEMBRANCE OF
MANY PUBLIC SERVICES AND
PRIVATE KINDNESSES

CONTENTS

BOOK THE FIRST
RECALLED TO LIFE

BOOK THE SECOND
THE GOLDEN THREAD

CONTENTS

BOOK THE THIRD
THE TRACK OF A STORM

WHEN I was acting, with my children and friends, in Mr. Wilkie Collins's drama of *The Frozen Deep,* I first conceived the main idea of this story. A strong desire was upon me then to embody it in my own person; and I traced out in my fancy the state of mind of which it would necessitate the presentation to an observant spectator, with particular care and interest.

As the idea became familiar to me, it gradually shaped itself into its present form. Throughout its execution, it has had complete possession of me; I have so far verified what is done and suffered in these pages, as that I have certainly done and suffered it all myself.

Whenever any reference (however slight) is made here to the condition of the French people before or during the Revolution, it is truly made, on the faith of trustworthy witnesses. It has been one of my hopes to add something to the popular and picturesque means of understanding that terrible time, though no one can hope to add anything to the philosophy of Mr. Carlyle's wonderful book.

TAVISTOCK HOUSE, LONDON
November, 1859

BOOK THE FIRST

Recalled to Life

1 The Period

IT WAS the best of times, it was the worst of times, it was the age of wisdom, it was the age of foolishness, it was the epoch of belief, it was the epoch of incredulity, it was the season of Light, it was the season of Darkness, it was the spring of hope, it was the winter of despair, we had everything before us, we had nothing before us, we were all going direct to Heaven, we were all going direct the other way—in short, the period was so far like the present period, that some of its noisiest authorities insisted on its being received, for good or for evil, in the superlative degree of comparison only.

There were a king with a large jaw, and a queen with a plain face, on the throne of England; there were a king with a large jaw, and a queen with a fair face, on the throne of France. In both countries it was clearer than crystal to the lords of the State preserves of loaves and fishes, that things in general were settled for ever.

It was the year of Our Lord one thousand seven hundred and seventy-five. Spiritual revelations were conceded to England at that favoured period, as at this. Mrs. Southcott had recently attained her five-and-twentieth blessed birthday, of whom a prophetic private in the Life Guards had heralded the sublime appearance by announcing that arrangements were made for the swallowing up of London and Westminster. Even the Cock-lane ghost had been laid only a round dozen of years, after rapping out its messages, as the spirits of this very year last past (supernaturally deficient in originality) rapped out theirs. Mere messages in the earthly order of events had lately come to the English Crown and People, from a congress of British subjects in America: which, strange to relate, have proved more important to the human race than any communications yet received through any of the chickens of the Cock-lane brood.

France, less favoured on the whole as to matters spiritual than her sister of the shield and trident, rolled with
exceeding smoothness down hill, making paper money
and spending it. Under the guidance of her Christian
pastors, she entertained herself, besides, with such humane achievements as sentencing a youth to have his
hands cut off, his tongue torn out with pincers, and his
body burned alive, because he had not kneeled down in
the rain to do honour to a dirty procession of monks
which passed within his view, at a distance of some fifty
or sixty yards. It is likely enough that, rooted in the
woods of France and Norway, there were growing trees,
when that sufferer was put to death, already marked by
the Woodman, Fate, to come down and be sawn into
boards, to make a certain movable framework with a sack
and a knife in it, terrible in history. It is likely enough
that in the rough outhouses of some tillers of the heavy
lands adjacent to Paris, there were sheltered from the
weather that very day, rude carts, bespattered with rustic
mire, snuffed about by pigs, and roosted in by poultry,
which the Farmer, Death, had already set apart to be his
tumbrils of the Revolution. But that Woodman and that
Farmer, though they work unceasingly, work silently, and
no one heard them as they went about with muffled tread:
the rather, forasmuch as to entertain any suspicion that
they were awake, was to be atheistical and traitorous.

In England, there was scarcely an amount of order and
protection to justify much national boasting. Daring bur-
glaries by armed men, and highway robberies, took place
in the capital itself every night; families were publicly
cautioned not to go out of town without removing their
furniture to upholsterers' warehouses for security; the
highwayman in the dark was a City tradesman in the
light, and, being recognised and challenged by his fellow-
tradesman whom he stopped in his character of "the Captain," gallantly shot him through the head and rode
away; the mail was waylaid by seven robbers, and the
guard shot three dead, and then got shot dead himself
by the other four, "in consequence of the failure of his
ammunition": after which the mail was robbed in peace;
that magnificent potentate, the Lord Mayor of London,
was made to stand and deliver on Turnham Green by
one highwayman, who despoiled the illustrious creature
in sight of all his retinue; prisoners in London gaols

fought battles with their turnkeys, and the majesty of the
law fired blunderbusses in among them, loaded with rounds
of shot and ball; thieves snipped off diamond crosses
from the necks of noble lords at Court drawing-rooms;
musketeers went into St. Giles's, to search for contraband
goods, and the mob fired on the musketeers, and the
musketeers fired on the mob, and nobody thought any
of these occurrences much out of the common way. In
the midst of them, the hangman, ever busy and ever
worse than useless, was in constant requisition; now, string-
ing up long rows of miscellaneous criminals; now, hanging a housebreaker on Saturday who had been taken on
Tuesday; now, burning people in the hand at Newgate
by the dozen, and now, burning pamphlets at the door of
Westminster Hall; to-day, taking the life of an atrocious
murderer, and to-morrow of a wretched pilferer who had
robbed a farmer's boy of sixpence.

All these things, and a thousand like them, came to pass
in and close upon the dear old year one thousand seven
hundred and seventy-five. Environed by them, while the
Woodman and the Farmer worked unheeded, those two
of the large jaws, and those other two of the plain and the
fair faces, trod with stir enough, and carried their divine
rights with a high hand. Thus did the year one thousand
seven hundred and seventy-five conduct their Greatnesses,
and myriads of small creatures—the creatures of this
chronicle among the rest—along the roads that lay before
them.

2 The Mail

IT WAS the Dover road that lay, on a Friday night
late in November, before the first of the persons with
whom this history has business. The Dover road lay, as to
him, beyond the Dover mail, as it lumbered up Shooter's
Hill. He walked uphill in the mire by the side of the
mail, as the rest of the passengers did; not because they

had the least relish for walking exercise, under the circumstances, but because the hill, and the harness, and the mud, and the mail, were all so heavy, that the horses had three times already come to a stop, besides once drawing the coach across the road, with the mutinous intent of taking it back to Blackheath. Reins and whip and coachman and guard, however, in combination, had read that article of war which forbade a purpose otherwise strongly in favour of the argument, that some brute animals are endued with Reason; and the team had capitulated and returned to their duty.

With drooping heads and tremulous tails, they mashed their way through the thick mud, floundering and stumbling between whiles, as if they were falling to pieces at the larger joints. As often as the driver rested them and brought them to a stand, with a wary "Wo-ho! so-ho then!" the near leader violently shook his head and everything upon it—like an unusually emphatic horse, denying that the coach could be got up the hill. Whenever the leader made this rattle, the passenger started, as a nervous passenger might, and was disturbed in mind.

There was a steaming mist in all the hollows, and it had roamed in its forlornness up the hill, like an evil spirit, seeking rest and finding none. A clammy and intensely cold mist, it made its slow way through the air in ripples that visibly followed and overspread one another, as the waves of an unwholesome sea might do. It was dense enough to shut out everything from the light of the coach-lamps but these its own workings, and a few yards of road; and the reek of the labouring horses steamed into it, as if they had made it all.

Two other passengers, besides the one, were plodding up the hill by the side of the mail. All three were wrapped to the cheek-bones and over the ears, and wore jack-boots. Not one of the three could have said, from anything he saw, what either of the other two was like; and each was hidden under almost as many wrappers from the eyes of the mind, as from the eyes of the body, of his two companions. In those days, travellers were very shy of being confidential on a short notice, for anybody on the road might be a robber or in league with robbers. As to the latter, when every posting-house and ale-house could produce somebody in "the Captain's" pay, ranging from the landlord to the lowest stable nondescript, it was the likeliest thing upon the cards. So the guard of the Dover mail thought to himself, that Friday night in November, one thousand seven hundred and seventy-five, lumbering up Shooter's Hill, as he stood on his own particular perch behind the mail, beating his feet, and keeping an eye and a hand on the arm-chest before him, where a loaded blunderbuss lay at the top of six or eight loaded horse-pistols, deposited on a substratum of cutlass.

The Dover mail was in its usual genial position that the guard suspected the passengers, the passengers suspected one another and the guard, they all suspected everybody else, and the coachman was sure of nothing but the horses; as to which cattle he could with a clear conscience have taken his oath on the two Testaments that they were not fit for the journey.

"Wo-ho!" said the coachman. "So, then! One more pull and you're at the top and be damned to you, for I have had trouble enough to get you to it!—Joe!"

"Halloa!" the guard replied.

"What o'clock do you make it, Joe?"

"Ten minutes, good, past eleven."

"My blood!" ejaculated the vexed coachman, "and not atop of Shooter's yet! Tst! Yah! Get on with you!"

The emphatic horse, cut short by the whip in a most decided negative, made a decided scramble for it, and the three other horses followed suit. Once more, the Dover mail struggled on, with the jack-boots of its passengers squashing along by its side. They had stopped when the coach stopped, and they kept close company with it. If any one of the three had had the hardihood to propose to another to walk on a little ahead into the mist and darkness, he would have put himself in a fair way of getting shot instantly as a highwayman.

The last burst carried the mail to the summit of the hill. The horses stopped to breathe again, and the guard got down to skid the wheel for the descent, and open the coach-door to let the passengers in.

"Tst! Joe!" cried the coachman in a warning voice, looking down from his box.

"What do you say, Tom?"

They both listened.

"I say a horse at a canter coming up, Joe."

"*I* say a horse at a gallop, Tom," returned the guard,

leaving his hold of the door, and mounting nimbly to his place. "Gentlemen! In the king's name, all of you!"

With this hurried adjuration, he cocked his blunder-buss, and stood on the offensive.

The passenger booked by this history was on the coach-step, getting in; the two other passengers were close be-hind him, and about to follow. He remained on the step, half in the coach and half out of it; they remained in the road below him. They all looked from the coachman to the guard, and from the guard to the coachman, and lis-tened. The coachman looked back and the guard looked back, and even the emphatic leader pricked up his ears and looked back, without contradicting.

The stillness consequent on the cessation of the rum-bling and labouring of the coach, added to the stillness of the night, made it very quiet indeed. The panting of the horses communicated a tremulous motion to the coach, as if it were in a state of agitation. The hearts of the passen-gers beat loud enough perhaps to be heard; but at any rate, the quiet pause was audibly expressive of people out of breath, and holding the breath, and having the pulses quickened by expectation.

The sound of a horse at a gallop came fast and furiously up the hill.

"So-ho!" the guard sang out, as loud as he could roar. "Yo there! Stand! I shall fire!"

The pace was suddenly checked, and, with much splash-ing and floundering, a man's voice called from the mist, "Is that the Dover mail?"

"Never you mind what it is!" the guard retorted. "What are you?"

"*Is* that the Dover mail?"

"Why do you want to know?"

"I want a passenger, if it is."

"What passenger?"

"Mr. Jarvis Lorry."

Our booked passenger showed in a moment that it was his name. The guard, the coachman, and the two other passengers eyed him distrustfully.

"Keep where you are," the guard called to the voice in the mist, "because, if I should make a mistake, it could never be set right in your lifetime. Gentleman of the name of Lorry answer straight."

"What is the matter?" asked the passenger, then, with mildly quavering speech. "Who wants me? Is it Jerry?"

("I don't like Jerry's voice, if it is Jerry," growled the guard to himself. "He's hoarser than suits me, is Jerry.")

"Yes, Mr. Lorry."

"What is the matter?"

"A despatch sent after you from over yonder. T. and Co."

"I know this messenger, guard," said Mr. Lorry, getting down into the road—assisted from behind more swiftly than politely by the other two passengers, who immediately scrambled into the coach, shut the door, and pulled up the window. "He may come close; there's nothing wrong."

"I hope there ain't, but I can't make so 'Nation sure of that," said the guard, in gruff soliloquy. "Hallo you!"

"Well! And hallo you!" said Jerry, more hoarsely than before.

"Come on at a footpace, d'ye mind me? And if you've got holsters to that saddle o' yourn, don't let me see your hand go nigh 'em. For I'm a devil at a quick mistake, and when I make one it takes the form of Lead. So now let's look at you."

The figures of a horse and rider came slowly through the eddying mist, and came to the side of the mail, where the passenger stood. The rider stooped, and, casting up his eyes at the guard, handed the passenger a small folded paper. The rider's horse was blown, and both horse and rider were covered with mud, from the hoofs of the horse to the hat of the man.

"Guard!" said the passenger, in a tone of quiet business confidence.

The watchful guard, with his right hand at the stock of his raised blunderbuss, his left at the barrel, and his eye on the horseman, answered curtly, "Sir."

"There is nothing to apprehend. I belong to Tellson's Bank. You must know Tellson's Bank in London. I am going to Paris on business. A crown to drink. I may read this?"

"If so be as you're quick, sir."

He opened it in the light of the coach-lamp on that side, and read—first to himself and then aloud: " 'Wait at Dover for Mam'selle.' It's not long, you see, guard. Jerry, say that my answer was, RECALLED TO LIFE."

Jerry started in his saddle. "That's a Blazing strange answer, too," said he, at his hoarsest.

"Take that message back, and they will know that I received this, as well as if I wrote. Make the best of your way. Good night."

With those words the passenger opened the coach-door and got in; not at all assisted by his fellow-passengers, who had expeditiously secreted their watches and purses in their boots, and were now making a general pretence of being asleep. With no more definite purpose than to escape the hazard of originating any other kind of action.

The coach lumbered on again, with heavier wreaths of mist closing round it as it began the descent. The guard soon replaced his blunderbuss in his arm-chest, and, having looked to the rest of its contents, and having looked to the supplementary pistols that he wore in his belt, looked to a smaller chest beneath his seat, in which there were a few smith's tools, a couple of torches, and a tinder-box. For he was furnished with that completeness that if the coach-lamps had been blown and stormed out, which did occasionally happen, he had only to shut himself up inside, keep the flint and steel sparks well off the straw, and get a light with tolerable safety and ease (if he were lucky) in five minutes.

"Tom!" softly over the coach-roof.

"Hallo, Joe."

"Did you hear the message?"

"I did, Joe."

"What did you make of it, Tom?"

"Nothing at all, Joe."

"That's coincidence, too," the guard mused, "for I made the same of it myself."

Jerry, left alone in the mist and darkness, dismounted meanwhile, not only to ease his spent horse, but to wipe the mud from his face, and shake the wet out of his hat-brim, which might be capable of holding about half a gallon. After standing with the bridle over his heavily-splashed arm, until the wheels of the mail were no longer within hearing and the night was quite still again, he turned to walk down the hill.

"After that there gallop from Temple Bar, old lady, I won't trust your fore-legs till I get you on the level," said this hoarse messenger, glancing at his mare. " 'Recalled to life.' That's a Blazing strange message. Much of that wouldn't do for you, Jerry! I say, Jerry! You'd be in a Blazing bad way, if recalling to life was to come into fashion, Jerry!"

3 *The Night Shadows*

A WONDERFUL fact to reflect upon, that every human creature is constituted to be that profound secret and mystery to every other. A solemn consideration, when I enter a great city by night, that every one of those darkly clustered houses encloses its own secret; that every room in every one of them encloses its own secret; that every beating heart in the hundreds of thousands of breasts there is, in some of its imaginings, a secret to the heart nearest it! Something of the awfulness, even of Death itself, is referable to this. No more can I turn the leaves of this dear book that I loved, and vainly hope in time to read it all. No more can I look into the depths of this unfathomable water, wherein, as momentary lights glanced into it, I have had glimpses of buried treasure and other things submerged. It was appointed that the book should shut with a spring, for ever and for ever, when I had read but a page. It was appointed that the water should be locked in an eternal frost, when the light was playing on its surface, and I stood in ignorance on the shore. My friend is dead, my neighbour is dead, my love, the darling of my soul, is dead; it is the inexorable consolidation and perpetuation of the secret that was always in that individuality, and which I shall carry in mine to my life's end. In any of the burial-places of this city through which I pass, is there a sleeper more inscrutable than its busy inhabitants are, in their innermost personality, to me, or than I am to them?

As to this, his natural and not to be alienated inheritance, the messenger on horseback had exactly the same possessions as the King, the first Minister of State, or the richest merchant in London. So with the three passengers shut up in the narrow compass of one lumbering old mail coach; they were mysteries to one another, as complete as if each had been in his own coach and six, or his own coach and sixty, with the breadth of a county between him and the next.

The messenger rode back at an easy trot, stopping pretty often at ale-houses by the way to drink, but evincing a tendency to keep his own counsel, and to keep his hat cocked over his eyes. He had eyes that assorted very well with that decoration, being of a surface black, with no depth in the colour or form, and much too near together —as if they were afraid of being found out in something, singly, if they kept too far apart. They had a sinister expression, under an old cocked-hat like a three-cornered spittoon, and over a great muffler for the chin and throat, which descended nearly to the wearer's knees. When he stopped for drink, he moved this muffler with his left hand, only while he poured his liquor in with his right; as soon as that was done, he muffled again.

"No, Jerry, no!" said the messenger, harping on one theme as he rode. "It wouldn't do for you, Jerry. Jerry, you honest tradesman, it wouldn't suit *your* line of business! Recalled—! Bust me if I don't think he'd been a drinking!"

His message perplexed his mind to that degree that he was fain, several times, to take off his hat to scratch his head. Except on the crown, which was raggedly bald, he had stiff, black hair, standing jaggedly all over it, and growing downhill almost to his broad, blunt nose. It was so like smith's work, so much more like the top of a strongly spiked wall than a head of hair, that the best of players at leap-frog might have declined him, as the most dangerous man in the world to go over.

While he trotted back with the message he was to deliver to the night watchman in his box at the door of Tellson's Bank, by Temple Bar, who was to deliver it to greater authorities within, the shadows of the night took such shapes to him as arose out of the message, and took such shapes to the mare as arose out of *her* private topics of uneasiness. They seemed to be numerous, for she shied at every shadow on the road.

What time, the mail-coach lumbered, jolted, rattled, and bumped upon its tedious way, with its three fellow-inscrutables inside. To whom, likewise, the shadows of the night revealed themselves, in the forms their dozing eyes and wandering thoughts suggested.

Tellson's Bank had a run upon it in the mail. As the bank passenger—with an arm drawn through the leathern strap, which did what lay in it to keep him from pounding against the next passenger, and driving him into his corner, whenever the coach got a special jolt—nodded in his place, with half-shut eyes, the little coach-windows, and the coach-lamp dimly gleaming through them, and the bulky bundle of opposite passenger, became the bank, and did a great stroke of business. The rattle of the harness was the chink of money, and more drafts were honoured in five minutes than even Tellson's, with all its foreign and home connection, ever paid in thrice the time. Then the strong-rooms underground, at Tellson's, with such of their valuable stores and secrets as were known to the passenger (and it was not a little that he knew about them), opened before him, and he went in among them with the great keys and the feebly-burning candle, and found them safe, and strong, and sound, and still, just as he had last seen them.

But, though the bank was almost always with him, and though the coach (in a confused way, like the presence of pain under an opiate) was always with him, there was another current of impression that never ceased to run, all through the night. He was on his way to dig some one out of a grave.

Now, which of the multitude of faces that showed themselves before him was the true face of the buried person, the shadows of the night did not indicate; but they were all the faces of a man of five-and-forty by years, and they differed principally in the passions they expressed, and in the ghastliness of their worn and wasted state. Pride, contempt, defiance, stubbornness, submission, lamentation, succeeded one another; so did varieties of sunken cheek, cadaverous colour, emaciated hands and figures. But the face was in the main one face, and every head was prematurely white. A hundred times the dozing passenger inquired of this spectre:

"Buried how long?"

The answer was always the same: "Almost eighteen years."

"You had abandoned all hope of being dug out?"

"Long ago."

"You know that you are recalled to life?"

"They tell me so."

"I hope you care to live?"

"I can't say."

"Shall I show her to you? Will you come and see her?"

The answers to this question were various and contradictory. Sometimes the broken reply was, "Wait! It would
kill me if I saw her too soon." Sometimes, it was given in
a tender rain of tears, and then it was, "Take me to her."
Sometimes it was staring and bewildered, and then it was,
"I don't know her. I don't understand."

After such imaginary discourse, the passenger in his
fancy would dig, and dig, dig—now with a spade, now
with a great key, now with his hands—to dig this wretched
creature out. Got out at last, with earth hanging about
his face and hair, he would suddenly fall away to dust.
The passenger would then start to himself, and lower the
window, to get the reality of mist and rain on his cheek.

Yet even when his eyes were opened on the mist and
rain, on the moving patch of light from the lamps, and
the hedge at the roadside retreating by jerks, the night
shadows outside the coach would fall into the train of the
night shadows within. The real banking-house by Temple
Bar, the real business of the past day, the real strong-
rooms, the real express sent after him, and the real message returned, would all be there. Out of the midst of them,
the ghostly face would rise, and he would accost it again.

"Buried how long?"

"Almost eighteen years."

"I hope you care to live?"

"I can't say."

Dig—dig—dig—until an impatient movement from one
of the two passengers would admonish him to pull up the
window, draw his arm securely through the leathern strap,
and speculate upon the two slumbering forms, until his
mind lost its hold of them, and they again slid away into
the bank and the grave.

"Buried how long?"

"Almost eighteen years."

"You had abandoned all hope of being dug out?"

"Long ago."

The words were still in his hearing as just spoken—distinctly in his hearing as ever spoken words had been in his
life—when the weary passenger started to the conscious-

ness of daylight, and found that the shadows of the night were gone.

He lowered the window, and looked out at the rising sun. There was a ridge of ploughed land, with a plough upon it where it had been left last night when the horses were unyoked; beyond, a quiet coppice-wood, in which many leaves of burning red and golden yellow still remained upon the trees. Though the earth was cold and wet, the sky was clear, and the sun rose bright, placid, and beautiful.

"Eighteen years!" said the passenger, looking at the sun. "Gracious Creator of day! To be buried alive for eighteen years!"

*   *   *   *   *   *   *   *

4 The Preparation

WHEN THE mail got successfully to Dover, in the course of the forenoon, the head drawer at the Royal George Hotel opened the coach-door as his custom was. He did it with some flourish of ceremony, for a mail journey from London in winter was an achievement to congratulate an adventurous traveller upon.

By that time, there was only one adventurous traveller left to be congratulated; for the two others had been set down at their respective roadside destinations. The mildewy inside of the coach, with its damp and dirty straw, its disagreeable smell, and its obscurity, was rather like a larger dog-kennel. Mr. Lorry, the passenger, shaking himself out of it in chains of straw, a tangle of shaggy wrapper, flapping hat, and muddy legs, was rather like a larger sort of dog.

"There will be a packet to Calais to-morrow, drawer?"

"Yes, sir, if the weather holds and the wind sets tolerable fair. The tide will serve pretty nicely at about two in the afternoon, sir. Bed, sir?"

"I shall not go to bed till night; but I want a bedroom, and a barber."

"And then breakfast, sir? Yes, sir. That way, sir, if you please. Show Concord! Gentleman's valise and hot water to Concord. Pull off gentleman's boots in Concord. (You will find a fine sea-coal fire, sir.) Fetch barber to Concord. Stir about there, now, for Concord!"

The Concord bedchamber being always assigned to a passenger by the mail, and passengers by the mail being always heavily wrapped up from head to foot, the room had the odd interest for the establishment of the Royal George, that although but one kind of man was seen to go into it, all kinds and varieties of men came out of it. Consequently, another drawer, and two porters, and several maids and the landlady, were all loitering by accident at various points of the road between the Concord and the coffee-room, when a gentleman of sixty, formally dressed in a brown suit of clothes, pretty well worn, but very well kept, with large square cuffs and large flaps to the pockets, passed along on his way to his breakfast.

The coffee-room had no other occupant, that forenoon, than the gentleman in brown. His breakfast-table was drawn before the fire, and as he sat, with its light shining on him, waiting for the meal, he sat so still, that he might have been sitting for his portrait.

Very orderly and methodical he looked, with a hand on each knee, and a loud watch ticking a sonorous sermon under his flapped waistcoat, as though it pitted its gravity and longevity against the levity and evanescence of the brisk fire. He had a good leg, and was a little vain of it, for his brown stockings fitted sleek and close, and were of a fine texture; his shoes and buckles, too, though plain, were trim. He wore an odd little sleek crisp flaxen wig, setting very close to his head; which wig, it is to be presumed, was made of hair, but which looked far more as though it were spun from filaments of silk or glass. His linen, though not of a fineness in accordance with his stockings, was as white as the tops of the waves that broke upon the neighbouring beach, or the specks of sail that glinted in the sunlight far at sea. A face habitually suppressed and quieted was still lighted up under the quaint wig by a pair of moist bright eyes that must have cost their owner, in years gone by, some pains to drill to the composed and reserved expression of Tellson's Bank. He had a healthy colour in his cheeks, and his face, though lined, bore few traces of anxiety. But, perhaps the confidential bachelor clerks in Tellson's Bank were principally occupied with the cares of other people; and perhaps second-hand cares, like second-hand clothes, come easily off and on.

Completing his resemblance to a man who was sitting for his portrait, Mr. Lorry dropped off to sleep. The arrival of his breakfast roused him, and he said to the drawer, as he moved his chair to it:

"I wish accommodation prepared for a young lady who may come here at any time to-day. She may ask for Mr. Jarvis Lorry, or she may only ask for a gentleman from Tellson's Bank. Please to let me know."

"Yes, sir. Tellson's Bank in London, sir?"

"Yes."

"Yes, sir. We have oftentimes the honour to entertain your gentlemen in their travelling backwards and forwards betwixt London and Paris, sir. A vast deal of travelling, sir, in Tellson and Company's House."

"Yes. We are quite a French House, as well as an English one."

"Yes, sir. Not much in the habit of such travelling yourself, I think, sir?"

"Not of late years. It is fifteen years since we—since I—came last from France."

"Indeed, sir? That was before my time here, sir. Before our people's time here, sir. The George was in other hands at that time, sir."

"I believe so."

"But I would hold a pretty wager, sir, that a House like Tellson and Company was flourishing, a matter of fifty, not to speak of fifteen years ago?"

"You might treble that, and say a hundred and fifty, yet not be far from the truth."

"Indeed, sir!"

Rounding his mouth and both his eyes, as he stepped backward from the table, the waiter shifted his napkin from his right arm to his left, dropped into a comfortable attitude, and stood surveying the guest while he ate and drank, as from an observatory or watch-tower, according to the immemorial usage of waiters in all ages.

When Mr. Lorry had finished his breakfast, he went out for a stroll on the beach. The little narrow, crooked town of Dover hid itself away from the beach, and ran its head into the chalk cliffs, like a marine ostrich. The beach was a desert of heaps of sea and stones tumbling wildly about, and the sea did what it liked, and what it liked was destruction. It thundered at the town, and thundered at the cliffs, and brought the coast down, madly. The air among the houses was of so strong a piscatory flavour that one might have supposed sick fish went up to be dipped in it, as sick people went down to be dipped in the sea. A little fishing was done in the port, and a quantity of strolling about by night, and looking seaward: particularly at those times when the tide made, and was near flood. Small tradesmen, who did no business whatever, sometimes unaccountably realised large fortunes, and it was remarkable that nobody in the neighbourhood could endure a lamplighter.

As the day declined into the afternoon, and the air, which had been at intervals clear enough to allow the French coast to be seen, became again charged with mist and vapour, Mr. Lorry's thoughts seemed to cloud too. When it was dark, and he sat before the coffee-room fire, awaiting his dinner as he had awaited his breakfast, his mind was busily digging, digging, digging, in the live red coals.

A bottle of good claret after dinner does a digger in the red coals no harm, otherwise than as it has a tendency to throw him out of work. Mr. Lorry had been idle a long time, and had just poured out his last glassful of wine with as complete an appearance of satisfaction as is ever to be found in an elderly gentleman of a fresh complexion who has got to the end of a bottle, when a rattling of wheels came up the narrow street, and rumbled into the inn-yard.

He set down his glass untouched. "This is Mam'selle!" said he.

In a very few minutes the waiter came in to announce that Miss Manette had arrived from London, and would be happy to see the gentleman from Tellson's.

"So soon?"

Miss Manette had taken some refreshment on the road, and required none then, and was extremely anxious to see the gentleman from Tellson's immediately, if it suited his pleasure and convenience.

The gentleman from Tellson's had nothing left for it but to empty his glass with an air of stolid desperation, settle his odd little flaxen wig at the ears, and follow the waiter to Miss Manette's apartment. It was a large, dark room, furnished in a funereal manner with black horsehair, and loaded with heavy dark tables. These had been oiled and oiled, until the two tall candles on the table in the middle of the room were gloomily reflected on every leaf; as if *they* were buried, in deep graves of black mahogany, and no light to speak of could be expected from them until they were dug out.

The obscurity was so difficult to penetrate that Mr. Lorry, picking his way over the well-worn Turkey carpet, supposed Miss Manette to be, for the moment, in some adjacent room, until, having got past the two tall candles, he saw, standing to receive him by the table between them and the fire, a young lady of not more than seventeen, in a riding-cloak, and still holding her straw travelling-hat by its ribbon in her hand. As his eyes rested on a short, slight, pretty figure, a quantity of golden hair, a pair of blue eyes that met his own with an inquiring look, and a forehead with a singular capacity (remembering how young and smooth it was) of lifting and knitting itself into an expression that was not quite one of perplexity, or wonder, or alarm, or merely of a bright fixed attention, though it included all the four expressions—as his eyes rested on these things, a sudden vivid likeness passed before him, of a child whom he had held in his arms on the passage across that very Channel, one cold time, when the hail drifted heavily and the sea ran high. The likeness passed away, like a breath along the surface of the gaunt pier-glass behind her, on the frame of which, a hospital procession of Negro cupids, several headless and all cripples, were offering black baskets of Dead Sea fruit to black divinities of the feminine gender—and he made his formal bow to Miss Manette.

"Pray take a seat, sir." In a very clear and pleasant young voice; a little foreign in its accent, but a very little indeed.

"I kiss your hand, miss," said Mr. Lorry, with the manners of an earlier date, as he made his formal bow again, and took his seat.

"I received a letter from the Bank, sir, yesterday, informing me that some intelligence—or discovery—"

"The word is not material, miss; either word will do."

"—respecting the small property of my poor father, whom I never saw—so long dead—"

Mr. Lorry moved in his chair, and cast a troubled look towards the hospital procession of Negro cupids. As if *they* had any help for anybody in their absurd baskets!

"—render it necessary that I should go to Paris, there to communicate with a gentleman of the Bank, so good as to be despatched to Paris for the purpose."

"Myself."

"As I was prepared to hear, sir."

She curtseyed to him (young ladies made curtseys in those days), with a pretty desire to convey to him that she felt how much older and wiser he was than she. He made her another bow.

"I replied to the Bank, sir, that as it was considered necessary, by those who know, and who are so kind as to advise me, that I should go to France, and that as I am an orphan and have no friend who could go with me, I should esteem it highly if I might be permitted to place myself, during the journey, under that worthy gentleman's protection. The gentleman had left London, but I think a messenger was sent after him to beg the favour of his waiting for me here."

"I was happy," said Mr. Lorry, "to be entrusted with the charge. I shall be more happy to execute it."

"Sir, I thank you indeed. I thank you very gratefully. It was told me by the Bank that the gentleman would explain to me the details of the business, and that I must prepare myself to find them of a surprising nature. I have done my best to prepare myself, and I naturally have a strong and eager interest to know what they are."

"Naturally," said Mr. Lorry. "Yes—I—"

After a pause, he added, again settling the crisp flaxen wig at the ears:

"It is very difficult to begin."

He did not begin, but, in his indecision, met her glance. The young forehead lifted itself into that singular expression—but it was pretty and characteristic, besides being singular—and she raised her hand, as if with an involuntary action she caught at, or stayed some passing shadow.

"Are you quite a stranger to me, sir?"

"Am I not?" Mr. Lorry opened his hands, and extended them outwards with an argumentative smile.

Between the eyebrows and just over the little feminine nose, the line of which was as delicate and fine as it was possible to be, the expression deepened itself as she took her seat thoughtfully in the chair by which she had hitherto remained standing. He watched her as she mused, and the moment she raised her eyes again, went on:

"In your adopted country, I presume, I cannot do better than address you as a young English lady, Miss Manette?"

"If you please, sir."

"Miss Manette, I am a man of business. I have a business charge to acquit myself of. In your reception of it, don't heed me any more than if I was a speaking machine —truly, I am not much else. I will, with your leave, relate to you, miss, the story of one of our customers."

"Story!"

He seemed wilfully to mistake the word she had repeated, when he added, in a hurry, "Yes, customers; in the banking business we usually call our connection our customers. He was a French gentleman; a scientific gentleman; a man of great acquirements—a Doctor."

"Not of Beauvais?"

"Why, yes, of Beauvais. Like Monsieur Manette, your father, the gentleman was of Beauvais. Like Monsieur Manette, your father, the gentleman was of repute in Paris. I had the honour of knowing him there. Our relations were business relations, but confidential. I was at that time in our French House, and had been—oh! twenty years."

"At that time—I may ask, at what time, sir?"

"I speak, miss, of twenty years ago. He married—an English lady—and I was one of the trustees. His affairs, like the affairs of many other French gentlemen and French families, were entirely in Tellson's hands. In a similar way I am, or I have been, trustee of one kind or other for scores of our customers. These are mere business relations, miss; there is no friendship in them; no particular interest, nothing like sentiment. I have passed from one to another, in the course of my business life, just as I pass from one of our customers to another in the course of my business day; in short, I have no feelings; I am a mere machine. To go on—"

"But this is my father's story, sir; and I begin to think" —the curiously roughened forehead was very intent upon him—"that when I was left an orphan through my mother's surviving my father only two years, it was you who brought me to England. I am almost sure it was you."

Mr. Lorry took the hesitating little hand that confidingly advanced to take his, and he put it with some ceremony to his lips. He then conducted the young lady straightway to her chair again, and, holding the chairback with his left hand, and using his right by turns to rub his chin, pull his wig at the ears, or point what he said, stood looking down into her face while she sat looking up into his.

"Miss Manette, it *was* I. And you will see how truly I spoke of myself just now, in saying I had no feelings, and that all the relations I hold with my fellow-creatures are mere business relations, when you reflect that I have never seen you since. No; you have been the ward of Tellson's House since, and I have been busy with the other business of Tellson's House since. Feelings! I have no time for them, no chance of them. I pass my whole life, miss, in turning an immense pecuniary mangle."

After this odd description of his daily routine of employment, Mr. Lorry flattened his flaxen wig upon his head with both hands (which was most unnecessary, for nothing could be flatter than its shining surface was before), and resumed his former attitude.

"So far, miss (as you have remarked), this is the story of your regretted father. Now comes the difference. If your father had not died when he did— Don't be frightened! How you start!"

She did, indeed, start. And she caught his wrist with both her hands.

"Pray," said Mr. Lorry, in a soothing tone, bringing his left hand from the back of the chair to lay it on the supplicatory fingers that clasped him in so violent a tremble: "pray control your agitation—a matter of business. As I was saying—"

Her look so discomposed him that he stopped, wandered, and began anew:

"As I was saying; if Monsieur Manette had not died; if he had suddenly and silently disappeared; if he had been spirited away; if it had not been difficult to guess to what dreadful place, though no art could trace him; if he had an enemy in some compatriot who could exercise a privilege that I in my own time have known the boldest people afraid to speak of in a whisper, across the water there; for instance, the privilege of filling up blank forms for the consignment of any one to the oblivion of a prison for any length of time; if his wife had implored the king, the queen, the court, the clergy, for any tidings of him, and all quite in vain—then the history of your father would have been the history of this unfortunate gentleman, the Doctor of Beauvais."

"I entreat you to tell me more, sir."

"I will. I am going to. You can bear it?"

"I can bear anything but the uncertainty you leave me in at this moment."

"You speak collectedly, and you—*are* collected. That's good!" (Though his manner was less satisfied than his words.) "A matter of business. Regard it as a matter of business—business that must be done. Now if this doctor's wife, though a lady of great courage and spirit, had suffered so intensely from this cause before her little child was born—"

"The little child was a daughter, sir?"

"A daughter. A—a—matter of business—don't be distressed. Miss, if the poor lady had suffered so intensely before her little child was born, that she came to the determination of sparing the poor child the inheritance of any part of the agony she had known the pains of, by rearing her in the belief that her father was dead— No, don't kneel! In Heaven's name why should you kneel to me?"

"For the truth. O dear, good, compassionate sir, for the truth!"

"A—a matter of business. You confuse me, and how can I transact business if I am confused? Let us be clear-headed. If you could kindly mention now, for instance, what nine times ninepence are, or how many shillings in twenty guineas, it would be so encouraging. I should be so much more at my ease about your state of mind."

Without directly answering to this appeal, she sat so still when he had gently raised her, and the hands that had not ceased to clasp his wrists were so much more steady than they had been, that she communicated some reassurance to Mr. Jarvis Lorry.

"That's right, that's right. Courage! Business! You have business before you; useful business. Miss Manette, your mother took this course with you. And when she died— I believe broken-hearted—having never slackened her unavailing search for your father, she left you, at two years old, to grow to be blooming, beautiful, and happy, without the dark cloud upon you of living in uncertainty whether your father soon wore his heart out in prison, or wasted there through many lingering years."

As he said the words he looked down, with admiring

pity, on the flowing golden hair; as if he pictured to himself
that it might have been already tinged with gray.

"You know that your parents had no great possession,
and that what they had was secured to your mother and
to you. There has been no new discovery, of money, or of
any other property; but—"

He felt his wrist held closer, and he stopped. The expression in the forehead, which had so particularly attracted his notice, and which was now immovable, had
deepened into one of pain and horror.

"But he has been—been found. He is alive. Greatly
changed, it is too probable; almost a wreck, it is possible;
though we will hope the best. Still, alive. Your father has
been taken to the house of an old servant in Paris, and we
are going there: I, to identify him if I can: you, to restore
him to life, love, duty, rest, comfort."

A shiver ran through her frame, and from it through
his. She said, in a low, distinct, awe-stricken voice, as if
she were saying it in a dream:

"I am going to see his ghost! It will be his ghost—not
him!"

Mr. Lorry quietly chafed the hands that held his arm.
"There, there, there! See now, see now! The best and the
worst are known to you, now. You are well on your way
to the poor wronged gentleman, and, with a fair sea voyage,
and a fair land journey, you will be soon at his dear side."

She repeated in the same tone, sunk to a whisper, "I
have been free, I have been happy, yet his ghost has never
haunted me!"

"Only one thing more," said Mr. Lorry, laying stress
upon it as a wholesome means of enforcing her attention.
"He has been found under another name; his own, long
forgotten or long concealed. It would be worse than useless now to inquire which; worse than useless to seek to
know whether he has been for years overlooked, or always
designedly held prisoner. It would be worse than useless
now to make any inquiries, because it would be dangerous.
Better not to mention the subject, anywhere or in any way,
and to remove him—for a while at all events—out of
France. Even I, safe as an Englishman, and even Tellson's,
important as they are to French credit, avoid all naming
of the matter. I carry about me not a scrap of writing
openly referring to it. This is a secret service altogether.
My credentials, entries, and memoranda are all compre-

hended in the one line, 'Recalled to Life,' which may mean anything. But what is the matter? She doesn't notice a word! Miss Manette!"

Perfectly still and silent, and not even fallen back in her chair, she sat under his hand, utterly insensible; with her eyes open and fixed upon him, and with that last expression looking as if it were carved or branded into her forehead. So close was her hold upon his arm, that he feared to detach himself lest he should hurt her; therefore he called out loudly for assistance without moving.

A wild-looking woman, whom, even in his agitation, Mr. Lorry observed to be all of a red colour, and to have red hair, and to be dressed in some extraordinary tight-fitting fashion, and to have on her head a most wonderful bonnet like a Grenadier wooden measure, and good measure too, or a great Stilton cheese, came running into the room in advance of the inn servants, and soon settled the question of his detachment from the poor young lady, by laying a brawny hand upon his chest, and sending him flying back against the nearest wall.

("I really think this must be a man!" was Mr. Lorry's breathless reflection, simultaneously with his coming against the wall.)

"Why, look at you all!" bawled this figure, addressing the inn servants. "Why don't you go and fetch things, instead of standing there staring at me? I am not so much to look at, am I? Why don't you go and fetch things? I'll let you know, if you don't bring smelling-salts, cold water, and vinegar, quick, I will."

There was an immediate dispersal for these restoratives, and she softly laid the patient on a sofa, and tended her with great skill and gentleness: calling her "my precious!" and "my bird!" and spreading her golden hair aside over her shoulders with great pride and care.

"And you in brown!" she said, indignantly turning to Mr. Lorry; "couldn't you tell her what you had to tell her, without frightening her to death? Look at her, with her pretty pale face and her cold hands. Do you call *that* being a banker?"

Mr. Lorry was so exceedingly disconcerted by a question so hard to answer, that he could only look on, at a distance, with much feeble sympathy and humility, while the strong woman, having banished the inn servants under the mysterious penalty of "letting them know" something not mentioned if they stayed there, staring, recovered her charge by a regular series of gradations, and coaxed her to lay her drooping head upon her shoulder.

"I hope she will do well now," said Mr. Lorry.

"No thanks to you in brown, if she does. My darling pretty!"

"I hope," said Mr. Lorry, after another pause of feeble sympathy and humility, "that you accompany Miss Manette to France?"

"A likely thing, too!" replied the strong woman. "If it was ever intended that I should go across salt water, do you suppose Providence would have cast my lot in an island?"

This being another question hard to answer, Mr. Jarvis Lorry withdrew to consider it.

*   *   *   *   *   *   *   *

5 *The Wine-Shop*

A LARGE cask of wine had been dropped and broken, in the street. The accident had happened in getting it out of a cart; the cask had tumbled out with a run, the hoops had burst, and it lay on the stones just outside the door of the wine-shop, shattered like a walnut-shell.

All the people within reach had suspended their business, or their idleness, to run to the spot and drink the wine. The rough, irregular stones of the street, pointing every way, and designed, one might have thought, expressly to lame all living creatures that approached them, had dammed it into little pools; these were surrounded, each by its own jostling group or crowd, according to its size. Some men kneeled down, made scoops of their two hands joined, and sipped, or tried to help women, who bent over their shoulders, to sip, before the wine had all run out between their fingers. Others, men and women, dipped in the puddles with little mugs of mutilated earthenware, or even with handkerchiefs from women's heads, which were squeezed dry into infants' mouths; others made small mud embankments, to stem the wine as it ran; others, directed by lookers-on up at high windows, darted here and there, to cut off little streams of wine that started away in new directions; others devoted themselves to the sodden and lee-dyed pieces of the cask, licking, and even champing the moister wine-rotted fragments with eager relish. There was no drainage to carry off the wine, and not only did it all get taken up, but so much mud got taken up along with it, that there might have been a scavenger in the street, if anybody acquainted with it could have believed in such a miraculous presence.

A shrill sound of laughter and of amused voices—voices of men, women, and children—resounded in the street while this wine game lasted. There was little roughness in the sport, and much playfulness. There was a special companionship in it, an observable inclination on the part of every one to join some other one, which led, especially among the luckier or lighter-hearted, to frolicsome embraces, drinking of healths, shaking of hands, and even joining of hands and dancing, a dozen together. When the wine was gone, and the places where it had been most abundant were raked into a gridiron pattern by fingers, these demonstrations ceased, as suddenly as they had broken out. The man who had left his saw sticking in the firewood he was cutting, set it in motion again; the woman who had left on a doorstep the little pot of hot ashes, at which she had been trying to soften the pain in her own starved fingers and toes, or in those of her child, returned to it; men with bare arms, matted locks, and cadaverous faces, who had emerged into the winter light from cellars, moved away, to descend again; and a gloom gathered on the scene that appeared more natural to it than sunshine.

The wine was red wine, and had stained the ground of the narrow street in the suburb of Saint Antoine, in Paris, where it was spilled. It had stained many hands, too, and many faces, and many naked feet, and many wooden shoes. The hands of the man who sawed the wood left red marks on the billets; and the forehead of the woman who nursed her baby was stained with the stain of the old rag she wound about her head again. Those who had been greedy with the staves of the cask, had acquired a tigerish smear about the mouth; and one tall joker so besmirched, his head more out of a long squalid bag of a nightcap than in it, scrawled upon a wall with his finger dipped in muddy wine-lees—BLOOD.

The time was to come, when that wine too would be spilled on the street-stones, and when the stain of it would be red upon many there.

And now that the cloud settled on Saint Antoine, which a momentary gleam had driven from his sacred countenance, the darkness of it was heavy—cold, dirt, sickness, ignorance, and want, were the lords in waiting on the saintly presence—nobles of great power all of them; but, most especially, the last. Samples of a people that had undergone a terrible grinding and re-grinding in the mill, and certainly not in the fabulous mill which ground old people young, shivered at every corner, passed in and out at every doorway, looked from every window, fluttered in every vestige of a garment that the wind shook. The mill which had worked them down was the mill that grinds young people old; the children had ancient faces and grave voices; and upon them, and upon the grown faces, and ploughed into every furrow of age and coming up afresh, was the sign, Hunger. It was prevalent everywhere. Hunger was pushed out of the tall houses, in the wretched clothing that hung upon poles and lines; Hunger was patched into them with straw and rag and wood and paper; Hunger was repeated in every fragment of the small modicum of fire-wood that the man sawed off; Hunger stared down from the smokeless chimneys, and started up from the filthy street that had no offal, among its refuse, of anything to eat. Hunger was the inscription on the baker's shelves, written in every small loaf of his scanty stock of bad bread; at the sausage-shop, in every dead-dog preparation that was offered for sale. Hunger rattled its dry bones among the roasting chestnuts in the turned cylinder; Hunger was shred into atomies in every farthing porringer of husky chips of potato, fried with some reluctant drops of oil.

Its abiding place was in all things fitted to it. A narrow winding street, full of offence and stench, with other narrow winding streets diverging, all peopled by rags and nightcaps, and all smelling of rags and nightcaps, and all visible things with a brooding look upon them that looked ill. In the hunted air of the people there was yet some wild-beast thought of the possibility of turning at bay. Depressed and slinking though they were, eyes of fire were not wanting among them; nor compressed lips, white with what they suppressed; nor foreheads knitted into the likeness of the gallows-rope they mused about enduring, or inflicting. The trade signs (and they were almost as many as the shops) were, all, grim illustrations of Want. The butcher and the porkman painted up only the leanest scrags of meat; the baker, the coarsest of meagre loaves. The people rudely pictured as drinking in the wine-shops, croaked over their scanty measures of thin wine and beer, and were glower-ingly confidential together. Nothing was represented in a flourishing condition, save tools and weapons; but, the cutler's knives and axes were sharp and bright, the smith's hammers were heavy, and the gunmaker's stock was mur-derous. The crippling stones of the pavement, with their many little reservoirs of mud and water, had no footways, but broke off abruptly at the doors. The kennel, to make amends, ran down the middle of the street—when it ran at all: which was only after heavy rains, and then it ran, by many eccentric fits, into the houses. Across the streets, at wide intervals, one clumsy lamp was slung by a rope and pulley; at night, when the lamplighter had let these down, and lighted, and hoisted them again, a feeble grove of dim wicks swung in a sickly manner overhead, as if they were at sea. Indeed they were at sea, and the ship and crew were in peril of tempest.

For, the time was to come, when the gaunt scarecrows of that region should have watched the lamplighter, in their idleness and hunger, so long as to conceive the idea of improving on his method, and hauling up men by those ropes and pulleys, to flare upon the darkness of their condi-tion. But, the time was not come yet; and every wind that blew over France shook the rags of the scarecrows in vain, for the birds, fine of song and feather, took no warning.

The wine-shop was a corner shop, better than most others in its appearance and degree, and the master of the wine-shop had stood outside it, in a yellow waistcoat and green breeches, looking on at the struggle for the lost wine. "It's not my affair," said he, with a final shrug of the shoul-ders. "The people from the market did it. Let them bring another."

There, his eyes happening to catch the tall joker writing up his joke, he called to him across the way:

"Say, then, my Gaspard, what do you do there?"

The fellow pointed to his joke with immense signifi-cance, as is often the way with his tribe. It missed its mark, and completely failed, as is often the way with his tribe too.

"What now? Are you a subject for the mad hospital?" said the wine-shop keeper, crossing the road, and obliterating the jest with a handful of mud, picked up for the purpose, and smeared over it. "Why do you write in the public streets? Is there—tell me thou—is there no other place to write such words in?"

In his expostulation he dropped his cleaner hand (perhaps accidentally, perhaps not) upon the joker's heart. The joker rapped it with his own, took a nimble spring upward, and came down in a fantastic dancing attitude, with one of his stained shoes jerked off his foot into his hand, and held out. A joker of an extremely, not to say wolfishly practical character he looked, under those circumstances.

"Put it on, put it on," said the other. "Call wine, wine; and finish there." With that advice, he wiped his soiled hand upon the joker's dress, such as it was—quite deliberately, as having dirtied the hand on his account; and then re-crossed the road and entered the wine-shop.

This wine-shop keeper was a bull-necked, martial-looking man of thirty, and he should have been of a hot temperament, for, although it was a bitter day, he wore no coat, but carried one slung over his shoulder. His shirt-sleeves were rolled up, too, and his brown arms were bare to the elbows. Neither did he wear anything more on his head than his own crisply-curling short dark hair. He was a dark man altogether, with good eyes and a good bold breadth between them. Good-humoured looking on the whole, but implacable-looking, too; evidently a man of a strong resolution and a set purpose; a man not desirable to be met, rushing down a narrow pass with a gulf on either side, for nothing would turn the man.

Madame Defarge, his wife, sat in the shop behind the counter as he came in. Madame Defarge was a stout woman of about his own age, with a watchful eye that seldom seemed to look at anything, a large hand heavily ringed, a steady face, strong features, and great composure of manner. There was a character about Madame Defarge, from which one might have predicated that she did not often make mistakes against herself in any of the reckonings over which she presided. Madame Defarge, being sensitive to cold, was wrapped in fur, and had a quantity of bright shawl twined about her head, though not to the concealment of her large earrings. Her knitting was before her, but she had laid it down to pick her teeth with a toothpick. Thus engaged, with her right elbow supported by her left hand, Madame Defarge said nothing when her lord came in, but coughed just one grain of cough. This, in combination with the lifting of her darkly defined eyebrows over her toothpick by the breadth of a line, suggested to her husband that he would do well to look round the shop among the customers, for any new customer who had dropped in while he stepped over the way.

The wine-shop keeper accordingly rolled his eyes about, until they rested upon an elderly gentleman and a young lady, who were seated in a corner. Other company were there: two playing cards, two playing dominoes, three standing by the counter lengthening out a short supply of wine. As he passed behind the counter, he took notice that the elderly gentleman said in a look to the young lady, "This is our man."

"What the devil do *you* do in that galley there?" said Monsieur Defarge to himself; "I don't know you."

But, he feigned not to notice the two strangers, and fell into discourse with the triumvirate of customers who were drinking at the counter.

"How goes it, Jacques?" said one of these three to Monsieur Defarge. "Is all the spilt wine swallowed?"

"Every drop, Jacques," answered Monsieur Defarge.

When this interchange of Christian name was effected, Madame Defarge, picking her teeth with her toothpick, coughed another grain of cough, and raised her eyebrows by the breadth of another line.

"It is not often," said the second of the three, addressing Monsieur Defarge, "that many of these miserable beasts know the taste of wine, or of anything but black bread and death. Is it not so, Jacques?"

"It is so, Jacques," Monsieur Defarge returned.

At this second interchange of the Christian name, Madame Defarge, still using her toothpick with profound composure, coughed another grain of cough, and raised her eyebrows by the breadth of another line.

The last of the three now said his say, as he put down his empty drinking vessel, and smacked his lips.

"Ah! So much the worse! A bitter taste it is that such

poor cattle always have in their mouths, and hard lives they live, Jacques. Am I right, Jacques?"

"You are right, Jacques," was the response of Monsieur Defarge.

This third interchange of the Christian name was completed at the moment when Madame Defarge put her toothpick by, kept her eyebrows up, and slightly rustled in her seat.

"Hold then! True!" muttered her husband. "Gentlemen —my wife!"

The three customers pulled off their hats to Madame Defarge, with three flourishes. She acknowledged their homage by bending her head, and giving them a quick look. Then she glanced in a casual manner round the wine-shop, took up her knitting with great apparent calmness and repose of spirit, and became absorbed in it.

"Gentlemen," said her husband, who had kept his bright eye observantly upon her, "good day. The chamber, furnished bachelor-fashion, that you wished to see, and were inquiring for when I stepped out, is on the fifth floor. The doorway of the staircase gives on the little courtyard close to the left here," pointing with his hand, "near to the window of my establishment. But, now that I remember, one of you has already been there, and can show the way. Gentlemen, adieu!"

They paid for their wine, and left the place. The eyes of Monsieur Defarge were studying his wife at her knitting, when the elderly gentleman advanced from his corner, and begged the favour of a word.

"Willingly, sir," said Monsieur Defarge, and quietly stepped with him to the door.

Their conference was very short, but very decided. Almost at the first word, Monsieur Defarge started and became deeply attentive. It had not lasted a minute, when he nodded and went out. The gentleman then beckoned to the young lady, and they, too, went out. Madame Defarge knitted with nimble fingers and steady eyebrows, and saw nothing.

Mr. Jarvis Lorry and Miss Manette, emerging from the wine-shop thus, joined Monsieur Defarge in the doorway to which he had directed his other company just before. It opened from a stinking little black courtyard, and was the general public entrance to a great pile of houses, inhabited by a great number of people. In the gloomy tile-paved entry to the gloomy tile-paved staircase, Monsieur Defarge bent down on one knee to the child of his old master, and put her hand to his lips. It was a gentle action, but not at all gently done; a very remarkable transformation had come over him in a few seconds. He had no good-humour in his face, nor any openness of aspect left, but had become a secret, angry, dangerous man.

"It is very high; it is a little difficult. Better to begin slowly." Thus Monsieur Defarge, in a stern voice, to Mr. Lorry, as they began ascending the stairs.

"Is he alone?" the latter whispered.

"Alone! God help him, who should be with him?" said the other, in the same low voice.

"Is he always alone, then?"

"Yes."

"Of his own desire?"

"Of his own necessity. As he was, when I first saw him after they found me and demanded to know if I would take him, and, at my peril, be discreet—as he was then, so he is now."

"He is greatly changed?"

"Changed!"

The keeper of the wine-shop stopped to strike the wall with his hand, and mutter a tremendous curse. No direct answer could have been half so forcible. Mr. Lorry's spirits grew heavier and heavier, as he and his two companions ascended higher and higher.

Such a staircase, with its accessories, in the older and more crowded parts of Paris, would be bad enough now; but, at that time, it was vile indeed to unaccustomed and unhardened senses. Every little habitation within the great foul nest of one high building—that is to say, the room or rooms within every door that opened on the general staircase—left its own heap of refuse on its own landing, besides flinging other refuse from its own windows. The uncontrollable and hopeless mass of decomposition so engendered would have polluted the air, even if poverty and deprivation had not loaded it with their intangible impurities; the two bad sources combined made it almost insupportable. Through such an atmosphere, by a steep dark shaft of dirt and poison, the way lay. Yielding to his own disturbance of mind, and to his young companion's agitation, which became greater every instant, Mr. Jarvis Lorry twice stopped to rest. Each of these stoppages was made at a doleful grating, by which any languishing good airs that were left uncorrupted seemed to escape, and all spoilt and sickly vapours seemed to crawl in. Through the rusted bars, tastes, rather than glimpses, were caught of the jumbled neighbourhood; and nothing within range, nearer or lower than the summits of the two great towers of Notre Dame, had any promise on it of healthy life or wholesome aspirations.

At last, the top of the staircase was gained, and they stopped for the third time. There was yet an upper staircase, of a steeper inclination and of contracted dimensions, to be ascended, before the garret story was reached. The keeper of the wine-shop, always going a little in advance, and always going on the side which Mr. Lorry took, as though he dreaded to be asked any questions by the young lady, turned himself about here, and, carefully feeling in the pockets of the coat he carried over his shoulder, took out a key.

"The door is locked then, my friend?" said Mr. Lorry, surprised.

"Ay. Yes," was the grim reply of Monsieur Defarge.

"You think it necessary to keep the unfortunate gentleman so retired?"

"I think it necessary to turn the key." Monsieur Defarge whispered it closer in his ear, and frowned heavily.

"Why?"

"Why! Because he has lived so long, locked up, that he would be frightened—rave—tear himself to pieces—die—come to I know not what harm—if his door was left open."

"Is it possible?" exclaimed Mr. Lorry.

"Is it possible?" repeated Defarge, bitterly. "Yes. And a beautiful world we live in, when it *is* possible, and when many other such things are possible, and not only possible, but done—done, see you!—under that sky there, every day. Long live the Devil. Let us go on."

This dialogue had been held in so very low a whisper, that not a word of it had reached the young lady's ears. But, by this time she trembled under such strong emotion, and her face expressed such deep anxiety, and, above all, such dread and terror, that Mr. Lorry felt it incumbent on him to speak a word or two of reassurance.

"Courage, dear miss! Courage! Business! The worst will be over in a moment; it is but passing the room-door, and the worst is over. Then, all the good you bring to him, all the relief, all the happiness you bring to him, begin. Let our good friend here assist you on that side. That's well, friend Defarge. Come, now. Business, business!"

They went up slowly and softly. The staircase was short, and they were soon at the top. There, as it had an abrupt turn in it, they came all at once in sight of three men, whose heads were bent down close together at the side of a door, and who were intently looking into the room to which the door belonged, through some chinks or holes in the wall. On hearing footsteps close at hand, these three turned, and rose, and showed themselves to be the three of one name who had been drinking in the wine-shop.

"I forgot them in the surprise of your visit," explained Monsieur Defarge. "Leave us, good boys; we have business here."

The three glided by, and went silently down.

There appearing to be no other door on that floor, and the keeper of the wine-shop going straight to this one when they were left alone, Mr. Lorry asked him in a whisper, with a little anger:

"Do you make a show of Monsieur Manette?"

"I show him, in the way you have seen, to a chosen few."

"Is that well?"

"*I* think it is well."

"Who are the few? How do you choose them?"

"I choose them as real men, of my name—Jacques is my name—to whom the sight is likely to do good. Enough: you are English; that is another thing. Stay there, if you please, a little moment."

With an admonitory gesture to keep them back, he stooped, and looked in through the crevice in the wall. Soon raising his head again, he struck twice or thrice upon the door—evidently with no other object than to make a noise there. With the same intention, he drew the key across it, three or four times, before he put it clumsily into the lock, and turned it as heavily as he could.

The door slowly opened inward under his hand, and he looked into the room and said something. A faint voice answered something. Little more than a single syllable could have been spoken on either side.

He looked back over his shoulder, and beckoned them to enter. Mr. Lorry got his arm securely round the daughter's waist, and held her; for he felt that she was sinking.

"A—a—a—business, business!" he urged, with a moisture that was not of business shining on his cheek. "Come in, come in!"

"I am afraid of it," she answered, shuddering.

"Of it? What?"

"I mean of him. Of my father."

Rendered in a manner desperate, by her state and by the beckoning of their conductor, he drew over his neck the arm that shook upon his shoulder, lifted her a little, and hurried her into the room. He set her down just within the door, and held her, clinging to him.

Defarge drew out the key, closed the door, locked it on the inside, took out the key again, and held it in his hand. All this he did, methodically, and with as loud and harsh an accompaniment of noise as he could make. Finally, he walked across the room with a measured tread to where the window was. He stopped there, and faced around.

The garret, built to be a depository for firewood and the like, was dim and dark: for the window of dormer shape was in truth a door in the roof, with a little crane over it for the hoisting up of stores from the street: unglazed, and closing up the middle in two pieces, like any other door of French construction. To exclude the cold, one half of this door was fast closed, and the other was opened but a very little way. Such a scanty portion of light was admitted through these means, that it was difficult, on first coming in, to see anything; and long habit alone could have slowly formed in any one, the ability to do any work requiring nicety in such obscurity. Yet, work of that kind was being done in the garret; for, with his back towards the door, and his face towards the window where the keeper of the wine-shop stood looking at him, a white-haired man sat on a low bench, stooping forward and very busy, making shoes.

*   *   *   *   *   *   *   *

6 *The Shoemaker*

"GOOD DAY!" said Monsieur Defarge, looking down at the white head that bent low over the shoemaking.

It was raised for a moment, and a very faint voice responded to the salutation, as if it were at a distance:

"Good day!"

"You are still hard at work, I see?"

After a long silence, the head was lifted for another moment, and the voice replied, "Yes—I am working." This time, a pair of haggard eyes had looked at the questioner, before the face had dropped again.

The faintness of the voice was pitiable and dreadful. It was not the faintness of physical weakness, though confinement and hard fare no doubt had their part in it. Its deplorable peculiarity was, that it was the faintness of solitude and disuse. It was like the last feeble echo of a sound made long and long ago. So entirely had it lost the life and resonance of the human voice, that it affected the senses like a once beautiful colour faded away into a poor weak stain. So sunken and suppressed it was, that it was like a voice underground. So expressive it was, of a hopeless and lost creature, that a famished traveller, wearied out by lonely wandering in a wilderness, would have remembered home and friends in such a tone before lying down to die.

Some minutes of silent work had passed, and the haggard eyes had looked up again; not with any interest or curiosity, but with a dull mechanical perception, beforehand, that the spot where the only visitor they were aware of had stood, was not yet empty.

"I want," said Defarge, who had not removed his gaze from the shoemaker, "to let in a little more light here. You can bear a little more?"

The shoemaker stopped his work; looked with a vacant air of listening, at the floor on one side of him; then similarly, at the floor on the other side of him; then upward at the speaker.

"What did you say?"

"You can bear a little more light?"

"I must bear it, if you let it in." (Laying the palest shadow of a stress upon the second word.)

The opened half-door was opened a little further, and secured at that angle for the time. A broad ray of light fell into the garret, and showed the workman with an unfinished shoe upon his lap, pausing in his labour. His few common tools and various scraps of leather were at his feet and on his bench. He had a white beard, raggedly cut, but not very long, a hollow face, and exceedingly bright eyes. The hollowness and thinness of his face would have caused them to look large, under his yet dark eyebrows and his confused white hair, though they had been really otherwise; but, they were naturally large, and looked unnaturally so. His yellow rags of shirt lay open at the throat, and showed his body to be withered and worn. He, and his old canvas frock, and his loose stockings, and all his poor tatters of clothes, had, in a long seclusion from direct light and air, faded down to such a dull uniformity of parchment-yellow, that it would have been hard to say which was which.

He had put up a hand between his eyes and the light, and the very bones of it seemed transparent. So he sat, with a steadfastly vacant gaze, pausing in his work. He never looked at the figure before him, without first looking down on this side of himself, then on that, as if he had lost the habit of associating place with sound; he never spoke, without first wandering in this manner, and forgetting to speak.

"Are you going to finish that pair of shoes to-day?" asked Defarge, motioning to Mr. Lorry to come forward.

"What did you say?"

"Do you mean to finish that pair of shoes to-day?"

"I can't say that I mean to. I suppose so. I don't know."

But, the question reminded him of his work, and he bent over it again.

Mr. Lorry came silently forward, leaving the daughter by the door. When he had stood, for a minute or two, by the side of Defarge, the shoemaker looked up. He showed no surprise at seeing another figure, but the unsteady fingers of one of his hands strayed to his lips as he looked at it (his lips and his nails were of the same pale lead-colour), and then the hand dropped to his work, and he once more bent over the shoe. The look and the action had occupied but an instant.

"You have a visitor, you see," said Monsieur Defarge.

"What did you say?"

"Here is a visitor."

The shoemaker looked up as before, but without removing a hand from his work.

"Come!" said Defarge. "Here is monsieur, who knows a well-made shoe when he sees one. Show him that shoe you are working at. Take it, monsieur."

Mr. Lorry took it in his hand.

"Tell monsieur what kind of shoe it is, and the maker's name."

There was a longer pause than usual, before the shoe-maker replied:

"I forget what it was you asked me. What did you say?"

"I said, couldn't you describe the kind of shoe, for monsieur's information?"

"It is a lady's shoe. It is a young lady's walking-shoe. It is in the present mode. I never saw the mode. I have had a pattern in my hand." He glanced at the shoe with some little passing touch of pride.

"And the maker's name?" said Defarge.

Now that he had no work to hold, he laid the knuckles of the right hand in the hollow of the left, and then the knuckles of the left hand in the hollow of the right, and then passed a hand across his bearded chin, and so on in regular changes, without a moment's intermission. The task of recalling him from the vacancy into which he always sank when he had spoken was like recalling some very weak person from a swoon, or endeavouring, in the hope of some disclosure, to stay the spirit of a fast-dying man.

"Did you ask me for my name?"

"Assuredly I did."

"One Hundred and Five, North Tower."

"Is that all?"

"One Hundred and Five, North Tower."

With a weary sound that was not a sigh, nor a groan, he bent to work again, until the silence was again broken.

"You are not a shoemaker by trade?" said Mr. Lorry, looking steadfastly at him.

His haggard eyes turned to Defarge as if he would have

transferred the question to him: but as no help came from that quarter, they turned back on the questioner when they had sought the ground.

"I am not a shoemaker by trade? No, I was not a shoemaker by trade. I—I learnt it here. I taught myself. I asked leave to—"

He lapsed away, even for minutes, ringing those measured changes on his hands the whole time. His eyes came slowly back, at last, to the face from which they had wandered; when they rested on it, he started, and resumed, in the manner of a sleeper that moment awake, reverting to a subject of last night.

"I asked leave to teach myself, and I got it with much difficulty after a long while, and I have made shoes ever since."

As he held out his hand for the shoe that had been taken from him, Mr. Lorry said, still looking steadfastly in his face:

"Monsieur Manette, do you remember nothing of me?"

The shoe dropped to the ground, and he sat looking fixedly at the questioner.

"Monsieur Manette"—Mr. Lorry laid his hand upon Defarge's arm—"do you remember nothing of this man? Look at him. Look at me. Is there no old banker, no old business, no old servant, no old time, rising in your mind, Monsieur Manette?"

As the captive of many years sat looking fixedly, by turns, at Mr. Lorry and Defarge, some long-obliterated marks of an actively intent intelligence in the middle of the forehead, gradually forced themselves through the black mist that had fallen on him. They were overclouded again, they were fainter, they were gone; but they had been there. And so exactly was the expression repeated on the fair young face of her who had crept along the wall to a point where she could see him, and where she now stood looking at him, with hands which at first had been only raised in frightened compassion, if not even to keep him off and shut out the sight of him, but which were now extending towards him, trembling with eagerness to lay the spectral face upon her warm young breast, and love it back to life and hope—so exactly was the expression repeated (though in stronger characters) on her fair young face, that it looked as though it had passed like a moving light, from him to her.

Darkness had fallen on him in its place. He looked at the two, less and less attentively, and his eyes in gloomy abstraction sought the ground and looked about him in the old way. Finally, with a deep long sigh, he took the shoe up, and resumed his work.

"Have you recognised him, monsieur?" asked Defarge in a whisper.

"Yes; for a moment. At first I thought it quite hopeless, but I have unquestionably seen, for a single moment, the face that I once knew so well. Hush! Let us draw further back. Hush!"

She had moved from the wall of the garret, very near to the bench on which he sat. There was something awful in his unconsciousness of the figure that could have put out its hand and touched him as he stooped over his labour.

Not a word was spoken, not a sound was made. She stood, like a spirit, beside him, and he bent over his work.

It happened, at length, that he had occasion to change the instrument in his hand, for his shoemaker's knife. It lay on that side of him which was not the side on which she stood. He had taken it up, and was stooping to work again, when his eyes caught the skirt of her dress. He raised them, and saw her face. The two spectators started forward, but she stayed them with a motion of her hand. She had no fear of his striking at her with the knife, though they had.

He stared at her with a fearful look, and after a while his lips began to form some words, though no sound proceeded from them. By degrees, in the pauses of his quick and laboured breathing, he was heard to say:

"What is this?"

With the tears streaming down her face, she put her two hands to her lips, and kissed them to him; then clasped them on her breast, as if she laid his ruined head there.

"You are not the gaoler's daughter?"

She sighed, "No."

"Who are you?"

Not yet trusting the tones of her voice, she sat down on the bench beside him. He recoiled, but she laid her hand upon his arm. A strange thrill struck him when she did so, and visibly passed over his frame; he laid the knife down softly, as he sat staring at her.

Her golden hair, which she wore in long curls, had been hurriedly pushed aside, and fell down over her neck. Advancing his hand by little and little, he took it up and looked at it. In the midst of the action he went astray, and, with another deep sigh, fell to work at his shoemaking.

But not for long. Releasing his arm, she laid her hand upon his shoulder. After looking doubtfully at it, two or three times, as if to be sure that it was really there, he laid down his work, put his hand to his neck, and took off a blackened string with a scrap of folded rag attached to it. He opened this, carefully, on his knee, and it contained a very little quantity of hair: not more than one or two long golden hairs, which he had, in some old day, wound off upon his finger.

He took her hair into his hand again, and looked closely at it. "It is the same. How can it be! When was it! How was it!"

As the concentrating expression returned to his forehead, he seemed to become conscious that it was in hers too. He turned her full to the light, and looked at her.

"She had laid her head upon my shoulder, that night when I was summoned out—she had a fear of my going, though I had none—and when I was brought to the North Tower they found these upon my sleeve. 'You will leave me them? They can never help me to escape in the body, though they may in the spirit.' Those were the words I said. I remember them very well."

He formed this speech with his lips many times before he could utter it. But when he did find spoken words for it, they came to him coherently, though slowly.

"How was this?—*Was it you?*"

Once more, the two spectators started, as he turned upon her with a frightful suddenness. But she sat perfectly still in his grasp, and only said, in a low voice, "I entreat you, good gentlemen, do not come near us, do not speak, do not move!"

"Hark!" he exclaimed. "Whose voice was that?"

His hands released her as he uttered this cry, and went up to his white hair, which they tore in a frenzy. It died out, as everything but his shoemaking did die out of him, and he refolded his little packet and tried to secure it in his breast; but he still looked at her, and gloomily shook his head.

"No, no, no; you are too young, too blooming. It can't be. See what the prisoner is. These are not the hands she knew, this is not the face she knew, this is not a voice she ever heard. No, no. She was—and he was—before the slow years of the North Tower—ages ago. What is your name, my gentle angel?"

Hailing his softened tone and manner, his daughter fell upon her knees before him, with her appealing hands upon his breast.

"O, sir, at another time you shall know my name, and who my mother was, and who my father, and how I never knew their hard, hard history. But I cannot tell you at this time, and I cannot tell you here. All that I may tell you, here and now, is, that I pray to you to touch me and to bless me. Kiss me, kiss me! O my dear, my dear!"

His cold white head mingled with her radiant hair, which warmed and lighted it as though it were the light of Freedom shining on him.

"If you hear in my voice—I don't know that it is so, but I hope it is—if you hear in my voice any resemblance to a voice that once was sweet music in your ears, weep for it, weep for it! If you touch, in touching my hair, anything that recalls a beloved head that lay on your breast when you were young and free, weep for it, weep for it! If, when I hint to you of a Home that is before us, where I will be true to you with all my duty and with all my faithful service, I bring back the remembrance of a Home long desolate, while your poor heart pined away, weep for it, weep for it!"

She held him closer round the neck, and rocked him on her breast like a child.

"If, when I tell you, dearest dear, that your agony is over, and that I have come here to take you from it, and that we go to England to be at peace and at rest, I cause you to think of your useful life laid waste, and of our native France so wicked to you, weep for it, weep for it! And if, when I shall tell you of my name, and of my father who is living, and of my mother who is dead, you learn that I have to kneel to my honoured father, and implore his pardon for having never for his sake striven all day and lain awake and wept all night, because the love of my poor mother hid his torture from me, weep for it, weep for it! Weep for her, then, and for me! Good gentlemen, thank God! I feel his sacred tears upon my face, and his sobs strike against my heart. O, see! Thank God for us, thank God!"

He had sunk in her arms, and his face dropped on her

breast: a sight so touching, yet so terrible in the tremendous wrong and suffering which had gone before it, that the two beholders covered their faces.

When the quiet of the garret had been long undisturbed, and his heaving breast and shaken form had long yielded to the calm that must follow all storms—emblem to humanity, of the rest and silence into which the storm called Life must hush at last—they came forward to raise the father and daughter from the ground. He had gradually dropped to the floor, and lay there in a lethargy, worn out. She had nestled down with him, that his head might lie upon her arm; and her hair drooping over him curtained him from the light.

"If, without disturbing him," she said, raising her hand to Mr. Lorry as he stooped over them, after repeated blowings of his nose, "all could be arranged for our leaving Paris at once, so that, from the very door, he could be taken away—"

"But, consider. Is he fit for the journey?" asked Mr. Lorry.

"More fit for that, I think, than to remain in this city, so dreadful to him."

"It is true," said Defarge, who was kneeling to look on and hear. "More than that; Monsieur Manette is, for all reasons, best out of France. Say, shall I hire a carriage and post-horses?"

"That's business," said Mr. Lorry, resuming on the shortest notice his methodical manners; "and if business is to be done, I had better do it."

"Then be so kind," urged Miss Manette, "as to leave us here. You see how composed he has become, and you cannot be afraid to leave him with me now. Why should you be? If you will lock the door to secure us from interruption, I do not doubt that you will find him, when you come back, as quiet as you leave him. In any case, I will take care of him until you return, and then we will remove him straight."

Both Mr. Lorry and Defarge were rather disinclined to this course, and in favour of one of them remaining. But, as there were not only carriage and horses to be seen to, but travelling papers; and as time pressed, for the day was drawing to an end, it came at last to their hastily dividing the business that was necessary to be done, and hurrying away to do it.

Then, as the darkness closed in, the daughter laid her head down on the hard ground close at the father's side, and watched him. The darkness deepened and deepened, and they both lay quiet, until a light gleamed through the chinks in the wall.

Mr. Lorry and Monsieur Defarge had made all ready for the journey, and had brought with them, besides travelling cloaks and wrappers, bread and meat, wine, and hot coffee. Monsieur Defarge put this provender, and the lamp he carried, on the shoemaker's bench (there was nothing else in the garret but a pallet bed), and he and Mr. Lorry roused the captive, and assisted him to his feet.

No human intelligence could have read the mysteries of his mind, in the scared blank wonder of his face. Whether he knew what had happened, whether he recollected what they had said to him, whether he knew that he was free, were questions which no sagacity could have solved. They tried speaking to him; but, he was so confused, and so very slow to answer, that they took fright at his bewilderment, and agreed for the time to tamper with him no more. He had a wild, lost manner of occasionally clasping his head in his hands, that had not been seen in him before; yet, he had some pleasure in the mere sound of his daughter's voice, and invariably turned to it when she spoke.

In the submissive way of one long accustomed to obey under coercion, he ate and drank what they gave him to eat and drink, and put on the cloak and other wrappings that they gave him to wear. He readily responded to his daughter's drawing her arm through his, and took—and kept—her hand in both his own.

They began to descend; Monsieur Defarge going first with the lamp, Mr. Lorry closing the little procession. They had not traversed many steps of the long main staircase when he stopped, and stared at the roof and round at the walls.

"You remember the place, my father? You remember coming up here?"

"What did you say?"

But, before she could repeat the question, he murmured an answer as if she had repeated it.

"Remember? No, I don't remember. It was so very long ago."

That he had no recollection whatever of his having been brought from his prison to that house was apparent to them. They heard him mutter, "One Hundred and Five, North Tower"; and when he looked about him, it evidently was for the strong fortress-walls which had long encom-passed him. On their reaching the courtyard he instinctively altered his tread, as being in expectation of a drawbridge; and when there was no drawbridge, and he saw the carriage waiting in the open street, he dropped his daughter's hand and clasped his head again.

No crowd was about the door; no people were discern-ible at any of the many windows; not even a chance passer-by was in the street. An unnatural silence and deser-tion reigned there. Only one soul was to be seen, and that was Madame Defarge—who leaned against the door-post, knitting, and saw nothing.

The prisoner had got into a coach, and his daughter had followed him, when Mr. Lorry's feet were arrested on the step by his asking, miserably, for his shoemaking tools and the unfinished shoes. Madame Defarge immediately called to her husband that she would get them, and went, knitting, out of the lamplight, through the courtyard. She quickly brought them down and handed them in— and immediately afterwards leaned against the door-post, knitting, and saw nothing.

Defarge got upon the box, and gave the word "To the Barrier!" The postilion cracked his whip, and they clat-tered away under the feeble over-swinging lamps.

Under the over-swinging lamps—swinging ever brighter in the better streets, and ever dimmer in the worse—and by lighted shops, gay crowds, illuminated coffee-houses, and theatre-doors, to one of the city gates. Soldiers with lanterns, at the guard-house there. "Your papers, travel-lers!" "See here then, Monsieur the Officer," said Defarge, getting down, and taking him gravely apart, "these are the papers of monsieur inside, with the white head. They were consigned to me, with him, at the—" He dropped his voice, there was a flutter among the military lanterns, and one of them being handed into the coach by an arm in uniform, the eyes connected with the arm looked, not an every-day or an every-night look, at monsieur with the white head. "It is well. Forward!" from the uniform. "Adieu!" from Defarge. And so, under a short grove of feebler and feebler over-swinging lamps, out under the great groves of stars.

Beneath that arch of unmoved and eternal lights; some,

so remote from this little earth that the learned tell us it is doubtful whether their rays have even yet discovered it, as a point in space where anything is suffered or done: the shadows of the night were broad and black. All through the cold and restless interval, until dawn, they once more whispered in the ears of Mr. Jarvis Lorry—sitting opposite the buried man who had been dug out, and wondering what subtle powers were for ever lost to him, and what were capable of restoration—the old inquiry:

"I hope you care to be recalled to life?"

And the old answer:

"I can't say."

BOOK THE SECOND

The Golden Thread

The Year

BOOK THE SECOND

1 Five Years Later

TELLSON'S BANK by Temple Bar was an old-fashioned place, even in the year one thousand seven hundred and eighty. It was very small, very dark, very ugly, very incommodious. It was an old-fashioned place, moreover, in the moral attribute that the partners in the House were proud of its smallness, proud of its darkness, proud of its ugliness, proud of its incommodiousness. They were even boastful of its eminence in those particulars, and were fired by an express conviction that, if it were less objectionable, it would be less respectable. This was no passive belief, but an active weapon which they flashed at more convenient places of business. Tellson's (they said) wanted no elbowroom, Tellson's wanted no light, Tellson's wanted no embellishment. Noakes and Co.'s might, or Snooks Brothers' might; but Tellson's, thank Heaven!—

Any one of these partners would have disinherited his son on the question of rebuilding Tellson's. In this respect the House was much on a par with the Country, which did very often disinherit its sons for suggesting improvements in laws and customs that had long been highly objectionable, but were only the more respectable.

Thus it had come to pass, that Tellson's was the triumphant perfection of inconvenience. After bursting open a door of idiotic obstinacy, with a weak rattle in its throat, you fell into Tellson's down two steps, and came to your senses in a miserable little shop, with two little counters, where the oldest of men made your cheque shake as if the wind rustled it, while they examined the signature by the dingiest of windows, which were always under a showerbath of mud from Fleet Street, and which were made the dingier by their own iron bars proper, and the heavy shadow of Temple Bar. If your business necessitated your seeing "the House," you were put into a species of Condemned Hold at the back, where you meditated on a mis-

spent life, until the House came with its hands in its
pockets, and you could hardly blink at it in the dismal twilight. Your money came out of, or went into, wormy old
wooden drawers, particles of which flew up your nose and
down your throat when they were opened and shut. Your
bank-notes had a musty odour, as if they were fast decom-
posing into rags again. Your plate was stowed away among
the neighbouring cesspools, and evil communications cor-
rupted its good polish in a day or two. Your deeds got into
extemporised strong-rooms made of kitchens and scul-
leries, and fretted all the fat out of their parchments into
the banking-house air. Your lighter boxes of family papers
went upstairs into a Barmecide room, that always had a
great dining-table in it and never had a dinner, and where,
even in the year one thousand seven hundred and eighty,
the first letters written to you by your old love, or by your
little children, were but newly released from the horror of
being ogled through the windows, by the heads exposed on
Temple Bar with an insensate brutality and ferocity worthy
of Abyssinia or Ashantee.

But indeed, at that time, putting to death was a recipe
much in vogue with all trades and professions, and not
least of all with Tellson's. Death is Nature's remedy for
all things, and why not Legislation's? Accordingly, the
forger was put to Death; the utterer of a bad note was put
to Death; the unlawful opener of a letter was put to
Death; the purloiner of forty shillings and sixpence was
put to Death; the holder of a horse at Tellson's door,
who made off with it, was put to Death; the coiner of a
bad shilling was put to Death; the sounders of three-
fourths of the notes in the whole gamut of Crime were
put to Death. Not that it did the least good in the way of
prevention—it might almost have been worth remarking
that the fact was exactly the reverse—but, it cleared off
(as to this world) the trouble of each particular case, and
left nothing else connected with it to be looked after. Thus,
Tellson's, in its day, like greater places of business, its
contemporaries, had taken so many lives, that, if the heads
laid low before it had been ranged on Temple Bar instead
of being privately disposed of, they would probably have
excluded what little light the ground floor had, in a rather
significant manner.

Cramped in all kinds of dim cupboards and hutches at
Tellson's, the oldest of men carried on the business gravely.

When they took a young man into Tellson's London house, they hid him somewhere till he was old. They kept him in a dark place, like a cheese, until he had the full Tellson flavour and blue-mould upon him. Then only was he permitted to be seen, spectacularly poring over large books, and casting his breeches and gaiters into the general weight of the establishment.

Outside Tellson's—never by any means in it, unless called in—was an odd-job-man, an occasional porter and messenger, who served as the live sign of the house. He was never absent during business hours, unless upon an errand, and then he was represented by his son: a grisly urchin of twelve, who was his express image. People understood that Tellson's, in a stately way, tolerated the odd-job-man. The house had always tolerated some person in that capacity, and time and tide had drifted this person to the post. His surname was Cruncher, and on the youthful occasion of his renouncing by proxy the works of darkness, in the easterly parish church of Hounsditch, he had received the added appellation of Jerry.

The scene was Mr. Cruncher's private lodging in Hangingsword Alley, Whitefriars: the time, half-past seven of the clock on a windy March morning, Anno Domini seventeen hundred and eighty. (Mr. Cruncher himself always spoke of the year of our Lord as Anna Dominoes: apparently under the impression that the Christian era dated from the invention of a popular game, by a lady who had bestowed her name upon it.)

Mr. Cruncher's apartments were not in a savoury neighbourhood, and were but two in number, even if a closet with a single pane of glass in it might be counted as one. But they were very decently kept. Early as it was, on the windy March morning, the room in which he lay abed was already scrubbed throughout; and between the cups and saucers arranged for breakfast, and the lumbering deal table, a very clean white cloth was spread.

Mr. Cruncher reposed under a patchwork counterpane, like a Harlequin at home. At first, he slept heavily, but, by degrees, began to roll and surge in bed, until he rose above the surface, with his spiky hair looking as if it must tear the sheets to ribbons. At which juncture, he exclaimed, in a voice of dire exasperation:

"Bust me, if she ain't at it agin!"

A woman of orderly and industrious appearance rose

from her knees in a corner, with sufficient haste and trepidation to show that she was the person referred to.

"What!" said Mr. Cruncher, looking out of bed for a boot. "You're at it agin, are you?"

After hailing the morn with this second salutation, he threw a boot at the woman as a third. It was a very muddy boot, and may introduce the odd circumstance connected with Mr. Cruncher's domestic economy, that, whereas he often came home after banking hours with clean boots, he often got up next morning to find the same boots covered with clay.

"What," said Mr. Cruncher, varying his apostrophe after missing his mark, "what are you up to, Aggerawayter?"

"I was only saying my prayers."

"Saying your prayers! You're a nice woman! What do you mean by flopping yourself down and praying agin me?"

"I was not praying against you; I was praying for you."

"You weren't. And if you were, I won't be took the liberty with. Here! Your mother's a nice woman, young Jerry, going a praying agin your father's prosperity. You've got a dutiful mother, you have, my son. You've got a religious mother, you have, my boy: going and flopping herself down, and praying that the bread-and-butter may be snatched out of the mouth of her only child."

Master Cruncher (who was in his shirt) took this very ill, and, turning to his mother, strongly deprecated any praying away of his personal board.

"And what do you suppose, you conceited female," said Mr. Cruncher, with unconscious inconsistency, "that the worth of *your* prayers may be? Name the price that you put *your* prayers at!"

"They only come from the heart, Jerry. They are worth no more than that."

"Worth no more than that," repeated Mr. Cruncher. "They ain't worth much, then. Whether or no, I won't be prayed agin, I tell you. I can't afford it. I'm not a-going to be made unlucky by *your* sneaking. If you must go flopping yourself down, flop in favour of your husband and child, and not in opposition to 'em. If I had had any but a unnat'ral wife, and this poor boy had had any but a unnat'ral mother, I might have made some money last week instead of being counterprayed and countermined and religiously circumwented into the worst of luck. B-u-u-ust me!" said Mr. Cruncher, who all this time had been putting on his clothes, "if I ain't, what with piety and one blowed thing and another, been choused this last week into as bad luck as ever a poor devil of a honest tradesman met with! Young Jerry, dress yourself, my boy, and while I clean my boots keep a eye upon your mother now and then, and if you see any signs of more flopping, give me a call. For, I tell you," here he addressed his wife once more, "I won't be gone agin, in this manner. I am as rickety as a hackney-coach, I'm as sleepy as laudanum, my lines is strained to that degree that I shouldn't know, if it wasn't for the pain in 'em, which was me and which somebody else, yet I'm none the better for it in pocket; and it's my suspicion that you've been at it from morning to night to prevent me from being the better for it in pocket, and I won't put up with it. Aggerawayter, and what do you say now!"

Growling, in addition, such phrases as "Ah! yes! You're religious, too. You wouldn't put yourself in opposition to the interests of your husband and child, would you? Not you!" and throwing off other sarcastic sparks from the whirling grindstone of his indignation, Mr. Cruncher betook himself to his boot-cleaning and his general preparation for business. In the meantime, his son, whose head was garnished with tenderer spikes, and whose young eyes stood close by one another, as his father's did, kept the required watch upon his mother. He greatly disturbed that poor woman at intervals, by darting out of his sleeping closet, where he made his toilet, with a suppressed cry of "You are going to flop, Mother. Halloa, Father!" and, after raising this fictitious alarm, darting in again with an undutiful grin.

Mr. Cruncher's temper was not at all improved when he came to his breakfast. He resented Mrs. Cruncher's saying grace with particular animosity.

"Now, Aggerawayter! What are you up to? At it agin?"

His wife explained that she had merely "asked a blessing."

"Don't do it!" said Mr. Cruncher, looking about, as if he rather expected to see the loaf disappear under the efficacy of his wife's petitions. "I ain't a going to be blest out of house and home. I won't have my wittles blest off my table. Keep still!"

Exceedingly red-eyed and grim, as if he had been up all night at a party which had taken anything but a convivial turn, Jerry Cruncher worried his breakfast rather than ate it, growling over it like any four-footed inmate of a menagerie. Towards nine o'clock he smoothed his ruffled aspect, and, presenting as respectful and business-like an exterior as he could overlay his natural self with, issued forth to the occupation of the day.

It could scarcely be called a trade, in spite of his favourite description of himself as "a honest tradesman." His stock consisted of a wooden stool, made out of a broken-backed chair cut down, which stool young Jerry, walking at his father's side, carried every morning to beneath the banking-house window that was nearest Temple Bar; where, with the addition of the first handful of straw that could be gleaned from any passing vehicle to keep the cold and wet from the odd-job-man's feet, it formed the encampment for the day. On this post of his, Mr. Cruncher was as well known to Fleet Street and the Temple, as the Bar itself—and was almost as ill-looking.

Encamped at a quarter before nine, in good time to touch his three-cornered hat to the oldest of men as they passed in to Tellson's, Jerry took up his station on this windy March morning, with young Jerry standing by him, when not engaged in making forays through the Bar, to inflict bodily and mental injuries of an acute description on passing boys who were small enough for his amiable purpose. Father and son, extremely like each other, looking silently on at the morning traffic in Fleet Street, with their two heads as near to one another as the two eyes of each were, bore a considerable resemblance to a pair of monkeys. The resemblance was not lessened by the accidental circumstance, that the mature Jerry bit and spat out straw, while the twinkling eyes of the youthful Jerry were as restlessly watchful of him as of everything else in Fleet Street.

The head of one of the regular indoor messengers attached to Tellson's establishment was put through the door, and the word was given:

"Porter wanted!"

"Hooray, Father! Here's an early job to begin with!"

Having thus given his parent God speed, young Jerry seated himself on the stool, entered on his reversionary interest in the straw his father had been chewing, and cogitated.

"Al-ways rusty! His fingers is al-ways rusty!" muttered young Jerry. "Where does my father get all that iron rust from? He don't get no iron rust here!"

2 *A Sight*

"YOU KNOW the Old Bailey well, no doubt?" said one of the oldest of clerks to Jerry the messenger.

"Yes, sir," returned Jerry, in something of a dogged manner. "I *do* know the Bailey."

"Just so. And you know Mr. Lorry."

"I know Mr. Lorry, sir, much better than I know the Bailey. Much better," said Jerry, not unlike a reluctant witness at the establishment in question, "than I, as a honest tradesman, wish to know the Bailey."

"Very well. Find the door where the witnesses go in, and show the doorkeeper this note for Mr. Lorry. He will then let you in."

"Into the court, sir?"

"Into the court."

Mr. Cruncher's eyes seemed to get a little closer to one another, and to interchange the inquiry, "What do you think of this?"

"Am I to wait in the court, sir?" he asked, as the result of that conference.

"I am going to tell you. The doorkeeper will pass the note to Mr. Lorry, and do you make any gesture that will attract Mr. Lorry's attention, and show him where you stand. Then what you have to do, is, to remain there until he wants you."

"Is that all, sir?"

"That's all. He wishes to have a messenger at hand. This is to tell him you are there."

As the ancient clerk deliberately folded and super-scribed the note, Mr. Cruncher, after surveying him in silence until he came to the blotting-paper stage, remarked:

"I suppose they'll be trying Forgeries this morning?"

"Treason!"

"That's quartering," said Jerry. "Barbarous!"

"It is the law," remarked the ancient clerk, turning his surprised spectacles upon him. "It is the law."

"It's hard in the law to spile a man, I think. It's hard enough to kill him, but it's wery hard to spile him, sir."

"Not at all," returned the ancient clerk. "Speak well of the law. Take care of your chest and voice, my good friend, and leave the law to take care of itself. I give you that advice."

"It's the damp, sir, what settles on my chest and voice," said Jerry. "I leave you to judge what a damp way of earning a living mine is."

"Well, well," said the old clerk; "we all have our various ways of gaining a livelihood. Some of us have damp ways, and some of us have dry ways. Here is the letter. Go along."

Jerry took the letter, and, remarking to himself with less internal deference than he made an outward show of, "You are a lean old one, too," made his bow, informed his son, in passing, of his destination, and went his way.

They hanged at Tyburn, in those days, so the street outside Newgate had not obtained one infamous notoriety that has since attached to it. But, the gaol was a vile place in which most kinds of debauchery and villainy were practised, and where dire diseases were bred, that came into court with the prisoners, and sometimes rushed straight from the dock at my Lord Chief Justice himself, and pulled him off the bench. It had more than once happened, that the Judge in the black cap pronounced his own doom as certainly as the prisoner's, and even died before him. For the rest, the Old Bailey was famous as a kind of deadly inn-yard, from which pale travellers set out continually, in carts and coaches, on a violent passage into the other world: traversing some two miles and a half of public street and road, and shaming few good citizens, if any. So powerful is use, and so desirable to be good use in the beginning. It was famous, too, for the pillory, a wise old institution, that inflicted a punishment of which no one could foresee the extent; also, for the whipping-post, another dear old institution, very humanising and softening to behold in action; also, for extensive transactions in blood-money, another fragment of ancestral wisdom, systematically leading to the most frightful mercenary crimes that could be committed under Heaven. Altogether, the Old Bailey, at that date, was a choice illustration of the precept that "Whatever is, is right"; an aphorism that would be as final as it is lazy, did it not include the troublesome consequence, that nothing that ever was, was wrong.

Making his way through the tainted crowd, dispersed up and down this hideous scene of action, with the skill of a man accustomed to make his way quietly, the messenger found out the door he sought, and handed in his letter through a trap in it. For people then paid to see the play at the Old Bailey, just as they paid to see the play in Bedlam—only the former entertainment was much the dearer. Therefore, all the Old Bailey doors were well guarded—except, indeed, the social doors by which the criminals got there, and those were always left wide open.

After some delay and demur, the door grudgingly turned on its hinges a very little way, and allowed Mr. Jerry Cruncher to squeeze himself into court.

"What's on?" he asked, in a whisper, of the man he found himself next to.

"Nothing yet."

"What's coming on?"

"The treason case."

"The quartering one, eh?"

"Ah!" returned the man, with a relish; "he'll be drawn on a hurdle to be half hanged, and then he'll be taken down and sliced before his own face, and then his inside will be taken out and burnt while he looks on, and then his head will be chopped off, and he'll be cut into quarters. That's the sentence."

"If he's found guilty, you mean to say?" Jerry added, by way of proviso.

"Oh! they'll find him guilty," said the other. "Don't you be afraid of that."

Mr. Cruncher's attention was here diverted to the doorkeeper, whom he saw making his way to Mr. Lorry, with the note in his hand. Mr. Lorry sat at a table, among the gentlemen in wigs: not far from a wigged gentleman, the prisoner's counsel, who had a great bundle of papers, before him: and nearly opposite another wigged gentleman with his hands in his pockets, whose whole attention, when Mr. Cruncher looked at him then or afterwards, seemed to be concentrated on the ceiling of the court. After some gruff coughing and rubbing of his chin and signing with his hand, Jerry attracted the notice of Mr. Lorry, who had stood up to look for him, and who quietly nodded and sat down again.

"What's *he* got to do with this case?" asked the man he had spoken with.

"Blest if I know," said Jerry.

"What have *you* got to do with it, then, if a person may inquire?"

"Blest if I know that either," said Jerry.

The entrance of the judge, and a consequent great stir and settling down in the court, stopped the dialogue. Presently, the dock became the central point of interest. Two gaolers, who had been standing there, went out, and the prisoner was brought in, and put to the bar.

Everybody present, except the one wigged gentleman who looked at the ceiling, stared at him. All the human breath in the place rolled at him, like a sea, or a wind, or a fire. Eager faces strained round pillars and corners, to get a sight of him; spectators in back rows stood up, not to miss a hair of him; people on the floor of the court laid their hands on the shoulders of the people before them, to help themselves, at anybody's cost, to a view of him—stood a-tiptoe, got upon ledges, stood upon next to nothing, to see every inch of him. Conspicuous among these latter, like an animated bit of the spiked wall of Newgate, Jerry stood: aiming at the prisoner the beery breath of a whet he had taken as he came along, and discharging it to mingle with the waves of other beer, and gin, and tea, and coffee, and what not that flowed at him, and already broke upon the great windows behind him in an impure mist and rain.

The object of all this staring and blaring was a young man of about five-and-twenty, well-grown and well-looking, with a sunburnt cheek and a dark eye. His condition was that of a young gentleman. He was plainly dressed in black, or very dark gray, and his hair, which was long and dark, was gathered in a ribbon at the back of his neck; more to be out of his way than for ornament. As an emotion of the mind will express itself through any covering of the body, so the paleness which his situation engendered came through the brown upon his cheek, showing the soul to be stronger than the sun. He was otherwise quite self-possessed, bowed to the judge, and stood quiet.

The sort of interest with which this man was stared and breathed at was not a sort that elevated humanity. Had he stood in peril of a less horrible sentence—had there been a chance of any one of its savage details being spared —by just so much would he have lost in his fascination. The form that was to be doomed to be so shamefully mangled was the sight; the immortal creature that was to be so butchered and torn asunder, yielded the sensation. Whatever gloss the various spectators put upon the interest, according to their several arts and powers of self-deceit, the interest was, at the root of it, ogreish.

Silence in the court! Charles Darnay had yesterday pleaded not guilty to an indictment denouncing him (with infinite jingle and jangle) for that he was a false traitor to our serene, illustrious, excellent and so forth, prince, our Lord the King, by reason of his having, on divers occasions, and by divers means and ways, assisted Lewis, the French King, in his wars against our said serene, illustrious, excellent, and so forth; that was to say, by coming and going, between the dominions of our said serene, illustrious, excellent, and so forth, and those of the said French Lewis, and wickedly, falsely, traitorously, and otherwise evil-adverbiously, revealing to the said French Lewis what forces our said serene, illustrious, excellent, and so forth, had in preparation to send to Canada and North America. This much, Jerry, with his head becoming more and more spiky as the law terms bristled it, made out with huge satisfaction, and so arrived circuitously at the understanding that the aforesaid, and over and over again aforesaid, Charles Darnay, stood there before him upon his trial; that the jury were swearing in; and that Mr. Attorney-General was making ready to speak.

The accused, who was (and who knew he was) being mentally hanged, beheaded, and quartered, by everybody there, neither flinched from the situation, nor assumed any theatrical air in it. He was quiet and attentive; watched the opening proceedings with a grave interest; and stood with his hands resting on the slab of wood before him, so composedly, that they had not displaced a leaf of the herbs with which it was strewn. The court was all bestrewn with herbs and sprinkled with vinegar, as a precaution against gaol air and gaol fever.

Over the prisoner's head there was a mirror, to throw the light down upon him. Crowds of the wicked and the wretched had been reflected in it, and had passed from its surface and this earth's together. Haunted in a most ghastly manner that abominable place would have been, if the glass could ever have rendered back its reflections, as the ocean is one day to give up its dead. Some passing thought of the infamy and disgrace for which it had been reserved may have struck the prisoner's mind. Be that as it may, a change in his position making him conscious of a bar of light across his face, he looked up; and when he saw the glass his face flushed, and his right hand pushed the herbs away.

It happened, that the action turned his face to that side of the court which was on his left. About on a level with his eyes, there sat, in that corner of the Judge's bench, two persons upon whom his look immediately rested; so immediately, and so much to the changing of his aspect, that all the eyes that were turned upon him, turned to them.

The spectators saw in the two figures, a young lady of little more than twenty, and a gentleman who was evidently her father; a man of a very remarkable appearance in respect of the absolute whiteness of his hair, and a certain indescribable intensity of face: not of an active kind, but pondering and self-communing. When this expression was upon him, he looked as if he were old; but when it was stirred and broken up—as it was now, in a moment, on his speaking to his daughter—he became a handsome man, not past the prime of life.

His daughter had one of her hands drawn through his arm, as she sat by him, and the other pressed upon it. She had drawn close to him, in her dread of the scene, and in her pity for the prisoner. Her forehead had been strikingly expressive of an engrossing terror and compassion that saw nothing but the peril of the accused. This had been so very noticeable, so very powerfully and naturally shown, that starers who had had no pity for him were touched by her; and the whisper went about: "Who are they?"

Jerry, the messenger, who had made his own observations, in his own manner, and who had been sucking the rust off his fingers in his absorption, stretched his neck to hear who they were. The crowd about him had pressed and passed the inquiry on to the nearest attendant, and from him it had been more slowly pressed and passed back; at last it got to Jerry:

"Witnesses."

"For which side?"

"Against."

"Against what side?"

"The prisoner's."

The Judge, whose eyes had gone in the general direction, recalled them, leaned back in his seat, and looked steadily at the man whose life was in his hand, as Mr. Attorney-General rose to spin the rope, grind the axe, and hammer the nails into the scaffold.

*   *   *   *   *   *   *   *

3   *A Disappointment*

MR. ATTORNEY-GENERAL had to inform the jury that the prisoner before them, though young in years, was old in the treasonable practices which claimed the forfeit of his life. That this correspondence with the public enemy was not a correspondence of to-day, or of yesterday, or even of last year, or of the year before. That, it was certain the prisoner had, for longer than that, been in the habit of passing and repassing between France and England, on secret business of which he could give no honest account. That, if it were in the nature of traitorous ways to thrive (which happily it never was), the real wickedness and guilt of his business might have remained undiscovered. That Providence, however, had put it into the heart of a person who was beyond fear and beyond reproach, to ferret out the nature of the prisoner's schemes, and, struck with horror, to disclose them to his Majesty's Chief Secretary of State and most honourable Privy Council. That this patriot would be produced before them. That his position and attitude were, on the whole, sublime. That he had been the prisoner's friend, but, at once in an auspicious and an evil hour detecting his infamy, had resolved to immolate the traitor he could no longer cherish in his bosom, on the sacred altar of his country. That, if statues were decreed in Britain, as in ancient Greece and Rome, to public benefactors, this shining citizen would assuredly have had one. That, as they were not so decreed, he probably would not have one. That Virtue, as had been

observed by the poets (in many passages which he well
knew the jury would have, word for word, at the tips of
their tongues; whereat the jury's countenances displayed a
guilty consciousness that they knew nothing about the passages), was in a manner contagious; more especially the
bright virtue known as patriotism, or love of country. That
the lofty example of this immaculate and unimpeachable
witness for the Crown, to refer to whom however unworth-
ily was an honour, had communicated itself to the prisoner's servant, and had engendered in him a holy
determination to examine his master's table-drawers and
pockets, and secrete his papers. That he (Mr. Attorney-
General) was prepared to hear some disparagement attempted of this admirable servant; but that, in a general
way, he preferred him to his (Mr. Attorney-General's)
brothers and sisters, and honoured him more than his (Mr.
Attorney-General's) father and mother. That he called with
confidence on the jury to come and do likewise. That the
evidence of these two witnesses, coupled with the documents of their discovering that would be produced, would
show the prisoner to have been furnished with lists of his
Majesty's forces, and of their disposition and preparation, both by sea and land, and would leave no doubt
that he had habitually conveyed such information to a
hostile power. That these lists could not be proved to be
in the prisoner's handwriting; but that it was all the same;
that, indeed, it was rather the better for the prosecution,
as showing the prisoner to be artful in his precautions.
That the proof would go back five years, and would show
the prisoner already engaged in these pernicious missions,
within a few weeks before the date of the very first action
fought between the British troops and the Americans.
That, for these reasons, the jury, being a loyal jury (as
he knew they were), and being a responsible jury (as *they*
knew they were), must positively find the prisoner guilty,
and make an end of him, whether they liked it or not. That
they never could lay their heads upon their pillows; that
they never could tolerate the idea of their wives laying their
heads upon their pillows; that they could never endure the
notion of their children laying their heads upon their pillows; in short, that there never more could be, for them or
theirs, any laying of heads upon pillows at all, unless the
prisoner's head was taken off. That head Mr. Attorney-
General concluded by demanding of them, in the name of

everything he could think of with a round turn in it, and
on the faith of his solemn asseveration that he already
considered the prisoner as good as dead and gone.

When the Attorney-General ceased, a buzz arose in the
court as if a cloud of great blue-flies were swarming about
the prisoner, in anticipation of what he was soon to become. When toned down again, the unimpeachable patriot
appeared in the witness-box.

Mr. Solicitor-General then, following his leader's lead,
examined the patriot: John Barsad, gentleman, by name.
The story of his pure soul was exactly what Mr. Attorney-
General had described it to be—perhaps, if it had a fault,
a little too exactly. Having released his noble bosom of its
burden, he would have modestly withdrawn himself, but
that the wigged gentleman with the papers before him, sitting not far from Mr. Lorry, begged to ask him a few
questions. The wigged gentleman sitting opposite, still
looking at the ceiling of the court.

Had he ever been a spy himself? No, he scorned the
base insinuation. What did he live upon? His property.
Where was his property? He didn't precisely remember
where it was. What was it? No business of anybody's. Had
he inherited it? Yes, he had. From whom? Distant relation. Very distant? Rather. Ever been in prison? Certainly
not. Never in a debtors' prison? Didn't see what that had
to do with it. Never in a debtors' prison?—Come, once
again. Never? Yes. How many times? Two or three times.
Not five or six? Perhaps. Of what profession? Gentleman.
Ever been kicked? Might have been. Frequently? No. Ever
kicked downstairs? Decidedly not; once received a kick
on the top of a staircase, and fell downstairs of his own
accord. Kicked on that occasion for cheating at dice?
Something to that effect was said by the intoxicated liar
who committed the assault, but it was not true. Swear it
was not true? Positively. Ever live by cheating at play?
Never. Ever live by play? Not more than other gentlemen
do. Ever borrow money of the prisoner? Yes. Ever pay
him? No. Was not this intimacy with the prisoner, in reality
a very slight one, forced upon the prisoner in coaches,
inns, and packets? No. Sure he saw the prisoner with these
lists? Certain. Knew no more about the lists? No. Had not
procured them himself, for instance? No. Expect to get
anything by this evidence? No. Not in regular government
pay and employment to lay traps? Oh dear no. Or to do

anything? Oh dear no. Swear that? Over and over again
No motives but motives of sheer patriotism? None what
ever.

The virtuous servant, Roger Cly, swore his way through
the case at a great rate. He had taken service with the
prisoner, in good faith and simplicity, four years ago. He
had asked the prisoner, aboard the Calais packet, if he
wanted a handy fellow, and the prisoner had engaged him
He had not asked the prisoner to take the handy fellow
as an act of charity—never thought of such a thing. He
began to have suspicions of the prisoner, and to keep an
eye upon him, soon afterwards. In arranging his clothes
while travelling, he had seen similar lists to these in the
prisoner's pockets, over and over again. He had taken these
lists from the drawer of the prisoner's desk. He had not
put them there first. He had seen the prisoner show these
identical lists to French gentlemen at Calais, and similar
lists to French gentlemen, both at Calais and Boulogne
He loved his country, and couldn't bear it, and had given
information. He had never been suspected of stealing a
silver teapot; he had been maligned respecting a mustard
pot, but it turned out to be only a plated one. He had
known the last witness seven or eight years; that was
merely a coincidence. He didn't call it a particularly curi
ous coincidence; most coincidences were curious. Neither
did he call it a curious coincidence that true patriotism
was *his* only motive too. He was a true Briton, and hoped
there were many like him.

The blue-flies buzzed again, and Mr. Attorney-General
called Mr. Jarvis Lorry.

"Mr. Jarvis Lorry, are you a clerk in Tellson's Bank?"

"I am."

"On a certain Friday night in November one thousand
seven hundred and seventy-five, did business occasion you
to travel between London and Dover by the mail?"

"It did."

"Were there any other passengers in the mail?"

"Two."

"Did they alight on the road in the course of the night?"

"They did."

"Mr. Lorry, look upon the prisoner. Was he one of
those two passengers?"

"I cannot undertake to say that he was."

"Does he resemble either of these two passengers?"

"Both were so wrapped up, and the night was so dark, and we were all so reserved, that I cannot undertake to say even that."

"Mr. Lorry, look again upon the prisoner. Supposing him wrapped up as those two passengers were, is there anything in his bulk and stature to render it unlikely that he was one of them?"

"No."

"You will not swear, Mr. Lorry, that he was not one of them?"

"No."

"So at least you say he may have been one of them?"

"Yes. Except that I remember them both to have been —like myself—timorous of highwaymen, and the prisoner has not a timorous air."

"Did you ever see a counterfeit of timidity, Mr. Lorry?"

"I certainly have seen that."

"Mr. Lorry, look once more upon the prisoner. Have you seen him, to your certain knowledge, before?"

"I have."

"When?"

"I was returning from France a few days afterwards, and at Calais, the prisoner came on board the packet-ship in which I returned, and made the voyage with me."

"At what hour did he come on board?"

"At a little after midnight."

"In the dead of the night. Was he the only passenger who came on board at that untimely hour?"

"He happened to be the only one."

"Never mind about 'happening,' Mr. Lorry. He was the only passenger who came on board in the dead of the night?"

"He was."

"Were you travelling alone, Mr. Lorry, or with any companion?"

"With two companions. A gentleman and lady. They are here."

"They are here. Had you any conversation with the prisoner?"

"Hardly any. The weather was stormy, and the passage long and rough, and I lay on a sofa, almost from shore to shore."

"Miss Manette!"

The young lady, to whom all eyes had been turned before, and were now turned again, stood up where she had sat. Her father rose with her, and kept her hand drawn through his arm.

"Miss Manette, look upon the prisoner."

To be confronted with such pity, and such earnest youth and beauty, was far more trying to the accused than to be confronted with all the crowd. Standing, as it were, apart with her on the edge of his grave, not all the staring curiosity that looked on could, for the moment, nerve him to remain quite still. His hurried right hand parcelled out the herbs before him into imaginary beds of flowers in a garden: and his efforts to control and steady his breathing shook the lips from which the colour rushed to his heart. The buzz of the great flies was loud again.

"Miss Manette, have you seen the prisoner before?"

"Yes, sir."

"Where?"

"On board of the packet-ship just now referred to, sir, and on the same occasion."

"You are the young lady just now referred to?"

"O! most unhappily, I am."

The plaintive tone of her compassion merged into the less musical voice of the judge, as he said something fiercely: "Answer the questions put to you, and make no remark upon them."

"Miss Manette, had you any conversation with the prisoner on that passage across the Channel?"

"Yes, sir."

"Recall it."

In the midst of a profound stillness, she faintly began: "When the gentleman came on board——"

"Do you mean the prisoner?" inquired the judge, knitting his brows.

"Yes, my Lord."

"Then say the prisoner."

"When the prisoner came on board, he noticed that my father," turning her eyes lovingly to him as he stood beside her, "was much fatigued and in a very weak state of health. My father was so reduced that I was afraid to take him out of the air, and I had made a bed for him on the deck near the cabin steps, and I sat on the deck at his side to take care of him. There were no other passengers that night, but we four. The prisoner was so good as to beg permission to advise me how I could shelter my father from the wind and weather, better than I had done. I had not known how to do it well, not understanding how the wind would set when we were out of the harbour. He did it for me. He expressed great gentleness and kindness for my father's state, and I am sure he felt it. That was the manner of our beginning to speak together."

"Let me interrupt you for a moment. Had he come on board alone?"

"No."

"How many were with him?"

"Two French gentlemen."

"Had they conferred together?"

"They had conferred together until the last moment, when it was necessary for the French gentlemen to be landed in their boat."

"Had any papers been handed about among them, similar to these lists?"

"Some papers had been handed about among them, but I don't know what papers."

"Like these in shape and size?"

"Possibly, but indeed I don't know, although they stood whispering very near to me: because they stood at the top of the cabin steps to have the light of the lamp that was hanging there; it was a dull lamp, and they spoke very low, and I did not hear what they said, and saw only that they looked at papers."

"Now, to the prisoner's conversation, Miss Manette."

"The prisoner was as open in his confidence with me—which arose out of my helpless situation—as he was kind, and good, and useful to my father. I hope," bursting into tears, "I may not repay him by doing him harm to-day."

Buzzing from the blue-flies.

"Miss Manette, if the prisoner does not perfectly understand that you give the evidence which it is your duty to give—which you must give—and which you cannot escape from giving—with great unwillingness, he is the only person present in that condition. Please to go on."

"He told me that he was travelling on business of a delicate and difficult nature which might get people into trouble, and that he was therefore travelling under an assumed name. He said that this business had, within a few days, taken him to France, and might, at intervals, take him backwards and forwards between France and England for a long time to come."

"Did he say anything about America, Miss Manette? Be particular."

"He tried to explain to me how that quarrel had arisen, and he said that, so far as he could judge, it was a wrong and foolish one on England's part. He added, in a jesting way, that perhaps George Washington might gain almost as great a name in history as George the Third. But there was no harm in his way of saying this: it was said laughingly, and to beguile the time."

Any strongly marked expression of face on the part of a chief actor in a scene of great interest to whom many eyes are directed will be unconsciously imitated by the spectators. Her forehead was painfully anxious and intent as she gave this evidence, and, in the pauses when she stopped for the judge to write it down, watched its effect upon the counsel for and against. Among the lookers-on there was the same expression in all quarters of the court; insomuch, that a great majority of the foreheads there might have been mirrors reflecting the witness, when the judge looked up from his notes to glare at that tremendous heresy about George Washington.

Mr. Attorney-General now signified to my Lord, that he deemed it necessary, as a matter of precaution and form, to call the young lady's father, Doctor Manette. Who was called accordingly.

"Doctor Manette, look upon the prisoner. Have you ever seen him before?"

"Once. When he called at my lodgings in London. Some three years, or three years and a half ago."

"Can you identify him as your fellow-passenger on board the packet, or speak to his conversation with your daughter?"

"Sir, I can do neither."

"Is there any particular and special reason for your being unable to do either?"

He answered, in a low voice, "There is."

"Has it been your misfortune to undergo a long imprisonment, without trial, or even accusation, in your native country, Doctor Manette?"

He answered, in a tone that went to every heart, "A long imprisonment."

"Were you newly released on the occasion in question?"

"They tell me so."

"Have you no remembrance of the occasion?"

"None. My mind is a blank, from some time—I cannot even say what time—when I employed myself, in my captivity, in making shoes, to the time when I found myself living in London with my dear daughter here. She had become familiar to me, when a gracious God restored my faculties; but, I am quite unable even to say how she had become familiar. I have no remembrance of the process."

Mr. Attorney-General sat down, and the father and daughter sat down together.

A singular circumstance then arose in the case. The object in hand being to show that the prisoner went down, with some fellow-plotter untracked, in the Dover mail on that Friday night in November five years ago, and got out of the mail in the night, as a blind, at a place where he did not remain, but from which he travelled back some dozen miles or more, to a garrison and dockyard, and there collected information; a witness was called to identify him as having been at the precise time required, in the coffee-room of an hotel in that garrison-and-dockyard town, waiting for another person. The prisoner's counsel was cross-examining this witness with no result, except that he had never seen the prisoner on any other occasion, when the wigged gentleman who had all this time been looking at the ceiling of the court, wrote a word or two on a little piece of paper, screwed it up, and tossed it to him. Opening this piece of paper in the next pause, the counsel looked with great attention and curiosity at the prisoner.

"You say again you are quite sure that it *was* the prisoner?"

The witness was quite sure.

"Did you ever see anybody very like the prisoner?"

Not so like (the witness said) as that he could be mistaken.

"Look well upon that gentleman, my learned friend there," pointing to him who had tossed the paper over, "and then look well upon the prisoner. How say you? Are they very like each other?"

Allowing for my learned friend's appearance being careless and slovenly if not debauched, they were sufficiently like each other to surprise, not only the witness, but everybody present, when they were thus brought into comparison. My Lord being prayed to bid my learned friend lay aside his wig, and giving no very gracious con-

sent, the likeness became much more remarkable. My
Lord inquired of Mr. Stryver (the prisoner's counsel),
whether they were next to try Mr. Carton (name of my
learned friend) for treason? But, Mr. Stryver replied to
my Lord, no; but he would ask the witness to tell him
whether what happened once might happen twice; whether
he would have been so confident if he had seen this illustration of his rashness sooner, whether he would be so confident, having seen it; and more. The upshot of which was,
to smash this witness like a crockery vessel, and shiver his
part of the case to useless lumber.

Mr. Cruncher had by this time taken quite a lunch of
rust off his fingers in his following of the evidence. He
had now to attend while Mr. Stryver fitted the prisoner's
case on the jury, like a compact suit of clothes; showing
them how the patriot, Barsad, was a hired spy and traitor,
an unblushing trafficker in blood, and one of the greatest
scoundrels upon earth since accursed Judas—which he
certainly did look rather like. How the virtuous servant,
Cly, was his friend and partner, and was worthy to be;
how the watchful eyes of those forgers and false swearers
had rested on the prisoner as a victim, because some family affairs in France, he being of French extraction, did
require his making those passages across the Channel—
though what those affairs were, a consideration for others
who were near and dear to him, forbade him, even for his
life, to disclose. How the evidence that had been warped
and wrested from the young lady, whose anguish in giving
it they had witnessed, came to nothing, involving the
mere little innocent gallantries and politenesses likely to
pass between any young gentleman and young lady so
thrown together—with the exception of that reference to
George Washington, which was altogether too extravagant
and impossible to be regarded in any other light than as a
monstrous joke. How it would be a weakness in the government to break down in this attempt to practise for popularity on the lowest national antipathies and fears, and
therefore Mr. Attorney-General had made the most of it;
how, nevertheless, it rested upon nothing, save that vile and
infamous character of evidence too often disfiguring such
cases, and of which the State Trials of this country were
full. But, there my Lord interposed (with as grave a face
as if it had not been true), saying that he could not sit upon
that Bench and suffer those allusions.

Mr. Stryver then called his few witnesses, and Mr. Cruncher had next to attend while Mr. Attorney-General turned the whole suit of clothes Mr. Stryver had fitted on the jury inside out; showing how Barsad and Cly were even a hundred times better than he had thought them, and the prisoner a hundred times worse. Lastly, came my Lord himself, turning the suit of clothes, now inside out, now outside in, but on the whole decidedly trimming and shaping them into grave-clothes for the prisoner.

And now, the jury turned to consider, and the great flies swarmed again.

Mr. Carton, who had so long sat looking at the ceiling of the court, changed neither his place nor his attitude, even in this excitement. While his learned friend, Mr. Stryver, massing his papers before him, whispered with those who sat near, and from time to time glanced anxiously at the jury; while all the spectators moved more or less, and grouped themselves anew; while even my Lord himself arose from his seat, and slowly paced up and down his platform, not unattended by a suspicion in the minds of the audience that his state was feverish; this one man sat leaning back, with his torn gown half off him, his untidy wig put on just as it had happened to light on his head after its removal, his hands in his pockets, and his eyes on the ceiling as they had been all day. Something especially reckless in his demeanour not only gave him a disreputable look, but so diminished the strong resemblance he undoubtedly bore to the prisoner (which his momentary earnestness, when they were compared together, had strengthened), that many of the lookers-on, taking note of him now, said to one another they would hardly have thought the two were so alike. Mr. Cruncher made the observation to his next neighbour, and added, "I'd hold half a guinea that *he* don't get no law work to do. Don't look like the sort of one to get any, do he?"

Yet, this Mr. Carton took in more of the details of the scene than he appeared to take in; for now, when Miss Manette's head dropped upon her father's breast, he was the first to see it, and to say audibly: "Officer! look to that young lady. Help the gentleman to take her out. Don't you see that she will fall!"

There was much commiseration for her as she was removed, and much sympathy with her father. It had evidently been a great distress to him to have the days of his imprisonment recalled. He had shown strong internal agitation when he was questioned, and that pondering or brooding look which made him old had been upon him, like a heavy cloud, ever since. As he passed out, the jury, who had turned back and paused a moment, spoke, through their foreman.

They were not agreed, and wished to retire. My Lord (perhaps with George Washington on his mind) showed some surprise that they were not agreed, but signified his pleasure that they should retire under watch and ward, and retired himself. The trial had lasted all day, and the lamps in the court were now being lighted. It began to be rumoured that the jury would be out a long while. The spectators dropped off to get refreshment, and the prisoner withdrew to the back of the dock, and sat down.

Mr. Lorry, who had gone out when the young lady and her father went out, now reappeared, and beckoned to Jerry: who, in the slackened interest, could easily get near him.

"Jerry, if you wish to take something to eat, you can. But, keep in the way. You will be sure to hear when the jury come in. Don't be a moment behind them, for I want you to take the verdict back to the bank. You are the quickest messenger I know, and will get to Temple Bar long before I can."

Jerry had just enough forehead to knuckle, and he knuckled it in acknowledgment of this communication and a shilling. Mr. Carton came up at the moment, and touched Mr. Lorry on the arm.

"How is the young lady?"

"She is greatly distressed; but her father is comforting her, and she feels the better for being out of court."

"I'll tell the prisoner so. It won't do for a respectable bank gentleman like you to be seen speaking to him publicly, you know."

Mr. Lorry reddened as if he were conscious of having debated the point in his mind, and Mr. Carton made his way to the outside of the bar. The way out of court lay in that direction, and Jerry followed him, all eyes, ears, and spikes.

"Mr. Darnay!"

The prisoner came forward directly.

"You will naturally be anxious to hear of the witness,

Miss Manette. She will do very well. You have seen the worst of her agitation."

"I am deeply sorry to have been the cause of it. Could you tell her so for me, with my fervent acknowledgments?"

"Yes, I could. I will, if you ask it."

Mr. Carton's manner was so careless as to be almost insolent. He stood, half turned from the prisoner, lounging with his elbow against the bar.

"I do ask it. Accept my cordial thanks."

"What," said Carton, still only half turned towards him, "do you expect, Mr. Darnay?"

"The worst."

"It's the wisest thing to expect, and the likeliest. But I think their withdrawing is in your favour."

Loitering on the way out of court not being allowed, Jerry heard no more: but left them—so like each other in feature, so unlike each other in manner—standing side by side, both reflected in the glass above them.

An hour and a half limped heavily away in the thief-and-rascal crowded passages below, even though assisted off with mutton pies and ale. The hoarse messenger, uncomfortably seated on a form after taking that refection, had dropped into a doze, when a loud murmur and a rapid tide of people setting up the stairs that led to the court carried him along with them.

"Jerry, Jerry!" Mr. Lorry was already calling at the door when he got there.

"Here, sir. It's a fight to get back again. Here I am, sir!"

Mr. Lorry handed him a paper through the throng. "Quick! Have you got it?"

"Yes, sir."

Hastily written on the paper was the word "Acquitted."

"If you had sent the message, 'Recalled to life,' again," muttered Jerry, as he turned, "I should have known what you meant, this time."

He had no opportunity of saying, or so much as thinking, anything else, until he was clear of the Old Bailey; for, the crowd came pouring out with a vehemence that nearly took him off his legs, and a loud buzz swept into the street as if the baffled blue-flies were dispersing in search of other carrion.

*　　*　　*　　*　　*　　*　　*　　*

4 Congratulatory

FROM THE dimly-lighted passages of the court, the last sediment of the human stew that had been boiling there all day was straining off, when Doctor Manette, Lucie Manette, his daughter, Mr. Lorry, the solicitor for the defence, and its counsel, Mr. Stryver, stood gathered round Mr. Charles Darnay—just released—congratulating him on his escape from death.

It would have been difficult, by a far brighter light, to recognise in Doctor Manette, intellectual of face and upright of bearing, the shoemaker of the garret in Paris. Yet, no one could have looked at him twice, without looking again: even though the opportunity of observation had not extended to the mournful cadence of his low grave voice, and to the abstraction that overclouded him fitfully, without any apparent reason. While one external cause, and that a reference to his long lingering agony, would always —as on the trial—evoke this condition from the depths of his soul, it was also in its nature to arise of itself, and to draw a gloom over him, as incomprehensible to those unacquainted with his story as if they had seen the shadow of the actual Bastille thrown upon him by a summer sun, when the substance was three hundred miles away.

Only his daughter had the power of charming this black brooding from his mind. She was the golden thread that united him to a Past beyond his misery, and to a Present beyond his misery: and the sound of her voice, the light of her face, the touch of her hand, had a strong beneficial influence with him almost always. Not absolutely always, for she could recall some occasions on which her power had failed; but they were few and slight, and she believed them over.

Mr. Darnay had kissed her hand fervently and gratefully, and had turned to Mr. Stryver, whom he warmly thanked. Mr. Stryver, a man of little more than thirty, but looking twenty years older than he was, stout, loud, red, bluff, and free from any drawback of delicacy, had a pushing way of shouldering himself (morally and physically) into companies and conversations, that argued well for his shouldering his way up in life.

He still had his wig and gown on, and he said, squaring himself at his late client to that degree that he squeezed the innocent Mr. Lorry clean out of the group: "I am glad to have brought you off with honour, Mr. Darnay. It was an infamous prosecution, grossly infamous; but not the less likely to succeed on that account."

"You have laid me under an obligation to you for life —in two senses," said his late client, taking his hand.

"I have done my best for you, Mr. Darnay; and my best is as good as another man's, I believe."

It clearly being incumbent on someone to say, "Much better," Mr. Lorry said it; perhaps not quite disinterestedly, but with the interested object of squeezing himself back again.

"You think so?" said Mr. Stryver. "Well! you have been present all day, and you ought to know. You are a man of business, too."

"And as such," quoth Mr. Lorry, whom the counsel learned in the law had now shouldered back into the group, just as he had previously shouldered him out of it, "as such I will appeal to Doctor Manette, to break up this conference and order us all to our homes. Miss Lucie looks ill, Mr. Darnay has had a terrible day, we are worn out."

"Speak for yourself, Mr. Lorry," said Stryver; "I have a night's work to do yet. Speak for yourself."

"I speak for myself," answered Mr. Lorry, "and for Mr. Darnay, and for Miss Lucie, and— Miss Lucie, do you not think I may speak for us all?" He asked her the question pointedly, and with a glance at her father.

His face had become frozen, as it were, in a very curious look at Darnay: an intent look, deepening into a frown of dislike and distrust, not even unmixed with fear. With this strange expression on him his thoughts had wandered away.

"My father," said Lucie, softly laying her hand on his. He slowly shook the shadow off, and turned to her.

"Shall we go home, my father?"

With a long breath, he answered, "Yes."

The friends of the acquitted prisoner had dispersed, under the impression—which he himself had originated—

that he would not be released that night. The lights were nearly all extinguished in the passages, the iron gates were being closed with a jar and a rattle, and the dismal place was deserted until to-morrow morning's interest of gallows, pillory, whipping-post, and branding-iron should re-people it. Walking between her father and Mr. Darnay, Lucie Manette passed into the open air. A hackney-coach was called, and the father and daughter departed in it.

Mr. Stryver had left them in the passages, to shoulder his way back to the robing-room. Another person, who had not joined the group, or interchanged a word with any one of them, but who had been leaning against the wall where its shadow was darkest, had silently strolled out after the rest, and had looked on until the coach drove away. He now stepped up to where Mr. Lorry and Mr. Darnay stood upon the pavement.

"So, Mr. Lorry! Men of business may speak to Mr. Darnay now?"

Nobody had made any acknowledgment of Mr. Carton's part in the day's proceedings; nobody had known of it. He was unrobed, and was none the better for it in appearance.

"If you knew what a conflict goes on in the business mind, when the business mind is divided between good-natured impulse and business appearances, you would be amused, Mr. Darnay."

Mr. Lorry reddened, and said, warmly, "You have mentioned that before, sir. We men of business, who serve a House, are not our own masters. We have to think of the House more than ourselves."

"*I* know, *I* know," rejoined Mr. Carton, carelessly. "Don't be nettled, Mr. Lorry. You are as good as another, I have no doubt: better, I dare say."

"And indeed, sir," pursued Mr. Lorry, not minding him, "I really don't know what you have to do with the matter. If you'll excuse me, as very much your elder, for saying so, I really don't know that it is your business."

"Business! Bless you, *I* have no business," said Mr. Carton.

"It is a pity you have not, sir."

"I think so, too."

"If you had," pursued Mr. Lorry, "perhaps you would attend to it."

"Lord love you, no!—I shouldn't," said Mr. Carton.

"Well, sir!" cried Mr. Lorry, thoroughly heated by his indifference, "business is a very good thing, and a very respectable thing. And, sir, if business imposes its restraints and its silences and impediments, Mr. Darnay as a young gentleman of generosity knows how to make allowance for that circumstance. Mr. Darnay, good-night, God bless you, sir! I hope you have been this day preserved for a prosperous and happy life.—Chair there!"

Perhaps a little angry with himself, as well as with the barrister, Mr. Lorry bustled into the chair, and was carried off to Tellson's. Carton, who smelt of port wine, and did not appear to be quite sober, laughed then, and turned to Darnay.

"This is a strange chance that throws you and me together. This must be a strange night to you, standing alone here with your counterpart on these street stones?"

"I hardly seem yet," returned Charles Darnay, "to belong to this world again."

"I don't wonder at it; it's not so long since you were pretty far advanced on your way to another. You speak faintly."

"I begin to think I *am* faint."

"Then why the devil don't you dine? I dined, myself, while those numskulls were deliberating which world you should belong to—this, or some other. Let me show you the nearest tavern to dine well at."

Drawing his arm through his own, he took him down Ludgate Hill to Fleet Street, and so, up a covered way, into a tavern. Here, they were shown into a little room, where Charles Darnay was soon recruiting his strength with a good plain dinner and good wine: while Carton sat opposite to him at the same table, with his separate bottle of port before him, and his fully half-insolent manner upon him.

"Do you feel, yet, that you belong to this terrestrial scheme again, Mr. Darnay?"

"I am frightfully confused regarding time and place; but I am so far mended as to feel that."

"It must be an immense satisfaction!"

He said it bitterly, and filled up his glass again: which was a large one.

"As to me, the greatest desire I have is to forget that I belong to it. It has no good in it for me—except wine like this—nor I for it. So we are not much alike in that particular. Indeed, I begin to think we are not much alike in any particular, you and I."

Confused by the emotion of the day, and feeling his being there with this double of coarse deportment to be like a dream, Charles Darnay was at a loss how to answer; finally, answered not at all.

"Now your dinner is done," Carton presently said, "why don't you call a health, Mr. Darnay; why don't you give your toast?"

"What health? What toast?"

"Why, it's on the tip of your tongue. It ought to be, it must be, I'll swear it's there."

"Miss Manette, then!"

"Miss Manette, then!"

Looking his companion full in the face while he drank the toast, Carton flung his glass over his shoulder against the wall, where it shivered to pieces; then rang the bell, and ordered in another.

"That's a fair young lady to hand to a coach in the dark, Mr. Darnay!" he said, filling his new goblet.

A slight frown and a laconic "Yes" were the answer.

"That's a fair young lady to be pitied by and wept for by! How does it feel? Is it worth being tried for one's life, to be the object of such sympathy and compassion, Mr. Darnay?"

Again Darnay answered not a word.

"She was mightily pleased to have your message, when I gave it her. Not that she showed she was pleased, but I suppose she was."

The allusion served as a timely reminder to Darnay that this disagreeable companion had, of his own free will, assisted him in the strait of the day. He turned the dialogue to that point, and thanked him for it.

"I neither want any thanks, nor merit any," was the careless rejoinder. "It was nothing to do, in the first place; and I don't know why I did it, in the second. Mr. Darnay, let me ask you a question."

"Willingly, and a small return for your good offices."

"Do you think I particularly like you?"

"Really, Mr. Carton," returned the other, oddly disconcerted, "I have not asked myself the question."

"But ask yourself the question now."

"You have acted as if you do; but I don't think you do."

"*I* don't think I do," said Carton. "I begin to have a very good opinion of your understanding."

"Nevertheless," pursued Darnay, rising to ring the bell, "there is nothing in that, I hope, to prevent my calling the reckoning, and our parting without ill-blood on either side."

Carton rejoining, "Nothing in life!" Darnay rang. "Do you call the whole reckoning?" said Carton. On his answering in the affirmative, "Then bring me another pint of this same wine, drawer, and come and wake me at ten."

The bill being paid, Charles Darnay rose and wished him good-night. Without returning the wish, Carton rose too, with something of a threat of defiance in his manner, and said, "A last word, Mr. Darnay: you think I am drunk?"

"I think you have been drinking, Mr. Carton."

"Think? You know I have been drinking."

"Since I must say so, I know it."

"Then you shall likewise know why. I am a disappointed drudge, sir. I care for no man on earth, and no man on earth cares for me."

"Much to be regretted. You might have used your talents better."

"May be so, Mr. Darnay; may be not. Don't let your sober face elate you, however; you don't know what it may come to. Good-night!"

When he was left alone, this strange being took up a candle, went to a glass that hung against the wall, and surveyed himself minutely in it.

"Do you particularly like the man?" he muttered, at his own image. "Why should you particularly like a man who resembles you? There is nothing in you to like; you know that. Ah, confound you! What a change you have made in yourself! A good reason for taking to a man, that he shows you what you have fallen away from, and what you might have been! Change places with him, and would you have been looked at by those blue eyes as he was, and commiserated by that agitated face as he was? Come on, and have it out in plain words! You hate the fellow."

He resorted to his pint of wine for consolation, drank it all in a few minutes, and fell asleep on his arms, with his hair straggling over the table, and a long winding-sheet in the candle dripping down upon him.

5 *The Jackal*

THOSE WERE drinking days, and most men drank hard. So very great is the improvement Time has brought about in such habits, that a moderate statement of the quantity of wine and punch which one man would swallow in the course of a night, without any detriment to his reputation as a perfect gentleman, would seem, in these days, a ridiculous exaggeration. The learned profession of the law was certainly not behind any other learned profession in its Bacchanalian propensities; neither was Mr. Stryver, already fast shouldering his way to a large and lucrative practice, behind his compeers in this particular, any more than in the drier parts of the legal race.

A favourite at the Old Bailey, and eke at the Sessions, Mr. Stryver had begun cautiously to hew away the lower staves of the ladder on which he mounted. Sessions and Old Bailey had now to summon their favourite, specially, to their longing arms; and shouldering itself towards the visage of the Lord Chief Justice in the Court of King's Bench, the florid countenance of Mr. Stryver might be daily seen, bursting out of the bed of wigs, like a great sunflower pushing its way at the sun from among a rank garden full of flaring companions.

It had once been noted at the Bar, that while Mr. Stryver was a glib man, and an unscrupulous, and a ready, and a bold, he had not that faculty of extracting the essence from a heap of statements, which is among the most striking and necessary of the advocate's accomplishments. But a remarkable improvement came upon him as to this. The more business he got, the greater his power seemed to grow of getting at its pith and marrow; and however late at night he sat carousing with Sydney Carton, he always had his points at his fingers' ends in the morning.

Sydney Carton, idlest and most unpromising of men, was Stryver's great ally. What the two drank together, between Hilary Term and Michaelmas, might have floated a king's ship. Stryver never had a case in hand, anywhere, but Carton was there, with his hands in his pockets, staring at the ceiling of the court; they went the same circuit, and even there they prolonged their usual orgies late into the night, and Carton was rumoured to be seen at broad day, going home stealthily and unsteadily to his lodging, like a dissipated cat. At last, it began to get about, among such as were interested in the matter, that although Sydney Carton would never be a lion, he was an amazingly good jackal, and that he rendered suit and service to Stryver in that humble capacity.

"Ten o'clock, sir," said the man at the tavern, whom he had charged to wake him—"ten o'clock, sir."

"*What's* the matter?"

"Ten o'clock, sir."

"What do you mean? Ten o'clock at night?"

"Yes, sir. Your honour told me to call you."

"Oh! I remember. Very well, very well."

After a few dull efforts to get to sleep again, which the man dexterously combated by stirring the fire continuously for five minutes, he got up, tossed his hat on, and walked out. He turned into the Temple, and, having revived himself by twice pacing the pavements of King's Bench Walk and Paper Buildings, turned into the Stryver chambers.

The Stryver clerk, who never assisted at these conferences, had gone home, and the Stryver principal opened the door. He had his slippers on, and a loose bed-gown, and his throat was bare for his greater ease. He had that rather wild, strained, seared marking about the eyes, which may be observed in all free livers of his class, from the portrait of Jeffries downward, and which can be traced, under various disguises of Art, through the portraits of every Drinking Age.

"You are a little late, Memory," said Stryver.

"About the usual time; it may be a quarter of an hour later."

They went into a dingy room lined with books and littered with papers, where there was a blazing fire. A kettle steamed upon the hob, and in the midst of the wreck of papers a table shone, with plenty of wine upon it, and brandy, and rum, and sugar, and lemons.

"You have had your bottle, I perceive, Sydney."

"Two to-night, I think. I have been dining with the day's client; or seeing him dine—it's all one!"

"That was a rare point, Sydney, that you brought to bear upon the identification. How did you come by it? When did it strike you?"

"I thought he was rather a handsome fellow, and I thought I should have been much the same sort of fellow, if I had had any luck."

Mr. Stryver laughed till he shook his precocious paunch.

"You and your luck, Sydney! Get to work, get to work."

Sullenly enough, the jackal loosened his dress, went into an adjoining room, and came back with a large jug of cold water, a basin, and a towel or two. Steeping the towels in the water, and partially wringing them out, he folded them on his head in a manner hideous to behold, sat down at the table, and said, "Now I am ready!"

"Not much boiling down to be done to-night, Memory," said Mr. Stryver, gaily, as he looked among his papers.

"How much?"

"Only two sets of them."

"Give me the worst first."

"There they are, Sydney. Fire away!"

The lion then composed himself on his back on a sofa on one side of the drinking-table, while the jackal sat at his own paper-bestrewn table proper, on the other side of it, with the bottles and glasses ready to his hand. Both resorted to the drinking-table without stint, but each in a different way; the lion for the most part reclining with his hands in his waistband, looking at the fire, or occasionally flirting with some lighter documents; the jackal, with knitted brows and intent face, so deep in his task, that his eyes did not even follow the hand he stretched out for his glass—which often groped about, for a minute or more, before it found the glass for his lips. Two or three times the matter in hand became so knotty, that the jackal found it imperative on him to get up, and steep his towels anew. From these pilgrimages to the jug and basin, he returned with such eccentricities of damp head-gear as no words can describe; which were made the more ludicrous by his anxious gravity.

At length the jackal had got together a compact repast for the lion, and proceeded to offer it to him. The lion took it with care and caution, made his selection from it, and his remarks upon it, and the jackal assisted both.

When the repast was fully discussed, the lion put his hands in his waistband again, and lay down to meditate. The jackal then invigorated himself with a bumper for his throttle, and a fresh application to his head, and applied himself to the collection of a second meal; this was administered to the lion in the same manner, and was not disposed of until the clocks struck three in the morning.

"And now we have done, Sydney, fill a bumper of punch," said Mr. Stryver.

The jackal removed the towels from his head, which had been steaming again, shook himself, yawned, shivered, and complied.

"You were very sound, Sydney, in the matter of those crown witnesses to-day. Every question told."

"I always am sound; am I not?"

"I don't gainsay it. What has roughened your temper? Put some punch to it and smooth it again."

With a deprecatory grunt, the jackal again complied.

"The old Sydney Carton of old Shrewsbury School," said Stryver, nodding his head over him as he reviewed him in the present and the past, "the old seesaw Sydney. Up one minute and down the next; now in spirits and now in despondency!"

"Ah!" returned the other, sighing: "yes! The same Sydney, with the same luck. Even then, I did exercises for other boys, and seldom did my own."

"And why not?"

"God knows. It was my way, I suppose."

He sat, with his hands in his pockets, and his legs stretched out before him, looking at the fire.

"Carton," said his friend, squaring himself at him with a bullying air, as if the fire-grate had been the furnace in which sustained endeavour was forged, and the one delicate thing to be done for the old Sydney Carton of old Shrewsbury School was to shoulder him into it, "your way is, and always was, a lame way. You summon no energy and purpose. Look at me."

"Oh, botheration!" returned Sydney, with a lighter and more good-humoured laugh. "Don't *you* be moral!"

"How have I done what I have done?" said Stryver; "how do I do what I do?"

"Partly through paying me to help you, I suppose. But it's not worth your while to apostrophise me, or the air, about it; what you want to do, you do. You were always in the front rank, and I was always behind."

"I had to get into the front rank; I was not born there, was I?"

"I was not present at the ceremony; but my opinion is you were," said Carton. At this, he laughed again, and they both laughed.

"Before Shrewsbury, and at Shrewsbury, and ever since Shrewsbury," pursued Carton, "you have fallen into your rank, and I have fallen into mine. Even when we were fellow-students in the Student Quarter of Paris, picking up French, and French law, and other French crumbs that we didn't get much good of, you were always somewhere, and I was always—nowhere."

"And whose fault was that?"

"Upon my soul, I am not sure that it was not yours. You were always driving and riving and shouldering and pressing, to that restless degree that I had no chance for my life but in rust and repose. It's a gloomy thing, however, to talk about one's own past, with the day breaking. Turn me in some other direction before I go."

"Well then! Pledge me to the pretty witness," said Stryver, holding up his glass. "Are you turned in a pleasant direction?"

Apparently not, for he became gloomy again.

"Pretty witness," he muttered, looking down into his glass. "I have had enough of witnesses to-day and to-night; who's your pretty witness?"

"The picturesque doctor's daughter, Miss Manette."

"*She* pretty?"

"Is she not?"

"No."

"Why, man alive, she was the admiration of the whole court!"

"Rot the admiration of the whole court! Who made the Old Bailey a judge of beauty? She was a golden-haired doll!"

"Do you know, Sydney," said Mr. Stryver, looking at him with sharp eyes, and slowly drawing a hand across his florid face: "do you know, I rather thought, at the time, that you sympathised with the golden-haired doll, and were quick to see what happened to the golden-haired doll?"

"Quick to see what happened! If a girl, doll or no doll,

swoons within a yard or two of a man's nose, he can see it without a perspective-glass. I pledge you, but I deny the beauty. And now I'll have no more drink; I'll get to bed."

When his host followed him out on the staircase with a candle, to light him down the stairs, the day was coldly looking in through its grimy windows. When he got out of the house, the air was cold and sad, the dull sky overcast, the river dark and dim, the whole scene like a lifeless desert. And wreaths of dust were spinning round and round before the morning blast, as if the desert-sand had risen far away, and the first spray of it in its advance had begun to overwhelm the city.

Waste forces within him, and a desert all around, this man stood still on his way across a silent terrace, and saw for a moment, lying in the wilderness before him, a mirage of honourable ambition, self-denial, and perseverance. In the fair city of this vision, there were airy galleries from which the loves and graces looked upon him, gardens in which the fruits of life hung ripening, waters of Hope that sparkled in his sight. A moment, and it was gone. Climbing into a high chamber in a well of houses, he threw himself down in his clothes on a neglected bed, and its pillow was wet with wasted tears.

Sadly, sadly, the sun rose; it rose upon no sadder sight than the man of good abilities and good emotions, incapable of their directed exercise, incapable of his own help and his own happiness, sensible of the blight on him, and resigning himself to let it eat him away.

*   *   *   *   *   *   *   *

6   *Hundreds of People*

THE QUIET lodgings of Doctor Manette were in a quiet street-corner not far from Soho Square. On the afternoon of a certain fine Sunday when the waves of four months had rolled over the trial for treason, and carried it, as to the public interest and memory, far out to sea, Mr. Jarvis Lorry walked along the sunny streets from

Clerkenwell, where he lived, on his way to dine with the Doctor. After several relapses into business-absorption, Mr. Lorry had become the Doctor's friend, and the quiet street-corner was the sunny part of his life.

On this certain fine Sunday, Mr. Lorry walked towards Soho, early in the afternoon, for three reasons of habit. Firstly, because, on fine Sundays, he often walked out, before dinner, with the Doctor and Lucie; secondly, because, on unfavourable Sundays, he was accustomed to be with them as the family friend, talking, reading, looking out of window, and generally getting through the day; thirdly, because he happened to have his own little shrewd doubts to solve, and knew how the ways of the Doctor's household pointed to that time as a likely time for solving them.

A quainter corner than the corner where the Doctor lived was not to be found in London. There was no way through it, and the front windows of the Doctor's lodging commanded a pleasant little vista of street that had a congenial air of retirement on it. There were few buildings then, north of the Oxford Road, and forest-trees flourished, and wild flowers grew, and the hawthorn blossomed in the now vanished fields. As a consequence, country airs circulated in Soho with vigorous freedom, instead of languishing into the parish like stray paupers without a settlement; and there was many a good south wall, not far off, on which the peaches ripened in their season.

The summer light struck into the corner brilliantly in the earlier part of the day; but, when the streets grew hot, the corner was in shadow, though not in shadow so remote but that you could see beyond it into a glare of brightness. It was a cool spot, staid but cheerful, a wonderful place for echoes, and a very harbour from the raging streets.

There ought to have been a tranquil bark in such an anchorage, and there was. The Doctor occupied two floors of a large still house, where several callings purported to be pursued by day, but whereof little was audible any day, and which was shunned by all of them at night. In a building at the back, attainable by a courtyard where a plane-tree rustled its green leaves, church-organs claimed to be made, and silver to be chased, and likewise gold to be beaten by some mysterious giant who had a golden arm starting out of the wall of the front hall—as if he had beaten himself precious, and menaced a similar conversion of all visitors. Very little of these trades, or of a lonely lodger rumoured to live upstairs, or of a dim coach-trimming maker asserted to have a counting-house below, was ever heard or seen. Occasionally, a stray workman, putting his coat on, traversed the hall, or a stranger peered about there, or a distant clink was heard across the courtyard, or a thump from the golden giant. These, however, were only the exceptions required to prove the rule that the sparrows in the plane-tree behind the house, and the echoes in the corner before it, had their own way from Sunday morning unto Saturday night.

Doctor Manette received such patients here as his old reputation, and its revival in the floating whispers of his story, brought him. His scientific knowledge, and his vigilance and skill in conducting ingenious experiments, brought him otherwise into moderate request, and he earned as much as he wanted.

These things were within Mr. Jarvis Lorry's knowledge, thoughts, and notice, when he rang the door-bell of the tranquil house in the corner, on the fine Sunday afternoon.

"Doctor Manette at home?"

Expected home.

"Miss Lucie at home?"

Expected home.

"Miss Pross at home?"

Possibly at home, but of a certainty impossible for handmaid to anticipate intentions of Miss Pross, as to admission or denial of the fact.

"As I am at home myself," said Mr. Lorry, "I'll go upstairs."

Although the Doctor's daughter had known nothing of the country of her birth, she appeared to have innately derived from it that ability to make much of little means, which is one of its most useful and most agreeable characteristics. Simple as the furniture was, it was set off by so many little adornments, of no value but for their taste and fancy, that its effect was delightful. The disposition of everything in the rooms, from the largest object to the least; the arrangement of colours, the elegant variety and contrast obtained by thrift in trifles, by delicate hands, clear eyes, and good sense, were at once so pleasant in themselves, and so expressive of their originator, that, as

Mr. Lorry stood looking about him, the very chairs and tables seemed to ask him, with something of that peculiar expression which he knew so well by this time, whether he approved?

There were three rooms on a floor, and, the doors by which they communicated being put open that the air might pass freely through them all, Mr. Lorry, smilingly observant of that fanciful resemblance which he detected all around him, walked from one to another. The first was the best room, and in it were Lucie's birds, and flowers, and books, and desk, and work-table, and box of water-colours; the second was the Doctor's consulting-room, used also as the dining-room; the third, changingly speckled by the rustle of the plane-tree in the yard, was the Doctor's bedroom, and there, in a corner, stood the disused shoemaker's bench and tray of tools, much as it had stood on the fifth floor of the dismal house by the wine-shop, in the suburb of Saint Antoine in Paris.

"I wonder," said Mr. Lorry, pausing in his looking about, "that he keeps that reminder of his sufferings about him!"

"And why wonder at that?" was the abrupt inquiry that made him start.

It proceeded from Miss Pross, the wild red woman, strong of hand, whose acquaintance he had first made at the Royal George Hotel at Dover, and had since improved.

"I should have thought—" Mr. Lorry began.

"Pooh! You'd have thought!" said Miss Pross; and Mr. Lorry left off.

"How do you do?" inquired that lady then—sharply, and yet as if to express that she bore him no malice.

"I am pretty well, I thank you," answered Mr. Lorry, with meekness; "how are you?"

"Nothing to boast of," said Miss Pross.

"Indeed?"

"Ah! Indeed!" said Miss Pross. "I am very much put out about my Ladybird."

"Indeed?"

"For gracious' sake say something else besides 'indeed,' or you'll fidget me to death," said Miss Pross: whose character (dissociated from stature) was shortness.

"Really, then?" said Mr. Lorry, as an amendment.

"Really is bad enough," returned Miss Pross, "but better. Yes, I am very much put out."

"May I ask the cause?"

"I don't want dozens of people who are not at all worthy of Ladybird, to come here looking after her," said Miss Pross.

"*Do* dozens come for that purpose?"

"Hundreds," said Miss Pross.

It was characteristic of this lady (as of some other people before her time and since) that whenever her original proposition was questioned, she exaggerated it.

"Dear me!" said Mr. Lorry, as the safest remark he could think of.

"I have lived with the darling—or the darling has lived with me, and paid me for it; which she certainly should never have done, you may take your affidavit, if I could have afforded to keep either myself or her for nothing—since she was ten years old. And it's really very hard," said Miss Pross.

Not seeing with precision what was very hard, Mr. Lorry shook his head; using that important part of himself as a sort of fairy cloak that would fit anything.

"All sorts of people who are not in the least degree worthy of the pet are always turning up," said Miss Pross. "When you began it—"

"*I* began it, Miss Pross?"

"Didn't you? Who brought her father to life?"

"Oh! If *that* was beginning it—" said Mr. Lorry.

"It wasn't ending it, I suppose? I say, when you began it, it was hard enough; not that I have any fault to find with Doctor Manette, except that he is not worthy of such a daughter, which is no imputation on him, for it was not to be expected that anybody should be, under any circumstances. But it really is doubly and trebly hard to have crowds and multitudes of people turning up after him (I could have forgiven him), to take Ladybird's affections away from me."

Mr. Lorry knew Miss Pross to be very jealous, but he also knew her by this time to be, beneath the surface of her eccentricity, one of those unselfish creatures—found only among women—who will, for pure love and admiration, bind themselves willing slaves, to youth when they have lost it, to beauty that they never had, to accomplishments that they were never fortunate enough to gain, to bright hopes that never shone upon their own sombre lives. He knew enough of the world to know that there is nothing in it better than the faithful service of the heart; so rendered and so free from any mercenary taint, he had such an exalted respect for it, that in the retributive arrangements made by his own mind—we all make such arrangements, more or less—he stationed Miss Pross much nearer to the lower Angels than many ladies immeasurably better got up both by Nature and Art, who had balances at Tellson's.

"There never was, nor will be, but one man worthy of Ladybird," said Miss Pross; "and that was my brother Solomon, if he hadn't made a mistake in life."

Here again: Mr. Lorry's inquiries into Miss Pross's personal history had established the fact that her brother Solomon was a heartless scoundrel who had stripped her of everything she possessed, as a stake to speculate with, and had abandoned her in her poverty for evermore, with no touch of compunction. Miss Pross's fidelity of belief in Solomon (deducting a mere trifle for this slight mistake) was quite a serious matter with Mr. Lorry, and had its weight in his good opinion of her.

"As we happen to be alone for the moment, and are both people of business," he said, when they had got back to the drawing-room and had sat down there in friendly relations, "let me ask you—does the Doctor, in talking with Lucie, never refer to the shoemaking time, yet?"

"Never."

"And yet keeps that bench and those tools beside him?"

"Ah!" returned Miss Pross, shaking her head. "But I don't say he don't refer to it within himself."

"Do you believe that he thinks of it much?"

"I do," said Miss Pross.

"Do you imagine—" Mr. Lorry had begun, when Miss Pross took him up short with:

"Never imagine anything. Have no imagination at all."

"I stand corrected; do you suppose—you go so far as to suppose, sometimes?"

"Now and then," said Miss Pross.

"Do you suppose," Mr. Lorry went on, with a laughing twinkle in his bright eye, as it looked kindly at her, "that Doctor Manette has any theory of his own, preserved through all those years, relative to the cause of his being so oppressed; perhaps, even to the name of his oppressor?"

"I don't suppose anything about it but what Ladybird tells me."

"And this is—?"

"That she thinks he has."

"Now don't be angry at my asking all these questions; because I am a mere dull man of business, and you are a woman of business."

"Dull?" Miss Pross inquired, with placidity.

Rather wishing his modest adjective away, Mr. Lorry replied, "No, no, no. Surely not. To return to business— Is it not remarkable that Doctor Manette, unquestionably innocent of any crime as we are all well assured he is, should never touch upon that question? I will not say with me, though he had business relations with me many years ago, and we are now intimate; I will say with the fair daughter to whom he is so devotedly attached, and who is so devotedly attached to him? Believe me, Miss Pross, I don't approach the topic with you, out of curiosity, but out of zealous interest."

"Well! To the best of my understanding, and bad's the best, you'll tell me," said Miss Pross, softened by the tone of the apology, "he is afraid of the whole subject."

"Afraid?"

"It's plain enough, I should think, why he may be. It's a dreadful remembrance. Besides that, his loss of himself grew out of it. Not knowing how he lost himself, or how he recovered himself, he may never feel certain of not losing himself again. That alone wouldn't make the subject pleasant, I should think."

It was a profounder remark than Mr. Lorry had looked for. "True," said he, "and fearful to reflect upon. Yet, a doubt lurks in my mind, Miss Pross, whether it is good for Doctor Manette to have that suppression always shut up within him. Indeed, it is this doubt and the uneasiness it sometimes causes me that has led me to our present confidence."

"Can't be helped," said Miss Pross, shaking her head. "Touch that string, and he instantly changes for the worse. Better leave it alone. In short, must leave it alone, like or no like. Sometimes, he gets up in the dead of the night, and will be heard, by us overhead there, walking up and down, walking up and down, in his room. Ladybird has learnt to know then that his mind is walking up and down, walking up and down, in his old prison. She hurries to him, and they go on together, walking up and down, walking up and down, until he is composed. But he never says a word of the true reason for his restlessness, to her, and she finds it best not to hint at it to him. In silence they go walking up and down together, walking up and down together, till her love and company have brought him to himself."

Notwithstanding Miss Pross's denial of her own imagination, there was a perception of the pain of being monotonously haunted by one sad idea, in her repetition of the phrase, walking up and down, which testified to her possessing such a thing.

The corner has been mentioned as a wonderful corner for echoes; it had begun to echo so resoundingly to the tread of coming feet, that it seemed as though the very mention of that weary pacing to and fro had set it going. "Here they are!" said Miss Pross, rising to break up the confidence; "and now we shall have hundreds of people pretty soon!"

It was such a curious corner in its acoustical properties, such a peculiar ear of a place, that as Mr. Lorry stood at the open window, looking for the father and daughter whose steps he heard, he fancied they would never approach. Not only would the echoes die away, as though the steps had gone; but, echoes of other steps that never came would be heard in their stead, and would die away for good when they seemed close at hand. However, father and daughter did at last appear, and Miss Pross was ready at the street door to receive them.

Miss Pross was a pleasant sight, albeit wild, and red, and grim, taking off her darling's bonnet when she came upstairs, and touching it up with the ends of her handkerchief, and blowing the dust off it, and folding her mantle ready for laying by, and smoothing her rich hair with as much pride as she could possibly have taken in her own hair if she had been the vainest and handsomest of women. Her darling was a pleasant sight too, embracing her and thanking her, and protesting against her taking so much trouble for her—which last she only dared to do playfully, or Miss Pross, sorely hurt, would have retired to her own chamber and cried. The Doctor was a pleasant sight too, looking on at them, and telling Miss Pross how she spoilt Lucie, in accents and with eyes that had as much spoiling in them as Miss Pross had, and would have had more if it were possible. Mr. Lorry was a pleasant sight too, beaming at all this in his little wig, and thanking his bachelor stars for having lighted him in his declining years to a Home. But, no Hundreds of people came to see the sights, and Mr. Lorry looked in vain for the fulfillment of Miss Pross's prediction.

Dinner-time, and still no Hundreds of people. In the arrangements of the little household, Miss Pross took charge of the lower regions, and always acquitted herself marvelously. Her dinners, of a very modest quality, were so well cooked and so well served, and so neat in their contrivances, half English and half French, that nothing could be better. Miss Pross's friendship being of the thoroughly practical kind, she had ravaged Soho and the adjacent provinces, in search of impoverished French, who, tempted by shillings and half-crowns, would impart culinary mysteries to her. From these decayed sons and daughters of Gaul, she had acquired such wonderful arts, that the woman and girl who formed the staff of domestics regarded her as quite a sorceress, or Cinderella's godmother: who would send out for a fowl, a rabbit, a vegetable or two from the garden, and change them into anything she pleased.

On Sundays, Miss Pross dined at the Doctor's table, but on other days persisted in taking her meals at unknown periods, either in the lower regions, or in her own room on the second floor—a blue chamber, to which no one but her Ladybird ever gained admittance. On this occasion, Miss Pross, responding to Ladybird's pleasant face and pleasant efforts to please her, unbent exceedingly; so the dinner was very pleasant, too.

It was an oppressive day, and, after dinner, Lucie proposed that the wine should be carried out under the plane-tree, and they should sit there in the air. As everything turned upon her, and revolved about her, they went out under the plane-tree, and she carried the wine down for the special benefit of Mr. Lorry. She had installed herself, some time before, as Mr. Lorry's cupbearer; and while they sat under the plane-tree, talking, she kept his glass replenished. Mysterious backs and ends of houses peeped at them as they talked, and the plane-tree whispered to them in its own way above their heads.

Still, the Hundreds of people did not present themselves. Mr. Darnay presented himself while they were sitting under the plane-tree, but he was only One.

Doctor Manette received him kindly, and so did Lucie. But, Miss Pross suddenly became afflicted with a twitching in the head and body, and retired into the house. She was not unfrequently the victim of this disorder, and she called it, in familiar conversation, "a fit of the jerks."

The Doctor was in his best condition, and looked specially young. The resemblance between him and Lucie was very strong at such times, and as they sat side by side, she leaning on his shoulder, and he resting his arm on the back of her chair, it was very agreeable to trace the likeness.

He had been talking all day, on many subjects, and with unusual vivacity. "Pray, Doctor Manette," said Mr. Darnay, as they sat under the plane-tree—and he said it in the natural pursuit of the topic in hand, which happened to be the old buildings of London—"have you seen much of the Tower?"

"Lucie and I have been there; but only casually. We have seen enough of it, to know that it teems with interest; little more."

"*I* have been there, as you remember," said Darnay, with a smile, though reddening a little angrily, "in another character, and not in a character that gives facilities for seeing much of it. They told me a curious thing when I was there."

"What was that?" Lucie asked.

"In making some alterations, the workmen came upon an old dungeon, which had been, for many years, built up and forgotten. Every stone of its inner wall was covered by inscriptions which had been carved by prisoners —dates, names, complaints, and prayers. Upon a corner stone in an angle of the wall, one prisoner, who seemed to have gone to execution, had cut, as his last work, three letters. They were done with some very poor instrument, and hurriedly, with an unsteady hand. At first, they were read as D. I. C.; but, on being more carefully examined, the last letter was found to be G. There was no record or legend of any prisoner with those initials, and many fruitless guesses were made what the name could have been. At length, it was suggested that the letters were not initials, but the complete word, DIG. The floor was examined very carefully under the inscription, and, in the earth beneath a stone, or tile, or some fragment of paving, were found the ashes of a paper, mingled with the ashes of a small leathern case or bag. What the unknown prisoner had written will never be read, but he had written something, and hidden it away to keep it from the gaoler."

"My father," exclaimed Lucie, "you are ill!"

He had suddenly started up, with his hand to his head. His manner and his look quite terrified them all.

"No, my dear, not ill. There are large drops of rain falling, and they made me start. We had better go in."

He recovered himself almost instantly. Rain was really falling in large drops, and he showed the back of his hand with rain-drops on it. But, he said not a single word in reference to the discovery that had been told of, and, as they went into the house, the business eye of Mr. Lorry either detected, or fancied it detected, on his face, as it turned toward Charles Darnay, the same singular look that had been upon it when it turned towards him in the passages of the Court House.

He recovered himself so quickly, however, that Mr. Lorry had doubts of his business eye. The arm of the golden giant in the hall was not more steady than he was, when he stopped under it to remark to them that he was not yet proof against slight surprises (if he ever would be), and that the rain had startled him.

Tea-time, and Miss Pross making tea, with another fit of the jerks upon her, and yet no Hundreds of people. Mr. Carton had lounged, but he made only Two.

The night was so very sultry, that although they sat with doors and windows open, they were overpowered by heat. When the tea-table was done with, they all moved to one of the windows, and looked out into the heavy twilight. Lucie sat by her father; Darnay sat beside her; Carton leaned against a window. The curtains were long and white, and some of the thunder-gusts that whirled into the corner caught them up to the ceiling, and waved them like spectral wings.

"The rain-drops are still falling, large, heavy, and few," said Doctor Manette. "It comes slowly."

"It comes surely," said Carton.

They spoke low, as people watching and waiting mostly do; as people in a dark room, watching and waiting for lightning, always do.

There was a great hurry in the streets, of people speeding away to get shelter before the storm broke; the wonderful corner for echoes resounded with the echoes of footsteps coming and going, yet not a footstep was there.

"A multitude of people, and yet a solitude!" said Darnay, when they had listened for a while.

"Is it not impressive, Mr. Darnay?" asked Lucie. "Sometimes, I have sat here of an evening, until I have fancied —but even the shade of a foolish fancy makes me shudder to-night, when all is so black and solemn—"

"Let us shudder too. We may know what it is."

"It will seem nothing to you. Such whims are only impressive as we originate them, I think; they are not to be communicated. I have sometimes sat alone here of an evening, listening, until I have made the echoes out to be the echoes of all the footsteps that are coming by and by into our lives."

"There is a great crowd coming one day into our lives, if that be so," Sydney Carton struck in, in his moody way.

The footsteps were incessant, and the hurry of them became more and more rapid. The corner echoed and re-echoed with the tread of feet; some, as it seemed, under the windows; some, as it seemed, in the room; some coming, some going, some breaking off, some stopping altogether; all in the distant streets, and not one within sight.

"Are all these footsteps destined to come to all of us, Miss Manette, or are we to divide them among us?"

"I don't know, Mr. Darnay; I told you it was a foolish fancy, but you asked for it. When I have yielded myself to it, I have been alone, and then I have imagined them the footsteps of the people who are to come into my life, and my father's."

"I take them into mine!" said Carton. "*I* ask no questions and make no stipulations. There is a great crowd bearing down upon us, Miss Manette, and I see them—by the lightning." He added the last words, after there had been a vivid flash which had shown him lounging in the window.

"And I hear them!" he added again, after a peal of thunder. "Here they come, fast, fierce, and furious!"

It was the rush and roar of rain that he typified, and it stopped him, for no voice could be heard in it. A memorable storm of thunder and lightning broke with that sweep of water, and there was not a moment's interval in crash, and fire, and rain, until after the moon rose at midnight.

The great bell of Saint Paul's was striking one in the cleared air, when Mr. Lorry, escorted by Jerry, high-booted and bearing a lantern, set forth on his return-passage to Clerkenwell. There were solitary patches of road on the way between Soho and Clerkenwell, and Mr. Lorry, mindful of footpads, always retained Jerry for this service: though it was usually performed a good two hours earlier.

"What a night it has been! Almost a night, Jerry," said Mr. Lorry, "to bring the dead out of their graves."

"I never see the night myself, master—nor yet I don't expect to—what would do that," answered Jerry.

"Good-night, Mr. Carton," said the man of business. "Good-night, Mr. Darnay. Shall we ever see such a night again, together!"

Perhaps. Perhaps, see the great crowd of people with its rush and roar, bearing down upon them, too.

---

7 *Monseigneur in Town*

MONSEIGNEUR, one of the great lords in power at the Court, held his fortnightly reception in his grand hotel in Paris. Monseigneur was in his inner room, his sanctuary of sanctuaries, the Holiest of Holiests to the crowd of worshippers in the suite of rooms without. Monseigneur was about to take his chocolate. Monseigneur could swallow a great many things with ease, and was by some few sullen minds supposed to be rather rapidly swallowing France; but, his morning's chocolate could not so much as get into the throat of Monseigneur without the aid of four strong men besides the cook.

Yes. It took four men, all four a-blaze with gorgeous decoration, and the chief of them unable to exist with fewer than two gold watches in his pocket, emulative of the noble and chaste fashion set by Monseigneur, to conduct the happy chocolate to Monseigneur's lips. One lac-

quey carried the chocolate-pot into the sacred presence;
a second milled and frothed the chocolate with the little
instrument he bore for that function; a third presented
the favoured napkin; a fourth (he of the two gold watches)
poured the chocolate out. It was impossible for Monseigneur to dispense with one of these attendants on the
chocolate and hold his high place under the admiring
Heavens. Deep would have been the blot upon his escutcheon if his chocolate had been ignobly waited on by only
three men; he must have died of two.

Monseigneur had been out at a little supper last night,
where the Comedy and the Grand Opera were charmingly
represented. Monseigneur was out at a little supper most
nights, with fascinating company. So polite and so impressible was Monseigneur, that the Comedy and the Grand
Opera had far more influence with him in the tiresome
articles of state affairs and state secrets, than the needs of
all France. A happy circumstance for France, as the like
always is for all countries similarly favoured!—always was
for England (by way of example), in the regretted days of
the merry Stuart who sold it.

Monseigneur had one truly noble idea of general public business, which was, to let everything go on in its own
way; of particular public business, Monseigneur had the
other truly noble idea that it must all go his way—tend to
his own power and pocket. Of his pleasures, general and
particular, Monseigneur had the other truly noble idea,
that the world was made for them. The text of his order
(altered from the original by only a pronoun, which is
not much) ran: "The earth and the fulness thereof are
mine, saith Monseigneur."

Yet, Monseigneur had slowly found that vulgar embarrassments crept into his affairs, both private and public; and he had, as to both classes of affairs, allied himself
perforce with a Farmer-General. As to finances public, because Monseigneur could not make anything at all of them,
and must consequently let them out to somebody who
could; as to finances private, because Farmer-Generals
were rich, and Monseigneur, after generations of great
luxury and expense, was growing poor. Hence Monseigneur had taken his sister from a convent, while there was
yet time to ward off the impending veil, the cheapest garment she could wear, and had bestowed her as a prize
upon a very rich Farmer-General, poor in family. Which

Farmer-General, carrying an appropriate cane with a golden apple on the top of it, was now among the company in the outer rooms, much prostrated before by mankind— always excepting superior mankind of the blood of Monseigneur, who, his own wife included, looked down upon him with the loftiest contempt.

A sumptuous man was the Farmer-General. Thirty horses stood in his stables, twenty-four male domestics sat in his halls, six body-women waited on his wife. As one who pretended to do nothing but plunder and forage where he could, the Farmer-General—howsoever his matrimonial relations conduced to social morality—was at least the greatest reality among the personages who attended at the hotel of Monseigneur that day.

For, the rooms, though a beautiful scene to look at, and adorned with every device of decoration that the taste and skill of the time could achieve, were, in truth, not a sound business; considered with any reference to the scarecrows in the rags and nightcaps elsewhere (and not so far off, either, but that the watching towers of Notre Dame, almost equi-distant from the two extremes, could see them both), they would have been an exceedingly uncomfortable business—if that could have been anybody's business, at the house of Monseigneur. Military officers destitute of military knowledge; naval officers with no idea of a ship; civil officers without a notion of affairs; brazen ecclesiastics, of the worst world worldly, with sensual eyes, loose tongues, and looser lives; all totally unfit for their several callings, all lying horribly in pretending to belong to them, but all nearly or remotely of the order of Monseigneur, and therefore foisted on all public employments from which anything was to be got; these were to be told off by the score and the score. People not immediately connected with Monseigneur or the State, yet equally unconnected with anything that was real, or with lives passed in travelling by any straight road to any true earthly end, were no less abundant. Doctors who made great fortunes out of dainty remedies for imaginary disorders that never existed, smiled upon their courtly patients in the ante-chambers of Monseigneur. Projectors who had discovered every kind of remedy for the little evils with which the State was touched, except the remedy of setting to work in earnest to root out a single sin, poured their distracting babble into any ears they could lay hold of, at the reception of Monseigneur. Unbelieving

Philosophers who were remodelling the world with words, and making card-towers of Babel to scale the skies with, talked with Unbelieving Chemists who had an eye on the transmutation of metals, at this wonderful gathering accumulated by Monseigneur. Exquisite gentlemen of the finest breeding, which was at that remarkable time—and has been since—to be known by its fruits of indifference to every natural subject of human interest, were in the most exemplary state of exhaustion, at the hotel of Monseigneur. Such homes had these various notabilities left behind them in the fine world of Paris, that the spies among the assembled devotees of Monseigneur—forming a goodly half of the polite company—would have found it hard to discover among the angels of that sphere one solitary wife, who, in her manners and appearance, owned to being a mother. Indeed, except for the mere act of bringing a troublesome creature into this world—which does not go far towards the realisation of the name of mother—there was no such thing known to the fashion. Peasant women kept the unfashionable babies close, and brought them up, and charming grandmammas of sixty dressed and supped as at twenty.

The leprosy of unreality disfigured every human creature in attendance upon Monseigneur. In the outermost room were half a dozen exceptional people who had had, for a few years, some vague misgiving in them that things in general were going rather wrong. As a promising way of setting them right, half of the half-dozen had become members of a fantastic sect of Convulsionists, and were even then considering within themselves whether they should foam, rage, roar, and turn cataleptic on the spot—thereby setting up a highly intelligible finger-post to the Future, for Monseigneur's guidance. Besides these Dervishes, were other three who had rushed into another sect, which mended matters with a jargon about "The Centre of Truth"; holding that Man had got out of the Centre of Truth—which did not need much demonstration—but had not got out of the Circumference, and that he was to be kept from flying out of the Circumference, and was even to be shoved back into the Centre, by fasting and seeing of spirits. Among these, accordingly, much discoursing with spirits went on—and it did a world of good which never became manifest.

But, the comfort was, that all the company at the grand

hotel of Monseigneur were perfectly dressed. If the Day of Judgment had only been ascertained to be a dress day, everybody there would have been eternally correct. Such frizzling and powdering and sticking up of hair, such delicate complexions artificially preserved and mended, such gallant swords to look at, and such delicate honour to the sense of smell, would surely keep anything going, for ever and ever. The exquisite gentlemen of the finest breeding wore little pendent trinkets that chinked as they languidly moved; these golden fetters rang like precious little bells; and what with that ringing, and with the rustle of silk and brocade and fine linen, there was a flutter in the air that fanned Saint Antoine and his devouring hunger far away.

Dress was the one unfailing talisman and charm used for keeping all things in their places. Everybody was dressed for a Fancy Ball that was never to leave off. From the Palace of the Tuileries, through Monseigneur and the whole Court, through the Chambers, the Tribunals of Justice, and all society (except the scarecrows), the Fancy Ball descended to the Common Executioner; who, in pursuance of the charm, was required to officiate "frizzled, powdered, in a gold-laced coat, pumps, and white silk stockings." At the gallows and the wheel—the axe was a rarity—Monsieur Paris, as it was the episcopal mode among his brother professors of the provinces, Monsieur Orleans, and the rest, to call him, presided in this dainty dress. And who among the company at Monseigneur's reception in that seventeen hundred and eightieth year of our Lord, could possibly doubt that a system rooted in a frizzled hangman, powdered, gold-laced, pumped, and white-silk stockinged, would see the very stars out!

Monseigneur having eased his four men of their burdens and taken his chocolate, caused the doors of the Holiest of Holiests to be thrown open, and issued forth. Then, what submission, what cringing and fawning, what servility, what abject humiliation! As to bowing down in body and spirit, nothing in that way was left for Heaven—which may have been one among other reasons why the worshippers of Monseigneur never troubled it.

Bestowing a word of promise here and a smile there, a whisper on one happy slave and a wave of the hand on another, Monseigneur affably passed through his rooms to the remote region of the Circumference of Truth. There, Monseigneur turned, and came back again, and so in the due course of time got himself shut up in his sanctuary by the chocolate sprites, and was seen no more.

The show being over, the flutter in the air became quite a little storm, and the precious little bells went ringing downstairs. There was soon but one person left of all the crowd, and he, with his hat under his arm and his snuff-box in his hand, slowly passed among the mirrors on his way out.

"I devote you," said this person, stopping at the last door on his way, and turning in the direction of the sanctuary, "to the Devil!"

With that, he shook the snuff from his fingers as if he had shaken the dust from his feet, and quietly walked downstairs.

He was a man of about sixty, handsomely dressed, haughty in manner, and with a face like a fine mask. A face of a transparent paleness; every feature in it clearly defined; one set expression on it. The nose, beautifully formed otherwise, was very slightly pinched at the top of each nostril. In those two compressions, or dints, the only little change that the face ever showed, resided. They persisted in changing colour sometimes, and they would be occasionally dilated and contracted by something like a faint pulsation; then, they gave a look of treachery, and cruelty, to the whole countenance. Examined with attention, its capacity of helping such a look was to be found in the line of the mouth, and the lines of the orbits of the eyes, being much too horizontal and thin; still, in the effect the face made, it was a handsome face, and a remarkable one.

Its owner went downstairs into the courtyard, got into his carriage, and drove away. Not many people had talked with him at the reception; he had stood in a little space apart, and Monseigneur might have been warmer in his manner. It appeared, under the circumstances, rather agreeable to him to see the common people dispersed before his horses, and often barely escaping from being run down. His man drove as if he were charging an enemy, and the furious recklessness of the man brought no check into the face, or to the lips, of the master. The complaint had sometimes made itself audible, even in that deaf city and dumb age, that, in the narrow streets without footways, the fierce patrician custom of hard driving endangered and maimed the mere vulgar in a barbarous manner. But, few cared enough for that to think of it a second time, and, in this matter, as in all others, the common wretches were left to get out of their difficulties as they could.

With a wild rattle and clatter, and an inhuman abandonment of consideration not easy to be understood in these days, the carriage dashed through streets and swept round corners, with women screaming before it, and men clutching each other and clutching children out of its way. At last, swooping at a street corner by a fountain, one of its wheels came to a sickening little jolt, and there was a loud cry from a number of voices, and the horses reared and plunged.

But for the latter inconvenience, the carriage probably would not have stopped; carriages were often known to drive on, and leave their wounded behind, and why not? But the frightened valet had got down in a hurry, and there were twenty hands at the horses' bridles.

"What has gone wrong?" said Monsieur, calmly looking out.

A tall man in a nightcap had caught up a bundle from among the feet of the horses, and had laid it on the basement of the fountain, and was down in the mud and wet, howling over it like a wild animal.

"Pardon, Monsieur the Marquis!" said a ragged and submissive man, "it is a child."

"Why does he make that abominable noise? Is it his child?"

"Excuse me, Monsieur the Marquis—it is a pity—yes."

The fountain was a little removed; for the street opened, where it was, into a space some ten or twelve yards square. As the tall man suddenly got up from the ground, and came running at the carriage, Monsieur the Marquis clapped his hand for an instant on his sword-hilt.

"Killed!" shrieked the man, in wild desperation, extending both arms at their length above his head, and staring at him. "Dead!"

The people closed round, and looked at Monsieur the Marquis. There was nothing revealed by the many eyes that looked at him but watchfulness and eagerness; there was no visible menacing or anger. Neither did the people say anything; after the first cry, they had been silent, and they remained so. The voice of the submissive man who had spoken was flat and tame in its extreme submission. Monsieur the Marquis ran his eyes over them all, as if they had been mere rats come out of their holes.

He took out his purse.

"It is extraordinary to me," said he, "that you people cannot take care of yourselves and your children. One or the other of you is for ever in the way. How do I know what injury you have done my horses? See! Give him that."

He threw out a gold coin for the valet to pick up, and all the heads craned forward that all the eyes might look down at it as it fell. The tall man called out again with a most unearthly cry, "Dead!"

He was arrested by the quick arrival of another man, for whom the rest made way. On seeing him, the miserable creature fell upon his shoulder, sobbing and crying, and pointing to the fountain, where some women were stooping over the motionless bundle, and moving gently about it. They were as silent, however, as the men.

"I know all, I know all," said the last comer. "Be a brave man, my Gaspard! It is better for the poor little plaything to die so, than to live. It has died in a moment, without pain. Could it have lived an hour as happily?"

"You are a philosopher, you there," said the Marquis smiling. "How do they call you?"

"They call me Defarge."

"Of what trade?"

"Monsieur the Marquis, vendor of wine."

"Pick up that, philosopher and vendor of wine," said the Marquis, throwing him another gold coin, "and spend it as you will. The horses there; are they right?"

Without deigning to look at the assemblage a second time, Monsieur the Marquis leaned back in his seat, and was just being driven away with the air of a gentleman who had accidentally broken some common thing, and had paid for it, and could afford to pay for it; when his ease was suddenly disturbed by a coin flying into his carriage, and ringing on its floor.

"Hold!" said Monsieur the Marquis. "Hold the horses! Who threw that?"

He looked to the spot where Defarge the vendor of wine had stood a moment before; but the wretched father was grovelling on his face on the pavement in that spot, and the figure that stood beside him was the figure of a dark stout woman, knitting.

"You dogs!" said the Marquis, but smoothly, and with

an unchanged front, except as to the spots on his nose. "I would ride over any of you very willingly, and exterminate you from the earth. If I knew which rascal threw at the carriage, and if that brigand were sufficiently near it, he should be crushed under the wheels."

So cowed was their condition, and so long and hard their experience of what such a man could do to them, within the law and beyond it, that not a voice, or a hand, or even an eye was raised. Among the men, not one. But the woman who stood knitting looked up steadily, and looked the Marquis in the face. It was not for his dignity to notice it; his contemptuous eyes passed over her, and over all the other rats; and he leaned back in his seat again, and gave the word "Go on!"

He was driven on, and other carriages came whirling by in quick succession; the Minister, the State-Projector, the Farmer-General, the Doctor, the Lawyer, the Ecclesiastic, the Grand Opera, the Comedy, the whole Fancy Ball, in a bright continuous flow, came whirling by. The rats had crept out of their holes to look on, and they remained looking on for hours; soldiers and police often passing between them and the spectacle, and making a barrier behind which they slunk, and through which they peeped. The father had long ago taken up his bundle and hidden himself away with it, when the women who had tended the bundle while it lay on the base of the fountain sat there watching the running of the water and the rolling of the Fancy Ball—when the one woman who had stood conspicuous, knitting, still knitted on with the steadfastness of Fate. The water of the fountain ran, the swift river ran, the day ran into evening, so much life in the city ran into death according to rule, time and tide waited for no man, the rats were sleeping close together in their dark holes again, the Fancy Ball was lighted up at supper, all things ran their course.

post-horses, poor fountain, all usual poor appoint-
ts. I had its poor people too. All its people were poor.

8 *Monseigneur in the Country*

A BEAUTIFUL landscape, with the corn bright in it,
but not abundant. Patches of poor rye where corn should
have been, patches of poor peas and beans, patches of
most coarse vegetable substitutes for wheat. On inanimate
nature, as on the men and women who cultivated it, a
prevalent tendency towards an appearance of vegetating
unwillingly—a dejected disposition to give up, and wither
away.

Monsieur the Marquis in his travelling carriage (which
might have been lighter), conducted by four post-horses
and two postilions, fagged up a steep hill. A blush on the
countenance of Monsieur the Marquis was no impeach-
ment of his high breeding; it was not from within; it was
occasioned by an external circumstance beyond his control
—the setting sun.

The sunset struck so brilliantly into the travelling carriage when it gained the hill-top, that its occupant was
steeped in crimson. "It will die out," said Monsieur the
Marquis, glancing at his hands, "directly."

In effect, the sun was so low that it dipped at the moment. When the heavy drag had been adjusted to the
wheel, and the carriage slid down hill, with a cinderous
smell, in a cloud of dust, the red glow departed quickly;
the sun and the Marquis going down together, there was no
glow left when the drag was taken off.

But, there remained a broken country, bold and open,
a little village at the bottom of the hill, a broad sweep and
rise beyond it, a church-tower, a windmill, a forest for the
chase, and a crag with a fortress on it used as a prison.
Round upon all these darkening objects as the night drew
on, the Marquis looked, with the air of one who was coming near home.

The village had its one poor street, with its poor brewery, poor tannery, poor tavern, poor stable-yard for relay

of post-horses, poor fountain, all usual poor appointments. It had its poor people too. All its people were poor, and many of them were sitting at their doors, shredding spare onions and the like for supper, while many were at the fountain, washing leaves, and grasses, and any such small yieldings of the earth that could be eaten. Expressive signs of what made them poor were not wanting; the tax for the state, the tax for the church, the tax for the lord, tax local and tax general, were to be paid here and to be paid there, according to solemn inscription in the little village, until the wonder was, that there was any village left unswallowed.

Few children were to be seen, and no dogs. As to the men and women, their choice on earth was stated in the prospect—Life on the lowest terms that could sustain it, down in the little village under the mill; or captivity and Death in the dominant prison on the crag.

Heralded by a courier in advance, and by the cracking of his postilions' whips, which twined snake-like about their heads in the evening air, as if he came attended by the Furies, Monsieur the Marquis drew up in his travelling carriage at the posting-house gate. It was hard by the fountain, and the peasants suspended their operations to look at him. He looked at them, and saw in them, without knowing it, the slow sure filing down of misery-worn face and figure that was to make the meagreness of Frenchmen an English superstition which should survive the truth through the best part of a hundred years.

Monsieur the Marquis cast his eyes over the submissive faces that drooped before him, as the like of himself had drooped before Monseigneur of the Court—only the difference was, that these faces drooped merely to suffer and not to propitiate—when a grizzled mender of the roads joined the group.

"Bring me hither that fellow!" said the Marquis to the courier.

The fellow was brought, cap in hand, and the other fellows closed round to look and listen, in the manner of the people at the Paris fountain.

"I passed you on the road?"

"Monseigneur, it is true. I had the honour of being passed on the road."

"Coming up the hill, and at the top of the hill, both?"

"Monseigneur, it is true."

"What did you look at, so fixedly?"

"Monseigneur, I looked at the man."

He stooped a little, and with his tattered blue cap pointed under the carriage. All his fellows stooped to look under the carriage.

"What man, pig? And why look there?"

"Pardon, Monseigneur; he swung by the chain of the shoe—the drag."

"Who?" demanded the traveller.

"Monseigneur, the man."

"May the Devil carry away these idiots! How do you call the man? You know all the men of this part of the country. Who was he?"

"Your clemency, Monseigneur! He was not of this part of the country. Of all the days of my life, I never saw him."

"Swinging by the chain? To be suffocated?"

"With your gracious permission, that was the wonder of it, Monseigneur. His head was hanging over—like this!"

He turned himself sideways to the carriage, and leaned back, with his face thrown up to the sky, and his head hanging down; then recovered himself, fumbled with his cap, and made a bow.

"What was he like?"

"Monseigneur, he was whiter than the miller. All covered with dust, white as a spectre, tall as a spectre!"

The picture produced an immense sensation in the little crowd; but all eyes, without comparing notes with other eyes, looked at Monsieur the Marquis. Perhaps, to observe whether he had any spectre on his conscience.

"Truly, you did well," said the Marquis, felicitously sensible that such vermin were not to ruffle him, "to see a thief accompanying my carriage, and not open that great mouth of yours. Bah! Put him aside, Monsieur Gabelle!"

Monsieur Gabelle was the postmaster, and some other taxing functionary united; he had come out with great obsequiousness to assist at this examination, and had held the examined by the drapery of his arm in an official manner.

"Bah! Go aside!" said Monsieur Gabelle.

"Lay hands on this stranger if he seeks to lodge in your village to-night, and be sure that his business is honest, Gabelle."

"Monsieur, I am flattered to devote myself to your orders."

"Did he run away, fellow?—Where is that accursed?"

The accursed was already under the carriage with some half-dozen particular friends, pointing out the chain with his blue cap. Some half-dozen other particular friends promptly hauled him out, and presented him breathless to Monsieur the Marquis.

"Did the man run away, dolt, when we stopped for the drag?"

"Monseigneur, he precipitated himself over the hillside, head first, as a person plunges into a river."

"See to it, Gabelle. Go on!"

The half-dozen who were peering at the chain were still among the wheels, like sheep; the wheels turned so suddenly that they were lucky to save their skins and bones; they had very little else to save or they might not have been so fortunate.

The burst with which the carriage started out of the village and up the rise beyond was soon checked by the steepness of the hill. Gradually, it subsided to a footpace, swinging and lumbering upward among the many sweet scents of a summer night. The postilions, with a thousand gossamer gnats circling about them in lieu of the Furies, quietly mended the points to the lashes of their whips; the valet walked by the horses; the courier was audible, trotting on ahead into the dim distance.

At the steepest point of the hill there was a little burial-ground, with a Cross and a new large figure of Our Saviour on it; it was a poor figure in wood, done by some inexperienced rustic carver, but he had studied the figure from the life—his own life, maybe—for it was dreadfully spare and thin.

To this distressful emblem of a great distress that had long been growing worse, and was not at its worst, a woman was kneeling. She turned her head as the carriage came up to her, rose quickly, and presented herself at the carriage-door.

"It is you, Monseigneur! Monseigneur, a petition."

With an exclamation of impatience, but with his unchangeable face, Monseigneur looked out.

"How, then! What is it? Always petitions!"

"Monseigneur. For the love of the great God! My husband, the forester."

"What of your husband, the forester? Always the same with you people. He cannot pay something?"

"He has paid all, Monseigneur. He is dead."

"Well! He is quiet. Can I restore him to you?"

"Alas, no, Monseigneur! But he lies yonder, under a little heap of poor grass."

"Well?"

"Monseigneur, there are so many little heaps of poor grass."

"Again, well?"

She looked an old woman, but was young. Her manner was one of passionate grief; by turns she clasped her veinous and knotted hands together with wild energy, and laid one of them on the carriage-door—tenderly, caressingly, as if it had been a human breast, and could be expected to feel the appealing touch.

"Monseigneur, hear me! Monseigneur, hear my petition! My husband died of want; so many die of want; so many more will die of want."

"Again, well? Can I feed them?"

"Monseigneur, the good God knows; but I don't ask it. My petition is that a morsel of stone or wood, with my husband's name, may be placed over him to show where he lies. Otherwise, the place will be quickly forgotten, it will never be found when I am dead of the same malady, I shall be laid under some other heap of poor grass. Monseigneur, they are so many, they increase so fast, there is so much want. Monseigneur! Monseigneur!"

The valet had put her away from the door, the carriage had broken into a brisk trot, the postilions had quickened the pace, she was left far behind, and Monseigneur, again escorted by the Furies, was rapidly diminishing the league or two of distance that remained between him and his château.

The sweet scents of the summer night rose all around him, and rose, as the rain falls, impartially, on the dusty, ragged, and toil-worn group at the fountain not far away, to whom the mender of roads, with the aid of the blue cap without which he was nothing, still enlarged upon his man like a spectre, as long as they could bear it. By degrees, as they could bear no more, they dropped off one by one, and the lights twinkled in little casements; which lights, as the casements darkened, and more stars came out, seemed to have shot up into the sky instead of having been extinguished.

The shadow of a large high-roofed house, and of many overhanging trees, was upon Monsieur the Marquis by that time; and the shadow was exchanged for the light of a flambeau, as his carriage stopped, and the great door of his château was opened to him.

"Monsieur Charles, whom I expect; is he arrived from England?"

"Monseigneur, not yet."

*　　*　　*　　*　　*　　*　　*　　*

9　*The Gorgon's Head*

IT WAS a heavy mass of building, that château of Monsieur the Marquis, with a large stone courtyard before it, and two stone sweeps of staircase meeting in a stone terrace before the principal door. A stony business altogether, with heavy stone balustrades, and stone urns, and stone flowers, and stone faces of men, and stone heads of lions, in all directions. As if the Gorgon's head had surveyed it, when it was finished, two centuries ago.

Up the broad flight of shallow steps, Monsieur the Marquis, flambeau preceded, went from his carriage, sufficiently disturbing the darkness to elicit loud remonstrance from an owl in the roof of the great pile of stable building away among the trees. All else was so quiet, that the flambeau carried up the steps, and the other flambeau held at the great door, burnt as if they were in a close room of state, instead of being in the open night-air. Other sound than the owl's voice there was none, save the falling of a fountain into its stone basin; for, it was one of those dark nights that hold their breath by the hour together, and then heave a long low sigh, and hold their breath again.

The great door clanged behind him, and Monsieur the Marquis crossed a hall grim with certain old boar-spears, swords, and knives of the chase; grimmer with certain heavy riding-rods and riding-whips, of which many a peasant, gone to his benefactor Death, had felt the weight when his lord was angry.

Avoiding the larger rooms, which were dark and made fast for the night, Monsieur the Marquis, with his flambeau-bearer going on before, went up the staircase to a door in a corridor. This thrown open, admitted him to his own private apartment of three rooms; his bedchamber and two others. High vaulted rooms with cool uncarpeted floors, great dogs upon the hearths for the burning of wood in winter time, and all luxuries befitting the state of a marquis in a luxurious age and country. The fashion of the last Louis but one, of the line that was never to break— the fourteenth Louis—was conspicuous in their rich furniture; but, it was diversified by many objects that were illustrations of old pages in the history of France.

A supper-table was laid for two, in the third of the rooms; a round room, in one of the château's four extinguisher-topped towers. A small lofty room, with its window wide open, and the wooden jalousie-blinds closed, so that the dark night only showed in slight horizontal lines of black, alternating with their broad lines of stone colour.

"My nephew," said the Marquis, glancing at the supper preparation; "they said he was not arrived."

Nor was he; but, he had been expected with Monseigneur.

"Ah! It is not probable he will arrive to-night; nevertheless, leave the table as it is. I shall be ready in a quarter of an hour."

In a quarter of an hour Monseigneur was ready, and sat down alone to his sumptuous and choice supper. His chair was opposite to the window, and he had taken his soup, and was raising his glass of Bordeaux to his lips, when he put it down.

"What is that?" he calmly asked, looking with attention at the horizontal lines of black and stone colour.

"Monseigneur? That?"

"Outside the blinds. Open the blinds."

It was done.

"Well?"

"Monseigneur, it is nothing. The trees and the night are all that are here."

The servant who spoke had thrown the blinds wide, had looked out into the vacant darkness, and stood, with that blank behind him, looking round for instructions.

"Good," said the imperturbable master. "Close them again."

That was done too, and the Marquis went on with his supper. He was half-way through it, when he again stopped with his glass in his hand, hearing the sound of wheels. It came on briskly, and came up to the front of the château.

"Ask who is arrived."

It was the nephew of Monseigneur. He had been some few leagues behind Monseigneur, early in the afternoon. He had diminished the distance rapidly, but not so rapidly as to come up with Monseigneur on the road. He had heard of Monseigneur, at the posting-houses, as being before him.

He was to be told (said Monseigneur) that supper awaited him then and there, and that he was prayed to come to it. In a little while he came. He had been known in England as Charles Darnay.

Monseigneur received him in a courtly manner, but they did not shake hands.

"You left Paris yesterday, sir?" he said to Monseigneur, as he took his seat at table.

"Yesterday. And you?"

"I come direct."

"From London?"

"Yes."

"You have been a long time coming," said the Marquis, with a smile.

"On the contrary; I come direct."

"Pardon me! I mean, not a long time on the journey; a long time intending the journey."

"I have been detained by"—the nephew stopped a moment in his answer—"various business."

"Without doubt," said the polished uncle.

So long as a servant was present, no other words passed between them. When coffee had been served and they were alone together, the nephew, looking at the uncle and meeting the eyes of the face that was like a fine mask, opened a conversation.

"I have come back, sir, as you anticipate, pursuing the object that took me away. It carried me into great and unexpected peril; but it is a sacred object, and if it had carried me to death I hope it would have sustained me."

"Not to death," said the uncle; "it is not necessary to say to death."

"I doubt, sir," returned the nephew, "whether, if it had carried me to the utmost brink of death, you would have cared to stop me there."

The deepened marks in the nose, and the lengthening of the fine straight lines in the cruel face, looked ominous as to that; the uncle made a graceful gesture of protest, which was so clearly a slight form of good breeding that it was not reassuring.

"Indeed, sir," pursued the nephew, "for anything I know, you may have expressly worked to give a more suspicious appearance to the suspicious circumstances that surrounded me."

"No, no, no," said the uncle, pleasantly.

"But, however that may be," resumed the nephew, glancing at him with deep distrust, "I know that your diplomacy would stop me by any means, and would know no scruple as to means."

"My friend, I told you so," said the uncle, with a fine pulsation in the two marks. "Do me the favour to recall that I told you so, long ago."

"I recall it."

"Thank you," said the Marquis—very sweetly indeed.

His tone lingered in the air, almost like the tone of a musical instrument.

"In effect, sir," pursued the nephew, "I believe it to be at once your bad fortune, and my good fortune, that has kept me out of a prison in France here."

"I do not quite understand," returned the uncle, sipping his coffee. "Dare I ask you to explain?"

"I believe that if you were not in disgrace with the Court, and had not been overshadowed by that cloud for years past, a letter *de cachet* would have sent me to some fortress indefinitely."

"It is possible," said the uncle, with great calmness. "For the honour of the family, I could even resolve to incommode you to that extent. Pray excuse me!"

"I perceive that, happily for me, the Reception of the day before yesterday was, as usual, a cold one," observed the nephew.

"I would not say happily, my friend," returned the uncle, with refined politeness; "I would not be sure of that. A good opportunity for consideration, surrounded by the advantages of solitude, might influence your destiny to far greater advantage than you influence it for yourself.

But it is useless to discuss the question. I am, as you say, at a disadvantage. These little instruments of correction, these gentle aids to the power and honour of families, these slight favours that might so incommode you, are only to be obtained now by interest and importunity. They are sought by so many, and they are granted (comparatively) to so few! It used not to be so, but France in all such things is changed for the worse. Our not remote ancestors held the right of life and death over the surrounding vulgar. From this room, many such dogs have been taken out to be hanged; in the next room (my bedroom), one fellow, to our knowledge, was poniarded on the spot for professing some insolent delicacy respecting his daughter—*his* daughter? We have lost many privileges; a new philosophy has become the mode; and the assertion of our station, in these days, might (I do not go so far as to say would, but might) cause us real inconvenience. All very bad, very bad!"

The Marquis took a gentle little pinch of snuff, and shook his head; as elegantly despondent as he could becomingly be of a country still containing himself, that great means of regeneration.

"We have so asserted our station, both in the old time and in the modern time also," said the nephew, gloomily, "that I believe our name to be more detested than any name in France."

"Let us hope so," said the uncle. "Detestation of the high is the involuntary homage of the low."

"There is not," pursued the nephew, in his former tone, "a face I can look at, in all this country round about us, which looks at me with any deference on it but the dark deference of fear and slavery."

"A compliment," said the Marquis, "to the grandeur of the family, merited by the manner in which the family has sustained its grandeur. Hah!" And he took another gentle little pinch of snuff, and lightly crossed his legs.

But, when his nephew, leaning an elbow on the table, covered his eyes thoughtfully and dejectedly with his hand, the fine mask looked at him sideways with a stronger concentration of keenness, closeness, and dislike, than was comportable with its wearer's assumption of indifference.

"Repression is the only lasting philosophy. The dark deference of fear and slavery, my friend," observed the

Marquis, "will keep the dogs obedient to the whip, as long as this roof," looking up to it, "shuts out the sky."

That might not be so long as the Marquis supposed. If a picture of the château as it was to be a very few years hence, and of fifty like it as they too were to be a very few years hence, could have been shown to him that night, he might have been at a loss to claim his own from the ghastly, fire-charred, plunder-wrecked ruins. As for the roof he vaunted, he might have found *that* shutting out the sky in a new way—to wit, for ever, from the eyes of the bodies into which its lead was fired, out of the barrels of a hundred thousand muskets.

"Meanwhile," said the Marquis, "I will preserve the honour and repose of the family, if you will not. But you must be fatigued. Shall we terminate our conference for the night?"

"A moment more."

"An hour, if you please."

"Sir," said the nephew, "we have done wrong, and are reaping the fruits of wrong."

"*We* have done wrong?" repeated the Marquis, with an inquiring smile, and delicately pointing, first to the nephew, then to himself.

"Our family; our honourable family, whose honour is of so much account to both of us, in such different ways. Even in my father's time, we did a world of wrong, injuring every human creature who came between us and our pleasure, whatever it was. Why need I speak of my father's time, when it is equally yours? Can I separate my father's twin brother, joint inheritor, and next successor, from himself?"

"Death has done that!" said the Marquis.

"And has left me," answered the nephew, "bound to a system that is frightful to me, responsible for it, but powerless in it; seeking to execute the last request of my dear mother's lips, and to obey the last look of my dear mother's eyes, which implored me to have mercy and to redress; and tortured by seeking assistance and power in vain."

"Seeking them from me, my nephew," said the Marquis, touching him on the breast with his forefinger—they were now standing by the hearth—"you will for ever seek them in vain, be assured."

Every fine straight line in the clear whiteness of his face was cruelly, craftily, and closely compressed, while he stood looking quietly at his nephew, with his snuff-box in his hand.

Once again he touched him on the breast, as though his finger were the fine point of a small sword, with which, in delicate finesse, he ran him through the body, and said:

"My friend, I will die, perpetuating the system under which I have lived."

When he had said it, he took a culminating pinch of snuff, and put his box in his pocket.

"Better to be a rational creature," he added then, after ringing a small bell on the table, "and accept your natural destiny. But you are lost, Monsieur Charles, I see."

"This property and France are lost to me," said the nephew sadly; "I renounce them."

"Are they both yours to renounce? France may be, but is the property? It is scarcely worth mentioning; but, is it yet?"

"I had no intention, in the words I used, to claim it yet. If it passed to me from you, to-morrow——"

"Which I have the vanity to hope is not probable."

"——or twenty years hence——"

"You do me too much honour," said the Marquis; "still, I prefer that supposition."

"I would abandon it, and live otherwise and elsewhere. It is little to relinquish. What is it but a wilderness of misery and ruin?"

"Hah!" said the Marquis, glancing round the luxurious room.

"To the eye it is fair enough, here; but seen in its integrity, under the sky, and by the daylight, it is a crumbling tower of waste, mismanagement, extortion, debt, mortgage, oppression, hunger, nakedness, and suffering."

"Hah!" said the Marquis again, in a well-satisfied manner.

"If it ever becomes mine, it shall be put into some hands better qualified to free it slowly (if such a thing is possible) from the weight that drags it down, so that the miserable people who cannot leave it and who have been wrung to the last point of endurance may, in another generation, suffer less; but it is not for me. There is a curse on it, and on all this land."

"And you?" said the uncle. "Forgive my curiosity; do you, under your new philosophy, graciously intend to live?"

"I must do, to live, what others of my countrymen, even

with nobility at their backs, may have to do some day—
work."

"In England, for example?"

"Yes. The family honour, sir, is safe from me in this
country. The family name can suffer from me in no other,
for I bear it in no other."

The ringing of the bell had caused the adjoining bedchamber to be lighted. It now shone brightly, through the
door of communication. The Marquis looked that way,
and listened for the retreating step of his valet.

"England is very attractive to you, seeing how indifferently you have prospered there," he observed then, turning his calm face to his nephew with a smile.

"I have already said, that for my prospering there, I am
sensible I may be indebted to you, sir. For the rest, it is my
refuge."

"They say, those boastful English, that it is the refuge
of many. You know a compatriot who has found a refuge
there? A Doctor?"

"Yes."

"With a daughter?"

"Yes."

"Yes," said the Marquis. "You are fatigued. Good-
night!"

As he bent his head in his most courtly manner, there
was a secrecy in his smiling face, and he conveyed an air
of mystery to those words, which struck the eyes and ears
of his nephew forcibly. At the same time, the thin straight
lines of the setting of the eyes, and the thin straight lips,
and the markings in the nose, curved with a sarcasm that
looked handsomely diabolic.

"Yes," repeated the Marquis. "A Doctor with a daughter. Yes. So commences the new philosophy! You are
fatigued. Good-night!"

It would have been of as much avail to interrogate any
stone face outside the château as to interrogate that face
of his. The nephew looked at him in vain, in passing on to
the door.

"Good-night!" said the uncle. "I look to the pleasure of
seeing you again in the morning. Good repose! Light
Monsieur my nephew to his chamber there!—And burn
Monsieur my nephew in his bed, if you will," he added to
himself, before he rang his little bell again, and summoned
his valet to his own bedroom.

The valet come and gone, Monsieur the Marquis walked to and fro in his loose chamber-robe, to prepare himself gently for sleep, that hot still night. Rustling about the room, his softly-slippered feet making no noise on the floor, he moved like a refined tiger: looked like some enchanted marquis of the impenitently wicked sort, in story, whose periodical change into tiger form was either just going off, or just coming on.

He moved from end to end of his voluptuous bedroom, looking again at the scraps of the day's journey that came unbidden into his mind; the slow toil up the hill at sunset, the setting sun, the descent, the mill, the prison on the crag, the little village in the hollow, the peasants at the fountain, and the mender of roads with his blue cap pointing out the chain under the carriage. That fountain suggested the Paris fountain, the little bundle lying on the step, the women bending over it, and the tall man with his arms up, crying, "Dead!"

"I am cool now," said Monsieur the Marquis, "and may go to bed."

So, leaving only one light burning on the large hearth, he let his thin gauze curtains fall around him, and heard the night break its silence with a long sigh as he composed himself to sleep.

The stone faces on the outer walls stared blindly at the black night for three heavy hours; for three heavy hours the horses in the stables rattled at their racks, the dogs barked, and the owl made a noise with very little resemblance in it to the noise conventionally assigned to the owl by men-poets. But it is the obstinate custom of such creatures hardly ever to say what is set down for them.

For three heavy hours, the stone faces of the château, lion and human, stared blindly at the night. Dead darkness lay on all the landscape, dead darkness added its own hush to the hushing dust on all the roads. The burial-place had got to the pass that its little heaps of poor grass were undistinguishable from one another; the figure on the Cross might have come down, for anything that could be seen of it. In the village, taxers and taxed were fast asleep. Dreaming, perhaps, of banquets, as the starved usually do, and of ease and rest, as the driven slave and the yoked ox may, its lean inhabitants slept soundly, and were fed and freed.

The fountain in the village flowed unseen and unheard,

and the fountain at the château dropped unseen and un-heard—both melting away, like the minutes that were fall-ing from the spring of Time—through three dark hours. Then, the gray water of both began to be ghostly in the light, and the eyes of the stone faces of the château were opened.

Lighter and lighter, until at last the sun touched the tops of the still trees, and poured its radiance over the hill. In the glow, the water of the château fountain seemed to turn to blood, and the stone faces crimsoned. The carol of the birds was loud and high, and, on the weather-beaten sill of the great window of the bedchamber of Monsieur the Marquis, one little bird sang its sweetest song with all its might. At this, the nearest stone face seemed to stare amazed, and, with opened mouth and dropped under-jaw, looked awestricken.

Now, the sun was full up, and movement began in the village. Casement windows opened, crazy doors were un-barred, and people came forth shivering—chilled, as yet, by the new sweet air. Then began the rarely lightened toil of the day among the village population. Some, to the foun-tain; some, to the fields; men and women here, to dig and delve; men and women there, to see to the poor livestock, and lead the bony cows out, to such pasture as could be found by the roadside. In the church and at the Cross, a kneeling figure or two; attendant on the latter prayers, the led cow, trying for a breakfast among the weeds at its foot.

The château awoke later, as became its quality, but awoke gradually and surely. First, the lonely boar-spears and knives of the chase had been reddened as of old; then, had gleamed trenchant in the morning sunshine; now, doors and windows were thrown open, horses in their stables looked round over their shoulders at the light and fresh-ness pouring in at doorways, leaves sparkled and rustled at iron-grated windows, dogs pulled hard at their chains, and reared impatient to be loosed.

All these trivial incidents belonged to the routine of life, and the return of morning. Surely, not so the ringing of the great bell of the château, nor the running up and down the stairs; nor the hurried figures on the terrace; nor the booting and tramping here and there and everywhere, nor the quick saddling of horses and riding away?

What winds conveyed this hurry to the grizzled mender of roads, already at work on the hilltop beyond the village, with his day's dinner (not much to carry) lying in a bundle that it was worth no cow's while to peck at, on a heap of stones? Had the birds, carrying some grains of it to a distance, dropped one over him as they sow chance seeds? Whether or no, the mender of roads ran, on the sultry morning, as if for his life, down the hill, knee-high in dust, and never stopped till he got to the fountain.

All the people of the village were at the fountain, standing about in their depressed manner, and whispering low, but showing no other emotions than grim curiosity and surprise. The led cows, hastily brought in and tethered to anything that would hold them, were looking stupidly on, or lying down chewing the cud of nothing particularly repaying their trouble, which they had picked up in their interrupted saunter. Some of the people of the château, and some of those of the posting-house, and all the taxing authorities, were armed more or less, and were crowded on the other side of the little street in a purposeless way, that was highly fraught with nothing. Already, the mender of roads had penetrated into the midst of a group of fifty particular friends, and was smiting himself in the breast with his blue cap. What did all this portend, and what portended the swift hoisting-up of Monsieur Gabelle behind a servant on horseback, and the conveying away of the said Gabelle (double-laden though the horse was), at a gallop, like a new version of the German ballad of Leonora?

It portended that there was one stone face too many, up at the château.

The Gorgon had surveyed the building again in the night, and had added the one stone face wanting; the stone face for which it had waited through about two hundred years.

It lay back on the pillow of Monsieur the Marquis. It was like a fine mask, suddenly startled, made angry, and petrified. Driven home into the heart of the stone figure attached to it was a knife. Round its hilt was a frill of paper, on which was scrawled:

"Drive him fast to his tomb. This, from JACQUES.*"*

*   *   *   *   *   *   *   *

10 *Two Promises*

MORE MONTHS, to the number of twelve, had come and gone, and Mr. Charles Darnay was established in England as a higher teacher of the French language who was conversant with French literature. In this age, he would have been a professor; in that age, he was a tutor. He read with young men who could find any leisure and interest for the study of a living tongue spoken all over the world, and he cultivated a taste for its stores of knowledge and fancy. He could write of them, besides, in sound English, and render them into sound English. Such masters were not at that time easily found; Princes that had been, and Kings that were to be, were not yet of the teacher class, and no ruined nobility had dropped out of Tellson's ledgers, to turn cooks and carpenters. As a tutor, whose attainments made the student's way unusually pleasant and profitable, and as an elegant translator who brought something to his work besides mere dictionary knowledge, young Mr. Darnay soon became known and encouraged. He was well acquainted, moreover, with the circumstances of his country, and those were of ever-growing interest. So, with great perseverance and untiring industry, he prospered.

In London, he had expected neither to walk on pavements of gold, nor lie on beds of roses; if he had had any such exalted expectation, he would not have prospered. He had expected labour, and he found it, and did it, and made the best of it. In this, his prosperity consisted.

A certain portion of his time was passed at Cambridge, where he read with undergraduates as a sort of tolerated smuggler who drove a contraband trade in European languages, instead of conveying Greek and Latin through the custom-house. The rest of his time he passed in London.

Now, from the days when it was always summer in Eden, to these days when it is mostly winter in fallen latitudes, the world of a man has invariably gone one way—

Charles Darnay's way—the way of the love of a woman.

He had loved Lucie Manette from the hour of his danger. He had never heard a sound so sweet and dear as the sound of her compassionate voice; he had never seen a face so tenderly beautiful, as hers when it was confronted with his own on the edge of the grave that had been dug for him. But, he had not yet spoken to her on the subject; the assassination at the deserted château far away beyond the heaving water and the long, long, dusty roads—the solid stone château which had itself become the mere mist of a dream—had been done a year, and he had never yet, by so much as a single spoken word, disclosed to her the state of his heart.

That he had his reasons for this, he knew full well. It was again a summer day when, lately arrived in London from his college occupation, he turned into the quiet corner in Soho, bent on seeking an opportunity of opening his mind to Doctor Manette. It was the close of the summer day, and he knew Lucie to be out with Miss Pross.

He found the Doctor reading in his arm-chair at a window. The energy which had at once supported him under his old sufferings and aggravated their sharpness had been gradually restored to him. He was now a very energetic man indeed, with great firmness of purpose, strength of resolution, and vigour of action. In his recovered energy he was sometimes a little fitful and sudden, as he had at first been in the exercise of his other recovered faculties; but, this had never been frequently observable, and had grown more and more rare.

He studied much, slept little, sustained a great deal of fatigue with ease, and was equably cheerful. To him, now entered Charles Darnay, at sight of whom he laid aside his book and held out his hand.

"Charles Darnay! I rejoice to see you. We have been counting on your return these three or four days past. Mr. Stryver and Sydney Carton were both here yesterday, and both made you out to be more than due."

"I am obliged to them for their interest in the matter," he answered, a little coldly as to them, though very warmly as to the Doctor. "Miss Manette—"

"Is well," said the Doctor, as he stopped short, "and your return will delight us all. She has gone out on some household matters, but will soon be home."

"Doctor Manette, I knew she was from home. I took the

opportunity of her being from home, to beg to speak to you."

There was a blank silence.

"Yes?" said the Doctor, with evident constraint. "Bring your chair here, and speak on."

He complied as to the chair, but appeared to find the speaking on less easy.

"I have had the happiness, Doctor Manette, of being so intimate here," so he at length began, "for some year and a half, that I hope the topic on which I am about to touch may not—"

He was stayed by the Doctor's putting out his hand to stop him. When he had kept it so a little while, he said, drawing it back:

"Is Lucie the topic?"

"She is."

"It is hard for me to speak of her at any time. It is very hard for me to hear her spoken of in that tone of yours, Charles Darnay."

"It is a tone of fervent admiration, true homage, and deep love, Doctor Manette!" he said deferentially.

There was another blank silence before her father rejoined:

"I believe it. I do you justice; I believe it."

His constraint was so manifest, and it was so manifest, too, that it originated in an unwillingness to approach the subject, that Charles Darnay hesitated.

"Shall I go on, sir?"

Another blank.

"Yes, go on."

"You anticipate what I would say, though you cannot know how earnestly I say it, how earnestly I feel it, without knowing my secret heart, and the hopes and fears and anxieties with which it has long been laden. Dear Doctor Manette, I love your daughter fondly, dearly, disinterestedly, devotedly. If ever there were love in the world, I love her. You have loved yourself; let your old love speak for me!"

The Doctor sat with his face turned away, and his eyes bent on the ground. At the last words, he stretched out his hand again, hurriedly, and cried:

"Not that, sir! Let that be! I adjure you, do not recall that!"

His cry was so like a cry of actual pain, that it rang in

Charles Darnay's ears long after he had ceased. He motioned with the hand he had extended, and it seemed to be an appeal to Darnay to pause. The latter so received it, and remained silent.

"I ask your pardon," said the Doctor, in a subdued tone, after some moments. "I do not doubt your loving Lucie; you may be satisfied of it."

He turned towards him in his chair, but did not look at him, or raise his eyes. His chin dropped upon his hand, and his white hair overshadowed his face.

"Have you spoken to Lucie?"

"No."

"Nor written?"

"Never."

"It would be ungenerous to affect not to know that your self-denial is to be referred to your consideration for her father. Her father thanks you."

He offered his hand; but his eyes did not go with it.

"I know," said Darnay, respectfully, "how can I fail to know, Doctor Manette, I who have seen you together from day to day, that between you and Miss Manette there is an affection so unusual, so touching, so belonging to the circumstances in which it has been nurtured, that it can have few parallels, even in the tenderness between a father and child. I know, Doctor Manette—how can I fail to know—that, mingled with the affection and duty of a daughter who has become a woman, there is, in her heart, towards you, all the love and reliance of infancy itself. I know that, as in her childhood she had no parent, so she is now devoted to you with all the constancy and fervour of her present years and character, united to the trustfulness and attachment of the early days in which you were lost to her. I know perfectly well that if you had been restored to her from the world beyond this life, you could hardly be invested, in her sight, with a more sacred character than that in which you are always with her. I know that when she is clinging to you, the hands of baby, girl, and woman, all in one, are around your neck. I know that in loving you she sees and loves her mother at her own age, sees and loves you at my age, loves her mother brokenhearted, loves you through your dreadful trial and in your blessed restoration. I have known this, night and day, since I have known you in your home."

Her father sat silent, with his face bent down. His

breathing was a little quickened; but he repressed all other signs of agitation.

"Dear Doctor Manette, always knowing this, always seeing her and you with this hallowed light about you, I have forborne, and forborne as long as it was in the nature of man to do it. I have felt, and do even now feel, that to bring my love—even mine—between you, is to touch your history with something not quite so good as itself. But I love her. Heaven is my witness that I love her!"

"I believe it," answered her father, mournfully. "I have thought so before now. I believe it."

"But, do not believe," said Darnay, upon whose ear the mournful voice struck with a reproachful sound, "that if my fortune were so cast as that, being one day so happy as to make her my wife, I must at any time put any separation between her and you, I could or would breathe a word of what I now say. Besides that I should know it to be hopeless, I should know it to be a baseness. If I had any such possibility, even at a remote distance of years, harboured in my thoughts, and hidden in my heart—if it ever had been there—if it ever could be there—I could not now touch this honoured hand."

He laid his own upon it as he spoke.

"No, dear Doctor Manette. Like you, a voluntary exile from France; like you, driven from it by its distractions, oppressions, and miseries; like you, striving to live away from it by my own exertions, and trusting in a happier future; I look only to sharing your fortunes, sharing your life and home, and being faithful to you to the death. Not to divide with Lucie her privilege as your child, companion, and friend; but to come in aid of it, and bind her closer to you, if such a thing can be."

His touch still lingered on her father's hand. Answering the touch for a moment, but not coldly, her father rested his hands upon the arms of his chair, and looked up for the first time since the beginning of the conference. A struggle was evidently in his face; a struggle with that occasional look which had a tendency in it to dark doubt and dread.

"You speak so feelingly and so manfully, Charles Darnay, that I thank you with all my heart, and will open all my heart—or nearly so. Have you any reason to believe that Lucie loves you?"

"None. As yet, none."

"Is it the immediate object of this confidence, that you may at once ascertain that, with my knowledge?"

"Not even so. I might not have the hopefulness to do it for weeks; I might (mistaken or not mistaken) have that hopefulness to-morrow."

"Do you seek any guidance from me?"

"I ask none, sir. But I have thought it possible that you might have it in your power, if you should deem it right, to give me some."

"Do you seek any promise from me?"

"I do seek that."

"What is it?"

"I well understand that, without you, I could have no hope. I well understand that, even if Miss Manette held me at this moment in her innocent heart—do not think I have the presumption to assume so much—I could retain no place in it against her love for her father."

"If that be so, do you see what, on the other hand, is involved in it?"

"I understand equally well, that a word from her father in any suitor's favour would outweigh herself and all the world. For which reason, Doctor Manette," said Darnay, modestly but firmly, "I would not ask that word, to save my life."

"I am sure of it. Charles Darnay, mysteries arise out of close love, as well as out of wide division; in the former case, they are subtle and delicate, and difficult to penetrate. My daughter Lucie is, in this one respect, such a mystery to me; I can make no guess at the state of her heart."

"May I ask, sir, if you think she is—" As he hesitated her father supplied the rest.

"Is sought by any other suitor?"

"It is what I meant to say."

Her father considered a little before he answered:

"You have seen Mr. Carton here, yourself. Mr. Stryver is here too, occasionally. If it be at all, it can only be by one of these."

"Or both," said Darnay.

"I had not thought of both; I should not think either likely. You want a promise from me. Tell me what it is."

"It is, that if Miss Manette should bring to you at any time, on her own part, such a confidence as I have ventured to lay before you, you will bear testimony to what I have said, and to your belief in it. I hope you may be able to think so well of me, as to urge no influence against me. I say nothing more of my stake in this; this is what I ask. The condition on which I ask it, and which you have an undoubted right to require, I will observe immediately."

"I give the promise," said the Doctor, "without any condition. I believe your object to be, purely and truthfully, as you have stated it. I believe your intention is to perpetuate, and not to weaken, the ties between me and my other and far dearer self. If she should ever tell me that you are essential to her perfect happiness, I will give her to you. If there were—Charles Darnay, if there were—"

The young man had taken his hand gratefully; their hands were joined as the Doctor spoke:

"—any fancies, any reasons, any apprehensions, anything whatsoever, new or old, against the man she really loved—the direct responsibility thereof not lying on his head—they should all be obliterated for her sake. She is everything to me; more to me than suffering, more to me than wrong, more to me— Well! This is idle talk."

So strange was the way in which he faded into silence, and so strange his fixed look when he had ceased to speak, that Darnay felt his own hand turn cold in the hand that slowly released and dropped it.

"You said something to me," said Doctor Manette, breaking into a smile. "What was it you said to me?"

He was at a loss how to answer, until he remembered having spoken of a condition. Relieved as his mind reverted to that, he answered:

"Your confidence in me ought to be returned with full confidence on my part. My present name, though but slightly changed from my mother's, is not, as you will remember, my own. I wish to tell you what that is, and why I am in England."

"Stop!" said the Doctor of Beauvais.

"I wish it, that I may the better deserve your confidence, and have no secret from you."

"Stop!"

For an instant, the Doctor even had his two hands at his ears; for another instant, even had his two hands laid on Darnay's lips.

"Tell me when I ask you, not now. If your suit should prosper, if Lucie should love you, you shall tell me on your marriage morning. Do you promise?"

"Willingly."

"Give me your hand. She will be home directly, and it is better she should not see us together to-night. Go! God bless you!"

It was dark when Charles Darnay left him, and it was an hour later and darker when Lucie came home; she hurried into the room alone—for Miss Pross had gone straight upstairs—and was surprised to find his reading-chair empty.

"My father!" she called to him. "Father dear!"

Nothing was said in answer, but she heard a low hammering sound in his bedroom. Passing lightly across the intermediate room, she looked in at his door and came running back frightened, crying to herself, with her blood all chilled, "What shall I do! What shall I do!"

Her uncertainty lasted but a moment; she hurried back, and tapped at his door, and softly called to him. The noise ceased at the sound of her voice, and he presently came out to her, and they walked up and down together for a long time.

She came down from her bed, to look at him in his sleep that night. He slept heavily, and his tray of shoemaking tools, and his old unfinished work, were all as usual.

11 *A Companion Picture*

"SYDNEY," said Mr. Stryver, on that self-same night, or morning, to his jackal; "mix another bowl of punch; I have something to say to you."

Sydney had been working double tides that night, and the night before, and the night before that, and a good many nights in succession, making a grand clearance among Mr. Stryver's papers before the setting in of the long vacation. The clearance was effected at last; the Stryver arrears were handsomely fetched up; everything was got rid of until November should come with its fogs atmospheric and fogs legal, and bring grist to the mill again.

Sydney was none the livelier and none the soberer for so

much application. It had taken a deal of extra wet-towelling to pull him through the night; a correspondingly extra quantity of wine had preceded the towelling; and he was in a very damaged condition, as he now pulled his turban off and threw it into the basin in which he had steeped it at intervals for the last six hours.

"Are you mixing that other bowl of punch?" said Stryver the portly, with his hands in his waistband, glancing round from the sofa where he lay on his back.

"I am."

"Now, look here! I am going to tell you something that will rather surprise you, and that perhaps will make you think me not quite as shrewd as you usually do think me. I intend to marry."

"*Do* you?"

"Yes. And not for money. What do you say now?"

"I don't feel disposed to say much. Who is she?"

"Guess."

"Do I know her?"

"Guess."

"I am not going to guess, at five o'clock in the morning, with my brains frying and sputtering in my head. If you want me to guess, you must ask me to dinner."

"Well, then, I'll tell you," said Stryver, coming slowly into a sitting posture. "Sydney, I rather despair of making myself intelligible to you, because you are such an insensible dog."

"And you," returned Sydney, busy concocting the punch, "are such a sensitive and poetical spirit."

"Come!" rejoined Stryver, laughing boastfully, "though I don't prefer any claim to being the soul of Romance (for I hope I know better), still I am a tenderer sort of fellow than *you*."

"You are a luckier, if you mean that."

"I don't mean that. I mean I am a man of more— more—"

"Say gallantry, while you are about it," suggested Carton.

"Well! I'll say gallantry. My meaning is that I am a man," said Stryver, inflating himself at his friend as he made the punch, "who cares more to be agreeable, who takes more pains to be agreeable, who knows better how to be agreeable, in a woman's society, than you do."

"Go on," said Sydney Carton.

"No; but before I go on," said Stryver, shaking his head in his bullying way, "I'll have this out with you. You've been at Doctor Manette's house as much as I have, or more than I have. Why, I have been ashamed of your moroseness there! Your manners have been of that silent and sullen and hang-dog kind, that, upon my life and soul, I have been ashamed of you, Sydney!"

"It should be very beneficial to a man in your practice at the bar, to be ashamed of anything," returned Sydney; "you ought to be much obliged to me."

"You shall not get off in that way," rejoined Stryver, shouldering the rejoinder at him; "no, Sydney, it's my duty to tell you—and I tell you to your face to do you good—that you are a de-vilish ill-conditioned fellow in that sort of society. You are a disagreeable fellow."

Sydney drank a bumper of the punch he had made, and laughed.

"Look at me!" said Stryver, squaring himself; "I have less need to make myself agreeable than you have, being more independent in circumstances. Why do I do it?"

"I never saw you do it yet," muttered Carton.

"I do it because it's politic; I do it on principle. And look at me! I get on!"

"You don't get on with your account of your matrimonial intentions," answered Carton, with a careless air; "I wish you would keep to that. As to me—will you never understand that I am incorrigible?"

He asked the question with some appearance of scorn.

"You have no business to be incorrigible," was his friend's answer, delivered in no very soothing tone.

"I have no business to be, at all, that I know of," said Sydney Carton. "Who is the lady?"

"Now, don't let my announcement of the name make you uncomfortable, Sydney," said Mr. Stryver, preparing him with ostentatious friendliness for the disclosure he was about to make, "because I know you don't mean half you say; and if you meant it all, it would be of no importance. I make this little preface, because you once mentioned the young lady to me in slighting terms."

"I did?"

"Certainly; and in these chambers."

Sydney Carton looked at his punch and looked at his complacent friend; drank his punch and looked at his complacent friend.

"You made mention of the young lady as a golden-haired doll. The young lady is Miss Manette. If you had been a fellow of any sensitiveness or delicacy of feeling in that kind of way, Sydney, I might have been a little resentful of your employing such a designation; but you are not. You want that sense altogether; therefore I am no more annoyed when I think of the expression, than I should be annoyed by a man's opinion of a picture of mine, who had no eye for pictures: or of a piece of music of mine, who had no ear for music."

Sydney Carton drank the punch at a great rate; drank it by bumpers, looking at his friend.

"Now you know all about it, Syd," said Mr. Stryver. "I don't care about fortune: she is a charming creature, and I have made up my mind to please myself: on the whole, I think I can afford to please myself. She will have in me a man already pretty well off, and a rapidly rising man, and a man of some distinction: it is a piece of good fortune for her, but she is worthy of good fortune. Are you astonished?"

Carton, still drinking the punch, rejoined, "Why should I be astonished?"

"You approve?"

Carton, still drinking the punch, rejoined, "Why should I not approve?"

"Well!" said his friend Stryver, "you take it more easily than I fancied you would, and are less mercenary on my behalf than I thought you would be; though, to be sure, you know well enough by this time that your ancient chum is a man of a pretty strong will. Yes, Sydney, I have had enough of this style of life, with no other as a change from it; I feel that it is a pleasant thing for a man to have a home when he feels inclined to go to it (when he doesn't, he can stay away), and I feel that Miss Manette will tell well in any station, and will always do me credit. So I have made up my mind. And now, Sydney, old boy, I want to say a word to *you* about *your* prospects. You are in a bad way, you know; you really are in a bad way. You don't know the value of money, you live hard, you'll knock up one of these days, and be ill and poor; you really ought to think about a nurse."

The prosperous patronage with which he said it, made him look twice as big as he was, and four times as offensive.

"Now, let me recommend you," pursued Stryver, "to

look it in the face. I have looked it in the face, in my different way; look it in the face, you, in your different way. Marry. Provide somebody to take care of you. Never mind your having no enjoyment of women's society, nor understanding of it, nor tact for it. Find out somebody. Find out some respectable woman with a little property—somebody in the landlady way, or lodging-letting way—and marry her, against a rainy day. That's the kind of thing for *you*. Now think of it, Sydney."

"I'll think of it," said Sydney.

*   *   *   *   *   *   *   *

12   *The Fellow of Delicacy*

MR. STRYVER having made up his mind to that magnanimous bestowal of good fortune on the Doctor's daughter, resolved to make her happiness known to her before he left town for the Long Vacation. After some mental debating of the point, he came to the conclusion that it would be as well to get all the preliminaries done with, and they could then arrange at their leisure whether he should give her his hand a week or two before Michaelmas Term, or in the little Christmas vacation between it and Hilary.

As to the strength of his case, he had not a doubt about it, but clearly saw his way to the verdict. Argued with the jury on substantial worldly grounds—the only grounds ever worth taking into account—it was a plain case, and had not a weak spot in it. He called himself for the plaintiff, there was no getting over his evidence, the counsel for the defendant threw up his brief, and the jury did not even turn to consider. After trying it, Stryver, C. J., was satisfied that no plainer case could be.

Accordingly, Mr. Stryver inaugurated the Long Vacation with a formal proposal to take Miss Manette to Vauxhall Gardens; that failing, to Ranelagh; that unaccountably failing too, it behoved him to present himself in Soho, and there declare his noble mind.

Towards Soho, therefore, Mr. Stryver shouldered his

way from the Temple, while the bloom of the Long Vacation's infancy was still upon it. Anybody who had seen him projecting himself into Soho while he was yet on Saint Dunstan's side of Temple Bar, bursting in his full-blown way along the pavement, to the jostlement of all weaker people, might have seen how safe and strong he was.

His way taking him past Tellson's, and he both banking at Tellson's and knowing Mr. Lorry as the intimate friend of the Manettes, it entered Mr. Stryver's mind to enter the bank, and reveal to Mr. Lorry the brightness of the Soho horizon. So, he pushed open the door with the weak rattle in its throat, stumbled down the two steps, got past the two ancient cashiers, and shouldered himself into the musty back closet where Mr. Lorry sat at great books ruled for figures, with perpendicular iron bars to his window as if that were ruled for figures too, and everything under the clouds were a sum.

"Halloa!" said Mr. Stryver. "How do you do? I hope you are well!"

It was Stryver's grand peculiarity that he always seemed too big for any place, or space. He was so much too big for Tellson's, that old clerks in distant corners looked up with looks of remonstrance, as though he squeezed them against the wall. The House itself, magnificently reading the paper quite in the far-off perspective, lowered displeased, as if the Stryver head had been butted into its responsible waistcoat.

The discreet Mr. Lorry said, in a sample tone of the voice he would recommend under the circumstances, "How do you do, Mr. Stryver? How do you do, sir?" and shook hands. There was a peculiarity in his manner of shaking hands, always to be seen in any clerk at Tellson's who shook hands with a customer when the House pervaded the air. He shook in a self-abnegating way, as one who shook for Tellson and Co.

"Can I do anything for you, Mr. Stryver?" asked Mr. Lorry, in his business character.

"Why, no, thank you; this is a private visit to yourself, Mr. Lorry; I have come for a private word."

"Oh indeed!" said Mr. Lorry, bending down his ear, while his eye strayed to the House afar off.

"I am going," said Mr. Stryver, leaning his arms confidentially on the desk: whereupon, although it was a large double one, there appeared to be not half desk enough for him: "I am going to make an offer of myself in marriage to your agreeable little friend, Miss Manette, Mr. Lorry."

"Oh dear me!" cried Mr. Lorry, rubbing his chin, and looking at his visitor dubiously.

"Oh dear me, sir?" repeated Stryver, drawing back. "Oh dear you, sir? What may your meaning be, Mr. Lorry?"

"My meaning," answered the man of business, "is, of course, friendly and appreciative, and that it does you the greatest credit, and—in short, my meaning is everything you could desire. But—really, you know, Mr. Stryver—" Mr. Lorry paused, and shook his head at him in the oddest manner, as if he were compelled against his will to add, internally, "you know there really is so much too much of you!"

"Well!" said Stryver, slapping the desk with his contentious hand, opening his eyes wider, and taking a long breath; "if I understand you, Mr. Lorry, I'll be hanged!"

Mr. Lorry adjusted his little wig at both ears as a means towards that end, and bit the feather of a pen.

"D——n it all, sir!" said Stryver, staring at him, "am I not eligible?"

"Oh dear yes! Yes. Oh yes, you're eligible!" said Mr. Lorry. "If you say eligible, you are eligible."

"Am I not prosperous?" asked Stryver.

"Oh! if you come to prosperous, you are prosperous," said Mr. Lorry.

"And advancing?"

"If you come to advancing, you know," said Mr. Lorry, delighted to be able to make another admission, "nobody can doubt that."

"Then what on earth is your meaning, Mr. Lorry?" demanded Stryver, perceptibly crestfallen.

"Well! I— Were you going there now?" asked Mr. Lorry.

"Straight!" said Stryver, with a plump of his fist on the desk.

"Then I think I wouldn't, if I was you."

"Why?" said Stryver. "Now, I'll put you in a corner," forensically shaking a forefinger at him. "You are a man of business and bound to have a reason. State your reason. Why wouldn't you go?"

"Because," said Mr. Lorry, "I wouldn't go on such an

object without having some cause to believe that I should succeed."

"D——n me!" cried Stryver, "but this beats everything."

Mr. Lorry glanced at the distant House, and glanced at the angry Stryver.

"Here's a man of business—a man of years—a man of experience—*in* a bank," said Stryver; "and having summed up three leading reasons for complete success, he says there's no reason at all! Says it with his head on!" Mr. Stryver remarked upon the peculiarity as if it would have been infinitely less remarkable if he had said it with his head off.

"When I speak of success, I speak of success with the young lady; and when I speak of causes and reasons to make success probable, I speak of causes and reasons that will tell as such with the young lady. The young lady, my good sir," said Mr. Lorry, mildly tapping the Stryver arm, "the young lady. The young lady goes before all."

"Then you mean to tell me, Mr. Lorry," said Stryver, squaring his elbows, "that it is your deliberate opinion that the young lady at present in question is a mincing fool?"

"Not exactly so. I mean to tell you, Mr. Stryver," said Mr. Lorry, reddening, "that I will hear no disrespectful word of that young lady from any lips; and that if I knew any man—which I hope I do not—whose taste was so coarse, and whose temper was so overbearing, that he could not restrain himself from speaking disrespectfully of that young lady at this desk, not even Tellson's should prevent my giving him a piece of my mind."

The necessity of being angry in a suppressed tone had put Mr. Stryver's blood-vessels into a dangerous state when it was his turn to be angry; Mr. Lorry's veins, methodical as their courses could usually be, were in no better state now it was his turn.

"That is what I mean to tell you, sir," said Mr. Lorry. "Pray let there be no mistake about it."

Mr. Stryver sucked the end of a ruler for a little while, and then stood hitting a tune out of his teeth with it, which probably gave him the toothache. He broke the awkward silence by saying:

"This is something new to me, Mr. Lorry. You deliberately advise me not to go up to Soho and offer myself—*myself*, Stryver of the King's Bench bar?"

"Do you ask me for my advice, Mr. Stryver?"

"Yes, I do."

"Very good. Then I give it, and you have repeated it correctly."

"And all I can say of it is," laughed Stryver with a vexed laugh, "that this—ha, ha!—beats everything past, present, and to come."

"Now understand me," pursued Mr. Lorry. "As a man of business, I am not justified in saying anything about this matter, for, as a man of business, I know nothing of it. But, as an old fellow, who has carried Miss Manette in his arms, who is the trusted friend of Miss Manette and of her father too, and who has a great affection for them both, I have spoken. The confidence is not of my seeking, recollect. Now, you think I may not be right?"

"Not I!" said Stryver, whistling. "I can't undertake to find third parties in common sense; I can only find it for myself. I suppose sense in certain quarters; you suppose mincing bread-and-butter nonsense. It's new to me, but you are right, I dare say."

"What I suppose, Mr. Stryver, I claim to characterise for myself. And understand me, sir," said Mr. Lorry quickly flushing again, "I will not—not even at Tellson's—have it characterised for me by any gentleman breathing."

"There! I beg your pardon!" said Stryver.

"Granted. Thank you. Well, Mr. Stryver, I was about to say: it might be painful to you to find yourself mistaken, it might be painful to Doctor Manette to have the task of being explicit with you, it might be very painful to Miss Manette to have the task of being explicit with you. You know the terms upon which I have the honour and happiness to stand with the family. If you please, committing you in no way, representing you in no way, I will undertake to correct my advice by the exercise of a little new observation and judgment expressly brought to bear upon it. If you should then be dissatisfied with it, you can but test its soundness for yourself; if, on the other hand, you should be satisfied with it, and it should be what it now is, it may spare all sides what is best spared. What do you say?"

"How long would you keep me in town?"

"Oh! It is only a question of a few hours. I could go to Soho in the evening, and come to your chambers afterwards."

"Then I say yes," said Stryver. "I won't go up there

now, I am not so hot upon it as that comes to; I say yes, and I shall expect you to look in to-night. Good-morning."

Then Mr. Stryver turned and burst out of the Bank, causing such a concussion of air on his passage through, that to stand up against it bowing behind the two counters, required the utmost remaining strength of the two ancient clerks. Those vulnerable and feeble persons were always seen by the public in the act of bowing, and were popularly believed, when they had bowed a customer out, still to keep on bowing in the empty office until they bowed another customer in.

The barrister was keen enough to divine that the banker would not have gone so far in his expression of opinion on any less solid ground than moral certainty. Unprepared as he was for the large pill he had to swallow, he got it down. "And now," said Mr. Stryver, shaking his forensic forefinger at the Temple in general, when it was down, "my way out of this is to put you all in the wrong."

It was a bit of the art of an Old Bailey tactician, in which he found great relief. "You shall not put me in the wrong, young lady," said Mr. Stryver; "I'll do that for you."

Accordingly, when Mr. Lorry called that night as late as ten o'clock, Mr. Stryver, among a quantity of books and papers littered out for the purpose, seemed to have nothing less on his mind than the subject of the morning. He even showed surprise when he saw Mr. Lorry, and was altogether in an absent and preoccupied state.

"Well!" said that good-natured emissary, after a full half-hour of bootless attempts to bring him round to the question. "I have been to Soho."

"To Soho?" repeated Mr. Stryver, coldly. "Oh to be sure! What am I thinking of!"

"And I have no doubt," said Mr. Lorry, "that I was right in the conversation we had. My opinion is confirmed, and I reiterate my advice."

"I assure you," returned Mr. Stryver, in the friendliest way, "that I am sorry for it on your account, and sorry for it on the poor father's account. I know this must always be a sore subject with the family; let us say no more about it."

"I don't understand you," said Mr. Lorry.

"I dare say not," rejoined Stryver, nodding his head in a smoothing and final way; "no matter, no matter."

"But it does matter," Mr. Lorry urged.

"No it doesn't; I assure you it doesn't. Having supposed that there was sense where there is no sense, and a laudable ambition where there is not a laudable ambition, I am well out of my mistake, and no harm is done. Young women have committed similar follies often before, and have repented them in poverty and obscurity often before. In an unselfish aspect, I am sorry that the thing is dropped, because it would have been a bad thing for me in a worldly point of view; in a selfish aspect, I am glad that the thing has dropped, because it would have been a bad thing for me in a worldly point of view—it is hardly necessary to say I could have gained nothing by it. There is no harm at all done. I have not proposed to the young lady, and, between ourselves, I am by no means certain, on reflection, that I ever should have committed myself to that extent. Mr. Lorry, you can not control the mincing vanities and giddinesses of empty-headed girls; you must not expect to do it, or you will always be disappointed. Now, pray say no more about it. I tell you, I regret it on account of others, but I am satisfied on my own account. And I am really very much obliged to you for allowing me to sound you, and for giving me your advice; you know the young lady better than I do; you were right, it never would have done."

Mr. Lorry was so taken aback, that he looked quite stupidly at Mr. Stryver shouldering him towards the door, with an appearance of showering generosity, forbearance, and good-will on his erring head. "Make the best of it, my dear sir," said Stryver; "say no more about it; thank you again for allowing me to sound you; good-night!"

Mr. Lorry was out in the night, before he knew where he was. Mr. Stryver was lying back on his sofa, winking at his ceiling.

13 *The Fellow of No Delicacy*

IF SYDNEY CARTON ever shone anywhere, he certainly never shone in the house of Doctor Manette. He had been there often, during a whole year, and had always been the same moody and morose lounger there. When he cared to talk, he talked well; but, the cloud of caring for nothing, which overshadowed him with such a fatal darkness, was very rarely pierced by the light within him.

And yet he did care something for the streets that environed that house, and for the senseless stones that made their pavements. Many a night he vaguely and unhappily wandered there, when wine had brought no transitory gladness to him; many a dreary daybreak revealed his solitary figure lingering there, and still lingering there when the first beams of the sun brought into strong relief, removed beauties of architecture in spires of churches and lofty buildings, as perhaps the quiet time brought some sense of better things, else forgotten and unattainable, into his mind. Of late, the neglected bed in the Temple Court had known him more scantily than ever; and often when he had thrown himself upon it no longer than a few minutes, he had got up again, and haunted that neighbourhood.

On a day in August, when Mr. Stryver (after notifying to his jackal that "he had thought better of that marrying matter") had carried his delicacy into Devonshire, and when the sight and scent of flowers in the City streets had some waifs of goodness in them for the worst, of health for the sickliest, and of youth for the oldest, Sydney's feet still trod those stones. From being irresolute and purposeless, his feet became animated by an intention, and, in the working out of that intention, they took him to the Doctor's door.

He was shown upstairs, and found Lucie at her work, alone. She had never been quite at her ease with him, and received him with some little embarrassment as he seated himself near her table. But, looking up at his face in the interchange of the first few common-places, she observed a change in it.

"I fear you are not well, Mr. Carton!"

"No. But the life I lead, Miss Manette, is not conducive to health. What is to be expected of, or by, such profligates?"

"Is it not—forgive me; I have begun the question on my lips—a pity to live no better life?"

"God knows it is a shame!"

"Then why not change it?"

Looking gently at him again, she was surprised and saddened to see that there were tears in his eyes. There were tears in his voice too, as he answered:

"It is too late for that. I shall never be better than I am. I shall sink lower, and be worse."

He leaned an elbow on her table, and covered his eyes with his hand. The table trembled in the silence that followed.

She had never seen him softened, and was much distressed. He knew her to be so, without looking at her, and said:

"Pray forgive me, Miss Manette. I break down before the knowledge of what I want to say to you. Will you hear me?"

"If it will do you any good, Mr. Carton, if it would make you happier, it would make me very glad!"

"God bless you for your sweet compassion!"

He unshaded his face after a little while, and spoke steadily.

"Don't be afraid to hear me. Don't shrink from anything I say. I am like one who died young. All my life might have been."

"No, Mr. Carton. I am sure that the best part of it might still be; I am sure that you might be much, much worthier of yourself."

"Say of you, Miss Manette, and although I know better—although in the mystery of my own wretched heart I know better—I shall never forget it!"

She was pale and trembling. He came to her relief with a fixed despair of himself which made the interview unlike any other that could have been holden.

"If it had been possible, Miss Manette, that you could

have returned the love of the man you see before you—self-flung away, wasted, drunken, poor creature of misuse as you know him to be—he would have been conscious this day and hour, in spite of his happiness, that he would bring you to misery, bring you to sorrow and repentance, blight you, disgrace you, pull you down with him. I know very well that you can have no tenderness for me; I ask for none; I am even thankful that it cannot be."

"Without it, can I not save you, Mr. Carton? Can I not recall you—forgive me again!—to a better course? Can I in no way repay your confidence? I know this is a confidence," she modestly said, after a little hesitation, and in earnest tears, "I know you would say this to no one else. Can I turn it to no good account for yourself, Mr. Carton?"

He shook his head.

"To none. No, Miss Manette, to none. If you will hear me through a very little more, all you can ever do for me is done. I wish you to know that you have been the last dream of my soul. In my degradation I have not been so degraded but that the sight of you with your father, and of this home made such a home by you, has stirred old shadows that I thought had died out of me. Since I knew you, I have been troubled by a remorse that I thought would never reproach me again, and have heard whispers from old voices impelling me upward, that I thought were silent forever. I have had unformed ideas of striving afresh, beginning anew, shaking off sloth and sensuality, and fighting out the abandoned fight. A dream, all a dream, that ends in nothing, and leaves the sleeper where he lay down, but I wish you to know that you inspired it."

"Will nothing of it remain? O Mr. Carton, think again! Try again!"

"No, Miss Manette; all through it, I have known myself to be quite undeserving. And yet I have had the weakness, and have still the weakness, to wish you to know with what a sudden mastery you kindled me, heap of ashes that I am, into fire—a fire, however, inseparable in its nature from myself, quickening nothing, lighting nothing, doing no service, idly burning away."

"Since it is my misfortune, Mr. Carton, to have made you more unhappy than you were before you knew me—"

"Don't say that, Miss Manette, for you would have reclaimed me, if anything could. You will not be the cause of my becoming worse."

"Since the state of your mind that you describe, is, at all events, attributable to some influence of mine—this is what I mean, if I can make it plain—can I use no influence to serve you? Have I no power for good, with you, at all?"

"The utmost good that I am capable of now, Miss Manette, I have come here to realise. Let me carry through the rest of my misdirected life the remembrance that I opened my heart to you, last of all the world; and that there was something left in me at this time which you could deplore and pity."

"Which I entreated you to believe again and again, most fervently, with all my heart, was capable of better things, Mr. Carton!"

"Entreat me to believe it no more, Miss Manette. I have proved myself, and I know better. I distress you; I draw fast to an end. Will you let me believe, when I recall this day, that the last confidence of my life was reposed in your pure and innocent breast, and that it lies there alone, and will be shared by no one?"

"If that will be a consolation to you, yes."

"Not even by the dearest one ever to be known to you?"

"Mr. Carton," she answered, after an agitated pause, "the secret is yours, not mine; and I promise to respect it."

"Thank you. And again, God bless you."

He put her hand to his lips, and moved towards the door.

"Be under no apprehension, Miss Manette, of my ever resuming this conversation by so much as a passing word. I will never refer to it again. If I were dead, that could not be surer than it is henceforth. In the hour of my death, I shall hold sacred the one good remembrance—and shall thank and bless you for it—that my last avowal of myself was made to you, and that my name, and faults, and miseries were gently carried in your heart. May it otherwise be light and happy!"

He was so unlike what he had ever shown himself to be, and it was so sad to think how much he had thrown away, and how much he every day kept down and perverted, that Lucie Manette wept mournfully for him as he stood looking back to her.

"Be comforted!" he said. "I am not worth such feeling, Miss Manette. An hour or two hence, and the low companions and low habits that I scorn but yield to, will render me less worth such tears as those, than any wretch who creeps along the streets. Be comforted! But, within myself, I shall always be, towards you, what I am now, though outwardly I shall be what you have heretofore seen me. The last supplication but one I make to you, is, that you will believe this of me."

"I will, Mr. Carton."

"My last supplication of all is this; and with it, I will relieve you of a visitor with whom I well know you have nothing in unison, and between whom and you there is an impassable space. It is useless to say it, I know, but it rises out of my soul. For you, and for any dear to you, I would do anything. If my career were of that better kind that there was any opportunity or capacity of sacrifice in it, I would embrace any sacrifice for you and for those dear to you. Try to hold me in your mind, at some quiet times, as ardent and sincere in this one thing. The time will come, the time will not be long in coming, when new ties will be formed about you—ties that will bind you yet more tenderly and strongly to the home you so adorn —the dearest ties that will ever grace and gladden you. O Miss Manette, when the little picture of a happy father's face looks up in yours, when you see your own bright beauty springing up anew at your feet, think now and then that there is a man who would give his life, to keep a life you love beside you!"

He said, "Farewell!" said a last "God bless you!" and left her.

---

14 *The Honest Tradesman*

TO THE EYES of Mr. Jeremiah Cruncher, sitting on his stool in Fleet Street with his grisly urchin beside him, a vast number and variety of objects in movement were every day presented. Who could sit upon anything in Fleet Street during the busy hours of the day, and not be dazed and deafened by two immense processions, one ever tending westward with the sun, the other ever tending eastward from the sun, both ever tending to the plains beyond the range of red and purple where the sun goes down!

With his straw in his mouth, Mr. Cruncher sat watching the two streams, like the heathen rustic who has for several centuries been on duty watching one stream—saving that Jerry had no expectation of their ever running dry. Nor would it have been an expectation of a hopeful kind, since a small part of his income was derived from the pilotage of timid women (mostly of a full habit and past the middle term of life) from Tellson's side of the tides to the opposite shore. Brief as such companionship was in every separate instance, Mr. Cruncher never failed to become so interested in the lady as to express a strong desire to have the honour of drinking her very good health. And it was from the gifts bestowed upon him towards the execution of this benevolent purpose, that he recruited his finances, as just now observed.

Time was, when a poet sat upon a stool in a public place, and mused in the sight of men. Mr. Cruncher, sitting on a stool in a public place, but not being a poet, mused as little as possible, and looked about him.

It fell out that he was thus engaged in a season when crowds were few, and belated women few, and when his affairs in general were so unprosperous as to awaken a strong suspicion in his breast that Mrs. Cruncher must have been "flopping" in some pointed manner, when an unusual concourse, pouring down Fleet Street westward, attracted his attention. Looking that way, Mr. Cruncher made out that some kind of funeral was coming along, and that there was popular objection to this funeral, which engendered uproar.

"Young Jerry," said Mr. Cruncher, turning to his offspring, "it's a buryin'."

"Hooroar, Father!" cried Young Jerry.

The young gentleman uttered this exultant sound with mysterious significance. The elder gentleman took the cry so ill, that he watched his opportunity, and smote the young gentleman on the ear.

"What d'ye mean? What are you hooroaring at? What do you want to conwey to your own father, you young Rip? This boy is a getting too many for *me!*" said Mr.

Cruncher, surveying him. "Him and his hooroars! Don't let me hear no more of you, or you shall feel some more of me. D'ye hear?"

"I warn't doing no harm," Young Jerry protested, rubbing his cheek.

"Drop it then," said Mr. Cruncher; "I won't have none of *your* no harms. Get atop of that there seat, and look at the crowd."

His son obeyed, and the crowd approached; they were bawling and hissing round a dingy hearse and dingy mourning coach, in which mourning coach there was only one mourner, dressed in the dingy trappings that were considered essential to the dignity of the position. The position appeared by no means to please him, however, with an increasing rabble surrounding the coach, deriding him, making grimaces at him, and incessantly groaning and calling out: "Yah! Spies! Tst! Yaha! Spies!" with many compliments too numerous and forcible to repeat.

Funerals had at all times a remarkable attraction for Mr. Cruncher; he always pricked up his senses, and became excited, when a funeral passed Tellson's. Naturally, therefore, a funeral with this uncommon attendance excited him greatly, and he asked of the first man who ran against him:

"What is it, brother? What's it about?"

"*I* don't know," said the man. "Spies! Yaha! Tst! Spies!"

He asked another man. "Who is it?"

"*I* don't know," returned the man, clapping his hands to his mouth nevertheless, and vociferating in a surprising heat and with the greatest ardour, "Spies! Yaha! Tst, tst! Spi-ies!"

At length, a person better informed on the merits of the case, tumbled against him, and from this person he learned that the funeral was the funeral of one Roger Cly.

"Was *he* a spy?" asked Mr. Cruncher.

"Old Bailey spy," returned his informant. "Yaha! Tst! Yah! Old Bailey Spi-i-es!"

"Why, to be sure!" exclaimed Jerry, recalling the Trial at which he had assisted. "I've seen him. Dead, is he?"

"Dead as mutton," returned the other, "and can't be too dead. Have 'em out, there! Spies! Pull 'em out, there! Spies!"

The idea was so acceptable in the prevalent absence of any idea, that the crowd caught it up with eagerness, and loudly repeating the suggestion to have 'em out, and to pull 'em out, mobbed the two vehicles so closely that they came to a stop. On the crowd's opening the coach doors, the one mourner scuffled out of himself and was in their hands for a moment; but he was so alert, and made such good use of his time, that in another moment he was scouring away up a by-street, after shedding his cloak, hat, long hatband, white pocket-handkerchief, and other symbolical tears.

These the people tore to pieces and scattered far and wide with great enjoyment, while the tradesmen hurriedly shut up their shops; for a crowd in those times stopped at nothing, and was a monster much dreaded. They had already got the length of opening the hearse to take the coffin out, when some brighter genius proposed, instead, its being escorted to its destination amidst general rejoicing. Practical suggestions being much needed, this suggestion, too, was received with acclamation, and the coach was immediately filled with eight inside and a dozen out, while as many people got on the roof of the hearse as could by any exercise of ingenuity stick upon it. Among the first of these volunteers was Jerry Cruncher himself, who modestly concealed his spiky head from the observation of Tellson's, in the further corner of the mourning coach.

The officiating undertakers made some protest against these changes in the ceremonies; but, the river being alarmingly near, and several voices remarking on the efficacy of cold immersion in bringing refractory members of the profession to reason, the protest was faint and brief. The remodelled procession started, with a chimney-sweep driving the hearse—advised by the regular driver, who was perched beside him, under close inspection, for the purpose —and with a pieman, also attended by his cabinet minister, driving the mourning coach. A bear-leader, a popular street character of the time, was impressed as an additional ornament, before the cavalcade had gone far down the Strand; and his bear, who was black and very mangy, gave quite an undertaking air to that part of the procession in which he walked.

Thus, with beer-drinking, pipe-smoking, song-roaring, and infinite caricaturing of woe, the disorderly procession went its way, recruiting at every step, and all the shops shutting up before it. Its destination was the old church of Saint Pancras, far off in the fields. It got there in course of time; insisted on pouring into the burial-ground; finally accomplished the interment of the deceased Roger Cly in its own way, and highly to its own satisfaction.

The dead man disposed of, and the crowd being under the necessity of providing some other entertainment for itself, another brighter genius (or perhaps the same) conceived the humour of impeaching casual passers-by, as Old Bailey spies, and wreaking vengeance on them. Chase was given to some scores of inoffensive persons who had never been near the Old Bailey in their lives, in the realisation of this fancy, and they were roughly hustled and maltreated. The transition to the sport of window-breaking, and thence to the plundering of public-houses, was easy and natural. At last, after several hours, when sundry summer-houses had been pulled down, and some area-railings had been torn up, to arm the more belligerent spirits, a rumour got about that the Guards were coming. Before this rumour, the crowd gradually melted away, and perhaps the Guards came, and perhaps they never came, and this was the usual progress of a mob.

Mr. Cruncher did not assist at the closing sports, but had remained behind in the churchyard, to confer and condole with the undertakers. The place had a soothing influence on him. He procured a pipe from a neighbouring public-house, and smoked it, looking in at the railings and maturely considering the spot.

"Jerry," said Mr. Cruncher, apostrophising himself in his usual way, "you see that there Cly that day, and you see with your own eyes that he was a young 'un and a straight made 'un."

Having smoked his pipe out, and ruminated a little longer, he turned himself about, that he might appear, before the hour of closing, on his station at Tellson's. Whether his meditations on mortality had touched his liver, or whether his general health had been previously at all amiss, or whether he desired to show a little attention to an eminent man, is not so much to the purpose, as that he made a short call upon his medical adviser—a distinguished surgeon—on his way back.

Young Jerry relieved his father with dutiful interest, and reported no job in his absence. The bank closed, the ancient clerks came out, the usual watch was set, and Mr. Cruncher and his son went home to tea.

"Now, I tell you where it is!" said Mr. Cruncher to his wife, on entering. "If, as a honest tradesman, my wenturs goes wrong to-night, I shall make sure that you're been praying agin me, and I shall work you for it the same as if I seen you do it."

The dejected Mrs. Cruncher shook her head.

"Why, you're at it afore my face!" said Mr. Cruncher, with signs of angry apprehension.

"I am saying nothing."

"Well, then; don't meditate nothing. You might as well flop as meditate. You may as well go agin me one way as another. Drop it altogether."

"Yes, Jerry."

"Yes, Jerry," repeated Mr. Cruncher, sitting down to tea. "Ah! It *is* yes, Jerry. That's about it. You may say yes, Jerry."

Mr. Cruncher had no particular meaning in these sulky corroborations, but made use of them, as people not unfrequently do, to express general ironical dissatisfaction.

"You and your yes, Jerry," said Mr. Cruncher, taking a bite out of his bread-and-butter, and seeming to help it down with a large invisible oyster out of his saucer. "Ah! I think so. I believe you."

"You are going out to-night?" asked his decent wife, when he took another bite.

"Yes, I am."

"May I go with you, father?" asked his son, briskly.

"No, you mayn't. I'm going—as your mother knows—a fishing. That's where I'm going to. Going a fishing."

"Your fishing-rod gets rayther rusty; don't it, Father?"

"Never you mind."

"Shall you bring any fish home, Father?"

"If I don't, you'll have short commons, to-morrow," returned the gentleman, shaking his head; "that's questions enough for you; I ain't a going out till you've been long a-bed."

He devoted himself during the remainder of the evening to keeping a most viligant watch on Mrs. Cruncher, and sullenly holding her in conversation that she might be prevented from meditating any petitions to his disadvantage. With this view, he urged his son to hold her in conversation also, and led the unfortunate woman a hard life by dwelling on any causes of complaint he could bring against her, rather than he would leave her for a moment to her own reflections. The devoutest person could have rendered no greater homage to the efficacy of an honest prayer than he

did in this distrust of his wife. It was as if a professed un-
believer in ghosts should be frightened by a ghost story.

"And mind you!" said Mr. Cruncher. "No games to-
morrow! If I, as a honest tradesman, succeed in providing
a jinte of meat or two, none of your not touching of it,
and sticking to bread. If I, as a honest tradesman, am able
to provide a little beer, none of your declaring on water.
When you go to Rome, do as Rome does. Rome will be
a ugly customer to you, if you don't. *I'm* your Rome, you
know."

Then he began grumbling again:

"With your flying into the face of your own wittles and
drink! I don't know how scarce you mayn't make the wittles
and drink here, by your flopping tricks and your unfeeling
conduct. Look at your boy; he *is* your'n, ain't he? He's as
thin as a lath. Do you call yourself a mother, and not know
that a mother's first duty is to blow her boy out?"

This touched Young Jerry on a tender place; who adjured his mother to perform her first duty, and, whatever
else she did or neglected, above all things to lay especial
stress on the discharge of that maternal function so affect-
ingly and delicately indicated by his other parent.

Thus the evening wore away with the Cruncher family,
until Young Jerry was ordered to bed, and his mother, laid
under similar injunctions, obeyed them. Mr. Cruncher
beguiled the earlier watches of the night with solitary pipes,
and did not start upon his excursion until nearly one
o'clock. Towards that small and ghostly hour, he rose up
from his chair, took a key out of his pocket, opened a
locked cupboard, and brought forth a sack, a crowbar of
convenient size, a rope and chain, and other fishing tackle
of that nature. Disposing these articles about him in skilful
manner, he bestowed a parting defiance on Mrs. Cruncher,
extinguished the light, and went out.

Young Jerry, who had only made a feint of undressing
when he went to bed, was not long after his father. Under
cover of the darkness he followed out of the room, followed
down the stairs, followed down the court, followed out into
the streets. He was in no uneasiness concerning his getting
into the house again, for it was full of lodgers, and the door
stood ajar all night.

Impelled by a laudable ambition to study the art and
mystery of his father's honest calling, Young Jerry, keeping
as close to house-fronts, walls, and doorways, as his eyes

were close to one another, held his honoured parent in view. The honoured parent, steering northward, had not gone far, when he was joined by another disciple of Izaak Walton, and the two trudged on together.

Within half an hour from the first starting, they were beyond the winking lamps, and the more than winking watchmen, and were out upon a lonely road. Another fisherman was picked up here—and that so silently, that if Young Jerry had been superstitious, he might have supposed the second follower of the gentle craft to have, all of a sudden, split himself in two.

The three went on, and Young Jerry went on, until the three stopped under a bank overhanging the road. Upon the top of the bank was a low brick wall, surmounted by an iron railing. In the shadow of bank and wall the three turned out of the road, and up a blind lane, of which the wall—there, risen to some eight or ten feet high—formed one side. Crouching down in a corner, peeping up the lane, the next object that Young Jerry saw was the form of his honoured parent, pretty well defined against a watery and clouded moon, nimbly scaling an iron gate. He was soon over, and then the second fisherman got over, and then the third. They all dropped softly on the ground within the gate, and lay there a little—listening perhaps. Then, they moved away on their hands and knees.

It was now Young Jerry's turn to approach the gate: which he did, holding his breath. Crouching down again in a corner there, and looking in, he made out the three fishermen creeping through some rank grass, and all the gravestones in the churchyard—it was a large churchyard that they were in—looking on like ghosts in white, while the church tower itself looked on like the ghost of a monstrous giant. They did not creep far, before they stopped and stood upright. And then they began to fish.

They fished with a spade, at first. Presently the honoured parent appeared to be adjusting some instrument like a great corkscrew. Whatever tools they worked with, they worked hard, until the awful striking of the church clock so terrified Young Jerry, that he made off, with his hair as stiff as his father's.

But, his long-cherished desire to know more about these matters not only stopped him in his running away, but lured him back again. They were still fishing perseveringly, when he peeped in at the gate for the second time;

but, now they seemed to have got a bite. There was a screwing and complaining sound down below, and their bent figures were strained, as if by a weight. By slow degrees the weight broke away the earth upon it, and came to the surface. Young Jerry very well knew what it would be; but, when he saw it, and saw his honoured parent about to wrench it open, he was so frightened, being new to the sight, that he made off again, and never stopped until he had run a mile or more.

He would not have stopped then for anything less necessary than breath, it being a spectral sort of race that he ran, and one highly desirable to get to the end of. He had a strong idea that the coffin he had seen was running after him; and, pictured as hopping on behind him, bolt upright, upon its narrow end, always on the point of overtaking him and hopping on at his side—perhaps taking his arm—it was a pursuer to shun. It was an inconsistent and ubiquitous fiend too, for, while it was making the whole night behind him dreadful, he darted out into the roadway to avoid dark alleys, fearful of its coming hopping out of them like a dropsical boy's-kite without tail and wings. It hid in doorways too, rubbing its horrible shoulders against doors, and drawing them up to its ears, as if it were laughing. It got into shadows on the road, and lay cunningly on its back to trip him up. All this time it was incessantly hopping on behind and gaining on him, so that when the boy got to his own door he had reason for being half dead. And even then it would not leave him, but followed him upstairs with a bump on every stair, scrambled into bed with him, and bumped down, dead and heavy, on his breast when he fell asleep.

From his oppressed slumber, Young Jerry in his closet was awakened after daybreak and before sunrise by the presence of his father in the family room. Something had gone wrong with him; at least, so Young Jerry inferred, from the circumstance of his holding Mrs. Cruncher by the ears, and knocking the back of her head against the headboard of the bed.

"I told you I would," said Mr. Cruncher, "and I did."

"Jerry, Jerry, Jerry!" his wife implored.

"You oppose yourself to the profit of the business," said Jerry, "and me and my partners suffer. You was to honour and obey; why the devil don't you?"

"I try to be a good wife, Jerry," the poor woman protested, with tears.

"Is it being a good wife to oppose your husband's business? Is it honouring your husband to dishonour his business? Is it obeying your husband to disobey him on the wital subject of his business?"

"You hadn't taken to the dreadful business then, Jerry."

"It's enough for you," retorted Mr. Cruncher, "to be the wife of an honest tradesman, and not to occupy your female mind with calculations when he took to his trade or when he didn't. A honouring and obeying wife would let his trade alone altogether. Call yourself a religious woman? If you're a religious woman, give me a irreligious one! You have no more nat'ral sense of duty than the bed of this here Thames River has of a pile, and similarly it must be knocked into you."

The altercation was conducted in a low tone of voice, and terminated in the honest tradesman's kicking off his clay-soiled boots, and lying down at his length on the floor. After taking a timid peep at him lying on his back, with his rusty hands under his head for a pillow, his son lay down too, and fell asleep again.

There was no fish for breakfast, and not much of anything else. Mr. Cruncher was out of spirits, and out of temper, and kept an iron pot-lid by him as a projectile for the correction of Mrs. Cruncher, in case he should observe any symptoms of her saying Grace. He was brushed and washed at the usual hour, and set off with his son to pursue his ostensible calling.

Young Jerry, walking with the stool under his arm at his father's side along sunny and crowded Fleet Street, was a very different Young Jerry from him of the previous night, running home through darkness and solitude from his grim pursuer. His cunning was fresh with the day, and his qualms were gone with the night—in which particulars it is not improbable that he had compeers in Fleet Street and the City of London, that fine morning.

"Father," said Young Jerry, as they walked along: taking care to keep at arm's length and to have the stool well between them: "what's a resurrection-man?"

Mr. Cruncher came to a stop on the pavement before he answered, "How should I know?"

"I thought you knowed everything, Father," said the artless boy.

"Hem! Well," returned Mr. Cruncher, going on again, and lifting off his hat to give his spikes free play, "he's a tradesman."

"What's his goods, Father?" asked the brisk Young Jerry.

"His goods," said Mr. Cruncher, after turning it over in his mind, "is a branch of scientific goods."

"Persons' bodies, ain't it, Father?" asked the lively boy.

"I believe it is something of that sort," said Mr. Cruncher.

"Oh, Father, I should so like to be a resurrection-man when I'm quite growed up!"

Mr. Cruncher was soothed, but shook his head in a dubious and moral way. "It depends upon how you dewelop your talents. Be careful to dewelop your talents, and never to say no more than you can help to nobody, and there's no telling at the present time what you may not come to be fit for." As Young Jerry, thus encouraged, went on a few yards in advance, to plant the stool in the shadow of the Bar, Mr. Cruncher added to himself: "Jerry, you honest tradesman, there's hopes wot that boy will yet be a blessing to you, and a recompense to you for his mother!"

*   *   *   *   *   *   *   *

15 *Knitting*

THERE HAD been earlier drinking than usual in the wine-shop of Monsieur Defarge. As early as six o'clock in the morning, sallow faces peeping through its barred windows had descried other faces within, bending over measures of wine. Monsieur Defarge sold a very thin wine at the best of times, but it would seem to have been an unusually thin wine that he sold at this time. A sour wine, moreover, or a souring, for its influence on the mood of those who drank it was to make them gloomy. No vivacious Bacchanalian flame leaped out of the pressed grape of Monsieur Defarge: but, a smouldering fire that burnt in the dark lay hidden in the dregs of it.

This had been the third morning in succession on which there had been early drinking at the wine-shop of Monsieur Defarge. It had begun on Monday, and here was Wednesday come. There had been more of early brooding than drinking; for, many men had listened and whispered and slunk about there from the time of the opening of the door, who could not have laid a piece of money on the counter to save their souls. These were to the full as interested in the place, however, as if they could have commanded whole barrels of wine; and they glided from seat to seat, and from corner to corner, swallowing talk in lieu of drink, with greedy looks.

Notwithstanding an unusual flow of company, the master of the wine-shop was not visible. He was not missed; for, nobody who crossed the threshold looked for him, nobody asked for him, nobody wondered to see only Madame Defarge in her seat, presiding over the distribution of wine, with a bowl of battered small coins before her, as much defaced and beaten out of their original impress as the small coinage of humanity from whose ragged pockets they had come.

A suspended interest and a prevalent absence of mind were perhaps observed by the spies who looked in at the wine-shop, as they looked in at every place, high and low, from the king's palace to the criminal's gaol. Games at cards languished, players at dominoes musingly built towers with them, drinkers drew figures on the tables with spilt drops of wine, Madame Defarge herself picked out the pattern on her sleeve with her toothpick, and saw and heard something inaudible and invisible a long way off.

Thus, Saint Antoine in this vinous feature of his, until midday. It was high noontide, when two dusty men passed through his streets and under his swinging lamps: of whom, one was Monsieur Defarge: the other a mender of roads in a blue cap. All adust and athirst, the two entered the wine-shop. Their arrival had lighted a kind of fire in the breast of Saint Antoine, fast spreading as they came along, which stirred and flickered in flames of faces at most doors and windows. Yet, no one had followed them, and no man spoke when they entered the wine-shop, though the eyes of every man there were turned upon them.

"Good-day, gentlemen!" said Monsieur Defarge.

It may have been a signal for loosening the general tongue. It elicited an answering chorus of "Good-day!"

"It is bad weather, gentlemen," said Defarge, shaking his head.

Upon which, every man looked at his neighbour, and then all cast down their eyes and sat silent. Except one man, who got up and went out.

"My wife," said Defarge aloud, addressing Madame Defarge; "I have travelled certain leagues with this good mender of roads, called Jacques. I met him—by accident—a day and a half's journey out of Paris. He is a good child, this mender of roads, called Jacques. Give him to drink, my wife!"

A second man got up and went out. Madame Defarge set wine before the mender of roads called Jacques, who doffed his blue cap to the company, and drank. In the breast of his blouse he carried some coarse dark bread; he ate of this between whiles, and sat munching and drinking near Madame Defarge's counter. A third man got up and went out.

Defarge refreshed himself with a draught of wine—but, he took less than was given to the stranger, as being himself a man to whom it was no rarity—and stood waiting until the countryman had made his breakfast. He looked at no one present, and no one now looked at him; not even Madame Defarge, who had taken up her knitting, and was at work.

"Have you finished your repast, friend?" he asked, in due season.

"Yes, thank you."

"Come, then! You shall see the apartment that I told you you could occupy. It will suit you to a marvel."

Out of the wine-shop into the street, out of the street into a courtyard, out of the courtyard up a steep staircase, out of the staircase into a garret—formerly the garret where a white-haired man sat on a low bench, stooping forward and very busy, making shoes.

No white-haired man was there now; but, the three men were there who had gone out of the wine-shop singly. And between them and the white-haired man afar off was the one small link, that they had once looked in at him through the chinks in the wall.

Defarge closed the door carefully, and spoke in a subdued voice:

"Jacques One, Jacques Two, Jacques Three! This is the

witness encountered by appointment, by me, Jacques Four. He will tell you all. Speak, Jacques Five!"

The mender of roads, blue cap in hand, wiped his swarthy forehead with it, and said, "Where shall I commence, monsieur?"

"Commence," was Monsieur Defarge's not unreasonable reply, "at the commencement."

"I saw him then, messieurs," began the mender of roads, "a year ago this running summer, underneath the carriage of the Marquis, hanging by the chain. Behold the manner of it. I leaving my work on the road, the sun going to bed, the carriage of the Marquis slowly ascending the hill, he hanging by the chain—like this."

Again the mender of roads went through the whole performance; in which he ought to have been perfect by that time, seeing that it had been the infallible resource and indispensable entertainment of his village during a whole year.

Jacques One struck in, and asked if he had ever seen the man before?

"Never," answered the mender of roads, recovering his perpendicular.

Jacques Three demanded how he afterwards recognized him then?

"By his tall figure," said the mender of roads, softly, and with his finger at his nose. "When Monsieur the Marquis demands that evening, 'Say, what is he like?' I make response, 'Tall as a spectre.'"

"You should have said, short as a dwarf," returned Jacques Two.

"But what did I know? The deed was not then accomplished, neither did he confide in me. Observe! Under those circumstances even, I do not offer my testimony. Monsieur the Marquis indicates me with his finger, standing near our little fountain, and says, 'To me! Bring that rascal!' My faith, messieurs, I offer nothing."

"He is right there, Jacques," murmured Defarge, to him who had interrupted. "Go on."

"Good!" said the mender of roads, with an air of mystery. "The tall man is lost, and he is sought—how many months? Nine, ten, eleven?"

"No matter the number," said Defarge. "He is well hidden, but at last he is unluckily found. Go on!"

"I am again at work upon the hillside, and the sun is

again about to go to bed. I am collecting my tools to descend to my cottage down in the village below, where it is already dark, when I raise my eyes, and see coming over the hill six soldiers. In the midst of them is a tall man with his arms bound—tied to his sides—like this!"

With the aid of his indispensable cap, he represented a man with his elbows bound fast at his hips, with cords that were knotted behind him.

"I stand aside, messieurs, by my heap of stones, to see the soldiers and their prisoner pass (for it is a solitary road, that, where any spectacle is well worth looking at), and at first, as they approach, I see no more than that they are six soldiers with a tall man bound, and that they are almost black to my sight—except on the side of the sun going to bed, where they have a red edge, messieurs. Also, I see that their long shadows are on the hollow ridge on the opposite side of the road, and are on the hill above it, and are like the shadows of giants. Also, I see that they are covered with dust, and that the dust moves with them as they come, tramp, tramp! But when they advance quite near to me, I recognise the tall man, and he recognises me. Ah, but he would be well content to precipitate himself over the hillside once again, as on the evening when he and I first encountered, close to the same spot!"

He described it as if he were there, and it was evident that he saw it vividly; perhaps he had not seen much in his life.

"I do not show the soldiers that I recognise the tall man; he does not show the soldiers that he recognises me; we do it, and we know it, with our eyes. 'Come on!' says the chief of that company, pointing to the village, 'bring him fast to his tomb!' and they bring him faster. I follow. His arms are swelled because of being bound so tight, his wooden shoes are large and clumsy, and he is lame. Because he is lame, and consequently slow, they drive him with their guns—like this!"

He imitated the action of a man's being impelled forward by the butt-ends of muskets.

"As they descend the hill like madmen running a race, he falls. They laugh and pick him up again. His face is bleeding and covered with dust, but he cannot touch it; thereupon they laugh again. They bring him into the village; all the village runs to look; they take him past the mill, and up to the prison; all the village sees the prison gate open in the darkness of night, and swallow him—like this!"

He opened his mouth as wide as he could, and shut it with a sounding snap of his teeth. Observant of his unwillingness to mar the effect by opening it again, Defarge said, "Go on, Jacques."

"All the village," pursued the mender of roads, on tip-toe and in a low voice, "withdraws; all the village whispers by the fountain; all the village sleeps; all the village dreams of that unhappy one, within the locks and bars of the prison on the crag, and never to come out of it, except to perish. In the morning, with my tools upon my shoulder, eating my morsel of black bread as I go, I make a circuit by the prison, on my way to my work. There I see him, high up, behind the bars of a lofty iron cage, bloody and dusty as last night, looking through. He has no hand free, to wave to me; I dare not call to him; he regards me like a dead man."

Defarge and the three glanced darkly at one another. The looks of all of them were dark, repressed, and revengeful, as they listened to the countryman's story; the manner of all of them, while it was secret, was authoritative too. They had the air of a rough tribunal; Jacques One and Two sitting on the old pallet-bed, each with his chin resting on his hand, and his eyes intent on the road-mender; Jacques Three, equally intent, on one knee behind them, with his agitated hand always gliding over the network of fine nerves about his mouth and nose; Defarge standing between them and the narrator, whom he had stationed in the light of the window, by turns looking from him to them, and from them to him.

"Go on, Jacques," said Defarge.

"He remains up there in his iron cage some days. The village looks at him by stealth, for it is afraid. But it always looks up, from a distance, at the prison on the crag; and in the evening, when the work of the day is achieved and it assembles to gossip at the fountain, all faces are turned towards the prison. Formerly, they were turned towards the posting-house; now, they are turned towards the prison. They whisper at the fountain, that although condemned to death he will not be executed; they say that petitions have been presented in Paris, showing that he was enraged and made mad by the death of his child; they say that a petition has been presented to the King himself.

What do I know? It is possible. Perhaps yes, perhaps no."

"Listen then, Jacques," Number One of that name sternly interposed. "Know that a petition was presented to the King and Queen. All here, yourself excepted, saw the King take it, in his carriage in the street, sitting beside the Queen. It is Defarge whom you see here, who, at the hazard of his life, darted out before the horses, with the petition in his hand."

"And once again listen, Jacques!" said the kneeling Number Three: his fingers ever wandering over and over those fine nerves, with a strikingly greedy air, as if he hungered for something—that was neither food nor drink; "the guard, horse and foot, surrounded the petitioner, and struck him blows. You hear?"

"I hear, messieurs."

"Go on then," said Defarge.

"Again; on the other hand, they whisper at the fountain," resumed the countryman, "that he is brought down into our country to be executed on the spot, and that he will very certainly be executed. They even whisper that because he has slain Monseigneur, and because Monseigneur was the father of his tenants—serfs—what you will—he will be executed as a parricide. One old man says at the fountain, that his right hand, armed with the knife, will be burnt off before his face; that, into wounds which will be made in his arms, his breast, and his legs, there will be poured boiling oil, melted lead, hot resin, wax, and sulphur; finally, that he will be torn limb from limb by four strong horses. That old man says, all this was actually done to a prisoner who made an attempt on the life of the late King, Louis Fifteen. But how do I know if he lies? I am not a scholar."

"Listen once again then, Jacques!" said the man with the restless hand and the craving air. "The name of that prisoner was Damiens, and it was all done in open day, in the open streets of this city of Paris; and nothing was more noticed in the vast concourse that saw it done, than the crowd of ladies of quality and fashion, who were full of eager attention to the last—to the last, Jacques, prolonged until nightfall, when he had lost two legs and an arm, and still breathed! And it was done—why, how old are you?"

"Thirty-five," said the mender of roads, who looked sixty.

"It was done when you were more than ten years old; you might have seen it."

"Enough!" said Defarge, with grim impatience. "Long live the Devil! Go on."

"Well! Some whisper this, some whisper that; they speak of nothing else; even the fountain appears to fall to that tune. At length, on Sunday night when all the village is asleep, come soldiers, winding down from the prison, and their guns ring on the stones of the little street. Workmen dig, workmen hammer, soldiers laugh and sing; in the morning, by the fountain, there is raised a gallows forty feet high, poisoning the water."

The mender of roads looked *through* rather than *at* the low ceiling, and pointed as if he saw the gallows somewhere in the sky.

"All work is stopped, all assemble there, nobody leads the cows out, the cows are there with the rest. At midday, the roll of drums. Soldiers have marched into the prison in the night, and he is in the midst of many soldiers. He is bound as before, and in his mouth there is a gag—tied so, with a tight string, making him look almost as if he laughed." He suggested it, by creasing his face with his two thumbs, from the corners of his mouth to his ears. "On the top of the gallows is fixed the knife, blade upwards, with its point in the air. He is hanged there forty feet high—and is left hanging, poisoning the water."

They looked at one another, as he used his blue cap to wipe his face, on which the perspiration had started afresh while he recalled the spectacle.

"It is frightful, messieurs. How can the women and the children draw water! Who can gossip of an evening, under that shadow! Under it, have I said? When I left the village, Monday evening as the sun was going to bed, and looked back from the hill, the shadow struck across the church, across the mill, across the prison—seemed to strike across the earth, messieurs, to where the sky rests upon it!"

The hungry man gnawed one of his fingers as he looked at the other three, and his finger quivered with the craving that was on him.

"That's all, messieurs. I left at sunset (as I had been warned to do), and I walked on, that night and half next day, until I met (as I was warned I should) this comrade. With him, I came on, now riding and now walking, through the rest of yesterday and through last night. And here you see me!"

After a gloomy silence, the first Jacques said, "Good! You have acted and recounted faithfully. Will you wait for us a little, outside the door?"

"Very willingly," said the mender of roads. Whom Defarge escorted to the top of the stairs, and, leaving seated there, returned.

The three had risen, and their heads were together when he came back to the garret.

"How say you, Jacques?" demanded Number One. "To be registered?"

"To be registered, as doomed to destruction," returned Defarge.

"Magnificent!" croaked the man with the craving.

"The château and all the race?" inquired the first.

"The château and all the race," returned Defarge. "Extermination."

The hungry man repeated, in a rapturous croak, "Magnificent!" and began gnawing another finger.

"Are you sure," asked Jacques Two, of Defarge, "that no embarrassment can arise from our manner of keeping the register? Without doubt it is safe, for no one beyond ourselves can decipher it; but shall we always be able to decipher it—or, I ought to say, will she?"

"Jacques," returned Defarge, drawing himself up, "if madame my wife undertook to keep the register in her memory alone, she would not lose a word of it—not a syllable of it. Knitted, in her own stitches and her own symbols, it will always be as plain to her as the sun. Confide in Madame Defarge. It would be easier for the weakest poltroon that lives, to erase himself from existence, than to erase one letter of his name or crimes from the knitted register of Madame Defarge."

There was a murmur of confidence and approval, and then the man who hungered asked: "Is this rustic to be sent back soon? I hope so. He is very simple; is he not a little dangerous?"

"He knows nothing," said Defarge; "at least nothing more than would easily elevate himself to a gallows of the same height. I charge myself with him; let him remain with me; I will take care of him, and set him on his road. He wishes to see the fine world—the King, the Queen, and Court; let him see them on Sunday."

"What?" exclaimed the hungry man, staring. "Is it a good sign, that he wishes to see royalty and nobility?"

"Jacques," said Defarge, "judiciously show a cat milk, if you wish her to thirst for it. Judiciously show a dog his natural prey, if you wish him to bring it down one day."

Nothing more was said, and the mender of roads, being found already dozing on the topmost stair, was advised to lay himself down on the pallet-bed and take some rest. He needed no persuasion, and was soon asleep.

Worse quarters than Defarge's wine-shop could easily have been found in Paris for a provincial slave of that degree. Saving for a mysterious dread of madame by which he was constantly haunted, his life was very new and agreeable. But, madame sat all day at her counter, so expressly unconscious of him, and so particularly determined not to perceive that his being there had any connection with anything below the surface, that he shook in his wooden shoes whenever his eye lighted on her. For, he contended with himself that it was impossible to foresee what that lady might pretend next; and he felt assured that if she should take it into her brightly ornamented head to pretend that she had seen him do a murder and afterwards flay the victim, she would infallibly go through with it until the play was played out.

Therefore, when Sunday came, the mender of roads was not enchanted (though he said he was) to find that madame was to accompany monsieur and himself to Versailles. It was additionally disconcerting to have madame knitting all the way there, in a public conveyance; it was additionally disconcerting yet, to have madame in the crowd in the afternoon, still with her knitting in her hands as the crowd waited to see the carriage of the King and Queen.

"You work hard, madame," said a man near her.

"Yes," answered Madame Defarge; "I have a good deal to do."

"What do you make, madame?"

"Many things."

"For instance—"

"For instance," returned Madame Defarge, composedly, "shrouds."

The man moved a little further away, as soon as he could, and the mender of roads fanned himself with his blue cap: feeling it mightily close and oppressive. If he needed a King and Queen to restore him, he was fortunate

in having his remedy at hand; for, soon the large-faced
King and the fair-faced Queen came in their golden coach,
attended by the shining Bull's Eye of their Court, a glittering multitude of laughing ladies and fine lords, and in
jewels and silks and powder and splendour and elegantly
spurning figures, and handsomely disdainful faces of both
sexes, the mender of roads bathed himself, so much to his
temporary intoxication, that he cried Long live the King,
Long live the Queen, Long live everybody and everything!
as if he had never heard of ubiquitous Jacques in his time.
Then, there were gardens, courtyards, terraces, fountains,
green banks, more King and Queen, more Bull's Eye, more
lords and ladies, more Long live they all! until he absolutely wept with sentiment. During the whole of this scene,
which lasted some three hours, he had plenty of shouting
and weeping and sentimental company, and throughout
Defarge held him by the collar, as if to restrain him from
flying at the objects of his brief devotion and tearing them
to pieces.

"Bravo!" said Defarge, clapping him on the back when
it was over, like a patron; "you are a good boy!"

The mender of roads was now coming to himself, and
was mistrustful of having made a mistake in his late demonstrations; but no.

"You are the fellow we want," said Defarge, in his ear;
"you make these fools believe that it will last for ever.
Then, they are the more insolent, and it is nearer ended."

"Hey!" cried the mender of roads, reflectively; "that's
true."

"These fools know nothing. While they despise your
breath, and would stop it for ever and ever, in you or in a
hundred like you rather than in one of their own horses or
dogs, they only know what your breath tells them. Let it
deceive them, then, a little longer; it cannot deceive them
too much."

Madame Defarge looked superciliously at the client, and
nodded in confirmation.

"As to you," said she, "you would shout and shed tears
for anything, if it made a show and a noise. Say! Would
you not?"

"Truly, madame, I think so. For the moment."

"If you were shown a great heap of dolls, and were set
upon them to pluck them to pieces and despoil them for

your own advantage, you would pick out the richest and gayest. Say! Would you not?"

"Truly yes, madame."

"Yes. And if you were shown a flock of birds, unable to fly, and were set upon them to strip them of their feathers for your own advantage, you would set upon the birds of the finest feathers; would you not?"

"It is true, madame."

"You have seen both dolls and birds to-day," said Madame Defarge, with a wave of her hand towards the place where they had last been apparent; "now, go home!"

*　　*　　*　　*　　*　　*　　*　　*

16　*Still Knitting*

MADAME DEFARGE and monsieur her husband returned amicably to the bosom of Saint Antoine, while a speck in a blue cap toiled through the darkness, and through the dust, and down the weary miles of avenues by the wayside, slowly tending towards that point of the compass where the château of Monsieur the Marquis, now in his grave, listened to the whispering trees. Such ample leisure had the stone faces, now, for listening to the trees and to the fountain, that the few village scarecrows who, in their quest for herbs to eat and fragments of dead stick to burn, strayed within sight of the great stone courtyard and terrace staircase, had it borne in upon their starved fancy that the expression of the faces was altered. A rumour just lived in the village—had a faint and bare existence there, as its people had—that when the knife struck home, the faces changed, from faces of pride to faces of anger and pain; also, that when that dangling figure was hauled up forty feet above the fountain, they changed again, and bore a cruel look of being avenged, which they would henceforth bear for ever. In the stone face over the great window of the bedchamber where the murder was done, two fine dints were pointed out in the sculptured nose, which everybody recognised, and which nobody had seen of old; and on the scarce occasions when two or three ragged peasants emerged from the crowd to take a hurried peep at Monsieur the Marquis petrified, a skinny finger would not have pointed to it for a minute, before they all started away among the moss and leaves, like the more fortunate hares who could find a living there.

Château and hut, stone face and dangling figure, the red stain on the stone floor, and the pure water in the village well—thousands of acres of land—a whole province of France—all France itself—lay under the night sky, concentrated into a faint hair-breadth line. So does a whole world, with all its greatnesses and littlenesses, lie in a twinkling star. And as mere human knowledge can split a ray of light and analyse the manner of its composition, so, sublimer intelligences may read in the feeble shining of this earth of ours every thought and act, every vice and virtue, of every responsible creature on it.

The Defarges, husband and wife, came lumbering under the starlight, in their public vehicle, to that gate of Paris whereunto their journey naturally tended. There was the usual stoppage at the barrier guard-house, and the usual lanterns came glancing forth for the usual examination and inquiry. Monsieur Defarge alighted; knowing one or two of the soldiery there, and one of the police. The latter he was intimate with, and affectionately embraced.

When Saint Antoine had again enfolded the Defarges in his dusky wings, and they, having finally alighted near the Saint's boundaries, were picking their way on foot through the black mud and offal of his streets, Madame Defarge spoke to her husband:

"Say then, my friend; what did Jacques of the police tell thee?"

"Very little to-night, but all he knows. There is another spy commissioned for our quarter. There may be many more, for all that he can say, but he knows of one."

"Eh well!" said Madame Defarge, raising her eyebrows with a cool business air. "It is necessary to register him. How do they call that man?"

"He is English."

"So much the better. His name?"

"Barsad," said Defarge, making it French by pronunciation. But, he had been so careful to get it accurately, that he then spelt it with perfect correctness.

"Barsad," repeated madame. "Good. Christian name?"

"John."

"John Barsad," repeated madame, after murmuring it once to herself. "Good. His appearance; is it known?"

"Age, about forty years; height, about five feet nine; black hair; complexion dark; generally, rather handsome visage; eyes dark, face thin, long, and sallow; nose aquiline, but not straight, having a peculiar inclination towards the left cheek; expression, therefore, sinister!"

"Eh my faith. It is a portrait!" said madame, laughing. "He shall be registered to-morrow."

They turned into the wine-shop, which was closed (for it was midnight) and where Madame Defarge immediately took her post at her desk, counted the small moneys that had been taken during her absence, examined the stock, went through the entries in the book, made other entries of her own, checked the serving man in every possible way, and finally dismissed him to bed. Then she turned out the contents of the bowl of money for the second time, and began knotting them up in her handkerchief, in a chain of separate knots, for safe keeping through the night. All this while, Defarge, with his pipe in his mouth, walked up and down, complacently admiring, but never interfering; in which condition, indeed, as to the business and his domestic affairs, he walked up and down through life.

The night was hot, and the shop, close shut and surrounded by so foul a neighbourhood, was ill-smelling. Monsieur Defarge's olfactory sense was by no means delicate, but the stock of wine smelt much stronger than it ever tasted, and so did the stock of rum and brandy and aniseed. He whiffed the compound of scents away, as he put down his smoked-out pipe.

"You are fatigued," said madame, raising her glance as she knotted the money. "There are only the usual odours."

"I am a little tired," her husband acknowledged.

"You are a little depressed, too," said madame, whose quick eyes had never been so intent on the accounts, but they had had a ray or two for him. "Oh, the men, the men!"

"But my dear!" began Defarge.

"But my dear!" repeated madame, nodding firmly; "but my dear! You are faint of heart to-night, my dear!"

"Well, then," said Defarge, as if a thought were wrung out of his breast, "it *is* a long time."

"It is a long time," repeated his wife; "and when is it not a long time? Vengeance and retribution require a long time; it is the rule."

"It does not take a long time to strike a man with lightning," said Defarge.

"How long," demanded madame, composedly, "does it take to make and store the lightning? Tell me."

Defarge raised his head thoughtfully, as if there were something in that too.

"It does not take a long time," said madame, "for an earthquake to swallow a town. Eh well! Tell me how long it takes to prepare the earthquake?"

"A long time, I suppose," said Defarge.

"But when it is ready, it takes place, and grinds to pieces everything before it. In the meantime, it is always preparing, though it is not seen or heard. That is your consolation. Keep it."

She tied a knot with flashing eyes, as if it throttled a foe.

"I tell thee," said madame, extending her right hand for emphasis, "that although it is a long time on the road, it is on the road and coming. I tell thee it never retreats, and never stops. I tell thee it is always advancing. Look around and consider the lives of all the world that we know, consider the faces of all the world that we know, consider the rage and discontent to which the Jacquerie addresses itself with more and more of certainty every hour. Can such things last? Bah! I mock you."

"My brave wife," returned Defarge, standing before her with his head a little bent, and his hands clasped at his back, like a docile and attentive pupil before his catechist, "I do not question all this. But it has lasted a long time, and it is possible—you know well, my wife, it is possible—that it may not come, during our lives."

"Eh well! How then?" demanded madame, tying another knot, as if there were another enemy strangled.

"Well!" said Defarge, with a half-complaining and half-apologetic shrug. "We shall not see the triumph."

"We shall have helped it," returned madame, with her extended hand in strong action. "Nothing that we do is done in vain. I believe, with all my soul, that we shall see the triumph. But even if not, even if I knew certainly not, show me the neck of an aristocrat and tyrant, and still I would—"

Then madame, with her teeth set, tied a very terrible knot indeed.

"Hold!" cried Defarge, reddening a little as if he felt

charged with cowardice; "I too, my dear, will stop at nothing."

"Yes! But it is your weakness that you sometimes need to see your victim and your opportunity, to sustain you. Sustain yourself without that. When the time comes, let loose a tiger and a devil; but wait for the time with the tiger and the devil chained—not shown—yet always ready."

Madame enforced the conclusion of this piece of advice by striking her little counter with her chain of money as if she knocked its brains out, and then gathering the heavy handkerchief under her arm in a serene manner, and observing that it was time to go to bed.

Next noontide saw the admirable woman in her usual place in the wine-shop, knitting away assiduously. A rose lay beside her, and if she now and then glanced at the flower, it was with no infraction of her usual preoccupied air. There were a few customers, drinking or not drinking, standing or seated, sprinkled about. The day was very hot, and heaps of flies, who were extending their inquisitive and adventurous perquisitions into all the glutinous little glasses near madame, fell dead at the bottom. Their decease made no impression on the other flies out promenading, who looked at them in the coolest manner (as if they themselves were elephants, or something as far removed), until they met the same fate. Curious to consider how heedless flies are!—perhaps they thought as much at Court that sunny summer day.

A figure entering at the door threw a shadow on Madame Defarge which she felt to be a new one. She laid down her knitting, and began to pin the rose in her headdress, before she looked at the figure.

It was curious. The moment Madame Defarge took up the rose, the customers ceased talking, and began gradually to drop out of the wine-shop.

"Good day, madame," said the new-comer.

"Good day, monsieur."

She said it aloud, but added to herself, as she resumed her knitting: "Hah! Good day, age about forty, height about five feet nine, black hair, generally rather handsome visage, complexion dark, eyes dark, thin long and sallow face, aquiline nose but not straight, having a peculiar inclination towards the left cheek which imparts a sinister expression! Good day, one and all!"

"Have the goodness to give me a little glass of old

cognac, and a mouthful of cool fresh water, madame."

Madame complied with a polite air.

"Marvelous cognac this, madame!"

It was the first time it had ever been so complimented, and Madame Defarge knew enough of its antecedents to know better. She said, however, that the cognac was flattered, and took up her knitting. The visitor watched her fingers for a few moments, and took the opportunity of observing the place in general.

"You knit with great skill, madame."

"I am accustomed to it."

"A pretty pattern too!"

"*You* think so?" said madame, looking at him with a smile.

"Decidedly. May one ask what it is for?"

"Pastime," said madame, looking at him with a smile, while her fingers moved nimbly.

"Not for use?"

"That depends. I may find a use for it one day. If I do—well," said madame, drawing a breath and nodding her head with a stern kind of coquetry, "I'll use it!"

It was remarkable: but the taste of Saint Antoine seemed to be decidedly opposed to a rose on the headdress of Madame Defarge. Two men had entered separately, and had been about to order drinks, when, catching sight of that novelty, they faltered, made a pretence of looking about as if for some friend who was not there, and went away. Nor, of those who had been there when this visitor entered, was there one left. They had all dropped off. The spy had kept his eyes open, but had been able to detect no sign. They had lounged away in a poverty-stricken, purposeless, accidental manner, quite natural and unimpeachable.

"JOHN," thought madame, checking off her work as her fingers knitted, and her eyes looked at the stranger. "Stay long enough, and I shall knit 'BARSAD' before you go."

"You have a husband, madame?"

"I have."

"Children?"

"No children."

"Business seems bad?"

"Business is very bad; the people are so poor."

"Ah, the unfortunate, miserable people! So oppressed, too—as you say."

"As *you* say," madame retorted, correcting him, and

deftly knitting an extra something into his name that boded
him no good.

"Pardon me: certainly it was I who said so, but you
naturally think so. Of course."

"*I* think?" returned madame, in a high voice. "I and my
husband have enough to do to keep this wine-shop open,
without thinking. All we think, here, is how to live. That is
the subject *we* think of, and it gives us, from morning to
night, enough to think about, without embarrassing our
heads concerning others. *I* think for others? No, no."

The spy, who was there to pick up any crumbs he could
find, or make, did not allow his baffled state to express itself in his sinister face; but, stood with an air of gossiping
gallantry, leaning his elbow on Madame Defarge's little
counter, and occasionally sipping his cognac.

"A bad business this, madame, of Gaspard's execution.
Ah! the poor Gaspard!" With a sigh of great compassion.

"My faith!" returned madame, coolly and lightly, "if
people use knives for such purposes, they have to pay for
it. He knew beforehand what the price of his luxury was;
he has paid the price."

"I believe," said the spy, dropping his soft voice to a
tone that invited confidence, and expressing an injured revolutionary susceptibility in every muscle of his wicked face:
"I believe there is much compassion and anger in this
neighbourhood, touching the poor fellow? Between ourselves."

"Is there?" asked madame, vacantly.

"Is there not?"

"—Here is my husband!" said Madame Defarge.

As the keeper of the wine-shop entered at the door, the
spy saluted him by touching his hat, and saying, with an
engaging smile, "Good day, Jacques!" Defarge stopped
short, and stared at him.

"Good day, Jacques!" the spy repeated; with not quite so
much confidence, or quite so easy a smile under the stare.

"You deceive yourself, monsieur," returned the keeper
of the wine-shop. "You mistake me for another. That is not
my name. I am Ernest Defarge."

"It is all the same," said the spy, airily, but discomfited
too; "good day!"

"Good day!" answered Defarge, drily.

"I was saying to madame, with whom I had the pleasure
of chatting when you entered, that they tell me there is—

and no wonder!—much sympathy and anger in Saint Antoine, touching the unhappy fate of poor Gaspard."

"No one has told me so," said Defarge, shaking his head. "I know nothing of it."

Having said it, he passed behind the little counter, and stood with his hand on the back of his wife's chair, looking over that barrier at the person to whom they were both opposed, and whom either of them would have shot with the greatest satisfaction.

The spy, well used to his business, did not change his unconscious attitude, but drained his little glass of cognac, took a sip of fresh water, and asked for another glass of cognac. Madame Defarge poured it out for him, took to her knitting again, and hummed a little song over it.

"You seem to know this quarter well; that is to say, better than I do?" observed Defarge.

"Not at all, but I hope to know it better. I am so profoundly interested in its miserable inhabitants."

"Hah!" muttered Defarge.

"The pleasure of conversing with you, Monsieur Defarge, recalls to me," pursued the spy, "that I have the honour of cherishing some interesting associations with your name."

"Indeed!" said Defarge, with much indifference.

"Yes, indeed. When Doctor Manette was released, you, his old domestic, had the charge of him, I know. He was delivered to you. You see I am informed of the circumstances?"

"Such is the fact, certainly," said Defarge. He had had it conveyed to him, in an accidental touch of his wife's elbow as she knitted and warbled, that he would do best to answer, but always with brevity.

"It was to you," said the spy, "that his daughter came; and it was from your care that his daughter took him, accompanied by a neat brown monsieur; how is he called?—in a little wig—Lorry—of the bank of Tellson and Company—over to England?"

"Such is the fact," repeated Defarge.

"Very interesting remembrances!" said the spy. "I have known Doctor Manette and his daughter, in England."

"Yes?" said Defarge.

"You don't hear much about them now?" said the spy.

"No," said Defarge.

"In effect," madame struck in, looking up from her work

and her little song, "we never hear about them. We received the news of their safe arrival, and perhaps another letter, or perhaps two; but, since then, they have gradually taken their road in life—we, ours—and we have held no correspondence."

"Perfectly so, madame," replied the spy. "She is going to be married."

"Going?" echoed madame. "She was pretty enough to have been married long ago. You English are cold, it seems to me."

"Oh! You know I am English."

"I perceive your tongue is," returned madame; "and what the tongue is, I suppose the man is."

He did not take the identification as a compliment; but he made the best of it, and turned it off with a laugh. After sipping his cognac to the end, he added:

"Yes, Miss Manette is going to be married. But not to an Englishman; to one who, like herself, is French by birth. And speaking of Gaspard (ah, poor Gaspard! It was cruel, cruel!), it is a curious thing that she is going to marry the nephew of Monsieur the Marquis, for whom Gaspard was exalted to that height of so many feet; in other words, the present Marquis. But he lives unknown in England, he is no Marquis there; he is Mr. Charles Darnay. D'Aulnais is the name of his mother's family."

Madame Defarge knitted steadily, but the intelligence had a palpable effect upon her husband. Do what he would, behind the little counter, as to the striking of a light and the lighting of his pipe, he was troubled, and his hand was not trustworthy. The spy would have been no spy if he had failed to see it, or to record it in his mind.

Having made, at least, this one hit, whatever it might prove to be worth, and no customers coming in to help him to any other, Mr. Barsad paid for what he had drunk, and took his leave: taking occasion to say, in a genteel manner, before he departed, that he looked forward to the pleasure of seeing Monsieur and Madame Defarge again. For some minutes after he had emerged into the outer presence of Saint Antoine, the husband and wife remained exactly as he had left them, lest he should come back.

"Can it be true," said Defarge, in a low voice, looking down at his wife as he stood smoking with his hand on the back of her chair, "what he has said of Ma'amselle Manette?"

"As he has said it," returned madame, lifting her eye-brows a little, "it is probably false. But it may be true."

"If it is—" Defarge began, and stopped.

"If it is?" repeated his wife.

"—And if it does come, while we live to see it triumph—I hope, for her sake, Destiny will keep her husband out of France."

"Her husband's destiny," said Madame Defarge, with her usual composure, "will take him where he is to go, and will lead him to the end that is to end him. That is all I know."

"But it is very strange—now, at least, is it not very strange"—said Defarge, rather pleading with his wife to induce her to admit it, "that, after all our sympathy for Monsieur her father, and herself, her husband's name should be proscribed under your hand at this moment, by the side of that infernal dog's who has just left us?"

"Stranger things than that will happen when it does come," answered madame. "I have them both here, of a certainty; and they are both here for their merits; that is enough."

She rolled up her knitting when she had said those words, and presently took the rose out of the handkerchief that was wound about her head. Either Saint Antoine had an instinctive sense that the objectionable decoration was gone, or Saint Antoine was on the watch for its disappearance; howbeit, the Saint took courage to lounge in, very shortly afterwards, and the wine-shop recovered its habitual aspect.

In the evening, at which season of all others Saint Antoine turned himself inside out, and sat on door-steps and window-ledges, and came to the corners of vile streets and courts, for a breath of air, Madame Defarge with her work in her hand was accustomed to pass from place to place and from group to group: a missionary—there were many like her—such as the world will do well never to breed again. All the women knitted. They knitted worthless things; but, the mechanical work was a mechanical substitute for eating and drinking: the hands moved for the jaws and the digestive apparatus: if the bony fingers had been still, the stomachs would have been more famine-pinched.

But, as the fingers went, the eyes went, and the thoughts. And as Madame Defarge moved on from group to group, all three went quicker and fiercer among every little knot of women that she had spoken with, and left behind.

Her husband smoked at his door, looking after her with admiration. "A great woman," said he, "strong woman, a grand woman, a frightfully grand woman!"

Darkness closed around, and then came the ringing of church bells and the distant beating of the military drums in the Palace Courtyard, as the women sat knitting, knitting. Darkness encompassed them. Another darkness was closing in as surely, when the church bells, then ringing pleasantly in many an airy steeple over France, should be melted into thunder cannon; when the military drums should be beating to drown a wretched voice, that night all-potent as the voice of Power and Plenty, Freedom and Life. So much was closing in about the women who sat knitting, knitting, that they their very selves were closing in around a structure yet unbuilt, where they were to sit knitting, knitting, counting dropping heads.

*   *   *   *   *   *   *   *

17 *One Night*

NEVER DID the sun go down with a brighter glory on the quiet corner of Soho, than one memorable evening when the Doctor and his daughter sat under the plane-tree together. Never did the moon rise with a milder radiance over great London, than on that night when it found them still seated under the tree, and shone upon their faces through its leaves.

Lucie was to be married to-morrow. She had reserved this last evening for her father, and they sat alone under the plane-tree.

"You are happy, my dear father?"

"Quite, my child."

They had said little, though they had been there a long time. When it was yet light enough to work and read, she had neither engaged herself in her usual work, nor had she read to him. She had employed herself in both ways, at his side under the tree, many and many a time; but this time was not quite like any other, and nothing could make it so.

"And I am very happy to-night, dear father. I am deeply happy in the love that Heaven has so blessed—my love for Charles, and Charles's love for me. But, if my life were not to be still consecrated to you, or if my marriage were so arranged as that it would part us, even by the length of a few of these streets, I should be more unhappy and self-reproachful now than I can tell you. Even as it is—"

Even as it was, she could not command her voice.

In the sad moonlight, she clasped him by the neck, and laid her face upon his breast. In the moonlight which is always sad, as the light of the sun itself is—as the light called human life is—as its coming and its going.

"Dearest dear! Can you tell me, this last time, that you feel quite, quite sure, no new affections of mine, and no new duties of mine, will ever interpose between us? *I* know it well, but do you know it? In your own heart, do you feel quite certain?"

Her father answered, with a cheerful firmness of conviction he could scarcely have assumed. "Quite sure, my darling! More than that," he added, as he tenderly kissed her: "my future is far brighter, Lucie, seen through your marriage, than it could have been—nay, than it ever was—without it."

"If I could hope *that,* my father!—"

"Believe it, love! Indeed it is so. Consider how natural and how plain it is, my dear, that it should be so. You, devoted and young, cannot fully appreciate the anxiety I have felt that your life should not be wasted—"

She moved her hand towards his lips, but he took it in his, and repeated the word.

"—wasted, my child—should not be wasted, struck aside from the natural order of things—for my sake. Your unselfishness cannot entirely comprehend how much my mind has gone on this; but, only ask yourself, how could my happiness be perfect, while yours was incomplete?"

"If I had never seen Charles, my father, I should have been quite happy with you."

He smiled at her unconscious admission that she would have been unhappy without Charles, having seen him; and replied:

"My child, you did see him, and it is Charles. If it had

not been Charles, it would have been another. Or, if it had been no other, I should have been the cause, and then the dark part of my life would have cast its shadow beyond myself, and would have fallen on you."

It was the first time, except at the trial, of her ever hearing him refer to the period of his suffering. It gave her a strange and new sensation while his words were in her ears; and she remembered it long afterwards.

"See!" said the Doctor of Beauvais, raising his hand towards the moon. "I have looked at her from my prison-window, when I could not bear her light. I have looked at her when it has been such torture to me to think of her shining upon what I had lost, that I have beaten my head against my prison-walls. I have looked at her, in a state so dull and lethargic, that I have thought of nothing but the number of horizontal lines I could draw across her at the full, and the number of perpendicular lines with which I could intersect them." He added in his inward and pondering manner, as he looked at the moon, "It was twenty either way, I remember, and the twentieth was difficult to squeeze in."

The strange thrill with which she heard him go back to that time deepened as he dwelt upon it; but, there was nothing to shock her in the manner of his reference. He only seemed to contrast his present cheerfulness and felicity with the dire endurance that was over.

"I have looked at her, speculating thousands of times upon the unborn child from whom I had been rent. Whether it was alive. Whether it had been born alive, or the poor mother's shock had killed it. Whether it was a son who would some day avenge his father. (There was a time in my imprisonment, when my desire for vengeance was unbearable.) Whether it was a son who would never know his father's story; who might even live to weigh the possibility of his father's having disappeared of his own will and act. Whether it was a daughter who would grow to be a woman."

She drew closer to him, and kissed his cheek and his hand.

"I have pictured my daughter, to myself, as perfectly forgetful of me—rather, altogether ignorant of me, and unconscious of me. I have cast up the years of her age, year after year. I have seen her married to a man who knew nothing of my fate. I have altogether perished from the remembrance of the living, and in the next generation my place was a blank."

"My father! Even to hear that you had such thoughts of a daughter who never existed strikes to my heart as if I had been that child."

"You, Lucie? It is out of the consolation and restoration you have brought to me that these remembrances arise, and pass between us and the moon on this last night.— What did I say just now?"

"She knew nothing of you. She cared nothing for you."

"So! But on other moonlight nights, when the sadness and the silence have touched me in a different way—have affected me with something as like a sorrowful sense of peace, as any emotion that had pain for its foundations could—I have imagined her as coming to me in my cell, and leading me out into the freedom beyond the fortress. I have seen her image in the moonlight often, as I now see you; except that I never held her in my arms: it stood between the little grated window and the door. But, you understand that that was not the child I am speaking of?"

"The figure was not; the—the—image; the fancy?"

"No. That was another thing. It stood before my disturbed sense of sight, but it never moved. The phantom that my mind pursued was another and more real child. Of her outward appearance I know no more than that she was like her mother. The other had that likeness too—as you have—but was not the same. Can you follow me, Lucie? Hardly, I think? I doubt you must have been a solitary prisoner to understand these perplexed distinctions."

His collected and calm manner could not prevent her blood from running cold, as he thus tried to anatomise his old condition.

"In that more peaceful state, I have imagined her, in the moonlight, coming to me and taking me out to show me that the home of her married life was full of her loving remembrance of her lost father. My picture was in her room, and I was in her prayers. Her life was active, cheerful, useful; but my poor history pervaded it all."

"I was that child, my father. I was not half so good, but in my love that was I."

"And she showed me her children," said the Doctor of Beauvais, "and they had heard of me, and had been taught to pity me. When they passed a prison of the State, they kept far from its frowning walls, and looked up at its bars, and spoke in whispers. She could never deliver me; I imagined that she always brought me back after showing me such things. But then, blessed with the relief of tears, I fell upon my knees, and blessed her."

"I am that child, I hope, my father. O my dear, my dear, will you bless me as fervently to-morrow?"

"Lucie, I recall these old troubles in the reason that I have to-night for loving you better than words can tell, and thanking God for my great happiness. My thoughts, when they were wildest, never rose near the happiness that I have known with you, and that we have before us."

He embraced her, solemnly commended her to Heaven, and humbly thanked Heaven for having bestowed her on him. By and by, they went into the house.

There was no one bidden to the marriage but Mr. Lorry; there was even to be no bridesmaid but the gaunt Miss Pross. The marriage was to make no change in their place of residence; they had been able to extend it, by taking to themselves the upper rooms formerly belonging to the apocryphal invisible lodger, and they desired nothing more.

Doctor Manette was very cheerful at the little supper. They were only three at table, and Miss Pross made the third. He regretted that Charles was not there; was more than half disposed to object to the loving little plot that kept him away; and drank to him affectionately.

So, the time came for him to bid Lucie good night, and they separated. But, in the stillness of the third hour of the morning, Lucie came downstairs again, and stole into his room; not free from unshaped fears, beforehand.

All things, however, were in their places; all was quiet; and he lay asleep, his white hair picturesque on the untroubled pillow, and his hands lying quiet on the coverlet. She put her needless candle in the shadow at a distance, crept up to his bed, and put her lips to his; then, leaned over him, and looked at him.

Into his handsome face the bitter waters of captivity had worn; but, he covered up their tracks with a determination so strong, that he held the mastery of them even in his sleep. A more remarkable face in its quiet, resolute, and guarded struggle with an unseen assailant was not to be beheld in all the wide dominions of sleep, that night.

She timidly laid her hand on his dear breast, and put up a prayer that she might ever be as true to him as her love aspired to be, and as his sorrows deserved. Then, she withdrew her hand, and kissed his lips once more, and went away. So the sunrise came, and the shadows of the leaves of the plane-tree moved upon his face, as softly as her lips had moved in praying for him.

18 *Nine Days*

THE MARRIAGE-DAY was shining brightly, and they were ready outside the closed door of the Doctor's room, where he was speaking with Charles Darnay. They were ready to go to church; the beautiful bride, Mr. Lorry, and Miss Pross—to whom the event, through a gradual process of reconcilement to the inevitable, would have been one of absolute bliss, but for the yet lingering consideration that her brother Solomon should have been the bridegroom.

"And so," said Mr. Lorry, who could not sufficiently admire the bride, and who had been moving round her to take in every point of her quiet, pretty dress; "and so it was for this, my sweet Lucie, that I brought you across the Channel, such a baby! Lord bless me! How little I thought what I was doing! How lightly I valued the obligation I was conferring on my friend Mr. Charles!"

"You didn't mean it," remarked the matter-of-fact Miss Pross, "and therefore how could you know it? Nonsense!"

"Really? Well; but don't cry," said the gentle Mr. Lorry.

"I am not crying," said Miss Pross; "*you* are."

"I, my Pross?" (By this time, Mr. Lorry dared to be pleasant with her; on occasion.)

"You were, just now; I saw you do it, and I don't wonder at it. Such a present of plate as you have made 'em is enough to bring tears into anybody's eyes. There's not a fork or a spoon in the collection," said Miss Pross, "that I didn't cry over, last night after the box came, till I couldn't see it."

"I am highly gratified," said Mr. Lorry, "though, upon

Scenes on these pages
are from the CBS-TV
presentation,
A TALE
OF TWO CITIES.

Chris Sarandon
plays the dual roles
of Charles Darnay
(as above) and
Sydney Carton.

Lucie Manette
(Alice Krige),
in love with
Charles Darnay.

Lucie Manette learns from Mr. Lorry that her father is alive.

Lucie and Dr. Manette traveling to London.

The execution of Gaspard (Bernard Hug), assassin of the wicked Marquis de St. Evrémonde.

Madame Defarge, in her wineshop, is busy with her sinister knitting.

The luxurious life of the aristocrats.

Tumbrils carry the doomed aristocrats to their deaths.

my honour, I had no intention of rendering those trifling articles of remembrance invisible to any one. Dear me! This is an occasion that makes a man speculate on all he has lost. Dear, dear, dear! To think that there might have been a Mrs. Lorry, any time these fifty years almost!"

"Not at all!" From Miss Pross.

"You think there never might have been a Mrs. Lorry?" asked the gentleman of that name.

"Pooh!" rejoined Miss Pross; "you were a bachelor in your cradle."

"Well!" observed Mr. Lorry, beamingly adjusting his little wig, "that seems probable, too."

"And you were cut out for a bachelor," pursued Miss Pross, "before you were put in your cradle."

"Then, I think," said Mr. Lorry, "that I was very un-handsomely dealt with, and that I ought to have had a voice in the selection of my pattern. Enough! Now, my dear Lucie," drawing his arm soothingly round her waist, "I hear them moving in the next room, and Miss Pross and I, as two formal folks of business, are anxious not to lose the final opportunity of saying something to you that you wish to hear. You leave your good father, my dear, in hands as earnest and as loving as your own; he shall be taken every conceivable care of: during the next fortnight, while you are in Warwickshire and thereabouts, even Tell-son's shall go to the wall (comparatively speaking) before him. And when, at the fortnight's end, he comes to join you and your beloved husband, on your other fortnight's trip in Wales, you shall say that we have sent him to you in the best health and in the happiest frame. Now I hear Somebody's step coming to the door. Let me kiss my dear girl with an old-fashioned bachelor blessing, before Some-body comes to claim his own."

For a moment, he held the fair face from him to look at the well-remembered expression on the forehead, and then laid the bright golden hair against his little brown wig, with a genuine tenderness and delicacy which, if such things be old-fashioned, were as old as Adam.

The door of the Doctor's room opened, and he came out with Charles Darnay. He was so deadly pale—which had not been the case when they went in together—that no vestige of colour was to be seen in his face. But, in the composure of his manner he was unaltered, except that to the shrewd glance of Mr. Lorry it disclosed some shadowy indication that the old air of avoidance and dread had lately passed over him, like a cold wind.

He gave his arm to his daughter, and took her downstairs to the chariot which Mr. Lorry had hired in honour of the day. The rest followed in another carriage, and soon, in a neighbouring church, where no strange eyes looked on, Charles Darnay and Lucie Manette were happily married.

Besides the glancing tears that shone among the smiles of the little group when it was done, some diamonds, very bright and sparkling, glanced on the bride's hand, which were newly released from the dark obscurity of one of Mr. Lorry's pockets. They returned home to breakfast, and all went well, and in due course the golden hair that had mingled with the poor shoemaker's white locks in the Paris garret were mingled with them again in the morning sunlight, on the threshold of the door at parting.

It was a hard parting, though it was not for long. But her father cheered her, and said at last, gently disengaging himself from her enfolding arms, "Take her, Charles! She is yours!"

And her agitated hand waved to them from a chaise window, and she was gone.

The corner being out of the way of the idle and curious, and the preparations having been very simple and few, the Doctor, Mr. Lorry, and Miss Pross were left quite alone. It was when they turned into the welcome shade of the cool old hall, that Mr. Lorry observed a great change to have come over the Doctor; as if the golden arm uplifted there had struck him a poisoned blow.

He had naturally repressed much, and some revulsion might have been expected in him when the occasion for repression was gone. But, it was the old scared lost look that troubled Mr. Lorry; and through his absent manner of clasping his head and drearily wandering away into his own room when they got upstairs, Mr. Lorry was reminded of Defarge the wine-shop keeper, and the starlight ride.

"I think," he whispered to Miss Pross, after anxious consideration, "I think we had best not speak to him just now, or at all disturb him. I must look in at Tellson's; so I will go there at once and come back presently. Then, we will take him a ride into the country, and dine there, and all will be well."

't was easier for Mr. Lorry to look in at Tellson's, than

to look out of Tellson's. He was detained two hours. When he came back, he ascended the old staircase alone, having asked no question of the servant; going thus into the Doctor's rooms, he was stopped by a low sound of knocking.

"Good God!" he said, with a start. "What's that?"

Miss Pross, with a terrified face, was at his ear. "O me, O me! All is lost!" cried she, wringing her hands. "What is to be told to Ladybird? He doesn't know me, and is making shoes!"

Mr. Lorry said what he could to calm her, and went himself into the Doctor's room. The bench was turned towards the light, as it had been when he had seen the shoemaker at his work before, and his head was bent down, and he was very busy.

"Doctor Manette. My dear friend, Doctor Manette!"

The Doctor looked at him for a moment—half inquiringly, half as if he were angry at being spoken to—and bent over his work again.

He had laid aside his coat and waistcoat; his shirt was open at the throat, as it used to be when he did that work; and even the old haggard, faded surface of face had come back to him. He worked hard—impatiently—as if in some sense of having been interrupted.

Mr. Lorry glanced at the work in his hand, and observed that it was a shoe of the old size and shape. He took up another that was lying by him, and asked what it was?

"A young lady's walking shoe," he muttered, without looking up. "It ought to have been finished long ago. Let it be."

"But, Doctor Manette. Look at me!"

He obeyed, in the old mechanically submissive manner, without pausing in his work.

"You know me, my dear friend? Think again. This is not your proper occupation. Think, dear friend!"

Nothing would induce him to speak more. He looked up, for an instant at a time, when he was requested to do so; but, no persuasion would extract a word from him. He worked, and worked, and worked, in silence, and words fell on him as they would have fallen on an echoless wall, or on the air. The only ray of hope that Mr. Lorry could discover, was, that he sometimes furtively looked up without being asked. In that, there seemed a faint expression of curiosity or perplexity—as though he were trying to reconcile some doubts in his mind.

Two things at once impressed themselves on Mr. Lorry, as important above all others; the first, that this must be kept secret from Lucie; the second that it must be kept secret from all who knew him. In conjunction with Miss Pross, he took immediate steps towards the latter precaution, by giving out that the Doctor was not well, and required a few days of complete rest. In aid of the kind deception to be practised on his daughter, Miss Pross was to write, describing his having been called away professionally, and referring to an imaginary letter of two or three hurried lines in his own hand, represented to have been addressed to her by the same post.

These measures, advisable to be taken in any case, Mr. Lorry took in the hope of his coming to himself. If that should happen soon, he kept another course in reserve; which was, to have a certain opinion that he thought the best, on the Doctor's case.

In the hope of his recovery, and of resort to this third course being thereby rendered practicable, Mr. Lorry resolved to watch him attentively, with as little appearance as possible of doing so. He therefore made arrangements to absent himself from Tellson's for the first time in his life, and took his post by the window in the same room.

He was not long in discovering that it was worse than useless to speak to him, since, on being pressed, he became worried. He abandoned that attempt in the first day, and resolved merely to keep himself always before him, as a silent protest against the delusion into which he had fallen, or was falling. He remained, therefore, in his seat near the window, reading and writing, and expressing in as many pleasant and natural ways as he could think of, that it was a free place.

Doctor Manette took what was given him to eat and drink, and worked on, that first day, until it was too dark to see—worked on, half an hour after Mr. Lorry could not have seen, for his life, to read or write. When he put his tools aside as useless, until morning, Mr. Lorry rose and said to him:

"Will you go out?"

He looked down at the floor on either side of him in the old manner, looked up in the old manner, and repeated in the old low voice:

"Out?"

"Yes; for a walk with me. Why not?"

He made no effort to say why not, and said not a word more. But, Mr. Lorry thought he saw, as he leaned forward on his bench in the dusk, with his elbows on his knees and his head in his hands, that he was in some misty way asking himself, "Why not?" The sagacity of the man of business perceived an advantage here, and determined to hold it.

Miss Pross and he divided the night into two watches, and observed him at intervals from the adjoining room. He paced up and down for a long time before he lay down; but, when he did finally lay himself down, he fell asleep. In the morning, he was up betimes, and went straight to his bench and to work.

On the second day, Mr. Lorry saluted him cheerfully by his name, and spoke to him on topics that had been of late familiar to them. He returned no reply, but it was evident that he heard what was said, and that he thought about it, however confusedly. This encouraged Mr. Lorry to have Miss Pross in with her work, several times during the day; at those times, they quietly spoke of Lucie, and of her father then present, precisely in the usual manner, and as if there were nothing amiss. This was done without any demonstrative accompaniment, not long enough or often enough to harass him; and it lightened Mr. Lorry's friendly heart to believe that he looked up oftener, and that he appeared to be stirred by some perception of inconsistencies surrounding him.

When it fell dark again, Mr. Lorry asked him as before: "Dear Doctor, will you go out?"

As before, he repeated, "Out?"

"Yes; for a walk with me. Why not?"

This time, Mr. Lorry feigned to go out when he could extract no answer from him, and, after remaining absent for an hour, returned. In the meanwhile, the Doctor had removed to the seat in the window, and had sat there looking down at the plane-tree; but, on Mr. Lorry's return, he slipped away to his bench.

The time went very slowly on, and Mr. Lorry's hope darkened, and his heart grew heavier again, and grew yet heavier and heavier every day. The third day came and went, the fourth, the fifth. Five days, six days, seven days, eight days, nine days.

With a hope ever darkening, and with a heart always growing heavier and heavier, Mr. Lorry passed through this anxious time. The secret was well kept, and Lucie was unconscious and happy; but he could not fail to observe that the shoemaker, whose hand had been a little out at first, was growing dreadfully skilful, and that he had never been so intent on his work, and that his hands had never been so nimble and expert, as in the dusk of the ninth evening.

---

19 *An Opinion*

WORN OUT by anxious watching, Mr. Lorry fell asleep at his post. On the tenth morning of his suspense, he was startled by the shining of the sun into the room where a heavy slumber had overtaken him when it was dark night.

He rubbed his eyes and roused himself; but he doubted, when he had done so, whether he was not still asleep. For, going to the door of the Doctor's room and looking in, he perceived that the shoemaker's bench and tools were put aside again, and that the Doctor himself sat reading at the window. He was in his usual morning dress, and his face (which Mr. Lorry could distinctly see), though still very pale, was calmly studious and attentive.

Even when he had satisfied himself that he was awake, Mr. Lorry felt giddily uncertain for some few moments whether the late shoemaking might not be a disturbed dream of his own; for, did not his eyes show him his friend before him in his accustomed clothing and aspect, and employed as usual; and was there any sign within their range, that the change of which he had so strong an impression had actually happened?

It was but the inquiry of his first confusion and astonishment, the answer being obvious. If the impression were not produced by a real corresponding and sufficient cause, how came he, Jarvis Lorry, there? How came he to have fallen asleep, in his clothes, on the sofa in Doctor Manette's consulting-room, and to be debating these points outside the Doctor's bedroom door in the early morning?

Within a few minutes, Miss Pross stood whispering at his side. If he had had any particle of doubt left, her talk would of necessity have resolved it; but he was by that time clear-headed, and had none. He advised that they should let the time go by until the regular breakfast-hour, and should then meet the Doctor as if nothing unusual had occurred. If he appeared to be in his customary state of mind, Mr. Lorry would then cautiously proceed to seek direction and guidance from the opinion he had been, in his anxiety, so anxious to obtain.

Miss Pross submitting herself to his judgment, the scheme was worked out with care. Having abundance of time for his usual methodical toilette, Mr. Lorry presented himself at the breakfast-hour in his usual white linen, and with his usual neat leg. The Doctor was summoned in the usual way, and came to breakfast.

So far as it was possible to comprehend him without overstepping those delicate and gradual approaches which Mr. Lorry felt to be the only safe advance, he at first supposed that his daughter's marriage had taken place yesterday. An incidental allusion, purposely thrown out, to the day of the week, and the day of the month, set him thinking and counting, and evidently made him uneasy. In all other respects, however, he was so composedly himself, that Mr. Lorry determined to have the aid he sought. And that aid was his own.

Therefore, when the breakfast was done and cleared away, and he and the Doctor were left together, Mr. Lorry said, feelingly:

"My dear Manette, I am anxious to have your opinion, in confidence, on a very curious case in which I am deeply interested; that is to say, it is very curious to me; perhaps, to your better information it may be less so."

Glancing at his hands, which were discoloured by his late work, the Doctor looked troubled, and listened attentively. He had already glanced at his hands more than once.

"Doctor Manette," said Mr. Lorry, touching him affectionately on the arm, "the case is the case of a particularly dear friend of mine. Pray give your mind to it, and advise me well for his sake—and above all, for his daughter's—his daughter's, my dear Manette."

"If I understand," said the Doctor, in a subdued tone, "some mental shock—?"

"Yes!"

"Be explicit," said the Doctor. "Spare no detail."

Mr. Lorry saw that they understood one another, and proceeded.

"My dear Manette, it is the case of an old and a prolonged shock, of great acuteness and severity to the affections, the feelings, the—the—as you express it—the mind. The mind. It is the case of a shock under which the sufferer was borne down, one cannot say for how long, because I believe he cannot calculate the time himself, and there are no other means of getting at it. It is the case of a shock from which the sufferer recovered, by a process that he cannot trace himself—as I once heard him publicly relate in a striking manner. It is the case of a shock from which he has recovered, so completely, as to be a highly intelligent man, capable of close application of mind, and great exertion of body, and of constantly making fresh additions to his stock of knowledge, which was already very large. But, unfortunately, there has been"—he paused and took a deep breath—"a slight relapse."

The Doctor, in a low voice, asked, "Of how long duration?"

"Nine days and nights."

"How did it show itself? I infer," glancing at his hands again, "in the resumption of some old pursuit connected with the shock?"

"That is the fact."

"Now, did you ever see him," asked the Doctor, distinctly and collectedly, though in the same low voice, "engaged in that pursuit originally?"

"Once."

"And when the relapse fell on him, was he in most respects—or in all respects—as he was then?"

"I think in all respects."

"You spoke of his daughter. Does his daughter know of the relapse?"

"No. It has been kept from her, and I hope will always be kept from her. It is known only to myself, and to one other who may be trusted."

The Doctor grasped his hand, and murmured, "That was very kind. That was very thoughtful!" Mr. Lorry grasped his hand in return, and neither of the two spoke for a little while.

"Now, my dear Manette," said Mr. Lorry, at length, in his most considerate and most affectionate way, "I am a

mere man of business, and unfit to cope with such intricate and difficult matters. I do not possess the kind of
information necessary; I do not possess the kind of intelligence; I want guiding. There is no man in this world on
whom I could so rely for right guidance, as on you. Tell
me, how does this relapse come about? Is there danger
of another? Could a repetition of it be prevented? How
should a repetition of it be treated? How does it come
about at all? What can I do for my friend? No man ever
can have been more desirous in his heart to serve a friend,
than I am to serve mine, if I knew how. But I don't know
how to originate in such a case. If your sagacity, knowledge, and experience could put me on the right track, I
might be able to do so much; unenlightened and undirected,
I can do so little. Pray discuss it with me; pray enable me
to see it a little more clearly, and teach me how to be a little
more useful."

Doctor Manette sat meditating after these earnest words
were spoken, and Mr. Lorry did not press him.

"I think it probable," said the Doctor, breaking silence
with an effort, "that the relapse you have described, my
dear friend, was not quite unforeseen by its subject."

"Was it dreaded by him?" Mr. Lorry ventured to ask.

"Very much." He said it with an involuntary shudder.

"You have no idea how such an apprehension weighs
on the sufferer's mind, and how difficult—how almost impossible—it is, for him to force himself to utter a word
upon the topic that oppresses him."

"Would he," asked Mr. Lorry, "be sensibly relieved if
he could prevail upon himself to impart that secret brooding to any one, when it is on him?"

"I think so. But it is, as I have told you, next to impossible. I even believe it—in some cases—to be quite impossible."

"Now," said Mr. Lorry, gently laying his hand on the
Doctor's arm again, after a short silence on both sides, "to
what would you refer this attack?"

"I believe," returned Doctor Manette, "that there had
been a strong and extraordinary revival of the train of
thought and remembrance that was the first cause of the
malady. Some intense associations of a most distressing
nature were vividly recalled, I think. It is probable that
there had long been a dread lurking in his mind, that those
associations would be recalled—say, under certain circum-

stances—say, on a particular occasion. He tried to prepare himself in vain; perhaps the effort to prepare himself made him less able to bear it."

"Would he remember what took place in the relapse?" asked Mr. Lorry, with natural hesitation.

The Doctor looked desolately round the room, shook his head, and answered, in a low voice, "Not at all."

"Now, as to the future," hinted Mr. Lorry.

"As to the future," said the Doctor, recovering firmness, "I should have great hope. As it pleased Heaven in its mercy to restore him so soon, I should have great hope. He, yielding under the pressure of a complicated something, long dreaded and long vaguely foreseen and contended against, and recovering after the cloud had burst and passed, I should hope that the worst was over."

"Well, well! That's good comfort. I am thankful!" said Mr. Lorry.

"I am thankful!" repeated the Doctor, bending his head with reverence.

"There are two other points," said Mr. Lorry, "on which I am anxious to be instructed. I may go on?"

"You cannot do your friend a better service." The Doctor gave him his hand.

"To the first, then. He is of a studious habit, and unusually energetic; he applies himself with great ardour to the acquisition of professional knowledge, to the conducting of experiments, to many things. Now, does he do too much?"

"I think not. It may be the character of his mind, to be always in singular need of occupation. That may be, in part, natural to it; in part, the result of affliction. The less it was occupied with healthy things, the more it would be in danger of turning in the unhealthy direction. He may have observed himself, and made the discovery."

"You are sure that he is not under too great a strain?"

"I think I am quite sure of it."

"My dear Manette, if he were overworked now——"

"My dear Lorry, I doubt if that could easily be. There has been a violent stress in one direction, and it needs a counter-weight."

"Excuse me, as a persistent man of business. Assuming for a moment that he *was* overworked; it would show itself in some renewal of this disorder?"

"I do not think so. I do not think," said Doctor Manette with the firmness of self-conviction, "that anything but the one train of association would renew it. I think that, henceforth, nothing but some extraordinary jarring of that chord could renew it. After what has happened, and after his recovery, I find it difficult to imagine any such violent sounding of that string again. I trust, and I almost believe, that the circumstances likely to renew it are exhausted."

He spoke with the diffidence of a man who knew how slight a thing would overset the delicate organisation of the mind, and yet with the confidence of a man who had slowly won his assurance out of personal endurance and distress. It was not for his friend to abate that confidence. He professed himself more relieved and encouraged than he really was, and approached his second and last point. He felt it to be the most difficult of all; but, remembering his old Sunday-morning conversation with Miss Pross, and remembering what he had seen in the last nine days, he knew that he must face it.

"The occupation resumed under the influence of this passing affliction so happily recovered from," said Mr. Lorry, clearing his throat, "we will call—Blacksmith's work, Blacksmith's work. We will say, to put a case and for the sake of illustration, that he had been used, in his bad time, to work at a little forge. We will say that he was unexpectedly found at his forge again. Is it not a pity that he should keep it by him?"

The Doctor shaded his forehead with his hand, and beat his foot nervously on the ground.

"He has always kept it by him," said Mr. Lorry, with an anxious look at his friend. "Now, would it not be better that he should let it go?"

Still, the Doctor, with shaded forehead, beat his foot nervously on the ground.

"You do not find it easy to advise me?" said Mr. Lorry. "I quite understand it to be a nice question. And yet I think—" And there he shook his head, and stopped.

"You see," said Doctor Manette, turning to him after an uneasy pause, "it is very hard to explain, consistently, the innermost workings of this poor man's mind. He once yearned so frightfully for that occupation, and it was so welcome when it came; no doubt it relieved his pain so much, by substituting the perplexity of the fingers for the perplexity of the brain, and by substituting, as he became

more practised, the ingenuity of the hands for the ingenuity
of the mental torture; that he has never been able to bear
the thought of putting it quite out of his reach. Even now,
when I believe he is more hopeful of himself than he has
ever been, and even speaks of himself with a kind of confidence, the idea that he might need that old employment,
and not find it, gives him a sudden sense of terror, like that
which one may fancy strikes to the heart of a lost child."

He looked like his illustration, as he raised his eyes to
Mr. Lorry's face.

"But may not—mind! I ask for information, as a plodding man of business who only deals with such material
objects as guineas, shillings, and bank-notes—may not the
retention of the thing involve the retention of the idea?
If the thing were gone, my dear Manette, might not the
fear go with it? In short, is it not a concession to the misgiving, to keep the forge?"

There was another silence.

"You see, too," said the Doctor, tremulously, "it is such
an old companion."

"I would not keep it," said Mr. Lorry, shaking his head,
for he gained in firmness as he saw the Doctor disquieted.
"I would recommend him to sacrifice it. I only want your
authority. I am sure it does no good. Come! Give me your
authority, like a dear good man. For his daughter's sake,
my dear Manette!"

Very strange to see what a struggle there was within
him.

"In her name, then, let it be done; I sanction it. But,
I would not take it away while he was present. Let it be
removed when he is not there; let him miss his old companion after an absence."

Mr. Lorry readily engaged for that, and the conference
was ended. They passed the day in the country, and the
Doctor was quite restored. On the three following days he
remained perfectly well, and on the fourteenth day he went
away to join Lucie and her husband. The precaution that
had been taken to account for his silence, Mr. Lorry had
previously explained to him, and he had written to Lucie
in accordance with it, and she had no suspicions.

On the night of the day on which he had left the house,
Mr. Lorry went into his room with a chopper, saw, chisel,
and hammer, attended by Miss Pross carrying a light.
There, with closed doors, and in a mysterious and guilty

manner, Mr. Lorry hacked the shoemaker's bench to pieces, while Miss Pross held the candle as if she were assisting at a murder—for which, indeed, in her grimness, she was no unsuitable figure. The burning of the body (previously reduced to pieces convenient for the purpose) was commenced without delay in the kitchen fire; and the tools, shoes, and leather were buried in the garden. So wicked do destruction and secrecy appear to honest minds, that Mr. Lorry and Miss Pross, while engaged in the commission of their deed and in the removal of its traces, almost felt, and almost looked, like accomplices in a horrible crime.

20 *A Plea*

WHEN THE newly-married pair came home, the first person who appeared, to offer his congratulations, was Sydney Carton. They had not been at home many hours when he presented himself. He was not improved in habits, or in looks, or in manner; but there was a certain rugged air of fidelity about him, which was new to the observation of Charles Darnay.

He watched his opportunity of taking Darnay aside into a window, and of speaking to him when no one overheard.

"Mr. Darnay," said Carton, "I wish we might be friends."

"We are already friends, I hope."

"You are good enough to say so, as a fashion of speech; but, I don't mean any fashion of speech. Indeed, when I say I wish we might be friends, I scarcely mean quite that, either."

Charles Darnay—as was natural—asked him, in all good-humour and good-fellowship, what he did mean?

"Upon my life," said Carton, smiling, "I find that easier to comprehend in my own mind, than to convey to yours. However, let me try. You remember a certain famous occasion when I was more drunk than—than usual?"

"I remember a certain famous occasion when you forced me to confess that you had been drinking."

"I remember it too. The curse of those occasions is heavy upon me, for I always remember them. I hope it may be taken into account one day, when all days are at an end for me! Don't be alarmed; I am not going to preach."

"I am not at all alarmed. Earnestness in you is anything but alarming to me."

"Ah!" said Carton, with a careless wave of his hand, as if he waved that away. "On the drunken occasion in question (one of a large number, as you know), I was insufferable about liking you, and not liking you. I wish you would forget it."

"I forgot it long ago."

"Fashion of speech again! But, Mr. Darnay, oblivion is not so easy to me, as you represent it to be to you. I have by no means forgotten it, and a light answer does not help me to forget it."

"If it was a light answer," returned Darnay, "I beg your forgiveness for it. I had no other object than to turn a slight thing, which, to my surprise, seems to trouble you too much, aside. I declare to you on the faith of a gentleman, that I have long dismissed it from my mind. Good Heaven, what was there to dismiss! Have I had nothing more important to remember, in the great service you rendered me that day?"

"As to the great service," said Carton, "I am bound to avow to you, when you speak of it in that way, that it was mere professional claptrap. I don't know that I cared what became of you, when I rendered it.—Mind! I say when I rendered it; I am speaking of the past."

"You make light of the obligation," returned Darnay, "but I will not quarrel with *your* light answer."

"Genuine truth, Mr. Darnay, trust me! I have gone aside from my purpose; I was speaking about our being friends. Now, you know me; you know I am incapable of all the higher and better flights of men. If you doubt it, ask Stryver, and he'll tell you so."

"I prefer to form my own opinion, without the aid of his."

"Well! At any rate you know me as a dissolute dog, who has never done any good, and never will."

"I don't know that you 'never will.' "

"But I do, and you must take my word for it. Well! If you could endure to have such a worthless fellow, and a fellow of such indifferent reputation, coming and going at odd times, I should ask that I might be permitted to come and go as a privileged person here; that I might be regarded as an useless (and I would add, if it were not for the resemblance I detected between you and me), an unornamental, piece of furniture, tolerated for its old service, and taken no notice of. I doubt if I should abuse the permission. It is a hundred to one if I should avail myself of it four times in a year. It would satisfy me, I dare say, to know that I had it."

"Will you try?"

"That is another way of saying that I am placed on the footing I have indicated. I thank you, Darnay. I may use that freedom with your name?"

"I think so, Carton, by this time."

They shook hands upon it, and Sydney turned away. Within a minute afterwards, he was, to all outward appearance, as unsubstantial as ever.

When he was gone, and in the course of an evening passed with Miss Pross, the Doctor, and Mr. Lorry, Charles Darnay made some mention of this conversation in general terms, and spoke of Sydney Carton as a problem of carelessness and recklessness. He spoke of him, in short, not bitterly or meaning to bear hard upon him, but as anybody might who saw him as he showed himself.

He had no idea that this could dwell in the thoughts of his fair young wife; but, when he afterwards joined her in their own room, he found her waiting for him with the old pretty lifting of the forehead strongly marked.

"We are thoughtful to-night!" said Darnay, drawing his arm about her.

"Yes, dearest Charles," with her hand on his breast, and the inquiring and attentive expression fixed upon him; "we are rather thoughtful to-night, for we have something on our mind to-night."

"What is it, my Lucie?"

"Will you promise not to press one question on me, if I beg you not to ask it?"

"Will I promise? What will I not promise to my Love?"

What, indeed, with his hand putting aside the golden hair from the cheek, and his other hand against the heart that beat for him!

"I think, Charles, poor Mr. Carton deserves more consideration and respect than you expressed for him tonight."

"Indeed, my own? Why so?"

"That is what you are not to ask me! But I think—I know—he does."

"If you know it, it is enough. What would you have me do, my Life?"

"I would ask you, dearest, to be very generous with him always, and very lenient on his faults when he is not by. I would ask you to believe that he has a heart he very, very seldom reveals, and that there are deep wounds in it. My dear, I have seen it bleeding."

"It is a painful reflection to me," said Charles Darnay, quite astounded, "that I should have done him any wrong. I never thought this of him."

"My husband, it is so. I fear he is not to be reclaimed; there is scarcely a hope that anything in his character or fortunes is reparable now. But, I am sure that he is capable of good things, gentle things, even magnanimous things."

She looked so beautiful in the purity of her faith in this lost man, that her husband could have looked at her as she was for hours.

"And, O my dearest Love!" she urged, clinging nearer to him, laying her head upon his breast, and raising her eyes to his, "remember how strong we are in our happiness, and how weak he is in his misery!"

The supplication touched him home. "I will always remember it, dear Heart! I will remember it as long as I live."

He bent over the golden head, and put the rosy lips to his, and folded her in his arms. If one forlorn wanderer then pacing the dark streets could have heard her innocent disclosure, and could have seen the drops of pity kissed away by her husband from the soft blue eyes so loving of that husband, he might have cried to the night—and the words would not have parted from his lips for the first time—

"God bless her for her sweet compassion!"

*　　*　　*　　*　　*　　*　　*　　*

21 *Echoing Footsteps*

A WONDERFUL corner for echoes, it has been re-marked, that corner where the Doctor lived. Ever busily winding the golden thread which bound her husband, and her father, and herself, and her old directress and companion, in a life of quiet bliss, Lucie sat in the still house in the tranquilly resounding corner, listening to the echoing footsteps of years.

At first, there were times, though she was a perfectly happy young wife, when her work would slowly fall from her hands, and her eyes would be dimmed. For there was something coming in the echoes, something light, afar off, and scarcely audible yet, that stirred her heart too much. Fluttering hopes and doubts—hope, of a love as yet un-known to her: doubts, of her remaining upon earth, to enjoy that new delight—divided her breast. Among the echoes then, there would arise the sound of footsteps at her own early grave; and thoughts of the husband who would be left so desolate, and who would mourn for her so much, swelled to her eyes, and broke like waves.

That time passed, and her little Lucie lay on her bosom. Then, among the advancing echoes, there was the tread of her tiny feet and the sound of her prattling words. Let greater echoes resound as they would, the young mother at the cradle side could always hear those coming. They came, and the shady house was sunny with a child's laugh, and the Divine friend of children, to whom in her trouble she had confided hers, seemed to take her child in His arms, as He took the child of old, and made it a sacred joy to her.

Ever busily winding the golden thread that bound them all together, weaving the service of her happy influence through the tissue of all their lives, and making it predomi-nate nowhere, Lucie heard in the echoes of years none but friendly and soothing sounds. Her husband's step was strong and prosperous among them; her father's firm and equal. Lo, Miss Pross, in harness of string, awakening the echoes, as an unruly charger, whip-corrected, snorting and pawing the earth under the plane-tree in the garden!

Even when there were sounds of sorrow among the rest, they were not harsh nor cruel. Even when golden hair, like her own, lay in a halo on a pillow round the worn face of a little boy, and he said, with a radiant smile, "Dear papa and mamma, I am very sorry to leave you both, and to leave my pretty sister; but I am called, and I must go!" those were not tears all of agony that wetted his young mother's cheek, as the spirit departed from her embrace that had been entrusted to it. Suffer them and forbid them not. They see my Father's face. O Father, blessed words!

Thus, the rustling of an Angel's wings got blended with the other echoes, and they were not wholly of earth, but had in them that breath of Heaven. Sighs of the winds that blew over a little garden-tomb were mingled with them also, and both were audible to Lucie, in a hushed murmur —like the breathing of a summer sea asleep upon a sandy shore—as the little Lucie, comically studious at the task of the morning, or dressing a doll at her mother's footstool, chattered in the tongues of the Two Cities that were blended in her life.

The echoes rarely answered to the actual tread of Sydney Carton. Some half-dozen times a year, at most, he claimed his privilege of coming in uninvited, and would sit among them through the evening, as he had once done often. He never came there heated with wine. And one other thing regarding him was whispered in the echoes, which has been whispered by all true echoes for ages and ages.

No man ever really loved a woman, lost her, and knew her with a blameless though an unchanged mind, when she was a wife and a mother, but her children had a strange sympathy with him—an instinctive delicacy of pity for him. What fine hidden sensibilities are touched in such a case, no echoes tell; but it is so, and it was so here. Carton was the first stranger to whom little Lucie held out her chubby arms, and he kept his place with her as she grew. The little boy had spoken of him, almost at the last. "Poor Carton! Kiss him for me!"

Mr. Stryver shouldered his way through the law, like some great engine forcing itself through turbid water, and dragged his useful friend in his wake, like a boat towed astern. As the boat so favoured is usually in a rough plight, and mostly under water, so, Sydney had a swamped life of it. But, easy and strong custom, unhappily so much easier and stronger in him than any stimulating sense of desert or disgrace, made it the life he was to lead; and he no more thought of emerging from his state of lion's jackal, than any real jackal may be supposed to think of rising to be a lion. Stryver was rich; had married a florid widow with property and three boys, who had nothing particularly shining about them but the straight hair of their dumpling heads.

These three young gentlemen, Mr. Stryver, exuding patronage of the most offensive quality from every pore, had walked before him like three sheep to the quiet corner in Soho, and had offered as pupils to Lucie's husband: delicately saying, "Halloa! here are three lumps of bread-and-cheese towards your matrimonial picnic, Darnay!" The polite rejection of the three lumps of bread-and-cheese had quite bloated Mr. Stryver with indignation, which he afterwards turned to account in the training of the young gentlemen, by directing them to beware of the pride of beggars, like that tutor-fellow. He was also in the habit of declaiming to Mrs. Stryver, over his full-bodied wine, on the arts Mrs. Darnay had once put in practice to "catch" him, and on the diamond-cut-diamond arts in himself, madam, which had rendered him "not to be caught." Some of his King's Bench familiars, who were occasionally parties to the full-bodied wine and the lie, excused him for the latter by saying that he had told it so often, that he believed it himself —which is surely such an incorrigible aggravation of an originally bad offence, as to justify any such offender's being carried off to some suitably retired spot, and there hanged out of the way.

These were among the echoes to which Lucie, sometimes pensive, sometimes amused and laughing, listened in the echoing corner, until her little daughter was six years old. How near to her heart the echoes of her child's tread came, and those of her own dear father's, always active and self-possessed, and those of her dear husband's, need not be told. Nor, how the slightest echo of their united home, directed by herself with such a wise and elegant thrift that it was more abundant than any waste, was music to her. Nor, how there were echoes all about her, sweet in her ears,

of the many times her father had told her that he found her
more devoted to him married (if that could be) than single,
and of the many times her husband had said to her that
no cares and duties seemed to divide her love for him or
her help to him, and asked her "What is the magic secret,
my darling, of your being everything to all of us, as if there
were only one of us, yet never seeming to be hurried, or to
have too much to do?"

But, there were other echoes, from a distance, that rumbled menacingly in the corner all through this space of
time. And it was now, about little Lucie's sixth birthday,
that they began to have an awful sound, as of a great storm
in France with a dreadful sea rising.

On a night in mid-July, one thousand seven hundred and
eighty-nine, Mr. Lorry came in late, from Tellson's, and sat
himself down by Lucie and her husband in the dark window. It was a hot, wild night, and they were all three reminded of the old Sunday night when they had looked
at the lightning from the same place.

"I began to think," said Mr. Lorry, pushing his brown
wig back, "that I should have to pass the night at Tellson's.
We have been so full of business all day, that we have not
known what to do first, or which way to turn. There is such
an uneasiness in Paris, that we have actually a run of confidence upon us! Our customers over there seem not to be
able to confide their property to us fast enough. There is
positively a mania among some of them for sending it to
England."

"That has a bad look," said Darnay.

"A bad look, you say, my dear Darnay? Yes, but we
don't know what reason there is in it. People are so unreasonable! Some of us at Tellson's are getting old, and we
really can't be troubled out of the ordinary course without
due occasion."

"Still," said Darnay, "you know how gloomy and threatening the sky is."

"I know that, to be sure," assented Mr. Lorry, trying
to persuade himself that his sweet temper was soured, and
that he grumbled, "but I am determined to be peevish
after my long day's botheration. Where is Manette?"

"Here he is," said the Doctor, entering the dark room at
the moment.

"I am quite glad you are at home; for these hurries and
forebodings, by which I have been surrounded all day long,

have made me nervous without reason. You are not going out, I hope?"

"No; I am going to play backgammon with you, if you like," said the Doctor.

"I don't think I do like, if I may speak my mind. I am not fit to be pitted against you to-night. Is the tea-board still there, Lucie? I can't see."

"Of course, it has been kept for you."

"Thank ye, my dear. The precious child is safe in bed?"

"And sleeping soundly."

"That's right; all safe and well! I don't know why anything should be otherwise than safe and well here, thank God; but I have been so put out all day, and I am not as young as I was! My tea, my dear! Thank ye. Now, come and take your place in the circle, and let us sit quiet, and hear the echoes about which you have your theory."

"Not a theory; it was a fancy."

"A fancy, then, my wise pet," said Mr. Lorry, patting her hand. "They are very numerous and very loud, though, are they not? Only hear them!"

Headlong, mad, and dangerous footsteps to force their way into anybody's life, footsteps not easily made clean again if once stained red, the footsteps raging in Saint Antoine afar off, as the little circle sat in the dark London window.

Saint Antoine had been, that morning, a vast dusky mass of scarecrows heaving to and fro, with frequent gleams of light above the billowy heads, where steel blades and bayonets shone in the sun. A tremendous roar arose from the throat of Saint Antoine, and a forest of naked arms struggled in the air like shrivelled branches of trees in a winter wind: all the fingers convulsively clutching at every weapon or semblance of a weapon that was thrown up from the depths below, no matter how far off.

Who gave them out, whence they last came, where they began, through what agency they crookedly quivered and jerked, scores at a time, over the heads of the crowd, like a kind of lightning, no eye in the throng could have told; but, muskets were being distributed—so were cartridges, powder, and ball, bars of iron and wood, knives, axes, pikes, every weapon that distracted ingenuity could discover or devise. People who could lay hold of nothing else, set themselves with bleeding hands to force stones and bricks out of their places in walls. Every pulse and heart in Saint Antoine was on high-fever strain and at high-fever heat. Every living creature there held life as of no account, and was demented with a passionate readiness to sacrifice it.

As a whirlpool of boiling waters has a centre point, so all this raging circled round Defarge's wine-shop, and every human drop in the caldron had a tendency to be sucked towards the vortex where Defarge himself, already begrimed with gunpowder and sweat, issued orders, issued arms, thrust this man back, dragged this man forward, disarmed one to arm another, laboured and strove in the thickest of the uproar.

"Keep near to me, Jacques Three," cried Defarge; "and do you, Jacques One and Two, separate and put yourselves at the head of as many of these patriots as you can. Where is my wife?"

"Eh, well! Here you see me!" said madame, composed as ever, but not knitting to-day. Madame's resolute right hand was occupied with an axe, in place of the usual softer implements, and in her girdle were a pistol and a cruel knife.

"Where do you go, my wife?"

"I go," said madame, "with you at present. You shall see me at the head of women, by and by."

"Come, then!" cried Defarge, in a resounding voice. "Patriots and friends, we are ready! The Bastille!"

With a roar that sounded as if all the breath in France had been shaped into the detested word, the living sea rose, wave on wave, depth on depth, and overflowed the city to that point. Alarm-bells ringing, drums beating, the sea raging and thundering on its new beach, the attack began.

Deep ditches, double drawbridge, massive stone walls, eight great towers, cannon, muskets, fire and smoke. Through the fire and through the smoke—in the fire and in the smoke, for the sea cast him up against a cannon, and on the instant he became a cannonier—Defarge of the wine-shop worked like a manful soldier, two fierce hours.

Deep ditch, single drawbridge, massive stone walls, eight great towers, cannon, muskets, fire and smoke. One draw-bridge down! "Work, comrades all, work! Work, Jacques One, Jacques Two, Jacques One Thousand, Jacques Two Thousand, Jacques Five-and-Twenty Thousand; in the name of all the Angels or the Devils—which you prefer—

work!" Thus Defarge of the wine-shop, still at his gun, which had long grown hot.

"To me, women!" cried madame his wife. "What! We can kill as well as the men when the place is taken!" And to her, with a shrill thirsty cry, trooping women variously armed, but all armed alike in hunger and revenge.

Cannon, muskets, fire and smoke; but, still the deep ditch, the single drawbridge, the massive stone walls, and the eight great towers. Slight displacements of the raging sea, made by the falling wounded. Flashing weapons, blazing torches, smoking waggon-loads of wet straw, hard work at neighbouring barricades in all directions, shrieks, volleys, execrations, bravery without stint, boom, smash and rattle, and the furious sounding of the living sea; but, still the deep ditch, and the single drawbridge, and the massive stone walls, and the eight great towers, and still Defarge of the wine-shop at his gun, grown doubly hot by the service of four fierce hours.

A white flag from within the fortress, and a parley—this dimly perceptible through the raging storm, nothing audible in it—suddenly the sea rose immeasurably wider and higher, and swept Defarge of the wine-shop over the lowered drawbridge, past the massive stone outer walls, in among the eight great towers surrendered!

So resistless was the force of the ocean bearing him on, that even to draw his breath or turn his head was as impracticable as if he had been struggling in the surf at the South Sea, until he was landed in the outer courtyard of the Bastille. There, against an angle of a wall, he made a struggle to look about him. Jacques Three was nearly at his side; Madame Defarge, still heading some of her women, was visible in the inner distance, and her knife was in her hand. Everywhere was tumult, exultation, deafening and maniacal bewilderment, astounding noise, yet furious dumb-show.

"The prisoners!"

"The records!"

"The secret cells!"

"The instruments of torture!"

"The prisoners!"

Of all these cries, and ten thousand incoherencies, "The prisoners!" was the cry most taken up by the sea that rushed in, as if there were an eternity of people, as well as of time and space. When the foremost billows rolled past, bearing the prison officers with them, and threatening them all with instant death if any secret nook remained undisclosed, Defarge laid his strong hand on the breast of one of these men—a man with a gray head, who had a lighted torch in his hand—separated him from the rest, and got him between himself and the wall.

"Show me the North Tower!" said Defarge. "Quick!"

"I will faithfully," replied the man, "if you will come with me. But there is no one there."

"What is the meaning of One Hundred and Five, North Tower?" asked Defarge. "Quick!"

"The meaning, monsieur?"

"Does it mean a captive, or a place of captivity? Or do you mean that I shall strike you dead?"

"Kill him!" croaked Jacques Three, who had come close up.

"Monsieur, it is a cell."

"Show it me!"

"Pass this way, then."

Jacques Three, with his usual craving on him, and evidently disappointed by the dialogue taking a turn that did not seem to promise bloodshed, held by Defarge's arm as he held the turnkey's. Their three heads had been close together during this brief discourse, and it had been as much as they could do to hear one another, even then: so tremendous was the noise of the living ocean, in its irruption into the fortress, and its inundation of the courts and passages and staircases. All around outside, too, it beat the walls with a deep, hoarse roar, from which, occasionally, some partial shouts of tumult broke and leaped into the air like spray.

Through gloomy vaults where the light of day had never shone, past hideous doors of dark dens and cages, down cavernous flights of steps, and again up steep rugged ascents of stone and brick, more like dry waterfalls than staircases, Defarge, the turnkey, and Jacques Three, linked hand and arm, went with all the speed they could make. Here and there, especially at first, the inundation started on them and swept by; but when they had done descending, and were winding and climbing up a tower, they were alone. Hemmed in here by the massive thickness of walls and arches, the storm within the fortress and without was only audible to them in a dull, subdued way, as if the noise out of which they had come had almost destroyed their sense of hearing.

The turnkey stopped at a low door, put a key in a clashing lock, swung the door slowly open, and said, as they all bent their heads and passed in:

"One Hundred and Five, North Tower!"

There was a small, heavily-grated, unglazed window high in the wall, with a stone screen before it, so that the sky could be only seen by stooping low and looking up. There was a small chimney, heavily barred across, a few feet within. There was a heap of old feathery wood-ashes on the hearth. There was a stool, and table, and a straw bed. There were the four blackened walls, and a rusted iron ring in one of them.

"Pass that torch slowly along these walls, that I may see them," said Defarge to the turnkey.

The man obeyed, and Defarge followed the light closely with his eyes.

"Stop!—Look here, Jacques!"

"A. M.!" croaked Jacques Three, as he read greedily.

"Alexandre Manette," said Defarge in his ear, following the letters with his swart forefinger, deeply engrained with gunpowder. "And here he wrote 'a poor physician.' And it was he, without doubt, who scratched a calendar on this stone. What is that in your hand? A crowbar? Give it me!"

He had still the linstock of his gun in his own hand. He made a sudden exchange of the two instruments, and turning on the worm-eaten stool and table, beat them to pieces in a few blows.

"Hold the light higher!" he said, wrathfully, to the turnkey. "Look among those fragments with care, Jacques. And see! Here is my knife," throwing it to him; "rip open that bed, and search the straw. Hold the light higher, you!"

With a menacing look at the turnkey he crawled upon the hearth, and, peering up the chimney, struck and prised at its sides with the crowbar, and worked at the iron grating across it. In a few minutes, some mortar and dust came dropping down, which he averted his face to avoid; and in it, and in the old wood-ashes, and in a crevice in the chimney into which his weapon had slipped or wrought itself, he groped with a cautious touch.

"Nothing in the wood, and nothing in the straw, Jacques?"

"Nothing."

"Let us collect them together, in the middle of the cell.
So! Light them, you!"

The turnkey fired the little pile, which blazed high and
hot. Stooping again to come out at the low-arched door,
they left it burning, and retraced their way to the courtyard; seeming to recover their sense of hearing as they
came down, until they were in the raging flood once more.

They found it surging and tossing, in quest of Defarge
himself. Saint Antoine was clamorous to have its wine-
shop keeper foremost in the guard upon the governor who
had defended the Bastille and shot the people. Otherwise,
the governor would not be marched to the Hôtel de Ville
for judgment. Otherwise, the governor would escape, and
the people's blood (suddenly of some value, after many
years of worthlessness) be unavenged.

In the howling universe of passion and contention that
seemed to encompass this grim old officer, conspicuous in
his gray coat and red decoration, there was but one quite
steady figure, and that was a woman's. "See, there is my
husband!" she cried, pointing him out. "See Defarge!" She
stood immovable close to the grim old officer, and remained immovable close to him; remained immovable
close to him through the streets, as Defarge and the rest
bore him along; remained immovable close to him when
he got near his destination, and began to be struck at from
behind; remained immovable close to him when the long-
gathering rain of stabs and blows fell heavy; was so close
to him when he dropped dead under it, that, suddenly animated, she put her foot upon his neck, and with her cruel
knife—long ready—hewed off his head.

The hour was come, when Saint Antoine was to execute
his horrible idea of hoisting up men for lamps to show
what he could be and do. Saint Antoine's blood was up,
and the blood of tyranny and domination by the iron hand
was down—down on the steps of the Hôtel de Ville where
the governor's body lay—down on the sole of the shoe of
Madame Defarge where she had trodden on the body to
steady it for mutilation. "Lower the lamp yonder!" cried
Saint Antoine, after glaring round for a new means of
death; "here is one of his soldiers to be left on guard!" The
swinging sentinel was posted, and the sea rushed on.

The sea of black and threatening waters, and of destructive upheaving of wave against wave, whose depths were
yet unfathomed and whose forces were yet unknown. The

remorseless sea of turbulently swaying shapes, voices of vengeance, and faces hardened in the furnaces of suffering until the touch of pity could make no mark on them.

But, in the ocean of faces where every fierce and furious expression was in vivid life, there were two groups of faces —each seven in number—so fixedly contrasting with the rest, that never did sea roll which bore more memorable wrecks with it. Seven faces of prisoners, suddenly released by the storm that had burst their tomb, were carried high overhead: all scared, all lost, all wondering and amazed, as if the Last Day were come, and those who rejoiced around them were lost spirits. Other seven faces there were, carried higher, seven dead faces, whose drooping eyelids and half-seen eyes awaited the Last Day. Impassive faces, yet with a suspended—not an abolished—expression on them; faces, rather, in a fearful pause, as having yet to raise the dropped lids of the eyes, and bear witness with the bloodless lips, "THOU DIDST IT!"

Seven prisoners released, seven gory heads on pikes, the keys of the accursed fortress of the eight strong towers, some discovered letters and other memorials of prisoners of old time, long dead of broken hearts—such, and such-like, the loudly echoing footsteps of Saint Antoine escort through the Paris streets in mid-July, one thousand seven hundred and eighty-nine. Now, Heaven defeat the fancy of Lucie Darnay, and keep these feet far out of her life! For, they are headlong, mad, and dangerous; and in the years so long after the breaking of the cask at Defarge's wine-shop door, they are not easily purified when once stained red.

*   *   *   *   *   *   *   *

22 *The Sea Still Rises*

HAGGARD Saint Antoine had had only one exultant week in which to soften his modicum of hard and bitter bread to such extent as he could, with the relish of fraternal embraces and congratulations, when Madame Defarge sat at her counter, as usual, presiding over the customers. Madame Defarge wore no rose in her head, for the great brotherhood of Spies had become, even in one short week, extremely chary of trusting themselves to the saint's mercies. The lamps across his streets had a portentously elastic swing with them.

Madame Defarge, with her arms folded, sat in the morning light and heat, contemplating the wine-shop and the street. In both, there were several knots of loungers, squalid and miserable, but now with a manifest sense of power enthroned on their distress. The raggedest night-cap, awry on the wretchedest head, had this crooked significance in it: "I know how hard it has grown for me, the wearer of this, to support life in myself; but do you know how easy it has grown for me, the wearer of this, to destroy life in you?" Every lean bare arm, that had been without work before, had this work always ready for it now, that it could strike. The fingers of the knitting women were vicious, with the experience that they could tear. There was a change in the appearance of Saint Antoine; the image had been hammering into this for hundreds of years, and the last finishing blows had told mightily on the expression.

Madame Defarge sat observing it, with such suppressed approval as was to be desired in the leader of the Saint Antoine women. One of her sisterhood knitted beside her. The short, rather plump wife of a starved grocer, and the mother of two children withal, this lieutenant had already earned the complimentary name of The Vengeance.

"Hark!" said The Vengeance. "Listen, then! Who comes?"

As if a train of powder laid from the outermost bound of the Saint Antoine Quarter to the wine-shop door, had been suddenly fired, a fast-spreading murmur came rushing along.

"It is Defarge," said madame. "Silence, patriots!"

Defarge came in breathless, pulled off a red cap he wore, and looked around him. "Listen, everywhere!" said madame again. "Listen to him!" Defarge stood, panting, against a background of eager eyes and open mouths, formed outside the door; all those within the wine-shop had sprung to their feet.

"Say then, my husband. What is it?"

"News from the other world!"

"How, then?" cried madame, contemptuously. "The other world?"

"Does everybody here recall old Foulon, who told the famished people that they might eat grass, and who died, and went to Hell?"

"Everybody!" from all throats.

"The news is of him. He is among us!"

"Among us!" from the universal throat again. "And dead?"

"Not dead! He feared us so much—and with reason—that he caused himself to be represented as dead, and had a grand mock-funeral. But they have found him alive, hiding in the country, and have brought him in. I have seen him but now, on his way to the Hôtel de Ville, a prisoner. I have said that he had reason to fear us. Say all! *Had* he reason?"

Wretched old sinner of more than threescore years and ten, if he had never known it yet, he would have known it in his heart of hearts if he could have heard the answering cry.

A moment of profound silence followed. Defarge and his wife looked steadfastly at one another. The Vengeance stooped, and the jar of a drum was heard as she moved it at her feet behind the counter.

"Patriots!" said Defarge, in a determined voice, "are we ready?"

Instantly Madame Defarge's knife was in her girdle; the drum was beating in the streets, as if it and a drummer had flown together by magic; and The Vengeance, uttering terrific shrieks, and flinging her arms about her head like all the forty Furies at once, was tearing from house to house, rousing the women.

The men were terrible, in the bloody-minded anger with which they looked from windows, caught up what arms they had, and came pouring down into the streets; but, the women were a sight to chill the boldest. From such household occupations as their bare poverty yielded, from their children, from their aged and their sick crouching on the bare ground famished and naked, they ran out with streaming hair, urging one another, and themselves, to madness with the wildest cries and actions. Villain Foulon taken, my sister! Old Foulon taken, my mother! Miscreant Foulon taken, my daughter! Then, a score of others ran into the midst of these, beating their breasts, tearing their hair, and screaming, Foulon alive! Foulon who told the starving people they might eat grass! Foulon who told my old father

that he might eat grass, when I had no bread to give him!
Foulon who told my baby it might suck grass, when these
breasts were dry with want! O mother of God, this Foulon!
O Heaven, our suffering! Hear me, my dead baby and my
withered father: I swear on my knees, on these stones, to
avenge you on Foulon! Husbands, and brothers, and young
men, Give us the blood of Foulon, Give us the head of
Foulon, Give us the heart of Foulon, Give us the body and
soul of Foulon, Rend Foulon to pieces, and dig him into
the ground, that grass may grow from him! With these cries,
numbers of the women, lashed into blind frenzy, whirled
about, striking and tearing at their own friends until they
dropped into a passionate swoon, and were only saved by
the men belonging to them from being trampled under foot.

Nevertheless, not a moment was lost; not a moment!
This Foulon was at the Hôtel de Ville, and might be loosed.
Never, if Saint Antoine knew his own sufferings, insults,
and wrongs! Armed men and women flocked out of the
Quarter so fast, and drew even these last dregs after them
with such a force of suction, that within a quarter of an
hour there was not a human creature in Saint Antoine's
bosom but a few old crones and the wailing children.

No. They were all by that time choking the Hall of Examination where this old man, ugly and wicked, was, and
overflowing into the adjacent open space and streets. The
Defarges, husband and wife, The Vengeance, and Jacques
Three were in the first press, and at no great distance from
him in the Hall.

"See!" cried madame, pointing with her knife. "See the
old villain bound with ropes. That was well done to tie a
bunch of grass upon his back. Ha, ha! That was well done.
Let him eat it now!" Madame put her knife under her arm,
and clapped her hands as at a play.

The people immediately behind Madame Defarge, explaining the cause of her satisfaction to those behind them,
and those again explaining to others, and those to others,
the neighbouring streets resounded with the clapping of
hands. Similarly, during two or three hours of drawl, and
the winnowing of many bushels of words, Madame Defarge's frequent expressions of impatience were taken up,
with marvelous quickness, at a distance: the more readily,
because certain men who had by some wonderful exercise
of agility climbed up the external architecture to look in
from the windows, knew Madame Defarge well, and acted

as a telegraph between her and the crowd outside the
building.

At length the sun rose so high that it struck a kindly ray
as of hope or protection, directly down upon the old prisoner's head. The favour was too much to bear; in an instant
the barrier of dust and chaff, that had stood surprisingly
long, went to the winds, and Saint Antoine got him!

It was known directly, to the furthest confines of the
crowd. Defarge had but sprung over a railing and a table,
and folded the miserable wretch in a deadly embrace—
Madame Defarge had but followed and turned her hand in
one of the ropes with which he was tied—The Vengeance
and Jacques Three were not yet up with them, and the men
at the windows had not yet swooped into the Hall, like
birds of prey from their high perches—when the cry
seemed to go up, all over the city, "Bring him out! Bring
him to the lamp!"

Down, and up, and head foremost on the steps of the
building; now, on his knees; now, on his feet; now, on his
back; dragged, and struck at, and stifled by the bunches of
grass and straw that were thrust into his face by hundreds
of hands; torn, bruised, panting, bleeding, yet always en-
treating and beseeching for mercy; now full of vehement
agony of action, with a small clear space about him as the
people drew one another back that they might see; now, a
log of dead wood drawn through a forest of legs; he was
hauled to the nearest street corner where one of the fatal
lamps swung, and there Madame Defarge let him go—as a
cat might have done to a mouse—and silently and composedly looked at him while they made ready, and while
he besought her: the women passionately screeching at him
all the time, and the men sternly calling out to have him
killed with grass in his mouth. Once, he went aloft, and
the rope broke, and they caught him shrieking; twice, he
went aloft, and the rope broke, and they caught him shrieking; then, the rope was merciful, and held him, and his
head was soon upon a pike, with grass enough in the mouth
for all Saint Antoine to dance at the sight of.

Nor was this the end of the day's bad work, for Saint
Antoine so shouted and danced his angry blood up, that
it boiled again, on hearing when the day closed in that the
son-in-law of the despatched, another of the people's
enemies and insulters, was coming into Paris under a guard
five hundred strong, in cavalry alone. Saint Antoine wrote

his crimes on flaring sheets of paper, seized him—would have torn him out of the breast of an army to bear Foulon company—set his head and heart on pikes, and carried the three spoils of the day, in wolf-procession, through the streets.

Not before dark night did the men and women come back to the children, wailing and breadless. Then, the miserable bakers' shops were beset by long files of them, patiently waiting to buy bad bread; and while they waited with stomachs faint and empty, they beguiled the time by embracing one another on the triumphs of the day, and achieving them again in gossip. Gradually, these strings of ragged people shortened and frayed away; and then poor lights began to shine in high windows, and slender fires were made in the streets, at which neighbours cooked in common, afterwards supping at their doors.

Scanty and insufficient suppers those, and innocent of meat, as of most other sauce to wretched bread. Yet, human fellowship infused some nourishment into the flinty viands, and struck some sparks of cheerfulness out of them. Fathers and mothers who had had their full share in the worst of the day played gently with their meagre children; and lovers, with such a world around them and before them, loved and hoped.

It was almost morning, when Defarge's wine-shop parted with its last knot of customers, and Monsieur Defarge said to madame his wife, in husky tones, while fastening the door:

"At last it is come, my dear!"

"Eh well!" returned madame. "Almost."

Saint Antoine slept, the Defarges slept: even The Vengeance slept with her starved grocer, and the drum was at rest. The drum's was the only voice in Saint Antoine that blood and hurry had not changed. The Vengeance, as custodian of the drum, could have wakened him up and had the same speech out of him as before the Bastille fell, or old Foulon was seized; not so with the hoarse tones of the men and women in Saint Antoine's bosom.

23 *Fire Rises*

THERE WAS a change on the village where the fountain fell, and where the mender of roads went forth daily to hammer out of the stones on the highway such morsels of bread as might serve for patches to hold his poor ignorant soul and his poor reduced body together. The prison on the crag was not so dominant as of yore; there were soldiers to guard it, but not many; there were officers to guard the soldiers, but not one of them knew what his men would do—beyond this: that it would probably not be what he was ordered.

Far and wide lay a ruined country, yielding nothing but desolation. Every green leaf, every blade of grass and blade of grain, was as shrivelled and poor as the miserable people. Everything was bowed down, dejected, oppressed, and broken. Habitations, fences, domesticated animals, men, women, children, and the soil that bore them—all worn out.

Monseigneur (often a most worthy individual gentleman) was a national blessing, gave a chivalrous tone to things, was a polite example of luxurious and shining life, and a great deal more to equal purpose; nevertheless, Monseigneur as a class had, somehow or other, brought things to this. Strange that Creation, designed expressly for Monseigneur, should be so soon wrung dry and squeezed out! There must be something short-sighted in the eternal arrangements, surely! Thus it was, however; and the last drop of blood having been extracted from the flints, and the last screw of the rack having been turned so often that its purchase crumbled, and it now turned and turned with nothing to bite, Monseigneur began to run away from a phenomenon so low and unaccountable.

But, this was not the change on the village, and on many a village like it. For scores of years gone by, Monseigneur had squeezed it and wrung it, and had seldom graced it with his presence except for the pleasures of the chase—

now, found in hunting the people; now, found in hunting the beasts, for whose preservation Monseigneur made edifying spaces of barbarous and barren wilderness. No. The change consisted in the appearance of strange faces of low caste, rather than in the disappearance of the high-caste, chiseled, and otherwise beatified and beatifying features of Monseigneur.

For, in these times, as the mender of roads worked, solitary, in the dust, not often troubling himself to reflect that dust he was and to dust he must return, being for the most part too much occupied in thinking how little he had for supper and how much more he would eat if he had it—in these times, as he raised his eyes from his lonely labour, and viewed the prospect, he would see some rough figure approaching on foot, the like of which was once a rarity in those parts, but was now a frequent presence. As it advanced, the mender of roads would discern without surprise that it was a shaggy-haired man, of almost barbarian aspect, tall, in wooden shoes that were clumsy even to the eyes of a mender of roads, grim, rough, swart, steeped in the mud and dust of many highways, dank with the marshy moisture of many low grounds, sprinkled with the thorns and leaves and moss of many byways through woods.

Such a man came upon him, like a ghost, at noon in the July weather, as he sat on his heap of stones under a bank, taking such shelter as he could get from a shower of hail.

The man looked at him, looked at the village in the hollow, at the mill, and at the prison on the crag. When he had identified these objects in what benighted mind he had, he said, in a dialect that was just intelligible:

"How goes it, Jacques?"

"All well, Jacques."

"Touch then!"

They joined hands, and the man sat down on the heap of stones.

"No dinner?"

"Nothing but supper now," said the mender of roads, with a hungry face.

"It is the fashion," growled the man. "I meet no dinner anywhere."

He took out a blackened pipe, filled it, lighted it with flint and steel, pulled at it until it was in a bright glow: then, suddenly held it from him and dropped something into it from between his finger and thumb, that blazed and went out in a puff of smoke.

"Touch then." It was the turn of the mender of roads to say it this time, after observing these operations. They again joined hands.

"To-night?" said the mender of roads.

"To-night," said the man, putting the pipe in his mouth.

"Where?"

"Here."

He and the mender of roads sat on the heap of stones looking silently at one another, with the hail driving in between them like a pigmy charge of bayonets, until the sky began to clear over the village.

"Show me!" said the traveller then, moving to the brow of the hill.

"See!" returned the mender of roads, with extended finger. "You go down here, and straight through the street, and past the fountain——"

"To the Devil with all that!" interrupted the other, rolling his eyes over the landscape. "*I* go through no streets and past no fountains. Well?"

"Well! About two leagues beyond the summit of that hill above the village."

"Good. When do you cease to work?"

"At sunset."

"Will you wake me, before departing? I have walked two nights without resting. Let me finish my pipe, and I shall sleep like a child. Will you wake me?"

"Surely."

The wayfarer smoked his pipe out, put it in his breast, slipped off his great wooden shoes, and lay down on his back on the heap of stones. He was fast asleep directly.

As the road-mender plied his dusty labour, and the hail-clouds, rolling away, revealed bright bars and streaks of sky which were responded to by silver gleams upon the landscape, the little man (who wore a red cap now, in place of his blue one) seemed fascinated by the figure on the heap of stones. His eyes were so often turned towards it, that he used his tools mechanically, and, one would have said, to very poor account. The bronze face, the shaggy black hair and beard, the coarse woollen red cap, the rough medley dress of homespun stuff and hairy skins of beasts, the powerful frame attenuated by spare living, and the sullen and desperate compression of the lips in sleep, inspired the mender of roads with awe. The traveller had travelled far, and his feet were foot-sore, and his ankles chafed and bleeding; his great shoes, stuffed with leaves and grass, had been heavy to drag over the many long leagues, and his clothes were chafed into holes, as he himself was into sores. Stooping down beside him, the road-mender tried to get a peep at secret weapons in his breast or where not; but, in vain, for he slept with his arms crossed upon him, and set as resolutely as his lips. Fortified towns with their stockades, guard-houses, gates, trenches, and drawbridges seemed, to the mender of roads, to be so much air as against this figure. And when he lifted his eyes from it to the horizon and looked around, he saw in his small fancy similar figures, stopped by no obstacle, tending to centres all over France.

The man slept on, indifferent to showers of hail and intervals of brightness, to sunshine on his face and shadow, to the pattering lumps of dull ice on his body and the diamonds into which the sun changed them, until the sun was low in the west, and the sky was glowing. Then, the mender of roads, having got his tools together and all things ready to go down into the village, roused him.

"Good!" said the sleeper, rising on his elbow. "Two leagues beyond the summit of the hill?"

"About."

"About. Good!"

The mender of roads went home, with the dust going on before him according to the set of the wind, and was soon at the fountain, squeezing himself in among the lean kine brought there to drink, and appearing even to whisper to them in his whispering to all the village. When the village had taken its poor supper, it did not creep to bed, as it usually did, but came out of doors again, and remained there. A curious contagion of whispering was upon it, and also, when it gathered together at the fountain in the dark, another curious contagion of looking expectantly at the sky in one direction only. Monsieur Gabelle, chief functionary of the place, became uneasy; went out on his housetop alone, and looked in that direction too; glanced down from behind his chimneys at the darkening faces by the fountain below, and sent word to the sacristan who kept the keys of the church, that there might be need to ring the tocsin by and by.

The night deepened. The trees environing the old château, keeping its solitary state apart, moved in a rising wind, as though they threatened the pile of building massive and dark in the gloom. Up the two terrace flights of steps the rain ran wildly, and beat at the great door, like a swift messenger rousing those within; uneasy rushes of wind went through the hall, among the old spears and knives, and passed lamenting up the stairs, and shook the curtains of the bed where the last Marquis had slept. East, west, north, and south, through the woods, four heavy-treading, unkempt figures crushed the high grass and cracked the branches, striding on cautiously to come together in the courtyard. Four lights broke out there, and moved away in different directions, and all was black again.

But, not for long. Presently, the château began to make itself strangely visible by some light of its own, as though it were growing luminous. Then, a flickering streak played behind the architecture of the front, picking out transparent places, and showing where balustrades, arches, and windows were. Then it soared higher, and grew broader and brighter. Soon, from a score of the great windows, flames burst forth, and the stone faces awakened, stared out of fire.

A faint murmur arose about the house from the few people who were left there, and there was a saddling of a horse and riding away. There was spurring and splashing through the darkness, and bridle was drawn in the space by the village fountain, and the horse in a foam stood at Monsieur Gabelle's door. "Help, Gabelle! Help, every one!" The tocsin rang impatiently, but other help (if that were any) there was none. The mender of roads, and two hundred and fifty particular friends, stood with folded arms at the fountain, looking at the pillar of fire in the sky. "It must be forty feet high," said they, grimly; and never moved.

The rider from the château, and the horse in a foam, clattered away through the village, and galloped up the stony steep, to the prison on the crag. At the gate, a group of officers were looking at the fire; removed from them, a group of soldiers. "Help, gentlemen-officers! The château is on fire; valuable objects may be saved from the flames by timely aid! Help, help!" The officers looked towards the soldiers who looked at the fire; gave no orders; and answered, with shrugs and biting of lips, "It must burn."

As the rider rattled down the hill again and through the street, the village was illuminating. The mender of roads, and the two hundred and fifty particular friends, inspired as one man and woman by the idea of lighting up, had darted into their houses, and were putting candles in every dull little pane of glass. The general scarcity of everything occasioned candles to be borrowed in a rather peremptory manner of Monsieur Gabelle; and in a moment of reluctance and hesitation on that functionary's part, the mender of roads, once so submissive to authority, had remarked that carriages were good to make bonfires with, and that post-horses would roast.

The château was left to itself to flame and burn. In the roaring and raging of the conflagration, a red-hot wind, driving straight from the infernal regions, seemed to be blowing the edifice away. With the rising and falling of the blaze, the stone faces showed as if they were in torment. When the great masses of stone and timber fell, the face with the two dints in the nose became obscured: anon struggled out of the smoke again, as if it were the face of the cruel Marquis, burning at the stake and contending with the fire.

The château burned; the nearest trees, laid hold of by the fire, scorched and shrivelled; trees at a distance, fired by the four fierce figures, begirt the blazing edifice with a new forest of smoke. Molten lead and iron boiled in the marble basin of the fountain; the water ran dry; the extinguisher tops of the towers vanished like ice before the heat, and trickled down into four rugged wells of flame. Great rents and splits branched out in the solid walls, like crystallisation; stupefied birds wheeled about and dropped into the furnace; four fierce figures trudged away, east, west, north, and south, along the night-enshrouded roads, guided by the beacon they had lighted, towards their next destination. The illuminated village had seized hold of the tocsin, and, abolishing the lawful ringer, rang for joy.

Not only that; but the village, light-headed with famine, fire, and bell-ringing, and bethinking itself that Monsieur Gabelle had to do with the collection of rent and taxes— though it was but a small instalment of taxes, and no rent at all, that Gabelle had got in those latter days—became impatient for an interview with him, and, surrounding his house, summoned him to come forth for personal conference. Whereupon, Monsieur Gabelle did heavily bar his door, and retire to hold counsel with himself. The result of that conference was that Gabelle again withdrew himself to his housetop behind his stack of chimneys; this time resolved, if his door was broken in (he was a small Southern man of retaliative temperament), to pitch himself head foremost over the parapet, and crush a man or two below.

Probably, Monsieur Gabelle passed a long night up there, with the distant château for fire and candle, and the beating at his door, combined with the joy-ringing, for music; not to mention his having an ill-omened lamp slung across the road before his posting-house gate, which the village showed a lively inclination to displace in his favour. A trying suspense, to be passing a whole summer night on the brink of the black ocean, ready to take that plunge into it upon which Monsieur Gabelle had resolved! But, the friendly dawn appearing at last, and the rush-candles of the village guttering out, the people happily dispersed, and Monsieur Gabelle came down bringing his life with him for that while.

Within a hundred miles, and in the light of other fires, there were other functionaries less fortunate, that night and other nights, whom the rising sun found hanging across once-peaceful streets, where they had been born and bred; also, there were other villages and townspeople less fortunate than the mender of roads and his fellows, upon whom the functionaries and soldiery turned with success, and whom they strung up in their turn. But, the fierce figures were steadily wending east, west, north, and south, be that as it would; and whosoever hung, fire burned. The altitude of the gallows that would turn to water and quench it, no functionary, by any stretch of mathematics, was able to calculate successfully.

*　　*　　*　　*　　*　　*　　*　　*

24 *Drawn to the Loadstone Rock*

IN SUCH risings of fire and risings of sea—the firm earth shaken by the rushes of an angry ocean which had now no ebb, but was always on the flow, higher and higher, to the terror and wonder of the beholders on the shore—three years of tempest were consumed. Three more birth-

days of little Lucie had been woven by the golden thread
into the peaceful tissue of the life of her home.

Many a night and many a day had its inmates listened
to the echoes in the corner, with hearts that failed them
when they heard the thronging feet. For, the footsteps had
become to their minds as the footsteps of a people, tumultuous under a red flag and with their country declared in
danger, changed into wild beasts, by terrible enchantment
long persisted in.

Monseigneur, as a class, had dissociated himself from
the phenomenon of his not being appreciated: of his being
so little wanted in France, as to incur considerable danger
of receiving his dismissal from it, and this life together.
Like the fabled rustic who raised the Devil with infinite
pains, and was so terrified at the sight of him that he could
ask the Enemy no question, but immediately fled; so, Monseigneur, after boldly reading the Lord's Prayer backwards
for a great number of years, and performing many other
potent spells for compelling the Evil One, no sooner beheld
him in his terrors than he took to his noble heels.

The shining Bull's Eye of the Court was gone, or it would
have been the mark for a hurricane of national bullets. It
had never been a good eye to see with—had long had the
mote in it of Lucifer's pride, Sardanapalus's luxury, and a
mole's blindness—but it had dropped out and was gone.
The Court, from that exclusive inner circle to its outermost
rotten ring of intrigue, corruption, and dissimulation, was
all gone together. Royalty was gone; had been besieged in
its Palace and "suspended," when the last tidings came
over.

The August of the year one thousand seven hundred and
ninety-two was come, and Monseigneur was by this time
scattered far and wide.

As was natural, the headquarters and great gathering-
place of Monseigneur, in London, was Tellson's Bank.
Spirits are supposed to haunt the places where their bodies
most resorted, and Monseigneur without a guinea haunted
the spot where his guineas used to be. Moreover, it was the
spot to which such French intelligence as was most to be
relied upon came quickest. Again: Tellson's was a mu-
nificent house, and extended great liberality to old customers who had fallen from their high estate. Again: those
nobles who had seen the coming storm in time, and anticipating plunder or confiscation, had made provident remit-

tances to Tellson's, were always to be heard of there by their needy brethren. To which must be added that every new-comer from France reported himself and his tidings at Tell-son's, almost as a matter of course. For such variety of reasons, Tellson's was at that time, as to French intelli-gence, a kind of High Exchange; and this was so well known to the public, and the inquiries made there were in consequence so numerous, that Tellson's sometimes wrote the latest news out in a line or so and posted it in the Bank windows, for all who ran through Temple Bar to read.

On a steaming, misty afternoon, Mr. Lorry sat at his desk, and Charles Darnay stood leaning on it, talking with him in a low voice. The penitential den once set apart for interviews with the House was now the news-exchange, and was filled to overflowing. It was within half an hour or so of the time of closing.

"But, although you are the youngest man that ever lived," said Charles Darnay, rather hesitating, "I must still suggest to you—"

"I understand. That I am too old?" said Mr. Lorry.

"Unsettled weather, a long journey, uncertain means of travelling, a disorganised country, a city that may not be even safe for you."

"My dear Charles," said Mr. Lorry, with cheerful con-fidence, "you touch some of the reasons for my going: not for my staying away. It is safe enough for me; nobody will care to interfere with an old fellow of hard upon fourscore when there are so many people there much better worth interfering with. As to its being a disorganised city, if it were not a disorganised city there would be no occasion to send somebody from our House here to our House there, who knows the city and the business, of old, and is in Tell-son's confidence. As to the uncertain travelling, the long journey, and the winter weather, if I were not prepared to submit myself to a few inconveniences for the sake of Tell-son's, after all these years, who ought to be?"

"I wish I were going myself," said Charles Darnay, somewhat restlessly, and like one thinking aloud.

"Indeed! You are a pretty fellow to object and advise!" exclaimed Mr. Lorry. "You wish you were going yourself? And you a Frenchman born? You are a wise counsellor."

"My dear Mr. Lorry, it is because I am a Frenchman born, that the thought (which I did not mean to utter here, however) has passed through my mind often. One cannot help thinking, having had some sympathy for the miserable people, and having abandoned something to them," he spoke here in his former thoughtful manner, "that one might be listened to, and might have the power to persuade to some restraint. Only last night, after you had left us, when I was talking to Lucie—"

"When you were talking to Lucie," Mr. Lorry repeated. "Yes. I wonder you are not ashamed to mention the name of Lucie! Wishing you were going to France at this time of day!"

"However, I am not going," said Charles Darnay, with a smile. "It is more to the purpose that you say you are."

"And I am, in plain reality. The truth is, my dear Charles," Mr. Lorry glanced at the distant House, and lowered his voice, "you can have no conception of the difficulty with which our business is transacted, and of the peril in which our books and papers over yonder are involved. The Lord above knows what the compromising consequence would be to numbers of people, if some of our documents were seized or destroyed; and they might be, at any time, you know, for who can say that Paris is not set afire to-day, or sacked to-morrow! Now, a judicious selection from these with the least possible delay, and the burying of them, or otherwise getting them out of harm's way, is within the power (without loss of precious time) of scarcely any one but myself, if any one. And shall I hang back, when Tellson's knows this and says this—Tellson's, whose bread I have eaten these sixty years—because I am a little stiff about the joints? Why, I am a boy, sir, to half a dozen old codgers here!"

"How I admire the gallantry of your youthful spirit, Mr. Lorry."

"Tut! Nonsense, sir!—And, my dear Charles," said Mr. Lorry, glancing at the House again, "you are to remember, that getting things out of Paris at this present time, no matter what things, is next to an impossibility. Papers and precious matters were this very day brought to us here (I speak in strict confidence; it is not business-like to whisper it, even to you), by the strangest bearers you can imagine, every one of whom had his head hanging on by a single hair as he passed the Barriers. At another time, our parcels would come and go, as easily as in business-like Old England; but now, everything is stopped."

"And do you really go to-night?"

"I really go to-night, for the case has become too pressing to admit of delay."

"And do you take no one with you?"

"All sorts of people have been proposed to me, but I
will have nothing to say to any of them. I intend to take
Jerry. Jerry has been my body-guard on Sunday nights for
a long time past, and I am used to him. Nobody will suspect Jerry of being anything but an English bull-dog, or of
having any design in his head but to fly at somebody who
touches his master."

"I must say again that I heartily admire your gallantry
and youthfulness."

"I must say again, nonsense, nonsense! When I have
executed this little commission, I shall, perhaps, accept Tellson's proposal to retire and live at my ease. Time enough,
then, to think about growing old."

This dialogue had taken place at Mr. Lorry's usual desk,
with Monseigneur swarming within a yard or two of it,
boastful of what he would do to avenge himself on the
rascal-people before long. It was too much the way of
Monseigneur under his reverses as a refugee, and it was
much too much the way of native British orthodoxy, to talk
of this terrible Revolution as if it were the one only harvest
ever known under the skies that had not been sown—as if
nothing had ever been done, or omitted to be done, that
had led to it—as if observers of the wretched millions in
France, and of the misused and perverted resources that
should have made them prosperous, had not seen it inevitably coming, years before, and had not in plain words recorded what they saw. Such vapouring, combined with the
extravagant plots of Monseigneur for the restoration of a
state of things that had utterly exhausted itself, and worn
out Heaven and earth as well as itself, was hard to be en-
dured without some remonstrance by any sane man who
knew the truth. And it was such vapouring all about his
ears, like a troublesome confusion of blood in his own
head, added to a latent uneasiness in his mind, which had
already made Charles Darnay restless, and which still kept
him so.

Among the talkers was Stryver, of the King's Bench Bar,
far on his way to state promotion, and, therefore, loud on
the theme: broaching to Monseigneur his devices for blowing the people up and exterminating them from the face of
the earth, and doing without them: and for accomplishing

many similar objects akin in their nature to the abolition of eagles by sprinkling salt on the tails of the race. Him, Darnay heard with a particular feeling of objection; and Darnay stood divided between going away that he might hear no more, and remaining to interpose his word, when the thing that was to be went on to shape itself out.

The House approached Mr. Lorry, and laying a soiled and unopened letter before him, asked if he had yet discovered any traces of the person to whom it was addressed? The House laid the letter down so close to Darnay that he saw the direction—the more quickly because it was his own right name. The address, turned into English, ran:

"Very pressing. To Monsieur heretofore the Marquis St. Evrémonde, of France. Confided to the cares of Messrs. Tellson and Co., Bankers, London, England."

On the marriage morning, Doctor Manette had made it his one urgent and express request to Charles Darnay, that the secret of this name should be—unless he, the Doctor, dissolved the obligation—kept inviolate between them. Nobody else knew it to be his name; his own wife had no suspicion of the fact; Mr. Lorry could have none.

"No," said Mr. Lorry, in reply to the House; "I have referred it, I think, to everybody now here, and no one can tell me where this gentleman is to be found."

The hands of the clock verging upon the hour of closing the Bank, there was a general set of the current of talkers past Mr. Lorry's desk. He held the letter out inquiringly; and Monseigneur looked at it, in the person of this plotting and indignant refugee; and Monseigneur looked at it, in the person of that plotting and indignant refugee; and This, That, and The Other, all had something disparaging to say, in French or in English, concerning the Marquis who was not to be found.

"Nephew, I believe—but in any case degenerate successor—of the polished Marquis who was murdered," said one. "Happy to say, I never knew him."

"A craven who abandoned his post," said another—this Monseigneur had been got out of Paris, legs uppermost and half suffocated, in a load of hay—"some years ago."

"Infected with the new doctrines," said a third, eyeing the direction through his glass in passing; "set himself in opposition to the last Marquis, abandoned the estates when he inherited them, and left them to the ruffian herd. They will recompense him now, I hope, as he deserves."

"Hey?" cried the blatant Stryver. "Did he though? Is that the sort of fellow? Let us look at his infamous name. D—n the fellow!"

Darnay, unable to restrain himself any longer, touched Mr. Stryver on the shoulder, and said:

"I know the fellow."

"Do you, by Jupiter?" said Stryver. "I am sorry for it."

"Why?"

"Why, Mr. Darnay? D'ye hear what he did? Don't ask why, in these times."

"But I do ask why."

"Then I tell you again, Mr. Darnay, I am sorry for it. I am sorry to hear you putting any such extraordinary questions. Here is a fellow, who, infected by the most pestilent and blasphemous code of deviltry that ever was known, abandoned his property to the vilest scum of the earth that ever did murder by wholesale, and you ask me why I am sorry that a man who instructs youth knows him? Well, but I'll answer you. I am sorry because I believe there is contamination in such a scoundrel. That's why."

Mindful of the secret, Darnay with great difficulty checked himself, and said: "You may not understand the gentleman."

"I understand how to put *you* in a corner, Mr. Darnay," said Bully Stryver, "and I'll do it. If this fellow is a gentleman, I *don't* understand him. You may tell him so, with my compliments. You may also tell him, from me, that after abandoning his worldly goods and position to this butcherly mob, I wonder he is not at the head of them. But, no, gentlemen," said Stryver, looking all round, and snapping his fingers, "I know something of human nature, and I tell you that you'll never find a fellow like this fellow, trusting himself to the mercies of such precious *protégés*. No, gentlemen; he'll always show 'em a clean pair of heels very early in the scuffle, and sneak away."

With those words, and a final snap of his fingers, Mr. Stryver shouldered himself into Fleet Street, amidst the general approbation of his hearers. Mr. Lorry and Charles Darnay were left alone at the desk, in the general departure from the Bank.

"Will you take charge of the letter?" said Mr. Lorry. "You know where to deliver it?"

"I do."

"Will you undertake to explain that we suppose it to

have been addressed here, on the chance of our knowing
where to forward it, and that it has been here some time?"

"I will do so. Do you start for Paris from here?"

"From here, at eight."

"I will come back, to see you off."

Very ill at ease with himself, and with Stryver and most
other men, Darnay made the best of his way into the quiet
of the Temple, opened the letter, and read it. These were
its contents:

"Prison of the Abbaye, Paris.
"June 21, 1792.

"Monsieur heretofore the Marquis,

"After having long been in danger of my life at the hands
of the village, I have been seized, with great violence and
indignity, and brought a long journey on foot to Paris. On
the road I have suffered a great deal. Nor is that all; my
house has been destroyed—razed to the ground.

"The crime for which I am imprisoned, Monsieur heretofore the Marquis, and for which I shall be summoned
before the tribunal, and shall lose my life (without your so
generous help) is, they tell me, treason against the majesty
of the people, in that I have acted against them for an emigrant. It is in vain I represent that I have acted for them,
and not against, according to your commands. It is in vain
I represent that, before the sequestration of emigrant property, I had remitted the imposts they had ceased to pay;
that I had collected no rent; that I had had recourse to no
process. The only response is, that I have acted for an emigrant, and where is that emigrant?

"Ah! most gracious Monsieur heretofore the Marquis,
where is that emigrant? I cry in my sleep where is he? I demand of Heaven, will he not come to deliver me? No answer. Ah! Monsieur heretofore the Marquis, I send my
desolate cry across the sea, hoping it may perhaps reach
your ears through the great bank of Tellson known at Paris!

"For the love of Heaven, of justice, of generosity, of the
honour of your noble name, I supplicate you, Monsieur
heretofore the Marquis, to succour and release me. My
fault is that I have been true to you. Oh! Monsieur heretofore the Marquis, I pray you be you true to me!

"From this prison here of horror, whence I every hour
tend nearer and nearer to destruction, I send you, Monsieur

heretofore the Marquis, the assurance of my dolorous and unhappy service.

> "Your afflicted
> *"Gabelle."*

The latent uneasiness in Darnay's mind was roused to vigorous life by this letter. The peril of an old servant and a good one, whose only crime was fidelity to himself and his family, stared him so reproachfully in the face that, as he walked to and fro in the Temple considering what to do, he almost hid his face from the passers-by.

He knew very well that in his horror of the deed which had culminated the bad deeds and bad reputation of the old family house, in his resentful suspicions of his uncle, and in the aversion with which his conscience regarded the crumbling fabric that he was supposed to uphold, he had acted imperfectly. He knew very well that in his love for Lucie, his renunciation of his social place, though by no means new to his own mind, had been hurried and incomplete. He knew that he ought to have systematically worked it out and supervised it, and that he had meant to do it, and that it had never been done.

The happiness of his own chosen English home, the necessity of being always actively employed, the swift changes and troubles of the time which had followed on one another so fast, that the events of this week annihilated the immature plans of last week, and the events of the week following made all new again; he knew very well, that to the force of these circumstances he had yielded—not without disquiet, but still without continuous and accumulating resistance. That he had watched the times for a time of action, and that they had shifted and struggled until the time had gone by, and the nobility were trooping from France by every highway and byway, and their property was in course of confiscation and destruction, and their very names were blotting out, was as well known to himself as it could be to any new authority in France that might impeach him for it.

But, he had oppressed no man, he had imprisoned no man; he was so far from having harshly exacted payment of his dues, that he had relinquished them of his own will, thrown himself on a world with no favour in it, won his own private place there, and earned his own bread. Monsieur Gabelle had held the impoverished and involved

estate on written instructions, to spare the people, to give
them what little there was to give—such fuel as the heavy
creditors would let them have in the winter, and such produce as could be saved from the same grip in the summer
—and no doubt he had put the fact in plea and proof, for
his own safety, so that it could not but appear now.

This favoured the desperate resolution Charles Darnay
had begun to make, that he would go to Paris.

Yes. Like the mariner in the old story, the winds and
streams had driven him within the influence of the Loadstone Rock, and it was drawing him to itself, and he must
go. Everything that arose before his mind drifted him on,
faster and faster, more and more steadily, to the terrible
attraction. His latent uneasiness had been that bad aims
were being worked out in his own unhappy land by bad
instruments, and that he who could not fail to know that
he was better than they, was not there, trying to do something to stay blood-shed, and assert the claims of mercy
and humanity. With this uneasiness half stifled, and half
reproaching him, he had been brought to the pointed comparison of himself with the brave old gentleman in whom
duty was so strong; upon that comparison (injurious to
himself) had instantly followed the sneers of Monseigneur,
which had stung him bitterly, and those of Stryver, which
above all were coarse and galling, for old reasons. Upon
those had followed Gabelle's letter: the appeal of an innocent prisoner, in danger of death, to his justice, honour,
and good name.

His resolution was made. He must go to Paris.

Yes. The Loadstone Rock was drawing him, and he
must sail on, until he struck. He knew of no rock; he saw
hardly any danger. The intention with which he had done
what he had done, even although he had left it incompleted,
presented it before him in an aspect that would be gratefully acknowledged in France on his presenting himself to
assert it. Then, that glorious vision of doing good, which is
so often the sanguine mirage of so many good minds, arose
before him, and he even saw himself in the illusion with
some influence to guide this raging Revolution that was
running so fearfully wild.

As he walked to and fro with his resolution made, he
considered that neither Lucie nor her father must know of
it until he was gone. Lucie should be spared the pain of
separation; and her father, always reluctant to turn his

thoughts towards the dangerous ground of old, should come to the knowledge of the step, as a step taken, and not in the balance of suspense and doubt. How much of the incompleteness of his situation was referable to her father, through the painful anxiety to avoid reviving old associations of France in his mind, he did not discuss with himself. But, that circumstance too had its influence in his course.

He walked to and fro, with thoughts very busy, until it was time to return to Tellson's and take leave of Mr. Lorry. As soon as he arrived in Paris he would present himself to this old friend, but he must say nothing of his intention now.

A carriage with post-horses was ready at the Bank door and Jerry was booted and equipped.

"I have delivered that letter," said Charles Darnay to Mr. Lorry. "I would not consent to your being charged with any written answer, but perhaps you will take a verbal one?"

"That I will, and readily," said Mr. Lorry, "if it is not dangerous."

"Not at all. Though it is to a prisoner in the Abbaye."

"What is his name?" said Mr. Lorry, with his open pocket-book in his hand.

"Gabelle."

"Gabelle. And what is the message to the unfortunate Gabelle in prison?"

"Simply, 'that he has received the letter, and will come.'"

"Any time mentioned?"

"He will start upon his journey to-morrow night."

"Any person mentioned?"

"No."

He helped Mr. Lorry to wrap himself in a number of coats and cloaks, and went out with him from the warm atmosphere of the old Bank, into the misty air of Fleet Street. "My love to Lucie, and to little Lucie," said Mr. Lorry at parting, "and take precious care of them till I come back." Charles Darnay shook his head and doubtfully smiled, as the carriage rolled away.

That night—it was the fourteenth of August—he sat up late, and wrote two fervent letters; one was to Lucie, explaining the strong obligation he was under to go to Paris, and showing her, at length, the reasons that he had, for feeling confident that he could become involved in no personal danger there; the other was to the Doctor, confiding

Lucie and their dear child to his care, and dwelling on the same topics with the strongest assurances. To both, he wrote that he would despatch letters in proof of his safety immediately after his arrival.

It was a hard day, that day of being among them, with the first reservation of their joint lives on his mind. It was a hard matter to preserve the innocent deceit of which they were profoundly unsuspicious. But, an affectionate glance at his wife, so happy and busy, made him resolute not to tell her what impended (he had been half moved to do it, so strange it was to him to act in anything without her quiet aid), and the day passed quickly away. Early in the evening he embraced her, and her scarcely less dear namesake, pretending that he would return by and by (an imaginary engagement took him out, and he had secreted a valise of clothes ready), and so he emerged into the heavy mist of the heavy street, with a heavier heart.

The unseen force was drawing him fast to itself, now, and all the tides and winds were setting straight and strong towards it. He left his two letters with a trusty porter, to be delivered half an hour before midnight, and no sooner; took horse for Dover; and began his journey. "For the love of Heaven, justice, of generosity, of the honour of your noble name!" was the poor prisoner's cry with which he strengthened his sinking heart, as he left all that was dear on earth behind him, and floated away for the Loadstone Rock.

BOOK THE THIRD

The Track of a Storm

1 *In Secret*

THE TRAVELLER fared slowly on his way, who fared towards Paris from England in the autumn of the year one thousand seven hundred and ninety-two. More than enough of bad roads, bad equipages, and bad horses he would have encountered to delay him, though the fallen and unfortunate King of France had been upon his throne in all his glory; but, the changed times were fraught with other obstacles than these. Every town-gate and village taxing-house had its band of citizen-patriots, with their national muskets in a most explosive state of readiness, who stopped all comers and goers, cross-questioned them, inspected their papers, looked for their names in lists of their own, turned them back, or sent them on, or stopped them and laid them in hold, as their capricious judgment or fancy deemed best for the dawning Republic One and Indivisible, of Liberty, Equality, Fraternity, or Death.

A very few French leagues of his journey were accomplished, when Charles Darnay began to perceive that for him along these country roads there was no hope of return until he should have been declared a good citizen at Paris. Whatever might befall now, he must on to his journey's end. Not a mean village closed upon him, not a common barrier dropped across the road behind him, but he knew it to be another iron door in the series that was barred between him and England. The universal watchfulness so encompassed him, that if he had been taken in a net, or were being forwarded to his destination in a cage, he could not have felt his freedom more completely gone.

This universal watchfulness not only stopped him on the highway twenty times in a stage, but retarded his progress twenty times in a day, by riding after him and taking him back, riding before him and stopping him by anticipation, riding with him and keeping him in charge. He had been days upon his journey in France alone, when he went to bed

tired out, in a little town on the high road, still a long way
from Paris.

Nothing but the production of the afflicted Gabelle's letter from his prison of the Abbaye would have got him on
so far. His difficulty at the guard-house in this small place
had been such that he felt his journey to have come to a
crisis. And he was, therefore, as little surprised as a man
could be, to find himself awakened at the small inn to
which he had been remitted until morning, in the middle
of the night.

Awakened by a timid local functionary and three armed
patriots in rough red caps and with pipes in their mouths,
who sat down on the bed.

"Emigrant," said the functionary, "I am going to send
you on to Paris, under an escort."

"Citizen, I desire nothing more than to get to Paris,
though I could dispense with the escort."

"Silence!" growled a red-cap, striking at the coverlet
with the butt-end of his musket. "Peace, aristocrat!"

"It is as the good patriot says," observed the timid functionary. "You are an aristocrat, and must have an escort—
and must pay for it."

"I have no choice," said Charles Darnay.

"Choice! Listen to him!" cried the same scowling red-
cap. "As if it was not a favour to be protected from the
lamp-iron!"

"It is always as the good patriot says," observed the
functionary. "Rise and dress yourself, emigrant."

Darnay complied, and was taken back to the guard-
house, where other patriots in rough red caps were smoking, drinking, and sleeping, by a watch-fire. Here he paid
a heavy price for his escort, and hence he started with it on
the wet, wet roads at three o'clock in the morning.

The escort were two mounted patriots in red caps and
tricoloured cockades, armed with national muskets and
sabres, who rode one on either side of him. The escorted
governed his own horse, but a loose line was attached to
his bridle, the end of which one of the patriots kept girded
round his wrist. In this state they set forth with the sharp
rain driving in their faces: clattering at a heavy dragoon
trot over the uneven town pavement, and out upon the
mire-deep roads. In this state they traversed without
change, except of horses and pace, all the mire-deep leagues
that lay between them and the capital.

They travelled in the night, halting an hour or two after daybreak, and lying by until the twilight fell. The escort were so wretchedly clothed, that they twisted straw round their bare legs, and thatched their ragged shoulders to keep the wet off. Apart from personal discomfort of being so attended, and apart from such considerations of present danger as arose from one of the patriots being chronically drunk, and carrying his musket very recklessly, Charles Darnay did not allow the restraint that was laid upon him to awaken any serious fears in his breast; for, he reasoned with himself that it could have no reference to the merits of an individual case that was not yet stated, and of representations, confirmable by the prisoner in the Abbaye, that were not yet made.

But when they came to the town of Beauvais—which they did at eventide, when the streets were filled with people—he could not conceal from himself that the aspect of affairs was very alarming. An ominous crowd gathered to see him dismount at the posting-yard, and many voices called out loudly, "Down with the emigrant!"

He stopped in the act of swinging himself out of his saddle, and, resuming it as his safest place, said:

"Emigrant, my friends! Do you not see me here, in France, of my own will?"

"You are a cursed emigrant," cried a farrier, making at him in a furious manner through the press, hammer in hand; "and you are a cursed aristocrat!"

The postmaster interposed himself between this man and the rider's bridle (at which he was evidently making), and soothingly said, "Let him be; let him be! He will be judged at Paris."

"Judged!" repeated the farrier, swinging his hammer. "Ay! and condemned as a traitor." At this the crowd roared approval.

Checking the postmaster, who was for turning his horse's head to the yard (the drunken patriot sat composedly in his saddle looking on, with the line round his wrist), Darnay said, as soon as he could make his voice heard:

"Friends, you deceive yourselves, or you are deceived. I am not a traitor."

"He lies!" cried the smith. "He is a traitor since the decree. His life is forfeit to the people. His cursed life is not his own!"

At the instant when Darnay saw a rush in the eyes of the

crowd, which another instant would have brought upon him, the postmaster turned his horse into the yard, the escort rode in close upon his horse's flanks, and the postmaster shut and barred the crazy double gates. The farrier struck a blow upon them with his hammer, and the crowd groaned; but, no more was done.

"What is this decree that the smith spoke of?" Darnay asked the postmaster, when he had thanked him, and stood beside him in the yard.

"Truly, a decree for selling the property of emigrants."

"When passed?"

"On the fourteenth."

"The day I left England!"

"Everybody says it is but one of several, and that there will be others—if there are not already—banishing all emigrants, and condemning all to death who return. That is what he meant when he said your life was not your own."

"But there are no such decrees yet?"

"What do I know!" said the postmaster, shrugging his shoulders; "there may be, or there will be. It is all the same. What would you have?"

They rested on some straw in a loft until the middle of the night, and then rode forward again when all the town was asleep. Among the many wild changes observable on familiar things which made this wild ride unreal, not the least was the seeming rarity of sleep. After long and lonely spurring over dreary roads, they would come to a cluster of poor cottages, not steeped in darkness, but all glittering with lights, and would find the people, in a ghostly manner in the dead of the night, circling hand in hand round a shrivelled tree of Liberty, or all drawn up together singing a Liberty song. Happily, however, there was sleep in Beauvais that night to help them out of it, and they passed on once more into solitude and loneliness: jingling through the untimely cold and wet, among impoverished fields that had yielded no fruits of the earth that year, diversified by the blackened remains of burnt houses, and by the sudden emergence from ambuscade, and sharp reining up across their way, of patriot patrols on the watch on all the roads.

Daylight at last found them before the wall of Paris. The barrier was closed and strongly guarded when they rode up to it.

"Where are the papers of this prisoner?" demanded a

resolute-looking man in authority, who was summoned out by the guard.

Naturally struck by the disagreeable word, Charles Darnay requested the speaker to take notice that he was a free traveller and French citizen, in charge of an escort which the disturbed state of the country had imposed upon him, and which he had paid for.

"Where," repeated the same personage, without taking any heed of him whatever, "are the papers of this prisoner?"

The drunken patriot had them in his cap, and produced them. Casting his eyes over Gabelle's letter, the same personage in authority showed some disorder and surprise, and looked at Darnay with a close attention.

He left escort and escorted without saying a word, however, and went into the guard-room; meanwhile, they sat upon their horses outside the gate. Looking about him while in this state of suspense, Charles Darnay observed that the gate was held by a mixed guard of soldiers and patriots, the latter far outnumbering the former; and that while ingress into the city for peasants' carts bringing in supplies, and for similar traffic and traffickers, was easy enough, egress, even for the homeliest people, was very difficult. A numerous medley of men and women, not to mention beasts and vehicles of various sorts, was waiting to issue forth; but, the previous identification was so strict, that they filtered through the barrier very slowly. Some of these people knew their turn for examination to be so far off, that they lay down on the ground to sleep or smoke, while others talked together, or loitered about. The red cap and tricolor cockade were universal, both among men and women.

When he had sat in his saddle some half-hour, taking note of these things, Darnay found himself confronted by the same man in authority, who directed the guard to open the barrier. Then he delivered to the escort, drunk and sober, a receipt for the escorted, and requested him to dismount. He did so, and the two patriots, leading his tired horse, turned and rode away without entering the city.

He accompanied his conductor into a guard-room, smelling of common wine and tobacco, where certain soldiers and patriots, asleep and awake, drunk and sober, and in various neutral states between sleeping and waking, drunkenness and sobriety, were standing and lying about. The light in the guard-house, half derived from the waning oil-lamps of the night, and half from the overcast day, was in a correspondingly uncertain condition. Some registers were lying open on a desk, and an officer of a coarse, dark aspect presided over these.

"Citizen Defarge," said he to Darnay's conductor, as he took a slip of paper to write on. "Is this the emigrant Evrémonde?"

"This is the man."

"Your age, Evrémonde?"

"Thirty-seven."

"Married, Evrémonde?"

"Yes."

"Where married?"

"In England."

"Without doubt. Where is your wife, Evrémonde?"

"In England."

"Without doubt. You are consigned, Evrémonde, to the prison of La Force."

"Just Heaven!" exclaimed Darnay. "Under what law, and for what offence?"

The officer looked up from his slip of paper for a moment.

"We have new laws, Evrémonde, and new offences, since you were here." He said it with a hard smile, and went on writing.

"I entreat you to observe that I have come here voluntarily, in response to that written appeal of a fellow-countryman which lies before you. I demand no more than the opportunity to do so without delay. Is not that my right?"

"Emigrants have no rights, Evrémonde," was the stolid reply. The officer wrote until he had finished, read over to himself what he had written, sanded it, and handed it to Defarge, with the words "In secret."

Defarge motioned with the paper to the prisoner that he must accompany him. The prisoner obeyed, and a guard of two armed patriots attended them.

"Is it you," said Defarge, in a low voice, as they went down the guard-house steps and turned into Paris, "who married the daughter of Doctor Manette, once a prisoner in the Bastille that is no more?"

"Yes," replied Darnay, looking at him with surprise.

"My name is Defarge, and I keep a wine-shop in the Quarter Saint Antoine. Possibly you have heard of me."

"My wife came to your house to reclaim her father? Yes!"

The word "wife" seemed to serve as a gloomy reminder to Defarge, to say with sudden impatience, "In the name of that sharp female newly born, and called La Guillotine, why did you come to France?"

"You heard me say why, a minute ago. Do you not believe it is the truth?"

"A bad truth for you," said Defarge, speaking with knitted brows, and looking straight before him.

"Indeed I am lost here. All here is so unprecedented, so changed, so sudden and unfair, that I am absolutely lost. Will you render me a little help?"

"None." Defarge spoke, always looking straight before him.

"Will you answer me a single question?"

"Perhaps. According to its nature. You can say what it is."

"In this prison that I am going to so unjustly, shall I have some free communication with the world outside?"

"You will see."

"I am not to be buried there, prejudged, and without any means of presenting my case?"

"You will see. But, what then? Other people have been similarly buried in worse prisons, before now."

"But never by me, Citizen Defarge."

Defarge glanced darkly at him for answer, and walked on in a steady and set silence. The deeper he sank into this silence, the fainter hope there was—or so Darnay thought —of his softening in any slight degree. He, therefore, made haste to say:

"It is of the utmost importance to me (you know, Citizen, even better than I, of how much importance) that I should be able to communicate to Mr. Lorry of Tellson's Bank, an English gentleman who is now in Paris, the simple fact, without comment, that I have been thrown into the prison of La Force. Will you cause that to be done for me?"

"I will do," Defarge doggedly rejoined, "nothing for you. My duty is to my country and the People. I am the sworn servant of both, against you. I will do nothing for you."

Charles Darnay felt it hopeless to entreat him further, and his pride was touched besides. As they walked on in silence, he could not but see how used the people were to the spectacle of prisoners passing along the streets. The very children scarcely noticed him. A few passers turned their heads, and a few shook their fingers at him as an aristocrat; otherwise, that a man in good clothes should be going to prison was no more remarkable than that a labourer in working clothes should be going to work. In one narrow, dark, and dirty street through which they passed, an excited orator, mounted on a stool, was addressing an excited audience on the crimes against the people, of the king and the royal family. The few words that he caught from this man's lips first made it known to Charles Darnay that the king was in prison, and that the foreign ambassadors had one and all left Paris. On the road (except at Beauvais) he had heard absolutely nothing. The escort and the universal watchfulness had completely isolated him.

That he had fallen among far greater dangers than those which had developed themselves when he left England, he of course knew now. That perils had thickened about him fast, and might thicken faster and faster yet, he of course knew now. He could not but admit to himself that he might not have made this journey, if he could have foreseen the events of a few days. And yet his misgivings were not so dark as, imagined by the light of this later time, they would appear. Troubled as the future was, it was the unknown future, and in its obscurity there was ignorant hope. The horrible massacre, days and nights long, which, within a few rounds of the clock, was to set a great mark of blood upon the blessed garnering time of harvest, was as far out of his knowledge as if it had been a hundred thousand years away. The "sharp female newly born, and called La Guillotine," was hardly known to him, or to the generality of people, by name. The frightful deeds that were to be soon done were probably unimagined at that time in the brains of the doers. How could they have a place in the shadowy conceptions of a gentle mind?

Of unjust treatment in detention and hardship, and in cruel separation from his wife and child, he foreshadowed the likelihood, or the certainty; but, beyond this, he dreaded nothing distinctly. With this on his mind, which was enough to carry into a dreary prison courtyard, he arrived at the prison of La Force.

A man with a bloated face opened the strong wicket, to whom Defarge presented "The Emigrant Evrémonde."

"What the Devil! How many more of them!" exclaimed the man with the bloated face.

Defarge took his receipt without noticing the exclamation, and withdrew, with his two fellow-patriots.

"What the Devil, I say again!" exclaimed the gaoler, left with his wife. "How many more!"

The gaoler's wife, being provided with no answer to the question, merely replied, "One must have patience, my dear!" Three turnkeys who entered, responsive to a bell she rang, echoed the sentiment, and one added, "For the love of Liberty"; which sounded in that place like an inappropriate conclusion.

The prison of La Force was a gloomy prison, dark and filthy, and with a horrible smell of foul sleep in it. Extraordinary how soon the noisome flavour of imprisoned sleep becomes manifest in all such places that are ill cared for!

"In secret, too," grumbled the gaoler, looking at the written paper. "As if I was not already full to bursting!"

He stuck the paper on a file, in an ill-humour, and Charles Darnay awaited his further pleasure for half an hour: sometimes, pacing to and fro in the strong arched room; sometimes, resting on a stone seat; in either case detained to be imprinted on the memory of the chief and his subordinates.

"Come!" said the chief, at length taking up his keys, "come with me, emigrant."

Through the dismal prison twilight, his new charge accompanied him by corridor and staircase, many doors clanging and locking behind them, until they came into a large, low, vaulted chamber, crowded with prisoners of both sexes. The women were seated at a long table, reading and writing, knitting, sewing, and embroidering; the men were for the most part standing behind their chairs, or lingering up and down the room.

In the instinctive association of prisoners with shameful crime and disgrace, the new-comer recoiled from this company. But the crowning unreality of his long unreal ride was their all at once rising to receive him, with every refinement of manner known to the time, and with all the engaging graces and courtesies of life.

So strangely clouded were these refinements by the prison manners and gloom, so spectral did they become in the inappropriate squalor and misery through which they were seen, that Charles Darnay seemed to stand in a company of the dead. Ghosts all! The ghost of beauty, the ghost of stateliness, the ghost of elegance, the ghost of pride, the ghost of frivolity, the ghost of wit, the ghost of youth, the ghost of age, all waiting their dismissal from the desolate shore, all turning on him eyes that were changed by the death they had died in coming there.

It struck him motionless. The gaoler standing at his side, and the other gaolers moving about, who would have been well enough as to appearance in the ordinary exercise of their functions, looked so extravagantly coarse contrasted with sorrowing mothers and blooming daughters who were there—with the apparitions of the coquette, the young beauty, and the mature woman delicately bred—that the inversion of all experience and likelihood which the scene of shadows presented, was heightened to its utmost. Surely, ghosts all. Surely, the long unreal ride some progress of disease that had brought him to these gloomy shades!

"In the name of the assembled companions in misfortune," said a gentleman of courtly appearance and address, coming forward, "I have the honour of giving you welcome to La Force, and of condoling with you on the calamity that has brought you among us. May it soon terminate happily! It would be an impertinence elsewhere, but it is not so here, to ask your name and condition?"

Charles Darnay roused himself, and gave the required information, in words as suitable as he could find.

"But I hope," said the gentleman, following the chief gaoler with his eyes, who moved across the room, "that you are not in secret?"

"I do not understand the meaning of the term, but I have heard them say so."

"Ah, what a pity! We so much regret it! But take courage; several members of our society have been in secret, at first, and it has lasted but a short time." Then he added, raising his voice, "I grieve to inform the society—in secret."

There was a murmur of commiseration as Charles Darnay crossed the room to a grated door where the gaoler awaited him, and many voices—among which, the soft and compassionate voices of women were conspicuous—gave him good wishes and encouragement. He turned at the grated door, to render the thanks of his heart; it closed under the gaoler's hand; and the apparitions vanished from his sight for ever.

The wicket opened on a stone staircase, leading upward. When they had ascended forty steps (the prisoner of half an hour already counted them), the gaoler opened a low black door, and they passed into a solitary cell. It struck cold and damp, but it was not dark.

"Yours," said the gaoler.

"Why am I confined alone?"

"How do I know!"

"I can buy pen, ink, and paper?"

"Such are not my orders. You will be visited, and can ask then. At present, you may buy your food, and nothing more."

There were, in the cell, a chair, a table, and a straw mattress. As the gaoler made a general inspection of these objects, and of the four walls, before going out, a wandering fancy wandered through the mind of the prisoner leaning against the wall opposite to him, that this gaoler was so unwholesomely bloated, both in face and person, as to look like a man who had been drowned and filled with water. When the gaoler was gone, he thought in the same wandering way, "Now am I left, as if I were dead." Stopping then, to look down at the mattress, he turned from it with a sick feeling, and thought, "And here in these crawling creatures is the first condition of the body after death.

"Five paces by four and a half, five paces by four and a half, five paces by four and a half." The prisoner walked to and fro in his cell, counting its measurement, and the roar of the city arose like muffled drums with a wild swell of voices added to them. "He made shoes, he made shoes, he made shoes." The prisoner counted the measurement again, and paced faster, to draw his mind with him from that latter repetition. "The ghosts that vanished when the wicket closed. There was one among them, the appearance of a lady dressed in black, who was leaning in the embrasure of a window, and she had a light shining upon her golden hair, and she looked like . . . Let us ride on again, for God's sake, through the illuminated villages with the people all awake! . . . He made shoes, he made shoes, he made shoes. . . . Five paces by four and a half." With such scraps tossing and rolling upward from the depths of his mind, the prisoner walked faster and faster, obstinately counting and counting; and the roar of the city changed to this extent—that it still rolled in like muffled drums, but with the wail of voices that he knew, in the swell that rose above them.

* * * * * * * *

2 *The Grindstone*

TELLSON'S BANK, established in the Saint Germain Quarter of Paris, was in a wing of a large house, approached by a courtyard and shut off from the street by a high wall and a strong gate. The house belonged to a great nobleman who had lived in it until he made a flight from the troubles, in his own cook's dress, and got across the borders. A mere beast of the chase flying from hunters, he was still in his metempsychosis no other than the same Monseigneur, the preparation of whose chocolate for whose lips had once occupied three strong men besides the cook in question.

Monseigneur gone, and the three strong men absolving themselves from the sin of having drawn his high wages, by being more than ready and willing to cut his throat on the altar of the dawning Republic one and indivisible of Liberty, Equality, Fraternity, or Death, Monseigneur's house had been first sequestrated, and then confiscated. For, all things moved so fast, and decree followed decree with that fierce precipitation, that now upon the third night of the autumn month of September, patriot emissaries of the law were in possession of Monseigneur's house, and had marked it with the tricolour, and were drinking brandy in its state apartments.

A place of business in London like Tellson's place of business in Paris would soon have driven the House out of its mind and into the Gazette. For, what would staid British responsibility and respectability have said to orange-trees in boxes in a bank courtyard, and even to a Cupid over the counter? Yet such things were. Tellson's had whitewashed the Cupid, but he was still to be seen on the ceiling, in the coolest linen, aiming (as he very often does) at money from morning to night. Bankruptcy must inevitably have come of this young pagan, in Lombard Street, London, and also of a curtained alcove in the rear of the immortal boy, and also of a looking-glass let into the wall, and also of clerks not at all old, who danced in public on the slightest provocation. Yet, a French Tellson's could get on with these things exceedingly well, and, as long as the times held together, no man had taken fright at them, and drawn out his money.

What money would be drawn out of Tellson's henceforth, and what would lie there, lost and forgotten; what plate and jewels would tarnish in Tellson's hiding-places, while the depositors rusted in prisons, and when they should have violently perished; how many accounts with Tellson's, never to be balanced in this world, must be carried over into the next; no man could have said, that night, any more than Mr. Jarvis Lorry could, though he thought heavily of these questions. He sat by a newly lighted wood fire (the blighted and unfruitful year was prematurely cold), and on his honest and courageous face there was a deeper shade than the pendent lamp could throw, or any object in the room distortedly reflect—a shade of horror.

He occupied rooms in the Bank, in his fidelity to the House of which he had grown to be a part, like strong root-ivy. It chanced that they derived a kind of security from the patriotic occupation of the main building, but the true-hearted old gentleman never calculated about that. All such circumstances were indifferent to him, so that he did his duty. On the opposite side of the courtyard, under a colonnade, was extensive standing for carriages—where, indeed, some carriages of Monseigneur yet stood. Against two of the pillars were fastened two great flaring flambeaux, and in the light of these, standing out in the open air, was a large grindstone: a roughly mounted thing which appeared to have hurriedly been brought there from some neighbouring smithy, or other workshop. Rising and looking out of window at these harmless objects, Mr. Lorry shivered, and retired to his seat by the fire. He had opened not only the glass window, but the lattice blind outside it, and he had closed both again, and he shivered through his frame.

From the streets beyond the high wall and the strong gate there came the usual night hum of the city, with now and then an indescribable ring to it, weird and unearthly, as if some unwonted sounds of a terrible nature were going up to Heaven.

"Thank God," said Mr. Lorry, clasping his hands, "that no one near and dear to me is in this dreadful town to-night. May He have mercy on all who are in danger!"

Soon afterwards, the bell at the great gate sounded, and he thought, "They have come back!" and sat listening. But, there was no loud irruption into the courtyard, as he had expected, and he heard the gate clash again, and all was quiet.

The nervousness and dread that were upon him inspired that vague uneasiness respecting the Bank which a great change would naturally awaken, with such feelings roused. It was well guarded, and he got up to go among the trusty people who were watching it, when his door suddenly opened, and two figures rushed in, at sight of which he fell back in amazement.

Lucie and her father! Lucie with her arms stretched out to him, and with that old look of earnestness so concentrated and intensified, that it seemed as though it had been stamped upon her face expressly to give force and power to it in this one passage of her life.

"What is this?" cried Mr. Lorry, breathless and confused. "What is the matter? Lucie! Manette! What has happened? What has brought you here? What is it?"

With the look fixed upon him, in her paleness and wildness, she panted out in his arms, imploringly, "O my dear friend! My husband!"

"Your husband, Lucie?"

"Charles."

"What of Charles?"

"Here."

"Here, in Paris?"

"Has been here some days—three or four—I don't know how many—I can't collect my thoughts. An errand of generosity brought him here unknown to us; he was stopped at the barrier, and sent to prison."

The old man uttered an irrepressible cry. Almost at the same moment, the bell of the great gate rang again, and a loud noise of feet and voices came pouring into the courtyard.

"What is that noise?" said the Doctor, turning towards the window.

"Don't look!" cried Mr. Lorry. "Don't look out! Manette, for your life, don't touch the blind!"

The Doctor turned, with his hand upon the fastening of the window, and said, with a cool bold smile:

"My dear friend, I have a charmed life in this city. I have been a Bastille prisoner. There is no patriot in Paris —in Paris? in France—who, knowing me to have been a prisoner in the Bastille, would touch me, except to overwhelm me with embraces, or carry me in triumph. My old pain has given me a power that has brought us through the barrier, and gained us news of Charles there, and brought us here. I knew it would be so; I knew I could help Charles out of all danger; I told Lucie so.—What is that noise?" His hand was again upon the window.

"Don't look!" cried Mr. Lorry, absolutely desperate. "No, Lucie, my dear, nor you!" He got his arm round her, and held her. "Don't be so terrified, my love. I solemnly swear to you that I know of no harm having happened to Charles; that I had no suspicion even of his being in this fatal place. What prison is he in?"

"La Force!"

"La Force! Lucie, my child, if ever you were brave and serviceable in your life—and you were always both—you will compose yourself now, to do exactly as I bid you; for more depends upon it than you can think, or I can say. There is no help for you in any action on your part to-night; you cannot possibly stir out. I say this, because what I must bid you to do for Charles's sake is the hardest thing to do of all. You must instantly be obedient, still, and quiet. You must let me put you in a room at the back here. You must leave your father and me alone for two minutes, and as there are Life and Death in the world you must not delay."

"I will be submissive to you. I see in your face that you know I can do nothing else than this. I know you are true."

The old man kissed her, and hurried her into his room, and turned the key; then, came hurrying back to the Doctor, and opened the window and partly opened the blind, and put his hand upon the Doctor's arm, and looked out with him into the courtyard.

Looked out upon a throng of men and women: not enough in number, or near enough, to fill the courtyard: not more than forty or fifty in all. The people in possession of the house had let them in at the gate, and they had rushed in to work at the grindstone; it had evidently been set up there for their purpose, as in a convenient and retired spot.

But, such awful workers, and such awful work!

The grindstone had a double handle, and turning at it madly were two men, whose faces, as their long hair flapped back when the whirlings of the grindstone brought their faces up, were more horrible and cruel than the visages of the wildest savages in their most barbarous disguise. False eyebrows and false moustaches were stuck upon them, and their hideous countenances were all bloody and sweaty, and all awry with howling, and all staring and glaring with beastly excitement and want of sleep. As these ruffians turned and turned, their matted locks now flung forward over their eyes, now flung backward over their necks, some women held wine to their mouths that they might drink; and what with dropping blood, and what with dropping wine, and what with the stream of sparks struck out of the stone, all their wicked atmosphere seemed gore and fire. The eye could not detect one creature in the group free from the smear of blood. Shouldering one another to get next at the sharpening-stone were men stripped to the waist, with the stain all over their limbs and bodies; men in all sorts of rags, with the stain upon those rags; men devilishly set off with spoils of women's lace and silk and ribbon, with the stain dyeing those trifles through and through. Hatchets, knives, bayonets, swords, all brought to be sharpened, were all red with it. Some of the hacked swords were tied to the wrists of those who carried them, with strips of linen and fragments of dress: ligatures various in kind, but all deep of the one colour. And as the frantic wielders of these weapons snatched them from the stream of sparks and tore away into the streets, the same red hue was red in their frenzied eyes—eyes which any unbrutalised beholder would have given twenty years of life to petrify with a well-directed gun.

All this was seen in a moment, as the vision of a drowning man, or of any human creature at any very great pass, could see a world if it were there. They drew back from the window, and the Doctor looked for explanation in his friend's ashy face.

"They are," Mr. Lorry whispered the words, glancing fearfully round at the locked room, "murdering the prisoners. If you are sure of what you say; if you really have the power you think you have—as I believe you have—make yourself known to these devils, and get taken to La Force. It may be too late, I don't know, but let it not be a minute later!"

Doctor Manette pressed his hand, hastened bareheaded out of the room, and was in the courtyard when Mr. Lorry regained the blind.

His streaming white hair, his remarkable face, and the impetuous confidence of his manner, as he put the weapons aside like water, carried him in an instant to the heart of the concourse at the stone. For a few moments there was a pause, and a hurry, and a murmur, and the unintelligible sound of his voice; and then Mr. Lorry saw him, surrounded by all, and in the midst of a line of twenty men long, all linked shoulder to shoulder, and hand to shoulder, hurried out with cries of—"Live the Bastille prisoner! Help for the Bastille prisoner's kindred in La Force! Room for the Bastille prisoner in front there! Save the prisoner Evrémonde at La Force!" and a thousand answering shouts.

He closed the lattice again with a fluttering heart, closed the window and the curtain, hastened to Lucie, and told her that her father was assisted by the people, and gone in search of her husband. He found her child and Miss Pross with her; but it never occurred to him to be surprised by their appearance until a long time afterwards, when he sat watching them in such quiet as the night knew.

Lucie had, by that time, fallen into a stupor on the floor at his feet, clinging to his hand. Miss Pross had laid the child down on his own bed, and her head had gradually fallen on the pillow beside her pretty charge. O the long, long night, with the moans of the poor wife! And O the long, long night, with no return of her father and no tidings!

Twice more in the darkness the bell at the great gate sounded, and the irruption was repeated, and the grindstone whirled and spluttered. "What is it?" cried Lucie, affrighted. "Hush! The soldiers' swords are sharpened there," said Mr. Lorry. "The place is national property now, and used as a kind of armoury, my love."

Twice more in all; but, the last spell of work was feeble and fitful. Soon afterwards the day began to dawn, and he softly detached himself from the clasping hand, and cautiously looked out again. A man, so besmeared that he

might have been a sorely wounded soldier creeping back
to consciousness on a field of slain, was rising from the
pavement by the side of the grindstone, and looking about
him with a vacant air. Shortly, this worn-out murderer
descried in the imperfect light one of the carriages of Monseigneur, and, staggering to that gorgeous vehicle, climbed
in at the door, and shut himself up to take his rest on its
dainty cushions.

The great grindstone, Earth, had turned when Mr. Lorry
looked out again, and the sun was red on the courtyard.
But, the lesser grindstone stood alone there in the calm
morning air, with a red upon it that the sun had never
given, and would never take away.

3 *The Shadow*

ONE OF the first considerations which arose in the
business mind of Mr. Lorry when business hours came
round, was this—that he had no right to imperil Tellson's
by sheltering the wife of an emigrant prisoner under the
Bank roof. His own possessions, safety, life, he would have
hazarded for Lucie and her child, without a moment's
demur; but the great trust he held was not his own, and
as to that business charge he was a strict man of business.

At first, his mind reverted to Defarge, and he thought of
finding out the wine-shop again and taking counsel with
its master in reference to the safest dwelling-place in the
distracted state of the city. But, the same consideration
that suggested him, repudiated him; he lived in the most
violent Quarter, and doubtless was influential there, and
deep in its dangerous workings.

Noon coming, and the Doctor not returning, and every
minute's delay tending to compromise Tellson's, Mr. Lorry
advised with Lucie. She said that her father had spoken
of hiring a lodging for a short term, in that Quarter, near
the banking-house. As there was no business objection to
this, and as he foresaw that even if it were all well with

Charles, and he were to be released, he could not hope to leave the city, Mr. Lorry went out in quest of such a lodging, and found a suitable one, high up in a removed by-street where the closed blinds in all the other windows of a high melancholy square of buildings marked deserted homes.

To this lodging he at once removed Lucie and her child, and Miss Pross: giving them what comfort he could, and much more than he had himself. He left Jerry with them, as a figure to fill a doorway that would bear considerable knocking on the head, and returned to his own occupations. A disturbed and doleful mind he brought to bear upon them, and slowly and heavily the day lagged on with him.

It wore itself out, and wore him out with it, until the Bank closed. He was again alone in his room of the previous night, considering what to do next, when he heard a foot upon the stair. In a few moments, a man stood in his presence, who, with a keenly observant look at him, addressed him by his name.

"Your servant," said Mr. Lorry. "Do you know me?"

He was a strongly made man with dark curling hair, from forty-five to fifty years of age. For answer he repeated, without any change of emphasis, the words:

"Do you know me?"

"I have seen you somewhere."

"Perhaps at my wine-shop?"

Much interested and agitated, Mr. Lorry said: "You come from Doctor Manette?"

"Yes. I come from Doctor Manette."

"And what says he? What does he send me?"

Defarge gave into his anxious hand an open scrap of paper. It bore the words in the Doctor's writing:

"Charles is safe, but I cannot safely leave this place yet. I have obtained the favour that the bearer has a short note from Charles to his wife. Let the bearer see his wife."

It was dated from La Force, within an hour.

"Will you accompany me," said Mr. Lorry, joyfully relieved after reading this note aloud, "to where his wife resides?"

"Yes," returned Defarge.

Scarcely noticing, as yet, in what a curiously reserved

and mechanical way Defarge spoke, Mr. Lorry put on his hat and they went down into the courtyard. There, they found two women, one knitting.

"Madame Defarge, surely!" said Mr. Lorry, who had left her in exactly the same attitude some seventeen years ago.

"It is she," observed her husband.

"Does madame go with us?" inquired Mr. Lorry, seeing that she moved as they moved.

"Yes. That she may be able to recognise the faces and know the persons. It is for their safety."

Beginning to be struck by Defarge's manner, Mr. Lorry looked dubiously at him, and led the way. Both the women followed; the second woman being The Vengeance.

They passed through the intervening streets as quickly as they might, ascended the staircase of the new domicile, were admitted by Jerry, and found Lucie weeping, alone. She was thrown into a transport by the tidings Mr. Lorry gave her of her husband, and clasped the hand that delivered his note—little thinking what it had been doing near him in the night, and might, but for a chance, have done to him.

"DEAREST—Take courage. I am well, and your father has influence around me. You cannot answer this. Kiss our child for me."

That was all the writing. It was so much, however, to her who received it, that she turned from Defarge to his wife, and kissed one of the hands that knitted. It was a passionate, loving, thankful, womanly action, but the hand made no response—dropped cold and heavy, and took to its knitting again.

There was something in its touch that gave Lucie a check. She stopped in the act of putting the note in her bosom, and, with her hands yet at her neck, looked terrified at Madame Defarge. Madame Defarge met the lifted eyebrows and forehead with a cold, impassive stare.

"My dear," said Mr. Lorry, striking in to explain; "there are frequent risings in the streets; and, although it is not likely they will ever trouble you, Madame Defarge wishes to see those whom she has the power to protect at such times, to the end that she may know them—that she may identify them. I believe," said Mr. Lorry, rather halting in his reassuring words, as the stony manner of all the three impressed itself upon him more and more, "I state the case, Citizen Defarge?"

Defarge looked gloomily at his wife, and gave no other answer than a gruff sound of acquiescence.

"You had better, Lucie," said Mr. Lorry, doing all he could to propitiate, by tone and manner, "have the dear child here, and our good Pross. Our good Pross, Defarge, is an English lady, and knows no French."

The lady in question, whose rooted conviction that she was more than a match for any foreigner was not to be shaken by distress and danger, appeared with folded arms, and observed in English to The Vengeance, whom her eyes first encountered, "Well, I am sure, Boldface! I hope *you* are pretty well!" She also bestowed a British cough on Madame Defarge; but, neither of the two took much heed of her.

"Is that his child?" said Madame Defarge, stopping in her work for the first time, and pointing her knitting-needle at little Lucie as if it were the finger of Fate.

"Yes, madame," answered Mr. Lorry; "this is our poor prisoner's darling daughter, and only child."

The shadow attendant on Madame Defarge and her party seemed to fall so threatening and dark on the child, that her mother instinctively kneeled on the ground beside her, and held her to her breast. The shadow attendant on Madame Defarge and her party seemed then to fall, threatening and dark, on both the mother and the child.

"It is enough, my husband," said Madame Defarge. "I have seen them. We may go."

But, the suppressed manner had enough of menace in it—not visible and presented, but indistinct and withheld —to alarm Lucie into saying, as she laid her appealing hand on Madame Defarge's dress:

"You will be good to my poor husband. You will do him no harm. You will help me to see him if you can?"

"Your husband is not my business here," returned Madame Defarge, looking down at her with perfect composure. "It is the daughter of your father who is my business here."

"For my sake, then, be merciful to my husband. For my child's sake! She will put her hands together and pray you to be merciful. We are more afraid of you than of these others."

Madame Defarge received it as a compliment, and looked at her husband. Defarge, who had been uneasily biting his thumb-nail and looking at her, collected his face into a sterner expression.

"What is it that your husband says in that little letter?" asked Madame Defarge, with a lowering smile. "Influence; he says something touching influence?"

"That my father," said Lucie, hurriedly taking the paper from her breast, but with her alarmed eyes on her questioner and not on it, "has much influence around him."

"Surely it will release him!" said Madame Defarge. "Let it do so."

"As a wife and mother," cried Lucie, most earnestly, "I implore you to have pity on me and not to exercise any power that you possess against my innocent husband, but to use it in his behalf. O sister-woman, think of me. As a wife and mother!"

Madame Defarge looked, coldly as ever, at the suppliant, and said, turning to her friend The Vengeance:

"The wives and mothers we have been used to see, since we were as little as this child, and much less, have not been greatly considered? We have known *their* husbands and fathers laid in prison and kept from them, often enough? All our lives, we have seen our sister-women suffer, in themselves and in their children, poverty, nakedness, hunger, thirst, sickness, misery, oppression and neglect of all kinds?"

"We have seen nothing else," returned The Vengeance.

"We have borne this a long time," said Madame Defarge, turning her eyes again upon Lucie. "Judge you! Is it likely that the trouble of one wife and mother would be much to us now?"

She resumed her knitting and went out. The Vengeance followed. Defarge went last, and closed the door.

"Courage, my dear Lucie," said Mr. Lorry, as he raised her. "Courage, courage! So far all goes well with us— much, much better than it has of late gone with many poor souls. Cheer up, and have a thankful heart."

"I am not thankless, I hope, but that dreadful woman seems to throw a shadow on me and on all my hopes."

"Tut, tut!" said Mr. Lorry; "what is this despondency in the brave little breast? A shadow indeed! No substance in it, Lucie."

But the shadow of the manner of these Defarges was dark upon himself, for all that, and in his secret mind it troubled him greatly.

* * * * * * * *

4 Calm in Storm

DOCTOR MANETTE did not return until the morning of the fourth day of his absence. So much of what had happened in that dreadful time as could be kept from the knowledge of Lucie was so well concealed from her, that not until long afterwards, when France and she were far apart, did she know that eleven hundred defenceless prisoners of both sexes and all ages had been killed by the populace; that four days and nights had been darkened by this deed of horror; and that the air around her had been tainted by the slain. She only knew that there had been an attack upon the prisons, that all political prisoners had been in danger, and that some had been dragged out by the crowd and murdered.

To Mr. Lorry, the Doctor communicated under an injunction of secrecy on which he had no need to dwell, that the crowd had taken him through a scene of carnage to the prison of La Force. That in the prison he had found a self-appointed tribunal sitting, before which the prisoners were brought singly, and by which they were rapidly ordered to be put forth to be massacred, or to be released, or (in a few cases) to be sent back to their cells. That presented by his conductors to this tribunal, he had announced himself by name and profession as having been for eighteen years a secret and unaccused prisoner in the Bastille; that one of the body so sitting in judgment had risen and identified him, and that this man was Defarge.

That hereupon he had ascertained, through the registers on the table, that his son-in-law was among the living prisoners, and had pleaded hard to the tribunal—of whom some members were asleep and some awake, some dirty with murder and some clean, some sober and some not—

for his life and liberty. That in the first frantic greetings lavished on himself as a notable sufferer under the overthrown system, it had been accorded to him to have Charles Darnay brought before the lawless court, and examined. That he seemed on the point of being at once released, when the tide in his favour met with some unexplained check (not intelligible to the Doctor), which led to a few words of secret conference. That the man sitting as president had then informed Doctor Manette that the prisoner must remain in custody, but should, for his sake, be held inviolate in safe custody. That immediately, on a signal, the prisoner was removed to the interior of the prison again; but, that he, the Doctor, had then so strongly pleaded for permission to remain and assure himself that his son-in-law was, through no malice or mischance, delivered to the concourse whose murderous yells outside the gate had often drowned the proceedings, that he had obtained the permission, and had remained in that Hall of Blood until the danger was over.

The sights he had seen there, with brief snatches of food and sleep by intervals, shall remain untold. The mad joy over the prisoners who were saved had astounded him scarcely less than the mad ferocity against those who were cut to pieces. One prisoner there was, he said, who had been discharged into the street free, but at whom a mistaken savage had thrust a pike as he passed out. Being besought to go to him and dress the wound, the Doctor had passed out at the same gate, and had found him in the arms of a company of Samaritans, who were seated on the bodies of their victims. With an inconsistency as monstrous as anything in this awful nightmare, they had helped the healer, and tended the wounded man with the gentlest solicitude—had made a litter for him and escorted him carefully from the spot—had then caught up their weapons and plunged anew into a butchery so dreadful, that the Doctor had covered his eyes with his hands, and swooned away in the midst of it.

As Mr. Lorry received these confidences, and as he watched the face of his friend, now sixty-two years of age, a misgiving arose within him that such dread experiences would revive the old danger. But, he had never seen his friend in his present aspect: he had never at all known him in his present character. For the first time the Doctor felt, now, that his suffering was strength and power. For the first time he felt that in that sharp fire he had slowly forged the iron which could break the prison door of his daughter's husband, and deliver him. "It all tended to a good end, my friend; it was not mere waste and ruin. As my beloved child was helpful in restoring me to myself, I will be helpful now in restoring the dearest part of herself to her; by the aid of Heaven I will do it!" Thus, Doctor Manette. And when Jarvis Lorry saw the kindled eyes, the resolute face, the calm strong look and bearing of the man whose life always seemed to him to have been stopped, like a clock, for so many years, and then set going again with an energy which had lain dormant during the cessation of its usefulness, he believed.

Greater things than the Doctor had at that time to contend with would have yielded before his persevering purpose. While he kept himself in his place, as a physician, whose business was with all degrees of mankind, bond and free, rich and poor, bad and good, he used his personal influence so wisely, that he was soon the inspecting physician of three prisons, and among them of La Force. He could now assure Lucie that her husband was no longer confined alone, but was mixed with the general body of prisoners; he saw her husband weekly, and brought sweet messages to her, straight from his lips; sometimes her husband himself sent a letter to her (though never by the Doctor's hand), but she was not permitted to write to him: for, among the many wild suspicions of plots in the prisons, the wildest of all pointed at emigrants who were known to have made friends or permanent connections abroad.

This new life of the Doctor's was an anxious life, no doubt; still, the sagacious Mr. Lorry saw that there was a new sustaining pride in it. Nothing unbecoming tinged the pride; it was a natural and worthy one; but he observed it as a curiosity. The Doctor knew, that up to that time, his imprisonment had been associated, in the minds of his daughter and his friend, with his personal affliction, deprivation, and weakness. Now that this was changed, and he knew himself to be invested through that old trial with forces to which they both looked for Charles's ultimate safety and deliverance, he became so far exalted by the change, that he took the lead and direction, and required them as the weak, to trust to him as the strong. The preceding relative positions of himself and Lucie were reversed, yet only as the liveliest gratitude and affection could reverse them, for he could have had no pride but in rendering some service to her who had rendered so much to him. "All curious to see," thought Mr. Lorry, in his amiably shrewd way, "but all natural and right; so, take the lead, my dear friend, and keep it; it couldn't be in better hands."

But, though the Doctor tried hard, and never ceased trying, to get Charles Darnay set at liberty, or at least to get him brought to trial, the public current of the time set too strong and fast for him. The new era began; the king was tried, doomed, and beheaded; the Republic of Liberty, Equality, Fraternity, or Death, declared for victory or death against the world in arms; the black flag waved night and day from the great towers of Notre Dame; three hundred thousand men, summoned to rise against the tyrants of the earth, rose from all the varying soils of France, as if the dragon's teeth had been sown broadcast, and had yielded fruit equally on hill and plain, on rock, in gravel, and alluvial mud, under the bright sky of the South and under the clouds of the North, in fell and forest, in the vineyards and the olive-grounds and among the cropped grass and the stubble of the corn, along the fruitful banks of the broad rivers, and in the sand of the sea-shore. What private solicitude could rear itself against the deluge of the Year One of Liberty—the deluge rising from below, not falling from above, and with the windows of Heaven shut, not opened!

There was no pause, no pity, no peace, no interval of relenting rest, no measurement of time. Though days and nights circled as regularly as when time was young, and the evening and morning were the first day, other count of time there was none. Hold of it was lost in the raging fever of a nation, as it is in the fever of one patient. Now, breaking the unnatural silence of a whole city, the executioner showed the people the head of the king—and now, it seemed almost in the same breath, the head of his fair wife which had had eight weary months of imprisoned widowhood and misery, to turn it gray.

And yet, observing the strange law of contradiction which obtains in all such cases, the time was long, while it flamed by so fast. A revolutionary tribunal in the capital, and forty or fifty thousand revolutionary committees all over the land; a law of the Suspected, which struck away all security for liberty or life, and delivered over any good and innocent person to any bad and guilty one, prisons gorged with people who had committed no offence, and could obtain no hearing; these things became the established order and nature of appointed things, and seemed to be ancient usage before they were many weeks old. Above all, one hideous figure grew as familiar as if it had been before the general gaze from the foundations of the world—the figure of the sharp female called La Guillotine.

It was the popular theme for jests; it was the best cure for headache, it infallibly prevented the hair from turning gray, it imparted a peculiar delicacy to the complexion, it was the National Razor which shaved close: who kissed La Guillotine looked through the little window and sneezed into the sack. It was the sign of the regeneration of the human race. It superseded the Cross. Models of it were worn on breasts from which the Cross was discarded, and it was bowed down to and believed in where the Cross was denied.

It sheared off heads so many, that it and the ground it most polluted were a rotten red. It was taken to pieces, like a toy-puzzle for a young Devil, and was put together again when the occasion wanted it. It hushed the eloquent, struck down the powerful, abolished the beautiful and good. Twenty-two friends of high public mark, twenty-one living and one dead, it had lopped the heads off, in one morning, in as many minutes. The name of the strong man of Old Scripture had descended to the chief functionary who worked it; but, so armed, he was stronger than his namesake, and blinder, and tore away the gates of God's own Temple every day.

Among these terrors, and the brood belonging to them, the Doctor walked with a steady head: confident in his power, cautiously persistent in his end, never doubting that he would save Lucie's husband at last. Yet the current of the time swept by, so strong and deep, and carried the time away so fiercely, that Charles had lain in prison one year and three months when the Doctor was thus steady and confident. So much more wicked and distracted had the Revolution grown in that December month, that the rivers of the South were encumbered with the bodies of the violently drowned by night, and prisoners were shot in lines and squares under the southern wintry sun. Still, the Doctor walked among the terrors with a steady hand. No man better known than he, in Paris at that day; no

man in a stranger situation. Silent, humane, indispensable
in hospital and prison, using his art equally among assas-
sins and victims, he was a man apart. In the exercise of his
skill, the appearance and the story of the Bastille Captive
removed him from all other men. He was not suspected or
brought in question, any more than if he had indeed been
recalled to life some eighteen years before, or were a Spirit
moving among mortals.

5 *The Wood-Sawyer*

ONE YEAR and three months. During all that time
Lucie was never sure, from hour to hour, but that the Guillotine would strike off her husband's head next day. Every
day, through the stony streets, the tumbrils now jolted
heavily, filled with Condemned. Lovely girls; bright women,
brown-haired, black-haired, and gray; youths; stalwart
men and old; gentle born and peasant born; all red wine
for La Guillotine, all daily brought into light from the dark
cellars of the loathsome prisons, and carried to her through
the streets to slake her devouring thirst. Liberty, equality,
fraternity, or death—the last, much the easiest to bestow,
O Guillotine!

If the suddenness of her calamity, and the whirling
wheels of the time, had stunned the Doctor's daughter into
awaiting the result in idle despair, it would but have been
with her as it was with many. But, from the hour when she
had taken the white head to her fresh young bosom in the
garret of Saint Antoine, she had been true to her duties.
She was truest to them in the season of trial, as all the
quietly loyal and good will always be.

As soon as they were established in their new residence,
and her father had entered on the routine of his avoca-
tions, she arranged the little household as exactly as if
her husband had been there. Everything had its appointed
place and its appointed time. Little Lucie she taught as
regularly as if they had all been united in their English

home. The slight devices with which she cheated herself in the show of a belief that they would soon be reunited— the little preparations for his speedy return, the setting aside of his chair and his books—these, and the solemn prayer at night for one dear prisoner especially, among the many unhappy souls in prison and the shadow of death— were almost the only outspoken reliefs of her heavy mind.

She did not greatly alter in appearance. The plain dark dresses, akin to mourning dresses, which she and her child wore, were as neat and as well attended to as the brighter clothes of happy days. She lost her colour, and the old and intent expression was a constant, not an occasional, thing; otherwise, she remained very pretty and comely. Sometimes, at night on kissing her father, she would burst into the grief she had repressed all day, and would say that her sole reliance, under Heaven, was on him. He always resolutely answered: "Nothing can happen to him without my knowledge, and I know that I can save him, Lucie."

They had not made the round of their changed life many weeks, when her father said to her, on coming home one evening:

"My dear, there is an upper window in the prison, to which Charles can sometimes gain access at three in the afternoon. When he can get to it—which depends on many uncertainties and incidents—he might see you in the street, he thinks, if you stood in a certain place that I can show you. But you will not be able to see him, my poor child, and even if you could, it would be unsafe for you to make a sign of recognition."

"O show me the place, my father, and I will go there every day."

From that time, in all weathers, she waited there two hours. As the clock struck two, she was there, and at four she turned resignedly away. When it was not too wet or inclement for her child to be with her, they went together; at other times she was alone; but she never missed a single day.

It was the dark and dirty corner of a small winding street. The hovel of a cutter of wood into lengths for burning was the only house at that end; all else was wall. On the third day of her being there, he noticed her.

"Good day, citizeness."

"Good day, citizen."

This mode of address was now prescribed by decree. It

had been established voluntarily some time ago, among the more thorough patriots; but, was now law for everybody.

"Walking here again, citizeness?"

"You see me, citizen!"

The wood-sawyer, who was a little man with a redundancy of gesture (he had once been a mender of roads), cast a glance at the prison, pointed at the prison, and putting his ten fingers before his face to represent bars, peeped through them jocosely.

"But it's not my business," said he. And went on sawing his wood.

Next day he was looking out for her, and accosted her the moment she appeared.

"What? Walking here again, citizeness?"

"Yes, citizen."

"Ah! A child too! Your mother, is it not, my little citizeness?"

"Do I say yes, Mamma?" whispered little Lucie, drawing close to her.

"Yes, dearest."

"Yes, citizen."

"Ah! But it's not my business. My work is my business. See my saw! I call it my Little Guillotine. La, la, la; La, la, la! And off his head comes!"

The billet fell as he spoke, and he threw it into a basket.

"I call myself the Samson of the firewood guillotine. See here again! Loo, loo, loo; Loo, loo, loo! And off *her* head comes! Now, a child. Tickle, tickle; Pickle, pickle! And off *its* head comes. All the family!"

Lucie shuddered as he threw two more billets into his basket, but it was impossible to be there while the wood-sawyer was at work, and not be in his sight. Thenceforth, to secure his good will, she always spoke to him first, and often gave him drink-money, which he readily received.

He was an inquisitive fellow, and sometimes when she had quite forgotten him in gazing at the prison roof and grates, and in lifting her heart up to her husband, she would come to herself to find him looking at her, with his knee on his bench and his saw stopped in its work. "But it's not my business!" he would generally say at those times, and would briskly fall to his sawing again.

In all weathers, in the snow and frost of winter, in the bitter winds of spring, in the hot sunshine of summer, in the rains of autumn, again in the snow and frost of winter,

Lucie passed two hours of every day at this place; and every day on leaving it, she kissed the prison wall. Her husband saw her (so she learned from her father) it might be once in five or six times: it might be twice or thrice running: it might be, not for a week or a fortnight together. It was enough, that he could and did see her when the chances served, and on that possibility she would have waited out the day, seven days a week.

These occupations brought her round to the December month, wherein her father walked among the terrors with a steady head. On a lightly-snowing afternoon she arrived at the usual corner. It was a day of some wild rejoicing, and a festival. She had seen the houses, as she came along, decorated with little pikes, and with little red caps stuck upon them; also, with tricoloured ribbons; also, with the standard inscription (tricoloured letters were the favourite), Republic One and Indivisible. Liberty, Equality, Fraternity, or Death!

The miserable shop of the wood-sawyer was so small, that its whole surface furnished very indifferent space for this legend. He had got somebody to scrawl it up for him, however, who had squeezed Death in with most inappropriate difficulty. On his house-top he displayed pike and cap, as a good citizen must, and in a window he had stationed his saw inscribed as his "Little Sainte Guillotine"—for the great sharp female was by that time popularly canonised. His shop was shut and he was not there, which was a relief to Lucie, and left her quite alone.

But, he was not far off, for presently she heard a troubled movement and a shouting coming along, which filled her with fear. A moment afterwards, and a throng of people came pouring round the corner by the prison wall, in the midst of whom was the wood-sawyer hand in hand with The Vengeance. There could not be fewer than five hundred people, and they were dancing like five thousand demons. There was no other music than their own singing. They danced to the popular Revolution song, keeping a ferocious time that was like a gnashing of teeth in unison. Men and women danced together, women danced together, men danced together, as hazard had brought them together. At first, they were a mere storm of coarse red caps and coarse woollen rags; but, as they filled the place, and stopped to dance about Lucie, some ghastly apparition of a dance-figure gone raving mad arose among them. They advanced, retreated, struck at one another's hands, clutched at one another's heads, spun round alone, caught one another and spun round in pairs, until many of them dropped. While those were down, the rest linked hand in hand, and all spun round together: then the ring broke, and in separate rings of two and four they turned and turned until they all stopped at once, began again, struck, clutched, and tore, and then reversed the spin, and all spun round another way. Suddenly they stopped again, paused, struck out the time afresh, formed into lines the width of the public way, and, with their heads low down and their hands high up, swooped screaming off. No fight could have been half so terrible as this dance. It was so emphatically a fallen sport—a something once innocent, delivered over to all devilry—a healthy pastime changed into a means of angering the blood, bewildering the senses, and steeling the heart. Such grace as was visible in it made it the uglier, showing how warped and perverted all things good by nature were become. The maidenly bosom bared to this, the pretty almost-child's head thus distracted, the delicate foot mincing in this slough of blood and dirt, were types of the disjointed time.

This was the Carmagnole. As it passed, leaving Lucie frightened and bewildered in the doorway of the woodsawyer's house, the feathery snow fell as quietly and lay as white and soft, as if it had never been.

"O my father!" for he stood before her when she lifted up the eyes she had momentarily darkened with her hand; "such a cruel, bad sight."

"I know, my dear, I know. I have seen it many times. Don't be frightened! Not one of them would harm you."

"I am not frightened for myself, my father. But when I think of my husband, and the mercies of these people—"

"We will set him above their mercies very soon. I left him climbing to the window, and I came to tell you. There is no one here to see. You may kiss your hand towards that highest shelving roof."

"I do so, Father, and I send him my soul with it."

"You cannot see him, my poor dear?"

"No, Father," said Lucie, yearning and weeping as she kissed her hand, "no."

A footstep in the snow. Madame Defarge. "I salute you, citizeness," from the Doctor. "I salute you, citizen." This in passing. Nothing more. Madame Defarge gone, like a shadow over the white road.

"Give me your arm, my love. Pass from here with an air of cheerfulness and courage, for his sake. That was well done"; they had left the spot; "it shall not be in vain. Charles is summoned for to-morrow."

"For to-morrow!"

"There is no time to lose. I am well prepared, but there are precautions to be taken, that could not be taken until he was actually summoned before the Tribunal. He has not received the notice yet, but I know that he will presently be summoned for to-morrow, and removed to the Conciergerie; I have timely information. You are not afraid?"

She could scarcely answer, "I trust in you."

"Do so, implicitly. Your suspense is nearly ended, my darling; he shall be restored to you within a few hours; I have encompassed him with every protection. I must see Lorry."

He stopped. There was a heavy lumbering of wheels within hearing. They both knew too well what it meant. One. Two. Three. Three tumbrils faring away with their dread loads over the hushing snow.

"I must see Lorry," the Doctor repeated, turning her another way.

The staunch old gentleman was still in his trust; had never left it. He and his books were in frequent requisition as to property confiscated and made national. What he could save for the owners, he saved. No better man living to hold fast by what Tellson's had in keeping, and to hold his peace.

A murky red and yellow sky, and a rising mist from the Seine, denoted the approach of darkness. It was almost dark when they arrived at the Bank. The stately residence of Monseigneur was altogether blighted and deserted. Above a heap of dust and ashes in the court ran the letters: National Property. Republic One and Indivisible. Liberty, Equality, Fraternity, or Death!

Who could that be with Mr. Lorry—the owner of the riding-coat upon the chair—who must not be seen? From whom, newly arrived, did he come out, agitated and surprised, to take his favourite in his arms? To whom did he appear to repeat her faltering words, when, raising his voice and turning his head towards the door of the room from which he had issued, he said: "Removed to the Conciergerie and summoned for to-morrow"?

*   *   *   *   *   *   *

6 *Triumph*

THE DREAD Tribunal of five judges, public prosecutor, and determined jury, sat every day. Their lists went forth every evening, and were read out by the gaolers of the various prisons to their prisoners. The standard gaoler-joke was, "Come out and listen to the evening paper, you inside there!"

"Charles Evrémonde, called Darnay!"

So at last began the evening paper at La Force.

When a name was called, its owner stepped apart into a spot reserved for those who were announced as being thus fatally recorded. Charles Evrémonde, called Darnay, had reason to know the usage; he had seen hundreds pass away so.

His bloated gaoler, who wore spectacles to read with, glanced over them to assure himself that he had taken his place, and went through the list, making a similar short pause at each name. There were twenty-three names, but only twenty were responded to; for one of the prisoners so summoned had died in gaol and been forgotten, and two had already been guillotined and forgotten. The list was read, in the vaulted chamber where Darnay had seen the associated prisoners on the night of his arrival. Every one of those had perished in the massacre; every human creature he had since cared for and parted with had died on the scaffold.

There were hurried words of farewell and kindness, but the parting was soon over. It was the incident of every day, and the society of La Force were engaged in the preparation of some games of forfeits and a little concert, for that evening. They crowded to the grates and shed tears there; but, twenty places in the projected entertainments had to be refilled, and the time was, at best, short to the lock-up hour, when the common rooms and corridors would be delivered over to the great dogs who kept watch there through the night. The prisoners were far from insensible or unfeeling; their ways arose out of a condition of the time. Similarly, though with a subtle difference, a species of fervour or intoxication, known, without doubt, to have led some persons to brave the guillotine unnecessarily, and to die by it, was not mere boastfulness, but a wild infection of the wildly shaken public mind. In seasons of pestilence, some of us will have a secret attraction to the disease—a terrible passing inclination to die of it. And all of us have like wonders hidden in our breasts, only needing circumstances to evoke them.

The passage to the Conciergerie was short and dark; the night in its vermin-haunted cells was long and cold. Next day, fifteen prisoners were put to the bar before Charles Darnay's name was called. All the fifteen were condemned, and the trials of the whole occupied an hour and a half.

"Charles Evrémonde, called Darnay," was at length arraigned.

His judges sat upon the bench in feathered hats; but the rough red cap and tricoloured cockade was the headdress otherwise prevailing. Looking at the jury and the turbulent audience, he might have thought that the usual order of things was reversed, and that the felons were trying the honest men. The lowest, cruelest, and worst populace of a city, never without its quantity of low, cruel, and bad, were the directing spirits of the scene: noisily commenting, applauding, disapproving, anticipating, and precipitating the result, without a check. Of the men, the greater part were armed in various ways; of the women, some wore knives, some daggers, some ate and drank as they looked on, many knitted. Among these last was one with a spare piece of knitting under her arm as she worked. She was in a front row, by the side of a man whom he had never seen since his arrival at the Barrier, but whom he directly remembered as Defarge. He noticed that she once or twice whispered in his ear, and that she seemed to be his wife; but, what he most noticed in the two figures was, that although they were posted as close to himself as they could be, they never looked towards him. They seemed to be waiting for something with a dogged determination, and they looked at the jury, but at nothing else. Under the President sat

Doctor Manette, in his usual quiet dress. As well as the prisoner could see, he and Mr. Lorry were the only men there, unconnected with the Tribunal, who wore their usual clothes, and had not assumed the coarse garb of the Carmagnole.

Charles Evrémonde, called Darnay, was accused by the public prosecutor as an emigrant, whose life was forfeit to the Republic, under the decree which banished all emigrants on pain of Death. It was nothing that the decree bore date since his return to France. There he was, and there was the decree; he had been taken in France, and his head was demanded.

"Take off his head!" cried the audience. "An enemy to the Republic!"

The President rang his bell to silence those cries, and asked the prisoner whether it was not true that he had lived many years in England?

Undoubtedly it was.

Was he not an emigrant then? What did he call himself?

Not an emigrant, he hoped, within the sense and spirit of the law.

Why not? the President desired to know.

Because he had voluntarily relinquished a title that was distasteful to him, and a station that was distasteful to him, and had left his country—he submitted before the word emigrant in the present acceptation by the Tribunal was in use—to live by his own industry in England, rather than on the industry of the overladen people of France.

What proof had he of this?

He handed in the names of two witnesses: Théophile Gabelle, and Alexandre Manette.

But he had married in England? the President reminded him.

True, but not an English woman.

A citizeness of France?

Yes. By birth.

Her name and family?

"Lucie Manette, only daughter of Doctor Manette, the good physician who sits there."

This answer had a happy effect upon the audience. Cries in exaltation of the well-known good physician rent the hall. So capriciously were the people moved, that tears immediately rolled down several ferocious countenances which had been glaring at the prisoner a moment before, as f with impatience to pluck him out into the streets and kill him.

On these few steps of his dangerous way, Charles Darnay had set his foot according to Doctor Manette's reiterated instructions. The same cautious counsel directed every step that lay before him, and had prepared every inch of his road.

The President asked, why had he returned to France when he did, and not sooner?

He had not returned sooner, he replied, simply because he had no means of living in France, save those he had resigned; whereas, in England, he lived by giving instruction in the French language and literature. He had returned when he did, on the pressing and written entreaty of a French citizen, who represented that his life was endangered by his absence. He had come back, to save a citizen's life, and to bear his testimony, at whatever personal hazard, to the truth. Was that criminal in the eyes of the Republic?

The populace cried enthusiastically, "No!" and the President rang his bell to quiet them. Which it did not, for they continued to cry "No!" until they left off, of their own will.

The President required the name of that citizen? The accused explained that the citizen was his first witness. He also referred with confidence to the citizen's letter, which had been taken from him at the Barrier, but which he did not doubt would be found among the papers then before the President.

The Doctor had taken care that it should be there—had assured him that it would be there—and at this stage of the proceedings it was produced and read. Citizen Gabelle was called to confirm it, and did so. Citizen Gabelle hinted, with infinite delicacy and politeness, that in the pressure of business imposed on the Tribunal by the multitudes of enemies of the Republic with which it had to deal, he had been slightly overlooked in his prison of the Abbaye—in fact, had rather passed out of the Tribunal's patriotic remembrance—until three days ago; when he had been summoned before it, and had been set at liberty on the jury's declaring themselves satisfied that the accusation against him was answered, as to himself, by the surrender of the citizen Evrémonde, called Darnay.

Doctor Manette was next questioned. His high personal

popularity, and the clearness of his answers, made a great impression; but, as he proceeded, as he showed that the accused was his first friend on his release from his long imprisonment; that the accused had remained in England, always faithful and devoted to his daughter and himself in their exile; that, so far from being in favour with the aristocrat government there, he had actually been tried for his life by it, as the foe of England and friend of the United States—as he brought these circumstances into view, with the greatest discretion and with the straightforward force of truth and earnestness, the jury and the populace became one. At last, when he appealed by name to Monsieur Lorry, an English gentleman then and there present, who, like himself, had been a witness on that English trial and could corroborate his account of it, the jury declared that they had heard enough, and that they were ready with their votes if the President were content to receive them.

At every vote (the jurymen voted aloud and individually), the populace set up a shout of applause. All the voices were in the prisoner's favour, and the President declared him free.

Then began one of those extraordinary scenes with which the populace sometimes gratified their fickleness, or their better impulses towards generosity and mercy, or which they regarded as some set-off against their swollen account of cruel rage. No man can decide now to which of these motives such extraordinary scenes were referable; it is probable, to a blending of all the three, with the second predominating. No sooner was the acquittal pronounced, than tears were shed as freely as blood at another time, and such fraternal embraces were bestowed upon the prisoner by as many of both sexes as could rush at him, that after his long and unwholesome confinement, he was in danger of fainting from exhaustion; none the less he knew very well that the very same people, carried by another current, would have rushed at him with the very same intensity, to rend him to pieces and strew him over the streets.

His removal, to make way for other accused persons who were to be tried, rescued him from these caresses for the moment. Five were to be tried together, next, as enemies of the Republic, forasmuch as they had not assisted it by word or deed. So quick was the Tribunal to compensate itself and the nation for a chance lost, that these five came down to him before he left the place, condemned to die

within twenty-four hours. The first of them told him so,
with the customary prison sign of Death—a raised finger—
and they all added in words, "Long live the Republic!"

The five had had, it is true, no audience to lengthen their
proceedings, for when he and Doctor Manette emerged
from the gate, there was a great crowd about it, in which
there seemed to be every face he had seen in court—except
two, for which he looked in vain. On his coming out, the
concourse made at him anew, weeping, embracing, and
shouting, all by turns and all together, until the very tide
of the river on the bank of which the mad scene was acted,
seemed to run mad, like the people on the shore.

They put him into a great chair they had among them,
and which they had taken either out of the court itself, or
one of its rooms or passages. Over the chair they had
thrown a red flag, and to the back of it they had bound a
pike with a red cap on its top. In this car of triumph, not
even the Doctor's entreaties could prevent his being carried
to his home on men's shoulders, with a confused sea of red
caps heaving about him, and casting up to sight from the
stormy deep such wrecks of faces, that he more than once
misdoubted his mind being in confusion, and that he was
in the tumbril on his way to the Guillotine.

In wild dreamlike procession, embracing whom they
met and pointing him out, they carried him on. Reddening
the snowy streets with the prevailing Republican colour, in
winding and tramping through them, as they had reddened
them below the snow with a deeper dye, they carried him
thus into the courtyard of the building where he lived. Her
father had gone on before, to prepare her, and when her
husband stood upon his feet, she dropped insensible in his
arms.

As he held her to his heart and turned her beautiful
head between his face and the brawling crowd, so that his
tears and her lips might come together unseen, a few of
the people fell to dancing. Instantly, all the rest fell to
dancing, and the courtyard overflowed with the Carmagnole. Then, they elevated into the vacant chair a young
woman from the crowd to be carried as the Goddess of
Liberty, and then swelling and overflowing out into the
adjacent streets, and along the river's bank, and over the
bridge, the Carmagnole absorbed them every one and
whirled them away.

After grasping the Doctor's hand, as he stood victorious

and proud before him; after grasping the hand of Mr.
Lorry, who came panting in breathless from his struggle
against the waterspout of the Carmagnole; after kissing
little Lucie, who was lifted up to clasp her arms round his
neck; and after embracing the ever-zealous and faithful
Pross who lifted her; he took his wife in his arms, and
carried her up to their rooms.

"Lucie! My own! I am safe."

"O dearest Charles, let me thank God for this on my
knees as I have prayed to Him."

They all reverently bowed their heads and hearts. When
she was again in his arms, he said to her:

"And now speak to your father, dearest. No other man
in all this France could have done what he has done for
me."

She laid her head upon her father's breast, as she had
lain his poor head on her own breast, long, long ago. He
was happy in the return he had made her, he was recom-
pensed for his suffering, he was proud of his strength. "You
must not be weak, my darling," he remonstrated; "don't
tremble so. I have saved him."

7   *A Knock at the Door*

"I HAVE saved him." It was not another of the
dreams in which he had often come back; he was really
here. And yet his wife trembled, and a vague but heavy
fear was upon her.

All the air around was so thick and dark, the people
were so passionately revengeful and fitful, the innocent
were so constantly put to death on vague suspicion and
black malice, it was so impossible to forget that many as
blameless as her husband, and as dear to others as he was
to her, every day shared the fate from which he had been
clutched, that her heart could not be as lightened of its
load as she felt it ought to be. The shadows of the wintry
afternoon were beginning to fall, and even now the dread-

ful carts were rolling through the streets. Her mind pursued them, looking for him among the condemned; and then she clung to his real presence and trembled more.

Her father, cheering her, showed a compassionate superiority to this woman's weakness, which was wonderful to see. No garret, no shoemaking, no One Hundred and Five, North Tower, now! He had accomplished the task he had set himself, his promise was redeemed, he had saved Charles. Let them all lean upon him.

Their housekeeping was of a very frugal kind: not only because that was the safest way of life, involving the least offence to the people, but because they were not rich, and Charles, throughout his imprisonment, had had to pay heavily for his bad food, and for his guard, and towards the living of the poorer prisoners. Partly on this account, and partly to avoid a domestic spy, they kept no servant; the citizen and citizeness who acted as porters at the courtyard gate rendered them occasional service; and Jerry (almost wholly transferred to them by Mr. Lorry) had become their daily retainer, and had his bed there every night.

It was an ordinance of the Republic One and Indivisible of Liberty, Equality, Fraternity, or Death, that on the door or doorpost of every house, the name of every inmate must be legibly inscribed in letters of a certain size, at a certain convenient height from the ground. Mr. Jerry Cruncher's name, therefore, duly embellished the doorpost down below; and, as the afternoon shadows deepened, the owner of that name himself appeared, from overlooking a painter whom Doctor Manette had employed to add to the list the name of Charles Evrémonde, called Darnay.

In the universal fear and distrust that darkened the time, all the usual harmless ways of life were changed. In the Doctor's little household, as in very many others, the articles of daily consumption that were wanted were purchased every evening, in small quantities and at various small shops. To avoid attracting notice, and to give as little occasion as possible for talk and envy, was the general desire.

For some months past, Miss Pross and Mr. Cruncher had discharged the office of purveyors; the former carrying the money; the latter, the basket. Every afternoon at about the time when the public lamps were lighted, they fared forth on this duty, and made and brought home such purchases as were needful. Although Miss Pross, through her long association with a French family, might have known as much of their language as of her own, if she had had a mind, she had no mind in that direction; consequently, she knew no more of that "nonsense" (as she was pleased to call it) than Mr. Cruncher did. So her manner of marketing was to plump a noun-substantive at the head of a shopkeeper without any introduction in the nature of an article, and, if it happened not to be the name of the thing she wanted, to look round for that thing, lay hold of it, and hold on by it until the bargain was concluded. She always made a bargain for it, by holding up, as a statement of its just price, one finger less than the merchant held up, whatever his number might be.

"Now, Mr. Cruncher," said Miss Pross, whose eyes were red with felicity; "if you are ready, I am."

Jerry hoarsely professed himself at Miss Pross's service. He had worn all his rust off long ago, but nothing would file his spiky head down.

"There's all manner of things wanted," said Miss Pross, "and we shall have a precious time of it. We want wine, among the rest. Nice toasts these red heads will be drinking, wherever we buy it."

"It will be much the same to your knowledge, miss, I should think," retorted Jerry, "whether they drink your health or the Old Un's."

"Who's he?" said Miss Pross.

Mr. Cruncher, with some difference, explained himself as meaning "Old Nick's."

"Ha!" said Miss Pross, "it doesn't need an interpreter to explain the meaning of these creatures. They have but one, and it's Midnight Murder, and Mischief!"

"Hush, dear! Pray, pray, be cautious!" cried Lucie.

"Yes, yes, yes, I'll be cautious," said Miss Pross; "but I may say among ourselves, that I do hope there will be no oniony and tobaccoey smotherings in the form of embracings all round, going on in the streets. Now, Ladybird, never you stir from that fire till I come back! Take care of the dear husband you have recovered, and don't move your pretty head from his shoulders as you have it now, till you see me again! May I ask a question, Doctor Manette, before I go?"

"I think you may take that liberty," the Doctor answered, smiling.

"For gracious' sake, don't talk about liberty; we have quite enough of that," said Miss Pross.

"Hush, dear! Again?" Lucie remonstrated.

"Well, my sweet," said Miss Pross, nodding her head emphatically, "the short and the long of it is, that I am a subject of His Most Gracious Majesty King George the Third." Miss Pross curtsied at the name. "And as such, my maxim is, Confound their politics, Frustrate their knavish tricks, On him our hopes we fix, God save the King!"

Mr. Cruncher, in an access of loyalty, growlingly repeated the words after Miss Pross, like somebody at church.

"I am glad you have so much of the Englishman in you, though I wish you had never taken that cold in your voice," said Miss Pross, approvingly. "But the question, Doctor Manette. Is there"—it was the good creature's way to affect to make light of anything that was a great anxiety with them all, and to come at it in this chance manner—"is there any prospect, yet, of our getting out of this place?"

"I fear not yet. It would be dangerous for Charles yet."

"Heigh-ho-hum!" said Miss Pross, cheerfully repressing a sigh as she glanced at her darling's golden hair in the light of the fire, "then we must have patience and wait: that's all. We must hold up our heads and fight low, as my brother Solomon used to say. Now, Mr. Cruncher!— Don't you move, Ladybird!"

They went out, leaving Lucie, and her husband, her father, and the child, by a bright fire. Mr. Lorry was expected back presently from the banking house. Miss Pross had lighted the lamp, but had put it aside in a corner, that they might enjoy the firelight undisturbed. Little Lucie sat by her grandfather with her hands clasped through his arm: and he, in a tone not rising much above a whisper, began to tell her a story of a great and powerful fairy who had opened a prison-wall and let out a captive who had once done the fairy a service. All was subdued and quiet, and Lucie was more at ease than she had been.

"What is that?" she cried, all at once.

"My dear!" said her father, stopping in his story, and laying his hand on hers, "command yourself. What a disordered state you are in! The least thing—nothing—startles you! *You*, your father's daughter!"

"I thought, my father," said Lucie, excusing herself, with a pale face and in a faltering voice, "that I heard strange feet upon the stairs."

"My love, the staircase is as still as Death."

As he said the word, a blow was struck upon the door.

"Oh Father, Father. What can this be! Hide Charles. Save him!"

"My child," said the Doctor, rising, and laying his hand upon her shoulder, "I *have* saved him. What weakness is this, my dear! Let me go to the door."

He took the lamp in his hand, crossed the two intervening outer rooms, and opened it. A rude clattering of feet over the floor, and four rough men in red caps, armed with sabres and pistols, entered the room.

"The Citizen Evrémonde, called Darnay," said the first.

"Who seeks him?" answered Darnay.

"I seek him. We seek him. I know you, Evrémonde; I saw you before the Tribunal to-day. You are again the prisoner of the Republic."

The four surrounded him, where he stood with his wife and child clinging to him.

"Tell me how and why am I again a prisoner?"

"It is enough that you return straight to the Conciergerie, and will know to-morrow. You are summoned for to-morrow."

Doctor Manette, whom this visitation had so turned into stone, that he stood with the lamp in his hand, as if he were a statue made to hold it, moved after these words were spoken, put the lamp down, and confronting the speaker, and taking him, not ungently, by the loose front of his red woollen shirt, said:

"You know him, you have said. Do you know me?"

"Yes, I know you, Citizen Doctor."

"We all know you, Citizen Doctor," said the other three.

He looked abstractedly from one to another, and said, in a lower voice, after a pause:

"Will you answer his question to me then? How does this happen?"

"Citizen Doctor," said the first, reluctantly, "he has been denounced to the section of Saint Antoine. This citizen," pointing out the second who had entered, "is from Saint Antoine."

"He is accused by Saint Antoine."

"Of what?" asked the Doctor.

"Citizen Doctor," said the first, with his former reluctance, "ask no more. If the Republic demands sacrifices from you, without doubt you as a good patriot will be happy to make them. The Republic goes before all. The People is supreme. Evrémonde, we are pressed."

"One word," the Doctor entreated. "Will you tell me who denounced him?"

"It is against rule," answered the first; "but you can ask him of Saint Antoine here."

The Doctor turned his eyes upon that man, who moved uneasily on his feet, rubbed his beard a little, and at length said:

"Well! Truly it is against rule. But he is denounced—and gravely—by the Citizen and Citizeness Defarge. And by one other."

"What other?"

"Do *you* ask, Citizen Doctor?"

"Yes."

"Then," said he of Saint Antoine, with a strange look, "you will be answered to-morrow. Now, I am dumb!"

---

8 *A Hand at Cards*

HAPPILY UNCONSCIOUS of the new calamity at home, Miss Pross threaded her way along the narrow streets and crossed the river by the bridge of the Pont-Neuf, reckoning in her mind the number of indispensable purchases she had to make. Mr. Cruncher, with the basket, walked at her side. They both looked to the right and to the left into most of the shops they passed, had a wary eye for all gregarious assemblages of people, and turned out of their road to avoid any very excited groups of talkers. It was a raw evening, and the misty river, blurred to the eye with blazing lights and to the ear with harsh noises, showed where the barges were stationed in which the smiths worked, making guns for the Army of the Republic. Woe to the man who played tricks with *that* Army, or got undeserved promotion in it! Better for him that his beard had never grown, for the National Razor shaved him close.

Having purchased a few small articles of grocery, and a

measure of oil for the lamp, Miss Pross bethought herself of the wine they wanted. After peeping into several wine-shops, she stopped at the sign of The Good Republican Brutus of Antiquity, not far from the National Palace, once (and twice) the Tuileries, where the aspect of things rather took her fancy. It had a quieter look than any other place of the same description they had passed, and, though red with patriotic caps, was not so red as the rest. Sounding Mr. Cruncher, and finding him of her opinion, Miss Pross resorted to The Good Republican Brutus of Antiquity, attended by her cavalier.

Slightly observant of the smoky lights; of the people, pipe in mouth, playing with limp cards and yellow dominoes; of the one bare-breasted, bare-armed, soot-begrimed workman reading a journal aloud, and of the others listening to him; of the weapons worn, or laid aside to be resumed; of the two or three customers fallen forward asleep, who in the popular high-shouldered shaggy black spencer looked, in that attitude, like slumbering bears or dogs; the two outlandish customers approached the counter, and showed what they wanted.

As their wine was measuring out, a man parted from another man in a corner, and rose to depart. In going, he had to face Miss Pross. No sooner did he face her, than Miss Pross uttered a scream, and clapped her hands.

In a moment, the whole company were on their feet. That somebody was assassinated by somebody vindicating a difference of opinion was the likeliest occurrence. Everybody looked to see somebody fall, but only saw a man and a woman standing staring at each other; the man with all the outward aspect of a Frenchman and a thorough Republican; the woman, evidently English.

What was said in this disappointing anti-climax, by the disciples of The Good Republican Brutus of Antiquity, except that it was something very voluble and loud, would have been as so much Hebrew or Chaldean to Miss Pross and her protector, though they had been all ears. But, they had no ears for anything in their surprise. For, it must be recorded, that not only was Miss Pross lost in amazement and agitation, but, Mr. Cruncher—though it seemed on his own separate and individual account—was in a state of the greatest wonder.

"What is the matter?" said the man who had caused Miss

Pross to scream; speaking in a vexed, abrupt voice (though in a low tone), and in English.

"Oh, Solomon, dear Solomon!" cried Miss Pross, clapping her hands again. "After not setting eyes upon you or hearing of you for so long a time, do I find you here!"

"Don't call me Solomon. Do you want to be the death of me?" asked the man, in a furtive, frightened way.

"Brother, brother!" cried Miss Pross, bursting into tears. "Have I ever been so hard with you that you ask me such a cruel question?"

"Then hold your meddlesome tongue," said Solomon, "and come out, if you want to speak to me. Pay for your wine, and come out. Who's this man?"

Miss Pross, shaking her loving and dejected head at her by no means affectionate brother, said through her tears, "Mr. Cruncher."

"Let him come out too," said Solomon. "Does he think me a ghost?"

Apparently, Mr. Cruncher did, to judge from his looks. He said not a word, however, and Miss Pross, exploring the depths of her reticule through her tears with great difficulty, paid for her wine. As she did so, Solomon turned to the followers of The Good Republican Brutus of Antiquity, and offered a few words of explanation in the French language, which caused them all to relapse into their former places and pursuits.

"Now," said Solomon, stopping at the dark street corner, "what do you want?"

"How dreadfully unkind in a brother nothing has ever turned my love away from!" cried Miss Pross, "to give me such a greeting, and show me no affection."

"There. Con-found it! There," said Solomon, making a dab at Miss Pross's lips with his own. "Now are you content?"

Miss Pross only shook her head and wept in silence.

"If you expect me to be surprised," said her brother Solomon, "I am not surprised; I knew you were here; I know of most people who are here. If you really don't want to endanger my existence—which I half believe you do—go your ways as soon as possible, and let me go mine. I am busy. I am an official."

"My English brother Solomon," mourned Miss Pross, casting up her tear-fraught eyes, "that had the makings in him of one of the best and greatest of men in his native country, an official among foreigners, and such foreigners! I would almost sooner have seen the dear boy lying in his—"

"I said so!" cried her brother, interrupting. "I knew it. You want to be the death of me. I shall be rendered Sus-spected by my own sister. Just as I am getting on!"

"The gracious and merciful Heavens forbid!" cried Miss Pross. "Far rather would I never see you again, dear Sol-omon, though I have ever loved you truly, and ever shall. Say but one affectionate word to me, and tell me there is nothing angry or estranged between us, and I will detain you no longer."

Good Miss Pross! As if the estrangement between them had come of any culpability of hers. As if Mr. Lorry had not known it for a fact, years ago, in the quiet corner in Soho, that this precious brother had spent her money and left her!

He was saying the affectionate word, however, with a far more grudging condescension and patronage than he could have shown if their relative merits and positions had been reversed (which is invariably the case, all the world over), when Mr. Cruncher, touching him on the shoulder, hoarsely and unexpectedly interposed with the following singular question:

"I say! Might I ask the favour? As to whether your name is John Solomon, or Solomon John?"

The official turned towards him with sudden distrust. He had not previously uttered a word.

"Come!" said Mr. Cruncher. "Speak out, you know." (Which, by the way, was more than he could do himself.) "John Solomon, or Solomon John? She calls you Solomon, and she must know, being your sister. And *I* know you're John, you know. Which of the two goes first? And regard-ing that name of Pross, likewise. That warn't your name over the water."

"What do you mean?"

"Well, I don't know all I mean, for I can't call to mind what your name was, over the water."

"No?"

"No. But I'll swear it was a name of two syllables."

"Indeed?"

"Yes. T'other one's was one syllable. I know you. You was a spy-witness at the Bailey. What, in the name of the

Father of Lies, own father to yourself, was you called at that time?"

"Barsad," said another voice, striking in.

"That's the name for a thousand pound!" cried Jerry.

The speaker who struck in was Sydney Carton. He had his hands behind him under the skirts of his riding-coat, and he stood at Mr. Cruncher's elbow as negligently as he might have stood at the Old Bailey itself.

"Don't be alarmed, my dear Miss Pross. I arrived at Mr. Lorry's, to his surprise, yesterday evening; we agreed that I would not present myself elsewhere until all was well, or unless I could be useful; I present myself here, to beg a little talk with your brother. I wish you had a better employed brother than Mr. Barsad. I wish for your sake Mr. Barsad was not a sheep of the prisons."

Sheep was a cant word of the time for a spy, under the gaolers. The spy, who was pale, turned paler, and asked him how he dared—

"I'll tell you," said Sydney. "I lighted on you, Mr. Barsad, coming out of the prison of the Conciergerie while I was contemplating the walls, an hour or more ago. You have a face to be remembered, and I remember faces well. Made curious by seeing you in that connection, and having a reason, to which you are no stranger, for associating you with the misfortunes of a friend now very unfortunate, I walked in your direction. I walked into the wine-shop here, close after you, and sat near you. I had no difficulty in deducing from your unreserved conversation, and the rumour openly going about among your admirers, the nature of your calling. And gradually, what I had done at random seemed to shape itself into a purpose, Mr. Barsad."

"What purpose?" the spy asked.

"It would be troublesome, and might be dangerous, to explain in the street. Could you favour me, in confidence, with some minutes of your company—at the office of Tellson's Bank, for instance?"

"Under a threat?"

"Oh! Did I say that?"

"Then, why should I go there?"

"Really, Mr. Barsad, I can't say, if you can't."

"Do you mean that you won't say, sir?" the spy irresolutely asked.

"You apprehend me very clearly, Mr. Barsad. I won't."

Carton's negligent recklessness of manner came power-

fully in aid of his quickness and skill, in such a business as
he had in his secret mind, and with such a man as he had
to do with. His practiced eye saw it, and made the most of
it.

"Now, I told you so," said the spy, casting a reproachful
look at his sister; "if any trouble comes of this, it's your
doing."

"Come, come, Mr. Barsad!" exclaimed Sydney. "Don't
be ungrateful. But for my great respect for your sister, I
might not have led up so pleasantly to a little proposal that
I wish to make for our mutual satisfaction. Do you go with
me to the Bank?"

"I'll hear what you have got to say. Yes, I'll go with
you."

"I propose that we first conduct your sister safely to the
corner of her own street. Let me take your arm, Miss Pross.
This is not a good city, at this time, for you to be out in,
unprotected; and as your escort knows Mr. Barsad, I will
invite him to Mr. Lorry's with us. Are we ready? Come
then!"

Miss Pross recalled soon afterwards, and to the end of
her life remembered, that as she pressed her hands on
Sydney's arm and looked up in his face, imploring him to
do no hurt to Solomon, there was a braced purpose in the
arm and a kind of inspiration in the eyes, which not only
contradicted his light manner, but changed and raised the
man. She was too much occupied then with fears for the
brother who so little deserved her affection, and with Sydney's friendly reassurances, adequately to heed what she
observed.

They left her at the corner of the street, and Carton led
the way to Mr. Lorry's, which was within a few minutes'
walk. John Barsad, or Solomon Pross, walked at his side.

Mr. Lorry had just finished his dinner, and was sitting
before a cheery little log or two of fire—perhaps looking
into their blaze for the picture of that younger elderly gentleman from Tellson's, who had looked into the red coals
at the Royal George at Dover, now a good many years ago.
He turned his head as they entered, and showed the surprise with which he saw a stranger.

"Miss Pross's brother, sir," said Sydney. "Mr. Barsad."

"Barsad?" repeated the old gentleman. "Barsad? I have
an association with the name—and with the face."

"I told you you had a remarkable face, Mr. Barsad," observed Carton, coolly. "Pray sit down."

As he took a chair himself, he supplied the link that Mr. Lorry wanted, by saying to him with a frown, "Witness at that trial." Mr. Lorry immediately remembered, and regarded his new visitor with an undisguised look of abhorrence.

"Mr. Barsad has been recognized by Miss Pross as the affectionate brother you have heard of," said Sydney, "and has acknowledged the relationship. I pass to worse news. Darnay has been arrested again."

Struck with consternation, the old gentleman exclaimed, "What do you tell me! I left him safe and free within these two hours, and am about to return to him!"

"Arrested for all that. When was it done, Mr. Barsad?"

"Just now, if at all."

"Mr. Barsad is the best authority possible, sir," said Sydney, "and I have it from Mr. Barsad's communication to a friend and brother sheep over a bottle of wine, that the arrest has taken place. He left the messengers at the gate, and saw them admitted by the porter. There is no earthly doubt that he is retaken."

Mr. Lorry's business eye read in the speaker's face that it was loss of time to dwell upon the point. Confused, but sensible that something might depend upon his presence of mind, he commanded himself, and was silently attentive.

"Now, I trust," said Sydney to him, "that the name and influence of Doctor Manette may stand him in as good stead to-morrow—you said he would be before the Tribunal to-morrow, Mr. Barsad?—"

"Yes; I believe so."

"—In as good stead to-morrow as to-day. But it may not be so. I own to you, I am shaken, Mr. Lorry, by Doctor Manette's not having the power to prevent this arrest."

"He may not have known of it beforehand," said Mr. Lorry.

"But that very circumstance would be alarming, when we remember how identified he is with his son-in-law."

"That's true," Mr. Lorry acknowledged, with his troubled hand at his chin, and his troubled eyes on Carton.

"In short," said Sydney, "this is a desperate time, when desperate games are played for desperate stakes. Let the Doctor play the winning game; I will play the losing one. No man's life here is worth purchase. Any one carried home by the people to-day may be condemned to-morrow. Now, the stake I have resolved to play for, in case of the worst, is a friend in the Conciergerie. And the friend I purpose to myself to win is Mr. Barsad."

"You need have good cards, sir," said the spy.

"I'll run them over. I'll see what I hold.—Mr. Lorry, you know what a brute I am; I wish you'd give me a little brandy."

It was put before him, and he drank off a glassful—drank off another glassful—pushed the bottle thoughtfully away.

"Mr. Barsad," he went on, in the tone of one who really was looking over a hand at cards: "Sheep of the prisons, emissary of Republican committees, now turnkey, now prisoner, always spy and secret informer, so much the more valuable here for being English that an Englishman is less open to suspicion of subornation in those characters than a Frenchman, represents himself to his employers under a false name. That's a very good card. Mr. Barsad, now in the employ of the republican French government, was formerly in the employ of the aristocratic English government, the enemy of France and freedom. That's an excellent card. Inference clear as day in this region of suspicion, that Mr. Barsad, still in the pay of the aristocratic English government, is the spy of Pitt, the treacherous foe of the Republic crouching in its bosom, the English traitor and agent of all mischief so much spoken of and so difficult to find. That's a card not to be beaten. Have you followed my hand, Mr. Barsad?"

"Not to understand your play," returned the spy, somewhat uneasily.

"I play my ace, denunciation of Mr. Barsad to the nearest Section Committee. Look over your hand, Mr. Barsad, and see what you have. Don't hurry."

He drew the bottle near, poured out another glassful of brandy, and drank it off. He saw that the spy was fearful of his drinking himself into a fit state for the immediate denunciation of him. Seeing it, he poured out and drank another glassful.

"Look over your hand carefully, Mr. Barsad. Take time."

It was a poorer hand than he suspected. Mr. Barsad saw losing cards in it that Sydney Carton knew nothing of. Thrown out of his honourable employment in England, through too much unsuccessful hard swearing there—not because he was wanted there: our English reasons for vaunting our superiority to secrecy and spies are of very modern date—he knew that he had crossed the Channel, and accepted service in France: first, as a tempter and an eavesdropper among his own countrymen there: gradually, as a tempter and an eavesdropper among the natives. He knew that under the overthrown government he had been a spy upon Saint Antoine and Defarge's wine-shop; had received from the watchful police such heads of information concerning Doctor Manette's imprisonment, release, and history, as should serve him for an introduction to familiar conversation with the Defarges; and tried them on Madame Defarge, and had broken down with them signally. He always remembered with fear and trembling that that terrible woman had knitted when he talked with her, and had looked ominously at him as her fingers moved. He had since seen her, in the Section of Saint Antoine, over and over again produce her knitted registers, and denounce people whose lives the guillotine then surely swallowed up. He knew, as every one employed as he was did, that he was never safe; that flight was impossible; that he was tied fast under the shadow of the axe; and that in spite of his utmost tergiversation and treachery in furtherance of the reigning terror, a word might bring it down upon him. Once denounced, and on such grave grounds as had just now been suggested to his mind, he foresaw that the dreadful woman of whose unrelenting character he had seen many proofs, would produce against him that fatal register, and would quash his last chance of life. Besides that all secret men are men soon terrified, here were surely cards enough of one black suit to justify the holder in growing rather livid as he turned them over.

"You scarcely seem to like your hand," said Sydney, with the greatest composure. "Do you play?"

"I think, sir," said the spy, in the meanest manner, as he turned to Mr. Lorry, "I may appeal to a gentleman of your years and benevolence to put it to this other gentleman, so much your junior, whether he can under any circumstances reconcile it to his station to play that ace of which he has spoken. I admit that *I* am a spy, and that it is considered a discreditable station—though it must be filled by somebody; but this gentleman is no spy, and why should he so demean himself as to make himself one?"

"I play my ace, Mr. Barsad," said Carton, taking the answer on himself, and looking at his watch, "without any scruple, in a very few minutes."

"I should have hoped, gentlemen both," said the spy, always striving to hook Mr. Lorry into the discussion, "that your respect for my sister——"

"I could not better testify my respect for your sister than by finally relieving her of her brother," said Sydney Carton.

"You think not, sir?"

"I have thoroughly made up my mind about it."

The smooth manner of the spy, curiously in dissonance with his ostentatiously rough dress, and probably with his usual demeanour, received such a check from the inscrutability of Carton—who was a mystery to wiser and honester men than he—that it faltered here and failed him. While he was at a loss, Carton said, resuming his former air of contemplating cards:

"And indeed, now I think again, I have a strong impression that I have another good card here, not yet enumerated. That friend and fellow-sheep, who spoke of himself as pasturing in the country prisons; who was he?"

"French. You don't know him," said the spy, quickly.

"French, eh?" repeated Carton, musing, and not appearing to notice him at all, though he echoed the word. "Well; he may be."

"Is, I assure you," said the spy; "though it's not important."

"Though it's not important," repeated Carton in the same mechanical way—"though it's not important— No, it's not important. No. Yet I know the face."

"I think not. I am sure not. It can't be," said the spy.

"It—can't—be," muttered Sydney Carton, retrospectively, and filling his glass (which fortunately was a small one) again. "Can't—be. Spoke good French. Yet like a foreigner, I thought?"

"Provincial," said the spy.

"No. Foreign!" cried Carton, striking his open hand on the table, as a light broke clearly on his mind. "Cly! Disguised, but the same man. We had that man before us at the Old Bailey."

"Now, there you are hasty, sir," said Barsad, with a smile that gave his aquiline nose an extra inclination to one side; "there you really give me an advantage over you. Cly (who I will unreservedly admit, at this distance of time, was a partner of mine) has been dead several years. I attended him in his last illness. He was buried in London, at the church of Saint Pancras-in-the-Fields. His unpopularity with the blackguard multitude at the moment prevented my following his remains, but I helped to lay him in his coffin."

Here Mr. Lorry became aware, from where he sat, of a most remarkable goblin shadow on the wall. Tracing it to its source, he discovered it to be caused by a sudden extraordinary rising and stiffening of all the risen and stiff hair on Mr. Cruncher's head.

"Let us be reasonable," said the spy, "and let us be fair. To show you how mistaken you are, and what an unfounded assumption yours is, I will lay before you a certificate of Cly's burial, which I happen to have carried in my pocket-book," with a hurried hand he produced and opened it, "ever since. There it is. Oh, look at it, look at it! You may take it in your hand; it's no forgery."

Here Mr. Lorry perceived the reflection on the wall to elongate, and Mr. Cruncher rose and stepped forward. His hair could not have been more violently on end, if it had been that moment dressed by the cow with the crumpled horn in the house that Jack built.

Unseen by the spy, Mr. Cruncher stood at his side, and touched him on the shoulder like a ghostly bailiff.

"That there Roger Cly, master," said Mr. Cruncher, with a taciturn and iron-bound visage. "So *you* put him in his coffin?"

"I did."

"Who took him out of it?"

Barsad leaned back in his chair, and stammered, "What do you mean?"

"I mean," said Mr. Cruncher, "that he warn't never in it. No! Not he! I'll have my head took off, if he was ever in it."

The spy looked round at the two gentlemen; they both looked in unspeakable astonishment at Jerry.

"I tell you," said Jerry, "that you buried paving-stones and earth in that there coffin. Don't go and tell *me* that you buried Cly. It was a take-in. Me and two more knows it."

"How do you know it?"

"What's that to you? Ecod!" growled Mr. Cruncher, "it's you I have got a old grudge again, is it, with your shameful impositions upon tradesmen! I'd catch hold of your throat and choke you for half a guinea."

Sydney Carton, who, with Mr. Lorry, had been lost in amazement at this turn of the business, here requested Mr. Cruncher to moderate and explain himself.

"At another time, sir," he returned, evasively, "the present time is ill-conwenient for explainin'. What I stand to is, that he knows well wot that there Cly was never in that there coffin. Let him say he was, in so much as a word of one syllable, and I'll either catch hold of his throat and choke him for half a guinea"—Mr. Cruncher dwelt upon this as quite a liberal offer—"or I'll out and announce him."

"Humph! I see one thing," said Carton. "I hold another card, Mr. Barsad. Impossible, here in raging Paris, with Suspicion filling the air, for you to outlive denunciation, when you are in communication with another aristocratic spy of the same antecedents as yourself, who, moreover, has the mystery about him of having feigned death and come to life again! A plot in the prisons, of the foreigner against the Republic. A strong card—a certain Guillotine card! Do you play?"

"No!" returned the spy. "I throw up. I confess that we were so unpopular with the outrageous mob, that I only got away from England at the risk of being ducked to death, and that Cly was so ferreted up and down that he never would have got away at all but for that sham. Though how this man knows it was a sham is a wonder of wonders to me."

"Never you trouble your head about this man," retorted the contentious Mr. Cruncher; "you'll have trouble enough with giving your attention to that gentleman. And look here! Once more"—Mr. Cruncher could not be restrained from making rather an ostentatious parade of his liberality—"I'd catch hold of your throat and choke you for half a guinea."

The sheep of the prisons turned from him to Sydney Carton, and said, with more decision, "It has come to a point. I go on duty soon, and can't overstay my time. You told me you had a proposal; what is it? Now, it is of no use asking too much of me. Ask me to do anything in my office, putting my head in great extra danger, and I had better trust my life to the chances of a refusal than the chances of consent. In short, I should make that choice. You talk of desperation. We are all desperate here. Remember! I may denounce you if I think proper, and I can swear my way through stone walls, and so can others. Now, what do you want with me?"

"Not very much. You are a turnkey at the Conciergerie?"

"I tell you once for all, there is no such thing as an escape possible," said the spy, firmly.

"Why need you tell me what I have not asked? You are a turnkey at the Conciergerie?"

"I am sometimes."

"You can be when you choose?"

"I can pass in and out when I choose."

Sydney Carton filled another glass with brandy, poured it slowly out upon the hearth, and watched it as it dropped. It being all spent, he said, rising:

"So far, we have spoken before these two, because it was as well that the merits of the cards should not rest solely between you and me. Come into the dark room here, and let us have one final word alone."

* * * * * * * *

9 *The Game Made*

WHILE SYDNEY CARTON and the sheep of the prisons were in the adjoining dark room, speaking so low that not a sound was heard, Mr. Lorry looked at Jerry in considerable doubt and mistrust. That honest tradesman's manner of receiving the look did not inspire confidence; he changed the leg on which he rested, as often as if he had fifty of those limbs, and were trying them all; he examined his finger-nails with a very questionable closeness of attention; and whenever Mr. Lorry's eye caught his, he was taken with that peculiar kind of short cough requiring the hollow of a hand before it, which is seldom, if ever, known to be an infirmity attendant on perfect openness of character.

"Jerry," said Mr. Lorry. "Come here."

Mr. Cruncher came forward sideways, with one of his shoulders in advance of him.

"What have you been, besides a messenger?"

After some cogitation, accompanied with an intent look at his patron, Mr. Cruncher conceived the luminous idea of replying, "Agricultooral character."

"My mind misgives me much," said Mr. Lorry, angrily, shaking his forefinger at him, "that you have used the respectable and great house of Tellson's as a blind, and that you have had an unlawful occupation of an infamous description. If you have, don't expect me to befriend you when you get back to England. If you have, don't expect me to keep your secret. Tellson's shall not be imposed upon."

"I hope, sir," pleaded the abashed Mr. Cruncher, "that a gentleman like yourself wot I've had the honour of odd jobbing till I'm gray at it, would think twice about harming of me, even if it wos so—I don't say it is, but even if it wos. And which it is to be took into account that if it wos, it wouldn't, even then, be all o' one side. There'd be two sides to it. There might be medical doctors at the present hour, a picking up their guineas where a honest tradesman don't pick up his fardens—fardens! no, nor yet his half fardens—half fardens! no, nor yet his quarter—a banking away like smoke at Tellson's and a cocking their medical eyes at that tradesman on the sly, a going in and going out to their own carriages—ah! equally like smoke, if not more so. Well, that 'ud be imposing, too, on Tellson's. For you cannot sarse the goose and not the gander. And here's Mrs. Cruncher, or leastways wos in the Old England times, and would be to-morrow, if cause given, a floppin' again the business to that degree as is ruinating—stark ruinating! Whereas them medical doctors' wives don't flop—catch 'em at it! Or, if they flop, their floppings goes in favour of more patients, and how can you rightly have one without t'other? Then, wot with undertakers, and wot with parish clerks, and wot with sextons, and wot with private watchmen (all awaricious and all in it), a man wouldn't get much by it, even if it wos so. And wot little a man did get, would never prosper with him, Mr. Lorry. He'd never have no good of it; he'd want all along to be out of the line, if he could see his way out, being once in—even if it wos so."

"Ugh!" cried Mr. Lorry, rather relenting, nevertheless. "I am shocked at the sight of you."

"Now, what I would humbly offer to you, sir," pursued Mr. Cruncher, "even if it wos so, which I don't say it is—"

"Don't prevaricate," said Mr. Lorry.

"No, I will *not*, sir," returned Mr. Cruncher, as if nothing were further from his thought or practice—"which I don't say it is—wot I would humbly offer to you, sir, would be this. Upon that there stool, at that there bar, sets that there boy of mine, brought up and growed up to be a man, wot will errand you, message you, general-light-job you, till your heels is where your head is, if such should be your wishes. If it wos so, which I still don't say it is (for I will not prewaricate to you, sir), let that there boy keep his father's place, and take care of his mother; don't blow upon that boy's father—do not do it, sir—and let that father go into the line of the reg'lar diggin', and make amends for what he would have un-dug—if it wos so—by diggin' of 'em in with a will, and with conwictions respectin' the futur' keepin' of 'em safe. That, Mr. Lorry," said Mr. Cruncher, wiping his forehead with his arm, as an announcement that he had arrived at the peroration of his discourse, "is wot I would respectfully offer to you, sir. A man don't see all this here goin' on dreadful round him, in the way of subjects without heads, dear me, plentiful enough fur to bring the price down to porterage and hardly that, without havin' his serious thoughts of things. And these here would be mine, if it wos so, entreatin' of you fur to bear in mind that wot I said just now, I up and said in the good cause when I might have kep' it back."

"That at least is true," said Mr. Lorry. "Say no more now. It may be that I shall yet stand your friend, if you deserve it, and repent in action—not in words. I want no more words."

Mr. Cruncher knuckled his forehead, as Sydney Carton and the spy returned from the dark room. "Adieu, Mr. Barsad," said the former; "our arrangement thus made, you have nothing to fear from me."

He sat down in a chair on the hearth, over against Mr. Lorry. When they were alone, Mr. Lorry asked him what he had done?

"Not much. If it should go ill with the prisoner, I have ensured access to him, once."

Mr. Lorry's countenance fell.

"It is all I could do," said Carton. "To propose too much would be to put this man's head under the axe, and, as he himself said, nothing worse could happen to him if he were denounced. It was obviously the weakness of the position. There is no help for it."

"But access to him," said Mr. Lorry, "if it should go ill before the Tribunal, will not save him."

"I never said it would."

Mr. Lorry's eyes gradually sought the fire; his sympathy with his darling, and the heavy disappointment of this second arrest, gradually weakened them; he was an old man now, overborne with anxiety of late, and his tears fell.

"You are a good man and a true friend," said Carton, in an altered voice. "Forgive me if I notice that you are affected. I could not see my father weep, and sit by, careless. And I could not respect your sorrow more, if you were my father. You are free from that misfortune, however."

Though he said the last words, with a slip into his usual manner, there was a true feeling and respect both in his tone and in his touch, that Mr. Lorry, who had never seen the better side of him, was wholly unprepared for. He gave him his hand, and Carton gently pressed it.

"To return to poor Darnay," said Carton. "Don't tell *her* of this interview, or this arrangement. It would not enable *her* to go to see him. She might think it was contrived, in case of the worst, to convey to him the means of anticipating the sentence."

Mr. Lorry had not thought of that, and he looked quickly at Carton to see if it were in his mind. It seemed to be; he returned the look, and evidently understood it.

"She might think a thousand things," Carton said, "and any of them would only add to her trouble. Don't speak of me to her. As I said to you when I first came, I had better not see her. I can put my hand out, to do any little helpful work for her that my hand can find to do, without that. You are going to her, I hope? She must be very desolate to-night."

"I am going now, directly."

"I am glad of that. She has such a strong attachment to you and reliance on you. How does she look?"

"Anxious and unhappy, but very beautiful."

"Ah!"

It was a long, grieving sound, like a sigh—almost like a sob. It attracted Mr. Lorry's eyes to Carton's face, which was turned to the fire. A light, or a shade (the old gentleman could not have said which), passed from it as swiftly as a change would sweep over a hillside on a wild bright day, and he lifted his foot to put back one of the little flaming logs, which was tumbling forward. He wore the white

riding-coat and top-boots then in vogue, and the light of the
fire touching their light surfaces made him look very pale,
with his long brown hair, all untrimmed, hanging loose
about him. His indifference to fire was sufficiently remarkable to elicit a word of remonstrance from Mr. Lorry; his
boot was still upon the hot embers of the flaming log, when
it had broken under the weight of his foot.

"I forgot it," he said.

Mr. Lorry's eyes were again attracted to his face. Taking
note of the wasted air which clouded the naturally handsome features, and having the expression of prisoners'
faces fresh in his mind, he was strongly reminded of that
expression.

"And your duties here have drawn to an end, sir?" said
Carton, turning to him.

"Yes. As I was telling you last night when Lucie came in
so unexpectedly, I have at length done all that I can do
here. I hoped to have left them in perfect safety, and then
to have quitted Paris. I have my Leave to Pass. I was
ready to go."

They were both silent.

"Yours is a long life to look back upon, sir?" said Carton, wistfully.

"I am in my seventy-eighth year."

"You have been useful all your life; steadily and constantly occupied; trusted, respected, and looked up to?"

"I have been a man of business, ever since I have been a
man. Indeed, I may say that I was a man of business when
a boy."

"See what a place you fill at seventy-eight. How many
people will miss you when you leave it empty!"

"A solitary old bachelor," answered Mr. Lorry, shaking
his head. "There is nobody to weep for me."

"How can you say that? Wouldn't *she* weep for you?
Wouldn't her child?"

"Yes, yes, thank God. I didn't quite mean what I said."

"It *is* a thing to thank God for; is it not?"

"Surely, surely."

"If you could say, with truth, to your own solitary heart,
to-night, 'I have secured to myself the love and attachment, the gratitude or respect, of no human creature; I
have won myself a tender place in no regard; I have done
nothing good or serviceable to be remembered by'; your

seventy-eight years would be seventy-eight heavy curses; would they not?"

"You say truly, Mr. Carton; I think they would be."

Sydney turned his eyes again upon the fire, and, after a silence of a few moments, said:

"I should like to ask you: Does your childhood seem far off? Do the days when you sat at your mother's knee seem days of very long ago?"

Responding to his softened manner, Mr. Lorry answered:

"Twenty years back, yes; at this time of my life, no. For, as I draw closer and closer to the end, I travel in the circle, nearer and nearer to the beginning. It seems to be one of the kind smoothings and preparings of the way. My heart is touched now, by many remembrances that had long fallen asleep, of my pretty young mother (and I so old!), and by many associations of the days when what we call the World was not so real with me, and my faults were not confirmed in me."

"I understand the feeling!" exclaimed Carton, with a bright flush. "And you are the better for it?"

"I hope so."

Carton terminated the conversation here, by rising to help him on with his outer coat. "But you," said Mr. Lorry, reverting to the theme, "you are young."

"Yes," said Carton. "I am not old, but my young way was never the way to age. Enough of me."

"And of me, I am sure," said Mr. Lorry. "Are you going out?"

"I'll walk with you to her gate. You know my vagabond and restless habits. If I should prowl about the streets a long time, don't be uneasy; I shall reappear in the morning. You go to the Court to-morrow?"

"Yes, unhappily."

"I shall be there, but only as one of the crowd. My spy will find a place for me. Take my arm, sir."

Mr. Lorry did so, and they went downstairs and out in the streets. A few minutes brought them to Mr. Lorry's destination. Carton left him there; but lingered at a little distance, and turned back to the gate again when it was shut, and touched it. He had heard of her going to the prison every day. "She came out here," he said, looking about him, "turned this way, must have trod on these stones often. Let me follow in her steps."

It was ten o'clock at night when he stood before the prison of La Force, where she had stood hundreds of times. A little wood-sawyer, having closed his shop, was smoking his pipe at his shop-door.

"Good night, citizen," said Sydney Carton, pausing in going by; for the man eyed him inquisitively.

"Good night, citizen."

"How goes the Republic?"

"You mean the Guillotine. Not ill. Sixty-three to-day. We shall mount to a hundred soon. Samson and his men complain sometimes, of being exhausted. Ha, ha, ha! He is so droll, that Samson. Such a barber!"

"Do you often go to see him——"

"Shave? Always. Every day. What a barber! You have seen him at work?"

"Never."

"Go and see him when he has a good batch. Figure this to yourself, citizen; he shaved the sixty-three to-day, in less than two pipes! Less than two pipes. Word of honour!"

As the grinning little man held out the pipe he was smoking, to explain how he timed the executioner, Carton was so sensible of a rising desire to strike the life out of him, that he turned away.

"But you are not English," said the wood-sawyer, "though you wear English dress?"

"Yes," said Carton, pausing again, and answering over his shoulder.

"You speak like a Frenchman."

"I am an old student here."

"Aha, a perfect Frenchman! Good night, Englishman."

"Good night, citizen."

"But go and see that droll dog," the little man persisted, calling after him. "And take a pipe with you!"

Sydney had not gone far out of sight, when he stopped in the middle of the street under a glimmering lamp, and wrote with his pencil on a scrap of paper. Then, traversing, with the decided step of one who remembered the way well, several dark and dirty streets—much dirtier than usual, for the best public thoroughfares remained uncleansed in those times of terror—he stopped at a chemist's shop, which the owner was closing with his own hands. A small, dim, crooked shop, kept in a tortuous, up-hill thoroughfare, by a small, dim, crooked man.

Giving this citizen, too, good night, as he confronted

him at his counter, he laid the scrap of paper before him. "Whew!" the chemist whistled softly, as he read it. "Hi! hi! hi!"

Sydney Carton took no heed, and the chemist said:

"For you, citizen?"

"For me."

"You will be careful to keep them separate, citizen? You know the consequences of mixing them?"

"Perfectly."

Certain small packets were made and given to him. He put them, one by one, in the breast of his inner coat, counted out the money for them, and deliberately left the shop. "There is nothing more to do," said he, glancing upward at the moon, "until to-morrow. I can't sleep."

It was not a reckless manner, the manner in which he said these words aloud under the fast-sailing clouds, nor was it more expressive of negligence than defiance. It was the settled manner of a tired man, who had wandered and struggled and got lost, but who at length struck into his road and saw its end.

Long ago, when he had been famous among his earliest competitors as a youth of great promise, he had followed his father to the grave. His mother had died, years before. These solemn words, which had been read at his father's grave, arose in his mind as he went down the dark streets, among the heavy shadows, with the moon and the clouds sailing on high above him. "I am the resurrection and the life, saith the Lord: he that believeth in me, though he were dead, yet shall he live: and whosoever liveth and believeth in me, shall never die."

In a city dominated by the axe, alone at night, with natural sorrow rising in him for the sixty-three who had been that day put to death, and for to-morrow's victims then awaiting their doom in the prisons, and still of to-morrow's and to-morrow's, the chain of association that brought the words home, like a rusty old ship's anchor from the deep, might have been easily found. He did not seek it, but repeated them and went on.

With a solemn interest in the lighted windows where the people were going to rest, forgetful through a few calm hours of the horrors surrounding them; in the towers of the churches, where no prayers were said, for the popular revulsion had even travelled that length of self-destruction from years of priestly impostors, plunderers, and profligates; in the distant burial-places, reserved, as they wrote upon the gates, for Eternal Sleep; in the abounding gaols; and in the streets along which the sixties rolled to a death which had become so common and material, that no sorrowful story of a haunting Spirit ever arose among the people out of all the working of the Guillotine; with a solemn interest in the whole life and death of the city settling down to its short nightly pause in fury; Sydney Carton crossed the Seine again for the lighted streets.

Few coaches were abroad, for riders in coaches were liable to be suspected, and gentility hid its head in red nightcaps, and put on heavy shoes, and trudged. But, the theatres were all well filled, and the people poured cheerfully out as he passed, and went chatting home. At one of the theatre doors, there was a little girl with a mother, looking for a way across the street through the mud. He carried the child over, and before the timid arm was loosed from his neck asked her for a kiss.

"I am the resurrection and the life, saith the Lord: he that believeth in me, though he were dead, yet shall he live: and whosoever liveth and believeth in me, shall never die."

Now that the streets were quiet, and the night wore on, the words were in the echoes of his feet, and were in the air. Perfectly calm and steady, he sometimes repeated them to himself as he walked; but he heard them always.

The night wore out, and, as he stood upon the bridge listening to the water as it splashed the river-walls of the Island of Paris, where the picturesque confusion of houses and cathedral shone bright in the light of the moon, the day came coldly, looking like a dead face out of the sky. Then, the night, with the moon and the stars, turned pale and died, and for a little while it seemed as if Creation were delivered over to Death's dominion.

But the glorious sun, rising, seemed to strike those words, that burden of the night, straight and warm to his heart in its long bright rays. And looking along them, with reverently shaded eyes, a bridge of light appeared to span the air between him and the sun, while the river sparkled under it.

The strong tide, so swift, so deep, and certain, was like a congenial friend in the morning stillness. He walked by the stream, far from the houses, and in the light and warmth of the sun fell asleep on the bank. When he awoke and was afoot again, he lingered there yet a little longer, watching an eddy that turned and turned purposeless, until the stream absorbed it, and carried it on to the sea.—"Like me!"

A trading-boat, with a sail of the softened colour of a dead leaf, then glided into his view, floated by him, and died away. As its silent track in the water disappeared, the prayer that had broken up out of his heart for a merciful consideration of all his poor blindness and errors, ended in the words, "I am the resurrection and the life."

Mr. Lorry was already out when he got back, and it was easy to surmise where the good old man was gone. Sydney Carton drank nothing but a little coffee, ate some bread, and, having washed and changed to refresh himself, went out to the place of trial.

The court was all astir and a-buzz, when the black sheep —whom many fell away from in dread—pressed him into an obscure corner among the crowd. Mr. Lorry was there, and Doctor Manette was there. She was there, sitting beside her father.

When her husband was brought in, she turned a look upon him, so sustaining, so encouraging, so full of admiring love and pitying tenderness, yet so courageous for his sake, that it called the healthy blood into his face, brightened his glance, and animated his heart. If there had been any eyes to notice the influence of her look on Sydney Carton, it would have been seen to be the same influence exactly.

Before that unjust Tribunal, there was little or no order of procedure, ensuring to any accused person any reasonable hearing. There could have been no such Revolution, if all laws, forms, and ceremonies had not first been so monstrously abused that the suicidal vengeance of the Revolution was to scatter them all to the winds.

Every eye was turned to the jury. The same determined patriots and good republicans as yesterday and the day before, and to-morrow and the day after. Eager and prominent among them, one man with a craving face, and his fingers perpetually hovering about his lips, whose appearance gave great satisfaction to the spectators. A life-thirsting, cannibal-looking, bloody-minded juryman, the Jacques Three of Saint Antoine. The whole jury, as a jury of dogs empanelled to try the deer.

Every eye then turned to the five judges and the public prosecutor. No favourable leaning in that quarter to-day. A fell, uncompromising, murderous business-meaning there. Every eye then sought some other eye in the crowd, and gleamed at it approvingly; and heads nodded at one another, before bending forward with a strained attention.

Charles Evrémonde, called Darnay. Released yesterday. Re-accused and retaken yesterday. Indictment delivered to him last night. Suspected and denounced enemy of the Republic, aristocrat, one of a family of tyrants, one of a race proscribed, for that they had used their abolished privileges to the infamous oppression of the people. Charles Evrémonde, called Darnay, in right of such proscription absolutely dead in law.

To this effect, in as few or fewer words, the public prosecutor.

The President asked, was the accused openly denounced or secretly?

"Openly, President."

"By whom?"

"Three voices. Ernest Defarge, wine-vendor of Saint Antoine."

"Good."

"Thérèse Defarge, his wife."

"Good."

"Alexandre Manette, physician."

A great uproar took place in the court, and in the midst of it, Doctor Manette was seen, pale and trembling, standing where he had been seated.

"President, I indignantly protest to you that this is a forgery and a fraud. You know the accused to be the husband of my daughter. My daughter, and those dear to her, are far dearer to me than my life. Who and where is the false conspirator who says that I denounce the husband of my child!"

"Citizen Manette, be tranquil. To fail in submission to the authority of the Tribunal would be to put yourself out of law. As to what is dearer to you than life, nothing can be so dear to a good citizen as the Republic."

Loud acclamations hailed this rebuke. The President rang his bell, and with warmth resumed.

"If the Republic should demand of you the sacrifice of your child herself, you would have no duty but to sacrifice her. Listen to what is to follow. In the meanwhile, be silent!"

Frantic acclamations were again raised. Doctor Manette sat down, with his eyes looking around, and his lips trembling; his daughter drew closer to him. The craving man on the jury rubbed his hands together, and restored the usual hand to his mouth.

Defarge was produced, when the court was quiet enough to admit of his being heard, and rapidly expounded the story of the imprisonment, and of his having been a mere boy in the Doctor's service, and of the release, and of the state of the prisoner when released and delivered to him. This short examination followed, for the court was quick with its work.

"You did good service at the taking of the Bastille, citizen?"

"I believe so."

Here, an excited woman screeched from the crowd: "You were one of the best patriots there. Why not say so? You were a cannonier that day there, and you were among the first to enter the accursed fortress when it fell. Patriots, I speak the truth!"

It was The Vengeance who, amidst the warm commendations of the audience, thus assisted the proceedings. The President rang his bell; but The Vengeance, warming with encouragement, shrieked, "I defy that bell!" wherein she was likewise much commended.

"Inform the Tribunal of what you did that day within the Bastille, citizen."

"I knew," said Defarge, looking down at his wife, who stood at the bottom of the steps on which he was raised, looking steadily up at him; "I knew that this prisoner, of whom I speak, had been confined in a cell known as One Hundred and Five, North Tower. I knew it from himself. He knew himself by no other name than One Hundred and Five, North Tower, when he made shoes under my care. As I serve my gun that day, I resolve, when the place shall fall, to examine that cell. It falls. I mount to the cell, with a fellow-citizen who is one of the jury, directed by a gaoler. I examine it, very closely. In a hole in the chimney, where a stone has been worked out and replaced, I find a written paper. This is that written paper. I have made it my business to examine some specimens of the writing of Doctor Manette. This is the writing of Doctor Manette. I confide this paper, in the writing of Doctor Manette, to the hands of the President."

"Let it be read."

In a dead silence and stillness—the prisoner under trial

looked lovingly at his wife, his wife only looking from him to look with solicitude at her father, Doctor Manette keeping his eyes fixed on the reader, Madame Defarge never taking hers from the prisoner, Defarge never taking his from his feasting wife, and all the other eyes there intent upon the Doctor, who saw none of them—the paper was read, as follows.

*   *   *   *   *   *   *   *

10 *The Substance of the Shadow*

"I, ALEXANDRE MANETTE, unfortunate physician, native of Beauvais, and afterwards resident in Paris, write this melancholy paper in my doleful cell in the Bastille, during the last month of the year 1767. I write it at stolen intervals, under every difficulty. I design to secrete it in the wall of the chimney, where I have slowly and laboriously made a place of concealment for it. Some pitying hand may find it there, when I and my sorrows are dust.

"These words are formed by the rusty iron point with which I write with difficulty in scrapings of soot and charcoal from the chimney, mixed with blood, in the last month of the tenth year of my captivity. Hope has quite departed from my breast. I know from terrible warnings I have noted in myself that my reason will not long remain unimpaired, but I solemnly declare that I am at this time in the possession of my right mind—that my memory is exact and circumstantial—and that I write the truth as I shall answer for these my last recorded words, whether they be ever read by men or not, at the Eternal Judgment-seat.

"One cloudy moonlight night, in the third week of December (I think the twenty-second of the month) in the year 1757, I was walking on a retired part of the quay by the Seine for the refreshment of the frosty air, at an hour's distance from my place of residence in the Street of the School of Medicine, when a carriage came along behind me, driven very fast. As I stood aside to let that carriage pass, apprehensive that it might otherwise run me down, a head was put out at the window, and a voice called to the driver to stop.

"The carriage stopped as soon as the driver could rein in his horse, and the same voice called to me by my name. I answered. The carriage was then so far in advance of me that the two gentlemen had time to open the door and alight before I came up with it. I observed that they were both wrapped in cloaks, and appeared to conceal themselves. As they stood side by side near the carriage door, I also observed that they both looked of about my own age, or rather younger, and that they were greatly alike, in stature, manner, voice, and (as far as I could see) face too.

" 'You are Doctor Manette?' said one.

" 'I am.'

" 'Doctor Manette, formerly of Beauvais,' said the other; 'the young physician, originally an expert surgeon, who within the last year or two has made a rising reputation in Paris?'

" 'Gentlemen,' I returned, 'I am that Doctor Manette of whom you speak so graciously.'

" 'We have been to your residence,' said the first, 'and not being so fortunate as to find you there, and being informed that you were probably walking in this direction, we followed, in the hope of overtaking you. Will you please to enter the carriage?'

"The manner of both was imperious, and they both moved, as these words were spoken, so as to place me between themselves and the carriage door. They were armed. I was not.

" 'Gentlemen,' said I, 'pardon me; but I usually inquire who does me the honour to seek my assistance, and what is the nature of the case to which I am summoned.'

"The reply to this was made by him who had spoken second. 'Doctor, your clients are people of condition. As to the nature of the case, our confidence in your skill assures us that you will ascertain it for yourself better than we can describe it. Enough. Will you please to enter the carriage?'

"I could do nothing but comply, and I entered it in silence. They both entered after me—the last springing in, after putting up the steps. The carriage turned about, and drove on at its former speed.

"I repeat this conversation exactly as it occurred. I have no doubt that it is, word for word, the same. I describe everything exactly as it took place, constraining my mind not to wander from the task. Where I make the broken marks that follow here, I leave off for the time, and put my paper in its hiding-place. . . .

"The carriage left the streets behind, passed the North Barrier, and emerged upon the country road. At two-thirds of a league from the Barrier—I did not estimate the distance at that time, but afterwards when I traversed it—it struck out of the main avenue, and presently stopped at a solitary house. We all three alighted, and walked, by a damp soft footpath in a garden where a neglected fountain had overflowed, to the door of the house. It was not opened immediately, in answer to the ringing of the bell, and one of my two conductors struck the man who opened it, with his heavy riding-glove, across the face.

"There was nothing in this action to attract my particular attention, for I had seen common people struck more commonly than dogs. But, the other of the two, being angry likewise, struck the man in like manner with his arm; the look and bearing of the brothers were then so exactly alike, that I then first perceived them to be twin brothers.

"From the time of our alighting at the outer gate (which we found locked, and which one of the brothers had opened to admit us, and had relocked), I had heard cries proceeding from an upper chamber. I was conducted to this chamber straight, the cries growing louder as we ascended the stairs, and I found a patient in a high fever of the brain, lying on a bed.

"The patient was a woman of great beauty, and young; assuredly not much past twenty. Her hair was torn and ragged, and her arms were bound to her sides with sashes and handkerchiefs. I noticed that these bonds were all portions of a gentleman's dress. On one of them, which was a fringed scarf for a dress of ceremony, I saw the armorial bearings of a noble, and the letter *E*.

"I saw this, within the first minute of my contemplation of the patient; for, in her restless strivings she had turned over on her face on the edge of the bed, had drawn the end of the scarf into her mouth, and was in danger of suffocation. My first act was to put out my hand to relieve her breathing; and in moving the scarf aside, the embroidery in the corner caught my sight.

"I turned her gently over, placed my hands upon her breast to calm her and keep her down, and looked into her face. Her eyes were dilated and wild, and she constantly uttered piercing shrieks, and repeated the words, 'My husband, my father, and my brother!' and then counted up to twelve, and said, 'Hush!' For an instant, and no more, she would pause to listen, and then the piercing shrieks would begin again, and she would repeat the cry, 'My husband, my father, and my brother!' and would count up to twelve, and say 'Hush!' There was no variation in the order, or the manner. There was no cessation, but the regular moment's pause, in the utterance of these sounds.

" 'How long,' I asked, 'has this lasted?'

"To distinguish the brothers, I will call them the elder and the younger; by the elder, I mean him who exercised the most authority. It was the elder who replied, 'Since about this hour last night.'

" 'She has a husband, a father, and a brother?'

" 'A brother.'

" 'I do not address her brother?'

"He answered with great contempt, 'No.'

" 'She has some recent association with the number twelve?'

"The younger brother impatiently rejoined, 'With twelve o'clock.'

" 'See, gentlemen,' said I, still keeping my hands upon her breast, 'how useless I am, as you have brought me! If I had known what I was coming to see, I could have come provided. As it is, time must be lost. There are no medicines to be obtained in this lonely place.'

"The elder brother looked to the younger, who said haughtily, 'There is a case of medicines here'; and brought it from a closet, and put it on the table. . . .

"I opened some of the bottles, smelt them, and put the stoppers to my lips. If I had wanted to use anything save narcotic medicines that were poisons in themselves, I would not have administered any of those.

" 'Do you doubt them?' asked the younger brother.

" 'You see, monsieur, I am going to use them,' I replied, and said no more.

"I made the patient swallow, with great difficulty, and after many efforts, the dose that I desired to give. As I intended to repeat it after a while, and as it was necessary to watch its influence, I then sat down by the side of the bed. There was a timid and suppressed woman in attendance (wife of the man downstairs), who had retreated into a corner. The house was damp and decayed, indifferently furnished—evidently, recently occupied and temporarily used. Some thick old hangings had been nailed up before the windows, to deaden the sound of the shrieks. They continued to be uttered in their regular succession, with the cry, 'My husband, my father, and my brother!' the counting up to twelve, and 'Hush!' The frenzy was so violent, that I had not unfastened the bandages restraining the arms, but, I had looked to them, to see that they were not painful. The only spark of encouragement in the case was, that my hand upon the sufferer's breast had this much soothing influence, that for minutes at a time it tranquillised the figure. It had no effect upon the cries: no pendulum could be more regular.

"For the reason that my hand had this effect (I assume), I had sat by the side of the bed for half an hour, with the two brothers looking on, before the elder said:

" 'There is another patient.'

"I was startled and asked, 'Is it a pressing case?'

" 'You had better see,' he carelessly answered; and took up a light. . . .

"The other patient lay in a back room across a second staircase, which was a species of loft over a stable. There was a low plastered ceiling to a part of it; the rest was open, to the ridge of the tiled roof, and there were beams across. Hay and straw were stored in that portion of the place, fagots for firing, and a heap of apples in sand. I had to pass through that part, to get at the other. My memory is circumstantial and unshaken. I try it with these details, and I see them all, in this my cell in the Bastille, near the close of the tenth year of my captivity, as I saw them all that night.

"On some hay on the ground, with a cushion thrown under his head, lay a handsome peasant boy—a boy of not more than seventeen at the most. He lay on his back, with his teeth set, his right hand clenched on his breast, and his glaring eyes looking straight upward. I could not see where his wound was, as I kneeled on one knee over him; but, I could see that he was dying of a wound from a sharp point.

" 'I am a doctor, my poor fellow,' said I. 'Let me examine it.'

" 'I do not want it examined,' he answered; 'let it be.'

"It was under his hand, and I soothed him to let me move his hand away. The wound was a sword-thrust, received from twenty to twenty-four hours before, but no skill could have saved him if it had been looked to without delay. He was then dying fast. As I turned my eyes to the elder brother, I saw him looking down at this handsome boy whose life was ebbing out, as if he were a wounded bird, or hare, or rabbit; not at all as if he were a fellow-creature.

" 'How has this been done, monsieur?' said I.

" 'A crazed young common dog! A serf! Forced my brother to draw upon him, and has fallen by my brother's sword—like a gentleman.'

"There was no touch of pity, sorrow, or kindred humanity in this answer. The speaker seemed to acknowledge that it was inconvenient to have that different order of creature dying there, and that it would have been better if he had died in the usual obscure routine of his vermin kind. He was quite incapable of any compassionate feeling about the boy, or about his fate.

"The boy's eyes had slowly moved to him as he had spoken, and they now slowly moved to me.

" 'Doctor, they are very proud, these nobles; but we common dogs are proud too, sometimes. They plunder us, outrage us, beat us, kill us; but we have a little pride left, sometimes. She—have you seen her, Doctor?'

"The shrieks and the cries were audible there, though subdued by the distance. He referred to them, as if she were lying in our presence.

"I said, 'I have seen her.'

" 'She is my sister, Doctor. They have had their shameful rights, these nobles, in the modesty and virtue of our sisters, many years, but we have had good girls among us. I know it, and have heard my father say so. She was a good girl. She was betrothed to a good young man, too; a tenant of his. We were all tenants of his—that man's who stands there. The other is his brother, the worst of a bad race.'

"It was with the greatest difficulty that the boy gathered bodily force to speak; but, his spirit spoke with a dreadful emphasis.

" 'We were so robbed by that man who stands there, as all we common dogs are by those superior beings—taxed by him without mercy, obliged to work for him without pay, obliged to grind our corn at his mill, obliged to feed scores of his tame birds on our wretched crops, and forbidden for our lives to keep a single tame bird of our own, pillaged and plundered to that degree that when we chanced to have a bit of meat, we ate it in fear, with the door barred and the shutters closed, that his people should not see it and take it from us—I say, we were so robbed, and hunted, and were made so poor, that our father told us it was a dreadful thing to bring a child into the world, and that what we should most pray for was that our women might be barren and our miserable race die out!'

"I had never before seen the sense of being oppressed, bursting forth like a fire. I had supposed that it must be latent in the people somewhere; but, I had never seen it break out, until I saw it in the dying boy.

" 'Nevertheless, Doctor, my sister married. He was ailing at that time, poor fellow, and she married her lover, that she might tend and comfort him in our cottage—our dog-hut, as that man would call it. She had not been married many weeks, when that man's brother saw her and admired her, and asked that man to lend her to him—for what are husbands among us! He was willing enough, but my sister was good and virtuous, and hated his brother with a hatred as strong as mine. What did the two then, to persuade her husband to use his influence with her, to make her willing?'

"The boy's eyes, which had been fixed on mine, slowly turned to the looker-on, and I saw in the two faces that all he said was true. The two opposing kinds of pride confronting one another, I can see, even in this Bastille; the gentleman's all negligent indifference; the peasant's, all trodden-down sentiment, and passionate revenge.

" 'You know, Doctor, that it is among the rights of these nobles to harness us common dogs to carts, and drive us. They so harnessed him and drove him. You know that it is among their rights to keep us in their grounds all night, quieting the frogs, in order that their noble sleep may not be disturbed. They kept him out in the unwholesome mists at night, and ordered him back into his harness in the day. But he was not persuaded. No! Taken out of harness one day at noon, to feed—if he could find food—he sobbed twelve times, once for every stroke of the bell, and died on her bosom.'

"Nothing human could have held life in the boy but his determination to tell all his wrong. He forced back the gathering shadows of death, as he forced his clenched right hand to remain clenched, and to cover his wound.

" 'Then, with that man's permission and even with his aid, his brother took her away; in spite of what I know she must have told his brother—and what that is, will not be long unknown to you, Doctor, if it is now—his brother took her away—for his pleasure and diversion, for a little while. I saw her pass me on the road. When I took the tidings home, our father's heart burst; he never spoke one of the words that filled it. I took my young sister (for I have another) to a place beyond the reach of this man, and where, at least, she will never be *his* vassal. Then, I tracked the brother here, and last night climbed in—a common dog, but sword in hand.—Where is the loft window? It was somewhere here?'

"The room was darkening to his sight; the world was narrowing around him. I glanced about me, and saw that the hay and straw were trampled over the floor, as if there had been a struggle.

" 'She heard me, and ran in. I told her not to come near us till he was dead. He came in and first tossed me some pieces of money; then struck at me with a whip. But I, though a common dog, so struck at him as to make him draw. Let him break into as many pieces as he will the sword that he stained with my common blood; he drew to defend himself—thrust at me with all his skill for his life.'

"My glance had fallen, but a few moments before, on the fragments of a broken sword, lying among the hay. That weapon was a gentleman's. In another place lay an old sword that seemed to have been a soldier's.

" 'Now, lift me up, Doctor; lift me up. Where is he?'

" 'He is not here,' I said, supporting the boy, and thinking that he referred to the brother.

" 'He! Proud as these nobles are, he is afraid to see me. Where is the man who was here? Turn my face to him.'

"I did so, raising the boy's head against my knee. But, invested for the moment with extraordinary power, he raised himself completely: obliging me to rise too, or I could not have still supported him.

" 'Marquis,' said the boy, turned to him with his eyes opened wide, and his right hand raised, 'in the days when all these things are to be answered for, I summon you and yours, to the last of your bad race, to answer for them. I mark this cross of blood upon you, as a sign that I do it. In the days when all these things are to be answered for, I summon your brother, the worst of the bad race, to answer for them separately. I mark this cross of blood upon him, as a sign that I do it.'

"Twice, he put his hand to the wound in his breast, and with his forefinger drew a cross in the air. He stood for an instant with the finger yet raised, and, as it dropped, he dropped with it, and I laid him down dead. . . .

"When I returned to the bedside of the young woman, I found her raving in precisely the same order and continuity. I knew that this might last for many hours, and that it would probably end in the silence of the grave.

"I repeated the medicines I had given her, and I sat at the side of the bed until the night was far advanced. She never abated the piercing quality of her shrieks, never stumbled in the distinctness or the order of her words. They were always 'My husband, my father, and my brother! One, two, three, four, five, six, seven, eight, nine, ten, eleven, twelve. Hush!'

"This lasted twenty-six hours from the time when I first saw her. I had come and gone twice, and was again sitting by her, when she began to falter. I did what little could be done to assist that opportunity, and by and by she sank into a lethargy, and lay like the dead.

"It was as if the wind and rain had lulled at last, after a long and fearful storm. I released her arms, and called the woman to assist me to compose her figure and the dress she had torn. It was then that I knew her condition to be that of one in whom the first expectations of being a mother have arisen; and it was then that I lost the little hope I had had of her.

" 'Is she dead?' asked the Marquis, whom I will still describe as the elder brother, coming booted into the room from his horse.

" 'Not dead,' said I; 'but like to die.'

" 'What strength there is in these common bodies!' he said, looking down at her with some curiosity.

" 'There is prodigious strength,' I answered him, 'in sorrow and despair.'

"He first laughed at my words, and then frowned at them. He moved a chair with his foot near to mine, ordered the woman away, and said in a subdued voice:

" 'Doctor, finding my brother in this difficulty with these hinds, I recommended that your aid should be invited. Your reputation is high, and, as a young man with your fortune to make, you are probably mindful of your interest. The things that you see here are things to be seen, and not spoken of.'

"I listened to the patient's breathing, and avoided answering.

" 'Do you honour me with your attention, Doctor?'

" 'Monsieur,' said I, 'in my profession, the communications of patients are always received in confidence.' I was guarded in my answer, for I was troubled in my mind with what I had heard and seen.

"Her breathing was so difficult to trace, that I carefully tried the pulse and the heart. There was life, and no more. Looking round as I resumed my seat, I found both the brothers intent upon me. . . .

"I write so with much difficulty, the cold is so severe, I am so fearful of being detected and consigned to an underground cell and total darkness, that I must abridge this narrative. There is no confusion or failure in my memory; it can recall, and could detail, every word that was ever spoken between me and those brothers.

"She lingered for a week. Towards the last, I could understand some few syllables that she said to me, by placing my ear close to her lips. She asked me where she was, and I told her; who I was, and I told her. It was in vain that I asked her for her family name. She faintly shook her head upon the pillow, and kept her secret, as the boy had done.

"I had no opportunity of asking her any question, until I had told the brothers she was sinking fast, and could not live another day. Until then, though no one was ever presented to her consciousness save the woman and myself, one or other of them had always jealously sat behind the curtain at the head of the bed when I was there. But when it came to that, they seemed careless what communication I might hold with her; as if—the thought passed through my mind—I were dying too.

"I always observed that their pride bitterly resented the younger brother's (as I call him) having crossed swords with a peasant, and that peasant a boy. The only consideration that appeared to affect the mind of either of them was the consideration that this was highly degrading to the family, and was ridiculous. As often as I caught the younger brother's eyes, their expression reminded me that he disliked me deeply, for knowing what I knew from the boy. He was smoother and more polite to me than the elder; but I saw this. I also saw that I was an incumbrance in the mind of the elder, too.

"My patient died, two hours before midnight—at a time,

by my watch, answering almost to the minute when I had first seen her. I was alone with her, when her forlorn young head drooped gently on one side, and all her earthly wrongs and sorrows ended.

"The brothers were waiting in a room downstairs, impatient to ride away. I had heard them, alone at the bedside, striking their boots with their riding-whips, and loitering up and down.

" 'At last she is dead?' said the elder, when I went in.

" 'She is dead,' said I.

" 'I congratulate you, my brother,' were his words as he turned round.

"He had before offered me money, which I had postponed taking. He now gave me a rouleau of gold. I took it from his hand, but laid it on the table. I had considered the question, and had resolved to accept nothing.

" 'Pray excuse me,' said I. 'Under the circumstances, no.'

"They exchanged looks, but bent their heads to me as I bent mine to them, and we parted without another word on either side. . . .

"I am weary, weary, weary—worn down by misery. I cannot read what I have written with this gaunt hand.

"Early in the morning, the rouleau of gold was left at my door in a little box, with my name on the outside. From the first, I had anxiously considered what I ought to do. I decided, that day, to write privately to the Minister, stating the nature of the two cases to which I had been summoned, and the place to which I had gone: in effect, stating all the circumstances. I knew what Court influence was, and what the immunities of the nobles were, and I expected that the matter would never be heard of; but I wished to relieve my own mind. I had kept the matter a profound secret, even from my wife; and this, too, I resolved to state in my letter. I had no apprehension whatever of my real danger; but I was conscious that there might be danger for others, if others were compromised by possessing the knowledge that I possessed.

"I was much engaged that day, and could not complete my letter that night. I rose long before my usual time next morning to finish it. It was the last day of the year. The letter was lying before me just completed, when I was told that a lady waited, who wished to see me. . . .

"I am growing more and more unequal to the task I have

set myself. It is so cold, so dark, my senses are so be-numbed, and the gloom upon me is so dreadful.

"The lady was young, engaging, and handsome, but not marked for long life. She was in great agitation. She pre-sented herself to me as the wife of the Marquis St. Evré-monde. I connected the title by which the boy had addressed the elder brother, with the initial letter embroi-dered on the scarf, and had no difficulty in arriving at the conclusion that I had seen that nobleman very lately.

"My memory is still accurate, but I cannot write the words of our conversation. I suspect that I am watched more closely than I was, and I know not at what times I may be watched. She had in part suspected, and in part discovered, the main facts of the cruel story, of her hus-band's share in it, and my being resorted to. She did not know that the girl was dead. Her hope had been, she said in great distress, to show her, in secret, a woman's sym-pathy. Her hope had been to avert the wrath of Heaven from a house that had long been hateful to the suffering many.

"She had reasons for believing that there was a young sister living, and her greatest desire was to help that sister. I could tell her nothing but that there was such a sister; beyond that, I knew nothing. Her inducement to come to me, relying on my confidence, had been the hope that I could tell her the name and place of abode. Whereas, to this wretched hour I am ignorant of both. . . .

"These scraps of paper fail me. One was taken from me, with a warning, yesterday. I must finish my record to-day.

"She was a good, compassionate lady, and not happy in her marriage. How could she be! The brother distrusted and disliked her, and his influence was all opposed to her; she stood in dread of him, and in dread of her husband too. When I handed her down to the door, there was a child, a pretty boy from two to three years old, in her carriage.

" 'For his sake, Doctor,' she said, pointing to him in tears, 'I would do all I can to make what poor amends I can. He will never prosper in his inheritance otherwise. I have a presentiment that if no other innocent atonement is made for this, it will one day be required of him. What I have left to call my own—it is little beyond the worth of a few jewels—I will make it the first charge of his life to bestow, with the compassion and lamenting of his dead mother, on this injured family, if the sister can be discovered.'

"She kissed the boy, and said, caressing him, 'It is for thine own dear sake. Thou wilt be faithful, little Charles?' The child answered her bravely, 'Yes!' I kissed her hand, and she took him in her arms, and went away caressing him. I never saw her more.

"As she had mentioned her husband's name in the faith that I knew it, I added no mention of it to my letter. I sealed my letter, and, not trusting it out of my own hands, delivered it myself that day.

"That night, the last night of the year, towards nine o'clock, a man in a black dress rang at my gate, demanded to see me, and softly followed my servant, Ernest Defarge, a youth, upstairs. When my servant came into the room where I sat with my wife—O my wife, beloved of my heart! My fair young English wife!—we saw the man, who was supposed to be at the gate, standing silent behind him.

"An urgent case in the Rue St. Honoré, he said. It would not detain me, he had a coach in waiting.

"It brought me here, it brought me to my grave. When I was clear of the house, a black muffler was drawn tightly over my mouth from behind, and my arms were pinioned. The two brothers crossed the road from a dark corner, and identified me with a single gesture. The Marquis took from his pocket the letter I had written, showed it me, burnt it in the light of a lantern that was held, and extinguished the ashes with his foot. Not a word was spoken. I was brought here, I was brought to my living grave.

"If it had pleased God to put it in the hard heart of either of the brothers, in all these frightful years, to grant me any tidings of my dearest wife—so much as to let me know by a word whether alive or dead—I might have thought that He had not quite abandoned them. But, now I believe that the mark of the red cross is fatal to them, and that they have no part in His mercies. And them and their descendants, to the last of their race, I, Alexandre Manette, unhappy prisoner, do this last night of the year 1767, in my unbearable agony, denounce to the times when all these things shall be answered for. I denounce them to Heaven and to earth."

A terrible sound arose when the reading of this document was done. A sound of craving and eagerness that had nothing articulate in it but blood. The narrative called up the most revengeful passions of the time, and there was not a head in the nation but must have dropped before it.

Little need, in presence of that tribunal and that auditory, to show how the Defarges had not made the paper public, with the other captured Bastille memorials borne in procession, and had kept it, biding their time. Little need to show that this detested family name had long been anathematised by Saint Antoine, and was wrought into the fatal register. The man never trod ground whose virtues and services would have sustained him in that place that day, against such denunciation.

And all the worse for the doomed man, that the denouncer was a well-known citizen, his own attached friend, the father of his wife. One of the frenzied aspirations of the populace was for imitations of the questionable public virtues of antiquity, and for sacrifices and self-immolations on the people's altar. Therefore when the President said (else had his own head quivered on his shoulders), that the good physician of the Republic would deserve better still of the Republic by rooting out an obnoxious family of aristocrats, and would doubtless feel a sacred glow and joy in making his daughter a widow and her child an orphan, there was wild excitement, patriotic fervour, not a touch of human sympathy.

"Much influence around him, has that Doctor?" murmured Madame Defarge, smiling to The Vengeance. "Save him now, my Doctor, save him!"

At every juryman's vote, there was a roar. Another and another. Roar and roar.

Unanimously voted. At heart and by descent an aristocrat, an enemy of the Republic, a notorious oppressor of the People. Back to the Conciergerie, and Death within four-and-twenty hours!

* * * * * * * *

11 Dusk

THE WRETCHED wife of the innocent man thus doomed to die fell under the sentence, as if she had been mortally stricken. But, she uttered no sound; and so strong was the voice within her, representing that it was she of all the world who must uphold him in his misery and not augment it, that it quickly raised her, even from that shock.

The judges having to take part in a public demonstration out of doors, the Tribunal adjourned. The quick noise and movement of the court's emptying itself by many passages had not ceased, when Lucie stood stretching out her arms towards her husband, with nothing in her face but love and consolation.

"If I might touch him! If I might embrace him once! O, good citizens, if you would have so much compassion for us!"

There was but a gaoler left, along with two of the four men who had taken him last night, and Barsad. The people had all poured out to the show in the streets. Barsad proposed to the rest, "Let her embrace him then; it is but a moment." It was silently acquiesced in, and they passed her over the seats in the hall to a raised place. where he, by leaning over the dock, could hold her in his arms.

"Farewell, dear darling of my soul. My parting blessing on my love. We shall meet again, where the weary are at rest!"

They were her husband's words, as he held her to his bosom.

"I can bear it, dear Charles. I am supported from above: don't suffer for me. A parting blessing for our child."

"I send it to her by you. I kiss her by you. I say farewell to her by you."

"My husband. No! A moment!" He was tearing himself apart from her. "We shall not be separated long. I feel that this will break my heart by and by; but I will do my duty while I can, and when I leave her, God will raise up friends for her, as He did for me."

Her father had followed her, and would have fallen on his knees to both of them, but that Darnay put out a hand and seized him, crying:

"No, no! What have you done, what have you done, that you should kneel to us! We know now what a struggle you made of old. We know now what you underwent when you suspected my descent, and when you knew it. We know now the natural antipathy you strove against, and conquered, for her dear sake. We thank you with all our hearts, and all our love and duty. Heaven be with you!"

Her father's only answer was to draw his hands through his white hair, and wring them with a shriek of anguish.

"It could not be otherwise," said the prisoner. "All things have worked together as they have fallen out. It was the always-vain endeavour to discharge my poor mother's trust that first brought my fatal presence near you. Good could never come of such evil, a happier end was not in nature to so unhappy a beginning. Be comforted, and forgive me. Heaven bless you!"

As he was drawn away, his wife released him, and stood looking after him with her hands touching one another in the attitude of prayer, and with a radiant look upon her face, in which there was even a comforting smile. As he went out at the prisoners' door, she turned, laid her head lovingly on her father's breast, tried to speak to him, and fell at his feet.

Then, issuing from the obscure corner from which he had never moved, Sydney Carton came and took her up. Only her father and Mr. Lorry were with her. His arm trembled as it raised her, and supported her head. Yet, there was an air about him that was not all of pity—that had a flush of pride in it.

"Shall I take her to a coach? I shall never feel her weight."

He carried her lightly to the door, and laid her tenderly down in a coach. Her father and their old friend got into it, and he took his seat beside the driver.

When they arrived at the gateway where he had paused in the dark not many hours before, to picture to himself on which of the rough stones of the street her feet had trodden, he lifted her again, and carried her up the staircase to their rooms. There, he laid her down on a couch, where her child and Miss Pross wept over her.

"Don't recall her to herself," he said, softly, to the latter, "she is better so. Don't revive her to consciousness, while she only faints."

"Oh, Carton, Carton, dear Carton!" cried little Lucie, springing up and throwing her arms passionately round him, in a burst of grief. "Now that you have come, I think you will do something to help mamma, something to save papa! Oh, look at her, dear Carton! Can you, of all the people who love her, bear to see her so?"

He bent over the child, and laid her blooming cheek against his face. He put her gently from him, and looked at her unconscious mother.

"Before I go," he said, and paused—"I may kiss her?"

It was remembered afterwards that when he bent down and touched her face with his lips, he murmured some words. The child, who was nearest to him, told them afterwards, and told her grandchildren when she was a handsome old lady, that she heard him say, "A life you love."

When he had gone out into the next room, he turned suddenly on Mr. Lorry and her father, who were following, and said to the latter:

"You had great influence but yesterday, Doctor Manette; let it at least be tried. These judges, and all the men in power, are very friendly to you, and very recognisant of your services; are they not?"

"Nothing connected with Charles was concealed from me. I had the strongest assurances that I should save him; and I did." He returned the answer in great trouble, and very slowly.

"Try them again. The hours between this and to-morrow afternoon are few and short, but try."

"I intend to try. I will not rest a moment."

"That's well. I have known such energy as yours do great things before now—though never," he added, with a smile and a sigh together, "such great things as this. But try! Of little worth as life is when we misuse it, it is worth that effort. It would cost nothing to lay down if it were not."

"I will go," said Doctor Manette, "to the Prosecutor and the President straight, and I will go to others whom it is better not to name. I will write too, and— But stay! There is a celebration in the streets, and no one will be accessible until dark."

"That's true. Well! It is a forlorn hope at the best, and not much the forlorner for being delayed till dark. I should like to know how you speed; though, mind! I expect nothing! When are you likely to have seen these dread powers, Doctor Manette?"

"Immediately after dark, I should hope. Within an hour or two from this."

"It will be dark soon after four. Let us stretch the hour or two. If I go to Mr. Lorry's at nine, shall I hear what you have done, either from our friend or from yourself?"

"Yes."

"May you prosper!"

Mr. Lorry followed Sydney to the outer door, and, touching him on the shoulder as he was going away, caused him to turn.

"I have no hope," said Mr. Lorry, in a sorrowful whisper.

"Nor have I."

"If any one of these men, or all of these men, were disposed to spare him—which is a large supposition; for what is his life, or any man's to them!—I doubt if they durst spare him after the demonstration in the court."

"And so do I. I heard the fall of the axe in that sound."

Mr. Lorry leaned his arm upon the doorpost, and bowed his face upon it.

"Don't despond," said Carton, very gently; "don't grieve. I encouraged Doctor Manette in this idea, because I felt that it might one day be consolatory to her. Otherwise, she might think 'his life was wantonly thrown away or wasted,' and that might trouble her."

"Yes, yes, yes," returned Mr. Lorry, drying his eyes, "you are right. But he will perish; there is no real hope."

"Yes. He will perish; there is no real hope," echoed Carton. And walked with a settled step, downstairs.

12 *Darkness*

SYDNEY CARTON paused in the street, not quite decided where to go. "At Tellson's banking-house at nine," he said, with a musing face. "Shall I do well, in the meantime, to show myself? I think so. It is best that these people should know there is such a man as I here; it is a sound precaution, and may be a necessary preparation. But care, care, care! Let me think it out!"

Checking his steps, which had begun to tend towards an object, he took a turn or two in the already darkening street, and traced the thought in his mind to its possible consequences. His first impression was confirmed. "It is best," he said, finally resolved, "that these people should know there is such a man as I here." And he turned his face towards Saint Antoine.

Defarge had described himself, that day, as the keeper of a wine-shop in the Saint Antoine suburb. It was not difficult, for one who knew the city well, to find his house without asking any question. Having ascertained its situation, Carton came out of those closer streets again, and dined at a place of refreshment and fell sound asleep after dinner. For the first time in many years, he had no strong drink. Since last night he had taken nothing but a little light thin wine, and last night he had dropped the brandy slowly down on Mr. Lorry's hearth like a man who had done with it.

It was as late as seven o'clock when he awoke refreshed, and went out into the streets again. As he passed along towards Saint Antoine, he stopped at a shop-window where there was a mirror, and slightly altered the disordered arrangement of his loose cravat, and his coat-collar, and his wild hair. This done he went on direct to Defarge's, and went in.

There happened to be no customer in the shop but Jacques Three, of the restless fingers and the croaking

voice. This man, whom he had seen upon the jury, stood
drinking at the little counter, in conversation with the
Defarges, man and wife. The Vengeance assisted in the
conversation, like a regular member of the establishment.

As Carton walked in, took his seat and asked (in very
indifferent French) for a small measure of wine, Madame
Defarge cast a careless glance at him, and then a keener,
and then a keener, and then advanced to him herself, and
asked him what it was he had ordered.

He repeated what he had already said.

"English?" asked Madame Defarge, inquisitively raising
her dark eyebrows.

After looking at her, as if the sound of even a single
French word were slow to express itself to him, he answered, in his former strong foreign accent, "Yes, madame, yes. I am English!"

Madame Defarge returned to her counter to get the
wine, and, as he took up a Jacobin journal and feigned
to pore over it puzzling out its meaning, he heard her say,
"I swear to you, like Evrémonde!"

Defarge brought him the wine, and gave him good evening.

"How?"

"Good evening."

"Oh! Good evening, citizen," filling his glass. "Ah! and
good wine. I drink to the Republic."

Defarge went back to the counter, and said, "Certainly,
a little like." Madame sternly retorted, "I tell you a good
deal like." Jacques Three pacifically remarked, "He is so
much in your mind, see you, madame." The amiable
Vengeance added, with a laugh, "Yes, my faith! And you
are looking forward with so much pleasure to seeing him
once more to-morrow!"

Carton followed the lines and words of his paper with a
slow forefinger, and with a studious and absorbed face.
They were all leaning their arms on the counter close together, speaking low. After a silence of a few moments,
during which they all looked towards him without disturbing his outward attention from the Jacobin editor, they
resumed their conversation.

"It is true what madame says," observed Jacques Three.
"Why stop? There is great force in that. Why stop?"

"Well, well," reasoned Defarge, "but one must stop
somewhere. After all, the question is still where?"

"At extermination," said madame.

"Magnificent!" croaked Jacques Three. The Vengeance, also, highly approved.

"Extermination is good doctrine, my wife," said Defarge, rather troubled; "in general, I say nothing against it. But this Doctor has suffered much; you have seen him to-day; you have observed his face when the paper was read."

"I have observed his face!" repeated madame, contemptuously and angrily. "Yes. I have observed his face. I have observed his face to be not the face of a true friend of the Republic. Let him take care of his face!"

"And you have observed, my wife," said Defarge, in a deprecatory manner, "the anguish of his daughter, which must be a dreadful anguish to him!"

"I have observed his daughter," repeated madame; "yes, I have observed his daughter, more times than one. I have observed her to-day, and I have observed her other days. I have observed her in the court, and I have observed her in the street by the prison. Let me but lift my finger—!" She seemed to raise it (the listener's eyes were always on his paper), and to let it fall with a rattle on the ledge before her, as if the axe had dropped.

"The citizeness is superb!" croaked the juryman.

"She is an angel!" said The Vengeance, and embraced her.

"As to thee," pursued madame, implacably, addressing her husband, "if it depended on thee—which, happily, it does not—thou wouldst rescue this man even now."

"No!" protested Defarge. "Not if to lift this glass would do it! But I would leave the matter there. I say, stop there."

"See you then, Jacques," said Madame Defarge, wrathfully; "and see you, too, my little Vengeance; see you both! Listen! For other crimes as tyrants and oppressors, I have this race a long time on my register, doomed to destruction and extermination. Ask my husband, is that so."

"It is so," asserted Defarge, without being asked.

"In the beginning of the great days, when the Bastille falls, he finds this paper of to-day, and he brings it home, and in the middle of the night when this place is clear and shut, we read it, here on this spot, by the light of this lamp. Ask him, is that so."

"It is so," asserted Defarge.

"That night, I tell him, when the paper is read through, and the lamp is burnt out, and the day is gleaming in above those shutters and between those iron bars, that I have now a secret to communicate. Ask him, is that so."

"It is so," assented Defarge again.

"I communicate to him that secret. I smite this bosom with these two hands as I smite it now, and I tell him, 'Defarge, I was brought up among the fishermen of the seashore, and that peasant family so injured by the two Evrémonde brothers, as that Bastille paper describes, is my family. Defarge, that sister of the mortally wounded boy upon the ground was my sister, that husband was my sister's husband, that unborn child was their child, that brother was my brother, that father was my father, those dead are my dead, and that summons to answer for those things descends to me!' Ask him, is that so."

"It is so," assented Defarge once more.

"Then tell wind and fire where to stop," returned madame; "but don't tell me."

Both her hearers derived a horrible enjoyment from the deadly nature of her wrath—the listener could feel how white she was, without seeing her—and both highly commended it. Defarge, a weak minority, interposed a few words for the memory of the compassionate wife of the Marquis; but only elicited from his own wife a repetition of her last reply. "Tell the wind and the fire where to stop; not me!"

Customers entered, and the group was broken up. The English customer paid for what he had had, perplexedly counted his change, and asked, as a stranger, to be directed towards the National Palace. Madame Defarge took him to the door, and put her arm on his, in pointing out the road. The English customer was not without his reflections then, that it might be a good deed to seize that arm, lift it, and strike under it sharp and deep.

But, he went his way, and was soon swallowed up in the shadow of the prison wall. At the appointed hour, he emerged from it to present himself in Mr. Lorry's room again, where he found the old gentleman walking to and fro in restless anxiety. He said he had been with Lucie until just now, and had only left her for a few minutes, to come and keep his appointment. Her father had not been seen, since he quitted the banking-house towards four o'clock. She had some faint hopes that his mediation might save Charles, but they were very slight. He had been more than five hours gone: where could he be?

Mr. Lorry waited until ten; but, Doctor Manette not returning, and he being unwilling to leave Lucie any longer, it was arranged that he should go back to her, and come to the banking-house again at midnight. In the meanwhile, Carton could wait alone by the fire for the Doctor.

He waited and waited, and the clock struck twelve; but Doctor Manette did not come back. Mr. Lorry returned, and found no tidings of him, and brought none. Where could he be?

They were discussing this question, and were almost building up some weak structure of hope on his prolonged absence, when they heard him on the stairs. The instant he entered the room, it was plain that all was lost.

Whether he had really been to any one, or whether he had been all that time traversing the streets, was never known. As he stood staring at them, they asked him no question, for his face told them everything.

"I cannot find it," said he, "and I must have it. Where is it?"

His head and throat were bare, and, as he spoke with a helpless look straying all around, he took his coat off, and let it drop on the floor.

"Where is my bench? I have been looking everywhere for my bench, and I can't find it. What have they done with my work? Time presses: I must finish those shoes."

They looked at one another, and their hearts died within them.

"Come, come!" said he, in a whimpering miserable way; "let me get to work. Give me my work."

Receiving no answer, he tore his hair, and beat his feet upon the ground, like a distracted child.

"Don't torture a poor forlorn wretch," he implored them, with a dreadful cry, "but give me my work! What is to become of us, if those shoes are not done to-night?"

Lost, utterly lost!

It was so clearly beyond hope to reason with him, or try to restore him, that—as if by agreement—they each put a hand upon his shoulder, and soothed him to sit down before the fire, with a promise that he should have his work presently. He sank into the chair, and brooded over the embers, and shed tears. As if all that had happened since the garret time were a momentary fancy, or a dream, Mr. Lorry saw him shrink into the exact figure that Defarge had had in keeping.

Affected, and impressed with terror as they both were, by this spectacle of ruin, it was not a time to yield to such emotions. His lonely daughter, bereft of her final hope and reliance, appealed to them both too strongly. Again, as if by agreement, they looked at one another with one meaning in their faces. Carton was the first to speak:

"The last chance is gone: it was not much. Yes; he had better be taken to her. But, before you go, will you, for a moment, steadily attend to me? Don't ask me why I make the stipulations I am going to make, and exact the promise I am going to exact; I have a reason—a good one."

"I do not doubt it," answered Mr. Lorry. "Say on."

The figure in the chair between them was all the time monotonously rocking itself to and fro, and moaning. They spoke in such a tone as they would have used if they had been watching by a sick-bed in the night.

Carton stooped to pick up the coat, which lay almost entangling his feet. As he did so, a small case in which the Doctor was accustomed to carry the list of his day's duties fell lightly on the floor. Carton took it up, and there was a folded paper in it. "We should look at this!" he said. Mr. Lorry nodded his consent. He opened it, and exclaimed, "Thank God!"

"What is it?" asked Mr. Lorry, eagerly.

"A moment! Let me speak of it in its place. First," he put his hand in his coat, and took another paper from it, "that is the certificate which enables me to pass out of this city. Look at it. You see—Sydney Carton, an Englishman?"

Mr. Lorry held it open in his hand, gazing in his earnest face.

"Keep it for me until to-morrow. I shall see him to-morrow, you remember, and I had better not take it into the prison."

"Why not?"

"I don't know; I prefer not to do so. Now, take this paper that Doctor Manette has carried about him. It is a similar certificate, enabling him and his daughter and her child, at any time, to pass the barrier and the frontier. You see?"

"Yes!"

"Perhaps he obtained it as his last and utmost precaution against evil, yesterday. When is it dated? But no matter; don't stay to look; put it up carefully with mine and your own. Now, observe! I never doubted until within this hour or two, that he had or could have such a paper. It is good, until recalled. But it may be soon recalled, and, I have reason to think, will be."

"They are not in danger?"

"They are in great danger. They are in danger of denunciation by Madame Defarge. I know it from her own lips. I have overheard words of that woman's, to-night, which have presented their danger to me in strong colours. I have lost no time, and since then, I have seen the spy. He confirms me. He knows that a wood-sawyer, living by the prison-wall, is under the control of the Defarges, and has been rehearsed by Madame Defarge as to his having seen *her*"—he never mentioned Lucie's name—"making signs and signals to prisoners. It is easy to foresee that the pretence will be the common one, a prison plot, and that it will involve her life—and perhaps her child's—and perhaps her father's—for both have been seen with her at that place. Don't look so horrified. You will save them all."

"Heaven grant I may, Carton! But how?"

"I am going to tell you how. It will depend on you, and it could depend on no better man. This new denunciation will certainly not take place until after to-morrow; probably not until two or three days afterwards; more probably a week afterwards. You know it is a capital crime, to mourn for, or sympathise with, a victim of the Guillotine. She and her father would unquestionably be guilty of this crime, and this woman (the inveteracy of whose pursuit cannot be described) would wait to add that strength to her case, and make herself doubly sure. You follow me?"

"So attentively, and with so much confidence in what you say, that for the moment I lose sight," touching the back of the Doctor's chair, "even of this distress."

"You have money, and can buy the means of travelling to the sea-coast as quickly as the journey can be made. Your preparations have been completed for some days, to return to England. Early to-morrow have your horses ready, so that they may be in starting trim at two o'clock in the afternoon."

"It shall be done!"

His manner was so fervent and inspiring, that Mr. Lorry caught the flame, and was as quick as youth.

"You are a noble heart. Did I say we could depend upon

no better man? Tell her, to-night, what you know of her danger as involving her child and her father. Dwell upon that, for she would lay her own fair head beside her husband's cheerfully." He faltered for an instant; then went on as before. "For the sake of her child and her father, press upon her the necessity of leaving Paris, with them and you, at that hour. Tell her that it was her husband's last arrangement. Tell her that more depends upon it than she dare believe, or hope. You think that her father, even in this sad state, will submit himself to her; do you not?"

"I am sure of it."

"I thought so. Quietly and steadily have all these arrangements made in the courtyard here, even to the taking of your own seat in the carriage. The moment I come to you, take me in, and drive away."

"I understand that I wait for you under all circumstances?"

"You have my certificate in your hand with the rest, you know, and will reserve my place. Wait for nothing but to have my place occupied, and then for England!"

"Why, then," said Mr. Lorry, grasping his eager but so firm and steady hand, "it does not all depend on one old man, but I shall have a young and ardent man at my side."

"By the help of Heaven you shall! Promise me solemnly that nothing will influence you to alter the course on which we now stand pledged to one another."

"Nothing, Carton."

"Remember these words to-morrow: change the course, or delay in it—for any reason—and no life can possibly be saved, and many lives must inevitably be sacrificed."

"I will remember them. I hope to do my part faithfully."

"And I hope to do mine. Now, good-bye!"

Though he said it with a grave smile of earnestness, and though he even put the old man's hand to his lips, he did not part from him then. He helped him so far to arouse the rocking figure before the dying embers, as to get a cloak and hat put upon it, and to tempt it forth to find where the bench and work were hidden that it still moaningly besought to have. He walked on the other side of it and protected it to the courtyard of the house where the afflicted heart—so happy in the memorable time when he had revealed his own desolate heart to it—outwatched the awful night. He entered the courtyard and remained there for a few moments alone, looking up at the light in the window of her room. Before he went away, he breathed a blessing towards it, and a farewell.

---

13 *Fifty-two*

IN THE black prison of the Conciergerie, the doomed of the day awaited their fate. They were in number as the weeks of the year. Fifty-two were to roll that afternoon on the life-tide of the city to the boundless everlasting sea. Be-before their cells were quit of them, new occupants were appointed; before their blood ran into the blood spilled yesterday, the blood that was to mingle with theirs to-morrow was already set apart.

Two score and twelve were told off. From the farmer-general of seventy, whose riches could not buy his life, to the seamstress of twenty, whose poverty and obscurity could not save her. Physical diseases, engendered in the vices and neglects of men, will seize on victims of all degrees; and the frightful moral disorder, born of unspeakable suffering, intolerable oppression, and heartless indifference, smote equally without distinction.

Charles Darnay, alone in a cell, had sustained himself with no flattering delusion since he came to it from the Tribunal. In every line of the narrative he had heard, he had heard his condemnation. He had fully comprehended that no personal influence could possibly save him, that he was virtually sentenced by the millions, and that units could avail him nothing.

Nevertheless, it was not easy, with the face of his beloved wife fresh before him, to compose his mind to what it must bear. His hold on life was strong, and it was very, very hard to loosen; by gradual efforts and degrees unclosed a little here, it clenched the tighter there; and when he brought his strength to bear on that hand and it yielded, this was closed again. There was a hurry, too, in all his thoughts, a turbulent and heated working of his heart, that contended against resignation. If, for a moment, he did feel resigned, then his wife and child, who had to live after him, seemed to protest and to make it a selfish thing.

But, all this was at first. Before long the consideration that there was no disgrace in the fate he must meet, and that numbers went the same road wrongfully, and trod it firmly every day, sprang up to stimulate him. Next followed the thought that much of the future peace of mind enjoyable by the dear ones depended on his quiet fortitude. So, by degrees he calmed into the better state, when he could raise his thoughts much higher, and draw comfort down.

Before it had set in dark on the night of his condemnation, he had travelled thus far on his last way. Being allowed to purchase the means of writing, and a light, he sat down to write until such time as the prison lamps should be extinguished.

He wrote a long letter to Lucie, showing her that he had known nothing of her father's imprisonment, until he had heard of it from herself, and that he had been as ignorant as she of his father's and uncle's responsibility for that misery, until the paper had been read. He had already explained to her that his concealment from herself of the name he had relinquished was the one condition—fully intelligible now—that her father had attached to their betrothal, and was the one promise he had still exacted on the morning of their marriage. He entreated her, for her father's sake, never to seek to know whether her father had become oblivious of the existence of the paper, or had had it recalled to him (for the moment, or for good), by the story of the Tower, on that old Sunday under the dear old plane-tree in the garden. If he had preserved any definite remembrance of it, there could be no doubt that he had supposed it destroyed with the Bastille, when he had found no mention of it among the relics of prisoners which the populace had discovered there, and which had been described to all the world. He besought her—though he added that he knew it was needless—to console her father, by impressing him through every tender means she could think of, with the truth that he had done nothing for which he could justly reproach himself, but had uniformly forgotten himself for their joint sakes. Next to her preservation of his own last grateful love and blessing, and her overcoming of her sorrow, to devote herself to their dear child, he adjured her, as they would meet in Heaven, to comfort her father.

To her father himself, he wrote in the same strain; but, he told her father that he expressly confided his wife and child to his care. And he told him this, very strongly, with the hope of rousing him from any despondency or dangerous retrospect towards which he foresaw he might be tending.

To Mr. Lorry, he commended them all, and explained his worldly affairs. That done, with many added sentences of grateful friendship and warm attachment, all was done. He never thought of Carton. His mind was so full of the others, that he never once thought of him.

He had time to finish these letters before the lights were put out. When he lay down on his straw bed, he thought he had done with this world.

But, it beckoned him back in his sleep, and showed itself in shining forms. Free and happy, back in the old house in Soho (though it had nothing in it like the real house), unaccountably released and light of heart, he was with Lucie again, and she told him it was all a dream, and he had never gone away. A pause of forgetfulness, and then he had even suffered, and had come back to her, dead and at peace, and yet there was no difference in him. Another pause of oblivion, and he awoke in the sombre morning, unconscious where he was or what had happened, until it flashed upon his mind, "this is the day of my death!"

Thus, had he come through the hours, to the day when the fifty-two heads were to fall. And now, while he was composed, and hoped that he could meet the end with quiet heroism, a new action began in his waking thoughts, which was very difficult to master.

He had never seen the instrument that was to terminate his life. How high it was from the ground, how many steps it had, where he would be stood, how he would be touched, whether the touching hands would be dyed red, which way his face would be turned, whether he would be the first, or might be the last: these and many similar questions, in no wise directed by his will, obtruded themselves over and over again, countless times. Neither were they connected with fear: he was conscious of no fear. Rather, they originated in a strange besetting desire to know what to do when the time came; a desire gigantically disproportionate to the few split moments to which it referred; a wondering that was more like the wondering of some other spirit within his, than his own.

The hours went on as he walked to and fro, and the clocks struck the numbers he would never hear again. Nine gone for ever, ten gone for ever, eleven gone for ever, twelve coming on to pass away. After a hard contest with that eccentric action of thought which had last perplexed him, he had got the better of it. He walked up and down, softly repeating their names to himself. The worst of the strife was over. He could walk up and down, free from distracting fancies, praying for himself and for them.

Twelve gone for ever.

He had been apprised that the final hour was three, and he knew he would be summoned some time earlier, inasmuch as the tumbrils jolted heavily and slowly through the streets. Therefore, he resolved to keep two before his mind, as the hour, and so to strengthen himself in the interval that he might be able, after that time, to strengthen others.

Walking regularly to and fro with his arms folded on his breast, a very different man from the prisoner who had walked to and fro at La Force, he heard one struck away from him, without surprise. The hour had measured like most other hours. Devoutly thankful to Heaven for his recovered self-possession, he thought, "There is but another now," and turned to walk again.

Footsteps in the stone passage outside the door. He stopped.

The key was put in the lock, and turned. Before the door was opened, or as it opened, a man said in a low voice, in English: "He has never seen me here; I have kept out of his way. Go you in alone; I wait near. Lose no time!"

The door was quickly opened and closed, and there stood before him face to face, quiet, intent upon him, with the light of a smile on his features, and a cautionary finger on his lip, Sydney Carton.

There was something so bright and remarkable in his look, that, for the first moment, the prisoner misdoubted him to be an apparition of his own imagining. But, he spoke, and it was his voice; he took the prisoner's hand, and it was his real grasp.

"Of all the people upon earth, you least expected to see me?" he said.

"I could not believe it to be you. I can scarcely believe

it now. You are not"—the apprehension came suddenly into his mind—"a prisoner?"

"No. I am accidentally possessed of a power over one of the keepers here, and in virtue of it I stand before you. I come from her—your wife, dear Darnay."

The prisoner wrung his hand.

"I bring you a request from her."

"What is it?"

"A most earnest, pressing, and emphatic entreaty, addressed to you in the most pathetic tones of the voice so dear to you, that you well remember."

The prisoner turned his face partly aside.

"You have no time to ask me why I bring it, or what it means; I have no time to tell you. You must comply with it—take off those boots you wear, and draw on these of mine."

There was a chair against the wall of the cell, behind the prisoner. Carton, pressing forward, had already, with the speed of lightning, got him down into it, and stood over him, barefoot.

"Draw on those boots of mine. Put your hands to them; put your will to them. Quick!"

"Carton, there is no escaping from this place; it never can be done. You will only die with me. It is madness."

"It would be madness if I asked you to escape; but do I? When I ask you to pass out at that door, tell me it is madness and remain here. Change that cravat for this of mine, that coat for this of mine. While you do it, let me take this ribbon from your hair, and shake out your hair like this of mine!"

With wonderful quickness, and with a strength both of will and action, that appeared quite supernatural, he forced all these changes upon him. The prisoner was like a young child in his hands.

"Carton! Dear Carton! It is madness. It cannot be accomplished, it never can be done, it has been attempted, and has always failed. I implore you not to add your death to the bitterness of mine."

"Do I ask you, my dear Darnay, to pass the door? When I ask that, refuse. There are pen and ink and paper on this table. Is your hand steady enough to write?"

"It was when you came in."

"Steady it again, and write what I shall dictate. Quick, friend, quick!"

Pressing his hand to his bewildered head, Darnay sat down at the table. Carton, with his right hand in his breast, stood close beside him.

"Write exactly as I speak."

"To whom do I address it?"

"To no one." Carton still had his hand in his breast.

"Do I date it?"

"No."

The prisoner looked up at each question. Carton, standing over him with his hand in his breast, looked down.

"'If you remember,'" said Carton, dictating, "'the words that passed between us, long ago, you will readily comprehend this when you see it. You do remember them, I know. It is not in your nature to forget them.'"

He was drawing his hand from his breast; the prisoner chancing to look up in his hurried wonder as he wrote, the hand stopped, closing upon something.

"Have you written 'forget them'?" Carton asked.

"I have. Is that a weapon in your hand?"

"No; I am not armed."

"What is it in your hand?"

"You shall know directly. Write on; there are but a few words more." He dictated again. "'I am thankful that the time has come, when I can prove them. That I do so is no subject for regret or grief.'" As he said these words with his eyes fixed on the writer, his hand slowly and softly moved down close to the writer's face.

The pen dropped from Darnay's fingers on the table, and he looked about him vacantly.

"What vapour is that?" he asked.

"Vapour?"

"Something that crossed me?"

"I am conscious of nothing; there can be nothing here. Take up the pen and finish. Hurry, hurry!"

As if his memory were impaired, or his faculties disordered, the prisoner made an effort to rally his attention. As he looked at Carton with clouded eyes and with an altered manner of breathing, Carton—his hand again in his breast—looked steadily at him.

"Hurry, hurry!"

The prisoner bent over the paper once more.

"'If it had been otherwise'"—Carton's hand was again watchfully and softly stealing down—"'I never should have used the longer opportunity. If it had been otherwise' "—the hand was at the prisoner's face—" 'I should but have had so much the more to answer for. If it had been otherwise—' " Carton looked at the pen and saw it was trailing off into unintelligible signs.

Carton's hand moved back to his breast no more. The prisoner sprang up with a reproachful look, but Carton's hand was close and firm at his nostrils, and Carton's left arm caught him round the waist. For a few seconds he faintly struggled with the man who had come to lay down his life for him; but, within a minute or so, he was stretched insensible on the ground.

Quickly, but with hands as true to the purpose as his heart was, Carton dressed himself in the clothes the prisoner had laid aside, combed back his hair, and tied it with the ribbon the prisoner had worn. Then, he softly called, "Enter there! Come in!" and the spy presented himself.

"You see?" said Carton, looking up, as he kneeled on one knee beside the insensible figure, putting the paper in the breast: "is your hazard very great?"

"Mr. Carton," the spy answered, with a timid snap of his fingers, "my hazard is not *that,* in the thick of business here, if you are true to the whole of your bargain."

"Don't fear me. I will be true to the death."

"You must be, Mr. Carton, if the tale of fifty-two is to be right. Being made right by you in that dress, I shall have no fear."

"Have no fear! I shall soon be out of the way of harming you, and the rest will soon be far from here, please God! Now, get assistance and take me to the coach."

"You?" said the spy nervously.

"Him, man, with whom I have exchanged. You go out at the gate by which you brought me in?"

"Of course."

"I was weak and faint when you brought me in, and I am fainter now you take me out. The parting interview has overpowered me. Such a thing has happened here, often, and too often. Your life is in your own hands. Quick! Call assistance!"

"You swear not to betray me?" said the trembling spy, as he paused for a last moment.

"Man, man!" returned Carton, stamping his foot; "have I sworn by no solemn vow already, to go through with this, that you waste the precious moments now? Take him yourself to the courtyard you know of, place him yourself in the carriage, show him yourself to Mr. Lorry, tell him yourself to give him no restorative but air, and to remember my words of last night, and his promise of last night, and drive away!"

The spy withdrew, and Carton seated himself at the table, resting his forehead on his hands. The spy returned immediately, with two men.

"How, then?" said one of them, contemplating the fallen figure. "So afflicted to find that his friend has drawn a prize in the lottery of Sainte Guillotine?"

"A good patriot," said the other, "could hardly have been more afflicted if the aristocrat had drawn a blank."

They raised the unconscious figure, placed it on a litter they had brought to the door, and bent to carry it away.

"The time is short, Evrémonde," said the spy, in a warning voice.

"I know it well," answered Carton. "Be careful of my friend, I entreat you, and leave me."

"Come, then, my children," said Barsad. "Lift him, and come away!"

The door closed, and Carton was left alone. Straining his powers of listening to the utmost, he listened for any sound that might denote suspicion or alarm. There was none. Keys turned, doors clashed, footsteps passed along distant passages: no cry was raised, or hurry made, that seemed unusual. Breathing more freely in a little while, he sat down at the table, and listened again until the clock struck two.

Sounds that he was not afraid of, for he divined their meaning, then began to be audible. Several doors were opened in succession, and finally his own. A gaoler, with a list in his hand, looked in, merely saying, "Follow me, Evrémonde!" and he followed into a large dark room, at a distance. It was a dark winter day, and what with the shadows within, and what with the shadows without, he could but dimly discern the others who were brought there to have their arms bound. Some were standing; some seated. Some were lamenting, and in restless motion; but, these were few. The great majority were silent and still, looking fixedly at the ground.

As he stood by the wall in a dim corner, while some of the fifty-two were brought in after him, one man stopped in passing, to embrace him, as having a knowledge of him. It thrilled him with a great dread of discovery; but the man went on. A very few moments after that, a young woman, with a slight girlish form, a sweet spare face in which there was no vestige of colour, and large widely opened patient eyes, rose from the seat where he had observed her sitting, and came to speak to him.

"Citizen Evrémonde," she said, touching him with her cold hand, "I am a poor little seamstress, who was with you in La Force."

He murmured for answer: "True. I forget what you were accused of?"

"Plots. Though the just Heaven knows I am innocent of any. Is it likely? Who would think of plotting with a poor little weak creature like me?"

The forlorn smile with which she said it so touched him, that tears started from his eyes.

"I am not afraid to die, Citizen Evrémonde, but I have done nothing. I am not unwilling to die, if the Republic which is to do so much good for us poor, will profit by my death; but I do not know how that can be, Citizen Evrémonde. Such a poor weak little creature!"

As the last thing on earth that his heart was to warm and soften to, it warmed and softened to this pitiable girl.

"I heard you were released, Citizen Evrémonde. I hoped it was true?"

"It was. But, I was again taken and condemned."

"If I may ride with you, Citizen Evrémonde, will you let me hold your hand? I am not afraid, but I am little and weak, and it will give me more courage."

As the patient eyes were lifted to his face, he saw a sudden doubt in them, and then astonishment. He pressed the work-worn, hunger-worn young fingers, and touched his lips.

"Are you dying for him?" she whispered.

"And his wife and child. Hush! Yes."

"Oh, you will let me hold your brave hand, stranger?"

"Hush! Yes, my poor sister; to the last."

The same shadows that are falling on the prison are falling, in that same hour of the early afternoon, on the Barrier with the crowd about it, when a coach going out of Paris drives up to be examined.

"Who goes here? Whom have we within? Papers!"

The papers are handed out, and read.

"Alexandre Manette. Physician. French. Which is he?"

This is he; this helpless, inarticulately murmuring, wandering old man pointed out.

"Apparently the Citizen-Doctor is not in his right mind? The Revolution-fever will have been too much for him?"

Greatly too much for him.

"Hah! Many suffer with it. Lucie. His daughter. French. Which is she?"

This is she.

"Apparently it must be. Lucie, the wife of Evrémonde; is it not?"

It is.

"Hah! Evrémonde has an assignation elsewhere. Lucie, her child. English. This is she?"

She and no other.

"Kiss me, child of Evrémonde. Now, thou hast kissed a good Republican; something new in thy family; remember it! Sydney Carton. Advocate. English. Which is he?"

He lies here, in this corner of the carriage. He, too, is pointed out.

"Apparently the English advocate is in a swoon?"

It is hoped he will recover in the fresher air. It is represented that he is not in strong health, and has separated sadly from a friend who is under the displeasure of the Republic.

"Is that all? It is not a great deal, that! Many are under the displeasure of the Republic, and must look out at the little window. Jarvis Lorry. Banker. English. Which is he?"

"I am he. Necessarily, being the last."

It is Jarvis Lorry who has replied to all the previous questions. It is Jarvis Lorry who has alighted and stands with his hands on the coach door, replying to a group of officials. They leisurely walk round the carriage and leisurely mount the box, to look at what little luggage it carries on the roof; the country-people hanging about press nearer to the coach doors and greedily stare in; a little child, carried by its mother, has its short arm held out for it, that it may touch the wife of an aristocrat who has gone to the Guillotine.

"Behold your papers, Jarvis Lorry, countersigned."

"One can depart, citizen?"

"One can depart. Forward, my postillions! A good journey!"

"I salute you, citizens.—And the first danger passed!"

These are again the words of Jarvis Lorry, as he clasps

his hands, and looks upward. There is terror in the carriage, there is weeping, there is the heavy breathing of the insensible traveller.

"Are we not going too slowly? Can they not be induced to go faster?" asks Lucie, clinging to the old man.

"It would seem like flight, my darling. I must not urge them too much; it would rouse suspicion."

"Look back, look back, and see if we are pursued!"

"The road is clear, my dearest. So far, we are not pursued."

Houses in twos and threes pass by us, solitary farms, ruinous buildings, dye-works, tanneries, and the like, open country, avenues of leafless trees. The hard uneven pavement is under us, the soft deep mud is on either side. Sometimes, we strike into the skirting mud, to avoid the stones that clatter us and shake us; sometimes we stick in ruts and sloughs there. The agony of our impatience is then so great, that in our wild alarm and hurry we are for getting out and running—hiding—doing anything but stopping.

Out of the open country, in again among ruinous buildings, solitary farms, dye-works, tanneries, and the like, cottages in twos and threes, avenues of leafless trees. Have these men deceived us, and taken us back by another road? Is not this the same place twice over? Thank Heaven, no. A village. Look back, look back, and see if we are pursued! Hush! the posting-house.

Leisurely, our four horses are taken out; leisurely, the coach stands in the little street, bereft of horses, and with no likelihood upon it of ever moving again; leisurely, the new horses come into visible existence, one by one; leisurely, the new postillions follow, sucking and plaiting the lashes of their whips; leisurely, the old postillions count their money, make wrong additions, and arrive at dissatisfied results. All the time, our overfraught hearts are beating at a rate that would far outstrip the fastest gallop of the fastest horses ever foaled.

At length the new postillions are in their saddles, and the old are left behind. We are through the village, up the hill, and down the hill, and on the low watery grounds. Suddenly, the postillions exchange speech with animated gesticulation, and the horses are pulled up, almost on their haunches. We are pursued?

"Ho! Within the carriage there. Speak then!"

"What is it?" asks Mr. Lorry, looking out at window.

"How many did they say?"

"I do not understand you."

"—At the last post. How many to the Guillotine to-day?"

"Fifty-two."

"I said so! A brave number! My fellow-citizen here would have it forty-two; ten more heads are worth having. The Guillotine goes handsomely. I love it. Hi forward. Whoop!"

The night comes on dark. He moves more; he is beginning to revive, and to speak intelligibly; he thinks they are still together; he asks him, by his name, what he has in his hand. O pity us, kind Heaven, and help us! Look out, look out, and see if we are pursued.

The wind is rushing after us, and the clouds are flying after us, and the moon is plunging after us, and the whole wild night is in pursuit of us; but, so far, we are pursued by nothing else.

*   *   *   *   *   *   *   *

14   *The Knitting Done*

IN THAT same juncture of time when the fifty-two awaited their fate, Madame Defarge held darkly ominous council with The Vengeance and Jacques Three of the Revolutionary Jury. Not in the wine-shop did Madame Defarge confer with these ministers, but in the shed of the wood-sawyer, erst a mender of roads. The sawyer himself did not participate in the conference, but abided at a little distance, like an outer satellite who was not to speak until required, or to offer an opinion until invited.

"But our Defarge," said Jacques Three, "is undoubtedly a good Republican? Eh?"

"There is no better," the voluble Vengeance protested in her shrill notes, "in France."

"Peace, little Vengeance," said Madame Defarge, laying her hand with a slight frown on her lieutenant's lips, "hear me speak. My husband, fellow-citizen, is a good

Republican and a bold man; he has deserved well of the Republic, and possesses its confidence. But my husband has his weaknesses, and he is so weak as to relent towards this Doctor."

"It is a great pity," croaked Jacques Three, dubiously shaking his head, with his cruel fingers at his hungry mouth; "it is not quite like a good citizen; it is a thing to regret."

"See you," said madame, "I care nothing for this Doctor, I. He may wear his head or lose it, for any interest I have in him; it is all one to me. But, the Evrémonde people are to be exterminated, and the wife and child must follow the husband and father."

"She has a fine head for it," croaked Jacques Three. "I have seen blue eyes and golden hair there, and they looked charming when Samson held them up." Ogre that he was, he spoke like an epicure.

Madame Defarge cast down her eyes, and reflected a little.

"The child also," observed Jacques Three, with a meditative enjoyment of his words, "has golden hair and blue eyes. And we seldom have a child there. It is a pretty sight!"

"In a word," said Madame Defarge, coming out of her short abstraction, "I cannot trust my husband in this matter. Not only do I feel, since last night, that I dare not confide to him the details of my projects; but also I feel that if I delay, there is danger of his giving warning, and then they might escape."

"That must never be," croaked Jacques Three; "no one must escape. We have not half enough as it is. We ought to have six score a day."

"In a word," Madame Defarge went on, "my husband has not my reason for pursuing this family to annihilation, and I have not his reason for regarding this Doctor with any sensibility. I must act for myself, therefore. Come hither, little citizen."

The wood-sawyer, who held her in the respect, and himself in the submission, of mortal fear, advanced with his hand to his red cap.

"Touching those signals, little citizen," said Madame Defarge, sternly, "that she made to the prisoners; you are ready to bear witness to them this very day?"

"Ay, ay, why not!" cried the sawyer. "Every day, in all

weathers, from two to four, always signalling, sometimes with the little one, sometimes without. I know what I know. I have seen with my eyes."

He made all manner of gestures while he spoke, as if in incidental imitation of some few of the great diversity of signals that he had never seen.

"Clearly plots," said Jacques Three. "Transparently!"

"There is no doubt of the jury?" inquired Madame Defarge, letting her eyes turn to him with a gloomy smile.

"Rely upon the patriotic jury, dear citizeness. I answer for my fellow-jurymen."

"Now, let me see," said Madame Defarge, pondering again. "Yet once more! Can I spare this Doctor to my husband? I have no feeling either way. Can I spare him?"

"He would count as one head," observed Jacques Three, in a low voice. "We really have not heads enough; it would be a pity, I think."

"He was signalling with her when I saw her," argued Madame Defarge; "I cannot speak of one without the other; and I must not be silent, and trust the case wholly to him, this little citizen here. For, I am not a bad witness."

The Vengeance and Jacques Three vied with each other in their fervent protestations that she was the most admirable and marvellous of witnesses. The little citizen, not to be outdone, declared her to be a celestial witness.

"He must take his chance," said Madame Defarge. "No, I cannot spare him! You are engaged at three o'clock; you are going to see the batch of to-day executed.—You?"

The question was addressed to the wood-sawyer, who hurriedly replied in the affirmative: seizing the occasion to add that he was the most ardent of Republicans, and that he would be in effect the most desolate of Republicans, if anything prevented him from enjoying the pleasure of smoking his afternoon pipe in the contemplation of the droll national barber. He was so very demonstrative herein, that he might have been suspected (perhaps was, by the dark eyes that looked contemptuously at him out of Madame Defarge's head) of having his small individual fears for his own personal safety, every hour in the day.

"I," said madame, "am equally engaged at the same place. After it is over—say at eight to-night—come you to me, in Saint Antoine, and we will give information against these people at my Section."

The wood-sawyer said he would be proud and flattered

to attend the citizeness. The citizeness looking at him, he became embarrassed, evaded her glance as a small dog would have done, retreated among his wood, and hid his confusion over the handle of the saw.

Madame Defarge beckoned the juryman and The Vengeance a little nearer to the door, and there expounded her further views of them thus:

"She will now be at home, awaiting the moment of his death. She will be mourning and grieving. She will be in a state of mind to impeach the justice of the Republic. She will be full of sympathy with its enemies. I will go to her."

"What an admirable woman; what an adorable woman!" exclaimed Jacques Three, rapturously. "Ah, my cherished!" cried The Vengeance; and embraced her.

"Take you my knitting," said Madame Defarge, placing it in her lieutenant's hands, "and have it ready for me in my usual seat. Keep me my usual chair. Go you there, straight, for there will probably be a greater concourse than usual, to-day."

"I willingly obey the orders of my chief," said The Vengeance with alacrity, and kissing her cheek. "You will not be late?"

"I shall be there before the commencement."

"And before the tumbrils arrive. Be sure you are there, my soul," said The Vengeance, calling after her, for she had already turned into the street, "before the tumbrils arrive!"

Madame Defarge slightly waved her hand, to imply that she heard, and might be relied upon to arrive in good time, and so went through the mud and round the corner of the prison wall. The Vengeance and the jury-man, looking after her as she walked away, were highly appreciative of her fine figure, and her superb moral endowments.

There were many women at that time, upon whom the time laid a dreadfully disfiguring hand; but, there was not one among them more to be dreaded than this ruthless woman, now taking her way along the streets. Of a strong and fearless character, and shrewd sense and readiness, of great determination, of that kind of beauty which not only seems to impart to its possessor firmness and animosity, but to strike into others an instinctive recognition of those qualities; the troubled time would have heaved her up, under any circumstances. But, imbued from her childhood with a brooding sense of wrong, and an inveterate hatred of a class, opportunity had developed her into a tigress. She was absolutely without pity. If she had ever had the virtue in her, it had quite gone out of her.

It was nothing to her, that an innocent man was to die for the sins of his forefathers; she saw, not him, but them. It was nothing to her, that his wife was to be made a widow and his daughter an orphan; that was insufficient punishment, because they were her natural enemies and her prey, and as such had no right to live. To appeal to her, was made hopeless by her having no sense of pity, even for herself. If she had been laid low in the streets, in any of the many encounters in which she had been engaged, she would not have pitied herself: nor, if she had been ordered to the axe to-morrow, would she have gone to it with any softer feeling than a fierce desire to change places with the man who sent her there.

Such a heart Madame Defarge carried under her rough robe. Carelessly worn, it was a becoming robe enough, in a certain weird way, and her dark hair looked rich under her coarse red cap. Lying hidden in her bosom was a loaded pistol. Lying hidden at her waist was a sharpened dagger. Thus accoutred, and walking with the confident tread of such a character, and with the supple freedom of a woman who had habitually walked in her girlhood, barefoot and bare-legged, on the brown sea-sand, Madame Defarge took her way along the streets.

Now, when the journey of the travelling coach, at that very moment waiting for the completion of its load, had been planned out last night, the difficulty of taking Miss Pross in it had much engaged Mr. Lorry's attention. It was not merely desirable to avoid overloading the coach, but it was of the highest importance that the time occupied in examining it and its passengers, should be reduced to the utmost; since their escape might depend on the saving of only a few seconds here and there. Finally, he had proposed, after anxious consideration, that Miss Pross and Jerry, who were at liberty to leave the city, would leave it at three o'clock in the lightest-wheeled conveyance known to that period. Unencumbered with luggage, they would soon overtake the coach, and, passing it and preceding it on the road, would order its horses in advance, and greatly facilitate its progress during the precious hours of the night, when delay was the most to be dreaded.

Seeing in this arrangement the hope of rendering real

service in that pressing emergency, Miss Pross hailed it with joy. She and Jerry had beheld the coach start, had known who it was that Solomon brought, had passed some ten minutes in tortures of suspense, and were now concluding their arrangements to follow the coach, even as Madame Defarge, taking her way through the streets, now drew nearer and nearer to the else-deserted lodging in which they held their consultation.

"Now what do you think, Mr. Cruncher," said Miss Pross, whose agitation was so great that she could hardly speak, or stand, or move, or live: "what do you think of our not starting from this courtyard? Another carriage having already gone from here to-day, it might awaken suspicion."

"My opinion, miss," returned Mr. Cruncher, "is as you're right. Likewise wot I'll stand by you, right or wrong."

"I am so distracted with fear and hope for our precious creatures," said Miss Pross, wildly crying, "that I am incapable of forming any plan. Are *you* capable of forming any plan, my dear good Mr. Cruncher?"

"Respectin' a future spear o' life, miss," returned Mr. Cruncher, "I hope so. Respectin' any present use o' this here blessed old head o' mine, I think not. Would you do me the favour, miss, to take notice o' two promises and wows wot it is my wishes fur to record in this here crisis?"

"Oh, for gracious' sake!" cried Miss Pross, still wildly crying, "record them at once, and get them out of the way, like an excellent man."

"First," said Mr. Cruncher, who was all in a tremble, and who spoke with an ashy and solemn visage, "them poor things well out o' this, never no more will I do it, never no more!"

"I am quite sure, Mr. Cruncher," returned Miss Pross, "that you never will do it again, whatever it is, and I beg you not to think it necessary to mention more particularly what it is."

"No, miss," returned Jerry, "it shall not be named to you. Second: them poor things well out o' this, and never no more will I interfere with Mrs. Cruncher's flopping, never no more!"

"Whatever housekeeping arrangement that may be," said Miss Pross, striving to dry her eyes and compose herself, "I have no doubt it is best that Mrs. Cruncher should have it entirely under her own superintendence.—O my poor darlings!"

"I go so far as to say, miss, morehover," proceeded Mr. Cruncher, with a most alarming tendency to hold forth as from a pulpit—"and let my words be took down and took to Mrs. Cruncher through yourself—that wot my opinions respectin' flopping has undergone a change, and that wot I only hope with all my heart as Mrs. Cruncher may be a flopping at the present time."

"There, there, there! I hope she is, my dear man," cried the distracted Miss Pross, "and I hope she finds it answering her expectations."

"Forbid it," proceeded Mr. Cruncher, with additional solemnity, additional slowness, and additional tendency to hold forth and hold out, "as anything wot I have ever said or done should be wisited on my earnest wishes for them poor creeturs now! Forbid it as we shouldn't all flop (if it was anyways conwenient) to get 'em out o' this here dismal risk! Forbid it, miss! Wot I say, for-*bid* it!" This was Mr. Cruncher's conclusion after a protracted but vain endeavour to find a better one.

And still Madame Defarge, pursuing her way along the streets, came nearer and nearer.

"If we ever get back to our native land," said Miss Pross, "you may rely upon my telling Mrs. Cruncher as much as I may be able to remember and understand of what you have so impressively said; and at all events you may be sure that I shall bear witness to your being thoroughly in earnest at this dreadful time. Now, pray let us think! My esteemed Mr. Cruncher, let us think!"

Still, Madame Defarge, pursuing her way along the streets, came nearer and nearer.

"If you were to go before," said Miss Pross, "and stop the vehicle and horses from coming here, and were to wait somewhere for me, wouldn't that be best?"

Mr. Cruncher thought it might be best.

"Where could you wait for me?" asked Miss Pross.

Mr. Cruncher was so bewildered that he could think of no locality but Temple Bar. Alas! Temple Bar was hundreds of miles away, and Madame Defarge was drawing very near indeed.

"By the cathedral door," said Miss Pross. "Would it be much out of the way, to take me in, near the great cathedral door between the two towers?"

"No, miss," answered Mr. Cruncher.

"Then, like the best of men," said Miss Pross, "go to the posting-house straight, and make that change."

"I am doubtful," said Mr. Cruncher, hesitating and shaking his head, "about leaving of you, you see. We don't know what may happen."

"Heaven knows we don't," returned Miss Pross, "but have no fear of me. Take me in at the cathedral, at three o'clock, or as near it as you can, and I am sure it will be better than our going from here. I feel certain of it. There! Bless you, Mr. Cruncher! Think—not of me, but of the lives that may depend on both of us!"

This exordium, and Miss Pross's two hands in quite agonised entreaty clasping his, decided Mr. Cruncher. With an encouraging nod or two, he immediately went out to alter the arrangements, and left her by herself to follow as she had proposed.

The having originated a precaution which was already in course of execution was a great relief to Miss Pross. The necessity of composing her appearance so that it should attract no special notice in the streets was another relief. She looked at her watch, and it was twenty minutes past two. She had no time to lose, but must get ready at once.

Afraid, in her extreme perturbation, of the loneliness of the deserted rooms, and of half-imagined faces peeping from behind every open door in them, Miss Pross got a basin of cold water and began laving her eyes, which were swollen and red. Haunted by her feverish apprehensions, she could not bear to have her sight obscured for a minute at a time by the dripping water, but constantly paused and looked around to see that there was no one watching her. In one of those pauses she recoiled and cried out, for she saw a figure standing in the room.

The basin fell to the ground broken, and the water flowed to the feet of Madame Defarge. By strange stern ways, and through much staining blood, those feet had come to meet that water.

Madame Defarge looked coldly at her, and said, "The wife of Evrémonde; where is she?"

It flashed upon Miss Pross's mind that the doors were all standing open, and would suggest the flight. Her first act was to shut them. There were four in the room, and she shut them all. She then placed herself before the door of the chamber which Lucie had occupied.

Madame Defarge's dark eyes followed her through this
rapid movement, and rested on her when it was finished.
Miss Pross had nothing beautiful about her; years had not
tamed the wildness, or softened the grimness, of her appearance; but, she too, was a determined woman in her
different way, and she measured Madame Defarge with her
eyes, every inch.

"You might, from your appearance, be the wife of Lucifer," said Miss Pross, in her breathing. "Nevertheless, you
shall not get the better of me. I am an Englishwoman."

Madame Defarge looked at her scornfully, but still with
something of Miss Pross's own perception that they two
were at bay. She saw a tight, hard, wiry woman before her,
as Mr. Lorry had seen in the same figure a woman with a
strong hand, in the years gone by. She knew full well that
Miss Pross was the family's devoted friend; Miss Pross
knew full well that Madame Defarge was the family's malevolent enemy.

"On my way yonder," said Madame Defarge, with a
slight movement of her hand towards the fatal spot, "where
they reserve my chair and my knitting for me, I am come
to make my compliments to her in passing. I wish to see
her."

"I know that your intentions are evil," said Miss Pross,
"and you may depend upon it, I'll hold my own against
them."

Each spoke in her own language; neither understood the
other's words; both were very watchful, and intent to deduce, from look and manner, what the unintelligible words
meant.

"It will do her no good to keep herself concealed from
me at this moment," said Madame Defarge. "Good patriots
will know what that means. Let me see her. Go tell her that
I wish to see her. Do you hear?"

"If those eyes of yours were bed-winches," returned
Miss Pross, "and I was an English four-poster, they
shouldn't loose a splinter of me. No, you wicked foreign
woman; I am your match."

Madame Defarge was not likely to follow these idiomatic remarks in detail; but, she so far understood them as
to perceive that she was set at naught.

"Woman imbecile and pig-like!" said Madame Defarge,
frowning. "I take no answer from you. I demand to see
her. Either tell her that I demand to see her, or stand out of

the way of the door and let me go to her!" This, with an angry explanatory wave of her right arm.

"I little thought," said Miss Pross, "that I should ever want to understand your nonsensical language; but I would give all I have, except the clothes I wear, to know whether you suspect the truth, or any part of it."

Neither of them for a single moment released the other's eyes. Madame Defarge had not moved from the spot where she stood when Miss Pross first became aware of her; but she now advanced one step.

"I am a Briton," said Miss Pross, "I am desperate. I don't care an English twopence for myself. I know that the longer I keep you here, the greater hope there is for my Ladybird. I'll not leave a handful of that dark hair upon your head, if you lay a finger on me!"

Thus Miss Pross, with a shake of her head and a flash of her eyes between every rapid sentence, and every rapid sentence a whole breath. Thus Miss Pross who had never struck a blow in her life.

But, her courage was of that emotional nature that it brought the irrepressible tears into her eyes. This was a courage that Madame Defarge so little comprehended as to mistake for weakness. "Ha, ha!" she laughed, "you poor wretch! What are you worth! I address myself to that Doctor." Then she raised her voice and called out, "Citizen Doctor! Wife of Evrémonde! Child of Evrémonde! Any person but this miserable fool, answer the Citizeness Defarge!"

Perhaps the following silence, perhaps some latent disclosure in the expression of Miss Pross's face, perhaps a sudden misgiving apart from either suggestion, whispered to Madame Defarge that they were gone. Three of the doors she opened swiftly, and looked in.

"Those rooms are all in disorder, there has been hurried packing, there are odds and ends upon the ground. There is no one in that room behind you! Let me look."

"Never!" said Miss Pross, who understood the request as perfectly as Madame Defarge understood the answer.

"If they are not in that room, they are gone, and can be pursued and brought back," said Madame Defarge to herself.

"As long as you don't know whether they are in that room or not, you are uncertain what to do," said Miss Pross to *her*self; "and you shall not know that, if I can prevent your knowing it; and know that, or not know that, you shall not leave here while I can hold you."

"I have been in the streets from the first, nothing has stopped me, I will tear you to pieces, but I will have you from that door," said Madame Defarge.

"We are alone at the top of a high house in a solitary courtyard, we are not likely to be heard, and I pray for bodily strength to keep you here, while every minute you are here is worth a hundred thousand guineas to my darling," said Miss Pross.

Madame Defarge made at the door. Miss Pross, on the instinct of the moment, seized her round the waist in both her arms, and held her tight. It was in vain for Madame Defarge to struggle and to strike; Miss Pross, with the vigorous tenacity of love, always so much stronger than hate, clasped her tight, and even lifted her from the floor in the struggle that they had. The two hands of Madame Defarge buffeted and tore her face; but, Miss Pross, with her head down, held her round the waist, and clung to her with more than the hold of a drowning woman.

Soon, Madame Defarge's hands ceased to strike, and felt at her encircled waist. "It is under my arm," said Miss Pross, in smothered tones, "you shall not draw it. I am stronger than you, I bless Heaven for it. I'll hold you till one or other of us faints or dies!"

Madame Defarge's hands were at her bosom. Miss Pross looked up, saw what it was, struck at it, struck out a flash and a crash, and stood alone—blinded with smoke.

All this was in a second. As the smoke cleared, leaving an awful stillness, it passed out on the air, like the soul of the furious woman whose body lay lifeless on the ground.

In the first fright and horror of her situation, Miss Pross passed the body as far from it as she could, and ran down the stairs to call for fruitless help. Happily, she bethought herself of the consequences of what she did, in time to check herself and go back. It was dreadful to go in at the door again; but she did go in, and even went near it, to get the bonnet and other things that she must wear. These she put on, out on the staircase, first shutting and locking the door and taking away the key. She then sat down on the stairs a few moments to breathe and to cry, and then got up and hurried away.

By good fortune she had a veil on her bonnet, or she

could hardly have gone along the streets without being stopped. By good fortune, too, she was naturally so peculiar in appearance as not to show disfigurement like any other woman. She needed both advantages, for the marks of griping fingers were deep in her face, and her hair was torn, and her dress (hastily composed with unsteady hands) was clutched and dragged a hundred ways.

In crossing the bridge, she dropped the door key in the river. Arriving at the cathedral some few minutes before her escort, and waiting there, she thought, what if the key were already taken in a net, what if it were identified, what if the door were opened and the remains discovered, what if she were stopped at the gate, sent to prison, and charged with murder! In the midst of these fluttering thoughts, the escort appeared, took her in, and took her away.

"Is there any noise in the streets?" she asked him.

"The usual noises," Mr. Cruncher replied; and looked surprised by the question and by her aspect.

"I don't hear you," said Miss Pross. "What do you say?"

It was in vain for Mr. Cruncher to repeat what he said; Miss Pross could not hear him. "So I'll nod my head," thought Mr. Cruncher, amazed, "at all events she'll see that." And she did.

"Is there any noise in the streets now?" asked Miss Pross again, presently.

Again Mr. Cruncher nodded his head.

"I don't hear it."

"Gone deaf in a hour?" said Mr. Cruncher, ruminating, with his mind much disturbed; "wot's come to her?"

"I feel," said Miss Pross, "as if there had been a flash and a crash, and that crash was the last thing I should ever hear in this life."

"Blest if she ain't in a queer condition!" said Mr. Cruncher, more and more disturbed. "Wot can she have been a takin', to keep her courage up? Hark! There's the roll of them dreadful carts! You can hear that, miss?"

"I can hear," said Miss Pross, seeing that he spoke to her, "nothing. O, my good man, there was first a great crash, and then a great stillness, and that stillness seems to be fixed and unchangeable, never to be broken any more as long as my life lasts."

"If she don't hear the roll of those dreadful carts, now very nigh their journey's end," said Mr. Cruncher, glancing over his shoulder, "it's my opinion that indeed she never will hear anything else in this world."

And indeed she never did.

*　　*　　*　　*　　*　　*　　*　　*

15 *The Footsteps Die Out For Ever*

ALONG THE Paris streets, the death-carts rumble, hollow and harsh. Six tumbrils carry the day's wine to La Guillotine. All the devouring and insatiate monsters imagined since imagination could record itself, are fused in the one realisation, Guillotine. And yet there is not in France, with its rich variety of soil and climate, a blade, a leaf, a root, a sprig, a peppercorn, which will grow to maturity under conditions more certain than those that have produced this horror. Crush humanity out of shape once more, under similar hammers, and it will twist itself into the same tortured forms. Sow the same seed of rapacious license and oppression over again, and it will surely yield the same fruit according to its kind.

Six tumbrils roll along the streets. Change these back again to what they were, thou powerful enchanter, Time, and they shall be seen to be the carriages of absolute monarchs, the equipages of feudal nobles, the toilettes of flaring Jezebels, the churches that are not my Father's house but dens of thieves, the huts of millions of starving peasants! No; the great magician who majestically works out the appointed order of the Creator never reverses his transformations. "If thou be changed into this shape by the will of God," say the seers to the enchanted, in the wise Arabian stories, "then remain so! But, if thou wear this form through mere passing conjuration, then resume thy former aspect!" Changeless and hopeless, the tumbrils roll along.

As the sombre wheels of the six carts go round, they seem to plough up a long crooked furrow among the populace in the streets. Ridges of faces are thrown to this side and to that, and the ploughs go steadily onward. So used are the regular inhabitants of the houses to the spectacle, that in many windows there are no people, and in some the occupation of the hands is not so much as suspended, while the eyes survey the faces in the tumbrils. Here and there, the inmate has visitors to see the sight; then he points his finger, with something of the complacency of a curator or authorised exponent, to this cart and to this, and seems to tell who sat here yesterday, and who there the day before.

Of the riders in the tumbrils, some observe these things, and all things on their last roadside, with an impassive stare; others, with a lingering interest in the ways of life and men. Some, seated with drooping heads, are sunk in silent despair; again, there are some so heedful of their looks that they cast upon the multitude such glances as they have seen in theatres, and in pictures. Several close their eyes, and think, or try to get their straying thoughts together. Only one, and he a miserable creature, of a crazed aspect, is so shattered and made drunk by horror, that he sings, and tries to dance. Not one of the whole number appeals, by look or gesture, to the pity of the people.

There is a guard of sundry horsemen riding abreast of the tumbrils, and faces are often turned up to some of them, and they are asked some questions. It would seem to be always the same question, for, it is always followed by a press of people towards the third cart. The horsemen abreast of that cart frequently point out one man in it with their swords. The leading curiosity is to know which is he; he stands at the back of the tumbril with his head bent down, to converse with a mere girl who sits on the side of the cart, and holds his hand. He has no curiosity or care for the scene about him, and always speaks to the girl. Here and there in the long street of St. Honoré, cries are raised against him. If they move him at all, it is only to a quiet smile, as he shakes his hair a little more loosely about his face. He cannot easily touch his face, his arms being bound.

On the steps of a church, awaiting the coming-up of the tumbrils, stands the spy and prison-sheep. He looks into the first of them: not there. He looks into the second: not there. He already asks himself, "Has he sacrificed me?" when his face clears, as he looks into the third.

"Which is Evrémonde?" says a man behind him.

"That. At the back there."

"With his hand in the girl's?"

"Yes."

The man cries, "Down, Evrémonde! To the Guillotine all aristocrats; Down, Evrémonde!"

"Hush, hush!" the spy entreats him, timidly.

"And why not, citizen?"

"He is going to pay the forfeit: it will be paid in five minutes more. Let him be at peace."

But the man continuing to exclaim, "Down, Evrémonde!" the face of Evrémonde is for a moment turned towards him. Evrémonde then sees the spy, and looks attentively at him, and goes his way.

The clocks are on the stroke of three, and the furrow ploughed among the populace is turning round, to come on into the place of execution, and end. The ridges thrown to this side and to that, now crumble in and close behind the last plough as it passes on, for all are following to the Guillotine. In front of it, seated in chairs, as in a garden of public diversion, are a number of women, busily knitting. On one of the foremost chairs stands The Vengeance, looking about for her friend.

"Thérèse!" she cries, in her shrill tones. "Who has seen her? Thérèse Defarge!"

"She never missed before," says a knitting-woman of the sisterhood.

"No; nor will she miss now," cries The Vengeance, petulantly. "Thérèse!"

"Louder," the woman recommends.

Ay! Louder, Vengeance, much louder, and still she will scarcely hear thee. Louder yet, Vengeance, with a little oath or so added, and yet it will hardly bring her. Send other women up and down to seek her, lingering somewhere; and yet, although the messengers have done dread deeds, it is questionable whether of their own will they will go far enough to find her!

"Bad Fortune!" cries The Vengeance, stamping her foot in the chair, "and here are the tumbrils! And Evrémonde will be despatched in a wink, and she not here! See her knitting in my hand, and her empty chair ready for her. I cry with vexation and disappointment!"

As The Vengeance descends from her elevation to do it, the tumbrils begin to discharge their loads. The ministers of Sainte Guillotine are robed and ready. Crash!—A head is held up, and the knitting-women who scarcely lifted their eyes to look at it a moment ago when it could think and speak, count One.

The second tumbril empties and moves on; the third comes up. Crash!—And the knitting-women, never faltering or pausing in their work, count Two.

The supposed Evrémonde descends, and the seamstress is lifted out next after him. He has not relinquished her patient hand in getting out, but still holds it as he promised. He gently places her with her back to the crashing engine that constantly whirrs up and falls, and she looks into his face and thanks him.

"But for you, dear stranger, I should not be so composed, for I am naturally a poor little thing, faint of heart; nor should I have been able to raise my thoughts to Him who was put to death, that we might have hope and comfort here to-day. I think you were sent to me by Heaven."

"Or you to me," says Sydney Carton. "Keep your eyes upon me, dear child, and mind no other object."

"I mind nothing while I hold your hand. I shall mind nothing when I let it go, if they are rapid."

"They will be rapid. Fear not!"

The two stand in the fast-thinning throng of victims, but they speak as if they were alone. Eye to eye, voice to voice, hand to hand, heart to heart, these two children of the Universal Mother, else so wide apart and differing, have come together on the dark highway, to repair home together, and to rest in her bosom.

"Brave and generous friend, will you let me ask you one last question? I am very ignorant, and it troubles me—just a little."

"Tell me what it is."

"I have a cousin, an only relative and an orphan, like myself, whom I love very dearly. She is five years younger than I, and she lives in a farmer's house in the south country. Poverty parted us, and she knows nothing of my fate—for I cannot write—and if I could, how should I tell her! It is better as it is."

"Yes, yes; better as it is."

"What I have been thinking as we came along, and what I am still thinking now, as I look into your kind strong face which gives me much support, is this: If the Republic really does good to the poor, and they come to be less hungry, and in all ways to suffer less, she may live a long time: she may even live to be old."

"What then, my gentle sister?"

"Do you think"—the uncomplaining eyes, in which there is so much endurance, fill with tears, and the lips part a little more and tremble—"that it will seem long to me, while I wait for her in the better land where I trust both you and I will be mercifully sheltered?"

"It cannot be, my child; there is no time there, and no trouble there."

"You comfort me so much! I am so ignorant. Am I to kiss you now? Is the moment come?"

"Yes."

She kisses his lips; he kisses hers; they solemnly bless each other. The spare hand does not tremble as he releases it; nothing worse than a sweet, bright constancy is in the patient face. She goes next before him—is gone; the knitting-women count Twenty-two.

"I am the Resurrection and the Life, saith the Lord: he that believeth in me, though he were dead, yet shall he live: and whosoever liveth and believeth in me shall never die."

The murmuring of many voices, the upturning of many faces, the pressing on of many footsteps in the outskirts of the crowd, so that it swells forward in a mass, like one great heave of water, all flashes away. Twenty-three.

THEY said of him, about the city that night, that it was the peacefullest man's face ever beheld there. Many added that he looked sublime and prophetic.

One of the most remarkable sufferers by the same axe—a woman—had asked at the foot of the same scaffold, not long before, to be allowed to write down the thoughts that were inspiring her. If he had given an utterance to his, and they were prophetic, they would have been these:

"I see Barsad, and Cly, Defarge, The Vengeance, the Juryman, the Judge, long ranks of the new oppressors who have risen on the destruction of the old, perishing by this retributive instrument, before it shall cease out of its present use. I see a beautiful city and a brilliant people rising from this abyss, and, in their struggles to be truly free, in their triumphs and defeats, through long long years to come, I see the evil of this time and of the previous time of which this is the natural birth, gradually making expiation for itself and wearing out.

"I see the lives for which I lay down my life, peaceful,

useful, prosperous and happy, in that England which I shall see no more. I see *her* with a child upon her bosom, who bears my name. I see her father, aged and bent, but otherwise restored, and faithful to all men in his healing office, and at peace. I see the good old man, so long their friend, in ten years' time enriching them with all he has, and passing tranquilly to his reward.

"I see that I hold a sanctuary in their hearts, and in the hearts of their descendants, generations hence. I see her, an old woman, weeping for me on the anniversary of this day. I see her and her husband, their course done, living side by side in their last earthly bed, and I know that each was not more honoured and held sacred in the other's soul, than I was in the souls of both.

"I see that child who lay upon her bosom and who bore my name, a man winning his way up in that path of life which once was mine. I see him winning it so well, that my name is made illustrious there by the light of his. I see the blots I threw upon it faded away. I see him, foremost of the just judges and honoured men, bringing a boy of my name, with a forehead that I know and golden hair, to this place —then fair to look upon, with not a trace of this day's disfigurement—and I hear him tell the child my story, with a tender and faltering voice.

"It is a far, far better thing that I do, than I have ever done; it is a far, far better rest that I go to than I have ever known."

AFTERWORD

THROUGHOUT the nineteenth century Europe was haunted by the specter of revolution. The flaming holocaust that had been born in France and poured its fiery floods over nearly all the rest of the Continent troubled the nightmares of the dominant classes with shuddering visions of an infuriated Jacquerie burning down châteaux, ferocious mobs tearing through the streets, howling tribunals, the rumbling of tumbrils, the hiss and thud of the guillotine, the bloodbaths of the Napoleonic Wars. The rulers of the nations had put back—or almost put back—the clock, but they had not solved the problems of social injustice and suffering. The Terror might rise again.

This was the foreboding burden of *A Tale of Two Cities,* sounding like a dreadful drum with deepening vibrancy through the accelerating rush and rising tumult of the fierce revolutionary violence it unfolded. If men turned their eyes from the miseries of emaciated toilers in mines and mills and factories, deafened their ears to the cries of exploited children, closed their hearts to sickness and poverty, there would be a hideous retribution. Wrong would generate wrong—blazing into all the horrors of revolution, engulfing both the innocent and the guilty in a sacrificial incandescence. Later readers of the novel have not always realized the degree to which Dickens was appealing to a troubled social conscience and a fear of social turmoil.

The danger was not imaginary. The July Revolution of 1830 had seen barricades again in Paris, and it was succeeded by risings in Belgium, Italy, Germany, and Poland. Suppression followed; but, beneath the surface, discontent seethed and bubbled. In 1848 the entire continent erupted. Revolutions swept Sicily, Lombardy, and Poland; republics were proclaimed in Venice and Rome; violence broke out in Budapest, Vienna, and Berlin; the boulevards and byways of Paris boiled with the bloodiest street-fighting Europe had known since 1793. Following the downfall of Napoleon III, the radicals and socialists proclaimed a Commune. The National Guard seized the cannon belonging to the regular army and refused to fire upon the crowd; during the Bloody Week of May 21 there were mob executions and then sanguinary reprisals.

England had suffered less from war and political turmoil than the Continent, but for that very reason, perhaps, her comfortable middle class was the more worried. Their fears of radicalism and revolt were not unlike those that agitated the United States during the depression of the 1930's and after the two world wars. Even during periods of prosperity, beneath England's fat padding of plush and horsehair, its ponderous walnut furniture, and its complacency over the millions of steel knives turned out at Sheffield and the miles of iron rails girdling the country, the age trembled as often as industrial unrest forced it to recall the hordes of misery festering in its foul slums. When might not the red fury, which had repeatedly laved Europe in flames, burst into fire at home?

The menace, indeed, again and again seemed imminent. The ranks of the hundreds of thousands thrown out of work by the economic dislocations that followed the peace of 1815 were swollen by more than 400,000 demobilized soldiers. Hungry laborers rioted; for the first time in English history habeas corpus was suspended; in the Peterloo Massacre a peaceful crowd demonstrating for parliamentary reform and repeal of the Corn Laws was ridden down by the militia; a band of extremists plotted to assassinate the entire cabinet, seize the Bank of England, and establish a provisional government.

A dozen years later there might have been revolution but for the passage of the Reform Bill of 1832. Disorder broke out all over England; for two days a mob held Bristol; in Scotland angry weavers stoned Sir Walter Scott's carriage, shouting "Burke Sir Walter." The close of the decade brought the Chartist agitation for universal suffrage and laboring-class representation in Parliament. In 1840 the cotton mills of Manchester were deserted while threatening jobless men filled the streets; all the North of England went out on one general strike, which the authorities put down by firing into the crowds. The next year a brickmakers' strike ended in bloody riots, and the year after that came a great strike in Lancashire, while in the South rebellious farm laborers set fire to ricks and barns. In 1845 the Irish potato blight and the prolonged rains that rotted the harvest on the ground reduced the poor to starvation. Only the repeal of the Corn Laws ended the danger of rebellion.

During the Crimean War conditions again grew ominous. The war was made an excuse for dropping all efforts at social planning: popular education, slum clearance, sanitation, hours and wages, factory conditions—every necessary amelioration. "The old cannon-smoke and blood-mists," Dickens summarized bitterly, were being allowed to "obscure the wrongs and sufferings of the people." In London there were bread riots in the East End, with dock laborers raising the black flag and looting bakers' shops. "Take my knowledge of things for what it may be worth a dozen years hence," Dickens prophesied. "The people will not bear for any length of time what they bear now." Unless a change were made there would be "such a shake in this country as was never seen on Earth since Samson pulled the Temple down upon his head."

Amid such social conflicts *A Tale of Two Cities* was born. Dickens wrote it not in a time of peace, prosperity, and stability, but of mass protest and imminent revolution. He first conceived the story shortly after a hundred people had been killed or wounded by the bomb with which Orsini attempted to assassinate Napoleon III. Even as the novel was being published, revolutions deposed the rulers of Parma, Tuscany, Modena, and Romagna, and there were insurrections in the Papal States. Only a year later, in four swift months, Garibaldi's Redshirts swarmed over all Sicily and triumphantly captured Naples. Everywhere the old tyrannies and injustices were crashing. Unless England's landowners, merchants, and industrialists took warning, might not their turn come next?

A Tale of Two Cities was thus not only a work of art, it was also a tract for the times, a conditional prophecy. The French Revolution had been the decisive upheaval that had destroyed the eighteenth-century world and shattered the power of the aristocracy in France, had shaken it even in the rest of Europe. It was the convulsive womb out of which the modern world had been born. But the changes it had wrought had been far from sufficient. With an "enormous black cloud of poverty in every town spreading and deepening every hour," as Dickens said, was it not clear that force and greed still had the upper hand over justice and love?

Among Dickens' novels *A Tale of Two Cities* was not the first in which he had dealt with the theme of revolt. In a way, indeed, that theme sounds like an angry tocsin throughout the entire body of his work. For all the high-spirited comedy that rollicks in his fiction and often wells up to towering heights of hilarity, his deepest driving forces are his sympathy for the misused and oppressed and his burning revolt against cruelty and injustice. Even in *Pickwick Papers,* the comic epic that brought him his early fame, there is no mistaking his scorn for the corruption of politics in the Eatanswill election, his hatred for the chicaneries of the law, and his indignant pity for the haggard debtors immured behind the bars of the Fleet Prison.

And repeatedly, thenceforth, in novel after novel, Dickens returned to the attack. At first the rumblings of revolt were hardly more than implicit—in those few scenes, for example, of *The Old Curiosity Shop* that paint the industrial North, with dark figures swarming among the blazing furnaces, "clustered by torchlight round their leaders, who told them, in stern language, of their wrongs, and urged them on to frightful cries and threats" until maddened men, "armed with sword and firebrand . . . rushed forth on errands of terror and destruction." The disorders only glimpsed here dominate *Barnaby Rudge,* boiling up in the mob fury of the Gordon Riots of 1780, the gutting of churches, the burning of Lord Mansfield's mansion, the storming of Newgate. These two hundred tumultuous pages are like the eruption of a subterranean volcano heaving flame and lava from the black depths within which they have been seething. When this novel was first published, amid Chartist agitation and industrial strife, many of Dickens' readers must have understood it in the way he meant it, as a portent of the dangers of their own time.

But the surrender of Newgate had sounded the alarm bell of no such national cataclysm as the fall of the Bastille. It was almost inevitable that eventually Dickens would return to the theme, seeking to embody it in a more powerful form; and hardly possible that if he did so he should overlook the French Revolution as the archetypal symbol both of his indictment and of his warning. Though in many ways *A Tale of Two Cities* is the least characteristic of his novels, in this sense it is central to Dickens' thought. It proclaims in a crescendo of trumpet blasts what sounds only in ominous undertones through the others, emerging in the paragraphs on the pestilence in *Dombey and Son,* Krook's death by spontaneous combustion in *Bleak House,* the threats of reality turning wolfish in *Hard Times,* the image of society as a jail that grows ever darker in *Little Dorrit, Great Expectations,* and *Our Mutual Friend.*

This prison image runs, indeed, through all Dickens' work, from the Fleet Prison of *Pickwick Papers* to the condemned cell in which the murderer in the unfinished *Mystery of Edwin Drood* was to await his death. In *A Tale of Two Cities* it is crucial. The eighteen years of unjust imprisonment Doctor Manette has spent in the Bastille have broken him and driven him mad. Though the Bastille prisoner may be "recalled to life" and precariously restored to sanity, the suffering past with all its weight of guilt and wrong cannot be blotted out. And Doctor Manette's sufferings become the symbol of the fate of the entire French people, confined within the walls of a cruel and unyielding social system. The fall of the Bastille is both a literal and a figurative statement of the violent destruction of that system.

The vision of the Revolution as inevitable retribution for the evil past illumines all its scenes of ferocity and bloodshed and reverberates in the concluding rumble of the death carts trundling to the guillotine. "Crush humanity out of shape once more, under similar hammers," Dickens exclaims, "and it will twist itself into the same tortured forms. Sow the same seed of rapacious license and oppression over again, and it will surely yield the same fruit according to its kind.

"Six tumbrils roll along the streets. Change these back again to what they were, thou powerful enchanter, Time, and they shall be seen to be the carriages of absolute monarchs, the equipages of feudal nobles, the toilettes of flaring Jezebels, the churches that are not my Father's house but dens of thieves, the huts of millions of starving peasants!" And, he might have added, the criminal dives of Whitechapel and Saffron Hill, Mr. Dombey's icy mansion, the smoke-blackened tenements of Coketown, the golden pomp of Mr. Merdle's feasts, the miners dying of fossy-jaw, the ponderous silver candelabra of Mr. Podsnap's board, and the mutilated children in jail-like factories.

The rising tumult of the revolutionary storm is portrayed

by Dickens with a strange and ambivalent mingling of sympathy and horror, of exultation and fear. Though as a merciful human being he sickens at the cruelty of mass murder, he understands this fury as "a wild infection of the wildly shaken public mind" and sees how it can be brought to gloat in a bath of blood. Even as he shudders back in fascinated terror, he is at the same time one of the mob, sharing its fierce lust of revenge and destruction. There is a dreadful compulsion in the Carmagnole, "a ghastly apparition of a dance-figure gone raving mad," "keeping a ferocious time . . . like a gnashing of teeth in unison," with dancers who "advanced, retreated, struck at one another's hands," spun, "clutched and tore," and then, "with their heads low down, and their hands high up, swooped screaming off." Horrible though they are, there is nothing strange about the emotions of these maddened people, at one moment weeping tears of sympathy and the next howling for more heads.

But furious as are the passions rolling through this tempestuous narrative, Dickens subjects them to a superb artistic control. Never had he previously plotted a novel with more skill, joined all its intricate details with more craftsmanship, prepared its successive revelations with more mastery. Published both in weekly and in monthly installments, it was so organized that every number incorporated some vital development in its organic growth. At the end of the eighth weekly installment, in the quiet little court off Soho where Doctor Manette dwells, there is the famous episode of the hosts of hurrying footsteps, which Lucie thinks of as the echoes of all those that are presently to come into their lives. A number of carefully spaced installments establish and underline Sydney Carton's attitude toward Darnay and the devotion to Lucie that will lead him to take Darnay's place in prison. Jerry Cruncher's knowledge of the pretended burial of the spy Roger Cly later gives Carton the weapon that enables him to blackmail the turnkey Barsad. An entire essay could be devoted to the scores of structural brilliances that articulate the novel.

It is pointless to complain—though Dickens' friend Forster did—that *A Tale of Two Cities* has none of the great triumphs of comedy that abound in his other novels, no Dick Swiveller or Sairey Gamp or Captain Cuttle or Flora Finching. Dickens was aiming at a different kind of novel; one might as well object that *Macbeth* has no Falstaff or Touchstone. A more cogent criticism might be that most of the characters, although vividly and sometimes power-fully drawn, have little psychological complexity or depth, although this would not be altogether true of Sydney Car-ton and Doctor Manette. Here again, however, Dickens was essaying another sort of novel: one, as he himself explained, whose characters should be expressed by the action, "more than they should express themselves, by dia-logue," or by introspection. Nevertheless, it must be con-ceded that the stripped brevity of the narrative and the consequent condensation of psychological portrayal result in a certain melodramatic thinness of characterization.

Melodramatic coincidences also flaw the otherwise splen-did structure of the book. Of all the women in France, Mme. Defarge, the wife of Doctor Manette's old servant, turns out also to be the younger sister of the wronged vic-tims of the Evrémonde family whose deaths the Doctor had witnessed. Of all the men Lucie might have married, she chances to fall in love with Charles Darnay, the inno-cent heir of that evil family. Of all the angry mob storming the Bastille, it is Defarge who finds the hidden papers that denounce Darnay to the revolutionary tribunal. Of all the turnkeys of the Paris jails, the one in charge of Darnay's cell at La Force is Barsad, against whom Carton has a damaging piece of knowledge. Last, and most staggering of all, Carton is almost Darnay's twin and can take his place on the scaffold. Even Dickens' consummate ingenuity in preparation cannot entirely mask these cumulative coin-cidences.

Though in its deepest sense the novel is not sentimental, it does on occasion fall into emotional overindulgence. The death of Sydney Carton is drenched in every organ chord to make it heartrending, with the timorous and pathetic little seamstress who detects his masquerade and precedes him to the guillotine, and the nobly mournful rhythms of his valedictory: "It is a far, far better thing I do, than I have ever done; it is a far, far better rest that I go to, than I have ever known." Far worse is the pathos of Lucie's prolonged words of comfort to her father in Defarge's gar-ret, when she cradles his white head on her breasts; there is something almost embarrassing in the obtrusive artifice of the refrain, "weep for it, weep for it," recurring in tearful cadence.

These defects in the book, however, are far outweighed by its triumphs, its dramatic force, the enormous power with which it renders the red phantasmagoria of revolution rushing past in hideous pageant, the terror and horror of helpless suffering and sacrifice, the grandeur of renunciation. There is the storming of the Bastille, with its seven gory heads on pikes, the attack on the Hôtel de Ville, with naked women beating their breasts in bloody-minded fury; the screaming outcries against Foulon, who told the starving people to eat grass: "Give us the blood of Foulon, Give us the head of Foulon, Give us the heart of Foulon, Give us the body and soul of Foulon, Rend Foulon to pieces, and dig him into the ground, that grass may grow from him!"

And, ever, like a tempest, the Terror rises, devouring new victims as it tears on its appalling way, swallowing those who were judges and jurymen, bathing the very ground beneath the guillotine in rivers of blood. Dickens well knows that in its course the Revolution has undergone a monstrous transformation and that the revolutionary mob has become a horde of howling demons. But he perceives, too, that the Revolution was the fatal fruit of centuries of oppression, a growth of historical necessity rooted in the unalterable past. Though the innocent suffered with the guilty, it embodied a tragic justice.

Ultimately, through the dying vision of Carton, Dickens looks into a future that at least partially redeems the agonies through which it came into being: "I see a beautiful city and a brilliant people rising from this abyss, and in their struggles to be truly free, in their triumphs and defeats, through long, long years to come, I see the evil of this time, and of the previous time of which this is the natural birth, gradually making expiation for itself and wearing out." The noble vision out of which the Revolution had been born would not die. In its close *A Tale of Two Cities* soars high above both the morbid terrors of the reactionary and the revengeful fury of the Jacobin. Dickens' revolutionary vision is creative, not destructive. It transcends anger and rebellion with hope and love.

EDGAR JOHNSON
The City College of the City
University of New York
July 4, 1962

SELECTED BIBLIOGRAPHY

WORKS BY CHARLES DICKENS

Sketches by Boz, 1836, 1839 Sketches and Stories
The Posthumous Papers of the Pickwick Club, 1837 Novel (Signet Classic 0451-517563)
Oliver Twist; or, the Parish Boy's Progress, 1838 Novel (Signet Classic 0451-516850)
The Life and Adventures of Nicholas Nickleby, 1839 Novel (Signet Classic 0451-516338)
The Old Curiosity Shop, 1841 Novel
Barnaby Rudge, 1841 Novel
American Notes: For General Circulation, 1842 Travel Book
A Christmas Carol: in Prose, 1843 Christmas Book
The Life and Adventures of Martin Chuzzlewit, 1844 Novel
The Chimes, 1844 Christmas Book
The Cricket on the Hearth, 1845 Christmas Book
Pictures from Italy, 1846 Travel Book
The Battle of Life: A Love Story, 1846 Christmas Book
Dealings with the Firm of Dombey and Son, 1848 Novel (Meridian Classic 0452-007550)
The Haunted Man and the Ghost's Bargain, 1848 Christmas Book
The Personal History of David Copperfield, 1850 Novel (Signet Classic 0451-519078)
A Child's History of England, 1852, 1853, 1854 History
Bleak House, 1853 Novel (Signet Classic 0451-520017)
Hard Times: For These Times, 1854 Novel (Signet Classic 0451-513355)
Little Dorrit, 1857 Novel (Meridian Classic 0452-008557)
The Lazy Tour of Two Idle Apprentices (with Wilkie Collins), 1857 Travel Book
Reprinted Pieces, 1858 Collection of Magazine Articles
A Tale of Two Cities, 1859 Novel (Signet Classic 0451-519590)
Great Expectations, 1861 Novel (Signet Classic 0451-520769)
The Uncommercial Traveler, 1861, 1868 Collection of Magazine Articles
Our Mutual Friend, 1865 Novel (Signet Classic 0451-518632)
"George Silverman's Explanation," 1868 Story
The Mystery of Edwin Drood (unfinished), 1870 Novel (Meridian Classic 0452-006880)

BIOGRAPHY AND CRITICISM

Butt, John, and Kathleen Tillotson. *Dickens at Work.* London: Methuen, 1957.

Chesterton, G. K. *Appreciations and Criticisms of the Works of Charles Dickens.* London: Dent; New York: Dutton, 1911.

————. *Charles Dickens: A Critical Study.* London: Methuen, 1906. Rpt. as *Charles Dickens: The Last of the Great Men.* Foreward by Alexander Woollcott. New York: The Press of the Reader's Club, 1942.

Cockshut, A. O. J. *The Imagination of Charles Dickens.* New York: New York Univ. Press, 1962.

Collins, P. A. W. *Dickens and Crime.* London: Macmillan; New York: St. Martin's Press, 1962.

————. *Dickens and Education.* London: Macmillan; New York: St. Martin's Press, 1963.

————, ed. *Dickens: The Critical Heritage.* New York: Barnes and Noble, 1971.

Fielding, K. J. *Charles Dickens: A Critical Introduction.* 2nd ed., enlarged. London: Longmans, 1965.

Ford, G. H. *Dickens and his Readers: Aspects of Novel Criticism Since 1836.* Princeton, N. J.: Princeton Univ. Press, 1955.

————, and Lauriat Lane, Jr., eds. *The Dickens Critics.* Ithaca, N. Y.: Cornell Univ. Press, 1961.

Forster, John. *The Life of Charles Dickens.* Ed., Annotated, with Intro. by J. W. T. Ley. London: Cecil Palmer; New York: Doubleday, Doran, 1928.

Garius, R. *The Dickens Theater: A Reassessment of the Novels.* New York and London: The Clarendon Press of Oxford Univ. Press, 1965.

Gissing, George. *Charles Dickens: A Critical Study.* New York: Dodd, Mead, 1904.

————. *Critical Studies of the Works of Charles Dickens.* New York: Greenberg, 1924.

Gross, John, and G. Pearson, eds. *Dickens and the Twentieth Century.* Toronto: Univ. of Toronto Press, 1962.

Hardy, Barbara. *The Moral Art of Dickens.* New York: Oxford Univ. Press, 1970.

House, Humphrey. *The Dickens World.* London and New York: Oxford Univ. Press, 1941.

Jackson, Thomas A. *Charles Dickens: Progress of a Radical.* New York: International Publishers, 1938.

Johnson, E. D. H. *Charles Dickens: An Introduction to His Novels.* New York: Random House, 1969.

Johnson, Edgar. *Charles Dickens: His Tragedy and Triumph.* 2 vols. New York: Simon and Schuster, 1952. Rev. and Abridged, 1 vol., New York: Viking, 1977.

Leavis, F. R., and Q. D. Leavis. *Dickens the Novelist.* New York: Pantheon, 1971.

MacKenzie, Norman, and Jeanne MacKenzie. *Dickens: A Life.* New York and London: Oxford Univ. Press, 1979.

Marcus, Steven. *Dickens: From Pickwick to Dombey.* New York: Basic Books, 1965.

Miller, J. Hillis. *Charles Dickens: The World of his Novels*. Cambridge: Harvard Univ. Press, 1958.

Monod, Sylvère. *Dickens the Novelist*. Intro. Edward Wagenknecht. Norman: Oklahoma Univ. Press, 1968.

Nisbet, Ada, and Blake Nevius, eds. *Dickens Centennial Essays*. Berkeley: Univ. of California Press, 1971.

Orwell, George. "Charles Dickens." In *The Collected Essays, Journalism and Letters of George Orwell*, I. Ed. Sonia Orwell and Ian Angus. Harmondsworth: Penguin, 1972, pp. 454-504.

Pearson, Hesketh. *Dickens, His Character, Comedy, and Career*. New York: Harper, 1949.

Pope-Hennessey, Una. *Charles Dickens*. London: Chatto & Windus, 1945.

Romano, John. *Dickens and Reality*. New York: Columbia Univ. Press, 1978.

Smith, Grahame. *Dickens, Money and Society*. Berkeley: Univ. of California Press, 1968.

Stewart, Garrett. *Dickens and the Trials of Imagination*. Cambridge: Harvard Univ. Press, 1974.

Stoehr, Taylor. *Dickens: The Dreamer's Stance*. Ithaca, N.Y.: Cornell Univ. Press, 1965.

Sucksmith, Harvey Peter. *The Narrative Art of Charles Dickens: The Rhetoric of Sympathy and Irony in his Novels*. New York and London: The Clarendon Press of Oxford Univ. Press, 1970.

Wagenknecht, Edward. *The Man Charles Dickens: A Victorian Portrait*. Rev. ed. Norman: Univ. of Oklahoma Press, 1966.

Wall, Stephen, ed. *Charles Dickens: A Critical Anthology*. Middlesex, England; Baltimore, Maryland: Penguin, 1970.

Williams, Raymond. *Culture and Society 1780-1950*. New York: Columbia Univ. Press, 1958.

Wilson, Angus. *The World of Charles Dickens*. London: Secker and Warburg; New York: Viking, 1970.

Wilson, Edmund. "Dickens: The Two Scrooges." In his *The Wound and the Bow*. New York: Oxford Univ. Press, 1947, pp. 1-104.

A NOTE ON THE TEXT

The text of this volume is taken from the "Charles Dickens" Edition of 1868–1870, which Dickens himself revised for the press, striking out or altering occasional words and making other minor changes. A few obvious errors that escaped his eye have been corrected.

Dickens originally published the novel in weekly installments in *All the Year Round* from April 30 to November 26, 1859, and cannily made an extra profit by also bringing it out from June through December in monthly numbers bound in his customary green paper covers. In this Signet Classic edition the end of a weekly installment is indicated by a row of asterisks, the end of a monthly installment, by a ruled line.

THE WORKS OF CHARLES DICKENS

BRITISH CLASSICS

- [ ] **TYPHOON AND OTHER TALES by Joseph Conrad.** (009367—$4.50)
- [ ] **LORD JIM by Joseph Conrad.** (511956—$1.95)
- [ ] **NOSTROMO by Joseph Conrad.** Foreword by F. R. Leavis. (520920—$3.95)
- [ ] **HEART OF DARKNESS and THE SECRET SHARER by Joseph Conrad.** Introduction by Albert J. Guerard. (520726—$1.95)*
- [ ] **FAR FROM THE MADDING CROWD by Thomas Hardy.** Afterword by James Wright Macalester. (521153—$2.95)
- [ ] **JUDE THE OBSCURE by Thomas Hardy.** Foreword by A. Alvarez. (517830—$2.95)
- [ ] **THE MAYOR OF CASTERBRIDGE by Thomas Hardy.** Afterword by Walter Allen. (512308—$1.95)
- [ ] **THE RETURN OF THE NATIVE by Thomas Hardy.** (519744—$2.25)*
- [ ] **TESS OF THE D'URBERVILLES by Thomas Hardy.** Afterword by Donald Hall. (519248—$2.95)*
- [ ] **KIM by Rudyard Kipling.** Introduction by Raymond Carney. (521447—$2.50)*
- [ ] **CAPTAINS COURAGEOUS by Rudyard Kipling.** Afterword by C. A. Bodelsen. (517512—$1.95)
- [ ] **THE JUNGLE BOOKS by Rudyard Kipling.** Afterword by Marcus Cunliffe. (521927—$3.50)
- [ ] **JUST SO STORIES by Rudyard Kipling.** (521803—$2.95)
- [ ] **KIDNAPPED by Robert Louis Stevenson.** (519728—$1.95)*
- [ ] **THE SHERLOCK HOLMES MYSTERIES by Sir Arthur Conan Doyle.** (521064—$3.50)

*Price slightly higher in Canada
†Not available in Canada

Buy them at your local

bookstore or use coupon

on next page for ordering.